# Intermediate Accounting

# Intermediate Accounting

**REVISED FOURTH EDITION**

**With Revised Chapter 17 for SFAS 158**

J. DAVID SPICELAND
*University of Memphis*

JAMES F. SEPE
*Santa Clara University*

LAWRENCE A. TOMASSINI
*The Ohio State University*

McGraw-Hill Irwin

Boston Burr Ridge, IL Dubuque, IA Madison, WI New York San Francisco St. Louis
Bangkok Bogotá Caracas Kuala Lumpur Lisbon London Madrid Mexico City
Milan Montreal New Delhi Santiago Seoul Singapore Sydney Taipei Toronto

The McGraw·Hill Companies

McGraw-Hill
Irwin

INTERMEDIATE ACCOUNTING
Published by McGraw-Hill/Irwin, a business unit of The McGraw-Hill Companies, Inc., 1221 Avenue of the Americas, New York, NY, 10020. 

This book is printed on acid-free paper.

1 2 3 4 5 6 7 8 9 0 DOW/DOW 0 9 8 7

ISBN-13: 978-0-07-128749-4
ISBN-10: 0-07-128749-3

www.mhhe.com

**Dedicated to:**

David's wife Charlene, daughters Denise and Jessica, and sons Michael David, Michael, and David
Jim's granddaughter Kaitlyn, and father Anthony Sepe
Larry's wife and children: Eve Tomassini, Nicholas, Anthony, and Katherine

Dear Colleagues,

As we wrap up work on the fourth edition of *Intermediate Accounting,* we'd like to thank each of you who adopted the third edition and the updated third edition. Thanks to users like you, sales of our third edition doubled over the previous edition, and our McGraw-Hill colleagues recognized our success by voting our book Revision of the Year for the second time running. More than awards or sales figures however, it's the positive response from so many of our fellow faculty that truly brand *Intermediate Accounting* a success. As intermediate accounting instructors ourselves, we know how crucial it is to choose the right textbook for your course and for your students. That's why, when we began work on the fourth edition, we wanted your input every step of the way.

Our partners at McGraw-Hill tell us they've rarely seen the kind of extraordinary feedback we received in preparing the fourth edition. More than 160 of you took the time to provide us with feedback on the book. Your suggestions were extremely valuable, but what struck us most was the tremendous enthusiasm of even the most critical review. Everyone, it seems, found something to like in *Intermediate Accounting,* as you'll see for yourself as you read this introductory preface. That enthusiasm doesn't stop with faculty; we received letters from students who, when their current books proved inadequate, bought *Intermediate Accounting* completely on their own initiative.

Our goal was to create the kind of textbook you would have written for yourself to use, and we continue our commitment to provide you and your students with the most readable, accurate, and up-to-date intermediate text available. We also pledge to continue to write the major ancillary materials that accompany the text ourselves, including the website materials. Last, we will continue to listen to you, our colleagues, in developing our text to help provide your students with the knowledge, skills, and competencies to meet the challenges of our evolving accounting profession.

Sincerely,

J. David Spiceland    James F. Sepe    Lawrence A. Tomassini

# About the Authors

## David Spiceland

David Spiceland is professor of accounting at the University of Memphis, where he teaches intermediate accounting and other financial accounting courses at the undergraduate and master's levels. He received his BS degree in finance from the University of Tennessee, his MBA from Southern Illinois University, and his PhD in accounting from the University of Arkansas.

Professor Spiceland's primary research interests are in earnings management and educational research. He has published articles in a variety of journals including *The Accounting Review, Accounting and Business Research, Journal of Financial Research,* and *Journal of Accounting Education*. David has received university and college awards and recognition for his teaching, research, and technological innovations in the classroom.

## Jim Sepe

Jim Sepe is an associate professor of accounting at Santa Clara University where he teaches primarily intermediate accounting in both the undergraduate and graduate programs. He previously taught at California Poly State University–San Luis Obispo and the University of Washington and has visited at Stanford University and the Rome campus of Loyola University of Chicago.

Professor Sepe received his BS from Santa Clara University, MBA from the University of California–Berkeley, and PhD from the University of Washington. His research interests concern financial reporting issues and the use of financial information by capital markets. He has published in *The Accounting Review,* the *Journal of Business Finance and Accounting, Financial Management,* the *Journal of Forensic Accounting,* the *Journal of Applied Business Research,* and the *Journal of Accounting Education*. He is a past recipient of the American Accounting Association's Competitive Manuscript Award and has served as a member of the editorial board of *The Accounting Review*.

Jim has received numerous awards for his teaching excellence and innovations in the classroom, including Santa Clara University's Brutocao Award for Excellence in Curriculum Innovation.

## Larry Tomassini

Larry Tomassini is professor of accounting and MIS and director of the accounting honors program at The Ohio State University. He has held several endowed chair positions during his academic career, including the Ernst & Young Distinguished Professor at the University of Illinois and the Peat Marwick Mitchell Centennial Professorship in Accounting at the University of Texas.

His research has been widely published in scholarly journals, including *The Accounting Review, Accounting Horizons, Journal of Accounting Research* and *Contemporary Accounting Research*. Dr. Tomassini is a reviewer for the *Journal of Financial Statement Analysis* and *Issues in Accounting Education*.

He teaches financial accounting courses at the undergraduate and master's levels. Recently, he has been director of the Ohio State Master of Accounting Program and vice president for Publications of the American Accounting Association.

Larry has been a pioneer in the use of Internet technology to support the teaching of accounting courses.

# Your Vehicle to Success

The cyclist may cross the finish line alone, but getting there takes the support of a dedicated team. Likewise, *Intermediate Accounting* is the work not just of its talented authors but of the more than 160 faculty reviewers who shared their insights, experience and opinions with us. Our reviewers helped us to build *Intermediate Accounting* into the vehicle that can carry your students to success in their accounting course, and we have the research to prove it: Spiceland was ranked #1 in improved student performance over a previous textbook, #1 in readability and tied for #1 in overall professor satisfaction.*

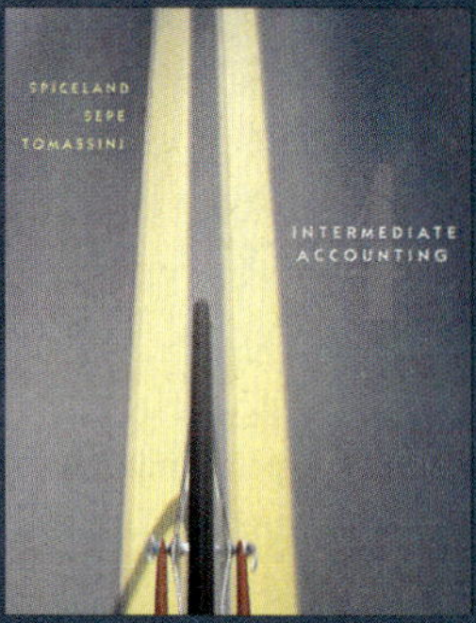


Our development process began in the spring of 2004, when we received the first of what would become more than 160 in-depth reviews of *Intermediate Accounting*. A blend of Spiceland users and non-users, these reviewers explained how they use textbooks in their teaching while many answered detailed questions about every one of Spiceland's 21 chapters. And the work of improving *Intermediate Accounting* is ongoing—even now, we're scheduling new symposia and reviewers' conferences to collect even more opinions from faculty.

*Intermediate Accounting* is the book that faculty all over the country (and the world) have been looking for and have helped shape. We are confident that, just as our users have made *Intermediate Accounting* a success, so will the book in turn prove to be a vital ingredient in your success as a teacher and in your students' success in their studies and their careers.

*Intermediate Accounting* was designed from the start to be not simply a textbook, but a complete learning system, encompassing textbook, key ancillaries, and online content, all of which are written by authors Spiceland, Sepe and Tomassini. The *Intermediate Accounting* learning system is built around five key attributes:

**"I am very impressed with this textbook and its supplements. The authors have carefully developed the book to meet the needs of a wide range of student learners. It is clearly written in understandable terms. There are many features available to provide your students with the best chance to master this material."**

*- Robert Gruber, University of Wisconsin—Whitewater*

**"It is a complete and concise learning system that reaches out to divergent learning styles of students. Bottom line, students learn accounting with this learning system."**

*- Janice Stoudemire, Midlands Technical College*

**"Well on its way to becoming the standard."**

*- John Garlick, Fayetteville State University*

*Results from an independent market survey of intermediate accounting professors July–September 2002 by Professional Research Group, LLC.

# in Intermediate Accounting

**Clarity:** Reviewers, instructors, and students all have hailed *Intermediate Accounting*'s ability to explain both simple and complex topics in language that is clear and approachable. Its highly acclaimed conversational writing style establishes a friendly dialogue between the text and each individual student. So readable is Spiceland that we've even received letters from students who bought the book themselves—despite their instructors using competing books in the course! No surprise that Spiceland was found to be the most readable intermediate accounting textbook in independent research.*

**A Decision-Making Perspective:** Recent events have focused public attention on the key role of accounting in providing information useful to decision makers. The CPA exam, too, is redirecting its focus to emphasize the professional skills needed to critically evaluate accounting method alternatives. *Intermediate Accounting* provides a decision maker's perspective to emphasize the professional judgment and critical thinking skills required of accountants today.

**Flexible Technology:** Today's accounting students have come of age in a digital world, and Spiceland's Learning System reflects that trend through its comprehensive technology package. The Coach tutorial software provides a browser-based, text-integrated multimedia environment in which to review concepts and take practice quizzes, while McGraw-Hill's Homework Manager™ offers infinite algorithmically generated practice problems in an online environment students can access whenever they want. Feedback in McGraw-Hill's Homework Manager™ is immediate, giving students an instant snapshot of their progress in mastering the material.

**Consistent Quality:** The *Intermediate Accounting* author team ensures seamless compatibility throughout the Spiceland learning package by writing every major supplement themselves: Coach, Study Guide, Instructor's Resource Manual, Solutions Manual, Test Bank, and website content are all created by authors Spiceland, Sepe, and Tomassini. The end-of-chapter material, too, is written by the author team and tested in their classrooms before being included in *Intermediate Accounting*. That dedication makes Spiceland users among the most satisfied of any intermediate accounting text.*

**A Commitment to Currency:** Few disciplines see the kind of rapid change that accounting experiences, and the Spiceland team is committed to keeping your course as up to date as possible. The fourth edition fully integrates all the latest FASB standards, including "Accounting Changes and Error Corrections," "*Exchanges of Nonmonetary Assets—An Amendment of APB Opinion No. 29,*" and "Share-Based Payment."

Rated the most satisfying textbook by students in independent research,* *Intermediate Accounting* has the quality, flexibility, and attention to detail your students need to master a challenging subject. It's their vehicle to success in your intermediate accounting course—and beyond.

**"This text … shows tremendous promise in getting the students to actually read the book. … The Spiceland text is so interesting, they might not even realize they are learning."**

*- Anonymous*

**"There are a number of computerized/web-based supplements to assist students along with a plethora of terrific examples in the chapters and within the end of chapter material."**

*- Angela Sandburg, Jacksonville State University*

**"This is one of the few texts that I am aware of that the authors actually are responsible for the problems. This adds so much consistency and continuity."**

*- Janice Stoudemire, Midlands Technical College*

**"Overall, I find the Spiceland end-of-chapter material far superior to that in Kieso in terms of quantity, especially as it relates to the diversity of the problem material."**

*- Chula King, University of West Florida*

*Results from an independent market survey of intermediate accounting professors July–September 2002 by Professional Research Group, LLC.

# What Stands Out in the Fourth Edition?

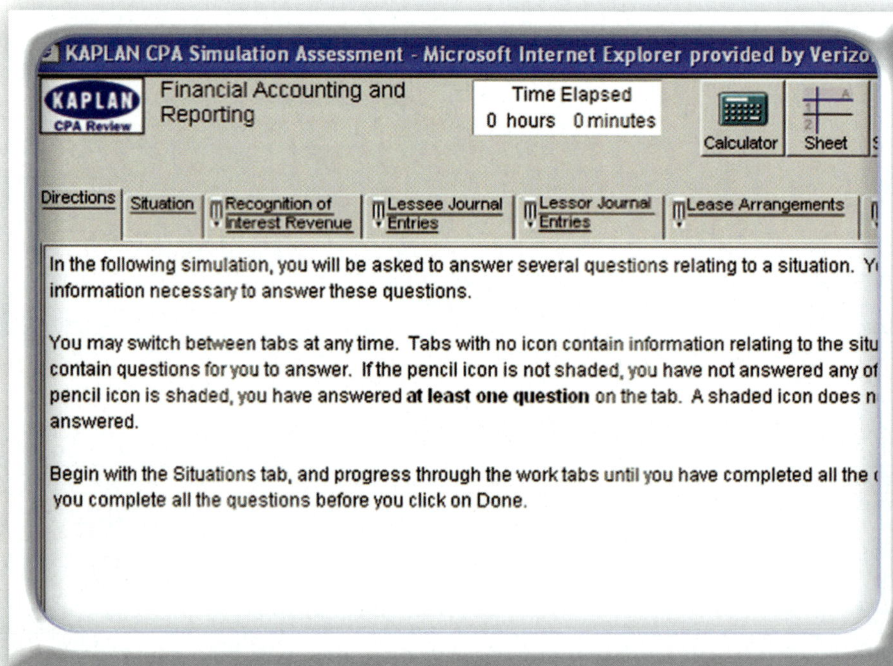


> **"Excellent feature! I cannot wait to work through these. Students should find them extremely valuable, especially if they plan to sit for the CPA exam."**
>
> *- Karen Foust, Tulane University*

## CPA Simulations

Students sitting for the new computerized CPA exam will confront an interface unlike any they've encountered before; from finding information in a research database to entering data into a spreadsheet, the CPA exam doesn't look or act like any other software program. Spiceland's new CPA Simulations allow students to practice intermediate accounting concepts in a web-based environment identical to that used in the actual CPA exam. There'll be no hesitation or confusion when your students sit for the real exam: they'll know exactly what they need to do.

KAPLAN
CPA Review

**Revising a book as successful as Intermediate Accounting takes judiciousness and a strong vision of what a textbook should be. New features aren't piled on for their own sake; only when our users consistently point out an opportunity for improvement does the Spiceland team take action. The result is a book that never loses its original strengths as it gains in usefulness and flexibility with each revision.**

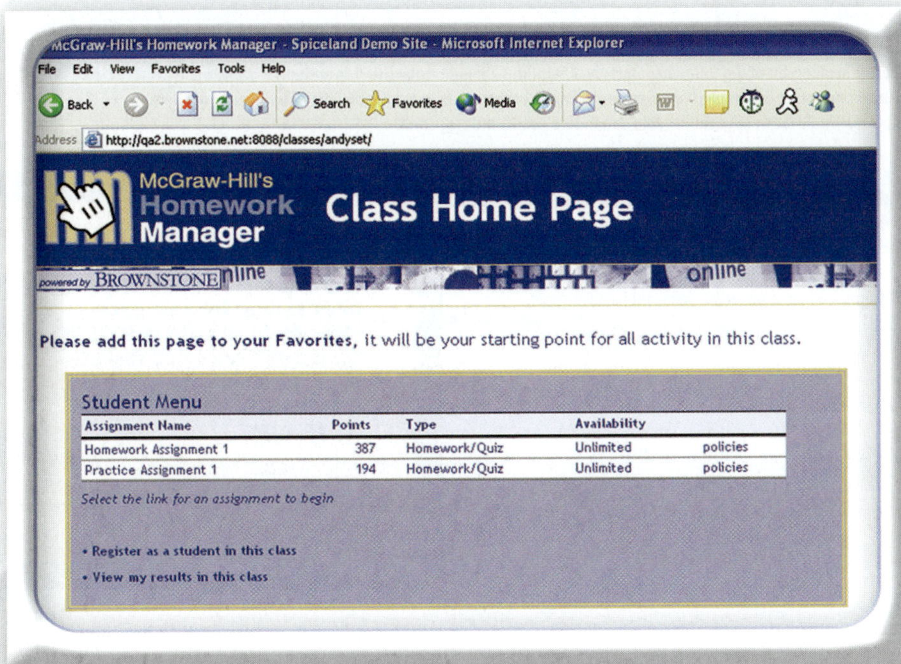


## McGraw-Hill's Homework Manager™

**McGraw-Hill's Homework Manager** is a web-based supplement that duplicates problem structures directly from the end-of-chapter material in *Intermediate Accounting*, using algorithms as needed to provide a limitless supply of online self-graded practice for students, or assignments and tests with unique versions of every problem. Assignments are graded automatically, with the results stored in your private gradebook. Detailed results let you see at a glance how each student does on an assignment or an individual problem—you can even see how many tries it took them to solve it. Students can use McGraw-Hill's Homework Manager on a schedule that's convenient to them, receiving guided feedback every step of the way.

> **"I believe Coach and Homework Manager are tremendous assets for my students."**
>
> *- Rebecca Shortridge, Northern Illinois University*

# How did we build a better book?

## BRIEF EXERCISES

**BE 3–1**
Current versus noncurrent classification
• LO2

Indicate whether each of the following assets and liabilities should be classified as current or noncurrent: (a) accounts receivable; (b) prepaid rent for the next six months; (c) note receivable due in two years; (d) note payable due in 90 days; (e) note payable due in five years; and (f) patent.

**BE 3–2**
Balance sheet classification
• LO3 LO4

The trial balance for K and J Nursery, Inc. listed the following acc… end of its fiscal year: cash, $16,000; accounts receivable, $11,000… $80,000; accounts payable, $14,000; wages payable, $9,000; intere… 18 months), $30,000; common stock, $50,000. Calculate total curr… would appear in the company's year-end balance sheet.

## Brief Exercises

A much-requested feature, the new Brief Exercises appear in the end-of-chapter material, where they offer the opportunity for concise, step-by-step reinforcement before moving on to more complex exercises, problems, and cases.

> **"I very much like the distinction between brief exercises and exercises ... I usually have to hunt for brief exercises that I can use quickly in class and I can't find them for some topics. In my opinion, they are a great selling point for your text."**
>
> *- David Roberts, Texas A&M University International*

CHAPTER 3 The Balance Sheet and Financial Disclosures 139

**E 3-17**
Multiple choice; CMA exam; Disclosures and the current ratio
• LO5 LO6 LO9

The following questions dealing with financial disclosures and the current ratio are adapted from questions that previously appeared on Certified Management Accountant (CMA) examinations. The CMA designation sponsored by the Institute of Management Accountants (www.imanet.org) provides members with an objective measure of knowledge and competence in the field of management accounting. Determine the response that best completes the statements or questions.

1. The Financial Accounting Standards Board has provided guidance on disclosures of transactions between related parties, for example, transactions between subsidiaries of a common parent. SFAS 57, *Related Party Disclosures,* requires all of the following disclosures except
   a. The nature of the relationship involved.
   b. A description of the transactions for each period an income statement is presented.

## CMA Exam Questions

Each chapter now includes a set of multiple choice questions pertaining to issues in those chapters that have appeared in previous Certified Management Accountants (CMA) exams. These not only provide your students with additional practice on questions in multiple choice format, but also make them aware of the alternative certification route many of them will take as they pursue careers in corporate accounting.

**There's more to making a book better than adding new features. Organizing and updating the content is one of the foremost challenges a textbook faces, and Intermediate Accounting undergoes continual refinement to ensure that the content is as fresh and as easy to present and teach as possible.**

# New Content Organization

A great many events have impacted accounting over the past few years, and *Intermediate Accounting* integrates every important development just where it belongs. Some examples include:

- Expanded coverage of Sarbanes-Oxley in Chapter 1, with additional coverage of SOX Section 404 in the internal control material of Chapter 7.
- The overview of the statement of cash flows has been expanded in Chapter 4.
- Chapter 10 has been rewritten to accommodate *FASB Statement No. 153*, "Exchanges of Nonmonetary Assets—An Amendment of *APB Opinion No. 29*."
- The previous Chapter 18, "Employee Benefit Plans," has been eliminated and its content integrated with companion topics in Chapters 17 and 19. A major impetus for the change is SFAS 123 (revised), "Share-Based Payment."
- Chapter 20, along with portions of several other chapters, has been revised and rewritten to reflect major changes in the way we report changes in accounting principles.
- The FedEx financial statements figure prominently in many of the text's key cases. In response to feedback from our users, we've moved them to their own appendix at the back of the book, making them easier to access.
- A feature of previous editions, the Present Value Tables have been moved to the back endsheets to make them easier for students and instructors to quickly find, regardless of which *Intermediate Accounting* configuration they are using.

For more details on the fourth edition's organization, see pages (xi–xii) of the Preface.

**"Of the chapters I reviewed, SST was equal or superior to the Kieso text...Had I done a review this thorough before our last textbook adoption decision, I would have recommended SST over Kieso. The organization and writing style is exceptional."**

*- Joe Morris,*
*Southeastern Louisiana University*

**"I absolutely agree with covering OPEB along with pensions, they are very similar."**

*- Barbara Muller,*
*Arizona State University*

# What Keeps Spiceland Users Coming Back?

## Financial Reporting Cases

Each chapter opens with a Financial Reporting Case that places the student in the role of the decision maker, engaging the student in an interesting situation related to the accounting issues to come. Then, the cases pose questions of the student in the role of decision maker. Marginal notations throughout the chapter point out locations where each question is addressed. Finally, the questions are answered at the end of the chapter.

## Decision Makers' Perspective

These sections appear throughout the text to illustrate how accounting information is put to work in today's firms. With the CPA exam placing greater focus on application of skills in realistic work settings, these discussions help your students gain an edge that will remain with them as they enter the workplace.

## Earnings Management

With 86 percent of intermediate accounting faculty teaching earnings management in their courses,* Spiceland's integrated coverage of this key topic throughout the book is especially helpful.

---

**FINANCIAL REPORTING CASE**

**Engineering Profits**

After graduating from college last year, two of your engineering-major friends started an Internet consulting practice. They began operations on July 1 and felt they did quite well during their first year. Now they would like to borrow $20,000 from a local bank to buy new computing equipment and office furniture. To support their loan application, the friends presented the bank with the following income statement for their first year of operations ending June 30:

| | | |
|---|---|---|
| Consulting revenue | | $96,000 |
| Operating expenses: | | |
| Salaries | $32,000 | |
| Rent | 9,000 | |
| Supplies | 4,800 | |
| Utilities | 3,000 | |
| Advertising | 1,200 | (50,000) |
| Net income | | $46,000 |

---

**"I think students will enjoy the real-world cases at the beginning of the chapters as well as the Decision Makers' Perspective."**

*- Rebecca Shortridge, Northern Illinois University*

holder with 15 shares would receive 3 additional shares and $9 in cash ($12

**DECISION MAKERS' PERSPECTIVE**

Profitability is the key to a company's long-run survival. A summary measur ity often used by investors and potential investors, particularly common shar return on shareholders' equity. This ratio measures the ability of company n generate net income from the resources that owners provide. The ratio is comp ing net income by average shareholders' equity. A variation of this ratio ofte a company has both preferred and common stock outstanding. The return to c holders' equity is calculated by subtracting dividends to preferred shareholde merator and using average common shareholders' equity as the denominator. ratio focuses on the profits generated on the assets provided by common shar

Although the ratio is useful when evaluating the effectiveness of managem ing resources provided by owners, analysts must be careful not to view it in isc out considering how the ratio is derived. Keep in mind that shareholders' equi of the book value of equity, equivalent to the book value of net assets. Book v quickly become out of line with market value

**"Very clearly lays out the issue, explaining all ramifications. Doesn't assume that [students] are bringing any knowledge to the table."**

*- Lorraine Stern, York College, CUNY*

### Earnings Quality

LO3 Financial analysts are concerned with more than just the bottom li ment—net income. The presentation of the components of net inco plemental disclosures provide clues to the user of the statement in an *quality*. Earnings quality is used as a framework for more in-depth c and nonoperating income.

The term **earnings quality** refers to the ability of reported earnin company's future earnings. After all, an income statement simply re ready have occurred. The relevance of any historical-based financial predictive value. To enhance predictive value, analysts try to separ *tory earnings* effects from its *permanent earnings*. Transitory earni transactions or events that are not likely to occur again in the forese likely to have a different impact on earnings in the future. Later in two items that, because of their transitory nature, are required to be re bottom of the income statement. Analysts begin their assessment of r

*quality refers ... bility of ... d earnings ... to predict a ... y's future ...*

**"I think that this discussion, and others like it in the text, is excellent. Being a former CFO, I spend a fair amount of time talking with students about how earnings can be managed, in the hands of a biased (unethical?) CFO."**

*- Ron Tilden, University of Washington, Bothell*

**In talking to so many intermediate accounting faculty, we didn't hear only how to improve the book—there was much, much more that both users and nonusers insisted we keep exactly as it was. Here are some of the features that have made Spiceland such a phenomenal success in its previous editions.**

ADDITIONAL CONSIDERATION

**Periodic Inventory System**

The principal alternative to the perpetual invento
system requires that the cost of merchandise pu
account called *purchases*. When inventory is
decreased and cost of goods sold is not recorde
determined and the inventory account is adjusted
For example, the purchase of $60,000 of me
Clothing is recorded as follows:

Purchases. . . . . . . . . . . . . . . . . . . . . . . . . . . . . . . . .
Accounts payable . . . . . . . . . . . . . . . . . . . . . . . .

No cost of goods sold entry is recorded when sales are made in the periodic system.
At the end of July, the amount of ending inventory is determined (either by means of a physical count of goods on hand or by estimation) to be $38,000 and cost of goods sold for the month is determined as follows:

| | |
|---|---|
| Beginning inventory | -0- |
| Plus: Purchases | 60,000 |
| Less: Ending inventory | (38,000) |
| Cost of goods sold | 22,000 |

djusts the
8,000):

60,000

> **"These help students understand the development of reporting rules from concepts."**
>
> *- Betty Chavis, California State University-Fullerton*

## Additional Consideration Boxes

These are "on the spot" considerations of important, but incidental or infrequent aspects of the primary topics to which they relate. Their parenthetical nature, highlighted by enclosure in Additional Consideration boxes, helps maintain an appropriate level of rigor of topic coverage without sacrificing clarity of explanation.

ETHICAL DILEMMA

The Raintree Cosmetic Company has several loans outstanding with a local bank. The debt agreements all contain a covenant stipulating that Raintree must maintain a current ratio of at least .9. Jackson Phillips, company controller, estimates that the 2006 year-end current assets and current liabilities will be $2,100,000 and $2,400,000, respec-
tively. These estimates provide a current ratio of o
will increase Raintree's borrowing costs as the loa
Jackson proposes to the company president tha
on credit before year-end. This will cause both c
crease by the same amount, but the current ratio
inventory will be used over the later part of 2007
housing costs and financing costs to increase.
Jackson is concerned about the ethics of his pr

> **"In light of all the accounting irregularities that have surfaced, ethics have become a hot topic and certainly something that needs to be stressed to students."**
>
> *- Irwin Uhr, Hunter College*

## Ethical Dilemmas

Because ethical ramifications of business decisions impact so many individuals as well as the core of our economy, Ethical Dilemmas are incorporated within the context of accounting issues as they are discussed. These features lend themselves very well to impromptu class discussions and debates.

## Broaden Your Perspective Cases

Finish each chapter with these powerful and effective cases, a great way to reinforce and expand concepts learned in the chapter.

BROADEN YOUR PERSPECTIVE

**Apply your critical-thinking ability to the knowledge you've gained. These cases will provide you a opportunity to develop your research, analysis, judgment, and communication skills. You will also wo with other students, integrate what you've learned, apply it in real-world situations, and consider i global and e ... levelop yo decision-ma**

Judgment Case 1–1
The development of accounting standards
● LO3

In 1934, Co ... mission bo
the power a ... s.

> **"This is where Spiceland seems to be well ahead of our current text."**
>
> *- Mary Jo Kranacher, York College, CUNY*

> **"I like the idea of having the students think, analyze and research issues. They are not just memorizing facts and procedures."**
>
> *- Kathleen Fitzpatrick, University of Toledo Community Technical College*

*Results from an independent market survey of intermediate accounting professors July–September 2002 by Professional Research Group, LLC.

# What's New in the Fourth Edition?

## Chapter 1
### Environment and Theoretical Structure of Financial Accounting

- Expanded Chapter 1 coverage of the Sarbanes-Oxley Act.
- Added a section on the debate between principles-based and rules-based approaches to accounting standard setting.
- Revised discussion of accounting principles to include the new FASB standard addressing the hierarchy of GAAP.*
- The FedEx financial statements previously located in an appendix to Chapter 1 are now located in an appendix at the end of the text, making them easier to find.*

## Chapter 2
### Review of the Accounting Process

Added additional end-of-chapter material on the conversion of cash to accrual income determination.*

## Chapter 3
### The Balance Sheet and Financial Disclosures

All real-world disclosure examples have been updated.*

## Chapter 4
### The Income Statement and Statement of Cash Flows

- Part B of Chapter 4 provides an overview of the statement of cash flows.
- Discussion of the indirect method of presenting cash flows from operating activities has been expanded to add more depth of coverage, including a new illustration.
- The concept review exercise is revised to include the indirect method, and new end-of-chapter materials have been added.
- Chapter 4 has been rewritten to reflect the new standard on accounting changes. Financial statements no longer will report a "cumulative effect of a change in accounting principle." Instead, most voluntary changes in accounting principle will be accounted for retrospectively. Changes in depreciation, depletion, and amortization methods are now accounted for in the same manner as a change in estimate.
- Discussion of comprehensive income is now expanded and reorganized to enhance students' grasp of this difficult concept.*

## Chapter 5
### Income Measurement and Profitability Analysis

Expanded the discussion of SEC's revenue recognition bulletin, SAB #101.*

## Chapter 6
### Time Value of Money Concepts

The future and present value tables previously located in an appendix to Chapter 6 are now located in an appendix at the end of the text.*

## Chapter 7
### Cash and Receivables

- Coverage of internal control has been expanded to include a discussion of the controversial Section 404 of Sarbanes-Oxley.
- Further material (including a real-world example) has been added to help students better understand accounting for sales returns.*

## Chapter 8
### Inventories – Measurement

The learning objectives are expanded to better reflect the key issues discussed in the chapter.*

## Chapter 9
### Inventories – Additional Issues

Coverage of changes in inventory methods is revised to reflect the new standard on accounting changes.

## Chapter 10
### Operational Assets – Acquisition and Disposition

Chapter 10 is rewritten to reflect FASB Statement No. 153, *Exchanges of Nonmonetary Assets—an amendment of* APB Opinion No. 29. This represents a significant simplification in accounting for nonmonetary exchanges by eliminating a major exception to fair value accounting when the exchange involves similar assets.

## Chapter 11
### Operational Assets – Utilization and Impairment

- The section on changes in depreciation, depletion, and amortization has been updated to reflect the new standard on accounting changes.
- New real-world examples of operational asset impairment, including goodwill, have been added.*

## Chapter 12
### Investments

- The discussion of fair value adjustments for available-for-sale securities uses a valuation account rather than the previous approach of increasing or decreasing the investment account directly. The primary advantage of this approach is its ability to deal with the situation when a bond is classified as available-for-sale to allow making a market adjustment separate from amortizing a discount or premium.*
- Coverage of comprehensive income has been significantly expanded within the context of the integrally-related discussions of reporting unrealized investment gains and losses and comprehensive income, including related discussion of difficult to convey, but essential, "reclassification adjustments."*
- To assist students in understanding the effects of fair value adjustments on financial statements, annotated T-account analysis sections accompanied by excerpted portions of financial statements affected have been added.*

**We received an unprecedented amount of feedback prior to writing the fourth edition of Intermediate Accounting. The following list of changes and improvements is a testament to our users and their commitment to making Intermediate Accounting the best book of its kind.**

Chapter

## 13

### Current Liabilities and Contingencies

Relocated discussions of paid future absences and bonuses from the previous Employee Benefits chapter to this chapter to provide a more meaningful perspective within the context of other accrued liabilities.*

Chapter

## 14

### Bonds and Long-Term Notes

Revised the discussion of liabilities to address the new way of reporting manditorily redeemable stock as a liability as called for by SFAS No. 150, *Accounting for Financial Instruments with Characteristics of both Liabilities and Equity.**

Chapter

## 15

### Leases

Utilized the discussion of leasehold improvements in this chapter to provide a synopsis of one of the most wide-spread accounting correction events ever that took place in 2005, at the same time reinforcing students' understanding of accounting for leasehold improvements.*

Chapter

## 16

### Accounting for Income Taxes

Expanded a Decision Makers' Perspective section of this chapter to point out that recent empirical evidence indicates that some companies use the deferred tax asset valuation allowance account to manage earnings upward to meet analyst forecasts.*

Chapter

## 17

### Pensions and Other Postretirement Benefits

Revised Chapter 17 to include new pension disclosures called for by SFAS No. 132 (revised 2003), *Employers' Disclosures about Pensions and Other Postretirement Benefits—an amendment of FASB Statements Nos. 87, 88, and 106*. Related to that pronouncement's requirement that pensions and OPEB now are to be presented together, postretirement benefits other than pensions are now presented as Part E of this chapter rather than in the previous Employee Benefits chapter. Combining pensions and OPEB avoids separation of two integrally related topics that are accounted for almost identically.*

Chapter

## 18

(previously 19)

### Shareholders' Equity

- Expanded coverage of comprehensive income to enhance students' grasp of the concept, and particularly at this juncture the distinction between (a) comprehensive income *created during the reporting period* and (b) comprehensive income *accumulated* over the current and prior periods. The explanation of other comprehensive income is offered as a parallel concept with "traditional" net income.*
- Modified the discussion of hybrid securities and the debt versus equity issue to address the new way of reporting manditorily redeemable stock called for by SFAS No. 150, *Accounting for Financial Instruments with Characteristics of both Liabilities and Equity.**

Chapter

## 19

(previously 20)

### Share-Based Compensation and Earnings Per Share

Statement No. 123 (revised 2004), *Share-Based Payment,* requires fair value accounting for employee stock options, eliminating altogether the popular intrinsic value approach and reducing reported earnings for most companies. Coverage of share-based compensation has been rewritten and moved to the new Chapter 19, preceding discussions of earnings per share. This move strengthens the short EPS chapter and combines two fundamentally related topics.*

Chapter

## 20

(previously 21)

### Accounting Changes and Error Corrections

Under *Accounting Changes and Error Corrections—a replacement of APB Opinion No. 20 and FASB Statement No. 3 (Proposed Statement of Financial Accounting Standards),* financial statements no longer will report a "cumulative effect of a change in accounting principle." Instead, most voluntary changes in accounting principle will be accounted for retrospectively. To accommodate the new approach, major portions of this chapter as well as lesser portions of five other chapters (4, 9, 11, 16, and 19) affected by this change have been rewritten.

Chapter

## 21

(previously 22)

### The Statement of Cash Flows Revisited

This chapter continues to be devoted entirely to in-depth coverage of the statement of cash flows to complement and extend the more fundamental presentation of the statement in Chapter 4, which has been expanded in this edition.

### Appendix A—Derivatives

### Appendix B—FedEx Financial Statements

> **"If you had organized these any other way, I probably would have suggested exactly the changes that you made."**
>
> *- David Roberts, Texas A&M University International*

* These items represent revisions to the 3e Update Edition.

# How Does Spiceland Help My Students Improve Their Performance?

## Online Learning Center (OLC)

www.mhhe.com/spiceland4e

Today's students are every bit as comfortable using a web browser as they are reading a printed book. That's why we offer an Online Learning Center (OLC) that follows **Intermediate Accounting** chapter by chapter. It doesn't require any building or maintenance on your part, and is ready to go the moment you and your students type in the URL.

As your students study, they can refer to the OLC Website for such benefits as:

- E-learning sessions
- Self-grading quizzes
- Electronic flash cards
- Communication tools
- Audio narrated PowerPoints
- News/References
- Real-world electronic cases
- Class activities and projects
- Alternate exercises and problems
- Check figures
- Career information
- Practice exams
- Toolbox
- FASB pronouncements, summaries and updates
- Accounting and financial information
- International accounting resources
- Text updates

A secured Instructor Resource Center stores your essential course materials to save you prep time before class. The Instructor's Resource Manual, Solutions, PowerPoint, Case Implementation Manual and sample syllabi are now just a couple of clicks away. You will also find useful packaging information and transition notes.

The OLC Website also serves as a doorway to other technology solutions such as PageOut, which is free to *Intermediate Accounting* adopters.

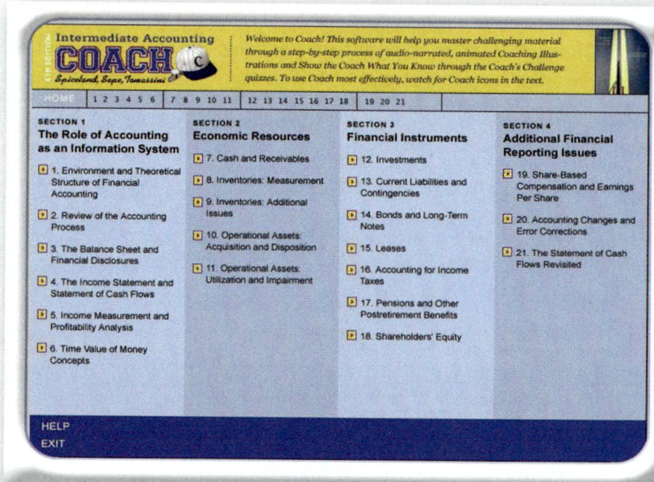


## Coach

Coach is our award-winning tutorial software designed to help students understand critical accounting concepts. First, Coach actually provides spoken, narrated feedback as it helps students work through problems, rather than acting as just a reservoir of content that couldn't fit in the text. Second, the concept, content, and execution of Coach have been driven by and are part of the philosophy of the text authors.

Coach helps students master challenging material through a clear, step-by-step model. **Coaching Illustrations** are animated illustrations and examples similar to those found in the text that walk students through difficult concepts in a step-by-step manner. Look for the Coach icon in the text to identify these illustrations. **Show the Coach What You Know** provides students with a fun and interactive way to quiz themselves on key terminology and concepts.

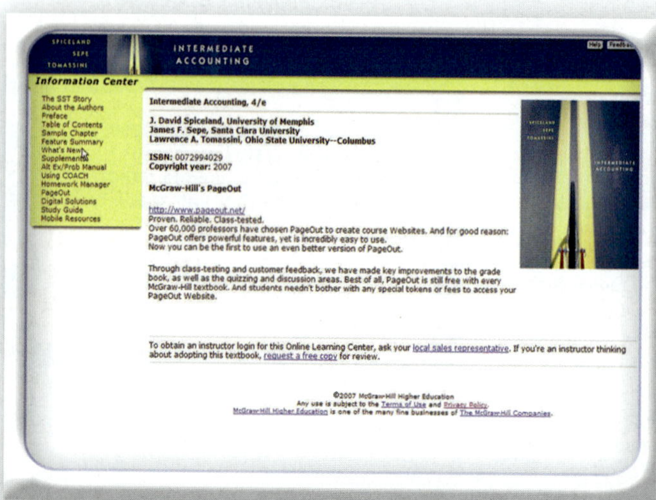


> **"It is wonderful. I have my students evaluate each course I teach and rate the resources used. Time after time, students rate Coach as their number one choice. They love the interaction."**
>
> *- Janice Stoudemire, Midlands Technical College*

**Intermediate Accounting's digital learning tools provide a comprehensive and cutting-edge environment for your students to practice in—and all digital content is prepared by the authors themselves.**

## McGraw-Hill's Homework Manager™

**McGraw-Hill's Homework Manager** is a web-based homework management system that gives you unparalleled power and flexibility in creating homework assignments, tests and quizzes. Homework Manager duplicates problem structures directly from the end-of-chapter material in your McGraw-Hill textbook, using algorithms to provide limitless variations of textbook problems. Use Homework Manager to supply online self-graded practice for students, or create assignments and tests with unique versions of every problem: Homework Manager can grade assignments automatically, provide instant feedback to students, and store all results in your private gradebook. Detailed results let you see at a glance how each student does and easily track the progress of every student in your course.

## McGraw-Hill's Homework Manager Plus™

**McGraw-Hill's Homework Manager Plus** combines the power of Homework Manager with the latest interactive learning technology to create a comprehensive, fully integrated online study package.

Students using Homework Manager Plus can access not only **Homework Manager** itself, but the Interactive Online Textbook as well. Far more than a textbook on a screen, this resource is completely integrated into Homework Manager, allowing students working on assignments to click a hotlink and instantly review the appropriate material in the textbook. **NetTutor** rounds out the package by offering live tutoring with a qualified expert in the course material, using our innovative virtual whiteboard to allow student and tutor to communicate in real time.

By including Homework Manager Plus with your textbook adoption, you're giving your students a vital edge as they progress through the course and ensuring that the help they need is never more than a mouse click away.

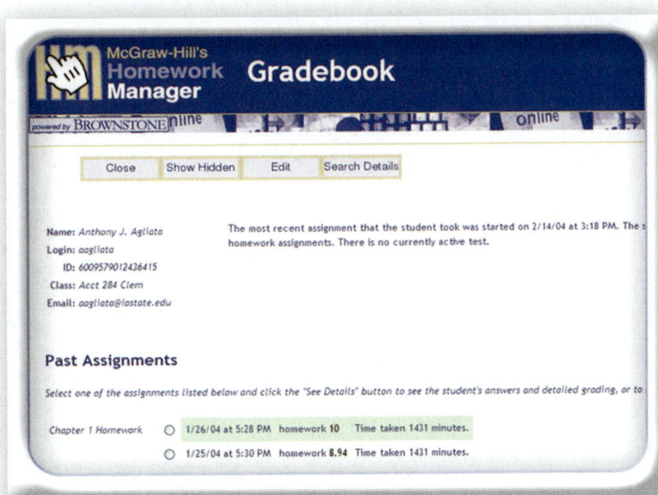

# How Does Spiceland Help Me Build a Better Course?

ALEKS®
A BETTER STATE OF KNOWLEDGE

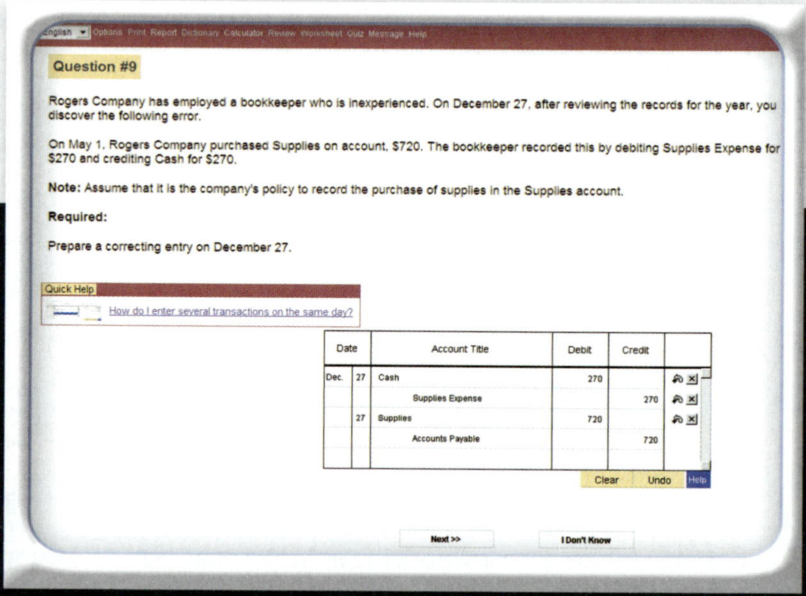


> **"The two [technology assets] that I find most exciting are Homework Manager and ALEKS. These alone are powerful reasons to choose this textbook."**
>
> *- Chula King, University of West Florida*

ALEKS for the Accounting Cycle uses innovative adaptive learning technology to provide individualized guided learning to each and every student. ALEKS defines the key concepts, offers explanations and opportunities to practice, analyzes and corrects errors, and moves on to new topics when the student is ready.

When a student completes an initial assessment with ALEKS, the system analyzes the student's responses and determines an individual knowledge state for that student with great efficiency. From then on, ALEKS sets an appropriate learning path for the student by carefully analyzing his or her responses and determining what material is ready to be learned next.

You'll see increased motivation and confidence in your students after they use ALEKS. You'll see improved performance in courses where ALEKS is deployed, as well as fewer drops. And you'll see it all with minimal effort on your part—that's how easy it is to integrate ALEKS into your course.

## What are the benefits of ALEKS for the Accounting Cycle?

- Intermediate accounting students can use ALEKS for a review of the accounting cycle. Since ALEKS is self-guided, you can reduce the time spent in your intermediate course reviewing material from financial accounting.
- ALEKS can be used as the curriculum for a bridge course between financial accounting and intermediate accounting.
- MBA students can use ALEKS for a self-guided review of accounting to prepare for their MBA program. Since it is online, students can do their work from anywhere in the world.

Contact your McGraw-Hill representative today and learn more about ALEKS, or email aleks@mcgraw-hill.com.

**From innovative self-guided assessment and guidance to complete online course solutions, McGraw-Hill/Irwin lets you take full advantage of everything the digital age has to offer.**

WebCT courses • campus • community

Bb Blackboard www.blackboard.com

## Flexible Online Course Content

No matter what platform you use, McGraw-Hill is committed to making your online course a success. We provide free, WebCT- and Blackboard-compatible course cartridges containing all the content you need.

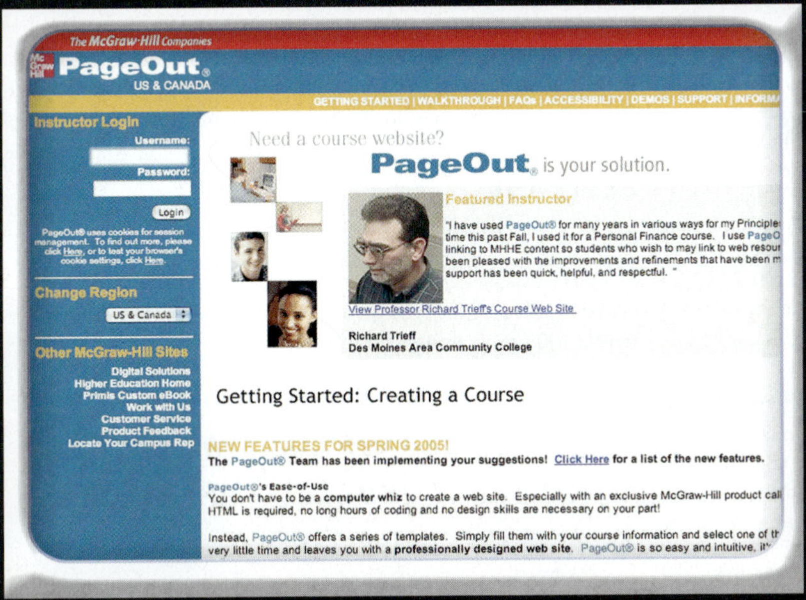


> **"The course I will use this text for is a 'blended' course ... partially online and partially on campus. This will be very useful."**
>
> *- Kathy Simons, Bryant College*

PageOut

## PageOut-McGraw-Hill's Course Management System

PageOut is the easiest way to create a Website for your accounting course.

There's no need for HTML coding, graphic design, or a thick how-to book. Just fill in a series of boxes with simple English and click on one of our professional designs. In no time, your course is online with a Website that contains your syllabus!

Should you need assistance in preparing your Website, we can help. Our team of product specialists is ready to take your course materials and build a custom Website to your specifications. You simply need to call a McGraw-Hill/Irwin PageOut specialist to start the process. Best of all, PageOut is free when you adopt *Intermediate Accounting*! To learn more, please visit **www.pageout.net.**

To see how these platforms can assist your online course, visit **www.mhhe.com**

# A GREAT LEARNING SYSTEM DOESN'T STOP WITH THE BOOK.

## INSTRUCTOR SUPPLEMENTS

### INSTRUCTOR'S RESOURCE MANUAL

*Volume 1 ISBN-13: 9780073130385 (ISBN-10: 0073130389)*
*Volume 2 ISBN-13: 9780073130453 (ISBN-10: 0073130451)*

This manual provides for each chapter: (a) a chapter overview; (b) a comprehensive lecture outline; (c) extensive teaching transparency masters that can be modified to suit an instructor's particular needs or preferences; (d) a variety of suggested class activities (real world, ethics, FedEx, professional development activities including research, analysis, communication and judgment, and others); and (e) an assignment chart indicating topic, learning objective, and estimated completion time for every question, exercise, problem, and case.

### CASE IMPLEMENTATION MANUAL

Most accounting instructors are not trained specifically to teach ethics, international accounting, group interaction techniques, Internet techniques, and writing. To assist instructors in adding one or more of these dimensions to their courses, our Case Implementation Manual is designed to provide instructional support for teaching cases in these areas. The manual is prepared in concert with the experts on our board of advisors, who offer the background material necessary to help students derive maximum benefit from these cases, as well as suggest how instructors can incorporate these cases to their best advantage. The Solutions Manual includes detailed solutions to every case. This manual is available on the text Website:
**www.mhhe.com/spiceland4e.**

### SOLUTIONS MANUAL

*Volume 1 ISBN-13: 9780073130477 (ISBN-10: 0073130478)*
*Volume 2 ISBN-13: 9780073130460 (ISBN-10: 007313046X)*

The Solutions Manual includes detailed solutions for every question, exercise, problem, and case in the text.

### SOLUTIONS TRANSPARENCIES

*Volume 1 ISBN-13: 9780073130187 (ISBN-10: 0073130184)*
*Volume 2 ISBN-13: 9780073130255 (ISBN-10: 0073130257)*

Acetate overhead transparencies for every question, exercise, problem, and case are provided in a large, readable typeface.

### INSTRUCTOR'S CD-ROM

*ISBN-13: 9780073130286 (ISBN-10: 0073130281)*

This all-in-one resource contains the Instructor's Resource Manual, Solutions Manual, Testbank Word files, Computerized TB, PowerPoint® slides, and Instructor Excel Templates.

### TESTBANK

*Volume 1 ISBN-13: 9780073130378 (ISBN-10: 0073130370)*
*Volume 2 ISBN-13: 9780073130484 (ISBN-10: 0073130486)*

Written by the authors, this comprehensive Testbank contains over 3,100 problems and true/false, multiple-choice, and essay questions.

### COMPUTERIZED TESTBANK WITH ALGORITHMIC PROBLEM GENERATOR

*ISBN-13: 9780073130347 (ISBN-10: 0073130346)*

New to the fourth edition computerized testbank is an algorithmic problem generator enabling instructors to create similarly structured problems with different values, allowing every student to be assigned a unique quiz or test. The user-friendly interface allows faculty to easily create different versions of the same test, change the answer order, edit or add questions, and even conduct online testing.

### AUDIO POWERPOINT SLIDES

The Audio PowerPoint slides are created by Jon Booker and Charles Caldwell of Tennessee Technological University and Susan Galbreath of David Lipscomb University. The slides include an accompanying audio lecture with notes and are available on the Online Learning Center (OLC) and Instructor's CD-ROM.

**Intermediate Accounting authors Spiceland, Sepe, and Tomassini know from their own years of teaching experience what separates a great textbook from a merely adequate one. Every component of the learning package must be imbued with the same style and approach, and that's why the Intermediate Accounting authors write every major ancillary themselves, whether printed or online. It's one more thing that sets Intermediate Accounting far above the competition.**

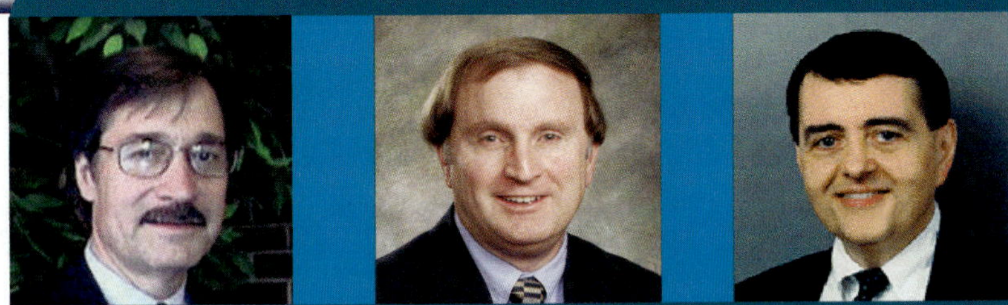

> **"I think this is amazing. Author involvement in all aspects of the text materials may be the single most important advantage of the Spiceland text over its competitors."**
>
> - Jennifer Gaver, University of Georgia

# STUDENT SUPPLEMENTS

## STUDY GUIDE

*Volume 1: ISBN-13: 9780073130354 (ISBN-10: 0073130354)*
*Volume 2: ISBN-13: 9780073130361 (ISBN-10: 0073130362)*

The Study Guide, written by the text authors, provides chapter summaries, detailed illustrations, and a wide variety of self-study questions, exercises, and multiple-choice problems (with solutions).

## WORKING PAPERS

*ISBN-13: 9780073130330 (ISBN-10: 0073130338)*

Working Papers provide students with formatted templates to aid them in doing homework assignments.

## EXCEL TEMPLATES

Selected end-of-chapter exercises and problems, marked in the text with an icon, can be solved using these Microsoft Excel templates, located on the OLC.

## UNDERSTANDING CORPORATE ANNUAL REPORTS

Sixth Edition, by William R. Pasewark

*ISBN-13: 9780073101811 (ISBN-10: 0073101818)*

This project provides students with instruction for obtaining an annual report from a publicly traded corporation and for making an industry or competitor comparison.

## ALTERNATE EXERCISES AND PROBLEMS

This online manual includes additional exercises and problems for each chapter in the text. Available on the OLC.

## COACH

This step-by-step, tutorial software is available on the OLC and integrated throughout the text to help students better understand intermediate accounting topics.

## PRACTICE SETS:

Grady Wholesale Practice Set: Review of the Accounting Cycle
*Instructor ISBN-13: 9780073130217 (ISBN-10: 0073130214)*
*Student ISBN-13: 9780073130194 (ISBN-10: 0073130192)*

Granite Bay Jet Ski Inc., Level 1
*Instructor ISBN 9780072947663 (ISBN-10: 0072947667)*
*Student ISBN 9780072957891 (ISBN-10: 0072957891)*

Granite Bay Jet Ski Inc., Level 2
*Instructor ISBN 9780073045184 (ISBN-10: 0073045187)*
*Student ISBN 9780073080161 (ISBN-10: 0073080160)*

# Acknowledgments


## Fourth Edition Reviewers

**Charlene Abendroth,** *California State University, Hayward*
**Marie Archambault,** *Marshall University*
**Peter Aghimien,** *Indiana University-South Bend*
**Tony Amoruso,** *West Virginia University*
**James Anderson,** *St. Cloud Tech College*
**Matt Anderson,** *Michigan State University*
**Florence Atiase,** *University of Texas at Austin*
**Craig Bain,** *Northern Arizona University*
**James Bannister,** *University of Hartford*
**Katherine Barker,** *Lander University*
**Homer Bates,** *University of North Florida*
**Daniel Bayak,** *Lehigh University*
**Jan Bell,** *California State University, Northridge*
**Whit Broome,** *University of Virginia-Charlottesville*
**Kevin Brown,** *Drexel University*
**John Brozovsky,** *Virginia Tech*
**Eddy Burks,** *Athens State University*
**Ronald Campbell,** *North Carolina A&T University*
**Al Case,** *Southern Oregon University*
**Joan Cezair,** *Fayetteville State University*
**Nandini Chandar,** *Rutgers University*
**Gyan Chandra,** *Miami University, Oxford, Ohio**
**Otto Chang,** *California State University, Santa Barbara*
**Kim Charland,** *Kansas State University*
**Betty Chavis,** *California State University, Fullerton*
**Alan Cherry,** *Loyola Marymount University*
**Steve Christian,** *Jackson Community College*
**Bryan Church,** *Georgia Institute of Technology*
**Marilyn G. Ciolino,** *Delgado Community College*
**Lynn Clements,** *Florida Southern College*
**Bob Cluskey,** *State University of West Georgia*
**Christie L. Comunale,** *Long Island University-C.W. Post Campus*
**Betty Conner,** *University of Colorado at Denver*
**Ellen Cook,** *U of Louisiana at Lafayette*
**Araya Debessay,** *University of Delaware*
**Marinus Debruine,** *Grand Valley State University*
**Larry Deppe,** *Weber State University*
**Judi Doing,** *University of Arizona*
**Orapin Duangploy,** *University of Houston Downtown*
**Wendy Duffy,** *Illinois State University*
**Tim Eaton,** *Marquette University*
**Jerry Engeholm,** *Pace University*
**Kathleen Fitzpatrick,** *University of Toledo Community Tech College*
**Sandra Fleak,** *Truman State University*
**Dick Fleischman,** *John Carroll University*
**Karen Foust,** *Tulane University*
**Clyde Galbraith,** *West Chester University of Pennsylvania*
**Susan Galbreath,** *David Lipscomb University*
**John Garlick,** *Fayetteville State University*
**Jennifer Gaver,** *University of Georgia*
**Nashwa George,** *Montclair State University*
**John Gillett,** *Bradley University*
**Sid Glandon,** *University of Texas at El Paso*
**Geoffrey Goldsmith,** *Belhaven College*
**Janet Greenlee,** *University of Dayton*
**Robert Gruber,** *University of Wisconsin-Whitewater*
**Amy Haas,** *Kingsborough Community College*
**Seth Hammer,** *Towson University*
**Coby Harmon,** *University of California, Santa Barbara*
**Charles Harter,** *North Dakota State University-Fargo*
**Robert Hatanaka,** *University of Hawaii at Manoa*
**Roger Hehman,** *University of Cincinnati-Blue Ash*
**Lyle Hicks,** *Danville Area Community College*
**Steve Hunt,** *Western Illinois University*
**Eliot Kamlet,** *Binghamton University*
**Ronald Kilgore,** *University of Tennessee-Martin*
**Chula King,** *University of West Florida*
**Gordon Klein,** *University of California Los Angeles*
**Larry Klein,** *Bentley College*
**David Knight,** *Boro of Manhattan Community College*
**Mary-Jo Kranacher,** *York College, CUNY*
**Jerry Krueze,** *Western Michigan University**

**As you know if you've read this far, Intermediate Accounting would not be what it is without the passionate feedback of our colleagues. Through your time and effort, we were able to create a learning system that truly responds to the needs of the market, and for that, we sincerely thank each of you.**

**Linda Kuechler,** *Daemen College*
**Tara Laken,** *Joliet Junior College*
**Jerry Lehman,** *Madison Area Technical College-Truax*
**Barbara Lippincott,** *University of Tampa*
**Susan Lynn,** *University of Baltimore*
**Mostafa Maksy,** *Northeastern Illinois University*
**Danny Matthews,** *Midwestern State University*
**Kevin McNelis,** *New Mexico State University*
**Wilda Meixner,** *Texas State University-San Marcos*
**Cathy Miller,** *University of Michigan-Flint*
**Bonnie Moe,** *University of Illinois-Springfield*
**Kathy Moffeit,** *State University of West Georgia*
**Jackie Moffitt,** *Louisiana State University*
**Louella Moore,** *Arkansas State University*
**Joe Moran,** *College of DuPage*
**Joe Morris,** *Southeastern Louisiana University*
**Barbara Muller,** *Arizona State University-West*
**Emeka Ofobike,** *University of Akron*
**Steven Onaitis,** *University of Pittsburgh-Pittsburgh*
**Janet C. Papiernik,** *Indiana University Purdue University Fort Wayne*
**Patricia Parker,** *Columbus State Community College*
**Sy Pearlman,** *California State University-Long Beach*
**Gary Pieroni,** *University of California Berkeley*
**Joanne Pinto,** *Montclair State University*
**Marion Posey,** *Pace University*
**Mike Prockton,** *Finger Lakes Community College*
**Judy Ramage,** *Christian Bros University*
**Donald Raux,** *Siena College*
**Sara Reiter,** *SUNY-Bingham*
**Randall Rentfro,** *Florida Atlantic University-Fort Lauderdale*
**David Roberts,** *Texas A & M University International*
**Luther Ross,** *Central Piedmont Community College*
**Eric Rothenburg,** *Kingsborough Community College*
**Marc Rubin,** *Miami University, Oxford, Ohio*
**John Rude,** *Bloomsburg University of Pennsylvania*
**Robert W. Rutledge,** *Texas State University*
**Maria Sanchez,** *Rider University*
**Angela Sandberg,** *Jacksonville State University*
**Alex Sannella,** *Rutgers University-Newark*
**Stanley Sauber,** *Brooklyn College*
**Gary Schader,** *Kean University*
**Carol G. Schaver,** *Louisiana Tech University*
**Paul Schloemer,** *Ashland University*
**Barbara Scofield,** *University of Texas Permian Basin*
**Jerry Scott,** *Ivy Tech State College*
**Michael Serif,** *Dowling College*
**Rebecca Shortridge,** *Ball State University*
**Kathy Simons,** *Bryant College*
**Lorraine Stern,** *York College, CUNY*
**Doug Stevens,** *Syracuse University*
**Janice Stoudemire,** *Midlands Technical College*
**Lynn Suberly,** *Valdosta State University**
**John Surdick,** *Xavier University*
**Debbie Tanju,** *University of Alabama at Birmingham*
**Peter Theuri,** *Northern Kentucky University*
**Ron Tilden,** *University of Washington, Bothell*
**Michael Toerner,** *Southern University-Baton Rouge*
**Michael Trebesh,** *Alma College*
**Richard A. Turpen,** *U of Alabama at Birmingham*
**Michael Tyler,** *Barry University*
**Irwin Uhr,** *Hunter College*
**Frank Urbancic,** *University of Southern Alabama*
**Herbert Vessel,** *Southern University-Baton Rouge*
**James Voss,** *Pennsylvania State Behrend-Erie*
**Larry Walther,** *University of Texas-Arlington**
**Weiman Wang,** *Tulane University*
**Scott White,** *Lindenwood University*
**Gloria Worthy,** *Southwest Tennessee Community College-Macon Campus*
**Suzanne Wright,** *Pennsylvania State University-University Park*
**Robert Wyatt,** *Drury University*
**Thomas Yandow,** *Norwich University*
**George Young,** *Florida Atlantic University-Fort Lauderdale*
**Kay Zekany,** *Ohio Northern University*
**Mary Zenner,** *College of Lake County*

* Completed in-depth review of Testbank

# Acknowledgments

## Fourth Edition Reviewers' Conference Attendees

**Reviewers' conferences give our authors a valuable opportunity to interact with textbook users face to face, hearing firsthand their successes and difficulties in the classroom. That feedback was particularly valuable in crafting the fourth edition of *Intermediate Accounting,* and the Spiceland team extends special thanks to all those who participated:**

**Tony Amoruso,** *West Virginia University*

**Matt Anderson,** *Michigan State University*

**James Bannister,** *University of Hartford*

**Kevin Brown,** *Drexel University*

**Gyan Chandra,** *Miami University, Oxford, Ohio*

**Araya Debessay,** *University of Delaware*

**Jerry Engeholm,** *Pace University*

**Sandra Fleak,** *Truman State University*

**Clyde Galbraith,** *West Chester University of Pennsylvania*

**Janet Greenlee,** *University of Dayton*

**Amy Haas,** *Kingsborough Community College*

**David Knight,** *Boro of Manhattan Community College*

**Mary-Jo Kranacher,** *York College, CUNY*

**Jackie Moffitt,** *Louisiana State University*

**Emeka Ofobike,** *University of Akron*

**Stephen Onaitis,** *University of Pittsburgh*

**Marion Posey,** *Pace University*

**Randall Rentfro,** *Florida Atlantic University-Fort Lauderdale*

**Eric Rothenburg,** *Kingsborough Community College*

**John Rude,** *Bloomsburg University of Pennsylvania*

**Maria Sanchez,** *Rider University*

**Gary Schader,** *Kean University*

**Paul Schloemer,** *Ashland University*

**Lorraine Stern,** *York College, CUNY*

**Doug Stevens,** *Syracuse University*

**Lynn Suberly,** *Valdosta State University*

**John Surdick,** *Xavier University*

**Peter Theuri,** *Northern Kentucky University*

**Irwin Uhr,** *Hunter College*

**George Young,** *Florida Atlantic University-Fort Lauderdale*

## Previous Edition Reviewers and Focus Group Attendees

**The Spiceland team also extends sincere thanks to the reviewers of our previous editions, without whose input we could not have made *Intermediate Accounting* the extraordinary success it has been.**

**Noel D. Addy, Jr.,** *Mississippi State University*

**Elsie Ameen,** *Sam Houston State University†*

**Anthony J. Amoruso,** *Virginia Tech*

**Matthew J. Anderson,** *Michigan State University†*

**Joseph N. Antenucci,** *Youngstown State University*

**Marie Archambault,** *Marshall University*

**Florence Atiase,** *University of Texas at Austin*

**Paul Bahnson,** *Boise State University†*

**Jane Baldwin,** *Baylor University*

**Anne Beatty,** *Pennsylvania State University*

**Daisy Beck,** *Louisiana State University at Baton Rouge†*

**Bruce Billings,** *Florida State University*

**Thomas Black,** *San Jose State University†*

**Robert Bloom,** *John Carroll University*

**L. Charles Bokemeier,** *Michigan State University*

**Laura D. Bolding,** *University of Texas at Dallas*

**Joseph F. Brazel III,** *Drexel University*

**Nat R. Briscoe,** *Northwestern State University†*

**Richard C. Brooks,** *West Virginia University*

**Helen Brubeck,** *San Jose State University*

**Lisa Bryant,** *The Ohio State University*

**Michael H. Brown,** *Abilene Christian University*

**Philip G. Buchanan,** *George Mason University*

**Maria Bullen,** *Georgia State University†*

**Albert R. Bundons,** *Johnson County Community College*

**Howard Bunsis,** *Eastern Michigan University*

**David Burgstahler,** *University of Washington*

**Suzanne Busch,** *California State University, Hayward†*

**Jane E. Campbell,** *Kennesaw State University*

**Nandini Chandar,** *Rutgers University*

**Raymond Chen,** *California State University, Northridge*

**Alan Cherry,** *Loyola Marymount University†*

**James Chiu,** *California State University, Northridge*

**Kwang-Hyun Chung,** *Pace University*

**Anna Cianci,** *University of Florida*

**Myrtle W. Clark,** *University of Kentucky*

**Stan Clark,** *University of Southern Mississippi*

**Janice Cobb,** *Texas Christian University*

**Karen M. Collins,** *Lehigh University*

**Elizabeth Conner,** *University of Colorado at Denver*

**Edward J. Conrad,** *University of Akron*

**Richard Cross,** *Bentley College*

**Ronald J. Daigle,** *Texas Tech University*

**David B. Davidson,** *California State University at Long Beach*

**Denise de la Rosa,** *Central Connecticut State University*

**Marinus DeBruine,** *Grand Valley State University*

**Lee Dexter,** *Minnesota State University at Moorhead*

**Orapin Duangploy,** *University of Houston-Downtown†*

**Joanne Duke,** *San Francisco State University†*

**Andrea Drake,** *University of Cincinnati*

**David Eichelberger,** *Austin Peay State University*

**Susan W. Eldridge,** *University of Texas at Austin*

**Richard Elmendorf,** *Metropolitan State College of Denver*

**Richard Fern,** *Eastern Kentucky University†*

**Daniel J. Flaherty,** *Southwest Texas State University*

**Richard K. Fleischman, Jr.,** *John Carroll University*

**Mary M. Fleming,** *California State University at Fullerton*

**Albert H. Frakes,** *Washington State University*

**Diana Franz,** *University of Toledo*

**Laurel Franzen,** *University of Texas at Dallas†*

**Robert N. Freeman,** *University of Texas at Austin*

**Lucille Genduso,** *Nova Southeastern University*

**Tae Ghil Ryu,** *Metropolitan State College of Denver*

**Sid Glandon,** *University of Texas at El Paso†*

**Janet L. Grange,** *Chicago State University*

**Sharron M. Graves,** *Stephen F. Austin State University*

**Wayne R. Guay,** *University of Pennsylvania*

**Daryl Guffey,** *Clemson University†*

**Abo Habib,** *Minnesota State University at Mankato*

**Marcia L. Halvorsen,** *University of Cincinnati*

**John G. Hamer,** *University of Massachusetts at Lowell*

**Coby J. Harmon,** *University of California at Santa Barbara*

**Donald R. Herrmann,** *Oregon State University*

**Hassan Hetzi,** *California State Polytechnic University at Pomona†*

**Julia Higgs,** *Florida Atlantic University†*

**Inam Hussain,** *Purdue University*

**Constance M. Hylton,** *George Mason University*

**Marianne L. James,** *California State University, Los Angeles*

**Jefferson P. Jones,** *Auburn University†*

**J. Edward Ketz**, *Pennsylvania State University*
**Kwangok Kim**, *University of Southern Indiana*
**Jerry G. Kreuze**, *Western Michigan University*
**Kenneth Lambert**, *University of Memphis*
**Ellen L. Landgraf**, *Loyola University at Chicago*
**E. John Larsen**, *University of Southern California*
**Doug Laufer**, *Metropolitan State College of Denver*
**Dave Law**, *Youngstown State University*
**Patsy L. Lee**, *University of Texas at Arlington*
**Wallace Leese**, *California State University at Chico†*
**Craig Lefanowicz**, *Michigan State University*
**Charles Leflar**, *University of Arkansas*
**Joseph Legoria**, *Mississippi State University†*
**Barbara Lippincott**, *University of South Florida†*
**Chao-Shin Liu**, *University of Notre Dame*
**Carolyn L. Lousteau**, *University of New Orleans†*
**Heidemarie Lundblad**, *California State University, Northridge*
**Gary A. Luoma**, *University of South Carolina†*
**Marc Massoud**, *Claremont McKenna†*
**Ralph J. McQuade**, *Bentley College*
**Wilda F. Meixner**, *Southwest Texas State University*
**Robert S. Milbrath**, *University of Houston†*
**John R. Mills**, *University of Nevada at Reno*
**George S. Minmier**, *University of Memphis*
**Jacquelyn Moffitt**, *Louisiana State University*
**Louella J. Moore**, *Arkansas State University*
**Kimberly K. Moreno**, *Virginia Tech†*
**Jan Morris**, *University of Houston at Clear Lake*
**Joseph L. Morris**, *Southeastern Louisiana University*
**Paula H. Morris**, *Kennesaw State University†*
**Richard M. Morton**, *Florida State University*
**Charles W. Murphy**, *Bunker Hill Community College*
**John D. Neill III**, *Abilene Christian University†*
**Linda Nichols**, *Texas Tech University†*
**Henry Norton**, *Metropolitan State College of Denver*
**Emeka Ofobike**, *University of Akron*
**Stephen Ostlund**, *Minnesota State University at Moorhead*
**Hong Pak**, *California State Polytechnic University at Pomona*
**William H. Parrott**, *University of South Florida*
**Robert W. Parry, Jr.**, *Indiana University†*
**Kirk Philipich**, *Ohio State University*
**Linda S. Perry**, *Texas A&M University*
**Marlene Plumlee**, *University of Utah*
**Kevin Poirier**, *Johnson and Wales University*
**Mary Ann Prater**, *Clemson University*
**Donald Putnam**, *California Polytechnic University at Pomona*
**Atul Rai**, *Florida State University†*
**Cecily Raiborn**, *Loyola University at New Orleans†*
**K.K. Raman**, *University of North Texas†*
**Randall Rentfro**, *Florida Atlantic University†*
**Vernon J. Richardson**, *University of Kansas*
**Richard A. Riley, Jr.**, *West Virginia University†*
**Paul J. Robertson**, *New Mexico State University*
**Mark Ross**, *Western Kentucky University†*
**Pamela Roush**, *University of Central Florida†*
**Marc Rubin**, *Miami University, Oxford, Ohio*
**John A. Rude**, *Bloomsburg University*
**Clayton Sager**, *University of Wisconsin-Whitewater*
**Maria Sanchez**, *Drexel University*
**Susan W. Scholz**, *University of Kansas*
**Paul Schwinghammer**, *Minnesota State University at Mankato*
**Robert J. Shepherd**, *University of California at Santa Cruz*
**Rebecca Shortridge**, *Ball State University*
**Joel Siegel**, *Queens College*
**John Sneed**, *University of Nebraska at Kearney*
**Will Snyder**, *San Diego State University†*
**Julie S. Sobery**, *Southern Illinois University at Carbondale*
**Vic Stanton**, *California State University, Hayward*
**Ronald Stone**, *California State University Northridge†*
**Janice Stoudemire**, *Midlands Technical College*
**William D. Stout**, *University of Louisville†*
**Charles Bruce Swindle**, *McNesse State University†*
**Paulette R. Tandy**, *University of Nevada at Las Vegas†*
**Diane Tanner**, *University of North Florida†*
**Gary K. Taylor**, *University of Alabama†*
**Peter Theuri**, *Northern Kentucky University†*
**Wayne Thomas**, *University of Oklahoma*
**Richard Townsend**, *University of Tennessee*
**Shobha Venkataraman**, *Drexel University*
**Larry Walther**, *University of Texas at Arlington*
**Bruce Wampler**, *University of Louisiana at Monroe†*
**Weiman Wang**, *Tulane University†*
**Andrea B. Weickgenannt**, *Northern Kentucky University*
**Thomas R. Weirich**, *Central Michigan University*
**Mike S. Wilkins**, *Texas A&M University*
**Arlette Wilson**, *Auburn University*
**Joni Young**, *University of New Mexico*

# We Are Grateful

We would like to acknowledge the following individuals: Maurice Hirsch, Jr., Southern Illinois University, James A. Schweikart, Rhode Island College, Mary E. Harston, St. Mary's University, Timothy J. Louwers, Louisiana State University, and Williams R. Pasewark, Texas Technological University, for assistance creating the Case Implementation Manual; Jon A. Booker and Charles W. Caldwell of Tennessee Technological University and Susan C. Galbreath of David Lipscomb University for crafting the PowerPoint Slides; and Jack E. Terry, ComSource Associates, for developing the Excel Templates.

Alice Sineath, Forsyth Community College and Marc Giullian, Montana State University-Bozeman made significant contributions to the accuracy of the text, end-of-chapter material, and solutions manual. In addition, we appreciate the help and guidance received from Tim Doupnik, University of South Carolina, for his contribution to the Global Perspective Boxes, and Tim Doupnik and Gary Meek, Oklahoma State University, for the direction provided on the Global Marketplace section in Chapter 1. Thank you, also, to Jim Lynch, partner, KPMG, for help with the new FASB standards.

We are most grateful for the talented assistance and support from the many people at McGraw-Hill/Irwin. We would particularly like to thank Brent Gordon, editorial director; Stewart Mattson, publisher; Tim Vertovec, executive editor; Heather Nagrocki, developmental editor; Melissa Larmon, marketing manager; Greg Patterson, regional sales manager; Elizabeth Mavetz, media technology producer; Pat Frederickson, lead project manager; Rose Hepburn, senior production supervisor; Keith McPherson, director of design; Adam Rooke, senior designer; Jeremy Cheshareck, photo research coordinator; Carol Loreth, senior supplement producer; Joyce Chappetto, media project manager; Judy Besser, administrative assistant; Dan Wiencek, senior copywriter; and Erwin Llereza, senior advertising designer.

Finally, we extend our thanks to Kaplan CPA Review for their assistance developing simulations for our inclusion in the end-of-chapter material, as well as FedEx Corporation for allowing us to use its Annual Report in Appendix B and throughout the text. We also acknowledge permission from the AICPA to adapt material from the Uniform CPA Examination, the IMA for permission to adapt material from the CMA Examination, and Dow Jones & Co., Inc. for permission to excerpt material from *The Wall Street Journal.*

David Spiceland Jim Sepe Larry Tomassini

† Previous Edition Focus Group Attendee

# Contents in Brief

# Contents

1 SECTION

## The Role of Accounting as an Information System

### 1 CHAPTER Environment and Theoretical Structure of Financial Accounting

### 2 CHAPTER Review of the Accounting Process

# 3 CHAPTER The Balance Sheet and Financial Disclosures

# 4 CHAPTER The Income Statement and Statement of Cash Flows

# 5 CHAPTER Income Measurement and Profitability Analysis

# 6 CHAPTER Time Value of Money Concepts



# 2 SECTION Economic Resources

# 7 CHAPTER Cash and Receivables

# 8 CHAPTER Inventories: Measurement

## 9 CHAPTER Inventories: Additional Issues

## 10 CHAPTER Operational Assets: Acquisition and Disposition

## 11 CHAPTER Operational Assets: Utilization and Impairment

# 3 SECTION Financial Instruments and Liabilities

## 12 CHAPTER Investments

## 13 CHAPTER Current Liabilities and Contingencies

# 14 CHAPTER Bonds and Long-Term Notes

# 15 CHAPTER Leases

## 16 CHAPTER Accounting for Income Taxes

## 17 CHAPTER Pensions and Other Postretirement Benefits

## 18 CHAPTER Shareholders' Equity



# 4 SECTION Additional Financial Reporting Issues

## 19 CHAPTER Share-Based Compensation and Earnings Per Share

## 20 CHAPTER Accounting Changes and Error Corrections

## 21 CHAPTER The Statement of Cash Flows Revisited

# Intermediate Accounting

# The Role of Accounting as an Information System

1

SECTION

# 1 CHAPTER

# Environment and Theoretical Structure of Financial Accounting

## OVERVIEW

The primary function of financial accounting is to provide relevant and reliable financial information to users external to the business enterprise. The focus of financial accounting is on the information needs of investors and creditors. These users make critical resource allocation decisions that affect the nation's economy. The primary means of conveying financial information to external users is through financial statements and related notes.

In this chapter you explore important topics such as the FASB's conceptual framework that serve as a foundation for a more detailed study of financial statements, the way the statement elements are measured, and the concepts underlying these measurements and related disclosures.

## LEARNING OBJECTIVES

**After studying this chapter, you should be able to:**

- LO1 Describe the function and primary focus of financial accounting.
- LO2 Explain the difference between cash and accrual accounting.
- LO3 Define generally accepted accounting principles (GAAP) and discuss the historical development of accounting standards.
- LO4 Explain why the establishment of accounting standards is characterized as a political process.
- LO5 Explain the purpose of the FASB's conceptual framework.
- LO6 Identify the objectives of financial reporting, the qualitative characteristics of accounting information, and the elements of financial statements.
- LO7 Describe the four basic assumptions underlying GAAP.
- LO8 Describe the four broad accounting principles that guide accounting practice.

# FINANCIAL REPORTING CASE

## Misguided Marketing Major

During a class break in your investments class, a marketing major tells the following story to you and some friends:

The chief financial officer of a large company is interviewing three candidates for the top accounting position with his firm. He asks each the same question:

| | |
|---|---|
| *CFO:* | What is two plus two? |
| *First candidate:* | Four. |
| *CFO:* | What is two plus two? |
| *Second candidate:* | Four. |
| *CFO:* | What is two plus two? |
| *Third candidate:* | What would you like it to be? |
| *CFO:* | You're hired. |

After you take some good-natured ribbing from the nonaccounting majors, your friend says, "Seriously, though, there must be ways the accounting profession prevents that kind of behavior. Aren't there some laws, or rules, or something? Are they based on some sort of theory, or are they just arbitrary?"

**By the time you finish this chapter, you should be able to respond appropriately to the questions posed in this case. Compare your response to the solution provided at the end of the chapter.**

### QUESTIONS

1. What should you tell your friend about the presence of accounting standards in the United States? Who has the authority for standard setting? Who has the responsibility? (page 9)
2. What is the economic and political environment in which standard setting occurs? (page 12)
3. What is the relationship among management, auditors, investors, and creditors that tends to preclude the "What would you like it to be?" attitude? (page 15)
4. In general, what is the conceptual framework that underlies accounting principles? (page 18)

# PART A FINANCIAL ACCOUNTING ENVIRONMENT

Have you ever received a C grade on a paper and thought you deserved better? In 1965 Fred Smith did. His term paper for an economics class proposed a revolutionary air freight delivery method that revolved around a "hub and spokes" system. The hub would be located in a middle-America location (Memphis was eventually chosen) with spokes radiating out to cities across the country. A package from Los Angeles, destined for New York, would be flown in on the Los Angeles spoke in a few hours to the hub location in Memphis. There it would be sorted and routed out on the return flight of the plane that had just brought in shipments from New York, arriving before dawn. Los Angeles to New York overnight!

"The concept is interesting and well formed, but in order to earn better than a 'C,' the idea must be feasible." —quote from a Yale University professor in response to Federal Express founder Fred Smith's paper proposing reliable overnight delivery service.

**FedEx Corporation**

Fred Smith had so much confidence in his idea that in 1971 he created a company called **Federal Express**. On April 17, 1973, when operations officially began, the company served 25 cities and delivered 186 packages. The company struggled at first, and it wasn't until three years later that it reported its first profit of $3.6 million. A quarter of a century later, Federal Express Corporation's annual profit exceeded $580 million and annual revenue topped $19 billion. Average package volume reached approximately 3.2 million daily worldwide.[1]

Many factors contributed to the success of Federal Express. The company's founder was visionary in terms of his package delivery system. The hub and spokes concept is now used throughout the air freight industry. A key factor contributing to the growth and success of Federal Express was its access to external capital (resources). At various times in the company's brief history, the ability to raise external capital from investors and creditors was critical to its phenomenal growth. For example, several bank loans provided financing in the early years, and in 1978, an initial public offering of the company's stock provided over $17 million in equity financing.

**Investors and creditors use information to assess risk and return.**

Investors and creditors use many different kinds of information before supplying capital to business enterprises like Federal Express. The information is used to assess the future risk and return of their potential investments in the enterprise.[2] For example, information about the enterprise's products and its management is of vital importance to this assessment. In addition, various kinds of financial information are extremely important to investors and creditors.

● LO1

**The primary focus of *financial accounting* is on the information needs of investors and creditors.**

You might think of accounting as a special "language" used to communicate financial information about a business to those who wish to use the information to make decisions. **Financial accounting,** in particular, is concerned with providing relevant financial information to various *external* users. The chart in Graphic 1–1 illustrates a number of financial information supplier groups as well as several external user groups. Of these groups, the primary focus of financial accounting is on the financial information provided by *profit-oriented companies to their present and potential investors and creditors.* The reason for this focus is discussed in a later section of this chapter. One external user group, often referred to as *financial intermediaries,* includes financial analysts, stockbrokers, mutual fund managers, and credit rating organizations. These users provide advice to investors and creditors and/or make investment-credit decisions on their behalf. The collapse of **Enron Corporation** in 2001 and other high profile accounting failures made immensely clear the importance of reporting reliable financial information.

On the other hand, **managerial accounting** deals with the concepts and methods used to provide information to an organization's *internal* users, that is, its managers. You study managerial accounting elsewhere in your curriculum.

---

[1]Vance Trimble, *Overnight Success* (New York: Crown Publishers, Inc., 1993).

[2]Risk refers to the variability of possible outcomes from an investment. Return is the amount received over and above the investment and usually is expressed as a percentage.

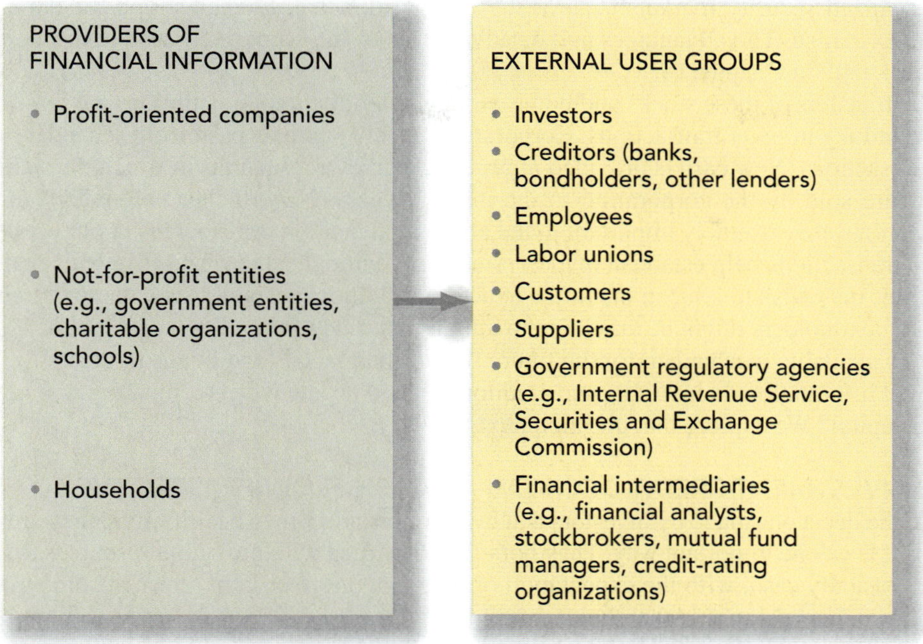


**GRAPHIC 1–1**
Financial Information Supplier Groups and External User Groups

**Financial statements convey financial information to external users.**

The primary means of conveying financial information to investors, creditors, and other external users is through financial statements and related disclosure notes. The financial statements most frequently provided are (1) the balance sheet or statement of financial position, (2) the income statement or statement of operations, (3) the statement of cash flows, and (4) the statement of shareholders' equity. As you progress through this text, you will review and expand your knowledge of the information in these financial statements, the way the elements in these statements are measured, and the concepts underlying these measurements and related disclosures. We use the term **financial reporting** to refer to the process of providing this information to external users. Keep in mind, though, that external users receive important financial information in a variety of other formats as well, including news releases and management forecasts, prospectuses, reports filed with regulatory agencies, and the president's letter.

**FedEx Corporation**

Appendix B located at the back of this text contains recent financial statements, including related disclosure notes, for **FedEx Corporation**, now the parent company of Federal Express. We occasionally refer to the FedEx financial statements to illustrate certain points. You also can refer to these statements as new topics are introduced in later chapters.

## The Economic Environment and Financial Reporting

**The *capital markets* provide a mechanism to help our economy allocate resources efficiently.**

In the United States, we have a highly developed free-enterprise economy with the majority of productive resources privately owned rather than government owned. It's important in this type of system that a mechanism exists to allocate the scarce resources of our society, both natural resources and labor, in an efficient manner. Resources should be allocated to private enterprises that will use them best to provide goods and services desired by society and not to enterprises that will waste them. The mechanisms that foster this efficient allocation of resources are the **capital markets.** We can think of the capital markets simply as a composite of all investors and creditors.

***Corporations* acquire capital from investors in exchange for ownership interest and from creditors by borrowing.**

The three primary forms of business organization are the sole proprietorship, the partnership, and the corporation. In the United States, sole proprietorships and partnerships outnumber corporations. However, the dominant form of business organization, in terms of the ownership of productive resources, is the **corporation.** The corporate form makes it easier for an enterprise to acquire resources through the capital markets. Investors provide resources, usually cash, to a corporation in exchange for evidence of ownership interest, that is, shares of stock. Creditors such as banks lend cash to the corporation. Also, creditors can lend the corporation cash through the medium of bonds. Stocks and bonds usually are traded on organized security markets such as the New York Stock Exchange and the American Stock Exchange. The advantages and disadvantages of the corporate form are discussed at greater length in Chapter 18.

**Secondary market transactions provide for the transfer of stocks and bonds among individuals and institutions.**

The transfers of these stocks and bonds among individuals and institutions are referred to as **secondary market** transactions. Corporations receive no new cash from secondary market transactions. New cash is provided in *primary* market transactions in which the shares or bonds are sold by the corporation to the initial owners. Nevertheless, secondary market transactions are extremely important to the efficient allocation of resources in our economy. These transactions help establish market prices for additional shares and for bonds that corporations may wish to issue in the future to acquire additional capital. Also, many shareholders and bondholders might be unwilling to initially provide resources to corporations if there were no available mechanism for the future sale of their stocks and bonds to others.

What information do investors and creditors need to decide which companies will be provided capital? We explore that question next.

## THE INVESTMENT-CREDIT DECISION—A CASH FLOW PERSPECTIVE

**Investors and creditors both are interested in earning a fair return on the resources provided.**

While the decisions made by investors and by creditors are somewhat different, they are similar in at least one important way. They both are concerned with providing resources to companies, usually cash, with the expectation of receiving more cash in return at some time in the future. A corporation's shareholders will receive cash from their investment through the ultimate sale of the ownership shares of stock. In addition, many corporations distribute cash to their shareholders in the form of periodic dividends. For example, if an investor provides a company with \$10,000 cash (that is, purchases ownership shares) at the end of 2005, receives \$400 in dividends from the company during 2006, and sells the ownership interest (shares) at the end of 2006 for \$10,600 (\$600 share price appreciation), the investment would have generated a **rate of return** of 10% for 2006, calculated as follows:

$$\frac{\$400 \text{ dividends} + \$600 \text{ share price appreciation}}{\$10{,}000 \text{ initial investment}} = 10\%$$

**The expected *rate of return* and uncertainty, or risk, of that return are key variables in the investment decision.**

Investors always are faced with more than one investment opportunity. There are many factors to consider before one of these opportunities is chosen. Two extremely important variables are the *expected rate of return* from each investment option, and the *uncertainty,* or *risk,* of that expected return. For example, consider the following two investment options:

1. Invest \$10,000 in a savings account insured by the U.S. government that will generate a 5% rate of return.
2. Invest \$10,000 in a profit-oriented company.

While the rate of return from option 1 is known with virtual certainty, the return from option 2 is uncertain. The amount and timing of the cash to be received in the future from option 2 are unknown. Investors require information about the company that will help them estimate the unknown return.

**A company will be able to provide a return to investors and creditors only if it can generate a profit from selling its products or services.**

In the long run, a company will be able to provide investors with a return only if it can generate a profit. That is, it must be able to use the resources provided by investors and creditors to generate cash receipts from selling a product or service that exceed the cash disbursements necessary to provide that product or service. If this excess can be generated, the marketplace is implicitly saying that society's resources have been efficiently allocated. The marketplace is assigning a value to the product or service that exceeds the value assigned to the resources used to produce that product or service.

**The objective of financial accounting is to provide investors and creditors with useful information for decision making.**

In summary, the primary objective of financial accounting is to provide investors and creditors with information that will help them make investment and credit decisions. More specifically, the information should help investors and creditors evaluate the *amounts, timing,* and *uncertainty* of the enterprise's future cash receipts and disbursements. The better this information is, the more efficient will be investor and creditor resource allocation decisions. Financial accounting, in providing key elements of the information set used by capital market participants, plays a vital societal role in the resource allocation process. The importance of this role to society explains why the primary focus of financial accounting is on the information needs of investors and creditors.

The Financial Accounting Standards Board, the current private sector body responsible for setting accounting standards in the United States, has published a conceptual framework for financial reporting (discussed later in this chapter). The first concept statement of the framework describes the specific objectives of external financial reporting. These objectives affirm the importance of the cash flow information needs of investors and creditors.

Throughout this text, you will be reminded of this cash flow perspective. For example, Chapter 4 describes certain events that are reported separately in the income statement due to the fact that these historical events have implications for future cash flows that are different from the normal operating activities. Separation of these events from normal operating activities provides financial statement users with information to more easily predict an enterprise's future cash flows.

## CASH VERSUS ACCRUAL ACCOUNTING

LO2

Even though predicting future cash flows is the primary objective, the model best able to achieve that objective is the **accrual accounting** model. A competing model is **cash basis accounting.** Each model produces a periodic measure of performance that could be used by investors and creditors for predicting future cash flows.

**Cash Basis Accounting.** Cash basis accounting produces a measure called **net operating cash flow.** This measure is the difference between cash receipts and cash disbursements during a reporting period from transactions related to providing goods and services to customers.

***Net operating cash flow** is the difference between cash receipts and cash disbursements from providing goods and services.*

Net operating cash flow is very easy to understand and all information required to measure it is factual. Also, it certainly relates to a variable of critical interest to investors and creditors. What could be better in helping to predict future cash flows from selling products and services than current cash flows from these activities? Remember, a company will be able to provide a return to investors and creditors only if it can use the capital provided to generate a positive net operating cash flow. However, there is a major drawback to using the current period's operating cash flow to predict future operating cash flows. Over the life of the company, net operating cash flow definitely is the variable of concern. However, over short periods of time, *operating cash flows may not be indicative of the company's long-run cash-generating ability* (that is, its ability to generate positive net operating cash flows in the future).

To demonstrate this, consider the following example. In Illustration 1–1 net operating cash flows are determined for the Carter Company during its first three years of operations.

Over the three-year period, Carter generated a positive net operating cash flow of $60,000. At the end of this three-year period, Carter has no outstanding debts. Because total sales and cash receipts over the three-year period were each $300,000, nothing is owed to Carter by customers. Also, at the beginning of the first year, Carter prepaid $60,000 for three years' rent on the facilities. There are no uncompleted transactions at the end of the three-year period. In that sense, we can view this three-year period as a micro version of the entire life of a company.

| | Year 1 | Year 2 | Year 3 | Total |
|---|---|---|---|---|
| Sales (on credit) | $100,000 | $100,000 | $100,000 | $300,000 |
| **Net Operating Cash Flows** | | | | |
| Cash receipts from customers | $ 50,000 | $125,000 | $125,000 | $300,000 |
| Cash disbursements: | | | | |
| Prepayment of three years' rent | (60,000) | –0– | –0– | (60,000) |
| Salaries to employees | (50,000) | (50,000) | (50,000) | (150,000) |
| Utilities | (5,000) | (15,000) | (10,000) | (30,000) |
| Net operating cash flow | $ (65,000) | $ 60,000 | $ 65,000 | $ 60,000 |

**ILLUSTRATION 1–1**
Cash Basis Accounting

The company incurred utility costs of $10,000 per year over the period. However, during the first year only $5,000 actually was paid, with the remainder being paid the second year. Employee salary costs of $50,000 were paid in full each year.

**Over short periods of time, operating cash flow may not be an accurate predictor of future operating cash flows.**

Is net operating cash flow for year 1 (negative $65,000) an accurate indicator of future cash-generating ability?[3] Obviously, it is not a good predictor of the positive net cash flows that occur in the next two years. Is the three-year pattern of net operating cash flows indicative of the company's year-by-year performance? No. But, if we measure the same activities by the accrual accounting model, we get a more accurate prediction of future operating cash flows and a more reasonable portrayal of the balanced operating performance of the company over the three years.

***Net income* is the difference between *revenues* and *expenses.***

**Accrual Accounting.** The accrual accounting model measures the entity's accomplishments and resource sacrifices during the period, regardless of when cash is received or paid. The accrual accounting model's measure of periodic accomplishments is called *revenues,* and the periodic measure of resource sacrifices is called *expenses.* The difference between revenues and expenses is *net income,* or net loss if expenses are greater than revenues.[4]

How would we measure revenues and expenses in this very simplistic situation? Illustration 1–2 offers a possible solution.

**ILLUSTRATION 1–2**

Accrual Accounting

**The accrual accounting model provides a measure of periodic performance called *net income,* the difference between revenues and expenses.**

**CARTER COMPANY**
**Income Statements**

| | Year 1 | Year 2 | Year 3 | Total |
|---|---|---|---|---|
| Revenues | $100,000 | $100,000 | $100,000 | $300,000 |
| Expenses: | | | | |
| Rent | 20,000 | 20,000 | 20,000 | 60,000 |
| Salaries | 50,000 | 50,000 | 50,000 | 150,000 |
| Utilities | 10,000 | 10,000 | 10,000 | 30,000 |
| Total expenses | 80,000 | 80,000 | 80,000 | 240,000 |
| Net Income | $ 20,000 | $ 20,000 | $ 20,000 | $ 60,000 |

**Net income is considered a better indicator of future operating cash flows than is current net operating cash flow.**

Net income of $20,000 for year 1 appears to be a reasonable predictor of the company's cash-generating ability as total net operating cash flow for the three-year period is a positive $60,000. Also, compare the three-year pattern of net operating cash flows in Illustration 1–1 to the three-year pattern of net income in Illustration 1–2. The net income pattern is more representative of the steady operating performance over the three-year period.[5]

While this example is somewhat simplistic, it allows us to see the motivation for using the accrual accounting model. Accrual income attempts to measure the accomplishments and sacrifices that occurred during the year, which may not correspond to cash inflows and outflows. For example, revenue for year 1 is the $100,000 in sales. This is a better measure of the company's accomplishments during year 1 than the $50,000 cash collected from customers.

Does this mean that information about cash flows from operating activities is not useful? No. Indeed, when combined with information about cash flows from investing and financing activities, this information provides valuable input into decisions made by investors and creditors. In fact, collectively, this cash flow information constitutes the statement of cash flows—one of the basic financial statements.[6]

---

[3] A negative cash flow is possible only if invested capital (i.e., owners contributed cash to the company in exchange for ownership interest) is sufficient to cover the cash deficiency. Otherwise, the company would have to either raise additional external funds or go bankrupt.

[4] Net income also includes gains and losses, which are discussed later in the chapter.

[5] Empirical evidence that accrual accounting provides a better measure of short-term performance than cash flows is provided by Patricia DeChow, "Accounting Earnings and Cash Flows as Measures of Firm Performance: The Role of Accrual Accounting," *Journal of Accounting and Economics* 18 (1994), pp. 3–42.

[6] The statement of cash flows is discussed in detail in Chapters 4 and 21.

# The Development of Financial Accounting and Reporting Standards

● LO3

**FINANCIAL REPORTING CASE**

Q1, p. 3

Accrual accounting is the financial reporting model used by the majority of profit-oriented companies and by many not-for-profit companies. The fact that companies use the same model is important to financial statement users. Investors and creditors use financial information to make their resource allocation decisions. It's critical that they be able to *compare* financial information among companies. To facilitate these comparisons, financial accounting employs a body of standards known as **generally accepted accounting principles**, often abbreviated as **GAAP** (and pronounced *gap*). GAAP are a dynamic set of both broad and specific guidelines that companies should follow when measuring and reporting the information in their financial statements and related notes. The more important broad principles or standards are discussed in a subsequent section of this chapter and revisited throughout the text in the context of accounting applications for which they provide conceptual support.[7] More specific standards, such as how to measure and report a lease transaction, receive more focused attention in subsequent chapters.

## HISTORICAL PERSPECTIVE AND STANDARDS

Pressures on the accounting profession to establish uniform accounting standards began to surface after the stock market crash of 1929. Some feel that insufficient and misleading financial statement information led to inflated stock prices and that this contributed to the stock market crash and the subsequent depression.

**The *Securities and Exchange Commission (SEC)* was created by Congress with the 1934 Securities Exchange Act.**

The 1933 Securities Act and the 1934 Securities Exchange Act were designed to restore investor confidence. The 1933 act sets forth accounting and disclosure requirements for initial offerings of securities (stocks and bonds). The 1934 act applies to secondary market transactions and mandates reporting requirements for companies whose securities are publicly traded on either organized stock exchanges or in over-the-counter markets.[8] The 1934 act also created the **Securities and Exchange Commission (SEC)**.

**The SEC has the authority to set accounting standards for companies, but has delegated the responsibility to the accounting profession.**

In the 1934 act, *Congress gave the SEC both the power and responsibility for setting accounting and reporting standards for companies whose securities are publicly traded.* However, the SEC, a government appointed body, has delegated the primary responsibility for setting accounting standards to the private sector. It is important to understand that the SEC delegated only the responsibility, not the authority, to set standards. The power still lies with the SEC. If the SEC does not agree with a particular standard issued by the private sector, it can force a change in the standard. In fact, it has done so in the past.

The SEC does issue its own accounting standards in the form of *Financial Reporting Releases (FRRs),* which regulate what must be reported by companies to the SEC itself. These standards usually agree with those previously issued by the private sector. To learn more about the SEC, consult its Internet site at www.sec.gov.[9]

**Early Standard Setting.** The first private sector body to assume the task of setting accounting standards was the **Committee on Accounting Procedure (CAP)**. The CAP was a committee of the **American Institute of Accountants (AIA)**. The AIA, which was renamed the **American Institute of Certified Public Accountants (AICPA)** in 1957, is the national organization of professional public accountants. From 1938 to 1959, the CAP issued 51 *Accounting Research Bulletins (ARBs)* which dealt with specific accounting and reporting problems. No theoretical framework for financial accounting was established. This approach of dealing with individual issues without a framework led to stern criticism of the accounting profession.

**The *Accounting Principles Board (APB)* followed the CAP.**

In 1959 the **Accounting Principles Board (APB)** replaced the CAP. Members of the APB also belonged to the AICPA. The APB operated from 1959 through 1973 and issued 31

[7]The terms *standards* and *principles* sometimes are used interchangeably.

[8]Reporting requirements for SEC registrants include Form 10-K, the annual report form, and Form 10-Q, the report that must be filed for the first three quarters of each fiscal year.

[9]In 2000, the SEC issued regulation FD (Fair Disclosure) which redefined how companies interact with analysts and the public in disclosing material information. Prior to regulation FD, companies often disclosed important information to a select group of analysts before disseminating the information to the general public. Now, this type of selective disclosure is prohibited. The initial disclosure of market-sensitive information must be made available to the general public.

*Accounting Principles Board Opinions (APBOs),* various *Interpretations,* and four *Statements.* The *Opinions* also dealt with specific accounting and reporting problems. Many *ARBs* and *APBOs* have not been superseded and still represent authoritative GAAP.

The APB's main effort to establish a theoretical framework for financial accounting and reporting was *APB Statement No. 4,* "Basic Concepts and Accounting Principles Underlying Financial Statements of Business Enterprises." Unfortunately, the effort was not successful.

The APB was composed of members of the accounting profession and was supported by their professional organization. Members participated in the activities of the board on a voluntary, part-time basis. The APB was criticized by industry and government for its inability to establish an underlying framework for financial accounting and reporting and for its inability to act quickly enough to keep up with financial reporting issues as they developed. Perhaps the most important flaw of the APB was a perceived lack of independence. Composed almost entirely of public accountants, the board was subject to the criticism that the clients of the represented public accounting firms were exerting self-interested pressure on the board and influencing their decisions. Other interest groups were underrepresented in the standard-setting process.

**The *FASB* currently sets accounting standards.**

**Current Standard Setting.** Criticism of the APB led to the creation in 1973 of the **Financial Accounting Standards Board (FASB)** and its supporting structure. The FASB differs from its predecessor in many ways. There are seven full-time members of the FASB, compared to 18–21 part-time members of the APB. While all of the APB members belonged to the AICPA, FASB members represent various constituencies concerned with accounting standards. Members have included representatives from the accounting profession, profit-oriented companies, accounting educators, and government. The APB was supported financially by the AICPA, while the FASB is supported by its parent organization, the **Financial Accounting Foundation (FAF).** The FAF is responsible for selecting the members of the FASB and its Advisory Council, ensuring adequate funding of FASB activities, and exercising general oversight of the FASB's activities.[10] The FASB is, therefore, an independent, private sector body whose members represent a broad constituency of interest groups.[11]

**The *Emerging Issues Task Force (EITF)* identifies financial reporting issues and attempts to resolve them without involving the FASB.**

In 1984, the FASB's **Emerging Issues Task Force (EITF)** was formed to provide more timely responses to emerging financial reporting issues. The EITF membership includes 15 individuals from public accounting and private industry, along with a representative from the FASB and an SEC observer. The membership of the task force is designed to include individuals who are in a position to be aware of emerging financial reporting issues. The task force considers these emerging issues and attempts to reach a consensus on how to account for them. If consensus can be reached, generally no FASB action is required. The task force disseminates its rulings in the form of *EITF Issues.* These pronouncements are considered part of generally accepted accounting principles.

If a consensus can't be reached, FASB involvement may be necessary. The EITF plays an important role in the standard-setting process by identifying potential problem areas and then acting as a filter for the FASB. This speeds up the standard-setting process and allows the FASB to focus on pervasive long-term problems.

**In addition to issuing specific accounting standards, the FASB has formulated a *conceptual framework* to provide an underlying theoretical and conceptual structure for accounting standards.**

One of the FASB's most important activities has been the formulation of a **conceptual framework.** The conceptual framework project, discussed in more depth later in this chapter, deals with theoretical and conceptual issues and provides an underlying structure for current and future accounting and reporting standards. The FASB has issued seven *Statements of Financial Accounting Concepts (SFACs)* to describe its conceptual framework. The board also has issued over 150 specific accounting standards, called *Statements of Financial Accounting Standards (SFASs),* as well as numerous FASB *Interpretations and Technical Bulletins.*[12]

---

[10]The FAF's primary sources of funding are contributions and the sales of the FASB's publications. The FAF is governed by trustees, the majority of whom are appointed from the membership of eight sponsoring organizations. These organizations represent important constituencies involved with the financial reporting process. For example, one of the founding organizations is the Association of Investment Management and Research (formerly known as the Financial Analysts Federation) which represents financial information *users,* and another is the Financial Executives International which represents financial information *preparers.* The FAF also raises funds to support the activities of the Government Accounting Standards Board (GASB).

[11]The FASB organization also includes the **Financial Accounting Standards Advisory Council** (FASAC). The major responsibility of the FASAC is to advise the FASB on the priorities of its projects, including the suitability of new projects that might be added to its agenda.

[12]For more information, go to the FASB's Internet site at www.fasb.org.

**GRAPHIC 1–2**
Accounting Standard Setting

HIERARCHY OF STANDARD-SETTING AUTHORITY

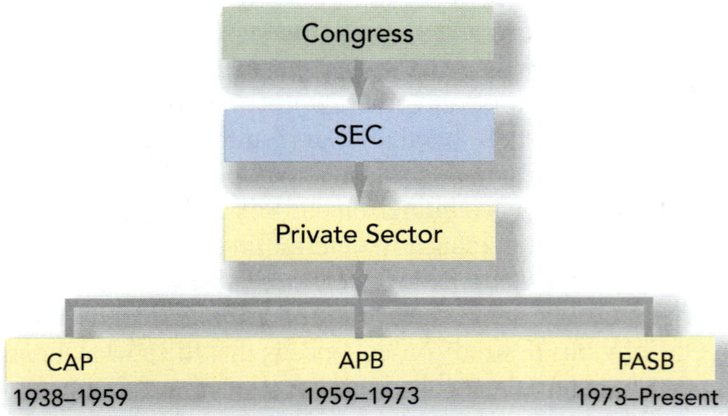


HIERARCHY OF GAAP

**In descending order of authority**

a. AICPA Accounting Research Bulletins and Accounting Principles Board Opinions that are not superseded by action of the FASB, FASB Statements of Financial Standards and Interpretations, FASB Statement 133 Implementation Issues, and FASB Staff Positions (also, SEC rules, interpretive releases, and Staff Accounting Bulletins for SEC registrants).
b. FASB Technical Bulletins and, if cleared by the FASB, AICPA Industry Audit and Accounting Guides and Statements of Position.
c. AICPA Accounting Standards Executive Committee Practice Bulletins that have been cleared by the FASB and consensus positions of the FASB Emerging Issues Task Force.
d. Implementation guides published by the FASB staff, AICPA accounting interpretations, and practices that are widely recognized and prevalent either generally or in the industry.

Graphic 1–2 summarizes this discussion on accounting standards. The top of the graphic shows the sources of accounting standards in order of authority. Congress gave the SEC the responsibility and authority to set accounting standards, specifically for companies whose securities are publicly traded. The SEC has delegated the task to various private sector bodies (currently the FASB) while retaining its legislated authority.

The lower portion of the graphic summarizes the framework for selecting the principles to be used in preparing financial statements in conformity with generally accepted accounting principles. The GAAP hierarchy includes the authoritative pronouncements and interpretations of the SEC, CAP, APB, and FASB, as well as AICPA industry guides, bulletins and interpretations. The FASB recently decided to categorize these various sources in descending order (a through d) of authority. Previously, this formalization of a hierarchy existed only in the auditing literature.[13]

## ADDITIONAL CONSIDERATION

Accounting standards and the standard-setting process discussed above relate to standards governing the measurement and reporting of information for profit-oriented organizations. In 1984, the **Government Accounting Standards Board (GASB)** was created to develop accounting standards for governmental units such as states and cities. The GASB operates under the oversight of the Financial Accounting Foundation and the Governmental Accounting Standards Advisory Council.

[13] The hierarchy presented here is based on an Exposure Draft entitled "The Hierarchy of Generally Accepted Accounting Principles," *Proposed Statement of Financial Accounting Standards,* (Norwalk, Conn.: FASB), April 28, 2005. The Standard was expected to be effective for fiscal periods beginning after September 15, 2005. The FASB's Concept Statements are not included in the hierarchy. They do not constitute GAAP, but provide a structure for evaluating current standards and for issuing new standards.

## THE ESTABLISHMENT OF ACCOUNTING STANDARDS—A POLITICAL PROCESS

● LO4

**FINANCIAL REPORTING CASE**

Q2, p. 3

The setting of accounting and reporting standards often has been characterized as a *political process.* Standards, particularly changes in standards, can have significant differential effects on companies, investors and creditors, and other interest groups. A change in an accounting standard or the introduction of a new standard can result in a substantial redistribution of wealth within our economy.

The role of the FASB in setting accounting standards is a complex one. Sound accounting principles can provide significant guidance in determining the appropriate method to measure and report an economic transaction. However, the FASB must gauge the potential economic consequences of a change in a standard to the various interest groups as well as to society as a whole. One obvious desired consequence is that the new standard will provide a better set of information to external users and thus improve the resource allocation process.

**The FASB must consider potential economic consequences of a change in an accounting standard or the introduction of a new standard.**

An example of possible adverse economic consequences is the issue of accounting for postretirement employee health care benefits. Many corporations guarantee to pay the health care and life insurance costs of their employees after retirement. Traditionally, these companies accounted for these benefits as expenses in the period in which they made payments to or on behalf of retired employees. In 1989, the FASB proposed that these costs be accounted for by recognizing expenses over the period of employment rather than after retirement.

Companies feared that the new standard would seriously depress their annual income, and as a result, they would be forced to reduce their health care costs for retirees to soften the effect of the new standard. A survey of 992 large companies found that during the two years following the adoption of the new standard, 79% of the companies surveyed changed their retiree medical plans. Of those, 78% increased retirees' share of costs and 1% eliminated all coverage.[14] As a specific example, **American Telephone and Telegraph Co.** in 1989 negotiated with its union to pay health care benefits to retirees only up to a maximum fixed amount, as opposed to unlimited medical benefits offered by many companies. Of course, AT&T's decision to limit retiree medical benefits may have been purely a business decision unrelated to the new reporting requirements.[15] Or, the new accounting standard may have caused companies like AT&T to reevaluate the costs and benefits of their postretirement packages. This issue is covered in depth in Chapter 17.

Carl Landegger, chairman of **The Black Clawson Company**, expressed his fear of the new accounting standard in open hearings before the FASB in 1989. The FASB reacted to these fears by modifying their originally proposed accounting treatment to ease possible adverse economic consequences to current and future retirees covered by these postretirement health care plans. The resulting standard, *SFAS 106,* "Employers' Accounting for Postretirement Benefits Other Than Pensions," was issued in 1990.

> **CARL LANDEGGER**
> If this becomes GAAP [generally accepted accounting principles], it will cause pain. It will cause evil. People will literally lose their health care benefits.[16]

Another example of the effect of economic consequences on standard setting is the highly controversial debate surrounding accounting for employee stock options. Employees often are given the option to buy shares in the future at a preset price as an integral part of their total compensation package. The accounting objective for any form of compensation is to report compensation expense during the period of service for which the compensation is given. At issue is the amount of compensation to be recognized as expense for stock options.

---

[14]Rod Coddington, "USA Snapshots," Hewitt Associates Survey of 992 Large Employers, *USA Today* (November 8, 1991).

[15]A change in an accounting standard does not directly affect the cash flow of a company. For example, changing from the cash to the accrual method of accounting for postretirement health care benefits does not *directly* change the amounts and timing of the cash payments the company has to make to retirees. However, real cash flow effects could result for a number of reasons. As a result of the change in a standard, (1) a company could alter the way it operates, (2) income tax payments could change, or (3) the new standard could cause the violation of a debt agreement thus increasing financing costs.

[16]Carl Landegger, reprinted in *Accounting Today* (October 23, 1989), p. 1.

Historically, options have been measured at their intrinsic value, which is the simple difference between the market price of the shares and the option price at which they can be acquired. For instance, an option that permits an employee to buy $60 stock for $42 has an intrinsic value of $18. The problem is that options for which the exercise price equals the market value of the underlying stock at the date of grant (which describes most plans) have no intrinsic value and thus result in zero compensation when measured this way, even though the fair value of the options can be quite substantial. To the FASB and many others, it seems counterintuitive to not record any compensation expense for arrangements that routinely provide a large part of the total compensation of executives.

**Public pressure sometimes prevails over conceptual merit in the standard-setting arena.**

In 1995, after lengthy debate, the FASB bowed to public pressure and consented to encourage, rather than require, companies to expense the fair value of employee stock options. Recently, nearly a decade later, the contentious issue resurfaced, and the FASB issued an exposure draft requiring companies to measure options at their fair values and to expense that amount over an appropriate service period. This issue is discussed at greater length in Chapter 19.

The most recent example of the political process at work in standard setting is the heated debate that occurred on the issue of accounting for business combinations. Back in 1996, the FASB added to its agenda a project to consider a possible revision in the practice of allowing two separate and distinct methods of accounting for business combinations, the pooling of interests method and the purchase method. A thorough explanation of the differences between these methods is beyond the scope of this text. For our discussion here, just note that a key issue in the debate related to goodwill, an intangible asset that arises only in business combinations accounted for using the purchase method. Under the then-existing standards, goodwill, like any other intangible asset, was amortized (expensed) over its estimated useful life thus reducing reported net income for several years following the acquisition. It was that negative impact on earnings that motivated many companies involved in a business combination to take whatever steps necessary to structure the transaction as a pooling of interests, thereby avoiding goodwill, its amortization to expense, and the resulting reduction in earnings.

**DENNIS POWELL—CISCO SYSTEMS, INC. VP**
Clearly the FASB listened and responded to extensive comments from the public and the financial community to make the purchase method of accounting more effective and realistic.[17]

As you might guess, when the FASB initially proposed eliminating the pooling method, many companies that were actively engaged in business acquisitions vigorously opposed the elimination of this means of avoiding goodwill. To support their opposition these companies argued that if they were required to use purchase accounting, many business combinations important to economic growth would prove unattractive due to the negative impact on earnings caused by goodwill amortization and would not be undertaken.

To satisfy opposition to its proposal, the FASB suggested several modifications over the years, but it wasn't until the year 2000 that a satisfactory compromise was reached. Specifically, under the new accounting standards issued in 2001[18], only the purchase method is acceptable, but to soften the impact, the resulting goodwill is *not* amortized. We discuss goodwill and its measurement in Chapters 10 and 11.

**The FASB undertakes a series of information-gathering steps before issuing a substantive accounting standard.**

The FASB's dilemma is to balance accounting considerations and political considerations resulting from perceived possible adverse economic consequences. To help solve this dilemma, the board undertakes a series of elaborate information-gathering steps before issuing a substantive accounting standard involving alternative accounting treatments for an economic transaction. These steps include open hearings, deliberations, and requests for written comments from interested parties. For example, 467 comment letters were received on the 1989 proposal concerning accounting for postretirement employee health care benefits. Graphic 1–3 outlines the FASB's standard-setting process.

[17]Jonathan Weil, "FASB Backs Down on Goodwill-Accounting Rules," *The Wall Street Journal* (December 7, 2000).
[18]"Business Combinations," *Statement of Financial Accounting Standards No. 141* (Norwalk, Conn.: FASB, 2001), and "Goodwill and Other Intangible Assets," *Statement of Financial Accounting Standards No. 142* (Norwalk, Conn.: FASB, 2001).

**GRAPHIC 1–3**
The FASB's Standard-Setting Process

| Step | Explanation |
|---|---|
| 1. Identification of problem | A measurement or reporting issue is identified by the Emerging Issues Task Force and placed on the FASB's agenda. |
| 2. The task force | A task force of approximately 15 knowledgeable persons is appointed to advise the Board on various matters. |
| 3. Research and analysis | The FASB's technical staff investigates the issue. |
| 4. *Discussion memorandum (DM)* | The DM, a detailed analysis of the problem along with alternative solutions, is prepared and disseminated to interested parties. |
| 5. Public response | Public hearings are held to discuss the issue and letters of response are sent to the FASB which then analyzes this feedback. |
| 6. *Exposure draft (ED)* | A preliminary draft of a proposed statement, called an exposure draft, is issued. The ED details the proposed treatment for the problem. |
| 7. Public response | Written responses to the ED are accepted and analyzed. The ED is revised, if necessary, depending on the board's analysis. |
| 8. *Statement* issued | An *SFAS* is issued if four of the seven FASB members support the revised ED. |

These steps are the FASB's attempt to acquire consensus as to the preferred method of accounting, as well as to anticipate adverse economic consequences. The board's process is similar to that of an elected political representative, a U.S. congresswoman for example, trying to determine consensus among her constituency before voting on a bill on the floor of the House of Representatives. For this reason, accounting standard setting is a political process.

## OUR GLOBAL MARKETPLACE

**Many U.S. and foreign companies operate and raise capital in more than one country.**

Advances in communication and transportation systems continue to expand the marketplace in which companies operate. The world economy is more integrated than ever, and many of the larger U.S. corporations are truly multinational in nature. These multinational corporations have their home in the United States but operate and perhaps raise capital in other countries. For example, **Coca-Cola**, **IBM**, **Colgate-Palmolive**, **Gillette**, and many other companies generate more than 50% of their revenue from foreign sales. It is not uncommon for even relatively small companies to transact business in many different countries.

Of course, many foreign corporations operate in the United States as well. In fact, companies such as **Columbia Records** and **Bridgestone Americas Holding** are owned by companies that reside in other countries. The financial marketplace also has taken on a global dimension, with many companies crossing geographic boundaries to raise capital. For example, nearly 500 foreign companies are listed on the New York Stock Exchange and nearly 400 foreign companies are listed on the London Stock Exchange. This expanded marketplace requires that company management understand the laws, customs, regulations, *and* accounting and reporting standards of many different countries.

**Toward Global Accounting Standards.** Most industrialized countries have organizations responsible for determining accounting and reporting standards. In some countries, the United Kingdom for instance, the responsible organization is a private sector body similar to the FASB in the United States. In other countries, such as France, the organization is a governmental body.

Accounting standards prescribed by these various groups are not the same. Standards differ from country to country for many reasons, including different legal systems, levels of inflation, culture, degrees of sophistication and use of capital markets, and political and economic ties with other countries. These differences can cause problems for multinational corporations. A company doing business in more than one country may find it difficult to comply with more than one set of accounting standards if there are important differences among the sets. It has been argued that different national accounting standards impair the ability of companies to raise capital in international markets.

In response to this problem, the **International Accounting Standards Committee (IASC)** was formed in 1973 to develop global accounting standards. The IASC in 2001 reorganized itself and created a new standard-setting body called the **International Accounting Standards Board (IASB).** The IASC now acts as an umbrella organization similar to the Financial Accounting Foundation (FAF) in the United States. This new global standard-setting structure is consistent with a recent FASB vision report attempting to identify an optimal standard-setting environment.[19] The IASB's objectives are (1) to develop a single set of high quality, understandable global accounting standards, (2) to promote the use of those standards, and (3) to bring about the convergence of national accounting standards and international accounting standards.

**The *International Accounting Standards Board (IASB)* is dedicated to developing a single set of global accounting standards.**

The IASC issued 41 International Accounting Standards (IASs). The IASB endorsed these standards when it was formed in 2001. Since then, the IASB has revised many of them and has issued six standards of its own, called **International Financial Reporting Standards (IFRSs).** Compliance with these standards is voluntary, since the IASB has no authority to enforce them. However, more and more countries are basing their national accounting standards on international accounting standards.[20] The International Organization of Securities Commissions (IOSCO) approved a resolution permitting its members to use these standards to prepare their financial statements for cross-border offerings and listings. Beginning in 2005, all listed companies in the European Union (EU) must prepare their consolidated financial statements using IFRS. Some 7,000 listed EU companies are affected.

***International Financial Reporting Standards* are gaining support around the globe.**

In the United States, the move toward convergence of accounting standards began in earnest with the cooperation of the FASB and the IASC on the earnings per share (EPS) issue. In 1994, the FASB and the IASC began working on projects leading toward the issuance of new standards for the computation of EPS. The intent of the FASB's project was to issue an EPS standard that would be compatible with the new international standard and, at the same time, simplify U.S. GAAP. Chapter 19 describes this standard.

In 2002, the FASB and IASB signed the so-called Norwalk Agreement, formalizing their commitment to convergence of U.S. GAAP and IFRS. Under this agreement, the boards pledged to remove existing differences between their standards and to coordinate their future standard-setting agendas so that major issues are worked on together. Recent standards issued by the FASB that you will encounter in our later discussions on share-based compensation, nonmonetary exchanges, and inventory costs are recent examples of this commitment to convergence.

**The commitment to narrowing differences between U.S. GAAP and international standards has influenced recent FASB standards.**

Global Perspectives are included throughout the text to emphasize that our economy does not operate in isolation and to introduce you to some of the differences and similarities in accounting and reporting practices around the world. In addition, your instructor may assign end-of-chapter international cases to further explore these differences and similarities.

## THE ROLE OF THE AUDITOR

**FINANCIAL REPORTING CASE**

Q3, p. 3

It is the responsibility of management to apply accounting standards when communicating with investors and creditors through financial statements. Another group, **auditors,** serves as an independent intermediary to help ensure that management has in fact appropriately applied GAAP in preparing the company's financial statements. Auditors examine (audit) financial statements to express a professional, independent opinion. The opinion reflects the auditors' assessment of the statements' "fairness," which is determined by the extent to which they are prepared in compliance with GAAP.

***Auditors* express an opinion on the compliance of financial statements with GAAP.**

**FedEx Corporation**

The report of the independent auditors for **FedEx Corporation**'s financial statements is in Appendix B. The first two paragraphs explain the scope of the audit, and the third states the auditors' opinion. After conducting its audit, the accounting firm **Ernst & Young LLP** stated that "In our opinion, the financial statements referred to above present fairly, . . . , in conformity with U.S. generally accepted accounting principles." This is known as a *clean*

[19] *International Accounting Standard Setting: A Vision for the Future* (Norwalk, Conn.: FASB, 1998).

[20] Helen Gernon and Gary Meek, *Accounting: An International Perspective* (New York: The McGraw-Hill Companies, 2001).

*opinion.* If there had been any material departures from GAAP or other problems that caused the auditors to question the fairness of the statements, the report would have been modified to inform readers.

**Auditors offer credibility to financial statements.**

The auditor adds credibility to the financial statements, increasing the confidence of capital market participants who rely on the information. Auditors, therefore, play an important role in the resource allocation process.

***Certified public accountants (CPAs)* are licensed by states to provide audit services.**

In most states, only individuals licensed as **certified public accountants (CPAs)** in the state can represent that the financial statements have been audited in accordance with generally accepted auditing standards. Requirements to be licensed as a CPA vary from state to state, but all states specify education, testing, and experience requirements. The testing requirement is to pass the Uniform CPA Examination.

## FINANCIAL REPORTING REFORM

**Sarbanes-Oxley**

The dramatic collapse of **Enron** in 2001 and the dismantling of the international public accounting firm of **Arthur Andersen** in 2002 severely shook U.S. capital markets. The credibility of the accounting profession itself as well as of corporate America was called into question. Public outrage over accounting scandals at high-profile companies like **WorldCom**, **Xerox**, **Merck**, **Adelphia Communications**, and others increased the pressure on lawmakers to pass measures that would restore credibility and investor confidence in the financial reporting process.

**PAUL SARBANES—U.S. SENATOR**
We confront an increasing crisis of confidence with the public's trust in our markets. If this continues, I think it poses a real threat to our economic health.[21]

Driven by these pressures, Congress acted swiftly and passed the *Public Company Accounting Reform and Investor Protection ACT of 2002*, commonly referred to as the *Sarbanes-Oxley Act* for the two congressmen who sponsored the bill. The legislation is comprehensive in its inclusion of the key players in the financial reporting process. The law provides for the regulation of auditors and the types of services they furnish to clients, increases accountability of corporate executives, addresses conflicts of interest for securities analysts, and provides for stiff criminal penalties for violators. Graphic 1–4 outlines the key provisions of the Act.

The changes imposed by the legislation are dramatic in scope and pose a significant challenge for the public accounting profession. At the same time, many maintain the changes were necessary to lessen the likelihood of corporate and accounting fraud and to restore investor confidence in the U.S. capital markets.

**WILLIAM J. MCDONOUGH—PCAOB CHAIRMAN**
This standard (*Auditing Standard No. 2*) is one of the most important and far-reaching auditing standards the board will ever adopt. In the past, internal controls were merely considered by auditors; now they will have to be tested and examined in detail. (as quoted in *PCAOBUS.org*, June 18, 2004).

Section 404 is perhaps the most controversial provision of the 2002 act. No one argues the importance of adequate internal controls. However, the costs of implementing this section of the act can be substantial. Not only are companies required to document internal controls and assess their adequacy, but their auditors, too, must provide an opinion on management's assessment. The Public Company Accounting Oversight Board's (PCAOB) *Auditing Standard No. 2* added an additional requirement that auditors express a second opinion on whether the company has maintained effective internal control over financial reporting.[22] We revisit Section 404 in Chapter 7 in the context of an introduction to internal controls.

---

[21] James Kuhnhenn, "Bush Vows to Punish Corporate Lawbreakers," *San Jose Mercury News* (July 9, 2002), p. 8A.

[22] "An Audit of Internal Control over Financial Reporting Performed in Conjunction with an Audit of Financial Statements," *Auditing Standard No. 2* (Washington, D.C.: PCAOB, 2004).

**GRAPHIC 1–4**

Public Company Accounting Reform and Investor Protection Act of 2002

**Key Provisions of the Act:**

- **Oversight board.** The five-member (two accountants) Public Company Accounting Oversight Board has the authority to establish standards dealing with auditing, quality control, ethics, independence and other activities relating to the preparation of audit reports, or can choose to delegate these responsibilities to the AICPA. Prior to the act, the AICPA set auditing standards. The SEC has oversight and enforcement authority.
- **Corporate executive accountability.** Corporate executives must personally certify the financial statements and company disclosures with severe financial penalties and the possibility of imprisonment for fraudulent misstatement.
- **Nonaudit services.** The law makes it unlawful for the auditors of public companies to perform a variety of nonaudit services for audit clients. Prohibited services include bookkeeping, internal audit outsourcing, appraisal or valuation services, and various other consulting services. Other nonaudit services, including tax services, require pre-approval by the audit committee of the company being audited.
- **Retention of work papers.** Auditors of public companies must retain all audit or review work papers for five years or face the threat of a prison term for willful violations.
- **Auditor rotation.** Lead audit partners are required to rotate every five years. Mandatory rotation of audit firms came under consideration.
- **Conflicts of interest.** Audit firms are not allowed to audit public companies whose chief executives worked for the audit firm and participated in that company's audit during the preceding year.
- **Hiring of auditor.** Audit firms are hired by the audit committee of the board of directors of the company, not by company management.
- **Internal control.** Section 404 of the act requires that company management document and assess the effectiveness of all internal control processes that could affect financial reporting. Company auditors express an opinion on whether management's assessment of the effectiveness of internal control is fairly stated. The PCAOB's *Auditing Standard No. 2* also requires that the company auditors express a second opinion on whether the company has maintained effective internal control over financial reporting.

**ROBERT HERZ—FASB CHAIRMAN**

Under a principles-based approach, one starts with laying out the key objectives of good reporting in the subject area and then provides guidance explaining the objective and relating it to some common examples. While rules are sometimes unavoidable, the intent is not to try to provide specific guidance or rules for every possible situation. Rather, if in doubt, the reader is directed back to the principles. (from his presentation to the FEI in 2002).

## A MOVE AWAY FROM RULES-BASED STANDARDS?

The accounting scandals at Enron and other companies also rekindled the debate over **principles-based**, or more recently termed **objectives-oriented**, versus **rules-based** accounting standards. In fact, a provision of the Sarbanes-Oxley Act required the SEC to study the issue and provide a report to Congress on its findings. That report, issued in July 2003, recommended that accounting standards be developed using an objectives-oriented approach.[23] The FASB also issued a proposal addressing this issue.[24]

**A principles-based, or objectives-oriented, approach to standard setting stresses professional judgment, as opposed to following a list of rules.**

An objectives-oriented approach to standard setting stresses using professional judgment, as opposed to following a list of rules when choosing the appropriate accounting treatment for a transaction. Lease accounting provides a useful example for comparing the two approaches. In Chapter 15 you will learn that a company records a long-term lease of an asset as either a *capital lease* or an *operating lease*. If a leasing arrangement is "in substance" the purchase of an asset with the lease

[23] "Study Pursuant to Section 108 (d) of the Sarbanes-Oxley Act of 2002 on the Adoption by the United States Financial Reporting System of a Principles-Based Accounting System," Securities and Exchange Commission (July 2003).

[24] "Principles-Based Approach to U.S. Standard Setting," *A Financial Accounting Standards Board Proposal* (Norwalk, Conn.: FASB, 2002).

payments effectively serving as payments for that purchase, we should account for the transaction that way. A capital lease requires that the property being leased be recorded as an asset and a liability to pay for the asset. No asset or liability is recorded for an operating lease. Therein lies the problem. Because company managers are aware that analysts view debt as indicative of financial risk, those managers often try to avoid reporting more debt than absolutely necessary. As a result, firms frequently stretch the limits of the rules to structure lease agreements so that they technically sidestep the FASB's detailed rules, principally four criteria provided in *SFAS No. 13,* for identifying capital leases that require recording a liability.

In contrast, the IASB employs an objectives-oriented approach to lease accounting in its *IAS 17.* In that standard, the focus is on professional judgment rather than specific rules to determine whether the leasing arrangement effectively transfers the "risk and rewards" of ownership. Professional judgment is then applied to determine if the risk and rewards have been transferred.

Which approach is more likely to capture the economic substance of the lease, rather than its form? The FASB's criteria were designed to aid the accountant in determining whether the risk and rewards of ownership have been transferred. Many would argue, though, that the result has been the opposite. Rather than use the criteria to enhance judgment, management and its accountants can use the rules as an excuse to avoid using professional judgment altogether and instead focus on the rules alone. Proponents of an objectives-oriented approach argue that its focus is squarely on professional judgment, there are few rules to sidestep, and we more likely will arrive at an appropriate accounting treatment. Detractors, on the other hand, argue that the absence of detailed rules opens the door to even more abuse. Even in the absence of intentional misuse, reliance on professional judgment could result in different interpretations for similar transactions, raising concerns about comparability.

The FASB is actively considering whether to move toward objectives-oriented standard setting. That the IASB primarily follows an objectives-oriented approach, coupled with the FASB's recent moves toward convergence of U.S. and international standards, hints at a leaning in that direction. Opposition, though, is ardent. The debate has by no means ended.

## PART B THE CONCEPTUAL FRAMEWORK

The increasing complexity of our business world creates growing pressure on the FASB to delicately balance the many constituents of the accounting standard-setting process. The task of the FASB is made less complex if there exists a set of cohesive objectives and fundamental concepts on which financial accounting and reporting can be based. A number of years after coming into existence in 1973, the FASB's efforts resulted in the establishment of these objectives and concepts.

**FINANCIAL REPORTING CASE**

Q4, p. 3

The **conceptual framework** has been described as a constitution, a coherent system of interrelated objectives and fundamentals that can lead to consistent standards and that prescribe the nature, function, and limits of financial accounting and reporting. The fundamentals are the underlying concepts of accounting, concepts that guide the selection of events to be accounted for, the measurement of those events, and the means of summarizing and communicating them to interested parties.[25]

● LO5

**The conceptual framework does not prescribe GAAP. It provides an underlying foundation for accounting standards.**

**FASB**
The *Concepts Statements* will guide the board in developing accounting standards by providing the board with a common foundation and basic reasoning on which to consider merits of alternatives.[26]

The FASB has disseminated this framework through seven Statements of Financial Accounting Concepts. *SFAC 4* deals with the objectives of financial reporting for nonprofit organizations, and *SFAC 3* was superseded by *SFAC 6,* which, with the other four statements, is dis-

[25]"Conceptual Framework for Financial Accounting and Reporting: Elements of Financial Statements and Their Measurement," *Discussion Memorandum* (Stamford, Conn.: FASB, 1976), p. 2.

[26]Introduction to "Objectives of Financial Reporting by Nonbusiness Organizations," *Statement of Financial Accounting Concepts No. 4* (Stamford, Conn.: FASB, 1980).

**GRAPHIC 1–5**
The Conceptual Framework

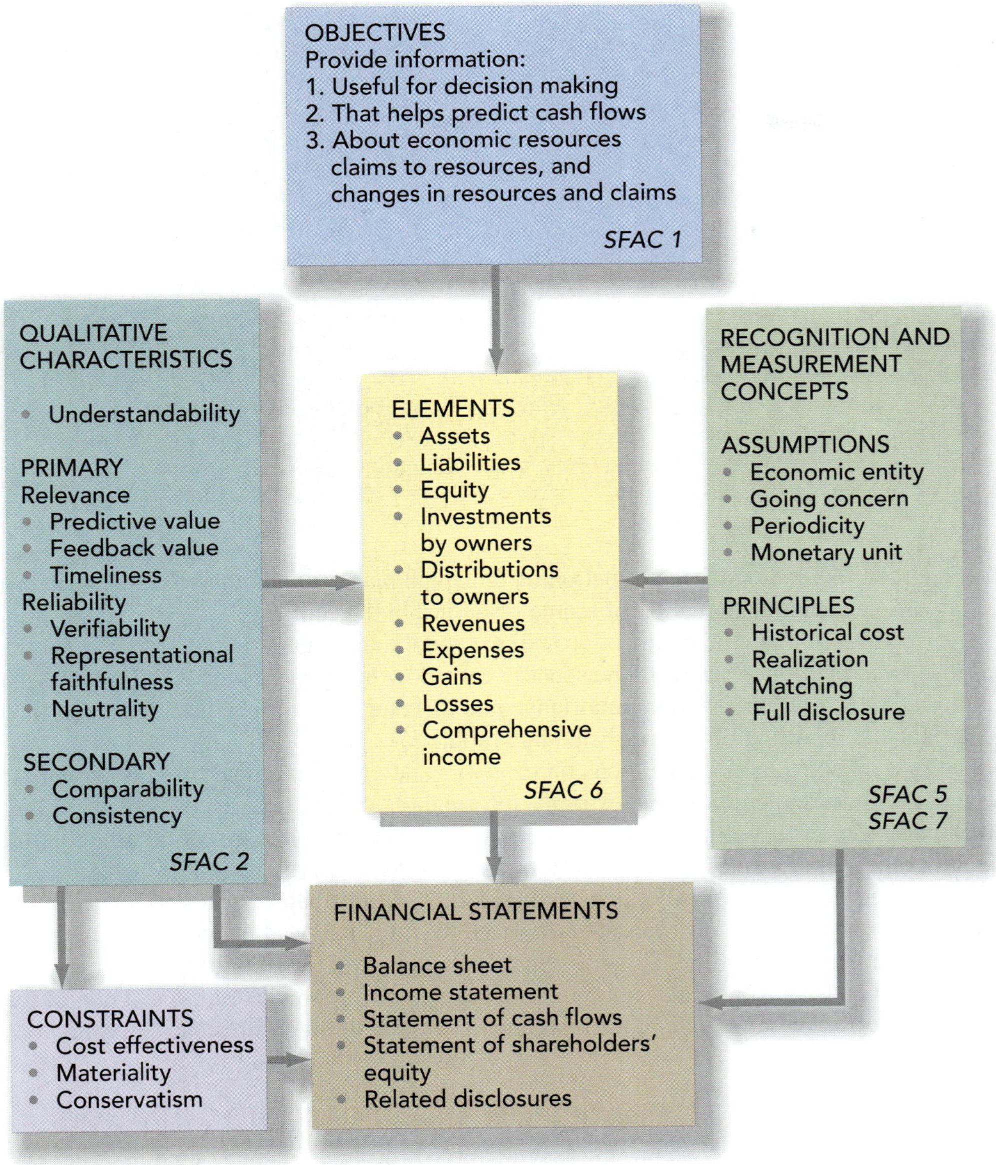


cussed below. It is important to realize that the conceptual framework provides structure and direction to financial accounting and reporting and does not directly prescribe GAAP.

The financial statements and their elements are most informative when they possess specific qualitative characteristics, subject to the constraints of materiality, cost effectiveness, and conservatism. Proper recognition and measurement of financial information rely on several assumptions and principles that underlie the financial reporting process.

The remainder of this chapter is devoted to discussions of the components of the conceptual framework that bear on financial statements as depicted in Graphic 1–5, beginning with the objectives of financial reporting.

## Objectives of Financial Reporting

● LO6

In specifying the overriding objectives of financial reporting, the board considered the economic, legal, political, and social environment in the United States. The objectives would be quite different in a socialist economy where the majority of productive resources are government owned.

Implicit in the objectives is an overall societal goal of serving the public interest by providing evenhanded financial and other information that, together with information from

**GRAPHIC 1–6**
Financial Reporting Objectives

1. Financial reporting should provide information that is useful to present and potential investors and creditors and other users in making rational investment, credit, and similar decisions.
   *The information should be comprehensible to those who have a reasonable understanding of business and economic activities and are willing to study the information with reasonable diligence.*
2. Financial reporting should provide information to help present and potential investors and creditors and other users to assess the amounts, timing, and uncertainty of prospective cash receipts.
   *Since investors' and creditors' cash flows are related to enterprise cash flows, financial reporting should provide information to help assess the amounts, timing, and uncertainty of prospective net cash inflows to the related enterprise.*
3. Financial reporting should provide information about the economic resources of an enterprise; the claims to those resources (obligations); and the effects of transactions, events, and circumstances that cause changes in resources and claims to those resources.
   *These are sources, direct or indirect, of future cash inflows and cash outflows.*

**The primary objective of financial reporting is to provide useful information for decision making.**

other sources, facilitates efficient functioning of capital markets and otherwise assists in promoting efficient capital allocation of scarce resources in the economy.[27]

***SFAC 1* establishes the objectives of financial reporting.**

The importance to our economy of providing capital market participants with information was discussed previously, as were the specific cash flow information needs of investors and creditors. *SFAC 1* articulates this importance and investor and creditor needs through three basic financial reporting objectives listed in Graphic 1–6.

The first objective specifies a focus on investors and creditors. In addition to the importance of investors and creditors as key users, information to meet their needs is likely to have general utility to other groups of external users who are interested in essentially the same financial aspects of a business as are investors and creditors.

***SFAC 1* affirms that investors and creditors are the primary external users of financial information.**

The second objective refers to the specific cash flow information needs of investors and creditors. The third objective emphasizes the need for information about economic resources and claims to those resources. This information would include not only the amount of resources and claims at a particular point in time but also changes in resources and claims that occur over periods of time. This information is key to predicting future cash flows.

## Qualitative Characteristics of Accounting Information

● LO6

To satisfy the stated objectives, information should possess certain characteristics. The purpose of *SFAC 2* is to outline the desired qualitative characteristics of accounting information.

**To be useful, information must make a difference in the decision process.**

Graphic 1–7 indicates these qualitative characteristics, presented in the form of a hierarchy of their perceived importance. Notice that the main focus, as stated in the first concept statement is on **decision usefulness**—the ability to be useful in decision making. **Understandability** means that users must understand the information within the context of the decision being made. This is a user-specific quality because users will differ in their ability to comprehend any set of information. The first stated financial reporting objective of *SFAC 1* is to provide comprehensible information to those who have a reasonable understanding of business and economic activities and are willing to study the information.

### PRIMARY QUALITATIVE CHARACTERISTICS

**To be useful for decision making, accounting information should be *relevant* and *reliable*.**

The primary decision-specific qualities that make accounting information useful are **relevance** and **reliability**. Both are critical. No matter how reliable, if information is not relevant to the decision at hand, it is useless. Conversely, relevant information is of little value if it cannot be relied on. Let's look closer at each of these two characteristics, including the components that make those qualities desirable. We also consider two secondary qualities—comparability and consistency.

[27]Introduction to "Objectives of Financial Reporting for Business Enterprises," *Statement of Financial Accounting Concepts No. 1* (Stamford, Conn.: FASB, 1978).

**GRAPHIC 1–7** Hierarchy of Desirable Characteristics of Accounting Information

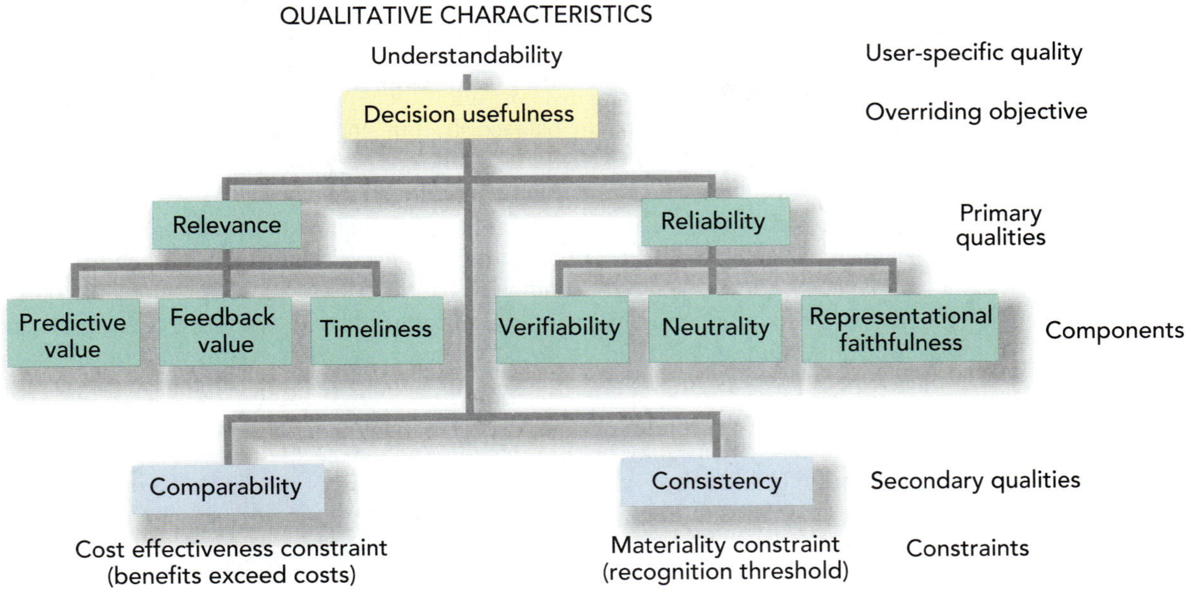


**Relevance.** To make a difference in the decision process, information must possess **predictive value** and/or **feedback value.** Generally, useful information will possess both qualities. For example, if net income and its components confirm investor expectations about future cash-generating ability, then net income has feedback value for investors. This confirmation can also be useful in predicting future cash-generating ability as expectations are revised.

This predictive ability is central to the concept of "earnings quality," the ability of reported earnings (income) to predict a company's future earnings. This is a concept we revisit frequently throughout this textbook in order to explore the impact on earnings quality of various topics under discussion. For instance, in Chapter 4 we discuss the contents of the income statement and certain classifications used in the statement from the perspective of helping analysts separate a company's transitory earnings from its permanent earnings. This separation is critical to a meaningful prediction of future earnings. In later chapters, we look at how various financial reporting decisions affect earnings quality.

**Timeliness** also is an important component of relevance. Information is timely when it is available to users early enough to allow its use in the decision process. The need for timely information requires that companies provide information to external users on a periodic basis. The SEC requires its registrants to submit financial statement information not only on an annual basis, but also quarterly for the first three quarters of each fiscal year.

**Information is *timely* if it is available to users before a decision is made.**

**Reliability.** **Reliability** is the extent to which information is *verifiable, representationally faithful,* and *neutral.* **Verifiability** implies a consensus among different measurers. For example, the historical cost of a piece of land to be reported in the balance sheet of a company is usually highly verifiable. The cost can be traced to an exchange transaction, the purchase of the land. However, the market value of that land is much more difficult to verify. Appraisers could differ in their assessment of market value. The term *objectivity* often is linked to verifiability. The historical cost of the land is objective but the land's market value is subjective, influenced by the measurer's past experience and prejudices. A measurement that is subjective is difficult to verify, which makes it more difficult for users to rely on.

**Representational faithfulness** exists when there is agreement between a measure or description and the phenomenon it purports to represent. For example, assume that the term *inventory* in a balance sheet of a retail company is understood by external users to represent items that are intended for sale in the ordinary course of business. If inventory includes, say, machines used to produce inventory, then it lacks representational faithfulness.

***Representational faithfulness* means agreement between a measure and a real-world phenomenon that the measure is supposed to represent.**

Several years ago, accountants used the term *reserve for doubtful accounts* to describe anticipated bad debts related to accounts receivable. For many, the term *reserve* means that a sum of money has been set aside for future bad debts. Because this was not the case, this term lacked representational faithfulness. The description "reserve. . . " now has been changed to "allowance for uncollectible accounts" or "allowance for doubtful accounts." In **FedEx Corporation**'s financial statements, the balance sheet in Appendix B reports *Receivables, less allowances of $151 million and $149 million* at the end of 2004 and 2003, respectively.

**FedEx Corporation**

**Accounting standards should not favor any particular groups or companies nor influence behavior in any specific way.**

Reliability assumes the information being relied on is neutral with respect to parties potentially affected. In that regard, **neutrality** is highly related to the establishment of accounting standards. You learned earlier that changes in accounting standards can lead to adverse economic consequences to certain companies, their investors and creditors, and other interest groups. Accounting standards should be established with overall societal goals and specific objectives in mind and should try not to favor particular groups or companies.

The FASB faces a difficult task in balancing neutrality and the consideration of economic consequences. A new accounting standard may favor one group of companies over others, but the FASB must convince the financial community that this was a consequence of the standard and not an objective used to set the standard. Donald Kirk, one of the members of the first group to serve on the FASB, stressed the importance of neutrality in the standard-setting process.

**DONALD KIRK**
If financial reporting is to be credible, there must be public confidence that the standard-setting system is credible, that selection of board members is based on merit and not the influence of special interests, and that standards are developed neutrally with the objective of relevant and reliable information, not purposeful manipulation.[28]

**A trade-off often is required between various degrees of relevance and reliability.**

The qualities of relevance and reliability often clash. For example, a net income forecast provided by the management of a company may possess a high degree of relevance to investors and creditors trying to predict future cash flows. However, a forecast necessarily contains subjectivity in the estimation of future events. GAAP presently do not require companies to provide forecasts of any financial variables.

### SECONDARY QUALITATIVE CHARACTERISTICS

**Accounting information should be *comparable* across different companies and over different time periods.**

Graphic 1–7 identifies two secondary qualitative characteristics important to decision usefulness—comparability and consistency. **Comparability** is the ability to help users see similarities and differences between events and conditions. We already have discussed the importance of the ability of investors and creditors to compare information across companies to make their resource allocation decisions. Closely related to comparability is the notion that **consistency** of accounting practices over time permits valid comparisons between different periods. The predictive and feedback value of information is enhanced if users can compare the performance of a company over time.[29] In the FedEx financial statements in Appendix B, notice that disclosure Note 1 includes a summary of significant accounting policies. A change in one of these policies would require disclosure in the financial statements and notes to restore comparability between periods.

**FedEx Corporation**

## Practical Boundaries (Constraints) to Achieving Desired Qualitative Characteristics

Most of us learn early in life that we can't get everything we desire. The latest electronic gadget may have all the qualitative characteristics that current technology can provide, but limited resources may lead us to purchase a fully functional model with fewer bells and whistles. **Cost effectiveness** also constrains the accounting choices we make. Specifically,

[28]Donald J. Kirk, chairman of the FASB, quoted in *Status Report,* December 23, 1986.

[29]Companies occasionally do change their accounting practices, which makes it difficult for users to make comparisons among different reporting periods. Chapter 4 and Chapter 20 describe the disclosures that a company makes in this situation to restore consistency among periods.

it's important that the benefits of endowing accounting information with all the qualitative characteristics we've discussed exceed the costs of doing so.

A related constraint on the type of information we provide is the concept of **materiality.** For an additional $20 you can add the latest enhancement to that electronic gadget you're considering. However, despite the higher specs, if you feel it will provide no discernible improvement in the performance of the product as you will use it, why pay the extra $20? In an accounting context, if a more costly way of providing information is not expected to have a material effect on decisions made by those using the information, the less costly method may be acceptable.

Cost effectiveness and materiality impart practical constraints on each of the qualitative characteristics of accounting information. Both suggest that a certain accounting treatment might be different from that dictated solely by consideration of desired qualities of information.

## COST EFFECTIVENESS

The costs of providing accounting information include those of gathering, processing, and disseminating information. There also are costs to users when interpreting information. In addition, costs include possible adverse economic consequences of implementing accounting standards. These costs in particular are difficult, if not impossible, to quantify.

**The costs of providing accounting information include any possible adverse economic consequences of accounting standards.**

An example of this is the standard that requires companies operating in more than one operating segment to disclose certain disaggregated financial information.[30] In addition to information gathering, processing, and dissemination costs, many companies feel that this reporting requirement imposes what could be called *competitive disadvantage costs.* These companies do not want their competitors to have the disaggregated data.

The perceived benefit from this or any accounting standard is increased *decision usefulness* of the information provided, which, hopefully, improves the resource allocation process. It is inherently impossible to quantify this benefit. The elaborate information-gathering process undertaken by the FASB in setting accounting standards is an attempt to assess both costs and benefits of a proposed accounting standard, even if in a subjective, nonquantifiable manner. In the case of reporting disaggregated information, the FASB decided that the perceived benefits of disclosing this information exceeded the costs of providing it.

**Information is *cost effective* only if the perceived benefit of increased *decision usefulness* exceeds the anticipated costs of providing that information.**

## MATERIALITY

Materiality is another pervasive constraint. Information is material if it can have an effect on a decision made by users. One consequence of considering materiality is that GAAP need not be followed if an item is immaterial. For example, GAAP requires that receivables be measured at their net realizable value. If bad debts are anticipated, they should be estimated and subtracted from the face amount of receivables for balance sheet measurement. This is called the *allowance method* of accounting for bad debts. However, if the amount of anticipated bad debts is not considered to be large enough to affect decisions made by users, the *direct write-off method* of accounting for bad debts can be used even though it is not a generally accepted technique. This method does not require estimation of bad debts for existing receivables.

**Information is *material* if it has an effect on decisions.**

The threshold for materiality will depend principally on the *relative* dollar amount of the transaction. For example, $10,000 in total anticipated bad debts for a multibillion dollar company like FedEx would not be considered material. The method used to account for these anticipated bad debts will not affect the decisions made by FedEx Corporation's financial statement users. This same $10,000 amount, however, could easily be material for a neighborhood pizza parlor. The FASB has been reluctant to establish any quantitative materiality guidelines. The threshold for materiality has been left to the subjective judgment of the company preparing the financial statements and its auditors.

Materiality is concerned not only with the dollar amount of an item but with the nature of the item as well. In 1999, the SEC issued *Staff Accounting Bulletin No. 99.*[31] The bulletin expresses the SEC's view that exclusive reliance on quantitative benchmarks to assess

---

[30]"Disclosures about Segments of an Enterprise and Related Information," *Statement of Financial Accounting Standards No. 131* (Norwalk, Conn.: FASB, 1997). The contents of this standard are described in the appendix to Chapter 3.

[31]"Materiality," *Staff Accounting Bulletin No. 99* (Washington, DC: SEC, August 1999).

**Professional judgment determines what amount is material in each situation.**

materiality in preparing financial statements is inappropriate. A number of other factors, including whether the item in question involves an unlawful transaction, should also be considered when determining materiality. For example, an activity such as the illegal payment of $10,000 to an official of a foreign government to secure a valuable contract would probably be considered material even if the amount is small relative to the size of the company.

### CONSERVATISM

***Conservatism* is a justification for some accounting practices, *not* a desired qualitative characteristic of accounting information.**

**Conservatism** is a practice followed in an attempt to ensure that uncertainties and risks inherent in business situations are adequately considered. It is a frequently cited characteristic of accounting information. Conservatism is not, however, a desired qualitative characteristic but a practical justification for some accounting choices. In that sense, conservatism serves as a third constraint on the achievement of various qualitative characteristics.[32]

The need for conservatism often is discussed in conjunction with the estimates required to comply with GAAP. For example, assume that a company estimated that its anticipated bad debts on existing receivables could be any number between $20,000 and $30,000, with the most likely amount being $25,000, and that these amounts are material. A conservative estimate would be $30,000, thus showing the lowest amount (of a range of possible values) in the balance sheet for net receivables and the highest expense (and therefore the lowest net income) in the income statement.

However, financial accounting information users could just as easily be misled by a conservative estimate as by an optimistic one. If $25,000 is the best estimate of anticipated bad debts, then that is the number that should be used. Conservatism is *not* a desirable characteristic nor is it an accounting principle. Nevertheless, there seem to be some accounting practices, such as the lower-of-cost-or-market method for measuring inventory (Chapter 9), that appear to be generated by a desire to be conservative. However, these practices are motivated by other accounting principles such as the realization principle as discussed later in this chapter. They also are influenced by practical realities of our legal system. Investors and creditors who lose money from stock purchases or loans are less likely to sue when bad news is exaggerated and good news is underestimated. While recognizing the role that conservatism plays in how information is reported, we also need to emphasize that it is not a desired characteristic from a qualitative standpoint. Instead, conservatism is a practical constraint on the extent to which other qualitative characteristics are instilled in accounting information.

Now that we've discussed the qualities that the elements of financial statements should possess, let's look more closely at the elements themselves.

## Elements of Financial Statements

● LO6

*SFAC 6* defines 10 elements of financial statements. These elements are "the building blocks with which financial statements are constructed—the classes of items that financial statements comprise."[33] They focus directly on items related to measuring performance and to reporting financial position. The definitions of these elements operationalize the resources, claims, and changes identified in the third objective of financial reporting in *SFAC 1*.[34] The *accrual accounting* model actually is embodied in the element definitions. The FASB recognized that accrual accounting produces information that is more successful in predicting future cash flows than is cash flow accounting.

**The 10 elements of financial statements defined in *SFAC 6* describe financial position and periodic performance.**

The 10 elements are: (1) assets, (2) liabilities, (3) equity, (4) investments by owners, (5) distributions to owners, (6) revenues, (7) expenses, (8) gains, (9) losses, and (10) comprehensive income.

You probably already know in general terms what most of these elements mean. But as you will see when they are discussed, it is helpful to have a deeper understanding of their meaning. You may recognize the first three elements—assets, liabilities, and equity—as those that portray the financial position of an enterprise.

[32]The FASB's hierarchy of qualitative characteristics does not specifically identify conservatism as a constraint. Most theorists include conservatism as one of the underlying accounting principles that guide accounting practice. Our classification recognizes its very real role in accounting choices as well as the practical motivation for those choices.

[33]"Elements of Financial Statements," *Statement of Financial Accounting Concepts No. 6* (Stamford, Conn.: FASB, 1985), par. 5.

[34]Graphic 1–6.

**Assets** are probable future economic benefits obtained or controlled by a particular entity as a result of past transactions or events.

*Assets* represent probable future economic benefits controlled by the enterprise.

A key characteristic of this definition is that an asset represents *probable* future economic benefits. A receivable is an asset only if it is probable that future benefits will result, that cash will be collected. The *controlled by* aspect of the definition also is important. The employees of a company certainly represent future economic benefits to a company. However, they are not owned or controlled by the company and do not qualify as assets.

**Liabilities** are probable future sacrifices of economic benefits arising from present obligations of a particular entity to transfer assets or provide services to other entities in the future as a result of past transactions or events.[35]

*Liabilities* represent obligations to other entities.

Most liabilities require the future payment of cash, the amount and timing of which are specified by a legally enforceable contract. Actually, though, a liability need not be payable in cash. Instead, it may require the company to transfer other assets or to provide services. For example, a warranty liability is created for the seller when a product is sold and the seller guarantees to fix or replace the product if it proves defective and it is probable that a material amount of product sold will, in fact, prove defective. A liability also need not be represented by a written agreement, nor be legally enforceable. For example, a company might choose to pay a terminated employee's salary for a period of time after termination even though not legally required to do so. The commitment creates a liability at the date of termination.

**Equity** or net assets, called **shareholders' equity** or **stockholders' equity** for a corporation, is the residual interest in the assets of an entity that remains after deducting liabilities.

Assets and liabilities are measured directly; equity is not. Equity is simply a residual amount. The accounting equation illustrates financial position.

$$\underbrace{\textbf{Assets} - \textbf{Liabilities}}_{\textit{Net Assets}} = \textbf{Equity}$$

*Equity* is a residual amount, the owners' interest in assets after subtracting liabilities.

For a corporation, equity arises primarily from two sources: (1) amounts *invested* by shareholders in the corporation and (2) amounts *earned* by the corporation on behalf of its shareholders. These two sources are reported as (1) **paid-in capital** and (2) **retained earnings.** We discuss this classification of shareholders' equity in more depth in Chapter 18.

The next two elements defined in *SFAC 6* deal with changes in equity from owner transactions.

**Investments by owners** are increases in equity resulting from transfers of resources (usually cash) to a company in exchange for ownership interest.

A corporation's issuance of ownership shares of stock in exchange for cash represents an investment by owners.

*Investments by owners* and *distributions to owners* are transactions describing any owner contribution to and withdrawal from the company.

**Distributions to owners** are decreases in equity resulting from transfers *to* owners.

A cash dividend paid by a corporation to its shareholders is the most common distribution to owners.

Revenues, gains, expenses, and losses describe changes in equity due to profit-generating transactions.

**Revenues** are inflows or other enhancements of assets or settlements of liabilities from delivering or producing goods, rendering services, or other activities that constitute the entity's ongoing major, or central, operations.

[35]In 2000, the FASB issued an exposure draft proposing a revision to the *Concept Statement No. 6* definition of a liability. The proposed amendment would expand the definition to also include as liabilities certain obligations that require or permit settlement by issuance of the issuer's equity shares and that do not establish an ownership interest. At the time this text was written, a final pronouncement had not been issued.

*Revenues* **are gross inflows resulting from providing goods or services to customers.**

A key characteristic is that revenues are inflows. The enterprise is acquiring something in exchange for providing goods and services to customers. Also, providing these goods and services represents a major operation of the enterprise.

On the other hand, if selling the item is not part of the central operations of the business but instead is only an incidental result of those operations, the inflow of assets would produce a gain rather than a revenue.

**Gains** are increases in equity from peripheral, or incidental, transactions of an entity.

FedEx earns revenue by providing a service, delivering packages, to its customers. If FedEx sold a piece of machinery used to deliver packages for an amount greater than its book value (original cost less depreciation recorded up to the date of sale), a gain would result. Gains are net inflows, the difference between the amount received and book value. Revenues are gross inflows, measured as the amount received or to be received for the goods or services without regard to the cost of providing the goods or services.

*Expenses* **are gross outflows incurred in generating revenues.**

**Expenses** are outflows or other using up of assets or incurrences of liabilities during a period from delivering or producing goods, rendering services, or other activities that constitute the entity's ongoing major, or central, operations.

A key characteristic is that expenses represent outflows of resources incurred in the process of generating revenues.

**Losses** represent decreases in equity arising from peripheral, or incidental, transactions of an entity.

If FedEx sold that piece of machinery used to deliver packages for *less* than its book value, a loss would result. So, losses are the opposite of gains—they are net *outflows* rather than net inflows. They differ from expenses by being net rather than gross outflows and by being peripheral, or incidental, transactions rather than major, or central, operations. Revenues plus gains less expenses and losses for a period equals **net income** or **net loss,** the so-called bottom line of the income statement.[36]

You should note that the definitions of these nine elements are in basic agreement with those used in practice. But, *SFAC 6* also introduced a new term, the 10th element, called *comprehensive income.*

**Comprehensive income** is the change in equity of a business enterprise during a period from transactions and other events and circumstances from nonowner sources. It includes all changes in equity during a period except those resulting from investments by owners and distributions to owners.

*Comprehensive income* **often does not equal net income.**

Under present GAAP, net income as reported in the income statement often doesn't equal comprehensive income. The difference is the treatment of certain changes in assets and liabilities *not* included in the determination of net income for the period in which they are recognized but instead reported collectively as a separate component of shareholders' equity in the balance sheet called accumulated other comprehensive income. For example, in your study of investments in Chapter 12, you will learn that for certain types of investments valued at fair values in the balance sheet, the changes in those values are not included in net income but rather in a separate component of shareholders' equity. Comprehensive income is discussed in Chapter 4.

**FedEx Corporation**

In the **FedEx Corporation** financial statements in Appendix B, the income statement for the most recent fiscal year reports net income of $838 million. The balance sheet for the most recent fiscal year shows accumulated other comprehensive income of $(46 million), and the statement of changes in stockholders' investment and comprehensive income provides the details of the change in this figure from the prior year.

[36]Some companies use the term *net earnings* instead of net income. If earnings are negative, the term used is *net loss.*

## Recognition and Measurement Concepts

Now that the various elements of financial statements have been identified, we discuss when they should be recognized (recorded) and how they should be measured. *SFAC 5* addresses these issues. **Recognition** refers to the process of admitting information into the basic financial statements. **Measurement** is the process of associating numerical amounts to the elements. For example, a revenue was previously defined as an inflow of assets from selling a good or providing a service. But, *when* should the revenue event be recorded, and at *what* amount?

### RECOGNITION

According to *SFAC 5,* an item should be recognized in the basic financial statements when it meets the following four criteria, subject to a cost effectiveness constraint and materiality threshold:

Recognition criteria.

1. *Definition.* The item meets the definition of an element of financial statements.
2. *Measurability.* The item has a relevant attribute measurable with sufficient reliability.
3. *Relevance.* The information about it is capable of making a difference in user decisions.
4. *Reliability.* The information is representationally faithful, verifiable, and neutral.[37]

These obviously are very general guidelines. The concept statement does not address *specific* recognition issues.

### MEASUREMENT

The question of measurement involves two choices: (1) the choice of a unit of measurement, and (2) the choice of an attribute to be measured. *SFAC 5* essentially confirmed existing practice in both of these areas. The monetary unit or measurement scale used in financial statements is nominal units of money without any adjustment for changes in purchasing power. In addition, the board acknowledged that different attributes such as historical cost, net realizable value, and present value of future cash flows are presently used to measure different financial statement elements, and that they expect that practice to continue. For example, property, plant, and equipment are measured at historical cost; accounts receivable are measured at their net realizable value; and most long-term liabilities, such as bonds, are measured at the present value of future cash payments.

*SFAC No. 7* provides a framework for using future cash flows in accounting measurements.

Present value measurements have long been associated with accounting valuation. However, because of its increased prominence, present value is the focus of a recent FASB concept statement that provides a framework for using future cash flows as the basis for accounting measurement and also asserts that the objective in valuing an asset or liability using present value is to approximate the fair value of that asset or liability.[38] We explore this objective in more depth in Chapter 6.

Answers to the recognition and measurement questions are imbedded in generally accepted accounting principles. *SFAC 5* confirmed some of the more important of these principles used in present practice. GAAP consist of broad principles and specific standards. The accrual accounting model is an example of a broad principle. Before addressing additional key broad principles, we look at some important assumptions that underlie those fundamental principles.

### UNDERLYING ASSUMPTIONS

● LO7

The four basic assumptions underlying GAAP are (1) the economic entity assumption, (2) the going concern assumption, (3) the periodicity assumption, and (4) the monetary unit assumption.

[37]"Recognition and Measurement in Financial Statements," *Statement of Financial Accounting Concepts No. 5* (Stamford, Conn.: FASB, 1984), par. 63.

[38]"Using Cash Flow Information and Present Value in Accounting Measurements," *Statement of Financial Accounting Concepts No. 7* (Norwalk, Conn.: FASB, 2000).

The *economic entity assumption* presumes that economic events can be identified specifically with an economic entity.

**Economic Entity Assumption.** An essential assumption is that all economic events can be identified with a particular economic entity. Investors desire information about an economic entity that corresponds to their ownership interest. For example, if you were considering buying some ownership stock in FedEx, you would want information on the various operating units that constitute FedEx. You would need information not only about their United States operations but also about their European and other international operations. Also, you would not want the information about FedEx combined with that of **United Parcel Service (UPS)**, another air freight company. These would be two separate *economic entities.* The financial information for the various companies (subsidiaries) in which FedEx owns a controlling interest (greater than 50% ownership of voting stock) should be combined with that of FedEx (the parent). The parent and its subsidiaries are separate *legal* entities but one *accounting* entity.

Another key aspect of this assumption is the distinction between the economic activities of owners and those of the company. For example, the economic activities of a sole proprietorship, Uncle Jim's Restaurant, should be separated from the activities of its owner, Uncle Jim. Uncle Jim's personal residence, for instance, is not an asset of the business.

Financial statements of a company presume the business is a *going concern.*

**Going Concern Assumption.** Another necessary assumption is that, in the absence of information to the contrary, it is anticipated that a business entity will continue to operate indefinitely. Accountants realize that the **going concern assumption** does not always hold since there certainly are many business failures. However, companies are begun with the hope of a long life, and many achieve that goal.

This assumption is critical to many broad and specific accounting principles. For example, the assumption provides justification for measuring many assets based on their historical costs. If it were known that an enterprise was going to cease operations in the near future, assets and liabilities would not be measured at their historical costs but at their current liquidation values. Similarly, depreciation of a building over an estimated life of 40 years presumes the business will operate that long.

The *periodicity assumption* allows the life of a company to be divided into artificial time periods to provide timely information.

**Periodicity Assumption.** The **periodicity assumption** relates to the qualitative characteristic of *timeliness.* External users need *periodic* information to make decisions. This need for periodic information requires that the economic life of an enterprise (presumed to be indefinite) be divided into artificial time periods for financial reporting. Corporations whose securities are publicly traded are required to provide financial information to the SEC on a quarterly and annual basis.[39] Financial statements often are prepared on a monthly basis for banks and others that might need more timely information.

For many companies, the annual time period (the fiscal year) used to report to external users is the calendar year. However, other companies have chosen a **fiscal year** that does not correspond to the calendar year. The accounting profession and the Securities and Exchange Commission advocate that companies adopt a fiscal year that corresponds to their natural business year. A natural business year is the 12-month period that ends when the business activities of a company reach their lowest point in the annual cycle. For example, many retailers, **Wal-Mart** for example, have adopted a fiscal year ending on January 31. Business activity in January generally is quite slow following the very busy Christmas period. We can see from the FedEx financial statements that the company's fiscal year ends on May 31. The **Campbell Soup Company**'s fiscal year ends in July; **Clorox**'s in June; and **Monsanto**'s in August.

**FedEx Corporation**

The *monetary unit assumption* states that financial statement elements should be measured in terms of the dollar.

**Monetary Unit Assumption.** Recall that to *measure* financial statement elements, a unit or scale of measurement must be chosen. Information would be difficult to use if, for example, assets were listed as "three machines, two trucks, and a building." A common denominator is needed to measure all elements. The dollar in the United States is the most appropriate common denominator to express information about financial statement elements and changes in those elements.

[39]The report that must be filed for the first three quarters of each fiscal year is Form 10-Q and the annual report is Form 10-K.

One problem with this assumption is that the monetary unit is presumed to be stable over time. That is, the value of the dollar, in terms of its ability to purchase certain goods and services, is constant over time. This obviously does not strictly hold. The U.S. economy has experienced periods of rapidly changing prices. To the extent that prices are unstable, and those machines, trucks and building were purchased at different times, the monetary unit used to measure them is not the same. The effect of changing prices on financial information generally is discussed elsewhere in your accounting curriculum, often in an advanced accounting course.

## ACCOUNTING PRINCIPLES

● LO8

There are four important broad accounting principles that provide significant guidance for accounting practice: (1) the historical cost principle, (2) the realization principle (also known as the *revenue recognition principle*), (3) the matching principle, and (4) the full-disclosure principle. These principles deal with the critical issues of recognition and measurement. The accrual accounting model is embodied in each of the principles.

**The *historical cost principle* states that asset and liability measurements should be based on the amount given or received in the exchange transaction.**

**Historical Cost Principle.** The FASB recognized in *SFAC 5* that elements in financial statements currently are measured by different attributes. In general, however, GAAP measure assets and liabilities based on their *original transaction value,* that is, their **historical costs.** For an asset, this is the fair value of what is given in exchange (usually cash) for the asset at its initial acquisition. For liabilities, it is the current cash equivalent received in exchange for assuming the liability. For example, if a company borrowed $1 million cash and signed an interest-bearing note promising to repay the cash in the future, the liability would be valued at $1 million, the cash received in exchange.[40]

**Historical cost measurement provides relevant cash flow information and also is highly verifiable.**

Why base measurement on historical costs? After all, the current value of a company's manufacturing plant might seem more relevant than its original cost. First, historical cost provides important cash flow information as it represents the cash or cash equivalent paid for an asset or received in exchange for the assumption of a liability. Second, because historical cost valuation is the result of an exchange transaction between two independent parties, the agreed on exchange value is objective and highly *verifiable.* Alternatives such as measuring an asset at its current market value involve *estimating* a selling price. An example given earlier in the chapter concerned the valuation of a parcel of land. Appraisers could easily differ in their assessment of current market value.

There are occasions where a departure from measuring an asset based on its historical cost is warranted. Some assets, for instance, are measured at their *net realizable value.* For example, if customers purchased goods or services on account for $10,000, the asset, accounts receivable, would initially be valued at $10,000, the original transaction value. Subsequently, if $2,000 in bad debts were anticipated, net receivables should be valued at $8,000, the net realizable value. Departures from historical cost measurement such as this provide more appropriate information in terms of the overall objective of providing information to aid in the prediction of future cash flows.

**A departure from historical cost valuation sometimes is appropriate.**

**Realization Principle.** Determining accounting income by the accrual accounting model is a challenging task. When to recognize revenue is critical to this determination. Revenues are inflows of assets resulting from providing a product or service to a customer. At what point is this event recognized by an increase in assets? The **realization principle** requires that two criteria be satisfied before revenue can be recognized:

**Revenue should be recognized when the earnings process is virtually complete and collection is reasonably assured.**

1. The earnings process is judged to be complete or virtually complete.
2. There is reasonable certainty as to the collectibility of the asset to be received (usually cash).

These criteria help ensure that a revenue event is not recorded until an enterprise has performed all or most of its earnings activities for a financially capable buyer. The primary earnings activity that triggers the recognition of revenue is known as the *critical event.* The

[40]This current cash equivalent for many liabilities also will equal the present value of future cash payments. This is illustrated in a subsequent chapter.

**Both revenue recognition criteria usually are met at the *point-of-sale*.**

critical event for many businesses occurs at the **point-of-sale.** This usually takes place when the goods or services sold to the buyer are *delivered* (i.e., title is transferred).

The *timing* of revenue recognition is a key element of earnings measurement. An income statement should report the results of all operating activities for the time period specified in the financial statements. A one-year income statement should report the company's accomplishments only for that one-year period. Revenue recognition criteria help ensure that a proper cut-off is made each reporting period and that exactly one year's activity is reported in that income statement. Not adhering to revenue recognition criteria could result in overstating revenue and hence net income in one reporting period and, consequently, understating revenue and net income in a subsequent period. Notice that revenue recognition criteria allow for the implementation of the accrual accounting model. Revenue should be recognized in the period it is earned, *not necessarily in the period in which cash is received.*

**Revenue is recognized when *earned*, regardless of when cash actually is received.**

Some revenue-producing activities call for revenue recognition over time, rather than at one particular point in time. For example, revenue recognition could take place *during* the earnings process for long-term construction contracts. We discuss revenue recognition in considerable depth in Chapter 5. That chapter also describes in more detail the concept of an earnings process and how it relates to performance measurement.

**Expenses are recognized in the same reporting period as the related revenues.**

**Matching Principle.** When are expenses recognized? The **matching principle** states that expenses are recognized in the same period as the related revenues. There is a cause-and-effect relationship between revenue and expense recognition implicit in this definition. In a given period, revenue is recognized according to the realization principle. The matching principle then requires that all expenses incurred in generating that same revenue also be recognized. The net result is a measure—net income—that matches current period accomplishments and sacrifices. This accrual-based measure provides a good indicator of future cash-generating ability.

Although the concept is straightforward, its implementation can be difficult. The difficulty arises in trying to identify cause-and-effect relationships. Many expenses are not incurred *directly* because of a revenue event. Instead, the expense is incurred to generate the revenue, but the association is indirect.

The matching principle is implemented by one of four different approaches, depending on the nature of the specific expense. Only the first approach involves an actual cause-and-effect relationship between revenue and expense. In the other three approaches, the relationship is indirect.

An expense can be recognized:

1. Based on an exact cause-and-effect relationship between a revenue and expense event.
2. By associating an expense with the revenues recognized in a specific time period.
3. By a systematic and rational allocation to specific time periods.
4. In the period incurred, without regard to related revenues.

**There is a direct relationship between some expenses and revenues.**

The first approach is appropriate for *cost of goods sold.* There is a definite cause-and-effect relationship between **Dell Inc.**'s revenue from the sale of personal computers and the costs to produce those computers. Commissions paid to salespersons for obtaining revenues also is an example of an expense recognized based on this approach.

**Some expenses are associated indirectly with revenues of a particular period.**

Unfortunately, for most expenses there is no obvious cause-and-effect relationship between a revenue and expense event. In other words, the revenue event does not directly *cause* expenses to be incurred. Many expenses, however, can be related to periods of time during which revenue is earned. For example, the monthly salary paid to an office worker is not directly related to any specific revenue event. The employee provides services during the month. The asset used to pay the employee, cash, provides benefits to the company only for that one month and *indirectly* relates to the revenue recognized in that same period.

**Some expenses are allocated to specific time periods.**

Some costs are incurred to acquire assets that provide benefits to the company for more than one reporting period. Refer again to the Carter Company example in Illustration 1–1 on page 7. At the beginning of year 1, $60,000 in rent was paid covering a three-year period. This asset, prepaid rent, helps generate revenues for more than one reporting period. In that example, we chose to "systematically and rationally" allocate rent expense equally to each of the three one-year periods rather than to charge the expense to year 1.

The fourth approach to expense recognition is called for in situations when costs are incurred but it is impossible to determine in which period or periods, if any, revenues will occur. For example, consider the cost of advertising. Advertising expenditures are made with the presumption that incurring that expense will generate incremental revenues. Let's say FedEx spends $1 million for a series of television commercials. It's difficult to determine when, how much, or even whether additional revenues occur as a result of that particular series of ads. Because of this difficulty, advertising expenditures are recognized as expense in the period incurred, with no attempt made to match them with revenues.

**Some expenses are recognized in the period incurred, without regard to related revenues.**

**The Full-Disclosure Principle.** Remember, the purpose of accounting is to provide information that is useful to decision makers. So, naturally, if there is accounting information not included in the primary financial statements that would benefit users, that information should be provided too. The **full-disclosure principle** means that the financial reports should include any information that could affect the decisions made by external users. Of course, the benefits of that information, as noted earlier, should exceed the costs of providing the information. Supplemental information is disclosed in a variety of ways, including:

**Any information useful to decision makers should be provided in the financial statements, subject to the cost effectiveness constraint.**

1. **Parenthetical comments** or **modifying comments** placed on the face of the financial statements.
2. **Disclosure notes** conveying additional insights about company operations, accounting principles, contractual agreements, and pending litigation.
3. **Supplemental financial statements** that report more detailed information than is shown in the primary financial statements.

**FedEx Corporation**

We find examples of these disclosures in the FedEx financial statements in Appendix B located at the back of this text. A parenthetical or modifying comment is provided in the common stockholders' investment section of the balance sheet with disclosure of the number of shares of stock authorized, issued, and outstanding. The statements include several notes as well as a supplemental statement disclosing information about the company's quarterly operating results. Notice that the **FedEx Corporation** financial statements include the following statement: "The accompanying notes are an integral part of these consolidated financial statements." We discuss and illustrate disclosure requirements as they relate to specific financial statement elements in later chapters as those elements are discussed.

Graphic 1–8 provides a summary of the accounting assumptions and principles that guide the recognition and measurement of accounting information.

**GRAPHIC 1–8**
Summary of Recognition and Measurement Concepts

| **Assumptions** | **Description** |
|---|---|
| Economic entity | All economic events can be identified with a particular economic entity. |
| Going concern | In the absence of information to the contrary, it is anticipated that a business entity will continue to operate indefinitely. |
| Periodicity | The life of a company can be divided into artificial time periods to provide timely information to external users. |
| Monetary unit | In the United States, financial statement elements should be measured in terms of the U.S. dollar. |
| **Principles** | |
| Historical cost | Asset and liability measurements should be based on the amount given or received in an exchange transaction. |
| Realization | Revenue should be recognized only after the earnings process is virtually complete and there is reasonable certainty of collecting the asset to be received from the customer. |
| Matching | Expenses should be recognized in the same reporting period as the related revenues. |
| Full disclosure | Any information that could change the decisions made by external users should be provided in the financial statements, subject to the cost effectiveness constraint. |

## Ethics in Accounting

***Ethics* deals with the ability to distinguish right from wrong.**

**Ethics** is a term that refers to a code or moral system that provides criteria for evaluating right and wrong. An ethical dilemma is a situation in which an individual or group is faced with a decision that tests this code. Many of these dilemmas are simple to recognize and resolve. For example, have you ever been tempted to call your professor and ask for an extension on the due date of an assignment by claiming a fictitious illness? Temptation like this will test your personal ethics.

Accountants, like others operating in the business world, are faced with many ethical dilemmas, some of which are complex and difficult to resolve. For instance, the capital markets' focus on periodic profits may tempt a company's management to bend or even break accounting rules to inflate reported net income. In these situations, technical competence is not enough to resolve the dilemma.

### ETHICS AND PROFESSIONALISM

One of the elements that many believe distinguishes a profession from other occupations is the acceptance by its members of a responsibility for the interests of those it serves. A high standard of ethical behavior is expected of those engaged in a profession. These standards often are articulated in a code of ethics. For example, law and medicine are professions that have their own codes of professional ethics. These codes provide guidance and rules to members in the performance of their professional responsibilities.

Public accounting has achieved widespread recognition as a profession. The AICPA, the national organization of professional certified public accountants, has its own Code of Professional Conduct which prescribes the ethical conduct members should strive to achieve. Similarly, the **Institute of Management Accountants (IMA)**—the primary national organization of accountants working in industry and government—has its own code of ethics, as does the **Institute of Internal Auditors**—the national organization of accountants providing internal auditing services for their own organizations.

### ANALYTICAL MODEL FOR ETHICAL DECISIONS

Ethical codes are informative and helpful. However, the motivation to behave ethically must come from within oneself and not just from the fear of penalties for violating professional codes. Presented below is a sequence of steps that provide a framework for analyzing ethical issues. These steps can help you apply your own sense of right and wrong to ethical dilemmas:[41]

**Step 1.** Determine the facts of the situation. This involves determining the who, what, where, when, and how.

**Step 2.** Identify the ethical issue and the stakeholders. Stakeholders may include shareholders, creditors, management, employees, and the community.

**Step 3.** Identify the values related to the situation. For example, in some situations confidentiality may be an important value that may conflict with the right to know.

**Step 4.** Specify the alternative courses of action.

**Step 5.** Evaluate the courses of action specified in step 4 in terms of their consistency with the values identified in step 3. This step may or may not lead to a suggested course of action.

**Step 6.** Identify the consequences of each possible course of action. If step 5 does not provide a course of action, assess the consequences of each possible course of action for all of the stakeholders involved.

**Step 7.** Make your decision and take any indicated action.

---

[41]Adapted from Harold Q. Langenderfer and Joanne W. Rockness, "Integrating Ethics into the Accounting Curriculum: Issues, Problems, and Solutions," *Issues in Accounting Education* (Spring 1989). These steps are consistent with those provided by the American Accounting Association's Advisory Committee on Professionalism and Ethics in their publication *Ethics in the Accounting Curriculum: Cases and Readings, 1990.*

## ETHICAL DILEMMA

You have recently been employed by a large retail chain that sells sporting goods. One of your tasks is to help prepare periodic financial statements for external distribution. The chain's largest creditor, National Savings & Loan, requires quarterly financial statements, and you are currently working on the statements for the three-month period ending June 30, 2006.

During the months of May and June, the company spent $1,200,000 on a large radio and TV advertising campaign. The $1,200,000 included the costs of producing the commercials as well as the radio and TV time purchased to run the commercials. All of the costs were charged to advertising expense. The company's chief financial officer (CFO) has asked you to prepare a June 30 adjusting entry to remove the costs from advertising expense and to set up an asset called *prepaid advertising* that will be expensed in July. The CFO explained that "This advertising campaign has produced significant sales in May and June and I think it will continue to bring in customers through the month of July. By recording the ad costs as an asset, we can match the cost of the advertising with the additional July sales. Besides, if we expense the advertising in May and June, we will show an operating loss on our income statement for the quarter. The bank requires that we continue to show quarterly profits in order to maintain our loan in good standing."

Ethical dilemmas are presented throughout the text. These dilemmas are designed to raise your consciousness on accounting issues with ethical ramifications. The analytical steps outlined above provide a framework with which to evaluate these situations. In addition, your instructor may assign end-of-chapter ethics cases for further discussion and application.

## FINANCIAL REPORTING CASE SOLUTION

1. **What should you tell your friend about the presence of accounting standards in the United States? Who has the authority for standard setting? Who has the responsibility?** *(p. 9)* In the United States we have a set of standards known as generally accepted accounting principles (GAAP). GAAP are a dynamic set of both broad and specific guidelines that companies should follow when measuring and reporting the information in their financial statements and related notes. The Securities and Exchange Commission has the authority to set accounting standards for companies whose securities are publicly traded but always has delegated the responsibility to the accounting profession. At present, the Financial Accounting Standards Board is the private sector body responsible for standard setting.
2. **What is the economic and political environment in which standard setting occurs?** *(p. 12)* The setting of accounting and reporting standards often has been characterized as a *political process*. Standards, particularly changes in standards, can have significant differential effects on companies, investors and creditors, and other interest groups. A change in an accounting standard or the introduction of a new standard can result in a substantial redistribution of wealth within our economy. The FASB must consider potential economic consequences of a change in an accounting standard or the introduction of a new standard.
3. **What is the relationship among management, auditors, investors, and creditors that tends to preclude the "What would you like it to be?" attitude?** *(p. 15)* It is the responsibility of management to apply accounting standards when communicating with investors and creditors through financial statements. Auditors serve as independent intermediaries to help ensure that the management-prepared statements are presented fairly in accordance with GAAP. In providing this assurance, the auditor precludes the "What would you like it to be?" attitude.
4. **In general, what is the conceptual framework that underlies accounting principles?** *(p. 18)* The conceptual framework is a coherent system of interrelated objectives and fundamentals that can lead to consistent standards and that prescribe the nature, function, and limits of financial accounting and reporting. The fundamentals are the underlying concepts

of accounting, concepts that guide the selection of events to be accounted for, the measurement of those events, and the means of summarizing and communicating them to interested parties. ■

## THE BOTTOM LINE

1. Financial accounting is concerned with providing relevant financial information to various external users. However, the primary focus is on the financial information provided by profit-oriented companies to their present and potential investors and creditors.
2. Cash basis accounting provides a measure of periodic performance called *net operating cash flow,* which is the difference between cash receipts and cash disbursements from transactions related to providing goods and services to customers. Accrual accounting provides a measure of performance called *net income,* which is the difference between revenues and expenses. Periodic net income is considered a better indicator of future operating cash flows than is current net operating cash flows.
3. Generally accepted accounting principles (GAAP) comprise a dynamic set of both broad and specific guidelines that companies follow when measuring and reporting the information in their financial statements and related notes. The Securities and Exchange Commission (SEC) has both the authority and responsibility to set accounting standards. However, the SEC has always delegated the responsibility to a private sector body, at this time the Financial Accounting Standards Board (FASB).
4. Accounting standards can have significant differential effects on companies, investors, creditors, and other interest groups. For this reason, the setting of accounting standards often has been characterized as a political process.
5. The FASB's conceptual framework is a set of cohesive objectives and fundamental concepts on which financial accounting and reporting standards will be based.
6. The objectives of financial reporting are concerned with providing information to help investors and creditors predict future cash flows. The primary decision-specific qualities that make accounting information useful are relevance and reliability. To be relevant, information must possess predictive value and/or feedback value and must be provided in a timely manner. The characteristics of reliable information are verifiability, representational faithfulness, and neutrality. The 10 elements of financial statements are assets, liabilities, equity, investments by owners, distributions to owners, revenues, expenses, gains, losses, and comprehensive income.
7. The four basic assumptions underlying GAAP are (1) the economic entity assumption, (2) the going concern assumption, (3) the periodicity assumption, and (4) the monetary unit assumption.
8. The four broad accounting principles that guide accounting practice are (1) the historical cost principle, (2) the realization principle, (3) the matching principle, and (4) the full-disclosure principle. ■

## QUESTIONS FOR REVIEW OF KEY TOPICS

**Q 1–1** What is the function and primary focus of financial accounting?

**Q 1–2** What is meant by the phrase *efficient allocation of resources*? What mechanism fosters the efficient allocation of resources in the United States?

**Q 1–3** Identify two important variables to be considered when making an investment decision.

**Q 1–4** What must a company do in the long run to be able to provide a return to investors and creditors?

**Q 1–5** What is the primary objective of financial accounting?

**Q 1–6** Define net operating cash flows. Briefly explain why periodic net operating cash flows may not be a good indicator of future operating cash flows.

**Q 1–7** What is meant by GAAP? Why should all companies follow GAAP in reporting to external users?

**Q 1–8** Explain the roles of the SEC and the FASB in the setting of accounting standards.

**Q 1–9** Explain the role of the auditor in the financial reporting process.

**Q 1–10** List three key provisions of the Sarbanes-Oxley Act of 2002. Order your list from most important to least important in terms of the likely long-term impact on the accounting profession and financial reporting.

**Q 1–11** Explain what is meant by *adverse economic consequences* of new or changed accounting standards.

**Q 1–12** Why does the FASB undertake a series of elaborate information-gathering steps before issuing a substantive accounting standard?

**Q 1–13** What is the purpose of the FASB's conceptual framework project?

**Q 1–14** Discuss the terms *relevance* and *reliability* as they relate to financial accounting information.

**Q 1–15** What are the components of relevant information? What are the components of reliable information?

**Q 1–16** Explain what is meant by: The benefits of accounting information must exceed the costs.

**Q 1–17** What is meant by the term *materiality* in financial reporting?

**Q 1–18** Briefly define the financial accounting elements: (1) assets, (2) liabilities, (3) equity, (4) investments by owners, (5) distributions to owners, (6) revenues, (7) expenses, (8) gains, (9) losses, and (10) comprehensive income.

**Q 1–19** What are the four basic assumptions underlying GAAP?

**Q 1–20** What is the going concern assumption?

**Q 1–21** Explain the periodicity assumption.

**Q 1–22** What are the four key broad accounting principles that guide accounting practice?

**Q 1–23** What are two important reasons to base the valuation of assets and liabilities on their historical cost?

**Q 1–24** Describe the two criteria that must be satisfied before revenue can be recognized.

**Q 1–25** What are the four different approaches to implementing the matching principle? Give an example of an expense that is recognized under each approach.

**Q 1–26** In addition to the financial statement elements arrayed in the basic financial statements, what are some other ways to disclose financial information to external users?

## BRIEF EXERCISES

**BE 1–1**
Accrual accounting
● LO2

Cash flows during the first year of operations for the Harman-Kardon Consulting Company were as follows: Cash collected from customers, $340,000; Cash paid for rent, $40,000; Cash paid to employees for services rendered during the year, $120,000; Cash paid for utilities, $50,000.

In addition, you determine that customers owed the company $60,000 at the end of the year and no bad debts were anticipated. Also, the company owed the gas and electric company $2,000 at year-end, and the rent payment was for a two-year period. Calculate accrual net income for the year.

**BE 1–2**
Sources of GAAP
● LO3

Identify the issuing organization for each of the following types of pronouncements: (a) Financial Reporting Releases, (b) Industry Accounting Guides, and (c) Statements of Financial Accounting Standards.

**BE 1–3**
Financial statement elements
● LO6

For each of the following items, identify the appropriate financial statement element or elements: (1) probable future sacrifices of economic benefits; (2) probable future economic benefits owned by the company; (3) inflows of assets from ongoing, major activities; (4) decrease in equity from peripheral or incidental transactions.

**BE 1–4**
Basic assumptions and principles
● LO6 through LO8

Listed below are several statements that relate to financial accounting and reporting. Identify the basic assumption, broad accounting principle, or pervasive constraint that applies to each statement.

1. **Sirius Satellite Radio Inc.** files its annual and quarterly financial statements with the SEC.
2. The president of **Applebee's International, Inc.** travels on the corporate jet for business purposes only and does not use the jet for personal use.
3. Jackson Manufacturing does not recognize revenue for unshipped merchandise even though the merchandise has been manufactured according to customer specifications.
4. Lady Jane Cosmetics depreciates the cost of equipment over their useful lives.

**BE 1–5**
Basic assumptions and principles
● LO6 through LO8

Identify the basic assumption or broad accounting principle that was violated in each of the following situations.

1. Astro Turf Company recognizes an expense, cost of goods sold, in the period the product is manufactured.
2. McCloud Drug Company owns a patent that it purchased three years ago for $2 million. The controller recently revalued the patent to its approximate market value of $8 million.
3. Philips Company pays the monthly mortgage on the home of its president, Larry Crosswhite, and charges the expenditure to miscellaneous expense.

**BE 1–6**
Basic assumptions and principles

● LO6 through LO8

For each of the following situations, (1) indicate whether you agree or disagree with the financial reporting practice employed and (2) state the basic assumption, pervasive constraint, or accounting principle that is applied (if you agree), or violated (if you disagree).

1. Winderl Corporation did not disclose that it was the defendant in a material lawsuit because the trial was still in progress.
2. Alliant Semiconductor Corporation files quarterly and annual financial statements with the SEC.
3. Reliant Pharmaceutical paid rent on its office building for the next two years and charged the entire expenditure to rent expense.
4. Rockville Engineering records revenue only after products have been shipped, even though customers pay Rockville 50% of the sales price in advance.

## EXERCISES

available with McGraw-Hill's Homework Manager www.mhhe.com/spiceland4e

**An alternate exercise and problem set is available on the text website: www.mhhe.com/spiceland4e**

**E 1–1**
Accrual accounting

● LO2

Listed below are several transactions that took place during the first two years of operations for the law firm of Pete, Pete, and Roy.

| | Year 1 | Year 2 |
|---|---|---|
| Amounts billed to customers for services rendered | $170,000 | $220,000 |
| Cash collected from customers | 160,000 | 190,000 |
| Cash disbursements: | | |
| Purchase of insurance policy | 60,000 | –0– |
| Salaries paid to employees for services rendered during the year | 90,000 | 100,000 |
| Utilities | 30,000 | 40,000 |

In addition, you learn that the company incurred utility costs of $35,000 in year one, that there were no liabilities at the end of year two, no anticipated bad debts on receivables, and that the insurance policy covers a three-year period.

**Required:**

1. Calculate the net operating cash flow for years 1 and 2.
2. Prepare an income statement for each year similar to Illustration 1–2 on page 8 according to the accrual accounting model.
3. Determine the amount of receivables from customers that the company would show in its year 1 and year 2 balance sheets prepared according to the accrual accounting model.

**E 1–2**
Accrual accounting

● LO2

Listed below are several transactions that took place during the second two years of operations for RPG Consulting.

| | Year 2 | Year 3 |
|---|---|---|
| Amounts billed to customers for services rendered | $350,000 | $450,000 |
| Cash collected from credit customers | 260,000 | 400,000 |
| Cash disbursements: | | |
| Payment of rent | 80,000 | –0– |
| Salaries paid to employees for services rendered during the year | 140,000 | 160,000 |
| Travel and entertainment | 30,000 | 40,000 |
| Advertising | 15,000 | 35,000 |

In addition, you learn that the company incurred advertising costs of $25,000 in year 2, owed the advertising agency $5,000 at the end of year 1, and there were no liabilities at the end of year 3. Also, there were no anticipated bad debts on receivables, and the rent payment was for a two-year period, year 2 and year 3.

**Required:**

1. Calculate accrual net income for both years.
2. Determine the amount due the advertising agency that would be shown as a liability on the RPG's balance sheet at the end of year 2.

**E 1–3**
Sources of GAAP

● LO3

Different organizations historically and currently have issued various pronouncements that constitute the body of generally accepted accounting principles. Presented below are some of these organizations as well as various authoritative pronouncements. Match each organization with the one or more pronouncement(s) with which it is associated.

| Organization | Pronouncements |
|---|---|
| 1. Accounting Principles Board | a. *Statements of Financial Accounting Concepts* |
| 2. Financial Accounting Standards Board | b. *Financial Reporting Releases* |
| 3. Securities and Exchange Commission | c. *Accounting Research Bulletins* |
| 4. Committee on Accounting Procedure | d. *Statements of Financial Accounting Standards* |
| 5. AICPA | e. *APBOs* |
| | f. *Industry Accounting Guides* |
| | g. *Technical Bulletins* |

**E 1–4**
Participants in establishing GAAP

● LO3

Three groups that participate in the process of establishing GAAP are users, preparers, and auditors. These groups are represented by various organizations. For each organization listed below, indicate which of these groups it primarily represents.

1. Securities and Exchange Commission
2. Financial Executives International
3. American Institute of Certified Public Accountants
4. Institute of Management Accountants
5. Association of Investment Management and Research

**E 1–5**
Financial statement elements

● LO6

For each of the items listed below, identify the appropriate financial statement element or elements.

1. Obligation to transfer cash or other resources as a result of a past transaction.
2. Dividends paid by a corporation to its shareholders.
3. Inflow of an asset from providing a good or service.
4. The financial position of a company.
5. Increase in equity during a period from nonowner transactions.
6. Increase in equity from peripheral or incidental transaction.
7. Sale of an asset used in the operations of a business for less than the asset's book value.
8. The owners' residual interest in the assets of a company.
9. An item owned by the company representing probable future benefits.
10. Revenues plus gains less expenses and losses.
11. An owner's contribution of cash to a corporation in exchange for ownership shares of stock.
12. Outflow of an asset related to the production of revenue.

**E 1–6**
Concepts; terminology; conceptual framework

● LO6

Listed below are several terms and phrases associated with the FASB's conceptual framework. Pair each item from List A (by letter) with the item from List B that is most appropriately associated with it.

| List A | List B |
|---|---|
| ____ 1. Predictive value | a. Decreases in equity resulting from transfers to owners. |
| ____ 2. Relevance | b. Requires consideration of the costs and value of information. |
| ____ 3. Timeliness | c. Important for making interfirm comparisons. |
| ____ 4. Distribution to owners | d. Applying the same accounting practices over time. |
| ____ 5. Feedback value | e. Along with relevance, a primary decision-specific quality. |
| ____ 6. Reliability | f. Agreement between a measure and the phenomenon it purports to represent. |
| ____ 7. Gain | g. Information is available prior to the decision. |
| ____ 8. Representational faithfulness | h. Pertinent to the decision at hand. |
| ____ 9. Comprehensive income | i. Implies consensus among different measurers. |
| ____ 10. Materiality | j. Information confirms expectations. |
| ____ 11. Comparability | k. The change in equity from nonowner transactions. |
| ____ 12. Neutrality | l. The process of admitting information into financial statements. |
| ____ 13. Recognition | m. Accounting information should not favor a particular group. |
| ____ 14. Consistency | n. Results if an asset is sold for more than its book value. |
| ____ 15. Cost effectiveness | o. Information is useful in predicting the future. |
| ____ 16. Verifiability | p. Concerns the relative size of an item and its effect on decisions. |

**E 1–7**
Multiple choice; conceptual framework

● LO6

The following questions dealing with the FASB's conceptual framework are adapted from questions that appeared on CPA examinations. Determine the response that best completes the statements or questions.

1. According to the FASB conceptual framework, which of the following situations violates the concept of reliability?
   a. Data on segments having the same expected risk and growth rates are reported to analysts estimating future profits.
   b. Financial statements are issued nine months late.

c. Management reports to stockholders regularly refer to new projects undertaken, but the financial statements never report project results.
d. Financial statements include property with a carrying amount increased to management's estimate of market value.

2. According to *Statements of Financial Accounting Concepts,* neutrality is an ingredient of

| | Reliability | Relevance |
|---|---|---|
| a. | Yes | Yes |
| b. | Yes | No |
| c. | No | Yes |
| d. | No | No |

3. According to the FASB conceptual framework, predictive value is an ingredient of

| | Relevance | Reliability |
|---|---|---|
| a. | No | No |
| b. | Yes | Yes |
| c. | No | Yes |
| d. | Yes | No |

4. According to the FASB conceptual framework, earnings
   a. Are the same as comprehensive income.
   b. Exclude certain gains and losses that are included in comprehensive income.
   c. Include certain gains and losses that are excluded from comprehensive income.
   d. Include certain losses that are excluded from comprehensive income.
5. According to the FASB conceptual framework, which of the following relates to both relevance and reliability?

| | Consistency | Verifiability |
|---|---|---|
| a. | Yes | Yes |
| b. | Yes | No |
| c. | No | Yes |
| d. | No | No |

**E 1–8**
Basic assumptions, principles, and constraints

● LO6 through LO8

Listed below are several terms and phrases associated with basic assumptions, underlying principles, and constraints. Pair each item from List A (by letter) with the item from List B that is most appropriately associated with it.

| List A | List B |
|---|---|
| ____ 1. Matching principle | a. The enterprise is separate from its owners and other entities. |
| ____ 2. Periodicity | b. A common denominator is the dollar. |
| ____ 3. Historical cost principle | c. The entity will continue indefinitely. |
| ____ 4. Materiality | d. Record expenses in the period the related revenue is recognized. |
| ____ 5. Realization principle | e. The original transaction value upon acquisition. |
| ____ 6. Going concern assumption | f. All information that could affect decisions should be reported. |
| ____ 7. Monetary unit assumption | g. The life of an enterprise can be divided into artificial time periods. |
| ____ 8. Economic entity assumption | h. Criteria usually satisfied at point of sale. |
| ____ 9. Full-disclosure principle | i. Concerns the relative size of an item and its effect on decisions. |

**E 1–9**
Basic assumptions and principles

● LO6 through LO8

Listed below are several statements that relate to financial accounting and reporting. Identify the basic assumption, broad accounting principle, or pervasive constraint that applies to each statement.

1. Jim Marley is the sole owner of Marley's Appliances. Jim borrowed $100,000 to buy a new home to be used as his personal residence. This liability was not recorded in the records of Marley's Appliances.
2. **Apple Computer, Inc.**, distributes an annual report to its shareholders.
3. **Hewlett-Packard Corporation** depreciates machinery and equipment over their useful lives.
4. Crosby Company lists land on its balance sheet at $120,000, its original purchase price, even though the land has a current market value of $200,000.
5. **Honeywell Corporation** records revenue when products are delivered to customers, even though the cash has not yet been received.
6. Liquidation values are not normally reported in financial statements even though many companies do go out of business.
7. **IBM Corporation**, a multibillion dollar company, purchased some small tools at a cost of $800. Even though the tools will be used for a number of years, the company recorded the purchase as an expense.

**E 1–10**
Basic assumptions and principles
● LO7 LO8

Identify the basic assumption or broad accounting principle that was violated in each of the following situations.

1. Pastel Paint Company purchased land two years ago at a price of $250,000. Because the value of the land has appreciated to $400,000, the company has valued the land at $400,000 in its most recent balance sheet.
2. Atwell Corporation has not prepared financial statements for external users for over three years.
3. The Klingon Company sells farm machinery. Revenue from a large order of machinery from a new buyer was recorded the day the order was received.
4. Don Smith is the sole owner of a company called Hardware City. The company recently paid a $150 utility bill for Smith's personal residence and recorded a $150 expense.
5. Golden Book Company purchased a large printing machine for $1,000,000 (a material amount) and recorded the purchase as an expense.
6. Ace Appliance Company is involved in a major lawsuit involving injuries sustained by some of its employees in the manufacturing plant. The company is being sued for $2,000,000, a material amount, and is not insured. The suit was not disclosed in the most recent financial statements because no settlement had been reached.

**E 1–11**
Basic assumptions and principles
● LO6 through LO8

For each of the following situations, indicate whether you agree or disagree with the financial reporting practice employed and state the basic assumption, pervasive constraint, or accounting principle that is applied (if you agree) or violated (if you disagree).

1. Wagner Corporation adjusted the valuation of all assets and liabilities to reflect changes in the purchasing power of the dollar.
2. Spooner Oil Company changed its method of accounting for oil and gas exploration costs from successful efforts to full cost. No mention of the change was included in the financial statements. The change had a material effect on Spooner's financial statements.
3. Cypress Manufacturing Company purchased machinery having a five-year life. The cost of the machinery is being expensed over the life of the machinery.
4. Rudeen Corporation purchased equipment for $180,000 at a liquidation sale of a competitor. Because the equipment was worth $230,000, Rudeen valued the equipment in its subsequent balance sheet at $230,000.
5. Davis Bicycle Company received a large order for the sale of 1,000 bicycles at $100 each. The customer paid Davis the entire amount of $100,000 on March 15. However, Davis did not record any revenue until April 17, the date the bicycles were delivered to the customer.
6. Gigantic Corporation purchased two small calculators at a cost of $32.00. The cost of the calculators was expensed even though they had a three-year estimated useful life.
7. Esquire Company provides financial statements to external users every three years.

**E 1–12**
Basic assumptions, principles, and constraints
● LO6 through LO8

Listed below are the basic assumptions, underlying principles, and constraints discussed in this chapter.

a. Economic entity assumption
b. Going concern assumption
c. Periodicity assumption
d. Monetary unit assumption
e. Historical cost principle
f. Realization principle
g. Matching principle
h. Full-disclosure principle
i. Cost effectiveness
j. Materiality
k. Conservatism

Identify by letter the assumption, principle, or constraint that relates to each statement or phrase below.

____ 1. Revenue is recognized only after certain criteria are satisfied.
____ 2. Information that could affect decision making should be reported.
____ 3. Cause-and-effect relationship between revenues and expenses.
____ 4. The basis for measurement of many assets and liabilities.
____ 5. Relates to the qualitative characteristic of timeliness.
____ 6. All economic events can be identified with a particular entity.
____ 7. The benefits of providing accounting information should exceed the cost of doing so.
____ 8. A consequence is that GAAP need not be followed in all situations.
____ 9. Not a qualitative characteristic, but a practical justification for some accounting choices.
____ 10. Assumes the entity will continue indefinitely.
____ 11. Inflation causes a violation of this assumption.

**E 1–13**
Multiple choice; concept statements, basic assumptions, principles
● LO5 through LO8

Determine the response that best completes the following statements or questions.

1. The primary objective of financial reporting is to provide information
   a. About a firm's economic resources and obligations.
   b. Useful in predicting future cash flows.
   c. Concerning the changes in financial position resulting from the income-producing efforts of the entity.
   d. About a firm's financing and investing activities.

2. *Statements of Financial Accounting Concepts* issued by the FASB
   a. Represent GAAP.
   b. Have been superseded by *SFAS*s.
   c. Are subject to approval of the SEC.
   d. Identify the conceptual framework within which accounting standards are developed.
3. In general, revenue is recognized as earned when the earning process is virtually complete and
   a. The sales price has been collected.
   b. A purchase order has been received.
   c. There is reasonable certainty as to the collectibility of the asset to be received.
   d. A contract has been signed.
4. In depreciating the cost of an asset, accountants are most concerned with
   a. Conservatism.
   b. The realization principle.
   c. Full disclosure.
   d. The matching principle.
5. The primary objective of the matching principle is to
   a. Provide full disclosure.
   b. Record expenses in the period that related revenues are recognized.
   c. Provide timely information to decision makers.
   d. Promote comparability between financial statements of different periods.
6. The separate entity assumption states that, in the absence of contrary evidence, all entities will survive indefinitely.
   a. True
   b. False

**E 1–14**
Multiple choice; CMA exam; concepts

● LO3 LO6

The following questions dealing with the environment and theoretical structure of financial accounting are adapted from questions that previously appeared on Certified Management Accountant (CMA) examinations. The CMA designation sponsored by the Institute of Management Accountants (**www.imanet.org**) provides members with an objective measure of knowledge and competence in the field of management accounting. Determine the response that best completes the statements or questions.

1. Accounting standard setting in the U.S. is
   a. Done primarily by the Securities and Exchange Commission.
   b. Done primarily by the private sector.
   c. The responsibility of the public sector.
   d. Done primarily by the International Accounting Standards Committee.
2. Reliability as used in accounting includes
   a. Determining the revenue first, then determining the costs incurred in earning that revenue.
   b. The entity's giving the same treatment to comparable transactions from period to period.
   c. Similar results being obtained by both the accountant and an independent party using the same measurement methods.
   d. The disclosure of all facts that may influence the judgment of an informed reader.
3. Recognition is the process of formally recording and reporting an item in the financial statements. In order for a revenue item to be recognized, it must be all of the following except
   a. Measurable.
   b. Relevant.
   c. Material.
   d. Realized or realizable.

## BROADEN YOUR PERSPECTIVE

**Apply your critical-thinking ability to the knowledge you've gained. These cases will provide you an opportunity to develop your research, analysis, judgment, and communication skills. You will also work with other students, integrate what you've learned, apply it in real-world situations, and consider its global and ethical ramifications. This practice will broaden your knowledge and further develop your decision-making abilities.**

**Judgment Case 1–1**
The development of accounting standards

● LO3

In 1934, Congress created the Securities and Exchange Commission (SEC) and gave the commission both the power and responsibility for setting accounting and reporting standards in the United States.

**Required:**

1. Explain the relationship between the SEC and the various private sector standard-setting bodies that have, over time, been delegated the responsibility for setting accounting standards.
2. Can you think of any reasons why the SEC has delegated this responsibility rather than set standards directly?

**Research Case 1–2**
Accessing SEC information through the Internet
● LO3

Internet access to the World Wide Web has provided a wealth of information accessible with our personal computers. Many chapters in this text contain Real World Cases that require you to access the web to research an accounting issue. The purpose of this case is to introduce you to the Internet home page of the Securities and Exchange Commission (SEC) and its EDGAR database.

**Required:**

1. Access the SEC home page on the Internet. The web address is www.sec.gov.
2. Choose the subaddress "About the SEC." What are the two basic objectives of the 1933 Securities Act?
3. Return to the SEC home page and access EDGAR. Describe the contents of the database.

**Research Case 1–3**
Accessing FASB information through the Internet
● LO4

The purpose of this case is to introduce you to the information available on the website of the Financial Accounting Standards Board (FASB).

**Required:**

Access the FASB home page on the Internet. The web address is www.fasb.org. Answer the following questions.

1. Describe the mission of the FASB.
2. Who are the current Board members? Briefly describe their backgrounds.
3. How are topics added to the FASB's technical agenda?
4. How many standards have been issued by the FASB? What topic is addressed in the most recently issued standard?
5. How many Exposure Drafts are currently outstanding? What topics do they address?

**Research Case 1–4**
Accounting standards in China
● LO3 LO4

Economic reforms in the People's Republic of China are moving that nation toward a market-driven economy. China's accounting practices must also change to accommodate the needs of potential investors. In an article entitled "Institutional Factors Influencing China's Accounting Reforms and Standards," Professor Bing Xiang analyzes the changes in the accounting environment of China during the recent economic reforms and their implications for the development of accounting reforms.

**Required:**

1. In your library or from some other source, locate the indicated article in *Accounting Horizons*, June 1998.
2. Briefly describe the economic reforms that led to the need for increased external financial reporting in China.
3. Conformity with International Accounting Standards was specified as an overriding objective in formulating China's accounting standards. What is the author's opinion of this objective?

**Communication Case 1–5**
Relevance and reliability
● LO6

Some theorists contend that companies that create pollution should report the social cost of that pollution in income statements. They argue that such companies are indirectly subsidized as the cost of pollution is borne by society while only production costs (and perhaps minimal pollution fines) are shown in the income statement. Thus, the product sells for less than would be necessary if all costs were included.

Assume that the FASB is considering a standard to include the social costs of pollution in the income statement. The process would require considering both relevance and reliability of the information produced by the new standard. Your instructor will divide the class into two to six groups depending on the size of the class. The mission of your group is to explain how the concepts of relevance and reliability relate to this issue.

**Required:**

Each group member should consider the question independently and draft a tentative answer prior to the class session for which the case is assigned.

In class, each group will meet for 10 to 15 minutes in different areas of the classroom. During that meeting, group members will take turns sharing their suggestions for the purpose of arriving at a single group treatment.

After the allotted time, a spokesperson for each group (selected during the group meetings) will share the group's solution with the class. The goal of the class is to incorporate the views of each group into a consensus answer to the question.

**Communication Case 1–6**
Accounting standard setting

● LO4

One of your friends is a financial analyst for a major stock brokerage firm. Recently she indicated to you that she had read an article in a weekly business magazine that alluded to the political process of establishing accounting standards. She had always assumed that accounting standards were established by determining the approach that conceptually best reflected the economics of a transaction.

**Required:**

Write a one to two-page article for a business journal explaining what is meant by the political process for establishing accounting standards. Be sure to include in your article a discussion of the need for the FASB to balance accounting considerations and economic consequences.

**Ethics Case 1–7**
The auditors' responsibility

● LO4

It is the responsibility of management to apply accounting standards when communicating with investors and creditors through financial statements. Another group, auditors, serves as an independent intermediary to help ensure that management has in fact appropriately applied GAAP in preparing the company's financial statements. Auditors examine (audit) financial statements to express a professional, independent opinion. The opinion reflects the auditors' assessment of the statements' fairness, which is determined by the extent to which they are prepared in compliance with GAAP.

Some feel that it is impossible for an auditor to give an independent opinion on a company's financial statements because the auditors' fees for performing the audit are paid by the company. In addition to the audit fee, quite often the auditor performs other services for the company such as preparing the company's income tax returns.

**Required:**

How might an auditor's ethics be challenged while performing an audit?

**Judgment Case 1–8**
Qualitative characteristics

● LO6

Generally accepted accounting principles do not require companies to disclose forecasts of any financial variables to external users. A friend, who is a finance major, is puzzled by this and asks you to explain why such relevant information is not provided to investors and creditors to help them predict future cash flows.

**Required:**

Explain to your friend why this information is not routinely provided to investors and creditors.

**Judgment Case 1–9**
GAAP, comparability, and the role of the auditor

● LO4 LO6

Mary McQuire is trying to decide how to invest her money. A friend recommended that she buy the stock of one of two corporations and suggested that she should compare the financial statements of the two companies before making a decision.

**Required:**

1. Do you agree that Mary will be able to compare the financial statements of the two companies?
2. What role does the auditor play in ensuring comparability of financial statements between companies?

**Judgment Case 1–10**
Cost effectiveness

● LO6

*Statement of Financial Accounting Concepts No. 2,* "Qualitative Characteristics of Accounting Information," includes a discussion of the pervasive constraint cost effectiveness. Assume that the FASB is considering revising an important accounting standard.

**Required:**

1. What is the desired benefit from revising an accounting standard?
2. What are some of the possible costs that could result from a revision of an accounting standard?
3. What does the FASB do in order to assess possible benefits and costs of a proposed revision of an accounting standard?

**Judgment Case 1–11**
The realization principle

● LO8

A new client, the Wolf Company, asks your advice concerning the point in time that the company should recognize revenue from the rental of its office buildings. Renters usually pay rent on a quarterly basis at the beginning of the quarter. The owners contend that the critical event that motivates revenue recognition should be the date the cash is received from renters. After all, the money is in hand and is very seldom returned.

**Required:**

1. Describe the two criteria that must be satisfied before revenue can be recognized.
2. Do you agree or disagree with the position of the owners of Wolf Company? Support your answer.

**Analysis Case 1–12**
The matching principle

● LO8

Revenues measure the accomplishments of a company during the period. Expenses are then matched with revenues to produce a periodic measure of performance called *net income.*

**Required:**

1. Explain what is meant by the phrase *matched with revenues.*
2. Describe the four approaches used to implement the matching principle and label them 1 through 4.
3. For each of the following, identify which matching approach should be used to recognize the cost as expense.
   a. The cost of producing a product.
   b. The cost of advertising.
   c. The cost of monthly rent on the office building.
   d. The salary of an office employee.
   e. Depreciation on an office building.

**Real World Case 1–13**
Elements; disclosures; Dell Inc.

● LO6 LO8

Selected financial statements from a recent annual report of **Dell Inc.** follow. Use these statements to answer the following questions.

**Required:**

1. The company's fiscal year ends on what date?
2. What amounts did Dell report for the following items for the fiscal year ended January 30, 2004?
   a. Total net revenues
   b. Total operating expenses
   c. Net income
   d. Total assets
   e. Total stockholders' equity
3. How many shares of common stock did the company have issued on January 30, 2004?
4. Why do you think Dell reports more than one year of data in its financial statements?

**DELL INC.**
**Consolidated Balance Sheets**
**($ in millions)**

| | January 30, 2004 | January 31, 2003 |
|---|---|---|
| **Assets** | | |
| Current assets: | | |
| Cash and cash equivalents | $ 4,317 | $ 4,232 |
| Short-term investments | 835 | 406 |
| Accounts receivable, net | 3,635 | 2,586 |
| Inventories | 327 | 306 |
| Other | 1,519 | 1,394 |
| Total current assets | 10,633 | 8,924 |
| Property, plant and equipment, net | 1,517 | 913 |
| Investments | 6,770 | 5,267 |
| Other noncurrent assets | 391 | 366 |
| Total assets | $19,311 | $15,470 |
| **Liabilities and Stockholders' Equity** | | |
| Current liabilities: | | |
| Accounts payable | $ 7,316 | $ 5,989 |
| Accrued and other | 3,580 | 2,944 |
| Total current liabilities | 10,896 | 8,933 |
| Long-term debt | 505 | 506 |
| Other noncurrent liabilities | 1,630 | 1,158 |
| Commitments and contingent liabilities (Note 7) | — | — |
| Total liabilities | 13,031 | 10,597 |
| Stockholders' equity: | | |
| Preferred stock and capital in excess of $.01 par value; shares issued and outstanding: none | — | — |
| Common stock and capital in excess of $.01 par value; shares authorized: 7,000; shares issued 2,721 and 2,681, respectively | 6,823 | 6,018 |
| Treasury stock, at cost; 165 and 102 shares, respectively | (6,539) | (4,539) |
| Retained earnings | 6,131 | 3,486 |
| Other comprehensive loss | (83) | (33) |
| Other | (52) | (59) |
| Total stockholders' equity | 6,280 | 4,873 |
| Total liabilities and stockholders' equity | $19,311 | $15,470 |

**Consolidated Statements of Income**
**($ in millions, except per share amounts)**

| | Fiscal Year Ended | |
|---|---|---|
| | **January 30, 2004** | **January 31, 2003** |
| Net revenue | $41,444 | $35,404 |
| Cost of revenue | 33,892 | 29,055 |
| Gross margin | 7,552 | 6,349 |
| Operating expenses: | | |
| Selling, general and administrative | 3,544 | 3,050 |
| Research, development and engineering | 464 | 455 |
| Special charges | — | — |
| Total operating expenses | 4,008 | 3,505 |
| Operating income | 3,544 | 2,844 |
| Investment and other income (loss), net | 180 | 183 |
| Income before income taxes | 3,724 | 3,027 |
| Income tax provision | 1,079 | 905 |
| Net income | $ 2,645 | $ 2,122 |
| Earnings per common share: | | |
| Basic | $ 1.03 | $ 0.82 |
| Diluted | $ 1.01 | $ 0.80 |
| Weighted-average shares outstanding: | | |
| Basic | $ 2,565 | $ 2,584 |
| Diluted | $ 2,619 | $ 2,644 |

# 2
CHAPTER

# Review of the Accounting Process

## OVERVIEW

Chapter 1 explained that the primary means of conveying financial information to investors, creditors, and other external users is through financial statements and related notes. The purpose of this chapter is to review the fundamental accounting process used to produce the financial statements. This review establishes a framework for the study of the concepts covered in intermediate accounting.

Actual accounting systems differ significantly from company to company. This chapter focuses on the many features that tend to be common to any accounting system.

## LEARNING OBJECTIVES

After studying this chapter, you should be able to:

- LO1 Analyze routine economic events—transactions—and record their effects on a company's financial position using the accounting equation format.
- LO2 Record transactions using the general journal format.
- LO3 Post the effects of journal entries to T-accounts and prepare an unadjusted trial balance.
- LO4 Identify and describe the different types of adjusting journal entries.
- LO5 Determine the required adjustments, record adjusting journal entries in general journal format, and prepare an adjusted trial balance.
- LO6 Describe the four basic financial statements.
- LO7 Explain the closing process.
- LO8 Convert from cash basis net income to accrual basis net income.

# FINANCIAL REPORTING CASE

## Engineering Profits

After graduating from college last year, two of your engineering-major friends started an Internet consulting practice. They began operations on July 1 and felt they did quite well during their first year. Now they would like to borrow $20,000 from a local bank to buy new computing equipment and office furniture. To support their loan application, the friends presented the bank with the following income statement for their first year of operations ending June 30:

| | | |
|---|---|---|
| Consulting revenue | | $96,000 |
| Operating expenses: | | |
| Salaries | $32,000 | |
| Rent | 9,000 | |
| Supplies | 4,800 | |
| Utilities | 3,000 | |
| Advertising | 1,200 | (50,000) |
| Net income | | $46,000 |

The bank officer noticed that there was no depreciation expense in the income statement and has asked your friends to revise the statement after making year-end adjustments. After agreeing to help, you discover the following information:

a. The friends paid $80,000 for equipment when they began operations. They think the equipment will be useful for five years.

b. They pay $500 a month to rent office space. In January, they paid a full year's rent in advance. This is included in the $9,000 rent expense.

c. Included in consulting revenue is $13,000 they received from a customer in June as a deposit for work to be performed in August.

**By the time you finish this chapter, you should be able to respond appropriately to the questions posed in this case. Compare your response to the solution provided at the end of the chapter.**

### QUESTIONS

1. What purpose do adjusting entries serve? (page 62)
2. What year-end adjustments are needed to revise the income statement? Did your friends do as well their first year as they thought? (page 62)

A solid foundation is vital to a sound understanding of intermediate accounting. So, we review the fundamental accounting process here to serve as a framework for the new concepts you will learn in this course.

Chapter 1 introduced the theoretical structure of financial accounting and the environment within which it operates. The primary function of financial accounting—to provide relevant and reliable financial information to external users—is accomplished by periodically disseminating financial statements and related notes. In this chapter we review the *process* used to identify, analyze, record, summarize, and then report the economic events affecting a company's financial position.

Keep in mind as you study this chapter that the accounting information systems businesses actually use are quite different from company to company. Larger companies generally use more complex systems than smaller companies use. The types of economic events affecting companies also cause differences in systems. We focus on the many features that tend to be common to all accounting systems.

**Computers are used to process accounting information. In this chapter we provide an overview of the basic model that underlies computer software programs.**

It is important to understand that this chapter and its appendixes are not intended to describe actual accounting systems. In most business enterprises, the sheer volume of data that must be processed precludes a manual accounting system. Fortunately, the computer provides a solution. *We describe and illustrate a manual accounting information system to provide an overview of the basic model that underlies the computer software programs actually used to process accounting information.*

Electronic data processing is fast, accurate, and affordable. Many large and medium-sized companies own or rent their own mainframe computers and company-specific data processing systems. Smaller companies can take advantage of technology with relatively inexpensive micro- and minicomputers and generalized data software packages such as QuickBooks and Peachtree Accounting Software. Enterprise Resource Planning (ERP) systems are now being installed in companies of all sizes. The objective of ERP is to create a customized software program that integrates all departments and functions across a company onto a single computer system that can serve the information needs of those different departments, including the accounting department.

## The Basic Model

***Economic events* cause changes in the financial position of the company.**

The first objective of any accounting system is to identify the **economic events** that can be expressed in financial terms by the system.[1] An economic event is any event that *directly* affects the financial position of the company. Recall from Chapter 1 that financial position comprises assets, liabilities, and owners' equity. Broad and specific accounting principles determine which events should be recorded, when the events should be recorded, and the dollar amount at which they should be measured.

***External events* involve an exchange between the company and another entity.**

Economic events can be classified as either external events or internal events. **External events** involve an exchange between the company and a separate economic entity. Examples are purchasing merchandise inventory for cash, borrowing cash from a bank, and paying salaries to employees. In each instance, the company receives something (merchandise, cash, and services) in exchange for something else (cash, assumption of a liability, and cash).

***Internal events* do not involve an exchange transaction but do affect the company's financial position.**

On the other hand, **internal events** directly affect the financial position of the company but don't involve an exchange transaction with another entity. Examples are the depreciation of machinery and the use of supplies. As we will see later in the chapter, these events must be recorded to properly reflect a company's financial position and results of operations in accordance with the accrual accounting model.

### THE ACCOUNTING EQUATION

● LO1

The **accounting equation** underlies the process used to capture the effect of economic events.

$$\text{Assets} = \text{Liabilities} + \text{Owners' Equity}$$

[1]There are many economic events that affect a company *indirectly* and are not recorded. For example, when the Federal Reserve changes its discount rate, it is an important economic event that can affect the company in many ways, but it is not recorded by the company.

The elements of the equation were defined in Chapter 1.

This general expression portrays the equality between the total economic resources of an entity (its assets)—shown on the left side of the equation—and the total claims to those resources (liabilities and equity)—shown on the right side. In other words, the resources of an enterprise are provided by creditors or owners.

The equation also implies that each economic event affecting this equation will have a dual effect because resources always must equal claims to those resources. For illustration, consider the events (we refer to these throughout the text as **transactions**) in Illustration 2–1.

**Each event, or *transaction,* has a dual effect on the accounting equation.**

**ILLUSTRATION 2–1**
Transaction Analysis

**1. An attorney invested $50,000 to open a law office.**
An investment by the owner causes both assets and owners' equity to increase.

| Assets | = | Liabilities | + | Owners' Equity |
|---|---|---|---|---|
| +$50,000 (cash) | | | | +$50,000 (investment by owner) |

**2. $40,000 was borrowed from a bank and a note payable was signed.**
This transaction causes assets and liabilities to increase. A bank loan increases cash and creates an obligation to repay it.

| Assets | = | Liabilities | + | Owners' Equity |
|---|---|---|---|---|
| +$40,000 (cash) | | +$40,000 (note payable) | | |

**3. Supplies costing $3,000 were purchased on account.**
Buying supplies on credit also increases both assets and liabilities.

| Assets | = | Liabilities | + | Owners' Equity |
|---|---|---|---|---|
| +$3,000 (supplies) | | +$3,000 (accounts payable) | | |

**4. Services were performed on account for $10,000.**
Transactions 4, 5, and 6 are revenue and expense transactions. Revenues and expenses (and gains and losses) are events that cause owners' equity to change. Revenues and gains describe inflows of assets, causing owners' equity to increase. Expenses and losses describe outflows of assets (or increases in liabilities), causing owners' equity to decrease.

| Assets | = | Liabilities | + | Owners' Equity |
|---|---|---|---|---|
| +$10,000 (receivables) | | | | +$10,000 (revenue) |

**5. Salaries of $5,000 were paid to employees.**

| Assets | = | Liabilities | + | Owners' Equity |
|---|---|---|---|---|
| −$5,000 (cash) | | | | −$5,000 (expense) |

**6. $500 of supplies were used.**

| Assets | = | Liabilities | + | Owners' Equity |
|---|---|---|---|---|
| −$500 (supplies) | | | | −$500 (expense) |

**7. $1,000 was paid on account to the supplies vendor.**
This transaction causes assets and liabilities to decrease.

| Assets | = | Liabilities | + | Owners' Equity |
|---|---|---|---|---|
| −$1,000 (cash) | | −$1,000 (accounts payable) | | |

Each transaction is analyzed to determine its effect on the equation and on the specific financial position elements.

The accounting equation can be expanded to include a column for each type of asset and liability and for each type of change in owners' equity.

As discussed in Chapter 1, owners of a corporation are its shareholders, so owners' equity for a corporation is referred to as shareholders' equity. Shareholders' equity for a corporation arises primarily from two sources: (1) amounts *invested* by shareholders in the corporation and (2) amounts *earned* by the corporation (on behalf of its shareholders). These are reported as (1) **paid-in capital** and (2) **retained earnings.** Retained earnings equals net income less distributions to shareholders (primarily dividends) since the inception of the corporation. Graphic 2–1 shows the basic accounting equation for a corporation with shareholders' equity expanded to highlight its composition. We use the corporate format throughout the remainder of the chapter.

**Owners' equity for a corporation, called *shareholders' equity,* is classified by source as either *paid-in capital* or *retained earnings.***

**GRAPHIC 2–1** Accounting Equation for a Corporation

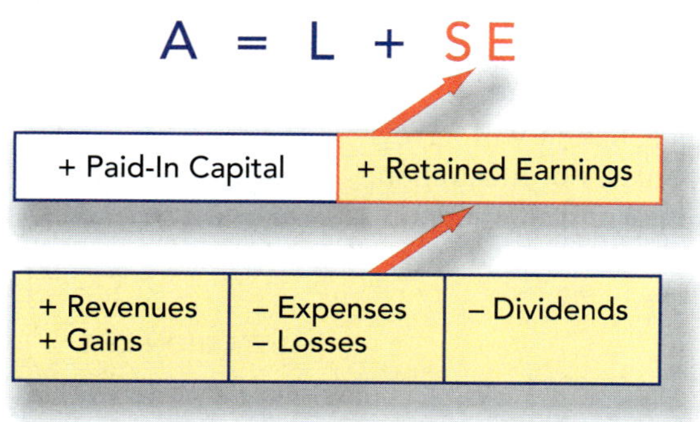


## ACCOUNT RELATIONSHIPS

All transactions could be recorded in columnar fashion as increases or decreases to elements of the accounting equation. However, even for a very small company with few transactions, this would become cumbersome. So, most companies use a process called the **double-entry system.** The term *double-entry* refers to the dual effect that each transaction has on the accounting equation.

*The double-entry system is used to process transactions.*

Elements of the accounting equation are represented by **accounts** which are contained in a **general ledger.** Increases and decreases in each element of a company's financial position are recorded in these accounts. A separate account is maintained for individual assets and liabilities, retained earnings, and paid-in capital. Also, to accumulate information needed for the income statement, we use separate accounts to keep track of the changes in retained earnings caused by revenues, expenses, gains, and losses. The number of accounts depends on the complexity of the company's operations.

*A general ledger is a collection of storage areas, called accounts, used to keep track of increases and decreases in financial position elements.*

An account includes the account title, an account number to aid the processing task, and columns or fields for increases, decreases, the cumulative balance, and the date. For instructional purposes we use **T-accounts** instead of formal ledger accounts. A T-account has space at the top for the account title and two sides for recording increases and decreases.

| Account Title | |
|---|---|
| | |

*In the double-entry system, debit means left side of an account and credit means right side of an account.*

For centuries, accountants have effectively used a system of **debits** and **credits** to increase and decrease account balances in the ledger. Debits merely represent the *left* side of the account and credits the *right* side, as shown below.

| Account Title | |
|---|---|
| debit side | credit side |

*Asset increases are entered on the debit side of accounts and decreases are entered on the credit side. Liability and equity account increases are credits and decreases are debits.*

Whether a debit or a credit represents an increase or a decrease depends on the type of account. Accounts on the left side of the accounting equation (assets) are *increased* (+) by *debit* entries and *decreased* (−) by *credit* entries. Accounts on the right side of the accounting equation (liabilities and shareholders' equity) are *increased* (+) by *credit* entries and *decreased* (−) by *debit* entries. This arbitrary, but effective, procedure ensures that for each transaction the net impact on the left sides of accounts always equals the net impact on the right sides of accounts.

For example, consider the bank loan in our earlier illustration. An asset, cash, increased by $40,000. Increases in assets are *debits.* Liabilities also increased by $40,000. Increases in liabilities are *credits.*

**Assets** = **Liabilities** + **Owners' Equity**

| Cash | |
|---|---|
| debit | credit |
| 40,000 | |
| + | |

| Note Payable | |
|---|---|
| debit | credit |
| | 40,000 |
| | + |

The debits equal the credits in every transaction (dual effect), so both before and after a transaction the accounting equation is in balance.

Prior exposure to the terms debit and credit probably comes from your experience with a bank account. For example, when a bank debits your checking account for service charges, it decreases your account balance. When you make a deposit, the bank credits your account, increasing your account balance. You must remember that from the bank's perspective, your bank account balance is a liability—it represents the amount that the bank owes you. There-

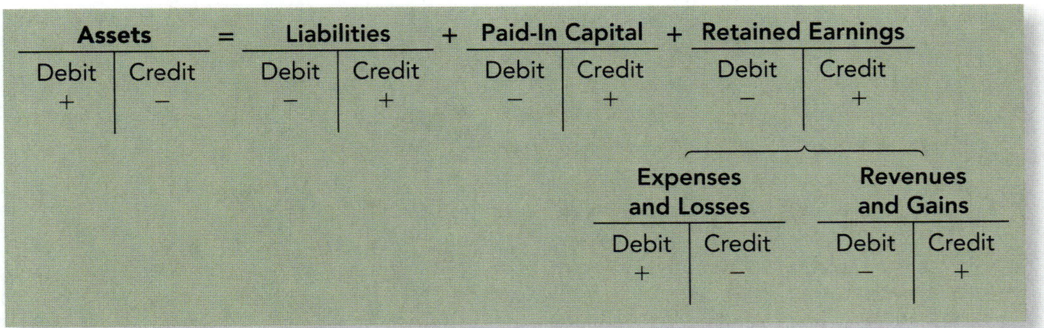


**GRAPHIC 2–2**
Accounting Equation, Debits and Credits, Increases and Decreases

fore, when the bank debits your account, it is decreasing its liability. When the bank credits your account, its liability increases.

Graphic 2–2 illustrates the relationship among the accounting equation, debits and credits, and the increases and decreases in financial position elements.

Notice that increases and decreases in retained earnings are recorded *indirectly.* For example, an expense represents a decrease in retained earnings, which requires a debit. That debit, however, is recorded in an appropriate expense account rather than in retained earnings itself. This allows the company to maintain a separate record of expenses incurred during an accounting period. The debit to retained earnings for the expense is recorded in a closing entry (reviewed later) at the end of the period, only after the expense total is reflected in the income statement. Similarly, an increase in retained earnings due to a revenue is recorded indirectly with a credit to a revenue account, which is later reflected as a credit to retained earnings.

The general ledger accounts serve as control accounts. Subsidiary accounts associated with a particular general ledger control account are maintained in separate subsidiary ledgers. For example, a subsidiary ledger for accounts receivable contains individual account receivable accounts for each of the company's credit customers. Subsidiary ledgers are discussed in more detail in Appendix 2C.

***Permanent accounts*** **represent the basic financial position elements of the accounting equation.**

***Temporary accounts*** **keep track of the changes in the retained earnings component of shareholders' equity.**

Each general ledger account can be classified as either *permanent* or *temporary.* **Permanent accounts** represent assets, liabilities, and shareholders' equity at a point in time. **Temporary accounts** represent changes in the retained earnings component of shareholders' equity for a corporation caused by revenue, expense, gain, and loss transactions. It would be cumbersome to record each revenue/expense, gain/loss transaction directly into the retained earnings account. The different types of events affecting retained earnings should be kept separate to facilitate the preparation of the financial statements. The balances in these temporary accounts are periodically, usually once a year, closed or zeroed out, and the net effect is recorded in the permanent retained earnings account. The temporary accounts need to be zeroed out to measure income on an annual basis. This closing process is discussed in a later section of this chapter.

## The Accounting Processing Cycle

Now that we've reviewed the basics of the double-entry system, let's look closer at the process used to identify, analyze, record, and summarize transactions and prepare financial statements. This section deals only with *external transactions,* those that involve an exchange transaction with another entity. Internal transactions are discussed in a later section.

The 10 steps in the accounting processing cycle are listed in Graphic 2–3:

We now discuss these steps in order.

**STEP 1: Obtain information about transactions from *source documents.***

The first step in the process is to *identify* external transactions affecting the accounting equation. An accountant usually does not directly witness business transactions. A mechanism is needed to relay the essential information about each transaction to the accountant. **Source documents** such as sales invoices, bills from suppliers, and cash register tapes serve this need.

These source documents usually identify the date and nature of each transaction, the participating parties, and the monetary terms. For example, a sales invoice identifies the date of

**GRAPHIC 2–3**
The Accounting Processing Cycle

**The Steps of the Accounting Processing Cycle**

1. Obtain information about external transactions from **source documents.**
2. **Analyze the transaction.**
3. Record the transaction in a **journal.**
4. **Post** from the journal to the general ledger accounts.
5. Prepare an **unadjusted trial balance.**
6. Record **adjusting entries** and post to the general ledger accounts.
7. Prepare an **adjusted trial balance.**
8. Prepare **financial statements.**
9. **Close** the temporary accounts to retained earnings (at year-end only).
10. Prepare a **post-closing trial balance** (at year-end only).

**STEP 2: Analyze the transaction.**

sale, the customer, the specific goods sold, the dollar amount of the sale, and the payment terms. With this information, the second step in the processing cycle, **transaction analysis**, can be accomplished. Transaction analysis is the process of reviewing the source documents to determine the dual effect on the accounting equation and the specific elements involved.

This process is summarized in Illustration 2–2 for the seven transactions described previously in Illustration 2–1.

**STEP 3: Record the transaction in a *journal*.**

The third step in the process is to record the transaction in a **journal.** Journals provide a chronological record of all economic events affecting a firm. Each journal entry is expressed in terms of equal debits and credits to accounts affected by the transaction being recorded. Debits and credits represent increases or decreases to specific accounts, depending on the type of account, as explained earlier. For example, for credit sales, a debit to accounts receivable and a credit to sales revenue is recorded in a sales journal.

A sales journal is an example of a **special journal** used to record a repetitive type of transaction. Appendix 2C discusses the use of special journals in more depth. In this chapter and throughout the text, we use the **general journal** format to record all transactions.

● LO2

Any type of transaction can be recorded in a general journal. It has a place for the date of the transaction, a place for account titles, account numbers, and supporting explanations, a place for debit entries, and a place for credit entries. A simplified journal entry is used throughout the text that lists the account titles to be debited and credited and the dollar amounts. A common convention is to list the debited accounts first, indent the credited accounts, and use the first of two columns for the debit amounts and the second column for the credit amounts. For example, the **journal entry** for the bank loan in Illustration 2–1, which requires a debit to cash and a credit to note payable, is recorded as follows:

**To record the borrowing of cash and the signing of a note payable.**

| | | |
|---|---|---|
| Cash | 40,000 | |
| Note payable | | 40,000 |

**STEP 4: *Post* from the journal to the general ledger accounts.**

Step 4 is to periodically transfer or *post* the debit and credit information from the journal to individual ledger accounts. Recall that a ledger is simply a collection of all of the company's various accounts. Each account provides a summary of the effects of all events and transactions on that individual account. This process is called **posting.** Posting involves transferring debits and credits recorded in individual journal entries to the specific accounts affected. As discussed earlier in the chapter, most accounting systems today are computerized, with the journal and ledger kept on disk. For these systems, the journal input information is automatically and instantly posted to the ledger accounts.

These first four steps in the processing cycle are illustrated using the external transactions in Illustration 2–3 which occurred during the month of July 2006, the first month of operations for Dress Right Clothing Corporation. The company operates a retail store that sells men's and women's clothing. Dress Right is organized as a corporation so owners' equity is classified by source as either paid-in capital or retained earnings.

The local bank requires that Dress Right furnish financial statements on a monthly basis. The transactions listed in the illustration are used to demonstrate the accounting processing cycle for the month of July 2006.

**ILLUSTRATION 2–2** Transaction Analysis, the Accounting Equation, and Debits and Credits

| Transaction | Transaction Analysis | Assets | = | Liabilities | + | Owners' Equity | Account Entry | | | | | |
|---|---|---|---|---|---|---|---|---|---|---|---|---|
| | | **Accounting Equation** | | | | | **Account** | **Debit** | **Credit** | **Account** | **Debit** | **Credit** |
| 1. An attorney invested $50,000 to open a law office. | Assets (cash) and owners' equity each increased by $50,000. | **+50,000** | | | | **+50,000** | **Cash** | 50,000 | | **Owners' Equity** | | 50,000 |
| | *Cumulative balances* | 50,000 | = | | | 50,000 | | | | | | |
| 2. $40,000 was borrowed from a bank and a note payable was signed. | Assets (cash) and liabilities (note payable) each increased by $40,000. | **+40,000** | | **+40,000** | | | **Cash** | 50,000<br>40,000 | | **Note Payable** | | 40,000 |
| | *Cumulative balances* | 90,000 | = | 40,000 | + | 50,000 | | | | | | |
| 3. Supplies costing $3,000 were purchased on account. | Assets (supplies) and liabilities (accounts payable) each increased by $3,000. | **+3,000** | | **+3,000** | | | **Supplies** | 3,000 | | **Accounts Payable** | | 3,000 |
| | *Cumulative balances* | 93,000 | = | 43,000 | + | 50,000 | | | | | | |
| 4. Services were performed on account for $10,000. | Assets (accounts receivable) and owners' equity (revenue) each increased by $10,000. | **+10,000** | | | | **+10,000** | **Accounts Receivable** | 10,000 | | **Owners' Equity (Revenue)** | | 10,000 |
| | *Cumulative balances* | 103,000 | = | 43,000 | + | 60,000 | | | | | | |
| 5. Salaries of $5,000 were paid to employees. | Assets (cash) decreased and owners' equity decreased (salaries expense increased) by $5,000. | **−5,000** | | | | **−5,000** | **Cash** | 50,000<br>40,000 | 5,000 | **Owners' Equity (Salaries Expense)** | 5,000 | |
| | *Cumulative balances* | 98,000 | = | 43,000 | + | 55,000 | | | | | | |
| 6. $500 of supplies were used. | Assets (supplies) decreased and owners' equity decreased (supplies expense increased) by $500. | **−500** | | | | **−500** | **Supplies** | 3,000 | 500 | **Owners' Equity (Supplies Expense)** | 500 | |
| | *Cumulative balances* | 97,500 | = | 43,000 | + | 54,500 | | | | | | |
| 7. $1,000 was paid on account to the supplies vendor. | Assets (cash) and liabilities (accounts payable) each decreased by $1,000. | **−1,000** | | **−1,000** | | | **Cash** | 50,000<br>40,000 | 5,000<br>1,000 | **Accounts Payable** | 1,000 | 3,000 |
| | *Cumulative balances* | 96,500 | = | 42,000 | + | 54,500 | | | | | | |

**ILLUSTRATION 2–3**
External Transactions for July 2006

| | | |
|---|---|---|
| July | 1 | Two individuals each invested $30,000 in the corporation. Each investor was issued 3,000 shares of common stock. |
| | 1 | Borrowed $40,000 from a local bank and signed two notes. The first note for $10,000 requires payment of principal and 10% interest in six months. The second note for $30,000 requires the payment of principal in two years. Interest at 10% is payable each year on July 1, 2007, and July 1, 2008. |
| | 1 | Paid $24,000 in advance for one year's rent on the store building. |
| | 1 | Purchased furniture and fixtures from Acme Furniture for $12,000 cash. |
| | 3 | Purchased $60,000 of clothing inventory on account from the Birdwell Wholesale Clothing Company. |
| | 6 | Purchased $2,000 of supplies for cash. |
| | 4–31 | Sold merchandise costing $20,000 for $35,000 cash. |
| | 9 | Sold clothing on account to St. Jude's School for Girls for $3,500. The clothing cost $2,000. |
| | 16 | Subleased a portion of the building to a jewelry store. Received $1,000 in advance for the first two months' rent beginning on July 16. |
| | 20 | Paid Birdwell Wholesale Clothing $25,000 on account. |
| | 20 | Paid salaries to employees for the first half of the month, $5,000. |
| | 25 | Received $1,500 on account from St. Jude's. |
| | 30 | The corporation paid its shareholders a cash dividend of $1,000. |

For each transaction, a source document provides the necessary information to complete steps two and three in the processing cycle, transaction analysis and recording the appropriate journal entry. Each transaction listed in Illustration 2–3 is analyzed below, preceded by the necessary journal entry.

To record the issuance of common stock.

| **July 1** | | |
|---|---|---|
| Cash . . . . . . . . . . . . . . . . . . . . . . . . . . . . . . . . . . . . . . . . . . . . . . | 60,000 | |
| Common stock . . . . . . . . . . . . . . . . . . . . . . . . . . . . . . . . . . . . . | | 60,000 |

This first transaction is an investment by owners that increases an asset, cash, and also increases shareholders' equity. Increases in assets are recorded as debits and increases in shareholders' equity are recorded as credits. We use the paid-in capital account called common stock because stock was issued in exchange for cash paid in.[2]

To record the borrowing of cash and the signing of notes payable.

| **July 1** | | |
|---|---|---|
| Cash . . . . . . . . . . . . . . . . . . . . . . . . . . . . . . . . . . . . . . . . . . . . . . | 40,000 | |
| Notes payable . . . . . . . . . . . . . . . . . . . . . . . . . . . . . . . . . . . . . | | 40,000 |

This transaction causes increases in both cash and the liability, notes payable. Increases in assets are debits and increases in liabilities are credits. The notes require payment of $40,000 in principal and $6,500 ([$10,000 × 10% × 6/12 = $500] + [$30,000 × 10% × 2 years = $6,000]) in interest. However, at this point we are concerned only with the external transaction that occurs when the cash is borrowed and the notes are signed. Later we discuss how the interest is recorded.

To record the payment of one year's rent in advance.

| **July 1** | | |
|---|---|---|
| Prepaid rent . . . . . . . . . . . . . . . . . . . . . . . . . . . . . . . . . . . . . . . . | 24,000 | |
| Cash . . . . . . . . . . . . . . . . . . . . . . . . . . . . . . . . . . . . . . . . . . . . | | 24,000 |

This transaction decreased cash (a credit) and increased an asset called prepaid rent, which is debited. Dress Right acquired the right to use the building for one full year. This is an asset because it represents a future benefit to the company. As we will see later, this asset expires over the one-year rental period.

[2]The different types of stock are discussed in Chapter 18.

| | | |
|---|---|---|
| **July 1** | | |
| Furniture and fixtures | 12,000 | |
| Cash | | 12,000 |

**To record the purchase of furniture and fixtures.**

This transaction increases one asset, furniture and fixtures, and decreases another, cash.

| | | |
|---|---|---|
| **July 3** | | |
| Inventory | 60,000 | |
| Accounts payable | | 60,000 |

**To record the purchase of merchandise inventory.**

This purchase of merchandise on account is recorded by a debit to inventory, an asset, and a credit to accounts payable, a liability. Increases in assets are debits, and increases in liabilities are credits.

The Dress Right Clothing Company uses the *perpetual inventory system* to keep track of its merchandise inventory. This system requires that the cost of merchandise purchased be recorded in inventory, an asset account. When inventory is sold, the inventory account is decreased by the cost of the item sold. The alternative method, the periodic system, is briefly discussed on the next page, and Chapters 8 and 9 cover the topic of inventory in depth.

| | | |
|---|---|---|
| **July 6** | | |
| Supplies | 2,000 | |
| Cash | | 2,000 |

**To record the purchase of supplies.**

The acquisition of supplies is recorded as a debit to the asset account supplies (an increase) and a credit to the asset cash (a decrease). Supplies are recorded as an asset because they represent future benefits.

| | | |
|---|---|---|
| **July 4–31** | | |
| Cash | 35,000 | |
| Sales revenue | | 35,000 |
| Cost of goods sold (expense) | 20,000 | |
| Inventory | | 20,000 |

**To record the month's cash sales and the cost of those sales.**

During the month of July, cash sales to customers totaled $35,000. The company's assets (cash) increase by this amount as does shareholders' equity. This increase in equity is recorded by a credit to the temporary account sales revenue.

At the same time, an asset, inventory, decreases and retained earnings decreases. Recall that expenses are outflows or using up of assets from providing goods and services. Dress Right incurred an expense equal to the cost of the inventory sold. The temporary account cost of goods sold increases. However, this increase in an expense represents a *decrease* in shareholders' equity—retained earnings—and accordingly the account is debited. Both of these transactions are *summary* transactions. Each sale made during the month requires a separate and similar entry.

| | | |
|---|---|---|
| **July 9** | | |
| Accounts receivable | 3,500 | |
| Sales revenue | | 3,500 |
| Cost of goods sold | 2,000 | |
| Inventory | | 2,000 |

**To record a credit sale and the cost of that sale.**

This transaction is similar to the cash sale above. The only difference is that the asset acquired in exchange for merchandise is accounts receivable rather than cash.

## ADDITIONAL CONSIDERATION

### Periodic Inventory System

The principal alternative to the perpetual inventory system is the periodic system. This system requires that the cost of merchandise purchased be recorded in a temporary account called *purchases.* When inventory is sold, the inventory account is not decreased and cost of goods sold is not recorded. Cost of goods sold for a period is determined and the inventory account is adjusted only at the end of a reporting period.

For example, the purchase of $60,000 of merchandise on account by Dress Right Clothing is recorded as follows:

| | | |
|---|---|---|
| Purchases | 60,000 | |
| Accounts payable | | 60,000 |

No cost of goods sold entry is recorded when sales are made in the periodic system.

At the end of July, the amount of ending inventory is determined (either by means of a physical count of goods on hand or by estimation) to be $38,000 and cost of goods sold for the month is determined as follows:

| | |
|---|---|
| Beginning inventory | -0- |
| Plus: Purchases | 60,000 |
| Less: Ending inventory | (38,000) |
| Cost of goods sold | 22,000 |

The following journal entry records cost of goods sold for the period and adjusts the inventory account to the actual amount on hand (in this case from zero to $38,000):

| | | |
|---|---|---|
| Cost of goods sold | 22,000 | |
| Inventory | 38,000 | |
| Purchases | | 60,000 |

Inventory is discussed in depth in Chapters 8 and 9.

**To record the receipt of rent in advance.**

**July 16**

| | | |
|---|---|---|
| Cash | 1,000 | |
| Unearned rent revenue (liability) | | 1,000 |

Cash increases by $1,000 so the cash account is debited. At this point, Dress Right does not recognize revenue even though cash has been received. Recall that the first criterion required for revenue recognition as stated in the realization principle is that the "earnings process is judged to be complete or virtually complete." Dress Right does not earn the revenue until it has provided the jewelry store with the use of facilities; that is, the revenue is earned as the rental period expires. On receipt of the cash, a liability called *unearned rent revenue* increases and is credited. This liability represents Dress Right's obligation to provide the use of facilities to the jewelry store.

**To record the payment of accounts payable.**

**July 20**

| | | |
|---|---|---|
| Accounts payable | 25,000 | |
| Cash | | 25,000 |

This transaction decreases both an asset (cash) and a liability (accounts payable). Decreases in assets are credits, and decreases in liabilities are debits.

**To record the payment of salaries for the first half of the month.**

**July 20**

| | | |
|---|---|---|
| Salaries expense | 5,000 | |
| Cash | | 5,000 |

Employees were paid for services rendered during the first half of the month. The cash expenditure did not create an asset since no future benefits result. Cash decreases and is credited; shareholders' equity decreases and is debited. The debit is recorded in the temporary account salaries expense.

**To record receipt of cash on account.**

**July 25**

| | | |
|---|---|---|
| Cash | 1,500 | |
| Accounts receivable | | 1,500 |

This transaction is an exchange of one asset, accounts receivable, for another asset, cash.

**To record the payment of a cash dividend.**

| | | |
|---|---|---|
| **July 30** | | |
| Retained earnings | 1,000 | |
| Cash | | 1,000 |

The payment of a cash dividend reduces both cash and retained earnings. An alternative is to debit a temporary account—dividends—that is closed to retained earnings at the end of the fiscal year along with the other temporary accounts.

**ILLUSTRATION 2–4**
The General Journal

**General Journal** **Page 1**

| Date 2006 | | Account Title and Explanation | Post Ref. | Debit | Credit |
|---|---|---|---|---|---|
| July | 1 | Cash | 100 | 60,000 | |
| | | Common stock | 300 | | 60,000 |
| | | *To record the issuance of common stock.* | | | |
| | 1 | Cash | 100 | 40,000 | |
| | | Notes payable | 220 | | 40,000 |
| | | *To record the borrowing of cash and the signing of notes payable.* | | | |
| | 1 | Prepaid rent | 130 | 24,000 | |
| | | Cash | 100 | | 24,000 |
| | | *To record the payment of one year's rent in advance.* | | | |
| | 1 | Furniture and fixtures | 150 | 12,000 | |
| | | Cash | 100 | | 12,000 |
| | | *To record the purchase of furniture and fixtures.* | | | |
| | 3 | Inventory | 140 | 60,000 | |
| | | Accounts payable | 210 | | 60,000 |
| | | *To record the purchase of merchandise inventory.* | | | |
| | 6 | Supplies | 125 | 2,000 | |
| | | Cash | 100 | | 2,000 |
| | | *To record the purchase of supplies.* | | | |
| | 4–31 | Cash | 100 | 35,000 | |
| | | Sales revenue | 400 | | 35,000 |
| | | *To record cash sales for the month.* | | | |
| | 4–31 | Cost of goods sold | 500 | 20,000 | |
| | | Inventory | 140 | | 20,000 |
| | | *To record the cost of cash sales.* | | | |
| | 9 | Accounts receivable | 110 | 3,500 | |
| | | Sales revenue | 400 | | 3,500 |
| | | *To record credit sale.* | | | |
| | 9 | Cost of goods sold | 500 | 2,000 | |
| | | Inventory | 140 | | 2,000 |
| | | *To record the cost of a credit sale.* | | | |
| | 16 | Cash | 100 | 1,000 | |
| | | Unearned rent revenue | 230 | | 1,000 |
| | | *To record the receipt of rent in advance.* | | | |
| | 20 | Accounts payable | 210 | 25,000 | |
| | | Cash | 100 | | 25,000 |
| | | *To record the payment of accounts payable.* | | | |
| | 20 | Salaries expense | 510 | 5,000 | |
| | | Cash | 100 | | 5,000 |
| | | *To record the payment of salaries for the first half of the month.* | | | |
| | 25 | Cash | 100 | 1,500 | |
| | | Accounts receivable | 110 | | 1,500 |
| | | *To record the receipt of cash on account.* | | | |
| | 30 | Retained earnings | 310 | 1,000 | |
| | | Cash | 100 | | 1,000 |
| | | *To record the payment of a cash dividend.* | | | |

Illustration 2–4 summarizes each of the transactions just discussed as they would appear in a general journal. In addition to the date, account titles, debit and credit columns, the journal also has a column titled Post Ref. (Posting Reference). This usually is a number assigned to the general ledger account that is being debited or credited. For purposes of this illustration, all asset accounts have been assigned numbers in the 100s, all liabilities are 200s, permanent shareholders' equity accounts are 300s, revenues are 400s, and expenses are 500s.

**ILLUSTRATION 2–5**
General Ledger Accounts

### Balance Sheet Accounts

**Cash 100**

| | | | |
|---|---|---|---|
| July 1 GJ1 | 60,000 | 24,000 | July 1 GJ1 |
| 1 GJ1 | 40,000 | 12,000 | 1 GJ1 |
| 4–31GJ1 | 35,000 | 2,000 | 6 GJ1 |
| 16 GJ1 | 1,000 | 25,000 | 20 GJ1 |
| 25 GJ1 | 1,500 | 5,000 | 20 GJ1 |
| | | 1,000 | 30 GJ1 |
| **July 31 Bal.** | **68,500** | | |

**Prepaid Rent 130**

| | | | |
|---|---|---|---|
| July 1 GJ1 | 24,000 | | |
| **July 31 Bal.** | **24,000** | | |

**Accounts Receivable 110**

| | | | |
|---|---|---|---|
| July 9 GJ1 | 3,500 | 1,500 | July 25 GJ1 |
| **July 31 Bal.** | **2,000** | | |

**Inventory 140**

| | | | |
|---|---|---|---|
| July 3 GJ1 | 60,000 | 20,000 | July 4–31 |
| | | 2,000 | 9 GJ1 |
| **July 31 Bal.** | **38,000** | | |

**Supplies 125**

| | | | |
|---|---|---|---|
| July 6 GJ1 | 2,000 | | |
| **July 31 Bal.** | **2,000** | | |

**Furniture and Fixtures 150**

| | | | |
|---|---|---|---|
| July 1 GJ1 | 12,000 | | |
| **July 31 Bal.** | **12,000** | | |

**Accounts Payable 210**

| | | | |
|---|---|---|---|
| July 20 GJ1 | 25,000 | 60,000 | July 3 GJ1 |
| | | **35,000** | **July 31 Bal.** |

**Notes Payable 220**

| | | | |
|---|---|---|---|
| | | 40,000 | July 1 GJ1 |
| | | **40,000** | **July 31 Bal.** |

**Unearned Rent Revenue 230**

| | | | |
|---|---|---|---|
| | | 1,000 | July 16 GJ1 |
| | | **1,000** | **July 31 Bal.** |

**Common Stock 300**

| | | | |
|---|---|---|---|
| | | 60,000 | July 1 GJ1 |
| | | **60,000** | **July 31 Bal.** |

**Retained Earnings 310**

| | | | |
|---|---|---|---|
| July 30 GJ1 | 1,000 | | |
| **July 31 Bal.** | **1,000** | | |

### Income Statement Accounts

**Sales Revenue 400**

| | | | |
|---|---|---|---|
| | | 35,000 | July 4–31 GJ1 |
| | | 3,500 | 9 GJ1 |
| | | **38,500** | **July 31 Bal.** |

**Cost of Goods Sold 500**

| | | | |
|---|---|---|---|
| July 4–31 GJ1 | 20,000 | | |
| July 9 GJ1 | 2,000 | | |
| **July 31 Bal.** | **22,000** | | |

**Salaries Expense 510**

| | | | |
|---|---|---|---|
| July 20 GJ1 | 5,000 | | |
| **July 31 Bal.** | **5,000** | | |

The ledger accounts also contain a posting reference, usually the page number of the journal in which the journal entry was recorded. This allows for easy cross-referencing between the journal and the ledger. Page 1 is used for Illustration 2–4.

● LO3

Step 4 in the processing cycle is to transfer the debit/credit information from the journal to the general ledger accounts. Illustration 2–5 contains the ledger accounts (in T-account form) for Dress Right *after* all of the general journal transactions have been posted. The reference GJ1 next to each of the posted amounts indicates that the source of the entry is page 1 of the general journal.

**STEP 5: Prepare an *unadjusted trial balance.***

Before financial statements are prepared and before adjusting entries are recorded (internal transactions) at the end of an accounting period, an **unadjusted trial balance** usually is prepared—step 5. A trial balance is simply a list of the general ledger accounts and their balances at a particular date. Its purpose is to check for completeness and to prove that the sum of the accounts with debit balances equals the sum of the accounts with credit balances, that is, the accounting equation is in balance. The fact that the debits and credits are equal does not necessarily mean that the equal balances are correct. The trial balance could contain offsetting errors. As we will see later in the chapter, this trial balance also facilitates the preparation of adjusting entries.

The unadjusted trial balance at July 31, 2006, for the Dress Right Clothing Corporation appears in Illustration 2–6. Notice that retained earnings has a debit balance of $1,000. This reflects the payment of the cash dividend to shareholders. The increases and decreases in retained earnings from revenue, expense, gain and loss transactions are recorded indirectly in temporary accounts. Before the start of the next year, these increases and decreases are transferred to the retained earnings account.

**ILLUSTRATION 2–6**
Unadjusted Trial Balance

**DRESS RIGHT CLOTHING CORPORATION**
**Unadjusted Trial Balance**
**July 31, 2006**

| Account Title | Debits | Credits |
|---|---|---|
| Cash | 68,500 | |
| Accounts receivable | 2,000 | |
| Supplies | 2,000 | |
| Prepaid rent | 24,000 | |
| Inventory | 38,000 | |
| Furniture and fixtures | 12,000 | |
| Accounts payable | | 35,000 |
| Notes payable | | 40,000 |
| Unearned rent revenue | | 1,000 |
| Common stock | | 60,000 |
| Retained earnings | 1,000 | |
| Sales revenue | | 38,500 |
| Cost of goods sold | 22,000 | |
| Salaries expense | 5,000 | |
| Totals | 174,500 | 174,500 |

At any time, the total of all debit balances should equal the total of all credit balances.

## CONCEPT REVIEW EXERCISE

**JOURNAL ENTRIES FOR EXTERNAL TRANSACTIONS**

The Wyndham Wholesale Company began operations on August 1, 2006. The following transactions took place during the month of August.

a. Owners invested $50,000 cash in the corporation in exchange for 5,000 shares of common stock.
b. Equipment is purchased for $20,000 cash.

c. On the first day of August, $6,000 rent on a building is paid for the months of August and September.
d. Merchandise inventory costing $38,000 is purchased on account. The company uses the perpetual inventory system.
e. $30,000 is borrowed from a local bank, and a note payable is signed.
f. Credit sales for the month are $40,000. The cost of merchandise sold is $22,000.
g. $15,000 is collected on account from customers.
h. $20,000 is paid on account to suppliers of merchandise.
i. Salaries of $7,000 are paid to employees for August.
j. A bill for $2,000 is received from the local utility company for the month of August.
k. $20,000 cash was loaned to another company, evidenced by a note receivable.
l. The corporation paid its shareholders a cash dividend of $1,000.

**Required:**

1. Prepare a journal entry for each transaction.
2. Prepare an unadjusted trial balance as of August 31, 2006.

**SOLUTION**

1. Prepare a journal entry for each transaction.
   a. The issuance of common stock for cash increases both cash and shareholders' equity (common stock).

| | | |
|---|---|---|
| Cash | 50,000 | |
| Common Stock | | 50,000 |

   b. The purchase of equipment increases equipment and decreases cash.

| | | |
|---|---|---|
| Equipment | 20,000 | |
| Cash | | 20,000 |

   c. The payment of rent in advance increases prepaid rent and decreases cash.

| | | |
|---|---|---|
| Prepaid rent | 6,000 | |
| Cash | | 6,000 |

   d. The purchase of merchandise on account increases both inventory and accounts payable.

| | | |
|---|---|---|
| Inventory | 38,000 | |
| Accounts payable | | 38,000 |

   e. Borrowing cash and signing a note increases both cash and note payable.

| | | |
|---|---|---|
| Cash | 30,000 | |
| Note payable | | 30,000 |

   f. The sale of merchandise on account increases both accounts receivable and sales revenue. Also, cost of goods sold increases and inventory decreases.

| | | |
|---|---|---|
| Accounts receivable | 40,000 | |
| Sales revenue | | 40,000 |
| Cost of goods sold | 22,000 | |
| Inventory | | 22,000 |

   g. The collection of cash on account increases cash and decreases accounts receivable.

| | | |
|---|---|---|
| Cash | 15,000 | |
| Accounts receivable | | 15,000 |

h. The payment of suppliers on account decreases both accounts payable and cash.

| | | |
|---|---|---|
| Accounts payable. . . . . . . . . . . . . . . . . . . . . . . . . . . . . . . . . . . . . . . . | 20,000 | |
| Cash . . . . . . . . . . . . . . . . . . . . . . . . . . . . . . . . . . . . . . . . . . . . . . . | | 20,000 |

i. The payments of salaries for the period increases salaries expense (decreases retained earnings) and decreases cash.

| | | |
|---|---|---|
| Salaries expense . . . . . . . . . . . . . . . . . . . . . . . . . . . . . . . . . . . . . . . . | 7,000 | |
| Cash . . . . . . . . . . . . . . . . . . . . . . . . . . . . . . . . . . . . . . . . . . . . . . . | | 7,000 |

j. The receipt of a bill for services rendered increases both an expense (utilities expense) and accounts payable.

| | | |
|---|---|---|
| Utilities expense. . . . . . . . . . . . . . . . . . . . . . . . . . . . . . . . . . . . . . . . | 2,000 | |
| Accounts payable. . . . . . . . . . . . . . . . . . . . . . . . . . . . . . . . . . . . . . | | 2,000 |

k. The lending of cash to another entity and the signing of a note increases note receivable and decreases cash.

| | | |
|---|---|---|
| Note receivable . . . . . . . . . . . . . . . . . . . . . . . . . . . . . . . . . . . . . . . . | 20,000 | |
| Cash . . . . . . . . . . . . . . . . . . . . . . . . . . . . . . . . . . . . . . . . . . . . . . . | | 20,000 |

l. Cash dividends paid to shareholders reduce both retained earnings and cash.

| | | |
|---|---|---|
| Retained earnings[3]. . . . . . . . . . . . . . . . . . . . . . . . . . . . . . . . . . . . . . | 1,000 | |
| Cash . . . . . . . . . . . . . . . . . . . . . . . . . . . . . . . . . . . . . . . . . . . . . . . | | 1,000 |

2. Prepare an unadjusted trial balance as of August 31, 2006.

| **Account Title** | **Debits** | **Credits** |
|---|---|---|
| Cash | 21,000 | |
| Accounts receivable | 25,000 | |
| Prepaid rent | 6,000 | |
| Inventory | 16,000 | |
| Note receivable | 20,000 | |
| Equipment | 20,000 | |
| Accounts payable | | 20,000 |
| Note payable | | 30,000 |
| Common stock | | 50,000 |
| Retained earnings | 1,000 | |
| Sales revenue | | 40,000 |
| Cost of goods sold | 22,000 | |
| Salaries expense | 7,000 | |
| Utilities expense | 2,000 | |
| Totals | 140,000 | 140,000 |

## Adjusting Entries

Step 6 in the processing cycle is to record in the general journal and post to the ledger accounts the effect of *internal events* on the accounting equation. These transactions do not involve an

**STEP 6: Record *adjusting entries* and post to the ledger accounts.**

[3]An alternative is to debit a temporary account—dividends—that is closed to retained earnings at the end of the fiscal year along with the other temporary accounts.

exchange transaction with another entity and, therefore, are not initiated by a source document. They are recorded *at the end of any period when financial statements are prepared.* These transactions are commonly referred to as **adjusting entries.**

FINANCIAL REPORTING CASE
Q1, p. 47

Even when all transactions and events are analyzed, corrected, journalized, and posted to appropriate ledger accounts, some account balances will require updating. Adjusting entries are required to implement the *accrual accounting model.* More specifically, these entries are required to satisfy the *realization principle* and the *matching principle.* Adjusting entries help ensure that all revenues earned in a period are recognized in that period, regardless of when the cash payment is received. Also, they enable a company to recognize all expenses incurred during a period, regardless of when cash payment is made. As a result, a period's income statement provides a more complete measure of a company's operating performance and a better measure for predicting future operating cash flows. The balance sheet also provides a more complete assessment of assets and liabilities as sources of future cash receipts and disbursements. You might think of adjusting entries as a method of bringing the company's financial information up to date before preparing the financial statements.

● LO4

Adjusting entries are necessary for three situations:

FINANCIAL REPORTING CASE
Q2, p. 47

1. **Prepayments,** sometimes referred to as *deferrals.*
2. **Accruals.**
3. **Estimates.**

## PREPAYMENTS

*Prepayments* are transactions in which the cash flow *precedes* expense or revenue recognition.

**Prepayments** occur when the cash flow *precedes* either expense or revenue recognition. For example, a company may buy supplies in one period but use them in a later period. The cash outflow creates an asset (supplies) which then must be expensed in a future period as the asset is used up. Similarly, a company may receive cash from a customer in one period but provide the customer with a good or service in a future period. For instance, magazine publishers usually receive cash in advance for magazine subscriptions. The cash inflow creates a liability (unearned revenue) that is recognized as revenue in a future period when it is earned.

*Prepaid expenses* represent assets recorded when a cash disbursement creates benefits beyond the current reporting period.

**Prepaid Expenses.** **Prepaid expenses** are the costs of assets acquired in one period and expensed in a future period. Whenever cash is paid, and it is not to (1) satisfy a liability or (2) pay a dividend or return capital to owners, it must be determined whether or not the payment creates future benefits or whether the payment benefits only the current period. The purchase of machinery, equipment, or supplies or the payment of rent in advance are examples of payments that create future benefits and should be recorded as assets. The benefits provided by these assets expire in future periods and their cost is expensed in future periods as related revenues are recognized.

The adjusting entry required for a prepaid expense is a *debit to an expense* and a *credit to an asset.*

To illustrate this concept, assume that a company paid a radio station $2,000 in July for advertising. If that $2,000 were for advertising provided by the radio station during the month of July, the entire $2,000 would be expensed in the same period as the cash disbursement. If, however, the $2,000 was a payment for advertising to be provided in a future period, say the month of August, then the cash disbursement creates an asset called *prepaid advertising.* An adjusting entry is required at the end of August to increase advertising expense (decrease shareholders' equity) and to decrease the asset prepaid advertising by $2,000. Assuming that the cash disbursement records a debit to an asset, as in this example, the adjusting entry for a prepaid expense is, therefore, a *debit to an expense* and a *credit to an asset.*

The unadjusted trial balance can provide a starting point for determining which adjusting entries are required for a period, particularly for prepayments. Review the July 31, 2006, unadjusted trial balance for the Dress Right Clothing Corporation in Illustration 2–6 on page 59 and try to anticipate the required adjusting entries for prepaid expenses.

● LO5

The first asset that requires adjustment is supplies, $2,000 of which were purchased during July. This transaction created an asset as the supplies will be used in future periods. The company could either track the supplies used or simply count the supplies at the end of the period and determine the dollar amount of supplies remaining. Assume that Dress Right determines that at the end of July, $1,200 of supplies remain. The following adjusting journal entry is required.

| July 31 | | |
|---|---|---|
| Supplies expense | 800 | |
| Supplies | | 800 |

To record the cost of supplies used during the month of July.

After this entry is recorded and posted to the ledger accounts, the supplies (asset) account is reduced to a $1,200 debit balance, and the supplies expense account will have an $800 debit balance.

**Supplies**

| | Debit | Credit |
|---|---|---|
| Beg. bal. | 0 | |
| | 2,000 | 800 |
| Bal. | 1,200 | |

The next prepaid expense requiring adjustment is rent. Recall that at the beginning of July, the company paid $24,000 to its landlord representing one year's rent in advance. As it is reasonable to assume that the rent services provided each period are equal, the monthly rent is $2,000. At the end of July 2006, one month's prepaid rent has expired and must be recognized as expense.

| July 31 | | |
|---|---|---|
| Rent expense ($24,000 ÷ 12) | 2,000 | |
| Prepaid rent | | 2,000 |

To record the cost of expired rent for the month of July.

After this entry is recorded and posted to the ledger accounts, the prepaid rent account will have a debit balance of $22,000, representing 11 remaining months at $2,000 a month, and the rent expense account will have a $2,000 debit balance.

**Prepaid Rent**

| | Debit | Credit |
|---|---|---|
| Beg. bal. | 0 | |
| | 24,000 | 2,000 |
| Bal. | 22,000 | |

The final prepayment involves the asset represented by furniture and fixtures that was purchased for $12,000. This asset has a long life but nevertheless will expire over time. For the previous two adjusting entries, it was fairly straightforward to determine the amount of the asset that expired during the period.

However, it is difficult, if not impossible, to determine how much of the benefits from using the furniture and fixtures expired during any particular period. Recall from Chapter 1 that one approach to implementing the matching principle is to "recognize an expense by a systematic and rational allocation to specific time periods."

Assume that the furniture and fixtures have a useful life of five years or 60 months and will be worthless at the end of that period, and that we choose to allocate the cost equally over the period of use. The amount of monthly expense, called *depreciation expense,* is $200 ($12,000 ÷ 60 months = $200), and the following adjusting entry is recorded.

| July 31 | | |
|---|---|---|
| Depreciation expense | 200 | |
| Accumulated depreciation—furniture and fixtures | | 200 |

To record depreciation of furniture and fixtures for the month of July.

The entry reduces an asset, furniture and fixtures, by $200. However, the asset account is not reduced directly. Instead, the credit is to an account called *accumulated depreciation.* This is a contra account to furniture and fixtures. The normal balance in a contra asset account will be a credit, that is, "contra," or opposite, to the normal debit balance in an asset account. The purpose of the contra account is to keep the original cost of the asset intact while reducing it indirectly. In the balance sheet, furniture and fixtures is reported net of accumulated depreciation. This topic is covered in depth in Chapter 11.

After this entry is recorded and posted to the ledger accounts, the accumulated depreciation account will have a credit balance of $200 and the depreciation expense account will have a $200 debit balance. If a required adjusting entry for a prepaid expense is not recorded, net income, assets, and shareholders' equity (retained earnings) will be overstated.

**Unearned Revenues.** **Unearned revenues** are created when a company receives cash from a customer in one period for goods or services that are to be provided in a future period. The cash receipt, an external transaction, is recorded as a debit to cash and a credit to a liability. This liability reflects the company's obligation to provide goods or services in the future.

*Unearned revenues* represent liabilities recorded when cash is received from customers in advance of providing a good or service.

To illustrate an unearned revenue transaction, assume that during the month of June a magazine publisher received $24 in cash for a 24-month subscription to a monthly magazine. The subscription begins in July. On receipt of the cash, the publisher records a liability,

**The adjusting entry required when unearned revenues are earned is a *debit to a liability* and a *credit to revenue.***

unearned subscription revenue, of $24. Subsequently, revenue of $1 is earned as each monthly magazine is published and mailed to the customer. An adjusting entry is required each month to increase shareholders' equity (revenue) to recognize the $1 in revenue earned and to decrease the liability. Assuming that the cash receipt records a credit to a liability, the adjusting entry for unearned revenues, therefore, is a *debit to a liability,* in this case unearned subscription revenue, and a *credit to revenue.*

Once again, the unadjusted trial balance provides information concerning unearned revenues. For Dress Right Clothing Corporation, the only unearned revenue in the trial balance is unearned rent revenue. Recall that the company subleased a portion of its building to a jewelry store for $500 per month. On July 16, the jewelry store paid Dress Right $1,000 in advance for the first two months' rent. The transaction was recorded as a debit to cash and a credit to unearned rent revenue.

At the end of July, how much of the $1,000 has been earned? Approximately one-half of one month's rent has been earned, or $250, requiring the following adjusting journal entry.

**To record the amount of unearned rent revenue earned during July.**

| | | |
|---|---|---|
| **July 31** | | |
| Unearned rent revenue . . . . . . . . . . . . . . . . . . . . . . . . . . . . . . . . . | 250 | |
| Rent revenue . . . . . . . . . . . . . . . . . . . . . . . . . . . . . . . . . . . . . . . | | 250 |

**Unearned Rent Revenue**

| | |
|---|---|
| | 0 Beg. bal. |
| 250 | 1,000 |
| | 750 End bal. |

After this entry is recorded and posted to the ledger accounts, the unearned rent revenue account is reduced to a credit balance of $750 for the remaining one and one-half months' rent, and the rent revenue account will have a $250 credit balance. If this entry is not recorded, net income and shareholders' equity (retained earnings) will be understated, and liabilities will be overstated.

**Alternative Approach to Record Prepayments.** The same end result can be achieved for prepayments by recording the external transaction directly into an expense or revenue account. In fact, many companies prefer this approach. For simplicity, bookkeeping instructions may require all cash payments for expenses to be debited to the appropriate expense account and all cash receipts for revenues to be credited to the appropriate revenue account. The adjusting entry then records the *unexpired* prepaid expense (asset) or *unearned* revenue (liability) as of the end of the period.

For example, on July 1, 2006, Dress Right paid $24,000 in cash for one year's rent on its building. The entry included a debit to prepaid rent. The company could have debited rent expense instead.

**Rent Expense**

| | |
|---|---|
| Beg. bal. 0 | |
| 24,000 | 22,000 |
| End bal. 2,000 | |

| | | |
|---|---|---|
| **Alternative Approach** | | |
| **July 1** | | |
| Rent expense . . . . . . . . . . . . . . . . . . . . . . . . . . . . . . . . . . . . . . . | 24,000 | |
| Cash . . . . . . . . . . . . . . . . . . . . . . . . . . . . . . . . . . . . . . . . . . . . | | 24,000 |

The adjusting entry then records the amount of prepaid rent as of the end of July, $22,000, and reduces rent expense to $2,000, the cost of rent for the month of July.

**Prepaid Rent**

| | |
|---|---|
| Beg. bal. 0 | |
| 22,000 | |
| End bal. 22,000 | |

| | | |
|---|---|---|
| **Alternative Approach** | | |
| **July 31** | | |
| Prepaid rent . . . . . . . . . . . . . . . . . . . . . . . . . . . . . . . . . . . . . . . | 22,000 | |
| Rent expense . . . . . . . . . . . . . . . . . . . . . . . . . . . . . . . . . . . . . . | | 22,000 |

The net effect of handling the transactions in this manner is the same as the previous treatment. Either way, the prepaid rent account will have a debit balance at the end of July of $22,000, and the rent expense account will have a debit balance of $2,000. What's important is that an adjusting entry is recorded to ensure the appropriate amounts are reflected in both the expense and asset *before financial statements are to be prepared.*

Similarly, the July 16 cash receipt from the jewelry store representing an advance for two months' rent could have been recorded by Dress Right as a credit to rent revenue instead of unearned rent revenue (a liability).

**Alternative Approach**
**July 16**

| | | |
|---|---|---|
| Cash | 1,000 | |
| Rent revenue | | 1,000 |

If Dress Right records the entire $1,000 as rent revenue in this way, it would then use the adjusting entry to record the amount of unearned revenue as of the end of July, $750, and reduce rent revenue to $250, the amount of revenue earned during the month of July.

**Alternative Approach**
**July 31**

| | | |
|---|---|---|
| Rent revenue | 750 | |
| Unearned rent revenue | | 750 |

## ACCRUALS

**Accruals** occur when the cash flow comes *after* either expense or revenue recognition. For example, a company often uses the services of another entity in one period and pays for them in a subsequent period. An expense must be recognized in the period incurred and an accrued liability recorded. Also, goods and services often are provided to customers on credit. In such instances, a revenue is recognized in the period earned and an asset, a receivable, is recorded.

*Accruals* involve transactions where the cash outflow or inflow takes place in a period subsequent to expense or revenue recognition.

Many accruals involve external transactions that automatically are recorded from a source document. For example, a sales invoice for a credit sale provides all the information necessary to record the debit to accounts receivable and the credit to sales revenue. However, there are some accruals that involve internal transactions and thus require adjusting entries. Because accruals involve recognition of expense or revenue before cash flow, the unadjusted trial balance will not be as helpful in identifying required adjusting entries as with prepayments.

**Accrued Liabilities.** For **accrued liabilities**, we are concerned with expenses incurred but not yet paid. Dress Right Clothing Corporation requires two adjusting entries for accrued liabilities at July 31, 2006.

*Accrued liabilities* represent liabilities recorded when an expense has been incurred prior to cash payment.

The first entry is for employee salaries for the second half of July. Recall that on July 20 the company paid employees $5,000 for salaries for the first half of the month. Salaries for the second half of July will probably be paid in early August. Nevertheless, the company incurred an expense in July for services provided to it by its employees. Also, there exists an obligation at the end of July to pay the salaries earned by employees. An adjusting entry is required to increase salaries expense (decrease shareholders' equity) and to increase liabilities for the salaries payable. The adjusting entry for an accrued liability always includes a *debit to an expense,* and a *credit to a liability.* Assuming that salaries for the second half of July are $5,500, the following adjusting entry is recorded.

The adjusting entry required to record an accrued liability is a ***debit to an expense*** and a ***credit to a liability.***

**July 31**

| | | |
|---|---|---|
| Salaries expense | 5,500 | |
| Salaries payable | | 5,500 |

To record accrued salaries at the end of July.

After this entry is recorded and posted to the general ledger, the salaries expense account will have a debit balance of $10,500 ($5,000 + 5,500), and the salaries payable account will have a credit balance of $5,500.

**Salaries Payable**

| | |
|---|---|
| | 0 Beg. bal. |
| | 5,500 |
| | 5,500 End bal. |

The unadjusted trial balance does provide information about the second required accrued liability entry. In the trial balance we can see a balance in the notes payable account of $40,000. The company borrowed this amount on July 1, 2006. Both notes require the payment of 10% interest. Whenever the trial balance reveals interest-bearing debt, and interest is not paid on the last day of the period, an adjusting entry is required for the amount of interest that has built up (accrued) since the last payment date or the last date interest was accrued. In this case, we calculate interest as follows:

$$\text{Principal} \times \text{Interest rate} \times \text{Time} = \text{Interest}$$
$$\$40{,}000 \times 10\% \times {}^{1}\!/_{12} = \$333 \text{ (rounded)}$$

To accrue interest expense for July on notes payable.

*Interest rates always are stated as the annual rate.* Therefore, the above calculation uses this annual rate multiplied by the principal amount multiplied by the amount of time outstanding, in this case one month or one-twelfth of a year.

| July 31 | | |
|---|---|---|
| Interest expense | 333 | |
| Interest payable | | 333 |

After this entry is recorded and posted to the ledger accounts, the interest expense account will have a debit balance of $333, and the interest payable account will have a credit balance of $333. Failure to record a required adjusting entry for an accrued liability will cause net income and shareholders' equity (retained earnings) to be overstated, and liabilities to be understated.[4]

*Accrued receivables* involve situations when the revenue is earned in a period prior to the cash receipt.

**Accrued Receivables.** **Accrued receivables** involve the recognition of revenue earned before cash is received. An example of an internal accrued revenue event is the recognition of interest earned on a loan to another entity. For example, assume that Dress Right loaned another corporation $30,000 at the beginning of August, evidenced by a note receivable. Terms of the note call for the payment of principal, $30,000, and interest at 8% in three months. An external transaction records the cash disbursement—a debit to note receivable and a credit to cash of $30,000.

The adjusting entry required to record an accrued revenue is a *debit to an asset,* a receivable, and a *credit to revenue.*

What adjusting entry would be required at the end of August? Dress Right needs to record the interest revenue earned but not yet received and the corresponding receivable. Interest receivable increases and interest revenue (shareholders' equity) also increases. The adjusting entry for accrued receivables always includes a *debit to an asset,* a receivable, and a *credit to revenue.* In this case, at the end of August Dress Right recognizes $200 in interest revenue ($\$30{,}000 \times 8\% \times {}^{1}\!/_{12}$) and makes the following adjusting entry. If this entry is not recorded, net income, assets, and shareholders' equity (retained earnings) will be understated.

To accrue interest revenue earned in August on note receivable.

| August 31 | | |
|---|---|---|
| Interest receivable | 200 | |
| Interest revenue | | 200 |

There are no accrued revenue adjusting entries required for Dress Right at the end of July.

The required adjusting entries for prepayments and accruals are recapped in Graphic 2–4. Each case involves recognizing an expense or revenue in a period that differs from the period in which cash was paid or received. These entries are necessary to properly measure operating performance and financial position according to the accrual accounting model.

**GRAPHIC 2–4**
Adjusting Entries

| | Adjusting Entries | | | |
|---|---|---|---|---|
| | Expenses | | Revenues | |
| | Debit | Credit | Debit | Credit |
| **Prepayments** (initially recorded as assets or liabilities) | Expense | Asset | Liability | Revenue |
| **Prepayments** (initially recorded as expenses or revenues) | Asset | Expense | Revenue | Liability |
| **Accruals** | Expense | Liability | Asset | Revenue |

[4]Dress Right Clothing is a corporation. Corporations are income-tax-paying entities. Income taxes—federal, state and local—are assessed on an annual basis and payments are made throughout the year. An additional adjusting entry would be required for Dress Right to accrue the amount of estimated income taxes payable that are applicable to the month of July. Accounting for income taxes is introduced in Chapter 4 and covered in depth in Chapter 16.

## ESTIMATES

A third classification of adjusting entries is **estimates.** Accountants often must make estimates of future events to comply with the accrual accounting model. For example, the calculation of depreciation expense requires an estimate of expected useful life of the asset being depreciated as well as its expected residual value. We discussed the adjusting entries for depreciation expense in the context of its being a prepayment, but it also could be thought of as an estimate.

**Accountants often must make *estimates* in order to comply with the accrual accounting model.**

One situation involving an estimate that does not fit neatly into either the prepayment or accrual classification is **bad debt expense.** Chapter 1 introduced briefly the allowance method of accounting for bad debts. This method requires an estimate of the amount of accounts receivable that will ultimately prove to be uncollectible. This estimate is required to properly match the bad debt expense with the revenue it helps generate as well as reflect the collectible portion of the receivable on the balance sheet.

The July 31, 2006, unadjusted trial balance for Dress Right shows a balance in accounts receivable of $2,000. Assume that the company's management felt that of this amount, only $1,500 would ultimately be collected. An adjusting entry is required to decrease accounts receivable and increase bad debt expense (decrease shareholders' equity) by $500. The adjusting entry is:

| | | |
|---|---|---|
| **July 31** | | |
| Bad debt expense .................................... | 500 | |
| Allowance for uncollectible accounts..................... | | 500 |

**To record bad debt expense for July.**

Notice that the accounts receivable account is not reduced directly. A contra account, called *allowance for uncollectible accounts,* is credited. After this entry is recorded and posted to the ledger accounts, bad debt expense will have a debit balance of $500 and the allowance for uncollectible accounts account will have a credit balance of $500.[5]

The contra account is used to keep intact in the accounts receivable account the total amount of receivables that are still outstanding. The allowance account will always have a credit balance equal to estimated bad debts on existing accounts receivable. Only when the account is actually written off as uncollectible would accounts receivable be reduced. At this point, the $500 is just an estimate. In the balance sheet, accounts receivable is shown net of the allowance account, in this case $1,500. Chapter 7 addresses the topics of accounts receivable and bad debts in more depth.

Illustration 2–7 recaps the July 31, 2006, adjusting entries for Dress Right Clothing Corporation as they would appear in a general journal.

● LO5

After the adjusting entries are posted to the general ledger accounts, the next step—step 7—in the processing cycle is to prepare an **adjusted trial balance.** The term adjusted refers to the fact that adjusting entries have now been posted to the accounts. Recall that the column titled Post Ref. (Posting Reference) is the number assigned to the general ledger account that is being debited or credited. Illustration 2–8 shows the July 31, 2006, adjusted trial balance for Dress Right Clothing Corporation.

[5]If the allowance for uncollectible accounts had a credit balance before the adjusting entry, say $150, then the adjusting entry would have required only a $350 debit to bad debt expense and credit to the allowance account.

**ILLUSTRATION 2–7**
The General Journal—Adjusting Entries

**DRESS RIGHT CLOTHING CORPORATION**
**General Journal** — **Page 2**

| Date 2006 | | Account Title and Explanation | Post Ref. | Debit | Credit |
|---|---|---|---|---|---|
| July | 31 | Supplies expense | 520 | 800 | |
| | | Supplies | 125 | | 800 |
| | | *To record the cost of supplies used during the month of July.* | | | |
| | 31 | Rent expense | 530 | 2,000 | |
| | | Prepaid rent | 130 | | 2,000 |
| | | *To record the cost of expired rent for the month of July.* | | | |
| | 31 | Depreciation expense | 540 | 200 | |
| | | Accumulated depreciation—furniture and fixtures | 155 | | 200 |
| | | *To record depreciation for furniture and fixtures for the month of July.* | | | |
| | 31 | Unearned rent revenue | 230 | 250 | |
| | | Rent revenue | 410 | | 250 |
| | | *To record the amount of unearned rent revenue earned during July.* | | | |
| | 31 | Salaries expense | 510 | 5,500 | |
| | | Salaries payable | 230 | | 5,500 |
| | | *To record accrued salaries at the end of July.* | | | |
| | 31 | Interest expense | 550 | 333 | |
| | | Interest payable | 240 | | 333 |
| | | *To accrue interest expense for July on notes payable.* | | | |
| | 31 | Bad debt expense | 560 | 500 | |
| | | Allowance for uncollectible accounts | 115 | | 500 |
| | | *To record bad debt expense for July.* | | | |

**ILLUSTRATION 2–8**
Adjusted Trial Balance

**STEP 7: Prepare an *adjusted trial balance.***

**DRESS RIGHT CLOTHING CORPORATION**
**Adjusted Trial Balance**
**July 31, 2006**

| Account Title | Debits | Credits |
|---|---|---|
| Cash | 68,500 | |
| Accounts receivable | 2,000 | |
| Allowance for uncollectible accounts | | 500 |
| Supplies | 1,200 | |
| Prepaid rent | 22,000 | |
| Inventory | 38,000 | |
| Furniture and fixtures | 12,000 | |
| Accumulated depreciation—furniture and fixtures | | 200 |
| Accounts payable | | 35,000 |
| Notes payable | | 40,000 |
| Unearned rent revenue | | 750 |
| Salaries payable | | 5,500 |
| Interest payable | | 333 |
| Common stock | | 60,000 |
| Retained earnings | 1,000 | |
| Sales revenue | | 38,500 |
| Rent revenue | | 250 |
| Cost of goods sold | 22,000 | |
| Salaries expense | 10,500 | |
| Supplies expense | 800 | |
| Rent expense | 2,000 | |
| Depreciation expense | 200 | |
| Interest expense | 333 | |
| Bad debt expense | 500 | |
| Totals | 181,033 | 181,033 |

## Concept Review Exercise

### Adjusting Entries

The Wyndham Wholesale Company needs to prepare financial statements at the end of August 2006 for presentation to its bank. An unadjusted trial balance as of August 31, 2006, was presented in a previous concept review exercise on page 61.

The following information also is available:

a. The company anticipates that of the $25,000 in accounts receivable from customers, $2,500 will *not* be collected.
b. The note payable requires the entire $30,000 in principal plus interest at 10% to be paid on July 31, 2007. The date of the loan is August 1, 2006.
c. Depreciation on the equipment for the month of August is $500.
d. The note receivable is dated August 16, 2006. The note requires the entire $20,000 in principal plus interest at 12% to be repaid in four months (the loan was outstanding for one-half month during August).
e. The prepaid rent of $6,000 represents rent for the months of August and September.

**Required:**

1. Prepare any necessary adjusting entries at August 31, 2006.
2. Prepare an adjusted trial balance as of August 31, 2006.
3. What is the total net effect on income (overstated or understated) if the adjusting entries are not made?

### Solution

1. Prepare any necessary adjusting entries at August 31, 2006.
   a. An adjusting entry is required to adjust allowance for uncollectible accounts to $2,500. Because there is no balance in the allowance account before adjustment, the adjusting entry must record a bad debt expense of $2,500.

| | | |
|---|---|---|
| Bad debt expense | 2,500 | |
| Allowance for uncollectible accounts | | 2,500 |

   b. An adjusting entry is required to accrue the interest expense on the note payable for the month of August. Accrued interest is calculated as follows:

$$\$30,000 \times 10\% \times 1/12 = \$250$$

| | | |
|---|---|---|
| Interest expense | 250 | |
| Interest payable | | 250 |

   c. Depreciation expense on the equipment must be recorded.

| | | |
|---|---|---|
| Depreciation expense | 500 | |
| Accumulated depreciation—equipment | | 500 |

   d. An adjusting entry is required for the one-half month of accrued interest revenue earned on the note receivable. Accrued interest is calculated as follows:

$$\$20,000 \times 12\% \times 1/12 \times 1/2 = \$100$$

| | | |
|---|---|---|
| Interest receivable | 100 | |
| Interest revenue | | 100 |

   e. An adjusting entry is required to recognize the amount of prepaid rent that expired during August.

| | | |
|---|---|---|
| Rent expense | 3,000 | |
| Prepaid rent | | 3,000 |

2. Prepare an adjusted trial balance as of August 31, 2006.

| Account Title | Debits | Credits |
|---|---|---|
| Cash | 21,000 | |
| Accounts receivable | 25,000 | |
| Allowance for uncollectible accounts | | 2,500 |
| Prepaid rent | 3,000 | |
| Inventory | 16,000 | |
| Interest receivable | 100 | |
| Note receivable | 20,000 | |
| Equipment | 20,000 | |
| Accumulated depreciation—equipment | | 500 |
| Accounts payable | | 20,000 |
| Interest payable | | 250 |
| Note payable | | 30,000 |
| Common stock | | 50,000 |
| Retained earnings | 1,000 | |
| Sales revenue | | 40,000 |
| Interest revenue | | 100 |
| Cost of goods sold | 22,000 | |
| Salaries expense | 7,000 | |
| Utilities expense | 2,000 | |
| Bad debt expense | 2,500 | |
| Interest expense | 250 | |
| Depreciation expense | 500 | |
| Rent expense | 3,000 | |
| Totals | 143,350 | 143,350 |

3. What is the effect on income (overstated or understated), if the adjusting entries are not made?

| Adjusting Entry | Income Overstated (understated) |
|---|---|
| Bad debt expense | $2,500 |
| Interest expense | 250 |
| Depreciation expense | 500 |
| Interest revenue | (100) |
| Rent expense | 3,000 |
| Net effect, income overstated by | $6,150 |

We now turn our attention to the preparation of financial statements.

## Preparing the Financial Statements

● LO6

**STEP 8: Preparation of *financial statements.***

The purpose of each of the steps in the processing cycle to this point is to provide information for step 8—preparation of the **financial statements.** The adjusted trial balance contains the necessary information. After all, the financial statements are the primary means of communicating financial information to external parties.

**The *income statement* is a *change* statement that summarizes the profit-generating transactions that caused shareholders' equity (retained earnings) to change during the period.**

### THE INCOME STATEMENT

The purpose of the **income statement** is to summarize the profit-generating activities of a company that occurred during a particular period of time. It is a *change* statement in that it reports the changes in shareholders' equity (retained earnings) that occurred during the period as a result of revenues, expenses, gains, and losses. Illustration 2–9 shows the income statement for Dress Right Clothing Corporation for the month of July 2006.

**ILLUSTRATION 2–9**
Income Statement

**DRESS RIGHT CLOTHING CORPORATION**
**Income Statement**
**For the Month of July 2006**

| | | |
|---|---|---|
| Sales revenue | | $38,500 |
| Cost of goods sold | | 22,000 |
| Gross profit | | 16,500 |
| Operating expenses: | | |
| Salaries | $10,500 | |
| Supplies | 800 | |
| Rent | 2,000 | |
| Depreciation | 200 | |
| Bad debt | 500 | |
| Total operating expenses | | 14,000 |
| Operating income | | 2,500 |
| Other income (expense): | | |
| Rent revenue | 250 | |
| Interest expense | (333) | (83) |
| Net income | | $ 2,417 |

The income statement indicates a profit for the month of July of $2,417. During the month, the company was able to increase its net assets (equity) from activities related to selling its product. Dress Right is a corporation and subject to the payment of income tax on its profits. We ignore this required accrual here and address income taxes in a later chapter.

The components of the income statement usually are classified, that is, grouped according to common characteristics. A common classification scheme is to separate operating items from nonoperating items, as we do in Dress Right's income statement. Operating items include revenues and expenses directly related to the principal revenue-generating activities of the company. For example, operating items for a manufacturing company include sales revenues from the sale of products and all expenses related to this activity. Companies that sell products like Dress Right often report a subtotal within operating income, sales less cost of goods sold, called *gross profit.* Nonoperating items include gains and losses and revenues and expenses from peripheral activities. For Dress Right Clothing, rent revenue and interest expense are nonoperating items because they do not relate to the principal revenue-generating activity of the company, selling clothes. In Chapter 4 we discuss the format and content of the income statement in more depth.

## THE BALANCE SHEET

**The *balance sheet* is a position statement that presents an organized list of assets, liabilities and equity at a particular point in time.**

The purpose of the **balance sheet** is to present the financial position of the company on a particular date. Unlike the income statement, which is a change statement reporting events that occurred *during a period of time,* the balance sheet is a statement that presents an organized list of assets, liabilities, and shareholders' equity *at a point in time.* To provide a quick overview, Illustration 2–10 shows the balance sheet for Dress Right Clothing at July 31, 2006.

**Balance sheet items usually are classified (grouped) according to common characteristics.**

As we do in the income statement, we group the balance sheet elements into meaningful categories. For example, most balance sheets include the classifications of **current assets** and **current liabilities.** Current assets are those assets that are cash, will be converted into cash, or will be used up within one year or the operating cycle, whichever is longer. Current liabilities are those liabilities that will be satisfied within one year or the operating cycle, whichever is longer. For a manufacturing company, the operating cycle refers to the period of time necessary to convert cash to raw materials, raw materials to a finished product, the finished product to receivables, and then finally receivables back to cash. For most companies, this period is less than a year.

Examples of assets not classified as current include property and equipment and long-term receivables and investments. The only noncurrent asset that Dress Right has at July 31, 2006, is furniture and fixtures, which is classified under the property and equipment category.

**ILLUSTRATION 2–10**
Balance Sheet

**DRESS RIGHT CLOTHING CORPORATION**
**Balance Sheet**
**At July 31, 2006**

| | | |
|---|---|---|
| **Assets** | | |
| Current assets: | | |
| Cash | | $ 68,500 |
| Accounts receivable | $ 2,000 | |
| Less: Allowance for uncollectible accounts | 500 | 1,500 |
| Supplies | | 1,200 |
| Inventory | | 38,000 |
| Prepaid rent | | 22,000 |
| Total current assets | | 131,200 |
| Property and equipment: | | |
| Furniture and fixtures | 12,000 | |
| Less: Accumulated depreciation | 200 | 11,800 |
| Total assets | | $143,000 |
| **Liabilities and Shareholders' Equity** | | |
| Current liabilities: | | |
| Accounts payable | | $ 35,000 |
| Salaries payable | | 5,500 |
| Unearned rent revenue | | 750 |
| Interest payable | | 333 |
| Note payable | | 10,000 |
| Total current liabilities | | 51,583 |
| Long-term liabilities: | | |
| Note payable | | 30,000 |
| Shareholders' equity: | | |
| Common stock, 6,000 shares issued and outstanding | $60,000 | |
| Retained earnings | 1,417* | |
| Total shareholders' equity | | 61,417 |
| Total liabilities and shareholders' equity | | $143,000 |

*Beginning retained earnings + Net income − Dividends
0 + $2,417 − 1,000 = $1,417

All liabilities not classified as current are listed as long term. Dress Right's liabilities at July 31, 2006, include the $30,000 note payable due to be paid in 23 months. This liability is classified as long term.

Shareholders' equity lists the *paid-in capital* portion of equity—common stock—and *retained earnings.* Notice that the income statement we looked at in Illustration 2–9 ties in to the balance sheet through retained earnings. Specifically, the revenue, expense, gain, and loss transactions that make up net income in the income statement ($2,417) become the major components of retained earnings. Later in the chapter we discuss the closing process we use to transfer, or close, these *temporary* income statement accounts to the *permanent* retained earnings account.

During the month, retained earnings, which increased by the amount of net income, also decreased by the amount of the cash dividend paid to shareholders, $1,000. The net effect of these two changes is an increase in retained earnings from zero at the beginning of the period to $1,417 ($2,417 − 1,000) at the end of the period and is also reported in the statement of shareholders' equity in Illustration 2–12 on page 73.

## THE STATEMENT OF CASH FLOWS

**The purpose of the *statement of cash flows* is to summarize the transactions that caused cash to change during the period.**

Similar to the income statement, the **statement of cash flows** also is a change statement, disclosing the events that caused cash to change during the period. The statement classifies all transactions affecting cash into one of three categories: (1) **operating activities,** (2) **investing activities,** and (3) **financing activities.** Operating activities are inflows and outflows of cash related to transactions entering into the determination of net income. Investing activities involve the acquisition and sale of (1) long-term assets used in the business and (2) non-operating investment assets. Financing activities involve cash inflows and outflows from transactions with creditors and owners.

The statement of cash flows for Dress Right for the month of July 2006 is shown in Illustration 2–11. As this is the first period of operations for Dress Right, the cash balance at the beginning of the period is zero. The net increase in cash of $68,500, therefore, equals the ending balance of cash disclosed in the balance sheet.

**ILLUSTRATION 2–11**
Statement of Cash Flows

**DRESS RIGHT CLOTHING CORPORATION**
**Statement of Cash Flows**
**For the Month of July 2006**

| | | |
|---|---|---|
| **Cash Flows from Operating Activities** | | |
| Cash inflows: | | |
| From customers | $36,500 | |
| From rent | 1,000 | |
| Cash outflows: | | |
| For rent | (24,000) | |
| For supplies | (2,000) | |
| To suppliers of merchandise | (25,000) | |
| To employees | (5,000) | |
| Net cash flows from operating activities | | $(18,500) |
| **Cash Flows from Investing Activities** | | |
| Purchase of furniture and fixtures | | (12,000) |
| **Cash Flows from Financing Activities** | | |
| Issue of common stock | $60,000 | |
| Increase in notes payable | 40,000 | |
| Payment of cash dividend | (1,000) | |
| Net cash flows from financing activities | | 99,000 |
| **Net increase in cash** | | $68,500 |

There are two generally accepted formats that can be used to report operating activities, the direct method and the indirect method. In Illustration 2–11 we use the direct method. These two methods are discussed and illustrated in subsequent chapters.

## THE STATEMENT OF SHAREHOLDERS' EQUITY

**The *statement of shareholders' equity* discloses the sources of changes in the permanent shareholders' equity accounts.**

The final statement, the **statement of shareholders' equity,** also is a change statement. It discloses the sources of the changes in the various permanent shareholders' equity accounts that occurred during the period. Illustration 2–12 shows the statement of shareholders' equity for Dress Right for the month of July 2006.[6]

**ILLUSTRATION 2–12**
Statement of Shareholders' Equity

**DRESS RIGHT CLOTHING CORPORATION**
**Statement of Shareholders' Equity**
**For the Month of July 2006**

| | Common Stock | Retained Earnings | Total Shareholders' Equity |
|---|---|---|---|
| Balance at July 1, 2006 | -0- | -0- | -0- |
| Issue of common stock | $60,000 | | $60,000 |
| Net income for July 2006 | | $2,417 | 2,417 |
| Less: Dividends | | (1,000) | (1,000) |
| Balance at July 31, 2006 | $60,000 | $1,417 | $61,417 |

[6]Some companies choose to disclose the changes in the retained earnings component of shareholders' equity in a separate statement or in a combined statement of income and retained earnings.

The individual profit-generating transactions causing retained earnings to change are summarized in the income statement. Therefore, the statement of shareholders' equity only shows the net effect of these transactions on retained earnings, in this case an increase of $2,417. In addition, the company paid its shareholders a cash dividend that reduced retained earnings.

## The Closing Process

**STEP 9: *Close* the temporary accounts to retained earnings (at year-end only).**

LO7

At the end of any interim reporting period, the accounting processing cycle is now complete. An interim reporting period is any period when financial statements are produced other than at the end of the fiscal year. However, at the end of the fiscal year, two final steps are necessary, closing the temporary accounts—step 9—and preparing a post-closing trial balance—step 10.

The **closing process** serves a *dual purpose:* (1) the temporary accounts (revenues, expenses, gains and losses) are reduced to *zero balances,* ready to measure activity in the upcoming accounting period, and (2) these temporary account balances are *closed (transferred) to retained earnings* to reflect the changes that have occurred in that account during the period. Often, an intermediate step is to close revenues and expenses to **income summary**; then income summary is closed to retained earnings. The use of the income summary account is just a bookkeeping convenience that provides a check that all temporary accounts have been properly closed (that is, the balance equals net income or loss).

To illustrate the closing process, assume that the fiscal year-end for Dress Right Clothing Corporation is July 31. Using the adjusted trial balance in Illustration 2–8, we can prepare the following general journal entries.

**To close the revenue accounts to income summary.**

| | | |
|---|---|---|
| **July 31** | | |
| Sales revenue | 38,500 | |
| Rent revenue | 250 | |
| Income summary | | 38,750 |

The first closing entry transfers the revenue account balances to income summary. Because revenue accounts have credit balances, they are debited to bring them to zero. After this entry is posted to the accounts, both revenue accounts have a zero balance.

**To close the expense accounts to income summary.**

| | | |
|---|---|---|
| **July 31** | | |
| Income summary | 36,333 | |
| Cost of goods sold | | 22,000 |
| Salaries expense | | 10,500 |
| Supplies expense | | 800 |
| Rent expense | | 2,000 |
| Depreciation expense | | 200 |
| Interest expense | | 333 |
| Bad debt expense | | 500 |

The second closing entry transfers the expense account balances to income summary. As expense accounts have debit balances, they are credited to bring them to zero. After this entry is posted to the accounts, the expense accounts have a zero balance and the income summary account has a credit balance equal to net income for the period, in this case $2,417.

**Income Summary**

| | | | |
|---|---|---|---|
| Expenses | 36,333 | 38,750 | Revenues |
| | | 2,417 | Net |

**To close the income summary account to retained earnings.**

| | | |
|---|---|---|
| **July 31** | | |
| Income summary | 2,417 | |
| Retained earnings | | 2,417 |

After this entry is posted to the accounts, the temporary accounts have zero balances and retained earnings has increased by the amount of the net income. It is important to remember that the temporary accounts are closed only at year-end and not at the end of any interim period. Closing the temporary accounts during the year would make it difficult to prepare the annual income statement.

After the closing entries are posted to the ledger accounts, a **post-closing trial balance** is prepared. The purpose of this trial balance is to verify that the closing entries were prepared and posted correctly and that the accounts are now ready for next year's transactions. Illustration 2–13 shows the post-closing trial balance for Dress Right at July 31, 2006, assuming a July 31 fiscal year-end.

**Step 10: Prepare a *post-closing trial balance* (at year-end only).**

**ILLUSTRATION 2–13**
Post-Closing Trial Balance

**DRESS RIGHT CLOTHING CORPORATION**
**Post-Closing Trial Balance**
**July 31, 2006**

| Account Title | Debits | Credits |
|---|---|---|
| Cash | 68,500 | |
| Accounts receivable | 2,000 | |
| Allowance for uncollectible accounts | | 500 |
| Supplies | 1,200 | |
| Prepaid rent | 22,000 | |
| Inventory | 38,000 | |
| Furniture and fixtures | 12,000 | |
| Accumulated depreciation—furniture and fixtures | | 200 |
| Accounts payable | | 35,000 |
| Notes payable | | 40,000 |
| Unearned rent revenue | | 750 |
| Salaries payable | | 5,500 |
| Interest payable | | 333 |
| Common stock | | 60,000 |
| Retained earnings | | 1,417 |
| Totals | 143,700 | 143,700 |

## CONCEPT REVIEW EXERCISE

### FINANCIAL STATEMENT PREPARATION AND CLOSING

Refer to the August 31, 2006, adjusted trial balance of the Wyndham Wholesale Company presented in a previous concept review exercise on page 70.

**Required:**

1. Prepare an income statement and a statement of shareholders' equity for the month ended August 31, 2006, and a classified balance sheet as of August 31, 2006.
2. Assume that August 31 is the company's fiscal year-end. Prepare the necessary closing entries and a post-closing trial balance.

### SOLUTION

1. Prepare an income statement and a statement of shareholders' equity for the month ended August 31, 2006, and a classified balance sheet as of August 31, 2006.

**WYNDHAM WHOLESALE COMPANY**
**Income Statement**
**For the Month of August 2006**

| | | |
|---|---|---|
| Sales revenue | | $40,000 |
| Cost of goods sold | | 22,000 |
| Gross profit | | 18,000 |
| Operating expenses: | | |
| Salaries | $7,000 | |
| Utilities | 2,000 | |
| Bad debt | 2,500 | |
| Depreciation | 500 | |
| Rent | 3,000 | |
| Total operating expenses | | 15,000 |
| Operating income | | 3,000 |
| Other income (expense): | | |
| Interest revenue | 100 | |
| Interest expense | (250) | (150) |
| Net income | | $ 2,850 |

**WYNDHAM WHOLESALE COMPANY**
**Statement of Shareholders' Equity**
**For the Month of August 2006**

| | Common Stock | Retained Earnings | Total Shareholders' Equity |
|---|---|---|---|
| Balance at August 1, 2006 | -0- | -0- | -0- |
| Issue of common stock | $50,000 | | $50,000 |
| Net income for August 2006 | | $2,850 | 2,850 |
| Less: Dividends | | (1,000) | (1,000) |
| Balance at August 31, 2006 | $50,000 | $1,850 | $51,850 |

**WYNDHAM WHOLESALE COMPANY**
**Balance Sheet**
**At August 31, 2006**

**Assets**

| | | |
|---|---|---|
| Current assets: | | |
| Cash | | $ 21,000 |
| Accounts receivable | $25,000 | |
| Less: Allowance for uncollectible accounts | 2,500 | 22,500 |
| Inventory | | 16,000 |
| Interest receivable | | 100 |
| Note receivable | | 20,000 |
| Prepaid rent | | 3,000 |
| Total current assets | | 82,600 |
| Property and equipment: | | |
| Equipment | 20,000 | |
| Less: Accumulated depreciation | 500 | 19,500 |
| Total assets | | $102,100 |

**Liabilities and Shareholders' Equity**

| | | |
|---|---|---|
| Current liabilities: | | |
| Accounts payable | | $ 20,000 |
| Interest payable | | 250 |
| Note payable | | 30,000 |
| Total current liabilities | | 50,250 |
| Shareholders' equity: | | |
| Common stock, 5,000 shares issued and outstanding | $50,000 | |
| Retained earnings | 1,850 | |
| Total shareholders' equity | | 51,850 |
| Total liabilities and shareholders' equity | | $102,100 |

2. Assume that August 31 is the company's fiscal year-end. Prepare the necessary closing entries and a post-closing trial balance.

| | | |
|---|---|---|
| **August 31** | | |
| Sales revenue | 40,000 | |
| Interest revenue | 100 | |
| Income summary | | 40,100 |
| **August 31** | | |
| Income summary | 37,250 | |
| Cost of goods sold | | 22,000 |
| Salaries expense | | 7,000 |
| Utilities expense | | 2,000 |
| Bad debt expense | | 2,500 |
| Interest expense | | 250 |
| Depreciation expense | | 500 |
| Rent expense | | 3,000 |
| **August 31** | | |
| Income summary | 2,850 | |
| Retained earnings | | 2,850 |

**To close the revenue accounts to income summary.**

**To close the expense accounts to income summary.**

**To close the income summary account to retained earnings.**

**Post-Closing Trial Balance**

| Account Title | Debits | Credits |
|---|---|---|
| Cash | 21,000 | |
| Accounts receivable | 25,000 | |
| Allowance for uncollectible accounts | | 2,500 |
| Prepaid rent | 3,000 | |
| Inventory | 16,000 | |
| Interest receivable | 100 | |
| Note receivable | 20,000 | |
| Equipment | 20,000 | |
| Accumulated depreciation—equipment | | 500 |
| Accounts payable | | 20,000 |
| Interest payable | | 250 |
| Note payable | | 30,000 |
| Common stock | | 50,000 |
| Retained earnings | | 1,850 |
| Totals | 105,100 | 105,100 |

## Conversion from Cash Basis to Accrual Basis

● LO8

In Chapter 1, we discussed and illustrated the differences between cash and accrual accounting. Cash basis accounting produces a measure called *net operating cash flow.* This measure is the difference between cash receipts and cash disbursements during a reporting period from transactions related to providing goods and services to customers. On the other hand, the accrual accounting model measures an entity's accomplishments and resource sacrifices during the period, regardless of when cash is received or paid. At this point, you might wish to review the material in Chapter 1 on pages 7 and 8 to reinforce your understanding of the motivation for using the accrual accounting model.

Adjusting entries, for the most part, are conversions from cash to accrual. Prepayments and accruals occur when cash flow precedes or follows expense or revenue recognition.

Accountants sometimes are called upon to convert cash basis financial statements to accrual basis financial statements, particularly for small businesses. You now have all of the tools you need to make this conversion. For example, if a company paid $20,000 cash for insurance during the fiscal year and you determine that there was $5,000 in prepaid insurance at the beginning of the year and $3,000 at the end of the year, then you can determine (accrual basis) *insurance expense* for the year. Prepaid insurance decreased by $2,000 during the year, so insurance expense must be $22,000 ($20,000 in cash paid *plus* the decrease in prepaid insurance). You can visualize as follows:

| | **Prepaid Insurance** |
|---|---|
| Balance, beginning of year | $ 5,000 |
| Plus: Cash paid | 20,000 |
| Less: Insurance expense | ? |
| Balance, end of year | $ 3,000 |

Insurance expense of $22,000 completes the explanation of the change in the balance of prepaid insurance. Prepaid insurance of $3,000 is reported as an asset in an accrual basis balance sheet.

Using T-accounts is a convenient approach for converting from cash to accrual. For example, if the amount of cash collected from customers during the year was $220,000, and you know that accounts receivable at the beginning of the year was $45,000 and $33,000 at the end of the year, you can use T-accounts to determine that sales revenue for the year must have been $208,000.

**Accounts Receivable**

| | | | |
|---|---|---|---|
| Beg. balance | 45,000 | | |
| Credit sales | ? | | |
| | | 220,000 | Cash collections |
| End balance | 33,000 | | |

**Sales Revenue**

| | | |
|---|---|---|
| | ? | Credit sales |

Illustration 2–14 provides an example of a conversion from cash basis net income to accrual basis net income.

**ILLUSTRATION 2–14**
Cash to Accrual

The Krinard Cleaning Services Company maintains its records on the cash basis, with one exception. The company reports equipment as an asset and records depreciation expense on the equipment. During 2006, Krinard collected $165,000 from customers, paid $92,000 in operating expenses, and recorded $10,000 in depreciation expense, resulting in net income of $63,000. The owner has asked you to convert this $63,000 in net income to full accrual net income. You are able to determine the following information about accounts receivable, prepaid expenses, and accrued liabilities:

| | **January 1, 2006** | **December 31, 2006** |
|---|---|---|
| Accounts receivable | $16,000 | $25,000 |
| Prepaid expenses | 7,000 | 4,000 |
| Accrued liabilities (for operating expenses) | 2,100 | 1,400 |

Accrual net income is $69,700, determined as follows:

| | |
|---|---|
| Cash basis net income | $63,000 |
| Add: Increase in accounts receivable | 9,000 |
| Deduct: Decrease in prepaid expenses | (3,000) |
| Add: Decrease in accrued liabilities | 700 |
| Accrual basis net income | $69,700 |

When converting from cash to accrual income, we add increases and deduct decreases in assets. For example, an increase in accounts receivable means that the company earned more revenue than cash collected, requiring the addition to cash basis income. Conversely, we add decreases and deduct increases in accrued liabilities. For example, a decrease in interest payable means that the company incurred less interest expense than the cash interest it paid, requiring the addition to cash basis income.

## FINANCIAL REPORTING CASE SOLUTION

1. **What purpose do adjusting entries serve?** *(p. 62)* Adjusting entries help ensure that only revenues actually earned in a period are recognized in that period, regardless of when cash is received. In this instance, for example, $13,000 cash has been received for services that haven't yet been performed. Also, adjusting entries enable a company to recognize all expenses incurred during a period, regardless of when cash is paid. Without depreciation, the friends' cost of using the equipment is not taken into account. Conversely, without adjustment, the cost of rent is overstated by $3,000 paid in advance for part of next year's rent.

   With adjustments, we get an accrual income statement that provides a more complete measure of a company's operating performance and a better measure for predicting future operating cash flows. Similarly, the balance sheet provides a more complete assessment of assets and liabilities as sources of future cash receipts and disbursements.
2. **What year-end adjustments are needed to revise the income statement? Did your friends do as well their first year as they thought?** *(p. 62)* Three year-end adjusting entries are needed:

| | | |
|---|---|---|
| 1. Depreciation expense ($80,000 ÷ 5 years) | 16,000 | |
| Accumulated depreciation—equipment | | 16,000 |
| 2. Prepaid rent ($500 × 6 months [July–Dec.]) | 3,000 | |
| Rent expense | | 3,000 |
| 3. Consulting revenue | 13,000 | |
| Unearned consulting revenue | | 13,000 |

No, your friends did not fare as well as their cash based statement would have indicated. With appropriate adjustments, their net income is actually only $20,000:

| | | |
|---|---|---|
| Consulting revenue ($96,000 − 13,000) | | $83,000 |
| Operating expenses: | | |
| Salaries | $32,000 | |
| Rent ($9,000 − 3,000) | 6,000 | |
| Supplies | 4,800 | |
| Utilities | 3,000 | |
| Advertising | 1,200 | |
| Depreciation | 16,000 | 63,000 |
| Net income | | $20,000 |

## THE BOTTOM LINE

1. The accounting equation underlies the process used to capture the effect of economic events. The equation (Assets = Liabilities + Owners' Equity) implies an equality between the total economic resources of an entity (its assets) and the total claims to those resources (liabilities and equity). It also implies that each economic event affecting this equation will have a dual effect because resources always must equal claims to those resources.
2. After determining the dual effect of external events on the accounting equation, the transaction is recorded in a journal. A journal is a chronological list of transactions in debit/credit form.
3. The next step in the processing cycle is to periodically transfer, or *post,* the debit and credit information from the journal to individual general ledger accounts. A general ledger is simply a collection of all of the company's various accounts. Each account

provides a summary of the effects of all events and transactions on that individual account. This process is called *posting.* An unadjusted trial balance is then prepared.

**4.** The next step in the processing cycle is to record in the general journal and post to the ledger accounts the effect of *internal events* on the accounting equation. These transactions do not involve an exchange transaction with another entity. They are recorded at the end of any period when financial statements must be prepared for external use. These transactions are commonly referred to as *adjusting entries.* After these entries are posted to the general ledger accounts, an adjusted trial balance is prepared.

**5.** Adjusting entries can be classified into three types: (1) prepayments, (2) accruals, and (3) estimates. Prepayments are transactions in which the cash flow *precedes* expense or revenue recognition. Accruals involve transactions where the cash outflow or inflow takes place in a period *subsequent* to expense or revenue recognition. Estimates for items such as future bad debts on receivables often are required to comply with the accrual accounting model.

**6.** The adjusted trial balance is used to prepare the financial statements. The four basic financial statements are: (1) the income statement, (2) the balance sheet, (3) the statement of cash flows, and (4) the statement of shareholders' equity. The purpose of the income statement is to summarize the profit-generating activities of the company that occurred during a particular period of time. The balance sheet presents the financial position of the company on a particular date. The statement of cash flows discloses the events that caused cash to change during the reporting period. The statement of shareholders' equity discloses the sources of the changes in the various permanent shareholders' equity accounts that occurred during the period.

**7.** At the end of the fiscal year, a final step in the accounting processing cycle, closing, is required. The closing process serves a *dual purpose:* (1) the temporary accounts (revenues and expenses) are reduced to *zero balances,* ready to measure activity in the upcoming accounting period, and (2) these temporary account balances are *closed (transferred) to retained earnings* to reflect the changes that have occurred in that account during the period. Often, an intermediate step is to close revenues and expenses to *income summary;* then *income summary* is closed to *retained earnings.*

**8.** Cash basis accounting produces a measure called *net operating cash flow.* This measure is the difference between cash receipts and cash disbursements during a reporting period from transactions related to providing goods and services to customers. On the other hand, the accrual accounting model measures an entity's accomplishments and resource sacrifices during the period, regardless of when cash is received or paid. Accountants sometimes are called upon to convert cash basis financial statements to accrual basis financial statements, particularly for small businesses. ■

## APPENDIX 2A Use of a Worksheet

A *worksheet* can be used as a tool to facilitate the preparation of adjusting and closing entries and the financial statements.

A **worksheet** often is used to organize the accounting information needed to prepare adjusting and closing entries and the financial statements. It is an informal tool only and is not part of the accounting system. There are many different ways to design and use worksheets. We will illustrate a representative method using the financial information for the Dress Right Clothing Corporation presented in the chapter. Computerized programs such as Lotus 1-2-3 and Excel facilitate the use of worksheets.

Illustration 2A–1 presents the completed worksheet. The worksheet is utilized after and instead of step 5 in the processing cycle, preparation of an unadjusted trial balance.

The first step is to enter account titles in column 1 and the unadjusted account balances in columns 2 and 3.

**Step 1.** The account titles as they appear in the general ledger are entered in column 1 and the balances of these accounts are copied onto columns 2 and 3, entitled Unadjusted Trial Balance. The accounts are copied in the same order as they appear in the general ledger, which usually is assets, liabilities, shareholders' equity permanent accounts, revenues, and expenses. The debit and credit columns are totaled to make sure that they balance. This procedure is repeated for each set of columns in the worksheet to check for accuracy.

**ILLUSTRATION 2A–1** Worksheet, Dress Right Clothing Corporation, July 2006

Microsoft Excel

Worksheet, Dress Right Clothing Corporation, July 2006

| | Account Title | Unadjusted Trial Balance Dr. | Unadjusted Trial Balance Cr. | Adjusting Entries Dr. | Adjusting Entries Cr. | Adjusted Trial Balance Dr. | Adjusted Trial Balance Cr. | Income Statement Dr. | Income Statement Cr. | Balance Sheet Dr. | Balance Sheet Cr. |
|---|---|---|---|---|---|---|---|---|---|---|---|
| 5 | Cash | 68,500 | | | | 68,500 | | | | 68,500 | |
| 6 | Accounts receivable | 2,000 | | | | 2,000 | | | | 2,000 | |
| 7 | Allowance for | | | | | | | | | | |
| 8 | uncollectible accounts | | 0 | | (7) 500 | | 500 | | | | 500 |
| 9 | Supplies | 2,000 | | | (1) 800 | 1,200 | | | | 1,200 | |
| 10 | Prepaid rent | 24,000 | | | (2) 2,000 | 22,000 | | | | 22,000 | |
| 11 | Inventory | 38,000 | | | | 38,000 | | | | 38,000 | |
| 12 | Furniture & fixtures | 12,000 | | | | 12,000 | | | | 12,000 | |
| 13 | Accumulated depreciation- | | | | | | | | | | |
| 14 | furniture & fixtures | | 0 | | (3) 200 | | 200 | | | | 200 |
| 15 | Accounts payable | | 35,000 | | | | 35,000 | | | | 35,000 |
| 16 | Note payable | | 40,000 | | | | 40,000 | | | | 40,000 |
| 17 | Unearned rent revenue | | 1,000 | (4) 250 | | | 750 | | | | 750 |
| 18 | Salaries payable | | 0 | | (5) 5,500 | | 5,500 | | | | 5,500 |
| 19 | Interest payable | | 0 | | (6) 333 | | 333 | | | | 333 |
| 20 | Common stock | | 60,000 | | | | 60,000 | | | | 60,000 |
| 21 | Retained earnings | 1,000 | | | | 1,000 | | | | 1,000 | |
| 22 | Sales revenue | | 38,500 | | | | 38,500 | | 38,500 | | |
| 23 | Rent revenue | | 0 | | (4) 250 | | 250 | | 250 | | |
| 24 | Cost of goods sold | 22,000 | | | | 22,000 | | 22,000 | | | |
| 25 | Salaries expense | 5,000 | | (5) 5,500 | | 10,500 | | 10,500 | | | |
| 26 | Supplies expense | 0 | | (1) 800 | | 800 | | 800 | | | |
| 27 | Rent expense | 0 | | (2) 2,000 | | 2,000 | | 2,000 | | | |
| 28 | Depreciation expense | 0 | | (3) 200 | | 200 | | 200 | | | |
| 29 | Interest expense | 0 | | (6) 333 | | 333 | | 333 | | | |
| 30 | Bad debt expense | 0 | | (7) 500 | | 500 | | 500 | | | |
| 31 | Totals | 174,500 | 174,500 | 9,583 | 9,583 | 181,033 | 181,033 | | | | |
| 32 | | | | | | | | | | | |
| 33 | Net Income | | | | | | | 2,417 | | | 2,417 |
| 34 | Totals | | | | | | | 38,750 | 38,750 | 144,700 | 144,700 |

Sheet1 / Sheet2 / Sheet3

Ready

The second step is to determine end-of-period adjusting entries and enter them in columns 4 and 5.

**Step 2.** The end-of-period adjusting entries are determined and entered directly on the worksheet in columns 4 and 5, entitled Adjusting Entries. The adjusting entries for Dress Right Clothing Corporation were discussed in detail in the chapter and exhibited in general journal form in Illustration 2–7 on page 68. You should refer back to this illustration and trace each of the entries to the worksheet. For worksheet purposes, the entries have been numbered from (1) to (7) for easy referencing.

For example, entry (1) records the cost of supplies used during the month of July with a debit to supplies expense and a credit to supplies for $800. A (1) is placed next to the $800 in the debit column in the supplies expense row as well as next to the $800 in the credit column in the supplies row. This allows us to more easily reconstruct the entry for general journal purposes and locate errors if the debit and credit columns do not balance.

The third step adds or deducts the effects of the adjusting entries on the account balances.

**Step 3.** The effects of the adjusting entries are added to or deducted from the account balances listed in the Unadjusted Trial Balance columns and copied across to columns 6 and 7, entitled Adjusted Trial Balance. For example, supplies had an unadjusted balance of $2,000. Adjusting entry (1) credited this account by $800, reducing the balance to $1,200.

The fourth step is to transfer the temporary retained earnings account balances to columns 8 and 9.

**Step 4.** The balances in the temporary retained earnings accounts, revenues and expenses, are transferred to columns 8 and 9, entitled Income Statement. The difference between the total debits and credits in these columns is equal to net income or net loss. In this case, because credits (revenues) exceed debits (expenses), a net income of $2,417 results. To balance the debits and credits in this set of columns, a $2,417 debit entry is made in the line labeled Net income.

The fifth step is to transfer the balances in the permanent accounts to columns 10 and 11.

**Step 5.** The balances in the permanent accounts are transferred to columns 10 and 11, entitled Balance Sheet. To keep the debits and credits equal in the worksheet, a $2,417 credit must be recorded to offset the $2,417 debit recorded in step 4 and labeled as net income. This credit represents the fact that when the temporary accounts are closed out to retained earnings, a $2,417 credit to retained earnings will result. The credit in column 11, therefore, represents an increase in retained earnings for the period, that is, net income.

After the worksheet is completed, the financial statements can be prepared directly from columns 8–11. The financial statements for Dress Right Clothing Corporation are shown in Illustrations 2–9 through 2–12. The accountant must remember to then record the adjusting entries in the general journal and post them to the general ledger accounts. An adjusted trial balance should then be prepared which should be identical to the one in the worksheet. At fiscal year-end, the income statement columns can then be used to prepare closing entries. ■

## APPENDIX 2B Reversing Entries

Accountants sometimes use **reversing entries** at the beginning of a reporting period. These optional entries remove the effects of some of the adjusting entries made at the end of the previous reporting period for the sole purpose of simplifying journal entries made during the new period. If the accountant does use reversing entries, these entries are recorded in the general journal and posted to the general ledger accounts on the first day of the new period.

Reversing entries are used most often with accruals. For example, the following adjusting entry for accrued salaries was recorded at the end of July 2006 for the Dress Right Clothing Corporation in the chapter:

To record accrued salaries at the end of July.

| | | |
|---|---|---|
| **July 31** | | |
| Salaries expense . . . . . . . . . . . . . . . . . . . . . . . . . . . . . . . . . . . . . . . . | 5,500 | |
| Salaries payable . . . . . . . . . . . . . . . . . . . . . . . . . . . . . . . . . . . . . . . . | | 5,500 |

If reversing entries are not used, when the salaries actually are paid in August, the accountant needs to remember to debit salaries payable and not salaries expense.

The account balances before and after salary payment can be seen below with the use of T-accounts.

| Salaries Expense | | | Salaries Payable | | |
|---|---|---|---|---|---|
| Bal. July 31 | 10,500 | | | 5,500 | Bal. July 31 |
| | | | (Cash Payment) 5,500 | | |
| | | | | -0- | Balance |

If the accountant for Dress Right employs reversing entries, the following entry is made on August 1, 2006:

| | | |
|---|---|---|
| **August 1** | | |
| Salaries payable | 5,500 | |
| Salaries expense | | 5,500 |

To reverse accrued salaries expense recorded at the end of July.

This entry reduces the salaries payable account to zero and reduces the salary expense account by $5,500. When salaries actually are paid in August, the debit is to salaries expense, thus increasing the account by $5,500.

| Salaries Expense | | | | Salaries Payable | | |
|---|---|---|---|---|---|---|
| Bal. July 31 | 10,500 | | | | 5,500 | Bal. July 31 |
| | | 5,500 | (Reversing entry) | 5,500 | | |
| (Cash payment) | 5,500 | | | | | |
| Balance | 10,500 | | | | -0- | Balance |

We can see that balances in the accounts after cash payment is made are identical. The use of reversing entries for accruals, which is optional, simply allows cash payments or cash receipts to be entered directly into the temporary expense or revenue accounts without regard to the accruals made at the end of the previous period. ■

APPENDIX 2C

# Subsidiary Ledgers and Special Journals

## Subsidiary Ledgers

The general ledger contains what are referred to as *control accounts.* In addition to the general ledger, a **subsidiary ledger** contains a group of subsidiary accounts associated with a particular general ledger control account. For example, there will be a subsidiary ledger for accounts receivable that keeps track of the increases and decreases in the account receivable balance for each of the company's customers purchasing goods or services on credit. After all of the postings are made from the appropriate journals, the balance in the accounts receivable control account should equal the sum of the balances in the accounts receivable subsidiary ledger accounts. Subsidiary ledgers also are used for accounts payable, plant and equipment, investments, and other accounts.

Accounting systems employ a *subsidiary ledger* which contains a group of subsidiary accounts associated with particular general ledger control accounts.

## Special Journals

An actual accounting system employs many different types of journals. The purpose of each journal is to record, in chronological order, the dual effect of a transaction in debit/credit form. The chapter used the general journal format to record each transaction. However, even for small companies with relatively few transactions, the general journal is used to record only a few types of transactions.[7]

For most external transactions, *special journals* are used to capture the dual effect of the transaction in debit/credit form.

The majority of transactions are recorded in **special journals.** These journals capture the dual effect of *repetitive* types of transactions. For example, cash receipts are recorded in a **cash receipts journal,** cash disbursements in a **cash disbursements journal,** credit sales in a **sales journal,** and the purchase of merchandise on account in a **purchases journal.**

[7]For example, end-of-period adjusting entries would be recorded in the general journal.

Special journals simplify the recording process in the following ways:

1. Journalizing the effects of a particular transaction is made more efficient through the use of specifically designed formats.
2. Individual transactions are not posted to the general ledger accounts but are accumulated in the special journals and a summary posting is made on a periodic basis.
3. The responsibility for recording journal entries for the repetitive types of transactions is placed on individuals who have specialized training in handling them.

The concepts of subsidiary ledgers and special journals are illustrated using the *sales journal* and the *cash receipts journal.*

## Sales Journal

**All credit sales are recorded in the *sales journal.***

The purpose of the **sales journal** is to record all credit sales. Cash sales are recorded in the cash receipts journal. Every entry in the sales journal has exactly the same effect on the accounts; the sales revenue account is credited and the accounts receivable control account is debited. Therefore, there is only one column needed to record the debit/credit effect of these transactions. Other columns are needed to capture information for updating the accounts receivable subsidiary ledger. Illustration 2C–1 presents the sales journal for Dress Right Clothing Corporation for the month of August 2006.

**ILLUSTRATION 2C–1**

Sales Journal, Dress Right Clothing Corporation, August 2006

**Page 1**

| Date | Accounts Receivable Subsidiary Account No. | Customer Name | Sales Invoice No. | Cr. Sales Revenue (400) Dr. Accounts Receivable (110) |
|---|---|---|---|---|
| 2006 | | | | |
| Aug. 5 | 801 | Leland High School | 10-221 | 1,500 |
| 9 | 812 | Mr. John Smith | 10-222 | 200 |
| 18 | 813 | Greystone School | 10-223 | 825 |
| 22 | 803 | Ms. Barbara Jones | 10-224 | 120 |
| 29 | 805 | Hart Middle School | 10-225 | 650 |
| | | | | 3,295 |

During the month of August, the company made five credit sales, totaling $3,295. This amount is posted as a debit to the accounts receivable control account, account number 110, and a credit to the sales revenue account, account number 400. The T-accounts for accounts receivable and sales revenue appear below. The reference SJ1 refers to page 1 of the sales journal.

**General Ledger**

| Accounts Receivable | 110 | |
|---|---|---|
| July 31 Balance | 2,000 | |
| Aug. 31 SJ1 | 3,295 | |

| Sales Revenue | | 400 |
|---|---|---|
| | 3,295 | Aug. 31 SJ1 |

In a computerized accounting system, as each transaction is recorded in the sales journal, the subsidiary ledger accounts for the customer involved will automatically be updated. For example, the first credit sale of the month is to Leland High School for $1,500. The sales invoice number for this sale is 10-221 and the customer's subsidiary account number is 801. As this transaction is entered, the subsidiary account 801 for Leland High School is debited for $1,500.

**Accounts Receivable Subsidiary Ledger**

| Leland High School | | | 801 |
|---|---|---|---|
| August 5 SJ1 | 1,500 | | |

As cash is collected from this customer, the cash receipts journal records the transaction with a credit to the accounts receivable control account and a debit to cash. At the same time, the accounts receivable subsidiary ledger account number 801 also is credited. After the postings are made from the special journals, the balance in the accounts receivable control account should equal the sum of the balances in the accounts receivable subsidiary ledger accounts.

## Cash Receipts Journal

The purpose of the **cash receipts journal** is to record all cash receipts, regardless of the source. Every transaction recorded in this journal produces a debit entry to the cash account with the credit to various other accounts. Illustration 2C–2 shows a cash receipts journal using transactions of the Dress Right Clothing Corporation for the month of August 2006.

***All cash receipts are recorded in the cash receipts journal.***

**ILLUSTRATION 2C–2**
Cash Receipts Journal, Dress Right Clothing Corporation, August 2006

**Page 1**

| Date | Explanation or Account Name | Dr. Cash (100) | Cr. Accounts Receivable (110) | Cr. Sales Revenue (400) | Cr. Other | Other Accounts |
|---|---|---|---|---|---|---|
| 2006 | | | | | | |
| Aug. 7 | Cash sale | 500 | | 500 | | |
| 11 | Borrowed cash | 10,000 | | | 10,000 | Note payable (220) |
| 17 | Leland High School | 750 | 750 | | | |
| 20 | Cash sale | 300 | | 300 | | |
| 25 | Mr. John Smith | 200 | 200 | | | |
| | | 11,750 | 950 | 800 | 10,000 | |

Because every transaction results in a debit to the cash account, No. 100, a column is provided for that account. At the end of August, an $11,750 debit is posted to the general ledger cash account with the source labeled CR1, cash receipts journal, page 1.

Because cash and credit sales are common, separate columns are provided for these accounts. At the end of August, a $950 credit is posted to the accounts receivable general ledger account, No. 110, and an $800 credit is posted to the sales revenue account, No. 400. Two additional credit columns are provided for uncommon cash receipt transactions, one for the credit amount and one for the account being credited. We can see that in August, Dress Right borrowed $10,000 requiring a credit to the note payable account, No. 220.

In addition to the postings to the general ledger control accounts, each time an entry is recorded in the accounts receivable column, a credit is posted to the accounts receivable subsidiary ledger account for the customer making the payment. For example, on August 17, Leland High School paid $750 on account. The subsidiary ledger account for Leland High School is credited for $750. ■

**Accounts Receivable Subsidiary Ledger**

| Leland High School | | | 801 |
|---|---|---|---|
| August 5 SJ1 | 1,500 | | |
| | | 750 | August 17 CR1 |

## QUESTIONS FOR REVIEW OF KEY TOPICS

**Q 2–1** Explain the difference between external events and internal events. Give an example of each type of event.

**Q 2–2** Each economic event or transaction will have a dual effect on financial position. Explain what is meant by this dual effect.

**Q 2–3** What is the purpose of a journal? What is the purpose of a general ledger?

**Q 2–4** Explain the difference between permanent accounts and temporary accounts. Why does an accounting system include both types of accounts?

**Q 2–5** Describe how debits and credits affect assets, liabilities, and permanent owners' equity accounts.

**Q 2–6** Describe how debits and credits affect temporary owners' equity accounts.

**Q 2–7** What is the first step in the accounting processing cycle? What role do source documents fulfill in this step?

**Q 2–8** Describe what is meant by transaction analysis.

**Q 2–9** Describe what is meant by posting, the fourth step in the processing cycle.

**Q 2–10** Describe the events that correspond to the following two journal entries:

| | | |
|---|---|---|
| 1. Inventory | 20,000 | |
| Accounts payable | | 20,000 |
| 2. Accounts receivable | 30,000 | |
| Sales revenue | | 30,000 |
| Cost of goods sold | 18,000 | |
| Inventory | | 18,000 |

**Q 2–11** What is an unadjusted trial balance? An adjusted trial balance?

**Q 2–12** Define adjusting entries and discuss their purpose.

**Q 2–13** Define closing entries and their purpose.

**Q 2–14** Define prepaid expenses and provide at least two examples.

**Q 2–15** Unearned revenues represent liabilities recorded when cash is received from customers in advance of providing a good or service. What adjusting journal entry is required at the end of a period to recognize the amount of unearned revenues that were earned during the period?

**Q 2–16** Define accrued liabilities. What adjusting journal entry is required to record accrued liabilities?

**Q 2–17** Describe the purpose of each of the four primary financial statements.

**Q 2–18** [Based on Appendix 2A] What is the purpose of a worksheet? In an 11-column worksheet similar to Illustration 2A–1, what would be the result of incorrectly transferring the balance in a liability account to column 9, the credit column under income statement?

**Q 2–19** [Based on Appendix 2B] Define reversing entries and discuss their purpose.

**Q 2–20** [Based on Appendix 2C] What is the purpose of special journals? In what ways do they simplify the recording process?

**Q 2–21** [Based on Appendix 2C] Explain the difference between the general ledger and a subsidiary ledger.

## BRIEF EXERCISES

**BE 2–1**
Transaction analysis
● LO1

The Marchetti Soup Company entered into the following transactions during the month of June: (1) purchased inventory on account for $165,000 (assume Marchetti uses a perpetual inventory system); (2) paid $40,000 in salaries to employees for work performed during the month; (3) sold merchandise that cost $120,000 to credit customers for $200,000; (4) collected $180,000 in cash from credit customers; and (5) paid suppliers of inventory $145,000. Analyze each transaction and show the effect of each on the accounting equation for a corporation.

**BE 2–2**
Journal entries
● LO2

Prepare journal entries for each of the transactions listed in BE 2–1.

**BE 2–3**
T-accounts
● LO3

Post the journal entries prepared in BE 2–2 to T-accounts. Assume that the opening balances in each of the accounts is zero except for cash, accounts receivable, and accounts payable that had opening balances of $65,000, $43,000, and $22,000 respectively.

**BE 2–4**
Journal entries
● LO2

Prepare journal entries for each of the following transactions for a company that has a fiscal year-end of December 31: (1) on October 1, $12,000 was paid for a one-year fire insurance policy; (2) on June 30 the company lent its chief financial officer $10,000; principal and interest at 6% are due in one year; and (3) equipment costing $60,000 was purchased at the beginning of the year for cash.

**BE 2–5**
Adjusting entries
● LO4 LO5

Prepare the necessary adjusting entries at December 31 for each of the items listed in BE 2–4. Depreciation on the equipment is $12,000 per year.

**BE 2–6**
Adjusting entries; income determination
● LO5

If the adjusting journal entries prepared in BE 2–5 were not made, would net income be higher or lower and by how much?

**BE 2–7**
Adjusting entries
● LO4 LO5

Prepare the necessary adjusting entries at its year-end of December 31, 2006, for the Jamesway Corporation for each of the following situations. No adjusting entries were made during the year.

1. On December 20, 2006, Jamesway received a $4,000 payment from a customer for services to be rendered early in 2007. Service revenue was credited.
2. On December 1, 2006, the company paid a local radio station $2,000 for 40 radio ads that were to be aired, 20 per month, throughout December and January. Prepaid advertising was debited.
3. Employee salaries for the month of December totaling $16,000 will be paid on January 7, 2007.
4. On August 31, 2006, Jamesway borrowed $60,000 from a local bank. A note was signed with principal and 8% interest to be paid on August 31, 2007.

**BE 2–8**
Income determination
● LO5

If none of the adjusting journal entries prepared in BE 2–7 were made, would assets, liabilities, and shareholders' equity on the 12/31/06 balance sheet be higher or lower and by how much?

**BE 2–9**
Financial statements
● LO6

The following account balances were taken from the 2006 adjusted trial balance of the Bowler Corporation: sales revenue, $325,000; cost of goods sold, $168,000; salaries expense; $45,000; rent expense, $20,000; depreciation expense, $30,000; and miscellaneous expense, $12,000. Prepare an income statement for 2006.

**BE 2–10**
Financial statements
● LO6

The following account balances were taken from the 2006 post-closing trial balance of the Bowler Corporation: cash, $5,000; accounts receivable, $10,000; inventory, $16,000; machinery and equipment, $100,000; accumulated depreciation—machinery and equipment, $40,000; accounts payable, $20,000; salaries payable, $12,000; retained earnings, $9,000; and common stock, $50,000. Prepare a 12/31/06 balance sheet.

**BE 2–11**
Closing entries
● LO7

The year-end adjusted trial balance of the Timmons Tool and Die Corporation included the following account balances: retained earnings, $220,000; sales revenue, $850,000; cost of goods sold, $580,000; salaries expense, $180,000; rent expense, $40,000; and interest expense, $15,000. Prepare the necessary closing entries.

**BE 2–12**
Cash versus accrual accounting
● LO8

Newman Consulting Company maintains its records on a cash basis. During 2006 the following cash flows were recorded: cash received from customers, $420,000; and cash paid for salaries, utilities, and advertising, $240,000, $35,000, and $12,000, respectively. You also determine that customers owed the company $52,000 and $60,000 at the beginning and end of the year, respectively, and that the company owed the utility company $6,000 and $4,000 at the beginning and end of the year, respectively. Determine accrual net income for the year.

## EXERCISES



**An alternate exercise and problem set is available on the text website: www.mhhe.com/spiceland4e**

**E 2–1**
Transaction analysis
● LO1

The following transactions occurred during March 2006 for the Wainwright Corporation. The company owns and operates a wholesale warehouse.

1. Issued 30,000 shares of common stock in exchange for $300,000 in cash.
2. Purchased equipment at a cost of $40,000. $10,000 cash was paid and a note payable was signed for the balance owed.
3. Purchased inventory on account at a cost of $90,000. The company uses the perpetual inventory system.
4. Credit sales for the month totaled $120,000. The cost of the goods sold was $70,000.
5. Paid $5,000 in rent on the warehouse building for the month of March.
6. Paid $6,000 to an insurance company for fire and liability insurance for a one-year period beginning April 1, 2006.
7. Paid $70,000 on account for the merchandise purchased in 3.
8. Collected $55,000 from customers on account.
9. Recorded depreciation expense of $1,000 for the month on the equipment.

**Required:**
Analyze each transaction and show the effect of each on the accounting equation for a corporation.
*Example:*

| | Assets | = Liabilities | + Paid-In Capital | + Retained Earnings |
|---|---|---|---|---|
| 1. | +300,000 (cash) | | + 300,000 (common stock) | |

**E 2–2**
Journal entries
● LO2

Prepare journal entries to record each of the transactions listed in Exercise 2–1.

**E 2–3**
T-accounts and trial balance
● LO3

Post the journal entries prepared in Exercise 2–2 to T-accounts. Assume that the opening balances in each of the accounts is zero. Prepare a trial balance from the ending account balances.

**E 2–4**
Journal entries
● LO2

The following transactions occurred during the month of June 2006 for the Stridewell Corporation. The company owns and operates a retail shoe store.

1. Issued 100,000 shares of common stock in exchange for $500,000 cash.
2. Purchased furniture and fixtures at a cost of $100,000. $40,000 was paid in cash and a note payable was signed for the balance owed.
3. Purchased inventory on account at a cost of $200,000. The company uses the perpetual inventory system.
4. Credit sales for the month totaled $280,000. The cost of the goods sold was $140,000.
5. Paid $6,000 in rent on the store building for the month of June.
6. Paid $3,000 to an insurance company for fire and liability insurance for a one-year period beginning June 1, 2006.
7. Paid $120,000 on account for the merchandise purchased in 3.
8. Collected $55,000 from customers on account.
9. Paid shareholders a cash dividend of $5,000.
10. Recorded depreciation expense of $2,000 for the month on the furniture and fixtures.
11. Recorded the amount of prepaid insurance that expired for the month.

**Required:**
Prepare journal entries to record each of the transactions listed above.

**E 2–5**
The accounting processing cycle
● LO2 through LO7

Listed below are several terms and phrases associated with the accounting processing cycle. Pair each item from List A (by letter) with the item from List B that is most appropriately associated with it.

| List A | List B |
|---|---|
| ____ 1. Source documents | a. Records the dual effect of a transaction in debit/credit form. |
| ____ 2. Transaction analysis | b. Internal events recorded at the end of a reporting period. |
| ____ 3. Journal | c. Primary means of disseminating information to external decision makers. |
| ____ 4. Posting | d. To zero out the owners' equity temporary accounts. |
| ____ 5. Unadjusted trial balance | e. Determine the dual effect on the accounting equation. |
| ____ 6. Adjusting entries | f. List of accounts and their balances before recording adjusting entries. |
| ____ 7. Adjusted trial balance | g. List of accounts and their balances after recording closing entries. |
| ____ 8. Financial statements | h. List of accounts and their balances after recording adjusting entries. |
| ____ 9. Closing entries | i. A means of organizing information: not part of the formal accounting system. |
| ____ 10. Post-closing trial balance | j. Transferring balances from the journal to the ledger. |
| ____ 11. Worksheet | k. Used to identify and process external transactions. |

**E 2–6**
Debits and credits
● LO2

Indicate whether a debit will increase (I) or decrease (D) each of the following accounts:

| Increase (I) or Decrease (D) | Account |
|---|---|
| 1. ____ | Inventory |
| 2. ____ | Depreciation expense |
| 3. ____ | Accounts payable |
| 4. ____ | Prepaid rent |
| 5. ____ | Sales revenue |
| 6. ____ | Common stock |
| 7. ____ | Wages payable |
| 8. ____ | Cost of goods sold |
| 9. ____ | Utility expense |
| 10. ____ | Equipment |

| | |
|---|---|
| 11. ____ | Accounts receivable |
| 12. ____ | Allowance for uncollectible accounts |
| 13. ____ | Bad debt expense |
| 14. ____ | Interest expense |
| 15. ____ | Interest revenue |
| 16. ____ | Gain on sale of equipment |

**E 2–7**
Transaction analysis; debits and credits

● LO2

Some of the ledger accounts for the Sanderson Hardware Company are numbered and listed below. For each of the October 2006 transactions numbered 1 through 12 below, indicate by account number which accounts should be debited and credited. The company uses the perpetual inventory system. Assume that appropriate adjusting entries were made at the end of September.

| | | |
|---|---|---|
| (1) Accounts payable | (2) Equipment | (3) Inventory |
| (4) Accounts receivable | (5) Cash | (6) Supplies |
| (7) Supplies expense | (8) Prepaid rent | (9) Sales revenue |
| (10) Retained earnings | (11) Note payable | (12) Common stock |
| (13) Unearned revenue | (14) Rent expense | (15) Wages payable |
| (16) Cost of goods sold | (17) Wage expense | (18) Interest expense |

| | Account(s) Debited | Account(s) Credited |
|---|---|---|
| *Example:* Purchased inventory for cash | 3 | 5 |

1. Paid a cash dividend.
2. Paid rent for the next three months.
3. Sold goods to customers on account.
4. Purchased inventory on account.
5. Purchased supplies for cash.
6. Paid employees wages for September.
7. Issued common stock in exchange for cash.
8. Collected cash from customers for goods sold in 3.
9. Borrowed cash from a bank and signed a note.
10. At the end of October, recorded the amount of supplies that had been used during the month.
11. Received cash for advance payment from customer.
12. Accrued employee wages for October.

**E 2–8**
Adjusting entries

● LO4 LO5

Prepare the necessary adjusting entries at December 31, 2006, for the Falwell Company for each of the following situations. Assume that no financial statements were prepared during the year and no adjusting entries were recorded.

1. A three-year fire insurance policy was purchased on July 1, 2006, for $12,000. The company debited insurance expense for the entire amount.
2. Depreciation on equipment totaled $15,000 for the year.
3. The company determined that accounts receivable in the amount of $6,500 will probably not be collected. The allowance for uncollectible accounts account has a credit balance of $2,000 before any adjustment.
4. Employee salaries of $18,000 for the month of December will be paid in early January 2007.
5. On November 1, 2006, the company borrowed $200,000 from a bank. The note requires principal and interest at 12% to be paid on April 30, 2007.
6. On December 1, 2006, the company received $3,000 in cash from another company that is renting office space in Falwell's building. The payment, representing rent for December and January, was credited to unearned rent revenue.

**E 2–9**
Adjusting entries

● LO4 LO5

Prepare the necessary adjusting entries at December 31, 2006, for the Microchip Company for each of the following situations. Assume that no financial statements were prepared during the year and no adjusting entries were recorded.

1. On October 1, 2006, Microchip lent $90,000 to another company. A note was signed with principal and 8% interest to be paid on September 30, 2007.
2. On November 1, 2006, the company paid its landlord $6,000 representing rent for the months of November through January. Prepaid rent was debited.
3. On August 1, 2006, collected $12,000 in advance rent from another company that is renting a portion of Microchip's factory. The $12,000 represents one year's rent and the entire amount was credited to rent revenue.
4. Depreciation on machinery is $4,500 for the year.
5. Vacation pay for the year that had been earned by employees but not paid to them or recorded is $8,000.
6. Microchip began the year with $2,000 in its asset account, supplies. During the year, $6,500 in supplies were purchased and debited to supplies. At year-end, supplies costing $3,250 remain on hand.

**E 2–10**
Financial statements and closing entries

● LO6 LO7

The December 31, 2006, adjusted trial balance for the Blueboy Cheese Corporation is presented below.

| Account Title | Debits | Credits |
|---|---|---|
| Cash | 21,000 | |
| Accounts receivable | 300,000 | |
| Allowance for uncollectible accounts | | 20,000 |
| Prepaid rent | 10,000 | |
| Inventory | 50,000 | |
| Equipment | 600,000 | |
| Accumulated depreciation—equipment | | 250,000 |
| Accounts payable | | 40,000 |
| Note payable (due in six months) | | 60,000 |
| Salaries payable | | 8,000 |
| Interest payable | | 2,000 |
| Common stock | | 400,000 |
| Retained earnings | | 100,000 |
| Sales revenue | | 800,000 |
| Cost of goods sold | 480,000 | |
| Salaries expense | 120,000 | |
| Rent expense | 30,000 | |
| Depreciation expense | 60,000 | |
| Interest expense | 4,000 | |
| Bad debt expense | 5,000 | |
| Totals | 1,680,000 | 1,680,000 |

**Required:**

1. Prepare an income statement for the year ended December 31, 2006, and a classified balance sheet as of December 31, 2006.
2. Prepare the necessary closing entries at December 31, 2006.

**E 2–11**
Closing entries

● LO7

American Chip Corporation's fiscal year-end is December 31. The following is a partial adjusted trial balance as of December 31, 2006.

| Account Title | Debits | Credits |
|---|---|---|
| Retained earnings | | 80,000 |
| Sales revenue | | 750,000 |
| Interest revenue | | 3,000 |
| Cost of goods sold | 420,000 | |
| Salaries expense | 100,000 | |
| Rent expense | 15,000 | |
| Depreciation expense | 30,000 | |
| Interest expense | 5,000 | |
| Insurance expense | 6,000 | |

**Required:**

Prepare the necessary closing entries at December 31, 2006.

**E 2–12**
Cash versus accrual accounting; adjusting entries

● LO4 LO8

The Righter Shoe Store Company prepares monthly financial statements for its bank. The November 30 and December 31, 2006, trial balances contained the following account information:

| | Nov. 30 | | Dec. 31 | |
|---|---|---|---|---|
| | Dr. | Cr. | Dr. | Cr. |
| Supplies | 1,500 | | 3,000 | |
| Prepaid insurance | 6,000 | | 4,500 | |
| Wages payable | | 10,000 | | 15,000 |
| Unearned rent revenue | | 2,000 | | 1,000 |

The following information also is known:

a. The December income statement reported $2,000 in supplies expense.
b. No insurance payments were made in December.
c. $10,000 was paid to employees during December for wages.
d. On November 1, 2006, a tenant paid Righter $3,000 in advance rent for the period November through January. Unearned rent revenue was credited.

**Required:**

1. What was the cost of supplies purchased during December?
2. What was the adjusting entry recorded at the end of December for prepaid insurance?

3. What was the adjusting entry recorded at the end of December for accrued wages?
4. What was the amount of rent revenue earned in December? What adjusting entry was recorded at the end of December for unearned rent?

**E 2–13**
External transactions and adjusting entries

● LO2 LO4 LO5

The following transactions occurred during 2006 for the Beehive Honey Corporation:

| | |
|---|---|
| Feb. 1 | Borrowed $12,000 from a bank and signed a note. Principal and interest at 10% will be paid on January 31, 2007. |
| Apr. 1 | Paid $3,600 to an insurance company for a two-year fire insurance policy. |
| July 17 | Purchased supplies costing $2,800 on account. The company records supplies purchased in an asset account. At the December 31, 2006, year-end, supplies costing $1,250 remained on hand. |
| Nov. 1 | A customer borrowed $6,000 and signed a note requiring the customer to pay principal and 8% interest on April 30, 2007. |

**Required:**
1. Record each transaction in general journal form. Omit explanations.
2. Prepare any necessary adjusting entries at the December 31, 2006, year-end. No adjusting entries were made during the year for any item.

**E 2–14**
Accrual accounting income determination

● LO4 LO8

During the course of your examination of the financial statements of the Hales Corporation for the year ended December 31, 2006, you discover the following:

a. An insurance policy covering three years was purchased on January 1, 2006, for $6,000. The entire amount was debited to insurance expense and no adjusting entry was made for this item.
b. During 2006, the company received a $1,000 cash advance from a customer for merchandise to be manufactured and shipped in 2007. The $1,000 was credited to sales revenue. No entry was made for the cost of merchandise.
c. There were no supplies listed in the balance sheet under assets. However, you discover that supplies costing $750 were on hand at December 31.
d. Hales borrowed $20,000 from a local bank on October 1, 2006. Principal and interest at 12% will be paid on September 30, 2007. No accrual was made for interest.
e. Net income reported in the 2006 income statement is $30,000 before reflecting any of the above items.

**Required:**
Determine the proper amount of net income for 2006.

**E 2–15**
Cash versus accrual accounting

● LO8

Stanley and Jones Lawn Service Company (S&J) maintains its books on a cash basis. However, the company recently borrowed $100,000 from a local bank and the bank requires S&J to provide annual financial statements prepared on an accrual basis. During 2006, the following cash flows were recorded:

| | | |
|---|---|---|
| Cash collected from customers | | $320,000 |
| Cash paid for: | | |
| Salaries | $180,000 | |
| Supplies | 25,000 | |
| Rent | 12,000 | |
| Insurance | 6,000 | |
| Miscellaneous | 20,000 | 243,000 |
| Net operating cash flow | | $ 77,000 |

You are able to determine the following information about accounts receivable, prepaid expenses, and accrued liabilities:

| | January 1, 2006 | December 31, 2006 |
|---|---|---|
| Accounts receivable | $32,000 | $27,000 |
| Prepaid insurance | -0- | 2,000 |
| Supplies | 1,000 | 1,500 |
| Accrued liabilities (for miscellaneous expenses) | 2,400 | 3,400 |

In addition, you learn that the bank loan was dated September 30, 2006, with principal and interest at 6% due in one year. Depreciation on the company's equipment is $10,000 for the year.

**Required:**
Prepare an accrual-based income statement for 2006. (Ignore income taxes)

**E 2–16**
Worksheet [Based on Appendix 2A]

● LO5

The December 31, 2006, unadjusted trial balance for the Wolkstein Drug Company is presented below. December 31 is the company's fiscal year-end.

| Account Title | Debits | Credits |
|---|---|---|
| Cash | 20,000 | |
| Accounts receivable | 35,000 | |
| Allowance for uncollectible accounts | | 2,000 |
| Prepaid rent | 5,000 | |
| Inventory | 50,000 | |
| Equipment | 100,000 | |
| Accumulated depreciation—equipment | | 30,000 |
| Accounts payable | | 23,000 |
| Wages payable | | -0- |
| Common stock | | 100,000 |
| Retained earnings | | 29,000 |
| Sales revenue | | 323,000 |
| Cost of goods sold | 180,000 | |
| Wage expense | 71,000 | |
| Rent expense | 30,000 | |
| Depreciation expense | -0- | |
| Utility expense | 12,000 | |
| Bad debt expense | 4,000 | |
| Totals | 507,000 | 507,000 |

The following year-end adjusting entries are required:

a. Depreciation expense for the year on the equipment is $10,000.
b. The company has determined that the allowance for uncollectible accounts should be $5,000.
c. Accrued wages payable at year-end should be $4,000.

**Required:**

1. Prepare and complete a worksheet similar to Illustration 2A–1.
2. Prepare an income statement for 2006 and a balance sheet as of December 31, 2006.

**E 2–17**
Reversing entries [Based on Appendix 2B]
● LO4

The employees of Xitrex, Inc., are paid each Friday. The company's fiscal year-end is June 30, which falls on a Wednesday for the current year. Wages are earned evenly throughout the five-day workweek, and $10,000 will be paid on Friday, July 2.

**Required:**

1. Prepare an adjusting entry to record the accrued wages as of June 30, a reversing entry on July 1, and an entry to record the payment of wages on July 2.
2. Prepare journal entries to record the accrued wages as of June 30 and the payment of wages on July 2 assuming a reversing entry is not made.

**E 2–18**
Reversing entries (Based on Appendix 2B)
● LO4

Refer to Exercise 2–9 and respond to the following requirements.

**Required:**

1. If Microchip's accountant employed reversing entries, which adjusting entries would she likely reverse at the beginning of the following year?
2. Prepare the adjusting entries at the end of 2006 for the adjustments you identified in requirement 1.
3. Prepare the appropriate reversing entries at the beginning of 2007.

**E 2–19**
Special journals [Based on Appendix 2C]
● LO2

The White Company's accounting system consists of a general journal (GJ), a cash receipts journal (CR), a cash disbursements journal (CD), a sales journal (SJ), and a purchases journal (PJ). For each of the following, indicate which journal should be used to record the transaction.

| Transaction | Journal |
|---|---|
| 1. Purchased merchandise on account. | ______ |
| 2. Collected an account receivable. | ______ |
| 3. Borrowed $20,000 and signed a note. | ______ |
| 4. Recorded depreciation expense. | ______ |
| 5. Purchased equipment for cash. | ______ |
| 6. Sold merchandise for cash (the sale only, not the cost of the merchandise). | ______ |
| 7. Sold merchandise on credit (the sale only, not the cost of the merchandise). | ______ |
| 8. Recorded accrued wages payable. | ______ |
| 9. Paid employee wages. | ______ |
| 10. Sold equipment for cash. | ______ |
| 11. Sold equipment on credit. | ______ |
| 12. Paid a cash dividend to shareholders. | ______ |
| 13. Issued common stock in exchange for cash. | ______ |
| 14. Paid accounts payable. | ______ |

## PROBLEMS



**An alternate exercise and problem set is available on the text website: www.mhhe.com/spiceland4e**

**P 2–1**
Accounting cycle through unadjusted trial balance

● LO2 LO3

Halogen Laminated Products Company began business on January 1, 2006. During January, the following transactions occurred:

| | | |
|---|---|---|
| Jan. | 1 | Issued common stock in exchange for $100,000 cash. |
| | 2 | Purchased inventory on account for $35,000 (the perpetual inventory system is used). |
| | 4 | Paid an insurance company $2,400 for a one-year insurance policy. |
| | 10 | Sold merchandise on account for $12,000. The cost of the merchandise was $7,000. |
| | 15 | Borrowed $30,000 from a local bank and signed a note. Principal and interest at 10% is to be repaid in six months. |
| | 20 | Paid employees $6,000 wages for the first half of the month. |
| | 22 | Sold merchandise for $10,000 cash. The cost of the merchandise was $6,000. |
| | 24 | Paid $15,000 to suppliers for the merchandise purchased on January 2. |
| | 26 | Collected $6,000 on account from customers. |
| | 28 | Paid $1,000 to the local utility company for January gas and electricity. |
| | 30 | Paid $4,000 rent for the building. $2,000 was for January rent, and $2,000 for February rent. |

**Required:**

1. Prepare general journal entries to record each transaction. Omit explanations.
2. Post the entries to T-accounts.
3. Prepare an unadjusted trial balance as of January 30, 2006.

**P 2–2**
Accounting cycle through unadjusted trial balance

● LO2 LO3

The following is the post-closing trial balance for the Whitlow Manufacturing Corporation as of December 31, 2005.

| Account Title | Debits | Credits |
|---|---|---|
| Cash | 5,000 | |
| Accounts receivable | 2,000 | |
| Inventory | 5,000 | |
| Equipment | 11,000 | |
| Accumulated depreciation—equipment | | 3,500 |
| Accounts payable | | 3,000 |
| Common stock | | 10,000 |
| Retained earnings | | 6,500 |
| Sales revenue | | -0- |
| Cost of goods sold | -0- | |
| Wage expense | -0- | |
| Rent expense | -0- | |
| Advertising expense | -0- | |
| Totals | 23,000 | 23,000 |

The following transactions occurred during January 2006:

| | | |
|---|---|---|
| Jan. | 1 | Sold merchandise for cash, $3,500. The cost of the merchandise was $2,000. The company uses the perpetual inventory system. |
| | 2 | Purchased equipment on account for $5,500 from the Strong Company. |
| | 4 | Received a $150 bill from the local newspaper for an advertisement that appeared in the paper on January 2. |
| | 8 | Sold merchandise on account for $5,000. The cost of the merchandise was $2,800. |
| | 10 | Purchased merchandise on account for $9,500. |
| | 13 | Purchased equipment for cash, $800. |
| | 16 | Paid the entire amount due to the Strong Company. |
| | 18 | Received $4,000 from customers on account. |
| | 20 | Paid $800 to the owner of the building for January's rent. |
| | 30 | Paid employees $3,000 for salaries for the month of January. |
| | 31 | Paid a cash dividend of $1,000 to shareholders. |

**Required:**

1. Set up T-accounts and enter the beginning balances as of January 1, 2006.
2. Prepare general journal entries to record each transaction. Omit explanations.
3. Post the entries to T-accounts.
4. Prepare an unadjusted trial balance as of January 31, 2006.

**P 2–3**
Adjusting entries

● LO4 LO5

eXcel

Pastina Company manufactures and sells various types of pasta to grocery chains as private label brands. The company's fiscal year-end is December 31. The unadjusted trial balance as of December 31, 2006, appears below.

| Account Title | Debits | Credits |
|---|---|---|
| Cash | 30,000 | |
| Accounts receivable | 40,000 | |
| Allowance for uncollectible accounts | | 3,000 |
| Supplies | 1,500 | |
| Inventory | 60,000 | |
| Note receivable | 20,000 | |
| Interest receivable | -0- | |
| Prepaid rent | 2,000 | |
| Prepaid insurance | -0- | |
| Equipment | 80,000 | |
| Accumulated depreciation—equipment | | 30,000 |
| Accounts payable | | 28,000 |
| Wages payable | | -0- |
| Note payable | | 50,000 |
| Interest payable | | -0- |
| Unearned revenue | | -0- |
| Common stock | | 60,000 |
| Retained earnings | | 24,500 |
| Sales revenue | | 148,000 |
| Interest revenue | | -0- |
| Cost of goods sold | 70,000 | |
| Wage expense | 18,900 | |
| Rent expense | 11,000 | |
| Depreciation expense | -0- | |
| Interest expense | -0- | |
| Supplies expense | 1,100 | |
| Insurance expense | 6,000 | |
| Bad debt expense | 3,000 | |
| Totals | 343,500 | 343,500 |

Information necessary to prepare the year-end adjusting entries appears below.

1. Depreciation on the equipment for the year is $10,000.
2. The company estimates that of the $40,000 in accounts receivable outstanding at year-end, $5,500 probably will not be collected.
3. Employee wages are paid twice a month, on the 22nd for wages earned from the 1st through the 15th, and on the 7th of the following month for wages earned from the 16th through the end of the month. Wages earned from December 16 through December 31, 2006, were $1,500.
4. On October 1, 2006, Pastina borrowed $50,000 from a local bank and signed a note. The note requires interest to be paid annually on September 30 at 12%. The principal is due in 10 years.
5. On March 1, 2006, the company lent a supplier $20,000 and a note was signed requiring principal and interest at 8% to be paid on February 28, 2007.
6. On April 1, 2006, the company paid an insurance company $6,000 for a two-year fire insurance policy. The entire $6,000 was debited to insurance expense.
7. $800 of supplies remained on hand at December 31, 2006.
8. A customer paid Pastina $2,000 in December for 1,500 pounds of spaghetti to be manufactured and delivered in January 2007. Pastina credited sales revenue.
9. On December 1, 2006, $2,000 rent was paid to the owner of the building. The payment represented rent for December and January 2007, at $1,000 per month.

**Required:**

Prepare the necessary December 31, 2006, adjusting journal entries.

**P 2–4**
Accounting cycle; adjusting entries through post-closing trial balance

● LO5 through LO7

eXcel

Refer to Problem 2–3 and complete the following steps:

1. Enter the unadjusted balances from the trial balance into T-accounts.
2. Post the adjusting entries prepared in Problem 2–3 to the accounts.
3. Prepare an adjusted trial balance.
4. Prepare an income statement and a statement of shareholders' equity for the year ended December 31, 2006, and a classified balance sheet as of December 31, 2006. Assume that no common stock was issued during the year and that $4,000 in cash dividends were paid to shareholders during the year.
5. Prepare closing entries and post to the accounts.
6. Prepare a post-closing trial balance.

**P 2–5**
Adjusting entries

● LO4 LO5

Howarth Company's fiscal year-end is December 31. Below are the unadjusted and adjusted trial balances for December 31, 2006.

| | Unadjusted | | Adjusted | |
|---|---|---|---|---|
| **Account Title** | **Debits** | **Credits** | **Debits** | **Credits** |
| Cash | 50,000 | | 50,000 | |
| Accounts receivable | 35,000 | | 35,000 | |
| Allowance for uncollectible accounts | | 2,000 | | 3,500 |
| Prepaid rent | 2,000 | | 1,200 | |
| Supplies | 1,500 | | 800 | |
| Inventory | 60,000 | | 60,000 | |
| Note receivable | 30,000 | | 30,000 | |
| Interest receivable | -0- | | 1,500 | |
| Equipment | 45,000 | | 45,000 | |
| Accumulated depreciation—equipment | | 15,000 | | 20,000 |
| Accounts payable | | 32,000 | | 32,000 |
| Wages payable | | -0- | | 6,200 |
| Note payable | | 50,000 | | 50,000 |
| Interest payable | | -0- | | 2,500 |
| Unearned rent revenue | | -0- | | 2,000 |
| Common stock | | 46,000 | | 46,000 |
| Retained earnings | | 20,000 | | 20,000 |
| Sales revenue | | 244,000 | | 244,000 |
| Rent revenue | | 6,000 | | 4,000 |
| Interest revenue | | -0- | | 1,500 |
| Cost of goods sold | 126,000 | | 126,000 | |
| Wage expense | 45,000 | | 51,200 | |
| Rent expense | 11,000 | | 11,800 | |
| Depreciation expense | -0- | | 5,000 | |
| Supplies expense | 1,100 | | 1,800 | |
| Interest expense | 5,400 | | 7,900 | |
| Bad debt expense | 3,000 | | 4,500 | |
| Totals | 415,000 | 415,000 | 431,700 | 431,700 |

**Required:**
Prepare the adjusting journal entries that were made at December 31, 2006.

**P 2–6**
Accounting cycle

● LO2 through LO7

*eXcel*

The general ledger of the Karlin Company, a consulting company, at January 1, 2006, contained the following account balances:

| **Account Title** | **Debits** | **Credits** |
|---|---|---|
| Cash | 30,000 | |
| Accounts receivable | 15,000 | |
| Allowance for uncollectible accounts | | 500 |
| Equipment | 20,000 | |
| Accumulated depreciation | | 6,000 |
| Salaries payable | | 9,000 |
| Common stock | | 40,000 |
| Retained earnings | | 9,500 |
| Total | 65,000 | 65,000 |

The following is a summary of the transactions for the year:

a. Sales of services, $100,000, of which $30,000 was on credit.
b. Collected on accounts receivable, $27,300.
c. Issued shares of common stock in exchange for $10,000 in cash.
d. Paid salaries, $50,000 (of which $9,000 was for salaries payable).
e. Paid miscellaneous expenses, $24,000.
f. Purchased equipment for $15,000 in cash.
g. Paid $2,500 in cash dividends to shareholders.

**Required:**

1. Set up the necessary T-accounts and enter the beginning balances from the trial balance.
2. Prepare a general journal entry for each of the summary transactions listed above.
3. Post the journal entries to the accounts.
4. Prepare an unadjusted trial balance.

5. Prepare and post adjusting journal entries. Accrued salaries at year-end amounted to $1,000. Depreciation for the year on the equipment is $2,000. The allowance for uncollectible accounts is estimated to be $1,500.
6. Prepare an adjusted trial balance.
7. Prepare an income statement for 2006 and a balance sheet as of December 31, 2006.
8. Prepare and post closing entries.
9. Prepare a post-closing trial balance.

**P 2–7**
Adjusting entries and income effects

● LO4 LO5

The information necessary for preparing the 2006 year-end adjusting entries for Vito's Pizza Parlor appears below. Vito's fiscal year-end is December 31.

a. On July 1, 2006, purchased $10,000 of **IBM Corporation** bonds at face value. The bonds pay interest twice a year on January 1 and July 1. The annual interest rate is 12%.
b. Vito's depreciable equipment has a cost of $30,000, a five-year life, and no salvage value. The equipment was purchased in 2004. The straight-line depreciation method is used.
c. On November 1, 2006, the bar area was leased to Jack Donaldson for one year. Vito's received $6,000 representing the first six months' rent and credited unearned rent revenue.
d. On April 1, 2006, the company paid $2,400 for a two-year fire and liability insurance policy and debited insurance expense.
e. On October 1, 2006, the company borrowed $20,000 from a local bank and signed a note. Principal and interest at 12% will be paid on September 30, 2007.
f. At year-end there is a $1,800 debit balance in the supplies (asset) account. Only $700 of supplies remain on hand.

**Required:**
1. Prepare the necessary adjusting journal entries at December 31, 2006.
2. Determine the amount by which net income would be misstated if Vito's failed to make these adjusting entries. (Ignore income tax expense.)

**P 2–8**
Adjusting entries

● LO4

Excalibur Corporation manufactures and sells video games for personal computers. The unadjusted trial balance as of December 31, 2006, appears below. December 31 is the company's fiscal year-end. The company uses the perpetual inventory system.

| Account Title | Debits | Credits |
|---|---|---|
| Cash | 23,300 | |
| Accounts receivable | 32,500 | |
| Allowance for uncollectible accounts | | 100 |
| Supplies | -0- | |
| Prepaid rent | -0- | |
| Inventory | 65,000 | |
| Equipment | 75,000 | |
| Accumulated depreciation—equipment | | 10,000 |
| Accounts payable | | 26,000 |
| Wages payable | | 3,000 |
| Note payable | | 30,000 |
| Common stock | | 80,000 |
| Retained earnings | | 16,050 |
| Sales revenue | | 180,000 |
| Cost of goods sold | 95,000 | |
| Interest expense | -0- | |
| Wage expense | 32,350 | |
| Rent expense | 14,000 | |
| Supplies expense | 2,000 | |
| Utility expense | 6,000 | |
| Bad debt expense | -0- | |
| Totals | 345,150 | 345,150 |

Information necessary to prepare the year-end adjusting entries appears below.

1. The equipment was purchased in 2004 and is being depreciated using the straight-line method over an eight-year useful life with no salvage value.
2. Accrued wages at year-end should be $4,500.
3. The company estimates that 2% of all year-end accounts receivable will probably not be collected.
4. The company borrowed $30,000 on September 1, 2006. The principal is due to be repaid in 10 years. Interest is payable twice a year on each August 31 and February 28 at an annual rate of 10%.
5. The company debits supplies expense when supplies are purchased. Supplies on hand at year-end cost $500.
6. Prepaid rent at year-end should be $1,000.

**Required:**
Prepare the necessary December 31, 2006, adjusting entries.

**P 2–9**
Cash versus accrual accounting

● LO8

Selected balance sheet information for the Wolf Company at November 30, and December 31, 2006, is presented below. The company uses the perpetual inventory system and all sales to customers are made on credit.

| | Nov. 30 | | Dec. 31 | |
|---|---|---|---|---|
| | Dr. | Cr. | Dr. | Cr. |
| Accounts receivable | 10,000 | | 3,000 | |
| Prepaid insurance | 5,000 | | 7,500 | |
| Inventory | 7,000 | | 6,000 | |
| Accounts payable | | 12,000 | | 15,000 |
| Wages payable | | 5,000 | | 3,000 |

The following cash flow information also is available:

a. Cash collected from credit customers—$80,000.
b. Cash paid for insurance—$5,000.
c. Cash paid to suppliers of inventory—$60,000 (the entire accounts payable amounts relate to inventory purchases).
d. Cash paid to employees for wages—$10,000.

**Required:**

1. Determine the following for the month of December:
   a. Sales revenue
   b. Cost of goods sold
   c. Insurance expense
   d. Wage expense
2. Prepare a summary journal entry to record the month's sales and cost of those sales.

**P 2–10**
Accounting cycle; unadjusted trial balance through closing

● LO4 LO5 LO7

The unadjusted trial balance as of December 31, 2006, for the Bagley Consulting Company appears below. December 31 is the company's fiscal year-end.

| Account Title | Debits | Credits |
|---|---|---|
| Cash | 8,000 | |
| Accounts receivable | 9,000 | |
| Allowance for uncollectible accounts | | 50 |
| Prepaid insurance | 3,000 | |
| Land | 200,000 | |
| Buildings | 50,000 | |
| Accumulated depreciation—buildings | | 20,000 |
| Equipment | 100,000 | |
| Accumulated depreciation—equipment | | 40,000 |
| Accounts payable | | 35,000 |
| Salaries payable | | -0- |
| Unearned rent revenue | | -0- |
| Common stock | | 200,000 |
| Retained earnings | | 56,450 |
| Sales revenue | | 90,000 |
| Interest revenue | | 3,000 |
| Rent revenue | | 7,500 |
| Salaries expense | 37,000 | |
| Bad debt expense | -0- | |
| Depreciation expense | -0- | |
| Insurance expense | -0- | |
| Utility expense | 30,000 | |
| Maintenance expense | 15,000 | |
| Totals | 452,000 | 452,000 |

**Required:**

1. Enter the account balances in T-accounts.
2. From the trial balance and information given, prepare adjusting entries and post to the accounts.
   a. The buildings have an estimated useful life of 50 years with no salvage value. The company uses the straight-line depreciation method.
   b. The equipment is depreciated at 10 percent of original cost per year.
   c. Prepaid insurance expired during the year, $1,500.

    d. It is estimated that 10% of the accounts receivable balance will be uncollectible.
    e. Accrued salaries at year-end, $1,500.
    f. Unearned rent revenue at year-end should be $1,200.
3. Prepare an adjusted trial balance.
4. Prepare closing entries.
5. Prepare a post-closing trial balance.

**P 2–11**
Accrual accounting; financial statements
● LO4 LO6

McGuire Corporation began operations in 2006. The company purchases computer equipment from manufacturers and then sells to retail stores. During 2006, the bookkeeper used a check register to record all cash receipts and cash disbursements. No other journals were used. The following is a recap of the cash receipts and disbursements made during the year.

| | |
|---|---|
| Cash receipts: | |
| Sale of common stock | $ 50,000 |
| Collections from customers | 320,000 |
| Borrowed from local bank on April 1, note signed requiring principal and interest at 12% to be paid on March 31, 2007 | 40,000 |
| Total cash receipts | $410,000 |
| Cash disbursements: | |
| Purchase of merchandise | $220,000 |
| Payment of salaries | 80,000 |
| Purchase of equipment | 30,000 |
| Payment of rent on building | 14,000 |
| Miscellaneous expenses | 10,000 |
| Total cash disbursements | $354,000 |

You are called in to prepare financial statements at December 31, 2006. The following additional information was provided to you:

1. Customers owed the company $22,000 at year-end. Of this amount, it was anticipated that $3,000 would probably not be collected. There were no actual bad debt write-offs in 2006.
2. At year-end, $30,000 was still due to suppliers of merchandise purchased on credit.
3. At year-end, merchandise inventory costing $50,000 still remained on hand.
4. Salaries owed to employees at year-end amounted to $5,000.
5. On December 1, $3,000 in rent was paid to the owner of the building used by McGuire. This represented rent for the months of December through February.
6. The equipment, which has a 10-year life and no salvage value, was purchased on January 1, 2006. Straight-line depreciation is used.

**Required:**

Prepare an income statement for 2006 and a balance sheet as of December 31, 2006.

**P 2–12**
Worksheet [Based on Appendix 2A]
● LO5
eXcel

Using the information from Problem 2–8, prepare and complete a worksheet similar to Illustration 2A–1. Use the information in the worksheet to prepare an income statement and a statement of shareholders' equity for 2006 and a balance sheet as of December 31, 2006. Cash dividends paid to shareholders during the year amounted to $6,000. Also prepare the necessary closing entries assuming that adjusting entries have been correctly posted to the accounts.

## BROADEN YOUR PERSPECTIVE

**Apply your critical-thinking ability to the knowledge you've gained. These cases will provide you an opportunity to develop your research, analysis, judgment, and communication skills. You also will work with other students, integrate what you've learned, apply it in real world situations, and consider its global and ethical ramifications. This practice will broaden your knowledge and further develop your decision-making abilities.**

**Judgment Case 2–1**
Cash versus accrual accounting; adjusting entries; Chapters 1 and 2

● LO8

You have recently been hired by David & Company, a small public accounting firm. One of the firm's partners, Alice Davis, has asked you to deal with a disgruntled client, Mr. Sean Pitt, owner of the city's largest hardware store. Mr. Pitt is applying to a local bank for a substantial loan to remodel his store. The bank requires accrual based financial statements but Mr. Pitt has always kept the company's records on a cash basis. He does not see the purpose of accrual based statements. His most recent outburst went something like this: "After all, I collect cash from customers, pay my bills in cash, and I am going to pay the bank loan with cash. And, I already show my building and equipment as assets and depreciate them. I just don't understand the problem."

**Required:**

1. Explain the difference between a cash basis and an accrual basis measure of performance.
2. Why, in most cases, does accrual basis net income provide a better measure of performance than net operating cash flow.
3. Explain the purpose of adjusting entries as they relate to the difference between cash and accrual accounting.

**Judgment Case 2–2**
Cash versus accrual accounting

● LO8

Refer to Case 2–1 above. Mr. Pitt has relented and agrees to provide you with the information necessary to convert his cash basis financial statements to accrual basis statements. He provides you with the following transaction information for the fiscal year ending December 31, 2006:

1. A comprehensive insurance policy requires a payment every year for the upcoming year. The last payment of $12,000 was made on September 1, 2006.
2. Mr. Pitt allows customers to pay using a credit card. At the end of the current year, various credit card companies owed Mr. Pitt $6,500. At the end of last year, customer credit card charges outstanding were $5,000.
3. Employees are paid once a month, on the 10th of the month following the work period. Cash disbursements to employees were $8,200 and $7,200 for January 10, 2007, and January 10, 2006, respectively.
4. Utility bills outstanding totaled $1,200 at the end of 2006 and $900 at the end of 2005.
5. A physical count of inventory is always taken at the end of the fiscal year. The merchandise on hand at the end of 2006 cost $35,000. At the end of 2005, inventory on hand cost $32,000.
6. At the end of 2005, Mr. Pitt did not have any bills outstanding to suppliers of merchandise. However, at the end of 2006, he owed suppliers $4,000.

**Required:**

1. Mr. Pitt's 2006 cash basis net income (including depreciation expense) is $26,000. Determine net income applying the accrual accounting model.
2. Explain the effect on Mr. Pitt's balance sheet of converting from cash to accrual. That is, would assets, liabilities, and owner's equity be higher or lower and by what amounts?

**Communication Case 2–3**
Adjusting entries

● LO4

"I don't understand," complained Chris, who responded to your bulletin board posting in your responsibilities as a tutor. The complaint was in response to your statements that recording adjusting entries is a critical step in the accounting processing cycle, and the two major classifications of adjusting entries are prepayments and accruals.

**Required:**

Respond to Chris.

1. When do prepayments occur? Accruals?
2. Describe the appropriate adjusting entry for prepaid expenses and for unearned revenues. What is the effect on net income, assets, liabilities, and shareholders' equity of not recording a required adjusting entry for prepayments?
3. Describe the required adjusting entry for accrued liabilities and for accrued receivables. What is the effect on net income, assets, liabilities, and shareholders' equity of not recording a required adjusting entry for accruals?

**Analysis Case 2–4**
Financial statement information

● LO6 LO8

**FedEx Corporation**

Refer to the financial statements and related disclosure notes of **FedEx Corporation** in Appendix B located at the back of this text.

**Required:**

1. Determine the amount of cash paid to or in behalf of employees for salaries and benefits during the 2004 fiscal year.
2. Assuming that spare parts and supplies are used for maintenance and repairs, determine the combined amount of cash paid for maintenance and repairs and spare parts, supplies, and fuel purchased during the 2004 fiscal year.
3. What is the amount of depreciation and amortization recorded during the 2004 fiscal year?

3

CHAPTER

# The Balance Sheet and Financial Disclosures

## OVERVIEW

Chapter 1 stressed the importance of the financial statements in helping investors and creditors predict future cash flows. The balance sheet, along with accompanying disclosures, provides relevant information useful in helping investors and creditors not only to predict future cash flows, but also to make the related assessments of liquidity and long-term solvency.

The purpose of this chapter is to provide an overview of the balance sheet and financial disclosures and to explore how this information is used by decision makers.

## LEARNING OBJECTIVES

**After studying this chapter, you should be able to:**

- LO1 Describe the purpose of the balance sheet and understand its usefulness and limitations.
- LO2 Distinguish among current and noncurrent assets and liabilities.
- LO3 Identify and describe the various balance sheet asset classifications.
- LO4 Identify and describe the two balance sheet liability classifications.
- LO5 Explain the purpose of financial statement disclosures.
- LO6 Explain the purpose of the management discussion and analysis disclosure.
- LO7 Explain the purpose of an audit and describe the content of the audit report.
- LO8 Describe the techniques used by financial analysts to transform financial information into forms more useful for analysis.
- LO9 Identify and calculate the common liquidity and financing ratios used to assess risk.

# FINANCIAL REPORTING CASE

## What's It Worth?

"I can't believe it. Why don't you accountants prepare financial statements that are relevant?" Your friend Jerry is a finance major and is constantly badgering you about what he perceives to be a lack of relevance of financial statements prepared according to generally accepted accounting principles. "For example, take a look at this balance sheet for Electronic Arts that I just downloaded off the Internet. Electronic Arts is the company in California that produces all those cool video games like NASCAR, NBA Live, and Madden NFL. Anyway, the shareholders' equity of the company according to the 2004 balance sheet is $2,678,358,000. But if you multiply the number of outstanding shares by the most recent stock price per share, the company's market value is over six times that amount. I thought financial statements were supposed to help investors and creditors value a company." You decide to look at the company's balance sheet and try to set Jerry straight.

**By the time you finish this chapter, you should be able to respond appropriately to the questions posed in this case. Compare your response to the solution provided at the end of the chapter.**

### QUESTIONS

1. Respond to Jerry's criticism that shareholders' equity does not represent the market value of the company. What information does the balance sheet provide? (page 103)
2. The usefulness of the balance sheet is enhanced by classifying assets and liabilities according to common characteristics. What are the classifications used in Electronic Arts' balance sheet and what elements do those categories include? (page 104)

**ELECTRONIC ARTS, INC**
**Consolidated Balance Sheets**
**As of March 31**
($ in 000s except share data)

| | 2004 | 2003 |
|---|---|---|
| **Assets** | | |
| Current assets: | | |
| Cash and cash equivalents | $2,149,885 | $ 949,995 |
| Short-term investments | 264,461 | 637,623 |
| Marketable equity securities | 1,225 | 1,111 |
| Receivables, net of allowances of $154,682 and $164,634, respectively | 211,916 | 82,083 |
| Inventories | 55,143 | 39,679 |
| Deferred income taxes | 84,312 | 117,180 |
| Other current assets | 143,865 | 83,466 |
| Total current assets | 2,910,807 | 1,911,137 |
| Property and equipment, net | 298,073 | 262,252 |
| Investments in affiliates | 14,332 | 20,277 |
| Goodwill | 91,977 | 86,031 |
| Other intangibles, net | 18,468 | 21,301 |
| Long-term deferred income taxes | 40,755 | 13,523 |
| Other assets | 26,199 | 45,012 |
| Total assets | $3,400,611 | $2,359,533 |
| **Liabilities and Shareholders' Equity** | | |
| Current liabilities: | | |
| Accounts payable | $ 114,087 | $ 106,329 |
| Accrued and other liabilities | 608,166 | 464,547 |
| Total current liabilities | 722,253 | 570,876 |
| Commitments and contingencies | — | — |
| Minority interest in consolidated joint venture | — | 3,918 |
| Shareholders' equity: | | |
| Preferred stock, $0.01 par value. 10,000,000 shares authorized | — | — |
| Common stock | | |
| Class A common stock, $0.01 par value. 400,000,000 shares authorized; 301,332,458 and 288,266,610 shares issued and outstanding, respectively | 3,013 | 2,883 |
| Class B common stock, $0.01 par value. 100,000,000 shares authorized; 200,130 and 225,130 shares issued and outstanding, respectively | 2 | 2 |
| Paid-in capital | 1,153,680 | 856,428 |
| Retained earnings | 1,501,184 | 923,892 |
| Accumulated other comprehensive income | 20,479 | 1,534 |
| Total shareholders' equity | 2,678,358 | 1,784,739 |
| Total liabilities and shareholders' equity | $3,400,611 | $2,359,533 |

The balance sheet, along with accompanying disclosures, provides a wealth of information to external decision makers. The information provided is useful not only in the prediction of future cash flows but also in the related assessments of liquidity and long-term solvency.

This chapter begins our discussion of the financial statements by providing an overview of the balance sheet and the financial disclosures that accompany the financial statements. The first part of the chapter describes the usefulness and limitations of the balance sheet and illustrates the content of the statement. The second part illustrates financial statement disclosures presented to external users in addition to the basic financial statements. In the third part we discuss how this information can be used by decision makers to assess business risk. That discussion introduces some common financial ratios used to assess liquidity and long-term solvency.

Chapter 4 continues this discussion of the financial statements with its coverage of the income statement and the statement of cash flows.

# THE BALANCE SHEET

PART A

The purpose of the **balance sheet** is to report a company's financial position on a particular date. Unlike the income statement, which is a change statement reporting events that occurred *during a period of time,* the balance sheet presents an organized array of assets, liabilities, and shareholders' equity *at a point in time.* It is a freeze frame or snapshot of financial position at the end of a particular day marking the end of an accounting period.

## Usefulness and Limitations

● LO1

**Carter Hawley Hale Stores (CHHS), Inc.**, was one of the largest department store retailers in the United States. In 1991, the company operated over 100 stores in the sunbelt regions of the country. The company's divisions included The Broadway and Emporium. During the 1980s, the company struggled financially and in February of 1991 declared bankruptcy. CHHS's February 2, 1991, quarterly balance sheet, filed with the SEC and made publicly available, disclosed the information in Graphic 3–1.

**GRAPHIC 3–1** Quarterly Balance Sheet—Carter Hawley Hale Stores, Inc.

**Balance Sheet (condensed)**
**At February 2, 1991**
($ in 000s)

| | |
|---|---|
| **Assets** | |
| Current assets | $1,154,064 |
| Property and equipment, net | 511,690 |
| Other assets | 89,667 |
| Total assets | $1,755,421 |
| **Liabilities** | |
| Current liabilities | $ 175,982 |
| Long-term liabilities | 1,852,066 |
| Total liabilities | 2,028,048 |
| **Shareholders' Equity** | (272,627) |
| Total liabilities and shareholders' equity | $1,755,421 |

The negative shareholders' equity includes negative retained earnings of nearly $1 billion resulting from operating losses incurred over a number of years.

By the summer of 1991, the company's stock price had dropped to $1 per share from a 1989 high of $8. In June 1991, the following (condensed) balance sheet information was reported to the bankruptcy court:

| | ($ in 000s) |
|---|---|
| Property | $1,596,312 |
| Debts | 1,112,989 |
| Excess of property over debts | $ 483,323 |

Has the financial position changed this dramatically from February to June? No. Differences in reporting requirements by the SEC and the bankruptcy court cause the apparent discrepancy. First, the property (assets) disclosed to the bankruptcy court does not include accounts receivable and debts do not include the related liabilities for which the receivables had been pledged as collateral. This accounts for the smaller asset and debt figures as compared to those disclosed in the February statement provided to the SEC.

FINANCIAL REPORTING CASE

Q1, p. 101

But the striking difference is that the *negative equity* of $272,627,000 disclosed in the SEC report becomes a *positive equity* (excess of assets over liabilities) of $483,323,000 in the information disclosed to the bankruptcy court. This positive equity, divided by the number of common shares outstanding, results in a per share value of nearly $16. Why the discrepancy? The answer relates to the valuation of property. In the balance sheet submitted to the SEC, these assets are valued based on their original cost. However, the bankruptcy court requires assets to be reported at market value.[1] The market value of CHHS's property, which

[1]The bankruptcy court requires market value information in order to assess, among other things, the ability of the company to pay its creditors if assets were liquidated.

includes some valuable land in locations like San Francisco, was significantly higher than its original cost.

**Assets minus liabilities, measured according to GAAP, is not likely to be representative of the market value of the entity.**

This example illustrates an important limitation of the balance sheet. *The balance sheet does not portray the market value of the entity* as a going concern, nor, as in the CHHS example, its liquidation value. Many assets, like land and buildings for example, are measured at their historical costs rather than their market values. Relatedly, many company resources including its trained employees, its experienced management team, and its reputation are not recorded as assets at all. Also, many items and amounts reported in the balance sheet are heavily reliant on estimates rather than determinable amounts. For example, companies estimate the amount of receivables they will be able to actually collect and the amount of warranty costs they will eventually incur for products already sold. For these and other reasons, a company's **book value,** its assets minus its liabilities as shown in the balance sheet, usually will not directly measure the company's market value.

Consider for example that near the end of 2004, the 30 companies constituting the Dow Jones Industrial Average had an average ratio of market value to book value of approximately 3.85. The ratio for **Johnson & Johnson**, one of the world's largest companies in the health care business, was approximately 6.0. Can you think of an important reason why Johnson & Johnson's market value would be six times higher than its book value? One reason is that Johnson & Johnson spends significant amounts, over $5.2 billion in 2004 alone, on research and development of new products. Many of the drugs, for example, that the company has developed have been successful, and yet the costs to discover and develop them are not represented in the balance sheet. Research and development costs are expensed in the period incurred, and not capitalized as an asset.

Despite these limitations, the balance sheet does have significant value. An important feature of the statement is that it describes many of the resources a company has available for generating future cash flows. Another way the statement's content is informative is in combination with income statement items. For example, the relation between net income and assets provides a measure of return that is useful in predicting future profitability. In fact, many of the amounts reported in either of the two statements are more informative when viewed relative to an amount from the other statement.[2]

**The balance sheet provides information useful for assessing future cash flows, liquidity, and long-term solvency.**

The balance sheet does not simply list assets and liabilities. Instead, assets and liabilities are classified (grouped) according to common characteristics. These classifications, which we explore in the next section, along with related disclosure notes, help the balance sheet to provide additional important information about liquidity and long-term solvency. **Liquidity** refers to the period of time before an asset is converted to cash or until a liability is paid. This information is useful in assessing a company's ability to pay its *current* obligations. **Long-term solvency** refers to the riskiness of a company with regard to the amount of liabilities in its capital structure. Other things being equal, the risk to an investor or creditor increases as the percentage of liabilities, relative to equity, increases.

Solvency also provides information about *financial flexibility*—the ability of a company to alter cash flows in order to take advantage of unexpected investment opportunities and needs. For example, the higher the percentage of a company's liabilities to its equity, the more difficult it typically will be to borrow additional funds either to take advantage of a promising investment opportunity or to meet obligations. In general, the lower the financial flexibility, the higher the risk is that the enterprise will fail. In a subsequent section of this chapter, we introduce some common ratios used to assess liquidity and long-term solvency.

In summary, even though the balance sheet does not *directly measure* the market value of the entity, it provides valuable information that can be used to help *judge* market value.

## Classifications

**FINANCIAL REPORTING CASE**

Q2, p. 101

The usefulness of the balance sheet is enhanced when assets and liabilities are grouped according to common characteristics. *The broad distinction made in the balance sheet is the current versus noncurrent classification of both assets and liabilities.* The remainder of Part

[2]We explore some of these relationships in Chapter 5.

A provides an overview of the balance sheet. We discuss each of the three primary elements of the balance sheet (assets, liabilities, and shareholders' equity) in the order they are reported in the statement as well as the classifications typically made within the elements. The balance sheet elements were defined in Chapter 1 as follows:

**The key classification of assets and liabilities in the balance sheet is the current versus noncurrent distinction.**

**Assets** are probable future economic benefits obtained or controlled by a particular entity as a result of past transactions or events.

**Liabilities** are probable future sacrifices of economic benefits arising from present obligations of a particular entity to transfer assets or provide services to other entities in the future as a result of past transactions or events.

**Equity** (or net assets), called **shareholders' equity** or **stockholders' equity** for a corporation, is the residual interest in the assets of an entity that remains after deducting liabilities.

**GRAPHIC 3–2** Classification of Elements within a Balance Sheet

**Assets**
Current assets
Investments and funds
Property, plant, and equipment
Intangible assets
Other assets
**Liabilities**
Current liabilities
Long-term liabilities
**Shareholders' Equity**
Paid-in capital
Retained earnings

Graphic 3–2 lists the balance sheet elements along with their subclassifications.

We intentionally avoid detailed discussion of the question of valuation in order to focus on an overview of the balance sheet. In later chapters we look closer at the nature and valuation of the specific assets and liabilities.

## ASSETS

● LO2

**Current Assets.** Current assets include cash and other assets that are reasonably expected to be converted to cash or consumed within the coming year, or within the normal operating cycle of the business if that's longer than one year. The **operating cycle** for a typical manufacturing company refers to the period of time necessary to convert cash to raw materials, raw materials to a finished product, the finished product to receivables, and then finally receivables back to cash. This concept is illustrated in Graphic 3–3.

**Current assets include cash and all other assets expected to become cash or be consumed within one year or the *operating cycle*, whichever is longer.**

In some businesses, such as shipbuilding or distilleries, the operating cycle extends far beyond one year. For example, if it takes two years to build an oil-carrying supertanker, then the shipbuilder will classify as current those assets that will be converted to cash or consumed within two years. But for most businesses the operating cycle will be shorter than one year. In these situations the one-year convention is used to classify both assets and liabilities. Where a company has no clearly defined operating cycle, the one-year convention is used.

Graphic 3–4 presents the current asset sections of **FedEx Corporation**'s 2004 and 2003 balance sheets that also appear in Appendix B, located at the back of this text. In keeping with common practice, the individual current assets are listed in the order of their liquidity (nearness to cash).

**GRAPHIC 3–3** Operating Cycle of a Typical Manufacturing Company

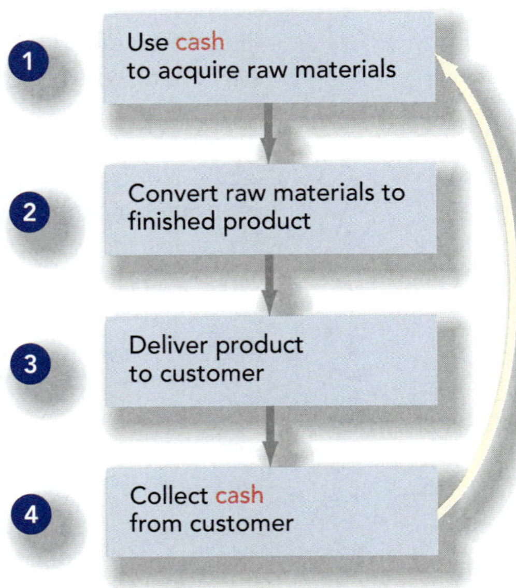


Cash and cash equivalents. The most liquid asset, cash, is listed first. Cash includes cash on hand and in banks that is available for use in the operations of the business and such items as bank drafts, cashier's checks, and money orders. **Cash equivalents** frequently include certain negotiable items such as commercial paper, money market funds, and U.S. treasury bills. These are highly liquid investments that can be quickly converted into cash. Most companies draw a distinction between investments classified as cash equivalents and the next category of current assets, short-term investments, according to the scheduled maturity of the investment. It is common practice to classify investments that have a maturity date of three months or less from the date of purchase

**GRAPHIC 3–4**
Current Assets—FedEx Corporation

**FedEx Corporation**

| | May 31 | |
|---|---|---|
| | **2004** | **2003** |
| (In millions) | | |
| **Assets** | | |
| Current Assets | | |
| Cash and cash equivalents | $1,046 | $ 538 |
| Receivables, less allowances of $151 and $149 | 3,027 | 2,627 |
| Spare parts, supplies, and fuel, less allowances of $124 and $101 | 249 | 228 |
| Deferred income taxes | 489 | 416 |
| Prepaid expenses and other | 159 | 132 |
| Total current assets | 4,970 | 3,941 |

● LO3

as cash equivalents. **FedEx Corporation**'s policy follows this practice and is disclosed in the summary of significant accounting policies disclosure note. The portion of the note from the company's 2004 financial statements is shown in Graphic 3–5.

**GRAPHIC 3–5**
Disclosure of Cash Equivalents—FedEx Corporation

**FedEx Corporation**

**Summary of Significant Accounting Policies (in part)**
Cash Equivalents. Cash equivalents in excess of current operating requirements are invested in short-term, interest-bearing instruments with maturities of three months or less at the date of purchase and are stated at cost, which approximates market value.

Cash that is restricted for a special purpose and not available for current operations should not be classified as a current asset. For example, if cash is being accumulated to repay a debt due in five years, the cash is classified as investments and funds, a noncurrent asset.[3]

***Investments are classified as current if management has the ability and intent to liquidate the investment in the near term.***

Short-term investments. Liquid investments not classified as cash equivalents are reported as either **short-term investments,** sometimes called *temporary investments* or *short-term marketable securities,* or investments and funds, a noncurrent asset. Investments in stock and debt securities of other corporations are included as short-term investments *if* the company has the ability and intent to sell those securities within the next 12 months or operating cycle, whichever is longer. If, for example, a company owns 1,000 shares of **IBM Corporation** stock and intends to hold those shares for several years, the stock is a long-term investment and should be classified as investments and funds.

For reporting purposes, investments in debt and equity securities are classified in one of three categories: (1) held to maturity, (2) trading securities, or (3) securities available for sale. We discuss these different categories and their accounting treatment in Chapter 12.

**FedEx Corporation**

Accounts receivable. **Accounts receivable** result from the sale of goods or services on credit. Notice in Graphic 3–4 that the FedEx receivables are valued less allowance, that is, net of the amount not expected to be collected. Accounts receivable often are referred to as *trade receivables* because they arise in the course of a company's normal trade. *Nontrade receivables* result from loans or advances by the company to other entities. When receivables are supported by a formal agreement or note that specifies payment terms they are called **notes receivable.**

Accounts receivable usually are due in 30 to 60 days, depending on the terms offered to customers and are, therefore, classified as current assets. Any receivable, regardless of the source, not expected to be collected within one year or the operating cycle, whichever is longer, is classified as investments and funds, a noncurrent asset.

[3]If the debt is due in the next year and classified as a current liability, then the cash also would be classified as current.

**Inventories.** **Inventories** include goods awaiting sale (finished goods), goods in the course of production (work in process), and goods to be consumed directly or indirectly in production (raw materials). Inventory for a wholesale or retail company consists only of finished goods, but the inventory of a manufacturer will include all three types of goods. Occasionally, a manufacturing company will report all three types of inventory directly in the balance sheet. More often, only the total amount of inventories is shown in the balance sheet and the balances of each type are shown in a disclosure note. For example, the note shown in Graphic 3–6 appears in the 2004 financial statements of **IBM Corporation**.

***Inventories*** **consist of assets that a retail or wholesale company acquires for resale or goods that manufacturers produce for sale.**

**GRAPHIC 3–6**
Inventories Disclosure—IBM Corporation

**E. Inventories**
($ in millions)

| | At Dec. 31 | |
|---|---|---|
| | **2004** | **2003** |
| Finished goods | $1,179 | $ 992 |
| Work in process and raw materials | 2,137 | 1,950 |
| | $3,316 | $2,942 |

Inventories are reported as current assets because they normally are sold within the operating cycle.

**FedEx Corporation** earns revenue by providing services to its customers rather than by selling goods. That is why there are no merchandise inventories listed in the company's balance sheet. Instead, the company shows an inventory of "spare parts, supplies and fuel." These assets will be *used* during the coming year in the process of earning service revenues.

**FedEx Corporation**

**Prepaid expenses.** Recall from Chapter 2 that a **prepaid expense** represents an asset recorded when an expense is paid in advance, creating benefits beyond the current period. Examples are prepaid rent and prepaid insurance. Even though these assets are not converted to cash, they would involve an outlay of cash if not prepaid.

Whether a prepaid expense is current or noncurrent depends on when its benefits will be realized. For example, if rent on an office building were prepaid for one year, then the entire prepayment is classified as a current asset. However, if rent were prepaid for a period extending beyond the coming year, a portion of the prepayment is classified as an other asset, a noncurrent asset.[4] **FedEx Corporation** combines prepaid expenses with other current assets in its balance sheet. Presumably, the "other" current asset category includes assets—such as short-term investments and nontrade receivables—that, because their amounts are not material, did not warrant separate disclosure.

**FedEx Corporation**

FedEx lists one other current asset in its balance sheet, "Deferred income taxes." This asset is discussed in Chapter 16.

When assets are expected to provide economic benefits beyond the next year, or operating cycle, they are reported as *noncurrent assets.* Typical classifications of noncurrent assets are (1) investments and funds, (2) property, plant, and equipment, and (3) intangible assets.

**Investments and Funds.** Most companies occasionally acquire assets that are not used directly in the operations of the business. These "nonoperating" assets include investments in equity and debt securities of other corporations, land held for speculation, noncurrent receivables, and cash set aside for special purposes (such as for future plant expansion). These assets are classified as noncurrent because management does not intend to convert the assets into cash in the next year (or the operating cycle if that's longer).

***Investments and funds*** **are nonoperating assets not used directly in operations.**

**Property, Plant, and Equipment.** Virtually all companies own assets classified as **property, plant, and equipment.** The common characteristics these assets share are that they are *tangible, long-lived, and used in the operations of the business.* Property, plant, and

**Tangible, long-lived assets used in the operations of the business are classified as** ***property, plant, and equipment.***

[4]Companies often include prepayments for benefits extending beyond one year as current assets when the amounts are not material.

equipment, along with intangible assets, generally are referred to as **operational assets.** They often are the primary revenue-generating assets of the business.

Property, plant, and equipment includes land, buildings, equipment, machinery, and furniture, as well as natural resources, such as mineral mines, timber tracts, and oil wells. These various assets usually are reported as a single amount in the balance sheet, with details provided in a note. They are reported at original cost less accumulated depreciation (or depletion for natural resources) to date. Quite often, a company will present only the net amount of property, plant, and equipment in the balance sheet and provide details in a disclosure note. Land often is listed as a separate item in this classification because it has an unlimited useful life and thus is not depreciated.

*Intangible assets* **generally represent exclusive rights that a company can use to generate future revenues.**

**Intangible Assets.** Some assets used in the operations of a business have no physical substance. These are appropriately called **intangible assets.** Generally, these represent the ownership of an exclusive right to something such as a product, a process, or a name. This right can be a valuable resource in generating future revenues. Patents, copyrights, and franchises are examples. They are reported in the balance sheet net of accumulated amortization. Some companies include intangible assets as part of property, plant, and equipment, while others report them either in a separate intangible asset classification or as other noncurrent assets.

Quite often, much of the value of intangibles is not reported in the balance sheet. For example, it would not be unusual for the historical cost of a patent to be significantly lower than its market value. As we discuss in Chapter 10, for internally developed intangibles, the costs that are included as part of historical cost are limited. Specifically, none of the research and development costs incurred in developing the intangible are included in cost.

**Other Assets.** Balance sheets often include a catch-all classification of noncurrent assets called **other assets.** This classification includes long-term prepaid expenses, called *deferred charges,* and any noncurrent asset not falling in one of the other classifications. For instance, if a company's noncurrent investments are not material in amount, they might be reported in the other asset classification rather than in a separate investments and funds category.

Graphic 3–7 reproduces the noncurrent asset section of **FedEx Corporation**'s 2004 and 2003 balance sheets. For FedEx, all other noncurrent assets are reported as other assets. This includes the intangible asset goodwill, prepaid pension costs, and intangible and other noncurrent assets.

**GRAPHIC 3–7**

Property, Plant, and Equipment and Other Assets—FedEx Corporation

**FedEx Corporation**

| | May 31 | |
|---|---|---|
| | **2004** | **2003** |
| (In millions) | | |
| **Assets** | | |
| Property and equipment, at cost | | |
| Aircraft and related equipment | 7,001 | 6,624 |
| Package handling and ground support equipment and vehicles | 5,296 | 5,013 |
| Computer and electronic equipment | 3,537 | 3,180 |
| Other | 4,477 | 4,200 |
| | 20,311 | 19,017 |
| Less accumulated depreciation and amortization | 11,274 | 10,317 |
| Net property and equipment | 9,037 | 8,700 |
| Other long-term assets | | |
| Goodwill | 2,802 | 1,063 |
| Prepaid pension cost | 1,127 | 1,269 |
| Intangible and other assets | 1,198 | 412 |
| Total other long-term assets | 5,127 | 2,744 |

We've seen how assets are grouped into current and noncurrent categories and that noncurrent assets always are subclassified further. Let's now turn our attention to liabilities. These, too, are separated into current and noncurrent (long-term) categories.

## LIABILITIES

Liabilities represent obligations to other entities. The information value of reporting these amounts is enhanced by classifying them as current liabilities and long-term liabilities. Graphic 3–8 shows the liability section of FedEx Corporation's 2004 and 2003 balance sheets.

● LO4

**GRAPHIC 3–8**
Liabilities—FedEx Corporation

**FedEx Corporation**

| | May 31 | |
|---|---|---|
| | **2004** | **2003** |
| (In millions) | | |
| **Liabilities** | | |
| Current liabilities | | |
| Current portion of long-term debt | $ 750 | $ 308 |
| Accrued salaries and employee benefits | 1,062 | 724 |
| Accounts payable | 1,615 | 1,168 |
| Accrued expenses | 1,305 | 1,135 |
| Total current liabilities | 4,732 | 3,335 |
| Long-term debt, less current portion | 2,837 | 1,709 |
| Other long-term liabilities | | |
| Deferred income taxes | 1,181 | 882 |
| Pension, postretirement healthcare and other benefit obligations | 768 | 657 |
| Self-insurance accruals | 591 | 536 |
| Deferred lease obligations | 503 | 466 |
| Deferred gains, principally related to aircraft transactions | 426 | 455 |
| Other liabilities | 60 | 57 |
| Total other long-term liabilities | 3,529 | 3,053 |

**Current Liabilities.** Current liabilities are those obligations that are expected to be satisfied through the use of current assets or the creation of other current liabilities. So, this classification includes all liabilities that are expected to be satisfied within one year or the operating cycle, whichever is longer. An exception is a liability that management intends to refinance on a long-term basis. For example, if management intends to refinance a six-month note payable by substituting a two-year note payable and has the ability to do so, then the liability would not be classified as current even though it's due within the coming year. This exception is discussed in more detail in Chapter 13.

**Current liabilities are expected to be satisfied within one year or the operating cycle, whichever is longer.**

The most common current liabilities are accounts payable, notes payable (short-term borrowings), unearned revenues, accrued liabilities, and the currently maturing portion of long-term debt. **Accounts payable** are obligations to suppliers of merchandise or of services purchased on *open account,* with payment usually due in 30 to 60 days. **Notes payable** are written promises to pay cash at some future date (I.O.U.s). Unlike accounts payable, notes usually require the payment of explicit interest in addition to the original obligation amount. Notes maturing in the next year or operating cycle, whichever is longer, will be classified as current liabilities. **Unearned revenues** represent cash received from a customer for goods or services to be provided in a future period.

**Current liabilities usually include *accounts and notes payable, unearned revenues, accrued liabilities,* and the *current maturities of long-term debt.***

**Accrued liabilities** represent obligations created when expenses have been incurred but will not be paid until a subsequent reporting period. Examples are accrued salaries payable, accrued interest payable, and accrued taxes payable. **FedEx Corporation** reported accrued liabilities at the end of 2004 in two categories: (1) accrued salaries and benefits of $1,062 million, and (2) accrued expenses of $1,305 million. In the disclosure note, shown in Graphic 3–9, the company provided the details.

Long-term notes, loans, mortgages, and bonds payable usually are reclassified and reported as current liabilities as they become payable within the next year (or operating cycle

**GRAPHIC 3–9**
Accrued Expenses Disclosure—FedEx Corporation

**FedEx Corporation**

**Note 5: Selected Current Liabilities**
The components of selected current liability captions were as follows (in millions):

| | May 31 | |
|---|---|---|
| | **2004** | **2003** |
| Accrued salaries and employee benefits | | |
| Salaries | $ 163 | $ 119 |
| Employee benefits | 496 | 227 |
| Compensated absences | 403 | 378 |
| | $1,062 | $ 724 |
| Accrued expenses | | |
| Self-insurance accruals | $ 442 | $ 401 |
| Taxes other than income taxes | 291 | 279 |
| Other | 572 | 455 |
| | $1,305 | $1,135 |

Current liabilities include the *current maturities of long-term debt.*

if that's longer).[5] Likewise, when long-term debt is payable in installments, the installment payable currently is reported as a current liability. For example, a $1,000,000 note payable requiring $100,000 in principal payments to be made in each of the next 10 years is classified as a $100,000 current liability—**current maturities of long-term debt**—and a $900,000 long-term liability.

Chapter 13 provides a more detailed analysis of current liabilities.

Noncurrent, or long-term liabilities, usually are those payable beyond the current year.

**Long-Term Liabilities.** Long-term liabilities are obligations that will *not* be satisfied in the next year or operating cycle, whichever is longer. They do not require the use of current assets or the creation of current liabilities for payment. Examples are long-term notes, bonds, pension obligations, and lease obligations.

But simply classifying a liability as long-term doesn't provide complete information to external users. For instance, long-term could mean anything from 2 to 20, 30, or 40 years. Payment terms, interest rates, and other details needed to assess the impact of these obligations on future cash flows and long-term solvency are reported in a disclosure note.

At the end of its 2004 fiscal year, FedEx Corporation reported long-term debt and other long-term liabilities. A disclosure note indicated that long-term debt consisted of notes and capital lease obligations. Other long-term liabilities included deferred income taxes, pension and other postretirement healthcare benefits, self-insurance accruals, deferred lease obligations, deferred gains, and other. These long-term liabilities are discussed in later chapters.

## SHAREHOLDERS' EQUITY

Shareholders' equity is composed of *paid-in capital* (invested capital) and *retained earnings* (earned capital).

Recall from our discussions in Chapters 1 and 2 that owners' equity is simply a residual amount derived by subtracting liabilities from assets. For that reason, it's also sometimes called net assets. Also recall that owners of a corporation are its shareholders, so owners' equity for a corporation is referred to as shareholders' equity or stockholders' equity. Shareholders' equity for a corporation arises primarily from two sources: (1) amounts *invested* by shareholders in the corporation, and (2) amounts *earned* by the corporation (on behalf of its shareholders). These are reported as (1) **paid-in capital** and (2) **retained earnings.** Retained earnings represents the accumulated net income earned since the inception of the corporation and not (yet) paid to shareholders as dividends.

Graphic 3–10 presents the shareholders' equity section of **FedEx Corporation**'s 2004 and 2003 balance sheets. The company calls this section common stockholders' investment.

[5]Payment can be with current assets or the creation of other current liabilities.

## GLOBAL PERSPECTIVE

### Balance Sheet

There are significant differences from country to country in the accounting methods used to measure balance sheet items. These differences, of course, also affect income statement amounts. For example, differences in inventory measurement methods affect the calculation of cost of goods sold as well as the inventory balance reported in the balance sheet. Many of these measurement differences are highlighted in the specific chapters that deal with the specific issues.

In terms of balance sheet presentation, the classification of assets and liabilities into current and noncurrent categories is prevalent globally. However, significant differences do exist, particularly with respect to terminology. In the United Kingdom, the term *stocks* refers to inventory. A U.S. investor would interpret stocks to mean investments in equity securities of other companies. In the United States, shareholders' equity is composed of paid-in capital and retained earnings. In many other countries, shareholders' equity is divided into capital and reserves. For example, in Germany, equity is divided into share capital, capital reserves, and revenue reserves. In India, liabilities whose existence is certain but whose value must be estimated, are called *provisions* and are listed separately.

Balance sheet presentation differences also exist. For example, a typical U.K. balance sheet begins with noncurrent assets, called *fixed assets.* Current assets are listed next and current liabilities are subtracted to arrive at net current assets, which is added to fixed assets. Long-term debt is then subtracted from this subtotal to arrive at net assets. The net assets total is equal to shareholders' interest, which is the last item reported in the balance sheet.

**GRAPHIC 3–10**
Shareholders' Equity—FedEx Corporation

**FedEx Corporation**

| (In millions, except shares) | May 31 | |
|---|---|---|
| | **2004** | **2003** |
| **Common Stockholders' Investment:** | | |
| Common stock, $0.10 par value; 800 million shares authorized; 300 million shares issued for 2004 and 299 million shares issued for 2003 | 30 | 30 |
| Additional paid-in capital | 1,079 | 1,088 |
| Retained earnings | 7,001 | 6,250 |
| Accumulated other comprehensive loss | (46) | (30) |
| | 8,064 | 7,338 |
| Less deferred compensation and treasury stock, at cost | 28 | 50 |
| Total common stockholders' investment | 8,036 | 7,288 |

From the inception of the corporation through May 31, 2004, FedEx has accumulated net income, less dividends, of $7,001 million, which is reported as *retained earnings*. The company's *paid-in capital* is represented by common stock and additional paid-in capital which collectively represent cash invested by shareholders in exchange for ownership interests. Information about the number of shares the company has authorized and how many shares have been issued also must be disclosed.

In addition to paid-in capital and retained earnings, shareholders' equity may include a few other equity components. For example, FedEx lists accumulated other comprehensive income, deferred compensation, and treasury stock. Accumulated other comprehensive income is discussed in Chapters 4, 12, and 18. Other equity components are addressed in later chapters, Chapter 18 in particular. We also discuss the concept of par value in Chapter 18.

# CONCEPT REVIEW EXERCISE

## BALANCE SHEET CLASSIFICATION

The following is a post-closing trial balance for the Sepia Paint Corporation at December 31, 2006, the end of the company's fiscal year:

| Account Title | Debits | Credits |
|---|---|---|
| Cash | 80,000 | |
| Accounts receivable | 200,000 | |
| Allowance for uncollectible accounts | | 20,000 |
| Inventories | 300,000 | |
| Prepaid expenses | 30,000 | |
| Note receivable (due in one month) | 60,000 | |
| Investments | 50,000 | |
| Land | 120,000 | |
| Buildings | 550,000 | |
| Machinery | 500,000 | |
| Accumulated depreciation—buildings and machinery | | 450,000 |
| Patent (net of amortization) | 50,000 | |
| Accounts payable | | 170,000 |
| Salaries payable | | 40,000 |
| Interest payable | | 10,000 |
| Note payable | | 100,000 |
| Bonds payable (due in 10 years) | | 500,000 |
| Common stock, no par | | 400,000 |
| Retained earnings | | 250,000 |
| Totals | 1,940,000 | 1,940,000 |

The $50,000 balance in the investment account consists of marketable equity securities of other corporations. The company's intention is to hold the securities for at least three years. The $100,000 note payable is an installment loan. $10,000 of the principal, plus interest, is due on each July 1 for the next 10 years. At the end of the year, 100,000 shares of common stock were issued and outstanding. The company has 500,000 shares of common stock authorized.

**Required:**

Prepare a classified balance sheet for the Sepia Paint Corporation at December 31, 2006.

## SOLUTION

**SEPIA PAINT CORPORATION**
**Balance Sheet**
**At December 31, 2006**

Assets

| | | |
|---|---|---|
| **Current assets:** | | |
| Cash | | $ 80,000 |
| Accounts receivable | $ 200,000 | |
| Less: Allowance for uncollectible amounts | (20,000) | 180,000 |
| Note receivable | | 60,000 |
| Inventories | | 300,000 |
| Prepaid expenses | | 30,000 |
| Total current assets | | 650,000 |
| **Investments** | | 50,000 |
| **Property, plant, and equipment:** | | |
| Land | 120,000 | |
| Buildings | 550,000 | |
| Machinery | 500,000 | |
| | 1,170,000 | |
| Less: Accumulated depreciation | (450,000) | |

| | | |
|---|---|---|
| Net property, plant, and equipment | | 720,000 |
| **Intangibles:** | | |
| Patent | | 50,000 |
| Total assets | | $1,470,000 |
| **Liabilities and Shareholders' Equity** | | |
| **Current liabilities:** | | |
| Accounts payable | | $ 170,000 |
| Salaries payable | | 40,000 |
| Interest payable | | 10,000 |
| Current maturities of long-term debt | | 10,000 |
| Total current liabilities | | 230,000 |
| **Long-term liabilities:** | | |
| Note payable | $ 90,000 | |
| Bonds payable | 500,000 | |
| Total long-term liabilities | | 590,000 |
| **Shareholders' equity:** | | |
| Common stock, no par, 500,000 shares authorized, 100,000 shares issued and outstanding | 400,000 | |
| Retained earnings | 250,000 | |
| Total shareholders' equity | | 650,000 |
| Total liabilities and shareholders' equity | | $1,470,000 |

The usefulness of the balance sheet, as well as the other financial statements, is significantly enhanced by financial statement disclosures. We now turn our attention to these disclosures.

# FINANCIAL DISCLOSURES

**PART B**

Financial statements are included in the annual report a company mails to its shareholders. They are, though, only part of the information provided. Critical to understanding the financial statements and to evaluating the firm's performance and financial health are disclosure notes and other information included in the annual report.

## Disclosure Notes

● LO5

Disclosure notes typically span several pages and explain or elaborate on the data presented in the financial statements themselves. Throughout this text you will encounter examples of items that usually are disclosed this way. For instance, information providing details of pension plans, leases, debt, and several assets is disclosed in the notes. Disclosures must include certain specific notes such as a summary of significant accounting policies, descriptions of subsequent events, and related-party transactions, but many notes are fashioned to suit the disclosure needs of the particular reporting enterprise. Actually, any explanation that contributes to investors' and creditors' understanding of the results of operations, financial position, or cash flows of the company should be included. Some common disclosures are made by some companies in the form of notes, while other companies disclose the same information as separate schedules or in other formats within the annual report. The specific format of disclosure is not important, only that the information is, in fact, disclosed. Let's take a look at just a few disclosure notes.

**The full-disclosure principle requires that financial statements provide all material, relevant information concerning the reporting entity.**

### SUMMARY OF SIGNIFICANT ACCOUNTING POLICIES

**The *summary of significant accounting policies* conveys valuable information about the company's choices from among various alternative accounting methods.**

There are many areas where management chooses from among equally acceptable alternative accounting methods. For example, management chooses whether to use accelerated or straight-line depreciation, whether to use FIFO, LIFO, or average cost to measure inventories, and whether the completed contract or percentage-of-completion method best reflects the performance of construction operations. It also defines which securities it considers to be cash equivalents and its policies regarding the timing of recognizing revenues. Typically, the first disclosure note consists of a summary of significant accounting policies that discloses the choices the company makes.[6] Graphic 3–11 shows you a portion of a typical summary note from a recent annual report of the **Starbucks Corporation**. FedEx Corporation reports the summary in its Note 1, shown in Appendix B located at the back of this text.

**FedEx Corporation**

**GRAPHIC 3–11** Summary of Significant Accounting Policies—Starbucks Corporation

**Note 1: Summary of Accounting Policies (in part)**

**Principles of Consolidation**

The consolidated financial statements reflect the financial position and operating results of Starbucks, which includes wholly owned subsidiaries and investees controlled by the Company.

**Cash Equivalents**

The Company considers all highly liquid instruments with a maturity of three months or less at the time of purchase to be cash equivalents.

**Inventories**

Inventories are stated at the lower of cost (primarily moving average cost) or market. The Company records inventory reserves for obsolete and slow-moving items and for estimated shrinkage between physical inventory counts.

**Property, Plant, and Equipment**

Property, plant, and equipment are carried at cost less accumulated depreciation. Depreciation of property, plant, and equipment which includes assets under capital leases, is provided on the straight-line method over estimated useful lives, generally ranging from two to seven years for equipment and 30 to 40 years for buildings. Leasehold improvements are amortized over the shorter of their estimated useful lives or the related lease life, generally 10 years.

**Revenue Recognition**

In most instances, retail store revenues are recognized when payment is tendered at the point of sale. Revenues from store value cards are recognized upon redemption. Until the redemption of store value cards, outstanding customer balances on such cards are included in "Deferred revenue" on the accompanying consolidated balance sheets.

Studying this note is an essential step in analyzing financial statements. Obviously, knowing which methods were used to derive certain accounting numbers is critical to assessing the adequacy of those amounts.

## SUBSEQUENT EVENTS

**A *subsequent event* is a significant development that takes place after the company's fiscal year-end but before the financial statements are issued.**

When an event that has a material effect on the company's financial position occurs after the fiscal year-end but before the financial statements actually are issued, the event is disclosed in a **subsequent event** disclosure note. Examples include the issuance of debt or equity securities, a business combination or the sale of a business, the sale of assets, an event that sheds light on the outcome of a loss contingency, or any other event having a material effect on operations. Graphic 3–12 illustrates the required disclosure by showing a note that **Costco Wholesale Corporation** included in its August 29, 2004, financial statements, announcing property damage and business interruption caused by hurricanes in Florida.

**GRAPHIC 3–12**

Subsequent Event—Costco Wholesale Corporation

**Note 11 Subsequent Event**

Subsequent to year-end, the Company experienced some business interruption in its Florida locations due to hurricane damage. With the exception of one warehouse, which has been closed since September 25, 2004, and is expected to reopen by November 22, 2004, all other warehouses incurred only minor damage and minimal disruption to their operations. Overall, the Company expects to incur losses in the range of $5 million to $7 million net of insurance recoveries.

We cover subsequent events in more depth in Chapter 13.

[6]"Disclosure of Accounting Policies," *Accounting Principles Board Opinion No. 22* (New York: AICPA, 1972).

## NOTEWORTHY EVENTS AND TRANSACTIONS

Some transactions and events occur only occasionally, but when they do occur are potentially important to evaluating a company's financial statements. In this category are related-party transactions, errors and irregularities, and illegal acts. The more frequent of these is related-party transactions.

Sometimes a company will engage in transactions with owners, management, families of owners or management, affiliated companies, and other parties that can significantly influence or be influenced by the company. The potential problem with **related-party transactions** is that their economic substance may differ from their legal form. For instance, borrowing or lending money at an interest rate that differs significantly from the market interest rate is an example of a transaction that could result from a related-party involvement. As a result of the potential for misrepresentation, financial statement users are particularly interested in more details about these transactions.

**The economic substance of *related-party* transactions should be disclosed, including dollar amounts involved.**

When related-party transactions occur, companies must disclose the nature of the relationship, provide a description of the transactions, and report the dollar amounts of transactions and any amounts due from or to related parties.[7] Graphic 3–13 shows a disclosure note from a recent annual report of **GAP Inc.** The note describes the company's relationship with Fisher Development, Inc., a general contractor wholly owned by the brother of GAP's chairman and his immediate family.

**GRAPHIC 3–13**
Related-Party Transactions Disclosure—GAP Inc.

We generally use a competitive bidding process for construction of new stores, expansions, relocations and major remodels (major store projects). In addition, we utilize a construction industry standard stipulated sum, non-exclusive agreement with our general contractors. As of January 31, 2004, we had 41 general contractors qualified to competitively bid in North America. Fisher Development, Inc. (FDI), a company that is wholly owned by the brother of Donald G. Fisher and the brother's immediate family, is one of our qualified general contractors. The stipulated sum agreement sets forth the terms under which our general contractors, including FDI, may act in connection with our construction activities. We paid approximately $4.2 million to FDI in fiscal 2003 for major store projects and other projects, which represents 15% of our total spent for all projects in fiscal 2003. On January 31, 2004, and February 1, 2003, amounts due to FDI were approximately $650,000 and $1.3 million, respectively. We paid $81 million and $416 million to FDI in fiscal 2002 and fiscal 2001, respectively. The Audit and Finance Committee of the Board reviews this relationship annually.

More infrequent are errors, irregularities, and illegal acts; however, when they do occur, their disclosure is important. The distinction between errors and **irregularities** is that errors are unintentional while irregularities are *intentional* distortions of financial statements.[8] Obviously, management fraud might cause a user to approach financial analysis from an entirely different and more cautious viewpoint.

Closely related to irregularities are **illegal acts** such as bribes, kickbacks, illegal contributions to political candidates, and other violations of the law. Accounting for illegal practices has been influenced by the Foreign Corrupt Practices Act passed by Congress in 1977. The Act is intended to discourage illegal business practices through tighter controls and also encourage better disclosure of those practices when encountered. The nature of such disclosures should be influenced by the materiality of the impact of illegal acts on amounts disclosed in the financial statements.[9] However, the SEC in *Staff Accounting Bulletin No. 99,*[10] expressed its view that exclusive reliance on quantitative benchmarks to assess materiality in preparing financial statements is inappropriate. A number of other factors, including whether the item in question involves an unlawful transaction, should also be considered when determining materiality.

---

[7] "Related Party Disclosures," *Statement of Financial Accounting Standards No. 57* (Stamford, Conn.: FASB, 1982).

[8] "The Auditor's Responsibility to Detect and Report Errors and Irregularities," *Statement on Auditing Standards No. 53* (New York: AICPA, 1988).

[9] "Illegal Acts by Clients," *Statement on Auditing Standards No. 54* (New York: AICPA, 1988).

[10] "Materiality," *Staff Accounting Bulletin No. 99* (Washington, DC: SEC, August 1999).

Disclosure notes for some financial statement elements are required. Others are provided when required by specific situations in the interest of full disclosure.

As you might expect, any disclosures of related-party transactions, irregularities, and illegal acts can be quite sensitive. Although auditors must be considerate of the privacy of the parties involved, that consideration cannot be subordinate to users' needs for full disclosure.

We've discussed only a few of the disclosure notes most frequently included in annual reports. Other common disclosures include details concerning earnings per share calculations, income taxes, property and equipment, contingencies, long-term debt, leases, pensions, stock options, changes in accounting methods, fair values of financial instruments, and exposure to market risk and credit risk. We discuss and illustrate these in later chapters in the context of related financial statement elements.

## Management Discussion and Analysis

● LO6

The management discussion and analysis provides a biased but informed perspective of a company's (a) operations, (b) liquidity, and (c) capital resources.

Each annual report includes a fairly lengthy discussion and analysis provided by the company's management. In this section, management provides its views on significant events, trends, and uncertainties pertaining to the company's (a) operations, (b) liquidity, and (c) capital resources. Although the **management discussion and analysis (MDA)** section may embody management's biased perspective, it can offer an informed insight that might not be available elsewhere. Graphic 3–14 contains part of the liquidity and capital resources portion of **The Walt Disney Company**'s MDA that followed a discussion of operations in its 2004 annual report.

**GRAPHIC 3–14**

Management Discussion and Analysis—Walt Disney Company

**Management Discussion and Analysis of Financial Condition and Results of Operations**
(In part: Liquidity and Capital Resources only)

Cash and cash equivalents increased by $459 million during the year ended September 30, 2004.

Capital expenditures for the Parks and Resorts segment are principally for theme park and resort expansion, new rides and attractions and recurring capital and capital improvements. The increase in domestic park spending in fiscal 2004 as compared to fiscal 2003 was primarily due to spending in anticipation of the 50th Anniversary Celebration which includes new attractions at Walt Disney World and Disneyland. The decrease in fiscal 2003 as compared to fiscal 2002 was primarily due to the completion in fiscal 2002 of a new resort facility at Walt Disney World. The international park spending in fiscal 2004, representing six months of Euro Disney and Hong Kong Disneyland capital expenditures following the implementation of FIN 46R, primarily relates to Hong Kong Disneyland construction. Our minority partner contributed $66 million which is included in financing activities.

The Company declared an annual dividend of $0.24 per share on December 1, 2004 related to fiscal 2004. The dividend is payable on January 6, 2005 to shareholders of record on December 10, 2004. During the fourth quarter of fiscal 2004, the Company repurchased 14.9 million shares of Disney common stock for approximately $335 million. No shares of Disney common stock were repurchased during fiscal 2003 and fiscal 2002. As of September 30, 2004, the Company was authorized to repurchase up to approximately 315 million shares of Company common stock.

We believe that the Company's financial condition is strong and that its cash balances, other liquid assets, operating cash flows, access to debt and equity capital markets and borrowing capacity, taken together, provide adequate resources to fund ongoing operating requirements and future capital expenditures related to the expansion of existing businesses and development of new projects.

## Management's Responsibilities

Auditors examine financial statements and the internal control procedures designed to support the content of those statements. Their role is to attest to the fairness of the financial statements based on that examination. However, management prepares and is responsible for the financial statements and other information in the annual report. To enhance the awareness of the users of financial statements concerning the relative roles of management and the auditor, annual reports include a management's responsibilities section that asserts the responsibility of management for the information contained in the annual report as well as an assessment of the company's internal control procedures.

Graphic 3–15 contains a portion of the statement of responsibility disclosure for **Cisco Systems, Inc.** included with the company's financial statements for the year ended July 31, 2004. Recall from our discussion of financial reporting reform in Chapter 1, that the *Sarbanes-Oxley Act of 2002* requires corporate executives to personally certify the financial statements. Submission of false statements carries a penalty of up to 20 years in jail. John Chambers, Cisco's president and chief executive officer, and Dennis Powell, the company's senior vice president and chief financial officer, signed the required certifications as well as the statement of responsibility. The last paragraph of the statement tells us that in the next fiscal year, the company's auditor will begin reporting on management's assertions as to the effectiveness of internal control as required by Section 404 of Sarbanes-Oxley.

**Statement of Responsibility (in part)**

Cisco's management has always assumed full accountability for maintaining compliance with our established financial accounting policies and for reporting our results with objectivity and the highest degree of integrity. It is critical for investors and other users of the consolidated financial statements to have confidence that the financial information that we provide is timely, complete, relevant, and accurate. Management is responsible for the fair presentation of Cisco's consolidated financial statements, prepared in accordance with generally accepted accounting principles (GAAP), and has full responsibility for their integrity and accuracy.

Management, with oversight of Cisco's Board of Directors, has established and maintains a strong ethical climate so that our affairs are conducted to the highest standards of personal and corporate conduct. Management also has established an effective system of internal control that provides reasonable assurance as to the integrity and accuracy of the consolidated financial statements. Cisco's policies and practices reflect corporate governance initiatives that are compliant with the listing requirements of NASDAQ and the corporate governance requirements of the Sarbanes-Oxley Act of 2002.

Our internal audit control function maintains critical oversight over the key areas of our business and financial processes and controls, and reports directly to our Audit Committee.

PricewaterhouseCoopers LLP, our independent registered public accounting firm, reports directly to the Audit Committee of the Board of Directors. PricewaterhouseCoopers LLP's accompanying report on our consolidated financial statements is based on its examination conducted in accordance with auditing standards generally accepted in the United States, including a review of our internal control structure for purposes of designing their audit procedures. At the end of our next fiscal year, our independent registered public accounting firm will report on our assertions as to the effectiveness of our internal control over financial reporting as required under Section 404 of the Sarbanes-Oxley Act of 2002. We are confident in the effectiveness of our internal controls and our ability to meet the requirements of this newly enacted legislation.

| | |
|---|---|
| John T. Chambers | Dennis D. Powell |
| President and Chief Executive Officer | Senior Vice President and Chief Financial Officer |

**GRAPHIC 3–15**
Management's Responsibilities—Cisco Systems, Inc.

**The management's responsibilities section avows the responsibility of management for the company's financial statements and internal control system.**

## Auditors' Report

LO7

One step in financial analysis should be an examination of the **auditors' report**. This is the report issued by the CPAs who audit the financial statements that informs users of the audit findings. Every audit report looks similar to the one prepared by **Deloitte & Touche LLP** for the financial statements of **Microsoft Corporation**, as shown in Graphic 3–16.

The reason for the similarities is that auditors' reports must be in exact compliance with the specifications of the AICPA and the PCAOB.[11] In most cases, including the report for

[11]"Reports on Audited Financial Statements," *Statement on Auditing Standards No. 58* (New York: AICPA, 1988), as amended by "Omnibus Statement on Auditing Standards—2000," *Statement on Auditing Standards No. 93* (New York: AICPA, 2000), and "References in Auditors' Reports to the Standards of the Public Company Accounting Oversight Board," *Auditing Standard No. 1* (Washington, D.C.: PCAOB, 2004).

**GRAPHIC 3–16**
Auditors' Report—Microsoft Corporation

**Report of Independent Registered Public Accounting Firm**

To the Board of Directors and Stockholders of Microsoft Corporation:

We have audited the accompanying consolidated balance sheets of Microsoft Corporation and subsidiaries as of June 30, 2003 and 2004, and the related consolidated statements of income, cash flows, and stockholders' equity for each of the three years in the period ended June 30, 2004. These financial statements are the responsibility of the Corporation's management. Our responsibility is to express an opinion on these financial statements based on our audits.

We conducted our audits in accordance with standards of the Public Company Accounting Oversight Board (United States). Those standards require that we plan and perform the audit to obtain reasonable assurance about whether the financial statements are free of material misstatement. An audit includes examining, on a test basis, evidence supporting the amounts and disclosures in the financial statements. An audit also includes assessing the accounting principles used and significant estimates made by management, as well as evaluating the overall financial statement presentation. We believe that our audits provide a reasonable basis for our opinion.

In our opinion, such consolidated financial statements present fairly, in all material respects, the financial position of Microsoft Corporation and subsidiaries as of June 30, 2003 and 2004, and the results of their operations and their cash flows for each of the three years in the period ended June 30, 2004 in conformity with accounting principles generally accepted in the United States of America.

As described in Note 13 to the financial statements, the Company retroactively adopted *Statement of Financial Accounting Standards No. 123,* "Accounting for Stock-Based Compensation," effective July 1, 2003.

Deloitte & Touche LLP
Seattle, Washington
August 24, 2004

The *auditors' report* provides the analyst with an independent and professional opinion about the fairness of the representations in the financial statements.

Microsoft, the auditors will be satisfied that the financial statements "present fairly" the financial position, results of operations, and cash flows and are "in conformity with generally accepted accounting principles." These situations prompt an **unqualified opinion.** Sometimes circumstances cause the auditors' report to include an explanatory paragraph in addition to the standard wording, even though the report is unqualified. Most notably, these include:

- *Lack of consistency* due to a change in accounting principle such that comparability is affected even though the auditor concurs with the desirability of the change.
- *Uncertainty* as to the ultimate resolution of a contingency for which a loss is material in amount but not necessarily probable or probable but not estimable.
- *Emphasis* of a matter concerning the financial statements that does not affect the existence of an unqualified opinion but relates to a significant event such as a related-party transaction.

The auditors' report calls attention to problems that might exist in the financial statements.

Some audits result in the need to issue other than an unqualified opinion, in which case the auditor will issue a (an):

- *Qualified opinion* This contains an exception to the standard unqualified opinion but not of sufficient seriousness to invalidate the financial statements as a whole.
- Examples of exceptions are (a) nonconformity with generally accepted accounting principles, (b) inadequate disclosures, and (c) a limitation or restriction of the scope of the examination.
- *Adverse opinion* This is necessary when the exceptions are so serious that a qualified opinion is not justified. Adverse opinions are rare because auditors usually are able to persuade management to rectify problems to avoid this undesirable report.
- *Disclaimer* An auditor will disclaim an opinion if insufficient information has been gathered to express an opinion.

During the course of each audit, the auditor is required to evaluate the company's ability to continue as a going concern for a reasonable time. If the auditor determines there is significant doubt, an explanation of the potential problem must be included in the auditors' report.[12]

**The auditor should assess the firm's ability to continue as a going concern.**

Obviously, the auditors' report is most informative when any of these deviations from the standard unqualified opinion are present. These departures from the norm should raise a red flag to a financial analyst and prompt additional search for information.

The auditors' report of **Trump Hotels & Casino Resorts, Inc.**, exhibited in Graphic 3–17, included a fourth paragraph after the standard first three paragraphs.

**GRAPHIC 3–17**
Going Concern Paragraph—Trump Hotels & Casino Resorts, Inc.

> The accompanying financial statements have been prepared assuming that Trump Hotels & Casino Resorts, Inc. will continue as a going concern. As more fully described in Note 1, the Company has experienced increased competition, has incurred recurring operating losses and has a working capital deficit at December 31, 2003. The Company is working on various alternatives to improve the Company's financial resources which are also described in Note 1. Absent the successful completion of one of these alternatives, the Company's operating results will increasingly become uncertain. These conditions raise substantial doubt about the Company's ability to continue as a going concern; however, the financial statements do not include any adjustments to reflect the possible future effects on the recoverability and classification of assets or the amounts and classification of liabilities that may result from the outcome of this uncertainty.

## Compensation of Directors and Top Executives

In the early 1990s, the compensation large U.S. corporations pay their top executives became an issue of considerable public debate and controversy. Shareholders, employees, politicians, and the public in general began to question the huge pay packages received by company officials at the same time that more and more rank and file employees were being laid off as a result of company cutbacks. Contributing to the debate was the realization that the compensation gap between executives and lower level employees was much wider than in Japan and most other industrial countries. During this time, it also became apparent that discovering exactly how much compensation corporations paid their top people was nearly impossible.

Part of the problem stemmed from the fact that disclosures of these amounts were meager; but a large part of the problem was that a substantial portion of executive pay often is in the form of stock options. Executive stock options give their holders the right to buy stock at a specified price, usually equal to the market price when the options are granted. When stock prices rise, executives can exercise their options and realize a profit. In some cases, options have made executive compensation seem extremely high. Stock options are discussed in depth in Chapter 19.

To help shareholders and others sort out the content of executive pay packages and better understand the commitments of the company in this regard, recent SEC requirements now provide for more disclosures on compensation to directors and executives, and in particular, concerning stock options. The **proxy statement** which must be sent each year to all shareholders, usually in the same mailing with the annual report, previously served primarily to invite shareholders to the meeting to elect board members and to vote on issues before the shareholders or to vote using an enclosed proxy card. Beginning with 1992 financial statements, the proxy statement assumed a larger role. Graphic 3–18 lists the information that the statement now also reports.

**The *proxy statement*, which is sent each year to all shareholders, contains disclosures on compensation to directors and executives.**

[12]"The Auditor's Consideration of an Entity's Ability to Continue as a Going Concern," *Statement on Auditing Standards No. 59* (New York: AICPA, 1988).

**GRAPHIC 3–18**
Proxy Statement Information

**A summary compensation table** that outlines how much directors and top executives are paid and what retirement benefits they will receive.
**A table of options granted** that reports information about options given to individually identified executives in the most recent year, including:
- The number of options and dates granted.
- The percentage of total options given to each top executive.
- The exercise price and expiration date of options.
- The company's estimate of the options' values.

**A table of options holdings** that reports information about all options currently held by individually identified executives, including:
- The number of options each executive owns and their value.
- The number of shares acquired in the most recent year by exercising options.
- The amount of profit realized from exercising options.

**GLOBAL PERSPECTIVE**

**Disclosure Practices around the World**

Most countries require specific disclosures by companies operating within their borders. Many of these disclosures are similar. However, the amount and types of required and voluntary disclosures differ from country to country. For example, in Israel, companies whose securities are publicly traded are required to disclose any receivable that exceeds 5 percent of total current assets. In Mexico, a disclosure reports the separate identification of long-term liabilities into the following categories: suppliers, affiliates, income tax, employees' profit sharing, and bank loans.

Several supplemental disclosures are uniquely European. These include information about shares and shareholders, certain employee disclosures, and environmental disclosures. An example of an environmental disclosure would be a discussion of safety measures adopted by the company in their manufacturing plants. In France, many enterprises are required to publish an annual social balance sheet. This report covers matters such as employment, training, health and safety conditions, employee benefits, and environmental issues. In general, European companies consider the full-disclosure concept to include a much broader set of information than do U.S. companies.

# PART C RISK ANALYSIS

## Using Financial Statement Information

● LO8

The overriding objective of financial reporting is providing information that investors and creditors can use to make decisions. Nevertheless, it's sometimes easy to lose sight of that objective while dealing with the intricacies that specific concepts and procedures can involve. In this part of the chapter we provide an overview of financial statement analysis and then demonstrate the use of ratios, a popular financial statement analysis technique, to analyze risk.

Investors, creditors, and others use information that companies provide in corporate financial reports to make decisions. Although the financial reports focus primarily on the past performance and the present financial condition of the reporting company, information users are most interested in the outlook for the future. Trying to gain a glimpse of the future from past and present data entails using various tools and techniques to formulate predictions. This is the goal of financial statement analysis.

*Comparative financial statements allow financial statement users to compare year-to-year financial position, results of operations, and cash flows.*

Financial statements are not presented in isolation. Every financial statement issued is accompanied by the corresponding financial statement of the preceding year, and often the previous two years. These are called **comparative financial statements.** They enable investors, creditors, and other users to compare year-to-year financial position, results of operations, and cash flows. These comparative data help an analyst detect and predict trends. Because operations often expand and contract in a cyclical fashion, analysis of any one year's data may not provide an accurate picture of a company.

Some analysts enhance their comparison by expressing each item as a percentage of that same item in the financial statements of another year (base amount) in order to more easily see year-to-year changes. This is referred to as **horizontal analysis.** Similarly, **vertical analysis** involves expressing each item in the financial statements as a percentage of an appropriate corresponding total, or base amount, but within the same year. For example, cash, inventory, and other assets can be restated as a percentage of total assets; net income and each expense can be restated as a percentage of revenues.

**No accounting numbers are meaningful in and of themselves.**

Regardless of the specific technique used, the essential point is that accounting numbers are virtually meaningless in isolation. Their value derives from comparison with other numbers. The most common way of comparing accounting numbers to evaluate the performance and risk of a firm is **ratio analysis.**

We use ratios every day. Batting averages indicate how well our favorite baseball players are performing. We evaluate basketball players by field goal percentage and rebounds per game. Speedometers measure the speed of our cars in terms of miles per hour. We compare grocery costs on the basis of price per pound or ounce. In each of these cases, the ratio is more meaningful than a single number by itself. Do 45 hits indicate satisfactory performance? It depends on the number of at-bats. Is $2 a good price for cheese? It depends on how many ounces the $2 buys. Ratios make these measurements meaningful.

**Evaluating information in ratio form allows analysts to control for size differences over time and among firms.**

Likewise, we can use ratios to help evaluate a firm's performance and financial position. Is net income of $4 million a cause for shareholders to celebrate? Probably not if shareholders' equity is $10 billion. But if shareholders equity is $10 million, that's a 40% return on equity! Although ratios provide more meaningful information than absolute numbers alone, the ratios are most useful when analyzed relative to some standard of comparison. That standard of comparison may be previous performance of the same company, the performance of a competitor company, or an industry average for the particular ratio.

Accountants should be conversant with ratio analysis for at least three reasons. First, when preparing financial statements, accountants should be familiar with the ways users will use the information provided to make better decisions concerning what and how to report. Second, when accountants participate in company decisions concerning operating and financing alternatives, they may find ratio analysis helpful in evaluating available choices. Third, during the planning stages of an audit, independent auditors often use ratio analysis to identify potential audit problems and determine the specific audit procedures that should be performed.

We introduce ratios related to risk analysis in this chapter and ratios related to profitability analysis in Chapter 5. You will also employ ratios in Decision Makers' Perspective sections of many of the chapters in this text. Analysis cases that benefit from ratio analysis are included in many of these chapters as well.

Investors and creditors use financial information to assess the future risk and return of their investments in business enterprises. The balance sheet provides information useful to this assessment. A key element of risk analysis is investigating a company's ability to pay its obligations when they come due. This type of risk often is referred to as **default risk.** Another aspect of risk is **operational risk** which relates more to how adept a company is at withstanding various events and circumstances that might impair its ability to earn profits. Obviously, these two types of risk are not completely independent of one another. Inability to earn profits certainly increases a company's chances of defaulting on its obligations. Conversely, regardless of a company's long-run prospects for generating profits, if it can't meet its obligations, the company's operations are at risk.

Assessing risk necessarily involves consideration of a variety of economywide risk factors such as inflation, interest rates, and the general business climate. Industrywide influences including competition, labor conditions, and technological forces also affect a company's risk profile. Still other risk factors are specific to the company itself. Financial ratios often are used in risk analysis to investigate a company's **liquidity** and **long-term solvency.** As we discuss some of the more common ratios in the following paragraphs, keep in mind the inherent relationship between risk and return and thus between our risk analysis in this chapter and our profitability analysis in Chapter 5.

## LIQUIDITY RATIOS

● LO9

Liquidity refers to the readiness of assets to be converted to cash. By comparing a company's liquid assets with its short-term obligations, we can obtain a general idea of the firm's ability to pay its short-term debts as they come due. Usually, current assets are thought of as the most liquid of a company's assets. Obviously, though, some are more liquid than others, so it's important also to evaluate the specific makeup of current assets. Two common measures of liquidity are (1) the current ratio and (2) the acid-test ratio (or quick ratio) calculated as follows:

$$\text{Current ratio} = \frac{\text{Current assets}}{\text{Current liabilities}}$$

$$\text{Acid-test ratio (or quick ratio)} = \frac{\text{Quick assets}}{\text{Current liabilities}}$$

*Working capital,* **the difference between current assets and current liabilities, is a popular measure of a company's ability to satisfy its short-term obligations.**

**Current Ratio.** Implicit in the definition of a current liability is the relationship between current assets and current liabilities. The difference between current assets and current liabilities is called **working capital.** By comparing a company's obligations that will shortly become due with the company's cash and other assets that, by definition, are expected to shortly be converted to cash, the ratio offers some indication as to ability to pay those debts. Although used in a variety of decisions, it is particularly useful to those considering whether to extend short-term credit. The **current ratio** is computed by dividing current assets by current liabilities. A current ratio of 2 indicates that the company has twice as many current assets available as current liabilities.

**FedEx Corporation**

**FedEx Corporation**'s working capital at the end of its 2004 fiscal year is $238 million consisting of current assets of $4,970 million (Graphic 3–4 on page 106) minus current liabilities of $4,732 million (Graphic 3–8 on page 109). The current ratio can be computed as follows:

$$\text{Current ratio} = \frac{\$4,970}{\$4,732} = 1.05$$

**Working capital may not present an accurate or complete picture of a company's liquidity.**

Care should be taken, however, in assessing liquidity based solely on working capital. Liabilities usually are paid with cash, not other components of working capital. A company could have difficulty paying its liabilities even with a current ratio significantly greater than 1.0. For example, if a significant portion of current assets consisted of inventories, and inventories usually are not converted to cash for several months, there could be a problem in paying accounts payable due in 30 days. On the other hand, a current ratio of less than 1.0 doesn't necessarily mean the company will have difficulty meeting its current obligations. A line of credit, for instance, which the company can use to borrow funds, provides financial flexibility. FedEx Corporation's 2004 annual report discloses $1 billion in credit agreements with banks. That also must be considered in assessing liquidity.

### ETHICAL DILEMMA

The Raintree Cosmetic Company has several loans outstanding with a local bank. The debt agreements all contain a covenant stipulating that Raintree must maintain a current ratio of at least .9. Jackson Phillips, company controller, estimates that the 2006 year-end current assets and current liabilities will be $2,100,000 and $2,400,000, respectively. These estimates provide a current ratio of only .875. Violation of the debt agreement will increase Raintree's borrowing costs as the loans are renegotiated at higher rates.

Jackson proposes to the company president that Raintree purchase inventory of $600,000 on credit before year-end. This will cause both current assets and current liabilities to increase by the same amount, but the current ratio will increase to .9. The extra $600,000 in inventory will be used over the later part of 2007. However, the purchase will cause warehousing costs and financing costs to increase.

Jackson is concerned about the ethics of his proposal. What do you think?

**Acid-Test Ratio (or Quick Ratio).** Some analysts like to modify the current ratio to consider only current assets that are readily available to pay current liabilities. One such variation in common use is the **acid-test ratio.** This ratio excludes inventories and prepaid items from current assets before dividing by current liabilities. The numerator, then, consists of cash, short-term investments, and accounts receivable, the "quick assets." By eliminating current assets less readily convertible into cash, the acid-test ratio provides a more rigorous indication of liquidity than does the current ratio.

**The *acid-test ratio* provides a more stringent indication of a company's ability to pay its current obligations.**

**FedEx Corporation**'s quick assets at the end of its 2004 fiscal year (in millions) total \$4,073 (\$1,046 + 3,027). The acid-test ratio can be computed as follows:

**FedEx Corporation**

$$\text{Acid-test ratio} = \frac{\$4{,}073}{\$4{,}732} = .86$$

Are these liquidity ratios adequate? It's difficult to say without some point of comparison. As indicated previously, common standards for such comparisons are industry averages for similar ratios or ratios of the same company in prior years. Industry averages for the above two ratios are as follows:

Industry Average

Current ratio = 1.15

Acid-test ratio = .95

FedEx Corporation's ratios are slightly less than the industry average. Is this an indication that liquidity is a problem for FedEx? Not necessarily, but it certainly would raise a red flag that calls for caution in analyzing other areas. Remember, each ratio is but one piece of the entire puzzle. For instance, profitability is perhaps the best indication of liquidity in the long run. We discuss ratios that measure profitability in Chapter 5.

Also, management may be very efficient in managing current assets so that, for example, receivables are collected faster than normal or inventory is sold faster than normal, making those assets more liquid than they otherwise would be. Higher turnover ratios, relative to that of a competitor or the industry, generally indicate a more liquid position for a given level of the current ratio. We discuss these turnover ratios in Chapter 5.

**Liquidity ratios should be assessed in the context of both profitability and efficiency of managing assets.**

## FINANCING RATIOS

● LO9

Investors and creditors, particularly long-term creditors, are vitally interested in a company's long-term solvency and stability. Financing ratios provide some indication of the riskiness of a company with regard to its ability to pay its long-term debts. Two common financing ratios are (1) the debt to equity ratio and (2) the times interest earned ratio. These ratios are calculated as follows:

$$\text{Debt to equity ratio} = \frac{\text{Total liabilities}}{\text{Shareholders' equity}}$$

$$\text{Times interest earned ratio} = \frac{\text{Net income} + \text{Interest expense} + \text{Taxes}}{\text{Interest expense}}$$

**Debt to Equity Ratio.** The **debt to equity ratio** compares resources provided by creditors with resources provided by owners. It is calculated by dividing total liabilities (current and noncurrent) by total shareholders' equity (including retained earnings).[13]

**The *debt to equity ratio* indicates the extent of reliance on creditors, rather than owners, in providing resources.**

The ratio provides a measure of creditors' protection in the event of insolvency. Other things being equal, the higher the ratio, the higher the risk. The higher the ratio, the greater the creditor claims on assets, so the higher the likelihood an individual creditor would not be paid in full if the company is unable to meet its obligations. Relatedly, a high ratio indicates not only more fixed interest obligations, but probably a higher *rate* of interest as well because lenders tend to charge higher rates as the level of debt increases.

[13]A commonly used variation of the debt to equity ratio is found by dividing total liabilities by *total assets* (or total equities), rather than by shareholders' equity only. Of course, in this configuration the ratio measures precisely the same attribute of the firm's capital structure but can be interpreted as the percentage of a company's total assets provided by funds from creditors, rather than by owners.

FedEx Corporation

**FedEx Corporation**'s total liabilities at the end of its 2004 fiscal year (in millions) are \$11,098 (current liabilities, \$4,732 + long-term debt, \$2,837 + other long-term liabilities, \$3,529—Graphic 3–8 on page 109), and shareholders' equity totals \$8,036 million (Graphic 3–10 on page 111). The debt to equity ratio can be computed as follows:

$$\text{Debt to equity ratio} = \frac{\$11,098}{\$8,036} = 1.38$$

As with all ratios, the debt to equity ratio is more meaningful if compared to some standard such as an industry or a competitor. For example, the debt to equity ratio for **United Parcel Service, Inc. (UPS)**, a major competitor, is 1.00, significantly lower than FedEx's ratio, indicating that UPS has less debt in its capital structure than does FedEx. Does this mean that UPS's default risk is less than that of FedEx? Other things equal—yes. Is that good? Not necessarily. As discussed in the next section, it may be that debt is being underutilized by UPS. More debt might increase the potential for return to shareholders, but the price would be higher risk. This is a fundamental trade-off faced by virtually all firms when trying to settle on the optimal capital structure.

**The debt to equity ratio indicates the extent of trading on the equity or *financial leverage*.**

**Relationship between risk and profitability.** The proportion of debt in the capital structure also is of interest to shareholders. After all, shareholders receive no return on their investments until after all creditor claims are paid. Therefore, the higher the debt to equity ratio, the higher the risk to shareholders. On the other hand, by earning a return on borrowed funds that exceeds the cost of borrowing the funds, a company can provide its shareholders with a total return higher than it could achieve by employing equity funds alone. This is referred to as favorable **financial leverage.**

For illustration, consider a newly formed corporation attempting to determine the appropriate mix of debt and equity. The initial capitalization goal is \$50 million. The capitalization mix alternatives have been narrowed to two: (1) \$10 million in debt and \$40 million in equity and (2) \$30 million in debt and \$20 million in equity.

Also assume that regardless of the capitalization mix chosen, the corporation will be able to generate a 16% annual return, *before payment of interest and income taxes,* on the \$50 million in assets acquired. In other words, income before interest and taxes will be \$8 million (16% × \$50 million). If the interest rate on debt is 8% and the income tax rate is 40%, comparative net income for the first year of operations for the two capitalization alternatives can be calculated as follows:

| | Alternative 1 | Alternative 2 |
|---|---|---|
| Income before interest and taxes | \$8,000,000 | \$8,000,000 |
| Less: Interest expense | (800,000)[a] | (2,400,000)[b] |
| Income before taxes | \$7,200,000 | \$5,600,000 |
| Less: Income tax expense (40%) | (2,880,000) | (2,240,000) |
| Net income | \$4,320,000 | \$3,360,000 |

[a]8% × \$10,000,000
[b]8% × \$30,000,000

Choose Alternative 1? Probably not. Although alternative 1 provides a higher net income, the return on the shareholders' equity (net income divided by shareholders' equity) is higher for alternative 2. Here's why:

**Favorable financial leverage means earning a return on borrowed funds that exceeds the cost of borrowing the funds.**

| | Alternative 1 | Alternative 2 |
|---|---|---|
| Return on shareholders' equity[14] = | $\frac{\$4,320,000}{\$40,000,000}$ | $\frac{\$3,360,000}{\$20,000,000}$ |
| = | 10.8% | 16.8% |

[14]If return is calculated on *average* shareholders' equity, we're technically assuming that all income is paid to shareholders in cash dividends, so that beginning, ending, and average shareholders' equity are the same. If we assume *no* dividends are paid, rates of return would be:

| | Alternative 1 | Alternative 2 |
|---|---|---|
| Return on shareholders' equity = | $\frac{\$4,320,000}{(\$44,320,000 + 40,000,000)/2}$ | $\frac{\$3,360,000}{(\$20,000,000 + 23,360,000)/2}$ |
| = | 10.25% | 15.50% |

In any case our conclusions are the same.

Alternative 2 generated a higher return for each dollar invested by shareholders. This is because the company leveraged its $20 million equity investment with additional debt. Because the cost of the additional debt (8%) is less than the return on assets invested (16%), the return to shareholders is higher. This is the essence of favorable financial leverage.

Be aware, though, leverage is not always favorable; the cost of borrowing the funds might exceed the returns they provide. If the return on assets turned out to be less than expected, the additional debt could result in a lower return on equity for alternative 2. If, for example, the return on assets invested (before interest and taxes) had been 6%, rather than 16%, alternative 1 would have provided the better return on equity:

| | Alternative 1 | Alternative 2 |
|---|---|---|
| Income before interest and taxes | $3,000,000 | $3,000,000 |
| Less: Interest expense | (800,000)[a] | (2,400,000)[b] |
| Income before taxes | $2,200,000 | $ 600,000 |
| Less: Income tax expense (40%) | (880,000) | (240,000) |
| Net income | $1,320,000 | $ 360,000 |

[a]8% × $10,000,000
[b]8% × $30,000,000

$$\text{Return on shareholders' equity}^{15} = \frac{\$1{,}320{,}000}{\$40{,}000{,}000} \qquad \frac{\$360{,}000}{\$20{,}000{,}000}$$

$$= 3.3\% \qquad 1.8\%$$

So, shareholders typically are faced with a tradeoff between the risk that high debt denotes and the potential for a higher return from having the higher debt. In any event, the debt to equity ratio offers a basis for making the choice.

**Times Interest Earned Ratio.** Another way to gauge the ability of a company to satisfy its fixed debt obligations is by comparing interest charges with the income available to pay those charges. The **times interest earned ratio** is designed to do this. It is calculated by dividing income before subtracting interest expense and income taxes by interest expense.

**The *times interest earned ratio* indicates the margin of safety provided to creditors.**

Bondholders, noteholders, and other creditors can measure the margin of safety they are accorded by a company's earnings. If income is many times greater than interest expense, creditors' interests are more protected than if income just barely covers this expense. For this purpose, income should be the amount available to pay interest which is income before subtracting interest and income taxes, calculated by adding back to net income the interest and taxes that were deducted.

As an example, **FedEx Corporation**'s 2004 financial statements report the following items:

**FedEx Corporation**

| | ($ in millions) |
|---|---|
| Net income | $ 838 |
| Interest expense | 136 |
| Income taxes | 481 |
| Income before interest and taxes | $1,455 |

The times interest earned ratio can be computed as follows:

$$\text{Times interest earned ratio} = \frac{\$1{,}455}{\$136} = 10.7 \text{ times}$$

[15]If we assume *no* dividends are paid, rates of return would be:

| | Alternative 1 | Alternative 2 |
|---|---|---|
| Return on shareholders' equity = | $\frac{\$1{,}320{,}000}{(\$41{,}320{,}000 + 40{,}000{,}000)/2}$ | $\frac{\$360{,}000}{(\$20{,}000{,}000 + 20{,}360{,}000)/2}$ |
| = | 3.25% | 1.78% |

In any case our conclusions are the same.

The ratio of 10.7 times indicates a considerable margin of safety for creditors. Income could decrease many times and the company would still be able to meet its interest payment obligations.[16] In comparison, UPS's times interest earned ratio for 2004 is 34 times. UPS has less interest-bearing debt in its capital structure than does FedEx and it earned slightly higher income.

Especially when viewed alongside the debt-equity ratio, the coverage ratio seems to indicate a comfortable safety cushion for creditors. It also indicates a degree of financial mobility if the company were to decide to raise new debt funds to "trade on the equity" and attempt to increase the return to shareholders through favorable financial leverage.

## FINANCIAL REPORTING CASE SOLUTION

1. **Respond to Jerry's criticism that shareholders' equity does not represent the market value of the company. What information does the balance sheet provide?** *(p. 103)* Jerry is correct. The financial statements are supposed to help investors and creditors value a company. However, the balance sheet is not intended to portray the market value of the entity. The assets of a company minus its liabilities as shown in the balance sheet (shareholders' equity) usually will not equal the company's market value for several reasons. For example, many assets are measured at their historical costs rather than their market values. Also, many company resources including its trained employees, its experienced management team, and its reputation are not recorded as assets at all. The balance sheet must be used in conjunction with other financial statements, disclosure notes, and other publicly available information.

   The balance sheet does, however, provide valuable information that can be used by investors and creditors to help determine market value. After all, it is the balance sheet that describes many of the resources a company has available for generating future cash flows. The balance sheet also provides important information about liquidity and long-term solvency.
2. **The usefulness of the balance sheet is enhanced by classifying assets and liabilities according to common characteristics. What are the classifications used in Electronic Arts' balance sheet and what elements do those categories include?** *(p. 104)*

   Electronic Arts' balance sheet contains the following classifications:

   Assets:
   - *Current assets* include cash and several other assets that are reasonably expected to be converted to cash or consumed within the coming year, or within the normal operating cycle of the business if that's longer than one year.
   - *Property and equipment* are the tangible long-lived assets used in the operations of the business. This category includes land, buildings, equipment, machinery, and furniture, as well as natural resources.
   - *Investments in affiliates* are investments in debt and equity securities of affiliated companies.
   - *Goodwill* is a unique intangible asset in that its cost can't be directly associated with any specifically identifiable right and is not separable from the company as a whole. It represents the unique value of the company as a whole over and above all identifiable tangible and intangible assets.
   - *Other intangibles* are assets that represent exclusive rights to something such as a product, a process, or a name. Patents, copyrights, and franchises are examples.
   - *Long-term deferred income taxes* result from temporary differences between taxable income and accounting income.

[16] Of course, interest is paid with cash, not with "income." The times interest earned ratio often is calculated by using cash flow from operations before subtracting either interest payments or tax payments as the numerator and interest payments as the denominator.

- *Other assets* is a "catch-all" classification of noncurrent assets and could include long-term prepaid expenses and any noncurrent asset not included in one of the other categories.

Liabilities:

*Current liabilities* are those obligations that are expected to be satisfied through the use of current assets or the creation of other current liabilities. Usually, this means liabilities that are expected to be paid within one year or the operating cycle, whichever is longer.

Shareholders' equity:

- *Common stock* and *paid-in capital* collectively equal the amounts invested by shareholders in the corporation.
- *Retained earnings* represents the accumulated net income earned since inception of the corporation and not yet paid out to shareholders as dividends.
- *Accumulated other comprehensive income* is the cumulative amount of other comprehensive income items. This topic is addressed in subsequent chapters. ■

## THE BOTTOM LINE

1. The balance sheet is a position statement that presents an organized array of assets, liabilities, and shareholders' equity at a particular point in time. The statement does not portray the market value of the entity. However, the information in the statement can be useful in assessing market value, as well as in providing important information about liquidity and long-term solvency.
2. Current assets include cash and other assets that are reasonably expected to be converted to cash or consumed during one year, or within the normal operating cycle of the business if the operating cycle is longer than one year. All other assets are classified as various types of noncurrent assets. Current liabilities are those obligations that are expected to be satisfied through the use of current assets or the creation of other current liabilities. All other liabilities are classified as long term.
3. In addition to cash and cash equivalents, current assets include short-term investments, accounts receivable, inventories, and prepaid expenses. Other asset classifications include investments and funds; property, plant, and equipment; intangible assets; and other assets.
4. Current liabilities include notes and accounts payable, unearned revenues, accrued liabilities, and the current maturities of long-term debt. Long-term liabilities include long-term notes, loans, mortgages, bonds, pension and lease obligations, as well as deferred income taxes.
5. Financial disclosures are used to convey additional information about the account balances in the basic financial statements as well as to provide supplemental information. This information is disclosed parenthetically in the basic financial statements or in notes or supplemental financial statements.
6. Annual financial statements will include management's discussion and analysis of key aspects of the company's business. The purpose of this disclosure is to provide external parties with management's insight into certain transactions, events, and circumstances that affect the enterprise, including their financial impact.
7. The purpose of an audit is to provide a professional, independent opinion as to whether or not the financial statements are prepared in conformity with GAAP. The audit report contains three paragraphs; the first two deal with the scope of the audit and the third paragraph states the auditors' opinion.
8. Financial analysts use various techniques to transform financial information into forms more useful for analysis. Horizontal analysis and vertical analysis provide a useful way of analyzing year-to-year changes. Ratio analysis allows analysts to control for size differences over time and among firms while investigating important relationships among financial variables.
9. The balance sheet provides information that can be useful in assessing risk. A key element of risk analysis is investigating a company's ability to pay its obligations when they come due. Liquidity ratios and financing ratios provide information about a company's ability to pay its obligations. ■

APPENDIX 3

# Reporting Segment Information

Many companies operate in several business segments as a strategy to achieve growth and to reduce operating risk through diversification.

Financial analysis of diversified companies is especially difficult. Consider, for example, a company that operates in several distinct business segments including computer peripherals, home health care systems, textiles, and consumer food products. The results of these distinctly different activities will be aggregated into a single set of financial statements, making difficult an informed projection of future performance. It may well be that the five-year outlook differs greatly among the areas of the economy represented by the different segments. To make matters worse for an analyst, the integrated financial statements do not reveal the relative investments in each of the business segments nor the success the company has had within each area. Given the fact that so many companies these days have chosen to balance their operating risks through diversification, aggregated financial statements pose a widespread problem for analysts, lending and credit officers, and other financial forecasters.

## Reporting by Operating Segment

To address the problem, the accounting profession requires companies engaged in more than one significant line of business to provide supplemental information concerning individual operating segments. The supplemental disaggregated data do not include complete financial statements for each reportable segment, only certain specified items.

Segment reporting facilitates the financial statement analysis of diversified companies.

Prior to 1997, *SFAS 14,* "Financial Reporting for Segments of a Business Enterprise," provided the specific reporting requirements for segment reporting.[17] *SFAS 14* applied the industry approach in determining reportable segments. The standard was the subject of much criticism because it allowed for inconsistent definitions of the term *industry* demonstrated by companies applying the standard. This inconsistency reduced the relevance and comparability of segment disclosures. In June 1997, the Financial Accounting Standards Board issued *SFAS 131* to replace *SFAS 14.*

### WHAT IS A REPORTABLE OPERATING SEGMENT?

The new standard employs a *management approach* in determining which segments of a company are reportable. This approach is based on the way that management organizes the segments within the enterprise for making operating decisions and assessing performance. The segments are, therefore, evident from the structure of the enterprise's internal organization.

More formally, the following characteristics define an **operating segment:**[18]

An operating segment is a component of an enterprise:

- That engages in business activities from which it may earn revenues and incur expenses (including revenues and expenses relating to transactions with other components of the same enterprise).
- Whose operating results are regularly reviewed by the enterprise's chief operating decision maker to make decisions about resources to be allocated to the segment and assess its performance.
- For which discrete financial information is available.

The FASB hopes that this new approach provides insights into the risk and opportunities management sees in the various areas of company operations. Also, reporting information based on the enterprise's internal organization should reduce the incremental cost to companies of providing the data. In addition, the board added quantitative thresholds to the definition of an operating segment to limit the number of reportable segments. Only segments of certain size (10% or more of total company revenues, assets, or net income) must be disclosed. However, a company must account for at least 75% of consolidated revenue through segment disclosures.

[17]"Financial Reporting for Segments of a Business Enterprise," *Statement of Financial Accounting Standards No. 14* (Stamford, CT: FASB, 1976).

[18]"Disclosures about Segments of an Enterprise and Related Information," *Statement of Financial Accounting Standards No. 131* (Norwalk, CT: FASB, 1997), par. 10.

## WHAT AMOUNTS ARE REPORTED BY AN OPERATING SEGMENT?

For areas determined to be reportable operating segments, the following disclosures are required:

a. General information about the operating segment.
b. Information about reported segment profit or loss, including certain revenues and expenses included in reported segment profit or loss, segments assets, and the basis of measurement.
c. Reconciliations of the totals of segment revenues, reported profit or loss, assets, and other significant items to corresponding enterprise amounts.
d. Interim period information.[19]

Graphic 3A–1 shows the business segment information reported by 3M Co. in its 2003 annual report.

**GRAPHIC 3A–1**
Business Segment Information Disclosure—3M Co.

**Business Segment Information**
($ in millions)

| | | Net Sales | Operating Income | Assets | Depr. and Amort. | Capital Expendit. |
|---|---|---|---|---|---|---|
| Health Care | **2003** | **$ 3,995** | **$1,027** | **$ 2,544** | **$ 169** | **$144** |
| | 2002 | 3,560 | 900 | 2,409 | 166 | 183 |
| | 2001 | 3,301 | 753 | 2,190 | 187 | 171 |
| Industrial | **2003** | **3,354** | **458** | **2,655** | **212** | **161** |
| | 2002 | 3,147 | 487 | 2,685 | 191 | 158 |
| | 2001 | 3,163 | 457 | 2,660 | 199 | 201 |
| Display and Graphics | **2003** | **2,962** | **885** | **2,570** | **159** | **126** |
| | 2002 | 2,228 | 534 | 2,476 | 135 | 84 |
| | 2001 | 1,997 | 372 | 1,619 | 169 | 117 |
| Consumer and Office | **2003** | **2,607** | **460** | **1,378** | **108** | **86** |
| | 2002 | 2,444 | 448 | 1,354 | 108 | 90 |
| | 2001 | 2,523 | 410 | 1,429 | 133 | 123 |
| Safety, Security and Protection Services | **2003** | **1,928** | **437** | **1,139** | **100** | **46** |
| | 2002 | 1,686 | 338 | 1,097 | 97 | 105 |
| | 2001 | 1,639 | 302 | 1,054 | 104 | 122 |
| Electro and Communications | **2003** | **1,818** | **255** | **1,568** | **138** | **43** |
| | 2002 | 1,831 | 253 | 1,633 | 135 | 77 |
| | 2001 | 2,107 | 215 | 1,768 | 136 | 148 |
| Transportation | **2003** | **1,538** | **389** | **872** | **68** | **64** |
| | 2002 | 1,388 | 333 | 846 | 66 | 58 |
| | 2001 | 1,306 | 270 | 828 | 63 | 70 |
| Corporate and Unallocated | **2003** | **30** | **(198)** | **4,874** | **10** | **7** |
| | 2002 | 48 | (247) | 2,829 | 56 | 8 |
| | 2001 | 18 | (506) | 3,058 | 98 | 28 |
| Total Company | **2003** | **$18,232** | **$3,713** | **$17,600** | **$ 964** | **$677** |
| | 2002 | 16,332 | 3,046 | 15,329 | 954 | 763 |
| | 2001 | 16,054 | 2,273 | 14,606 | 1,089 | 980 |

[19]Ibid., par. 25.

## REPORTING BY GEOGRAPHIC AREA

In today's global economy it is sometimes difficult to distinguish domestic and foreign companies. Most large U.S. firms conduct significant operations in other countries in addition to having substantial export sales from this country. Differing political and economic environments from country to country means risks and associated rewards sometimes vary greatly among the various operations of a single company. For instance, manufacturing facilities in a South American country embroiled in political unrest pose different risks from having a plant in Vermont, or even Canada. Without disaggregated financial information, these differences cause problems for analysts.

*SFAS 131* requires an enterprise to report certain geographic information unless it is impracticable to do so. This information includes:

a. Revenues from external customers (1) attributed to the enterprise's country of domicile and (2) attributed to all foreign countries in total from which the enterprise derives revenues, and
b. Long-lived assets other than financial instruments, long-term customer relationships of a financial institution, mortgage and other servicing rights, deferred policy acquisition costs, and deferred tax assets (1) located in the enterprise's country of domicile and (2) located in all foreign countries in total in which the enterprise holds assets.[20]

3M reported its geographic area information separately in a table reproduced in Graphic 3A–2. Notice that both the business segment (Graphic 3A–1) and geographic information disclosures include a reconciliation to company totals. For example, in both graphics, year 2003 net sales of both the segments and the geographic areas are reconciled to the company's total net sales of $18,232 ($ in millions).

**GRAPHIC 3A–2** Geographic Area Information Disclosure—3M Company

**Geographic Area Information** ($ in millions)

| | | United States | Europe and Middle East | Asia Pacific | Latin America, Africa and Canada | Other Unallocated | Total Company |
|---|---|---|---|---|---|---|---|
| Net sales to customers | 2003 | $7,581 | $4,624 | $4,335 | $1,651 | $ 41 | $18,232 |
| | 2002 | 7,426 | 4,035 | 3,431 | 1,392 | 48 | 16,332 |
| | 2001 | 7,523 | 3,960 | 3,043 | 1,494 | 34 | 16,054 |
| Operating income | 2003 | $1,213 | $ 800 | $1,373 | $ 436 | $(109) | $ 3,713 |
| | 2002 | 1,180 | 685 | 1,009 | 390 | (218) | 3,046 |
| | 2001 | 1,028 | 571 | 807 | 360 | (493) | 2,273 |
| Property, plant, and equipment—net | 2003 | $3,342 | $1,231 | $ 724 | $ 312 | $ — | $ 5,609 |
| | 2002 | 3,523 | 1,136 | 676 | 286 | — | 5,621 |
| | 2001 | 3,675 | 974 | 634 | 332 | — | 5,615 |

**FedEx Corporation**

For another example of both business segment and geographic area disclosures, see the **FedEx Corporation** segment information in Appendix B, located at the back of this text.

## INFORMATION ABOUT MAJOR CUSTOMERS

**Revenues from major customers must be disclosed.**

Some companies in the defense industry derive substantial portions of their revenues from contracts with the Defense Department. When cutbacks occur in national defense or in specific defense systems, the impact on a company's operations can be considerable. Obviously, financial analysts are extremely interested in information concerning the extent to which a

[20]Ibid., par. 38.

company's prosperity depends on one or more major customers such as in the situation described here. For this reason, if 10% or more of the revenue of an enterprise is derived from transactions with a single customer, the enterprise must disclose that fact, the total amount of revenue from each such customer, and the identity of the operating segment or segments earning the revenue. The identity of the major customer or customers need not be disclosed, although companies routinely provide that information. In its 2003 annual report, 3M did not report any major customer information. As an example of this type of disclosure, **Procter & Gamble Company**'s business segment disclosure included information on its largest customer, **Wal-Mart**, as shown in Graphic 3A–3. ■

**Note 12. Segment Information (in part)**
The Company's largest customer, Wal-Mart Stores, Inc. and its affiliates, accounted for 17%, 18% and 17% of consolidated net sales in 2004, 2003, and 2002, respectively. These sales occurred primarily in the United States.

**GRAPHIC 3A–3**
Major Customer Disclosure—Procter & Gamble Company

**GLOBAL PERSPECTIVE**

There is more international uniformity regarding disaggregated disclosures than with many other accounting issues. Many countries adopted *International Accounting Standard No. 14*, "Reporting Financial Information by Segment," issued in 1981 by the International Accounting Standards Committee. Under this standard, companies report revenues, identifiable assets and capital expenditures for both industry segments and geographic segments. In 2005, the IASB converged IAS 14 with SFAS 131, adopting the management approach found in U.S. GAAP.

# QUESTIONS FOR REVIEW OF KEY TOPICS

**Q 3–1** Describe the purpose of the balance sheet.

**Q 3–2** Explain why the balance sheet does not portray the market value of the entity.

**Q 3–3** Define current assets and list the typical asset categories included in this classification.

**Q 3–4** Define current liabilities and list the typical liability categories included in this classification.

**Q 3–5** Describe what is meant by an operating cycle for a typical manufacturing company.

**Q 3–6** Explain the difference(s) between investments in equity securities classified as current assets versus those classified as noncurrent assets.

**Q 3–7** Describe the common characteristics of assets classified as property, plant, and equipment and identify some assets included in this classification.

**Q 3–8** Distinguish between property, plant, and equipment and intangible assets.

**Q 3–9** Explain how each of the following liabilities would be classified in the balance sheet:

- A note payable of $100,000 due in five years.
- A note payable of $100,000 payable in annual installments of $20,000 each, with the first installment due next year.

**Q 3–10** Define the terms *paid-in-capital* and *retained earnings.*

**Q 3–11** Disclosure notes are an integral part of the information provided in financial statements. In what ways are the notes critical to understanding the financial statements and to evaluating the firm's performance and financial health?

**Q 3–12** A summary of the company's significant accounting policies is a required disclosure. Why is this disclosure important to external financial statement users?

**Q 3–13** Define a subsequent event.

**Q 3–14** Every annual report includes an extensive discussion and analysis provided by the company's management. Specifically, which aspects of the company must this discussion address? Isn't management's perspective too biased to be of use to investors and creditors?

**Q 3–15** The auditors' report provides the analyst with an independent and professional opinion about the fairness of the representations in the financial statements. What are the four main types of opinion an auditor might issue? Describe each.

**Q 3–16** What is a proxy statement? What information does it provide?

**Q 3–17** Define the terms *working capital, current ratio,* and *acid-test ratio* (or *quick ratio*).

**Q 3–18** Show the calculation of the following financing ratios: (1) the debt to equity ratio, and (2) the times interest earned ratio.

**Q 3–19** (Based on Appendix 3) Segment reporting facilitates the financial statement analysis of diversified companies. What determines whether an operating segment is a reportable segment for this purpose?

**Q 3–20** (Based on Appendix 3) For segment reporting purposes, what amounts are reported by each operating segment?

## BRIEF EXERCISES

**BE 3–1**
Current versus noncurrent classification
● LO2

Indicate whether each of the following assets and liabilities should be classified as current or noncurrent: (a) accounts receivable; (b) prepaid rent for the next six months; (c) note receivable due in two years; (d) note payable due in 90 days; (e) note payable due in five years; and (f) patent.

**BE 3–2**
Balance sheet classification
● LO3 LO4

The trial balance for K and J Nursery, Inc. listed the following account balances at December, 31, 2006, the end of its fiscal year: cash, $16,000; accounts receivable, $11,000; inventories, $25,000; equipment (net), $80,000; accounts payable, $14,000; wages payable, $9,000; interest payable, $1,000; note payable (due in 18 months), $30,000; common stock, $50,000. Calculate total current assets and total current liabilities that would appear in the company's year-end balance sheet.

**BE 3–3**
Balance sheet classification
● LO3 LO4

Refer to the situation described in BE 3–2. Determine the year-end balance in retained earnings for K and J Nursery, Inc.

**BE 3–4**
Balance sheet preparation
● LO2 through LO4

Refer to the situation described in BE 3–2. Prepare a classified balance sheet for K and J Nursery, Inc. The equipment originally cost $140,000.

**BE 3–5**
Balance sheet preparation
● LO2 through LO4

The following is a December 31, 2006, post-closing trial balance for Culver City Lighting, Inc. Prepare a classified balance sheet for the company.

| Account Title | Debits | Credits |
|---|---|---|
| Cash | 55,000 | |
| Accounts receivable | 39,000 | |
| Inventories | 45,000 | |
| Prepaid insurance | 15,000 | |
| Equipment | 100,000 | |
| Accumulated depreciation—equipment | | 34,000 |
| Patent, net | 40,000 | |
| Accounts payable | | 12,000 |
| Interest payable | | 2,000 |
| Note payable (due in 10, equal annual installments) | | 100,000 |
| Common stock | | 70,000 |
| Retained earnings | | 76,000 |
| Totals | 294,000 | 294,000 |

**BE 3–6**
Balance sheet classification
● LO2 through LO4

You have been asked to review the December 31, 2006, balance sheet for Champion Cleaning. After completing your review, you list the following three items for discussion with your superior:

1. An investment of $30,000 is included in current assets. Management has indicated that it has no intention of liquidating the investment in 2007.
2. A $100,000 note payable is listed as a long-term liability, but you have determined that the note is due in 10, equal annual installments with the first installment due on March 31, 2007.

3. Unearned revenue of $60,000 is included as a current liability even though only two-thirds will be earned in 2007.

Determine the appropriate classification of each of these items.

**BE 3–7**
Balance sheet preparation; missing elements
● LO2 through LO4

The following information is taken from the balance sheet of Raineer Plumbing: cash and cash equivalents, $40,000; accounts receivable, $120,000; inventories, ?; total current assets, $235,000; property, plant, and equipment (net), ?; total assets, $400,000; accounts payable, $32,000; note payable (due in two years), $50,000; common stock; $100,000; and retained earnings, ?. Determine the missing amounts.

**BE 3–8**
Financial disclosures
● LO5

For each of the following note disclosures, indicate whether the disclosure would likely appear in (A) the summary of significant accounts policies or (B) a separate note: (1) depreciation method; (2) contingency information; (3) significant issuance of common stock after the fiscal year-end; (4) cash equivalent designation; (5) long-term debt information; and (6) inventory costing method.

**BE 3–9**
Calculating ratios
● LO9

Refer to the trial balance information in BE 3–5. Calculate the (a) current ratio, (b) acid-test ratio, and (c) debt to equity ratio.

**BE 3–10**
Effect of decisions on ratios
● LO9

At the end of 2006, Barker Corporation's preliminary trial balance indicated a current ratio of 1.2. Management is contemplating paying some of its accounts payable balance before the end of the fiscal year. Explain the effect this transaction would have on the current ratio. Would your answer be the same if the preliminary trial balance indicated a current ratio of .8?

**BE 3–11**
Calculating ratios; solving for unknowns
● LO9

The current asset section of Stibbe Pharmaceutical Company's balance sheet included cash of $20,000 and accounts receivable of $40,000. The only other current asset is inventories. The company's current ratio is 2.0 and its acid-test ratio is 1.5. Determine the ending balance in inventories and total current liabilities.

## EXERCISES

available with McGraw-Hill's Homework Manager www.mhhe.com/spiceland4e

**An alternate exercise and problem set is available on the text website: www.mhhe.com/spiceland4e**

**E 3–1**
Balance sheet; missing elements
● LO3 LO4 LO8

The following December 31, 2006, fiscal year-end account balance information is available for the Stonebridge Corporation:

| | |
|---|---|
| Cash and cash equivalents | $ 5,000 |
| Accounts receivable (net) | 20,000 |
| Inventories | 60,000 |
| Property, plant, and equipment (net) | 120,000 |
| Accounts payable | 44,000 |
| Wages payable | 15,000 |
| Paid-in-capital | 100,000 |

The only asset not listed is short-term investments. The only liabilities not listed are a $30,000 note payable due in two years and related accrued interest of $1,000 due in four months. The current ratio at year-end is 1.5:1.

**Required:**

Determine the following at December 31, 2006:

1. Total current assets
2. Short-term investments
3. Retained earnings

**E 3–2**
Balance sheet classification
● LO3 LO4

The following are the typical classifications used in a balance sheet:

a. Current assets
b. Investments and funds
c. Property, plant, and equipment
d. Intangible assets
e. Other assets
f. Current liabilities
g. Long-term liabilities
h. Paid-in-capital
i. Retained earnings

**Required:**

For each of the following balance sheet items, use the letters above to indicate the appropriate classification category. If the item is a contra account, place a minus sign before the chosen letter.

1. ____ Equipment
2. ____ Accounts payable
3. ____ Allowance for uncollectible accounts
4. ____ Land, held for investment
5. ____ Note payable, due in 5 years
6. ____ Unearned rent revenue
7. ____ Note payable, due in 6 months
8. ____ Income less dividends, accumulated
9. ____ Investment in XYZ Corp., long-term
10. ____ Inventories
11. ____ Patent
12. ____ Land, in use
13. ____ Accrued liabilities
14. ____ Prepaid rent
15. ____ Common stock
16. ____ Building, in use
17. ____ Cash
18. ____ Taxes payable

**E 3–3**
Balance sheet classification

● LO3 LO4

The following are the typical classifications used in a balance sheet:

a. Current assets
b. Investments and funds
c. Property, plant, and equipment
d. Intangible assets
e. Other assets
f. Current liabilities
g. Long-term liabilities
h. Paid-in-capital
i. Retained earnings

**Required:**

For each of the following 2006 balance sheet items, use the letters above to indicate the appropriate classification category. If the item is a contra account, place a minus sign before the chosen letter.

1. ____ Accrued interest payable
2. ____ Franchise
3. ____ Accumulated depreciation
4. ____ Prepaid insurance, for 2008
5. ____ Bonds payable, due in 10 years
6. ____ Current maturities of long-term debt
7. ____ Note payable, due in three months
8. ____ Long-term receivables
9. ____ Bond sinking fund, will be used to retire bonds in 10 years
10. ____ Supplies
11. ____ Machinery
12. ____ Land, in use
13. ____ Unearned revenue
14. ____ Copyrights
15. ____ Preferred stock
16. ____ Land, held for speculation
17. ____ Cash equivalents
18. ____ Wages payable

**E 3–4**
Balance sheet preparation

● LO2 through LO4

The following is a December 31, 2006, post-closing trial balance for the Jackson Corporation.

| Account Title | Debits | Credits |
|---|---|---|
| Cash | 40,000 | |
| Accounts receivable | 34,000 | |
| Inventories | 75,000 | |
| Prepaid rent | 16,000 | |
| Marketable securities (short term) | 10,000 | |
| Machinery | 145,000 | |
| Accumulated depreciation—machinery | | 11,000 |
| Patent (net of amortization) | 83,000 | |
| Accounts payable | | 8,000 |
| Wages payable | | 4,000 |
| Taxes payable | | 32,000 |
| Bonds payable (due in 10 years) | | 200,000 |
| Common stock | | 100,000 |
| Retained earnings | | 48,000 |
| Totals | 403,000 | 403,000 |

**Required:**

Prepare a classified balance sheet for Jackson Corporation at December 31, 2006.

**E 3–5**
Balance sheet preparation

● LO2 through LO4

The following is a December 31, 2006, post-closing trial balance for the Valley Pump Corporation.

| Account Title | Debits | Credits |
|---|---|---|
| Cash | 25,000 | |
| Accounts receivable | 56,000 | |
| Inventories | 81,000 | |
| Interest payable | | 10,000 |
| Marketable securities | 44,000 | |
| Land | 120,000 | |
| Buildings | 300,000 | |
| Accumulated depreciation—buildings | | 100,000 |
| Equipment | 75,000 | |

| | | |
|---|---|---|
| Accumulated depreciation—equipment | | 25,000 |
| Copyright (net of amortization) | 12,000 | |
| Prepaid expenses | 32,000 | |
| Accounts payable | | 65,000 |
| Unearned revenues | | 20,000 |
| Notes payable | | 250,000 |
| Allowance for uncollectible accounts | | 5,000 |
| Common stock | | 200,000 |
| Retained earnings | | 70,000 |
| Totals | 745,000 | 745,000 |

**Additional information:**

1. The $120,000 balance in the land account consists of $100,000 for the cost of land where the plant and office buildings are located. The remaining $20,000 represents the cost of land being held for speculation.
2. The $44,000 in the marketable securities account represents an investment in the common stock of another corporation. Valley intends to sell one-half of the stock within the next year.
3. The notes payable account consists of a $100,000 note due in six months and a $150,000 note due in three annual installments of $50,000 each, with the first payment due in August of 2007.

**Required:**

Prepare a classified balance sheet for the Valley Pump Corporation at December 31, 2006.

**E 3–6**
Balance sheet preparation; errors

● LO2 through LO4

The following balance sheet for the Los Gatos Corporation was prepared by a recently hired accountant. In reviewing the statement you notice several errors.

**LOS GATOS CORPORATION**
**Balance Sheet**
**At December 31, 2006**

| | |
|---|---|
| **Assets** | |
| Cash | $ 40,000 |
| Accounts receivable | 80,000 |
| Inventories | 55,000 |
| Machinery (net) | 120,000 |
| Franchise (net) | 30,000 |
| Total assets | $325,000 |
| **Liabilities and Shareholders' Equity** | |
| Accounts payable | $ 50,000 |
| Allowance for uncollectible accounts | 5,000 |
| Note payable | 55,000 |
| Bonds payable | 110,000 |
| Shareholders' equity | 105,000 |
| Total liabilities and shareholders' equity | $325,000 |

**Additional information:**

1. Cash includes a $20,000 bond sinking fund to be used for repayment of the bonds payable in 2010.
2. The cost of the machinery is $190,000.
3. Accounts receivable includes a $20,000 note receivable from a customer due in 2009.
4. The note payable includes accrued interest of $5,000. Principal and interest are both due on February 1, 2007.
5. The company began operations in 2001. Income less dividends since inception of the company totals $35,000.
6. 50,000 shares of no par common stock were issued in 2001. 100,000 shares are authorized.

**Required:**

Prepare a corrected, classified balance sheet.

**E 3–7**
Balance sheet; current versus noncurrent classification

● LO2 through LO4

Cone Corporation is in the process of preparing its December 31, 2006, balance sheet. There are some questions as to the proper classification of the following items:

a. $50,000 in cash set aside in a savings account to pay bonds payable. The bonds mature in 2010.
b. Prepaid rent of $24,000, covering the period January 1, 2007, through December 31, 2008.
c. Note payable of $200,000. The note is payable in annual installments of $20,000 each, with the first installment payable on March 1, 2007.
d. Accrued interest payable of $12,000 related to the note payable.
e. Investment in marketable securities of other corporations, $80,000. Cone intends to sell one-half of the securities in 2007.

**Required:**
Prepare a partial classified balance sheet to show how each of the above items should be reported.

**E 3–8**
Balance sheet preparation; cash versus accrual accounting; Chapters 2 and 3

● LO2 through LO4

The following is the balance sheet of Korver Supply Company at December 31, 2005.

**KORVER SUPPLY COMPANY**
**Balance Sheet**
**At December 31, 2005**

| | |
|---|---|
| **Assets** | |
| Cash | $120,000 |
| Accounts receivable | 300,000 |
| Inventories | 200,000 |
| Furniture and fixtures, net | 150,000 |
| Total assets | $770,000 |
| **Liabilities and Shareholders' Equity** | |
| Accounts payable (for merchandise) | $190,000 |
| Note payable | 200,000 |
| Interest payable | 6,000 |
| Common stock | 100,000 |
| Retained earnings | 274,000 |
| Total liabilities and shareholders' equity | $770,000 |

Transactions during 2006 were as follows:

| | | |
|---|---|---|
| 1. | Sales to customers on account | $800,000 |
| 2. | Cash collected from customers | 780,000 |
| 3. | Purchase of merchandise on account | 550,000 |
| 4. | Cash payment to suppliers | 560,000 |
| 5. | Cost of merchandise sold | 500,000 |
| 6. | Cash paid for operating expenses | 160,000 |
| 7. | Cash paid for interest on note | 12,000 |

The note payable is dated June 30, 2005 and is due on June 30, 2007. Interest at 6% is payable annually on June 30. Depreciation on the furniture and fixtures for the year is $20,000. The furniture and fixtures originally cost $300,000.

**Required:**
Prepare a classified balance sheet at December 21, 2006 (ignore income taxes).

**E 3–9**
Financial disclosures

● LO5

The following are typical disclosures that would appear in the notes accompanying financial statements. For each of the items listed, indicate where the disclosure would likely appear—either in (A) the significant accounting policies note or (B) a separate note.

| | | |
|---|---|---|
| 1. | Inventory costing method | A |
| 2. | Information on related party transactions | ____ |
| 3. | Composition of property, plant, and equipment | ____ |
| 4. | Depreciation method | ____ |
| 5. | Subsequent event information | ____ |
| 6. | Basis of revenue recognition on long-term contracts | ____ |
| 7. | Important merger occurring after year-end | ____ |
| 8. | Composition of receivables | ____ |

**E 3–10**
Disclosure notes

● LO5

Hallergan Company produces car and truck batteries that it sells primarily to auto manufacturers. Dorothy Hawkins, the company's controller, is preparing the financial statements for the year ended December 31, 2006. Hawkins asks for your advice concerning the following information that has not yet been included in the statements. The statements will be issued on February 28, 2007.

1. Hallergan leases its facilities from the brother of the chief executive officer.
2. On January 8, 2007, Hallergan entered into an agreement to sell a tract of land that it had been holding as an investment. The sale, which resulted in a material gain, was completed on February 2, 2007.
3. Hallergan uses the straight-line method to determine depreciation on all of the company's depreciable assets.
4. On February 8, 2007, Hallergan completed negotiations with its bank for a $10,000,000 line of credit.
5. Hallergan uses the first-in, first-out (FIFO) method to value inventory.

**Required:**
For each of the above items, discuss any additional disclosures that Hawkins should include in Hallergan's financial statements.

**E 3–11**
Multiple choice; financial disclosures
● LO5

The following questions dealing with disclosures are adapted from questions that appeared on CPA examinations. Determine the response that best completes the statements or questions.

1. What is the purpose of information presented in notes to the financial statements?
   a. To provide disclosure required by generally accepted accounting principles.
   b. To correct improper presentation in the financial statements.
   c. To provide recognition of amounts not included in the totals of the financial statements.
   d. To present management's responses to auditor comments.
2. Which of the following information should be disclosed in the summary of significant accounting policies?
   a. Refinancing of debt subsequent to the balance sheet date.
   b. Guarantees of indebtedness of others.
   c. Criteria for determining which investments are treated as cash equivalents.
   d. Adequacy of pension plan assets relative to vested benefits.
3. Which of the following facts concerning fixed assets should be included in the summary of significant accounting policies?

| | Depreciation Method | Composition |
|---|---|---|
| a. | No | Yes |
| b. | Yes | Yes |
| c. | Yes | No |
| d. | No | No |

**E 3–12**
Concepts; terminology
● LO2 through LO5 LO7

Listed below are several terms and phrases associated with the balance sheet and financial disclosures. Pair each item from List A (by letter) with the item from List B that is most appropriately associated with it.

| List A | List B |
|---|---|
| ____ 1. Balance sheet | a. Will be satisfied through the use of current assets. |
| ____ 2. Liquidity | b. Items expected to be converted to cash or consumed within one year or the operating cycle. |
| ____ 3. Current assets | c. The statements are presented fairly in conformity with GAAP. |
| ____ 4. Operating cycle | d. An organized array of assets, liabilities and equity. |
| ____ 5. Current liabilities | e. Important to a user in comparing financial information across companies. |
| ____ 6. Cash equivalent | f. Scope limitation or a departure from GAAP. |
| ____ 7. Intangible asset | g. Recorded when an expense is incurred but not yet paid. |
| ____ 8. Working capital | h. Relates to the amount of time before an asset is converted to cash or a liability is paid. |
| ____ 9. Accrued liabilities | i. Occurs after the fiscal year-end but before the statements are issued. |
| ____ 10. Summary of significant accounting policies | j. Cash to cash. |
| ____ 11. Subsequent events | k. One-month U.S. Treasury bill. |
| ____ 12. Unqualified opinion | l. Current assets minus current liabilities. |
| ____ 13. Qualified opinion | m. Lacks physical substance. |

**E 3–13**
Calculating ratios
● LO9

The 2006 balance sheet for Hallbrook Industries, Inc. is shown below.

**HALLBROOK INDUSTRIES, INC.**
**Balance Sheet**
**December 31, 2006**
($ in 000s)

| | |
|---|---|
| **Assets** | |
| Cash | $ 200 |
| Short-term investments | 150 |
| Accounts receivable | 200 |
| Inventories | 350 |
| Property, plant, and equipment (net) | 1,000 |
| Total assets | $1,900 |
| **Liabilities and Shareholders' Equity** | |
| Current liabilities | $ 400 |
| Long-term liabilities | 350 |
| Paid-in capital | 750 |
| Retained earnings | 400 |
| Total liabilities and shareholders' equity | $1,900 |

The company's 2006 income statement reported the following amounts ($ in 000s):

| | |
|---|---|
| Net sales | $4,600 |
| Interest expense | 40 |
| Income tax expense | 100 |
| Net income | 160 |

**Required:**

Determine the following ratios for 2006:

1. Current ratio
2. Acid-test ratio
3. Debt to equity ratio
4. Times interest earned ratio

**E 3–14**
Calculating ratios; solve for unknowns

● LO9

The current asset section of the Excalibur Tire Company's balance sheet consists of cash, marketable securities, accounts receivable, and inventories. The December 31, 2006, balance sheet revealed the following:

| | |
|---|---|
| Inventories | $ 840,000 |
| Total assets | $2,800,000 |
| Current ratio | 2.25 |
| Acid-test ratio | 1.2 |
| Debt to equity ratio | 1.8 |

**Required:**

Determine the following 2006 balance sheet items:

1. Current assets
2. Shareholders' equity
3. Noncurrent assets
4. Long-term liabilities

**E 3–15**
Effect of management decisions on ratios

● LO9

Most decisions made by management impact the ratios analysts use to evaluate performance. Indicate (by letter) whether each of the actions listed below will immediately increase (I), decrease (D), or have no effect (N) on the ratios shown. Assume each ratio is less than 1.0 before the action is taken.

| Action | Current Ratio | Acid-Test Ratio | Debt to Equity Ratio |
|---|---|---|---|
| 1. Issuance of long-term bonds | ____ | ____ | ____ |
| 2. Issuance of short-term notes | ____ | ____ | ____ |
| 3. Payment of accounts payable | ____ | ____ | ____ |
| 4. Purchase of inventory on account | ____ | ____ | ____ |
| 5. Purchase of inventory for cash | ____ | ____ | ____ |
| 6. Purchase of equipment with a 4-year note | ____ | ____ | ____ |
| 7. Retirement of bonds | ____ | ____ | ____ |
| 8. Sale of common stock | ____ | ____ | ____ |
| 9. Write-off of obsolete inventory | ____ | ____ | ____ |
| 10. Purchase of short-term investment for cash | ____ | ____ | ____ |
| 11. Decision to refinance on a long-term basis some currently maturing debt | ____ | ____ | ____ |

**E 3–16**
Multiple choice; ratio analysis

● LO8 LO9

The following questions dealing with ratio analysis are adapted from questions that appeared on CPA examinations. Determine the response that best completes the statements or questions.

1. At December 30, 2006, Vida Co. had cash of $200,000, a current ratio of 1.5:1 and a quick ratio of .5:1. On December 31, 2006, all cash was used to reduce accounts payable. How did these cash payments affect the ratios?

| | Current Ratio | Quick Ratio |
|---|---|---|
| a. | Increased | Decreased |
| b. | Increased | No Effect |
| c. | Decreased | Increased |
| d. | Decreased | No Effect |

2. In analyzing a company's financial statements, which financial statement would a potential investor primarily use to assess the company's liquidity and financial flexibility?
   a. Balance sheet.
   b. Income statement.
   c. Statement of retained earnings.
   d. Statement of cash flows.

**E 3-17**
Multiple choice; CMA exam; Disclosures and the current ratio

● LO5 LO6 LO9

The following questions dealing with financial disclosures and the current ratio are adapted from questions that previously appeared on Certified Management Accountant (CMA) examinations. The CMA designation sponsored by the Institute of Management Accountants (www.imanet.org) provides members with an objective measure of knowledge and competence in the field of management accounting. Determine the response that best completes the statements or questions.

1. The Financial Accounting Standards Board has provided guidance on disclosures of transactions between related parties, for example, transactions between subsidiaries of a common parent. SFAS 57, *Related Party Disclosures,* requires all of the following disclosures except
   a. The nature of the relationship involved.
   b. A description of the transactions for each period an income statement is presented.
   c. The dollar amounts of transactions for each period an income statement is presented.
   d. The effect on the cash flow statement for each period a cash flow statement is presented.
2. The Management's Discussion and Analysis (MD&A) section of an annual report
   a. Includes the company president's letter.
   b. Covers three financial aspects of a firm's business: liquidity, capital resources, and results of operations.
   c. Is a technical analysis of past results and a defense of those results by management.
   d. Covers marketing and product line issues.
3. Windham Company has current assets of $400,000 and current liabilities of $500,000. Windham Company's current ratio would be increased by
   a. The purchase of $100,000 of inventory on account.
   b. The payment of $100,000 of accounts payable.
   c. The collection of $100,000 of accounts receivable.
   d. Refinancing a $100,000 long-term loan with short-term debt.

**E 3–18**
[Based on Appendix 3]
Segment reporting

● LO5

The Canton Corporation operates in four distinct business segments. The segments, along with 2006 information on revenues, assets and net income, are listed below ($ in millions):

| Segment | Revenues | Assets | Net Income |
|---|---|---|---|
| Pharmaceuticals | $2,000 | $1,000 | $200 |
| Plastics | 3,000 | 1,500 | 270 |
| Farm equipment | 2,500 | 1,250 | 320 |
| Electronics | 500 | 250 | 40 |
| Total company | $8,000 | $4,000 | $830 |

**Required:**

1. For which segments must Canton report supplementary information according to *SFAS No. 131?*
2. What amounts must be reported for the segments you identified in requirement 1?

# PROBLEMS

available with McGraw-Hill's Homework Manager www.mhhe.com/spiceland4e

**An alternate exercise and problem set is available on the text website: www.mhhe.com/spiceland4e**

**P 3–1**
Balance sheet preparation

● LO2 through LO4

Presented below is a list of balance sheet accounts presented in alphabetical order.

| | |
|---|---|
| Accounts payable | Inventories |
| Accounts receivable | Land (in use) |
| Accumulated depreciation—buildings | Long-term investments |
| Accumulated depreciation—equipment | Notes payable (due in 6 months) |
| Allowance for uncollectible accounts | Notes receivable (due in 2 years) |
| Bond sinking fund | Patent |
| Bonds payable (due in 10 years) | Preferred stock |
| Buildings | Prepaid expenses |
| Cash | Rent payable (current) |
| Common stock | Retained earnings |
| Copyright | Short-term investments |
| Equipment | Taxes payable |
| Interest receivable (due in three months) | Wages payable |

**Required:**

Prepare a classified balance sheet ignoring monetary amounts.

**P 3–2**
Balance sheet preparation; missing elements

● LO2 through LO4

The data listed below are taken from a recent balance sheet of **Amdahl Corporation**. Some amounts, indicated by question marks, have been intentionally omitted.

| | ($ in 000s) |
|---|---|
| Cash and cash equivalents | $ 239,186 |
| Short-term investments | 353,700 |
| Accounts receivable (net of allowance) | 504,944 |
| Inventories | ? |
| Prepaid expenses (current) | 83,259 |
| Total current assets | 1,594,927 |
| Long-term receivables | 110,800 |
| Property and equipment (net) | ? |
| Total assets | ? |
| Notes payable and short-term debt | 31,116 |
| Accounts payable | ? |
| Accrued liabilities | 421,772 |
| Other current liabilities | 181,604 |
| Total current liabilities | 693,564 |
| Long-term debt and deferred taxes | ? |
| Total liabilities | 956,140 |
| Shareholders' equity | 1,370,627 |

**Required:**

1. Determine the missing amounts.
2. Prepare Amdahl's classified balance sheet.

**P 3–3**
Balance sheet preparation

● LO2 through LO4

eXcel

The following is a December 31, 2006, post-closing trial balance for Almway Corporation.

| Account Title | Debits | Credits |
|---|---|---|
| Cash | 45,000 | |
| Investments | 110,000 | |
| Accounts receivable | 60,000 | |
| Inventories | 200,000 | |
| Prepaid insurance | 9,000 | |
| Land | 90,000 | |
| Buildings | 420,000 | |
| Accumulated depreciation—buildings | | 100,000 |
| Equipment | 110,000 | |
| Accumulated depreciation—equipment | | 60,000 |
| Patents (net of amortization) | 10,000 | |
| Accounts payable | | 75,000 |
| Notes payable | | 130,000 |
| Interest payable | | 20,000 |
| Bonds payable | | 240,000 |
| Common stock | | 300,000 |
| Retained earnings | | 129,000 |
| Totals | 1,054,000 | 1,054,000 |

**Additional information:**

1. The investment account includes an investment in common stock of another corporation of $30,000 which management intends to hold for at least three years. The balance of these investments are intended to be sold in the coming year.
2. The land account includes land which cost $25,000 that the company has not used and is currently listed for sale.
3. The cash account includes $15,000 set aside in a fund to pay bonds payable that mature in 2009 and $23,000 set aside in a three-month Treasury bill.
4. The notes payable account consists of the following:
   a. a $30,000 note due in six months.
   b. a $50,000 note due in six years.
   c. a $50,000 note due in five annual installments of $10,000 each, with the next installment due February 15, 2007.
5. The $60,000 balance in accounts receivable is net of an allowance for uncollectible accounts of $8,000.
6. The common stock account represents 100,000 shares of no par value common stock issued and outstanding. The corporation has 500,000 shares authorized.

**Required:**

Prepare a classified balance sheet for the Almway Corporation at December 31, 2006.

**P 3–4**
Balance sheet preparation

● LO2 through LO4

excel

The following is a December 31, 2006, post-closing trial balance for the Weismuller Publishing Company.

| Account Title | Debits | Credits |
|---|---|---|
| Cash | 65,000 | |
| Accounts receivable | 160,000 | |
| Inventories | 285,000 | |
| Prepaid expenses | 148,000 | |
| Machinery and equipment | 320,000 | |
| Accumulated depreciation—equipment | | 110,000 |
| Investments | 140,000 | |
| Accounts payable | | 60,000 |
| Interest payable | | 20,000 |
| Unearned revenue | | 80,000 |
| Taxes payable | | 30,000 |
| Notes payable | | 200,000 |
| Allowance for uncollectible accounts | | 16,000 |
| Common stock | | 400,000 |
| Retained earnings | | 202,000 |
| Totals | 1,118,000 | 1,118,000 |

**Additional information:**

1. Prepaid expenses include $120,000 paid on December 31, 2006, for a two-year lease on the building that houses both the administrative offices and the manufacturing facility.
2. Investments include $30,000 in Treasury bills purchased on November 30, 2006. The bills mature on January 30, 2007. The remaining $110,000 includes investments in marketable equity securities that the company intends to sell in the next year.
3. Unearned revenue represents customer prepayments for magazine subscriptions. Subscriptions are for periods of one year or less.
4. The notes payable account consists of the following:
   a. a $40,000 note due in six months.
   b. a $100,000 note due in six years.
   c. a $60,000 note due in three annual installments of $20,000 each, with the next installment due August 31, 2007.
5. The common stock account represents 400,000 shares of no par value common stock issued and outstanding. The corporation has 800,000 shares authorized.

**Required:**

Prepare a classified balanced sheet for the Weismuller Publishing Company at December 31, 2006.

**P 3–5**
Balance sheet preparation

● LO2 through LO4

excel

The following is a June 30, 2006, post-closing trial balance for Excell Company.

| Account Title | Debits | Credits |
|---|---|---|
| Cash | 83,000 | |
| Short-term investments | 65,000 | |
| Accounts receivable | 280,000 | |
| Prepaid expenses | 32,000 | |
| Land | 75,000 | |
| Buildings | 320,000 | |
| Accumulated depreciation—buildings | | 160,000 |
| Equipment | 265,000 | |
| Accumulated depreciation—equipment | | 120,000 |
| Accounts payable | | 173,000 |
| Accrued expenses | | 45,000 |
| Notes payable | | 100,000 |
| Mortgage payable | | 250,000 |
| Common stock | | 100,000 |
| Retained earnings | | 172,000 |
| Totals | 1,120,000 | 1,120,000 |

**Additional information:**

1. The short-term investments account includes $18,000 in U.S. treasury bills purchased in May. The bills mature in July.

2. The accounts receivable account consists of the following:

| | | |
|---|---|---|
| a. | Amounts owed by customers | $225,000 |
| b. | Allowance for uncollectible accounts—trade customers | (15,000) |
| c. | Nontrade note receivable (due in three years) | 65,000 |
| d. | Interest receivable on note (due in four months) | 5,000 |
| | Total | $280,000 |

3. The notes payable account consists of two notes of $50,000 each. One note is due on September 30, 2006, and the other is due on November 30, 2007.
4. The mortgage payable is payable in *semiannual* installments of $5,000 each plus interest. The next payment is due on October 31, 2006. Interest has been properly accrued and is included in accrued expenses.
5. Five hundred thousand shares of no par common stock are authorized, of which 200,000 shares have been issued and are outstanding.
6. The land account includes $50,000 representing the cost of the land on which the company's office building resides. The remaining $25,000 is the cost of land that the company is holding for investment purposes.

**Required:**

Prepare a classified balance sheet for the Excell Company at June 30, 2006.

**P 3–6**
Balance sheet preparation; errors
• LO2 through LO4

The following balance sheet for the Hubbard Corporation was prepared by the company:

**HUBBARD CORPORATION**
**Balance Sheet**
**At December 31, 2006**

| Assets | |
|---|---|
| Buildings | $ 750,000 |
| Land | 250,000 |
| Cash | 60,000 |
| Accounts receivable (net) | 120,000 |
| Inventories | 240,000 |
| Machinery | 280,000 |
| Patent (net) | 100,000 |
| Investment in marketable equity securities | 60,000 |
| Total assets | $1,860,000 |
| **Liabilities and Shareholders' Equity** | |
| Accounts payable | $ 215,000 |
| Accumulated depreciation | 255,000 |
| Notes payable | 500,000 |
| Appreciation of inventories | 80,000 |
| Common stock, authorized and issued 100,000 shares of no par stock | 430,000 |
| Retained earnings | 380,000 |
| Total liabilities and shareholders' equity | $1,860,000 |

**Additional information:**

1. The buildings, land, and machinery are all stated at cost except for a parcel of land that the company is holding for future sale. The land originally cost $50,000 but, due to a significant increase in market value, is listed at $120,000. The increase in the land account was credited to retained earnings.
2. Marketable equity securities consist of stocks of other corporations and are recorded at cost, $20,000 of which will be sold in the coming year. The remainder will be held indefinitely.
3. Notes payable are all long-term. However, a $100,000 note requires an installment payment of $25,000 due in the coming year.
4. Inventories are recorded at current resale value. The original cost of the inventories is $160,000.

**Required:**

Prepare a corrected classified balance sheet for the Hubbard Corporation at December 31, 2006.

**P 3–7**
Balance sheet preparation
• LO2 through LO4

Presented below is the balance sheet for HHD, Inc., at December 31, 2006.

| | | | |
|---|---|---|---|
| Current assets | $ 600,000 | Current liabilities | $ 400,000 |
| Investments | 500,000 | Long-term liabilities | 1,100,000 |
| Property, plant, and equipment | 2,000,000 | Shareholders' equity | 1,800,000 |
| Intangible assets | 200,000 | | |
| Total assets | $3,300,000 | Total liabilities and shareholders' equity | $3,300,000 |

The captions shown in the summarized statement above include the following:

a. Current assets: cash, $150,000; accounts receivable, $200,000; inventories, $225,000; and prepaid insurance, $25,000.
b. Investments: investments in common stock, short term, $90,000, and long term, $160,000; and bond sinking fund, $250,000.
c. Property, plant, and equipment: buildings, $1,500,000 less accumulated depreciation, $600,000; equipment, $500,000 less accumulated depreciation, $200,000; and land, $800,000.
d. Intangible assets: patent, $110,000; and copyright, $90,000.
e. Current liabilities: accounts payable, $100,000; notes payable, short term, $150,000, and long term, $90,000; and taxes payable, $60,000.
f. Long-term liabilities: bonds payable due 2011.
g. Shareholders' equity: preferred stock, $450,000; common stock, $1,000,000; retained earnings, $350,000.

**Required:**

Prepare a corrected classified balance sheet for HHD, Inc., at December 31, 2006.

**P 3–8**
**Balance sheet preparation**
● LO2 through LO4

Melody Lane Music Company was started by John Ross early in 2006. Initial capital was acquired by issuing shares of common stock to various investors and by obtaining a bank loan. The company operates a retail store that sells records, tapes, and compact discs. Business was so good during the first year of operations that John is considering opening a second store on the other side of town. The funds necessary for expansion will come from a new bank loan. In order to approve the loan, the bank requires financial statements.

John asks for your help in preparing the balance sheet and presents you with the following information for the year ending December 31, 2006:

a. Cash receipts consisted of the following:

| | |
|---|---|
| From customers | $360,000 |
| From issue of common stock | 100,000 |
| From bank loan | 100,000 |

b. Cash disbursements were as follows:

| | |
|---|---|
| Purchase of inventory | $300,000 |
| Rent | 15,000 |
| Salaries | 30,000 |
| Utilities | 5,000 |
| Insurance | 3,000 |
| Purchase of equipment and furniture | 40,000 |

c. The bank loan was made on March 31, 2006. A note was signed requiring payment of interest and principal on March 31, 2007. The interest rate is 12%.
d. The equipment and furniture were purchased on January 3, 2006, and have an estimated useful life of 10 years with no anticipated salvage value. Depreciation per year is $4,000.
e. Inventories on hand at the end of the year cost $100,000.
f. Amounts owed at December 31, 2006, were as follows:

| | |
|---|---|
| To suppliers of inventory | $20,000 |
| To the utility company | 1,000 |

g. Rent on the store building is $1,000 per month. On December 1, 2006, four months' rent was paid in advance.
h. Net income for the year was $76,000. Assume that the company is not subject to federal, state, or local income tax.

**Required:**

Prepare a balance sheet at December 31, 2006.

# BROADEN YOUR PERSPECTIVE

**Apply your critical-thinking ability to the knowledge you've gained. These cases will provide you an opportunity to develop your research, analysis, judgment, and communication skills. You also will work with other students, integrate what you've learned, apply it in real world situations, and consider its global and ethical ramifications. This practice will broaden your knowledge and further develop your decision-making abilities.**

**Communication Case 3–1**
Current versus noncurrent classification

● LO2

A first-year accounting student is confused by a statement made in a recent class. Her instructor stated that the assets listed in the balance sheet of the **IBM Corporation** include computers that are classified as current assets as well as computers that are classified as noncurrent assets. In addition, the instructor stated that investments in marketable securities of other corporations could be classified in the balance sheet as either current or noncurrent assets.

**Required:**

Explain to the student the distinction between current and noncurrent assets pertaining to the IBM computers and the investments in marketable securities.

**Analysis Case 3–2**
Current versus noncurrent classification

● LO2

The usefulness of the balance sheet is enhanced when assets and liabilities are grouped according to common characteristics. The broad distinction made in the balance sheet is the current versus noncurrent classification of both assets and liabilities.

**Required:**

1. Discuss the factors that determine whether an asset or liability should be classified as current or noncurrent in a balance sheet.
2. Identify six items that under different circumstances could be classified as either current or noncurrent. Indicate the factors that would determine the correct classification.

**Communication Case 3–3**
Inventory or property, plant, and equipment

● LO2 LO3

The Red Hen Company produces, processes, and sells fresh eggs. The company is in the process of preparing financial statements at the end of its first year of operations and has asked for your help in determining the appropriate treatment of the cost of its egg-laying flock. The estimated life of a laying hen is approximately two years, after which they are sold to soup companies.

The controller considers the company's operating cycle to be two years and wants to present the cost of the egg-producing flock as inventory in the current asset section of the balance sheet. He feels that the hens are "goods awaiting sale." The chief financial officer does not agree with this treatment. He thinks that the cost of the flock should be classified as property, plant, and equipment because the hens are used in the production of product—the eggs.

The focus of this case is the balance sheet presentation of the cost of the egg-producing flock. Your instructor will divide the class into two to six groups depending on the size of the class. The mission of your group is to reach consensus on the appropriate presentation.

**Required:**

1. Each group member should deliberate the situation independently and draft a tentative argument prior to the class session for which the case is assigned.
2. In class, each group will meet for 10 to 15 minutes in different areas of the classroom. During that meeting, group members will take turns sharing their suggestions for the purpose of arriving at a single group treatment.
3. After the allotted time, a spokesperson for each group (selected during the group meetings) will share the group's solution with the class. The goal of the class is to incorporate the views of each group into a consensus approach to the situation.

**Judgment Case 3–4**
Balance sheet; errors

● LO2 through LO5

You recently joined the internal auditing department of Marcus Clothing Corporation. As one of your first assignments, you are examining a balance sheet prepared by a staff accountant.

**MARCUS CLOTHING CORPORATION**
**Balance Sheet**
**At December 31, 2006**

| | | |
|---|---|---|
| **Assets** | | |
| Current assets: | | |
| Cash | | $ 137,000 |
| Accounts receivable, net | | 80,000 |
| Note receivable | | 53,000 |
| Inventories | | 240,000 |
| Investments | | 66,000 |
| Total current assets | | 576,000 |
| Other assets: | | |
| Land | $200,000 | |
| Equipment, net | 320,000 | |
| Prepaid expenses | 27,000 | |
| Patent | 22,000 | |
| Total other assets | | 569,000 |
| Total assets | | $1,145,000 |

**Liabilities and Shareholders' Equity**

| | | |
|---|---|---|
| Current liabilities: | | |
| Accounts payable | | $ 125,000 |
| Salaries payable | | 32,000 |
| Total current liabilities | | 157,000 |
| Long-term liabilities: | | |
| Note payable | $100,000 | |
| Bonds payable | 300,000 | |
| Interest payable | 20,000 | |
| Total long-term liabilities | | 420,000 |
| Shareholders' equity: | | |
| Common stock | 500,000 | |
| Retained earnings | 68,000 | |
| Total shareholders' equity | | 568,000 |
| Total liabilities and shareholders' equity | | $1,145,000 |

In the course of your examination you uncover the following information pertaining to the balance sheet:

1. The company rents its facilities. The land that appears in the statement is being held for future sale.
2. The note receivable is due in 2008. The balance of $53,000 includes $3,000 of accrued interest. The next interest payment is due in July 2007.
3. The note payable is due in installments of $20,000 per year. Interest on both the notes and bonds is payable annually.
4. The company's investments consist of marketable equity securities of other corporations. Management does not intend to liquidate any investments in the coming year.

**Required:**

Identify and explain the deficiencies in the statement prepared by the company's accountant. Include in your answer items that require additional disclosure, either on the face of the statement or in a note.

**Judgment Case 3–5**
Financial disclosures

● LO5

You recently joined the auditing staff of Best, Best, and Krug, CPAs. You have been assigned to the audit of Clearview, Inc., and have been asked by the audit senior to examine the balance sheet prepared by Clearview's accountant.

**CLEARVIEW, INC.**
**Balance Sheet**
**At December 31, 2006**
($ in millions)

**Assets**

| | | |
|---|---|---|
| Current assets: | | |
| Cash | | $ 10.5 |
| Accounts receivable | | 112.1 |
| Inventories | | 220.6 |
| Prepaid expenses | | 5.5 |
| Total current assets | | 348.7 |
| Investments | | 22.0 |
| Property, plant, and equipment, net | | 486.9 |
| Total assets | | $857.6 |

**Liabilities and Shareholders' Equity**

| | | |
|---|---|---|
| Current liabilities: | | |
| Accounts payable | | $ 83.5 |
| Accrued taxes and interest | | 25.5 |
| Current maturities of long-term debt | | 20.0 |
| Total current liabilities | | 129.0 |
| Long-term liabilities: | | 420.0 |
| Total liabilities | | 549.0 |
| Shareholders' equity: | | |
| Common stock | $100.0 | |
| Retained earnings | 208.6 | |
| Total shareholders' equity | | 308.6 |
| Total liabilities and shareholders' equity | | $857.6 |

**Required:**

Identify the items in the statement that most likely would require further disclosure either on the face of the statement or in a note. Further identify those items that would require disclosure in the significant accounting policies note.

**Real World Case 3–6**
Balance sheet and significant accounting policies disclosure

- LO3 through LO5 LO9

The balance sheet and disclosure of significant accounting policies taken from the 2004 annual report of **International Business Machines Corporation (IBM)** appear below. Use this information to answer the following questions:

1. What are the asset classifications contained in IBM's balance sheet?
2. What amounts did IBM report for the following items for 2004:
   a. Total assets
   b. Current assets
   c. Current liabilities
   d. Total shareholders' equity
   e. Retained earnings
   f. Inventories
3. What is the par value of IBM's common stock? How many shares of common stock are authorized and issued at the end of 2004?
4. Compute IBM's current ratio for 2004.
5. Identify the following items:
   a. The company's inventory valuation method.
   b. The company's depreciation method.
   c. The definition of cash equivalents.

**CONSOLIDATED STATEMENT OF FINANCIAL POSITION**
**INTERNATIONAL BUSINESS MACHINES CORPORATION**
**and Subsidiary Companies**
($ in millions)

| | | At December 31: | |
|---|---|---|---|
| | **Notes** | **2004** | **2003** |
| **Assets** | | | |
| Current assets: | | | |
| Cash and cash equivalents | | $ 10,053 | $ 7,290 |
| Marketable securities | D | 517 | 357 |
| Notes and accounts receivable—trade (net of allowances of $277 in 2004 and $352 in 2003) | | 10,522 | 10,026 |
| Short-term financing receivables (net of allowances of $681 in 2004 and $733 in 2003) | F | 15,801 | 17,583 |
| Other accounts receivable (net of allowances of $13 in 2004 and $16 in 2003) | | 1,813 | 1,314 |
| Inventories | E | 3,316 | 2,942 |
| Deferred taxes | P | 2,229 | 2,542 |
| Prepaid expenses and other current assets | | 2,719 | 2,608 |
| Total current assets | | 46,970 | 44,662 |
| Plant, rental machines, and other property | G | 36,385 | 36,153 |
| Less: Accumulated depreciation | G | 21,210 | 21,464 |
| Plant, rental machines, and other property—net | G | 15,175 | 14,689 |
| Long-term financing receivables | F | 10,950 | 10,741 |
| Prepaid pension assets | W | 20,394 | 18,426 |
| Investments and sundry assets | H | 5,468 | 7,294 |
| Goodwill | I | 8,437 | 6,921 |
| Intangible assets—net | I | 1,789 | 1,724 |
| Total assets | | $109,183 | $104,457 |
| **Liabilities and Stockholders' Equity** | | | |
| Current liabilities: | | | |
| Taxes | P | $ 4,728 | $ 5,475 |
| Short-term debt | K & L | 8,099 | 6,646 |
| Accounts payable | | 9,444 | 8,460 |
| Compensation and benefits | | 3,804 | 3,671 |
| Deferred income | | 7,175 | 6,492 |
| Other accrued expenses and liabilities | | 6,548 | 6,879 |
| Total current liabilities | | 39,798 | 37,623 |

| | | | |
|---|---|---|---|
| Long-term debt | K & L | 14,828 | 16,986 |
| Retirement and nonpension postretirement benefit obligations | W | 15,883 | 14,251 |
| Other liabilities | M | 8,927 | 7,733 |
| Total liabilities | | 79,436 | 76,593 |
| Contingencies and commitments | O | | |
| Stockholders' equity: | N | | |
| Common stock, par value $.20 per share and additional paid-in capital | | 18,355 | 16,269 |
| Shares authorized: 4,687,500,000 | | | |
| Shares issued (2004–1,962,687,087; 2003–1,937,393,604) | | | |
| Retained earnings | | 44,525 | 37,525 |
| Treasury stock, at cost (shares: 2004–317, 094,633; 2003–242,884,969) | | (31,072) | (24,034) |
| Accumulated gains and (losses) not affecting retained earnings | | (2,061) | (1,896) |
| Total stockholders' equity | | 29,747 | 27,864 |
| Total liabilities and stockholders' equity | | $109,183 | $104,457 |

**NOTES TO CONSOLIDATED FINANCIAL STATEMENTS**
**INTERNATIONAL BUSINESS MACHINES CORPORATION**
**AND SUBSIDIARY COMPANIES**

**A. Significant accounting policies (in part)**

*Revenue*

The company recognizes revenue when it is realized or realizable and earned. The company considers revenue realized or realizable and earned when it has persuasive evidence of an arrangement, the product has been shipped or the services provided to the customer, the sales price is fixed or determinable and collectibility is reasonably assured. The company reduces revenue for estimated client returns, stock rotation, price protection, rebates, and other similar allowances.

*Cash Equivalents*

All highly liquid investments with a maturity of three months or less at date of purchase are carried at fair value and considered to be cash equivalents.

*Inventories*

Raw materials, work in process, and finished goods are stated at the lower of average cost or net realizable value.

*Depreciation*

Plant, rental machines and other property are carried at cost, and depreciated over their estimated useful lives using the straight-line method.

**Judgment Case 3–7**
Post fiscal year-end events

● LO5

The fiscal year-end for the Northwest Distribution Corporation is December 31. The company's 2006 financial statements were issued on March 15, 2007. The following events occurred between December 31, 2006, and March 15, 2007.

1. On January 22, 2007, the company negotiated a major merger with Blandon Industries. The merger will be completed by the middle of 2007.
2. On February 3, 2007, Northwest negotiated a $10 million long-term note with the Credit Bank of Ohio. The amount of the note is material.
3. On February 25, 2007, a flood destroyed one of the company's manufacturing plants causing $600,000 of uninsured damage.

**Required:**

Determine the appropriate treatment of each of these events in the 2006 financial statements of Northwest Distribution Corporation.

**Research Case 3–8**
Related party disclosures; locate and extract relevant information and authoritative support for a financial reporting issue; Enron Corporation

● LO5

**Enron Corporation** was a darling in the energy-provider arena and in January of 2001 its stock price rose above $100 per share. A collapse of investor confidence in 2001 and revelations of accounting irregularities led to one of the largest bankruptcies in U.S. history. By the end of the year, its stock price had plummeted to less than $1 per share. Investigations and lawsuits followed. One problem area concerned transactions with related parties that were not adequately disclosed in the company's financial statements. Critics stated that the lack of information about these transactions made it difficult for analysts following Enron to identify problems the company was experiencing.

**Required:**

1. Consult the Summaries of FASB pronouncements at **www.fasb.org** or access the pronouncements from some other source. What authoritative pronouncement requires the disclosure of related-party transactions? When did the requirement become effective?
2. Describe the disclosures required for related-party transactions.

3. Use Edgarscan (**edgarscan.pwcglobal.com**) or another method to locate the December 31, 2000, financial statements of Enron. Search for the related-party disclosure. Briefly describe the relationship central to the numerous transactions described.
4. Why is it important that companies disclose related-party transactions? Use the Enron disclosure of the sale of dark fiber inventory in your answer.

**Research Case 3–9**
Disclosure of debt covenants

● LO5

Classifying a liability as short or long term provides useful cash flow information to financial statement users. Additional cash flow information is contained in a disclosure note that provides information about the payment terms, interest rates, collateral, and scheduled maturity amounts of long-term debt. Quite often, debt agreements contain certain constraints placed by the lender on the borrower in order to protect the lender's investment. Many of these constraints, called *debt covenants,* are based on accounting information. Professors Press and Weintrop in "Financial Statement Disclosure of Accounting-Based Debt Covenants" investigate the adequacy of debt covenant disclosures in financial statements.

**Required:**

1. In your library or from some other source, locate the indicated article in *Accounting Horizons,* March 1991.
2. Describe the two types of accounting-based debt covenants—affirmative covenants and negative covenants—discussed by the authors.
3. What is the authors' conclusion about the adequacy of disclosure of accounting-based covenants in financial statements?

**International Case 3–10**
Comparison of audit reports in the U.K. and the United States

● LO7

**British Airways Plc** is the largest international passenger airline in the world. The following is the Report of the Auditors accompanying the company's 2004 financial statements:

**Independent Auditors' Report to the Members of British Airways Plc**
We have audited the group's financial statements for the year ended March 31, 2004 which comprise the Consolidated Profit and Loss Account, Consolidated Balance Sheet, Company Balance Sheet, Consolidated Cash Flow Statement, Statement of Total Recognized Gains and Losses, Reconciliation of Movements in Shareholders' Funds, and the related notes 1 to 46. These financial statements have been prepared on the basis of the accounting policies set out therein.

**Respective responsibilities of directors and auditors (in part)**
The directors are responsible for preparing the annual report, including the financial statements which are required to be prepared in accordance with applicable United Kingdom law and accounting standards as set out in the statement of directors' responsibilities in relation to the financial statements. Our responsibility is to audit the financial statements in accordance with relevant legal and regulatory requirements, United Kingdom Auditing Standards and the Listing Rules of the Financial Services Authority. We report to you our opinion as to whether the financial statements give a true and fair view and whether the financial statements have been properly prepared in accordance with the Companies Act.

**Basis of audit opinion**
We conducted our audit in accordance with United Kingdom Auditing Standards issued by the Auditing Practices Board. An audit includes examination, on a test basis, of evidence relevant to the amounts and disclosures in the financial statements. It also includes an assessment of the significant estimates and judgments made by the directors in the preparation of the financial statements and of whether the accounting policies are appropriate to the group's circumstances, consistently applied and adequately disclosed.
We planned and performed our audit so as to obtain all the information and explanations which we considered necessary in order to provide us with sufficient evidence to give reasonable assurance that the financial statements are free from material misstatement, whether caused by fraud or other irregularity or error. In forming our opinion we also evaluated the overall adequacy of the presentation of information in the financial statements.

**Opinion**
In our opinion the financial statements give a true and fair view of the state of affairs of the Company and of the Group at March 31, 2004 and of the profit of the group for the year then ended; and the financial statements have been properly prepared in accordance with the Companies Act of 1985.
Ernst & Young
Registered Auditor
London
May 17, 2004

**Required:**

Compare the auditors' report in the United Kingdom with that of the United States.

**Real World Case 3–11**
Disclosures; proxy statement

● LO5 LO7

EDGAR, the Electronic Data Gathering, Analysis, and Retrieval system, performs automated collection, validation, indexing, and forwarding of submissions by companies and others who are required by law to file forms with the SEC. All publicly traded domestic companies use EDGAR to make the majority of their filings. (Some foreign companies file voluntarily.) Form 10-K or 10-KSB, which includes the annual report, is required to be filed on EDGAR. The SEC makes this information available on the Internet.

**Required:**

1. Access EDGAR on the Internet. The web address is **www.sec.gov**. Edgarscan (**edgarscan. pwcglobal. com**) from PricewaterhouseCoopers makes the process of accessing data from EDGAR easier.
2. Search for the **Briggs & Stratton Corp.**, a company engaged in the production of engines and power equipment in the United States. Access the 10-K filing for the fiscal year ended June 27, 2004. Search or scroll to find the disclosure notes and audit report.
3. Answer the following questions:
   a. Describe the subsequent event disclosed by the company.
   b. Which firm is the company's auditor? What type of opinion did the auditor render? Does the audit report contain any explanatory paragraphs?
4. Access the proxy statement filed with the SEC on September 9, 2004 (the proxy statement designation is Def 14A) and answer the following questions:
   a. What is the principal position of J. S. Shiely?
   b. What was the annual compensation paid to Mr. Shiely?

**Judgment Case 3–12**
Debt versus equity

● LO8

A common problem facing any business entity is the debt versus equity decision. When funds are required to obtain assets, should debt or equity financing be used? This decision also is faced when a company is initially formed. What will be the mix of debt versus equity in the initial capital structure? The characteristics of debt are very different from those of equity as are the financial implications of using one method of financing as opposed to the other.

Cherokee Plastics Corporation is formed by a group of investors to manufacture household plastic products. Their initial capitalization goal is $50,000,000. That is, the incorporators have decided to raise $50,000,000 to acquire the initial operating assets of the company. They have narrowed down the financing mix alternatives to two:

1. All equity financing.
2. $20,000,000 in debt financing and $30,000,000 in equity financing.

No matter which financing alternative is chosen, the corporation expects to be able to generate a 10% annual return, before payment of interest and income taxes, on the $50,000,000 in assets acquired. The interest rate on debt would be 8%. The effective income tax rate will be approximately 50%.

Alternative 2 will require specified interest and principal payments to be made to the creditors at specific dates. The interest portion of these payments (interest expense) will reduce the taxable income of the corporation and hence the amount of income tax the corporation will pay. The all-equity alternative requires no specified payments to be made to suppliers of capital. The corporation is not legally liable to make distributions to its owners. If the board of directors does decide to make a distribution, it is not an expense of the corporation and does not reduce taxable income and hence the taxes the corporation pays.

**Required:**

1. Prepare abbreviated income statements that compare first-year profitability for each of the two alternatives.
2. Which alternative would be expected to achieve the highest first-year profits? Why?
3. Which alternative would provide the highest rate of return on shareholders' equity? Why?
4. What other related implications of the decision should be considered?

**Analysis Case 3–13**
Obtain and critically evaluate an actual annual report

● LO5 LO7 through LO9

Financial reports are the primary means by which corporations report their performance and financial condition. Financial statements are one component of the annual report mailed to their shareholders and to interested others.

**Required:**

Obtain an annual report from a corporation with which you are familiar. Using techniques you learned in this chapter and any analysis you consider useful, respond to the following questions:

1. Do the firm's auditors provide a clean opinion on the financial statements?
2. Has the company made changes in any accounting methods it uses?
3. Have there been any subsequent events, errors and irregularities, illegal acts, or related-party transactions that have a material effect on the company's financial position?
4. What are two trends in the company's operations or capital resources that management considers significant to the company's future?
5. Is the company engaged in more than one significant line of business? If so, compare the relative profitability of the different segments.
6. How stable are the company's operations?
7. Has the company's situation deteriorated or improved with respect to liquidity, solvency, asset management, and profitability?

**Note:** You can obtain a copy of an annual report from a local company, from a friend who is a shareholder, from the investor relations department of the corporation, from a friendly stockbroker, or from EDGAR (Electronic Data Gathering, Analysis, and Retrieval) on the Internet (**www.sec.gov** or through Edgarscan at **edgarscan.pwcglobal.com**).

**Analysis Case 3–14**
Obtain and compare annual reports from companies in the same industry

● LO5 LO8 LO9

Insight concerning the performance and financial condition of a company often comes from evaluating its financial data in comparison with other firms in the same industry.

**Required:**

Obtain annual reports from three corporations in the same primary industry. Using techniques you learned in this chapter and any analysis you consider useful, respond to the following questions:

1. Are there differences in accounting methods that should be taken into account when making comparisons?
2. How do earnings trends compare in terms of both the direction and stability of income?
3. Which of the three firms had the greatest earnings relative to resources available?
4. Which corporation has made most effective use of financial leverage?
5. Of the three firms, which seems riskiest in terms of its ability to pay short-term obligations? Long-term obligations?

**Note:** You can obtain copies of annual reports from friends who are shareholders, from the investor relations department of the corporations, from a friendly stockbroker, or from EDGAR (Electronic Data Gathering, Analysis, and Retrieval) on the Internet (**www.sec.gov** or through Edgarscan at **edgarscan.pwcglobal.com**).

**Analysis Case 3–15**
Balance sheet information

● LO3 through LO5

**FedEx Corporation**

Refer to the financial statements and related disclosure notes of **FedEx Corporation** in Appendix B, located at the back of this text.

**Required:**

1. What categories does the company use to classify its assets? Its liabilities?
2. Why are "Spare parts, supplies and fuel" shown as a current asset?
3. Explain the current liability "current portion of long-term debt."
4. What purpose do the disclosure notes serve?
5. What method does the company use to depreciate its property and equipment?
6. Does the company report any subsequent events or related party transactions in its disclosure notes?

**Analysis Case 3–16**
[Based on Appendix 3]
Segment reporting concepts

● LO5

Levens Co. operates in several distinct business segments. The company does not have any reportable foreign operations or major customers.

**Required:**

1. What is the purpose of operating segment disclosures?
2. Define an operating segment.
3. List the amounts to be reported by operating segment.

**Ethics Case 3–17**
[Based on Appendix 3]
Segment reporting

● LO5

You are in your third year as an accountant with McCarver-Lynn Industries, a multidivisional company involved in the manufacturing, marketing, and sales of surgical prosthetic devices. After the fiscal year-end, you are working with the controller of the firm to prepare supplemental business segment disclosures. Yesterday you presented her with the following summary information:

| | ($ in millions) | | | | | |
|---|---|---|---|---|---|---|
| | **Domestic** | **Union of South Africa** | **Egypt** | **France** | **Denmark** | **Total** |
| Revenues | $ 845 | $222 | $265 | $343 | $311 | $1,986 |
| Capital expenditures | 145 | 76 | 88 | 21 | 42 | 372 |
| Assets | 1,005 | 301 | 290 | 38 | 285 | 1,919 |

Upon returning to your office after lunch, you find the following memo:

*Nice work. Let's combine the data this way*

| | ($ in millions) | | | |
|---|---|---|---|---|
| | **Domestic** | **Africa** | **Europe** | **Total** |
| Revenues | $845 | $487 | $654 | $1,986 |
| Capital expenditures | 145 | 164 | 63 | 372 |
| Assets | 1,005 | 591 | 323 | 1,919 |

*Some of our shareholders might react unfavorably to our recent focus on South African operations.*

**Required:**

Do you perceive an ethical dilemma? What would be the likely impact of following the controller's suggestions? Who would benefit? Who would be injured?

# 4

CHAPTER

# The Income Statement and Statement of Cash Flows

## OVERVIEW

The purpose of the income statement is to summarize the profit-generating activities that occurred during a particular reporting period. The purpose of the statement of cash flows is to provide information about the cash receipts and cash disbursements of an enterprise that occurred during the period.

This chapter has a twofold purpose: (1) to consider important issues dealing with income statement content, presentation, and disclosure and (2) to provide an *overview* of the statement of cash flows, which is covered in depth in Chapter 21.

## LEARNING OBJECTIVES

After studying this chapter, you should be able to:

- LO1 Explain the difference between net income and comprehensive income and how we report components of the difference.
- LO2 Discuss the importance of income from continuing operations and describe its components.
- LO3 Describe earnings quality and how it is impacted by management practices to manipulate earnings.
- LO4 Discuss the components of operating and nonoperating income and their relationship to earnings quality.
- LO5 Define what constitutes discontinued operations and describe the appropriate income statement presentation for these transactions.
- LO6 Define extraordinary items and describe the appropriate income statement presentation for these transactions.
- LO7 Describe the measurement and reporting requirements for a change in accounting principle.
- LO8 Explain the accounting treatments of changes in estimates and correction of errors.
- LO9 Define earnings per share (EPS) and explain required disclosures of EPS for certain income statement components.
- LO10 Describe the purpose of the statement of cash flows.
- LO11 Identify and describe the various classifications of cash flows presented in a statement of cash flows.

# FINANCIAL REPORTING CASE

## Precision Castparts Corporation

Your friend, Becky Morgan, has just received a generous gift from her grandfather. Accompanying a warm letter were 200 shares of stock of Precision Castparts Corporation, a worldwide manufacturer of complex metal components and products, along with the most recent financial statements of the company. Becky knows that you are an accounting major and pleads with you to explain some items in the company's income statement. "I remember studying the income statement in my introductory accounting course," says Becky, "but I am still confused. What is this item *discontinued operations?* And how about *restructuring costs?* These don't sound good. Are these something I should worry about?" You agree to try to help.

**PRECISION CASTPARTS CORPORATION**
**Income Statements**
**Years Ended March 31**
($ in millions)

| | 2004 | 2003 | 2002 |
|---|---|---|---|
| Net sales | $2,175 | $2,077 | $2,448 |
| Operating costs and expenses: | | | |
| Cost of goods sold | 1,679 | 1,587 | 1,898 |
| Selling and administrative | 204 | 180 | 199 |
| Restructuring costs | 12 | 22 | 16 |
| Other | 2 | – | 90 |
| Total operating costs and expenses | 1,897 | 1,789 | 2,203 |
| Operating income | 278 | 288 | 245 |
| Other income (expense): | | | |
| Interest expense | (54) | (56) | (66) |
| Other | (11) | 14 | – |
| Income before taxes | 213 | 246 | 179 |
| Income tax expense | 77 | 85 | 97 |
| Income from continuing operations | 136 | 161 | 82 |
| Loss from discontinued operations, net of tax | 18 | 37 | 39 |
| Net income | $ 118 | $ 124 | $ 43 |

(continued)

(concluded)

By the time you finish this chapter, you should be able to respond appropriately to the questions posed in this case. Compare your response to the solution provided at the end of the chapter.

## QUESTIONS

1. How would you explain restructuring costs to Becky? Are they necessarily a negative? (page 164)
2. In addition to discontinued operations, what other events sometimes are reported separately in the income statement that you might tell Becky about? Why are these events reported separately? (page 168)
3. Explain to Becky what is meant by discontinued operations and describe to her how one is reported in an income statement. (page 170)

In Chapter 1 we discussed the critical role of financial accounting information in allocating resources within our economy. Ideally, resources should be allocated to private enterprises that will (1) provide the goods and services our society desires and (2) at the same time provide a fair rate of return to those who supply the resources. A company will be able to achieve these goals only if it can use the resources society provides to generate revenues from selling products and services that exceed the expenses necessary to provide those products and services (that is, generate a profit).

The income statement displays a company's operating performance, that is, its net profit or loss, during the reporting period.

The purpose of the **income statement,** sometimes called the **statement of operations** or **statement of earnings,** is to summarize the profit-generating activities that occurred during a particular reporting period. Many investors and creditors perceive it as the statement most useful for predicting future profitability (future cash-generating ability).

The purpose of the **statement of cash flows** is to provide information about the cash receipts and cash disbursements of an enterprise that occurred during a period. In describing cash flows, the statement provides valuable information about the operating, investing, and financing activities that occurred during the period.

The *income statement* and *statement of cash flows* report changes that occurred during a particular reporting period.

Unlike the balance sheet, which is a position statement, the income statement and the statement of cash flows are *change* statements. The income statement reports the changes in shareholders' equity (retained earnings) that occurred during the reporting period as a result of revenues, expenses, gains, and losses. The statement of cash flows also is a change statement, disclosing the events that caused cash to change during the period.

This chapter is divided into two parts. The first part describes the content and presentation of the income statement and related disclosure issues. The second part provides an overview of the statement of cash flows.

# PART A THE INCOME STATEMENT AND COMPREHENSIVE INCOME

Before we discuss the specific components of an income statement in much depth, let's take a quick look at the general makeup of the statement. Graphic 4–1 offers a comprehensive statement for a hypothetical manufacturing company that you can refer to as we proceed through the chapter. At this point, our objective is only to gain a general perspective of the items reported and classifications contained in corporate income statements.

We'll look closer at the components of net income, but first we should consider the notion of net income itself and how it fits within the concept of comprehensive income.

## Comprehensive Income

LO1

Accounting professionals have engaged in an ongoing debate concerning which transactions should be included as components of periodic income. For instance, some argue that certain changes in shareholders' equity besides those attributable to traditional net income should be

**GRAPHIC 4–1**
Income Statement

**Income Statements**
(in millions, except earnings per share)

| | | Years Ended June 30 | |
|---|---|---|---|
| | | **2006** | **2005** |
| Income from Continuing Operations | Sales revenue | $1,450.6 | $1,380.0 |
| | Cost of goods sold | 832.6 | 800.4 |
| | Gross profit | 618.0 | 579.6 |
| | Operating expenses: | | |
| | Selling | 123.5 | 110.5 |
| | General and administrative | 147.8 | 139.1 |
| | Research and development | 55.0 | 65.0 |
| | Restructuring costs | 125.0 | — |
| | Total operating expenses | 451.3 | 314.6 |
| | Operating income | 166.7 | 265.0 |
| | Other income (expense): | | |
| | Interest income | 12.4 | 11.1 |
| | Interest expense | (25.9) | (24.8) |
| | Gain on sale of investments | 18.0 | 19.0 |
| | Income from continuing operations before income taxes and extraordinary item | 171.2 | 270.3 |
| | Income tax expense | 59.9 | 94.6 |
| | Income from continuing operations before extraordinary item | 111.3 | 175.7 |
| Separately Reported Items | Discontinued operations: | | |
| | Loss from operations of discontinued component (including gain on disposal in 2006 of $47) | (7.6) | (45.7) |
| | Income tax benefit | 2.0 | 13.0 |
| | Loss on discontinued operations | (5.6) | (32.7) |
| | Income before extraordinary item | 105.7 | 143.0 |
| | Extraordinary gain, net of $11 in tax expense | — | 22.0 |
| | Net income | $ 105.7 | $ 165.0 |
| Earnings per Share | **Earnings per common share—basic:** | | |
| | Income from continuing operations before extraordinary item | $ 2.14 | $ 3.38 |
| | Discontinued operations | (.11) | (.62) |
| | Extraordinary gain | — | .42 |
| | Net income | $ 2.03 | $ 3.18 |
| | **Earnings per common share—diluted:** | | |
| | Income from continuing operations before extraordinary item | $ 2.06 | $ 3.25 |
| | Discontinued operations | (.11) | (.62) |
| | Extraordinary gain | — | .42 |
| | Net income | $ 1.95 | $ 3.05 |

included in the determination of income. In what might be viewed as a compromise, the FASB decided to maintain the traditional view of net income, but to require companies also to report an expanded version of income called **comprehensive income** to include four types of gains and losses that traditionally haven't been included in income statements. Let's consider what that means.

## OTHER COMPREHENSIVE INCOME

***Comprehensive income*** **is the total change in equity for a reporting period other than from transactions with owners.**

The calculation of net income omits certain types of gains and losses that are included in comprehensive income. As one example, in Chapter 12 you will learn that certain investments are reported in the balance sheet at their fair values, but that the gains and losses resulting from adjusting those investments to fair value are *not* included in net income. Instead, they are reported as a separate component of shareholders' equity, **other comprehensive income (loss).**

Companies must report both net income and comprehensive income and reconcile the difference between the two.[1] Be sure to remember that net income actually is a part of comprehensive income. The reconciliation simply extends net income to include other comprehensive income items, reported net of tax, as shown in Illustration 4–1.

**ILLUSTRATION 4–1**
Comprehensive Income

| | | ($ in millions) |
|---|---|---|
| Net income | | $xxx |
| Other comprehensive income: | | |
| Net unrealized holding gains (losses) from investments (net of tax)* | $ x | |
| Gains (losses) from and amendments to postretirement benefit plans (net of tax)† | (x) | |
| Deferred gains (losses) from derivatives (net of tax)‡ | (x) | |
| Gains (losses) from foreign currency translation (net of tax)§ | x | xx |
| Comprehensive income | | $xxx |

*Changes in the market value of securities available-for-sale (described in Chapter 12).
†Gains and losses due to revising assumptions or market returns differing from expectations and prior service cost from amending the plan (described in Chapter 17).
‡When a derivative designated as a cash flow hedge is adjusted to fair value, the gain or loss is deferred as a component of comprehensive income and included in earnings later, at the same time as earnings are affected by the hedged transaction (described in the Derivatives Appendix to the text).
§Gains or losses from changes in foreign currency exchange rates. The amount could be an addition to or reduction in shareholders' equity. (This item is discussed elsewhere in your accounting curriculum.)

**Comprehensive income includes net income as well as other gains and losses that change shareholders' equity but are not included in traditional net income.**

The actual terminology used by companies for the four other comprehensive income items varies considerably. For instance, net unrecognized losses on pensions often are referred to as *minimum pension liability adjustments,* deferred gains (losses) from derivatives are sometimes called *derivative mark-to-market adjustments* or *changes in fair value of derivatives,* and gains (losses) from foreign currency translation are often identified as *foreign currency translation adjustments*.

## FLEXIBILITY IN REPORTING

**Reporting comprehensive income can be accomplished with a separate statement or by including the information in either the income statement or the statement of changes in shareholders' equity.**

The presentation shown in Illustration 4–1 can be (a) included as an extension to the income statement, (b) reported (exactly the same way) as a separate statement of comprehensive income, usually as part of a disclosure note, or (c) included in the statement of changes in shareholders' equity (Chapter 18). Each component of other comprehensive income can be displayed net of tax, as in Illustration 4–1, or alternatively, before tax with one amount shown for the aggregate income tax expense (or benefit).[2] A recent survey of reporting practices of 600 large public companies indicates that, of those companies that had other comprehensive income items, 84% chose to include the presentation of comprehensive income in their statements of changes in shareholders' equity.[3]

[1]"Reporting Comprehensive Income," *Statement of Financial Accounting Standards No. 130* (Norwalk, Conn.: FASB, 1997).
[2]The standard does not require the reporting of comprehensive earnings per share.
[3]*Accounting Trends and Techniques—2004* (New York: AICPA, 2004), p. 452.

Many, though, such as **Nacco Industries, Inc.**, and **Foster Wheeler Ltd.**, choose to present comprehensive income as an extension to their income statements. The **FedEx Corporation** statements of changes in stockholders' investment and comprehensive income in Appendix B, located at the back of this text, provides an example of a presentation of comprehensive income in that statement. On the other hand, in its 2006 financial statements, **Shire Pharmaceuticals** chose to use the separate statement approach, as shown in Graphic 4–2.

**FedEx Corporation**

**GRAPHIC 4–2**
Comprehensive Income Presented as a Separate Statement—Shire Pharmaceuticals

**SHIRE PHARMACEUTICALS GROUP**
**Consolidated Statements of Comprehensive Income**
**(In millions of dollars)**

| Year to December 31, | 2006 | 2005 | 2004 |
|---|---|---|---|
| Net (loss)/income | 278.2 | (578.4) | 236.3 |
| Other comprehensive income: | | | |
| Foreign currency translation | 18.1 | (56.0) | 46.8 |
| Unrealized holding (loss)/gain on available-for-sale securities | (1.8) | (1.0) | 27.0 |
| Realized gain on available-for-sale securities | — | (3.5) | (20.9) |
| Other comprehensive income (loss) | 16.3 | (60.5) | 52.9 |
| Comprehensive (loss)/income | 294.5 | (638.9) | 289.2 |

## ACCUMULATED OTHER COMPREHENSIVE INCOME

In addition to reporting comprehensive income that occurs in the current reporting period, we must also report these amounts on a cumulative basis in the balance sheet. This is consistent with the way we report net income that occurs in the current reporting period in the income statement and also report accumulated net income (that hasn't been distributed as dividends) in the balance sheet as retained earnings. Similarly, we report other comprehensive income as it occurs in the current reporting period and also report **accumulated other comprehensive income** (or **loss**) in the balance sheet. This is demonstrated in Graphic 4–2A for Shire Pharmaceuticals.

**The cumulative total of other comprehensive income (or comprehensive loss) is reported as accumulated other comprehensive income (or loss), an additional component of shareholders' equity that is displayed separately.**

**GRAPHIC 4–2A**
Shareholders' Equity—Shire Pharmaceuticals

**SHIRE PHARMACEUTICALS GROUP**
**Consolidated Balance Sheets (in part)**
**Years Ended December 31**

| (In millions of dollars) | 2006 | 2005 |
|---|---|---|
| Shareholders' Equity: | | |
| Common stock | 43.7 | 42.7 |
| Exchangeable shares | 59.4 | 101.2 |
| Treasury stock | (94.8) | (2.8) |
| Additional paid-in capital | 1,493.2 | 1,327.5 |
| Accumulated other comprehensive income | 87.8 | 71.5 |
| Retained earnings | 353.0 | 107.2 |
| Total shareholders' equity | 1,942.3 | 1,647.3 |

Referring to the numbers reported in Graphic 4–2, we can reconcile the changes in both retained earnings and accumulated other comprehensive income (loss):

Accumulated other comprehensive income increased by $16.3 million, from $71.5 million to $87.8 million.

| ($ in millions) | Retained Earnings | Accumulated Other Comprehensive Income (Loss) |
|---|---|---|
| Balance, 12/31/05 | $107.2 | $71.5 |
| Add: Net income | 278.2 | |
| Deduct Dividends | (32.4) | |
| Other comprehensive income | | 16.3 |
| Balance, 12/31/06 | $353.0 | $87.8 |

To further understand the relationship between net income and other comprehensive income, consider another example. Suppose Philips Corporation began 2006 with retained earnings of $600 million and accumulated other comprehensive income of $34 million. Let's also assume that net income for 2006, before considering the gain discussed below, is $100 million, of which $40 million was distributed to shareholders as dividends. Now assume that Philips purchased shares of IBM stock for $90 million during the year and sold them at year-end for $100 million. In that case, Philips would include the realized gain of $10 million in determining net income, If the income tax rate is 40%, net income includes a $6 million net-of-tax gain from the sale. This means that shareholders' equity, specifically retained earnings, also will include the $6 million.

| ($ in millions) | Retained Earnings | Accumulated Other Comprehensive Income |
|---|---|---|
| Balance, 12/31/05 | $600 | $34 |
| Net income ($100 + 6) | 106 | |
| Dividends | (40) | |
| Other comprehensive income | | –0– |
| Balance, 12/31/06 | $666 | $34 |

On the other hand, what if the shares are not sold before the end of the fiscal year but the year-end fair value is $100 million? In that case, the *unrealized* gain of $10 million is not included in net income. Instead, $6 million net-of-tax gain is considered a component of *other comprehensive income (loss)* for 2006 and results in an increase in *accumulated other comprehensive income (loss),* rather than retained earnings, in the 2006 balance sheet. The total of retained earnings and accumulated other comprehensive income is $700 million either way, as demonstrated below.

If the shares are *not* sold, the *unrealized* gain is part of other comprehensive income.

| ($ in millions) | Retained Earnings | Accumulated Other Comprehensive Income |
|---|---|---|
| Balance, 12/31/05 | $600 | $34 |
| Net income | 100 | |
| Dividends | (40) | |
| Other comprehensive income | | 6 |
| Balance, 12/31/06 | $660 | $40 |

Net income and comprehensive income are identical for an enterprise that has no other comprehensive income items. Our focus in the remainder of this chapter is on the measurement and reporting of net income in an income statement. Components of other comprehensive income are described in subsequent chapters.

## Income from Continuing Operations

● LO2

The need to provide information to help analysts predict future cash flows emphasizes the importance of properly reporting the amount of income from the entity's continuing operations. Clearly, it is the operating transactions that probably will continue into the future that are the best predictors of future cash flows. The components of **income from continuing**

**operations** are revenues, expenses (including income taxes), gains, and losses, excluding those related to discontinued operations and extraordinary items.[4]

**Income from continuing operations includes the revenues, expenses, gains and losses that will probably continue in future periods.**

## REVENUES, EXPENSES, GAINS, AND LOSSES

Revenues are inflows of resources resulting from providing goods or services to customers. For merchandising companies like **Wal-Mart**, the main source of revenue is sales revenue derived from selling merchandise. Service firms such as **FedEx** and **State Farm Insurance** generate revenue by providing services.

Expenses are outflows of resources incurred while generating revenue. They represent the costs of providing goods and services. The *matching principle* is a key player in the way we measure expenses. We attempt to establish a causal relationship between revenues and expenses. If causality can be determined, expenses are reported in the same period that the related revenue is recognized. If a causal relationship cannot be established, we either relate the expense to a particular period, allocate it over several periods, or expense it as incurred.

Gains and losses are increases or decreases in equity from peripheral or incidental transactions of an entity. In general, these gains and losses are those changes in equity that do not result directly from operations but nonetheless are related to those activities. For example, gains and losses from the routine sale of equipment, buildings, or other operating assets and from the sale of investment assets normally would be included in income from continuing operations. Later in the chapter we discuss certain gains and losses that are excluded from continuing operations.

## INCOME TAX EXPENSE

**_Income tax expense_ is shown as a separate expense in the income statement.**

Income taxes represent a major expense to a corporation, and accordingly, income tax expense is given special treatment in the income statement. Income taxes are levied on tax payers in proportion to the amount of taxable income that is reported to taxing authorities. Like individuals, corporations are income-tax-paying entities.[5] Because of the importance and size of **income tax expense** (sometimes called *provision for income taxes*), it always is reported as a separate expense in corporate income statements.

Federal, state, and sometimes local taxes are assessed annually and usually are determined by first applying a designated percentage (or percentages), the tax rate (or rates), to **taxable income.** Taxable income comprises revenues, expenses, gains, and losses as measured according to the regulations of the appropriate taxing authority.

Many of the components of taxable income and income reported in the income statement coincide. But sometimes tax rules and GAAP differ with respect to when and even whether a particular revenue or expense is included in income. When tax rules and GAAP differ regarding the timing of revenue or expense recognition, the actual payment of taxes may occur in a period different from when income tax expense is reported in the income statement. A common example is when a corporation takes advantage of tax laws by legally deducting more depreciation in the early years of an asset's life in its federal income tax return than it reports in its income statement. The amount of tax actually paid in the early years is less than the amount that is found by applying the tax rate to the reported GAAP income before taxes. We discuss this and other issues related to accounting for income taxes in Chapter 16. At this point, consider income tax expense to be simply a percentage of income before taxes.

**While the actual measurement of income tax expense can be complex, at this point we can consider income tax expense to be a simple percentage of income before taxes.**

## OPERATING VERSUS NONOPERATING INCOME

**A distinction often is made between _operating_ and _nonoperating_ income.**

Many corporate income statements distinguish between **operating** income and **nonoperating** income within continuing operations. Operating income includes revenues and expenses directly related to the principal revenue-generating activities of the company. For example, operating income for a manufacturing company includes sales revenues from the sale of products and all expenses related to this activity. Nonoperating income includes gains and losses and revenues and expenses related to peripheral or incidental activities of the company. For example, income from investments, gains and losses from the sale of operating assets and from investments, interest and dividend revenue, and interest expense are included

[4]These two separately reported items are addressed in a subsequent section.

[5]Partnerships are not tax-paying entities. Their taxable income or loss is included in the taxable income of the individual partners.

in nonoperating income.[6] *Other income (expense)* often is used in income statements as the classification heading for nonoperating items. A financial institution like a bank considers interest revenue and interest expense to be a part of operating income because they relate to the principal revenue-generating activities for that type of business.

Graphic 4–3 presents the 2004 and 2003 income statements for **FedEx Corporation**. Notice that FedEx distinguishes between operating and nonoperating income. Nonoperating revenues, expenses, gains and losses, and income tax expense (called provision for income taxes) are added to or subtracted from operating income to arrive at net income. As FedEx has no separately reported items, *income from continuing operations equals net income*.[7]

**GRAPHIC 4–3**

Income Statements—FedEx Corporation

**FedEx Corporation**

**Income Statements**
(In millions, except per share amounts)

| | Year Ended May 31 | |
|---|---|---|
| | **2004** | **2003** |
| Revenues | $24,710 | $22,487 |
| Operating expenses: | | |
| Salaries and employee benefits | 10,728 | 9,778 |
| Purchased transportation | 2,407 | 2,155 |
| Rentals and landing fees | 1,918 | 1,803 |
| Depreciation and amortization | 1,375 | 1,351 |
| Fuel | 1,481 | 1,349 |
| Maintenance and repairs | 1,523 | 1,398 |
| Business realignment costs | 435 | — |
| Other | 3,403 | 3,182 |
| | 23,270 | 21,016 |
| Operating income | 1,440 | 1,471 |
| Other income (expense): | | |
| Interest expense | (136) | (124) |
| Interest income | 20 | 6 |
| Other, net | (5) | (15) |
| | (121) | (133) |
| Income before income taxes | 1,319 | 1,338 |
| Provision for income taxes | 481 | 508 |
| Net income | $ 838 | $ 830 |
| Earnings per common share | | |
| Basic | $2.80 | $2.79 |
| Diluted | $2.76 | $2.74 |

Now let's consider the formats used to report the components of net income.

## INCOME STATEMENT FORMATS

A *single-step* income statement format groups all revenues and gains together and all expenses and losses together.

No specific standards dictate how income from continuing operations must be displayed, so companies have considerable latitude in how they present the components of income from continuing operations. This flexibility has resulted in a considerable variety of income statement presentations. However, we can identify two general approaches, the single-step and the multiple-step formats, that might be considered the two extremes, with the income statements of most companies falling somewhere in between.

The **single-step** format first lists all the revenues and gains included in income from continuing operations. Then, expenses and losses are grouped, subtotaled, and subtracted—in a

[6]Even though these activities are nonoperating, they are still included in continuing operations because they *generally* are expected to continue in future periods.

[7]In a later section we discuss items that are reported separately from continuing operations—discontinued operations and extraordinary items.

single step—from revenues and gains to derive income from continuing operations. Operating and nonoperating items are not separately classified. Illustration 4–2 shows an example of a single-step income statement for a hypothetical manufacturing company, Maxwell Gear Corporation.

**ILLUSTRATION 4–2**
Single-Step Income Statement

**MAXWELL GEAR CORPORATION**
**Income Statement**
**For the Year Ended December 31, 2006**

| | | |
|---|---|---|
| Revenues and gains: | | |
| Sales | | $573,522 |
| Interest and dividends | | 26,400 |
| Gain on sale of operating assets | | 5,500 |
| Total revenues and gains | | 605,422 |
| Expenses and losses: | | |
| Cost of goods sold | $302,371 | |
| Selling | 47,341 | |
| General and administrative | 24,888 | |
| Research and development | 16,300 | |
| Interest | 6,200 | |
| Loss on sale of investments | 8,322 | |
| Income taxes | 80,000 | |
| Total expenses and losses | | 485,422 |
| Net income | | $120,000 |

The **multiple-step** format reports a series of intermediate subtotals such as gross profit, operating income, and income before taxes. The overview income statements presented in Graphic 4–1 and the **FedEx Corporation** income statements in Graphic 4–3 are variations of the multiple-step format. Illustration 4–3 presents a multiple-step income statement for the Maxwell Gear Corporation.

**A *multiple-step* income statement format includes a number of intermediate subtotals before arriving at income from continuing operations.**

**ILLUSTRATION 4–3**
Multiple-Step Income Statement

**MAXWELL GEAR CORPORATION**
**Income Statement**
**For the Year Ended December 31, 2006**

| | | |
|---|---|---|
| Sales revenue | | $573,522 |
| Cost of goods sold | | 302,371 |
| Gross profit | | 271,151 |
| Operating expenses: | | |
| Selling | $47,341 | |
| General and administrative | 24,888 | |
| Research and development | 16,300 | |
| Total operating expenses | | 88,529 |
| Operating income | | 182,622 |
| Other income (expense): | | |
| Interest and dividend revenue | 26,400 | |
| Gain on sale of operating assets | 5,500 | |
| Interest expense | (6,200) | |
| Loss on sale of investments | (8,322) | |
| Total other income, net | | 17,378 |
| Income before income taxes | | 200,000 |
| Income tax expense | | 80,000 |
| Net income | | $120,000 |

**In addition to net income, the components of the income statement and their presentation also are important to financial statement users in their assessment of earnings quality.**

An advantage of the single-step format is its simplicity. Revenues and expenses are not classified or prioritized. A primary advantage of the multiple-step format is that, by separately classifying operating and nonoperating items, it provides information that might be useful in analyzing trends. Similarly, the classification of expenses by function also provides useful information. For example, reporting gross profit for merchandising companies highlights the important relationship between sales revenue and cost of goods sold. It is important to note that this issue is one of presentation. The bottom line, net income, is the same regardless of the format used. A recent survey of income statements of 600 large public companies indicates that the multiple-step format is used more than three times as often as the single-step format.[8] We use the multiple-step format for illustration purposes throughout the remainder of this chapter.

Before we investigate separately reported items, let's take a closer look at the components of both operating and nonoperating income and their relationship to earnings quality.

## Earnings Quality

● LO3

Financial analysts are concerned with more than just the bottom line of the income statement—net income. The presentation of the components of net income and the related supplemental disclosures provide clues to the user of the statement in an assessment of *earnings quality*. Earnings quality is used as a framework for more in-depth discussions of operating and nonoperating income.

***Earnings quality* refers to the ability of reported earnings (income) to predict a company's future earnings.**

The term **earnings quality** refers to the ability of reported earnings (income) to predict a company's future earnings. After all, an income statement simply reports on events that already have occurred. The relevance of any historical-based financial statement hinges on its predictive value. To enhance predictive value, analysts try to separate a company's *transitory earnings* effects from its *permanent earnings*. Transitory earnings effects result from transactions or events that are not likely to occur again in the foreseeable future, or that are likely to have a different impact on earnings in the future. Later in the chapter we address two items that, because of their transitory nature, are required to be reported separately at the bottom of the income statement. Analysts begin their assessment of permanent earnings with income before these two items, that is, income from continuing operations.

It would be a mistake, though, to assume income from continuing operations reflects permanent earnings entirely. In other words, there may be transitory earnings effects included in income from continuing operations. In a sense, the phrase *continuing* may be misleading.

### MANIPULATING INCOME AND INCOME SMOOTHING

A *Fortune* magazine article "Hocus-Pocus: How IBM Grew 27% a Year" contained a subtitle "Do you want to believe in the IBM miracle? Then don't look too closely at the numbers."[10] The article is highly critical of IBM's earnings management practices that allowed the company to report earnings per share growth of 27% per year from 1994 through 1999 with only minimal growth in revenues. The article's author attributes the increase in earnings per share to share buybacks, the sale of assets, and gains in pension fund assets, not a growth in permanent earnings.

**KEN SCHAPIRO—CONDOR CAPITAL MANAGEMENT**
IBM has run out of easy things to do to generate earnings growth. Now they have to do the hard stuff.[9]

An often-debated contention is that, within GAAP, managers have the power, to a limited degree, to manipulate reported company income. And the manipulation is not always in the direction of higher income. One author states that "Most executives prefer to report earnings that follow a smooth, regular, upward path. They hate to report declines, but they also want to avoid increases that vary wildly from year to year; it's better to have two years of 15% earnings

[8] *Accounting Trends and Techniques-2004* (New York: AICPA, 2004), p. 331.
[9] Bethany McLean, "Hocus-Pocus: How IBM Grew 27% a Year," *Fortune*, June 26, 2000, p. 168.
[10] Ibid.

**ARTHUR LEVITT, JR.**
While the problem of earnings management is not new, it has swelled in a market that is unforgiving of companies that miss their estimates. I recently read of one major U.S. company that failed to meet its so-called numbers by one penny and lost more than six percent of its stock value in one day.[12]

increases than a 30% gain one year and none the next. As a result, some companies 'bank' earnings by understating them in particularly good years and use the banked profits to polish results in bad years."[11]

**Many believe that corporate earnings management practices reduce the quality of reported earnings.**

Many believe that manipulating income reduces earnings quality because it can mask permanent earnings. A recent *BusinessWeek* issue was devoted entirely to the topic of earnings management. The issue, entitled "Corporate Earnings: Who Can You Trust," contains articles that are highly critical of corporate America's earnings manipulation practices. Arthur Levitt, Jr., former Chairman of the Securities and Exchange Commission, has been outspoken in his criticism of corporate earnings management practices and their effect on earnings quality. In an article appearing in the *CPA Journal,* he states,

> Increasingly, I have become concerned that the motivation to meet Wall Street earnings expectations may be overriding commonsense business practices. Too many corporate managers, auditors, and analysts are participants in a game of nods and winks. In the zeal to satisfy consensus earnings estimates and project a smooth earnings path, wishful thinking may be winning the day over faithful representation. As a result, I fear that we are witnessing an erosion in the *quality of earnings*, and therefore, the quality of financial reporting. Managing may be giving way to manipulation; integrity may be losing out to illusion. (emphasis added)[13]

How do managers manipulate income? Two major methods are (1) income shifting and (2) income statement classification. Income shifting is achieved by accelerating or delaying the recognition of revenues or expenses. For example, a practice called "channel stuffing" accelerates revenue recognition by persuading distributors to purchase more of your product than necessary near the end of a reporting period. The most common income statement classification manipulation involves the inclusion of recurring operating expenses in "special charge" categories such as restructuring costs (discussed below).[14] This practice sometimes is referred to as "big bath" accounting, a reference to cleaning up company balance sheets. Asset reductions, or the incurrence of liabilities, for these restructuring costs result in large reductions in income that might otherwise appear as normal operating expenses either in the current or future years.

Mr. Levitt would like to see various rule changes by standard setters to improve the transparency of financial statements. He does not want to eliminate necessary flexibility in financial reporting, but would like to make it easier for financial statement users to "see through the numbers" to the future. A key to a meaningful assessment of a company's future profitability is to understand the events reported in the income statement and their relationship with future earnings. Let's now revisit the components of operating income.

## OPERATING INCOME AND EARNINGS QUALITY

● LO4

Should all items of revenue and expense included in operating income be considered indicative of a company's permanent earnings? No, not necessarily. Sometimes, for example, operating expenses include some unusual items that may or may not continue in the future. Look closely at the 2004 and 2003 partial income statements of **Ciena Corporation**, a supplier of application-focused communications networking equipment, software and services, presented in Graphic 4–4. What items appear unusual? Certainly "Restructuring costs,"

[11]Ford S. Worthy, "Manipulating Profits: How It's Done," *Fortune*, June 25, 1984, p. 50.
[12]Arthur Levitt, Jr., "The Numbers Game," *The CPA Journal*, December 1998, p. 16.
[13]Ibid, p. 14.
[14]John J. Wild, Leopold A. Bernstein, and K.R. Subramanyam, *Financial Statement Analysis*, Seventh Edition, 2001, McGraw-Hill/Irwin, Burr Ridge, Illinois, p. 123.

"Goodwill impairment," "Long-lived asset impairment," and "In-process research and development" require further investigation. We discuss restructuring costs first.

**GRAPHIC 4–4**
Partial Income Statements—Ciena Corporation

**Income Statements (in part)**
($ in thousands)

| | Year Ended October 31, | |
|---|---|---|
| | **2004** | **2003** |
| Total revenue | $298,707 | $283,136 |
| Cost of goods sold | 226,954 | 210,091 |
| Gross profit | 71,753 | 73,045 |
| Operating expenses: | | |
| Research and development | 198,850 | 199,699 |
| Selling and marketing | 108,259 | 103,193 |
| General and administrative | 30,975 | 55,255 |
| Amortization of intangible assets | 30,839 | 17,870 |
| In-process research and development | 30,200 | 2,800 |
| Restructuring costs | 57,107 | 13,575 |
| Goodwill impairment | 371,712 | — |
| Long-lived asset impairment | 15,926 | 47,176 |
| Total operating expenses | 843,868 | 439,568 |
| Operating loss | (772,115) | (366,523) |

**FINANCIAL REPORTING CASE**
Q1, p. 154

*Restructuring costs* **include costs associated with shutdown or relocation of facilities or downsizing of operations.**

**Restructuring Costs.** When a company reorganizes its operations to attain greater efficiency, it often incurs significant associated costs. Facility closings and related employee layoffs translate into costs incurred for severance pay and relocation costs. These **restructuring costs** appear regularly on corporate income statements. In fact, a recent survey reports that in 2003, of the 600 companies surveyed, 219 (37%) included restructuring costs in their income statements.[15] For instance, let's consider our Ciena Corporation example. A disclosure note accompanying the company's financial statements indicates a 2004 closure of its San Jose, California, facility. Workforce reduction and lease termination costs were the primary expenses incurred. Graphic 4–5 reports a portion of the disclosure note related to the restructuring costs incurred during the fourth quarter of 2004.

**GRAPHIC 4–5**
Disclosure of Restructuring Costs—Ciena Corporation

**Restructuring costs (in part)**
During the fourth quarter of fiscal 2004, Ciena recorded a restructuring charge of $5.4 million related to a workforce reduction of approximately 119 employees, and $25.8 million primarily related to the exiting of Ciena's San Jose, CA, facility.

**Prior to 2003, restructuring costs were recognized (expensed) in the period the decision to restructure was made, not in the period or periods in which the actual activities took place.**

Prior to 2003, when a company restructured its operations, it estimated the future costs associated with the restructuring and expensed the costs in the period in which the decision to restructure was made. An offsetting liability was recorded. Later expenditures were charged against this liability as they occurred. The rationale for expensing now an estimate of future expenditures was to match the restructuring costs with the decision to restructure and not with the period or periods in which the actual activities take place or when the benefits (if any) are realized.

What if the estimates turned out to be incorrect?

[15]*Accounting Trends and Techniques–2004* (New York: AICPA, 2004), p. 346.

**Levi Strauss & Co.**, the famous jeans manufacturer, reported the following item as part of operating expenses in its 2000 and 1999 income statements ($ in thousands):

| | 2000 | 1999 |
|---|---|---|
| Restructuring costs | $(33,144) | $497,683 |

Why the negative expense in 2000? A review of the company's disclosure note reveals that in 1998 and 1999 it recorded restructuring costs that included estimated employee-related expenses and estimated facilities expenses associated with a plan to reduce capacity. However, in 2000, Levi lowered its estimate of the total costs associated with the restructuring and recorded an adjustment that increased income. As we discuss later in this chapter and throughout the text, when an estimate is changed in a reporting period after the period the estimate was made, the company should record the effect of the change in the current period rather than restate prior years' financial statements to correct the estimate.

The appearance of restructuring costs in corporate income statements increased significantly in the 1980s and 1990s. Many U.S. companies reacted to increased competition by streamlining their operations. The popular term heard often is *downsizing.* The SEC became concerned about the frequency with which companies were accruing restructuring costs in the manner described above. One of the chief concerns was that some companies purposely expensed large costs currently in an effort to manipulate future income. For example, employee relocation costs incurred in conjunction with a restructuring may produce future benefits to a company through greater operating efficiency. If so, accrual prior to any action may result in premature expense recognition of these costs.

**A new standard requires that restructuring costs be recognized only in the period incurred.**

The FASB responded to the SEC's concern in June 2002 with *SFAS No. 146.*[16] The Standard prohibits management from recognizing a liability for a cost associated with an exit or disposal activity unless and until a liability actually *has been incurred.* No longer can a company accrue restructuring costs in the period the company commits to an exit plan, unless the costs actually have been incurred. As an example, suppose terminated employees are to receive termination benefits, but only after they remain with the employer beyond a minimum retention period. In that case, a liability for termination benefits, and corresponding expense, should be accrued in the period(s) the employees render their service. On the other hand, if future service beyond a minimum retention period is not required, the benefits are recognized at the time the company communicates the arrangement to employees. In either case, the liability and expense are recorded at the point they are deemed incurred. Similarly, costs associated with closing facilities and relocating employees are recognized when goods or services associated with those activities are received and not accrued at the commitment date.

**BUSINESSWEEK**

Of course, companies have always taken write-offs and restructuring charges. But nervous regulators and investors fear that such multiyear write-offs are increasingly distorting corporate earnings—so much so, in fact, that some question whether the underlying meaning of profit numbers and their value as a true reflection of corporate performance is getting trampled.[17]

**Fair value is the objective for the initial measurement of a liability associated with restructuring costs.**

The Standard also establishes that fair value is the objective for initial measurement of the liability, and that a liability's fair value often will be measured by determining the present value of future estimated cash outflows. We discuss such present value calculations at length in later chapters, particularly in Chapters 6 and 14.

A major benefit of the new requirements is that liabilities accrued as a result of restructuring activities now comply with the definition of a liability in *Statement of Financial Concepts No. 6* and therefore are accounted for consistent with other liabilities. The new Standard also significantly reduces the possibility that restructuring costs can be used as a method to manipulate earnings.

**Should restructuring costs be considered part of a company's permanent earnings stream?**

Now that we understand the nature of restructuring costs, we can address the important question: Should

[16]"Accounting for Costs Associated with Exit or Disposal Activities," *Statement of Financial Accounting Standards No. 146* (Norwalk, Conn.: FASB, 2002).

[17]Nanette Byrnes, Richard A. Melcher, and Debra Sparks, "Earnings Hocus-Pocus: How Companies Come Up with the Numbers They Want," *BusinessWeek,* October 5, 1998, p. 135.

financial statement users consider these costs part of a company's permanent earnings stream, or are they transitory in nature? There is no easy answer. Ciena incurred restructuring costs in both 2003 and 2004. Will the company incur these costs again in the near future? Consider the following facts. During the 13-year period from 1991 through 2003, the Dow Jones Industrial 30 companies reported 83 restructuring charges in their collective income statements. That is an average of approximately 2.75 per company. But the average is deceiving. Six of the 30 companies reported no restructuring charges during that period. However, **DuPont** incurred restructuring charges in 10 of the 13 years, and **Alcoa** reported restructuring charges in 9 of their 13 income statements. An analyst must interpret restructuring charges in light of a company's past history in this area. Information in disclosure notes describing the restructuring and management plans related to the business involved also can be helpful.

Two other expenses in Ciena's income statement for 2004 that warrant additional scrutiny are *goodwill impairment* and *long-lived asset impairment.* These items involve what is referred to as *asset impairment* losses or charges. Any operational asset, whether tangible or intangible, should be written down if there has been a significant impairment of value. We explore operational assets in Chapters 10 and 11. After discussing this topic in more depth in those chapters, we revisit the concept of earnings quality as it relates to asset impairment. Also worthy of notice is the expense *in-process research and development.* This controversial expense that results from certain business combinations is addressed in Chapter 10.

Is it possible that financial analysts might look favorably at a company in the year it incurs a substantial restructuring charge or other unusual expense such as an asset impairment loss? Perhaps so, if they view management as creating higher profits in future years through operating efficiencies. Would analysts then reward that company again in future years when those operating efficiencies materialize? Certainly, this double halo effect might provide an attractive temptation to the management of some companies.

**ARTHUR LEVITT, JR.**

When a company decides to restructure, management and employees, investors and creditors, customers and suppliers all want to understand the expected effects. We need, of course, to ensure that financial reporting provides this information. But this should not lead to flushing all the associated costs—and maybe a little extra—through the financial statements.[18]

There are other operating expenses that also call into question this issue of earnings quality. For example, in Chapter 9 we discuss the write-down of inventory to comply with the lower-of-cost-or-market rule. Earnings quality also is influenced by the way income from investments is recorded (Chapter 12) and in the manner companies account for their pension plans (Chapter 17). In each case, after discussing these issues, we revisit this concept of earnings quality.

Earnings quality is affected by revenue issues as well as the expense issues we discussed. As an example, suppose that toward the end of its fiscal year, a company loses a major customer that can't be replaced. That would mean the current year's revenue figures contain a transitory component equal to the revenue generated from sales to that customer. Of course, in addition to its effect on revenues, losing the customer would have implications for the transitory/permanent nature of expenses and the bottom line net income. And, the pressure on companies to meet their earnings numbers often has led to premature revenue recognition, reducing the quality of the current period's earnings. Accelerating revenue recognition has caused problems for many companies.

For example, **Lucent Technologies'** revenue recognition practices recently attracted the attention of the SEC. Nine current and former employees were charged with securities fraud for improperly recognizing sales of $1.15 billion in fiscal 2000. The SEC accused the former employees of falsely inflating its revenues through aggressive sales practices, including the filing of false documents on sales to **Winstar Communications**, which later went bankrupt. The SEC also has pressed civil charges and a federal grand jury has indicated **McKesson**

[18]Arthur Levitt, Jr., "The Numbers Game," *The CPA Journal,* December 1998, p. 16.

**Corporation**'s former CFO for backdating a $20 million software sale by one month to meet the quarterly earnings target.[19]

We save these issues for Chapter 5 in which we discuss revenue recognition in considerable depth. Now, though, let's discuss earnings quality issues related to *nonoperating* items.

## NONOPERATING INCOME AND EARNINGS QUALITY

Most of the components of earnings in an income statement relate directly to the ordinary, continuing operations of the company. Some, though, such as interest and gains or losses are only tangentially related to normal operations. These we refer to as nonoperating items. Some nonoperating items have generated considerable discussion with respect to earnings quality, notably gains and losses generated either from the sale of operational assets or from the sale of investments. For example, as the stock market boom reached its height late in the year 2000, many companies recorded large gains from sale of investments that had appreciated significantly in value. How should those gains be interpreted in terms of their relationship to future earnings? Are they transitory or permanent? Let's consider an example.

**Gains and losses from the sale of operational assets and investments often can significantly inflate or deflate current earnings.**

**Intel Corporation** is the world's largest manufacturer of semiconductors. Graphic 4–6 shows the nonoperating section of Intel's income statements for the 2000 and 1999 fiscal years. In 2000, income before taxes increased by approximately 35% from the prior year. But notice that the *gains on investments, net* (net means net of losses) increased from $883 million to over $3.7 billion, accounting for a large portion of the increase in income. Some analysts questioned the quality of Intel's 2000 earnings because of these large gains.

**GRAPHIC 4–6**
Income Statements (in part)—Intel Corporation

**Income Statements (in part)**
(in millions)

| | Years Ended December 30 | |
|---|---|---|
| | **2000** | **1999** |
| Operating income | 10,395 | 9,767 |
| Gains on investments, net | 3,759 | 883 |
| Interest and other, net | 987 | 578 |
| Income before taxes | 15,141 | 11,228 |

Consider also **Cisco Systems'** 2004 earnings of $8.168 billion. This figure included over $3 billion in investment income, approximately half of which resulted from gains generated from the sale of securities. Can Cisco sustain these gains? Should they be considered part of permanent earnings or are they transitory? **Coca-Cola Company** has been criticized for manipulating its profits through the timely sale of bottling companies. The company often invests in weaker bottlers, enhances their operations, and then sells them for a profit. Are these gains an integral part of the soft-drink business or are they transitory blips in earnings? There are no easy answers to these questions.

Companies often voluntarily provide a **pro forma earnings** number when they announce annual or quarterly earnings. These pro forma earnings numbers are management's estimation of permanent earnings. For example, **Hewlett-Packard Company**, a leading global provider of computer peripherals, announced on November 16, 2004, that its income for the fiscal year ended April 1, 2004, was $3.497 billion. The company also announced that its *pro forma net income* (which, in this case, excludes restructuring charges, amortization of intangibles, acquisition-related charges, and in-process research and development) for the year was $4.067 billion. These pro forma earnings numbers are controversial as they represent management's biased view of permanent earnings and should be interpreted in that light. Nevertheless, these disclosures do provide additional information to the financial community.

**Many companies voluntarily provide *pro forma earnings*—management's assessment of permanent earnings.**

The Sarbanes-Oxley Act addressed pro forma earnings in its Section 401. One of the act's important provisions requires that if pro forma earnings are included in any periodic or other

[19]Jeffrey Marshall, "The Perils of Revenue Recognition," *Financial Executive,* July–August 2004.

The Sarbanes-Oxley Act requires a reconciliation between pro forma earnings and earnings determined according to GAAP.

report filed with the SEC or in any public disclosure or press release, the company also must provide a reconciliation with earnings determined according to generally accepted accounting principles.[20]

We now turn our attention to two income statement items—discontinued operations and extraordinary items—that, because of their nature, are more obviously not part of a company's permanent earnings and, appropriately, are excluded from continuing operations.

FINANCIAL REPORTING CASE

Q2, p. 154

## Separately Reported Items

The information in the income statement is useful if it can help users predict the future. Toward this end, users should be made aware of events reported in the income statement that are not likely to occur again in the foreseeable future.

GAAP require that certain transactions be reported separately in the income statement, below income from continuing operations.

There are two types of events that, if they have a material effect[21] on the income statement, require separate reporting and disclosure: (1) discontinued operations and (2) extraordinary items.[22] In fact, these are the only two events that are allowed to be reported below continuing operations. Although a company has considerable flexibility in reporting income from *continuing operations,* the presentation order of these two is mandated as follows:[23]

| | |
|---|---|
| Income from continuing operations before income taxes and extraordinary items | $xxx |
| Income tax expense | xx |
| Income from continuing operations before extraordinary items | xxx |
| Discontinued operations, net of $xx in taxes | xx |
| Extraordinary items, net of $xx in taxes[24] | xx |
| Net income | $xxx |

The objective is to separately report all the income effects of each of these items. That's why we include the income tax effect of each item in this separate presentation rather than report them as part of the income tax expense. The process of associating income tax effects with the income statement components that create them is referred to as *intraperiod tax allocation*. We address this process in the next section.

Until recently, there were three possible separately reported items. The third item, the *cumulative effect of a change in accounting principle*, was eliminated by a new accounting standard in 2005. Previously, the cumulative effect on the income of previous years from having used the old method rather than the new method was included in the income statement of the year of change as a separately reported item. The new standard requires retrospective treatment. We no longer report the entire effect in the year of the change. Instead, we retrospectively recast prior years' financial statements when we report those statements again (in comparative statements, for example). In other words, those statements are made to appear as if the newly adopted accounting method had been used in those years. We discuss the retrospective approach later in this chapter and in subsequent chapters.

### INTRAPERIOD INCOME TAX ALLOCATION

**Intraperiod tax allocation** associates (allocates) income tax expense (or income tax benefit if there is a loss) with each major component of income that causes it.[25] More specifically, income tax is allocated to income from continuing operations and each of the two separately reported items. For example, assume a company experienced an extraordinary gain during

[20]The Congress of the United States of America, *The Sarbanes-Oxley Act of 2002,* Section 401 (b) (2), Washington, D.C., 2004.

[21]The concept of materiality was discussed in Chapter 1. If the effect on the income statement is not material, these items are included in income from continuing operations.

[22]"Reporting Results of Operations," *Accounting Principles Board Opinion No. 30* (New York: AICPA, 1973).

[23]The presentation of these separately reported items is the same for single-step and multiple-step income statement formats. The single-step versus multiple-step distinction applies to items included in income from continuing operations.

[24]Companies that report discontinued operations and extraordinary items often show a subtotal after discontinued operations. This is not required.

[25]*Intraperiod* tax allocation concerns the association of income tax with income statement components. *Interperiod* tax allocation, covered in Chapter 16, addresses the problem created when taxable income does not equal income before taxes as determined by GAAP because of differences in the timing of revenue or expense recognition.

the year.[26] The amount of income tax expense deducted from income from continuing operations is the amount of income tax expense that the company would have incurred *if there were no extraordinary gain*. The effect on income taxes caused by the extraordinary item is deducted from the extraordinary gain itself in the income statement. Illustration 4–4 demonstrates this concept.

The Maxwell Gear Corporation had income from continuing operations before income tax expense of $200,000 and an extraordinary gain of $60,000 in 2006. The income tax rate is 40% on all items of income or loss. Therefore, the company's total income tax expense is $104,000 (40% × $260,000).

**ILLUSTRATION 4–4**
Intraperiod Tax Allocation

How should the company allocate the tax expense between income from continuing operations and the extraordinary gain? A partial income statement, beginning with income from continuing operations before income tax expense, *ignoring* intraperiod tax allocation, is shown in Illustration 4–4A.

| | |
|---|---|
| Income before income taxes and extraordinary item | $200,000 |
| Income tax expense | (104,000) |
| Income before extraordinary item | 96,000 |
| Extraordinary gain (gross) | 60,000 |
| Net income | $156,000 |

**ILLUSTRATION 4–4A**
Income Statement Presented *Incorrectly*—No Intraperiod Tax Allocation (extraordinary gain)

The deficiency of this presentation is that the apparent contribution to net income of (a) income before the extraordinary gain (that is, income from continuing operations) and (b) the extraordinary gain, is misleading. If the extraordinary gain had not occurred, income tax expense would not have been $104,000 but rather $80,000 (40% × $200,000). Similarly, the net benefit of the extraordinary gain is not $60,000, but rather $36,000 ($60,000 minus 40% × $60,000). The total tax expense of $104,000 must be *allocated*, $80,000 to continuing operations and $24,000 (40% × $60,000) to the extraordinary gain. The appropriate income statement presentation appears in Illustration 4–4B.

| | |
|---|---|
| Income before income taxes and extraordinary item | $200,000 |
| Income tax expense | (80,000) |
| Income before extraordinary item | 120,000 |
| Extraordinary gain, net of $24,000 tax expense | 36,000 |
| Net income | $156,000 |

**ILLUSTRATION 4–4B**
Income Statement Presented *Correctly*—Intraperiod Tax Allocation (extraordinary gain)

Net income is $156,000 either way. Intraperiod tax allocation is not an issue of measurement but an issue of presentation. The $120,000 income before extraordinary gain properly reflects income from continuing operations *including* the appropriate tax effects. Also, notice that income tax expense represents taxes that relate to the total of all of the revenue, expense, gain, and loss items included in continuing operations. Each of the items following continuing operations (discontinued operations and extraordinary items) are presented *net of their tax effect*. No items included in the computation of income from continuing operations are reported net of tax.

**The two items reported separately below income from continuing operations are presented net of the related income tax effect.**

[26]The criteria for classifying gains and losses as extraordinary are discussed in a later section of this chapter.

In the illustration, the extraordinary gain caused additional income tax expense to be incurred. What if the company had experienced an extraordinary loss of $60,000 instead of an extraordinary gain? In that case, rather than creating additional tax, the loss actually decreases tax due to its reducing taxable income by $60,000. The company's total income tax expense would be $56,000 [40% × ($200,000 − 60,000)].

The extraordinary loss *decreased* the amount of tax the company otherwise would have had to pay by $24,000. This is commonly referred to as a *tax benefit*. A partial income statement, beginning with income from continuing operations before income tax expense, *ignoring* intraperiod tax allocation is shown in Illustration 4–4C.

**ILLUSTRATION 4–4C**
Income Statement Presented *Incorrectly*—No Intraperiod Tax Allocation (extraordinary loss)

| | |
|---|---|
| Income before income taxes and extraordinary item | $200,000 |
| Income tax expense | (56,000) |
| Income before extraordinary item | 144,000 |
| Extraordinary loss (gross) | (60,000) |
| Net income | $ 84,000 |

Once again, income before the extraordinary loss (that is, income from continuing operations) is misleading. If the extraordinary loss had not occurred, income tax expense would not have been $56,000 but rather $80,000 (40% × $200,000). The total tax expense of $56,000 must be *allocated*, $80,000 tax expense to continuing operations and $24,000 tax benefit to the extraordinary loss. The appropriate income statement presentation appears in Illustration 4–4D.

**ILLUSTRATION 4–4D**
Income Statement Presented *Correctly*—Intraperiod Tax Allocation (extraordinary loss)

| | |
|---|---|
| Income before income taxes and extraordinary item | $200,000 |
| Income tax expense | (80,000) |
| Income before extraordinary item | 120,000 |
| Extraordinary loss, net of $24,000 tax benefit | (36,000) |
| Net income | $ 84,000 |

Now that we have seen how to report items net of their related tax effects, let's look closer at the two items reported net of tax below income from continuing operations: discontinued operations and extraordinary items.

## DISCONTINUED OPERATIONS

● LO5

**FINANCIAL REPORTING CASE**

Q3, p. 154

**Smithfield Foods, Inc.**, is the largest hog producer and pork processor in the world and the fifth largest beef producer in the United States. Prior to 2005, the company operated in four segments; pork, beef, hog production, and international. In 2004, though, Smithfield decided to discontinue the international segment and accordingly sold **Schneider Corporation** its meat and other food products subsidiary located in Canada.[27] The transaction is an example of a **discontinued operation.**

**What Constitutes an Operation?** For many years *APBO No. 30*[28] provided authoritative guidance for accounting and reporting of discontinued operations. This Opinion defined

[27]The primary reason companies discontinue operations often is that the line of business is no longer profitable. This was not the case with Smithfield's Canadian subsidiary sold in 2004 that had been generating a profit.

[28]"Reporting Results of Operations," *Opinions of the Accounting Principles Board No. 30* (New York: AICPA, 1973).

***SFAS NO. 144***

. . . a component of an entity comprises operations and cash flows that can be clearly distinguished, operationally and for financial reporting purposes, from the rest of the entity.[29]

an operation as a "segment of a business." A segment could be either a separate line of business or a separate class of customer. *SFAS No. 144,* issued in 2001, replaces the term segment of a business with *component of an entity.* A component of an entity comprises operations and cash flows that can be clearly distinguished, operationally and for financial reporting purposes, from the rest of the entity.

**SFAS No. 144 considers an operation to be a *component of an entity* whose operations and cash flows can be clearly distinguished from the rest of the entity.**

If a component of an entity has either been disposed of or classified as held for sale, we report the results of its operations separately in discontinued operations if two conditions are met:

1. The operations and cash flows of the component have been (or will be) eliminated from the ongoing operations.
2. The entity will not have any significant continuing involvement in the operations of the component after the disposal transaction.

Notice that the definition of an operation is significantly broadened with *SFAS No. 144.* A component of an entity may be a reportable segment or operating segment, a reporting unit, a subsidiary, or an asset group. For example, suppose Chadwick Industries operates a chain of 12 restaurants in the Southeast and also has a division that engages in the production of canned goods sold to retailers. Previously, either the restaurant chain or the canned goods division would qualify as an operation for purposes of reporting discontinued operations, but an individual restaurant within the chain or a manufacturing plant in the canned goods division would not qualify. Now, though, under *SFAS No. 144,* it could if it represents a component of the company with "operations and cash flows that can be clearly distinguished, operationally and for financial reporting purposes," from the rest of the restaurants or plants.

Remember, too, that the second condition for being reported separately as a discontinued operation is that the entity will not have any significant continuing involvement in the operations of the component after the disposal transaction. As an example, let's say Scooter's Barbecue franchises restaurants to independent owners but also has several company-owned restaurants. If Scooter's commits to a plan to sell its company-owned restaurants to an existing franchisee, the way it reports the transaction would depend on the terms of the agreement. If the franchise agreement requires Scooter's to maintain significant continuing involvement in the operations of the restaurants after they are sold, Scooter's will not report this transaction as a discontinued operation. On the other hand, if no continuing involvement is indicated, Scooter's will report the transaction separate from its franchising operations as a discontinued operation.[30] We see how in the next section.

**Reporting Discontinued Operations.** By definition, the income or loss stream from an identifiable discontinued operation no longer will continue. If Smithfield Foods had not separately reported the results of discontinuing its businesses, its 2004 and 2003 comparative income statements (in condensed form) would have appeared as in Illustration 4–5A.

The company generated net income of $227.1 million and $26.3 million in 2004 and 2003, respectively. However, an analyst concerned with Smithfield's future profitability is more interested in the 2004 and 2003 results after separating the effects of the discontinued operation from the results of operations that will continue. This information might have a significant impact on the analyst's assessment of future profitability.

Now let's compare these with the actual income statements Smithfield reported and reproduced (in condensed form) in Illustration 4–5B.

Compare the two income statements for their ability to predict future profitability. The income statements in Illustration 4–5B separately report the net-of-tax income effects of the discontinued operation. The 2004 revenues, expenses, gains, losses, and income tax related

**The net-of-tax income effects of a discontinued operation are reported separately in the income statement, below income from continuing operations.**

[29]"Accounting for the Impairment or Disposal of Long-Lived Assets," *Statement of Financial Accounting Standards No. 144* (Norwalk, Conn.: FASB, 2001), par. 41.
[30]Ibid., pgs. A25 and A27.

**ILLUSTRATION 4–5A**
Income Statements Presented Incorrectly *without* Separate Reporting of Discontinued Operations

**SMITHFIELD FOODS, INC**
**Income Statements**
**Years Ended May 2**

| | ($ in millions) | |
|---|---|---|
| | **2004** | **2003** |
| Net sales | $10,107.3 | $7,904.5 |
| Costs and expenses | 9,760.1 | 7,865.3 |
| Income before income taxes | 347.2 | 39.2 |
| Income tax expense | 120.1 | 12.9 |
| Net income | $ 227.1 | $ 26.3 |

**ILLUSTRATION 4–5B**
Income Statements Presented Correctly *with* Separate Reporting of Discontinued Operations

**SMITHFIELD FOODS, INC**
**Income Statements**
**Years Ended May 2**

| | ($ in millions) | |
|---|---|---|
| | **2004** | **2003** |
| Net sales | $9,267.0 | $7,135.4 |
| Costs and expenses | 9,020.2 | 7,118.9 |
| Income before income taxes | 246.8 | 16.5 |
| Income tax expense | 84.1 | 4.6 |
| Income from continuing operations | 162.7 | 11.9 |
| Discontinued operations: | | |
| Income from discontinued operations, net of tax of $9.0 in 2004 and $8.3 in 2003 | 15.4 | 14.4 |
| Gain on sale of Schneider, net of tax of $27.0 | 49.0 | — |
| Net income | $ 227.1 | $ 26.3 |

to the *discontinued* operation have been removed from *continuing* operations and reported separately for both 2004 and 2003.[31] Otherwise, as in Illustration 4–5A, it would appear that the company's profitability increased $200.8 million from $26.3 million to $227.1 million, and that its revenue increased by 28%, from $7,904.5 million to $10,107.3 million. However, a key in the assessment of profitability is the comparison of the company's performance from *continuing* operations. That comparison reveals an increase in revenue of 30% and an increase in profit of $150.8 million ($11.9 to $162.7). This provides a different picture of Smithfield's future profitability.

Sometimes a discontinued component actually has been sold by the end of a reporting period as in the case of Smithfield. Often, though, the component is being held for sale but the disposal transaction has not been completed as of the end of the reporting period. We consider these two possibilities next.

**When the component has been sold.** When its reporting period ended in 2004, Smithfield had sold its Canadian subsidiary. In such situations, when the discontinued component is sold before the end of the reporting period, the reported income effects of a discontinued operation will include two elements:

[31]Even though the operation was discontinued in 2004, it is important for comparative purposes to separate the effects for any prior years presented. This allows an apples-to-apples comparison of income from *continuing* operations. So, in comparative income statements reporting three years, the 2003 and 2002 income statements would be reclassified and the income from discontinued operations presented as a separately reported item.

1. Operating income or loss (revenues, expenses, gains and losses) of the component from the beginning of the reporting period to the disposal date.
2. Gain or loss on disposal.

These two elements can be combined or reported separately, net of their tax effects. Notice in Illustration 4–5B that Smithfield Foods chose to report the two elements separately. If combined, the gain or loss component must be indicated. In our illustrations to follow, we combine the income effects. Illustration 4–6 describes a situation in which the discontinued component is sold before the end of the reporting period.

**ILLUSTRATION 4–6**
Discontinued Operations—Gain on Disposal

The Duluth Holding Company has several operating divisions. In October 2006, management decided to sell one of its divisions that qualifies as a separate component according to *SFAS No. 144*. The division was sold on December 18, 2006, for a net selling price of $14,000,000. On that date, the assets of the division had a book value of $12,000,000. For the period January 1 through disposal, the division reported a pretax operating loss of $4,200,000. The company's income tax rate is 40% on all items of income or loss. Duluth generated after-tax profits of $22,350,000 from its continuing operations.

Duluth's income statement for the year 2006, beginning with income from continuing operations, would be reported as follows:

| | | |
|---|---|---|
| Income from continuing operations | | $22,350,000 |
| Discontinued operations: | | |
| Loss from operations of discontinued component (including gain on disposal of $2,000,000*) | $(2,200,000)† | |
| Income tax benefit | 880,000‡ | |
| Loss on discontinued operations | | (1,320,000) |
| Net income | | $21,030,000 |

*Net selling price of $14 million less book value of $12 million
†Operating loss of $4.2 million less gain on disposal of $2 million
‡$2,200,000 × 40%

Notice that a tax *benefit* occurs because a *loss* reduces taxable income, saving the company $880,000. On the other hand, had there been *income* from operations of $2,200,000, the $880,000 income tax effect would have represented additional income tax expense.

For comparison purposes, the net of tax operating income or loss of the discontinued component for any prior years included in the comparative income statements also are separately reported as discontinued operations.

**When the component is considered held for sale.** What if a company has decided to discontinue a component but, when the reporting period ends, the component has not yet been sold? If the situation indicates that the component is likely to be sold within a year, the component is considered "held for sale."[32] In that case, the income effects of the discontinued operation still are reported, but the two components of the reported amount are modified as follows:

**If a component to be discontinued has not yet been sold, its income effects, including any impairment loss, usually still are reported separately as discontinued operations.**

1. Operating income or loss (revenues, expenses, gains and losses) of the component from the beginning of the reporting period *to the end of the reporting period*.
2. An "impairment loss" if the carrying value of the assets of the component is more than fair value minus cost to sell.

The balance sheet is affected, too. The assets of the component considered held for sale are reported at the lower of their carrying amount (book value) or fair value minus cost to

[32]There are six criteria designed to determine whether the component is likely to be sold and therefore considered "held for sale." "Accounting for the Impairment or Disposal of Long-Lived Assets," *Statement of Financial Accounting Standards No. 144* (Norwalk, Conn.: FASB, 2001). In Chapter 11 we discuss this standard and the held for sale criteria in the context of accounting for the impairment of operational assets.

sell. And, because it's not in use, an operational asset classified as held for sale is no longer reported as part of property, plant and equipment and is not depreciated or amortized.

The two income elements can be combined or reported separately, net of their tax effects. In addition, if the amounts are combined and there is an impairment loss, the loss must be disclosed, either parenthetically on the face of the statement or in a disclosure note. Consider the example in Illustration 4–7.

**ILLUSTRATION 4–7**
Discontinued Operations—Impairment Loss

The Duluth Holding Company has several operating divisions. In October 2006, management decided to sell one of its divisions that qualifies as a separate component according to *SFAS No. 144*. On December 31, 2006, the end of the company's fiscal year, the division had not yet been sold. On that date, the assets of the division had a book value of $12,000,000 and a fair value, minus anticipated costs to sell, of $9,000,000. For the year, the division reported a pre-tax operating loss of $4,200,000. The company's income tax rate is 40% on all items of income or loss. Duluth generated after-tax profits of $22,350,000 from its continuing operations.

Duluth's income statement for 2006, beginning with income from continuing operations, would be reported as follows:

| | | |
|---|---|---|
| Income from continuing operations | | $22,350,000 |
| Discontinued operations: | | |
| Loss from operations of discontinued component (including impairment loss of $3,000,000) | $(7,200,000)* | |
| Income tax benefit | 2,880,000† | |
| Loss on discontinued operations | | (4,320,000) |
| Net income | | $18,030,000 |

*Operating loss of $4.2 million plus impairment loss of $3 million
†$7,200,000 × 40%

A disclosure note would provide additional details about the discontinued component, including the identity of the component, the major classes of assets and liabilities of the component, the reason for the discontinuance, and the expected manner of disposition. Also, the net-of-tax operating income or loss of the component being discontinued is also reported separate from continuing operations for any prior year that is presented for comparison purposes along with the 2006 income statement.

In the above illustration, if the fair value of the division's assets minus cost to sell exceeded the book value of $12,000,000, there is no impairment loss and the income effects of the discontinued operation would include only the operating loss of $4,200,000, less the income tax benefit.[33]

**Interim reporting.** Remember that companies whose ownership shares are publicly traded in the United States must file quarterly reports with the Securities and Exchange Commission. If a component of an entity is considered held for sale at the end of a quarter, the income effects of the discontinued component must be separately reported in the quarterly income statement. These effects would include the operating income or loss for the quarter as well as an impairment loss if the component's assets have a book value more than fair value minus cost to sell. If the assets are impaired and written down, any gain or loss on disposal in a subsequent quarter is determined relative to the new, written-down book value.

Let's now turn our attention to the second separately reported item, extraordinary gains and losses.

## EXTRAORDINARY ITEMS

● LO6

Occasionally, an unusual event may occur that materially affects the current year's income but is highly unlikely to occur again in the foreseeable future. If such an item is allowed to

[33]In the following year when the component is sold, the income effects must also be reported as a discontinued operation. Prior to SFAS No. 144, operating results for the subsequent period were estimated and considered in determining the income effect for the year the segment was deemed held for sale. This is no longer the case.

simply alter net income without pointing out its extraordinary nature, earnings quality is seriously compromised and investors and creditors may be misled into basing predictions of future income on current income that includes the nonrecurring event. For that reason, **extraordinary items** are "red flagged" in an income statement by being reported separately, net of tax, and appropriately labeled. Extraordinary items are material events and transactions that are both:

1. Unusual in nature
2. Infrequent in occurrence[34]

*Extraordinary items* are material gains and losses that are both *unusual in nature* and *infrequent in occurrence.*

These criteria must be considered in light of the environment in which the entity operates. There obviously is a considerable degree of subjectivity involved in the determination. The concepts of unusual and infrequent require judgment. In making these judgments, an accountant should keep in mind the overall objective of the income statement. The key question is how the event relates to a firm's future profitability. If it is judged that the event, because of its unusual nature and infrequency of occurrence, *is not likely to occur again*, separate reporting is warranted.

Companies often experience *unexpected* events that are not considered extraordinary items. The loss of a major customer or the death of the company president are unexpected events that likely will affect a company's future but are both normal risks of operating a business that could recur in the future. Other gains and losses from unexpected events that are *not* considered extraordinary include the effects of a strike, including those against competitors and major suppliers, and the adjustment of accruals on long-term contracts.[35]

The determination of whether an item is unusual and infrequent should consider the environment in which the company operates.

A key point in the definition of an extraordinary item is that determining whether an event satisfies *both* criteria depends on the environment in which the firm operates. The environment includes factors such as the type of products or services sold and the geographical location of the firm's operations. What is extraordinary for one firm may not be extraordinary for another firm. For example, a loss caused by a hurricane in Florida may not be judged to be extraordinary. However, hurricane damage in New York may indeed be unusual and infrequent.

Companies frequently sell subsidiary companies. Generally, the gain or loss is reported as a nonoperating item in the income statement or as a discontinued operation if the subsidiary is considered a component of the entity according to *SFAS No. 144.* In contrast, though, consider the disclosure note from recent financial statements of **El Paso Energy Corporation** shown in Graphic 4–7.

**GRAPHIC 4–7**
Extraordinary Gain Disclosure—El Paso Energy Corporation

**3. Extraordinary Gain**
During the first quarter, we sold East Tennessee Natural Gas and Sea Robin Pipeline Company to comply with an FTC order related to our merger with Sonat. Net proceeds from the sales were $457 million and we recognized an extraordinary gain of $89 million, net of income taxes of $60 million.

Why was the gain on sale of two subsidiary companies considered an extraordinary item? We can only speculate as to the company's reasoning, but it seems likely that the unusual nature of the sale, to comply with an order from the Federal Trade Commission, resulted in the conclusion by the company that such a gain was unlikely to occur again in the foreseeable future.

Logic and reasoning must be applied to the determination of whether or not an event is extraordinary. Keep in mind that the income statement should be a guide to predicting the future. If it is extremely unlikely that a material gain or loss will occur again in the future, the quality of earnings is improved and the usefulness of the income statement in predicting the future is enhanced if the income effects of that gain or loss are reported separately.

[34]"Reporting Results of Operations," *Accounting Principles Board Opinions No. 30* (New York: AICPA, 1973), par. 20.
[35]Ibid, par. 23.

Extraordinary gains and losses are presented, net of tax, in the income statement below discontinued operations.

As shown previously on page 168, the net-of-tax effects of extraordinary gains and losses are presented in the income statement below discontinued operations. In addition, a disclosure note is necessary to describe the nature of the event and the tax effects, if they are not indicated on the face of the income statement.[36]

### UNUSUAL OR INFREQUENT ITEMS

The income effect of an event that is either unusual or infrequent should be reported as a separate component of continuing operations.

If the income effect of an event is material and the event is either unusual or infrequent—but not both—the item should be *included in continuing operations* but reported as a separate income statement component. Recall the Ciena Corporation example in Graphic 4–4 on page 164. Restructuring costs and the impairment of goodwill and long-lived assets included in that company's continuing operations are examples of this type of event. The events may be unusual or infrequent, but, by their nature, they could occur again in the foreseeable future. However, rather than include these items with other gains and losses or with other expenses, they are reported as a separate line item in the income statement.[37] This method of reporting, including note disclosure, enhances earnings quality by providing information to the statement user to help assess the events' relationship with future profitability.

As we discussed earlier, the cumulative effect of a change in accounting principle no longer is reported as a separate item in the income statement. A new standard requires that we retrospectively adjust prior financial statements instead. As a result, the income statement and other financial statements are affected by these changes differently than before. In the next section, we explore the way various types of accounting changes are reported.

## Accounting Changes

Accounting changes fall into one of three categories: (1) a change in an accounting principle, (2) a change in estimate, or (3) a change in reporting entity. The correction of an error is another adjustment that is accounted for similarly. A brief overview of each is provided here. We cover accounting changes in detail in Chapter 20.

### CHANGE IN ACCOUNTING PRINCIPLE

● LO7

A change in accounting principle refers to a change from one acceptable accounting method to another. There are many situations in which there are alternative treatments for similar transactions. Common examples of these situations include the choice between FIFO, LIFO, and average cost for the measurement of inventory and among alternative revenue recognition methods.

Occasionally, a company will change from one generally accepted treatment to another. When these changes in accounting principles occur, information lacks consistency, hampering the ability of external users to compare financial information among reporting periods. If, for example, inventory and cost of goods sold are measured in one reporting period using LIFO and the FIFO method in a subsequent period, inventory, cost of goods sold, and hence, net income for the two periods are not comparable. Difficulties created by inconsistency and lack of comparability are alleviated by the way we report accounting changes.

Voluntary changes in accounting principles are accounted for retrospectively by revising prior years' financial statements.

There is more than one approach that could be used to account for a change in accounting principle. A new accounting standard requires that voluntary accounting changes be accounted for retrospectively.[38] Previously, the cumulative effect on the income of prior years from having used the old method rather than the new method was included in the income statement of the year of change as a separately reported item. We no longer report the entire effect in the year of the change. Instead, we retrospectively recast prior years' financial statements when we report those statements again (in comparative statements, for example). For

[36]For several years the FASB required companies to report material gains and losses from the early extinguishment of debt as extraordinary items. This is no longer the case and now these gains and losses are subject to the same criteria as other gains and losses for such treatment; namely, that they be both (a) unusual in nature and (b) infrequent in occurrence.

[37]These items are *not* reported net of tax. Only the two separately reported items—discontinued operations and extraordinary items—are reported net of tax.

[38]"Accounting Changes and Error Corrections—A Replacement of APB Opinion No. 20 and FASB Statement No. 3," *Statement of Financial Accounting Standards No. 154,* (Norwalk, Conn.: FASB, 2005).

each year reported in the comparative statements, we revise the balance of each account affected. In other words, we make those statements appear as if the newly adopted accounting method had been applied all along. Then, a journal entry is created to adjust all account balances affected to what those amounts would have been. In addition, if retained earnings is one of the accounts whose balance requires adjustment, that adjustment is made to the beginning balance of retained earnings for the earliest period reported on the comparative statements of shareholders' equity.[39]

Let's suppose that in 2006 the Dearborn Corporation switched from the LIFO inventory method to FIFO. Along with its 2006 statements, Dearborn presents two additional years of income statements and statements of shareholders' equity (2005 and 2004) as well as a 2005 balance sheet for comparative purposes. Here are the steps Dearborn would follow to account for the change.

1. The comparative financial statements are revised. For all three years—2004, 2005, and 2006—income statements will appear as if FIFO had been applied all along. Dearborn uses its new method, FIFO, to determine cost of goods sold, income tax expense, and net income in 2006 and recalculates the 2004 and 2005 numbers from LIFO to FIFO. Similarly, inventory and retained earnings in each year's balance sheet are reported using the newly adopted FIFO method. In its statements of shareholders' equity, Dearborn reports retained earnings each year as if it had used FIFO all along. Because 2004 is the earliest year reported, beginning retained earnings that year is revised to reflect the cumulative income effect of the difference in inventory methods for all years prior to 2004.
2. The appropriate accounts are adjusted. Dearborn will create a journal entry to adjust the book balances from their current LIFO amounts to what those balances would have been using FIFO. Since differences in cost of goods sold and income are reflected in retained earnings, as are the income tax effects, the journal entry updates these accounts.
3. A disclosure note provides additional information. Dearborn must provide clear justification that the change to FIFO is appropriate in a disclosure note. The note also indicates the effects of the change on items not reported on the face of the primary statements, as well as any per share amounts affected for the current period and all prior periods presented.

We will see these steps demonstrated in Chapter 9 in the context of our discussion of inventory methods. We'll revisit accounting changes in depth in Chapter 20.

## CHANGE IN DEPRECIATION, AMORTIZATION, OR DEPLETION METHOD

A change in depreciation, amortization, or depletion method is considered to be a change in accounting estimate that is achieved by a change in accounting principle. We account for these changes prospectively, exactly as we would any other change in estimate. We discuss and illustrate this approach in the next section.

**Changes in depreciation, amortization, or depletion methods are accounted for the same way as a change in accounting estimate.**

## CHANGE IN ACCOUNTING ESTIMATE

● LO8

Estimates are a necessary aspect of accounting. A few of the more common accounting estimates are the amount of future bad debts on existing accounts receivable, the useful life and residual value of a depreciable asset, and future warranty expenses.

Because estimates require the prediction of future events, it's not unusual for them to turn out to be wrong. When an estimate is modified as new information comes to light, accounting for the change in estimate is quite straightforward. We do not revise prior years' financial statements to reflect the new estimate. Instead, we merely incorporate the new estimate in any related accounting determinations from that point on.[40]

**A *change in accounting estimate* is reflected in the financial statements of the current period and future periods.**

Consider the example in Illustration 4–8.

[39]Sometimes a lack of information makes it impracticable to report a change retrospectively so the new method is simply applied prospectively, that is, we simply use the new method from now on. Also, if a new standard specifically requires prospective accounting, that requirement is followed.

[40]If the original estimate had been based on erroneous information or calculations or had not been made in good faith, the revision of that estimate would constitute the correction of an error.

**ILLUSTRATION 4–8**
Change in Accounting Estimate

The Maxwell Gear Corporation purchased machinery in 2003 for $2 million. The useful life of the machinery was estimated to be 10 years with no residual value. The straight-line depreciation method was used in 2003 through 2005, with a full year of depreciation taken in 2003. In 2006, the company revised the useful life of the machinery to eight years.

Neither depreciation expense nor accumulated depreciation reported in prior years is restated. No account balances are adjusted. Rather, in 2006 and later years, the adjusting entry to record depreciation expense simply will reflect the new useful life. In 2006, the entry is:

| | | |
|---|---|---|
| Depreciation expense (below) | 280,000 | |
| Accumulated depreciation | | 280,000 |

| | | |
|---|---|---|
| | $2,000,000 | Cost |
| $200,000 | | Previous annual depreciation ($2,000,000 ÷ 10 years) |
| × 3 years | 600,000 | Depreciation to date (2003–2005) |
| | $1,400,000 | Book value as of 1/1/06 |
| | ÷ 5 yrs. | Estimated remaining life (8 years − 3 years) |
| | $ 280,000 | New annual depreciation |

When a company makes a change in an estimate that affects several future periods, such as revising its estimate of an asset's useful life, the company reports in a disclosure note the effect of that change on the current year's income before extraordinary items, net income, and earnings per share. That disclosure isn't necessary for more routine changes such as revising estimates regarding uncollectible accounts, unless the effect of the change is material.

A recent annual report of **NationsRent, Inc.** provides us an example. The company operates a nationwide network of equipment rental locations offering a broad selection of equipment primarily to the construction and industrial segments of the equipment rental industry. Graphic 4–8 reproduces the disclosure note that described a change in the useful life and residual values for certain of its rental assets.

**GRAPHIC 4–8**
Change in Estimate—NationsRent, Inc.

**2. Change in Depreciation Estimate**
Effective July 1, the Company revised the estimated service lives and residual values for certain of its rental assets to better allocate depreciation expense over the time that such assets are in its rental fleet. This change decreased the estimated service lives and increased the residual values for certain rental assets. The change in estimate resulted in a decrease in rental equipment depreciation expense of approximately $9,800,000 and a decrease in net loss of approximately $6,000,000, or $0.10 per diluted share, for the current year.

As we discussed in a previous section, a change in depreciation, amortization, or depletion method is considered a change in estimate resulting from a change in principle. For that reason, we account for such a change prospectively, similar to the way we account for other changes in estimate. One difference is that most changes in estimate do not require a company to justify the change. However, this change in estimate is a result of changing an accounting principle and therefore requires a clear justification as to why the new method is preferable. Illustration 4–9 provides an example.

A disclosure note reports the effect on net income and earnings per share along with clear justification for changing depreciation methods.

## CHANGE IN REPORTING ENTITY

A third type of change—the **change in reporting entity**—involves the preparation of financial statements for an accounting entity other than the entity that existed in the previous period.[41] For example, if Company A acquired Company B during 2006, consolidated financial

[41]In Chapter 20 we discuss the different types of situations that result in a change in accounting entity.

**ILLUSTRATION 4–9**
Change in Depreciation Method

The Maxwell Gear Corporation uses the double-declining balance (DDB) depreciation method for most of its equipment. In 2006, for consistency with other firms in the industry, the company switched from the DDB method to straight-line depreciation for a large group of equipment purchased at the beginning of 2004. Maxwell purchased this equipment at a cost of $50 million. The machinery has an expected useful life of five years and no estimated residual value.

When the change occurs, the company does not revise either depreciation expense or accumulated depreciation reported in prior years. No account balances are adjusted. Rather, in 2006 and later years, its adjusting entry to record depreciation expense simply will reflect the new depreciation method (straight-line). In 2006, the adjusting entry is ($ in millions):

| | | |
|---|---|---|
| Depreciation expense (below) . . . . . . . . . . . . . . | 6 | |
| Accumulated depreciation . . . . . . . . . . . . . . | | 6 |

DDB depreciation:

| | |
|---|---|
| 2004 | $20 ($50 × 40%*) |
| 2005 | 12 ([$50 − 20] × 40%*) |
| Total | $32 |

*Double the straight-line rate for five years [(1/5 = 20%) × 2 = 40%]

| | |
|---|---|
| $50 | Cost |
| 32 | Depreciation to date, DDB (2004–2005) |
| $18 | Undepreciated cost as of 1/1/06 |
| ÷ 3 yrs. | Remaining life (5 years − 2 years) |
| $ 6 | New annual depreciation |

statements are generally required that combine the statements of the two companies as if they were a single reporting entity. The combined financial statements for A and B for 2006 would not be comparable to the financial statements of the separate companies for 2005.[42]

**A *change in reporting entity* requires that financial statements of prior periods be *retrospectively* restated.**

A change in reporting entity is reported by restating all previous periods' financial statements presented for comparative purposes as if the new reporting entity existed in those periods. In other words, in our example, the financial statements are presented as if A and B had been combined in prior years. In addition, in the first set of financial statements issued after the change, a disclosure note is required that describes the nature of the change, the reason it occurred, and the effect of the change on net income, income before extraordinary items, and related per share amounts for all periods presented.

## Correction of Accounting Errors

● LO8

Errors occur when transactions are either recorded incorrectly or not recorded at all. We briefly discuss the correction of errors here as an overview and in later chapters in the context of the effect of errors on specific chapter topics. In addition, Chapter 20 provides comprehensive coverage of the correction of errors.

Accountants employ various control mechanisms to ensure that transactions are accounted for correctly. In spite of this, errors occur. When errors do occur, they can affect any one or several of the financial statement elements on any of the financial statements a company prepares. In fact, many kinds of errors simultaneously affect more than one financial statement. When errors are discovered, they should be corrected.

Most errors are discovered in the same year that they are made. These errors are simple to correct. The original erroneous journal entry is reversed and the appropriate entry is recorded. If an error is discovered in a year subsequent to the year the error is made, accounting

[42]The issuance of *SFAS 94,* "Consolidation of All Majority-Owned Subsidiaries," resulted in hundreds of reporting entities being altered to include previously unconsolidated finance subsidiaries.

treatment depends on whether or not the error is material with respect to its effect on the financial statements. In practice, the vast majority of errors are not material and are, therefore, simply corrected in the year discovered.

### PRIOR PERIOD ADJUSTMENTS

After its financial statements are published and distributed to shareholders, Roush Distribution Company discovers an error in the statements. What does it do? *Material* errors discovered after the year the error is made are rare. The correction of these errors is considered to be a **prior period adjustment**.[43] A prior period adjustment refers to an addition to or reduction in the beginning retained earnings balance in a statement of shareholders' equity (or statement of retained earnings if that's presented instead).

When it's discovered that the ending balance of retained earnings in the period prior to the discovery of an error was incorrect as a result of that error, the balance is corrected. However, simply reporting a corrected amount might cause misunderstanding for someone familiar with the previously reported amount. Explicitly reporting a prior period adjustment on the statement of shareholders' equity (or statement of retained earnings) avoids this confusion.

In addition to reporting the prior period adjustment to retained earnings, previous years' financial statements that are incorrect as a result of the error are retrospectively restated to reflect the correction. Also, a disclosure note communicates the impact of the error on income.

## Earnings per Share Disclosures

● LO9

As we discussed in Chapter 3, financial statement users often use summary indicators, called *ratios,* to more efficiently make comparisons among different companies and over time for the same company. Besides highlighting important relationships among financial statement variables, ratios also accommodate differences in company size.

One of the most widely used ratios is **earnings per share (EPS),** which shows the amount of income earned by a company expressed on a per share basis. Companies report both **basic** and **diluted** EPS. Basic EPS is computed by dividing income available to common stockholders (net income less any preferred stock dividends) by the weighted-average number of common shares outstanding for the period. Diluted EPS reflects the potential dilution that could occur for companies that have certain securities outstanding that are convertible into common shares or stock options that could create additional common shares if the options were exercised. These items could cause EPS to decrease (become diluted). Because of the complexity of the calculation and the importance of EPS to investors, we devote a substantial portion of Chapter 19 to this topic. At this point, we focus on the financial statement presentation of EPS.

**All corporations whose common stock is publicly traded must disclose EPS.**

**FedEx Corporation**

All corporations whose common stock is publicly traded must report EPS on the face of the income statement. In Graphic 4–3 on page 160, **FedEx Corporation** discloses both basic ($2.80 in 2004) and diluted ($2.76 in 2004) EPS in its income statements for all years presented.

**Companies must disclose per share amounts for (1) income before any separately reported items, (2) each separately reported item, and (3) net income.**

When the income statement includes one or both of the separately reported items, per share amounts are reported separately for both income before these items and net income, as well as for both discontinued operations and extraordinary items. We see this demonstrated in recent income statements of **Noble International, LTD.**, a full-service provider of tailored laser welded blanks for the automotive industry, partially reproduced in Graphic 4–9.

[43]"Prior Period Adjustments," *Statement of Financial Accounting Standards No. 16* (Stamford, Conn.: FASB, 1977).

**GRAPHIC 4–9**
EPS Disclosures—Noble International, LTD.

**NOBLE INTERNATIONAL LTD.**
**Consolidated Statements of Income (in part)**
**For the Year Ended December 31**

| ($ in thousands, except per share amounts) | 2003 | 2002 |
|---|---|---|
| Income from continuing operations before extraordinary item | $9,134 | $ 4,061 |
| Loss from discontinued operations, net of tax | (3,898) | (17,231) |
| Income (loss) before extraordinary item | 5,236 | (13,170) |
| Extraordinary gain, net of tax | — | 315 |
| Net income | $5,236 | $(12,855) |
| Basic earnings (loss) per common share: | | |
| Income from continuing operations before extraordinary item | $ 1.17 | $ 0.57 |
| Loss from discontinued operations | (0.50) | (2.46) |
| Extraordinary gain | — | 0.05 |
| Net income (loss) | $ 0.67 | $ (1.84) |
| Diluted earnings (loss) per common share: | | |
| Income from continuing operations before extraordinary item | $ 1.09 | $ 0.57 |
| Loss from discontinued operations | (0.43) | (2.41) |
| Extraordinary gain | — | 0.04 |
| Net income (loss) | $ 0.66 | $ (1.80) |

## GLOBAL PERSPECTIVE

### The Income Statement

There are significant differences from country to country in the presentation and content of the income statement as well as in the accounting methods used to measure income statement amounts. Many of the measurement differences are highlighted in the specific chapters that deal with the specific issues. For example, differences in inventory measurement methods, differences in the treatment of goodwill, and differences in the method used to value and depreciate property and equipment are but three of the areas where global practices differ widely.

There also are many differences in the presentation and content of the income statement. Here are just a few examples:

1. *The title of the statement.* For example, in the United Kingdom (U.K.) it's called the Group Profit and Loss Account.
2. *Revenue terminology.* In a number of countries (e.g., the U.K. and Denmark), sales revenue is referred to as *turnover.*
3. *The treatment of extraordinary gains and losses.* In some countries certain extraordinary gains and losses are not included in the income statement, but are shown as direct adjustments to shareholders' equity. In other countries, extraordinary gains and losses are shown in the income statement at their gross amounts, not net of tax. In Korea, accounting principles specify certain transactions that must be reported as extraordinary.
4. *The treatment of a change in accounting principle.* In some countries, a change in accounting principle is treated as an adjustment to retained earnings. Under IFRSs, changes in accounting principle are accounted for retrospectively, consistent with U.S. GAAP.

## CONCEPT REVIEW EXERCISE

**INCOME STATEMENT PRESENTATION**

The Lippincott Construction Company builds office buildings. It also owns and operates a chain of motels throughout the Northwest. On September 30, 2006, the company decided to sell the entire motel business for $40 million. The sale was completed on December 15,

2006. Income statement information for 2006 is provided below for the two components of the company.

| | ($ in millions) | |
|---|---|---|
| | Construction Component | Motel Component |
| Sales revenue | $450.0 | $200.0 |
| Operating expenses | 226.0 | 210.0 |
| Other income (loss)* | 16.0 | (30.0) |
| Income (loss) before income taxes | $240.0 | $ (40.0) |
| Income tax expense (benefit)† | 96.0 | (16.0) |
| Net income (loss) | $144.0 | $ (24.0) |

*For the motel component, the entire Other income (loss) amount represents the loss on sale of assets of the component for $40 million when their book value was $70 million.
†A 40% tax rate applies to all items of income or loss.

In addition to the revenues and expenses of the construction and motel components, Lippincott experienced a before-tax loss of $20 million to its construction business from damage to buildings and equipment caused by volcanic activity at Mount St. Helens. The event was considered unusual and infrequent.

**Required:**

Prepare a 2006 income statement for the Lippincott Construction Company including EPS disclosures. There were 100 million shares of common stock outstanding throughout 2006. The company had no potential common shares outstanding.

## SOLUTION

**LIPPINCOTT CONSTRUCTION COMPANY**
**Income Statement**
**For the Year Ended December 31, 2006**
($ in millions, except per share amounts)

| | | |
|---|---|---|
| Sales revenue | | $450.0 |
| Operating expenses | | 226.0 |
| Operating income | | 224.0 |
| Other income | | 16.0 |
| Income from continuing operations before income taxes and extraordinary item | | 240.0 |
| Income tax expense | | 96.0 |
| Income from continuing operations before extraordinary item | | 144.0 |
| Discontinued operations: | | |
| Loss from operations of discontinued motel component (including loss on disposal of $30) | $(40) | |
| Income tax benefit | 16 | |
| Loss on discontinued operations | | (24.0) |
| Income before extraordinary item | | 120.0 |
| Extraordinary loss from volcano damage, net of $8.0 tax benefit | | (12.0) |
| Net income | | $108.0 |
| **Earnings per share:** | | |
| Income from continuing operations before extraordinary item | | $ 1.44 |
| Discontinued operations | | (.24) |
| Extraordinary loss | | (.12) |
| Net income | | $ 1.08 |

Now that we have discussed the presentation and content of the income statement, we turn our attention to the statement of cash flows.

# THE STATEMENT OF CASH FLOWS

**PART B**

● LO10

In addition to the income statement and the balance sheet, a **statement of cash flows (SCF)** is an essential component within the set of basic financial statements.[44] Specifically, when a balance sheet and an income statement are presented, a statement of cash flows is required for each income statement period. The purpose of the SCF is to provide information about the cash receipts and cash disbursements of an enterprise that occurred during a period. Similar to the income statement, it is a *change* statement, summarizing the transactions that caused cash to change during a reporting period. The term *cash* refers to *cash plus cash equivalents.* Cash equivalents, discussed in Chapter 3, include highly liquid (easily converted to cash) investments such as Treasury bills. Chapter 21 is devoted exclusively to the SCF. A brief overview is provided here.

***A statement of cash flows* is presented for each period for which results of operations are provided.**

## Usefulness of the Statement of Cash Flows

We discussed the difference between cash and accrual accounting in Chapter 1. It was pointed out and illustrated that over short periods of time, operating cash flows may not be indicative of the company's long-run cash-generating ability, and that accrual-based net income provides a more accurate prediction of future operating cash flows. Nevertheless, information about cash flows from operating activities, when combined with information about cash flows from other activities, can provide information helpful in assessing future profitability, liquidity, and long-term solvency. After all, a company must pay its debts with cash, not with income.

Of particular importance is the amount of cash generated from operating activities. In the long run, a company must be able to generate positive cash flow from activities related to selling its product or service. These activities must provide the necessary cash to pay debts, provide dividends to shareholders, and provide for future growth.

## Classifying Cash Flows

● LO11

A list of cash flows is more meaningful to investors and creditors if they can determine the type of transaction that gave rise to each cash flow. Toward this end, the statement of cash flows classifies all transactions affecting cash into one of three categories: (1) operating activities, (2) investing activities, and (3) financing activities.

### OPERATING ACTIVITIES

The inflows and outflows of cash that result from activities reported in the income statement are classified as cash flows from **operating activities.** In other words, this classification of cash flows includes the elements of net income reported on a cash basis rather than an accrual basis.[45]

***Operating activities* are inflows and outflows of cash related to the transactions entering into the determination of net operating income.**

Cash inflows include cash received from:

1. Customers from the sale of goods or services.
2. Interest and dividends from investments.

These amounts may differ from sales and investment income reported in the income statement. For example, sales revenue measured on the accrual basis reflects revenue earned during the period, not necessarily the cash actually collected. Revenue will not equal cash collected from customers if receivables from customers or unearned revenue changed during the period.

Cash outflows include cash paid for:

1. The purchase of inventory.
2. Salaries, wages, and other operating expenses.
3. Interest on debt.
4. Income taxes.

[44]"Statement of Cash Flows," *Statement of Financial Accounting Standards No. 95* (Stamford, Conn.: FASB, 1987).

[45]Cash flows related to gains and losses from the sale of assets shown in the income statement are reported as investing activities in the SCF.

**GLOBAL PERSPECTIVE**

**The Statement of Cash Flows**

Many other countries also require either the presentation of a statement of cash flows or a similar statement based on funds flows (for example, working capital). The international trend, however, is moving toward the U.S. practice of requiring cash flow statements. IFRSs require a statement of cash flows.

Likewise, these amounts may differ from the corresponding accrual expenses reported in the income statement. Expenses are reported when incurred, not necessarily when cash is actually paid for those expenses. Also, some revenues and expenses, like depreciation expense, don't affect cash at all and aren't reported in the statement of cash flows.

The difference between the inflows and outflows is called *net cash flows from operating activities.* This is equivalent to net income if the income statement had been prepared on a cash basis rather than an accrual basis.

**By the *direct method,* the cash effect of each operating activity is reported directly in the SCF.**

**Direct and Indirect Methods of Reporting.** Two generally accepted formats can be used to report operating activities, the direct method and the indirect method. Under the **direct method,** the cash effect of each operating activity is reported directly in the statement. For example, *cash received from customers* is reported as the cash effect of sales activities. Income statement transactions that have no cash flow effect, such as depreciation, are simply not reported.

**By the indirect method, cash flow from operating activities is derived indirectly by starting with reported net income and adding or subtracting items to convert that amount to a cash basis.**

By the **indirect method,** on the other hand, we arrive at net cash flow from operating activities indirectly by starting with reported net income and working backwards to convert that amount to a cash basis. Two types of adjustments to net income are needed. First, components of net income that do not affect cash are reversed. That means that noncash revenues and gains are subtracted, while noncash expenses and losses are added. For example, depreciation expense does not reduce cash, but it is subtracted in the income statement. To reverse this, then, we add back depreciation expense to net income to get back to the amount that we would have had if depreciation had not been subtracted.

Second, we make adjustments for changes in assets and liabilities during the period that indicate that amounts included as components of net income are not the same as cash flows for those components. For instance, suppose accounts receivable increases during the period because cash collected from customers is less than sales revenue. This increase in accounts receivable would then be subtracted from net income to arrive at *cash flow from operating activities.* In the indirect method, positive adjustments to net income are made for decreases in related assets and increases in related liabilities, while negative adjustments are made for increases in those assets and decreases in those liabilities.

To contrast the direct and indirect methods further, consider the example in Illustration 4–10.

**Direct Method.** Let's begin with the direct method of presentation. We illustrated this method previously in Chapter 2. In that chapter, specific cash transactions were provided and we simply included them in the appropriate cash flow category in the SCF. Here, we start with account balances, so the direct method requires a bit more reasoning.

From the income statement, we see that ALC's net income has four components. Three of those—service revenue, administrative expenses, and income tax expense—affect cash flows, but not by the accrual amounts reported in the income statement. One component—depreciation—reduces net income but not cash; it's simply an allocation over time of a prior year's expenditure for a depreciable asset. So, to report these operating activities on a cash basis, rather than an accrual basis, we take the three items that affect cash and adjust the amounts to reflect cash inflow rather than revenue earned and cash outflows rather than expenses incurred. Let's start with service revenue.

**ILLUSTRATION 4–10**
Contrasting the Direct and Indirect Methods of Presenting Cash Flows from Operating Activities

Arlington Lawn Care (ALC) began operations at the beginning of 2006. ALC's 2006 income statement and its year-end balance sheet are shown below ($ in thousands).

**ARLINGTON LAWN CARE**
**Income Statement**
**For the Year Ended December 31, 2006**

| | | |
|---|---|---|
| Service revenue | | $90 |
| Operating expenses: | | |
| Administrative | $32 | |
| Depreciation | 8 | |
| Total operating expenses | | 40 |
| Income before income taxes | | 50 |
| Income tax expense | | 15 |
| Net income | | $35 |

Net income is $35,000, but cash flow from these same activities is not necessarily the same amount.

**ARLINGTON LAWN CARE**
**Balance Sheet**
**At December 31, 2006**

| Assets | | Liabilities and Shareholders' Equity | |
|---|---|---|---|
| Current assets: | | Current liabilities: | |
| Cash | $ 63 | Accounts payable* | $ 7 |
| Accounts receivable | 12 | Income taxes payable | 15 |
| Total current assets | 75 | Total current liabilities | 22 |
| Equipment | 40 | Shareholders' equity: | |
| Less: Accumulated depreciation | (8) | Common stock | 50 |
| Total assets | $107 | Retained earnings | 35 |
| | | Total liabilities and shareholders' equity | $107 |

*For administrative expenses

Changes in assets and liabilities can indicate that cash inflows are different from revenues and cash outflows are different from expenses.

Service revenue is $90,000, but ALC did not collect that much cash from its customers. We know that because accounts receivable increased from $0 to $12,000, so ALC must have collected to date only $78,000 of the amount earned.

**Accounts Receivable**

| | | | |
|---|---|---|---|
| Beg. bal. | 0 | | |
| Revenue | 90 | | |
| | | 78 | Cash |
| End bal | 12 | | |

Similarly, administrative expenses of $32,000 were incurred, but $7,000 of that hasn't yet been paid because accounts payable increased by $7,000. That means cash paid thus far for administrative expenses was only $25,000. The other expense, income tax, was $15,000, but that's the amount by which income taxes payable increased so no cash has yet been paid for income taxes.

We can report ALC's cash flows from operating activities using the direct method as shown Illustration 4–10A.

**ILLUSTRATION 4–10A**
Direct Method of Presenting Cash Flows from Operating Activities

By the direct method, we report the components of net income on a cash basis.

**ARLINGTON LAWN CARE**
**Statement of Cash Flows**
**For the Year Ended December 31, 2006**

| | ($ in thousands) |
|---|---|
| **Cash Flows from Operating Activities** | |
| Cash received from customers* | $78 |
| Cash paid for administrative expenses† | (25) |
| Net cash flows from operating activities | $53 |

*Service revenue of $90,000, less increase of $12,000 in accounts receivable.
†Administrative expenses of $32,000, less increase of $7 thousand in accounts payable.

Depreciation expense does not reduce cash, but it is subtracted in the income statement. So, we add back depreciation expense to net income to eliminate it.

**Indirect Method.** To report operating cash flows using the indirect method, we take a different approach. We start with ALC's net income but realize that the $35,000 includes both cash and noncash components. We need to adjust net income, then, to eliminate the noncash effects so that we're left with only the cash flows. We start by eliminating the only noncash component of net income in our illustration—depreciation expense. Depreciation of $8,000 was subtracted in the income statement, so we simply add it back in to eliminate it.

We make adjustments for changes in assets and liabilities that indicate that components of net income are not the same as cash flows.

That leaves us with the three components that do affect cash but not by the amounts reported. For those, we need to make adjustments to net income to cause it to reflect cash flows rather than accrual amounts. For instance, we saw earlier that only $78,000 cash was received from customers even though $90,000 revenue is reflected in net income. That means we need to include an adjustment to reduce net income by $12,000, the increase in accounts receivable. In a similar manner, we include adjustments for the changes in accounts payable and income taxes payable to cause net income to reflect cash payments rather than expenses incurred. Because more was subtracted in the income statement for these two expenses than cash paid, we need to add back the differences—the increases in the liabilities for these expenses. Note that if these liabilities had decreased, we would have subtracted, rather than added, the changes.

Cash flows from operating activities using the indirect method are shown in Illustration 4–10B.

**ILLUSTRATION 4–10B**
Indirect Method of Presenting Cash Flows from Operating Activities

By the indirect method, we start with net income and work backwards to convert that amount to a cash basis.

**ARLINGTON LAWN CARE**
**Statement of Cash Flows**
**For the Year Ended December 31, 2006**

| | ($ in thousands) | |
|---|---|---|
| **Cash Flows from Operating Activities** | | |
| Net income | | $35 |
| *Adjustments for noncash effects:* | | |
| Depreciation expense | $ 8 | |
| Increase in accounts receivable | (12) | |
| Increase in accounts payable | 7 | |
| Increase in income taxes payable | 15 | 18 |
| Net cash flows from operating activities | | $53 |

Both the direct and the indirect methods produce the same net cash flows from operating activities; they are merely alternative approaches to reporting the cash flows. The FASB, in *SFAS 95,* stated its preference for the direct method. However, while both methods are used in practice, the indirect method is used much more frequently.

The choice of presentation method for cash flow from operating activities has no effect on how investing activities and financing activities are reported. We now look at how cash flows are classified into those two categories.

## INVESTING ACTIVITIES

*Investing activities* involve the acquisition and sale of (1) long-term assets used in the business and (2) nonoperating investment assets.

Cash flows from **investing activities** include inflows and outflows of cash related to the acquisition and disposition of long-term assets used in the operations of the business (such as property, plant, and equipment) and investment assets (except those classified as cash equivalents). The purchase and sale of inventories are not considered investing activities. Inventories are purchased for the purpose of being sold as part of the company's operations, so their purchase and sale are included with operating activities rather than investing activities.

Cash outflows from investing activities include cash paid for:

1. The purchase of long-term assets used in the business.
2. The purchase of investment securities like stocks and bonds of other entities (other than those classified as cash equivalents).
3. Loans to other entities.

Later, when the assets are disposed of, cash inflow from the sale of the assets (or collection of loans and notes) also is reported as cash flows from investing activities. As a result, cash inflows from these transactions are considered investing activities:

1. The sale of long-term assets used in the business.
2. The sale of investment securities (other than cash equivalents).
3. The collection of a nontrade receivable (excluding the collection of interest, which is an operating activity).

*Net cash flows from investing activities* represents the difference between the inflows and outflows. The only investing activity indicated in Illustration 4–10 is ALC's investment of $40,000 cash for equipment.

## FINANCING ACTIVITIES

**Financing activities** relate to the external financing of the company. Cash inflows occur when cash is borrowed from creditors or invested by owners. Cash outflows occur when cash is paid back to creditors or distributed to owners. The payment of interest to a creditor, however, is classified as an operating activity.

*Financing activities involve cash inflows and outflows from transactions with creditors (excluding trade creditors) and owners.*

Cash inflows include cash received from:

1. Owners when shares are sold to them.
2. Creditors when cash is borrowed through notes, loans, mortgages, and bonds.

Cash outflows include cash paid to:

1. Owners in the form of dividends or other distributions.
2. Owners for the reacquisition of shares previously sold.
3. Creditors as repayment of the principal amounts of debt (excluding trade payables that relate to operating activities).

*Net cash flows from financing activities* is the difference between the inflows and outflows. The only financing activity indicated in Illustration 4–10 is ALC's receipt of $50,000 cash from issuing common stock.

## NONCASH INVESTING AND FINANCING ACTIVITIES

As we just discussed, the statement of cash flows provides useful information about the investing and financing activities in which a company is engaged. Even though these primarily result in cash inflows and cash outflows, there may be significant investing and financing activities occurring during the period that do not involve cash flows at all. In order to provide complete information about these activities, the SCF shows any significant *noncash* investing and financing activities (that is, noncash exchanges). An example is the acquisition of equipment (an investing activity) by issuing either a long-term note payable or equity securities (a financing activity). These noncash activities are reported either in a separate schedule or in a note.

*Significant investing and financing transactions not involving cash also are reported.*

An illustration of a statement of cash flows is provided in the following concept review exercise.

# CONCEPT REVIEW EXERCISE

## STATEMENT OF CASH FLOWS

Dublin Enterprises, Inc. (DEI) owns a chain of retail electronics stores located in shopping malls. The following are the company's 2006 income statement and comparative balance sheets ($ in millions):

**Income Statement**
**For the Year Ended December 31, 2006**

| | |
|---|---|
| Revenue | $2,100 |
| Cost of goods sold | 1,400 |
| Gross profit | 700 |

| | | |
|---|---|---|
| Operating expenses: | | |
| Selling and administrative | $ 355 | |
| Depreciation | 85 | |
| Total operating expenses | | 440 |
| Income before income taxes | | 260 |
| Income tax expense | | 78 |
| Net income | | $ 182 |

| **Comparative Balance Sheets** | **12/31/06** | **12/31/05** |
|---|---|---|
| **Assets:** | | |
| Cash | $ 300 | $ 220 |
| Accounts receivable (net) | 227 | 240 |
| Inventory | 160 | 120 |
| Property, plant & equipment | 960 | 800 |
| Less: Accumulated depreciation | (405) | (320) |
| Total assets | $1,242 | $1,060 |
| **Liabilities and shareholders' equity:** | | |
| Accounts payable | $ 145 | $ 130 |
| Payables for selling and admin. expenses | 147 | 170 |
| Income taxes payable | 95 | 50 |
| Long-term debt | –0– | 100 |
| Common stock | 463 | 400 |
| Retained earnings | 392 | 210 |
| Total liabilities and shareholders' equity | $1,242 | $1,060 |

**Required:**

1. Prepare DEI's 2006 statement of cash flows using the direct method.
2. Prepare the cash flows from operating activities section of DEI's 2006 statement of cash flows using the indirect method.

**SOLUTION**

1. Prepare DEI's 2006 statement of cash flows using the direct method.

**DUBLIN ENTERPRISES, INC.**
**Statement of Cash Flows**
**For the Year Ended December 31, 2006**
($ in millions)

| | | |
|---|---|---|
| **Cash Flows from Operating Activities** | | |
| Collections from customers[1] | $2,113 | |
| Purchase of inventory[2] | (1,425) | |
| Payment of selling and administrative expenses[3] | (378) | |
| Payment of income taxes[4] | (33) | |
| Net cash flows from operating activities | | $277 |
| **Cash Flows from Investing Activities** | | |
| Purchase of property, plant, and equipment | | (160) |
| **Cash Flows from Financing Activities** | | |
| Issuance of common stock | 63 | |
| Payment on long-term debt | (100) | |
| Net cash flows from financing activities | | (37) |
| Net increase in cash | | 80 |
| Cash, January 1 | | 220 |
| Cash, December 31 | | $300 |

[1]Sales revenue of $2,100 million, plus $13 million decrease in accounts receivable (net).
[2]Cost of goods sold of $1,400 million, plus $40 million increase in inventory, less $15 million increase in accounts payable.
[3]Selling & administrative expenses of $355 million, plus $23 million decrease in payables for selling & administrative expenses.
[4]Income tax expense of $78 million, less $45 million increase in income taxes payable.

2. Prepare the cash flows from operating activities section of DEI's 2006 statement of cash flows using the indirect method.

**DUBLIN ENTERPRISES, INC.**
**Statement of Cash Flows**
**For the Year Ended December 31, 2006**
($ in millions)

| | | |
|---|---|---|
| **Cash Flows from Operating Activities** | | |
| Net Income | $182 | |
| *Adjustments for noncash effects:* | | |
| Depreciation expense | 85 | |
| Decrease in accounts receivable (net) | 13 | |
| Increase in inventory | (40) | |
| Increase in accounts payable | 15 | |
| Increase in income taxes payable | 45 | |
| Decrease in payables for selling and administrative expenses | (23) | |
| Net cash flows from operating activities | | $277 |

## FINANCIAL REPORTING CASE SOLUTION

1. **How would you explain restructuring costs to Becky? Are they necessarily a negative?** *(p. 164)* Restructuring costs include employee severance and termination benefits plus other costs associated with the shutdown or relocation of facilities or downsizing of operations. It's not necessarily bad. In fact, the objective is to make operations more efficient. The costs are incurred now in hopes of better earnings later. Prior to 2003, when a company restructured its operations, it estimated the future costs associated with the restructuring and expensed the costs in the period in which the decision to restructure was made. An offsetting liability was recorded. Later expenditures were charged against this liability as they occurred.
2. **In addition to discontinued operations, what other events sometimes are reported separately in the income statement that you might tell Becky about? Why are these items reported separately?** *(p. 168)* In addition to discontinued operations, extraordinary items also are reported separately in the income statement when they are present. The predictive ability of an income statement is significantly enhanced if normal and recurrent transactions are separated from unusual and nonrecurrent items. The income statement is a historical report, summarizing the most recent profit-generating activities of a company. The information in the statement is useful if it can help users predict the future. Toward this end, users should be made aware of events reported in the income statement that are not likely to occur again in the foreseeable future.
3. **Explain to Becky what is meant by discontinued operations and describe to her how one is reported in an income statement.** *(p. 170)* A discontinued operation occurs when a company decides to discontinue a separate component. A component of an entity comprises operations and cash flows that can be clearly distinguished, operationally and for financial reporting purposes, from the rest of the entity. The net-of-tax effect of discontinued operations is separately reported below income from continuing operations. If the component has been disposed of by the end of the reporting period, the income effects include: (1) income or loss from operations of the discontinued component from the beginning of the reporting period through the disposal date and (2) gain or loss on disposal of the component's assets. If the component has not been disposed of by the end of the reporting period, the income effects include: (1) income or loss from operations of the discontinued component from the beginning of the reporting period through the end of the reporting period, and (2) an impairment loss if the fair value minus cost to sell of the component's assets is less than their carrying amount (book value). ■

# THE BOTTOM LINE

1. The FASB's Concept Statement 6 defines the term *comprehensive income* as the change in equity from nonowner transactions. The calculation of net income, however, excludes certain transactions that are included in comprehensive income. To convey the relationship between the two measures, companies must report both net income and comprehensive income and reconcile the difference between the two. The presentation can be (a) included as an extension to the income statement, (b) reported (exactly the same way) as a separate statement of comprehensive income, or (c) included in the statement of changes in shareholders' equity.
2. The components of income from continuing operations are revenues, expenses (including income taxes), gains, and losses, excluding those related to discontinued operations and extraordinary items. Companies often distinguish between operating and nonoperating income within continuing operations.
3. The term *earnings quality* refers to the ability of reported earnings (income) to predict a company's future earnings. The relevance of any historical-based financial statement hinges on its predictive value. To enhance predictive value, analysts try to separate a company's *transitory earnings* effects from its *permanent earnings*. Many believe that manipulating income reduces earnings quality because it can mask permanent earnings. Two major methods used by managers to manipulate earnings are (1) income shifting and (2) income statement classification.
4. Analysts begin their assessment of permanent earnings with income from continuing operations. It would be a mistake to assume income from continuing operations reflects permanent earnings entirely. In other words, there may be transitory earnings effects included in both operating and nonoperating income.
5. A discontinued operation refers to the disposal or a planned disposal of a component of the entity. A component of an entity comprises operations and cash flows that can be clearly distinguished, operationally and for financial reporting purposes, from the rest of the company. The net-of-tax effects of discontinued operations are separately reported below income from continuing operations.
6. Extraordinary items are material gains and losses that are both unusual in nature and infrequent in occurrence. The net-of-tax effects of extraordinary items are presented in the income statement below discontinued operations, if any.
7. Most voluntary changes in accounting principles are reported retrospectively. This means revising all previous periods' financial statements to appear as if the newly adopted accounting method had been applied all along. Some changes are reported prospectively. These include: (a) changes in the method of depreciation, amortization, or depletion, (b) some changes in principle for which retrospective application is impracticable, and (c) a few changes for which an authoritative pronouncement requires prospective application.
8. A change in accounting estimate is treated currently and prospectively, rather than by recasting prior years' financial statements to correct the estimate. In other words, the new estimate merely is used from that point on. Most errors are discovered in the same year that they are made. These errors are simple to correct. However, material errors discovered in a year subsequent to the year the error was made are considered prior period adjustments. The correction of the error is accounted for by restating prior years' financial statements, causing an adjustment to beginning of period retained earnings.
9. Earnings per share (EPS) is the amount of income achieved during a period expressed per share of common stock outstanding. The EPS must be disclosed for income from continuing operations and for each item below continuing operations.
10. When a company provides a set of financial statements that reports both financial position and results of operations, a statement of cash flows is reported for each period for which results of operations are provided. The purpose of the statement is to provide information about the cash receipts and cash disbursements that occurred during the period.
11. To enhance the usefulness of the information, the statement of cash flows classifies all transactions affecting cash into one of three categories: (1) operating activities, (2) investing activities, or (3) financing activities. ■

# QUESTIONS FOR REVIEW OF KEY TOPICS

**Q 4–1** The income statement is a change statement. Explain what is meant by this.

**Q 4–2** Define comprehensive income. What are the three ways companies can present the reconciliation between net income and comprehensive income?

**Q 4–3** What transactions are included in income from continuing operations? Briefly explain why it is important to segregate income from continuing operations from other transactions affecting net income.

**Q 4–4** Distinguish between operating and nonoperating income in relation to the income statement.

**Q 4–5** Briefly explain the difference between the single-step and multiple-step income statement formats.

**Q 4–6** Explain what is meant by the term earnings quality.

**Q 4–7** What are restructuring costs and where are they reported in the income statement?

**Q 4–8** Define intraperiod tax allocation. Why is the process necessary?

**Q 4–9** Define what is meant by a component of an entity in the context of reporting the results of discontinued operations. How are discontinued operations reported in the income statement?

**Q 4–10** Define extraordinary items.

**Q 4–11** How should extraordinary gains and losses be reported in the income statement?

**Q 4–12** What is meant by a change in accounting principle? Describe the accounting treatment for a change in accounting principle.

**Q 4–13** Define earnings per share (EPS). For which income statement items must EPS be disclosed?

**Q 4–14** Accountants very often are required to make estimates, and very often those estimates prove incorrect. In what period(s) is the effect of a change in an accounting estimate reported?

**Q 4–15** The correction of a material error discovered in a year subsequent to the year the error was made is considered a prior period adjustment. Briefly describe the accounting treatment for prior period adjustments.

**Q 4–16** Describe the purpose of the statement of cash flows.

**Q 4–17** Identify and briefly describe the three categories of cash flows reported in the statement of cash flows.

**Q 4–18** Explain what is meant by noncash investing and financing activities pertaining to the statement of cash flows. Give an example of one of these activities.

**Q 4–19** Distinguish between the direct method and the indirect method for reporting the results of operating activities in the statement of cash flows.

# BRIEF EXERCISES

**BE 4–1**
Comprehensive income
● LO1

O'Reilly Beverage Company reported net income of $650,000 for 2006. In addition, the company deferred a $60,000 pretax loss on derivatives and had pretax net unrealized holding gains on investment securities of $40,000. Prepare a statement of comprehensive income for 2006. The company's income tax rate is 40%.

**BE 4–2**
Single-step income statement
● LO2

The adjusted trial balance of Pacific Scientific Corporation on December 31, 2006, the end of the company's fiscal year, contained the following income statement items ($ in millions): sales revenue, $2,106; cost of goods sold, $1,240; selling expenses, $126; general and administrative expenses, $105; interest expense, $35; and gain on sale of investments, $45. Income tax expense has not yet been accrued. The income tax rate is 40%. Prepare a single-step income statement for 2006. Ignore EPS disclosures.

**BE 4–3**
Multiple-step income statement
● LO2 LO4

Refer to the situation described in BE 4–2. If the company's accountant prepared a multiple-step income statement, what amount would appear in that statement for (a) operating income and (b) nonoperating income?

**BE 4–4**
Multiple-step income statement
● LO2 LO4

Refer to the situation described in BE 4–2. Prepare a multiple-step income statement for 2006. Ignore EPS disclosures.

**BE 4–5**
Multiple-step income statement
● LO2 LO4

The following is a partial year-end adjusted trial balance.

| Account Title | Debits | Credits |
|---|---|---|
| Sales revenue | | 300,000 |
| Loss on sale of investments | 22,000 | |
| Interest revenue | | 4,000 |
| Loss from flood damage (unusual and infrequent) | 50,000 | |
| Cost of goods sold | 160,000 | |
| General and administrative expenses | 40,000 | |
| Restructuring costs | 50,000 | |
| Selling expenses | 25,000 | |
| Income tax expense | 0 | |

Income tax expense has not yet been accrued. The income tax rate is 40%. Determine the following: (a) operating income (loss), (b) income (loss) before any separately reported items, and (c) net income (loss).

**BE 4–6**
Separately reported items
● LO4 LO6 LO9

The following are partial income statement account balances taken from the December 31, 2006, year-end trial balance of White and Sons, Inc.: restructuring costs, $300,000; interest revenue, $40,000; loss from earthquake (unusual and infrequent), $400,000; and loss on sale of investments, $50,000. Income tax expense has not yet been accrued. The income tax rate is 40%. Prepare the lower portion of the 2006 income statement beginning with $850,000 income before income taxes and extraordinary item. Include appropriate basic EPS disclosures. The company had 100,000 shares of common stock outstanding throughout the year.

**BE 4–7**
Discontinued operations
● LO5

On December 31, 2006, the end of the fiscal year, California Microtech Corporation completed the sale of its semiconductor business for $10 million. The business segment qualifies as a component of the entity according to *SFAS No. 144.* The book value of the assets of the segment was $8 million. The operating loss of the segment during 2006 was $3.6 million. Pretax income from continuing operations for the year totaled $5.8 million. The income tax rate is 30%. Prepare the lower portion of the 2006 income statement beginning with pretax income from continuing operations. Ignore EPS disclosures.

**BE 4–8**
Discontinued operations
● LO5

Refer to the situation described in BE 4–7. Assume that the semiconductor segment was not sold during 2006 but was held for sale at year-end. The estimated fair value of the segment's assets, less costs to sell, on December 31 was $10 million. Prepare the lower portion of the 2006 income statement beginning with pretax income from continuing operations. Ignore EPS disclosures.

**BE 4–9**
Discontinued operations
● LO5

Refer to the situation described in BE 4–8. Assume instead that the estimated fair value of the segment's assets, less costs to sell, on December 31 was $7 million rather than $10 million. Prepare the lower portion of the 2006 income statement beginning with pretax income from continuing operations. Ignore EPS disclosures.

**BE 4–10**
Accounting change
● LO7

The Korver Company decided to change its inventory costing method from average to FIFO. The depreciation method also was changed from double-declining balance to straight line. Identify the type of accounting change for these two changes and briefly describe the difference in accounting treatment between the two, if any.

**BE 4–11**
Accounting change
● LO8

Powell Manufacturing purchased machinery for $300,000 at the beginning of 2004. A six-year life was estimated and no residual value was anticipated. Straight-line depreciation is used. At the beginning of 2006, the estimated useful life was revised to 10 years in total. What type of accounting change is this? Determine depreciation for 2006.

**BE 4–12**
Statement of cash flows; direct method
● LO11

The following are summary cash transactions that occurred during the year for Hilliard Healthcare Co. (HHC):

| | |
|---|---|
| Cash received from: | |
| Customers | $660,000 |
| Interest on note receivable | 12,000 |
| Collection of note payable | 100,000 |
| Sale of land | 40,000 |
| Issuance of common stock | 200,000 |
| Cash paid for: | |
| Interest on note payable | 18,000 |
| Purchase of equipment | 120,000 |
| Operating expenses | 440,000 |
| Dividends to shareholders | 30,000 |

Prepare the cash flows from operating activities section of HHC's statement of cash flows using the direct method.

**BE 4–13**
Statement of cash flows; investing and financing activities
● LO11

Refer to the situation described in BE 4–12. Prepare the cash flows from investing and financing activities sections of HHC's statement of cash flows.

**BE 4–14**
Statement of cash flows; indirect method
● LO11

Net income of Mansfield Company was $45,000. The accounting records reveal depreciation expense of $80,000 as well as increases in prepaid rent, salaries payable, and income taxes payable of $60,000, $15,000, and $12,000, respectively. Prepare the cash flows from operating activities section of Mansfield's statement of cash flows using the indirect method.

# EXERCISES

available with McGraw-Hill's Homework Manager www.mhhe.com/spiceland4e

**An alternate exercise and problem set is available on the text website: www.mhhe.com/spiceland4e**

**E 4–1**
Comprehensive income
● LO1

The Massoud Consulting Group reported net income of $1,354,000 for its fiscal year ended December 31, 2006. In addition, during the year the company experienced a foreign currency translation adjustment gain of $240,000 and had unrealized losses on investment securities of $80,000. The company's effective tax rate on all items affecting comprehensive income is 30%. Each component of other comprehensive income is displayed net of tax.

Required:
1. Prepare a combined statement of income and comprehensive income for 2006, beginning with net income.
2. Prepare a separate statement of comprehensive income for 2006.

**E 4–2**
Income statement format; single step and multiple step
● LO2

The following is a partial trial balance for the Green Star Corporation as of December 31, 2006:

| Account Title | Debits | Credits |
|---|---|---|
| Sales revenue | | 1,300,000 |
| Interest revenue | | 30,000 |
| Gain on sale of equipment | | 50,000 |
| Cost of goods sold | 720,000 | |
| Salaries expense | 160,000 | |
| Depreciation expense | 50,000 | |
| Interest expense | 40,000 | |
| Rent expense | 25,000 | |
| Income tax expense | 130,000 | |

100,000 shares of common stock were outstanding throughout 2006.

Required:
1. Prepare a single-step income statement for 2006, including EPS disclosures.
2. Prepare a multiple-step income statement for 2006, including EPS disclosures.

**E 4–3**
Income statement format; single step and multiple step
● LO2 LO4 LO6

The following is a partial trial balance for General Lighting Corporation as of December 31, 2006:

| Account Title | Debits | Credits |
|---|---|---|
| Sales revenue | | 2,350,000 |
| Rental revenue | | 80,000 |
| Loss on sale of equipment | 22,500 | |
| Loss from flood damage (event is both unusual and infrequent) | 120,000 | |
| Cost of goods sold | 1,200,300 | |
| Loss from write-down of inventory due to obsolescence | 200,000 | |
| Salaries expense | 300,000 | |
| Depreciation expense | 100,000 | |
| Interest expense | 90,000 | |
| Rent expense | 50,000 | |

300,000 shares of common stock were outstanding throughout 2006. Income tax expense has not yet been accrued, The income tax rate is 40%.

Required:
1. Prepare a single-step income statement for 2006, including EPS disclosures.
2. Prepare a multiple-step income statement for 2006, including EPS disclosures.

**E 4–4**
Multiple-step statement of income and comprehensive income

● LO1 LO2 LO6

The trial balance for Lindor Corporation, a manufacturing company, for the year ended December 31, 2006, included the following comprehensive income accounts:

| Account Title | Debits | Credits |
|---|---|---|
| Sales revenue | | 2,300,000 |
| Gain on early debt extinguishment (unusual and infrequent) | | 400,000 |
| Cost of goods sold | 1,400,000 | |
| Selling and administrative expenses | 420,000 | |
| Interest expense | 40,000 | |
| Unrealized holding gains on investment securities | | 80,000 |

The trial balance does not include the accrual for income taxes. Lindor's income tax rate is 30%. One million shares of common stock were outstanding throughout 2006.

**Required:**
Prepare a combined multiple-step statement of income and comprehensive income for 2006, including appropriate EPS disclosures.

**E 4–5**
Income statement presentation; intraperiod tax allocation

● LO2 LO6

The following *incorrect* income statement was prepared by the accountant of the Axel Corporation:

**AXEL CORPORATION**
**Income Statement**
**For the Year Ended December 31, 2006**

| | | |
|---|---|---|
| Revenues and gains: | | |
| Sales | | $592,000 |
| Interest and dividends | | 32,000 |
| Gain from early extinguishment of debt | | 86,000 |
| Total revenues and gains | | 710,000 |
| Expenses and losses: | | |
| Cost of goods sold | $325,000 | |
| Selling expenses | 67,000 | |
| Administrative expenses | 87,000 | |
| Interest | 26,000 | |
| Restructuring costs | 55,000 | |
| Income taxes | 60,000 | |
| Total expenses and losses | | 620,000 |
| Net Income | | $ 90,000 |
| Earnings per share | | $ 0.90 |

**Required:**
Prepare a multiple-step income statement for 2006 applying generally accepted accounting principles. The income tax rate is 40%. The gain from early extinguishment of debt is considered an unusual and infrequent event.

**E 4–6**
Discontinued operations

● LO5

Chance Company had two operating divisions, one manufacturing farm equipment and the other office supplies. Both divisions are considered separate components as defined by *SFAS No. 144.* The farm equipment component had been unprofitable, and on September 1, 2006, the company adopted a plan to sell the assets of the division. The actual sale was effected on December 15, 2006, at a price of $600,000. The book value of the division's assets was $1,000,000, resulting in a before-tax loss of $400,000 on the sale.

The division incurred before-tax operating losses of $130,000 from the beginning of the year through December 15. The income tax rate is 40%. Chance's after-tax income from its continuing operations is $350,000.

**Required:**
Prepare an income statement for 2006 beginning with income from continuing operations. Include appropriate EPS disclosures assuming that 100,000 shares of common stock were outstanding throughout the year.

**E 4–7**
Income statement presentation; discontinued operations; restructuring charges

● LO2 LO4 LO5

Esquire Comic Book Company had income before tax of $1,000,000 in 2006 *before* considering the following material items:

1. Esquire sold one of its operating divisions, which qualified as a separate component according to *SFAS No. 144.* The before-tax loss on disposal was $350,000. The division generated before-tax operating income from the beginning of the year through disposal of $500,000. Neither the loss on disposal nor the operating income is included in the $1,000,000 before-tax income the company generated from its other divisions.
2. The company incurred restructuring costs of $80,000 during the year.

**Required:**
Prepare a 2006 income statement for Esquire beginning with income from continuing operations. Assume an income tax rate of 40%. Ignore EPS disclosures.

**E 4–8**
Discontinued operations; disposal in subsequent year

● LO5

Kandon Enterprises, Inc. has two operating divisions, one manufactures machinery and the other breeds and sells horses. Both divisions are considered separate components as defined by *SFAS No. 144.* The horse division has been unprofitable, and on November 15, 2006, Kandon adopted a formal plan to sell the division. The sale was completed on April 30, 2007. At December 31, 2006, the component was considered held for sale.

On December 31, 2006, the company's fiscal year-end, the book value of the assets of the horse division was $250,000. On that date, the fair value of the assets, less costs to sell, was $200,000. The before-tax operating loss of the division for the year was $140,000. The company's effective tax rate is 40%. The after-tax income from continuing operations for 2006 was $400,000.

**Required:**
1. Prepare a partial income statement for 2006 beginning with income from continuing operations. Ignore EPS disclosures.
2. Repeat requirement 1 assuming that the estimated net sales price of the horse division's assets was $400,000, instead of $200,000.

**E 4–9**
Discontinued operations; disposal in subsequent year; solving for unknown

● LO5

On September 17, 2006, Ziltech, Inc. entered into an agreement to sell one of its divisions that qualifies as a component of the entity according to *SFAS No. 144.* By December 31, 2006, the company's fiscal year-end, the division had not yet been sold, but was being held for sale. The net fair value (fair value minus costs to sell) of the division's assets at the end of the year was $11 million. The pretax operating income of the division during 2006 was $4 million. Pretax income from continuing operations for the year totaled $14 million. The income tax rate is 40%. Ziltech reported net income for the year of $7.2 million.

**Required:**
Determine the book value of the division's assets on December 31, 2006.

**E 4–10**
Accounting change

● LO8

Canliss Milling Company purchased machinery on January 2, 2004, for $800,000. A five-year life was estimated and no residual value was anticipated. Canliss decided to use the straight-line depreciation method and recorded $160,000 in depreciation in 2004 and 2005. Early in 2006, the company revised the *total* estimated life of the machinery to eight years.

**Required:**
1. What type of accounting change is this?
2. Briefly describe the accounting treatment for this change.
3. Determine depreciation for 2006.

**E 4–11**
Accounting change

● LO7

[This is a variation of the previous exercise]

Canliss Milling Company purchased machinery on January 2, 2004, for $800,000. A five-year life was estimated and no residual value was anticipated. Canliss decided to use the double-declining balance method and recorded depreciation of $320,000 in 2004 and $192,000 in 2005. Early in 2006, the company changed its depreciation method to the straight-line method.

**Required:**
1. Briefly describe the way Canliss should report this accounting change in the 2005–2006 comparative financial statements.
2. Prepare any 2006 journal entry related to the change.

**E 4–12**
Earnings per share

● LO9

The Esposito Import Company had 1 million shares of common stock outstanding during 2006. Its income statement reported the following items: income from continuing operations, $5 million; loss from discontinued operations, $1.6 million; extraordinary gain, $2.2 million. All of these amounts are net of tax.

**Required:**
Prepare the 2006 EPS presentation for the Esposito Import Company.

**E 4–13**
Multiple choice; income statement presentation

● LO2 LO4 through LO7

The following questions dealing with income statement presentation are adapted from questions that appeared in CPA examinations. Determine the response that best completes the statements or questions.

1. In Baer Food Co.'s 2006 single-step income statement, the section titled Revenues consisted of the following:

| | |
|---|---|
| Net sales revenue | $187,000 |
| Results from discontinued operations: | |
| Income from discontinued component, net of tax | 12,000 |
| Interest revenue | 10,200 |
| Gain on sale of equipment | 4,700 |
| Extraordinary gain (net of $750 tax effect) | 1,500 |
| Total revenues | $215,400 |

In the revenues section of the 2006 income statement, Baer Food should have reported total revenues of:

a. $216,300
b. $215,400

c. $203,700
d. $201,900

2. A transaction that is unusual but *not* infrequent should be reported separately as a(an)
   a. Extraordinary item, net of applicable income taxes.
   b. Extraordinary item, but *not* net of applicable income taxes.
   c. Component of income from continuing operations, net of applicable income taxes.
   d. Component of income from continuing operations, but *not* net of applicable income taxes.

**E 4–14**
Statement of cash flows; classifications

• LO11

The statement of cash flows classifies all cash inflows and outflows into one of the three categories shown below and lettered from a through c. In addition, certain transactions that do not involve cash are reported in the statement as noncash investing and financing activities, labeled d.

a. Operating activities
b. Investing activities
c. Financing activities
d. Noncash investing and financing activities

**Required:**

For each of the following transactions, use the letters above to indicate the appropriate classification category.

1. ____ Purchase of equipment for cash.
2. ____ Payment of employee salaries.
3. ____ Collection of cash from customers.
4. ____ Cash proceeds from a note payable.
5. ____ Purchase of common stock of another corporation for cash.
6. ____ Issuance of common stock for cash.
7. ____ Sale of machinery for cash.
8. ____ Payment of interest on note payable.
9. ____ Issuance of bonds payable in exchange for land and building.
10. ____ Payment of cash dividends to shareholders.
11. ____ Payment of principal on note payable.

**E 4–15**
Statement of cash flows preparation

• LO11

The following summary transactions occurred during 2006 for Bluebonnet Bakers:

| | |
|---|---|
| **Cash Received from:** | |
| Customers | $380,000 |
| Interest on note receivable | 6,000 |
| Principal on note receivable | 50,000 |
| Sale of investments | 30,000 |
| Proceeds from note payable | 100,000 |
| **Cash Paid for:** | |
| Purchase of inventory | 160,000 |
| Interest on note payable | 5,000 |
| Purchase of equipment | 85,000 |
| Salaries to employees | 90,000 |
| Principal on note payable | 25,000 |
| Payment of dividends to shareholders | 20,000 |

The balance of cash and cash equivalents at the beginning of 2006 was $17,000.

**Required:**

Prepare a statement of cash flows for 2006 for Bluebonnet Bakers. Use the direct method for reporting operating activities.

**E 4–16**
Statement of cash flows directly from transactions

• LO11

The following transactions occurred during March 2006 for the Wainwright Corporation. The company owns and operates a wholesale warehouse. [These are the same transactions analyzed in Exercise 2–1, when we determined their effect on elements of the accounting equation.]

1. Issued 30,000 shares of capital stock in exchange for $300,000 in cash.
2. Purchased equipment at a cost of $40,000. $10,000 cash was paid and a note payable was signed for the balance owed.
3. Purchased inventory on account at a cost of $90,000. The company uses the perpetual inventory system.
4. Credit sales for the month totaled $120,000. The cost of the goods sold was $70,000.
5. Paid $5,000 in rent on the warehouse building for the month of March.
6. Paid $6,000 to an insurance company for fire and liability insurance for a one-year period beginning April 1, 2006.
7. Paid $70,000 on account for the merchandise purchased in 3.
8. Collected $55,000 from customers on account.
9. Recorded depreciation expense of $1,000 for the month on the equipment.

**Required:**

1. Analyze each transaction and classify each as a financing, investing and/or operating activity (a transaction can represent more than one type of activity). In doing so, also indicate the cash effect of each, if any. If there is no cash effect, simply place a check mark (✔) in the appropriate column(s).
*Example:*

| Financing | Investing | Operating |
|---|---|---|
| 1. $300,000 | | |

2. Prepare a statement of cash flows. Assume the cash balance at the beginning of the month was $40,000.

**E 4–17**
Multiple choice; statement of cash flows
● LO10 LO11

The following questions dealing with the statement of cash flows are adapted from questions that appeared in CPA examinations. Determine the response that best completes the statements or questions.

1. The primary purpose of a statement of cash flows is to provide relevant information about
   a. Differences between net income and associated cash receipts and disbursements.
   b. An enterprise's ability to generate future positive net cash flows.
   c. The cash receipts and cash disbursements of an enterprise during a period.
   d. An enterprise's ability to meet cash operating needs.
2. In a statement of cash flows, proceeds from issuing equity instruments should be classified as cash inflows from
   a. Lending activities.
   b. Operating activities.
   c. Investing activities.
   d. Financing activities.
3. In a statement of cash flows, payments to acquire debt instruments of other entities (other than cash equivalents) should be classified as cash outflows for
   a. Operating activities.
   b. Investing activities.
   c. Financing activities.
   d. Lending activities.

**E 4–18**
Statement of cash flows; indirect method
● LO11

Presented below is the 2006 income statement and comparative balance sheet information for Tiger Enterprises.

**TIGER ENTERPRISES**
**Income Statement**
**For the Year Ended December 31, 2006**

| ($ in thousands) | | |
|---|---|---|
| Sales revenue | | $7,000 |
| Operating expenses: | | |
| Cost of goods sold | $3,360 | |
| Depreciation | 240 | |
| Insurance | 100 | |
| Administrative & other | 1,800 | |
| Total operating expenses | | 5,500 |
| Income before income taxes | | 1,500 |
| Income tax expense | | 600 |
| Net income | | $ 900 |

| **Balance Sheet Information** ($ in thousands) | **Dec. 31, 2006** | **Dec. 31, 2005** |
|---|---|---|
| **Assets:** | | |
| Cash | $ 300 | $ 200 |
| Accounts receivable | 750 | 830 |
| Inventory | 640 | 600 |
| Prepaid insurance | 50 | 20 |
| Plant and equipment | 2,100 | 1,800 |
| Less: Accumulated depreciation | (840) | (600) |
| Total assets | $3,000 | $2,850 |
| **Liabilities and Shareholders' Equity:** | | |
| Accounts payable | $ 300 | $ 360 |
| Payables for administrative & other expenses | 300 | 400 |
| Income taxes payable | 200 | 150 |
| Note payable (due 12/31/2007) | 800 | 600 |
| Common stock | 900 | 800 |
| Retained earnings | 500 | 540 |
| Total liabilities and shareholders' equity | $3,000 | $2,850 |

**Required:**
Prepare Tiger's statement of cash flows, using the indirect method to present cash flows from operating activities.

**E 4–19**
Statement of cash flows; direct method
● LO11

Refer to the situation described in E 4–18.

**Required:**
Prepare the cash flows from operating activities section of Tiger's 2006 statement of cash flows using the direct method. Assume that all purchases and sales of inventory are on account, and that there are no anticipated bad debts for accounts receivable. (Hint: Use T-accounts for the pertinent items to isolate the information needed for the statement.)

**E 4–20**
Concepts; terminology
● LO1 through LO11

Listed below are several terms and phrases associated with income statement presentation and the statement of cash flows. Pair each item from List A (by letter) with the item from List B that is most appropriately associated with it.

| List A | List B |
|---|---|
| ____ 1. Intraperiod tax allocation | a. Unusual, infrequent, and material gains and losses. |
| ____ 2. Comprehensive income | b. Starts with net income and works backwards to convert to cash. |
| ____ 3. Extraordinary items | c. Reports the cash effects of each operating activity directly on the statement. |
| ____ 4. Operating income | d. Correction of a material error of a prior period. |
| ____ 5. An operation (according to SFAS 144) | e. Related to the external financing of the company. |
| ____ 6. Earnings per share | f. Associates tax with income statement item. |
| ____ 7. Prior period adjustment | g. Total nonowner change in equity. |
| ____ 8. Financing activities | h. Related to the transactions entering into the determination of net income. |
| ____ 9. Operating activities (SCF) | i. Related to the acquisition and disposition of long-term assets. |
| ____ 10. Investing activities | j. Required disclosure for publicly traded corporation. |
| ____ 11. Direct method | k. A component of an entity. |
| ____ 12. Indirect method | l. Directly related to principal revenue-generating activities. |

**E 4–21**
Multiple choice; CMA exam; income statement
● LO2 LO5 LO6

The following questions dealing with the income statement are adapted from questions that previously appeared on Certified Management Accountant (CMA) examinations. The CMA designation sponsored by the Institute of Management Accountants (**www.imanet.org**) provides members with an objective measure of knowledge and competence in the field of management accounting. Determine the response that best completes the statements or questions.

1. In a multiple-step income statement for a retail company, all of the following are included in the operating section except
   a. Sales.
   b. Cost of goods sold.
   c. Dividend revenue.
   d. Administrative and selling expenses.
2. Which one of the following items is included in the determination of income from continuing operations?
   a. Discontinued operations.
   b. Extraordinary loss.
   c. Cumulative effect of a change in an accounting principle.
   d. Unusual loss from a write-down of inventory.
3. When reporting extraordinary items,
   a. Each item (net of tax) is presented on the face of the income statement separately as a component of net income for the period.
   b. Each item is presented exclusive of any related income tax.
   c. Each item is presented as an unusual item within income from continuing operations.
   d. All extraordinary gains or losses that occur in a period are summarized as total gains and total losses, then offset to present the net extraordinary gain or loss.

## PROBLEMS

available with McGraw-Hill's Homework Manager www.mhhe.com/spiceland4e

**An alternate exercise and problem set is available on the text website: www.mhhe.com/spiceland4e**

**P 4–1**
Multiple-step statement of income and comprehensive income
● LO1 LO2 LO4 LO6 LO8
eXcel

Duke Company's records show the following account balances at December 31, 2006:

| | |
|---|---|
| Sales | $15,000,000 |
| Cost of goods sold | 9,000,000 |
| General and administrative expenses | 1,000,000 |
| Selling expenses | 500,000 |
| Interest expense | 700,000 |

Income tax expense has not yet been determined. The following events also occurred during 2006:

1. $300,000 in restructuring costs were incurred in connection with plant closings.
2. The company operates a factory in South America. During the year, the foreign government took over (expropriated) the factory and paid Duke $1,000,000, which was one-fourth of the book value of the assets involved.
3. Inventory costing $400,000 was written off as obsolete. Material losses of this type were incurred twice in the last 10 years.
4. It was discovered that depreciation expense for 2005 was understated by $50,000 due to a mathematical error.
5. The company experienced a foreign currency translation adjustment loss of $200,000 and had unrealized gains on investment securities of $180,000.

**Required:**

Prepare a combined multiple-step statement of income and comprehensive income for 2006. The company's effective tax rate on all items affecting comprehensive income is 40%. Each component of other comprehensive income should be displayed net of tax. Ignore EPS disclosures.

**P 4–2**
Comparative income statements; multiple-step format

● LO2 LO4 through LO6 LO9

Selected information about income statement accounts for the Reed Company are presented below (the company's fiscal year ends on December 31):

| | 2006 | 2005 |
|---|---|---|
| Sales | $4,400,000 | $3,500,000 |
| Cost of goods sold | 2,860,000 | 2,000,000 |
| Administrative expenses | 800,000 | 675,000 |
| Selling expenses | 360,000 | 312,000 |
| Interest revenue | 150,000 | 140,000 |
| Interest expense | 200,000 | 200,000 |
| Loss on sale of assets of discontinued component | 50,000 | — |

On July 1, 2006, the company adopted a plan to discontinue a division that qualifies as a component of an entity as defined in *SFAS No. 144.* The assets of the component were sold on September 30, 2006 for $50,000 less than their book value. Results of operations for the component (*included* in the above account balances) were as follows:

| | 1/1/06–9/30/06 | 2005 |
|---|---|---|
| Sales | $400,000 | $500,000 |
| Cost of goods sold | (290,000) | (320,000) |
| Administrative expenses | (50,000) | (40,000) |
| Selling expenses | (20,000) | (30,000) |
| Operating income before taxes | $ 40,000 | $110,000 |

In addition to the account balances above, several events occurred during 2006 that have *not* yet been reflected in the above accounts:

1. A fire caused $50,000 in uninsured damages to the main office building. The fire was considered to be an infrequent but not unusual event.
2. $5 million face value of bonds payable were re-purchased (paid off) prior to maturity resulting in a loss of $100,000. The amount of the loss is material and the event is considered unusual and infrequent.
3. Inventory that had cost $40,000 had become obsolete because a competitor introduced a better product. The inventory was sold as scrap for $5,000.
4. Income taxes have not yet been accrued.

**Required:**

Prepare a multiple-step income statement for the Reed Company for 2006, showing 2005 information in comparative format, including income taxes computed at 40% and EPS disclosures assuming 300,000 shares of common stock.

**P 4–3**
Discontinued operations

● LO5

The following condensed income statements of the Jackson Holding Company are presented for the two years ended December 31, 2006 and 2005:

| | 2006 | 2005 |
|---|---|---|
| Sales | $15,000,000 | $9,600,000 |
| Cost of goods sold | 9,200,000 | 6,000,000 |
| Gross profit | 5,800,000 | 3,600,000 |
| Operating expenses | 3,200,000 | 2,600,000 |
| Operating income | 2,600,000 | 1,000,000 |
| Gain on sale of division | 600,000 | — |

| | | |
|---|---|---|
| | 3,200,000 | 1,000,000 |
| Income tax expense | 1,280,000 | 400,000 |
| Net income | $ 1,920,000 | $ 600,000 |

On October 15, 2006, Jackson entered into a tentative agreement to sell the assets of one of its divisions. The division comprises operations and cash flows that can be clearly distinguished, operationally and for financial reporting purposes, from the rest of the company. The division was sold on December 31, 2006, for $5,000,000. Book value of the division's assets was $4,400,000. The division's contribution to Jackson's operating income before-tax for each year was as follows:

| | |
|---|---|
| 2006 | $400,000 loss |
| 2005 | $300,000 loss |

Assume an income tax rate of 40%.

**Required:**

1. Prepare revised income statements according to generally accepted accounting principles, beginning with income from continuing operations before income taxes. Ignore EPS disclosures.
2. Assume that by December 31, 2006, the division had not yet been sold but was considered held for sale. The fair value of the division's assets on December 31 was $5,000,000. How would the presentation of discontinued operations be different from your answer to requirement 1?
3. Assume that by December 31, 2006, the division had not yet been sold but was considered held for sale. The fair value of the division's assets on December 31 was $3,900,000. How would the presentation of discontinued operations be different from your answer to requirement 1?

**P 4–4**
Income statement presentation

● LO5 LO6 LO8

For the year ending December 31, 2006, Micron Corporation had income from continuing operations before taxes of $1,200,000 before considering the following transactions and events. All of the items described below are before taxes and the amounts should be considered material.

1. During 2006, Micron decided to call in an outstanding issue of bonds. As a result, the firm recognized a gain on the early extinguishment of bonds of $400,000. The event is considered unusual and infrequent.
2. In November of 2006, Micron sold its Waffle House restaurant chain that qualified as a component of an entity. The company had adopted a plan to sell the chain in May of 2006. The operating income of the chain from January 1, 2006, through November was $160,000 and the loss on sale of the chain's assets was $300,000.
3. In 2006, Micron sold one of its six factories for $1,200,000. At the time of the sale, the factory had a carrying value of $1,100,000. The factory was not considered a component of the entity.
4. In 2004, Micron's accountant omitted the annual adjustment for patent amortization expense of $120,000. The error was not discovered until December, 2006.

**Required:**

1. Prepare Micron's income statement, beginning with income from continuing operations before taxes, for the year ended December 31, 2006. Assume an income tax rate of 30%. Ignore EPS disclosures.
2. Briefly explain the motivation for segregating certain income statement events from income from continuing operations.

**P 4–5**
Statement of cash flows

● LO11

The Diversified Portfolio Corporation provides investment advice to customers. A condensed income statement for the year ended December 31, 2006, appears below:

| | |
|---|---|
| Service revenue | $900,000 |
| Operating expenses | 700,000 |
| Income before income taxes | 200,000 |
| Income tax expense | 80,000 |
| Net income | $120,000 |

The following balance sheet information also is available:

| | 12/31/06 | 12/31/05 |
|---|---|---|
| Cash | $275,000 | $ 70,000 |
| Accounts receivable | 120,000 | 100,000 |
| Accounts payable (operating expenses) | 70,000 | 60,000 |
| Income taxes payable | 10,000 | 15,000 |

In addition, the following transactions took place during the year:

1. Common stock was issued for $100,000 in cash.
2. Long-term investments were sold for $50,000 in cash. The original cost of the investments also was $50,000.

3. $80,000 in cash dividends was paid to shareholders.
4. The company has no outstanding debt, other than those payables listed above.
5. Operating expenses include $30,000 in depreciation expense.

**Required:**

1. Prepare a statement of cash flows for 2006 for the Diversified Portfolio Corporation. Use the direct method for reporting operating activities.
2. Prepare the cash flows from operating activities section of Diversified's 2006 statement of cash flows using the indirect method.

**P 4–6**
Income statement presentation; unusual items
● LO4 LO6 LO8

The preliminary 2006 income statement of Alexian Systems, Inc., is presented below:

**ALEXIAN SYSTEMS, INC.**
**Income Statement**
**For the Year Ended December 31, 2006**
($ in millions, except earnings per share)

| | |
|---|---|
| Revenues and gains: | |
| Net sales | $425 |
| Interest | 3 |
| Other income | 126 |
| Total revenues and gains | 554 |
| Expenses: | |
| Cost of goods sold | 270 |
| Selling and administrative | 154 |
| Income taxes | 52 |
| Total expenses | 476 |
| Net Income | $ 78 |
| Earnings per share | $3.90 |

**Additional information:**

1. Selling and administrative expenses include $26 million in restructuring costs.
2. Included in other income is an extraordinary gain of $120 million. The remaining $6 million is from the gain on sale of operating assets.
3. Cost of goods sold was increased by $5 million to correct an error in the calculation of 2005's ending inventory. The amount is material.

**Required:**

For each of the three additional facts listed above, discuss the appropriate presentation of the item described. Do not prepare a revised statement.

**P 4–7**
Income statement presentation; unusual items
● LO4 LO6 LO8

[This is a variation of the previous problem focusing on income statement presentation.]

**Required:**

Refer to the information presented in Problem 4–6. Prepare a revised income statement for 2006 reflecting the additional facts. Use a multiple-step format. Assume that an income tax rate of 40% applies to all income statement items, and that 20 million shares of common stock were outstanding throughout the year.

**P 4–8**
Income statement—comprehensive
● LO2 LO4 through LO6 LO9

Rembrandt Paint Company had the following income statement items for the year ended December 31, 2006 ($ in 000s):

| | | | |
|---|---|---|---|
| Net sales | $18,000 | Cost of goods sold | $10,500 |
| Interest income | 200 | Selling and administrative expenses | 2,500 |
| Interest expense | 350 | Restructuring costs | 800 |
| Extraordinary gain | 3,000 | | |

In addition, during the year the company completed the disposal of its plastics business and incurred a loss from operations of $1.6 million and a gain on disposal of the component's assets of $2 million. 500,000 shares of common stock were outstanding throughout 2006. Income tax expense has not yet been accrued. The income tax rate is 30% on all items of income (loss).

**Required:**

Prepare a multiple-step income statement for 2006, including EPS disclosures.

**P 4–9**
Integration of financial statements; Chapters 3 and 4
● LO11

The chief accountant for Grandview Corporation provides you with the company's 2006 statement of cash flows and income statement. The accountant has asked for your help with some missing figures in the company's comparative balance sheets. These financial statements are shown below ($ in millions).

**GRANDVIEW CORPORATION**
**Statement of Cash Flows**
**For the Year Ended December 31, 2006**

| | | |
|---|---|---|
| **Cash Flows from Operating Activities:** | | |
| Collections from customers | $71 | |
| Payment to suppliers | (30) | |
| Payment of general & administrative expenses | (18) | |
| Payment of income taxes | (9) | |
| Net cash flows from operating activities | | $14 |
| **Cash Flows from Investing Activities:** | | |
| Sale of equipment | | 40 |
| **Cash Flows from Financing Activities:** | | |
| Issuance of common stock | 10 | |
| Payment of dividends | (3) | |
| Net cash flows from financing activities | | 7 |
| Net increase in cash | | $61 |

**GRANDVIEW CORPORATION**
**Income Statement**
**For the Year Ended December 31,2006**

| | | |
|---|---|---|
| Sales revenue | | $80 |
| Cost of goods sold | | 32 |
| Gross profit | | 48 |
| Operating expenses: | | |
| General and administrative | $18 | |
| Depreciation | 10 | |
| Total operating expenses | | 28 |
| Operating income | | 20 |
| Other income: | | |
| Gain on sale of equipment | | 15 |
| Income before income taxes | | 35 |
| Income tax expense | | 7 |
| Net income | | $28 |

**GRANDVIEW CORPORATION**
**Balance Sheets**
**At December 31**

| | 2006 | 2005 |
|---|---|---|
| **Assets:** | | |
| Cash | $120 | $ ? |
| Accounts receivable | ? | 84 |
| Inventory | 60 | ? |
| Property, plant & equipment | 150 | 200 |
| Less: Accumulated depreciation | (40) | ? |
| Total assets | ? | ? |
| **Liabilities and Shareholders' Equity:** | | |
| Accounts payable to suppliers | $ 40 | $ 30 |
| Payables for selling & admin. expenses | 9 | 9 |
| Income taxes payable | 22 | ? |
| Common stock | 240 | 230 |
| Retained earnings | ? | 47 |
| Total liabilities and shareholders' equity | ? | ? |

**Required:**

1. Calculate the missing amounts.
2. Prepare the operating activities section of Grandview's 2006 statement of cash flows using the indirect method.

# BROADEN YOUR PERSPECTIVE

**Apply your critical-thinking ability to the knowledge you've gained. These cases will provide you an opportunity to develop your research, analysis, judgment, and communication skills. You also will work with other students, integrate what you've learned, apply it in real world situations, and consider its global and ethical ramifications. This practice will broaden your knowledge and further develop your decision-making abilities.**

**Judgment Case 4–1**
Earnings quality

● LO3 LO4

The financial community in the United States has become increasingly concerned with the quality of reported company earnings.

**Required:**

1. Define the term *earnings quality*.
2. Explain the distinction between permanent and transitory earnings as it relates to the concept of earnings quality.
3. How do earnings management practices affect the quality of earnings?
4. Assume that a manufacturing company's annual income statement included a large gain from the sale of investment securities. What factors would you consider in determining whether or not this gain should be included in an assessment of the company's permanent earnings?

**Judgment Case 4–2**
Restructuring costs

● LO4

The appearance of restructuring costs in corporate income statements increased significantly in the 1980s and 1990s.

**Required:**

1. What types of costs are included in restructuring costs?
2. When are restructuring costs recognized?
3. How would you classify restructuring costs in a multi-step income statement?
4. What factors would you consider in determining whether or not restructuring costs should be included in an assessment of a company's permanent earnings?

**Judgment Case 4–3**
Earnings management

● LO3 LO4

Companies often are under pressure to meet or beat Wall Street earnings projections in order to increase stock prices and also to increase the value of stock options. Some resort to earnings management practices to artificially create desired results.

**Required:**

Is *earnings management* always intended to produce higher income? Explain.

**Real World Case 4–4**
Earnings quality and pro forma earnings

● LO4

[The solution to this case requires access to company data via the Internet.]

**Cisco Systems, Inc.**, the world's largest networking products company, announced on May 8, 2001, that its *pro forma earnings* for the quarter ended April 28, 2001, were $230 million. They also disclosed that actual earnings for the quarter, determined according to generally accepted accounting principles, were a *loss* of $2.69 billion.

**Required:**

1. What is meant by the term *pro forma earnings* in this context?
2. How do pro forma earnings relate to the concept of earnings quality?
3. Access the company's 10-Q (quarterly report) for the quarter ended April 28, 2001. You can go to the company's Internet site, EDGAR, or Edgarscan (**edgarscan.pwcglobal.com**). Using the company's income statement for the quarter and disclosure notes, reconcile the GAAP loss of $2.69 billion to the pro forma earnings figure of $230 million. Remember that both of these earnings (loss) figures are net of tax.

**Communication Case 4–5**
Income statement presentation of gain

● LO6

McMinville Corporation manufactures paper products. In 2002, the company purchased several large tracts of timber for $22 million with the intention of harvesting the timber rather than buying this critical raw material from outside suppliers. However, in 2006, McMinville abandoned the idea and all of the timber tracts were sold for $31 million. Net income for 2006, before considering this event, is $17.5 million and the company's effective tax rate is 30%.

The focus of this case is the income statement presentation of the gain on the sale of the timber tracts. Your instructor will divide the class into two to six groups depending on the size of the class. The mission of your group is to reach consensus on the appropriate income statement presentation of the gain.

**Required:**

Each group member should deliberate the situation independently and draft a tentative argument prior to the class session for which the case is assigned.

In class, each group will meet for 10 to 15 minutes in different areas of the classroom. During that meeting, group members will take turns sharing their suggestions for the purpose of arriving at a single group treatment.

After the allotted time, a spokesperson for each group (selected during the group meetings) will share the group's solution with the class. The goal of the class is to incorporate the views of each group into a consensus approach to the situation.

**Communication Case 4–6**
Income statement presentation

● LO6

**Carter Hawley Hale Stores (CHHS), Inc.** was one of the largest department store retailers in the United States. At the end of fiscal 1989, the company operated 113 stores in the sunbelt regions of the country. The company's divisions included The Broadway, with 43 stores in Southern California and 11 stores in the southwest, and Emporium, with 22 stores in the greater San Francisco Bay Area.

On October 17, 1989, a 7.1 Richter scale earthquake caused significant amounts of monetary damage to the San Francisco Bay Area. This was the largest earthquake to hit the Bay Area since the quake of 1906 destroyed much of San Francisco. California is lined with many active earthquake faults. Hundreds of small earthquakes occur each year throughout the state.

The Emporium division of CHHS suffered extensive damage as a result of the October 17 earthquake. Twelve of the twenty-two stores were closed for varying periods of time, with the Oakland store hardest hit. In total, uninsured damage was $27.5 million ($16.5 million after tax benefits).

For the fiscal year ending August 4, 1990, CHHS reported an after-tax loss of $9.47 million *before* considering the earthquake loss. Total revenues for the year were $2.857 billion.

**Required:**

Assume that you are the CHHS controller. The chief financial officer of CHHS has asked you to prepare a short report (1–2 pages) in memo form giving your recommendation as to the proper reporting of the earthquake damage costs in the income statement for the year ending August 4, 1990. Explain why your recommendation is appropriate. Be sure to include in your report any references to authoritative pronouncements that support your recommendation.

**Ethics Case 4–7**
Income statement presentation of unusual loss

● LO4

After a decade of consistent income growth, the Cranor Corporation sustained a before-tax loss of $8.4 million in 2006. The loss was primarily due to $10 million in expenses related to a product recall. Cranor manufactures medical equipment, including x-ray machines. The recall was attributable to a design flaw in the manufacture of the company's new line of machines.

The company controller, Jim Dietz, has suggested that the loss should be included in the 2006 income statement as an extraordinary item. "If we report it as an extraordinary item, our income from continuing operations will actually show an increase from the prior year. The stock market will appreciate the continued growth in ongoing profitability and will discount the one-time loss. And our bonuses are tied to income from continuing operations, not net income."

The chief executive officer asked Jim to justify this treatment. "I know we have had product recalls before and, of course, they do occur in our industry," Jim replied, "but we have never had a recall of this magnitude, and we fixed the design flaw and upgraded our quality control procedures."

**Required:**

Discuss the ethical dilemma faced by Jim Dietz and the company's chief executive officer.

**Research Case 4–8**
Locate and extract relevant information and authoritative support for a financial reporting issue; treatment of losses from terrorist attacks

● LO6

Yesterday you watched a TV special on the terrorist attacks of September 11, 2001. Those attacks resulted in a tragic loss of life and property. Today in your intermediate accounting class, your professor discussed the measurement and reporting of separately reported items, including extraordinary gains and losses. A classmate asked her if companies that sustained significant losses as a result of the attacks reported those losses as extraordinary items in their income statements. She asked the class to think about it and to formulate an answer for the next class period. She also mentioned that there is an Emerging Issues Task Force Issue that addresses this question and suggested you do some research.

**Required:**

1. Do you think that the terrorist attacks of September 11 constitute an "extraordinary" event?
2. Obtain the EITF Issue on accounting for the impact of the terrorist attacks. You might gain access through FARS, the FASB Financial Accounting Research System, from your school library, or some other source.
3. Why did the EITF address this issue and not the FASB itself?
4. What did your research reveal? What reasons did the EITF provide for its conclusion?

**Judgment Case 4–9**
Income statement presentation

● LO4 through LO7

Each of the following situations occurred during 2006 for one of your audit clients:

1. The write-off of inventory due to obsolescence.
2. Discovery that depreciation expenses were omitted by accident from 2005's income statement.
3. The useful lives of all machinery were changed from eight to five years.
4. The depreciation method used for all equipment was changed from the declining-balance to the straight-line method.
5. Ten million dollars face value of bonds payable were repurchased (paid off) prior to maturity resulting in a material loss of $500,000. The company considers the event unusual and infrequent.
6. Restructuring costs were incurred.

7. The Stridewell Company, a manufacturer of shoes, sold all of its retail outlets. It will continue to manufacture and sell its shoes to other retailers. A loss was incurred in the disposition of the retail stores. The retail stores are considered components of the entity.
8. The inventory costing method was changed from FIFO to average cost.

**Required:**

1. For each situation, identify the appropriate reporting treatment from the list below (consider each event to be material):
   a. As an extraordinary item.
   b. As an unusual or infrequent gain or loss.
   c. As a prior period adjustment.
   d. As a change in accounting principle.
   e. As a discontinued operation.
   f. As a change in accounting estimate.
   g. As a change in accounting estimate achieved by a change in accounting principle.
2. Indicate whether each situation would be included in the income statement in continuing operations (CO) or below continuing operations (BC), or if it would appear as an adjustment to retained earnings (RE). Use the format shown below to answer requirements 1 and 2.

| Situation | Treatment (a–g) | Financial Statement Presentation (CO, BC, or RE) |
|---|---|---|
| 1. | | |
| 2. | | |
| 3. | | |
| 4. | | |
| 5. | | |
| 6. | | |
| 7. | | |
| 8. | | |

**Judgment Case 4–10**
Income statement presentation

● LO4 through LO8

The following events occurred during 2006 for various audit clients of your firm. Consider each event to be independent and the effect of each event to be material.

1. A manufacturing company recognized a loss on the sale of equipment used in its manufacturing operations.
2. An automobile manufacturer sold all of the assets related to its financing component. The operations of the financing business can be clearly distinguished from the rest of the entity.
3. A company changed its depreciation method from the double-declining-balance method to the straight-line method.
4. Due to obsolescence, a company engaged in the manufacture of high-technology products incurred a loss on the write-down of inventory.
5. One of your clients discovered that 2005's depreciation expense was overstated. The error occurred because of a miscalculation of depreciation for the office building.
6. A cosmetics company decided to discontinue the manufacture of a line of women's lipstick. Other cosmetic lines will be continued. A loss was incurred on the sale of assets related to the lipstick product line. The operations of the discontinued line cannot be distinguished from the rest of the cosmetics business.

**Required:**

Discuss the 2006 financial statement presentation of each of the above events. Do not consider earnings per share disclosures.

**International Case 4–11**
Comparison of income statement presentation in the U.K. and the United States

● LO1 LO3

**Cadbury Schweppes** is a major global manufacturer of beverages and confectionery located in Great Britain whose products are sold in over 170 countries. Presented below is a recent company income statement:

**CADBURY SCHWEPPES PLC**
**Group Profit and Loss Account**
**For the 52 Weeks Ended 28 December 2003**
(in millions of pounds)

| | Before Exceptional Items | Exceptional Items | Total |
|---|---|---|---|
| Turnover | | | |
| Continuing operations | 5,564 | — | 5,564 |
| Acquisitions | 877 | — | 877 |
| | 6,441 | — | 6,441 |

| | | | |
|---|---|---|---|
| Operating costs | (5,389) | (353) | (5,742) |
| Continuing operations | 954 | (230) | 724 |
| Acquisitions | 98 | (123) | (25) |
| Group operating profit | 1,052 | (353) | 699 |
| Share of operating profit in associates | 51 | — | 51 |
| Total operating profit including associates | 1,103 | (353) | 750 |
| Loss on disposal of fixed assets | — | (7) | (7) |
| Profit on sale of subsidiaries and investments | — | 2 | 2 |
| Profit on ordinary activities before interest | 1,103 | (358) | 745 |
| Net interest | (181) | — | (181) |
| Profit on ordinary activities before taxes | 922 | (358) | 564 |
| Taxation | (254) | 81 | (173) |
| Profit on ordinary activities | 668 | (277) | 391 |
| Equity minority interests | (4) | — | (4) |
| Nonequity minority interests | (21) | — | (21) |
| Profit for the financial year | 643 | (277) | 366 |
| Dividends to ordinary shareholders | | | (242) |
| Profit retained | | | 124 |

**Required:**

Describe the differences between income statement presentation in the United Kingdom with that of the United States.

**Judgment Case 4–12**
Management incentives for change
● LO7

It has been suggested that not all accounting choices are made by management in the best interest of fair and consistent financial reporting.

**Required:**

What motivations can you think of for management's choice of accounting methods?

**Research Case 4–13**
Changes in accounting principles
● LO7

When a company changes an accounting principle, justification for the change is required in a disclosure note. Quite often, the stated justification is that the new accounting method is a more appropriate way to measure the related economic transaction. However, there are those that feel management makes accounting changes in order to manipulate earnings. Professors Pincus and Wasley in "The Incidence of Accounting Changes and Characteristics of Firms Making Accounting Changes" investigate accounting changes and possible motivations for making them.

**Required:**

1. In your library or from some other source, locate the indicated article in *Accounting Horizons,* June 1994.
2. What is the most frequent type of voluntary accounting change?
3. What inferences do the authors make about the use of voluntary accounting changes to manipulate earnings and what conclusion do they reach?

**Integrating Case 4–14**
Balance sheet and income statement; Chapters 3 and 4
● LO4 LO6

Rice Corporation is negotiating a loan for expansion purposes and the bank requires financial statements. Before closing the accounting records for the year ended December 31, 2006, Rice's controller prepared the following financial statements:

**RICE CORPORATION**
**Balance Sheet**
**At December 31, 2006**
($ in 000s)

| | |
|---|---|
| **Assets** | |
| Cash | $ 275 |
| Marketable securities | 78 |
| Accounts receivable | 487 |
| Inventories | 425 |
| Allowance for uncollectible accounts | (50) |
| Property and equipment, net | 160 |
| Total assets | $1,375 |
| **Liabilities and Shareholders' Equity** | |
| Accounts payable and accrued liabilities | $420 |
| Notes payable | 200 |
| Common stock | 260 |
| Retained earnings | 495 |
| Total liabilities and shareholders' equity | $1,375 |

**RICE CORPORATION**
**Income Statement**
**For the Year Ended December 31, 2006**
($ in 000s)

| | | |
|---|---|---|
| Net sales | | $1,580 |
| Expenses: | | |
| Cost of goods sold | $755 | |
| Selling and administrative | 385 | |
| Miscellaneous | 129 | |
| Income taxes | 100 | |
| Total expenses | | 1,369 |
| Net income | | $ 211 |

***Additional information:***

1. The company's common stock is traded on an organized stock exchange.
2. The investment portfolio consists of short-term investments valued at $57,000. The remaining investments will not be sold until the year 2008.
3. Miscellaneous expense represents the before-tax loss from damages caused by an earthquake. The event is considered to be both unusual and infrequent.
4. Notes payable consist of two notes:
   Note 1: $80,000 face value dated September 30, 2006. Principal and interest at 10% are due on September 30, 2007.
   Note 2: $120,000 face value dated April 30, 2006. Principal is due in two equal installments of $60,000 plus interest on the unpaid balance. The two payments are scheduled for April 30, 2007, and April 30, 2008.
   Interest on both loans has been correctly accrued and is included in accrued liabilities on the balance sheet and selling and administrative expenses on the income statement.
5. Selling and administrative expenses include a $90,000 charge incurred by the company in restructuring some of its operations. The amount of the charge is material.

**Required:**

Identify and explain the deficiencies in the presentation of the statements prepared by the company's controller. Do not prepare corrected statements. Include in your answer a list of items which require additional disclosure, either on the face of the statement or in a note.

**Analysis Case 4–15**
Income statement information

- LO2

Refer to the income statements of **FedEx Corporation** in Appendix B located at the back of this text.

**Required:**

1. What was the percentage increase or decrease in the company's net income from 2003 to 2004? From 2002 to 2003?
2. Using 2004 data, what is the company's approximate income tax rate?
3. Using 2004 data, what is the percentage of net income relative to revenue dollars?

**Real World Case 4–16**
Income statement information

- LO2 LO4 through LO6

EDGAR, the Electronic Data Gathering, Analysis, and Retrieval system, performs automated collection, validation, indexing, and forwarding of submissions by companies and others who are required by law to file forms with the U.S. Securities and Exchange Commission (SEC). All publicly traded domestic companies use EDGAR to make the majority of their filings. (Some foreign companies file voluntarily.) Form 10-K or 10-KSB, which includes the annual report, is required to be filed on EDGAR. The SEC makes this information available on the Internet.

**Required:**

1. Access EDGAR on the Internet. The web address is **www.sec.gov**. Edgarscan (**edgarscan. pwcglobal. com**) from PricewaterhouseCoopers makes the process of accessing data from EDGAR easier.
2. Search for a public company with which you are familiar. Access the most recent 10-K filing. Search or scroll to find the financial statements and related notes.
3. Answer the following questions related to the company's income statement:
   a. Does the company use the single-step or multiple-step format, or a variation?
   b. Does the income statement contain any separately reported items in any year presented (discontinued operation or extraordinary item)? If it does, describe the event that caused the item. (Hint: there should be a related disclosure note.)
   c. Describe the trend in net income over the years presented.
4. Repeat requirements 2 and 3 for two additional companies.

**Trueblood Accounting Case 4–17**

Restructuring costs

● LO4

The following Trueblood case is recommended for use with this chapter. The case provides an excellent opportunity for class discussion, group projects, and writing assignments. The case, along with Professor's Discussion Material, can be obtained from the Deloitte Foundation at its website: www.deloitte.com/us/truebloodcases.

**Case 04-5:** ***Alchemist, Inc.***

This case concerns the amount and timing of restructuring costs.

# CPA SIMULATION 4–1

**Best Consultants**

Financial Statements

Test your knowledge of the concepts discussed in this chapter, practice critical professional skills necessary for career success, and prepare for the computer-based CPA exam by accessing our CPA simulations at the text website: **www.mhhe.com/spiceland4e.**

The Best Consultants simulation tests your knowledge of (a) the content and structure of the income statement, (b) the reporting of discontinued operations and comprehensive income, (c) the difference between cash and accrual income statement items addressed in Chapters 1 and 2, and (d) the transactions that cause a change in retained earnings discussed in Chapters 2 and 19.

As on the CPA exam itself, you will be asked to use tools including a spreadsheet, a calculator, and professional accounting standards, to conduct research, derive solutions, and communicate conclusions related to these issues in a simulated environment headed by the following interactive tabs:

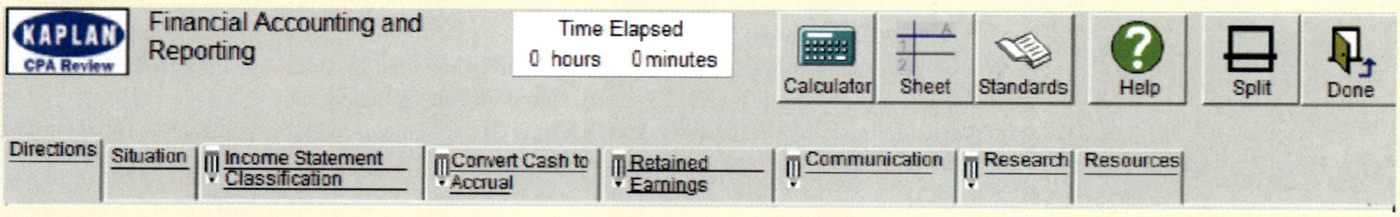


Specific tasks in the simulation include:

- Converting income statement items from a cash to accrual basis.
- Demonstrating your knowledge of the content and structure of the income statement.
- Understanding the transactions that affect retained earnings.
- Communicating various aspects of the reporting requirements for discontinued operations.
- Researching the disclosure requirements for the presentation of comprehensive income.

# 5
CHAPTER

# Income Measurement and Profitability Analysis

## OVERVIEW

Key to income measurement is the timing of revenue and expense recognition. The matching principle states that we recognize expenses in the period we recognize the related revenues. The timing of revenue recognition, therefore, is critical to income measurement. The focus of this chapter is revenue recognition. We also continue our discussion of financial statement analysis.

## LEARNING OBJECTIVES

After studying this chapter, you should be able to:

- LO1 Discuss the general objective of the timing of revenue recognition, list the two general criteria that must be satisfied before revenue can be recognized, and explain why these criteria usually are satisfied at a specific point in time.
- LO2 Describe the installment sales and cost recovery methods of recognizing revenue for certain installment sales and explain the unusual conditions under which these methods might be used.
- LO3 Discuss the implications for revenue recognition of allowing customers the right of return.
- LO4 Identify situations that call for the recognition of revenue over time and distinguish between the percentage-of-completion and completed contract methods of recognizing revenue for long-term contracts.
- LO5 Discuss the revenue recognition issues involving software and franchise sales.
- LO6 Identify and calculate the common ratios used to assess profitability.

## You Don't Have to Be a Rocket Scientist

"Good news! I got the job," she said, closing the door behind her.

Your sister, an aerospace engineer, goes on to explain that she accepted a position at Lockheed Martin Corporation, a world leader in the design, development, manufacture, and servicing of aircraft, spacecraft and launch vehicles, missiles, electronics, and information and telecommunication systems. She will supervise a long-term government contract beginning Tuesday.

"I got the salary I was asking for too," she continued. "Mr. Watson, my supervisor, also said I'll be getting a bonus tied to the gross profit on the project. It didn't hit me until I left his office, though, that this project will take two and a half years to complete. I hope I don't have to wait that long to get my bonus." Pointing to a page where she's circled part of a disclosure note, your sister hands you Lockheed's annual report. "I can't believe they wait that long to record income on all these multiyear projects. You're the accountant in the family; is that what this note is telling us?"

> *Sales and earnings (in part)*
> Sales and anticipated profits under long-term fixed-price production contracts are recorded on a percentage of completion basis . . .

**By the time you finish this chapter, you should be able to respond appropriately to the questions posed in this case. Compare your response to the solution provided at the end of the chapter.**

### QUESTIONS

1. Does your sister have to wait two and a half years to get her bonus? Explain. (page 224)
2. How are gross profits recognized using the percentage-of-completion method? (page 225)
3. Are there other situations in which revenue is recognized at times other than when a product is delivered? (page 217)

# PART A REVENUE RECOGNITION

Revenue recognition criteria help ensure that an income statement reflects the actual accomplishments of a company for the period.

In Chapter 4 we discussed the *nature of income* and its presentation in the income statement. In this chapter we turn our attention to the *measurement* of periodic accounting income. Of primary interest here is the timing of revenue recognition. This is an important issue not only in its own right but also because the matching principle states that expenses should be recognized in the period in which the related revenues are recognized.

Why is the timing of revenue recognition so important? An income statement should report the results of operations only for the time period specified in the report. That is, a one-year income statement should report the company's accomplishments and sacrifices (revenues and expenses) only for that one-year period.[1] Revenue recognition criteria help ensure that a proper cutoff is made each period and that no more than one year's activity is reported in the annual income statement. Revenues reflect positive inflows from activities, activities that generate cash flows. By comparing these activity levels period to period, a user can better assess future activities and thus future cash flows.

Our objective, then, is to recognize revenue in the period or periods that the revenue-generating activities of the company are performed. But we also must consider that recognizing revenue presumes that an asset (usually cash) has been received or will be received in exchange for the goods or services sold. Our judgment as to the collectibility of the cash from the sale of a product or service will, therefore, impact the timing of revenue recognition. These two concepts of performance and collectibility are captured by the general guidelines for revenue recognition in the realization principle.

● LO1

The **realization principle** requires that two criteria be satisfied before revenue can be recognized (recorded):[2]

1. The earnings process is judged to be complete or virtually complete *(the earnings process refers to the activity or activities performed by the company to generate revenue).*
2. There is reasonable certainty as to the collectibility of the asset to be received (usually cash).

The first criterion indicates that revenue is recognized at a point in time at or near the end of the earnings process. We sometimes encounter situations when strictly adhering to this criterion would violate our overriding objective of recognizing revenue in the period or periods that the revenue-generating activities of the company are performed. Later in this chapter we discuss situations when revenue is recognized over time, rather than at one particular point in time.

Even with this guideline, revenue recognition continues to be a controversial issue. For instance, Former SEC Chairman Arthur Levitt identified revenue recognition as a popular way for companies to manage their earnings, primarily prematurely.

**CBS MARKETWATCH**
If corporate information is no longer reliable, investors are left twisting in the wind. Suddenly, the financial assumptions you've used to calculate a stock's value become bogus.[3]

Premature revenue recognition reduces the quality of reported earnings and can cause serious problems for the reporting company.

Premature revenue recognition reduces the quality of reported earnings, particularly if those revenues never materialize. Many sad stories have surfaced involving companies forced to revise earnings numbers due to a restatement of revenues. The case of **Krispy Kreme Doughnuts** offers a prime example. In January 2005, the company announced that it would be restating its earnings for the last three quarters of fiscal 2004. Investors were already alarmed by the recent filing of a lawsuit that alleged the company routinely

[1]In addition to reporting on an annual basis, companies often provide information quarterly and, on occasion, monthly. The SEC requires its registrants to provide information on a quarterly and annual basis. This information, referred to as *interim financial statements*, pertains to any financial report covering a period of less than one year. The key accounting issues related to the presentation of interim statements are discussed in Appendix 5.

[2]These criteria are addressed in SFAC 5, "Recognition and Measurement in Financial Statements," *Statement of Financial Accounting Concepts No. 5* (Stamford, Conn.: FASB, 1984).

[3]Deborah Adamson, "What investors should fear the most," *CBS.MarketWatch.com,* April 30,2001.

**ARTHUR LEVITT, JR.**
Lastly, companies try to boost earnings by manipulating the recognition of revenue. Think about a bottle of fine wine. You wouldn't pop the cork on that bottle before it was ready. But some companies are doing this with their revenue . . .[4]

padded sales by doubling shipments to wholesale customers at the end of the quarter. In the two-day period following the announced restatement, the company's stock price dropped over 20% in value!

As part of its crackdown on earnings management, the SEC issued *Staff Accounting Bulletin No. 101*,[5] summarizing the SEC's views on revenue. The Bulletin provides additional criteria for judging whether or not the realization principle is satisfied:

1. Persuasive evidence of an arrangement exists.
2. Delivery has occurred or services have been rendered.
3. The seller's price to the buyer is fixed or determinable.
4. Collectibility is reasonably assured.

*SEC Staff Accounting Bulletin (SAB) No. 101* **provides general and specific guidelines for revenue recognition.**

In addition to these four criteria, *SAB 101* also poses a number of revenue recognition questions relating to each of the criteria. The questions provide the facts of the scenario and then the SEC offers its interpretive response. These responses and supporting explanations provide guidance to companies with similar revenue recognition issues. For example, the following question relates to the delivery and performance criteria:

---

**Facts:** Company A receives purchase orders for products it manufactures. At the end of its fiscal quarters, customers may not yet be ready to take delivery of the products for various reasons. These reasons may include, but are not limited to, a lack of available space for inventory, having more than sufficient inventory in their distribution channel, or delays in customers' production schedules.

**Questions:** May Company A recognize revenue for the sale of its products once it has completed manufacturing if it segregates the inventory of the products in its own warehouse from its own products? May Company A recognize revenue for the sale if it ships the products to a third-party warehouse but (1) Company A retains title to the product and (2) payment by the customer is dependent upon ultimate delivery to a customer-specified site?

---

How would you answer these questions? The SEC's response is generally, no. It believes that delivery generally is not considered to have occurred unless the customer has taken title and assumes the risk and rewards of ownership of the specific products in the customer's purchase order or sales agreement. Typically this occurs when a product is delivered to the customer's delivery site.[6]

Soon after *SAB No. 101* was issued, many companies changed their revenue recognition methods. In most cases, the changes resulted in a deferral of revenue recognition. As a case in point, consider the change made by **Brown & Sharpe Manufacturing Company**, a multinational manufacturer of metrology products, described in a disclosure note, displayed in Graphic 5–1.

**2. Accounting Change (in part)**
In 2000, the Company adopted *SEC Staff Accounting Bulletin No. 101 (SAB 101)*. As a result of adopting *SAB 101*, the Company changed the way it recognizes revenue for machines sold to customers. Prior to the adoption of *SAB 101*, the Company recognized revenue when the machines were shipped and title passed to the customer. Effective as of January 1, 2001, the Company recognizes revenue for machines sold to customers once the performance of machines is accepted by the customers.

**GRAPHIC 5–1**
Disclosure of Change in Revenue Recognition Policy—Brown & Sharpe Manufacturing Company

[4]Arthur Levitt, Jr., "The Numbers Game," *The CPA Journal*, December 1998, p. 18.
[5]"Revenue Recognition in Financial Statements," *Staff Accounting Bulletin No. 101* (Washington, DC: SEC, December 1999).
[6]Ibid, p. 5.

**ETHICAL DILEMMA**

The Precision Parts Corporation manufactures automobile parts. The company has reported a profit every year since the company's inception in 1980. Management prides itself on this accomplishment and believes one important contributing factor is the company's incentive plan that rewards top management a bonus equal to a percentage of operating income *if the operating income goal for the year is achieved.* However, 2006 has been a tough year, and prospects for attaining the income goal for the year are bleak.

Tony Smith, the company's chief financial officer, has determined a way to increase December sales by an amount sufficient to boost operating income over the goal for the year and earn bonuses for all top management. A reputable customer ordered $120,000 of parts to be shipped on January 15, 2007. Tony told the rest of top management "I know we can get that order ready by December 31 even though it will require some production line overtime. We can then just leave the order on the loading dock until shipment. I see nothing wrong with recognizing the sale in 2006, since the parts will have been manufactured and we do have a firm order from a reputable customer." The company's normal procedure is to ship goods f.o.b. destination and to recognize sales revenue when the customer receives the parts.

In requiring customer acceptance as part of the agreement, revenue recognition is delayed until this part of the earnings process is completed. Many of the changes in revenue recognition companies made in response to *SAB No. 101* are related to service revenue. We discuss some of these later in the chapter.

The central issue in most decisions concerning when to record revenue is judging when the earnings process is substantially complete and whether it is reasonably certain that a determinable amount of cash is collectible. Sometimes this decision is straightforward, as when **Intel Corporation** sells **Dell Inc.** a microprocessor. Other times, though, consideration must be given to whether (a) a customer in a risky transaction will actually pay, (b) a customer will exercise its right to return a purchased product, (c) it is reasonable to wait several years to recognize revenue on a long-term project, or (d) other atypical situations should justify altering the timing of revenue recognition. We'll discuss these variations on the timing decision in Part A of this chapter. First, though, it might be helpful to look at the overview of the variations provided in Graphic 5–2.

In January 2002, the FASB disseminated a proposal for a new project addressing revenue recognition.[7] The board is partnering with the International Accounting Standards Board to develop a comprehensive statement on revenue recognition that is conceptually based and framed in terms of principles. At the time this text was published, no new pronouncements had yet resulted from the project.

## Completion of the Earnings Process within a Single Reporting Period

### WHEN COLLECTIBILITY IS REASONABLY CERTAIN

**While revenue usually is earned during a period of time, revenue often is recognized at one specific point in time when both revenue recognition criteria are satisfied.**

Consider the timing of revenue recognition for a typical manufacturing company that sells its products on credit. Usually the buyer is given a length of time, say 30 days, to pay for the goods after they have been delivered. Graphic 5–3 shows several alternative points in time during the earnings process that could be considered the critical event for revenue recognition. It should be pointed out that revenue actually is earned *throughout* the earnings process. The critical event is the point in time when the realization principle is satisfied.[8]

[7] "Revenue Recognition," *Proposal for a New Agenda Project,* (Norwalk, Conn.: FASB, 2002). A project update was provided by the FASB on December 24, 2004.

[8] As you will learn later in this chapter, revenue often is not only earned throughout an earnings process, but also is recognized during the process rather than at one particular point in time.

**GRAPHIC 5–2**
Revenue Recognition

| Nature of the Revenue | Usually Recognize Revenue for: Sale of a Product | Sale of a Service |
|---|---|---|
| **Substantive completion of the earnings process can be identified with a specific point in time within a single reporting period:** | | |
| Collectibility of cash is reasonably certain. | When product is delivered (title transfers) | When the key activity is performed |
| Collectibility of cash is ***not*** reasonably certain: | | |
| • Because payments are significantly uncertain | When cash is collected (installment sales or cost recovery method) | When cash is collected (installment sales or cost recovery method) |
| • Because reliable estimates of product returns are unavailable | When critical event occurs that reduces product return uncertainty | Not applicable |
| • Because the product sold is out on consignment | When the consignee sells the product to the ultimate consumer | Not applicable |
| **Substantive completion of the earnings process occurs over more than one reporting period:** | | |
| Reasonably dependable estimates of progress are available. | Each period during the earning process (e.g., long-term construction contract) in proportion to its percentage of completion—usually the fraction of costs incurred to date | Each period during the earning process (e.g., rental period) in proportion to its percentage of performance—usually the fraction of time transpired |
| Dependable estimates of progress are not available. | At the completion of the project | Not applicable |
| **Industry-specific revenue:** | | |
| Franchise sales: | | |
| • Initial franchise fee | Not applicable | When initial services are "substantially performed" |
| • Continuing franchise fees | Not applicable | As services are performed |
| Computer software sales | As each product component (e.g., initial product; upgrade) is delivered | As each service component (e.g., customer support) is delivered |

**We usually recognize revenue at or near the completion of the earnings process unless collectibility is an issue.**

**Sometimes, it is more meaningful to recognize revenue over time in proportion to the performance of the activity.**

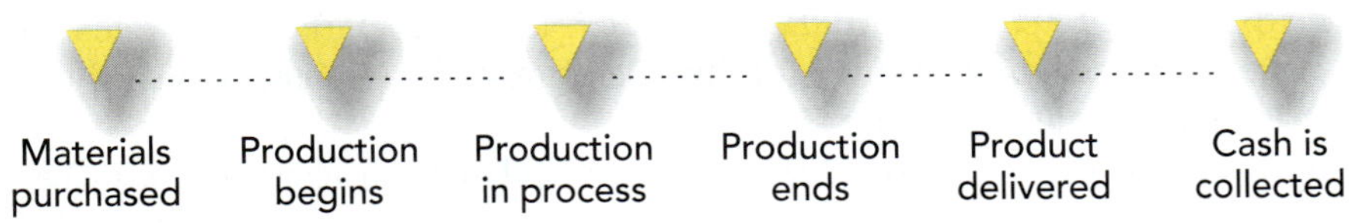


**GRAPHIC 5–3**
Earnings Process for a Typical Manufacturing Company

The product delivery date occurs when legal title to the goods passes from seller to buyer. This occurs either on the date the product is shipped from the seller's facility or when the goods actually are received by the buyer, depending on the terms of the sales agreement. If the

**The point of delivery refers to the date legal title to the product passes from seller to buyer.**

goods are shipped *f.o.b. (free on board) shipping point,* then legal title to the goods changes hands at the point of shipment when the seller delivers the goods to the common carrier (for example, a trucking company) and the purchaser is responsible for shipping costs and transit insurance. On the other hand, if the goods are shipped *f.o.b. destination,* the seller is responsible for shipping and legal title does not pass until the goods arrive at the customer's location.[9]

Let's consider the date production ends. At that point, it might be said that the earnings process is virtually complete. After all, the majority of the costs that must be expended to generate revenue have been incurred. The product has been produced and the remaining tasks are to sell the product and collect the cash.

However, at this point there usually exists significant uncertainty as to the collectibility of the asset to be received. We don't know if the product will be sold or the selling price or the buyer if eventually sold. Because of these uncertainties, revenue recognition usually is delayed until the point of product delivery. At that point we know the product has been sold, the price, and the buyer. The only remaining uncertainty involves the ultimate cash collection, which usually can be accounted for by estimating and recording allowances for possible return of the product and for uncollectibility of the cash, that is, bad debts. Both of these estimates are discussed in Chapter 7. As we discuss in the next section, significant uncertainty at point of product delivery related to either collectibility or product return causes a delay in revenue recognition.

**Revenue from the sale of products usually is recognized at the point of product delivery.**

In addition, at the point of delivery, legal title to the goods is transferred. A critical element of the contract between buyer and seller—product delivery—is now fulfilled and the earnings process normally is virtually complete.

Sometimes, a sales agreement requires additional, important performance steps to be performed by the seller. In this case, the earnings process is not virtually complete until those steps are performed. Graphic 5–1 on page 213 illustrates a situation where the seller, Brown & Sharpe, delays revenue recognition beyond delivery of machines until the performance of the machines has been accepted by the buyer. Customer acceptance is an important part of the agreement between buyer and seller.

**For service revenue, if there is one final service that is critical to the earnings process, revenues and costs are deferred and recognized after this service has been performed.**

**FedEx Corporation**

Service revenue, too, often is recognized at a point in time if there is one final activity that is deemed critical to the earnings process. In this case, all revenue and costs are deferred until this final activity has been performed. For example, a moving company will pack, load, transport, and deliver household goods for a fixed fee. Although packing, loading, and transporting all are important to the earning process, delivery is the culminating event of the earnings process. So, the entire service fee is recognized as revenue after the goods have been delivered. FedEx recognizes revenue in this manner. The Company's Summary of Significant Accounting Policies disclosure note indicates that "Revenue is recognized upon delivery of shipments." As with the sale of product, estimates of uncollectible amounts must be made for service revenue provided to customers on a credit basis.

**United Airlines** (and other major airlines) provide another example. Do you ever add miles to your frequent flyer mileage program by accumulating miles with a credit card or long-distance phone services? For example, you can obtain a **Citibank** credit card and earn one frequent flyer mile on United Airlines for every $1 charged on the card. Or if you use **MCI** long-distance, you can earn one mile for every $1 in long-distance charges. When you accumulate enough miles, you earn a free flight on United. Citibank and MCI must pay United Airlines for the frequent flyer miles it gives its customers. So, when does United Airlines recognize revenue for the miles it provides to customers of Citibank and MCI?

Until recently, United recognized revenue as the miles were sold. But, is United actually selling a product—miles? No, it is providing a service by flying customers of Citibank and MCI. The SEC's *Staff Accounting Bulletin No. 101,* discussed earlier, motivated United to change its revenue recognition policy for the sale of mileage. Graphic 5–4 shows a disclosure describing the change in policy.

United is recognizing "a portion of revenue" (probably a significant portion) when the final critical activity takes place, specifically "when the transportation is provided." While not specifically mentioned, the nondeferred portion of the revenue is recognized earlier to coincide with, and offset, the costs of administering the program.

[9]We discuss this aspect of title transfer in Chapter 7.

**Accounting Changes (in part)**
During the first quarter of 2000, United changed its method of accounting for the sale of mileage to participating partners in its Mileage Plus program, in accordance with *Staff Accounting Bulletin No. 101,* "Revenue Recognition in Financial Statements." Under the new accounting method, a portion of revenue from the sale of mileage (previously recognized in other revenue) is deferred and recognized as passenger revenue when the transportation is provided.

**GRAPHIC 5–4**
Disclosure of Change in Revenue Recognition Policy—United Airlines, Inc.

## SIGNIFICANT UNCERTAINTY OF COLLECTIBILITY

FINANCIAL REPORTING CASE

Q3, p. 211

Recognizing revenue at a specific point in time as described in the previous section assumes we are able to make reasonable estimates of amounts due from customers that potentially might be uncollectible. For product sales, this also includes amounts not collectible due to customers returning the products they purchased. Otherwise, we would violate one of the requirements of the revenue realization principle we discussed earlier that there must be reasonable certainty as to the collectibility of cash from the customer. Now, in this section, we address a few situations when uncertainties could cause a delay in recognizing revenue from a sale of a product or service. One such situation occasionally occurs when products (or services) are sold on an installment basis.

● LO2

**Installment Sales.** Customers sometimes are allowed to pay for purchases in installments over a long period of time. Many large retail stores, for instance, such as **Sears** and **J.C. Penney** sell certain products on an installment plan. Increasing the length of time allowed for payment usually increases the inevitable uncertainty about whether the store actually will collect a receivable. Is the uncertainty sufficient in an installment sale to cause Sears to delay recognizing revenue and related expenses beyond the point of sale? Usually, it's not.

**At times, revenue recognition is delayed due to a high degree of uncertainty related to ultimate cash collection.**

In most situations, the increased uncertainty concerning the collection of cash from installment sales can be accommodated satisfactorily by estimating uncollectible amounts. If, however, the installment sale creates significant uncertainty concerning cash collection, making impossible a reasonable assessment of future bad debts, then revenue and expense recognition should be delayed. For example, real estate sales often are made on an installment basis with relatively small down payments and long payment periods, perhaps 25 years or more. These payment characteristics, combined with the general speculative nature of many of these transactions, may translate into significant uncertainty concerning the collectibility of the installment receivable.[10] In fact, *SFAS No. 66* requires that the installment sales method (discussed below) be applied to a retail land sale that meets certain criteria.[11]

When extreme uncertainty exists regarding the ultimate collectibility of cash, we delay recognizing revenue and related expenses using one of two accounting techniques, the **installment sales method** or the **cost recovery method**. *We emphasize that these methods should be used only in situations involving exceptional uncertainty.* As an example, **Rouse Company** acquires, develops, and manages income-producing properties throughout the United States and develops and sells land for residential, commercial, and other uses. Graphic 5–5 shows the company's revenue recognition disclosure note included with recent annual financial statements. The note indicates that the preferred method is to recognize revenue upon delivery (full accrual method), but that in certain circumstances, one of these two alternative methods could be used.

**The installment sales and cost recovery methods are only used in unusual circumstances.**

### Installment sales method.

To deal with the uncertainty of collection, the **installment sales method** recognizes revenue and costs only when cash payments are received. Each payment is assumed to be composed of two components: (1) a partial recovery of the cost of the item sold and (2) a gross profit component. These components are determined by the gross profit percentage applicable to the sale. For example, if the gross profit percentage

**The *installment sales method* recognizes the gross profit by applying the gross profit percentage on the sale to the amount of cash actually received.**

[10]For income tax purposes, the installment sales method applies only to gains from the sale of certain types of properties. The tax law requires the use of the installment sales method for these transactions unless a taxpayer elects not to use the method.

[11]"Accounting for Sales of Real Estate," *Statement of Financial Accounting Standards No. 66* (Stamford, Conn.: FASB, 1982).

**GRAPHIC 5–5**

Disclosure of Revenue Recognition Policy—Rouse Company

**Revenue recognition and related matters (in part)**
Revenues from land sales are recognized using the full accrual method provided that various criteria relating to the terms of the transactions and any subsequent involvement by us with the land sold are met. Revenues relating to transactions that do not meet the established criteria are deferred and recognized when the criteria are met or using the installment or cost recovery methods, as appropriate in the circumstances.

(gross profit ÷ sales price) is 40%, then 60% of each dollar collected represents cost recovery and the remaining 40% is gross profit. Consider the example in Illustration 5–1.

**ILLUSTRATION 5–1**

Installment Sales Method

On November 1, 2006, the Belmont Corporation, a real estate developer, sold a tract of land for $800,000. The sales agreement requires the customer to make four equal annual payments of $200,000 plus interest on each November 1, beginning November 1, 2006. The land cost $560,000 to develop. The company's fiscal year ends on December 31.

**Gross profit recognition, installment sales method**

The gross profit of $240,000 ($800,000 − 560,000) represents 30% of the sales price ($240,000 ÷ $800,000). The collection of cash and the recognition of gross profit under the installment method are summarized below. We ignore the collection of interest charges and the recognition of interest revenue to concentrate on the collection of the $800,000 sales price and the recognition of gross profit on the sale.

| Date | Cash Collected | Cost Recovery (70%) | Gross Profit (30%) |
|---|---|---|---|
| Nov. 1, 2006 | $200,000 | $140,000 | $ 60,000 |
| Nov. 1, 2007 | 200,000 | 140,000 | 60,000 |
| Nov. 1, 2008 | 200,000 | 140,000 | 60,000 |
| Nov. 1, 2009 | 200,000 | 140,000 | 60,000 |
| Totals | $800,000 | $560,000 | $240,000 |

This illustrates that the gross profit recognized in a period will be equal to the gross profit percentage multiplied by the period's cash collection. The following journal entries are recorded (interest charges ignored):

**Inventory is credited for the portion of the receivable that represents the cost of the land sold. The difference is deferred gross profit.**

| | | |
|---|---|---|
| **November 1, 2006** | | |
| Installment receivables | 800,000 | |
| Inventory | | 560,000 |
| Deferred gross profit | | 240,000 |
| *To record installment sale.* | | |

The first entry records the installment receivable and the reduction of inventory. The difference between the $800,000 selling price and the $560,000 cost of sales represents the gross profit on the sale of $240,000. As it will be recognized only as collections are made, it is recorded in an account called *deferred gross profit.* This is a contra account to the installment receivable. It will be reduced to zero as the payments are received.[12]

[12]Accountants sometimes record installment sales in the following manner:

| | | |
|---|---|---|
| Installment sales receivable | 800,000 | |
| Installment sales | | 800,000 |
| *To record installment sales.* | | |
| Cost of installment sales | 560,000 | |
| Inventory | | 560,000 |
| *To record the cost of installment sales.* | | |

Then at the end of the period, the following adjusting/closing entry is recorded:

| | | |
|---|---|---|
| Installment sales | 800,000 | |
| Cost of installment sales | | 560,000 |
| Deferred gross profit on installment sales | | 240,000 |

The text entries concentrate on the effect of the transactions and avoid this unnecessary procedural complexity.

| | | |
|---|---|---|
| **November 1, 2006** | | |
| Cash . . . . . . . . . . . . . . . . . . . . . . . . . . . . . . . . . . . . . . . . . . . . . | 200,000 | |
| Installment receivables . . . . . . . . . . . . . . . . . . . . . . . . . . . . . . . | | 200,000 |
| *To record cash collection from installment sale.* | | |
| Deferred gross profit . . . . . . . . . . . . . . . . . . . . . . . . . . . . . . . . . . | 60,000 | |
| Realized gross profit. . . . . . . . . . . . . . . . . . . . . . . . . . . . . . . . . | | 60,000 |
| *To recognize gross profit from installment sale.* | | |

**When payments are received, gross profit is recognized, calculated by applying the gross profit percentage to the cash collected (30% × $200,000).**

The second set of entries records the collection of the first installment and recognizes the gross profit component of the payment, $60,000. Journal entries to record the remaining three payments are identical.

At the end of 2006, the balance sheet would report the following:

| | |
|---|---|
| Installment receivables | $600,000 |
| Less: Deferred gross profit | (180,000) |
| Installment receivables (net) | $420,000 |

The net amount of the receivable reflects the portion of the remaining payments that represents cost recovery (70% × $600,000). The installment receivables are classified as current assets if they will be collected within one year (or within the company's operating cycle, if longer); otherwise, they are classified as noncurrent assets.

The income statement for 2006 would report a gross profit from installment sales of $60,000. Sales and cost of goods sold usually are not reported in the income statement, just the resulting gross profit. But if installment sales are significant, the 2006 income statement in this illustration would report sales of $200,000 and cost of goods sold of $140,000.

## ADDITIONAL CONSIDERATION

We discuss the problem of accounting for bad debts in significant depth in Chapter 7. However, bad debts related to receivables on sales accounted for using the installment method create a unique problem. Assume that in the example described in Illustration 5–1, the Belmont Corporation collected the first payment but the customer was unable to make the remaining payments. Typically, the seller would repossess the item sold and make the following journal entry:

| | | |
|---|---|---|
| Repossessed inventory . . . . . . . . . . . . . . . . . . . . . . . . . . . . . . | 420,000 | |
| Deferred gross profit. . . . . . . . . . . . . . . . . . . . . . . . . . . . . . . . . | 180,000 | |
| Installment receivable . . . . . . . . . . . . . . . . . . . . . . . . . . . . . | | 600,000 |

This entry removes the receivable and the remaining deferred gross profit and records the repossessed land in an inventory account. The entry assumes that the land's current fair value is equal to the net receivable of $420,000. If the land's fair value at the date of repossession is less than $420,000, a loss on repossession is recorded (debited).

**Cost recovery method.** In situations where there is an extremely high degree of uncertainty regarding the ultimate cash collection on an installment sale, an even more conservative approach, the **cost recovery method,** can be used. This method defers all gross profit recognition until the cost of the item sold has been recovered. The gross profit recognition

## GLOBAL PERSPECTIVE

Many countries follow the U.S. practice of recognizing revenue on installment sales at date of sale, unless the installment sale creates a situation where there is significant uncertainty concerning cash collection, in which case revenue and expense recognition are delayed. There are, however, some countries where accounting procedures do not differentiate between installment and other credit sales.

The *cost recovery method* defers all gross profit recognition until cash equal to the cost of the item sold has been received.

pattern applying the cost recovery method to the Belmont Corporation situation used in Illustration 5–1 is shown below.

Gross profit recognition, cost recovery method

| Date | Cash Collected | Cost Recovery | Gross Profit |
|---|---|---|---|
| Nov. 1, 2006 | $200,000 | $200,000 | $ –0– |
| Nov. 1, 2007 | 200,000 | 200,000 | –0– |
| Nov. 1, 2008 | 200,000 | 160,000 | 40,000 |
| Nov. 1, 2009 | 200,000 | –0– | 200,000 |
| Totals | $800,000 | $560,000 | $240,000 |

The journal entries using this method are similar to those by the installment sales method except that $40,000 in gross profit is recognized in 2008 and $200,000 in 2009.

The cost recovery initial journal entry is identical to the installment sales method.

When payments are received, gross profit is recognized only after cost has been fully recovered.

| | | |
|---|---|---|
| **November 1, 2006** | | |
| Installment receivables | 800,000 | |
| Inventory | | 560,000 |
| Deferred gross profit | | 240,000 |
| *To record installment sale.* | | |
| **November 1, 2006, 2007, 2008, and 2009** | | |
| Cash | 200,000 | |
| Installment receivables | | 200,000 |
| *To record cash collection from installment sale.* | | |
| **November 1, 2006 and 2007** | | |
| No entry for gross profit. | | |
| **November 1, 2008** | | |
| Deferred gross profit | 40,000 | |
| Realized gross profit | | 40,000 |
| *To recognize gross profit from installment sale.* | | |
| **November 1, 2009** | | |
| Deferred gross profit | 200,000 | |
| Realized gross profit | | 200,000 |
| *To recognize gross profit from installment sale.* | | |

## Concept Review Exercise

### Installment Sales

Boatwright Implements, Inc., manufactures and sells farm machinery. For most of its sales, revenue and cost of sales are recognized at the delivery date. In 2006, it sold a cotton baler to a new customer for $100,000. The cost of the machinery was $60,000. Payment will be made in five annual installments of $20,000 each, with the first payment due in 2006. Boatwright usually does not allow its customers to pay in installments. Due to the unusual nature of the payment terms and the uncertainty of collection of the installment payments, Boatwright is considering alternative methods of recognizing profit on this sale.

**Required:**

Ignoring interest charges, prepare a table showing the gross profit to be recognized from 2006 through 2010 on the sale using the following three methods:

1. Point of delivery revenue recognition.
2. The installment sales method.
3. The cost recovery method.

SOLUTION

| | Point of Delivery | Installment Sales Method (40% × cash collection) | Cost Recovery Method |
|---|---|---|---|
| 2006 | $40,000 | $ 8,000 | $ –0– |
| 2007 | –0– | 8,000 | –0– |
| 2008 | –0– | 8,000 | –0– |
| 2009 | –0– | 8,000 | 20,000 |
| 2010 | –0– | 8,000 | 20,000 |
| Totals | $40,000 | $40,000 | $40,000 |

● LO3

**Right of Return.** Retailers usually give their customers the right to return merchandise if they are not satisfied. In most situations, even though the right to return merchandise exists, revenues and expenses can be appropriately recognized at point of delivery. Based on past experience, a company usually can estimate the returns that will result for a given volume of sales. These estimates are used to reduce both sales and cost of goods sold in anticipation of returns. The purpose of the estimates is to avoid overstating gross profit in the period of sale and understating gross profit in the period of return. The specific accounting treatment for sales returns is illustrated in Chapter 7 in conjunction with discussing the valuation of accounts receivable.

Because the return of merchandise can retroactively negate the benefits of having made a sale, the seller must meet certain criteria before revenue is recognized in situations when the **right of return** exists. The most critical of these criteria is that the seller must be able to make reliable estimates of future returns.[13] In certain situations, these criteria are not satisfied at the point of delivery of the product. For example, manufacturers of semiconductors like **Intel Corporation** and **Motorola Corporation** usually sell their products through independent distributor companies. Economic factors, competition among manufacturers, and rapid obsolescence of the product motivate these manufacturers to grant the distributors the right of return if they are unable to sell the semiconductors. So, revenue recognition often is deferred beyond the delivery point to the date the products actually are sold by the distributor to an end user.

As an example, the disclosure note shown in Graphic 5–6 appeared in a recent annual report of Intel Corporation.

**Revenue Recognition**
The company recognizes net revenue when the earnings process is complete, as evidenced by an agreement with the customer, transfer of title and acceptance, if applicable, as well as fixed pricing and probable collectibility. Because of frequent sales price reductions and rapid technology obsolescence in the industry, sales made to distributors under agreements allowing price protection and/or right of return are deferred until the distributors sell the merchandise.

GRAPHIC 5–6
Disclosure of Revenue Recognition Policy—Intel Corporation

For Intel, the event critical to revenue recognition is *not* the delivery of the product to the buyer but the ultimate sale of the product by the buyer (the distributor company) to an end user.

Any time a company recognizes revenue at a point other than the point of delivery, the revenue recognition method used is disclosed in the summary of significant accounting policies. Intel's disclosure note is an example. Graphic 5–7, a disclosure note from a recent financial statement of **Amdahl Corporation**, a manufacturer of mainframe computers, provides another example.

**Notes: Revenue Recognition (in part)**
Revenue from equipment sales is generally recognized when equipment has been shipped, installed, and financing arrangements have been completed.

GRAPHIC 5–7
Disclosure of Revenue Recognition Policy—Amdahl Corporation

[13]Other, less critical criteria are listed in "Revenue Recognition When Right of Return Exists," *Statement of Financial Accounting Standards No. 48* (Stamford, Conn.: FASB, 1981).

As the note indicates, revenue is delayed beyond the point of product delivery. Amdahl waits until the product has been properly installed and financing has been arranged by the buyer. Why does Amdahl delay revenue recognition? Until the product has been installed and financing arranged, there is a high degree of uncertainty concerning the possibility the product might be returned. Also, installation is an important part of the agreement between Amdahl and its customers.

**Consignment Sales.** Sometimes a company arranges for another company to sell its product under **consignment**. The "consignor" physically transfers the goods to the other company (the consignee), but the consignor retains legal title. If the consignee can't find a buyer within an agreed-upon time, the consignee returns the goods to the consignor. However, if a buyer is found, the consignee remits the selling price (less commission and approved expenses) to the consignor.

Because the consignor retains the risks and rewards of ownership of the product and title does not pass to the consignee, the consignor does not record a sale (revenue and related expenses) until the consignee sells the goods and title passes to the eventual customer. Of course, that means goods on consignment are still part of the consignor's inventory. As an example, **Intuit, Inc.** provides business and financial management software solutions for small businesses, accounting professionals and consumers. Its flagship products include QuickBooks and TurboTax. Some of the company's product is sold using consignment arrangements. Graphic 5–8 shows a portion of their revenue recognition disclosure note that was included in a recent annual report.

**GRAPHIC 5–8**
Disclosure of Revenue Recognition Policy—Intuit, Inc.

**Product Revenue (in part)**
We typically recognize revenue from the sale of our packaged software products and supplies when we ship the product. We sell some of our QuickBooks and Consumer Tax products on consignment to a limited number of resellers. We recognize revenue for these consignment transactions only when the end-user sale has occurred.

Up until now, we've focused on revenue-generating activities in which some specific event (e.g., delivery, collection, product performance, and resale) indicates that the earnings process is substantially completed and significant uncertainties have been alleviated, prompting us to recognize revenue and related expenses. We now turn our attention to situations in which it's desirable to recognize revenue over more than one reporting period—before a specific event indicates the earnings process is substantially completed.

## Completion of the Earnings Process over Multiple Reporting Periods

Revenue recognition at a single point in time, when an earnings process is virtually complete, is inappropriate for certain types of service revenue activities and also, usually, for long-term contracts.

### SERVICE REVENUE EARNED OVER TIME

**Service revenue often is recognized over time, in proportion to the amount of service performed.**

In a previous section we saw that many service activities encompass some final activity that is deemed critical to the earnings process. In these cases, we recognize revenue when that activity occurs. However, in many instances, service revenue activities occur over extended periods and recognizing revenue at any single date within that period would be inappropriate. Instead, it's more meaningful to recognize revenue over time in proportion to the performance of the activity.

As an example, consider the revenue a property owner earns when renting office space. If a landlord charges a tenant $12,000 in rent for the upcoming year, it would seem logical to recognize $1,000 of rent revenue each month over the one-year period (i.e., straight-line method) since services performed are similar over the period. The landlord recognizes rent revenue in proportion to the passage of time. Likewise, **Gold's Gym** will recognize revenue from a two-year membership ratably over the 24-month membership period.

A similar situation occurs if you buy a season pass to Disney World. When would **Walt Disney Co.** recognize revenue for the $515 it collects for the sale of a 365-day pass? Rationalizing that a pass can be used any number of times during the season, thus making it difficult to determine when service is provided, many companies once recognized all revenue from the sale of season passes on the date of sale. However, the SEC's *Staff Accounting Bulletin No. 101,* discussed earlier in the chapter, motivated most of these companies to change their revenue recognition policy. For example, Graphic 5–9 provides a disclosure note **Six Flags, Inc.** included in a recent annual report. Notice that the company now recognizes revenue *over time*, based on the anticipated usage of the season pass over the operating season.

**Revenue Recognition (in part)**
. . . the provisions of *SAB No 101* did change the accounting policies that the Company uses to recognize revenue from multi-admission tickets and season passes during the year. The Company's accounting policy as of January 1, 2000, recognizes the revenue from multi-admission tickets and season passes over the operating season on a usage basis rather than upon receipt.

**GRAPHIC 5–9**
Disclosure of Revenue Recognition Policy—Six Flags, Inc.

## LONG-TERM CONTRACTS

● LO4

Another activity in which it is desirable to recognize revenue over time is one involving a long-term contract. The types of companies that make use of long-term contracts are many and varied. A recent survey of reporting practices of 600 large public companies indicates that one in every six companies engages in long-term contracts.[14] And they are not just construction companies. In fact, even services such as research, installation, and consulting often are contracted for on a long-term basis. Graphic 5–10 lists just a sampling of companies that use long-term contracts, many of which you might recognize.

| Company | Type of Industry or Product |
|---|---|
| Oracle Corp. | Computer software, license and consulting fees |
| Lockheed Martin Corporation | Aircraft, missiles, and spacecraft |
| Datatec Systems, Inc. | Integrated computer systems design |
| Newport News Shipbuilding, Inc. | Shipbuilding |
| Nortel Networks Corp. | Networking solutions and services to support the Internet |
| Hamilton McGregor International Inc. | Construction, medical facilities |
| SBA Communications Corp. | Telecommunications |
| Layne Christensen Company | Water supply services and geotechnical construction |
| Kaufman & Broad Home Corp. | Commercial and residential construction |
| Raytheon Company | Defense electronics |
| Foster Wheeler Corp. | Construction, petroleum and chemical facilities |
| Halliburton | Construction, energy services |
| Morrison Knudsen Corp. | Construction, facilities including electric utilities |
| Allied Products Corp. | Large metal stamping presses |

**GRAPHIC 5–10**
Companies Engaged in Long-Term Contracts

The general revenue recognition criteria described in the realization principle suggest that revenue should be recognized when a long-term project is finished (that is, when the earnings process is virtually complete). This is known as the **completed contract method** of revenue recognition. The problem with this method is that all revenues, expenses, and resulting

**The *completed contract method* recognizes revenue at a point in time when the earnings process is complete.**

[14]*Accounting Trends and Techniques—2004* (New York: AICPA, 2001), p. 432.

**FINANCIAL REPORTING CASE**

Q1, p. 211

income from the project are recognized in the period in which the project is completed; no revenues or expenses are reported in the income statements of earlier reporting periods in which much of the work may have been performed. Net income should provide a measure of periodic accomplishment to help predict future accomplishments. Clearly, income statements prepared using the completed contract method do not fairly report each period's accomplishments when a project spans more than one reporting period. Much of the earnings process is far removed from the point of delivery.

The *percentage-of-completion method* allocates a share of a project's revenues and expenses to each reporting period during the contract period.

The **percentage-of-completion method** of revenue recognition for long-term projects is designed to help address this problem. This method recognizes revenue (and expenses) over time by allocating a share of the project's expected revenues and expenses to each period in which the earnings process occurs, that is, the contract period. Although the contract usually specifies total revenues, the project's expenses are not known until completion. Consequently, it is necessary for a company to estimate the project's future costs at the end of each reporting period to estimate total gross profit to be earned on the project.

Illustration 5–2 provides information to compare accounting for long-term contracts using the completed contract and percentage-of-completion methods.

**ILLUSTRATION 5–2**
Completed Contract and Percentage-of-Completion Methods Compared

At the beginning of 2006, the Harding Construction Company received a contract to build an office building for $5 million. The project is estimated to take three years to complete. According to the contract, Harding will bill the buyer in installments over the construction period according to a prearranged schedule. Information related to the contract is as follows:

| | 2006 | 2007 | 2008 |
|---|---|---|---|
| Construction costs incurred during the year | $1,500,000 | $1,000,000 | $1,600,000 |
| Construction costs incurred in prior years | –0– | 1,500,000 | 2,500,000 |
| Cumulative construction costs | 1,500,000 | 2,500,000 | 4,100,000 |
| Estimated costs to complete at end of year | 2,250,000 | 1,500,000 | –0– |
| Total estimated and actual construction costs | $3,750,000 | $4,000,000 | $4,100,000 |
| Billings made during the year | $1,200,000 | $2,000,000 | $1,800,000 |
| Cash collections during year | 1,000,000 | 1,400,000 | 2,600,000 |

Construction costs include the labor, materials, and overhead costs directly related to the construction of the building. Notice how the total of estimated and actual construction costs changes from period to period. Cost revisions are typical in long-term contracts where costs are estimated over long periods of time.

The completed contract method recognizes no income until project completion.

**Completed Contract Method.** With both the completed contract and percentage-of-completion methods, all costs of construction are recorded in an asset account called **construction in progress**. This account is equivalent to the asset work-in-process inventory in a manufacturing company. For the completed contract method, *no revenues or expenses related to this project are recognized in 2006 and 2007.* Construction in progress will show a balance of $1,500,000 and $2,500,000 at the end of 2006 and 2007, respectively, and $4,100,000 when the project is completed in 2008. This asset is then "sold" and revenue of $5,000,000 and cost of construction (similar to cost of goods sold) of $4,100,000 (gross profit of $900,000) are recognized in 2008.

The completed contract method does not properly portray a company's performance over the construction period.

Does this solution capture the reality of the situation? To the contrary, it seems to suggest that the construction company was idle or unproductive for two years and then produced a sizable profit the third year. For this reason, the percentage-of-completion method is preferable, and the completed contract method should be used only "when lack of dependable estimates or inherent hazards cause forecasts to be doubtful. . ."[15]

[15] "Long-Term Construction-Type Contracts," *Accounting Research Bulletin No. 45* (New York: AICPA 1955).

**Percentage-of-Completion Method.** The percentage-of-completion method recognizes a portion of the estimated gross profit each period based on progress to date. Progress to date depends on three factors:

1. The costs incurred to date.
2. The most recent estimate of the project's total cost.
3. The most recent gross profit estimate.

FINANCIAL REPORTING CASE

Q2, p. 211

Let's first focus on the calculation of periodic gross profit for each of the three years of construction. We then address the gross profit components—revenue and cost of construction. Progress to date usually is assumed to be the *proportion of the project's cost incurred to date divided by total estimated costs.* This fraction, the estimated percentage of completion, is assumed to be a measure of progress. It should be mentioned that this measure is based on costs and could differ significantly from an estimate of physical progress made by an engineer or architect. Companies use this method, often referred to as the cost-to-cost method of estimating a percentage-of-completion, more frequently than estimates of physical progress. In a recent disclosure note shown in Graphic 5–11, **SBA Communications** indicates it uses the cost-to-cost method "because management considers total cost to be the best available measure of progress . . . "

**Progress to date can be estimated as the proportion of the project's cost incurred to date divided by total estimated costs, or by relying on an engineer's or architect's estimate.**

**Revenue Recognition (in part)**
Revenue from construction projects is recognized on the percentage-of-completion method of accounting, determined by the percentage of cost incurred to date compared to management's estimated total anticipated cost for each contract. This method is used because management considers total cost to be the best available measure of progress on the contracts.

GRAPHIC 5–11
Disclosure of Revenue Recognition Policy—SBA Communications Corp.

The objective of determining a percentage of completion is to measure activity or project accomplishment to date. If the cost-to-cost approach does not properly parallel this accomplishment, then another method should be used. For example, the construction of a road might encounter a particularly difficult section of terrain requiring abnormal costs to be incurred without much progress being made on the road. In such a case, the cost-to-cost method might not adequately reflect how much of the project has actually been completed.

Illustration 5–2A shows the calculation of gross profit for each of the years for our Harding Construction Company example.

| | 2006 | 2007 | 2008 |
|---|---|---|---|
| Contract price | $5,000,000 | $5,000,000 | $5,000,000 |
| Actual costs to date | 1,500,000 | 2,500,000 | 4,100,000 |
| Estimated costs to complete | 2,250,000 | 1,500,000 | –0– |
| Total project cost | 3,750,000 | 4,000,000 | 4,100,000 |
| Total gross profit (estimated for 2006 and 2007, actual in 2008)—Contract price minus total costs | $1,250,000 | $1,000,000 | $ 900,000 |
| Percentage-of-completion—actual costs to date | $1,500,000 | $2,500,000 | (project is |
| divided by the estimated total project cost | $3,750,000 | $4,000,000 | complete) |
| | **= 40%** | **= 62.5%** | **100%** |
| Total project gross profit | $1,250,000 | $1,000,000 | $ 900,000 |
| Multiplied by the estimated % of completion | 40% | 62.5% | 100% |
| Gross profit earned to date | $ 500,000 | $ 625,000 | $ 900,000 |
| Less gross profit recognized in previous periods | –0– | (500,000) | (625,000) |
| Gross profit recognized currently | $ 500,000 | $ 125,000 | $ 275,000 |

ILLUSTRATION 5–2A
Percentage-of-Completion Method—Allocation of Gross Profit to Each Period

At the end of each period, the revised project gross profit estimate is multiplied by the revised estimate of the percentage of completion. The result is the estimated gross profit earned from inception to date. The current period's gross profit is calculated by subtracting from this amount the gross profit recognized in previous periods.

Income statements are more informative if the sales revenue and cost components of gross profit are reported rather than the net figure alone. So, the income statement for each year will report the appropriate revenue and cost of construction amounts. For example, in 2006 the gross profit of $500,000 consists of revenue of $2,000,000 (40% multiplied by the $5,000,000 contract price) and $1,500,000 in cost of construction. In subsequent periods, revenue is calculated by multiplying the percentage of completion by the contract price and then subtracting revenue recognized in prior periods. The cost of construction is the difference between revenue and gross profit. In most cases, cost of construction also equals the construction costs incurred during the period.[16] The table in Illustration 5–2B shows the revenue and cost of construction recognized in each of the three years of our example. Of course, as you can see in this illustration, we could have initially determined gross profit by first calculating revenue and then subtracting cost of construction.

**ILLUSTRATION 5–2B**

Percentage-of-Completion Method—Allocation of Revenue and Cost of Construction to Each Period

| | | |
|---|---|---|
| **2006** | | |
| Revenue recognized ($5,000,000 × 40%) | | $2,000,000 |
| Cost of construction | | 1,500,000 |
| Gross profit | | $ 500,000 |
| **2007** | | |
| Revenue recognized to date ($5,000,000 × 62.5%) | $3,125,000 | |
| Less: Revenue recognized in 2006 | (2,000,000) | |
| Revenue recognized | | $1,125,000 |
| Cost of construction | | 1,000,000 |
| Gross profit | | $ 125,000 |
| **2008** | | |
| Revenue recognized to date ($5,000,000 × 100%) | $5,000,000 | |
| Less: Revenue recognized in 2006 and 2007 | (3,125,000) | |
| Revenue recognized | | $1,875,000 |
| Cost of construction | | 1,600,000 |
| Gross profit | | $ 275,000 |

## A COMPARISON OF THE TWO METHODS—INCOME RECOGNITION

A period-by-period comparison of the gross profit patterns produced by each method of revenue recognition is presented below:

| | Percentage-of-Completion | Completed Contract |
|---|---|---|
| Gross profit recognized | | |
| 2006 | $500,000 | –0– |
| 2007 | 125,000 | –0– |
| 2008 | 275,000 | $900,000 |
| Total gross profit | $900,000 | $900,000 |

Although both methods yield identical gross profit of $900,000 for the entire three-year period, the timing differs. The completed contract method defers all gross profit to 2008, when

[16] Cost of construction does not equal the construction costs incurred during the year when a loss is projected on the entire project. This case is illustrated later in the chapter.

the project is completed. Obviously, the percentage-of-completion method provides a better measure of the company's economic activity and progress over the three-year period. That's why the percentage-of-completion method is preferred, and, as mentioned above, the completed contract method should be used only in situations where the company is unable to make dependable estimates of future costs necessary to apply the percentage-of-completion method.[17]

The percentage-of-completion method provides a more realistic measure of a project's periodic profitability, and is almost always used.

Our discussion to this point has concentrated on income recognition. Notice that *the amount billed and the cash actually received have no effect on income recognition.* We now turn our attention to the balance sheet effect of accounting for long-term construction contracts.

**Balance Sheet Effects Compared.** Summary journal entries for *both* the percentage-of-completion and completed contract methods are shown in Illustration 5–2C for construction costs, billings, and cash receipts.

**ILLUSTRATION 5–2C** Journal Entries—Costs, Billings, and Receipts

| | 2006 | | 2007 | | 2008 | |
|---|---|---|---|---|---|---|
| Construction in progress | 1,500,000 | | 1,000,000 | | 1,600,000 | |
| Cash, materials, etc. | | 1,500,000 | | 1,000,000 | | 1,600,000 |
| *To record construction costs.* | | | | | | |
| Accounts receivable | 1,200,000 | | 2,000,000 | | 1,800,000 | |
| Billings on construction contract | | 1,200,000 | | 2,000,000 | | 1,800,000 |
| *To record progress billings.* | | | | | | |
| Cash | 1,000,000 | | 1,400,000 | | 2,600,000 | |
| Accounts receivable | | 1,000,000 | | 1,400,000 | | 2,600,000 |
| *To record cash collections.* | | | | | | |

Notice that periodic billings are credited to **billings on construction contract.** This account is a contra account to the asset construction in progress. At the end of each period, the balances in these two accounts are compared. If the net amount is a debit, it is reported in the balance sheet as an asset. Conversely, if the net amount is a credit, it is reported as a liability.[18]

*Billings on construction contract* is subtracted from construction in progress to determine balance sheet presentation.

A debit balance essentially represents an unbilled receivable. The construction company is incurring construction costs (and recognizing gross profit using the percentage-of-completion method) for which it will be paid by the buyer. If the construction company bills the buyer an amount exactly equal to these costs (and profits recognized) then the accounts receivable balance properly reflects the claims of the construction company. If, however, the amount billed is less than the costs incurred (plus profits recognized) the difference represents the remaining claim to cash.

On the other hand, if the amount billed exceeds the costs incurred (plus profits recognized), then the overbilled accounts receivable overstate the amount of the claim to cash earned to that date and must be reported as a liability. This is similar to the situation when a customer pays for a product or service in advance. The advance is properly shown as a liability representing the obligation to provide the good or service in the future.

Accounting under each of the methods is precisely the same to this point. But, as explained earlier, gross profit (revenue less cost of construction) is recognized differently by the two approaches. The entries shown in Illustration 5–2D are the additional journal entries required using the percentage-of-completion method to recognize periodic revenue and cost of construction and to close the construction contract accounts (construction in progress and billings on construction contracts) and for the completed contract method at the end of the

Under the completed contract method, profit is recognized only at the completion of the project.

[17]For income tax purposes, the completed contract method may be used for home construction contracts and certain other real estate construction contracts. All other contracts must use the percentage-of-completion method.

[18]If the company is engaged in more than one long-term contract, all contracts for which construction in progress exceeds billings are grouped together and all contracts for which billings exceed construction in progress also are grouped. This could result in the presentation of both an asset and a liability in the balance sheet.

project to recognize revenue and cost of construction and to close the construction contract accounts.

**ILLUSTRATION 5–2D** Journal Entries—Profit Recognition and Closing

| | 2006 | | 2007 | | 2008 | |
|---|---|---|---|---|---|---|
| **Percentage-of-Completion** | | | | | | |
| Construction in progress (gross profit) . . . | 500,000 | | 125,000 | | 275,000 | |
| Cost of construction . . . . . . . . . . . . . . . . | 1,500,000 | | 1,000,000 | | 1,600,000 | |
| Revenue from long-term contracts . . . | | 2,000,000 | | 1,125,000 | | 1,875,000 |
| *To record gross profit.* | | | | | | |
| Billings on construction contract. . . . . . . | | | | | 5,000,000 | |
| Construction in progress . . . . . . . . . . . | | | | | | 5,000,000 |
| *To close accounts.* | | | | | | |
| **Completed Contract** | | | | | | |
| Construction in progress (gross profit) . . . | | | | | 900,000 | |
| Cost of construction . . . . . . . . . . . . . . . . | | | | | 4,100,000 | |
| Revenue from long-term contracts . . . | | | | | | 5,000,000 |
| *To record gross profit.* | | | | | | |
| Billings on construction contract. . . . . . . | | | | | 5,000,000 | |
| Construction in progress . . . . . . . . . . . | | | | | | 5,000,000 |
| *To close accounts.* | | | | | | |

Why debit construction in progress for the amount of gross profit recognized? In the typical manufacturing situation, inventory prior to sale is stated at cost. The difference between the historical cost of the inventory and its sales price (the gross profit) is not recognized until product delivery. In other words, assets are not increased until the inventory is sold.

The percentage-of-completion method departs from historical cost and recognizes a portion of the markup between the cost and the selling price of inventory prior to delivery. In our illustration, at the end of 2006 the total estimated cost is $3,750,000 and the estimated markup to sales price is $1,250,000. The inventory is increased by $500,000 which represents 40% of this total markup. The completed contract method recognizes the actual markup when the project is completed.

The construction in progress account and the billings on construction contracts account before closing entries are illustrated below for both methods using T-accounts:

Construction in progress includes periodic profit by the percentage-of-completion method.

**Percentage-of-Completion** — Construction in Progress

| | Debit | Credit |
|---|---|---|
| 2006 construction costs | 1,500,000 | |
| 2006 gross profit | 500,000 | |
| End balance, 2006 | 2,000,000 | |
| 2007 construction costs | 1,000,000 | |
| 2007 gross profit | 125,000 | |
| End balance, 2007 | 3,125,000 | |
| 2008 construction costs | 1,600,000 | |
| 2008 gross profit | 275,000 | |
| Balance, before closing | 5,000,000 | |

**Completed Contract** — Construction in Progress

| | Debit | Credit |
|---|---|---|
| 2006 construction costs | 1,500,000 | |
| End balance, 2006 | 1,500,000 | |
| 2007 construction costs | 1,000,000 | |
| End balance, 2007 | 2,500,000 | |
| 2008 construction costs | 1,600,000 | |
| 2008 gross profit | 900,000 | |
| Balance, before closing | 5,000,000 | |

Billings are the same by either method.

**Billings on Construction Contract** (Percentage-of-Completion)

| Debit | Credit | |
|---|---|---|
| | 1,200,000 | 2006 billings |
| | 2,000,000 | 2007 billings |
| | 1,800,000 | 2008 billings |
| | 5,000,000 | Balance, before closing |

**Billings on Construction Contract** (Completed Contract)

| Debit | Credit | |
|---|---|---|
| | 1,200,000 | 2006 billings |
| | 2,000,000 | 2007 billings |
| | 1,800,000 | 2008 billings |
| | 5,000,000 | Balance, before closing |

### GLOBAL PERSPECTIVE

There are significant differences among countries in the method used to recognize profit on long-term contracts. Practices in many countries, such as the U.K., Norway, Brazil, and Japan are similar to the United States. The percentage-of-completion method is preferred and the completed contract method can be used only in unusual situations. IFRSs require use of the percentage-of-completion method when certain criteria are met.

The balance sheet presentation for the construction-related accounts by both methods is shown in Illustration 5–2E.

**ILLUSTRATION 5–2E**
Balance Sheet Presentation

**Balance Sheet (End of Year)**

| | 2006 | 2007 |
|---|---|---|
| **Percentage-of-Completion:** | | |
| Current assets: | | |
| Accounts receivable | $200,000 | $800,000 |
| Costs and profit ($2,000,000) in excess of billings ($1,200,000) | 800,000 | |
| Current liabilities: | | |
| Billings ($3,200,000) in excess of costs and profit ($3,125,000) | | $ 75,000 |
| **Completed Contract:** | | |
| Current assets: | | |
| Accounts receivable | $200,000 | $800,000 |
| Costs ($1,500,000) in excess of billings ($1,200,000) | $300,000 | |
| Current liabilities: | | |
| Billings ($3,200,000) in excess of costs ($2,500,000) | | $700,000 |

Disclosure of the method used to account for long-term contracts will appear in the summary of significant accounting policies.

The first disclosure note to any set of financial statements usually is a summary of significant accounting policies. This note discloses the method the company uses to account for its long-term contracts. As an example of this, Graphic 5–12 shows the disclosure note that appeared in a recent annual report of **Fluor Corporation**.

**GRAPHIC 5–12**
Disclosure of Revenue Recognition Policy for Construction Contracts—Fluor Corporation

***Notes:* Engineering and Construction Contracts (in part)**
The company recognizes engineering and construction contract revenues using the percentage-of-completion method, based primarily on contract costs incurred to date compared with total estimated contract costs. . . . Changes to total estimated contract costs or losses, if any, are recognized in the period in which they are determined. Revenues recognized in excess of amounts billed are classified as current assets under contract work in progress. Amounts billed to clients in excess of revenues recognized to date are classified as current liabilities under advance billings on contracts.

**Long-Term Contract Losses.** The Harding Construction Company example above involves a situation in which a profit was realized on the construction contract. Unfortunately, losses sometimes occur on long-term contracts. As a prelude to the following discussion, notice in Graphic 5–12 that Fluor Corporation recognizes losses "in the period in which they are determined."

**Periodic loss occurs for profitable project.** At times, a loss must be recognized in at least one period over the life of the project even though the project as a whole is profitable. We determine the loss in precisely the same way we determined the profit in profitable years. For example, assume the same $5 million contract for Harding Construction Company described in Illustration 5–2 but with the following cost information:

| | 2006 | 2007 | 2008 |
|---|---|---|---|
| Construction costs incurred during the year | $1,500,000 | $1,260,000 | $1,840,000 |
| Construction costs incurred in prior years | –0– | 1,500,000 | 2,760,000 |
| Cumulative construction costs | 1,500,000 | 2,760,000 | 4,600,000 |
| Estimated costs to complete at end of year | 2,250,000 | 1,840,000 | –0– |
| Total estimated and actual construction costs | $3,750,000 | $4,600,000 | $4,600,000 |

At the end of 2006, gross profit of $500,000 (revenue of $2,000,000 less cost of construction of $1,500,000) is recognized as previously determined.

At the end of 2007, the company still forecasts a profit of $400,000 ($5,000,000 − $4,600,000) on the project and, at that time, the project is estimated to be 60% complete ($2,760,000 ÷ $4,600,000). Applying this percentage to the anticipated gross profit of $400,000 results in a gross profit *to date* of $240,000. But remember, a gross profit of $500,000 was recognized in 2006.

This situation is treated as a *change in accounting estimate* because it resulted from a change in the estimation of costs to complete at the end of 2006. Costs to complete—$4,600,000—were much higher than the end of 2006 estimate of $3,750,000. Recall from our discussion of changes in accounting estimates in Chapter 4 that we don't go back and restate the prior year's gross profit. Instead, the 2007 income statement would report *a loss of $260,000* ($500,000 − 240,000). The loss consists of revenue of $1,000,000 ($5,000,000 × 60% = $3,000,000 less 2006 revenue of $2,000,000) less cost of construction of $1,260,000 (cost incurred in 2007). The following journal entry records the loss:

**Recognized losses on long-term contracts reduce the construction in progress account.**

| | | |
|---|---|---|
| Cost of construction | 1,260,000 | |
| Revenue from long-term contracts | | 1,000,000 |
| Construction in progress (loss) | | 260,000 |

The 2008 income statement would report a gross profit of $160,000 determined as follows:

| | |
|---|---|
| Project gross profit | $400,000 |
| Less: Gross profit recognized in prior periods ($500,000 − 260,000) | (240,000) |
| 2008 gross profit | $160,000 |

The 2008 gross profit comprises $2,000,000 in revenue ($5,000,000 less revenue of $3,000,000 recognized in 2006 and 2007) and $1,840,000 in cost of construction (cost incurred in 2008).

Of course, by the completed contract method, no profit or loss is recorded in 2006 or 2007. Instead, a $400,000 gross profit (revenue of $5,000,000 and cost of construction of $4,600,000) is recognized in 2008.

**Loss is projected on the entire project.** A more conservative approach is indicated when a loss actually is projected on the entire contract. Again consider the Harding Construction Company example but with the following cost information:

| | 2006 | 2007 | 2008 |
|---|---|---|---|
| Construction costs incurred during the year | $1,500,000 | $1,260,000 | $2,440,000 |
| Construction costs incurred in prior years | –0– | 1,500,000 | 2,760,000 |
| Cumulative construction costs | 1,500,000 | 2,760,000 | 5,200,000 |
| Estimated costs to complete at end of year | 2,250,000 | 2,340,000 | –0– |
| Total estimated and actual construction costs | $3,750,000 | $5,100,000 | $5,200,000 |

At the end of 2007, revised costs indicate a loss of $100,000 for the entire project ($5,000,000 − 5,100,000). In this situation, the *total* anticipated loss must be recognized in 2007 for both the percentage-of-completion method and the completed contract method. As a gross profit of $500,000 was recognized in 2006 using the percentage-of-completion method, *a $600,000 loss is recognized in 2007*. Once again, this situation is treated as a change in accounting estimate with no restatement of 2006 income. If the completed contract method is used, because no gross profit is recognized in 2006 the $100,000 loss for the project is recognized in 2007.

**An estimated loss on a long-term contract is fully recognized in the first period the loss is anticipated, regardless of the revenue recognition method used.**

If the loss is not recognized in 2007, construction in progress would be valued at an amount greater than the company expects to realize from the contract. The construction in progress account is reduced to $2,660,000 ($2,760,000 in costs to date less $100,000 loss recognized to date). This amount combined with the estimated costs to complete of $2,340,000 equals the realizable contract price of $5,000,000. Recognizing losses on long-term projects in the period the losses become known is equivalent to measuring inventory at the lower of cost or market.

**Comparison of Periodic Gross Profit (Loss), Loss on Entire Contract.** The pattern of gross profit (loss) over the contract period for the two methods is summarized in the following table. Notice that an unanticipated increase in costs of $100,000 causes a further loss of $100,000 to be recognized in 2008.

| | Percentage-of-Completion | Completed Contract |
|---|---|---|
| Gross profit (loss) recognized: | | |
| 2006 | $ 500,000 | –0– |
| 2007 | (600,000) | $(100,000) |
| 2008 | (100,000) | (100,000) |
| Total project loss | $(200,000) | $(200,000) |

The table in Illustration 5–2F shows the revenue and cost of construction recognized in each of the three years using the percentage-of-completion method.

| | | |
|---|---|---|
| **2006** | | |
| Revenue recognized ($5,000,000 × 40%) | | $2,000,000 |
| Costs of construction | | 1,500,000 |
| Gross profit | | $ 500,000 |
| **2007** | | |
| Revenue recognized to date ($5,000,000 × 54.12%)* | $2,706,000 | |
| Less: Revenue recognized in 2006 | (2,000,000) | |
| Revenue recognized | | $ 706,000 |
| Cost of construction† | | 1,306,000 |
| Loss | | $ (600,000) |
| **2008** | | |
| Revenue recognized to date ($5,000,000 × 100%) | $5,000,000 | |
| Less: Revenue recognized in 2006 and 2007 | (2,706,000) | |
| Revenue recognized | | $2,294,000 |
| Cost of construction† | | 2,394,000 |
| Loss | | $ (100,000) |

*$2,760,000 ÷ $5,100,000 = 54.12%
†The difference between revenue and loss

**ILLUSTRATION 5–2F**
Percentage-of-Completion Method: Allocation of Revenue and Cost of Construction to Each Period—Loss on Entire Project

Revenue is recognized in the usual way by multiplying a percentage of completion by the total contract price. In situations where a loss is expected on the entire project, cost of construction for the period will no longer be equal to cost incurred during the period. The easiest way to compute cost of construction is to add the amount of the recognized loss to the amount of revenue recognized. For example, in 2007 revenue recognized of $706,000 is added to the loss of $600,000 to arrive at the cost of construction of $1,306,000.[19]

The journal entries to record the losses in 2007 and 2008 are as follows:

Recognized losses on long-term contracts reduce the construction in progress account.

| | | |
|---|---|---|
| **2007** | | |
| Cost of construction | 1,306,000 | |
| Revenue from long-term contracts | | 706,000 |
| Construction in progress (loss) | | 600,000 |
| **2008** | | |
| Cost of construction | 2,394,000 | |
| Revenue from long-term contracts | | 2,294,000 |
| Construction in progress (loss) | | 100,000 |

Using the completed contract method, no revenue or cost of construction is recognized until the contract is complete. In 2007, a loss on long-term contracts (an income statement account) of $100,000 is recognized. In 2008, the income statement will report revenue of $5,000,000 and cost of construction of $5,100,000, thus reporting the additional loss of $100,000. The journal entries to record the losses in 2007 and 2008 are as follows:

| | | |
|---|---|---|
| **2007** | | |
| Loss on long-term contracts | 100,000 | |
| Construction in progress (loss) | | 100,000 |
| **2008** | | |
| Cost of construction | 5,100,000 | |
| Revenue from long-term contracts | | 5,000,000 |
| Construction in progress (loss) | | 100,000 |

You can see from this that use of the percentage-of-completion method in this case produces a large overstatement of income in 2006 and a large understatement in 2007 caused by a change in the estimation of future costs. Recall that if a company feels that it is unable to make dependable forecasts of future costs, the completed contract method should be used.

## CONCEPT REVIEW EXERCISE

### LONG-TERM CONSTRUCTION CONTRACTS

During 2006, the Samuelson Construction Company began construction on an office building for the City of Gernon. The contract price is $8,000,000 and the building will take approximately 18 months to complete. Completion is scheduled for early in 2008. The company's fiscal year ends on December 31.

The following is a year-by-year recap of construction costs incurred and the estimated costs to complete the project as of the end of each year. Progress billings and cash collections also are indicated.

[19]The cost of construction also can be determined as follows:

| | | |
|---|---|---|
| Loss to date (100% recognized) | | $ 100,000 |
| Add: | | |
| Remaining total project cost, not including the loss ($5,100,000 − 100,000) | $5,000,000 | |
| Multiplied by the percentage of completion | × .5412* | 2,706,000 |
| Total | | 2,806,000 |
| Less: Cost of construction recognized in 2006 | | (1,500,000) |
| Cost of construction recognized in 2007 | | $1,306,000 |

*$2,760,000 ÷ $5,100,000

| | 2006 | 2007 | 2008 |
|---|---|---|---|
| Construction costs incurred during the year | $1,500,000 | $4,500,000 | $1,550,000 |
| Construction costs incurred in prior years | –0– | 1,500,000 | 6,000,000 |
| Cumulative construction costs | 1,500,000 | 6,000,000 | 7,550,000 |
| Estimated costs to complete at end of year | 4,500,000 | 1,500,000 | –0– |
| Total estimated and actual construction costs | $6,000,000 | $7,500,000 | $7,550,000 |
| Billings made during the year | $1,400,000 | $5,200,000 | $1,400,000 |
| Cash collections during year | 1,000,000 | 4,000,000 | 3,000,000 |

**Required:**

1. Determine the amount of gross profit or loss to be recognized in each of the three years applying both the percentage-of-completion and completed contract methods.
2. Prepare the necessary summary journal entries for each of the three years to account for construction costs incurred, recognized revenue and cost of construction, contract billings, and cash collections and to close the construction accounts in 2008 using the percentage-of-completion method only.
3. Prepare a partial balance sheet for 2006 and 2007 to include all construction-related accounts using the percentage-of-completion method.

**SOLUTION**

1. Determine the amount of gross profit or loss to be recognized in each of the three years applying both the percentage-of-completion and completed contract methods.

| | Percentage-of-Completion Method | | |
|---|---|---|---|
| | 2006 | 2007 | 2008 |
| Contract price | $8,000,000 | $8,000,000 | $8,000,000 |
| Less: costs to complete | 6,000,000 | $7,500,000 | 7,550,000 |
| Total estimated gross profit to date | 2,000,000 | 500,000 | 450,000 |
| Multiplied by % of completion* | 25% | 80% | 100% |
| Gross profit recognized to date | 500,000 | 400,000 | 450,000 |
| Less gross profit recognized in prior years | –0– | (500,000) | (400,000) |
| Gross profit (loss) recognized | $ 500,000 | $ (100,000) | $ 50,000 |

*Estimates of percentage-of-completion:

| 2006 | 2007 | 2008 |
|---|---|---|
| $\frac{1,500,000}{6,000,000} = 25\%$ | $\frac{6,000,000}{7,500,000} = 80\%$ | Project complete |

| | Completed Contract Method | | |
|---|---|---|---|
| | 2006 | 2007 | 2008 |
| Gross profit recognized | –0– | –0– | $450,000 |

2. Prepare the necessary summary journal entries for each of the three years to account for construction costs incurred, recognized revenue and cost of construction, contract billings, and cash collections and to close the construction accounts in 2008 using the percentage-of-completion method only.

| | 2006 | | 2007 | | 2008 | |
|---|---|---|---|---|---|---|
| Construction in progress . . . . . . . . . . . . . | 1,500,000 | | 4,500,000 | | 1,550,000 | |
| Cash, materials, etc. . . . . . . . . . . . . . . | | 1,500,000 | | 4,500,000 | | 1,550,000 |
| *To record construction costs.* | | | | | | |
| Construction in progress (gross profit). . . | 500,000 | | | | 50,000 | |
| Cost of construction . . . . . . . . . . . . . . . . | 1,500,000 | | | | 1,550,000 | |
| Revenue from long-term contracts (below) . . . . . . . . . . . . . . . | | 2,000,000 | | | | 1,600,000 |
| *To record gross profit.* | | | | | | |

| | 2006 | | 2007 | | 2008 | |
|---|---|---|---|---|---|---|
| Cost of construction . . . . . . . . . . . . . . . . | | | 4,500,000 | | | |
| Revenue from long-term contracts (below) . . . . . . . . . . . . . . . | | | | 4,400,000 | | |
| Construction in progress (loss). . . . . . . | | | | 100,000 | | |
| *To record loss.* | | | | | | |
| Accounts receivable . . . . . . . . . . . . . . . . | 1,400,000 | | 5,200,000 | | 1,400,000 | |
| Billings on construction contract. . . . . | | 1,400,000 | | 5,200,000 | | 1,400,000 |
| *To record progress billings.* | | | | | | |
| Cash. . . . . . . . . . . . . . . . . . . . . . . . . . . . | 1,000,000 | | 4,000,000 | | 3,000,000 | |
| Accounts receivable . . . . . . . . . . . . . . | | 1,000,000 | | 4,000,000 | | 3,000,000 |
| *To record cash collections.* | | | | | | |
| Billings on construction contract. . . . . . . | | | | | 8,000,000 | |
| Construction in progress . . . . . . . . . . . | | | | | | 8,000,000 |
| *To close accounts.* | | | | | | |

**Revenue recognized:**

| | | |
|---|---|---|
| 2006: | $8,000,000 × 25% = | $2,000,000 |
| 2007: | $8,000,000 × 80% = | $6,400,000 |
| | Less: Revenue recognized in 2006 | (2,000,000) |
| | Revenue recognized in 2007 | $4,400,000 |
| 2008: | $8,000,000 × 100% = | $8,000,000 |
| | Less: Revenue recognized in 2006 and 2007 | (6,400,000) |
| | Revenue recognized in 2008 | $1,600,000 |

3. Prepare a partial balance sheet for 2006 and 2007 to include all construction related accounts using the percentage-of-completion method.

**Balance Sheet**
**(End of Year)**

| | 2006 | 2007 |
|---|---|---|
| Current assets: | | |
| Accounts receivable | $400,000 | $1,600,000 |
| Costs and profit ($2,000,000) in excess of billings ($1,400,000) | 600,000 | |
| Current liabilities: | | |
| Billings ($6,600,000) in excess of costs and profit ($6,400,000) | | 200,000 |

## Industry-Specific Revenue Issues

● LO5 The previous sections addressed situations when revenue is recognized either at a point in time after the earnings process is virtually complete or over time during the earnings process. We now look at two industry-specific situations, software and franchise sales, that require revenue recognition using a combination of the two approaches.

### SOFTWARE REVENUE RECOGNITION

We all know how important personal computers and the software to run them have become in our daily lives. The software industry is a key economic component of our economy. **Microsoft** alone reported revenues in excess of $36 billion for its 2004 fiscal year.

The recognition of software revenues was a controversial issue throughout the 1990s. The controversy stemmed from the way software vendors typically package their products. It is not unusual for these companies to sell multiple software deliverables in a bundle for a lump-sum contract price. The bundle often includes product, upgrades, postcontract customer support, and other services. The critical accounting question concerns the timing of revenue recognition.

The American Institute of Certified Public Accountants (AICPA) issued a Statement of Position (SOP) in 1991 providing guidance in this area. However, inconsistencies in practice led to a new SOP in 1997.[20] *SOP 97-2* indicates that if an arrangement includes multiple elements, the revenue from the arrangement should be allocated to the various elements based on the relative fair values of the individual elements, "regardless of any separate prices stated within the contract for each element."[21]

For example, suppose that a vendor sold software to a customer for $100,000. As part of the contract, the vendor promises to provide technical support over the next six months. Prior to the issuance of *SOP 97-2,* some vendors were recognizing the entire $100,000 as revenue when the initial software was delivered. Now, the $100,000 contract price must be allocated based on fair values. So, the seller might recognize $80,000 in revenue initially and defer the remaining $20,000 and recognize it ratably over the next six months. In its 2004 balance sheet, Microsoft reported a liability for unearned (deferred) software revenue of $8.177 billion.

**Generally, a portion of the proceeds received from the sale of software is deferred and recognized as revenue in future periods.**

In 1998, *SOP 98-9*[22] amended certain paragraphs of *SOP 97-2* related to the methodology used to allocate the contract price in certain circumstances. Graphic 5–13 contains a portion of Microsoft Corporation's unearned revenue disclosure note explaining the changes it made in the allocation of revenue from the sale of its Windows and Office operating systems to comply with *SOP 98-9.*

**GRAPHIC 5–13**
Disclosure of Unearned Revenue Policy—Microsoft Corporation

**Unearned Revenue (in part)**
End users receive certain elements of the Company's products over a period of time. These elements include items such as browser technologies and technical support. Consequently, Microsoft's earned revenue reflects the recognition of fair value of these elements over the product's life cycle. Upon adoption of *SOP 98-9* during the fourth quarter of fiscal 1999, the Company was required to change the methodology of attributing fair value to undelivered elements. The percentages of undelivered elements in relation to the total arrangement decreased, reducing the amount of Windows and Office revenue treated as unearned, and increasing the amount of revenue recognized upon shipment. The percentage of revenue recognized ratably decreased from a range of 20% to 35% to a range of approximately 15% to 25% of Windows desktop operating systems.

It is interesting to note that some analysts questioned the quality of Microsoft's earnings because of their revenue recognition policy. Specifically, Microsoft was criticized for deferring excessive amounts of revenue. As you can see in the disclosure note, it now recognizes more revenue currently and defers less than it had in the past.

The accounting treatment of the cost of developing computer software is discussed in Chapter 10.

## FRANCHISE SALES

The use of franchise arrangements has become increasingly popular in the United States over the past 30 years. Many retail outlets for fast food, restaurants, motels, and auto rental agencies are operated as franchises. In the franchise arrangements, the **franchisor**, for example **McDonald's Corporation**, grants to the **franchisee**, quite often an individual, the right to sell the franchisor's products and use its name for a specified period of time. The restaurant where you ate your last Big Mac was probably owned and operated by an individual under a franchise agreement, not by McDonald's Corporation.

---

[20]"Software Revenue Recognition," *Statement of Position 97-2* (New York: AICPA, 1997).

[21]Ibid, p. 14.

[22]"Modification of SOP 97-2, Software Revenue Recognition With Respect to Certain Transactions," *Statement of Position 98-9* (New York: AICPA, 1998).

The fees to be paid by the franchisee to the franchisor usually comprise (1) the *initial franchise fee* and (2) *continuing franchise fees.* The services to be performed by the franchisor in exchange for the initial franchise fee, in addition to the right to use its name and sell its products, might include assistance in finding a location, constructing the facilities, and training employees. The initial franchise fee usually is a fixed amount, but it may be payable in installments.

The continuing franchise fees are paid to the franchisor for continuing rights as well as for advertising and promotion and other services provided over the life of the franchise agreement. These fees sometimes are a fixed annual or monthly amount, a percentage of the volume of business done by the franchise, or a combination of both.

> **FASB**
> Franchise fee revenue from an individual franchise sale ordinarily shall be recognized, with an appropriate provision for estimated uncollectible amounts, when all material services or conditions relating to the sale have been substantially performed or satisfied by the franchisor.[23]

*Continuing franchise fees are recognized over time as the services are performed.*

The continuing franchise fees usually do not present any accounting difficulty and are recognized by the franchisor as revenue *over time* in the periods the services are performed by the franchisor, which generally corresponds to the periods they are received. The challenging revenue recognition issue pertains to the initial franchise fee. In the early 1960s and 1970s, many franchisors recognized the entire initial franchise fee as revenue in the period in which the contract was signed. In many cases, there were significant services to be performed and the fee was collectible in installments over an extended period of time creating uncertainty as to cash collection.

*Initial franchise fees generally are recognized at a point in time when the earnings process is virtually complete.*

Specific guidelines for revenue recognition of the initial franchise fee are provided by *SFAS 45.* You should notice the similarity of these specific guidelines with those of the general revenue recognition guidelines we've discussed previously. A key to these conditions is the concept of *substantial performance.* It requires that substantially all of the initial services of the franchisor required by the franchise agreement be performed before the initial franchise fee can be recognized as revenue. The term *substantial* requires professional judgment on the part of the accountant. In situations when the initial franchise fee is collectible in installments, even after substantial performance has occurred, the installment sales or cost recovery methods should be used for profit recognition, if a reasonable estimate of uncollectibility cannot be made.

Consider the example in Illustration 5–3.

**ILLUSTRATION 5–3**
Franchise Sales

On March 31, 2006, the Red Hot Chicken Wing Corporation entered into a franchise agreement with Thomas Keller. In exchange for an initial franchise fee of $50,000, Red Hot will provide initial services to include the selection of a location, construction of the building, training of employees, and consulting services over several years. $10,000 is payable on March 31, 2006, with the remaining $40,000 payable in annual installments which include interest at an appropriate rate. In addition, the franchisee will pay continuing franchise fees of $1,000 per month for advertising and promotion provided by Red Hot, beginning immediately after the franchise begins operations. Thomas Keller opened his Red Hot franchise for business on September 30, 2006.

**Initial Franchise Fee.** Assuming that the initial services to be performed by Red Hot subsequent to the contract signing are substantial but that collectibility of the installment receivable is reasonably certain, the following journal entry is recorded:

[23]"Accounting for Franchise Fee Revenue," *Statement of Financial Accounting Standards No. 45* (Stamford, Conn.: FASB, 1981).

| | | |
|---|---|---|
| **March 31, 2006** | | |
| Cash ............................................. | 10,000 | |
| Note receivable ....................................... | 40,000 | |
| Unearned franchise fee revenue ........................ | | 50,000 |
| *To record franchise agreement and down payment.* | | |

**Revenue from initial franchise services is deferred until the services are rendered.**

The unearned franchise fee revenue would then be recognized when the initial services have been performed. This could occur in increments or at one point in time, depending on the circumstances.[24] For example, in our illustration, if substantial performance was deemed to have occurred when the franchise began operations, the following entry would be recorded:

| | | |
|---|---|---|
| **Sept. 30, 2006** | | |
| Unearned franchise fee revenue ........................... | 50,000 | |
| Franchise fee revenue ................................. | | 50,000 |
| *To recognize franchise fee revenue.* | | |

If collectibility of the installment receivable is uncertain and there is no basis for estimating uncollectible amounts, the initial entry would record a credit to deferred franchise fee revenue which is then recognized as being earned using either the installment sales or cost recovery methods.

**Continuing Franchise Fees.** Continuing franchise fee revenue is recognized on a monthly basis as follows:

| | | |
|---|---|---|
| Cash (or accounts receivable) ............................ | 1,000 | |
| Service revenue ....................................... | | 1,000 |
| *To recognize continuing franchise fee revenue.* | | |

Expenses incurred by the franchisor in providing these continuing franchise services should be recognized in the same periods as the service revenue.

Other unique industry-specific revenue recognition situations exist besides those we have discussed. The FASB and AICPA have issued detailed revenue recognition standards for such industries as insurance, record and music, cable television, and motion pictures.[25] These industry standards are beyond the scope of this text. However, in each case, the objective is the same: to recognize revenue in the period or periods that the revenue-generating activities of the company are performed.

### ADDITIONAL CONSIDERATION

In certain circumstances, revenue is recognized at the completion of the production process (before delivery). This approach generally is used by companies that deal in precious metals, and "... agricultural, mineral, and other products, units of which are interchangeable and have an immediate marketability at quoted prices. . . ."[26] This is called the *production basis* of recognizing revenue and is accomplished by writing inventory up from cost to market value.

Recall that in a typical manufacturing situation, revenue is not recognized at the completion of the production process due to significant uncertainty as to the collectibility of the asset to be received. We don't know if the product will be sold, nor the selling price,

[24]Franchise agreements sometimes require that any payments made to the franchisor will be refunded if the franchise fails to open. If this condition is present, it would be an important factor in deciding whether to recognize revenue before the franchise opens.

[25]"Accounting and Reporting by Insurance Enterprises," *Statement of Financial Accounting Standards No. 60* (Stamford, Conn.: FASB, 1982), "Financial Reporting in the Record and Music Industry," *Statement of Financial Accounting Standards No. 50* (Stamford, Conn.: FASB, 1981), "Financial Reporting by Cable Television Companies," *Statement of Financial Accounting Standards No. 51* (Stamford, Conn.: FASB, 1981), "Accounting by Producers or Distributors of Films," *Statement of Position 00-2* (New York: AICPA, 2000).

[26]"Restatement and Revision of Accounting Research Bulletins," *Accounting Research Bulletin No. 43* (New York: AICPA, 1953), Chapter 4, par. 16.

nor the buyer if eventually sold. These uncertainties are not significant when there is immediate marketability at quoted market prices for products like precious metals.

In cases when the production basis of recognizing revenue is used, full disclosure of the fact is required.

# PART B PROFITABILITY ANALYSIS

Chapter 3 provided an overview of financial statement analysis and introduced some of the common ratios used in risk analysis to investigate a company's liquidity and long-term solvency. We now introduce ratios related to profitability analysis.

## ACTIVITY RATIOS

LO6

One key to profitability is how well a company manages and utilizes its assets. Some ratios are designed to evaluate a company's effectiveness in managing assets. Of particular interest is the activity, or turnover ratios, of certain assets; that is, the frequency with which those assets are replaced. The greater the number of times an asset turns over—the higher the ratio—the less cash a company must devote to that asset, and the more cash it can commit to other purposes. In other words, if these turnover ratios increase, fewer assets are required to maintain a given level of activity (revenue). Activity ratios do not measure profitability directly. However, they are important factors affecting profitability.

*Activity ratios* measure a company's efficiency in managing its assets.

Although, in concept, the activity or turnover can be measured for any asset, activity ratios are most frequently calculated for accounts receivable, inventory, and total assets. These ratios are calculated as follows:

$$\text{Receivables turnover ratio} = \frac{\text{Net sales}}{\text{Average accounts receivable (net)}}$$

$$\text{Inventory turnover ratio} = \frac{\text{Cost of goods sold}}{\text{Average inventory}}$$

$$\text{Asset turnover ratio} = \frac{\text{Net sales}}{\text{Average total assets}}$$

The *receivables turnover ratio* offers an indication of how quickly a company is able to collect its accounts receivable.

**Receivables Turnover.** The **receivables turnover ratio** is calculated by dividing a period's net credit sales by the average net accounts receivable. Because income statements seldom distinguish between cash sales and credit sales, this ratio usually is computed using total net sales as the numerator. The denominator, average accounts receivable, is determined by adding beginning and ending net accounts receivable (gross accounts receivable less allowance for uncollectible accounts) and dividing by two.

The receivables turnover ratio provides an indication of a company's efficiency in collecting receivables. The ratio shows the number of times during a period that the average accounts receivable balance is collected. The higher the ratio, the shorter the average time between credit sales and cash collection.

The *average collection period* indicates the average age of accounts receivable.

A convenient extension is the **average collection period**. This measure is computed simply by dividing 365 days by the receivables turnover ratio. The result is an approximation of the number of days the average accounts receivable balance is outstanding.

$$\text{Average collection period} = \frac{365}{\text{Receivables turnover ratio}}$$

Monitoring the receivables turnover ratio (and average collection period) over time can provide useful information about a company's future prospects. For example, a decline in the receivables turnover ratio (an increase in the average collection period) could be an indication of customer dissatisfaction with the company's products. Another possible explanation is that the company has changed its credit policy and is granting extended credit terms in order to maintain customers. Ratio analysis does not explain what might be wrong. It does provide information that highlights areas for further investigation.

**Inventory Turnover.** An important activity measure for a merchandising company (a retail, wholesale, or manufacturing company) is the **inventory turnover ratio.** The ratio shows the number of times the average inventory balance is sold during a reporting period. It indicates how quickly inventory is sold. The more frequently a business is able to sell, or turn over, its inventory, the lower its investment in inventory must be for a given level of sales. The ratio is computed by dividing the period's cost of goods sold by the average inventory balance. The denominator, average inventory, is determined by adding beginning and ending inventory and dividing by two.[27]

**The *inventory turnover ratio* measures a company's efficiency in managing its investment in inventory.**

A relatively high ratio, say compared to a competitor, usually is desirable. A high ratio indicates comparative strength, perhaps caused by a company's superior sales force, the existence of highly popular products, or maybe a successful advertising campaign. However, it might also be caused by a relatively low inventory level, which could mean stockouts and lost sales in the future. As with any ratio, care must be taken in evaluating this ratio.

On the other hand, a relatively low ratio, or a decrease in the ratio over time, usually is perceived to be unfavorable. Too much capital may be tied up in inventory. A relatively low ratio may result from overstocking, the presence of obsolete items, or poor marketing and sales efforts.

Similar to the receivables turnover, we can divide the inventory turnover ratio into 365 days to compute the **average days in inventory.** This measure indicates the number of days it normally takes to sell inventory.

$$\text{Average days in inventory} = \frac{365}{\text{Inventory turnover ratio}}$$

**Asset Turnover.** A broad measure of asset efficiency is the **asset turnover ratio.** The ratio is computed by dividing a company's net sales or revenues by the average total assets available for use during a period. The denominator, average assets, is determined by adding beginning and ending total assets and dividing by two. The asset turnover ratio provides an indication of how efficiently a company utilizes all of its assets to generate revenue.

**The *asset turnover ratio* measures a company's efficiency in using assets to generate revenue.**

Industry standards are particularly important when evaluating asset turnover. Some industries are characterized by low turnover but typically make up for it with higher profit margins. Others have low profit margins but compensate with high turnover. Grocery stores typically have relatively low profit margins but relatively high asset turnover. In comparison, a manufacturer of specialized equipment will have a higher profit margin but a lower asset turnover ratio. But again, this ratio is best evaluated in conjunction with profit margin on sales. We do this in the next section.

## PROFITABILITY RATIOS

● LO6

A fundamental element of an analyst's task is to develop an understanding of a firm's profitability. Profitability ratios attempt to measure a company's ability to earn an adequate return relative to sales or resources devoted to operations. Resources devoted to operations can be defined as total assets or only those assets provided by owners, depending on the evaluation objective.

Three common profitability measures are (1) the profit margin on sales, (2) the return on assets, and (3) the return on shareholders' equity. These ratios are calculated as follows:

**Profitability ratios assist in evaluating various aspects of a company's profit-making activities.**

$$\text{Profit margin on sales} = \frac{\text{Net income}}{\text{Net sales}}$$

$$\text{Return on assets} = \frac{\text{Net income}}{\text{Average total assets}}$$

$$\text{Return on shareholders' equity} = \frac{\text{Net income}}{\text{Average shareholders' equity}}$$

[27]Notice the consistency in the measure used for the numerator and denominator of the two turnover ratios. For the receivables turnover ratio, both numerator and denominator are based on sales dollars, whereas they are both based on cost for the inventory turnover ratio.

When calculating profitability ratios, analysts adjust net income for any transitory income effects.

Notice that for all of the profitability ratios, our numerator is net income. Recall our discussion in Chapter 4 on earnings quality. The relevance of any historical-based financial statement hinges on its predictive value. To enhance predictive value, analysts try to separate a company's *transitory earnings* effects from its *permanent earnings*. Analysts begin their assessment of permanent earnings with income from continuing operations. Then, adjustments are made for transitory income effects, if any, included in income from continuing operations. It is this adjusted number that we use as the numerator in these ratios.

The *profit margin on sales* measures the amount of net income achieved per sales dollar.

**Profit Margin on Sales.** The **profit margin on sales** is simply net income divided by net sales. The ratio measures an important dimension of a company's profitability. It indicates the portion of each dollar of revenue that is available to cover expenses. It offers a measure of the company's ability to withstand either higher expenses or lower revenues.

As we discussed in the previous section, what is considered to be a desirable profit margin is highly sensitive to the nature of the business activity. For instance, you would expect a specialty shop to have a higher profit margin than, say, **Wal-Mart**. A low profit margin can be compensated for by a high asset turnover rate, and vice versa.

**Return on Assets.** The **return on assets (ROA)** indicates a company's overall profitability. The ratio expresses income as a percentage of the average total assets available to generate that income. Because total assets are partially financed with debt and partially by equity funds, this is an inclusive way of measuring earning power that ignores specific sources of financing.

Recall from our previous discussion that a company's return on assets is related to both profit margin and asset turnover. Specifically, profitability can be achieved by either a high profit margin, high turnover, or a combination of the two.[28] In fact, the return on assets can actually be calculated by multiplying the profit margin ratio by the asset turnover ratio.

$$\text{Return on assets} = \text{Profit margin on sales} \times \text{Asset turnover}$$

$$= \frac{\text{Net income}}{\text{Net sales}} \times \frac{\text{Net sales}}{\text{Average total assets}}$$

The decomposition of return on assets illustrates why some companies with relatively small profit margins can be very profitable if they have high asset turnover. Alternatively, companies with relatively low asset turnover ratios can be profitable if they are able to sustain large profit margins.

**ADDITIONAL CONSIDERATION**

The return on assets ratio often is computed as follows:

$$\text{Return on assets} = \frac{\text{Net income} + \text{Interest expense } (1 - \text{Tax rate})}{\text{Average total assets}}$$

The reason for adding back interest expense (net of tax) is that interest represents a return to suppliers of debt capital and should not be deducted in the computation of net income when computing the return on total assets. In other words, the numerator is the total amount of income available to both debt and equity capital.

The *return on shareholders' equity* measures the return to suppliers of equity capital.

**Return on Shareholders' Equity.** One measure of profitability is the ability of management to generate net income from the resources owners provide. Sometimes viewed by shareholders as the key criterion of profitability, the ratio is obtained by dividing net income by average shareholders' equity.

When the **return on shareholders' equity** is greater than the return on assets, management is using assets funded by debt to increase the income available for shareholders. This concept, known as *financial leverage,* was discussed in Chapter 3.

[28]This notion is sometimes referred to as the Du Pont analysis because the Du Pont Company was a pioneer in emphasizing this relationship.

**ADDITIONAL CONSIDERATION**

Sometimes when this ratio is calculated, shareholders' equity is viewed more narrowly to include only common shareholders. In that case, preferred stock is excluded from the denominator, and preferred dividends are deducted from net income in the numerator. The resulting rate of return on common shareholders' equity focuses on profits generated on resources provided by common shareholders.

Graphic 5–14 provides a recap of the activity and profitability ratios.

**GRAPHIC 5–14**
Activity and Profitability Ratios

**Activity ratios**

Receivables turnover $= \dfrac{\text{Net sales}}{\text{Average accounts receivable (net)}}$

Average collection period $= \dfrac{365}{\text{Receivables turnover ratio}}$

Inventory turnover $= \dfrac{\text{Cost of goods sold}}{\text{Average inventory}}$

Average days in inventory $= \dfrac{365}{\text{Inventory turnover ratio}}$

Asset turnover $= \dfrac{\text{Net sales}}{\text{Average total assets}}$

**Profitability ratios**

Profit margin on sales $= \dfrac{\text{Net income}}{\text{Net sales}}$

Return on assets $= \dfrac{\text{Net income}}{\text{Average total assets}}$

Return on shareholders' equity $= \dfrac{\text{Net income}}{\text{Average shareholders' equity}}$

## Profitability Analysis—An Illustration

To illustrate the computation of the activity and profitability ratios, we analyze two well-known pharmaceutical companies, **Bristol-Myers Squibb (BMS)** and **Merck & Co., Inc.** The operations of these two companies are similar in terms of their involvement in pharmaceutical and other health care products. Illustration 5–4A presents selected financial statement information for the two companies.

On the surface, it appears that Merck was more profitable than BMS. Merck's 2003 net income was $6.831 billion compared to $3.106 billion for BMS. But that's not the whole story. Even though both are very large companies, Merck is larger than BMS in terms of total assets. Illustration 5–4B presents a comparison of the various activity and profitability ratios for 2003. Notice that net income for Merck includes $241 million in income from discontinued operations. The profitability ratios in our illustration are calculated using income from continuing operations of $6.590 billion ($6,831 − $241).

BMS's receivables and inventory turnover ratios are significantly higher than Merck's. A possible cause is the different mix of products sold by the two companies. BMS is more diversified than Merck in terms of its product lines and markets that it serves. BMS's receivables and inventory turnovers are also higher than the industry average.

**ILLUSTRATION 5–4A**

Selected Financial Information for Bristol-Myers Squibb and Merck & Co., Inc.

**Balance Sheet**
($ in millions)

| | BMS | | Merck | |
|---|---|---|---|---|
| | **2003** | **2002** | **2003** | **2002** |
| Accounts receivable (net) | $ 3,646 | $ 2,968 | $ 4,024 | $ 5,424 |
| Inventories | 1,600 | 1,608 | 2,554 | 2,964 |
| Total assets | 27,470 | 25,022 | 40,587 | 47,561 |
| Total liabilities | 17,684 | 16,266 | 25,011 | 29,361 |
| Total shareholders' equity | 9,786 | 8,756 | 15,576 | 18,200 |
| Two-year averages: | | | | |
| Accounts receivable (net) | $ 3,307 | | $ 4,724 | |
| Inventories | 1,604 | | 2,759 | |
| Total assets | 26,246 | | 44,074 | |
| Total shareholders' equity | 9,271 | | 16,888 | |
| Income Statement—2003 | | | | |
| Net sales | $20,894 | | $22,486 | |
| Cost of goods sold | 7,592 | | 4,315 | |
| Net income | 3,106 | | 6,831* | |

*Includes $241 in income from discontinued operations.

**ILLUSTRATION 5–4B**

Activity and Profitability Ratios—Bristol-Myers Squibb (BMS) and Merck & Co., Inc.

| | | BMS | Merck | Industry Average* |
|---|---|---|---|---|
| **Activity ratios:** | | | | |
| Receivables turnover | = | $\frac{20,894}{3,307} = 6.32$ | $\frac{22,486}{4,724} = 4.76$ | 6.06 |
| Average collection period | = | $\frac{365}{6.32} =$ 58 days | $\frac{365}{4.76} =$ 77 days | 60 days |
| Inventory turnover | = | $\frac{7,592}{1,604} = 4.73$ | $\frac{4,315}{2,759} = 1.56$ | 2.55 |
| Average days in inventory | = | $\frac{365}{4.73} =$ 77 days | $\frac{365}{1.56} =$ 234 days | 143 days |
| Asset turnover | = | $\frac{20,894}{26,246} = .80$ | $\frac{22,486}{44,074} = .51$ | .65 |
| **Profitability ratios:** | | | | |
| Profit margin on sales | = | $\frac{3,106}{20,894} = .15$ | $\frac{6,590}{22,486} = .29$ | .18 |
| Return on assets | = | $\frac{3,106}{26,246} = .12$ | $\frac{6,590}{44,074} = .15$ | .12 |
| Return on shareholders' equity | = | $\frac{3,106}{9,271} = .34$ | $\frac{6,590}{16,888} = .39$ | .24 |

*Source: Reuters

Merck's return on shareholders' equity and return on assets are higher than BMS's and the ratios of both companies equal or exceed the industry average. As shown below, Merck's higher return on assets can be attributed to higher profit margin.

| | Profit Margin | × | Asset Turnover | | Return on Assets |
|---|---|---|---|---|---|
| **BMS:** | .15 | × | .80 | = | 12% |
| **Merck:** | .29 | × | .51 | = | 15% |

Both companies produced a higher return on shareholders' equity than return on assets. This means that they were both able to use assets funded by debt to increase the income available for shareholders. This is an example of favorable financial leverage to which we referred earlier.

The essential point of our discussion here, and in Part C of Chapter 3, is that raw accounting numbers alone mean little to decision makers. The numbers gain value when viewed in relation to other numbers. Similarly, the financial ratios formed by those relationships provide even greater perspective when compared with similar ratios of other companies, or relatedly, with averages for several companies in the same industry. Accounting information is useful in making decisions. Financial analysis that includes comparisons of financial ratios enhances the value of that information.

## FINANCIAL REPORTING CASE SOLUTION

1. **Does your sister have to wait two and a half years to get her bonus? Explain.** *(p. 224)* No. The *general* revenue recognition criteria would suggest that revenue and costs should be recognized when a project is finished. The difficulty this would create is that all revenues, expenses, and resulting profit from the project are recognized when the project is completed; no revenues or expenses would be reported in the income statements of earlier reporting periods in which much of the work may have been performed. The percentage-of-completion method of revenue recognition for long-term projects addresses this problem. A share of the project's profit is allocated to each period in which the earnings process occurs. This is two and a half years in this instance.
2. **How are gross profits recognized using the percentage-of-completion method?** *(p. 225)* The percentage-of-completion method recognizes part of the estimated gross profit each period. The amount recognized is based on progress to date which is estimated as the fraction of the project's cost incurred to date divided by total estimated costs. The estimated percentage of completion is multiplied by the revised project gross profit estimate. This yields the estimated gross profit earned from the beginning of the project. The gross profit recognized is calculated by subtracting from this amount the gross profit recognized in previous periods.
3. **Are there other situations in which revenue is recognized at times other than when a product is delivered?** *(p. 217)* Yes, revenue recognition sometimes is delayed until after the product is delivered. These situations involve either the possibility of product returns or bad debts. In most cases, product returns and bad debt are estimated and revenues are recognized when a product is delivered. However, in situations involving an abnormal degree of uncertainty about cash collection caused by potential returns or bad debts, revenue recognition *after* delivery sometimes is appropriate. ■

## THE BOTTOM LINE

**1.** The objective of revenue recognition is to recognize revenue in the period or periods that the revenue-generating activities of the company are performed. Also, judgment as to the collectibility of the cash from the sale of a product or service will impact the timing of revenue recognition. These two concepts of performance and collectibility are captured by the general guidelines for revenue recognition in the realization principle which requires that revenue should be recognized only after (1) the earnings process is virtually complete and (2) there is reasonable certainty of collecting the asset to be received (usually cash) from the customer. For the sale of product, these criteria usually are satisfied at the point of product delivery. At that point, the majority of the productive activities have taken place and any remaining uncertainty concerning asset collection can be accounted for by estimating possible returns and bad debts. Also, service revenue often is recognized at a point in time if there is one final activity that is deemed critical to the earnings process.

2. The installment sales method recognizes gross profit in collection periods by applying the gross profit percentage on the sale to the amount of cash actually received. The cost recovery method defers all gross profit recognition until cash has been received equal to the cost of the item sold. These methods of recognizing revenue should only be used in situations where there is an unusually high degree of uncertainty regarding the ultimate cash collection on an installment sale.
3. In most situations, even though the right to return merchandise exists, revenues and expenses can be appropriately recognized at point of delivery. Based on past experience, a company usually can estimate the returns that will result for a given volume of sales. These estimates reduce both sales and cost of goods sold in anticipation of returns. Revenue cannot be recognized at the point of delivery unless the seller is able to make reliable estimates of future returns. Otherwise, revenue recognition is deferred beyond the delivery point.
4. Revenue recognition at a single point in time when the earnings process is virtually complete is inappropriate for certain types of service revenue activities and also, usually, for long-term contracts. The completed contract method recognizes revenues and expenses on long-term construction and other long-term contracts at a point in time when the project is complete. This method is only used in unusual situations. The preferable method for recognizing revenues and expenses for long-term contracts is the percentage-of-completion method, which recognizes revenues over time by assigning a share of the project's revenues and costs to each reporting period during the project.
5. Industry guidelines require that the lump-sum contract price for software be allocated to the various elements of the package based on the relative fair values of the individual elements. Generally, this results in a deferral of a portion of the proceeds that are then recognized as revenue in future periods. The use of franchise arrangements has become increasingly popular. The fees to be paid by the franchisee to the franchisor usually are composed of (1) the initial franchise fee and (2) continuing franchise fees. *SFAS 45* requires that the franchisor has substantially performed the services promised in the franchise agreement and that the collectibility of the initial franchise fee is reasonably assured before the initial fee can be recognized as revenue. The continuing franchise fees are recognized by the franchisor as revenue over time in the periods the services are performed by the franchisor.
6. Activity and profitability ratios provide information about a company's profitability. Activity ratios include the receivables turnover ratio, the inventory turnover ratio, and the asset turnover ratio. Profitability ratios include the profit margin on sales, the return on assets, and the return on shareholders' equity. ■

## APPENDIX 5 INTERIM REPORTING

***Interim reports** are issued for periods of less than a year, typically as quarterly financial statements.*

Financial statements covering periods of less than a year are called *interim reports.* Companies registered with the SEC, which includes most public companies, must submit quarterly reports.[29] Though there is no requirement to do so, most also mail quarterly reports to their shareholders and typically include abbreviated, unaudited interim reports as supplemental information within their annual reports. For instance, Graphic 5A–1 shows the quarterly information disclosed in the 2004 annual report of **Microsoft Corporation**.

***Interim reporting** serves to enhance the timeliness of financial information.*

For accounting information to be useful to decision makers, it must be available on a timely basis. One of the objectives of interim reporting is to enhance the timeliness of financial information. In addition, quarterly reports provide investors and creditors with additional insight on the seasonality of business operations that might otherwise get lost in annual reports.

[29]Quarterly reports are filed with the SEC on form 10-Q. Annual reports to the SEC are on form 10-K.

**GRAPHIC 5A–1**
Interim Data in Annual Report—Microsoft Corporation

**Quarterly Information**
($ in millions, except per share amounts) (Unaudited)

| Quarter Ended | Sep. 30 | Dec. 31 | Mar. 31 | June 30 |
|---|---|---|---|---|
| **Fiscal 2003** | | | | |
| Revenue | $7,746 | $ 8,541 | $7,835 | $8,065 |
| Gross profit | 6,402 | 6,404 | 6,561 | 6,761 |
| Net income | 2,041 | 1,865 | 2,142 | 1,483(1) |
| Basic earnings per share | 0.19 | 0.17 | 0.20 | 0.14 |
| Diluted earnings per share | 0.19 | 0.17 | 0.20 | 0.14 |
| **Fiscal 2004** | | | | |
| Revenue | $8,215 | $10,153 | $9,175 | $9,292 |
| Gross profit | 6,735 | 7,809 | 7,764 | 7,811 |
| Net income | 2,614 | 1,549(2) | 1,315(3) | 2,690 |
| Basic earnings per share | 0.24 | 0.14 | 0.12 | 0.25 |
| Diluted earnings per share | 0.24 | 0.14 | 0.12 | 0.25 |

(1) Includes charges of $750 (pretax) million related to the Time Warner settlement and $1.15 billion in impairments of investments.
(2) Includes stock-based compensation charges of $2.2 billion for the employee stock option transfer program.
(3) Includes charges of $2.53 billion (pretax) related to the Sun Microsystems Inc. settlement and a fine imposed by the European Commission.

However, the downside to the benefits is the relative unreliability of interim reporting. With a shorter reporting period, questions associated with estimation and allocation are magnified. For example, certain expenses often benefit an entire year's operations and yet are incurred primarily within a single interim period. Similarly, should smaller companies use lower tax rates in the earlier quarters and higher rates in later quarters as higher tax brackets are reached? Another result of shorter reporting periods is the intensified effect of major events such as discontinued operations or extraordinary items. A second quarter casualty loss, for instance, that would reduce annual profits by 10% might reduce second quarter profits by 40% or more. Is it more realistic to allocate such a loss over the entire year? These and similar questions tend to hinge on the way we view an interim period in relation to the fiscal year. More specifically, should each interim period be viewed as a *discrete* reporting period or as an *integral part* of the annual period?

**The fundamental debate regarding interim reporting centers on the choice between the *discrete* and *integral part* approaches.**

## Reporting Revenues and Expenses

Existing practice and current reporting requirements for interim reporting generally follow the viewpoint that interim reports are an integral part of annual statements, although the discrete approach is applied to some items. Most revenues and expenses are recognized using the same accounting principles applicable to annual reporting. Some modifications are necessary to help cause interim statements to relate better to annual statements. This is most evident in the way costs and expenses are recognized. Most are recognized in interim periods as incurred. But when an expenditure clearly benefits more than just the period in which it is incurred, the expense should be allocated among the periods benefited on an allocation basis consistent with the company's annual allocation procedures. For example, annual repair expenses, property tax expense, and advertising expenses incurred in the first quarter that clearly benefit later quarters are assigned to each quarter through the use of accruals and deferrals. Costs and expenses subject to year-end adjustments, such as depreciation and bad debt expense, are estimated and allocated to interim periods in a systematic way. Similarly, income tax expense at each interim date should be based on estimates of the effective tax rate for the whole year. This would mean, for example, that if the estimated effective rate has changed since the previous interim period(s), the tax expense that period would be determined as the new rate times the cumulative pretax income to date, less the total tax expense reported in previous interim periods.

**With only a few exceptions, the same accounting principles applicable to annual reporting are used for interim reporting.**

## Reporting Unusual Items

**Discontinued operations and extraordinary items are reported entirely within the interim period in which they occur.**

On the other hand, major events such as discontinued operations or extraordinary items should be reported separately in the interim period in which they occur. That is, these amounts should not be allocated among individual quarters within the fiscal year. The same is true for items that are unusual or infrequent but not both. Notice that treatment of these items is more consistent with the discrete view than the integral part view.

## Earnings Per Share

**Quarterly EPS calculations follow the same procedures as annual calculations.**

A second item that is treated in a manner consistent with the discrete view is earnings per share. EPS calculations for interim reports follow the same procedures as annual calculations that you will study in Chapter 19. The calculations are based on conditions actually existing during the particular interim period rather than on conditions estimated to exist at the end of the fiscal year.

## Reporting Accounting Changes

**Accounting changes made in an interim period are reported by retrospectively applying the changes to prior financial statements.**

Recall from Chapter 4 that we account for a change in accounting principle retrospectively, meaning we recast prior years' financial statements when we report those statements again in comparative form. In other words, we make those statements appear as if the newly adopted accounting method had been used in those prior years. It's the same with interim reporting. We retrospectively report a change made during an interim period in similar fashion. Then in financial reports of subsequent interim periods of the same fiscal year, we disclose how that change affected (a) income from continuing operations, (b) net income, and (c) related per share amounts for the postchange interim period

## Minimum Disclosures

Complete financial statements are not required for interim period reporting, but certain minimum disclosures are required as follows:[30]

- Sales, income taxes, extraordinary items, and net income.
- Earnings per share.
- Seasonal revenues, costs, and expenses.
- Significant changes in estimates for income taxes.
- Discontinued operations, extraordinary items, and unusual or infrequent items.
- Contingencies.
- Changes in accounting principles or estimates.
- Significant changes in financial position.

When fourth quarter results are not separately reported, material fourth quarter events, including year-end adjustments, should be reported in disclosure notes to annual statements. ■

# QUESTIONS FOR REVIEW OF KEY TOPICS

**Q 5–1** What are the two general criteria that must be satisfied before a company can recognize revenue?

**Q 5–2** Explain why, in most cases, a seller recognizes revenue when it delivers its product rather than when it produces the product.

**Q 5–3** Revenue recognition for most installment sales occurs at the point of delivery of the product or service. Under what circumstances would a seller delay revenue recognition for installment sales beyond the delivery date?

**Q 5–4** Distinguish between the installment sales method and the cost recovery method of accounting for certain installment sales.

[30]"Interim Financial Reporting," *Accounting Principles Board Opinion No 28* (New York: AICPA, 1973).

**Q 5–5** How does a company report deferred gross profit resulting from the use of the installment sales method in its balance sheet?

**Q 5–6** Revenue recognition for most product sales that allow the right of return occurs at the point of product delivery. Under what circumstances would revenue recognition be delayed?

**Q 5–7** Describe a consignment sale. When does a consignor recognize revenue for a consignment sale?

**Q 5–8** Service revenue is recognized either at one point in time or over extended periods. Explain the rationale for recognizing revenue using these two approaches.

**Q 5–9** Distinguish between the percentage-of-completion and completed contract methods of accounting for long-term contracts with respect to income recognition. Under what circumstances should a company use the completed contract method?

**Q 5–10** Periodic billings to the customer for a long-term construction contract are recorded as billings on construction contract. How is this account reported in the balance sheet?

**Q 5–11** When is an estimated loss on a long-term contract recognized using the percentage-of-completion method? The completed contract method?

**Q 5–12** Briefly describe the guidelines provided by SOPs 97-2 and 98-9 for recognizing revenue from the sale of software.

**Q 5–13** Briefly describe the guidelines provided by SFAS 45 for the recognition of revenue by a franchisor for an initial franchise fee.

**Q 5–14** Show the calculation of the following activity ratios: (1) the receivables turnover ratio, (2) the inventory turnover ratio, and (3) the asset turnover ratio. What information about a company do these ratios offer?

**Q 5–15** Show the calculation of the following profitability ratios: (1) the profit margin on sales, (2) the return on assets, and (3) the return on shareholders' equity. What information about a company do these ratios offer?

**Q 5–16** [Based on Appendix 5] Interim reports are issued for periods of less than a year, typically as quarterly financial statements. Should these interim periods be viewed as separate periods or integral parts of the annual period?

## BRIEF EXERCISES

**BE 5–1**
Point of delivery recognition

● LO1

On July 1, 2006, Apache Company sold a parcel of undeveloped land to a construction company for $3,000,000. The book value of the land on Apache's books was $1,200,000. Terms of the sale required a down payment of $150,000 and 19 annual payments of $150,000 plus interest at an appropriate interest rate due on each July 1 beginning in 2007. Apache has no significant obligations to perform services after the sale. How much gross profit will Apache recognize in both 2006 and 2007 assuming point of delivery profit recognition?

**BE 5–2**
Installment sales method

● LO2

Refer to the situation described in BE 5–1. How much gross profit will Apache recognize in both 2006 and 2007 applying the installment sales method?

**BE 5–3**
Cost recovery method

● LO2

Refer to the situation described in BE 5–1. How much gross profit will Apache recognize in both 2006 and 2007 applying the cost recovery method?

**BE 5–4**
Installment sales method

● LO2

Refer to the situation described in BE 5–1. What should be the balance in the deferred gross profit account at the end of 2007 applying the installment sales method?

**BE 5–5**
Right of return

● LO3

Meyer Furniture sells office furniture mainly to corporate clients. Customers who return merchandise within 90 days for any reason receive a full refund. Discuss the issues Meyer must consider in determining its revenue recognition policy.

**BE 5–6**
Percentage-of-completion method; profit recognition

● LO4

A construction company entered into a fixed-price contract to build an office building for $20 million. Construction costs incurred during the first year were $6 million and estimated costs to complete at the end of the year were $9 million. How much gross profit will the company recognize in the first year using the percentage-of-completion method? How much revenue will appear in the company's income statement?

**BE 5–7**
Percentage-of-completion method; balance sheet
● LO4

Refer to the situation described in BE 5–6. During the first year the company billed its customer $7 million of which $5 million was collected before year-end. What would appear in the year-end balance sheet related to this contract?

**BE 5–8**
Completed contract method
● LO4

Refer to the situation described in BE 5–6. The building was completed during the second year. Construction costs incurred during the second year were $10 million. How much gross profit will the company recognize in first year and in the second year applying the completed contract method?

**BE 5–9**
Percentage-of-completion and completed contract methods; loss on entire project
● LO4

Franklin Construction entered into a fixed-price contract to build a freeway-connecting ramp for $30 million. Construction costs incurred the first year were $16 million and estimated costs to complete at the end of the year were $17 million. How much gross profit or loss will Franklin recognize the first year applying the percentage-of-completion method? Applying the completed contract method?

**BE 5–10**
Revenue recognition; franchise sales
● LO5

Collins, Inc. entered into a 10-year franchise agreement with an individual. For an initial franchise fee of $40,000, Collins agrees to assist in design and construction of the franchise location and in all other necessary start-up activities. Also, in exchange for advertising and promotional services, the franchisee agrees to pay continuing franchise fees equal to 5% of revenue generated by the franchise. When should Collins recognize revenue for the initial and continuing franchise fees?

**BE 5–11**
Receivables and inventory turnover ratios
● LO6

Universal Calendar Company began the year with accounts receivable and inventory balances of $100,000 and $80,000, respectively. Year-end balances for these accounts were $120,000 and $60,000, respectively. Sales for the year of $600,000 generated a gross profit of $200,000. Calculate the receivables and inventory turnover ratios for the year.

**BE 5–12**
Profitability ratios
● LO6

The 2006 income statement for Anderson TV and Appliance reported sales revenue of $420,000 and net income of $65,000. Average total assets for 2006 was $800,000. Shareholders' equity at the beginning of the year was $500,000 and $20,000 was paid to shareholders as dividends. There were no other shareholders' equity transactions that occurred during the year. Calculate the profit margin on sales, return on assets, and return on shareholders' equity for 2006.

**BE 5–13**
Inventory turnover ratio
● LO6

During 2006, Rogue Corporation reported sales revenue of $600,000. Inventory at both the beginning and end of the year totaled $75,000. The inventory turnover ratio for the year was 6.0. What amount of gross profit did the company report in its income statement for 2006?

## EXERCISES

available with McGraw-Hill's Homework Manager www.mhhe.com/spiceland4e

**An alternative exercise and problem set is available on the text website: www.mhhe.com/spiceland4e**

**E 5–1**
Installment sales method
● LO2

Charter Corporation, which began business in 2006, appropriately uses the installment sales method of accounting for its installment sales. The following data were obtained for sales made during 2006 and 2007:

| | 2006 | 2007 |
|---|---|---|
| Installment sales | $360,000 | $350,000 |
| Cost of installment sales | 234,000 | 245,000 |
| Cash collections on installment sales during: | | |
| 2006 | 150,000 | 100,000 |
| 2007 | — | 120,000 |

**Required:**
1. How much gross profit should Charter recognize in 2006 and 2007 from installment sales?
2. What should be the balance in the deferred gross profit account at the end of 2006 and 2007?

**E 5–2**
Installment sales method; journal entries
● LO2

[This is a variation of the previous exercise focusing on journal entries.]

Charter Corporation, which began business in 2006, appropriately uses the installment sales method of accounting for its installment sales. The following data were obtained for sales during 2006 and 2007:

| | 2006 | 2007 |
|---|---|---|
| Installment sales | $360,000 | $350,000 |
| Cost of installment sales | 234,000 | 245,000 |
| Cash collections on installment sales during: | | |
| 2006 | 150,000 | 100,000 |
| 2007 | — | 120,000 |

**Required:**

Prepare summary journal entries for 2006 and 2007 to account for the installment sales and cash collections. The company uses the perpetual inventory system.

**E 5–3**
Installment sales; alternative recognition methods

● LO2

On July 1, 2006, the Foster Company sold inventory to the Slate Corporation for $300,000. Terms of the sale called for a down payment of $75,000 and three annual installments of $75,000 due on each July 1, beginning July 1, 2007. Each installment also will include interest on the unpaid balance applying an appropriate interest rate. The inventory cost Foster $120,000. The company uses the perpetual inventory system.

**Required:**

1. Compute the amount of gross profit to be recognized from the installment sale in 2006, 2007, 2008, and 2009 using point of delivery revenue recognition. Ignore interest charges.
2. Repeat requirement 1 applying the installment sales method.
3. Repeat requirement 1 applying the cost recovery method.

**E 5–4**
Journal entries; point of delivery, installment sales, and cost recovery methods

● LO1 LO2

[This is a variation of the previous exercise focusing on journal entries.]

On July 1, 2006, the Foster Company sold inventory to the Slate Corporation for $300,000. Terms of the sale called for a down payment of $75,000 and three annual installments of $75,000 due on each July 1, beginning July 1, 2007. Each installment also will include interest on the unpaid balance applying an appropriate interest rate. The inventory cost Foster $120,000. The company uses the perpetual inventory system.

**Required:**

1. Prepare the necessary journal entries for 2006 and 2007 using point of delivery revenue recognition. Ignore interest charges.
2. Repeat requirement 1 applying the installment sales method.
3. Repeat requirement 1 applying the cost recovery method.

**E 5–5**
Installment sales and cost recovery methods; solve for unknowns

● LO2

Wolf Computer Company began operations in 2006. The company allows customers to pay in installments for many of its products. Installment sales for 2006 were $1,000,000. If revenue is recognized at the point of delivery, $600,000 in gross profit would be recognized in 2006. If the company instead uses the cost recovery method, $100,000 in gross profit would be recognized in 2006.

**Required:**

1. What was the amount of cash collected on installment sales in 2006?
2. What amount of gross profit would be recognized if the company uses the installment sales method?

**E 5–6**
Real estate sales; gain recognition

● LO1 LO2

On April 1, 2006, the Apex Corporation sold a parcel of underdeveloped land to the Applegate Construction Company for $2,400,000. The book value of the land on Apex's books was $480,000. Terms of the sale required a down payment of $120,000 and 19 annual payments of $120,000 plus interest at an appropriate interest rate due on each April 1 beginning in 2007. Apex has no significant obligations to perform services after the sale.

**Required:**

1. Prepare the necessary entries for Apex to record the sale, receipt of the down payment, and receipt of the first installment assuming that Apex is able to make a reliable estimate of possible uncollectible amounts (that is, point of delivery profit recognition is used). Ignore interest charges.
2. Repeat requirement 1 assuming that Apex cannot make a reliable estimate of possible uncollectible amounts and decides to use the installment sales method for profit recognition.

**E 5–7**
Long-term contract; percentage-of-completion and completed contract methods

● LO4

**Nortel Networks** contracted to provide a customer with Internet infrastructure for $2,000,000. The project began in 2006 and was completed in 2007. Data relating to the contract are summarized below:

| | 2006 | 2007 |
|---|---|---|
| Costs incurred during the year | $ 300,000 | $1,575,000 |
| Estimated costs to complete as of 12/31 | 1,200,000 | –0– |
| Billings during the year | 380,000 | 1,620,000 |
| Cash collections during the year | 250,000 | 1,750,000 |

**Required:**

1. Compute the amount of gross profit or loss to be recognized in 2006 and 2007 using the percentage-of-completion method.
2. Compute the amount of gross profit or loss to be recognized in 2006 and 2007 using the completed contract method.

3. Prepare a partial balance sheet to show how the information related to this contract would be presented at the end of 2006 using the percentage-of-completion method.
4. Prepare a partial balance sheet to show how the information related to this contract would be presented at the end of 2006 using the completed contract method.

**E 5–8**
Long-term contract; percentage of completion and completed contract methods

● LO4

On June 15, 2006, Sanderson Construction entered into a long-term construction contract to build a baseball stadium in Washington D.C. for $220 million. The expected completion date is April 1 of 2008, just in time for the 2008 baseball season. Costs incurred and estimated costs to complete at year-end for the life of the contract are as follows ($ in millions):

| | 2006 | 2007 | 2008 |
|---|---|---|---|
| Costs incurred during the year | $ 40 | $80 | $50 |
| Estimated costs to complete as of 12/31 | 120 | 60 | — |

**Required:**
1. Determine the amount of gross profit or loss to be recognized in each of the three years using the percentage-of-completion method.
2. How much revenue will Sanderson report in its 2006 and 2007 income statements related to this contract using the percentage-of-completion method?
3. Determine the amount of gross profit or loss to be recognized in each of the three years using the completed contract method.
4. Suppose the estimated costs to complete at the end of 2007 are $80 million instead of $60 million. Determine the amount of gross profit or loss to be recognized in 2007 using the percentage-of-completion method.

**E 5–9**
Percentage-of-completion method; loss projected on entire project

● LO4

On February 1, 2006, Arrow Construction Company entered into a three-year construction contract to build a bridge for a price of $8,000,000. During 2006, costs of $2,000,000 were incurred with estimated costs of $4,000,000 yet to be incurred. Billings of $2,500,000 were sent and cash collected was $2,250,000.

In 2007, costs incurred were $2,500,000 with remaining costs estimated to be $3,600,000. 2007 billings were $2,750,000 and $2,475,000 cash was collected. The project was completed in 2008 after additional costs of $3,800,000 were incurred. The company's fiscal year-end is December 31. Arrow uses the *percentage-of-completion* method.

**Required:**
1. Calculate the amount of gross profit or loss to be recognized in each of the three years.
2. Prepare journal entries for 2006 and 2007 to record the transactions described (credit various accounts for construction costs incurred).
3. Prepare a partial balance sheet to show the presentation of the project as of December 31, 2006 and 2007.

**E 5–10**
Completed contract method; loss projected on entire project

● LO4

[This is a variation of the previous exercise focusing on the completed contract method.]

On February 1, 2006, Arrow Construction Company entered into a three-year construction contract to build a bridge for a price of $8,000,000. During 2006, costs of $2,000,000 were incurred with estimated costs of $4,000,000 yet to be incurred. Billings of $2,500,000 were sent and cash collected was $2,250,000.

In 2007, costs incurred were $2,500,000 with remaining costs estimated to be $3,600,000. 2007 billings were $2,750,000 and $2,475,000 cash was collected. The project was completed in 2008 after additional costs of $3,800,000 were incurred. The company's fiscal year-end is December 31. Arrow uses the *completed contract* method.

**Required:**
1. Calculate the amount of gross profit or loss to be recognized in each of the three years.
2. Prepare journal entries for 2006 and 2007 to record the transactions described (credit various accounts for construction costs incurred).
3. Prepare a partial balance sheet to show the presentation of the project as of December 31, 2006 and 2007.

**E 5–11**
Income (loss) recognition; percentage-of-completion and completed contract methods compared

● LO4

Brady Construction Company contracted to build an apartment complex for a price of $5,000,000. Construction began in 2006 and was completed in 2008. The following are a series of independent situations, numbered 1 through 6, involving differing costs for the project. All costs are stated in thousands of dollars.

| | Costs Incurred During Year | | | Estimated Costs to Complete (As of the End of the Year) | | |
|---|---|---|---|---|---|---|
| Situation | 2006 | 2007 | 2008 | 2006 | 2007 | 2008 |
| 1 | 1,500 | 2,100 | 900 | 3,000 | 900 | — |
| 2 | 1,500 | 900 | 2,400 | 3,000 | 2,400 | — |
| 3 | 1,500 | 2,100 | 1,600 | 3,000 | 1,500 | — |
| 4 | 500 | 3,000 | 1,000 | 3,500 | 875 | — |
| 5 | 500 | 3,000 | 1,300 | 3,500 | 1,500 | — |
| 6 | 500 | 3,000 | 1,800 | 4,600 | 1,700 | — |

**Required:**

Copy and complete the following table.

| | Gross Profit (Loss) Recognized | | | | | |
|---|---|---|---|---|---|---|
| | Percentage-of-Completion | | | Completed Contract | | |
| **Situation** | **2006** | **2007** | **2008** | **2006** | **2007** | **2008** |
| 1 | | | | | | |
| 2 | | | | | | |
| 3 | | | | | | |
| 4 | | | | | | |
| 5 | | | | | | |
| 6 | | | | | | |

**E 5–12**
Percentage-of-completion method; solve for unknowns

● LO4

In 2006, Long Construction Corporation began construction work under a three-year contract. The contract price is $1,600,000. Long uses the percentage-of-completion method for financial reporting purposes. The financial statement presentation relating to this contract at December 31, 2006, is as follows:

| Balance Sheet | | |
|---|---|---|
| Accounts receivable (from construction progress billings) | | $30,000 |
| Construction in progress | $100,000 | |
| Less: Billings on construction contract | (94,000) | |
| Cost of uncompleted contracts in excess of billings | | 6,000 |

| Income Statement | |
|---|---|
| Income (before tax) on the contract recognized in 2006 | $20,000 |

**Required:**

1. What was the cost of construction actually incurred in 2006?
2. How much cash was collected in 2006 on this contract?
3. What was the estimated cost to complete as of the end of 2006?
4. What was the estimated percentage of completion used to calculate income in 2006?

*(AICPA adapted)*

**E 5–13**
Revenue recognition; software

● LO5

Easywrite Software Company shipped software to a customer on July 1, 2006. The arrangement with the customer also requires the company to provide technical support over the next 12 months and to ship an expected software upgrade on January 1, 2007. The total contract price is $243,000, and Easywrite estimates that the individual fair values of the components of the arrangement if sold separately would be:

| | |
|---|---|
| Software | $210,000 |
| Technical support | 30,000 |
| Upgrade | 30,000 |

**Required:**

1. Determine the timing of revenue recognition for the $243,000.
2. Assume that the $243,000 contract price was paid in advance on July 1, 2006. Prepare a journal entry to record the cash receipt. Do not worry about the cost of the items sold.

**E 5–14**
Revenue recognition; franchise sales

● LO5

On October 1, 2006, the Submarine Sandwich Company entered into a franchise agreement with an individual. In exchange for an initial franchise fee of $300,000, Submarine will provide initial services to the franchisee to include assistance in design and construction of the building, help in training employees, help in obtaining financing, and management advice over the first five years of the 10-year franchise agreement.

10% of the initial franchise fee is payable on October 1, 2006, with the remaining $270,000 payable in nine equal annual installments beginning on October 1, 2007. These installments will include interest at an appropriate rate. The franchise opened for business on January 15, 2007.

**Required:**

Assume that the initial services to be performed by Submarine Sandwich subsequent to October 1, 2006, are substantial and that collectibility of the installment receivable is reasonably certain. Substantial performance of the initial services is deemed to have occurred when the franchise opened. Prepare the necessary journal entries for the following dates (ignoring interest charges):

1. October 1, 2006
2. January 15, 2007

**E 5–15**
Multiple choice; revenue recognition

● LO2 LO4

The following questions dealing with revenue recognition are adapted from questions that appeared on CPA examinations. Determine the response that best completes the statements or questions.

1. Drew Co. produces expensive equipment for sale on installment contracts. When there is doubt about eventual collectibility, the income recognition method *least* likely to overstate income is

a. At the time the equipment is completed.
b. The installment method.
c. The cost recovery method.
d. At the time of delivery.

2. Hill Company began operations on January 1, 2006, and appropriately uses the installment method of accounting. Data available for 2006 are as follows:

| | |
|---|---|
| Installment accounts receivable | $500,000 |
| Installment sales | 900,000 |
| Cost of goods sold, as a percentage of sales | 60% |

Using the installment method, Hill's realized gross profit for 2006 would be
a. $360,000
b. $240,000
c. $200,000
d. $160,000

Questions 3 and 4 are based on the following data pertaining to Pell Co.'s construction jobs, which commenced during 2006:

| | Project 1 | Project 2 |
|---|---|---|
| Contract price | $420,000 | $300,000 |
| Cost incurred during 2006 | 240,000 | 280,000 |
| Estimated costs to complete | 120,000 | 40,000 |
| Billed to customers during 2006 | 150,000 | 270,000 |
| Received from customers during 2006 | 90,000 | 250,000 |

3. If Pell used the completed contract method, what amount of gross profit (loss) would Pell report in its 2006 income statement?
a. $(20,000)
b. $0
c. $340,000
d. $420,000

4. If Pell used the percentage-of-completion method, what amount of gross profit (loss) would Pell report in its 2006 income statement?
a. $(20,000)
b. $20,000
c. $22,500
d. $40,000

**E 5–16**
Concepts; terminology
● LO2 through LO6

Listed below are several terms and phrases associated with revenue recognition and profitability analysis. Pair each item from List A (by letter) with the item from List B that is most appropriately associated with it.

| List A | List B |
|---|---|
| ____ 1. Inventory turnover | a. Net income divided by net sales. |
| ____ 2. Return on assets | b. Defers recognition until cash collected equals cost. |
| ____ 3. Return on shareholders' equity | c. Defers recognition until project is complete. |
| ____ 4. Profit margin on sales | d. Net income divided by assets. |
| ____ 5. Cost recovery method | e. Risks and rewards of ownership retained by seller. |
| ____ 6. Percentage-of-completion method | f. Contra account to construction in progress. |
| ____ 7. Completed contract method | g. Net income divided by shareholders' equity. |
| ____ 8. Asset turnover | h. Cost of goods sold divided by inventory. |
| ____ 9. Receivables turnover | i. Recognition is in proportion to work completed. |
| ____ 10. Right of return | j. Recognition is in proportion to cash received. |
| ____ 11. Billings on construction contract | k. Net sales divided by assets. |
| ____ 12. Installment sales method | l. Net sales divided by accounts receivable. |
| ____ 13. Consignment sales | m. Could cause the deferral of revenue recognition beyond delivery point. |

**E 5–17**
Inventory turnover; calculation and evaluation
● LO6

The following is a portion of the condensed income statement for Rowan, Inc., a manufacturer of plastic containers:

| | | |
|---|---|---|
| Net sales | | $2,460,000 |
| Less: Cost of goods sold: | | |
| Inventory, January 1 | $ 630,000 | |
| Net purchases | 1,900,000 | |
| Inventory, December 31 | (690,000) | 1,840,000 |
| Gross profit | | $ 620,000 |

**Required:**

1. Determine Rowan's inventory turnover.
2. What information does this ratio provide?

**E 5–18**
Evaluating efficiency of asset management

● LO6

The 2006 income statement of Anderson Medical Supply Company reported net sales of $8 million, cost of goods sold of $4.8 million, and net income of $800,000. The following table shows the company's comparative balance sheets for 2006 and 2005:

| | ($ in 000s) | |
|---|---|---|
| | **2006** | **2005** |
| **Assets** | | |
| Cash | $ 300 | $ 380 |
| Accounts receivable | 700 | 500 |
| Inventory | 900 | 700 |
| Property, plant, and equipment (net) | 2,400 | 2,120 |
| Total assets | $4,300 | $3,700 |
| **Liabilities and Shareholders' Equity** | | |
| Current liabilities | $ 960 | $ 830 |
| Bonds payable | 1,200 | 1,200 |
| Paid-in capital | 1,000 | 1,000 |
| Retained earnings | 1,140 | 670 |
| Total liabilities and shareholders' equity | $4,300 | $3,700 |

Some industry averages for Anderson's line of business are

| | |
|---|---|
| Inventory turnover | 5 times |
| Average collection period | 25 days |
| Asset turnover | 1.8 times |

**Required:**

Assess Anderson's asset management relative to its industry.

**E 5–19**
Profitability ratios

● LO6

The following condensed information was reported by Peabody Toys, Inc., for 2006 and 2005:

| | ($ in 000s) | |
|---|---|---|
| | **2006** | **2005** |
| **Income statement information** | | |
| Net sales | $5,200 | $4,200 |
| Net income | 180 | 124 |
| **Balance sheet information** | | |
| Current assets | $ 800 | $ 750 |
| Property, plant, and equipment (net) | 1,100 | 950 |
| Total assets | $1,900 | $1,700 |
| Current liabilities | $ 600 | $ 450 |
| Long-term liabilities | 750 | 750 |
| Paid-in capital | 400 | 400 |
| Retained earnings | 150 | 100 |
| Liabilities and shareholders' equity | $1,900 | $1,700 |

**Required:**

1. Determine the following ratios for 2006:
   a. Profit margin on sales
   b. Return on assets
   c. Return on shareholders' equity
2. Determine the amount of dividends paid to shareholders during 2006.

**E 5–20**
Multiple choice; CMA exam; revenue recognition; percentage-of-completion method

● LO1 LO4

The following questions dealing with income measurement are adapted from questions that previously appeared on Certified Management Accountant (CMA) examinations. The CMA designation sponsored by the Institute of Management Accountants (www.imanet.org) provides members with an objective measure of knowledge and competence in the field of management accounting. Determine the response that best completes the statements or questions.

1. On May 28, Markal Company purchased a tooling machine from Arens and Associates for $1,000,000 payable as follows: 50 percent at the transaction closing date and 50 percent due June 28. The cost of the machine to Arens is $800,000. Markal paid Arens $500,000 at the transaction closing date and took

possession of the machine. On June 10, Arens determined that a change in the business environment has created a great deal of uncertainty regarding the collection of the balance due from Markal, and the amount is probably uncollectible. Arens and Markal have a fiscal year-end of May 31. The revenue recognized by Arens and Associates on May 28 is

a. $200,000.
b. $800,000.
c. $1,000,000.
d. $0.

2. The percentage-of-completion method of accounting for long-term construction contracts is an exception to the?
   a. Matching principle.
   b. Going-concern assumption.
   c. Economic-entity assumption.
   d. Revenue recognition principle.
3. Roebling Construction signed a $24 million contract on August 1, 2005 with the city of Candu to construct a bridge over the Vine River. Roebling's estimated cost of the bridge on that date was $18 million. The bridge was to be completed by April 2008. Roebling uses the percentage-of-completion method for income recognition. Roebling's fiscal year ends May 31. Data regarding the bridge contract are presented in the schedule below.

| | **At May 31** ($000 omitted) | |
|---|---|---|
| | **2006** | **2007** |
| Actual costs to date | $ 6,000 | $15,000 |
| Estimated costs to complete | 12,000 | 5,000 |
| Progress billings to date | 5,000 | 14,000 |
| Cash collected to date | 4,000 | 12,000 |

The gross profit or loss recognized in the fiscal year ended May 31, 2006 from this bridge contract is

a. $6,000,000 gross profit.
b. $2,000,000 gross profit.
c. $3,000,000 gross profit.
d. $1,000,000 gross profit.

**E 5–21**
Interim financial statements; income tax expense [Based on Appendix 5]

● LO1

Joplin Laminating Corporation reported income before income taxes during the first three quarters and management's estimates of the annual effective tax rate at the end of each quarter as shown below:

| | | **Quarter** | |
|---|---|---|---|
| | **First** | **Second** | **Third** |
| Income before income taxes | $50,000 | $40,000 | $100,000 |
| Estimated annual effective tax rate | 34% | 30% | 36% |

**Required:**
Determine the income tax expense to be reported in the income statement in each of the three quarterly reports.

**E 5–22**
Interim reporting; recognizing expenses [Based on Appendix 5]

● LO1

Security-Rand Corporation determines executive incentive compensation at the end of its fiscal year. At the end of the first quarter, management estimated that the amount will be $300 million. Depreciation expense for the year is expected to be $60 million. Also during the quarter, the company realized a gain of $23 million from selling two of its manufacturing plants.

**Required:**
What amounts for these items should be reported in the first quarter's income statement?

**E 5–23**
Interim financial statements; reporting expenses [Based on Appendix 5]

● LO1

Shields Company is preparing its interim report for the second quarter ending June 30. The following payments were made during the first two quarters:

| **Expenditure** | **Date** | **Amount** |
|---|---|---|
| Annual advertising | January | $800,000 |
| Property tax for the fiscal year | February | 350,000 |
| Annual equipment repairs | March | 260,000 |
| Extraordinary casualty loss | April | 185,000 |
| Research and development | May | 96,000 |

**Required:**
For each expenditure indicate the amount that would be reported in the quarterly income statements for the periods ending March 31, June 30, September 30, and December 31.

# PROBLEMS



**An alternative exercise and problem set is available on the text website: www.mhhe.com/spiceland4e**

**P 5–1**
Income statement presentation; installment sales method (Chapters 4 and 5)
● LO2

Reagan Corporation computed income from continuing operations before income taxes of $4,200,000 for 2006. The following material items have not yet been considered in the computation of income:

1. The company sold equipment and recognized a gain of $50,000. The equipment had been used in the manufacturing process and was replaced by new equipment.
2. In December, the company received a settlement of $1,000,000 for a lawsuit it had filed based on antitrust violations of a competitor. The settlement was considered to be an unusual and infrequent event.
3. Inventory costing $400,000 was written off as obsolete. Material losses of this type were incurred twice in the last eight years.
4. It was discovered that depreciation expense on the office building of $50,000 per year was not recorded in either 2005 or 2006.

In addition, you learn that *included* in revenues is $400,000 from installment sales made during the year. The cost of these sales is $240,000. At year-end, $100,000 in cash had been collected on the related installment receivables. Because of considerable uncertainty regarding the collectibility of receivables from these sales, the company's accountant should have used the installment sales method to recognize revenue and gross profit on these sales.

Also, the company's income tax rate is 40% and there were 1 million shares of common stock outstanding throughout the year.

**Required:**

Prepare an income statement for 2006 beginning with income from continuing operations before income taxes. Include appropriate EPS disclosures.

**P 5–2**
Installment sales and cost recovery methods
● LO2
eXcel

Ajax Company appropriately accounts for certain sales using the installment sales method. The perpetual inventory system is used. Information related to installment sales for 2006 and 2007 is as follows:

| | 2006 | 2007 |
|---|---|---|
| Sales | $300,000 | $400,000 |
| Cost of sales | 180,000 | 280,000 |
| Customer collections on: | | |
| 2006 sales | 120,000 | 100,000 |
| 2007 sales | | 150,000 |

**Required:**

1. Calculate the amount of gross profit that would be recognized each year from installment sales.
2. Prepare all necessary journal entries for each year.
3. Repeat requirements 1 and 2 assuming that Ajax uses the cost recovery method to account for its installment sales.

**P 5–3**
Installment sales; alternative recognition methods
● LO2
eXcel

On August 31, 2006, the Silva Company sold merchandise to the Bendix Corporation for $500,000. Terms of the sale called for a down payment of $100,000 and four annual installments of $100,000 due on each August 31, beginning August 31, 2007. Each installment also will include interest on the unpaid balance applying an appropriate interest rate. The book value of the merchandise on Silva's books on the date of sale was $300,000. The perpetual inventory system is used. The company's fiscal year-end is December 31.

**Required:**

1. Prepare a table showing the amount of gross profit to be recognized in each of the five years of the installment sale applying each of the following methods:
   a. Point of delivery revenue recognition.
   b. Installment sales method.
   c. Cost recovery method.
2. Prepare journal entries for each of the five years applying the three revenue recognition methods listed in requirement 1. Ignore interest charges.
3. Prepare a partial balance sheet as of the end of 2006 and 2007 listing the items related to the installment sale applying each of the three methods listed in requirement 1.

**P 5–4**
Percentage-of-completion method
● LO4
eXcel

In 2006, the Westgate Construction Company entered into a contract to construct a road for Santa Clara County for $10,000,000. The road was completed in 2008. Information related to the contract is as follows:

| | 2006 | 2007 | 2008 |
|---|---|---|---|
| Cost incurred during the year | $2,400,000 | $3,600,000 | $2,200,000 |
| Estimated costs to complete as of year-end | 5,600,000 | 2,000,000 | –0– |
| Billings during the year | 2,000,000 | 4,000,000 | 4,000,000 |
| Cash collections during the year | 1,800,000 | 3,600,000 | 4,600,000 |

Westgate uses the percentage-of-completion method of accounting for long-term construction contracts.

**Required:**

1. Calculate the amount of gross profit to be recognized in each of the three years.
2. Prepare all necessary journal entries for each of the years (credit *various accounts* for construction costs incurred).
3. Prepare a partial balance sheet for 2006 and 2007 showing any items related to the contract.
4. Calculate the amount of gross profit to be recognized in each of the three years assuming the following costs incurred and costs to complete information:

| | 2006 | 2007 | 2008 |
|---|---|---|---|
| Costs incurred during the year | $2,400,000 | $3,800,000 | $3,200,000 |
| Estimated costs to complete as of year-end | 5,600,000 | 3,100,000 | –0– |

5. Calculate the amount of gross profit to be recognized in each of the three years assuming the following costs incurred and costs to complete information:

| | 2006 | 2007 | 2008 |
|---|---|---|---|
| Costs incurred during the year | $2,400,000 | $3,800,000 | $3,900,000 |
| Estimated costs to complete as of year-end | 5,600,000 | 4,100,000 | –0– |

**P 5–5**
Completed contract method
● LO4

[This is a variation of the previous problem modified to focus on the completed contract method.]

**Required:**

Complete the requirements of Problem 5–4 assuming that Westgate Construction uses the completed contract method.

**P 5–6**
Construction accounting; loss projected on entire project
● LO4
eXcel

Curtiss Construction Company, Inc. entered into a fixed-price contract with Axelrod Associates on July 1, 2006, to construct a four-story office building. At that time, Curtiss estimated that it would take between two and three years to complete the project. The total contract price for construction of the building is $4,000,000. Curtiss appropriately accounts for this contract under the completed contract method in its financial statements. The building was completed on December 31, 2008. Estimated percentage of completion, *accumulated* contract costs incurred, estimated costs to complete the contract, and *accumulated* billings to Axelrod under the contract were as follows:

| | At 12-31-06 | At 12-31-07 | At 12-31-08 |
|---|---|---|---|
| Percentage of completion | 10% | 60% | 100% |
| Costs incurred to date | $ 350,000 | $2,500,000 | $4,250,000 |
| Estimated costs to complete | 3,150,000 | 1,700,000 | –0– |
| Billings to Axelrod, to date | 720,000 | 2,170,000 | 3,600,000 |

**Required:**

1. Prepare schedules to compute gross profit or loss to be recognized as a result of this contract for each of the three years.
2. Assuming Curtiss uses the percentage-of-completion method of accounting for long-term construction contracts, compute gross profit or loss to be recognized in each of the three years.
3. Assuming the percentage-of-completion method, compute the amount to be shown in the balance sheet at the end of 2006 and 2007 as either cost in excess of billings or billings in excess of costs.

*(AICPA adapted)*

**P 5–7**
Franchise sales; installment sales method
● LO2 LO5

Olive Branch Restaurant Corporation sells franchises throughout the western states. On January 30, 2006, the company entered into the following franchise agreement with Jim and Tammy Masters:

1. The initial franchise fee is $1.2 million. $200,000 is payable immediately and the remainder is due in 10, $100,000 installments plus 10% interest on the unpaid balance each January 30, beginning January 30, 2007. The 10% interest rate is an appropriate market rate.
2. In addition to allowing the franchisee to use the franchise name for the 10-year term of the agreement, in exchange for the initial fee Olive Branch agrees to assist the franchisee in selecting a location, obtaining financing, designing and constructing the restaurant building, and training employees.
3. All of the initial down payment of $200,000 is to be refunded by Olive Branch and the remaining obligation canceled if, for any reason, the franchisee fails to open the franchise.
4. In addition to the initial franchise fee, the franchisee is required to pay a monthly fee of 3% of franchise sales for advertising, promotion, menu planning, and other continuing services to be provided by Olive Branch over the life of the agreement. This fee is payable on the 10th of the following month.

Substantial performance of the initial services provided by Olive Branch, which are significant, is deemed to have occurred when the franchise opened on September 1, 2006. Franchise sales for the month of September 2006 were $40,000.

**Required:**

1. Assuming that collectibility of the installment receivable is reasonably certain, prepare the necessary journal entries for Olive Branch on the following dates (ignore interest charges on the installment receivable and the costs of providing franchise services):
   a. January 30, 2006
   b. September 1, 2006
   c. September 30, 2006
   d. January 30, 2007
2. Assume that significant uncertainty exists as to the collection of the installment receivable and that Olive Branch elects to recognize initial franchise fee revenue using the installment sales method. Prepare the necessary journal entries for the dates listed in requirement 1 (ignore interest charges on the installment receivable and the costs of providing franchise services).

**P 5–8**
Calculating activity and profitability ratios

● LO6

Financial statements for Askew Industries for 2006 are shown below:

**2006 Income Statement**

| | ($ in 000s) |
|---|---|
| Sales | $9,000 |
| Cost of goods sold | (6,300) |
| Gross profit | 2,700 |
| Operating expenses | (2,000) |
| Interest expense | (200) |
| Tax expense | (200) |
| Net income | $ 300 |

**Comparative Balance Sheets**

| | Dec. 31 | |
|---|---|---|
| | **2006** | **2005** |
| **Assets** | | |
| Cash | $ 600 | $ 500 |
| Accounts receivable | 600 | 400 |
| Inventory | 800 | 600 |
| Property, plant, and equipment (net) | 2,000 | 2,100 |
| | $4,000 | $3,600 |
| **Liabilities and Shareholders' Equity** | | |
| Current liabilities | $1,100 | $ 850 |
| Bonds payable | 1,400 | 1,400 |
| Paid-in capital | 600 | 600 |
| Retained earnings | 900 | 750 |
| | $4,000 | $3,600 |

**Required:**

Calculate the following ratios for 2006.

1. Inventory turnover ratio
2. Average days in inventory
3. Receivables turnover ratio
4. Average collection period
5. Asset turnover ratio
6. Profit margin on sales
7. Return on assets
8. Return on shareholders' equity

**P 5–9**
Use of ratios to compare two companies in the same industry

● LO6

Presented below are condensed financial statements adapted from those of two actual companies competing in the pharmaceutical industry—**Johnson and Johnson (J&J)** and **Pfizer, Inc.** ($ in millions, except per share amounts).

**Required:**

Evaluate and compare the two companies by responding to the following questions.

Note: Because two-year comparative statements are not provided, you should use year-end balances in place of average balances as appropriate.

1. Which of the two companies appears more efficient in collecting its accounts receivable and managing its inventory?
2. Which of the two firms had greater earnings relative to resources available?

3. Have the two companies achieved their respective rates of return on assets with similar combinations of profit margin and turnover?
4. From the perspective of a common shareholder, which of the two firms provided a greater rate of return?

**Balance Sheets**
($ in millions, except per share data)

| | J&J | Pfizer |
|---|---|---|
| **Assets:** | | |
| Cash | $ 5,377 | $ 1,520 |
| Short-term investments | 4,146 | 10,432 |
| Accounts receivable (net) | 6,574 | 8,775 |
| Inventories | 3,588 | 5,837 |
| Other current assets | 3,310 | 3,177 |
| Current assets | 22,995 | 29,741 |
| Property, plant, and equipment (net) | 9,846 | 18,287 |
| Intangibles and other assets | 15,422 | 68,747 |
| Total assets | $48,263 | $116,775 |
| **Liabilities and Shareholders' Equity:** | | |
| Accounts payable | $ 4,966 | $ 2,601 |
| Short-term notes | 1,139 | 8,818 |
| Other current liabilities | 7,343 | 12,238 |
| Current liabilities | 13,448 | 23,657 |
| Long-term debt | 2,955 | 5,755 |
| Other long-term liabilities | 4,991 | 21,986 |
| Total liabilities | 21,394 | 51,398 |
| Capital stock (par and additional paid-in capital) | 3,120 | 67,050 |
| Retained earnings | 30,503 | 29,382 |
| Accumulated other comprehensive income (loss) | (590) | 195 |
| Less: treasury stock and other equity adjustments | (6,164) | (31,250) |
| Total shareholders' equity | 26,869 | 65,377 |
| Total liabilities and shareholders' equity | $48,263 | $116,775 |

**Income Statements**

| | J&J | Pfizer |
|---|---|---|
| Net sales | $41,862 | $ 45,188 |
| Cost of goods sold | 12,176 | 9,832 |
| Gross profit | 29,686 | 35,356 |
| Operating expenses | 19,763 | 28,486 |
| Other (income) expense—net | (385) | 3,610 |
| Income before taxes | 10,308 | 3,260 |
| Tax expense | 3,111 | 1,621 |
| Net income | $ 7,197 | $ 1,639* |
| Basic net income per share | $ 2.42 | $ .22 |

*This is before income from discontinued operations.

**P 5–10**
Creating a balance sheet from ratios; Chapters 3 and 5
● LO6

Cadux Candy Company's income statement for the year ended December 31, 2006, reported interest expense of $2 million and income tax expense of $12 million. Current assets listed in its balance sheet include cash, accounts receivable, and inventories. Property, plant, and equipment is the company's only noncurrent asset. Financial ratios for 2006 are listed below. Profitability and turnover ratios with balance sheet items in the denominator were calculated using year-end balances rather than averages.

| | |
|---|---|
| Debt to equity ratio | 1.0 |
| Current ratio | 2.0 |
| Acid-test ratio | 1.0 |
| Times interest earned ratio | 17 times |
| Return on assets | 10% |
| Return on shareholders' equity | 20% |
| Profit margin on sales | 5% |
| Gross profit margin (gross profit divided by net sales) | 40% |
| Inventory turnover | 8 times |
| Receivables turnover | 20 times |

**Required:**

Prepare a December 31, 2006, balance sheet for the Cadux Candy Company.

**P 5–11**
Compare two companies in the same industry; Chapters 3 and 5

● LO6

Presented below are condensed financial statements adapted from those of two actual companies competing as the primary players in a specialty area of the food manufacturing and distribution industry. ($ in millions, except per share amounts.)

**Balance Sheets**

| **Assets** | **Metropolitan** | **Republic** |
|---|---|---|
| Cash | $ 179.3 | $ 37.1 |
| Accounts receivable (net) | 422.7 | 325.0 |
| Short-term investments | — | 4.7 |
| Inventories | 466.4 | 635.2 |
| Prepaid expenses and other current assets | 134.6 | 476.7 |
| Current assets | $1,203.0 | $1,478.7 |
| Property, plant, and equipment (net) | 2,608.2 | 2,064.6 |
| Intangibles and other assets | 210.3 | 464.7 |
| Total assets | $4,021.5 | $4,008.0 |
| **Liabilities and Shareholders' Equity** | | |
| Accounts payable | $ 467.9 | $ 691.2 |
| Short-term notes | 227.1 | 557.4 |
| Accruals and other current liabilities | 585.2 | 538.5 |
| Current liabilities | $1,280.2 | $1,787.1 |
| Long-term debt | 535.6 | 542.3 |
| Deferred tax liability | 384.6 | 610.7 |
| Other long-term liabilities | 104.0 | 95.1 |
| Total liabilities | $2,304.4 | $3,035.2 |
| Common stock (par and additional paid-in capital) | 144.9 | 335.0 |
| Retained earnings | 2,476.9 | 1,601.9 |
| Less: treasury stock | (904.7) | (964.1) |
| Total liabilities and shareholders' equity | $4,021.5 | $4,008.0 |

**Income Statements**

| | | |
|---|---|---|
| Net sales | $5,698.0 | $7,768.2 |
| Cost of goods sold | (2,909.0) | (4,481.7) |
| Gross profit | $2,789.0 | $3,286.5 |
| Operating expenses | (1,743.7) | (2,539.2) |
| Interest expense | (56.8) | (46.6) |
| Income before taxes | $ 988.5 | $ 700.7 |
| Tax expense | (394.7) | (276.1) |
| Net income | $ 593.8 | $ 424.6 |
| Net income per share | $ 2.40 | $ 6.50 |

**Required:**

Evaluate and compare the two companies by responding to the following questions.

Note: Because comparative statements are not provided you should use year-end balances in place of average balances as appropriate.

1. Which of the two firms had greater earnings relative to resources available?
2. Have the two companies achieved their respective rates of return on assets with similar combinations of profit margin and turnover?
3. From the perspective of a common shareholder, which of the two firms provided a greater rate of return?
4. Which company is most highly leveraged and which has made most effective use of financial leverage?
5. Of the two companies, which appears riskier in terms of its ability to pay short-term obligations?
6. How efficiently are current assets managed?
7. From the perspective of a creditor, which company offers the most comfortable margin of safety in terms of its ability to pay fixed interest charges?

**P 5–12**
Interim financial reporting (Based on Appendix 5)

● LO1

Branson Electronics Company is a small, publicly traded company preparing its first quarter interim report to be mailed to shareholders. The following information for the quarter has been compiled:

| | | |
|---|---|---|
| Revenues | | $180,000 |
| Cost of goods sold | | 35,000 |
| Operating expenses: | | |
| Fixed | $59,000 | |
| Variable | 48,000 | 107,000 |

Fixed operating expenses include payments of $50,000 to an advertising firm to promote the firm through various media throughout the year. The income tax rate for the firm's level of operations in the first quarter is 30%, but management estimates the effective rate for the entire year will be 36%.

**Required:**

Prepare the income statement to be included in Branson's first quarter interim report.

# BROADEN YOUR PERSPECTIVE

**Apply your critical-thinking ability to the knowledge you've gained. These cases will provide you an opportunity to develop your research, analysis, judgment, and communication skills. You also will work with other students, integrate what you've learned, apply it in real world situations, and consider its global and ethical ramifications. This practice will broaden your knowledge and further develop your decision-making abilities.**

**Real World Case 5–1**
Chainsaw Al; Revenue recognition and earnings management

● LO1

In May 2001, the Securities and Exchange Commission sued the former top executives at Sunbeam, charging the group with financial reporting fraud that allegedly cost investors billions in losses. **Sunbeam Corporation** is a recognized designer, manufacturer, and marketer of household and leisure products, including Coleman, Eastpak, First Alert, Grillmaster, Mixmaster, Mr. Coffee, Oster, Powermate, and Campingaz. In the mid-1990s, Sunbeam needed help: its profits had declined by over 80% percent, and in 1996, its stock price was down over 50% from its high. To the rescue: Albert Dunlap, also known as "Chainsaw Al" based on his reputation as a ruthless executive known for his ability to restructure and turn around troubled companies, largely by eliminating jobs.

The strategy appeared to work. In 1997, Sunbeam's revenues had risen by 18 percent. However, in April 1998, the brokerage firm of **Paine Webber** downgraded Sunbeam's stock recommendation. Why the downgrade? Paine Webber had noticed unusually high accounts receivable, massive increases in sales of electric blankets in the third quarter 1997, which usually sell best in the fourth quarter, as well as unusually high sales of barbeque grills for the fourth quarter. Soon after, Sunbeam announced a first quarter loss of $44.6 million, and Sunbeam's stock price fell 25 percent.

It eventually came to light that Dunlap and Sunbeam had been using a "bill and hold" strategy with retail buyers. This involved selling products at large discounts to retailers before they normally would buy and then holding the products in third-party warehouses, with delivery at a later date.

Many felt Sunbeam had deceived shareholders by artificially inflating earnings and the company's stock price. A class-action lawsuit followed, alleging that Sunbeam and Dunlap violated federal securities laws, suggesting the motivation to inflate the earnings and stock price was to allow Sunbeam to complete hundreds of millions of dollars of debt financing in order to complete some ongoing mergers. Shareholders alleged damages when Sunbeam's subsequent earnings decline caused a huge drop in the stock price.

**Required:**

1. How might Sunbeam's 1997 "bill and hold" strategy have contributed to artificially high earnings in 1997?
2. How would the strategy have led to the unusually high accounts receivable Paine Webber noticed?
3. How might Sunbeam's 1997 "bill and hold" strategy have contributed to a 1998 earnings decline?
4. How does earnings management of this type affect earnings quality?

**Judgment Case 5–2**
Revenue recognition

● LO1

Revenue earned by a business enterprise is recognized for accounting purposes at different times, according to the circumstances. In some situations revenue is recognized approximately as it is earned in the economic sense. In other situations revenue is recognized at point of delivery.

**Required:**

1. Explain and justify why revenue often is recognized as earned at point of delivery.
2. Explain in what situations it would be useful to recognize revenue as the productive activity takes place.
3. At what times, other than those included in (1) and (2) above, may it be appropriate to recognize revenue?

**Judgment Case 5–3**
Revenue recognition; trade-ins

● LO1

Apex Computer Company manufactures and sells large, mainframe computers. The computers range in price from $1 to $3 million and gross profit averages 40% of sales price. The company has a liberal trade-in policy. Customers are allowed to trade in their computers for a new generation machine anytime within three years of sale. The trade-in allowance granted will vary depending on the number of years between original sale and trade-in. However, in all cases, the allowance is expected to be approximately 25% higher than the prevailing market price of the computer.

As an example, in 2006 a customer who purchased a computer in 2004 for $2 million (the computer cost Apex $1,200,000 to manufacture) decided to trade it in for a new computer. The sales price of the new computer was $2.5 million and a trade-in allowance of $600,000 was granted on the old machine. As a result of the trade-in allowance, the customer had to pay only $1.9 million ($2.5 million less $600,000) for the new computer. The old computer taken back by Apex had a resale value of $480,000. The new computer cost $1.5 million to manufacture. The company accounted for the trade-in by recognizing revenue of $2,380,000 ($1.9 million received in cash + $480,000 value of old computer).

**Required:**

Does the company's revenue recognition policy for trade-ins seem appropriate? If not, describe the problem created by the liberal trade-in policy.

**Communication Case 5–4**
Revenue recognition

● LO1

Jerry's Ice Cream Parlor is considering a marketing plan to increase sales of ice cream cones. The plan will give customers a free ice cream cone if they buy 10 ice cream cones at regular prices. Customers will be issued a card that will be punched each time an ice cream cone is purchased. After 10 punches, the card can be turned in for a free cone.

Jerry Donovan, the company's owner, is not sure how the new plan will affect accounting procedures. He realizes that the company will be incurring costs each time a free ice cream cone is awarded, but there will be no corresponding revenue or cash inflow.

The focus of this case is the matching of revenues and expenses related to the free ice cream cones that will be awarded if the new plan is adopted. Your instructor will divide the class into two to six groups depending on the size of the class. The mission of your group is to reach consensus on the appropriate accounting treatment for the new plan.

**Required:**

1. Each group member should deliberate the situation independently and draft a tentative argument prior to the class session for which the case is assigned.
2. In class, each group will meet for 10–15 minutes in different areas of the classroom. During that meeting, group members will take turns sharing their suggestions for the purpose of arriving at a single group treatment.
3. After the allotted time, a spokesperson for each group (selected during the group meetings) will share the group's solution with the class. The goal of the class is to incorporate the views of each group into a consensus approach to the situation.

**Research Case 5–5**
Long-term contract accounting

● LO4

A recent article in *Accounting Horizons* describes the current accounting practices and disclosures for long-term contracts for the Fortune 500 companies.

**Required:**

In your library or from some other source, locate the indicated article in *Accounting Horizons,* September, 2004, and answer the following questions:

1. How many firms reported the use of one of the two long-term contract accounting methods?
2. Approximately half of the firms are in which industry?
3. How many firms reported the use of the percentage-of-completion method? The completed contract method?
4. What is the most frequently used approach to estimating a percentage-of-completion?

**Ethics Case 5–6**
Revenue recognition

● LO1

Horizon Corporation manufactures personal computers. The company began operations in 1999 and reported profits for the years 2001 through 2004. Due primarily to increased competition and price slashing in the industry, 2005's income statement reported a loss of $20 million. Just before the end of the 2006 fiscal year, a memo from the company's chief financial officer to Jim Fielding, the company controller, included the following comments:

*If we don't do something about the large amount of unsold computers already manufactured, our auditors will require us to write them off. The resulting loss for 2006 will cause a violation of our debt covenants and force the company into bankruptcy. I suggest that you ship half of our inventory to J.B. Sales, Inc., in Oklahoma City. I know the company's president and he will accept the merchandise and acknowledge the shipment as a purchase. We can record the sale in 2006 which will boost profits to an acceptable level. Then J.B. Sales will simply return the merchandise in 2007 after the financial statements have been issued.*

**Required:**

Discuss the ethical dilemma faced by Jim Fielding.

**Judgment Case 5–7**
Revenue recognition; installment sale

● LO1 LO2

On October 1, 2006, the Marshall Company sold a large piece of machinery to the Hammond Construction Company for $80,000. The cost of the machine was $40,000. Hammond made a down payment of $10,000 and agreed to pay the remaining balance in seven equal monthly installments of $10,000, plus interest at 12% on the unpaid balance, beginning November 1.

**Required:**

1. Identify three alternative methods for recognizing revenue and costs for the situation described and compute the amount of gross profit that would be recognized in 2006 using each method.
2. Discuss the circumstances under which each of the three methods would be used.

**Judgment Case 5–8**
Revenue recognition; *SAB 101* questions

● LO1

As part of its crackdown on earnings management, the SEC issued *Staff Accounting Bulletin No. 101* to provide additional guidance on when revenue should be recognized. Consider the following situations posed by the SEC and, for each, discuss whether or not you believe it is appropriate to recognize revenue.

1. **Facts:** Company M is a discount retailer. It generates revenue from annual membership fees it charges customers to shop at its stores and from the sale of products at a discount price to those customers. The membership arrangements with retail customers require the customer to pay the entire membership fee (e.g., $35) at the outset of the arrangement. However, the customer has the unilateral right to cancel the arrangement at any time during its term and receive a full refund of the initial fee. Based on historical data collected over time for a large number of homogeneous transactions, Company M estimates that approximately 40% of the customers will request a refund before the end of the membership contract term. Company M's data for the past five years indicates that significant variations between actual and estimated cancellations have not occurred, and Company M does not expect significant variations to occur in the foreseeable future.
   **Question:** May Company M recognize revenue for the membership fees and accrue the costs to provide membership services at the outset of the arrangement?
2. **Facts:** Company Z enters into an arrangement with Customer A to deliver Company Z's products to Customer A on a consignment basis. Pursuant to the terms of the arrangement, Customer A is a consignee, and title to the products does not pass from Company Z to Customer A until Customer A consumes the products in its operations. Company Z delivers product to Customer A under the terms of their arrangement.
   **Question:** May Company Z recognize revenue upon delivery of its product to Customer A?
3. **Facts:** Company R is a retailer that offers "layaway" sales to its customers. Company R retains the merchandise, sets it aside in its inventory, and collects a cash deposit from the customer. Although Company R may set a time period within which the customer must finalize the purchase, Company R does not require the customer to enter into an installment note or other fixed payment commitment or agreement when the initial deposit is received. The merchandise generally is not released to the customer until the customer pays the full purchase price. In the event that the customer fails to pay the remaining purchase price, the customer forfeits its cash deposit. In the event the merchandise is lost, damaged, or destroyed, Company R either must refund the cash deposit to the customer or provide replacement merchandise.
   **Question:** When may Company R recognize revenue for merchandise sold under its layaway program?

**Research Case 5–9**
Locate and extract relevant information and authoritative support for a financial reporting issue; revenue recognition; right of return

● LO3

Many companies sell products allowing their customers the right to return merchandise if they are not satisfied. Because the return of merchandise can retroactively negate the benefits of having made a sale, the seller must meet certain criteria before revenue is recognized in situations when the right of return exists. *SFAS No. 48,* "Revenue Recognition When Right of Return Exists," lists the criteria, the most critical of which is that the seller must be able to make reliable estimates of future returns.

**Required:**

1. Obtain the original *SFAS No. 48.* You might gain access through FARS, the FASB Financial Accounting Research System, from your school library, or some other source.
2. What factors does the standard discuss that may impair the ability to make a reasonable estimate of returns?
3. List all six criteria that must be met before revenue can be recognized when the right of return exists.
4. Using Edgarscan (**edgarscan.pwcglobal.com**) access the 10-K reports for the most recent fiscal year for **Hewlett Packard Company** and for **Advanced Micro Devices, Inc.** Search for the revenue recognition policy to determine when these two companies recognize revenue for product sales allowing customers the right of return.
5. Using your answers to requirements 2 and 3, speculate as to why the two revenue recognition policies differ.

**Judgment Case 5–10**
Revenue recognition; service sales

● LO1 LO4

Each of the following situations concerns revenue recognition for services.

1. **Delta Airlines** books a reservation for a roundtrip flight to Orlando for Ming Tsai on April 12. Delta charges the $425 to Tsai's Visa card on April 13 and receives the cash from Visa on May 1. The roundtrip flight commences on May 15. The ticket is nonrefundable.
2. Highlife Ski Resort in Colorado sells a season pass to Larry Werner on October 15. Highlife usually opens its season just after Thanksgiving and stays open until approximately April 30.
3. Dixon Management requires tenants to sign a three-year lease and charges $5,000 per month for one floor in its midtown high-rise. In addition to the monthly fee, payable at the beginning of each month, tenants pay a nonrefundable fee of $12,000 to secure the lease.

4. Janora Hawkins, attorney, agrees to accept an accident victim's case. Hawkins will be paid on a contingency basis. That is, if she wins the case, she will receive 30% of the total settlement. The case commences on July 15 and is settled successfully on August 28. On September 15 Hawkins receives her contingency payment of $60,000.

**Required:**
For each of the above situations, determine the appropriate timing of revenue recognition.

**Judgment Case 5–11**
Revenue recognition; long-term construction contracts
● LO4

Two accounting students were discussing the alternative methods of accounting for long-term construction contracts. The discussion focused on which method was most like the typical revenue recognition method of recognizing revenue at point of product delivery. Bill argued that the completed contract method was preferable because it was analogous to recognizing revenue at the point of delivery. John disagreed and supported the percentage-of-completion method, stating that it was analogous to accruing revenue during the earnings process, that is, as the work was performed.

**Required:**
Discuss the arguments made by both students. Which argument do you support? Why?

**Communication Case 5–12**
Percentage-of-completion and completed contract methods
● LO4

Willingham Construction is in the business of building high-priced, custom, single-family homes. The company, headquartered in Anaheim, California, operates throughout the Southern California area. The construction period for the average home built by Willingham is six months, although some homes have taken as long as nine months.

You have just been hired by Willingham as the assistant controller and one of your first tasks is to evaluate the company's revenue recognition policy. The company presently uses the completed contract method for all of its projects and management is now considering a switch to the percentage-of-completion method.

**Required:**
Write a 1- to 2-page memo to Virginia Reynolds, company controller, describing the differences between the percentage-of-completion and completed contract methods. Be sure to include references to GAAP as they pertain to the choice of method. Do not address the differential effects on income taxes nor the effect on the financial statements of switching between methods.

**International Case 5–13**
Comparison of revenue recognition in Sweden and the United States
● LO1 LO4

**Electrolux,** headquartered in Sweden, is the European leader in food-service equipment and the second largest producer in the world. The revenue recognition disclosure, included in a recent financial statement, is reproduced below.

> **General Accounting and Valuation Principles (in part)**
> Revenue recognition
> Sales are recorded net of VAT (value-added tax), specific sales taxes, returns, and trade discounts. Revenues arise almost exclusively from sales of finished products. Sales are recognized when the significant risks and rewards connected with ownership of the goods have been transferred to the buyer and the Group retains neither a continuing right to dispose of the goods nor effective control of those goods and when the amount of revenue can be measured reliably. This means that sales are recorded when goods have been put at the disposal of the customers in accordance with the agreed terms of delivery. Revenues from services are recorded when the service has been performed.

**Required:**
On the basis of the information the disclosures provide, compare revenue recognition in Sweden with that in the United States.

**Trueblood Accounting Case 5–14**
Revenue recognition; license agreement
● LO1

The following Trueblood case is recommended for use with this chapter. The case provides an excellent opportunity for class discussion, group projects, and writing assignments. The case, along with Professor's Discussion Material, can be obtained from the Deloitte Foundation at its website: **www.deloitte.com/us/truebloodcases**.

**Case 04-7:** ***Lighthouse***
This case concerns the appropriate timing of revenue recognition for a bundled product and service.

**Real World Case 5–15**
Revenue recognition; franchise sales
● LO5

EDGAR, the Electronic Data Gathering, Analysis, and Retrieval system, performs automated collection, validation, indexing, and forwarding of submissions by companies and others who are required by law to file forms with the U.S. Securities and Exchange Commission (SEC). All publicly traded domestic companies use EDGAR to make the majority of their filings. (Some foreign companies file voluntarily.) Form 10-K or 10-KSB, which include the annual report, is required to be filed on EDGAR. The SEC makes this information available on the Internet.

**Required:**
1. Access EDGAR on the Internet. The web address is **www.sec.gov**. Edgarscan (**edgarscan.pwcglobal.com**) from PricewaterhouseCoopers makes the process of accessing data from EDGAR easier.
2. Search for **Jack in the Box, Inc.** Access the most recent 10-K filing. Search or scroll to find the financial statements and related notes.

3. Answer the following questions related to the company's revenue recognition policies:
   a. When does the company recognize initial franchise license fee revenue?
   b. How are continuing fees determined?
4. Repeat requirements 2 and 3 for two additional companies that you suspect also earn revenues through the sale of franchise rights. Compare their revenue recognition policies with the policies of Jack in the Box.

**Analysis Case 5–16**
Evaluating profitability and asset management; obtain and compare annual reports from companies in the same industry

● LO6

Performance and profitability of a company often are evaluated using the financial information provided by a firm's annual report in comparison with other firms in the same industry. Ratios are useful in this assessment.

**Required:**

Obtain annual reports from two corporations in the same primary industry. Using techniques you learned in this chapter and any analysis you consider useful, respond to the following questions:

1. How do earnings trends compare in terms of both the direction and stability of income?
2. Which of the two firms had greater earnings relative to resources available?
3. How efficiently are current assets managed?
4. Has each of the companies achieved its respective rate of return on assets with similar combinations of profit margin and turnover?
5. Are there differences in accounting methods that should be taken into account when making comparisons?

**Note:** You can obtain copies of annual reports from friends who are shareholders, the investor relations department of the corporations, from a friendly stockbroker, or from EDGAR (Electronic Data Gathering, Analysis, and Retrieval) on the Internet (**www.sec.gov** or through Edgarscan at **edgarscan.pwcglobal.com**).

**Judgment Case 5–17**
Relationships among ratios; Chapters 3 and 5

● LO6

You are a part-time financial advisor. A client is considering an investment in common stock of a waste recycling firm. One motivation is a rumor the client heard that the company made huge investments in a new fuel creation process. Unable to confirm the rumor, your client asks you to determine whether the firm's assets had recently increased significantly.

Because the firm is small, information is sparse. Last quarter's interim report showed total assets of $324 million, approximately the same as last year's annual report. The only information more current than that is a press release last week in which the company's management reported "record net income for the year of $21 million, representing a 14.0% return on shareholders' equity. Performance was enhanced by the Company's judicious use of financial leverage on a debt/equity ratio of 2 to 1."

**Required:**

Use the information available to provide your client with an opinion as to whether the waste recycling firm invested in the new fuel creation process during the last quarter of the year.

**Integrating Case 5–18**
Using ratios to test reasonableness of data; Chapters 3 and 5

● LO6

You are a new staff accountant with a large regional CPA firm, participating in your first audit. You recall from your auditing class that CPAs often use ratios to test the reasonableness of accounting numbers provided by the client. Since ratios reflect the relationships among various account balances, if it is assumed that prior relationships still hold, prior years' ratios can be used to estimate what current balances should approximate. However, you never actually performed this kind of analysis until now. The CPA in charge of the audit of Covington Pike Corporation brings you the list of ratios shown below and tells you these reflect the relationships maintained by Covington Pike in recent years.

Profit margin on sales = 5%
Return on assets = 7.5%
Gross profit margin = 40%
Inventory turnover ratio = 6 times
Receivables turnover ratio = 25
Acid-test ratio = .9
Current ratio = 2 to 1
Return on shareholders' equity = 10%
Debt to equity ratio = 1/3
Times interest earned ratio = 12 times

Jotted in the margins are the following notes:

- Net income $15,000
- Only one short-term note ($5,000); all other current liabilities are trade accounts
- Property, plant, and equipment are the only noncurrent assets
- Bonds payable are the only noncurrent liabilities
- The effective interest rate on short-term notes and bonds is 8%
- No investment securities
- Cash balance totals $15,000

**Required:**

You are requested to approximate the current year's balances in the form of a balance sheet and income statement, to the extent the information allows. Accompany those financial statements with the calculations you use to estimate each amount reported.

**Analysis Case 5–19**
Revenue recognition; profitability analysis

● LO1 LO6

**FedEx Corporation**

Refer to the financial statements and related disclosure notes of **FedEx Corporation** in Appendix B located at the back of this text.

**Required:**

1. What method does the company use to recognize revenue?
2. What percentage of total 2004 revenues was generated by international operations? (Hint: see Note 13.)
3. Compute the following ratios for 2004:
   a. Receivables turnover ratio
   b. Profit margin on sales
   c. Return on assets
   d. Return on shareholders' equity

# CPA SIMULATION 5–1

**Leonard Brothers**
Revenue Recognition

KAPLAN
**CPA Review**

Test your knowledge of the concepts discussed in this chapter, practice critical professional skills necessary for career success, and prepare for the computer-based CPA exam by accessing our CPA simulations at the text website: **www.mhhe.com/spiceland4e.**

The Leonard Brothers simulation tests your knowledge of various revenue recognition issues and methods, including (a) the installment sales method, (b) revenue recognition for long-term contracts, and (c) accounting for franchise sales.

As on the CPA exam itself, you will be asked to use tools including a spreadsheet, a calculator, and professional accounting standards, to conduct research, derive solutions, and communicate conclusions related to these issues in a simulated environment headed by the following interactive tabs:

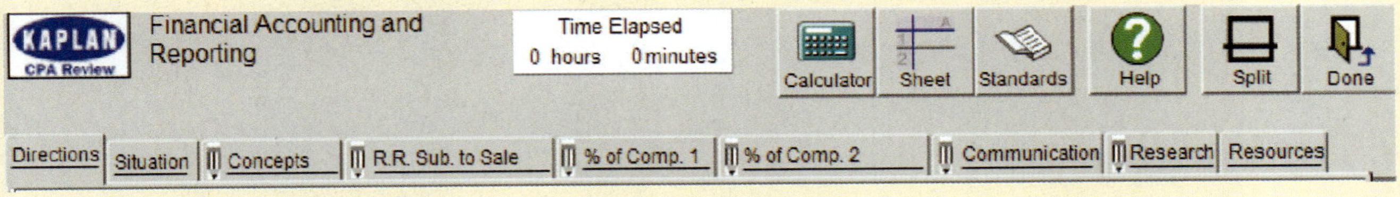


Specific tasks in the simulation address:

- Applying judgment in determining the revenue recognition method appropriate in various situations.
- Demonstrating an understanding of the installment sales method.
- Determining the appropriate journal entries for a long-term contract accounted for using the percentage-of-completion method.
- Analyzing the effect on the income statement and balance sheet of applying the percentage-of-completion method.
- Communicating the financial statement effects of using the percentage-of-completion method.
- Researching the accounting treatment and disclosure requirements for franchise sales.

6

CHAPTER

# Time Value of Money Concepts

## OVERVIEW

Time value of money concepts, specifically future value and present value, are essential in a variety of accounting situations. These concepts and the related computational procedures are the subjects of this chapter. Present values and future values of *single amounts* and present values and future values of *annuities* (series of equal periodic payments) are described separately but shown to be interrelated.

## LEARNING OBJECTIVES

After studying this chapter, you should be able to:

- LO1 Explain the difference between simple and compound interest.
- LO2 Compute the future value of a single amount.
- LO3 Compute the present value of a single amount.
- LO4 Solve for either the interest rate or the number of compounding periods when present value and future value of a single amount are known.
- LO5 Explain the difference between an ordinary annuity and an annuity due situation.
- LO6 Compute the future value of both an ordinary annuity and an annuity due.
- LO7 Compute the present value of an ordinary annuity, an annuity due, and a deferred annuity.
- LO8 Solve for unknown values in annuity situations involving present value.
- LO9 Briefly describe how the concept of the time value of money is incorporated into the valuation of bonds, long-term leases, and pension obligations.

# FINANCIAL REPORTING CASE

## The Winning Ticket

Al Castellano had been buying California State lottery tickets for 15 years at his neighborhood grocery store. On Sunday, June 24, 2005, his world changed. When he awoke, opened the local newspaper, and compared his lottery ticket numbers with Saturday night's winning numbers, he couldn't believe his eyes. All of the numbers on his ticket matched the winning numbers. He went outside for a walk, came back into the kitchen and checked the numbers again. He woke his wife Carmen, told her what had happened, and they danced through their apartment. Al, a 66-year-old retired supermarket clerk, and Carmen, a 62-year-old semiretired secretary, had won the richest lottery in California's history, $141 million!

On Monday when Al and Carmen claimed their prize, their ecstasy was waned slightly when they were informed that they would soon be receiving a check for approximately $43 million. When the Castellanos purchased the lottery ticket, they indicated that they would like to receive any lottery winnings in one lump payment rather than in 26 equal annual installments beginning now. They knew beforehand that the State of California is required to withhold 31% of lottery winnings for federal income tax purposes, but this reduction was way more than 31%.

Source: This case is adapted from an actual situation.

**By the time you finish this chapter, you should be able to respond appropriately to the questions posed in this case. Compare your response to the solution provided at the end of the chapter.**

### QUESTIONS

1. Why were the Castellanos to receive $43 million rather than the $141 million lottery prize? (page 280)
2. What interest rate did the State of California use to calculate the $43 million lump-sum payment? (page 286)
3. What are some of the accounting applications that incorporate the time value of money into valuation? (page 288)

# PART A BASIC CONCEPTS

## Time Value of Money

The *time value of money* means that money can be invested today to earn interest and grow to a larger dollar amount in the future.

The key to solving the problem described in the financial reporting case is an understanding of the concept commonly referred to as the **time value of money.** This concept means that money invested today will grow to a larger dollar amount in the future. For example, $100 invested in a savings account at your local bank yielding 6% annually will grow to $106 in one year. The difference between the $100 invested now—the present value of the investment—and its $106 future value represents the time value of money.

This concept has nothing to do with the worth or buying power of those dollars. Prices in our economy can change. If the inflation rate were higher than 6%, then the $106 you would have in the savings account actually would be worth less than the $100 you had a year earlier. The time value of money concept concerns only the growth in the dollar amounts of money.

Time value of money concepts are useful in valuing several assets and liabilities.

The concepts you will learn in this chapter are useful in solving many business decisions such as, for example, the determination of the lottery award presented in the financial reporting case. More important, the concepts also are necessary when valuing assets and liabilities for financial reporting purposes. As you will see in this and subsequent chapters, most accounting applications that incorporate the time value of money involve the concept of present value. The valuation of leases, bonds, pension obligations, and certain notes receivable and payable are a few prominent examples. It is important that you master the concepts and tools we review here. This knowledge is essential to the remainder of your accounting education.

### SIMPLE VERSUS COMPOUND INTEREST

● LO1

*Interest* is the amount of money paid or received in excess of the amount borrowed or lent.

**Interest** is the "rent" paid for the use of money for some period of time. In dollar terms, it is the amount of money paid or received in excess of the amount of money borrowed or lent. If you lent the bank $100 today and "received" $106 a year from now, your interest earned would be $6. Interest also can be expressed as a rate at which money will grow. In this case, that rate is 6%. It is this interest that gives money its time value.

**Simple interest** is computed by multiplying an initial investment times both the applicable interest rate and the period of time for which the money is used. For example, simple interest earned each year on a $1,000 investment paying 10% is $100 ($1,000 × 10%).

*Compound interest* includes interest not only on the initial investment but also on the accumulated interest in previous periods.

**Compound interest** results in increasingly larger interest amounts for each period of the investment. The reason is that interest is now being earned not only on the initial investment amount but also on the accumulated interest earned in previous periods.

For example, Cindy Johnson invested $1,000 in a savings account paying 10% interest *compounded* annually. How much interest will she earn each year, and what will be her investment balance after three years?

| Date | Interest (Interest rate × Outstanding balance = Interest) | Balance |
|---|---|---|
| Initial deposit | | $1,000 |
| End of year 1 | 10% × $1,000 = $100 | $1,100 |
| End of year 2 | 10% × $1,100 = $110 | $1,210 |
| End of year 3 | 10% × $1,210 = $121 | $1,331 |

With compound interest at 10% annually, the $1,000 investment would grow to $1,331 at the end of the three-year period. Of course, if Cindy withdrew the interest earned each year, she would earn only $100 in interest each year, that is, the amount of simple interest. If the investment period had been 20 years, 20 individual calculations would be needed. However, calculators, computer programs, and compound interest tables make these calculations much easier.

Most banks compound interest more frequently than once a year. Daily compounding is common for savings accounts. More rapid compounding has the effect of increasing the actual rate, which is called the **effective rate,** at which money grows per year. It is important to note that interest is typically stated as an annual rate regardless of the length of the compounding period involved. In situations when the compounding period is less than a year, the interest rate per compounding period is determined by dividing the annual rate by the number of periods. Assuming an annual rate of 12%:

Interest rates are typically stated as annual rates.

| Compounded | Interest Rate Per Compounding Period |
|---|---|
| Semiannually | 12% ÷ 2 = 6% |
| Quarterly | 12% ÷ 4 = 3% |
| Monthly | 12% ÷ 12 = 1% |

As an example, now let's assume Cindy Johnson invested $1,000 in a savings account paying 10% interest *compounded* twice a year. There are two six-month periods paying interest at 5% (the annual rate divided by two periods). How much interest will she earn the first year, and what will be her investment balance at the end of the year?

The *effective yield* is the rate at which money actually will grow during a full year.

| Date | Interest (Interest rate × Outstanding balance = Interest) | Balance |
|---|---|---|
| Initial deposit | | $1,000.00 |
| After six months | 5% × $1,000 = $50.00 | $1,050.00 |
| End of year 1 | 5% × $1,050 = $52.50 | $1,102.50 |

The $1,000 would grow by $102.50, the interest earned, to $1,102.50, $2.50 more than if interest were compounded only once a year. The effective annual interest rate, often referred to as the annual *yield,* is 10.25% ($102.50 ÷ $1,000).

## Valuing a Single Cash Flow Amount

### FUTURE VALUE OF A SINGLE AMOUNT

● LO2

In the first Cindy example, in which $1,000 was invested for three years at 10% compounded annually, the $1,331 is referred to as the **future value (FV).** A time diagram is a useful way to visualize this relationship, with 0 indicating the date of the initial investment.

Future value of a single amount.

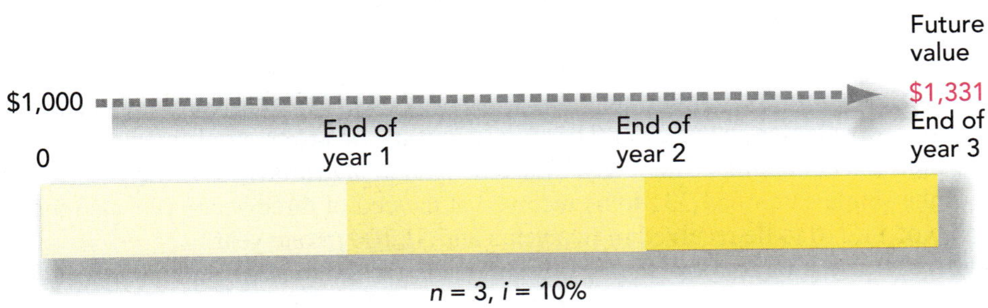


The future value after one year can be calculated as $1,000 × 1.10 (1.00 + .10) = $1,100. After three years, the future value is $1,000 × 1.10 × 1.10 × 1.10 = $1,331. In fact, the future value of any invested amount can be determined as follows:

$$FV = I\,(1 + i)^n$$

The *future value* of a single amount is the amount of money a dollar will grow to at some point in the future.

where: FV = Future value of the invested amount
I = Amount invested at the beginning of the period
$i$ = Interest rate
$n$ = Number of compounding periods

The future value can be determined by using Table 1, Future Value of $1, located at the end of this textbook. The table contains the future value of $1 invested for various periods of time, $n$, and at various rates, $i$.

**GRAPHIC 6–1**
Future Value of $1 (excerpt from Table 1)

| | Interest Rates (*i*) | | | | | |
|---|---|---|---|---|---|---|
| **Periods (*n*)** | **7%** | **8%** | **9%** | **10%** | **11%** | **12%** |
| 1 | 1.07000 | 1.08000 | 1.09000 | 1.10000 | 1.11000 | 1.12000 |
| 2 | 1.14490 | 1.16640 | 1.18810 | 1.21000 | 1.23210 | 1.25440 |
| 3 | 1.22504 | 1.25971 | 1.29503 | 1.33100 | 1.36763 | 1.40493 |
| 4 | 1.31080 | 1.36049 | 1.41158 | 1.46410 | 1.51807 | 1.57352 |
| 5 | 1.40255 | 1.46933 | 1.53862 | 1.61051 | 1.68506 | 1.76234 |
| 6 | 1.50073 | 1.58687 | 1.67710 | 1.77156 | 1.87041 | 1.97382 |
| 7 | 1.60578 | 1.71382 | 1.82804 | 1.94872 | 2.07616 | 2.21068 |
| 8 | 1.71819 | 1.85093 | 1.99256 | 2.14359 | 2.30454 | 2.47596 |

With this table, it's easy to determine the future value of any invested amount simply by multiplying it by the table value at the *intersection* of the column for the desired rate and the row for the number of compounding periods. Graphic 6–1 contains an excerpt from Table 1.

The table shows various values of $(1 + i)^n$ for different combinations of $i$ and $n$. From the table you can find the future value factor for three periods at 10% to be 1.331. This means that $1 invested at 10% compounded annually will grow to approximately $1.33 in three years. So, the future value of $1,000 invested for three years at 10% is $1,331:

FV = I × FV factor
FV = $1,000 × 1.331* = $1,331
*Future value of $1; $n = 3$, $i = 10\%$

The future value function in financial calculators or in computer spreadsheet programs calculates future values in the same way. Determining future values (and present values) electronically avoids the need for tables such as those in the chapter appendix. It's important to remember that the $n$ in the future value formula refers to the number of compounding periods, not necessarily the number of years. For example, suppose you wanted to know the future value *two* years from today of $1,000 invested at 12% with *quarterly* compounding. The number of periods is therefore eight and the compounding rate is 3% (12% annual rate divided by four, the number of quarters in a year). The future value factor from Table 1 is 1.26677, so the future value is $1,266.77 ($1,000 × 1.26677).[1]

## PRESENT VALUE OF A SINGLE AMOUNT

● LO3

The *present value* of a single amount is today's equivalent to a particular amount in the future.

The example used to illustrate future value reveals that $1,000 invested today is equivalent to $1,100 received after one year, $1,210 after two years, or $1,331 after three years, assuming 10% interest compounded annually. Thus, the $1,000 investment (I) is the **present value (PV)** of the single sum of $1,331 to be received at the end of three years. It is also the present value of $1,210 to be received in two years and $1,100 in one year.

Remember that the future value of a present amount is the present amount *times* $(1 + i)^n$. Logically, then, that computation can be reversed to find the *present value* of a future amount to be the future amount *divided* by $(1 + i)^n$. We substitute PV for I (invested amount) in the future value formula above.

$$FV = PV\,(1 + i)^n$$

$$PV = \frac{FV}{(1 + i)^n}$$

[1]When interest is compounded more frequently than once a year, the effective annual interest rate, or yield, can be determined using the following equation:

$$\text{Yield} = (1 + \frac{i}{p})^p - 1$$

with $i$ being the annual interest rate and $p$ the number of compounding periods per year. In this example, the annual yield would be 12.55%, calculated as follows:

$$\text{Yield} = (1 + \frac{.12}{4})^4 - 1 = 1.1255 - 1 = .1255$$

Determining the yield is useful when comparing returns on investment instruments with different compounding period length.

In our example,

$$PV = \frac{\$1{,}331}{(1 + .10)^3} = \frac{\$1{,}331}{1.331} = \$1{,}000$$

Of course, dividing by $(1 + i)^n$ is the same as multiplying by its reciprocal, $1/(1 + i)^n$.

$$PV = \$1{,}331 \times \frac{1}{(1 + .10)^3} = \$1{,}331 \times .75131 = \$1{,}000$$

As with future value, these computations are simplified by using calculators, computer programs, or present value tables. Table 2, Present Value of \$1, located at the end of this textbook provides the solutions of $1/(1 + i)^n$ for various interest rates ($i$) and compounding periods ($n$). These amounts represent the present value of \$1 to be received at the *end* of the different periods. The table can be used to find the present value of any single amount to be received in the future by *multiplying* that amount by the value in the table that lies at the *intersection* of the column for the appropriate rate and the row for the number of compounding periods.[2] Graphic 6–2 contains an excerpt from Table 2.

**GRAPHIC 6–2**
Present Value of \$1 (excerpt from Table 2)

| | Interest Rates (*i*) | | | | | |
|---|---|---|---|---|---|---|
| **Periods (*n*)** | **7%** | **8%** | **9%** | **10%** | **11%** | **12%** |
| 1 | .93458 | .92593 | .91743 | .90909 | .90090 | .89286 |
| 2 | .87344 | .85734 | .84168 | .82645 | .81162 | .79719 |
| 3 | .81630 | .79383 | .77218 | .75131 | .73119 | .71178 |
| 4 | .76290 | .73503 | .70843 | .68301 | .65873 | .63552 |
| 5 | .71299 | .68058 | .64993 | .62092 | .59345 | .56743 |
| 6 | .66634 | .63017 | .59627 | .56447 | .53464 | .50663 |
| 7 | .62275 | .58349 | .54703 | .51316 | .48166 | .45235 |
| 8 | .58201 | .54027 | .50187 | .46651 | .43393 | .40388 |

Notice that the farther into the future the \$1 is to be received, the less valuable it is now. This is the essence of the concept of the time value of money. Given a choice between \$1,000 now and \$1,000 three years from now, you would choose to have the money now. If you have it now, you could put it to use. But the choice between, say, \$740 now and \$1,000 three years from now would depend on your time value of money. If your time value of money is 10%, you would choose the \$1,000 in three years, because the \$740 invested at 10% for three years would grow to only \$984.94 [\$740 × 1.331 (FV of \$1, $i$ = 10%, $n$ = 3)]. On the other hand, if your time value of money is 11% or higher, you would prefer the \$740 now. Presumably, you would invest the \$740 now and have it grow to \$1,012.05 (\$740 × 1.36763) in three years.

Using the present value table above, the present value of \$1,000 to be received in three years assuming a time value of money of 10% is \$751.31 [\$1,000 × .75131 (PV of \$1, $i$ = 10% and $n$ = 3)]. Because the present value of the future amount, \$1,000, is higher than \$740 we could have today, we again determine that with a time value of money of 10%, the \$1,000 in three years is preferred to the \$740 now.

In our earlier example, \$1,000 now is equivalent to \$1,331 in three years, assuming the time value of money is 10%. Graphically, the relation between the present value and the future value can be viewed this way:

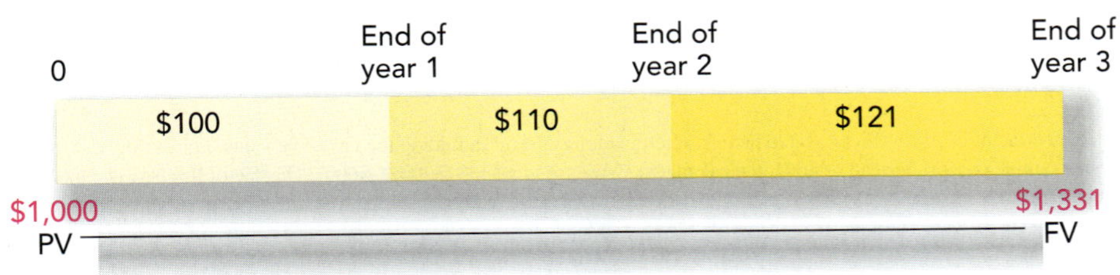


[2]The factors in Table 2 are the reciprocals of those in Table 1. For example, the future value factor for 10%, three periods is 1.331, while the present value factor is .75131. \$1 ÷ 1.331 = \$.75131, and \$1 ÷ .75131 = \$1.331.

**The calculation of future value requires the addition of interest, while the calculation of present value requires the removal of interest.**

**Accountants use PV calculations much more frequently than FV.**

While the calculation of future value of a single sum invested today requires the *inclusion* of compound interest, present value problems require the *removal* of compound interest. The process of computing present value *removes* the $331 of interest earned over the three-year period from the future value of $1,331, just as the process of computing future value *adds* $331 of interest to the present value of $1,000 to arrive at the future value of $1,331.

As we demonstrate later in this chapter and in subsequent chapters, present value calculations are incorporated into accounting valuation much more frequently than future value.

## SOLVING FOR OTHER VALUES WHEN FV AND PV ARE KNOWN

● LO4

There are four variables in the process of adjusting single cash flow amounts for the time value of money: the present value (PV), the future value (FV), the number of compounding periods ($n$), and the interest rate ($i$). If you know any three of these, the fourth can be determined. Illustration 6–1 solves for an unknown interest rate and Illustration 6–2 determines an unknown number of periods.

### Determining the Unknown Interest Rate

| **ILLUSTRATION 6–1** Determining $i$ When PV, FV, and $n$ Are Known | Suppose a friend asks to borrow $500 today and promises to repay you $605 two years from now. What is the annual interest rate you would be agreeing to? |
|---|---|

The following time diagram illustrates the situation:

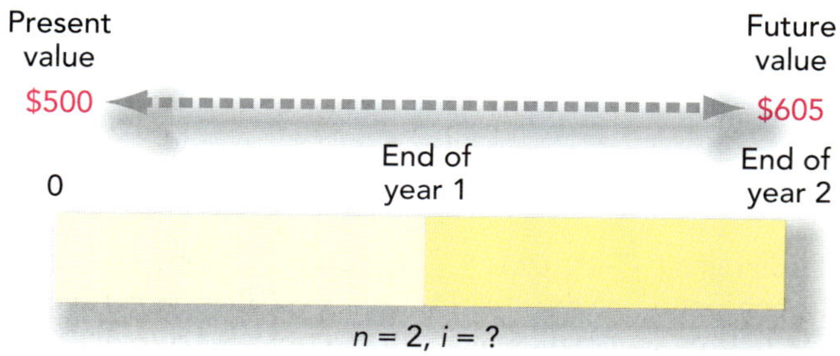


The interest rate is the discount rate that will provide a present value of $500 when discounting $605 to be received in two years:

**The unknown variable is the interest rate.**

$500 (present value) = $605 (future value) × ?*
*Present value of $1: $n = 2$, $i = ?$

Rearranging algebraically, we find that the present value table factor is .82645.

$500 (present value) ÷ $605 (future value) = .82645*
*Present value of $1: $n = 2$, $i = ?$

When you consult the present value table, Table 2, you search row two ($n = 2$) for this value and find it in the 10% column. So the effective interest rate is 10%. Notice that the computed factor value exactly equals the table factor value.[3]

[3]If the calculated factor lies between two table factors, interpolation is useful in finding the unknown value. For example, if the future value in our example is $600, instead of $605, the calculated PV factor is .83333 ($500 ÷ $600). This factor lies between the 9% factor of .84168 and the 10% factor of .82645. The total difference between these factors is .01523 (.84168 − .82645). The difference between the calculated factor of .83333 and the 10% factor of .82645 is .00688. This is 45% of the difference between the 9% and 10% factors:

$$\frac{.00688}{.01523} = .45$$

Therefore, the interpolated interest rate is 9.55% (10 − .45).

## Determining the Unknown Number of Periods

You want to invest $10,000 today to accumulate $16,000 for graduate school. If you can invest at an interest rate of 10% compounded annually, how many years will it take to accumulate the required amount?

**ILLUSTRATION 6–2**
Determining $n$ When PV, FV, and $i$ Are Known

The following time diagram illustrates the situation:

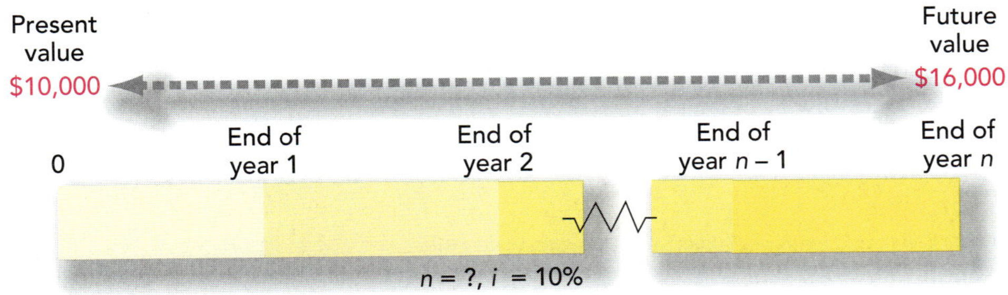


The number of years is the value of $n$ that will provide a present value of $10,000 when discounting $16,000 at a rate of 10%:

$10,000 (present value) = $16,000 (future value) × ?*
*Present value of $1; $n$ = ?, $i$ = 10%

The unknown variable is the number of periods.

Rearranging algebraically, we find that the present value table factor is .625.

$10,000 (present value) ÷ $16,000 (future value) = .625*
*Present value of $1: $n$ = ?, $i$ = 10%

When you consult the present value table, Table 2, you search the 10% column ($i$ = 10%) for this value and find .62092 in row five. So it would take approximately five years to accumulate $16,000 in the situation described.

**ADDITIONAL CONSIDERATION**

Solving for the unknown factor in either of these examples could just as easily be done using the future value tables. The number of years is the value of $n$ that will provide a present value of $10,000 when discounting $16,000 at a discount rate of 10%.

$16,000 (future value) = $10,000 (present value) × ?*
*Future value of $1: $n$ = ?, $i$ = 10%

Rearranging algebraically, the future value table factor is 1.6.

$16,000 (future value) ÷ $10,000 (present value) = 1.6*
*Future value of $1: $n$ = ?, $i$ = 10%

When you consult the future value table, Table 1, you search the 10% column ($i$ = 10%) for this value and find 1.61051 in row five. So it would take approximately five years to accumulate $16,000 in the situation described.

## CONCEPT REVIEW EXERCISE

**VALUING A SINGLE CASH FLOW AMOUNT**

Using the appropriate table, answer each of the following independent questions.

1. What is the future value of $5,000 at the end of six periods at 8% compound interest?
2. What is the present value of $8,000 to be received eight periods from today assuming a compound interest rate of 12%?

3. What is the present value of $10,000 to be received two *years* from today assuming an annual interest rate of 24% and *monthly* compounding?
4. If an investment of $2,000 grew to $2,520 in three periods, what is the interest rate at which the investment grew? Solve using both present and future value tables.
5. Approximately how many years would it take for an investment of $5,250 to accumulate to $15,000, assuming interest is compounded at 10% annually? Solve using both present and future value tables.

**SOLUTION**

1. FV = $5,000 × 1.58687* = $7,934

   *Future value of $1: $n = 6$, $i = 8\%$ (from Table 1)
2. PV = $8,000 × .40388* = $3,231

   *Present value of $1: $n = 8$, $i = 12\%$ (from Table 2)
3. PV = $10,000 × .62172* = $6,217

   *Present value of $1: $n = 24$, $i = 2\%$ (from Table 2)
4. Using present value table,

   $$\frac{\$2{,}000}{\$2{,}520} = .7937^*$$

   *Present value of $1: $n = 3$, $i = ?$ (from Table 2, $i$ approximately **8%**)

   Using future value table,

   $$\frac{\$2{,}520}{\$2{,}000} = 1.260^*$$

   *Future value of $1: $n = 3$, $i = ?$ (from Table 1, $i$ approximately **8%**)
5. Using present value table,

   $$\frac{\$5{,}250}{\$15{,}000} = .35^*$$

   *Present value of $1: $n = ?$, $i = 10\%$ (from Table 2, $n$ approximately **11 years**)

   Using future value table,

   $$\frac{\$15{,}000}{\$5{,}250} = 2.857^*$$

   *Future value of $1: $n = ?$. $i = 10\%$ (from Table 1, $n$ approximately **11 years**)

## Preview of Accounting Applications of Present Value Techniques—Single Cash Amount

Kile Petersen switched off his television set immediately after watching the Super Bowl game and swore to himself that this would be the last year he would watch the game on his 10-year-old 20-inch TV set. "Next year, a big screen TV," he promised himself. Soon after, he saw an advertisement in the local newspaper from Slim Jim's TV and Appliance offering a Philips 60-inch large screen television on sale for $1,800. And the best part of the deal was that Kile could take delivery immediately but would not have to pay the $1,800 for one whole year! "In a year, I can easily save the $1,800," he thought.

In the above scenario, the seller, Slim Jim's TV and Appliance, records a sale when the TV is delivered to Kile. How should the company value its receivable and corresponding sales revenue? We provide a solution to this question at the end of this section on page 276. The following discussion will help you to understand that solution.

*Monetary assets and monetary liabilities* **are valued at the present value of future cash flows.**

Many assets and most liabilities are monetary in nature. **Monetary assets** include money and claims to receive money, the amount of which is fixed or determinable. Examples include cash and most receivables. **Monetary liabilities** are obligations to pay amounts of cash, the amount of which is fixed or determinable. Most liabilities are monetary. For example, if you borrow money from a bank and sign a note payable, the amount of cash to be repaid to the bank is fixed. Monetary receivables and payables are valued based on the fixed amount of cash to be received or paid in the future with proper reflection of the time value of money. In other words, we value most receivables and payables at the present value of future cash flows, reflecting an appropriate time value of money.[4]

The example in Illustration 6–3 demonstrates this concept.

[4] "Interest on Receivables and Payables," *Accounting Principles Board Opinion No. 21* (New York: AICPA, 1971).

**Explicit Interest**
The Stridewell Wholesale Shoe Company manufactures athletic shoes for sale to retailers. The company recently sold a large order of shoes to Harmon Sporting Goods for $50,000. Stridewell agreed to accept a note in payment for the shoes requiring payment of $50,000 in one year plus interest at 10%.

**ILLUSTRATION 6–3**
Valuing a Note: One Payment, Explicit Interest

How should Stridewell value the note receivable and corresponding sales revenue earned? How should Harmon value the note payable and corresponding inventory purchased? As long as the interest rate explicitly stated in the agreement properly reflects the time value of money, the answer is $50,000, the face value of the note. It's important to realize that this amount also equals the present value of future cash flows at 10%. Future cash flows equal $55,000, $50,000 in note principal plus $5,000 in interest ($50,000 × 10%). Using a time diagram:

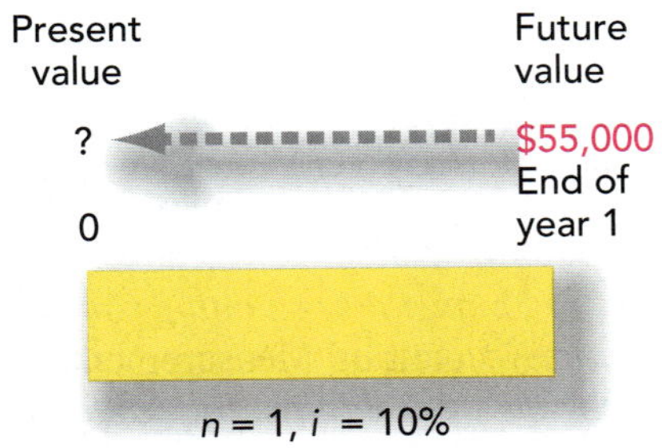


In equation form, we can solve for present value as follows:

$55,000 (future value) × .90909* = $50,000 (present value)
*Present value of $1: $n = 1$, $i = 10\%$

By calculating the present value of $55,000 to be received in one year, the interest of $5,000 is removed from the future value, resulting in a proper note receivable/sales revenue value of $50,000 for Stridewell and a $50,000 note payable/inventory value for Harmon.

While most notes, loans, and mortgages explicitly state an interest rate that will properly reflect the time value of money, there can be exceptions. Consider the example in Illustration 6–4.

**No Explicit Interest**
The Stridewell Wholesale Shoe Company recently sold a large order of shoes to Harmon Sporting Goods. Terms of the sale require Harmon to sign a noninterest-bearing note of $60,500 with payment due in two years.

**ILLUSTRATION 6–4**
Valuing a Note: One Payment, No Explicit Interest

How should Stridewell and Harmon value the note receivable/payable and corresponding sales revenue/inventory? Even though the agreement states a noninterest-bearing note, the $60,500 does, in fact, include interest for the two-year period of the loan. We need to remove the interest portion of the $60,500 to determine the portion that represents the sales price of the shoes. We do this by computing the present value. The following time diagram illustrates the situation assuming that a rate of 10% reflects the appropriate interest rate for a loan of this type:

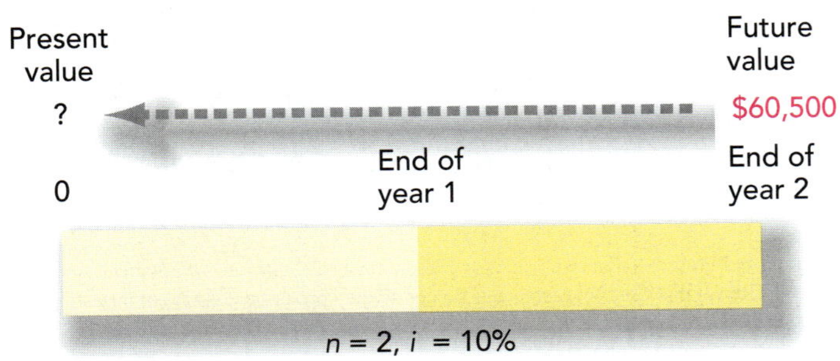

Again, using the present value of $1 table,

$60,500 (future value) × .82645* = $50,000 (present value)
*Present value of $1: $n = 2$, $i = 10\%$

Both the note receivable for Stridewell and the note payable for Harmon initially will be valued at $50,000. The difference of $10,500 ($60,500 − 50,000) represents interest revenue/expense to be recognized over the life of the note. The appropriate journal entries are illustrated in later chapters.

Now can you answer the question posed in the scenario at the beginning of this section? Assuming that a rate of 10% reflects the appropriate interest rate in this situation, Slim Jim's TV and Appliance records a receivable and sales revenue of $1,636 which is the present value of the $1,800 to be received from Kile Petersen one year from the date of sale.

$1,800 (future value) × .90909* = $1,636 (present value)
*Present value of $1: $n = 1$, $i = 10\%$ (from Table 2)

## Expected Cash Flow Approach

***SFAC No. 7***

***SFAC No. 7* provides a framework for using future cash flows in accounting measurements.**

Present value measurement has long been integrated with accounting valuation and is specifically addressed in several accounting standards. Because of its increased importance, the FASB in 2000 issued *Statement of Financial Accounting Concepts No. 7*, "Using Cash Flow Information and Present Value in Accounting Measurements."[5] This statement provides a framework for using future cash flows as the basis for accounting measurement and asserts that the objective in valuing an asset or liability using present value is to approximate the fair value of that asset or liability. Key to that objective is determining the present value of future cash flows associated with the asset or liability, *taking into account any uncertainty concerning the amounts and timing of the cash flows.* Although future cash flows in many instances are contractual and certain, the amounts and timing of cash flows are less certain in other situations.

For example, lease payments are provided in the contract between lessor and lessee. On the other hand, the future cash flows to be paid to settle a pending lawsuit may be highly uncertain. Traditionally, the way uncertainty has been considered in present value calculations has been by discounting the "best estimate" of future cash flows applying a discount rate that has been adjusted to reflect the uncertainty or risk of those cash flows. With the approach described by *SFAC No. 7,* though, the adjustment for uncertainty or risk of cash flows is applied to the cash flows, not the discount rate. This new *expected cash flow approach* incorporates specific probabilities of cash flows into the analysis. Consider Illustration 6–5.

Compare the approach described in Illustration 6–5 to the traditional approach that uses the present value of the most likely estimate of $200 million and ignores information about cash flow probabilities.

**The risk-free rate of interest is used when applying the expected cash flow approach to the calculation of present value.**

The discount rate used to determine present value when applying the expected cash flow approach should be the *risk-free rate of interest*. Other elements of uncertainty are incorporated into the determination of the probability-weighted expected cash flows. In the traditional approach, elements of uncertainty are incorporated into a risk-adjusted discount rate.

> ***SFAC NO. 7***
> "While many accountants do not routinely use the expected cash flow approach, expected cash flows are inherent in the techniques used in some accounting measurements, like pensions, other postretirement benefits, and some insurance obligations."[6]

The FASB expects that the traditional approach to calculating present value will continue to be used in many situations, particularly those where future cash flows are contractual. The Board also believes that the expected cash flow approach is more appropriate in more complex situa-

[5]"Using Cash Flow Information and Present Value in Accounting Measurements," *Statement of Financial Accounting Concepts No. 7* (Norwalk, Conn.: FASB, 2000). Recall that Concept Statements do not directly prescribe GAAP, but instead provide structure and direction to financial accounting.
[6]Ibid., para. 48.

**ILLUSTRATION 6–5**
Expected Cash Flow Approach

LDD Corporation faces the likelihood of having to pay an uncertain amount in five years in connection with an environmental cleanup. The future cash flow estimate is in the range of $100 million to $300 million with the following estimated probabilities:

| Loss Amount | Probability |
|---|---|
| $100 million | 10% |
| $200 million | 60% |
| $300 million | 30% |

The expected cash flow, then, is $220 million:

| | |
|---|---|
| $100 × 10% = | $ 10 million |
| 200 × 60% = | 120 million |
| 300 × 30% = | 90 million |
| | $220 million |

If the risk-free rate of interest is 5%, LDD will report a liability of $172,376,600, the present value of the expected cash outflow:

| |
|---|
| $220,000,000 |
| × .78353* |
| $172,376,600 |

*Present value of $1, $n = 5$, $i = 5\%$ (from Table 2)

tions. In fact, the Board has incorporated the concepts developed in *SFAC No. 7* into recent standards on asset retirement obligations, impairment losses, and business combinations. In Chapter 10 we illustrate the use of the expected cash flow approach as it would be applied to the measurement of an asset retirement obligation. In Chapter 13, we use the approach to measure the liability associated with a loss contingency.

## Basic Annuities

**PART B**

● LO5

The previous examples involved the receipt or payment of a single future amount. Financial instruments frequently involve multiple receipts or payments of cash. If the same amount is to be received or paid each period, the cash flows are referred to as an **annuity.** A common annuity encountered in practice is a loan on which periodic interest is paid in equal amounts. For example, bonds typically pay interest semiannually in an amount determined by multiplying a stated rate by a fixed principal amount. Some loans and most leases are paid in equal installments during a specified period of time.

*In an ordinary annuity cash flows occur at the end of each period.*

An agreement that creates an annuity can produce either an **ordinary annuity** or an **annuity due** (sometimes referred to as an annuity in advance) situation. The first cash flow (receipt or payment) of an ordinary annuity is made one compounding period *after* the date on which the agreement begins. The final cash flow takes place on the *last* day covered by the agreement. For example, an installment note payable dated December 31, 2006, might require the debtor to make three equal annual payments, with the first payment due on December 31, 2007, and the last one on December 31, 2009. The following time diagram illustrates an ordinary annuity:

*Ordinary annuity.*

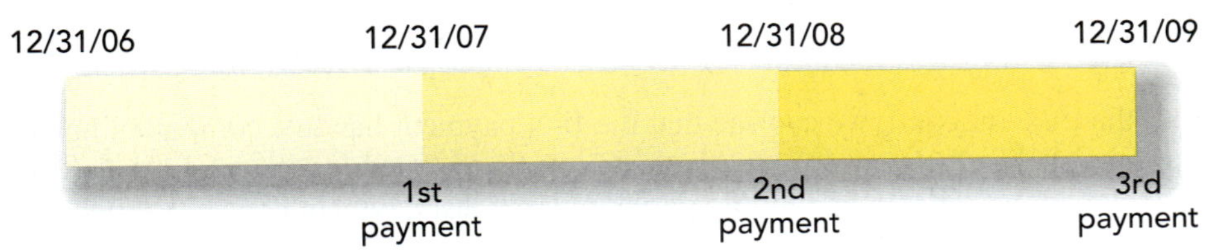


*In an annuity due cash flows occur at the beginning of each period.*

The first payment of an annuity due is made on the *first* day of the agreement, and the last payment is made one period *before* the end of the agreement. For example, a three-year lease of a building that begins on December 31, 2006, and ends on December 31, 2009, may require the first year's lease payment in advance on December 31, 2006. The third and last payment would take place on December 31, 2008, the beginning of the third year of the lease. The following time diagram illustrates this situation:

Annuity due.

## Future Value of an Annuity

### FUTURE VALUE OF AN ORDINARY ANNUITY

Let's first consider the future value of an ordinary annuity in Illustration 6–6.

**ILLUSTRATION 6–6**
Future Value of an Ordinary Annuity

Sally Rogers wants to accumulate a sum of money to pay for graduate school. Rather than investing a single amount today that will grow to a future value, she decides to invest $10,000 a year over the next three years in a savings account paying 10% interest compounded annually. She decides to make the first payment to the bank one year from today.

The following time diagram illustrates this ordinary annuity situation. Time 0 is the start of the first period.

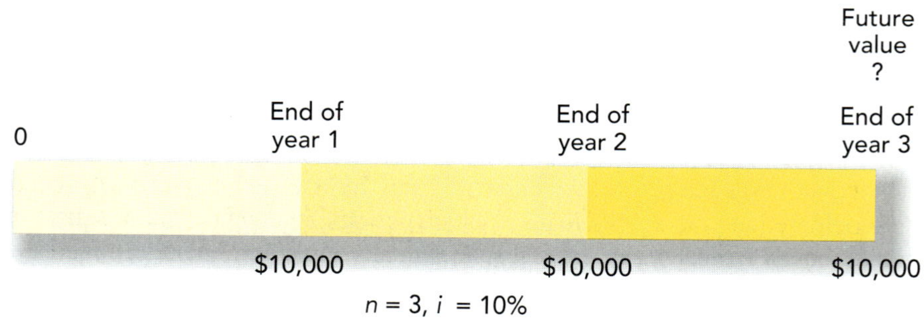


Using the FV of $1 factors from Table 1, we can calculate the future value of this annuity by calculating the future value of each of the individual payments as follows:

| | Payment | | FV of $1 $i$ = 10% | | Future Value (at the end of year 3) | $n$ |
|---|---|---|---|---|---|---|
| First payment | $10,000 | × | 1.21 | = | $12,100 | 2 |
| Second payment | 10,000 | × | 1.10 | = | 11,000 | 1 |
| Third payment | 10,000 | × | 1.00 | = | 10,000 | 0 |
| Total | | | 3.31 | | $33,100 | |

In the future value of an ordinary annuity, the last cash payment will not earn any interest.

From the time diagram, we can see that the first payment has two compounding periods to earn interest. The factor used, 1.21, is the FV of $1 invested for two periods at 10%. The second payment has one compounding period and the last payment does not earn any interest because it is invested on the last day of the three-year annuity period. Therefore, the factor used is 1.00.

● LO6

This illustration shows that it's possible to calculate the future value of the annuity by separately calculating the FV of each payment and then adding these amounts together. Fortunately, that's not necessary. Table 3, Future Value of an Ordinary Annuity, located at the end of this textbook simplifies the computation by summing the individual FV of $1 factors for various factors of *n* and *i*. Graphic 6–3 contains an excerpt from Table 3.

**GRAPHIC 6–3**
Future Value of an Ordinary Annuity of $1 (excerpt from Table 3)

| | Interest Rates (*i*) | | | | | |
|---|---|---|---|---|---|---|
| **Periods (*n*)** | **7%** | **8%** | **9%** | **10%** | **11%** | **12%** |
| 1 | 1.0000 | 1.0000 | 1.0000 | 1.0000 | 1.0000 | 1.0000 |
| 2 | 2.0700 | 2.0800 | 2.0900 | 2.1000 | 2.1100 | 2.1200 |
| 3 | 3.2149 | 3.2464 | 3.2781 | 3.3100 | 3.3421 | 3.3744 |
| 4 | 4.4399 | 4.5061 | 4.5731 | 4.6410 | 4.7097 | 4.7793 |
| 5 | 5.7507 | 5.8666 | 5.9847 | 6.1051 | 6.2278 | 6.3528 |
| 6 | 7.1533 | 7.3359 | 7.5233 | 7.7156 | 7.9129 | 8.1152 |
| 7 | 8.6540 | 8.9228 | 9.2004 | 9.4872 | 9.7833 | 10.0890 |
| 8 | 10.2598 | 10.6366 | 11.0285 | 11.4359 | 11.8594 | 12.2997 |

The future value of $1 at the end of each of three periods invested at 10% is shown in Table 3 to be $3.31. We can simply multiply this factor by $10,000 to derive the FV of our ordinary annuity (FVA):

FVA = $10,000 (annuity amount) × 3.31* = $33,100

*Future value of an ordinary annuity of $1: *n* = 3, *i* = 10%

## FUTURE VALUE OF AN ANNUITY DUE

Let's modify the previous illustration to create an annuity due in Illustration 6–7.

**ILLUSTRATION 6–7**
Future Value of an Annuity Due

Sally Rogers wants to accumulate a sum of money to pay for graduate school. Rather than investing a single amount today that will grow to a future value, she decides to invest $10,000 a year over the next three years in a savings account paying 10% interest compounded annually. She decides to make the first payment to the bank immediately. How much will Sally have available in her account at the end of three years?

The following time diagram depicts the situation. Again, note that 0 is the start of the first period.

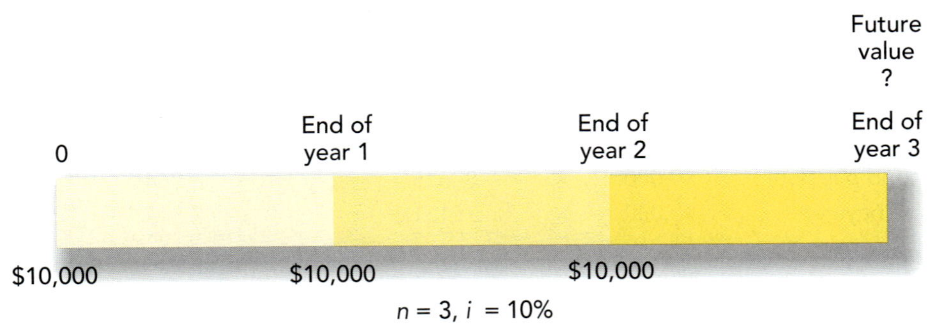


The future value can be found by separately calculating the FV of each of the three payments and then summing those individual future values:

**In the future value of an annuity due, the last cash payment will earn interest.**

| | Payment | | FV of $1 $i$ = 10% | | Future Value (at the end of year 3) | $n$ |
|---|---|---|---|---|---|---|
| First payment | $10,000 | × | 1.331 | = | $13,310 | 3 |
| Second payment | 10,000 | × | 1.210 | = | 12,100 | 2 |
| Third payment | 10,000 | × | 1.100 | = | 11,000 | 1 |
| Total | | | 3.641 | | $36,410 | |

And, again, this same future value can be found by using the future value of an annuity due (FVAD) factor from Table 5, Future Value of an Annuity Due, located at the end of this textbook, as follows:

FVAD = $10,000 (annuity amount) × 3.641* = $36,410

*Future value of an annuity due of $1: $n$ = 3, $i$ = 10%

Of course, if *unequal* amounts are invested each year, we can't solve the problem by using the annuity tables. The future value of each payment would have to be calculated separately.

## Present Value of an Annuity

### PRESENT VALUE OF AN ORDINARY ANNUITY

LO7

You will learn in later chapters that liabilities and receivables, with the exception of certain trade receivables and payables, are reported in financial statements at their present values. Most of these financial instruments specify equal periodic interest payments or installment payments. As a result, the most common accounting applications of the time value of money involve determining present value of annuities. As in the future value applications we discussed above, an annuity can be either an ordinary annuity or an annuity due. Let's look at an ordinary annuity first.

**FINANCIAL REPORTING CASE**

Q1, p. 267

On page 278, we determined that Sally Rogers could accumulate $33,100 for graduate school by investing $10,000 at the end of each of three years at 10%. The $33,100 is the future value of the ordinary annuity described. Another alternative is to invest one single amount at the beginning of the three-year period. (See Illustration 6–8.) This single amount will equal the present value at the beginning of the three-year period of the $33,100 future value. It will also equal the present value of the $10,000 three-year annuity.

**ILLUSTRATION 6–8**
Present Value of an Ordinary Annuity

Sally Rogers wants to accumulate a sum of money to pay for graduate school. She wants to invest a single amount today in a savings account earning 10% interest compounded annually that is equivalent to investing $10,000 at the end of each of the next three years.

The present value can be found by separately calculating the PV of each of the three payments and then summing those individual present values:

| | Payment | | PV of $1 $i$ = 10% | | Present Value (at the beginning of year 1) | $n$ |
|---|---|---|---|---|---|---|
| First payment | $10,000 | × | .90909 | = | $ 9,091 | 1 |
| Second payment | 10,000 | × | .82645 | = | 8,264 | 2 |
| Third payment | 10,000 | × | .75131 | = | 7,513 | 3 |
| Total | | | 2.48685 | | $24,868 | |

A more efficient method of calculating present value is to use Table 4, Present Value of an Ordinary Annuity, located at the end of this textbook. Graphic 6–4 contains an excerpt from Table 4.

Using Table 4, we calculate the PV of the ordinary annuity (PVA) as follows:

PVA = $10,000 (annuity amount) × 2.48685* = $24,868

*Present value of an ordinary annuity of $1: $n$ = 3, $i$ = 10%

**GRAPHIC 6–4**
Present Value of an Ordinary Annuity of $1 (excerpt from Table 4)

| | Interest Rates (*i*) | | | | | |
|---|---|---|---|---|---|---|
| **Periods (*n*)** | **7%** | **8%** | **9%** | **10%** | **11%** | **12%** |
| 1 | 0.93458 | 0.92593 | 0.91743 | 0.90909 | 0.90090 | 0.89286 |
| 2 | 1.80802 | 1.78326 | 1.75911 | 1.73554 | 1.71252 | 1.69005 |
| 3 | 2.62432 | 2.57710 | 2.53129 | 2.48685 | 2.44371 | 2.40183 |
| 4 | 3.38721 | 3.31213 | 3.23972 | 3.16987 | 3.10245 | 3.03735 |
| 5 | 4.10020 | 3.99271 | 3.88965 | 3.79079 | 3.69590 | 3.60478 |
| 6 | 4.76654 | 4.62288 | 4.48592 | 4.35526 | 4.23054 | 4.11141 |
| 7 | 5.38929 | 5.20637 | 5.03295 | 4.86842 | 4.71220 | 4.56376 |
| 8 | 5.97130 | 5.74664 | 5.53482 | 5.33493 | 5.14612 | 4.96764 |

## ADDITIONAL CONSIDERATION

As previously mentioned, financial calculators can be used to solve future and present value problems. For example, a Texas Instruments model BA-35 has the following pertinent keys:

N  % *i*  PV  FV  PMT  CPT

These keys are defined as follows:

N = Number of periods
% *i* = Interest rate
PV = Present value
FV = Future value
PMT = Annuity payments
CPT = Compute button

To illustrate its use, assume that you need to determine the present value of a 10-period ordinary annuity of $200 using a 10% interest rate. You would enter 10 = *N*, 10 = % *i*, 200 = PMT, then press CPT and PV to obtain the answer of $1,229.

Many professionals choose to use spreadsheet software, such as Excel, to solve time value of money problems. These spreadsheets can be used in a variety of ways. A template can be created using the formulas shown in Graphic 6–5 on page 291. An alternative is to use the software's built-in financial functions. For example, Excel has a function called PV that calculates the present value of an ordinary annuity. To use the function, you would select the pull-down menu for "insert," click on "function" and choose the category called "financial." Scroll down to PV and double click. You will then be asked to input the necessary variables—interest rate, the number of periods, and the payment amount.

The relationship between the present value and the future value of the annuity can be depicted graphically as follows:

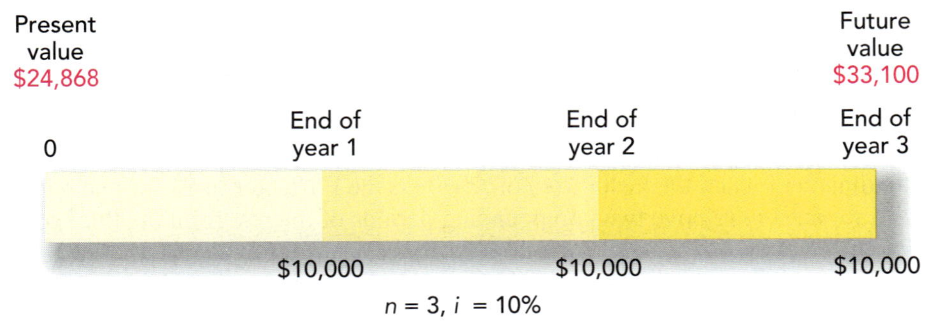


Relationship between present value and future value—ordinary annuity

This can be interpreted in several ways:

1. $10,000 invested at 10% at the end of each of the next three years will accumulate to $33,100 at the end of the third year.
2. $24,868 invested at 10% now will grow to $33,100 after three years.
3. Someone whose time value of money is 10% would be willing to pay $24,868 now to receive $10,000 at the end of each of the next three years.
4. If your time value of money is 10%, you should be indifferent with respect to paying/receiving (a) $24,868 now, (b) $33,100 three years from now, or (c) $10,000 at the end of each of the next three years.

**ADDITIONAL CONSIDERATION**

We also can verify that these are the present value and future value of the same annuity by calculating the present value of a single cash amount of $33,100 three years hence:

$$PV = \$33{,}100 \text{ (future value)} \times .75131^* = \$24{,}868$$

*Present value of $1: $n = 3$, $i = 10\%$

## PRESENT VALUE OF AN ANNUITY DUE

**ILLUSTRATION 6–9**
Present Value of an Annuity Due

In the previous illustration, suppose that the three equal payments of $10,000 are to be made at the *beginning* of each of the three years. Recall from the illustration on page 280 that the future value of this annuity is $36,410. What is the present value?

The following time diagram depicts this situation:

Present value of an annuity due.

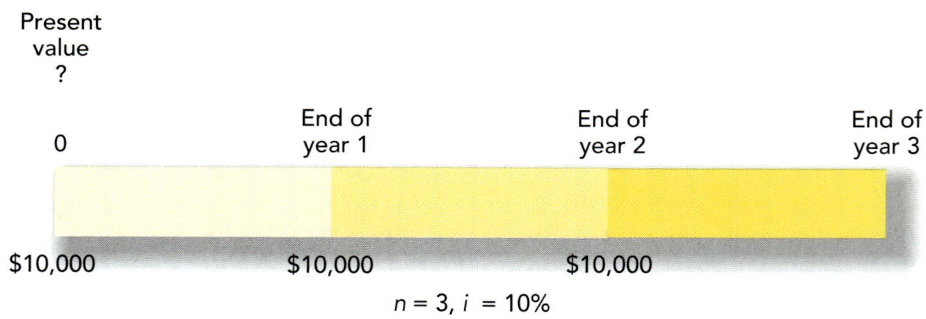


Once again, using individual PV factors of $1 from Table 2, the PV of the annuity due can be calculated as follows:

| | Payment | | PV of $1 $i = 10\%$ | | Present Value (at the beginning of year 1) | $n$ |
|---|---|---|---|---|---|---|
| First payment | $10,000 | × | 1.00000 | = | $10,000 | 0 |
| Second payment | 10,000 | × | .90909 | = | 9,091 | 1 |
| Third payment | 10,000 | × | .82645 | = | 8,264 | 2 |
| Total | | | 2.73554 | | $27,355 | |

In the present value of an annuity due, no interest needs to be removed from the first cash payment.

The first payment does not contain any interest since it is made on the first day of the three-year annuity period. Therefore, the factor used is 1.00. The second payment has one compounding period and the factor used of .90909 is the PV factor of $1 for one period and 10%, and we need to remove two compounding periods of interest from the third payment. The factor used of .82645 is the PV factor of $1 for two periods and 10%.

The relationship between the present value and the future value of the annuity can be depicted graphically as follows:

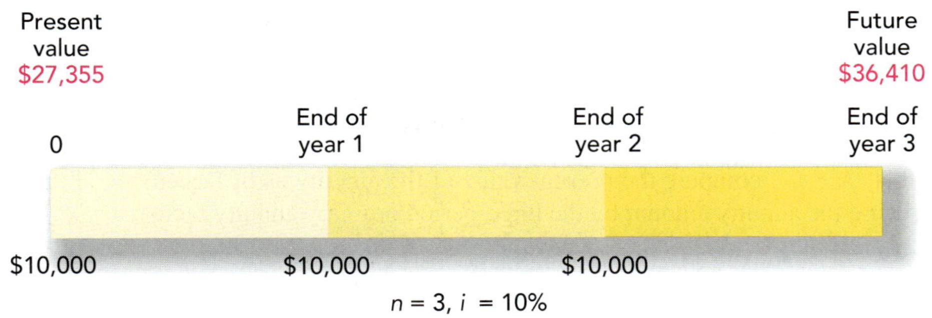


**Relationship between present value and future value—annuity due.**

Using Table 6, Present Value of an Annuity Due, located at the end of this book, we can more efficiently calculate the PV of the annuity due (PVAD):

$$PVAD = \$10{,}000 \text{ (annuity amount)} \times 2.73554^* = \$27{,}355$$

*Present value of an annuity due of $1: $n = 3$, $i = 10\%$

To better understand the relationship between Tables 4 and 6, notice that the PVAD factor for three periods, 10%, from Table 6 is 2.73554. This is simply the PVA factor for two periods, 10%, of 1.73554, plus 1.0. The addition of 1.0 reflects the fact that the first payment does not require the removal of any interest.

## PRESENT VALUE OF A DEFERRED ANNUITY

**A *deferred annuity* exists when the first cash flow occurs more than one period after the date the agreement begins.**

Accounting valuations often involve the present value of annuities in which the first cash flow is expected to occur more than one time period after the date of the agreement. As the inception of the annuity is deferred beyond a single period, this type of annuity is referred to as a **deferred annuity**.[7]

At January 1, 2006, you are considering acquiring an investment that will provide three equal payments of $10,000 each to be received at the end of three consecutive years. However, the first payment is not expected until *December 31, 2008*. The time value of money is 10%. How much would you be willing to pay for this investment?

**ILLUSTRATION 6–10**
Deferred Annuity

The following time diagram depicts this situation:

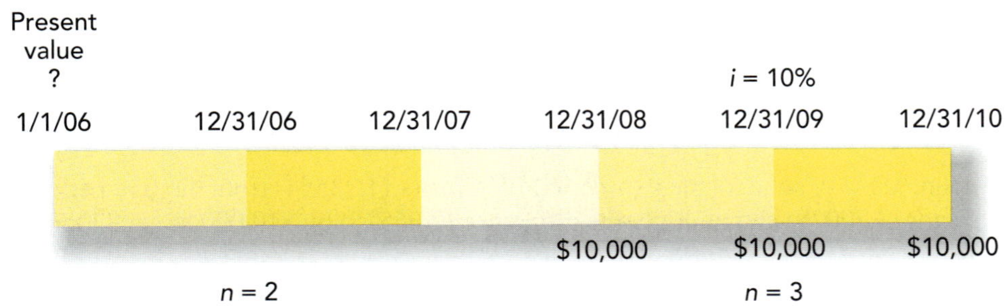


**Cash flows for a deferred annuity.**

The present value of the annuity can be calculated by summing the present values of the three individual cash flows, each discounted to today's PV:

| | Payment | | PV of \$1 $i = 10\%$ | | Present Value | $n$ |
|---|---|---|---|---|---|---|
| First payment | \$10,000 | × | .75131 | = | \$ 7,513 | 3 |
| Second payment | 10,000 | × | .68301 | = | 6,830 | 4 |
| Third payment | 10,000 | × | .62092 | = | 6,209 | 5 |
| | | | | | \$20,552 | |

[7]The future value of a deferred annuity is the same as the future amount of an annuity not deferred. That is because there are no interest compounding periods prior to the beginning of the annuity period.

A more efficient way of calculating the present value of a deferred annuity involves a two-step process:

1. Calculate the PV of the annuity as of the beginning of the annuity period.
2. Discount the single amount calculated in (1) to its present value *as of today.*

In this case, we compute the present value of the annuity as of December 31, 2007, by multiplying the annuity amount by the three-period ordinary annuity factor:

PVA = \$10,000 (annuity amount) × 2.48685* = \$24,868
*Present value of an ordinary annuity of \$1: $n = 3$, $i = 10\%$

This is the present value as of December 31, 2007. This single amount is then reduced to present value as of January 1, 2006, by making the following calculation:

PV = \$24,868 (future amount) × .82645* = \$20,552
*Present value of \$1: $n = 2$, $i = 10\%$

The following time diagram illustrates this two-step process:

**Present value of a deferred annuity—two-step process.**

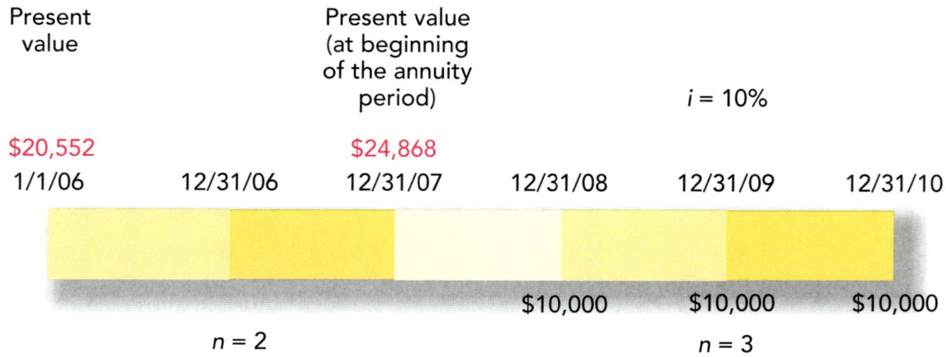


If you recall the concepts you learned in this chapter, you might think of other ways the present value of a deferred annuity can be determined. Among them:

1. Calculate the PV of an annuity due, rather than an ordinary annuity, and then discount that amount three periods rather than two:

   PVAD = \$10,000 (annuity amount) × 2.73554* = \$27,355
   *Present value of an annuity due of \$1: $n = 3$, $i = 10\%$

   This is the present value as of December 31, 2008. This single amount is then reduced to present value as of January 1, 2006 by making the following calculation:

   PV = \$27,355 × .75131* = \$20,552
   *Present value of \$1: $n = 3$, $i = 10\%$

2. From Table 4, subtract the two-period PVA factor (1.73554) from the five-period PVA factor (3.79079) and multiply the difference (2.05525) by \$10,000 to get \$20,552.

## Solving for Unknown Values in Present Value Situations

● LO8

In present value problems involving annuities, there are four variables: (1) present value of an ordinary annuity (PVA) or present value of an annuity due (PVAD), (2) the amount of each annuity payment, (3) the number of periods, *n*, and (4) the interest rate, *i*. If you know any three of these, the fourth can be determined.

**ILLUSTRATION 6–11**
Determining the Annuity Amount When Other Variables Are Known

Assume that you borrow \$700 from a friend and intend to repay the amount in four equal annual installments beginning one year from today. Your friend wishes to be reimbursed for the time value of money at an 8% annual rate. What is the required annual payment that must be made (the annuity amount), to repay the loan in four years?

The following time diagram illustrates the situation:

Determining the unknown annuity amount—ordinary annuity

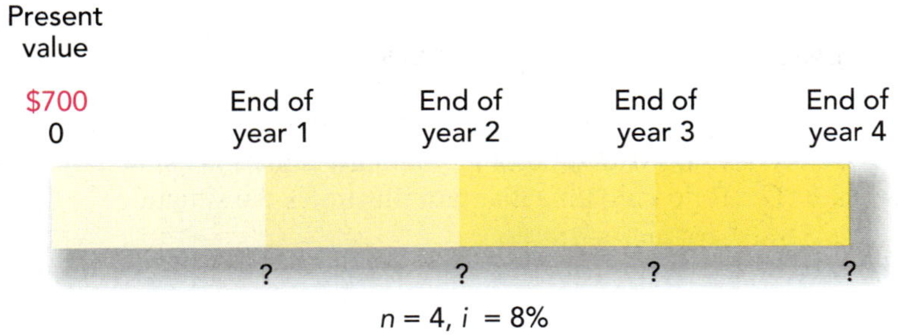


The required payment is the annuity amount that will provide a present value of $700 when discounting that amount at a discount rate of 8%:

The unknown variable is the annuity amount.

$700 (present value) = 3.31213* × annuity amount

Rearranging algebraically, we find that the annuity amount is $211.34.

$700 (present value) ÷ 3.31213* = $211.34 (annuity amount)
*Present value of an ordinary annuity of $1: $n = 4$, $i = 8\%$

You would have to make four annual payments of $211.34 to repay the loan. Total payments of $845.36 (4 × $211.34) would include $145.36 in interest ($845.36 − 700.00).

**ILLUSTRATION 6–12**
Determining $n$ When Other Variables Are Known

Assume that you borrow $700 from a friend and intend to repay the amount in equal installments of $100 per year over a period of years. The payments will be made at the end of each year beginning one year from now. Your friend wishes to be reimbursed for the time value of money at a 7% annual rate. How many years would it take before you repaid the loan?

Once again, this is an ordinary annuity situation because the first payment takes place one year from now. The following time diagram illustrates the situation:

Determining the unknown number of periods—ordinary annuity

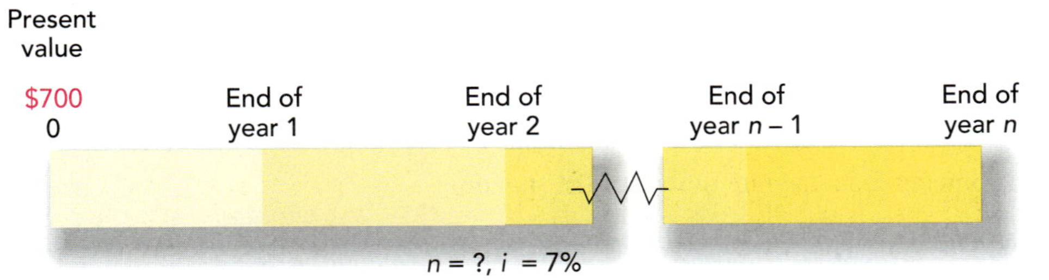


The number of years is the value of $n$ that will provide a present value of $700 when discounting $100 at a discount rate of 7%:

The unknown variable is the number of periods.

$700 (present value) = $100 (annuity amount) × ?*
*Present value of an ordinary annuity of $1: $n$ = ?, $i = 7\%$

Rearranging algebraically, we find that the PVA table factor is 7.0.

$700 (present value) ÷ $100 (annuity amount) = 7.0*
*Present value of an ordinary annuity of $1: $n$ = ?, $i = 7\%$

When you consult the PVA table, Table 4, you search the 7% column ($i = 7\%$) for this value and find 7.02358 in row 10. So it would take approximately 10 years to repay the loan in the situation described.

**ILLUSTRATION 6–13**
**Determining *i* When Other Variables Are Known**

Suppose that a friend asked to borrow $331 today (present value) and promised to repay you $100 (the annuity amount) at the end of each of the next four years. What is the annual interest rate implicit in this agreement?

**FINANCIAL REPORTING CASE**
Q2, p. 267

First of all, we are dealing with an ordinary annuity situation as the payments are at the end of each period. The following time diagram illustrates the situation:

*Determining the unknown interest rate—ordinary annuity.*

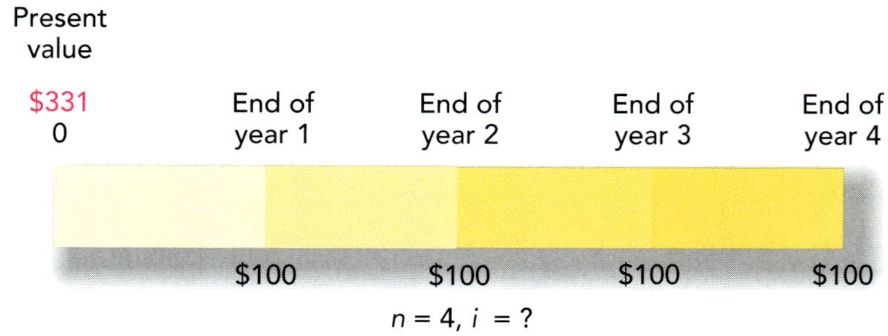


The interest rate is the discount rate that will provide a present value of $331 when discounting the $100 four-year ordinary annuity:

*The unknown variable is the interest rate.*

$331 (present value) = $100 (annuity amount) × ?*
*Present value of an ordinary annuity of $1: $n = 4, i = ?$

Rearranging algebraically, we find that the PVA table factor is 3.31.

$331 (present value) ÷ $100 (annuity amount) = 3.31*
*Present value of an ordinary annuity of $1: $n = 4, i = ?$

When you consult the PVA table, Table 4, you search row four ($n = 4$) for this value and find it in the 8% column. So the effective interest rate is 8%.

**ILLUSTRATION 6–14**
**Determining *i* When Other Variables Are Known—Unequal Cash Flows**

Suppose that you borrowed $400 from a friend and promised to repay the loan by making three annual payments of $100 at the end of each of the next three years plus a final payment of $200 at the end of year four. What is the interest rate implicit in this agreement?

The following time diagram illustrates the situation:

*Determining the unknown interest rate—unequal cash flows*

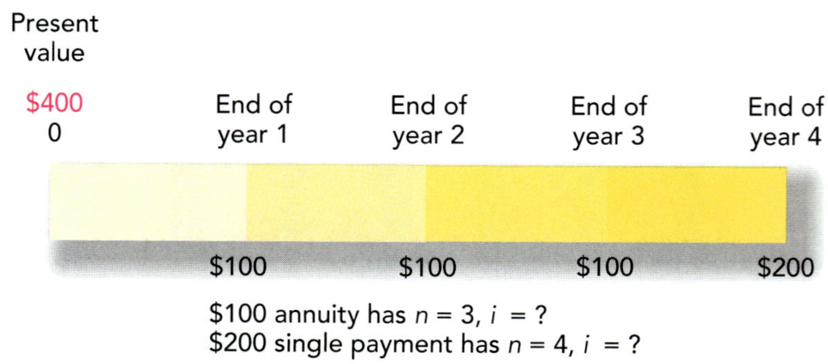


The interest rate is the discount rate that will provide a present value of $400 when discounting the $100 three-year ordinary annuity plus the $200 to be received in four years:

*The unknown variable is the interest rate.*

$400 (present value) = $100 (annuity amount) × ?* + $200 (single payment) × ?†
*Present value of an ordinary annuity of $1: $n = 3, i = ?$
†Present value of $1: $n = 4, i = ?$

This equation involves two unknowns and is not as easily solved as the two previous examples. One way to solve the problem is to trial-and-error the answer. For example, if we assumed $i$ to be 9%, the total PV of the payments would be calculated as follows:

$$PV = \$100\ (2.53129^*) + \$200\ (.70843^\dagger) = \$395$$

*Present value of an ordinary annuity of \$1: $n = 3$, $i = 9\%$
†Present value of \$1: $n = 4$, $i = 9\%$

Because the present value computed is less than the \$400 borrowed, using 9% removes too much interest. Recalculating PV with $i = 8\%$ results in a PV of \$405. This indicates that the interest rate implicit in the agreement is between 8% and 9%.

## Concept Review Exercise

### Annuities

Using the appropriate table, answer each of the following independent questions.

1. What is the future value of an annuity of \$2,000 invested at the *end* of each of the next six periods at 8% interest?
2. What is the future value of an annuity of \$2,000 invested at the *beginning* of each of the next six periods at 8% interest?
3. What is the present value of an annuity of \$6,000 to be received at the *end* of each of the next eight periods assuming an interest rate of 10%?
4. What is the present value of an annuity of \$6,000 to be received at the *beginning* of each of the next eight periods assuming an interest rate of 10%?
5. Jane bought a \$3,000 audio system and agreed to pay for the purchase in 10 equal annual installments of \$408 beginning one year from today. What is the interest rate implicit in this agreement?
6. Jane bought a \$3,000 audio system and agreed to pay for the purchase in 10 equal annual installments beginning one year from today. The interest rate is 12%. What is the amount of the annual installment?
7. Jane bought a \$3,000 audio system and agreed to pay for the purchase by making nine equal annual installments beginning one year from today plus a lump-sum payment of \$1,000 at the end of 10 periods. The interest rate is 10%. What is the required annual installment?
8. Jane bought an audio system and agreed to pay for the purchase by making four equal annual installments of \$800 beginning one year from today plus a lump-sum payment of \$1,000 at the end of five years. The interest rate is 12%. What was the cost of the audio system? (Hint: What is the present value of the cash payments?)
9. Jane bought an audio system and agreed to pay for the purchase by making five equal annual installments of \$1,100 beginning four years from today. The interest rate is 12%. What was the cost of the audio system? (Hint: What is the present value of the cash payments?)

### Solution

1. $FVA = \$2,000 \times 7.3359^* = \$14,672$

   *Future value of an ordinary annuity of \$1: $n = 6$, $i = 8\%$ (from Table 3)

2. $FVAD = \$2,000 \times 7.9228^* = \$15,846$

   *Future value of an annuity due of \$1: $n = 6$, $i = 8\%$ (from Table 5)

3. $PVA = \$6,000 \times 5.33493^* = \$32,010$

   *Present value of ordinary annuity of \$1: $n = 8$, $i = 10\%$ (from Table 4)

4. $PVAD = \$6,000 \times 5.86842^* = \$35,211$

   *Present value of an annuity due of \$1: $n = 8$, $i = 10\%$ (from Table 6)

5. $\dfrac{\$3,000}{\$408} = 7.35^*$

   *Present value of an ordinary annuity of \$1: $n = 10$, $i = ?$ (from Table 4, $i$ approximately 6%)

6. Each annuity payment $= \dfrac{\$3,000}{5.65022^*} = \$531$

   *Present value of an ordinary annuity of \$1: $n = 10$, $i = 12\%$ (from Table 4)

7. $$\text{Each annuity payment} = \frac{\$3{,}000 - [\text{PV of }\$1{,}000\ (n = 10, i = 10\%)]}{5.75902^*}$$

$$\text{Each annuity payment} = \frac{\$3{,}000 - (\$1{,}000 \times .38554^\dagger)}{5.75902^*}$$

$$\text{Each annuity payment} = \frac{\$2{,}614}{5.75902^*} = \$454$$

*Present value of an ordinary annuity of $1: $n = 9$, $i = 10\%$ (from Table 4)
†Present value of $1: $n = 10$, $i = 10\%$ (from Table 2)

8. $PV = \$800 \times 3.03735^* + \$1{,}000 \times .56743^\dagger = \$2{,}997$

*Present value of an ordinary annuity of $1: $n = 4$, $i = 12\%$ (from Table 4)
†Present value of $1: $n = 5$, $i = 12\%$ (from Table 2)

9. $PVA = \$1{,}100 \times 3.60478^* = \$3{,}965$

*Present value of an ordinary annuity of $1: $n = 5$, $i = 12\%$ (from Table 4)

This is the present value three years from today (the beginning of the five-year ordinary annuity). This single amount is then reduced to present value as of today by making the following calculation:

$PV = \$3{,}965 \times .71178^\dagger = \$2{,}822$

†Present value of $1: $n = 3$, $i = 12\%$, (from Table 2)

## Preview of Accounting Applications of Present Value Techniques—Annuities

● LO9

The time value of money has many applications in accounting. Most of these applications involve the concept of present value. Because financial instruments typically specify equal periodic payments, these applications quite often involve annuity situations. For example, let's consider one accounting situation using both an ordinary annuity and the present value of a single amount (long-term bonds), one using an annuity due (long-term leases), and a third using a deferred annuity (pension obligations).

**FINANCIAL REPORTING CASE**

Q3, p. 267

### VALUATION OF LONG-TERM BONDS

You will learn in Chapter 14 that a long-term bond usually requires the issuing (borrowing) company to repay a specified amount at maturity and make periodic stated interest payments over the life of the bond. The *stated* interest payments are equal to the contractual stated rate multiplied by the face value of the bonds. At the date the bonds are issued (sold), the marketplace will determine the price of the bonds based on the *market* rate of interest for investments with similar characteristics. The market rate at date of issuance may not equal the bonds' stated rate in which case the price of the bonds (the amount the issuing company actually is borrowing) will not equal the bonds' face value. Bonds issued at more than face value are said to be issued at a premium, while bonds issued at less than face value are said to be issued at a discount. Consider the example in Illustration 6–15.

**ILLUSTRATION 6–15**
Valuing a Long-Term Bond Liability

On June 30, 2006, Fumatsu Electric issued 10% stated rate bonds with a face amount of $200 million. The bonds mature on June 30, 2026 (20 years). The market rate of interest for similar issues was 12%. Interest is paid semiannually (5%) on June 30 and December 31, beginning December 31, 2006. The interest payment is $10 million (5% × $200 million). What was the price of the bond issue?

To determine the price of the bonds, we calculate the present value of the 40-period annuity (40 semiannual interest payments of $10 million) and the lump-sum payment of $200 million paid at maturity using the semiannual market rate of interest of 6%. In equation form,

$$\text{PVA} = \$10 \text{ million (annuity amount)} \times 15.04630^{*} = \$150{,}463{,}000$$
$$\text{PV} = \$200 \text{ million (lump sum)} \times .09722^{\dagger} = \underline{19{,}444{,}000}$$
$$\text{Price of the bond issue} = \underline{\underline{\$169{,}907{,}000}}$$

*Present value of an ordinary annuity of $1: $n = 40$, $i = 6\%$
†Present value of $1: $n = 40$, $i = 6\%$

The bonds will sell for $169,907,000, which represents a discount of $30,093,000 ($200,000,000 − 169,907,000). The discount results from the difference between the semi-annual stated rate of 5% and the market rate of 6%. Fumatsu records a $169,907,000 increase in cash and a corresponding liability for bonds payable. We discuss and illustrate the specific accounts used to record this transaction in Chapter 14.

## VALUATION OF LONG-TERM LEASES

Companies frequently acquire the use of assets by leasing rather than purchasing them. Leases usually require the payment of fixed amounts at regular intervals over the life of the lease. You will learn in Chapter 15 that certain long-term, noncancelable leases are treated in a manner similar to an installment sale by the lessor and an installment purchase by the lessee. In other words, the lessor records a receivable and the lessee records a liability for the several installment payments. For the lessee, this requires that the leased asset and corresponding lease liability be valued at the present value of the lease payments. Consider the example in Illustration 6–16.

On January 1, 2006, the Stridewell Wholesale Shoe Company signed a 25-year noncancelable lease agreement for an office building. Terms of the lease call for Stridewell to make annual lease payments of $10,000 at the *beginning* of each year, with the first payment due on January 1, 2006. Assuming an interest rate of 10% properly reflects the time value of money in this situation, how should Stridewell value the asset acquired and the corresponding lease liability if it is to be treated in a manner similar to an installment purchase?

**ILLUSTRATION 6–16**
Valuing a Long-Term Lease Liability

Once again, by computing the present value of the lease payments, we remove the portion of the payments that represents interest, leaving the portion that represents payment for the asset itself. Because the first payment is due immediately, as is common for leases, this is an annuity due situation. In equation form:

**Certain long-term leases require the recording of an asset and corresponding liability at the present value of future lease payments.**

$$\text{PVAD} = \$10{,}000 \text{ (annuity amount)} \times 9.98474^{*} = \$99{,}847$$

*Present value of an annuity due of $1: $n = 25$, $i = 10\%$

Stridewell initially will value the leased asset and corresponding lease liability at $99,847.

| | | |
|---|---|---|
| Leased office building | 99,847 | |
| Lease payable | | 99,847 |

**Journal entry at the inception of a lease**

The difference between this amount and total future cash payments of $250,000 ($10,000 × 25) represents the interest that is implicit in this agreement. That difference is recorded as interest over the life of the lease.

## VALUATION OF PENSION OBLIGATIONS

Pension plans are important compensation vehicles used by many U.S. companies. These plans are essentially forms of deferred compensation as the pension benefits are paid to employees after they retire. You will learn in Chapter 17 that some pension plans create obligations during employees' service periods that must be paid during their retirement periods. These obligations are funded during the employment period. This means companies contribute cash to pension funds annually with the intention of accumulating sufficient funds to pay employees the retirement benefits they have earned. The amounts contributed are determined using estimates of retirement benefits. The actual amounts paid to employees during retirement depend on many factors including future compensation levels and length of life. Consider Illustration 6–17.

**ILLUSTRATION 6–17**
Valuing a Pension Obligation

On January 1, 2006, the Stridewell Wholesale Shoe Company hired Sammy Sossa. Sammy is expected to work for 25 years before retirement on December 31, 2030. Annual retirement payments will be paid at the end of each year during his retirement period, expected to be 20 years. The first payment will be on December 31, 2031. During 2006 Sammy earned an annual retirement benefit estimated to be \$2,000 per year. The company plans to contribute cash to a pension fund that will accumulate to an amount sufficient to pay Sammy this benefit. Assuming that Stridewell anticipates earning 6% on all funds invested in the pension plan, how much would the company have to contribute at the end of 2006 to pay for pension benefits earned in 2006?

To determine the required contribution, we calculate the present value on December 31, 2006, of the deferred annuity of \$2,000 that begins on December 31, 2031, and is expected to end on December 31, 2050.

The following time diagram depicts this situation:

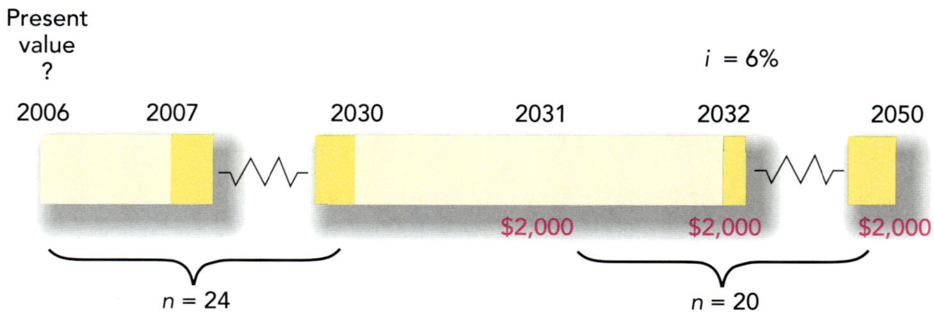


We can calculate the present value of the annuity using a two-step process. The first step computes the present value of the annuity as of December 31, 2030, by multiplying the annuity amount by the 20-period ordinary annuity factor:

PVA = \$2,000 (annuity amount) × 11.46992* = \$22,940

*Present value of an ordinary annuity of \$1: $n = 20$, $i = 6\%$

This is the present value as of December 31, 2030. This single amount is then reduced to present value as of December 31, 2006, by a second calculation:

PV = \$22,940 (future amount) × .24698* = \$5,666

*Present value of \$1: $n = 24$, $i = 6\%$

Stridewell would have to contribute \$5,666 at the end of 2006 to fund the estimated pension benefits earned by its employee in 2006. Viewed in reverse, \$5,666 invested now at 6% will accumulate a fund balance of \$22,940 at December 31, 2030. If the fund balance remains invested at 6%, \$2,000 can be withdrawn each year for 20 years before the fund is depleted.

Among the other situations you'll encounter using present value techniques are valuing notes (Chapters 10 and 14) and postretirement benefits (Chapter 17).

## Summary of Time Value of Money Concepts

Graphic 6–5 summarizes the time value of money concepts discussed in this chapter.

**GRAPHIC 6–5**
Summary of Time Value of Money Concepts

| Concept | Summary | Formula | Table |
|---|---|---|---|
| Future value (FV) of $1 | The amount of money that a dollar will grow to at some point in the future. | $FV = \$1\,(1+i)^n$ | 1 |
| Present value (PV) of $1 | The amount of money today that is equivalent to a given amount to be received or paid in the future. | $PV = \dfrac{\$1}{(1+i)^n}$ | 2 |
| Future value of an ordinary annuity (FVA) of $1 | The future value of a series of equal-sized cash flows with the first payment taking place at the end of the first compounding period. | $FVA = \dfrac{(1+i)^n - 1}{i}$ | 3 |
| Present value of an ordinary annuity (PVA) of $1 | The present value of a series of equal-sized cash flows with the first payment taking place at the end of the first compounding period. | $PVA = \dfrac{1 - \dfrac{1}{(1+i)^n}}{i}$ | 4 |
| Future value of an annuity due (FVAD) of $1 | The future value of a series of equal-sized cash flows with the first payment taking place at the beginning of the annuity period. | $FVAD = \left[\dfrac{(1+i)^n - 1}{i}\right] \times (1+i)$ | 5 |
| Present value of an annuity due (PVAD) of $1 | The present value of a series of equal-sized cash flows with the first payment taking place at the beginning of the annuity period. | $PVAD = \left[\dfrac{1 - \dfrac{1}{(1+i)^n}}{i}\right] \times (1+i)$ | 6 |

## FINANCIAL REPORTING CASE SOLUTION

1. **Why were the Castellanos to receive $43 million rather than the $141 million lottery prize?** (page 280) The Castellanos chose to receive their lottery winnings in one lump payment immediately rather than in 26 equal annual installments beginning immediately. The state calculates the present value of the 26 equal payments, withholds the necessary federal income tax, and pays the Castellanos the remainder.
2. **What interest rate did the State of California use to calculate the $43 million lump-sum payment?** (p. 286) The equal payment is determined by dividing $141 million by 26 periods:

| | |
|---|---|
| $141 million ÷ 26 = | $5,423,077 |
| Less: 31% federal income tax | (1,681,154) |
| Net-of-tax payment | $3,741,923 |

Since the first payment is made immediately, this is an annuity due situation. We must find the interest rate that provides a present value of $43 million. There is no 26 period row in Table 6. We can subtract the first payment from the $43 million since it is paid immediately and solve using the 25-period ordinary annuity table (that is, the 25 remaining annual payments beginning in one year):

$$\text{PVA factor} = \frac{\$43{,}000{,}000 - 3{,}741{,}923}{\$3{,}741{,}923} = 10.4914^*$$

*Present value of an ordinary annuity of $1: $n = 25$, $i = ?$ (from Table 4, $i$ = approximately 8%)

So, the interest rate used by the state was approximately 8%.

3. **What are some of the accounting applications that incorporate the time value of money into valuation?** (p. 288) Accounting applications that incorporate the time value of money techniques into valuation include the valuation of long-term notes receivable and various long-term liabilities that include bonds, notes, leases, pension obligations, and postretirement benefits other than pensions. We study these in detail in later chapters. ■

## THE BOTTOM LINE

1. A dollar today is worth more than a dollar to be received in the future. The difference between the present value of cash flows and their future value represents the time value of money. Interest is the rent paid for the use of money over time.
2. The future value of a single amount is the amount of money that a dollar will grow to at some point in the future. It is computed by *multiplying* the single amount by $(1 + i)^n$, where $i$ is the interest rate and $n$ the number of compounding periods. The Future Value of $1 table allows for the calculation of future value for any single amount by providing the factors for various combinations of $i$ and $n$.
3. The present value of a single amount is the amount of money today that is equivalent to a given amount to be received or paid in the future. It is computed by *dividing* the future amount by $(1 + i)^n$. The Present Value of $1 table simplifies the calculation of the present value of any future amount.
4. There are four variables in the process of adjusting single cash flow amounts for the time value of money: present value (PV), future value (FV), $i$ and $n$. If you know any three of these, the fourth can be computed easily.
5. An annuity is a series of equal-sized cash flows occurring over equal intervals of time. An ordinary annuity exists when the cash flows occur at the end of each period. An annuity due exists when the cash flows occur at the beginning of each period.
6. The future value of an ordinary annuity (FVA) is the future value of a series of equal-sized cash flows with the first payment taking place at the end of the first compounding period. The last payment will not earn any interest since it is made at the end of the annuity period. The future value of an annuity due (FVAD) is the future value of a series of equal-sized cash flows with the first payment taking place at the beginning of the annuity period (the beginning of the first compounding period).
7. The present value of an ordinary annuity (PVA) is the present value of a series of equal-sized cash flows with the first payment taking place at the end of the first compounding period. The present value of an annuity due (PVAD) is the present value of a series of equal-sized cash flows with the first payment taking place at the beginning of the annuity period. The present value of a deferred annuity is the present value of a series of equal-sized cash flows with the first payment taking place more than one time period after the date of the agreement.
8. In present value problems involving annuities, there are four variables: PVA or PVAD, the annuity amount, the number of compounding periods ($n$) and the interest rate ($i$). If you know any three of these, you can determine the fourth.
9. Most accounting applications of the time value of money involve the present values of annuities. The initial valuation of long-term bonds is determined by calculating the present value of the periodic stated interest payments and the present value of the lump-sum payment made at maturity. Certain long-term leases require the lessee to compute the present value of future lease payments to value the leased asset and corresponding lease obligation. Also, pension plans require the payment of deferred annuities to retirees. ■

## QUESTIONS FOR REVIEW OF KEY TOPICS

**Q 6–1** Define interest.

**Q 6–2** Explain compound interest.

**Q 6–3** What would cause the annual interest rate to be different from the annual effective rate or yield?

**Q 6–4** Identify the three items of information necessary to calculate the future value of a single amount.

**Q 6–5** Define the present value of a single amount.

**Q 6–6** Explain the difference between monetary and nonmonetary assets and liabilities.

**Q 6–7** What is an annuity?

**Q 6–8** Explain the difference between an ordinary annuity and an annuity due.

**Q 6–9** Explain the relationship between Table 2, Present Value of $1, and Table 4, Present Value of an Ordinary Annuity.

**Q 6–10** Prepare a time diagram for the present value of a four-year ordinary annuity of $200. Assume an interest rate of 10% per year.

**Q 6–11** Prepare a time diagram for the present value of a four-year annuity due of $200. Assume an interest rate of 10% per year.

**Q 6–12** What is a deferred annuity?

**Q 6–13** Assume that you borrowed $500 from a friend and promised to repay the loan in five equal annual installments beginning one year from today. Your friend wants to be reimbursed for the time value of money at an 8% annual rate. Explain how you would compute the required annual payment.

**Q 6–14** Compute the required annual payment in Question 6–13.

**Q 6–15** Explain how the time value of money concept is incorporated into the valuation of long-term leases.

## BRIEF EXERCISES

**BE 6–1**
Simple versus compound interest
● LO1

Fran Smith has two investment opportunities. The interest rate for both investments is 8%. Interest on the first investment will compound annually while interest on the second will compound quarterly. Which investment opportunity should Fran choose? Why?

**BE 6–2**
Future value; single amount
● LO2

Bill O'Brien would like to take his wife, Mary, on a trip three years from now to Europe to celebrate their 40th anniversary. He has just received a $20,000 inheritance from an uncle and intends to invest it for the trip. Bill estimates the trip will cost $23,500 and he believes he can earn 5% interest, compounded annually, on his investment. Will he be able to pay for the trip with the accumulated investment amount?

**BE 6–3**
Future value; solving for unknown; single amount
● LO4

Refer to the situation described in BE 6–2. Assume that the trip will cost $26,600. What interest rate, compounded annually, must Bill earn to accumulate enough to pay for the trip?

**BE 6–4**
Present value; single amount
● LO3

John has an investment opportunity that promises to pay him $16,000 in four years. He could earn a 6% annual return investing his money elsewhere. What is the maximum amount he would be willing to invest in this opportunity?

**BE 6–5**
Present value; solving for unknown; single amount
● LO4

Refer to the situation described in BE 6–4. Suppose the opportunity requires John to invest $13,200 today. What is the interest rate John would earn on this investment?

**BE 6–6**
Future value; ordinary annuity
● LO6

Leslie McCormack is in the spring quarter of her freshman year of college. She and her friends already are planning a trip to Europe after graduation in a little over three years. Mary would like to contribute to a savings account over the next three years in order to accumulate enough money to take the trip. Assuming an interest rate of 4%, compounded quarterly, how much will she accumulate in three years by depositing $500 at the *end* of each of the next 12 quarters, beginning three months from now?

**BE 6–7**
Future value; annuity due
● LO6

Refer to the situation described in BE 6–6. How much will Leslie accumulate in three years by depositing $500 at the *beginning* of each of the next 12 quarters?

**BE 6–8**
Present value; ordinary annuity
● LO7

Canliss Mining Company borrowed money from a local bank. The note the company signed requires five annual installment payments of $10,000 beginning one year from today. The interest rate on the note is 7%. What amount did Canliss borrow?

**BE 6–9**
Present value; annuity due
● LO7

Refer to the situation described in BE 6–8. What amount did Canliss borrow assuming that the first $10,000 payment was due immediately?

**BE 6–10**
Deferred annuity
● LO7

Refer to the situation described in BE 6–8. What amount did Canliss borrow assuming that the first of the five annual $10,000 payments was not due for three years?

**BE 6–11**
Solve for unknown; annuity
● LO8

Kingsley Toyota borrowed $100,000 from a local bank. The loan requires Kingsley to pay 10 equal annual installments beginning one year from today. Assuming an interest rate of 8%, what is the amount of each annual installment payment?

**BE 6–12**
Price of a bond
● LO9

On December 31, 2006, Interlink Communications issued 6% stated rate bonds with a face amount of $100 million. The bonds mature on December 31, 2036. Interest is payable annually on each December 31, beginning in 2007. Determine the price of the bonds on December 31, 2006, assuming that the market rate of interest for similar bonds was 7%.

**BE 6–13**
Lease payment
● LO9

On September 30, 2006, Ferguson Imports leased a warehouse. Terms of the lease require Ferguson to make 10 annual lease payments of $55,000 with the first payment due immediately. Accounting standards require the company to record a lease liability when recording this type of lease. Assuming an 8% interest rate, at what amount should Ferguson record the lease liability on September 30, 2006, before the first payment is made?

## EXERCISES



**An alternate exercise and problem set is available on the text website: www.mhhe.com/spiceland4e**

**E 6–1**
Future value; single amount
● LO2

Determine the future value of the following single amounts:

| | Invested Amount | Interest Rate | No. of Periods |
|---|---|---|---|
| 1. | $15,000 | 6% | 12 |
| 2. | 20,000 | 8 | 10 |
| 3. | 30,000 | 12 | 20 |
| 4. | 50,000 | 4 | 12 |

**E 6–2**
Present value; single amount
● LO3

Determine the present value of the following single amounts:

| | Future Amount | Interest Rate | No. of Periods |
|---|---|---|---|
| 1. | $20,000 | 7% | 10 |
| 2. | 14,000 | 8 | 12 |
| 3. | 25,000 | 12 | 20 |
| 4. | 40,000 | 10 | 8 |

**E 6–3**
Present value; multiple, unequal amounts
● LO3

Determine the combined present value as of December 31, 2006, of the following four payments to be received at the *end* of each of the designated years, assuming an annual interest rate of 8%.

| Payment | Year Received |
|---|---|
| $5,000 | 2007 |
| 6,000 | 2008 |
| 8,000 | 2010 |
| 9,000 | 2012 |

**E 6–4**
Future value; single amounts
● LO2

Determine the future value of $10,000 under each of the following sets of assumptions:

| | Annual Rate | Period Invested | Interest Compounded |
|---|---|---|---|
| 1. | 10% | 10 years | Semiannually |
| 2. | 12 | 5 years | Quarterly |
| 3. | 24 | 30 months | Monthly |

**E 6–5**
Future value; annuities
● LO6

Wiseman Video plans to make four annual deposits of $2,000 each to a special building fund. The fund's assets will be invested in mortgage instruments expected to pay interest at 12% on the fund's balance. Using the appropriate annuity table, determine how much will be accumulated in the fund on December 31, 2009, under each of the following situations:

1. The first deposit is made on December 31, 2006, and interest is compounded annually.
2. The first deposit is made on December 31, 2005, and interest is compounded annually.
3. The first deposit is made on December 31, 2005, and interest is compounded quarterly.
4. The first deposit is made on December 31, 2005, interest is compounded annually, *and* interest earned is withdrawn at the end of each year.

**E 6–6**
Present value; annuities
● LO7

Using the appropriate present value table and assuming a 12% annual interest rate, determine the present value on December 31, 2006, of a five-period annual annuity of $5,000 under each of the following situations:

1. The first payment is received on December 31, 2007, and interest is compounded annually.
2. The first payment is received on December 31, 2006, and interest is compounded annually.
3. The first payment is received on December 31, 2007, and interest is compounded quarterly.

**E 6–7**
Solving for unknowns; single amounts
● LO4

For each of the following situations involving single amounts, solve for the unknown (?). Assume that interest is compounded annually. ($i$ = interest rate, and $n$ = number of years)

| | Present Value | Future Value | *i* | *n* |
|---|---|---|---|---|
| 1. | ? | $ 40,000 | 10% | 5 |
| 2. | $36,289 | 65,000 | ? | 10 |
| 3. | 15,884 | 40,000 | 8 | ? |
| 4. | 46,651 | 100,000 | ? | 8 |
| 5. | 15,376 | ? | 7 | 20 |

**E 6–8**
Solve for unknowns; annuities
● LO8

For each of the following situations involving annuities, solve for the unknown (?). Assume that interest is compounded annually and that all annuity amounts are received at the *end* of each period. ($i$ = interest rate, and $n$ = number of years)

| | Present Value | Annuity Amount | *i* | *n* |
|---|---|---|---|---|
| 1. | ? | $ 3,000 | 8% | 5 |
| 2. | $242,980 | 75,000 | ? | 4 |
| 3. | 161,214 | 20,000 | 9 | ? |
| 4. | 500,000 | 80,518 | ? | 8 |
| 5. | 250,000 | ? | 10 | 4 |

**E 6–9**
Future value; solving for annuities and single amount
● LO4 LO8

John Rider wants to accumulate $100,000 to be used for his daughter's college education. He would like to have the amount available on December 31, 2011. Assume that the funds will accumulate in a certificate of deposit paying 8% interest compounded annually.

**Required:**
Answer each of the following independent questions.

1. If John were to deposit a single amount, how much would he have to invest on December 31, 2006?
2. If John were to make five equal deposits on each December 31, beginning on December 31, 2007, what is the required deposit?
3. If John were to make five equal deposits on each December 31, beginning on December 31, 2006, what is the required deposit?

**E 6–10**
Future and present value
● LO3 LO6 LO7

Answer each of the following independent questions.

1. Alex Meir recently won a lottery and has the option of receiving one of the following three prizes: (1) $64,000 cash immediately, (2) $20,000 cash immediately and a six-period annuity of $8,000 beginning one year from today, or (3) a six-period annuity of $13,000 beginning one year from today. Assuming an interest rate of 6%, which option should Alex choose?
2. The Weimer Corporation wants to accumulate a sum of money to repay certain debts due on December 31, 2015. Weimer will make annual deposits of $100,000 into a special bank account at the end of each of 10 years beginning December 31, 2006. Assuming that the bank account pays 7% interest compounded annually, what will be the fund balance after the last payment is made on December 31, 2015?

**E 6–11**
Noninterest-bearing note; single payment
● LO3

The Field Detergent Company sold merchandise to the Abel Company on June 30, 2006. Payment was made in the form of a noninterest-bearing note requiring Abel to pay $85,000 on June 30, 2008. Assume that a 10% interest rate properly reflects the time value of money in this situation.

**Required:**
Calculate the amount at which Field should record the note receivable and corresponding sales revenue on June 30, 2006.

**E 6–12**
Solving for unknown annuity payment
● LO8

Don James purchased a new automobile for $20,000. Don made a cash down payment of $5,000 and agreed to pay the remaining balance in 30 monthly installments, beginning one month from the date of purchase. Financing is available at a 24% *annual* interest rate.

**Required:**
Calculate the amount of the required monthly payment.

**E 6–13**
Solving for unknown interest rate
● LO8

Lang Warehouses borrowed $100,000 from a bank and signed a note requiring 20 annual payments of $13,388 beginning one year from the date of the agreement.

**Required:**
Determine the interest rate implicit in this agreement.

**E 6–14**
Solving for unknown annuity amount
● LO8

Sandy Kupchack just graduated from State University with a bachelors degree in history. During her four years at the U, Sandy accumulated $12,000 in student loans. She asks for your help in determining the amount of the *quarterly* loan payment. She tells you that the loan must be paid back in five years and that the annual interest rate is 8%. Payments begin in three months.

**Required:**
Determine Sandy's quarterly loan payment.

**E 6–15**
Price of a bond
● LO9

On September 30, 2006, the San Fillipo Corporation issued 8% stated rate bonds with a face amount of $300 million. The bonds mature on September 30, 2026 (20 years). The market rate of interest for similar bonds was 10%. Interest is paid semiannually on March 31 and September 30.

**Required:**
Determine the price of the bonds on September 30, 2006.

**E 6–16**
Deferred annuities
● LO7

Lincoln Company purchased merchandise from Grandville Corp. on September 30, 2006. Payment was made in the form of a noninterest-bearing note requiring Lincoln to make six annual payments of $5,000 on each September 30, beginning on September 30, 2009.

**Required:**
Calculate the amount at which Lincoln should record the note payable and corresponding purchases on September 30, 2006, assuming that an interest rate of 10% properly reflects the time value of money in this situation.

**E 6–17**
Deferred annuities; solving for annuity amount
● LO7 LO8

On April 1, 2006, John Vaughn purchased appliances from the Acme Appliance Company for $1,200. In order to increase sales, Acme allows customers to pay in installments and will defer any payments for six months. John will make 18 equal monthly payments, beginning October 1, 2006. The annual interest rate implicit in this agreement is 24%.

**Required:**
Calculate the monthly payment necessary for John to pay for his purchases.

**E 6–18**
Lease payments
● LO9

On June 30, 2006, Fly-By-Night Airlines leased a jumbo jet from **Boeing Corporation**. The terms of the lease require Fly-By-Night to make 20 annual payments of $400,000 on each June 30. Accounting standards require this lease to be recorded as a liability for the present value of scheduled payments. Assume that a 7% interest rate properly reflects the time value of money in this situation.

**Required:**
1. At what amount should Fly-By-Night record the lease liability on June 30, 2006, assuming that the first payment will be made on June 30, 2007?
2. At what amount should Fly-By-Night record the lease liability on June 30, 2006, *before* any payments are made, assuming that the first payment will be made on June 30, 2006?

**E 6–19**
Concepts; terminology
● LO1 through LO3 LO5

Listed below are several terms and phrases associated with concepts discussed in the chapter. Pair each item from List A (by letter) with the item from List B that is most appropriately associated with it.

| List A | List B |
|---|---|
| ____ 1. Interest | a. First cash flow occurs one period after agreement begins. |
| ____ 2. Monetary asset | b. The rate at which money will actually grow during a year. |
| ____ 3. Compound interest | c. First cash flow occurs on the first day of the agreement. |
| ____ 4. Simple interest | d. The amount of money that a dollar will grow to. |
| ____ 5. Annuity | e. Amount of money paid/received in excess of amount borrowed/lent. |
| ____ 6. Present value of a single amount | f. Obligation to pay a sum of cash, the amount of which is fixed. |
| ____ 7. Annuity due | g. Money can be invested today and grow to a larger amount. |
| ____ 8. Future value of a single amount | h. No fixed dollar amount attached. |
| ____ 9. Ordinary annuity | i. Computed by multiplying an invested amount by the interest rate. |
| ____ 10. Effective rate or yield | j. Interest calculated on invested amount plus accumulated interest. |
| ____ 11. Nonmonetary asset | k. A series of equal-sized cash flows. |
| ____ 12. Time value of money | l. Amount of money required today that is equivalent to a given future amount. |
| ____ 13. Monetary liability | m. Claim to receive a fixed amount of money. |

**E 6–20**
Multiple choice; CMA exam; time value of money concepts

● LO2 LO6 LO7 LO9

The following questions dealing with the time value of money are adapted from questions that previously appeared on Certified Management Accountant (CMA) examinations. The CMA designation sponsored by the Institute of Management Accountants (**www.imanet.org**) provides members with an objective measure of knowledge and competence in the field of management accounting. Determine the response that best completes the statements or questions.

1. Essex Corporation is evaluating a lease that takes effect on March 1. The company must make eight equal payments, with the first payment due on March 1. The concept most relevant to the evaluation of the lease is
   a. The present value of an annuity due.
   b. The present value of an ordinary annuity.
   c. The future value of an annuity due.
   d. The future value of an ordinary annuity.
2. Janet Taylor Casual Wear has $75,000 in a bank account as of December 31, 2004. If the company plans on depositing $4,000 in the account at the end of each of the next 3 years (2005, 2006, 2007) and all amounts in the account earn 8% per year, what will the account balance be at December 31, 2007? Ignore the effect of income taxes.

| | 8% Interest Rate Factors | |
|---|---|---|
| Period | Future Value of an Amount of $1 | Future Value of an Ordinary Annuity of $1 |
| 1 | 1.08 | 1.00 |
| 2 | 1.17 | 2.08 |
| 3 | 1.26 | 3.25 |
| 4 | 1.36 | 4.51 |

   a. $87,000.
   b. $88,000.
   c. $96,070.
   d. $107,500.

# PROBLEMS

available with McGraw-Hill's Homework Manager www.mhhe.com/spiceland4e

**An alternate exercise and problem set is available on the text website: www.mhhe.com/spiceland4e**

**P 6–1**
Analysis of alternatives

● LO3 LO7

Esquire Company needs to acquire a molding machine to be used in its manufacturing process. Two types of machines that would be appropriate are presently on the market. The company has determined the following:

> Machine A could be purchased for $48,000. It will last 10 years with annual maintenance costs of $1,000 per year. After 10 years the machine can be sold for $5,000.
> Machine B could be purchased for $40,000. It also will last 10 years and will require maintenance costs of $4,000 in year three, $5,000 in year six, and $6,000 in year eight. After 10 years, the machine will have no salvage value.

**Required:**

Determine which machine Esquire should purchase. Assume an interest rate of 8% properly reflects the time value of money in this situation and that maintenance costs are paid at the end of each year. Ignore income tax considerations.

**P 6–2**
Present and future value
● LO6 LO7 LO9

Johnstone Company is facing several decisions regarding investing and financing activities. Address each decision independently.

1. On June 30, 2006, the Johnstone Company purchased equipment from Genovese Corp. Johnstone agreed to pay Genovese $10,000 on the purchase date and the balance in five annual installments of $8,000 on each June 30 beginning June 30, 2007. Assuming that an interest rate of 10% properly reflects the time value of money in this situation, at what amount should Johnstone value the equipment?
2. Johnstone needs to accumulate sufficient funds to pay a $400,000 debt that comes due on December 31, 2011. The company will accumulate the funds by making five equal annual deposits to an account paying 6% interest compounded annually. Determine the required annual deposit if the first deposit is made on December 31, 2006.
3. On January 1, 2006, Johnstone leased an office building. Terms of the lease require Johnstone to make 20 annual lease payments of $120,000 beginning on January 1, 2006. A 10% interest rate is implicit in the lease agreement. At what amount should Johnstone record the lease liability on January 1, 2006, *before* any lease payments are made?

**P 6–3**
Analysis of alternatives
● LO3 LO7

Harding Company is in the process of purchasing several large pieces of equipment from Danning Machine Corporation. Several financing alternatives have been offered by Danning:

1. Pay $1,000,000 in cash immediately.
2. Pay $420,000 immediately and the remainder in 10 annual installments of $80,000, with the first installment due in one year.
3. Make 10 annual installments of $135,000 with the first payment due immediately.
4. Make one lump-sum payment of $1,500,000 five years from date of purchase.

**Required:**

Determine the best alternative for Harding, assuming that Harding can borrow funds at an 8% interest rate.

**P 6–4**
Investment analysis
● LO3 LO7

John Wiggins is contemplating the purchase of a small restaurant. The purchase price listed by the seller is $800,000. John has used past financial information to estimate that the net cash flows (cash inflows less cash outflows) generated by the restaurant would be as follows:

| Years | Amount |
|---|---|
| 1–6 | $80,000 |
| 7 | 70,000 |
| 8 | 60,000 |
| 9 | 50,000 |
| 10 | 40,000 |

If purchased, the restaurant would be held for 10 years and then sold for an estimated $700,000.

**Required:**

Assuming that John desires a 10% rate of return on this investment, should the restaurant be purchased? (Assume that all cash flows occur at the end of the year.)

**P 6–5**
Investment decision; varying rates
● LO3 LO7
eXcel

John and Sally Claussen are contemplating the purchase of a hardware store from John Duggan. The Claussens anticipate that the store will generate cash flows of $70,000 per year for 20 years. At the end of 20 years, they intend to sell the store for an estimated $400,000. The Claussens will finance the investment with a variable rate mortgage. Interest rates will increase twice during the 20-year life of the mortgage. Accordingly, the Claussens' desired rate of return on this investment varies as follows:

| | |
|---|---|
| Years 1–5 | 8% |
| Years 6–10 | 10% |
| Years 11–20 | 12% |

**Required:**

What is the maximum amount the Claussens should pay John Duggan for the hardware store? (Assume that all cash flows occur at the end of the year.)

**P 6–6**
Solving for unknowns
● LO8
eXcel

The following situations should be considered independently.

1. John Jamison wants to accumulate $60,000 for a down payment on a small business. He will invest $30,000 today in a bank account paying 8% interest compounded annually. Approximately how long will it take John to reach his goal?
2. The Jasmine Tea Company purchased merchandise from a supplier for $28,700. Payment was a noninterest-bearing note requiring Jasmine to make five annual payments of $7,000 beginning one year from the date of purchase. What is the interest rate implicit in this agreement?

3. Sam Robinson borrowed $10,000 from a friend and promised to pay the loan in 10 equal annual installments beginning one year from the date of the loan. Sam's friend would like to be reimbursed for the time value of money at a 9% annual rate. What is the annual payment Sam must make to pay back his friend?

**P 6–7**
Solving for unknowns
● LO8
eXcel

Lowlife Company defaulted on a $250,000 loan that was due on December 31, 2006. The bank has agreed to allow Lowlife to repay the $250,000 by making a series of equal annual payments beginning on December 31, 2007.

**Required:**
1. Calculate the required annual payment if the bank's interest rate is 10% and four payments are to be made.
2. Calculate the required annual payment if the bank's interest rate is 8% and five payments are to be made.
3. If the bank's interest rate is 10%, how many annual payments of $51,351 would be required to repay the debt?
4. If three payments of $104,087 are to be made, what interest rate is the bank charging Lowlife?

**P 6–8**
Deferred annuities
● LO7

On January 1, 2006, the Montgomery company agreed to purchase a building by making six payments. The first three are to be $25,000 each, and will be paid on December 31, 2006, 2007, and 2008. The last three are to be $40,000 each and will be paid on December 31, 2009, 2010, and 2011. Montgomery borrowed other money at a 10% annual rate.

**Required:**
1. At what amount should Montgomery record the note payable and corresponding cost of the building on January 1, 2006?
2. How much interest expense on this note will Montgomery recognize in 2006?

**P 6–9**
Deferred annuities
● LO7

John Roberts is 55 years old and has been asked to accept early retirement from his company. The company has offered John three alternative compensation packages to induce John to retire:
1. $180,000 cash payment to be paid immediately.
2. A 20-year annuity of $16,000 beginning immediately.
3. A 10-year annuity of $50,000 beginning at age 65.

**Required:**
Which alternative should John choose assuming that he is able to invest funds at a 7% rate?

**P 6–10**
Noninterest-bearing note; annuity and lump-sum payment
● LO3 LO7

On January 1, 2006, The Barrett Company purchased merchandise from a supplier. Payment was a noninterest-bearing note requiring five annual payments of $20,000 on each December 31 beginning on December 31, 2006, and a lump-sum payment of $100,000 on December 31, 2010. A 10% interest rate properly reflects the time value of money in this situation.

**Required:**
Calculate the amount at which Barrett should record the note payable and corresponding merchandise purchased on January 1, 2006.

**P 6–11**
Solving for unknown lease payment
● LO8 LO9

Benning Manufacturing Company is negotiating with a customer for the lease of a large machine manufactured by Benning. The machine has a cash price of $800,000. Benning wants to be reimbursed for financing the machine at an 8% annual interest rate.

**Required:**
1. Determine the required lease payment if the lease agreement calls for 10 equal annual payments beginning immediately.
2. Determine the required lease payment if the first of 10 annual payments will be made one year from the date of the agreement.
3. Determine the required lease payment if the first of 10 annual payments will be made immediately and Benning will be able to sell the machine to another customer for $50,000 at the end of the 10-year lease.

**P 6–12**
Solving for unknown lease payment; compounding periods of varying length
● LO9

(This is a variation of the previous problem focusing on compounding periods of varying length.)

Benning Manufacturing Company is negotiating with a customer for the lease of a large machine manufactured by Benning. The machine has a cash price of $800,000. Benning wants to be reimbursed for financing the machine at a 12% annual interest rate over the five-year lease term.

**Required:**
1. Determine the required lease payment if the lease agreement calls for 10 equal semiannual payments beginning six months from the date of the agreement.
2. Determine the required lease payment if the lease agreement calls for 20 equal quarterly payments beginning immediately.
3. Determine the required lease payment if the lease agreement calls for 60 equal monthly payments beginning one month from the date of the agreement. The present value of an ordinary annuity factor for $n = 60$ and $i = 1\%$ is 44.9550.

**P 6–13**
Lease vs. buy alternatives
● LO3 LO7 LO9

Kiddy Toy Corporation needs to acquire the use of a machine to be used in its manufacturing process. The machine needed is manufactured by Lollie Corp. The machine can be used for 10 years and then sold for $10,000 at the end of its useful life. Lollie has presented Kiddy with the following options:

1. *Buy machine.* The machine could be purchased for $160,000 in cash. All maintenance and insurance costs, which approximate $5,000 per year, would be paid by Kiddy.
2. *Lease machine.* The machine could be leased for a 10-year period for an annual lease payment of $25,000 with the first payment due immediately. All maintenance and insurance costs will be paid for by the Lollie Corp. and the machine will revert back to Lollie at the end of the 10-year period.

**Required:**

Assuming that a 12% interest rate properly reflects the time value of money in this situation and that all maintenance and insurance costs are paid at the end of each year, determine which option Kiddy should choose. Ignore income tax considerations.

**P 6–14**
Deferred annuities; pension obligation
● LO7 LO9

Three employees of the Horizon Distributing Company will receive annual pension payments from the company when they retire. The employees will receive their annual payments for as long as they live. Life expectancy for each employee is 15 years beyond retirement. Their names, the amount of their annual pension payments, and the date they will receive their first payment are shown below:

| Employee | Annual Payment | Date of First Payment |
|---|---|---|
| Tinkers | $20,000 | 12/31/09 |
| Evers | 25,000 | 12/31/10 |
| Chance | 30,000 | 12/31/11 |

**Required:**

1. Compute the present value of the pension obligation to these three employees as of December 31, 2006. Assume an 11% interest rate.
2. The company wants to have enough cash invested at December 31, 2009, to provide for all three employees. To accumulate enough cash, they will make three equal annual contributions to a fund that will earn 11% interest compounded annually. The first contribution will be made on December 31, 2006. Compute the amount of this required annual contribution.

# BROADEN YOUR PERSPECTIVE

**Apply your critical-thinking ability to the knowledge you've gained. These cases will provide you an opportunity to develop your research, analysis, judgment, and communication skills. You also will work with other students, integrate what you've learned, apply it in real world situations, and consider its global and ethical ramifications. This practice will broaden your knowledge and further develop your decision-making abilities.**

**Analysis Case 6–1**
Present value of an annuity
● LO7

On a rainy afternoon two years ago, John Smiley left work early to attend a family birthday party. Eleven minutes later, a careening truck slammed into his SUV on the freeway causing John to spend two months in a coma. Now he can't hold a job or make everyday decisions and is in need of constant care. Last week, the 40-year old Smiley won an out-of-court settlement from the truck driver's company. He was awarded payment for all medical costs and attorney fees, plus a lump-sum settlement of $2,330,716. At the time of the accident, John was president of his family's business and earned approximately $200,000 per year. He had anticipated working 25 more years before retirement.[8]

John's sister, an acquaintance of yours from college, has asked you to explain to her how the attorneys came up with the settlement amount. "They said it was based on his lost future income and a 7% rate of some kind," she explained. "But it was all 'legal-speak' to me."

**Required:**

How was the amount of the lump-sum settlement determined? Create a calculation that might help John's sister understand.

**Analysis Case 6–2**
Bonus alternatives; present value analysis
● LO3 LO7

Sally Hamilton has performed well as the chief financial officer of the Maxtech Computer Company and has earned a bonus. She has a choice among the following three bonus plans:

1. A $50,000 cash bonus paid now.
2. A $10,000 annual cash bonus to be paid each year over the next six years, with the first $10,000 paid now.
3. A three-year $22,000 annual cash bonus with the first payment due three years from now.

[8] This case is based on actual events.

**Required:**
Evaluate the three alternative bonus plans. Sally can earn a 6% annual return on her investments.

**Communication Case 6–3**
Present value of annuities
● LO7

Harvey Alexander, an all-league professional football player, has just declared free agency. Two teams, the San Francisco 49ers and the Dallas Cowboys, have made Harvey the following offers to obtain his services:

49ers: $1 million signing bonus payable immediately and an annual salary of $1.5 million for the five-year term of the contract.

Cowboys: $2.5 million signing bonus payable immediately and an annual salary of $1 million for the five-year term of the contract.

With both contracts, the annual salary will be paid in one lump-sum at the end of the football season.

**Required:**
You have been hired as a consultant to Harvey's agent, Phil Marks, to evaluate the two contracts. Write a short letter to Phil with your recommendation including the method you used to reach your conclusion. Assume that Harvey has no preference between the two teams and that the decision will be based entirely on monetary considerations. Also assume that Harvey can invest his money and earn an 8% annual return.

**Ethics Case 6–4**
Rate of return
● LO1

The Damon Investment Company manages a mutual fund composed mostly of speculative stocks. You recently saw an ad claiming that investments in the funds have been earning a rate of return of 21%. This rate seemed quite high so you called a friend who works for one of Damon's competitors. The friend told you that the 21% return figure was determined by dividing the two-year appreciation on investments in the fund by the average investment. In other words, $100 invested in the fund two years ago would have grown to $121 ($21 ÷ $100 = 21%).

**Required:**
Discuss the ethics of the 21% return claim made by the Damon Investment Company.

**Judgment Case 6–5**
Replacement decision
● LO3 LO7

Hughes Corporation is considering replacing a machine used in the manufacturing process with a new, more efficient model. The purchase price of the new machine is $150,000 and the old machine can be sold for $100,000. Output for the two machines is identical; they will both be used to produce the same amount of product for five years. However, the annual operating costs of the old machine are $18,000 compared to $10,000 for the new machine. Also, the new machine has a salvage value of $25,000, but the old machine will be worthless at the end of the five years.

**Required:**
Should the company sell the old machine and purchase the new model? Assume that an 8% rate properly reflects the time value of money in this situation and that all operating costs are paid at the end of the year. Ignore the effect of the decision on income taxes.

**Real World Case 6–6**
Zero-coupon notes
● LO3 LO9

**Sanmina-SCI Corporation** is a leading, independent global provider of customized, integrated electronics manufacturing services. The company's 2004 financial statements included the following information in the long-term debt disclosure note :

| | ($ in thousands) | |
|---|---|---|
| | **2004** | **2003** |
| Zero-coupon subordinated bonds, due 2020 | $608,092 | $584,473 |

Zero-coupon bonds pay no interest. The disclosure stated that bonds with a $1.66 billion maturity value were issued on September 12, 2000, for $751.8 million. The maturity value indicates the amount that the company will pay bondholders in 2020. Each individual bond has a maturity value (face amount) of $1,000. The company is accreting the issue price to maturity value using the bond's effective interest rate computed on a semiannual basis. Since their issuance, the company has repurchased $360.6 million in maturity value of these bonds.

**Required:**
1. Determine the effective interest rate on the bonds.
2. Determine the issue price of one, $1,000 maturity-value bond.

**Analysis Case 6–7**
Time value of money applications
● LO9
**FedEx Corporation**

Refer to the financial statements and related disclosure notes of **FedEx Corporation** in Appendix B located at the back of this text.

**Required:**
1. Identify the various liabilities that are valued by applying the time value of money concept.
2. What rate is used to value pension obligations?

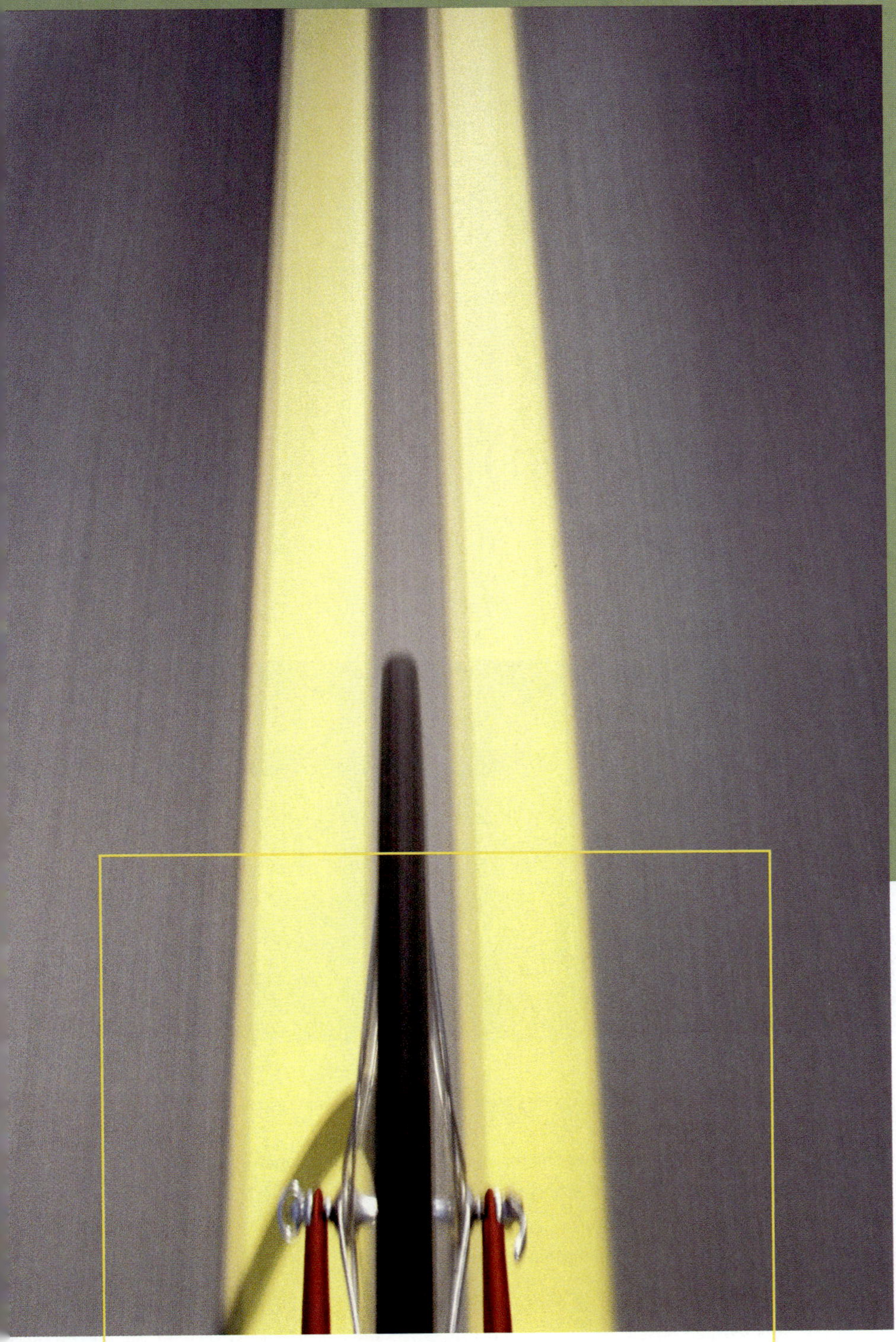

# Economic Resources

2

SECTION

7

CHAPTER

# Cash and Receivables

## OVERVIEW

We begin our study of assets by looking at cash and receivables—the two assets typically listed first in a balance sheet. Internal control and classification in the balance sheet are key issues we address in consideration of cash. For receivables, the key issues are valuation and the related income statement effects of transactions involving accounts receivable and notes receivable.

## LEARNING OBJECTIVES

After studying this chapter, you should be able to:

- LO1 Define what is meant by internal control and describe some key elements of an internal control system for cash receipts and disbursements.
- LO2 Explain the possible restrictions on cash and their implications for classification in the balance sheet.
- LO3 Distinguish between the gross and net methods of accounting for cash discounts.
- LO4 Describe the accounting treatment for merchandise returns.
- LO5 Describe the accounting treatment of anticipated uncollectible accounts receivable.
- LO6 Describe the two approaches to estimating bad debts.
- LO7 Describe the accounting treatment of short-term notes receivable.
- LO8 Differentiate between the use of receivables in financing arrangements accounted for as a secured borrowing and those accounted for as a sale.
- LO9 Describe the variables that influence a company's investment in receivables and calculate the key ratios used by analysts to monitor that investment.

# FINANCIAL REPORTING CASE

## What Does It All Mean?

Your roommate, Todd Buckley, was surfing the net looking for information about his future employer, Cisco Systems. Todd, an engineering major, recently accepted a position with Cisco, the world's largest provider of hardware, software, and services that drive the Internet. He noticed an article on TheStreet.com entitled "Cisco Triples Bad-Account Provision." "This doesn't look good," Todd grumbled. "The article says that my new employer's deadbeat account column has more than tripled in the span of a year. I guess all those dot-com companies are not paying their bills. But this sentence is confusing. 'For the fiscal first quarter Cisco moved $275 million from operating cash to cover potential nonpayments from failed customers.' Did they actually move cash and if so, where did they move it and why?"

You studied accounting for bad debts in your intermediate accounting class and are confident you can help. After reading the article, you comfort Todd. "First of all, the term *provision* just means expense, and no, Cisco didn't move any cash. The company uses what is called the *allowance method* to account for its bad debts, and it looks like it simply recorded $275 million in expense for the quarter and increased the allowance for uncollectible accounts." Todd was not happy with your answer. "Provisions! allowance method! uncollectible accounts! I want you to help me understand, not make things worse." "Okay," you offer, "let's start at the beginning."

**By the time you finish this chapter, you should be able to respond appropriately to the questions posed in this case. Compare your response to the solution provided at the end of the chapter.**

### QUESTIONS

1. Explain the allowance method of accounting for bad debts. (page 314)
2. What approaches might Cisco have used to arrive at the $275 million bad debt provision? (page 315)
3. Are there any alternatives to the allowance method? (page 317)

In the earlier chapters of this text, we studied the underlying measurement and reporting concepts for the basic financial statements presented to external decision makers. Now we turn our attention to the elements of those financial statements. Specifically, we further explore the elements of the balance sheet including the income statement effects of transactions involving these elements. We first address assets, then liabilities, and finally shareholders' equity. This chapter focuses on the current assets **cash and cash equivalents** and **receivables**.

# PART A CASH AND CASH EQUIVALENTS

**Cash** includes currency and coins, balances in checking accounts, and items acceptable for deposit in these accounts, such as checks and money orders received from customers. These forms of cash represent amounts readily available to pay off debt or to use in operations without any legal or contractual restriction.

Managers typically invest temporarily idle cash to earn interest on those funds rather than keep an unnecessarily large checking account. These amounts are essentially equivalent to cash because they can quickly become available for use as cash. So, short-term, highly liquid investments that can be readily converted to cash with little risk of loss are viewed as cash equivalents. For financial reporting we make no distinction between cash in the form of currency or bank account balances and amounts held in cash equivalent investments.

**A company's policy concerning which short-term, highly liquid investments it classifies as cash equivalents should be described in a disclosure note.**

**Cash equivalents** include such things as certain money market funds, treasury bills, and commercial paper. To be classified as cash equivalents, these investments must have a maturity date no longer than three months *from the date of purchase.* Companies are permitted flexibility in designating cash equivalents and must establish individual policies regarding which short-term, highly liquid investments are classified as cash equivalents. A company's policy should be consistent with the usual motivation for acquiring certain types of investments. The policy should be disclosed in the notes to the financial statements. Graphic 7–1 shows a note from a recent annual report of the **Sears, Roebuck and Co.** that provides a description of the company's cash equivalents.

**GRAPHIC 7–1**
Disclosure of Cash Equivalents—Sears, Roebuck and Co.

**Summary of Significant Accounting Policies (in part)**
**Cash and Cash Equivalents**
Cash equivalents include all highly liquid investments with original maturities of three months or less at the date of purchase. Such investments may include, but are not limited to, commercial paper, United States federal, state and municipal government securities, floating rate notes, repurchase agreements using the previously mentioned securities as collateral, and money market funds.

The measurement and reporting of cash and cash equivalents are largely straightforward because cash generally presents no measurement problems. It is the standard medium of exchange and the basis for measuring assets and liabilities. Cash and cash equivalents usually are combined and reported as a single amount in the balance sheet. However, cash that is not available for use in current operations because it is restricted for a special purpose usually is classified in one of the noncurrent asset categories. Restricted cash is discussed later in this chapter.

All assets must be safeguarded against possible misuse. However, cash is the most liquid asset and the asset most easily expropriated. As a result, a system of internal control of cash is a key accounting issue.

## Internal Control

LO1

The success of any business enterprise depends on an effective system of **internal control**. Internal control refers to a company's plan to (a) encourage adherence to company policies and procedures, (b) promote operational efficiency, (c) minimize errors and theft, and (d) enhance the reliability and accuracy of accounting data. From a financial accounting perspective, the focus is on controls intended to improve the accuracy and reliability of accounting information and to safeguard the company's assets.

Recall from our discussion in Chapter 1 that Section 404 of the *Sarbanes-Oxley Act of 2002* requires that companies not only document their internal controls and assess their adequacy, but that their auditors must provide an opinion on management's assessment. The Public Company Accounting Oversight Board's *Auditing Standard No. 2* further requires the auditor to express its own opinion on whether the company has maintained effective internal control over financial reporting.

**The Sarbanes-Oxley Act requires a company to document and assess its internal controls. Auditors express an opinion on management's assessment.**

Many companies have incurred significant costs in an effort to comply with the requirements of Section 404. A cottage industry of consulting firms and software products has arisen to help these companies. A framework for designing an internal control system is provided by the **Committee of Sponsoring Organizations (COSO)** of the Treadway Commission.[1] Formed in 1985, the organization is dedicated to improving the quality of financial reporting through, among other things, effective internal controls.

COSO defines internal control as a process, effected by an entity's board of directors, management and other personnel, designed to provide reasonable assurance regarding the achievement of objectives in the following categories:

- Effectiveness and efficiency of operations.
- Reliability of financial reporting.
- Compliance with applicable laws and regulations.[2]

A critical aspect of an internal control system is the *separation of duties*. Individuals that have physical responsibility for assets should not also have access to accounting records. For example, if the same individual has control of both the supplies inventory and the accounting records, the theft of supplies could be concealed by a reduction of the supplies account.

**Employees involved in recordkeeping should not also have physical access to the assets.**

As cash is the most liquid of all assets, a well-designed and functioning system of internal control must surround all cash transactions. Separation of duties is critical. Ideally, those who handle cash should not be involved in or have access to accounting records nor be involved in the reconciliation of cash book balances to bank balances.

## INTERNAL CONTROL PROCEDURES—CASH RECEIPTS

Consider the cash receipt process. Most nonretail businesses receive payment for goods by checks received through the mail. An approach to internal control over cash receipts might include the following steps:

1. Employee A opens the mail each day and prepares a multicopy listing of all checks including the amount and payor's name.
2. Employee B takes the checks, along with one copy of the listing, to the person responsible for depositing the checks in the company's bank account.
3. A second copy of the check listing is sent to the accounting department where the receipts are entered into the records.

The amount received should equal the amount deposited as verified by comparison with the bank-generated deposit slip and the amount recorded in the accounting records. This helps ensure accuracy as well as safeguard cash against theft.

## INTERNAL CONTROL PROCEDURES—CASH DISBURSEMENTS

Proper controls for cash disbursements should be designed to prevent any unauthorized payments and ensure that disbursements are recorded in the proper general ledger and subsidiary ledger accounts. Important elements of a cash disbursement control system include:

1. All disbursements, other than very small disbursements from petty cash, should be made by check. This provides a permanent record of all disbursements.

[1]The sponsoring organizations include the AICPA, the Financial Executives International, the Institute of Internal Auditors, the National Association of Accountants, and the Institute of Management Accountants.

[2]www.coso.org.

2. All expenditures should be *authorized* before a check is prepared. For example, a vendor invoice for the purchase of inventory should be compared with the purchase order and receiving report to ensure the accuracy of quantity, price, part numbers, and so on. This process should include verification of the proper ledger accounts to be debited.
3. Checks should be signed only by authorized individuals.

Responsibilities for check signing, check writing, check mailing, cash disbursement documentation, and recordkeeping ideally should be separated whenever possible.

An important part of any system of internal control of cash is the periodic reconciliation of book balances and bank balances to the correct balance. In addition, a petty cash system is employed by many business enterprises. We cover these two topics in Appendix 7 beginning on page 332.

## Restricted Cash and Compensating Balances

● LO2

We discussed the classification of assets and liabilities in Chapter 3. You should recall that only cash available for current operations or to satisfy current liabilities is classified as a current asset. Cash that is restricted in some way and not available for current use usually is reported as *investments and funds* or *other assets.*

Restrictions on cash can be informal, arising from management's intent to use a certain amount of cash for a specific purpose. For example, a company may set aside funds for future plant expansion. This cash, if material, should be classified as investments and funds or other assets. Sometimes restrictions are contractually imposed. Debt instruments, for instance, frequently require the borrower to set aside funds (often referred to as a sinking fund) for the future payment of a debt. In these instances, the restricted cash is classified as investments and funds or other assets if the debt is classified as noncurrent. On the other hand, if the liability is current, the restricted cash also is classified as current. Disclosure notes should describe any material restrictions of cash.

**The effect of a *compensating balance* is a higher effective interest rate on the debt.**

Banks frequently require cash restrictions in connection with loans or loan commitments (lines of credit). Typically, the borrower is asked to maintain a specified balance in a low-interest or noninterest-bearing account at the bank (creditor). The required balance usually is some percentage of the committed amount (say 2% to 5%). These are known as **compensating balances** because they compensate the bank for granting the loan or extending the line of credit.

A compensating balance results in the borrower's paying an effective interest rate higher than the stated rate on the debt. For example, suppose that a company borrows $10,000,000 from a bank at an interest rate of 12%. If the bank requires a compensating balance of $2,000,000 to be held in a noninterest-bearing checking account, the company really is borrowing only $8,000,000 (the loan less the compensating balance). This means an effective interest rate of 15% ($1,200,000 interest divided by $8,000,000 cash available for use).

**A material compensating balance must be disclosed regardless of the classification of the cash.**

The classification and disclosure of a compensating balance depends on the nature of the restriction and the classification of the related debt.[3] If the restriction is legally binding, the cash is classified as either current or noncurrent (investments and funds or other assets) depending on the classification of the related debt. In either case, note disclosure is appropriate.

If the compensating balance arrangement is informal with no contractual agreement that restricts the use of cash, the compensating balance can be reported as part of cash and cash equivalents, with note disclosure of the arrangement. Graphic 7–2 provides an example of a note disclosure of a compensating balance for **Rag Shops, Inc.**, a company that operates a chain of retail craft and fabric stores in a number of eastern states.

[3] "Amendments to Regulations S-X and Related Interpretations and Guidelines Regarding the Disclosure of Compensating Balances and Short-Term Borrowing Arrangements," *Accounting Series Release No. 148,* Securities and Exchange Commission (November 13, 1973).

**Note 9—Credit Facility (in part)**
The Company maintains a $10 million credit facility with a bank. The credit facility is renewable annually on or before each December 31 and currently consists of a discretionary unsecured line of credit for direct borrowings and the issuance and refinance of letters of credit. Borrowings under the line of credit bear interest at the bank's prime rate of 4% which remained constant throughout the nine months ended May 29, 2004. The facility requires the Company to maintain a compensating balance of $400,000 . . .

**GRAPHIC 7–2**
Disclosure of Compensating Balances—Rag Shops, Inc.

## DECISION MAKERS' PERSPECTIVE

Cash often is referred to as a *nonearning* asset because it earns no interest. For this reason, managers invest idle cash in either cash equivalents or short-term investments, both of which provide a return. Management's goal is to hold the minimum amount of cash necessary to conduct normal business operations, meet its obligations, and take advantage of opportunities. Too much cash reduces profits through lost returns, while too little cash increases risk. This tradeoff between risk and return is an ongoing choice made by internal decision makers. Whether the choice made is appropriate is an ongoing assessment made by investors and creditors.

**Companies hold cash to pay for planned and unplanned transactions and to satisfy compensating balance requirements.**

A company must have cash available for the compensating balances we discussed in the previous section as well as for planned disbursements related to normal operating, investing, and financing cash flows. However, because cash inflows and outflows can vary from planned amounts, a company needs an additional cash cushion as a precaution against that contingency. The size of the cushion depends on the company's ability to convert cash equivalents and short-term investments into cash quickly, along with its short-term borrowing capacity.

Liquidity is a measure of a company's cash position and overall ability to obtain cash in the normal course of business. A company is assumed to be liquid if it has sufficient cash or is capable of converting its other assets to cash in a relatively short period of time so that current needs can be met. Frequently, liquidity is measured with respect to the ability to pay currently maturing debt. The current ratio is one of the most common ways of measuring liquidity and is calculated by dividing current assets by current liabilities. By comparing liabilities that must be satisfied in the near term with assets that either are cash or will be converted to cash in the near term we have a base measure of a company's liquidity. We can refine the measure by adjusting for the implicit assumption of the current ratio that all current assets are equally liquid. In the acid-test or quick ratio, the numerator consists of "quick assets," which include only cash and cash equivalents, short-term investments, and accounts receivable. By eliminating inventories and prepaid expenses, the current assets that are less readily convertible into cash, we get a more precise indication of a company's short-term solvency than with the current ratio. We discussed and illustrated these liquidity ratios in Chapter 3.

**A liquidity ratio is but one indication of a company's liquidity.**

We should evaluate the adequacy of any ratio in the context of the industry in which the company operates and other specific circumstances. Bear in mind, though, that industry averages are only one indication of acceptability and any ratio is but one indication of liquidity. Profitability, for instance, is perhaps the best long-run indication of liquidity. And a company may be very efficient in managing its current assets so that, say, receivables are more liquid than they otherwise would be. The receivables turnover ratio we discuss in Part B of this chapter offers a measure of management's efficiency in this regard.

**A manager should actively monitor the company's cash position.**

There are many techniques that a company can use to manage cash balances. A discussion of these techniques is beyond the scope of this text. However, it is sufficient here to understand that management must make important decisions related to cash that have a direct impact on a company's profitability and risk. Because the lack of prudent cash management can lead to the failure of an otherwise sound company, it is essential that managers as well as outside investors and creditors maintain close vigil over this facet of a company's health. ■

# PART B CURRENT RECEIVABLES

**Receivables** represent a company's claims to the future collection of cash, other assets, or services. Receivables resulting from the sale of goods or services on account are called **accounts receivable** and often are referred to as *trade receivables. Nontrade receivables* are those other than trade receivables and include tax refund claims, interest receivable, and loans by the company to other entities including stockholders and employees. When a receivable, trade or nontrade, is accompanied by a formal promissory note, it is referred to as a note receivable. We consider notes receivable after first discussing accounts receivable.

An account receivable and an account payable are two sides of the same coin.

As you study receivables, realize that one company's claim to the future collection of cash corresponds to another company's (or individual's) obligation to pay cash. One company's account receivable will be the mirror image of another company's account payable—the measurement issues are identical. Chapter 13 addresses accounts payable and other current liabilities.

## Accounts Receivable

Accounts receivable are current assets because, by definition, they will be converted to cash within the normal operating cycle.

Most businesses provide credit to their customers, either because it's not practical to require immediate cash payment or to encourage customers to purchase the company's product or service. Accounts receivable are *informal* credit arrangements supported by an invoice and normally are due in 30 to 60 days after the sale. They almost always are classified as *current* assets because their normal collection period, even if longer than a year, is part of, and therefore less than, the operating cycle.

Typically, revenue and related accounts receivable are recognized at the point of delivery of the product or service.

The point at which accounts receivable are recognized depends on the earnings process of the company. We discussed the realization principle in Chapter 5 and the criteria that must be met before revenue can be recognized. Recall that revenue can be recognized only after the earnings process is *virtually complete* and *collection* from the customer is *reasonably certain.* For the typical credit sale, these criteria are satisfied at the point of delivery of the product or service, so revenue and the related receivable are recognized at that time.

### INITIAL VALUATION OF ACCOUNTS RECEIVABLE

We know from prior discussions that receivables should be recorded at the present value of future cash receipts using a realistic interest rate. So, a $10,000 sale on credit due in 30 days should result in a receivable valued at the present value of the $10,000. In other words, the interest portion of the $10,000 due in 30 days should be removed and recognized as interest revenue over the 30-day period, not as sales revenue at date of delivery of the product. If the monthly interest rate is 2%, the receivable would be valued at $9,804, calculated by multiplying the future cash payment of $10,000 by the present value of $1 factor for one period at 2% (.98039).

The typical account receivable is valued at the amount expected to be received, not the present value of that amount.

However, because the difference between the future and present values of accounts receivable often is immaterial, *APB Opinion 21* specifically excludes accounts receivable from the general rule that receivables be recorded at present value.[4] Therefore, accounts receivable initially are valued at the exchange price agreed on by the buyer and seller. In our example, both the account receivable and sales revenue would be recorded at $10,000. Let's discuss two aspects of accounts receivable related to their initial valuation—trade discounts and cash discounts.

**Trade Discounts.** Companies frequently offer **trade discounts** to customers, usually a percentage reduction from the list price. Trade discounts can be a way to change prices without publishing a new catalog or to disguise real prices from competitors. They also are used to give quantity discounts to large customers. For example, a manufacturer might list a machine part at $2,500 but sell it to a customer at list less a 10% discount. The trade discount of $250 is not recognized directly when recording the transaction. The discount is recognized indirectly by recording the sale at the net of discount price of $2,250, not at the list price.

[4] "Interest on Receivables and Payables," *Accounting Principles Board Opinion No. 21* (New York: AICPA, 1971).

**Cash Discounts.** Be careful to distinguish a *trade* discount from a *cash* discount. **Cash discounts,** often called *sales discounts,* represent reductions not in the selling price of a good or service but in the amount to be paid by a credit customer if paid within a specified period of time. It is a discount intended to provide incentive for quick payment.

***Cash discounts* reduce the amount to be paid if remittance is made within a specified short period of time.**

● LO3

The amount of the discount and the time period within which it's available usually are conveyed by cryptic terms like 2/10, n/30 (meaning a 2% discount if paid within 10 days, otherwise full payment within 30 days). There are two ways to record cash discounts, the gross method and the net method. Conceptually, the **gross method** views a discount not taken by the customer as part of sales of revenue. On the other hand, the **net method** considers sales revenue to be the net amount, after discount, and any discounts not taken by the customer as interest revenue. The discounts are viewed as compensation to the seller for providing financing to the customer. With both methods, discounts *taken* reduce sales revenue. Consider the example in Illustration 7–1.

**ILLUSTRATION 7–1**
Cash Discounts

The Hawthorne Manufacturing Company offers credit customers a 2% cash discount if the sales price is paid within 10 days. Any amounts not paid within 10 days are due in 30 days. These repayment terms are stated as 2/10, n/30. On October 5, 2006, Hawthorne sold merchandise at a price of $20,000. The customer paid $13,720 ($14,000 less the 2% cash discount) on October 14 and the remaining balance of $6,000 on November 4.

The appropriate journal entries to record the sale and cash collection, comparing the gross and net methods are as follows:

| Gross Method | | | Net Method | | |
|---|---|---|---|---|---|
| **October 5, 2006** | | | | | |
| Accounts receivable .... | 20,000 | | Accounts receivable ..... | 19,600 | |
| Sales revenue........ | | 20,000 | Sales revenue ........ | | 19,600 |
| **October 14, 2006** | | | | | |
| Cash................. | 13,720 | | Cash ................. | 13,720 | |
| Sales discounts ........ | 280 | | Accounts receivable ... | | 13,720 |
| Accounts receivable .. | | 14,000 | | | |
| **November 4, 2006** | | | | | |
| Cash................. | 6,000 | | Cash ................. | 6,000 | |
| Accounts receivable .. | | 6,000 | Accounts receivable ... | | 5,880 |
| | | | Interest revenue ...... | | 120 |

**By either method, net sales is reduced by discounts *taken.***

**Discounts *not* taken are included in sales revenue using the gross method and interest revenue using the net method.**

Notice that by using the gross method, we record the revenue and related receivable at the full $20,000 price. On remittance within the discount period, the $280 discount is recorded as a debit to an account called *sales discounts.* This is a contra account to sales revenue and is deducted from sales revenue to derive the net sales reported in the income statement. For payments made after the discount period, cash is simply increased and accounts receivable decreased by the gross amount originally recorded.

**The *gross method* views cash discounts *not* taken as part of sales revenue.**

Under the net method, we record revenue and the related accounts receivable at the agreed on price *less* the 2% discount applied to the entire price. Payments made within the discount period are recorded as debits to cash and credits to accounts receivable for the amount received. If a customer loses a discount by failing to pay within the discount period, the discount not taken is recorded as interest revenue. In this case, $120 in cash (2% × $6,000) is interest.

**The *net method* considers cash discounts *not* taken as interest revenue.**

Total revenue in the 2006 income statement would be the same by either method:

**Revenue comparison of the gross method and the net method**

| | Gross Method | Net Method |
|---|---|---|
| Sales | $20,000 | $19,600 |
| Less: Sales discounts | (280) | -0- |
| Net sales revenue | 19,720 | 19,600 |
| Interest revenue | 0 | 120 |
| Total revenue | $19,720 | $19,720 |

Which is correct? Conceptually, the net method usually reflects the reality of the situation—the real price is $19,600 and $120 is an interest penalty for not paying promptly. The net price usually is the price expected by the seller because the discount usually reflects a hefty interest cost that prudent buyers are unwilling to bear. Consider Illustration 7–1. Although the discount rate is stated as 2%, the effective rate really is 36.5%. The buyer must pay 2% of the price to delay payment an additional 20 days beyond the 10-day discount period. To convert this 20-day rate to an annual rate, we multiply by 365/20:

$$2\% \times 365/20 = 36.5\% \text{ effective rate}$$

Understandably, most buyers try to take the discount if at all possible.

The difference between the two methods, in terms of the effect of the transactions on income, is in the timing of the recognition of any discounts not taken. The gross method recognizes discounts not taken as revenue when the sale is made. The net method recognizes them as revenue after the discount period has passed and the cash is collected. These two measurement dates could be in different reporting periods.

From a practical standpoint, the effect on the financial statements of the difference between the two methods usually is immaterial. As a result, most companies use the gross method because it's easier and doesn't require adjusting entries for discounts not taken.

## SUBSEQUENT VALUATION OF ACCOUNTS RECEIVABLE

Following the initial valuation of an account receivable, two situations possibly could cause the cash ultimately collected to be less than the initial valuation of the receivable: (1) the customer could return the product, or (2) the customer could default and not pay the agreed on sales price. When accounting for sales and accounts receivable, we anticipate these possibilities.

● LO4

**Sales Returns.** Customers frequently are given the right to return the merchandise they purchase if they are not satisfied. We discussed how this policy affects revenue recognition in Chapter 5. We now discuss it from the perspective of asset valuation.

Recognizing *sales returns* when they occur could result in an overstatement of income in the period of the related sale.

When merchandise is returned for a refund or for credit to be applied to other purchases, the situation is called a **sales return.** When practical, a dissatisfied customer might be given a special price reduction as an incentive to keep the merchandise purchased.[5] Returns are common and often substantial in some industries such as food products, publishing, and retailing. In these cases, recognizing returns and allowances only as they occur could cause profit to be overstated in the period of the sale and understated in the return period. For example, assume merchandise is sold to a customer for $10,000 in December 2006, the last month in the selling company's fiscal year, and that the merchandise cost $6,000. If all of the merchandise is returned in 2007 after financial statements for 2006 are issued, gross profit will be overstated in 2006 and understated in 2007 by $4,000. Assets at the end of 2006 also will be overstated by $4,000 because a $10,000 receivable would be recorded instead of $6,000 in inventory.

To avoid misstating the financial statements, when amounts are material, returns should be anticipated by subtracting an allowance for estimated returns. For an example, refer to Illustration 7–2.

The allowance for sales returns is a contra account to accounts receivable. When returns actually occur in the following reporting period, the allowance for sales returns is debited. In this way, income is not reduced in the return period but in the period of the sales revenue.[6]

The perpetual inventory system records increases (debits) and decreases (credits) in the inventory account as they occur. The inventory of $78,000 in the first set of entries represents merchandise actually returned and on hand, while the inventory of $42,000 in the second set of entries represents an estimate of the cost of merchandise expected to be returned. This later amount is included in the period-end inventory in the company's balance sheet even though the actual merchandise belongs to other entities.

---

[5]Price reductions sometimes are referred to as *sales allowances* and are distinguished from situations when the products actually are returned for a refund or credit (sales returns).

[6]Of course, if the allowance for sales returns is estimated incorrectly, income in both the period of the sale and the return will be misstated.

**ILLUSTRATION 7–2**
Sales Returns

During 2006, its first year of operations, the Hawthorne Manufacturing Company sold merchandise on account for $2,000,000. This merchandise cost $1,200,000 (60% of the selling price). Industry experience indicates that 10% of all sales will be returned. Customers returned $130,000 in sales during 2006, prior to making payment.

The entries to record sales and merchandise returned during the year, *assuming that a perpetual inventory system is used,* are as follows:

| | | |
|---|---|---|
| **Sales** | | |
| Accounts receivable | 2,000,000 | |
|   Sales revenue | | 2,000,000 |
| Cost of goods sold (60% × $2,000,000) | 1,200,000 | |
|   Inventory | | 1,200,000 |
| **Returns** | | |
| Sales returns (actual returns) | 130,000 | |
|   Accounts receivable | | 130,000 |
| Inventory | 78,000 | |
|   Cost of goods sold (60% × $130,000) | | 78,000 |

At the end of 2006, the company would anticipate the remaining estimated returns using the following adjusting entries:

| | | |
|---|---|---|
| **Adjusting Entries** | | |
| Sales returns ([10% × $2,000,000] − $130,000) | 70,000 | |
|   Allowance for sales returns | | 70,000 |
| Inventory—estimated returns | 42,000 | |
|   Cost of goods sold (60% × $70,000) | | 42,000 |

**If sales returns are material, they should be estimated and recorded in the same period as the related sales.**

Quite often, a customer will return merchandise because it has been damaged during shipment or is defective. This possibility must be anticipated in a company's estimate of returns. As you will study in Chapter 9, inventory is valued at the lower-of-cost-or-market. Therefore, damaged or defective merchandise returned from a customer must be written down to market value.

Assuming that the estimates of future returns are correct, the following (summary) journal entry would be recorded in 2007:

| | | |
|---|---|---|
| Allowance for sales returns | 70,000 | |
|   Accounts receivable | | 70,000 |

**If the estimate of future sales returns turns out to be wrong, the new estimate is incorporated into accounting determinations in the next period.**

What happens if the estimate of future returns turns out to be more or less than $70,000? Remember from previous discussions that when an estimate turns out to be wrong, we don't revise prior years' financial statements to reflect the new estimate. Instead, we merely incorporate the new estimate in any related accounting determinations from that point on. Suppose in our illustration that in 2007 actual returns from 2006 sales are $60,000, instead of $70,000. If that happens, the allowance account will have a $10,000 balance and the inventory account will have a $6,000 balance ($10,000 × 60%) representing inventory that was not returned as anticipated. These balances can be used to offset actual returns in 2007 from 2007 sales. As a result, the 2007 adjusting entry to record estimated returns would be $10,000 ($6,000 in cost of goods sold/inventory) less than if the 2006 estimate had been correct. Similarly, if actual returns are $80,000, the 2007 adjusting entry will be $10,000 ($6,000) higher than if the 2006 estimate had been correct.

**Experience guides firms when estimating returns.**

How do companies estimate returns? Principally they rely on past history, taking into account any changes that might affect future experience. For example, changes in customer base, payment terms offered to customers, and overall economic conditions might suggest that future returns will differ from past returns. The task of estimating returns is made easier for many large retail companies whose fiscal year-end is the end of January. Since retail companies generate a large portion of their annual sales during the Christmas season, most returns from these sales would already have been accounted for by the end of January.

**Metro-Goldwyn-Mayer Inc., (MGM)** is engaged in the production and distribution of motion picture and television programs and experiences returns in the home video market. Graphic 7-3 describes the company's approach to estimating returns.

**GRAPHIC 7–3**
Disclosure of Sales Returns Policy-Metro-Goldwyn-Mayer, Inc.

**Summary of Significant Accounting Policies (in part)**
**Sales Returns**
In the home video market, the Company calculates an estimate of future returns of product. In determining the estimate of product sales that will be returned, the company performs an analysis that considers historical returns, changes in customer demand and current economic trends. Based on this information, a percentage of each sale is reserved provided that the customer has the right of return.

**If sales returns are immaterial, they can be recorded as they occur.**

In some industries, returns typically are small and infrequent. Companies in these industries usually simply record returns in the period they occur because the effect on income measurement and asset valuation is immaterial. In a few situations, significant uncertainty as to future collection is created by the right of return. In those cases, revenue recognition is deferred until the uncertainty is resolved. We discussed this possibility in Chapter 5.

● LO5

**FINANCIAL REPORTING CASE**
Q1, p. 305

**The use of the *allowance method* is an attempt to satisfy the matching principle in accounting for bad debts.**

**Uncollectible Accounts Receivable.** Companies that extend credit to customers know that it's unlikely that all customers will fully pay their accounts. **Bad debt expense** is an inherent cost of granting credit. It's an operating expense incurred to boost sales. As a result, even when specific customer accounts haven't been proven uncollectible by the end of the reporting period, the expense properly should be matched with sales revenue in the income statement for that period.[7] Likewise, as it's not expected that all accounts receivable will be collected, the balance sheet should report only the expected net realizable value of the asset, that is, the amount of cash the company expects to actually collect from customers. An estimate is therefore needed to record bad debt expense and the related reduction of accounts receivable. In an adjusting entry, we record bad debt expense and reduce accounts receivable indirectly by crediting a contra account (allowance for uncollectible accounts) to accounts receivable for an estimate of the amount that eventually will prove uncollectible. This approach to accounting for bad debts is known as the **allowance method.**

● LO6

There are two ways commonly used to arrive at this estimate of future bad debts—the income statement approach and the balance sheet approach. Illustration 7–3 is used to demonstrate both approaches. As you proceed through the illustration, remember that the two approaches represent alternative ways to estimate the *amount* of future bad debts. Except for the amounts, the accounting entries are identical.

**ILLUSTRATION 7–3**
Bad Debts

The Hawthorne Manufacturing Company sells its products offering 30 days' credit to its customers. During 2006, its first year of operations, the following events occurred:

| | |
|---|---|
| Sales on credit | $1,200,000 |
| Cash collections from credit customers | (895,000) |
| Accounts receivable, end of year | $ 305,000 |

There were no specific accounts determined to be uncollectible in 2006. The company anticipates that 2% of all credit sales will ultimately become uncollectible.

**Bad debt expense is estimated as a percentage of net credit sales.**

**Income statement approach.** Using the **income statement approach,** we estimate bad debt expense as a percentage of each period's net credit sales. This percentage usually is determined by reviewing the company's recent history of the relationship between credit sales and actual bad debts. For a relatively new company, this percentage may be obtained by referring to other sources such as industry averages.

[7]Some consider bad debts to be a contra (reduction) to revenue rather than an operating expense.

Under the income statement approach, the Hawthorne Manufacturing Company would make the following adjusting journal entry at the end of 2006:

**FINANCIAL REPORTING CASE**

Q2, p. 305

| | | |
|---|---|---|
| Bad debt expense (2% × $1,200,000) | 24,000 | |
| Allowance for uncollectible accounts | | 24,000 |

Allowance for uncollectible accounts is a contra account to accounts receivable. In the current asset section of the 2006 balance sheet, accounts receivable would be reported *net* of the allowance, as follows:

| | |
|---|---|
| Accounts receivable | $305,000 |
| Less: Allowance for uncollectible accounts | (24,000) |
| Net accounts receivable | $281,000 |

Quite often, companies report the allowance for uncollectible accounts (sometimes called *allowance for doubtful accounts*) parenthetically or alongside the accounts receivable account title separated by a dash or a comma. For example, **FedEx Corporation** reported the following under current assets in its comparative balance sheets for 2004 and 2003:

**FedEx Corporation**

| | ($ in millions) | |
|---|---|---|
| | **2004** | **2003** |
| Receivables—less allowances of $151 and $149 | $3,027 | $2,627 |

The $3,027 million figure at the end of 2004 is the company's estimate of the net realizable value of accounts receivable. Actual (gross) accounts receivable at the end of 2004 were $3,178 million ($3,027 + $151).

It's important to notice that the income statement approach focuses on the current year's credit sales. The effect on the balance sheet—the allowance for uncollectible accounts and hence net accounts receivable—is an incidental result of estimating the expense. An alternative is to focus on the balance sheet amounts instead. We look at this approach next.

**Using the *income statement approach,* the balance sheet amount is an indirect outcome of estimating bad debt expense.**

**Balance sheet approach.** Using the **balance sheet approach** to estimate future bad debts, we determine bad debt expense by estimating the net realizable value of accounts receivable to be reported in the balance sheet. In other words, the allowance for uncollectible accounts is determined. Bad debt expense is an indirect outcome of adjusting the allowance account to the desired balance.

**Using the *balance sheet approach,* bad debt expense is an incidental result of estimating the net realizable value of accounts receivable.**

For the Hawthorne Manufacturing Company example in Illustration 7–3, the company would estimate the amount of uncollectible accounts that will result from the $305,000 in accounts receivable outstanding at the end of 2006. This could be done by analyzing each customer account, by applying a percentage to the entire outstanding receivable balance, or by applying different percentages to accounts receivable balances depending on the length of time outstanding. This latter approach normally employs an **accounts receivable aging schedule.** For example, the aging schedule for Hawthorne's 2006 year-end accounts receivable is shown in Illustration 7–3A.

**ETHICAL DILEMMA**

The management of the Auto Parts Division of the Santana Corporation receives a bonus if the division's income achieves a specific target. For 2006 the target will be achieved by a wide margin. Mary Beth Williams, the controller of the division, has been asked by Philip Stanton, the head of the division's management team, to try to reduce this year's income and "bank" some of the profits for future years. Mary Beth suggests that the division's bad debt expense as a percentage of net credit sales for 2006 be increased from 3% to 5%. She believes that 3% is the more accurate estimate but knows that both the corporation's internal auditors as well as the external auditors allow some flexibility when estimates are involved. Does Mary Beth's proposal present an ethical dilemma?

**ILLUSTRATION 7–3A**
Accounts Receivable Aging Schedule

The schedule assumes older accounts are more likely to prove uncollectible.

| Customer | Accounts Receivable 12/31/06 | 0–60 Days | 61–90 Days | 91–120 Days | Over 120 Days |
|---|---|---|---|---|---|
| Axel Manufacturing Co. | $ 20,000 | $ 14,000 | $ 6,000 | | |
| Banner Corporation | 33,000 | | 20,000 | $10,000 | $ 3,000 |
| Dando Company | 60,000 | 50,000 | 10,000 | | |
| . . . . | . . | . . | . . | . . | . . |
| . . . . | . . | . . | . . | . . | . . |
| Xicon Company | 18,000 | 10,000 | 4,000 | 3,000 | 1,000 |
| Totals | $305,000 | $220,000 | $50,000 | $25,000 | $10,000 |

Higher estimated default percentages are applied to groups of older receivables.

**Summary**

| Age Group | Amount | Estimated Percent Uncollectible | Estimated Allowance |
|---|---|---|---|
| 0–60 days | $220,000 | 5% | $11,000 |
| 61–90 days | 50,000 | 10% | 5,000 |
| 91–120 days | 25,000 | 20% | 5,000 |
| Over 120 days | 10,000 | 45% | 4,500 |
| Allowance for uncollectible accounts | | | $25,500 |

The schedule classifies the year-end receivable balances according to their length of time outstanding. Presumably, the longer an account has been outstanding the more likely it will prove uncollectible. Based on past experience or other sources of information, a percentage is applied to age group totals.

The 2006 entry to record bad debts adjusts the balance in the allowance for uncollectible accounts to this required amount of $25,500. Because it is the first year of operations for Hawthorne and the beginning balance in the allowance account is zero, the adjusting entry would *debit* bad debt expense and *credit* allowance for uncollectible accounts for $25,500.

**Allowance**

| | Debit | Credit |
|---|---|---|
| Beg. bal. | | 4,000 |
| Adj. entry | | 21,500 |
| Bal. | | 25,500 |

To illustrate the concept further, let's suppose that this was not the first year of operations and the allowance account prior to the adjusting entry had a *credit* balance of $4,000. Then the amount of the entry would be $21,500—the amount necessary to adjust a credit balance of $4,000 to a credit balance of $25,500. Similarly, if the allowance account prior to the adjusting entry had a *debit* balance[8] of $4,000, then the amount of the entry would be $29,500.

Some companies use a combination of approaches in estimating bad debts. For example, Hawthorne could decide to accrue bad debts on a monthly basis using the income statement approach and then employ the balance sheet approach at the end of the year based on an aging of receivables. Each month an adjusting entry would record a debit to bad debt expense and a credit to allowance for uncollectible accounts equal to 2% of credit sales. In our illustration, the monthly accruals for 2006 would result in the following account balances at the end of 2006:

**Accounts Receivable**

| Debit | Credit |
|---|---|
| 305,000 | |

**Bad Debt Expense**

| Debit | Credit |
|---|---|
| 24,000 | |

**Allowance for Uncollectible Accounts**

| Debit | Credit |
|---|---|
| | 24,000 |

[8] A debit balance could result if the amount of receivables actually written off (discussed below) during the period exceeds the beginning credit balance in the allowance account.

At the end of the year, if the aging revealed a required allowance of $25,500, the following adjusting entry would be recorded:

| | | |
|---|---|---|
| Bad debt expense | 1,500 | |
| Allowance for uncollectible accounts | | 1,500 |

This entry adjusts the allowance account to the required amount.

In the 2006 balance sheet, accounts receivable would be reported net of the allowance, as follows:

| | |
|---|---|
| Accounts receivable | $305,000 |
| Less: Allowance for uncollectible accounts | (25,500) |
| Net accounts receivable | $279,500 |

**When accounts are deemed uncollectible.** The actual write-off of a receivable occurs when it is determined that all or a portion of the amount due will not be collected. Using the allowance method, the write-off is recorded as a debit to allowance for uncollectible accounts and a credit to accounts receivable. In our illustration, assume that actual bad debts in 2007 were $25,000. These write-offs would be recorded (in a summary journal entry) as follows:

| | | |
|---|---|---|
| Allowance for uncollectible accounts | 25,000 | |
| Accounts receivable | | 25,000 |

Net realizable value is not affected directly by the write-offs.

The write-off of an account receivable reduces both receivables and the allowance, thus having no effect on income or financial position.

| | |
|---|---|
| Accounts receivable | $280,000 |
| Less: Allowance for uncollectible accounts | (500) |
| Net accounts receivable | $279,500 |

Of course, actual bad debts will tend to differ from estimates. However, the year in which the estimate is made, 2006 in this case, is unaffected by the incorrect estimate. If the prior year's estimate of bad debts is too low, then, using the balance sheet approach, bad debt expense in the subsequent year will be increased. If the estimate is too high, then bad debt expense in the subsequent year will be decreased. For example, in our illustration, the allowance at the end of 2006 is $25,500. Actual bad debts related to 2006 receivables are $25,000. 2006's financial information cannot be changed. Instead, the $500 credit balance in allowance for uncollectible accounts will cause 2007's bad debt expense to be less than if 2006's estimate of bad debts had been correct.

**When previously written-off accounts are collected.** Occasionally, a receivable that has been written off will be collected in part or in full. When this happens, the receivable and the allowance should be reinstated. In other words, the entry to write off the account simply is reversed. The collection is then recorded the usual way as a debit to cash and a credit to accounts receivable. This process ensures that the company will have a complete record of the payment history of the customer. For example, assume that in our illustration, $1,200 that was previously written off is collected. The following journal entries record the event:

Recoveries of accounts receivable previously written off require the reinstatement of both the receivable and the allowance.

| | | | |
|---|---|---|---|
| Accounts receivable | 1,200 | | To reinstate the receivable previously written off. |
| Allowance for uncollectible accounts | | 1,200 | |
| Cash | 1,200 | | To record the cash collection. |
| Accounts receivable | | 1,200 | |

**Direct write-off of uncollectible accounts.** If uncollectible accounts are not anticipated or are immaterial, or if it's not possible to reliably estimate uncollectible accounts, an allowance for uncollectible accounts is not appropriate. In these few cases, adjusting entries are not recorded and any bad debts that do arise simply are written off as bad debt expense. A $750 uncollectible account would be recorded as follows:

FINANCIAL REPORTING CASE

Q3, p. 305

| | | |
|---|---|---|
| Bad debt expense . . . . . . . . . . . . . . . . . . . . . . . . . . . . . . . . . . . | 750 | |
| Accounts receivable . . . . . . . . . . . . . . . . . . . . . . . . . . . . . . . . . | | 750 |

**The *direct write-off method* is used only rarely for financial reporting, but it is the required method for income tax purposes.**

This approach is known as the **direct write-off method.** Of course, if the sale that generated this receivable occurred in a previous reporting period, the matching principle is violated. Operating expenses would have been understated and assets overstated in that period. This is why the direct write-off method of accounting for uncollectible accounts is not permitted by GAAP except in limited circumstances. Specifically, the allowance method must be used if it is probable that a material amount of receivables will not be collected and the amount can be reasonably estimated.[9] For federal income tax purposes, however, the direct write-off method is the required method for most companies and the allowance method is not permitted.

Graphic 7–4 summarizes the key issues involving measuring and reporting accounts receivable.

**GRAPHIC 7–4**
Measuring and Reporting Accounts Receivable

| | |
|---|---|
| **Recognition** | Depends on the earnings process; for most credit sales, revenue and the related receivables are recognized at the point of delivery. |
| **Initial valuation** | Initially recorded at the exchange price agreed upon by the buyer and seller. |
| **Subsequent valuation** | Initial valuation reduced by:<br>1. Allowance for sales returns<br>2. Allowance for uncollectible accounts:<br>—The income statement approach<br>—The balance sheet approach |
| **Classification** | Almost always classified as a current asset. |

**GLOBAL PERSPECTIVE**

In the United States, bad debts are estimated and the allowance for uncollectibles is deducted from the face amount of receivables. Globally, the practice of estimating bad debts is standard. Most countries also establish an allowance, or reserve, for bad debts that reduces receivables to net realizable value.

# CONCEPT REVIEW EXERCISE

## UNCOLLECTIBLE ACCOUNTS RECEIVABLE

The Hawthorne Manufacturing Company sells its products, offering 30 days' credit to its customers. Uncollectible amounts are estimated by accruing a monthly charge to bad debt expense equal to 2% of credit sales. At the end of the year, the allowance for uncollectible accounts is adjusted based on an aging of accounts receivable. The company began 2007 with the following balances in its accounts:

| | |
|---|---|
| Accounts receivable | $305,000 |
| Allowance for uncollectible accounts | (25,500) |

During 2007, sales on credit were $1,300,000, cash collections from customers were $1,250,000, and actual write-offs of accounts were $25,000. An aging of accounts receivable at the end of 2007 indicates a required allowance of $30,000.

[9] "Accounting for Contingencies," *Statement of Financial Accounting Standards No. 5* (Stamford, Conn.: FASB, 1975), par. 8.

**Required:**

1. Determine the balances in accounts receivable and allowance for uncollectible accounts at the end of 2007.
2. Determine bad debt expense for 2007.
3. Prepare journal entries for the monthly accrual of bad debts (in summary form), the write-off of receivables, and the year-end adjusting entry for bad debts.

**SOLUTION**

1. Determine the balances in accounts receivable and allowance for uncollectible accounts at the end of 2007.

| | |
|---|---|
| Accounts receivable: | |
| Beginning balance | $ 305,000 |
| Add: Credit sales | 1,300,000 |
| Less: Cash collections | (1,250,000) |
| Write-offs | (25,000) |
| Ending balance | $ 330,000 |

| | |
|---|---|
| Allowance for uncollectible accounts: | |
| Beginning balance | $ 25,500 |
| Add: Bad debt expense recorded monthly (2% × $1,300,000) | 26,000 |
| Less: Write-offs | (25,000) |
| Balance before year-end adjustment | 26,500 |
| Year-end adjustment | 3,500* |
| Ending balance | $ 30,000 |

*Required allowance of $30,000 less $26,500 already in allowance account.

2. Determine bad debt expense for 2007.

Bad debt expense would be $29,500 (monthly accrual of $26,000 plus year-end adjustment of an additional $3,500).

3. Prepare journal entries for the monthly accrual of bad debts (in summary form), the write-off of receivables, and the year-end adjusting entry for bad debts.

| | | |
|---|---|---|
| Bad debt expense (2% × $1,300,000) | 26,000 | |
| Allowance for uncollectible accounts | | 26,000 |
| *Monthly accrual of 2% of credit sales—summary entry.* | | |
| Allowance for uncollectible accounts | 25,000 | |
| Accounts receivable | | 25,000 |
| *Write-off of accounts receivable as they are determined uncollectible.* | | |
| Bad debt expense | 3,500 | |
| Allowance for uncollectible accounts | | 3,500 |
| *Year-end adjusting entry for bad debts.* | | |

## Notes Receivable

**Notes receivable** are formal credit arrangements between a creditor (lender) and a debtor (borrower). Notes arise from loans to other entities including affiliated companies and to stockholders and employees, from the extension of the credit period to trade customers, and occasionally from the sale of merchandise, other assets, or services. Notes receivable are classified as either current or noncurrent depending on the expected payment date(s).

Our examples below illustrate short-term notes. When the term of a note is longer than a year, it is reported as a long-term note. Long-term notes receivable are discussed in conjunction with long-term notes payable in Chapter 14.

● LO7

## INTEREST-BEARING NOTES

The typical note receivable requires the payment of a specified face amount, also called *principal,* at a specified maturity date or dates. In addition, interest is paid at a stated percentage of the face amount. Interest on notes is calculated as:

Face amount × Annual rate × Fraction of the annual period

For an example, consider Illustration 7–4.

**ILLUSTRATION 7–4**
Note Receivable

The Stridewell Wholesale Shoe Company manufactures athletic shoes that it sells to retailers. On May 1, 2006, the company sold shoes to Harmon Sporting Goods. Stridewell agreed to accept a $700,000, 6-month, 12% note in payment for the shoes. Interest is payable at maturity.
Stridewell would account for the note as follows:*

| | | |
|---|---|---|
| **May 1, 2006** | | |
| Note receivable | 700,000 | |
| Sales revenue | | 700,000 |
| *To record the sale of goods in exchange for a note receivable.* | | |
| **November 1, 2006** | | |
| Cash ($700,000 + $42,000) | 742,000 | |
| Interest revenue ($700,000 × 12% × 6/12) | | 42,000 |
| Note receivable | | 700,000 |
| *To record the collection of the note at maturity.* | | |

*To focus on recording the note we intentionally omit the entry required for the cost of the goods sold if the perpetual inventory system is used.

If the sale in the illustration occurs on August 1, 2006, and the company's fiscal year-end is December 31, a year-end adjusting entry accrues interest earned.

| | | |
|---|---|---|
| **December 31, 2006** | | |
| Interest receivable | 35,000 | |
| Interest revenue ($700,000 × 12% × 5/12) | | 35,000 |

The February 1 collection is then recorded as follows:

| | | |
|---|---|---|
| **February 1, 2007** | | |
| Cash ($700,000 + [$700,000 × 12% × 6/12]) | 742,000 | |
| Interest revenue ($700,000 × 12% × 1/12) | | 7,000 |
| Interest receivable (accrued at December 31) | | 35,000 |
| Note receivable | | 700,000 |

## NONINTEREST-BEARING NOTES

Sometimes a receivable assumes the form of a so-called **noninterest-bearing note**. The name is a misnomer, though. Noninterest-bearing notes actually do bear interest, but the interest is deducted (or discounted) from the face amount to determine the cash proceeds made available to the borrower at the outset. For example, the preceding note could be packaged as a $700,000 noninterest-bearing note, with a 12% discount rate. In that case, the $42,000 interest would be discounted at the outset rather than explicitly stated. As a result, the selling price of the shoes would have been only $658,000. Assuming a May 1, 2006 sale, the transaction is recorded as follows:[10]

[10]The entries shown assume the note is recorded by the gross method. By the net method, the interest component is netted against the face amount of the note as follows:

| | | |
|---|---|---|
| **May 1, 2006** | | |
| Note receivable | 658,000 | |
| Sales revenue | | 658,000 |
| **November 1, 2006** | | |
| Cash | 700,000 | |
| Note receivable | | 658,000 |
| Interest revenue ($700,000 × 12% × 6/12) | | 42,000 |

| | | |
|---|---|---|
| **May 1, 2006** | | |
| Note receivable (face amount) | 700,000 | |
| Discount on note receivable ($700,000 × 12% × 6/12) | | 42,000 |
| Sales revenue (difference) | | 658,000 |
| **November 1, 2006** | | |
| Discount on note receivable | 42,000 | |
| Interest revenue | | 42,000 |
| Cash | 700,000 | |
| Note receivable (face amount) | | 700,000 |

**The discount becomes interest revenue in a noninterest-bearing note.**

The discount on note receivable is a contra account to the note receivable account. That is, the note receivable would be reported in the balance sheet net (less) any remaining discount. The discount represents future interest revenue that will be recognized as it is earned over time. The sales revenue under this arrangement is only $658,000, but the interest is calculated as the discount rate times the $700,000 face amount. This causes the *effective* interest rate to be higher than the 12% stated rate.

**When interest is discounted from the face amount of a note, the effective interest rate is higher than the stated discount rate.**

| | |
|---|---|
| $ 42,000 | Interest for 6 months |
| ÷ $658,000 | Sales price |
| = 6.38% | Rate for 6 months |
| × 2* | To annualize the rate |
| = 12.76% | Effective interest rate |

*Two 6-month periods

If the sale occurs on August 1, the December 31, 2006, adjusting entry and the entry to record the cash collection on February 1, 2007, are recorded as follows:

| | | |
|---|---|---|
| **December 31, 2006** | | |
| Discount on note receivable | 35,000 | |
| Interest revenue ($700,000 × 12% × 5/12) | | 35,000 |
| **February 1, 2007** | | |
| Discount on note receivable | 7,000 | |
| Interest revenue ($700,000 × 12% × 1/12) | | 7,000 |
| Cash | 700,000 | |
| Note receivable (face amount) | | 700,000 |

In the December 31, 2006, balance sheet, the note receivable is shown at $693,000, face amount ($700,000) less remaining discount ($7,000).

**Metro-Goldwyn-Mayer Inc., (MGM)** licenses its television programs to networks. The disclosure note shown in Graphic 7–5 describes the company's revenue recognition policy for its license agreements and the use of noninterest-bearing notes.

**Revenue Recognition (in part)**
Revenues from television licensing, together with related costs, are recognized when the feature film or television program is available to the licensee for telecast. Long-term, noninterest-bearing receivables arising from licensing agreements are discounted to present value in accordance with *Accounting Principles Board (APB) Opinion No. 21,* "Interest on Receivables and Payables."

**GRAPHIC 7–5**
Disclosure of Revenue Recognition for License Agreements—Metro-Goldwyn-Mayer, Inc.

**Notes Received Solely for Cash.** If a note with an unrealistic interest rate—even a noninterest-bearing note—is received *solely* in exchange for cash, the cash paid to the issuer is considered to be its present value.[11] Even if this means recording interest at a ridiculously

**When a noninterest-bearing note is received solely in exchange for cash, the amount of cash exchanged is the basis for valuing the note.**

[11]This assumes that no other present or future considerations are included in the agreement. For example, a noninterest-bearing note might be given to a vendor in exchange for cash *and* a promise to provide future inventories at prices lower than anticipated market prices. The issuer values the note at the present value of cash payments using a realistic interest rate, and the difference between present value and cash payments is recognized as interest revenue over the life of the note. This difference also increases future inventory purchases to realistic market prices.

low or zero rate, the amount of cash exchanged is the basis for valuing the note. When a noncash asset is exchanged for a note with a low stated rate, we can argue that its real value is less than it's purported to be, but we can't argue that the present value of a sum of cash currently exchanged is less than that sum. If the noninterest-bearing note in the previous example had been received solely in exchange for $700,000 cash, the transaction would be recorded as follows:

| | | |
|---|---|---|
| Note receivable (face amount) . . . . . . . . . . . . . . . . . . . . . . . . . . . . | 700,000 | |
| Cash (given). . . . . . . . . . . . . . . . . . . . . . . . . . . . . . . . . . . . . . . . | | 700,000 |

### SUBSEQUENT VALUATION OF NOTES RECEIVABLE

Similar to accounts receivable, if a company anticipates bad debts on short-term notes receivable, it uses an allowance account to reduce the receivable to net realizable value. The process of recording bad debt expense is the same as with accounts receivable.

Long-term notes present a more significant measurement problem. The longer the duration of the note, the more likely are bad debts. One of the more difficult measurement problems facing banks and other lending institutions is the estimation of bad debts on their long-term notes (loans). As an example, **Wells Fargo & Company,** a large bank holding company, reported the following in the asset section of a recent balance sheet:

| | December 31 (in millions) | |
|---|---|---|
| | **2004** | **2003** |
| Loans | $287,586 | $253,073 |
| Allowance for loan losses | (3,762) | (3,891) |
| Net loans | $283,824 | $249,182 |

A disclosure note, reproduced in Graphic 7–6, describes Wells Fargo's loan loss policy.

**GRAPHIC 7–6**

Disclosure of Allowance for Loan Losses—Wells Fargo & Company

**Allowance for Loan Losses**

The allowance for loan losses is management's estimate of credit losses inherent in the loan portfolio, including unfunded commitments, at the balance sheet date. Our determination of the allowance, and the resulting provision, is based on judgments and assumptions, including (1) general economic conditions, (2) loan portfolio composition, (3) loan loss experience, (4) management's evaluation of credit risk relating to pools of loans and individual borrowers, (5) sensitivity analysis and expected loss models, and (6) observations from our internal auditors, internal loan review staff or our banking regulators.

When it becomes probable that a creditor will be unable to collect all amounts due according to the contractual terms of a note, the receivable is considered **impaired.** When a creditor's investment in a note receivable becomes impaired for any reason, the receivable is remeasured as the discounted present value of currently expected cash flows at the loan's original effective rate. Impairments of receivables are discussed in Appendix 12B.

## Financing with Receivables

LO8

Receivables, like any other asset, can be sold or used as collateral for debt. In fact, many companies avoid the difficulties of servicing (billing and collecting) receivables by transferring them to financial institutions. This practice also shortens those companies' operating cycles by providing cash to the companies immediately rather than having them wait until credit customers pay the amounts due. Of course, the financial institution will require compensation for providing this service, usually interest and/or a finance charge.

Responding to these desires, financial institutions have developed a wide variety of ways for companies to use their receivables to obtain immediate cash. The methods differ with respect to which rights and risks are retained by the *transferor* (the original holder of the receivables) and those passed on to the *transferee* (the new holder, the financial institution). Despite this diversity, any of these methods can be described as either:

1. A secured borrowing.
2. A sale of receivables.

When a company chooses between a borrowing or a sale, the critical element is the extent to which it (the transferor) is willing to *surrender control over the assets transferred*. The distinction for some arrangements is not always obvious. For such situations the FASB has provided guidelines. Specifically, the transferor is determined to have surrendered control over the receivables if and only if all of the following conditions are met:[12]

a. The transferred assets have been isolated from the transferor—put presumptively beyond the reach of the transferor and its creditors, even in bankruptcy or other receivership.
b. Each transferee has the right to pledge or exchange the assets it received.
c. The transferor does not maintain effective control over the transferred assets through either (1) an agreement that the transferor repurchase or redeem them before their maturity or (2) the ability to cause the transferee to return specific assets.

If the transferor is deemed to have surrendered control over the receivables, the arrangement is accounted for as a sale; otherwise as a secured borrowing.

If all of the above conditions are *not* met, the transferor treats the transaction as *a secured borrowing*. In that case the company records a liability with the receivables serving as collateral.

On the other hand, if each of the three conditions is met, the transferor treats the transaction as a *sale* and accounts for it in the same manner as the sale of any other asset. That is, the transferor "derecognizes" (removes) the receivables from its books, records the proceeds received (usually cash), and recognizes the difference as either a gain or loss (usually a loss) on the sale. On the other side of the transaction, the transferee recognizes the receivables obtained and measures them at their fair value. Let's now look in more detail at these two possibilities.

## SECURED BORROWING

As defined in the previous section, companies sometimes use receivables as collateral for loans. You may already be familiar with the concept of **assigning** or **pledging** receivables as collateral if you or someone you know has a mortgage on a home. The bank or other financial institution holding the mortgage will require that, if the homeowner defaults on the mortgage payments, the home be sold and the proceeds used to pay off the mortgage debt. Similarly, in the case of an assignment of receivables, nonpayment of a debt will require the proceeds from collecting the assigned receivables to go directly toward repayment of the debt.

Usually, the amount borrowed is less than the amount of receivables assigned. The difference provides some protection for the lender to allow for possible uncollectible accounts. Also, the assignee (transferee) usually charges the assignor an up-front finance charge in addition to stated interest on the collateralized loan. The receivables might be collected either by the assignor or the assignee, depending on the details of the arrangement. Illustration 7–5 provides an example.

In Santa Teresa's December 31, 2006, balance sheet, the company would report the receivables and note payable together as follows:

| | |
|---|---|
| ***Current assets:*** | |
| Accounts receivable assigned ($620,000 − 400,000) | $220,000 |
| Less: Liability—financing arrangement ($500,000 − 400,000) | (100,000) |
| Equity in accounts receivable assigned | $120,000 |

[12]"Accounting for Transfers and Servicing of Financial Assets and Extinguishments of Liabilities," *Statement of Financial Accounting Standards No. 140* (Norwalk, Conn.: FASB, 2000). The standard replaces *SFAS 125*.

**ILLUSTRATION 7–5**

Assignment of Accounts Receivable

At the end of November 2006, Santa Teresa Glass Company had outstanding accounts receivable of $750,000. On December 1, 2006, the company borrowed $500,000 from Finance Affiliates and signed a promissory note. Interest at 12% is payable monthly. The company assigned $620,000 of its receivables as collateral for the loan. Finance Affiliates charges a finance fee equal to 1.5% of the accounts receivable assigned.

Santa Teresa Glass records the borrowing as follows:

| | | |
|---|---|---|
| Cash (difference) | 490,700 | |
| Finance charge expense* (1.5% × $620,000) | 9,300 | |
| Liability—financing arrangement | | 500,000 |

Santa Teresa will continue to collect the receivables, record any discounts, sales returns, and bad debt write-offs, but will remit the cash to Finance Affiliates, usually on a monthly basis. When $400,000 of the receivables assigned are collected in December, Santa Teresa Glass records the following entries:

| | | |
|---|---|---|
| Cash | 400,000 | |
| Accounts receivable | | 400,000 |
| Interest expense ($500,000 × 12% × 1/12) | 5,000 | |
| Liability—financing arrangement | 400,000 | |
| Cash | | 405,000 |

*In theory, this fee should be allocated over the entire period of the loan rather than recorded as an expense in the initial period. However, amounts usually are small and the loan period usually is short. For expediency, then, we expense the entire fee immediately.

Netting a liability against a related asset usually is not allowed by GAAP. However, in this case, we deduct the note payable from the accounts receivable assigned because, by contractual agreement, the note will be paid with cash collected from the receivables. In Santa Teresa's financial statements, the arrangement also is described in a disclosure note.

A variation of assigning specific receivables occurs when trade receivables in general rather than specific receivables are pledged as collateral. The responsibility for collection of the receivables remains solely with the company. This variation is referred to as a **pledging** of accounts receivable. No special accounting treatment is needed and the arrangement is simply described in a disclosure note. For example, Graphic 7–7 shows a portion of the long-term debt disclosure note included in recent financial statements of **Lyondell Chemical Company**, a global chemical company.

**GRAPHIC 7–7**

Disclosure of Receivables Used as Collateral—Lyondell Chemical Company

**Long-Term Debt (in part)**

At year-end, the interest rate under the new inventory-based revolving credit facility was LIBOR plus 2.5%. The new revolving credit facility is secured by a lien on all inventory and certain personal property including a pledge of accounts receivable.

## SALE OF RECEIVABLES

Two popular arrangements used for the sale of receivables are *factoring* and *securitization.*

In recent years, the sale of accounts receivable has become an increasingly popular method of financing. Traditionally a technique used by companies in a few industries or with poor credit ratings, the sale of receivables is now a common occurrence for many different types of companies. For example, **Delta Air Lines**, **Phillips Petroleum**, **Unocal**, **IBM**, **Sears**, and **Raytheon** all sell receivables. The two most common types of selling arrangements are **factoring** and **securitization.** We'll now discuss each type.

A **factor** is a financial institution that buys receivables for cash, handles the billing and collection of the receivables, and charges a fee for this service. Actually, credit cards like VISA and Mastercard are forms of factoring arrangements. The seller relinquishes all rights to the future cash receipts in exchange for cash from the buyer (the *factor*).

As an example, Graphic 7–8 shows an excerpt from a recent advertisement of **Bankers Mutual Capital Corporation**, a financial institution that offers factoring as one of its services.

**Accounts Receivable Factoring**
Accounts receivable factoring is the selling of your invoices (accounts receivable) for cash versus waiting 30–60 days to be paid by your customer. Factoring will get you the working capital you need now and improve your cash flow. Bankers will advance 65%–80% against the invoice you generate and pay you the balance less our fee (typically 3%–6%) when the invoice is paid.

**GRAPHIC 7–8**

Advertisement of Factoring Service—Bankers Mutual Capital Corporation

Notice that the factor, Bankers Mutual, advances only between 65%–80% of the factored receivables. The remaining balance is retained as security until all of the receivables are collected and then remitted to the transferor, net of the factor's fee. The fee charged by this factor ranges from 3%–6%. The range depends on, among other things, the quality of the receivables and the length of time before payment is required.

Another popular arrangement used to sell receivables is a **securitization.** In a typical accounts receivable securitization, the company creates a special purpose entity (SPE), usually a trust or a subsidiary. The SPE buys a pool of trade receivables, credit card receivables, or loans from the company, and then sells related securities, for example bonds or commercial paper, that are backed (collateralized) by the receivables.

As an example of a securitization, Graphic 7–9 shows a portion of the disclosure note included in recent financial statements of **Sears, Roebuck and Co.** describing its securitization of credit card receivables.

**Note 1—Summary of Significant Accounting Policies (in part)**
**Accounting for Credit Card Securitizations**
Credit card securitizations are utilized as a part of the Company's overall funding strategy. Sears sells certain of its credit card receivables to various subsidiaries that in turn transfer those balances to master trusts (trusts). The trusts then securitize the receivable balances by issuing certificates representing undivided interests in the trusts receivables to both outside investors and to the Company (as a retained interest).

**GRAPHIC 7–9**

Disclosure of Credit Card Securitizations—Sears, Roebuck and Co.

The specific accounting treatment for the sale of receivables using factoring and securitization arrangements depends on the amount of risk the factor assumes, in particular whether it buys the receivables **without recourse** or **with recourse.**

**Sale without Recourse.** When a company sells accounts receivable **without recourse,** the buyer assumes the risk of uncollectibility. This means the buyer has no *recourse* to the seller if customers don't pay the receivables. In that case, the seller simply accounts for the transaction as a sale of an asset. As we discussed above, the buyer charges a fee for providing this service, usually a percentage of the book value of receivables. Because the fee reduces the proceeds the seller receives from selling the asset, the seller records a loss on sale of assets. The typical factoring arrangement is made without recourse. Illustration 7–6 provides an example.

**The buyer assumes the risk of uncollectibility when accounts receivable are sold *without recourse.***

**Sale with Recourse.** When a company sells accounts receivable **with recourse,** the seller retains the risk of uncollectibility. In effect, the seller guarantees that the buyer will be paid even if some receivables prove to be uncollectible. In Illustration 7–6, even if the receivables were sold with recourse, as long as the three conditions for sale treatment are met, Santa Teresa Glass would still account for the transfer as a sale. The only difference would be the additional requirement that Santa Teresa record the estimated fair value of the recourse obligation as a liability. The recourse obligation is the estimated amount that Santa Teresa will have to pay Finance Affiliates as a reimbursement for uncollectible receivables. Assuming that this amount is estimated at $5,000, the entry recorded by Santa Teresa appears in Illustration 7–6A.

**The seller retains the risk of uncollectibility when accounts receivable are sold *with recourse.***

**ILLUSTRATION 7–6**
Accounts Receivable Factored without Recourse

At the end of November 2006, the Santa Teresa Glass Company had outstanding accounts receivable of $750,000. In December 2006, the company factored $600,000 of accounts receivable to Finance Affiliates. The transfer was made without recourse. Finance Affiliates remits 90% of the factored receivables to Santa Teresa and retains the remaining 10%. When Finance Affiliates collects the receivables, it remits to Santa Teresa the retained amount, less a 4% fee (4% of the total factored amount).

Santa Teresa Glass records the transfer as follows:

The factor's fee is recorded as a loss.

| | | |
|---|---|---|
| Cash (90% × $600,000) | 540,000 | |
| Loss on sale of receivables (4% × $600,000) | 24,000 | |
| Receivable from factor (10% × $600,000 = $60,000 − 24,000 fee) | 36,000 | |
| Accounts receivable (balance sold) | | 600,000 |

**ILLUSTRATION 7–6A**
Accounts Receivable Factored with Recourse

| | | |
|---|---|---|
| Cash (90% × $600,000) | 540,000 | |
| Loss on sale of receivables (4% × $600,000 + 5,000) | 29,000 | |
| Receivable from factor (10% × $600,000 = $60,000 − 24,000 fee) | 36,000 | |
| Recourse liability | | 5,000 |
| Accounts receivable (balance sold) | | 600,000 |

Notice that the estimated recourse liability increases the loss on sale. If the factor collects all of the receivables, Santa Teresa eliminates the recourse liability and increases income (reduces the loss).

If the three conditions for sale treatment are not met, the transfer of receivables is accounted for as a secured borrowing.

If the three conditions for sale treatment were not met, the transfer of receivables would be accounted for as a secured borrowing, as demonstrated in Illustration 7–5. Recently, Sears Roebuck changed its accounting method for the securitization of credit card receivables. Previously, they were accounted for as sales, but now, because the *SFAS No. 140* sale conditions are not met, Sears accounts for the securitizations as secured borrowings. Notice in Graphic 7–9A that the change caused Sears to record over $8 billion in receivables and related secured borrowings.

**GRAPHIC 7–9A**
Disclosure of Credit Card Securitizations—Sears, Roebuck and Co.

**Note 1—Summary of Significant Accounting Policies (in part)**
**Accounting for Credit Card Securitizations**
On March 31, 2003, the Company adopted the requirements of *SFAS No. 140,* "Accounting for Transfers and Servicing of Financial Assets and Extinguishments of Liabilities," which superceded *SFAS No. 125.* Under *SFAS No. 125,* the Company's securitization transactions were accounted for as sales of receivables. *SFAS No. 140* established new conditions for a securitization to be accounted for as a sale of receivables. Accordingly, the Company recorded in the balance sheet approximately $8.1 billion of previously unconsolidated securitized credit card receivables and related securitization borrowings in the second quarter of 2001.

## DISCOUNTING A NOTE

The transfer of a note receivable to a financial institution is called *discounting.*

Similar to accounts receivable, a note receivable can be used to obtain immediate cash from a financial institution either by pledging the note as collateral for a loan or by selling the note. The transfer of a note is referred to as **discounting.** The financial institution accepts the note and gives the seller cash equal to the maturity value of the note reduced by a discount. The discount is computed by applying a discount rate to the maturity value and represents the financing fee the financial institution charges for the transaction. Illustration 7–7 provides an example of the calculation of the proceeds received by the transferor.

Similar to accounts receivable, if the three conditions for sale treatment are met, Stridewell would account for the transfer as a sale. If the conditions are not met, it is treated as a secured borrowing. For example, if the sale conditions are met, Illustration 7–7A shows the appropriate journal entries.

On December 31, 2006, the Stridewell Wholesale Shoe Company sold land in exchange for a nine-month, 10% note. The note requires the payment of $200,000 *plus* interest on September 30, 2007. The company's fiscal year-end is December 31. The 10% rate properly reflects the time value of money for this type of note. On March 31, 2007, Stridewell discounted the note at the Bank of the East. The bank's discount rate is 12%.

Because the note had been outstanding for three months before it's discounted at the bank, Stridewell first records the interest that has accrued prior to being discounted:

**ILLUSTRATION 7–7**
Discounting a Note Receivable

**March 31, 2007**

| | | |
|---|---|---|
| Interest receivable | 5,000 | |
| Interest revenue ($200,000 × 10% × 3/12) | | 5,000 |

STEP 1: Accrue interest earned on the note receivable prior to its being discounted.

Next, the value of the note if held to maturity is calculated. Then the discount for the time remaining to maturity is deducted to determine the cash proceeds from discounting the note:

| | |
|---|---|
| $200,000 | Face amount |
| 15,000 | Interest to maturity ($200,000 × 10% × 9/12) |
| 215,000 | Maturity value |
| (12,900) | Discount ($215,000 × 12% × 6/12) |
| $202,100 | Cash proceeds |

STEP 2: Add interest to maturity to calculate maturity value.

STEP 3: Deduct discount to calculate cash proceeds.

**ILLUSTRATION 7–7A**
Discounted Note Treated as a Sale

| | | |
|---|---|---|
| Cash (proceeds determined above) | 202,100 | |
| Loss on sale of note receivable (difference) | 2,900 | |
| Note receivable (face amount) | | 200,000 |
| Interest receivable (accrued interest determined above) | | 5,000 |

Record a loss (or gain) for difference between the cash proceeds and the note's book value.

# CONCEPT REVIEW EXERCISE

## FINANCING WITH RECEIVABLES

The Hollywood Lumber Company obtains financing from the Midwest Finance Company by factoring (or discounting) its receivables. During June 2006, the company factored $1,000,000 of accounts receivable to Midwest. The transfer was made *without* recourse. The factor, Midwest Finance, remits 80% of the factored receivables and retains 20%. When the receivables are collected by Midwest, the retained amount, less a 3% fee (3% of the total factored amount), will be remitted to Hollywood Lumber.

In addition, on June 30, 2006, Hollywood discounted a note receivable without recourse. The note, which originated on March 31, 2006, requires the payment of $150,000 *plus* interest at 8% on March 31, 2007. Midwest's discount rate is 10%. The company's fiscal year-end is December 31.

**Required:**

Prepare journal entries for Hollywood Lumber for the factoring of accounts receivable and the note receivable discounted on June 30. Assume that the required criteria are met and the transfers are accounted for as sales.

## SOLUTION

**The Factoring of Receivables**

| | | |
|---|---|---|
| Cash (80% × $1,000,000) | 800,000 | |
| Loss on sale of receivables (3% × $1,000,000) | 30,000 | |
| Receivable from factor (20% × $1,000,000 − 30,000 fee) | 170,000 | |
| Accounts receivable (balance sold) | | 1,000,000 |

**The Note Receivable Discounted**

| | | |
|---|---|---|
| Interest receivable | 3,000 | |
| Interest revenue ($150,000 × 8% × 3/12) | | 3,000 |
| Cash (proceeds determined below) | 149,850 | |
| Loss on sale of note receivable (difference) | 3,150 | |
| Note receivable (face amount) | | 150,000 |
| Interest receivable (accrued interest determined above) | | 3,000 |

**Add interest to maturity to calculate maturity value.**

**Deduct discount to calculate cash proceeds.**

| | |
|---|---|
| $150,000 | Face amount |
| 12,000 | Interest to maturity ($150,000 × 8%) |
| 162,000 | Maturity value |
| (12,150) | Discount ($162,000 × 10% × 9/12) |
| $149,850 | Cash proceeds |

In summary, there are several ways receivables can be used as a method of financing. However, each of these arrangements can be categorized as either a secured borrowing or as an outright sale of the receivables. Graphic 7–10 provides a visual summary of the possibilities.

**GRAPHIC 7–10**
Accounting for the Financing of Receivables

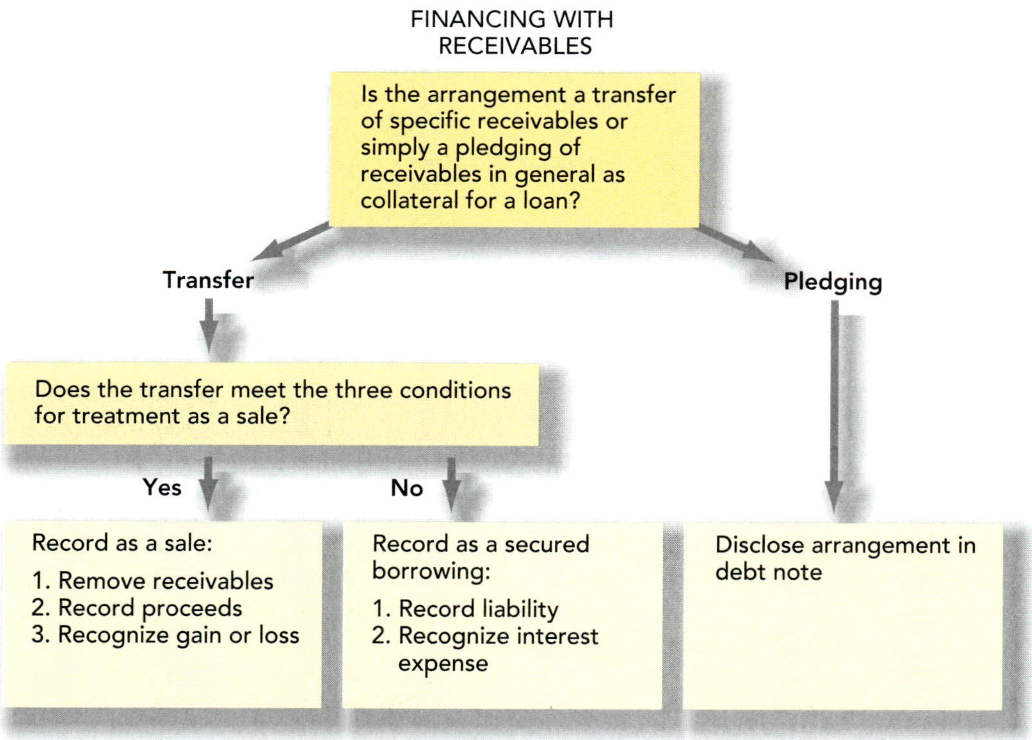

## DECISION MAKERS' PERSPECTIVE

### Receivables Management

• LO9

A company's investment in receivables is influenced by several variables, including the level of sales, the nature of the product or service sold, and credit and collection policies. These variables are, of course, related. For example, a change in credit policies could affect sales. In fact, more liberal credit policies—allowing customers a longer time to pay or offering cash discounts for early payment—often are initiated with the specific objective of increasing sales volume.

Management's choice of credit and collection policies often involves trade-offs. For example, offering cash discounts may increase sales volume, accelerate customer payment, and reduce bad debts. These benefits are not without cost. The cash discounts reduce the amount of cash collected from customers who take advantage of the discounts. Extending payment terms also may increase sales volume. However, this creates an increase in the required investment in receivables and may increase bad debts.

Management must evaluate the costs and benefits of any change in credit and collection policies.

The ability to use receivables as a method of financing also offers management alternatives. Assigning, factoring, and discounting receivables are alternative methods of financing operations that must be evaluated relative to other financing methods such as lines of credit or other types of short-term borrowing.

Investors, creditors, and financial analysts can gain important insights by monitoring a company's investment in receivables. Chapter 5 introduced the receivables turnover ratio and the related average collection period, ratios designed to monitor receivables. Recall that these ratios are calculated as follows:

$$\text{Receivables turnover ratio} = \frac{\text{Net sales}}{\text{Average accounts receivable (net)}}$$

$$\text{Average collection period} = \frac{\text{365 days}}{\text{Receivables turnover ratio}}$$

The turnover ratio shows the number of times during a period that the average accounts receivable balance is collected, and the average collection period is an approximation of the number of days the average accounts receivable balance is outstanding.

As a company's sales grow, receivables also will increase. If the percentage increase in receivables is greater than the percentage increase in sales, the receivables turnover ratio will decline (the average collection period will increase). This could indicate customer dissatisfaction with the product or that the company has extended too generous payment terms in order to attract new customers, which, in turn, could increase sales returns and bad debts.

These ratios also can be used to compare the relative effectiveness of companies in managing the investment in receivables. Of course, it would be meaningless to compare the receivables turnover ratio of a computer products company such as **IBM** with that of, say, a food products company like **Hershey.** A company selling high-priced, low-volume products like mainframe computers generally will grant customers longer payment terms than a company selling lower priced, higher volume food products. Graphic 7–11 lists the 2004 receivables turnover ratio for some well-known companies. The differences are as expected, given the nature of the companies' products.

**GRAPHIC 7–11** Receivables Turnover Ratios

| Company | 2004 Receivables Turnover Ratio |
|---|---|
| IBM | 4.26 |
| Johnson & Johnson | 5.12 |
| Caterpillar | 5.44 |
| Hershey | 7.09 |
| Intel | 7.91 |
| Sara Lee | 10.34 |

Let's compute the 2004 receivables turnover ratio and the average collection period for two companies in the same industry, **Dell** and **Apple Computer.**

Balance sheet and income statement information—Dell and Apple

($ in millions)

| | Dell | | Apple | |
|---|---|---|---|---|
| | 2004 | 2003 | 2004 | 2003 |
| Accounts receivable (net) | $3,635 | $2,586 | $774 | $766 |
| Two-year averages | $ 3,111 | | $ 770 | |
| Net sales—2004 | $41,444 | | $8,279 | |

Receivables turnover and average collection period—Dell and Apple

| | Dell | Apple | Industry Average |
|---|---|---|---|
| Receivables turnover | $= \frac{\$41,444}{\$3,111} = 13.32$ | $\frac{\$8,279}{\$770} = 10.75$ | 8.0 |
| Average collection period | $= \frac{365}{13.32} = 27$ days | $\frac{365}{10.75} = 34$ days | 46 days |

On average, it takes Apple seven days longer than Dell to collect its receivables. Both companies take less time to collect receivables than the industry average.

Academic research also has shown receivables information to be useful in financial statement analysis. Professors Lev and Thiagarajan empirically demonstrated the importance of a set of 12 fundamental variables in valuing companies' common stock. The set of variables included accounts receivable (change in accounts receivable minus change in sales) and allowance for uncollectible accounts (change in accounts receivable minus change in the allowance). Motivation for the receivables variable was that disproportionate increases in accounts receivable (relative to sales increases) can indicate difficulties in selling products, reflected in more lenient credit policies. The allowance variable was expected to indicate inadequate bad debt provisions. Both were found to be significant indicators of stock returns during high inflation years.[13]

## Earnings Quality

In May 2001 the Securities and Exchange Commission sued the former top executives at **Sunbeam,** charging the company with financial reporting fraud that allegedly cost investors billions in losses. In the mid-1990s, Sunbeam needed help: its profits had declined significantly as did its stock price, and in 1996, the company reported a loss from continuing operations of $198 million. To the rescue comes Albert Dunlap, also known as "Chainsaw Al," based on his reputation as a ruthless executive known for his ability to restructure and turn around troubled companies, largely by eliminating jobs.

The strategy appeared to work. In 1997, Sunbeam's revenues had risen by 18% and profits were back in the black with income from continuing operations of $123 million. However, in April 1998, **PaineWebber Inc.** downgraded Sunbeam's stock recommendation. Why the downgrade? PaineWebber had noticed unusually high accounts receivable, massive increases in sales of electric blankets in the third quarter 1997, which usually sell best in the fourth quarter, as well as unusually high sales of barbecue grills for the fourth quarter. Soon after, Sunbeam announced a first quarter loss of $44.6 million, and Sunbeam's stock price fell 25%.

It eventually came to light that Dunlap and Sunbeam had been using a "bill and hold" strategy with retail buyers. This involved selling products at large discounts to retailers before they normally would buy and then holding the products in third-party warehouses, with delivery at a later date. According to an article in *Barron's*, much of the variation in Sunbeam's income from 1996 to 1997 reflected *a discretionary use of accruals* to accelerate expenses to 1996.[14]

**Bad debt expense is one of a variety of discretionary accruals that provide management with the opportunity to manipulate income.**

Bad debt expense, and the corresponding allowance for uncollectible accounts, is one of several so-called discretionary accruals that directly impact a company's income. Other discretionary accruals include warranty expenses, discretionary compensation expenses such as bonuses, sales returns, and restructuring costs. Each of these accruals requires estimates of future events, thus providing management the opportunity to shift income among reporting periods. For example, if management overestimates bad debt expense in one period, a company will report lower profit that period and higher profit in a later period.

**ARTHUR LEVITT, JR.**
A third illusion played by some companies is using unrealistic assumptions to estimate . . . such items as sales returns, loan losses or warranty costs. In doing so, they stash accruals in cookie jars during good times and reach into them when needed in the bad times.[15]

Recall our discussion in Chapter 4 concerning earnings quality. We learned that managers have the ability, to a limited degree, to manipulate reported income and that many observers believe this practice diminishes earnings quality because it can mask permanent earnings. Former SEC Chairman Arthur Levitt listed discretionary accruals, which he called "Miscellaneous Cookie Jar Reserves," as one of the most popular methods companies use to manipulate income.

Financial analysts must be alert to the effect of discretionary accruals on income. Abnormal fluctuations in these items should raise a red flag, motivating further investigation. In the

[13]B. Lev and S. R. Thiagarajan, "Fundamental Information Analysis," *Journal of Accounting Research 31,* no. 2 (Autumn 1993). The main conclusion of the study was that fundamental variables, not just earnings, are useful in firm valuation, particularly when examined in the context of macroeconomic conditions such as inflation.

[14]Jonathan Laing, "Dangerous Games," *Barron's* (June 8, 1998).

[15]Arthur Levitt, Jr., "The Numbers Game," *The CPA Journal*, December, 1998, p. 16.

Sunbeam example, for instance, red flags in the 1996 income statement included a variety of unusual expenses and a large increase in general and administrative expenses. The balance sheet reported an increase of 44% in current liabilities from the prior year. This increase was caused by activities that included a significant accrual for restructuring costs and a large increase in the accrued warranty liability. The allowance for uncollectible accounts also increased by 30%. The marketplace was less than vigilant in noting and interpreting these signs. ■

## FINANCIAL REPORTING CASE SOLUTION

1. **Explain the allowance method of accounting for bad debts.** *(p. 314)* The allowance method estimates future bad debts in order to (1) match bad debt expense with related revenues and (2) report accounts receivable in the balance sheet at net realizable value. In an adjusting entry, we record bad debt expense and reduce accounts receivable indirectly by crediting a contra account to accounts receivable for an estimate of the amount that eventually will prove uncollectible.
2. **What approaches might Cisco have used to arrive at the $275 million bad debt provision?** *(p. 315)* There are two ways commonly used to arrive at an estimate of future bad debts, the income statement approach and the balance sheet approach. Using the income statement approach, we estimate bad debt expense as a percentage of each period's net credit sales. The balance sheet approach determines bad debt expense by estimating the net realizable value of accounts receivable. In other words, the allowance for uncollectible accounts is determined and bad debt expense is an indirect outcome of adjusting the allowance account to the desired balance.
3. **Are there any alternatives to the allowance method?** *(p. 317)* An alternative to the allowance method is the direct write-off method. Using this method, adjusting entries are not recorded and any bad debt that does arise simply is written off as bad debt expense. Of course, if the sale that generated this receivable occurred in a previous reporting period, this violates the matching principle. Operating expenses would have been understated and assets overstated that period. This is why the direct write-off method is not permitted by GAAP except in limited circumstances. ■

## THE BOTTOM LINE

1. Internal control refers to the plan designed to encourage adherence to company policies and procedures; promote operational efficiency; minimize irregularities, errors, thefts or fraud; and maximize the reliability and accuracy of accounting data. Key elements of an internal control system for cash receipts and disbursements include separation of record-keeping from control of cash duties and the periodic preparation of a bank reconciliation.
2. Cash can be informally restricted by management for a particular purpose. Restrictions also can be contractually imposed. If restricted cash is available for current operations or to pay current liabilities, it's classified as a current asset; otherwise, it's classified as investments and funds or other assets.
3. The gross method of accounting for cash discounts considers a discount not taken as part of sales revenue. The net method considers a discount not taken as interest revenue.
4. When merchandise returns are anticipated, an allowance for sales returns should be recorded as a contra account to accounts receivable and sales revenue also should be reduced by the anticipated sales returns.
5. Uncollectible accounts receivable should be anticipated in order to match bad debt expense with revenues generated. Likewise, accounts receivable should be reduced by an allowance for uncollectible accounts to report accounts receivable at net realizable value.

6. There are two approaches to estimating future bad debts. The income statement approach estimates bad debt expense based on the notion that a certain percentage of each period's credit sales will prove to be uncollectible. The balance sheet approach to estimating future bad debts indirectly determines bad debt expense by directly estimating the net realizable value of accounts receivable at the end of the period.
7. Notes receivable are formal credit arrangements between a creditor (lender) and a debtor (borrower). The typical note receivable requires the payment of a specified face amount, also called principal, at a specified maturity date or dates. In addition, interest is paid at a stated percentage of the face amount. Interest on notes is calculated by multiplying the face amount by the annual rate by the fraction of the annual period.
8. A wide variety of methods exists for companies to use their receivables to obtain immediate cash. These methods can be described as either:
   a. A secured borrowing
   b. A sale of receivables

   If three conditions indicating surrender of control are met, the transferor accounts for the transfer of receivables as a sale; otherwise as a secured borrowing.
9. A company's investment in receivables is influenced by several related variables, to include the level of sales, the nature of the product or service, and credit and collection policies. Investors, creditors, and financial analysts can gain important insights by monitoring a company's investment in receivables. The receivables turnover and average collection period ratios are designed to monitor receivables. ■

# APPENDIX 7 CASH CONTROLS

## Bank Reconciliation

One of the most important tools used in the control of cash is the **bank reconciliation.** Since all cash receipts are deposited into the bank account and cash disbursements are made by check, the bank account provides a separate record of cash. It's desirable to periodically compare the bank balance with the balance in the company's own records and reconcile any differences.

From your own personal experience, you know that the ending balance in your checking account reported on the monthly bank statement you receive rarely equals the balance you have recorded in your checkbook. Differences arise from two types of items: timing differences and errors.

**Differences between the cash book and bank balance occur due to differences in the timing of recognition of certain transactions and errors.**

*Timing differences* occur when the company and the bank record transactions at different times. At any point in time the company may have adjusted the cash balance for items of which the bank is not yet aware. Likewise, the bank may have adjusted its record of that balance by items of which the company is not yet aware. For example, checks written and cash deposits are not all processed by the bank in the same month that they are recorded by the company. Also, the bank may adjust the company's account for items such as service charges that the company is not aware of until the bank statement is received.

*Errors* can be made either by the company or the bank. For example, a check might be written for $210 but recorded on the company's books as a $120 disbursement; a deposit of $500 might be processed incorrectly by the bank as a $50 deposit. In addition to serving as a safeguard of cash, the bank reconciliation also uncovers errors such as these and helps ensure that the proper cash balance is reported in the balance sheet.

**STEP 1: Adjust the bank balance to the corrected cash balance.**

Bank reconciliations include adjustments to the balance per bank for timing differences involving transactions already reflected in the company's accounting records that have not yet been processed by the bank. These adjustments usually include *checks outstanding* and *deposits outstanding*. In addition, the balance per bank would be adjusted for any bank errors discovered. These adjustments produce an adjusted bank balance that represents the corrected cash balance.

**STEP 2: Adjust the book balance to the corrected cash balance.**

The balance per books is similarly adjusted for timing differences involving transactions already reflected by the bank of which the company is unaware until the bank statement is

**Step 1: Adjustments to Bank Balance:**

1. *Add deposits outstanding.* These represent cash amounts received by the company and debited to cash that have not been deposited in the bank by the bank statement cutoff date and cash receipts deposited in the bank near the end of the period that are not recorded by the bank until after the cutoff date.
2. *Deduct checks outstanding.* These represent checks written and recorded by the company as credits to cash that have not yet been processed by the bank before the cutoff date.
3. *Bank errors.* These will either be increases or decreases depending on the nature of the error.

**Step 2: Adjustments to Book Balance:**

1. *Add collections made by the bank* on the company's behalf and other increases in cash that the company is unaware of until the bank statement is received.
2. *Deduct service and other charges* made by the bank that the company is unaware of until the bank statement is received.
3. *Deduct NSF* (nonsufficient funds) *checks.* These are checks previously deposited for which the payors do not have sufficient funds in their accounts to cover the amount of the checks. The checks are returned to the company whose responsibility it is to seek payment from payors.
4. *Company errors.* These will either be increases or decreases depending on the nature of the error.

**GRAPHIC 7A–1**

Bank Reconciliation—Reconciling Items

Bank balance
+ Deposits outstanding
− Checks outstanding
± Errors
Corrected balance

Book balance
+ Collections by bank
− Service charges
− NSF checks
± Errors
Corrected balance

The two corrected balances must equal.

received. These would include service charges, charges for NSF (nonsufficient funds) checks, and collections made by the bank on the company's behalf. In addition, the balance per books is adjusted for any company errors discovered, resulting in an adjusted book balance that will also represent the corrected cash balance. *Each of these adjustments requires a journal entry to correct the book balance.* Only adjustments to the book balance require journal entries. Graphic 7A–1 recaps these reconciling items.

To demonstrate the bank reconciliation process, consider Illustration 7A–1.

The next step is to prepare adjusting journal entries to reflect each of the adjustments to the balance per books. These represent amounts the company was not previously aware of. No adjusting entries are needed for the adjustments to the balance per bank because the company has already recorded these items. However, the bank needs to be notified of any errors discovered.

| | | |
|---|---|---|
| Cash | 1,120 | |
| Notes receivable | | 1,000 |
| Interest revenue | | 120 |

To record the receipt of principal and interest on note collected directly by the bank.

| | | |
|---|---|---|
| Miscellaneous expense (bank service charges) | 80 | |
| Accounts receivable (NSF checks) | 2,187 | |
| Accounts payable (error in check to supplier) | 1,000 | |
| Cash | | 3,267 |

To record credits to cash revealed by the bank reconciliation.

After these entries are posted, the general ledger cash account will equal the corrected balance of $33,129.

## Petty Cash

Most companies keep a small amount of cash on hand to pay for low-cost items such as postage, office supplies, delivery charges, and entertainment expenses. It would be inconvenient, time consuming, and costly to process a check each time these small payments are made. A petty cash fund provides a more efficient way to handle these payments.

**ILLUSTRATION 7A–1**
Bank Reconciliation

The Hawthorne Manufacturing Company maintains a general checking account at the First Pacific Bank. First Pacific provides a bank statement and canceled checks once a month. The cutoff date is the last day of the month. The bank statement for the month of May is summarized as follows:

| | |
|---|---|
| Balance, May 1, 2006 | $32,120 |
| Deposits | 82,140 |
| Checks processed | (78,433) |
| Service charges | (80) |
| NSF checks | (2,187) |
| Note payment collected by bank (includes $120 interest) | 1,120 |
| Balance, May 31, 2006 | $34,680 |

The company's general ledger cash account has a balance of $35,276 at the end of May. A review of the company records and the bank statement reveals the following:

1. Cash receipts not yet deposited totaled $2,965.
2. A deposit of $1,020 was made on May 31 that was not credited to the company's account until June.
3. All checks written in April have been processed by the bank. Checks written in May that had not been processed by the bank total $5,536.
4. A check written for $1,790 was incorrectly recorded by the company as a $790 disbursement. The check was for payment to a supplier of raw materials.

The bank reconciliation prepared by the company appears as follows:

| **Step 1: Bank Balance to Corrected Balance** | |
|---|---|
| Balance per bank statement | $34,680 |
| Add: Deposits outstanding | 3,985* |
| Deduct: Checks outstanding | (5,536) |
| Corrected cash balance | $33,129 |

| **Step 2: Book Balance to Corrected Balance** | |
|---|---|
| Balance per books | $35,276 |
| Add: Note collected by bank | 1,120 |
| Deduct: | |
| Service charges | (80) |
| NSF checks | (2,187) |
| Error—understatement of check | (1,000) |
| Corrected cash balance | $33,129 |

*$2,965 + 1,020 = $3,985

The petty cash fund always should have cash and receipts that together equal the amount of the fund.

A petty cash fund is established by transferring a specified amount of cash from the company's general checking account to an employee designated as the petty cash custodian. The amount of the fund should approximate the expenditures made from the fund during a relatively short period of time (say a week or a month). The custodian disburses cash from the fund when the appropriate documentation is presented, such as a receipt for the purchase of office supplies. At any point in time, the custodian should be in possession of cash and appropriate receipts that sum to the amount of the fund. The receipts serve as the basis for recording appropriate expenses each time the fund is replenished. Consider the example in Illustration 7A–2.

In journal entry form, the transaction to establish the fund would be recorded as follows:

A petty cash fund is established by writing a check to the custodian.

| **May 1, 2006** | | |
|---|---|---|
| Petty Cash | 200 | |
| Cash (checking account) | | 200 |

**ILLUSTRATION 7A–2**
Petty Cash Fund

On May 1, 2006, the Hawthorne Manufacturing Company established a $200 petty cash fund. John Ringo is designated as the petty cash custodian. The fund will be replenished at the end of each month. On May 1, 2006, a check is written for $200 made out to John Ringo, petty cash custodian. During the month of May, John paid bills totaling $160 summarized as follows:

| | |
|---|---|
| Postage | $ 40 |
| Office supplies | 35 |
| Delivery charges | 55 |
| Entertainment | 30 |
| Total | $160 |

No entries are recorded at the time the actual expenditures are made from the fund. The expenditures are recorded when reimbursement is requested at the end of the month. At that time, a check is written to John Ringo, petty cash custodian, for the total of the fund receipts, $160 in this case. John cashes the check and replenishes the fund to $200. In journal entry form, replenishing the fund would be recorded as follows:

| **May 31, 2006** | | |
|---|---|---|
| Postage expense | 40 | |
| Office supplies expense | 35 | |
| Delivery expense | 55 | |
| Entertainment expense | 30 | |
| Cash (checking account) | | 160 |

**The appropriate expense accounts are debited when the petty cash fund is reimbursed.**

The petty cash account is not debited when replenishing the fund. If, however, the size of the fund is increased at time of replenishment, the account is debited for the increase. Similarly, petty cash would be credited if the size of the fund is decreased.

To maintain the control objective of separation of duties, the petty cash custodian should not be involved in the process of writing or approving checks, nor in recordkeeping. In addition, management should arrange for surprise counts of the fund. ■

## QUESTIONS FOR REVIEW OF KEY TOPICS

**Q 7–1** Define cash equivalents.

**Q 7–2** Explain the primary functions of internal controls procedures in the accounting area. What is meant by separation of duties?

**Q 7–3** What are the responsibilities of management described in Section 404 of the Sarbanes-Oxley Act? What are the responsibilities of the company's auditor?

**Q 7–4** Define a compensating balance. How are compensating balances reported in financial statements?

**Q 7–5** Explain the difference between a trade discount and a cash discount.

**Q 7–6** Distinguish between the gross and net methods of accounting for cash discounts.

**Q 7–7** Briefly explain the accounting treatment for sales returns.

**Q 7–8** Explain the typical way companies account for uncollectible accounts receivable (bad debts). When is it permissible to record bad debt expense only when receivables actually prove uncollectible?

**Q 7–9** Briefly explain the difference between the income statement approach and the balance sheet approach to estimating bad debts.

**Q 7–10** Is any special accounting treatment required for the assigning of accounts receivable in general as collateral for debt?

**Q 7–11** Explain any possible differences between accounting for accounts receivable factored without recourse and those factored with recourse.

**Q 7–12** What is meant by the discounting of a note receivable? Describe the four-step process used to account for discounted notes.

**Q 7–13** What are the key variables that influence a company's investment in receivables? Describe the two ratios used by financial analysts to monitor a company's investment in receivables.

**Q 7–14** (Based on Appendix 7) In a two-step bank reconciliation, identify the items that might be necessary to adjust the bank balance to the corrected cash balance. Identify the items that might be necessary to adjust the book balance to the corrected cash balance.

**Q 7–15** (Based on Appendix 7) How is a petty cash fund established? How is the fund replenished?

## BRIEF EXERCISES

**BE 7–1**
Internal control
● LO1

Janice Dodds opens the mail for the Ajax Plumbing Company. She lists all customer checks on a spreadsheet that includes the name of the customer and the check amount. The checks, along with the spreadsheet, are then sent to Jim Seymour in the accounting department who records the checks and deposits them daily in the company's checking account. How could the company improve its internal control procedure for the handling of its cash receipts?

**BE 7–2**
Cash and cash equivalents
● LO2

The following items appeared on the year-end trial balance of Consolidated Freight Corporation: cash in a checking account, U.S. Treasury bills that mature in six months, undeposited customer checks, cash in a savings account, and currency and coins. Which of these items would be included in the company's balance sheet as cash and cash equivalents?

**BE 7–3**
Cash discounts; gross method
● LO3

On December 28, 2006, Tristar Communications sold 10 units of its new satellite uplink system to various customers for $25,000 each. The terms of each sale were 1/10, n/30. Tristar uses the gross method to account for sales discounts. In what year will income before tax be affected assuming that all customers paid the net-of-discount amount on January 6, 2007? By how much?

**BE 7–4**
Cash discounts; net method
● LO3

Refer to the situation described in BE 7–3. Answer the questions assuming that Tristar uses the net method to account for sales discounts.

**BE 7–5**
Sales returns
● LO4

During 2006, its first year of operations, Hollis Industries recorded sales of $10,600,000 and experienced returns of $720,000. Cost of goods sold totaled $6,360,000 (60% of sales). The company estimates that 8% of all sales will be returned. Prepare the year-end adjusting journal entries to account for anticipated sales returns.

**BE 7–6**
Uncollectible accounts; income statement approach
● LO5 LO6

The following information relates to a company's accounts receivable: accounts receivable balance at the beginning of the year, $300,000; allowance for uncollectible accounts at the beginning of the year, $25,000 (credit balance); credit sales during the year, $1,500,000; accounts receivable written off during the year; $16,000, cash collections from customers; $1,450,000. Assuming the company estimates bad debts at an amount equal to 2% of credit sales, calculate (1) bad debt expense for the year and (2) the year-end balance in the allowance for uncollectible accounts.

**BE 7–7**
Uncollectible accounts; balance sheet approach
● LO5 LO6

Refer to the situation described in BE 7–6. Answer the two questions assuming the company estimates that future bad debts will equal 10% of the year-end balance in accounts receivable.

**BE 7–8**
Uncollectible accounts; solving for unknown
● LO5 LO6

A company's year-end balance in accounts receivable is $2,000,000. The allowance for uncollectible accounts had a beginning-of-year credit balance of $30,000. An aging of accounts receivable at the end of the year indicates a required allowance of $38,000. If bad debt expense for the year was $40,000, what was the amount of bad debts written off during the year?

**BE 7–9**
Uncollectible accounts; solving for unknown
● LO5 LO6

Refer to the situation described in BE 7–8. If credit sales for the year were $8,200,000 and $7,950,000 was collected from credit customers, what was the beginning-of-year balance in accounts receivable?

**BE 7–10**
Note receivable
● LO7

On December 1, 2006, Davenport Company sold merchandise to a customer for $20,000. In payment for the merchandise, the customer signed a 6% note requiring the payment of interest and principal on March 1, 2007. How much interest revenue will the company recognize during 2006? In 2007?

**BE 7–11**
Factoring of accounts receivable
● LO8

Logitech Corporation transferred $100,000 of accounts receivable to a local bank. The transfer was made without recourse. The local bank remits 85% of the factored amount to Logitech and retains the remaining 15%. When the bank collects the receivables, it will remit to Logitech the retained amount less a fee equal to 3% of the total amount factored. What is the effect of this transaction on the company's assets, liabilities, and income before income taxes?

**BE 7–12**
Factoring of accounts receivable
● LO8

Refer to the situation described in BE 7–11. Assuming that the sale criteria are not met, describe how Logitech would account for the transfer.

**BE 7–13**
Discounting a note
● LO8

On March 31, Dower Publishing discounted a $30,000 note at a local bank. The note was dated February 28 and required the payment of the principal amount and interest at 6% on May 31. The bank's discount rate is 8%. How much cash will Dower receive from the bank on March 31?

**BE 7–14**
Receivables turnover
● LO9

Camden Hardware's credit sales for the year were $320,000. Accounts receivable at the beginning and end of the year were $50,000 and $70,000, respectively. Calculate the accounts receivable turnover ratio and the average collection period for the year.

## EXERCISES

available with McGraw-Hill's Homework Manager www.mhhe.com/spiceland4e

**An alternate exercise and problem set is available on the text website: www.mhhe.com/spiceland4e**

**E 7–1**
Cash and cash equivalents; restricted cash
● LO2

The controller of the Red Wing Corporation is in the process of preparing the company's 2006 financial statements. She is trying to determine the correct balance of cash and cash equivalents to be reported as a current asset in the balance sheet. The following items are being considered:

a. Balances in the company's accounts at the First National Bank; checking $13,500, savings $22,100.
b. Undeposited customer checks of $5,200.
c. Currency and coins on hand of $580.
d. Savings account at the East Bay Bank with a balance of $400,000. This account is being used to accumulate cash for future plant expansion (in 2008).
e. $20,000 in a checking account at the East Bay Bank. The balance in the account represents a 20% compensating balance for a $100,000 loan with the bank. Red Wing may not withdraw the funds until the loan is due in 2009.
f. U.S. Treasury bills; 2-month maturity bills totaling $15,000, and 7-month bills totaling $20,000.

**Required:**
1. Determine the correct balance of cash and cash equivalents to be reported in the current asset section of the 2006 balance sheet.
2. For each of the items not included in your answer to requirement 1, explain the correct classification of the item.

**E 7–2**
Cash and cash equivalents
● LO2

Delta Automotive Corporation has the following assets listed in its 12/31/06 trial balance:

| | |
|---|---|
| Cash in bank—checking account | $22,500 |
| U.S. Treasury bills (mature in 30 days)* | 5,000 |
| Cash on hand (currency and coins) | 1,350 |
| U.S Treasury bills (mature in six months)* | 10,000 |
| Undeposited customer checks | 1,840 |

*Purchased on 11/30/06

**Required:**
1. Determine the correct balance of cash and cash equivalents to be reported in the current asset section of the 2006 balance sheet.
2. For each of the items not included in your answer to requirement 1, explain the correct classification of the item.

**E 7–3**
Trade and cash discounts; the gross method and the net method compared
● LO3

Tracy Company, a manufacturer of air conditioners, sold 100 units to Thomas Company on November 17, 2006. The units have a list price of $600 each, but Thomas was given a 30% trade discount. The terms of the sale were 2/10, n/30.

**Required:**

1. Prepare the journal entries to record the sale on November 17 (ignore cost of goods) and payment on November 26, 2006, assuming that the gross method of accounting for cash discounts is used.
2. Prepare the journal entries to record the sale on November 17 (ignore cost of goods) and payment on December 15, 2006, assuming that the gross method of accounting for cash discounts is used.
3. Repeat requirements 1 and 2 assuming that the net method of accounting for cash discounts is used.

**E 7–4**
Cash discounts; the gross method
● LO3

Harwell Company manufactures automobile tires. On July 15, 2006, the company sold 1,000 tires to the Nixon Car Company for $50 each. The terms of the sale were 2/10, n/30. Harwell uses the gross method of accounting for cash discounts.

**Required:**

1. Prepare the journal entries to record the sale on July 15 (ignore cost of goods) and payment on July 23, 2006.
2. Prepare the journal entries to record the sale on July 15 (ignore cost of goods) and payment on August 15, 2006.

**E 7–5**
Cash discounts; the net method
● LO3

[This is a variation of the previous exercise modified to focus on the net method of accounting for cash discounts.]

Harwell Company manufactures automobile tires. On July 15, 2006, the company sold 1,000 tires to the Nixon Car Company for $50 each. The terms of the sale were 2/10, n/30. Harwell uses the net method of accounting for cash discounts.

**Required:**

1. Prepare the journal entries to record the sale on July 15 (ignore cost of goods) and payment on July 23, 2006.
2. Prepare the journal entries to record the sale on July 15 (ignore cost of goods) and payment on August 15, 2006.

**E 7–6**
Uncollectible accounts; allowance method vs. direct write-off method
● LO5 LO6

Johnson Company uses the allowance method to account for uncollectible accounts receivable. Bad debt expense is established as a percentage of credit sales. For 2006, net credit sales totaled $4,500,000, and the estimated bad debt percentage is 1.5%. The allowance for uncollectible accounts had a credit balance of $42,000 at the beginning of 2006 and $40,000, after adjusting entries, at the end of 2006.

**Required:**

1. What is bad debt expense for 2006?
2. Determine the amount of accounts receivable written off during 2006.
3. If the company uses the direct write-off method, what would bad debt expense be for 2006?

**E 7–7**
Uncollectible accounts; allowance method; balance sheet approach
● LO5 LO6

Colorado Rocky Cookie Company offers credit terms to its customers. At the end of 2006, accounts receivable totaled $625,000. The allowance method is used to account for uncollectible accounts. The allowance for uncollectible accounts had a credit balance of $32,000 at the beginning of 2006 and $21,000 in receivables were written off during the year as uncollectible. Also, $1,200 in cash was received in December from a customer whose account previously had been written off. The company estimates bad debts by applying a percentage of 10% to accounts receivable at the end of the year.

**Required:**

1. Prepare journal entries to record the write-off of receivables, the collection of $1,200 for previously written off receivables, and the year-end adjusting entry for bad debt expense.
2. How would accounts receivable be shown in the 2006 year-end balance sheet?

**E 7–8**
Uncollectible accounts; allowance method and direct write-off method compared; solving for unknown
● LO6

Castle Company provides estimates for its uncollectible accounts. The allowance for uncollectible accounts had a credit balance of $17,280 at the beginning of 2006 and a $22,410 credit balance at the end of 2006 (after adjusting entries). If the direct write-off method had been used to account for uncollectible accounts (bad debt expense equals actual write-offs), the income statement for 2006 would have included bad debt expense of $17,100 and revenue of $2,200 from the collection of previously written off bad debts.

**Required:**

Determine bad debt expense for 2006 according to the allowance method.

**E 7–9**
Uncollectible accounts; allowance method; solving for unknowns
● LO5 LO6

**Microsoft Corporation** reported the following information in its 2004 financial statements ($ in millions):

| | 2004 | 2003 |
|---|---|---|
| Balance Sheet: | | |
| Accounts receivable, net | $ 5,890 | $5,196 |
| 2004 Income statement: | | |
| Sales revenue | $36,835 | |

A note disclosed that the allowance for uncollectible accounts had a balance of $166 million and $242 million at the end of 2004 and 2003, respectively. Bad debt expense for 2004 was $44 million.

**Required:**

Determine the amount of cash collected from customers during 2004.

**E 7–10**
Note receivable

● LO7

On June 30, 2006, the Esquire Company sold some merchandise to a customer for $30,000. In payment, Esquire agreed to accept a 6% note requiring the payment of interest and principal on March 31, 2007. The 6% rate is appropriate in this situation.

**Required:**

1. Prepare journal entries to record the sale of merchandise (omit any entry that might be required for the cost of the goods sold), the December 31, 2006, interest accrual, and the March 31 collection.
2. If the December 31 adjusting entry for the interest accrual is not prepared, by how much will income before income taxes be over- or understated in 2006 and 2007?

**E 7–11**
Noninterest-bearing note receivable

● LO7

[This is a variation of the previous exercise modified to focus on a noninterest-bearing note.]

On June 30, 2006, the Esquire Company sold some merchandise to a customer for $30,000 and agreed to accept as payment a noninterest-bearing note with an 8% discount rate requiring the payment of $30,000 on March 31, 2007. The 8% rate is appropriate in this situation.

**Required:**

1. Prepare journal entries to record the sale of merchandise (omit any entry that might be required for the cost of the goods sold), the December 31, 2006, interest accrual, and the March 31 collection.
2. What is the *effective* interest rate on the note?

**E 7–12**
Interest-bearing note receivable; solving for unknown rate

● LO7

On January 1, 2006, the Apex Company exchanged some shares of common stock it had been holding as an investment for a note receivable. The note principal plus interest is due on January 1, 2007. The 2006 income statement reported $2,200 in interest revenue from this note and a $6,000 gain on sale of investment in stock. The stock's book value was $16,000. The company's fiscal year ends on December 31.

**Required:**

1. What is the note's effective interest rate?
2. Reconstruct the journal entries to record the sale of the stock on January 1, 2006, and the adjusting entry to record interest revenue at the end of 2006. The company records adjusting entries only at year-end.

**E 7–13**
Multiple choice; accounts receivable

● LO5 LO6

The following questions dealing with accounts receivable are adapted from questions that appeared on CPA examinations. Determine the response that best completes the statements or questions.

1. When the allowance method of recognizing uncollectible accounts is used, the entry to record the write-off of a specific account:
   a. Decreases both accounts receivable and the allowance for uncollectible accounts.
   b. Decreases accounts receivable and increases the allowance for uncollectible accounts.
   c. Increases the allowance for uncollectible accounts and decreases net income.
   d. Decreases both accounts receivable and net income.
2. The following information pertains to Tara Co.'s accounts receivable at December 31, 2006:

| Days Outstanding | Amount | Estimated % Uncollectible |
|---|---|---|
| 0–60 | $120,000 | 1% |
| 61–120 | 90,000 | 2 |
| Over 120 | 100,000 | 6 |
| | $310,000 | |

   During 2006, Tara wrote off $7,000 in receivables and recovered $4,000 that had been written off in prior years. Tara's December 31, 2005, allowance for uncollectible accounts was $22,000. Under the aging method, what amount of allowance for uncollectible accounts should Tara report at December 31, 2006?
   a. $9,000
   b. $10,000
   c. $13,000
   d. $19,000
3. Mill Co.'s allowance for uncollectible accounts was $100,000 at the end of 2006 and $90,000 at the end of 2005. For the year ended December 31, 2006, Mill reported bad debt expense of $16,000 in its income statement. What amount did Mill debit to the appropriate account in 2006 to write off actual bad debts?
   a. $6,000
   b. $10,000
   c. $16,000
   d. $26,000

4. At January 1, 2006, Jamin Co. had a credit balance of $260,000 in its allowance for uncollectible accounts. Based on past experience, 2% of Jamin's credit sales have been uncollectible. During 2006, Jamin wrote off $325,000 of uncollectible accounts. Credit sales for 2006 were $9,000,000. In its December 31, 2006, balance sheet, what amount should Jamin report as allowance for uncollectible accounts?
   a. $115,000
   b. $180,000
   c. $245,000
   d. $440,000

**E 7–14**
Assigning of specific accounts receivable
● LO8

On June 30, 2006, the High Five Surfboard Company had outstanding accounts receivable of $600,000. On July 1, 2006, the company borrowed $450,000 from the Equitable Finance Corporation and signed a promissory note. Interest at 10% is payable monthly. The company assigned specific receivables totaling $600,000 as collateral for the loan. Equitable Finance charges a finance fee equal to 1.8% of the accounts receivable assigned.

**Required:**
Prepare the journal entry to record the borrowing on the books of High Five Surfboard.

**E 7–15**
Factoring of accounts receivable without recourse
● LO8

Mountain High Ice Cream Company transferred $60,000 of accounts receivable to the Prudential Bank. The transfer was made *without recourse*. Prudential remits 90% of the factored amount to Mountain High and retains 10%. When the bank collects the receivables, it will remit to Mountain High the retained amount less a 2% fee (2% of the total factored amount).

**Required:**
Prepare the journal entry to record the transfer on the books of Mountain High assuming that the sale criteria are met.

**E 7–16**
Factoring of accounts receivable with recourse
● LO8

[This is a variation of the previous exercise modified to focus on factoring with recourse.]

Mountain High Ice Cream Company transferred $60,000 of accounts receivable to the Prudential Bank. The transfer was made *with recourse*. Prudential remits 90% of the factored amount to Mountain High and retains 10%. When the bank collects the receivables, it will remit to Mountain High the retained amount less a 2% fee (2% of the total factored amount). Mountain High anticipates a $3,000 recourse obligation.

**Required:**
Prepare the journal entry to record the transfer on the books of Mountain High assuming that the sale criteria are met.

**E 7–17**
Discounting a note receivable
● LO8

Selkirk Company obtained a $15,000 note receivable from a customer on January 1, 2006. The note, along with interest at 10%, is due on July 1, 2006. On February 28, 2006, Selkirk discounted the note at Unionville Bank. The bank's discount rate is 12%.

**Required:**
Prepare the journal entries required on February 28, 2006, to accrue interest and to record the discounting (round all calculations to the nearest dollar) for Selkirk. Assume that the discounting is accounted for as a sale.

**E 7–18**
Multiple choice; financing with receivables
● LO7 LO8

The following questions dealing with financing with receivables are adapted from questions that appeared on CPA examinations. Determine the response that best completes the statements or questions.

1. Gar Co. factored its receivables without recourse with Ross Bank. Gar received cash as a result of this transaction, which is best described as a:
   a. Loan from Ross collateralized by Gar's accounts receivable.
   b. Loan from Ross to be repaid by the proceeds from Gar's accounts receivable.
   c. Sale of Gar's accounts receivable to Ross, with the risk of uncollectible accounts retained by Gar.
   d. Sale of Gar's accounts receivable to Ross, with the risk of uncollectible accounts transferred to Ross.
2. Roth, Inc. received from a customer a one-year, $500,000 note bearing annual interest of 8%. After holding the note for six months, Roth discounted the note at Regional Bank at an effective interest rate of 10%. What amount of cash did Roth receive from the bank?
   a. $540,000
   b. $523,810
   c. $513,000
   d. $495,238

**E 7–19**
Concepts; terminology
● LO1 through LO8

Listed below are several terms and phrases associated with cash and receivables. Pair each item from List A (by letter) with the item from List B that is most appropriately associated with it.

| List A | List B |
|---|---|
| ____ 1. Internal control | a. Restriction on cash. |
| ____ 2. Trade discount | b. Cash discount not taken is sales revenue. |
| ____ 3. Cash equivalents | c. Includes separation of duties. |
| ____ 4. Allowance for uncollectibles | d. Bad debt expense a % of credit sales. |
| ____ 5. Cash discount | e. Recognizes bad debts as they occur. |
| ____ 6. Balance sheet approach | f. Sale of receivables to a financial institution. |
| ____ 7. Income statement approach | g. Include highly liquid investments. |
| ____ 8. Net method | h. Estimate of bad debts. |
| ____ 9. Compensating balance | i. Reduction in amount paid by credit customer. |
| ____ 10. Discounting | j. Reduction below list price. |
| ____ 11. Gross method | k. Cash discount not taken is interest revenue. |
| ____ 12. Direct write-off method | l. Bad debt expense determined by estimating realizable value. |
| ____ 13. Factoring | m. Sale of note receivable to a financial institution. |

**E 7–20**
Receivables; transaction analysis

● LO3 LO5 through LO8

Weldon Corporation's fiscal year ends December 31. The following is a list of transactions involving receivables that occurred during 2006:

| | |
|---|---|
| Mar. 17 | Accounts receivable of $1,700 were written off as uncollectible. The company uses the allowance method. |
| 30 | Loaned an officer of the company $20,000 and received a note requiring principal and interest at 7% to be paid on March 30, 2007. |
| May 30 | Discounted the $20,000 note at a local bank. The bank's discount rate is 8%. The note was discounted without recourse and the sale criteria are met. |
| June 30 | Sold merchandise to the Blankenship Company for $12,000. Terms of the sale are 2/10, n/30. Weldon uses the gross method to account for cash discounts. |
| July 8 | The Blankenship Company paid its account in full. |
| Aug. 31 | Sold stock in a nonpublic company with a book value of $5,000 and accepted a $6,000 noninterest-bearing note with a discount rate of 8%. The $6,000 payment is due on February 28, 2007. The stock has no ready market value. |
| Dec. 31 | Bad debt expense is estimated to be 2% of credit sales for the year. Credit sales for 2006 were $700,000. |

**Required:**

1. Prepare journal entries for each of the above transactions (round all calculations to the nearest dollar).
2. Prepare any additional year-end adjusting entries indicated.

**E 7–21**
Ratio analysis

● LO9

**Cisco Systems** is the world's largest provider of hardware, software, and services that drive the Internet. The company reported the following information in its financial statements for three successive quarters during the 2004 fiscal year ($in millions):

| | Three Months Ended | | |
|---|---|---|---|
| | **5/01/04 (Q3)** | **1/24/04 (Q2)** | **10/25/03 (Q1)** |
| Balance sheets: | | | |
| Accounts receivable, net | $1,540 | $2,040 | $1,388 |
| Income statements: | | | |
| Sales revenue | $5,620 | $5,398 | $5,101 |

**Required:**

Compute the receivables turnover ratio and the average collection period for the second and third quarters. Assume that each quarter consists of 91 days.

**E 7–22**
Ratio analysis; solve for unknown

● LO9

The current asset section of the Moorcroft Outboard Motor Company's balance sheet reported the following amounts:

| | **12/31/06** | **12/31/05** |
|---|---|---|
| Accounts receivable, net | $400,000 | $300,000 |

The average collection period for 2006 is 50 days.

**Required:**

Determine net sales for 2006.

**E 7–23**
Multiple choice: CMA exam: uncollectible accounts

● LO5 LO6

The following questions dealing with receivables are adapted from questions that previously appeared on Certified Management Accountant (CMA) examinations. The CMA designation sponsored by the Institute of Management Accountants (**www.imanet.org**) provides members with an objective measure of knowledge and competence in the field of management accounting. Determine the response that best completes the statements or questions.

1. Bad debt expense must be estimated in order to satisfy the matching principle when expenses are recorded in the same periods as the related revenues. In estimating bad debt expense for a period, companies generally accrue
   a. Either an amount based on a percentage of total sales or an amount based on a percentage of accounts receivable after adjusting for any balance in the allowance for doubtful accounts.
   b. A percentage of total sales.
   c. Either an amount based on a percentage of credit sales or an amount based on a percentage of accounts receivable after adjusting for any balance in the allowance for doubtful accounts.
   d. An amount equal to last year's bad debt expense.

Questions 2 through 3 are based on the following information.

Madison Corporation uses the allowance method to value its accounts receivable and is making the annual adjustments at fiscal year-end, November 30. The proportion of uncollectible accounts is estimated based on past experience, which indicates 1.5% of net credit sales will be uncollectible. Total sales for the year were $2,000,000 of which $200,000 were cash transactions. Madison has determined that the Norris Corporation accounts receivable balance of $10,000 is uncollectible and will write off this account before year-end adjustments are made. Listed below are Madison's account balances at November 30 prior to any adjustments and the $10,000 write-off.

| | |
|---|---|
| Sales | $2,000,000 |
| Accounts receivable | 750,000 |
| Sales discounts | 125,000 |
| Allowance for doubtful accounts | 16,500 |
| Sales returns and allowances | 175,000 |
| Bad debt expense | 0 |

2. The entry to write off Norris Corporation's accounts receivable balance of $10,000 will
   a. Increase total assets and decrease net income.
   b. Decrease total assets and net income.
   c. Have no effect on total assets and decrease net income.
   d. Have no effect on total assets and net income.
3. As a result of the November 30 adjusting entry to provide for bad debts, the allowance for doubtful accounts will
   a. Increase by $30,000.
   b. Increase by $25,500.
   c. Increase by $22,500.
   d. Decrease by $22,500.

**E 7–24**
Petty cash (Based on Appendix 7)

● LO1

Loucks Company established a $200 petty cash fund on October 2, 2006. The fund is replenished at the end of each month. At the end of October 2006, the fund contained $37 in cash and the following receipts:

| | |
|---|---|
| Office supplies | $76 |
| Lunch with client | 48 |
| Postage | 20 |
| Miscellaneous | 19 |

**Required:**
Prepare the necessary general journal entries to establish the petty cash fund on October 2 and to replenish the fund on October 31.

**E 7–25**
Bank reconciliation (Based on Appendix 7)

● LO1

Jansen Company's general ledger showed a checking account balance of $23,820 at the end of May 2006. The May 31 cash receipts of $2,340, included in the general ledger balance, were placed in the night depository at the bank on May 31 and were processed by the bank on June 1. The bank statement dated May 31, 2006, showed bank service charges of $38. All checks written by the company had been processed by the bank by May 31 and were listed on the bank statement except for checks totaling $1,890.

**Required:**
Prepare a bank reconciliation as of May 31, 2006. [*Hint:* You will need to compute the balance that would appear on the bank statement.]

**E 7–26**
Bank reconciliation and adjusting entries (Based on Appendix 7)

● LO1

Harrison Company maintains a checking account at the First National City Bank. The bank provides a bank statement along with canceled checks on the last day of each month. The July 2006 bank statement included the following information:

| | |
|---|---|
| Balance, July 1, 2006 | $ 55,678 |
| Deposits | 179,500 |
| Checks processed | (192,610) |
| Service charges | (30) |

| | |
|---|---|
| NSF checks | (1,200) |
| Monthly loan payment deducted directly by bank from account (includes $320 in interest) | (3,320) |
| Balance, July 31, 2006 | $ 38,018 |

The company's general ledger account had a balance of $38,918 at the end of July. Deposits outstanding totaled $6,300 and all checks written by the company were processed by the bank except for those totaling $8,420. In addition, a $2,000 July deposit from a credit customer was recorded as a $200 debit to cash and credit to accounts receivable, and a check correctly recorded by the company as a $30 disbursement was incorrectly processed by the bank as a $300 disbursement.

Required:

1. Prepare a bank reconciliation for the month of July.
2. Prepare the necessary journal entries at the end of July to adjust the general ledger cash account.

## PROBLEMS

available with McGraw-Hill's Homework Manager www.mhhe.com/spiceland4e

**An alternate exercise and problem set is available on the text website: www.mhhe.com/spiceland4e**

**P 7–1**
Uncollectible accounts; allowance method; income statement and balance sheet approach

● LO5 LO6

excel

Swathmore Clothing Corporation grants its customers 30 days' credit. The company uses the allowance method for its uncollectible accounts receivable. During the year, a monthly bad debt accrual is made by multiplying 3% times the amount of credit sales for the month. At the fiscal year-end of December 31, an aging of accounts receivable schedule is prepared and the allowance for uncollectible accounts is adjusted accordingly.

At the end of 2005, accounts receivable were $574,000 and the allowance account had a credit balance of $54,000. Accounts receivable activity for 2006 was as follows:

| | |
|---|---|
| Beginning balance | $ 574,000 |
| Credit sales | 2,620,000 |
| Collections | (2,483,000) |
| Write-offs | (68,000) |
| Ending balance | $ 643,000 |

The company's controller prepared the following aging summary of year-end accounts receivable:

| | Summary | |
|---|---|---|
| **Age Group** | **Amount** | **Percent Uncollectible** |
| 0–60 days | $430,000 | 4% |
| 61–90 days | 98,000 | 15 |
| 91–120 days | 60,000 | 25 |
| Over 120 days | 55,000 | 40 |
| Total | $643,000 | |

Required:

1. Prepare a summary journal entry to record the monthly bad debt accrual and the write-offs during the year.
2. Prepare the necessary year-end adjusting entry for bad debt expense.
3. What is total bad debt expense for 2006? How would accounts receivable appear in the 2006 balance sheet?

**P 7–2**
Uncollectible accounts

● LO5

**Amdahl Corporation** manufactures large-scale, high performance computer systems. In a recent annual report, the balance sheet included the following information (dollars in thousands):

| | Current Year | Previous Year |
|---|---|---|
| Current assets: | | |
| Receivables, net of allowances of $5,042 and $6,590 in the previous year | $504,944 | $580,640 |

In addition, the income statement reported sales revenue of $2,158,755 (dollars in thousands) for the current year. All sales are made on a credit basis. The statement of cash flows indicates that cash collected from customers during the current year was $2,230,065 (dollars in thousands). There were no recoveries of accounts receivable previously written off.

**Required:**

1. Compute the following (dollar amounts in thousands):
   a. The amount of uncollectibles written off by Amdahl during the current year.
   b. The amount of bad debt expense that Amdahl would include in its income statement for the current year.
   c. The approximate percentage that Amdahl used to estimate uncollectibles for the current year, assuming that it uses the income statement approach.
2. Suppose that Amdahl had used the direct write-off method to account for uncollectibles. Compute the following (dollars in thousands):
   a. The accounts receivable information that would be included in the year-end balance sheet.
   b. The amount of bad debt expense that Amdahl would include in its income statement for the current year.

**P 7–3**
Uncollectible accounts

● LO5 LO6

eXcel

Raintree Cosmetic Company sells its products to customers on a credit basis. An adjusting entry for bad debt expense is recorded only at December 31, the company's fiscal year-end. The 2005 balance sheet disclosed the following:

| | |
|---|---|
| Current assets: | |
| Receivables, net of allowance for uncollectible accounts of $30,000 | $432,000 |

During 2006, credit sales were $1,750,000, cash collections from customers $1,830,000, and $35,000 in accounts receivable were written off. In addition, $3,000 was collected from a customer whose account was written off in 2005. An aging of accounts receivable at December 31, 2006, reveals the following:

| Age Group | Percentage of Year-End Receivables in Group | Percent Uncollectible |
|---|---|---|
| 0–60 days | 65% | 4% |
| 61–90 days | 20 | 15 |
| 91–120 days | 10 | 25 |
| Over 120 days | 5 | 40 |

**Required:**

1. Prepare summary journal entries to account for the 2006 write-offs and the collection of the receivable previously written off.
2. Prepare the year-end adjusting entry for bad debts according to each of the following situations:
   a. Bad debt expense is estimated to be 3% of credit sales for the year.
   b. Bad debt expense is estimated by computing net realizable value of the receivables. The allowance for uncollectible accounts is estimated to be 10% of the year-end balance in accounts receivable.
   c. Bad debt expense is estimated by computing net realizable value of the receivables. The allowance for uncollectible accounts is determined by an aging of accounts receivable.
3. For situations (a)–(c) in requirement 2 above, what would be the net amount of accounts receivable reported in the 2006 balance sheet?

**P 7–4**
Notes receivable; solving for unknowns

● LO7

Cypress Oil Company's December 31, 2006, balance sheet listed $645,000 of notes receivable and $16,000 of interest receivable included in current assets. The following notes make up the notes receivable balance:

| | |
|---|---|
| Note 1 | Dated 8/31/06, principal of $300,000 and interest at 10% due on 2/28/07. |
| Note 2 | Dated 6/30/06, principal of $150,000 and interest due 3/31/07. |
| Note 3 | $200,000 face value noninterest-bearing note dated 9/30/06, due 3/31/07. Note was issued in exchange for merchandise. |

The company records adjusting entries only at year-end. There were no other notes receivable outstanding during 2006.

**Required:**

1. Determine the rate used to discount the noninterest-bearing note.
2. Determine the explicit interest rate on Note 2.
3. What is the amount of interest revenue that appears in the company's 2006 income statement related to these notes?

**P 7–5**
Factoring versus assigning of accounts receivable

● LO8

Lonergan Company occasionally uses its accounts receivable to obtain immediate cash. At the end of June 2006, the company had accounts receivable of $780,000. Lonergan needs approximately $500,000 to capitalize on a unique investment opportunity. On July 1, 2006, a local bank offers Lonergan the following two alternatives:

a. Borrow $500,000, sign a note payable, and assign the entire receivable balance as collateral. At the end of each month, a remittance will be made to the bank that equals the amount of receivables collected plus 12% interest on the unpaid balance of the note at the beginning of the period.

b. Transfer $550,000 of specific receivables to the bank without recourse. The bank will charge a 2% finance charge on the amount of receivables transferred. The bank will collect the receivables directly from customers. The sale criteria are met.

**Required:**

1. Prepare the journal entries that would be recorded on July 1 for each of the alternatives.
2. Assuming that 80% of all June 30 receivables are collected during July, prepare the necessary journal entries to record the collection and the remittance to the bank.
3. For each alternative, explain any required note disclosures that would be included in the July 31, 2006, financial statements.

**P 7–6**
Factoring of accounts receivable; without recourse

● LO8

Samson Wholesale Beverage Company regularly factors its accounts receivable with the Milpitas Finance Company. On April 30, 2006, the company transferred $800,000 of accounts receivable to Milpitas. The transfer was made without recourse. Milpitas remits 90% of the factored amount and retains 10%. When Milpitas collects the receivables, it remits to Samson the retained amount less a 4% fee (4% of the total factored amount).

**Required:**

Prepare journal entries for Samson Wholesale Beverage for the transfer of accounts receivable on April 30 assuming the sale criteria are met.

**P 7–7**
Miscellaneous receivable transactions

● LO3 LO4 LO7 LO8

Evergreen Company sells lawn and garden products to wholesalers. The company's fiscal year-end is December 31. During 2006, the following transactions related to receivables occurred:

| | |
|---|---|
| Feb. 28 | Sold merchandise to Lennox, Inc. for $10,000 and accepted a 10%, 7-month note. 10% is an appropriate rate for this type of note. |
| Mar. 31 | Sold merchandise to Maddox Co. and accepted a noninterest-bearing note with a discount rate of 10%. The $8,000 payment is due on March 31, 2007. |
| Apr. 3 | Sold merchandise to Carr Co. for $7,000 with terms 2/10, n/30. Evergreen uses the gross method to account for cash discounts. |
| 11 | Collected the entire amount due from Carr Co. |
| 17 | A customer returned merchandise costing $3,200. Evergreen reduced the customer's receivable balance by $5,000, the sales price of the merchandise. Sales returns are recorded by the company as they occur. |
| 30 | Transferred receivables of $50,000 to a factor without recourse. The factor charged Evergreen a 1% finance charge on the receivables transferred. The sale criteria are met. |
| June 30 | Discounted the Lennox, Inc., note at the bank. The bank's discount rate is 12%. The note was discounted without recourse. |
| Aug. 31 | Lennox, Inc., paid the note amount plus interest to the bank. |

**Required:**

1. Prepare the necessary journal entries for Evergreen for each of the above dates. For transactions involving the sale of merchandise, ignore the entry for the cost of goods sold (round all calculations to the nearest dollar).
2. Prepare any necessary adjusting entries at December 31, 2006. Adjusting entries are only recorded at year-end (round all calculations to the nearest dollar).
3. Prepare a schedule showing the effect of the journal entries in requirements 1 and 2 on 2006 income before taxes.

**P 7–8**
Discounting a note receivable

● LO8

eXcel

Descriptors are provided below for six situations involving notes receivable being discounted at a bank. In each case, the maturity date of the note is December 31, 2006, and the principal and interest are due at maturity. For each, determine the proceeds received from the bank on discounting the note.

| Note | Note Face Value | Date of Note | Interest Rate | Date Discounted | Discount Rate |
|---|---|---|---|---|---|
| 1 | $50,000 | 3/31/06 | 8% | 6/30/06 | 10% |
| 2 | 50,000 | 3/31/06 | 8 | 9/30/06 | 10 |
| 3 | 50,000 | 3/31/06 | 8 | 9/30/06 | 12 |
| 4 | 80,000 | 6/30/06 | 6 | 10/31/06 | 10 |
| 5 | 80,000 | 6/30/06 | 6 | 10/31/06 | 12 |
| 6 | 80,000 | 6/30/06 | 6 | 11/30/06 | 10 |

**P 7–9**
Bank reconciliation and adjusting entries; cash and cash equivalents (Based on Appendix 7)

● LO1

The bank statement for the checking account of Management Systems, Inc. (MSI) showed a December 31, 2006, balance of $14,632.12. Information that might be useful in preparing a bank reconciliation is as follows:

a. Outstanding checks were $1,320.25.
b. The December 31, 2006, cash receipts of $575 were not deposited in the bank until January 2, 2007.
c. One check written in payment of rent for $246 was correctly recorded by the bank but was recorded by MSI as a $264 disbursement.
d. In accordance with prior authorization, the bank withdrew $450 directly from the checking account as payment on a mortgage note payable. The interest portion of that payment was $350. MSI has made no entry to record the automatic payment.

e. Bank service charges of $14 were listed on the bank statement.
f. A deposit of $875 was recorded by the bank on December 13, but it did not belong to MSI. The deposit should have been made to the checking account of MIS, Inc.
g. The bank statement included a charge of $85 for an NSF check. The check was returned with the bank statement and the company will seek payment from the customer.
h. MSI maintains a $200 petty cash fund that was appropriately reimbursed at the end of December.
i. According to instructions from MSI on December 30, the bank withdrew $10,000 from the account and purchased U.S. Treasury bills for MSI. MSI recorded the transaction in its books on December 31 when it received notice from the bank. Half of the Treasury bills mature in two months and the other half in six months.

**Required:**
1. Prepare a bank reconciliation for the MSI checking account at December 31, 2006. You will have to compute the balance per books.
2. Prepare any necessary adjusting journal entries indicated.
3. What amount would MSI report as cash and cash equivalents in the current asset section of the December 31, 2006, balance sheet?

**P 7–10**
Bank reconciliation and adjusting entries (Based on Appendix 7)

● LO1

eXcel

El Gato Painting Company maintains a checking account at American Bank. Bank statements are prepared at the end of each month. The November 30, 2006, reconciliation of the bank balance is as follows:

| | | |
|---|---|---|
| Balance per bank, November 30 | | $3,231 |
| Add: Deposits outstanding | | 1,200 |
| Less: Checks outstanding | | |
| #363 | $123 | |
| #365 | 201 | |
| #380 | 56 | |
| #381 | 86 | |
| #382 | 340 | (806) |
| Adjusted balance per bank, November 30 | | $3,625 |

The company's general ledger checking account showed the following for December:

| | |
|---|---|
| Balance, December 1 | $ 3,625 |
| Receipts | 42,650 |
| Disbursements | (41,853) |
| Balance, December 31 | $ 4,422 |

The December bank statement contained the following information:

| | |
|---|---|
| Balance, December 1 | $ 3,231 |
| Deposits | 43,000 |
| Checks processed | (41,918) |
| Service charges | (22) |
| NSF checks | (440) |
| Balance, December 31 | $ 3,851 |

The checks that were processed by the bank in December include all of the outstanding checks at the end of November except for check #365. In addition, there are some December checks that had not been processed by the bank by the end of the month. Also, you discover that check #411 for $320 was correctly recorded by the bank but was incorrectly recorded on the books as a $230 disbursement for advertising expense. Included in the bank's deposits is a $1,300 deposit incorrectly credited to the company's account. The deposit should have been posted to the credit of the Los Gatos Company. The NSF checks have not been redeposited and the company will seek payment from the customers involved.

**Required:**
1. Prepare a bank reconciliation for the El Gato checking account at December 31, 2006.
2. Prepare any necessary adjusting journal entries indicated.

# BROADEN YOUR PERSPECTIVE

**Apply your critical-thinking ability to the knowledge you've gained. These cases will provide you an opportunity to develop your research, analysis, judgment, and communication skills. You also will work with other students, integrate what you've learned, apply it in real world situations, and consider its global and ethical ramifications. This practice will broaden your knowledge and further develop your decision-making abilities.**

**Judgment Case 7–1**
Accounts and notes receivable
● LO5 LO6 LO8

Magrath Company has an operating cycle of less than one year and provides credit terms for all of its customers. On April 1, 2006, the company factored, without recourse, some of its accounts receivable.

Magrath uses the allowance method to account for uncollectible accounts. During 2006, some accounts were written off as uncollectible and other accounts previously written off as uncollectible were collected.

**Required:**

1. How should Magrath account for and report the accounts receivable factored on April 1, 2006? Why is this accounting treatment appropriate?
2. How should Magrath account for the collection of the accounts previously written off as uncollectible?
3. What are the two basic approaches to estimating uncollectible accounts under the allowance method? What is the rationale for each approach?

*(AICPA adapted)*

**Communication Case 7–2**
Uncollectible accounts
● LO5

You have been hired as a consultant by a parts manufacturing firm to provide advice as to the proper accounting methods the company should use in some key areas. In the area of receivables, the company president does not understand your recommendation to use the allowance method for uncollectible accounts. She stated, "Financial statements should be based on objective data rather than the guesswork required for the allowance method. Besides, since my uncollectibles are fairly constant from period to period, with significant variations occurring infrequently, the direct write-off method is just as good as the allowance method."

**Required:**

Draft a one-page response in the form of a memo to the president in support of your recommendation for the company to use the allowance method.

**Judgment Case 7–3**
Accounts receivable
● LO3 LO7 LO8

Hogan Company uses the net method of accounting for sales discounts. Hogan offers trade discounts to various groups of buyers.

On August 1, 2006, Hogan factored some accounts receivable on a without recourse basis. Hogan incurred a finance charge.

Hogan also has some notes receivable bearing an appropriate rate of interest. The principal and total interest are due at maturity. The notes were received on October 1, 2006, and mature on September 30, 2007. Hogan's operating cycle is less than one year.

**Required:**

1. a. Using the net method, how should Hogan account for the sales discounts at the date of sale? What is the rationale for the amount recorded as sales under the net method?
   b. Using the net method, what is the effect on Hogan's sales revenues and net income when customers do not take the sales discounts?
2. What is the effect of trade discounts on sales revenues and accounts receivable? Why?
3. How should Hogan account for the accounts receivable factored on August 1, 2006? Why?
4. How should Hogan report the effects of the interest-bearing notes receivable in its December 31, 2006, balance sheet and its income statement for the year ended December 31, 2006? Why?

*(AICPA adapted)*

**Ethics Case 7–4**
Uncollectible accounts
● LO5

You have recently been hired as the assistant controller for Stanton Industries, a large, publicly held manufacturing company. Your immediate superior is the controller who, in turn, is responsible to the vice president of finance.

The controller has assigned you the task of preparing the year-end adjusting entries. In the receivables area, you have prepared an aging of accounts receivable and have applied historical percentages to the balances of each of the age categories. The analysis indicates that an appropriate balance for the allowance for uncollectible accounts is $180,000. The existing balance in the allowance account prior to any adjusting entry is a $20,000 credit balance.

After showing your analysis to the controller, he tells you to change the aging category of a large account from over 120 days to current status and to prepare a new invoice to the customer with a revised date that agrees with the new aging category. This will change the required allowance for uncollectible accounts from

$180,000 to $135,000. Tactfully, you ask the controller for an explanation for the change and he tells you "We need the extra income, the bottom line is too low."

Required:

1. What is the effect on income before taxes of the change requested by the controller?
2. Discuss the ethical dilemma you face. Consider your options and responsibilities along with the possible consequences of any action you might take.

**Judgment Case 7–5**
Internal control

● LO1

For each of the following independent situations, indicate the apparent internal control weaknesses and suggest alternative procedures to eliminate the weaknesses.

1. John Smith is the petty cash custodian. John approves all requests for payment out of the $200 fund which is replenished at the end of each month. At the end of each month, John submits a list of all accounts and amounts to be charged and a check is written to him for the total amount. John is the only person ever to tally the fund.
2. All of the company's cash disbursements are made by check. Each check must be supported by an approved voucher which is in turn supported by the appropriate invoice and, for purchases, a receiving document. The vouchers are approved by Dean Leiser, the chief accountant, after reviewing the supporting documentation. Betty Hanson prepares the checks for Leiser's signature. Leiser also maintains the company's check register (the cash disbursements journal) and reconciles the bank account at the end of each month.
3. Fran Jones opens the company's mail and makes a listing of all checks and cash received from customers. A copy of the list is sent to Jerry McDonald who maintains the general ledger accounts. Fran prepares and makes the daily deposit at the bank. Fran also maintains the subsidiary ledger for accounts receivable which is used to generate monthly statements to customers.

**Real World Case 7–6**
Bad debts

● LO5

**Cirrus Logic, Inc.** is a leading designer and manufacturer of advanced integrated circuits that integrate algorithms and mixed-signal processing for mass storage, communications, consumer electronics, and industrial markets. The company's 2004 financial statements contained the following information:

| | ($ in thousands) | |
|---|---|---|
| **Balance sheets** | **2004** | **2003** |
| Current assets: | | |
| Accounts receivable, net | $ 19,804 | $ 22,712 |
| **Income statements** | **2004** | **2003** |
| Net sales | $196,338 | $261,999 |

In addition, the statement of cash flows disclosed that accounts receivable decreased during 2004 by $2,908 (in thousands). This indicates that cash received from customers was $2,908 (in thousands) more than accrual sales revenue. Also, a disclosure note reported that the allowance for uncollectible accounts (in thousands) was $696 and $977 at the end of 2004 and 2003, respectively.

Required:

1. What is the amount of accounts receivable due from customers at the end of 2004 and 2003?
2. Assuming that all sales are made on a credit basis, determine the amount of bad debt expense for 2004 and the amount of actual bad debt write-offs made in 2004.

**Real World Case 7–7**
Receivables; bad debts

● LO5

EDGAR, the Electronic Data Gathering, Analysis, and Retrieval system, performs automated collection, validation, indexing, and forwarding of submissions by companies and others who are required by law to file forms with the U.S. Securities and Exchange Commission (SEC). All publicly traded domestic companies use EDGAR to make the majority of their filings. (Some foreign companies file voluntarily.) Form 10-K or 10-KSB, which include the annual report, is required to be filed on EDGAR. The SEC makes this information available on the Internet.

Required:

1. Access EDGAR on the Internet. The web address is **www.sec.gov**. Edgarscan (**edgarscan.pwcglobal.com**) from Pricewaterhouse Coopers makes the process of accessing data from EDGAR easier.
2. Search for **Avon Products, Inc.** Access the 10-K filing for the most recent fiscal year. Search or scroll to find the financial statements.
3. Answer the following questions related to the company's accounts receivable and bad debts:
   a. What is the amount of gross trade accounts receivable at the end of the year?
   b. What is the amount of bad debt expense for the year? (*Hint:* check the statement of cash flows.)
   c. Determine the amount of actual bad debt write-offs made during the year. Assume that all bad debts relate only to trade accounts receivable.
   d. Using only information from the balance sheets, income statements, and your answer to requirement 3.c., determine the amount of cash collected from customers during the year. Assume

that all sales are made on a credit basis, that the company provides no allowances for sales returns, that no previously written-off receivables were collected, and that all sales relate to trade accounts receivable.

**Integrating Case 7–8**
Change in estimate of bad debts

● LO5

McLaughlin Corporation uses the allowance method to account for bad debts. At the end of the company's fiscal year, accounts receivable are analyzed and the allowance for uncollectible accounts is adjusted. At the end of 2006, the company reported the following amounts:

| | |
|---|---|
| Accounts receivable | $10,850,000 |
| Less: Allowance for uncollectible accounts | (450,000) |
| Accounts receivable, net | $10,400,000 |

In 2007, it was determined that $1,825,000 of year-end 2006 receivables had to be written off as uncollectible. This was due in part to the fact that Hughes Corporation, a long-standing customer that had always paid its bills, unexpectedly declared bankruptcy in 2007. Hughes owed McLaughlin $1,400,000. At the end of 2006, none of the Hughes receivable was considered uncollectible.

**Required:**

Describe the appropriate accounting treatment and required disclosures for McLaughlin's underestimation of bad debts at the end of 2006.

**Analysis Case 7–9**
Financing with receivables

● LO8

Financial institutions have developed a wide variety of methods for companies to use their receivables to obtain immediate cash. The methods differ with respect to which rights and risks are retained by the transferor (the original holder of the receivable) and those passed on to the transferee (the new holder, usually a financial institution).

**Required:**

1. Describe the alternative methods available for companies to use their receivables to obtain immediate cash.
2. Discuss the alternative accounting treatments for these methods.

**Research Case 7–10**
Locate and extract relevant information and authoritative support for a financial reporting issue; financing with receivables

● LO8

You are spending the summer working for a local wholesale furniture company, Samson Furniture, Inc. The company is considering a proposal from a local financial institution, Old Reliant Financial, to factor Samson's receivables. The company controller is unfamiliar with the most recent FASB pronouncement that deals with accounting for the transfer of financial assets and has asked you to do some research. The controller wants to make sure the arrangement with the financial institution is structured in such a way as to allow the factoring to be accounted for as a sale.

Old Reliant has offered to factor all of the company's receivables on a "without recourse" basis. Old Reliant will remit to Samson 90% of the factored amount, collect the receivables from Samson's customers, and retain the remaining 10% until all of the receivables have been collected. When Old Reliant collects all of the receivables, it will remit to Samson the retained amount, less a 4% fee (4% of the total factored amount).

**Required:**

1. Explain the meaning of the term *without recourse.*
2. Obtain the FASB standard on accounting for the transfer of financial assets. You might gain access through FARS, the FASB Financial Accounting Research System, from your school library, or some other source.
3. What conditions must be met for a transfer of receivables to be accounted for as a sale? What is the specific citation that Samson would rely on in applying that accounting treatment?
4. Assuming that the conditions for treatment as a sale are met, prepare Samson's journal entry to record the factoring of $400,000 of receivables.
5. An agreement that both entitles and obligates the transferor, Samson, to repurchase or redeem transferred assets from the transferee, Old Reliant, maintains the transferor's effective control over those assets and the transfer is accounted for as a secured borrowing, not a sale, if and only if what conditions are met?

**Analysis Case 7–11**
Compare receivables management using ratios

● LO9

The table below contains selected financial information included in the 2004 financial statements of **Sara Lee Corporation** and **Tyson Foods, Inc.**

| ($ in millions) | Sara Lee | | Tyson Foods | |
|---|---|---|---|---|
| | 2004 | 2003 | 2004 | 2003 |
| **Balance sheet:** | | | | |
| Accounts receivable, net | $ 1,929 | $ 1,857 | $ 1,240 | $ 1,280 |
| **Income statement:** | | | | |
| Net sales | 19,566 | 18,291 | 26,441 | 24,549 |

**Required:**

1. Calculate the 2004 receivables turnover ratio and average collection period for both companies. Evaluate the management of each company's investment in receivables.
2. Obtain annual reports from three corporations in the same primary industry and compare the management of each company's investment in receivables.

**Note:** You can obtain copies of annual reports from your library, from friends who are shareholders, from the investor relations department of the corporations, from a friendly stockbroker, or from EDGAR (Electronic Data Gathering, Analysis, and Retrieval) on the Internet (**www.sec.gov** or through Edgarscan at **edgarscan.pwcglobal.com**).

**Analysis Case 7–12**
Reporting cash and receivables

● LO2 LO5

**FedEx Corporation**

Refer to the financial statements and related disclosure notes of **FedEx Corporation** in Appendix B located at the back of this text.

**Required:**

1. What is FedEx's policy for designating investments as cash equivalents?
2. Determine the gross amount of receivables outstanding at May 31, 2004, and May 31, 2003.
3. What amount of receivables were written off during the 2004 fiscal year? Assume that no previously written-off receivables were collected during the year and that allowances relate only to allowances for uncollectible accounts. (*Hint:* check the statement of cash flows.)

8

CHAPTER

# Inventories: Measurement

## OVERVIEW

The next two chapters continue our study of assets by investigating the measurement and reporting issues involving inventories and the related expense—cost of goods sold. Inventory refers to the assets a company (1) intends to sell in the normal course of business, (2) has in production for future sale, or (3) uses currently in the production of goods to be sold.

## LEARNING OBJECTIVES

After studying this chapter, you should be able to:

- LO1 Explain the difference between a perpetual inventory system and a periodic inventory system.
- LO2 Explain which physical quantities of goods should be included in inventory.
- LO3 Determine the expenditures that should be included in the cost of inventory.
- LO4 Differentiate between the specific identification, FIFO, LIFO, and average cost methods used to determine the cost of ending inventory and cost of goods sold.
- LO5 Discuss the factors affecting a company's choice of inventory method.
- LO6 Understand supplemental LIFO disclosures and the effect of LIFO liquidations on net income.
- LO7 Calculate the key ratios used by analysts to monitor a company's investment in inventories.
- LO8 Determine ending inventory using the dollar-value LIFO inventory method.

# FINANCIAL REPORTING CASE

## Inventory Measurement at Ford Motor Company

A recent article in the financial section of your local newspaper reported on the labor negotiations between Ford Motor Company and the United Auto Workers. When you showed the article to a friend, he said, "I'll bet Ford uses LIFO to value its inventories. That way they can report lower profits and give them an edge in the negotiations." This aroused your curiosity and led you to download from the Internet Ford's most recent financial statements, which contained the following disclosure note:

*Note 6. Inventories*

Inventories at December 31 were as follows (in millions):

| | 2004 | 2003 |
|---|---|---|
| Raw materials, work in process, and supplies | $ 3,968 | $3,813 |
| Finished products | 6,798 | 5,338 |
| Total inventories | $10,766 | $9,151 |

Inventories are stated at the lower of cost or market. About one-fourth of inventories were determined under the last-in, first-out (LIFO) method. The cost of the remaining inventories were determined primarily by the first-in, first-out (FIFO) method. If the FIFO method had been used instead of LIFO, inventories would have been higher by $1,001 million and $996 million at the end of 2004 and 2003, respectively.

**By the time you finish this chapter, you should be able to respond appropriately to the questions posed in this case. Compare your response to the solution provided at the end of the chapter.**

### QUESTIONS

1. What inventory methods does Ford use to value its inventories? Is this permissible according to GAAP? (page 368)
2. What is the purpose of the disclosure information that reports what LIFO inventories would have been if valued at FIFO? (page 370)
3. Is your friend correct in his assertion that by using LIFO, Ford was able to report lower profits in 2004? (page 375)

# PART A RECORDING AND MEASURING INVENTORY

Inventories consist of assets that a retail or wholesale company acquires for resale or goods that manufacturers produce for sale.

Inventory refers to the assets a company (1) intends to sell in the normal course of business, (2) has in production for future sale (work in process), or (3) uses currently in the production of goods to be sold (raw materials). The computers produced by **Apple Computer** that are intended for sale to customers are inventory, as are partially completed components in the assembly lines of Apple's Cupertino facility, and the computer chips and memory modules that will go into computers produced later. The computers *used* by Apple to maintain its accounting system, however, are classified and accounted for as plant and equipment. Similarly, the stocks and bonds a securities dealer holds for sale are inventory, whereas Apple would classify the securities it holds as investments.

Proper accounting for inventories is essential for manufacturing, wholesale, and retail companies (enterprises that earn revenue by selling goods). Inventory usually is one of the most valuable assets listed in the balance sheet for these firms. Cost of goods sold—the expense recorded when inventory is sold—typically is the largest expense in the income statement. For example, a recent balance sheet for **Sara Lee Corporation** reported inventories of $2,779 billion, which represented 19% of total assets. The company's income statement reported cost of goods sold of $12 billion representing 67% of all expenses.

An important objective in inventory accounting is to match the appropriate cost of goods sold with sales revenue.

In this and the following chapter we discuss the measurement and reporting issues involving **inventory**, an asset, and the related expense, **cost of goods sold**. Inventory represents *quantities* of goods acquired, manufactured, or in the process of being manufactured. The inventory amount in the balance sheet at the end of an accounting period represents the cost of the inventory still on hand, and cost of goods sold in the income statement represents the cost of the inventory sold during the period. The historical cost principle and matching principle offer guidance for measuring inventory and cost of goods sold, but as we will see in this and the next chapter, it's usually difficult to measure inventory (cost of goods sold) at the exact cost of the actual physical quantities on hand (sold). Fortunately, accountants can use one of several techniques to approximate the desired result and satisfy our measurement objectives.

## Types of Inventory

### MERCHANDISING INVENTORY

Wholesale and retail companies purchase goods that are primarily in finished form. These companies are intermediaries in the process of moving goods from the manufacturer to the end-user. They often are referred to as merchandising companies and their inventory as merchandise inventory. *The cost of merchandise inventory includes the purchase price plus any other costs necessary to get the goods in condition and location for sale.* We discuss the concept of condition and location and the types of costs that typically constitute inventory later in this chapter.

### MANUFACTURING INVENTORIES

Inventory for a manufacturing company consists of *raw materials, work in process,* and *finished goods.*

Unlike merchandising companies, manufacturing companies actually produce the goods they sell to wholesalers, retailers, or other manufacturers. Inventory for a manufacturer consists of (1) raw materials, (2) work in process, and (3) finished goods. **Raw materials** represent the cost of components purchased from other manufacturers that will become part of the finished product. For example, Apple's raw materials inventory includes semiconductors, circuit boards, plastic, and glass that go into the production of personal computers.

The cost of *work in process* and *finished goods* includes the cost of raw materials, direct labor, and an allocated portion of manufacturing overhead.

**Work-in-process** inventory refers to the products that are not yet complete. The cost of work in process includes the cost of raw materials used in production, the cost of labor that can be directly traced to the goods in process, and an allocated portion of other manufacturing costs, called *manufacturing overhead.* Overhead costs include electricity and other utility costs to operate the manufacturing facility, depreciation of manufacturing equipment, and many other manufacturing costs that cannot be directly linked to the production of specific goods. Once the manufacturing process is completed, these costs that have accumulated in work in process are transferred to **finished goods.**

Manufacturing companies generally disclose, either in a note or directly in the balance sheet, the dollar amount of each inventory category. For example, **IBM Corporation**'s note disclosure of inventory category was shown on page 107. **Sara Lee Corporation** reports inventory categories directly in the balance sheet, as illustrated in Graphic 8–1.

The inventory accounts and the cost flows for a typical manufacturing company are shown using T-accounts in Graphic 8–2. The costs of raw materials used, direct labor applied, and manufacturing overhead applied, flow into work in process and then to finished goods. When the goods are sold, the cost of those goods flows to cost of goods sold.

**GRAPHIC 8–1** Inventories Disclosure—Sara Lee Corporation

**Balance Sheet**

| | ($ in millions) | |
|---|---|---|
| | **2004** | **2003** |
| Current assets: | | |
| Inventories | | |
| Finished goods | $1,921 | $1,810 |
| Work in process | 397 | 405 |
| Materials and supplies | 461 | 489 |
| Total | $2,779 | $2,704 |

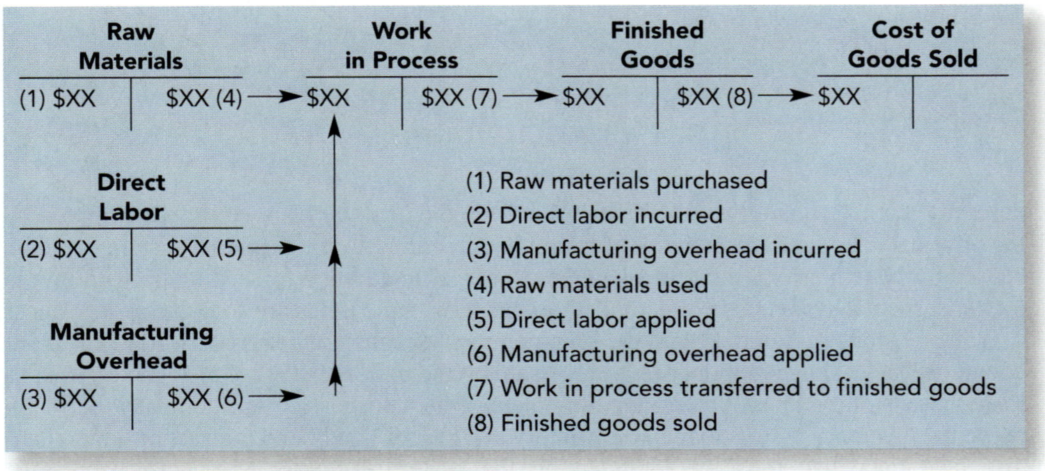


**GRAPHIC 8–2**
Inventory Components and Cost Flow for a Manufacturing Company

**The costs of inventory units follow their physical movement from one stage of activity to another.**

We focus here primarily on merchandising companies (wholesalers and retailers). Still, most of the accounting principles and procedures discussed here also apply to manufacturing companies. The unique problems involved with accumulating the direct costs of raw materials and labor and with allocating manufacturing overhead are addressed in managerial and cost accounting textbooks.

## Perpetual Inventory System

Two accounting systems are used to record transactions involving inventory: the **perpetual inventory system** and the **periodic inventory system**. The perpetual system was introduced in Chapter 2. The system is aptly termed perpetual because the account *inventory* is continually adjusted for each change in inventory, whether it's caused by a purchase, a sale, or a return of merchandise by the company to its supplier (a *purchase return* for the buyer, a *sales return* for the seller).[1] The cost of goods sold account, along with the inventory account, is adjusted each time goods are sold or are returned by a customer. This concept is applied to the Lothridge Wholesale Beverage Company for which inventory information is provided in Illustration 8–1. This hypothetical company also will be used in the next several illustrations.

**A *perpetual inventory system* continuously records both changes in inventory quantity and inventory cost.**

An important feature of a perpetual system is that it is designed to track inventory quantities from their acquisition to their sale. If the system is accurate, it allows management to determine how many goods are on hand on any date without having to take a physical count. However, physical counts of inventory usually are made anyway, either at the end of the fiscal year or on a sample basis throughout the year, to verify that the perpetual system is

[1] We discussed accounting for sales returns in Chapter 7.

**ILLUSTRATION 8–1**
Perpetual Inventory System

The Lothridge Wholesale Beverage Company purchases soft drinks from producers and then sells them to retailers. The company begins 2006 with merchandise inventory of $120,000 on hand. During 2006 additional merchandise is purchased on account at a cost of $600,000. Sales for the year, all on account, totaled $820,000. The cost of the soft drinks sold is $540,000. Lothridge uses the perpetual inventory system to keep track of both inventory quantities and inventory costs.

The following summary journal entries record the inventory transactions for the Lothridge Company:

| | | |
|---|---|---|
| **2006** | | |
| Inventory | 600,000 | |
| Accounts payable | | 600,000 |
| *To record the purchase of merchandise inventory.* | | |
| **2006** | | |
| Accounts receivable | 820,000 | |
| Sales revenue | | 820,000 |
| *To record sales on account.* | | |
| Cost of goods sold | 540,000 | |
| Inventory | | 540,000 |
| *To record the cost of sales.* | | |

correctly tracking quantities. Differences between the quantity of inventory determined by the physical count and the quantity of inventory according to the perpetual system could be caused by system errors, theft, breakage, or spoilage. In addition to keeping up with inventory, a perpetual system also directly determines how many items are sold during a period.

**A perpetual inventory system tracks both inventory quantities and inventory costs.**

You are probably familiar with the scanning mechanisms used at grocery store checkout counters. The scanners not only record the sale on the cash register but also can be used to track the sale of merchandise for inventory management purposes. For a company to use the perpetual inventory system to record inventory and cost of goods sold transactions, merchandise cost data also must be included on the system. That is, when merchandise is purchased/sold, the system must be able to record not only the addition/reduction in inventory quantity but also the addition/reduction in the *cost* of inventory.

## Periodic Inventory System

**A *periodic inventory system* adjusts inventory and records cost of goods sold only at the end of each reporting period.**

A **periodic inventory system** is not designed to track either the quantity or cost of merchandise. The merchandise inventory account balance is not adjusted as purchases and sales are made but only periodically at the end of a reporting period. A physical count of the period's ending inventory is made and costs are assigned to the quantities determined. Merchandise purchases, purchase returns, purchase discounts, and freight-in (purchases plus freight-in less returns and discounts equals net purchases) are recorded in temporary accounts and the period's cost of goods sold is determined at the end of the period by combining the temporary accounts with the inventory account:

**Cost of goods sold equation**

$$\text{Beginning inventory} + \text{Net purchases} - \text{Ending inventory} = \text{Cost of goods sold}$$

The cost of goods sold equation assumes that all inventory quantities not on hand at the end of the period were sold. This may not be the case if inventory items were either damaged or stolen. If damaged and stolen inventory are identified, they must be removed from beginning inventory or purchases before calculating cost of goods sold and then classified as a separate expense item.

Illustration 8–2 looks at the periodic system using the Lothridge Wholesale Beverage Company example.

**ILLUSTRATION 8–2**
Periodic Inventory System

The Lothridge Wholesale Beverage Company purchases soft drinks from producers and then sells them to retailers. The company began 2006 with merchandise inventory of $120,000 on hand. During 2006 additional merchandise was purchased on account at a cost of $600,000. Sales for the year, all on account, totaled $820,000. Lothridge uses a periodic inventory system. A physical count determined the cost of inventory at the end of the year to be $180,000.

The following journal entries summarize the inventory transactions for 2006. Of course, each individual transaction would actually be recorded as incurred:

| | | |
|---|---|---|
| **2006** | | |
| Purchases | 600,000 | |
| Accounts payable | | 600,000 |
| *To record the purchase of merchandise inventory.* | | |
| **2006** | | |
| Accounts receivable | 820,000 | |
| Sales revenue | | 820,000 |
| *To record sales on account.* | | |

**No entry is recorded for the cost of inventory sold.**

Because cost of goods sold isn't determined automatically and continually by the periodic system, it must be determined indirectly after a physical inventory count. Cost of goods sold for 2006 is determined as follows:

| | |
|---|---|
| Beginning inventory | $120,000 |
| Plus: Purchases | 600,000 |
| Cost of goods available for sale | 720,000 |
| Less: Ending inventory (per physical count) | (180,000) |
| Cost of goods sold | $540,000 |

The following journal entry combines the components of cost of goods sold into a single expense account and updates the balance in the inventory account:

| | | |
|---|---|---|
| **December 31, 2006** | | |
| Cost of goods sold | 540,000 | |
| Inventory (ending) | 180,000 | |
| Inventory (beginning) | | 120,000 |
| Purchases | | 600,000 |
| *To adjust inventory, close the purchases account, and record cost of goods sold.* | | |

This entry adjusts the inventory account to the correct period-end amount, closes the temporary purchases account, and records the residual as cost of goods sold. Now let's compare the two inventory accounting systems.

## A Comparison of the Perpetual and Periodic Inventory Systems

LO1

Beginning inventory plus net purchases during the period is the cost of goods available for sale. The main difference between a perpetual and a periodic system is that the periodic system allocates cost of goods available for sale between ending inventory and cost of goods sold (periodically) *at the end of the period.* In contrast, the perpetual system performs this allocation by decreasing inventory and increasing cost of goods sold (perpetually) *each time goods are sold.*

The impact on the financial statements of choosing one system over the other generally is not significant. The choice between the two approaches usually is motivated by management control considerations as well as the comparative costs of implementation. Perpetual systems can provide more information about the dollar amounts of inventory levels on a continuous basis. They also facilitate the preparation of interim financial statements by providing fairly accurate information without the necessity of a physical count of inventory.

A perpetual system provides more timely information but generally is more costly.

On the other hand, a perpetual system may be more expensive to implement than a periodic system. This is particularly true for inventories consisting of large numbers of low-cost items. Perpetual systems are more workable with inventories of high-cost items such as construction equipment or automobiles. However, with the help of computers and electronic sales devices such as cash register scanners, the perpetual inventory system is now available to many small businesses that previously could not afford them and is economically feasible for a broader range of inventory items than before.

The periodic system is less costly to implement during the period but requires a physical count before ending inventory and cost of goods sold can be determined. This makes the preparation of interim financial statements more costly unless an inventory estimation technique is used.[2] And, perhaps most importantly, the inventory monitoring features provided by a perpetual system are not available. However, it is important to remember that a perpetual system involves the tracking of both inventory quantities *and* costs. Many companies that determine costs only periodically employ systems to constantly monitor inventory quantities.

## What Is Included in Inventory?

### PHYSICAL QUANTITIES INCLUDED IN INVENTORY

LO2

Regardless of the system used, the measurement of inventory and cost of goods sold starts with determining the physical quantities of goods. Typically, determining the physical quantity that should be included in inventory is a simple matter because it consists of items in the possession of the company. However, in some situations the identification of items that should be included in inventory is more difficult. Consider, for example, goods in transit, goods on consignment, and sales returns.

**Goods in Transit.** At the end of a reporting period, it's important to ensure a proper inventory cutoff. This means determining the ownership of goods that are in transit between the company and its customers as well as between the company and its suppliers. For example, in December 2006, the Lothridge Wholesale Beverage Company sold goods to the Jabbar Company. The goods were shipped on December 29, 2006, and arrived at Jabbar's warehouse on January 3, 2007. The fiscal year-end for both companies is December 31.

Should the merchandise shipped to Jabbar be recorded as a sale by Lothridge and a purchase by Jabbar in 2006 and thus included in Jabbar's 2006 ending inventory? Should recording the sale/purchase be delayed until 2007 and the merchandise be included in Lothridge's 2006 ending inventory? The answer depends on who owns the goods at December 31. Ownership depends on the terms of the agreement between the two companies. If the goods are shipped **f.o.b. (free on board) shipping point,** then legal title to the goods changes hands at the point of shipment when the seller delivers the goods to the common carrier (for example, a trucking company), and the purchaser is responsible for shipping costs and transit insurance. In that case, Lothridge records the sale and inventory reduction in 2006 and Jabbar records a 2006 purchase and includes the goods in 2006 ending inventory even though the company is not in physical possession of the goods on the last day of the fiscal year.

Inventory shipped *f.o.b. shipping point* is included in the purchaser's inventory as soon as the merchandise is shipped.

On the other hand, if the goods are shipped **f.o.b. destination,** the seller is responsible for shipping and legal title does not pass until the goods arrive at their destination (the customer's location). In our example, if the goods are shipped f.o.b. destination, Lothridge includes the merchandise in its 2006 ending inventory and the sale is recorded in 2007. Jabbar records the purchase in 2007.

Inventory shipped *f.o.b. destination* is included in the purchaser's inventory only after it reaches the purchaser's destination.

[2] In Chapter 9 we discuss inventory estimation techniques that avoid the necessity of a physical count to determine ending inventory and cost of goods sold.

**Goods on Consignment.** Sometimes a company arranges for another company to sell its product under **consignment**. The goods are physically transferred to the other company (the consignee), but the transferor (consignor) retains legal title. If the consignee can't find a buyer, the goods are returned to the consignor. If a buyer is found, the consignee remits the selling price (less commission and approved expenses) to the consignor.

As we discussed in Chapter 5, because risk is retained by the consignor, the sale is not complete (revenue is not recognized) until an eventual sale to a third party occurs. As a result, goods held on consignment generally are not included in the consignee's inventory. While in stock, they belong to the consignor and should be included in inventory of the consignor even though not in the company's physical possession. A sale is recorded by the consignor only when the goods are sold by the consignee and title passes to the customer.

Goods held on *consignment* are included in the inventory of the consignor until sold by the consignee.

**Sales Returns.** Recall from our discussions in Chapters 5 and 7 that when the right of return exists, a seller must be able to estimate those returns before revenue can be recognized. The adjusting entry for estimated sales returns reduces sales revenue and accounts receivable. At the same time, cost of goods sold is reduced and inventory is increased (see Illustration 7–2 on page 313). As a result, a company includes in inventory the cost of merchandise it anticipates will be returned.

Now that we've considered which goods are part of inventory, let's examine the types of costs that should be associated with those inventory quantities.

## EXPENDITURES INCLUDED IN INVENTORY

● LO3

As mentioned earlier, the cost of inventory includes all necessary expenditures to acquire the inventory and bring it to its desired *condition* and *location* for sale or for use in the manufacturing process. Obviously, the cost includes the purchase price of the goods. But usually the cost of acquiring inventory also includes freight charges on incoming goods borne by the buyer; insurance costs incurred by the buyer while the goods are in transit (if shipped f.o.b. shipping point); and the costs of unloading, unpacking, and preparing merchandise inventory for sale or raw materials inventory for use.[3] The costs included in inventory are called **product costs**. They are associated with products and expensed as cost of goods sold only when the related products are sold.[4]

Expenditures necessary to bring inventory to its *condition* and *location* for sale or use are included in its cost.

Shipping charges on outgoing goods are related to the selling activity and are reported as a selling expense when incurred, not as part of inventory cost.

Shipping charges on outgoing goods are selling expenses, not part of inventory cost.

**Freight-In on Purchases.** Freight-in on purchases is commonly included in the cost of inventory. These costs clearly are necessary to get the inventory in location for sale or use and can generally be associated with particular goods. Freight costs are added to the inventory account in a perpetual system. In a periodic system, freight costs generally are added to a temporary account called **freight-in** or **transportation-in**, which is added to purchases in determining net purchases. The account is closed to cost of goods sold along with purchases and other components of cost of goods sold at the end of the reporting period. (See Illustration 8–4 on page 361.) From an accounting system perspective, freight-in also could be added to the purchases account. From a control perspective, by recording freight-in as a separate item, management can more easily track its freight costs. The same perspectives pertain to purchases returns and purchase discounts, which are discussed next.

The cost of *freight-in* paid by the purchaser generally is part of the cost of inventory.

**Purchase Returns.** In Chapter 7 we discussed merchandise returns from the perspective of the selling company. We now address returns from the buyer's point of view. You may recall that the seller views a return as a reduction of net sales. Likewise, a buyer views a return as a reduction of net purchases. When the buyer returns goods to the seller, a **purchase**

A *purchase return* represents a reduction of net purchases.

[3]A new FASB standard clarifies the language in *Accounting Research Bulletin No. 43* by requiring that abnormal amounts of certain costs be recognized as current period expenses rather than being included in the cost of inventory, specifically idle facility costs, freight, handling costs, and waste materials (spoilage). "Inventory Costs—An Amendment of *ARB No. 43*, Chapter 4," *Statement of Financial Accounting Standards No. 151* (Norwalk, Conn.: FASB, 2004).

[4]For practical reasons, though, some of these expenditures often are not included in inventory cost and are treated as **period costs**. They often are immaterial or it is impractical to associate the expenditures with particular units of inventory (for example, unloading and unpacking costs). Period costs are not associated with products and are expensed in the *period* incurred.

**return** is recorded. In a perpetual inventory system, this means a reduction in both inventory and accounts payable (if the account has not yet been paid) at the time of the return. In a periodic system an account called *purchase returns* temporarily accumulates these amounts. Purchase returns are subtracted from purchases when determining net purchases. The account is closed to cost of goods sold at the end of the reporting period.

*Purchase discounts* represent reductions in the amount to be paid if remittance is made within a designated period of time.

**Purchase Discounts.** Cash discounts also were discussed from the seller's perspective in Chapter 7. These discounts really are quick-payment discounts because they represent reductions in the amount to be paid by the buyer in the event payment is made within a specified period of time. The amount of the discount and the time period within which it's available are conveyed by cryptic terms like 2/10, n/30 (meaning a 2% discount if paid within 10 days, otherwise full payment within 30 days). As with the seller, the purchaser can record these **purchase discounts** using either the **gross method** or the **net method.** Consider Illustration 8–3 which is similar to the cash discount illustration in Chapter 7.

**ILLUSTRATION 8–3**
Purchase Discounts

On October 5, 2006, the Lothridge Wholesale Beverage Company purchased merchandise at a price of $20,000. The repayment terms are stated as 2/10, n/30. Lothridge paid $13,720 ($14,000 less the 2% cash discount) on October 14 and the remaining balance of $6,000 on November 4. Lothridge employs a periodic inventory system.

The gross and net methods of recording the purchase and cash payment are compared as follows:

By either method, net purchases is reduced by discounts taken.

Discounts not taken are included as purchases using the gross method and as interest expense using the net method.

| Gross Method | | | Net Method | | |
|---|---|---|---|---|---|
| **October 5, 2006** | | | | | |
| Purchases* | 20,000 | | Purchases* | 19,600 | |
| Accounts payable | | 20,000 | Accounts payable | | 19,600 |
| **October 14, 2006** | | | | | |
| Accounts payable | 14,000 | | Accounts payable | 13,720 | |
| Purchase discounts* | | 280 | Cash | | 13,720 |
| Cash | | 13,720 | | | |
| **November 4, 2006** | | | | | |
| Accounts payable | 6,000 | | Accounts payable | 5,880 | |
| Cash | | 6,000 | Interest expense | 120 | |
| | | | Cash | | 6,000 |

*The inventory account is used in a perpetual system.

The *gross method* views discounts not taken as part of inventory cost.

The *net method* considers discounts not taken as interest expense.

Conceptually, the gross method views a discount not taken as part of the cost of inventory. The net method considers the cost of inventory to include the net, after-discount amount, and any discounts not taken are reported as *interest expense*.[5] The discount is viewed as compensation to the seller for providing financing to the buyer.

Purchase discounts recorded under the gross method are subtracted from purchases when determining net purchases. The account is a temporary account that is closed to cost of goods sold at the end of the reporting period. Under the perpetual inventory system, purchase discounts are treated as a reduction in the inventory account.

The effect on the financial statements of the difference between the two methods usually is immaterial. Net income over time will be the same using either method. There will, however, be a difference in gross profit between the two methods equal to the amount of discounts not taken. In the preceding illustration, $120 in discounts not taken is included as interest expense using the net method and cost of goods sold using the gross method.

Illustration 8–4 compares the perpetual and periodic inventory systems, using the net method.

[5]An alternative treatment is to debit an expense account called *purchase discounts lost* rather than interest expense. This enables a company to more easily identify the forgone discounts.

**ILLUSTRATION 8–4**
Inventory Transactions—Perpetual and Periodic Systems

The Lothridge Wholesale Beverage Company purchases soft drinks from producers and then sells them to retailers. The company began 2006 with merchandise inventory of $120,000 on hand. During 2006 additional merchandise is purchased on account at a cost of $600,000. Lothridge's suppliers offer credit terms of 2/10, n/30. All discounts were taken. Lothridge uses the net method to record purchase discounts. All purchases are made f.o.b. shipping point. Freight charges paid by Lothridge totaled $16,000. Merchandise with a net of discount cost of $20,000 was returned to suppliers for credit. Sales for the year, all on account, totaled $830,000. The cost of the soft drinks sold is $550,000. $154,000 of inventory remained on hand at the end of 2006.

The above transactions are recorded in summary form according to both the perpetual and periodic inventory systems as follows:

($ in 000s)

| Perpetual System | | | Periodic System | | |
|---|---|---|---|---|---|
| | | | **Purchases** | | |
| Inventory ($600 × 98%) . . . | 588 | | Purchases ($600 × 98%) . . . . . | 588 | |
| Accounts payable. . . . . . | | 588 | Accounts payable . . . . . . . . | | 588 |
| | | | **Freight** | | |
| Inventory . . . . . . . . . . . . . | 16 | | Freight-in . . . . . . . . . . . . . . . | 16 | |
| Cash . . . . . . . . . . . . . . . . | | 16 | Cash . . . . . . . . . . . . . . . . . . | | 16 |
| | | | **Returns** | | |
| Accounts payable . . . . . . . | 20 | | Accounts payable. . . . . . . . . . | 20 | |
| Inventory . . . . . . . . . . . | | 20 | Purchase returns . . . . . . . . . | | 20 |
| | | | **Sales** | | |
| Accounts receivable . . . . . | 830 | | Accounts receivable . . . . . . . . | 830 | |
| Sales revenue . . . . . . . . . | | 830 | Sales revenue . . . . . . . . . . . | | 830 |
| Cost of goods sold . . . . . . | 550 | | No entry | | |
| Inventory . . . . . . . . . . . | | 550 | | | |
| | | | **End of period** | | |
| No Entry. . . . . . . . . . . . . | | | | | |
| | | | Cost of goods sold (below) . . . | 550 | |
| | | | Inventory (ending). . . . . . . . . | 154 | |
| | | | Purchase returns. . . . . . . . . . | 20 | |
| | | | Inventory (beginning). . . . . . | | 120 |
| | | | Purchases . . . . . . . . . . . . . | | 588 |
| | | | Freight-in . . . . . . . . . . . . . | | 16 |

**Supporting Schedule:**

| Cost of goods sold: | | |
|---|---|---|
| Beginning inventory . . . . . . . . | | $120 |
| Purchases . . . . . . . . . . . . . . . . | $588 | |
| Less: Returns. . . . . . . . . . . . | (20) | |
| Plus: Freight-in . . . . . . . . . . | 16 | |
| Net purchases. . . . . . . . . . . . . | | 584 |
| Cost of goods available . . . . . | | 704 |
| Less: Ending inventory . . . . | | (154) |
| Cost of goods sold. . . . . . . . . | | $550 |

## Inventory Cost Flow Assumptions

Regardless of whether the perpetual or periodic system is used, it's necessary to assign dollar amounts to the physical quantities of goods sold and goods remaining in ending inventory. Unless each item of inventory is specifically identified and traced through the system, assigning dollars is accomplished by making an assumption regarding how goods (and their associated costs) flow through the system. We examine the common cost flow assumptions next. In previous illustrations, dollar amounts of the cost of goods sold and the cost of ending inventory were assumed known. However, if various portions of inventory are acquired at different costs, we need a way to decide which units were sold and which remain in inventory. Illustration 8–5 will help explain.

**ILLUSTRATION 8–5**
Cost Flow

**Goods available for sale include beginning inventory plus purchases.**

The Browning Company began 2006 with $22,000 of inventory. The cost of beginning inventory (BI) is composed of 4,000 units purchased for $5.50 each. Merchandise transactions during 2006 were as follows:

**Purchases**

| Date of Purchase | Units | Unit Cost* | Total Cost |
|---|---|---|---|
| Jan.17 | 1,000 | $6.00 | $ 6,000 |
| Mar. 22 | 3,000 | 7.00 | 21,000 |
| Oct. 15 | 3,000 | 7.50 | 22,500 |
| Totals | 7,000 | | $49,500 |

**Sales**

| Date of Sale | Units |
|---|---|
| Jan. 10 | 2,000 |
| Apr. 15 | 1,500 |
| Nov. 20 | 3,000 |
| Total | 6,500 |

*includes purchase price and cost of freight.

As the data show, 7,000 units were purchased during 2006 at various prices and 6,500 units were sold. What is the cost of the 6,500 units sold? If all units, including beginning inventory, were purchased at the same price, then the answer would be simple. However, that rarely is the case.

The year started with 4,000 units, 7,000 units were purchased, and 6,500 units were sold. This means 4,500 units remain in ending inventory. This allocation of units available for sale is depicted in Graphic 8–3.

**GRAPHIC 8–3**
Allocation of Units Available

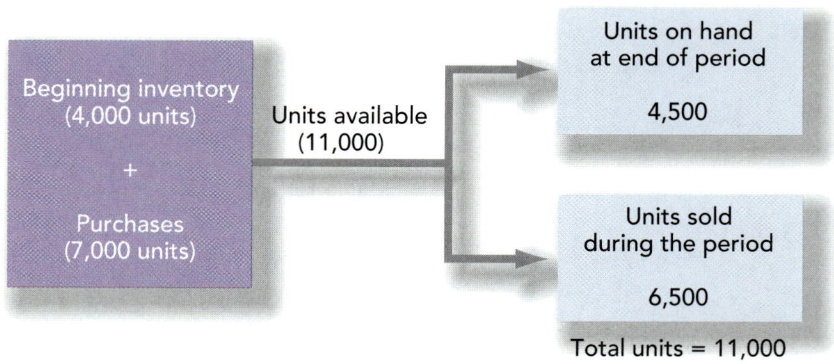


If a periodic system is used, what is the cost of the 4,500 units in ending inventory? In other words, which of the 11,000 (4,000 + 7,000) units available for sale were sold? Are they the more expensive ones bought toward the end of the year, or the less costly ones acquired before prices increased? Using the numbers given, let's consider the question as follows:

| | |
|---|---|
| Beginning inventory (4,000 units @ $5.50) | $22,000 |
| Plus: Purchases (7,000 units @ various prices) | 49,500 |
| Cost of goods available for sale (11,000 units) | $71,500 |
| Less: Ending inventory (4,500 units @ ?) | ? |
| Cost of goods sold (6,500 units @ ?) | ? |

The $71,500 in cost of goods available for sale must be allocated to ending inventory and cost of goods sold. The allocation decision is depicted in Graphic 8–4.

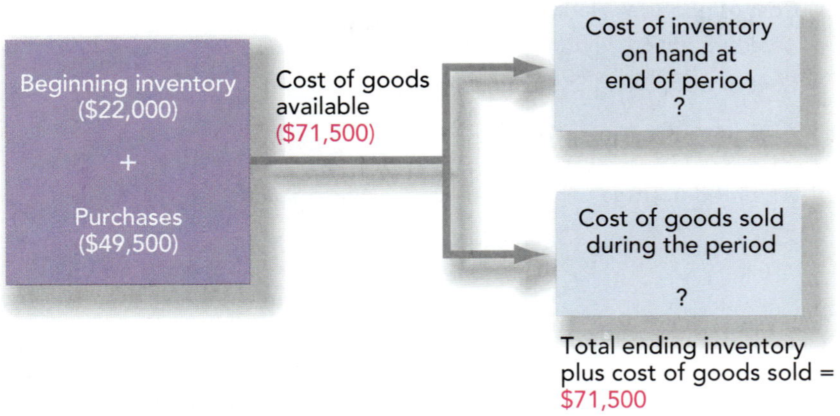


**GRAPHIC 8–4**
Allocation of Cost of Goods Available

Let's turn our attention now to the various inventory methods that can be used to achieve this allocation.

## SPECIFIC IDENTIFICATION

● LO4

It's sometimes possible for each unit sold during the period or each unit on hand at the end of the period to be matched with its actual cost. Actual costs can be determined by reference to the invoice representing the purchase of the item. This method is used frequently by companies selling unique, expensive products with low sales volume which makes it relatively easy and economically feasible to associate each item with its actual cost. For example, automobiles have unique serial numbers that can be used to match a specific auto with the invoice identifying the actual purchase price.

The **specific identification method,** however, is not feasible for many types of products either because items are not uniquely identifiable or because it is too costly to match a specific purchase price with each item sold or each item remaining in ending inventory. Most companies use cost flow methods to determine cost of goods sold and ending inventory. Cost flow methods are based on assumptions about how inventory might flow in and out of a company. However, it's important to note that the actual flow of a company's inventory does not have to correspond to the cost flow assumed. The various motivating factors that influence management's choice among alternative methods are discussed later in this chapter. We now explore the three most common cost flow methods: average cost, first-in, first-out (FIFO) and last-in, first-out (LIFO).

## AVERAGE COST

The **average cost method** assumes that cost of goods sold and ending inventory consist of a mixture of all the goods available for sale. The average unit cost applied to goods sold or to ending inventory is not simply an average of the various unit costs of purchases during the period but an average unit cost *weighted* by the number of units acquired at the various unit costs.

The *average cost method* assumes that items sold and items in ending inventory come from a mixture of all the goods available for sale.

**Periodic Average Cost.** In a periodic inventory system, this weighted average is calculated at the end of the period as follows:

$$\text{Weighted-average unit cost} = \frac{\text{Cost of goods available for sale}}{\text{Quantity available for sale}}$$

The calculation of average cost is demonstrated in Illustration 8–5A using data from Illustration 8–5.

Cost of goods sold also could be determined directly by multiplying the weighted-average unit cost of $6.50 by the number of units sold ($6.50 × 6,500 = $42,250).

**Perpetual Average Cost.** The weighted-average unit cost in a perpetual inventory system becomes a moving-average unit cost. A new weighted-average unit cost is calculated

**ILLUSTRATION 8–5A**
Average Cost—Periodic Inventory System

| | |
|---|---|
| Beginning inventory (4,000 units @ $5.50) | $22,000 |
| Plus: Purchases (7,000 units @ various prices) | 49,500 |
| Cost of goods available for sale (11,000 units) | 71,500 |
| Less: Ending inventory (determined below) | (29,250) |
| Cost of goods sold (6,500 units) | $42,250 |

**Cost of Ending Inventory:**

$$\text{Weighted-average unit cost} = \frac{\$71{,}500}{11{,}000 \text{ units}} = \$6.50$$

4,500 units × $6.50 = $29,250

In a perpetual inventory system, the average cost method is applied by computing a moving-average unit cost each time additional inventory is purchased.

each time additional units are *purchased*. The new average is determined after each purchase by (1) summing the cost of the previous inventory balance and the cost of the new purchase, and (2) dividing this new total cost (cost of goods available for sale) by the number of units on hand (the inventory units that are available for sale). This average is then used to cost any units sold before the next purchase is made. The moving-average concept is applied in Illustration 8–5B.

**ILLUSTRATION 8–5B** Average Cost—Perpetual Inventory System

| Date | Purchased | Sold | Balance |
|---|---|---|---|
| Beginning inventory | 4,000 @ $5.50 = $22,000 | | 4,000 @ $5.50 = $22,000 |
| Jan. 10 | | 2,000 @ $5.50 = $ 11,000 | 2,000 @ $5.50 = $11,000 |
| Jan. 17 | 1,000 @ $6.00 = $6,000 | | $11,000 + $6,000 = $17,000 |
| | | | 2,000 + 1,000 = 3,000 units |
| | $\left[\frac{\$17{,}000}{3{,}000 \text{ units}} = \$5.667\text{/unit}\right]$ | | |
| Mar. 22 | 3,000 @ $7.00 = $21,000 | | $17,000 + $21,000 = $38,000 |
| | $\left[\frac{\$38{,}000}{6{,}000 \text{ units}} = \$6.333\text{/unit}\right]$ | | 3,000 + 3,000 = 6,000 units |
| Apr. 15 | | 1,500 @ $6.333 = $ 9,500 | 4,500 @ $6.333 = $28,500 |
| Oct. 15 | 3,000 @ $7.50 = $22,500 | | $28,500 + $22,500 = $51,000 |
| | $\left[\frac{\$51{,}000}{7{,}500 \text{ units}} = \$6.80\text{/unit}\right]$ | | 4,500 + 3,000 = 7,500 units |
| Nov. 20 | | 3,000 @ $6.80 = $ 20,400 | 4,500 @ $6.80 = **$30,600** |
| | Total cost of goods sold | = **$40,900** | |

On January 17 the new average of $5.667 (rounded) is calculated by dividing the $17,000 cost of goods available ($11,000 from beginning inventory + $6,000 purchased on January 17) by the 3,000 units available (2,000 units from beginning inventory + 1,000 units acquired on January 17). The average is updated to $6.333 (rounded) with the March 22 purchase. The 1,500 units sold on April 15 are then costed at the average cost of $6.333.

Periodic average cost and perpetual average cost generally produce different allocations to cost of goods sold and ending inventory.

The *first-in, first-out (FIFO) method* assumes that items sold are those that were acquired first.

## FIRST-IN, FIRST-OUT (FIFO)

The **first-in, first-out (FIFO) method** assumes that units sold are the first units acquired. Beginning inventory is sold first, followed by purchases during the period in the chronological order of their acquisition. In our illustration, 6,500 units were sold during 2006. Applying FIFO, these would be the 4,000 units in beginning inventory, the 1,000 units purchased on January 17, and 1,500 of the 3,000 units from the March 22 purchase. By default, ending inventory consists of the most recently acquired units. In this case, the 4,500 units in ending inventory consist of the 3,000 units purchased on October 15, and 1,500 of the 3,000 units purchased on March 22. Graphically, the flow is as follows:

**Ending inventory applying FIFO consists of the most recently acquired items.**

| Units Available | | |
|---|---|---|
| BI | 4,000 | 6,500 units sold |
| Jan. 17 | 1,000 | |
| Mar. 22 | 1,500 | |
| Mar. 22 | 1,500 | 4,500 units in ending inventory |
| Oct. 15 | 3,000 | |
| Total | 11,000 | |

**FIFO flow**

**Periodic FIFO.** Recall that we determine physical quantities on hand in a periodic inventory system by taking a physical count. Costing the 4,500 units in ending inventory this way automatically gives us the cost of goods sold as well. Using the numbers from our illustration, we determine cost of goods sold to be $38,500 by subtracting the $33,000 ending inventory from $71,500 cost of goods available for sale as shown in Illustration 8–5C.

**ILLUSTRATION 8–5C**
FIFO—Periodic Inventory System

| | |
|---|---|
| Beginning inventory (4,000 units @ $5.50) | $22,000 |
| Plus: Purchases (7,000 units @ various prices) | 49,500 |
| Cost of goods available for sale (11,000 units) | 71,500 |
| Less: Ending inventory (determined below) | (33,000) |
| Cost of goods sold (6,500 units) | $38,500 |

**Cost of Ending Inventory:**

| Date of Purchase | Units | Unit Cost | Total Cost |
|---|---|---|---|
| Mar. 22 | 1,500 | $7.00 | $10,500 |
| Oct. 15 | 3,000 | 7.50 | 22,500 |
| Total | 4,500 | | $33,000 |

Of course, the 6,500 units sold could be costed directly as follows:

| Date of Purchase | Units | Unit Cost | Total Cost |
|---|---|---|---|
| Beg. inv. | 4,000 | $5.50 | $22,000 |
| Jan. 17 | 1,000 | 6.00 | 6,000 |
| Mar. 22 | 1,500 | 7.00 | 10,500 |
| Total | 6,500 | | $38,500 |

**Perpetual FIFO.** The same ending inventory and cost of goods sold amounts are always produced in a perpetual inventory system as in a periodic inventory system when FIFO is used. This is because the same units and costs are first in and first out whether cost of goods sold is determined as each sale is made or at the end of the period as a residual amount. The application of FIFO in a perpetual system is shown in Illustration 8–5D.

## LAST-IN, FIRST-OUT (LIFO)

**The *last-in, first-out (LIFO) method* assumes that items sold are those that were most recently acquired.**

The **last-in, first-out (LIFO) method** assumes that the units sold are the most recent units purchased. In our illustration, the 6,500 units assumed sold would be the 6,500 units acquired

**ILLUSTRATION 8–5D**
FIFO—Perpetual Inventory System

| Date | Purchased | Sold | Balance | |
|---|---|---|---|---|
| Beginning inventory | 4,000 @ $5.50 = $22,000 | | 4,000 @ $5.50 = $22,000 | |
| Jan. 10 | | 2,000 @ $5.50 = $11,000 | 2,000 @ $5.50 = $11,000 | |
| Jan. 17 | 1,000 @ $6.00 = $6,000 | | 2,000 @ $5.50<br>1,000 @ $6.00 | $17,000 |
| Mar. 22 | 3,000 @ $7.00 = $21,000 | | 2,000 @ $5.50<br>1,000 @ $6.00<br>3,000 @ $7.00 | $38,000 |
| Apr. 15 | | 1,500 @ $5.50 = $ 8,250 | 500 @ $5.50<br>1,000 @ $6.00<br>3,000 @ $7.00 | $29,750 |
| Oct. 15 | 3,000 @ $7.50 = $22,500 | | 500 @ $5.50<br>1,000 @ $6.00<br>3,000 @ $7.00<br>3,000 @ $7.50 | $52,250 |
| Nov. 20 | | 500 @ $5.50 +<br>1,000 @ $6.00 +<br>1,500 @ $7.00 = $19,250 | 1,500 @ $7.00<br>3,000 @ $7.50 | **$33,000** |
| | Total cost of goods sold | = **$38,500** | | |

most recently: the 3,000 units acquired on October 15, the 3,000 units acquired on March 22, and 500 of the 1,000 units purchased on January 17. Ending inventory, then, consists of the units acquired first; in this case, the 4,000 units from beginning inventory and 500 of the 1,000 units purchased on January 17. Graphically, the flow is as follows:

Ending inventory applying LIFO consists of the items acquired first.

LIFO flow

| Units Available | | |
|---|---|---|
| BI | 4,000 | 4,500 units in ending inventory |
| Jan. 17 | 500 | |
| Jan. 17 | 500 | 6,500 units sold |
| Mar. 22 | 3,000 | |
| Oct. 15 | 3,000 | |
| Total | 11,000 | |

**Periodic LIFO.** The cost of ending inventory determined to be $25,000 (calculated below) by the LIFO assumption and using a periodic system is subtracted from cost of goods available for sale to arrive at the cost of goods sold of $46,500 as shown in Illustration 8–5E.

**ILLUSTRATION 8–5E**
LIFO—Periodic Inventory System

| | |
|---|---|
| Beginning inventory (4,000 units @ $5.50) | $22,000 |
| Plus: Purchases (7,000 units @ various prices) | 49,500 |
| Cost of goods available for sale (11,000 units) | 71,500 |
| Less: Ending inventory (determined below) | (25,000) |
| Cost of goods sold (6,500 units) | $46,500 |

**Cost of Ending Inventory:**

| Date of Purchase | Units | Unit Cost | Total Cost |
|---|---|---|---|
| Beginning inventory | 4,000 | $5.50 | $22,000 |
| Jan. 17 | 500 | 6.00 | 3,000 |
| Total | 4,500 | | $25,000 |

The 6,500 sold could be costed directly as follows:

| Date of Purchase | Units | Unit Cost | Total Cost |
|---|---|---|---|
| Jan. 17 | 500 | $6.00 | $ 3,000 |
| Mar. 22 | 3,000 | 7.00 | 21,000 |
| Oct. 15 | 3,000 | 7.50 | 22,500 |
| Total | 6,500 | | $46,500 |

**Perpetual LIFO.** The application of LIFO in a perpetual system is shown in Illustration 8–5F. Each time inventory is purchased or sold, the LIFO layers are adjusted. For example, after the March 22 purchase, we have three layers of inventory at different unit costs listed in the chronological order of their purchase. When 1,500 units are sold on April 15, we assume they come from the most recent layer of 3,000 units purchased at $7.00.

**ILLUSTRATION 8–5F**
LIFO—Perpetual Inventory System

| Date | Purchased | Sold | Balance | |
|---|---|---|---|---|
| Beginning inventory | 4,000 @ $5.50 = $22,000 | | 4,000 @ $5.50 = $22,000 | |
| Jan. 10 | | 2,000 @ $5.50 = $11,000 | 2,000 @ $5.50 = $11,000 | |
| Jan. 17 | 1,000 @ $6.00 = $6,000 | | 2,000 @ $5.50<br>1,000 @ $6.00 | $17,000 |
| Mar. 22 | 3,000 @ $7.00 = $21,000 | | 2,000 @ $5.50<br>1,000 @ $6.00<br>3,000 @ $7.00 | $38,000 |
| Apr. 15 | | 1,500 @ $7.00 = $10,500 | 2,000 @ $5.50<br>1,000 @ $6.00<br>1,500 @ $7.00 | $27,500 |
| Oct. 15 | 3,000 @ $7.50 = $22,500 | | 2,000 @ $5.50<br>1,000 @ $6.00<br>1,500 @ $7.00<br>3,000 @ $7.50 | $50,000 |
| Nov. 20 | | 3,000 @ $7.50 = $22,500 | 2,000 @ $5.50<br>1,000 @ $6.00<br>1,500 @ $7.00 | $27,500 |
| | Total cost of goods sold | = $44,000 | | |

Notice that $44,000 of the cost of goods available for sale is allocated to cost of goods sold by perpetual LIFO and $27,500 to ending inventory (the balance after the last transaction), which is different from the periodic LIFO result of $46,500 and $25,000. Unlike FIFO, applying LIFO in a perpetual inventory system will generally result in an ending inventory and cost of goods sold different from the allocation arrived at applying LIFO in a periodic system. Periodic LIFO applies the last-in, first-out concept to total sales and total purchases only at the conclusion of the reporting period. Perpetual LIFO applies the same concept, but several times during the period—every time a sale is made.

**Perpetual LIFO generally results in cost of goods sold and inventory amounts that are different from those obtained by applying periodic LIFO.**

For example, when 2,000 units are sold on January 10, perpetual LIFO costs those units at $5.50, the beginning inventory unit cost. Periodic LIFO, by contrast, would be applied at year-end. By the end of the year, enough purchases have been made that the beginning inventory would be assumed to remain intact, and the January 10 units sold would be costed at a more recent price.

## COMPARISON OF COST FLOW METHODS

The three cost flow methods are compared below assuming a periodic inventory system.

Comparison of cost flow methods

| | Average | FIFO | LIFO |
|---|---|---|---|
| Cost of goods sold | $42,250 | $38,500 | $46,500 |
| Ending inventory | 29,250 | 33,000 | 25,000 |
| Total | $71,500 | $71,500 | $71,500 |

Notice that the average cost method in this example produces amounts that fall in between the FIFO and LIFO amounts for both cost of goods sold and ending inventory. This will usually be the case. Whether it will be FIFO or LIFO that produces the highest or lowest value of cost of goods sold and ending inventory depends on the pattern of the actual unit cost changes during the period.

If unit costs are increasing, LIFO will result in a higher cost of goods sold and lower ending inventory than FIFO.

During periods of generally rising costs, as in our example, FIFO results in a lower cost of goods sold than LIFO because the lower costs of the earliest purchases are assumed sold. LIFO cost of goods sold will include the more recent higher cost purchases. On the other hand, FIFO ending inventory includes the most recent higher cost purchases which results in a higher ending inventory than LIFO. LIFO ending inventory includes the lower costs of the earliest purchases. Conversely, if costs are declining, then FIFO will result in a higher cost of goods sold and lower ending inventory than LIFO.[6]

**Financial Reporting Case**

Q1, p. 353

A company must disclose the inventory method(s) it uses.

Each of the three methods is permissible according to generally accepted accounting principles and frequently is used. Also, a company need not use the same method for all of its inventory. For example, **International Paper Company** uses LIFO for its raw materials and finished pulp and paper products, and both the FIFO and average cost methods for other inventories. Because of the importance of inventories and the possible differential effects of different methods on the financial statements, a company must identify in a disclosure note the method(s) it uses. The chapter's opening case included an example of this disclosure for **Ford Motor Company**, and you will encounter additional examples later in the chapter.

Graphic 8–5 shows the results of a survey of inventory methods used by 600 large public companies in 2003 and 1973.[7] FIFO is the most popular method in both periods, but there has been a dramatic increase in the use of LIFO since the earlier period. Notice that the column total for the number of companies is greater than 600, indicating that many companies included in this sample do use multiple methods.

**Graphic 8–5**
Inventory Cost Flow Methods Used in Practice

| | 2003 | | 1973 | |
|---|---|---|---|---|
| | # of Companies | % of Companies | # of Companies | % of Companies |
| FIFO | 384 | 46% | 394 | 43% |
| LIFO | 251 | 30 | 150 | 16 |
| Average | 167 | 20 | 235 | 25 |
| Other* | 31 | 4 | 148 | 16 |
| Total | 833 | 100% | 927 | 100% |

*"Other" includes the specific identification method and miscellaneous less popular methods.

**GLOBAL PERSPECTIVE**

Inventory measurement techniques vary widely across different countries. In Mexico an acceptable technique is to use the latest purchase price to measure ending inventory. IFRSs do not permit the use of LIFO.

[6]The differences between the various methods also hold when a perpetual inventory system is used.

[7]*Accounting Trends and Techniques—2004* and *1974* (New York, New York: AICPA, 2004 and 1974)

● LO5

## DECISION MAKERS' PERSPECTIVE—Factors Influencing Method Choice

What factors motivate companies to choose one method over another? What factors have caused the increased popularity of LIFO? Choosing among alternative accounting methods is a complex issue. Often such choices are not made in isolation but in such a way that the combination of inventory cost flow assumptions, depreciation methods, pension assumptions, and other choices meet a particular objective. Also, many believe managers sometimes make these choices to maximize their own personal benefits rather than those of the company or its external constituents. But regardless of the motive, the impact on reported numbers is an important consideration in each choice of method. The inventory choice determines (a) how closely reported costs reflect the actual physical flow of inventory, (b) the timing of reported income and income tax expense, and (c) how well costs are matched with associated revenues.

**Physical Flow.** If a company wanted to choose a method that most closely approximates specific identification, then the actual physical flow of inventory in and out of the company would motivate the choice of method.

A company is not required to choose an inventory method that approximates actual physical flow.

For example, companies often attempt to sell the oldest goods in inventory first for some of their products. This certainly is the case with perishable goods such as many grocery items. The FIFO method best mirrors the physical flow in these situations. The average cost method might be used for liquids such as chemicals where items sold are taken from a mixture of inventory acquired at different times and different prices. There are very few inventories that actually flow in a LIFO manner. It is important for you to understand that there is no requirement that companies choose an inventory method that approximates actual physical flow and few companies make the choice on this basis. In fact, as we discuss next, the effect of inventory method on income and income taxes is the primary motivation that influences method choice.

**Income Taxes and Net Income.** If the unit cost of inventory changes during a period, the inventory method chosen can have a significant effect on the amount of income reported by the company to external parties and also on the amount of income taxes paid to the Internal Revenue Service (IRS) and state and local taxing authorities. Over the entire life of a company, cost of goods sold for all years will equal actual costs of items sold regardless of the inventory method used. However, as we have discussed, different inventory methods can produce significantly different results in each particular year.

When prices rise and inventory quantities are not decreasing, LIFO produces a higher cost of goods sold and therefore lower net income than the other methods. The company's income tax returns will report a lower taxable income using LIFO and lower taxes will be paid currently. Taxes are not reduced permanently, only deferred. The reduced amount will be paid to the taxing authorities when either the unit cost of inventory or the quantity of inventory subsequently declines. However, we know from our discussion of the time value of money that it is advantageous to save a dollar today even if it must be paid back in the future. Recall from the recent survey results exhibited earlier that the popularity of LIFO increased significantly between 1973 and 2003. The main reason for this increased popularity is attributable to high inflation (increasing prices) during the 1970s which motivated many companies to switch to LIFO in order to gain this tax benefit.

Many companies choose LIFO in order to reduce income taxes in periods when prices are rising.

A corporation's taxable income comprises revenues, expenses (including cost of goods sold), gains, and losses measured according to the regulations of the appropriate taxing authority. Income before tax as reported in the income statement does not always equal taxable income. In some cases, differences are caused by the use of different measurement methods.[8] However, IRS regulations, which determine federal taxable income, require that if a company uses LIFO to measure taxable income, the company also must use LIFO for external financial reporting. This is known as the **LIFO conformity rule** with respect to inventory methods.

[8]For example, a corporation can take advantage of incentives offered by Congress by deducting more depreciation in the early years of an asset's life in its federal income tax return than it reports in its income statement.

**GLOBAL PERSPECTIVE**

In the United States, if a company uses LIFO for tax purposes, the same method must be used for financial reporting, but differences might exist for other accounting choices. Other countries require much closer conformity of accounting practice and tax laws.

**If a company uses LIFO to measure its taxable income, IRS regulations require that LIFO also be used to measure income reported to investors and creditors (the *LIFO conformity rule*).**

Because of the LIFO conformity rule, to obtain the tax advantages of using LIFO in periods of rising prices, lower net income is reported to shareholders, creditors, and other external parties. The income tax motivation for using LIFO may be offset by a desire to report higher net income. Reported net income could have an effect on a corporation's share price,[9] on bonuses paid to management, or on debt agreements with lenders. For example, research has indicated that the managers of companies with bonus plans tied to income measures are more likely to choose accounting methods that maximize their bonuses (often those that increase net income).[10]

**FINANCIAL REPORTING CASE**

Q2, p. 353

In 1981, the LIFO conformity rule was liberalized to permit LIFO users to present designated supplemental disclosures, allowing a company to report in a note the effect of using another method on inventory valuation rather than LIFO. For example, Graphic 8–6 shows the note provided in a recent annual report by **Alcoa, Inc.**, a leading producer of aluminum, disclosing its use of LIFO for part of its inventories. A second note provides the supplemental LIFO disclosures.[11]

● LO6

**GRAPHIC 8–6**
Inventories Disclosure—Alcoa, Inc.

**Summary of Significant Accounting Policies**
**Inventory Valuation**
Inventories are carried at the lower of cost or market, with cost for a substantial portion of U.S. and Canadian inventories determined under the last-in, first-out (LIFO) method. The cost of other inventories is principally determined using the average-cost method.

**G. Inventories (in part)**
Approximately 46% of total inventories at December 31, 2003, were valued on a LIFO basis. If valued on an average-cost basis, total inventories would have been $558 and $514 million higher at the end of 2003 and 2002, respectively.

**Proponents of LIFO argue that it results in a better match of revenues and expenses.**

**LIFO Liquidations.** Earlier in the text, we demonstrated the importance of matching revenues and expenses in creating an income statement that is useful in predicting future cash flows. If prices change during a period, then LIFO generally will provide a better match of revenues and expenses. Sales reflect the most recent selling prices, and cost of goods sold includes the costs of the most recent purchases. Graphic 8–7 shows the **General Mills, Inc.** disclosure that was included in its summary of significant accounting policies.

**GRAPHIC 8–7**
Inventory Policy Disclosure—General Mills, Inc.

**(C) Inventories (in part)**
Inventories are valued at the lower of cost or market. We generally use LIFO as the preferred method of valuing inventory because we believe that it is a better match with current revenues.

---

[9]The concept of capital market efficiency has been debated for many years. In an efficient capital market, the market is not fooled by differences in accounting method choice that do not translate into real cash flow differences. The only apparent cash flow difference caused by different inventory methods is the amount of income taxes paid currently. In an efficient market, we would expect the share price of a company that switched its method to LIFO and saved tax dollars to increase even though it reported lower net income than if LIFO had not been adopted. Research on this issue is mixed. For example, see William E. Ricks, "Market's Response to the 1974 LIFO Adoptions," *Journal of Accounting Research* (Autumn 1982), and Robert Moren Brown, "Short-Range Market Reaction to Changes to LIFO Using Preliminary Earnings Announcement Dates," *Journal of Accounting Research* (Spring 1980).

[10]For example, see P. M. Healy, "The Effect of Bonus Schemes on Accounting Decisions," *Journal of Accounting and Economics* (April 1985), and D. Dhaliwal, G. Salamon, and E. Smith, "The Effect of Owner Versus Management Control on the Choice of Accounting Methods," *Journal of Accounting and Economics* (July 1982).

[11]Alcoa uses both the LIFO and average cost methods. Earlier in the chapter we pointed out that a company need not use the same inventory method for all of its inventories.

For the same reason, though, inventory costs in the balance sheet with LIFO generally are out of date because they reflect old purchase transactions. It is not uncommon for a company's LIFO inventory balance to be based on unit costs actually incurred several years earlier.

This distortion sometimes carries over to the income statement as well. When inventory quantities decline during a period, then these out-of-date inventory layers are liquidated and the cost of goods sold will partially match noncurrent costs with current selling prices. If costs have been increasing (decreasing), LIFO liquidations produce higher (lower) net income than would have resulted if the liquidated inventory were included in cost of goods sold at current costs. The paper profits (losses) caused by including out of date, low (high) costs in cost of goods sold is referred to as the effect on income of liquidations of LIFO inventory.

To illustrate this problem, consider the example in Illustration 8–6.

**ILLUSTRATION 8–6**
LIFO Liquidation

National Distributors, Inc., uses the LIFO inventory method. The company began 2006 with inventory of 10,000 units that cost $20 per unit. During 2006, 30,000 units were purchased for $25 each and 35,000 units were sold.

National's LIFO cost of goods sold for 2006 consists of:

| | |
|---|---|
| 30,000 units @ $25 per unit = | $750,000 |
| 5,000 units @ $20 per unit = | $100,000 |
| 35,000 | $850,000 |

Included in cost of goods sold are 5,000 units from beginning inventory that have now been liquidated. If the company had purchased at least 35,000 units, no liquidation would have occurred. Then cost of goods sold would have been $875,000 (35,000 units × $25 per unit) instead of $850,000. The difference between these two cost of goods sold figures is $25,000 ($875,000 − 850,000). This is the before tax income effect of the LIFO liquidation. Assuming a 40% income tax rate, the net effect of the liquidation is to increase net income by $15,000 [$25,000 × (1 − .40)]. The lower the costs of the units liquidated, the more severe the effect on income.

A material effect on net income of LIFO layer liquidation must be disclosed in a note.

A company must disclose in a note any material effect of **LIFO liquidation** on net income. For example, Graphic 8–8 shows the disclosure that accompanies recent financial statements of **Ethyl Corporation**, a manufacturer of fuels and lubricants.

**GRAPHIC 8–8**
LIFO Liquidation Disclosure—Ethyl Corporation

**8. Inventories (in part)**
During 2003 and 2001, TEL inventory quantities were reduced resulting in a liquidation of LIFO layers. The effect of these liquidations increased net income by $100,000 in 2003 and $800,000 in 2001. During 2002, petroleum additive inventory quantities were reduced resulting in a liquidation of LIFO layers and increasing net income by $300,000.

In our illustration, National Distributors, Inc. would disclose that LIFO liquidations increased income by $15,000 in 2006, assuming that this effect on income is considered material.

We've discussed several factors that influence companies in their choice of inventory method. A company could be influenced by the actual physical flow of its inventory, by the effect of inventory method on reported net income and the amount of income taxes payable currently, or by a desire to provide a better match of expenses with revenues. You've seen that the direction of the change in unit costs determines the effect of using different methods on net income and income taxes. While the United States has experienced persistent inflation for many years (increases in the general price-level), the prices of many goods and services have experienced periods of declining prices (for example, personal computers). ■

**ADDITIONAL CONSIDERATION**

### LIFO Reserves

Many companies use LIFO for external reporting and income tax purposes but maintain their internal records using FIFO or average cost. The reasons for doing this might include: (1) the high recordkeeping costs of the LIFO method, (2) the existence of contractual agreements such as bonus or profit sharing plans that prohibit the use of LIFO in the calculation of net income, and (3) the need for FIFO or average cost information for pricing decisions.

Generally, the conversion to LIFO is performed at the end of the period and not entered into the company's records. However, some companies enter the results of the conversion—the difference between the internal method and LIFO—directly into the accounts as a contra account to inventory. This contra account is called either the LIFO reserve or the LIFO allowance.

Occasionally, such companies report ending inventory valued using the internal method less the LIFO reserve or allowance to arrive at LIFO inventory reported in the balance sheet. For example, General Motors recently reported the following in a note:

| **Inventories** ($ in millions) | **2004** | **2003** |
|---|---|---|
| Total inventories at FIFO | $13,159 | $12,541 |
| Less LIFO allowance | 1,442 | 1,581 |
| Total inventories, at LIFO cost | $11,717 | $10,960 |

Note that this is merely another way of presenting the supplemental non-LIFO disclosures discussed previously.

## CONCEPT REVIEW EXERCISE

### INVENTORY COST FLOW METHODS

The Rogers Company began 2006 with an inventory of 10 million units of its principal product. These units cost $5 each. The following inventory transactions occurred during the first six months of 2006.

| **Date** | **Transaction** |
|---|---|
| Feb. 15 | Purchased, on account, 5 million units at a cost of $6.50 each. |
| Mar. 20 | Sold, on account, 8 million units at a selling price of $12 each. |
| Apr. 30 | Purchased, on account, 5 million units at a cost of $7 each. |

On June 30, 2006, 12 million units were on hand.

**Required:**

1. Prepare journal entries to record the above transactions. The company uses a periodic inventory system.
2. Prepare the required adjusting entry on June 30, 2006, applying each of the following inventory methods:
   a. Average
   b. FIFO
   c. LIFO
3. Repeat requirement 1 assuming that the company uses a perpetual inventory system.

### SOLUTION

1. Prepare journal entries to record the above transactions. The company uses a periodic inventory system.

| **February 15** | ($ in millions) | |
|---|---|---|
| Purchases (5 million × $6.50) | 32.5 | |
| Accounts payable | | 32.5 |
| *To record the purchase of inventory.* | | |

| | | |
|---|---|---|
| **March 20** | | |
| Accounts receivable (8 million × $12) | 96 | |
| Sales revenue | | 96 |
| *To record sales on account.* | | |
| **No entry is recorded for the cost of inventory sold.** | | |
| **April 30** | | |
| Purchases (5 million × $7) | 35 | |
| Accounts payable | | 35 |
| *To record the purchase of inventory.* | | |

2. Prepare the required adjusting entry on June 30, 2006, applying each method.

| | | ($ in millions) | | | | | |
|---|---|---|---|---|---|---|---|
| **Date** | **Journal entry** | **Average** | | **FIFO** | | **LIFO** | |
| June 30 | Cost of goods sold (determined below) | 47.0 | | 40.0 | | 54.5 | |
| | Inventory (ending—determined below) | 70.5 | | 77.5 | | 63.0 | |
| | Inventory (beginning – [10 million @ $5]) | | 50.0 | | 50.0 | | 50.0 |
| | Purchases ($32.5 million + 35 million) | | 67.5 | | 67.5 | | 67.5 |

**Calculation of Ending Inventory and Cost of Goods Sold:**

a. Average:

| | ($ in millions) |
|---|---|
| Beginning inventory (10 million units @ $5.00) | $ 50.0 |
| Plus: Purchases (10 million units @ various prices) | 67.5 |
| Cost of goods available for sale (20 million units) | 117.5 |
| Less: Ending inventory (determined below) | (70.5) |
| Cost of goods sold | $ 47.0 |

Cost of ending inventory:

$$\text{Weighted-average unit cost} = \frac{\$117.5}{20 \text{ million units}} = \$5.875$$

12 million units × $5.875 = $70.5 million

b. FIFO:

| | |
|---|---|
| Cost of goods available for sale (20 million units) | $117.5 |
| Less: Ending inventory (determined below) | (77.5) |
| Cost of goods sold | $ 40.0 |

Cost of ending inventory:

| Date of Purchase | Units | Unit Cost | Total Cost |
|---|---|---|---|
| April 30 | 5 million | $7.00 | $35.0 |
| Feb. 15 | 5 million | 6.50 | 32.5 |
| Beg. inv. | 2 million | 5.00 | 10.0 |
| Total | 12 million | | $77.5 |

c. LIFO:

| | |
|---|---|
| Cost of goods available for sale (20 million units) | $117.5 |
| Less: Ending inventory (determined below) | (63.0) |
| Cost of goods sold | $ 54.5 |

Cost of ending inventory:

| Date of Purchase | Units | Unit Cost | Total Cost |
|---|---|---|---|
| Beg. inv. | 10 million | $5.00 | $50.0 |
| Feb. 15 | 2 million | 6.50 | 13.0 |
| Total | 12 million | | $63.0 |

3. Repeat requirement 1 assuming that the company uses a perpetual inventory system.

| | ($ in millions) | |
|---|---|---|
| **February 15** | | |
| Inventory (5 million units × $6.50) | 32.5 | |
| Accounts payable | | 32.5 |
| *To record the purchase of inventory.* | | |
| **April 30** | | |
| Inventory (5 million units × $7.00) | 35.0 | |
| Accounts payable | | 35.0 |
| *To record the purchase of inventory.* | | |

| | ($ in millions) | | | | | |
|---|---|---|---|---|---|---|
| **Journal Entries—March 20** | **Average** | | **FIFO** | | **LIFO** | |
| Accounts receivable (8 million × $12) | 96.0 | | 96.0 | | 96.0 | |
| Sales revenue | | 96.0 | | 96.0 | | 96.0 |
| *To record sales on account.* | | | | | | |
| Cost of goods sold (determined below) | 44.0 | | 40.0 | | 47.5 | |
| Inventory (determined below) | | 44.0 | | 40.0 | | 47.5 |
| *To record cost of goods sold.* | | | | | | |

**Calculation of Cost of Goods Sold:**

a. Average:
Cost of goods sold:

| | ($, except unit costs, in millions) | | |
|---|---|---|---|
| **Date** | **Purchased** | **Sold** | **Balance** |
| Beg. inv. | 10 million @ $5.00 | | 10 million @ $5.00 = $50.0 |
| Feb. 15 | 5 million @ $6.50 | | $50 + 32.5 = $82.5 |
| | $\frac{\$82.5}{15 \text{ million units}} = \$5.50/\text{unit}$ | | |
| Mar. 20 | | 8 million @ $5.50 = $44.0 | |

b. FIFO:
Cost of goods sold:

| Units Sold | Cost of Units Sold | Total Cost |
|---|---|---|
| 8 million (from BI) | $5.00 | $40.0 |

c. LIFO:
Cost of goods sold:

| Units Sold | Cost of Units Sold | Total Cost |
|---|---|---|
| 5 million (from Feb. 15 purchase) | $6.50 | $32.5 |
| 3 million (from beg. inventory) | 5.00 | 15.0 |
| 8 million | | $47.5 |

## DECISION MAKERS' PERSPECTIVE

### Inventory Management

Managers closely monitor inventory levels to (1) ensure that the inventories needed to sustain operations are available, and (2) hold the cost of ordering and carrying inventories to the lowest possible level.[12] Unfortunately, these objectives often conflict with one another. Companies must maintain sufficient quantities of inventory to meet customer demand. However, maintaining inventory is costly. Fortunately, a variety of tools are available, including computerized inventory control systems and the outsourcing of inventory component production, to help balance these conflicting objectives.[13]

**A company should maintain sufficient inventory quantities to meet customer demand while at the same time minimizing inventory ordering and carrying costs.**

A **just-in-time (JIT) system** is another valuable technique that many companies have adopted to assist them with inventory management. JIT is a system used by a manufacturer to coordinate production with suppliers so that raw materials or components arrive just as they are needed in the production process. Have you ever ordered a personal computer from **Dell Inc.**? If so, the PC you received was not manufactured until you placed your order, and many of the components used in the production of your PC were not even acquired by Dell until then as well. This system enables Dell to maintain relatively low inventory balances. At the same time, the company's efficient production techniques, along with its excellent relationships with suppliers ensuring prompt delivery of components, enables Dell to quickly meet customer demand. In its January 28, 2005, fiscal year-end financial statements, Dell reported an inventory balance of $459 million. With this relatively low investment in inventory, Dell was able to generate over $49 billion in sales revenue. To appreciate the advantage this provides, compare these numbers with **Hewlett Packard (HP)**, a company that includes PCs among its wide variety of technology products. For its fiscal year ended October 31, 2004, HP reported product revenue of $54 billion. However, to achieve this level of sales, HP's investment in inventory was over $7 billion.

It is important for a financial analyst to evaluate a company's effectiveness in managing its inventory. As we discussed in Chapter 5, one key to profitability is how well a company utilizes its assets. This evaluation is influenced by the company's inventory method choice. The choice of inventory method is an important and complex management decision. The many factors affecting this decision were discussed in a previous section. The inventory method also affects the analysis of a company's liquidity and profitability by investors, creditors, and financial analysts. Analysts must make adjustments when evaluating companies that use different inventory methods. During periods of rising prices, we would expect a company using FIFO to report higher income than a LIFO or average cost company. If one of the companies being analyzed uses LIFO, precise adjustments can often be made using the supplemental disclosures provided by many LIFO companies. Recall that the LIFO conformity rule was liberalized to permit LIFO users to report in a note the effect of using a method other than LIFO for inventory valuation.

**FINANCIAL REPORTING CASE**

Q3, p. 353

For example, the disclosure note exhibited in Graphic 8–6 on page 370 reveals that **Alcoa Inc.** uses both the LIFO and average-cost inventory methods with 46% of its inventories valued using LIFO. **Alcan, Inc.**, Alcoa's major competitor, values all of its inventory using the average-cost method. Financial statement values for the two companies for 2003 are as follows ($ in millions):

[12]The cost of carrying inventory includes the possible loss from the write-down of obsolete inventory. We discuss inventory write-downs in Chapter 9. There are analytical models available to determine the appropriate amount of inventory a company should maintain. A discussion of these models is beyond the scope of this text.

[13]Eugene Brigham and Joel Houston, *Fundamentals of Financial Management,* 8th Edition, 1998, The Dryden Press, Orlando, Florida, p. 632.

| | Alcoa, Inc. | | Alcan, Inc. | |
|---|---|---|---|---|
| | 2003 | 2002 | 2003 | 2002 |
| **Balance sheet:** | | | | |
| Inventories | $ 2,524 | $ 2,414 | $ 1,706 | $ 1,587 |
| **Income statement:** | | | | |
| Net sales | 21,504 | 20,351 | 13,640 | 12,296 |
| Cost of goods sold | 17,138 | 16,327 | 10,802 | 9,716 |

Supplemental LIFO disclosures can be used to convert LIFO inventory and cost of goods sold amounts.

We can convert Alcoa's inventory and cost of goods sold to a 100% average cost basis before comparing the two companies by using the information provided in Graphic 8–6. Inventories recorded at LIFO were lower by approximately $558 million at December 31, 2003, and $514 million at December 31, 2002, than if they had been valued at average cost:

| | 2003 | 2002 |
|---|---|---|
| Inventories (as reported) | $2,524 | $2,414 |
| Add: conversion to average cost | 558 | 514 |
| Inventories (100% average cost) | $3,082 | $2,928 |

Cost of goods sold for 2003 would have been $44 million lower had Alcoa used average cost instead of LIFO. While beginning inventory would have been $514 million higher, ending inventory also would have been higher by $558 million. An increase in beginning inventory causes an increase in cost of goods sold, but an increase in ending inventory causes a decrease in cost of goods sold. Purchases for 2003 are the same regardless of the inventory valuation method used. Cost of goods sold for 2003 would have been $17,094 million ($17,138 − 44) if average cost had been used for all inventories.

We can now use the 100% average cost amounts to compare the two companies. Since cost of goods sold is lower by $44 million, income taxes and net income require adjustment before calculating any profitability ratio. Also, the converted inventory amounts can be used to compute liquidity ratios.

● LO7

One important profitability indicator using cost of goods sold is **gross profit** or **gross margin**, which highlights the important relationship between net sales revenue and cost of goods sold. The **gross profit ratio** is computed as follows:

$$\text{Gross profit ratio} = \frac{\text{Gross profit}}{\text{Net sales}}$$

The *gross profit ratio* indicates the percentage of each sales dollar available to cover other expenses and provide a profit.

The higher the ratio, the higher is the markup a company is able to achieve on its products. For example, a product that costs $100 that is sold for $150 provides a gross profit of $50 ($150 − 100) and a gross profit ratio of 33% ($50 ÷ $150). If that same product can be sold for $200, the gross profit increases to $100 and the gross profit ratio increases to 50% ($100 ÷ $200) and more dollars are available to cover expenses other than cost of goods sold.

The 2003 gross profit ($ in millions), for Alcoa, using the 100% average cost amounts, is $4,410 ($21,504 − 17,094) and the gross profit ratio is 21% ($4,410 ÷ $21,504). The ratio for Alcan also is 21% [($13,640 − 10,802) = $2,838 ÷ $13,640]. The ratio for both companies is less than the industry average of 27%.

Monitoring this ratio over time can provide valuable insights. For example, a declining ratio could indicate that the company is unable to offset rising costs with corresponding increases in sales price, or that sales prices are declining without a commensurate reduction in costs. In either case, the decline in the ratio has important implications for future profitability.

Chapter 5 introduced an important ratio, the **inventory turnover ratio**, which is designed to evaluate a company's effectiveness in managing its investment in inventory. The ratio shows the number of times the average inventory balance is sold during a reporting period. The more frequently a business is able to sell or turn over its inventory, the lower its investment in inventory must be for a given level of sales. Usually, the higher the ratio the more profitable a company will be. Monitoring the inventory turnover ratio over time can highlight potential problems. A declining ratio generally is unfavorable and could be caused by the presence of obsolete or slow-moving products, or poor marketing and sales efforts.

Recall that the ratio is computed as follows:

$$\text{Inventory turnover ratio} = \frac{\text{Cost of goods sold}}{\text{Average inventory}}$$

We can divide the inventory turnover ratio into 365 days to compute the **average days in inventory**, which indicates the average number of days it normally takes to sell inventory.

For Alcoa, the inventory turnover ratio for 2003 is 5.69 ($17,094 ÷ [($3,082 + 2,928) ÷ 2]) and the average days inventory is 64 days (365 ÷ 5.69). This compares to a turnover of 6.56 ($10,802 ÷ [($1,706 + 1,587) ÷ 2]) and an average days inventory of 56 days (365 days ÷ 6.56) for Alcan. It takes eight more days, on average, for Alcoa to turn over its inventory. Alcan's inventory turnover ratio is higher than the industry average of 6.19, while Alcoa's is lower.

Inventory increases that outrun increases in cost of goods sold might indicate difficulties in generating sales. These inventory buildups may also indicate that a company has obsolete or slow-moving inventory. This proposition was tested in an important academic research study. Professors Lev and Thiagarajan empirically demonstrated the importance of a set of 12 fundamental variables in valuing companies' common stock. The set of variables included inventory (change in inventory minus change in sales). The inventory variable was found to be a significant indicator of stock returns, particularly during high and medium inflation years.[14]

### Earnings Quality

Changes in the ratios we discussed above often provide information about the quality of a company's current period earnings. For example, a slowing turnover ratio combined with higher than normal inventory levels may indicate the potential for decreased production, obsolete inventory, or a need to decrease prices to sell inventory (which will then decrease gross profit ratios and net income).

The choice of which inventory method to use also affects earnings quality, particularly in times of rapidly changing prices. Earlier in this chapter we discussed the effect of a LIFO liquidation on company profits. A LIFO liquidation profit (or loss) reduces the quality of current period earnings. Fortunately for analysts, companies must disclose these profits or losses, if material. In addition, LIFO cost of goods sold determined using a periodic inventory system is more susceptible to manipulation than is FIFO. Year-end purchases can have a dramatic effect on LIFO cost of goods sold in rapid cost-change environments. Recall again our discussion in Chapter 4 concerning earnings quality. Many believe that manipulating income reduces earnings quality because it can mask permanent earnings. Inventory write-downs and changes in inventory method are two additional inventory-related techniques a company could use to manipulate earnings. We discuss these issues in the next chapter. ■

## METHODS OF SIMPLIFYING LIFO

**PART B**

The LIFO method described and illustrated to this point is called *unit LIFO*[15] because the last-in, first-out concept is applied to individual units of inventory. One problem with unit LIFO is that it can be very costly to implement. It requires records of each unit of inventory. The costs of maintaining these records can be significant, particularly when a company has numerous individual units of inventory and when unit costs change often during a period.

**The recordkeeping costs of unit LIFO can be significant.**

In the previous section, a second disadvantage of unit LIFO was identified—the possibility that LIFO layers will be liquidated if the quantity of a particular inventory unit declines below its beginning balance. Even if a company's total inventory quantity is stable or increasing, if the quantity of any particular inventory unit declines, unit LIFO will liquidate all

**Another disadvantage of unit LIFO is the possibility of LIFO liquidation.**

---

[14]B. Lev and S. R. Thiagarajan, "Fundamental Information Analysis," *Journal of Accounting Research* (Autumn 1993). The main conclusion of the study was that fundamental variables, not just earnings, are useful in firm valuation, particularly when examined in the context of macroeconomic conditions such as inflation.

[15]Unit LIFO sometimes is called *specific goods LIFO*.

or a portion of a LIFO layer of inventory. When inventory quantity declines in a period of rising costs, noncurrent lower costs will be included in cost of goods sold and matched with current selling prices, resulting in LIFO liquidation profit.

This part of the chapter discusses techniques that can be used to significantly reduce the recordkeeping costs of LIFO and to minimize the probability of LIFO inventory layers being liquidated. Specifically, we discuss the use of inventory pools and the dollar-value LIFO method.

## LIFO Inventory Pools

A pool consists of inventory units grouped according to natural physical similarities.

The objectives of using **LIFO inventory pools** are to simplify recordkeeping by grouping inventory units into pools based on physical similarities of the individual units and to reduce the risk of LIFO layer liquidation. For example, a glass company might group its various grades of window glass into a single window pool. Other pools might be auto glass and sliding door glass. A lumber company might pool its inventory into hardwood, framing lumber, paneling, and so on.

The average cost for all of the pool purchases during the period is applied to the current year's LIFO layer.

This allows a company to account for a few inventory pools rather than every specific type of inventory separately. Within pools, all purchases during a period are considered to have been made at the same time and at the same cost. Individual unit costs are converted to an average cost for the pool. If the quantity of ending inventory for the pool increases, then ending inventory will consist of the beginning inventory plus a single layer added during the period at the average acquisition cost for that pool.

Here's an example. Let's say Diamond Lumber Company has a rough-cut lumber inventory pool that includes three types: oak, pine, and maple. The beginning inventory consisted of the following:

| | Quantity (Board Feet) | Cost (Per Foot) | Total Cost |
|---|---|---|---|
| Oak | 16,000 | $2.20 | $35,200 |
| Pine | 10,000 | 3.00 | 30,000 |
| Maple | 14,000 | 2.40 | 33,600 |
| | 40,000 | | $98,800 |

The average cost for this pool is $2.47 per board foot ($98,800 ÷ 40,000 board feet). Now assume that during the next reporting period Diamond sold 46,000 board feet of lumber and purchased 50,000 board feet as follows:

| | Quantity (Board Feet) | Cost (Per Foot) | Total Cost |
|---|---|---|---|
| Oak | 20,000 | $2.25 | $ 45,000 |
| Pine | 14,000 | 3.00 | 42,000 |
| Maple | 16,000 | 2.50 | 40,000 |
| | 50,000 | | $127,000 |

The average cost for this pool is $2.54 per board foot ($127,000 ÷ 50,000 board feet). Because the quantity of inventory for the pool increased by 4,000 board feet (50,000 purchased less 46,000 sold), ending inventory will include the beginning inventory and a LIFO layer consisting of the 4,000 board feet increase. We would add this LIFO layer at the average cost of purchases made during the period, $2.54. The ending inventory of $108,960 now consists of two layers:

| | Quantity (Board Feet) | Cost (Per Foot) | Total Cost |
|---|---|---|---|
| Beginning inventory | 40,000 | $2.47 | $ 98,800 |
| LIFO layer added | 4,000 | 2.54 | 10,160 |
| Ending inventory | 44,000 | | $108,960 |

Despite the advantages of LIFO inventory pools, it's easy to imagine situations in which its benefits are not achieved. Suppose, for instance, that a company discontinues a certain product included in one of its pools. The old costs that existed in prior layers of inventory would be recognized as cost of goods sold and produce LIFO liquidation profit. Even if the product is replaced with another product, the replacement may not be similar enough to be included in the same inventory pool. In fact, the process itself of having to periodically redefine pools as changes in product mix occur, can be expensive and time consuming. The dollar-value LIFO approach helps overcome these problems.

## Dollar-Value LIFO

LO8

**Dollar-value LIFO (DVL)** gained such widespread popularity during the 1960s and 1970s that most LIFO applications are now based on this approach. DVL extends the concept of inventory pools by allowing a company to combine a large variety of goods into one pool. Physical units are not used in calculating ending inventory. Instead, the inventory is viewed as a quantity of value instead of a physical quantity of goods. Instead of layers of units from different purchases, the DVL inventory pool is viewed as comprising layers of dollar value from different years.

**A DVL pool is made up of items that are likely to face the same cost change pressures.**

Because the physical characteristics of inventory items are not relevant to DVL, an inventory pool is identified in terms of economic similarity rather than physical similarity. Specifically, a pool should consist of those goods that are likely to be subject to the same cost change pressures.

### ADVANTAGES OF DVL

The DVL method has important advantages. First, it simplifies the recordkeeping procedures compared to unit LIFO because no information is needed about unit flows. Second, it minimizes the probability of the liquidation of LIFO inventory layers, even more so than the use of pools alone, through the aggregation of many types of inventory into larger pools. In addition, the method can be used by firms that do not replace units sold with new units of the same kind. For firms whose products are subject to annual model changes, for example, the items in one year's inventory are not the same as the prior year's. Under pooled LIFO, the new replacement items must be substantially identical to previous models to be included in the same pool. Under DVL, no distinction is drawn between the old and new merchandise on the basis of their physical characteristics, so a much broader range of goods can be included in the pool. That is, the acquisition of the new items is viewed as replacement of the dollar value of the old items. Because the old layers are maintained, this approach retains the benefits of LIFO by matching the most recent acquisition cost of goods with sales measured at current selling prices.

### COST INDEXES

In either the unit LIFO approach or the pooled LIFO approach, we determine whether a new LIFO layer was added by comparing the ending quantity with the beginning quantity. The focus is on *units* of inventory. Under DVL, we determine whether a new LIFO layer was added by comparing the ending dollar amount with the beginning dollar amount. The focus is on inventory *value,* not units. However, if the price level has changed, we need a way to determine whether an observed increase is a real increase (an increase in the quantity of inventory) or one caused by an increase in prices. So before we compare the beginning and ending inventory amounts, we need to deflate inventory amounts by any increase in prices so that both the beginning and ending amounts are measured in terms of the same price level. We accomplish this by using cost indexes. A cost index for a particular layer year is determined as follows:

$$\text{Cost index in layer year} = \frac{\text{Cost in layer year}}{\text{Cost in base year}}$$

**The cost index for the base year (the year DVL is initially adopted) is set at 1.00.**

The base year is the year in which the DVL method is adopted and the layer year is any subsequent year in which an inventory layer is created. The cost index for the base year is set at 1.00. Subsequent years' indexes reflect cost changes relative to the base year. For example, if a "basket" of inventory items cost $120 at the end of the current year, and $100 at the end of the base year, the cost index for the current year would be: \$120 ÷ \$100 = 120%, or 1.20. This index simply tells us that costs in the layer year are 120% of what they were in the base year (i.e., costs increased by 20%).

There are several techniques that can be used to determine an index for a DVL pool. An external index like the Consumer Price Index or the Producer Price Index can be used. However, in most cases these indexes would not properly reflect cost changes for any individual DVL pool. Instead, most companies use an internally generated index. These indexes can be calculated using one of several techniques such as the *double-extension method* or the *link-chain method*. A discussion of these methods is beyond the scope of this text. In our examples and illustrations, we assume cost indexes are given.

## THE DVL INVENTORY ESTIMATION TECHNIQUE

The starting point in DVL is determining the current year's ending inventory valued at year-end costs.

DVL estimation begins with the determination of the current year's ending inventory valued in terms of year-end costs. It's not necessary for a company using DVL to track the item-by-item cost of purchases during the year. All that's needed is to take the physical quantities of goods on hand at the end of the year and apply year-end costs. Let's say the Hanes Company adopted the dollar-value LIFO method on January 1, 2006, when the inventory value was \$400,000. The 2006 ending inventory valued at year-end costs is \$441,000, and the cost index for the year is 1.05 (105%).

What is the 2006 ending inventory valued at DVL cost? The first step is to convert the ending inventory from year-end costs to base year costs so we can see if there was a real increase in inventory rather than an illusory one caused by price increases. We divide the ending inventory by the year's cost index to get an amount that can be compared directly with beginning inventory.

STEP 1: Convert ending inventory valued at year-end cost to base year cost.

$$\text{Ending inventory at } \textit{base year} \text{ cost} = \frac{\$441{,}000}{1.05} = \$420{,}000$$

The \$420,000 reflects the 2006 ending inventory deflated to base year cost.

Next we compare the \$420,000 ending inventory at base year cost to the beginning inventory, also at base year cost, of \$400,000. The \$20,000 increase in base-year dollars signifies a real increase in inventory quantity during the year. Applying the LIFO concept, ending inventory at base year cost consists of the beginning inventory layer of \$400,000 plus a \$20,000 2006 layer. These are the hypothetical costs of the layers as if each was acquired at base year prices.

STEP 2: Identify the layers of ending inventory and the years they were created.

Once the layers are identified, each is restated to prices existing when the layers were acquired. Each layer is multiplied by the cost index for the year it was acquired. The costs are totaled to obtain ending inventory at DVL cost.[16]

STEP 3: Convert each layer's base year cost to layer year cost using the cost index for the year it was acquired.

| Date | Ending Inventory at Base Year Cost | × | Cost Index | = | Ending Inventory at DVL Cost |
|---|---|---|---|---|---|
| 1/1/06 | \$400,000 | | 1.00 | | \$400,000 |
| 2006 layer | 20,000 | | 1.05 | | 21,000 |
| Totals | \$420,000 | | | | \$421,000 |

If we determined that inventory quantity had decreased during the year, then there would have been no 2006 layer added. The most recently added layer, in this case the beginning inventory layer, would be decreased to the inventory valuation determined in step 1. Once a layer of inventory or a portion of a layer is used (that is, sold) it cannot be replaced. In our example, if the base year layer is reduced to \$380,000, it will never be increased. Future increases in inventory quantity will result in new layers being added. This situation is illustrated in the concept review exercise that follows.

[16]It is important to note that the costs of the year's layer are only an approximation of actual acquisition cost. DVL assumes that all inventory quantities added during a particular year were acquired at a single cost.

# CONCEPT REVIEW EXERCISE

## DOLLAR-VALUE LIFO

On January 1, 2006, the Johnson Company adopted the dollar-value LIFO method. The inventory value on this date was $500,000. Inventory data for 2006 through 2009 are as follows:

| Date | Ending Inventory at Year-End Costs | Cost Index |
|---|---|---|
| 12/31/06 | $556,500 | 1.05 |
| 12/31/07 | 596,200 | 1.10 |
| 12/31/08 | 615,250 | 1.15 |
| 12/31/09 | 720,000 | 1.25 |

CHECK WITH THE COACH

**Required:**
Calculate Johnson's ending inventory for the years 2006 through 2009.

SOLUTION

**JOHNSON COMPANY**

| Date | Ending Inventory at Year-End Cost | Step 1: Ending Inventory at Base Year Cost | Step 2: Inventory Layers at Base Year Cost | Step 3: Inventory Layers Converted to Acquisition Year Cost | Ending Inventory At DVL Cost |
|---|---|---|---|---|---|
| 1/1/06 | $500,000 (base year) | $\frac{\$500,000}{1.00} = \$500,000$ | $500,000 (base) | $500,000 × 1.00 = $500,000 | **$500,000** |
| 12/31/06 | 556,500 | $\frac{\$556,500}{1.05} = \$530,000$ | $500,000 (base) | $500,000 × 1.00 = $500,000 | |
| | | | 30,000 (2006) | 30,000 × 1.05 = 31,500 | **531,500** |
| 12/31/07 | 596,200 | $\frac{\$596,200}{1.10} = \$542,000$ | $500,000 (base) | $500,000 × 1.00 = $500,000 | |
| | | | 30,000 (2006) | 30,000 × 1.05 = 31,500 | |
| | | | 12,000 (2007) | 12,000 × 1.10 = 13,200 | **544,700** |
| 12/31/08 | 615,250 | $\frac{\$615,250}{1.15} = \$535,000$* | $500,000 (base) | $500,000 × 1.00 = $500,000 | |
| | | | 30,000 (2006) | 30,000 × 1.05 = 31,500 | |
| | | | 5,000 (2007) | 5,000 × 1.10 = 5,500 | **537,000** |
| 12/31/09 | 720,000 | $\frac{\$720,000}{1.25} = \$576,000$ | $500,000 (base) | $500,000 × 1.00 = $500,000 | |
| | | | 30,000 (2006) | 30,000 × 1.05 = 31,500 | |
| | | | 5,000 (2007) | 5,000 × 1.10 = 5,500 | |
| | | | 41,000 (2009) | 41,000 × 1.25 = 51,250 | **588,250** |

*Since inventory declined during 2008 (from $542,000 to $535,000 at base year costs), no new layer is added. Instead the most recently acquired layer, 2007, is reduced to arrive at the $535,000 ending inventory at base year cost.

# FINANCIAL REPORTING CASE SOLUTION

1. **What inventory methods does Ford use to value its inventories? Is this permissible according to GAAP?** *(p. 368)* Ford uses the LIFO inventory method to value about one-fourth of its inventories. The cost of the remaining inventories is determined primarily by the FIFO method. Yes, both of these methods are permissible according to generally accepted accounting principles.
2. **What is the purpose of the disclosure information that reports what LIFO inventories would have been if valued at FIFO?** *(p. 370)* The LIFO conformity rule requires that if a company uses LIFO to measure taxable income, it also must use LIFO for external financial reporting. Ford does this. However, in 1981, the LIFO conformity rule was liberalized to allow LIFO users to provide supplemental disclosure of the effect on inventories of using another method on inventory valuation rather than LIFO. Ford's disclosure note offers this additional information.

3. **Is your friend correct in his assertion that by using LIFO, Ford was able to report lower profits in 2004?** *(p. 375)* Yes. If Ford had used FIFO instead of LIFO for its LIFO inventories, income before taxes in all prior years, including 2004, would have been higher by $1,001 million (the increase in 2004 ending inventory). In 2004 alone, income before taxes would have been *higher* by $5 million. Here's why. The increase in ending inventory of $1,001 million *decreases* cost of goods sold, but the increase in beginning inventory of $996 million *increases* cost of goods sold, resulting in a net decrease in cost of goods sold of $5 million. ■

## THE BOTTOM LINE

1. In a perpetual inventory system, inventory is continually adjusted for each change in inventory. Cost of goods sold is adjusted each time goods are sold or returned by a customer. A periodic inventory system adjusts inventory and records cost of goods sold only at the end of a reporting period.
2. Generally, determining the physical quantity that should be included in inventory is a simple matter, because it consists of items in the possession of the company. However, at the end of a reporting period it's important to determine the ownership of goods that are in transit between the company and its customers as well as between the company and its suppliers. Also, goods on consignment should be included in inventory of the consignor even though the company doesn't have physical possession of the goods. In addition, a company anticipating sales returns includes in inventory the cost of merchandise it estimates will be returned.
3. The cost of inventory includes all expenditures necessary to acquire the inventory and bring it to its desired condition and location for sale or use. Generally, these expenditures include the purchase price of the goods reduced by any returns and purchase discounts, plus freight-in charges.
4. Once costs are determined, the cost of goods available for sale must be allocated between cost of goods sold and ending inventory. Unless each item is specifically identified and traced through the system, the allocation requires an assumption regarding the flow of costs. First-in, first-out (FIFO) assumes that units sold are the first units acquired. Last-in, first-out (LIFO) assumes that the units sold are the most recent units purchased. The average cost method assumes that cost of goods sold and ending inventory consist of a mixture of all the goods available for sale.
5. A company's choice of inventory method will be influenced by (a) how closely cost flow reflects the actual physical flow of its inventory, (b) the timing of income tax expenses, and (c) how costs are matched with revenues.
6. The LIFO conformity rule requires that if a company uses LIFO to measure taxable income, it also must use LIFO for external financial reporting. LIFO users often provide supplemental disclosures describing the effect on inventories of using another method on inventory valuation rather than LIFO. If a company uses LIFO and inventory quantities decline during a period, then out of date inventory layers are liquidated and the cost of goods sold will partially match noncurrent costs with current selling prices. If costs have been increasing (decreasing), LIFO liquidations produce higher (lower) net income than would have resulted if the liquidated inventory were included in cost of goods sold at current costs. The paper profits (losses) caused by including out of date, low (high) costs in cost of goods sold is referred to as the effect on income of liquidations of LIFO inventory
7. Investors, creditors, and financial analysts can gain important insights by monitoring a company's investment in inventories. The gross profit ratio, inventory turnover ratio, and average days in inventory are designed to monitor inventories.
8. The dollar-value LIFO method converts ending inventory at year-end cost to base year cost using a cost index. After identifying the layers in ending inventory with the years they were created, each year's base year cost measurement is converted to layer year cost measurement using the layer year's cost index. The layers are then summed to obtain total ending inventory at cost. ■

# QUESTIONS FOR REVIEW OF KEY TOPICS

**Q 8–1** Describe the three types of inventory of a manufacturing company.

**Q 8–2** What is the main difference between a perpetual inventory system and a periodic inventory system?

**Q 8–3** The Cloud Company employs a perpetual inventory system and the McKenzie Corporation uses a periodic system. Describe the differences between the two systems in accounting for the following events: (1) purchase of merchandise, (2) sale of merchandise, (3) return of merchandise to supplier, and (4) payment of freight charge on merchandise purchased. Indicate which accounts would be debited and credited for each event.

**Q 8–4** The Bockner Company shipped merchandise to Laetner Corporation on December 28, 2006. Laetner received the shipment on January 3, 2007. December 31 is the fiscal year-end for both companies. The merchandise was shipped f.o.b. shipping point. Explain the difference in the accounting treatment of the merchandise if the shipment had instead been designated f.o.b. destination.

**Q 8–5** What is a consignment arrangement? Explain the accounting treatment of goods held on consignment.

**Q 8–6** Distinguish between the gross and net methods of accounting for purchase discounts.

**Q 8–7** The Esquire Company employs a periodic inventory system. Indicate the effect (increase or decrease) of the following items on cost of goods sold:

1. Beginning inventory
2. Purchases
3. Ending inventory
4. Purchase returns
5. Freight-in

**Q 8–8** Identify four methods of assigning cost to ending inventory and cost of goods sold and briefly explain the difference in the methods.

**Q 8–9** It's common in the electronics industry for unit costs of raw materials inventories to decline over time. In this environment, explain the difference between LIFO and FIFO, in terms of the effect on income and financial position. Assume that inventory quantities remain the same for the period.

**Q 8–10** Explain why proponents of LIFO argue that it provides a better match of revenue and expenses. In what situation would it not provide a better match?

**Q 8–11** Explain what is meant by the Internal Revenue Service conformity rule with respect to the inventory method choice.

**Q 8–12** Describe the ratios used by financial analysts to monitor a company's investment in inventories.

**Q 8–13** What is a LIFO inventory pool? How is the cost of ending inventory determined when pools are used?

**Q 8–14** Identify two advantages of dollar-value LIFO compared with unit LIFO.

**Q 8–15** The Austin Company uses the dollar-value LIFO inventory method with internally developed price indexes. Assume that ending inventory at year-end cost has been determined. Outline the remaining steps used in the dollar-value LIFO computations.

# BRIEF EXERCISES

**BE 8–1**
Determining ending inventory; periodic system

● LO1

A company began its fiscal year with inventory of $186,000. Purchases and cost of goods sold for the year were $945,000 and $982,000, respectively. What was the amount of ending inventory?

**BE 8–2**
Perpetual system; journal entries

● LO1

Litton Industries uses a perpetual inventory system. The company began its fiscal year with inventory of $267,000. Purchases of merchandise on account during the year totaled $845,000. Merchandise costing $902,000 was sold on account for $1,420,000. Prepare the journal entries to record these transactions.

**BE 8–3**
Goods in transit

● LO2

Kelly Corporation shipped goods to a customer f.o.b. destination on December 29, 2006. The goods arrived at the customer's location in January. In addition, one of Kelly's major suppliers shipped goods to Kelly f.o.b. shipping point on December 30. The merchandise arrived at Kelly's location in January. Which shipments should be included in Kelly's December 31 inventory?

**BE 8–4**
Purchase discounts; gross method
● LO3

On December 28, 2006, Videotech Corporation (VTC) purchased 10 units of a new satellite uplink system from Tristar Communications for $25,000 each. The terms of each sale were 1/10, n/30. VTC uses the gross method to account for purchase discounts and a perpetual inventory system. VTC paid the net-of-discount amount on January 6, 2007. Prepare the journal entries on December 28 and January 6 to record the purchase and payment.

**BE 8–5**
Purchase discounts; net method
● LO3

Refer to the situation described in BE 8–4. Prepare the necessary journal entries assuming that VTC uses the net method to account for purchase discounts.

**BE 8–6**
Inventory cost flow methods; periodic system
● LO4

Samuelson and Messenger (S&M) began 2006 with 200 units of its one product. These units were purchased near the end of 2005 for $25 each. During the month of January, 100 units were purchased on January 8 for $28 each and another 200 units were purchased on January 19 for $30 each. Sales of 125 units and 100 units were made on January 10 and January 25, respectively. There were 275 units on hand at the end of the month. S&M uses a *periodic* inventory system. Calculate ending inventory and cost of goods sold for January using (1) FIFO, and (2) average cost.

**BE 8–7**
Inventory cost flow methods; perpetual system
● LO4

Refer to the situation described in BE 8–6. S&M uses a *perpetual* inventory system. Calculate ending inventory and cost of goods sold for January using (1) FIFO, and (2) average cost.

**BE 8–8**
LIFO method
● LO4

Esquire, Inc. uses the LIFO method to value its inventory. Inventory at January 1, 2006, was $500,000 (20,000 units at $25 each). During 2006, 80,000 units were purchased, all at the same price of $30 per unit. 85,000 units were sold during 2006. Esquire uses a periodic inventory system. Calculate the December 31, 2006, ending inventory and cost of goods sold for 2006.

**BE 8–9**
LIFO method
● LO4

AAA Hardware uses the LIFO method to value its inventory. Inventory at the beginning of the year consisted of 10,000 units of the company's one product. These units cost $15 each. During the year, 60,000 units were purchased at a cost of $18 each and 64,000 units were sold. Near the end of the fiscal year, management is considering the purchase of an additional 5,000 units at $18. What would be the effect of this purchase on income before income taxes? Would your answer be the same if the company used FIFO instead of LIFO?

**BE 8–10**
LIFO liquidation
● LO6

Refer to the situation described in BE 8–8. Assuming an income tax rate of 40%, what is LIFO liquidation profit or loss that the company would report in a disclosure note accompanying its financial statements?

**BE 8–11**
Supplemental LIFO disclosures
● LO6

**Albertsons, Inc.** reported inventories of $3,035 million and $2,973 million in its 2004 and 2003 balance sheets, respectively. Cost of goods sold for 2004 was $25,306 million. The company uses both the LIFO and FIFO inventory methods. A disclosure note reported that if FIFO had been used exclusively, inventory would have been higher by $576 million and $589 million at the end of 2004 and 2003, respectively. Calculate cost of goods sold assuming the exclusive use of FIFO.

**BE 8–12**
Ratio analysis
● LO7

Selected financial statement data for Schmitzer, Inc. is shown below:

| | 2006 | 2005 |
|---|---|---|
| Balance sheet: | | |
| Inventories | 60,000 | 48,000 |
| Ratios: | | |
| Gross profit ratio for 2006 | 40% | |
| Inventory turnover ratio for 2006 | 5 | |

What was the amount of net sales for 2006?

**BE 8–13**
Dollar-value LIFO
● LO8

At the beginning of 2006, a company adopts the dollar-value LIFO inventory method for its one inventory pool. The pool's value on that date was $1,400,000. The 2006 ending inventory valued at year-end costs was $1,664,000 and the year-end cost index was 1.04. Calculate the inventory value at the end of 2006 using the dollar-value LIFO method.

# EXERCISES



**An alternate exercise and problem set is available on the text website: www.mhhe.com/spiceland4e**

**E 8–1**
Perpetual inventory system; journal entries
● LO1

John's Specialty Store uses a perpetual inventory system. The following are some inventory transactions for the month of May, 2006:

1. John's purchased merchandise on account for $5,000. Freight charges of $300 were paid in cash.
2. John's returned some of the merchandise purchased in (1). The cost of the merchandise was $600 and John's account was credited by the supplier.
3. Merchandise costing $2,800 was sold for $5,200 in cash.

**Required:**
Prepare the necessary journal entries to record these transactions.

**E 8–2**
Periodic inventory system; journal entries
● LO1

[This is a variation of the previous exercise modified to focus on the periodic inventory system.]

John's Specialty Store uses a periodic inventory system. The following are some inventory transactions for the month of May, 2006:

1. John's purchased merchandise on account for $5,000. Freight charges of $300 were paid in cash.
2. John's returned some of the merchandise purchased in (1). The cost of the merchandise was $600 and John's account was credited by the supplier.
3. Merchandise costing $2,800 was sold for $5,200 in cash.

**Required:**
Prepare the necessary journal entries to record these transactions.

**E 8–3**
Determining cost of goods sold; periodic inventory system
● LO1

Askew Company uses a periodic inventory system. The June 30, 2006, year-end trial balance for the company contained the following information:

| Account | Debit | Credit |
|---|---|---|
| Merchandise inventory, 7/1/05 | 32,000 | |
| Sales | | 380,000 |
| Sales returns | 12,000 | |
| Purchases | 240,000 | |
| Purchase discounts | | 6,000 |
| Purchase returns | | 10,000 |
| Freight-in | 17,000 | |
| Freight-out | 13,000 | |

In addition, you determine that the June 30, 2006, inventory balance is $40,000.

**Required:**

1. Calculate the cost of goods sold for the Askew Company for the year ending June 30, 2006.
2. Prepare the year-end adjusting entry to record cost of goods sold.

**E 8–4**
Perpetual and periodic inventory systems compared
● LO1

The following information is available for the Johnson Corporation for 2006:

| | |
|---|---|
| Beginning inventory | $ 25,000 |
| Merchandise purchases (on account) | 155,000 |
| Freight charges on purchases (paid in cash) | 10,000 |
| Merchandise returned to supplier (for credit) | 12,000 |
| Ending inventory | 30,000 |
| Sales (on account) | 250,000 |
| Cost of merchandise sold | 148,000 |

**Required:**
Applying both a perpetual and a periodic inventory system, prepare the journal entries that summarize the transactions that created these balances. Include all end-of-period adjusting entries indicated.

**E 8–5**
Periodic inventory system; missing data
● LO1

The Playa Company uses a periodic inventory system. The following information is taken from Playa's records. Certain data have been intentionally omitted. ($ in thousands)

| | 2006 | 2007 | 2008 |
|---|---|---|---|
| Beginning inventory | ? | ? | 225 |
| Cost of goods sold | 627 | 621 | ? |
| Ending inventory | ? | 225 | 216 |
| Cost of goods available for sale | 876 | ? | 800 |
| Purchases (gross) | 630 | ? | 585 |
| Purchase discounts | 18 | 15 | ? |
| Purchase returns | 24 | 30 | 14 |
| Freight-in | 13 | 32 | 16 |

**Required:**
Determine the missing numbers. Show computations where appropriate.

**E 8–6**
Purchase discounts; the gross method

● LO3

On July 15, 2006, the Nixon Car Company purchased 1,000 tires from the Harwell Company for $50 each. The terms of the sale were 2/10, n/30. Nixon uses a periodic inventory system and the *gross* method of accounting for purchase discounts.

**Required:**
1. Prepare the journal entries to record the purchase on July 15 and payment on July 23, 2006.
2. Prepare the journal entry to record the payment on August 15, 2006.
3. If Nixon instead uses a perpetual inventory system, explain any changes to the journal entries created in requirements 1 and 2.

**E 8–7**
Purchase discounts; the net method

● LO3

[This is a variation of the previous exercise modified to focus on the net method of accounting for purchase discounts.]

On July 15, 2006, the Nixon Car Company purchased 1,000 tires from the Harwell Company for $50 each. The terms of the sale were 2/10, n/30. Nixon uses a periodic inventory system and the *net* method of accounting for purchase discounts.

**Required:**
1. Prepare the journal entries to record the purchase on July 15 and payment on July 23, 2006.
2. Prepare the journal entry to record the payment on August 15, 2006.
3. If Nixon instead uses a perpetual inventory system, explain any changes to the journal entries created in requirements 1 and 2.

**E 8–8**
Trade and purchase discounts; the gross method and the net method compared

● LO3

Tracy Company, a manufacturer of air conditioners, sold 100 units to Thomas Company on November 17, 2006. The units have a list price of $500 each, but Thomas was given a 30% trade discount. The terms of the sale were 2/10, n/30. Thomas uses a periodic inventory system.

**Required:**
1. Prepare the journal entries to record the purchase by Thomas on November 17 and payment on November 26, 2006, using the gross method of accounting for purchase discounts.
2. Prepare the journal entry to record the payment on December 15, 2006, using the gross method of accounting for purchase discounts.
3. Repeat requirements 1 and 2 using the net method of accounting for purchase discounts.

**E 8–9**
Goods in transit

● LO2

The Kwok Company's inventory balance on December 31, 2006, was $165,000 (based on a 12/31/06 physical count) *before* considering the following transactions:
1. Goods shipped to Kwok f.o.b. destination on December 20, 2006, were received on January 4, 2007. The invoice cost was $30,000.
2. Goods shipped to Kwok f.o.b. shipping point on December 28, 2006, were received on January 5, 2007. The invoice cost was $17,000.
3. Goods shipped from Kwok to a customer f.o.b. destination on December 27, 2006, were received by the customer on January 3, 2007. The sales price was $40,000 and the merchandise cost $22,000.
4. Goods shipped from Kwok to a customer f.o.b. destination on December 26, 2006, were received by the customer on December 30, 2006. The sales price was $20,000 and the merchandise cost $13,000.
5. Goods shipped from Kwok to a customer f.o.b. shipping point on December 28, 2006, were received by the customer on January 4, 2007. The sales price was $25,000 and the merchandise cost $12,000.

**Required:**
Determine the correct inventory amount to be reported in Kwok's 2006 balance sheet.

**E 8–10**
Goods in transit; consignment

● LO2

The December 31, 2006, year-end inventory balance of the Raymond Corporation is $210,000. You have been asked to review the following transactions to determine if they have been correctly recorded.
1. Goods shipped to Raymond f.o.b. destination on December 26, 2006, were received on January 2, 2007. The invoice cost of $30,000 *is* included in the preliminary inventory balance.
2. At year-end, Raymond held $14,000 of merchandise on consignment from the Harrison Company. This merchandise *is* included in the preliminary inventory balance.
3. On December 29, merchandise costing $6,000 was shipped to a customer f.o.b. shipping point and arrived at the customer's location on January 3, 2007. The merchandise is *not* included in the preliminary inventory balance.
4. At year-end, Raymond had merchandise costing $15,000 on consignment with the Joclyn Corporation. The merchandise is *not* included in the preliminary inventory balance.

**Required:**
Determine the correct inventory amount to be reported in Raymond's 2006 balance sheet.

**E 8–11**
Inventory cost flow methods; periodic system
● LO1 LO4

Altira Corporation uses a periodic inventory system. The following information related to its merchandise inventory during the month of August 2006 is available:

| | |
|---|---|
| Aug. 1 | Inventory on hand—2,000 units; cost $6.10 each. |
| 8 | Purchased 10,000 units for $5.50 each. |
| 14 | Sold 8,000 units for $12.00 each. |
| 18 | Purchased 6,000 units for $5.00 each. |
| 25 | Sold 7,000 units for $11.00 each. |
| 31 | Inventory on hand—3,000 units. |

**Required:**

Determine the inventory balance Altira would report in its August 31, 2006, balance sheet and the cost of goods sold it would report in its August 2006 income statement using each of the following cost flow methods:

1. First-in, first-out (FIFO)
2. Last-in, first-out (LIFO)
3. Average cost

**E 8–12**
Inventory cost flow methods; perpetual system
● LO1 LO4

[This is a variation of the previous exercise modified to focus on the perpetual inventory system and alternative cost flow methods.]

Altira Corporation uses a perpetual inventory system. The following transactions affected its merchandise inventory during the month of August 2006:

| | |
|---|---|
| Aug. 1 | Inventory on hand—2,000 units; cost $6.10 each. |
| 8 | Purchased 10,000 units for $5.50 each. |
| 14 | Sold 8,000 units for $12.00 each. |
| 18 | Purchased 6,000 units for $5.00 each. |
| 25 | Sold 7,000 units for $11.00 each. |
| 31 | Inventory on hand—3,000 units. |

**Required:**

Determine the inventory balance Altira would report in its August 31, 2006, balance sheet and the cost of goods sold it would report in its August 2006 income statement using each of the following cost flow methods:

1. First-in, first-out (FIFO)
2. Last-in, first-out (LIFO)
3. Average cost

**E 8–13**
Comparison of FIFO and LIFO; periodic system
● LO1 LO4

Alta Ski Company's inventory records contained the following information regarding its latest ski model. The company uses a periodic inventory system.

| | |
|---|---|
| Beginning inventory, January 1, 2006 | 600 units @ $80 each |
| Purchases: | |
| January 15 | 1,000 units @ $95 each |
| January 21 | 800 units @ $100 each |
| Sales: | |
| January 5 | 400 units @ $120 each |
| January 22 | 800 units @ $130 each |
| January 29 | 400 units @ $135 each |
| Ending inventory, January 31, 2006 | 800 units |

**Required:**

1. Which method, FIFO or LIFO, will result in the highest cost of goods sold figure for January 2006? Why? Which method will result in the highest ending inventory balance? Why?
2. Compute cost of goods sold for January and the ending inventory using both the FIFO and LIFO methods.

**E 8–14**
Average cost method; periodic and perpetual systems
● LO1 LO4

The following information is taken from the inventory records of the CNB Company:

| | |
|---|---|
| Beginning inventory, 9/1/06 | 5,000 units @ $10.00 |
| Purchases: | |
| 9/7 | 3,000 units @ $10.40 |
| 9/25 | 8,000 units @ $10.75 |
| Sales: | |
| 9/10 | 4,000 units |
| 9/29 | 5,000 units |

7,000 units were on hand at the end of September.

**Required:**

1. Assuming that CNB uses a periodic inventory system and employs the average cost method, determine cost of goods sold for September and September's ending inventory.
2. Repeat requirement 1 assuming that the company uses a perpetual inventory system.

**E 8–15**
FIFO, LIFO, and average cost methods
● LO1 LO4

Causwell Company began 2006 with 10,000 units of inventory on hand. The cost of each unit was $5.00. During 2006 an additional 30,000 units were purchased at a single unit cost, and 20,000 units remained on hand at the end of 2006 (20,000 units therefore were sold during 2006). Causwell uses a periodic inventory system. Cost of goods sold for 2006, applying the average cost method, is $115,000. The company is interested in determining what cost of goods sold would have been if the FIFO or LIFO methods were used.

**Required:**

1. Determine the cost of goods sold for 2006 using the FIFO method. [*Hint:* Determine the cost per unit of 2006 purchases.]
2. Determine the cost of goods sold for 2006 using the LIFO method.

**E 8–16**
Multiple choice; inventory measurement
● LO1 LO2 LO4

The following questions dealing with inventory measurement are adapted from questions that appeared on CPA examinations. Determine the response that best completes the statements or questions.

1. Herc Co.'s inventory at December 31, 2006, was $1,500,000 based on a physical count priced at cost, and before any adjustment for the following:
   - Merchandise costing $90,000, shipped f.o.b. shipping point from a vendor on December 30, 2006, was received and recorded on January 5, 2007.
   - Goods in the shipping area were excluded from inventory although shipment was not made until January 4, 2007. The goods, billed to the customer f.o.b. shipping point on December 30, 2006, had a cost of $120,000.

   What amount should Herc report as inventory in its December 31, 2006, balance sheet?
   a. $1,500,000
   b. $1,590,000
   c. $1,620,000
   d. $1,710,000

Items 2 and 3 are based on the following:

During 2006, Metro Co., which maintains a perpetual inventory system, recorded the following information pertaining to its inventory:

| | Units | Unit Cost | Total Cost | Units on Hand |
|---|---|---|---|---|
| Balance on 1/1/06 | 1,000 | $1 | $1,000 | 1,000 |
| Purchased on 1/7/06 | 600 | 3 | 1,800 | 1,600 |
| Sold on 1/20/06 | 900 | | | 700 |
| Purchased on 1/25/06 | 400 | 5 | 2,000 | 1,100 |

2. Under the moving-average inventory method, what amount should Metro report as inventory at January 31, 2006?
   a. $2,640
   b. $3,225
   c. $3,300
   d. $3,900
3. Under the LIFO method, what amount should Metro report as inventory at January 31, 2006?
   a. $1,300
   b. $2,700
   c. $3,900
   d. $3,400
4. According to the net method, which of the following items would be included in the cost of inventory?

| | Freight Costs | Purchase Discounts Not Taken |
|---|---|---|
| a. | Yes | No |
| b. | Yes | Yes |
| c. | No | Yes |
| d. | No | No |

**E 8–17**
LIFO liquidation
● LO4 LO6

The Reuschel Company began 2006 with inventory of 10,000 units at a cost of $7 per unit. During 2006, 50,000 units were purchased for $8.50 each. Sales for the year totaled 54,000 units leaving 6,000 units on hand at the end of 2006. Reuschel uses a periodic inventory system and the LIFO inventory cost method.

**Required:**
1. Calculate cost of goods sold for 2006.
2. From a financial reporting perspective, what problem is created by the use of LIFO in this situation? Describe the disclosure required to report the effects of this problem.

**E 8–18**
Ratio analysis
● LO7

The table below contains selected financial information from the 2003 financial statements of **Maytag Corporation** and **Whirlpool Corporation** ($ in millions):

| | Maytag | | Whirlpool | |
|---|---|---|---|---|
| | **2003** | **2002** | **2003** | **2002** |
| Net sales | $4,792 | $4,666 | $12,176 | $11,016 |
| Cost of goods sold | 3,932 | 3,661 | 9,407 | 8,464 |
| Year-end inventory | 468 | 468 | 1,340 | 1,089 |

**Required:**
Calculate and compare the 2003 gross profit ratio, the inventory turnover ratio, and the average days in inventory for the two companies.

**E 8–19**
Dollar-value LIFO
● LO8

On January 1, 2006, the Haskins Company adopted the dollar-value LIFO method for its one inventory pool. The pool's value on this date was $660,000. The 2006 and 2007 ending inventory valued at year-end costs were $690,000 and $760,000, respectively. The appropriate cost indexes are 1.04 for 2006 and 1.08 for 2007:

**Required:**
Calculate the inventory value at the end of 2006 and 2007 using the dollar-value LIFO method.

**E 8–20**
Dollar-value LIFO
● LO8

Mercury Company has only one inventory pool. On December 31, 2006, Mercury adopted the dollar-value LIFO inventory method. The inventory on that date using the dollar-value LIFO method was $200,000. Inventory data are as follows:

| Year | Inventory at Year-End Costs | Inventory at Base Year Costs |
|---|---|---|
| 2007 | $231,000 | $220,000 |
| 2008 | 299,000 | 260,000 |
| 2009 | 300,000 | 250,000 |

**Required:**
Compute the inventory at December 31, 2007, 2008, and 2009, using the dollar-value LIFO method.

*(AICPA adapted)*

**E 8–21**
Multiple choice; dollar-value LIFO
● LO8

The following questions dealing with dollar-value LIFO are adapted from questions that appeared on CPA examinations. Determine the response that best completes the statements or questions.

1. Walt Co. adopted the dollar-value LIFO inventory method as of January 1, 2006, when its inventory was valued at $500,000. Walt's entire inventory constitutes a single pool. Using a relevant cost index of 1.10, Walt determined that its December 31, 2006, inventory was $577,500 at current year cost, and $525,000 at base year cost. What was Walt's dollar-value LIFO inventory at December 31, 2006?
   a. $525,000
   b. $527,500
   c. $552,500
   d. $577,500
2. Brock Co. adopted the dollar-value LIFO inventory method as of January 1, 2005. A single inventory pool and an internally computed cost index are used to compute Brock's LIFO inventory layers. Information about Brock's dollar value inventory follows:

| | Inventory | | |
|---|---|---|---|
| **Date** | **At Base Year Cost** | **At Current Year Cost** | **At Dollar-Value LIFO** |
| 1/1/05 | $40,000 | $40,000 | $40,000 |
| 2005 layer | 5,000 | 14,000 | 6,000 |
| 12/31/05 | 45,000 | 54,000 | 46,000 |
| 2006 layer | 15,000 | 26,000 | ? |
| 12/31/06 | $60,000 | $80,000 | ? |

What was Brock's dollar-value LIFO inventory at December 31, 2006?
   a. $80,000
   b. $74,000
   c. $66,000
   d. $60,000

**E 8–22**
Concepts; terminology
● LO1 through LO5

Listed below are several terms and phrases associated with inventory measurement. Pair each item from List A (by letter) with the item from List B that is most appropriately associated with it.

| List A | List B |
|---|---|
| ____ 1. Perpetual inventory system | a. Legal title passes when goods are delivered to common carrier. |
| ____ 2. Periodic inventory system | b. Goods are transferred to another company but title remains with transferor. |
| ____ 3. F.o.b. shipping point | c. Purchase discounts not taken are included in inventory cost. |
| ____ 4. Gross method | d. If LIFO is used for taxes, it must be used for financial reporting. |
| ____ 5. Net method | e. Items sold are those acquired first. |
| ____ 6. Cost index | f. Items sold are those acquired last. |
| ____ 7. F.o.b. destination | g. Purchase discounts not taken are considered interest expense. |
| ____ 8. FIFO | h. Used to convert ending inventory at year-end cost to base year cost. |
| ____ 9. LIFO | i. Continuously records changes in inventory. |
| ____ 10. Consignment | j. Items sold come from a mixture of goods acquired during the period. |
| ____ 11. Average cost | k. Legal title passes when goods arrive at location. |
| ____ 12. IRS conformity rule | l. Adjusts inventory at the end of the period. |

**E 8–23**
Multiple choice; CMA exam; inventory measurement
● LO1 LO4

The following questions dealing with inventory are adapted from questions that previously appeared on Certified Management Accountant (CMA) examinations. The CMA designation sponsored by the Institute of Management Accountants (www.imanet.org) provides members with an objective measure of knowledge and competence in the field of management accounting. Determine the response that best completes the statements or questions.

Questions 1 through 3 are based on the following information. Thomas Engine Company is a wholesaler of marine engine parts. The activity of carburetor 2642J during the month of March is presented below.

| Date | Balance or Transaction | Units | Unit Cost | Unit Sales Price |
|---|---|---|---|---|
| Mar. 1 | Inventory | 3,200 | $64.30 | $86.50 |
| 4 | Purchase | 3,400 | 64.75 | 87.00 |
| 14 | Sales | 3,600 | | 87.25 |
| 25 | Purchase | 3,500 | 66.00 | 87.25 |
| 28 | Sales | 3,450 | | 88.00 |

1. If Thomas uses a first-in, first-out perpetual inventory system, the total cost of the inventory for carburetor 2642J at March 31 is
   a. $196,115.
   b. $197,488.
   c. $201,300.
   d. $263,825.
2. If Thomas uses a last-in, first-out periodic inventory system, the total cost of the inventory for carburetor 2642J at March 31 is
   a. $196,115.
   b. $197,488.
   c. $201,300.
   d. $268,400
3. If Thomas uses a last-in, first-out perpetual inventory system, the total cost of the inventory for carburetor 2642J at March 31 is
   a. $196,200.
   b. $197,488.
   c. $263,863.
   d. $268,400

## PROBLEMS

available with McGraw-Hill's Homework Manager www.mhhe.com/spiceland4e

**An alternate exercise and problem set is available on the text website: www.mhhe.com/spiceland4e**

**P 8–1**
Various inventory transactions; journal entries
● LO1 through LO3

James Company began the month of October with inventory of $15,000. The following inventory transactions occurred during the month:

a. The company purchased merchandise on account for $22,000 on October 12, 2006. Terms of the purchase were 2/10, n/30. James uses the net method to record purchases. The merchandise was shipped f.o.b. shipping point and freight charges of $500 were paid in cash.

b. On October 18 the company returned merchandise costing $3,000. The return reduced the amount owed to the supplier. The merchandise returned came from beginning inventory, not from the October 12 purchase.
c. On October 31, James paid for the merchandise purchased on October 12.
d. During October merchandise costing $18,000 was sold on account for $28,000.
e. It was determined that inventory on hand at the end of October cost $16,060.

**Required:**

1. Assuming that the James Company uses a periodic inventory system, prepare journal entries for the above transactions including the adjusting entry at the end of October to record cost of goods sold.
2. Assuming that the James Company uses a perpetual inventory system, prepare journal entries for the above transactions.

**P 8–2**
Items to be included in inventory

● LO2

The following inventory transactions took place near December 31, 2006, the end of the Rasul Company's fiscal year-end:

1. On December 27, 2006, merchandise costing $2,000 was shipped to the Myers Company on consignment. The shipment arrived at Myers's location on December 29, but none of the merchandise was sold by the end of the year. The merchandise was *not* included in the 2006 ending inventory.
2. On January 5, 2007, merchandise costing $8,000 was received from a supplier and recorded as a purchase on that date and *not* included in the 2006 ending inventory. The invoice revealed that the shipment was made f.o.b. shipping point on December 28, 2006.
3. On December 29, 2006, the company shipped merchandise costing $12,000 to a customer f.o.b. destination. The goods, which arrived at the customer's location on January 4, 2007, were *not* included in Rasul's 2006 ending inventory. The sale was recorded in 2006.
4. Merchandise costing $4,000 was received on December 28, 2006, on consignment from the Aborn Company. A purchase was *not* recorded and the merchandise was *not* included in 2006 ending inventory.
5. Merchandise costing $6,000 was received and recorded as a purchase on January 8, 2007. The invoice revealed that the merchandise was shipped from the supplier on December 28, 2006, f.o.b. destination. The merchandise was *not* included in 2006 ending inventory.

**Required:**

State whether the company correctly accounted for each of the above transactions. Give the reason for your answer.

**P 8–3**
Costs included in inventory

● LO2 LO3

Reagan Corporation is a wholesale distributor of truck replacement parts. Initial amounts taken from Reagan's records are as follows:

| | | |
|---|---|---|
| Inventory at December 31 (based on a physical count of goods in Reagan's warehouse on December 31) | | $1,250,000 |
| Accounts payable at December 31: | | |
| **Vendor** | **Terms** | **Amount** |
| Baker Company | 2%, 10 days, net 30 | $ 265,000 |
| Charlie Company | Net 30 | 210,000 |
| Dolly Company | Net 30 | 300,000 |
| Eagler Company | Net 30 | 225,000 |
| Full Company | Net 30 | — |
| Greg Company | Net 30 | — |
| | | $1,000,000 |
| Sales for the year | | $9,000,000 |

**Additional information:**

1. Parts held by Reagan on consignment from Charlie, amounting to $155,000, were included in the physical count of goods in Reagan's warehouse and in accounts payable at December 31.
2. Parts totaling $22,000, which were purchased from Full and paid for in December, were sold in the last week of the year and appropriately recorded as sales of $28,000. The parts were included in the physical count of goods in Reagan's warehouse on December 31 because the parts were on the loading dock waiting to be picked up by customers.
3. Parts in transit on December 31 to customers, shipped f.o.b. shipping point on December 28, amounted to $34,000. The customers received the parts on January 6 of the following year. Sales of $40,000 to the customers for the parts were recorded by Reagan on January 2.
4. Retailers were holding goods on consignment from Reagan, which had a cost of $210,000 and a retail value of $250,000.
5. Goods were in transit from Greg to Reagan on December 31. The cost of the goods was $25,000, and they were shipped f.o.b. shipping point on December 29.

6. A freight bill in the amount of $2,000 specifically relating to merchandise purchased in December, all of which was still in the inventory at December 31, was received on January 3. The freight bill was not included in either the inventory or in accounts payable at December 31.
7. All the purchases from Baker occurred during the last seven days of the year. These items have been recorded in accounts payable and accounted for in the physical inventory at cost before discount. Reagan's policy is to pay invoices in time to take advantage of all discounts, adjust inventory accordingly, and record accounts payable net of discounts.

**Required:**

Prepare a schedule of adjustments to the initial amounts using the format shown below. Show the effect, if any, of each of the transactions separately and if the transactions would have no effect on the amount shown, state *none*.

| | Inventory | Accounts Payable | Sales |
|---|---|---|---|
| Initial amounts | $1,250,000 | $1,000,000 | $9,000,000 |
| Adjustments—increase (decrease): | | | |
| 1. | | | |
| 2. | | | |
| 3. | | | |
| 4. | | | |
| 5. | | | |
| 6. | | | |
| 7. | | | |
| Total adjustments | | | |
| Adjusted amounts | $ | $ | $ |

*(AICPA adapted)*

**P 8–4**
Various inventory transactions; determining inventory and cost of goods

● LO1 through LO4

Johnson Corporation began 2006 with inventory of 10,000 units of its only product. The units cost $8 each. The company uses a periodic inventory system and the LIFO cost method. The following transactions occurred during 2006:

a. Purchased 50,000 additional units at a cost of $10 per unit. Terms of the purchases were 2/10, n/30, and 60% of the purchases were paid for within the 10-day discount period. The company uses the gross method to record purchase discounts. The merchandise was purchased f.o.b. shipping point and freight charges of $.50 per unit were paid by Johnson.
b. 1,000 units purchased during the year were returned to suppliers for credit. Johnson was also given credit for the freight charges of $.50 per unit it had paid on the original purchase. The units were defective and were returned two days after they were received.
c. Sales for the year totaled 45,000 units at $18 per unit.
d. On December 28, 2006, Johnson purchased 5,000 additional units at $10 each. The goods were shipped f.o.b. destination and arrived at Johnson's warehouse on January 4, 2007.
e. 14,000 units were on hand at the end of 2006.

**Required:**

1. Determine ending inventory and cost of goods sold for 2006.
2. Assuming that operating expenses other than those indicated in the above transactions amounted to $150,000, determine income before income taxes for 2006.

**P 8–5**
Various inventory costing methods

● LO1 LO4

eXcel

Ferris Company began 2006 with 6,000 units of its principal product. The cost of each unit is $8. Merchandise transactions for the month of January 2006 are as follows:

| | Purchases | | |
|---|---|---|---|
| **Date of Purchase** | **Units** | **Unit Cost*** | **Total Cost** |
| Jan. 10 | 5,000 | $ 9 | $ 45,000 |
| Jan. 18 | 6,000 | 10 | 60,000 |
| Totals | 11,000 | | $105,000 |

*Includes purchase price and cost of freight.

| Sales | |
|---|---|
| **Date of Sale** | **Units** |
| Jan. 5 | 3,000 |
| Jan. 12 | 2,000 |
| Jan. 20 | 4,000 |
| Total | 9,000 |

8,000 units were on hand at the end of the month.

**Required:**

Calculate January's ending inventory and cost of goods sold for the month using each of the following alternatives:

1. FIFO, periodic system
2. LIFO, periodic system
3. LIFO, perpetual system
4. Average cost, periodic system
5. Average cost, perpetual system

**P 8–6**
Various inventory costing methods; gross profit ratio
● LO1 LO4
eXcel

Topanga Group began operations early in 2006. Inventory purchase information for the quarter ended March 31, 2006, for Topanga's only product is provided below. The unit costs include the cost of freight. The company uses a periodic inventory system.

| Date of Purchase | Units | Unit Cost | Total Cost |
|---|---|---|---|
| Jan. 7 | 5,000 | $4.00 | $ 20,000 |
| Feb. 16 | 12,000 | 4.50 | 54,000 |
| March 22 | 17,000 | 5.00 | 85,000 |
| Totals | 34,000 | | $159,000 |

Sales for the quarter, all at $7.00 per unit, totaled 20,000 units leaving 14,000 units on hand at the end of the quarter.

**Required:**

1. Calculate the Topanga's gross profit ratio for the first quarter using:
   a. FIFO
   b. LIFO
   c. Average cost
2. Comment on the relative effect of each of the three inventory methods on the gross profit ratio.

**P 8–7**
Various inventory costing methods
● LO1 LO4
eXcel

Carlson Auto Dealers Inc. sells a handmade automobile as its only product. Each automobile is identical; however, they can be distinguished by their unique ID number. At the beginning of 2006, Carlson had three cars in inventory, as follows:

| Car ID | Cost |
|---|---|
| 203 | $60,000 |
| 207 | 60,000 |
| 210 | 63,000 |

During 2006, each of the three autos sold for $90,000. Additional purchases (listed in chronological order) and sales for the year were as follows:

| Car ID | Cost | Selling Price |
|---|---|---|
| 211 | $63,000 | $ 90,000 |
| 212 | 63,000 | 93,000 |
| 213 | 64,500 | not sold |
| 214 | 66,000 | 96,000 |
| 215 | 69,000 | 100,500 |
| 216 | 70,500 | not sold |
| 217 | 72,000 | 105,000 |
| 218 | 72,300 | 106,500 |
| 219 | 75,000 | not sold |

**Required:**

1. Calculate 2006 ending inventory and cost of goods sold assuming the company uses the specific identification inventory method.
2. Calculate ending inventory and cost of goods sold assuming FIFO and a periodic inventory system.
3. Calculate ending inventory and cost of goods sold assuming LIFO and a periodic inventory system.
4. Calculate ending inventory and cost of goods sold assuming the average cost method and a periodic inventory system.

**P 8–8**
Supplemental LIFO disclosures
● LO4 LO6

**Caterpillar, Inc.** is one of the world's largest manufacturers of construction, mining, agricultural, and forestry machinery. The following disclosure note is included in the company's 2004 financial statements:

**D. Inventories** ($ in millions)
Inventories are stated at the lower of cost or market. Cost is principally determined using the last-in, first-out, (LIFO) method. The value of inventories on the LIFO basis represented about 80% of total inventories at December 31, 2004, 2003, and 2002.

If the FIFO (first-in, first-out) method had been in use, inventories would have been $2,124, $1,863, and $1,977 higher than reported at December 31, 2004, 2003, and 2002, respectively

If inventories valued at LIFO cost had been valued at FIFO cost, net income would have been $191 million higher in 2004 and $83 million lower in 2003.

Required:

1. Approximate the company's effective income tax rate for the year ended December 31, 2004.
2. Why might the information contained in the disclosure note be useful to a financial analyst?
3. Using the income tax rate calculated in 1, how much higher (lower) would retained earnings have been at the end of 2004 if Caterpillar had used the FIFO inventory method for all of its inventory?

**P 8–9**
LIFO liquidation
● LO4 LO6

Taylor Corporation has used a periodic inventory system and the LIFO cost method since its inception in 2006. The company began 2006 with the following inventory layers (listed in chronological order of acquisition):

| | |
|---|---|
| 10,000 units @ $15 | $150,000 |
| 15,000 units @ $20 | 300,000 |
| Beginning inventory | $450,000 |

During 2006, 30,000 units were purchased for $25 per unit. Due to unexpected demand for the company's product, 2006 sales totaled 40,000 units at various prices, leaving 15,000 units in ending inventory.

Required:

1. Calculate cost of goods sold for 2006.
2. Determine the amount of LIFO liquidation profit that the company must report in a disclosure note to its 2006 financial statements. Assume an income tax rate of 40%.
3. If the company decided to purchase an additional 10,000 units at $25 per unit at the end of the year, how much income tax currently payable would be saved?

**P 8–10**
Dollar-value LIFO
● LO8
eXcel

On January 1, 2006, the Taylor Company adopted the dollar-value LIFO method. The inventory value for its one inventory pool on this date was $400,000. Inventory data for 2006 through 2008 are as follows:

| Date | Ending Inventory at Year-End Costs | Cost Index |
|---|---|---|
| 12/31/06 | $441,000 | 1.05 |
| 12/31/07 | 487,200 | 1.12 |
| 12/31/08 | 510,000 | 1.20 |

Required:
Calculate Taylor's ending inventory for 2006, 2007, and 2008.

**P 8–11**
Dollar-value LIFO
● LO8

Kingston Company uses the dollar-value LIFO method of computing inventory. An external price index is used to convert ending inventory to base year. The company began operations on January 1, 2006, with an inventory of $150,000. Year-end inventories at year-end costs and cost indexes for its one inventory pool were as follows:

| Year Ended December 31 | Inventory at Year-End Costs | Cost Index (Relative to Base Year) |
|---|---|---|
| 2006 | $200,000 | 1.08 |
| 2007 | 245,700 | 1.17 |
| 2008 | 235,980 | 1.14 |
| 2009 | 228,800 | 1.10 |

Required:
Calculate inventory amounts at the end of each year.

**P 8–12**
Dollar-value LIFO

● LO8

On January 1, 2006, Avondale Lumber adopted the dollar-value LIFO inventory method. The inventory value for its one inventory pool on this date was $260,000. An internally generated cost index is used to convert ending inventory to base year. Year-end inventories at year-end costs and cost indexes for its one inventory pool were as follows:

| Year Ended December 31 | Inventory at Year-End Costs | Cost Index (Relative to Base Year) |
|---|---|---|
| 2006 | $340,000 | 1.02 |
| 2007 | 350,000 | 1.06 |
| 2008 | 400,000 | 1.07 |
| 2009 | 430,000 | 1.10 |

**Required:**
Calculate inventory amounts at the end of each year.

# BROADEN YOUR PERSPECTIVE

**Apply your critical-thinking ability to the knowledge you've gained. These cases will provide you an opportunity to develop your research, analysis, judgment, and communication skills. You also will work with other students, integrate what you've learned, apply it in real world situations, and consider its global and ethical ramifications. This practice will broaden your knowledge and further develop your decision-making abilities.**

**Judgment Case 8–1**
Riding the Merry-Go-Round

● LO7

Merry-Go-Round Enterprises, the clothing retailer for dedicated followers of young men's and women's fashion, was looking natty as a company. It was March 1993, and the Joppa, Maryland-based outfit had just announced the acquisition of Chess King, a rival clothing chain, a move that would give it the biggest share of the young men's clothing market. Merry-Go-Round told brokerage firm analysts that the purchase would add $13 million, or 15 cents a share, to profits for the year. So some Wall Street analysts raised their earnings estimates for Merry-Go-Round. The company's stock rose $2.25, or 15 percent, to $17 on the day of the Chess King news. Merry-Go-Round was hot—$100 of its stock in January 1988 was worth $804 five years later. In 1993 the chain owned 1,460 stores in 44 states, mostly under the Cignal, Chess King, and Merry-Go-Round names.

Merry-Go-Round's annual report for the fiscal year ended January 30, 1993, reported a 15% sales growth, to $877.5 million from $761.2 million. A portion of the company's balance sheet is reproduced below:

| | Jan. 30, 1993 | Feb. 1, 1992 |
|---|---|---|
| **Assets** | | |
| Cash and cash equivalents | $40,115,000 | $29,781,000 |
| Marketable securities | — | 9,703 |
| Receivables | 6,466,000 | 6,195 |
| Merchandise inventories | 82,197,000 | 59,971,000 |

But Merry-Go-Round spun out. The company lost $544,000 in the first six months of 1993, compared with earnings of $13.5 million in the first half of 1992. In the fall of 1992, Leonard "Boogie" Weinglass, Merry-Go-Round's flamboyant founder and chairman who had started the company in 1968, boarded up his Merry-Go-Ranch in Aspen, Colorado, and returned to management after a 12-year hiatus. But the pony-tailed, shirtsleeved entrepreneur—the inspiration for the character Boogie in the movie *Diner*—couldn't save his company from bankruptcy. In January 1994, the company filed for Chapter 11 protection in Baltimore. Shares crumbled below $3.

**Required:**
In retrospect, can you identify any advance warning at the date of the financial statements of the company's impending bankruptcy?
[Adapted from Jonathan Burton, "Due Diligence," *Worth,* June 1994, pp. 89–96.]

**Judgment Case 8–2**
The specific identification inventory method; inventoriable costs

● LO3 LO4

Happlia Co. imports household appliances. Each model has many variations and each unit has an identification number. Happlia pays all costs for getting the goods from the port to its central warehouse in Des Moines. After repackaging, the goods are consigned to retailers. A retailer makes a sale, simultaneously buys the appliance from Happlia, and pays the balance due within one week.

To alleviate the overstocking of refrigerators at a Minneapolis retailer, some were reshipped to a Kansas City retailer where they were still held in inventory at December 31, 2006. Happlia paid the costs of this reshipment. Happlia uses the specific identification inventory costing method.

**Required:**

1. In regard to the specific identification inventory costing method:
   a. Describe its key elements.
   b. Discuss why it is appropriate for Happlia to use this method.
2. a. What general criteria should Happlia use to determine inventory carrying amounts at December 31, 2006?
   b. Give four examples of costs included in these inventory carrying amounts.
3. What costs should be reported in Happlia's 2006 income statement? Ignore lower of cost or market considerations.

*(AICPA adapted)*

**Communication Case 8–3**
LIFO versus FIFO
● LO4 LO5

You have just been hired as a consultant to Tangier Industries, a newly formed company. The company president, John Meeks, is seeking your advice as to the appropriate inventory method Tangier should use to value its inventory and cost of goods sold. Mr. Meeks has narrowed the choice to LIFO and FIFO. He has heard that LIFO might be better for tax purposes, but FIFO has certain advantages for financial reporting to investors and creditors. You have been told that the company will be profitable in its first year and for the foreseeable future.

**Required:**

Prepare a report for the president describing the factors that should be considered by Tangier in choosing between LIFO and FIFO.

**Communication Case 8–4**
LIFO versus FIFO
● LO4 LO5

An accounting intern for a local CPA firm was reviewing the financial statements of a client in the electronics industry. The intern noticed that the client used the FIFO method of determining ending inventory and cost of goods sold. When she asked a colleague why the firm used FIFO instead of LIFO, she was told that the client used FIFO to minimize its income tax liability. This response puzzled the intern because she thought that LIFO would minimize income tax liability.

**Required:**

What would you tell the intern to resolve the confusion?

**Judgment Case 8–5**
Goods in transit
● LO2

At the end of 2006, the Biggie Company performed its annual physical inventory count. John Lawrence, the manager in charge of the physical count, was told that an additional $22,000 in inventory that had been sold and was in transit to the customer should be included in the ending inventory balance. John was of the opinion that the merchandise shipped should be excluded from the ending inventory since Biggie was not in physical possession of the merchandise.

**Required:**

Discuss the situation and indicate why John's opinion might be incorrect.

**Ethics Case 8–6**
Profit manipulation
● LO4

In 2005 the Moncrief Company purchased from Jim Lester the right to be the sole distributor in the western states of a product called Zelenex. In payment, Moncrief agreed to pay Lester 20% of the gross profit recognized from the sale of Zelenex in 2006.

Moncrief uses a periodic inventory system and the LIFO inventory method. Late in 2006, the following information is available concerning the inventory of Zelenex:

| | |
|---|---|
| Beginning inventory, 1/1/06 (10,000 units @ $30) | $ 300,000 |
| Purchases (40,000 units @ $30) | 1,200,000 |
| Sales (35,000 units @ $60) | $2,100,000 |

By the end of the year, the purchase price of Zelenex had risen to $40 per unit. On December 28, 2006, three days before year-end, Moncrief is in a position to purchase 20,000 additional units of Zelenex at the $40 per unit price. Due to the increase in purchase price, Moncrief will increase the selling price in 2007 to $80 per unit. Inventory on hand before the purchase, 15,000 units, is sufficient to meet the next six months' sales and the company does not anticipate any significant changes in purchase price during 2007.

**Required:**

1. Determine the effect of the purchase of the additional 20,000 units on the 2006 gross profit from the sale of Zelenex and the payment due to Jim Lester.
2. Discuss the ethical dilemma Moncrief faces in determining whether or not the additional units should be purchased.

**Real World Case 8–7**
Effects of inventory valuation methods; LIFO and FIFO
● LO4 LO6

Income statement and balance sheet information abstracted from a recent annual report of **Safeway, Inc.**, one of the world's largest food retailers, appears below:

**Balance Sheets**
($ in millions)

| | At Dec. 31, | |
|---|---|---|
| | **2004** | **2003** |
| Current assets: | | |
| Merchandise inventories | $2,741 | $2,642 |

**Income Statements**
($ in millions)

| | For the Year Ended Dec. 31, | |
|---|---|---|
| | **2004** | **2003** |
| Net sales | $35,823 | $35,727 |
| Cost of goods sold | 25,228 | 25,003 |
| Gross profit | $10,595 | $10,724 |

The significant accounting policies note disclosure contained the following:

**Merchandise Inventories**
Merchandise inventory of $1,943 million at year-end 2004 and $1,903 million at year-end 2003 is valued at the lower of cost on a last-in, first-out ("LIFO") basis or market value. Such LIFO inventory had a replacement or current cost of $1,992 million at year-end 2004 and $1,967 million at year-end 2003. All remaining inventory is valued at the lower of cost on a first-in, first-out ("FIFO") basis or market value. The FIFO cost of inventory approximates replacement or current cost.

**Required:**
1. Why is Safeway disclosing the replacement or current cost of its LIFO inventory?
2. Assuming that year-end replacement/current cost figures approximate FIFO inventory values, estimate what the beginning and ending inventory balances for the 2004 fiscal year would have been if Safeway had used FIFO for all of its inventories.
3. Estimate the effect on cost of goods sold (that is, would it have been greater or less and by how much?) for the 2004 fiscal year if Safeway had used FIFO for all of its inventories.

**Real World Case 8–8**
Effects of inventory valuation methods

● LO4 LO5 LO7

EDGAR, the Electronic Data Gathering, Analysis, and Retrieval system, performs automated collection, validation, indexing, and forwarding of submission by companies and others who are required by law to file forms with the U.S. Securities and Exchange Commission (SEC). All publicly traded domestic companies use EDGAR to make the majority of their filings. (Some foreign companies file voluntarily.) Form 10-K or 10-KSB, which includes the annual report, is required to be filed on EDGAR. The SEC makes this information available on the Internet.

**Required:**
1. Access EDGAR on the Internet. The web address is **www.sec.gov**. Edgarscan (**edgarscan.pwcglobal.com**) from Pricewaterhouse Coopers makes the process of accessing data from EDGAR easier.
2. Search for **Whole Foods Market, Inc.** Access the 10-K filing for the most recent fiscal year. Search or scroll to find the financial statements and related notes.
3. Answer the following questions related to the company's inventories:
   a. What method(s) does the company use to value its inventories?
   b. Calculate what cost of sales would have been for the year if the company had used FIFO to value its inventories.
   c. Calculate inventory turnover for the year using the reported numbers.

**International Case 8–9**
Comparison of inventory valuation in the Netherlands and the U.S.A.

● LO3 LO4

**Heineken**, based in Amsterdam, is one of the world's largest international beverage companies, selling its products in some 150 countries. The current assets disclosure note included in recent financial statements of the company is reproduced below. The note provides information on the company's method of valuing inventory (stocks).

**Current Assets (in part)**
Stocks purchased from third parties are stated at replacement cost, based on prices from current purchase contracts and latest prices as at balance sheet date. Finished products and work in process are stated at manufactured cost based on replacement cost and taking into account the product stage reached.

**Required:**
On the basis of the information the note provides, compare inventory valuation in the Netherlands with that in the United States.

**Communication Case 8–10**
Dollar-value LIFO method
● LO8

Maxi Corporation uses the unit LIFO inventory method. The costs of the company's products have been steadily rising since the company began operations in 1996 and cost increases are expected to continue. The chief financial officer of the company would like to continue using LIFO because of its tax advantages. However, the controller, Sally Hamel, would like to reduce the recordkeeping costs of LIFO that have steadily increased over the years as new products have been added to the company's product line. Sally suggested the use of the dollar-value LIFO method. The chief financial officer has asked Sally to describe the dollar-value LIFO procedure.

**Required:**
Describe the dollar-value LIFO procedure.

**Research Case 8–11**
Locate and extract relevant information and authoritative support for a financial reporting issue; product financing arrangement
● LO2 LO3

You were recently hired to work in the controller's office of the Balboa Lumber Company. Your boss, Alfred Eagleton, took you to lunch during your first week and asked a favor. "Things have been a little slow lately, and we need to borrow a little cash to tide us over. Our inventory has been building up and the CFO wants to pledge the inventory as collateral for a short-term loan. But I have a better idea." Mr. Eagleton went on to describe his plan. "On July 1, 2006, the first day of the company's third quarter, we will sell $100,000 of inventory to the Harbaugh Corporation for $160,000. Harbaugh will pay us immediately and then we will agree to repurchase the merchandise in two months for $164,000. The $4,000 is Harbaugh's fee for holding the inventory and for providing financing. I already checked with Harbaugh's controller and he has agreed to the arrangement. Not only will we obtain the financing we need, but the third quarter's before-tax profits will be increased by $56,000, the gross profit on the sale less the $4,000 fee. Go research the issue and make sure we would not be violating any specific accounting standards related to product financing arrangements."

**Required:**
1. Obtain the original FASB Standard on accounting for product financing arrangements. You might gain access through FARS, the FASB Financial Accounting Research System, from your school library, or some other source. Determine the appropriate treatment of product financing arrangements like the one proposed by Mr. Eagleton.
2. Prepare the journal entry to record the "sale" of the inventory and subsequent repurchase.

**Analysis Case 8–12**
Compare inventory management using ratios
● LO7

The table below contains selected financial information included in the 2004 financial statements of **General Motors** and **Ford Motor Company**:

| | ($ in millions) | | | |
|---|---|---|---|---|
| | **General Motors** | | **Ford Motor Company** | |
| | **2004** | **2003** | **2004** | **2003** |
| **Balance sheet:** | | | | |
| Inventories | $11,717 | $10,960 | $10,766 | $9,151 |
| | **2004** | | **2004** | |
| **Income statement:** | | | | |
| Net sales | $193,517 | | $147,134 | |
| Cost of goods sold | 159,951 | | 135,856 | |

Disclosure notes reveal that both companies use the LIFO inventory method to value the majority of their inventories.

**Required:**
1. Calculate the 2004 gross profit ratio, inventory turnover ratio, and average days in inventory for both companies. Evaluate the management of each company's investment in inventory. Industry averages for these ratios are as follows:

| | |
|---|---|
| Gross profit | 18% |
| Inventory turnover | 11.56 |
| Average days in inventory | 32 |

2. Obtain annual reports from three corporations in an industry other than autos and compare the management of each company's investment in inventory.

**Note:** You can obtain copies of annual reports from your library, from friends who are shareholders, from the investor relations department of the corporations, from a friendly stockbroker, or from EDGAR (Electronic Data Gathering, Analysis, and Retrieval) on the Internet (**www.sec.gov** or through Edgarscan at **edgarscan.pwcglobal.com**).

**Trueblood Accounting Case 8–13**
Inventory valuation

● LO3

The following Trueblood case is recommended for use with this chapter. The case provides an excellent opportunity for class discussions, group projects, and writing assignments. The case, along with Professor's Discussion Material, can be obtained from the Deloitte Foundation at its website: **www.deloitte.com/us/truebloodcases.**

**Case 02-09: *GrassChopper***

This case concerns an exclusive supply agreement and the valuation of inventory.

**Analysis Case 8–14**
Reporting of inventories

● LO4

**FedEx Corporation**

Refer to the financial statements and related disclosure notes of **FedEx Corporation** in Appendix B located at the back of this text.

**Required:**

1. Why does merchandise inventory not appear in FedEx's balance sheet? Does the balance sheet report any type of inventory?
2. What method does FedEx use to value its inventory?

# 9 CHAPTER

# Inventories: Additional Issues

## OVERVIEW

We covered most of the principal measurement and reporting issues involving the asset inventory and the corresponding expense cost of goods sold in the previous chapter. In this chapter we complete our discussion of inventory measurement by explaining the lower-of-cost-or-market rule used to value inventories. In addition, we investigate inventory estimation techniques, methods of simplifying LIFO, changes in inventory method, and inventory errors.

## LEARNING OBJECTIVES

**After studying this chapter, you should be able to:**

- LO1 Understand and apply the lower-of-cost-or-market rule used to value inventories.
- LO2 Estimate ending inventory and cost of goods sold using the gross profit method.
- LO3 Estimate ending inventory and cost of goods sold using the retail inventory method, applying the various cost flow methods.
- LO4 Explain how the retail inventory method can be made to approximate the lower-of-cost-or-market rule.
- LO5 Determine ending inventory using the dollar-value LIFO retail inventory method.
- LO6 Explain the appropriate accounting treatment required when a change in inventory method is made.
- LO7 Explain the appropriate accounting treatment required when an inventory error is discovered.

# FINANCIAL REPORTING CASE

## Does It Count?

Today you drove over to Sears to pick up a few items. Yesterday, your accounting professor had discussed inventory measurement issues and the different methods (FIFO, LIFO, and average) used by companies to determine ending inventory and cost of goods sold. You can't imagine actually counting the inventory in all of the Sears stores around the country. "There must be some way they can avoid counting all of that inventory every time they want to produce financial statements," you tell your dog when you get home. "I think I'll go check their financial statements on the Internet to see what kind of inventory method they use." You find the following in the summary of significant accounting policies included in Sears's most recent financial statements:

> **Merchandise Inventories (in part):**
> Approximately 88% of merchandise inventories are valued at the lower of cost or market, with cost determined using the retail inventory method (RIM) under the last-in, first-out (LIFO) cost flow assumption. To estimate the effects of inflation on inventories, the Company utilizes internally developed price indices.

**By the time you finish this chapter, you should be able to respond appropriately to the questions posed in this case. Compare your response to the solution provided at the end of the chapter.**

### QUESTIONS

1. Sears values its inventory at the lower of cost or market. What does that mean? Under what circumstances might Sears be justified in reporting its inventory at less than cost? (page 402)
2. How does Sears avoid counting all its inventory every time it produces financial statements? What are internal price indices used for? (page 419)

# PART A REPORTING—LOWER OF COST OR MARKET

In the previous chapter you learned that there are several methods a company could use to determine the cost of inventory at the end of a period and the corresponding cost of goods sold for the period. You also learned that it is important for a company to disclose the inventory method that it uses. Otherwise, investors and creditors would be unable to meaningfully compare accounting information from company to company. This disclosure typically is made in the summary of significant accounting policies accompanying the financial statements. **Coca-Cola Company**'s inventory method disclosure is shown in Graphic 9–1.

**GRAPHIC 9–1**
Disclosure of Inventory Method—Coca-Cola Company

**Summary of Significant Accounting Policies (in part) Inventories**
Inventories consist primarily of raw materials, supplies, concentrates and syrups and are valued at the lower of cost or market. We determine cost on the basis of average cost or first-in, first-out methods.

● LO1

**FINANCIAL REPORTING CASE**

Q1, p. 401

The disclosure indicates that Coca-Cola uses both the average cost and FIFO methods to determine the cost of its inventories. Notice that inventories actually are valued at the *lower of cost or market.* Assets are initially valued at their historical costs, but a departure from cost is warranted when the utility of an asset (its probable future economic benefits) is no longer as great as its cost. Accounts receivable, for example, are valued at net realizable value by reducing initial valuation with an allowance for uncollectible accounts.

The LCM approach to valuing inventory is required by GAAP.

The utility, or benefits, a company receives from inventory result from the ultimate sale of the goods. So deterioration, obsolescence, changes in price levels, or any situation that might compromise the inventory's salability impairs that utility. The **lower-of-cost-or-market (LCM)** approach to valuing inventory was developed to avoid reporting inventory at an amount greater than the benefits it can provide. Reporting inventories at LCM causes losses to be recognized in the period the value of inventory declines below its cost rather than in the period in that the goods ultimately are sold. LCM is not an optional approach to valuing inventory; it is required by GAAP.

The tremendous growth of the Internet that took place during the decade of the 90s allowed companies that produced products that support the Internet to become extremely profitable. **Cisco Systems, Inc.**, the world's largest networking products company, is one of those companies. In 1993, Cisco reported $649 million in sales revenue. By 2000, sales had reached nearly $19 billion! Growth rates of 50% year-to-year were commonplace. The company's market capitalization (price per share of common stock multiplied by the number of common shares outstanding) soared to over $500 billion. To keep pace with this growth in sales, inventories swelled from $71 million in 1993 to over $2.5 billion in 2000.

At the end of 2000, corporate spending on Internet infrastructure took a drastic downturn. Many dot-com companies went bankrupt, and companies like Cisco saw their fantastic growth rates nosedive. Early in 2001, the company reported its first-ever quarterly loss and, due to declining demand for its products, recorded an inventory write-down in excess of $2 billion. The company's once lofty market capitalization dropped to just over $100 billion.

**CISCO POSTS $5BN LOSS ON HUGE WRITE-DOWNS**
Technology giant Cisco Systems posted on Tuesday a third-quarter net loss of $2.69 billion, its first ever, following a write-down of inventory, restructuring costs and a sharp drop-off in corporate spending.

. . . and a write-down of over $2 billion for excess inventory.

Cisco said 80 percent of the inventory charge relates to raw materials, such as semiconductor memories, optical components, . . .

"Most of the excess inventory cannot be sold as it is custom built for Cisco," chief financial officer Mr. Larry Carter said in a conference call.[1]

[1]Fiona Buffini, "Cisco Posts $5bn Loss on Huge Writedowns," *Financial Review,* May 9, 2001.

## Determining Market Value

From the preceding discussion, you might interpret the term *market* to mean the amount that could be realized if the inventory were sold. However, *Accounting Research Bulletin No. 43* defines market for LCM purposes as the inventory's current replacement cost (by purchase or reproduction) except that market should not:

***Replacement cost (RC)* generally means the cost to replace the item by purchase or manufacture.**

a. Exceed the net realizable value (that is, estimated selling price in the ordinary course of business less reasonably predictable costs of completion and disposal).
b. Be less than net realizable value reduced by an allowance for an approximately normal profit margin.

In effect, we have a ceiling and a floor between which market (that is, replacement cost) must fall. **Net realizable value (NRV)** represents the upper limit and **net realizable value less a normal profit margin (NRV − NP)** provides the lower limit. If **replacement cost (RC)** is within the range, it represents market; if it is above the ceiling or below the floor, the ceiling or the floor becomes market. As a result, the designated market value is the number that falls in the middle of the three possibilities: replacement cost, net realizable value, and net realizable value less a normal profit margin. The designated market value is compared with cost, and the lower of the two is used to value inventory.

**The ceiling of *net realizable value (NRV)* and the floor of *net realizable value less a normal profit margin (NRV − NP)* establish a range within which the market must fall.**

Let's see how the LCM rule is applied in Illustration 9–1 and then we will discuss its theoretical merit.

Notice that the designated market value is the middle amount of the three market possibilities. This number is then compared to cost and the lower of the two is the final inventory value. For item A, cost is lower than market. For each of the other items, the designated market is lower than cost, requiring an adjustment to the carrying value of inventory. We discuss the adjustment procedure later in the chapter. First though, let's consider the conceptual justification of the LCM rule.

**Theoretical Merits.** What is the logic for designating replacement cost as the principal meaning of market value in the LCM rule? First, a change in replacement cost usually is a good indicator of the direction of change in selling price. If replacement cost declines, selling price usually will decline, or already has declined. Another reason is that if previously acquired inventory is revalued at its replacement cost, then the profit margin realized on its sale will likely approximate the profit margin realizable on the sale of newly acquired items.

The upper limit placed on replacement cost prevents inventory from being valued at an amount above what can be realized from its sale. The lower limit prevents inventory from being valued at an amount below what can be realized from its sale after considering normal profit margin. For example, consider item D in our illustration. If item D is valued at its replacement cost of $37 without considering the ceiling or floor, a loss of $53 ($90 cost less $37) would be recognized. If the item is subsequently sold at its current selling price less usual disposal costs (NRV = $76), then a gross profit of $39 ($76 less $37) would be recognized. This is much higher than its normal profit of $20 (20% × $100) and causes a shifting of income from the period the inventory loss is recognized to the period the item is sold. The ceiling and floor prohibit this kind of profit distortion.

On the other hand, critics of LCM contend that the method causes losses to be recognized that haven't actually occurred. Others maintain that it introduces needless inconsistency in order to be conservative. Inconsistency is created because LCM recognizes decreases in market value as they occur, but not increases.

**Some accountants complain that LCM promotes conservatism at the expense of consistency.**

**GLOBAL PERSPECTIVE**

The technique of valuing inventories at the lower of cost or market is fairly standard around the globe. However, differences exist in the designation of market. In the United States, market is defined as replacement cost, constrained by the ceiling of net realizable value and the floor of net realizable value less a normal profit margin. In many other countries, for example in New Zealand market value is defined as net realizable value. The IASB's *International Accounting Standard 2* also defines market as net realizable value.

**ILLUSTRATION 9–1**
Lower of Cost or Market

The Collins Company has five inventory items on hand at the end of 2006. The year-end unit costs (determined by applying the average cost method), current unit selling prices, and estimated disposal (selling) costs for each of the items are presented below. The gross profit ratio for each of the products is 20% of selling price.

| Item | Cost | Replacement Cost | Selling Price | Estimated Disposal Costs |
|---|---|---|---|---|
| A | $ 50 | $55 | $100 | $15 |
| B | 100 | 90 | 120 | 20 |
| C | 80 | 70 | 85 | 20 |
| D | 90 | 37 | 100 | 24 |
| E | 95 | 92 | 110 | 24 |

The determination of inventory value is a two-step process: first, determine the designated market value and second, compare the designated market value to cost. The lower of the two is the LCM inventory value.

Inventory is valued at the lower of cost or the designated market value.

| Item | (1) RC | (2) NRV | (3) NRV − NP | (4) Designated Market Value [Middle Value of (1), (2) and (3)] | (5) Cost | Inventory Value [Lower of (4) and (5)] |
|---|---|---|---|---|---|---|
| A | $55 | $ 85 | $65 | $65 | $ 50 | $50 |
| B | 90 | 100 | 76 | 90 | 100 | 90 |
| C | 70 | 65 | 48 | 65 | 80 | 65 |
| D | 37 | 76 | 56 | 56 | 90 | 56 |
| E | 92 | 86 | 64 | 86 | 95 | 86 |

RC = Current replacement cost.
NRV = Estimated selling price less estimated disposal costs.
NRV − NP = NRV less a normal profit margin.

Example for item B:

| | | |
|---|---|---|
| Selling price | $120 | |
| Less: Disposal costs | (20) | |
| NRV | 100 | |
| Less: Normal profit | (24) | ($120 selling price × 20%) |
| NRV − NP | $ 76 | |

The practice of recognizing decreases but not increases is not simply an application motivated by conservatism. Recall our discussions in previous chapters on revenue recognition and the realization principle. Recognizing increases in the value of inventory prior to sale would, in most cases, violate the realization principle. Assume that merchandise costing $100 has a net realizable value of $150. Recognizing the increase in value would increase pretax income by $50. This is equivalent to recognizing revenue of $150, cost of goods sold of $100, and gross profit of $50. Either way, pretax income is increased in a period prior to sale of the product. Prior to sale, there usually exists significant uncertainty as to the collectibility of the asset to be received. We don't know if the product will be sold, nor the selling price, or the buyer if eventually sold.

The LCM rules stated in *ARB No. 43* are intended as a guide rather than a literal rule. In practice, companies frequently define market as net realizable value. This is a number that often is easier to estimate than replacement cost. Also, assuming the NRV does not change, when the item is sold, there will be neither gross profit nor additional loss. The entire effect on income is recognized in the period the realizable value drops below cost.

**ETHICAL DILEMMA**

The Hartley Paper Company, owned and operated by Bill Hartley, manufactures and sells different types of computer paper. The company has reported profits in the majority of years since the company's inception in 1965 and is projecting a profit in 2006 of $65,000, down from $96,000 in 2005.

Near the end of 2006, the company is in the process of applying for a bank loan. The loan proceeds will be used to replace manufacturing equipment necessary to modernize the manufacturing operation. In preparing the financial statements for the year, the chief accountant, Don Davis, mentioned to Bill Hartley that approximately $40,000 of paper inventory has become obsolete and should be written off as a loss in 2006. Bill is worried that the write-down would lower 2006 income to a level that might cause the bank to refuse the loan. Without the loan, it would be difficult for the company to compete. This could cause decreased future business and employees might have to be laid off. Bill is considering waiting until 2007 to write down the inventory. Don Davis is contemplating his responsibilities in this situation.

## APPLYING LOWER OF COST OR MARKET

Lower of cost or market can be applied to individual inventory items, to logical categories of inventory, or to the entire inventory. A major product line can be considered a logical category of inventory. For income tax purposes, the lower-of-cost-or-market rule must be applied on an individual item basis.

**The LCM rule can be applied to individual inventory items, logical inventory categories, or the entire inventory.**

**ARB NO. 43**

The most common practice is to apply the *lower of cost or market rule* separately to each item of the inventory. However, if there is only one end-product category the cost utility of the total stock—the inventory in its entirety—may have the greatest significance for accounting purposes.

Similarly, where more than one major product or operational category exists, the application of the *lower of cost or market, whichever is lower* rule to the total of items included in such major categories may result in the most useful determination of income.[2]

Let's return to our illustration and assume the unit amounts pertain to 1,000 units of each inventory item. Also, let's say items A–B and items C–E are two collections of similar items that can be considered logical categories of inventory. Illustration 9–1A compares the LCM valuation accounting to each of three possible applications.

The final LCM inventory value is different for each of the three applications. The inventory value is $347,000 if LCM is applied to each item, $357,000 if it is applied to product line categories, and $362,000 if applied to the entire inventory. Applying LCM to groups of inventory items will usually cause a higher inventory valuation than if applied on an item-by-item basis because group application permits decreases in the market value of some items to be offset by increases in others. Each approach is acceptable but should be applied consistently from one period to another.

## ADJUSTING COST TO MARKET

When a company applies the LCM rule and a material write-down of inventory is required, the company has two choices of how to record the reduction. One way found in practice is to report the loss as a separate item in the income statement. An alternative is to include the loss as part of the cost of goods sold.

| | | | | | | |
|---|---|---|---|---|---|---|
| Loss on reduction to LCM .... | xx | | or | Cost of goods sold........ | xx | |
| Inventory* ............... | | xx | | Inventory*............. | | xx |

*Or, inventory can be reduced indirectly with a credit to an allowance account.

[2]"Restatement and Revision of Accounting Research Bulletins," *Accounting Research Bulletin No. 43* (New York: AICPA, 1953), Ch. 4, par. 11.

**ILLUSTRATION 9–1A**

LCM Determination—Application at Different Levels of Aggregation

| | | | Lower-of-Cost-or-Market | | |
|---|---|---|---|---|---|
| **Item** | **Cost** | **Designated Market Value** | **By Individual Items** | **By Product Line** | **By Total Inventory** |
| A | $ 50,000 | $ 65,000 | $ 50,000 | | |
| B | 100,000 | 90,000 | 90,000 | | |
| Total A + B | $150,000 | $155,000 | | $150,000 | |
| C | $ 80,000 | $ 65,000 | 65,000 | | |
| D | 90,000 | 56,000 | 56,000 | | |
| E | 95,000 | 86,000 | 86,000 | | |
| Total C, D, & E | $265,000 | $207,000 | | 207,000 | |
| Total | $415,000 | $362,000 | $347,000 | $357,000 | $362,000 |

**The preferable way to report a loss from an inventory write-down is as a separate item in the income statement.**

Recording the write-down as a separate item more accurately reports the event that occurred—a loss from holding inventory during a period when inventory value declined. Including this holding loss as part of cost of goods sold has the same effect on reported earnings, but distorts the relationship between sales and cost of goods sold. Conceptually, cost of goods sold should include only the cost of goods actually sold during the period. Even so, many companies do include the "holding loss" in cost of goods sold.

Recall from our introductory discussion to this chapter that **Cisco Systems, Inc.**, recently recorded an inventory write-down in excess of $2 billion. To understand how the relationship between sales and cost of goods sold can be distorted, let's consider the top part of the company's income statements for the first quarter of 2001 and 2000 shown in Graphic 9–2.

**GRAPHIC 9–2**

Partial Income Statements—Cisco Systems, Inc.

**INCOME STATEMENTS (IN PART)**
**For the Three Months Ended,**
($ in millions)

| | **April 28, 2001** | **April 29, 2000** |
|---|---|---|
| Net sales | $4,728 | $4,933 |
| Cost of sales | 4,400 | 1,761 |
| Gross profit | 328 | 3,172 |

**Reporting a loss from an inventory write-down as part of cost of goods sold distorts the relationship between sales and cost of goods sold.**

Using the information in the statements, the gross profit ratio dropped from 64% ($3,172 ÷ $4,933) in 2000 to 7% ($328 ÷ $4,728) in 2001. An analyst might conclude that there was a significant deterioration in the markup the company was able to achieve on its products. However, this assessment is premature. A disclosure note included in the financial statements for the first quarter of 2001 reported that during the quarter Cisco recorded "an excess inventory charge of $2.25 billion classified as cost of sales." We get a more accurate portrayal of the company's gross profit ratio if we reduce the cost of goods sold by the inventory charge (write-down):

| | |
|---|---|
| Sales | $4,728 |
| Adjusted cost of sales ($4,400 – 2,250) | 2,150 |
| Adjusted gross profit | 2,578 |
| Adjusted gross profit ratio | 55% |

Cisco's gross profit ratio did decline from the prior year, but not nearly as drastically as the reported financial statement information would lead us to believe.

Regardless of which method we use to record the write-down, the reduced inventory value becomes the new cost basis for subsequent reporting, and if the inventory value later recovers prior to its sale, we do not write it back up.[3]

**ADDITIONAL CONSIDERATION**

In very limited circumstances, businesses are allowed under GAAP to carry inventory at a market value above cost. *ARB 43* restricted this approach generally to companies that deal in precious metals, and ". . . agricultural, mineral, and other products, units of which are interchangeable and have an immediate marketability at quoted prices . . ."[4] Writing inventory up to market value means recognizing revenue for the increase. This is called the *production basis* of recognizing revenue. In rare cases when the method is appropriate, full disclosure of the fact that inventory is valued at market is required.

## CONCEPT REVIEW EXERCISE

### LOWER OF COST OR MARKET

The Strand Company sells four products that can be grouped into two major categories. Information necessary to apply the LCM rule at the end of 2006 for each of the four products is presented below. The normal profit margin for each of the products is 25% of selling price. The company records any losses from adjusting cost to market as separate income statement items and reduces inventory directly.

| Product | Cost | Replacement Cost | Selling Price | Disposal Costs |
|---|---|---|---|---|
| 101 | $ 80,000 | $ 85,000 | $160,000 | $30,000 |
| 102 | 175,000 | 160,000 | 200,000 | 25,000 |
| 201 | 160,000 | 140,000 | 180,000 | 50,000 |
| 202 | 45,000 | 20,000 | 60,000 | 22,000 |

Products 101 and 102 are in category A and products 201 and 202 are in category B.

**Required:**

1. Determine the designated market value for each of the four products according to the LCM rule.
2. Determine the amount of the loss from write-down of inventory that would be required, applying the LCM rule to:
   a. Individual items
   b. Major categories
   c. The entire inventory

### SOLUTION

1. Determine the designated market value for each of the four products according to the LCM rule.

| | (1) | (2) | (3) | (4) |
|---|---|---|---|---|
| Product | RC | NRV (Selling Price Less Disposal Costs) | NRV − NP | Designated Market Value [Middle Value of (1), (2) & (3)] |
| 101 | $ 85,000 | $130,000 | $ 90,000 | $ 90,000 |
| 102 | 160,000 | 175,000 | 125,000 | 160,000 |
| 201 | 140,000 | 130,000 | 85,000 | 130,000 |
| 202 | 20,000 | 38,000 | 23,000 | 23,000 |

[3]The SEC, in its *Staff Accounting Bulletin No. 100,* "Restructuring and Impairment Charges" (Washington, DC: SEC, November, 1999), paragraph B.B., reaffirmed the provisions of *Accounting Research Bulletin No. 43* on this issue. For interim reporting purposes, however, recoveries of losses on the same inventory in subsequent interim periods of the same fiscal year through market price recoveries should be recognized as gains in the later interim period, not to exceed the previously recognized losses.

[4]"Restatement and Revision of Accounting Research Bulletins," *Accounting Research Bulletin No. 43* (New York: AICPA, 1953), Ch. 4, par. 16.

Calculation of NRV − NP:

| Product | NRV | NP | NRV − NP |
|---|---|---|---|
| 101 | $130,000 | $40,000<br>(25% × $160,000) | $ 90,000 |
| 102 | 175,000 | 50,000<br>(25% × $200,000) | 125,000 |
| 201 | 130,000 | 45,000<br>(25% × $180,000) | 85,000 |
| 202 | 38,000 | 15,000<br>(25% × $ 60,000) | 23,000 |

2. Determine the amount of the loss from write-down of inventory that would be required.

| | | | Lower-of-Cost-or-Market | | |
|---|---|---|---|---|---|
| **Product** | **Cost** | **Designated Market Value** | **By Individual Products** | **By Category** | **By Total Inventory** |
| 101 | $ 80,000 | $ 90,000 | $ 80,000 | | |
| 102 | 175,000 | 160,000 | 160,000 | | |
| Total 101 + 102 | $255,000 | $250,000 | | $250,000 | |
| 201 | $160,000 | $130,000 | 130,000 | | |
| 202 | 45,000 | 23,000 | 23,000 | | |
| Total 201 + 202 | $205,000 | $153,000 | | 153,000 | |
| Total | $460,000 | $403,000 | $393,000 | $403,000 | $403,000 |

The LCM value for both the category application and the entire inventory application are identical because, in this particular case, market is below cost for both of the categories.

Amount of loss from write-down using individual items:

$460,000 − 393,000 = **$67,000**

Amount of loss from write-down using categories or the entire inventory:

$460,000 − 403,000 = **$57,000**

# PART B INVENTORY ESTIMATION TECHNIQUES

The Southern Wholesale Company distributes approximately 100 products throughout the state of Mississippi. Southern uses a periodic inventory system and takes a physical count of inventory once a year at its fiscal year-end. A recent fire destroyed the entire inventory in one of Southern's warehouses. How can the company determine the dollar amount of inventory destroyed when submitting an insurance claim to obtain reimbursement for the loss?

Home Improvement Stores, Inc., sells over 1,000 different products to customers in each of its 17 retail stores. The company uses a periodic inventory system and takes a physical count of inventory once a year at its fiscal year-end. Home Improvement's bank has asked for monthly financial statements as a condition attached to a recent loan. Can the company avoid the costly procedure of counting inventory at the end of each month to determine ending inventory and cost of goods sold?

These are just two examples of situations when it is either impossible or infeasible to determine the dollar amount of ending inventory by taking a count of the physical quantity of inventory on hand at the end of a period. Fortunately, companies can estimate inventory in these situations by either the gross profit method or the retail inventory method.

## The Gross Profit Method

The **gross profit method**, also known as the **gross margin method**, is useful in situations where estimates of inventory are desirable. The technique is valuable in a variety of situations:

● LO2

1. In determining the cost of inventory that has been lost, destroyed, or stolen.
2. In estimating inventory and cost of goods sold for interim reports, avoiding the expense of a physical inventory count.
3. In auditors' testing of the overall reasonableness of inventory amounts reported by clients.
4. In budgeting and forecasting.

However, the gross profit method provides only an approximation of inventory and is not acceptable according to generally accepted accounting principles for annual financial statements.

**The *gross profit method* is not acceptable for the preparation of annual financial statements.**

The technique relies on a relationship you learned in the previous chapter—ending inventory and cost of goods sold always equal the cost of goods available for sale. Even when inventory is unknown, we can estimate it because accounting records usually indicate the cost of goods available for sale (beginning inventory plus net purchases), and the cost of goods sold can be estimated from available information. So by subtracting the cost of goods sold estimate from the cost of goods available for sale, we obtain an estimate of ending inventory. Let's compare that with the way inventory and cost of goods sold normally are determined.

Usually, in a periodic inventory system, ending inventory is known from a physical count and cost of goods sold is *derived* as follows:

| | |
|---|---|
| Beginning inventory | (from the accounting records) |
| Plus: Net purchases | (from the accounting records) |
| Goods available for sale | |
| Less: Ending inventory | (from a physical count) |
| Cost of goods sold | |

However, when using the gross profit method, the ending inventory is *not* known. Instead, the amount of sales is known—from which we can estimate the cost of goods sold—and ending inventory is the amount calculated.

| | |
|---|---|
| Beginning inventory | (from the accounting records) |
| Plus: Net purchases | (from the accounting records) |
| Goods available for sale | |
| Less: Cost of goods sold | (estimated) |
| Ending inventory | (estimated) |

So, a first step in estimating inventory is to estimate cost of goods sold. This estimate relies on the historical relationship among (a) net sales, (b) cost of goods sold, and (c) gross profit. Gross profit, you will recall, is simply net sales minus cost of goods sold. So, if we know what net sales are, and if we know what percentage of net sales the gross profit is, we can fairly accurately estimate cost of goods sold. Companies often sell products that have similar gross profit ratios. As a result, accounting records usually provide the information necessary to estimate the cost of ending inventory, even when a physical count is impractical. Let's use the gross profit method to solve the problem of Southern Wholesale Company introduced earlier in the chapter. Suppose the company began 2006 with inventory of $600,000, and on March 17 a warehouse fire destroyed the entire inventory. Company records indicate net purchases of $1,500,000 and net sales of $2,000,000 prior to the fire. The gross profit ratio in each of the previous three years has been very close to 40%. Illustration 9–2 shows how Southern can estimate the cost of the inventory destroyed for its insurance claim.

### A WORD OF CAUTION

The gross profit method provides only an estimate. The key to obtaining good estimates is the reliability of the gross profit ratio. The ratio usually is estimated from relationships between sales and cost of goods sold. However, the current relationship may differ from the past. In

**ILLUSTRATION 9–2**
Gross Profit Method

| | | |
|---|---|---|
| Beginning inventory (from records) | | $ 600,000 |
| Plus: Net purchases (from records) | | 1,500,000 |
| Goods available for sale | | 2,100,000 |
| Less: Cost of goods sold: | | |
| Net sales | $2,000,000 | |
| Less: Estimated gross profit of 40% | (800,000) | |
| Estimated cost of goods sold* | | (1,200,000) |
| Estimated ending inventory | | $ 900,000 |

*Alternatively, cost of goods sold can be calculated as $2,000,000 × (1 − .40) = $1,200,000.

**The key to obtaining good estimates is the reliability of the gross profit ratio.**

that case, all available information should be used to make necessary adjustments. For example, the company may have made changes in the markup percentage of some of its products. Very often different products have different markups. In these situations, a blanket ratio should not be applied across the board. The accuracy of the estimate can be improved by grouping inventory into pools of products that have similar gross profit relationships rather than using one gross profit ratio for the entire inventory.

The company's cost flow assumption should be implicitly considered when estimating the gross profit ratio. For example, if LIFO is used and the relationship between cost and selling price has changed for recent acquisitions, this would suggest a ratio different from one where the average cost method was used. Another difficulty with the gross profit method is that it does not explicitly consider possible theft or spoilage of inventory. The method assumes that if the inventory was not sold, then it must be on hand at the end of the period. Suspected theft or spoilage would require an adjustment to estimates obtained using the gross profit method.

### ADDITIONAL CONSIDERATION

The gross profit ratio is, by definition, a percentage of sales. Sometimes, though, the gross profit is stated as a percentage of cost instead. In that case, it is referred to as the **markup on cost**. For instance, a 66⅔% markup on cost is equivalent to a gross profit ratio of 40%. Here's why:

A gross profit ratio of 40% can be formulated as:

$$\text{Sales} = \text{Cost} + \text{Gross profit}$$
$$100\% = 60\% + 40\%$$

Now, expressing gross profit as a percentage of cost we get:

$$\text{Gross profit \%} \div \text{Cost \%} = \text{Gross profit as a \% of cost}$$
$$40\% \div 60\% = 66\tfrac{2}{3}\%$$

Conversely, gross profit as a percentage of cost can be converted to gross profit as a percentage of sales (the gross profit ratio) as follows:

$$\text{Gross profit as a \% of sales} = \frac{\text{Gross profit as a \% of cost}}{1 + \text{Gross profit as a \% of cost}}$$

$$\frac{66\tfrac{2}{3}\%}{1 + 66\tfrac{2}{3}\%} = 40\%$$

Be careful to note which way the percentage is being stated. If stated as a markup on cost, it can be converted to the gross profit ratio, and the gross profit method can be applied the usual way.

## The Retail Inventory Method

● LO3

The **retail inventory method** is similar to the gross profit method in that it relies on the relationship between cost and selling price to estimate ending inventory and cost of goods sold.

As the name implies, the method is used by many retail companies such as **Dayton Hudson**, **Wal-Mart**, **Sears Roebuck**, **Saks**, **J.C. Penney**, and **May Department Stores**. Certain retailers like auto dealers and jewelry stores, whose inventory consists of few, high-priced items, can economically use the specific identification inventory method. However, high-volume retailers selling many different items at low unit prices find the retail inventory method ideal, although with the advent of bar coding on more and more retail merchandise, use of the method is declining. Similar to the gross profit method, its principal benefit is that a physical count of inventory is not required to estimate ending inventory and cost of goods sold.

The retail method tends to provide a more accurate estimate than the gross profit method because it's based on the current **cost-to-retail percentage** rather than on a historical gross profit ratio.

The *retail inventory method* uses the *cost-to-retail percentage* based on a current relationship between cost and selling price.

The increased reliability in the estimate of the cost percentage is achieved by comparing cost of goods available for sale with goods available for sale *at current selling prices*. So, to use the technique, a company must maintain records of inventory and purchases not only at cost, but also at current selling price. We refer to this as *retail information*. In its simplest form, the retail inventory method estimates the amount of ending inventory (at retail) by subtracting sales (at retail) from goods available for sale (at retail). This estimated ending inventory at retail is then converted to cost by multiplying it by the cost-to-retail percentage. This ratio is found by dividing goods available for sale at *cost* by goods available for sale at *retail*.

Let's use the retail inventory method to solve the problem of the Home Improvement Store introduced earlier in the chapter. Suppose the company's bank has asked for monthly financial statements as a condition attached to a loan dated May 31, 2006. To avoid a physical count of inventory, the company intends to use the retail inventory method to estimate ending inventory and cost of goods sold for the month of June. Using data available in its accounting records, Illustration 9–3 shows how Home Improvement can estimate ending inventory and cost of goods sold for June.

**ILLUSTRATION 9–3**
Retail Method

| | Cost | Retail |
|---|---|---|
| Beginning inventory | $ 60,000 | $100,000 |
| Plus: Net purchases | 287,200 | 460,000 |
| Goods available for sale | $347,200 | $560,000 |
| Cost-to-retail percentage: $\frac{\$347,200}{\$560,000} = 62\%$ | | |
| Less: Net sales | | (400,000) |
| Estimated ending inventory at retail | | $160,000 |
| Estimated ending inventory at cost (62% × $160,000) | (99,200) | |
| Estimated cost of goods sold—goods available for sale (at cost) minus ending inventory (at cost) equals cost of goods sold | $248,000 | |

Goods available for sale (at retail) minus net sales equals estimated ending inventory (at retail).

Unlike the gross profit method, the retail inventory method is acceptable for external financial reporting if the results of applying the method are sufficiently close to what would have been achieved using a more rigorous determination of the cost of ending inventory. Also, it's allowed by the Internal Revenue Service as a method that can be used to determine cost of goods sold for income tax purposes.[5] Another advantage of the method is that different cost flow methods can be explicitly incorporated into the estimation technique. In other words, we can modify the application of the method to estimate ending inventory and cost of goods sold to approximate average cost, lower-of-average-cost-or-market (conventional method) and LIFO. (The FIFO retail method is possible but used less frequently in practice.) We illustrate these variations later in the chapter.

The retail inventory method can be used for financial reporting and income tax purposes.

[5]The retail method is acceptable for external reporting and for tax purposes because it tends to provide a better estimate than the gross profit method. The retail method uses a current cost-to-retail percentage rather than a historical gross profit ratio.

Like the gross profit method, the retail inventory method also can be used to estimate the cost of inventory lost, stolen, or destroyed; for testing the overall reasonableness of physical counts; in budgeting and forecasting as well as in generating information for interim financial statements. Even though the retail method provides fairly accurate estimates, a physical count of inventory usually is performed at least once a year to verify accuracy and detect spoilage, theft, and other irregularities.

## RETAIL TERMINOLOGY

Changes in the selling prices must be included in the determination of ending inventory at retail.

Our example above is simplified in that we implicitly assumed that the selling prices of beginning inventory and of merchandise purchased did not change from date of acquisition to the end of the period. This frequently is an unrealistic assumption. The terms in Graphic 9–3 are associated with changing retail prices of merchandise inventory.

**GRAPHIC 9–3**
Terminology Used in Applying the Retail Method

| | |
|---|---|
| **Initial markup** | Original amount of markup from cost to selling price. |
| **Additional markup** | Increase in selling price subsequent to initial markup. |
| **Markup cancellation** | Elimination of an additional markup. |
| **Markdown** | Reduction in selling price below the original selling price. |
| **Markdown cancellation** | Elimination of a markdown. |

To illustrate, assume that a product purchased for $6 is initially marked up $4, from $6 to $10, the original selling price. If the selling price is subsequently increased to $12, the additional markup is $2. If the selling price is then subsequently decreased to $10.50, the markup cancellation is $1.50. We refer to the net effect of the changes ($2.00 − 1.50 = $.50) as the **net markup.** Graphic 9-4A depicts these events.

**GRAPHIC 9–4A**
Retail Inventory Method Terminology

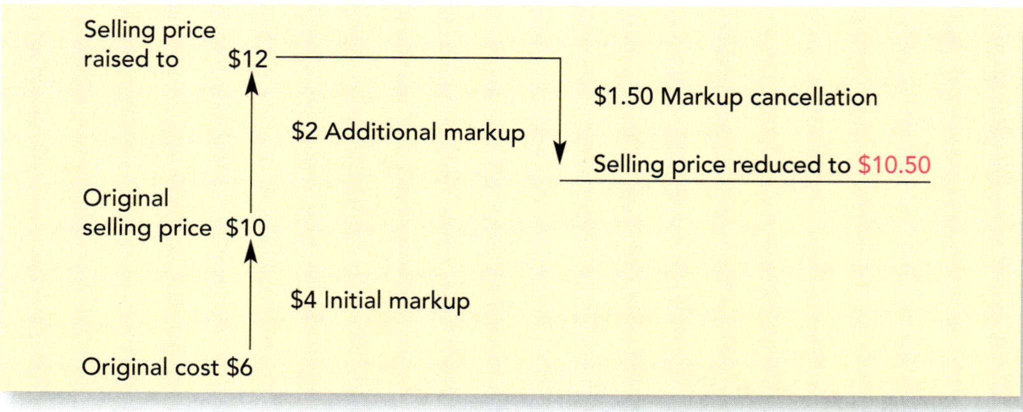


Now let's say the selling price of the product purchased for $6 and initially marked up to $10, is reduced to $7. The markdown is $3. If the selling price is later increased to $8, the markdown cancellation is $1. The net effect of the change ($3 − 1 = $2) is the **net markdown**. Graphic 9-4B depicts this possibility.

**GRAPHIC 9–4B**
Retail Inventory Method Terminology

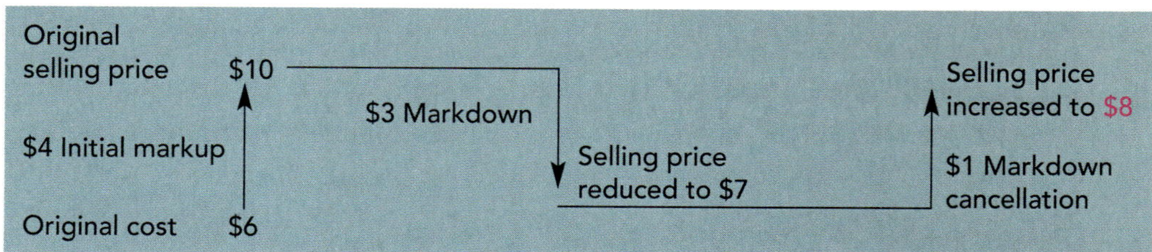

When applying the retail inventory method, *net markups and net markdowns must be included in the determination of ending inventory at retail.* We now continue our illustration of the retail inventory method, but expand it to incorporate markups and markdowns as well as to approximate cost by each of the alternative inventory cost flow methods.

**Net markups and net markdowns are included in the retail column to determine ending inventory at retail.**

## COST FLOW METHODS

Let's continue the Home Improvement Stores example into July with Illustration 9–4 and see how the retail inventory method can be used to approximate different cost flow assumptions. We'll also use the same illustration to see how the retail method can be modified to approximate lower of cost or market.

**ILLUSTRATION 9–4**

The Retail Inventory Method—Various Cost Flow Methods

Home Improvement Stores, Inc., uses a periodic inventory system and the retail inventory method to estimate ending inventory and cost of goods sold. The following data are available from the company's records for the month of July 2006:

| | Cost | Retail |
|---|---|---|
| Beginning inventory | $ 99,200 | $160,000 |
| Net purchases | 305,280[1] | 470,000[2] |
| Net markups | | 10,000 |
| Net markdowns | | 8,000 |
| Net sales | | 434,000[3] |

[1]Purchases at cost less returns, plus freight-in.
[2]Original selling price of purchased goods less returns at retail.
[3]Gross sales less returns.

**Approximating Average Cost.** Recall that the average cost method assumes that cost of goods sold and ending inventory each consist of a *mixture* of all the goods available for sale. So when we use the retail method to approximate average cost, the cost-to-retail percentage should be based on the weighted averages of the costs and retail amounts for *all* goods available for sale. This is achieved by calculating the cost-to-retail percentage by dividing the total cost of goods available for sale by total goods available for sale at retail. When this average percentage is applied to ending inventory at retail, we get an estimate of ending inventory at average cost. If you look back to our simplified example for the month of June, you'll notice that we used this approach there. So, our ending inventory and cost of goods sold estimates for June were estimates of average cost.[6]

**To approximate average cost, the cost-to-retail percentage is determined for *all* goods available for sale.**

Now, we use the retail inventory method to approximate average costs for July. Notice in Illustration 9–5 that both markups and markdowns are included in the determination of goods available for sale at retail.

● LO4

**Approximating Average LCM—The Conventional Retail Method.** Recall from our discussion earlier in the chapter that, however costs are determined, inventory should be reported in the balance sheet at LCM. Fortunately, we can apply the retail inventory method in such a way that LCM is approximated. This method often is referred to as the **conventional retail method.** We apply the method by *excluding markdowns from the calculation of the cost-to-retail percentage.* Markdowns still are subtracted in the retail column but only after the percentage is calculated. To approximate lower of average cost or market, the retail method is modified as shown in Illustration 9–6.

**To approximate LCM, markdowns are not included in the calculation of the cost-to-retail percentage.**

Notice that by not subtracting net markdowns from the denominator, the cost-to-retail percentage is lower than it was previously (63.2% versus 64%). This always will be the case when markdowns exist. As a result, the cost approximation of ending inventory always will be less when markdowns exist. To understand why this lower amount approximates LCM, we need to realize that markdowns usually occur when obsolescence, spoilage, overstocking, price declines, or competition has lessened the utility of the merchandise. To recognize

[6]We also implicitly assumed no net markups or markdowns.

**ILLUSTRATION 9–5**
Retail Method—Average Cost

| | Cost | Retail |
|---|---|---|
| Beginning inventory | $ 99,200 | $160,000 |
| Plus: Net purchases | 305,280 | 470,000 |
| Net markups | | 10,000 |
| Less: Net markdowns | | (8,000) |
| Goods available for sale | 404,480 | 632,000 |
| Cost-to-retail percentage: $\frac{\$404,480}{\$632,000} = \underline{\underline{64\%}}$ | | |
| Less: Net sales | | (434,000) |
| Estimated ending inventory at retail | | $198,000 |
| Estimated ending inventory at cost (64% × $198,000) | (126,720) | |
| Estimated cost of goods sold | $277,760 | |

**ILLUSTRATION 9–6**
Retail Method—Average Cost, LCM

| | Cost | Retail |
|---|---|---|
| Beginning inventory | $ 99,200 | $160,000 |
| Plus: Net purchases | 305,280 | 470,000 |
| Net markups | | 10,000 |
| | | 640,000 |
| Cost-to-retail percentage: $\frac{\$404,480}{\$640,000} = \underline{\underline{63.2\%}}$ | | |
| Less: Net markdowns | | (8,000) |
| Goods available for sale | 404,480 | 632,000 |
| Less: Net sales | | (434,000) |
| Estimated ending inventory at retail | | $198,000 |
| Estimated ending inventory at cost (63.2% × $198,000) | (125,136) | |
| Estimated cost of goods sold | $279,344 | |

The logic for using this approximation is that a markdown is evidence of a reduction in the utility of inventory.

this decline in utility in the period it occurs, as LCM does, we exclude net markdowns from the calculation of the cost-to-retail (market) percentage. It should be emphasized that this approach provides only an *approximation* of what ending inventory might be as opposed to applying the LCM rule in the more exact way described earlier in the chapter.

Also notice that the ending inventory at retail is the same using both approaches ($198,000). This will be the case regardless of the cost flow method used because in all approaches this amount reflects the ending inventory at current retail prices.

The LCM variation is not generally used in combination with LIFO. This does not mean that a company using LIFO ignores the LCM rule. Any obsolete or slow-moving inventory that has not been marked down by year-end can be written down to market after the estimation of inventory using the retail method. This is usually not a significant problem. If prices are rising, LIFO ending inventory includes old lower priced items whose costs are likely to be lower than current market. The LCM variation could be applied to the FIFO method.

**The LIFO Retail Method.** The last-in, first-out (LIFO) method assumes that units sold are those most recently acquired. When there's a net increase in inventory quantity during a period, the use of LIFO results in ending inventory that includes the beginning inventory as well as one or more additional layers added during the period. When there's a net decrease in inventory quantity, LIFO layer(s) are liquidated. In applying LIFO to the retail method in the simplest way, we assume that the retail prices of goods remained stable during the period. This assumption, which is relaxed later in the chapter, allows us to look at the beginning and ending inventory in dollars to determine if inventory quantity has increased or decreased.

We'll use the numbers from our previous example to illustrate using the retail method to approximate LIFO so we can compare the results with those of the conventional retail method. Recall that beginning inventory at retail is $160,000 and ending inventory at retail is $198,000. If we assume stable retail prices, inventory quantity must have increased during the year. This means ending inventory includes the beginning inventory layer of $160,000 ($99,200 at cost) as well as some additional merchandise purchased during the period. To estimate total ending inventory at LIFO cost, we also need to determine the inventory layer added during the period. When using the LIFO retail method, we assume no more than one inventory layer is added per year if inventory increases.[7] Each layer will carry its own cost-to-retail percentage.

**If inventory at retail increases during the year, a new layer is added.**

Illustration 9–7 shows how Home Improvement Stores would estimate total ending inventory and cost of goods sold for the period using the LIFO retail method. The beginning inventory layer carries a cost-to-retail percentage of 62% ($99,200 ÷ $160,000). The layer of inventory added during the period is $38,000 at retail, which is determined by subtracting beginning inventory at retail from ending inventory at retail ($198,000 − 160,000). This layer will be converted to cost by multiplying it by its own cost-to-retail percentage reflecting the *current* period's ratio of cost to retail amounts, in this case 64.68%.

**ILLUSTRATION 9–7**
LIFO Retail Method

| | Cost | Retail |
|---|---|---|
| Beginning inventory | $ 99,200 | $160,000 |
| Plus: Net purchases | 305,280 | 470,000 |
| Net markups | | 10,000 |
| Less: Net markdowns | | (8,000) |
| Goods available for sale (excluding beginning inventory) | 305,280 | 472,000 |
| Goods available for sale (including beginning inventory) | 404,480 | 632,000 |
| Beginning inventory cost-to-retail percentage: $\frac{\$99,200}{\$160,000} = 62\%$ | | |
| July cost-to-retail percentage: $\frac{\$305,280}{\$472,000} = 64.68\%$ | | |
| Less: Net sales | | (434,000) |
| Estimated ending inventory at retail | | $198,000 |

Estimated ending inventory at cost:

| | Retail | | Cost | |
|---|---|---|---|---|
| Beginning inventory | $160,000 × 62.00% | = | $ 99,200 | |
| Current period's layer | 38,000 × 64.68% | = | 24,578 | |
| Total | $198,000 | | $123,778 | (123,778) |
| Estimated cost of goods sold | | | | $280,702 |

**Beginning inventory is excluded from the calculation of the cost-to-retail percentage.**

**Each layer has its own cost-to-retail percentage.**

The next period's (August's) beginning inventory will include the two distinct layers (June and July), each of which carries its own unique cost-to-retail percentage. Notice in the illustration that both net markups and net markdowns are included in the calculation of the current period's cost-to-retail percentage.

[7]Of course, any number of layers at different costs can actually be added through the years. When using the regular LIFO method, rather than LIFO retail, we would keep track of each of those layers.

## OTHER ISSUES PERTAINING TO THE RETAIL METHOD

To focus on the key elements of the retail method, we've so far ignored some of the details of the retail process. Fundamental elements such as returns and allowances, discounts, freight, spoilage, and shortages can complicate the retail method.

Recall that net purchases is found by adding freight-in to purchases and subtracting both purchase returns and purchase discounts. When these components are considered separately in the retail method, purchase returns are deducted from purchases on both the cost and retail side (at different amounts) and freight-in is added only to the cost side in determining net purchases. If the gross method is used to record purchases, purchase discounts taken also are deducted in determining the cost of net purchases.

**If sales are recorded net of employee discounts, the discounts are added to sales.**

Likewise, net sales is found by subtracting sales returns from sales. However, sales discounts are *not* subtracted because to do so would cause the inventory to be overstated. Sales discounts do not represent an adjustment in selling price but a financial incentive for customers to pay early. On the other hand, when sales are recorded net of employee discounts, the discounts are *added* to net sales before sales are deducted in the retail column.

For example, suppose an item of merchandise purchased for $6 is initially marked up to $10. Original selling price is therefore $10. When the item is sold, we deduct sales of $10 from the retail column. But if the item is sold to an employee for $7 (a $3 employee discount) and recorded as a $7 sale, the $3 employee discount must be added back to sales so the full $10 is deducted from goods available at retail to arrive at ending inventory at retail.

We also need to consider spoilage, breakage, and theft. So far we've assumed that by subtracting goods sold from goods available for sale, we find ending inventory. It's possible, though, that some of the goods available for sale were lost to such shortages and therefore do not remain in ending inventory.

**Normal shortages are deducted in the retail column *after* the calculation of the cost-to-retail percentage.**

**Abnormal shortages are deducted in both the cost and retail columns *before* the calculation of the cost-to-retail percentage.**

To take these shortages into account when using the retail method, we deduct the retail value of inventory lost due to spoilage, breakage, or theft in the retail column. These losses are expected for most retail ventures so they are referred to as *normal shortages* (spoilage, breakage, etc.), and are deducted in the retail column *after* the calculation of the cost-to-retail percentage. Because these losses are anticipated, they are included implicitly in the determination of selling prices. Including normal spoilage in the calculation of the percentage would distort the normal relationship between cost and retail. *Abnormal shortages* should be deducted in both the cost and retail columns *before* the calculation of the cost-to-retail percentage. These losses are not anticipated and are not included in the determination of selling prices.

We recap the treatment of special elements in the application of the retail method in Graphic 9–5 and illustrate the use of some of them in the concept review exercise that follows.

**GRAPHIC 9–5** Recap of Other Retail Method Elements

| Element | Treatment |
|---|---|
| **Before calculating the cost-to-retail percentage:** | |
| Freight-in | *Added* in the cost column. |
| Purchase returns | *Deducted* in both the cost and retail columns. |
| Purchase discounts taken (if gross method used to record purchases) | *Deducted* in the cost column. |
| Abnormal shortages (spoilage, breakage, theft) | *Deducted* in both the cost and retail columns. |
| **After calculating the cost-to-retail percentage:** | |
| Normal shortages (spoilage, breakage, theft) | *Deducted* in the retail column. |
| Employee discounts (if sales recorded net of discounts) | *Added* to net sales. |

# CONCEPT REVIEW EXERCISE

## RETAIL INVENTORY METHOD

The Henderson Company uses the retail inventory method to estimate ending inventory and cost of goods sold. The following data for 2006 are available in Henderson's accounting records:

| | Cost | Retail |
|---|---|---|
| Beginning inventory | $ 8,000 | $12,000 |
| Purchases | 68,000 | 98,000 |
| Freight-in | 3,200 | |
| Purchase returns | 3,000 | 4,200 |
| Net markups | | 6,000 |
| Net markdowns | | 2,400 |
| Normal spoilage | | 1,800 |
| Net sales | | 92,000 |

The company records sales net of employee discounts. These discounts for 2006 totaled $2,300.

**Required:**

1. Estimate Henderson's ending inventory and cost of goods sold for the year using the average cost method.
2. Estimate Henderson's ending inventory and cost of goods sold for the year using the conventional retail method (LCM, average cost).
3. Estimate Henderson's ending inventory and cost of goods sold for the year using the LIFO retail method.

## SOLUTION

1. Estimate Henderson's ending inventory and cost of goods sold for the year using the average cost method.

| | | | Cost | Retail |
|---|---|---|---|---|
| Beginning inventory | | | $ 8,000 | $ 12,000 |
| Plus: Purchases | | | 68,000 | 98,000 |
| Freight-in | | | 3,200 | |
| Less: Purchase returns | | | (3,000) | (4,200) |
| Plus: Net markups | | | | 6,000 |
| Less: Net markdowns | | | | (2,400) |
| Goods available for sale | | | $76,200 | $109,400 |
| Cost-to-retail percentage: $\frac{\$76,200}{\$109,400} = 69.65\%$ | | | | |
| Less: Normal spoilage | | | | (1,800) |
| Sales: | | | | |
| Net sales | $92,000 | | | |
| Add back employee discounts | 2,300 | | | (94,300) |
| Estimated ending inventory at retail | | | | $ 13,300 |
| Estimated ending inventory at cost (69.65% × $13,300) | | | (9,263) | |
| Estimated cost of goods sold | | | $66,937 | |

2. Estimate Henderson's ending inventory and cost of goods sold for the year using the conventional retail method (LCM, average cost).

| | Cost | Retail |
|---|---|---|
| Beginning inventory | $ 8,000 | $ 12,000 |
| Plus: Purchases | 68,000 | 98,000 |
| Freight-in | 3,200 | |
| Less: Purchase returns | (3,000) | (4,200) |
| Plus: net markups | | 6,000 |
| | | 111,800 |
| Cost-to-retail percentage: $\frac{\$76,200}{\$111,800} = 68.16\%$ | | |
| Less: Net markdowns | | (2,400) |
| Goods available for sale | 76,200 | 109,400 |
| Less: Normal spoilage | | (1,800) |
| Sales: | | |
| Net sales $92,000 | | |
| Add back employee discounts 2,300 | | (94,300) |
| Estimated ending inventory at retail | | $ 13,300 |
| Estimated ending inventory at cost (68.16% × $13,300) | (9,065) | |
| Estimated cost of goods sold | $67,135 | |

3. Estimate Henderson's ending inventory and cost of goods sold for the year using the LIFO retail method.

| | Cost | Retail |
|---|---|---|
| Beginning inventory | $ 8,000 | $ 12,000 |
| Plus: Purchases | 68,000 | 98,000 |
| Freight-in | 3,200 | |
| Less: Purchase returns | (3,000) | (4,200) |
| Plus: Net markups | | 6,000 |
| Less: Net markdowns | | (2,400) |
| Goods available for sale (excluding beginning inventory) | 68,200 | 97,400 |
| Goods available for sale (including beginning inventory) | 76,200 | 109,400 |
| Cost-to-retail percentage: $\frac{\$68,200}{\$97,400} = 70.02\%$ | | |
| Less: Normal spoilage | | (1,800) |
| Sales: | | |
| Net sales $92,000 | | |
| Add back employee discounts 2,300 | | (94,300) |
| Estimated ending inventory at retail | | $ 13,300 |

Estimated ending inventory at cost:

| | Retail | | Cost | |
|---|---|---|---|---|
| Beginning inventory | $12,000 × 66.67%* | = | $8,000 | |
| Current period's layer | 1,300 × 70.02% | = | 910 | |
| Total | $13,300 | | $8,910 | (8,910) |
| Estimated cost of goods sold | | | | $67,290 |

*$8,000 ÷ $12,000 = 66.67%

# DOLLAR-VALUE LIFO RETAIL

**PART C**

● LO5

In our earlier illustration of the LIFO retail method, we assumed that the retail prices of the inventory remained stable during the period. If you recall, we compared the ending inventory (at retail) with the beginning inventory (at retail) to see if inventory had increased. If the dollar amount of ending inventory exceeded the beginning amount, we assumed a new LIFO layer had been added. But this isn't necessarily true. It may be that the dollar amount of ending inventory exceeded the beginning amount simply because prices increased, without an actual change in the quantity of goods. So, to see if there's been a "real" increase in quantity, we need a way to eliminate the effect of any price changes before we compare the ending inventory with the beginning inventory. Fortunately, we can accomplish this by combining two methods we've already discussed—the LIFO retail method (Part B of this chapter) and dollar-value LIFO (previous chapter). The combination is called the **dollar-value LIFO retail method.**

**FINANCIAL REPORTING CASE**

Q2, p. 401

To illustrate, we return to the Home Improvement Stores situation (Illustration 9–7) in which we applied LIFO retail. We keep the same inventory data, but change the illustration from the month of July to the fiscal year 2006. This allows us to build into Illustration 9–7A a significant change in retail prices over the year of 10% (an increase in the retail price index from 1 to 1.10). We follow the LIFO retail procedure up to the point of comparing the ending inventory with the beginning inventory. However, because prices have risen, the apparent increase in inventory is only partly due to an additional layer of inventory and partly due to the increase in retail prices. The real increase is found by deflating the ending inventory amount to beginning of the year prices before comparing beginning and ending amounts. We did this with the dollar-value LIFO technique discussed in the previous chapter.[8]

**Using the retail method to approximate LIFO is referred to as the *dollar-value LIFO retail method.***

**ILLUSTRATION 9–7A**

The Dollar-Value LIFO Retail Method

| | Cost | Retail |
|---|---|---|
| Beginning inventory | $ 99,200 | $160,000 |
| Plus: Net purchases | 305,280 | 470,000 |
| Net markups | | 10,000 |
| Less: Net markdowns | | (8,000) |
| Goods available for sale (excluding beginning inventory) | 305,280 | 472,000 |
| Goods available for sale (including beginning inventory) | 404,480 | 632,000 |
| Base layer cost-to-retail percentage: $\frac{\$99,200}{\$160,000} = 62\%$ | | |
| 2006 layer cost-to-retail percentage: $\frac{\$305,280}{\$472,000} = 64.68\%$ | | |
| Less: Net sales | | (434,000) |
| Ending inventory at current year retail prices | | $198,000 |
| Estimated ending inventory at cost (calculated below) | (113,430) | |
| Estimated cost of goods sold | $291,050 | |

| Ending Inventory at Year-End Retail Prices | Step 1 Ending Inventory at Base Year Retail Prices | Step 2 Inventory Layers at Base Year Retail Prices | Step 3 Inventory Layers Converted to Cost |
|---|---|---|---|
| $198,000 → (determined above) | $\frac{\$198,000}{1.10} = \$180,000$ → | $180,000 | |
| | | 160,000 (base) × 1.00 × .62 | = $ 99,200 |
| | | $ 20,000 (2006) × 1.10 × .6468 = | 14,230 |
| Total ending inventory at dollar-value LIFO retail cost | | | $113,430 |

**Base year retail amounts are converted to layer year retail and then to cost.**

[8]The index used here is analogous to the cost index used in regular DVL except that it reflects the change in retail prices rather than in acquisition costs.

**Each layer year carries its unique retail price index and its unique cost-to-retail percentage.**

In this illustration, a $20,000 year 2006 layer is added to the base layer. Two adjustments are needed to convert this amount to LIFO cost. Multiplying by the 2006 price index (1.10) converts it from its base year retail to 2006 retail. Multiplying by the 2006 cost-to-retail percentage (.6468) converts it from its 2006 retail to 2006 cost. The two steps are combined in our illustration. The base year inventory also is converted to cost. The two layers are added to derive ending inventory at dollar-value LIFO retail cost.

When additional layers are added in subsequent years, their LIFO amounts are determined the same way. For illustration, let's assume ending inventory in 2007 is $226,200 at current retail prices and the price level has risen to 1.16. Also assume that the cost-to-retail percentage for 2007 net purchases is 63%. In Illustration 9–7B, the ending inventory is converted to base year retail (step 1). This amount is apportioned into layers, each at base year retail (step 2). Layers then are converted to layer year costs (step 3).

**ILLUSTRATION 9–7B**
The Dollar-Value LIFO Retail Inventory Method

**Base year retail amounts are converted to layer year retail and then to cost.**

| Ending Inventory at Year-End Retail Prices | Step 1 Ending Inventory at Base Year Retail Prices | Step 2 Inventory Layers at Base Year Retail Prices | Step 3 Inventory Layers Converted to LIFO Cost |
|---|---|---|---|
| $226,200 (assumed) → | $226,200 / 1.16 = $195,000 → | $195,000 | |
| | | 160,000 (base) × 1.00 × .62 = | $ 99,200 |
| | | 20,000 (2006) × 1.10 × .6468 = | 14,230 |
| | | $ 15,000 (2007) × 1.16 × .63 = | 10,962 |
| Total ending inventory at dollar-value LIFO retail cost | | | $124,392 |

Now, let's assume that ending inventory in 2007 is $204,160 at current retail prices (instead of $226,200) and the price level has risen to 1.16. Also assume that the cost-to-retail percentage for 2007 net purchases is 63%. Step 1 converts the ending inventory to a base year price of $176,000 ($204,160 ÷ 1.16). A comparison to the beginning inventory at base year prices of $180,000 ($160,000 base year layer + $20,000 2006 layer) indicates that inventory *decreased* during 2007. In this case, no 2007 layer is added and 2007 ending inventory at dollar-value LIFO retail of $110,584 is determined in Illustration 9–7C.

**ILLUSTRATION 9–7C**
The Dollar-Value LIFO Retail Inventory Method

| Ending Inventory at Year-End Retail Prices | Step 1 Ending Inventory at Base Year Retail Prices | Step 2 Inventory Layers at Base Year Retail Prices | Step 3 Inventory Layers Converted to LIFO Cost |
|---|---|---|---|
| $204,160 (assumed) → | $204,160 / 1.16 = $176,000 → | $176,000 | |
| | | 160,000 (base) × 1.00 × .62 = | $ 99,200 |
| | | 16,000 (2006) × 1.10 × .6468 = | 11,384 |
| Total ending inventory at dollar-value LIFO retail cost | | | $110,584 |

A portion of the 2006 inventory layer has been liquidated—reduced from $20,000 to $16,000 at base year prices—to reduce total inventory at base year prices to $176,000.

As we mentioned earlier in this section, many high-volume retailers selling many different items use the retail method. **J.C. Penney Company, Inc.**, for example, uses the dollar-value LIFO variation of the retail method. Graphic 9–6 shows the inventory disclosure note included in the company's recent financial statements.

Notice that J.C. Penney uses an internal index to adjust for changing prices and that the lower-of-cost-or-market rule is determined on an aggregate basis for similar types of merchandise.

**Summary of Significant Accounting Policies (in part) Merchandise Inventories**
Inventories are valued primarily at the lower of cost (using the last-in, first-out, or LIFO, method) or market, determined by the retail method for department stores and store support centers and average cost for Catalog/Internet and regional warehouses. The lower of cost or market is determined on an aggregate basis for similar types of merchandise. To estimate the effects of inflation/deflation on ending inventory, an internal index measuring price changes from the beginning to the end of the year is calculated.

**GRAPHIC 9–6**
Disclosure of Inventory Method—J.C. Penney Company, Inc.

## CONCEPT REVIEW EXERCISE

### DOLLAR-VALUE LIFO RETAIL METHOD

On January 1, 2006, the Nicholson Department Store adopted the dollar-value LIFO retail inventory method. Inventory transactions at both cost and retail and cost indexes for 2006 and 2007 are as follows:

| | 2006 | | 2007 | |
|---|---|---|---|---|
| | **Cost** | **Retail** | **Cost** | **Retail** |
| Beginning inventory | $16,000 | $24,000 | | |
| Net purchases | 42,000 | 58,500 | 45,000 | 58,700 |
| Net markups | | 3,000 | | 2,400 |
| Net markdowns | | 1,500 | | 1,100 |
| Net sales | | 56,000 | | 57,000 |
| Price index: | | | | |
| January 1, 2006 | 1.00 | | | |
| December 31, 2006 | 1.08 | | | |
| December 31, 2007 | 1.15 | | | |

**Required:**
Estimate the 2006 and 2007 ending inventory and cost of goods sold using the dollar-value LIFO retail inventory method.

**SOLUTION**

| | 2006 | | 2007 | |
|---|---|---|---|---|
| | **Cost** | **Retail** | **Cost** | **Retail** |
| Beginning inventory | $16,000 | $24,000 | $17,456 | $28,000 |
| Plus: Net purchases | 42,000 | 58,500 | 45,000 | 58,700 |
| Net markups | | 3,000 | | 2,400 |
| Less: Net markdowns | | (1,500) | | (1,100) |
| Goods available for sale (excluding beg. inv.) | 42,000 | 60,000 | 45,000 | 60,000 |
| Goods available for sale (including beg. inv.) | 58,000 | 84,000 | 62,456 | 88,000 |

Base layer

Cost-to-retail percentage: $\frac{\$16,000}{\$24,000} = 66.67\%$

2006

Cost-to-retail percentage: $\frac{\$42,000}{\$60,000} = 70\%$

2007

Cost-to-retail percentage: $\frac{\$45,000}{\$60,000} = 75\%$

| | 2006 Cost | 2006 Retail | 2007 Cost | 2007 Retail |
|---|---|---|---|---|
| Less: Net sales | | (56,000) | | (57,000) |
| Estimated ending inv. at current year retail prices | | $28,000 | | $31,000 |
| Less: Estimated ending inventory at cost (below) | (17,456) | | (18,345) | |
| Estimated cost of goods sold | $40,544 | | $44,111 | |

**2006**

| Ending Inventory at Year-End Retail Prices | Step 1 Ending Inventory at Base Year Retail Prices | Step 2 Inventory Layers at Base Year Retail Prices | Step 3 Inventory Layers Converted to Cost |
|---|---|---|---|
| $28,000 (above) | $\frac{\$28,000}{1.08}$ = $25,926 | $24,000 (base) × 1.00 × 66.67% = | $16,000 |
| | | 1,926 (2006) × 1.08 × 70.00% = | 1,456 |
| Total ending inventory at dollar-value LIFO retail cost | | | $17,456 |

**2007**

| Ending Inventory at Year-End Retail Prices | Step 1 Ending Inventory at Base Year Retail Prices | Step 2 Inventory Layers at Base Year Retail Prices | Step 3 Inventory Layers Converted to Cost |
|---|---|---|---|
| $31,000 (above) | $\frac{\$31,000}{1.15}$ = $26,957 | $24,000 (base) × 1.00 × 66.67% = | $16,000 |
| | | 1,926 (2006) × 1.08 × 70.00% = | 1,456 |
| | | 1,031 (2007) × 1.15 × 75.00% = | 889 |
| Total ending inventory at dollar-value LIFO retail cost | | | $18,345 |

# PART D CHANGE IN INVENTORY METHOD AND INVENTORY ERRORS

## Change in Inventory Method

● LO6

Accounting principles should be applied consistently from period to period to allow for comparability of operating results. However, changes within a company as well as changes in the external economic environment may require a company to change an accounting method. As we mentioned in Chapter 8, high inflation in the 1970s motivated many companies to switch to the LIFO inventory method.

Specific accounting treatment and disclosures are prescribed for companies that change accounting principles. Chapter 4 introduced the subject of accounting changes and Chapter 20 provides in-depth coverage of the topic. Here we provide an overview of how changes in inventory methods are reported.

### MOST INVENTORY CHANGES

Changes in inventory methods, other than a change to LIFO, are accounted for retrospectively.

Recall from our discussion in Chapter 4 that most voluntary changes in accounting principles are reported retrospectively. This means reporting all previous periods' financial statements as if the new method had been used in all prior periods. Changes in inventory methods, other than a change to LIFO, are treated this way. We discuss the *to LIFO* exception in the next section. In Chapter 4 we outlined the steps a company undertakes to account for a change in inventory method. We demonstrate those steps using a real world example in Illustrations 9–8 and 9–8A.

Step 1: Revise Comparative Financial Statements

The first step is to revise prior years' financial statements. That is, for each year reported in the comparative statements, McKesson makes those statements appear as if the newly adopted accounting method (100% FIFO) had been applied all along. In its balance sheets, McKesson would report 2004 inventory by its newly adopted method, 100% FIFO, and also would revise the amounts it reported last year for its 2003 inventory. In its income statements, cost of goods sold also would reflect the new method in both 2004 and 2003 as shown in Illustration 9–8A.

In its statements of shareholders' equity, McKesson would report retained earnings each year as if it had used FIFO all along, and for the earliest year reported, it would revise begin-

McKesson Corporation is a Fortune 100 company producing products and services in the healthcare industry. In a note accompanying its 2004 financial statements, the company disclosed that it uses the LIFO inventory method for 90% of its inventories and FIFO for the remainder. The company's balance sheets reported inventories of $6,735 million and $6,023 million at the end of 2004 and 2003, respectively. The inventory disclosure note reports that if the FIFO method had been used to value the entire inventory, instead of just 10% of it, inventories would have been $6,982 million and $6,241 million at the end of 2004 and 2003, respectively. Partial income statements for 2004 and 2003 are as follows:

**ILLUSTRATION 9–8**
Change in Inventory Method

**McKESSON CORPORATION**
**Partial Income Statements**
**For the Years Ended March 31,**

| ($ in millions) | 2004 | 2003 |
|---|---|---|
| Sales revenue | $69,506 | $57,121 |
| Cost of goods sold | 66,258 | 54,018 |
| Gross profit | 3,248 | 3,103 |
| Operating expenses | 2,265 | 2,170 |
| Operating income | $ 983 | $ 933 |

Let's suppose that in 2004 McKesson decided to value all of its inventories using the FIFO method.

**ILLUSTRATION 9–8A**
Income statements—100% FIFO

**McKESSON CORPORATION**
**Partial Income Statements**
**For the Years Ended March 31,**

| ($ in millions) | 2004 | 2003 |
|---|---|---|
| Sales revenue | $69,506 | $57,121 |
| Cost of goods sold | 66,229 | 54,022 |
| Gross profit | 3,277 | 3,099 |
| Operating expenses | 2,265 | 2,170 |
| Operating income | $ 1,012 | $ 929 |

2004 cost of goods sold of $66,229 million is $29 million less on a 100% FIFO basis. Here's why. McKesson's note reported that beginning inventory is $218 million higher ($6,241 – 6,023), and ending inventory also is higher by $247 million ($6,982 – 6,735). An increase in beginning inventory causes an increase in cost of goods sold, but an increase in ending inventory causes a decrease in cost of goods sold. The net effect of the two adjustments ($247 – 218) is the $29 million decrease in 2004 cost of goods sold.

McKesson would report 2004 cost of goods sold by its newly adopted method, 100% FIFO.

In a similar manner, 2003 cost of goods sold would be adjusted to $54,022 million. A note included in McKesson's 2003 financial statements reports that 2002 ending inventory of $6,022 million would have been $6,244 million on an all FIFO basis. 2003's beginning inventory would be $222 million higher ($6,244 – 6,022) and ending inventory for 2003 would be $218 million higher ($6,241 – 6,023). The net effect of the two adjustments ($222 – 218) is that 2003 cost of goods sold would be $4 million higher.

McKesson would increase the amount it reported last year for its cost of goods sold as if 100% FIFO had been used.

ning retained earnings that year to reflect the cumulative income effect of the difference in inventory methods for all prior years. We see this step illustrated in Chapter 20 after you have studied the statement of shareholders' equity in more depth.

Step 2: The appropriate accounts are adjusted.

McKesson also would create a journal entry to adjust the book balances from their current amounts to what those balances would have been using 100% FIFO. Since differences in cost of goods sold and income are reflected in retained earnings, as are the income tax effects, the journal entry updates inventory, retained earnings, and the appropriate income tax account. We ignore the income tax effects here and include those effects in an illustration in

**Inventory at the beginning of 2004 would be $218 million higher if FIFO is used to value the entire inventory.**

Chapter 20. The journal entry below, *ignoring income taxes,* adjusts the April 1, 2004 (end of the 2003 fiscal year, beginning of 2004) inventory to the 100% FIFO inventory amount of $6,241 million.

| | ($ in millions) | |
|---|---|---|
| Inventory ($6,241 − 6,023) . . . . . . . . . . . . . . . . . . . . . . . . . . . . . . . | 218 | |
| Retained earnings. . . . . . . . . . . . . . . . . . . . . . . . . . . . . . . . . . . . | | 218 |

**Step 3: A disclosure note provides additional information.**

McKesson must provide in a disclosure note clear justification that the change to 100% FIFO is appropriate. The note also would indicate the effects of the change on items not reported on the face of the primary statements, as well as any per share amounts affected for the current period and all prior periods presented.

We see an example of such a note in a recent annual report of **Schweitzer-Maudit International, Inc.**, the world's largest supplier of fine papers to the tobacco industry, when it changed its inventory method from LIFO to FIFO. Graphic 9–7 shows the disclosure note that described the change.

**GRAPHIC 9–7**

Disclosure of Change in Inventory Method–Schweitzer-Maudit International, Inc.

**Note 3. Accounting Change (in part)**

In the fourth quarter of 2003, the Company's U.S. business segment changed its method of accounting for inventories for financial reporting purposes from the LIFO method to the FIFO method. Management of the Company believes the FIFO method is preferable to the LIFO method. Due to recent low inflationary trends and because inventory physical movement is on a FIFO basis, management of the Company believes that FIFO accounting provides a better matching of costs and revenues.

As required, this change in accounting method has been retroactively applied by restating the accompanying 2002 and 2001 financial statements. The cumulative net income effect of this change in accounting method of $3.8 as of December 31, 2000, the earliest date included in the accompanying financial statements, is reflected as an adjustment to increase previously reported retained earnings in the Consolidated Statements of Changes in Stockholders' Equity. Assuming the Company's U.S. business segment had remained on the LIFO method of inventory valuation for financial reporting purposes, the Company estimates that full year 2003 operating profit would have been unfavorably impacted by approximately $2 million, and net income, therefore, would have been lower by approximately $1.2 million, or a reduction in both basic and diluted net income per share of approximately $0.08.

## CHANGE TO THE LIFO METHOD

**Accounting records usually are inadequate for a company changing to *LIFO* to report the change retrospectively.**

When a company changes *to the LIFO inventory method* from any other method, it usually is impossible to calculate the income effect on prior years. To do so would require assumptions as to when specific LIFO inventory layers were created in years prior to the change. As a result, a company changing to LIFO usually does not report the change retrospectively. Instead, the LIFO method simply is used from that point on. The base year inventory for all future LIFO determinations is the beginning inventory in the year the LIFO method is adopted.[9]

A disclosure note is needed to explain (a) the nature of and justification for the change, (b) the effect of the change on current year's income and earnings per share, and (c) why retrospective application was impracticable. When **General Cable Corporation** adopted the LIFO inventory method, it reported the change in the note shown in Graphic 9–8.

As we discussed in Chapter 8, an important motivation for using LIFO in periods of rising costs is that it produces higher cost of goods sold and lowers income and income taxes. Notice in the disclosure note that the switch to LIFO caused an *increase* in income in the year of the switch indicating an environment of decreasing costs. General Cable had reasons other than an immediate reduction in its tax bill for switching to LIFO.

[9]A change to LIFO is handled the same way for income tax purposes.

**Inventories (in part)**

As of January 1, General Cable changed its accounting method for its North American non-metal inventories from the FIFO method to the LIFO method. The impact of the change was an increase in operating income of $6.4 million, or $0.12 of earnings per share on both a basic and diluted basis during the year. The cumulative effect of the change on prior years was not determinable. The Company believes that the change to the LIFO accounting method for its North American non-metal inventories more accurately reflects the impact of both volatile raw material prices and ongoing cost productivity initiatives, conforms the accounting for all North American inventories and provides a more comparable basis of accounting with direct competitors in North America who are on LIFO for the majority of their inventories.

**GRAPHIC 9–8**
Change in Inventory Method Disclosure—General Cable Corporation

| Company | FIFO EPS | LIFO EPS | % Effect of the Switch |
|---|---|---|---|
| DuPont | $6.27 | $5.10 | −18.7 |
| Eastman Kodak | 1.68 | 1.54 | −8.3 |
| Firestone Tire | 2.40 | 1.53 | −36.2 |
| Florida Steel | 4.61 | 3.96 | −14.1 |
| Marathon Oil | 4.84 | 4.32 | −10.7 |
| Std. Oil of Ohio | 2.27 | 2.02 | −11.0 |
| Stokely Van Camp | 3.69 | 2.70 | −26.8 |

**GRAPHIC 9–9**
Income Effect of Change to LIFO—1974 Examples

Recall from Chapter 8 that inflation was extremely high in 1974 causing hundreds of companies to switch to LIFO. These companies were likely motivated by the opportunity to lower their income taxes. Graphic 9–9 lists the earnings per share (EPS) effect of the switch from FIFO to LIFO for just a few of the hundreds of companies that switched to LIFO in 1974.

**ADDITIONAL CONSIDERATION**

When changing from one generally accepted accounting principle to another, a company must justify that the change results in financial information that more properly portrays operating results and financial position. For income tax purposes, a company generally must obtain consent from the Internal Revenue Service before changing an accounting method. A special form also must be filed with the IRS when a company intends to adopt the LIFO inventory method. When a company changes from LIFO for tax purposes, it can't change back to LIFO until five tax returns have been filed using the non-LIFO method.

## Inventory Errors

● LO7

Accounting errors must be corrected when they are discovered. In Chapter 4 we briefly discussed the correction of accounting errors and Chapter 20 provides in-depth coverage. Here we provide an overview of the accounting treatment and disclosures in the context of inventory errors. Inventory errors include the over- or understatement of ending inventory due to a mistake in physical count or a mistake in pricing inventory quantities. Also, errors include the over- or understatement of purchases which could be caused by the cutoff errors described in Chapter 8.

If an inventory error is discovered in the same accounting period it occurred, the original erroneous entry should simply be reversed and the appropriate entry recorded. This situation presents no particular reporting problem.

**For material errors, previous years' financial statements are retrospectively restated.**

**Incorrect balances are corrected.**

**A correction of retained earnings is reported as a prior period adjustment.**

If a *material* inventory error is discovered in an accounting period subsequent to the period in which the error was made, any previous years' financial statements that were incorrect as a result of the error are retrospectively restated to reflect the correction.[10] And, of course, any account balances that are incorrect as a result of the error are corrected by journal entry. If, due to an error affecting net income, retained earnings is one of the incorrect accounts, the correction is reported as a prior period adjustment to the beginning balance on the statement of shareholders' equity.[11] In addition, a disclosure note is needed to describe the nature of the error and the impact of its correction on net income, income before extraordinary items, and earnings per share.

**A disclosure note describes the nature and the impact of the error.**

When analyzing inventory errors, it's helpful to visualize the way cost of goods sold, net income, and retained earnings are determined (see Graphic 9–10). Beginning inventory and net purchases are *added* in the calculation of cost of goods sold. If either of these is overstated (understated) then cost of goods sold would be overstated (understated). On the other hand, ending inventory is *deducted* in the calculation of cost of goods sold, so if ending inventory is overstated (understated) then cost of goods sold is understated (overstated). Of course, errors that affect income also will affect income taxes. In the illustration that follows, we ignore the tax effects of the errors and focus on the errors themselves rather than their tax aspects.

**GRAPHIC 9–10**

Visualizing the Effect of Inventory Errors

| | | |
|---|---|---|
| Beginning inventory | | |
| Plus: Net purchases | | |
| Less: Ending inventory | Revenues | |
| Cost of goods sold → | Less: Cost of goods sold | |
| | Less: Other expenses | Beginning retained earnings |
| | Net income → | Plus: Net income |
| | | Less: Dividends |
| | | Ending retained earnings |

Let's look at an example in Illustration 9–9.

## WHEN THE INVENTORY ERROR IS DISCOVERED THE FOLLOWING YEAR

**Previous years' financial statements are retrospectively restated.**

First, let's assume the error is discovered in 2006. The 2005 financial statements that were incorrect as a result of the error are retrospectively restated to reflect the correct inventory amount, cost of goods sold, net income, and retained earnings when those statements are reported again for comparative purposes in the 2006 annual report. The following journal entry, ignoring income taxes, corrects the error.

**A journal entry corrects any incorrect account balance.**

| | | |
|---|---|---|
| Retained earnings | 800,000 | |
| Inventory | | 800,000 |

**When retained earnings requires correction, a prior period adjustment is made on the statement of shareholders' equity.**

Because retained earnings is one of the accounts that is incorrect, when the error is discovered in 2006, the correction to that account is reported as a prior period adjustment to the 2006 beginning retained earnings balance in Barton's statement of shareholders' equity (or statement of retained earnings). Prior period adjustments do not flow through the income statement but directly adjust retained earnings. This adjustment is illustrated in Chapter 20.

[10]If the effect of the error is not material, it is simply corrected in the year of discovery.

[11]The prior period adjustment is applied to beginning retained earnings for the year following the error, or for the earliest year being reported in the comparative financial statements when the error occurs prior to the earliest year presented. The retained earnings balances in years after the first year also are adjusted to what those balances would be if the error had not occurred, but a company may choose not to explicitly report those adjustments as separate line items.

**ILLUSTRATION 9–9**
Inventory Error Correction

The Barton Company uses a periodic inventory system. At the end of 2005, a mathematical error caused an $800,000 overstatement of ending inventory. Ending inventories for 2006 and 2007 are correctly determined.

The way we correct this error depends on when the error is discovered. Assuming that the error is not discovered until after 2006, the 2005 and 2006 effects of the error, ignoring income tax effects, are shown below. The overstated and understated amounts are $800,000 in each instance.

**Analysis: U = Understated O = Overstated**

| 2005 | | 2006 | |
|---|---|---|---|
| Beginning inventory | | Beginning inventory | O |
| Plus: Net purchases | | Plus: Net purchases | |
| Less: Ending inventory | O | Less: Ending inventory | |
| Cost of goods sold | U | Cost of goods sold | O |
| Revenues | | Revenues | |
| Less: Cost of goods sold | U | Less: Cost of goods sold | O |
| Less: Other expenses | | Less: Other expenses | |
| Net income | O | Net income | U |
| ↓ | | ↓ | |
| Retained earnings | O | Retained earnings | *corrected* |

## WHEN THE INVENTORY ERROR IS DISCOVERED SUBSEQUENT TO THE FOLLOWING YEAR

If the error isn't discovered until 2007, the 2006 financial statements also are retrospectively restated to reflect the correct cost of goods sold and net income even though no correcting entry would be needed at that point. Inventory and retained earnings would not require adjustment. The error has self-corrected and no prior period adjustment is needed.

Also, a disclosure note in Barton's annual report should describe the nature of the error and the impact of its correction on each year's net income (overstated by $800,000 in 2005; understated by $800,000 in 2006), income before extraordinary items (same as net income in this case), and earnings per share.

**A disclosure note describes the nature of the error and the impact of the correction on income.**

# CONCEPT REVIEW EXERCISE

**INVENTORY ERRORS**

In 2006, the controller of the Fleischman Wholesale Beverage Company discovered the following material errors related to the 2004 and 2005 financial statements:

a. Inventory at the end of 2004 was understated by $50,000.
b. Late in 2005, a $3,000 purchase was incorrectly recorded as a $33,000 purchase. The invoice has not yet been paid.
c. Inventory at the end of 2005 was overstated by $20,000.

The company uses a periodic inventory system.

**Required:**

1. Assuming that the errors were discovered after the 2005 financial statements were issued, analyze the effect of the errors on 2004 and 2005 cost of goods sold, net income, and retained earnings. Ignore income taxes.
2. Prepare a journal entry to correct the errors.

SOLUTION

1. **Analysis: U = Understated O = Overstated**

| 2004 | | 2005 | |
|---|---|---|---|
| Beginning inventory | | Beginning inventory | U-50,000 |
| Plus: Net purchases | | Plus: Net purchases | O-30,000 |
| Less: Ending inventory | U-50,000 | Less: Ending inventory | O-20,000 |
| Cost of goods sold | O-50,000 | Cost of goods sold | U-40,000 |
| Revenues | | Revenues | |
| Less: Cost of goods sold | O-50,000 | Less: Cost of goods sold | U-40,000 |
| Less: Other expenses | | Less: Other expenses | |
| Net income | U-50,000 | Net income | O-40,000 |
| ↓ | | ↓ | |
| Retained earnings | U-50,000 | Retained earnings | U-10,000 |

2. Prepare a journal entry to correct the errors.

| | | |
|---|---|---|
| Accounts payable | 30,000 | |
| Inventory | | 20,000 |
| Retained earnings | | 10,000 |

## Earnings Quality

A change in the accounting method a company uses to value inventory is one way managers can artificially manipulate income. However, this method of income manipulation is transparent. As we learned in a previous section, the effect on income of switching from one inventory method to another must be disclosed. That disclosure restores comparability between periods and enhances earnings quality.

**Inventory write-downs often are cited as a method used to shift income between periods.**

On the other hand, inventory write-downs are included in the broader category of "big bath" accounting techniques some companies use to manipulate earnings. By overstating the write-down, profits are increased in future periods as the inventory is used or sold. When the demand for many high technology products decreased significantly in late 2000 and early 2001, several companies, including **Sycamore Networks**, **Lucent Technologies**, and **JDS Uniphase**, recorded large inventory write-offs, some in the billions of dollars. In the introduction to this chapter, we discussed the over $2 billion inventory write-off recorded by **Cisco Systems**. Certainly these write-offs reflected the existing economic environment. However, some analysts questioned the size of some of the write-offs. For example, William Schaff, an investment officer at Bay Isle Financial noted that Cisco's write-off was approximately equal to the balance of inventory on hand at the end of the previous quarter and about equal to the cost of goods actually sold during the quarter.

**WILLIAM SCHAFF—BAY ISLE FINANCIAL**
I have nothing on which to base these theories other than the fact that writing off a whole quarter's inventory seems a bit much to just shrug off. It's very disturbing.[12]

A financial analyst must carefully consider the effect of any significant asset write-down on the assessment of a company's permanent earnings.

## FINANCIAL REPORTING CASE SOLUTION

1. **Sears values its inventory at the lower of cost or market. What does that mean? Under what circumstances might Sears be justified in reporting its inventory at less than cost?** *(p. 402)* A departure from historical cost is warranted when the probable benefits to be re-

[12]William Schaff, "What Is the Definition of an Earnings Bath," *Information Week Online,* April 24, 2001.

ceived from any asset drop below the asset's cost. The benefits from inventory result from the ultimate sale of the goods. Deterioration, obsolescence, and changes in price levels are situations that might cause the benefits to be received from sale to drop below cost. The lower-of-cost-or-market approach recognizes losses in the period when the value of the inventory declines below its cost rather than in the period in which the goods ultimately are sold.

2. **How does Sears avoid counting all its inventory every time it produces financial statements? What are internal price indices used for?** *(p. 419)* Sears uses the dollar-value LIFO retail inventory method. The retail inventory estimation technique avoids the counting of ending inventory by keeping track of goods available for sale not only at cost but also at retail prices. Each period's sales, at sales prices, are deducted from the retail amount of goods available for sale to arrive at ending inventory at retail. This amount is then converted to cost using a cost-to-retail percentage.

   The dollar-value LIFO retail method uses a price index to first convert ending inventory at retail to base year prices. Yearly LIFO layers are then determined and each layer is converted to that year's current year retail prices using the year's price index and then to cost using the layer's cost-to-retail percentage. For the price index, Sears uses an internally generated index rather than an external price index. ■

## The Bottom Line

1. Inventory is valued at the lower of cost or market (LCM). The designated market value in the LCM rule is the middle number of replacement cost (RC), net realizable value (NRV), and net realizable value less a normal profit margin (NRV − NP).
2. The gross profit method estimates cost of goods sold which is then subtracted from cost of goods available for sale to estimate ending inventory. The estimate of cost of goods sold is determined by subtracting an estimate of gross profit from net sales. The estimate of gross profit is determined by multiplying the historical gross profit ratio times net sales.
3. The retail inventory method determines the amount of ending inventory at retail by subtracting sales for the period from goods available for sale at retail. Ending inventory at retail is then converted to *cost* by multiplying it by the cost-to-retail percentage, which is based on a current relationship between cost and selling price.
4. By the conventional retail method, we estimate average cost at lower of cost or market. Average cost is estimated by including beginning inventory in the calculation of the cost-to-retail percentage. LCM is estimated by excluding markdowns from the calculation. Markdowns are subtracted in the retail column after the percentage is calculated.
5. By the LIFO retail method, ending inventory includes the beginning inventory plus the current year's layer. To determine layers, we compare ending inventory at retail to beginning inventory at retail and assume that no more than one inventory layer is added if inventory increases. Each layer carries its own cost-to-retail percentage which is used to convert each layer from retail to cost. The dollar-value LIFO retail inventory method combines the LIFO retail method and the dollar-value LIFO method (Chapter 8) to estimate LIFO from retail prices when the price level has changed.
6. Most changes in inventory methods are reported retrospectively. This means revising all previous periods' financial statements to appear as if the newly adopted inventory method had been applied all along. An exception is a change to the LIFO method. In this case, it usually is impossible to calculate the income effect on prior years. To do so would require assumptions as to when specific LIFO inventory layers were created in years prior to the change. As a result, a company changing to LIFO usually does not report the change retrospectively. Instead, the LIFO method simply is used from that point on.
7. If a material inventory error is discovered in an accounting period subsequent to the period in which the error is made, previous years' financial statements that were incorrect as a result of the error are retrospectively restated to reflect the correction. Account balances are corrected by journal entry. A correction of retained earnings is reported as a prior period adjustment to the beginning balance in the statement of shareholders' equity. In addition, a disclosure note is needed to describe the nature of the error and the impact of its correction on income. ■

# APPENDIX 9 PURCHASE COMMITMENTS

*Purchase commitments protect the buyer against price increases and provide a supply of product.*

**Purchase commitments** are contracts that obligate a company to purchase a specified amount of merchandise or raw materials at specified prices on or before specified dates. Companies enter into these agreements to make sure they will be able to obtain important inventory as well as to protect against increases in purchase price. However, if the purchase price decreases before the agreement is exercised, the commitment has the disadvantage of requiring the company to purchase inventory at a higher than market price. If this happens, a loss on the purchase commitment is recorded.

Purchases made pursuant to a purchase commitment are recorded at the lower of contract price or market price on the date the contract is executed.

Because purchase commitments create the possibility of this kind of loss, the loss occurs when the market price falls below the commitment price rather than when the inventory eventually is sold. This means recording the loss when the product is purchased or, if the commitment is still outstanding, at the end of the reporting period. In other words, purchases are recorded at market price when that price is lower than the contract price, and a loss is recognized for the difference. Also, losses are recognized for any purchase commitments outstanding at the end of a reporting period when market price is less than contract price. In effect, the LCM rule is applied to purchase commitments. This is best understood by the example in Illustration 9A–1.

**ILLUSTRATION 9A–1**
Purchase Commitments

In July 2006, the Lassiter Company signed two purchase commitments. The first requires Lassiter to purchase inventory for $500,000 by November 15, 2006. The second requires the company to purchase inventory for $600,000 by February 15, 2007. Lassiter's fiscal year-end is December 31. The company uses a perpetual inventory system.

## Contract Period within Fiscal Year

The contract period for the first commitment is contained within a single fiscal year. Lassiter would record the purchase at the contract price if the market price at date of acquisition is at least *equal to* the contract price of $500,000.[13]

If market price is equal to or greater than the contract price, the purchase is recorded at the contract price.

| | | |
|---|---|---|
| Inventory (contract price) | 500,000 | |
| Cash (or accounts payable) | | 500,000 |

If the market price at acquisition is *less* than the contract price, inventory is recorded at the market price and a loss is recognized.[14] For example, if the market price is $425,000, the following entry records the purchase:

If market price is less than the contract price, the purchase is recorded at the market price.

| | | |
|---|---|---|
| Inventory (market price) | 425,000 | |
| Loss on purchase commitment | 75,000 | |
| Cash (or accounts payable) | | 500,000 |

The objective of this treatment is to associate the loss with the period in which the price declines rather than with the period in which the company eventually sells the inventory. This is the same objective as the LCM rule you studied in the chapter.

## Contract Period Extends beyond Fiscal Year

Now let's consider Lassiter's second purchase commitment that is outstanding at the end of the fiscal year 2006 (that is, the purchases have not yet been made). If the market price at the end of the year is at least *equal* to the contract price of $600,000, no entry is recorded. However, if the market price at year-end is *less* than the contract price, a loss must be recognized

[13]In each of the following situations, if a periodic inventory system is used *purchases* is debited instead of *inventory*.

[14]Recall from the LCM discussion in the chapter that the preferred method of recording losses from inventory write-downs is to recognize the loss as a separate item in the income statement, rather than as an increase in cost of goods sold.

to satisfy the LCM objective of associating the loss with the period in which the price declines rather than with the period in which the company eventually sells the inventory. Let's say the year-end market price of the inventory for Lassiter's second purchase commitment is $540,000. The following adjusting entry is recorded:

| | | |
|---|---|---|
| **December 31, 2006** | | |
| Estimated loss on purchase commitment ($600,000 − 540,000) . . . | 60,000 | |
| Estimated liability on purchase commitment. . . . . . . . . . . . . . . | | 60,000 |

**If the market price at year-end is less than the contract price a loss is recorded for the difference.**

At this point, the loss is an *estimated* loss. The actual loss, if any, will not be known until the inventory actually is purchased. The best estimate of the market price on date of purchase is the current market price, in this case $540,000. Because no inventory has been acquired, we can't credit inventory for the LCM loss. Instead, a liability is credited because, in a sense, the loss represents an obligation to the seller of the inventory to purchase inventory above market price.

**A liability is credited for estimated losses on purchase commitments.**

The entry to record the actual purchase on or before February 15, 2007, will vary depending on the market price of the inventory at date of purchase. If the market price is unchanged or has increased from the year-end price, the following entry is made:

| | | |
|---|---|---|
| Inventory (accounting cost) . . . . . . . . . . . . . . . . . . . . . . . . . . . . . | 540,000 | |
| Estimated liability on purchase commitment. . . . . . . . . . . . . . . . . . | 60,000 | |
| Cash (or accounts payable) . . . . . . . . . . . . . . . . . . . . . . . . . . . . | | 600,000 |

**If market price on purchase date has not declined from year-end price, the purchase is recorded at the year-end market price.**

Even if the market price of the inventory increases, there is no recovery of the $60,000 loss recognized in 2006. Remember that when the LCM rule is applied, the reduced inventory value, in this case the reduced value of purchases, is considered to be the new cost and any recovery of value is ignored.

If the market price declines even further from year-end levels, an additional loss is recognized. For example, if the market price of the inventory covered by the commitment declines to $510,000, the following entry is recorded:

| | | |
|---|---|---|
| Inventory (market price) . . . . . . . . . . . . . . . . . . . . . . . . . . . . . . . | 510,000 | |
| Loss on purchase commitment ($540,000 − 510,000) . . . . . . . . . . | 30,000 | |
| Estimated liability on purchase commitment. . . . . . . . . . . . . . . . . . | 60,000 | |
| Cash (or accounts payable) . . . . . . . . . . . . . . . . . . . . . . . . . . . . | | 600,000 |

**If market price on purchase date declines from year-end price, the purchase is recorded at the market price.**

The total loss on this purchase commitment of $90,000 is thus allocated between 2006 and 2007 according to when the decline in value of the inventory covered by the commitment occurred.

If there are material amounts of purchase commitments outstanding at the end of a reporting period, the contract details are disclosed in a note. This disclosure is required even if no loss estimate has been recorded. ■

## QUESTIONS FOR REVIEW OF KEY TOPICS

**Q 9–1** Explain the lower-of-cost-or-market approach to valuing inventory.

**Q 9–2** What is the meaning of market in the lower-of-cost-or-market rule?

**Q 9–3** What are the various ways the LCM determination can be made?

**Q 9–4** Describe the preferred method of adjusting from cost to market for material inventory write-downs.

**Q 9–5** Explain the gross profit method of estimating ending inventory.

**Q 9–6** The Rider Company uses the gross profit method to estimate ending inventory and cost of goods sold. The cost percentage is determined based on historical data. What factors could cause the estimate of ending inventory to be overstated?

**Q 9–7** Explain the retail inventory method of estimating ending inventory.

**Q 9–8** Both the gross profit method and the retail inventory method provide a way to estimate ending inventory. What is the main difference between the two estimation techniques?

Q 9–9 Define each of the following retail terms: initial markup, additional markup, markup cancellation, markdown, markdown cancellation.

Q 9–10 Explain how to estimate the average cost of inventory when using the retail inventory method.

Q 9–11 What is the conventional retail method?

Q 9–12 Explain the LIFO retail inventory method.

Q 9–13 Discuss the treatment of freight-in, net markups, normal spoilage, and employee discounts in the application of the retail inventory method.

Q 9–14 Explain the difference between the retail inventory method using LIFO and the dollar-value LIFO retail method.

Q 9–15 Describe the accounting treatment for a change in inventory method other than to LIFO.

Q 9–16 When a company changes its inventory method to LIFO, an exception is made for the way accounting changes usually are reported. Explain the difference in the accounting treatment of a change *to* the LIFO inventory method from other inventory method changes.

Q 9–17 Explain the accounting treatment of material inventory errors discovered in an accounting period subsequent to the period in which the error is made.

Q 9–18 It is discovered in 2006 that ending inventory in 2004 was understated. What is the effect of the understatement on the following:

| | |
|---|---|
| 2004: | Cost of goods sold |
| | Net income |
| | Ending retained earnings |
| 2005: | Net purchases |
| | Cost of goods sold |
| | Net income |
| | Ending retained earnings |

Q 9–19 (Based on Appendix 9) Define purchase commitments. What is the advantage(s) of these agreements to buyers?

Q 9–20 (Based on Appendix 9) Explain how the lower-of-cost-or-market rule is applied to purchase commitments.

## BRIEF EXERCISES

**BE 9–1**
Lower of cost or market
• LO1

Ross Electronics has one product in its ending inventory. Per unit data consist of the following: cost, $20; replacement cost, $18; selling price, $30; disposal costs, $4. The normal profit margin is 30% of selling price. What unit value should Ross use when applying the LCM rule to ending inventory?

**BE 9–2**
Lower of cost or market
• LO1

SLR Corporation has 1,000 units of each of its two products in its year-end inventory. Per unit data for each of the products are as follows:

| | Product 1 | Product 2 |
|---|---|---|
| Cost | $50 | $30 |
| Replacement cost | 48 | 26 |
| Selling price | 70 | 36 |
| Disposal costs | 6 | 4 |
| Normal profit margin | 10 | 8 |

Determine the balance sheet carrying value of SLR's inventory assuming that the LCM rule is applied to individual products. What is the before-tax income effect of the LCM adjustment?

**BE 9–3**
Gross profit method
• LO2

On February 26 a hurricane destroyed the entire inventory stored in a warehouse owned by the Rockford Corporation. The following information is available from the records of the company's periodic inventory system: beginning inventory, $220,000; purchases and net sales from the beginning of the year through February 26, $400,000 and $600,000, respectively; gross profit ratio, 30%. Estimate the cost of the inventory destroyed by the hurricane using the gross profit method.

**BE 9–4**
Gross profit method; solving for unknown
• LO2

Adams Corporation estimates that it lost $75,000 in inventory from a recent flood. The following information is available from the records of the company's periodic inventory system: beginning inventory, $150,000; purchases and net sales from the beginning of the year through the date of the flood, $450,000 and $700,000, respectively. What is the company's gross profit ratio?

**BE 9–5**
Retail inventory method; average cost
● LO3

Kiddie World uses a periodic inventory system and the retail inventory method to estimate ending inventory and cost of goods sold. The following data are available for the quarter ending September 30, 2006:

| | Cost | Retail |
|---|---|---|
| Beginning inventory | $300,000 | $ 450,000 |
| Net purchases | 861,000 | 1,210,000 |
| Freight-in | 22,000 | |
| Net markups | | 48,000 |
| Net markdowns | | 18,000 |
| Net sales | | 1,200,000 |

Estimate ending inventory and cost of goods sold (average cost).

**BE 9–6**
Retail inventory method; LIFO
● LO3

Refer to the situation described in BE 9–5. Estimate ending inventory and cost of goods sold (LIFO).

**BE 9–7**
Conventional retail method
● LO4

Refer to the situation described in BE 9–5. Estimate ending inventory and cost of goods sold using the conventional method (average cost and the LCM approximation).

**BE 9–8**
Conventional retail method
● LO4

Roberson Corporation uses a periodic inventory system and the retail inventory method. Accounting records provided the following information for the 2006 fiscal year:

| | Cost | Retail |
|---|---|---|
| Beginning inventory | $220,000 | $ 400,000 |
| Net purchases | 640,000 | 1,180,000 |
| Freight-in | 17,800 | |
| Net markups | | 16,000 |
| Net markdowns | | 6,000 |
| Normal spoilage | | 3,000 |
| Net sales | | 1,300,000 |

The company records sales to employees net of discounts. These discounts totaled $15,000 for the year. Estimate ending inventory and cost of goods sold using the conventional method (average cost and the LCM approximation).

**BE 9–9**
Dollar-value LIFO retail
● LO5

On January 1, 2006, Sanderson Variety Store adopted the dollar-value LIFO retail inventory method. Accounting records provided the following information:

| | Cost | Retail |
|---|---|---|
| Beginning inventory | $ 40,800 | $ 68,000 |
| Net purchases | 155,440 | 270,000 |
| Net markups | | 6,000 |
| Net markdowns | | 8,000 |
| Net sales | | 250,000 |
| Retail price index, end of year | | 1.02 |

Calculate the inventory value at the end of the year using the dollar-value LIFO retail method.

**BE 9–10**
Dollar-value LIFO retail
● LO5

Refer to the situation described in BE 9–9. During 2007, purchases at cost and retail were $168,000 and $301,000, respectively. Net markups, net markdowns, and net sales for the year were $3,000, $4,000, and $280,000, respectively. The retail price index at the end of 2007 was 1.06. Calculate the inventory value at the end of 2007 using the dollar-value LIFO retail method.

**BE 9–11**
Change in inventory costing methods
● LO6

In 2006, Hopyard Lumber changed its inventory method from LIFO to FIFO. Inventory at the end of 2005 of $127,000 would have been $145,000 if FIFO had been used. Inventory at the end of 2006 is $162,000 using the new FIFO method but would have been $151,000 if the company had continued to use LIFO. Describe the steps Hopyard should take to report this change. What is the effect of the change on 2006 cost of goods sold?

**BE 9–12**
Change in inventory costing methods
● LO6

In 2006, Wade Window and Glass changed its inventory method from FIFO to LIFO. Inventory at the end of 2005 is $150,000. Describe the steps Wade Window and Glass should take to report this change.

**BE 9–13**
Inventory error
● LO7

In 2006, Winslow International, Inc.'s controller discovered that ending inventories for 2004 and 2005 were overstated by $200,000 and $500,000, respectively. Determine the effect of the errors on retained earnings at January 1, 2006. (Ignore income taxes.)

**BE 9–14**
Inventory error
● LO7

Refer to the situation described in BE 9–13. What steps would be taken to report the error in the 2006 financial statements?

# EXERCISES



**An alternate exercise and problem set is available on the text website: www.mhhe.com/spiceland4e**

**E 9–1**
Lower of cost or market
● LO1

Herman Company has three products in its ending inventory. Specific per unit data for each of the products are as follows:

| | Product 1 | Product 2 | Product 3 |
|---|---|---|---|
| Cost | $20 | $ 90 | $50 |
| Replacement cost | 18 | 85 | 40 |
| Selling price | 40 | 120 | 70 |
| Disposal costs | 6 | 40 | 10 |
| Normal profit margin | 5 | 30 | 12 |

**Required:**
What unit values should Herman use for each of its products when applying the LCM rule to ending inventory?

**E 9–2**
Lower of cost or market
● LO1

Tatum Company has four products in its inventory. Information about the December 31, 2006, inventory is as follows:

| Product | Total Cost | Total Replacement Cost | Total Net Realizable Value |
|---|---|---|---|
| 101 | $120,000 | $110,000 | $100,000 |
| 102 | 90,000 | 85,000 | 110,000 |
| 103 | 60,000 | 40,000 | 50,000 |
| 104 | 30,000 | 28,000 | 50,000 |

The normal gross profit percentage is 25% of *cost.*

**Required:**
1. Determine the balance sheet inventory carrying value at December 31, 2006, assuming the LCM rule is applied to individual products.
2. Assuming that Tatum recognizes an inventory write-down as a separate income statement item, determine the amount of the loss.

**E 9–3**
Gross profit method
● LO2

On September 22, 2006, a flood destroyed the entire merchandise inventory on hand in a warehouse owned by the Rocklin Sporting Goods Company. The following information is available from the records of the company's periodic inventory system:

| | |
|---|---|
| Inventory, January 1, 2006 | $140,000 |
| Net purchases, January 1 through September 22 | 370,000 |
| Net sales, January 1 through September 22 | 550,000 |
| Gross profit ratio | 25% |

**Required:**
Estimate the cost of inventory destroyed in the flood using the gross profit method.

**E 9–4**
Gross profit method
● LO2

On November 21, 2006, a fire at Hodge Company's warehouse caused severe damage to its entire inventory of Product Tex. Hodge estimates that all usable damaged goods can be sold for $12,000. The following information was available from the records of Hodge's periodic inventory system:

| | |
|---|---|
| Inventory, November 1 | $100,000 |
| Net purchases from November 1, to the date of the fire | 140,000 |
| Net sales from November 1, to the date of the fire | 220,000 |

Based on recent history, Hodge's gross profit ratio on Product Tex is 35% of net sales.

**Required:**
Calculate the estimated loss on the inventory from the fire, using the gross profit method.

*(AICPA adapted)*

**E 9–5**
Gross profit method
• LO2

A fire destroyed a warehouse of the Goren Group, Inc., on May 4, 2006. Accounting records on that date indicated the following:

| | |
|---|---|
| Merchandise inventory, January 1, 2006 | $1,900,000 |
| Purchases to date | 5,800,000 |
| Freight-in | 400,000 |
| Sales to date | 8,200,000 |

The gross profit ratio has averaged 20% of sales for the past four years.

**Required:**
Use the gross profit method to estimate the cost of the inventory destroyed in the fire.

**E 9–6**
Gross profit method; solving for unknown cost percentage
• LO2

National Distributing Company uses a periodic inventory system to track its merchandise inventory and the gross profit method to estimate ending inventory and cost of goods sold for interim periods. Net purchases for the month of August were $31,000. The July 31 and August 31, 2006, financial statements contained the following information:

**Income Statements**
**For the Months Ending**

| | August 31, 2006 | July 31, 2006 |
|---|---|---|
| Net sales | $50,000 | $40,000 |

**Balance Sheets**
**At**

| | August 31, 2006 | July 31, 2006 |
|---|---|---|
| Assets: | | |
| Merchandise inventory | $28,000 | $27,000 |

**Required:**
Determine the company's cost percentage.

**E 9–7**
Retail inventory method; average cost
• LO3

San Lorenzo General Store uses a periodic inventory system and the retail inventory method to estimate ending inventory and cost of goods sold. The following data are available for the month of October 2006:

| | Cost | Retail |
|---|---|---|
| Beginning inventory | $35,000 | $50,000 |
| Net purchases | 19,120 | 31,600 |
| Net markups | | 1,200 |
| Net markdowns | | 800 |
| Net sales | | 32,000 |

**Required:**
Estimate the average cost of ending inventory and cost of goods sold for October. Do not approximate LCM.

**E 9–8**
Conventional retail method
• LO4

Campbell Corporation uses the retail method to value its inventory. The following information is available for the year 2006:

| | Cost | Retail |
|---|---|---|
| Merchandise inventory, January 1, 2006 | $190,000 | $280,000 |
| Purchases | 600,000 | 840,000 |
| Freight-in | 8,000 | |
| Net markups | | 20,000 |
| Net markdowns | | 4,000 |
| Net sales | | 800,000 |

**Required:**
Determine the December 31, 2006, inventory that approximates average cost, lower of cost or market.

**E 9–9**
Retail inventory method; LIFO
• LO3

Crosby Company owns a chain of hardware stores throughout the state. The company uses a periodic inventory system and the retail inventory method to estimate ending inventory and cost of goods sold. The following data are available for the three months ending March 31, 2006:

| | Cost | Retail |
|---|---|---|
| Beginning inventory | $160,000 | $280,000 |
| Net purchases | 607,760 | 840,000 |
| Net markups | | 20,000 |
| Net markdowns | | 4,000 |
| Net sales | | 800,000 |

**Required:**
Estimate the LIFO cost of ending inventory and cost of goods sold for the three months ending March 31, 2006. Assume stable retail prices during the period.

**E 9–10**
Conventional retail method; normal spoilage

● LO4

Almaden Valley Variety Store uses the retail inventory method to estimate ending inventory and cost of goods sold. Data for 2006 are as follows:

| | Cost | Retail |
|---|---|---|
| Beginning inventory | $ 12,000 | $ 20,000 |
| Purchases | 102,600 | 165,000 |
| Freight-in | 3,480 | |
| Purchase returns | 4,000 | 7,000 |
| Net markups | | 6,000 |
| Net markdowns | | 3,000 |
| Normal spoilage | | 4,200 |
| Net sales | | 152,000 |

**Required:**
Estimate the ending inventory and cost of goods sold for 2006, applying the conventional retail method (average, LCM).

**E 9–11**
Conventional retail method; employee discounts

● LO3 LO4

LeMay Department Store uses the retail inventory method to estimate ending inventory for its monthly financial statements. The following data pertain to one of its largest departments for the month of March 2006:

| | Cost | Retail |
|---|---|---|
| Beginning inventory | $ 40,000 | $ 60,000 |
| Purchases | 207,000 | 400,000 |
| Freight-in | 14,488 | |
| Purchase returns | 4,000 | 6,000 |
| Net markups | | 5,800 |
| Net markdowns | | 3,500 |
| Normal breakage | | 6,000 |
| Net sales | | 280,000 |
| Employee discounts | | 1,800 |

Sales are recorded net of employee discounts.

**Required:**
1. Compute estimated ending inventory and cost of goods sold for March applying the conventional retail method (average, LCM).
2. Recompute the cost-to-retail percentage using the average cost method and ignoring LCM considerations.

**E 9–12**
Retail inventory method; solving for unknowns

● LO3

Adams Corporation uses a periodic inventory system and the retail inventory method to estimate ending inventory and cost of goods sold. The following data are available for the month of September 2006:

| | Cost | Retail |
|---|---|---|
| Beginning inventory | $21,000 | $35,000 |
| Net purchases | 10,500 | ? |
| Net markups | | 4,000 |
| Net markdowns | | 1,000 |
| Net sales | | ? |

The company used the average cost flow method and estimated inventory at the end of September to be $17,437.50. If the company had used the LIFO cost flow method, the cost-to-retail percentage would have been 50%.

**Required:**
Compute net purchases at retail and net sales for the month of September.

**E 9–13**
Multiple choice; LCM; inventory estimation techniques

● LO1 through LO3

The following questions dealing with the lower-of-cost-or-market rule for valuing inventory and inventory estimation techniques are adapted from questions that appeared on CPA examinations. Determine the response that best completes the statements or questions.

1. Which of the following statements are correct when a company applying the lower-of-cost-or-market method reports its inventory at replacement cost?

I. The original cost is less than replacement cost.
II. The net realizable value is greater than replacement cost.

a. I only.
b. II only.
c. Both I and II.
d. Neither I nor II.

2. Moss Co. has determined its December 31, 2006, inventory on a FIFO basis to be $400,000. Information pertaining to that inventory follows:

| | |
|---|---|
| Estimated selling price | $408,000 |
| Estimated cost of disposal | 20,000 |
| Normal profit margin | 60,000 |
| Current replacement cost | 360,000 |

Moss records losses that result from applying the lower-of-cost-or-market rule. At December 31, 2006, what should be the net carrying amount of Moss's inventory?

a. $400,000
b. $388,000
c. $360,000
d. $328,000

3. Hutch, Inc. uses the conventional retail inventory method to account for inventory. The following information relates to 2006 operations:

| | Cost | Retail |
|---|---|---|
| Beginning inventory and purchases | $600,000 | $920,000 |
| Net markups | | 40,000 |
| Net markdowns | | 60,000 |
| Sales | | 780,000 |

What amount should be reported as cost of goods sold for 2006?

a. $480,000
b. $487,500
c. $520,000
d. $525,000

4. The following information is available for Cooke Company in 2006:

| | |
|---|---|
| Net sales | $1,800,000 |
| Freight-in | 45,000 |
| Purchase discounts | 25,000 |
| Ending inventory | 120,000 |

The gross margin is 40% of net sales. What is the cost of goods available for sale?

a. $840,000
b. $960,000
c. $1,200,000
d. $1,220,000

**E 9–14**
Dollar-value LIFO retail
● LO5

On January 1, 2006, the Brunswick Hat Company adopted the dollar-value LIFO retail method. The following data are available for 2006:

| | Cost | Retail |
|---|---|---|
| Beginning inventory | $ 71,280 | $132,000 |
| Net purchases | 112,500 | 255,000 |
| Net markups | | 6,000 |
| Net markdowns | | 11,000 |
| Net sales | | 232,000 |
| Retail price index, 12/31/06 | | 1.04 |

**Required:**
Calculate the estimated ending inventory and cost of goods sold for 2006.

**E 9–15**
Dollar-value LIFO retail
● LO5

Canova Corporation adopted the dollar-value LIFO retail method on January 1, 2006. On that date, the cost of the inventory on hand was $15,000 and its retail value was $18,750. Information for 2006 and 2007 is as follows:

| Date | Ending Inventory at Retail | Retail Price Index | Cost-to-Retail Percentage |
|---|---|---|---|
| 12/31/06 | $25,000 | 1.25 | 82% |
| 12/31/07 | 28,600 | 1.30 | 85 |

**Required:**
1. What is the cost-to-retail percentage for the inventory on hand at 1/1/06?
2. Calculate the inventory value at the end of 2006 and 2007 using the dollar-value LIFO retail method.

**E 9–16**
Dollar-value LIFO retail
● LO5

Lance-Hefner Specialty Shoppes decided to use the dollar-value LIFO retail method to value its inventory. Accounting records provide the following information:

| | Cost | Retail |
|---|---|---|
| Merchandise inventory, January 1, 2006 | $160,000 | $250,000 |
| Net purchases | 350,200 | 510,000 |
| Net markups | | 7,000 |
| Net markdowns | | 2,000 |
| Net sales | | 380,000 |

Pertinent retail price indexes are as follows:

| | |
|---|---|
| January 1, 2006 | 1.00 |
| December 31, 2006 | 1.10 |

**Required:**
Determine ending inventory and cost of goods sold.

**E 9–17**
Dollar-value LIFO retail; solving for unknowns
● LO5

Bosco Company adopted the dollar-value LIFO retail method at the beginning of 2006. Information for 2006 and 2007 is as follows, with certain data intentionally omitted:

| | Inventory | | | |
|---|---|---|---|---|
| Date | Cost | Retail | Retail Price Index | Cost-to-Retail Percentage |
| Inventory, 1/1/06 | $21,000 | $28,000 | 1.00 | ? |
| Inventory, 12/31/06 | 22,792 | 33,600 | 1.12 | ? |
| 2007 net purchases | 60,000 | 88,400 | | |
| 2007 net sales | | 80,000 | | |
| Inventory, 12/31/07 | ? | ? | 1.20 | |

**Required:**
Determine the missing data.

**E 9–18**
Change in inventory costing methods
● LO6

In 2006, CPS Company changed its method of valuing inventory from the FIFO method to the average cost method. At December 31, 2005, CPS's inventories were $32 million (FIFO). CPS's records indicated that the inventories would have totaled $23.8 million at December 31, 2005, if determined on an average cost basis.

**Required:**
1. Prepare the journal entry to record the adjustment. (Ignore income taxes.)
2. Briefly describe other steps CPS should take to report the change.

**E 9–19**
Change in inventory costing methods
● LO6

Goddard Company has used the FIFO method of inventory valuation since it began operations in 2003. Goddard decided to change to the average cost method for determining inventory costs at the beginning of 2006. The following schedule shows year-end inventory balances under the FIFO and average cost methods:

| Year | FIFO | Average Cost |
|---|---|---|
| 2003 | $45,000 | $54,000 |
| 2004 | 78,000 | 71,000 |
| 2005 | 83,000 | 78,000 |

**Required:**
1. Ignoring income taxes, prepare the 2006 journal entry to adjust the accounts to reflect the average cost method.
2. How much higher or lower would cost of goods sold be in the 2005 revised income statement?

**E 9–20**
Error correction; inventory error
● LO7

During 2006, WMC Corporation discovered that its ending inventories reported in its financial statements were misstated by the following amounts:

| | | |
|---|---|---|
| 2004 | understated by | $120,000 |
| 2005 | overstated by | 150,000 |

WMC uses a periodic inventory system and the FIFO cost method.

**Required:**
1. Determine the effect of these errors on retained earnings at January 1, 2006, before any adjustments. Explain your answer. (Ignore income taxes.)
2. Prepare a journal entry to correct the error.
3. What other step(s) would be taken in connection with the error?

**E 9–21**
Inventory errors

● LO7

For each of the following inventory errors occurring in 2006, determine the effect of the error on 2006's cost of goods sold, net income, and retained earnings. Assume that the error is not discovered until 2007 and that a periodic inventory system is used. Ignore income taxes.

U = understated O = overstated NE = no effect

| | Cost of Goods Sold | Net Income | Retained Earnings |
|---|---|---|---|
| (Example) 1. Overstatement of ending inventory | U | O | O |
| 2. Overstatement of purchases | | | |
| 3. Understatement of beginning inventory | | | |
| 4. Freight-in charges are understated | | | |
| 5. Understatement of ending inventory | | | |
| 6. Understatement of purchases | | | |
| 7. Overstatement of beginning inventory | | | |
| 8. Understatement of purchases plus understatement of ending inventory by the same amount | | | |

**E 9–22**
Inventory error

● LO7

In 2006, the internal auditors of Development Technologies, Inc. discovered that a $4 million purchase of merchandise in 2006 was recorded in 2005 instead. The physical inventory count at the end of 2005 was correct.

**Required:**
Prepare the journal entry needed in 2006 to correct the error. Also, briefly describe any other measures Development Technologies would take in connection with correcting the error. (Ignore income taxes.)

**E 9–23**
Multiple choice; dollar-value LIFO retail, inventory errors

● LO5 LO7

The following questions dealing with dollar-value LIFO retail and inventory errors are adapted from questions that appeared on CPA examinations. Determine the response that best completes the statements or questions.

1. On December 31, 2005, Jason Company adopted the dollar-value LIFO retail inventory method. Inventory data for 2006 are as follows:

| | LIFO Cost | Retail |
|---|---|---|
| Inventory, 12/31/05 | $360,000 | $500,000 |
| Inventory, 12/31/06 | ? | 660,000 |
| Increase in price level for 2006 | | 10% |
| Cost to retail ratio for 2006 | | 70% |

Under the LIFO retail method, Jason's inventory at December 31, 2006, should be
a. $437,000
b. $462,000
c. $472,000
d. $483,000

2. Bren Co.'s beginning inventory at January 1, 2006, was understated by $26,000, and its ending inventory was overstated by $52,000. As a result, Bren's cost of goods sold for 2006 was
a. Understated by $26,000.
b. Overstated by $26,000.
c. Understated by $78,000.
d. Overstated by $78,000.

**E 9–24**
Concepts; terminology

● LO1 through LO7

Listed below are several terms and phrases associated with inventory measurement. Pair each item from List A (by letter) with the item from List B that is most appropriately associated with it.

| List A | List B |
|---|---|
| ____ 1. Gross profit ratio | a. Reduction in selling price below the original selling price. |
| ____ 2. Cost-to-retail percentage | b. Beginning inventory is not included in the calculation of the cost-to-retail percentage. |
| ____ 3. Additional markup | c. Deducted in the retail column after the calculation of the cost-to-retail percentage. |
| ____ 4. Markdown | d. Requires base year retail to be converted to layer year retail and then to cost. |
| ____ 5. Net markup | e. Gross profit divided by net sales. |
| ____ 6. Retail method, FIFO and LIFO | f. Material inventory error discovered in a subsequent year. |
| ____ 7. Conventional retail method | g. Must be added to sales if sales are recorded net of discounts. |
| ____ 8. Change from LIFO | h. Deducted in the retail column to arrive at goods available for sale at retail. |
| ____ 9. Dollar-value LIFO retail | i. Divide cost of goods available for sale by goods available at retail. |
| ____ 10. Normal spoilage | j. Average cost, LCM. |
| ____ 11. Requires retrospective restatement | k. Added to the retail column to arrive at goods available for sale. |
| ____ 12. Employee discounts | l. Increase in selling price subsequent to initial markup. |
| ____ 13. Net markdowns | m. Ceiling in the determination of market. |
| ____ 14. Net realizable value | n. Accounting change requiring retrospective treatment. |

**E 9–25**
Multiple choice; CMA exam; conventional retail method; inventory errors

● LO4 LO7

The following questions dealing with inventory are adapted from questions that previously appeared on Certified Management Accountant (CMA) examinations. The CMA designation sponsored by the Institute of Management Accountants (www.imanet.org) provides members with an objective measure of knowledge and competence in the field of management accounting. Determine the response that best completes the statements or questions.

1. All sales and purchases for the year at Ross Corporation are credit transactions. Ross uses a perpetual inventory system. During the year, it shipped certain goods that were correctly excluded from ending inventory although the sale was not recorded. Which one of the following statements is correct?
   a. Accounts receivable was not affected, inventory was not affected, sales were understated, and cost of goods sold was understated.
   b. Accounts receivable was understated, inventory was not affected, sales were understated, and cost of goods sold was understated.
   c. Accounts receivable was understated, inventory was overstated, sales were understated, and cost of goods sold was overstated.
   d. Accounts receivable was understated, inventory was not affected, sales were understated, and cost of goods sold was not affected.
2. During the year 1 year-end physical inventory count at Tequesta Corporation, $40,000 worth of inventory was counted twice. Assuming that the year 2 year-end inventory was correct, the result of the year 1 error was that
   a. Year 1 retained earnings was understated, and year 2 ending inventory was correct.
   b. Year 1 cost of goods sold was overstated, and year 2 income was understated.
   c. Year 1 income was overstated, and year 2 ending inventory was overstated.
   d. Year 1 cost of goods sold was understated, and year 2 retained earnings was correct.
3. The following FCL Corporation inventory information is available for the year ended December 31:

| | Cost | Retail |
|---|---|---|
| Beginning inventory at 1/1 | $35,000 | $100,000 |
| Net purchases | 55,000 | 110,000 |
| Net markups | | 15,000 |
| Net markdowns | | 25,000 |
| Net sales | | 150,000 |

   The December 31 ending inventory at cost using the conventional (lower of average cost or market) retail inventory method equals
   a. $17,500
   b. $20,000
   c. $27,500
   d. $50,000

**E 9–26**
Purchase commitments (Based on Appendix 9)

● LO1

On October 6, 2006, the Elgin Corporation signed a purchase commitment to purchase inventory for $60,000 on or before March 31, 2007. The company's fiscal year-end is December 31. The contract was exercised on March 21, 2007, and the inventory was purchased for cash at the contract price. On the purchase date of March 21, the market price of the inventory was $54,000. The market price of the inventory on December 31, 2006, was $56,000. The company uses a perpetual inventory system.

**Required:**
1. Prepare the necessary adjusting journal entry (if any is required) on December 31, 2006.
2. Prepare the journal entry to record the purchase on March 21, 2007.

**E 9–27**
Purchase commitments (Based on Appendix 9)

● LO1

In March 2006, the Phillips Tool Company signed two purchase commitments. The first commitment requires Phillips to purchase inventory for $100,000 by June 15, 2006. The second commitment requires the company to purchase inventory for $150,000 by August 20, 2006. The company's fiscal year-end is June 30. Phillips uses a periodic inventory system.

The first commitment is exercised on June 15, 2006, when the market price of the inventory purchased was $85,000. The second commitment was exercised on August 20, 2006, when the market price of the inventory purchased was $120,000.

**Required:**
Prepare the journal entries required on June 15, June 30, and August 20, 2006, to account for the two purchase commitments. Assume that the market price of the inventory related to the outstanding purchase commitment was $140,000 at June 30.

## PROBLEMS

available with McGraw-Hill's Homework Manager www.mhhe.com/spiceland4e

**An alternate exercise and problem set is available on the text website: www.mhhe.com/spiceland4e**

**P 9–1**
Lower of cost or market
● LO1
eXcel

Decker Company has five products in its inventory. Information about the December 31, 2006, inventory follows.

| Product | Quantity | Unit Cost | Unit Replacement Cost | Unit Selling Price |
|---|---|---|---|---|
| A | 1,000 | $10 | $12 | $16 |
| B | 800 | 15 | 11 | 18 |
| C | 600 | 3 | 2 | 8 |
| D | 200 | 7 | 4 | 6 |
| E | 600 | 14 | 12 | 13 |

The selling cost for each product consists of a 15 percent sales commission. The normal profit percentage for each product is 40 percent of the selling price.

**Required:**

1. Determine the balance sheet inventory carrying value at December 31, 2006, assuming the LCM rule is applied to individual products.
2. Determine the balance sheet inventory carrying value at December 31, 2006, assuming the LCM rule is applied to the entire inventory. Also, assuming that Decker recognizes an inventory write-down as a separate income statement item, determine the amount of the loss.

**P 9–2**
Lower of cost or market
● LO1

Almaden Hardware Store sells two distinct types of products, tools and paint products. Information pertaining to its 2006 year-end inventory is as follows:

| Inventory, by Product Type | Quantity | Per Unit Cost | Designated Market |
|---|---|---|---|
| Tools: | | | |
| Hammers | 100 | $ 5.00 | $5.50 |
| Saws | 200 | 10.00 | 9.00 |
| Screwdrivers | 300 | 2.00 | 2.60 |
| Paint products: | | | |
| 1-gallon cans | 500 | 6.00 | 5.00 |
| Paint brushes | 100 | 4.00 | 4.50 |

**Required:**

1. Determine the balance sheet inventory carrying value at year-end, assuming the LCM rule is applied to (a) individual products, (b) product type, and (c) total inventory.
2. Assuming that the company recognizes an inventory write-down as a separate income statement item, for each of the LCM applications determine the amount of the loss.

**P 9–3**
Gross profit method
● LO2

Smith Distributors, Inc., supplies ice cream shops with various toppings for making sundaes. On November 17, 2006, a fire resulted in the loss of all of the toppings stored in one section of the warehouse. The company must provide its insurance company with an estimate of the amount of inventory lost. The following information is available from the company's accounting records:

| | Fruit Toppings | Marshmallow Toppings | Chocolate Toppings |
|---|---|---|---|
| Inventory, January 1, 2006 | $ 20,000 | $ 7,000 | $ 3,000 |
| Net purchases through Nov. 17 | 150,000 | 36,000 | 12,000 |
| Net sales through Nov. 17 | 200,000 | 55,000 | 20,000 |
| Historical gross profit ratio | 20% | 30% | 35% |

**Required:**

1. Calculate the estimated cost of each of the toppings lost in the fire.
2. What factors could cause the estimates to be over- or understated?

**P 9–4**
Retail inventory method; various cost methods

● LO3 LO4

Sparrow Company uses the retail inventory method to estimate ending inventory and cost of goods sold. Data for 2006 are as follows:

| | Cost | Retail |
|---|---|---|
| Beginning inventory | $ 90,000 | $180,000 |
| Purchases | 355,000 | 580,000 |
| Freight-in | 9,000 | |
| Purchase returns | 7,000 | 11,000 |
| Net markups | | 16,000 |
| Net markdowns | | 12,000 |
| Normal spoilage | | 3,000 |
| Abnormal spoilage | 4,800 | 8,000 |
| Sales | | 540,000 |
| Sales returns | | 10,000 |

The company records sales net of employee discounts. Discounts for 2006 totaled $4,000.

**Required:**

Estimate Sparrow's ending inventory and cost of goods sold for the year using the retail inventory method and the following applications:

1. Average cost
2. Conventional (average, LCM)

**P 9–5**
Retail inventory method; conventional and LIFO

● LO3 LO4

eXcel

Alquist Company uses the retail method to estimate its ending inventory. Selected information about its year 2006 operations is as follows:

a. January 1, 2006, beginning inventory had a cost of $100,000 and a retail value of $150,000.
b. Purchases during 2006 cost $1,387,500 with an original retail value of $2,000,000.
c. Freight costs were $10,000 for incoming merchandise and $25,000 for outgoing (sold) merchandise.
d. Net additional markups were $300,000 and net markdowns were $150,000.
e. Based on prior experience, shrinkage due to shoplifting was estimated to be $15,000 of retail value.
f. Merchandise is sold to employees at a 20% of selling price discount. Employee sales are recorded in a separate account at the net selling price. The balance in this account at the end of 2006 is $250,000.
g. Sales to customers totaled $1,750,000 for the year.

**Required:**

1. Estimate ending inventory and cost of goods sold using the conventional retail method (average, LCM).
2. Estimate ending inventory and cost of goods sold using the LIFO retail method. (Assume stable prices.)

**P 9–6**
Retail inventory method

● LO3 LO4

eXcel

Grand Department Store, Inc., uses the retail inventory method to estimate ending inventory for its monthly financial statements. The following data pertain to a single department for the month of October 2006:

| | |
|---|---|
| Inventory, October 1, 2006: | |
| At cost | $ 20,000 |
| At retail | 30,000 |
| Purchases (exclusive of freight and returns): | |
| At cost | 100,151 |
| At retail | 146,495 |
| Freight-in | 5,100 |
| Purchase returns: | |
| At cost | 2,100 |
| At retail | 2,800 |
| Additional markups | 2,500 |
| Markup cancellations | 265 |
| Markdowns (net) | 800 |
| Normal spoilage and breakage | 4,500 |
| Sales | 135,730 |

**Required:**

1. Using the conventional retail method, prepare a schedule computing estimated lower-of-cost-or-market inventory for October 31, 2006.
2. A department store using the conventional retail inventory method estimates the cost of its ending inventory as $29,000. An accurate physical count reveals only $22,000 of inventory at lower of cost or market. List the factors that may have caused the difference between computed inventory and the physical count.

*(AICPA adapted)*

**P 9–7**
Retail method—average cost and LCM

● LO3 LO4

Smith-Kline Company maintains inventory records at selling prices as well as at cost. For 2006, the records indicate the following data:

| | ($ in 000s) | |
|---|---|---|
| | **Cost** | **Retail** |
| Beginning inventory | $ 80 | $ 125 |
| Purchases | 671 | 1,006 |
| Freight-in on purchases | 30 | |
| Purchase returns | 1 | 2 |
| Net markups | | 4 |
| Net markdowns | | 8 |
| Net sales | | 916 |

**Required:**
Use the retail method to approximate cost of ending inventory in each of the following ways:
1. Average cost
2. Average (LCM) cost

**P 9–8**
Dollar-value LIFO retail method

● LO5

[This is a variation of the previous problem, modified to focus on the dollar-value LIFO retail method.]

Smith-Kline Company maintains inventory records at selling prices as well as at cost. For 2006, the records indicate the following data:

| | ($ in 000s) | |
|---|---|---|
| | **Cost** | **Retail** |
| Beginning inventory | $ 80 | $ 125 |
| Purchases | 671 | 1,006 |
| Freight-in on purchases | 30 | |
| Purchase returns | 1 | 2 |
| Net markups | | 4 |
| Net markdowns | | 8 |
| Net sales | | 916 |

**Required:**
Assuming the price level increased from 1.00 at January 1 to 1.10 at December 31, 2006, use the dollar-value LIFO retail method to approximate cost of ending inventory and cost of goods sold.

**P 9–9**
Dollar-value LIFO retail

● LO5

On January 1, 2006, HGC Camera Store adopted the dollar-value LIFO retail inventory method. Inventory transactions at both cost and retail, and cost indexes for 2006 and 2007 are as follows:

| | **2006** | | **2007** | |
|---|---|---|---|---|
| | **Cost** | **Retail** | **Cost** | **Retail** |
| Beginning inventory | $28,000 | $ 40,000 | | |
| Net purchases | 85,000 | 108,000 | 90,000 | 114,000 |
| Freight-in | 2,000 | | 2,500 | |
| Net markups | | 10,000 | | 8,000 |
| Net markdowns | | 2,000 | | 2,200 |
| Net sales to customers | | 100,000 | | 104,000 |
| Sales to employees (net of 20% discount) | | 2,400 | | 4,000 |
| Price Index: | | | | |
| January 1, 2006 | 1.00 | | | |
| December 31, 2006 | 1.06 | | | |
| December 31, 2007 | 1.10 | | | |

**Required:**
Estimate the 2006 and 2007 ending inventory and cost of goods sold using the dollar-value LIFO retail inventory method.

**P 9–10**
Retail inventory method; various applications

● LO3 through LO5

eXcel

Raleigh Department Store converted from the conventional retail method to the LIFO retail method on January 1, 2004, and is now considering converting to the dollar-value LIFO retail inventory method. Management requested, during your examination of the financial statements for the year ended December 31, 2006, that you furnish a summary showing certain computations of inventory costs for the past three years. Available information follows:

a. The inventory at January 1, 2004, had a retail value of $45,000 and a cost of $27,500 based on the conventional retail method.
b. Transactions during 2004 were as follows:

| | Cost | Retail |
|---|---|---|
| Gross purchases | $282,000 | $490,000 |
| Purchase returns | 6,500 | 10,000 |
| Purchase discounts | 5,000 | |
| Gross sales | | 492,000 |
| Sales returns | | 5,000 |
| Employee discounts | | 3,000 |
| Freight-in | 26,500 | |
| Net markups | | 25,000 |
| Net markdowns | | 10,000 |

Sales to employees are recorded net of discounts.

c. The retail value of the December 31, 2005, inventory was $56,100, the cost-to-retail percentage for 2005 under the LIFO retail method was 62%, and the appropriate price index was 102% of the January 1, 2005, price level.

d. The retail value of the December 31, 2006, inventory was $48,300, the cost-to-retail percentage for 2006 under the LIFO retail method was 61%, and the appropriate price index was 105% of the January 1, 2005, price level.

**Required:**

1. Prepare a schedule showing the computation of the cost of inventory at December 31, 2004, based on the conventional retail method.
2. Prepare a similar schedule as in requirement 1 based on the LIFO retail method.
3. Same requirement as (1) for December 31, 2005 and 2006, based on the dollar-value LIFO retail method.

*(AICPA adapted)*

**P 9–11**
Change in methods
● LO6

Rockwell Corporation uses a periodic inventory system and has used the FIFO cost method since inception of the company in 1974. In 2006, the company decided to switch to the average cost method. Data for 2006 are as follows:

| | | |
|---|---|---|
| Beginning inventory, FIFO (5,000 units @ $30) | | $150,000 |
| Purchases: | | |
| 5,000 units @ $36 | $180,000 | |
| 5,000 units @ $40 | 200,000 | 380,000 |
| Cost of goods available for sale | | $530,000 |
| Sales for 2006 (8,000 units @ $70) | | $560,000 |

Additional Information:

a. The company's effective income tax rate is 40% for all years.

b. If the company had used the average cost method prior to 2006, ending inventory for 2005 would have been $130,000.

c. 7,000 units remained in inventory at the end of 2006.

**Required:**

1. Ignoring income taxes, prepare the 2006 journal entry to adjust the accounts to reflect the average cost method.
2. What is the effect of the change in methods on 2006 net income?

**P 9–12**
Inventory errors
● LO7

You have been hired as the new controller for the Ralston Company. Shortly after joining the company in 2006, you discover the following errors related to the 2004 and 2005 financial statements:

a. Inventory at 12/31/04 was understated by $6,000.

b. Inventory at 12/31/05 was overstated by $9,000.

c. On 12/31/05, inventory was purchased for $3,000. The company did not record the purchase until the inventory was paid for early in 2006. At that time, the purchase was recorded by a debit to purchases and a credit to cash.

The company uses a periodic inventory system.

**Required:**

1. Assuming that the errors were discovered after the 2005 financial statements were issued, analyze the effect of the errors on 2005 and 2004 cost of goods sold, net income, and retained earnings. (Ignore income taxes.)
2. Prepare a journal entry to correct the errors.
3. What other step(s) would be taken in connection with the error?

**P 9–13**
Inventory errors
● LO7

The December 31, 2006, inventory of Tog Company, based on a physical count, was determined to be $450,000. Included in that count was a shipment of goods that cost $50,000 received from a supplier at the end of the month. The purchase was recorded and paid for in 2007. Another supplier shipment costing

$20,000 was correctly recorded as a purchase in 2006. However, the merchandise, shipped FOB shipping point, was not received until 2007 and was incorrectly omitted from the physical count. A third purchase, shipped from a supplier FOB shipping point on December 28, 2006, did not arrive until January 3, 2007. The merchandise, which cost $80,000, was not included in the physical count and the purchase has not yet been recorded.

The company uses a periodic inventory system.

**Required:**

1. Determine the correct December 31, 2006, inventory balance and, assuming that the errors were discovered after the 2006 financial statements were issued, analyze the effect of the errors on 2006 cost of goods sold, net income, and retained earnings. (Ignore income taxes.)
2. Prepare a journal entry to correct the errors.

**P 9–14**
Purchase commitments (Based on Appendix 9)

● LO1

In November 2006, the Brunswick Company signed two purchase commitments. The first commitment requires Brunswick to purchase 10,000 units of inventory at $10 per unit by December 15, 2006. The second commitment requires the company to purchase 20,000 units of inventory at $11 per unit by March 15, 2007. Brunswick's fiscal year-end is December 31. The company uses a periodic inventory system. Both contracts were exercised on their expiration date.

**Required:**

1. Prepare the journal entry to record the December 15 purchase for cash assuming the following alternative unit market prices on that date:
   a. $10.50
   b. $ 9.50
2. Prepare any necessary adjusting entry at December 31, 2006, for the second purchase commitment assuming the following alternative unit market prices on that date:
   a. $12.50
   b. $10.30
3. Assuming that the unit market price on December 31 was $10.30, prepare the journal entry to record the purchase on March 15, 2007, assuming the following alternative unit market prices on that date:
   a. $11.50
   b. $10.00

## BROADEN YOUR PERSPECTIVE

**Apply your critical-thinking ability to the knowledge you've gained. These cases will provide you an opportunity to develop your research, analysis, judgment, and communication skills. You also will work with other students, integrate what you've learned, apply it in real world situations, and consider its global and ethical ramifications. This practice will broaden your knowledge and further develop your decision-making abilities.**

**Judgment Case 9–1**
Inventoriable costs; lower of cost or market; retail inventory method

● LO1 LO3 LO4

Hudson Company, which is both a wholesaler and a retailer, purchases its inventories from various suppliers.

Additional facts for Hudson's wholesale operations are as follows:

a. Hudson incurs substantial warehousing costs.
b. Hudson uses the lower-of-cost-or-market method. The replacement cost of the inventories is below the net realizable value and above the net realizable value less the normal profit margin. The original cost of the inventories is above replacement cost and below the net realizable value.

Additional facts for Hudson's retail operations are as follows:

a. Hudson determines the estimated cost of its ending inventories held for sale at retail using the conventional retail inventory method, which approximates lower of average cost or market.
b. Hudson incurs substantial freight-in costs.
c. Hudson has net markups and net markdowns.

**Required:**

1. Theoretically, how should Hudson account for the warehousing costs related to its wholesale inventories? Why?
2. a. In general, why is the lower-of-cost-or-market method used to value inventory?
   b. At which amount should Hudson's wholesale inventories be reported in the balance sheet? Explain the application of the lower-of-cost-or-market method in this situation.
3. In the calculation of the cost-to-retail percentage used to determine the estimated cost of its ending retail inventories, how should Hudson treat

a. Freight-in costs?
b. Net markups?
c. Net markdowns?

4. Why does Hudson's retail inventory method approximate lower of average cost or market?

*(AICPA adapted)*

**Communication Case 9–2**
Lower of cost or market

● LO1

The lower-of-cost-or-market approach to valuing inventory is a departure from the accounting principle of reporting assets at their historical costs. There are those who believe that inventory, as well as other assets, should be valued at market, regardless of whether market is above or below cost.

The focus of this case is the justification for the lower-of-cost-or-market rule for valuing inventories. Your instructor will divide the class into two to six groups depending on the size of the class. The mission of your group is to defend the lower-of-cost-or-market approach against the alternatives of valuing inventory at either historical cost or market value.

**Required:**

1. Each group member should consider the situation independently and draft a tentative argument prior to the class session for which the case is assigned.
2. In class, each group will meet for 10 to 15 minutes in different areas of the classroom. During that meeting, group members will take turns sharing their suggestions for the purpose of arriving at a single group argument.
3. After the allotted time, a spokesperson for each group (selected during the group meetings) will share the group's solution with the class. The goal of the class is to incorporate the views of each group into a consensus approach to the situation.

**Integrating Case 9–3**
Unit LIFO and LCM

● LO1

York Co. sells one product, which it purchases from various suppliers. York's trial balance at December 31, 2006, included the following accounts:

| | |
|---|---|
| Sales (33,000 units @ $16) | $528,000 |
| Sales discounts | 7,500 |
| Purchases | 368,900 |
| Purchase discounts | 18,000 |
| Freight-in | 5,000 |
| Freight-out | 11,000 |

York Co.'s inventory purchases during 2006 were as follows:

| | Units | Cost per Unit | Total Cost |
|---|---|---|---|
| Beginning inventory | 8,000 | $8.20 | $ 65,600 |
| Purchases, quarter ended March 31 | 12,000 | 8.25 | 99,000 |
| Purchases, quarter ended June 30 | 15,000 | 7.90 | 118,500 |
| Purchases, quarter ended September 30 | 13,000 | 7.50 | 97,500 |
| Purchases, quarter ended December 31 | 7,000 | 7.70 | 53,900 |
| | 55,000 | | $434,500 |

**Additional Information:**

a. York's accounting policy is to report inventory in its financial statements at the lower of cost or market, applied to total inventory. Cost is determined under the last-in, first-out (LIFO) method.
b. York has determined that, at December 31, 2006, the replacement cost of its inventory was $8 per unit and the net realizable value was $8.80 per unit. York's normal profit margin is $1.05 per unit.

**Required:**

1. Prepare York's schedule of cost of goods sold, with a supporting schedule of ending inventory. York uses the direct method of reporting losses from market decline of inventory.
2. Explain the rule of lower of cost or market and its application in this situation.

*(AICPA adapted)*

**Judgment Case 9–4**
The dollar-value LIFO method; the retail inventory method

● LO3 LO4

Huddell Company, which is both a wholesaler and retailer, purchases merchandise from various suppliers. The dollar-value LIFO method is used for the wholesale inventories.

Huddell determines the estimated cost of its retail ending inventories using the conventional retail inventory method, which approximates lower of average cost or market.

**Required:**

1. a. What are the advantages of using the dollar-value LIFO method as opposed to the traditional LIFO method?
   b. How does the application of the dollar-value LIFO method differ from the application of the traditional LIFO method?

2. a. In the calculation of the cost-to-retail percentage used to determine the estimated cost of its ending inventories, how should Huddell use
      - Net markups?
      - Net markdowns?
   b. Why does Huddell's retail inventory method approximate lower of average cost or market?

*(AICPA adapted)*

**Communication Case 9–5**
Retail inventory method
● LO3 LO4

The Brenly Paint Company, your client, manufactures paint. The company's president, Mr. Brenly, decided to open a retail store to sell paint as well as wallpaper and other items that would be purchased from other suppliers. He has asked you for information about the retail method of estimating inventories at the retail store.

**Required:**
Prepare a report to the president explaining the retail method of estimating inventories.

**Analysis Case 9–6**
Change in inventory method
● LO6

Generally accepted accounting principles should be applied consistently from period to period. However, changes within a company, as well as changes in the external economic environment, may force a company to change an accounting method. The specific reporting requirements when a company changes from one generally accepted inventory method to another depend on the methods involved.

**Required:**
Explain the accounting treatment for a change in inventory method (a) not involving LIFO, (b) from the LIFO method, and (c) to the LIFO method. Explain the logic underlying those treatments. Also, describe how disclosure requirements are designed to address the departure from consistency and comparability of changes in accounting principle.

**Real World Case 9–7**
Change in inventory method
● LO6

On January 16, 2001, **Pennzoil-Quaker State Company** made the following announcement:

---

Houston (January 16, 2001)—Pennzoil-Quaker State Company (NYSE: PZL) announced today that it has changed its inventory costing method from last-in, first-out (LIFO) to moving average cost for all products previously on the LIFO method. The new method is expected to provide a better matching of raw material costs to product selling prices, producing a more accurate measure of operating results for the Company's businesses.

The change will require the Company to restate its historical reported earnings. Recurring earnings per share are expected to be reduced in pro forma 1998 to 24 cents from 48 cents, increased in 1999 to 61 cents from 49 cents, and increased in the first nine months of 2000 by a total of 17 cents.

---

**Required:**
1. Why does GAAP require Pennzoil-Quaker State to retrospectively adjust historical reported earnings for this type of accounting change?
2. Assuming that the quantity of inventory remained stable during the first nine months of 2000, did the cost of Pennzoil-Quaker State's inventory move up or down during that period?

**Real World Case 9–8**
Change in inventory method
● LO6

EDGAR, the Electronic Data Gathering, Analysis, and Retrieval system, performs automated collection, validation, indexing, and forwarding of submissions by companies and others who are required by law to file forms with the U.S. Securities and Exchange Commission (SEC). All publicly traded domestic companies use EDGAR to make the majority of their filings. (Some foreign companies file voluntarily.) Form 10-K or 10-KSB, which includes the annual report, is required to be filed on EDGAR. The SEC makes this information available on the Internet.

**Required:**
1. Access EDGAR on the Internet. The web address is **www.sec.gov**. Edgarscan (**edgarscan.pwcglobal.com**) from Pricewaterhouse Coopers makes the process of accessing data from EDGAR easier.
2. Search for **Eagle Supply Group, Inc.** Access the 10-K filing for the fiscal year ended June 30, 2003. Search or scroll to find the financial statements and related notes.
3. Answer the following questions related to the company's inventories:
   a. Describe the change made in the company's method of accounting for inventories.
   b. What was the effect of the change on retained earnings as of July 1, 2000?
   c. What was the effect of the change on 2002's previously reported net income?

**Communication Case 9–9**
Change in inventory method; disclosure note
● LO6

Mayfair Department Stores, Inc., operates over 30 retail stores in the Pacific Northwest. Prior to 2006, the company used the FIFO method to value its inventory. In 2006, Mayfair decided to switch to the dollar-value LIFO retail inventory method. One of your responsibilities as assistant controller is to prepare the disclosure note describing the change in method that will be included in the company's 2006 financial statements. Kenneth Meier, the controller, provided the following information:

a. Internally developed retail price indexes are used to adjust for the effects of changing prices.
b. If the change had not been made, cost of goods sold for the year would have been $22 million lower. The company's income tax rate is 40% and there were 100 million shares of common stock outstanding during 2006.
c. The cumulative effect of the change on prior years' income is not determinable.
d. The reasons for the change were (a) to provide a more consistent matching of merchandise costs with sales revenue, and (b) the new method provides a more comparable basis of accounting with competitors that also use the LIFO method.

**Required:**

1. Prepare for Kenneth Meier the disclosure note that will be included in the 2006 financial statements.
2. Explain why the "cumulative effect of the change on prior years' income is not determinable."

**Judgment Case 9–10**
Inventory errors
● LO7

Some inventory errors are said to be self-correcting in that the error has the opposite financial statement effect in the period following the error, thereby correcting the original account balance errors.

**Required:**

Despite this self-correcting feature, discuss why these errors should not be ignored and describe the steps required to account for the error correction.

**Ethics Case 9–11**
Overstatement of ending inventory
● LO7

Danville Bottlers is a wholesale beverage company. Danville uses the FIFO inventory method to determine the cost of its ending inventory. Ending inventory quantities are determined by a physical count. For the fiscal year-end June 30, 2006, ending inventory was originally determined to be $3,265,000. However, on July 17, 2006, John Howard, the company's controller, discovered an error in the ending inventory count. He determined that the correct ending inventory amount should be $2,600,000.

Danville is a privately owned corporation with significant financing provided by a local bank. The bank requires annual audited financial statements as a condition of the loan. By July 17, the auditors had completed their review of the financial statements which are scheduled to be issued on July 25. They did not discover the inventory error.

John's first reaction was to communicate his finding to the auditors and to revise the financial statements before they are issued. However, he knows that his and his fellow workers' profit-sharing plans are based on annual pretax earnings and that if he revises the statements, everyone's profit-sharing bonus will be significantly reduced.

**Required:**

1. Why will bonuses be negatively affected? What is the effect on pretax earnings?
2. If the error is not corrected in the current year and is discovered by the auditors during the following year's audit, how will it be reported in the company's financial statements?
3. Discuss the ethical dilemma John Howard faces.

**Analysis Case 9–12**
Purchase commitments
(Based on Appendix 9)
● LO1

The management of the Esquire Oil Company believes that the wholesale price of heating oil that they sell to homeowners will increase again as the result of increased political problems in the Middle East. The company is currently paying $.80 a gallon. If they are willing to enter an agreement in November 2006 to purchase a million gallons of heating oil during the winter of 2007, their supplier will guarantee the price at $.80 per gallon. However, if the winter is a mild one, Esquire would not be able to sell a million gallons unless they reduced their retail price and thereby increase the risk of a loss for the year. On the other hand, if the wholesale price did increase substantially, they would be in a favorable position with respect to their competitors. The company's fiscal year-end is December 31.

**Required:**

Discuss the accounting issues related to the purchase commitment that Esquire is considering.

# CPA SIMULATION 9–1

**Central Engines**
Inventory Costing Methods

KAPLAN CPA Review

Test your knowledge of the concepts discussed in this chapter, practice critical professional skills necessary for career success, and prepare for the computer-based CPA exam by accessing our CPA simulations at the text website: **www.mhhe.com/spiceland4e**.

The Central Engines simulation tests your knowledge of (a) the differential effects on financial statements of the various inventory costing methods, the difference between the gross and net method of accounting for purchase discounts, and LIFO liquidations that you studied in Chapter 8 and (b) the lower-of-cost or market approach to valuing inventory covered in this chapter.

As on the CPA exam itself, you will be asked to use tools including a spreadsheet, a calculator, and professional accounting standards to conduct research, derive solutions, and communicate conclusions related to these issues in a simulated environment headed by the following interactive tabs:

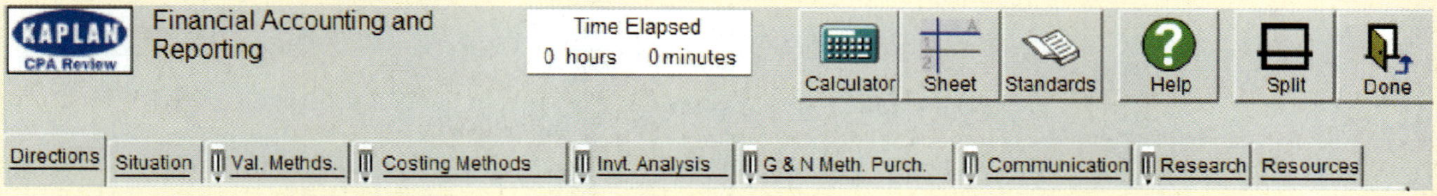


Specific tasks in the simulation address:

- Demonstrating your knowledge of the effect on inventory and cost of goods sold of using different cost flow assumptions.
- Understanding the implications of using LIFO versus FIFO to value inventory.
- Analyzing the effects of differing cost flow assumptions on numerous financial statement elements
- Understanding the differences between the gross and net method of accounting for purchase discounts.
- Communicating the effect of a LIFO liquidation on financial statements.
- Researching the application of the lower-of-cost-or market approach to valuing inventory.

## CPA SIMULATION 9–2

**Ohio Valley Pet Company**
Inventory

KAPLAN
CPA Review

Test your knowledge of the concepts discussed in this chapter, practice critical professional skills necessary for career success, and prepare for the computer-based CPA exam by accessing our CPA simulations at the text website: **www.mhhe.com/spiceland4e.**

The Ohio Valley Pet Company simulation tests your knowledge of (a) the costs to be included in inventory and the inventory turnover ratio addressed in Chapter 8, (b) the application of the lower-of-cost-or-market approach to valuing inventory, inventory estimation techniques, and inventory errors covered in this chapter, and (c) accounting for purchase commitments covered in the Appendix to this chapter.

As on the CPA exam itself, you will be asked to use tools including a spreadsheet, a calculator, and professional accounting standards, to conduct research, derive solutions, and communicate conclusions related to these issues in a simulated environment headed by the following interactive tabs:

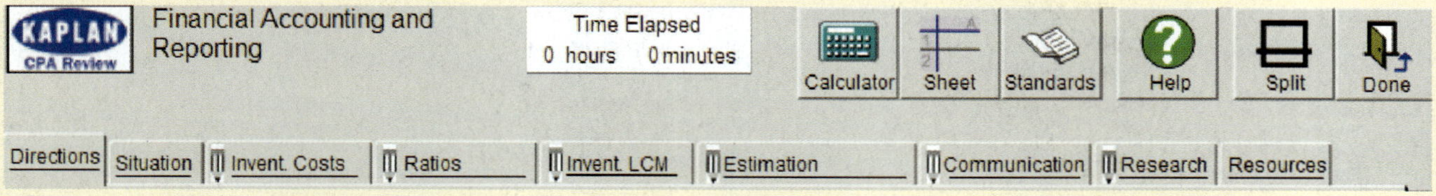


Specific tasks in the simulation address:

- Determining whether or not certain costs should be included in inventory.
- Analyzing the effect of various transactions on the inventory turnover ratio.
- Applying the lower-of-cost-or-market approach to valuing inventory.
- Understanding the retail inventory method and the gross profit method used for estimating ending inventory.
- Communicating the effects of inventory errors on financial statement elements.
- Researching how to report an unrealized loss on an outstanding purchase commitment.

10

CHAPTER

# Operational Assets: Acquisition and Disposition

## OVERVIEW

This chapter and the one that follows address the measurement and reporting issues involving operational assets. Operational assets include tangible and intangible long-term assets that are used in the production of goods and services. This chapter covers the valuation at date of acquisition and the disposition of these assets. In Chapter 11 we discuss the allocation of the cost of operational assets to the periods benefited by their use, the treatment of expenditures made over the life of these assets to maintain and improve them, and the impairment of operational assets.

## LEARNING OBJECTIVES

**After studying this chapter, you should be able to:**

- LO1 Identify the various costs included in the initial cost of property, plant, and equipment, natural resources, and intangible assets.
- LO2 Determine the initial cost of individual operational assets acquired as a group for a lump-sum purchase price.
- LO3 Determine the initial cost of an operational asset acquired in exchange for a deferred payment contract.
- LO4 Determine the initial cost of operational assets acquired in exchange for equity securities or through donation.
- LO5 Calculate the fixed-asset turnover ratio used by analysts to measure how effectively managers use property, plant, and equipment.
- LO6 Explain how to account for dispositions and exchanges for other nonmonetary assets.
- LO7 Identify the items included in the cost of a self-constructed asset and determine the amount of capitalized interest.
- LO8 Explain the difference in the accounting treatment of costs incurred to purchase intangible assets versus the costs incurred to internally develop intangible assets.

# FINANCIAL REPORTING CASE

## A Disney Adventure

"Now I'm really confused," confessed Stan, your study partner, staring blankly at the Walt Disney Company balance sheet that your professor handed out last week. "I thought that interest is always expensed in the income statement. Now I see that Disney is capitalizing interest. I'm not even sure what *capitalize* means! And what about this other account called *goodwill?* The balance of $16,966 million in 2004 is unchanged from last year. I thought those kinds of assets lose their value gradually over time. I believe amortization is the correct term." "That's right," you tell Stan, "amortization is the correct term, and if you hadn't missed class today, we wouldn't be having this conversation. Let's take a look at the Disney financial statements and the disclosure note on capitalized interest and I'll try to explain it all to you."

**Borrowings (in part):**
The Company capitalizes interest on assets constructed for its theme parks, resort and other property, and on theatrical and television productions in process. In 2004, 2003, and 2002, total interest capitalized was $35 million, $33 million, and $36 million, respectively.

**By the time you finish this chapter, you should be able to respond appropriately to the questions posed in this case. Compare your response to the solution provided at the end of the chapter.**

### QUESTIONS

1. Describe to Stan what it means to capitalize an expenditure. What is the general rule for determining which costs are capitalized when an operational asset is acquired? (page 453)
2. Which costs might be included in the initial cost of equipment? (page 455)
3. In what situations is interest capitalized rather than expensed? (page 471)
4. What is the three-step process used to determine the amount of interest capitalized? (page 472)
5. What is goodwill and how is it measured? Why didn't the amount of goodwill in Disney's 2004 balance sheet change from the prior year? (page 461)

**General Motors Corporation** has significant investments in the production facilities it uses to manufacture the automobiles it sells. On the other hand, the principal revenue-producing assets of **Microsoft Corporation** are the copyrights on its computer software that permit it the exclusive rights to earn profits from those products. Timber reserves provide major revenues to **Boise Cascade**. From a reporting perspective, we classify GM's production facilities as property, plant, and equipment;[1] Microsoft's copyrights as intangible assets, and Boise Cascade's timber reserves as natural resources. Together, these three noncurrent assets constitute **operational assets,** a term used to describe the broad category of *long-term, revenue-producing assets.* Unlike manufacturers, many service firms and merchandising companies rely primarily on people or investments in inventories rather than on operational assets to generate revenues. Even nonmanufacturing firms, though, typically have at least modest investments in buildings, equipment, and other operational assets.

The measurement and reporting issues pertaining to this group of assets include valuation at date of acquisition, disposition, the treatment of expenditures made over the life of these assets to maintain and improve them, the allocation of cost to reporting periods that benefit from their use, and impairment. The allocation of asset cost over time is called *depreciation* for plant and equipment, *amortization* for intangible assets, and *depletion* for natural resources. We focus on initial valuation and disposition in this chapter, and subsequent expenditures, cost allocation, and impairment in the next chapter.

# PART A VALUATION AT ACQUISITION

## Types of Operational Assets

For financial reporting purposes, operational assets typically are classified in two categories:

1. **Property, plant, and equipment.** Assets in this category include land, buildings, equipment, machinery, autos, and trucks. **Natural resources** such as oil and gas deposits, timber tracts, and mineral deposits also are included.
2. **Intangible assets.** Unlike other operational assets, these lack physical substance and the extent and timing of their future benefits typically are highly uncertain. They include patents, copyrights, trademarks, franchises, and goodwill.

Of course, every company maintains its own unique mix of operational assets. The way these assets are classified and combined for reporting purposes also varies from company to company. As an example, a recent **Tyson Foods, Inc.**, balance sheet reported net property, plant, and equipment of $3,964 million and $4,039 million at the end of fiscal 2004 and 2003, respectively. A disclosure note, shown in Graphic 10–1, provided the details.

In practice, some companies report intangibles as part of property, plant, and equipment. Some include intangible assets in the other asset category in the balance sheet, and others show intangibles as a separate balance sheet category. For example, **K-Swiss, Inc.**, manufacturer of an array of athletic footwear, reported intangibles as a separate category in a recent balance sheet:

| | ($ in thousands) | |
|---|---|---|
| **Assets (in part):** | **2004** | **2003** |
| Intangible assets | $4,700 | $7,301 |

The disclosure note shown in Graphic 10-2 provided the details.

Before we examine in detail specific operational assets, you should find it helpful to study the overview provided by Graphic 10–3 on page 454.

[1]These are sometimes called *plant assets* or *fixed assets.*

**Property, Plant, and Equipment and Depreciation (in part):**
The major categories of property, plant, and equipment and accumulated depreciation, at cost, at October 2, 2004, and September 27, 2003, are as follows:

| | ($ in millions) | |
|---|---|---|
| | 2004 | 2003 |
| Land | $ 111 | $ 113 |
| Buildings and leasehold improvements | 2,307 | 2,293 |
| Machinery and equipment | 3,981 | 3,886 |
| Land improvements and other | 194 | 184 |
| Buildings and equipment under construction | 218 | 177 |
| | 6,811 | 6,653 |
| Less: accumulated depreciation | 2,847 | 2,614 |
| Net property, plant, and equipment | $3,964 | $4,039 |

**GRAPHIC 10–1**
Property, Plant, and Equipment—Tyson Foods, Inc.

**Note C—Intangible Assets (in part)**
Intangible assets as of December 31 consist of the following (in thousands):

| | 2004 | 2003 |
|---|---|---|
| Goodwill | $4,618 | $4,772 |
| Trademarks | 2,761 | 5,382 |
| Other | 8 | 8 |
| Less: Accumulated amortization | (2,687) | (2,861) |
| | $4,700 | $7,301 |

**GRAPHIC 10–2**
Intangible Assets—K-Swiss, Inc.

## Costs to Be Capitalized

● LO1

Operational assets can be acquired through purchase, exchange, lease, donation, self-construction, or a business combination. We address acquisitions through leasing in Chapter 15 and acquisitions through business combinations later in this chapter and in Chapter 12.

The initial valuation of operational assets usually is quite simple. We know from prior study that assets are valued on the basis of their original costs. In Chapter 8 we introduced the concept of condition and location in determining the cost of inventory. This concept applies to the valuation of operational assets as well. The initial cost of an operational asset includes the purchase price and all expenditures necessary to bring the asset to its desired condition and location for use.

**FINANCIAL REPORTING CASE**

Q1, p. 451

**The initial cost of an operational asset includes the purchase price and all expenditures necessary to bring the asset to its desired condition and location for use.**

Our objective in identifying the costs of an asset is to distinguish the expenditures that produce future benefits from those that produce benefits only in the current period. The costs in the second group are recorded as expenses, but those in the first group are *capitalized.* That is, they are recorded as an asset and expensed in future periods.[2]

The distinction is not trivial. This point was unmistakably emphasized in the summer of 2002 when **WorldCom, Inc.** disclosed that it had improperly capitalized nearly $4 billion in expenditures related to the company's telecom network. This massive fraud resulted in one of the largest financial statement restatements in history and triggered the collapse of the once powerful corporation. Capitalizing rather than expensing these expenditures caused a

[2]Exceptions are land and certain intangible assets that have indefinite useful lives. Costs to acquire these assets also produce future benefits and therefore are capitalized, but unlike other operational assets, their costs are not systematically expensed in future periods as depreciation or amortization.

**GRAPHIC 10–3**

Operational Assets and Their Acquisition Costs

| Asset | Description | Typical Acquisition Costs |
|---|---|---|
| **Property, plant, and equipment** | Productive assets that derive their value from long-term use in operations rather than from resale. | All expenditures necessary to get the asset in condition and location for its intended use. |
| Equipment | Broad term that includes machinery, computers and other office equipment, vehicles, furniture, and fixtures. | Purchase price (less discounts), taxes, transportation, installation, testing, trial runs, reconditioning. |
| Land | Real property used in operations (land held for speculative investment or future use is reported as investments or other assets). | Purchase price, attorney's fees, title, recording fees, commissions, back taxes, mortgages, liens, clearing, filling, draining, removing old buildings. |
| Land improvements | Enhancements to property such as parking lots, driveways, private roads, fences, landscaping, and sprinkler systems. | Separately identifiable costs. |
| Buildings | Structures that include warehouses, plant facilities, and office buildings. | Purchase price, attorney's fees, commissions, reconditioning. |
| Natural resources | Productive assets that are physically consumed in operations such as timber, mineral deposits, and oil and gas reserves. | Acquisition, exploration, development, and restoration costs. |
| **Intangible Assets** | Productive assets that lack physical substance and have long-term but typically uncertain benefits. | All expenditures necessary to get the asset in the location and condition for its intended use. |
| Patents | Exclusive 20-year right to manufacture a product or use a process. | Purchase price, legal fees, filing fees, not including internal R&D. |
| Copyrights | Exclusive right to benefit from a creative work such as a song, film, painting, photograph, or book. | Purchase price, legal fees, filing fees, not including internal R&D. |
| Trademarks (tradenames) | Exclusive right to display a word, a slogan, a symbol, or an emblem that distinctively identifies a company, product, or a service. | Purchase price, legal fees, filing fees, not including internal R&D. |
| Franchises | A contractual arrangement under which a franchisor grants the franchisee the exclusive right to use the franchisor's trademark or tradename. | Franchise fee plus any legal fees. |
| Goodwill | The unique value of the company as a whole over and above all identifiable assets. | Excess of the purchase price of the company over the fair value of the net assets acquired. |

substantial overstatement of reported income for 2001 and the first quarter of 2002, in fact, producing impressive profits where losses should have been reported. If the deception had not been discovered, not only would income for 2001 and 2002 have been overstated, but income for many years into the future would have been understated as the fraudulent capitalized assets were depreciated. Of course, the balance sheet also would have overstated the assets and equity of the company.

## PROPERTY, PLANT, AND EQUIPMENT

**FINANCIAL REPORTING CASE**

Q2, p. 451

**Cost of Equipment.** Equipment is a broad term that encompasses machinery used in manufacturing, computers and other office equipment, vehicles, furniture, and fixtures. The cost of equipment includes the purchase price plus any sales tax (less any discounts received from the seller), transportation costs paid by the buyer to transport the asset to the location in which it will be used, expenditures for installation, testing, legal fees to establish title, and any other costs of bringing the asset to its condition and location for use. To the extent that these costs can be identified and measured, they should be included in the asset's initial valuation rather than expensed currently.

Although most costs can be identified easily, others are more difficult. For example, the costs of training personnel to operate machinery could be considered a cost necessary to make the asset ready for use. However, because it is difficult to measure the amount of training costs associated with specific assets, these costs usually are expensed. Consider Illustration 10–1.

**ILLUSTRATION 10–1**
Initial Cost of Equipment

Central Machine Tools purchased an industrial lathe to be used in its manufacturing process. The purchase price was $62,000. Central paid a freight company $1,000 to transport the machine to its plant location plus $300 shipping insurance. In addition, the machine had to be installed and mounted on a special platform built specifically for the machine at a cost of $1,200. After installation, several trial runs were made to ensure proper operation. The cost of these trials including wasted materials was $600. At what amount should Central capitalize the lathe?

| | |
|---|---:|
| Purchase price | $62,000 |
| Freight and handling | 1,000 |
| Insurance during shipping | 300 |
| Special foundation | 1,200 |
| Trial runs | 600 |
| | $65,100 |

Each of the expenditures described was necessary to bring the machine to its condition and location for use and should be capitalized and expensed in the future periods in which the asset is used.

**Cost of Land.** The cost of land also should include each expenditure needed to get the land ready for its intended use. These include the purchase price plus closing costs such as fees for the attorney, real estate agent commissions, title and title search, and recording. If the property is subject to back taxes, liens, mortgages, or other obligations, these amounts are included also. In addition, any expenditures such as clearing, filling, draining, and even removing old buildings that are needed to prepare the land for its intended use are part of the land's cost. Proceeds from the sale of salvaged materials from old buildings torn down after purchase reduce the cost of land. Illustration 10–2 provides an example.

**Land improvements.** It's important to distinguish between the cost of land and the cost of **land improvements** because land has an indefinite life and land improvements usually do not. Examples of land improvements include the cost of parking lots, driveways, and private roads and the costs of fences and lawn and garden sprinkler systems. Costs of these assets are separately identified and capitalized. We depreciate their cost over periods benefited by their use.

**The costs of *land improvements* are capitalized and depreciated.**

**ILLUSTRATION 10–2**
Initial Cost of Land

The Byers Structural Metal Company purchased a six-acre tract of land and an existing building for $500,000. The company plans to raze the old building and construct a new office building on the site. In addition to the purchase price, the company made the following expenditures at closing of the purchase:

| | |
|---|---|
| Title insurance | $ 3,000 |
| Commissions | 16,000 |
| Property taxes | 6,000 |

Shortly after closing, the company paid a contractor $10,000 to tear down the old building and remove it from the site. An additional $5,000 was paid to grade the land. The $6,000 in property taxes included $4,000 of delinquent taxes paid by Byers on behalf of the seller and $2,000 attributable to the portion of the current fiscal year after the purchase date. What should be the capitalized cost of the land?

| | |
|---|---|
| Capitalized cost of land: | |
| Purchase price of land (and building to be razed) | $500,000 |
| Title insurance | 3,000 |
| Commissions | 16,000 |
| Delinquent property taxes | 4,000 |
| Cost of removing old building | 10,000 |
| Cost of grading | 5,000 |
| Total cost of land | $538,000 |

Two thousand dollars of the property taxes relate only to the current period and should be expensed. Other costs were necessary to acquire the land and are capitalized.

**Cost of Buildings.** The cost of acquiring a building usually includes realtor commissions and legal fees in addition to the purchase price. Quite often a building must be refurbished, remodeled, or otherwise modified to suit the needs of the new owner. These reconditioning costs are part of the building's acquisition cost. When a building is constructed rather than purchased, unique accounting issues are raised. We discuss these in the "Self-Constructed Assets" section of this chapter.

**Cost of Natural Resources.** **Natural resources** that provide long-term benefits are reported as property, plant, and equipment. These include timber tracts, mineral deposits, and oil and gas deposits. They can be distinguished from other assets by the fact that their benefits are derived from their physical consumption. For example, mineral deposits are physically diminishing as the minerals are extracted from the ground and either sold or used in the production process.[3] On the contrary, equipment, land, and buildings produce benefits for a company through their *use* in the production of goods and services. Unlike those of natural resources, their physical characteristics usually remain unchanged during their useful lives.

**The cost of a natural resource includes the *acquisition costs* for the use of land, the *exploration* and *development costs* incurred before production begins, and *restoration costs* incurred during or at the end of extraction.**

Sometimes a company buys natural resources from another company. In that case, initial valuation is simply the purchase price plus any other costs necessary to bring the asset to condition and location for use. More frequently, though, the company will develop these assets. In this situation, the initial valuation can include (a) acquisition costs, (b) exploration costs, (c) development costs, and (d) restoration costs. **Acquisition costs** are the amounts paid to acquire the rights to explore for undiscovered natural resources or to extract proven natural resources. **Exploration costs** are expenditures such as drilling a well, or excavating a mine, or any other costs of searching for natural resources. **Development costs** are incurred after the resource has been discovered but before production begins. They include a variety of costs such as expenditures for tunnels, wells, and shafts. It is not unusual for the cost of a natural resource, either purchased or developed, also to include estimated **restoration costs.** These are costs to restore land or other property to its original condition after extraction of the natural resource ends. Because restoration expenditures occur later—after

[3]Because of this characteristic, natural resources sometimes are called *wasting assets*.

production begins—they initially represent an obligation incurred in conjunction with an asset retirement. Restoration costs are one example of *asset retirement obligations,* the topic of the next subsection.

On the other hand, the costs of heavy equipment and other assets a company uses during drilling or excavation usually are not considered part of the cost of the natural resource itself. Instead, they are considered depreciable plant and equipment. However, if an asset used in the development of a natural resource cannot be moved and has no alternative use, its depreciable life is limited by the useful life of the natural resource.

**Asset Retirement Obligations.** Sometimes a company incurs obligations associated with the disposition of an operational asset, often as a result of acquiring that asset. For example, an oil and gas exploration company might be required to restore land to its original condition after extraction is completed. Until recently, there was considerable diversity in the ways companies accounted for these obligations. Some companies recognized these **asset retirement obligations** (AROs) gradually over the life of the asset while others did not recognize the obligations until the asset was retired or sold.

**As asset retirement obligation (ARO) is measured at fair value and is recognized as a liability and corresponding increase in asset valuation.**

*SFAS No. 143* now requires that an existing legal obligation associated with the retirement of a tangible, long-lived asset be recognized as a liability and measured at fair value. When the liability is credited, the offsetting debit is to the related operational asset.[4] These retirement obligations could arise in connection with several types of operational assets. We introduce the topic here because they are most likely with natural resources. Let's consider some of the provisions of this new accounting standard.

**Scope.** AROs arise only from *legal* obligations associated with the retirement of a tangible long-lived asset that result from the acquisition, construction, or development and (or) normal operation of a long-lived asset.

**Recognition.** A retirement obligation might arise at the inception of an asset's life or during its operating life. For instance, an offshore oil-and-gas production facility typically incurs its removal obligation when it begins operating. On the other hand, a landfill or a mining operation might incur a reclamation obligation gradually over the life of the asset as space is consumed with waste or as the mine is excavated.

**Measurement.** A company recognizes the fair value of an ARO in the period it's incurred. The liability increases the valuation of the operational asset. Usually, the fair value is estimated by calculating the present value of estimated future cash outflows.

**Present value calculations.** Traditionally, the way uncertainty has been considered in present value calculations has been by discounting the "best estimate" of future cash flows applying a discount rate that has been adjusted to reflect the uncertainty or risk of those cash flows. That's not the approach we take here. Instead, we follow the approach described in the FASB's Concept Statement No. 7[5] which is to adjust the cash flows, not the discount rate, for the uncertainty or risk of those cash flows. This **expected cash flow approach** incorporates specific probabilities of cash flows into the analysis. We use a discount rate equal to the *credit-adjusted risk free rate.* The higher a company's credit risk, the higher will be the discount rate. All other uncertainties or risks are incorporated into the cash flow probabilities. We first considered an illustration of this approach in Chapter 6. Illustration 10–3 demonstrates the approach in connection with the acquisition of a natural resource.

As we discuss in Chapter 11, the cost of the coal mine is allocated to future periods as *depletion* using a depletion rate based on the estimated amount of coal discovered. The $600,000 cost of the excavation equipment, less any anticipated residual value, is allocated to future periods as *depreciation.*

[4]"Accounting for Asset Retirement Obligations," *Statement of Financial Accounting Standards No. 143* (Norwalk, Conn.: FASB, 2001).

[5]"Using Cash Flow Information and Present Value in Accounting Measurements," *Statement of Financial Accounting Concepts No. 7* (Norwalk, Conn.: FASB, 2000).

**ILLUSTRATION 10–3**
Cost of Natural Resources

The Jackson Mining Company paid $1,000,000 for the right to explore for a coal deposit on 500 acres of land in Pennsylvania. Costs of exploring for the coal deposit totaled $800,000 and intangible development costs incurred in digging and erecting the mine shaft were $500,000. In addition, Jackson purchased new excavation equipment for the project at a cost of $600,000. After the coal is removed from the site, the equipment will be sold.

Jackson is required by its contract to restore the land to a condition suitable for recreational use after it extracts the coal. The company has provided the following three cash flow possibilities (A, B and C) for the restoration costs to be paid in three years, after extraction is completed:

| | Cash Outflow | Probability |
|---|---|---|
| A | $500,000 | 30% |
| B | 600,000 | 50% |
| C | 700,000 | 20% |

The company's credit-adjusted risk free interest rate is 8%.
Total capitalized cost for the coal deposit is:

| | |
|---|---|
| Purchase of rights to explore | $1,000,000 |
| Exploration costs | 800,000 |
| Development costs | 500,000 |
| Restoration costs | 468,360* |
| Total cost of coal deposit | $2,768,360 |

*Present value of expected cash outflow for restoration costs (asset retirement obligation):
$500,000 × 30% = $150,000
600,000 × 50% = 300,000
700,000 × 20% = 140,000
$590,000 × .79383 = $468,360
(.79383 is the present value of $1, $n$ = 3, $i$ = 8%)

**Journal Entries:**

| | | |
|---|---|---|
| Coal mine (determined above) | 2,768,360 | |
| Cash ($1,000,000 + 800,000 + 500,000) | | 2,300,000 |
| Asset retirement liability (determined above) | | 468,360 |
| Excavation equipment | 600,000 | |
| Cash (cost) | | 600,000 |

The difference between the asset retirement liability of $468,360 and the probability-weighted expected cash outflow of $590,000 is recognized as accretion expense, an operating expense, over the three-year excavation period. This process increases the liability to $590,000 by the end of the excavation period.

| Year | Accretion Expense | Increase in Balance | Asset Retirement Obligation |
|---|---|---|---|
| | | | 468,360 |
| 1 | 8% (468,360) = 37,469 | 37,469 | 505,829 |
| 2 | 8% (505,829) = 40,466 | 40,466 | 546,295 |
| 3 | 8% (546,295) = 43,705* | 43,705 | 590,000 |

*rounded

If the actual restoration costs are more (less) than the $590,000, a loss (gain) on retirement of the obligation is recognized for the difference.

**St. Mary Land & Exploration Company** is engaged in the exploration, development, acquisition, and production of natural gas and crude oil. In 2003, St. Mary adopted the provisions of *SFAS No. 143* and, as a result, reported a $25 million asset retirement obligation in its balance sheet. Graphic 10–4 describes the company's adoption and provides a summary of the requirements of the standard.

**GRAPHIC 10–4**
Disclosure of Asset Retirement Obligations—St. Mary Land & Exploration Company

**9. Asset Retirement Obligations (in part)**
Effective January 1, 2003, the Company adopted the provisions of *SFAS No. 143,* "Accounting for Asset Retirement Obligations." *SFAS No. 143* generally applies to legal obligations associated with the retirement of long-lived assets that result from the acquisition, construction, development and/or the normal operation of a long-lived asset. *SFAS No. 143* requires the Company to recognize an estimated liability for costs associated with the abandonment of its oil and gas properties. As of January 1, 2003, the Company recognized the future cost to abandon oil and gas properties over the estimated economic life of the oil and gas properties in accordance with the provisions of *SFAS No. 143.* A liability for the fair value of an asset retirement obligation with a corresponding increase to the carrying value of the related long-lived asset is recorded at the time a well is completed or acquired. The increase in carrying value is included in proved oil and gas properties on the consolidated balance sheets. The Company depletes the amount added to proved oil and gas property costs and recognizes accretion expense in connection with the discounted liability over the remaining life of the respective oil and gas properties.

The estimated liability is based on historical experience in abandoning wells, estimated economic lives, external estimates as to the cost to abandon the wells in the future, and federal and state regulatory requirements. The liability is discounted using a credit-adjusted risk-free rate of approximately 7.25%. Revisions to the liability could occur due to changes in estimated abandonment costs or well economic lives, or if federal or state regulators enact new requirements regarding the abandonment of wells.

**Asset retirement obligations could result from the acquisition of many different types of tangible operational assets, not just natural resources.**

It is important to understand that asset retirement obligations could result from the acquisition of many different types of tangible operational assets, not just natural resources. For example, **Dow Chemical Company** reported a $57 million asset retirement liability in its 2004 balance sheet related to anticipated demolition and remediation activities at its manufacturing sites in the United States, Germany, and France.

Sometimes, after exploration or development, it becomes apparent that continuing the project is economically infeasible. If that happens, any costs incurred are expensed rather than capitalized. An exception is in the oil and gas industry, where we have two generally accepted accounting alternatives for accounting for projects that prove unsuccessful. We discuss these alternatives in Appendix 10.

## INTANGIBLE ASSETS

***Intangible assets* generally represent exclusive rights that provide benefits to the owner.**

**Intangible assets** include such items as patents, copyrights, trademarks, franchises, and goodwill. Despite their lack of physical substance, these assets can be extremely valuable resources for a company. For example, **Interbrand Sampson**, the world's leading branding consulting company, recently estimated the value of the **Coca-Cola** trademark to be $67 billion.[6] In general, intangible assets refer to the ownership of exclusive rights that provide benefits to the owner in the production of goods and services.

The issues involved in accounting for intangibles are similar to those of other operational assets. One key difference, though, is that the future benefits that we attribute to intangible assets usually are much less certain than those attributed to tangible operational assets. For example, will the new toy for which a company acquires a patent be accepted by the market? If so, will it be a blockbuster like Beanie Babies or Rubik's Cube, or will it be only a moderate success? Will it have lasting appeal like Barbie dolls, or will it be a short-term fad? In short, it's often very difficult to anticipate the timing, and even the existence, of future benefits attributable to many intangible assets. In fact, this uncertainty is a discriminating characteristic of intangible assets that perhaps better distinguishes them from tangible assets than their lack of physical substance. After all, other assets, too, do not exist physically but are not considered intangible assets. Accounts receivable and prepaid expenses, for example, have no physical substance and yet are reported among tangible assets.

[6]This $67 billion represents an estimate of the market value to the company at the time the estimate was made, not the historical cost valuation that appears in the balance sheet of Coca-Cola.

**Intangible assets with finite useful lives are amortized; intangible assets with indefinite useful lives are not amortized.**

Companies can either (1) *purchase* intangible assets from other entities (existing patent, copyright, trademark, or franchise rights) or (2) *develop* intangible assets internally (say, develop a new product or process that is then patented). In either case, we amortize its cost, unless it has an indefinite useful life.[7] Also, just like other operational assets, intangibles are subject to asset impairment rules. We discuss amortization and impairment in Chapter 11. In this chapter, we consider the acquisition cost of intangibles.

**Purchased intangibles are valued at their original cost.**

The initial valuation of purchased intangibles usually is quite simple. We value a purchased intangible at its original cost, which includes its purchase price and all other costs necessary to bring it to condition and location for intended use. For example, if a company purchases a patent from another entity, it might pay legal fees and filing fees in addition to the purchase price. We value intangible assets acquired in exchange for stock, or for other nonmonetary assets, or with deferred payment contracts exactly as we do other operational assets. Let's look briefly at the costs of purchasing some of the more common intangible assets.

**Patents.** A **patent** is an exclusive right to manufacture a product or to use a process. This right is granted by the U.S. Patent Office for a period of 20 years. In essence, the holder of a patent has a monopoly on the use, manufacture, or sale of the product or process. If a patent is purchased from an inventor or another individual or company, the amount paid is its initial valuation. The cost might also include such other costs as legal and filing fees to secure the patent. Holders of patents often need to defend a patent in court against infringement. Any attorney fees and other costs of successfully defending a patent are added to the patent account.

When a patent is *developed internally,* the research and development costs of doing so are expensed as incurred. We discuss research and development in more detail in a later section. We capitalize legal and filing fees to secure the patent, even if internally developed.

**Copyrights.** A **copyright** is an exclusive right of protection given to a creator of a published work, such as a song, film, painting, photograph, or book. Copyrights are protected by law and give the creator the exclusive right to reproduce and sell the artistic or published work for the life of the creator plus 70 years. Accounting for the costs of copyrights is virtually identical to that of patents.

**Trademarks.** A **trademark,** also called **tradename,** is an exclusive right to display a word, a slogan, a symbol, or an emblem that distinctively identifies a company, a product, or a service. The trademark can be registered with the U.S. Patent Office which protects the trademark from use by others for a period of 10 years. The registration can be renewed for an indefinite number of 10-year periods, so a trademark is an example of an intangible asset whose useful life could be indefinite.

**Trademarks or tradenames often are considered to have indefinite useful lives.**

Trademarks or tradenames often are acquired through a business combination. As an example, in 2002, **Hewlett-Packard Company (HP)** acquired all of the outstanding stock of **Compaq Computer Corporation** for $24 billion. Of that amount, $1.4 billion was assigned to the Compaq tradename. HP stated in a disclosure note that this ". . . intangible asset will not be amortized because it has an indefinite remaining useful life based on many factors and considerations, including the length of time that the Compaq name has been in use, the Compaq brand awareness and market position and the plans for continued use of the Compaq brand within a portion of HP's overall product portfolio."

Trademarks can be very valuable. The estimated value of $67 billion for the Coca-Cola trademark mentioned previously is a good example. Note that the cost of the trademark reported in the balance sheet is far less than the estimate of its worth to the company. The Coca-Cola Company's 2004 balance sheet disclosed trademarks at a cost of only $2 billion.

***Franchise* operations are among the most common ways of doing business.**

**Franchises.** A **franchise** is a contractual arrangement under which the franchisor grants the franchisee the exclusive right to use the franchisor's trademark or tradename within a geographical area, usually for a specified period of time. Many popular retail businesses such as fast food outlets, automobile dealerships, and motels are franchises. For example, the last time you ordered a hamburger at McDonald's, you were probably dealing with a franchise.

[7] "Goodwill and Other Intangible Assets," *Statement of Financial Accounting Standards No. 142* (Norwalk, Conn.: FASB, 2001).

The owner of that McDonald's outlet paid **McDonald's Corporation** a fee in exchange for the exclusive right to use the McDonald's name and to sell its products within a specified geographical area. In addition, many franchisors provide other benefits to the franchisee, such as participating in the construction of the retail outlet, training of employees, and national advertising.

Payments to the franchisor usually include an initial payment plus periodic payments over the life of the franchise agreement. The franchisee capitalizes as an intangible asset, franchise, the initial franchise fee plus any legal costs associated with the contract agreement. The asset is then amortized over the life of the franchise agreement. The periodic payments usually relate to services provided by the franchisor on a continuing basis and are expensed as incurred.

Most purchased intangibles are *specifically identifiable.* That is, cost can be directly associated with a specific intangible right. An exception is goodwill, which we discuss next.

**Goodwill.** Goodwill is a unique intangible asset in that its cost can't be directly associated with any specifically identifiable right and it is not separable from the company itself. It represents the unique value of a company as a whole over and above its identifiable tangible and intangible assets. Goodwill can emerge from a company's clientele and reputation, its trained employees and management team, its favorable business location, and any other unique features of the company that can't be associated with a specific asset.

*Goodwill* can only be purchased through the acquisition of another company.

FINANCIAL REPORTING CASE

Q5, p. 451

Because goodwill can't be separated from a company, it's not possible for a buyer to acquire it without also acquiring the whole company or a substantial portion of it. Goodwill will appear as an asset in a balance sheet only when it was purchased in connection with the acquisition of another company. In that case, the capitalized cost of goodwill equals the purchase price of the company less the fair value of the net assets acquired. The fair value of the net assets equals the fair value of all identifiable tangible and intangible assets less the market value of any liabilities of the selling company assumed by the buyer. Goodwill is a residual asset; it's the amount left after other assets are identified and valued. Consider Illustration 10–4.

*Goodwill* is the excess of the purchase price over the fair market value of the net assets acquired.

ILLUSTRATION 10–4

Goodwill

The Smithson Corporation acquired all of the outstanding common stock of the Rider Corporation in exchange for $18 million cash.* Smithson assumed all of Rider's long-term debts which have a fair value of $12 million at the date of acquisition. The fair values of all identifiable assets of Rider are as follows ($ in millions):

| | |
|---|---|
| Receivables | $ 5 |
| Inventory | 7 |
| Property, plant, and equipment | 9 |
| Patent | 4 |
| Total | $25 |

The cost of the goodwill resulting from the acquisition is $5 million:

| | | |
|---|---|---|
| Purchase price | | $18 |
| Less: fair value of net assets | | |
| Assets | $25 | |
| Less: liabilities assumed | (12) | (13) |
| Goodwill | | $ 5 |

The Smithson Corporation records the acquisition as follows:

| | | |
|---|---|---|
| Receivables (fair value) | 5 | |
| Inventory (fair value) | 7 | |
| Property, plant, and equipment (fair value) | 9 | |
| Patent (fair value) | 4 | |
| Goodwill (difference) | 5 | |
| Liabilities (fair value) | | 12 |
| Cash (purchase price) | | 18 |

*Determining the amount a purchaser is willing to pay for a company in excess of the identifiable net assets is a question of determining the value of a company as a whole. This question is addressed in most introductory and advanced finance textbooks.

**GLOBAL PERSPECTIVE**

In the United States, goodwill is capitalized and not amortized. Internationally, the treatment of goodwill varies. Some countries, such as Japan, capitalize and amortize goodwill. *International Financial Reporting Standard 3,* issued in 2004 by the IASB, requires goodwill to be recognized as an asset. As in the United States, goodwill is not amortized and must be tested annually for impairment. Beginning in 2005, publicly traded companies in the European Union and Australia will prepare their consolidated financial statements applying this standard.

**ADDITIONAL CONSIDERATION**

It's possible for the fair value of net assets to be greater than the purchase price. The fact that the sum of the separate values of the assets is greater than their combined values indicates that bringing them together actually reduced their value. This effect is rare and often is referred to as *negative goodwill.* Some accountants have argued that this negative amount should be disclosed in the balance sheet as a deduction from other assets. GAAP generally requires the simpler treatment of recognizing the acquired assets at their combined purchase price instead of their individual fair values.

Of course, a company can develop its own goodwill through advertising, training, and other efforts. In fact, most do. However, a company must expense all such costs incurred in the internal generation of goodwill. By not capitalizing these items, accountants realize that the matching principle is violated because many of these expenditures do result in significant future benefits. Also, it's difficult to compare two companies when one has purchased goodwill and the other has not. But imagine how difficult it would be to associate these expenditures with any objective measure of goodwill. In essence, we have a situation where the characteristic of reliability overshadows relevance.

**Goodwill, along with other intangible assets with indefinite useful lives, is not amortized.**

As we discussed in Chapter 1, recent accounting standards have significantly changed the way we account for business combinations. Before these new standards became effective in 2001, we amortized (expensed over time) goodwill just like any other intangible asset. This no longer is the case. Now, just like for other intangible assets that have indefinite useful lives, *we do not amortize goodwill.* This makes it imperative that companies make every effort to identify specific intangibles other than goodwill that they acquire in a business combination since goodwill is the amount left after other assets are identified.

***SFAS 141* requires that in a business combination an intangible asset must be recognized as an asset apart from goodwill if it arises from contractual or other legal rights or is separable.**

In keeping with that goal, *SFAS 141* provides guidelines for determining which intangibles should be separately recognized and valued. Specifically, an intangible should be recognized as an asset apart from goodwill if it arises from contractual or other legal rights or is capable of being separated from the acquired entity. Possibilities are patents, trademarks, copyrights, and franchise agreements, and such items as customer lists, license agreements, order backlogs, employment contracts, and noncompetition agreements.[8] In past years, some of these intangibles, if present in a business combination, often were included in the cost of goodwill.[9]

## Lump-Sum Purchases

● LO2

It's not unusual for a group of operational assets to be acquired for a single sum. If these assets are indistinguishable, for example 10 identical delivery trucks purchased for a lump-sum price of $150,000, valuation is obvious. Each of the trucks would be valued at $15,000 ($150,000 ÷ 10). However, if the lump-sum purchase involves different assets, it's necessary to allocate the lump-sum acquisition price among the separate items. The assets acquired may have different characteristics and different useful lives. For example, the

[8]"Business Combinations," *Statement of Financial Accounting Standards No. 141* (Norwalk, Conn.: FASB, 2001).

[9]An assembled workforce is an example of an intangible that is not recognized as a separate asset. A workforce does not represent a contractual or legal right, nor is it separable from the company as a whole.

acquisition of a factory may include assets that are significantly different such as land, building, and equipment.

The allocation is made in proportion to the individual assets' relative market values. This process is best explained by an example in Illustration 10–5.

**ILLUSTRATION 10–5**
Lump-Sum Purchase

The Smyrna Hand & Edge Tools Company purchased an existing factory for a single sum of $2,000,000. The price included title to the land, the factory building, and the manufacturing equipment in the building, a patent on a process the equipment uses, and inventories of raw materials. An independent appraisal estimated the market values of the assets (if purchased separately) at $330,000 for the land, $550,000 for the building, $660,000 for the equipment, $440,000 for the patent and $220,000 for the inventories. The lump-sum purchase price of $2,000,000 is allocated to the separate assets as follows:

| | Market Values | |
|---|---|---|
| Land | $ 330,000 | 15% |
| Building | 550,000 | 25 |
| Equipment | 660,000 | 30 |
| Patent | 440,000 | 20 |
| Inventories | 220,000 | 10 |
| Total | $2,200,000 | 100% |

| | | | |
|---|---|---|---|
| Land | (15% × $2,000,000) | 300,000 | |
| Building | (25% × $2,000,000) | 500,000 | |
| Equipment | (30% × $2,000,000) | 600,000 | |
| Patent | (20% × $2,000,000) | 400,000 | |
| Inventories | (10% × $2,000,000) | 200,000 | |
| Cash | | | 2,000,000 |

**The total purchase price is allocated in proportion to the relative market values of the assets acquired.**

The relative market value percentages are multiplied by the lump-sum purchase price to determine the initial valuation of each of the separate assets. Notice that the lump-sum purchase includes inventories, which is not an operational asset. The procedure used here to allocate the purchase price in a lump-sum acquisition pertains to any type of asset mix, not just to operational assets.

**ETHICAL DILEMMA**

Grandma's Cookie Company purchased a factory building. The company controller, Don Nelson, is in the process of allocating the lump-sum purchase price between land and building. Don suggests to the company's chief financial officer, Judith Prince, that they fudge a little by allocating a disproportionately higher share of the price to land. Don reasons that this will reduce depreciation expense, boost income, increase their profit-sharing bonus, and hopefully, increase the price of the company's stock. Judith has some reservations about this because the higher reported income will also cause income taxes to be higher than they would be if a correct allocation of the purchase price is made.

What are the ethical issues? What stakeholders' interests are in conflict?

## Noncash Acquisitions

Companies sometimes acquire operational assets without paying cash but instead by issuing debt or equity securities, receiving donated assets, or exchanging other assets. *The controlling principle in each of these situations is that in any noncash transaction (not just those dealing with operational assets), the components of the transaction are recorded at their fair values.* The first indicator of fair value is the fair value of the assets, debt, or equity securities given. Sometimes the fair value of the assets received is used when their fair value is more clearly evident than the fair value of the assets given.

**Assets acquired in noncash transactions are valued at the fair value of the assets given or the fair value of the assets received, whichever is more clearly evident.**

## DEFERRED PAYMENTS

● LO3

A company can acquire an operational asset by giving the seller a promise to pay cash in the future and thus creating a liability, usually a note payable. The initial valuation of the asset is, again, quite simple as long as the note payable explicitly requires the payment of interest at a realistic interest rate. For example, suppose a machine is acquired for \$15,000 and the buyer signs a note requiring the payment of \$15,000 sometime in the future *plus* interest in the meantime at a realistic interest rate. The machine would be valued at \$15,000 and the transaction recorded as follows:

| | | |
|---|---|---|
| Machine | 15,000 | |
| Note payable | | 15,000 |

We know from our discussion of the time value of money in Chapter 6 that most liabilities are valued at the present value of future cash payments, reflecting an appropriate time value of money. As long as the note payable explicitly contains a realistic interest rate, the present value will equal the face value of the note, \$15,000 in our previous example. This also should be equal to the fair value of the machine purchased. On the other hand, when an interest rate is not specified or is unrealistic, determining the cost of the asset is less straightforward. In that case, the accountant should look beyond the form of the transaction and record its substance. Consider Illustration 10–6.

**ILLUSTRATION 10–6**
Asset Acquired with Debt—Present Value of Note Indicative of Fair Value

On January 2, 2006, the Midwestern Steam Gas Corporation purchased an industrial furnace. In payment, Midwestern signed a noninterest-bearing note requiring \$50,000 to be paid on December 31, 2007. If Midwestern had borrowed cash to buy the furnace, the bank would have required an interest rate of 10%.

**Some portion of the payment(s) required by a noninterest-bearing note in reality is interest.**

On the surface, it might appear that Midwestern is paying \$50,000 for the furnace, the eventual cash payment. However, when you note that the agreement specifies no interest even though the payment won't be made for two years, it becomes obvious that a portion of the \$50,000 payment is not actually payment for the furnace, but instead is interest on the note. At what amount should Midwestern value the furnace and the related note payable?

**Noncash transactions are recorded at the fair value of the items exchanged.**

The answer is fair value, as it is for any noncash transaction. This might be the fair value of the furnace or the fair value of the note. Let's say, in this situation, that the furnace is custom-built, so its cash price is unavailable. But Midwestern can determine the fair value of the note payable by computing the present value of the cash payments at the appropriate interest rate of 10%. The amount actually paid for the machine, then, is the present value of the cash flows called for by the loan agreement, discounted at the market rate—10% in this case.

$$PV = \$50,000\ (.82645^{*}) = \$41,323$$

*Present value of \$1: $n = 2$, $i = 10\%$ (from Table 2)

So the furnace should be recorded at its *real* cost, \$41,323, as follows:[10]

**The economic essence of a transaction should prevail over its outward appearance.**

| | | |
|---|---|---|
| Furnace (determined above) | 41,323 | |
| Discount on note payable (difference) | 8,677 | |
| Note payable (face amount) | | 50,000 |

Notice that the note also is recorded at \$41,323, its present value, but this is accomplished by using a contra account, called *discount on note payable,* for the difference between the

[10]The entry shown assumes the note is recorded using the gross method. By the net method, a discount account is not used and the note is simply recorded at present value.

| | | |
|---|---|---|
| Machine | 41,323 | |
| Note payable | | 41,323 |

face amount of the note ($50,000) and its present value ($41,323). The difference of $8,677 is the portion of the eventual $50,000 payment that represents interest and is recognized as interest expense over the life of the note.

Assuming that Midwestern's fiscal year-end is December 31 and that adjusting entries are recorded only at the end of each year, the company would record the following entries at the end of 2006 and 2007 to accrue interest and the payment of the note:

| | | |
|---|---|---|
| **December 31, 2006** | | |
| Interest expense ($41,323 × 10%) | 4,132 | |
| Discount on note payable | | 4,132 |
| **December 31, 2007** | | |
| Interest expense ([$41,323 + 4,132]* × 10%) | 4,545 | |
| Discount on note payable | | 4,545 |
| Note payable (face amount) | 50,000 | |
| Cash | | 50,000 |

*The 2006 unpaid interest increases the amount owed by $4,132.

**Note payable**

| | | | |
|---|---|---|---|
| Jan. 1, 2006 | | 50,000 | |
| | 50,000 | | Dec. 31, 2007 |
| Bal. 12/31/07 | | 0 | |

**Discount on note payable**

| | | | |
|---|---|---|---|
| | 8,677 | Jan. 1, 2006 | |
| Dec. 31, 2006 | | 4,132 | |
| Dec. 31, 2007 | | 4,545 | |
| | 0 | Bal. 12/31/07 | |

Sometimes, the fair value of an asset acquired in a noncash transaction is readily available from price lists, previous purchases, or otherwise. In that case, this fair value may be more clearly evident than the fair value of the note and it would serve as the best evidence of the exchange value of the transaction. As an example, let's consider Illustration 10–7.

**ILLUSTRATION 10–7**
**Noninterest-Bearing Note—Fair Value of Asset Is Known**

On January 2, 2006, Dennison, Inc. purchased a machine and signed a noninterest-bearing note in payment. The note requires the company to pay $100,000 on December 31, 2008. Dennison is not sure what interest rate appropriately reflects the time value of money. However, price lists indicate the machine could have been purchased for cash at a price of $79,383.

Dennison records both the asset and liability at $79,383 on January 2:

| | | |
|---|---|---|
| Machine (cash price) | 79,383 | |
| Discount on note payable (difference) | 20,617 | |
| Note payable (face amount) | | 100,000 |

In this situation, we infer the present value of the note from the fair value of the asset. Again, the difference between the note's $79,383 present value and the cash payment of $100,000 represents interest. We can determine the interest rate that is implicit in the agreement as follows:

$$\$79{,}383 \text{ (present value)} = \$100{,}000 \text{ (face amount)} \times \text{PV factor}$$

$$\$79{,}383 \div \$100{,}000 = .79383^*$$

*Present value of $1: $n = 3$, $i = ?$ (from Table 2, $i = 8\%$)

We refer to the 8% rate as the *implicit rate of interest.* Dennison records interest each year at 8% in the same manner as demonstrated in Illustration 10–6 and discussed in greater depth in Chapter 14.

We now turn our attention to the acquisition of operational assets acquired in exchange for equity securities or through donation.

## ISSUANCE OF EQUITY SECURITIES

● LO4

The most common situation in which equity securities are issued for operational assets occurs when small companies incorporate and the owner or owners contribute assets to the new corporation in exchange for ownership securities, usually common stock. Because the common shares are not publicly traded, it's difficult to determine their fair value. In that case, the fair value of the assets received by the corporation is probably the better indicator of the transaction's exchange value. In other situations, particularly those involving corporations whose stock is actively traded, the market value of the shares is the best indication of fair value. Consider Illustration 10–8.

**ILLUSTRATION 10–8**
Asset Acquired by Issuing Equity Securities

On March 31, 2006, the Elcorn Company issued 10,000 shares of its nopar common stock in exchange for land. On the date of the transaction, the market value of the common stock was $20 per share. The journal entry to record this transaction is:

| | | |
|---|---|---|
| Land . . . . . . . . . . . . . . . . . . . . . . . . . . . . . . . . . . . . . . . . . . . . . | 200,000 | |
| Common stock (10,000 shares × $20) . . . . . . . . . . . . . . . . . . . . . . | | 200,000 |

Assets acquired by issuing common stock are valued at the fair value of the securities or the fair value of the assets, whichever is more clearly evident.

If the market value of the common stock had not been reliably determinable, the value of the land as determined through an independent appraisal would be used as the cost of the land and the value of the common stock.

## DONATED ASSETS

*Donated assets* are recorded at their fair values.

On occasion, companies acquire operational assets through donation. The donation usually is an enticement to do something that benefits the donor. For example, the developer of an industrial park might pay some of the costs of building a manufacturing facility to entice a company to locate in its park. Companies record assets donated by unrelated parties at their fair values based on either an available market price or an appraisal value. This should not be considered a departure from historical cost valuation. Instead, it is equivalent to the donor contributing cash to the company and the company using the cash to acquire the asset.

Revenue is credited for the amount paid by an unrelated party.

As the recipient records the asset at its fair value, what account receives the offsetting credit? Over the years, there has been disagreement over this question. Should the recipient increase its paid-in capital—the part of shareholders' equity representing investments in the firm? Or, should the donated asset be considered revenue? *SFAS 116* requires that donated assets be recorded as *revenue.*[11] Recall that revenues generally are inflows of assets from delivering or producing goods, rendering services, or from other activities that constitute the entity's ongoing major or central operations. The rationale is that the company receiving the donation is performing a service for the donor in exchange for the asset donated.

Corporations occasionally receive donations from governmental units. A local governmental unit might provide land or pay all or some of the cost of a new office building or manufacturing plant to entice a company to locate within its geographical boundaries. For example, the city of San Jose, California, recently paid a significant portion of the cost of a new office building for **IBM Corporation**. *SFAS 116 does not apply to transfers of assets from governmental units.* However, it is the opinion of the authors that this type of donation also should be accounted for as revenue by the recipient. In the IBM example, the new office building, located in downtown San Jose, brought jobs to a revitalized downtown area and increased revenues to the city. The City of San Jose did not receive an equity interest in IBM through its donation, but significantly benefited nevertheless.

Illustration 10–9 provides an example. In this illustration, we assume that, even though the donation is from a governmental unit, *SFAS 116* guidelines apply.

**ILLUSTRATION 10–9**
Asset Donation

Elcorn Enterprises decided to relocate its office headquarters to the city of Westmont. The city agreed to pay 20% of the $20 million cost of building the headquarters in order to entice Elcorn to relocate. The building was completed on May 3, 2006. Elcorn paid its portion of the cost of the building in cash. Elcorn records the transaction as follows:

| | | |
|---|---|---|
| Building . . . . . . . . . . . . . . . . . . . . . . . . . . . . . . . . . . . . . . . . . . | 20,000,000 | |
| Cash . . . . . . . . . . . . . . . . . . . . . . . . . . . . . . . . . . . . . . . . . . . | | 16,000,000 |
| Revenue—donation of asset (20% × $20 million) . . . . . . . . . . . . . | | 4,000,000 |

Operational assets also can be acquired in an exchange. Because an exchange transaction inherently involves a disposition of one operational asset as it is given up in exchange for another, we cover these transactions in Part B, Dispositions and Exchanges.

[11] "Accounting for Contributions Received and Contributions Made," *Statement of Financial Accounting Standards No. 116* (Norwalk, Conn.: FASB, 1993).

## DECISION MAKERS' PERSPECTIVE

The operational asset acquisition decision is among the most significant decisions that management must make. A decision to acquire a new fleet of airplanes or to build or purchase a new office building or manufacturing plant could influence a company's performance for many years.

These decisions, often referred to as **capital budgeting** decisions, require management to forecast all future net cash flows (cash inflows minus cash outflows) generated by the operational asset(s). These cash flows are then used in a model to determine if the future cash flows are sufficient to warrant the capital expenditure. One such model, the net present value model, compares the present value of future net cash flows with the required initial acquisition cost of the asset(s). If the present value is higher than the acquisition cost, the asset is acquired. You have studied or will study capital budgeting in considerable depth in a financial management course. The introduction to the time value of money concept in Chapter 6 provided you with important tools necessary to evaluate capital budgeting decisions.

A key to profitability is how well a company manages and utilizes its assets. Financial analysts often use activity, or turnover, ratios to evaluate a company's effectiveness in managing assets. This concept was illustrated with receivables and inventory in previous chapters. Operational assets—particularly property, plant, and equipment (PP&E)—usually are a company's primary revenue-generating assets. Their efficient use is critical to generating a satisfactory return to owners. One ratio analysts often use to measure how effectively managers use PP&E is the **fixed-asset turnover ratio.** This ratio is calculated as follows:

● LO5

*The fixed-asset turnover ratio measures a company's effectiveness in managing property, plant, and equipment.*

$$\text{Fixed-asset turnover ratio} = \frac{\text{Net sales}}{\text{Average fixed assets}}$$

The ratio indicates the level of sales generated by the company's investment in fixed assets. The denominator usually is the book value (cost less accumulated depreciation and depletion) of property, plant, and equipment.[12]

As with other turnover ratios, we can compare a company's fixed-asset turnover with that of its competitors, with an industry average, or with the same company's ratio over time. Let's compare the fixed-asset turnover ratios for **Dell** and **Apple**, the same two companies we used in Chapter 7 to illustrate accounts receivable turnover.

($ in millions)

| | Dell | | Apple | |
|---|---|---|---|---|
| | **2004** | **2003** | **2004** | **2003** |
| Property, plant, and equipment (net) | $1,517 | $913 | $707 | $669 |
| Net sales—2004 | $41,444 | | $8,279 | |

The 2004 fixed-asset turnover for Dell is 34 ($41,444 ÷ [($1,517 + 913) ÷ 2]) compared to Apple's turnover of 12 ($8,279 ÷ [($707 + 669) ÷ 2]). Dell is able to generate nearly three times as much as Apple in sales dollars for each dollar invested in fixed assets. ■

# DISPOSITIONS AND EXCHANGES

**PART B**

● LO6

After using operational assets, companies will sell, retire, or exchange those assets. Accounting for exchanges differs somewhat from accounting for sales and retirements because they involve both an acquisition and a disposition. So let's look first at sales and retirements and then we'll address accounting for exchanges. Be sure to note that in each case, the companies should record depreciation, depletion, or amortization up to the date of disposition or exchange.

[12] If intangible assets are significant, their book value could be added to the denominator to produce a turnover that reflects all operational assets. The use of book value provides an approximation of the company's current investment in these assets.

# Dispositions

When selling operational assets for monetary consideration (cash or a receivable), the seller recognizes a gain or loss for the difference between the consideration received and the book value of the asset sold. Illustration 10–10 provides an example.

**ILLUSTRATION 10–10**
Sale of Operational Asset

**A gain or loss is recognized for the difference between the consideration received and the asset's book value.**

The Robosport Company sold for $6,000 machinery that originally cost $20,000. Depreciation of $12,000 had been recorded up to the date of sale. Since the $8,000 book value of the asset ($20,000 − 12,000) exceeds the $6,000 consideration Robosport received, the company recognizes a $2,000 loss. The sale is recorded as follows:

| | | |
|---|---|---|
| Cash (selling price) | 6,000 | |
| Accumulated depreciation (account balance) | 12,000 | |
| Loss on disposal of machinery (difference) | 2,000 | |
| Machinery (account balance) | | 20,000 |

Retirements (or abandonments) are treated similarly. The only difference is that there will be no monetary consideration received. A loss is recorded for the remaining book value of the asset.

**Operational assets to be disposed of by sale are classified as held for sale and measured at the lower of book value or fair value less cost to sell.**

When an operational asset is to be disposed of by *sale,* we classify it as "held for sale" and report it at the lower of its book value or fair value less any cost to sell.[13] If the fair value less cost to sell is below book value, we recognize an impairment loss. Operational assets classified as held for sale are not depreciated or amortized. Recall from your study of discontinued operations in Chapter 4 that this treatment is the same one we employed in accounting for a component of an entity that is held for sale. We cover this topic in more depth in the impairment section of Chapter 11.

**ADDITIONAL CONSIDERATION**

**Involuntary Conversions**

Occasionally companies dispose of operational assets unintentionally. These so-called involuntary conversions include destruction by fire, earthquake, flood, or other catastrophe and expropriation by a governmental body.

Usually, the company receives a cash settlement from an insurance company for destroyed assets or from the governmental body for expropriated assets. The company often immediately reinvests this cash in similar assets. Nevertheless, involuntary conversions are treated precisely the same as voluntary conversions. That is, the proceeds are recorded, the book value of the lost assets are removed, and a gain or loss is recognized for the difference.

# Exchanges

Sometimes a company will acquire an operational asset in exchange for another operational asset. This frequently involves a trade-in by which a new asset is acquired in exchange for an old asset, and cash is given to equalize the fair values of the assets exchanged. The basic principle followed in these nonmonetary asset[14] exchanges is to value the asset received at fair value. This can be the fair value of the asset(s) given up or the fair value of the asset(s) received plus (or minus) any cash exchanged. We first look to the fair value of the asset given up. However, in a trade-in, quite often the fair value of the new asset is more clearly evident than the second-hand value of the asset traded in. A gain or loss is recognized for the

[13]"Accounting for the Impairment or Disposal of Long-Lived Assets," *Statement of Financial Accounting Standards No. 144* (Norwalk, Conn.: FASB, 2001)

[14]Monetary items are assets and liabilities whose *amounts are fixed,* by contract or otherwise, in terms of a specific number of dollars. Others are considered nonmonetary.

difference between the fair value of the asset given up and its book value. See the example in Illustration 10–11.

**ILLUSTRATION 10–11**
Nonmonetary Asset Exchange

The Elcorn Company traded its laser equipment for the newer air-cooled ion lasers manufactured by American Laser Corporation. The old equipment had a book value of $100,000 (cost of $500,000 less accumulated depreciation of $400,000) and a fair value of $150,000. To equalize the fair values of the assets exchanged, in addition to the old machinery, Elcorn paid American Laser $430,000 in cash. This means that the fair value of the new laser equipment is $580,000. We know this because American Laser was willing to trade the new lasers in exchange for old lasers worth $150,000 plus $430,000 in cash. The following journal entry records the transaction:

| | | |
|---|---|---|
| Laser equipment—new ($150,000 + 430,000) | 580,000 | |
| Accumulated depreciation | 400,000 | |
| Laser equipment—old | | 500,000 |
| Cash | | 430,000 |
| Gain ($150,000 − 100,000) | | 50,000 |

The new laser equipment is recorded at $580,000, the fair value of the old equipment, $150,000, plus the cash given of $430,000. This also equals the fair value of the new lasers. Elcorn recognizes a gain of $50,000, which is simply the difference between the old equipment's fair value of $150,000 and its $100,000 book value.

**An operational asset received in an exchange of nonmonetary assets generally is valued at fair value.**

Until recently, the accounting treatment of nonmonetary asset exchanges depended on a number of factors including (1) whether the assets exchanged were similar or dissimilar, (2) whether a gain or loss was indicated in the exchange, and (3) whether cash was given or received. A new accounting standard[15] simplified accounting for exchanges of operational assets by requiring the use of fair value except in rare situations in which the fair value cannot be determined or the exchange lacks commercial substance.[16]

In either of these circumstances, the asset(s) acquired are valued at the *book value* of the asset(s) given up plus (or minus) any cash exchanged—not fair value—and no gain is recognized. Let's discuss each of these situations.

## FAIR VALUE NOT DETERMINABLE

It would be unusual for a company not to be able to reasonably determine fair value of either asset in an exchange. Nevertheless, if the situation does occur, the company would simply use the book value of the asset given up plus (minus) any cash given (received) to value the asset acquired. For example, if fair value had not been determinable in Illustration 10–11, Elcorn would have recorded the exchange as follows:

| | | |
|---|---|---|
| Equipment—new ($100,000 + 430,000) | 530,000 | |
| Accumulated depreciation | 400,000 | |
| Equipment—old | | 500,000 |
| Cash | | 430,000 |

**If we cannot determine the fair value of either asset in the exchange, the asset received is valued at the book value of the asset given.**

The new equipment is valued at the book value of the old equipment ($100,000) plus the cash given ($430,000). No gain is recognized.

## EXCHANGE LACKS COMMERCIAL SUBSTANCE

If we record an exchange at fair value, then a gain or loss is recognized for the difference between the fair value and book value of the asset(s) given up. To preclude the possibility of companies engaging in exchanges of appreciated assets solely to be able to recognize gains, fair value can only be used in legitimate exchanges that have commercial substance.

**Fair value can only be used in nonmonetary exchanges that have commercial substance.**

[15]"Exchanges of Nonmonetary Assets—an amendment of *APB Opinion No. 29," Statement of Financial Accounting Standards No. 153* (Norwalk, Conn.: FASB, 2004).

[16]There is a third situation, not involving operational assets, which precludes the use of fair value in a nonmonetary exchange. The transaction is an exchange of inventories to facilitate sales to customers other than the parties to the exchange.

A nonmonetary exchange is considered to have commercial substance if the company (1) expects a change in future cash flows as a result of the exchange and (2) that expected change is significant relative to the fair value of the assets exchanged. Otherwise, the exchange does not have commercial substance, book value is used to value the asset(s) acquired, and no gain is recognized.

## Concept Review Exercise

### Exchanges

The MD Corporation recently acquired new equipment to be used in its production process. In exchange, the company traded in an existing asset that had an original cost of $60,000 and accumulated depreciation on the date of the exchange of $45,000. In addition, MD paid $40,000 cash to the equipment manufacturer. The fair value of the old equipment is $17,000.

**Required:**

1. Prepare the journal entry MD would use to record the exchange transaction assuming that the transaction has commercial substance.
2. Prepare the journal entry MD would use to record the exchange transaction assuming that the transaction does *not* have commercial substance.

### Solution

1. Prepare the journal entry MD would use to record the exchange transaction assuming that the transaction has commercial substance.

| | | |
|---|---|---|
| Equipment—new ($17,000 + 40,000) | 57,000 | |
| Accumulated depreciation (account balance) | 45,000 | |
| Cash (amount paid) | | 40,000 |
| Equipment—old (account balance) | | 60,000 |
| Gain ($17,000 fair value − $15,000 book value) | | 2,000 |

2. Prepare the journal entry MD would use to record the exchange transaction assuming that the transaction does *not* have commercial substance.

| | | |
|---|---|---|
| Equipment—new ($15,000 + 40,000) | 55,000 | |
| Accumulated depreciation (account balance) | 45,000 | |
| Cash (amount paid) | | 40,000 |
| Equipment—old (account balance) | | 60,000 |

## Part C SELF-CONSTRUCTED ASSETS AND RESEARCH AND DEVELOPMENT

Two types of expenditures relating to operational assets whose accounting treatment has generated considerable controversy are interest costs pertaining to self-constructed assets and amounts spent for research and development. We now consider those expenditures and why those controversies have developed.

### Self-Constructed Assets

● LO7

A company might decide to construct an operational asset for its own use rather than buy an existing one. For example, a retailer like **Nordstrom** might decide to build its own store rather than purchase an existing building. A manufacturing company like **Intel** could construct its own manufacturing facility. In fact, Nordstrom and Intel are just two of the many companies that self-construct assets. Other recognizable examples include **Walt Disney**, **Sears**, and **Caterpillar**. Quite often these companies act as the main contractor and then subcontract most of the actual construction work.

The critical accounting issue in these instances is identifying the cost of the self-constructed asset. The task is more difficult than for purchased assets because there is no external transaction to establish an exchange price. Actually, two difficulties arise in connection with assigning costs to self-constructed assets: (1) determining the amount of the company's indirect manufacturing costs (overhead) to be allocated to the construction and (2) deciding on the proper treatment of interest (actual or implicit) incurred during construction.

## OVERHEAD ALLOCATION

**The cost of a self-constructed asset includes identifiable materials and labor and a portion of the company's manufacturing overhead costs.**

One difficulty of associating costs with self-constructed assets is the same difficulty encountered when determining cost of goods manufactured for sale. The costs of material and direct labor usually are easily identified with a particular construction project and are included in cost. However, the treatment of manufacturing overhead cost and its allocation between construction projects and normal production is a controversial issue.

Some accountants advocate the inclusion of only the *incremental* overhead costs in the total cost of construction. That is, the asset's cost would include only those additional costs that are incurred because of the decision to construct the asset. This would exclude such indirect costs as depreciation and the salaries of supervisors that would be incurred whether or not the construction project is undertaken. If, however, a new construction supervisor was hired specifically to work on the project, then that salary would be included in asset cost.

Others advocate assigning overhead on the same basis that is used for a regular manufacturing process. That is, all overhead costs are allocated both to production and to self-constructed assets based on the relative amount of a chosen cost driver (for example, labor hours) incurred. This is known as the *full-cost approach* and is the generally accepted method used to determine the cost of a self-constructed asset.

## INTEREST CAPITALIZATION

**FINANCIAL REPORTING CASE**

Q3, p. 451

To reiterate, the cost of an asset includes all costs necessary to get the asset ready for its intended use. Unlike one purchased from another company, a self-constructed asset requires time to create it. During this construction period, the project must be financed in some way. This suggests the question as to whether interest costs during the construction period are one of the costs of acquiring the asset itself or simply costs of financing the asset. On the one hand, we might point to interest charges to finance inventories during their period of manufacture or to finance the purchase of plant assets from others and argue that construction period interest charges are merely costs of financing the asset that should be expensed as incurred like all other interest costs. On the other hand, we might argue that self-constructed assets are different in that during the construction period, they are not yet ready for their intended use for producing revenues. And, so, in keeping with both the historical cost principle and the matching concept, all costs during this period, including interest, should be capitalized and then allocated as depreciation during later periods when the assets are providing benefits.

**Only assets that are constructed as discrete projects qualify for interest capitalization.**

**Qualifying Assets.** Generally accepted accounting principles are consistent with the second argument. Specifically, interest is capitalized during the construction period for (a) assets built for a company's own use as well as for (b) assets constructed *as discrete projects* for sale or lease (a ship or a real estate development, for example). This excludes from interest capitalization consideration inventories that are routinely manufactured in large quantities on a repetitive basis and assets that already are in use or are ready for their intended use.[17] Interest costs incurred during the productive life of the asset are expensed as incurred.

**Only interest incurred during the construction period is eligible for capitalization.**

Prior to 1979, when this treatment was mandated by *SFAS 34,* many companies treated construction-period interest costs as a cost of obtaining funds and not a cost of obtaining an asset. Accordingly, interest costs were expensed rather than capitalized. In fact, prior to the early 1970s, few companies other than utilities capitalized interest. Utilities have long been motivated to do so by the desire to increase their asset bases on which regulated utility rates are determined. Nonregulated companies began to follow suit during the economic slowdown of the early 1970s as a way to decrease expenses and bolster profits. *SFAS 34* was an attempt to address the diversity of accounting practice. Now all companies capitalize interest incurred during the construction of a qualified asset.

[17]"Capitalization of Interest Costs," *Statement of Financial Accounting Standards No. 34* (Stamford, Conn.: FASB, 1979).

The interest capitalization period begins when construction begins and the first expenditure is made as long as interest costs are actually being incurred.

**Period of Capitalization.** The capitalization period for a self-constructed asset starts with the first expenditure (materials, labor, or overhead) and ends either when the asset is substantially complete and ready for use or when interest costs no longer are being incurred. Interest costs incurred can pertain to borrowings other than those obtained specifically for the construction project. However, interest costs can't be imputed; actual interest costs must be incurred.

**Average Accumulated Expenditures.** Because we consider interest to be a necessary cost of getting a self-constructed asset ready for use, the amount capitalized is only that portion of interest cost incurred during the construction period that *could have been avoided* if expenditures for the asset had not been made. In other words, if construction had not been undertaken, debt incurred for the project would not have been necessary and/or other interest-bearing debt could have been liquidated or employed elsewhere.

*Average accumulated expenditures* approximates the average debt necessary for construction.

As a result, interest should be determined for only the construction expenditures actually incurred during the capitalization period. And unless all expenditures are made at the outset of the period, it's necessary to determine the *average* amount outstanding during the period. This is the amount of debt that would be required to finance the expenditures and thus the amount on which interest would accrue. For instance, if a company accumulated $1,500,000 of construction expenditures fairly evenly throughout the construction period, the average expenditures would be:

| | |
|---|---|
| Total accumulated expenditures incurred evenly throughout the period | $1,500,000 |
| | ÷ 2 |
| Average accumulated expenditures | $ 750,000 |

Average accumulated expenditures is determined by time-weighting individual expenditures made during the construction period.

At the beginning of the period, no expenditures have accumulated, so no interest has accrued (on the equivalent amount of debt). But, by the end of the period interest is accruing on the total amount, $1,500,000. On average, then, interest accrues on half the total or $750,000.

If expenditures are not incurred evenly throughout the period, a simple average is insufficient. In that case, a weighted average is determined by time-weighting individual expenditures or groups of expenditures by the number of months from their incurrence to the end of the construction period. This is demonstrated in Illustration 10–12.

**ILLUSTRATION 10–12**
Interest Capitalization

On January 1, 2006, the Mills Conveying Equipment Company began construction of a building to be used as its office headquarters. The building was completed on June 30, 2007. Expenditures on the project, mainly payments to subcontractors, were as follows:

| | |
|---|---|
| January 3, 2006 | $ 500,000 |
| March 31, 2006 | 400,000 |
| September 30, 2006 | 600,000 |
| Accumulated expenditures at December 31, 2006 (before interest capitalization) | $1,500,000 |
| January 31, 2007 | 600,000 |
| April 30, 2007 | 300,000 |

On January 2, 2006, the company obtained a $1 million construction loan with an 8% interest rate. The loan was outstanding during the entire construction period. The company's other interest-bearing debt included two long-term notes of $2,000,000 and $4,000,000 with interest rates of 6% and 12%, respectively. Both notes were outstanding during the entire construction period.

**FINANCIAL REPORTING CASE**

Q4, p. 451

The weighted-average accumulated expenditures by the end of 2006 are:

| | | |
|---|---|---|
| January 3, 2006 | $500,000 × $^{12}/_{12}$ = | $500,000 |
| March 31, 2006 | 400,000 × $^{9}/_{12}$ = | 300,000 |
| September 30, 2006 | 600,000 × $^{3}/_{12}$ = | 150,000 |
| Average accumulated expenditures for 2006 | = | $950,000 |

Again notice that the average accumulated expenditures are less than the total accumulated expenditures of $1,500,000. If Mills had borrowed exactly the amount necessary to finance the project, it would not have incurred interest on a loan of $1,500,000 for the whole year but only on an average loan of $950,000. The next step is to determine the interest to be capitalized for the average accumulated expenditures.

**STEP 1: Determine the average accumulated expenditures.**

**Interest Rates.** In this situation, debt financing was obtained specifically for the construction project, and the amount borrowed is sufficient to cover the average accumulated expenditures. To determine the interest capitalized, then, we simply multiply the construction loan rate of 8% by the average accumulated expenditures.

**STEP 2: Calculate the amount of interest to be capitalized.**

Interest capitalized for 2006 = $950,000 × 8% = $76,000

Notice that this is the same answer we would get by assuming separate 8% construction loans were made for each expenditure at the time each expenditure was made:

**The amount of interest capitalized is determined by multiplying an interest rate by the average accumulated expenditures.**

| Loans | | Annual Rate | | Portion of Year Outstanding | | Interest |
|---|---|---|---|---|---|---|
| $500,000 | × | 8% | × | 12/12 | = | $40,000 |
| 400,000 | × | 8% | × | 9/12 | = | 24,000 |
| 600,000 | × | 8% | × | 3/12 | = | 12,000 |
| Interest capitalized for 2006 | | | | | | $76,000 |

The interest of $76,000 is added to the cost of the building, bringing accumulated expenditures at December 31, 2006, to $1,576,000 ($1,500,000 + 76,000). The remaining interest cost incurred but not capitalized is expensed.

It should be emphasized that interest capitalization does not require that funds actually be borrowed for this specific purpose, only that the company does have outstanding debt. The presumption is that even if the company doesn't borrow specifically for the project, funds from other borrowings must be diverted to finance the construction. Either way—directly or indirectly—interest costs are incurred. In our illustration, for instance, even without the construction loan, interest would be capitalized because other debt was outstanding. The capitalized interest would be the average accumulated expenditures multiplied by the weighted-average rate on these other loans. The weighted-average interest rate on all debt other than the construction loan would be 10%, calculated as follows:[18]

| Loans | | Rate | | Interest |
|---|---|---|---|---|
| $2,000,000 | × | 6% | = | $120,000 |
| 4,000,000 | × | 12% | = | 480,000 |
| $6,000,000 | | | | $600,000 |

$$\text{Weighted-average rate: } \frac{\$600{,}000}{\$6{,}000{,}000} = 10\%$$

This is a weighted average because total interest is $600,000 on total debt of $6,000,000.

## ADDITIONAL CONSIDERATION

The weighted-average rate isn't used for 2006 in our illustration because the specific construction loan is sufficient to cover the average accumulated expenditures. If the specific construction loan had been insufficient to cover the average accumulated expenditures, its 8% interest rate would be applied to the average accumulated expenditures up to the amount of the specific borrowing, and any remaining average accumulated expenditures in excess of specific borrowings would be multiplied by the

[18]The same result can be obtained simply by multiplying the individual debt interest rates by the relative amount of debt at each rate. In this case, one-third of total debt is at 6% and two-thirds of the total debt is at 12% (1/3 × 6% + 2/3 × 12% = 10%).

weighted-average rate on all other outstanding interest-bearing debt. Suppose, for illustration, that the 8% construction loan had been only $500,000 rather than $1,000,000. We would calculate capitalized interest using both the specific rate and the weighted-average rate:

| | Average Accumulated Expenditures | | Rate | | Interest |
|---|---|---|---|---|---|
| Total | $950,000 | | | | |
| Specific borrowing | 500,000 | × | 8% | = | $40,000 |
| Excess | $450,000 | × | 10% | = | 45,000 |
| Capitalized interest | | | | | $85,000 |

In our illustration, it's necessary to use this approach in 2007.

**Interest capitalized is limited to interest incurred.**

It's possible that the amount of interest calculated to be capitalized exceeds the amount of interest actually incurred. If that's the case, we limit the interest capitalized to the actual interest incurred. In our illustration, total interest cost incurred during 2006 far exceeds the $76,000 of capitalized interest calculated, so it's not necessary to limit the capitalized amount.

**STEP 3: Compare calculated interest with actual interest incurred.**

| Loans | | Rate | | Actual Interest | Calculated Interest |
|---|---|---|---|---|---|
| $1,000,000 | × | 8% | = | $ 80,000 | |
| 2,000,000 | × | 6% | = | 120,000 | |
| 4,000,000 | × | 12% | = | 480,000 | |
| | | | | $680,000 | $76,000 |

Use lower amount

Continuing the example based on the information in Illustration 10–12, let's determine the amount of interest capitalized during 2007 for the building. The total accumulated expenditures by the end of the project are:

| | |
|---|---|
| Accumulated expenditures at the beginning of 2007 (including interest capitalization) | $1,576,000 |
| January 31, 2007 | 600,000 |
| April 30, 2007 | 300,000 |
| Accumulated expenditures at June 30, 2007 (before 2007 interest capitalization) | $2,476,000 |

The weighted-average accumulated expenditures by the end of the project are:

**STEP 1: Determine the average accumulated expenditures.**

| | | |
|---|---|---|
| January 1, 2007 | $1,576,000 × $\frac{6}{6}$ = | $1,576,000 |
| January 31, 2007 | 600,000 × $\frac{5}{6}$ = | 500,000 |
| April 30, 2007 | 300,000 × $\frac{2}{6}$ = | 100,000 |
| Average accumulated expenditures for 2007 | | $2,176,000 |

Notice that the 2007 expenditures are weighted relative to the construction period of six months because the project was finished on June 30, 2007. Interest capitalized for 2007 would be $98,800, calculated as follows:

**STEP 2: Calculate the amount of interest to be capitalized.**

| | Average Accumulated Expenditures | | Annual Rate | | Fraction of Year | | |
|---|---|---|---|---|---|---|---|
| | $2,176,000 | | | | | | |
| Specific borrowing | 1,000,000 | × | 8% | × | $\frac{6}{12}$ | = | $40,000 |
| Excess | $1,176,000 | × | 10% | × | $\frac{6}{12}$ | = | 58,800 |
| Capitalized interest | | | | | | | $98,800 |

Multiplying by six-twelfths reflects the fact that the interest rates are annual rates (12-month rates) and the construction period is only 6 months.

| Loans | | Annual Rate | Actual Interest | Calculated Interest |
|---|---|---|---|---|
| $1,000,000 | × | 8% × 6/12 = | $ 40,000 | |
| 2,000,000 | × | 6% × 6/12 = | 60,000 | |
| 4,000,000 | × | 12% × 6/12 = | 240,000 | |
| | | | $340,000 | $98,800 |
| | | | | Use lower amount |

STEP 3: Compare calculated interest with actual interest incurred.

For the first six months of 2007, $98,800 of interest would be capitalized, bringing the total capitalized cost of the building to $2,574,800 ($2,476,000 + 98,800), and $241,200 in interest would be expensed ($340,000 − 98,800).

**ADDITIONAL CONSIDERATION**

To illustrate how the actual interest limitation might come into play, let's assume the nonspecific borrowings in our illustration were $200,000 and $400,000 (instead of $2,000,000 and $4,000,000). Our comparison would change as follows:

| Loans | | Annual Rate | Actual Interest | Calculated Interest |
|---|---|---|---|---|
| $1,000,000 | × | 8% × 6/12 = | $40,000 | |
| 200,000 | × | 6% × 6/12 = | 6,000 | |
| 400,000 | × | 12% × 6/12 = | 24,000 | |
| | | | $70,000 | $98,800 |
| | | | Use lower amount | |

The method of determining interest to capitalize that we've discussed is called the **specific interest method** because we use rates from specific construction loans to the extent of specific borrowings before using the average rate of other debt. Sometimes, though, it's difficult to associate specific borrowings with projects. In these situations, it's acceptable to just use the weighted-average rate on all interest-bearing debt, including all construction loans. This is known as the **weighted-average method**. In our illustration, for example, if the $1,000,000, 8% loan had not been specifically related to construction, we would calculate a single weighted-average rate as shown below.

Weighted-average method

| Loans | | Rate | | Interest |
|---|---|---|---|---|
| $1,000,000 | × | 8% | = | $ 80,000 |
| 2,000,000 | × | 6% | = | 120,000 |
| 4,000,000 | × | 12% | = | 480,000 |
| $7,000,000 | | | | $680,000 |

$$\text{Weighted-average rate: } \frac{\$680{,}000}{\$7{,}000{,}000} = 9.7\%$$

If we were using the weighted-average method rather than the specific interest method, we would simply multiply this single rate times the average accumulated expenditures to determine capitalizable interest.

If material, the amount of interest capitalized during the period must be disclosed.

**Disclosure.** For an accounting period in which interest costs are capitalized, both the total amount of interest costs incurred and the amount that has been capitalized should be

**GLOBAL PERSPECTIVE**

The accounting principles of most countries permit some form of interest capitalization; Japan and Brazil are exceptions. However, differences do exist as to the situations when interest can be capitalized. IFRSs allow the capitalization of interest on inventories that require a substantial period of time to bring them to condition for sale. Differences also exist as to the amount of interest to be capitalized. In Argentina imputed interest on the company's equity may be capitalized.

disclosed. Graphic 10–5 shows an interest capitalization disclosure note that was included in a recent annual report of **Carnival Corporation**, the world's largest cruise company.

**GRAPHIC 10–5**
Capitalized Interest Disclosure—Carnival Corporation

**Note 4—Property and Equipment (in part)**
Capitalized interest, primarily on our ships under construction, amounted to $26 million, $49 million, and $39 million in fiscal 2004, 2003, and 2002, respectively. Amounts related to ships under construction include progress fees, capitalized interest, construction oversight costs and various owner supplied items.

## RESEARCH AND DEVELOPMENT (R&D)

● LO8

For years the practice was to allow companies to either expense or capitalize R&D costs, but in 1974 the FASB issued *SFAS 2* which now requires all research and development costs to be charged to expense when incurred.[19] This was a controversial standard opposed by many companies who preferred delaying the recognition of these expenses until later years when presumably the expenditures bear fruit.

**Most R&D costs are expensed in the periods incurred.**

**R&D costs entail a high degree of uncertainty of future benefits and are difficult to match with future revenues.**

A company undertakes an R&D project because it believes the project will eventually provide benefits that exceed the current expenditures. Unfortunately, though, it's difficult to predict which individual research and development projects will ultimately provide benefits. In fact, only 1 in 10 actually reach commercial production. Moreover, even for those projects that pan out, a direct relationship between research and development costs and specific future revenue is difficult to establish. In other words, even if R&D costs do lead to future benefits, it's difficult to objectively determine the size of the benefits and in which periods the costs should be expensed if they are capitalized. These are the issues that prompted the FASB to require immediate expensing.

The FASB's approach is certain in most cases to understate assets and overstate current expense because at least some of the R&D expenditures will likely produce future benefits.

**Determining R&D Costs.** *SFAS 2* distinguishes research and development as follows:

**Research** is planned search or critical investigation aimed at discovery of new knowledge with the hope that such knowledge will be useful in developing a new product or service or a new process or technique or in bringing about a significant improvement to an existing product or process.
**Development** is the translation of research findings or other knowledge into a plan or design for a new product or process or for a significant improvement to an existing product or process whether intended for sale or use.[20]

R&D costs include salaries, wages, and other labor costs of personnel engaged in R&D activities, the costs of materials consumed, equipment, facilities, and intangibles used in R&D projects, the costs of services performed by others in connection with R&D activities,

[19] "Accounting for Research and Development Costs," *Statement of Financial Accounting Standards No. 2* (Stamford, Conn.: FASB, 1974), par. 12.
[20] Ibid., par. 8.

and a reasonable allocation of indirect costs related to those activities. General and administrative costs should not be included unless they are clearly related to the R&D activity.

If an operational asset is purchased specifically for a single R&D project, its cost is considered R&D and expensed immediately even though the asset's useful life extends beyond the current year. However, the cost of an operational asset that has an alternative future use beyond the current R&D project is *not* a current R&D expense. Instead, the depreciation or amortization of these alternative-use assets is included as R&D expenses in the current and future periods the assets are used for R&D activities.

**R&D expense includes the depreciation and amortization of operational assets used in R&D activities.**

In general, R&D costs pertain to activities that occur prior to the start of commercial production, and costs of starting commercial production and beyond are not R&D costs. Graphic 10–6 captures this concept with a time line beginning with the start of an R&D project and ending with the ultimate sale of a developed product or the use of a developed process. The graphic also provides examples of activities typically included as R&D and examples of activities typically excluded from R&D.[21]

**GRAPHIC 10–6**
Research and Development Expenditures

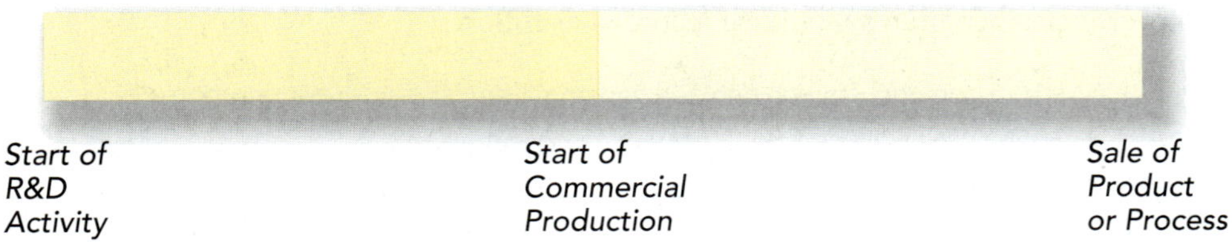


*Examples of R&D Costs:*

- Laboratory research aimed at discovery of new knowledge
- Searching for applications of new research findings or other knowledge
- Design, construction, and testing of preproduction prototypes and models
- Modification of the formulation or design of a product or process

*Examples of Non-R&D Costs:*

- Engineering follow-through in an early phase of commercial production
- Quality control during commercial production including routine testing of products
- Routine ongoing efforts to refine, enrich, or otherwise improve on the qualities of an existing product
- Adaptation of an existing capability to a particular requirement or customer's need as a part of a continuing commercial activity

**Costs incurred *before* the start of commercial production are all expensed as R&D.**

**Costs incurred *after* commercial production begins would be either expensed or included in the cost of inventory.**

Costs incurred before the start of commercial production are all expensed as R&D. The costs incurred after commercial production begins would be either expensed or treated as manufacturing overhead and included in the cost of inventory. Let's look at an example in Illustration 10–13.

The salaries and wages, supplies consumed, and payments to others for R&D services are expensed in 2006 as R&D. The equipment is capitalized and the 2006 depreciation is expensed as R&D. Even though the costs to develop the patented product are expensed, the filing and legal costs for the patent are capitalized and amortized in future periods just as similar costs are capitalized for purchased intangibles. Amortization of the patent is discussed in Chapter 11.

**Filing and legal costs for patents, copyrights, and other developed intangibles are capitalized and amortized in future periods.**

[21]Ibid., par. 9 and 10.

**ILLUSTRATION 10–13**
Research and Development Costs

The Askew Company made the following cash expenditures during 2006 related to the development of a new industrial plastic:

| | |
|---|---|
| R&D salaries and wages | $10,000,000 |
| R&D supplies consumed during 2006 | 3,000,000 |
| Purchase of R&D equipment | 5,000,000 |
| Patent filing and legal costs | 100,000 |
| Payments to others for services performed in connection with R&D activities | 1,200,000 |
| Total | $19,300,000 |

The project resulted in a new product to be manufactured in 2007. A patent was filed with the U.S. Patent Office. The equipment purchased will be employed in other projects. Depreciation on the equipment for 2006 was $500,000.

The various expenditures would be recorded as follows:

| | | |
|---|---|---|
| R&D expense ($10,000,000 + 3,000,000 + 1,200,000) | 14,200,000 | |
| Cash | | 14,200,000 |
| *To record R&D expenses.* | | |
| Equipment | 5,000,000 | |
| Cash | | 5,000,000 |
| *To record the purchase of equipment.* | | |
| R&D expense | 500,000 | |
| Accumulated depreciation—equipment | | 500,000 |
| *To record R&D depreciation.* | | |
| Patent | 100,000 | |
| Cash | | 100,000 |
| *To capitalize the patent filing and legal costs.* | | |

| Expenditures reconciliation: | |
|---|---|
| Recorded as R&D | $14,200,000 |
| Capitalized as equipment | 5,000,000 |
| Capitalized as patent | 100,000 |
| Total expenditures | $19,300,000 |

**GAAP require disclosure of total R&D expense incurred during the period.**

GAAP require that total R&D expense incurred must be disclosed either as a line item in the income statement or in a disclosure note. For example, **Microsoft** reported $6.299 billion of R&D expense on the face of its 2004 income statement. In our illustration, total R&D expense disclosed in 2006 would be $14,700,000 ($14,200,000 in expenditures and $500,000 in depreciation). Note that if Askew later sells this patent to another company for, say, $15 million, the buyer would capitalize the entire purchase price rather than only the filing and legal costs. Once again, the reason for the apparent inconsistency in accounting treatment of internally generated intangibles and externally purchased intangibles is the difficulty of associating costs and benefits.

**R&D Performed for Others.** The requirements of *SFAS 2* do not apply to companies that perform R&D for other companies under contract. In these situations, the R&D costs are capitalized as inventory and carried forward into future years until the project is completed. Of course, justification is that the benefits of these expenditures are the contract fees that are determinable and are earned over the term of the project. Income from these contracts can be recognized using either the percentage-of-completion or completed contract method. We discussed these alternatives in Chapter 5.

Another exception pertains to a company that develops computer software. Expenditures made after the software is determined to be technologically feasible but before it is ready for

**GLOBAL PERSPECTIVE**

Unlike the United States, many other countries, including Japan, Korea, and Brazil, permit companies to capitalize research and development costs as intangible assets. *International Accounting Standard 38* requires research to be expensed immediately, but development costs must be capitalized when certain criteria have been met.

commercial production are capitalized. Costs incurred before technological feasibility is established are expensed as incurred. We discuss software development costs below.

**Start-Up Costs.** For its fiscal year ended February 1, 2004, **Home Depot, Inc.** opened 175 new stores throughout the world. The company incurred a variety of one-time pre-opening costs for salaries of employees supervising construction, training, travel, and relocation of employees totaling $86 million. In fact, whenever a company introduces a new product or service, or commences business in a new territory or with a new customer, it incurs similar **start-up costs.** As with R&D expenditures, a company must expense all the costs related to a company's start-up activities in the period incurred, rather than capitalize those costs as an asset. Start-up costs also include **organization costs** related to organizing a new entity, such as legal fees and state filing fees to incorporate.[22]

**Start-up costs are expensed in the period incurred.**

**ADDITIONAL CONSIDERATION**

**Development Stage Enterprises**

A development stage enterprise is a new business that has either not commenced its principal operations or has begun its principal operations but has not generated significant revenues. Prior to *SFAS 7*,[23] many of these companies recorded an asset for the normal operating costs incurred during the development stage. This asset was then expensed over a period of time beginning with the commencement of operations.

*SFAS 7* requires that these enterprises comply with the same generally accepted accounting principles that apply to established operating companies in determining whether a cost is to be charged to expense when incurred or capitalized and expensed in future periods. Therefore, normal operating costs incurred during the development stage are expensed, not capitalized. *SFAS 7* does allow development stage enterprises to provide items of supplemental information to help financial statement readers more readily assess their future cash flows.

**Software Development Costs.** The computer software industry has become a large and important U.S. business over the last two decades. Relative newcomers such as **Microsoft** and **Adobe Systems**, as well as traditional hardware companies like **IBM**, are leaders in this multibillion dollar industry. A significant expenditure for these companies is the cost of developing software. Prior to 1985, some companies were capitalizing software development costs and expensing them in future periods and others were expensing these costs in the period incurred.

In 1985, the FASB issued *SFAS 86,* which requires all companies to expense costs incurred to develop or purchase computer software to be sold, leased, or otherwise marketed as R&D costs until **technological feasibility** of the product has been established.[24] The Statement does not address the accounting treatment of costs incurred to develop computer software to be used internally. We account for these costs in a similar manner, however. Costs incurred during the preliminary project stage are expensed as R&D. After the application development stage is reached (for example, at the coding stage or installation stage), we

**GAAP require the capitalization of software development costs incurred after *technological feasibility* is established.**

[22]"Reporting on the Costs of Start-Up Activities," *Statement of Position 98-5* (New York: AICPA, 1998).

[23]"Accounting and Reporting by Development Stage Enterprises," *Statement of Financial Accounting Standards No. 7* (Stamford, Conn.: FASB, 1975).

[24]"Accounting for the Costs of Computer Software to be Sold, Leased, or Otherwise Marketed," *Statement of Financial Accounting Standards No. 86* (Stamford, Conn.: FASB, 1985).

capitalize any further costs.[25] We generally capitalize the costs of computer software *purchased* for internal use.

Technological feasibility is established "when the enterprise has completed all planning, designing, coding, and testing activities that are necessary to establish that the product can be produced to meet its design specifications including functions, features, and technical performance requirements."[26] Costs incurred after technological feasibility but before the product is available for general release to customers are capitalized as an intangible asset. These costs include coding and testing costs and the production of product masters. Similar to the treatment of such costs under *SFAS 2,* costs incurred after the product release date usually are not R&D expenditures. Graphic 10–7 shows the R&D time line introduced earlier in the chapter and adds the point of establishment of technological feasibility. Only the costs incurred between technological feasibility and the product release date are capitalized.

**GRAPHIC 10–7**
Research and Development Expenditures—Computer Software

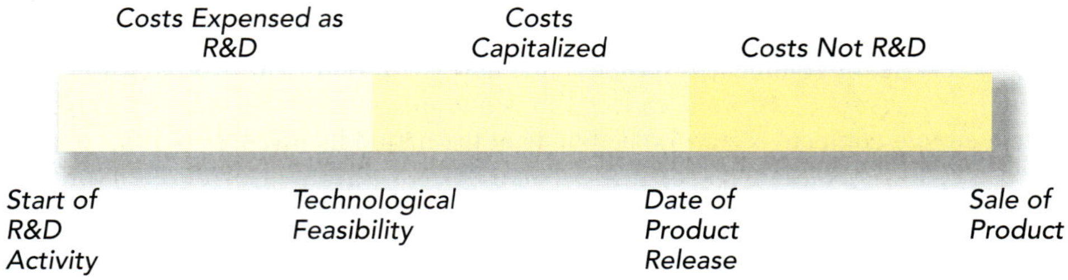


The amortization of capitalized computer software development costs begins when the product is available for general release to customers. The periodic amortization percentage is the greater of (1) the ratio of current revenues to current and anticipated revenues (percentage-of-revenue method) or (2) the straight-line percentage over the useful life of the asset, as shown in Illustration 10–14.

**ILLUSTRATION 10–14**
Software Development Costs

The Astro Corporation develops computer software graphics programs for sale. A new development project begun in 2005 reached technological feasibility at the end of June 2006, and the product was available for release to customers early in 2007. Development costs incurred in 2006 prior to June 30 were $1,200,000 and costs incurred from June 30 to the product availability date were $800,000. 2007 revenues from the sale of the new product were $3,000,000 and the company anticipates an additional $7,000,000 in revenues. The economic life of the software is estimated at four years.

Astro Corporation would expense the $1,200,000 in costs incurred prior to the establishment of technological feasibility and capitalize the $800,000 in costs incurred between technological feasibility and the product availability date. 2007 amortization of the intangible asset, software development costs, is calculated as follows:

1. Percentage-of-revenue method:

$$\frac{\$3{,}000{,}000}{\$3{,}000{,}000 + 7{,}000{,}000} = 30\% \times \$800{,}000 = \$240{,}000$$

2. Straight-line method:

$$\tfrac{1}{4} \text{ or } 25\% \times \$800{,}000 = \$200{,}000.$$

The percentage-of-revenue method is used because it produces the greater amortization, $240,000.

Graphic 10–8 shows the software disclosure included in a recent annual report of **Computer Associates International, Inc.** The note provides a good summary of the accounting treatment of software development costs.

[25] "Accounting for the Costs of Computer Software Developed or Obtained for Internal Use," *Statement of Position 98-1* (New York: AICPA, 1998).

[26] "Accounting for the Costs of Computer Software to Be Sold, Leased, or Otherwise Marketed," *Statement of Financial Accounting Standards No. 86* (Stamford, Conn.: FASB, 1985), par. 4.

**Capitalized Software Costs and Other Identified Intangible Assets (in part)**
In accordance with *SFAS No. 86,* "Accounting for the Costs of Computer Software to Be Sold, Leased, or Otherwise Marketed," internally generated software development costs associated with new products and significant enhancements to existing software products are expensed as incurred until technological feasibility has been established. Internally generated software development costs of $44 million, $40 million, and $53 million were capitalized during fiscal years 2004, 2003, and 2002, respectively. The Company recorded amortization of $40 million, $35 million, and $32 million for the fiscal years ended March 31, 2004, 2003, and 2002, respectively. Annual amortization of capitalized software costs is the greater of the amount computed using (i) the ratio that current gross revenue for a software product bears to the total of current and anticipated future revenue for that software product or (ii) the straight-line method over the remaining estimated economic life of the software product, generally estimated to be five years.

**GRAPHIC 10–8**
Software Disclosure—Computer Associates International, Inc.

Why do generally accepted accounting principles allow this exception to the general rule of expensing all R&D? We could attribute it to the political process. Software is a very important industry to our economy and perhaps its lobbying efforts resulted in the standard allowing software companies to capitalize certain R&D costs.

We could also attribute the exception to the nature of the software business. Recall that R&D costs in general are expensed in the period incurred for two reasons: (1) they entail a high degree of uncertainty of future benefits, and (2) they are difficult to match with future benefits. With software, there is an important identifiable engineering milestone, technological feasibility. When this milestone is attained, the probability of the software product's success increases significantly. And because the useful life of software is fairly short (one to four years in most cases), it is much easier to determine the periods of increased revenues than for R&D projects in other industries. Compare this situation with, say, the development of a new drug. Even after the drug has been developed, it must go through extensive testing to meet FDA (Food and Drug Administration) approval, which may never be attained. If attained, the useful life of the drug could be anywhere from a few months to many years.

**Purchased Research and Development and Earnings Quality.** It is not unusual for one company to buy another company in order to obtain technology developed or in the process of being developed by the acquired company. When one company buys another, we allocate the purchase price to tangible and intangible assets as well as to **in-process research and development**. To do this, we must distinguish between *developed* technology (an intangible asset) and *in-process* R&D. Using terminology adopted in accounting for software development costs, if *technological feasibility* has been achieved, the value of that technology is considered "developed." The amount we attribute to developed technology is capitalized and amortized. The amount we attribute to in-process R&D, though, is expensed (written off), in the period of the acquisition.[27]

**In a business acquisition, the amount allocated to developed technology is capitalized and amortized, but the amount allocated to *in-process research and development,* is expensed (written off), in the period of the acquisition.**

As an example, in 2003 **IBM Corporation** acquired 100% of the shares of **Rational Software Corporation** for $2,163 million. IBM allocated the purchase price as follows ($ in millions):

| | |
|---|---|
| Tangible assets | $1,341 |
| Developed technology | 229 |
| Other identifiable intangible assets | 212 |
| In-process research and development | 9 |
| Goodwill | 1,405 |
| | 3,196 |
| Less: Liabilities assumed | (1,033) |
| Total | $2,163 |

[27]The FASB has been working on a project involving business combinations. This project is expected to result in a standard that would be effective for fiscal years beginning December 31, 2006. One of the FASB's tentative conclusions is to require that in-process research and development costs would no longer be expensed in the period of acquisition but instead would be recorded as an asset measured at fair value.

Note that the Rational acquisition included a $229 million allocation to developed technology and only $9 million to in-process R&D. At the time of the acquisition, Rational was an established company with few new development projects underway resulting in the relatively small amount of in-process R&D. In the late 1990s, many technology-motivated acquisitions included allocations to in-process R&D that exceeded 75% of the purchase price. Graphic 10–9 shows some examples.

**GRAPHIC 10–9**
Percentages of In-Process R&D

| Acquiring Company | Acquired Company | Percentage of Purchase Price Allocated to In-Process R&D |
|---|---|---|
| Adobe Systems | Ares Software | 95% |
| 3Com | Axon Networks | 80 |
| Sphinx Pharmaceutical | Genesis Pharmaceutical | 100 |
| Cisco Systems | Lightstream | 80 |
| H&R Block | Spry | 78 |

A profusion of large-percentage write-offs caused the SEC to scrutinize the amounts allocated to in-process R&D and, in some cases, require the write-offs to be reduced. For example, the $37 billion acquisition of **MCI** by **WorldCom** originally included a $7 billion amount allocated to in-process R&D. The SEC convinced WorldCom to reduce this amount to $3.1 billion.

**An analyst must decide whether to consider in-process R&D expenses as transitory in nature or as a part of permanent earnings.**

Should financial statement users consider in-process R&D expenses as part of a company's permanent earnings stream, or are they transitory in nature? Consider the fact that significant in-process R&D expenses appear regularly in the income statements of **Cisco**, **Sun Microsystems**, and other high-technology companies. In a manner similar to such items as restructuring costs and losses from inventory write-downs, a financial analyst must carefully consider the nature of these expenses in an assessment of a company's permanent earnings.

The immediate expensing of in-process R&D is another example of "big bath" accounting techniques some companies use to manipulate earnings. By writing off large amounts of the purchase price, companies significantly reduce earnings in the year of acquisition. However, the larger the write-off, the smaller the amount allocated to goodwill. Until 2001, goodwill was capitalized and amortized over periods ranging from 3 to 10 years for most technology companies. The immediate write-off of a portion of the purchase price increased earnings for years into the future by reducing the amount of goodwill amortization.

**BUSINESSWEEK**
". . . The aim of many of today's giant write-offs is to front-load expenses. Charge off three years of expenses all at once, and by definition future earnings will be better. It's akin to making three years of mortgage payments at once, then claiming your income has grown."[28]

As you learned earlier in this chapter, recent accounting standards significantly changed the accounting treatment of goodwill, eliminating the practice of amortizing goodwill. Will this change in accounting standards reduce companies' desire to write off large amounts of purchase price as in-process R&D? There is no easy answer to this question. Even though goodwill is no longer subject to periodic amortization, it is still subject to the impairment of value rules that we discuss in Chapter 11. These rules could result in large future write-downs of the cost of goodwill. Companies may still be motivated to write-off immediately as much of the purchase price of a business acquisition as possible to avoid any future income reductions.

[28]"Earnings Hocus-Pocus: How Companies Come Up with the Numbers They Want," *BusinessWeek* (October 5, 1998), p. 135.

## FINANCIAL REPORTING CASE SOLUTION

1. **Describe to Stan what it means to capitalize an expenditure. What is the general rule for determining which costs are capitalized when an operational asset is acquired?** (p. 453) To capitalize an expenditure simply means to record it as an asset. All expenditures other than payments to shareholders and debt repayments are either expensed as incurred or capitalized. In general, the choice is determined by whether the expenditure benefits more than just the current period. Exceptions to this general principle are discussed in the chapter. The initial cost of an operational asset includes all expenditures necessary to bring the asset to its desired condition and location for use.
2. **Which costs might be included in the initial cost of equipment?** (p. 455) In addition to the purchase price, the cost of equipment might include the cost of transportation, installation, testing, and legal fees to establish title.
3. **In what situations is interest capitalized rather than expensed?** (p. 471) Interest is capitalized only for assets constructed for a company's own use or for assets constructed as discrete products for sale or lease. For example, Walt Disney capitalizes interest on assets constructed for its theme parks, resorts and other property, and on theatrical and television productions in process. During the construction period, interest is considered a cost necessary to get the asset ready for its intended use.
4. **What is the three-step process used to determine the amount of interest capitalized?** (p. 472) The first step is to determine the average accumulated expenditures for the period. The second step is to multiply the average accumulated expenditures by an appropriate interest rate or rates to determine the amount of interest capitalized. A final step compares the interest determined in step two with actual interest incurred. Interest capitalized is limited to the amount of interest incurred.
5. **What is goodwill and how is it measured? Why didn't the amount of goodwill in Disney's 2004 balance sheet change from the prior year?** (p. 461) Goodwill represents the unique value of a company as a whole over and above its identifiable tangible and intangible assets. Because goodwill can't be separated from a company, it's not possible for a buyer to acquire it without also acquiring the whole company or a substantial portion of it. Goodwill will appear as an asset in a balance sheet only when it was purchased in connection with the acquisition of another company. In that case, the capitalized cost of goodwill equals the purchase price of the company less the fair value of the net assets acquired. Goodwill is a residual asset; it's the amount left after other assets are identified and valued. Recent accounting standards have significantly changed the way we account for goodwill. Before these new standards became effective in 2001, we amortized (expensed over time) goodwill just like any other intangible asset. This no longer is the case. Now, just like for other intangible assets that have indefinite useful lives, we do not amortize goodwill. That is why the amount of goodwill in Disney's 2004 balance sheet did not change from the prior year. ■

## THE BOTTOM LINE

1. The initial cost of an operational asset acquired in an exchange transaction includes the purchase price and all expenditures necessary to bring the asset to its desired condition and location for use. The cost of a natural resource includes the acquisition costs for the use of land, the exploration and development costs incurred before production begins, and restoration costs incurred during or at the end of extraction. Purchased intangibles are valued at their original cost to include the purchase price and legal and filing fees.
2. If a lump-sum purchase involves different assets, it is necessary to allocate the lump-sum acquisition price among the separate items according to some logical allocation method. A widely used allocation method is to divide the lump-sum purchase price according to the individual assets' relative market values.

3. Assets acquired in exchange for deferred payment contracts are valued at their fair value or the present value of payments using a realistic interest rate.
4. Assets acquired through the issuance of equity securities are valued at the fair value of the securities if known; if not known, the fair value of the assets received is used. Donated assets are valued at their fair value.
5. A key to profitability is how well a company manages and utilizes its assets. Financial analysts often use activity, or turnover, ratios to evaluate a company's effectiveness in managing its assets. Operational assets—particularly property, plant, and equipment (PP&E)—usually are a company's primary revenue-generating assets. Their efficient use is critical to generating a satisfactory return to owners. One ratio that analysts often use to measure how effectively managers use PP&E is the fixed-asset turnover ratio. This ratio is calculated by dividing net sales by average fixed assets.
6. When an operational asset is sold, a gain or loss is recognized for the difference between the consideration received and the asset's book value. The basic principle used for nonmonetary exchanges is to value the asset(s) received based on the fair value of the asset(s) given up. In certain situations, the valuation of the asset(s) received is based on the book value of the asset(s) given up.
7. The cost of a self-constructed asset includes identifiable materials and labor and a portion of the company's manufacturing overhead costs. In addition, GAAP provide for the capitalization of interest incurred during construction. The amount of interest capitalized is equal to the average accumulated expenditures for the period multiplied by the appropriate interest rates, not to exceed actual interest incurred.
8. Research and development costs incurred to internally develop an intangible asset are expensed in the period incurred. Filing and legal costs for developed intangibles are capitalized. ■

## APPENDIX 10 OIL AND GAS ACCOUNTING

Chapter 1 characterized the establishment of accounting and reporting standards as a political process. Standards, particularly changes in standards, can have significant differential effects on companies, investors and creditors, and other interest groups. The FASB must consider potential economic consequences of a change in an accounting standard or the introduction of a new standard. The history of oil and gas accounting provides a good example of this political process and the effect of possible adverse economic consequences on the standard-setting process.

There are two generally accepted methods that companies can use to account for oil and gas exploration costs. The **successful efforts method** requires that exploration costs that are known *not* to have resulted in the discovery of oil or gas (sometimes referred to as *dry holes*) be included as expenses in the period the expenditures are made. The alternative, the **full-cost method,** allows costs incurred in searching for oil and gas within a large geographical area to be capitalized as assets and expensed in the future as oil and gas from the successful wells are removed from that area. Both of these methods are widely used. Illustration 10A–1 compares the two alternatives.

**ILLUSTRATION 10A–1**
Oil and Gas Accounting

The Shannon Oil Company incurred $2,000,000 in exploration costs for each of 10 oil wells drilled in 2006 in west Texas. Eight of the 10 wells were dry holes.

The accounting treatment of the $20 million in total exploration costs will vary significantly depending on the accounting method used. The summary journal entries using each of the alternative methods are as follows:

| Successful Efforts | | | Full Cost | | |
|---|---|---|---|---|---|
| Oil deposit | 4,000,000 | | Oil deposit | 20,000,000 | |
| Exploration expense | 16,000,000 | | Cash | | 20,000,000 |
| Cash | | 20,000,000 | | | |

Using the full-cost method, Shannon would capitalize the entire $20 million which is expensed as oil from the two successful wells is depleted. On the other hand, using the successful efforts method, the cost of the unsuccessful wells is expensed in 2006, and only the $4 million cost related to the successful wells is capitalized and expensed in future periods as the oil is depleted.

In 1977 the FASB attempted to establish uniformity in the accounting treatment of oil and gas exploration costs. *SFAS 19* was issued requiring all companies to use the successful efforts method.[29]

*SFAS 19* met with criticism from the oil and gas companies that were required to switch from full cost to successful efforts accounting. These companies felt that the switch would seriously depress their reported income over time. As a result, they argued, their ability to raise capital in the securities markets would be inhibited, which would result in a cutback of new exploration. The fear that the standard would cause domestic companies to significantly reduce oil and gas exploration and thus increase our dependence on foreign oil was compelling to the U.S. Congress, the SEC, and the Department of Energy.

**Many feared that the implementation of *SFAS 19* would cause a significant cutback in the exploration for new oil and gas in the United States.**

Extensive pressure from Congress, the SEC, and affected companies forced the FASB to rescind *Standard 19.* Presently, oil and gas companies can use either the successful efforts or full-cost method to account for oil and gas exploration costs. Of course, the method used must be disclosed. For example, Graphic 10A–1 shows how **ChevronTexaco Corp.**, disclosed their use of the successful efforts method in a note to recent financial statements.

**Properties, Plant and Equipment**
The successful efforts method is used for oil and gas exploration and production activities.

**GRAPHIC 10A–1**
Oil and Gas Accounting Disclosure—ChevronTexaco Corp.

[29]"Financial Accounting and Reporting by Oil and Gas Producing Companies," *Statement of Financial Accounting Standards No. 19* (Stamford, Conn.: FASB, 1977).

## QUESTIONS FOR REVIEW OF KEY TOPICS

**Q 10–1** Define operational assets and explain the difference between tangible and intangible operational assets.

**Q 10–2** What is included in the original cost of an operational asset acquired in an exchange transaction?

**Q 10–3** Identify the costs associated with the initial valuation of a developed natural resource.

**Q 10–4** Briefly summarize the accounting treatment for intangible assets, explaining the difference between purchased and internally developed intangible assets.

**Q 10–5** What is goodwill and how is it measured?

**Q 10–6** Explain the method generally used to allocate the cost of a lump-sum purchase to the individual assets acquired.

**Q 10–7** When an operational asset is acquired and a note payable is assumed, explain how acquisition cost of the asset is determined when the interest rate for the note is less than the current market rate for similar notes.

**Q 10–8** Explain how operational assets acquired in exchange for equity securities are valued.

**Q 10–9** Explain how operational assets acquired through donation are valued.

**Q 10–10** When an operational asset is disposed of, how is gain or loss on disposal computed?

**Q 10–11** What is the basic principle for valuing operational assets acquired in exchange for other nonmonetary assets?

**Q 10–12** Identify the two exceptions to valuing operational assets acquired in nonmonetary exchanges at the fair value of the asset(s) given up.

**Q 10–13** In what situations is interest capitalized?

**Q 10–14** Define average accumulated expenditures and explain how it is computed.

**Q 10–15** Explain the difference between the specific interest method and the weighted-average method in determining the amount of interest to be capitalized.

**Q 10–16** Define R&D according to *SFAS 2.*

**Q 10–17** Explain the accounting treatment of equipment acquired for use in R&D projects.

**Q 10–18** Explain the accounting treatment of costs incurred to develop computer software.

**Q 10–19** Explain the difference in the accounting treatment of the cost of developed technology and the cost of in-process R&D in an acquisition.

**Q 10–20** (Based on Appendix 10) Explain the difference between the successful efforts and the full-cost methods of accounting for oil and gas exploration costs.

# BRIEF EXERCISES

**BE 10–1**
Acquisition cost; machine
● LO1

Beaverton Lumber purchased a milling machine for $35,000. In addition to the purchase price, Beaverton made the following expenditures: freight, $1,500; installation, $3,000; testing, $2,000; personal property tax on the machine for the first year, $500. What is the initial cost of the machine?

**BE 10–2**
Acquisition cost; land and building
● LO1

Fullerton Waste Management purchased land and a warehouse for $600,000. In addition to the purchase price, Fullerton made the following expenditures related to the acquisition: broker's commission, $30,000; title insurance, $3,000; miscellaneous closing costs, $6,000. The warehouse was immediately demolished at a cost of $18,000 in anticipation of the building of a new warehouse. Determine the amounts Fullerton should capitalize as the cost of the land and the building.

**BE 10–3**
Lump-sum acquisition
● LO2

Refer to the situation described in BE 10–2. Assume that Fullerton decides to use the warehouse rather than demolishing it. An independent appraisal estimates the market values of the land and warehouse at $420,000 and $280,000, respectively. Determine the amounts Fullerton should capitalize as the cost of the land and the building.

**BE 10–4**
Cost of a natural resource
● LO1

Smithson Mining operates a silver mine in Nevada. Acquisition, exploration, and development costs totaled $5.6 million. After the silver is extracted in approximately five years, Smithson is obligated to restore the land to its original condition, including constructing a wildlife preserve. The company's controller has provided the following three cash flow possibilities for the restoration costs: (1) $500,000, 20% probability; (2) $550,000, 45% probability; and (3) $650,000, 35% probability. The company's credit-adjusted, risk-free rate of interest is 6%. What is the initial cost of the silver mine?

**BE 10–5**
Cost of a natural resource
● LO1

Refer to the situation described in BE 10–4. What is the carrying value of the asset retirement liability at the end of one year? Assuming that the actual restoration costs incurred after extraction is completed are $596,000, what amount of gain or loss will Smithson recognize on retirement of the liability?

**BE 10–6**
Goodwill
● LO1

Pro-tech Software acquired all of the outstanding stock of Reliable Software for $14 million. The book value of Reliable's net assets (assets minus liabilities) was $8.3 million. The fair values of Reliable's assets and liabilities equaled their book values with the exception of certain intangible assets whose fair values exceeded book values by $2.5 million. Calculate the amount paid for goodwill.

**BE 10–7**
Acquisition cost; noninterest-bearing note
● LO3

On June 30, Kimberly Farms purchased custom-made harvesting machinery from a local producer. In payment, Kimberly signed a noninterest-bearing note requiring the payment of $60,000 in two years. The fair value of the machinery is not known, but an 8% interest rate properly reflects the time value of money for this type of loan agreement. At what amount will Kimberly initially value the machinery? How much interest expense will Kimberly recognize in its income statement for this note for the year ended December 31?

**BE 10–8**
Acquisition cost; issuance of equity securities
● LO4

Shackelford Corporation acquired a patent from its founder, Jim Shackelford, in exchange for 50,000 shares of the company's nopar common stock. On the date of the exchange, the common stock had a market value of $22 per share. Determine the cost of the patent.

**BE 10–9**
Fixed-asset turnover ratio; solve for unknown
● LO5

The balance sheets of Pinewood Resorts reported net fixed assets of $740,000 and $940,000 at the end of 2005 and 2006, respectively. The fixed-asset turnover ratio for 2006 was 3.25. Calculate Pinewood's net sales for 2006.

**BE 10–10**
Disposal of operational assets
● LO6

Lawler Clothing sold manufacturing equipment for $16,000. Lawler originally purchased the equipment for $80,000, and depreciation through the date of sale totaled $71,000. What was the gain or loss on the sale of the equipment?

**BE 10–11**
Nonmonetary exchange
● LO6

Calaveras Tire exchanged machinery for two pickup trucks. The book value and fair value of the machinery were $20,000 (original cost of $65,000 less accumulated depreciation of $45,000) and $17,000, respectively. To equalize fair values, Calaveras received $8,000 in cash. At what amount will Calaveras value the pickup trucks? How much gain or loss will the company recognize on the exchange?

**BE 10–12**
Nonmonetary exchange
● LO6

Refer to the situation described in BE 10–11. Answer the questions assuming that the fair value of the machinery was $24,000, instead of $17,000.

**BE 10–13**
Nonmonetary exchange
● LO6

Refer to the situation described in BE 10–11. Answer the questions assuming that the exchange lacks commercial substance.

**BE 10–14**
Interest capitalization
● LO7

A company constructs a building for its own use. Construction began on January 2 and ended on December 28. The expenditures for construction were as follows: January 2, $500,000; March 31, $600,000; June 30, $400,000; October 30, $600,000. To help finance construction, the company arranged a 7% construction loan on January 2 for $700,000. The company's other borrowings, outstanding for the whole year, consisted of a $3 million loan and a $5 million note with interest rates of 8% and 6%, respectively. Assuming the company uses the *specific interest method,* calculate the amount of interest capitalized for the year.

**BE 10–15**
Interest capitalization
● LO7

Refer to the situation described in BE 10–14. Assuming the company uses the *weighted-average method,* calculate the amount of interest capitalized for the year.

**BE 10–16**
Research and development
● LO8

Maxtor Technology incurred the following costs during the year related to the creation of a new type of personal computer monitor:

| | |
|---|---|
| Salaries | $220,000 |
| Depreciation on R&D facilities and equipment | 125,000 |
| Utilities and other direct costs incurred for the R&D facilities | 66,000 |
| Patent filing and related legal costs | 22,000 |
| Payment to another company for performing a portion of the development work | 120,000 |
| Costs of adapting the new monitor for the specific needs of a customer | 80,000 |

What amount should Maxtor report as research and development expense in its income statement?

## EXERCISES

available with McGraw-Hill's Homework Manager www.mhhe.com/spiceland4e

**An alternate exercise and problem set is available on the text website: www.mhhe.com/spiceland4e**

**E 10–1**
Acquisition costs; land and building
● LO1

On March 1, 2006, Beldon Corporation purchased land as a factory site for $60,000. An old building on the property was demolished, and construction began on a new building that was completed on December 15, 2006. Costs incurred during this period are listed below:

| | |
|---|---|
| Demolition of old building | $ 4,000 |
| Architect's fees (for new building) | 12,000 |
| Legal fees for title investigation of land | 2,000 |
| Property taxes on land (for period beginning March 1, 2006) | 3,000 |
| Construction costs | 500,000 |
| Interest on construction loan | 5,000 |

Salvaged materials resulting from the demolition of the old building were sold for $2,000.

**Required:**
Determine the amounts that Beldon should capitalize as the cost of the land and the new building.

**E 10–2**
Acquisition cost; machinery

● LO1

Oaktree Company purchased a new machine and made the following expenditures:

| | |
|---|---|
| Purchase price | $45,000 |
| Sales tax | 2,200 |
| Freight charges for shipment of machine | 700 |
| Insurance on the machine for the first year | 900 |
| Installation of machine | 1,000 |

The machine, including sales tax, was purchased on open account, with payment due in 30 days. The other expenditures listed above were paid in cash.

**Required:**
Prepare the necessary journal entries to record the above expenditures.

**E 10–3**
Cost of a natural resource

● LO1

Jackpot Mining Company operates a copper mine in central Montana. The company paid $1,000,000 in 2006 for the mining site and spent an additional $600,000 to prepare the mine for extraction of the copper. After the copper is extracted in approximately four years, the company is required to restore the land to its original condition, including repaving of roads and replacing a greenbelt. The company has provided the following three cash flow possibilities for the restoration costs:

| | Cash Outflow | Probability |
|---|---|---|
| 1 | $300,000 | 25% |
| 2 | 400,000 | 40% |
| 3 | 600,000 | 35% |

To aid extraction, Jackpot purchased some new equipment on July 1, 2006, for $120,000. After the copper is removed from this mine, the equipment will be sold. The credit-adjusted, risk-free rate of interest is 10%.

**Required:**
1. Determine the cost of the copper mine.
2. Prepare the journal entries to record the acquisition costs of the mine and the purchase of equipment.

**E 10–4**
Intangibles

● LO1

Freitas Corporation was organized early in 2006. The following expenditures were made during the first few months of the year:

| | |
|---|---|
| Attorneys' fees in connection with the organization of the corporation | $ 12,000 |
| State filing fees and other incorporation costs | 3,000 |
| Purchase of a patent | 20,000 |
| Legal and other fees for transfer of the patent | 2,000 |
| Purchase of furniture | 30,000 |
| Pre-opening salaries | 40,000 |
| Total | $107,000 |

**Required:**
Prepare a summary journal entry to record the $107,000 in cash expenditures.

**E 10–5**
Goodwill

● LO1

On March 31, 2006, the Wolfson Corporation acquired all of the outstanding common stock of Barney Corporation for $17,000,000 in cash. The book values and fair values of Barney's assets and liabilities were as follows:

| | Book Value | Fair Value |
|---|---|---|
| Current assets | $ 6,000,000 | $ 7,500,000 |
| Property, plant, and equipment | 11,000,000 | 14,000,000 |
| Other assets | 1,000,000 | 1,500,000 |
| Current liabilities | 4,000,000 | 4,000,000 |
| Long-term liabilities | 6,000,000 | 5,500,000 |

**Required:**
Calculate the amount paid for goodwill.

**E 10–6**
Goodwill

● LO1

Johnson Corporation purchased all of the outstanding common stock of Smith Corporation for $11,000,000 in cash. The book value of Smith's net assets (assets minus liabilities) was $7,800,000. The fair values of all of Smith's assets and liabilities were equal to their book values with the following exceptions:

| | Book Value | Fair Value |
|---|---|---|
| Receivables | $1,300,000 | $1,100,000 |
| Property, plant, and equipment | 8,000,000 | 9,400,000 |
| Intangible assets | 200,000 | 1,200,000 |

**Required:**
Calculate the amount paid for goodwill.

**E 10–7**
Multiple choice; operational assets

● LO1

The following questions dealing with operational assets are adapted from questions that appeared on CPA examinations. Determine the response that best completes the statements or questions.

1. On December 1, 2006, Boyd Co. purchased a $400,000 tract of land for a factory site. Boyd razed an old building on the property and sold the materials it salvaged from the demolition. Boyd incurred additional costs and realized salvage proceeds during December 2006 as follows:

| | |
|---|---|
| Demolition of old building | $50,000 |
| Legal fees for purchase contract and recording of ownership | 10,000 |
| Title guarantee insurance | 12,000 |
| Proceeds from sale of salvaged materials | 8,000 |

In its December 31, 2006, balance sheet, Boyd should report a balance in the land account of
a. $464,000
b. $460,000
c. $442,000
d. $422,000

2. On October 1, 2006, Shaw Corp. purchased a machine for $126,000 that was placed in service on November 30, 2006. Shaw incurred additional costs for this machine, as follows:

| | |
|---|---|
| Shipping | $3,000 |
| Installation | 4,000 |
| Testing | 5,000 |

In Shaw's December 31, 2006, balance sheet, the machine's cost should be reported as
a. $126,000
b. $129,000
c. $133,000
d. $138,000

3. Hy Corp. bought Patent A for $40,000 and Patent B for $60,000. Hy also paid acquisition costs of $5,000 for Patent A and $7,000 for Patent B. Both patents were challenged in legal actions. Hy paid $20,000 in legal fees for a successful defense of Patent A and $30,000 in legal fees for an unsuccessful defense of Patent B. What amount should Hy capitalize for patents?
a. $162,000
b. $112,000
c. $65,000
d. $45,000

**E 10–8**
Lump-sum acquisition

● LO2

Pinewood Company purchased two buildings on four acres of land. The lump-sum purchase price was $900,000. According to independent appraisals, the fair market values were $450,000 (building A) and $250,000 (building B) for the buildings and $300,000 for the land.

**Required:**
Determine the initial valuation of the buildings and the land.

**E 10–9**
Acquisition cost; noninterest-bearing note

● LO3

On January 1, 2006, Byner Company purchased a used tractor. Byner paid $5,000 down and signed a noninterest-bearing note requiring $25,000 to be paid on December 31, 2008. The fair value of the tractor is not determinable. An interest rate of 10% properly reflects the time value of money for this type of loan agreement. The company's fiscal year-end is December 31.

**Required:**
1. Prepare the journal entry to record the acquisition of the tractor. Round computations to the nearest dollar.
2. How much interest expense will the company include in its 2006 and 2007 income statements for this note?
3. What is the amount of the liability the company will report in its 2006 and 2007 balance sheets for this note?

**E 10–10**
Acquisition cost; issuance of equity securities and donation

● LO4

On February 1, 2006, the Xilon Corporation issued 5,000 shares of its nopar common stock in exchange for five acres of land located in the city of Monrovia. On the date of the acquisition, Xilon's common stock had a market value of $18 per share. An office building was constructed on the site by an independent contractor. The building was completed on November 2, 2006, at a cost of $600,000. Xilon paid $400,000 in cash and the remainder was paid by the city of Monrovia.

**Required:**
Prepare the journal entries to record the acquisition of the land and the building, assuming that *SFAS 116* guidelines apply.

**E 10–11**
Fixed-asset turnover ratio

● LO 5

**Intel Corporation** reported the following information in its 2004 financial statements ($ in millions):

| | 2004 | 2003 |
|---|---|---|
| **Balance sheets** | | |
| Property, plant, and equipment (net) | $15,768 | $16,661 |
| **Income statement** | | |
| Net sales for 2004 | $34,209 | |

**Required:**
1. Calculate Intel's 2004 fixed-asset turnover ratio.
2. How would you interpret this ratio?

**E 10–12**
Disposal of operational asset

● LO6

Funseth Farms, Inc. purchased a tractor in 2003 at a cost of $30,000. The tractor was sold for $3,000 in 2006. Depreciation recorded through the disposal date totaled $26,000.

**Required:**
1. Prepare the journal entry to record the sale.
2. Assuming that the tractor was sold for $10,000, prepare the journal entry to record the sale.

**E 10–13**
Nonmonetary exchange

● LO6

Cedric Company recently traded in an older model computer for a new model. The old model's book value was $180,000 (original cost of $400,000 less $220,000 in accumulated depreciation) and its fair value was $200,000. Cedric paid $60,000 to complete the exchange.

**Required:**
Prepare the journal entry to record the exchange.

**E 10–14**
Nonmonetary exchange

● LO6

[This is a variation of the previous exercise.]

**Required:**
Assume the same facts as in Exercise 10–13, except that the fair value of the old equipment is $170,000. Prepare the journal entry to record the exchange.

**E 10–15**
Nonmonetary exchange

● LO6

The Bronco Corporation exchanged land for a patent. The land had a book value of $120,000 and a fair value of $150,000. Bronco paid the owner of the patent $10,000 to complete the exchange.

**Required:**
1. What is the fair value of the patent?
2. Prepare the journal entry to record the exchange.

**E 10–16**
Nonmonetary exchange

● LO6

[This is a variation of the previous exercise.]

**Required:**
Assume the same facts as in Exercise 10–15 except that Bronco *received* $10,000 from the owner of the patent to complete the exchange.
1. What is the fair value of the patent?
2. Prepare the journal entry to record the exchange.

**E 10–17**
Nonmonetary exchange

● LO6

The Tinsley Company exchanged land that it had been holding for future plant expansion for a more suitable parcel located farther from residential areas. Tinsley carried the land at its original cost of $30,000. According to an independent appraisal, the land currently is worth $72,000. Tinsley gave $14,000 in cash to complete the transaction.

**Required:**
1. What is the fair value of the new parcel of land received by Tinsley?
2. Prepare the journal entry to record the exchange.
3. Prepare the journal entry to record the exchange assuming the exchange lacks commercial substance.

**E 10–18**
Acquisition cost; multiple methods

● LO1 LO3 LO4

Connors Corporation acquired manufacturing equipment for use in its assembly line. Below are four *independent* situations relating to the acquisition of the equipment.
1. The equipment was purchased on account for $25,000. Credit terms were 2/10, n/30. Payment was made within the discount period and the company records the purchases of equipment net of discounts.
2. Connors gave the seller a noninterest-bearing note. The note required payment of $27,000 one year from date of purchase. The fair value of the equipment is not determinable. An interest rate of 10% properly reflects the time value of money in this situation.
3. Connors traded in old equipment that had a book value of $6,000 (original cost of $14,000 and accumulated depreciation of $8,000) and paid cash of $22,000. The old equipment had a fair value of $2,500 on the date of the exchange.
4. Connors issued 1,000 shares of its nopar common stock in exchange for the equipment. The market value of the common stock was not determinable. The equipment could have been purchased for $24,000 in cash.

**Required:**

For each of the above situations, prepare the journal entry required to record the acquisition of the equipment. Round computations to the nearest dollar.

**E 10–19**
Interest capitalization

● LO7

On January 1, 2006, the Marjlee Company began construction of an office building to be used as its corporate headquarters. The building was completed early in 2007. Construction expenditures for 2006, which were incurred evenly throughout the year, totaled $6,000,000. Marjlee had the following debt obligations which were outstanding during all of 2006:

| | |
|---|---|
| Construction loan, 10% | $1,500,000 |
| Long-term note, 9% | 2,000,000 |
| Long-term note, 6% | 4,000,000 |

**Required:**

Calculate the amount of interest capitalized for the building using the specific interest method.

**E 10–20**
Interest capitalization

● LO7

On January 2, 2006, the Shagri Company began construction on a new manufacturing facility for its own use. The building was completed in 2007. The only interest-bearing debt the company had outstanding during 2006 was long-term bonds with a carrying value of $10,000,000 and an effective interest rate of 8%. Construction expenditures incurred during 2006 were as follows:

| | |
|---|---|
| January 2 | $500,000 |
| March 1 | 600,000 |
| July 31 | 480,000 |
| September 30 | 600,000 |
| December 31 | 300,000 |

**Required:**

Calculate the amount of interest capitalized for 2006.

**E 10–21**
Interest capitalization

● LO7

On January 2, 2006, the Highlands Company began construction on a new manufacturing facility for its own use. The building was completed in 2007. The company borrowed $1,500,000 at 8% on January 2 to help finance the construction. In addition to the construction loan, Highlands had the following debt outstanding throughout 2006:

$5,000,000, 12% bonds
$3,000,000, 8% long-term note

Construction expenditures incurred during 2006 were as follows:

| | |
|---|---|
| January 2 | $ 600,000 |
| March 31 | 1,200,000 |
| June 30 | 800,000 |
| September 30 | 600,000 |
| December 31 | 400,000 |

**Required:**

Calculate the amount of interest capitalized for 2006 using the specific interest method.

**E 10–22**
Research and development

● LO8

In 2006, Space Technology Company modified its model Z2 satellite to incorporate a new communication device. The company made the following expenditures:

| | |
|---|---|
| Basic research to develop the technology | $2,000,000 |
| Engineering design work | 680,000 |
| Development of a prototype device | 300,000 |
| Acquisition of equipment | 60,000 |
| Testing and modification of the prototype | 200,000 |
| Legal and other fees for patent application on the new communication system | 40,000 |
| Legal fees for successful defense of the new patent | 20,000 |
| Total | $3,300,000 |

The equipment will be used on this and other research projects. Depreciation on the equipment for 2006 is $10,000.

During your year-end review of the accounts related to intangibles, you discover that the company has capitalized all of the above as costs of the patent. Management contends that the device simply represents an improvement of the existing communication system of the satellite and, therefore, should be capitalized.

**Required:**

Prepare correcting entries that reflect the appropriate treatment of the expenditures.

**E 10–23**
Research and development

● LO8

Delaware Company incurred the following research and development costs during 2006:

| | |
|---|---|
| Salaries and wages for lab research | $ 400,000 |
| Materials used in R&D projects | 200,000 |
| Purchase of equipment | 900,000 |
| Fees paid to outsiders for R&D projects | 320,000 |
| Patent filing and legal costs for a developed product | 65,000 |
| Salaries, wages, and supplies for R&D work performed for another company under a contract | 350,000 |
| Total | $2,235,000 |

The equipment has a seven-year life and will be used for a number of research projects. Depreciation for 2006 is $120,000.

**Required:**
Calculate the amount of research and development expense that Delaware should report in its 2006 income statement.

**E 10–24**
Multiple choice; operational assets

● LO6 through LO8

The following questions dealing with operational assets are adapted from questions that appeared on CPA examinations. Determine the response that best completes the statements or questions.

1. Dahl Co. traded a delivery van and $5,000 cash for a newer van owned by West Corp. The following information relates to the values of the vans on the exchange date:

| | Book Value | Fair Value |
|---|---|---|
| Old van | $30,000 | $45,000 |
| New van | 40,000 | 50,000 |

Dahl's income tax rate is 30%. What amount should Dahl report as gain on exchange of the vans.
a. $15,000
b. $1,000
c. $700
d. $0

2. Heller Co. incurred the following costs in 2006:

| | |
|---|---|
| Research and development services performed by Kay Corp. for Heller | $150,000 |
| Testing for evaluation of new products | 125,000 |
| Laboratory research aimed at discovery of new knowledge | 185,000 |

What amount should Heller report as research and development expense in its income statement for the year ended December 31, 2006?
a. $125,000
b. $150,000
c. $335,000
d. $460,000

3. During 2006, Bay Co. constructed machinery for its own use and for sale to customers. Bay Co. routinely manufactures machinery for sale. Bank loans financed these assets both during construction and after construction was complete. How much of the interest incurred should be reported as interest expense in the 2006 income statement?

| | Interest Incurred for Machinery for Own Use | Interest Incurred for Machinery Held for Sale |
|---|---|---|
| a. | All interest incurred | All interest incurred |
| b. | All interest incurred | Interest incurred after completion |
| c. | Interest incurred after completion | Interest incurred after completion |
| d. | Interest incurred after completion | All interest incurred |

4. Cole Co. began constructing a new building for its own use in January 2006. During 2006, Cole incurred interest of $50,000 on specific construction debt and $20,000 on other borrowings. Interest computed on the weighted-average amount of accumulated expenditures for the building during 2006 was $40,000. What amount of interest cost should Cole capitalize?
a. $20,000
b. $40,000
c. $50,000
d. $70,000

**E 10–25**
Concepts; terminology

● LO1 LO4 LO6 LO7

Listed below are several terms and phrases associated with operational assets. Pair each item from List A (by letter) with the item from List B that is most appropriately associated with it.

| List A | List B |
|---|---|
| ____ 1. Depreciation | a. Exclusive right to display a word, a symbol, or an emblem. |
| ____ 2. Depletion | b. Exclusive right to benefit from a creative work. |
| ____ 3. Amortization | c. Operational assets that represent rights. |
| ____ 4. Average accumulated expenditures | d. The allocation of cost for natural resources. |
| ____ 5. Revenue—donation of asset | e. Purchase price less fair market value of net identifiable assets. |
| ____ 6. Nonmonetary exchange | f. The allocation of cost for plant and equipment. |
| ____ 7. Natural resources | g. Approximation of average amount of debt if all construction funds were borrowed. |
| ____ 8. Intangible assets | h. Account credited when assets are donated to a corporation. |
| ____ 9. Copyright | i. The allocation of cost for intangible assets. |
| ____ 10. Trademark | j. Basic principle is to value assets acquired using fair value of assets given. |
| ____ 11. Goodwill | k. Wasting assets. |

**E 10–26**
Software development costs

● LO8

Early in 2006, the Excalibur Company began developing a new software package to be marketed. The project was completed in December 2006 at a cost of $6 million. Of this amount, $4 million was spent before technological feasibility was established. Excalibur expects a useful life of five years for the new product with total revenues of $10 million. During 2007, revenue of $4 million was recognized.

**Required:**

1. Prepare a journal entry to record the 2006 development costs.
2. Calculate the required amortization for 2007.
3. At what amount should the computer software costs be reported in the December 31, 2007, balance sheet?

**E 10–27**
Multiple choice; CMA exam; acquisition costs; nonmonetary exchange

● LO1 LO6

The following questions dealing with operational assets are adapted from questions that previously appeared on Certified Management Accountant (CMA) examinations. The CMA designation sponsored by the Institute of Management Accountants (**www.imanet.org**) provides members with an objective measure of knowledge and competence in the field of management accounting. Determine the response that best completes the statements or questions.

1. Pearl Corporation acquired manufacturing machinery on January 1 for $9,000. During the year, the machine produced 1,000 units, of which 600 were sold. There was no work-in-process inventory at the beginning or at the end of the year. Installation charges of $300 and delivery charges of $200 were also incurred. The machine is expected to have a useful life of five years with an estimated salvage value of $1,500. Pearl uses the straight-line depreciation method. The original cost of the machinery to be recorded in Pearl's books is
   a. $9,500.
   b. $9,300.
   c. $9,200.
   d. $9,000.

Questions 2 and 3 are based on the following information. Harper is contemplating exchanging a machine used in its operations for a similar machine on May 31. Harper will exchange machines with either Austin Corporation or Lubin Company. The data relating to the machines are presented below.

| | Harper | Austin | Lubin |
|---|---|---|---|
| Original cost of the machine | $162,500 | $180,000 | $150,000 |
| Accumulated depreciation thru May 31 | 98,500 | 70,000 | 65,000 |
| Fair value at May 31 | 80,000 | 95,000 | 60,000 |

2. If Harper exchanges its used machine and $15,000 cash for Austin's used machine, the gain that Harper should recognize from this transaction for financial reporting purposes would be
   a. $0
   b. $2,526
   c. $15,000
   d. $16,000
3. If Harper exchanges its used machine for Lubin's used machine and also receives $20,000 cash, the gain that Harper should recognize from this transaction for financial reporting purposes would be
   a. $0
   b. $4,000
   c. $16,000
   d. $25,000

**E 10–28**
Full-cost and successful efforts methods compared. (Based on Appendix 10)

● LO1

The Manguino Oil Company incurred exploration costs in 2006 searching and drilling for oil as follows:

| | |
|---|---|
| Well 101 | $ 50,000 |
| Well 102 | 60,000 |
| Well 103 | 80,000 |
| Wells 104–108 | 260,000 |
| Total | $450,000 |

It was determined that Wells 104–108 were dry holes and were abandoned. Wells 101, 102, and 103 were determined to have sufficient oil reserves to be commercially successful.

**Required:**

1. Prepare a summary journal entry to record the indicated costs assuming that the company uses the full-cost method of accounting for exploration costs. All of the exploration costs were paid in cash.
2. Prepare a summary journal entry to record the indicated costs assuming that the company uses the successful efforts method of accounting for exploration costs. All of the exploration costs were paid in cash.

## PROBLEMS

available with McGraw-Hill's Homework Manager www.mhhe.com/spiceland4e

**An alternate exercise and problem set is available on the text website: www.mhhe.com/spiceland4e**

**P 10–1**
Acquisition costs

● LO1 through LO4

eXcel

Tristar Production Company began operations on September 1, 2006. Listed below are a number of transactions that occurred during its first four months of operations.

1. On September 1, the company acquired five acres of land with a building that will be used as a warehouse. Tristar paid $100,000 in cash for the property. According to appraisals, the land had a fair market value of $75,000 and the building had a fair market value of $45,000.
2. On September 1, Tristar signed a $40,000 noninterest-bearing note to purchase equipment. The $40,000 payment is due on September 1, 2007. Assume that 8% is a reasonable interest rate.
3. On September 15, a truck was donated to the corporation. Similar trucks were selling for $2,500.
4. On September 18, the company paid its lawyer $3,000 for organizing the corporation.
5. On October 10, Tristar purchased machinery for cash. The purchase price was $15,000 and $500 in freight charges also were paid.
6. On December 2, Tristar acquired various items of office equipment. The company was short of cash and could not pay the $5,500 normal cash price. The supplier agreed to accept 200 shares of the company's nopar common stock in exchange for the equipment. The market value of the stock is not readily determinable.
7. On December 10, the company acquired a tract of land at a cost of $20,000. It paid $2,000 down and signed a 10% note with both principal and interest due in one year. Ten percent is an appropriate rate of interest for this note.

**Required:**

Prepare journal entries to record each of the above transactions.

**P 10–2**
Acquisition costs; land and building

● LO1 LO2 LO7

On January 1, 2006, the Blackstone Corporation purchased a tract of land (site number 11) with a building for $600,000. Additionally, Blackstone paid a real estate broker's commission of $36,000, legal fees of $6,000, and title insurance of $18,000. The closing statement indicated that the land value was $500,000 and the building value was $100,000. Shortly after acquisition, the building was razed at a cost of $75,000.

Blackstone entered into a $3,000,000 fixed-price contract with Barnett Builders, Inc., on March 1, 2006, for the construction of an office building on land site 11. The building was completed and occupied on September 30, 2007. Additional construction costs were incurred as follows:

| | |
|---|---|
| Plans, specifications, and blueprints | $12,000 |
| Architects' fees for design and supervision | 95,000 |

To finance the construction cost, Blackstone borrowed $3,000,000 on March 1, 2006. The loan is payable in 10 annual installments of $300,000 plus interest at the rate of 14%. Blackstone's average amounts of accumulated building construction expenditures were as follows:

| | |
|---|---|
| For the period March 1 to December 31, 2006 | $ 900,000 |
| For the period January 1 to September 30, 2007 | 2,300,000 |

**Required:**

1. Prepare a schedule that discloses the individual costs making up the balance in the land account in respect of land site 11 as of September 30, 2007.

2. Prepare a schedule that discloses the individual costs that should be capitalized in the office building account as of September 30, 2007.

*(AICPA adapted)*

**P 10–3**
Acquisition costs

● LO1 LO4 LO6

The plant asset and accumulated depreciation accounts of Pell Corporation had the following balances at December 31, 2005:

| | Plant Asset | Accumulated Depreciation |
|---|---|---|
| Land | $ 350,000 | $ — |
| Land improvements | 180,000 | 45,000 |
| Building | 1,500,000 | 350,000 |
| Machinery and equipment | 1,158,000 | 405,000 |
| Automobiles | 150,000 | 112,000 |

Transactions during 2006 were as follows:

a. On January 2, 2006, machinery and equipment were purchased at a total invoice cost of $260,000, which included a $5,500 charge for freight. Installation costs of $27,000 were incurred.
b. On March 31, 2006, a machine purchased for $58,000 in 2002 was sold for $36,500. Depreciation recorded through the date of sale totaled $24,650.
c. On May 1, 2006, expenditures of $50,000 were made to repave parking lots at Pell's plant location. The work was necessitated by damage caused by severe winter weather.
d. On November 1, 2006, Pell acquired a tract of land with an existing building in exchange for 10,000 shares of Pell's common stock that had a market price of $38 per share. Pell paid legal fees and title insurance totaling $23,000. Shortly after acquisition, the building was razed at a cost of $35,000 in anticipation of new building construction in 2007.
e. On December 31, 2006, Pell purchased a new automobile for $15,250 cash and trade-in of an old automobile purchased for $18,000 in 2002. Depreciation on the old automobile recorded through December 31, 2006, totaled $13,500. The market value of the old automobile was $3,750.

**Required:**

1. Prepare a schedule analyzing the changes in each of the plant assets during 2006, with detailed supporting computations.
2. Prepare a schedule showing the gain or loss from each asset disposal that would be recognized in Pell's income statement for the year ended December 31, 2006.

*(AICPA adapted)*

**P 10–4**
Intangibles

● LO1 LO8

The Horstmeyer Corporation commenced operations early in 2006. A number of expenditures were made during 2006 that were debited to one account called *intangible asset.* A recap of the $644,000 balance in this account at the end of 2006 is as follows:

| Date | Transaction | Amount |
|---|---|---|
| 2/3/06 | State incorporation fees and legal costs related to organizing the corporation | $ 7,000 |
| 3/1/06 | Fire insurance premium for three-year period | 6,000 |
| 3/15/06 | Purchased a copyright | 20,000 |
| 4/30/06 | Research and development costs | 40,000 |
| 6/15/06 | Legal fees for filing a patent on a new product resulting from an R&D project | 3,000 |
| 9/30/06 | Legal fee for successful defense of patent developed above | 12,000 |
| 10/13/06 | Entered into a 10-year franchise agreement with franchisor | 40,000 |
| Various | Advertising costs | 16,000 |
| 11/30/06 | Purchase of all of the outstanding common stock of Stiltz Corp. | 500,000 |
| | Total | $644,000 |

The total purchase price of the Stiltz Corp. stock was debited to this account. The market value of Stiltz Corp.'s assets and liabilities on the date of the purchase were as follows:

| | |
|---|---|
| Receivables | $100,000 |
| Equipment | 350,000 |
| Patent | 150,000 |
| Total assets | 600,000 |
| Note payable assumed | (220,000) |
| Market value of net assets | $380,000 |

**Required:**

Prepare the necessary journal entries to clear the intangible asset account and to set up accounts for separate intangibles, other types of assets, and expenses indicated by the transactions.

**P 10–5**
Acquisition costs; journal entries

● LO1 LO3 LO6 LO8

Consider each of the transactions below. All of the expenditures were made in cash.

1. The Edison Company spent $12,000 during the year for experimental purposes in connection with the development of a new product.
2. In April, the Marshall Company lost a patent infringement suit and paid the plaintiff $7,500.
3. In March, the Cleanway Laundromat bought equipment. Cleanway paid $6,000 down and signed a noninterest-bearing note requiring the payment of $18,000 in nine months. The cash price for this equipment was $23,000.
4. On June 1, the Jamsen Corporation installed a sprinkler system throughout the building at a cost of $28,000.
5. The Mayer Company, plaintiff, paid $12,000 in legal fees in November, in connection with a successful infringement suit on its patent.
6. The Johnson Company traded its old machine with an original cost of $7,400 and a book value of $3,000 plus cash of $8,000 for a new one that had a fair value of $10,000.

**Required:**
Prepare journal entries to record each of the above transactions.

**P 10–6**
Nonmonetary exchange

● LO6

Southern Company owns a building that it leases. The building's fair value is $1,400,000 and its book value is $800,000 (original cost of $2,000,000 less accumulated depreciation of $1,200,000). Southern exchanges this for another building owned by the Eastern Company. The building's book value on Eastern's books is $950,000 (original cost of $1,600,000 less accumulated depreciation of $650,000). Eastern also gives Southern $140,000 to complete the exchange.

**Required:**
Prepare the journal entries to record the exchange on the books of both Southern and Eastern.

**P 10–7**
Nonmonetary exchange

● LO6

On September 3, 2006, the Robers Company exchanged operational assets with Phifer Corporation. The facts of the exchange are as follows:

| | Robers' Asset | Phifer's Asset |
|---|---|---|
| Original cost | $120,000 | $140,000 |
| Accumulated depreciation | 55,000 | 63,000 |
| Fair value | 75,000 | 70,000 |

To equalize the exchange, Phifer paid Robers $5,000 in cash.

**Required:**
Record the exchange for both Robers and Phifer.

**P 10–8**
Interest capitalization; specific interest method

● LO7

eXcel

On January 1, 2006, the Mason Manufacturing Company began construction of a building to be used as its office headquarters. The building was completed on September 30, 2007.

Expenditures on the project were as follows:

| | |
|---|---|
| January 3, 2006 | $1,000,000 |
| March 1, 2006 | 600,000 |
| June 30, 2006 | 800,000 |
| October 1, 2006 | 600,000 |
| January 31, 2007 | 270,000 |
| April 30, 2007 | 585,000 |
| August 31, 2007 | 900,000 |

On January 2, 2006, the company obtained a $3 million construction loan with a 10% interest rate. The loan was outstanding all of 2006 and 2007. The company's other interest-bearing debt included two long-term notes of $4,000,000 and $6,000,000 with interest rates of 6% and 8%, respectively. Both notes were outstanding during all of 2006 and 2007. The company's fiscal year-end is December 31.

**Required:**

1. Calculate the amount of interest that Mason should capitalize in 2006 and 2007 using the specific interest method.
2. What is the total cost of the building?
3. Calculate the amount of interest expense that will appear in the 2006 and 2007 income statements.

**P 10–9**
Interest capitalization; weighted-average method

● LO7

eXcel

[This is a variation of the previous problem, modified to focus on the weighted-average interest method.]

**Required:**
Refer to the facts in Problem 10–8 and answer the following questions:

1. Calculate the amount of interest that Mason should capitalize in 2006 and 2007 using the weighted-average method.
2. What is the total cost of the building?
3. Calculate the amount of interest expense that will appear in the 2006 and 2007 income statements.

**P 10–10**
Research and development

• LO8

In 2006, Starsearch Corporation began work on three research and development projects. One of the projects was completed and commercial production of the developed product began in December. The company's fiscal year-end is December 31. All of the following 2006 expenditures were included in the R&D expense account:

| | |
|---|---|
| Salaries and wages for: | |
| Lab research | $ 300,000 |
| Design and construction of preproduction prototype | 160,000 |
| Quality control during commercial production | 20,000 |
| Materials and supplies consumed for: | |
| Lab research | 60,000 |
| Construction of preproduction prototype | 30,000 |
| Purchase of equipment | 600,000 |
| Patent filing and legal fees for completed project | 40,000 |
| Payments to others for research | 120,000 |
| Total | $1,330,000 |

$200,000 of equipment was purchased solely for use in one of the projects. After the project is completed, the equipment will be abandoned. The remaining $400,000 in equipment will be used on future R&D projects. The useful life of equipment is five years. Assume that all of the equipment was acquired at the beginning of the year.

**Required:**
Prepare journal entries to reflect the appropriate treatment of the expenditures.

# BROADEN YOUR PERSPECTIVE

**Apply your critical-thinking ability to the knowledge you've gained. These cases will provide you an opportunity to develop your research, analysis, judgment, and communication skills. You also will work with other students, integrate what you've learned, apply it in real world situations, and consider its global and ethical ramifications. This practice will broaden your knowledge and further develop your decision-making abilities.**

**Judgment Case 10–1**
Acquisition costs

• LO1 LO3 LO6

A company may acquire operational assets for cash, in exchange for a deferred payment contract, by exchanging other operational assets, or by a combination of these methods.

**Required:**
1. Identify six types of costs that should be capitalized as the cost of a parcel of land. For your answer, assume that the land has an existing building that is to be removed in the immediate future in order that a new building can be constructed on the site.
2. At what amount should a company record an operational asset acquired in exchange for a deferred payment contract?
3. In general, at what amount should operational assets received in exchange for other nonmonetary assets be valued? Specifically, at what amount should a company value a new machine acquired by exchanging an older, similar machine and paying cash?

*(AICPA adapted)*

**Research Case 10–2**
Locate and extract relevant information and cite authoritative support for a financial reporting issue; restoration costs; asset retirement obligation

• LO1

Your client, Hazelton Mining, recently entered into an agreement to obtain the rights to operate a coal mine in West Virginia for $15 million. Hazelton incurred development costs of $6 million in preparing the mine for extraction, which began on July 1, 2006. The contract requires Hazelton to restore the land and surrounding area to its original condition after extraction is complete in three years.

The company controller, Alice Cushing, is not sure how to account for the restoration costs and has asked your advice. Alice is aware of a recent accounting pronouncement addressing this issue, but is not sure of its provisions. She has narrowed down the possible cash outflows for the restoration costs to four possibilities:

| Cash Outflow | Probability |
|---|---|
| $3 million | 20% |
| 4 million | 30% |
| 5 million | 25% |
| 6 million | 25% |

Alice also informs you that the company's credit-adjusted risk-free interest rate is 9%. Before responding to Alice, you need to research the issue.

**Required:**

1. Obtain the original FASB Standard on accounting for asset retirement obligations. You might gain access through FARS, the FASB Financial Accounting Research System, from your school library, or some other source. Explain the basic treatment of asset retirement obligations.
2. Determine the capitalized cost of the coal mine.
3. Prepare a summary journal entry to record the acquisition costs of the mine.
4. How much accretion expense will the company record in its income statement for the fiscal year 2006, related to this transaction?
5. Explain to Alice how Hazelton would account for the restoration if the restoration costs differed from the recorded liability in three years. By way of explanation, prepare the journal entry to record the payment of the retirement obligation in three years assuming that the actual restoration costs were $4.7 million.
6. Describe to Alice the necessary disclosure requirements for the obligation.

**Judgment Case 10–3**
Self-constructed assets
● LO7

Chilton Peripherals manufactures printers, scanners, and other computer peripheral equipment. In the past, the company purchased equipment used in manufacturing from an outside vendor. In March 2006, Chilton decided to design and build equipment to replace some obsolete equipment. A section of the manufacturing plant was set aside to develop and produce the equipment. Additional personnel were hired for the project. The equipment was completed and ready for use in September.

**Required:**

1. In general, what costs should be capitalized for a self-constructed asset?
2. Discuss two alternatives for the inclusion of overhead costs in the cost of the equipment constructed by Chilton. Which alternative is generally accepted for financial reporting purposes?
3. Under what circumstance(s) would interest be included in the cost of the equipment?

**Judgment Case 10–4**
Interest capitalization
● LO7

*SFAS 34* provides guidelines for the inclusion of interest in the initial cost of an operational asset.

**Required:**

1. What assets qualify for interest capitalization? What assets do not qualify for interest capitalization?
2. Over what period should interest be capitalized?
3. Explain average accumulated expenditures.
4. Explain the two methods that could be used to determine the appropriate interest rate(s) to be used in capitalizing interest.
5. Describe the three steps used to determine the amount of interest capitalized during a reporting period.

**Research Case 10–5**
Goodwill
● LO1

Accounting for purchased goodwill has been a controversial issue for many years. In the United States, the amount of purchased goodwill is capitalized and not amortized. Globally, the treatment of goodwill varies significantly, with some countries not recognizing goodwill as an asset. Professors Johnson and Petrone, in "Is Goodwill an Asset?" discuss this issue.

**Required:**

1. In your library or from some other source, locate the indicated article in *Accounting Horizons,* September 1998.
2. Does goodwill meet the FASB's definition of an asset?
3. What are the key concerns of those that believe goodwill is not an asset?

**Real World Case 10–6**
Property, plant, and equipment; intangibles
● LO1

**Coca-Cola Company** reported the following amounts in the asset section of its balance sheets for the years ended December 31, 2004 and 2003:

| | ($ in millions) | |
|---|---|---|
| | **2004** | **2003** |
| Property, plant, and equipment, net | $6,091 | $6,097 |
| Intangible assets, net* | 702 | 981 |

*These are the company's finite life intangibles.

In addition, the 2004 statement of cash flows reported the following items ($ in millions):

| | |
|---|---|
| Depreciation and amortization | $893 |
| Additions to property and equipment | 755 |
| Proceeds from sale of equipment | 341 |

**Required:**

Assuming that no new intangible assets were acquired or sold during 2004, what was the gain or loss recognized in 2004 from the sale of property, plant, and equipment?

**Judgment Case 10–7**
Goodwill

● LO1

Athena Paper Corporation acquired for cash 100% of the outstanding common stock of Georgia, Inc., a supplier of wood pulp. The purchase price of $4,500,000 was significantly higher than the book value of Georgia's net assets (assets less liabilities) of $2,800,000. The Athena controller recorded the difference of $1,700,000 as an asset, goodwill.

**Required:**

1. Discuss the meaning of the term *goodwill.*
2. In what situation would the Athena controller be correct in her valuation of goodwill?

**Judgment Case 10–8**
Research and development

● LO8

Prior to 1974, accepted practice was for companies to either expense or capitalize R&D costs. In 1974, the FASB issued *SFAS 2* which now requires all research and development costs to be charged to expense when incurred. This was a controversial standard, opposed by many companies who preferred delaying the recognition of these expenses until later years when presumably the expenditures bear fruit.

Several research studies have been conducted to determine if the standard had any impact on the behavior of companies. One interesting finding was that, prior to *SFAS 2,* companies that expensed R&D costs were significantly larger than those companies that capitalized R&D costs.

**Required:**

1. Explain the FASB's logic in deciding to require all companies to expense R&D costs in the period incurred.
2. Identify possible reasons to explain why, prior to *SFAS 2,* companies that expensed R&D costs were significantly larger than those companies that capitalized R&D costs.

**Judgment Case 10–9**
Research and development

● LO8

Clonal, Inc., a biotechnology company, developed and patented a diagnostic product called Trouver. Clonal purchased some research equipment to be used exclusively for Trouver and subsequent research projects. Clonal defeated a legal challenge to its Trouver patent, and began production and marketing operations for the project.

Corporate headquarters' costs were allocated to Clonal's research division as a percentage of the division's salaries.

**Required:**

1. How should the equipment purchased for Trouver be reported in Clonal's income statements and statements of financial position?
2. a. Describe the matching principle.
   b. Describe the accounting treatment of research and development costs and consider whether this is consistent with the matching principle. What is the justification for the accounting treatment of research and development costs?
3. How should corporate headquarters' costs allocated to the research division be classified in Clonal's income statements? Why?
4. How should the legal expenses incurred in defending Trouver's patent be reported in Clonal's financial statements?

*(AICPA adapted)*

**Communication Case 10–10**
Research and development

● LO8

The focus of this case is the situation described in Case 10–9. What is the appropriate accounting for R&D costs? Do you believe that (1) capitalization is the correct treatment of R&D costs, (2) expensing is the correct treatment of R&D costs, or (3) that companies should be allowed to choose between expensing and capitalizing R&D costs?

**Required:**

1. Develop a list of arguments in support of your view prior to the class session for which the case is assigned. Do not be influenced by the method required by the FASB. Base your opinion on the conceptual merit of the options.
2. In class, your instructor will pair you (and everyone else) with a classmate who also has independently developed a position.
   a. You will be given three minutes to argue your view to your partner. Your partner likewise will be given three minutes to argue his or her view to you. During these three-minute presentations, the listening partner is not permitted to speak.
   b. Then after each person has had a turn attempting to convince his or her partner, the two partners will have a three-minute discussion in which they will decide which alternative is more convincing and arguments will be merged into a single view for each pair.
3. After the allotted time, a spokesperson for each of the three alternatives will be selected by the instructor. Each spokesperson will field arguments from the class as to the appropriate alternative. The class will then discuss the merits of the alternatives and attempt to reach a consensus view, though a consensus is not necessary.

**Trueblood Accounting Case 10–11**
Acquisition Costs

● LO1

The following Trueblood case is recommended for use with this chapter. The case provides an excellent opportunity for class discussion, group projects, and writing assignments. The case, along with Professor's Discussion Material, can be obtained from the Deloitte Foundation at its website: **www.deloitte.com/us/truebloodcases**.

**Case 02-1:** ***Cost Capitalization at Crispy Crust***

This case concerns the treatment of acquisition, construction, and carrying costs incurred in the preparation of new restaurants.

**Communication Case 10–12**
Research and development

● LO8

Thomas Plastics is in the process of developing a revolutionary new plastic valve. A new division of the company was formed to develop, manufacture, and market this new product. As of year-end (December 31, 2006), the new product has not been manufactured for sale; however, prototype units were built and are in operation.

Throughout 2006, the new division incurred a variety of costs. These costs included expenses (including salaries of administrative personnel) and market research costs. In addition, approximately $500,000 in equipment (estimated useful life of 10 years) was purchased for use in developing and manufacturing the new valve. Approximately $200,000 of this equipment was built specifically for developing the design of the new product; the remaining $300,000 of the equipment was used to manufacture the preproduction prototypes and will be used to manufacture the new product once it is in commercial production.

The president of the company, Sally Rogers, has been told that research and development costs must be expensed as incurred, but she does not understand this treatment. She believes the research will lead to a profitable product and to increased future revenues. Also, she wonders how to account for the $500,000 of equipment purchased by the new division. "I thought I understood accounting," she growled. "Explain to me why expenditures that benefit our future revenues are expensed rather than capitalized!"

**Required:**

Write a one- to two-page report to Sally Rogers explaining the generally accepted accounting principles relevant to this issue. The report should also address the treatment of the equipment purchases.

*(AICPA adapted)*

**Ethics Case 10–13**
Research and development

● LO8

Mayer Biotechnical, Inc., develops, manufactures, and sells pharmaceuticals. Significant research and development (R&D) expenditures are made for the development of new drugs and the improvement of existing drugs. During 2006, $220 million was spent on R&D. Of this amount, $30 million was spent on the purchase of equipment to be used in a research project involving the development of a new antibiotic.

The controller, Alice Cooper, is considering capitalizing the equipment and depreciating it over the five-year useful life of the equipment at $6 million per year, even though the equipment likely will be used on only one project. The company president has asked Alice to make every effort to increase 2006 earnings because in 2007 the company will be seeking significant new financing from both debt and equity sources. "I guess we might use the equipment in other projects later," Alice wondered to herself.

**Required:**

1. Assuming that the equipment was purchased at the beginning of 2006, by how much would Alice's treatment of the equipment increase before tax earnings as opposed to expensing the equipment cost?
2. Discuss the ethical dilemma Alice faces in determining the treatment of the $30 million equipment purchase.

**International Case 10–14**
Comparison of operational asset valuation in the Netherlands and the United States

● LO1

**Heineken**, based in Amsterdam, is one of the world's largest international beverage companies, selling its products in some 150 countries. Operational asset disclosures accompanying a recent annual report are reproduced below.

**Intangible Fixed Assets (in part)**

Goodwill is calculated as the difference between the cost of an acquisition and its net asset value. Goodwill is carried at cost less accumulated amortization and impairment. Amortization is calculated by the straight-line method based on the expected economic life of the assets concerned, subject to a maximum of 20 years. Other intangible fixed assets satisfying the applicable criteria are capitalized and amortized by the straight-line method over three years. Costs of internally developed brands, patents and licenses and research and development are expensed.

**Fixed Assets (in part)**

Except for land, which is not depreciated, tangible fixed assets are stated at replacement cost less accumulated depreciation. The replacement cost is based on appraisals by internal and external experts, taking into account technical and economic developments. Other factors taken into account include the experience gained in the construction of breweries throughout the world.

**Required:**

On the basis of the information the disclosures provide, compare operational asset valuation in the Netherlands with that in the United States.

**Analysis Case 10–15**
Fixed-asset turnover ratio

● LO5

**National Semiconductor Corporation,** headquartered in Santa Clara, California, is a global semiconductor manufacturer. The company's 2004 fixed-asset turnover ratio, using the average book value of property, plant, and equipment (PP&E) as the denominator, was approximately 2.87. Additional information taken from the company's 2004 annual report is as follows:

| | ($ in millions) |
|---|---|
| Book value of PP&E—beginning of 2004 | $681 |
| Purchases of PP&E during 2004 | 215 |
| Depreciation of PP&E for 2004 | 196 |

There were no dispositions of PP&E during 2004.

**Required:**

1. How is the fixed-asset turnover ratio computed? How would you interpret National's ratio of 2.87?
2. Use the data to determine National's net sales for 2004.
3. Obtain annual reports from three corporations in the same primary industry as National (Intel Corporation and Advanced Micro Devices are two well-known competitors) and compare the management of each company's investment in property, plant, and equipment.

   **Note:** You can obtain copies of annual reports from your library, from friends who are shareholders, from the investor relations department of the corporations, from a friendly stockbroker, or from EDGAR (Electronic Data Gathering, Analysis, and Retrieval) on the Internet (**www.sec.gov** or through Edgarscan at **edgarscan.pwcglobal.com**).

**Judgment Case 10–16**
Computer software costs

● LO8

The Elegant Software Company recently completed the development and testing of a new software program that provides the ability to transfer data from among a variety of operating systems. The company believes this product will be quite successful and capitalized all of the costs of designing, developing, coding, and testing the software. These costs will be amortized over the expected useful life of the software on a straight-line basis.

**Required:**

1. Was Elegant correct in its treatment of the software development costs? Why?
2. Explain the appropriate method for determining the amount of periodic amortization for any capitalized software development costs.

**Real World Case 10–17**
Operational assets

● LO1 LO7

EDGAR, the Electronic Data Gathering, Analysis, and Retrieval system, performs automated collection, validation, indexing, and forwarding of submissions by companies and others who are required by law to file forms with the U.S. Securities and Exchange Commission (SEC). All publicly traded domestic companies use EDGAR to make the majority of their filings. (Some foreign companies file voluntarily.) Form 10-K or 10-KSB, which includes the annual report, is required to be filed on EDGAR. The SEC makes this information available on the Internet.

**Required:**

1. Access EDGAR on the Internet. The web address is **www.sec.gov**. Edgarscan (**edgarscan.pwcglobal.com**) from PricewaterhouseCoopers makes the process of accessing data from EDGAR easier.
2. Search for **Home Depot, Inc.** Access the 10-K filing for the most recent fiscal year. Search or scroll to find the financial statements and related notes.
3. Answer the following questions related to the company's operational assets:
   a. Name the different types of operational assets the company lists in its balance sheet under property, plant, and equipment.
   b. How much cash was used for the acquisition of property, plant, and equipment during the year?
   c. What was the amount of interest capitalized during the year?
   d. Compute the fixed-asset turnover ratio for the fiscal year.

**Analysis Case 10–18**
Reporting operational assets

● LO1 LO5

**FedEx Corporation**

Refer to the financial statements and related disclosure notes of **FedEx Corporation** in Appendix B located at the back of this text.

**Required:**

1. What categories of operational assets does FedEx report in its 2004 balance sheet?
2. How much interest did FedEx capitalize in 2004?
3. How much cash was used in 2004 to purchase property and equipment? How does this compare with purchases in previous years?
4. The fixed-asset turnover ratio for **United Parcel Service**, FedEx's chief competitor, for the year ended December 31, 2004, is 2.43. How does this compare with FedEx's ratio? What is the ratio intended to measure?

# 11 CHAPTER

# Operational Assets: Utilization and Impairment

## OVERVIEW

This chapter completes our discussion of accounting for operational assets. We address the allocation of the cost of these assets to the periods benefited by their use.

The usefulness of most operational assets is consumed as the assets are applied to the production of goods or services. Cost allocation corresponding to this consumption of usefulness is known as *depreciation* for plant and equipment, *depletion* for natural resources, and *amortization* for intangibles.

We also consider the treatment of expenditures incurred subsequent to acquisition and the impairment of operational assets.

## LEARNING OBJECTIVES

After studying the chapter you should be able to:

- LO1 Explain the concept of cost allocation as it pertains to operational assets.
- LO2 Determine periodic depreciation using both time-based and activity-based methods.
- LO3 Calculate the periodic depletion of a natural resource.
- LO4 Calculate the periodic amortization of an intangible asset.
- LO5 Explain the appropriate accounting treatment required when a change is made in the service life or residual value of an operational asset.
- LO6 Explain the appropriate accounting treatment required when a change in depreciation, amortization, or depletion method is made.
- LO7 Explain the appropriate treatment required when an error in accounting for an operational asset is discovered.
- LO8 Identify situations that involve a significant impairment of the value of operational assets and describe the required accounting procedures.
- LO9 Discuss the accounting treatment of repairs and maintenance, additions, improvements, and rearrangements to operational assets.

# Financial Reporting Case

## What's in a Name?

"I don't understand this at all," your friend Penny Lane moaned. "Depreciation, depletion, amortization; what's the difference? Aren't they all the same thing?" Penny and you are part of a class team working on a case involving OfficeMax Incorporated, formerly known as Boise Cascade Corporation. Part of the project involves comparing reporting methods over a three-year period. "Look at these disclosure notes from last year's annual report. Besides mentioning those three terms, they also talk about a charge for asset impairment. How is that different?" Penny showed you the disclosure notes.

> **Property and Equipment (in part)**
> Most of our paper and wood products manufacturing facilities determine depreciation by the units-of-production method; other operations use the straight-line method over the estimated useful lives of the assets.
>
> For our longer-rotation timberland properties, we calculate depletion rates at the end of each year based on the total estimated volume of timber that is mature enough to be harvested and processed. We amortize logging roads over their expected useful lives or as related timber is harvested.
>
> **Long-Lived Asset Impairment (in part)**
> We account for the impairment of long-lived assets in all of our segments in accordance with SFAS No. 144, Accounting for the Impairment or Disposal of Long-Lived Assets. An impairment of a long-lived asset exists when the carrying value of an asset exceeds its fair value and when the carrying value is not recoverable through future operations. We review the carrying value of long-lived assets for impairment when events or changes in circumstances indicate that the carrying amount of assets may not be recoverable. In December, we recorded a $14.7 million pretax charge for the write-down of impaired assets at our plywood and lumber operations in Yakima, Washington.

**By the time you finish this chapter, you should be able to respond appropriately to the questions posed in this case. Compare your response to the solution provided at the end of the chapter.**

### QUESTIONS

1. Is Penny correct? Do the terms *depreciation*, *depletion*, and *amortization* all mean the same thing? (page 504)
2. What is the units-of-production method? How is it used by this company? (page 508)
3. Explain how asset impairment differs from depreciation, depletion, and amortization. How are impairment losses measured for tangible operational assets with finite useful lives? (page 523)

# PART A DEPRECIATION, DEPLETION, AND AMORTIZATION

## Cost Allocation—an Overview

● LO1

Operational assets are purchased with the expectation that they will provide future benefits, usually for several years. Specifically, they are acquired to be used as part of the revenue-generating operations. Logically, then, the costs of acquiring the assets should be allocated to expense during the reporting periods benefited by their use. That is, their costs are matched with the revenues they help generate.

Let's suppose that a company purchases a used delivery truck for $8,200 to be used to deliver product to customers. The company estimates that five years from the acquisition date the truck will be sold for $2,200. The cost of using the truck during the five-year period is $6,000 ($8,200 − 2,200). The situation is portrayed in Graphic 11–1.

**GRAPHIC 11–1**
Cost Allocation for an Operational Asset

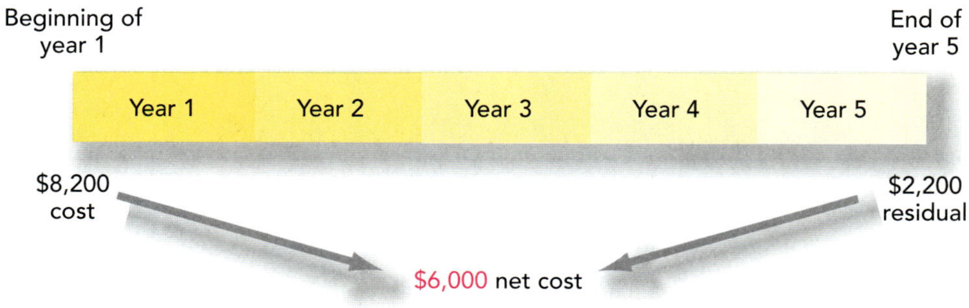


Theoretically, the matching principle requires that the $6,000 be allocated to the five individual years of asset use in direct proportion to the role the asset played in revenue production. However, very seldom is there a clear-cut relationship between the use of operational assets and revenue production. In other words, we can't tell precisely the portion of the total benefits of the asset that was consumed in any particular period. As a consequence, we must resort to arbitrary allocation methods to approximate a matching of expense with revenue. Contrast this situation with the $24,000 prepayment of one year's rent on an office building at $2,000 per month. In that case, we know precisely that the benefits of the asset, prepaid rent, are consumed at a rate of $2,000 per month.

**FINANCIAL REPORTING CASE**
Q1, p. 503

Cost allocation for operational assets is known as **depreciation** for plant and equipment, **depletion** for natural resources, and **amortization** for intangibles. The process often is confused with measuring a decline in fair value of an asset. For example, let's say our delivery truck purchased for $8,200 can be sold for $5,000 at the end of one year but we intend to keep it for the full five-year estimated life. It has experienced a decline in value of $3,200 ($8,200 − 5,000). However, *depreciation is a process of cost allocation, not valuation.* We would not record depreciation expense of $3,200 for year one of the truck's life. Instead, we would distribute the cost of the asset, less any anticipated residual value, over the estimated useful life in a systematic and rational manner that attempts to match revenues with the *use* of the asset, not the decline in its value. After all, the truck is purchased to be used in operations, not to be sold.

**Depreciation, depletion, and amortization are processes that attempt to satisfy the matching principle.**

The specific accounting treatment depends on the intended use of the asset. For assets used in the manufacture of a product, for example, depreciation, depletion, or amortization is considered a product cost to be included as part of the cost of inventory. Eventually, when the product is sold, it becomes part of the cost of goods sold. For assets *not* used in production, primarily plant and equipment and certain intangibles used in the selling and administrative functions of the company, periodic depreciation or amortization is reported as expense in the income statement. You might recognize this distinction as the difference between a product cost and a period cost. When a product cost is reported as an expense (cost of goods sold) depends on when the product is sold; when a period cost is reported as an expense depends on the reporting period in which it is incurred.

**Depreciation, depletion, and amortization for an asset used to manufacture a product is an overhead cost included in the cost of inventory.**

# Measuring Cost Allocation

The process of cost allocation for operational assets requires that three factors be established at the time the asset is put into use. These factors are:

1. **Service life**—the estimated use that the company expects to receive from the asset.
2. **Allocation base**—the value of the usefulness that is expected to be consumed.
3. **Allocation method**—the pattern in which the usefulness is expected to be consumed.

Let's consider these one at a time.

## SERVICE LIFE

The **service life,** or **useful life,** of an operational asset is the amount of use that the company expects to obtain from the asset before disposing of it. This use can be expressed in units of time, or in units of activity. For example, the estimated service life of a delivery truck could be expressed in terms of years or in terms of the number of miles that the company expects the truck to be driven before disposition. We use the terms service life and useful life interchangeably throughout the chapter.

**The *service life,* or *useful life,* of an operational asset can be expressed in units of time or in units of activity.**

Physical life provides the upper bound for service life of tangible operational assets. Physical life will vary according to the purpose for which the asset is acquired and the environment in which it is operated. For example, a diesel powered electric generator may last for many years if it is used only as an emergency backup or for only a few years if it is used regularly.

**Expected obsolescence can shorten service life below physical life.**

The service life of a tangible operational asset may be less than physical life for a variety of reasons. For example, the expected rate of technological change may shorten service life. If suppliers are expected to develop new technologies that are more efficient, the company may keep an asset for a period of time much shorter than physical life. Likewise, if the company sells its product in a market that frequently demands new products, the machinery and equipment used to produce products may be useful only for as long as its output can be sold. Similarly, a mineral deposit might be projected to contain 4 million tons of a mineral, but it may be economically feasible with existing extraction methods to mine only 2 million tons. For intangible assets, legal or contractual life often is a limiting factor. For instance, a patent might be capable of providing enhanced profitability for 50 years, but the legal life of a patent is only 20 years.

Management intent also may shorten the period of an asset's usefulness below its physical, legal, or contractual life. For example, a company may have a policy of using its delivery trucks for a three-year period and then trading the trucks for new models.

Companies quite often disclose the range of service lives for different categories of operational assets. For example, Graphic 11–2 shows how **IBM Corporation** disclosed its service lives in a note accompanying recent financial statements.

**Depreciation and Amortization (in part)**

The estimated useful lives of depreciable properties generally are as follows: buildings, 50 years; building equipment, 20 years; land improvements, 20 years; plant, laboratory and office equipment, 2 to 15 years; and computer equipment, 1.5 to 5 years.

**GRAPHIC 11–2**
Service Life Disclosure—International Business Machines Corporation

## ALLOCATION BASE

The total amount of cost to be allocated over an asset's service life is called its **allocation base.** The amount is the difference between the initial value of the asset at its acquisition (its cost) and its **residual value.** Residual or salvage value is the amount the company expects to receive for the asset at the end of its service life less any anticipated disposal costs. In our delivery truck example above, the allocation base is $6,000 ($8,200 cost less $2,200 anticipated residual value).

***Allocation base* is the difference between the cost of the asset and its anticipated *residual value.***

In certain situations, residual value can be estimated by referring to a company's prior experience or to publicly available information concerning resale values of various types of assets. For example, if a company intends to trade its delivery trucks in three years for the new model, approximations of the three-year residual value for that type of truck can be obtained from used truck blue books.

However, estimating residual value for many operational assets can be very difficult due to the uncertainty about the future. For this reason, along with the fact that residual values often are immaterial, many companies simply assume a residual value of zero. Companies usually do not disclose estimated residual values.

### ALLOCATION METHOD

The *allocation method* used should be systematic and rational and correspond to the pattern of asset use.

In determining how much cost to allocate to periods of an asset's use, a method should be selected that corresponds to the pattern of the loss of the asset's usefulness. *ARB 43* states that the chosen method should allocate the asset's cost "as equitably as possible to the periods during which services are obtained from [its] use." The bulletin further specifies that the method should produce a cost allocation in a "systematic and rational manner."[1] The objective is to try to allocate cost to the period in an amount that is proportional to the amount of benefits generated by the asset during the period relative to the total benefits provided by the asset during its life.

In practice, there are two general approaches that attempt to obtain this systematic and rational allocation. The first approach allocates the cost base according to the *passage of time.* Methods following this approach are referred to as **time-based** methods. The second approach allocates an asset's cost base using a measure of the asset's *input* or *output.* This is an **activity-based** method. We compare these approaches first in the context of depreciation. Later we see that depletion of natural resources typically follows an activity-based approach and the amortization of intangibles typically follows a time-based approach.

## Depreciation of Operational Assets

LO2

To demonstrate and compare the most common depreciation methods, we refer to the situation described in Illustration 11–1.

**ILLUSTRATION 11–1**
Depreciation Methods

The Hogan Manufacturing Company purchased a machine for $250,000. The company expects the service life of the machine to be five years. During that time, it is expected that the machine will produce 140,000 units. The anticipated residual value is $40,000. The machine was disposed of after five years of use. Actual production during the five years of the asset's life was:

| Year | Units Produced |
|---|---|
| 1 | 24,000 |
| 2 | 36,000 |
| 3 | 46,000 |
| 4 | 8,000 |
| 5 | 16,000 |
| Total | 130,000 |

### TIME-BASED DEPRECIATION METHODS

The *straight-line depreciation method* allocates an equal amount of depreciable base to each year of the asset's service life.

**Straight-Line Method.** By far the most easily understood and widely used depreciation method is **straight line.** By this approach, an equal amount of depreciable base is allocated to each year of the asset's service life. The depreciable base is simply divided by the number of years in the asset's life to determine annual depreciation. In our illustration, the straight-line annual depreciation is $42,000, calculated as follows:

[1]"Restatement and Revision of Accounting Research Bulletins," *Accounting Research Bulletin No. 43* (New York: AICPA, 1953), Ch. 9.

$$\frac{\$250{,}000 - 40{,}000}{5 \text{ years}} = \$42{,}000 \text{ per year}$$

**Accelerated Methods.** Using the straight-line method implicitly assumes that the benefits derived from the use of the asset are the same each year. In some situations it might be more appropriate to assume that the asset will provide greater benefits in the early years of its life than in the later years. In these cases, a more appropriate matching of depreciation with revenues is achieved with a declining pattern of depreciation, with higher depreciation in the early years of the asset's life and lower depreciation in later years. An accelerated depreciation method also would be appropriate when benefits derived from the asset are approximately equal over the asset's life, but repair and maintenance costs increase significantly in later years. The early years incur higher depreciation and lower repairs and maintenance expense, while the later years have lower depreciation and higher repairs and maintenance. Two commonly used ways to achieve such a declining pattern are the sum-of-the-years'-digits method and declining balance methods.

***Accelerated depreciation methods* are appropriate when the asset is more useful in its earlier years.**

Sum-of-the-years'-digits method. The **sum-of-the-years'-digits (SYD) method** has no logical foundation other than the fact that it accomplishes the objective of accelerating depreciation in a systematic manner. This is achieved by multiplying the depreciable base by a fraction that declines each year and results in depreciation that decreases by the same amount each year. The denominator of the fraction remains constant and is the sum of the digits from one to *n*, where *n* is the number of years in the asset's service life. For example, if there are five years in the service life, the denominator is the sum of 1, 2, 3, 4, and 5, which equals 15.[2] The numerator decreases each year; it begins with the value of *n* in the first year and decreases by one each year until it equals one in the final year of the asset's estimated service life. The annual fractions for an asset with a five-year life are: 5/15, 4/15, 3/15, 2/15, and 1/15. We calculate depreciation for the five years of the machine's life using the sum-of-the-years'-digits method in Illustration 11–1A.

**The *SYD method* multiplies depreciable base by a declining fraction.**

**ILLUSTRATION 11–1A**
Sum-of-the-Years'-Digits Depreciation

| Year | Depreciable Base | × | Depreciation Rate per Year | = | Depreciation | Book Value End of Year |
|---|---|---|---|---|---|---|
| 1 | $210,000 | | 5/15* | | $ 70,000 | $180,000 |
| 2 | 210,000 | | 4/15 | | 56,000 | 124,000 |
| 3 | 210,000 | | 3/15 | | 42,000 | 82,000 |
| 4 | 210,000 | | 2/15 | | 28,000 | 54,000 |
| 5 | 210,000 | | 1/15 | | 14,000 | 40,000 |
| Totals | | | 15/15 | | $210,000 | |

$$^{*}\frac{n(n+1)}{2} = \frac{5(5+1)}{2} = 15$$

Declining balance methods. As an alternative, an accelerated depreciation pattern can be achieved by various declining balance methods. Rather than multiplying a constant balance by a declining fraction as we do in SYD depreciation, we multiply a constant fraction by a declining balance each year. Specifically, we multiply a constant percentage rate times the decreasing book value (cost less accumulated depreciation) of the asset (*not depreciable base*) at the beginning of the year. Because the rate remains constant while the book value declines, annual depreciation is less each year.

***Declining balance depreciation methods* multiply beginning-of-year book value, not depreciable base, by an annual rate that is a multiple of the straight-line rate.**

The rates used are multiples of the straight-line rate. The straight-line rate is simply one, divided by the number of years in the asset's service life. For example, the straight-line rate for an asset with a five-year life is one-fifth, or 20%. Various multiples used in practice are 125%, 150%, or 200% of the straight-line rate. When 200% is used as the multiplier, the

[2]A formula useful when calculating the denominator is $n(n + 1)/2$.

method is known as the **double-declining-balance (DDB) method** because the rate used is twice the straight-line rate.

In our illustration, the double-declining-balance rate would be 40% (two times the straight-line rate of 20%). Depreciation is calculated in Illustration 11–1B for the five years of the machine's life using the double-declining-balance method.

**ILLUSTRATION 11–1B**
Double-Declining-Balance Depreciation

| Year | Book Value Beginning of Year | × | Depreciation Rate per Year | = | Depreciation | Book Value End of Year |
|---|---|---|---|---|---|---|
| 1 | $250,000 | | 40% | | $100,000 | $150,000 |
| 2 | 150,000 | | 40 | | 60,000 | 90,000 |
| 3 | 90,000 | | 40 | | 36,000 | 54,000 |
| 4 | 54,000 | | | | 14,000* | 40,000 |
| 5 | 40,000 | | | | — | 40,000 |
| Total | | | | | $210,000 | |

*Amount necessary to reduce book value to residual value.

Notice that in the fourth year depreciation expense is a plug amount that reduces book value to the expected residual value (book value beginning of year, $54,000, minus expected residual value, $40,000, = $14,000). There is no depreciation expense in year 5 since book value has already been reduced to the expected residual value. Declining balance methods often allocate the asset's depreciable base over fewer years than the expected service life.

It is not uncommon for a company to switch from accelerated to straight line approximately halfway through an asset's useful life as part of the company's planned depreciation approach.

**Switch from Accelerated to Straight Line.** The result of applying the double-declining-balance method in our illustration produces an awkward result in the later years of the asset's life. By using the double-declining-balance method in our illustration, no depreciation expense is recorded in year 5 even though the asset is still producing benefits. In practice, many companies switch to the straight-line method approximately halfway through an asset's useful life.

In our illustration, the company would switch to straight line in either year 3 or year 4. Assuming the switch is made at the beginning of year 4, because the book value at the beginning of that year is $54,000, an additional $14,000 ($54,000 − 40,000 in residual value) of depreciation must be recorded. Applying the straight-line concept, $7,000 ($14,000 divided by two remaining years) in depreciation is recorded in both year 4 and year 5.

It should be noted that this switch to straight line is not a change in depreciation method requiring reporting as a change in an accounting principle. The switch is part of the company's planned depreciation approach.

## ACTIVITY-BASED DEPRECIATION METHODS

*Activity-based depreciation methods* estimate service life in terms of some measure of productivity.

The most logical way to allocate an asset's cost to periods of an asset's use is to measure the usefulness of the asset in terms of its productivity. For example, we could measure the service life of a machine in terms of its *output* (for example, the estimated number of units it will produce) or in terms of its *input* (for example, the number of hours it will operate). We have already mentioned that one way to measure the service life of a vehicle is to estimate the number of miles it will operate. The most common activity-based method is called the **units-of-production method.**

**FINANCIAL REPORTING CASE**

Q2, p. 503

The measure of output used is the estimated number of units (pounds, items, barrels, etc.) to be produced by the machine. We could also use a measure of input such as the number of hours the machine is expected to operate. By the units-of-production method, we first compute the average depreciation rate per unit by dividing the depreciable base by the number of units expected to be produced. This per unit rate is then multiplied by the number of units produced each period. In our illustration, the depreciation rate per unit is $1.50, computed as follows:

$$\frac{\$250{,}000 - 40{,}000}{140{,}000 \text{ units}} = \$1.50 \text{ per unit}$$

**The *units-of-production method* computes a depreciation rate per measure of activity and then multiplies this rate by actual activity to determine periodic depreciation.**

Each unit produced will require an additional $1.50 of depreciation to be recorded. As we are estimating service life based on units produced rather than in years, depreciation is not constrained by time. However, total depreciation is constrained by the asset's cost and the anticipated residual value. In our illustration, suppose the company intended to dispose of the asset at the end of five years. Depreciation for year five must be modified. Depreciation expense would be a residual amount necessary to bring the book value of the asset down to residual value. Depreciation for the five years is determined in Illustration 11–1C using the units-of-production method. Notice that the last year's depreciation expense is a plug amount that reduces book value to the expected residual value.

**ILLUSTRATION 11–1C**
Units-of-Production Depreciation

| Year | Units Produced | × | Depreciation Rate per Unit | = | Depreciation | Book Value End of Year |
|---|---|---|---|---|---|---|
| 1 | 24,000 | | $1.50 | | $ 36,000 | $214,000 |
| 2 | 36,000 | | 1.50 | | 54,000 | 160,000 |
| 3 | 46,000 | | 1.50 | | 69,000 | 91,000 |
| 4 | 8,000 | | 1.50 | | 12,000 | 79,000 |
| 5 | 16,000 | | | | 39,000* | 40,000 |
| Totals | 130,000 | | | | $210,000 | |

*Amount necessary to reduce book value to residual value.

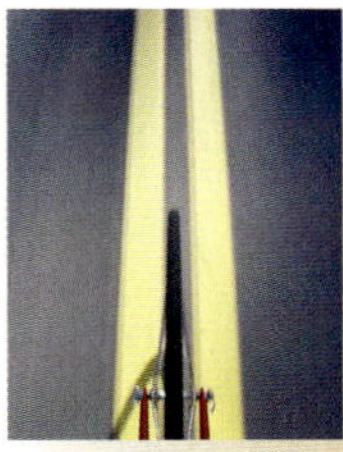

## DECISION MAKERS' PERSPECTIVE—Selecting a Depreciation Method

Illustration 11–1D compares periodic depreciation calculated using each of the alternatives we discussed and illustrated.

**ILLUSTRATION 11–1D**
Comparison of Various Depreciation Methods

| Year | Straight Line | Sum-of-the-Years' Digits | Double-Declining Balance | Units of Production |
|---|---|---|---|---|
| 1 | $ 42,000 | $ 70,000 | $100,000 | $ 36,000 |
| 2 | 42,000 | 56,000 | 60,000 | 54,000 |
| 3 | 42,000 | 42,000 | 36,000 | 69,000 |
| 4 | 42,000 | 28,000 | 14,000 | 12,000 |
| 5 | 42,000 | 14,000 | 0 | 39,000 |
| Total | $210,000 | $210,000 | $210,000 | $210,000 |

**All methods provide the same total depreciation over an asset's life.**

Theoretically, using an activity-based depreciation method provides a better matching of revenues and expenses. Clearly, the productivity of a plant asset is more closely associated with the benefits provided by that asset than the mere passage of time. Also, these methods allow for random patterns of depreciation to correspond with the random patterns of asset use.

**Activity-based methods are theoretically superior to time-based methods but often are impractical to apply in practice.**

However, activity-based methods quite often are either infeasible or too costly to use. For example, buildings don't have an identifiable measure of productivity. Even for machinery, there may be an identifiable measure of productivity such as machine hours or units produced, but it frequently is more costly to determine each period than it is to simply measure the passage of time. For these reasons, most companies use time-based depreciation methods.

Graphic 11–3 shows the results of a recent survey of depreciation methods used by large public companies.[3]

[3] *Accounting Trends and Techniques—2004* (New York: AICPA, 2004), p. 409.

**GRAPHIC 11–3**
Use of Various Depreciation Methods

| Depreciation Method | Number of Companies |
|---|---|
| Straight line | 580 |
| Declining balance | 22 |
| Sum-of-the-years'-digits | 7 |
| Accelerated method—not specified | 41 |
| Units of production | 30 |
| Other | 4 |

Why do so many companies use the straight-line method as opposed to other time-based methods? Many companies perhaps consider the benefits derived from the majority of plant assets to be realized approximately evenly over these assets' useful lives. Certainly a contributing factor is that straight line is the easiest method to understand and apply.

Another motivation is the positive effect on reported income. Straight-line depreciation produces a higher net income than accelerated methods in the early years of an asset's life. In Chapter 8 we pointed out that reported net income can affect bonuses paid to management or debt agreements with lenders.

**A company does not have to use the same depreciation method for both financial reporting and income tax purposes.**

Conflicting with the desire to report higher profits is the desire to reduce taxes by reducing taxable income. An accelerated method serves this objective by reducing taxable income more in the early years of an asset's life than straight line. You probably recall a similar discussion from Chapter 8 in which the benefits were described of using the LIFO inventory method during periods of increasing costs. However, remember that the LIFO conformity rule requires companies using LIFO for income tax reporting to also use LIFO for financial reporting. *No such conformity rule exists for depreciation methods.* Income tax regulations allow firms to use different approaches to computing depreciation in their tax returns and in their financial statements. The method used for tax purposes is therefore not a constraint in the choice of depreciation methods for financial reporting. As a result, most companies use the straight-line method for financial reporting and the Internal Revenue Service's prescribed accelerated method (discussed in Appendix 11A) for income tax purposes. For example, Graphic 11–4 shows **Merck & Co.**'s depreciation policy as reported in a disclosure note accompanying recent financial statements.

**GRAPHIC 11–4**
Depreciation Method Disclosure—Merck & Co.

> **Summary of Accounting Policies (in part):**
> **Depreciation**
> Depreciation is provided over the estimated useful lives of the assets, principally using the straight-line method. For tax purposes, accelerated methods are used.

It is not unusual for a company to use different depreciation methods for different classes of assets. For example, Graphic 11–5 illustrates the **International Paper Company** depreciation policy disclosure contained in a note accompanying recent financial statements. ■

**GLOBAL PERSPECTIVE**

In the United States, income tax regulations allow firms to use different approaches in computing depreciation in their tax returns and financial statements. Internationally, in a number of countries, such as Japan, depreciation rates for financial reporting must be the same as those used for income tax purposes. International Financial Reporting Standards require depreciation to be determined on a systematic basis over the useful life of the asset, as in the United States.

**Summary of Accounting Policies (in part):**
**Plants, Properties, and Equipment**
Plants, properties, and equipment are stated at cost, less accumulated depreciation. The units-of-production method of depreciation is used for major pulp and paper mills and certain wood products facilities, and the straight-line method for other plants and equipment.

**GRAPHIC 11–5**
Depreciation Method Disclosure—International Paper Company

## CONCEPT REVIEW EXERCISE

**DEPRECIATION METHODS**

The Sprague Company purchased a fabricating machine on January 1, 2006, at a net cost of \$130,000. At the end of its four-year useful life, the company estimates that the machine will be worth \$30,000. Sprague also estimates that the machine will run for 25,000 hours during its four-year life. The company's fiscal year ends on December 31.

**Required:**
Compute depreciation for 2006 through 2009 using each of the following methods:

1. Straight line.
2. Sum-of-the-years'-digits.
3. Double-declining balance.
4. Units of production (using machine hours). Actual production was as follows:

| Year | Machine Hours |
|---|---|
| 2006 | 6,000 |
| 2007 | 8,000 |
| 2008 | 5,000 |
| 2009 | 7,000 |

**SOLUTION**

1. Straight line.

$$\frac{\$130{,}000 - 30{,}000}{4 \text{ years}} = \$25{,}000 \text{ per year}$$

2. Sum-of-the-years'-digits.

| Year | Depreciable Base | × | Depreciation Rate per Year | = | Depreciation |
|---|---|---|---|---|---|
| 2006 | \$100,000 | | 4/10 | | \$ 40,000 |
| 2007 | 100,000 | | 3/10 | | 30,000 |
| 2008 | 100,000 | | 2/10 | | 20,000 |
| 2009 | 100,000 | | 1/10 | | 10,000 |
| Total | | | | | \$100,000 |

3. Double-declining balance.

| Year | Book Value Beginning of Year | × | Depreciation Rate per Year | = | Depreciation | Book Value End of Year |
|---|---|---|---|---|---|---|
| 2006 | \$130,000 | | 50% | | \$ 65,000 | \$65,000 |
| 2007 | 65,000 | | 50 | | 32,500 | 32,500 |
| 2008 | 32,500 | | | | 2,500* | 30,000 |
| 2009 | 30,000 | | | | — | 30,000 |
| Total | | | | | \$100,000 | |

*Amount necessary to reduce book value to residual value.

4. Units of production (using machine hours).

| Year | Machine Hours | × | Depreciation Rate per Hour | = | Depreciation | Book Value End of Year |
|---|---|---|---|---|---|---|
| 2006 | 6,000 | | $4* | | $ 24,000 | $106,000 |
| 2007 | 8,000 | | 4 | | 32,000 | 74,000 |
| 2008 | 5,000 | | 4 | | 20,000 | 54,000 |
| 2009 | 7,000 | | | | 24,000† | 30,000 |
| Total | | | | | $100,000 | |

*($130,000 − 30,000)/25,000 hours = $4 per hour.
†Amount necessary to reduce book value to residual value.

## Group and Composite Depreciation Methods

*Group and composite depreciation methods* **aggregate assets to reduce the record-keeping costs of determining periodic depreciation.**

As you might imagine, depreciation records could become quite cumbersome and costly if a company has hundreds, or maybe thousands, of depreciable assets. However, the burden can be lessened if the company uses the group or composite method to depreciate assets collectively rather than individually. The two methods are the same except for the way the collection of assets is aggregated for depreciation. The **group depreciation method** defines the collection as depreciable assets that share similar service lives and other attributes. For example, group depreciation could be used for fleets of vehicles or collections of machinery. The **composite depreciation method** is used when assets are physically dissimilar but are aggregated anyway to gain the convenience of group depreciation. For instance, composite depreciation can be used for all of the depreciable assets in one manufacturing plant, even though individual assets in the composite may have widely diverse service lives.

Both approaches are similar in that they involve applying a single straight-line rate based on the average service lives of the assets in the group or composite.[4] The process is demonstrated using Illustration 11–2.

**ILLUSTRATION 11–2**
Group Depreciation

The Express Delivery Company began operations in 2006. It will depreciate its fleet of delivery vehicles using the group method. The cost of vehicles purchased early in 2006, along with residual values, estimated lives, and straight-line depreciation per year by type of vehicle, are as follows:

| Asset | Cost | Residual Value | Depreciable Base | Estimated Life (yrs.) | Depreciation per Year (straight line) |
|---|---|---|---|---|---|
| Vans | $150,000 | $30,000 | $120,000 | 6 | $20,000 |
| Trucks | 120,000 | 16,000 | 104,000 | 5 | 20,800 |
| Wagons | 60,000 | 12,000 | 48,000 | 4 | 12,000 |
| Totals | $330,000 | $58,000 | $272,000 | | $52,800 |

The *group depreciation* rate is determined by dividing the depreciation per year by the total cost. The group's *average service* life is calculated by dividing the depreciable base by the depreciation per year:

$$\text{Group depreciation rate} = \frac{\$52{,}800}{\$330{,}000} = 16\%$$

$$\text{Average service life} = \frac{\$272{,}000}{\$52{,}800} = 5.15 \text{ years (rounded)}$$

[4]A declining balance method could also be used with either the group or composite method by applying a multiple (e.g., 200%) to the straight-line group or composite rate.

If there are no changes in the assets contained in the group, depreciation of $52,800 per year (16% × $330,000) will be recorded for 5.15 years. This means the depreciation in the sixth year will be $7,920 (.15 of a full year's depreciation = 15% × $52,800), which depreciates the cost of the group down to its estimated residual value. In other words, the group will be depreciated over the average service life of the assets in the group.

**The depreciation rate is applied to the total cost of the group or composite for the period.**

In practice, there very likely will be changes in the assets constituting the group as new assets are added and others are retired or sold. Additions are recorded by increasing the group asset account for the cost of the addition. Depreciation is determined by multiplying the group rate by the total cost of assets in the group for that period. Once the group or composite rate and the average service life are determined, they normally are continued despite the addition and disposition of individual assets. This implicitly assumes that the service lives of new assets approximate those of individual assets they replace.

Because depreciation records are not kept on an individual asset basis, dispositions are recorded under the assumption that the book value of the disposed item exactly equals any proceeds received and no gain or loss is recorded. For example, if a delivery truck in the above illustration that cost $15,000 is sold for $3,000 in the year 2009, the following journal entry is recorded:

**No gain or loss is recorded when a group or composite asset is retired or sold.**

| | | |
|---|---|---|
| Cash | 3,000 | |
| Accumulated depreciation (difference) | 12,000 | |
| Vehicles | | 15,000 |

Any actual gain or loss is included in the accumulated depreciation account. This practice generally will not distort income as the unrecorded gains tend to offset unrecorded losses.

The group and composite methods simplify the recordkeeping of depreciable assets. This simplification justifies any immaterial errors in income determination. Graphic 11–6 shows a disclosure note accompanying recent financial statements of the **El Paso Natural Gas Company** describing the use of the group depreciation method for its regulated property.

**GRAPHIC 11–6**
Disclosure of Depreciation Method—El Paso Natural Gas Company

**Property, Plant, and Equipment (in part)**
We use the group method to depreciate regulated property, plant, and equipment. Under this method, assets with similar lives and other characteristics are grouped and depreciated as one asset. For aircraft, we apply the depreciation rates to the total cost of the group until its net book value equals its salvage value. Currently, our depreciation rates vary from 2 to 33 percent. Using these rates, the average remaining depreciable lives of these assets range from 1 to 40 years.

When we retire regulated property, plant, and equipment, we charge accumulated depreciation and amortization for the original cost, plus the cost of retirement, less its salvage value. We do not recognize a gain or loss unless we sell an entire operating unit.

Additional group-based depreciation methods, the retirement and replacement methods, are discussed in Appendix 11B.

## Depletion of Natural Resources

● LO3

Allocation of the cost of natural resources is called **depletion**. Because the usefulness of natural resources generally is directly related to the amount of the resources extracted, the activity-based units-of-production method is widely used to calculate periodic depletion. Service life is therefore the estimated amount of natural resource to be extracted (for example, tons of mineral or barrels of oil).

Depletion base is cost less any anticipated residual value. Residual value could be significant if cost includes land that has a value after the natural resource has been extracted.

The example in Illustration 11–3 was first introduced in Chapter 10.

**ILLUSTRATION 11–3**
Depletion of Natural Resources

The Jackson Mining Company paid $1,000,000 for the right to explore for a coal deposit on 500 acres of land in Pennsylvania. Costs of exploring for the coal deposit totaled $800,000 and intangible development costs incurred in digging and erecting the mine shaft were $500,000. In addition, Jackson purchased new excavation equipment for the project at a cost of $600,000. After the coal is removed from the site, the equipment will be sold for an anticipated residual value of $60,000.

The company geologist estimates that 1 million tons of coal will be extracted over the three-year period. During 2006, 300,000 tons were extracted. Jackson is required by its contract to restore the land to a condition suitable for recreational use after it extracts the coal.

In Chapter 10 on page 458 we determined that the capitalized cost of the natural resource, coal mine, including the restoration costs, is $2,768,360. Since there is no residual value to the land, the depletion base equals cost and the depletion rate per ton is calculated as follows:

**Depletion of the cost of natural resources usually is determined using the units-of-production method.**

$$\text{Depletion per ton} = \frac{\text{Depletion base}}{\text{Estimated extractable tons}}$$

$$\text{Depletion per ton} = \frac{\$2,768,360}{1,000,000 \text{ tons}} = \$2.76836 \text{ per ton}$$

For each ton of coal extracted, $2.768360 in depletion is recorded. In 2006, the following journal entry records depletion.

| | | |
|---|---|---|
| Depletion ($2.76836 × 300,000 tons) | 830,508 | |
| Coal mine | | 830,508 |

Notice that the credit is to the asset, coal mine, rather than to a contra account, accumulated depletion. Although this approach is traditional, the use of a contra account is acceptable.

Depletion is a product cost and is included in the cost of the inventory of coal, just as the depreciation on manufacturing equipment is included in inventory cost. The depletion is then included in cost of goods sold in the income statement when the coal is sold.

What about depreciation on the $600,000 cost of excavation equipment? If the equipment can be moved from the site and used on future projects, the equipment's depreciable base should be allocated over its useful life. If the asset is not movable, as in our illustration, then it should be depreciated over its useful life or the life of the natural resource, whichever is shorter.

**The units-of-production method often is used to determine depreciation and amortization on assets used in the extraction of natural resources.**

Quite often, companies use the units-of-production method to calculate depreciation and amortization on assets used in the extraction of natural resources. The activity base used is the same as that used to calculate depletion, the estimated recoverable natural resource. In our illustration, the depreciation rate would be $.54 per ton, calculated as follows.

$$\text{Depreciation per ton} = \frac{\$600,000 - 60,000}{1,000,000 \text{ tons}} = \$.54 \text{ per ton}$$

In 2006, $162,000 in depreciation ($.54 × 300,000 tons) is recorded and also included as part of the cost of the coal inventory.

The summary of significant accounting policies disclosure accompanying recent financial statements of **ConocoPhilips** shown in Graphic 11–7 provides a good summary of depletion, amortization, and depreciation for natural resource properties.

**GRAPHIC 11–7**
Depletion Method Disclosure—ConocoPhilips

**Summary of Significant Accounting Policies (in part)**
Depletion and Amortization—Leasehold costs of producing properties are depleted using the units-of-production method based on estimated proved oil and gas reserves. Amortization of intangible development costs is based on the units-of-production method using estimated proved developed oil and gas reserves.

Depreciation and amortization of properties, plants and equipment on producing oil and gas properties, certain pipeline assets, and on Syncrude mining operations are determined by the units-of-production method.

ADDITIONAL CONSIDERATION

**Percentage Depletion**

Depletion of cost less residual value required by GAAP should not be confused with percentage depletion (also called *statutory depletion*) allowable for income tax purposes for oil, gas, and most mineral natural resources. Under these tax provisions, a producer is allowed to deduct a fixed percentage of gross income as depletion expense without regard to the cost of the natural resource. Over the life of the asset, percentage depletion could exceed the asset's cost. The percentage allowed varies according to the type of natural resource.

Because percentage depletion usually differs from cost depletion, a difference between taxable income and financial reporting income before tax results. These differences are discussed in Chapter 16.

# Amortization of Intangible Assets

● LO4

Let's turn now to a third type of long-lived asset—intangible assets. As for most other operational assets, we allocate the cost of an intangible asset over its service or useful life. However, for the few intangible assets with indefinite useful lives, amortization is inappropriate.

## INTANGIBLE ASSETS SUBJECT TO AMORTIZATION

**The cost of an intangible asset with a *finite* useful life is *amortized.***

Allocating the cost of intangible assets is called **amortization.** For an intangible asset with a finite useful life, we allocate its capitalized cost less any estimated residual value to periods in which the asset is expected to contribute to the company's revenue-generating activities. This requires that we determine the asset's useful life, its amortization base (cost less estimated residual value), and the appropriate allocation method, similar to our depreciating tangible assets.

**Useful Life.** Legal, regulatory, or contractual provisions often limit the useful life of an intangible asset. On the other hand, useful life might sometimes be less than the asset's legal or contractual life. For example, the useful life of a patent would be considerably less than its legal life of 20 years if obsolescence were expected to limit the longevity of a protected product.

**Residual Value.** We discussed the cost of intangible assets in Chapter 10. The expected residual value of an intangible asset usually is zero. This might not be the case, though, if at the end of its useful life to the reporting entity the asset will benefit another entity. For example, if Quadra Corp. has a commitment from another company to purchase one of Quadra's patents at the end of its useful life at a determinable price, we use that price as the patent's residual value.

**Allocation Method.** The method of amortization should reflect the pattern of use of the asset in generating benefits. Most companies use the straight-line method. We discussed and illustrated a unique approach to determining the periodic amortization of software development costs in Chapter 10. Recall that the periodic amortization percentage for software development costs is the *greater* of (1) the ratio of current revenues to current and anticipated revenues (percentage of revenue method), or (2) the straight-line percentage over the useful life of the asset.

**Intel Corporation** reported several intangible assets in a recent balance sheet. A note, shown in Graphic 11–8, disclosed the range of estimated useful lives and the use of the straight-line method of allocation.

Like depletion, amortization expense traditionally is credited to the asset account itself rather than to accumulated amortization. However, the use of a contra account is acceptable. Notice in Graphic 11–8 that Intel uses an accumulated amortization contra account. Let's look at an example in Illustration 11–4.

Similar to depreciation, amortization is either a product cost or a period cost depending on the use of the asset. For intangibles used in the manufacture of a product, amortization is

**Graphic 11–8**

Intangible Asset Useful Life Disclosure—Intel Corporation

**Summary of Significant Accounting Policies (in part)**
**Identified Intangible Assets**
Acquisition-related intangibles include developed technology, trademarks and customer lists, and are amortized on a straight-line basis over periods ranging from 2 to 6 years. Intellectual property assets primarily represent rights acquired under technology licenses and are amortized over the periods of benefit, ranging from 2 to 10 years, generally on a straight-line basis. All identified intangible assets are classified within other assets on the balance sheet. In the quarter following the period in which identified intangible assets become fully amortized, the fully amortized balances are removed from the gross asset and accumulated amortization amounts.

**Illustration 11–4**

Amortization of Intangibles

Hollins Corporation began operations in 2006. Early in January, the company purchased a franchise from Ajax Industries for $200,000. The franchise agreement is for a period of 10 years. In addition, Hollins purchased a patent for $50,000. The remaining legal life of the patent is 13 years. However, due to expected technological obsolescence, the company estimates that the useful life of the patent is only 8 years. Hollins uses the straight-line amortization method for all intangible assets. The company's fiscal year-end is December 31.

The journal entries to record a full year of amortization for these intangibles are as follows:

| | | |
|---|---|---|
| Amortization expense ($200,000 ÷ 10 years) . . . . . . . . . . . . . . . . . . | 20,000 | |
| Franchise . . . . . . . . . . . . . . . . . . . . . . . . . . . . . . . . . . . . . . . . . . | | 20,000 |
| *To record amortization of franchise.* | | |
| Amortization expense ($50,000 ÷ 8 years) . . . . . . . . . . . . . . . . . . . . . | 6,250 | |
| Patent . . . . . . . . . . . . . . . . . . . . . . . . . . . . . . . . . . . . . . . . . . . | | 6,250 |
| *To record amortization of patent.* | | |

a product cost and is included in the cost of inventory (and doesn't become an expense until the inventory is sold). For intangible assets not used in production, such as the franchise cost in our illustration, periodic amortization is expensed in the period incurred.

## INTANGIBLE ASSETS NOT SUBJECT TO AMORTIZATION

**The cost of an intangible asset with an *indefinite* useful life is *not* amortized**

An intangible asset that is determined to have an indefinite useful life is not subject to periodic amortization. Useful life is considered indefinite if there is no foreseeable limit on the period of time over which the asset is expected to contribute to the cash flows of the entity.[5]

Indefinite does not necessarily mean permanent. For example, suppose Collins Corporation acquired a trademark in conjunction with the acquisition of a tire company. Collins plans to continue to produce the line of tires marketed under the acquired company's trademark. Recall from our discussion in Chapter 10 that trademarks have a legal life of 10 years, but the registration can be renewed for an indefinite number of 10-year periods. The life of the purchased trademark is initially considered to be indefinite and the cost of the trademark is not amortized. However, if after several years management decides to phase out production of the tire line over the next three years, Collins would amortize the remaining book value over a three-year period.

**Trademarks or tradenames often are considered to have indefinite useful lives.**

Recall the **Hewlett-Packard Company (HP)** acquisition of **Compaq Computer Corporation** discussed in Chapter 10. HP allocated $1.4 million of the purchase price to Compaq's tradename, which is not being amortized. Graphic 11–9 provides another example in a disclosure made by **Staples, Inc.**, in a recent annual report.

**Goodwill is an intangible asset whose cost is *not* expensed through periodic amortization.**

Goodwill is the most common intangible asset with an indefinite useful life. Recall that goodwill is measured as the difference between the purchase price of a company and the fair value of all of the identifiable net assets (tangible and intangible assets minus the fair value of liabilities assumed). Does this mean that goodwill and other intangible assets with indefinite useful lives will remain in a company's balance sheet at their original capitalized values

[5]"Goodwill and Other Intangible Assets," *Statement of Financial Accounting Standards* No. 142 (Norwalk, Conn.: FASB, 2001), par. B45.

**Goodwill and Intangible Assets (in part)**
Intangible assets not subject to amortization, which include registered trademarks and tradenames, were $153.0 million and $144.6 million at January 29, 2005 and January 31, 2004, respectively.

**GRAPHIC 11–9**
Indefinite Life Intangibles Disclosure—Staples, Inc.

indefinitely? Not necessarily. Like other operational assets, intangibles are subject to the impairment of value rules we discuss in a subsequent section of this chapter. In fact, indefinite life intangibles must be tested for impairment annually, or more frequently if events or circumstances indicate that the asset might be impaired.

# ADDITIONAL ISSUES

**PART B**

In this part of the chapter, we discuss the following issues related to cost allocation:

1. Partial periods
2. Changes in estimates
3. Change in depreciation method
4. Error correction
5. Impairment of value

## Partial Periods

Only in textbooks are operational assets purchased and disposed of at the very beginning or very end of a company's fiscal year. When acquisition and disposal occur at other times, a company theoretically must determine how much depreciation, depletion, and amortization to record for the part of the year that each asset actually is used.

Let's repeat the Hogan Manufacturing Company illustration used earlier in the chapter but modify it in Illustration 11–5 to assume that the asset was acquired *during* the company's fiscal year.

On April 1, 2006, the Hogan Manufacturing Company purchased a machine for $250,000. The company expects the service life of the machine to be five years and the anticipated residual value is $40,000. The machine was disposed of after five years of use. The company's fiscal year-end is December 31. Partial-year depreciation is recorded based on the number of months the asset is in service.

**ILLUSTRATION 11–5**
Depreciation Methods—Partial Year

Notice that no information is provided on the estimated output of the machine. Partial-year depreciation presents a problem only when time-based depreciation methods are used. In an activity-based method, the rate per unit of output simply is multiplied by the actual output for the period, regardless of the length of that period.

Depreciation per year of the asset's life calculated earlier in the chapter for the various time-based depreciation methods is shown in Illustration 11–5A.

Illustration 11–5B shows how Hogan would depreciate the machinery by these three methods assuming an April 1 acquisition date.

Notice that 2006 depreciation is three-quarters of the full year's depreciation for the first year of the asset's life, because the asset was used nine months, or 3/4 of the year. The remaining one-quarter of the first year's depreciation is included in 2007's depreciation along with 3/4 of the depreciation for the second year of the asset's life. This calculation is not necessary for the straight-line method because a full year's depreciation is the same for each year of the asset's life.

Usually, the above procedure is impractical or at least cumbersome. As a result, most companies adopt a simplifying assumption, or convention, for computing partial year's

**ILLUSTRATION 11–5A**
Yearly Depreciation

| Year | Straight Line | Sum-of-the-Years'-Digits | Double-Declining Balance |
|---|---|---|---|
| 1 | $ 42,000 | $ 70,000 | $100,000 |
| 2 | 42,000 | 56,000 | 60,000 |
| 3 | 42,000 | 42,000 | 36,000 |
| 4 | 42,000 | 28,000 | 14,000 |
| 5 | 42,000 | 14,000 | 0 |
| Total | $210,000 | $210,000 | $210,000 |

**ILLUSTRATION 11–5B** Partial-Year Depreciation

| Year | Straight Line | Sum-of-the-Years'-Digits | Double-Declining Balance |
|---|---|---|---|
| 2006 | $42,000 × 3/4 = **$ 31,500** | $70,000 × 3/4 = **$ 52,500** | $100,000 × 3/4 = **$ 75,000** |
| 2007 | **$ 42,000** | $70,000 × 1/4 = $ 17,500 | $100,000 × 1/4 = $ 25,000 |
| | | +56,000 × 3/4 = 42,000 | +60,000 × 3/4 = 45,000 |
| | | **$ 59,500** | **$ 70,000*** |
| 2008 | **$ 42,000** | $56,000 × 1/4 = $ 14,000 | $60,000 × 1/4 = $ 15,000 |
| | | +42,000 × 3/4 = 31,500 | +36,000 × 3/4 = 27,000 |
| | | **$ 45,500** | **$ 42,000** |
| 2009 | **$ 42,000** | $42,000 × 1/4 = $ 10,500 | $36,000 × 1/4 = $ 9,000 |
| | | +28,000 × 3/4 = 21,000 | +14,000 × 3/4 = 10,500 |
| | | **$ 31,500** | **$ 19,500** |
| 2010 | **$ 42,000** | $28,000 × 1/4 = $ 7,000 | $14,000 × 1/4 = **$ 3,500** |
| | | +14,000 × 3/4 = 10,500 | |
| | | **$ 17,500** | |
| 2011 | $42,000 × 1/4 = **$ 10,500** | $14,000 × 1/4 = **$ 3,500** | |
| Totals | **$210,000** | **$210,000** | **$210,000** |

*Could also be determined by multiplying the book value at the beginning of the year by twice the straight-line rate: ($250,000 − 75,000) × 40% = $70,000.

depreciation and use it consistently. A common convention is to record one-half of a full year's depreciation in the year of acquisition and another half year in the year of disposal. This is known as the **half-year convention.**[6]

## CONCEPT REVIEW EXERCISE

### DEPLETION AND AMORTIZATION

**Part A:**

On March 29, 2006, the Horizon Energy Corporation purchased the mineral rights to a coal deposit in New Mexico for $2 million. Development costs and the present value of estimated land restoration costs totaled an additional $3.4 million. The company removed 200,000 tons of coal during 2006 and estimated that an additional 1,600,000 tons would be removed over the next 15 months.

[6]Another common method is the modified half-year convention. This method records a full year's depreciation when the asset is acquired in the first half of the year or sold in the second half. No depreciation is recorded if the asset is acquired in the second half of the year or sold in the first half. These half-year conventions are simple and, in most cases, will not result in material differences from a more precise calculation.

**Required:**
Compute depletion on the mine for 2006.

**SOLUTION**

| **Cost of Coal Mine:** | ($ in millions) |
|---|---|
| Purchase price of mineral rights | $2.0 |
| Development and restoration costs | 3.4 |
| | $5.4 |

**Depletion:**

$$\text{Depletion per ton} = \frac{\$5.4 \text{ million}}{1.8 \text{ million tons*}} = \$3 \text{ per ton}$$

*200,000 + 1,600,000

$$2006 \text{ depletion} = \$3 \times 200{,}000 \text{ tons} = \$600{,}000$$

**Part B:**
On October 1, 2006, Advanced Micro Circuits, Inc., completed the purchase of Zotec Corporation for $200 million. Included in the allocation of the purchase price were the following identifiable intangible assets ($ in millions), along with the allocated amounts and estimated useful lives:

| Intangible Asset | Allocated Amount | Useful Life (in years) |
|---|---|---|
| Patent | $10 | 5 |
| Developed technology | 50 | 4 |
| Customer list | 10 | 2 |

In addition, $100 million was allocated to tangible assets and $30 million to goodwill. Straight-line amortization is used for all purchased intangibles.

During 2006, Advanced finished work on a software development project. Development costs incurred after technological feasibility was achieved and before the product release date totaled $2 million. The software was available for release to the general public on September 29, 2006. During the last three months of the year, revenue from the sale of the software was $4 million. The company estimates that the software will generate an additional $36 million in revenue over the next 45 months.

**Required:**
Compute amortization for purchased intangibles and software development costs for 2006.

**SOLUTION**

**Amortization of Purchased Intangibles:**

| | |
|---|---|
| Patent | $10 million / 5 = $2 million × 3/12 year = $.5 million |
| Developed technology | $50 million / 4 = $12.5 million × 3/12 year = $3.125 million |
| Customer list | $10 million / 2 = $5 million × 3/12 year = $1.25 million |
| Goodwill | The cost of goodwill is not amortized. |

**Amortization of Software Development Costs:**

(1) Percentage-of-revenue method:

$$\frac{\$4 \text{ million}}{(\$4 \text{ million} + 36 \text{ million})} = 10\% \times \$2 \text{ million} = \$200{,}000$$

(2) Straight-line:

$$\frac{3 \text{ months}}{48 \text{ months}} \text{ or } 6.25\% \times \$2 \text{ million} = \$125{,}000$$

Advanced will use the percentage-of-revenue method since it produces the greater amortization, $200,000.

## Changes in Estimates

● LO5

The calculation of depreciation, depletion, or amortization requires estimates of both service life and residual value. It's inevitable that at least some estimates will prove incorrect. Chapter 4 introduced the topic of changes in estimates along with coverage of changes in accounting principles and the correction of errors. Here and in subsequent sections of this chapter, we provide overviews of the accounting treatment and disclosures required for these changes and errors when they involve operational assets.

**A change in estimate should be reflected in the financial statements of the current period and future periods.**

Changes in estimates are accounted for prospectively. When a company revises a previous estimate based on new information, prior financial statements are not restated. Instead, the company merely incorporates the new estimate in any related accounting determinations from then on. So, it usually will affect some aspects of both the balance sheet and the income statement in the current and future periods. And a disclosure note should describe the effect of a change in estimate on income before extraordinary items, net income, and related per-share amounts for the current period.

Consider the example in Illustration 11–6.

**ILLUSTRATION 11–6**
Change in Accounting Estimate

On January 1, 2004, the Hogan Manufacturing Company purchased a machine for $250,000. The company expects the service life of the machine to be five years and its anticipated residual value to be $40,000. The company's fiscal year-end is December 31 and the straight-line depreciation method is used for all depreciable assets. During 2006, the company revised its estimate of service life from five to eight years and also revised estimated residual value to $22,000.

For 2004 and 2005, depreciation is $42,000 per year [($250,000 − 40,000) ÷ 5 years] or $84,000 for the two years. However, with the revised estimate, depreciation for 2006 and subsequent years is determined by allocating the book value remaining at the beginning of 2006 less the revised residual value equally over the remaining service life of six years (8 − 2). The remaining book value at the beginning of 2006 is $166,000 ($250,000 − 84,000) and depreciation for 2006 and subsequent years is recorded as follows:

| | | |
|---|---|---|
| Depreciation expense (below) | 24,000 | |
| Accumulated depreciation | | 24,000 |

| | | |
|---|---|---|
| | $250,000 | Cost |
| $42,000 | | Old annual depreciation ($210,000 ÷ 5 years) |
| × 2 years | 84,000 | Depreciation to date (2004–2005) |
| | 166,000 | Book value as of 1/1/06 |
| | 22,000 | Less revised residual value |
| | 144,000 | Revised depreciable base |
| | ÷ 6 | Estimated remaining life (8 years − 2 years) |
| | $ 24,000 | New annual depreciation |

The asset's book value is depreciated down to the anticipated residual value of $22,000 at the end of the revised eight-year service life. In addition, a note discloses the effect of the change in estimate on income, if material. The before-tax effect is an increase in income of $18,000 (depreciation of $42,000 if the change had not been made, less $24,000 depreciation after the change). **BMC Software, Inc.** recently revised the service lives for capitalized software costs. Graphic 11–10 shows the note that disclosed the change.

## Changes in Depreciation, Amortization, or Depletion Method

● LO6

Recall from our discussion in Chapter 4 that a recent accounting standard requires that a change in depreciation, amortization, or depletion method be considered a change in ac-

**Software Development Costs and Related Assets (in part)**

The capitalized software costs are amortized over the products estimated economic lives, which historically have typically been five years, beginning upon the declaration of the underlying products as generally available for sale. As discussed below, the Company revised the estimated economic lives for certain software products as of January 1, 2003, such that the capitalized costs for the majority of products will be amortized over an estimated life of three years.

These changes in estimated economic lives resulted in an additional $12.4 million and $36.8 million of amortization expense in the years ended March 31, 2003 and 2004, respectively, and reduced basic and diluted earnings per share for the years ended March 31, 2003 and 2004 by $0.03 per share and $0.14 per share, respectively.

**GRAPHIC 11–10**

Change in Estimate Disclosure—BMC Software, Inc.

counting estimate that is achieved by a change in accounting principle. We account for these changes prospectively, exactly as we would any other change in estimate. One difference is that most changes in estimate do not require a company to justify the change. However, this change in estimate is a result of changing an accounting principle and therefore requires a clear justification as to why the new method is preferable. Consider the example in Illustration 11–7.

On January 1, 2004, the Hogan Manufacturing Company purchased a machine for $250,000. The company expects the service life of the machine to be five years and its anticipated residual value to be $30,000. The company's fiscal year-end is December 31 and the double-declining-balance (DDB) depreciation method is used. During 2006, the company switched from the DDB to the straight-line method. In 2006, the adjusting entry is:

| | | |
|---|---|---|
| Depreciation expense (below) | 20,000 | |
| Accumulated depreciation | | 20,000 |

DDB depreciation:

| | |
|---|---|
| 2004 | $100,000 ($250,000 × 40%*) |
| 2005 | 60,000 ([$250,000 − 100,000] × 40%*) |
| Total | $160,000 |

*Double the straight-line rate for 5 years ([1/5 = 20%] × 2 = 40%)

| | |
|---|---|
| $250,000 | Cost |
| 160,000 | Depreciation to date, DDB (2004–2005) |
| 90,000 | Undepreciated cost as of 1/1/06 |
| 30,000 | Less residual value |
| 60,000 | Depreciable base |
| ÷ 3 yrs. | Remaining life (5 years − 2 years) |
| $ 20,000 | New annual depreciation |

A disclosure note reports the effect of the change on net income and earnings per share along with clear justification for changing depreciation methods.

**ILLUSTRATION 11–7**

Change in Depreciation Method

Frequently, when a company changes depreciation method, the change will be effective only for assets placed in service after that date. Of course, that means depreciation schedules do not require revision because the change does not affect assets depreciated in prior periods. A disclosure note still is required to provide justification for the change and to report the effect of the change in the current year's income. Graphic 11–11 provides an example of this type of change in depreciation method made by **Dow Chemical**.

**Changes in depreciation, amortization, or depletion methods are accounted for the same way as a change in accounting estimate.**

**GRAPHIC 11–11**
Change in Depreciation Method for Newly Acquired Assets—The Dow Chemical Company

> **Note B: Accounting Change (in part)**
> For property released to operations at the beginning of the current fiscal year, the company changed from an accelerated method to the straight-line method of depreciation. The change reflects the Company's engineering and maintenance practices which result in property not being subject to high maintenance costs or substantially reduced productivity in the later years of its useful life. In addition, the change to the straight-line method conforms to predominant industry practice. This change did not have a material effect on current income.

## Error Correction

• LO7 Errors involving operational assets include computational errors in the calculation of depreciation, depletion, or amortization and mistakes made in determining whether expenditures should be capitalized or expensed. These errors can affect many years. For example, let's say a major addition to an operational asset should be capitalized but incorrectly is expensed. Not only is income in the year of the error understated, but subsequent years' income is overstated because depreciation is omitted.

Recall from our discussion of inventory errors in Chapter 9 that if a material error is discovered in an accounting period subsequent to the period in which the error is made, any previous years' financial statements that were incorrect as a result of the error are retrospectively restated to reflect the correction. Any account balances that are incorrect as a result of the error are corrected by journal entry. If retained earnings is one of the incorrect accounts, the correction is reported as a *prior period adjustment* to the beginning balance in the statement of shareholders' equity.[7] In addition, a disclosure note is needed to describe the nature of the error and the impact of its correction on net income, income before extraordinary items, and earnings per share.

Here is a summary of the treatment of material errors occurring in a previous year:

- Previous years' financial statements are retrospectively restated.
- Account balances are corrected.
- If retained earnings requires correction, the correction is reported as a prior period adjustment.
- A note describes the nature of the error and the impact of the correction on income.

Consider Illustration 11–8. The 2004 and 2005 financial statements that were incorrect as a result of the error are *retrospectively restated* to report the addition to the patent and to reflect the correct amount of amortization expense, assuming both statements are reported again for comparative purposes in the 2006 annual report.

Because retained earnings is one of the accounts incorrect as a result of the error, a correction to that account of $180,000 is reported as a prior period adjustment to the 2006 beginning retained earnings balance in Hathaway's comparative statements of shareholders' equity. Assuming that 2005 is included with 2006 in the comparative statements, a correction would be made to the 2005 beginning retained earnings balance as well. That prior period adjustment, though, would be for the pre-2005 difference: $300,000 − 60,000 = $240,000.

Also, a disclosure note accompanying Hathaway's 2006 financial statements should describe the nature of the error and the impact of its correction on each year's net income (understated by $240,000 in 2004 and overstated by $60,000 in 2005), income before extraordinary items (same as net income), and earnings per share.

Chapter 20 provides in-depth coverage of changes in estimates and methods, and of accounting errors. We cover the tax effect of these changes and errors in that chapter.

---

[7]The prior period adjustment is applied to beginning retained earnings for the year following the error, or for the earliest year being reported in the comparative financial statements when the error occurs prior to the earliest year presented. The retained earnings balances in years after the first year also are adjusted to what those balances would be if the error had not occurred, but a company may choose not to explicitly report those adjustments as separate line items.

**ILLUSTRATION 11–8**
Error Correction

In 2006, the controller of the Hathaway Corporation discovered an error in recording $300,000 in legal fees to successfully defend a patent infringement suit in 2004. The $300,000 was charged to legal fee expense but should have been capitalized and amortized over the five-year remaining life of the patent. Straight-line amortization is used by Hathaway for all intangibles.

**Analysis**

($ in thousands)

| | Correct (Should Have Been Recorded) | | | Incorrect (As Recorded) | | |
|---|---|---|---|---|---|---|
| 2004 | Patent | 300 | | Expense | 300 | |
| | Cash | | 300 | Cash | | 300 |
| 2004 | Expense | 60 | | Amortization entry omitted | | |
| | Patent | | 60 | | | |
| 2005 | Expense | 60 | | Amortization entry omitted | | |
| | Patent | | 60 | | | |

During the two-year period, amortization expense was *understated* by $120 thousand, but other expenses were *overstated* by $300 thousand, so net income during the period was *understated* by $180 thousand (ignoring income taxes). This means retained earnings is currently *understated* by that amount.

Patent is understated by $180 thousand.

| | ($ in thousands) | |
|---|---|---|
| Patent | 180 | |
| Retained earnings | | 180 |

*To correct incorrect accounts.*

Sometimes, the analysis is easier if you re-create the entries actually recorded incorrectly and those that would have been recorded if the error hadn't occurred, and then compare them.

## Impairment of Value

● LO8

Depreciation, depletion, and amortization reflect a gradual consumption of the benefits inherent in an operational asset. An implicit assumption in allocating the cost of an asset over its useful life is that there has been no significant reduction in the anticipated total benefits or service potential of the asset. Situations can arise, however, that cause a significant decline or impairment of those benefits or service potentials. An extreme case would be the destruction of a plant asset—say a building destroyed by fire—before the asset is fully depreciated. The remaining carrying value of the asset in that case should be written off as a loss. Sometimes, though, the impairment of future value is more subtle.

**FINANCIAL REPORTING CASE**

Q3, p. 503

The way we recognize and measure an impairment loss differs depending on whether the operational assets are to be held and used or are being held to be sold. Accounting is different, too, for operational assets with finite lives and those with indefinite lives. We consider those differences now.

### OPERATIONAL ASSETS TO BE HELD AND USED

An increasingly common occurrence in practice is the partial write-down of operational assets that remain in use. For example, in the second quarter of 2001, **American Airlines** reduced the carrying value (book value) of certain aircraft by $685 million. The write-down reflected the significant reduction in demand for air travel that occurred even before the September 11, 2001, terrorist attacks on the World Trade Center and the Pentagon.

Conceptually, there is considerable merit for a policy requiring the write-down of an operational asset when there has been a significant decline in value. A write-down can provide important information about the future cash flows that a company can generate from using the asset. However, in practice, this process is very subjective. Even if it appears certain that significant impairment of value has occurred, it often is difficult to measure the amount of the required write-down.

An operational asset held for use should be written down if there has been a significant impairment of value.

For example, let's say a company purchased $2,000,000 of equipment to be used in the production of a new type of laser printer. Depreciation is determined using the straight-line method over a useful life of six years and the residual value is estimated at $200,000. At the beginning of year 3, the machine's book value has been reduced by accumulated depreciation to $1,400,000 [$2,000,000 − ($300,000 × 2)]. At that time, new technology is developed causing a significant reduction in the selling price of the new laser printer as well as a reduction in anticipated demand for the product. Management estimates that the equipment will be useful for only two more years and will have no significant residual value.

This situation is not simply a matter of a change in the estimates of useful life and residual value. Management must decide if the events occurring in year 3 warrant a write-down of the asset below $1,400,000. A write-down would be appropriate if the company decided that it would be unable to fully recover this amount through future use.

For operational assets to be held and used, different guidelines apply to (1) tangible operational assets and intangible operational assets with finite useful lives (subject to depreciation, depletion, or amortization) and (2) intangible operational assets with indefinite useful lives (not subject to amortization).

**Tangible Operational Assets and Finite Life Intangibles.** *SFAS No. 144*[8] provides guidelines for when to recognize and how to measure impairment losses of long-lived tangible assets and intangible assets with finite useful lives. For purposes of this recognition and measurement, assets are grouped at the lowest level for which identifiable cash flows are largely independent of the cash flows of other assets.

**Tangible operational assets and finite life intangibles are tested for impairment only when events or changes in circumstances indicate book value may not be recoverable.**

Recognition. It would be impractical to test all assets or asset groups for impairment at the end of every reporting period. *SFAS 144* requires investigation of possible impairment only if events or changes in circumstances indicate that the book value of the asset or asset group may not be recoverable. This might happen from:

a. A significant decrease in market price.
b. A significant adverse change in how the asset is being used or in its physical condition.
c. A significant adverse change in legal factors or in the business climate.
d. An accumulation of costs significantly higher than the amount originally expected for the acquisition or construction of an asset.
e. A current-period loss combined with a history of losses or a projection of continuing losses associated with the asset.
f. A realization that the asset will be disposed of significantly before the end of its estimated useful life.[9]

**STEP 1—An impairment loss is required only when the undiscounted sum of future cash flows is less than book value.**

Measurement. Determining whether to record an impairment loss and actually recording the loss is a two-step process. The first step is a recoverability test—an impairment loss is required only when the undiscounted sum of estimated future cash flows from an asset is less than the asset's book value. The measurement of impairment loss—step 2—is the difference between the asset's book value and its fair value. If an impairment loss is recognized, the written-down book value becomes the new cost base for future cost allocation. Later recovery of an impairment loss is prohibited.

**STEP 2—The impairment loss is the excess of book value over fair value.**

Let's look closer at the measurement process (step two). Fair value is the amount at which the asset could be bought or sold in a current transaction between willing parties. Quoted market prices could be used if they're available. If fair value is not determinable, it must be estimated.

The process is best described by an example. Consider Illustration 11–9.

[8]"Accounting for the Impairment of Long-Lived Assets and for Long-Lived Assets to Be Disposed Of," *Statement of Financial Accounting Standards* No. 144 (Norwalk, Conn.: FASB, 2001). This standard retains the fundamental provisions of its predecessor, SFAS No. 121.

[9]Ibid., par. 8.

**ILLUSTRATION 11–9**
Impairment Loss—Tangible Operational Asset

The Dakota Corporation operates several factories that manufacture medical equipment. Near the end of the company's 2006 fiscal year, a change in business climate related to a competitor's innovative products indicated to management that the $170 million book value of the assets of one of Dakota's factories may not be recoverable.

Management is able to identify cash flows from this factory and estimates that future cash flows over the remaining useful life of the factory will be $150 million. The fair value of the factory's assets is not readily available but is estimated to be $135 million.

**Change in circumstances.** The change in business climate related to a competitor's innovative products requires investigation of possible impairment.

**Step 1. Recoverability.** Because book value of $170 million exceeds undiscounted future cash flows of $150 million, an impairment loss is indicated.

**Step 2. Measurement of impairment loss.** The impairment loss is $35 million, determined as follows:

| | |
|---|---|
| Book value | $170 million |
| Fair value | 135 million |
| Impairment loss | $ 35 million |

The loss normally is reported in the income statement as a separate item included in operating expenses.

The present value of future cash flows often is used as a measure of fair value.

Because the fair value of the factory assets was not readily available to Dakota in Illustration 11–9, the $135 million had to be estimated. One method that can be used to estimate fair value is to compute the discounted present value of future cash flows expected from the asset. Keep in mind that we use *undiscounted* estimates of cash flows in step one to determine whether an impairment loss is indicated, but *discounted* estimates of cash flows to determine the amount of the loss. In calculating present value, either a traditional approach or an expected cash flow approach can be used. The traditional approach is to incorporate risk and uncertainty into the discount rate. Recall from discussions in previous chapters that the expected cash flow approach incorporates risk and uncertainty instead into a determination of a probability-weighted cash flow expectation, and then discounts this expected cash flow using a risk-free interest rate. We discussed and illustrated the expected cash flow approach in previous chapters.

A disclosure note is needed to describe the impairment loss. The note should include a description of the impaired asset or asset group, the facts and circumstances leading to the impairment, the amount of the loss if not separately disclosed on the face of the income statement, and the method used to determine fair value.

In its quarter ended September 30, 2004, **AT&T Corporation** reported an asset impairment charge of $11 billion. In July, the company had announced a strategic change in its business, shifting its focus away from traditional consumer services and toward business markets and emerging technologies. This change was the triggering event that required an asset impairment review. Graphic 11–12 shows the disclosure note from AT&T's quarterly financial statements that describes the impairment.

Intangible assets with indefinite useful lives should be tested for impairment at least annually.

**Indefinite Life Intangible Assets Other than Goodwill.** Intangible assets with indefinite useful lives should be tested for impairment annually, or more frequently if events or changes in circumstances indicate that the asset may be impaired. The measurement of an impairment loss for indefinite life intangibles other than goodwill is a one-step process. We compare the fair value of the asset with its book value. If book value exceeds fair value, an impairment loss is recognized for the difference. Notice that we omit the recoverability test with these assets. Because we anticipate cash flows to continue indefinitely, recoverability is not a good indicator of impairment.

If book value exceeds fair value, an impairment loss is recognized for the difference.

Similar to tangible operational assets and finite life intangibles, if an impairment loss is recognized, the written-down book value becomes the new cost base for future cost allocation. Recovery of the impairment loss is prohibited. Disclosure requirements also are similar.

**GRAPHIC 11–12**
Asset Impairment Disclosure—AT&T Corporation

**Note 5. Asset Impairment and Other Charges (in part)**
As a result of this strategic change, we performed an evaluation of our long-lived assets, including property, plant and equipment (PP&E) and internal-use software (IUS) (the asset group) as of July 1, 2004, as this strategic change created a "triggering event" necessitating such a review. In assessing impairments for long-lived assets we follow the provisions of *SFAS No. 144,* "Accounting for the Impairment or Disposal of Long-Lived Assets." We operate an integrated telecommunications network; therefore, we performed our testing of the asset group at the entity level, as this is the lowest level for which identifiable cash flows are available.

In performing the test, we determined that the total of the expected future undiscounted cash flows directly related to the existing service potential of the asset group was less than the carrying value of the asset group; therefore, an impairment charge was required. The impairment charges of $11,389 million represented the difference between the fair values of the asset group and its carrying values and are included within asset impairment and net restructuring and other charges in the consolidated statements of operations. The impairment charges resulted from sustained pricing pressure and the evolution of services toward newer technologies in the business market as well as changes in the regulatory environment, which led to a shift away from traditional consumer services.

**Goodwill.** Recall that goodwill is a unique intangible asset. Unlike other assets, its cost (a) can't be directly associated with any specific identifiable right and (b) is not separable from the company as a whole. Because of these unique characteristics, we can't measure the impairment of goodwill the same way as other operational assets. *SFAS No. 142*[10] provides guidelines for impairment, which while similar to general impairment guidelines, are specific to goodwill. Let's compare the two-step process for measuring goodwill impairment with the two-step process for measuring impairment for tangible operational assets and finite-life intangibles.

**STEP 1—A goodwill impairment loss is indicated when the fair value of the *reporting* unit is less than its book value.**

In Step 1, for all classifications of operational assets, we decide whether a write-down due to impairment is required by determining whether the value of an asset has fallen below its book value. However, in this comparison, the value of assets for tangible operational assets and finite-life intangibles is considered to be value in use as measured by the sum of undiscounted cash flows expected from the asset. But due to its unique characteristics, the value of goodwill is not associated with any specific cash flows and must be measured in a unique way. By its very nature, goodwill is inseparable from a particular *reporting unit.* So, for this step, we compare the value of the reporting unit itself with its book value. If the fair value of the reporting unit is less than its book value, an impairment loss is indicated. A reporting unit is an operating segment of a company or a component of an operating segment for which discrete financial information is available and segment management regularly reviews the operating results of that component.

If goodwill is tested for impairment at the same time as other operational assets of the reporting unit, the other assets must be tested first and any impairment loss and asset write-down recorded prior to testing goodwill.

**STEP 2—A goodwill impairment loss is measured as the excess of the book value of the goodwill over its "implied" fair value.**

In Step 2, for all classifications of operational assets, if impairment is indicated from step 1, we measure the amount of impairment as the excess of the book value of the asset over its fair value. However, unlike for most other operational assets, the fair value of goodwill cannot be measured directly (market value, present value of associated cash flows, etc.) and so must be "implied" from the fair value of the reporting unit that acquired the goodwill.

The implied fair value of goodwill is calculated in the same way that goodwill is determined in a business combination. That is, it's a residual amount measured by subtracting the fair value of all identifiable net assets from the purchase price using the unit's previously determined fair value as the purchase price.[11] An example is provided in Illustration 11–10.

[10]"Goodwill and Other Intangible Assets," *Statement of Financial Accounting Standards* No. 142 (Norwalk, Conn.: FASB, 2001).
[11]The impairment loss recognized cannot exceed the book value of goodwill.

**ILLUSTRATION 11–10**
Impairment Loss—Goodwill

In 2005, the Upjane Corporation acquired Pharmacopia Corporation for $500 million. Upjane recorded $100 million in goodwill related to this acquisition because the fair value of the net assets of Pharmacopia was $400 million. After the acquisition, Pharmacopia continues to operate as a separate company and is considered a reporting unit.

Upjane performs a goodwill impairment test at the end of every fiscal year. At the end of 2006, the book value of Pharmacopia's net assets is $440 million, including the $100 million in goodwill. On that date, the fair value of Pharmacopia has dropped to $350 million and the fair value of all of its identifiable tangible and intangible assets, excluding goodwill, is $325 million.

**Step 1. Recoverability.** Because book value of the net assets of $440 million exceeds fair value of the reporting unit of $350 million, an impairment loss is indicated.

**Step 2. Measurement of impairment loss.** The impairment loss is $75 million, determined as follows:

| | |
|---|---|
| **Determination of implied goodwill:** | |
| Fair value of Pharmacopia | $350 million |
| Fair value of Pharmacopia's net assets (excluding goodwill) | 325 million |
| Implied value of goodwill | $ 25 million |
| **Measurement of impairment loss:** | |
| Book value of goodwill | $100 million |
| Implied value of goodwill | 25 million |
| Impairment loss | $ 75 million |

**Goodwill should be tested for impairment at least annually.**

Similar to other intangible assets with indefinite useful lives, goodwill should be tested for impairment on an annual basis and in between annual test dates if events or circumstances indicate that the fair value of the reporting unit is below its book value.

The acquiring company in a business combination often pays for the acquisition using its own stock. In the late 1990s, the stock prices of many companies were unusually high. These often-inflated stock prices meant high purchase prices for many acquisitions and, in many cases, incredibly high values allocated to goodwill. When stock prices retreated in 2000 and 2001, it became obvious that the book value of goodwill for many companies would never be recovered. Some examples of multibillion dollar goodwill impairment losses are shown in Graphic 11–13.

**GRAPHIC 11–13**
Goodwill Impairment Losses

| Company | Goodwill Impairment Loss |
|---|---|
| AOL Time Warner | $54 billion |
| JDS Uniphase | 50 billion |
| Nortel Networks | 12 billion |
| Lucent Technologies | 4 billion |
| Vivendi Universal SA | 15 billion (Euro dollars) |

**Intel Corporation** provides a more recent example. At the end of the company's 2003 fiscal year, it recorded a $611 million goodwill impairment loss relating to its Wireless Communications and Computing Group. Graphic 11–14 describes the circumstances of the impairment and provides a good summary of accounting for goodwill impairment.

## OPERATIONAL ASSETS TO BE SOLD

We have been discussing the recognition and measurement for the impairment of value of assets to be held and used. We also test for impairment of operational assets held for sale. These are operational assets management has actively committed to sell immediately in their present condition and for which sale is probable.

**GRAPHIC 11–14**
Goodwill Impairment Disclosure—Intel Corporation

**Note 16. Goodwill (in part)**
During the fourth quarter of 2003, the company completed its annual impairment review for goodwill and found indicators of impairment for the Wireless Communications and Computing Group (WCCG) reporting unit. The WCCG business, comprised primarily of flash memory products and cellular baseband chipsets, has not performed as management had expected. In the fourth quarter of 2003, it became apparent that WCCG was now expected to grow more slowly than previously projected. A slower-than-expected rollout of products and slower-than-expected customer acceptance of our products in the baseband chipset business, as well as a delay in the transition to next-generation phone networks, have pushed out the forecasts for sales into high-end data cell phones. These factors resulted in lower growth expectations for the reporting unit and triggered the goodwill impairment.

The impairment review requires a two-step process. The first step of the review compares the fair value of the reporting units with substantial goodwill against their aggregate carrying values, including goodwill. The company estimated the fair value of the WCCG and ICG reporting units using the income method of valuation, which includes the use of estimated discounted cash flows. Based on the comparison, the carrying value of the WCCG reporting unit exceeded the fair value. Accordingly, the company performed the second step of the test, comparing the implied fair value of the WCCG reporting unit's goodwill with the carrying amount of that goodwill. Based on this assessment, the company recorded a non-cash impairment charge of $611 million, which is included as a component of operating income in the all other category for segment reporting purposes.

**For operational assets held for sale, if book value exceeds fair value less cost to sell, an impairment loss is recognized for the difference.**

An operational asset or group of assets classified as held for sale is measured at the lower of its book value or fair value less cost to sell. An impairment loss is recognized for any write-down to fair value less cost to sell.[12] Except for including the cost to sell, notice the similarity to impairment of assets to be held and used. We don't depreciate or amortize these assets while classified as held for sale and report them separately in the balance sheet. Recall from our discussion of discontinued operations in Chapter 4 that similar rules apply for a component of an entity that is classified as held for sale.[13]

Graphic 11–15 summarizes the guidelines for the recognition and measurement of impairment of losses.

## IMPAIRMENT LOSSES AND EARNINGS QUALITY

What do in-process research and development expenditures, losses from the write-down of inventory, and restructuring costs have in common? The presence of any of these items in a corporate income statement presents a challenge to an analyst trying to determine a company's permanent earnings—those likely to continue in the future. We discussed each of these issues in prior chapters.

**An analyst must decide whether to consider asset impairment losses as transitory in nature or as a part of permanent earnings.**

We now can add asset impairment losses to the list of "big bath" accounting techniques some companies use to manipulate earnings. By writing off large amounts of operational assets, companies significantly reduce earnings in the year of the write-off but are able to increase future earnings by lowering future depreciation, depletion, or amortization. Here's how. We measure the impairment loss as the difference between an asset's book value and its fair value. However, in most cases, fair value must be estimated, and the estimation process usually involves a forecast of future net cash flows the company expects to generate from the asset's use. If a company underestimates future net cash flows, fair value is understated. This has two effects: (1) current year's income is unrealistically low due to the impairment loss being overstated and (2) future income is unrealistically high because depreciation, depletion, and amortization are based on understated asset values.

[12]If the asset is unsold at the end of a subsequent reporting period, a gain is recognized for any increase in fair value less cost to sell, but not in excess of the loss previously recognized.

[13]A component of an entity comprises operations and cash flows that can be clearly distinguished, operationally and for financial reporting purposes, from the rest of the entity. One objective of *SFAS No. 144* is to establish a single accounting model, based on the framework developed in *SFAS No. 121,* for long-lived assets to be disposed of by sale.

**GRAPHIC 11–15**
Summary of Operational Asset Impairment Guidelines

| Type of Operational Asset | When to Test for Impairment | Impairment Test |
|---|---|---|
| **To Be Held and Used:** | | |
| Tangible and finite-life intangibles | When events or circumstances indicate book value may not be recoverable | Step 1—An impairment loss is required only when book value is not recoverable (undiscounted sum of estimated future cash flows less than book value). Step 2—The impairment loss is the excess of book value over fair value. |
| Indefinite life intangibles (other than goodwill) | At least annually, or more frequently if indicated | If book value exceeds fair value, an impairment loss is recognized for the difference. |
| Goodwill | At least annually, or more frequently if indicated | Step 1—A loss is indicated when the fair value of the reporting unit is less than its book value. Step 2—An impairment loss is measured as the excess of book value over implied fair value. |
| **To Be Sold** | When considered held for sale | If book value exceeds fair value less cost to sell, an impairment loss is recognized for the difference. |

**PART C**

# SUBSEQUENT EXPENDITURES

Now that we have acquired and measured operational assets, we can address accounting issues incurred subsequent to their acquisition. This part of the chapter deals with the treatment of expenditures made over the life of these assets to maintain and/or improve them.

## Expenditures Subsequent to Acquisition

● LO9

Many operational assets require expenditures to repair, maintain, or improve them. These expenditures can present accounting problems if they are material. In general, a choice must be made between capitalizing the expenditures by either increasing the asset's book value or creating a new asset, or expensing them in the period in which they are incurred. Conceptually, we can refer to the matching principle that requires the capitalization of expenditures that are expected to produce benefits beyond the current fiscal year. Expenditures that simply maintain a given level of benefits are expensed in the period they are incurred.

Expenditures related to operational assets can increase future benefits in the following ways:

1. An extension of the *useful life* of the asset.
2. An increase in the *operating efficiency* of the asset resulting in either an increase in the quantity of goods or services produced or a decrease in future operating costs.
3. An increase in the *quality* of the goods or services produced by the asset.

**GLOBAL PERSPECTIVE**

In the United States, accounting for operational assets subsequent to initial acquisition is based on the historical cost of the asset, and revaluations to reflect changes in market values, other than in asset impairment situations, generally are not permitted. Internationally, the requirements of *IAS 16* deviate significantly from U.S. GAAP by allowing firms to revalue assets at balance sheet dates subsequent to initial valuation.

Theoretically, expenditures that cause any of these results should be capitalized initially and then expensed in future periods through depreciation, depletion, or amortization. This permits the matching of the expenditure with the future benefits. Of course, materiality is an important factor in the practical application of this approach.

Many companies do not capitalize any expenditure unless it exceeds a predetermined amount that is considered material.

For expediency, many companies set materiality thresholds for the capitalization of any expenditure. For example, a company might decide to expense all expenditures under $200 regardless of whether or not future benefits are increased. Judgment is required to determine the appropriate materiality threshold as well as the appropriate treatment of expenditures over $200. There often are practical problems in capitalizing these expenditures. For example, even if future benefits are increased by the expenditure, it may be difficult to determine how long the benefits will last. It's important for a company to establish a policy for treating these expenditures and apply it consistently.

We classify subsequent expenditures as (1) repairs and maintenance, (2) additions, (3) improvements, or (4) rearrangements.

## REPAIRS AND MAINTENANCE

Expenditures for *repairs and maintenance* generally are expensed when incurred.

These expenditures are made to *maintain* a given level of benefits provided by the asset and do not *increase* future benefits. For example, the cost of an engine tune-up or the repair of an engine part for a delivery truck allows the truck to continue its productive activity. If the maintenance is not performed, the truck will not provide the benefits originally anticipated. In that sense, future benefits are provided; without the repair, the truck will no longer operate. The key, though, is that future benefits are not provided *beyond those originally anticipated.* Expenditures for these activities should be expensed in the period incurred.

### ADDITIONAL CONSIDERATION

If repairs and maintenance costs are seasonal, interim financial statements may be misstated. For example, suppose annual maintenance is performed on a company's fleet of delivery trucks. The annual income statement correctly includes one year's maintenance expense. However, for interim reporting purposes, if the entire expenditure is made in one quarter, should that quarter's income statement include as expense the entire cost of the annual maintenance? If these expenditures can be anticipated, they should be accrued evenly throughout the year by crediting an allowance account. The allowance account is then debited when the maintenance is performed.

## ADDITIONS

The costs of *additions* usually are capitalized.

As the term implies, **additions** involve adding a new major component to an existing asset and should be capitalized because future benefits are increased. For example, adding a refrigeration unit to a delivery truck increases the capability of the truck, thus increasing its future benefits. Other examples include the construction of a new wing on a building and the addition of a security system to an existing building.

The capitalized cost includes all necessary expenditures to bring the addition to a condition and location for use. For a building addition, this might include the costs of tearing down and removing a wall of the existing building. The capitalized cost of additions are depreciated over the remaining useful life of the original asset or its own useful life, whichever is shorter.

## IMPROVEMENTS

The costs of *improvements* usually are capitalized.

Expenditures classified as **improvements** involve the replacement of a major component of an operational asset. The replacement can be a new component with the same characteristics as the old component or a new component with enhanced operating capabilities. For example, an existing refrigeration unit in a delivery truck could be replaced with a new but similar unit or with a new and improved refrigeration unit. In either case, the cost of the improvement usually increases future benefits and should be capitalized by increasing the book value of the related asset (the delivery truck) and depreciated over the useful life of the improved asset. There are three methods used to record the cost of improvements.

1. *Substitution.* The improvement can be recorded as both (1) a disposition of the old component and (2) the acquisition of the new component. This approach is conceptually appealing but it is practical only if the original cost and accumulated depreciation of the old component can be separately identified.
2. *Capitalization of new cost.* Another way to record an improvement is to include the cost of the improvement (net of any consideration received from the disposition of the old component) as a debit to the related asset account, without removing the original cost and accumulated depreciation of the original component. This approach is acceptable only if the book value of the original component has been reduced to an immaterial amount through prior depreciation.
3. *Reduction of accumulated depreciation.* Another way to increase an asset's book value is to leave the asset account unaltered but decrease its related accumulated depreciation. The argument for this method is that many improvements extend the useful life of an asset and are equivalent to a partial recovery of previously recorded depreciation. This approach produces the same book value as the capitalization of cost to the asset account. Cost and accumulated depreciation will differ under the two methods.

The three methods are compared in Illustration 11–11.

**ILLUSTRATION 11–11**
Improvements

The Palmer Corporation replaced the air conditioning system in one of its office buildings that it leases to tenants. The cost of the old air conditioning system, $200,000, is included in the cost of the building. However, the company has separately depreciated the air conditioning system. Depreciation recorded up to the date of replacement totaled $160,000. The old system was removed and the new system installed at a cost of $230,000, which was paid in cash. Parts from the old system were sold for $12,000.

Accounting for the improvement differs depending on the alternative chosen.

| | | | |
|---|---|---|---|
| Cash | 12,000 | | ***Substitution*** **(1) Disposition of old component.** |
| Accumulated depreciation—buildings | 160,000 | | |
| Loss on disposal (difference) | 28,000 | | |
| Buildings | | 200,000 | |
| Buildings | 230,000 | | **(2) Acquisition of new component.** |
| Cash | | 230,000 | |
| Buildings | 218,000 | | ***Capitalization of new cost*** |
| Cash ($230,000 – 12,000) | | 218,000 | |
| Accumulated depreciation—buildings | 218,000 | | ***Reduction of accumulated depreciation*** |
| Cash ($230,000 – 12,000) | | 218,000 | |

## REARRANGEMENTS

Expenditures made to restructure an asset without addition, replacement, or improvement are termed **rearrangements.** The objective is to create a new capability for the asset and not necessarily to extend its useful life. Examples include the rearrangement of machinery on the production line to increase operational efficiency and the relocation of a company's operating plant or office building. If these expenditures are material and they clearly increase future benefits, they should be capitalized and expensed in the future periods benefited. If the expenditures are not material or if it's not certain that future benefits have increased, they should be expensed in the period incurred.

**The costs of material *rearrangements* should be capitalized if they clearly increase future benefits.**

Graphic 11–16 provides a summary of the accounting treatment for the various types of expenditures related to tangible operational assets.

## COSTS OF DEFENDING INTANGIBLE RIGHTS

Repairs, additions, improvements, and rearrangements generally relate to tangible operational assets. A possible significant expenditure incurred subsequent to the acquisition of intangible assets is the cost of defending the right that gives the asset its value. If an intangible

**The costs incurred to *successfully* defend an intangible right should be capitalized.**

**GRAPHIC 11–16**
Expenditures Subsequent to Acquisition

| Type of Expenditure | Definition | Usual Accounting Treatment |
|---|---|---|
| Repairs and maintenance | Expenditures to maintain a given level of benefits | Expense in the period incurred |
| Additions | The addition of a new major component to an existing asset | Capitalize and depreciate over the remaining useful life of the original asset or its own useful life, whichever is shorter |
| Improvements | The replacement of a major component | Capitalize and depreciate over the useful life of the improved asset |
| Rearrangements | Expenditures to restructure an asset without addition, replacement, or improvement | If expenditures are material and clearly increase future benefits, capitalize and depreciate over the future periods benefited |

right is *successfully* defended, the litigation costs should be capitalized and amortized over the remaining useful life of the related intangible. This is the appropriate treatment of these expenditures even if the intangible asset was originally developed rather than purchased.

**The costs incurred to *unsuccessfully* defend an intangible right should be expensed.**

If the defense of an intangible right is *unsuccessful,* then the litigation costs should be expensed as incurred because they provide no future benefit. In addition, the book value of any intangible asset should be reduced to realizable value. For example, if a company is unsuccessful in defending a patent infringement suit, the patent's value may be eliminated. The book value of the patent should be written off as a loss.

## FINANCIAL REPORTING CASE SOLUTION

1. **Is Penny correct? Do the terms *depreciation, depletion,* and *amortization* all mean the same thing?** *(p. 504)* Penny is correct. Each of these terms refers to the cost allocation of operational assets over their service lives. The term *depreciation* is used for plant and equipment, *depletion* for natural resources, and *amortization* for intangibles.
2. **What is the units-of-production method? How is it used by this company?** *(p. 508)* The units-of-production method is an activity-based method that computes a depreciation (or depletion or amortization) rate per measure of activity and then multiplies this rate by actual activity to determine periodic cost allocation. The method is used by this company to (1) depreciate its paper and wood products manufacturing facilities, (2) measure depletion of the cost of timber harvested, and (3) measure amortization of the cost of logging roads. The cost of logging roads is an intangible asset because the company does not own the roads. The company has incurred costs to upgrade the roads to make them serviceable and has the right to use them in its timber operations.
3. **Explain how asset impairment differs from depreciation, depletion, and amortization. How are impairment losses measured for tangible operational assets with finite useful lives?** *(p. 523)* Depreciation, depletion, and amortization reflect a gradual consumption of the benefits inherent in an operational asset. An implicit assumption in allocating the cost of an asset over its useful life is that there has been no significant reduction in the anticipated total benefits or service potential of the asset. Situations can arise, however, that cause a significant decline or *impairment* of those benefits or service potentials. Determining whether to record an impairment loss for a tangible operational asset and actually recording the loss is a two-step process. The first step is a recoverability test—an impairment loss is required only when the undiscounted sum of estimated future cash flows from an asset is less than the asset's book value. The measurement of impairment loss—step 2—is the difference between the asset's book value and its fair value. If an impairment loss is recognized, the written-down book value becomes the new cost base for future cost allocation. ■

## THE BOTTOM LINE

1. The use of operational assets represents a consumption of benefits, or service potentials, inherent in the assets. The matching principle requires that the cost of these inherent benefits or service potentials that were consumed be recognized as an expense. As there very seldom is a direct relationship between the use of operational assets and revenue production, accounting resorts to arbitrary allocation methods to achieve a matching of expenses with revenues.
2. The allocation process for plant and equipment is called *depreciation.* Time-based depreciation methods estimate service life in years and then allocate depreciable base, cost less estimated residual value, using either a straight-line or accelerated pattern. Activity-based depreciation methods allocate the depreciable base by estimating service life according to some measure of productivity.
3. The allocation process for natural resources is called *depletion.* The activity-based method called units-of-production usually is used to determine periodic depletion.
4. The allocation process for intangible assets is called *amortization.* For an intangible asset with a finite useful life, the capitalized cost less any estimated residual value must be allocated to periods in which the asset is expected to contribute to the company's revenue-generating activities. An intangible asset that is determined to have an indefinite useful life is not subject to periodic amortization. Goodwill is perhaps the most typical intangible asset with an indefinite useful life.
5. A change in either the service life or residual value of an operational asset should be reflected in the financial statements of the current period and future periods by recalculating periodic depreciation, depletion, or amortization.
6. A change in depreciation, depletion, or amortization method is considered a change in accounting estimate that is achieved by a change in accounting principle. We account for these changes prospectively, exactly as we would any other change in estimate. One difference is that most changes in estimate do not require a company to justify the change. However, this change in estimate is a result of changing an accounting principle and therefore requires a clear justification as to why the new method is preferable.
7. A material error in accounting for an operational asset that is discovered in a year subsequent to the year of the error requires that previous years' financial statements that were incorrect as a result of the error are retrospectively restated to reflect the correction. Any account balances that are incorrect as a result of the error are corrected by journal entry. If retained earnings is one of the incorrect accounts, the correction is reported as a prior period adjustment to the beginning balance in the statement of shareholders' equity. In addition, a disclosure note is needed to describe the nature of the error and the impact of its correction on income.
8. Conceptually, there is considerable merit for a policy requiring the write-down of an operational asset when there has been a *significant* decline in value below carrying value (book value). The write-down provides important information about the future cash flows to be generated from the use of the asset. However, in practice this policy is very subjective. *SFAS 144* establishes guidance for when to recognize and how to measure impairment losses of tangible operational assets and intangible operational assets that have finite useful lives. *SFAS 142* provides additional guidance for the recognition and measurement of impairment for indefinite life intangibles and goodwill.
9. Expenditures for repairs and maintenance generally are expensed when incurred. The costs of additions and improvements usually are capitalized. The costs of material rearrangements should be capitalized if they clearly increase future benefits. ■

## APPENDIX 11A

## COMPARISON WITH MACRS (TAX DEPRECIATION)

Depreciation for financial reporting purposes is an attempt to distribute the cost of the asset, less any anticipated residual value, over the estimated useful life in a systematic and rational manner that attempts to match revenues with the use of the asset. Depreciation for income tax purposes is influenced by the revenue needs of government as well as the desire to influence economic behavior. For example, accelerated depreciation schedules currently allowed are intended to provide incentive for companies to expand and modernize their facilities thus stimulating economic growth.

The federal income tax code allows taxpayers to compute depreciation for their tax returns on assets acquired after 1986 using the **modified accelerated cost recovery system (MACRS).**[14] Key differences between the calculation of depreciation for financial reporting and the calculation using MACRS are:

1. Estimated useful lives and residual values are not used in MACRS.
2. Firms can't choose among various accelerated methods under MACRS.
3. A half-year convention is used in determining the MACRS depreciation rates.

Under MACRS, each asset is placed within a recovery period category. The six categories for personal property are 3, 5, 7, 10, 15, and 20 years. For example, the 5-year category includes most machinery and equipment, automobiles, and light trucks.

Depending on the category, fixed percentage rates are applied to the original cost of the asset. The rates for the 5-year asset category are as follows:

| Year | Rate |
|---|---|
| 1 | 20.00% |
| 2 | 32.00 |
| 3 | 19.20 |
| 4 | 11.52 |
| 5 | 11.52 |
| 6 | 5.76 |
| Total | 100.00% |

These rates are equivalent to applying the double-declining-balance method with a switch to straight-line in the year straight line yields an equal or higher deduction than DDB. In most cases, the half-year convention is used regardless of when the asset is placed in service.[15] The first-year rate of 20% for the five-year category is one-half of the DDB rate for an asset with a five-year life (2 × 20%). The sixth year rate of 5.76% is one-half of the straight-line rate established in year 4, the year straight-line depreciation exceeds DDB depreciation.

Companies have the option to use the straight-line method for the entire tax life of the asset, applying the half-year convention, rather than using MACRS depreciation schedules. Because of the differences discussed above, tax depreciation for a given year will likely be different from GAAP depreciation. ■

# APPENDIX 11B RETIREMENT AND REPLACEMENT METHODS OF DEPRECIATION

**Retirement** and **replacement** depreciation methods occasionally are used to depreciate relatively low-valued assets with short service lives. Under either approach, an aggregate asset account that represents a group of similar assets is increased at the time the initial collection is acquired.

[14]For assets acquired between 1981 and 1986, tax depreciation is calculated using the accelerated cost recovery system (ACRS), which is similar to MACRS. For assets acquired before 1981, tax depreciation can be calculated using any of the depreciation methods discussed in the chapter. Residual values are used in the calculation of depreciation for pre-1981 assets.

[15]In certain situations, mid-quarter and mid-month conventions are used.

## Retirement Method

Using the **retirement depreciation method,** the asset account also is increased for the cost of subsequent expenditures. When an item is disposed of, the asset account is credited for its cost, and depreciation expense is recorded for the difference between cost and proceeds received, if any. No other entries are made for depreciation. As a consequence, one or more periods may pass without any expense recorded. For example, the following entry records the purchase of 100 handheld calculators at $50 acquisition cost each:

**The *retirement depreciation method* records depreciation when assets are disposed of and measures depreciation as the difference between the proceeds received and cost.**

| | | |
|---|---|---|
| Calculators (100 × $50) | 5,000 | |
| Cash | | 5,000 |
| *To record the acquisition of calculators.* | | |

If 20 new calculators are acquired at $45 each, the asset account is increased.

| | | |
|---|---|---|
| Calculators (20 × $45) | 900 | |
| Cash | | 900 |
| *To record additional calculator acquisitions.* | | |

Thirty calculators are disposed of (retired) by selling them secondhand to a bookkeeping firm for $5 each. The following entry reflects the retirement method:

| | | |
|---|---|---|
| Cash (30 × $5) | 150 | |
| Depreciation expense (difference) | 1,350 | |
| Calculators (30 × $50) | | 1,500 |
| *To record the sale/depreciation of calculators.* | | |

Notice that the retirement system assumes a FIFO cost flow approach in determining the cost of assets, $50 each, that were disposed.

## Replacement Method

By the **replacement depreciation method,** the initial acquisition of assets is recorded the same way as by the retirement method; that is, the aggregate cost is increased. However, depreciation expense is the amount paid for new or replacement assets. Any proceeds received from asset dispositions reduces depreciation expense. For our example, the acquisition of 20 new calculators at $45 each is recorded as depreciation as follows:

**By the *replacement method,* depreciation is recorded when assets are replaced.**

| | | |
|---|---|---|
| Depreciation expense (20 × $45) | 900 | |
| Cash | | 900 |
| *To record the replacement/depreciation of calculators.* | | |

The sale of the old calculators is recorded as a reduction of depreciation:

| | | |
|---|---|---|
| Cash (30 × $5) | 150 | |
| Depreciation expense | | 150 |
| *To record the sale of calculators.* | | |

The asset account balance remains the same throughout the life of the aggregate collection of assets.

Because these methods are likely to produce aggregate expense measurements that differ from individual calculations, retirement and replacement methods are acceptable only in situations where the distortion in depreciation expense does not have a material effect on income. These methods occasionally are encountered in regulated industries such as utilities. ■

## QUESTIONS FOR REVIEW OF KEY TOPICS

**Q 11–1** Explain the similarities in and differences among depreciation, depletion, and amortization.

**Q 11–2** Depreciation is a process of cost allocation, not valuation. Explain this statement.

**Q 11–3** Identify and define the three characteristics of an asset that must be established to determine periodic depreciation, depletion, or amortization.

**Q 11–4** Discuss the factors that influence the estimation of service life for a depreciable asset.

**Q 11–5** What is meant by depreciable base? How is it determined?

**Q 11–6** Briefly differentiate between activity-based and time-based allocation methods.

**Q 11–7** Briefly differentiate between the straight-line depreciation method and accelerated depreciation methods.

**Q 11–8** Why are time-based depreciation methods used more frequently than activity-based methods?

**Q 11–9** What are some factors that could explain the predominant use of the straight-line depreciation method?

**Q 11–10** Briefly explain the differences and similarities between the group approach and composite approach to depreciating aggregate assets.

**Q 11–11** Define depletion and compare it with depreciation.

**Q 11–12** Compare and contrast amortization of intangible assets with depreciation and depletion.

**Q 11–13** What are some of the simplifying conventions a company can use to calculate depreciation for partial years?

**Q 11–14** Explain the accounting treatment required when a change is made to the estimated service life of a machine.

**Q 11–15** Explain the accounting treatment and disclosures required when a change is made in depreciation method.

**Q 11–16** Explain the steps required to correct an error in accounting for an operational asset that is discovered in a year subsequent to the year the error was made.

**Q 11–17** Explain what is meant by the impairment value of an operational asset. How should these impairments be accounted for?

**Q 11–18** Explain the differences in the accounting treatment of repairs and maintenance, additions, improvements, and rearrangements.

## BRIEF EXERCISES

**BE 11–1**
Cost allocation
• LO1

At the beginning of its fiscal year, Koeplin Corporation purchased a machine for $50,000. At the end of the year, the machine had a fair value of $32,000. Koeplin's controller recorded depreciation expense of $18,000 for the year, the decline in the machine's value. Why is this an incorrect approach to measuring periodic depreciation?

**BE 11–2**
Depreciation methods
• LO2

On January 1, 2006, Canseco Plumbing Fixtures purchased equipment for $30,000. Residual value at the end of an estimated four-year service life is expected to be $2,000. The company expects the machine to operate for 10,000 hours. Calculate depreciation expense for 2006 and 2007 using each of the following depreciation methods: (a) straight line, (b) sum-of-the-years'-digits, (c) double-declining balance, and (d) units-of-production using machine hours. The machine operated for 2,200 and 3,000 hours in 2006 and 2007, respectively.

**BE 11–3**
Depreciation methods; partial years
• LO2

Refer to the situation described in BE 11–2. Assume the machine was purchased on March 31, 2006, instead of January 1. Calculate depreciation expense for 2006 and 2007 using each of the following depreciation methods: (a) straight line, (b) sum-of-the-years'-digits, and (c) double-declining balance.

**BE 11–4**
Group depreciation
• LO2

Mondale Winery depreciates its equipment using the group method. The cost of equipment purchased in 2006 totaled $425,000. The estimated residual value of the equipment was $40,000 and the group depreciation rate was determined to be 18%. What is the annual depreciation for the group? If equipment that cost $42,000 is sold in 2007 for $35,000, what amount of gain or loss will the company recognize for the sale?

**BE 11–5**
Depletion
• LO3

Fitzgerald Oil and Gas incurred costs of $8.25 million for the acquisition and development of a natural gas deposit. The company expects to extract 3 million cubic feet of natural gas during a four-year period. Natural gas extracted during year 1 and year 2 were 700,000 and 800,000 cubic feet, respectively. What was the depletion for year 1 and year 2?

**BE 11–6**
Amortization
• LO4

On June 28 Lexicon Corporation acquired 100% of the common stock of Gulf & Eastern. The purchase price allocation included the following items: $4 million, patent; $3 million, developed technology; $2 million, in-process research and development; $5 million, goodwill. Lexicon's policy is to amortize intangible assets using the straight-line method, no residual value, and a five-year useful life. What is the total amount of expenses (ignoring taxes) that would appear in Lexicon's income statement for the year ended December 31 related to these items?

**BE 11–7**
Change in estimate; useful life of equipment
● LO5

At the beginning of 2004, Robotics, Inc. acquired a manufacturing facility for $12 million. $9 million of the purchase price was allocated to the building. Depreciation for 2004 and 2005 was calculated using the straight-line method, a 25-year useful life, and a $1 million residual value. In 2006, the estimates of useful life and residual value were changed to 20 years and $500,000, respectively. What is depreciation on the building for 2006?

**BE 11–8**
Change in principle; change in depreciation method
● LO5

Refer to the situation described in BE 11–7. Assume that instead of changing the useful life and residual value, in 2006 the company switched to the double-declining-balance depreciation method. How should Robotics account for the change? What is depreciation on the building for 2006?

**BE 11–9**
Error correction
● LO7

Refer to the situation described in BE 11–7. Assume that 2004 depreciation was incorrectly recorded as $32,000. This error was discovered in 2006. How should Robotics account for the error? What is depreciation on the building for 2006 assuming no change in estimate of useful life or residual value?

**BE 11–10**
Impairment; tangible operational assets
● LO8

Collison and Ryder Company (C&R) has been experiencing declining market conditions for its sportswear division. Management decided to test the operational assets of the division for possible impairment. The test revealed the following: book value of division's assets, $26.5 million; fair value of division's assets, $21 million; sum of estimated future cash flows generated from the division's assets, $28 million. What amount of impairment loss should C&R recognize?

**BE 11–11**
Impairment; tangible operational assets
● LO8

Refer to the situation described in BE 11–10. Assume that the sum of estimated future cash flows is $24 million instead of $28 million. What amount of impairment loss should C&R recognize?

**BE 11–12**
Impairment; goodwill
● LO8

WebHelper, Inc. acquired 100% of the outstanding stock of Silicon Chips Corporation (SCC) for $45 million, of which $15 million was allocated to goodwill. At the end of the current fiscal year, the annual impairment test revealed the following: fair value of SCC, $40 million; fair value of SCC's net assets (excluding goodwill), $31 million; book value of SCC's net assets (including goodwill), $42 million. What amount of impairment loss should WebHelper recognize?

**BE 11–13**
Impairment; goodwill
● LO8

Refer to the situation described in BE 11–12. Assume that the fair value of SCC is $44 million instead of $40 million. What amount of impairment loss should WebHelper recognize?

**BE 11–14**
Subsequent expenditures
● LO9

Demmert Manufacturing incurred the following expenditures during the current fiscal year: annual maintenance on its machinery, $5,400; remodeling of offices, $22,000; rearrangement of the shipping and receiving area resulting in an increase in productivity, $35,000; addition of a security system to the manufacturing facility, $25,000. How should Demmert account for each of these expenditures?

# EXERCISES

available with McGraw-Hill's Homework Manager www.mhhe.com/spiceland4e

**An alternate exercise and problem set is available on the text website: www.mhhe.com/spiceland4e**

**E 11–1**
Depreciation methods
● LO2

On January 1, 2006, the Excel Delivery Company purchased a delivery van for $33,000. At the end of its five-year service life, it is estimated that the van will be worth $3,000. During the five-year period, the company expects to drive the van 100,000 miles.

**Required:**

Calculate annual depreciation for the five-year life of the van using each of the following methods. Round all computations to the nearest dollar.

1. Straight line.
2. Sum-of-the-years' digits.
3. Double-declining balance.
4. Units of production using miles driven as a measure of output, and the following actual mileage:

| Year | Miles |
|---|---|
| 2006 | 22,000 |
| 2007 | 24,000 |
| 2008 | 15,000 |
| 2009 | 20,000 |
| 2010 | 21,000 |

**E 11–2**
Depreciation methods

● LO2

On January 1, 2006, the Allegheny Corporation purchased machinery for $115,000. The estimated service life of the machinery is 10 years and the estimated residual value is $5,000. The machine is expected to produce 220,000 units during its life.

**Required:**

Calculate depreciation for 2006 and 2007 using each of the following methods. Round all computations to the nearest dollar.

1. Straight line.
2. Sum-of-the-years' digits.
3. Double-declining balance.
4. One hundred fifty percent declining balance.
5. Units of production (units produced in 2006, 30,000; units produced in 2007, 25,000).

**E 11–3**
Depreciation methods; partial years

● LO2

[This is a variation of the previous exercise modified to focus on depreciation for partial years.]

On October 1, 2006, the Allegheny Corporation purchased machinery for $115,000. The estimated service life of the machinery is 10 years and the estimated residual value is $5,000. The machine is expected to produce 220,000 units during its life.

**Required:**

Calculate depreciation for 2006 and 2007 using each of the following methods. Partial-year depreciation is calculated based on the number of months the asset is in service. Round all computations to the nearest dollar.

1. Straight line.
2. Sum-of-the-years' digits.
3. Double-declining balance.
4. One hundred fifty percent declining balance.
5. Units of production (units produced in 2006, 10,000; units produced in 2007, 25,000).

**E 11–4**
Depreciation methods; asset addition

● LO2

Funseth Company purchased a five-story office building on January 1, 2004, at a cost of $5,000,000. The building has a residual value of $200,000 and a 30-year life. The straight-line depreciation method is used. On June 30, 2006, construction of a sixth floor was completed at a cost of $1,650,000.

**Required:**

Calculate the depreciation on the building and building addition for 2006 and 2007 assuming that the addition did not change the life or residual value of the building.

**E 11–5**
Depreciation methods; solving for unknowns

● LO2

For each of the following depreciable assets, determine the missing amount (?). Abbreviations for depreciation methods are SL for straight line, SYD for sum-of-the-years' digits, and DDB for double-declining balance.

| Asset | Cost | Residual Value | Service Life (Years) | Depreciation Method | Depreciation (Year 2) |
|---|---|---|---|---|---|
| A | ? | $20,000 | 5 | DDB | $24,000 |
| B | $ 40,000 | ? | 8 | SYD | 7,000 |
| C | 65,000 | 5,000 | ? | SL | 6,000 |
| D | 230,000 | 10,000 | 10 | ? | 22,000 |
| E | 200,000 | 20,000 | 8 | 150%DB | ? |

**E 11–6**
Multiple choice; cost allocation

● LO2 through LO4

The following questions dealing with depreciation, depletion, and amortization are adapted from questions that appeared on CPA examinations. Determine the response that best completes the statements or questions.

1. In January 2006, Vorst Co. purchased a mineral mine for $2,640,000 with removable ore estimated at 1,200,000 tons. After it has extracted all the ore, Vorst will be required by law to restore the land to its original condition. The present value of the estimated restoration expenditures is $180,000. Vorst believes it will be able to sell the property afterwards for $300,000. During 2006, Vorst incurred $360,000 of development costs preparing the mine for production and removed and sold 60,000 tons of ore. In its 2006 income statement, what amount should Vorst report as depletion?
   a. $135,000
   b. $144,000
   c. $150,000
   d. $159,000

2. South Co. purchased a machine that was installed and placed in service on January 1, 2006, at a cost of $240,000. Salvage value was estimated at $40,000. The machine is being depreciated over 10 years by the double-declining-balance method. For the year ended December 31, 2007, what amount should South report as depreciation expense?
   a. $48,000
   b. $38,400
   c. $32,000
   d. $21,600
3. A machine with a five-year estimated service life and an estimated 10% residual value was acquired on January 1, 2004. On December 31, 2007, accumulated depreciation, using the sum-of-the-years'-digits method, would be
   a. (Original cost less residual value) multiplied by 1/15.
   b. (Original cost less residual value) multiplied by 14/15.
   c. Original cost multiplied by 14/15.
   d. Original cost multiplied by 1/15.
4. Mark Co. bought a franchise from Fred Co. on January 1, 2006, for $204,000. An independent consultant retained by Mark estimated that the remaining life of the franchise was 40 years. Its unamortized cost on Fred's books at January 1, 2006, was $68,000. What amount should be amortized for the year ended December 31, 2006?
   a. $5,100
   b. $4,080
   c. $4,000
   d. $1,700

**E 11–7**
Group depreciation
● LO2

Highsmith Rental Company purchased an apartment building early in 2006. There are 20 apartments in the building and each is furnished with major kitchen appliances. The company has decided to use the group depreciation method for the appliances. The following data are available:

| Appliance | Cost | Residual Value | Service Life (in Years) |
|---|---|---|---|
| Stoves | $15,000 | $3,000 | 6 |
| Refrigerators | 10,000 | 1,000 | 5 |
| Dishwashers | 8,000 | 500 | 4 |

In 2009, three new refrigerators costing $2,700 were purchased for cash. The old refrigerators, which originally cost $1,500, were sold for $200.

**Required:**
1. Calculate the group depreciation rate, group life, and depreciation for 2006.
2. Prepare the journal entries to record the purchase of the new refrigerators and the sale of the old refrigerators.

**E 11–8**
Double-declining-balance method; switch to straight line
● LO2

On January 2, 2006, the Jackson Company purchased equipment to be used in its manufacturing process. The equipment has an estimated life of eight years and an estimated residual value of $30,625. The expenditures made to acquire the asset were as follows:

| | |
|---|---|
| Purchase price | $154,000 |
| Freight charges | 2,000 |
| Installation charges | 4,000 |

Jackson's policy is to use the double-declining-balance (DDB) method of depreciation in the early years of the equipment's life and then switch to straight line halfway through the equipment's life.

**Required:**
1. Calculate depreciation for each year of the asset's eight-year life.
2. Discuss the accounting treatment of the depreciation on the equipment.

**E 11–9**
Depletion
● LO3

On April 17, 2006, the Loadstone Mining Company purchased the rights to a coal mine. The purchase price plus additional costs necessary to prepare the mine for extraction of the coal totaled $4,500,000. The company expects to extract 900,000 tons of coal during a four-year period. During 2006, 240,000 tons were extracted and sold immediately.

**Required:**
1. Calculate depletion for 2006.
2. Discuss the accounting treatment of the depletion calculated in requirement 1.

**E 11–10**
Cost of a natural resource; depletion and depreciation; Chapters 10 and 11

● LO2 LO3

[This exercise is a continuation of Exercise 10–3 in Chapter 10 focusing on depletion and depreciation.]

Jackpot Mining Company operates a copper mine in central Montana. The company paid $1,000,000 in 2006 for the mining site and spent an additional $600,000 to prepare the mine for extraction of the copper. After the copper is extracted in approximately four years, the company is required to restore the land to its original condition, including repaving of roads and replacing a greenbelt. The company has provided the following three cash flow possibilities for the restoration costs:

| | Cash Outflow | Probability |
|---|---|---|
| 1 | $300,000 | 25% |
| 2 | 400,000 | 40% |
| 3 | 600,000 | 35% |

To aid extraction, Jackpot purchased some new equipment on July 1, 2006, for $120,000. After the copper is removed from this mine, the equipment will be sold for an estimated residual amount of $20,000. There will be no residual value for the copper mine. The credit-adjusted risk-free rate of interest is 10%.

The company expects to extract 10 million pounds of copper from the mine. Actual production was 1.6 million pounds in 2006 and 3 million pounds in 2007.

**Required:**

1. Compute depletion and depreciation on the mine and mining equipment for 2006 and 2007. The units-of-production method is used to calculate depreciation.
2. Discuss the accounting treatment of the depletion and depreciation on the mine and mining equipment.

**E 11–11**
Amortization

● LO4

Janes Company provided the following information on intangible assets:

a. A patent was purchased from the Lou Company for $700,000 on January 1, 2004. Janes estimated the remaining useful life of the patent to be 10 years. The patent was carried on Lou's accounting records at a net book value of $350,000 when Lou sold it to Janes.
b. During 2006, a franchise was purchased from the Rink Company for $500,000. The contractual life of the franchise is 10 years and Janes records a full year of amortization in the year of purchase.
c. Janes incurred research and development costs in 2006 as follows:

| | |
|---|---|
| Materials and supplies | $140,000 |
| Personnel | 180,000 |
| Indirect costs | 60,000 |
| Total | $380,000 |

d. Effective January 1, 2006, based on new events that have occurred, Janes estimates that the remaining life of the patent purchased from Lou is only five more years.

**Required:**

1. Prepare the entries necessary in 2004 and 2006 to reflect the above information.
2. Prepare a schedule showing the intangible asset section of Janes's December 31, 2006, balance sheet.

**E 11–12**
Patent amortization

● LO4

On January 2, 2006, David Corporation purchased a patent for $500,000. The remaining legal life is 12 years, but the company estimated that the patent will be useful only for eight years. In January 2008, the company incurred legal fees of $45,000 in successfully defending a patent infringement suit. The successful defense did not change the company's estimate of useful life.

**Required:**

Prepare journal entries related to the patent for 2006, 2007, and 2008.

**E 11–13**
Change in estimate; useful life of patent

● LO4 LO5

Van Frank Telecommunications has a patent on a cellular transmission process. The company has amortized the patent on a straight-line basis since 2002, when it was acquired at a cost of $9 million at the beginning of that year. Due to rapid technological advances in the industry, management decided that the patent would benefit the company over a total of six years rather than the nine-year life being used to amortize its cost. The decision was made at the end of 2006 (before adjusting and closing entries).

**Required:**

Prepare the appropriate adjusting entry for patent amortization in 2006 to reflect the revised estimate.

**E 11–14**
Change in estimate; useful life and residual value of equipment

● LO2 LO5

Wardell Company purchased a minicomputer on January 1, 2004, at a cost of $40,000. The computer was depreciated using the straight-line method over an estimated five-year life with an estimated residual value of $4,000. On January 1, 2006, the estimate of useful life was changed to a total of 10 years, and the estimate of residual value was changed to $900.

**Required:**

1. Prepare the appropriate adjusting entry for depreciation in 2006 to reflect the revised estimate.
2. Repeat requirement 1 assuming that the company uses the sum-of-the-years'-digits method instead of the straight-line method.

**E 11–15**
Change in principle; change in depreciation methods

● LO2 LO5

Alteran Corporation purchased a machine for $1.5 million in 2003. The machine is being depreciated over a 10-year life using the sum-of-the-years'-digits method. The residual value is expected to be $300,000. At the beginning of 2006, Alteran decided to change to the straight-line depreciation method for this machine.

**Required:**
Prepare the 2006 depreciation adjusting entry.

**E 11–16**
Change in principle; change in depreciation methods

● LO2 LO6

For financial reporting, Clinton Poultry Farms has used the declining-balance method of depreciation for conveyor equipment acquired at the beginning of 2003 for $2,560,000. Its useful life was estimated to be six years, with a $160,000 residual value. At the beginning of 2006, Clinton decides to change to the straight-line method. The effect of this change on depreciation for each year is as follows:

| | ($ in 000s) | | |
|---|---|---|---|
| **Year** | **Straight Line** | **Declining Balance** | **Difference** |
| 2003 | $ 400 | $ 640 | $240 |
| 2004 | 400 | 550 | 150 |
| 2005 | 400 | 460 | 60 |
| | $1,200 | $1,650 | $450 |

**Required:**
1. Briefly describe the way Clinton should report this accounting change in the 2005–2006 comparative financial statements.
2. Prepare any 2006 journal entry related to the change.

**E 11–17**
Error correction

● LO2 LO7

In 2006, internal auditors discovered that PKE Displays, Inc., had debited an expense account for the $350,000 cost of a machine purchased on January 1, 2003. The machine's life was expected to be five years with no residual value. Straight-line depreciation is used by PKE.

**Required:**
1. Prepare the appropriate correcting entry assuming the error was discovered in 2006 before the adjusting and closing entries. (Ignore income taxes.)
2. Assume the error was discovered in 2008 after the 2007 financial statements are issued. Prepare the appropriate correcting entry.

**E 11–18**
Impairment; tangible operational assets

● LO8

Chadwick Enterprises, Inc., operates several restaurants throughout the Midwest. Three of its restaurants located in the center of a large urban area have experienced declining profits due to declining population. The company's management has decided to test the operational assets of the restaurants for possible impairment. The relevant information for these assets is presented below.

| | |
|---|---|
| Book value | $6.5 million |
| Estimated undiscounted sum of future cash flows | 4.0 million |
| Fair value | 3.5 million |

**Required:**
1. Determine the amount of the impairment loss.
2. Repeat requirement 1 assuming that the estimated undiscounted sum of future cash flows is $6.8 million and fair value is $5 million.

**E 11–19**
Impairment; goodwill

● LO8

In 2004, Alliant Corporation acquired Centerpoint, Inc. for $300 million, of which $50 million was allocated to goodwill. Alliant tests for goodwill impairment at the end of each year. At the end of 2006, management has provided the following information:

| | |
|---|---|
| Fair value of Centerpoint, Inc. | $220 million |
| Fair value of Centerpoint's net assets (excluding goodwill) | 200 million |
| Book value of Centerpoint's net assets (including goodwill) | 250 million |

**Required:**
1. Determine the amount of the impairment loss.
2. Repeat requirement 1 assuming that the fair value of Centerpoint is $270 million.

**E 11–20**
Subsequent expenditures

● LO9

Belltone Company made the following expenditures related to its 10-year-old manufacturing facility:
1. The heating system was replaced at a cost of $250,000. The cost of the old system was not known. The company accounts for improvements as reductions of accumulated depreciation.
2. A new wing was added at a cost of $750,000. The new wing substantially increases the productive capacity of the plant.
3. Annual building maintenance was performed at a cost of $14,000.
4. All of the machinery on the assembly line in the plant was rearranged at a cost of $50,000. The rearrangement clearly increases the productive capacity of the plant.

**Required:**

Prepare journal entries to record each of the above expenditures.

**E 11–21**
Depreciation methods; disposal of operational asset; Chapters 10 and 11

● LO2

Howarth Manufacturing Company purchased a lathe on June 30, 2002, at a cost of $80,000. The residual value of the lathe was estimated to be $5,000 at the end of a five-year life. The lathe was sold on March 31, 2006, for $17,000. Howarth uses the straight-line depreciation method for all of its plant and equipment. Partial-year depreciation is calculated based on the number of months the asset is in service.

**Required:**

1. Prepare the journal entry to record the sale.
2. Assuming that Howarth had instead used the sum-of-the-years'-digits depreciation method, prepare the journal entry to record the sale.

**E 11–22**
Multiple choice; operational assets

● LO2 LO4 LO5 LO8 LO9

The following questions involving operational assets are adapted from questions that appeared on CPA examinations. Determine the response that best completes the statements or questions.

1. In January 2004, Winn Corp. purchased equipment at a cost of $500,000. The equipment had an estimated residual value of $100,000, an estimated eight-year useful life, and was being depreciated by the straight-line method. Two years later, it became apparent to Winn that this equipment suffered a permanent impairment of value. In January 2006, management determined the carrying amount should be only $175,000, with a two-year remaining useful life, and the residual value should be reduced to $25,000. In Winn's December 31, 2006, balance sheet, the equipment should be reported at a carrying amount of
   a. $350,000
   b. $175,000
   c. $150,000
   d. $100,000
2. On January 1, 2003, Lane, Inc., acquired equipment for $100,000 with an estimated 10-year useful life. Lane estimated a $10,000 residual value and used the straight-line method of depreciation. During 2007, after its 2006 financial statements had been issued, Lane determined that, due to obsolescence, this equipment's remaining useful life was only four years and its residual value would be $4,000. In Lane's December 31, 2007, balance sheet, what was the carrying amount of this asset?
   a. $51,500
   b. $49,000
   c. $41,500
   d. $39,000
3. On January 1, 2003, Taft Co. purchased a patent for $714,000. The patent is being amortized over its remaining legal life of 15 years expiring on January 1, 2018. During 2006, Taft determined that the economic benefits of the patent would not last longer than 10 years from the date of acquisition. What amount should be reported in the balance sheet for the patent, net of accumulated amortization, at December 31, 2006?
   a. $428,400
   b. $489,600
   c. $504,000
   d. $523,600
4. During 2005, Yvo Corp. installed a production assembly line to manufacture furniture. In 2006, Yvo purchased a new machine and rearranged the assembly line to install this machine. The rearrangement did not significantly increase the estimated useful life of the assembly line, but it did result in significantly more efficient production. The following expenditures were incurred in connection with this project:

| | |
|---|---|
| Machine | $75,000 |
| Labor to install machine | 14,000 |
| Parts added in rearranging the assembly line to provide future benefits | 40,000 |
| Labor and overhead to rearrange the assembly line | 18,000 |

   What amount of the above expenditures should be capitalized in 2006?
   a. $147,000
   b. $107,000
   c. $89,000
   d. $75,000

**E 11–23**
Concepts; terminology

● LO1 through LO6 LO8

Listed below are several items and phrases associated with depreciation, depletion, and amortization. Pair each item from List A (by letter) with the item from List B that is most appropriately associated with it.

| List A | List B |
|---|---|
| ____ 1. Depreciation | a. Cost allocation for natural resource. |
| ____ 2. Service life | b. Accounted for prospectively. |
| ____ 3. Depreciable base | c. When there has been a significant decline in value. |
| ____ 4. Activity-based methods | d. The amount of use expected from an operational asset. |
| ____ 5. Time-based methods | e. Estimates service life in units of output. |
| ____ 6. Double-declining balance | f. Cost less residual value. |
| ____ 7. Group method | g. Cost allocation for plant and equipment. |
| ____ 8. Composite method | h. Does not subtract residual value from cost. |
| ____ 9. Depletion | i. Accounted for in the same way as a change in estimate. |
| ____ 10. Amortization | j. Aggregates assets that are similar. |
| ____ 11. Change in useful life | k. Aggregates assets that are physically unified. |
| ____ 12. Change in depreciation method | l. Cost allocation for an intangible asset. |
| ____ 13. Write-down of asset | m. Estimates service life in years. |

**E 11–24**
Multiple choice; CMA exam; depletion; amortization; subsequent expenditures

● LO3 LO4 LO9

The following questions dealing with the environment and theoretical structure of financial accounting are adapted from questions that previously appeared on Certified Management Accountant (CMA) examinations. The CMA designation sponsored by the Institute of Management Accountants (**www.imanet.org**) provides members with an objective measure of knowledge and competence in the field of management accounting. Determine the response that best completes the statements or questions.

1. WD Mining Company purchased a section of land for $600,000 in 1989 to develop a zinc mine. The mine began operating in 1997. At that time, management estimated that the mine would produce 200,000 tons of quality ore. A total of 100,000 tons of ore was mined and processed from 1997 through December 31, 2004. During January 2005, a very promising vein was discovered. The revised estimate of ore still to be mined was 250,000 tons. Estimated salvage value for the mine land was $100,000 in both 1997 and 2005. Assuming that 10,000 tons of ore was mined in 2005, the computation WD Mining company should use to determine the amount of depletion to record in 2005 would be
   a. (($600,000 − $100,000)/450,000 tons) × 10,000 tons.
   b. (($600,000 − $100,000)/350,000 tons) × 10,000 tons.
   c. (($600,000 − $100,000 − $250,000)/350,000 tons) × 10,000 tons.
   d. (($600,000 − $100,000 − $250,000)/250,000 tons) × 10,000 tons.
2. Costs that are capitalized with regard to a patent include
   a. Legal fees of obtaining the patent, incidental costs of obtaining the patent, and costs of successful patent infringement suits.
   b. Legal fees of obtaining the patent, incidental costs of obtaining the patent, and research and development costs incurred on the invention that is patented.
   c. Legal fees of obtaining the patent, costs of successful patent infringement suits, and research and development costs incurred on the invention that is patented.
   d. Incidental costs of obtaining the patent, costs of successful and unsuccessful patent infringement suits, and the value of any signed patent licensing agreement.
3. On September 1, year 1, for $4,000,000 cash and $2,000,000 notes payable, Norbend Corporation acquired the net assets of Crisholm Company, which had a fair value of $5,496,000 on that date. Norbend's management is of the opinion that the goodwill generated has an indefinite life. During the year-end audit for year 3 after all adjusting entries have been made, the goodwill is determined to be worthless. The amount of the write-off as of December 31, year 3 should be
   a. $504,000.
   b. $478,800.
   c. $466,200.
   d. $474,600.

**E 11–25**
Retirement and replacement depreciation (Based on Appendix 11B)

● LO2

Cadillac Construction Company uses the retirement method to determine depreciation on its small tools. During 2004, the first year of the company's operations, tools were purchased at a cost of $8,000. In 2006, tools originally costing $2,000 were sold for $250 and replaced with new tools costing $2,500.

**Required:**

1. Prepare journal entries to record each of the above transactions.
2. Repeat requirement 1 assuming that the company uses the replacement depreciation method instead of the retirement method.

## PROBLEMS

available with McGraw-Hill's Homework Manager www.mhhe.com/spiceland4e

**An alternate exercise and problem set is available on the text website: www.mhhe.com/spiceland4e**

**P 11–1**
Depreciation methods; change in methods
● LO2 LO6

The fact that generally accepted accounting principles allow companies flexibility in choosing between certain allocation methods can make it difficult for a financial analyst to compare periodic performance from firm to firm.

Suppose you were a financial analyst trying to compare the performance of two companies. Company A uses the double-declining-balance depreciation method. Company B uses the straight-line method. You have the following information taken from the 12/31/06 year-end financial statements for Company B:

| | |
|---|---|
| **Income Statement** | |
| Depreciation expense | $ 10,000 |
| **Balance Sheet** | |
| Assets: | |
| Plant and equipment, at cost | $200,000 |
| Less: Accumulated depreciation | (40,000) |
| Net | $160,000 |

You also determine that all of the assets constituting the plant and equipment of Company B were acquired at the same time, and that all of the $200,000 represents depreciable assets. Also, all of the depreciable assets have the same useful life and residual values are zero.

**Required:**

1. In order to compare performance with Company A, estimate what B's depreciation expense would have been for 2006 if the double-declining-balance depreciation method had been used by Company B since acquisition of the depreciable assets.
2. If Company B decided to switch depreciation methods in 2006 from the straight line to the double-declining-balance method, prepare the 2006 adjusting journal entry to record depreciation for the year.

**P 11–2**
Comprehensive problem; Chapters 10 and 11
● LO2 LO4
eXcel

At December 31, 2005, Cord Company's plant asset and accumulated depreciation and amortization accounts had balances as follows:

| Category | Plant Asset | Accumulated Depreciation and Amortization |
|---|---|---|
| Land | $ 175,000 | $ — |
| Buildings | 1,500,000 | 328,900 |
| Machinery and equipment | 1,125,000 | 317,500 |
| Automobiles and trucks | 172,000 | 100,325 |
| Leasehold improvements | 216,000 | 108,000 |
| Land improvements | — | — |

**Depreciation methods and useful lives:**
Buildings—150% declining balance; 25 years.
Machinery and equipment—Straight line; 10 years.
Automobiles and trucks—150% declining balance; 5 years, all acquired after 2002.
Leasehold improvements—Straight line.
Land improvements—Straight line.

Depreciation is computed to the nearest month and residual values are immaterial. *Transactions during 2006 and other information:*

a. On January 6, 2006, a plant facility consisting of land and building was acquired from King Corp. in exchange for 25,000 shares of Cord's common stock. On this date, Cord's stock had a market price of $50 a share. Current assessed values of land and building for property tax purposes are $187,500 and $562,500, respectively.
b. On March 25, 2006, new parking lots, streets, and sidewalks at the acquired plant facility were completed at a total cost of $192,000. These expenditures had an estimated useful life of 12 years.
c. The leasehold improvements were completed on December 31, 2002, and had an estimated useful life of eight years. The related lease, which would terminate on December 31, 2008, was renewable for an additional four-year term. On April 29, 2006, Cord exercised the renewal option.
d. On July 1, 2006, machinery and equipment were purchased at a total invoice cost of $325,000. Additional costs of $10,000 for delivery and $50,000 for installation were incurred.
e. On August 30, 2006, Cord purchased a new automobile for $12,500.

f. On September 30, 2006, a truck with a cost of $24,000 and a carrying amount of $9,100 on date of sale was sold for $11,500. Depreciation for the nine months ended September 30, 2006, was $2,650.
g. On December 20, 2006, a machine with a cost of $17,000 and a carrying amount of $2,975 at date of disposition was scrapped without cash recovery.

**Required:**
1. Prepare a schedule analyzing the changes in each of the plant asset accounts during 2006. This schedule should include columns for beginning balance, increase, decrease, and ending balance for each of the plant asset accounts. Do not analyze changes in accumulated depreciation and amortization.
2. For each asset category, prepare a schedule showing depreciation or amortization expense for the year ended December 31, 2006. Round computations to the nearest whole dollar.

*(AICPA adapted)*

**P 11–3**
Depreciation methods
● LO2
eXcel

[This problem is a continuation of Problem 10–3 in Chapter 10 focusing on depreciation.]

**Required:**
For each asset classification, prepare a schedule showing depreciation expense for the year ended December 31, 2006, using the following depreciation methods and useful lives:

Land improvements—Straight line; 15 years.
Building—150% declining balance; 20 years.
Machinery and equipment—Straight line; 10 years.
Automobiles—150% declining balance; 3 years.

Depreciation is computed to the nearest month and no residual values are used.

*(AICPA adapted)*

**P 11–4**
Partial-year depreciation; asset addition; increase in useful life
● LO2 LO9

On April 1, 2004, the KB Toy Company purchased equipment to be used in its manufacturing process. The equipment cost $48,000, has an eight-year useful life, and has no residual value. The company uses the straight-line depreciation method for all manufacturing equipment.

On January 4, 2006, $12,350 was spent to repair the equipment and to add a feature that increased its operating efficiency. Of the total expenditure, $2,000 represented ordinary repairs and annual maintenance and $10,350 represented the cost of the new feature. In addition to increasing operating efficiency, the total useful life of the equipment was extended to 10 years.

**Required:**
Prepare journal entries for the following:
1. Depreciation for 2004 and 2005.
2. The 2006 expenditure.
3. Depreciation for 2006.

**P 11–5**
Operational assets; comprehensive
● LO2

The Thompson Corporation, a manufacturer of steel products, began operations on October 1, 2004. The accounting department of Thompson has started the fixed-asset and depreciation schedule presented below. You have been asked to assist in completing this schedule. In addition to ascertaining that the data already on the schedule are correct, you have obtained the following information from the company's records and personnel:

a. Depreciation is computed from the first of the month of acquisition to the first of the month of disposition.
b. Land A and Building A were acquired from a predecessor corporation. Thompson paid $812,500 for the land and building together. At the time of acquisition, the land had an appraised value of $72,000 and the building had an appraised value of $828,000.
c. Land B was acquired on October 2, 2004, in exchange for 3,000 newly issued shares of Thompson's common stock. At the date of acquisition, the stock had a par value of $5 per share and a fair market value of $25 per share. During October 2004, Thompson paid $10,400 to demolish an existing building on this land so it could construct a new building.
d. Construction of Building B on the newly acquired land began on October 1, 2005. By September 30, 2006, Thompson had paid $210,000 of the estimated total construction costs of $300,000. Estimated completion and occupancy are July 2007.
e. Certain equipment was donated to the corporation by the city. An independent appraisal of the equipment when donated placed the fair value at $16,000 and the residual value at $2,000.
f. Machine A's total cost of $110,000 includes installation charges of $550 and normal repairs and maintenance of $11,000. Residual value is estimated at $5,500. Machine A was sold on February 1, 2006.
g. On October 1, 2005, Machine B was acquired with a down payment of $4,000 and the remaining payments to be made in 10 annual installments of $4,000 each beginning October 1, 2006. The prevailing interest rate was 8%.

**THOMPSON CORPORATION**
**Fixed Asset and Depreciation Schedule**
**For Fiscal Years Ended September 30, 2005, and September 30, 2006**

| Assets | Acquisition Date | Cost | Residual | Depreciation Method | Estimated Life in Years | Depreciation for Year Ended 9/30 2005 | Depreciation for Year Ended 9/30 2006 |
|---|---|---|---|---|---|---|---|
| Land A | 10/1/04 | $**(1)** | N/A | N/A | N/A | N/A | N/A |
| Building A | 10/1/04 | **(2)** | $47,500 | SL | **(3)** | $14,000 | $**(4)** |
| Land B | 10/2/04 | **(5)** | N/A | N/A | N/A | N/A | N/A |
| Building B | Under construction | 210,000 to date | — | SL | 30 | — | **(6)** |
| Donated Equipment | 10/2/04 | **(7)** | 2,000 | 150% Declining balance | 10 | **(8)** | **(9)** |
| Machine A | 10/2/04 | **(10)** | 5,500 | Sum-of-the-years'-digits | 10 | **(11)** | **(12)** |
| Machine B | 10/1/05 | **(13)** | — | SL | 15 | — | **(14)** |

N/A = not applicable

**Required:**

Supply the correct amount for each numbered item on the schedule. Round each answer to the nearest dollar.

*(AICPA adapted)*

**P 11–6**
Depreciation methods; partial-year depreciation; sale of assets

● LO2

excel

On March 31, 2006, the Herzog Company purchased a factory complete with machinery and equipment. The allocation of the total purchase price of $1,000,000 to the various types of assets along with estimated useful lives and residual values are as follows:

| Asset | Cost | Estimated Residual Value | Estimated Useful Life in Years |
|---|---|---|---|
| Land | $ 100,000 | N/A | N/A |
| Building | 500,000 | none | 25 |
| Machinery | 240,000 | 10% of cost | 8 |
| Equipment | 160,000 | $13,000 | 6 |
| Total | $1,000,000 | | |

On June 29, 2007, machinery included in the March 31, 2006, purchase that cost $100,000 was sold for $80,000. Herzog uses the straight-line depreciation method for buildings and machinery and the sum-of-the-years'-digits method for equipment. Partial-year depreciation is calculated based on the number of months an asset is in service.

**Required:**

1. Compute depreciation expense on the building, machinery, and equipment for 2006.
2. Prepare the journal entries to record (1) depreciation on the machinery sold on June 29, 2007, and (2) the sale of machinery.
3. Compute depreciation expense on the building, remaining machinery, and equipment for 2007.

**P 11–7**
Depletion; change in estimate

● LO3 LO5

excel

In 2006, the Marion Company purchased land containing a mineral mine for $1,600,000. Additional costs of $600,000 were incurred to develop the mine. Geologists estimated that 400,000 tons of ore would be extracted. After the ore is removed, the land will have a resale value of $100,000.

To aid in the extraction, Marion built various structures and small storage buildings on the site at a cost of $150,000. These structures have a useful life of 10 years. The structures cannot be moved after the ore has been removed and will be left at the site. In addition, new equipment costing $80,000 was purchased and installed at the site. Marion does not plan to move the equipment to another site, but estimates that it can be sold at auction for $4,000 after the mining project is completed.

In 2006, 50,000 tons of ore were extracted and sold. In 2007, the estimate of total tons of ore in the mine was revised from 400,000 to 487,500. During 2007, 80,000 tons were extracted, of which 60,000 tons were sold.

**Required:**

1. Compute depletion and depreciation of the mine and the mining facilities and equipment for 2006 and 2007. Marion uses the units-of-production method to determine depreciation on mining facilities and equipment.
2. Compute the book value of the mineral mine, structures, and equipment as of December 31, 2007.
3. Discuss the accounting treatment of the depletion and depreciation on the mine and mining facilities and equipment.

**P 11–8**
Amortization

● LO4

The following information concerns the intangible assets of Epstein Corporation:

a. On June 30, 2006, Epstein completed the purchase of the Johnstone Corporation for $2,000,000 in cash. The fair value of the net identifiable assets of Johnstone was $1,700,000.
b. Included in the assets purchased from Johnstone was a patent that was valued at $80,000. The remaining legal life of the patent was 13 years, but Epstein believes that the patent will only be useful for another eight years.
c. Epstein acquired a franchise on October 1, 2006, by paying an initial franchise fee of $200,000. The contractual life of the franchise is 10 years.

**Required:**

1. Prepare year-end adjusting journal entries to record amortization expense on the intangibles at December 31, 2006.
2. Prepare the intangible asset section of the December 31, 2006, balance sheet.

**P 11–9**
Straight-line depreciation; change in useful life and residual value

● LO2 LO5

The property, plant, and equipment section of the Jasper Company's December 31, 2005, balance sheet contained the following:

| | | |
|---|---|---|
| Property, plant, and equipment: | | |
| Land | | $120,000 |
| Building | $840,000 | |
| Less: Accumulated depreciation | (200,000) | 640,000 |
| Equipment | 180,000 | |
| Less: Accumulated depreciation | ? | ? |
| Total property, plant, and equipment | | ? |

The land and building were purchased at the beginning of 2001. Straight-line depreciation is used and a residual value of $40,000 for the building is anticipated.

The equipment is comprised of the following three machines:

| Machine | Cost | Date Acquired | Residual Value | Life in Years |
|---|---|---|---|---|
| 101 | $70,000 | 1/1/03 | $7,000 | 10 |
| 102 | 80,000 | 6/30/04 | 8,000 | 8 |
| 103 | 30,000 | 9/1/05 | 3,000 | 9 |

The straight-line method is used to determine depreciation on the equipment. On March 31, 2006, Machine 102 was sold for $52,500. Early in 2006, the useful life of machine 101 was revised to seven years in total, and the residual value was revised to zero.

**Required:**

1. Calculate the accumulated depreciation on the equipment at December 31, 2005.
2. Prepare the journal entry to record the sale of machine 102. Also prepare the journal entry to record 2006 depreciation on machine 102 up to the date of sale.
3. Prepare the 2006 year-end adjusting journal entries to record depreciation on the building and equipment.

**P 11–10**
Accounting changes; three accounting situations

● LO2 LO5 LO6

Described below are three independent and unrelated situations involving accounting changes. Each change occurs during 2006 before any adjusting entries or closing entries are prepared.

a. On December 30, 2002, Rival Industries acquired its office building at a cost of $1,000,000. It has been depreciated on a straight-line basis assuming a useful life of 40 years and no residual value. However, plans were finalized in 2006 to relocate the company headquarters at the end of 2011. The vacated office building will have a residual value at that time of $700,000.
b. At the beginning of 2002, the Hoffman Group purchased office equipment at a cost of $330,000. Its useful life was estimated to be 10 years with no residual value. The equipment has been depreciated by the sum-of-the-years'-digits method. On January 1, 2006, the company changed to the straight-line method.
c. At the beginning of 2006, Jantzen Specialties, which uses the sum-of-the-years'-digits method, changed to the straight-line method for newly acquired buildings and equipment. The change increased current year net income by $445,000.

**Required:**

For each situation:

1. Identify the type of change.
2. Prepare any journal entry necessary as a direct result of the change as well as any adjusting entry for 2006 related to the situation described. (Ignore income tax effects.)
3. Briefly describe any other steps that should be taken to appropriately report the situation.

**P 11–11**
Error correction; change in depreciation method

● LO2 LO6 LO7

Collins Corporation purchased office equipment at the beginning of 2004 and capitalized a cost of $2,000,000. This cost figure included the following expenditures:

| | |
|---|---|
| Purchase price | $1,850,000 |
| Freight charges | 30,000 |
| Installation charges | 20,000 |
| Annual maintenance charge | 100,000 |
| Total | $2,000,000 |

The company estimated an eight-year useful life for the equipment. No residual value is anticipated. The double-declining-balance method was used to determine depreciation expense for 2004 and 2005.

In 2006, after the 2005 financial statements were issued, the company decided to switch to the straight-line depreciation method for this equipment. At that time, the company's controller discovered that the original cost of the equipment incorrectly included one year of annual maintenance charges for the equipment.

**Required:**

1. Ignoring income taxes, prepare the appropriate correcting entry for the equipment capitalization error discovered in 2006.
2. Ignoring income taxes, prepare any 2006 journal entry(s) related to the change in depreciation methods.

**P 11–12**
Depreciation and amortization; impairment of operational assets

● LO2 LO4 LO8

At the beginning of 2004, Metatec, Inc. acquired Ellison Technology Corporation for $600 million. In addition to cash, receivables, and inventory, the following allocations were made:

| | |
|---|---|
| Plant and equipment (depreciable assets) | $150 million |
| Patent | 40 million |
| Goodwill | 100 million |

The plant and equipment are depreciated over a 10-year useful life on a straight-line basis. There is no estimated residual value. The patent is estimated to have a 5-year useful life, no residual value, and is amortized using the straight-line method.

At the end of 2006, a change in business climate indicated to management that the operational assets of Ellison might be impaired. The following amounts have been determined:

| | |
|---|---|
| Plant and equipment: | |
| Undiscounted sum of future cash flows | $ 80 million |
| Fair value | 60 million |
| Patent: | |
| Undiscounted sum of future cash flows | $ 20 million |
| Fair value | 13 million |
| Goodwill: | |
| Fair value of Ellison Technology | $450 million |
| Fair value of Ellison's net assets (excluding goodwill) | 390 million |
| Book value of Ellison's net assets (including goodwill) | 470 million* |

*After first recording any impairment losses on plant and equipment and the patent.

**Required:**

1. Compute the book value of the plant and equipment and patent at the end of 2006.
2. When should the plant and equipment and the patent be tested for impairment?
3. When should goodwill be tested for impairment?
4. Determine the amount of any impairment loss to be recorded, if any, for the three assets.

# BROADEN YOUR PERSPECTIVE

**Apply your critical-thinking ability to the knowledge you've gained. These cases will provide you an opportunity to develop your research, analysis, judgment, and communication skills. You also will work with other students, integrate what you've learned, apply it in real world situations, and consider its global and ethical ramifications. This practice will broaden your knowledge and further develop your decision-making abilities.**

**Analysis Case 11–1**
Depreciation, depletion, and amortization

● LO1

The terms depreciation, depletion, and amortization all refer to the process of allocating the cost of an operational asset to the periods the asset is used.

**Required:**

Discuss the differences between depreciation, depletion, and amortization as the terms are used in accounting for operational assets.

**Communication Case 11–2**
Depreciation

● LO1

At a recent luncheon, you were seated next to Mr. Hopkins, the president of a local company that manufactures bicycle parts. He heard that you were a CPA and made the following comments to you:

---

Why is it that I am forced to recognize depreciation expense in my company's income statement when I know that I could sell many of my operational assets for more than I paid for them? I thought that the purpose of the balance sheet was to reflect the value of my business and that the purpose of the income statement was to report the net change in value or wealth of a company. It just doesn't make sense to penalize my profits when there hasn't been any loss in value from using the operational assets.

---

At the conclusion of the luncheon, you promised to send him a short explanation of the rationale for current depreciation practices.

**Required:**
Prepare a letter to Mr. Hopkins. Explain the accounting concept of depreciation and include a brief example in your explanation showing that over the life of the asset the change in value approach to depreciation and the allocation of cost approach will result in the same total effect on income.

**Judgment Case 11–3**
Straight-line method; composite depreciation

● LO1 LO2

Portland Co. uses the straight-line depreciation method for depreciable assets. All assets are depreciated individually except manufacturing machinery, which is depreciated by the composite method.

**Required:**
1. What factors should have influenced Portland's selection of the straight-line depreciation method?
2. a. What benefits should derive from using the composite method rather than the individual basis for manufacturing machinery?
   b. How should Portland have calculated the manufacturing machinery's annual depreciation in its first year of operation?

*(AICPA adapted)*

**Judgment Case 11–4**
Depreciation

● LO1 LO2

At the beginning of the year, Patrick Company acquired a computer to be used in its operations. The computer was delivered by the supplier, installed by Patrick, and placed into operation. The estimated useful life of the computer is five years, and its estimated residual value is significant.

**Required:**
1. a. What costs should Patrick capitalize for the computer?
   b. What is the objective of depreciation accounting?
2. What is the rationale for using accelerated depreciation methods?

*(AICPA adapted)*

**Judgment Case 11–5**
Capitalize or expense; materiality

● LO9

Redline Publishers, Inc., produces various manuals ranging from computer software instructional booklets to manuals explaining the installation and use of large pieces of industrial equipment. At the end of 2006, the company's balance sheet reported total assets of $62 million and total liabilities of $40 million. The income statement for 2006 reported net income of $1.1 million, which represents an approximate 3% increase from the prior year. The company's effective income tax rate is 30%.

Near the end of 2006, a variety of expenditures were made to overhaul the company's manufacturing equipment. None of these expenditures exceeded $750, the materiality threshold the company has set for the capitalization of any such expenditure. Even though the overhauls extended the service life of the equipment, the expenditures were expensed, not capitalized.

John Henderson, the company's controller, is worried about the treatment of the overhaul expenditures. Even though no individual expenditure exceeded the $750 materiality threshold, total expenditures were $70,000.

**Required:**
Should the overhaul expenditures be capitalized or expensed?

**Communication Case 11–6**
Capitalize or expense; materiality

● LO9

The focus of the case is the situation described in the previous case. Your instructor will divide the class into two to six groups depending on the size of the class. The mission of your group is to determine the treatment of the overhaul expenditures.

**Required:**
1. Each group member should deliberate the situation independently and draft a tentative argument prior to the class session for which the case is assigned.
2. In class, each group will meet for 10 to 15 minutes in different areas of the classroom. During the meeting, group members will take turns sharing their suggestions for the purpose of arriving at a single group treatment.
3. After the allotted time, a spokesperson for each group (selected during the group meetings) will share the group's solution with the class. The goal of the class is to incorporate the views of each group into a consensus approach to the situation.

**Integrating Case 11–7**
Errors; change in estimate; change in principle; inventory and operational assets

● LO5 through LO7

Whaley Distributors is a wholesale distributor of electronic components. Financial statements for the year ended December 31, 2006, reported the following amounts and subtotals ($ in millions):

| | Assets | Liabilities | Shareholders' Equity | Net Income | Expenses |
|---|---|---|---|---|---|
| 2005 | $640 | $330 | $310 | $210 | $150 |
| 2006 | $820 | $400 | $420 | $230 | $175 |

In 2007 the following situations occurred or came to light:

a. Internal auditors discovered that ending inventories reported in the financial statements the two previous years were misstated due to faulty internal controls. The errors were in the following amounts:

| | |
|---|---|
| 2005 inventory | Overstated by $12 million |
| 2006 inventory | Understated by $10 million |

b. A patent costing $18 million at the beginning of 2005, expected to benefit operations for a total of six years, has not been amortized since acquired.

c. Whaley's conveyer equipment has been depreciated by the sum-of-the-years'-digits (SYD) method since constructed at the beginning of 2005 at a cost of $30 million. It has an expected useful life of five years and no expected residual value. At the beginning of 2007, Whaley decided to switch to straight-line depreciation.

**Required:**

For each situation:

1. Prepare any journal entry necessary as a direct result of the change or error correction as well as any adjusting entry for 2007 related to the situation described. (Ignore tax effects.)
2. Determine the amounts to be reported for each of the items shown above from the 2005 and 2006 financial statements when those amounts are reported again in the 2007, 2006, and 2005 comparative financial statements.

**Judgment Case 11–8**
Accounting changes

● LO5 LO6

There are various types of accounting changes, each of which is required to be reported differently.

**Required:**

1. What type of accounting change is a change from the sum-of-the-years'-digits method of depreciation to the straight-line method for previously recorded assets? Under what circumstances does this type of accounting change occur?
2. What type of accounting change is a change in the expected service life of an asset arising because of more experience with the asset? Under what circumstances does this type of accounting change occur?

*(AICPA adapted)*

**Trueblood Accounting Case 11–9**
Impairment

● LO8

The following Trueblood case is recommended for use with this chapter. The case provides an excellent opportunity for class discussion, group projects, and writing assignments. The case, along with Professor's Discussion Material, can be obtained from the Deloitte & Touche Foundation at its website: www.deloitte.com/us/truebloodcases.

**Case 04-3: *Home Computer, Inc.***

The objectives of this case are (a) to determine if Home Computer should recognize an impairment loss for operational assets and, if so, (b) to calculate the amount of the loss.

**Research Case 11–10**
Locate and extract relevant information and cite authoritative support for a financial reporting issue; impairment of operational assets

● LO8

The company controller, Barry Melrose, has asked for your help in interpreting accounting standards for the recognition and measurement of impairment losses for operational assets. "We have a significant amount of goodwill on our books from last year's acquisition of Comcast Corporation. Also, I think we may have a problem with the assets of some of our factories out West. And one of our divisions is currently considering disposing of a large group of depreciable assets."

Your task as assistant controller is to research the issue.

**Required:**

1. Obtain the original FASB Standards on accounting for the impairment of operational assets. You might gain access through FARS, the FASB Financial Accounting Research System, from your school library, or some other source.
2. When should operational assets be tested for impairment?
3. Explain the processes for measuring an impairment loss for operational assets to be held and used.
4. What are the specific criteria that must be met for an asset or asset group to be classified as held for sale?
5. Explain the processes for measuring an impairment loss for operational assets classified as held for sale.

**Ethics Case 11–11**
Asset impairment

● LO8

At the beginning of 2004, the Healthy Life Food Company purchased equipment for $42 million to be used in the manufacture of a new line of gourmet frozen foods. The equipment was estimated to have a 10-year service life and no residual value. The straight-line depreciation method was used to measure depreciation for 2004 and 2005.

Late in 2006, it became apparent that sales of the new frozen food line were significantly below expectations. The company decided to continue production for two more years (2007 and 2008) and then discontinue the line. At that time, the equipment will be sold for minimal scrap values.

The controller, Heather Meyer, was asked by Harvey Dent, the company's chief executive officer (CEO), to determine the appropriate treatment of the change in service life of the equipment. Heather determined that there has been an impairment of value requiring an immediate write-down of the equipment of $12,900,000. The remaining book value would then be depreciated over the equipment's revised service life.

The CEO does not like Heather's conclusion because of the effect it would have on 2006 income. "Looks like a simple revision in service life from 10 years to 5 years to me," Dent concluded. "Let's go with it that way, Heather."

**Required:**

1. What is the difference in before-tax income between the CEO's and Heather's treatment of the situation?
2. Discuss Heather Meyer's ethical dilemma.

**Judgment Case 11–12**
Earnings management and operational assets

● LO5 LO6

Companies often are under pressure to meet or beat Wall Street earnings projections in order to increase stock prices and also to increase the value of stock options. Some resort to earnings management practices to artificially create desired results.

**Required:**

1. How can a company manage earnings by changing its depreciation method? Is this an effective technique to manage earnings?
2. How can a company manage earnings by changing the estimated useful lives of depreciable assets? Is this an effective technique to manage earnings?
3. Using a fictitious example and numbers you make up, describe in your own words how asset impairment losses could be used to manage earnings. How might that benefit the company?

**Judgment Case 11–13**
Subsequent expenditures

● LO9

The Cummings Company charged various expenditures made during 2006 to an account called repairs and maintenance expense. You have been asked by your supervisor in the company's internal audit department to review the expenditures to determine if they were appropriately recorded. The amount of each of the transactions included in the account is considered material.

1. Engine tune-up and oil change on the company's 12 delivery trucks—$1,300.
2. Rearrangement of machinery on the main production line—$5,500. It is not evident that the rearrangement will increase operational efficiency.
3. Installation of aluminum siding on the manufacturing plant—$32,000.
4. Replacement of the old air conditioning system in the manufacturing plant with a new system—$120,000.
5. Replacement of broken parts on three machines—$1,500.
6. Annual painting of the manufacturing plant—$11,000.
7. Purchase of new forklift to move finished product to the loading dock—$6,000.
8. Patching leaks in the roof of the manufacturing plant—$6,500. The repair work did not extend the useful life of the roof.

**Required:**

For each of the transactions listed above, indicate whether the expenditure is appropriately charged to the repair and maintenance expense account, and if not, indicate the proper account to be charged.

**Real World Case 11–14**
Disposition and depreciation

● LO1

**International Business Machines Corporation (IBM)** reported the following in the asset section of its balance sheets for the years ended December 31, 2004 and 2003.

| | 2004 | 2003 |
|---|---|---|
| ($ in millions) | | |
| Plant, rental machines, and other property | $36,385 | $36,153 |
| Less: Accumulated depreciation | 21,210 | 21,464 |
| Plant, rental machines, and other property—net | $15,175 | $14,689 |

The following note was included as a part of the Significant Accounting Policies disclosure note in IBM's 2004 financial statements:

**Depreciation**
Plant, rental machines, and other property are carried at cost, and depreciated over their estimated useful lives using the straight-line method.

Also, Note G disclosed that the total cost of plant, rental machines, and other property included $840 million and $865 million in land and land improvements at the end of 2004 and 2003, respectively. In addition, the statement of cash flows for the year ended December 31, 2004, reported the following as cash flows from investing activities:

| ($ in millions) | |
|---|---|
| Payments for plant, rental machines, and other property | $(5,368) |
| Proceeds from disposition of plant, rental machines, and other property | 1,311 |

The statement of cash flows also reported 2004 depreciation of $3,959 million.

**Required:**

1. Assume that all plant, rental machines, and other property acquired during 2004 were purchased for cash. Determine the amount of gain or loss from dispositions of plant, rental machines, and other property recognized during 2004.
2. Assume that the entire amount reported in Note G as land and land improvements represents assets that are not depreciated. What is the approximate average service life of IBM's depreciable assets?

**Real World Case 11–15**
Depreciation and depletion method; asset impairment; subsequent expenditures

- LO2 LO3 LO8 LO9

EDGAR, the Electronic Data Gathering, Analysis, and Retrieval system, performs automated collection, validation, indexing, and forwarding of submissions by companies and others who are required by law to file forms with the U.S. Securities and Exchange Commission (SEC). All publicly traded domestic companies use EDGAR to make the majority of their filings. (Some foreign companies file voluntarily.) Form 10-K or 10-KSB, which includes the annual report, is required to be filed on EDGAR. The SEC makes this information available on the Internet.

**Required:**

1. Access EDGAR on the Internet. The web address is www.sec.gov. Edgarscan (edgarscan. pwcglobal. com) from PricewaterhouseCoopers makes the process of accessing data from EDGAR easier.
2. Search for ChevronTexaco Corporation. Access the 10-K filing for most recent fiscal year. Search or scroll to find the financial statements and related notes.
3. Answer the following questions related to the company's operational assets:
   a. Describe the company's depreciation and depletion policies.
   b. Describe the company's policy for subsequent expenditures made for operational assets.

**Analysis Case 11–16**
Depreciation and amortization

- LO2 LO4

**FedEx Corporation**

Refer to the financial statements and related disclosure notes of FedEx Corporation in Appendix B located at the back of this text.

**Required:**

1. What amount of depreciation and amortization did the company report in 2004?
2. What depreciation method is used for financial reporting purposes and what are the service lives and residual values of depreciable assets? What depreciation method is used for income tax purposes?

## CPA SIMULATION 11–1

**Yamashita Kyle**
Operational Assets

KAPLAN CPA Review

Test your knowledge of the concepts discussed in this chapter, practice critical professional skills necessary for career success, and prepare for the computer-based CPA exam by accessing our CPA simulations at the text website: www.mhhe.com/spiceland4e.

The Yamashita Kyle simulation tests your knowledge of (a) depreciation methods including group depreciation, and the measurement of impairment of value for tangible, operational assets covered in this chapter, and (b) accounting for the disposal of operational assets, the capitalization of interest, and research and development expenditures discussed in Chapter 10.

As on the CPA exam itself, you will be asked to use tools including a spreadsheet, a calculator, and professional accounting standards, to conduct research, derive solutions, and communicate conclusions related to these issues in a simulated environment headed by the following interactive tabs:

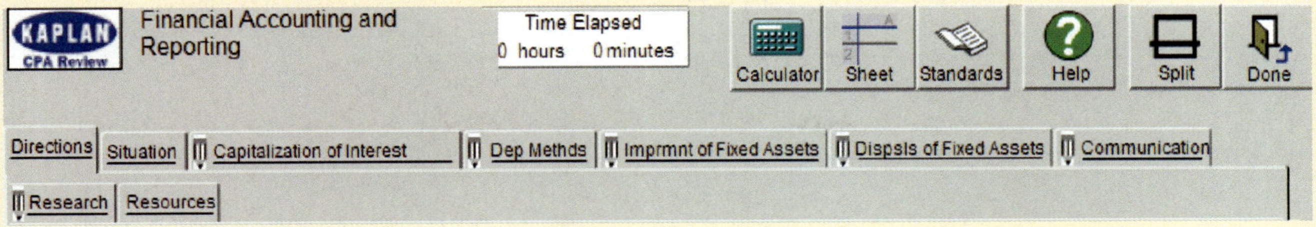


Specific tasks in the simulation address:

- Testing your knowledge of various aspects of accounting for interest capitalization.
- Calculating the appropriate amount of depreciation, applying several depreciation methods.
- Understanding the appropriate steps involved in determining the amount of impairment loss to recognize for a tangible, operational asset.
- Determining the appropriate income statement effect of the disposal of operational assets.
- Communicating your understanding of (1) the treatment of expenditures subsequent to the acquisition of operational assets and (2) the situations that require the capitalization of interest.
- Researching various items related to the measurement and reporting of operational assets, including useful lives, group depreciation, and research and development expenditures.

# Financial Instruments and Liabilities

3

SECTION

12

CHAPTER

# Investments

## OVERVIEW

In this chapter, you will learn that investments that companies make in the stock and debt securities of other companies are accounted for differently depending on the nature of the investments. For instance, you'll see that investment securities categorized as securities held-to-maturity are reported at amortized cost, while securities available-for-sale and trading securities are reported at their fair values.

We also discuss the equity method—a completely different way to record and report investments in stock when specific characteristics indicate that the investor can significantly influence the operating and financial policies of the investee.

## LEARNING OBJECTIVES

**After studying this chapter, you should be able to:**

- LO1 Demonstrate how to identify and account for investments classified for reporting purposes as held-to-maturity.
- LO2 Demonstrate how to identify and account for investments classified for reporting purposes as available-for-sale.
- LO3 Demonstrate how to identify and account for investments classified for reporting purposes as trading securities.
- LO4 Explain what constitutes significant influence by the investor over the operating and financial policies of the investee.
- LO5 Demonstrate the way investments are recorded and reported by the equity method.
- LO6 Explain the adjustments made in the equity method when the fair value of the net assets underlying an investment exceeds their book value at acquisition.

# FINANCIAL REPORTING CASE

## A Case of Coke

You are the lone accounting major in your five-member group in your Business Policy class. A part of the case your group is working on is the analysis of the financial statements of the Coca-Cola Company.

The marketing major in the group is confused by the following disclosure note from Coca-Cola's 2004 annual report:

**Note 8: Financial Instruments (in part)**
CERTAIN DEBT AND MARKETABLE EQUITY SECURITIES
Investments in debt and marketable equity securities, other than investments accounted for by the equity method, are categorized as either trading, available-for-sale or held-to-maturity. On December 31, 2003 and 2002, we had no trading securities. Securities categorized as available-for-sale are stated at fair value, with unrealized gains and losses, net of deferred income taxes, reported as a component of accumulated other comprehensive income. Debt securities categorized as held-to-maturity are stated at amortized cost.

On December 31, 2004, available-for-sale and held-to-maturity securities consisted of the following (in millions)

| | | Gross Unrealized | | |
|---|---|---|---|---|
| **December 31, 2004** | **Cost** | **Gains** | **Losses** | **Estimated Fair Value** |
| *Available-for-sale securities* | | | | |
| Equity securities | $ 144 | $146 | $ (2) | $ 288 |
| Other debt securities | 5 | – | (1) | 4 |
| | $ 149 | $146 | $ (3) | $ 292 |
| *Held-to-maturity securities* | | | | |
| Bank and corporate debt | $4,479 | $ – | $ – | $4,479 |
| Other debt securities | 107 | $ – | $ – | 107 |
| | $4,586 | $ – | $ – | $4,586 |

"They say unrealized gains and losses are reported as part of comprehensive income? I don't see these gains and losses on the income statement," he complained. "Maybe comprehensive income is something else altogether. And held-to-maturity securities—why are they treated differently?"

**By the time you finish this chapter, you should be able to respond appropriately to the questions posed in this case. Compare your response to the solution provided at the end of the chapter.**

### QUESTIONS

1. How should you respond? Why are held-to-maturity securities treated differently from other investment securities? (page 562)
2. Why are unrealized gains and losses on available-for-sale securities not reported on the income statement? (page 564)
3. What is comprehensive income? (page 564)
4. Anticipate his next question and explain why Coke accounts for some of its investments by the equity method and what that means. (page 576)

Most companies invest in financial instruments issued by other companies. For some investors, these investments represent ongoing affiliations with the companies whose securities are acquired. For instance, in 2004 **Kmart** acquired all the common stock of **Sears** to become the nation's third-largest retailer. **Microsoft** invested $600 million in nationwide wireless phone company **Nextel Communications Inc.,** gaining access to wireless Internet users. Some investments, though, are made not to obtain a favorable business relationship with another firm but simply to earn a return from the dividends or interest the securities pay or from increases in the market prices of the securities—the same prospective rewards that might motivate you to buy stocks, bonds, or other investment securities. With such diversity in investment objectives, it's understandable that no single accounting method is adequate to report every investment. As you'll discover when reading this chapter, investments are accounted for in six ways, depending on the nature of the investment relationship. Before we discuss these in detail, see the quick overview of the six approaches in Graphic 12–1.

**GRAPHIC 12–1**
Reporting Categories for Investments

| Characteristics of the Investment | Reporting Method |
|---|---|
| **The investor *controls* the investee:** The investor owns *more than 50% of the voting stock* of the investee | **Consolidation**—financial statements are combined as if a single company |
| **The investor can *"significantly influence"* the operating and financial policies of the investee:** Typically the investor owns *between 20% and 50% of the voting stock* of the investee | **Equity method**—cost adjusted for subsequent growth of the investee |
| **The investor *cannot* "significantly influence" the operating and financial policies of the investee:** Investments in debt securities for which the investor has the "positive intent and ability" to *hold to maturity* | **Held-to-maturity**—investment reported at amortized cost |
| Investments *not* held in active trading account for immediate resale nor to be held to maturity | **Securities available-for-sale**—investment reported at fair value (with unrealized gains and losses excluded from earnings and reported in shareholders' equity) |
| Investments held in *active trading account* for immediate resale | **Trading securities**—investment reported at fair value (with unrealized gains and losses included in earnings) |
| Fair value of the investments *not* determinable | **Cost method**—investment reported at cost |

We discuss the last four categories in Part A of the chapter. The equity method is described in Part B, as well as an abbreviated discussion of consolidated statements.

## PART A ACCOUNTING FOR INVESTMENT SECURITIES

To finance its operations and often the expansion of those operations, a corporation raises funds by selling equity securities (common and preferred stock) and debt securities (bonds and notes). These securities are purchased as investments by individual investors, mutual funds, and also by other corporations. In later chapters we discuss equity and debt securities from the perspective of the issuing company. Our focus in this chapter is on the corporations that invest in securities issued by other corporations as well as those issued by governmental units (bonds, Treasury bills, and Treasury bonds).

For reporting purposes, all investments in *debt* securities and investments in *equity* securities that have readily determinable fair values (except those for which the equity method or consolidation is appropriate) are classified in one of three categories and accounted for differently depending on the classification as shown in Graphic 12–2.[1]

**GRAPHIC 12–2**
Reporting Categories for Investments in Marketable Securities

| Reporting Category | Classification Criteria |
|---|---|
| Held-to-maturity | Debt securities for which the investor has the positive intent and ability to hold to maturity |
| Securities available-for-sale | Debt or equity securities not classified as either securities held-to-maturity or trading securities (typically securities whose sale depends on market factors and financial conditions of the company) |
| Trading securities | Debt or equity securities held for immediate resale |

For all three categories, we include in the determination of earnings *realized* gains and losses—those that arise when securities are sold. Similarly, we include investment income (dividends and interest) in the determination of earnings for all three categories. The differences in accounting treatment among the categories of securities arise with respect to *unrealized* gains and losses, those that arise from holding securities during a period when their market values change.

As you know, the purpose of accounting is to provide information useful in making decisions. What's most relevant for that purpose is not necessarily the same for each investment a company might make. For example, day-to-day changes in market value are less descriptive of investment success for an investment in corporate bonds that management *fully intends to hold until the bonds mature* than for an investment in the common stock of another corporation *acquired with the hope of profiting from market price changes.* Let's examine the three reporting classifications, one by one.

## Securities to Be Held to Maturity

● LO1

Unlike a share of stock, a bond or other debt security has a specified date on which it matures. On its maturity date, the "face amount" is paid to investors. In the meantime, interest equal to a specified percentage of the face amount is paid to investors on specified interest dates. However, even though the maturity amount is fixed and interest payments are fixed, this doesn't mean the market value of the security doesn't change. On the contrary, if "market" rates of interest *rise* after a fixed-rate security is purchased, the value of the now-below-market, fixed-interest payments declines. So, the market value of the investment falls. Conversely, if "market" rates of interest *fall* after a fixed-rate security is purchased, the fixed interest payments become relatively attractive, so the market value of the investment rises.

**The market value of a fixed-rate investment moves in the opposite direction of market rates of interest.**

The Board (FASB) deliberately chose to make the held-to-maturity category restrictive because it believes that the use of amortized cost must be justified for each investment in a debt security. At acquisition, an entity should establish the positive intent and ability to hold a security to maturity, which is distinct from the mere absence of intent to sell.[2]

Are these movements in market price relevant? Not if the investor has no intention of selling the investment before maturity. Increases and decreases in the market value between the time a debt security is acquired and the day it matures to a prearranged maturity value are less important if sale before maturity isn't an alternative. For this reason, if an investor has the "positive intent and ability"

**Changes in market value are less relevant to an investor who will hold a security to its maturity regardless of those changes.**

[1] "Accounting for Certain Investments in Debt and Equity Securities," *Statement of Financial Accounting Standards No. 115* (Norwalk, Conn.: FASB, 1993).
[2] Ibid., par. 46.

to hold the securities to maturity, investments in debt securities are classified as **held-to-maturity** and reported at amortized *cost* in the balance sheet.

A debt security is *not* classified as held-to-maturity if the investor might sell it in response to changes in market prices or interest rates, to meet the investor's liquidity needs, or similar factors. For instance, an investment would not be classified as held-to-maturity if the investor might sell it to achieve favorable tax treatment. An investment in securities to be "held to maturity" by the investor is demonstrated in Illustration 12–1.

**ILLUSTRATION 12–1**
Held-to-Maturity Securities

On January 1, 2006, United Intergroup, Inc. purchased as an investment $700,000 of 12% bonds. Because the 12% stated rate was less than the rate paid by other companies on similar bonds, say 14%, United was able to buy the securities at a "discounted" price of $666,633. Interest of $42,000 [$700,000 × (12% ÷ 2)] is receivable semiannually on June 30 and December 31.

**Purchase of Investment.** The journal entry to record the *purchase* of investment securities is:

All investment securities are initially recorded at cost.

| | | |
|---|---|---|
| **January 1** | | |
| Investment in bonds (face amount) | 700,000 | |
| Discount on bond investment (difference) | | 33,367 |
| Cash (price paid for the bonds) | | 666,633 |

**Investment Revenue.** Interest accrues on bonds, or any other interest-bearing security for that matter, at a *constant percentage* of the investment each period. Of course, under the concept of *accrual accounting,* the periodic effective interest is unaffected by when the cash interest actually is received. Recording interest each period as the *effective market rate of interest multiplied by the outstanding balance of the investment* (during the interest period) is referred to as the effective interest method. This simply is an application of the accrual concept, consistent with accruing all revenues as they are earned, regardless of when cash is received.

The effective interest on debt is the *market rate of interest multiplied by the outstanding balance of the debt.*

Continuing our example, the initial investment is $666,633. Since the effective interest rate is 14%, interest recorded as *revenue* to the investor for the first six-month interest period is $46,664:

| | | | | |
|---|---|---|---|---|
| $666,633 | × | [14% ÷ 2] | = | $46,664 |
| Outstanding balance | | Effective rate | | Effective interest |

However, the bond security calls for semiannual interest payments of only $42,000—the *stated* rate (6%) times the *face amount* ($700,000). As always, when only a portion of revenue is received, the remainder becomes an asset—in this case an addition to the existing investment. So the difference, $4,664, increases the investment and is reflected as a reduction in the discount (a valuation account). The journal entry to record the interest received for the first six months as *investment revenue* is:

The "unreceived" portion of the effective interest increases the existing investment.

Dividend and interest income from all investment securities is included in earnings.

| | | |
|---|---|---|
| **June 30** | | |
| Cash (stated rate × face amount) | 42,000 | |
| Discount on bond investment (difference) | 4,664 | |
| Investment revenue (market rate × outstanding balance) | | 46,664 |

The amortized cost of the investment now is $700,000 − ($33,367 − 4,664) = $671,297, which is higher than the original investment. Because the balance of the investment increases each period, the dollar amount of interest revenue (market rate × outstanding balance) also will increase each period. We discuss this in much greater detail in Chapter 14.

**Reporting Investments in Securities to Be Held to Maturity.** Securities to be held to maturity are recorded at cost as illustrated above, and holding gains or losses from market price changes are ignored. So if the market value of the investment were to increase from

$666,633 at January 1 to, say, $680,000 at June 30, we would ignore that holding gain and report the investment in a balance sheet at that date at its amortized cost of $671,297 as determined above:

| | |
|---|---|
| Investment in bonds | $700,000 |
| *Less:* Discount on bond investment | 28,703 |
| Book value (amortized cost) | $671,297 |

We will revisit our discussion of investments in debt securities to be "held to maturity" in Chapter 14, "Bonds and Long-Term Notes." This way we can more readily see that accounting by the company that issues bonds and by the company that invests in those bonds is opposite but parallel; that is, each side of the transaction is the mirror image of the other. When we resume our discussion of bond investments at that point, be sure to notice that we continue the same numerical illustration we began in this chapter.

Let's turn our attention now to accounting and reporting for investments referred to as "securities available-for-sale" and "trading securities." These include investments in *debt* securities that are not classified as held-to-maturity and *equity* securities that have *readily determinable fair values.* You'll notice that, unlike held-to-maturity securities, we report investments in the other two categories at their fair market values.

Graphic 12–3 provides a description from a recent annual report of how **United Community Financial Corporation** accounts for its investments in each of the three reporting categories.

**Note (in part): Investment and Mortgage-Backed Securities**
Securities are classified as available for sale, held to maturity, or trading upon their acquisition. Securities classified as available for sale are carried at an estimated fair value with the unrealized holding gain or loss reflected as a component of equity, net of taxes. Securities classified as held to maturity are carried at amortized cost. Securities classified as trading are carried at estimated fair value with the market value adjustment reflected in the income statement. . . . Realized gains and losses on the sale of debt securities are recorded based on the amortized cost of the securities sold.

**GRAPHIC 12–3**
Investments in Securities to Be Held to Maturity—United Community Financial Corporation

Obviously, not all investments are intended to be held to maturity. When an investment is acquired to be held for an *unspecified period of time,* we classify the investment as either (a) "securities available-for-sale" or (b) "trading securities." The trading securities category concerns primarily banks and other financial institutions who frequently buy and sell securities expecting to earn profits on short-term changes in price. On the other hand, securities available for sale is a more general classification that includes all investments other than trading securities or securities to be held to maturity. So, we'll discuss the less restrictive securities available-for-sale category first.

## Securities Available-for-Sale

LO2

The Board concluded that fair value information is more relevant than amortized cost information, in part because it reflects the effects of a management decision to buy a financial asset at a specific time and then continue to hold it for an unspecified period of time.[3]

When you or I buy stock in a corporation, say **Coca-Cola,** we hope the market value will rise before we sell it. We also might look forward to the cash dividends Coca-Cola pays its shareholders every three months. We may even have fairly defined criteria for when we plan to sell the stock, or we may intend to wait and see what happens to market prices. In either case, our investment is available to sell given the right combination of market factors and our own cash situation. So it often is, too, with companies who invest in the securities of other corporations or

[3] Ibid., par. 51.

**Investments in securities to be held for an *unspecified period of time* are reported at their fair values.**

governmental entities. When a company acquires an investment, not for an active trading account (as a financial institution might) or to be held to maturity (which of course couldn't be stock because it has no maturity date), the company classifies its investment as **securities available-for-sale.** Because these securities are not expressly intended to be held to some scheduled maturity date, the investment is reported in a balance sheet at the *fair market value* of the investment securities on the reporting date. Just like any investment, regardless of how we classify it, the investment is initially recorded at its cost—that is, the total amount paid for the securities including any brokerage fees. But then, when a balance sheet is prepared, this type of investment is written up or down to its fair value, or "marked to market."

**FINANCIAL REPORTING CASE**

Q1, p. 557

Be sure to notice that mark-to-market accounting is a departure from historical costs, which is the way most assets are reported in balance sheets. Why the difference? For these investments, fair value information is more relevant than for other assets intended primarily to be used in company operations, like buildings, land and equipment, or for investments to be *held to maturity.*[4] For instance, consider an investment in debt. As interest rates rise or fall, the fair value of the investment will decrease or increase. Movements in fair values are less relevant if the investment is to be held to maturity; the investor receives the same contracted interest payments and principal at maturity, regardless of changes in fair value. This is similar to changes in the fair values of operational assets, typically intended to be held throughout their productive lives.

**Fair values are less relevant for investments to be held to maturity.**

## ADDITIONAL CONSIDERATION

### No More Cherry Picking

One motivation of the FASB when deciding to move to mark-to-market accounting for investments was to curtail what it perceived as (and the SEC insisted was) a common practice at the time—"cherry picking." This refers to a company carefully choosing when and which of its securities to sell. Specifically, it means selling a security that had risen in value in order to realize a gain or not selling a security that had declined in value in order not to realize a loss, or even choosing to realize a loss in good years in order to "smooth" income.

As just argued, market values and changes in market value are less relevant to an investor who will hold a security to its maturity regardless of value changes. On the other hand, for investments of unspecified length, changes in market values, and thus market returns, provide an indication of management's success in deciding when to acquire the investment, when to sell it, whether to invest in fixed-rate or variable-rate securities, and whether to invest in long-term or short-term securities. Accounting for securities available for sale is demonstrated in Illustration 12–2.

**ILLUSTRATION 12–2**
Investment in Securities Available-for-Sale

American Capital buys and sells both debt and equity securities of other companies as investments. The following transactions during 2006 pertain to American's investment portfolio. Assume American Capital buys securities, *not* intending to profit from short-term changes in price and *not* intending to hold debt securities to maturity. The securities are properly classified as available-for-sale. The company's fiscal year-end is December 31.

| | | |
|---|---|---|
| November 1 | Purchased ABM Corporation 10% notes for $120 million (face amount). | |
| November 30 | Received cash interest of $1 million on the investment in ABM Corporation notes, calculated as $120 million × 10% × 1⁄12 year. | |
| December 1 | Sold the ABM Corporation notes for $123 million. | |
| December 21 | Acquired two new investments costing: | |
| | Millington Industries common shares | $30 million |
| | Bartlett Corporation common shares | 20 million |
| December 31 | The market prices of the investments are: | |
| | Millington Industries common shares | $35 million |
| | Bartlett Corporation common shares | 19 million |

[4]Investments to be held to maturity, of course, include only debt securities.

**Purchase of Investment.** The journal entry to record the purchase of investment securities is:

| **November 1** | ($ in millions) | |
|---|---|---|
| Investment in ABM notes | 120 | |
| Cash | | 120 |

All investment securities are initially recorded at cost.

**Investment Revenue.** The journal entry to record the cash interest is:

| **November 30** | ($ in millions) | |
|---|---|---|
| Cash ($120 million × 10% × 1⁄12 year) | 1 | |
| Investment revenue | | 1 |

Dividend and interest income is included in earnings.

**Sale of Investments.** The journal entry to record the sale of the ABM Corporation notes is:

| **December 1** | ($ in millions) | |
|---|---|---|
| Cash | 123 | |
| Investment in ABM notes | | 120 |
| Gain on sale of investments | | 3 |

Realized gains and losses are included in earnings.

**Purchase of Investments.** The journal entry to record the purchase of investment securities is:

| **December 21** | ($ in millions) | |
|---|---|---|
| Investment in Millington shares | 30 | |
| Investment in Bartlett shares | 20 | |
| Cash | | 50 |

All investment securities are initially recorded at cost.

**Adjusting Investments to Fair Value.** Reporting investments at their fair values means adjusting their carrying amounts for changes in fair value after their acquisition (or since the last reporting date if they were held at that time). These changes are called "unrealized holding gains and losses" because they haven't yet been realized through the sale of the securities. They must be recorded (or updated) any time financial statements are prepared for external use. The journal entry to adjust the investments in our illustration to fair market value at year-end is:

| ($ in millions) **Available-for-Sale Securities** | **Cost** | **Fair Value** | **Unrealized Gain (Loss)** |
|---|---|---|---|
| Millington Industries shares | $30 | $35 | $5 |
| Bartlett Corporation shares | 20 | 19 | (1) |
| Totals | $50 | $54 | $4* |

| **December 31** | | |
|---|---|---|
| Fair value adjustment (calculated above) | 4 | |
| Net unrealized holding gains and losses | | 4 |

*The $4 million balance in the accumulated unrealized holding gains and losses is reported as *accumulated other comprehensive income*, a component of shareholders' equity in the 2006 balance sheet. The $4 million *change* in the accumulated balance is reported as 2006 *other comprehensive income*.

Notice that we record the increase in fair value *indirectly* by debiting a valuation account, fair value adjustment, rather than directly debiting the investment account itself.[5]

All investment securities (except those held to maturity) are adjusted to their fair values on each reporting date.

| | |
|---|---|
| Securities available-for-sale | $50 |
| Plus: Fair value adjustment | 4 |
| | $54 |

The other half of the adjusting entry is a shareholders' equity account, net unrealized holding gains or losses. The reason for this is explained in the next section.

## ADDITIONAL CONSIDERATION

### When the Fair Value Isn't Readily Determinable

The fair value of equity securities is considered "readily determinable" if selling prices are currently available on a securities exchange.

If the fair value of an equity security is *not* readily determinable, an investment in that security is carried and reported at cost (except when the equity method described in Part B of this chapter is appropriate). Any dividends received would be recognized as investment revenue, and a gain or loss would be reported only when actually realized, which is when the investment is sold.

Having a readily determinable fair value is not a requirement for *debt* securities to be reported at fair value. Even though some debt securities don't trade regularly, their fair values can be reasonably estimated by determining the discounted present value of their interest and principal payments. You learned how to do this in Chapter 6 and will gain considerably more exposure to the process in Chapter 14.

**Reporting Investments in Securities Available-for-Sale.** Investments in securities *available-for-sale* are reported in a balance sheet at fair value. Holding gains and losses from retaining securities during periods of price change are *not* included in the determination of income for the period. Instead, they are accumulated and reported as a separate component of shareholders' equity, as part of Other Comprehensive Income. That is, an unrealized holding gain would increase shareholders' equity; an unrealized holding loss would decrease shareholders' equity.

FINANCIAL REPORTING CASE

Q2, p. 557

By definition, these securities are *not* acquired for the purpose of profiting from short-term market price changes, so gains and losses from holding these securities while prices change are not considered relevant performance measures to be included in earnings. This, in fact, is the argument made by the FASB. A by-product of this treatment is the avoidance of earnings volatility that would come from adjusting earnings for gains and losses as they occur. Opponents of this view argue that this amounts to a form of "income smoothing" that lessens earnings quality. This counterargument suggests that periodic gains and losses from holding securities during periods of changes in market value are, indeed, relevant measures of the performance of management that can, at its discretion, choose whether or not to realize the gains and losses by selling the securities.

On the 2006 balance sheet, investments available-for-sale are reported at the *fair value* of the investment securities ($35 + 19 = $54 million), but the *net* unrealized holding gain ($5 − 1 = $4 million) is not reported in the income statement. Instead, it's reported in the balance sheet as a separate component of shareholders' equity, specifically as part of accumulated *other comprehensive income.*

FINANCIAL REPORTING CASE

Q3, p. 557

**Comprehensive income,** as you may recall from Chapter 4, is a more expansive view of the change in shareholders' equity than traditional net income. In fact, it encompasses all changes in equity *other than from transactions with owners.*[6] So, in addition to net income, comprehensive income includes up to four other changes in equity as indicated in Illustration 12–2A.

[5] An acceptable alternative to increasing (or decreasing) an investment to fair value *indirectly* as we've done here is to debit (or credit) the investment account directly. This, however, would be inconvenient for a debt security, like an investment in bonds, classified as available-for-sale, because of the difficulty in amortizing its cost separately from fair market adjustments.

[6] Transactions with owners primarily include dividends and the sale or purchase of shares of the company's stock.

| | ($ in millions) | |
|---|---|---|
| Net income | | $xxx |
| Other comprehensive income: | | |
| Net unrealized holding gains (losses) from investments (net of tax)* | $ 4 | |
| Gains (losses) from and amendments to postretirement benefit plans (net of tax)† | (x) | |
| Deferred gains (losses) from derivatives (net of tax)‡ | x | |
| Gains (losses) from foreign currency translation (net of tax)§ | x | xx |
| Comprehensive income | | $xxx |

**ILLUSTRATION 12–2A**
Comprehensive Income

Comprehensive income includes net income as well as other gains and losses that change shareholders' equity but are not included in traditional net income.

*Changes in the market value of securities available-for-sale.
†Gains and losses due to revising assumptions or market returns differing from expectations and prior service cost from amending the plan (described in Chapter 17).
‡When a derivative designated as a cash flow hedge is adjusted to fair value, the gain or loss is deferred as a component of comprehensive income and included in earnings later, at the same time as earnings are affected by the hedged transaction (described in the Derivatives Appendix to the text).
§Gains or losses from changes in foreign currency exchange rates. The amount could be an addition to or reduction in shareholders' equity. (This item is discussed elsewhere in your accounting curriculum.)

To communicate the relationship between the two measures, companies must report both net income and comprehensive income and reconcile the difference between the two.[7] We see the impact on financial statements of the transactions in Illustration 12–2B.

| | | ($ in millions) |
|---|---|---|
| **Income Statement** | | |
| **Revenues** | | $ ♦ |
| **Expenses** | | (♦) |
| **Other Income (Expense)** | | |
| Investment revenue | | 1 |
| Gain on sale of investments | | 3 |
| **Net Income** | | $ ♦ |
| **Other Comprehensive Income*** | | |
| Unrealized holding gain on investments† | | $ 4 |
| **Balance Sheet** | | |
| **Assets** | | |
| Securities available-for-sale | $50 | |
| Plus: Fair value adjustment | 4 | $ 54 |
| **Liabilities** | | |
| Not affected | | |
| **Shareholders' Equity** | | |
| *Accumulated other comprehensive income* | | |
| Net unrealized holding gain (loss) | | $ 4 |
| **Statement of Cash Flows** | | |
| **Operating Activities** | | |
| Investment revenue | | $ 1 |
| **Investing Activities** | | |
| Purchase of investment securities | | $120 |
| Sale of investment securities | | $123 |
| **Financing Activities** | | |
| Not affected | | |

**ILLUSTRATION 12–2B**
Reporting Securities Available-for-Sale

Only realized gains and losses are reported in the income statement.

Comprehensive income other than net income includes unrealized holding gains and losses that occur *during the reporting period.*

Securities available-for-sale are reported at fair value.

Shareholders' equity includes net unrealized holding gains or losses *accumulated over the current and prior periods.*

Cash flows from buying and selling securities are classified as investing activities.

*Can be reported either (a) as an extension of the income statement, (b) as a separate statement in a disclosure note, or (c) as part of the statement of shareholders' equity.
†Unlike for trading securities, unrealized holding gains and losses for securities available-for-sale are not included in income but, instead, as a component of *other comprehensive income.*

[7]*Statement of Financial Accounting Standards No. 130,* "Reporting Comprehensive Income," (Norwalk, Conn.: FASB, 1997).

| Retained earnings Jan. 1 | Acc. other compr. income, Jan. 1 |
|---|---|
| Net income (less div.) | Other compr. income |
| Retained earnings, Dec. 31 | Acc. other compr. income, Dec. 31 |

In addition to reporting the unrealized holding gains or losses that occur in the current reporting period, $4 million in this instance, we must also report these amounts on a cumulative basis in the balance sheet. This is consistent with the way we report net income and retained earnings. Comprehensive income includes (a) net income and (b) other comprehensive income. We report net income that occurs in the current reporting period in the income statement and also report *accumulated* net income (that hasn't been distributed as dividends) in the balance sheet as retained earnings. Similarly, we report other comprehensive income as it occurs in the current reporting period (see Illustration 12–2A) and also report *accumulated* other comprehensive income in the balance sheet. After completion of the 2006 transactions listed in Illustration 12–2, the account balances are those shown in Illustration 12–2B.

Individual securities available for sale are classified as either current or noncurrent assets, depending on how long they're likely to be held. An example from the 2004 annual report of **Cisco Systems** is shown in Graphic 12–4.

**GRAPHIC 12–4**

Investments in Securities Available-for-Sale—Cisco Systems

**2. Summary of Significant Accounting Policies (in part)**

The Company's investments comprise U.S. government notes and bonds; corporate notes, bonds, and asset-backed securities; municipal notes and bonds; and publicly traded equity securities. Investments with original or remaining maturities of more than three months and less than one year are considered to be short-term. These investments are held in the custody of a major financial institution. The specific identification method is used to determine the cost basis of fixed income securities disposed of. The weighted-average method is used to determine the cost basis of publicly traded equity securities disposed of. At July 31, 2004 and July 26, 2003, the Company's investments were classified as available-for-sale. These investments are recorded in the Consolidated Balance Sheets at fair value. Unrealized gains and losses on these investments are included as a separate component of accumulated other comprehensive income, net of tax.

**7. Investments (in part)**

The following tables summarize the Company's investments (in millions):

| July 31, 2004 | Amortized Cost | Gross Unrealized Gains | Gross Unrealized Losses | Fair Value |
|---|---|---|---|---|
| Fixed Income securities: | | | | |
| U.S. government notes and bonds | $ 4,408 | $ 9 | $(20) | $ 4,397 |
| Corporate notes, bonds, and asset-backed securities | 9,333 | 14 | (42) | 9,305 |
| Municipal notes and bonds | 710 | — | (1) | 709 |
| Total fixed income securities | 14,451 | 23 | (63) | 14,411 |
| Publicly traded equity securities | 755 | 387 | (8) | 1,134 |
| Total | $15,206 | $410 | $(71) | $15,545 |
| Reported as: | | | | |
| Short-term investments | | | | $ 4,947 |
| Investments | | | | 10,598 |
| Total | | | | $15,545 |

**ADDITIONAL CONSIDERATION**

Be sure to note that the effect on *total* shareholders' equity is precisely the same as if the holding gains and losses had been included in earnings. The difference is that, if included in earnings, the impact would be an increase or decrease in retained earnings rather than a separate component of shareholders' equity. You might think of it this way. Accumulated other comprehensive income accumulates other comprehensive income just as retained earnings *accumulates* traditional net income (that hasn't been distributed as dividends).

**Selling Securities Previously Adjusted to Fair Value.** To see how to record the sale of a security that was previously adjusted to fair value, let's assume the Millington shares are sold on June 9, 2007, for $36 million. The fair value of the shares has risen $6 million since the investment was acquired for $30 million. Five million dollars of that increase occurred in 2006 but that gain wasn't recognized in 2006 earnings because it wasn't yet realized by selling the investment. Now, the entire $6 million gain is recognized in 2007 when it is actually realized:

| **June 9, 2007**[8] | ($ in millions) | |
|---|---|---|
| Cash ............................................. | 36 | |
| Investment in Millington shares (cost) ..................... | | 30 |
| Gain on sale of investments (difference)................... | | 6 |

**Gains and losses from securities available-for-sale are included in earnings when they are realized by selling the securities.**

**Purchase of Investments.** Now suppose American buys common stock of Eads Industries for $45 million on October 7.

| **October 7, 2007** | ($ in millions) | |
|---|---|---|
| Investment in Eads shares ............................... | 45 | |
| Cash ............................................. | | 45 |

**We initially record all investment securities at cost.**

**Subsequent Adjustments to Fair Value.** At December 31, 2007, the market prices of the investments are: Bartlett Corporation shares, $16 million, and Eads Industries shares, $46 million.

**December 31, 2007**

| ($ in millions) **Securities Available-for-Sale** | **Cost** | **Fair Value** | **Unrealized Gain (Loss)** |
|---|---|---|---|
| Bartlett Corporation shares | $20 | $16 | $(4) |
| Eads Industries shares | 45 | 46 | 1 |
| Totals | $65 | $62 | $(3) |

Moving from a positive $4 (2006) to a negative $3 requires a reduction of $7:

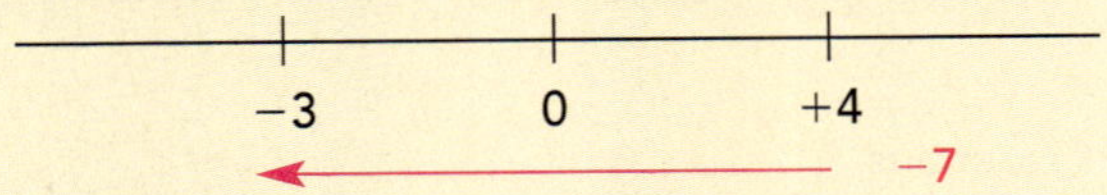


| | | |
|---|---|---|
| Net unrealized holding gains and losses ($4 credit to $3 debit).... | 7 | |
| Fair value adjustment ($4 debit to $3 credit).................. | | 7 |

**We need to report a $3 million accumulated net *loss*, but last year's balance was a $4 million net *gain*, so we need to change the balance by $7 million.**

**The fair value adjustment to the securities available-for-sale account also needs to be changed by $7 million to a credit balance of $3 million.**

After the 2007 transactions and adjusting entry, these are the account balances:

**Assets**

| **Securities Available-for-Sale** | | |
|---|---|---|
| 2006 Balance | 50 | 30 Sale |
| Purchase | 45 | |
| 2007 Balance | 65 | |

| **Fair Value Adjustment** | | | |
|---|---|---|---|
| 2006 Balance | 4 | 7 | Other compr. income |
| | | 3 | 2007 Balance |

| | |
|---|---|
| Securities available-for-sale | $65 |
| Less: Fair value adjustment | (3) |
| | $62 |

**We report the $7 million *change* in the net unrealized holding gains and losses as 2007 *other comprehensive income.***

**After the fair value adjustment, the securities available-for-sale are reported at fair value, $62 million.**

[8]Alternatively, a company could choose to make an additional entry at the time of sale that would reverse out (a) the fair value adjustment related to the security sold and (b) the portion of the accumulated net unrealized holding gains and losses related to the security sold:

| | | |
|---|---|---|
| Net unrealized holding gains and losses (related to Millington shares).................. | 5 | |
| Fair value adjustment (December 31 adjustment to Millington shares) .................. | | 5 |

The effect of this second entry, though, is accomplished as part of the December 31 market value adjustment as it is demonstrated later.

The $3 million debit balance in the account is reported as *accumulated other comprehensive loss,* a negative component of shareholders' equity in the 2007 balance sheet.

**Shareholders' Equity**
**Accumulated Other Comprehensive Income**

**Net Unrealized Holding Gains and Losses**

| | | | |
|---|---|---|---|
| | | 4 | 2006 Balance |
| Other compr. income | 7 | | |
| 2007 Balance | 3 | | |

**Financial Statement Presentation.** The 2007 financial statements will include the amounts shown in Illustration 12–2C.

**ILLUSTRATION 12–2C**
Reporting Securities Available-for-Sale

Only realized gains and losses are reported in the income statement.

Securities available-for-sale are reported at fair value.

Shareholders' equity includes net unrealized holding gains or losses *accumulated over the current and prior periods.*

Cash flows from buying and selling securities are classified as investing activities.

**Income Statement**

| | | ($ in millions) |
|---|---|---|
| **Revenues** | | $ ♦ |
| **Expenses** | | (♦) |
| **Other Income (Expense)** | | |
| Gain on sale of investments | | $ 6 |
| **Net Income** | | $ ♦ |
| **Other Comprehensive Income*** | | |
| Unrealized holding loss on investments† | | $ 7 |
| **Balance Sheet** | | |
| **Assets** | | |
| Securities available-for-sale | $65 | |
| Less: Fair value adjustment | (3) | $62 |
| **Liabilities** | | |
| Not affected | | |
| **Shareholders' Equity** | | |
| *Accumulated other comprehensive income* | | |
| Net unrealized holding gain (loss) | | $ (3) |
| **Statement of Cash Flows** | | |
| **Operating Activities** | | |
| None | | |
| **Investing Activities** | | |
| Purchase of investment securities | | $45 |
| Sale of investment securities | | 36 |
| **Financing Activities** | | |
| Not affected | | |

*Can be reported either (a) as an extension of the income statement, (b) as a separate statement in a disclosure note, or (c) as part of the statement of shareholders' equity.
†Unlike for trading securities, unrealized holding gains and losses for securities available-for-sale are not included in income but, instead, as a component of *other comprehensive income.*

**Bartlett shares**

| | |
|---|---|
| Cost | $20 |
| Loss | (1) |
| FV 2006 | $19 |
| Loss | (3) |
| FV 2007 | $16 |

**Eads shares**

| | |
|---|---|
| Cost | $45 |
| Gain | 1 |
| FV 2007 | $46 |

**Millington shares**

| | |
|---|---|
| Cost | $30 |
| 2006 Gain | 5 |
| FV 2006 | $35 |
| 2007 Gain | 1 |
| Sale price | $36 |

**Reclassification Adjustment.** Let's look closer at the $7 million negative amount reported for 2007 as other comprehensive income. It actually is composed of three amounts:

| | $ in millions |
|---|---|
| 1. An additional $3 million unrealized loss from the drop during 2007 in the value of the Bartlett shares (from the $19 million fair value last year to the $16 million value now). | $(3) |
| 2. A $1 million unrealized gain from the increase during 2007 in the value of the Eads shares acquired this year (from their $45 million cost to their current $46 million value). | 1 |
| 3. A reclassification adjustment: the "reversal" of the $5 million unrealized gain reported in 2006 on the Millington shares reported again this year as part of the gain realized when the shares were sold. | (5) |
| Other comprehensive income for 2007 | $(7) |

Components one and two are relatively intuitive. Each represents a change in the fair value of American Capital's investment portfolio while holding securities available-for-sale during 2007.

The third component, however, needs further examination. We saw earlier that a $5 million unrealized holding gain was reported in 2006 on the Millington shares because the shares had risen in value from a $30 million cost to $35 million at the end of 2006. The shares increased in value another $1 million and were sold during 2007 for $36 million, and a gain was recorded for the entire $6 million increase in value because that was the amount realized through the sale of the shares. Recall, though, that comprehensive income includes both net income and other comprehensive income. Net income in 2007 includes the $6 million realized gain. However, $5 million of that gain already has been reported in comprehensive income—as an unrealized holding gain in 2006. Isn't that double-counting? Yes it is, unless we compensate by reducing comprehensive income by the $5 million portion of the 2007 realized gain that already has been reported. That's what the third component does; it reduces this year's comprehensive income by the amount that was reported last year to keep it from being reported twice.

$5 million of the realized gain was reported previously and shouldn't be reported again.

| | | |
|---|---|---|
| Cash | 36 | |
| 2006 gain | | 5 |
| 2007 gain | | 1 |
| Investment | | 30 |

This adjustment takes no additional action. It's automatically accomplished each period when we compare the cost of the portfolio with its fair value. Remember, we compared the $65 million cost with the $62 million fair value to see that balances in the fair value adjustment and the net unrealized gains and losses accounts needed to be a negative $3 million. Comparing that with the positive $4 million existing balances indicated that we needed the $7 million reduction. As shown above, that $7 million already includes the $5 million adjustment.

Because the cost and fair value of the Millington shares no longer are included in the $65 million and $62 million portfolio amounts, elimination of the previous holding gain is automatically a part of the $7 million reduction in comprehensive income.

In Illustration 12–2C, we simply reported the total $7 million negative *other comprehensive income.* It's common practice, though, to separately report the current period's net unrealized holding gains or losses and the adjustment for the reclassification of previously reported holding gains and losses.[9] Doing so would cause our statement of comprehensive income to appear as follows:

**Other Comprehensive Income**

| | |
|---|---|
| Unrealized holding gains (losses) on investments | $(2) |
| Reclassification adjustment of 2006 unrealized gain included in 2007 net income | (5) |
| Net unrealized holding gains (losses) | $(7) |

The $7 million reduction in other comprehensive income includes the $2 million 2007 net unrealized loss ($3 − 1) and the embedded reversal of the $5 million 2006 unrealized gain that's also included in the 2007 realized gain.

It usually is called a *reclassification adjustment* because we are reclassifying an amount ($5 million in this instance) from what otherwise would appear as a 2007 holding loss to a disclosure that a portion of the *2007 realized gain* was reported previously as a *2006 holding gain.*

**Impairment of Investments.** Occasionally, the fair value of a security will decline for a specific reason that's judged to be "other than temporary." For instance, a bankruptcy filing might indicate a degradation in the creditworthiness of the issuer of bonds. An investor holding the bonds as an investment might conclude that a drop in the market price of the bonds is an other-than-temporary impairment. In that case, when the investment is written down to its fair value, the amount of the write-down should be treated as though it were a realized loss (meaning it's included in income for the period). After the other-than-temporary write-down, the normal treatment of unrealized gains or losses is resumed; that is, changes in fair value are reported as a separate component of shareholders' equity. In the 2002 fourth quarter, **Texas Instruments** recorded a $638 million write-down of investment securities due to a decline in market value the company considered other than temporary.

A loss inherent in an "other-than-temporary" impairment is recognized in earnings even though the security hasn't been sold.

[9]If not separately reported within the statement in which comprehensive income is reported, components must be separately reported in the disclosure note pertaining to comprehensive income per "Reporting Comprehensive Income," *Statement of Financial Accounting Standards No. 130,* (Norwalk, Conn.: FASB, 1997).

## Trading Securities

● LO3

Trading securities are actively managed in a trading account for the purpose of profiting from short-term price changes.

Some companies—primarily financial institutions—actively and frequently buy and sell securities expecting to earn profits on short-term differences in price. Investments in debt or equity securities acquired principally for the purpose of selling them in the near term are classified as **trading securities.** The holding period for trading securities generally is measured in hours and days rather than months or years. By definition, these are short-term investments to be reported among the investor's current assets.

The approach used to account for trading securities differs from how we account for securities available-for-sale in one major respect. Specifically, we report unrealized holding gains or losses on trading securities in the income statement as if they actually had been realized. Keep in mind as you study this section that relatively few investments are classified this way because, typically, only banks and other financial operations invest in securities in the manner and for the purpose necessary to be categorized as trading securities.

**ADDITIONAL CONSIDERATION**

**Bankers' Objections**

Perhaps the strongest objections to mark-to-market accounting when *SFAS No. 115* was being proposed came from the banking and insurance industries. Their concern was the volatile impact on earnings from reporting unrealized gains and losses on assets (trading securities) while not being permitted to mark liabilities to market as well. These objections were (and are) not merely self-interested urgings; there is an ongoing academic debate concerning this apparent inconsistency.

Holding gains and losses for trading securities are *included in earnings.*

When securities are actively managed, as trading securities are, with the expressed intent of profiting from short-term market price changes, the gains and losses that result from holding securities during market price changes are appropriate measures of success or lack of success in that endeavor. For that reason, it's appropriate to report these holding gains and losses in earnings for the period of change, even if they haven't yet been realized through the sale of the securities. To see how, let's modify our illustration to assume the investment securities we considered earlier in Illustration 12–2 are trading securities, rather than securities available-for-sale. Consider Illustration 12–3:

**ILLUSTRATION 12–3**
Investments in Trading Securities

American Capital buys and sells both debt and equity securities of other companies as investments. The following transactions during 2006 pertain to the investment portfolio. Assume American Capital frequently and actively buys and sells both debt and equity securities, intending to profit from short-term differences in price. The company's fiscal year-end is December 31.

| | | |
|---|---|---|
| November 18 | Purchased ABM Corporation 10% notes for $120 million (face amount). | |
| November 30 | Received cash interest of $1 million on the investment in ABM Corporation notes, calculated as $120 million × 10% × 1/12 year. | |
| December 1 | Sold the ABM Corporation notes for $123 million. | |
| December 21 | Acquired two new investments costing: | |
| | Millington Industries shares | $30 million |
| | Bartlett Corporation shares | 20 million |
| December 31 | The market prices of the investments are: | |
| | Millington Industries shares | $35 million |
| | Bartlett Corporation shares | 19 million |

**Purchase of Investment.** The journal entry to record the purchase of investment securities is recorded in precisely the same way for trading securities as for investments classified as available-for-sale:

| **November 18** | ($ in millions) | |
|---|---|---|
| Investment in ABM notes | 120 | |
| Cash | | 120 |

All investment securities are initially recorded at cost.

**Investment Revenue.** The journal entry to record the cash interest is:

| **November 30** | ($ in millions) | |
|---|---|---|
| Cash ($120 million × 10% × 1/12 year) | 1 | |
| Investment revenue | | 1 |

Dividend and interest income is included in earnings.

**Sale of Investments.** The journal entry to record the sale of the ABM Corporation notes is:

| **December 1** | ($ in millions) | |
|---|---|---|
| Cash | 123 | |
| Investment in ABM notes | | 120 |
| Gain on sale of investments | | 3 |

Realized gains and losses are included in earnings.

**Purchase of Investments.** The journal entry to record the purchase is:

| **December 21** | ($ in millions) | |
|---|---|---|
| Investment in Millington shares | 30 | |
| Investment in Bartlett shares | 20 | |
| Cash | | 50 |

All investment securities are initially recorded at cost.

**Adjusting Investments to Fair Value.** Although it's acceptable to record the changes in fair value *indirectly* by debiting a valuation account as we did in the previous section for securities available-for-sale, companies that invest in trading securities typically do not because the investments turn over quickly. Instead they record fair value adjustments directly to the investment accounts as demonstrated in the following journal entries:

| **December 31** | ($ in millions) | |
|---|---|---|
| Investment in Millington shares | 5 | |
| Unrealized holding gain on investments ($35 − 30) | | 5 |
| Unrealized holding loss on investments ($19 − 20) | 1 | |
| Investment in Bartlett shares | | 1 |

All investment securities (except those held to maturity) are adjusted to their fair values on each reporting date.

The key difference in reporting trading securities as opposed to securities available-for-sale is that we report unrealized holding gains or losses as part of current earnings as explained next.

**Financial Statement Presentation.** For *trading securities* unrealized holding gains and losses are included in earnings of the period the changes in value occur. In the balance sheet, the investments in our illustration are reported at the *fair value* of the investment securities ($35 + 19 = $54 million), and the *net* unrealized holding gain ($5 − 1 = $4 million) is reported in the income statement. The 2006 financial statements will include the amounts shown in Illustration 12–3A.

**ILLUSTRATION 12–3A**
Reporting Trading Securities

Unrealized holding gains and losses on trading securities as well as realized gains and losses are reported in the income statement.

Trading securities are reported at fair value.

Cash flows from buying and selling trading securities are classified as operating activities.

| Income Statement | ($ in millions) |
|---|---|
| **Other Income (Expense)** | |
| Investment revenue | $ 1 |
| Gain on sale of investments | 3 |
| Net unrealized holding gain on investments | 4 |
| **Other Comprehensive Income** | |
| none | |
| **Balance Sheet** | |
| **Assets** | |
| Trading securities at fair value (cost $50) | $ 54 |
| **Statement of Cash Flows** | |
| **Operating Activities** | |
| Investment revenue | $ 1 |
| Purchase of trading securities* | (120) |
| Sale of trading securities* | 123 |

*Inflows and outflows of cash from buying and selling trading securities typically are considered operating activities because financial institutions that routinely transact in trading securities consider them an appropriate part of their normal operations.

## Transfers between Reporting Categories

A transfer of a security between reporting categories is accounted for at fair value and in accordance with *the new reporting classification.*

At acquisition, an investor assigns debt and equity securities to one of the three reporting classifications—held-to-maturity, available-for-sale, or trading. At each reporting date, the appropriateness of the classification is reassessed. For instance, if the investor no longer has the ability to hold certain securities to maturity and will now hold them for resale, those securities would be reclassified. When a security is reclassified between two reporting categories, the security is transferred at its fair value on the date of transfer. Any unrealized holding gain or loss at reclassification should be accounted for *in a manner consistent with the classification into which the security is being transferred.* A summary is provided in Graphic 12–5.

**GRAPHIC 12–5**
Transfer between Investment Categories

| Transfer from: | To: | Unrealized Gain or Loss from Transfer at Fair Market Value |
|---|---|---|
| Either of the other | Trading | Include in current earnings |
| Trading | Either of the other | There is none (already recognized in earnings) |
| Held-to-maturity | Available-for-sale | Report as a separate component of shareholders' equity (in Other Comprehensive Income) |
| Available-for-sale | Held-to-maturity | Don't write off any existing unrealized holding gain or loss, but amortize it to earnings over the remaining life of the security (fair value amount becomes the security's amortized cost basis). |

Reclassifications are quite unusual, so when they occur, disclosure notes should describe the circumstances that resulted in the transfers. Other footnote disclosures are described in a later section.

## CONCEPT REVIEW EXERCISE

### VARIOUS INVESTMENT SECURITIES

Diversified Services, Inc., offers a variety of business services, including financial services through its escrow division. Diversified entered into the following investment activities during the last month of 2006 and the first week of 2007. Diversified's fiscal year ends on December 31. The only securities held by Diversified at December 1 were 12 million common shares of Shelby Laminations, Inc., purchased in November for $48 million and classified as available-for-sale.

**2006**

Dec. 1 Purchased $30 million of 12% bonds of Vince-Gill Amusement Corporation and $24 million of 10% bonds of Eastern Waste Disposal Corporation, both at face value and both to be held until they mature. Interest on each bond issue is payable semiannually on November 30 and May 31.

9 Sold one-half of the Shelby Laminations common shares for $25 million.

29 Received cash dividends of $1.5 million from the Shelby Laminations common shares.

30 Purchased U.S. Treasury bonds for $5.8 million as trading securities hoping to earn profits on short-term differences in prices.

31 Recorded the necessary adjusting entry(s) relating to the investments.

The year-end market price of the Shelby Laminations common stock was $4.25 per share. The fair values of the bond investments were $32 million for Vince-Gill Amusement Corporation and $20 million for Eastern Waste Disposal Corporation. A sharp rise in short-term interest rates on the last day of the year caused the fair value of the Treasury bonds to fall to $5.7 million.

**2007**

Jan. 7 Sold the remaining Shelby Laminations common shares for $26 million.

**Required:**

Prepare the appropriate journal entry for each transaction or event and show the amounts that would be reported in the company's 2006 income statement relative to these investments.

### SOLUTION

**2006**

Dec. 1 Purchased $30 million of 12% bonds of Vince-Gill Amusement Corporation and $24 million of 10% bonds of Eastern Waste Disposal Corporation, both at face value and both to be held until they mature. Interest on each bond issue is payable semiannually on November 30 and May 31.

| | ($ in millions) | |
|---|---|---|
| Investment in Vince-Gill Amusement bonds | 30 | |
| Investment in Eastern Waste Disposal bonds | 24 | |
| Cash | | 54 |

Dec. 9 Sold one-half of the Shelby Laminations common shares for $25 million.

| | ($ in millions) | |
|---|---|---|
| Cash (selling price) | 25 | |
| Investment in Shelby Laminations common shares ($48 × ½) | | 24 |
| Gain on sale of investments (difference) | | 1 |

Dec. 29 Received cash dividends of $1.5 million from the Shelby Laminations common shares.

| | ($ in millions) | |
|---|---|---|
| Cash | 1.5 | |
| Investment revenue | | 1.5 |

Dec. 30 Purchased U.S. Treasury bonds for $5.8 million as trading securities, hoping to earn profits on short-term differences in prices.

| | ($ in millions) | |
|---|---|---|
| Investment in U.S. Treasury bonds. . . . . . . . . . . . . . . . . . . . . . . . . . | 5.8 | |
| Cash . . . . . . . . . . . . . . . . . . . . . . . . . . . . . . . . . . . . . . . . . . . . . | | 5.8 |

Dec. 31 Recorded the necessary adjusting entry(s) relating to the investments.

| **Accrued Interest (one month)** | ($ in millions) | |
|---|---|---|
| Investment revenue receivable—Vince-Gill Amusement ($30 million × 12% × 1/12) . . . . . . . . . . . . . . . . . . . . . . . . . . . . . . . | 0.3 | |
| Investment revenue receivable—Eastern Waste Disposal ($24 million × 10% × 1/12) . . . . . . . . . . . . . . . . . . . . . . . . . . . . . . . | 0.2 | |
| Investment revenue . . . . . . . . . . . . . . . . . . . . . . . . . . . . . . . . . | | 0.5 |
| **Fair Value Adjustments** | | |
| Unrealized holding loss on investments ($5.7 − 5.8 million) . . . . . . | 0.1 | |
| Investment in U.S. Treasury bonds. . . . . . . . . . . . . . . . . . . . . . . . | | 0.1 |
| Fair value adjustment. . . . . . . . . . . . . . . . . . . . . . . . . . . . . . . . . . | 1.5 | |
| Net unrealized holding gains and losses on securities available-for-sale ([12 million shares × ½ × $4.25] − [$48 million × ½]) . . . . . . . . . . . . . . . . . . . . . . . . . . . . . . . . . . . . | | 1.5 |

Note: Securities held-to-maturity are not adjusted to fair value.

| **Reported in the 2006 Income Statement:** | ($ in millions) |
|---|---|
| Investment revenue ($1.5 + 0.5) | $2.0 |
| Gain on sale of investments (Shelby) | 1.0 |
| Unrealized holding loss on investments (trading securities) | (0.1) |

Note: The unrealized holding gain for the Shelby Laminations common shares is not included in income because it pertains to securities available-for-sale rather than trading securities.

**2007**

Jan. 7 Sold the remaining Shelby Laminations common shares for $26 million.

| | ($ in millions) | |
|---|---|---|
| Cash (selling price) . . . . . . . . . . . . . . . . . . . . . . . . . . . . . . . . . . . . . . . . | 26 | |
| Investment in Shelby Laminations common shares (cost: ½ × $48) . . . | | 24 |
| Gain on sale of investments (difference) . . . . . . . . . . . . . . . . . . . . . . . | | 2 |

## Financial Statement Presentation and Disclosure

Trading securities are current assets by definition. Held-to-maturity and available-for-sale securities are either current or noncurrent depending on when they are expected to mature or to be sold. However, it's not necessary that a company report individual amounts for the three categories of investments—held-to-maturity, available-for-sale, or trading—on the face of the balance sheet as long as that information is presented in the disclosure notes.[10]

On the statement of cash flows, inflows and outflows of cash from buying and selling trading securities typically are considered operating activities because for companies that routinely transact in trading securities (financial institutions), trading in those securities constitutes an appropriate part of the companies' normal operations. But because held-to-maturity and available-for-sale securities are not purchased and held principally to be sold in

[10]*Statement of Financial Accounting Standards No. 115,* "Accounting for Certain Investments in Debt and Equity Securities," (Norwalk, Conn.: FASB, 1993), par. 18.

the near term, cash flows from the purchase, sale, and maturity of these securities are considered investing activities.

Investors should disclose the following in the disclosure notes for each year presented:

- Aggregate fair value.
- Gross realized and unrealized holding gains.
- Gross realized and unrealized holding losses.
- Change in net unrealized holding gains and losses.
- Amortized cost basis by major security type.

Information about maturities should be reported for debt securities by disclosing the fair value and cost for at least four maturity groupings: (a) within 1 year, (b) after 1 year through 5 years, (c) after 5 years through 10 years, and (d) after 10 years.[11] A disclosure note from **Microsoft**'s 2004 annual report (Graphic 12–6) provides an example.

**GRAPHIC 12–6**

Disclosures of Investment Securities—Microsoft Corporation

The maturities of debt securities at June 30, 2004, were as follows:

| (In millions) | Cost Basis | Estimated Fair Value |
|---|---|---|
| Due in one year or less | $37,348 | $37,388 |
| Due after one year through five years | 14,077 | 14,064 |
| Due after five years through ten years | 5,636 | 5,665 |
| Due after ten years | 4,994 | 4,956 |
| Total | $62,055 | $62,073 |

# THE EQUITY METHOD

**PART B**

When a company invests in the equity securities (primarily common stock) of another company, the investor can benefit either (a) *directly* through dividends and/or market price appreciation or (b) *indirectly* through the creation of desirable operating relationships with the investee. The way we report a company's investment in the stock of another company depends on the nature of the relationship between the investor and the investee.

For reporting purposes, we classify the investment relationship in one of three ways, and account for the investment differently depending on the classification, as shown in Graphic 12–7:

**GRAPHIC 12–7**

Reporting Classifications for Investment Relationships

| Classification | Reporting Method |
|---|---|
| The investor *cannot* significantly influence the investee (usually < 20% equity ownership) | Varies by reporting category (see Part A of this chapter) |
| The investor can significantly influence the operating and financial policies of the investee (usually 20%–50% equity ownership) | Equity method |
| The investor controls the investee (usually >50% equity ownership) | Consolidation |

**The *equity method* is used when an investor can't control, but can significantly influence, the investee.**

We focused on the first classification in Part A of this chapter. Now, let's turn our attention to the second classification—the **equity method**. A detailed discussion of the third classification—consolidated financial statements—is beyond the scope of this book. That

[11]Ibid., par. 20.

**FINANCIAL REPORTING CASE**

Q4, p. 557

discussion often is a major focus of the advanced accounting course or is taught as a separate consolidations course. In this chapter, we'll briefly overview the subject only to provide perspective to aspects of the equity method that purposely mimic some effects of consolidation. Let's do that now, before addressing the specifics of the equity method.

## How the Equity Method Relates to Consolidated Financial Statements

If a company acquires more than 50% of the voting stock of another company, it's said to have a controlling interest because by voting those shares, the investor actually can control the company acquired. The investor is referred to as the *parent;* the investee is termed the *subsidiary.* For reporting purposes (although not legally), the parent and subsidiary are considered to be a single reporting entity, and their financial statements are *consolidated.* Both companies continue to operate as separate legal entities and the subsidiary reports separate financial statements. However, because of the controlling interest, the parent company reports consolidated financial statements.

*Consolidated financial statements* combine the individual elements of the parent and subsidiary statements.

The acquired company's assets are included in consolidated financial statements at their fair values and the difference between the acquisition price and fair value of the acquired net assets is recorded as goodwill.

**Consolidated financial statements** combine the separate financial statements of the parent and the subsidiary each period into a single aggregate set of financial statements as if there were only one company. This entails an item-by-item combination of the parent and subsidiary statements (after first eliminating any amounts that are shared by the separate financial statements).[12] For instance, if the parent has $8 million cash and the subsidiary has $3 million cash, the consolidated balance sheet would report $11 million cash.

Two aspects of the consolidation process are of particular interest to us in understanding the equity method. First, in consolidated financial statements, the acquired company's assets are included in the financial statements at their fair values rather than their book values. Second, if the acquisition price is more than the fair value of the acquired net assets (assets less liabilities), that difference is recorded as an intangible asset—goodwill.[13] We'll return to the discussion of these two aspects when we reach the point in our discussion of the equity method where their influence is felt. As we'll see, the equity method is in many ways a partial consolidation.

We use the equity method when the investor can't control the investee but can exercise significant influence over the operating and financial policies of an investee.

## What Is Significant Influence?

● LO4

Usually an investor can exercise *significant influence* over the investee when it owns between 20% and 50% of the investee's voting shares.

When effective control is absent, the investor still may be able to exercise significant influence over the operating and financial policies of the investee. This would be the case if the investor owns a large percentage of the outstanding shares relative to other shareholders. By voting those shares as a block, decisions often can be swayed in the direction the investor desires. When significant influence exists, the investment should be accounted for by the equity method. It should be presumed, in the absence of evidence to the contrary, that the investor exercises **significant influence** over the investee when it owns between 20% and 50% of the investee's voting shares.[14]

**ADDITIONAL CONSIDERATION**

It's possible that a company that owns over 20% of the voting shares cannot exercise significant influence over the investee. If, for instance, another company or a small group of shareholders owns 51% or more of the shares, that company controls the

[12]This avoids double counting those amounts in the consolidated statements. For example, amounts owed by one company to the other are represented by accounts payable in one set of financial statements and accounts receivable in the other. These amounts are not included in the statements of the consolidated entity because a company can't "owe itself."

[13]This is the usual case because most companies are worth more than the sum of the values of individual components of the company due to reputation, longevity, managerial expertise, customer loyalty, or a host of other possibilities.

[14]Shareholders are the owners of the corporation. By voting their shares, it is they who determine the makeup of the board of directors—who, in turn, appoint officers—who, in turn, manage the company. Common stock usually is the class of shares given voting privileges. However, a corporation can create classes of preferred shares that also have voting rights. This is discussed at greater length in Chapter 18.

investee regardless of how other investors vote their shares. *FASB Interpretation No. 35* provides this and other examples of indications that an investor may be unable to exercise significant influence:

- The investee challenges the investor's ability to exercise significant influence (through litigation or complaints to regulators).
- The investor surrenders significant shareholder rights in a signed agreement.
- The investor is unable to acquire sufficient information about the investee to apply the equity method.
- The investor tries and fails to obtain representation on the board of directors of the investee.[15]

In such cases, the equity method would be inappropriate.

Conversely, it's also possible that a company that owns *less than* 20% of the voting shares *is* able to exercise significant influence over the investee. Ability to exercise significant influence with less than 20% ownership might be indicated, for example, by having an officer of the investor corporation on the board of directors of the investee corporation or by having, say, 18% of the voting shares while no other investor owns more than ½%. In such cases the equity method would be appropriate. **Amazon.com** provided the following example in a recent disclosure note:

**Note 6—Investments**

At December 31, 2000, the Company's equity-method investees and the Company's approximate ownership interest in each investee, based on outstanding shares, were as follows:

| Company | Percentage Ownership |
|---|---|
| Basis Technology | 11% |
| Drugstore.com | 21 |
| Eziba.com | 20 |
| Greenlight.com | 5 |
| Kozmo.com | 16 |

Although the Company's ownership percentage for Basis Technology, Greenlight.com and Kozmo.com is below 20%, the Company's representation on the investees' Board of Directors and the impact of commercial arrangements result in the Company having significant influence over the operations of each investee.

## A Single Entity Concept

● LO5

**The investor's ownership interest in individual assets and liabilities of the investee is represented by a single investment account.**

Much like consolidation, the equity method views the investor and investee collectively as a special type of single entity (as if the two companies were one company). However, using the equity method, the investor doesn't include separate financial statement items of the investee on an item-by-item basis as in consolidation. Instead, the investor reports its equity interest in the investee as a single investment account.

**The investment account is adjusted to reflect the investor's share of both increases and decreases in the investee's net assets.**

Under the equity method, the investor recognizes investment income equal to its percentage share (based on stock ownership) of the net income earned by the investee rather than the portion of that net income received as cash dividends. The rationale for this approach is the presumption of the equity method that the fortunes of the investor and investee are sufficiently intertwined that as the investee prospers, the investor prospers proportionately. Stated differently, as the investee earns additional net assets, the investor's share of those net assets increases.

Initially, the investment is recorded at cost. The carrying amount of this investment subsequently is:

[15]"Criteria for Applying the Equity Method of Accounting for Investments in Common Stock," *FASB Interpretation No. 35* (Stamford, Conn.: FASB, 1981).

- Increased by the investor's percentage share of the investee's net income (or decreased by its share of a loss).
- Decreased by dividends paid.

Let's look at the example in Illustration 12–4.

**ILLUSTRATION 12–4**
Equity Method

On January 2, 2006, American Capital Corporation purchased 25% of the outstanding common shares of Embassy Message Corporation for $200 million. The following information is available regarding Embassy Message Corporation during 2006:

| | ($ in millions) |
|---|---|
| Net assets at acquisition:* | |
| Fair value | $600 |
| Book value | 480 |
| 2006 net income | 100 |
| 2006 dividends declared and paid | 24 |

When a company invests in shares of another corporation, the asset initially is recorded at cost. In accordance with the cost principle, the recorded amount includes any brokerage fees or commissions paid to acquire the shares.

The *cost principal* governs the acquisition of assets.

| **Initial Acquisition** | ($ in millions) | |
|---|---|---|
| Investment in equity securities (cost of shares) | 200 | |
| Cash | | 200 |

Following the acquisition, the investment account is adjusted for the investor's percentage share of net income reported by the investee.†

As the investee earns additional net assets, the investment in those net assets increases.

| **Investee Net Income** | | |
|---|---|---|
| Investment in equity securities | 25 | |
| Investment revenue (25% share of $100 million earned) | | 25 |

As the investee prospers, the investor prospers proportionately.

Adjusting the investment account reflects the equity method's presumption that as the investee earns additional net assets, the investor's equity interest in those net assets increases proportionately. This reasoning also supports recognizing investment revenue as the investee earns net income, not when those earnings actually are distributed as dividends.

In fact, when the investor actually receives dividends, the investment account is *reduced* accordingly:

As the investee distributes net assets as dividends, the investment in those net assets declines.

| **Dividends** | | |
|---|---|---|
| Cash (25% share of $24 million dividends paid) | 6 | |
| Investment in equity securities | | 6 |

Because investment revenue is recognized as it is earned by the investee, it would be inappropriate to recognize revenue again as earnings are distributed as dividends. Instead, we view the dividend distribution as a *reduction of the investee's net assets,* indicating that the investor's equity interest in those net assets declines proportionately.

*Recall that net assets are equivalent to shareholders' equity. Each is what's left over after creditor claims have been subtracted from assets:
Assets − Liabilities = Shareholders' equity
(Assets − Liabilities: Net assets)

†If any portion of the investee's net income was reported by the investee as an extraordinary item, the investor also would report the same proportion of its share as an extraordinary item. In this illustration, for instance, if $4 million, or 4%, of Embassy Message Corporation's income had been reported as an extraordinary gain, then American Capital Corporation would report 4% of its $25 million share, or $1 million, as an extraordinary gain as well.

## Further Adjustments

● LO6

When the investor's expenditure to acquire an investment exceeds the book value of the underlying net assets acquired, additional adjustments to both the investment account and investment revenue might be needed. The purpose is to approximate the effects of consolidation, without actually consolidating financial statements. More specifically, both the investment account and investment revenue are adjusted for differences between net income reported by the investee and what that amount would have been if consolidation procedures had been followed. Let's look closer at what that means.

As mentioned earlier, consolidated financial statements report (a) the acquired company's assets at their fair market values rather than their book values and (b) goodwill for the excess of the acquisition price over the fair value of the identifiable net assets acquired.

The first of these two consequences of the consolidation process usually has an effect on income, and it's the income effect that we're interested in when applying the equity method. First, increasing asset balances to their fair values usually will result in higher expenses. For instance, if buildings, equipment, or other depreciable assets are written up to higher values, depreciation expense will be higher during their remaining useful lives. Likewise, if the recorded amount of inventory is increased, cost of goods sold will be higher when the inventory is sold. However, if it's land that's increased, there is no income effect because we don't depreciate land.

On the other hand, recording goodwill will not result in higher expenses. Goodwill is an intangible asset, but one whose cost usually is not charged to earnings.[16] As a consequence, then, of increasing asset balances to fair value but not of recording goodwill, expenses will rise and income will fall. It is this negative effect on income that the equity method seeks to imitate.

Recall that our illustration provides the following information regarding Embassy Message Corporation's net assets at the time American Capital Corporation pays $200 million for a 25% interest in the company:

| **Net Assets at Acquisition:** | ($ in millions) |
|---|---|
| Fair value | $600 |
| Book value | 480 |

Let's assume that (a) two-thirds of the difference between the book value of the net assets and their fair market value is attributable to depreciable assets having a fair market value in excess of their undepreciated cost and (b) the remaining third is attributable to land having a fair market value in excess of its cost. We can determine the portion of these differences that American Capital purchased with its $200 million investment and, therefore, any additional amounts to be expensed as shown in Graphic 12–8.

**GRAPHIC 12–8**
Source of Differences between the Investment and the Book Value of Net Assets Acquired

| | **Investee Net Assets** ↓ | **Net Assets Purchased** ↓ | **($ in millions) Difference Attributed to:** ↓ | |
|---|---|---|---|---|
| Cost | | $200 | | |
| | | | *Goodwill:* | $50 |
| Fair value | $600 × 25% = | $150 | | |
| | | | *Undervaluation of:* | |
| | | | *Depreciable assets* (⅔) | $20 |
| | | | *Land* (⅓) | $10 |
| Book value | $480 × 25% = | $120 | | |

Notice in Graphic 12–8 that American Capital paid $200 million for identifiable net assets worth $150 million, and the $50 million difference is attributable to goodwill. Similarly, the identifiable net assets worth $150 million have a book value of only $120 million, and we assumed the $30 million difference is attributable to undervalued depreciable assets ($20 million) and land ($10 million).

[16]Beginning in 2002, goodwill is not amortized periodically to expense. Only if the asset's value is subsequently judged to be impaired is all or a portion of the recorded amount charged against earnings. "Goodwill and Other Intangible Assets," *Statement of Financial Accounting Standards No. 141* (Norwalk, Conn.: FASB, 2001). For review, see Chapter 11.

**Amortization of Additional Depreciation.** Remember, we assumed that two-thirds of the difference between the book value of the net assets and their fair market value is attributable to depreciable assets having a fair market value in excess of their undepreciated cost, or ($150 − 120 million) × ⅔ = $20 million. Let's also assume that these depreciable assets have an average remaining useful life of 10 years, and are being depreciated by the straight-line method. Investment revenue and the investment both would be reduced by the negative income effect of the "extra depreciation" the higher fair value would cause:

| **Additional Depreciation** | ($ in millions) | |
|---|---|---|
| Investment revenue ($20 million ÷ 10 years) | 2 | |
| Investment in equity shares | | 2 |

We would need to record this adjustment in each of the next nine years as well, since the average remaining useful life is 10 years.[17]

**No Amortization of Land.** On the contrary, the remaining $10 million difference between the book value of the net assets and their fair market value has no effect on earnings. Unlike buildings and equipment, land is not an asset we depreciate. As a result, writing up the land from book value to fair value (as would occur in consolidation) would not cause higher expenses, so as we mimic consolidation here in the equity method, we have no need to adjust Investment revenue or the Investment in equity securities.

**No Amortization of Goodwill.** Recall from Chapter 11 that goodwill, unlike most other intangible assets, should not be amortized. In that sense, goodwill resembles land. Expenses are unaffected by whether goodwill is recorded or not. So acquiring goodwill ($50 million in our example) will not cause higher expenses, so we have no need to adjust Investment revenue or the Investment in equity securities.

## Reporting the Investment

The market value of the investment shares at the end of the reporting period is not reported when using the equity method. The investment account is reported at its original cost, increased by the investor's share of the investee's net income (adjusted for additional expenses like depreciation), and decreased by the portion of those earnings actually received as dividends. In other words, the investment account represents the investor's share of the investee's net assets initially acquired, adjusted for the investor's share of the subsequent increase in the investee's net assets (net assets earned and not yet distributed as dividends).

**The carrying amount of the investment is its initial cost plus the investor's equity in the undistributed earnings of the investee.**

**Investment in Equity Securities**
($ in millions)

| | | | |
|---|---|---|---|
| Cost | 200 | | |
| Share of income | 25 | | |
| | | 6 | Dividends |
| | | 2 | Depreciation |
| Balance | 217 | | |

**When the Investee Reports a Net Loss.** Our illustration assumed the investee earned net income. If the investee reports a *net loss* instead, the investment account would be *decreased* by the investor's share of the investee's net loss (adjusted for additional expenses).

[17]If the $20 million difference between fair value and book value had been attributable to undervalued inventory rather than undervalued depreciable assets, we would adjust Investment revenue and the Investment in equity securities by the entire $20 million the first year. The reasoning is that inventory usually is sold within a year—unlike buildings and equipment that last several years. So, if inventory is increased by $20 million, cost of goods sold will be $20 million higher the first year.

**When the Investment Is Acquired in Mid-Year.** Obviously, we've simplified the illustration by assuming the investment was acquired at the beginning of 2006, entailing a full year's income, dividends, and amortization. In the more likely event that an investment is acquired sometime after the beginning of the year, the application of the equity method is easily modified to include the appropriate fraction of each of those amounts. For example, if the investment in our illustration had been acquired on October 1 rather than January 2, we would simply record income, dividends, and amortization for three months, or 3/12 of the year. This would result in the following adjustments to the investment account:

**Investment in Equity Securities**
($ in millions)

| | | |
|---|---|---|
| Cost | 200.00 | |
| Share of income (3/12 × $25) | 6.25 | |
| | | 1.50 (3/12 × $6) Dividends* |
| | | .50 (3/12 × $2) Depreciation |
| Balance | 204.25 | |

*This example assumes quarterly dividends and that the dividend was declared for the October 1–December 31 quarter. Investors receive the entire amount of any dividends declared while they own stock, regardless of how long they have held the shares.

**Changes in the investment account the first year are adjusted for the fraction of the year the investor has owned the investment.**

**ADDITIONAL CONSIDERATION**

It's possible that the investor's proportionate share of investee losses could exceed the carrying amount of the investment. If this happens, the investor should discontinue applying the equity method until the investor's share of subsequent investee earnings has equaled losses not recognized during the time the equity method was discontinued. This avoids reducing the investment account below zero.

**Amazon.com** reported its investments in affiliated companies for which it exercised significant influence using the equity method as shown in Graphic 12–9.

**GRAPHIC 12–9**
Equity Method—Amazon.com

In millions

| December 31 | 2003 | 2002 |
|---|---|---|
| Total current assets | $1,820,809 | $1,615,676 |
| Fixed assets, net | 224,285 | 239,398 |
| Goodwill, net | 69,121 | 70,811 |
| Other intangibles, net | 518 | 3,460 |
| Equity investments | 14,831 | 15,442 |
| Other assets | 32,469 | 45,662 |
| Total assets | $2,162,033 | $1,990,449 |

## What If Conditions Change?

**A Change from the Equity Method to Another Method.** When the investor's level of influence changes, it may be necessary to change from the equity method to another method. This could happen, for instance, if a sale of shares causes the investor's ownership interest to fall from, say, 25% to 15%, resulting in the equity method no longer being appropriate.[18] Another example is provided by **Sprint**, which in February 2001 agreed to end its exclusive alliance with **EarthLink** and relinquished its seats on EarthLink's board of directors.

[18]When a portion of an equity method investment is sold, the investor removes from the investment account the appropriate proportion of the carrying value and records a gain or loss for the difference between that amount and the selling price.

As a result, Sprint discontinued using the equity method for its investment in EarthLink. When this situation happens, *no adjustment* is made to the remaining carrying amount of the investment. Instead, the equity method is simply discontinued and the new method applied from then on. The balance in the investment account when the equity method is discontinued would serve as the new cost basis for writing the investment up or down to market value on the next set of financial statements.

**A Change from Another Method to the Equity Method.** On the other hand, when a change *to* the equity method is appropriate, because the investor's ownership interest rises from 15% to 25%, the investment account should be retroactively adjusted to the balance that would have existed if the equity method always had been used. As income also would have been different, retained earnings would be adjusted as well. For example, assume it's determined that an investor's share of investee net income, reduced by dividends, was $4 million during a period when the equity method was not used, but additional purchases of shares cause the equity method to be appropriate now. The following journal entry would record the change:

Both the investment and retained earnings would be increased by the investor's share of the undistributed earnings in years prior to a change to the equity method.

| | ($ in millions) | |
|---|---|---|
| Investment in equity securities | 4 | |
| Retained earnings (investment revenue from the equity method) | | 4 |

In addition to the adjustment of account balances, financial statements would be restated to the equity method for each year reported in the annual report for comparative purposes. Also, the income effect for years prior to those shown in the comparative statements is reported on the statement of retained earnings as an adjustment to beginning retained earnings of the earliest year reported. A disclosure note also should describe the change. Reporting accounting changes is described in more detail in Chapter 20.

**ADDITIONAL CONSIDERATION**

**Effect on Deferred Income Taxes**

Investment revenue is recorded by the equity method when income is earned by the investee, but that revenue is not taxed until it's actually received as cash dividends. This creates a temporary difference between book income and taxable income. You will learn in Chapter 16 that the investor must report a deferred tax liability for the income tax that ultimately will be paid when the income eventually is received as dividends.

### IF AN EQUITY METHOD INVESTMENT IS SOLD

When an investment being reported by the equity method is sold, a gain or loss is recognized if the selling price is more or less than the carrying amount (book value) of the investment. For example, let's continue our illustration and assume American Capital Corporation sells its investment in Embassy Message Corporation at the end of 2006 for $234 million. A journal entry would record a gain as follows:

When an equity method investment is sold, a gain or loss is recognized for the difference between its selling price and its carrying amount.

| | ($ in millions) | |
|---|---|---|
| Cash (proceeds from sale) | 234 | |
| Investment in equity securities (balance) | | 217 |
| Gain on sale of investment (difference) | | 17 |

## CONCEPT REVIEW EXERCISE

**THE EQUITY METHOD**

Delta Apparatus bought 40% of Clay Crating Corp.'s outstanding common shares on January 2, 2006, for $540 million. The carrying amount of Clay Crating's net assets (shareholders' equity) at the purchase date totaled $900 million. Book values and fair values were the same for all financial statement items except for inventory and buildings, for which fair values exceeded book values by $25 million and $225 million, respectively. All inventory on hand at the acquisition date was sold during 2006. The buildings have average remaining useful lives of 18 years. During 2006, Clay Crating reported net income of $220 million and paid an $80 million cash dividend.

**Required:**

1. Prepare the appropriate journal entries during 2006 for the investment.
2. Determine the amounts relating to the investment that Delta Apparatus should report in the 2006 financial statements:
   a. As an investment in the balance sheet.
   b. As investment revenue in the income statement.
   c. Among investing activities in the statement of cash flows.

**SOLUTION**

1. Prepare the appropriate journal entries during 2006 for the investment.

| | ($ in millions) | |
|---|---|---|
| **Purchase** | | |
| Investment in Clay Crating shares | 540 | |
| Cash | | 540 |
| **Net income** | | |
| Investment in Clay Crating shares (40% × $220 million) | 88 | |
| Investment revenue | | 88 |
| **Dividends** | | |
| Cash (40% × $80 million) | 32 | |
| Investment in Clay Crating shares | | 32 |
| **Inventory** | | |
| Investment revenue (higher cost of goods sold during 2006 if beginning inventory had been adjusted to fair value) | 10 | |
| Investment in Clay Crating shares (40% × $25 million) | | 10 |
| **Buildings** | | |
| Investment revenue ([$225 million × 40%] ÷ 18 years) | 5 | |
| Investment in Clay Crating shares | | 5 |

| | Investee Net Assets ↓ | Net Assets Purchased ↓ | Difference Attributed to ↓ | |
|---|---|---|---|---|
| Cost | | $540 | | |
| | | | Goodwill: | $80 [difference] |
| Fair value | $1,150† × 40% = | $460 | | |
| | | | Undervaluation of inventory | $10 [$25 × 40%] |
| Book value | $ 900 × 40% = | $360 | | |
| | | | Undervaluation of buildings | $90 [$225 × 40%] |

†($900 + 25 + 225)

2. Determine the amounts that Delta Apparatus should report in the 2006 financial statements:
   a. As an investment in the balance sheet:

**Investment in Clay Crating Shares**
($ in millions)

| | | | |
|---|---|---|---|
| Cost | 540 | | |
| Share of income | 88 | | |
| | | 32 | Dividends |
| | | 10 | Inventory |
| | | 5 | Buildings |
| Balance | 581 | | |

b. As investment revenue in the income statement:

| | | | | |
|---|---|---|---|---|
| $88 million | − | [$10 + 5] million | = | $73 million |
| (share of income) | | (adjustments) | | |

c. In the statement of cash flows:

- Among investing activities: $540 million cash outflow
- Among operating activities: $32 million cash inflow

## DECISION MAKERS' PERSPECTIVE

Corporations invest in other corporations for a variety of reasons.

The way we account for investments has considerable impact on both the valuation of corporate assets and income determination. Consequently, it is critical that both managers and external decision makers clearly understand those impacts and make decisions accordingly.

Managerial decisions concerning investments in other corporations are motivated by a variety of factors. Short-term investments in actively traded securities are common among banks, insurance companies, and other financial institutions. Manufacturing, merchandising, and nonfinancial service firms are more likely to make short-term investments to optimize the use of temporarily idle cash. Substantial portfolios of long-term securities are prominent among financial institutions who must keep large amounts of funds invested for long periods. Other firms, though, invest long term to derive any number of operating benefits such as creating desirable relationships with suppliers or customers. The way we report a company's investment in the stock of another company depends on the nature of the relationship between the investor and the investee. That is, the choice is dictated by the situation; it's not a discretionary matter.

The way an investment is accounted for impacts reported income as well as various financial ratios.

By and large, the way we account for an investment has little effect on a company's cash flows. On the other hand, profits companies report often are significantly impacted by methods used to account for investments. For example, suppose Investor Company owns 20% of Investee Company. Investee's net income is $1 million. Suppose also that Investee distributes one-half its earnings as dividends. (Thus, Investor receives 20% × $1 million × ½ = $100,000.) Also assume the fair value of Investor's investment in Investee's common stock increased by $250,000 during the year. The investment revenue Investor includes on its income statement varies greatly depending on whether the investment is reported as a trading security, a security held for sale, or an investment accounted for by the equity method. The variation is shown in Graphic 12–10.

**GRAPHIC 12–10**

Variation in Earnings by Method Used to Account for Investments

Which accounting method causes reported income to be highest?

| | Accounting Method Used | | |
|---|---|---|---|
| | **Trading Security** | **Security Held for Sale** | **Equity Method** |
| Share of Investee income* | $100,000 | $100,000 | $200,000 |
| Increase in Investee's fair value† | 250,000 | 0 | 0 |
| Investor's investment income | $350,000 | $100,000 | $200,000 |

*Recognized whether received as dividends or not by the equity method; only if received as dividends otherwise.
†Reported in income for trading securities, component of shareholders' equity for securities available for sale, and not recognized at all for equity-method investments.

Thus, despite the lack of real impact on cash flows, the accounting method affects net income, including calculations of earnings per share and any rate of return ratios. When analyzing a company's profitability, lenders and investors should be alert to the way accounting methods affect reported net income. Clearly, managerial intent plays a crucial role in classifying securities. This discretion introduces the possibility of earnings management (manipulation of income) which has obvious implications for earnings quality. As an analyst, you would want to be particularly wary if the method changes from one year to the next. Companies have been known to adjust their ownership percentage, and therefore their method of accounting, suspiciously in concert with the prosperity of an investee.

Actually, the equity method was designed in part to prevent the manipulation of income that would be possible if investing corporations recognized income only when received as dividends, even when they have significant influence over investees. This would create the possibility that an investing corporation can dictate when and if dividends are paid, effectively manipulating the timing of income recognition. The equity method limits that potential method of managing earnings but given the discretion management has in classifying investments, creates other potential abuses. ■

**Accounting methods intended to limit the opportunities for income manipulation sometimes actually create other opportunities.**

## Financial Instruments and Investment Derivatives

A **financial instrument** is defined as:

- Cash,
- Evidence of an *ownership interest* in an entity,[19]
- A contract that (a) imposes on one entity an obligation to *deliver* cash (say accounts payable) or another financial instrument and (b) conveys to the second entity a right to *receive* cash (say accounts receivable) or another financial instrument, or
- A contract that (a) imposes on one entity an obligation to *exchange* financial instruments on potentially unfavorable terms (say the issuer of a stock option) and (b) conveys to a second entity a right to *exchange* other financial instruments on potentially favorable terms (say the holder of a stock option).[20]

An entirely new class of financial instruments has emerged in recent years in response to the desire of firms to manage risks. In fact, these financial instruments would not exist in their own right, but have been created solely to hedge against risks created by other financial instruments or by transactions that have yet to occur but are anticipated. Financial futures, interest rate swaps, forward contracts, and options have become commonplace.[21] These financial instruments often are called **derivatives** because they "derive" their values or contractually required cash flows from some other security or index. For instance, an option to buy an asset in the future at a preset price has a value that is dependent on, or derived from, the value of the underlying asset. Their rapid acceptance as indispensable components of the corporate capital structure has left the accounting profession scrambling to keep pace.

**_Derivatives_ are financial instruments that "derive" their values from some other security or index.**

The urgency to establish accounting standards for financial instruments has been accelerated by headline stories in the financial press reporting multimillion-dollar losses on exotic derivatives by **Enron Corporation**, **Procter & Gamble**, **Orange County** (California), **Piper Jaffrey**, and **Gibson Greetings**, to mention a few. The headlines have tended to focus attention on the misuse of these financial instruments rather than their legitimate use in

**GLOBAL PERSPECTIVE**

No other country reports its investments exactly like we do in the United States. Most countries report short-term investments at lower of cost or market. Some, including Argentina and Israel, report at fair value.

Most countries report noncurrent investments (other than equity method investees) at some variation of cost, but methods vary widely, ranging from unadjusted historical cost (China) to fair market value (New Zealand).

However, International Financial Reporting Standards (IAS 39) classify investments as available-for-sale, trading, or held-to-maturity as we do in the U.S. Available-for-sale and trading securities are carried at fair value and unrealized gains and losses are treated the same way as in the U.S.

[19]This category includes not just shares of stock, but also partnership agreements and stock options.

[20]"Disclosure of Information about Financial Instruments with Off-Balance-Sheet Risk and Financial Instruments with Concentrations of Credit Risk," *Statement of Financial Accounting Standards No. 105,* (Stamford, Conn.: FASB, 1990), par. 6.

[21]Interest rate futures were traded for the first time in 1975 on the Chicago Board of Trade. Interest rate swaps were invented in the early 1980s. They now comprise over 70% of derivatives in use.

managing risk. So maligned in the press have been derivatives that, in a recent conference, James Leisenring, then the FASB's vice chairman, facetiously defined a derivative as "any investment that lost money this year."

The FASB's ongoing financial instruments project is expected to lead to a consistent framework for accounting for all financial instruments.

Actually, the FASB has been involved since 1986 in a project to provide a consistent framework for resolving financial instrument accounting issues, including those related to derivatives and other "off-balance-sheet" instruments. The financial instruments project has three separate but related parts: disclosure, recognition and measurement, and distinguishing between liabilities and equities. Unfortunately, issues to be resolved are extremely complex and will likely require several years to resolve. To help fill the disclosure gap in the meantime, the FASB has offered a series of temporary, "patchwork" solutions. These are primarily in the form of additional disclosures for financial instruments. More recently, the FASB has tackled the issues of recognition and measurement. We discuss these requirements in Appendix A after we've spent some time with the measurement issues necessary to understand accounting for derivatives.

## FINANCIAL REPORTING CASE SOLUTION

1. **How should you respond? Why are held-to-maturity securities treated differently from other investment securities?** *(p. 562)* You should explain that if an investor has the positive intent and ability to hold the securities to maturity, investments in debt securities are classified as held-to-maturity and reported at amortized cost in the balance sheet. Increases and decreases in market value are not reported in the financial statements. The reasoning is that the changes are irrelevant to an investor who will hold a security to its maturity regardless of those changes. Changes in the market value between the time a debt security is acquired and the day it matures to a prearranged maturity value aren't important if sale before maturity isn't an alternative.
2. **Why are unrealized gains and losses not reported on the income statement?** *(p. 564)* Available-for-sale securities are *not* acquired for the purpose of profiting from short-term market price changes, so the argument made by the FASB is that gains and losses from holding these securities while prices change are not considered relevant performance measures to be included in earnings.
3. **What is comprehensive income?** *(p. 564)* Comprehensive income is a more expansive view of the change in shareholders' equity than traditional net income. In fact, it encompasses all changes in equity other than from transactions with owners. In addition to net income, comprehensive income includes up to four other changes in equity.
4. **Anticipate his next question and explain why Coke accounts for some of its investments by the equity method and what that means.** *(p. 576)* When an investor does not have "control," but still is able to exercise *significant influence* over the operating and financial policies of the investee, the investment should be accounted for by the equity method. Apparently Coke owns between 20% and 50% of the voting shares of some of the companies it invests in. By the equity method, Coke recognizes investment income in an amount equal to its percentage share of the net income earned by those companies, instead of the amount of that net income it receives as cash dividends. The rationale is that as the investee earns additional net assets, Coke's share of those net assets increases. ■

## THE BOTTOM LINE

1. Investment securities are classified for reporting purposes as held-to-maturity, available-for-sale, or trading securities. If an investor has the positive intent and ability to hold the securities to maturity, investments in debt securities are classified as held-to-maturity and reported at amortized cost in the balance sheet. These investments are recorded at cost, and holding gains or losses from market price changes are ignored.
2. Investments in debt and equity securities that don't fit the definitions of the other reporting categories are classified as available-for-sale. They are reported at their fair values.

Holding gains and losses from retaining securities during periods of price change are not included in the determination of income for the period; they are reported as a separate component of shareholders' equity.

3. Investments in debt or equity securities acquired principally for the purpose of selling them in the near term are classified as trading securities. They are reported at their fair values. Holding gains and losses for trading securities are included in earnings.
4. When an investor is able to exercise significant influence over the operating and financial policies of the investee, the investment should be accounted for by the equity method. Usually an investor can exercise significant influence when it owns between 20% and 50% of the investee's voting shares.
5. By the equity method, the investor recognizes investment income equal to its percentage share (based on share ownership) of the net income earned by the investee, rather than the portion of that net income received as cash dividends. The investment account is adjusted for the investor's percentage share of net income reported by the investee. When the investor actually receives dividends, the investment account is reduced accordingly.
6. When the cost of an investment exceeds the book value of the underlying net assets acquired, both the investment account and investment revenue are adjusted for differences between net income reported by the investee and what that amount would have been if consolidation procedures had been followed. ■

APPENDIX 12A

# OTHER INVESTMENTS (SPECIAL PURPOSE FUNDS, INVESTMENTS IN LIFE INSURANCE POLICIES)

## Special Purpose Funds

It's often convenient for companies to set aside money to be used for specific purposes. You learned about one such special purpose fund in Chapter 7 when we discussed petty cash funds. Recall that a petty cash fund is money set aside to conveniently make small expenditures using currency rather than having to follow the time-consuming, formal procedures normally used to process checks. Similar funds sometimes are used to pay interest, payroll, or other short-term needs. Like petty cash, these short-term special purpose funds are reported as current assets.

**Some special purpose funds—like petty cash—are current assets.**

Special purpose funds also are sometimes established to serve longer term needs. It's common, for instance, to periodically set aside cash into a fund designated to repay bonds and other long-term debt. Such funds usually accumulate cash over the debt's term to maturity and are composed of the company's periodic contributions plus interest or dividends from investing the money in various return-generating investments. In fact, some debt contracts require the borrower to establish such a fund to repay the debt. In similar fashion, management might voluntarily choose to establish a fund to accumulate money to expand facilities, provide for unexpected losses, to buy back shares of stock, or any other special purpose that might benefit from an accumulation of funds. Of course, these funds that won't be used within the upcoming operating cycle are noncurrent assets. They are reported as part of investments and funds. The same criteria for classifying securities into reporting categories that we discussed previously should be used to classify securities in which funds are invested. Any investment revenue from these funds is reported as such on the income statement.

**A special purpose fund can be established for virtually any purpose.**

**Noncurrent special purpose funds are reported within the category *investments and funds.***

## Investments in Life Insurance Policies

Companies frequently buy life insurance policies on the lives of their key officers. Under normal circumstances, the company pays the premium for the policy and as beneficiary, receives the proceeds when the officer dies. Of course, the objective is to compensate the company for the untimely loss of a valuable resource in the event the officer dies. However, some types of life insurance policies can be surrendered while the insured is still alive in exchange for a determinable amount of money, called the **cash surrender value**. In effect, a

**Certain life insurance policies can be surrendered while the insured is still alive in exchange for its *cash surrender value.***

portion of each premium payment is not used by the insurance company to pay for life insurance coverage, but instead is invested on behalf of the insured company in a fixed-income investment. Accordingly, the cash surrender value increases each year by the portion of premiums invested plus interest on the previous amount invested. This is simply a characteristic of whole life insurance, unlike term insurance whose lower premiums provide death benefits only.

Part of each insurance premium represents an increase in the cash surrender value.

From an accounting standpoint, the periodic insurance premium should not be expensed in its entirety. Rather, part of each premium payment, the investment portion, is recorded as an asset. Illustration 12A–1 provides an example. ■

**ILLUSTRATION 12A–1**
Cash Surrender Value

Several years ago, American Capital acquired a $1 million insurance policy on the life of its chief executive officer, naming American Capital as beneficiary. Annual premiums are $18,000, payable at the beginning of each year. In 2006, the cash surrender value of the policy increased according to the contract from $5,000 to $7,000. The CEO died at the end of 2006.

Part of the annual premium represents a build-up in the cash surrender value.

| | | |
|---|---|---|
| Insurance expense (difference) | 16,000 | |
| Cash surrender value of life insurance ($7,000 – 5,000) | 2,000 | |
| Cash (2006 premium) | | 18,000 |

*To record insurance expense and the increase in the investment.*

The cash surrender value is considered to be a noncurrent investment and would be reported in the investments and funds section of the balance sheet. Of course when the insured officer dies, the corporation receives the death benefit of the insurance policy, and the cash surrender value ceases to exist because canceling the policy no longer is an option. The corporation recognizes a gain for the amount of the death benefit less the cash surrender value:

When the death benefit is paid, the cash surrender value becomes null and void.

| | | |
|---|---|---|
| Cash (death benefit) | 1,000,000 | |
| Cash surrender value of life insurance (balance) | | 7,000 |
| Gain on life insurance settlement (difference) | | 993,000 |

*To record the proceeds at death.*

# APPENDIX 12B IMPAIRMENT OF A RECEIVABLE DUE TO A TROUBLED DEBT RESTRUCTURING

When a creditor's receivable becomes impaired due to a troubled debt restructuring or for any other reason, the receivable is remeasured based on the discounted present value of currently expected cash flows at the loan's original effective rate (regardless of the extent to which expected cash receipts have been reduced).

When the original terms of a debt agreement are changed as a result of financial difficulties experienced by the debtor (borrower), the new arrangement is referred to as a **troubled debt restructuring**. We discuss troubled debt restructurings in much more detail in Chapter 14. The essential point here is that such an arrangement involves some concessions on the part of the creditor (lender), resulting in the impairment of the creditor's asset: the investment in a receivable.

## When the Receivable Is Settled Outright

Sometimes a receivable in a troubled debt restructuring is actually settled at the time of the restructuring with the receipt of cash (or a noncash asset), or even shares of the debtor's stock. In that case, the creditor simply records a loss for the difference between the carrying amount of the receivable and the fair value of the asset(s) or equity securities received. Illustration 12B–1 provides an example.

First Prudent Bank is owed $30 million by Brillard Properties under a 10% note with two years remaining to maturity. Due to financial difficulties of the developer, the previous year's interest ($3 million) was not received. The bank agrees to settle the receivable (and accrued interest receivable) in exchange for property having a fair market value of $20 million.

| | ($ in millions) | |
|---|---|---|
| Land (fair market value) | 20 | |
| Loss on troubled debt restructuring | 13 | |
| Accrued interest receivable (10% × $30 million) | | 3 |
| Note receivable (balance) | | 30 |

For most active lenders, a troubled debt restructuring unfortunately is not both unusual and infrequent; so usually the loss is not reported as an extraordinary loss.

**ILLUSTRATION 12B–1**
Debt Settled at the Time of a Restructuring

The carrying amount of the receivable is $33 million

## When the Receivable Is Continued, but with Modified Terms

In the previous example we assumed that First Prudent Bank agreed to accept property in full settlement of the receivable. In a troubled debt restructuring, it is more likely that the bank would allow the receivable to continue but with the terms of the debt agreement modified to make it easier for the debtor to comply. The lender might agree to reduce or delay the scheduled interest payments. Or, it may agree to reduce or delay the maturity amount. Often a troubled debt restructuring will call for some combination of these concessions.

As one of many possibilities, suppose the bank agrees to (1) forgive the interest accrued from last year, (2) reduce the two remaining interest payments from $3 million each to $2 million each, and (3) reduce the face amount from $30 million to $25 million. Clearly, the bank's investment in the receivable has been impaired. The extent of impairment is the difference between the $33 million carrying amount of the receivable (the present value of the receivable's cash flows prior to the restructuring) and the present value of the revised cash flows discounted at the loan's original effective rate (10%). See Illustration 12B–2 for a demonstration.

After restructuring, the lender still records interest annually at the 10% effective rate. ■

Brillard Properties owes First Prudent Bank $30 million under a 10% note with two years remaining to maturity. Due to financial difficulties of the developer, the previous year's interest ($3 million) was not paid. First Prudent Bank agrees to:
1. Forgive the interest accrued from last year.
2. Reduce the remaining two interest payments to $2 million each.
3. Reduce the principal to $25 million.

**Analysis**

| | | | |
|---|---|---|---|
| **Previous Value** | | | |
| Accrued interest | (10% × $30,000,000) | $ 3,000,000 | |
| Principal | | 30,000,000 | |
| Carrying amount of the receivable | | | $33,000,000 |
| **New Value** | | | |
| Interest | $ 2 million × 1.73554* = | $ 3,471,080 | |
| Principal | $25 million × 0.82645† = | 20,661,250 | |
| Present value of the receivable | | | (24,132,330) |
| **Loss** | | | $ 8,867,670 |

*Present value of an ordinary annuity of $1: $n = 2$, $i = 10\%$
†Present value of $1: $n = 2$, $i = 10\%$

**Journal Entry**

| | | |
|---|---|---|
| Loss on troubled debt restructuring (to balance) | 8,867,670 | |
| Accrued interest receivable (10% × $30,000,000) | | 3,000,000 |
| Note receivable ($30,000,000 − 24,132,330) | | 5,867,670 |

**ILLUSTRATION 12B–2**
Receivable Impaired by Troubled Debt Restructuring—Terms Modified

The discounted present value of the cash flows prior to the restructuring was the same as the receivable's carrying amount.

The discounted present value of the cash flows after the restructuring is less.

The difference is a loss.

# QUESTIONS FOR REVIEW OF KEY TOPICS

**Q 12–1** All investments in *debt* securities and investments in *equity* securities that have readily determinable fair values (except those for which the equity method or consolidation is appropriate) are classified for reporting purposes in one of three categories and accounted for differently depending on the classification. What are these three categories?

**Q 12–2** When market rates of interest *rise* after a fixed-rate security is purchased, the value of the now-below-market, fixed-interest payments declines, so the market value of the investment falls. On the other hand, if market rates of interest *fall* after a fixed-rate security is purchased, the fixed-interest payments become relatively attractive, and the market value of the investment rises. How are these price changes reflected in the investment account for a security classified as held-to-maturity?

**Q 12–3** When is the fair value of an equity security considered to be readily determinable? How is an investment in an equity security reported if its fair value is *not* readily determinable?

**Q 12–4** When an investment is acquired to be held for an unspecified period of time as opposed to being held to maturity, it is reported at the fair value of the investment securities on the reporting date. Why?

**Q 12–5** Reporting an investment at its fair value means adjusting its carrying amount for changes in fair value after its acquisition (or since the last reporting date if it was held at that time). Such changes are called unrealized holding gains and losses because they haven't yet been realized through the sale of the security. If the security is classified as available-for-sale, how are unrealized holding gains and losses reported?

**Q 12–6** What is "comprehensive income"? Its composition varies from company to company but may include which financial items?

**Q 12–7** Why are holding gains and losses treated differently for trading securities and securities available-for-sale?

**Q 12–8** The market value of Helig Forestry and Mining Corporation common stock dropped 6⅛ points when the federal government passed new legislation banning one of the company's primary techniques for extracting ore. Harris Corporation owns shares of Helig and classifies its investment as securities available-for-sale. How should the decline in market value be handled by Harris?

**Q 12–9** Western Die-Casting Company holds an investment in unsecured bonds of LGB Heating Equipment, Inc. When the investment was acquired, management's intention was to hold the bonds for resale. Now management has the positive intent and ability to hold the bonds to maturity. How should the reclassification of the investment be accounted for?

**Q 12–10** Is it necessary for an investor to report individual amounts for the three categories of investments— held-to-maturity, available-for-sale, or trading—in the financial statements? What information should be disclosed about these investments?

**Q 12–11** Under what circumstances is the equity method used to account for an investment in stock?

**Q 12–12** The equity method has been referred to as a *one-line consolidation.* What might prompt this description?

**Q 12–13** In the application of the equity method, how should dividends from the investee be accounted for? Why?

**Q 12–14** The fair value of depreciable assets of Penner Packaging Company exceeds their book value by $12 million. The assets' average remaining useful life is 10 years. They are being depreciated by the straight-line method. Finest Foods Industries buys 40% of Penner's common shares. When adjusting investment revenue and the investment by the equity method, how will the situation described affect those two accounts?

**Q 12–15** Superior Company owns 40% of the outstanding stock of Bernard Company. During 2006, Bernard paid a $100,000 cash dividend on its common shares. What effect did this dividend have on Superior's 2006 financial statements?

**Q 12–16** Sometimes an investor's level of influence changes, making it necessary to change from the equity method to another method. How should the investor account for this change in accounting method?

**Q 12–17** Define a financial instrument. Provide three examples of current liabilities that represent financial instruments.

**Q 12–18** Some financial instruments are called derivatives. Why?

**Q 12–19** (Based on Appendix 12A) Northwest Carburetor Company established a fund in 2003 to accumulate money for a new plant scheduled for construction in 2006. How should this special purpose fund be reported in Northwest's balance sheet?

**Q 12–20** (Based on Appendix 12A) Whole-life insurance policies typically can be surrendered while the insured is still alive in exchange for a determinable amount of money called the *cash surrender value.* When a company buys a life insurance policy on the life of a key officer to protect the company against the untimely loss of a valuable resource in the event the officer dies, how should the company account for the cash surrender value?

**Q 12–21** (Based on Appendix 12B) Marshall Companies, Inc., holds a note receivable from a former subsidiary. Due to financial difficulties, the former subsidiary has been unable to pay the previous year's interest on the note. Marshall agreed to restructure the debt by both delaying and reducing remaining cash payments. The concessions impair the creditor's investment in the receivable. How is this impairment recorded?

## BRIEF EXERCISES

**BE 12–1**
Securities held-to-maturity; bond investment; effective interest
● LO1

Lance Brothers Enterprises acquired $720,000 of 3% bonds, dated July 1, on July 1, 2006, as a long-term investment. Management has the positive intent and ability to hold the bonds until maturity. The market interest rate (yield) was 4% for bonds of similar risk and maturity. Lance Brothers paid $600,000 for the investment in bonds and will receive interest semiannually on June 30 and December 31. Prepare the journal entries (a) to record Lance Brothers' investment in the bonds on July 1, 2006, and (b) to record interest on December 31, 2006, at the effective (market) rate.

**BE 12–2**
Purchase and sale of investment securities
● LO2

CPS, Inc. purchased 2,000 shares of **Walt Disney** common stock at $27 per share and paid a brokerage fee of $900. The company sold the shares three months later for $29 per share, paying a brokerage fee on the sale of $950. What are the journal entries CPS recorded for the purchase and the sale?

**BE 12–3**
Securities available-for-sale; adjusting entry
● LO2

For several years Fister Links Products has held shares of **Microsoft** common stock, considered by the company to be securities available-for-sale. The shares were acquired at a cost of $500,000. Their fair value last year was $610,000 and is $670,000 this year. At what amount will the investment be reported in this year's balance sheet? What adjusting entry is required to accomplish this objective?

**BE 12–4**
Classification of securities; reporting
● LO2
**FedEx Corporation**

Adams Industries holds 40,000 shares of **FedEx** common stock. On December 31, 2005, and December 31, 2006, the market value of the stock is $95 and $100 per share, respectively. What is the appropriate reporting category for this investment and at what amount will it be reported in the 2006 balance sheet?

**BE 12–5**
Trading securities
● LO3

S&L Financial buys and sells securities expecting to earn profits on short-term differences in price. On December 27, 2006, S&L purchased **Coca-Cola** common shares for $875,000 and sold the shares on January 3, 2007, for $880,000. At December 31, the shares had a fair value of $873,000. What pretax amounts did S&L include in its 2006 and 2007 earnings as a result of this investment?

**BE 12–6**
Trading securities
● LO3

S&L Financial buys and sells securities which it classifies as available-for-sale. On December 27, 2006, S&L purchased **Coca-Cola** common shares for $875,000 and sold the shares on January 3, 2007, for $880,000. At December 31, the shares had a fair value of $873,000. What pretax amounts did S&L include in its 2006 and 2007 earnings as a result of this investment?

**BE 12–7**
Equity method
● LO4 LO5

Turner Company owns 40% of the outstanding stock of ICA Company. During the current year, ICA paid a $5 million cash dividend on its common shares. What effect did this dividend have on Turner's 2006 financial statements?

**BE 12–8**
Equity method
● LO4 LO5

Turner Company owns 10% of the outstanding stock of ICA Company. During the current year, ICA paid a $5 million cash dividend on its common shares. What effect did this dividend have on Turner's 2006 financial statements?

**BE 12–9**
Equity method
● LO6

The fair value of Wallis, Inc.'s depreciable assets exceeds their book value by $50 million. The assets have an average remaining useful life of 15 years and are being depreciated by the straight-line method. Park Industries buys 30% of Wallis's common shares. When Park adjusts its investment revenue and the investment by the equity method, how will the situation described affect those two accounts?

**BE 12–10**
Impairment
● LO5

LED Corporation owns 100,000 shares of Branch Pharmaceuticals common stock and classifies its investment as securities available-for-sale. The market price of Branch's stock fell over 30%, by 4.5 points when the FDA banned one of the company's principal drugs. What journal entry should LED record to account for the decline in market value? How should the decline be reported?

**BE 12–11**
Change in principle; change to the equity method
● LO5

At the beginning of 2006, Pioneer Products' ownership interest in the common stock of LLB Co. increased to the point that it became appropriate to begin using the equity method of accounting for the investment. The balance in the investment account was $44 million at the time of the change but would have been $56 million if Pioneer had used the equity method and the account had been adjusted for investee net income and dividends. How should Pioneer report the change? Would your answer be the same if Pioneer is changing *from* the equity method rather than *to* the equity method?

# EXERCISES

available with McGraw-Hill's Homework Manager www.mhhe.com/spiceland4e

**An alternate exercise and problem set is available on the text website: www.mhhe.com/spiceland4e**

**E 12–1**
Securities held-to-maturity; bond investment; effective interest
● LO1

Tanner-UNF Corporation acquired as a long-term investment $240 million of 6% bonds, dated July 1, on July 1 2006. Company management has the positive intent and ability to hold the bonds until maturity. The market interest rate (yield) was 8% for bonds of similar risk and maturity. Tanner-UNF paid $200 million for the bonds. The company will receive interest semiannually on June 30 and December 31. As a result of changing market conditions, the fair value of the bonds at December 31, 2006, was $210 million.

**Required:**

1. Prepare the journal entry to record Tanner-UNF's investment in the bonds on July 1, 2006.
2. Prepare the journal entries by Tanner-UNF to record interest on December 31, 2006, at the effective (market) rate.
3. At what amount will Tanner-UNF report its investment in the December 31, 2006, balance sheet? Why?
4. Suppose Moody's bond rating agency downgraded the risk rating of the bonds motivating Tanner-UNF to sell the investment on January 2, 2007, for $190 million. Prepare the journal entry to record the sale.

**E 12–2**
Securities held-to-maturity
● LO1

FF&T Corporation is a confectionery wholesaler that frequently buys and sells securities to meet various investment objectives. The following selected transactions relate to FF&T's investment activities during the last two months of 2006. At November 1, FF&T held $48 million of 20-year, 10% bonds of Convenience, Inc., purchased May 1, 2006, at face value. Management has the positive intent and ability to hold the bonds until maturity. FF&T's fiscal year ends on December 31.

| | | |
|---|---|---|
| Nov. | 1 | Received semiannual interest of $2.4 million from the Convenience, Inc., bonds. |
| Dec. | 1 | Purchased 12% bonds of Facsimile Enterprises at their $30 million face value, to be held until they mature in 2019. Semiannual interest is payable May 31 and November 30. |
| | 31 | Purchased U.S. Treasury bills that mature in two months for $8.9 million. |
| | 31 | Recorded any necessary adjusting entry(s) relating to the investments. |

The fair values of the investments at December 31 were:

| | |
|---|---|
| Convenience bonds | $44.7 million |
| Facsimile Enterprises bonds | 30.9 million |
| U.S. Treasury bills | 8.9 million |

**Required:**

Prepare the appropriate journal entry for each transaction or event.

**E 12–3**
Purchase and sale of investment securities
● LO2 LO3

Shott Farm Supplies Corporation purchased 800 shares of General Motors stock at $50 per share and paid a brokerage fee of $1,200. Two months later, the shares were sold for $53 per share. The brokerage fee on the sale was $1,300.

**Required:**

Prepare entries for the purchase and the sale.

**E 12–4**
Securities available-for-sale; adjusting entries
● LO2

Loreal-American Corporation purchased several marketable securities during 2006. At December 31, 2006, the company had the investments in common stock listed below. None was held at the last reporting date, December 31, 2005, and all are considered securities available-for-sale.

| | Cost | Fair Value | Unrealized Holding Gain (Loss) |
|---|---|---|---|
| Short term: | | | |
| Blair, Inc. | $ 480,000 | $ 405,000 | $(75,000) |
| ANC Corporation | 450,000 | 480,000 | 30,000 |
| Totals | $ 930,000 | $ 885,000 | $(45,000) |
| Long term: | | | |
| Drake Corporation | $ 480,000 | $ 560,000 | $ 80,000 |
| Aaron Industries | 720,000 | 660,000 | (60,000) |
| Totals | $1,200,000 | $1,220,000 | $ 20,000 |

**Required:**

1. Prepare appropriate adjusting entries at December 31, 2006.
2. What amounts would be reported in the income statement at December 31, 2006, as a result of these adjusting entries?

**E 12–5**
Classification of securities; adjusting entries

● LO2

On February 18, 2006, Union Corporation purchased 10,000 shares of IBM common stock as a long-term investment at $60 per share. On December 31, 2006, and December 31, 2007, the market value of IBM stock is $58 and $61 per share, respectively.

**Required:**

1. What is the appropriate reporting category for this investment? Why?
2. Prepare the adjusting entry for December 31, 2006.
3. Prepare the adjusting entry for December 31, 2007.

**E 12–6**
Various transactions related to securities available-for-sale

● LO2

Construction Forms Corporation buys securities to be available for sale when circumstances warrant, not to profit from short-term differences in price and not necessarily to hold debt securities to maturity. The following selected transactions relate to investment activities of Construction Forms whose fiscal year ends on December 31. No investments were held by Construction Forms at the beginning of the year.

**2006**

| | |
|---|---|
| Mar. 2 | Purchased 1 million Platinum Gauges, Inc., common shares for $31 million, including brokerage fees and commissions. |
| Apr. 12 | Purchased $20 million of 10% bonds at face value from Zenith Wholesale Corporation. |
| July 18 | Received cash dividends of $2 million on the investment in Platinum Gauges, Inc., common shares. |
| Oct. 15 | Received semiannual interest of $1 million on the investment in Zenith bonds. |
| 16 | Sold the Zenith bonds for $21 million. |
| Nov. 1 | Purchased 500,000 LTD International preferred shares for $40 million, including brokerage fees and commissions. |
| Dec. 31 | Recorded the necessary adjusting entry(s) relating to the investments. The market prices of the investments are $32 per share for Platinum Gauges, Inc., and $74 per share for LTD International preferred shares. |

**2007**

| | |
|---|---|
| Jan. 23 | Sold half the Platinum Gauges, Inc., shares for $32 per share. |
| Mar. 1 | Sold the LTD International preferred shares for $76 per share. |

**Required:**

1. Prepare the appropriate journal entry for each transaction or event.
2. Show the amounts that would be reported in the company's 2006 income statement relative to these investments.

**E 12–7**
Securities available-for-sale; journal entries

● LO2

On January 2, 2006, Sanborn Tobacco, Inc. bought 5% of Jackson Industry's capital stock for $90 million as a temporary investment. Sanborn classified the securities acquired as available-for-sale. Jackson Industry's net income for the year ended December 31, 2006, was $120 million. The fair value of the shares held by Sanborn was $98 million at December 31, 2006. During 2006, Jackson declared a dividend of $60 million.

**Required:**

1. Prepare all appropriate journal entries related to the investment during 2006.
2. Indicate the effect of this investment on 2006 income before taxes.

**E 12–8**
Various transactions relating to trading securities

● LO3

Rantzow-Lear Company buys and sells securities expecting to earn profits on short-term differences in price. The company's fiscal year ends on December 31. The following selected transactions relating to Rantzow-Lear's trading account occurred during December 2006 and the first week of 2007.

**2006**

| | |
|---|---|
| Dec. 17 | Purchased 100,000 Grocers' Supply Corporation preferred shares for $350,000. |
| 28 | Received cash dividends of $2,000 from the Grocers' Supply Corporation preferred shares. |
| 31 | Recorded any necessary adjusting entry relating to the Grocers' Supply Corporation preferred shares. The market price of the stock was $4 per share. |

**2007**

| | |
|---|---|
| Jan. 5 | Sold the Grocers' Supply Corporation preferred shares for $395,000. |

**Required:**

1. Prepare the appropriate journal entry for each transaction.
2. Indicate any amounts that Rantzow-Lear Company would report in its 2006 balance sheet and income statement as a result of this investment.

**E 12–9**
Various investment securities

● LO1 LO2 LO3

At December 31, 2006, Hull-Meyers Corp. had the following investments that were purchased during 2006, its first year of operations:

| | Cost | Fair Value |
|---|---|---|
| **Trading Securities:** | | |
| Security A | $ 900,000 | $ 910,000 |
| Security B | 105,000 | 100,000 |
| Totals | $1,005,000 | $1,010,000 |
| **Securities Available-for-Sale:** | | |
| Security C | $ 700,000 | $ 780,000 |
| Security D | 900,000 | 915,000 |
| Totals | $1,600,000 | $1,695,000 |
| **Securities to Be Held-to-Maturity:** | | |
| Security E | $ 490,000 | $ 500,000 |
| Security F | 615,000 | 610,000 |
| Totals | $1,105,000 | $1,110,000 |

No investments were sold during 2006. All securities except Security D and Security F are considered short-term investments. None of the market changes is considered permanent.

**Required:**

Determine the following amounts at December 31, 2006.

1. Investments reported as current assets.
2. Investments reported as noncurrent assets.
3. Unrealized gain (or loss) component of income before taxes.
4. Unrealized gain (or loss) component of shareholders' equity.

**E 12–10**
Securities available-for-sale; adjusting entries
● LO2

The accounting records of Jamaican Importers, Inc. at January 1, 2006, included the following:

| | |
|---|---|
| **Assets:** | |
| Investment in IBM common shares | $1,345,000 |
| Less: Fair value adjustment | (145,000) |
| | $1,200,000 |
| **Shareholders' Equity:** | |
| Accumulated unrealized holding gains and losses | $ 145,000 |

No changes occurred during 2006 in the investment portfolio.

**Required:**

Prepare appropriate adjusting entry(s) at December 31, 2006, assuming the market value of the IBM common shares was:

1. $1,175,000
2. $1,275,000
3. $1,375,000

**E 12–11**
Securities available-for-sale; fair value adjustment
● LO2

The investments of Harlon Enterprises included the following cost and fair value amounts:

| ($ in millions) | | Fair Value, Dec. 31 | |
|---|---|---|---|
| **Securities Available-for-Sale** | **Cost** | **2006** | **2007** |
| A Corporation shares | $ 20 | $14 | na |
| B Corporation bonds | 35 | 35 | $ 37 |
| C Corporation shares | 15 | na | 14 |
| D Industries shares | 45 | 46 | 50 |
| Totals | $115 | $95 | $101 |

Harlon Enterprises sold its holdings of A Corporation shares on June 1, 2007, for $15 million. On September 12, it purchased the C Corporation shares.

**Required:**

1. What is the effect of the sale of the A Corporation shares and the purchase of the C Corporation shares on Harlon's 2007 pretax earnings?
2. At what amount should Harlon's securities available-for-sale portfolio be reported in its 2007 balance sheet? What adjusting entry is needed to accomplish this? What is the effect of the adjustment on Harlon's 2007 pretax earnings?

**E 12–12**
Multiple choice; investment securities
● LO1 LO2 LO3

The following questions dealing with investments are adapted from questions that appeared in recent CPA examinations. Determine the response that best completes the statements or questions.

1. Nola Co. has adopted *Statement of Financial Accounting Standards No. 115*, "Accounting for Certain Investments in Debt and Equity Securities." Nola has a portfolio of marketable equity securities that it

does not intend to sell in the near term. How should Nola classify these securities, and how should it report unrealized gains and losses from these securities?

| Classify as | Report as a |
|---|---|
| a. Trading securities | Component of income from continuing operations |
| b. Available-for-sale | Separate component of shareholders' equity |
| c. Trading securities | Separate component of shareholders' equity |
| d. Available-for-sale | Component of income from continuing operations |

2. Kale Co. has adopted *Statement of Financial Accounting Standards No. 115,* "Accounting for Certain Investments in Debt and Equity Securities." Kale purchased bonds at a discount on the open market as an investment and intends to hold these bonds to maturity. Kale should account for these bonds at:
   a. Cost
   b. Amortized cost
   c. Fair value
   d. Lower of cost or market

**E 12–13**
Investment securities and equity method investments compared

● LO2 LO4

As a long-term investment, Painters' Equipment Company purchased 20% of AMC Supplies, Inc.'s 400,000 shares for $480,000 at the beginning of the fiscal year of both companies. On the purchase date, the fair value and book value of AMC's net assets were equal. During the year, AMC earned net income of $250,000 and distributed cash dividends of 25 cents per share. At year-end, the fair value of the shares is $505,000.

**Required:**
1. Assume no significant influence was acquired. Prepare the appropriate journal entries from the purchase through the end of the year.
2. Assume significant influence was acquired. Prepare the appropriate journal entries from the purchase through the end of the year.

**E 12–14**
Equity method; purchase; investee income; dividends

● LO4 LO5

As a long-term investment at the beginning of the fiscal year, Florists International purchased 30% of Nursery Supplies, Inc.'s 8 million shares for $56 million. The fair value and book value of the shares were the same at that time. During the year, Nursery Supplies earned net income of $40 million and distributed cash dividends of $1.25 per share. At the end of the year, the fair value of the shares is $52 million.

**Required:**
Prepare the appropriate journal entries from the purchase through the end of the year.

**E 12–15**
Change in principle; change to the equity method

● LO5

The Trump Companies, Inc. has ownership interests in several public companies. At the beginning of 2006, the company's ownership interest in the common stock of Milken Properties increased to the point that it became appropriate to begin using the equity method of accounting for the investment. The balance in the investment account was $31 million at the time of the change. Accountants working with company records determined that the balance would have been $48 million if the account had been adjusted for investee net income and dividends as prescribed by the equity method.

**Required:**
1. Prepare the journal entry to record the change in principle.
2. Briefly describe other steps Trump should take to report the change.
3. Suppose Trump is changing *from* the equity method rather than *to* the equity method. How would your answers to requirements 1 and 2 differ?

**E 12–16**
Error corrections; investment

● LO1 LO2 LO3

On December 12, 2006, an investment costing $80,000 was sold for $100,000. The total of the sale proceeds was credited to the investment account.

**Required:**
1. Prepare the journal entry to correct the error assuming it is discovered before the books are adjusted or closed in 2006. (Ignore income taxes.)
2. Prepare the journal entry to correct the error assuming it is not discovered until early 2007. (Ignore income taxes.)

**E 12–17**
Equity method; adjustment for depreciation

● LO5 LO6

Fizer Pharmaceutical paid $68 million on January 2, 2006, for 4 million shares of Carne Cosmetics common stock. The investment represents a 25% interest in the net assets of Carne and gave Fizer the ability to exercise significant influence over Carne's operations. Fizer received dividends of $1 per share on December 21, 2006, and Carne reported net income of $40 million for the year ended December 31, 2006. The market value of Carne's common stock at December 31, 2006, was $18.50 per share.

- The book value of Carne's net assets was $192 million.
- The fair market value of Carne's depreciable assets exceeded their book value by $32 million. These assets had an average remaining useful life of eight years.
- The remainder of the excess of the cost of the investment over the book value of net assets purchased was attributable to goodwill.

**Required:**

Prepare all appropriate journal entries related to the investment during 2006.

**E 12–18**
Equity method
● LO5 LO6

On January 1, 2006, Cameron, Inc. bought 20% of the outstanding common stock of Lake Construction Company for $300 million cash. At the date of acquisition of the stock, Lake's net assets had a fair value of $900 million. Their book value was $800 million. The difference was attributable to the fair value of Lake's buildings and its land exceeding book value, each accounting for one-half of the difference. Lake's net income for the year ended December 31, 2006, was $150 million. During 2006, Lake declared and paid cash dividends of $30 million. The buildings have a remaining life of 10 years.

**Required:**

1. Prepare all appropriate journal entries related to the investment during 2006, assuming Cameron accounts for this investment by the equity method.
2. Determine the amounts to be reported by Cameron:
   a. As an investment in Cameron's 2006 balance sheet.
   b. As investment revenue in the income statement.
   c. Among investing activities in the statement of cash flows.

**E 12–19**
Multiple choice; CPA exam; equity method
● LO5

The following questions dealing with the equity method are adapted from questions that appeared on previous CPA examinations. Determine the response that best completes the statements or questions. Questions 1–3 are based on the following information.

Grant, Inc. acquired 30% of South Co's voting stock for $200,000 on January 2, 2006. Grant's 30% interest in South gave Grant the ability to exercise significant influence over South's operating and financial policies. During 2006, South earned $80,000 and paid dividends of $50,000. South reported earnings of $100,000 for the six months ended June 30, 2007, and $200,000 for the year ended December 31, 2007. On July 1, 2007, Grant sold half of its stock in South for $150,000 cash. South paid dividends of $60,000 on October 1, 2007.

1. Before income taxes, what amount should Grant include in its 2006 income statement as a result of the investment?
   a. $15,000
   b. $24,000
   c. $50,000
   d. $80,000
2. In Grant's December 31, 2006, balance sheet, what should be the carrying amount of this investment?
   a. $200,000
   b. $209,000
   c. $224,000
   d. $230,000
3. In its 2007 income statement, what amount should Grant report as gain from the sale of half of its investment?
   a. $24,500
   b. $30,500
   c. $35,000
   d. $45,500

**E 12–20**
Multiple choice; CMA exam; investments
● LO1 LO2

The following questions dealing with investments are adapted from questions that previously appeared on Certified Management Accountant (CMA) examinations. The CMA designation sponsored by the Institute of Management Accountants (**www.imanet.org**) provides members with an objective measure of knowledge and competence in the field of management accounting. Determine the response that best completes the statements or questions.

1. An investment in available-for-sale securities is valued on the balance sheet at
   a. The cost to acquire the asset.
   b. Accumulated income minus accumulated dividends since acquisition.
   c. Fair value.
   d. The par or stated value of the securities.

Questions 2 and 3 are based on the following information concerning Monahan Company's portfolio of debt securities at May 31, year 2 and May 31, year 3. All of the debt securities were purchased by Monahan during June, year 1. Prior to June, year 1, Monahan had no investments in debt or equity securities.

| As of May 31, Year 2 | Amortized Cost | Fair Value |
|---|---|---|
| Cleary Company bonds | $164,526 | $168,300 |
| Beauchamp Industry bonds | 204,964 | 205,200 |
| Morrow Inc. bonds | 305,785 | 285,200 |
| Total | $675,275 | $658,700 |

| As of May 31, Year 3 | Amortized Cost | Fair Value |
|---|---|---|
| Cleary Company bonds | $152,565 | $147,600 |
| Beauchamp Industry bonds | 193,800 | 204,500 |
| Morrow Inc. bonds | 289,130 | 291,400 |
| Total | $635,495 | $643,500 |

2. Assuming that the above securities are properly classified as available-for-sale securities under SFAS 115, *Accounting for Certain Investments in Debt and Equity Securities,* the unrealized holding gain or loss as of May 31, year 3 would be
   a. recognized as an $8,005 unrealized holding gain on the income statement.
   b. recognized in other comprehensive income by a year-end credit of $8,005.
   c. recognized in other comprehensive income by a year-end debit of $8,005.
   d. not recognized.
3. Assuming that the above securities are properly classified as held-to-maturity securities under SFAS 115, *Accounting for Certain Investments in Debt and Equity Securities,* the unrealized holding gain or loss as of May 31, year 2 would be
   a. recognized as an $8,005 unrealized holding gain on the income statement.
   b. recognized in other comprehensive income by a year-end credit of $8,005.
   c. recognized in other comprehensive income by a year-end debit of $8,005.
   d. not recognized.

**E 12–21**
Life insurance policy (Based on Appendix 12A)

Edible Chemicals Corporation owns a $4 million whole life insurance policy on the life of its CEO, naming Edible Chemicals as beneficiary. The annual premiums are $70,000 and are payable at the beginning of each year. The cash surrender value of the policy was $21,000 at the beginning of 2006.

**Required:**
1. Prepare the appropriate 2006 journal entry to record insurance expense and the increase in the investment assuming the cash surrender value of the policy increased according to the contract to $27,000.
2. The CEO died at the end of 2006. Prepare the appropriate journal entry.

**E 12–22**
Life insurance policy (Based on Appendix 12A)

Below are two unrelated situations relating to life insurance.

**Required:**
Prepare the appropriate journal entry for each situation.
1. Ford Corporation owns a whole life insurance policy on the life of its president. Ford Corporation is the beneficiary. The insurance premium is $25,000. The cash surrender value increased during the year from $2,500 to $4,600.
2. Petroleum Corporation received a $250,000 life insurance settlement when its CEO died. At that time, the cash surrender value was $16,000.

**E 12–23**
Impairment of securities available-for-sale; troubled debt restructuring (Based on Appendix 12B)
● LO2

At January 1, 2006, Clayton Hoists, Inc. owed Third BancCorp $12 million, under a 10% note due December 31, 2007. Interest was paid last on December 31, 2004. Clayton was experiencing severe financial difficulties and asked Third BancCorp to modify the terms of the debt agreement. After negotiation Third BancCorp agreed to:
- Forgive the interest accrued for the year just ended.
- Reduce the remaining two years' interest payments to $1 million each.
- Reduce the principal amount to $11 million.

**Required:**
Prepare the journal entries by Third BancCorp necessitated by the restructuring of the debt at
1. January 1, 2006.
2. December 31, 2006.
3. December 31, 2007.

**E 12–24**
Impairment of securities available-for-sale; troubled debt restructuring (Based on Appendix 12B)
● LO2

At January 1, 2006, NCI Industries, Inc. was indebted to First Federal Bank under a $240,000, 10% unsecured note. The note was signed January 1, 2002, and was due December 31, 2007. Annual interest was last paid on December 31, 2004. NCI was experiencing severe financial difficulties and negotiated a restructuring of the terms of the debt agreement. First Federal agreed to reduce last year's interest and the remaining two years' interest payments to $11,555 each and delay all payments until December 31, 2007, the maturity date.

**Required:**
Prepare the journal entries by First Federal Bank necessitated by the restructuring of the debt at
1. January 1, 2006.
2. December 31, 2006.
3. December 31, 2007.

# PROBLEMS

available with McGraw-Hill's Homework Manager www.mhhe.com/spiceland4e

**An alternate exercise and problem set is available on the text website: www.mhhe.com/spiceland4e**

**P 12–1**
Securities held-to-maturity; bond investment; effective interest

● LO1

Fuzzy Monkey Technologies, Inc. purchased as a long-term investment $80 million of 8% bonds, dated January 1, on January 1, 2006. Management has the positive intent and ability to hold the bonds until maturity. For bonds of similar risk and maturity the market yield was 10%. The price paid for the bonds was $66 million. Interest is received semiannually on June 30 and December 31. Due to changing market conditions, the fair value of the bonds at December 31, 2006, was $70 million.

**Required:**

1. Prepare the journal entry to record Fuzzy Monkey's investment on January 1, 2006.
2. Prepare the journal entry by Fuzzy Monkey to record interest on June 30, 2006 (at the effective rate).
3. Prepare the journal entries by Fuzzy Monkey to record interest on December 31, 2006 (at the effective rate).
4. At what amount will Fuzzy Monkey report its investment in the December 31, 2006, balance sheet? Why?

**P 12–2**
Securities available-for-sale; bond investment; effective interest

● LO2

(Note: This problem is a variation of the preceding problem, modified to cause the investment to be in securities available-for-sale.)

Fuzzy Monkey Technologies, Inc. purchased as a long-term investment $80 million of 8% bonds, dated January 1, on January 1, 2006. Management intends to have the investment available for sale when circumstances warrant. For bonds of similar risk and maturity the market yield was 10%. The price paid for the bonds was $66 million. Interest is received semiannually on June 30 and December 31. Due to changing market conditions, the fair value of the bonds at December 31, 2006, was $70 million.

**Required:**

1. Prepare the journal entry to record Fuzzy Monkey's investment on January 1, 2006.
2. Prepare the journal entry by Fuzzy Monkey to record interest on June 30, 2006 (at the effective rate).
3. Prepare the journal entries by Fuzzy Monkey to record interest on December 31, 2006 (at the effective rate).
4. At what amount will Fuzzy Monkey report its investment in the December 31, 2006, balance sheet? Why? Prepare any entry necessary to achieve this reporting objective.

**P 12–3**
Various transactions related to securities available-for-sale

● LO2

The following selected transactions relate to investment activities of Ornamental Insulation Corporation. The company buys securities, *not* intending to profit from short-term differences in price and *not* necessarily to hold debt securities to maturity, but to have them available for sale when circumstances warrant. Ornamental's fiscal year ends on December 31. No investments were held by Ornamental on December 31, 2005.

**2006**

| | |
|---|---|
| Feb. 21 | Acquired Distribution Transformers Corporation common shares costing $400,000. |
| Mar. 18 | Received cash dividends of $8,000 on the investment in Distribution Transformers common shares. |
| Sep. 1 | Acquired $900,000 of American Instruments' 10% bonds at face value. |
| Oct. 20 | Sold the Distribution Transformers shares for $425,000. |
| Nov. 1 | Purchased M&D Corporation common shares costing $1,400,000. |
| Dec. 31 | Recorded any necessary adjusting entry(s) relating to the investments. The market prices of the investments are: |

| | |
|---|---|
| American Instruments bonds | $ 850,000 |
| M&D Corporation shares | $1,460,000 |

(Hint: Interest must be accrued for the American Instruments' bonds.)

**2007**

| | |
|---|---|
| Jan. 20 | Sold the M&D Corporation shares for $1,485,000. |
| Mar. 1 | Received semiannual interest of $45,000 on the investment in American Instruments bonds. |
| Aug. 12 | Acquired Vast Communication common shares costing $650,000. |
| Sept. 1 | Received semiannual interest of $45,000 on the investment in American Instruments bonds. |
| Dec. 31 | Recorded any necessary adjusting entry(s) relating to the investments. The market prices of the investments are: |

| | |
|---|---|
| Vast Communication shares | $670,000 |
| American Instruments bonds | $830,000 |

**Required:**

1. Prepare the appropriate journal entry for each transaction or event during 2006.
2. Indicate any amounts that Ornamental Insulation would report in its 2006 balance sheet and income statement as a result of these investments.
3. Prepare the appropriate journal entry for each transaction or event during 2007.
4. Indicate any amounts that Ornamental Insulation would report in its 2007 balance sheet and income statement as a result of these investments.

**P 12–4**
Various transactions relating to trading securities

● LO3

American Surety and Fidelity buys and sells securities expecting to earn profits on short-term differences in price. For the first 11 months of the year, gains from selling trading securities totaled $8 million, losses were $11 million, and the company had earned $5 million in investment revenue. The following selected transactions relate to American's trading account during December, 2006, and the first week of 2007. The company's fiscal year ends on December 31. No trading securities were held by American on December 1, 2006.

**2006**

Dec. 12 Purchased FF&G Corporation bonds for $12 million.
13 Purchased 2 million Ferry Intercommunications common shares for $22 million.
15 Sold the FF&G Corporation bonds for $12.1 million.
22 Purchased U.S. Treasury bills for $56 million and Treasury bonds for $65 million.
23 Sold half the Ferry Intercommunications common shares for $10 million.
26 Sold the U.S. Treasury bills for $57 million.
27 Sold the Treasury bonds for $63 million.
28 Received cash dividends of $200,000 from the Ferry Intercommunications common shares.
31 Recorded any necessary adjusting entry(s) and closing entries relating to the investments. The market price of the Ferry Intercommunications stock was $10 per share.

**2007**

Jan. 2 Sold the remaining Ferry Intercommunications common shares for $10.2 million.
5 Purchased Warehouse Designs Corporation bonds for $34 million.

**Required:**

1. Prepare the appropriate journal entry for each transaction or event during 2006.
2. Indicate any amounts that American would report in its 2006 balance sheet and income statement as a result of these investments.
3. Prepare the appropriate journal entry for each transaction or event during 2007.

**P 12–5**
Securities held-to-maturity, securities available for sale, and trading securities

● LO1 LO2 LO3

eXcel

Amalgamated General Corporation is a consulting firm that also offers financial services through its credit division. From time to time the company buys and sells securities intending to earn profits on short-term differences in price. The following selected transactions relate to Amalgamated's investment activities during the last quarter of 2006 and the first month of 2007. The only securities held by Amalgamated at October 1 were $30 million of 10% bonds of Kansas Abstractors, Inc. purchased on May 1 at face value. The company's fiscal year ends on December 31.

**2006**

Oct. 18 Purchased 2 million preferred shares of Millwork Ventures Company for $58 million as a speculative investment to be sold under suitable circumstances.
31 Received semiannual interest of $1.5 million from the Kansas Abstractors bonds.
Nov. 1 Purchased 10% bonds of Holistic Entertainment Enterprises at their $18 million face value, to be held until they mature in 2013. Semiannual interest is payable April 30 and October 31.
1 Sold the Kansas Abstractors bonds for $28 million because rising interest rates are expected to cause their fair value to continue to fall.
Dec. 1 Purchased 12% bonds of Household Plastics Corporation at their $60 million face value, to be held until they mature in 2023. Semiannual interest is payable May 31 and November 30.
20 Purchased U. S. Treasury bonds for $5.6 million as trading securities, hoping to earn profits on short-term differences in prices.
21 Purchased 4 million common shares of NXS Corporation for $44 million as trading securities, hoping to earn profits on short-term differences in prices.
23 Sold the Treasury bonds for $5.7 million.
29 Received cash dividends of $3 million from the Millwork Ventures Company preferred shares.
31 Recorded any necessary adjusting entry(s) and closing entries relating to the investments. The market price of the Millwork Ventures Company preferred stock was $27.50 per share and $11.50 per share for the NXS Corporation common. The fair values of the bond investments were $58.7 million for Household Plastics Corporation and $16.7 million for Holistic Entertainment Enterprises.

**2007**

Jan. 7 Sold the NXS Corporation common shares for $43 million.

**Required:**

Prepare the appropriate journal entry for each transaction or event.

**P 12–6**
Securities available-for-sale; fair value adjustment; reclassification adjustment
● LO2

At December 31, 2006, the investments in securities available-for-sale of Beale Developments were reported at $78 million:

| | | |
|---|---|---|
| Securities available-for-sale | $74 | |
| Plus: Fair value adjustment | 4 | $78 |

During the year, Beale sold its investment in Schwab Pharmaceuticals, which had cost $25 million, for $28 million. Those shares had a fair value at December 31, 2006, of $27 million. No other investments were sold. At December 31, 2007, the investments in securities available-for-sale included the cost and fair value amounts shown below.

| ($ in millions) Securities Available-for-Sale | Cost | Fair Value | Unrealized Gain (Loss) |
|---|---|---|---|
| Daisy Theaters, Inc. shares | $40 | $42 | $2 |
| Orpheum Entertainment bonds | 9 | 12 | 3 |
| Totals | $49 | $54 | $5 |

**Required:**

1. At what amount should Beale report its securities available-for-sale in its December 31, 2007, balance sheet?
2. What journal entry is needed to enable the investment to be reported at this amount?
3. What is the amount of the reclassification adjustment to 2007 other comprehensive income? Show how the reclassification adjustment should be reported.

**P 12–7**
Investment securities and equity method investments compared
● LO2 LO4 LO5 LO6
*eXcel*

On January 4, 2006, Runyan Bakery paid $324 million for 10 million shares of Lavery Labeling Company common stock. The investment represents a 30% interest in the net assets of Lavery and gave Runyan the ability to exercise significant influence over Lavery's operations. Runyan received dividends of $2.00 per share on December 15, 2006, and Lavery reported net income of $160 million for the year ended December 31, 2006. The market value of Lavery's common stock at December 31, 2006, was $31 per share. On the purchase date, the book value of Lavery's net assets was $800 million and:

a. The fair market value of Lavery's depreciable assets, with an average remaining useful life of six years, exceeded their book value by $80 million.
b. The remainder of the excess of the cost of the investment over the book value of net assets purchased was attributable to goodwill.

**Required:**

1. Prepare all appropriate journal entries related to the investment during 2006, assuming Runyan accounts for this investment by the equity method.
2. Prepare the journal entries required by Runyan, assuming that the 10 million shares represents a 10% interest in the net assets of Lavery rather than a 30% interest.

**P 12–8**
Equity method
● LO5 LO6
*eXcel*

Northwest Paperboard Company, a paper and allied products manufacturer, was seeking to gain a foothold in Canada. Toward that end, the company bought 40% of the outstanding common shares of Vancouver Timber and Milling, Inc. on January 2, 2006, for $400 million.

At the date of purchase, the book value of Vancouver's net assets was $775 million. The book values and fair values for all balance sheet items were the same except for inventory and plant facilities. The fair value exceeded book value by $5 million for the inventory and by $20 million for the plant facilities.

The estimated useful life of the plant facilities is 16 years. All inventory acquired was sold during 2006.

Vancouver reported net income of $140 million for the year ended December 31, 2006. Vancouver paid a cash dividend of $30 million.

**Required:**

1. Prepare all appropriate journal entries related to the investment during 2006.
2. What amount should Northwest report as its income from its investment in Vancouver for the year ended December 31, 2006?
3. What amount should Northwest report in its balance sheet as its investment in Vancouver?
4. What should Northwest report in its statement of cash flows regarding its investment in Vancouver?

**P 12–9**
Equity method
● LO5 LO6

On January 2, 2006, Miller Properties paid $19 million for 1 million shares of Marlon Company's 6 million outstanding common shares. Miller's CEO became a member of Marlon's board of directors during the first quarter of 2006.

The carrying amount of the Marlon's net assets was $66 million. Miller estimated the fair value of those net assets to be the same except for a patent valued at $24 million over cost. The remaining amortization period for the patent is 10 years.

Marlon reported earnings of $12 million and paid dividends of $6 million during 2006. On December 31, 2006, Marlon's common stock was trading on the NYSE at $18.50 per share.

**Required:**

1. When considering whether to account for its investment in Marlon under the equity method, what criteria should Miller's management apply?
2. Assume Miller accounts for its investment in Marlon using the equity method. Ignoring income taxes, determine the amounts related to the investment to be reported in its 2006:
   a. Income statement.
   b. Balance sheet.
   c. Statement of cash flows.

**P 12–10**
Classifying investments

● LO1 through LO5

Indicate (by letter) the way each of the investments listed below most likely should be accounted for based on the information provided.

| Item | Reporting Category |
|---|---|
| ____ 1. 35% of the nonvoting preferred stock of American Aircraft Company. | T. Trading securities |
| ____ 2. Treasury bills to be held to maturity. | M. Securities held-to-maturity |
| ____ 3. Two-year note receivable from affiliate. | A. Securities available-for-sale |
| ____ 4. Accounts receivable. | E. Equity method |
| ____ 5. Treasury bond maturing in one week. | C. Consolidation |
| ____ 6. Common stock held in trading account for immediate resale. | N. None of these |
| ____ 7. Bonds acquired to profit from short-term differences in price. | |
| ____ 8. 35% of the voting common stock of Computer Storage Devices Company. | |
| ____ 9. 90% of the voting common stock of Affiliated Peripherals, Inc. | |
| ____ 10. Corporate bonds of Primary Smelting Company to be sold if interest rates fall ½%. | |
| ____ 11. 25% of the voting common stock of Smith Foundries Corporation: 51% family-owned by Smith family; fair value determinable. | |
| ____ 12. 17% of the voting common stock of Shipping Barrels Corporation: Investor's CEO on the board of directors of Shipping Barrels Corporation. | |

**P 12–11**
Impairment of securities available-for-sale; troubled debt restructuring (Based on Appendix 12B)

● LO2

eXcel

At January 1, 2006, Rothschild Chair Company, Inc. was indebted to First Lincoln Bank under a $20 million, 10% unsecured note. The note was signed January 1, 2000, and was due December 31, 2009. Annual interest was last paid on December 31, 2004. Rothschild Chair Company was experiencing severe financial difficulties and negotiated a restructuring of the terms of the debt agreement.

**Required:**

Prepare all journal entries by First Lincoln Bank to record the restructuring and any remaining transactions relating to the debt under each of the independent circumstances below:

1. First Lincoln Bank agreed to settle the debt in exchange for land having a fair market value of $16 million but carried on Rothschild Chair Company's books at $13 million.
2. First Lincoln Bank agreed to (a) forgive the interest accrued from last year, (b) reduce the remaining four interest payments to $1 million each, and (c) reduce the principal to $15 million.
3. First Lincoln Bank agreed to defer all payments (including accrued interest) until the maturity date and accept $27,775,000 at that time in settlement of the debt.

## BROADEN YOUR PERSPECTIVE

**Apply your critical-thinking ability to the knowledge you've gained. These cases will provide you an opportunity to develop your research, analysis, judgment, and communication skills. You also will work with other students, integrate what you've learned, apply it in real world situations, and consider its global and ethical ramifications. This practice will broaden your knowledge and further develop your decision-making abilities.**

**Real World Case 12–1**
Sprint's investments

● LO2

The following disclosure note appeared in the 2004 annual report of the **Sprint Corporation**.

**Investments in Equity Securities (in part)**

The cost of investments in marketable equity securities, primarily consisting of **EarthLink** common stock, was $90 million and $134 million at year-end 2004 and 2003, respectively. Accumulated unrealized holding gains were $42 million (net of $25 million tax) at year-end 2004. Comparatively, at year-end 2003, the accumulated unrealized holding gains were $38 million (net of $23 million tax). Accumulated unrealized holding gains were included in Accumulated other comprehensive income (loss) on the Consolidated Balance Sheets.

At year-end 2004, Sprint held 12.3 million shares of EarthLink common stock, down from 18.9 million shares at year-end 2003. These securities were reflected in Other assets on the Consolidated Balance Sheets.

In the 2004 fourth quarter, . . . , 5.6 million shares were used to settle . . . forward contracts. Sprint sold an additional 1.0 million shares in the open market. Sprint recognized a $10.8 million gain on these transactions.

**Required:**

1. From the information provided by the disclosure note, determine the amount at which Sprint reported its investment in Earthlink common stock in its 2004 balance sheet.
2. What would have been Sprint's journal entry to reflect the 2004 fair value of the investments? Ignore taxes.
3. The note indicates that Sprint sold one million shares, producing a $10.8 million gain. Does this imply that the securities involved had not previously been adjusted to fair value? Why? What would have been the journal entry to record the sale of the one million shares in 2004 if we assume that $1.5 million of the gain pertained to those shares and that Sprint used the average cost method to determine the cost of the shares sold?

**Research Case 12–2**
Reporting securities available-for-sale; obtain and critically evaluate an annual report

● LO2

Investments in common stocks potentially affect each of the various financial statements as well as the disclosure notes that accompany those statements.

**Required:**

1. Locate a recent annual report of a public company that includes a footnote that describes an investment in securities available-for-sale. You can use EdgarScan at **edgarscan.pwcglobal.com**.
2. Under what caption are the investments reported in the comparative balance sheets? Are they reported as current or noncurrent assets?
3. Are realized gains or losses reported in the comparative income statements?
4. Are unrealized gains or losses reported in the comparative statements and shareholders' equity?
5. Are unrealized gains or losses identifiable in the comparative balance sheets? If so, under what caption? Why are unrealized gains or losses reported here rather than in the income statements?
6. Are cash flow effects of these investments reflected in the company's comparative statements of cash flows? If so, what information is provided by this disclosure?
7. Does the footnote provide information not available in the financial statements?

**Integrating Case 12–3**
How was the adoption of *SFAS 115* an exception to the usual method of accounting for changes in accounting principle?

● LO1 LO2 LO3

In Chapter 4 you learned that most changes in accounting principle require retrospective application of the new method in years prior to the change. Some changes mandated by new FASB accounting standards require neither of those approaches, and instead require or permit *prospective* application of the new standard. An example of this exception is *SFAS 115*, "Accounting for Certain Investments in Debt and Equity Securities." Recall that the standard requires that certain investments that previously were reported at lower of cost or market were required by the new standard to be reported instead at their fair values.

**Required:**

Explain how *SFAS 115* is an exception to the general method of accounting for changes in accounting principle.

**Trueblood Accounting Case 12–4**
Equity method

● LO2

The following Trueblood case is recommended for use with this chapter. The case provides an excellent opportunity for class discussion, group projects, and writing assignments. The case, along with Professor's Discussion Material, can be obtained from the Deloitte Foundation at its website: **www.deloitte.com/us/truebloodcases**.

**Case: 03–10: *Painless, Inc.***

This case gives students an opportunity to discuss whether and how the equity method should ever be applied to preferred stock investments.

**International Case 12–5**
Comparison of investment accounting in France and the United States

● LO1 through LO5

**Renault** is the largest automobile manufacturer in France. The investment disclosures accompanying financial statements in Renault's 2003 annual report are reproduced below:

**Accounting Policies (in part)**
*N. Securities*
**Equity securities**
Equity investments in non-consolidated companies are carried in the balance sheet at acquisition cost less any provisions. The corresponding dividends are recorded in the year of distribution.

Provisions are established when the value in use of the investments falls below acquisition cost. The value in use is determined on the basis of profitability prospects, the commercial outlets the investment represents for the Group, and the share in net assets.

**Debt securities**
Debt securities consist entirely of fixed-rate securities acquired to be held on a long-term basis, usually until maturity. They are hedged by interest rate futures for durable protection against foreign exchange exposure, or by long-term financing to ensure they can be held until maturity.

Discounts and premiums are spread over the remaining life of the security on a straight-line basis. Provisions for amortization are established when the issuer is likely to default.

**Marketable securities**
Marketable securities are valued at acquisition cost excluding related expenses and accrued interest for bonds, or at market value if this is lower.

**Required:**
On the basis of the information the disclosures provide, compare accounting for investments in France with that in the United States.

**Research Case 12–6**
Researching the way investments are reported; retrieving information from the Internet

● LO1 LO2 LO3

All publicly traded domestic companies use EDGAR, the Electronic Data Gathering, Analysis, and Retrieval system, to make the majority of their filings with the SEC. You can access EDGAR on the Internet at **www.sec.gov**, or you can use EdgarScan at **edgarscan.pwcglobal.com**.

**Required:**
1. Search for a public company with which you are familiar. Access its most recent 10-K filing. Search or scroll to find financial statements and related notes.
2. Answer the following questions. (If the chosen company does not report investments in the securities of other companies, choose another company.)
   a. What is the amount and classification of any investment securities reported in the balance sheet? Are unrealized gains or losses reported in the shareholders' equity section?
   b. Are any investments reported by the equity method?
   c. What amounts from these investments are reported in the comparative income statements? Has that income increased or decreased over the years reported?
   d. Are any acquisitions or disposals of investments reported in the statement of cash flows?

**Real World Case 12–7**
Merck's investments

● LO2

Corporations frequently invest in securities issued by other corporations. Some investments are acquired to secure a favorable business relationship with another company. On the other hand, others are intended only to earn an investment return from the dividends or interest the securities pay or from increases in the market prices of the securities—the same motivations that might cause you to invest in stocks, bonds, or other securities. This diversity in investment objectives means no single accounting method is adequate to report every investment.

**Merck & Co., Inc.** invests in securities of other companies. Access the most recent financial statements of Merck using EdgarScan (**edgarscan.pwcglobal.com/**).

**Required:**
1. What is the amount and classification of any investment securities reported on the balance sheet? In which current and noncurrent asset categories are investments reported by Merck? What criteria are used to determine the classifications?
2. How are unrealized gains or losses reported? realized gains and losses?
3. Are any investments reported by the equity method?
4. What amounts from these investments are reported in the comparative income statements?
5. Are cash flow effects of these investments reflected in the company's comparative statements of cash flows? If so, what information is provided by this disclosure?

**Real World Case 12–8**
Comprehensive income—Microsoft

● LO2

As required by *SFAS No. 115,* **Microsoft Corporation** reports its investments available-for-sale at the *fair value* of the investment securities. The *net* unrealized holding gain is not reported in the income statement. Instead, it's reported as part of Other comprehensive income in shareholders' equity.

Comprehensive income is a broader view of the change in shareholders' equity than traditional net income, encompassing all changes in equity from nonowner transactions. Microsoft chose to report its Other comprehensive income as a separate statement in a disclosure note in its 2004 annual report.

**Other Comprehensive Income**
The changes in the components of other comprehensive income are as follows:
($ in millions)

| Year Ended June 30 | 2002 | 2003 | 2004 |
|---|---|---|---|
| Net gains (losses) on derivative instruments | $ (91) | $ (102) | $ 101 |
| Net unrealized investment gains/(losses): | | | |
| Unrealized holding gains, net of tax effect of $(955) in 2002, $610 in 2003, and $(994) in 2004 | (1,774) | 1,132 | (1,846) |
| Reclassification adjustment for losses included in net income, net of tax effect of $958 in 2002, $60 in 2003, and $524 in 2004 | 1,779 | 111 | 973 |
| Net unrealized investment gains/(losses) | 5 | 1,243 | (873) |
| Translation adjustments and other | 82 | 116 | 51 |
| Other comprehensive income/(loss) | $ (4) | $1,257 | $ (721) |

**Required:**

1. The note indicates Unrealized holding losses during 2004 in the amount of $1,846 million. Is this the amount Microsoft would include as a separate component of shareholders' equity? Explain.
2. What does Microsoft mean by the term, "Reclassification adjustment for gains included in net income"?
3. Microsoft's disclosure note refers to "Translation adjustments and other." What might the "other" components of Other comprehensive income be?

## CPA SIMULATION 12–1

**Barbados Investments**
Investments

KAPLAN CPA Review

Test your knowledge of the concepts discussed in this chapter, practice critical professional skills necessary for career success, and prepare for the computer-based CPA exam by accessing our CPA simulations at the text website: **www.mhhe.com/spiceland4e**.

The Barbados Investments simulation tests your knowledge of a) the way we classify investment securities among the categories of trading securities, available-for-sale securities, and those held-to-maturity, b) how we account for those investments, c) the way accounting for investments affects comprehensive income, and d) the appropriate use of the equity method.

As on the CPA exam itself, you will be asked to use tools including a spreadsheet, a calculator, and professional accounting standards, to conduct research, derive solutions, and communicate conclusions related to these issues in a simulated environment headed by the following interactive tabs:

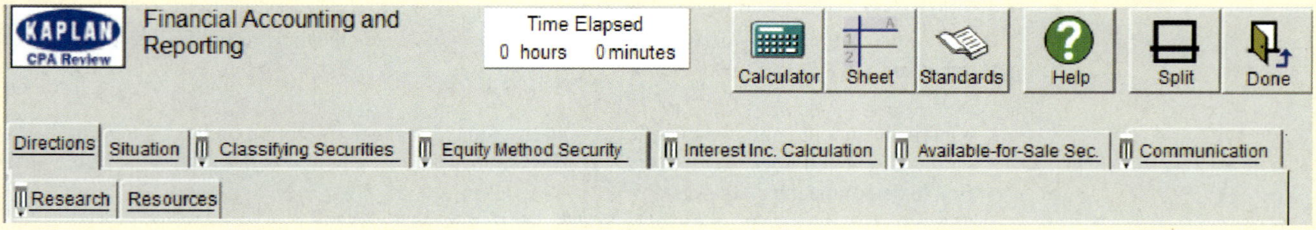

Specific tasks in the simulation include:

- Analyzing various transactions involving investment securities and determining their appropriate balance sheet classification.
- Applying judgment in the application of the equity method.
- Determining the amount of interest revenue to be reported from a debt investment.
- Demonstrating an understanding of comprehensive income and how it is affected by investments in securities.
- Communicating the way we account for investments using the equity method.
- Researching the financial reporting ramifications of changing the classification of investment securities.

13

CHAPTER

# Current Liabilities and Contingencies

## OVERVIEW

With the discussion of investments in Chapter 12, we concluded our six-chapter coverage of assets that began in Chapter 7. This is the first of six chapters devoted to liabilities. Here we focus on short-term liabilities. Bonds and long-term notes are discussed in Chapter 14. Obligations relating to leases, income taxes, pensions, and other postretirement benefits are the subjects of the following four chapters. In Part A of this chapter, we discuss liabilities that are classified appropriately as current. In Part B we turn our attention to situations in which there is uncertainty as to whether an obligation really exists. These are designated as loss contingencies.

## LEARNING OBJECTIVES

**After studying this chapter, you should be able to:**

- LO1 Define liabilities and distinguish between current and long-term liabilities.
- LO2 Account for the issuance and payment of various forms of notes and record the interest on the notes.
- LO3 Characterize accrued liabilities and liabilities from advance collection and describe when and how they should be recorded.
- LO4 Determine when a liability can be classified as a noncurrent obligation.
- LO5 Identify situations that constitute contingencies and the circumstances under which they should be accrued.
- LO6 Demonstrate the appropriate accounting treatment for contingencies, including unasserted claims and assessments.

# FINANCIAL REPORTING CASE

## Dinstuhl's Dad

"My dad is confused," your friend Buzz Dinstuhl proclaimed at the office one morning. "You see, we're competing against each other in that investment game I told you about, and one of his hot investments is Syntel Microsystems. When he got their annual report yesterday afternoon, he started analyzing it, you know, really studying it closely. Then he asked me about this part here." Buzz pointed to the current liability section of the balance sheet and related disclosure note:

SYNTEL MICROSYSTEMS, INC.
Balance Sheet
December 31, 2006 and 2005
($ in millions)

| Current Liabilities | 2006 | 2005 |
|---|---|---|
| Accounts payable | $233.5 | $241.6 |
| Short-term borrowings (Note 3) | 187.0 | 176.8 |
| Accrued liabilities | 65.3 | 117.2 |
| Accrued loss contingency | 76.9 | – |
| Other current liabilities | 34.6 | 45.2 |
| Current portion of long-term debt | 44.1 | 40.3 |
| Total current liabilities | $641.4 | $621.1 |

**Note 3: Short-Term Borrowings (in part)**
The components of short-term borrowings and their respective weighted average interest rates at the end of the period are as follows:

$ in millions

| | 2006 | | 2005 | |
|---|---|---|---|---|
| | Amount | Average Interest Rate | Amount | Average Interest Rate |
| Commercial paper | $ 34.0 | 5.2% | $ 27.1 | 5.3% |
| Bank loans | 218.0 | 5.5 | 227.7 | 5.6 |
| Amount reclassified to long-term liabilities | (65.0) | – | (78.0) | – |
| Total short-term borrowings | $187.0 | | $176.8 | |

The Company maintains bank credit lines sufficient to cover outstanding short-term borrowings. As of December 31, 2006, the Company had $200.0 million fee-paid lines available.

At December 31, 2006 and 2005, the Company classified $65.0 million and $78.0 million, respectively, of commercial paper and bank notes as long-term debt. The Company has the intent and ability, through formal renewal agreements, to renew these obligations into future periods.

(continued)

(concluded)

**Note 6: Contingencies (in part)**
Between 2004 and 2005, the Company manufactured cable leads that, the Company has learned, contribute to corrosion of linked components with which they are installed. At December 31, 2006, the Company accrued $132.0 million in anticipation of remediation and claims settlement deemed probable, of which $76.9 million is considered a current liability.

"So, what's the problem?" you asked.

"Well, he thinks I'm some sort of financial wizard because I'm in the business."

"And because you tell him so all the time," you interrupted.

"Maybe so, but he's been told that current liabilities are riskier than long-term liabilities, and now he's focusing on that. He can't see why some long-term debt is reported here in the current section. And it also looks like some is reported the other way around; some current liabilities reported as long term. Plus, the contingency amount seems like it's not even a contractual liability. Then he wants to know what some of those terms mean. Lucky for me, I had to leave before I had to admit I didn't know the answers. You're the accounting graduate; help me out."

**By the time you finish this chapter, you should be able to respond appropriately to the questions posed in this case. Compare your response to the solution provided at the end of the chapter.**

## QUESTIONS

1. What are accrued liabilities? What is commercial paper? (page 617)
2. Why did Syntel Microsystems include some long-term debt in the current liability section? (page 622)
3. Did they also report some current amounts as long-term debt? Explain. (page 623)
4. Must obligations be known contractual debts in order to be reported as liabilities? (page 626)
5. Is it true that current liabilities are riskier than long-term liabilities? (page 636)

# PART A CURRENT LIABILITIES

**Liabilities and owners' equity accounts represent specific sources of a company's assets.**

Before a business can invest in an asset it first must acquire the money to pay for it. This can happen in either of two ways—funds can be provided by owners or the funds must be borrowed. You may recognize this as a description of the basic accounting equation: liabilities and owners' equity on the right-hand side of the equation represent the two basic sources of the assets on the left-hand side. You studied assets in the chapters leading to this one and you will study owners' equity later. This chapter and the next four describe the various liabilities that constitute creditors' claims on a company's assets.

## Characteristics of Liabilities

Entities routinely incur most liabilities to acquire the funds, goods, and services they need to operate and just as routinely settle the liabilities they incur.[1]

**Most liabilities obligate the debtor to pay cash at specified times and result from legally enforceable agreements.**

You already know what liabilities are. You encounter them every day. The multibillion dollar national debt we hear discussed almost daily is a liability of all of us. Our creditors are the individuals and institutions that have bought debt securities from (loaned money to) our government. Similarly, when businesses issue notes and bonds, their creditors are the banks, individuals, and organizations that exchange cash for those securities. If you are paying for a car or a home with monthly payments, you have a personal liability. Each of these obligations represents the most common type of liability—one to be

[1] "Elements of Financial Statements," *Statement of Financial Accounting Concepts No. 6* (Stamford, Conn.: FASB, 1985), par. 38.

paid in cash and for which the amount and timing are specified by a legally enforceable contract.

However, to be reported as a **liability,** an obligation need not be payable in cash. Instead, it may require the company to transfer other assets or to provide services. It also need not be represented by a written agreement nor be legally enforceable. Even the amount and timing of repayment need not be precisely known. From a financial reporting perspective, a liability has three essential characteristics. Liabilities:

**Some liabilities are not contractual obligations and may not be payable in cash.**

LO1

1. Are *probable, future* sacrifices of economic benefits.
2. Arise from *present* obligations (to transfer goods or provide services) to other entities.
3. Result from *past* transactions or events.[2]

Notice that the definition of a liability involves the present, the future, and the past. It is a present responsibility to sacrifice assets in the future because of a transaction or other event that already has happened.

Later in the chapter we'll discuss several liabilities that possess these characteristics but have elements of uncertainty regarding the amount and timing of payments and sometimes even their existence.

## What Is a Current Liability?

In a classified balance sheet, liabilities are categorized as either **current liabilities** or long-term liabilities. Listing financial statement elements by classification provides additional clarification concerning the nature of those elements. In the case of liabilities, the additional information provided by the classification relates to their relative riskiness. Will payment require the use of current assets and reduce the amount of liquid funds available for other uses? If so, are sufficient liquid funds available to pay currently maturing obligations in addition to meeting current operating needs? Or is the due date comfortably in the future, permitting resources to be used for other purposes without risking default or without compromising operating efficiency? Classifying liabilities as either current or long term helps investors and creditors assess the riskiness of a business's obligations in this regard. In this chapter, we focus on current liabilities. The next three chapters address liabilities classified as long term.

**Classifying liabilities as either current or long term helps investors and creditors assess the relative risk of a business's liabilities.**

We often characterize current liabilities as obligations payable within one year or within the firm's operating cycle, whichever is longer. This general definition usually applies. However, a more discriminating definition identifies current liabilities as those expected to be satisfied with *current assets* or by the creation of other *current liabilities.*[3]

***Current liabilities* are expected to require current assets and usually are payable within one year.**

As you study the liabilities discussed in this chapter, you should be aware that a practical expediency usually affects the way current liabilities are reported on the balance sheet. Conceptually, liabilities should be recorded at their present values. In other words, the amount recorded is the present value of all anticipated future cash payments resulting from the debt (specifically, principal and interest payments). This is due to the time value of money.[4] However, in practice, liabilities payable within one year ordinarily are recorded instead at their maturity amounts.[5] The inconsistency usually is inconsequential because the relatively short-term maturity of current liabilities makes the interest or time value component immaterial.

**Current liabilities ordinarily are reported at their maturity amounts.**

The most common obligations reported as current liabilities are accounts payable, notes payable, commercial paper, income tax liability, accrued liabilities, and contingencies. Liabilities related to income taxes are the subject of Chapter 16. We discuss the others here.

Before we examine specific current liabilities, let's use the current liability section of the balance sheet of **General Mills, Inc.,** and related disclosure notes to overview the chapter and to provide perspective on the liabilities we discuss (Graphic 13–1).

[2]Ibid.

[3]Committee on Accounting Procedure, American Institute of CPAs, *Accounting Research and Terminology Bulletin, Final Edition* (New York: AICPA, August 1961), p. 21.

[4]You learned the concept of the time value of money and the mechanics of present value calculations in Chapter 6.

[5]In fact, those arising in connection with suppliers in the normal course of business and due within a year are specifically exempted from present value reporting by "Interest on Receivables and Payables," *Accounting Principles Board Opinion No. 21* (New York: AICPA, August 1971), par. 3.

**GRAPHIC 13–1**

Current Liabilities—General Mills

**In practice, there is little uniformity regarding precise captions used to describe current liabilities or in the extent to which accounts are combined into summary captions. These are representative and fairly typical.**

**Amounts reported on the face of the balance sheet seldom are sufficient to adequately describe current liabilities. Additional descriptions are provided in disclosure notes.**

**GENERAL MILLS, INC.**
**Excerpt from Balance Sheet** ($ in millions)
**May 30, 2004 and May 25, 2003**

**Liabilities**

| **Current Liabilities:** | **2004** | **2003** |
|---|---|---|
| Accounts payable | $1,145 | $1,303 |
| Current portion of long-term debt | 233 | 105 |
| Notes payable | 583 | 1,236 |
| Other current liabilities | 796 | 800 |
| Total current liabilities | $2,757 | $3,444 |

**8. Notes Payable**

The components of notes payable and their respective weighted average interest rates at the end of the period are as follows:

| | **2004** | | **2003** | |
|---|---|---|---|---|
| Dollars in millions: | **Note Payable** | **Weighted Average Interest Rate** | **Note Payable** | **Weighted Average Interest Rate** |
| U.S. commercial paper | $441 | 1.2% | $1,415 | 1.4% |
| Canadian commercial paper | 159 | 2.1 | 28 | 3.3 |
| Euro commercial paper | 499 | 2.1 | 527 | 1.5 |
| Financial institutions | 234 | 6.7 | 366 | 1.4 |
| Amount reclassified to long-term debt | (750) | — | (1,100) | — |
| Total notes payable | $583 | | $1,236 | |

To ensure availability of funds, we maintain bank credit lines sufficient to cover our outstanding short-term borrowings. As of May 30, 2004, we had $1.85 billion fee-paid lines and $264 million uncommitted, no-fee lines available in the U.S. and Canada.

In the third quarter of fiscal 2004, we entered into an agreement for a new $750 million credit facility, expiring in January 2009. That facility replaced a $1.1 billion, 364-day facility, which expired January 22, 2004. The new credit facility, along with our existing $1.1 billion multiyear facility that expires January 2006, brings our total committed back-up credit amount to $1.85 billion. These revolving credit agreements provide us with the ability to refinance short-term borrowings on a long-term basis; accordingly, a portion of our notes payable has been reclassified to long-term debt.

You may want to refer back to portions of Graphic 13–1 as corresponding liabilities are described later in the chapter. We discuss accounts payable and notes payable first.

# Open Accounts and Notes

Many businesses buy merchandise or supplies on credit. Most also find it desirable to borrow cash from time to time to finance their activities. In this section we discuss the liabilities these borrowing activities create: namely, trade accounts and trade notes, bank loans, and commercial paper.

## ACCOUNTS PAYABLE AND TRADE NOTES PAYABLE

**Buying merchandise on account in the ordinary course of business creates *accounts payable.***

**Accounts payable** are obligations to suppliers of merchandise or of services purchased on *open account.* Most trade credit is offered on open account. This means that the only formal credit instrument is the invoice. Because the time until payment usually is short (often 30, 45, or 60 days), these liabilities typically are noninterest-bearing and are reported at their face amounts. As shown in Graphic 13–1, General Mills's largest current liability in 2004 was accounts payable, $1,145 million. The key accounting considerations relating to accounts payable are determining their existence and ensuring that they are recorded in the appropriate accounting period. You studied these issues and learned how cash discounts are handled during your study of inventories in Chapter 8.

**Trade notes payable** differ from accounts payable in that they are formally recognized by a written promissory note. Often these are of a somewhat longer term than open accounts and sometimes they bear interest.

**About 30% of General Mills's current liabilities are in the form of trade credit.**

## SHORT-TERM NOTES PAYABLE

The most common way for a corporation to obtain temporary financing is to arrange a short-term bank loan. When a company borrows cash from a bank and signs a promissory note (essentially an IOU), the firm's liability is reported as *notes payable* (sometimes *bank loans* or *short-term borrowings*). About two-thirds of bank loans are short term, but because many are routinely renewed, some tend to resemble long-term debt. In fact, in some cases we report them as long-term financing (as you'll see later in the chapter).

Very often, smaller firms are unable to tap into the major sources of long-term financing to the extent necessary to provide for their capital needs. So they must rely heavily on short-term financing. Even large companies typically utilize short-term debt as a significant and indispensable component of their capital structure. One reason is that short-term funds usually offer lower interest rates than long-term debt. Perhaps most importantly, corporations desire flexibility. As a rule, managers want as many financing alternatives as possible.

**Credit Lines.** Usually short-term bank loans are arranged under an existing **line of credit** with a bank or group of banks. These can be noncommitted or committed lines of credit. A *noncommitted* line of credit is an informal agreement that permits a company to borrow up to a prearranged limit without having to follow formal loan procedures and paperwork. Banks sometimes require the company to maintain a compensating balance on deposit with the bank, say, 5% of the line of credit.[6] The 2004 annual report of **Kerr-McGee Corporation** illustrates a noncommitted line of credit (Graphic 13–2).

**A *line of credit* allows a company to borrow cash without having to follow formal loan procedures and paperwork.**

**Note 9: Debt (in part)**
At year-end 2004, the company had available unused bank lines of credit and revolving credit facilities of $1.55 billion. The company has arrangements to maintain compensating balances with certain banks that provide credit.

**GRAPHIC 13–2**
Disclosure of Credit Lines—Kerr-McGee Corporation

A *committed* line of credit is a more formal agreement that usually requires the firm to pay a commitment fee to the bank. A typical annual commitment fee is ¼% of the total committed funds. Banks often require smaller firms to keep compensating balances in the bank. A disclosure note in the 2004 annual report of the **Walgreen Co.** describes a committed line of credit as shown in Graphic 13–3.

**A *committed* line of credit is a formal arrangement usually requiring a commitment fee and sometimes a compensating balance.**

**Short-Term Borrowings (in part)**
At August 31, 2004, the company had a syndicated bank line of credit facility of $200 million to support the company's short-term commercial paper program. The company pays a nominal facility fee to the financing bank to keep this line of credit facility active.

**GRAPHIC 13–3**
Disclosure of Committed Line of Credit—Walgreen Company

General Mills's disclosure notes that we looked at in Graphic 13–1 indicate that the company has both noncommitted and committed lines of credit.

[6] A compensating balance is a deposit kept by a company in a low-interest or noninterest-bearing account at the bank. The required deposit usually is some percentage of the committed amount or the amount used (say, 2% to 5%). The effect of the compensating balance is to increase the borrower's effective interest rate and the bank's effective rate of return.

**Interest.** When a company borrows money, it pays the lender **interest** in return for using the lender's money during the term of the loan. You might think of the interest as the "rent" paid for using money. Interest is stated in terms of a percentage rate to be applied to the face amount of the loan. Because the stated rate typically is an annual rate, when calculating interest for a short-term note we must adjust for the fraction of the annual period the loan spans. Interest on notes is calculated as:

Face amount × Annual rate × Time to maturity

This is demonstrated in Illustration 13–1.

**ILLUSTRATION 13–1**
Note Issued for Cash

● LO2

Interest on notes is calculated as:
Face amount × Annual rate × Time to maturity

On May 1, Affiliated Technologies, Inc., a consumer electronics firm borrowed $700,000 cash from First BancCorp under a noncommitted short-term line of credit arrangement and issued a six-month, 12% promissory note. Interest was payable at maturity.

| | | |
|---|---|---|
| **May 1** | | |
| Cash | 700,000 | |
| Notes payable | | 700,000 |
| **November 1** | | |
| Interest expense ($700,000 × 12% × 6/12) | 42,000 | |
| Notes payable | 700,000 | |
| Cash ($700,000 + 42,000) | | 742,000 |

Sometimes a bank loan assumes the form of a so-called **noninterest-bearing note.** Obviously, though, no bank will lend money without interest. Noninterest-bearing loans actually do bear interest, but the interest is deducted (or discounted) from the face amount to determine the cash proceeds made available to the borrower at the outset. For example, the preceding note could be packaged as a $700,000 noninterest-bearing note, with a 12% discount rate. In that case, the $42,000 interest would be discounted at the outset, rather than explicitly stated:[7]

The proceeds of the note are reduced by the interest in a noninterest-bearing note.

| | | |
|---|---|---|
| **May 1** | | |
| Cash (difference) | 658,000 | |
| Discount on notes payable ($700,000 × 12% × 6/12) | 42,000 | |
| Notes payable (face amount) | | 700,000 |
| **November 1** | | |
| Interest expense | 42,000 | |
| Discount on notes payable | | 42,000 |
| Notes payable (face amount) | 700,000 | |
| Cash | | 700,000 |

Notice that the amount borrowed under this arrangement is only $658,000, but the interest is calculated as the discount rate times the $700,000 face amount. This causes the *effective* interest rate to be higher than the 12% stated rate:

When interest is discounted from the face amount of a note, the effective interest rate is higher than the stated discount rate.

$$\frac{\$42{,}000 \text{ Interest for 6 months}}{\$658{,}000 \text{ Amount borrowed}} = 6.38\% \text{ Rate for 6 months}$$

[7]Be sure to understand that we are actually recording the note at $658,000, not $700,000, but are recording the interest portion separately in a contra-liability account, discount on notes payable. The entries shown reflect the gross method. By the net method, the interest component is netted against the face amount of the note as follows:

| | | |
|---|---|---|
| **May 1** | | |
| Cash | 658,000 | |
| Notes payable | | 658,000 |
| **November 1** | | |
| Interest expense ($700,000 × 12% × 6/12) | 42,000 | |
| Notes payable | 658,000 | |
| Cash | | 700,000 |

To annualize:

$$6.38\% \times 12/6 = 12.76\% \text{ Effective interest rate}$$

We studied short-term notes from the perspective of the lender (note receivable) in Chapter 7.

**Secured Loans.** Sometimes short-term loans are *secured,* meaning a specified asset of the borrower is pledged as collateral or security for the loan. Although many kinds of assets can be pledged, the secured loans most frequently encountered in practice are secured by inventory or accounts receivable. For example, **Collins Industries, Inc.,** which sells vehicle chassis to major vehicle manufacturers, disclosed the secured notes described in Graphic 13–4.

**Inventory or accounts receivable often are pledged as security for short-term loans.**

**Note 4: Chassis Floorplan Notes Payable (in part)**
Chassis floorplan notes are payable to a financing subsidiary of a chassis manufacturer. These notes are secured by the related chassis and are payable upon the earlier of the date the Company sells the chassis or 180 days from the date of the note.

**GRAPHIC 13–4**
Disclosure of Notes Secured by Inventory—Collins Industries, Inc.

When accounts receivable serve as collateral, we refer to the arrangement as *pledging* accounts receivable. Sometimes, the receivables actually are sold outright to a finance company as a means of short-term financing. This is called *factoring* receivables.[8]

## COMMERCIAL PAPER

Some large corporations obtain temporary financing by issuing **commercial paper,** often purchased by other companies as a short-term investment. Commercial paper refers to unsecured notes sold in minimum denominations of $25,000 with maturities ranging from 30 to 270 days (beyond 270 days the firm would be required to file a registration statement with the SEC). Interest often is discounted at the issuance of the note. Usually commercial paper is issued directly to the buyer (lender) and is backed by a line of credit with a bank (see the **Walgreens** disclosure note in Graphic 13–3). This allows the interest rate to be lower than in a bank loan. Commercial paper has become an increasingly popular way for large companies to raise funds, the total amount having expanded over fivefold in the last decade.

**Large, highly rated firms sometimes sell *commercial paper* to borrow funds at a lower rate than through a bank loan.**

**FINANCIAL REPORTING CASE**
Q1, p. 612

**GLOBAL PERSPECTIVE**

The financial market is becoming increasingly multinational. World markets have grown dramatically in the last decade. The commercial unification of European countries, the introduction of the Euro, and the fall of communism in portions of Europe and Asia are both causes and symptoms of the heightened globalization of the capital marketplace.

Companies wishing to reduce their exposure to risk and to widen their choices of funding sources are taking advantage of the broader opportunities the global environment provides. Increasingly, U.S. corporate debt is displaying a multinational dimension, with statements of financial position often reporting short-term to intermediate-term loans in several different countries. Loans from foreign banks that are denominated in dollars are called Eurodollar loans. Also, foreign loans frequently are denominated in the currency of the lender (Swiss franc, Euro, and so on). When loans must be repaid in foreign currencies a new element of risk is introduced. This is because if exchange rates change, the number of dollars representing the foreign currency that must be repaid differs from the number of dollars representing the foreign currency borrowed. We discuss hedging against this risk exposure in the previous chapter and in Appendix A at the back of the book.[9]

**Corporations often have loans from banks in many different countries.**

[8]Both methods of accounts receivable financing were discussed in Chapter 7, "Cash and Receivables."

[9]Elsewhere in your accounting curriculum, often in advanced accounting, you will learn how foreign-currency-denominated loans are translated into dollars in U.S. financial statements.

The name *commercial paper* refers to the fact that a paper certificate traditionally is issued to the lender to signify the obligation, although there is a trend toward total computerization of paper sold directly to the lender so that no paper is created. Since commercial paper is a form of notes payable, recording its issuance and payment is exactly the same as our earlier illustration.

In a statement of cash flows, the cash a company receives from using notes to borrow funds as well as the cash it uses to repay the notes are reported among cash flows from financing activities. Most of the other liabilities we study in this chapter are integrally related to a company's primary operations and thus are part of operating activities. We discuss long-term notes in the next chapter.

## Accrued Liabilities

● LO3

**Accrued liabilities** represent expenses already incurred but not yet paid (accrued expenses). These liabilities are recorded by adjusting entries at the end of the reporting period, prior to preparing financial statements. You learned how to record accrued liabilities in your study of introductory accounting and you reinforced your understanding in Chapter 2. Common examples are salaries and wages payable, income taxes payable, and interest payable.

### ACCRUED INTEREST PAYABLE

Liabilities accrue for expenses that are incurred but not yet paid.

Accrued interest payable arises in connection with notes like those discussed earlier in this chapter (as well as other forms of debt). For example, to continue Illustration 13–1, let's assume the fiscal period for Affiliated Technologies ends on June 30, two months after the six-month note is issued. The issuance of the note, intervening adjusting entry, and note payment would be recorded as shown in Illustration 13–1A.

**ILLUSTRATION 13–1A**

Note with Accrued Interest

At June 30, two months' interest has accrued and is recorded to avoid misstating expenses and liabilities on the June 30 financial statements.

| | | |
|---|---|---|
| **Issuance of Note on May 1** | | |
| Cash | 700,000 | |
| Note payable | | 700,000 |
| **Accrual of Interest on June 30** | | |
| Interest expense ($700,000 × 12% × 2/12) | 14,000 | |
| Interest payable | | 14,000 |
| **Note Payment on November 1** | | |
| Interest expense ($700,000 × 12% × 4/12) | 28,000 | |
| Interest payable (from adjusting entry) | 14,000 | |
| Note payable | 700,000 | |
| Cash ($700,000 + 42,000) | | 742,000 |

### SALARIES, COMMISSIONS, AND BONUSES

Compensation for employee services can be in the form of hourly wages, salary, commissions, bonuses, stock compensation plans, or pensions.[10] Accrued liabilities arise in connection with compensation expense when employee services have been performed as of a financial statement date, but employees have yet to be paid. These accrued expenses/accrued liabilities are recorded by adjusting entries at the end of the reporting period, prior to preparing financial statements.

**Vacations, Sick Days, and Other Paid Future Absences.** Suppose a firm grants two weeks of paid vacation each year to nonsalaried employees. Some take their vacations during the year earned and are compensated then. Some wait. Is the compensation an expense during the year earned for only those who actually are paid that year for their absence? When you recall what you've learned about accrual accounting, you probably conclude otherwise.

[10]Pensions are discussed in Chapter 17, and stock-based compensation plans are discussed in Chapter 19.

An employer should accrue an expense and the related liability for employees' compensation for future absences (such as vacation pay) if the obligation meets four conditions. These conditions, all of which must be met for accrual, are listed in Graphic 13–5.

**GRAPHIC 13–5**
Conditions for Accrual of Paid Future Absences

1. The obligation is attributable to employees' services already performed.
2. The paid absence can be taken in a later year—the benefit vests (will be compensated even if employment is terminated) or the benefit can be accumulated over time.
3. Payment is probable.
4. The amount can be reasonably estimated.

If these conditions look familiar, it's because they are simply the characteristics of a liability we discussed earlier, adapted to relate to a potential obligation for future absences of employees. Also, be sure to recognize the consistency of these conditions with accruing loss contingencies only when the obligation is both (a) probable and (b) can be reasonably estimated. The situation is demonstrated in Illustration 13–2.

**ILLUSTRATION 13–2**
Paid Future Absences

Davidson-Getty Chemicals has 8,000 employees. Each employee earns two weeks of paid vacation per year. Vacation time not taken in the year earned can be carried over to subsequent years. During 2006, 2,500 employees took both weeks' vacation, but at the end of the year, 5,500 employees had vacation time carryovers as follows:

| Employees | Vacation Weeks Earned but Not Taken | Total Carryover Weeks |
|---|---|---|
| 2,500 | 0 | 0 |
| 2,000 | 1 | 2,000 |
| 3,500 | 2 | 7,000 |
| 8,000 | | 9,000 |

During 2006, compensation averaged $600 a week per employee.

**When Vacations Were Taken in 2006**

| | | |
|---|---|---|
| Salaries and wages expense (2,500 × 2 wks. × $600) + (2,000 × 1 wk. × $600) | 4,200,000 | |
| Cash (or wages payable) | | 4,200,000 |

**December 31, 2006 (adjusting entry)**

| | | |
|---|---|---|
| Salaries and wages expense (9,000 carryover weeks × $600) | 5,400,000 | |
| Liability—compensated future absences | | 5,400,000 |

When the necessary conditions are met, compensated future absences are accrued in the year the compensation is earned.

The liability for paid absences usually is accrued at the existing wage rate rather than at a rate estimated to be in effect when absences occur.[11] So, if wage rates have risen, the difference between the accrual and the amount paid increases compensation expense that year. For example, let's assume all the carryover vacation time is taken in 2007 and the actual amount paid to employees is $5,700,000:

**When Year 2006 Vacations Are Taken in 2007**

| | | |
|---|---|---|
| Liability—compensated future absences (account balance) | 5,400,000 | |
| Salaries and wages expense (difference) | 300,000 | |
| Cash (or salaries and wages payable) (given) | | 5,700,000 |

[11] Actually, *SFAS 43* is silent on how the liability should be measured. In practice, most companies choose the current rate because it avoids estimates and usually produces a lower expense and liability.

Customary practice should be considered when deciding whether an obligation exists.

Company policy and actual practice should be considered when deciding whether the rights to payment for absences have been earned by services already rendered. Consider an illustrative situation. Suppose scientists in a private laboratory are eligible for paid sabbaticals every seven years. Should a liability be accrued at the end of a scientist's sixth year? No—if sabbatical leave is granted only to perform research beneficial to the employer. Yes—if past practice indicates that sabbatical leave is intended to provide unrestricted compensated absence for past service and other conditions are met.

Custom and practice also influence whether unused rights to paid absences expire or can be carried forward. Obviously, if rights vest (payable even if employment is terminated) they haven't expired. But holiday time, military leave, maternity leave, and jury time typically do not accumulate if unused, so a liability for those benefits usually is not accrued. On the other hand, if it's customary that a particular paid absence, say holiday time, can be carried forward—if employees work on holidays, in this case—a liability is accrued if it's probable that employees will be compensated in a future year.

Accrual of sick pay is not required, but is permitted.

Interestingly, sick pay quite often meets the conditions for accrual but is specifically excluded by *SFAS 43,* "Accounting for Compensated Absences," from mandatory accrual. Its exclusion is because future absence depends on future illness, which usually is not a certainty. However, similar to other forms of paid absences, the decision of whether to accrue nonvesting sick pay should be based on actual policy and practice. If company policy or custom is that employees are paid sick pay even when their absences are not due to illness, it's appropriate to record a liability for unused sick pay. For example, some companies routinely allow unused sick pay benefits to be accumulated and paid at retirement (or to beneficiaries if death comes before retirement). If each condition is met except that the company finds it impractical to reasonably estimate the amount of compensation for future absences, a disclosure note should describe the situation.

A wide variety of bonus plans provide compensation tied to performance other than stock prices.

Bonuses sometimes take the place of permanent annual raises.

**Annual Bonuses.** Sometimes compensation packages include annual bonuses tied to performance objectives designed to provide incentive to executives. The most common performance measures are earnings per share, net income, and operating income, each being used by about a quarter of firms having bonus plans. Nonfinancial performance measures, such as customer satisfaction and product or service quality, also are used by about 13% of these firms.[12] In recent years, **annual bonuses** have been gaining in use, not just for executives, but for nonmanagerial personnel as well. Unfortunately for employees, bonuses often take the place of annual raises. This allows a company to increase employee pay without permanently locking in the increases in salaries. Bonuses are compensation expense of the period they are earned.

## Liabilities from Advance Collections

Liabilities are created when amounts are received that will be returned or remitted to others. Deposits and advances from customers and collections for third parties are cases in point.

### DEPOSITS AND ADVANCES FROM CUSTOMERS

Collecting cash from a customer as a refundable deposit or as an advance payment for products or services creates a liability to return the deposit or to supply the products or services.[13]

**Refundable Deposits.** In some businesses it's typical to require customers to pay cash as a deposit that will be refunded when a specified event occurs. You probably have encountered such situations. When apartments are rented, security or damage deposits often are collected. Utility companies frequently collect deposits when service is begun. Similarly, deposits sometimes are required on returnable containers, to be refunded when the containers are returned. The situation is demonstrated in Illustration 13–3.

[12] C. D. Ittner, D. F. Larker, and M. V. Rajan, "The Choice of Performance Measures in Annual Bonus Contracts," Working Paper, The Wharton School, University of Pennsylvania (August 1995).

[13] *SFAC 6* specifically identifies customer advances and deposits as liabilities under the definition provided in that statement. "Elements of Financial Statements," *Statement of Financial Accounting Concepts No. 6* (Stamford, CT: FASB, 1985), par. 197.

**ILLUSTRATION 13–3**
Refundable Deposits

Rancor Chemical Company sells combustible chemicals in expensive, reusable containers. Customers are charged a deposit for each container delivered and receive a refund when the container is returned. Deposits collected on containers delivered during the year were $300,000. Deposits are forfeited if containers are not returned within one year. Ninety percent of the containers were returned within the allotted time. Deposits charged are twice the actual cost of containers. The inventory of containers remains on the company's books until deposits are forfeited.

| | | |
|---|---|---|
| **When Deposits Are Collected** | | |
| Cash | 300,000 | |
| Liability—refundable deposits | | 300,000 |
| **When Containers Are Returned*** | | |
| Liability—refundable deposits | 270,000 | |
| Cash | | 270,000 |
| **When Deposits Are Forfeited*** | | |
| Liability—refundable deposits | 30,000 | |
| Revenue—sale of containers | | 30,000 |
| Cost of goods sold | 15,000 | |
| Inventory of containers | | 15,000 |

When a deposit becomes nonrefundable, inventory should be reduced to reflect the fact that the containers won't be returned.

*Of course, not all containers are returned at the same time, nor does the allotted return period expire at the same time for all containers not returned. These entries summarize the several individual returns and forfeitures.

**Advances from Customers.** At times, businesses require advance payments from customers that will be applied to the purchase price when goods are delivered or services provided. Gift certificates, magazine subscriptions, layaway deposits, special order deposits, and airline tickets are examples. These customer advances represent liabilities until the related product or service is provided. For instance, one of the largest liabilities reported by **Readers Digest Association, Inc.,** is deferred revenue from the sale of magazine subscriptions ($403 million in 2004). Advances are demonstrated in Illustration 13–4.

**ILLUSTRATION 13–4**
Customer Advance

Tomorrow Publications collects magazine subscriptions from customers at the time subscriptions are sold. Subscription revenue is recognized over the term of the subscription. Tomorrow collected $20 million in subscription sales during its first year of operations. At December 31, the average subscription was one-fourth expired.

| | ($ in millions) | |
|---|---|---|
| **When Advance Is Collected** | | |
| Cash | 20 | |
| Unearned subscriptions revenue | | 20 |
| **When Product Is Delivered** | | |
| Unearned subscriptions revenue | 5 | |
| Subscriptions revenue | | 5 |

A customer advance produces an obligation that is satisfied when the product or service is provided.

The **New York Times Company** described its recognition of revenue from newspaper subscriptions in the disclosure note shown in Graphic 13–6.

**GRAPHIC 13–6**
Disclosure of Advances from Customers—The New York Times Company

**Note 1: Summary of Significant Accounting Policies (in part)**
Proceeds from subscriptions are deferred at the times of sale as unexpired subscriptions and are included in revenues on a pro rata basis over the terms of the subscriptions.

Like refundable deposits, customer advances forfeited (for instance, gift certificates not redeemed) create revenue when they are deemed forfeited. Liability accounts produced by customer deposits and advances are classified as current or long-term liabilities depending on when the obligation is expected to be satisfied.

### COLLECTIONS FOR THIRD PARTIES

Companies often make collections for third parties from customers or from employees and periodically remit these amounts to the appropriate governmental (or other) units. Amounts collected this way represent liabilities until remitted.

Sales taxes collected from customers represent liabilities until remitted.

An example is sales taxes. For illustration, assume a state sales tax rate of 4% and local sales tax rate of 3%. Adding the tax to a $100 sale creates a $7 liability until the tax is paid:

| | | |
|---|---|---|
| Cash (or accounts receivable) | 107 | |
| Sales revenue | | 100 |
| Sales taxes payable ([4% + 3%] × $100) | | 7 |

Amounts collected from employees in connection with payroll also represent liabilities until remitted.

Payroll-related deductions such as withholding taxes, Social Security taxes, employee insurance, employee contributions to retirement plans, and union dues also create current liabilities until the amounts collected are paid to appropriate parties. These payroll-related liabilities are explored further in the appendix to this chapter.

Although recorded in separate liability accounts, accrued liabilities usually are combined and reported under a single caption or perhaps two accrued liability captions in the balance sheet.

## A Closer Look at the Current and Noncurrent Classification

● LO4

Given a choice, do you suppose management would prefer to report an obligation as a current liability or as a noncurrent liability? Other things being equal, most would choose the noncurrent classification. The reason is that in most settings outsiders (like banks, bondholders, and shareholders) consider debt that is payable currently to be riskier than debt that need not be paid for some time. Relatedly, the long-term classification enables the company to report higher working capital (current assets minus current liabilities) and a higher current ratio (current assets/current liabilities). Working capital and the current ratio often are explicitly restricted in loan contracts. As you study this section, you should view the classification choice from this perspective. That is, the question is not so much "What amount should be reported as a current liability?" but rather "What amount can be excluded from classification as a current liability?"

### CURRENT MATURITIES OF LONG-TERM DEBT

**FINANCIAL REPORTING CASE**

Q2, p. 612

The currently maturing portion of a long-term debt must be reported as a current liability.

Long-term obligations (bonds, notes, lease liabilities, deferred tax liabilities) usually are reclassified and reported as current liabilities when they become payable within the upcoming year (or operating cycle, if longer than a year). For example, a 20-year bond issue is reported as a long-term liability for 19 years but normally is reported as a current liability on the balance sheet prepared during the 20th year of its term to maturity.[14] General Mills reported $233 million of its long-term debt as a current liability in 2004 (see Graphic 13–1, page 614).

### OBLIGATIONS CALLABLE BY THE CREDITOR

Long-term liabilities that are due on demand—by terms of the contract or violation of contract covenants—must be reported as current liabilities.

The requirement to classify currently maturing debt as a current liability includes debt that is *callable* (in other words, due on demand) *by the creditor* in the upcoming year (or operating cycle, if longer), even if the debt is not expected to be called. The current liability classification also is intended to include situations in which the creditor has the right to demand payment because an *existing violation* of a provision of the debt agreement makes it callable (say, working capital has fallen below a contractual minimum). This also includes situations in which debt is not yet callable but will be callable within the year if an existing violation

[14]Debt to be refinanced is an exception we discuss later.

is not corrected within a specified grace period (unless it's probable the violation will be corrected within the grace period or waived by the creditor).[15]

## WHEN SHORT-TERM OBLIGATIONS ARE EXPECTED TO BE REFINANCED

FINANCIAL REPORTING CASE

Q3, p. 612

Reconsider the 20-year bond issue we discussed earlier. Normally we would reclassify it as a current liability on the balance sheet prepared during its 20th year. But suppose a second 20-year bond issue is sold specifically to refund the first issue when it matures. Do we have a long-term liability for 19 years, a current liability for a year, and then another long-term liability? Or, do we have a single 40-year, long-term liability? If we look beyond the outward form of the transactions, the substance of the events obviously supports a single, continuing, noncurrent obligation. The concept of substance over form influences the classification of obligations expected to be refinanced.

**Short-term obligations can be reported as noncurrent liabilities if the company (a) *intends* to refinance on a long-term basis and (b) demonstrates the *ability* to do so by a refinancing agreement or by actual financing.**

Short-term obligations (including the callable obligations we discussed in the previous section) that are expected to be refinanced on a long-term basis can be reported as noncurrent, rather than current, liabilities only if two conditions are met. The firm (1) must intend to refinance on a long-term basis and (2) must actually have demonstrated the ability to do so. Ability to refinance on a long-term basis can be demonstrated by either an existing refinancing agreement or by actual financing prior to the issuance of the financial statements.[16] An example will provide perspective (Illustration 13–5).

**ILLUSTRATION 13–5**
Short-Term Obligations that Are Expected to Be Refinanced on a Long-Term Basis

Brahm Bros. Ice Cream had $12 million of notes that mature in May 2007 and also had $4 million of bonds issued in 1981 that mature in February 2007. On December 31, 2006, the company's fiscal year-end, management intended to refinance both on a long-term basis.

On February 7, 2007, the company issued $4 million of 20-year bonds, applying the proceeds to repay the bond issue that matured that month. In early March, prior to the actual issuance of the 2006 financial statements, Brahm Bros. negotiated a line of credit with a commercial bank for up to $7 million any time during 2007. Any borrowings will mature two years from the date of borrowing. Interest is at the prime London interbank borrowing rate.*

| | December 31, 2006 |
|---|---|
| **Classification** | ($ in 000s) |
| **Current Liabilities** | |
| Notes payable | $5,000 |
| **Long-Term Liabilities** | |
| Notes payable | $7,000 |
| Bonds payable | 4,000 |

Management's ability to refinance the bonds on a long-term basis was demonstrated by actual financing prior to the issuance of the financial statements. Ability to refinance $7 million of the notes is demonstrated by a refinancing agreement. The remaining $5 million must be reported as a current liability.

*This is a widely available rate often used as a basis for establishing interest rates on lines of credit.

If shares of stock had been issued to refinance the bonds in the illustration, the bonds still would be excluded from classification as a current liability. The specific form of the long-term refinancing (bonds, bank loans, equity securities) is irrelevant when determining the appropriate classification. Requiring companies to actually demonstrate the ability to refinance on a long-term basis in addition to merely intending to do so avoids intentional or unintentional understatements of current liabilities.

It's important to remember that several weeks usually pass between the end of a company's fiscal year and the date the financial statements for that year actually are issued.

[15] "Classification of Obligations That Are Callable by the Creditor," *Statement of Financial Accounting Standards No. 78* (Stamford, Conn.: FASB, 1983).

[16] "Classification of Obligations Expected to Be Refinanced," *Statement of Financial Accounting Standards No. 6* (Stamford, Conn.: FASB, 1975).

Events occurring during that period can be used to clarify the nature of financial statement elements at the reporting date. Here we consider refinancing agreements and actual securities transactions to support a company's ability to refinance on a long-term basis. Later in the chapter we use information that becomes available during this period to decide how loss contingencies are reported.

## CONCEPT REVIEW EXERCISE

### CURRENT LIABILITIES

The following selected transactions relate to liabilities of Southern Communications, Inc., for portions of 2006 and 2007. Southern's fiscal year ends on December 31.

**Required:**
Prepare the appropriate journal entries for these transactions.

**2006**

| | |
|---|---|
| July 1 | Arranged an uncommitted short-term line of credit with First City Bank amounting to $25,000,000 at the bank's prime rate (11.5% in July). The company will pay no commitment fees for this arrangement. |
| Aug. 9 | Received a $30,000 refundable deposit from a major customer for copper-lined mailing containers used to transport communications equipment. |
| Oct. 7 | Received most of the mailing containers covered by the refundable deposit and a letter stating that the customer will retain containers represented by $2,000 of the deposit and forfeits that amount. The cost of the forfeited containers was $1,500. |
| Nov. 1 | Borrowed $7 million cash from First City Bank under the line of credit arranged in July and issued a nine-month promissory note. Interest at the prime rate of 12% was payable at maturity. |
| Dec. 31 | Recorded appropriate adjusting entries for the liabilities described above. |

**2007**

| | |
|---|---|
| Feb. 12 | Using the unused portion of the credit line as support, issued $9 million of commercial paper and issued a six-month promissory note. Interest was discounted at issuance at a 10% discount rate. |
| Aug. 1 | Paid the 12% note at maturity. |
| 12 | Paid the commercial paper at maturity. |

### SOLUTION

**2006**

**July 1**
No entry is made for a line of credit until a loan actually is made. The existence and terms of the line would be described in a disclosure note.

| | Debit | Credit |
|---|---|---|
| **August 9** | | |
| Cash | 30,000 | |
| Liability—refundable deposits | | 30,000 |
| **October 7** | | |
| Liability—refundable deposits | 30,000 | |
| Cash | | 28,000 |
| Revenue—sale of containers | | 2,000 |
| Cost of goods sold | 1,500 | |
| Inventory of containers | | 1,500 |
| **November 1** | | |
| Cash | 7,000,000 | |
| Notes payable | | 7,000,000 |
| **December 31** | | |
| Interest expense ($7,000,000 × 12% × 2/12) | 140,000 | |
| Interest payable | | 140,000 |

**2007**

| | | |
|---|---|---|
| **February 12** | | |
| Cash ($9,000,000 − [$9,000,000 × 10% × $\frac{6}{12}$]) | 8,550,000 | |
| Discount on notes payable (difference) | 450,000 | |
| Note payable | | 9,000,000 |

Note that the effective interest rate is [($9,000,000 × 10% × $\frac{6}{12}$) ÷ $8,550,000] × $\frac{12}{6}$ = $450,000 ÷ $8,550,000 × 2 = 10.53%.

| | | |
|---|---|---|
| **August 1** | | |
| Interest expense ($7,000,000 × 12% × $\frac{7}{12}$) | 490,000 | |
| Interest payable (from adjusting entry) | 140,000 | |
| Note payable (face amount) | 7,000,000 | |
| Cash ($7,000,000 + $630,000) | | 7,630,000 |
| **August 12** | | |
| Interest expense ($9,000,000 × 10% × $\frac{6}{12}$) | 450,000 | |
| Discount on notes payable | | 450,000 |
| Note payable (face amount) | 9,000,000 | |
| Cash ($8,550,000 + $450,000) | | 9,000,000 |

# CONTINGENCIES

**PART B**

The feature that distinguishes the contingencies we discuss in this part of the chapter from the liabilities we discussed previously is uncertainty as to whether an obligation really exists. The existing uncertainty will be resolved only when some future event occurs (or doesn't occur). We will discuss gain contingencies, too, because of their similarity to loss contingencies.

## Loss Contingencies

● LO5

**Ford Motor Company's** financial statements recently indicated potential obligations from pending lawsuits (shown in Graphic 13–7).

**GRAPHIC 13–7**
Disclosure of Pending Litigation—Ford Motor Company

**Note 12: Litigation and Claims (in part)**
Various legal actions, governmental investigations and proceedings and claims are pending or may be instituted or asserted in the future against the company and its subsidiaries, including those arising out of alleged defects in the company's products, governmental regulations relating to safety, emissions and fuel economy, financial services, intellectual property rights, product warranties and environmental matters. Certain of the pending legal actions are, or purport to be, class actions. Some of the foregoing matters involve or may involve compensatory, punitive, or antitrust or other treble damage claims in very large amounts, or demands for recall campaigns, environmental remediation programs, sanctions, or other relief which, if granted, would require very large expenditures.

The disclosure indicates that if certain events occur, "very large expenditures" would result. Do these contingencies represent liabilities of Ford? Certainly the liabilities *may* exist on the date of the financial statements. But how likely is an unfavorable outcome? Also, precise amounts of any obligations Ford may have are unknown. But can the amounts be estimated? These are the key questions addressed by accounting standards for loss contingencies.

*A loss contingency* **involves an existing uncertainty as to whether a loss really exists, where the uncertainty will be resolved only when some future event occurs.**

A **loss contingency** is an existing, uncertain situation involving potential loss depending on whether some future event occurs. Whether a contingency is accrued and reported as a liability depends on (a) the likelihood that the confirming event will occur and (b) what can be determined about the amount of loss. Consider an IRS assessment of additional income taxes for prior years, pending at year-end, for which the outcome will not be known until after the financial statements are issued. We must assess the likelihood that the company will pay the back taxes and if so, how much they will pay.

Note that the cause of the uncertainty must occur before the statement date. In this case, the prior years' operations for which the tax liability is questioned occurred before the current accounting period ended. Otherwise, regardless of the likelihood of the eventual outcome, no liability could have existed at the statement date. Recall that one of the essential characteristics of a liability is that it results "from past transactions or events."

**FINANCIAL REPORTING CASE**

Q4, p. 612

Accounting standards require that the likelihood that the future event(s) will confirm the incurrence of the liability be (somewhat arbitrarily) categorized as probable, reasonably possible, or remote:[17]

*Likelihood That a Liability Exists*

Probable—Confirming event is likely to occur.
Reasonably possible—The chance the confirming event will occur is more than remote but less than likely.
Remote—The chance the confirming event will occur is slight.

● LO6

Also key to reporting a contingent liability is its dollar amount. The amount of the potential loss is classified as either known, reasonably estimable, or not reasonably estimable. A liability is accrued if it is both probable that the confirming event will occur and the amount can be at least reasonably estimated. A general depiction of the accrual of a loss contingency is:

*Accrual of a Loss Contingency—Liability*

| | | |
|---|---|---|
| Loss (or expense) ........................................ | x,xxx | |
| Liability ........................................ | | x,xxx |

**ADDITIONAL CONSIDERATION**

If one amount within a range of possible loss appears better than other amounts within the range, that amount is accrued. When no amount within the range appears more likely than others, the *minimum* amount should be *recorded* and the possible *additional loss* should be *disclosed.*[18]

In a recent annual report (Graphic 13–8), **Union Pacific** reported a loss contingency it had accrued for a claim against it by government agencies for which the company deemed payment was both probable and reasonably estimable.

**GRAPHIC 13–8**
Accrual of Loss Contingency—Union Pacific

**9. Commitments and Contingencies (in part)**
We accrue the cost of remediation where our obligation is probable and such costs can be reasonably estimated. As of December 31, 2004 and 2003, we had a liability of $201 million and $187 million, respectively, accrued for future environmental costs, of which $50 million and $57 million were recorded in current liabilities as accrued casualty costs.

It's important to note that some loss contingencies don't involve liabilities at all. Some contingencies when resolved cause a noncash asset to be impaired, so accruing it means reducing the related asset rather than recording a liability:

*Accrual of a Loss Contingency—Asset Impairment*

| | | |
|---|---|---|
| Loss (or expense) ........................................ | x,xxx | |
| Asset (or valuation account) ............................ | | x,xxx |

[17]"Accounting for Contingencies," *Statement of Financial Accounting Standards No. 5* (Stamford, Conn.: FASB, 1975).
[18]"Reasonable Estimation of the Amount of the Loss," *FASB Interpretation No. 14* (Stamford, Conn.: FASB, 1976).

The most common loss contingency of this type is an uncollectible receivable. You have recorded these before without knowing you were accruing a loss contingency (*Debit:* bad debt expense; *Credit:* allowance for uncollectible accounts).

If one or both of these criteria is not met, but there is at least a reasonable possibility that the loss will occur, a disclosure note should describe the contingency. It also should provide an estimate of the possible loss or range of loss, if possible. If an estimate cannot be made, a statement to that effect is needed.

**A loss contingency is disclosed in notes to the financial statements if there is at least a reasonable possibility that the loss will occur.**

**Varian Medical Systems, Inc.** designs and manufactures cancer therapy systems. VMS felt that the loss contingency from an investment was reasonably possible and accordingly did not accrue a liability but provided the information noted in Graphic 13–9.

**GRAPHIC 13–9**
Disclosure of Loss Contingency—VMS, Inc.

**Note 9 (in part)**
. . . we agreed to invest $5 million in a consortium to participate in the acquisition of a minority interest in dpiX LLC ("dpiX"), which supplies us with amorphous silicon based thin-film transistor arrays. Based on information provided by dpiX, management currently believes it is reasonably possible that we will recognize a loss of up to $5 million on this investment beginning in the fourth quarter of fiscal year 2001 and continuing through fiscal year 2002.

Graphic 13–10 highlights appropriate accounting treatment for each possible combination of (a) the likelihood of an obligation's being confirmed and (b) the determinability of its dollar amount.

**GRAPHIC 13–10**
Accounting Treatment of Loss Contingencies

| | Dollar Amount of Potential Loss | | |
|---|---|---|---|
| **Likelihood** | **Known** | **Reasonably Estimable** | **Not Reasonably Estimable** |
| Probable | Liability accrued and disclosure note | Liability accrued and disclosure note | Disclosure note only |
| Reasonably possible | Disclosure note only | Disclosure note only | Disclosure note only |
| Remote | No disclosure required* | No disclosure required* | No disclosure required* |

*Except for certain guarantees and other specified off-balance-sheet risk situations discussed in the next chapter.

**A loss contingency is accrued only if a loss is probable and the amount can reasonably be estimated.**

## PRODUCT WARRANTIES AND GUARANTEES

**Manufacturer's Original Warranty.** Satisfaction guaranteed! Your money back if not satisfied! If anything goes wrong in the first five years or 50,000 miles . . . ! Three-year guarantee! These and similar promises accompany most consumer goods. The reason—to boost sales. It follows, then, that any costs of making good on such guarantees should be recorded as expenses in the same accounting period the products are sold (matching principle). The obstacle is that much of the cost usually occurs later, sometimes years later. This is a loss contingency. There may be a future sacrifice of economic benefits (cost of satisfying the guarantee) due to an existing circumstance (the guaranteed products have been sold) that depends on an uncertain future event (customer claim).

**Most consumer products are accompanied by a guarantee.**

As you might expect, meeting the accrual criteria is more likely for some types of loss contingencies than for others. For instance, the outcome of pending litigation is particularly difficult to predict. On the other hand, the criteria for accrual almost always are met for some types of loss contingencies. Product warranties (or product guarantees) inevitably entail costs. And while we usually can't predict the liability associated with an individual sale, reasonably accurate estimates of the *total* liability for a period usually are possible, based on

The contingent liability for product warranties almost always is accrued.

prior experience. So the contingent liability for warranties and guarantees usually is accrued. The estimated warranty (guarantee) liability is credited and warranty (guarantee) expense is debited in the reporting period in which the product under warranty is sold. This is demonstrated in Illustration 13–6.

**ILLUSTRATION 13–6**
Product Warranty

Caldor Health, a supplier of in-home health care products, introduced a new therapeutic chair carrying a two-year warranty against defects. Estimates based on industry experience indicate warranty costs of 3% of sales during the first 12 months following the sale and 4% the next 12 months. During December 2006, its first month of availability, Caldor sold $2 million of the chairs.

The costs of satisfying guarantees should be recorded as expenses in the same accounting period the products are sold.

**During December**

| | | |
|---|---|---|
| Cash (and accounts receivable) | 2,000,000 | |
| Sales revenue | | 2,000,000 |

**December 31, 2006 (adjusting entry)**

| | | |
|---|---|---|
| Warranty expense ([3% + 4%] × $2,000,000) | 140,000 | |
| Estimated warranty liability | | 140,000 |

When customer claims are made and costs are incurred to satisfy those claims, the liability is reduced (let's say $61,000 in 2007):

| | | |
|---|---|---|
| Estimated warranty liability | 61,000 | |
| Cash, wages payable, parts and supplies, etc. | | 61,000 |

Estimates of warranty costs cannot be expected to be precise. However, if the estimating method is monitored and revised when necessary, overestimates and underestimates should cancel each other over time. The estimated liability may be classified as current or as part current and part long-term, depending on when costs are expected to be incurred.

**Expected Cash Flow Approach.** In Chapter 6, you learned of a framework for using future cash flows as the basis for measuring assets and liabilities, introduced by the FASB in 2000 with *Statement of Financial Accounting Concepts No. 7*, "Using Cash Flow Information and Present Value in Accounting Measurements."[19] The approach described in the Concept Statement offers a way to take into account *any uncertainty concerning the amounts and timing of the cash flows*. Although future cash flows in many instances are contractual and certain, the amounts and timing of cash flows are less certain in other situations, such as warranty obligations.

*SFAC No. 7* provides a framework for using future cash flows in accounting measurements.

As demonstrated in Illustration 13–6, the traditional way of measuring a warranty obligation is to report the "best estimate" of future cash flows, ignoring the time value of money on the basis of immateriality. However, when the warranty obligation spans more than one year and we can associate probabilities with possible cash flow outcomes, the approach described by *SFAC No. 7* offers a more plausible estimate of the warranty obligation. This new "expected cash flow approach" incorporates specific probabilities of cash flows into the analysis. In Chapter 6, we discussed the expected cash flow approach to determining present value. Illustration 13–7 provides an example.

**Extended Warranty Contracts.** It's difficult these days to buy a CD player, a digital camera, a car, or almost any durable consumer product without being asked to buy an extended warranty agreement. An extended warranty provides warranty protection beyond the manufacturer's original warranty. Because an extended warranty is priced and sold separately from the warranted product, it essentially constitutes a separate sales transaction. The accounting question is "when should the revenue from the sale be recognized?"

[19]"Using Cash Flow Information and Present Value in Accounting Measurements," *Statement of Financial Accounting Concepts No. 7* (Norwalk, Conn.: FASB, 2000). Recall that Concept Statements do not directly prescribe GAAP, but instead provide structure and direction to financial accounting.

**ILLUSTRATION 13–7**
Product Warranty

Caldor Health, a supplier of in-home health care products, introduced a new therapeutic chair carrying a two-year warranty against defects. During December of 2006, its first month of availability, Caldor sold $2 million of the chairs. Industry experience indicates the following probability distribution for the potential warranty costs:

| Warranty Costs | Probability |
|---|---|
| **2007** | |
| $50,000 | 20% |
| $60,000 | 50% |
| $70,000 | 30% |
| **2008** | |
| $70,000 | 20% |
| $80,000 | 50% |
| $90,000 | 30% |

Probabilities are associated with possible cash outcomes.

An arrangement with a service firm requires that costs for the two-year warranty period be settled at the end of 2007 and 2008. The risk-free rate of interest is 5%. Applying the estimated cash flow approach, at the end of the 2006 fiscal year, Caldor would record a warranty liability (and expense) of $131,564, calculated as follows:

| | | |
|---|---|---|
| $50,000 × 20% = | $10,000 | |
| 60,000 × 50% = | 30,000 | |
| 70,000 × 30% = | 21,000 | |
| | $61,000 | |
| | × .95238* | $ 58,095 |
| $70,000 × 20% = | $14,000 | |
| 80,000 × 50% = | 40,000 | |
| 90,000 × 30% = | 27,000 | |
| | $81,000 | |
| | × .90703† | 73,469 |
| | | $131,564 |

*Present value of $1, $n = 1$, $i = 5\%$ (from Table 2)
†Present value of $1, $n = 2$, $i = 5\%$ (from Table 2)

The probability-weighted cash outcomes provide the expected cash flows.

The present value of the expected cash flows is the estimated liability.

**December 31, 2006 (adjusting entry)**

| | | |
|---|---|---|
| Warranty expense | 131,564 | |
| Estimated warranty liability (calculated above) | | 131,564 |

By the accrual concept, revenue is recognized when earned, not necessarily when cash is received. Because the earning process for an extended warranty continues during the contract period, revenue should be recognized over the same period. So, revenue from separately priced extended warranty contracts is deferred as a liability at the time of sale and recognized on a straight-line basis over the contract period. Notice that this is similar to an advance payment for products or services that, as we discussed earlier, creates a liability to supply the products or services. We demonstrate accounting for extended warranties in Illustration 13–8.

Remember that the costs incurred to satisfy customer claims under the extended warranties also will be recorded during the same three-year period, achieving a proper matching of revenues and expenses. If sufficient historical evidence indicates that the costs of satisfying customer claims will be incurred on other than a straight-line basis, revenue should be recognized by the same pattern (proportional to the costs).[20]

[20]"Accounting for Separately Priced Extended Warranty and Product Maintenance Contracts," *FASB Technical Bulletin 90-1*, 1990.

**ILLUSTRATION 13–8**
Extended Warranty

**The manufacturer's warranty covers 2006. Revenue from the extended warranty is recognized during the three years of the contract period.**

Brand Name Appliances sells major appliances that carry a one-year manufacturer's warranty. Customers are offered the opportunity at the time of purchase to also buy a three-year extended warranty for an additional charge. On January 3, 2006, Brand Name sold a $60 extended warranty.

| | | |
|---|---|---|
| **January 3, 2006** | | |
| Cash (or accounts receivable) | 60 | |
| Unearned revenue—extended warranties | | 60 |
| **December 31, 2007, 2008, 2009 (adjusting entries)** | | |
| Unearned revenue—extended warranties | 20 | |
| Revenue—extended warranties ($60 ÷ 3) | | 20 |

## PREMIUMS

Cash rebates have become commonplace. Cash register receipts, bar codes, rebate coupons, or other proofs of purchase often can be mailed to the manufacturer for cash rebates. Sometimes promotional offers promise premiums other than cash (like toys, dishes, and utensils) to buyers of certain products. Of course the purpose of these premium offers is to stimulate sales. So it follows that the estimated amount of the cash rebates or the cost of noncash premiums estimated to be given out represents both an expense and an estimated liability in the reporting period the product is sold. Like a manufacturer's warranty, this loss contingency almost always meets accrual criteria. Premiums are illustrated in Illustration 13–9.

**ILLUSTRATION 13–9**
Premiums

**The costs of promotional offers should be recorded as expenses in the same accounting period the products are sold.**

CMX Corporation offered $2 cash rebates on a particular model of hand-held hair dryers. To receive the rebate, customers must mail in a rebate certificate enclosed in the package plus the cash register receipt. Previous experience indicates that 30% of coupons will be redeemed. One million hair dryers were sold in 2006 and total payments to customers were $225,000.

| | | |
|---|---|---|
| Promotional expense (30% × $2 × 1,000,000) | 600,000 | |
| Estimated premium liability | | 600,000 |
| *To record the estimated liability for premiums.* | | |
| Estimated premium liability | 225,000 | |
| Cash | | 225,000 |
| *To record payments to customers for coupons.* | | |

The remaining liability of $375,000 is reported in the 2006 balance sheet and is reduced as future rebates are paid. The liability should be classified as current or long term depending on when future rebates are expected to be paid.

Of course, if premiums actually are included in packages of products sold, no contingent liability is created. For example, the costs of toys in Cracker Jack boxes and cereal boxes, and phone cards and compact discs in drink cartons are simply expenses of the period the product is sold, for which the amount is readily determinable.

### ADDITIONAL CONSIDERATION

Cents-off coupons are a popular marketing tool. Coupons clipped from newspapers, from mail offers, or included in packages are redeemable for cash discounts at the time promoted items are purchased. Issuing the coupons creates a contingent liability to be recorded in the period the coupons are issued. However, because the hoped-for sales don't materialize until later, a question arises as to when the related expense should be recognized. Logically, since the purpose of coupon offers is to stimulate sales, the expense properly should be deferred until the coupons are redeemed (when the sales occur).

**Illustration**

On December 18, 2006, Craft Foods distributed coupons in newspaper inserts offering 50 cents off the purchase price of one of its cereal brands when coupons are presented to retailers. Retailers are reimbursed by Craft for the face amount of coupons plus 10% for handling. Previous experience indicates that 20% of coupons will be redeemed. Coupons issued had a total face amount of $1,000,000 and total payments to retailers in 2006 were $50,000. Retailers were paid $170,000 in 2007.

| | | |
|---|---|---|
| Promotional expense (redeemed in 2006) | 50,000 | |
| Cash | | 50,000 |
| *To record payments to retailers for coupons in 2006.* | | |
| Deferred promotional expense (an asset) | 170,000 | |
| Estimated coupon liability ([20% × $1,000,000 × 1.10] − $50,000) | | 170,000 |
| *To record the estimated liability for coupons in 2006.* | | |
| Estimated coupon liability | 170,000 | |
| Cash | | 170,000 |
| Promotional expense (redeemed in 2007) | 170,000 | |
| Deferred promotional expense | | 170,000 |
| *To record payments to retailers for coupons in 2007.* | | |

This situation, though prevalent, is not addressed by promulgated accounting standards. In practice, most firms either (a) recognize the entire expense with the liability in the period the coupons are issued, like we record premiums, or (b) recognize no liability in the period the coupons are issued, recording the expense when reimbursements are made. One reason is that the same coupons are reissued periodically, making it difficult to associate specific reimbursements with specific offers. Another reason is that the time lag between the time a merchant receives a coupon from customers and the time it's presented to the manufacturer for reimbursement prevents appropriate apportionment of the expense.

## LITIGATION CLAIMS

Pending litigation similar to that disclosed by **Ford** in Graphic 13–7 on page 625 is not unusual. In fact, the majority of medium and large corporations annually report loss contingencies due to litigation. By far the most common disclosure is nonspecific regarding the actual litigation but uses wording similar to this contingency disclosure from an annual report of **Sun Microsystems** (Graphic 13–11).

**Note 10: Commitments and Contingencies (in part)**
From time to time and in the ordinary course of business, the Company may be subject to various claims, charges, and litigation. In the opinion of management, final judgments from such pending claims, charges, and litigation, if any, against the Company would not have a material adverse effect on its consolidated financial position, results of operations, or cash flows.

**GRAPHIC 13–11**
Disclosure of Litigation Contingencies—Sun Microsystems, Inc.

In practice, accrual of a loss from pending or ongoing litigation is rare. Imagine why. Suppose you are chief financial officer of Feinz Foods. Feinz is the defendant in a $44 million class action suit. The company's legal counsel informally advises you that chances that the company will emerge victorious in the lawsuit are quite doubtful. Counsel feels the company might lose $30 million. Now suppose you decide to accrue a $30 million loss in your financial statements. Later, in the courtroom, your disclosure that Feinz management feels it is probable that the company will lose $30 million would be welcome ammunition for the opposing legal counsel. Understanding this, most companies rely on the knowledge that in today's legal environment the outcome of litigation is highly uncertain, making likelihood predictions difficult. Companies usually do not record a loss until after the ultimate settlement has been reached or negotiations for settlement are substantially completed. Instead, disclosure notes typically describe the specifics of the litigation along with whether management feels an adverse outcome would materially affect the financial position of the company. As you can see in Graphic 13–12, **ExxonMobil Corporation,** in a recent quarterly report, disclosed but did not accrue damages from a lawsuit it lost, even after the award was affirmed by trial court, because the company was appealing the verdict.

**GRAPHIC 13–12**
Disclosure of a Lawsuit—ExxonMobil

**17. Litigation and Other Contingencies (in part)**
On May 22, 2001, a state court jury in New Orleans, Louisiana, returned a verdict against the corporation and three other entities in a case brought by a landowner claiming damage to his property. The jury awarded the plaintiff $56 million in compensatory damages and $1 billion in punitive damages. The award has been affirmed by the trial court, and the corporation is in the process of taking an appeal to the Louisiana Fourth Circuit Court of Appeals. The ultimate outcome is not expected to have a materially adverse effect upon the corporation's operations or financial condition.

## SUBSEQUENT EVENTS

It's important to remember several weeks usually pass between the end of a company's fiscal year and the date the financial statements for that year actually are issued. Events occurring during this period can be used to clarify the nature of financial statement elements at the report date. This situation can be represented by the following time line:

**When the cause of a loss contingency occurs before the year-end, a clarifying event before financial statements are issued can be used to determine how the contingency is reported.**

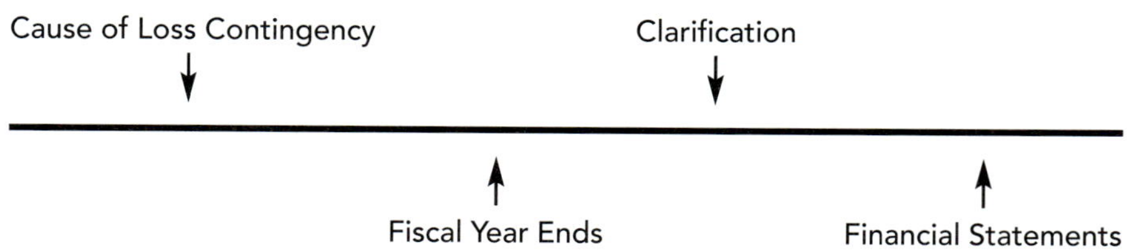


For instance, if information becomes available that sheds light on a claim that existed when the fiscal year ended, that information should be used in determining the probability of a loss contingency materializing and in estimating the amount of the loss. The settlement of a lawsuit after the March 31 report date of **Measurement Specialties, Inc.** apparently influenced its accrual of a loss contingency (Graphic 13–13).

**GRAPHIC 13–13**
Accrual of Litigation Contingency—Measurement Specialties, Inc.

**15. Commitments and Contingencies (in part)**
On May 18, 2004, the Company reached an agreement in principle with the SEC which would resolve the commission's investigation of the Company. As of March 31, 2004, the Company has provided an accrual of $2,100,000.

For a loss contingency to be accrued, the cause of the lawsuit must have occurred before the accounting period ended. It's not necessary that the lawsuit actually was filed during that reporting period.

Sometimes, the cause of a loss contingency occurs after the end of the year but before the financial statements are issued:

**If an event giving rise to a contingency occurs after the year-end, a liability should not be accrued.**

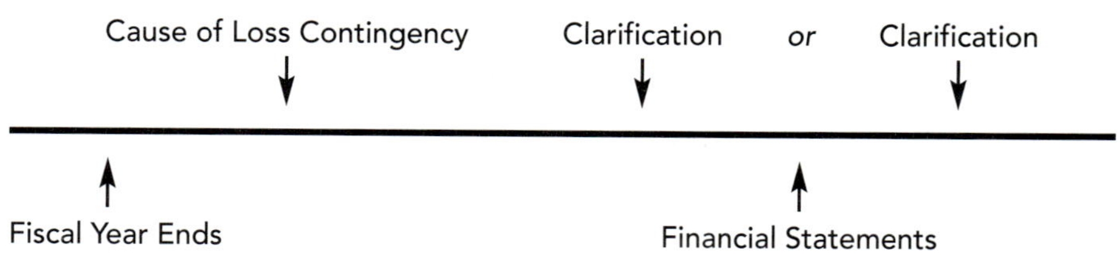

When a contingency comes into existence after the year-end, a liability cannot be accrued because it didn't exist at the end of the year. However, if the failure to disclose the possible loss would cause the financial statements to be misleading, the situation should be described in a disclosure note, including the effect of the possible loss on key accounting numbers affected.[21]

In fact, *any* event occurring after the fiscal year-end but before the financial statements are issued that has a material effect on the company's financial position must be disclosed in a subsequent events disclosure note. Examples are an issuance of debt or equity securities, a business combination, and discontinued operations.

A disclosure note of the **Dow Chemical Company** from its 2000 annual report is shown in Graphic 13–14 and describes an event that will occur in the first quarter of fiscal 2001.

**S. Merger with Union Carbide Corporation**
On February 6, 2001, the Company completed its merger with Union Carbide in a tax-free, stock-for-stock transaction. Dow issued 1.611 shares of common stock for each share of Union Carbide common stock outstanding, or approximately 219 million shares.

**GRAPHIC 13–14**
Subsequent Events—Dow Chemical Company

## UNASSERTED CLAIMS AND ASSESSMENTS

It must be probable that an unasserted claim or assessment or an unfiled lawsuit will occur before considering whether and how to report the possible loss.

Even if a claim has yet to be made when the financial statements are issued, a contingency may warrant accrual or disclosure. However, an unfiled lawsuit or an unasserted claim or assessment need not be disclosed unless it is *probable that the suit, claim, or assessment will occur.* If it is probable, then the likelihood of an unfavorable outcome and the feasibility of estimating a dollar amount should be considered in deciding whether and how to report the possible loss.

For example, the IRS may be in the process of auditing a company's tax returns but has not proposed a deficiency assessment. If management feels an assessment is probable, the possible tax assessment might need to be reported. An estimated loss and contingent liability would be accrued if an unfavorable outcome is probable and the amount can be reasonably estimated. However, note disclosure alone would be appropriate if an unfavorable settlement is only reasonably possible, and no action is needed if chances of that outcome are remote. Notice that when the claim or assessment is unasserted as yet, a two-step process is involved in deciding how it should be reported:

1. Is a claim or assessment probable? (If the answer to this question is no, no disclosure is needed; skip step 2.)
2. Only if a claim or assessment is probable should we evaluate (a) the likelihood of an unfavorable outcome and (b) whether the dollar amount can be estimated.

If the conclusion of step 1 is that the claim or assessment *is not* probable, no further action is required. If the conclusion of step 1 is that the claim or assessment *is* probable, the decision as to whether or not a liability is accrued or disclosed is precisely the same as when the claim or assessment already has been asserted.

As described in a recent disclosure note (see Graphic 13–15), **Union Pacific** felt that some unasserted claims meet the criteria for accrual under this two-step decision process.

**12. Commitments and Contingencies (in part)**
The Corporation and its subsidiaries periodically enter into financial and other commitments in connection with their businesses. It is not possible at this time for the Corporation to determine fully the effect of all unasserted claims on its consolidated financial condition, results of operations or liquidity; however, to the extent possible, where unasserted claims can be estimated and where such claims are considered probable, the Corporation has recorded a liability.

**GRAPHIC 13–15**
Unasserted Claims—Union Pacific Corporation

[21]"Accounting for Contingencies," *Statement of Financial Accounting Standards No. 5* (Stamford, Conn.: FASB, 1975), par. 11.

**Accrued loss contingencies meet the *SFAC 6* definition of liabilities.**

Notice that the treatment of contingent liabilities is consistent with the accepted definition of liabilities as (a) probable, future sacrifices of economic benefits (b) that arise from present obligations to other entities and (c) that result from past transactions or events.[22] The inherent uncertainty involved with contingent liabilities means additional care is required to determine whether future sacrifices of economic benefits are probable and whether the amount of the sacrifices can be quantified.

## Gain Contingencies

**Gain contingencies are not accrued.**

A gain contingency is an uncertain situation that might result in a gain. For example, in a pending lawsuit, one side—the defendant—faces a loss contingency; the other side—the plaintiff—has a gain contingency. As we discussed earlier, loss contingencies are accrued when the event confirming the obligation is probable and the amount can reasonably be estimated. However, gain contingencies are not accrued. The nonparallel treatment of gain contingencies follows the same conservative reasoning that motivates reporting some assets at lower of cost or market. Specifically, it's desirable to anticipate losses, but recognizing gains should await their realization.

Though gain contingencies are not recorded in the accounts, they are disclosed in notes to the financial statements. Care should be taken that the disclosure note not give "misleading implications as to the likelihood of realization."[23]

## Concept Review Exercise

### Contingencies

Hanover Industries manufactures and sells food products and food processing machinery. While preparing the December 31, 2006, financial statements for Hanover, the following information was discovered relating to contingencies and possible adjustments to liabilities. Hanover's 2006 financial statements were issued on April 1, 2007.

a. On November 12, 2006, a former employee filed a lawsuit against Hanover alleging age discrimination and asking for damages of $750,000. At December 31, 2006, Hanover's attorney indicated that the likelihood of losing the lawsuit was possible but not probable. On March 5, 2007, Hanover agreed to pay the former employee $125,000 in return for withdrawing the lawsuit.

b. After a tax audit of the 2005 return, the IRS has questioned some expenses paid to a major stockholder. At April, 2007, the IRS has not yet made an assessment of additional taxes, but Hanover feels it will. Hanover's accountants and legal counsel believe the deductions were appropriate but that if an assessment is made, there is a reasonable possibility that subsequent court action would result in an additional tax liability of $55,000.

c. Hanover grants a one-year warranty for each processing machine sold. Past experience indicates that the costs of satisfying warranties are approximately 2% of sales. During 2006, sales of processing machines totaled $21,300,000. 2006 expenditures for warranty repair costs were $178,000 related to 2006 sales and $220,000 related to 2005 sales. The January 1, 2006, balance of the warranty liability account was $250,000.

d. Hanover is the plaintiff in a $600,000 lawsuit filed in 2005 against Ansdale Farms for failing to deliver on contracts for produce. The suit is in final appeal. Legal counsel advises that it is probable that Hanover will prevail and will be awarded $300,000.

e. Included with certain food items sold in 2006 were coupons redeemable for a kitchen appliance at the rate of five coupons per appliance. During 2006, 30,000 coupons were issued and 5,000 coupons were redeemed. Although this is the first such promotion in years, past experience indicates that 60% of coupons are never redeemed. An inventory of kitchen appliances is maintained, and a count shows that 1,000 are on hand at December 31, 2006, with a normal retail value of $20,000 and a cost to Hanover of $8,000.

---

[22] "Elements of Financial Statements," *Statement of Financial Accounting Concepts No. 6* (Stamford, Conn.: FASB, 1985).

[23] "Accounting For Contingencies," *Statement of Financial Accounting Standards No. 5* (Stamford, Conn.: FASB, 1975), par. 17.

**Required:**

1. Determine the appropriate means of reporting each situation. Briefly explain your reasoning.
2. Prepare any necessary journal entries and state whether a disclosure note is needed.

**SOLUTION**

a. This is a loss contingency. Hanover can use the information occurring after the end of the year in determining appropriate disclosure. The cause for the suit existed at the end of the year. Hanover should accrue the $125,000 loss because an agreement has been reached confirming the loss and the amount is known.

| | | |
|---|---|---|
| Loss—litigation | 125,000 | |
| Liability—litigation | | 125,000 |

A disclosure note also is appropriate.

b. At the time financial statements are issued, an IRS claim is as yet unasserted. However, an assessment is probable. Thus, (a) the likelihood of an unfavorable outcome and (b) whether the dollar amount can be estimated are considered. No accrual is necessary because an unfavorable outcome is not probable. But because an unfavorable outcome is reasonably possible, a disclosure note is appropriate.

*Note:* If the likelihood of a claim being asserted is not probable, disclosure is not required even if an unfavorable outcome is thought to be probable in the event of an assessment and the amount is estimable.

c. The contingency for warranties should be accrued because it is probable that expenditures will be made and the amount can be estimated from past experience. When customer claims are made and costs are incurred to satisfy those claims the liability is reduced.

| | | |
|---|---|---|
| Warranty expense (2% × $21,300,000) | 426,000 | |
| Estimated warranty liability | | 426,000 |
| Estimated warranty liability ($178,000 + 220,000) | 398,000 | |
| Cash, wages payable, parts and supplies, etc. | | 398,000 |

The liability at December 31, 2006, would be reported as $278,000:

**Warranty Liability**
(in 000s)

| | | | |
|---|---|---|---|
| | | 250 | Balance, Jan. 1 |
| | | 426 | 2006 expense |
| 2006 expenditures | 398 | | |
| | | 278 | Balance, Dec. 31 |

A disclosure note also is appropriate.

d. This is a gain contingency. Gain contingencies cannot be accrued even if the gain is probable and reasonably estimable. The gain should be recognized only when realized. It can be disclosed, but care should be taken to avoid misleading language regarding the realizability of the gain.

e. The contingency for premiums should be accrued because it is probable that coupons will be redeemed and the amount can be estimated from past experience. When coupons are redeemed and appliances are issued, the liability is reduced.

| | | |
|---|---|---|
| Promotional expense (40% × [30,000 ÷ 5] × $8*) | 19,200 | |
| Estimated premium liability | | 19,200 |
| Estimated premium liability ([5,000 ÷ 5] × $8*) | 8,000 | |
| Inventory of premiums | | 8,000 |

*$8,000 ÷ 1,000 = $8

The liability at December 31, 2006, would be reported as $11,200:

**Premium Liability**

| | | | |
|---|---|---|---|
| | | 19,200 | 2006 expense |
| 2006 expenditures | 8,000 | | |
| | | 11,200 | Balance, Dec. 31 |

A disclosure note also is appropriate.

## DECISION MAKERS' PERSPECTIVE

*An analyst of risk should be concerned with a company's ability to meet its short-term obligations.*

Current liabilities impact a company's liquidity. Liquidity refers to a company's cash position and overall ability to obtain cash in the normal course of business. A company is said to be liquid if it has sufficient cash (or other assets convertible to cash in a relatively short time) to pay currently maturing debts. Because the lack of liquidity can cause the demise of an otherwise healthy company, it is critical that managers as well as outside investors and creditors maintain close scrutiny of this aspect of a company's well-being.

Keeping track of the current ratio is one of the most common ways of doing this. The current ratio is intended as a measure of short-term solvency and is determined by dividing current assets by current liabilities.

**FINANCIAL REPORTING CASE**

Q5, p. 612

When we compare liabilities that must be satisfied in the near term with assets that either are cash or will be converted to cash in the near term, we get a useful measure of a company's liquidity. A ratio of 1 to 1 or higher often is considered a rule-of-thumb standard, but like other ratios, acceptability should be evaluated in the context of the industry in which the company operates and other specific circumstances. Keep in mind, though, that industry averages are only one indication of adequacy and that the current ratio is but one indication of liquidity.

*A manager should actively monitor a company's liquidity.*

We can adjust for the implicit assumption of the current ratio that all current assets are equally liquid. The acid-test, or quick, ratio is similar to the current ratio but is based on a more conservative measure of assets available to pay current liabilities. Specifically, the numerator, quick assets, includes only cash and cash equivalents, short-term investments, and accounts receivable. By eliminating current assets such as inventories and prepaid expenses that are less readily convertible into cash, the acid-test ratio provides a more rigorous indication of a company's short-term solvency than does the current ratio.

*A liquidity ratio is but one indication of a company's liquidity.*

If either of these liquidity ratios is less than that of the industry as a whole, does that mean that liquidity is a problem? Perhaps; perhaps not. It does, though, raise a red flag that suggests caution when assessing other areas. It's important to remember that each ratio is but one piece of the puzzle. For example, profitability is probably the best long-run indication of liquidity. Also, management may be very efficient in managing current assets so that some current assets—receivables or inventory—are more liquid than they otherwise would be and more readily available to satisfy liabilities. The turnover ratios discussed in earlier chapters help measure the efficiency of asset management in this regard.

*Analysts should be alert for efforts to manipulate measures of liquidity.*

Given the actual and perceived importance of a company's liquidity in the minds of analysts, it's not difficult to adopt a management perspective and imagine efforts to manipulate the ratios that measure liquidity. For instance, a company might use its economic muscle or persuasive powers to influence the timing of accounts payable recognition by asking suppliers to change their delivery schedules. Because accounts payable is included in the denominator in most measures of liquidity, such as the current ratio, the timing of their recognition could mean the difference between an unacceptable ratio and an acceptable one, or between violating a debt covenant and compliance. For example, suppose a company with a current ratio of 1.25 (current assets of $5 million and current liabilities of $4 million) is in violation of a debt covenant requiring a minimum current ratio of 1.3. By delaying the delivery of $1 million of inventory, the ratio would increase to 1.33 (current assets of $4 million and current liability of $3 million).

It is important for creditors and analysts to be attentive for evidence of activities that would indicate timing strategies, such as unusual variations in accounts payable levels. You might notice that such timing strategies are similar to earnings management techniques we discussed previously—specifically, manipulating the timing of revenue and expense recognition in order to "smooth" income over time.

In the next chapter, we continue our discussion of liabilities. Our focus will shift from current liabilities to long-term liabilities in the form of bonds and long-term notes. ■

## FINANCIAL REPORTING CASE SOLUTION

1. **What are accrued liabilities? What is commercial paper?** *(p. 617)* Accrued liabilities are reported for expenses already incurred but not yet paid (accrued expenses). These include salaries and wages payable, income taxes payable, and interest payable. Commercial paper is a form of notes payable sometimes used by large corporations to obtain temporary financing. It is sold to other companies as a short-term investment. It represents unsecured notes sold in minimum denominations of $25,000 with maturities ranging from 30 to 270 days. Typically, commercial paper is issued directly to the buyer (lender) and is backed by a line of credit with a bank.
2. **Why did Syntel Microsystems include some long-term debt in the current liability section?** *(p. 622)* Syntel Microsystems did include some long-term debt in the current liability section. The currently maturing portion of a long-term debt must be reported as a current liability. Amounts are reclassified and reported as current liabilities when they become payable within the upcoming year.
3. **Did they also report some current amounts as long-term debt? Explain.** *(p. 623)* Yes they did. It is permissible to report short-term obligations as noncurrent liabilities if the company (a) intends to refinance on a long-term basis and (b) demonstrates the ability to do so by a refinancing agreement or by actual financing. As the disclosure note explains, this is the case for a portion of Syntel's currently payable debt.
4. **Must obligations be known contractual debts in order to be reported as liabilities?** *(p. 626)* No. From an accounting perspective, it is not necessary that obligations be known, legally enforceable debts to be reported as liabilities. They must only be probable and the dollar amount reasonably estimable.
5. **Is it true that current liabilities are riskier than long-term liabilities?** *(p. 636)* Other things being equal, current liabilities generally are considered riskier than long-term liabilities. For that reason, management usually would rather report a debt as long term. Current debt, though, is not necessarily risky. The liquidity ratios we discussed in the chapter attempt to measure liquidity. Remember, any such measure must be assessed in the context of other factors: industry standards, profitability, turnover ratios, and risk management activities, to name a few. ■

## THE BOTTOM LINE

1. Liabilities are present obligations to sacrifice assets in the future because of something that already has occurred. Current liabilities are expected to require current assets (or the creation of other current liabilities) and usually are payable within one year.
2. Short-term bank loans usually are arranged under an existing line of credit with a bank or group of banks. When interest is discounted from the face amount of a note (a so-called noninterest-bearing note), the effective interest rate is higher than the stated discount rate. Large, highly rated firms sometimes sell commercial paper directly to the buyer (lender) to borrow funds at a lower rate than through a bank loan.
3. Accrued liabilities are recorded by adjusting entries for expenses already incurred, but for which cash has yet to be paid (accrued expenses). Familiar examples are salaries and wages payable, income taxes payable, and interest payable.
4. Short-term obligations can be reported as noncurrent liabilities if the company (a) intends to refinance on a long-term basis and (b) demonstrates the ability to do so by actual financing or a formal agreement to do so.

5. A loss contingency is an existing, uncertain situation involving potential loss depending on whether some future event occurs. Whether a contingency is accrued and reported as a liability depends on (a) the likelihood that the confirming event will occur and (b) what can be determined about the amount of loss. It is accrued if it is both probable that the confirming event will occur and the amount can be at least reasonably estimated.
6. A clarifying event before financial statements are issued, but after the year-end, can be used to determine how the contingency is reported. An unasserted suit, claim, or assessment warrants accrual or disclosure if it is probable it will be asserted. A gain contingency is a contingency that might result in a gain. A gain contingency is not recognized until it actually is realized. ■

# APPENDIX 13 PAYROLL-RELATED LIABILITIES

All firms incur liabilities in connection with their payrolls. These arise primarily from legal requirements to withhold taxes from employees' paychecks and from payroll taxes on the firms themselves. Some payroll-related liabilities result from voluntary payroll deductions of amounts payable to third parties.

## EMPLOYEES' WITHHOLDING TAXES

Employers are required by law to withhold federal (sometimes state) income taxes and Social Security taxes from employees' paychecks and remit these to the Internal Revenue Service. The amount withheld for federal income taxes is determined by a tax table furnished by the IRS and varies according to the amount earned and the number of exemptions claimed by the employee. Also, the Federal Insurance Contributions Act (FICA) requires employers to withhold a percentage of each employee's earnings up to a specified maximum. Both the percentage and the maximum are changed intermittently. As this text went to print, the deduction for Social Security was 6.2% of the first $90,000 an employee earns. Additionally, a deduction for Medicare tax was 1.45% with no limit on the base amount. The employer also must pay an equal (matching) amount on behalf of the employee.

## VOLUNTARY DEDUCTIONS

Besides the required deductions for income taxes and Social Security taxes, employees often authorize their employers to deduct other amounts from their paychecks. These deductions might include union dues, contributions to savings or retirement plans, and insurance premiums. Amounts deducted this way represent liabilities until paid to the appropriate organizations.

## EMPLOYERS' PAYROLL TAXES

One payroll tax mentioned earlier is the employer's matching amount of FICA taxes. The employer also must pay federal and state unemployment taxes on behalf of its employees. The Federal Unemployment Tax Act (FUTA) requires a tax of 6.2% of the first $7,000 earned by each employee. This amount is reduced by a 5.4% (maximum) credit for contributions to state unemployment programs, so the net federal rate often is .8%.[24] In many states the state rate is 5.4% but may be reduced by merit ratings affected by the employer's employment experience.

## FRINGE BENEFITS

In addition to salaries and wages, withholding taxes, and payroll taxes, many companies provide employees a variety of fringe benefits. Most commonly, employers pay all or part of employees' insurance premiums and/or contributions to retirement income plans.

Representative payroll-related liabilities are presented in Illustration 13A–1.

As you study the illustration, you should note the similarity among all payroll-related liabilities. Amounts withheld—voluntarily or involuntarily—from paychecks are liabilities

[24] All states presently have unemployment tax programs.

**ILLUSTRATION 13A–1**
Payroll-Related Liabilities

Crescent Lighting and Fixtures' payroll for the second week in January was $100,000. The following deductions, fringe benefits, and taxes apply:

| | |
|---|---|
| Federal income taxes to be withheld | $20,000 |
| State income taxes to be withheld | 3,000 |
| Medical insurance premiums (Blue Cross)—70% paid by employer | 1,000 |
| Employee contribution to voluntary retirement plan (Fidelity Investments)—contributions matched by employer | 4,000 |
| Union dues (Local No. 222)—paid by employees | 100 |
| Life insurance premiums (Prudential Life)—100% paid by employer | 200 |
| Social Security tax rate | 6.2% |
| Medicare tax rate | 1.45% |
| Federal unemployment tax rate (after state deduction) | 0.80% |
| State unemployment tax rate | 5.40% |

| | | |
|---|---|---|
| Salaries and wages expense (total amount earned) | 100,000 | |
| Withholding taxes payable (federal income tax) | | 20,000 |
| Withholding taxes payable (state income tax) | | 3,000 |
| Social Security taxes payable (6.2%) | | 6,200 |
| Medicare taxes payable (1.45%) | | 1,450 |
| Payable to Blue Cross (insurance premiums—30%) | | 300 |
| Payable to Fidelity Investments (employees' investment) | | 4,000 |
| Payable to Local No. 222 (union dues) | | 100 |
| Salaries and wages payable (net pay) | | 64,950 |
| Payroll tax expense (total) | 13,850 | |
| Social Security taxes payable (employer's matching amount) | | 6,200 |
| Medicare taxes payable (employer's matching amount) | | 1,450 |
| FUTA payable (federal unemployment tax: .8%) | | 800 |
| State unemployment tax payable (5.4%) | | 5,400 |
| Salaries and wages expense (fringe benefits) | 4,900 | |
| Payable to Blue Cross (insurance premiums—70%) | | 700 |
| Payable to Fidelity Investments (matching amount) | | 4,000 |
| Payable to Prudential Life (insurance premiums) | | 200 |

**Amounts withheld from paychecks represent liabilities until remitted to third parties.**

**The employer's share of FICA and unemployment taxes constitute the employer's payroll tax expense.**

**Fringe benefits are part of salaries and wages expense and represent liabilities until remitted to third parties.**

until turned over to appropriate third parties. Payroll taxes and expenses for fringe benefits are incurred as a result of services performed by employees and also are liabilities until paid to appropriate third parties. ■

# QUESTIONS FOR REVIEW OF KEY TOPICS

**Q 13–1** What are the essential characteristics of liabilities for purposes of financial reporting?

**Q 13–2** What distinguishes current liabilities from long-term liabilities?

**Q 13–3** Bronson Distributors owes a supplier $100,000 on open account. The amount is payable in three months. What is the theoretically correct way to measure the reportable amount for this liability? In practice, how will it likely be reported? Why?

**Q 13–4** Bank loans often are arranged under existing lines of credit. What is a line of credit? How does a noncommitted line of credit differ from a committed line?

**Q 13–5** Banks sometimes loan cash under noninterest-bearing notes. Is it true that banks lend money without interest?

**Q 13–6** How does commercial paper differ from a bank loan? Why is the interest rate often less for commercial paper?

**Q 13–7** Salaries of $5,000 have been earned by employees by the end of the period but will not be paid to employees until the following period. How should the expense and related liability be recorded? Why?

**Q 13–8** Under what conditions should an employer accrue an expense and the related liability for employees' compensation for future absences? How do company custom and practice affect the accrual decision?

**Q 13–9** How are refundable deposits and customer advances similar? How do they differ?

**Q 13–10** Amounts collected for third parties represent liabilities until remitted. Provide several examples of this kind of collection.

**Q 13–11** Consider the following liabilities of Future Brands, Inc., at December 31, 2006, the company's fiscal year-end. Should they be reported as current liabilities or long-term liabilities?

1. \$77 million of 8% notes are due on May 31, 2010. The notes are callable by the Company's bank, beginning March 1, 2007.
2. \$102 million of 8% notes are due on May 31, 2011. A debt covenant requires Future to maintain a current ratio (ratio of current assets to current liabilities) of at least 2 to 1. Future is in violation of this requirement but has obtained a waiver from the bank until May 2007, since both companies feel Future will correct the situation during the first half of 2007.

**Q 13–12** Long-term obligations usually are reclassified and reported as current liabilities when they become payable within the upcoming year (or operating cycle, if longer than a year). So, a 25-year bond issue is reported as a long-term liability for 24 years but normally is reported as a current liability on the balance sheet prepared during the 25th year of its term to maturity. Name a situation in which this would not be the case.

**Q 13–13** Define a loss contingency. Provide three examples.

**Q 13–14** List and briefly describe the three categories of likelihood that a future event(s) will confirm the incurrence of the liability for a loss contingency.

**Q 13–15** Under what circumstances should a loss contingency be accrued?

**Q 13–16** Suppose the analysis of a loss contingency indicates that an obligation is not probable. What accounting treatment if any is warranted?

**Q 13–17** Name two loss contingencies that almost always are accrued.

**Q 13–18** Distinguish between the accounting treatment of a manufacturer's warranty and an extended warranty. Why the difference?

**Q 13–19** At December 31, the end of the reporting period, the analysis of a loss contingency indicates that an obligation is only reasonably possible, though its dollar amount is readily estimable. During February, before the financial statements are issued, new information indicates the loss is probable. What accounting treatment is warranted?

**Q 13–20** After the end of the reporting period, a contingency comes into existence. Under what circumstances, if any, should the contingency be reported in the financial statements for the period ended?

**Q 13–21** Suppose the Environmental Protection Agency is in the process of investigating Ozone Ruination Limited for possible environmental damage but has not proposed a penalty as of December 31, 2006, the company's fiscal year-end. Describe the two-step process involved in deciding how this unasserted assessment should be reported.

**Q 13–22** You are the plaintiff in a lawsuit. Your legal counsel advises that your eventual victory is inevitable. "You will be awarded \$12 million," your attorney confidently asserts. Describe the appropriate accounting treatment.

## BRIEF EXERCISES

**BE 13–1**
Bank loan; accrued interest

● LO2 LO3

On October 1, Eder Fabrication borrowed \$60 million and issued a nine-month, 12% promissory note. Interest was payable at maturity. Prepare the journal entry for the issuance of the note and the appropriate adjusting entry for the note at December 31, the end of the reporting period.

**BE 13–2**
Non-interest-bearing note; accrued interest

● LO2 LO3

On October 1, Eder Fabrication borrowed \$60 million and issued a nine-month promissory note. Interest was discounted at issuance at a 12% discount rate. Prepare the journal entry for the issuance of the note and the appropriate adjusting entry for the note at December 31, the end of the reporting period.

**BE 13–3**
Determining accrued interest

● LO2 LO3

On July 1, Orcas Lab issued a \$100,000, 12%, 8-month note. Interest is payable at maturity. What is the amount of interest expense that should be recorded in a year-end adjusting entry if the fiscal year-end is (a) December 31 and (b) September 30.

**BE 13–4**
Commercial paper
● LO2

Branch Corporation issued $12 million of commercial paper on March 1 on a nine-month note. Interest was discounted at issuance at a 9% discount rate. Prepare the journal entry for the issuance of the commercial paper and its repayment at maturity.

**BE 13–5**
Non-interest-bearing note; effective interest rate
● LO2

Life.com issued $10 million of commercial paper on April 1 on a nine-month note. Interest was discounted at issuance at a 6% discount rate. What is the effective interest rate on the commercial paper?

**BE 13–6**
Advance collection
● LO3

On December 12, 2006, Pace Electronics received $24,000 from a customer toward a cash sale of $240,000 of diodes to be completed on January 16, 2007. What journal entries should Pace record on December 12 and January 16?

**BE 13–7**
Sales tax
● LO3

During December, Rainey Equipment made a $600,000 credit sale. The state sales tax rate is 6% and the local sales tax rate is 1.5%. Prepare the appropriate journal entry.

**BE 13–8**
Warranties
● LO5 LO6

Right Medical introduced a new implant that carries a five-year warranty against manufacturer's defects. Based on industry experience with similar product introductions, warranty costs are expected to approximate 1% of sales. Sales were $15 million and actual warranty expenditures were $20,000 for the first year of selling the product. What amount (if any) should Right report as a liability at the end of the year?

**BE 13–9**
Product recall
● LO5 LO6

Consultants notified management of Goo Goo Baby Products that a crib toy poses a potential health hazard. Counsel indicated that a product recall is probable and is estimated to cost the company $5.5 million. How will this affect the company's income statement and balance sheet this period?

**BE 13–10**
Contingency
● LO5 LO6

Skill Hardware is the plaintiff in a $16 million lawsuit filed against a supplier. The litigation is in final appeal and legal counsel advises that it is virtually certain that Skill will win the lawsuit and be awarded $12 million. How should Skill account for this event?

**BE 13–11**
Contingency
● LO5 LO6

Bell International can estimate the amount of loss that will occur if a foreign government expropriates some company property. Expropriation is considered reasonably possible. How should Bell report the loss contingency?

**BE 13–12**
Contingencies
● LO5 LO6

Household Solutions manufactures kitchen storage products. During the year, the company became aware of potential costs due to (1) a possible product defect that is reasonably possible and can be reasonably estimated, (2) a safety hazard that is probable and cannot be reasonably estimated, and (3) a new product warranty that is probable and can be reasonably estimated. Which, if any, of these costs should be accrued?

**BE 13–13**
Unasserted assessment
● LO5 LO6

At March 13, 2007, the Environmental Protection Agency is in the process of investigating a possible emissions leak last summer at a facility of Now Chemical. The EPA has not yet proposed a penalty assessment. Now's fiscal year ends on December 31, 2006, and its financial statements are published in March, 2007. Management feels an assessment is *reasonably possible,* and if an assessment is made an unfavorable settlement of $13 million is *probable.* What, if any, action should Now take for its financial statements?

## EXERCISES

available with McGraw-Hill's Homework Manager www.mhhe.com/spiceland4e

**An alternate exercise and problem set is available on the text website: www.mhhe.com/spiceland4e**

**E 13–1**
Bank loan; accrued interest
● LO2 LO3

On November 1, 2006, Quantum Technology, a geothermal energy supplier, borrowed $8 million cash to fund a geological survey. The loan was made by Nevada BancCorp under a noncommitted short-term line of credit arrangement. Quantum issued a nine-month, 12% promissory note. Interest was payable at maturity. Quantum's fiscal period is the calendar year.

**Required:**

1. Prepare the journal entry for the issuance of the note by Quantum Technology.
2. Prepare the appropriate adjusting entry for the note by Quantum on December 31, 2006.
3. Prepare the journal entry for the payment of the note at maturity.

**E 13–2**
Determining accrued interest in various situations

● LO2 LO3

On July 1, 2006, Ross-Livermore Industries issued nine-month notes in the amount of $200 million. Interest is payable at maturity.

**Required:**
Determine the amount of interest expense that should be recorded in a year-end adjusting entry under each of the following independent assumptions:

| | Interest Rate | Fiscal Year-End |
|---|---|---|
| 1. | 12% | December 31 |
| 2. | 10% | September 30 |
| 3. | 9% | October 31 |
| 4. | 6% | January 31 |

**E 13–3**
Multiple choice; CPA exam; current liabilities

● LO3 LO4

The following questions dealing with current liabilities are adapted from questions that appeared on past CPA examinations. Determine the response that best completes the statements or questions.

1. Black Co. requires advance payments with special orders for machinery constructed to customer specifications. These advances are nonrefundable. Information for 2006 is as follows:

| | |
|---|---|
| Customer advances—balance 12/31/05 | $118,000 |
| Advances received with orders in 2006 | 184,000 |
| Advances applied to orders shipped in 2006 | 164,000 |
| Advances applicable to orders canceled in 2006 | 50,000 |

In Black's December 31, 2006, balance sheet, what amount should be reported as a current liability for advances from customer?
a. $0.
b. $88,000.
c. $138,000.
d. $148,000.

2. Which of the following is generally associated with payables classified as accounts payable?

| | Periodic Payment of Interest | Secured by Collateral |
|---|---|---|
| a. | No | No |
| b. | No | Yes |
| c. | Yes | No |
| d. | Yes | Yes |

**E 13–4**
Short-term notes

● LO2

The following selected transactions relate to liabilities of United Insulation Corporation. United's fiscal year ends on December 31.

**Required:**
Prepare the appropriate journal entries through the maturity of each liability.

| | |
|---|---|
| **2006** | |
| Jan. 13 | Negotiated a revolving credit agreement with Parish Bank that can be renewed annually upon bank approval. The amount available under the line of credit is $20 million at the bank's prime rate. |
| Feb. 1 | Arranged a three-month bank loan of $5 million with Parish Bank under the line of credit agreement. Interest at the prime rate of 10% was payable at maturity. |
| May 1 | Paid the 10% note at maturity. |
| Dec. 1 | Supported by the credit line, issued $10 million of commercial paper on a nine-month note. Interest was discounted at issuance at a 9% discount rate. |
| 31 | Recorded any necessary adjusting entry(s). |
| **2007** | |
| Sept. 1 | Paid the commercial paper at maturity. |

**E 13–5**
Paid future absences

● LO3

JWS Transport Company's employees earn vacation time at the rate of 1 hour per 40-hour work period. The vacation pay vests immediately (that is, an employee is entitled to the pay even if employment terminates). During 2006, total wages paid to employees equaled $404,000, including $4,000 for vacations actually taken in 2006 but not including vacations related to 2006 that will be taken in 2007. All vacations earned before 2006 were taken before January 1, 2006. No accrual entries have been made for the vacations. No overtime premium and no bonuses were paid during the period.

**Required:**
Prepare the appropriate adjusting entry for vacations earned but not taken in 2006.

**E 13–6**
Paid future absences
● LO3

On January 1, 2006, Poplar Fabricators Corporation agreed to grant its employees two weeks' vacation each year, with the stipulation that vacations earned each year can be taken the following year. For the year ended December 31, 2006, Poplar Fabricators' employees each earned an average of $900 per week. Seven hundred vacation weeks earned in 2006 were not taken during 2006.

**Required:**

1. Prepare the appropriate adjusting entry for vacations earned but not taken in 2006.
2. Suppose wage rates for employees have risen by an average of 5 percent by the time vacations actually are taken in 2007. Also, assume wages earned in 2007 (including vacations earned and taken in 2007) were $31 million. Prepare a journal entry that summarizes 2007 wages and the payment for 2006 vacations taken in 2007.

**E 13–7**
Customer advances; sales taxes
● LO3

Bavarian Bar and Grill opened for business in November 2006. During its first two months of operation, the restaurant sold gift certificates in various amounts totaling $5,200, mostly as Christmas presents. They are redeemable for meals within two years of the purchase date, although experience within the industry indicates that 80% of gift certificates are redeemed within one year. Certificates totaling $1,300 were presented for redemption during 2006 for meals having a total price of $2,100. The sales tax rate on restaurant sales is 4%, assessed at the time meals (not gift certificates) are purchased. Sales taxes will be remitted in January.

**Required:**

1. Prepare the appropriate journal entries (in summary form) for the gift certificates sold during 2006 (keeping in mind that, in actuality, each sale of a gift certificate or a meal would be recorded individually).
2. Determine the liability for gift certificates to be reported on the December 31, 2006, balance sheet.
3. What is the appropriate classification (current or noncurrent) of the liabilities at December 31, 2006? Why?

**E 13–8**
Customer deposits
● LO3

Diversified Semiconductors sells perishable electronic components. Some must be shipped and stored in reusable protective containers. Customers pay a deposit for each container received. The deposit is equal to the container's cost. They receive a refund when the container is returned. During 2006, deposits collected on containers shipped were $850,000.

Deposits are forfeited if containers are not returned within 18 months. Containers held by customers at January 1, 2006, represented deposits of $530,000. In 2006, $790,000 was refunded and deposits forfeited were $35,000.

**Required:**

1. Prepare the appropriate journal entries for the deposits received and returned during 2006.
2. Determine the liability for refundable deposits to be reported on the December 31, 2006, balance sheet.

**E 13–9**
Various transactions involving advance collections
● LO3

The following selected transactions relate to liabilities of Interstate Farm Implements for December of 2006. Interstate's fiscal year ends on December 31.

**Required:**

Prepare the appropriate journal entries for these transactions.

1. On December 15, received $7,500 from Bradley Farms toward the purchase of a $98,000 tractor to be delivered on January 6, 2007.
2. During December, received $25,500 of refundable deposits relating to containers used to transport equipment parts.
3. During December, credit sales totaled $800,000. The state sales tax rate is 5% and the local sales tax rate is 2%. (This is a summary journal entry for the many individual sales transactions for the period.)

**E 13–10**
Current—noncurrent classification of debt
● LO1 LO4

A recent annual report of **Sprint Corporation** contained a rather lengthy narrative entitled "Review of Segmental Results of Operation." The narrative noted that short-term notes payable and commercial paper outstanding at the end of the year aggregated $756 million and that during the following year "This entire balance will be replaced by the issuance of long-term debt or will continue to be refinanced under existing long-term credit facilities."

**Required:**

How did Sprint report the debt in its balance sheet? Why?

**E 13–11**
Current—noncurrent classification of debt
● LO1 LO4

At December 31, 2006, Newman Engineering's liabilities include the following:

1. $10 million of 9% bonds were issued for $10 million on May 31, 1985. The bonds mature on May 31, 2017, but bondholders have the option of calling (demanding payment on) the bonds on May 31, 2007. However, the option to call is not expected to be exercised, given prevailing market conditions.
2. $14 million of 8% notes are due on May 31, 2010. A debt covenant requires Newman to maintain current assets at least equal to 175% of its current liabilities. On December 31, 2006, Newman is in violation of this covenant. Newman obtained a waiver from National City Bank until June 2007,

having convinced the bank that the company's normal 2 to 1 ratio of current assets to current liabilities will be reestablished during the first half of 2007.

3. $7 million of 11% bonds were issued for $7 million on August 31, 1975. The bonds mature on July 31, 2007. Sufficient cash is expected to be available to retire the bonds at maturity.

**Required:**

What portion of the debt can be excluded from classification as a current liability (that is, reported as a noncurrent liability)? Explain.

**E 13–12**
Warranties

● LO5 LO6

Cupola Awning Corporation introduced a new line of commercial awnings in 2006 that carry a two-year warranty against manufacturer's defects. Based on their experience with previous product introductions, warranty costs are expected to approximate 3% of sales. Sales and actual warranty expenditures for the first year of selling the product were:

| Sales | Actual Warranty Expenditures |
|---|---|
| $5,000,000 | $37,500 |

**Required:**

1. Does this situation represent a loss contingency? Why or why not? How should Cupola account for it?
2. Prepare journal entries that summarize sales of the awnings (assume all credit sales) and any aspects of the warranty that should be recorded during 2006.
3. What amount should Cupola report as a liability at December 31, 2006?

**E 13–13**
Extended warranties

● LO5 LO6

Carnes Electronics sells consumer electronics that carry a 90-day manufacturer's warranty. At the time of purchase, customers are offered the opportunity to also buy a two-year extended warranty for an additional charge. During 2006, Carnes received $412,000 for these extended warranties (approximately evenly throughout the year).

**Required:**

1. Does this situation represent a loss contingency? Why or why not? How should it be accounted for?
2. Prepare journal entries that summarize sales of the extended warranties (assume all credit sales) and any aspects of the warranty that should be recorded during 2006.

**E 13–14**
Contingency; product recall

● LO5 LO6

Sound Audio manufactures and sells audio equipment for automobiles. Engineers notified management in December 2006 of a circuit flaw in an amplifier that poses a potential fire hazard. An intense investigation indicated that a product recall is virtually certain, estimated to cost the company $2 million. The fiscal year ends on December 31.

**Required:**

1. Should this loss contingency be accrued, disclosed only, or neither? Explain.
2. What loss, if any, should Sound Audio report in its 2006 income statement?
3. What liability, if any, should Sound Audio report in its 2006 balance sheet?
4. Prepare any journal entry needed.

**E 13–15**
Impairment of accounts receivable

● LO5 LO6

The Manda Panda Company uses the allowance method to account for bad debts. At the beginning of 2006, the allowance account had a credit balance of $75,000. Credit sales for 2006 totaled $2,400,000 and the year-end accounts receivable balance was $490,000. During this year, $73,000 in receivables were determined to be uncollectible. Manda Panda anticipates that 3% of all credit sales will ultimately become uncollectible. The fiscal year ends on December 31.

**Required:**

1. Does this situation describe a loss contingency? Explain.
2. What is the bad debt expense that Manda Panda should report in its 2006 income statement?
3. Prepare the appropriate journal entry to record the contingency.
4. What is the net realizable value (book value) Manda Panda should report in its 2006 balance sheet?

**E 13–16**
Premiums

● LO5 LO6

Drew-Richards iMusic is a regional music media reseller. As a promotion, it offered $5 cash rebates on specific CDs. Customers must mail in a proof-of-purchase seal from the package plus the cash register receipt to receive the rebate. Experience suggests that 70% of the rebates will be claimed. Twenty thousand of the CDs were sold in 2006. Total rebates to customers in 2006 were $22,000 and were recorded as promotional expense when paid. The fiscal year ends on December 31.

**Required:**

1. What is the promotional expense that Drew-Richards should report in its 2006 income statement?
2. What is the premium liability that Drew-Richards should report in its 2006 balance sheet?
3. Prepare the appropriate journal entry to record the contingency.

**E 13–17**
Unasserted assessment

● LO6

At April 1, 2007, the IRS is in the process of auditing the tax returns of Shu Lamination, Inc. for the previous three years, but has not proposed a deficiency assessment. Shu's fiscal year ends on December 31, 2006. The company's financial statements are published in April 2007.

**Required:**

For each of the following scenarios, determine the appropriate way to report the situation. Explain your reasoning and prepare any necessary journal entry.

1. Management feels an assessment is *reasonably possible,* and if an assessment is made an unfavorable settlement of $13 million is *reasonably possible.*
2. Management feels an assessment is *reasonably possible,* and if an assessment is made an unfavorable settlement of $13 million is *probable.*
3. Management feels an assessment is *probable,* and if an assessment is made an unfavorable settlement of $13 million is *reasonably possible.*
4. Management feels an assessment is *probable,* and if an assessment is made an unfavorable settlement of $13 million is *probable.*

**E 13–18**
Various transactions involving contingencies

● LO5 LO6

The following selected transactions relate to contingencies of Classical Tool Makers, Inc., which began operations in July 2006. Classical's fiscal year ends on December 31. Financial statements are published in April 2007.

**Required:**

Prepare the appropriate journal entries to record any amounts that should be recorded as a result of each of these contingencies and indicate whether a disclosure note is indicated.

1. Classical's products carry a one-year warranty against manufacturer's defects. Based on previous experience, warranty costs are expected to approximate 4% of sales. Sales were $2 million (all credit) for 2006. Actual warranty expenditures were $30,800 and were recorded as warranty expense when incurred.
2. Although no customer accounts have been shown to be uncollectible, Classical estimates that 2% of credit sales will eventually prove uncollectible.
3. In December 2006, the State of Tennessee filed suit against Classical, seeking penalties for violations of clean air laws. On January 23, 2007, Classical reached a settlement with state authorities to pay $1.5 million in penalties.
4. Classical is the plaintiff in a $4 million lawsuit filed against a supplier. The suit is in final appeal and attorneys advise that it is virtually certain that Classical will win the case and be awarded $2.5 million.
5. In November 2006, Classical became aware of a design flaw in an industrial saw that poses a potential electrical hazard. A product recall appears unavoidable. Such an action would likely cost the company $500,000.
6. Classical offered $25 cash rebates on a new model of jigsaw. Customers must mail in a proof-of-purchase seal from the package plus the cash register receipt to receive the rebate. Experience suggests that 60% of the rebates will be claimed. Ten thousand of the jigsaws were sold in 2006. Total rebates to customers in 2006 were $105,000 and were recorded as promotional expense when paid.

**E 13–19**
Multiple choice; CPA exam; contingencies

● LO5 LO6

The following questions dealing with current liabilities are adapted from questions that appeared on past CPA examinations. Determine the response that best completes the statements or questions.

1. During 2006, Smith Co. filed suit against West, Inc., seeking damages for patent infringement. At December 31, 2006, Smith's legal counsel believed that it was probable that Smith would be successful against West for an estimated amount in the range of $75,000 to $150,000, with all amounts in the range considered equally likely. In March 2007, Smith was awarded $100,000 and received full payment thereof. In its 2006 financial statements, issued in February 2007, how should this award be reported?
   a. As a receivable and revenue of $100,000.
   b. As a receivable and deferred revenue of $100,000.
   c. As a disclosure of a contingent gain of $100,000.
   d. As a disclosure of a contingent gain of an undetermined amount in the range of $75,000 to $150,000.
2. Vadis Co. sells appliances that include a three-year warranty. Service calls under the warranty are performed by an independent mechanic under a contract with Vadis. Based on experience, warranty costs are estimated at $30 for each machine sold. When should Vadis recognize these warranty costs?
   a. Evenly over the life of the warranty.
   b. When the service calls are performed.
   c. When payments are made to the mechanic.
   d. When the machines are sold.
3. Management can estimate the amount of loss that will occur if a foreign government expropriates some company assets. If expropriation is reasonably possible, a loss contingency should be
   a. Disclosed but not accrued as a liability.
   b. Disclosed and accrued as a liability.
   c. Accrued as liability but not disclosed.
   d. Neither accrued as a liability nor disclosed.

4. In December 2006, Mill Co. began including one coupon in each package of candy that it sells and offering a toy in exchange for 50 cents and five coupons. The toys cost Mill 80 cents each. Eventually 60% of the coupons will be redeemed. During December, Mill sold 110,000 packages of candy and no coupons were redeemed. In its December 31, 2006, balance sheet, what amount should Mill report as estimated liability for coupons?
   a. $3,960
   b. $10,560
   c. $19,800
   d. $52,800

**E 13–20**
Disclosures of liabilities

● LO1 through LO6

Indicate (by letter) the way each of the items listed below should be reported on a balance sheet at December 31, 2006.

| Item | Reporting Method |
|---|---|
| ____ 1. Commercial paper. | N. Not reported |
| ____ 2. Noncommitted line of credit. | C. Current liability |
| ____ 3. Customer advances. | L. Long-term liability |
| ____ 4. Estimated warranty cost. | D. Disclosure note only |
| ____ 5. Accounts payable. | A. Asset |
| ____ 6. Long-term bonds that will be callable by the creditor in the upcoming year unless an existing violation is not corrected (there is a reasonable possibility the violation will be corrected within the grace period). | |
| ____ 7. Note due March 3, 2007. | |
| ____ 8. Interest accrued on note, Dec. 31, 2006. | |
| ____ 9. Short-term bank loan to be paid with proceeds of sale of common stock. | |
| ____ 10. A determinable gain that is contingent on a future event that appears extremely likely to occur in three months. | |
| ____ 11. Unasserted assessment of back taxes that probably will be asserted, in which case there would probably be a loss in six months. | |
| ____ 12. Unasserted assessment of back taxes with a reasonable possibility of being asserted, in which case there would probably be a loss in 13 months. | |
| ____ 13. A determinable loss from a past event that is contingent on a future event that appears extremely likely to occur in three months. | |
| ____ 14. Bond sinking fund. | |
| ____ 15. Long-term bonds callable by the creditor in the upcoming year that are not expected to be called. | |

**E 13–21**
Warranty expense; change in estimate

● LO5 LO6

Woodmier Lawn Products introduced a new line of commercial sprinklers in 2005 that carry a one-year warranty against manufacturer's defects. Because this was the first product for which the company offered a warranty, trade publications were consulted to determine the experience of others in the industry. Based on that experience, warranty costs were expected to approximate 2% of sales. Sales of the sprinklers in 2005 were $2.5 million. Accordingly, the following entries relating to the contingency for warranty costs were recorded during the first year of selling the product:

| | | |
|---|---|---|
| **Accrued liability and expense** | | |
| Warranty expense (2% × $2,500,000) | 50,000 | |
| Estimated warranty liability | | 50,000 |
| **Actual expenditures (summary entry)** | | |
| Estimated warranty liability | 23,000 | |
| Cash, wages payable, parts and supplies, etc. | | 23,000 |

In late 2006, the company's claims experience was evaluated and it was determined that claims were far more than expected—3% of sales rather than 2%.

**Required:**

1. Assuming sales of the sprinklers in 2006 were $3.6 million and warranty expenditures in 2006 totaled $88,000, prepare any journal entries related to the warranty.
2. Assuming sales of the sprinklers were discontinued after 2005, prepare any journal entry(s) in 2006 related to the warranty.

**E 13–22**
Change in accounting estimate

● LO3

The Commonwealth of Virginia filed suit in October 2004 against Northern Timber Corporation, seeking civil penalties and injunctive relief for violations of environmental laws regulating forest conservation. When the 2005 financial statements were issued in 2006, Northern had not reached a settlement with state authorities, but legal counsel advised Northern Timber that it was probable the ultimate settlement would be $1,000,000 in penalties. The following entry was recorded:

| | | |
|---|---|---|
| Loss—litigation | 1,000,000 | |
| Liability—litigation | | 1,000,000 |

Late in 2006, a settlement was reached with state authorities to pay a total of $600,000 to cover the cost of violations.

**Required:**

1. Prepare any journal entries related to the change.
2. Briefly describe other steps Northern should take to report the change.

**E 13–23**
Contingency; Dow Chemical Company disclosure

● LO5 LO6

The **Dow Chemical Company** provides chemical, plastic, and agricultural products and services to various consumer markets. The following excerpt is taken from the disclosure notes of Dow's 2003 annual report ($ in millions):

> At December 31, 2003, the Company had accrued obligations of $381 for environmental remediation and restoration costs, including $40 for the remediation of Superfund sites. This is management's best estimate of the costs for remediation and restoration with respect to environmental matters for which the Company has accrued liabilities, although the ultimate cost with respect to these particular matters could range up to twice that amount. Inherent uncertainties exist in these estimates primarily due to unknown conditions, changing governmental regulations and legal standards regarding liability, and evolving technologies for handling site remediation and restoration.

**Required:**

Does the excerpt describe a loss contingency? Under what conditions would Dow accrue such a contingency? What journal entry did Dow use to record the provision (loss)?

**E 13–24**
Multiple choice; CMA exam; current liabilities and contingencies

● LO5 LO6

The following questions dealing with current liabilities and contingencies are adapted from questions that previously appeared on Certified Management Accountant (CMA) examinations. The CMA designation sponsored by the Institute of Management Accountants (**www.imanet.org**) provides members with an objective measure of knowledge and competence in the field of management accounting. Determine the response that best completes the statements or questions.

1. An employee has the right to receive compensation for future paid leave, and the payment of compensation is probable. If the obligation relates to rights that vest but the amount cannot be reasonably estimated, the employer should
   a. Accrue a liability with proper disclosure.
   b. Not accrue a liability nor disclose the situation.
   c. Accrue a liability; however, the additional disclosure is not required.
   d. Not accrue a liability; however, disclosure is required.
2. The accrual of a contingent liability and the related loss should be recorded when the
   a. Loss resulting from a future event may be material in relation to income.
   b. Future event that gives rise to the liability is unusual in nature and nonrecurring.
   c. Amount of the loss resulting from the event is reasonably estimated and the occurrence of the loss is probable.
   d. Event that gives rise to the liability is unusual and its occurrence is probable.
3. For the past 3 months, Kenton Inc. has been negotiating a labor contract with potentially significant wage increases. Before completing the year-end financial statements on November 30, Kenton determined that the contract was likely to be signed in the near future. Kenton has estimated that the effect of the new contract will cost the company either $100,000, $200,000, or $300,000. Also Kenton believes that each estimate has an equal chance of occurring and that the likelihood of the new contract being retroactive to the fiscal year ended November 30 is probable. According to SFAS 5, Kenton should
   a. Do nothing because no loss will occur if the contract is never signed.
   b. Disclose each loss contingency amount in the notes to the November 30 financial statements.
   c. Accrue $100,000 in the income statement, and disclose the nature of the contingency and the additional loss exposure.
   d. Follow conservatism and accrue $300,000 in the income statement, and disclose the nature of the contingency.
4. Lister Company intends to refinance a portion of its short-term debt next year and is negotiating a long-term financing agreement with a local bank. This agreement will be noncancelable and will extend for 2 years. The amount of short-term debt that Lister Company can exclude from its statement of financial position at December 31
   a. May exceed the amount available for refinancing under the agreement.
   b. Depends on the demonstrated ability to consummate the refinancing.

c. Must be adjusted by the difference between the present value and the market value of the short-term debt.
d. Is reduced by the proportionate change in the working capital ratio.

**E 13–25**
Payroll-related liabilities (Based on Appendix 13)
● LO3

Lee Financial Services pays employees monthly. Payroll information is listed below for January 2006, the first month of Lee's fiscal year. Assume that none of the employees exceeded any relevant wage base.

| | |
|---|---|
| Salaries | $500,000 |
| Federal income taxes to be withheld | 100,000 |
| Federal unemployment tax rate | 0.80% |
| State unemployment tax rate (after FUTA deduction) | 5.40% |
| Social Security (FICA) tax rate | 7.65% |

**Required:**
Prepare the appropriate journal entries to record salaries and wages expense and payroll tax expense for the January 2006 pay period.

## PROBLEMS

available with McGraw-Hill's Homework Manager www.mhhe.com/spiceland4e

**An alternate exercise and problem set is available on the text website: www.mhhe.com/spiceland4e**

**P 13–1**
Bank loan; accrued interest
● LO2 LO3
eXcel

Blanton Plastics, a household plastic product manufacturer, borrowed $14 million cash on October 1, 2006, to provide working capital for year-end production. Blanton issued a four-month, 12% promissory note to N,C&I Bank under a prearranged short-term line of credit. Interest on the note was payable at maturity. Each firm's fiscal period is the calendar year.

**Required:**
1. Prepare the journal entries to record (a) the issuance of the note by Blanton Plastics and (b) N,C&I Bank's receivable on October 1, 2006.
2. Prepare the journal entries by both firms to record all subsequent events related to the note through January 31, 2007.
3. Suppose the face amount of the note was adjusted to include interest (a noninterest-bearing note) and 12% is the bank's stated discount rate. Prepare the journal entries to record the issuance of the noninterest-bearing note by Blanton Plastics on October 1, 2006, the adjusting entry at December 31, and payment of the note at maturity. What would be the effective interest rate?

**P 13–2**
Various transactions involving liabilities
● LO1 through LO4
eXcel

Camden Biotechnology began operations in September 2006. The following selected transactions relate to liabilities of the company for September 2006 through March 2007. Camden's fiscal year ends on December 31. Its financial statements are issued in April.

**2006**
a. On September 5, opened checking accounts at Second Commercial Bank and negotiated a short-term line of credit of up to $15,000,000 at the bank's prime rate (10.5% at the time). The company will pay no commitment fees.
b. On October 1, borrowed $12 million cash from Second Commercial Bank under the line of credit and issued a five-month promissory note. Interest at the prime rate of 10% was payable at maturity. Management planned to issue 10-year bonds in February to repay the note.
c. Received $2,600 of refundable deposits in December for reusable containers used to transport and store chemical-based products.
d. For the September–December period, sales on account totaled $4,100,000. The state sales tax rate is 3% and the local sales tax rate is 3%. (This is a summary journal entry for the many individual sales transactions for the period.)
e. Recorded the adjusting entry for accrued interest.

**2007**
f. In February, issued $10 million of 10-year bonds at face value and paid the bank loan on the March 1 due date.
g. Half of the storage containers covered by refundable deposits were returned in March. The remaining containers are expected to be returned during the next six months.

**Required:**
1. Prepare the appropriate journal entries for these transactions.
2. Prepare the current and long-term liability sections of the December 31, 2006, balance sheet. Trade accounts payable on that date were $252,000.

**P 13–3**
Current—noncurrent classification of debt
● LO1 LO4

The balance sheet at December 31, 2006, for Nevada Harvester Corporation includes the liabilities listed below:

a. 11% bonds with a face amount of $40 million were issued for $40 million on October 31, 1997. The bonds mature on October 31, 2017. Bondholders have the option of calling (demanding payment on) the bonds on October 31, 2007, at a redemption price of $40 million. Market conditions are such that the call is not expected to be exercised.
b. Management intended to refinance $6 million of its 10% notes that mature in May 2007. In early March, prior to the actual issuance of the 2006 financial statements, Nevada Harvester negotiated a line of credit with a commercial bank for up to $5 million any time during 2007. Any borrowings will mature two years from the date of borrowing.
c. Noncallable 12% bonds with a face amount of $20 million were issued for $20 million on September 30, 1985. The bonds mature on September 30, 2007. Sufficient cash is expected to be available to retire the bonds at maturity.
d. A $12 million 9% bank loan is payable on October 31, 2012. The bank has the right to demand payment after any fiscal year-end in which Nevada Harvester's ratio of current assets to current liabilities falls below a contractual minimum of 1.7 to 1 and remains so for six months. That ratio was 1.45 on December 31, 2006, due primarily to an intentional temporary decline in inventory levels. Normal inventory levels will be reestablished during the first quarter of 2007.

**Required:**

1. Determine the amount that can be excluded from classification as a current liability (that is, reported as a noncurrent liability) for each. Explain the reasoning behind your classifications.
2. Prepare the liability section of a classified balance sheet and any necessary footnote disclosure for Nevada Harvester at December 31, 2006. Accounts payable and accruals are $22 million.

**P 13–4**
Various liabilities
● LO1 through LO4

The unadjusted trial balance of the Manufacturing Equitable at December 31, 2006, the end of its fiscal year, included the following account balances. Manufacturing's 2006 financial statements were issued on April 1, 2007.

| | |
|---|---|
| Accounts receivable | $ 92,500 |
| Accounts payable | 35,000 |
| Bank notes payable | 600,000 |
| Mortgage note payable | 1,200,000 |

Other information:

a. The bank notes, issued August 1, 2006, are due on July 31, 2007, and pay interest at a rate of 10%, payable at maturity.
b. The mortgage note is due on March 1, 2007. Interest at 9% has been paid up to December 31 (assume 9% is a realistic rate). Manufacturing intended at December 31, 2006, to refinance the note on its due date with a new 10-year mortgage note. In fact, on March 1, Manufacturing paid $250,000 in cash on the principal balance and refinanced the remaining $950,000.
c. Included in the accounts receivable balance at December 31, 2006, were two subsidiary accounts that had been overpaid and had credit balances totaling $18,000. The accounts were of two major customers who were expected to order more merchandise from Manufacturing and apply the overpayments to those future purchases.
d. On November 1, 2006, Manufacturing rented a portion of its factory to a tenant for $30,000 per year, payable in advance. The payment for the 12 months ended October 31, 2007, was received as required and was credited to rent revenue.

**Required:**

1. Prepare any necessary adjusting journal entries at December 31, 2006, pertaining to each item of other information (a–d).
2. Prepare the current and long-term liability sections of the December 31, 2006, balance sheet.

**P 13–5**
Bonus compensation
● LO3

Sometimes compensation packages include bonuses designed to provide performance incentives to employees. The difficulty a bonus can cause accountants is not an accounting problem, but a math problem. The complication is that the bonus formula sometimes specifies that the calculation of the bonus is based in part on the bonus itself. This occurs anytime the bonus is a percentage of income because expenses are components of income, and the bonus is an expense.

Regalia Fashions has an incentive compensation plan through which a division manager receives a bonus equal to 10% of the division's net income. Division income in 2006 before the bonus and income tax was $150,000. The tax rate is 30%.

**Required:**

1. Express the bonus formula as one or more algebraic equation(s).*

*Remember when you were studying algebra, and you wondered if you would ever use it?

2. Using these formulas calculate the amount of the bonus.
3. Prepare the adjusting entry to record the bonus compensation.
4. Bonus arrangements take many forms. Suppose the bonus specifies that the bonus is 10% of the division's income before tax, but after the bonus itself. Calculate the amount of the bonus.

**P 13–6**
Various contingencies
● LO5 LO6

Eastern Manufacturing is involved with several situations that possibly involve contingencies. Each is described below. Eastern's fiscal year ends December 31, and the 2006 financial statements are issued on March 15, 2007.

a. Eastern is involved in a lawsuit resulting from a dispute with a supplier. On February 3, 2007, judgment was rendered against Eastern in the amount of $107 million plus interest, a total of $122 million. Eastern plans to appeal the judgment and is unable to predict its outcome though it is not expected to have a material adverse effect on the company.
b. In November, 2005, the State of Nevada filed suit against Eastern, seeking civil penalties and injunctive relief for violations of environmental laws regulating hazardous waste. On January 12, 2007, Eastern reached a settlement with state authorities. Based upon discussions with legal counsel, the Company feels it is probable that $140 million will be required to cover the cost of violations. Eastern believes that the ultimate settlement of this claim will not have a material adverse effect on the company.
c. Eastern is the plaintiff in a $200 million lawsuit filed against United Steel for damages due to lost profits from rejected contracts and for unpaid receivables. The case is in final appeal and legal counsel advises that it is probable that Eastern will prevail and be awarded $100 million.
d. At March 15, 2007, the IRS is in the process of auditing Eastern's tax returns for 2004–2005, but has not proposed a deficiency assessment. Management feels an assessment is reasonably possible, and if an assessment is made an unfavorable settlement of up to $33 million is reasonably possible.

**Required:**
1. Determine the appropriate means of reporting each situation. Explain your reasoning.
2. Prepare any necessary journal entries and disclosure notes.

**P 13–7**
Frequent flyer program
● LO5 LO6

Northeast Airlines operates a frequent flyer marketing program under which mileage credits are earned by flying on Northeast. The program was designed to retain and increase the business of frequent travelers by offering incentives for their continued patronage. Awards are issued to members at the 20,000 miles level. All awards have an expiration date three years from the date earned. Experience indicates that 25% of free travel earned will actually be redeemed. Northeast accounts for its frequent flyer obligation on the accrual basis using the incremental cost method. The incremental costs include food, beverage, and an additional cost per passenger that is based on engineering formulas to determine the average fuel cost per pound per hour. Northeast's liability for free travel at the beginning of 2006 was $25 million. The incremental cost of free travel taken (redeemed) in 2006 was $8 million. The costs of free travel earned for miles traveled in 2006 are estimated to be $40 million. The fiscal year ends on December 31.

**Required:**
1. Is it appropriate for Northeast to account for its frequent flyer program on the accrual basis? Why?
2. What is the expense that Northeast should report in its 2006 income statement?
3. What is the liability that Northeast should report in its 2006 balance sheet?
4. Prepare the appropriate journal entry to record the year-end accrual of the 2006 expense.

**P 13–8**
Expected cash flow approach; product recall
● LO6
eXcel

The Heinrich Tire Company recalled a tire in its subcompact line in December 2006. Costs associated with the recall were originally thought to approximate $50 million. Now, though, while management feels it is probable the company will incur substantial costs, all discussions indicate that $50 million is an excessive amount. Based on prior recalls in the industry, management has provided the following probability distribution for the potential loss:

| Loss Amount | Probability |
|---|---|
| $40 million | 20% |
| $30 million | 50% |
| $20 million | 30% |

An arrangement with a consortium of distributors requires that all recall costs be settled at the end of 2007. The risk-free rate of interest is 5%.

**Required:**
1. Applying the estimated cash flow approach of *SFAC No. 7,* estimate Heinrich's liability at the end of the 2006 fiscal year.
2. Prepare the journal entry to record the contingent liability (and loss).
3. Prepare the journal entry to accrue interest on the liability at the end of 2007.
4. Prepare the journal entry to pay the liability at the end of 2007, assuming the actual cost is $30 million. Heinrich records an additional loss if the actual costs are higher or a gain if the costs are lower.

**P 13–9**
Subsequent events
● LO6

Lincoln Chemicals became involved in investigations by the U.S. Environmental Protection Agency in regard to damages connected to waste disposal sites. Below are four possibilities regarding the timing of (A) the alleged damage caused by Lincoln, (B) an investigation by the EPA, (C) the EPA assessment of penalties, and (D) ultimate settlement. In each case, assume that Lincoln is unaware of any problem until an investigation is begun. Also assume that once the EPA investigation begins, it is probable that a damage assessment will ensue and that once an assessment is made by the EPA, it is reasonably possible that a determinable amount will be paid by Lincoln.

**Required:**

For each case, decide whether (a) a loss should be accrued in the financial statements with an explanatory note, (b) a disclosure note only should be provided, or (c) no disclosure is necessary.

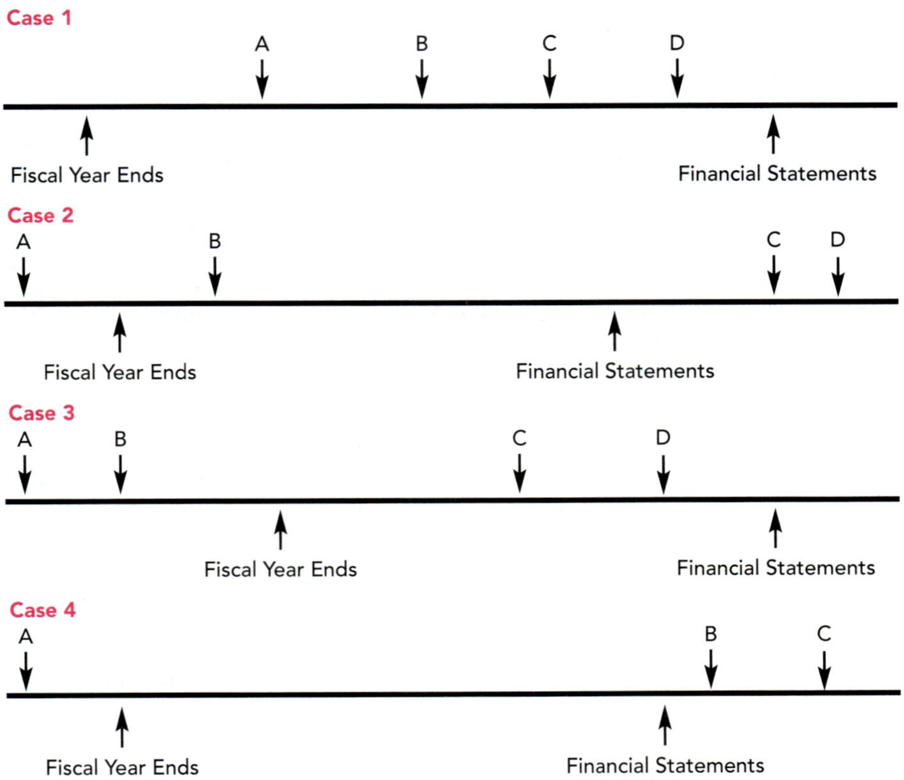


**P 13–10**
Concepts; terminology
● LO1 through LO4

Listed below are several terms and phrases associated with current liabilities. Pair each item from List A (by letter) with the item from List B that is most appropriately associated with it.

| List A | List B |
|---|---|
| ____ 1. Face amount × Interest rate × Time. | a. Informal agreement |
| ____ 2. Payable with current assets. | b. Secured loan |
| ____ 3. Short-term debt to be refinanced with common stock. | c. Refinancing prior to the issuance of the financial statements |
| ____ 4. Present value of interest plus present value of principal. | d. Accounts payable |
| ____ 5. Noninterest-bearing. | e. Accrued liabilities |
| ____ 6. Noncommitted line of credit. | f. Commercial paper |
| ____ 7. Pledged accounts receivable. | g. Current liabilities |
| ____ 8. Reclassification of debt. | h. Long-term liability |
| ____ 9. Purchased by other corporations. | i. Usual valuation of liabilities |
| ____ 10. Expenses not yet paid. | j. Interest on debt |
| ____ 11. Liability until refunded. | k. Customer advances |
| ____ 12. Applied against purchase price. | l. Customer deposits |

**P 13–11**
Payroll-related liabilities (Based on Appendix 13)
● LO3

Alamar Petroleum Company offers its employees the option of contributing up to 5% of their wages or salaries, with the contribution being matched by Alamar. The company also pays 80% of medical and life insurance premiums. Deductions relating to these plans and other payroll information for the first biweekly payroll period of February are listed below.

| | |
|---|---|
| Wages and salaries | $2,000,000 |
| Employee contribution to voluntary retirement plan | 84,000 |
| Medical insurance premiums | 42,000 |
| Life insurance premiums | 9,000 |
| Federal income taxes to be withheld | 400,000 |
| Local income taxes to be withheld | 53,000 |
| Payroll taxes: | |
| Federal unemployment tax rate | 0.80% |
| State unemployment tax rate (after FUTA deduction) | 5.40% |
| Social Security tax rate | 6.2% |
| Medicare tax rate | 1.45% |

**Required:**

Prepare the appropriate journal entries to record salaries and wages expense and payroll tax expense for the biweekly pay period. Assume that no employee's cumulative wages exceed the relevant wage bases.

# BROADEN YOUR PERSPECTIVE

**Apply your critical-thinking ability to the knowledge you've gained. These cases will provide you an opportunity to develop your research, analysis, judgment, and communication skills. You also will work with other students, integrate what you've learned, apply it in real world situations, and consider its global and ethical ramifications. This practice will broaden your knowledge and further develop your decision-making abilities.**

**Research Case 13–1**
Bank loan; accrued interest
● LO1 LO2

A fellow accountant has solicited your opinion regarding the classification of short-term obligations repaid prior to being replaced by a long-term security. Cheshire Foods, Inc., issued $5,000,000 of short-term commercial paper during 2005 to finance construction of a plant. At September 30, 2006, Cheshire's fiscal year-end, the company intends to refinance the commercial paper by issuing long-term bonds. However, because Cheshire temporarily has excess cash, in November 2006 it liquidates $2,000,000 of the commercial paper as the paper matures. In December 2006, the company completes a $10,000,000 long-term bond issue. Later during December, it issues its September 30, 2006 financial statements. The proceeds of the long-term bond issue are to be used to replenish $2,000,000 in working capital, to pay $3,000,000 of commercial paper as it matures in January 2007, and to pay $5,000,000 of construction costs expected to be incurred later that year to complete the plant.

You initially are hesitant because you don't recall encountering a situation in which short-term obligations were repaid prior to being replaced by a long-term security. However, you are encouraged by remembering that this general topic is covered by an FASB pronouncement to which you have access: "Classification of Obligations Expected to Be Refinanced," *Statement of Financial Accounting Standards No. 6* (Stamford, Conn.: FASB, 1975). Also, "Classification of Obligation Repaid Prior to Being Replaced by a Long-Term Security," *FASB Interpretation No. 8,* addresses this situation specifically.

**Required:**

Determine how the $5,000,000 of commercial paper should be classified by consulting the FASB standard. Before doing so, formulate your own opinion on the proper treatment.

**Real World Case 13–2**
Returnable containers
● LO1 LO3

The **Zoo Doo Compost Company** processes a premium organic fertilizer made with the help of the animals at the Memphis Zoo. Zoo Doo is sold in a specially designed plastic pail that may be kept and used for household chores or returned to the seller. The fertilizer is sold for $12.50 per two-gallon pail (including the $1.76 cost of the pail). For each pail returned, Zoo Doo donates $1 to the Memphis Zoo and the pail is used again.[25]

**Required:**

The founder and president of this start-up firm has asked your opinion on how to account for the donations to be made when fertilizer pails are returned. (Ignore any tax implications.)

**Research Case 13–3**
Relationship of liabilities to assets and owners' equity
● LO1

*SFAC No. 6* states that "an entity's assets, liabilities, and equity (net assets) all pertain to the same set of probable future economic benefits." Explain this statement.

[25]Case based on Kay McCullen, "Take The Zoo Home With You!" *Head Lions,* July 1991 and a conversation with the Zoo Doo Compost Company president, Pierce Ledbetter.

**Judgment Case 13–4**
Paid future absences

● LO3

Cates Computing Systems develops and markets commercial software for personal computers and workstations. Three situations involving compensation for possible future absences of Cates's employees are described below.

a. Cates compensates employees at their regular pay rate for time absent for military leave, maternity leave, and jury time. Employees are allowed predetermined absence periods for each type of absence.
b. Members of the new product development team are eligible for three months' paid sabbatical leave every four years. Five members of the team have just completed their fourth year of participation.
c. Company policy permits employees four paid sick days each year. Unused sick days can accumulate and can be carried forward to future years.

**Required:**

1. What are the conditions that require accrual of an expense and related liability for employees' compensation for future absences?
2. For each of the three situations, indicate the circumstances under which accrual of an expense and related liability is warranted.

**Ethics Case 13–5**
Outdoors R Us

● LO1

Outdoors R Us owns several membership-based campground resorts throughout the Southwest. The company sells campground sites to new members, usually during a get-acquainted visit and tour. The campgrounds offer a wider array of on-site facilities than most. New members sign a multiyear contract, pay a down payment, and make monthly installment payments. Because no credit check is made and many memberships originate on a spur-of-the-moment basis, cancellations are not uncommon.

Business has been brisk during its first three years of operations, and since going public in 1998, the market value of its stock has tripled. The first sign of trouble came in 2006 when the new sales dipped sharply.

One afternoon, two weeks before the end of the fiscal year, Diane Rice, CEO, and Gene Sun, controller, were having an active discussion in Sun's office.

*Sun:* I've thought more about our discussion yesterday. Maybe something can be done about profits.
*Rice:* I hope so. Our bonuses and stock value are riding on this period's performance.
*Sun:* We've been recording unearned revenues when new members sign up. Rather than recording liabilities at the time memberships are sold, I think we can justify reporting sales revenue for all memberships sold.
*Rice:* What will be the effect on profits?
*Sun:* I haven't run the numbers yet, but let's just say very favorable.

**Required:**

1. Why do you think liabilities had been recorded previously?
2. Is the proposal ethical?
3. Who would be affected if the proposal is implemented?

**Trueblood Accounting Case 13–6**
Evaluation of a loss contingency

● LO5 LO6

The following Trueblood case is recommended for use with this chapter. The case provides an excellent opportunity for class discussion, group projects, and writing assignments. The case, along with Professor's Discussion Material, can be obtained from the Deloitte Foundation at its website: **www.deloitte.com/us/truebloodcases**.

**Case 02-3: *Frequent Fixer***

This case gives students the opportunity to determine the accounting for product recall campaigns.

**Communication Case 13–7**
Exceptions to the general classification guideline; group interaction

● LO4

Domestic Transfer and Storage is a large trucking company headquartered in the Midwest. Rapid expansion in recent years has been financed in large part by debt in a variety of forms. In preparing the financial statements for 2007, questions have arisen regarding the way certain of the liabilities are to be classified in the company's classified balance sheet.

A meeting of several members of the accounting area is scheduled for tomorrow, April 8, 2007. You are confident that that meeting will include the topic of debt classification. You want to appear knowledgeable at the meeting, but realizing it's been a few years since you have dealt with classification issues, you have sought out information you think relevant. Questionable liabilities at the company's fiscal year-end (January 31, 2007) include the following:

a. $15 million of 9% commercial paper is due on July 31, 2007. Management intends to refinance the paper on a long-term basis. In early April, 2007, Domestic negotiated a credit agreement with a commercial bank for up to $12 million any time during the next three years, any borrowings from which will mature two years from the date of borrowing.
b. $17 million of 11% notes were issued on June 30, 2004. The notes are due on November 30, 2007. The company has investments of $20 million classified as "available for sale."
c. $25 million of 10% notes were due on February 28, 2007. On February 21, 2007, the company issued 30-year, 9.4% bonds in a private placement to institutional investors.
d. Recently, company management has considered reducing debt in favor of a greater proportion of equity financing. $20 million of 12% bonds mature on July 31, 2007. Discussions with underwriters, which

began on January 4, 2007, resulted in a contractual arrangement on March 15 under which new common shares will be sold in July for approximately $20 million.

In order to make notes to yourself in preparation for the meeting concerning the classification of these items, you decide to discuss them with a colleague. Specifically, you want to know what portion of the debt can be excluded from classification as a current liability (that is, reported as a noncurrent liability) and why.

**Required:**

1. What is the appropriate classification of each liability? Develop a list of arguments in support of your view prior to the class session for which the case is assigned.
2. In class, your instructor will pair you (and everyone else) with a classmate (who also has independently developed a position). You will be given three minutes to argue your view to your partner. Your partner likewise will be given three minutes to argue his or her view to you. During these three-minute presentations, the listening partner is not permitted to speak.
3. Then after each person has had a turn attempting to convince his or her partner, the two partners will have a three-minute discussion to decide which classifications are more convincing. Arguments will be merged into a single view for each pair.
4. After the allotted time, a spokesperson for each of the four liabilities will be selected by the instructor. Each spokesperson will field arguments from the class as to the appropriate classification. The class then will discuss the merits of the classification and attempt to reach a consensus view, though a consensus is not necessary.

**Communication Case 13–8**
Various contingencies

● LO5 LO6

"I see an all-nighter coming on," Gayle grumbled. "Why did Mitch just now give us this assignment?" Your client, Western Manufacturing is involved with several situations that possibly involve contingencies. The assignment Gayle refers to is to draft appropriate accounting treatment for each situation described below in time for tomorrow's meeting of the audit group. Western's fiscal year is the calendar year 2006, and the 2006 financial statements are issued on March 15, 2007.

1. During 2006, Western experienced labor disputes at three of its plants. Management hopes an agreement will soon be reached. However negotiations between the Company and the unions have not produced an acceptable settlement and, as a result, strikes are ongoing at these facilities since March 1, 2007. It is virtually certain that material costs will be incurred but the amount of possible costs cannot be reasonably ascertained.
2. In accordance with a 2004 contractual agreement with A. J. Conner Company, Western is entitled to $37 million for certain fees and expense reimbursements. These were written off as bad debts in 2005. A. J. Conner has filed for bankruptcy. The bankruptcy court on February 4, 2007, ordered A. J. Conner to pay $23 million immediately upon consummation of a proposed merger with Garner Holding Group.
3. Western warrants most products it sells against defects in materials and workmanship for a period of a year. Based on their experience with previous product introductions, warranty costs are expected to approximate 2% of sales. A warranty liability of $39 million was reported at December 31, 2005. Sales of warranted products during 2006 were $2,100 million and actual warranty expenditures were $40 million. Expenditures in excess of the existing liability were debited to warranty expense.
4. Western is involved in a suit filed in January 2007 by Crump Holdings seeking $88 million, as an adjustment to the purchase price in connection with the Company's sale of its textile business in 2006. The suit alleges that Western misstated the assets and liabilities used to calculate the purchase price for the textile division. Legal counsel advises that it is reasonably possible that Western could end up losing an indeterminable but material amount not expected to have a material adverse effect on the Company's financial position.

**Required:**

1. Determine the appropriate means of reporting each situation.
2. In a memo to the audit manager, Mitch Riley, explain your reasoning. Include any necessary journal entries and drafts of appropriate disclosure notes.

**Judgment Case 13–9**
Loss contingency and full disclosure

● LO5 LO6

In the March 2007 meeting of Valleck Corporation's board of directors, a question arose as to the way a possible obligation should be disclosed in the forthcoming financial statements for the year ended December 31. A veteran board member brought to the meeting a draft of a disclosure note that had been prepared by the controller's office for inclusion in the annual report. Here is the note:

> On May 9, 2006, the United States Environmental Protection Agency (EPA) issued a Notice of Violation (NOV) to Valleck alleging violations of the Clean Air Act. Subsequently, in June 2006, the EPA commenced a civil action with respect to the foregoing violation seeking civil penalties of approximately $853,000. The EPA alleges that Valleck exceeded applicable volatile organic substance emission limits. The Company estimates that the cost to achieve compliance will be $190,000; in addition the Company expects to settle the EPA lawsuit for a civil penalty of $205,000 which will be paid in 2009.

"Where did we get the $205,000 figure?" he asked. On being informed that this is the amount negotiated last month by company attorneys with the EPA, the director inquires, "Aren't we supposed to report a liability for that in addition to the note?"

**Required:**

Explain whether Valleck should report a liability in addition to the note. Why or why not? For full disclosure, should anything be added to the disclosure note itself?

**Communication Case 13–10**
Change in loss contingency; write a memo

● LO5 LO6

Late in 2006, you and two other officers of Curbo Fabrications Corporation just returned from a meeting with officials of The City of Jackson. The meeting was unexpectedly favorable even though it culminated in a settlement with city authorities that required your company pay a total of $475,000 to cover the cost of violations of city construction codes. Jackson had filed suit in November 2004, against Curbo Fabrications Corporation, seeking civil penalties and injunctive relief for violations of city construction codes regulating earthquake damage standards. Alleged violations involved several construction projects completed during the previous three years. When the financial statements were issued in 2005, Curbo had not reached a settlement with state authorities, but legal counsel had advised the Company that it was probable the ultimate settlement would be $750,000 in penalties. The following entry had been recorded:

| | | |
|---|---|---|
| Loss—litigation | 750,000 | |
| Liability—litigation | | 750,000 |

The final settlement, therefore, was a pleasant surprise. While returning from the meeting, your conversation turned to reporting the settlement in the 2006 financial statements. You drew the short straw and were selected to write a memo to Janet Zeno, the financial vice president, advising the proper course of action.

**Required:**

Write the memo. Include descriptions of any journal entries related to the change in amounts. Briefly describe other steps Curbo should take to report the settlement.

**Research Case 13–11**
Researching the way contingencies are reported; retrieving information from the Internet

● LO5 LO6

EDGAR (Electronic Data Gathering, Analysis, and Retrieval system) performs automated collection, validation, indexing, acceptance, and forwarding of submissions by companies and others who are required by law to file forms with the U.S. Securities and Exchange Commission (SEC). All publicly traded domestic companies use EDGAR to make the majority of their filings. Form 10-K, which includes the annual report, is required to be filed on EDGAR. The SEC makes this information available on the Internet.

**Required:**

1. Access EDGAR on the Internet using EdgarScan at: **edgarscan.pwcglobal.com**.
2. Search for a public company with which you are familiar. Access its most recent 10-K filing. Search or scroll to find the financial statements and related notes.
3. Specifically, look for any contingency(s) reported in the disclosure notes. Identify the nature of the contingency(s) described and explain the reason(s) the loss or losses was or was not accrued.
4. Repeat requirements 2 and 3 for two additional companies.

**Communication Case 13–12**
Accounting changes

● LO5 LO6

Kevin Brantly is a new hire in the controller's office of Fleming Home Products. Two events occurred in late 2006 that the company had not previously encountered. The events appear to affect two of the company's liabilities, but there is some disagreement concerning whether they also affect financial statements of prior years. Each change occurred during 2006 before any adjusting entries or closing entries were prepared. The tax rate for Fleming is 40% in all years.

- Fleming Home Products introduced a new line of commercial awnings in 2005 that carry a one-year warranty against manufacturer's defects. Based on industry experience, warranty costs were expected to approximate 3% of sales. Sales of the awnings in 2005 were $3,500,000. Accordingly, warranty expense and a warranty liability of $105,000 were recorded in 2005. In late 2006, the company's claims experience was evaluated and it was determined that claims were far fewer than expected—2% of sales rather than 3%. Sales of the awnings in 2006 were $4,000,000 and warranty expenditures in 2006 totaled $91,000.
- In November 2004, the State of Minnesota filed suit against the company, seeking penalties for violations of clean air laws. When the financial statements were issued in 2005, Fleming had not reached a settlement with state authorities, but legal counsel advised Fleming that it was probable the company would have to pay $200,000 in penalties. Accordingly, the following entry was recorded:

| | | |
|---|---|---|
| Loss—litigation | 200,000 | |
| Liability—litigation | | 200,000 |

Late in 2006, a settlement was reached with state authorities to pay a total of $350,000 in penalties.

**Required:**

Kevin's supervisor, perhaps unsure of the answer, perhaps wanting to test Kevin's knowledge, e-mails the message, "Kevin, send me a memo on how we should handle our awning warranty and that clean air suit."

Wanting to be accurate, Kevin consults his reference materials. What will he find? Prepare the memo requested.

**Real World Case 13–13**
Frequent flyer miles

● LO1 LO3

Most airlines offer a frequent flyer program under which passengers can earn free travel. **Northwest Airlines Corporation** described its program in a recent annual report:

> **Frequent Flyer Program (in part):** The Company utilizes a number of estimates in accounting for its WorldPerks frequent flyer program. The Company accounts for the frequent flyer program obligations by recording a liability for the estimated incremental cost of flight awards expected to be redeemed on Northwest and other airline partners. Customers are expected to redeem their mileage, and a liability is recorded, when their accounts accumulate the minimum number of miles needed to obtain one flight award.
>
> The number of estimated travel awards outstanding and expected to be redeemed at December 31, 2004, 2003, and 2002 was approximately 3.8, 7.2, and 7.8 million, respectively. Northwest recorded a liability for these estimated awards of $215 million, $119 million and $127 million at December 31, 2004, 2003 and 2002, respectively.

| | ($ in millions) | |
|---|---|---|
| **Current Liabilities** | **2004** | **2003** |
| Air traffic liability | $1,468 | $1,272 |
| Accrued compensation and benefits | 895 | 950 |
| Accounts payable | 566 | 540 |
| Collections as agent | 135 | 111 |
| Accrued aircraft rent | 267 | 268 |
| Other accrued liabilities | 417 | 405 |
| Current maturities of long-term debt | 696 | 668 |
| Current obligations under capital leases | 53 | 65 |
| | 4,497 | 4,279 |

**Required:**

1. Why does Northwest's frequent flyer program produce a liability?
2. Is incremental cost the appropriate measure of the liability? Why?
3. Is the liability current, long-term, or both?
4. Prepare journal entry appropriate to recognize Northwest's expense and liability assuming the liability for the frequent flyer program is included in the Air Traffic liability.

**Real World Case 13–14**
Superfund liability

● LO5 LO6

The Comprehensive Environmental Response, Compensation, and Liability Act (CERCLA), commonly known as Superfund, created a tax on the chemical and petroleum industries and provided broad Federal authority to respond directly to releases or threatened releases of hazardous substances that may endanger public health or the environment. Because pharmaceutical production in years prior to the Act is one source of concern, many drug makers face potential liability for environmental remediation. A disclosure note from the 2004 annual report of **Merck & Co.** reports the Company's response:

> **Note 9: Contingencies and Environmental Liabilities (in part)**
> A worldwide survey was initially performed to assess all sites for potential contamination resulting from past industrial activities. Where assessment indicated that physical investigation was warranted, such investigation was performed, providing a better evaluation of the need for remedial action. Where such need was identified, remedial action was then initiated. Estimates of the extent of contamination at each site were initially made at the pre-investigation stage and liabilities for the potential cost of remediation were accrued at that time. As more definitive information became available during the course of investigations and/or remedial efforts at each site, estimates were refined and accruals were adjusted accordingly. These estimates and related accruals continue to be refined annually.
>
> In management's opinion, the liabilities for all environmental matters that are probable and reasonably estimable have been accrued and totaled $127.5 million and $158.1 million at December 31, 2004 and 2003, respectively. These liabilities are undiscounted, do not consider potential recoveries from insurers or other parties and will be paid out over the periods of remediation for the applicable sites, which are expected to occur primarily over the next 15 years.

Merck's expenditures for remediation and environmental costs were $30.3 million in 2004.

**Required:**

1. From an accounting perspective, what necessitated the accrual?
2. Why is the accrued amount different in 2004 from the year before?
3. Relying on the information provided by the disclosure note, re-create the journal entry Merck recorded to adjust the liability.

**Ethics Case 13–15**
Profits guaranteed

● LO5

This was Joel Craig's first visit to the controller's corner office since being recruited for the senior accountant position in May. Because he'd been directed to bring with him his preliminary report on year-end adjustments, Craig presumed he'd done something wrong in preparing the report. That he had not was Craig's first surprise. His second surprise was his boss's request to reconsider one of the estimated expenses.

S & G Fasteners was a new company, specializing in plastic industrial fasteners. All products carry a generous long-term warranty against manufacturer's defects. "Don't you think 4% of sales is a little high for our warranty expense estimate?" his boss wondered. "After all, we're new at this. We have little experience with product introductions. I just got off the phone with Blanchard (the company president). He thinks we'll have trouble renewing our credit line with the profits we're projecting. The pressure's on."

**Required:**

1. Should Craig follow his boss's suggestion?
2. Does revising the warranty estimate pose an ethical dilemma?
3. Who would be affected if the suggestion is followed?

**International Case 13–16**
Accounting for current liabilities and contingencies in other countries

● LO1 through LO6

The International Accounting Standards Board (IASB) seeks to narrow worldwide differences in accounting practices and the presentation of financial information. The IASB has worked toward uniformity for many years, but harmonization has by no means been achieved. In the area of accounting for current liabilities and contingencies, significant differences exist from country to country. The differences impact the financial position and the ability of analysts to assess risk in countries where these benefits are significant.

**Required:**

Choose a country other than the United States and:

1. Locate a recent annual report of a non-U.S. company.
2. Determine the way that country reports current liabilities on its balance sheet. Include in your analysis:
   a. Whether they are reported as a separate classification of liabilities or whether they are netted against current assets.
   b. Whether and how details are reported in disclosure notes.
3. Determine the way that country reports contingencies. Include in your analysis:
   a. Under what conditions are loss contingencies accrued.
   b. Whether gain contingencies can be accrued or reported in disclosure notes.

**Note:** You can obtain copies of annual reports by contacting the investor relations department of the corporation, from a friendly stockbroker, from EDGAR, the Electronic Data Gathering and Retrieval service of the SEC, through EdgarScan at **edgarscan.pwcglobal.com/**, or often from the company's website.

**Analysis Case 13–17**
Analyzing financial statements; liquidity ratios

● LO1

IGF Foods Company is a large, primarily domestic, consumer foods company involved in the manufacture, distribution and sale of a variety of food products. Industry averages are derived from Troy's *The Almanac of Business and Industrial Financial Ratios.* Following are the 2006 and 2005 comparative balance sheets for IGF. (The financial data we use are from actual financial statements of a well-known corporation, but the company name used is fictitious and the numbers and dates have been modified slightly.)

**IGF FOODS COMPANY**
**Comparative Balance Sheets**
**Years Ended December 31, 2006 and 2005**
($ in millions)

| | 2006 | 2005 |
|---|---|---|
| **Assets** | | |
| Current assets: | | |
| Cash | $ 48 | $ 142 |
| Accounts receivable | 347 | 320 |
| Marketable securities | 358 | — |
| Inventories | 914 | 874 |
| Prepaid expenses | 212 | 154 |
| Total current assets | $1,879 | $1,490 |
| Property, plant, and equipment (net) | 2,592 | 2,291 |
| Intangibles (net) | 800 | 843 |
| Other assets | 74 | 60 |
| Total assets | $5,345 | $4,684 |

| Liabilities and Shareholders' Equity | | |
|---|---|---|
| Current liabilities: | | |
| Accounts payable | $ 254 | $ 276 |
| Accrued liabilities | 493 | 496 |
| Notes payable | 518 | 115 |
| Current portion of long-term debt | 208 | 54 |
| Total current liabilities | $1,473 | $ 941 |
| Long-term debt | 534 | 728 |
| Deferred income taxes | 407 | 344 |
| Total liabilities | $2,414 | $2,013 |
| Shareholders' equity: | | |
| Common stock | 180 | 180 |
| Additional paid-in capital | 21 | 63 |
| Retained earnings | 2,730 | 2,428 |
| Total shareholders' equity | $2,931 | $2,671 |
| Total liabilities and shareholders' equity | $5,345 | $4,684 |

Liquidity refers to a company's cash position and overall ability to obtain cash in the normal course of business. A company is said to be liquid if it has sufficient cash or is capable of converting its other assets to cash in a relatively short period of time so that currently maturing debts can be paid.

**Required:**

1. Calculate the current ratio for IGF for 2006. The average ratio for the stocks listed on the New York Stock Exchange in a comparable time period was 1.5. What information does your calculation provide an investor?
2. Calculate IGF's acid-test or quick ratio for 2006. The ratio for the stocks listed on the New York Stock Exchange in a comparable time period was .80. What does your calculation indicate about IGF's liquidity?

**Analysis Case 13–18**
Reporting current liabilities; liquidity

● LO1

**FedEx Corporation**

Refer to the financial statements and related disclosure notes of **FedEx Corporation** in Appendix B at the back of the book. At the end of its 2004 fiscal year, FedEx reported current liabilities of $4.7 billion on its balance sheet.

**Required:**

1. What are the four components of current liabilities?
2. Are current assets sufficient to cover current liabilities? What is the current ratio for 2004? How does the ratio compare with 2003?
3. FedEx reported accrued expenses among its current liabilities. What were the two largest accrued expenses in 2004 aside from "other"? What are accrued expenses and when does FedEx record them?

# 14 CHAPTER

# Bonds and Long-Term Notes

## OVERVIEW

This chapter continues the presentation of liabilities. Specifically, the discussion focuses on the accounting treatment of long-term liabilities. Long-term notes and bonds are discussed, as well as the extinguishment of debt and debt convertible into stock.

## LEARNING OBJECTIVES

After studying this chapter, you should be able to:

- LO1 Identify the underlying characteristics of debt instruments and describe the basic approach to accounting for debt.
- LO2 Account for bonds issued at par, at a discount, or at a premium, recording interest at the effective rate or by the straight-line method.
- LO3 Characterize the accounting treatment of notes, including installment notes, issued for cash or for noncash consideration.
- LO4 Describe the disclosures appropriate to long-term debt in its various forms.
- LO5 Record the early extinguishment of debt and its conversion into equity securities.

# FINANCIAL REPORTING CASE

## Service Leader, Inc.

The mood is both upbeat and focused on this cool October morning. Executives and board members of Service Leader, Inc., are meeting with underwriters and attorneys to discuss the company's first bond offering in its 20-year history. You are attending in the capacity of company controller and two-year member of the board of directors. The closely held corporation has been financed entirely by equity, internally generated funds, and short-term bank borrowings.

Bank rates of interest, though, have risen recently and the company's unexpectedly rapid, but welcome, growth has prompted the need to look elsewhere for new financing. Under consideration are 15-year, 6.25% first mortgage bonds with a principal amount of $70 million. The bonds would be callable at 103 any time after June 30, 2008, and convertible into Service Leader common stock at the rate of 45 shares per $1,000 bond.

Other financing vehicles have been discussed over the last two months, including the sale of additional stock, nonconvertible bonds, and unsecured notes. This morning *The Wall Street Journal* indicated that market rates of interest for debt similar to the bonds under consideration are about 6.5%.

**By the time you finish this chapter, you should be able to respond appropriately to the questions posed in this case. Compare your response to the solution provided at the end of the chapter.**

### QUESTIONS

1. What does it mean that the bonds are "first mortgage" bonds? What effect does that have on financing? (page 663)
2. From Service Leader's perspective, why are the bonds callable? What does that mean? (page 663)
3. How will it be possible to sell bonds paying investors 6.25% when other, similar investments will provide the investors a return of 6.5%? (page 665)
4. Would accounting differ if the debt were designated as notes rather than bonds? (page 675)
5. Why might the company choose to make the bonds convertible into common stock? (page 684)

# The Nature of Long-Term Debt

● LO1

A company must raise funds to finance its operations and often the expansion of those operations. Presumably, at least some of the necessary funding can be provided by the company's own operations, though some funds must be provided by external sources. Ordinarily, external financing includes some combination of equity and debt funding. We explore debt financing first.

**Liabilities signify *creditors' interest* in a company's assets.**

In the present chapter, we focus on debt in the form of bonds and notes. The following three chapters deal with liabilities also, namely those arising in connection with leases (Chapter 15), deferred income taxes (Chapter 16), and pensions and employee benefits (Chapter 17). Some employee benefits create equity rather than debt, which are discussed in Chapter 19. In Chapter 18, we examine shareholders' interest arising from external *equity* financing. In Chapter 21, we see that cash flows from both debt and equity financing are reported together in a statement of cash flows as "cash flows from financing activities."

As you read this chapter, you will find the focus to be on the liability side of the transactions we examine. Realize, though, that the mirror image of a liability is an asset (bonds payable/investment in bonds, note payable/note receivable, etc.). So as we discuss accounting for debts from the viewpoint of the issuers of the debt instruments, we also will take the opportunity to see how the lender deals with the corresponding asset. Studying the two sides of the same transaction in tandem will emphasize their inherent similarities.

**A note payable and a note receivable are two sides of the same coin.**

Accounting for a liability is a relatively straightforward concept. This is not to say that all debt instruments are unchallenging, "plain vanilla" loan agreements. Quite the contrary, the financial community continually devises increasingly exotic ways to flavor financial instruments in the attempt to satisfy the diverse and evolving tastes of both debtors and creditors.

Packaging aside, a liability requires the future payment of cash in specified (or estimated) amounts, at specified (or projected) dates. As time passes, interest accrues on debt. As a general rule, the periodic interest is the effective interest rate times the amount of the debt outstanding during the period. This same principle applies regardless of the specific form of the liability—note payable, bonds payable, lease liability, pension obligation, or other debt instruments. Also, as a general rule, long-term liabilities are reported at their present values. The present value of a liability is the present value of its related cash flows (principal and/or interest payments), discounted at the effective rate of interest at issuance.

**Periodic interest is the effective interest rate times the amount of the debt outstanding during the interest period.**

We begin our study of long-term liabilities by examining accounting for bonds. We follow that section with a discussion of debt in the form of notes in Part B. It's important to note that, although particulars of the two forms of debt differ, the basic approach to accounting for each type is precisely the same. In Part C, we look at various ways bonds and notes are retired or converted into other securities.

## PART A BONDS

**A bond issue divides a large liability into many smaller liabilities.**

A company can borrow cash from a bank or other financial institution by signing a promissory note. We discuss notes payable later in the chapter. Medium- and large-sized corporations often choose to borrow cash by issuing bonds. In fact, the most common form of corporate debt is bonds. A bond issue, in effect, breaks down a large debt (large corporations often borrow hundreds of millions of dollars at a time) into manageable parts—usually $1,000 or $5,000 units. This avoids the necessity of finding a single lender who is both willing and able to loan a large amount of money at a reasonable interest rate. So rather than signing a $400 million note to borrow cash from a financial institution, a company may find it more economical to sell 400,000 $1,000 bonds to many lenders—theoretically up to 400,000 lenders.

**Corporations issuing bonds are obligated to repay a stated amount at a specified *maturity date* and periodic *interest* between the issue date and maturity.**

**Bonds** obligate the issuing corporation to repay a stated amount (variously referred to as the *principal, par value, face amount,* or *maturity value*) at a specified *maturity date.* Maturities for bonds typically range from 10 to 40 years. In return for the use of the money borrowed, the company also agrees to pay *interest* to bondholders between the issue date and maturity. The periodic interest is a stated percentage of face amount (variously referred to as the *stated rate, coupon rate,* or *nominal rate*). Ordinarily, interest is paid semiannually on designated interest dates beginning six months after the day the bonds are "dated."

## The Bond Indenture

The specific promises made to bondholders are described in a document called a **bond indenture.** Because it would be impractical for the corporation to enter into a direct agreement with each of the many bondholders, the bond indenture is held by a trustee, usually a commercial bank or other financial institution, appointed by the issuing firm to represent the rights of the bondholders. If the company fails to live up to the terms of the bond indenture, the trustee may bring legal action against the company on behalf of the bondholders.

A *bond indenture* describes the specific promises made to bondholders.

Most corporate bonds are debenture bonds. A **debenture bond** is secured only by the "full faith and credit" of the issuing corporation. No specific assets are pledged as security. Investors in debentures usually have the same standing as the firm's other general creditors. So in case of bankruptcy, debenture holders and other general creditors would be treated equally. An exception is the **subordinated debenture,** which as the name implies, is not entitled to receive any liquidation payments until the claims of other specified debt issues are satisfied.

Liquidation rights affect a bond issue's effective interest rate.

A **mortgage bond,** on the other hand, is backed by a lien on specified real estate owned by the issuer. Because a mortgage bond is considered less risky than debentures, it typically will command a lower interest rate.

FINANCIAL REPORTING CASE

Q1, p. 661

Today most corporate bonds are registered bonds. Interest checks are mailed directly to the owner of the bond, whose name is registered with the issuing company. Years ago, it was typical for bonds to be structured as **coupon bonds** (sometimes called *bearer bonds*). The name of the owner of a coupon bond was not registered. Instead, to collect interest on a coupon bond the holder actually clipped an attached coupon and redeemed it in accordance with instructions in the indenture. A carryover effect of this practice is that we still often see the term *coupon rate* in reference to the stated interest rate on bonds.

Bonds are not always retired by a single-sum payment at a specific maturity date. The bond indenture also might provide for their redemption through a call feature, by serial payments, through sinking fund provisions, or by conversion.

Most corporate bonds are **callable** (or redeemable). The call feature allows the issuing company to buy back, or call, outstanding bonds from bondholders before their scheduled maturity date. This feature affords the company some protection against being stuck with relatively high-cost debt in the event interest rates fall during the period to maturity. The call price must be prespecified and often exceeds the bond's face amount (a call premium), sometimes declining as maturity is approached.

FINANCIAL REPORTING CASE

Q2, p. 661

For example, financial statements of **Emhart Corporation** included this footnote disclosure:

> The Company's 9¼% (9.65% effective interest rate, after discount) sinking fund debentures are callable at prices decreasing from 105% of face amount currently to 100% in 2006.

"No call" provisions usually prohibit calls during the first few years of a bond's life. Very often, calls are mandatory. That is, the corporation may be required to redeem the bonds on a prespecified, year-by-year basis. Bonds requiring such sinking fund redemptions often are labeled *sinking fund debentures.*

Mandatory sinking fund redemptions retire a bond issue gradually over its term to maturity.

The **sinking fund** typically is administered by a trustee who repurchases bonds in the open market. If insufficient willing sellers are found, the trustee must exercise the bonds' call feature to buy the required amount of bonds, using a lottery approach to select bonds for call from among existing bondholders.

**Serial bonds** provide a more structured (and less popular) way to retire bonds on a piecemeal basis. Serial bonds are retired in installments during all or part of the life of the issue. Each bond has its own specified maturity date. So for a typical 30-year serial issue, 25 to 30 separate maturity dates might be assigned to specific portions of the bond issue.

**Convertible bonds** are retired as a consequence of bondholders choosing to convert them into shares of stock. We look closer at convertible bonds a little later in the chapter.

## Recording Bonds at Issuance

LO2 Bonds represent a liability to the corporation that issues the bonds and an asset to a company that buys the bonds as an investment. Each side of the transaction is the mirror image of the other.[1] This is demonstrated in Illustration 14–1.

**ILLUSTRATION 14–1**
Bonds Sold at Face Amount

On January 1, 2006, Masterwear Industries issued $700,000 of 12% bonds. Interest of $42,000 is payable semiannually on June 30 and December 31. The bonds mature in three years (an unrealistically short maturity to shorten the illustration). The entire bond issue was sold in a private placement to United Intergroup, Inc., at the face amount.

**At Issuance (January 1)**

| | | |
|---|---|---|
| **Masterwear (Issuer)** | | |
| Cash | 700,000 | |
| Bonds payable (face amount) | | 700,000 |
| **United (Investor)** | | |
| Investment in bonds (face amount) | 700,000 | |
| Cash | | 700,000 |

### BONDS ISSUED BETWEEN INTEREST DATES

**All bonds sell at their price plus any interest that has accrued since the last interest date.**

We assumed that the bonds in the previous example were sold on the day they were dated (date printed in the indenture contract). But suppose a weak market caused a delay in selling the bonds until two months after that date (four months before semiannual interest was to be paid). In that case, the buyer would be asked to pay the seller **accrued interest** for two months in addition to the price of the bonds. For illustration, assume Masterwear was unable to sell the bonds in the previous example until March 1—two months after they are dated. This variation is shown in Illustration 14–1A. United would pay the price of the bonds ($700,000) plus $14,000 accrued interest:

| $700,000 | × | 12% | × | 2/12 | = | $14,000 |
|---|---|---|---|---|---|---|
| Face amount | | Annual rate | | Fraction of the annual period | | Accrued interest |

**ILLUSTRATION 14–1A**
Bonds Sold at Face Amount between Interest Dates

**At Issuance (March 1)**

| | | |
|---|---|---|
| **Masterwear (Issuer)** | | |
| Cash (price plus accrued interest) | 714,000 | |
| Bonds payable (face amount) | | 700,000 |
| Interest payable (accrued interest determined above) | | 14,000 |
| **United (Investor)** | | |
| Investment in bonds (face amount) | 700,000 | |
| Interest receivable (accrued interest determined above) | 14,000 | |
| Cash (price plus accrued interest) | | 714,000 |

When Masterwear pays semiannual interest on June 30, a full six months' interest is paid. But having received two months' accrued interest in advance, Masterwear's *net* interest expense will be four months' interest, for the four months the bonds have been outstanding at that time. Likewise, when United receives six months' interest—after holding the bonds for only four months—United will net only the four months' interest to which it is entitled:

[1]You should recall from Chapter 12 that investments in bonds that are to be held to maturity by the investor are reported at amortized cost, which is the method described here. However, also remember that investments in debt securities *not* to be held to maturity are reported at the fair value of the securities held, as described in Chapter 12.

**At the First Interest Date (June 30)**

| | | |
|---|---|---|
| **Masterwear (Issuer)** | | |
| Interest expense (6 mo. − 2 mo. = 4 mo.) | 28,000 | |
| Interest payable[2] (accrued interest determined above) | 14,000 | |
| Cash (stated rate × face amount) | | 42,000 |
| **United (Investor)** | | |
| Cash (stated rate × face amount) | 42,000 | |
| Interest receivable (accrued interest determined above) | | 14,000 |
| Interest revenue (6 mo. − 2 mo. = 4 mo.) | | 28,000 |

**Since the investor will hold the bonds for only four months before receiving six months' interest, two months' accrued interest must be added to the price paid.**

**The issuer incurs interest expense, and the investor earns interest revenue, for only the four months the bonds are outstanding.**

## DETERMINING THE SELLING PRICE

The price of a bond issue at any particular time is not necessarily equal to its face amount. The $700,000, 12% bond issue in the previous illustration, for example, may sell for more than face amount (at a **premium**) or less than face amount (at a **discount**), depending on how the 12% *stated* interest rate compares with the prevailing *market* or *effective rate* of interest (for securities of similar risk and maturity). For instance, if the 12% bonds are competing in a market in which similar bonds are providing a 14% return, the bonds could be sold only at a price less than $700,000. On the other hand, if the market rate is only 10%, the 12% stated rate would seem relatively attractive and the bonds would sell at a premium over face amount. The reason the stated rate often differs from the market rate, resulting in a discount or premium, is the inevitable delay between the date the terms of the issue are established and the date the issue comes to market.

**FINANCIAL REPORTING CASE**

Q3, p. 661

In addition to the characteristic terms of a bond agreement as specified in the indenture, the market rate for a specific bond issue is influenced by the creditworthiness of the company issuing the bonds. To evaluate the risk and quality of an individual bond issue, investors rely heavily on bond ratings provided by **Standard & Poor's Corporation** and by **Moody's Investors Service, Inc.** See the bond ratings in Graphic 14–1.

**Other things being equal, the lower the perceived riskiness of the corporation issuing bonds, the higher the price those bonds will command.**

**GRAPHIC 14–1**
Bond Ratings*

| | S&P | Moody's |
|---|---|---|
| Investment Grades: | | |
| Highest | AAA | Aaa |
| High | AA | Aa |
| Medium | A | A |
| Minimum investment grade | BBB | Baa |
| "Junk" Ratings: | | |
| Speculative | BB | Ba |
| Very speculative | B | B |
| Default or near default | CCC | Caa |
| | CC | Ca |
| | C | C |
| | D | |

*Adapted from *Bond Record* (New York: Moody's Investors Service, monthly) and *Bond Guide* (New York: Standard & Poor's Corporation, monthly).

---

[2]Some accountants prefer to credit interest expense, rather than interest payable, when the bonds are sold. When that is done, this entry would require simply a debit to interest expense and a credit to cash for $42,000. The interest expense account would then reflect the same *net* debit of four months' interest ($42,000 − $14,000).

**Interest Expense**

| | |
|---|---|
| | 2 months |
| 6 months | |
| 4 months | |

Similarly, the investor could debit interest revenue, rather than interest receivable when buying the bonds.

**A bond issue will be priced by the marketplace to yield the market rate of interest for securities of similar risk and maturity.**

Forces of supply and demand cause a bond issue to be *priced to yield the market rate.* In other words, an investor paying that price will earn an effective rate of return on the investment equal to the market rate. The price is calculated as the present value of all the cash flows required of the bonds, where the discount rate used in the present value calculation is the market rate. Specifically, the price will be the present value of the periodic cash interest payments (face amount × stated rate) plus the present value of the principal payable at maturity, both discounted at the market rate.

Bonds priced at a discount are described in Illustration 14–2.

**ILLUSTRATION 14–2**

Bonds Sold at a Discount

**Because interest is paid semiannually, the present value calculations use:**
**a. one-half the stated rate (6%),**
**b. one-half the market rate (7%), and**
**c. 6 (3 × 2) semiannual periods.**

On January 1, 2006, Masterwear Industries issued $700,000 of 12% bonds, dated January 1. Interest of $42,000 is payable semiannually on June 30 and December 31. The bonds mature in three years. The market yield for bonds of similar risk and maturity is 14%. The entire bond issue was purchased by United Intergroup, Inc.

**Calculation of the Price of the Bonds**

| | | | **Present Values** |
|---|---|---|---|
| Interest | $ 42,000 × 4.76654* | = | $200,195 |
| Principal | $700,000 × 0.66634† | = | 466,438 |
| Present value (price) of the bonds | | | $666,633 |

*Present value of an ordinary annuity of $1: $n = 6$, $i = 7\%$ (Table 4).
†Present value of $1: $n = 6$, $i = 7\%$ (Table 2).
Note: Present value tables are provided at the end of this textbook. If you need to review the concept of the time value of money, refer to the discussions in Chapter 6.

The calculation is illustrated in Graphic 14–2.

**GRAPHIC 14–2**

Cash Flows from a Bond Issue

**Because of the time value of money, the present value of the future cash flows is less than $952,000.**

**Dates of Cash Flows**

| | | | | | |
|---|---|---|---|---|---|
| 1. June 30, 2006 | $ 42,000 | | | | |
| 2. December 31, 2006 | 42,000 | | | | |
| 3. June 30, 2007 | 42,000 | | | | |
| 4. December 31, 2007 | 42,000 | | | | |
| 5. June 30, 2008 | 42,000 | | | | Total Future |
| 6. December 31, 2008 | 42,000 | | $700,000 | | Cash Flows |
| | $252,000 | + | $700,000 | = | $952,000 |

Present Value discounted at 7%

| | | | | | Present Value of Cash Flows |
|---|---|---|---|---|---|
| January 1, 2006 | $200,195 | + | $466,438 | = | $666,633 |

Although the cash flows total $952,000, the present value of those future cash flows as of January 1, 2006, is only $666,633. This is due to the time value of money.

***Journal Entries at Issuance—Bonds Sold at a Discount***

| | | |
|---|---|---|
| **Masterwear (Issuer)** | | |
| Cash (price calculated above) | 666,633 | |
| Discount on bonds payable (difference) | 33,367 | |
| Bonds payable (face amount) | | 700,000 |
| **United (Investor)** | | |
| Investment in bonds (face amount) | 700,000 | |
| Discount on bond investment (difference) | | 33,367 |
| Cash (price calculated above) | | 666,633 |

When bond prices are quoted in financial media, they typically are stated in terms of a percentage of face amount. Thus, a price quote of 98 means a $1,000 bond will sell for $980; a bond priced at 101 will sell for $1,010.

## Determining Interest—Effective Interest Method

**The *effective interest* on debt is the market rate of interest multiplied by the outstanding balance of the debt.**

Interest accrues on an outstanding debt at a constant percentage of the debt each period. Of course, under the concept of accrual accounting, the periodic effective interest is not affected by the time at which the cash interest actually is paid. Recording interest each period as the *effective market rate of interest multiplied by the outstanding balance of the debt* (during the interest period) is referred to as the **effective interest method.** Although giving this a label—the effective interest method—implies some specialized procedure, this simply is an application of the accrual concept, consistent with accruing all expenses as they are incurred.

Continuing our example, we determined that the amount of debt when the bonds are issued is $666,633. Since the effective interest rate is 14%, interest recorded (as expense to the issuer and revenue to the investor) for the first six-month interest period is $46,664:

| $666,633 | × | [14% ÷ 2] | = | $46,664 |
|---|---|---|---|---|
| Outstanding balance | | Effective rate | | Effective interest |

However, the bond indenture calls for semiannual interest payments of only $42,000—the *stated* rate (6%) times the *face amount* ($700,000). As always, when only a portion of an expense is paid, the remainder becomes a liability—in this case an addition to the already outstanding liability. So the difference, $4,664, increases the liability and is reflected as a reduction in the discount (a valuation account). This is illustrated in Graphic 14–3.

Interest accrues on the outstanding debt at the effective rate. Interest paid is the amount specified in the bond indenture—the stated rate times the face amount. These amounts and the change in the outstanding debt are recorded as follows:

**GRAPHIC 14–3**
Change in Debt When Effective Interest Exceeds Cash Paid

| | Outstanding Balance | | Account Balances: Bonds Payable (face amount) | | Account Balances: Discount on Bonds Payable |
|---|---|---|---|---|---|
| January 1 | $666,633 | = | $700,000 | less | $33,367 |
| Interest accrued at 7% | 46,664 | | | | |
| Portion of interest paid | (42,000) | | | | (4,664) |
| June 30 | $671,297 | = | $700,000 | less | $28,703 |

**The unpaid portion of the effective interest increases the existing liability.**

*Journal Entries—The Interest Method*

**At the First Interest Date (June 30)**

| | | |
|---|---|---|
| **Masterwear (Issuer)** | | |
| Interest expense (market rate × outstanding balance) | 46,664 | |
| Discount on bonds payable (difference) | | 4,664 |
| Cash (stated rate × face amount) | | 42,000 |
| **United (Investor)** | | |
| Cash (stated rate × face amount) | 42,000 | |
| Discount on bond investment (difference) | 4,664 | |
| Interest revenue (market rate × outstanding balance) | | 46,664 |

**The effective interest is calculated each period as the market rate times the amount of the debt outstanding during the interest period.**

Because the balance of the debt changes each period, the dollar amount of interest (balance × rate) also will change each period. To keep up with the changing amounts, it usually is convenient to prepare a schedule that reflects the changes in the debt over its term to maturity. An amortization schedule for the situation under discussion is shown in Graphic 14–4.

Amounts for the journal entries each interest date are found in the first three columns of the schedule. Traditionally, this schedule has been referred to as an **amortization schedule**—a

**GRAPHIC 14–4**
Amortization Schedule—Discount

| Date | Cash Interest | Effective Interest | Increase in Balance | Outstanding Balance |
|---|---|---|---|---|
| | (6% × Face amount) | (7% × Outstanding balance) | (Discount reduction) | |
| 1/1/06 | | | | 666,633 |
| 6/30/06 | 42,000 | .07 (666,633) = 46,664 | 4,664 | 671,297 |
| 12/31/06 | 42,000 | .07 (671,297) = 46,991 | 4,991 | 676,288 |
| 6/30/07 | 42,000 | .07 (676,288) = 47,340 | 5,340 | 681,628 |
| 12/31/07 | 42,000 | .07 (681,628) = 47,714 | 5,714 | 687,342 |
| 6/30/08 | 42,000 | .07 (687,342) = 48,114 | 6,114 | 693,456 |
| 12/31/08 | 42,000 | .07 (693,456) = 48,544* | 6,544 | 700,000 |
| | 252,000 | 285,367 | 33,367 | |

*Rounded.

Since less cash is paid each period than the effective interest, the unpaid difference increases the outstanding balance of the debt.

reference to alleged amortization of the discount.[3] This is an apparent carryover from earlier days when the discount was considered to be an asset to be amortized. To the contrary, the discount is a valuation account, having no existence apart from the related debt. As you learned in the previous paragraphs, changes in its balance are the derived result of changes in the outstanding debt, when portions of periodic accrued interest go unpaid.[4]

However, because this terminology is so prevalent in practice, we too will use the label *amortization schedule*. Be sure to realize, though, that this label is a misnomer—nothing is being amortized. The essential point to remember is that the effective interest method is a straightforward application of the accrual concept, whereby interest expense (or revenue) is accrued periodically at the effective rate. It involves neither deferring expenses (or revenues) nor amortizing deferrals.

Terms such as *unamortized or deferred discount or premium* and *to amortize discount or premium* are carryovers from the days when debt discount was considered to be an amortizable asset and do not describe accurately either the assets or liabilities and events involved or the interest method of accounting for them.[5]

A liability should be reported at its present value.

Determining interest in this manner has a convenient side effect. It results in reporting the liability at the present value of future cash payments—the appropriate valuation method for any liability.[6] This is obvious at issuance; we actually calculated the present value to be $666,633. What perhaps is not quite as obvious is that the outstanding amount of debt each subsequent period (shown in the right-hand column of the amortization schedule) is still the present value of the remaining cash flows, discounted at the original rate.

## ADDITIONAL CONSIDERATION

Although the reported amount each period is the **present value** of the bonds, at any date after issuance this amount is not necessarily equal to the **market value** of the bonds. This is because the **market** rate of interest will not necessarily remain the same as the rate implicit in the original issue price (the effective rate). Of course, for negotiable financial instruments, the issue price is the market price at any given time. Differences between market values and present values based on the original rate are holding gains and losses. If we were to use the market rate to revalue bonds on each reporting

[3] You learned in earlier chapters that amortization is the accounting process of reducing an asset or liability by periodic write-downs or payments [*SFAC 6*, par. 142].

[4] Or as we see later, the debt changes when periodic interest is overpaid. This occurs when debt is sold at a premium, rather than at a discount.

[5] "Elements of Financial Statements," *Statement of Financial Accounting Concepts No. 6*, par. 36 (Stamford, Conn.: FASB, 1985), par. 239.

[6] "Interest on Receivables and Payables," *APB Opinion No. 21* (New York: AICPA, 1971).

date—that is, recalculate the present value using the market rate—the reported amount always would be the market value. Some accountants contend that reporting market values and resultant holding gains and losses would provide more meaningful information than reporting debt at its present value, discounted at the original rate. Reporting debt at market values is not presently permitted by GAAP except in certain specialized industries like the mutual fund and insurance industries. Certainly the market value of existing debt is information considered by management in refinancing decisions.

## ZERO-COUPON BONDS

A zero-coupon bond pays no interest. Instead, it offers a return in the form of a "deep discount" from the face amount. For illustration, let's look at the zero-coupon bonds offered by **General Mills, Inc.** in 2002. Two billion, two hundred thirty million dollars face amount of the 20-year securities sold for $1.501 million. As the amortization schedule in Graphic 14–5 demonstrates, they were priced to yield 2%.

**GRAPHIC 14–5**
Zero-Coupon Securities—General Mills, Inc.

| ($ in millions) | Cash Interest | Effective Interest | Increase in Balance | Outstanding Balance* |
|---|---|---|---|---|
| | (0% × Face amount) | (2% × Outstanding debt) | (Discount reduction) | |
| | | | | 1,501 |
| 2002 | 0 | .02 (1,501) = 30 | 30 | 1,531 |
| 2003 | 0 | .02 (1,531) = 31 | 31 | 1,561 |
| 2004 | 0 | .02 (1,561) = 31 | 31 | 1,593 |
| ◆ | ◆ | ◆ | ◆ | ◆ |
| ◆ | ◆ | ◆ | ◆ | ◆ |
| ◆ | ◆ | ◆ | ◆ | ◆ |
| 2021 | 0 | .02 (2,143) = 43 | 43 | 2,186 |
| 2022 | 0 | .02 (2,186) = 44 | 44 | 2,230 |
| | | 729 | 729 | |

*Some numbers appear not to total because the underlying calculations are not rounded.

Zero-coupon bonds provide us a convenient opportunity to reinforce a key concept we just learned: that we accrue the interest expense (or revenue) each period at the effective rate regardless of how much cash interest actually is paid (zero in this case). An advantage of issuing zero-coupon bonds or notes is that the corporation can deduct for tax purposes the annual interest expense (see schedule) but has no related cash outflow until the bonds mature. However, the reverse is true for investors in "zeros." Investors receive no periodic cash interest, even though annual interest revenue is reportable for tax purposes. So those who invest in zero-coupon bonds usually have tax-deferred or tax-exempt status, such as pension funds, individual retirement accounts (IRAs), and charitable organizations. Zero-coupon bonds and notes are gaining popularity but still constitute a relatively small proportion of corporate debt.

## BONDS SOLD AT A PREMIUM

In Illustration 14–2, Masterwear Industries sold the bonds at a price that would yield an effective rate higher than the stated rate. The result was a discount. On the other hand, if the 12% bonds had been issued when the market yield for bonds of similar risk and maturity was *lower* than the stated rate, say 10%, the issue would have been priced at a *premium.* Because the 12% rate would seem relatively attractive in a 10% market, the bonds would command an issue price of more than $700,000, calculated in Illustration 14–3.

**ILLUSTRATION 14–3**

Bonds Sold at a Premium

**Because interest is paid *semiannually*, the present value calculations use:**

**a. one-half the stated rate (6%),**

**b. one-half the market rate (5%), and**

**c. 6 (3 × 2) semiannual periods.**

On January 1, 2006, Masterwear Industries issued $700,000 of 12% bonds, dated January 1. Interest of $42,000 is payable semiannually on June 30 and December 31. The bonds mature in three years. The market yield for bonds of similar risk and maturity is 10%. The entire bond issue was purchased by United Intergroup, Inc.

**Calculation of the Price of the Bonds**

| | | | **Present Values** |
|---|---|---|---|
| Interest | $42,000 × 5.07569* | = | $213,179 |
| Principal | $700,000 × 0.74622† | = | 522,354 |
| Present value (price) of the bonds | | | $735,533 |

*Present value of an ordinary annuity of $1: $n = 6$, $i = 5\%$.
†Present value of $1: $n = 6$, $i = 5\%$.

***Journal Entries at Issuance—Bonds Sold at Premium***

| | | |
|---|---|---|
| **Masterwear (Issuer)** | | |
| Cash (price calculated above) | 735,533 | |
| Bonds payable (face amount) | | 700,000 |
| Premium on bonds payable (difference) | | 35,533 |
| **United (Investor)** | | |
| Investment in bonds (face amount) | 700,000 | |
| Premium on bond investment (difference) | 35,533 | |
| Cash (price calculated above) | | 735,533 |

Interest on bonds sold at a premium is determined in precisely the same manner as on bonds sold at a discount. Again, interest is the effective interest rate applied to the debt outstanding during each period (balance at the end of the previous interest period), and the cash paid is the stated rate times the face amount, as shown in Graphic 14–6:

**GRAPHIC 14–6**

Amortization Schedule—Premium

**Since *more* cash is paid each period than the effective interest, the debt outstanding is reduced by the overpayment.**

| Date | Cash Interest | Effective Interest | Decrease in Balance | Outstanding Balance |
|---|---|---|---|---|
| | (6% × Face amount) | (5% × Outstanding balance) | (Premium reduction) | |
| 1/1/06 | | | | 735,533 |
| 6/30/06 | 42,000 | .05 (735,533) = 36,777 | 5,223 | 730,310 |
| 12/31/06 | 42,000 | .05 (730,310) = 36,516 | 5,484 | 724,826 |
| 6/30/07 | 42,000 | .05 (724,826) = 36,241 | 5,759 | 719,067 |
| 12/31/07 | 42,000 | .05 (719,067) = 35,953 | 6,047 | 713,020 |
| 6/30/08 | 42,000 | .05 (713,020) = 35,651 | 6,349 | 706,671 |
| 12/31/08 | 42,000 | .05 (706,671) = 35,329* | 6,671 | 700,000 |
| | 252,000 | 216,467 | 35,533 | |

*Rounded.

Notice that the debt declines each period. This is because the effective interest each period is less than the cash interest paid. The overpayments each period reduce the amount owed. Remember, this is precisely the opposite of when debt is sold at a discount, when the effective interest each period is more than the cash paid, and the underpayment of interest adds to the amount owed.

**ADDITIONAL CONSIDERATION**

The preceding illustrations describe bonds sold at a discount and at a premium. The same concepts apply to bonds sold at face amount. But some of the procedures would be unnecessary. For instance, calculating the present value of the interest and the principal always will give us the face amount when the effective rate and the stated rate are the same:

**Calculation of the Price of the Bonds**

| | | **Present Values** |
|---|---|---|
| Interest | \$42,000 × 4.91732* = | \$206,528 |
| Principal | \$700,000 × 0.70496† = | 493,472 |
| Present value (price) of the bonds | | \$700,000 |

*Present value of an ordinary annuity of \$1: $n = 6$, $i = 6\%$.
†Present value of \$1: $n = 6$, $i = 6\%$.

## WHEN FINANCIAL STATEMENTS ARE PREPARED BETWEEN INTEREST DATES

When an accounting period ends between interest dates, it is necessary to record interest that has accrued since the last interest date. As an example, refer again to Illustration 14–2 on page 666. If the fiscal years of Masterwear and United end on October 31 and interest was last paid and recorded on June 30, four months' interest must be accrued in a year-end adjusting entry. Because interest is recorded for only a portion of a semiannual period, amounts recorded are simply the amounts shown in the amortization schedule (Graphic 14–4, p. 668) times the appropriate fraction of the semiannual period (in this case 4/6).

**Any interest that has accrued since the last interest date must be recorded by an adjusting entry prior to preparing financial statements.**

**At October 31**

| | | |
|---|---|---|
| **Masterwear (Issuer)** | | |
| Interest expense (4/6 × 46,991) | 31,327 | |
| Discount on bonds payable (4/6 × 4,991) | | 3,327 |
| Interest payable (4/6 × 42,000) | | 28,000 |
| **United (Investor)** | | |
| Interest receivable (4/6 × 42,000) | 28,000 | |
| Discount on bond investment (4/6 × 4,991) | 3,327 | |
| Interest revenue (4/6 × 46,991) | | 31,327 |

***Adjusting Entries—To Accrue Interest***

**To avoid understating interest in the financial statements, four months' interest is recorded at the end of the reporting period.**

Two months later, when semiannual interest is paid next, the remainder of the semiannual interest is allocated to the first two months of the next accounting year—November and December:

**At the December 31 Interest Date**

| | | |
|---|---|---|
| **Masterwear (Issuer)** | | |
| Interest expense (2/6 × 46,991) | 15,664 | |
| Interest payable (from adjusting entry) | 28,000 | |
| Discount on bonds payable (2/6 × 4,991) | | 1,664 |
| Cash (stated rate × face amount) | | 42,000 |
| **United (Investor)** | | |
| Cash (stated rate × face amount) | 42,000 | |
| Discount on bond investment (2/6 × 4,991) | 1,664 | |
| Interest receivable (from adjusting entry) | | 28,000 |
| Interest revenue (2/6 × 46,991) | | 15,664 |

**Of the six-months' interest paid December 31, only the November and December interest is expensed in the new fiscal year.**

## The Straight-Line Method—A Practical Expediency

In some circumstances the profession permits an exception to the conceptually appropriate method of determining interest for bond issues. A company is allowed to determine interest indirectly by allocating a discount or a premium equally to each period over the term to maturity—if doing so produces results that are not materially different from the usual (and preferable) interest method.[7] The decision should be guided by whether the **straight-line method** would tend to mislead investors and creditors in the particular circumstance.

By the straight-line method, the discount in Illustration 14–2 and Graphic 14–4 would be allocated equally to the six semiannual periods (three years):

$33,367 ÷ 6 periods = $5,561 per period

*Journal Entries—Straight-Line Method*

**By the straight-line method, interest (expense and revenue) is a plug figure, resulting from calculating the amount of discount reduction.**

**At Each of the Six Interest Dates**

| | | |
|---|---|---|
| **Masterwear (Issuer)** | | |
| Interest expense (to balance) | 47,561 | |
| Discount on bonds payable (discount ÷ 6 periods) | | 5,561 |
| Cash (stated rate × face amount) | | 42,000 |
| **United (Investor)** | | |
| Cash (stated rate × face amount) | 42,000 | |
| Discount on bond investment (discount ÷ 6 periods) | 5,561 | |
| Interest revenue (to balance) | | 47,561 |

Allocating the discount or premium equally over the life of the bonds by the straight-line method results in a constant dollar amount of interest each period. An amortization schedule, then, would serve little purpose. For example, if we prepared one for the straight-line method in this situation, it would provide the same amounts each period as shown in Graphic 14–7.

**GRAPHIC 14–7**
Amortization Schedule—Straight-Line Method

**By the straight-line method, the amount of the discount to be reduced periodically is calculated, and the recorded interest is the plug figure.**

| | Cash Interest | Recorded Interest | | Increase in Balance | Outstanding Balance |
|---|---|---|---|---|---|
| | (6% × Face amount) | (Cash + Discount reduction) | | ($33,367 ÷ 6) | |
| 1/1/06 | | | | | 666,633 |
| 6/30/06 | 42,000 | (42,000 + 5,561) = | 47,561 | 5,561 | 672,194 |
| 12/31/06 | 42,000 | (42,000 + 5,561) = | 47,561 | 5,561 | 677,755 |
| 6/30/07 | 42,000 | (42,000 + 5,561) = | 47,561 | 5,561 | 683,316 |
| 12/31/07 | 42,000 | (42,000 + 5,561) = | 47,561 | 5,561 | 688,877 |
| 6/30/08 | 42,000 | (42,000 + 5,561) = | 47,561 | 5,561 | 694,438 |
| 12/31/08 | 42,000 | (42,000 + 5,561) = | 47,561 | 5,561 | 700,000* |
| | 252,000 | | 285,366 | 33,366 | |

*Rounded.

**Determining interest by allocating the discount (or premium) on a straight-line basis is a practical expediency permitted in some situations by the materiality concept.**

Remember, constant dollar amounts are not produced when the effective interest method is used. By that method, the dollar amounts of interest vary over the term to maturity because the percentage rate of interest remains constant but is applied to a changing debt balance.

Also, be sure to realize that the straight-line method is not an alternative method of determining interest in a conceptual sense. Instead, it is an application of the materiality concept, by which an appropriate application of GAAP (e.g., the effective interest method) can be bypassed for reasons of practical expediency in situations when doing so has no material effect

[7]Ibid.

on the results. Based on the frequency with which the straight-line method is used in practice, we can infer that managers very frequently conclude that its use has no material impact on investors' decisions.

## CONCEPT REVIEW EXERCISE

### ISSUING BONDS AND RECORDING INTEREST

On January 1, 2006, the Meade Group issued $8,000,000 of 11% bonds, dated January 1. Interest is payable semiannually on June 30 and December 31. The bonds mature in four years. The market yield for bonds of similar risk and maturity is 10%.

**Required:**

1. Determine the price these bonds sold for to yield the 10% market rate and record their issuance by the Meade Group.
2. Prepare an amortization schedule that determines interest at the effective rate and record interest on the first interest date, June 30, 2006.

### SOLUTION

1. Determine the price these bonds sold for to yield the 10% market rate and record their issuance by the Meade Group.

**Calculation of the Price of the Bonds**

There are eight semiannual periods and one-half the market rate is 5%.

| | | | |
|---|---|---|---|
| Interest | $440,000 × 6.46321* | = | $2,843,812 |
| Principal | $8,000,000 × 0.67684† | = | 5,414,720 |
| Present value (price) of the bonds | | | $8,258,532 |

*Present value of an ordinary annuity of $1: $n = 8$, $i = 5\%$.
†Present value of $1: $n = 8$, $i = 5\%$.

*Journal Entry at Issuance*

| | | |
|---|---|---|
| Cash (price calculated above) | 8,258,532 | |
| Bonds payable (face amount) | | 8,000,000 |
| Premium on bonds payable (difference) | | 258,532 |

2. Prepare an amortization schedule that determines interest at the effective rate and record interest on the first interest date, June 30, 2006.

**Amortization Schedule**

| Date | Cash Interest | Effective Interest | | Decrease in Balance | Outstanding Balance |
|---|---|---|---|---|---|
| | (5.5% × Face amount) | (5% × Outstanding balance) | | (Premium reduction) | |
| 1/1/06 | | | | | 8,258,532 |
| 6/30/06 | 440,000 | .05 (8,258,532) = | 412,927 | 27,073 | 8,231,459 |
| 12/31/06 | 440,000 | .05 (8,231,459) = | 411,573 | 28,427 | 8,203,032 |
| 6/30/07 | 440,000 | .05 (8,203,032) = | 410,152 | 29,848 | 8,173,184 |
| 12/31/07 | 440,000 | .05 (8,173,184) = | 408,659 | 31,341 | 8,141,843 |
| 6/30/08 | 440,000 | .05 (8,141,843) = | 407,092 | 32,908 | 8,108,935 |
| 12/31/08 | 440,000 | .05 (8,108,935) = | 405,447 | 34,553 | 8,074,382 |
| 6/30/09 | 440.000 | .05 (8,074,382) = | 403,719 | 36,281 | 8,038,101 |
| 12/31/09 | 440,000 | .05 (8,038,101) = | 401,899* | 38,101 | 8,000,000 |
| | 3,520,000 | | 3,261,468 | 258,532 | |

*Rounded.

*More cash is paid each period than the effective interest, so the debt outstanding **is** reduced by the "overpayment."*

| | | |
|---|---|---|
| Interest expense (5% × $8,258,532) | 412,927 | |
| Premium on bonds payable (difference) | 27,073 | |
| Cash (5.5% × $8,000,000) | | 440,000 |
| *To record interest* | | |

## Debt Issue Costs

Rather than sell bonds directly to the public, corporations usually sell an entire issue to an underwriter who then resells them to other security dealers and the public. By committing to purchase bonds at a set price, an investment house such as **Salomon Smith Barney**, **Goldman Sachs**, and **Merrill Lynch** is said to underwrite any risks associated with a new issue. The underwriting fee is the spread between the price the underwriter pays and the resale price.

Alternatively, the issuing company may choose to sell the debt securities directly to a single investor (as we assumed in previous illustrations)—often a pension fund or an insurance company. This is referred to as *private placement.* Issue costs are less because privately placed securities are not subject to the costly and lengthy process of registering with the SEC that is required of public offerings. Underwriting fees also are avoided.

**Costs of issuing debt securities are recorded as a debit to an asset account, "debt issue costs," and amortized to expense over the term to maturity.**

With either publicly or privately sold debt, the issuing company will incur costs in connection with issuing bonds or notes, such as legal and accounting fees and printing costs, in addition to registration and underwriting fees. These **debt issue costs** are recorded *separately* and are amortized over the term of the related debt. GAAP requires a debit to an asset account—debt issue costs. The asset is allocated to expense, usually on a straight-line basis.

For example, let's assume issue costs in Illustration 14–3 had been $12,000. The entries for the issuance of the bonds would include a separate asset account for the issue costs:

**The premium (or discount) is unaffected by debt issue costs because they are recorded in a separate account.**

| | | |
|---|---|---|
| Cash (price minus issue costs) | 723,533 | |
| Debt issue costs | 12,000 | |
| Bonds payable (face amount) | | 700,000 |
| Premium on bonds payable (price minus face amount) | | 35,533 |

Semiannual amortization of the asset would be:

| | | |
|---|---|---|
| Debt issue expense ($12,000 ÷ 6) | 2,000 | |
| Debt issue costs | | 2,000 |

### ADDITIONAL CONSIDERATION

The treatment of issue costs just described is required by APB Opinion No. 21. A conceptually more appealing treatment would be to reduce the recorded amount of the debt by the debt issue costs instead of recording the costs separately as an asset. The cost of these services reduces the net cash the issuing company receives from the sale of the financial instrument. A lower [net] amount is borrowed at the same cost, increasing the effective interest rate. However, unless the recorded amount of the debt is reduced by the issue costs, the higher rate is not reflected in a higher recorded interest expense.[8] The actual increase in the effective interest rate would be reflected in the interest expense if the issue cost is allowed to reduce the premium (or increase the discount) on the debt:

| | | |
|---|---|---|
| Cash (price calculated above) | 723,533 | |
| Bonds payable (face amount) | | 700,000 |
| Premium on bonds payable (difference) | | 23,533 |

Also, this approach is consistent with the treatment of issue costs when equity securities are sold. You will see in Chapter 18 that the effect of share issue costs is to reduce the amount credited to stock accounts.

This treatment also is suggested by the FASB in *SFAC 6.* Remember, though, that concept statements do not constitute GAAP, so until a new FASB standard is issued to supersede *APB Opinion 21,* the generally accepted practice is to record debt issue costs as assets.

[8]When the same amortization method is used for both, net income is unaffected by whether the cost is amortized as a separate debt issue expense or is reflected in a higher interest expense.

The corporate bond is the basic long-term debt instrument for most large companies. But for many small and medium-sized firms, the debt instrument often used is a *note.* We discuss notes next.

# LONG-TERM NOTES

**PART B**

When a company borrows cash from a bank and signs a promissory note (essentially an IOU), the firm's liability is reported as a *note payable.* Or a note might be issued in exchange for a noncash asset—perhaps to purchase equipment on credit. In concept, notes are accounted for in precisely the same way as bonds. In fact, we could properly substitute notes payable for bonds payable in each of our previous illustrations.

● LO3

**FINANCIAL REPORTING CASE**

Q4, p. 661

## Note Issued for Cash

The interest rate stated in a note is likely to be equal to the market rate because the rate usually is negotiated at the time of the loan. So discounts and premiums are less likely than on bonds. Accounting for a note issued for cash is demonstrated in Illustration 14–4.

**ILLUSTRATION 14–4**

Note Issued for Cash

On January 1, 2006, Skill Graphics, Inc., a product-labeling and graphics firm, borrowed $700,000 cash from First BancCorp and issued a three-year, $700,000 promissory note. Interest of $42,000 was payable semiannually on June 30 and December 31.

| | | |
|---|---|---|
| **At Issuance** | | |
| **Skill Graphics (Borrower)** | | |
| Cash | 700,000 | |
| Notes payable (face amount) | | 700,000 |
| **First BancCorp (Lender)** | | |
| Notes receivable (face amount) | 700,000 | |
| Cash | | 700,000 |
| **At Each of the Six Interest Dates** | | |
| **Skill Graphics (Borrower)** | | |
| Interest expense | 42,000 | |
| Cash (stated rate × face amount) | | 42,000 |
| **First BancCorp (Lender)** | | |
| Cash (stated rate × face amount) | 42,000 | |
| Interest revenue | | 42,000 |
| **At Maturity** | | |
| **Skill Graphics (Borrower)** | | |
| Notes payable | 700,000 | |
| Cash (face amount) | | 700,000 |
| **First BancCorp (Lender)** | | |
| Cash (face amount) | 700,000 | |
| Notes receivable | | 700,000 |

## Note Exchanged for Assets or Services

Occasionally the *stated* interest rate is not indicative of the *market* rate at the time a note is negotiated. The value of the asset (cash or noncash) or service exchanged for the note establishes the market rate.[9] For example, let's assume Skill Graphics purchased a package-labeling

[9]If the debt instrument is negotiable and a dependable exchange price is readily available, the market value of the debt may be better evidence of the value of the transaction than the value of a noncash asset, particularly if it has no established cash selling price. The value of the asset or the debt, whichever is considered more reliable, should be used to record the transaction (*APB 21*).

machine from Hughes–Barker Corporation by issuing a 12%, $700,000, three-year note that requires interest to be paid semiannually. Let's also assume that the machine could have been purchased at a cash price of $666,633. You probably recognize this numerical situation as the one used earlier to illustrate bonds sold at a discount (Illustration 14–2). Reference to the earlier example will confirm that exchanging this $700,000 note for a machine with a cash price of $666,633 implies an annual market rate of interest of 14%. That is, 7% is one-half the discount rate that yields a present value of $666,633 for the note's cash flows (interest plus principal):

| | | | Present Values |
|---|---|---|---|
| Interest | $ 42,000 × 4.76654* | = | $200,195 |
| Principal | $700,000 × 0.66634† | = | 466,438 |
| Present value of the note | | | $666,633 |

*Present value of an ordinary annuity of $1: $n = 6, i = 7\%$.
†Present value of $1: $n = 6, i = 7\%$.

This is referred to as the **implicit rate of interest**—the rate implicit in the agreement. It may be that the implicit rate is not apparent. Sometimes the value of the asset (or service) is not readily determinable, but the interest rate stated in the transaction is unrealistic relative to the rate that would be expected in a similar transaction under similar circumstances. Deciding what the appropriate rate should be is called *imputing* an interest rate.

A basic concept of accounting is *substance over form.*

For example, suppose the machine exchanged for the 12% note is custom-made for Skill Graphics so that no customary cash price is available with which to work backwards to find the implicit rate. In that case, the appropriate rate would have to be found externally. It might be determined, for instance, that a more realistic interest rate for a transaction of this type, at this time, would be 14%. Then it would be apparent that Skill Graphics actually paid less than $700,000 for the machine and that part of the face amount of the note in effect makes up for the lower than normal interest rate. You learned early in your study of accounting that the economic essence of a transaction should prevail over its outward appearance. In keeping with this basic precept, the accountant should look beyond the *form* of this transaction and record its *substance.* The amount actually paid for the machine is the present value of the cash flows called for by the loan agreement, discounted at the market rate—imputed in this case to be 14%. So both the asset acquired and the liability used to purchase it should be recorded at the real cost, $666,633.

## ADDITIONAL CONSIDERATION

For another example, let's assume the more realistic interest rate for a transaction of this type is, say, 16%. In that case we would calculate the real cost of the machine by finding the present value of both the interest and the principal, discounted at half the 16% rate:

| | | | Present Values |
|---|---|---|---|
| Interest | $42,000 × 4.62288* | = | $194,161 |
| Principal | $700,000 × 0.63017† | = | 441,119 |
| Present value of the note | | | $635,280 |

*Present value of an ordinary annuity of $l: $n = 6, i = 8\%$.
†Present value of $1: $n = 6, i = 8\%$.

Both the asset acquired and the liability used to purchase it would be recorded at $635,280.

The accounting treatment is the same whether the amount is determined directly from the market value of the machine (and thus the note) or indirectly as the present value of the note (and thus the value of the asset):[10]

*Journal Entries at Issuance—Note with Unrealistic Interest Rate*

| | | |
|---|---|---|
| **Skill Graphics (Buyer/Issuer)** | | |
| Machinery (cash price) | 666,633 | |
| Discount on note payable (difference) | 33,367 | |
| Notes payable (face amount) | | 700,000 |
| **Hughes–Barker (Seller/Lender)** | | |
| Notes receivable (face amount) | 700,000 | |
| Discount on note receivable (difference) | | 33,367 |
| Sales revenue (cash price) | | 666,633 |

Likewise, whether the effective interest rate is determined as the rate implicit in the agreement, given the asset's market value, or whether the effective rate is imputed as the appropriate interest rate if the asset's value is unknown, both parties to the transaction should record periodic interest (interest expense to the borrower, interest revenue to the lender) at the effective rate, rather than the stated rate.

*Journal Entries—The Interest Method*

**The effective interest (expense to the issuer; revenue to the investor) is calculated each period as the effective rate times the amount of the debt outstanding during the interest period.**

| **At the First Interest Date (June 30)** | | |
|---|---|---|
| **Skill Graphics (Borrower)** | | |
| Interest expense (effective rate × outstanding balance) | 46,664 | |
| Discount on notes payable (difference) | | 4,664 |
| Cash (stated rate × face amount) | | 42,000 |
| **Hughes–Barker (Seller/Lender)** | | |
| Cash (stated rate × face amount) | 42,000 | |
| Discount on notes receivable (difference) | 4,664 | |
| Interest revenue (effective rate × outstanding balance) | | 46,664 |

The interest expense (interest revenue for the lender) varies as the balance of the note changes over time. See the amortization schedule in Graphic 14–8.[11]

## Installment Notes

You may have recently purchased a car, or maybe a house. If so, unless you paid cash, you signed a note promising to pay the purchase price over, say, four years for the car, or 30 years for the house. Car and house notes usually call for payment in monthly installments rather than by a single amount at maturity. Corporations, too, often borrow using installment notes. Typically, installment payments are equal amounts each period. Each payment includes both

[10]The method shown is the *gross method.* Alternatively, the *net method* can be used as follows:

| | | |
|---|---|---|
| **Skill Graphics (Buyer/Issuer)** | | |
| Machinery (cash price) | 666,633 | |
| Notes payable (face amount) | | 666,633 |
| **Hughes–Barker (Seller/Lender)** | | |
| Notes receivable (face amount) | 666,633 | |
| Sales revenue (cash price) | | 666,633 |

Under the gross method the note is recorded at the face amount and a contra account, called *discount on note payable,* is recorded for the difference between face value and present value. This discount represents the interest to be recognized over the term of the loan. As payments are made, the note is reduced by the full amount of the payment. Interest revenue (and interest expense) are recognized by a reduction in the discount on note and a credit to interest revenue (debit to interest expense). After the last payment, the discount and note accounts both will be zero. Over the term of the note, the note is shown net of the discount in the balance sheet.

[11]The creation of amortization schedules is simplified by an electronic spreadsheet such as Microsoft Excel.

**GRAPHIC 14–8**
Amortization Schedule—Note

**Since less cash is paid each period than the effective interest, the unpaid difference (the discount reduction) increases the outstanding balance of the debt.**

| Date | Cash Interest | Effective Interest | Increase in Balance | Outstanding Balance |
|---|---|---|---|---|
| | (6% × Face amount) | (7% × Outstanding balance) | (Discount reduction) | |
| 1/1/06 | | | | 666,633 |
| 6/30/06 | 42,000 | .07 (666,633) = 46,664 | 4,664 | 671,297 |
| 12/31/06 | 42,000 | .07 (671,297) = 46,991 | 4,991 | 676,288 |
| 6/30/07 | 42,000 | .07 (676,288) = 47,340 | 5,340 | 681,628 |
| 12/31/07 | 42,000 | .07 (681,628) = 47,714 | 5,714 | 687,342 |
| 6/30/08 | 42,000 | .07 (687,342) = 48,114 | 6,114 | 693,456 |
| 12/31/08 | 42,000 | .07 (693,456) = 48,544* | 6,544 | 700,000 |
| | 252,000 | 285,367 | 33,367 | |

*Rounded.

an amount that represents interest and an amount that represents a reduction of the outstanding balance. The periodic reduction of the balance is sufficient that at maturity the note is completely paid. This amount is easily calculated by dividing the amount of the loan by the appropriate discount factor for the present value of an annuity. The installment payment amount that would pay the note above is:

| | | | | |
|---|---|---|---|---|
| $666,633 | ÷ | 4.76654 | = | $139,857 |
| Amount of loan | | (from Table 4 $n = 6, i = 7.0\%$) | | Installment payment |

Consider Graphic 14–9.

**GRAPHIC 14–9**
Amortization Schedule—Installment Note

**Each installment payment includes interest on the outstanding debt at the effective rate. The remainder of each payment reduces the outstanding balance.**

| Date | Cash Payment | Effective Interest | Decrease in Debt | Outstanding Balance |
|---|---|---|---|---|
| | | (7% × Outstanding balance) | | |
| 1/1/06 | | | | 666,633 |
| 6/30/06 | 139,857 | .07 (666,633) = 46,664 | 93,193 | 573,440 |
| 12/31/06 | 139,857 | .07 (573,440) = 40,141 | 99,716 | 473,724 |
| 6/30/07 | 139,857 | .07 (473,724) = 33,161 | 106,696 | 367,028 |
| 12/31/07 | 139,857 | .07 (367,028) = 25,692 | 114,165 | 252,863 |
| 6/30/08 | 139,857 | .07 (252,863) = 17,700 | 122,157 | 130,706 |
| 12/31/08 | 139,857 | .07 (130,706) = 9,151* | 130,706 | 0 |
| | 839,142 | 172,509 | 666,633 | |

*Rounded.

The procedure is the same as for a note whose principal is paid at maturity, but the periodic cash payments are larger and there is no lump-sum payment at maturity. We calculated the amount of the payments so that after covering the interest on the existing debt each period, the excess would exactly amortize the debt to zero at maturity (rather than to a designated maturity amount).

For installment notes, the outstanding balance of the note does not eventually become its face amount as it does for notes with designated maturity amounts. Instead, at the maturity date the balance is zero. Consequently, the significance is lost of maintaining separate balances for the face amount (in a note account) and the discount (or premium). So an installment note typically is recorded at its net carrying amount in a single note payable (or receivable) account:

| | | |
|---|---|---|
| **Skill Graphics (Buyer/Issuer)** | | |
| Machinery | 666,633 | |
| Note payable | | 666,633 |
| **Hughes–Barker (Seller/Lender)** | | |
| Note receivable | 666,633 | |
| Sales revenue | | 666,633 |

*Journal Entries at Issuance—Installment Note*

| | | |
|---|---|---|
| **At the First Interest Date (June 30)** | | |
| **Skill Graphics (Borrower)** | | |
| Interest expense (effective rate × outstanding balance) | 46,664 | |
| Note payable (difference) | 93,193 | |
| Cash (installment payment calculated above) | | 139,857 |
| **Hughes–Barker (Seller/Lender)** | | |
| Cash (installment payment calculated above) | 139,857 | |
| Note receivable (difference) | | 93,193 |
| Interest revenue (effective rate × outstanding balance) | | 46,664 |

**Each payment includes both an amount that represents interest and an amount that represents a reduction of principal.**

**ADDITIONAL CONSIDERATION**

You will learn in the next chapter that the liability associated with a capital lease is accounted for the same way as this installment note. In fact, if the asset described above had been leased rather than purchased, the cash payments would be designated lease payments rather than installment loan payments, and a virtually identical amortization schedule would apply.

The reason for the similarity is that we view a capital lease as being, in substance, equivalent to an installment purchase/sale. Naturally, then, accounting treatment of the two essentially identical transactions should be consistent. Be sure to notice the parallel treatment as you study leases in the next chapter.

## Financial Statement Disclosures

● LO4

In the balance sheet, long-term debt (liability for the debtor; asset for the creditor) typically is reported as a single amount, net of any discount or increased by any premium, rather than at its face amount accompanied by a separate valuation account for the discount or premium. Any portion of the debt to be paid (received) during the upcoming year, or operating cycle if longer, should be reported as a current amount.

**Supplemental disclosure is required of the fair value of bonds, notes, and other financial instruments.**

The fair value of financial instruments must be disclosed either in the body of the financial statements or in disclosure notes.[12] These fair values are available for bonds and other securities traded on market exchanges in the form of quoted market prices. On the other hand, financial instruments not traded on market exchanges require other evidence of market value. For example, the market value of a note payable might be approximated by the present value of principal and interest payments using a current discount rate commensurate with the risks involved.

For all long-term borrowings, disclosures also should include the aggregate amounts maturing and sinking fund requirements (if any) for each of the next five years.[13] To comply, **Procter & Gamble**'s 2004 annual report stated:

[12] "Disclosures About Fair Values of Financial Instruments," *Statement of Financial Accounting Standards No. 107* (Norwalk, Conn.: FASB, 1991).

[13] "Disclosure of Long-Term Obligations," *Statement of Financial Accounting Standards No. 47* (Stamford, Conn.: FASB, 1981), par. 10b.

The fair value and scheduled amounts should be disclosed for the next five years.

**($ in millions)**

The fair value of the long-term debt was $13,168 and $12,396 June 30, 2004 and 2003, respectively. Long-term debt maturities during the next five years are as follows:

2005—$1,518; 2006—$2,625; 2007—$1,433; 2008—$972 and 2009—$1,150.

Borrowing is a financing activity; lending is an investing activity.

Paying or receiving interest is an operating activity.

In a statement of cash flows, issuing bonds or notes are reported as cash flows from financing activities by the issuer (borrower) and cash flows from investing activities by the investor (lender). Similarly, when the debt is repaid, the issuer (borrower) reports the cash outflow as a financing activity while the investor (lender) reports it as a cash inflow from investing activities. However, because both interest expense and interest revenue are components of the income statement, both parties to the transaction report cash payments for interest among operating activities.

## DECISION MAKERS' PERSPECTIVE

Business decisions involve risk. Failure to properly consider risk in those decisions is one of the most costly, yet one of the most common mistakes investors and creditors can make. Long-term debt is one of the first places decision makers should look when trying to get a handle on risk.

Generally speaking, debt increases risk.

To evaluate a firm's risk, you might start by calculating its debt to equity ratio.

In general, debt increases risk. As an owner, debt would place you in a subordinate position relative to creditors because the claims of creditors must be satisfied first in case of liquidation. In addition, debt requires payment, usually on specific dates. Failure to pay debt interest and principal on a timely basis may result in default and perhaps even bankruptcy. The debt to equity ratio, total liabilities/shareholders' equity, often is calculated to measure the degree of risk. Other things being equal, the higher the debt to equity ratio, the higher the risk. The type of risk this ratio measures is called *default risk* because it presumably indicates the likelihood a company will default on its obligations.

As a manager, you would try to create favorable financial leverage to earn a return on borrowed funds in excess of the cost of borrowing the funds.

Debt also can be an advantage. It can be used to enhance the return to shareholders. This concept, known as leverage, was described and illustrated in Chapter 3. If a company earns a return on borrowed funds in excess of the cost of borrowing the funds, shareholders are provided with a total return greater than what could have been earned with equity funds alone. This desirable situation is called *favorable financial leverage.* Unfortunately, leverage is not always favorable. Sometimes the cost of borrowing the funds exceeds the returns they generate. This illustrates the typical risk-return trade-off faced by shareholders.

As an external analyst or a manager, you are concerned with a company's ability to repay debt.

Creditors demand interest payments as compensation for the use of their capital. Failure to pay interest as scheduled may cause several adverse consequences, including bankruptcy. Therefore, another way to measure a company's ability to pay its obligations is by comparing interest payments with income available to pay those charges. The times interest earned ratio does this by dividing income before subtracting interest expense or income tax expense by interest expense.

Two points about this ratio are important. First, because interest is deductible for income tax purposes, income before interest and taxes is a better indication of a company's ability to pay interest than is income after interest and taxes (i.e., net income). Second, income before interest and taxes is a rough approximation for cash flow generated from operations. The primary concern of decision makers is, of course, the cash available to make interest payments. In fact, this ratio often is computed by dividing cash flow generated from operations by interest payments.

For illustration, let's compare the ratios for **Coca-Cola** and **PepsiCo.** Graphic 14–10 on the next page provides condensed financial statements adapted from 2004 annual reports of those companies.

The debt to equity ratio is higher for PepsiCo:

$$\text{Debt to equity ratio} = \frac{\text{Total liabilities}}{\text{Shareholders' equity}}$$

**GRAPHIC 14–10**
Condensed Financial Statements—Coca-Cola, PepsiCo

| Balance Sheets | ($ in millions) | |
|---|---|---|
| | **Coca-Cola** | **PepsiCo** |
| **Assets** | | |
| Current assets | $12,094 | $ 8,639 |
| Property, plant, and equipment (net) | 6,091 | 8,149 |
| Intangibles and other assets | 13,142 | 11,199 |
| Total assets | $31,327 | $27,987 |
| **Liabilities and Shareholders' Equity** | | |
| Current liabilities | $10,971 | $ 6,752 |
| Long-term liabilities | 4,421 | 7,712 |
| Total liabilities | $15,392 | $14,464 |
| Shareholders' equity | 15,935 | 13,523 |
| Total liabilities and shareholders' equity | $31,327 | $27,987 |
| **Income Statements** | | |
| Net sales | $21,962 | $29,261 |
| Cost of goods sold | (7,638) | (13,406) |
| Gross profit | $14,324 | $15,855 |
| Operating expenses | (7,906) | (10,142) |
| Interest expense | (196) | (167) |
| Income before taxes | $ 6,222 | $ 5,546 |
| Tax expense | (1,375) | (1,334) |
| Net income | $ 4,847 | $ 4,212 |

The debt to equity ratio indicates the extent of trading on the equity, or financial leverage.

$$\text{Coca-Cola} = \frac{\$15,392}{\$15,935} = .97$$

$$\text{PepsiCo} = \frac{\$14,464}{\$13,523} = 1.07$$

Remember, that's not necessarily a positive or a negative. Let's look closer. When the return on shareholders' equity is greater than the return on assets, management is using debt funds to enhance the earnings for shareholders. Both firms do this. We calculate return on assets as follows:

The rate of return on assets indicates profitability without regard to how resources are financed.

$$\text{Rate of return on assets} = \frac{\text{Net income}}{\text{Total assets}}$$

$$\text{Coca-Cola} = \frac{\$4,847}{\$31,327} = 15.5\%$$

$$\text{PepsiCo} = \frac{\$4,212}{\$27,987} = 15.0\%$$

The return on assets indicates a company's overall profitability, ignoring specific sources of financing. In this regard, Coca-Cola's profitability exceeds that of PepsiCo. That advantage disappears when we compare return to shareholders:

The rate of return on shareholders' equity indicates the effectiveness of employing resources provided by owners.

$$\text{Rate of return on shareholders' equity} = \frac{\text{Net income}}{\text{Shareholders' equity}}$$

$$\text{Coca-Cola} = \frac{\$4,847}{\$15,935} = 30.4\%$$

$$\text{PepsiCo} = \frac{\$4,212}{\$13,523} = 31.1\%$$

**GLOBAL PERSPECTIVE**

Capital markets are operating more and more as a global marketplace. Firms competing for international resources, such as debt funding, include domestic corporations, multinational corporations, as well as foreign corporations and joint ventures. This poses several problems for lenders and other resource providers attempting to evaluate alternatives across international boundaries.

One persistent problem is the lack of uniformity in accounting standards used to produce the financial statements being compared. The gap has narrowed in recent years, but analysts must be aware of differences in accounting methods from country to country. Other considerations are being familiar with the accounting consequences of translating results from abroad into dollars, institutional, political, cultural, and tax differences, and identifying appropriate international industry standards for comparison.

PepsiCo's higher leverage has been used to provide a return to shareholders roughly equal to Coca-Cola, even though its return on assets is less. PepsiCo increased its return to shareholders 2.07 times (31.1%/15.0%) the return on assets. Coca-Cola increased its return to shareholders 1.96 times (30.4%/15.5%) the return on assets. Interpret this with caution, though. PepsiCo's higher leverage means higher risk as well. In down times, PepsiCo's return to shareholders will suffer proportionally more than will Coca-Cola's.

From the perspective of a creditor, we might look at which company offers the most comfortable margin of safety in terms of its ability to pay fixed interest charges:

The times interest earned ratio indicates the margin of safety provided to creditors.

$$\text{Times interest earned ratio} = \frac{\text{Net income plus interest plus taxes}}{\text{Interest}}$$

$$\text{Coca-Cola} = \frac{\$4{,}847 + 196 + 1{,}375}{\$196} = 32.7 \text{ times}$$

$$\text{PepsiCo} = \frac{\$4{,}212 + 167 + 1{,}334}{\$167} = 34.2 \text{ times}$$

In this regard, both firms provide an adequate margin of safety. The interest coverage ratios seem to indicate an ample safety cushion for creditors, particularly when considered in conjunction with their debt-equity ratios.

Decision makers should be alert to gains and losses that have nothing to do with a company's normal operating activities.

Liabilities also can have misleading effects on the income statement. Decision makers should look carefully at gains and losses produced by early extinguishment of debt. These have nothing to do with a company's normal operating activities. Unchecked, corporate management can be tempted to schedule debt buybacks to provide discretionary income in down years or even losses in up years to smooth income over time.

Outside analysts as well as managers should actively monitor risk management activities.

Alert investors and lenders also look outside the financial statements for risks associated with "off-balance-sheet" financing and other commitments that don't show up on the face of financial statements but nevertheless expose a company to risk. Relatedly, most companies attempt to actively manage the risk associated with these and other obligations. It is important for top management to understand and closely monitor risk management strategies. Some of the financial losses that have grabbed headlines in recent years, were permitted by a lack of oversight and scrutiny by senior management of companies involved. It is similarly important for investors and creditors to become informed about risks companies face and how well-equipped those companies are in managing that risk. The supplemental disclosures designed to communicate the degree of risk associated with the financial instruments we discuss in this chapter contribute to that understanding. We examine the significance of lease commitments in the next chapter. ■

## CONCEPT REVIEW EXERCISE

**NOTE WITH AN UNREALISTIC INTEREST RATE**

Cameron-Brown, Inc., constructed for Harmon Distributors a warehouse that was completed and ready for occupancy on January 2, 2006. Harmon paid for the warehouse by issuing a

$900,000, four-year note that required 7% interest to be paid on December 31 of each year. The warehouse was custom-built for Harmon, so its cash price was not known. By comparison with similar transactions, it was determined that an appropriate interest rate was 10%.

**Required:**

1. Prepare the journal entry for Harmon's purchase of the warehouse on January 2, 2006.
2. Prepare (a) an amortization schedule for the four-year term of the note and (b) the journal entry for Harmon's first interest payment on December 31, 2006.
3. Suppose Harmon's note had been an installment note to be paid in four equal payments. What would be the amount of each installment if payable (a) at the end of each year, beginning December 31, 2006? or (b) at the beginning of each year, beginning on January 2, 2006?

**SOLUTION**

1. Prepare the journal entry for Harmon's purchase of the warehouse on January 2, 2006.

| | | | Present Values |
|---|---|---|---|
| Interest | $63,000 × 3.16987* | = | $199,702 |
| Principal | $900,000 × 0.68301† | = | 614,709 |
| Present value of the note | | | $814,411 |

*Present value of an ordinary annuity of $1: $n = 4$, $i = 10\%$.
†Present value of $1: $n = 4$, $i = 10\%$.

| | | |
|---|---|---|
| Warehouse (price determined above) | 814,411 | |
| Discount on notes payable (difference) | 85,589 | |
| Notes payable (face amount) | | 900,000 |

2. Prepare (a) an amortization schedule for the four-year term of the note and (b) the journal entry for Harmon's first interest payment on December 31, 2006.

a.

| Dec. 31 | Cash Interest | Effective Interest | | Increase in Balance | Outstanding Balance |
|---|---|---|---|---|---|
| | (7% × Face amount) | (10% × Outstanding balance) | | (Discount reduction) | |
| | | | | | 814,411 |
| 2006 | 63,000 | .10 (814,411) = | 81,441 | 18,441 | 832,852 |
| 2007 | 63,000 | .10 (832,852) = | 83,285 | 20,285 | 853,137 |
| 2008 | 63,000 | .10 (853,137) = | 85,314 | 22,314 | 875,451 |
| 2009 | 63,000 | .10 (875,451) = | 87,549* | 24,549 | 900,000 |
| | 252,000 | | 337,589 | 85,589 | |

*Rounded.

Each period the unpaid interest increases the outstanding balance of the debt.

b.

| | | |
|---|---|---|
| Interest expense (effective rate × outstanding balance) | 81,441 | |
| Discount on notes payable (difference) | | 18,441 |
| Cash (stated rate × face amount) | | 63,000 |

The effective interest is the market rate times the amount of the debt outstanding during the year.

3. Suppose Harmon's note had been an installment note to be paid in four equal payments. What would be the amount of each installment if payable (a) at the end of each year, beginning December 31, 2006? or (b) at the beginning of each year, beginning on January 2, 2006?

a. $814,411 Amount of loan ÷ 3.16987 (from Table 4 $n = 4$, $i = 10\%$) = $256,923 Installment payment

b. $814,411 Amount of loan ÷ 3.48685 (from Table 6 $n = 4$, $i = 10\%$) = $233,566 Installment payment

Because money has a time value, installment payments delayed until the end of each period must be higher than if the payments are made at the beginning of each period.

# PART C DEBT RETIRED EARLY, CONVERTIBLE INTO STOCK, OR PROVIDING AN OPTION TO BUY STOCK

## Early Extinguishment of Debt

● LO5

As the previous illustration demonstrated, debt paid in installments is systematically retired over the term to maturity so that at the designated maturity date the outstanding balance is zero. When a maturity amount is specified as in our earlier illustrations, any discount or premium has been systematically reduced to zero as of the maturity date and the debt is retired simply by paying the maturity amount. However, a gain or a loss may result when debt is retired before its scheduled maturity.

Earlier we noted that a call feature accompanies most bonds to protect the issuer against declining interest rates. Even when bonds are not callable, the issuing company can retire bonds early by purchasing them on the open market. Regardless of the method, when debt of any type is retired prior to its scheduled maturity date, the transaction is referred to as **early extinguishment of debt.**

**Any difference between the outstanding debt and the amount paid to retire that debt represents either a gain or a loss.**

To record the extinguishment, the account balances pertinent to the debt obviously must be removed from the books. Of course cash is credited for the amount paid—the call price or market price. The difference between the carrying amount of the debt and the reacquisition price represents either a gain or a loss on the early extinguishment of debt. Let's continue an earlier example to illustrate the retirement of debt prior to its scheduled maturity (Illustration 14–5):

**ILLUSTRATION 14–5**
Early Extinguishment of Debt

On January 1, 2007, Masterwear Industries called its $700,000, 12% bonds when their carrying amount was $676,288. The indenture specified a call price of $685,000. The bonds were issued previously at a price to yield 14%.

| | | |
|---|---|---|
| Bonds payable (face amount) | 700,000 | |
| Loss on early extinguishment[14] ($685,000 − $676,288) | 8,712 | |
| Discount on bonds payable ($700,000 − $676,288) | | 23,712 |
| Cash (call price) | | 685,000 |

## Convertible Bonds

**FINANCIAL REPORTING CASE**

Q5, p. 661

Sometimes corporations include a convertible feature as part of a bond offering. **Convertible bonds** can be converted into (that is, exchanged for) shares of stock at the option of the bondholder. Among the reasons for issuing convertible bonds rather than straight debt are (a) to sell the bonds at a higher price (which means a lower effective interest cost),[15] (b) to use as a medium of exchange in mergers and acquisitions, and (c) to enable smaller firms or debt-heavy companies to obtain access to the bond market. Sometimes convertible bonds serve as an indirect way to issue stock when there is shareholder resistance to direct issuance of additional equity.

**Convertible bonds can be exchanged for shares of stock at the option of the investor.**

**Convertible bonds have features of both debt and equity.**

Central to each of these reasons for issuing convertible debt is that the conversion feature is attractive to investors. This hybrid security has features of both debt and equity. The owner has a fixed-income security that can become common stock if and when the firm's prosperity makes that feasible. This increases the investor's upside potential while limiting the downside risk. The conversion feature has monetary value. Just how valuable it is depends on both the conversion terms and market conditions. But from an accounting perspective the question raised is how to account for its value. To evaluate the question, consider Illustration 14–6.

[14]For several years the FASB required companies to report gains and losses from early extinguishment of debt as extraordinary items, but no longer. Now, these gains and losses are subject to the same criteria as other gains and losses for such treatment; namely, that they be both (a) unusual and (b) infrequent. *Statement of Financial Accounting Standards No. 145,* "Rescission of FASB Statements No. 4, 44, and 64, Amendment of FASB Statement No. 13, and Technical Corrections" (Norwalk, Conn.: FASB, 2002).

[15]Remember, there is an inverse relationship between bond prices and interest rates. When the price is higher, the rate (yield) is lower, and vice versa.

**ILLUSTRATION 14–6**
Convertible Bonds

On January 1, 2006, HTL Manufacturers issued $100 million of 8% convertible debentures due 2016 at 103 (103% of face value). The bonds are convertible at the option of the holder into $1 par common stock at a conversion ratio of 40 shares per $1,000 bond. HTL recently issued nonconvertible, 20-year, 8% debentures at 98.

It would appear that the conversion feature is valued by the market at $5 million—the difference between the market value of the convertible bonds, $103 million, and the market value of the nonconvertible bonds, $98 million. Some accountants argue that we should record the value of the conversion option in a shareholders' equity account ($5 million in this case) and the debt value in the bond accounts ($100 million bonds payable less $2 million discount). In fact, *SFAS 150* indicates that convertible securities and similar securities will be dealt with in phase 2 of the FASB's project on hybrid securities.[16] In the meantime, the currently accepted practice is to record the entire issue price as debt in precisely the same way as for nonconvertible bonds.[17] Treating the features as two inseparable parts of a single security avoids the practical difficulty of trying to measure the separate values of the debt and the conversion option. We sidestepped this difficulty in our illustration by assuming that HTL had recently issued nonconvertible bonds that were otherwise similar to the convertible bonds.

**Because of the inseparability of their debt and equity features, the entire issue price of convertible bonds is recorded as debt, as if they are nonconvertible bonds.**

***Journal Entry at Issuance—Convertible Bonds***

| | ($ in millions) | |
|---|---|---|
| Cash (103% × $100 million) | 103 | |
| Convertible bonds payable (face amount) | | 100 |
| Premium on bonds payable (difference) | | 3 |

**The value of the conversion feature is not separately recorded.**

Since we make no provision for the separate value of the conversion option, all subsequent entries, including the periodic reduction of the premium, are exactly the same as if these were nonconvertible bonds. So the illustrations and examples of bond accounting we discussed earlier would pertain equally to nonconvertible or convertible bonds.

*SFAS 150* did address accounting for "freestanding" hybrid securities. It requires that stock or other financial instruments that a company is obligated to buy back (manditorily redeemable) must be reported in the balance sheet as a liability, not as shareholders' equity.

## WHEN THE CONVERSION OPTION IS EXERCISED

If and when the bondholder exercises his or her option to convert the bonds into shares of stock, the bonds are removed from the accounting records and the new shares issued are recorded at the same amount (in other words, at the book value of the bonds). To illustrate, assume that half the convertible bonds issued by HTL Manufacturers are converted at a time when the remaining unamortized premium is $2 million:

***Journal Entry at Conversion***

| | ($ in millions) | |
|---|---|---|
| Convertible bonds payable (½ the account balance) | 50 | |
| Premium on bonds payable (½ the account balance) | 1 | |
| Common stock [(50,000 bonds × 40 shares) × $1 par] | | 2 |
| Paid-in capital—excess of par (to balance) | | 49 |

**The 2 million shares issued are recorded at the $51 million book value of the bonds retired.**

**ADDITIONAL CONSIDERATION**

The method just described is referred to as the *book value method,* since the new shares are recorded at the book value of the bonds being redeemed. It is by far the most popular method in practice. Another acceptable approach, the *market value*

[16] "Accounting for Certain Financial Instruments with Characteristics of Both Liabilities and Equity," *Statement of Financial Accounting Standards No. 150* (Norwalk, Conn.: FASB, 2003).

[17] "Accounting for Convertible Debt and Debt Issued with Stock Purchase Warrants," *Accounting Principles Board Opinion No. 14* (New York: APB, 1969).

*method,* records the new shares at the market value of the shares themselves or of the bonds, whichever is more determinable. Because the market value most likely will differ from the book value of the bonds, a gain or loss on conversion will result. Assume for illustration that the market value of HTL's stock is $30 per share at the time of the conversion:

| | ($ in millions) | |
|---|---|---|
| Convertible bonds payable (1/2 the account balance) . . . . . . . . . . | 50 | |
| Premium on bonds payable (1/2 the account balance) . . . . . . . . . . | 1 | |
| Loss on conversion of bonds (to balance) . . . . . . . . . . . . . . . . . . . | 9 | |
| Common stock [(50,000 bonds × 40 shares) × $1 par] . . . . . . . . | | 2 |
| Paid-in capital in excess of par [(50,000 × 40 shares) × $29] . . . | | 58 |

If a single investor had purchased the 50,000 bonds being converted, that company would record the conversion as follows:

| | ($ in millions) | |
|---|---|---|
| Investment in common stock . . . . . . . . . . . . . . . . . . . . . . . . . . . . . | 51 | |
| Investment in convertible bonds (account balance) . . . . . . . . . . . | | 50 |
| Premium on bond investment (account balance) . . . . . . . . . . . . . | | 1 |

### INDUCED CONVERSION

Investors often are reluctant to convert bonds to stock, even when share prices have risen significantly since the convertible bonds were purchased. This is because the market price of the convertible bonds will rise along with market prices of the stock. So companies sometimes try to induce conversion. The motivation might be to reduce debt and become a better risk to potential lenders or achieve a lower debt-to-equity ratio.

One way is through the call provision. As we noted earlier, most corporate bonds are callable by the issuing corporation. When the specified call price is less than the conversion value of the bonds (the market value of the shares), calling the convertible bonds provides bondholders with incentive to convert. Bondholders will choose the shares rather than the lower call price.

**Any additional consideration provided to induce conversion of convertible debt is recorded as an expense of the period.**

Occasionally, corporations may try to encourage voluntary conversion by offering an added inducement in the form of cash, stock warrants, or a more attractive conversion ratio. When additional consideration is provided to induce conversion, the fair value of that consideration is considered an expense incurred to bring about the conversion.[18]

## Bonds with Detachable Warrants

Another (less common) way to sweeten a bond issue is to include **detachable stock purchase warrants** as part of the security issue. A stock warrant gives the investor an option to purchase a stated number of shares of common stock at a specified *option price,* often within a given period of time. Like a conversion feature, warrants usually mean a lower interest rate and often enable a company to issue debt when borrowing would not be feasible otherwise.

**The issue price of bonds with detachable warrants is allocated between the two different securities on the basis of their market values.**

However, unlike a conversion feature, warrants can be separated from the bonds. This means they can be exercised independently or traded in the market separately from bonds, having their own market price. In essence, two different securities—the bonds and the warrants—are sold as a package for a single issue price. Accordingly, the issue price is allocated between the two different securities on the basis of their market values. If the independent market value of only one of the two securities is reliably determinable, that value establishes the allocation. This is demonstrated in Illustration 14–7.

[18]"Induced Conversions of Convertible Debt," *Statement of Financial Accounting Standards No. 84* (Stamford, Conn.: FASB, 1985).

**ILLUSTRATION 14–7**
Bonds with Detachable Warrants

On January 1, 2006, HTL Manufacturers issued $100 million of 8% debentures due 2013 at 103 (103% of face value). Accompanying each bond were 20 warrants. Each warrant permitted the holder to buy one share of $1 par common stock at $25 per share. Shortly after issuance, the warrants were listed on the exchange at $3 per warrant.

| | ($ in millions) | |
|---|---|---|
| Cash (103% × $100 million) | 103 | |
| Discount on bonds payable (difference) | 3 | |
| Bonds payable (face amount) | | 100 |
| Paid-in capital—stock warrants outstanding* (100,000 bonds × 20 warrants × $3) | | 6 |

*Reported as part of shareholders' equity rather than as a liability.

## ADDITIONAL CONSIDERATION

Market imperfections may cause the separate market values not to sum to the issue price of the package. In this event, allocation is achieved on the basis of the **relative market values** of the two securities. Let's say the bonds have a separate market price of $940 per bond (priced at 94):

**Market Values**

| | | |
|---|---|---|
| Bonds (100,000 bonds × $940) | $ 94 | 94% |
| Warrants (100,000 bonds × 20 warrants × $3) | 6 | 6 |
| Total | $100 | 100% |

**Proportion of Issue Price Allocated to Bonds:**

$103 million × 94% = $96,820,000

**Proportion of Issue Price Allocated to Warrants:**

$103 million × 6% = $6,180,000

| | ($ in millions) | |
|---|---|---|
| Cash (103% × $100 million) | 103.00 | |
| Discount on bonds payable ($100 million − $96.82 million) | 3.18 | |
| Bonds payable (face amount) | | 100.00 |
| Paid-in capital—stock warrants outstanding | | 6.18 |

Notice that this is the same approach we used in Chapter 10 to allocate a single purchase price to two or more assets bought for that single price. We also will allocate the total selling price of two equity securities sold for a single issue in proportion to their relative market values in Chapter 18.

If one-half of the warrants (1 million) in Illustration 14–7 are exercised when the market value of HTL's common stock is $30 per share, 1 million shares would be issued for one warrant each plus the exercise price of $25 per share.

*Journal Entry at Exercise of Detachable Warrants*

| | ($ in millions) | |
|---|---|---|
| Cash (1,000,000 warrants × $25) | 25 | |
| Paid-in capital—stock warrants outstanding (1,000,000 warrants × $3) | 3 | |
| Common stock (1,000,000 shares × $1 par per share) | | 1 |
| Paid-in capital—excess of par (to balance) | | 27 |

The $30 market value at the date of exercise is not used in valuing the additional shares issued. The new shares are recorded at the total of the previously measured values of both the warrants and the shares.

# CONCEPT REVIEW EXERCISE

## ISSUANCE AND EARLY EXTINGUISHMENT OF DEBT

The disclosure notes to the 2006 financial statements of Olswanger Industries included the following:

---

**Note 12: Bonds**

On October 3, 2005, the Corporation sold bonds with an aggregate principal amount of $500,000,000 bearing a 14% interest rate. The bonds will mature on September 15, 2015 and are unsecured subordinated obligations of the Corporation. Interest is payable semiannually on March 15 and September 15. The Corporation may redeem the bonds at any time beginning September 15, 2005, as a whole or from time to time in part, through maturity, at specified redemption prices ranging from 112% of principal in declining percentages of principal amount through 2012 when the percentage is set at 100% of principal amount. The cost of issuing the bonds, totaling $11,000,000, and the discount of $5,000,000 are being amortized over the life of the bonds, using the straight-line method and the interest method, respectively. Amortization of these items for the year ended December 31, 2006, was $960,000 and $252,000, respectively.

During the year ended December 31, 2006, the Corporation repurchased, in open market transactions, $200,000,000 in face amount of the bonds for $224,000,000, including accrued interest. The unamortized cost of issuing these bonds and the unamortized discount, $3,972,000 and $1,892,000, respectively, have been deducted in the current period.

---

From the information provided by Olswanger in Note 12, you should be able to recreate some of the journal entries the company recorded in connection with this bond issue.

**Required:**

1. Prepare the journal entry for the issuance of these bonds on October 3, 2005. (Be sure to include accrued interest for the half-month period between September 15 and October 3.)
2. Prepare the journal entry for the repurchase of these bonds, assuming the date of repurchase was November 15, 2006. The accrued interest for the two-month period between September 15 and November 15 would be $200,000,000 × 14% × 2⁄12 = $4,667,000 (rounded). Assume the entry to accrue interest was recorded separately, so the cash paid to repurchase the bonds was $219,333,000 [$224,000,000 (amount given) – $4,667,000].

## SOLUTION

1. Prepare the journal entry for the issuance of these bonds on October 3, 2005.

| | ($ in 000s) | |
|---|---|---|
| Cash (to balance) | 486,916 | |
| Bond issue costs (given in note) | 11,000 | |
| Discount on bonds payable (given in note) | 5,000 | |
| Bonds payable (face amount—given in note) | | 500,000 |
| Interest payable (accrued interest—see below*) | | 2,916 |

*Accrued interest: $500,000 × 14% × .05/12 = $2,916

2. Prepare the journal entry for the repurchase of these bonds, assuming the date of repurchase was November 15, 2006.

| | ($ in 000s) | |
|---|---|---|
| Bonds payable (face amount repurchased) | 200,000 | |
| Loss on early extinguishment (to balance) | 25,197 | |
| Discount on bonds payable (given in note) | | 1,892 |
| Bond issue costs (given in note) | | 3,972 |
| Cash (given in requirement 2) | | 219,333 |

## FINANCIAL REPORTING CASE SOLUTION

1. **What does it mean that the bonds are first mortgage bonds? What effect does that have on financing?** *(p. 663)* A mortgage bond is backed by a lien on specified real estate owned by the issuer. This makes it less risky than unsecured debt, so Service Leader can expect to be able to sell the bonds at a higher price (lower interest rate).
2. **From Service Leader's perspective, why are the bonds callable? What does that mean?** *(p. 663)* The call feature gives Service Leader some protection against being stuck with relatively high-cost debt in case interest rates fall during the 15 years to maturity. Service Leader can buy back, or call, the bonds from bondholders before the 15-year maturity date, after June 30, 2008. The call price is prespecified at 103 percent of the face value—$1,030 per $1,000 bond.
3. **How will it be possible to sell bonds paying investors 6.25% when other, similar investments will provide the investors a return of 6.5%?** *(p. 665)* Service Leader will be able to sell its 6.25% bonds in a 6.5% market only by selling them at a discounted price, below face amount. Bonds are priced by the marketplace to yield the market rate of interest for securities of similar risk and maturity. The price will be the present value of all the periodic cash interest payments (face amount × stated rate) plus the present value of the principal payable at maturity, both discounted at the market rate.
4. **Would accounting differ if the debt were designated as notes rather than bonds?** *(p. 675)* No. Other things being equal, whether they're called bonds, notes, or some other form of debt, the same accounting principles apply. They will be recorded at present value and interest will be recorded at the market rate over the term to maturity.
5. **Why might the company choose to make the bonds convertible into common stock?** *(p. 684)* Convertible bonds can be converted at the option of the bondholders into shares of stock. Sometimes the motivation for issuing convertible bonds rather than straight debt is to use the bonds as a medium of exchange in mergers and acquisitions, as a way for smaller firms or debt-heavy companies to obtain access to the bond market, or as an indirect way to issue stock when there is shareholder resistance to direct issuance of additional equity. None of these seems pertinent to Service Leader. The most likely reason is to sell at a higher price. The conversion feature is attractive to investors. Investors have a fixed-income security that can become common stock if circumstances make that attractive. The investor has additional possibilities for higher returns, with downside risk limited by the underlying debt. ■

## THE BOTTOM LINE

1. A liability requires the future payment of cash in specified amounts at specified dates. As time passes, interest accrues on debt at the effective interest rate times the amount of the debt outstanding during the period. This same principle applies regardless of the specific form of the liability.
2. Forces of supply and demand cause a bond to be priced to yield the market rate, calculated as the present value of all the cash flows required, where the discount rate is the market rate. Interest accrues at the effective market rate of interest multiplied by the outstanding balance (during the interest period). A company is permitted to allocate a discount or a premium equally to each period over the term to maturity if doing so produces results that are not materially different from the interest method.
3. In concept, notes are accounted for in precisely the same way as bonds. When a note is issued with an unrealistic interest rate, the effective market rate is used both to determine the amount recorded in the transaction and to record periodic interest thereafter.

4. On the balance sheet, disclosure should include, for all long-term borrowings, the aggregate amounts maturing and sinking fund requirements (if any) for each of the next five years. Supplemental disclosures are needed for (a) off-balance-sheet credit or market risk, (b) concentrations of credit risk, and (c) the fair value of financial instruments.
5. A gain or loss on early extinguishment of debt should be recorded for the difference between the reacquisition price and the carrying amount of the debt. Convertible bonds are accounted for as straight debt, but the value of the equity feature is recorded separately for bonds issued with detachable warrants. ■

# APPENDIX 14 TROUBLED DEBT RESTRUCTURING

A respected real estate developer, Brillard Properties, was very successful developing and managing a number of properties in the southeastern United States. To finance these investments, the developer had borrowed hundreds of millions of dollars from several regional banks. For years, events occurred as planned. The investments prospered. Cash flow was high. Interest payments on the debt were timely and individual loans were repaid as they matured.

Almost suddenly, however, the real estate climate in the region soured. Investments that had provided handsome profits now did not provide the cash flow necessary to service the debt. Bankers who had loaned substantial funds to Brillard now faced a dilemma. Because contractual interest payments were unpaid, the bankers had the legal right to demand payment, which would force the developer to liquidate all or a major part of the properties to raise the cash. Sound business practice? Not necessarily.

If creditors force liquidation, they then must share among themselves the cash raised from selling the properties—at forced sale prices. Believing the developer's financial difficulties were caused by temporary market forces, not by bad management, the bankers felt they could minimize their losses by *restructuring* the debt agreements, rather than by forcing liquidation.

When changing the original terms of a debt agreement is motivated by financial difficulties experienced by the debtor (borrower), the new arrangement is referred to as a **troubled debt restructuring**. By definition, a troubled debt restructuring involves some concessions on the part of the creditor (lender). A troubled debt restructuring may be achieved in either of two ways:

1. The debt may be *settled* at the time of the restructuring.
2. The debt may be *continued,* but with *modified terms.*

## Debt Is Settled

In the situation described above, one choice the bankers had was to try to actually settle the debt outright at the time of the troubled debt restructuring. For instance, a bank holding a \$30 million note from the developer might agree to accept a property valued at, let's say, \$20 million as final settlement of the debt. In that case, the developer has a \$10 million gain equal to the difference between the carrying amount of the debt and the fair value of the property transferred. The debtor may need to adjust the carrying amount of an asset to its fair value prior to recording its exchange for a debt. The developer in our example, for instance, would need to change the recorded amount for the property specified in the exchange agreement if it is carried at an amount other than its \$20 million fair market value. In such an instance, an ordinary gain or loss on disposition of assets should be recorded as shown in Illustration 14A–1.

In all areas of accounting, a noncash transaction is recorded at fair value.

The payment to settle a debt in a troubled debt restructuring might be cash, or a noncash asset (as in the example here), or even shares of the debtor's stock. An example of shares of stock being given in exchange for debt forgiveness is the celebrated reorganization of TWA in 1992 (since acquired by American Airlines), when creditors received a 55% stake in the company's common shares in return for forgiving about \$1 billion of the airline's \$1.5 billion debt. In any case, the debtor's gain is the difference between the carrying amount of the debt and the fair value of the asset(s) or equity securities transferred.

**ILLUSTRATION 14A–1**
Debt Settled

First Prudent Bank agrees to settle Brillard's $30 million debt in exchange for property having a fair market value of $20 million. The carrying amount of the property on Brillard's books is $17 million:

| | ($ in millions) | |
|---|---|---|
| Land ($20 million minus $17 million) | 3 | |
| Gain on disposition of assets | | 3 |
| Note payable (carrying amount) | 30 | |
| Gain on troubled debt restructuring | | 10 |
| Land (fair value) | | 20 |

**An asset is adjusted to fair value prior to recording its exchange for a debt.**

## Debt Is Continued, but with Modified Terms

We assumed in the previous example that First Prudent Bank agreed to accept property in full settlement of the debt. A more likely occurrence would be that the bank allows the debt to continue, but modifies the terms of the debt agreement to make it easier for the debtor to comply. The bank might agree to reduce or delay the scheduled *interest payments.* Or, it may agree to reduce or delay the *maturity amount.* Often a troubled debt restructuring will call for some combination of these concessions.

Let's say the stated interest rate on the note in question is 10% and annual interest payments of $3 million (10% × $30 million) are payable in December of each of two remaining years to maturity. Also assume that the developer was unable to pay the $3 million interest payment for the year just ended. This means that the amount owed—the carrying amount (or book value) of the debt—is $33 million ($30 million plus one year's accrued interest).

**The carrying amount of a debt is the current balance of the primary debt plus any accrued (unpaid) interest.**

According to generally accepted accounting principles, the way the debtor accounts for the restructuring depends on the extent of the reduction in cash payments called for by the restructured arrangement. More specifically, the accounting procedure depends on whether, under the new agreement, total cash payments (a) are *less than* the carrying amount of the debt or (b) still *exceed* the carrying amount of the debt.

**Two quite different situations are created when the terms of a debt are modified, depending on whether the cash payments are reduced to the extent that interest is eliminated.**

### WHEN TOTAL CASH PAYMENTS ARE LESS THAN THE CARRYING AMOUNT OF THE DEBT

By the original agreement, the debtor was to pay at maturity the $30 million loaned, plus enough periodic interest to provide a 10% effective rate of return. If the new agreement calls for less cash than the $33 million now owed, interest is presumed to have been eliminated.

As one of many possibilities, suppose the bank agrees to (1) forgive the interest accrued from last year, (2) reduce the two remaining interest payments from $3 million each to $2 million each, and (3) reduce the face amount from $30 million to $25 million. Clearly, the debtor will pay less by the new agreement than by the original one. In fact, if we add up the total payments called for by the new agreement, the total [($2 million × 2) plus $25 million] is less than the $33 million carrying amount. Because the $29 million does not exceed the amount owed, the restructured debt agreement no longer provides interest on the debt. Actually, the new payments are $4 million short of covering the debt itself. So, after the debt restructuring, no interest expense is recorded. All subsequent cash payments are considered to be payment of the debt itself. Consider Illustration 14A–2.

**ILLUSTRATION 14A–2**
Cash Payments Less than the Debt

Brillard Properties owes First Prudent Bank $30 million under a 10% note with two years remaining to maturity. Due to financial difficulties of the developer, the previous year's interest ($3 million) was not paid. First Prudent Bank agrees to:

1. Forgive the interest accrued from last year.
2. Reduce the remaining two interest payments to $2 million each.
3. Reduce the principal to $25 million.

| **Analysis:** | | |
|---|---|---|
| | Carrying amount | $30 million + $3 million = $33 million |
| | Future payments | ($2 million × 2) + $25 million = 29 million |
| | Gain | $ 4 million |

(continued)

**ILLUSTRATION 14A–2**
Concluded

| Carrying Amount | | |
|---|---|---|
| Before Restr. | Adj. | After Restr. |
| $30 | (1) | $29 |
| 3 | (3) | 0 |
| $33 | (4) | $29 |

| | ($ in millions) | |
|---|---|---|
| Accrued interest payable (10% × $30 million) . . . . . . . . . . . . . . . . . . | 3 | |
| Note payable ($30 million − $29 million). . . . . . . . . . . . . . . . . . . . . . | 1 | |
| Gain on debt restructuring . . . . . . . . . . . . . . . . . . . . . . . . . . . . . . | | 4 |

After restructuring, no interest expense is recorded. All cash payments are considered to be payment of the note itself.

When the total future cash payments are less than the carrying amount of the debt, the difference is recorded as a gain at the date of restructure. No interest should be recorded thereafter. That is, all subsequent cash payments result in reductions of principal.

The $25 million payment at maturity reduces the note to zero.

| **At Each of the Two Interest Dates** | ($ in millions) | |
|---|---|---|
| Note payable . . . . . . . . . . . . . . . . . . . . . . . . . . . . . . . . . . . . . . | 2 | |
| Cash (revised "interest" amount) . . . . . . . . . . . . . . . . . . . . . . . . . | | 2 |
| **At Maturity** | | |
| Note payable . . . . . . . . . . . . . . . . . . . . . . . . . . . . . . . . . . . . . . | 25 | |
| Cash (revised principal amount) . . . . . . . . . . . . . . . . . . . . . . . . . . | | 25 |

## WHEN TOTAL CASH PAYMENTS EXCEED THE CARRYING AMOUNT OF THE DEBT

Let's modify the example in the previous section. Now suppose the bank agrees to delay the due date for all cash payments until maturity and accept $34,333,200 at that time in full settlement of the debt. Rather than just reducing the cash payments as in the previous illustration, the payments are delayed. It is not the nature of the change that creates the need to account differently for this situation, but the amount of the total cash payments under the agreement relative to the carrying amount of the debt. This situation is demonstrated in Illustration 14A–3.

**ILLUSTRATION 14A–3**
Cash Payments More than the Debt

The discount rate that equates the present value on the debt ($33 million) and its future value ($34,333,200) is the effective rate of interest.

Brillard Properties owes First Prudent Bank $30 million under a 10% note with two years remaining to maturity. Due to Brillard's financial difficulties, the previous year's interest ($3 million) was not paid. First Prudent Bank agrees to:

1. Delay the due date for all cash payments until maturity.
2. Accept $34,333,200 at that time in full settlement of the debt.

| **Analysis:** | | | |
|---|---|---|---|
| | Future payments | | $34,333,200 |
| | Carrying amount | $30 million + $3 million = | 33,000,000 |
| | Interest | | $ 1,333,200 |

**Calculation of the New Effective Interest Rate**

- $33,000,000 ÷ $34,333,200 = .9612, the Table 2 value for $n = 2$, $i = ?$
- In row 2 of Table 2, the number .9612 is in the 2% column. So, this is the new effective interest rate.

As long as cash payments exceed the amount owed there will be interest—although at a lower effective rate.

Now the total payments called for by the new agreement, $34,333,200, exceed the $33 million carrying amount. Because the payments exceed the amount owed, the restructured debt agreement still provides interest on the debt—but less than before the agreement was revised. No longer is the effective rate 10%. The accounting objective now is to determine what the new effective rate is and *record interest for the remaining term of the loan at that new, lower rate,* as shown in Illustration 14A–3.

Unpaid interest is accrued at the effective rate times the carrying amount of the note.

Because the total future cash payments are not less than the carrying amount of the debt, no reduction of the existing debt is necessary and no entry is required at the time of the debt restructuring. Even though no cash is paid until maturity under the restructured debt agreement, interest expense still is recorded annually—but at the new rate.

| | | |
|---|---|---|
| **At the End of the First Year** | | |
| Interest expense [2% × ($30,000,000 + 3,000,000)] . . . . . . . . . . . . | 660,000 | |
| Accrued interest payable . . . . . . . . . . . . . . . . . . . . . . . . . . . . | | 660,000 |
| **At the End of the Second Year** | | |
| Interest expense [2% × ($30,000,000 + 3,660,000)] . . . . . . . . . . . . | 673,200 | |
| Accrued interest payable . . . . . . . . . . . . . . . . . . . . . . . . . . . . | | 673,200 |
| **At Maturity (End of the Second Year)** | | |
| Note payable . . . . . . . . . . . . . . . . . . . . . . . . . . . . . . . . . . . . | 30,000,000 | |
| Accrued interest payable ($3,000,000 + 660,000 + 673,200) . . . . . . | 4,333,200 | |
| Cash (required by new agreement) . . . . . . . . . . . . . . . . . . . . . . | | 34,333,200 |

**The carrying amount of the debt is increased by the unpaid interest from the previous year.**

**The total of the accrued interest account plus the note account is equal to the amount scheduled to be paid at maturity.**

## ADDITIONAL CONSIDERATION

To keep up with the changing amounts, it may be convenient to prepare an amortization schedule for the debt.

| Year | Cash Interest | Effective Interest | | Increase in Balance | Outstanding Balance |
|---|---|---|---|---|---|
| | | (2% × Outstanding balance) | | | |
| | | | | | 33,000,000 |
| 1 | 0 | .02 (33,000,000) = | 660,000 | 660,000 | 33,660,000 |
| 2 | 0 | .02 (33,660,000) = | 673,200 | 673,200 | 34,333,200 |
| | 0 | | 1,333,200 | 1,333,200 | |

An amortization schedule is particularly helpful if there are several years remaining to maturity.

In our example, the restructured debt agreement called for a single cash payment at maturity ($34,333,200). If more than one cash payment is required (as in the agreement in our earlier example), calculating the new effective rate is more difficult. The concept would remain straightforward: (1) determine the interest rate that provides a present value of all future cash payments that is equal to the current carrying amount and (2) record the interest at that rate thereafter. Mechanically, though, the computation by hand would be cumbersome, requiring a time-consuming trial-and-error calculation. Since our primary interest is understanding the concepts involved, we will avoid the mathematical complexities of such a situation.

You also should be aware that when a restructuring involves modification of terms, accounting for a liability by the debtor, as described in this section, and accounting for a receivable by the creditor, which was described in Chapter 12, are inconsistent. You may recall that when a creditor's investment in a receivable becomes impaired, due to a troubled debt restructuring or for any other reason, the receivable is remeasured based on the discounted present value of currently expected cash flows at the loan's original effective rate (regardless of the extent to which expected cash receipts have been reduced). For ease of comparison, the example in this chapter (Illustration 14A–3) describes the same situation as the example in Chapter 12 (Illustration 12B–2). There is no conceptual justification for the asymmetry between debtors' and creditors' accounting for troubled debt restructurings. The FASB will likely reconsider debtors' accounting in the future.[19] ■

[19] "Accounting by Creditors for Impairment of a Loan," *Statement of Financial Accounting Standards No. 114* (Norwalk, Conn.: FASB, 1993), par. 63.

## QUESTIONS FOR REVIEW OF KEY TOPICS

**Q 14–1** How is periodic interest determined for outstanding liabilities? For outstanding receivables? How does the approach compare from one form of debt instrument (say bonds payable) to another (say notes payable)?

**Q 14–2** As a general rule, how should long-term liabilities be reported on the debtor's balance sheet?

**Q 14–3** How are bonds and notes the same? How do they differ?

**Q 14–4** What information is contained in a bond indenture? What purpose does it serve?

**Q 14–5** Why will bonds always sell at their price plus any interest that has accrued since the last interest date?

**Q 14–6** On January 1, 2006, Brandon Electronics issued $85 million of 11.5% bonds, dated January 1. The market yield for bonds of maturity issued by similar firms in terms of riskiness is 12.25%. How can Brandon sell debt paying only 11.5% in a 12.25% market?

**Q 14–7** How is the price determined for a bond (or bond issue)?

**Q 14–8** A zero-coupon bond pays no interest. Explain.

**Q 14–9** When bonds are issued at a premium the debt declines each period. Explain.

**Q 14–10** Compare the two commonly used methods of determining interest on bonds.

**Q 14–11** *APB Opinion No. 21* requires that debt issue costs be recorded separately and amortized over the term of the related debt. Describe a logical alternative to this accounting treatment.

**Q 14–12** When a note's stated rate of interest is unrealistic relative to the market rate, the concept of substance over form should be employed. Explain.

**Q 14–13** Mandatorily redeemable shares obligate the issuing company to buy back the shares in exchange for cash or other assets. Where in the balance sheet are these securities reported?

**Q 14–14** How does an installment note differ from a note for which the principal is paid as a single amount at maturity?

**Q 14–15** Long-term debt can be reported either (a) as a single amount, net of any discount or increased by any premium or (b) at its face amount accompanied by a separate valuation account for the discount or premium. Any portion of the debt to be paid during the upcoming year, or operating cycle if longer, should be reported as a current amount. Regarding amounts to be paid in the future, what additional disclosures should be made in connection with long-term debt?

**Q 14–16** Early extinguishment of debt often produces a gain or a loss. How is the gain or loss determined?

**Q 14–17** What criteria are used to classify a gain or loss on early extinguishment of debt as an extraordinary item in the income statement?

**Q 14–18** Both convertible bonds and bonds issued with detachable warrants have features of both debt and equity. How does the accounting treatment differ for the two hybrid securities? Why is the accounting treatment different?

**Q 14–19** At times, companies try to induce voluntary conversion by offering an added incentive—maybe cash, stock warrants, or a more favorable conversion ratio. How is such an inducement accounted for? How is it measured?

**Q 14–20** (Based on Appendix 14) When the original terms of a debt agreement are changed because of financial difficulties experienced by the debtor (borrower), the new arrangement is referred to as a *troubled debt restructuring.* Such a restructuring can take a variety of forms. For accounting purposes, these possibilities are categorized. What are the accounting classifications of troubled debt restructurings?

**Q 14–21** (Based on Appendix 14) Pratt Industries owes First National Bank $5 million but, due to financial difficulties, is unable to comply with the original terms of the loan. The bank agrees to settle the debt in exchange for land having a fair market value of $3 million. The carrying amount of the property on Pratt's books is $2 million. For the reporting period in which the debt is settled, what amount(s) will Pratt report on its income statement in connection with the troubled debt restructuring?

**Q 14–22** (Based on Appendix 14) The way a debtor accounts for the restructuring depends on the extent of the reduction in cash payments called for by the restructured arrangement. Describe, in general, the accounting procedure for the two basic cases: when, under the new agreement, total cash payments (a) are less than the carrying amount of the debt or (b) still exceed the carrying amount of the debt.

## BRIEF EXERCISES

**BE 14–1**
Accrued interest
● LO1

On April 1, 2006, Holiday Brands issued $30 million of 6%, 30-year bonds, dated January 1, 2006, for $27.5 million (plus accrued interest). What was the amount of accrued interest that was included in the proceeds received from the bond issue?

**BE 14–2**
Determining the price of bonds
● LO2

A company issued 5%, 20-year bonds with a face amount of $80 million. The market yield for bonds of similar risk and maturity is 6%. Interest is paid semiannually. At what price did the bonds sell?

**BE 14–3**
Determining the price of bonds
● LO2

A company issued 6%, 15-year bonds with a face amount of $75 million. The market yield for bonds of similar risk and maturity is 6%. Interest is paid semiannually. At what price did the bonds sell?

**BE 14–4**
Determining the price of bonds
● LO2

A company issued 5%, 20-year bonds with a face amount of $100 million. The market yield for bonds of similar risk and maturity is 4%. Interest is paid semiannually. At what price did the bonds sell?

**BE 14–5**
Effective interest on bonds
● LO2

On January 1, a company issued 7%, 15-year bonds with a face amount of $90 million for $82,218,585 to yield 8%. Interest is paid semiannually. What was interest expense at the effective interest rate on June 30, the first interest date?

**BE 14–6**
Effective interest on bonds
● LO2

On January 1, a company issued 3%, 20-year bonds with a face amount of $80 million for $69,033,776 to yield 4%. Interest is paid semiannually. What was the interest expense at the effective interest rate on the December 31 annual income statement?

**BE 14–7**
Straight-line interest on bonds
● LO2

On January 1, a company issued 3%, 20-year bonds with a face amount of $80 million for $69,033,776 to yield 4%. Interest is paid semiannually. What was the straight-line interest expense on the December 31 annual income statement?

**BE 14–8**
Investment in bonds
● LO2

On January 1, a company purchased 3%, 20-year corporate bonds for $69,033,776 as an investment. The bonds have a face amount of $80 million and are priced to yield 4%. Interest is paid semiannually. Prepare the journal entry to record revenue at the effective interest rate on December 31, the second interest payment date.

**BE 14–9**
Note with unrealistic interest rate
● LO3

Snipes Construction paid for earth-moving equipment by issuing a $300,000, 3-year note that specified 2% interest to be paid on December 31 of each year. The equipment's retail cash price was unknown, but it was determined that a reasonable interest rate was 5%. At what amount should Snipes record the equipment and the note? What journal entry should it record for the transaction?

**BE 14–10**
Installment note
● LO3

On January 1, a company borrowed cash by issuing a $300,000, 5%, installment note to be paid in three equal payments at the end of each year beginning December 31. What would be the amount of each installment? Prepare the journal entry for the second installment payment.

**BE 14–11**
Early extinguishment; effective interest
● LO5

A company retired $60 million of its 6% bonds at 102 ($61.2 million) before their scheduled maturity. At the time, the bonds had a remaining discount of $2 million. Prepare the journal entry to record the redemption of the bonds.

**BE 14–12**
Bonds with detachable warrants
● LO5

Hoffman Corporation issued $60 million of 5%, 20-year bonds at 102. Each of the 60,000 bonds was issued with 10 detachable stock warrants, each of which entitled the bondholder to purchase, for $20, one share of $1 par common stock. At the time of sale, the market value of the common stock was $25 per share and the market value of each warrant was $5. Prepare the journal entry to record the issuance of the bonds.

**BE 14–13**
Convertible bonds
● LO5

Hoffman Corporation issued $60 million of 5%, 20-year bonds at 102. Each of the 60,000 bonds was convertible into one share of $1 par common stock. Prepare the journal entry to record the issuance of the bonds.

## EXERCISES



**An alternative exercise and problem set is available on the text website: www.mhhe.com/spiceland4e**

**E 14–1**
Accrued interest
● LO1

On March 1, 2006, Brown-Ferring Corporation issued $100 million of 12% bonds, dated January 1, 2006, for $99 million (plus accrued interest). The bonds mature on December 31, 2025, and pay interest semiannually on June 30 and December 31. Brown-Ferring's fiscal period is the calendar year.

**Required:**

1. Determine the amount of accrued interest that was included in the proceeds received from the bond sale.
2. Prepare the journal entry for the issuance of the bonds by Brown-Ferring.

**E 14–2**
Bond valuation
● LO2

Your investment department has researched possible investments in corporate debt securities. Among the available investments are the following $100 million bond issues, each dated January 1, 2006. Prices were determined by underwriters at different times during the last few weeks.

| | Company | Bond Price | Stated Rate |
|---|---|---|---|
| 1. | BB Corp. | $109 million | 11% |
| 2. | DD Corp. | $100 million | 10% |
| 3. | GG Corp. | $ 91 million | 9% |

Each of the bond issues matures on December 31, 2025, and pays interest semiannually on June 30 and December 31. For bonds of similar risk and maturity, the market yield at January 1, 2006, is 10%.

**Required:**

Other things being equal, which of the bond issues offers the most attractive investment opportunity at the prices stated? the least attractive? Why?

**E 14–3**
Determine the price of bonds in various situations
● LO2

Determine the price of a $1 million bond issue under each of the following independent assumptions:

| | Maturity | Interest Paid | Stated Rate | Effective (market) Rate |
|---|---|---|---|---|
| 1. | 10 years | annually | 10% | 12% |
| 2. | 10 years | semiannually | 10% | 12% |
| 3. | 10 years | semiannually | 12% | 10% |
| 4. | 20 years | semiannually | 12% | 10% |
| 5. | 20 years | semiannually | 12% | 12% |

**E 14–4**
Determine the price of bonds; issuance; effective interest; no amortization schedule
● LO2

The Bradford Company issued 10% bonds, dated January 1, with a face amount of $80 million on January 1, 2006. The bonds mature in 2015 (10 years). For bonds of similar risk and maturity, the market yield is 12%. Interest is paid semiannually on June 30 and December 31.

**Required:**

1. Determine the price of the bonds at January 1, 2006.
2. Prepare the journal entry to record their issuance by The Bradford Company on January 1, 2006.
3. Prepare the journal entry to record interest on June 30, 2006 (at the effective rate). (Do not prepare an amortization schedule.)
4. Prepare the journal entry to record interest on December 31, 2006 (at the effective rate). (Do not prepare an amortization schedule.)

**E 14–5**
Investor; effective interest; no amortization schedule
● LO2

The Bradford Company sold the entire bond issue described in the previous exercise to Saxton-Bose Corporation.

**Required:**

1. Prepare the journal entry to record the purchase of the bonds by Saxton-Bose on January 1, 2006.
2. Prepare the journal entry to record interest revenue on June 30, 2006 (at the effective rate). (Do not prepare an amortization schedule.)
3. Prepare the journal entry to record interest revenue on December 31, 2006 (at the effective rate). (Do not prepare an amortization schedule.)

**E 14–6**
Determine the price of bonds; issuance; effective interest; financial statement effects
● LO2

Myriad Solutions, Inc. issued 10% bonds, dated January 1, with a face amount of $320 million on January 1, 2006. The bonds mature in 2016 (10 years). For bonds of similar risk and maturity the market yield is 12%. Interest is paid semiannually on June 30 and December 31.

**Required:**

1. Determine the price of the bonds at January 1, 2006.
2. What would be the net amount of the liability Myriad would report in its balance sheet at December 31, 2006?
3. What would be the amount related to the bonds that Myriad would report in its income statement for the year ended December 31, 2006?
4. What would be the amount related to the bonds that Myriad would report in its statement of cash flows for the year ended December 31, 2006?

**E 14–7**
Determine the price of bonds; issuance; effective interest; no amortization schedule
● LO2

The Gorman Group issued $900,000 of 13% bonds on June 30, 2006. The bonds were dated on June 30 and mature on June 30, 2026 (20 years). The market yield for bonds of similar risk and maturity is 12%. Interest is paid semiannually on December 31 and June 30.

**Required:**

1. Determine the price of the bonds at June 30, 2006.
2. Prepare the journal entry to record their issuance by The Gorman Group on June 30, 2006.
3. Prepare the journal entry to record interest on December 31, 2006 (at the effective rate). (Do not prepare an amortization schedule.)
4. Prepare the journal entry to record interest on June 30, 2007 (at the effective rate). (Do not prepare an amortization schedule.)

**E 14–8**
Determine the price of bonds; issuance; straight-line method

● LO2

Universal Foods issued 10% bonds, dated January 1, with a face amount of $150 million on January 1, 2006. The bonds mature on December 31, 2020 (15 years). The market rate of interest for similar issues was 12%. Interest is paid semiannually on June 30 and December 31. Universal uses the straight-line method.

**Required:**

1. Determine the price of the bonds at January 1, 2006.
2. Prepare the journal entry to record their issuance by Universal Foods on January 1, 2006.
3. Prepare the journal entry to record interest on June 30, 2006.
4. Prepare the journal entry to record interest on December 31, 2013.

**E 14–9**
Investor; straight-line method

● LO2

Universal Foods sold the entire bond issue described in the previous exercise to Wang Communications.

**Required:**

1. Prepare the journal entry to record the purchase of the bonds by Wang Communications on January 1, 2006.
2. Prepare the journal entry to record interest revenue on June 30, 2006.
3. Prepare the journal entry to record interest revenue on December 31, 2013.

**E 14–10**
Issuance of bonds; effective interest; no amortization schedule

● LO2

Federal Semiconductors issued 11% bonds, dated January 1, with a face amount of $800 million on January 1, 2006. The bonds sold for $739,814,813 and mature in 2025 (20 years). For bonds of similar risk and maturity the market yield was 12%. Interest is paid semiannually on June 30 and December 31.

**Required:**

1. Prepare the journal entry to record their issuance by Federal on January 1, 2006.
2. Prepare the journal entry to record interest on June 30, 2006 (at the effective rate). (Do not prepare an amortization schedule.)
3. Prepare the journal entry to record interest on December 31, 2006 (at the effective rate). (Do not prepare an amortization schedule.)

**E 14–11**
Issuance of bonds; effective interest; amortization schedule

● LO2

National Orthopedics Co. issued 9% bonds, dated January 1, with a face amount of $500,000 on January 1, 2006. The bonds mature in 2009 (4 years). For bonds of similar risk and maturity the market yield was 10%. Interest is paid semiannually on June 30 and December 31.

**Required:**

1. Determine the price of the bonds at January 1, 2006.
2. Prepare the journal entry to record their issuance by National on January 1, 2006.
3. Prepare an amortization schedule that determines interest at the effective rate each period.
4. Prepare the journal entry to record interest on June 30, 2006.
5. Prepare the appropriate journal entries at maturity on December 31, 2009.

**E 14–12**
Bonds; effective interest; no amortization schedule; adjusting entry

● LO2

On February 1, 2006, Strauss-Lombardi issued 9% bonds, dated February 1, with a face amount of $800,000. The bonds sold for $731,364 and mature on January 31, 2026 (20 years). The market yield for bonds of similar risk and maturity was 10%. Interest is paid semiannually on July 31 and January 31. Strauss-Lombardi's fiscal year ends December 31.

**Required:**

1. Prepare the journal entry to record their issuance by Strauss-Lombardi on February 1, 2006.
2. Prepare the journal entry to record interest on July 31, 2006 (at the effective rate). (Do not prepare an amortization schedule.)
3. Prepare the adjusting entry to accrue interest on December 31, 2006.
4. Prepare the journal entry to record interest on January 31, 2007.

**E 14–13**
Bonds; straight-line method; adjusting entry

● LO2

On March 1, 2006, Stratford Lighting issued 14% bonds, dated March 1, with a face amount of $300,000. The bonds sold for $294,000 and mature on February 28, 2026 (20 years). Interest is paid semiannually on August 31 and February 28. Stratford uses the straight-line method and its fiscal year ends December 31.

**Required:**

1. Prepare the journal entry to record the issuance of the bonds by Stratford Lighting on March 1, 2006.
2. Prepare the journal entry to record interest on August 31, 2006.
3. Prepare the journal entry to accrue interest on December 31, 2006.
4. Prepare the journal entry to record interest on February 28, 2007.

**E 14–14**
Multiple choice; CPA exam; bonds

● LO2

The following questions dealing with bonds are adapted from past CPA examinations. Determine the response that best completes the statements or questions.

1. On January 1, 2007, Oak Co. issued 400 of its 8%, $1,000 bonds at 97 plus accrued interest. The bonds are dated October 1, 2006, and mature on October 1, 2012. Interest is payable semiannually on April 1 and October 1. Accrued interest for the period October 1, 2006, to January 1, 2007, amounted to $8,000. On January 1, 2007, what amount should Oak report as bonds payable, net of discount?
   a. $380,000
   b. $388,000
   c. $388,300
   d. $392,000
2. On December 31, 2006, Moss Co. issued $1,000,000 of 11% bonds at 109. Each $1,000 bond was issued with 50 detachable stock warrants, each of which entitled the bondholder to purchase one share of $5 par common stock for $25. Immediately after issuance, the market value of each warrant was $4. On December 31, 2006, what amount should Moss record as discount or premium for issuance of bonds?
   a. $40,000 premium
   b. $90,000 premium
   c. $110,000 discount
   d. $200,000 discount
3. A bond issued on June 1, 2006, has interest payment dates of April 1 and October 1. Bond interest expense for the year ended December 31, 2006, is for a period of
   a. Three months
   b. Four months
   c. Six months
   d. Seven months

**E 14–15**
Note with unrealistic interest rate

● LO3

Amber Mining and Milling, Inc., contracted with Truax Corporation to have constructed a custom-made lathe. The machine was completed and ready for use on January 1, 2006. Amber paid for the lathe by issuing a $600,000, three-year note that specified 4% interest, payable annually on December 31 of each year. The cash market price of the lathe was unknown. It was determined by comparison with similar transactions that 12% was a reasonable rate of interest.

**Required:**

1. Prepare the journal entry on January 1, 2006, for Amber Mining and Milling's purchase of the lathe.
2. Prepare an amortization schedule for the three-year term of the note.
3. Prepare the journal entries to record (a) interest for each of the three years and (b) payment of the note at maturity.

**E 14–16**
Installment note

● LO3

American Food Services, Inc., acquired a packaging machine from Barton and Barton Corporation. Barton and Barton completed construction of the machine on January 1, 2006. In payment for the $4 million machine, American Food Services issued a four-year installment note to be paid in four equal payments at the end of each year. The payments include interest at the rate of 10%.

**Required:**

1. Prepare the journal entry for American Food Services' purchase of the machine on January 1, 2006.
2. Prepare an amortization schedule for the four-year term of the installment note.
3. Prepare the journal entry for the first installment payment on December 31, 2006.
4. Prepare the journal entry for the third installment payment on December 31, 2008.

**E 14–17**
Early extinguishment

● LO5

The balance sheet of Indian River Electronics Corporation as of December 31, 2005, included 12.25% bonds having a face amount of $90 million. The bonds had been issued in 1998 and had a remaining discount of $3 million at December 31, 2005. On January 1, 2006, Indian River Electronics called the bonds before their scheduled maturity at the call price of 102.

**Required:**

Prepare the journal entry by Indian River Electronics to record the redemption of the bonds at January 1, 2006.

**E 14–18**
Convertible bonds

● LO5

On January 1, 2006, Gless Textiles issued $12 million of 9%, 10-year convertible bonds at 101. The bonds pay interest on June 30 and December 31. Each $1,000 bond is convertible into 40 shares of Gless's $1 par common stock. Century Services purchased 10% of the issue as an investment.

**Required:**

1. Prepare the journal entries for the issuance of the bonds by Gless and the purchase of the bond investment by Century.
2. Prepare the journal entries for the June 30, 2010, interest payment by both Gless and Century assuming both use the straight-line method.

3. On July 1, 2011, when Gless's common stock had a market price of $33 per share, Century converted the bonds it held. Prepare the journal entries by both Gless and Century for the conversion of the bonds (book value method).

**E 14–19**
Bonds with detachable warrants

● LO5

On August 1, 2006, Limbaugh Communications issued $30 million of 10% nonconvertible bonds at 104. The bonds are due on July 31, 2026. Each $1,000 bond was issued with 20 detachable stock warrants, each of which entitled the bondholder to purchase, for $60, one share of Limbaugh Communications' $10 par common stock. Interstate Containers purchased 20% of the bond issue. On August 1, 2006, the market value of the common stock was $58 per share and the market value of each warrant was $8.

In February, 2017, when Limbaugh's common stock had a market price of $72 per share and the unamortized discount balance was $1 million, Interstate Containers exercised the warrants it held.

**Required:**

1. Prepare the journal entries on August 1, 2006, to record (a) the issuance of the bonds by Limbaugh and (b) the investment by Interstate.
2. Prepare the journal entries for both Limbaugh and Interstate in February, 2017, to record the exercise of the warrants.

**E 14–20**
New debt issues; offerings announcements

● LO2

When companies offer new debt security issues, they publicize the offerings in the financial press and on internet sites. Assume the following were among the debt offerings reported in December 2003:

**New Securities Issues**

**Corporate**

**National Equipment Transfer Corporation**—$200 million bonds via lead managers Second Tennessee Bank N.A. and Morgan, Dunavant & Co., according to a syndicate official. Terms: maturity, Dec. 15, 2009; coupon 7.46%; issue price, par; yield, 7.46%; noncallable, debt ratings: Ba-1 (Moody's Investors Service, Inc.), BBB+ (Standard & Poor's).

**IgWig Inc.**—$350 million of notes via lead manager Stanley Brothers, Inc., according to a syndicate official. Terms: maturity, Dec. 1, 2011; coupon, 6.46%; Issue price, 99; yield, 6.56%; call date, NC; debt ratings: Baa-1 (Moody's Investors Service, Inc.), A (Standard & Poor's).

**Required:**

1. Prepare the appropriate journal entries to record the sale of both issues to underwriters. Ignore share issue costs and assume no accrued interest.
2. Prepare the appropriate journal entries to record the first semiannual interest payment for both issues.

**E 14–21**
Error in amortization schedule

● LO1 LO2

Wilkins Food Products, Inc. acquired a packaging machine from Lawrence Specialists Corporation. Lawrence completed construction of the machine on January 1, 2004. In payment for the machine Wilkins issued a three-year installment note to be paid in three equal payments at the end of each year. The payments include interest at the rate of 10%.

Lawrence made a conceptual error in preparing the amortization schedule which Wilkins failed to discover until 2006. The error had caused Wilkins to understate interest expense by $45,000 in 2004 and $40,000 in 2005.

**Required:**

1. Determine which accounts are incorrect as a result of these errors at January 1, 2006, before any adjustments. Explain your answer. (Ignore income taxes.)
2. Prepare a journal entry to correct the error.
3. What other step(s) would be taken in connection with the error?

**E 14–22**
Error correction; accrued interest on bonds

● LO1 LO2

At the end of 2005, Majors Furniture Company failed to accrue $61,000 of interest expense that accrued during the last five months of 2005 on bonds payable. The bonds mature in 2019. The discount on the bonds is amortized by the straight-line method. The following entry was recorded on February 1, 2006, when the semiannual interest was paid:

| | | |
|---|---|---|
| Interest expense | 73,200 | |
| Discount on bonds payable | | 1,200 |
| Cash | | 72,000 |

**Required:**

Prepare any journal entry necessary to correct the error as well as any adjusting entry for 2006 related to the situation described. (Ignore income taxes.)

**E 14–23**
Multiple choice; CMA exam; long-term debt
● LO2

The following questions dealing with long-term debt are adapted from questions that previously appeared on Certified Management Accountant (CMA) examinations. The CMA designation sponsored by the Institute of Management Accountants (www.imanet.org) provides members with an objective measure of knowledge and competence in the field of management accounting. Determine the response that best completes the statements or questions.

Questions 1 and 2 are based on the following information. On January 1, Matthew Company issued 7% term bonds with a face amount of $1,000,000 due in 8 years. Interest is payable semiannually on January 1 and July 1. On the date of issue, investors were willing to accept an effective interest rate of 6%.

1. The bonds were issued on January 1 at
   a. a premium.
   b. an amortized value.
   c. book value.
   d. a discount.
2. Assume the bonds were issued on January 1 for $1,062,809. Using the effective interest amortization method, Matthew Company recorded interest expense for the 6 months ended June 30 in the amount of
   a. $35,000.
   b. $70,000.
   c. $63,769.
   d. $31,884.
3. A bond issue sold at a premium is valued on the statement of financial position at the
   a. maturity value.
   b. maturity value plus the unamortized portion of the premium.
   c. cost at the date of investment.
   d. maturity value less the unamortized portion of the premium.

**E 14–24**
Troubled debt restructuring; debt settled (Based on Appendix 14)

At January 1, 2006, Transit Developments owed First City Bank Group $600,000, under an 11% note with three years remaining to maturity. Due to financial difficulties, Transit was unable to pay the previous year's interest.

First City Bank Group agreed to settle Transit's debt in exchange for land having a fair market value of $450,000. Transit purchased the land in 2002 for $325,000.

**Required:**
Prepare the journal entry(s) to record the restructuring of the debt by Transit Developments.

**E 14–25**
Troubled debt restructuring; modification of terms (Based on Appendix 14)

At January 1, 2006, Brainard Industries, Inc., owed Second BancCorp $12 million under a 10% note due December 31, 2008. Interest was paid last on December 31, 2004. Brainard was experiencing severe financial difficulties and asked Second BancCorp to modify the terms of the debt agreement. After negotiation Second BancCorp agreed to:

a. Forgive the interest accrued for the year just ended.
b. Reduce the remaining two years' interest payments to $1 million each and delay the first payment until December 31, 2007.
c. Reduce the unpaid principal amount to $11 million.

**Required:**
Prepare the journal entries by Brainard Industries, Inc., necessitated by the restructuring of the debt at (1) January 1, 2006, (2) December 31, 2007, and (3) December 31, 2008.

**E 14–26**
Troubled debt restructuring; modification of terms (Based on Appendix 14)

At January 1, 2006, NCI Industries, Inc., was indebted to First Federal Bank under a $240,000, 10% unsecured note. The note was signed January 1, 2002, and was due December 31, 2007. Annual interest was last paid on December 31, 2004. NCI was experiencing severe financial difficulties and negotiated a restructuring of the terms of the debt agreement. First Federal agreed to reduce last year's interest and the remaining two years' interest payments to $11,555 each and delay all payments until December 31, 2007, the maturity date.

**Required:**
Prepare the journal entries by NCI Industries, Inc., necessitated by the restructuring of the debt at: (1) January 1, 2006; (2) December 31, 2006; and (3) December 31, 2007.

# PROBLEMS

available with McGraw-Hill's Homework Manager www.mhhe.com/spiceland4e

**An alternate exercise and problem set is available on the text website: www.mhhe.com/spiceland4e**

**P 14–1**
Determining the price of bonds; discount and premium; issuer and investor

On January 1, 2006, Instaform, Inc., issued 10% bonds with a face amount of $50 million, dated January 1. The bonds mature in 2025 (20 years). The market yield for bonds of similar risk and maturity is 12%. Interest is paid semiannually.

● LO2

**Required:**

1. Determine the price of the bonds at January 1, 2006, and prepare the journal entry to record their issuance by Instaform.
2. Assume the market rate was 9%. Determine the price of the bonds at January 1, 2006, and prepare the journal entry to record their issuance by Instaform.
3. Assume Broadcourt Electronics purchased the entire issue in a private placement of the bonds. Using the data in requirement 2, prepare the journal entry to record their purchase by Broadcourt.

**P 14–2**
Accrued interest; effective interest; financial statement effects

● LO2

On March 1, 2006, Baddour, Inc. issued 10% bonds, dated January 1, with a face amount of $160 million. The bonds were priced at $140 million (plus accrued interest) to yield 12%. Interest is paid semiannually on June 30 and December 31. Baddour's fiscal year ends September 30.

**Required:**

1. What amount(s) related to the bonds would Baddour report in its balance sheet at September 30, 2006?
2. What amount(s) related to the bonds would Baddour report in its income statement for the year ended September 30, 2006?
3. What amount(s) related to the bonds would Baddour report in its statement of cash flows for the year ended September 30, 2006?

**P 14–3**
Straight-line and effective interest compared

● LO2

eXcel

On January 1, 2006, Bradley Recreational Products issued $100,000, 9%, four-year bonds. Interest is paid semiannually on June 30 and December 31. The bonds were issued at $96,768 to yield an annual return of 10%.

**Required:**

1. Prepare an amortization schedule that determines interest at the effective interest rate.
2. Prepare an amortization schedule by the straight-line method.
3. Prepare the journal entries to record interest expense on June 30, 2008, by each of the two approaches.
4. Explain why the pattern of interest differs between the two methods.
5. Assuming the market rate is still 10%, what price would a second investor pay the first investor on June 30, 2008, for $10,000 of the bonds?

**P 14–4**
Bond amortization schedule

● LO2

On January 1, 2006, Tennessee Harvester Corporation issued debenture bonds that pay interest semiannually on June 30 and December 31. Portions of the bond amortization schedule appear below:

| Payment | Cash Interest | Effective Interest | Increase in Balance | Outstanding Balance |
|---|---|---|---|---|
| | | | | 6,627,273 |
| 1 | 320,000 | 331,364 | 11,364 | 6,638,637 |
| 2 | 320,000 | 331,932 | 11,932 | 6,650,569 |
| 3 | 320,000 | 332,528 | 12,528 | 6,663,097 |
| 4 | 320,000 | 333,155 | 13,155 | 6,676,252 |
| 5 | 320,000 | 333,813 | 13,813 | 6,690,065 |
| 6 | 320,000 | 334,503 | 14,503 | 6,704,568 |
| ~ | ~ | ~ | ~ | ~ |
| ~ | ~ | ~ | ~ | ~ |
| ~ | ~ | ~ | ~ | ~ |
| 38 | 320,000 | 389,107 | 69,107 | 7,851,247 |
| 39 | 320,000 | 392,562 | 72,562 | 7,923,809 |
| 40 | 320,000 | 396,191 | 76,191 | 8,000,000 |

**Required:**

1. What is the face amount of the bonds?
2. What is the initial selling price of the bonds?
3. What is the term to maturity in years?
4. Interest is determined by what approach?
5. What is the stated annual interest rate?
6. What is the effective annual interest rate?
7. What is the total cash interest paid over the term to maturity?
8. What is the total effective interest expense recorded over the term to maturity?

**P 14–5**
Issuer and investor; effective interest; amortization schedule; adjusting entries

● LO2

eXcel

On February 1, 2006, Cromley Motor Products issued 9% bonds, dated February 1, with a face amount of $80 million. The bonds mature on January 31, 2010 (4 years). The market yield for bonds of similar risk and maturity was 10%. Interest is paid semiannually on July 31 and January 31. Barnwell Industries acquired $80,000 of the bonds as a long-term investment. The fiscal years of both firms end December 31.

**Required:**

1. Determine the price of the bonds issued on February 1, 2006.
2. Prepare amortization schedules that indicate (a) Cromley's effective interest expense and (b) Barnwell's effective interest revenue for each interest period during the term to maturity.

3. Prepare the journal entries to record (a) the issuance of the bonds by Cromley and (b) Barnwell's investment on February 1, 2006.
4. Prepare the journal entries by both firms to record all subsequent events related to the bonds through January 31, 2008.

**P 14–6**
Issuer and investor; straight-line method; adjusting entries
● LO2

On April 1, 2006, Western Communications, Inc., issued 12% bonds, dated March 1, 2006, with face amount of $30 million. The bonds sold for $29.3 million and mature on February 28, 2009. Interest is paid semiannually on August 31 and February 28. Stillworth Corporation acquired $30,000 of the bonds as a long-term investment. The fiscal years of both firms end December 31, and both firms use the straight-line method.

**Required:**

1. Prepare the journal entries to record (a) issuance of the bonds by Western and (b) Stillworth's investment on April 1, 2006.
2. Prepare the journal entries by both firms to record all subsequent events related to the bonds through maturity.

**P 14–7**
Issuer and investor; effective interest; no amortization schedule
● LO2
eXcel

McWherter Instruments sold $400 million of 8% bonds, dated January 1, on January 1, 2006. The bonds mature on December 31, 2025 (20 years). For bonds of similar risk and maturity, the market yield was 10%. Interest is paid semiannually on June 30 and December 31. Blanton Technologies, Inc., purchased $400,000 of the bonds as a long-term investment.

**Required:**

1. Determine the price of the bonds issued on January 1, 2006.
2. Prepare the journal entries to record (a) their issuance by McWherter and (b) Blanton's investment on January 1, 2006.
3. Prepare the journal entries by (a) McWherter and (b) Blanton to record interest on June 30, 2006 (at the effective rate). (Do not prepare an amortization schedule.)
4. Prepare the journal entries by (a) McWherter and (b) Blanton to record interest on December 31, 2006 (at the effective rate). (Do not prepare an amortization schedule.)

**P 14–8**
Zero-coupon bonds
● LO2

On January 1, 2006, Darnell Window and Pane issued $18 million of 10-year, zero-coupon bonds for $5,795,518.

**Required:**

1. Prepare the journal entry to record the bond issue.
2. Determine the effective rate of interest.
3. Prepare the journal entry to record annual interest expense at December 31, 2006.
4. Prepare the journal entry to record annual interest expense at December 31, 2007.
5. Prepare the journal entry to record the extinguishment at maturity.

**P 14–9**
Notes exchanged for assets
● LO3

At the beginning of the year, Lambert Motors issued the three notes described below.

1. The company issued a two-year, 12%, $600,000 note in exchange for a tract of land. The current market rate of interest is 12%.
2. Lambert acquired some office equipment with a fair market value of $94,643 by issuing a one-year, $100,000 note. The stated interest on the note is 6%.
3. The company purchased a building by issuing a three-year installment note. The note is to be repaid in equal installments of $1 million per year beginning one year hence. The current market rate of interest is 12%.

**Required:**

Prepare the journal entries to record each of the three transactions and the interest expense at the end of the first year for each.

**P 14–10**
Note with unrealistic interest rate
● LO3

At January 1, 2006, Brant Cargo acquired equipment by issuing a five-year, $150,000 (payable at maturity), 4% note. The market rate of interest for notes of similar risk is 10%.

**Required:**

1. Prepare the journal entry for Brant Cargo to record the purchase of the equipment.
2. Prepare the journal entry for Brant Cargo to record the interest at December 31, 2006.
3. Prepare the journal entry for Brant Cargo to record the interest at December 31, 2007.

**P 14–11**
Noninterest-bearing installment note
● LO3

At the beginning of 2006, VHF Industries acquired a machine with a fair market value of $6,074,700 by issuing a four-year, noninterest-bearing note in the face amount of $8 million. The note is payable in four annual installments of $2 million at the end of each year.

**Required:**

1. What is the effective rate of interest implicit in the agreement?
2. Prepare the journal entry to record the purchase of the machine.
3. Prepare the journal entry to record the first installment payment at December 31, 2006.
4. Prepare the journal entry to record the second installment payment at December 31, 2007.

5. Suppose the market value of the machine was unknown at the time of purchase, but the market rate of interest for notes of similar risk was 11%. Prepare the journal entry to record the purchase of the machine.

**P 14–12**
Note and installment note with unrealistic interest rate
● LO3

eXcel

Braxton Technologies, Inc., constructed a conveyor for A&G Warehousers that was completed and ready for use on January 1, 2006. A&G paid for the conveyor by issuing a $100,000, four-year note that specified 5% interest to be paid on December 31 of each year. The conveyor was custom-built for A&G, so its cash price was unknown. By comparison with similar transactions it was determined that a reasonable interest rate was 10%.

**Required:**

1. Prepare the journal entry for A&G's purchase of the conveyor on January 1, 2006.
2. Prepare an amortization schedule for the four-year term of the note.
3. Prepare the journal entry for A&G's third interest payment on December 31, 2008.
4. If A&G's note had been an installment note to be paid in four equal payments at the end of each year beginning December 31, 2006, what would be the amount of each installment?
5. Prepare an amortization schedule for the four-year term of the installment note.
6. Prepare the journal entry for A&G's third installment payment on December 31, 2008.

**P 14–13**
Early extinguishment of debt
● LO2 LO5

Three years ago American Insulation Corporation issued 10 percent, $800,000, 10-year bonds for $770,000. Debt issue costs were $3,000. American Insulation exercised its call privilege and retired the bonds for $790,000. The corporation uses the straight-line method both to determine interest and to amortize debt issue costs.

**Required:**

Prepare the journal entry to record the call of the bonds.

**P 14–14**
Early extinguishment; effective interest
● LO2 LO5

The long-term liability section of Twin Digital Corporation's balance sheet as of December 31, 2005, included 12% bonds having a face amount of $20 million and a remaining discount of $1 million. Disclosure notes indicate the bonds were issued to yield 14%.

Interest is recorded at the effective interest rate and paid on January 1 and July 1 of each year. On July 1, 2006, Twin Digital retired the bonds at 102 ($20.4 million) before their scheduled maturity.

**Required:**

1. Prepare the journal entry by Twin Digital to record the semiannual interest on July 1, 2006.
2. Prepare the journal entry by Twin Digital to record the redemption of the bonds on July 1, 2006.

**P 14–15**
Investments in bonds; accrued interest; sale
● LO1 LO2 LO4

The following transactions relate to bond investments of Livermore Laboratories. The company's fiscal year ends on December 31. Livermore uses the straight-line method to determine interest.

| | | |
|---|---|---|
| **2006** | | |
| July | 1 | Purchased $16 million of Bracecourt Corporation 10% debentures, due in 20 years (June 30, 2026), for $15.7 million. Interest is payable on January 1 and July 1 of each year. |
| Oct. | 1 | Purchased $30 million of 12% Framm Pharmaceuticals debentures, due May 31, 2016, for $31,160,000 plus accrued interest. Interest is payable on June 1 and December 1 of each year. |
| Dec. | 1 | Received interest on the Framm bonds. |
| | 31 | Accrued interest. |
| **2007** | | |
| Jan. | 1 | Received interest on the Bracecourt bonds. |
| June | 1 | Received interest on the Framm bonds. |
| July | 1 | Received interest on the Bracecourt bonds. |
| Sept. | 1 | Sold $15 million of the Framm bonds at 101 plus accrued interest. |
| Dec. | 1 | Received interest on the remaining Framm bonds. |
| | 31 | Accrued interest. |
| **2008** | | |
| Jan. | 1 | Received interest on the Bracecourt bonds. |
| Feb. | 28 | Sold the remainder of the Framm bonds at 102 plus accrued interest. |
| Dec. | 31 | Accrued interest. |

**Required:**

Prepare the appropriate journal entries for these long-term bond investments.

**P 14–16**
Debt issue costs; issuance; expensing; early extinguishment
● LO1 LO2 LO5

Cupola Fan Corporation issued 10%, $400,000, 10-year bonds for $385,000 on June 30, 2006. Debt issue costs were $1,500. Interest is paid semiannually on December 31 and June 30. One year from the issue date (July 1, 2007), the corporation exercised its call privilege and retired the bonds for $395,000. The corporation uses the straight-line method both to determine interest and to amortize debt issue costs.

**Required:**

1. Prepare the journal entry to record the issuance of the bonds.
2. Prepare the journal entries to record the payment of interest and amortization of debt issue costs on December 31, 2006.

3. Prepare the journal entries to record the payment of interest and amortization of debt issue costs on June 30, 2007.
4. Prepare the journal entries to record the call of the bonds.

**P 14–17**
Concepts; terminology
- LO 1 through LO5

Listed below are several terms and phrases associated with long-term debt. Pair each item from List A (by letter) with the item from List B that is most appropriately associated with it.

| List A | List B |
|---|---|
| ____ 1. Effective rate times balance | a. Straight-line method |
| ____ 2. Promises made to bondholders | b. Discount |
| ____ 3. Present value of interest plus present value of principal | c. Liquidation payments after other claims satisfied |
| | d. Name of owner not registered |
| ____ 4. Call feature | e. Premium |
| ____ 5. Debt issue costs | f. Checks are mailed directly |
| ____ 6. Market rate higher than stated rate | g. No specific assets pledged |
| ____ 7. Coupon bonds | h. Bond indenture |
| ____ 8. Convertible bonds | i. Backed by a lien |
| ____ 9. Market rate less than stated rate | j. Interest expense |
| ____ 10. Stated rate times face amount | k. May become stock |
| ____ 11. Registered bonds | l. Legal, accounting, printing |
| ____ 12. Debenture bond | m. Protection against falling rates |
| ____ 13. Mortgage bond | n. Periodic cash payments |
| ____ 14. Materiality concept | o. Bond price |
| ____ 15. Subordinated debenture | |

**P 14–18**
Early extinguishment
- LO2 LO5

The long-term liability section of Eastern Post Corporation's balance sheet as of December 31, 2005, included 10% bonds having a face amount of $40 million and a remaining premium of $6 million. On January 1, 2006, Eastern Post retired some of the bonds before their scheduled maturity.

**Required:**

Prepare the journal entry by Eastern Post to record the redemption of the bonds under each of the independent circumstances below:

1. Eastern Post called half the bonds at the call price of 102 (102% of face amount).
2. Eastern Post repurchased $10 million of the bonds on the open market at their market price of $10.5 million.

**P 14–19**
Convertible bonds; induced conversion; bonds with detachable warrants
- LO2 LO5

Bradley-Link's December 31, 2006, balance sheet included the following items:

| | ($ in millions) |
|---|---|
| **Long-Term Liabilities** | |
| 9.6% convertible bonds, callable at 101 beginning in 2007, due 2010 (net of unamortized discount of $2) [note 8] | $198 |
| 10.4% registered bonds callable at 104 beginning in 2016, due 2020 (net of unamortized discount of $1) [note 8] | 49 |
| **Shareholders' Equity** | |
| Paid-in capital—stock warrants outstanding | 4 |

**Note 8: Bonds (in part)**
The 9.6% bonds were issued in 1993 at 97.5 to yield 10%. Interest is paid semiannually on June 30 and December 31. Each $1,000 bond is convertible into 40 shares of the Company's $1 par common stock.

The 10.4% bonds were issued in 1997 at 102 to yield 10%. Interest is paid semiannually on June 30 and December 31. Each $1,000 bond was issued with 40 detachable stock warrants, each of which entitles the holder to purchase one share of the Company's $1 par common stock for $25, beginning 2007.

On January 3, 2007, when Bradley-Link's common stock had a market price of $32 per share, Bradley-Link called the convertible bonds to force conversion. 90% were converted; the remainder were acquired at the call price. When the common stock price reached an all-time high of $37 in December of 2007, 40% of the warrants were exercised.

**Required:**

1. Show the journal entries that were recorded when each of the two bond issues was originally sold in 1993 and 1997.
2. Prepare the journal entry to record (book value method) the conversion of 90% of the convertible bonds in January 2007 and the retirement of the remainder.

3. Assume Bradley-Link induced conversion by offering $150 cash for each bond converted. Prepare the journal entry to record (book value method) the conversion of 90% of the convertible bonds in January 2007.
4. Assume Bradley-Link induced conversion by modifying the conversion ratio to exchange 45 shares for each bond rather than the 40 shares provided in the contract. Prepare the journal entry to record (book value method) the conversion of 90% of the convertible bonds in January 2007.
5. Prepare the journal entry to record the exercise of the warrants in December 2007.

**P 14–20**
Troubled debt restructuring (Based on Appendix 14)

At January 1, 2006, Rothschild Chair Company, Inc., was indebted to First Lincoln Bank under a $20 million, 10% unsecured note. The note was signed January 1, 2003, and was due December 31, 2009. Annual interest was last paid on December 31, 2004. Rothschild Chair Company was experiencing severe financial difficulties and negotiated a restructuring of the terms of the debt agreement.

**Required:**

Prepare all journal entries by Rothschild Chair Company, Inc., to record the restructuring and any remaining transactions relating to the debt under each of the independent circumstances below:

1. First Lincoln Bank agreed to settle the debt in exchange for land having a fair market value of $16 million but carried on Rothschild Chair Company's books at $13 million.
2. First Lincoln Bank agreed to (a) forgive the interest accrued from last year, (b) reduce the remaining four interest payments to $1 million each, and (c) reduce the principal to $15 million.
3. First Lincoln Bank agreed to defer all payments (including accrued interest) until the maturity date and accept $27,775,000 at that time in settlement of the debt.

# BROADEN YOUR PERSPECTIVE

**Apply your critical-thinking ability to the knowledge you've gained. These cases will provide you an opportunity to develop your research, analysis, judgment, and communication skills. You also will work with other students, integrate what you've learned, apply it in real world situations, and consider its global and ethical ramifications. This practice will broaden your knowledge and further develop your decision-making abilities.**

**Communication Case 14–1**
Convertible securities and warrants; concepts

● LO5

It is not unusual to issue long-term debt in conjunction with an arrangement under which lenders receive an option to buy common stock during all or a portion of the time the debt is outstanding. Sometimes the vehicle is convertible bonds; sometimes warrants to buy stock accompany the bonds and are separable. Interstate Chemical is considering these options in conjunction with a planned debt issue.

"You mean we have to report $7 million more in liabilities if we go with convertible bonds? Makes no sense to me," your CFO said. "Both ways seem pretty much the same transaction. Explain it to me, will you?"

**Required:**

Write a memo. Include in your explanation each of the following:

1. The differences in accounting for proceeds from the issuance of convertible bonds and of debt instruments with separate warrants to purchase common stock.
2. The underlying rationale for the differences.
3. Arguments that could be presented for the alternative accounting treatment.

**Real World Case 14–2**
Zero-coupon debt; Hewlett-Packard Company

The 2004 annual report of **Hewlett-Packard Company** reports zero-coupon notes issued at the end of its 1997 fiscal year. One billion, eight hundred million dollars face amount of 20-year debt sold for $968 million, a price to yield 3.149%. In fiscal 2002, HP repurchased $257 million in face value of the notes for a purchase price of $127 million, resulting in a gain on the early extinguishment of debt.

**Required:**

1. What journal entry did Hewlett-Packard use to record the sale in 1997?
2. Using an electronic spreadsheet, prepare an amortization schedule for the notes. Assume interest is calculated annually and use numbers expressed in millions of dollars; that is, the face amount is $1,800.
3. What was the effect on HP's earnings in 1998? Explain.
4. From the amortization schedule, determine the book value of the debt at the end of 2002.
5. What journal entry did Hewlett-Packard use to record the early extinguishment of debt in 2002, assuming the purchase was made at the end of the year?

**Communication Case 14–3**
Is convertible debt a liability or is it shareholders' equity? Group Interaction

● LO1 LO2 LO5

Some financial instruments can be considered compound instruments in that they have features of both debt and shareholders' equity. The most common example encountered in practice is convertible debt—bonds or notes convertible by the investor into common stock. A topic of debate for several years has been whether:

**View 1:** Issuers should account for an instrument with both liability and equity characteristics entirely as a liability or entirely as an equity instrument depending on which characteristic governs.

**View 2:** Issuers should account for an instrument as consisting of a liability component and an equity component that should be accounted for separately.

In considering this question, you should disregard what you know about the current position of the FASB on the issue. Instead, focus on conceptual issues regarding the practicable and theoretically appropriate treatment, unconstrained by GAAP. Also, focus your deliberations on convertible bonds as the instrument with both liability and equity characteristics.

**Required:**

1. Which view do you favor? Develop a list of arguments in support of your view prior to the class session for which the case is assigned.
2. In class, your instructor will pair you (and everyone else) with a classmate (who also has independently developed an argument).
   a. You will be given three minutes to argue your view to your partner. Your partner likewise will be given three minutes to argue his or her view to you. During these three-minute presentations, the listening partner is not permitted to speak.
   b. After each person has had a turn attempting to convince his or her partner, the two partners will have a three-minute discussion in which they will decide which view is more convincing. Arguments will be merged into a single view for each pair.
3. After the allotted time, a spokesperson for each of the two views will be selected by the instructor. Each spokesperson will field arguments from the class in support of that view's position and list the arguments on the board. The class then will discuss the merits of the two lists of arguments and attempt to reach a consensus view, though a consensus is not necessary.

**Analysis Case 14–4**
Issuance of bonds

● LO2

The following appeared in the October 15, 2005, issue of the *Financial World Journal*:

This announcement is not an offer of securities for sale or an offer to buy securities.
New Issue October 15, 2005

**$750,000,000**
**CRAFT FOODS, INC.**
**7.75% Debentures Due October 1, 2015**
Price 99.57%
plus accrued interest if any from date of issuance

Copies of the prospectus and the related prospectus supplement may be obtained from such of the undersigned as may legally offer these securities under applicable securities laws.

**Keegan Morgan & Co. Inc.**
**Coldwell Bros. & Co.**
**Robert Stacks & Co.**
**Sherwin-William & Co.**

**Required:**

1. Explain what is being described by the announcement.
2. Can you think of a psychological reason for the securities to be priced as they are?
3. What are the accounting considerations for Craft Foods, Inc.? Describe how Craft recorded the sale.

**Judgment Case 14–5**
Noninterest-bearing debt

● LO3

While reading a recent issue of *Health & Fitness,* a trade journal, Brandon Wilde noticed an ad for equipment he had been seeking for use in his business. The ad offered oxygen therapy equipment under the following terms:

Model BL 44582
$204,000 zero interest loan
Quarterly payments of $17,000 for only 3 years

The ad captured Wilde's attention, in part because he recently had been concerned that the interest charges incurred by his business were getting out of line. The price, though, was somewhat higher than prices for this model he had seen elsewhere.

**Required:**

Advise Mr. Wilde on the purchase he is considering.

**Judgment Case 14–6**
Noninterest-bearing note exchanged for cash and other privileges

● LO3

The Jaecke Group, Inc., manufactures various kinds of hydraulic pumps. In June 2006, the company signed a four-year purchase agreement with one of its main parts suppliers, Hydraulics, Inc. Over the four-year period, Jaecke has agreed to purchase 100,000 units of a key component used in the manufacture of its pumps. The agreement allows Jaecke to purchase the component at a price lower than the prevailing market price at the time of purchase. As part of the agreement, Jaecke will lend Hydraulics $200,000 to be repaid after four years with no stated interest (the prevailing market rate of interest for a loan of this type is 10%).

Jaecke's chief accountant has proposed recording the note receivable at $200,000. The parts inventory purchase from Hydraulics over the next four years will then be recorded at the actual prices paid.

**Required:**

Do you agree with the accountant's valuation of the note and his intention to value the parts inventory acquired over the four-year period of the agreement at actual prices paid? If not, how would you account for the initial transaction and the subsequent inventory purchases?

**Communication Case 14–7**
Note receivable exchanged for cash and other services

● LO3

The Pastel Paint Company recently loaned $300,000 to KIX 96, a local radio station. The radio station signed a noninterest-bearing note requiring the $300,000 to be repaid in three years. As part of the agreement, the radio station will provide Pastel with a specified amount of free radio advertising over the three-year term of the note.

The focus of this case is the valuation of the note receivable by Pastel Paint Company and the treatment of the "free" advertising provided by the radio station. Your instructor will divide the class into two to six groups depending on the size of the class. The mission of your group is to reach consensus on the appropriate note valuation and accounting treatment of the free advertising.

**Required:**

1. Each group member should deliberate the situation independently and draft a tentative argument prior to the class session for which the case is assigned.
2. In class, each group will meet for 10 to 15 minutes in different areas of the classroom. During that meeting, group members will take turns sharing their suggestions for the purpose of arriving at a single group treatment.
3. After the allotted time, a spokesperson for each group (selected during the group meetings) will share the group's solution with the class. The goal of the class is to incorporate the views of each group into a consensus approach to the situation.

**Analysis Case 14–8**
Issuance, extinguishment, and conversion of bonds

● LO2 LO5

On January 1, 2005, Brewster Company issued 2,000 of its five-year, $1,000 face amount, 11% bonds dated January 1 at an effective annual interest rate (yield) of 9%. Brewster uses the effective interest method of amortization. On December 31, 2006, the 2,000 bonds were extinguished early through acquisition in the open market by Brewster for $1,980,000. On July 1, 2005, Brewster issued 5,000 of its six-year, $1,000 face amount, 10% convertible bonds dated July 1 at an effective annual interest rate (yield) of 12%. The convertible bonds are convertible at the option of the investor into Brewster's common stock at a ratio of 10 shares of common stock for each bond. Brewster used the effective interest method of amortization. On July 1, 2006, an investor in Brewster's convertible bonds tendered 1,500 bonds for conversion into 15,000 shares of Brewster's common stock which had a market value of $105 per share at the date of the conversion.

**Required:**

1. a. Were the 11% bonds issued at par, at a discount, or at a premium? Why?
   b. Would the amount of interest expense for the 11% bonds using the effective interest method of amortization be higher in the first or second year of the life of the bonds issue? Why?
2. a. How should gain or loss on early extinguishment of debt be determined? Does the early extinguishment of the 11% bonds result in a gain or loss? Why?
   b. How should Brewster report the early extinguishment of the 11% bonds on the 2006 income statement?
3. a. Would recording the conversion of the 10% convertible bonds into common stock under the book value method affect net income? What is the rationale for the book value method?
   b. Would recording the conversion of the 10% convertible bonds into common stock under the market value method affect net income? What is the rationale for the market value method?

*(AICPA adapted)*

**Ethics Case 14–9**
Debt for equity swaps; have your cake and eat it too

● LO1 LO5

The cloudy afternoon mirrored the mood of the conference of division managers. Claude Meyer, assistant to the controller for Hunt Manufacturing, wore one of the gloomy faces that was just emerging from the conference room. "Wow, I knew it was bad, but not that bad," Claude thought to himself. "I don't look forward to sharing those numbers with shareholders."

The numbers he discussed with himself were fourth quarter losses which more than offset the profits of the first three quarters. Everyone had known for some time that poor sales forecasts and production delays had wreaked havoc on the bottom line, but most were caught off guard by the severity of damage.

Later that night he sat alone in his office, scanning and rescanning the preliminary financial statements on his computer monitor. Suddenly his mood brightened. "This may work," he said aloud, though no one could hear. Fifteen minutes later he congratulated himself, "Yes!"

The next day he eagerly explained his plan to Susan Barr, controller of Hunt for the last six years. The plan involved $300 million in convertible bonds issued three years earlier.

*Meyer:* By swapping stock for the bonds, we can eliminate a substantial liability from the balance sheet, wipe out most of our interest expense, and reduce our loss. In fact, the book value of the bonds is significantly less than the market value of the stock we'd issue. I think we can produce a profit.

*Barr:* But Claude, our bondholders are not inclined to convert the bonds.

*Meyer:* Right. But, the bonds are callable. As of this year, we can call the bonds at a call premium of 1%. Given the choice of accepting that redemption price or converting to stock, they'll all convert. We won't have to pay a cent. And, since no cash will be paid, we won't pay taxes either.

**Required:**

Do you perceive an ethical dilemma? What would be the impact of following up on Claude's plan? Who would benefit? Who would be injured?

**Judgment Case 14–10**
Analyzing financial statements; financial leverage; interest coverage

● LO1

IGF Foods Company is a large, primarily domestic, consumer foods company involved in the manufacture, distribution, and sale of a variety of food products. Industry averages are derived from Troy's *The Almanac of Business and Industrial Financial Ratios.* Following are the 2006 and 2005 comparative income statements and balance sheets for IGF. (The financial data we use are from actual financial statements of a well-known corporation, but the company name is fictitious and the numbers and dates have been modified slightly to disguise the company's identity.)

**IGF FOODS COMPANY**
**Years Ended December 31, 2006 and 2005**
($ in millions)

| Comparative Income Statements | 2006 | 2005 |
|---|---|---|
| Net sales | $6,440 | $5,800 |
| Cost of goods sold | (3,667) | (3,389) |
| Gross profit | 2,773 | 2,411 |
| Operating expenses | (1,916) | (1,629) |
| Operating income | 857 | 782 |
| Interest expense | (54) | (53) |
| Income from operations before tax | 803 | 729 |
| Income taxes | (316) | (287) |
| Net income | $ 487 | $ 442 |
| **Comparative Balance Sheets** | | |
| **Assets** | | |
| Total current assets | $1,879 | $1,490 |
| Property, plant, and equipment (net) | 2,592 | 2,291 |
| Intangibles (net) | 800 | 843 |
| Other assets | 74 | 60 |
| Total assets | $5,345 | $4,684 |
| **Liabilities and Shareholders' Equity** | | |
| Total current liabilities | $1,473 | $ 941 |
| Long-term debt | 534 | 728 |
| Deferred income taxes | 407 | 344 |
| Total liabilities | 2,414 | 2,013 |
| Shareholders' equity: | | |
| Common stock | 180 | 180 |
| Additional paid-in capital | 21 | 63 |
| Retained earnings | 2,730 | 2,428 |
| Total shareholders' equity | 2,931 | 2,671 |
| Total liabilities and shareholders' equity | $5,345 | $4,684 |

Long-term solvency refers to a company's ability to pay its long-term obligations. Financing ratios provide investors and creditors with an indication of this element of risk.

**Required:**

1. Calculate the debt to equity ratio for IGF for 2006. The average ratio for the stocks listed on the New York Stock Exchange in a comparable time period was 1.0. What information does your calculation provide an investor?
2. Is IGF experiencing favorable or unfavorable financial leverage?

3. Calculate IGF's times interest earned ratio for 2006. The coverage for the stocks listed on the New York Stock Exchange in a comparable time period was 5.1. What does your calculation indicate about IGF's risk?

**Real World Case 14–11**

Researching the way long-term debt is reported; retrieving information from the Internet

- LO1 through LO4

EDGAR, the Electronic Data Gathering. Analysis, and Retrieval system, performs automated collection, validation, indexing, acceptance and forwarding of submissions by companies and others who are required by law to file forms with the U.S. Securities and Exchange Commission (SEC). All publicly traded domestic companies use EDGAR to make the majority of their filings. (Some foreign companies do so voluntarily.) Form 10-K, including the annual report, is required to be filed on EDGAR. The SEC makes this information available on the Internet.

**Required:**

1. Access EDGAR on the Internet using EdgarScan at: **edgarscan.pwcglobal.com**.
2. Search for Procter & Gamble. Access its 2004 10-K filing. Search or scroll to find the financial statements and related notes.
3. What is the total debt (including current liabilities and deferred taxes) reported on the balance sheet? How has that amount changed over the most recent two years?
4. Compare the total liabilities (including current liabilities and deferred taxes) with the shareholders' equity and calculate the debt to equity ratio for the most recent two years. Has the proportion of debt financing and equity financing changed recently?
5. Does P&G obtain more financing through notes, bonds, or commercial paper? Are required debt payments increasing or decreasing over time? Is any long-term debt classified as short-term or vice versa? Why?

# CPA SIMULATION 14–1

**Ace Company**

Long-Term Debt

KAPLAN CPA Review

Test your knowledge of the concepts discussed in this chapter, practice critical professional skills necessary for career success, and prepare for the computer-based CPA exam by accessing our CPA simulations at the text website: **www.mhhe.com/spiceland4e.**

The Ace Company simulation tests your knowledge of a) the way we account for and report bonds from the perspective of both the issuer and investor, b) reporting the cash flows related to bonds, and c) capitalization of interest on funds provided by bonds and used to construct a building, as we studied in Chapter 10.

As on the CPA exam itself, you will be asked to use tools including a spreadsheet, a calculator, and professional accounting standards, to conduct research, derive solutions, and communicate conclusions related to these issues in a simulated environment headed by the following interactive tabs:

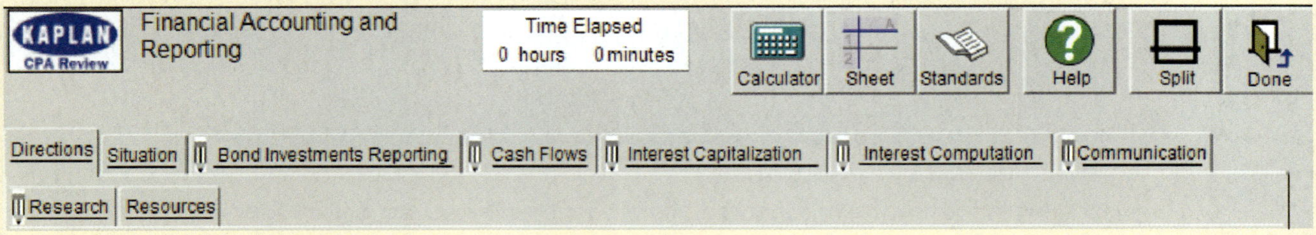


Specific tasks in the simulation include:

- Determining the selling price of bonds and analyzing the way an investor should report an investment in bonds.
- Applying judgment in the classification of cash flows from bond transactions on a statement of cash flows.
- Determining the amount of interest to be capitalized as part of the cost of an asset constructed with funding provided by bonds.
- Demonstrating an understanding of the way interest is calculated on debt.
- Communicating the way we account for convertible debt and debt with detachable warrants.
- Researching the way early extinguishments of debt is reported.

15

CHAPTER

# Leases

## OVERVIEW

In the previous chapter, we saw how companies account for their long-term debt. The focus of that discussion was *bonds* and *notes*. In this chapter we continue our discussion of debt, but we now turn our attention to liabilities arising in connection with *leases*. Leases that produce such debtor/creditor relationships are referred to as *capital* leases by the lessee and as either *direct financing* or *sales-type* leases by the lessor. We also will see that some leases do not produce debtor/creditor relationships, but instead are accounted for as rental agreements. These are designated as *operating* leases.

### LEARNING OBJECTIVES

**After studying this chapter, you should be able to:**

- LO1 Identify and describe the operational, financial, and tax objectives that motivate leasing.
- LO2 Explain why some leases constitute rental agreements and some represent purchases/sales accompanied by debt financing.
- LO3 Explain the basis for each of the criteria and conditions used to classify leases.
- LO4 Record all transactions associated with operating leases by both the lessor and lessee.
- LO5 Describe and demonstrate how both the lessee and lessor account for a nonoperating lease.
- LO6 Describe and demonstrate how the lessor accounts for a sales-type lease.
- LO7 Explain how lease accounting is affected by the residual value of a leased asset.
- LO8 Describe the way a bargain purchase option affects lease accounting.
- LO9 Explain the impact on lease accounting of executory costs, the discount rate, initial direct costs, and contingent rentals.
- LO10 Explain sale-leaseback agreements and other special leasing arrangements and their accounting treatment.

# FINANCIAL REPORTING CASE

## It's a Hit!

"Don't get too comfortable with those big numbers," said Aaron Sanchez, controller for your new employer. "It's likely our revenues will take a hit over the next couple of years as more of our customers lease our machines rather than buy them."

You've just finished your first look at Higher Graphics' third quarter earnings report. Like most companies in your industry, HG leases its labeling machines to some customers and sells them to others. Eager to understand the implications of your new supervisor's concerns, you pull out your old intermediate accounting book and turn to the leases chapter.

**By the time you finish this chapter, you should be able to respond appropriately to the questions posed in this case. Compare your response to the solution provided at the end of the chapter.**

### QUESTIONS

1. How would HG's revenues "take a hit" as a result of more customers leasing rather than buying labeling machines? (page 717)
2. Under what kind of leasing arrangements would the "hit" not occur? (page 726)

# PART A ACCOUNTING BY THE LESSOR AND LESSEE

We all are familiar with leases. If you ever have leased an apartment, you know that a lease is a contractual arrangement by which a **lessor** (owner) provides a **lessee** (user) the right to use an asset for a specified period of time. In return for this right, the lessee agrees to make stipulated, periodic cash payments during the term of the lease. An apartment lease is a typical rental agreement in which the fundamental rights and responsibilities of ownership are retained by the lessor; the lessee merely uses the asset temporarily. Businesses, too, lease assets under similar arrangements. These are referred to as **operating leases.** Many contracts, though, are formulated outwardly as leases, but in reality are installment purchases/sales. These are called **capital leases** (**direct financing** or **sales-type leases** to the lessor). Graphic 15–1 compares the possibilities.

An apartment lease is a typical rental agreement referred to as an *operating lease.*

**GRAPHIC 15–1**
Basic Lease Classifications

| Lessee | Lessor |
|---|---|
| Operating lease | Operating lease |
| Capital lease | Direct financing lease |
| | Sales-type lease |

After looking at some of the possible advantages of leasing assets rather than buying them in certain circumstances, we will explore differences in leases further.

### DECISION MAKERS' PERSPECTIVE—Advantages of Leasing

● LO1

When a young entrepreneur started a computer training center a few years ago, she had no idea how fast her business would grow. Now, while she knows she needs computers, she doesn't know how many. Just starting out, she also has little cash with which to buy them.

The U.S. Navy once leased a fleet of tankers to avoid asking Congress for appropriations.

The mutual funds department of a large investment firm often needs new computers and peripherals—fast. The department manager knows he can't afford to wait up to a year, the time it sometimes takes, to go through company channels to obtain purchase approval.

An established computer software publisher recently began developing a new line of business software. The senior programmer has to be certain he's testing the company's products on the latest versions of computer hardware. And yet he views large expenditures on equipment subject to rapid technological change and obsolescence as risky business.

Leasing can facilitate asset acquisition.

Each of these individuals is faced with different predicaments and concerns. The entrepreneur is faced with uncertainty and cash flow problems, the department manager with time constraints and bureaucratic control systems, the programmer with fear of obsolescence. Though their specific concerns differ, these individuals have all met their firms' information technology needs with the same solution: each has decided to lease the computers rather than buy them.

The number one method of external financing by U.S. businesses is leasing.

Computers are by no means the only assets obtained through leasing arrangements. To the contrary, leasing has grown to be the most popular method of external financing of corporate assets in America. The airplane in which you last flew probably was leased, as was the gate from which it departed. Your favorite retail outlet at the local shopping mall likely leases the space it operates. Many companies actually exist for the sole purpose of acquiring assets and leasing them to others. And, leasing often is a primary method of "selling" a firm's products. **IBM** and **Boeing** are familiar examples.

In light of its popularity, you may be surprised that leasing usually is more expensive than buying. Of course, the higher apparent cost of leasing is because the lessor usually shoulders at least some of the financial and risk burdens that a purchaser normally would assume. So, why the popularity?

**Tax incentives often motivate leasing.**

The lease decisions described above are motivated by operational incentives. Tax and market considerations also motivate firms to lease. Sometimes leasing offers tax saving advantages over outright purchases. For instance, a company with little or no taxable income—maybe a business just getting started, or one experiencing an economic downturn—will get little benefit from depreciation deductions. But the company can benefit *indirectly* by leasing assets rather than buying. By allowing the *lessor* to retain ownership and thus benefit from depreciation deductions, the lessee often can negotiate lower lease payments. Lessees with sufficient taxable income to take advantage of the depreciation deductions, but still in lower tax brackets than lessors, also can achieve similar indirect tax benefits.

**Leasing sometimes is used as a means of off-balance-sheet financing.**

The desire to obtain "off-balance-sheet financing" also is sometimes a leasing stimulus. When funds are borrowed to purchase an asset, the liability has a detrimental effect on the company's debt-equity ratio and other quantifiable indicators of riskiness. Similarly, the purchased asset increases total assets and correspondingly lowers calculations of the rate of return on assets. Despite research that indicates otherwise, management actions continue to reflect a belief that the financial market is naive and is fooled by off-balance-sheet financing.[1] Managers continue to avoid reporting assets and liabilities by leasing rather than buying and by constructing lease agreements in such a way that capitalizing the assets and liabilities is not required.[2]

**Operational, tax, and financial market incentives often make leasing an attractive alternative to purchasing.**

Whether or not there is any real effect on security prices, sometimes off-balance-sheet financing helps a firm avoid exceeding contractual limits on designated financial ratios (like the debt to equity ratio, for instance).[3] When the operational, tax, and financial market advantages are considered, the *net* cost of leasing often is less than the cost of purchasing. ■

## Capital Leases and Installment Notes Compared

● LO2

You learned in the previous chapter how to account for an installment note. To a great extent, then, you already have learned how to account for a capital lease. To illustrate, let's recall the situation described in the previous chapter. We assumed that Skill Graphics purchased a package-labeling machine from Hughes–Barker Corporation by issuing a three-year installment note that required six semiannual installment payments of $139,857 each. That arrangement provided for the purchase of the $666,633 machine as well as interest at an annual rate of 14% (7% twice each year). Remember, too, that each installment payment consisted of part interest (7% times the outstanding balance) and part payment for the machine (the remainder of each payment).

Now let's suppose that Skill Graphics instead acquired the package-labeling machine from Hughes–Barker Corporation under a three-year *lease* that required six semiannual rental payments of $139,857 each. Obviously, the fundamental nature of the transaction remains the same regardless of whether it is negotiated as an installment purchase or as a lease. So, it would be inconsistent to account for this lease in a fundamentally different way than for an installment purchase:

---

[1]A comprehensive research study commissioned by the FASB offers strong evidence that managers try to structure leases as operating leases to avoid balance sheet effects, but also that the securities market behaves as if it sees through these attempts. That is, leases have the same effect on the market whether they are reflected as assets and liabilities on the balance sheet or are merely reported in the disclosure notes. These are conclusions of A. Rashad Abdel-khalik, "The Economic Effects on Leases of FASB *Statement No. 13,* Accounting for Leases," *Research Report* (Stamford, Conn.: FASB, 1981).

[2]You will learn later in the chapter that accounting standards are designed to identify lease arrangements that, despite their outward appearance, are in reality purchases of assets. Assets acquired by these arrangements, *capital leases,* are required to be recorded as well as the related lease liability. Managers often structure lease terms so that capitalization requirements are avoided.

[3]It is common for debt agreements, particularly long-term ones, to include restrictions on the debtor as a way to provide some degree of protection to the creditor. Sometimes a minimum level is specified for current assets relative to current liabilities, net assets, debt as a ratio of equity, or many other financial ratios. Often a restriction is placed on dividend payments, share repurchases, or other activities that might impede the debtor's ability to repay the debt. Typically, the debt becomes due on demand when the debtor becomes in violation of such a debt covenant, often after a specified grace period.

***Comparison of a Note and Capital Lease***

**In keeping with the basic accounting concept of substance over form, accounting for a capital lease parallels that for an installment purchase.**

| **At Inception (January 1)** | | |
|---|---|---|
| **Installment Note** | | |
| Machinery. . . . . . . . . . . . . . . . . . . . | 666,633 | |
| Note payable . . . . . . . . . . . . . . . . . . | | 666,633 |
| **Capital Lease** | | |
| Leased machinery . . . . . . . . . . . . . . . . | 666,633 | |
| Lease payable. . . . . . . . . . . . . . . . . . | | 666,633 |

Consistent with the nature of the transaction, interest expense accrues each period at the effective rate times the outstanding balance:

***Interest Compared for a Note and Capital Lease***

**Each payment includes both an amount that represents interest and an amount that represents a reduction of principal.**

| **At the First Semiannual Payment Date (June 30)** | | |
|---|---|---|
| **Installment Note** | | |
| Interest expense (7% × $666,633) . . . . . . . . | 46,664 | |
| Note payable (difference). . . . . . . . . . . . | 93,193 | |
| Cash (installment payment) . . . . . . . . . . . | | 139,857 |
| **Capital Lease** | | |
| Interest expense (7% × $666,633) . . . . . . . . | 46,664 | |
| Lease payable (difference) . . . . . . . . . . . | 93,193 | |
| Cash (rental payment) . . . . . . . . . . . . . . | | 139,857 |

Because the lease payable balance declines with each payment, the interest becomes less each period. An amortization schedule is convenient to track the changing amounts as shown in Graphic 15–2.

**GRAPHIC 15–2**
Lease Amortization Schedule

**Each rental payment includes interest on the outstanding balance at the effective rate. The remainder of each payment reduces the outstanding balance.**

| Date | Payments | Effective Interest | | Decrease in Balance | Outstanding Balance |
|---|---|---|---|---|---|
| | | (7% × Outstanding balance) | | | |
| | | | | | 666,633 |
| 1 | 139,857 | .07(666,633) = | 46,664 | 93,193 | 573,440 |
| 2 | 139,857 | .07(573,440) = | 40,141 | 99,716 | 473,724 |
| 3 | 139,857 | .07(473,724) = | 33,161 | 106,696 | 367,028 |
| 4 | 139,857 | .07(367,028) = | 25,692 | 114,165 | 252,863 |
| 5 | 139,857 | .07(252,863) = | 17,700 | 122,157 | 130,706 |
| 6 | 139,857 | .07(130,706) = | 9,151* | 130,706 | 0 |
| | 839,142 | | 172,509 | 666,633 | |

*Rounded.

You should recognize this as essentially the same amortization schedule we used in the previous chapter in connection with our installment note example. The reason for the similarity is that we view a capital lease as being, in substance, equivalent to an installment purchase. So naturally the accounting treatment of the two essentially identical transactions should be consistent.

## Lease Classification

A lease is accounted for as either a rental agreement or a purchase/sale accompanied by debt financing. The choice of accounting method hinges on the nature of the leasing arrangement.

**A basic concept of accounting is substance over form.**

**Capital leases** are agreements that we identify as being formulated outwardly as leases, but which are in reality installment purchases. Sometimes the true nature of an arrangement is obvious. For example, a 10-year noncancelable lease of a computer with a 10-year useful life, by which title passes to the lessee at the end of the lease term, obviously more nearly represents a purchase than a rental agreement. But what if the terms of the contract do not transfer title, and the lease term is for only seven years of the asset's 10-year life? Suppose contractual terms permit the lessee to obtain title under certain prearranged conditions? What if compensation provided by the lease contract is nearly equal to the value of the asset under lease? These situations are less clear-cut.

Professional judgment is needed to differentiate between leases that represent rental agreements and those that in reality are installment purchases/sales. The essential question is whether the usual risks and rewards of ownership have been transferred to the lessee. But judgment alone is likely to lead to inconsistencies in practice. The desire to encourage consistency in practice motivated the FASB to provide guidance for distinguishing between the two fundamental types of leases.[4] As you study the classification criteria in the following paragraphs, keep in mind that some leases clearly fit the classifications we give them, but others fall in a gray area somewhere between the two extremes. For those, we end up forcing them into one category or the other by somewhat arbitrary criteria.

**Accounting for leases attempts to see through the legal form of the agreements to determine their economic substance.**

## CLASSIFICATION CRITERIA

● LO3

A lessee should classify a lease transaction as a capital lease if it includes a noncancelable lease term and one or more of the four criteria listed in Graphic 15–3 are met.[5] Otherwise, it is an operating lease.

**GRAPHIC 15–3**
Criteria for Classification as a Capital Lease

1. The agreement specifies that ownership of the asset transfers to the lessee.
2. The agreement contains a bargain purchase option.
3. The noncancelable lease term is equal to 75% or more of the expected economic life of the asset.
4. The present value of the minimum lease payments is equal to or greater than 90% of the fair value of the asset.

Let's look closer at these criteria.

**Criterion 1: Transfer of ownership.**

Since our objective is to determine when the risks and rewards of ownership have been transferred to the lessee, the first criterion is self-evident. If legal title passes to the lessee during, or at the end of, the lease term, obviously ownership attributes are transferred.

**Criterion 2: Bargain purchase option.**

A **bargain purchase option (BPO)** is a provision in the lease contract that gives the lessee the option of purchasing the leased property at a bargain price. This is defined as a price sufficiently lower than the expected fair value of the property (when the option becomes exercisable) that the exercise of the option appears reasonably assured at the inception of the lease. Because exercise of the option appears reasonably assured, transfer of ownership is expected. So the logic of the second criterion is similar to that of the first. Applying criterion 2 in practice, though, often is more difficult because it is necessary to make a judgment now about whether a future option price will be a bargain.

**Criterion 3: Lease term is 75% of economic life.**

If an asset is leased for most of its useful life, then most of the benefits and responsibilities of ownership are transferred to the lessee. We presume, quite arbitrarily, that 75% or more of the **expected economic life** of the asset is an appropriate threshold point for this purpose.

Although the intent of this criterion is fairly straightforward, implementation sometimes is troublesome. First, the lease term may be uncertain. It may be renewable beyond its initial term. Or the lease may be cancelable after a designated noncancelable period. When either is an issue, we ordinarily consider the lease term to be the noncancelable[6] term of the lease

---

[4] "Accounting for Leases," *Statement of Financial Accounting Standards No. 13* (Stamford, Conn.: FASB, 1980), par. 7.

[5] Noncancelable in this context does not preclude the agreement from specifying that the lease is cancelable after a designated noncancelable lease term. If no portion of the lease term is noncancelable, it is an operating lease. Later in this section, we discuss treatment of any cancelable portion of the lease term.

[6] Noncancelable in this context is a lease that is cancelable only by (a) the occurrence of some remote contingency, (b) permission of the lessor, (c) a new lease with the same lessor, or (d) payment by the lessee of a penalty in an amount such that continuation of the lease appears, at inception, reasonably assured. "Accounting for Leases: Sale and Leaseback Transactions Involving Real Estate, Sales-Type Leases of Real Estate, Definition of the Lease Term, Initial Direct Costs of Direct Financing Leases," *Statement of Financial Accounting Standards No. 98* (Stamford, Conn.: FASB, 1988), par. 22.

plus any periods covered by **bargain renewal options**.[7] A bargain renewal option gives the lessee the option to renew the lease at a bargain rate. That is, the rental payment is sufficiently lower than the expected fair rental of the property at the date the option becomes exercisable that exercise of the option appears reasonably assured.

**ADDITIONAL CONSIDERATION**

Periods covered by bargain renewal options are not included in the lease term if a **bargain purchase option** is present. This is because the lease term should not extend beyond the date a bargain purchase option becomes exercisable. For example, assume a BPO allows a lessee to buy a leased delivery truck at the end of the noncancelable five-year lease term. Even if an option to renew the lease beyond that date is considered to be a bargain renewal option, that extra period would not be included as part of the lease term. Remember, we presume the BPO will be exercised after the initial five-year term, making the renewal option irrelevant.

Another implementation issue is estimating the economic life of the leased property. This is the estimated remaining time the property is expected to be economically usable for its intended purpose, with normal maintenance and repairs, at the inception of the lease. Estimates of the economic life of leased property are subject to the same uncertainty limitations of most estimates. This uncertainty presents the opportunity to arrive at estimates that cause this third criterion not to be met.

Finally, if the inception of the lease occurs during the last 25% of an asset's economic life, this third criterion does not apply. This is consistent with the basic premise of this criterion that most of the risks and rewards of ownership occur during the first 75% of an asset's life.

Criterion 4: Present value of payments is 90% of fair value.

If the lease payments required by a lease contract substantially pay for a leased asset, it is logical to identify the arrangement as a lease equivalent to an installment purchase. This situation is considered to exist when the present value of the **minimum lease payments** is equal to or greater than 90% of the fair value of the asset at the inception of the lease. In general, minimum lease payments are payments the lessee is required to make in connection with the lease. We look closer at the make-up of minimum lease payments later in the chapter.

The 90% recovery criterion often is the decisive one. As mentioned earlier, lessees often try to avoid writing a lease agreement that will require recording an asset and liability. When this is an objective, it usually is relatively easy to avoid meeting the first three criteria. However, when the underlying motive for the lease agreement is that the lessee substantively acquire the asset, it is more difficult to avoid meeting the 90% recovery criterion without defeating that motive. New ways, though, continually are being devised to structure leases to avoid meeting this criterion. Later we will look at some popular devices that are used.

Again consistent with the basic premise that most of the risks and rewards of ownership occur during the first 75% of an asset's life, this fourth criterion does not apply if the inception of the lease occurs during the last 25% of an asset's economic life.

## ADDITIONAL LESSOR CONDITIONS

As we saw in the previous section, the lessee accounts for a capital lease as if an asset were purchased—records both an asset and a liability at the inception of the lease. Consistency would suggest that the lessor in the same lease transaction should record the sale of an asset. Indeed, consistency is a goal of the FASB's lease accounting standards. The four classification criteria discussed in the previous section apply to both parties to the transaction, lessees and lessors. However, a fundamental difference is that for a lessor to record the sale side of

[7]If applicable, the lease term also should include (a) periods for which failure to renew the lease imposes a penalty on the lessee in an amount such that renewal appears reasonably assured, (b) periods covered by ordinary renewal options during which a guarantee by the lessee of the lessor's debt directly or indirectly related to the leased property is expected to be in effect or a loan from the lessee to the lessor directly or indirectly related to the leased property is expected to be outstanding, (c) periods covered by ordinary renewal options preceding the date that a bargain purchase option is exercisable, or (d) periods representing renewals or extensions of the lease at the lessor's option. "Accounting for Leases: Sale and Leaseback Transactions Involving Real Estate, Sales-Type Leases of Real Estate, Definition of the Lease Term, Initial Direct Costs of Direct Financing Leases," *Statement of Financial Accounting Standards No. 98* (Stamford, Conn.: FASB, 1988), par. 22.

the transaction, it is necessary also to satisfy the conditions of the realization principle we discussed in Chapter 5. In particular, the FASB specifies that for the lessor to record a lease as a direct financing lease or a sales-type lease, two conditions must be met in addition to one of the four classification criteria. These are listed in Graphic 15–4.

1. The collectibility of the lease payments must be reasonably predictable.
2. If any costs to the lessor have yet to be incurred, they are reasonably predictable. (Performance by the lessor is substantially complete.)

**GRAPHIC 15–4**
Additional Conditions for Classification as a Nonoperating Lease by the Lessor

In the case of a sales-type lease (discussed later in Part A of this chapter) in which the lessor recognizes sales revenue, the reason for these additional conditions is apparent; collectibility of payments and substantial completion of the earnings process are conditions of the revenue realization principle. This logic is extended to agreements classified as direct financing leases. Although sales revenue is not recorded in a direct financing lease, the leased asset is removed from the lessor's books and is replaced by a receivable.

**Additional lessor conditions for classification as a nonoperating lease are consistent with criteria of the revenue realization principle.**

Although uniformity of classification is a goal of lease accounting standards, it is obvious that the additional conditions allow inconsistencies.[8] Indeed, in lease negotiations an objective of the parties involved often is to devise terms that will result in a sale by the lessor but an operating lease by the lessee.[9]

In the remaining sections of Part A of this chapter we consider, in order, operating leases, direct financing leases (capital leases to the lessee), and sales-type leases (capital leases to the lessee).

## Operating Leases

**FINANCIAL REPORTING CASE**
Q1, p. 711

If a lease does not meet any of the criteria for a capital lease it is considered to be more in the nature of a rental agreement and is referred to as an **operating lease.**[10] We assume that the fundamental rights and responsibilities of ownership are retained by the lessor and that the lessee merely is using the asset temporarily. In keeping with that presumption, a sale is not recorded by the lessor; a purchase is not recorded by the lessee. Instead, the periodic rental payments are accounted for merely as rent by both parties to the transaction—rent revenue by the lessor, rent expense by the lessee.

● LO4

Let's look at an example that illustrates the relatively straightforward accounting for operating leases. The earlier example comparing a capital lease to an installment purchase assumed rental payments at the *end* of each period. A more typical leasing arrangement requires rental payments at the *beginning* of each period. This more realistic payment schedule is assumed in Illustration 15–1.

Journal entries for Illustration 15–1 are shown in Illustration 15–1A.

In an operating lease, rent is recognized on a straight-line basis unless another systematic method more clearly reflects the benefits of the asset's use. So, if rental payments are uneven—for instance, if rent increases are scheduled—the total scheduled payments ordinarily would be expensed equally (straight-line basis) over the lease term.[11]

### ADVANCE PAYMENTS

Often lease agreements call for advance payments to be made at the inception of the lease that represent prepaid rent. For instance, it is common for a lessee to pay a bonus in return for negotiating more favorable lease terms. Such payments are recorded as prepaid rent and allocated (normally on a straight-line basis) to rent expense/rent revenue over the lease term. So the rent that is periodically reported in those cases consists of the periodic rent payments themselves plus an allocated portion of prepaid rent. This is demonstrated in Illustration 15–1B.

[8] "Accounting for Leases," *Statement of Financial Accounting Standards No. 13* (Stamford, Conn.: FASB, 1980).
[9] Later in the chapter we discuss ways this is done.
[10] The term *operating lease* got its name long ago when a lessee routinely received from the lessor an operator along with leased equipment.
[11] "Accounting for Operating Leases With Scheduled Rent Increases," *FASB Technical Bulletin 85-3* (Stamford, Conn.: FASB, 1985), par. 1.

**ILLUSTRATION 15–1**
Application of Classification Criteria

On January 1, 2006, Sans Serif Publishers, Inc., a computer services and printing firm, leased a color copier from CompuDec Corporation.

The lease agreement specifies four annual payments of $100,000 beginning January 1, 2006, the inception of the lease, and at each January 1 through 2009. The useful life of the copier is estimated to be six years.

Before deciding to lease, Sans Serif considered purchasing the copier for its cash price of $479,079. If funds were borrowed to buy the copier, the interest rate would have been 10%.

How should this lease be classified? We apply the four classification criteria:

| | |
|---|---|
| 1. Does the agreement specify that ownership of the asset transfers to the lessee? | No |
| 2. Does this agreement contain a bargain purchase option? | No |
| 3. Is the lease term equal to 75% or more of the expected economic life of the asset? | No<br>(4 yrs < 75% of 6 yrs) |
| 4. Is the present value of the minimum lease payments equal to or greater than 90% of the fair value of the asset? | No<br>($348,685 < 90% of $479,079)<br>$100,000 × 3.48685* = $348,685<br>Lease payments / Present value |

Since none of the four classification criteria is met, this is an operating lease.

*Present value of an annuity due of $1: $n = 4$, $i = 10\%$. Recall from Chapter 6 that we refer to periodic payments at the beginning of each period as an *annuity due*.

**ILLUSTRATION 15–1A**
Journal Entries for an Operating Lease

At the beginning of the year, the rent payments are prepaid rent to the lessee and unearned rent to the lessor.

The lessor retains the asset on its books, and accordingly records depreciation on the asset.

The operating lease described in Illustration 15–1 is recorded as follows:

**At Each of the Four Payment Dates**

| | | |
|---|---|---|
| **Sans Serif Publishers, Inc. (Lessee)** | | |
| Prepaid rent | 100,000 | |
| Cash | | 100,000 |
| **CompuDec Corporation (Lessor)** | | |
| Cash | 100,000 | |
| Unearned rent revenue | | 100,000 |

**At the End of Each Year**

| | | |
|---|---|---|
| **Sans Serif Publishers, Inc. (Lessee)** | | |
| Rent expense | 100,000 | |
| Prepaid rent | | 100,000 |
| **CompuDec Corporation (Lessor)** | | |
| Unearned rent revenue | 100,000 | |
| Rent revenue | | 100,000 |
| Depreciation expense | x,xxx | |
| Accumulated depreciation | | x,xxx |

Sometimes advance payments include security deposits that are refundable at the expiration of the lease or prepayments of the last period's rent. A refundable security deposit is recorded as a long-term receivable (by the lessee) and liability (by the lessor) unless it is not expected to be returned. A prepayment of the last period's rent is recorded as prepaid rent and allocated to rent expense/rent revenue during the last period of the lease term.

At times, lease agreements call for uneven rent payments during the term of the lease. One way this can occur is when the initial payment (or maybe several payments) is waived. This is called a **rent abatement.**

Alternatively, rent payments may be scheduled to increase periodically over the lease term. In any event, the total rent over the term of the lease is allocated to individual periods on a straight-line basis. This means the (temporarily) unpaid portion of rent expense must be credited to deferred rent expense payable until later in the lease term when rent payments exceed rent expense.

**ILLUSTRATION 15–1B**

Journal Entries—Operating Lease with Advance Payment

Assume Sans Serif paid a $40,000 bonus (advance payment) at the inception of the lease described in Illustration 15–1 in return for lower periodic payments—$90,000 each.

| | | |
|---|---|---|
| **At the Inception of the Lease** | | |
| **Sans Serif Publishers, Inc. (Lessee)** | | |
| Prepaid rent (bonus payment) | 40,000 | |
| Cash | | 40,000 |
| **CompuDec Corporation (Lessor)** | | |
| Cash | 40,000 | |
| Unearned rent revenue (bonus payment) | | 40,000 |
| **At Each of the Four Payment Dates** | | |
| **Sans Serif Publishers, Inc. (Lessee)** | | |
| Prepaid rent (annual rent payment) | 90,000 | |
| Cash | | 90,000 |
| **CompuDec Corporation (Lessor)** | | |
| Cash | 90,000 | |
| Unearned rent revenue (annual rent payment) | | 90,000 |
| **At the End of Each Year** | | |
| **Sans Serif Publishers, Inc. (Lessee)** | | |
| Rent expense (annual rent) | 90,000 | |
| Prepaid rent | | 90,000 |
| Rent expense (bonus allocation) | 10,000 | |
| Prepaid rent ($40,000 ÷ 4) | | 10,000 |
| **CompuDec Corporation (Lessor)** | | |
| Unearned rent revenue | 90,000 | |
| Rent revenue (annual rent) | | 90,000 |
| Unearned rent revenue ($40,000 ÷ 4) | 10,000 | |
| Rent revenue (bonus allocation) | | 10,000 |
| Depreciation expense | x,xxx | |
| Accumulated depreciation | | x,xxx |

**Advance payments in operating leases are deferred and allocated to rent over the lease term.**

**Rent comprises the periodic rent payments plus an allocated portion of the advance payment.**

## LEASEHOLD IMPROVEMENTS

**The cost of a *leasehold improvement* is depreciated over its useful life to the lessee.**

Sometimes a lessee will make improvements to leased property that reverts back to the lessor at the end of the lease. If a lessee constructs a new building or makes modifications to existing structures, that cost represents an asset just like any other capital expenditure. Like other assets, its cost is allocated as depreciation expense over its useful life to the lessee, which will be the shorter of the physical life of the asset or the lease term.[12] Theoretically, such assets can be recorded in accounts descriptive of their nature, such as buildings or plant. In practice, the traditional account title used is **leasehold improvements**.[13] In any case, the undepreciated cost usually is reported in the balance sheet under the caption *property, plant, and equipment.* Movable assets like office furniture and equipment that are not attached to the leased property are not considered leasehold improvements.

**Hundreds of firms in 2005 corrected the way they accounted for leases.**

During 2005 hundreds of companies, particularly in the retail and restaurant industries, underwent one of the most widespread accounting correction events ever. Corrections were in the way these companies, including **Pep Boys**, **Ann Taylor**, **Target**, and **Domino's Pizza**, had allocated the cost of leasehold improvements. Rather than expensing leasehold improvements properly over the lease terms, these firms for years had inappropriately expensed the

[12]If the agreement contains an option to renew, and the likelihood of renewal is uncertain, the renewal period is ignored.

[13]Also, traditionally, depreciation sometimes is labeled amortization when in connection with leased assets and leasehold improvements. This is of little consequence. Remember, both depreciation and amortization refer to the process of allocating an asset's cost over its useful life.

cost over the longer estimated useful lives of the properties. Prompting the sweeping revisions was a Securities and Exchange Commission letter on February 7, 2005, urging companies to follow long-standing accounting standards in this area. A result of the improper practices was to defer expense, thereby accelerating earnings. For instance, **McDonald's Corp.** recorded a charge of $139 million in its 2004 fourth quarter to adjust for the difference.

Let's turn our attention now to accounting for leases that meet the criteria and conditions for classification as nonoperating leases by both the lessee and the lessor.

## Nonoperating Leases—Lessee and Lessor

LO5

A lease that transfers substantially all of the benefits and risks incident to ownership of property should be accounted for as the acquisition of an asset and the incurrence of an obligation by the lessee and as a sale or financing by the lessor.[14]

In the operating lease illustration, we assumed Sans Serif leased a copier directly from its manufacturer. Now let's assume a financial intermediary provided financing by acquiring the copier and leasing it to the user. And to temporarily avoid unnecessary confusion that adjusting entries might create, the example in Illustration 15–2 on the next page assumes that the inception of the lease, as well as subsequent rental payments, are made at the end of both companies' fiscal years.[15]

Traditionally, the lessee uses the **net method** to record leases, and the lessor uses the **gross method.**[16] As you study the entries in Illustration 15–2, keep in mind that both methods achieve the same result, and theoretically either method could be used.

**A leased asset is recorded by the lessee at the present value of the *minimum lease payments* or the asset's fair value, whichever is lower.**

The amount recorded (capitalized) by the lessee is the present value of the **minimum lease payments.** However, if the fair value of the asset is lower than this amount, the recorded value of the asset should be limited to fair value. Unless the lessor is a manufacturer or dealer, the fair value typically will be the lessor's cost ($479,079 in this case). However, if considerable time has elapsed between the purchase of the property by the lessor and the inception of the lease, the fair value might be different. When the lessor is a manufacturer or dealer, the fair value of the property at the inception of the lease ordinarily will be its normal selling price (reduced by any volume or trade discounts). We study this situation (a sales-type lease) later. In unusual cases, market conditions may cause fair value to be less than the normal selling price.

**Interest is a function of time. It accrues at the effective rate on the balance outstanding during the period.**

Be sure to note that the entire $100,000 first rental payment is applied to principal reduction.[17] Because it occurred at the inception of the lease, no interest had yet accrued. Subsequent rental payments include interest on the outstanding balance as well as a residual portion that reduces that outstanding balance. As of the second rental payment date, one year's interest has accrued on the $379,079 balance outstanding during 2007, recorded as in Illustration 15–2A.

Notice that by either the net method (lessee) or the gross method (lessor), the outstanding balance is reduced by $62,092—the portion of the $100,000 payment remaining after interest is covered. The lease liability is reduced directly; the reduction in the net receivable is the combined effect of reducing the gross receivable by $100,000 and unearned interest revenue, a valuation (contra) account, by $37,908.[18]

---

[14] "Accounting for Leases," *Statement of Financial Accounting Standards No. 13* (Stamford, Conn.: FASB, 1980).

[15] We relax this assumption and consider accrued interest in a later section.

[16] *SFAS 13* does not specifically mandate the methods to be used, but illustrations provided in the Standard portray the net method for the lessee and the gross method for the lessor. As indicated later in the chapter, both the lessee and the lessor must report in disclosure notes *both* the gross and net amounts of the lease.

[17] Another way to view this is to think of the first $100,000 as a down payment with the remaining $379,079 financed by 5 (i.e., 6 − 1) *year-end* lease payments.

[18] Note that unearned interest revenue is not a liability, as you might assume from the account title. Unlike other unearned revenue accounts for which the cash is received in advance of the revenue being earned (and thus a liability), this account represents interest revenue that will be both received and earned periodically over the lease term. The account is analogous to the discount on notes receivable or on bond investment when those investments are recorded by the gross method.

**ILLUSTRATION 15–2**
Nonoperating Leases

On December 31, 2006, Sans Serif Publishers, Inc., leased a copier from First LeaseCorp. First LeaseCorp purchased the equipment from CompuDec Corporation at a cost of $479,079.

The lease agreement specifies annual payments beginning December 31, 2006, the inception of the lease, and at each December 31 through 2011. The six-year lease term is equal to the estimated useful life of the copier.

First LeaseCorp routinely acquires electronic equipment for lease to other firms. The interest rate in these financing arrangements is 10%.

Since the lease term is equal to the expected useful life of the copier (>75%), the transaction must be recorded by the lessee as a **capital lease.**[19] If we assume also that collectibility of the lease payments and any costs to the lessor that are yet to be incurred are reasonably predictable, this qualifies also as a **direct financing lease** to First LeaseCorp. To achieve its objectives, First LeaseCorp must (a) recover its $479,079 investment as well as (b) earn interest revenue at a rate of 10%. So, the lessor determined that annual rental payments would be $100,000:

Rental payments are calculated such that their present value is equal to the lessor's cost.

$479,079 ÷ 4.79079* = $100,000
Lessor's cost | Rental payments

*Present value of an annuity due of $1: $n = 6$, $i = 10\%$.

Of course, Sans Serif Publishers, Inc., views the transaction from the other side. The price the lessee pays for the copier is the present value of the rental payments:

$100,000 × 4.79079* = $479,079
Rental payments | Lessee's cost

*Present value of an annuity due of $1: $n = 6$, $i = 10\%$.

*Journal Entries at Inception—Direct Financing Lease*

**Direct Financing Lease (December 31, 2006)†**

| | | |
|---|---|---|
| **Sans Serif Publishers, Inc. (Lessee)** | | |
| Leased equipment (present value of lease payments) | 479,079 | |
| Lease payable (present value of lease payments) | | 479,079 |
| **First LeaseCorp (Lessor)** | | |
| Lease receivable (gross sum of lease payments)* | 600,000 | |
| Unearned interest revenue (difference) | | 120,921 |
| Inventory of equipment (lessor's cost) | | 479,079 |

LESSEE

| Net Payable |
|---|
| $479,079 |

LESSOR

| Gross Rec'ble | Unearned Interest | Net Rec'ble |
|---|---|---|
| $600,000 | (120,921) | $479,079 |

**First Lease Payment (December 31, 2006)†**

| | | |
|---|---|---|
| **Sans Serif Publishers, Inc. (Lessee)** | | |
| Lease payable | 100,000 | |
| Cash | | 100,000 |
| **First LeaseCorp (Lessor)** | | |
| Cash | 100,000 | |
| Lease receivable | | 100,000 |

LESSEE

| Net Payable |
|---|
| $479,079 |
| (100,000) |
| $379,079 |

LESSOR

| Gross Rec'ble | Unearned Interest | Net Rec'ble |
|---|---|---|
| $600,000 | (120,921) | $479,079 |
| (100,000) | 0 | (100,000) |
| $500,000 | (120,921) | $379,079 |

*In the disclosure notes, the lease receivable is reported as the lessor's gross investment in the lease.
†Of course, the entries to record the lease and the first payment could be combined into a single entry since they occur at the same time.

The amortization schedule in Graphic 15–5 shows how the lease balance and the effective interest change over the six-year lease term.

Each rental payment after the first includes both an amount that represents interest and an amount that represents a reduction of principal. The periodic reduction of principal is sufficient that, at the end of the lease term, the outstanding balance is zero.

[19]The fourth criterion also is met. The present value of lease payments ($479,079) is 100% (>90%) of the fair value of the copier ($479,079). Meeting any one of the four criteria is sufficient.

**ILLUSTRATION 15–2A**

Journal Entries for the Second Lease Payment

LESSEE

| | Net Payable |
|---|---|
| | $479,079 |
| | (100,000) |
| | $379,079 |
| | (62,092) |
| | $316,987 |

LESSOR

| Gross Rec'ble | Unearned Interest | Net Rec'ble |
|---|---|---|
| $600,000 | (120,921) | $479,079 |
| (100,000) | 0 | (100,000) |
| $500,000 | (120,921) | $379,079 |
| (100,000) | 37,908 | (62,092) |
| $400,000 | (83,013) | $316,987 |

**Second Lease Payment (December 31, 2007)**

| | | |
|---|---|---|
| **Sans Serif Publishers, Inc. (Lessee)** | | |
| Interest expense [10% × ($479,079 − 100,000)] | 37,908 | |
| Lease payable (difference) | 62,092 | |
| Cash (rental payment) | | 100,000 |
| **First LeaseCorp (Lessor)** | | |
| Cash (rental payment) | 100,000 | |
| Lease receivable | | 100,000 |
| Unearned interest revenue | 37,908 | |
| Interest revenue [10% × ($600,000 − 120,921 − 100,000)] | | 37,908 |

**GRAPHIC 15–5**

Lease Amortization Schedule

**The first rental payment includes no interest.**

**The total of the cash payments ($600,000) provides for:**
1. **Payment for the copier ($479,079).**
2. **Interest ($120,921) at an effective rate of 10%.**

| Dec. 31 | Payments | Effective Interest | Decrease in Balance | Outstanding Balance |
|---|---|---|---|---|
| | | (10% × Outstanding balance) | | |
| 2006 | | | | 479,079 |
| 2006 | 100,000 | | 100,000 | 379,079 |
| 2007 | 100,000 | .10 (379,079) = 37,908 | 62,092 | 316,987 |
| 2008 | 100,000 | .10 (316,987) = 31,699 | 68,301 | 248,686 |
| 2009 | 100,000 | .10 (248,686) = 24,869 | 75,131 | 173,555 |
| 2010 | 100,000 | .10 (173,555) = 17,355 | 82,645 | 90,910 |
| 2011 | 100,000 | .10 (90,910) = 9,090* | 90,910 | 0 |
| | 600,000 | 120,921* | 479,079 | |

*Adjusted for rounding of other numbers in the schedule.

An interesting aspect of the amortization schedule that you may want to note at this point relates to a disclosure requirement that we discuss at the end of the chapter. Among other things, the lessee and lessor must report separately the current and noncurrent portions of the outstanding lease balance. Both amounts are provided by the amortization schedule. For example, if we want the amounts to report on the 2007 balance sheet, refer to the next row of the schedule. The portion of the 2008 payment that represents principal ($68,301) is the *current* (as of December 31, 2007) balance. The *noncurrent* amount is the balance outstanding after the 2008 reduction ($248,686). These amounts are the current and noncurrent lease liability for the lessee and the current and noncurrent net investment for the lessor.

## DEPRECIATION

Depreciation is recorded for leased assets in a manner consistent with the lessee's usual policy for depreciating its operational assets.

**Because a capital lease assumes the lessee purchased the asset, the lessee depreciates its cost.**

**End of Each Year**

| | | |
|---|---|---|
| **Sans Serif Publishers, Inc. (Lessee)** | | |
| Depreciation expense ($479,079 ÷ 6 years*) | 79,847 | |
| Accumulated depreciation | | 79,847 |

*If the lessee depreciates assets by the straight-line method.

**Depreciation Period.** The lessee normally should depreciate a leased asset over the term of the lease. However, if ownership transfers or a bargain purchase option is present (i.e., either of the first two classification criteria is met), the asset should be depreciated over its useful life. This means depreciation is recorded over the useful life of the asset to the lessee.

The depreciation period is restricted to the lease term unless the lease provides for transfer of title or a BPO.

A description of leased assets and related depreciation provided in a recent disclosure note (Graphic 15–6) of **Kroger Company** is representative of leased asset disclosures.

**GRAPHIC 15–6**
Disclosure of Leased Assets—Kroger Company

**6. PROPERTY, PLANT AND EQUIPMENT, NET**
Property, plant and equipment, net consists of:

| | 2003 | 2002 |
|---|---|---|
| Land | $ 1,519 | $ 1,357 |
| Buildings and land improvements | 4,435 | 3,947 |
| Equipment | 7,745 | 7,583 |
| Leasehold improvements | 3,555 | 3,176 |
| Construction-in-progress | 636 | 802 |
| Leased property under capital leases | 535 | 564 |
| | 18,425 | 17,429 |
| Accumulated depreciation and amortization | (7,247) | (6,881) |
| Total | $11,178 | $10,548 |

Accumulated depreciation for leased property under capital leases was $246 at January 31, 2004 and $248 at February 1, 2003.

## ACCRUED INTEREST

If a company's reporting period ends at any time between payment dates, it is necessary to record (as an adjusting entry) any interest that has accrued since interest was last recorded. We purposely avoided this step in the previous illustration by assuming that the lease agreement specified rental payments on December 31—the end of the reporting period. But if payments were made on another date, or if the company's fiscal year ended on a date other than December 31, accrued interest would be recorded prior to preparing financial statements. For example, if the inception of the lease had been a day later (January 1, 2006) and rental payments were made on January 1 of each year, the effective interest amounts shown in the lease amortization schedule still would be appropriate but would be recorded one day prior to the actual rental payment. For instance, the second cash payment of $100,000 would occur on January 1, 2006, but the interest component of that payment ($37,908) would be accrued a day earlier as shown in Illustration 15–2B.

At each financial statement date, any interest that has accrued since interest was last recorded must be accrued for all liabilities and receivables, including those relating to leases.

Notice that this is consistent with recording accrued interest on any debt, whether in the form of a note, a bond, or a lease.

We assumed in this illustration that First LeaseCorp bought the copier for $479,079 and then leased it for the same price. There was no profit on the "sale" itself. The only income derived by the lessor was interest revenue earned over the lease term. In effect, First LeaseCorp financed the purchase of the copier by Sans Serif Publishers. This type of lease is a direct financing lease. This kind of leasing is a thriving industry. It is a profitable part of operations for banks and other financial institutions (Citicorp is one of the largest). Some leasing companies do nothing else. Often leasing companies, like **IBM Credit Corporation**, are subsidiaries of larger corporations, formed for the sole purpose of conducting financing activities for their parent corporations.

**ILLUSTRATION 15–2B**

Journal Entries When Interest Is Accrued Prior to the Lease Payment

LESSEE

| | Net Payable |
|---|---|
| | $479,079 |
| | (100,000) |
| | $379,079 |
| | (62,092) |
| | $316,987 |

LESSOR

| Gross Rec'ble | Unearned Interest | Net Rec'ble |
|---|---|---|
| $600,000 | (120,921) | $479,079 |
| (100,000) | 0 | (100,000) |
| $500,000 | (120,921) | $379,079 |
| (100,000) | 37,908 | (62,092) |
| $400,000 | (83,013) | $316,987 |

**December 31, 2007 (to accrue interest)**

| | | |
|---|---|---|
| **Sans Serif Publishers, Inc. (Lessee)** | | |
| Interest expense [10% × ($479,079 − 100,000)] | 37,908 | |
| Interest payable | | 37,908 |
| **First LeaseCorp (Lessor)** | | |
| Unearned interest revenue | 37,908 | |
| Interest revenue [10% × ($479,079 − 100,000)] | | 37,908 |

**Second Lease Payment (January 1, 2008)**

| | | |
|---|---|---|
| **Sans Serif Publishers, Inc. (Lessee)** | | |
| Interest payable (from adjusting entry above) | 37,908 | |
| Lease payable (difference) | 62,092 | |
| Cash (rental payment) | | 100,000 |
| **First LeaseCorp (Lessor)** | | |
| Cash (rental payment) | 100,000 | |
| Lease receivable | | 100,000 |

# CONCEPT REVIEW EXERCISE

## DIRECT FINANCING LEASE

United Cellular Systems leased a satellite transmission device from Pinnacle Leasing Services on January 1, 2007. Pinnacle paid $625,483 for the transmission device. Its fair market value is $625,483.

**Terms of the Lease Agreement and Related Information:**

| | |
|---|---|
| Lease term | 3 years (6 semiannual periods) |
| Semiannual rental payments | $120,000 − beginning of each period |
| Economic life of asset | 3 years |
| Interest rate | 12% |

**Required:**

1. Prepare the appropriate entries for both United Cellular Systems and Pinnacle Leasing Services on January 1, the inception of the lease.
2. Prepare an amortization schedule that shows the pattern of interest expense for United Cellular Systems and interest revenue for Pinnacle Leasing Services over the lease term.
3. Prepare the appropriate entries to record the second lease payment on July 1, 2007, and adjusting entries on December 31, 2007 (the end of both companies' fiscal years).

## SOLUTION

1. Prepare the appropriate entries for both United Cellular Systems and Pinnacle Leasing Services on January 1, the inception of the lease.

Calculation of the present value of minimum lease payments.

**Present value of periodic rental payments:**

$$(\$120,000 \times 5.21236^*) = \$625,483$$

*Present value of an annuity due of $1: $n = 6$, $i = 6\%$.

**January 1, 2007**

| | | |
|---|---|---|
| **United Cellular Systems (Lessee)** | | |
| Leased equipment (calculated above) | 625,483 | |
| Lease payable (calculated above) | | 625,483 |
| Lease payable | 120,000 | |
| Cash (rental payment) | | 120,000 |

| | | |
|---|---|---|
| **Pinnacle Leasing Services (Lessor)** | | |
| Lease receivable ($120,000 × 6) | 720,000 | |
| Unearned interest revenue ($720,000 − 625,483) | | 94,517 |
| Inventory of equipment (lessor's cost) | | 625,483 |
| Cash (rental payment) | 120,000 | |
| Lease receivable | | 120,000 |

2. Prepare an amortization schedule that shows the pattern of interest expense for United Cellular Systems and interest revenue for Pinnacle Leasing Services over the lease term.

| Date | Payments | Effective Interest | Decrease in Balance | Outstanding Balance |
|---|---|---|---|---|
| | | (6% × Outstanding balance) | | |
| 1/1/07 | | | | 625,483 |
| 1/1/07 | 120,000 | | 120,000 | 505,483 |
| 7/1/07 | 120,000 | .06 (505,483) = 30,329 | 89,671 | 415,812 |
| 1/1/08 | 120,000 | .06 (415,812) = 24,949 | 95,051 | 320,761 |
| 7/1/08 | 120,000 | .06 (320,761) = 19,246 | 100,754 | 220,007 |
| 1/1/09 | 120,000 | .06 (220,007) = 13,200 | 106,800 | 113,207 |
| 7/1/09 | 120,000 | .06 (113,207) = 6,793* | 113,207 | 0 |
| | 720,000 | 94,517 | 625,483 | |

*Adjusted for rounding of other numbers in the schedule.

3. Prepare the appropriate entries to record the second lease payment on July 1, 2007, and adjusting entries on December 31, 2007 (the end of both companies' fiscal years).

| | | |
|---|---|---|
| **July 1, 2007** | | |
| **United Cellular Systems (Lessee)** | | |
| Interest expense [6% × ($625,483 − 120,000)] | 30,329 | |
| Lease payable (difference) | 89,671 | |
| Cash (rental payment) | | 120,000 |
| **Pinnacle Leasing Services (Lessor)** | | |
| Cash (rental payment) | 120,000 | |
| Lease receivable (rental payment) | | 120,000 |
| Unearned interest revenue | 30,329 | |
| Interest revenue [6% × ($625,483 − 120,000)] | | 30,329 |
| **December 31, 2007** | | |
| **United Cellular Systems (Lessee)** | | |
| Interest expense (6% × $415,812: from schedule) | 24,949 | |
| Interest payable | | 24,949 |
| Depreciation expense ($625,483 ÷ 3 years) | 208,494 | |
| Accumulated depreciation | | 208,494 |
| **Pinnacle Leasing Services (Lessor)** | | |
| Unearned interest revenue | 24,949 | |
| Interest revenue (6% × $415,812: from schedule) | | 24,949 |

Let's turn our attention now to situations in which the lessors are manufacturers or retailers and use lease arrangements as a means of selling their products.

## Sales-Type Leases

LO6

A **sales-type lease** differs from a direct financing lease in only one respect. In addition to interest revenue earned over the lease term, the lessor receives a manufacturer's or dealer's profit on the "sale" of the asset.[20] This additional profit exists when the fair value of the asset (usually the present value of the minimum lease payments, or "selling price") exceeds the cost or carrying value of the asset sold. Accounting for a sales-type lease is the same as for a direct financing lease except for recognizing the profit at the inception of the lease.[21]

**FINANCIAL REPORTING CASE**

Q2, p. 711

To illustrate, let's modify our previous illustration. Assume all facts are the same except Sans Serif Publishers leased the copier directly from CompuDec Corporation, rather than through the financing intermediary. Also assume CompuDec's cost of the copier was $300,000. If you recall that the lease payments (their present value) provide a selling price of $479,079, you see that CompuDec receives a gross profit on the sale of $479,079 − 300,000 = $179,079. This sales-type lease is demonstrated in Illustration 15–3.

**ILLUSTRATION 15–3**
Sales-Type Lease

On December 31, 2006, Sans Serif Publishers, Inc., leased a copier from CompuDec Corporation at a price of $479,079.

The lease agreement specifies annual payments of $100,000 beginning December 31, 2006, the inception of the lease, and at each December 31 through 2011. The six-year lease term is equal to the estimated useful life of the copier.

CompuDec manufactured the copier at a cost of $300,000.

CompuDec's interest rate for financing the transaction is 10%.

**Sales-Type Lease***

**CompuDec Corporation (Lessor)**

| | | |
|---|---|---|
| Lease receivable ($100,000 × 6) | 600,000 | |
| Cost of goods sold (lessor's cost) | 300,000 | |
| Sales revenue (present value of the minimum lease payments) | | 479,079 |
| Unearned interest revenue ($600,000 − 479,079) | | 120,921 |
| Inventory of equipment (lessor's cost) | | 300,000 |

| | |
|---|---|
| Sales revenue | $479,079 |
| − COGS | 300,000 |
| Dealer's profit | $179,079 |

**First Lease Payment***

**CompuDec Corporation (Lessor)**

| | | |
|---|---|---|
| Cash | 100,000 | |
| Lease receivable | | 100,000 |

Remember, no interest has accrued when the first payment is made at the inception of the lease.

*Of course, the entries to record the lease and the first payment could be combined into a single entry:

| | | |
|---|---|---|
| Lease receivable ($600,000 − $100,000) | 500,000 | |
| Cost of goods sold | 300,000 | |
| Cash | 100,000 | |
| Unearned interest revenue | | 120,921 |
| Sales revenue | | 479,079 |
| Inventory of equipment | | 300,000 |

Recording a sales-type lease is similar to recording a sale of merchandise on account:

| | | |
|---|---|---|
| A/R | {price} | |
| Sales rev | | {price} |
| COGS | {cost} | |
| Inventory | | {cost} |

You should recognize the similarity between recording both the revenue and cost components of this sale by lease and recording the same components of other sales transactions. As in the sale of any product, gross profit is the difference between sales revenue and cost of goods sold.

All entries other than the entry at the inception of the lease, which includes the gross profit on the sale, are the same for a sales-type lease and a direct financing lease.

Accounting by the lessee is not affected by how the lessor classifies the lease. All lessee entries are precisely the same as in the previous illustration of a direct financing lease.

Graphic 15–7 shows the relationships among various lease components, using dollar amounts from the previous illustration.

[20]A lessor need not be a manufacturer or a dealer for the arrangement to qualify as a sales-type lease. The existence of a profit (or loss) on the sale is the distinguishing factor.

[21]It is possible that the asset's carrying value will exceed its fair value, in which case a dealer's loss should be recorded.

**GLOBAL PERSPECTIVE**

In Japan and Italy, there are no accounting requirements regarding nonoperating leases. All leases in those countries are accounted for as operating leases by both lessees and lessors. Most other industrial nations differentiate between operating and nonoperating leases. The criteria for drawing the distinction, though, vary widely from country to country. Similar to U.S. GAAP, IAS 17, "Leases," also distinguishes between operating and nonoperating (finance) leases. Although conceptually similar, IAS 17 provides less specific guidance than U.S. GAAP in classifying leases.

**GRAPHIC 15–7**
Lease Payment Relationships

| Lessor: | | Lessee: |
|---|---|---|
| **SALES-TYPE LEASE** | | **CAPITAL LEASE** |
| **Gross Investment in Lease*** | **$600,000** | **Minimum Lease Payments** |
| | Less:<br>Interest during lease term<br>($120,921) | |
| | Equals: | |
| **Selling Price**<br>(present value of payments) | **$479,079** | **Purchase Price**<br>(present value of payments) |
| | Less:<br>Profit on sale†<br>($179,079) | |
| | Equals: | |
| **Cost to Lessor** | **$300,000** | **(irrelevant to lessee)** |

*The lessor's gross investment in the lease also would include any *unguaranteed* residual value in addition to the minimum lease payments. Also, any residual value guaranteed by the lessee is included in the minimum lease payments (both companies). We address these issues later in the chapter.
†If profit is zero, this would be a direct financing lease.

**The difference between the total payments and their present value (selling price of the asset) represents interest.**

**If the price is higher than the cost to the lessor, the lessor realizes a profit on the sale.**

**PART B**

# RESIDUAL VALUE AND BARGAIN PURCHASE OPTIONS

## Residual Value

The **residual value** of leased property is an estimate of what its commercial value will be at the end of the lease term. In our previous examples of nonoperating leases, we assumed that the residual value was negligible. But now let's consider the economic effect of a leased asset that does have a residual value and how that will affect the way both the lessee and the lessor account for the lease agreement.

● LO7

Suppose the copier leased in Illustration 15–3 was expected to be worth $60,000 at the end of the six-year lease term. Should this influence the lessor's (CompuDec) calculation of periodic rental payments? Other than the possible influence on rental payments, should the lessee (Sans Serif Publishers) be concerned with the residual value of the leased assets? The answer to both questions is maybe. We'll use modified Illustration 15–4 to see why.

In deciding whether the residual value affects how the lease is recorded, the first question that influences the answer is "Who gets the residual value?"

**ILLUSTRATION 15–4**
Residual Value

On December 31, 2006, Sans Serif Publishers, Inc., leased a color copier from CompuDec Corporation at a price of $479,079. The lease agreement specifies annual payments beginning December 31, 2006, the inception of the lease, and at each December 31 through 2011. The estimated useful life of the copier is seven years. At the end of the six-year lease term the copier is expected to be worth $60,000.

CompuDec manufactured the copier at a cost of $300,000.*
CompuDec's interest rate for financing the transaction is 10%.

*This provision is to be consistent with Illustration 15–3 which described a sales-type lease. However, our discussion of the effect of a residual value would be precisely the same if our illustration were of a direct financing lease (for instance, if the lessor's cost were $479,079) except that, of course, neither sales revenue nor cost of goods sold would be recorded in a direct financing lease.

## WHO GETS THE RESIDUAL VALUE?

If the *lessee* obtains title, the lessor's computation of rental payments is unaffected by any residual value.

**Lessee Obtains Title.** Consider CompuDec (the lessor) first. Suppose Sans Serif will own the copier at the end of the lease term—by transfer of title or by the expected exercise of a bargain purchase option. In that case, it is Sans Serif, not CompuDec, who will benefit by the residual value. So the lessor can't count on the $60,000 residual value to help recover its $479,079 investment. The lessor's computation of rental payments of $100,000 therefore is unaffected by the residual value.

On the other side of the transaction, the residual value influences the lessee only by the fact that depreciation calculations reflect a reduced depreciable amount. However, in determining the amount to capitalize as a leased asset and to record as a lease liability, the residual value is ignored. The capitalized amount is simply the present value of the minimum lease payments.

If the lessor retains title, the amount to be recovered through periodic lease payments is reduced by the present value of the residual amount.

**Lessor Retains Title.** On the other hand, if CompuDec retains title to the asset, then it would anticipate receiving the $60,000 residual value at the conclusion of the lease term. That amount would contribute to the total amount to be recovered by the lessor and would reduce the amount needed to be recovered from the lessee through periodic rental payments. The amount of each payment would be reduced from $100,000 to $92,931, calculated in Illustration 15–4A.

**ILLUSTRATION 15–4A**
Lessor's Calculation of Rental Payments When Lessor Retains Residual Value

| | |
|---|---|
| Amount to be recovered (fair market value) | $479,079 |
| Less: Present value of the residual value ($60,000 × .56447*) | (33,868) |
| Amount to be recovered through periodic rental payments | $445,211 |
| Rental payments at the beginning of each of the next six years: ($445,211 ÷ 4.79079†) | $ 92,931 |

*Present value of $1: $n = 6$, $i = 10\%$.
†Present value of an annuity due of $1: $n = 6$, $i = 10\%$.

On the other side of the transaction, the lessee (Sans Serif Publishers) considers the purchase price of the copier to include, at a minimum, the present value of the periodic rental payments ($445,211):

$$\underset{\text{Rental payments}}{\$92{,}931} \times 4.79079^{*} = \underset{\text{Present value}}{\$445{,}211^{\dagger}}$$

*Present value of an annuity due of $1: $n = 6$, $i = 10\%$.
†The multiplication actually produces $445,212.9. We use $445,211 to be consistent with the lessor's calculation ($445,211 ÷ 4.79079 = $92,931). The difference is due to rounding.

Whether or not the lessee's cost also includes an amount due to the residual value depends on whether the residual value is viewed as an additional "payment" by the lessee. It is viewed as an additional payment when the lessee *guarantees* the residual value to be a particular amount at the end of the lease term.

## WHEN THE RESIDUAL VALUE IS GUARANTEED BY THE LESSEE

Sometimes the lease agreement includes a guarantee by the lessee that the lessor will recover a specified residual value when custody of the asset reverts back to the lessor at the end of the lease term. This not only reduces the lessor's risk but also provides incentive to the lessee to exercise a higher degree of care in maintaining the leased asset than it otherwise might. The lessee promises to return not only the property but also sufficient cash to provide the lessor with a minimum combined value. In effect, the guaranteed residual value is an additional lease payment that is to be paid in property, or cash, or both. As such, it is included in the minimum lease payments and affects the amount the lessee records as both a leased asset and a lease liability, as shown in Illustration 15–4B.

**ILLUSTRATION 15–4B**
Lessee's Calculation of the Present Value of Minimum Lease Payments Including a Guaranteed Residual Value

| | |
|---|---|
| Present value of periodic rental payments ($92,931 × 4.79079*) | $445,211 |
| Plus: Present value of the residual value ($60,000 × .56447)† | 33,868 |
| Present value of minimum lease payments (Recorded as a leased asset and a lease liability) | $479,079 |

*Present value of an annuity due of $1: $n = 6$, $i = 10\%$.
†Present value of $1: $n = 6$, $i = 10\%$.

You should notice that the lessee's calculation of the amount to capitalize is precisely the reverse of the lessor's calculation of periodic rental payments. This is because when the residual value is guaranteed, both view it as an additional lease payment. In accordance with *SFAS 13,* the guaranteed residual value is a component of the minimum lease payments for both the lessor and lessee.[22] We see in Graphic 15–8 how this affects the accounting for the lease as reflected in the lease amortization schedule for CompuDec and Sans Serif.

**GRAPHIC 15–8**
Amortization Schedule with Residual Value

| Dec. 31 | Payments | Effective Interest (10% × Outstanding balance) | Decrease in Balance | Outstanding Balance |
|---|---|---|---|---|
| 2006 | | | | 479,079 |
| 2006 | 92,931 | | 92,931 | 386,148 |
| 2007 | 92,931 | .10 (386,148) = 38,615 | 54,316 | 331,832 |
| 2008 | 92,931 | .10 (331,832) = 33,183 | 59,748 | 272,084 |
| 2009 | 92,931 | .10 (272,084) = 27,208 | 65,723 | 206,361 |
| 2010 | 92,931 | .10 (206,361) = 20,636 | 72,295 | 134,066 |
| 2011 | 92,931 | .10 (134,066) = 13,407 | 79,524 | 54,542 |
| 2012 | 60,000 | .10 (54,542) = 5,458* | 54,542 | 0 |
| | 617,586 | 138,507 | 479,079 | |

*Adjusted for rounding of other numbers in the schedule.

As long as the asset (and its residual value) revert back to the lessor, the lessor views the residual value as an additional component of its investment in the lease.

The lessee views it as an additional payment only if the residual value is guaranteed by the lessee.

Be aware of several points the amortization schedule reveals. First, the six periodic cash payments are now $92,931 as we calculated previously. Notice also that we now include the $60,000 residual value as an additional lease payment. Despite the different composition of the minimum lease payments, their present value ($479,079) is the same as when we assumed $100,000 periodic payments and no residual value. However, the effective interest

[22]Later you will see that when the residual value is *not* guaranteed, it is *not* considered a component of minimum lease payments for either the lessor or the lessee; but it still is considered a part of the lessor's gross investment in the lease and affects the amount of periodic lease payments.

that will be recorded over the lease term (as interest expense by the lessee and interest revenue by the lessor) now is more: $138,507. (It was $120,921 before.) The higher interest reflects the fact that payments are farther in the future, causing the outstanding lease balances (and interest on those balances) to be higher during the lease term. Also, note that the total of the lease payments now is more: $617,586. (It was $600,000 before.) This total is referred to as the lessor's **gross investment in the lease** and, as shown in Illustration 15–4C, initially is recorded by the lessor as the lease receivable:[23]

**The lessor's *gross investment in the lease* is the total of periodic rental payments and any residual value.**

**ILLUSTRATION 15–4C**

Sales-Type Lease with Guaranteed Residual Value

| | |
|---|---|
| Sales revenue | $479,079 |
| – COGS | 300,000 |
| Dealer's profit | $179,079 |

**Sales-Type Lease, December 31, 2006**

| | | |
|---|---|---|
| **Sans Serif Publishers, Inc. (Lessee)** | | |
| Leased equipment (present value of lease payments) | 479,079 | |
| Lease payable (present value of lease payments) | | 479,079 |
| **CompuDec Corporation (Lessor)** | | |
| Lease receivable [($92,931 × 6) + $60,000] | 617,586 | |
| Cost of goods sold (lessor's cost) | 300,000 | |
| Sales revenue (present value of minimum lease payments*) | | 479,079 |
| Unearned interest revenue ($617,586 – 479,079) | | 138,507 |
| Inventory of equipment (lessor's cost) | | 300,000 |

**First Lease Payment, December 31, 2006**

| | | |
|---|---|---|
| **Sans Serif Publishers, Inc. (Lessee)** | | |
| Lease payable | 92,931 | |
| Cash | | 92,931 |
| **CompuDec Corporation (Lessor)** | | |
| Cash | 92,931 | |
| Lease receivable | | 92,931 |

*Minimum lease payments include the residual value because it's guaranteed.

Notice, too, that the timing of the $60,000 payment is December 31, 2012, the end of the lease term. Remember, the final periodic cash payment on December 31, 2011, is at the beginning of the final year. The journal entries that accompany this final cash payment are shown in Illustration 15–4D.

**ILLUSTRATION 15–4D**

Entries to Accompany Final Periodic Payment

**The residual value reduces the asset's depreciable cost to $419,079.**

**As the outstanding balance becomes less toward the end of the lease term, the portion of each payment that represents interest also becomes less.**

**December 31, 2011**

| | | |
|---|---|---|
| **Sans Serif Publishers, Inc. (Lessee)** | | |
| Depreciation expense [($479,079 – 60,000)* ÷ 6 years] | 69,847 | |
| Accumulated depreciation | | 69,847 |
| Interest expense (10% × outstanding balance) | 13,407 | |
| Lease payable (difference) | 79,524 | |
| Cash (rental payment) | | 92,931 |
| **CompuDec Corporation (Lessor)** | | |
| Cash (rental payment) | 92,931 | |
| Lease receivable | | 92,931 |
| Unearned interest revenue | 13,407 | |
| Interest revenue (10% × outstanding balance) | | 13,407 |

*The depreciable cost is reduced by the lessee-guaranteed residual value.

[23]Under the net method, the net investment in the lease ($479,079) would be recorded as the lessor's lease receivable.

At December 31, 2012, the lessee's book value of the fully depreciated copier is its $60,000 estimated residual value. If we assume that the actual residual value also is at least $60,000, then the lessee is not obligated to pay cash in addition to returning the copier to the lessor (demonstrated in Illustration 15–4E).[24]

**ILLUSTRATION 15–4E**
End of Lease Term—Actual Residual Value Equals the Guaranteed Amount

| December 31, 2012 | | |
|---|---|---|
| **Sans Serif Publishers, Inc. (Lessee)** | | |
| Depreciation expense [($479,079 − 60,000)* ÷ 6 years] | 69,847 | |
| Accumulated depreciation | | 69,847 |
| Interest expense (10% × outstanding balance) | 5,458 | |
| Lease payable (difference) | 54,542 | |
| Accumulated depreciation (account balance) | 419,079 | |
| Leased equipment (account balance) | | 479,079 |
| **CompuDec Corporation (Lessor)** | | |
| Inventory of equipment (residual value) | 60,000 | |
| Lease receivable (account balance) | | 60,000 |
| Unearned interest revenue (account balance) | 5,458 | |
| Interest revenue (10% × outstanding balance) | | 5,458 |

*The depreciable cost is reduced by the lessee-guaranteed residual value.

**The sixth and final depreciation charge increases the balance in accumulated depreciation to $419,079.**

**The copier is reinstated on the books of the lessor at its fair value at the end of the lease term.**

However, if we assume that the actual residual value at December 31, 2012, is only $25,000, then the lessee is required to pay $35,000 cash to the lessor in addition to returning the copier. The lessee records this payment as a loss.[25]

## WHEN THE RESIDUAL VALUE IS NOT GUARANTEED

The previous example demonstrates that when the residual value is guaranteed, both the lessor and lessee view it as a component of minimum lease payments. But what if the lessee does *not* guarantee the residual value? In that case, the lessee is not obligated to make any payments other than the periodic rental payments. As a result, the present value of the minimum lease payments—recorded as a leased asset and a lease liability—is simply the present value of periodic rental payments ($445,211). The same is true when the residual value is guaranteed by a third-party guarantor. (Insurance companies sometimes assume this role.)

**If the lessee doesn't guarantee the residual value, the asset and liability are recorded as the PV of periodic rental payments only.**

From the lessor's perspective, the residual value is a component of minimum lease payments only if it is guaranteed (by either the lessee or a third-party guarantor). Yet, even if it is not guaranteed, the residual value is viewed as a component of the lessor's gross investment in the lease. So, if we modify the previous illustration to assume the residual value is not guaranteed, the lessor's gross investment still is $617,586 [($92,931 × 6) + $60,000], but the sales revenue is only $445,211—the present value of the minimum lease payments. In other words, sales revenue includes the present value only of the periodic rental payments, not the unguaranteed residual value. Cost of goods sold is similarly reduced by the present value of the unguaranteed residual value, as shown in Illustration 15–4F.

**The lessor's minimum lease payments include a residual value only if it is guaranteed (by either the lessee or a third party guarantor).**

Sales revenue does not include the unguaranteed residual value because the revenue to be recovered from the lessee is lease payments only. The remainder of the lessor's gross investment is to be recovered—not from payment by the lessee (as is presumed when the residual value is guaranteed), but by selling, re-leasing, or otherwise obtaining value from the asset when it reverts back to the lessor. You might want to view the situation this way: The portion of the asset sold is the portion not represented by the unguaranteed residual value. So, both the asset's cost and its selling price are reduced by the present value of the portion not sold.

**When the lessee doesn't guarantee the residual value, the lessee's net liability and the lessor's net receivable will differ because the former does not include the unguaranteed residual amount.**

[24]If the actual value is *more* than the estimated residual value, the lessor may realize a gain if and when the asset subsequently is sold, but the potential gain does not affect the entries at the end of the lease term.

[25]Sometimes by mutual agreement the lessee will sell the leased asset at the end of the lease term and remit the proceeds (plus any deficiency under the guarantee) to the lessor.

**ILLUSTRATION 15–4F**

Sales-Type Lease with Unguaranteed Residual Value

**Dealer's profit is the same as when the residual value is guaranteed because both sales revenue and COGS are reduced by the same amounts.**

| Sales-Type Lease | | |
|---|---|---|
| **Sans Serif Publishers, Inc. (Lessee)** | | |
| Leased equipment (present value of lease payments) | 445,211 | |
| Lease payable (present value of lease payments) | | 445,211 |
| **CompuDec Corporation (Lessor)** | | |
| Lease receivable [($92,931 × 6) + $60,000] | 617,586 | |
| Cost of goods sold ($300,000 − 33,868) | 266,132 | |
| Sales revenue ($479,079 − 33,868)* | | 445,211 |
| Unearned interest revenue ($617,586 − 479,079) | | 138,507 |
| Inventory of equipment (lessor's cost) | | 300,000 |
| **First Lease Payment** | | |
| **Sans Serif Publishers, Inc. (Lessee)** | | |
| Lease payable | 92,931 | |
| Cash | | 92,931 |
| **CompuDec Corporation (Lessor)** | | |
| Cash | 92,931 | |
| Lease receivable | | 92,931 |

*Also can be calculated as the present value of the lessor's minimum lease payments, which do not include the unguaranteed residual value.

The lessor's net lease receivable is $479,079, as described in an earlier amortization schedule, even when the residual value is not guaranteed. However, the lessee's lease liability would be only $445,211 at the inception of the lease and would become zero with the final payment at the beginning of the final year, with reductions occurring in accordance with the pattern described by the schedule in Graphic 15–9.

**GRAPHIC 15–9**

Lessee's Amortization Schedule—Residual Value Not Guaranteed

**Because the lessee does not guarantee the residual value, the lessee does not consider it to be an additional lease payment.**

| Dec. 31 | Payments | Effective Interest | Decrease in Balance | Outstanding Balance |
|---|---|---|---|---|
| | | (10% × Outstanding balance) | | |
| 2006 | | | | 445,211 |
| 2006 | 92,931 | | 92,931 | 352,280 |
| 2007 | 92,931 | .10 (352,280) = 35,228 | 57,703 | 294,577 |
| 2008 | 92,931 | .10 (294,577) = 29,458 | 63,473 | 231,104 |
| 2009 | 92,931 | .10 (231,104) = 23,110 | 69,821 | 161,283 |
| 2010 | 92,931 | .10 (161,283) = 16,128 | 76,803 | 84,480 |
| 2011 | 92,931 | .10 (84,480) = 8,451* | 84,480 | 0 |
| | 557,586 | 112,375* | 445,211* | |

*Adjusted for rounding of other numbers in the schedule.

When the residual value is not guaranteed, the lessor bears any loss that results from the actual residual value of the leased asset being less than the original estimate.

Graphic 15–10 summarizes the effect of the residual value of a leased asset for each of the various possibilities regarding the nature of the residual value.

## Bargain Purchase Options

● LO8

We mentioned earlier that a **bargain purchase option (BPO)** is a provision of some lease contracts that gives the lessee the option of purchasing the leased property at a bargain price. We discussed BPOs in the context of how they affect the classification of leases, but none of our earlier illustrations included a situation in which a BPO was present. You should have

**GRAPHIC 15–10**
Effect of a Residual Value: A Summary

Is the **residual value** of a leased asset included in:

| | the Lessor's | | the Lessee's |
|---|---|---|---|
| | (a) Gross Investment in Lease *Computation of Payments* | (b) Minimum Lease Payments *Sales Revenue* | (c) Minimum Lease Payments *Asset & Liability* |
| **Lessee** gets the residual value (by transfer of title or the expected exercise of a bargain purchase option) | No | No | No |
| **Lessor** gets the residual value (title does *not* transfer; *no* bargain purchase option) | | | |
| • Residual value is not guaranteed | Yes | No | No |
| • Residual value is guaranteed by the lessee. | Yes | Yes | Yes |
| • Residual value is guaranteed by a third party guarantor. | Yes | Yes | No |

(a) if included in the lessor's gross investment in the lease, the residual value is part of the computation by the **lessor** of the amount of the periodic rental payments
(b) the present value of the lessor's minimum lease payments is sales revenue in a sales-type lease
(c) the present value of the lessee's minimum lease payments is the amount to be capitalized as an asset and a liability

noted that a bargain price is defined in such a way that an additional cash payment is expected when a BPO is included in the agreement. Remember, a bargain price is one that is sufficiently below the property's expected fair value that the exercise of the option appears reasonably assured. Because exercise of the option appears at the inception of the lease to be reasonably assured, payment of the option price is expected to occur when the option becomes exercisable.

**When a BPO is present, both the lessor and the lessee view the option price as an additional lease payment.**

The logic applied to lessee-guaranteed residual values in the previous section applies here too. The expectation that the option price will be paid effectively adds an additional cash flow to the lease for both the lessee and the lessor. That additional payment is included as a component of minimum lease payments for both the lessor and the lessee. It therefore (a) reduces the amount of the periodic rent payments the *lessor* must receive from the lessee and (b) is included in the computation of the amount to be capitalized (as an asset and liability) by the *lessee*. In fact, the way a BPO is included in these calculations is precisely the same way that a lessee-guaranteed residual value is included. This is demonstrated in Graphic 15–11.

**GRAPHIC 15–11**
Effect of a Bargain Purchase Option

✔ The **lessor,** when computing periodic rental payments, *subtracts* the present value of the BPO from the amount to be recovered (fair market value) to determine the amount that must be recovered from the lessee through the periodic rent payments.
✔ The **lessee** *adds* the present value of the BPO price to the present value of periodic payments when computing the amount to be recorded as a leased asset and a lease liability.

To emphasize the similarity in the way a lessee-guaranteed[26] residual value and a BPO affect the calculations, let's assume the $60,000 in our last illustration is an option price that could be paid by Sans Serif at the conclusion of the lease to purchase the copier. To make

[26]The lessee-guaranteed qualification here refers to what you learned in the previous section: a residual value is part of the lessee's minimum lease payments only when guaranteed by the lessee; the lessor includes in its computation of rent payments any residual values that revert to the lessor—guaranteed or not.

this a "bargain" purchase option let's say the residual value at the same time is expected now to be $75,000. This situation is assumed in Illustration 15–5.

**ILLUSTRATION 15–5**
Bargain Purchase Option

**The lessor's selling price is reduced by the present value of the BPO price to determine the amount that must be recovered from the periodic rental payments.**

On December 31, 2006, Sans Serif Publishers, Inc., leased a color copier from CompuDec Corporation at a price of $479,079. The lease agreement specifies annual payments beginning December 31, 2006, the inception of the lease, and at each December 31 through 2011. The estimated useful life of the copier is seven years. At the end of the six-year lease term the copier is expected to be worth $75,000 and Sans Serif has the option to purchase it for $60,000 on that date. The residual value after seven years is zero.[27]

CompuDec manufactured the copier at a cost of $300,000.
CompuDec's interest rate for financing the transaction is 10%.

| | |
|---|---|
| Amount to be recovered (fair market value) | $479,079 |
| Less: Present value of the BPO price ($60,000 × .56447*) | (33,868) |
| Amount to be recovered through periodic rental payments | $445,211 |
| Rental payments at the beginning of each of the next six years: ($445,211 ÷ 4.79079†) | $ 92,931 |

*Present value of $1: $n = 6$, $i = 10\%$.
†Present value of an annuity due of $1: $n = 6$, $i = 10\%$.

When you compare the way the *BPO* affected the lessor's (CompuDec's) calculation with the way the lessee-guaranteed residual value affected the calculation earlier, you see that they are exactly the same. That's the case also for the lessee (Sans Serif Publishers) as shown in Illustration 15–5A.

**ILLUSTRATION 15–5A**
Lessee's Calculation of the Present Value of Minimum Lease Payments When a BPO Is Present

| | |
|---|---|
| Present value of periodic rental payments ($92,931 × 4.79079*) | $445,211 |
| Plus: Present value of the BPO price ($60,000 × .56447†) | 33,868 |
| Present value of minimum lease payments (recorded as a leased asset and a lease liability) | $479,079 |

*Present value of an annuity due of $1: $n = 6$, $i = 10\%$.
†Present value of $1: $n = 6$, $i = 10\%$.

**Because a BPO is expected to be exercised, its exercise price is viewed as one more cash payment.**

**When a BPO is present, the residual value becomes irrelevant.**

You should recognize this as the same calculation we used when there was no BPO but the residual value was guaranteed and so was considered an additional lease payment. A question you might have at this point is: Why are we now ignoring the residual value? Earlier it was considered an additional lease payment. Yet, now we view the BPO price as an additional lease payment but ignore the residual value. The reason is obvious when you recall an essential characteristic of a BPO—it's expected to be exercised. So, when it is exercised, title to the leased asset passes to the lessee and with title, any residual value. And remember, when the lessee gets the residual value it is ignored by both parties to the lease.

The lease amortization schedule for CompuDec and Sans Serif when a BPO is included in the lease agreement (Graphic 15–12) should look familiar to you also.

Recording the exercise of the option is similar to recording the periodic rent payments. That is, a portion of the payment covers interest for the year, and the remaining portion reduces the outstanding balance (to zero with this last payment), as shown in Illustration 15–5B.

[27]Our discussion of the effect of a bargain purchase option would be precisely the same if our illustration were of a direct financing lease (for instance, if the lessor's cost were $479,079) except that, of course, neither sales revenue nor cost of goods sold would be recorded in a direct financing lease.

**GRAPHIC 15–12**
Amortization Schedule—with BPO

| Dec. 31 | Payments | Effective Interest | Decrease in Balance | Outstanding Balance |
|---|---|---|---|---|
| | | (10% × Outstanding balance) | | |
| 2006 | | | | 479,079 |
| 2006 | 92,931 | | 92,931 | 386,148 |
| 2007 | 92,931 | .10 (386,148) = 38,615 | 54,316 | 331,832 |
| 2008 | 92,931 | .10 (331,832) = 33,183 | 59,748 | 272,084 |
| 2009 | 92,931 | .10 (272,084) = 27,208 | 65,723 | 206,361 |
| 2010 | 92,931 | .10 (206,361) = 20,636 | 72,295 | 134,066 |
| 2011 | 92,931 | .10 (134,066) = 13,407 | 79,524 | 54,542 |
| 2012 | 60,000 | .10 (54,542) = 5,458* | 54,542 | 0 |
| | 617,586 | 138,507 | 479,079 | |

*Adjusted for rounding of other numbers in the schedule.

**Both the lessor and lessee view the BPO price ($60,000) as an additional cash payment.**

**ILLUSTRATION 15–5B**
Journal Entries—with BPO

| December 31, 2012 | | |
|---|---|---|
| **Sans Serif Publishers, Inc. (Lessee)** | | |
| Depreciation expense ($479,079* ÷ 7 years) | 68,440 | |
| Accumulated depreciation | | 68,440 |
| Interest expense (10% × $54,542) | 5,458 | |
| Lease payable (difference) | 54,542 | |
| Cash (BPO price) | | 60,000 |
| **CompuDec Corporation (Lessor)** | | |
| Cash (BPO price) | 60,000 | |
| Lease receivable (account balance) | | 60,000 |
| Unearned interest revenue (account balance) | 5,458 | |
| Interest revenue (10% × outstanding balance) | | 5,458 |

*The residual value is zero after the full seven-year useful life.

**The depreciation entries reflect the fact that the lessee anticipates using the copier for its full seven-year life.**

Note that depreciation also is affected by the BPO. As pointed out earlier, the lessee normally depreciates a leased asset over the term of the lease. But if ownership transfers by contract or by the expected exercise of a bargain purchase option, the asset should be depreciated over the asset's useful life. This reflects the fact that the lessee anticipates using the leased asset for its full useful life. In this illustration, the copier is expected to be useful for seven years, so depreciation is $68,440 ($479,079 ÷ 7 years).

**The cash payment expected when the BPO is exercised represents part interest, part principal just like the other cash payments.**

## WHEN A BPO IS EXERCISABLE BEFORE THE END OF THE LEASE TERM

We assumed in this example that the BPO was exercisable on December 31, 2012—the end of the lease term. This assumption was convenient to illustrate the similarity between how a residual value and a BPO are dealt with when accounting for leases. It also is a very realistic assumption. Sometimes, though, the lease contract specifies that a BPO becomes exercisable before the designated lease term ends. Since a BPO is expected to be exercised, the lease term ends for accounting purposes when the option becomes exercisable. For example, let's say the BPO in the previous example could be exercised a year earlier—at the end of the fifth year. The effect this would have on accounting for the lease is to change the lease term from six years to five. All calculations would be modified accordingly. Stated differently, minimum lease payments include only the periodic cash payments specified in the agreement that occur prior to the date a BPO becomes exercisable. (We assume the option is exercised at that time and the lease ends.)

**The length of the lease term is limited to the time up to when a bargain purchase option becomes exercisable.**

We have seen how minimum lease payments are affected by a residual value and by a bargain purchase option. Let's now consider how maintenance, insurance, taxes, and other costs usually associated with ownership (called *executory costs*) affect minimum lease payments.

**ETHICAL DILEMMA**

"I know we had discussed that they're supposed to be worth $24,000 when our purchase option becomes exercisable," Ferris insisted. "That's why we agreed to the lease terms. But, Jenkins, you know how fast computers become dated. We can make a good case that they'll be worth only $10,000 in three years."

The computers to which Ferris referred were acquired by lease. The lease meets none of the criteria for classification as a capital lease except that it contains an apparent bargain purchase option. Under the lease option, the computers can be purchased for $10,000 after three years.

"We could avoid running up our debt that way," Jenkins agreed.

How could debt be avoided?
Do you perceive an ethical problem?

# PART C OTHER LEASE ACCOUNTING ISSUES

## Executory Costs

LO9

One of the responsibilities of ownership that is transferred to the lessee in a capital lease is the responsibility to pay for maintenance, insurance, taxes, and any other costs usually associated with ownership. These are referred to as **executory costs.** Lease agreements usually are written in such a way that these costs are borne by the lessee. These expenditures simply are expensed by the lessee as incurred: repair expense, insurance expense, property tax expense, and so on. Let's return, for example, to Illustration 15–2. Now, suppose that a $2,000 per year maintenance agreement was arranged with an outside service for the leased copier. Sans Serif (the lessee) would expense this fee each year as incurred:

The lessee simply expenses executory costs as incurred.

| | | |
|---|---|---|
| Maintenance expense | 2,000 | |
| Cash (annual fee) | | 2,000 |

Any portion of rental payments that represents maintenance, insurance, taxes, or other executory costs is not considered part of minimum lease payments.

The lessor is unaffected by executory costs paid by the lessee.

Sometimes, as an expediency, a lease contract will specify that the lessor is to pay executory costs, but that the lessee will reimburse the lessor through higher rental payments. When rental payments are inflated for this reason, these executory costs are excluded in determining the minimum lease payments. They still are expensed by the lessee, even though paid through the lessor. For demonstration, let's modify Illustration 15–2 to assume the periodic rental payments were increased to $102,000 with the provision the lessor (First LeaseCorp) pays the maintenance fee. We do this in Illustration 15–6.

## Discount Rate

An important factor in the overall lease equation that we've glossed over until now is the discount rate used in present value calculations. Because lease payments occur in future periods, we must consider the time value of money when evaluating their present value. The rate is important because it influences virtually every amount reported in connection with the lease by both the lessor and the lessee.

The lessee uses the lower of the interest rate implicit in the lease or the lessee's own incremental borrowing rate.

One rate is implicit in the lease agreement. This is the effective interest rate the lease payments provide the lessor over and above the price at which the asset is sold under the lease. It is the desired rate of return the lessor has in mind when deciding the size of the rental payments. (Refer to our earlier calculations of the periodic rental payments.) Usually the lessee is aware of the lessor's implicit rate or can infer it from the asset's fair market value.[28] When the lessor's implicit rate is unknown, the lessee should use its own incremental borrowing rate.

[28]The corporation laws of some states, Florida for instance, actually require the interest rate to be expressly stated in the lease agreement.

On December 31, 2006, Sans Serif Publishers, Inc., leased a copier from First LeaseCorp. First LeaseCorp purchased the equipment from CompuDec Corporation at a cost of $479,079.

- Six annual payments of $102,000 beginning December 31, 2006.
- Payments include $2,000 which First LeaseCorp will use to pay an annual maintenance fee.
- The interest rate in these financing arrangements is 10%.
- Capital lease to Sans Serif.
- Direct financing lease to First LeaseCorp.

**Second Payment (December 31, 2007)**

| | | |
|---|---|---|
| **Sans Serif Publishers, Inc. (Lessee)** | | |
| Maintenance expense (2007 fee) | 2,000 | |
| Prepaid maintenance (paid in 2006) | | 2,000 |
| Interest expense [10% × ($479,079 − 100,000)] | 37,908 | |
| Lease payable (difference) | 62,092 | |
| Prepaid maintenance (2008 fee) | 2,000 | |
| Cash (rental payment) | | 102,000 |
| **First LeaseCorp (Lessor)** | | |
| Cash (rental payment) | 102,000 | |
| Lease receivable | | 100,000 |
| Maintenance fee payable* | | 2,000 |
| Unearned interest revenue | 37,908 | |
| Interest revenue [10% × ($600,000 − 120,921 − 100,000)] | | 37,908 |

*This assumes the $2,000 maintenance fee has not yet been paid to the outside maintenance service.

**ILLUSTRATION 15–6**
Rental Payments Including Executory Costs Paid by the Lessor

**Executory costs that are included in periodic rental payments to be paid by the lessor are, in effect, indirectly paid by the lessee—and expensed by the lessee.**

**Amounts recorded for periodic interest and the periodic reduction of principal are unaffected by executory costs.**

This is the rate the lessee would expect to pay a bank if funds were borrowed to buy the asset. When the lessor's implicit rate *is* known, the lessee should use the lower of the two rates.[29]

## WHEN THE LESSEE'S INCREMENTAL BORROWING RATE IS LESS THAN THE LESSOR'S IMPLICIT RATE

Instances are few in which the lessee actually would use its incremental borrowing rate. Here's why. We noted earlier that, like any other asset, a leased asset should not be recorded at more than its fair market value. Look what happens to the present value payments if Sans Serif uses a discount rate less than the 10% rate implicit in Illustration 15–6 (let's say 9%):

| | | |
|---|---|---|
| $100,000 × 4.88965* | = | $488,965 |
| Rental payments | | Lessee's cost |

*Present value of an annuity due of $1: $n = 6$, $i = 9\%$.

But remember, the fair market value of the copier was $479,079. The $100,000 amount for the rental payments was derived by the lessor, contemplating a market value of $479,079 and a desired interest rate of return (implicit rate) of 10%. So, using a discount rate lower than the lessor's implicit rate usually would result in the present value of minimum lease payments being more than the fair market value.

This conclusion does not hold when the leased asset has an unguaranteed residual value. You will recall that the lessor's determinations always include any residual value that accrues to the lessor; but when the lessee doesn't guarantee the residual value, it is *not* included in the lessee's present value calculations. Combining two previous examples, let's modify our demonstration of an unguaranteed residual value (Illustration 15–6) to assume the lessee's incremental borrowing rate was 9%. Because the residual value was expected to contribute to the lessor's recovery of the $479,079 fair market value, the rental payments were only $92,931. But, the lessee would ignore the unguaranteed residual value and calculate its cost of the leased asset to be $454,400.

[29]*Incremental borrowing rate* refers to the fact that lending institutions tend to view debt as being increasingly risky as the level of debt increases. Thus, additional (i.e., incremental) debt is likely to be loaned at a higher interest rate than existing debt, other things being equal.

| $92,931 × 4.88965* | = | $454,400 |
|---|---|---|
| Rental payments | | Lessee's cost |

*Present value of an annuity due of $1: $n = 6$, $i = 9\%$.

In this case, the present value of minimum lease payments would be *less than* the fair market value even though a lower discount rate is used. But again, if there is no residual value, or if the lessee guarantees the residual value, or if the unguaranteed residual value is relatively small, a discount rate lower than the lessor's implicit rate will result in the present value of minimum lease payments being more than the fair market value.

## WHEN THE LESSOR'S IMPLICIT RATE IS UNKNOWN

What if the lessee is unaware of the lessor's implicit rate? This is a logical question in light of the rule that says the lessee should use its own incremental borrowing rate when the lessor's implicit rate is unknown to the lessee. But in practice the lessor's implicit rate usually is known. Even if the lessor chooses not to explicitly disclose the rate, the lessee usually can deduce the rate using information he knows about the value of the leased asset and the lease payments. After all, in making the decision to lease rather than buy, the lessee typically becomes quite knowledgeable about the asset.

Even so, it is possible that a lessee might be unable to derive the lessor's implicit rate. This might happen, for example, if the leased asset has a relatively high residual value. Remember, a residual value (guaranteed or not) is an ingredient in the lessor's calculation of the rental payments. Sometimes it may be hard for the lessee to identify the residual value estimated by the lessor if the lessor chooses not to make it known.[30] The longer the lease term or the more risk of obsolescence the leased asset is subject to, the less of a factor the residual value typically is.

### ADDITIONAL CONSIDERATION

As pointed out earlier, the management of a lessee company sometimes will try to structure a lease to avoid the criteria that would cause the lease to be classified as a capital lease in order to gain the questionable advantages of off-balance-sheet financing. On the other hand, a *lessor* normally would prefer recording a **nonoperating** lease, other things being equal. Two ways sometimes used to structure a lease to qualify as an operating lease by the lessee, but as a nonoperating lease by the lessor are: (1) cause the two parties to use different interest rates and (2) avoid including the residual value in the lessee's minimum lease payments. Let's see how they work:

**1. Cause the Two Parties to Use Different Interest Rates.**

It was pointed out earlier that a lessee sometimes can claim to be unable to determine the lessor's implicit rate. Not knowing the lessor's implicit rate would permit the lessee to use its own incremental borrowing rate. If higher than the lessor's implicit rate, the present value it produces may cause the 90% of fair value criterion **not** to be met for the lessee (thus an operating lease) even though the criterion is met for the lessor (thus a nonoperating lease).

**2. Avoid Including the Residual Value in the Lessee's Minimum Lease Payments.**

The residual value, if guaranteed by the lessee or by a third party guarantor, is included in the minimum lease payments by the lessor when applying the 90% of fair value criterion and thus increases the likelihood that it is met. However, when the residual value is guaranteed by a third-party guarantor and not by the lessee, it is **not** included in the lessee's minimum lease payments. So, if a residual value is sufficiently large and guaranteed by a third-party guarantor, it may cause the 90% of fair value criterion to be met by the lessor, but not by the lessee.

Both schemes are unintentionally encouraged by lease accounting rules. As long as arbitrary cutoff points are used (90% of fair value in this case), maneuvers will be devised to circumvent them.

[30]Disclosure requirements provide that the lessor company must disclose the components of its investments in nonoperating leases, which would include any estimated residual values. But the disclosures are aggregate amounts, not amounts of individual leased assets.

## Lessor's Initial Direct Costs

The costs incurred by the lessor that are associated directly with originating a lease and are essential to acquire that lease are referred to as **initial direct costs.** They include legal fees, commissions, evaluating the prospective lessee's financial condition, and preparing and processing lease documents. The method of accounting for initial direct costs depends on the nature of the lease. Remember, a lessor can classify a lease as (1) an operating lease, (2) a direct financing lease, or (3) a sales-type lease. The accounting treatment for initial direct costs by each of the three possible lease types is summarized below.

1. For *operating leases,* initial direct costs are recorded as assets and amortized over the term of the lease. Since the only revenue an operating lease produces is rental revenue, and that revenue is recognized over the lease term, initial direct costs also are automatically recognized over the lease term to match these costs with the rent revenues they help generate.
2. In *direct financing leases,* interest revenue is earned over the lease term, so initial direct costs are matched with the interest revenues they help generate. Therefore, initial direct costs are not expensed at the outset but are deferred and recognized over the lease term. This can be accomplished by reducing the lessor's *unearned interest revenue* by the total of initial direct costs. Then, as unearned interest revenue is recognized over the lease term at a constant effective rate, the initial direct costs are recognized at the same rate (that is, proportionally).
3. For *sales-type leases,* initial direct costs are expensed at the inception of the lease. Since the usual reason for a sales-type lease is for a manufacturer or a dealer to sell its product, it's reasonable to recognize the costs of creating the transaction as a selling expense in the period of the sale.

## Contingent Rentals

Sometimes rental payments may be increased (or decreased) at some future time during the lease term, depending on whether or not some specified event occurs. Usually the contingency is related to revenues, profitability, or usage above some designated level. For example, a recent annual report of **Wal-Mart Stores** included the note re-created in Graphic 15–13.

**9 Commitments (in part)**
Certain of the leases provide for contingent additional rentals based on percentage of sales. The additional rentals amounted to $46 million, $51 million and $63 million in 2004, 2003 and 2002, respectively.

**GRAPHIC 15–13**
Disclosure of Contingent Rentals—Wal-Mart Stores

Contingent rentals are *not* included in the minimum lease payments because they are not determinable at the inception of the lease. Instead, they are included as components of income when (and if) they occur. Increases or decreases in rental payments that are dependent only on the passage of time are not contingent rentals; these are part of minimum lease payments.

Although contingent rentals are not included in minimum lease payments, they are reported in disclosure notes by both the lessor and lessee.

## A Brief Summary

Leasing arrangements often are complex. In studying this chapter you've encountered several features of lease agreements that alter the way we make several of the calculations needed to account for leases. Graphic 15–14 provides a concise review of the essential lease accounting components, using calculations from a hypothetical lease situation to provide a numerical perspective.

**GRAPHIC 15–14** Lease Terms and Concepts: A Summary

**Lease Situation for Calculations**

($ in 000s)

| | | | |
|---|---|---|---|
| Lease term (years) | 4 | Lessor's cost | $300 |
| Asset's useful life (years) | 5 | Residual value: | |
| Lessor's implicit rate (known by lessee) | 12% | Guaranteed by lessee | $8 |
| Lessee's incremental borrowing rate | 13% | Guaranteed by third party[a] | $6 |
| Rental payments (including executory costs) at the beginning of each year | $102 | Unguaranteed | $5 |
| | | Executory costs paid annually by lessor | $2 |
| | | Bargain purchase option | none |
| | | Initial direct costs | 3 |

| Amount | Description | Calculation |
|---|---|---|
| **Lessor's:** | | |
| Gross investment in the lease[b] | Total of periodic rental payments[c] plus any residual value that reverts to the lessor (guaranteed or not) or plus BPO price[d] | ($100 × 4) + ($8 + 6 + 5) = $419 |
| Net investment in the lease | Present value of the gross investment (discounted at lessor's rate) plus any initial direct costs in a direct financing lease | ($100 × 3.40183[e]) + ($19 × .63552[f]) = $352[g] |
| Unearned interest revenue | Gross investment − Net investment | $419 − 352 = $67 |
| Minimum lease payments | Total of periodic rental payments[c] plus residual value guaranteed to the lessor (by lessee and/or by third party) or plus BPO price[d] | ($100 × 4) + ($8 + 6) = $414 |
| Sales revenue | Present value of lessor's minimum lease payments; also, net investment − present value of unguaranteed residual value | ($100 × 3.40183[e]) + ($14 × .63552[f]) = $349; also: $352 − ($5 × .63552) = $349 |
| Cost of goods sold | Lessor's cost − Present value of unguaranteed residual value | $300 − ($5 × .63552[f]) = $297 |
| Dealer's profit | Sales revenue − Cost of goods sold; also, Net investment − Lessor's cost | $349 − 297 = $52; also, $352 − 300 = $52 |
| **Lessee's:** | | |
| Minimum lease payments | Total of periodic rental payments[c] plus residual value guaranteed by lessee or plus BPO price[d] | ($100 × 4) + $8 = $408 |
| Leased asset | Present value of minimum lease payments (using lower of lessor's rate and lessee's incremental borrowing rate); cannot exceed fair value | ($100 × 3.40183[e]) + ($8 × .63552[f]) = $345 |
| Lease liability at inception | Same as leased asset | ($100 × 3.40183[e]) + ($8 × .63552[f]) = $345 |

[a]Beyond any amount guaranteed by the lessee (amount guaranteed is $8 + 6 minus any amount paid by the lessee).
[b]This is the amount to be recovered by the lessor and therefore is used in the calculation of periodic lease payments. It also is the lease receivable at the inception of lease.
[c]Any portion of rental payments that represents maintenance, insurance, taxes, or other executory costs is not considered part of minimum lease payments. In this case, rentals are reduced as follows: $102 − 2 = $100.
[d]In this context, a residual value and a BPO price are mutually exclusive: if a BPO exists, any residual value is expected to remain with the lessee and is not considered an additional payment.
[e]Present value of annuity due of $1: $n = 4$, $i = 12\%$.
[f]Present value of $1: $n = 4$, $i = 12\%$.
[g]Since this is a sales-type lease ($352 − 300 = $52 dealer's profit), initial direct costs are expensed at the lease's inception and do not increase the net investment in the lease.

## Lease Disclosures

Lease disclosure requirements are quite extensive for both the lessor and lessee. Virtually all aspects of the lease agreement must be disclosed. For *all* leases (a) a general description of the leasing arrangement is required as well as (b) minimum future payments, in the aggregate and for each of the five succeeding fiscal years. Other required disclosures are specific to the type of lease and include: residual values, contingent rentals, unearned interest, sublease rentals, and executory costs. Some representative examples are shown in Graphics 15–15 (lessor) and 15–16 (lessee) on page 742.

**IBM** is a manufacturer that relies heavily on leasing as a means of selling its products. Its disclosure of sales-type leases is shown in Graphic 15–15.

**GRAPHIC 15–15**
Lessor Disclosure of Sales-Type Leases—IBM Corporation

**F Financing Receivables (in part)**
(dollars in millions)

| At December 31: | 2003 | 2002 |
|---|---|---|
| **Short term:** | | |
| **Net investment in sales-type leases** | **$ 5,940** | **$ 5,779** |
| Commercial financing receivables | 5,653 | 4,972 |
| Customer loans receivable | 5,235 | 4,462 |
| Installment payment receivables | 657 | 698 |
| Other non-Global Financing related | 98 | 85 |
| Total | $17,583 | $15,996 |
| **Long term:** | | |
| **Net investment in sales-type leases** | **$ 6,010** | **$ 6,505** |
| Commercial financing receivables | 197 | 462 |
| Customer loans receivable | 4,300 | 4,179 |
| Installment payment receivables | 217 | 273 |
| Other non-Global Financing related | 17 | 21 |
| Total | $10,741 | $11,440 |

Net investment in sales-type leases is for leases that relate principally to IBM equipment and are generally for terms ranging from two to five years. Net investment in sales-type leases includes unguaranteed residual values of $845 million and $821 million at December 31, 2003 and 2002, respectively, and is reflected net of unearned income of $1,227 million and $1,330 million and of allowance for uncollectible accounts of $337 million and $361 million at those dates, respectively.

**Wal-Mart Stores** leases facilities under both operating and capital leases. Its long-term obligations under these lease agreements are disclosed in a note to its financial statements (see Graphic 15–16).

### DECISION MAKERS' PERSPECTIVE—Financial Statement Impact

As indicated in the Decision Makers' Perspective at the beginning of the chapter, leasing can allow a firm to conserve assets, to avoid some risks of owning assets, and to obtain favorable tax benefits. These advantages are desirable. It also was pointed out earlier that some firms try to obscure the realities of their financial position through off-balance-sheet financing or by avoiding violating terms of contracts that limit the amount of debt a company can have. Accounting guidelines are designed to limit the ability of firms to hide financial realities. Nevertheless, investors and creditors should be alert to the impact leases can have on a company's financial position and on its risk. ■

Leasing sometimes is used as a means of off-balance-sheet financing.

**GRAPHIC 15–16**

Lessee Disclosure of Leases—Wal-Mart Stores

**Note 9 Commitments (in part)**

The Company and certain of its subsidiaries have long-term leases for stores and equipment. Rentals (including, for certain leases, amounts applicable to taxes, insurance, maintenance, other operating expenses and contingent rentals) under all operating leases were $1.1 billion, $1.1 billion, and $1.0 billion in 2004, 2003, and 2002, respectively. Aggregate minimum annual rentals at January 31, 2004, under non-cancelable leases are as follows (in millions):

| Fiscal Year | Operating Leases | Capital Leases |
|---|---|---|
| 2005 | $ 665 | $ 430 |
| 2006 | 651 | 427 |
| 2007 | 599 | 419 |
| 2008 | 553 | 411 |
| 2009 | 519 | 397 |
| Thereafter | 5,678 | 3,002 |
| Total minimum rentals | $8,665 | 5,086 |
| Less estimated executory costs | | 44 |
| Net minimum lease payments | | 5,042 |
| Less imputed interest at rates ranging from 4.2% to 14.0% | | 1,849 |
| Present value of minimum lease payments | | $3,193 |

## BALANCE SHEET AND INCOME STATEMENT

Lease liabilities affect the debt to equity ratio and the rate of return on assets.

Lease transactions identified as nonoperating impact several of a firm's financial ratios. Because we record liabilities for capital leases, the debt-equity ratio (liabilities divided by shareholders' equity) is immediately impacted. Because we also record leased assets, the immediate impact on the rate of return on assets (net income divided by assets) is negative, but the lasting effect depends on how leased assets are utilized to enhance future net income. As illustrated in this chapter, the financial statement impact of a capital lease is no different from that of an installment purchase.

Do operating leases create long-term commitments equivalent to liabilities?

Even operating leases, though, can significantly affect risk. Operating leases represent long-term commitments that can become a problem if business declines and cash inflows drop off. For example, long-term lease commitments became a big problem for **Businessland** in the early 1990s. The company's revenues declined but it was saddled with lease commitments for numerous facilities the company no longer occupied. Its stock's market price declined from $11.88 to $.88 in one year.

The net income difference between treating a lease as a capital lease versus an operating lease generally is not significant.

Whether leases are capitalized or treated as operating leases affects the income statement as well as the balance sheet. However, the impact generally is not significant. Over the life of a lease, total expenses are equal regardless of the accounting treatment of a lease. If the lease is capitalized, total expenses comprise interest and depreciation. The total of these equals the total amount of rental payments, which would constitute rent expense if not capitalized. There is, however, a timing difference between lease capitalization and operating lease treatment, but the timing difference usually isn't great.

The difference in impact on the balance sheet between capital leases and operating leases is significant.

The more significant difference between capital leases and operating leases is the impact on the balance sheet. As mentioned above, a capital lease adds to both the asset and liability side of the balance sheet; operating leases do not affect the balance sheet at all. How can external financial statement users adjust their analysis to incorporate the balance sheet differences between capital and operating leases? A frequently offered suggestion is to capitalize all noncancelable lease commitments, including those related to operating leases. Some financial analysts, in fact, do this on their own to get a better feel for a company's actual debt position.

To illustrate, refer to Graphic 15–16, which reveals the operating lease commitments disclosed by **Wal-Mart Stores**. If these lease arrangements were considered nonoperating, these payments would be capitalized (reported at the present value of all future payments). By making some reasonable assumptions, we can estimate the present value of all future payments to be made on existing operating leases. For example, the interest rates used by Wal-Mart to discount rental payments on capital leases range from 4.2% to 14.0%. If we use the approximate average rate of 10%, and make certain other assumptions, we can determine the debt equivalent of the operating lease commitments as shown in Graphic 15–17.

**GRAPHIC 15–17**
Estimating the Debt Equivalent of Operating Lease Commitments

**Capitalized Value or Debt Equivalent of Wal-Mart's Operating Leases**

| Fiscal Years | Operating Leases | PV Factor 10% | Present Value |
|---|---|---|---|
| 2005 | $ 665 | .909 | $ 604 |
| 2006 | 651 | .826 | 538 |
| 2007 | 599 | .751 | 450 |
| 2008 | 553 | .683 | 378 |
| 2009 | 519 | .621 | 322 |
| Thereafter | 5,678 | .386* | 2,192 |
| Total minimum rentals | $8,665 | | $4,484 |

*This is the PV factor for $i$ = 10%, $n$ = 10, which treats payments after 2009 as occurring in 2014, an assumption due to not knowing precise dates of specific payments after 2009.

If capitalized, these operating lease commitments would add $4,484 million to Wal-Mart's liabilities and approximately $4,484 to the company's assets.[31] Let's look at the impact this would have on the company's debt to equity ratio and its return on assets ratio using selected financial statement information taken from Wal-Mart's annual report for the fiscal year ending January 31, 2004, shown below:

| | ($ in millions) |
|---|---|
| Total assets | $104,912 |
| Total liabilities | 61,289 |
| Total shareholders' equity | 43,623 |
| Net income | 9,054 |

The debt to equity and return on assets ratios are calculated in Graphic 15–18 without considering the capitalization of operating leases and then again after adding $4,484 million to both total assets and total liabilities. In the calculation of return on assets, we use only the year-end total assets rather than the average total assets for the year. Also, we assume no impact on income.

**GRAPHIC 15–18**
Ratios with and without Capitalization of Operating Leases

| | ($ in millions) Without Capitalization | With Capitalization |
|---|---|---|
| Debt to equity ratio | $\frac{\$61{,}289}{\$43{,}623} = 1.40$ | $\frac{\$65{,}773}{\$43{,}623} = 1.51$ |
| Return on assets | $\frac{\$9{,}054}{\$104{,}912} = 8.6\%$ | $\frac{\$9{,}054}{\$109{,}396} = 8.3\%$ |

[31] If these operating leases were capitalized, both assets and liabilities would increase by the same amount at inception of the lease. However, in later years, the leased asset account balance and the lease liability account will, generally, not be equal. The leased asset account is reduced by depreciation and the lease liability account is reduced (amortized) down to zero using the effective interest method.

The debt to equity ratio rises from 1.40 to 1.51, and the return on assets ratio declines from 8.6% to 8.3%.

### STATEMENT OF CASH FLOW IMPACT

Operating leases are not reported on a statement of cash flows at the lease's inception.

**Operating Leases.** Remember, lease payments for operating leases represent rent—expense to the lessee, revenue for the lessor. These amounts are included in net income, so both the lessee and lessor report cash payments for operating leases in a statement of cash flows as cash flows from operating activities.

The interest portion of a capital lease payment is a cash flow from operating activities and the principal portion is a cash flow from financing activities.

**Capital Leases and Direct Financing Leases.** You've learned in this chapter that capital leases are agreements that we identify as being formulated outwardly as leases, but which are in reality installment purchases, so we account for them as such. Each rental payment (except the first if paid at inception) includes both an amount that represents interest and an amount that represents a reduction of principal. In a statement of cash flows, then, the lessee reports the interest portion as a cash outflow from operating activities and the principal portion as a cash outflow from financing activities. On the other side of the transaction, the lessor in a direct financing lease reports the interest portion as a cash inflow from operating activities and the principal portion as a cash inflow from investing activities. Both the lessee and lessor report the lease at its inception as a noncash investing/financing activity.

Cash receipts from a sales-type lease are cash flows from operating activities.

**Sales-Type Leases.** A sales-type lease differs from a direct-financing lease for the lessor in that we assume the lessor is actually selling its product. Consistent with reporting sales of products under installment sales agreements rather than lease agreements, the lessor reports cash receipts from a sales-type lease as cash inflows from operating activities.

## CONCEPT REVIEW EXERCISE

### VARIOUS LEASE ACCOUNTING ISSUES

*(This is an extension of the previous Concept Review Exercise.)*
United Cellular Systems leased a satellite transmission device from Satellite Technology Corporation on January 1, 2007. Satellite Technology paid $500,000 for the transmission device. Its retail value is $653,681.

**Terms of the Lease Agreement and Related Information:**

| | |
|---|---|
| Lease term | 3 years (6 semiannual periods) |
| Semiannual rental payments | $123,000—beginning of each period |
| Economic life of asset | 4 years |
| Implicit interest rate<br>(Also lessee's incremental borrowing rate) | 12% |
| Unguaranteed residual value | $40,000 |
| Regulatory fees paid by lessor | $3,000/twice each year (included in rentals) |
| Lessor's initial direct costs | $4,500 |
| Contingent rental payments | Additional $4,000 if revenues exceed a specified base |

**Required:**

1. Prepare an amortization schedule that describes the pattern of interest expense over the lease term for United Cellular Systems.
2. Prepare an amortization schedule that describes the pattern of interest revenue over the lease term for Satellite Technology.
3. Prepare the appropriate entries for both United Cellular Systems and Satellite Technology on January 1 and June 30, 2007.
4. Prepare the appropriate entries for both United Cellular Systems and Satellite Technology on December 31, 2009 (the end of the lease term), assuming the device is returned to the lessor and its actual residual value is $14,000 on that date.

1. Prepare an amortization schedule that describes the pattern of interest expense over the lease term for United Cellular Systems.

**SOLUTION**

**Calculation of the Present Value of Minimum Lease Payments:**

Present value of periodic rental payments excluding executory costs of $3,000:

($120,000 × 5.21236*) = $625,483

*Present value of an annuity due of $1: $n = 6$, $i = 6\%$.

Note: The *unguaranteed* residual value is excluded from minimum lease payments for both the lessee and lessor.

| Date | Payments | Effective Interest | Decrease in Balance | Outstanding Balance |
|---|---|---|---|---|
| | | (6% × Outstanding balance) | | |
| 1/1/07 | | | | 625,483 |
| 1/1/07 | 120,000 | | 120,000 | 505,483 |
| 6/30/07 | 120,000 | .06 (505,483) = 30,329 | 89,671 | 415,812 |
| 1/1/08 | 120,000 | .06 (415,812) = 24,949 | 95,051 | 320,761 |
| 6/30/08 | 120,000 | .06 (320,761) = 19,246 | 100,754 | 220,007 |
| 1/1/09 | 120,000 | .06 (220,007) = 13,200 | 106,800 | 113,207 |
| 6/30/09 | 120,000 | .06 (113,207) = 6,793* | 113,207 | 0 |
| | 720,000 | 94,517 | 625,483 | |

*Adjusted for rounding of other numbers in the schedule.

2. Prepare an amortization schedule that describes the pattern of interest revenue over the lease term for Satellite Technology.

**Calculation of the Lessor's Net Investment:**

| | |
|---|---|
| Present value of periodic rental payments excluding executory costs of $3,000 ($120,000 × 5.21236*) | $625,483 |
| Plus: Present value of the unguaranteed residual value ($40,000 × .70496†) | 28,198 |
| Lessor's net investment in lease | $653,681 |

*Present value of an annuity due of $1: $n = 6$, $i = 6\%$.

†Present value of $1: $n = 6$, $i = 6\%$.

Note: The *unguaranteed* residual value is excluded from minimum lease payments, but is part of the lessor's gross and net investment in the lease.

| Date | Payments | Effective Interest | Decrease in Balance | Outstanding Balance |
|---|---|---|---|---|
| | | (6% × Outstanding balance) | | |
| 1/1/07 | | | | 653,681 |
| 1/1/07 | 120,000 | | 120,000 | 533,681 |
| 6/30/07 | 120,000 | .06 (533,681) = 32,021 | 87,979 | 445,702 |
| 1/1/08 | 120,000 | .06 (445,702) = 26,742 | 93,258 | 352,444 |
| 6/30/08 | 120,000 | .06 (352,444) = 21,147 | 98,853 | 253,591 |
| 1/1/09 | 120,000 | .06 (253,591) = 15,215 | 104,785 | 148,806 |
| 6/30/09 | 120,000 | .06 (148,806) = 8,928 | 111,072 | 37,734 |
| 12/31/09 | 40,000 | .06 (37,734) = 2,266* | 37,734 | 0 |
| | 760,000 | 106,319 | 653,681 | |

*Adjusted for rounding of other numbers in the schedule.

3. Prepare the appropriate entries for both United Cellular Systems and Satellite Technology on January 1 and June 30, 2007.

**January 1, 2007**

**United Cellular Systems (Lessee)**

| | | |
|---|---|---|
| Leased equipment (calculated above) | 625,483 | |
| Lease payable (calculated above) | | 625,483 |
| Lease payable (payment less executory costs) | 120,000 | |
| Regulatory fees expense (executory costs) | 3,000 | |
| Cash (rental payment) | | 123,000 |

| | | |
|---|---|---|
| **Satellite Technology (Lessor)** | | |
| Lease receivable [($120,000 × 6) + $40,000[a]] | 760,000 | |
| Cost of goods sold [$500,000 − ($40,000[a] × .70496)] | 471,802 | |
| Sales revenue (present value of minimum lease payments[b]) | | 625,483 |
| Unearned interest revenue ($760,000 − 653,681) | | 106,319 |
| Inventory of equipment (lessor's cost) | | 500,000 |
| Selling expense | 4,500 | |
| Cash (initial direct costs) | | 4,500 |
| Cash (rental payment) | 123,000 | |
| Regulatory fees payable (or cash) | | 3,000 |
| Lease receivable (payment less executory costs) | | 120,000 |

[a]This is the unguaranteed residual value.
[b]Also, $653,681 − ($40,000[a] × .70496).

| June 30, 2007 | | |
|---|---|---|
| **United Cellular Systems (Lessee)** | | |
| Interest expense [6% × ($625,483 − 120,000)] | 30,329 | |
| Lease payable (difference) | 89,671 | |
| Regulatory fees expense (annual fee) | 3,000 | |
| Cash (rental payment) | | 123,000 |
| **Satellite Technology (Lessor)** | | |
| Cash (lease payment) | 123,000 | |
| Regulatory fees payable (or cash) | | 3,000 |
| Lease receivable (payment less executory costs) | | 120,000 |
| Unearned interest revenue | 32,021 | |
| Interest revenue [6% × ($653,681 − 120,000)] | | 32,021 |

4. Prepare the appropriate entries for both United Cellular Systems and Satellite Technology on December 31, 2009 (the end of the lease term), assuming the device is returned to the lessor and its actual residual value is $14,000 on that date.

| December 31, 2009 | | |
|---|---|---|
| **United Cellular Systems (Lessee)** | | |
| Depreciation expense ($625,483 ÷ 3 years) | 208,494 | |
| Accumulated depreciation | | 208,494 |
| Accumulated depreciation (account balance) | 625,483 | |
| Leased equipment (account balance) | | 625,483 |
| **Satellite Technology (Lessor)** | | |
| Inventory of equipment (actual residual value) | 14,000 | |
| Loss on leased assets ($40,000 − 14,000) | 26,000 | |
| Lease receivable (account balance) | | 40,000 |
| Unearned interest revenue (account balance) | 2,266 | |
| Interest revenue (6% × $37,734: from schedule) | | 2,266 |

# PART D SPECIAL LEASING ARRANGEMENTS

## Sale-Leaseback Arrangements

LO10

In a **sale-leaseback transaction**, the owner of an asset sells it and immediately leases it back from the new owner. Sound strange? Maybe, but this arrangement is common. In a sale-leaseback transaction two things happen:

1. The seller-lessee receives cash from the sale of the asset.
2. The seller-lessee pays periodic rent payments to the buyer-lessor to retain the use of the asset.

What motivates this kind of arrangement? The two most common reasons are: (1) If the asset had been financed originally with debt and interest rates have fallen, the sale-leaseback transaction can be used to effectively refinance at a lower rate. (2) The most likely motivation for a sale-leaseback transaction is to generate cash.

## CAPITAL LEASES

Illustration 15–7 demonstrates a sale-leaseback involving a capital lease. The sale and simultaneous leaseback of the warehouses should be viewed as a single borrowing transaction. Although there appear to be two separate transactions, look closer at the substance of the agreement. Teledyne still retains the use of the warehouses that it had prior to the sale-leaseback. What is different? Teledyne has $900,000 cash and a noncancelable obligation to make annual payments of $133,155. In substance, Teledyne simply has borrowed $900,000 to be repaid over 10 years along with 10% interest. From the perspective of substance over form, we do not immediately recognize the $300,000 gain on the sale of the warehouses but defer the gain to be recognized over the term of the lease (or the useful life of the asset if title is expected to transfer outright or by the exercise of a BPO), demonstrated in Illustration 15–7A.

**Recording a sale-leaseback transaction follows the basic accounting concept of substance over form.**

**ILLUSTRATION 15–7**
Sale-Leaseback

Teledyne Distribution Center was in need of cash. Its solution: sell its four warehouses for $900,000, then lease back the warehouses to obtain their continued use. The warehouses had a carrying value on Teledyne's books of $600,000 (original cost $950,000). Other information:

1. The sale date is December 31, 2006.
2. The noncancelable lease term is 10 years and requires annual payments of $133,155 beginning December 31, 2006. The estimated remaining useful life of the warehouses is 10 years.
3. The annual rental payments (present value $900,000) provides the lessor with a 10% rate of return on the financing arrangement.* Teledyne's incremental borrowing rate is 10%.
4. Teledyne depreciates its warehouses on a straight-line basis.

| | | |
|---|---|---|
| *$133,155 × | 6.75902 | = $900,000 ($899,997.30 rounded) |
| Rent payments | (from Table 6) $n = 10, i = 10\%$ | Present value |

**ILLUSTRATION 15–7A**
Recording a Sale-Leaseback

| | | |
|---|---|---|
| **December 31, 2006** | | |
| Cash | 900,000 | |
| Accumulated depreciation ($950,000 – 600,000) | 350,000 | |
| Warehouses (cost) | | 950,000 |
| Deferred gain on sale-leaseback (difference) | | 300,000 |
| Leased warehouses (present value of lease payments) | 900,000 | |
| Lease payable (present value of lease payments) | | 900,000 |
| Lease payable | 133,155 | |
| Cash | | 133,155 |
| **December 31, 2007** | | |
| Interest expense [10% × ($900,000 – 133,155)] | 76,685 | |
| Lease payable (difference) | 56,470 | |
| Cash (rental payment) | | 133,155 |
| Depreciation expense ($900,000 ÷ 10 years) | 90,000 | |
| Accumulated depreciation | | 90,000 |
| Deferred gain on sale-leaseback ($300,000 ÷ 10 years) | 30,000 | |
| Depreciation expense | | 30,000 |

**The gain on sale-leaseback is deferred and recognized over the lease term as a reduction of depreciation expense.**

Since the lease term is equal to the expected useful life of the warehouses (>75%), the leaseback must be recorded by the lessee as a capital lease.[32] There typically is an interdependency between the lease terms and the price at which the asset is sold. The earnings

[32]The fourth criterion also is met. The present value of lease payments ($900,000) is 100% (>90%) of the fair value of the warehouses ($900,000). Meeting any one of the four criteria is sufficient.

process is not complete at the time of sale but is completed over the term of the lease. So, viewing the sale and the leaseback as a single transaction is consistent with the realization principle. Look closely at the 2007 entries to see the net effect of recording the sale leaseback this way. Amortizing the deferred gain over the lease term as a reduction of depreciation expense decreases depreciation each year to $60,000.[33] Interest expense is $76,685. If Teledyne had *not* sold the warehouses ($600,000 carrying value) and had borrowed $900,000 cash by issuing an installment note, the 2007 effect would have been virtually identical:

**Depreciating the carrying value of the warehouses over their remaining useful life produces depreciation equal to the net depreciation recorded in a sale-leaseback.**

| **December 31, 2007** | | |
|---|---|---|
| Interest expense [10% × ($900,000 − 133,155)] | 76,685 | |
| Note payable (difference) | 56,470 | |
| Cash (installment payment) | | 133,155 |
| Depreciation expense ($600,000 ÷ 10 years) | 60,000 | |
| Accumulated depreciation | | 60,000 |

The deferred gain is reported on the balance sheet as a valuation (contra) account, offsetting the leased asset. The 2007 balance sheet effect of the sale-leaseback transaction and a $900,000 installment note are compared in Graphic 15–19. Once again, the effect is virtually identical.

**GRAPHIC 15–19**
Comparison of a Sale-Leaseback and a Purchase

| | Sale-Leaseback | Retain Asset; Borrow Cash |
|---|---|---|
| **Assets** | | |
| Leased asset | $900,000 | $950,000 |
| Less: Accumulated depreciation | (90,000) | (410,000) |
| Less: Deferred gain ($300,000 − 30,000) | (270,000) | |
| | $540,000 | $540,000 |
| **Liabilities** | | |
| Lease payable ($900,000 − 133,155 − 56,470) | $710,375 | |
| Note payable ($900,000 − 133,155 − 56,470) | | $710,375 |

Accounting by the buyer/lessor is no different in a sale-leaseback transaction than another lease transaction. That is, it records a lease in accordance with the usual lease guidelines.

## OPERATING LEASES

If the leaseback portion of the previous sale-leaseback transaction were classified as an operating lease, the gain still would be deferred but would be recognized as a reduction of rent expense rather than depreciation. There is no leased asset to depreciate.[34]

| **December 31, 2007** | | |
|---|---|---|
| Deferred gain on sale-leaseback ($300,000 ÷ 10 years) | 30,000 | |
| Rent expense | | 30,000 |

Those of you with a healthy sense of skepticism will question whether the leaseback portion of our sale-leaseback situation could qualify as an operating lease. After all, the 10-year lease term is equal to the 10-year remaining useful life. But when you remember that neither the third (75% of economic life) nor the fourth (90% recovery) classification criterion applies if the inception of the lease occurs during the last 25% of an asset's economic life, you

[33] If depreciation is over the useful life of the leased asset rather than the lease term because ownership is expected to transfer to the lessee, amortization of the deferred gain also would be over the useful life. If a leaseback of land is a capital lease, the amortization of the deferred gain is recorded as revenue.

[34] The deferred gain would be reported as a deferred liability since it could not be offset against a leased asset.

see the possibility of an operating lease. Suppose, for instance, that the original useful life of the warehouses was 40 years. In that case, the current lease term would occur during the last 25% of an asset's economic life and we would have an operating lease.

### LOSSES ON SALE-LEASEBACKS

In a sale-leaseback, any gain on the sale of the asset is deferred and amortized. However, a real loss on the sale of the property is recognized immediately—not deferred. A real loss means the fair value is less than the carrying amount of the asset. On the other hand, if the fair value exceeds the carrying amount, but the asset is sold to the buyer/lessor for less than the carrying amount, an artificial loss is produced that is probably in substance a prepayment of rent and should be deferred and amortized.

## Real Estate Leases

Some leases involve land—exclusively or in part. The concepts we discussed in the chapter also relate to **real estate leases.** But the fact that land has an unlimited life causes us to modify how we account for some leases involving real estate.

### LEASES OF LAND ONLY

Because the useful life of land is indefinite, the risks and rewards of ownership cannot be presumed transferred from the lessor to the lessee unless title to the land is expected to transfer—outright or by the expected exercise of a bargain purchase option (criterion 1 or criterion 2). Since the useful life is undefined, the third and fourth criteria are not applicable. Relatedly, because the leased asset is land, depreciation is inappropriate.

Only the first (title transfers) and second (BPO) classification criteria apply in a land lease.

### LEASES OF LAND AND BUILDING

When the leased property includes both land and a building and the lease transfers ownership or is expected to by exercise of a BPO, the lessee should record each leased asset separately. The present value of the minimum lease payments is allocated between the leased land and leased building accounts on the basis of their relative market values.

When neither of the first two criteria is met, the question arises as to whether the third and fourth criteria apply. Because they logically should apply to the building (because its life is limited) but not to the land (because its life is unlimited), the profession employs an arbitrary guideline. If the fair value of the land is less than 25% of the combined fair value, it is in effect ignored and both the lessee and the lessor treat the land and building as a single unit. The single leased asset is depreciated as if land were not involved. If the fair value of the land is 25% or more of the combined fair value, both the lessee and the lessor treat the land and building as two separate leases. Thus, the land lease is an operating lease, and the building lease is classified and accounted for in the manner described in the chapter.

When (a) the leased property includes both land and a building, (b) neither of the first two criteria is met, and (c) the fair value of the land is 25% or more of the combined fair value, both the lessee and the lessor treat the land as an operating lease and the building as any other lease.

### LEASES OF ONLY PART OF A BUILDING

Some of the most common of leases involve leasing only part of a building. For instance, businesses frequently lease space in an office building or individual stores in a shopping mall. Practical difficulties arise when applying lease accounting procedures in these situations. What is the cost of the third shop from the entrance in a $14 million mall? What is the fair value of a sixth floor office suite in a 40-floor office complex? Despite practical difficulties, usual lease accounting treatment applies. It may, however, be necessary to employ real estate appraisals or replacement cost information to arrive at reasonable estimates of cost or fair value.

Usual lease accounting procedures apply to leases that involve only part of a building, although extra effort may be needed to arrive at reasonable estimates of cost and fair value.

## Leveraged Leases

In a **leveraged lease,** a third-party, long-term creditor provides nonrecourse financing for a lease agreement between a lessor and lessee. The term *leveraged* refers to the fact that the lessor acquires title to the asset after borrowing a large part of the investment.

From the lessee's perspective, accounting for a leveraged lease is not distinguishable from accounting for a nonleveraged lease. Accounting for leveraged leases by the lessor is similar

A *leveraged lease* involves significant long-term, nonrecourse financing by a third-party creditor.

A lessor records its investment (receivable) net of the nonrecourse debt and reports income from the lease only in those years when the receivable exceeds the liability.

to that for nonleveraged leases. A lessor records its investment (receivable) net of the nonrecourse debt. The lessor's liability to the lender should be offset against its lease receivable from the lessee because its role is in substance that of a mortgage broker. That is, the lessor earns income by serving as an agent for a firm wishing to acquire property and a lender seeking an investment. The lessor borrows enough cash from the lender to acquire the property, which is in turn leased to the lessee under a capital lease. Payments from the lessee are applied to the note held by the lender. The note may be assumed by the lessee *without recourse* such that the lessor is absolved of responsibility for its payment. In order to qualify for favorable treatment under the tax code, the lessor must maintain at least a minimum percentage of equity position in the asset. Also, the lessor should report income from the lease only in those years when the receivable exceeds the liability.

## FINANCIAL REPORTING CASE SOLUTION

1. **How would HG's revenues "take a hit" as a result of more customers leasing than buying mainframes?** *(p. 717)* When HG leases machines under operating leases, it reports revenue as it collects "rent" over the lease term. When HG sells machines, on the other hand, it recognizes revenue "up front" in the year of sales. Actually, total revenues are not necessarily less with a lease, but are spread out over the several years of the lease term. This delays the recognition of revenues, creating the "hit" in the reporting periods in which a shift to leasing occurs.
2. **Under what kind of leasing arrangements would the "hit" not occur?** *(p. 726)* The hit will not occur when HG leases its machines under sales-type leases. In those cases, despite the fact that the contract specifies a lease, in effect, HG actually sells its machines under the arrangement. Consequently, HG will recognize sales revenue (and cost of goods sold) at the inception of the lease. The amount recognized is roughly the same as if customers actually buy the machines. As a result, the income statement will not receive the hit created by the substitution of operating leases for outright sales. ■

## THE BOTTOM LINE

1. Leasing is used as a means of off-balance-sheet financing and to achieve operational and tax objectives.
2. In keeping with the concept of substance over form, a lease is accounted for as either a rental agreement or a purchase/sale accompanied by debt financing.
3. A lessee should classify a lease transaction as a capital lease if it is noncancelable and if one or more of four classification criteria are met. Otherwise, it is an operating lease. A lessor records a lease as a direct financing lease or a sales-type lease only if two conditions relating to revenue realization are met in addition to one of the four classification criteria.
4. In an operating lease a sale is not recorded by the lessor; a purchase is not recorded by the lessee. Instead, the periodic rental payments are accounted for merely as rent revenue by the lessor, rent expense by the lessee.
5. In a capital lease the lessee records a leased asset at the present value of the minimum lease payments. A nonoperating lease is recorded by the lessor as a sales-type lease or direct financing lease, depending on whether the lease provides the lessor a dealer's profit.
6. A sales-type lease requires recording sales revenue and cost of goods sold by the lessor at the inception of the lease. All other entries are the same as in a direct financing lease.
7. A lessee-guaranteed residual value is included as a component of minimum lease payments for both the lessor and the lessee. An unguaranteed residual value is not (but is part of the lessor's gross investment in the lease).
8. A bargain purchase option is included as a component of minimum lease payments for both the lessor and the lessee. The lease term effectively ends when the BPO is exercisable.

9. Executory costs (maintenance, insurance, taxes, and any other costs usually associated with ownership) are expenses of the lessee. Any costs incurred by the lessor that are associated directly with originating a lease and are essential to acquire that lease are called *initial direct costs* and are expensed in accordance with the matching principle. To find the present value of minimum lease payments to capitalize as an asset and liability, the lessee usually uses a discount rate equal to the lower of the rate implicit in the lease agreement and its own incremental borrowing rate. Contingent rentals are *not* included in the minimum lease payments because they are not determinable at the inception of the lease.
10. A gain on the sale of an asset in a sale leaseback arrangement is deferred and amortized over the lease term (or asset life if title is expected to transfer to the lessee). The lease portion of the transaction is evaluated and accounted for like any lease. ■

## QUESTIONS FOR REVIEW OF KEY TOPICS

**Q 15–1** The basic concept of "substance over form" influences lease accounting. Explain.

**Q 15–2** How is interest determined in a nonoperating lease transaction. How does the approach compare to other forms of debt (say bonds payable or notes payable)?

**Q 15–3** How are leases and installment notes the same? How do they differ?

**Q 15–4** A lessee should classify a lease transaction as a capital lease if it is noncancelable and one or more of four classification criteria are met. Otherwise, it is an operating lease. What are these criteria?

**Q 15–5** What is a bargain purchase option? How does it differ from other purchase options?

**Q 15–6** Lukawitz Industries leased equipment to Seminole Corporation for a four-year period, at which time possession of the leased asset will revert back to Lukawitz. The equipment cost Lukawitz $4 million and has an expected useful life of six years. Its normal sales price is $5.6 million. The present value of the minimum lease payments for both the lessor and lessee is $5.2 million. The first payment was made at the inception of the lease. Collectibility of the remaining lease payments is reasonably assured, and Lukawitz has no material cost uncertainties. How should this lease be classified (a) by Lukawitz Industries (the lessor) and (b) by Seminole Corporation (the lessee)? Why?

**Q 15–7** Can the present value of minimum lease payments differ between the lessor and lessee? If so, how?

**Q 15–8** Compare the way a bargain purchase option and a residual value are treated by the lessee when determining minimum lease payments.

**Q 15–9** What are executory costs? How are they accounted for by the lessee in a capital lease when paid by the lessee? When paid by the lessor? Explain.

**Q 15–10** The discount rate influences virtually every amount reported in connection with a lease by both the lessor and the lessee. What is the lessor's discount rate when determining the present value of minimum lease payments? What is the lessee's discount rate?

**Q 15–11** A lease might specify that rental payments may be increased (or decreased) at some future time during the lease term depending on whether or not some specified event occurs such as revenues or profits exceeding some designated level. Under what circumstances are contingent rentals included or excluded from minimum lease payments? If excluded, how are they recognized in income determination?

**Q 15–12** The lessor's initial direct costs often are substantial. What are initial direct costs?

**Q 15–13** When are initial direct costs recognized in an operating lease? In a direct financing lease? In a sales-type lease? Why?

**Q 15–14** In a sale-leaseback transaction the owner of an asset sells it and immediately leases it back from the new owner. This dual transaction should be viewed as a single borrowing transaction. Why?

**Q 15–15** Explain how the general classification criteria are applied to leases that involve land.

**Q 15–16** What are the guidelines for determining when a material amount of land is involved in a lease?

**Q 15–17** How does a leveraged lease differ from a nonleveraged lease?

## BRIEF EXERCISES

**BE 15–1**
Operating lease
● LO4

At the beginning of its fiscal year, Lakeside, Inc. leased office space to LTT Corporation under a seven-year operating lease agreement. The contract calls for quarterly rent payments of $25,000 each. The office building was acquired by Lakeside at a cost of $2 million and was expected to have a useful life of 25 years with no residual value. What will be the effect of the lease on LTT's earnings for the first year (ignore taxes)?

**BE 15–2**
Operating lease

● LO4

In the situation described in the previous brief exercise, what will be the effect of the lease on Lakeside's earnings for the first year (ignore taxes)?

**BE 15–3**
Operating lease; advance payment

● LO4

Ward Products leased office space under a 10-year operating lease agreement. The lease specified 120 monthly rent payments of $5,000 each, beginning at the inception of the lease. In addition to the first rent payment, Ward also paid a $100,000 advance payment at the lease's inception. What will be the effect of the lease on Ward's earnings for the first year (ignore taxes)?

**BE 15–4**
Lease classification

● LO3 LO5

Corinth Co. leased equipment to Athens Corporation for an eight-year period, at which time possession of the leased asset will revert back to Corinth. The equipment cost Corinth $16 million and has an expected useful life of 12 years. Its normal sales price is $22.4 million. The present value of the minimum lease payments for both the lessor and lessee is $20.4 million. The first payment was made at the inception of the lease. Collectibility of the remaining lease payments is reasonably assured, and Corinth has no material cost uncertainties. How should Athens classify this lease? Why?

**BE 15–5**
Lease classification

● LO3 LO5

In the situation described in BE 15-4, how should Corinth classify this lease? Why?

**BE 15–6**
Net investment in leases

● LO5

The 2004 annual report of the **Sonic Corporation** reported minimum lease payments receivable of $10,313,000 and a net investment in direct financing leases of $7,161,000. What accounts for the difference between these two amounts? Explain.

**BE 15–7**
Nonoperating lease; calculate interest

● LO5

A lease agreement calls for quarterly lease payments of $5,376 over a 10-year lease term, with the first payment at July 1, the lease's inception. The interest rate is 8%. Both the fair value and the cost of the asset to the lessor are $150,000. What would be the amount of interest expense the lessee would record in conjunction with the second quarterly payment at October 1? What would be the amount of interest revenue the lessor would record in conjunction with the second quarterly payment at October 1?

**BE 15–8**
Capital lease; lessee; balance sheet effects

● LO5

A lease agreement that qualifies as a capital lease calls for annual lease payments of $26,269 over a six-year lease term, with the first payment at January 1, the lease's inception. The interest rate is 5%. If lessee's fiscal year is the calendar year, what would be the amount of the lease liability that the lessee would report in its balance sheet at the end of the first year? What would be the interest payable?

**BE 15–9**
Capital lease; lessee; income statement effects

● LO5

In the situation described in BE 15–8, what would be the pretax amounts related to the lease that the lessee would report in its income statement for the year ended December 31?

**BE 15–10**
Sales-type lease; lessor; income statement effects

● LO6

In the situation described in BE 15–8, assume the asset being leased cost the lessor $125,000 to produce. Determine the price at which the lessor is "selling" the asset (present value of the lease payments). What would be the pretax amounts related to the lease that the lessor would report in its income statement for the year ended December 31?

**BE 15–11**
Sales-type lease; lessor; calculate lease payments

● LO6

Manning Imports is contemplating an agreement to lease equipment to a customer for five years. Manning normally sells the asset for a cash price of $100,000. Assuming that 8% is a reasonable rate of interest, what must be the amount of quarterly lease payments (beginning at the inception of the lease) in order for Manning to recover its normal selling price as well as be compensated for financing the asset over the lease term?

**BE 15–12**
Guaranteed residual value; direct financing lease

● LO5 through LO7

On January 1, James Industries leased equipment to a customer for a four-year period, at which time possession of the leased asset will revert back to James. The equipment cost James $700,000 and has an expected useful life of six years. Its normal sales price is $700,000. The residual value after four years, guaranteed by the lessee, is $100,000. Lease payments are due on December 31 of each year, beginning with the first payment at the end of the first year. Collectibility of the remaining lease payments is reasonably assured, and there are no material cost uncertainties. The interest rate is 5%. Calculate the amount of the annual lease payments.

**BE 15–13**
Bargain purchase option; lessor; direct financing lease

● LO5 LO6 LO8

Ace Leasing acquires equipment and leases it to customers under long-term direct financing leases. Universal earns interest under these arrangements at a 6% annual rate. Ace leased a machine it purchased for $600,000 under an arrangement that specified annual payments beginning at the inception of the lease for five years. The lessee had the option to purchase the machine at the end of the lease term for $100,000 when it was expected to have a residual value of $160,000. Calculate the amount of the annual lease payments.

# EXERCISES

available with McGraw-Hill's Homework Manager www.mhhe.com/spiceland4e

**An alternative exercise and problem set is available on the text website: www.mhhe.com/spiceland4e**

**E 15–1**
Operating lease

● LO4

On January 1, 2006, Nath-Langstrom Services, Inc., a computer software training firm, leased several computers from ComputerWorld Corporation under a two-year operating lease agreement. The contract calls for four rent payments of $10,000 each, payable semiannually on June 30 and December 31 each year. The computers were acquired by ComputerWorld at a cost of $90,000 and were expected to have a useful life of six years with no residual value.

**Required:**
Prepare the appropriate entries for both (a) the lessee and (b) the lessor from the inception of the lease through the end of 2006. (Use straight-line depreciation.)

**E 15–2**
Operating lease; advance payment; leasehold improvement

● LO4

On January 1, 2006, Winn Heat Transfer leased office space under a three-year operating lease agreement. The arrangement specified three annual rent payments of $80,000 each, beginning January 1, 2006, the inception of the lease, and at each January 1 through 2008. Winn also paid a $96,000 advance payment at the inception of the lease in addition to the first $80,000 rent payment. With permission of the owner, Winn made structural modifications to the building before occupying the space at a cost of $180,000. The useful life of the building and the structural modifications were estimated to be 30 years with no residual value.

**Required:**
Prepare the appropriate entries for Winn Heat Transfer from the inception of the lease through the end of 2006. Winn's fiscal year is the calendar year. Winn uses straight-line depreciation.

**E 15–3**
Multiple choice; CPA exam; operating leases

● LO4

The following questions dealing with various topics in this chapter are adapted from previous CPA examinations. Determine the response that best completes the statements or questions.

1. On January 2, 2005, Ral Co. leased land and building from an unrelated lessor for a 10-year term. The lease has a renewal option for an additional 10 years, but Ral has not reached a decision with regard to the renewal option. In early January 2005, Ral completed the following improvements to the property:

| Description | Estimated Life | Cost |
|---|---|---|
| Sales office | 10 years | $47,000 |
| Warehouse | 25 years | $75,000 |
| Parking lot | 15 years | $18,000 |

   Amortization of leasehold improvements for 2006 should be
   a. $7,000
   b. $8,900
   c. $12,200
   d. $14,000

2. As an inducement to enter a lease, Graf Co., a lessor, granted Zep, Inc., a lessee, 12 months of free rent under a five-year operating lease. The lease was effective on January 1, 2006, and provides for monthly rental payments to begin January 1, 2007. Zep made the first rental payment on December 30, 2006. In its 2006 income statement, Graf should report rental revenue in an amount equal to
   a. Zero.
   b. Cash received during 2006.
   c. One-fourth of the total cash to be received over the life of the lease.
   d. One-fifth of the total cash to be received over the life of the lease.

(Note: Exercises 4, 5, and 6 are three variations of the same basic situation.)

**E 15–4**
Capital lease; lessee

● LO5

Manufacturers Southern leased high-tech electronic equipment from Edison Leasing on January 1, 2006. Edison purchased the equipment from International Machines at a cost of $112,080.

| Related Information: | |
|---|---|
| Lease term | 2 years (8 quarterly periods) |
| Quarterly rental payments | $15,000—beginning of each period |
| Economic life of asset | 2 years |
| Fair value of asset | $112,080 |
| Implicit interest rate | 8% |
| (Also lessee's incremental borrowing rate) | |

**Required:**

Prepare a lease amortization schedule and appropriate entries for Manufacturers Southern from the inception of the lease through January 1, 2007. Depreciation is recorded at the end of each fiscal year (December 31) on a straight-line basis.

**E 15–5**
Direct financing lease; lessor
● LO5

Edison Leasing leased high-tech electronic equipment to Manufacturers Southern on January 1, 2006. Edison purchased the equipment from International Machines at a cost of $112,080.

| Related Information: | |
|---|---|
| Lease term | 2 years (8 quarterly periods) |
| Quarterly rental payments | $15,000—beginning of each period |
| Economic life of asset | 2 years |
| Fair value of asset | $112,080 |
| Implicit interest rate | 8% |
| (Also lessee's incremental borrowing rate) | |

**Required:**

Prepare a lease amortization schedule and appropriate entries for Edison Leasing from the inception of the lease through January 1, 2007. Edison's fiscal year ends December 31.

**E 15–6**
Sales-type lease; lessor
● LO6

Manufacturers Southern leased high-tech electronic equipment from International Machines on January 1, 2006. International Machines manufactured the equipment at a cost of $85,000.

| Related Information: | |
|---|---|
| Lease term | 2 years (8 quarterly periods) |
| Quarterly rental payments | $15,000—beginning of each period |
| Economic life of asset | 2 years |
| Fair value of asset | $112,080 |
| Implicit interest rate | 8% |
| (Also lessee's incremental borrowing rate) | |

**Required:**

1. Show how International Machines determined the $15,000 quarterly rental payments.
2. Prepare appropriate entries for International Machines to record the lease at its inception, January 1, 2006, and the second rental payment on April 1, 2006.

**E 15–7**
Capital lease
● LO5

American Food Services, Inc., leased a packaging machine from Barton and Barton Corporation. Barton and Barton completed construction of the machine on January 1, 2006. The lease agreement for the $4 million (fair market value) machine specified four equal payments at the end of each year. The useful life of the machine was expected to be four years with no residual value. Barton and Barton's implicit interest rate was 10% (also American Food Services' incremental borrowing rate).

**Required:**

1. Prepare the journal entry for American Food Services at the inception of the lease on January 1, 2006.
2. Prepare an amortization schedule for the four-year term of the lease.
3. Prepare the journal entry for the first lease payment on December 31, 2006.
4. Prepare the journal entry for the third lease payment on December 31, 2008.

(Note: You may wish to compare your solution to this exercise with that of Exercise 14–16 which deals with a parallel situation in which the packaging machine was acquired with an installment note.)

(Note: Exercises 8, 9, and 10 are three variations of the same situation.)

**E 15–8**
Capital lease; lessee; balance sheet and income statement effects
● LO5

On June 30, 2006, Georgia-Atlantic, Inc. leased a warehouse facility from IC Leasing Corporation. The lease agreement calls for Georgia-Atlantic to make semiannual lease payments of $562,907 over a three-year lease term, payable each June 30 and December 31, with the first payment at June 30, 2006. Georgia-Atlantic's incremental borrowing rate is 10%, the same rate IC uses to calculate lease payment amounts. Depreciation is recorded on a straight-line basis at the end of each fiscal year. The fair value of the warehouse is $3 million.

**Required:**

1. Determine the present value of the lease payments at June 30, 2006 (to the nearest $000) that Georgia-Atlantic uses to record the leased asset and lease liability.

2. What pretax amounts related to the lease would Georgia-Atlantic report in its balance sheet at December 31, 2006?
3. What pretax amounts related to the lease would Georgia-Atlantic report in its income statement for the year ended December 31, 2006?

**E 15–9**
Direct financing lease; lessor; balance sheet and income statement effects

● LO5

On June 30, 2006, Georgia-Atlantic, Inc. leased a warehouse facility from IC Leasing Corporation. The lease agreement calls for Georgia-Atlantic to make semiannual lease payments of $562,907 over a three-year lease term, payable each June 30 and December 31, with the first payment at June 30, 2006. Georgia-Atlantic's incremental borrowing rate is 10%, the same rate IC used to calculate lease payment amounts. IC purchased the warehouse from Builders, Inc. at a cost of $3 million.

**Required:**
1. What pretax amounts related to the lease would IC report in its balance sheet at December 31, 2006?
2. What pretax amounts related to the lease would IC report in its income statement for the year ended December 31, 2006?

**E 15–10**
Sales-type lease; lessor; balance sheet and income statement effects

● LO6

On June 30, 2006, Georgia-Atlantic, Inc. leased a warehouse facility from Builders, Inc. The lease agreement calls for Georgia-Atlantic to make semiannual lease payments of $562,907 over a three-year lease term, payable each June 30 and December 31, with the first payment at June 30, 2006. Georgia-Atlantic's incremental borrowing rate is 10%, the same rate Builders used to calculate lease payment amounts. Builders constructed the warehouse at a cost of $2.5 million.

**Required:**
1. Determine the price at which Builders is "selling" the warehouse (present value of the lease payments) at June 30, 2006 (to the nearest $000).
2. What pretax amounts related to the lease would Builders report in its balance sheet at December 31, 2006?
3. What pretax amounts related to the lease would Builders report in its income statement for the year ended December 31, 2006?

**E 15–11**
Lessor calculation of annual rental payments; lessee calculation of asset and liability

● LO5 LO6

Each of the three independent situations below describes a nonoperating lease in which annual rental payments are payable at the beginning of each year. The lessee is aware of the lessor's implicit rate of return.

| | Situation | | |
|---|---|---|---|
| | 1 | 2 | 3 |
| Lease term (years) | 10 | 20 | 4 |
| Lessor's rate of return | 11% | 9% | 12% |
| Lessee's incremental borrowing rate | 12% | 10% | 11% |
| Fair market value of leased asset | $600,000 | $980,000 | $185,000 |

**Required:**
For each situation, determine:
a. The amount of the annual rental payments as calculated by the lessor.
b. The amount the lessee would record as a leased asset and a lease liability.

**E 15–12**
Lessor calculation of annual rental payments; lessee calculation of asset and liability

● LO5 LO6

(Note: This is a variation of the previous exercise modified to assume rental payments are at the end of each period.)

Each of the three independent situations below describes a nonoperating lease in which annual rental payments are payable at the *end* of each year. The lessee is aware of the lessor's implicit rate of return.

| | Situation | | |
|---|---|---|---|
| | 1 | 2 | 3 |
| Lease term (years) | 10 | 20 | 4 |
| Lessor's rate of return | 11% | 9% | 12% |
| Lessee's incremental borrowing rate | 12% | 10% | 11% |
| Fair market value of leased asset | $600,000 | $980,000 | $185,000 |

**Required:**
For each situation, determine:
a. The amount of the annual rental payments as calculated by the lessor.
b. The amount the lessee would record as a leased asset and a lease liability.

**E 15–13**
Calculation of annual lease payments; residual value

● LO5 through LO7

Each of the four independent situations below describes a nonoperating lease in which annual rental payments are payable at the beginning of each year. Determine the annual rental payments for each:

| | Situation | | | |
|---|---|---|---|---|
| | 1 | 2 | 3 | 4 |
| Lease term (years) | 4 | 7 | 5 | 8 |
| Lessor's rate of return | 10% | 11% | 9% | 12% |
| Fair market value of leased asset | $50,000 | $350,000 | $75,000 | $465,000 |
| Lessor's cost of leased asset | $50,000 | $350,000 | $45,000 | $465,000 |
| Residual value: | | | | |
| Guaranteed by lessee | 0 | $ 50,000 | 0 | $ 30,000 |
| Unguaranteed | 0 | 0 | $ 7,000 | $ 15,000 |

**E 15–14**
Lease concepts; direct financing leases; guaranteed and unguaranteed residual value

● LO5 through LO7

Each of the four independent situations below describes a direct financing lease in which annual rental payments of $100,000 are payable at the beginning of each year. Each is a capital lease for the lessee. Determine the following amounts at the inception of the lease:

A. The lessor's:
   1. Minimum lease payments
   2. Gross investment in the lease
   3. Net investment in the lease
   4. Unearned interest revenue

B. The lessee's:
   5. Minimum lease payments
   6. Leased asset
   7. Lease liability

| | Situation | | | |
|---|---|---|---|---|
| | 1 | 2 | 3 | 4 |
| Lease term (years) | 7 | 7 | 8 | 8 |
| Lessor's and lessee's discount rate | 9% | 11% | 10% | 12% |
| Residual value: | | | | |
| Guaranteed by lessee | 0 | $50,000 | 0 | $40,000 |
| Unguaranteed | 0 | 0 | $50,000 | $60,000 |

**E 15–15**
Calculation of annual lease payments; BPO

● LO5 through LO8

For each of the three independent situations below determine the amount of the annual rental payments. Each describes a nonoperating lease in which annual rental payments are payable at the beginning of each year. Each lease agreement contains an option that permits the lessee to acquire the leased asset at an option price sufficiently lower than the expected market value that the exercise of the option appears reasonably certain.

| | Situation | | |
|---|---|---|---|
| | 1 | 2 | 3 |
| Lease term (years) | 5 | 12 | 4 |
| Lessor's rate of return | 12% | 11% | 9% |
| Fair market value of leased asset | $60,000 | $420,000 | $185,000 |
| Lessor's cost of leased asset | $50,000 | $420,000 | $145,000 |
| Bargain purchase option: | | | |
| Option price | $10,000 | $ 50,000 | $ 22,000 |
| Exercisable at end of year: | 5 | 5 | 3 |

**E 15–16**
Capital lease; bargain purchase option; lessee

● LO5 through LO8

Federated Fabrications leased a tooling machine on December 31, 2005, for a three-year period. The lease agreement specified annual payments of $36,000 beginning with the first payment at the inception of the lease, and each December 31 through 2007. The company had the option to purchase the machine on December 30, 2008, for $45,000 when its fair value was expected to be $60,000. The machine's estimated useful life was six years with no salvage value. Federated depreciates assets by the straight-line method. The company was aware that the lessor's implicit rate of return was 12%, which was less than Federated's incremental borrowing rate.

**Required:**

1. Calculate the amount Federated should record as a leased asset and lease liability for this capital lease.
2. Prepare an amortization schedule that describes the pattern of interest expense for Federated over the lease term.
3. Prepare the appropriate entries for Federated from the inception of the lease through the end of the lease term.

**E 15–17**
Bargain purchase option; lessor; direct financing lease

● LO5 through LO8

Universal Leasing leases electronic equipment to a variety of businesses. The company's primary service is providing alternate financing by acquiring equipment and leasing it to customers under long-term direct financing leases. Universal earns interest under these arrangements at a 10% annual rate.

The company leased an electronic typesetting machine purchased for $30,900 to a local publisher, Desktop Inc., on December 31, 2005. The lease contract specified annual payments of $8,000 beginning December 31, 2005, the inception of the lease, and each December 31 through 2007 (three-year lease term). The publisher had the option to purchase the machine on December 30, 2008, for $12,000 when it was expected to have a residual value of $16,000.

**Required:**

1. Show how Universal calculated the $8,000 annual rental payments for this direct financing lease.
2. Prepare an amortization schedule that describes the pattern of interest revenue for Universal Leasing over the lease term.
3. Prepare the appropriate entries for Universal Leasing from the inception of the lease through the end of the lease term.

**E 15–18**
Executory costs; lessor and lessee

● LO5 through LO7 LO9

On December 31, 2005, NRC Credit Corporation leased equipment to Brand Services under a direct financing lease designed to earn NRC a 12% rate of return for providing long-term financing. The lease agreement specified:

a. 10 annual payments of $55,000 (including executory costs) beginning December 31, 2005, the inception of the lease.
b. The estimated useful life of the leased equipment is 10 years with no residual value. Its cost to NRC was $316,412.
c. The lease qualifies as a capital lease to Brand.
d. A 10-year service agreement with Quality Maintenance Company was negotiated to provide maintenance of the equipment as required. Payments of $5,000 per year are specified, beginning December 31, 2005. NRC was to pay this executory cost as incurred, but lease payments reflect this expenditure.
e. A partial amortization schedule, appropriate for both the lessee and lessor, follows:

| Dec. 31 | Payments | Effective Interest | Decrease in Balance | Outstanding Balance |
|---|---|---|---|---|
| | | (12% × Outstanding balance) | | |
| | | | | 316,412 |
| 2005 | 50,000 | | 50,000 | 266,412 |
| 2006 | 50,000 | .12 (266,412) = 31,969 | 18,031 | 248,381 |
| 2007 | 50,000 | .12 (248,381) = 29,806 | 20,194 | 228,187 |

**Required:**

Prepare the appropriate entries for both the lessee and lessor to record:

1. The lease at its inception.
2. The second lease payment and depreciation (straight line) on December 31, 2006.

**E 15–19**
Executory costs plus management fee; lessor and lessee

● LO5 through LO7 LO9

Refer to the lease agreement described in the previous exercise. Assume the contract specified that NRC (the lessor) was to pay, not only the $5,000 maintenance fees, but also insurance of $700 per year, and was to receive a $250 management fee for facilitating service and paying executory costs. The lessee's rental payments were increased to include an amount sufficient to reimburse executory costs plus NRC's fee.

**Required:**

Prepare the appropriate entries for both the lessee and lessor to record the **second** lease payment, executory costs, and depreciation (straight line) on December 31, 2006.

**E 15–20**
Multiple choice; CPA exam; nonoperating leases

● LO5 LO6 LO9

The following questions dealing with various topics in this chapter are adapted from previous CPA examinations. Determine the response that best completes the statements or questions.

1. On December 31, 2005, Roe Co. leased a machine from Colt for a five-year period. Equal annual payments under the lease are $105,000 (including $5,000 annual executory costs) and are due on December 31 of each year. The first payment was made on December 31, 2005, and the second payment was made on December 31, 2006. The five lease payments are discounted at 10% over the lease term. The present value of minimum lease payments at the inception of the lease and before the first annual payment was $417,000. The lease is appropriately accounted for as a capital lease by Roe. In its December 31, 2006, balance sheet, Roe should report a lease liability of
   a. $317,000
   b. $315,000
   c. $285,300
   d. $248,700
2. Winn Co. manufactures equipment that is sold or leased. On December 31, 2006, Winn leased equipment to Bart for a five-year period ending December 31, 2011, at which date ownership of the leased asset will be transferred to Bart. Equal payments under the lease are $22,000 (including $2,000 executory costs) and are due on December 31 of each year. The first payment was made on December 31, 2006. Collectibility of the remaining lease payments is reasonably assured, and Winn has no material cost uncertainties. The normal sales price of the equipment is $77,000, and cost is $60,000. For the year ended December 31, 2006, what amount of income should Winn realize from the lease transaction?

a. $17,000
b. $22,000
c. $23,000
d. $33,000

3. At the inception of a capital lease, the guaranteed residual value should be
   a. Included as part of minimum lease payments at present value.
   b. Included as part of minimum lease payments at future value.
   c. Included as part of minimum lease payments only to the extent that guaranteed residual value is expected to exceed estimated residual value.
   d. Excluded from minimum lease payments.

**E 15–21**
Lessor's initial direct costs; operating, direct financing and sales-type leases

● LO4 through LO6 LO9

Terms of a lease agreement and related facts were:

a. Leased asset had a retail cash selling price of $100,000. Its useful life was six years with no residual value (straight-line depreciation).
b. Annual rental payments at the beginning of each year were $20,873, beginning January 1.
c. Lessor's implicit rate when calculating annual rental payments was 10%.
d. Costs of negotiating and consummating the completed lease transaction incurred by the lessor were $2,062.
e. Collectibility of the rent payments by the lessor was reasonably predictable and there were no costs to the lessor that were yet to be incurred.

**Required:**

Prepare the appropriate entries for the lessor to record the lease, the initial payment at its inception, and at the December 31 fiscal year-end under each of the following three independent assumptions:

1. The lease term is three years and the lessor paid $100,000 to acquire the asset (operating lease).
2. The lease term is six years and the lessor paid $100,000 to acquire the asset (direct financing lease). Also assume that adjusting the net investment by initial direct costs reduces the effective rate of interest to 9%.
3. The lease term is six years and the lessor paid $85,000 to acquire the asset (sales-type lease).

**E 15–22**
Lessor's initial direct costs; operating lease

● LO4 LO9

The following relate to an operating lease agreement:

a. The lease term is 3 years, beginning January 1, 2006.
b. The leased asset cost the lessor $800,000 and had a useful life of eight years with no residual value. The lessor uses straight-line depreciation for its depreciable assets.
c. Annual rental payments at the beginning of each year were $137,000.
d. Costs of negotiating and consummating the completed lease transaction incurred by the lessor were $2,400.

**Required:**

Prepare the appropriate entries for the lessor from the inception of the lease through the end of the lease term.

**E 15–23**
Lessor's initial direct costs; direct financing lease

● LO5 LO9

Terms of a lease agreement and related facts were:

a. Costs of negotiating and consummating the completed lease transaction incurred by the lessor were $4,242.
b. The retail cash selling price of the leased asset was $500,000. Its useful life was three years with no residual value.
c. Collectibility of the rent payments by the lessor was reasonably predictable and there were no costs to the lessor that were yet to be incurred.
d. The lease term is three years and the lessor paid $500,000 to acquire the asset (direct financing lease).
e. Annual rental payments at the beginning of each year were $184,330.
f. Lessor's implicit rate when calculating annual rental payments was 11%.

**Required:**

1. Prepare the appropriate entries for the lessor to record the lease and related payments at its inception, January 1, 2006.
2. Calculate the effective rate of interest revenue after adjusting the net investment by initial direct costs.
3. Record any entry(s) necessary at December 31, 2006, the fiscal year-end.

**E 15–24**
Lessor's initial direct costs; sales-type lease

● LO6 LO9

The lease agreement and related facts indicate the following:

a. Leased equipment had a retail cash selling price of $300,000. Its useful life was five years with no residual value.
b. Collectibility of the rent payments by the lessor was reasonably predictable and there were no costs to the lessor that were yet to be incurred.
c. The lease term is five years and the lessor paid $265,000 to acquire the equipment (sales-type lease).
d. Lessor's implicit rate when calculating annual rental payments was 8%.
e. Annual rental payments beginning January 1, 2006, the inception of the lease, were $69,571.
f. Costs of negotiating and consummating the completed lease transaction incurred by the lessor were $7,500.

**Required:**

Prepare the appropriate entries for the lessor to record:

1. The lease and the initial payment at its inception.
2. Any entry(s) necessary at December 31, 2006, the fiscal year-end.

**E 15–25**
Sale-leaseback; capital lease

● LO10

To raise operating funds, Signal Aviation sold an airplane on January 1, 2006, to a finance company for $770,000. Signal immediately leased the plane back for a 13-year period, at which time ownership of the airplane will transfer to Signal. The airplane has a fair value of $800,000. Its cost and its carrying value were $620,000. Its useful life is estimated to be 15 years. The lease requires Signal to make payments of $102,771 to the finance company each January 1. Signal depreciates assets on a straight-line basis. The lease has an implicit rate of 11%.

**Required:**

Prepare the appropriate entries for Signal on:

1. January 1, 2006, to record the sale-leaseback.
2. December 31, 2006, to record necessary adjustments.

**E 15–26**
Sale-leaseback; operating lease

● LO10

To raise operating funds, National Distribution Center sold its office building to an insurance company on January 1, 2006, for $800,000 and immediately leased the building back. The operating lease is for the final 12 years of the building's estimated 50-year useful life. The building has a fair value of $800,000 and a carrying amount of $650,000 (its original cost was $1 million). The rental payments of $100,000 are payable to the insurance company each December 31. The lease has an implicit rate of 9%.

**Required:**

Prepare the appropriate entries for National Distribution Center on:

1. January 1, 2006, to record the sale-leaseback.
2. December 31, 2006, to record necessary adjustments.

**E 15–27**
Multiple choice; CPA exam; other lease accounting issues

● LO4 LO10

The following questions dealing with various topics in this chapter are adapted from previous CPA examinations. Determine the response that best completes the statements or questions.

1. Able sold its headquarters building at a gain and simultaneously leased back the building. The lease was reported as a capital lease. At the time of sale, the gain should be reported as
   a. Operating income.
   b. An extraordinary item, net of income tax.
   c. A separate component of shareholders' equity.
   d. An asset valuation allowance.
2. On January 1, 2006, Wren Co. leased a building to Brill under an operating lease for 10 years at $50,000 per year, payable the first day of each lease year. Wren paid $15,000 to a real estate broker as a finder's fee. The building is depreciated $12,000 per year. For 2006, Wren incurred insurance and property tax expense totaling $9,000. Wren's net rental income for 2006 should be
   a. $27,500
   b. $29,000
   c. $35,000
   d. $36,500

**E 15–28**
Concepts; terminology

● LO3 through LO9

Listed below are several terms and phrases associated with leases. Pair each item from List A (by letter) with the item from List B that is most appropriately associated with it.

| List A | List B |
|---|---|
| ____ 1. Effective rate times balance. | a. PV of BPO price. |
| ____ 2. Realization principle. | b. Lessor's net investment. |
| ____ 3. Minimum lease payments plus unguaranteed residual value. | c. Lessor's gross investment. |
| ____ 4. Periodic rent payments plus lessee-guaranteed residual value. | d. Operating lease. |
| ____ 5. PV of minimum lease payments plus PV of unguaranteed residual value. | e. Depreciable assets. |
| ____ 6. Initial direct costs. | f. Loss to lessee. |
| ____ 7. Rent revenue. | g. Executory costs. |
| ____ 8. Bargain purchase option. | h. Depreciation longer than lease term. |
| ____ 9. Leasehold improvements. | i. Disclosure only. |
| ____ 10. Cash to satisfy residual value guarantee. | j. Interest expense. |
| ____ 11. Capital lease expense. | k. Additional lessor conditions. |
| ____ 12. Deducted in lessor's computation of rental payments. | l. Lessee's minimum lease payments. |
| ____ 13. Title transfers to lessee. | m. Purchase price less than fair market value. |
| ____ 14. Contingent rentals. | n. Sales-type lease selling expense. |
| ____ 15. Rent payments plus lessee-guaranteed and third-party-guaranteed residual value. | o. Lessor's minimum lease payments. |

**E 15–29**
Real estate lease; land and building
● LO10

On January 1, 2006, Cook Textiles leased a building with two acres of land from Peck Development. The lease is for 10 years at which time Cook has an option to purchase the property for $100,000. The building has an estimated life of 20 years with a residual value of $150,000. The lease calls for Cook to assume all costs of ownership and to make annual payments of $200,000 due at the beginning of each year. On January 1, 2006, the estimated value of the land was $400,000. Cook uses the straight-line method of depreciation and pays 10% interest on borrowed money. Peck's implicit rate is unknown.

**Required:**
Prepare Cook Company's journal entries related to the lease in 2006.

**E 15–30**
Multiple choice; CMA exam; leases
● LO7 LO9 LO10

The following questions dealing with leases are adapted from questions that previously appeared on Certified Management Accountant (CMA) examinations. The CMA designation sponsored by the Institute of Management Accountants (www.imanet.org) provides members with an objective measure of knowledge and competence in the field of management accounting. Determine the response that best completes the statements or questions.

1. For a direct-financing lease, the gross investment (lease payments receivable) recorded by the lessor is equal to the
   a. Present value of the minimum lease payments minus the unguaranteed residual value accruing to the lessor at the end of the lease term.
   b. Lower of 90% of the present value of the minimum lease payments or the fair value of the leased asset.
   c. Difference between the fair value of the leased asset and the unearned interest revenue.
   d. Minimum lease payments plus the unguaranteed residual value accruing to the lessor at the end of the lease term.
2. Initial direct costs incurred by the lessor under a sales-type lease should be
   a. Deferred and allocated over the economic life of the leased property.
   b. Expensed in the period incurred.
   c. Deferred and allocated over the term of the lease in proportion to the recognition of rental income.
   d. Added to the gross investment in the lease and amortized over the term of the lease as a yield adjustment.
3. Howell Corporation, a publicly traded corporation, is the lessee in a leasing agreement with Brandon Inc. to lease land and a building. If the lease contains a bargain purchase option, Howell should record the land and the building as a(n)
   a. Operating lease and capital lease, respectively.
   b. Capital lease and operating lease, respectively.
   c. Capital lease but recorded as a single unit.
   d. Capital lease but separately classified.

# PROBLEMS

available with McGraw-Hill's Homework Manager www.mhhe.com/spiceland4e

**An alternate exercise and problem set is available on the text website: www.mhhe.com/spiceland4e**

**P 15–1**
Operating lease; scheduled rent increases
● LO4

On January 1, 2006, Sweetwater Furniture Company leased office space under a 21-year operating lease agreement. The contract calls for annual rent payments on December 31 of each year. The payments are $10,000 the first year and increase by $500 per year. Benefits expected from using the office space are expected to remain constant over the lease term.

**Required:**
Record Sweetwater's rent payment at December 31, 2010 (the fifth rent payment) and December 31, 2020 (the 15th rent payment).

**P 15–2**
Lease amortization schedule
● LO5 LO7

On January 1, 2006, National Insulation Corporation (NIC) leased office space under a capital lease. Rental payments are made annually. Title does not transfer to the lessee and there is no bargain purchase option. Portions of the lessee's lease amortization schedule appear below:

| Jan. 1 | Payments | Effective Interest | Decrease in Balance | Outstanding Balance |
|---|---|---|---|---|
| 2006 | | | | 192,501 |
| 2006 | 20,000 | | 20,000 | 172,501 |
| 2007 | 20,000 | 17,250 | 2,750 | 169,751 |
| 2008 | 20,000 | 16,975 | 3,025 | 166,726 |
| 2009 | 20,000 | 16,673 | 3,327 | 163,399 |
| 2010 | 20,000 | 16,340 | 3,660 | 159,739 |
| 2011 | 20,000 | 15,974 | 4,026 | 155,713 |

| Jan. 1 | Payments | Effective Interest | Decrease in Balance | Outstanding Balance |
|---|---|---|---|---|
| — | — | — | — | — |
| — | — | — | — | — |
| — | — | — | — | — |
| 2023 | 20,000 | 7,364 | 12,636 | 61,006 |
| 2024 | 20,000 | 6,101 | 13,899 | 47,107 |
| 2025 | 20,000 | 4,711 | 15,289 | 31,818 |
| 2026 | 35,000 | 3,182 | 31,818 | 0 |

**Required:**
1. What is NIC's lease liability at the inception of the lease (after the first payment)?
2. What amount would NIC record as a leased asset?
3. What is the lease term in years?
4. What is the asset's residual value expected at the end of the lease term?
5. How much of the residual value is guaranteed by the lessee?
6. What is the effective annual interest rate?
7. What is the total amount of minimum lease payments?
8. What is the total effective interest expense recorded over the term of the lease?

**P 15–3**
Direct financing and sales-type lease; lessee and lessor

● LO3 LO5 LO6

Rand Medical manufactures lithotripters. Lithotripsy uses shock waves instead of surgery to eliminate kidney stones. Physicians' Leasing purchased a lithotripter from Rand for $2,000,000 and leased it to Mid-South Urologists Group, Inc., on January 1, 2006.

| **Lease Description:** | |
|---|---|
| Quarterly rental payments | $130,516—beginning of each period |
| Lease term | 5 years (20 quarters) |
| No residual value; no BPO | |
| Economic life of lithotripter | 5 years |
| Implicit interest rate and lessee's incremental borrowing rate | 12% |
| Fair value of asset | $2,000,000 |

Collectibility of the rental payments is reasonably assured, and there are no lessor costs yet to be incurred.

**Required:**
1. How should this lease be classified by Mid-South Urologists Group and by Physicians' Leasing?
2. Prepare appropriate entries for both Mid-South Urologists Group and Physicians' Leasing from the inception of the lease through the second rental payment on April 1, 2006. Depreciation is recorded at the end of each fiscal year (December 31).
3. Assume Mid-South Urologists Group leased the lithotripter directly from the manufacturer, Rand Medical, which produced the machine at a cost of $1.7 million. Prepare appropriate entries for Rand Medical from the inception of the lease through the second rental payment on April 1, 2006.

**P 15–4**
Capital lease

● LO5

At the beginning of 2006, VHF Industries acquired a machine with a fair market value of $6,074,700 by signing a four-year lease. Rentals are payable in four annual payments of $2 million at the end of each year.

**Required:**
1. What is the effective rate of interest implicit in the agreement?
2. Prepare the lessee's journal entry at the inception of the lease.
3. Prepare the journal entry to record the first lease payment at December 31, 2006.
4. Prepare the journal entry to record the second lease payment at December 31, 2007.
5. Suppose the market value of the machine and the lessor's implicit rate were unknown at the time of the lease, but that the lessee's incremental borrowing rate of interest for notes of similar risk was 11%. Prepare the lessee's entry at the inception of the lease.

(Note: You may wish to compare your solution to this problem with that of Problem 14–11, which deals with a parallel situation in which the machine was acquired with an installment note.)
(Note: Problems 5, 6, and 7 are three variations of the same basic situation.)

**P 15–5**
Capital lease; lessee; financial statement effects

● LO5

Werner Chemical, Inc. leased a protein analyzer on September 30, 2006. The five-year lease agreement calls for Werner to make quarterly lease payments of $391,548, payable each September 30, December 31, March 31, June 30, with the first payment at September 30, 2006. Werner's incremental borrowing rate is 12%. Depreciation is recorded on a straight-line basis at the end of each fiscal year. The useful life of the equipment is five years.

**Required:**
1. Determine the present value of the lease payments at September 30, 2006 (to the nearest $000).
2. What pretax amounts related to the lease would Werner report in its balance sheet at December 31, 2006?

3. What pretax amounts related to the lease would Werner report in its income statement for the year ended December 31, 2006?
4. What pretax amounts related to the lease would Werner report in its statement of cash flows for the year ended December 31, 2006?

**P 15–6**
Direct financing lease; lessor; financial statement effects

● LO5

Abbott Equipment leased a protein analyzer to Werner Chemical, Inc. on September 30, 2006. Abbott purchased the machine from NutraLabs, Inc. at a cost of $6 million. The five-year lease agreement calls for Werner to make quarterly lease payments of $391,548, payable each September 30, December 31, March 31, June 30, with the first payment at September 30, 2006. Abbot's implicit interest rate is 12%.

**Required:**
1. What pretax amounts related to the lease would Abbott report in its balance sheet at December 31, 2006?
2. What pretax amounts related to the lease would Abbott report in its income statement for the year ended December 31, 2006?
3. What pretax amounts related to the lease would Abbott report in its statement of cash flows for the year ended December 31, 2006?

**P 15–7**
Sales-type lease; lessor; financial statement effects

● LO6

NutraLabs, Inc. leased a protein analyzer to Werner Chemical, Inc. on September 30, 2006. NutraLabs manufactured the machine at a cost of $5 million. The five-year lease agreement calls for Werner to make quarterly lease payments of $391,548, payable each September 30, December 31, March 31, June 30, with the first payment at September 30, 2006. NutraLabs' implicit interest rate is 12%.

**Required:**
1. Determine the price at which NutraLabs is "selling" the equipment (present value of the lease payments) at September 30, 2006 (to the nearest $000).
2. What pretax amounts related to the lease would NutraLabs report in its balance sheet at December 31, 2006?
3. What pretax amounts related to the lease would NutraLabs report in its income statement for the year ended December 31, 2006?
4. What pretax amounts related to the lease would NutraLabs report in its statement of cash flows for the year ended December 31, 2006?

(Note: Problems 8, 9, and 10 are three variations of the same basic situation.)

**P 15–8**
Guaranteed residual value; direct financing lease

● LO3 LO5 LO7

eXcel

On December 31, 2006, Rhone-Metro Industries leased equipment to Western Soya Co. for a four-year period ending December 31, 2010, at which time possession of the leased asset will revert back to Rhone-Metro. The equipment cost Rhone-Metro $365,760 and has an expected useful life of six years. Its normal sales price is $365,760. The lessee-guaranteed residual value at December 31, 2010, is $25,000. Equal payments under the lease are $100,000 and are due on December 31 of each year. The first payment was made on December 31, 2006. Collectibility of the remaining lease payments is reasonably assured, and Rhone-Metro has no material cost uncertainties. Western Soya's incremental borrowing rate is 12%. Western Soya knows the interest rate implicit in the lease payments is 10%. Both companies use straight-line depreciation.

**Required:**
1. Show how Rhone-Metro calculated the $100,000 annual rental payments.
2. How should this lease be classified (a) by Western Soya Co. (the lessee) and (b) by Rhone-Metro Industries (the lessor)? Why?
3. Prepare the appropriate entries for both Western Soya Co. and Rhone-Metro on December 31, 2006.
4. Prepare an amortization schedule(s) describing the pattern of interest over the lease term for the lessee and the lessor.
5. Prepare all appropriate entries for both Western Soya and Rhone-Metro on December 31, 2007 (the second rent payment and depreciation).
6. Prepare the appropriate entries for both Western Soya and Rhone-Metro on December 31, 2010 assuming the equipment is returned to Rhone-Metro and the actual residual value on that date is $1,500.

**P 15–9**
Unguaranteed residual value; executory costs; sales-type lease

● LO6 LO7 LO9

eXcel

Rhone-Metro Industries manufactures equipment that is sold or leased. On December 31, 2006, Rhone-Metro leased equipment to Western Soya Co. for a four-year period ending December 31, 2010, at which time possession of the leased asset will revert back to Rhone-Metro. The equipment cost $300,000 to manufacture and has an expected useful life of six years. Its normal sales price is $365,760. The expected residual value of $25,000 at December 31, 2010, is not guaranteed. Equal payments under the lease are $104,000 (including $4,000 executory costs) and are due on December 31 of each year. The first payment was made on December 31, 2006. Collectibility of the remaining lease payments is reasonably assured, and Rhone-Metro has no material cost uncertainties. Western Soya's incremental borrowing rate is 12%. Western Soya knows the interest rate implicit in the lease payments is 10%. Both companies use straight-line depreciation.

**Required:**

1. Show how Rhone-Metro calculated the $104,000 annual rental payments.
2. How should this lease be classified (a) by Western Soya Co. (the lessee) and (b) by Rhone-Metro Industries (the lessor)? Why?
3. Prepare the appropriate entries for both Western Soya Co. and Rhone-Metro on December 31, 2006.
4. Prepare an amortization schedule(s) describing the pattern of interest over the lease term for the lessee and the lessor.
5. Prepare the appropriate entries for both Western Soya and Rhone-Metro on December 31, 2007 (the second rent payment and depreciation).
6. Prepare the appropriate entries for both Western Soya and Rhone-Metro on December 31, 2010, assuming the equipment is returned to Rhone-Metro and the actual residual value on that date is $1,500.

**P 15–10**
Bargain purchase option exercisable before lease term ends; executory costs; sales-type lease

● LO3 LO6 LO8 LO9

Rhone-Metro Industries manufactures equipment that is sold or leased. On December 31, 2006, Rhone-Metro leased equipment to Western Soya Co. for a noncancelable stated lease term of four years ending December 31, 2010, at which time possession of the leased asset will revert back to Rhone-Metro. The equipment cost $300,000 to manufacture and has an expected useful life of six years. Its normal sales price is $365,760. The expected residual value of $25,000 at December 31, 2010, is not guaranteed. Western Soya Co. can exercise a bargain purchase option on December 30, 2009, at an option price of $10,000. Equal payments under the lease are $134,960 (including $4,000 annual executory costs) and are due on December 31 of each year. The first payment was made on December 31, 2006. Collectibility of the remaining lease payments is reasonably assured, and Rhone-Metro has no material cost uncertainties. Western Soya's incremental borrowing rate is 12%. Western Soya knows the interest rate implicit in the lease payments is 10%. Both companies use straight-line depreciation.

Hint: A lease term ends for accounting purposes when an option becomes exercisable if it's expected to be exercised (i.e., a BPO).

**Required:**

1. Show how Rhone-Metro calculated the $134,960 annual rental payments.
2. How should this lease be classified (a) by Western Soya Co. (the lessee) and (b) by Rhone-Metro Industries (the lessor)? Why?
3. Prepare the appropriate entries for both Western Soya Co. and Rhone-Metro on December 31, 2006.
4. Prepare an amortization schedule(s) describing the pattern of interest over the lease term for the lessee and the lessor.
5. Prepare the appropriate entries for both Western Soya and Rhone-Metro on December 31, 2007 (the second rent payment and depreciation).
6. Prepare the appropriate entries for both Western Soya and Rhone-Metro on December 30, 2009, assuming the BPO is exercised on that date.

**P 15–11**
Operating lease to lessee—nonoperating lease to lessor

● LO3 LO4 LO5 LO7

Allied Industries manufactures high performance conveyers that often are leased to industrial customers. On December 31, 2006, Allied leased a conveyer to Poole Carrier Corporation for a three-year period ending December 31, 2009, at which time possession of the leased asset will revert back to Allied. Equal payments under the lease are $200,000 and are due on December 31 of each year. The first payment was made on December 31, 2006. Collectibility of the remaining lease payments is reasonably assured, and Allied has no material cost uncertainties. The conveyer cost $450,000 to manufacture and has an expected useful life of six years. Its normal sales price is $659,805. The expected residual value of $150,000 at December 31, 2009, is guaranteed by United Assurance Group. Poole Carrier's incremental borrowing rate and the interest rate implicit in the lease payments are 10%.

**Required:**

1. Show how Allied Industries calculated the $200,000 annual rental payments.
2. How should this lease be classified (a) by Allied (the lessor) and (b) by Poole (the lessee)? Why?
3. Prepare the appropriate entries for both Poole and Allied on December 31, 2006.
4. Prepare an amortization schedule(s) describing the pattern of interest over the lease term.
5. Prepare the appropriate entries for both Poole and Allied on December 31, 2007, 2008, and 2009, assuming the conveyer is returned to Allied at the end of the lease and the actual residual value on that date is $105,000.

**P 15–12**
Lease concepts; direct financing leases; guaranteed and unguaranteed residual value

● LO3 LO5 LO7

Each of the four independent situations below describes a direct financing lease in which annual rental payments of $10,000 are payable at the beginning of each year. Each is a capital lease for the lessee. Determine the following amounts at the inception of the lease:

A. The lessor's:
   1. Minimum lease payments
   2. Gross investment in the lease
   3. Net investment in the lease
   4. Unearned interest revenue

B. The lessee's:
 5. Minimum lease payments
 6. Leased asset
 7. Lease liability

| | Situation | | | |
|---|---|---|---|---|
| | 1 | 2 | 3 | 4 |
| Lease term (years) | 4 | 4 | 4 | 4 |
| Asset's useful life (years) | 4 | 5 | 5 | 5 |
| Lessor's implicit rate (known by lessee) | 11% | 11% | 11% | 11% |
| Lessee's incremental borrowing rate | 11% | 12% | 11% | 12% |
| Residual value: | | | | |
| Guaranteed by lessee | 0 | $4,000 | 0 | 0 |
| Guaranteed by third party | 0 | 0 | $4,000 | 0 |
| Unguaranteed | 0 | 0 | 0 | $4,000 |

**P 15–13**
Lease concepts

● LO3 LO5 LO7

Four independent situations are described below. For each, annual rental payments of $100,000 (not including any executory costs paid by lessor) are payable at the beginning of each year. Each is a nonoperating lease for both the lessor and lessee. Determine the following amounts at the inception of the lease:

A. The lessor's:
 1. Minimum lease payments
 2. Gross investment in the lease
 3. Net investment in the lease
 4. Unearned interest revenue
 5. Sales revenue
 6. Cost of goods sold
 7. Dealer's profit

B. The lessee's:
 8. Minimum lease payments
 9. Leased asset
 10. Lease liability

| | Situation | | | |
|---|---|---|---|---|
| | 1 | 2 | 3 | 4 |
| Lease term (years) | 4 | 5 | 6 | 4 |
| Lessor's cost | $369,175 | $433,809 | $500,000 | $400,000 |
| Asset's useful life (years) | 6 | 7 | 7 | 5 |
| Lessor's implicit rate (known by lessee) | 10% | 12% | 9% | 10% |
| Lessee's incremental borrowing rate | 9% | 10% | 11% | 12% |
| Residual value: | | | | |
| Guaranteed by lessee | 0 | $ 53,000 | $ 40,000 | $ 60,000 |
| Guaranteed by third party* | 0 | 0 | 0 | $ 50,000 |
| Unguaranteed | $ 30,000 | 0 | $ 35,000 | $ 40,000 |
| Executory costs paid annually by lessor | $ 1,000 | $ 8,000 | $ 5,000 | $ 10,000 |

*Over and above any amount guaranteed by the lessee (after a deductible equal to any amount guaranteed by the lessee).

**P 15–14**
Executory costs; lessor and lessee

● LO3 LO5 LO9

Branif Leasing leases mechanical equipment to industrial consumers under direct financing leases that earn Branif a 10% rate of return for providing long-term financing. A lease agreement with Branson Construction specified 20 annual payments of $100,000 beginning December 31, 2005, the inception of the lease. The estimated useful life of the leased equipment is 20 years with no residual value. Its cost to Branif was $936,500. The lease qualifies as a capital lease to Branson. Maintenance of the equipment was contracted for through a 20-year service agreement with Midway Service Company requiring 20 annual payments of $3,000 beginning December 31, 2005. Both companies use straight-line depreciation.

**Required:**

Prepare the appropriate entries for both the lessee and lessor to record the second lease payment and depreciation on December 31, 2006, under each of three independent assumptions:

1. The lessee pays executory costs as incurred.
2. The contract specifies that the lessor pays executory costs as incurred. The lessee's rental payments were increased to $103,000 to include an amount sufficient to reimburse these costs.
3. The contract specifies that the lessor pays executory costs as incurred. The lessee's rental payments were increased to $103,300 to include an amount sufficient to reimburse these costs plus a 10% management fee for Branif.

**P 15–15**
Sales-type lease; bargain purchase option exercisable before lease term ends; lessor and lessee

● LO3 LO5 LO6 LO7 LO8

eXcel

Mid-South Auto Leasing leases vehicles to consumers. The attraction to customers is that the company can offer competitive prices due to volume buying and requires an interest rate implicit in the lease that is one percent below alternate methods of financing. On September 30, 2006, the company leased a delivery truck to a local florist, Anything Grows.

The lease agreement specified quarterly payments of $3,000 beginning September 30, 2006, the inception of the lease, and each quarter (December 31, March 31, and June 30) through June 30, 2009 (three-year lease term). The florist had the option to purchase the truck on September 29, 2008, for $6,000 when it was expected to have a residual value of $10,000. The estimated useful life of the truck is four years. Mid-South Auto Leasing's quarterly interest rate for determining payments was 3% (approximately 12% annually). Mid-South paid $25,000 for the truck. Both companies use straight-line depreciation. Anything Grows' incremental interest rate is 12%.

Hint: A lease term ends for accounting purposes when an option becomes exercisable if it's expected to be exercised (i.e., a BPO).

**Required:**

1. Calculate the amount of dealer's profit that Mid-South would recognize in this sales-type lease. (Be careful to note that, although payments occur on the last calendar day of each quarter, since the first payment was at the inception of the lease, payments represent an annuity due.)
2. Prepare the appropriate entries for Anything Grows and Mid-South on September 30, 2006.
3. Prepare an amortization schedule(s) describing the pattern of interest expense for Anything Grows and interest revenue for Mid-South Auto Leasing over the lease term.
4. Prepare the appropriate entries for Anything Grows and Mid-South Auto Leasing on December 31, 2006.
5. Prepare the appropriate entries for Anything Grows and Mid-South on September 29, 2008, assuming the bargain purchase option was exercised on that date.

**P 15–16**
Lessee-guaranteed residual value; third-party-guaranteed residual value; unguaranteed residual value; executory costs; different interest rates for lessor and lessee

● LO3 LO5 LO7 LO9

On December 31, 2005, Yard Art Landscaping leased a delivery truck from Branch Motors. Branch paid $40,000 for the truck. Its retail value is $45,114.

The lease agreement specified annual payments of $11,000 beginning December 31, 2005, the inception of the lease, and at each December 31 through 2008. Branch Motors' interest rate for determining payments was 10%. At the end of the four-year lease term (December 31, 2009) the truck was expected to be worth $15,000. The estimated useful life of the truck is five years with no salvage value. Both companies use straight-line depreciation.

Yard Art guaranteed a residual value of $6,000. Guarantor Assurance Corporation was engaged to guarantee a residual value of $11,000, but with a deductible equal to any amount paid by the lessee ($11,000 reduced by any amount paid by the lessee). Yard Art's incremental borrowing rate is 9%.

A $1,000 per year maintenance agreement was arranged for the truck with an outside service firm. As an expediency, Branch Motors agreed to pay this fee. It is, however, reflected in the $11,000 rental payments.

Collectibility of the rent payments by Yard Arts is reasonably predictable and there are no costs to the lessor that are yet to be incurred.

**Required:**

1. How should this lease be classified by Yard Art Landscaping (the lessee)? Why?
2. Calculate the amount Yard Arts Landscaping would record as a leased asset and a lease liability.
3. How should this lease be classified by Branch Motors (the lessor)? Why?
4. Show how Branch Motors calculated the $11,000 annual rental payments.
5. Calculate the amount Branch Motors would record as sales revenue.
6. Prepare the appropriate entries for both Yard Arts and Branch Motors on December 31, 2005.
7. Prepare an amortization schedule that describes the pattern of interest expense over the lease term for Yard Arts.
8. Prepare an amortization schedule that describes the pattern of interest revenue over the lease term for Branch Motors.
9. Prepare the appropriate entries for both Yard Arts and Branch Motors on December 31, 2006.
10. Prepare the appropriate entries for both Yard Arts and Branch Motors on December 31, 2008 (the final rent payment).
11. Prepare the appropriate entries for both Yard Arts and Branch Motors on December 31, 2009 (the end of the lease term), assuming the truck is returned to the lessor and the actual residual value of the truck was $4,000 on that date.

**P 15–17**
Initial direct costs; direct financing lease

● LO3 LO5 LO9

eXcel

Bidwell Leasing purchased a single-engine plane for its fair market value of $645,526 and leased it to Red Baron Flying Club on December 31, 2005.

Terms of the lease agreement and related facts were:

a. Eight annual payments of $110,000 beginning December 31, 2005, the inception of the lease, and at each December 31 through 2012. Bidwell Leasing's implicit interest rate was 10%. The estimated useful life of the plane is eight years. Payments were calculated as follows:

| | | |
|---|---|---|
| Amount to be recovered (fair market value) | | $645,526 |
| Rent payments at the beginning of each of the next eight years: ($645,526 ÷ 5.86842*) | $110,000 | |

*Present value of an annuity due of $1: $n = 8$, $i = 10\%$.

b. Red Baron's incremental borrowing rate is 11%.

c. Costs of negotiating and consummating the completed lease transaction incurred by Bidwell Leasing were $18,099.

d. Collectibility of the rent payments by Bidwell Leasing is reasonably predictable and there are no costs to the lessor that are yet to be incurred.

**Required:**

1. How should this lease be classified (a) by Bidwell Leasing (the lessor) and (b) by Red Baron (the lessee)?
2. Prepare the appropriate entries for both Red Baron Flying Club and Bidwell Leasing on December 31, 2005.
3. Prepare an amortization schedule that describes the pattern of interest expense over the lease term for Red Baron Flying Club.
4. Determine the effective rate of interest for Bidwell Leasing for the purpose of recognizing interest revenue over the lease term.
5. Prepare an amortization schedule that describes the pattern of interest revenue over the lease term for Bidwell Leasing.
6. Prepare the appropriate entries for both Red Baron and Bidwell Leasing on December 31, 2006 (the second rent payment). Both companies use straight-line depreciation.
7. Prepare the appropriate entries for both Red Baron and Bidwell Leasing on December 31, 2012 (the final rent payment).

**P 15–18**
Initial direct costs; sales-type lease

● LO3 LO6 LO9

(Note: This problem is a variation of the preceding problem, modified to cause the lease to be a sales-type lease.)

Bidwell Leasing purchased a single-engine plane for $400,000 and leased it to Red Baron Flying Club for its fair market value of $645,526 on December 31, 2005.

Terms of the lease agreement and related facts were:

a. Eight annual payments of $110,000 beginning December 31, 2005, the inception of the lease, and at each December 31 through 2012. Bidwell Leasing's implicit interest rate was 10%. The estimated useful life of the plane is eight years. Payments were calculated as follows:

| | | |
|---|---|---|
| Amount to be recovered (fair market value) | | $645,526 |
| Rent payments at the beginning of each of the next eight years: ($645,526 ÷ 5.86842*) | $110,000 | |

*Present value of an annuity due of $1: $n = 8$, $i = 10\%$.

b. Red Baron's incremental borrowing rate is 11%.

c. Costs of negotiating and consummating the completed lease transaction incurred by Bidwell Leasing were $18,099.

d. Collectibility of the rent payments by Bidwell Leasing is reasonably predictable and there are no costs to the lessor that are yet to be incurred.

**Required:**

1. How should this lease be classified (a) by Bidwell Leasing (the lessor) and (b) by Red Baron (the lessee)?
2. Prepare the appropriate entries for both Red Baron Flying Club and Bidwell Leasing on December 31, 2005.
3. Prepare an amortization schedule that describes the pattern of interest expense over the lease term for Red Baron Flying Club.
4. Prepare the appropriate entries for both Red Baron and Bidwell Leasing on December 31, 2006 (the second rent payment). Both companies use straight-line depreciation.
5. Prepare the appropriate entries for both Red Baron and Bidwell Leasing on December 31, 2012 (the final rent payment).

**P 15–19**
Sale-leaseback

● LO5 LO10

To raise operating funds, North American Courier Corporation sold its building on January 1, 2006, to an insurance company for $500,000 and immediately leased the building back. The lease is for a 10-year period ending December 31, 2015, at which time ownership of the building will revert to North American Courier. The building has a carrying amount of $400,000 (original cost $1,000,000). The lease requires North American to make payments of $88,492 to the insurance company each December 31. The building had a total original useful life of 30 years with no residual value and is being depreciated on a straight-line basis. The lease has an implicit rate of 12%.

**Required:**

1. Prepare the appropriate entries for North American on (a) January 1, 2006, to record the sale-leaseback and (b) December 31, 2006, to record necessary adjustments.
2. Show how North American's December 31, 2006, balance sheet and income statement would reflect the sale-leaseback.

**P 15–20**
Real estate lease; land and building
● LO10

On January 1, 2006, Cook Textiles leased a building with two acres of land from Peck Development. The lease is for 10 years. No purchase option exists and the property will revert to Peck at the end of the lease. The building and land combined have a fair market value on January 1, 2006, of $1,450,000 and the building has an estimated life of 20 years with a residual value of $150,000. The lease calls for Cook to assume all costs of ownership and to make annual payments of $200,000 due at the beginning of each year. On January 1, 2006, the estimated value of the land was $400,000. Cook uses the straight-line method of depreciation and pays 10% interest on borrowed money. Peck's implicit rate is unknown.

**Required:**

1. Prepare journal entries for Cook Textiles for 2006. Assume the land could be rented without the building for $59,000 each year.
2. Assuming the land had a fair market value on January 1, 2006, of $200,000 and could be rented alone for $30,000, prepare journal entries for Cook Textiles for 2006.

# BROADEN YOUR PERSPECTIVE

**Apply your critical-thinking ability to the knowledge you've gained. These cases will provide you an opportunity to develop your research, analysis, judgment, and communication skills. You also will work with other students, integrate what you've learned, apply it in real world situations, and consider its global and ethical ramifications. This practice will broaden your knowledge and further develop your decision-making abilities.**

**Analysis Case 15–1**
Reporting leases; off-balance-sheet financing
● LO1 through LO5
**FedEx Corporation**

Refer to the financial statements and related disclosure notes of **FedEx Corporation** in the appendix at the end of this book. Management's Discussion and Analysis states that "Generally, management's practice in recent years with respect to funding new aircraft acquisitions has been to finance such aircraft through long-term lease transactions that qualify as off-balance-sheet operating leases under applicable accounting rules."

**Required:**

1. What does FedEx's management mean when it says some leases "qualify as off-balance-sheet" financing?
2. See Note 7 in the disclosure notes. What is FedEx's capital lease liability?
3. If the operating leases were capitalized, approximately how much would that increase the capital lease liability?
4. What effect would that have on the company's debt-equity ratio?

**Research Case 15–2**
Locate and extract relevant information and authoritative support for a financial reporting issue; capital lease; sublease of a leased asset
● LO1 through LO5

"I don't see that in my intermediate accounting text I saved from college," you explain to another member of the accounting division of Dowell Chemical Corporation. "This will take some research." Your comments pertain to the appropriate accounting treatment of a proposed sublease of warehouses Dowell has used for product storage.

Dowell leased the warehouses one year ago on December 31. The five-year lease agreement called for Dowell to make quarterly lease payments of $2,398,303, payable each December 31, March 31, June 30, and September 30, with the first payment at the lease's inception. As a capital lease, Dowell had recorded the leased asset and liability at $40 million, the present value of the lease payments at 8%. Dowell records depreciation on a straight-line basis at the end of each fiscal year.

Today, Jason True, Dowell's controller, explained a proposal to sublease the underused warehouses to American Tankers, Inc. for the remaining four years of the lease term. American Tankers would be substituted as lessee under the original lease agreement. As the new lessee, it would become the primary obligor under the agreement, but Dowell would be secondarily liable for fulfilling the obligations under the lease agreement. Indications are that it would be reasonably possible, though not likely, that American Tankers would default and Dowell would be required to fulfill those obligations. "Check on how we would need to account for this and get back to me," he had said.

**Required:**

1. After the first full year under the warehouse lease, what is the balance in Dowell's lease liability? An amortization schedule will be helpful in determining this amount.
2. After the first full year under the warehouse lease, what is the carrying amount (after accumulated depreciation) of Dowell's leased warehouses?

3. Obtain the original FASB Standard on accounting for leases. You might gain access from the FASB website at www.fasb.org/st/, through FARS, the FASB Financial Accounting Research System, from your school library, or some other source. Determine the appropriate accounting treatment for the proposed sublease. What is the specific citation that Dowell would rely on in applying that accounting treatment?
4. What, if any, journal entry would Dowell record in connection with the sublease?
5. What, if any, disclosure would Dowell provide in its financial statements in connection with the sublease? Why?

**Communication Case 15–3**
Classification issues; lessee accounting; group interaction

● LO3 LO7 LO8

Interstate Automobiles Corporation leased 40 vans to VIP Transport under a four-year noncancelable lease on December 30, 2005. Information concerning the lease and the vans follows:

a. Equal annual lease payments of $300,000 are due on December 31 each year. The first payment was made December 31, 2005. Interstate's implicit interest rate is 10% and known by VIP.
b. VIP has the option to purchase all of the vans at the end of the lease for a total of $290,000. The vans' estimated residual value is $300,000 at the end of the lease term and $50,000 at the end of 7 years, the estimated life of each van.
c. VIP estimates the fair value of the vans to be $1,240,000. Interstate's cost was $1,050,000.
d. VIP's incremental borrowing rate is 11%.
e. VIP will pay the executory costs (maintenance, insurance, and other fees not included in the annual lease payments) of $1,000 per year. The depreciation method is straight-line.
f. The collectibility of the lease payments is reasonably predictable, and there are no important cost uncertainties.

Your instructor will divide the class into two to six groups depending on the size of the class. The mission of your group is to assess the proper recording and reporting of the lease described.

**Required:**

1. Each group member should deliberate the situation independently and draft a tentative argument prior to the class session for which the case is assigned.
2. In class, each group will meet for 10 to 15 minutes in different areas of the classroom. During that meeting, group members will take turns sharing their suggestions for the purpose of arriving at a single group treatment.
3. After the allotted time, a spokesperson for each group (selected during the group meetings) will share the group's solution with the class. The goal of the class is to incorporate the views of each group into a consensus approach to the situation.
   Specifically, you should address:
   a. Identify potential advantages to VIP of leasing the vans rather than purchasing them.
   b. How should the lease be classified by VIP? by Interstate?
   c. Regardless of your response to previous requirements, suppose VIP recorded the lease on December 31, 2005, as a capital lease in the amount of $1,100,000. What would be the appropriate journal entries related to the capital lease for the second lease payment on December 31, 2006?

**International Case 15–4**
Comparison of lease accounting in the U.K. and the United States

● LO1 through LO6

One of the world's largest petroleum and petrochemical groups is the British Petroleum Company p.l.c. (BP), based in London. Lease disclosures accompanying BP's 2003 financial statements are reproduced below:

***Accounting Policies (in part)***
**Leases**
Assets held under leases which result in group companies receiving substantially all risks and rewards of ownership (finance leases) are capitalized as tangible fixed assets at the estimated present value of underlying lease payments. The corresponding finance lease obligation is included with borrowings. Rentals under operating leases are charged against income as incurred.

| ***Note 27: Finance Debt (in part)*** | (£ million) | |
|---|---|---|
| **Obligations under Finance Leases** | **2003** | **2002** |
| Minimum future lease payments payable within: | | |
| 1 year | 127 | 106 |
| 2 to 5 years | 979 | 836 |
| Thereafter | 3,528 | 3,481 |
| | 4,634 | 4,423 |
| Less finance charges | 2,452 | 2,417 |
| Net obligations | 2,182 | 2,006 |

**Required:**

On the basis of the information the disclosures provide, compare lessee accounting for leases in the United Kingdom with that in the United States.

**Judgment Case 15–5**
Debt equivalent of operating leases

- LO1 through LO6

At December 31, 2004, **American Airlines** had 231 jet aircraft under operating leases and 94 aircraft under capital leases. Lease disclosures accompanying American's 2004 financial statements are reproduced below:

**Note 5. Leases (in part)**
American leases various types of equipment and property, primarily aircraft and airport facilities. The future minimum lease payments required under capital leases, together with the present value of such payments, and future minimum lease payments required under operating leases that have initial or remaining non-cancelable lease terms in excess of one year as of December 31, 2004, were (in millions):

| Year Ending December 31, | Capital Leases | Operating Leases |
|---|---|---|
| 2005 | $ 211 | $ 1,066 |
| 2006 | 233 | 999 |
| 2007 | 187 | 982 |
| 2008 | 225 | 931 |
| 2009 | 174 | 838 |
| 2010 and subsequent | 950 | 7,525 |
| | 1,980 | $12,341 |
| Less amount representing interest | 815 | |
| Present value of net minimum lease payments | $1,165 | |

American's capital lease liability is reported among other debt on the balance sheet. The company's debt totaled $25,567 million. Some analysts might consider operating lease commitments as equivalent to debt when assessing financial risk. If American's operating leases were considered capital leases, lease payments would be capitalized at the present value of all future payments.

**Required:**

1. If the interest rate used by American to discount rental payments on capital leases is 12% and rentals after 2009 are payable approximately evenly over the following 9 years (approximated as $7,525 ÷ $838), what is the debt equivalent of the operating lease commitments?
2. If operating lease commitments are considered equivalent to debt, what percentage of American's debt is represented by lease liabilities?

**Real World Case 15–6**
Lease concepts

- LO1 through LO6

**Safeway, Inc.**, is one of the world's largest food retailers, operating 1,871 stores in the United States and Canada. Approximately two-thirds of the premises that the company occupies are leased. Its financial statements and disclosure notes revealed the following information:

**Balance Sheet**
($ in millions)

| | 2004 | 2003 |
|---|---|---|
| **Assets** | | |
| Property: | | |
| Property under capital lease | $773.8 | $758.1 |
| Less: Accumulated amortization | (230.9) | (181.6) |
| **Liabilities** | | |
| Current liabilities: | | |
| Current obligations under capital leases | 42.8 | 50.5 |
| Long-term debt: | | |
| Obligation under capital leases | 654.0 | 668.3 |

**Required:**

1. Discuss some possible reasons why Safeway leases rather than purchases most of its premises.
2. The net asset "property under capital lease" has a 2004 balance of $542.9 million ($773.8 − 230.9). Liabilities for capital leases total $696.8 ($42.8 + 654.0). Why do the asset and liability amounts differ?

3. Prepare a 2005 summary entry to record Safeway's lease payments, which were $112 million.
4. Assuming that all property under capital lease is depreciated over the life of the lease, and that all 2004 amortization (depreciation) applied to leased assets held at the beginning of the year, what is the average life of Safeway's capital leases?
5. What is the approximate average interest rate on Safeway's capital leases? (Hint: See Req. 3)

**Ethics Case 15–7**
Leasehold improvements
● LO3

American Movieplex, a large movie theater chain, leases most of its theater facilities. In conjunction with recent operating leases, the company spent $28 million for seats and carpeting. The question being discussed over breakfast on Wednesday morning was the length of the depreciation period for these leasehold improvements. The company controller, Sarah Keene, was surprised by the suggestion of Larry Person, her new assistant.

*Keene:* Why 25 years? We've never depreciated leasehold improvements for such a long period.
*Person:* I noticed that in my review of back records. But during our expansion to the Midwest, we don't need expenses to be any higher than necessary.
*Keene:* But isn't that a pretty rosy estimate of these assets' actual life? Trade publications show an average depreciation period of 12 years.

**Required:**
1. How would increasing the depreciation period affect American Movieplex's income?
2. Does revising the estimate pose an ethical dilemma?
3. Who would be affected if Person's suggestion is followed?

**Research Case 15–8**
Researching lease disclosures; retrieving information from the Internet
● LO3 LO4 LO5

EDGAR, the Electronic Data Gathering, Analysis, and Retrieval system, performs automated collection, validation, indexing, acceptance, and forwarding of submissions by companies and others who are required by law to file forms with the U.S. Securities and Exchange Commission (SEC). All publicly traded domestic companies use EDGAR to make the majority of their filings. (Some foreign companies do so voluntarily.) Form 10-K which includes the annual report, is required to be filed on EDGAR. The SEC makes this information available on the Internet.

**Required:**
1. Access EDGAR on the Internet using EdgarScan at: **edgarscan.pwcglobal.com.**
2. Search for a company with which you are familiar and which you believe leases some of its facilities. (Retail firms and airlines are good candidates.) Access the company's most recent 10-K filing. Search or scroll to find the financial statements and related notes.
3. From the disclosure notes, determine the total capital lease obligation of the firm. What percentage does this represent of total liabilities (including current liabilities and deferred taxes) reported on the balance sheet?
4. Compare the company's rental commitments over the next five years and beyond five years for capital leases and operating leases. If operating leases were capitalized, would the company's reported debt change significantly?
5. Repeat steps 2–4 for another firm in the same industry. Are leasing practices similar between the two firms?

**Real World Case 15–9**
Sale-leaseback; FedEx
● LO10

**FedEx Corporation,** the world's largest express transportation company, leases much of its aircraft, land, facilities, and equipment. A portion of those leases are part of sale and leaseback arrangements. An excerpt from FedEx's 2004 disclosure notes describes the company's handling of gains from those arrangements:

> **Deferred Gains.**
> Gains on the sale and leaseback of aircraft and other property and equipment are deferred and amortized ratably over the life of the lease as a reduction of rent expense.

**Required:**
1. Why should companies defer gains from sale-leaseback arrangements?
2. Based on the information provided in the disclosure note, determine whether the leases in the leaseback portion of the arrangements are considered by FedEx to be capital leases or operating leases. Explain.

**Communication Case 15–10**
Where's the gain?
● LO1 LO2 LO3 LO10

General Tools is seeking ways to maintain and improve cash balances. As company controller, you have proposed the sale and leaseback of much of the company's equipment. As seller-lessee, General Tools would retain the right to essentially all of the remaining use of the equipment. The term of the lease would be six years. A gain would result on the sale portion of the transaction. The lease portion would be classified appropriately as a capital lease.

You previously convinced your CFO of the cash flow benefits of the arrangement, but now he doesn't understand the way you will account for the transaction. "I really had counted on that gain to bolster this period's earnings. What gives?" he wondered. "Put it in a memo, will you? I'm having trouble following what you're saying to me."

**Required:**

Write a memo to your CFO. Include discussion of each of these points:

1. How the sale portion of the sale-leaseback transaction should be accounted for at the lease's inception.
2. How the gain on the sale portion of the sale-leaseback transaction should be accounted for during the lease.
3. How the leaseback portion of the sale-leaseback transaction should be accounted for at the lease's inception.
4. The conceptual basis for capitalizing certain long-term leases.

**Trueblood Case 15–11**
Lease incentives

- LO1 through LO4

The following Trueblood case is recommended for use with this chapter. The case provides an excellent opportunity for class discussion, group projects, and writing assignments. The case, along with Professor's Discussion Material, can be obtained from the Deloitte Foundation at its website: **www.deloitte.com/us/truebloodcases.**

**Case 04-6: *Power Station***

This case gives students the opportunity to use their judgment in evaluating appropriate lease accounting for the sale and leaseback of equipment.

## CPA SIMULATION 15–1

**GA Company**
Leases

KAPLAN
**CPA Review**

Test your knowledge of the concepts discussed in this chapter, practice critical professional skills necessary for career success, and prepare for the computer-based CPA exam by accessing our CPA simulations at the text website: **www.mhhe.com/spiceland4e.**

The GA Company simulation tests your knowledge of a) the way we account for and report leases from the perspective of both the lessor and lessee, b) how lease accounting is influenced by bargain purchase options and guaranteed residual value, and c) accounting for sale-leaseback arrangements.

As on the CPA exam itself, you will be asked to use tools including a spreadsheet, a calculator, and professional accounting standards, to conduct research, derive solutions, and communicate conclusions related to these issues in a simulated environment headed by the following interactive tabs:

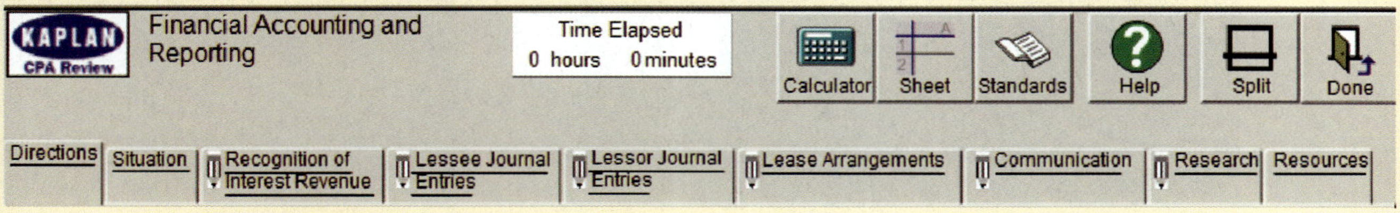


Specific tasks in the simulation include:

- Complete a worksheet pertaining to interest revenue recognition on a sales-type lease.
- Demonstrating an understanding of the way a lessee accounts for a capital lease.
- Demonstrating an understanding of the way a lessor accounts for a sales-type lease.
- Applying judgment in deciding how bargain purchase options, residual value, and sale-leaseback arrangements affect lease accounting.
- Communicating the criteria applied when classifying leases.
- Researching whether sale leaseback treatment is appropriate in a specific situation described.

# 16 CHAPTER

# Accounting for Income Taxes

## OVERVIEW

In this chapter we explore the financial accounting and reporting standards for the effects of income taxes. The discussion defines and illustrates temporary differences, which are the basis for recognizing deferred tax assets and deferred tax liabilities, as well as nontemporary differences, which have no deferred tax consequences. You will learn how to adjust deferred tax assets and deferred tax liabilities when tax laws or rates change. We also discuss accounting for operating loss carrybacks and carryforwards and intraperiod tax allocation.

## LEARNING OBJECTIVES

**After studying this chapter, you should be able to:**

- LO1 Describe the types of temporary differences that cause deferred tax liabilities and determine the amounts needed to record periodic income taxes.
- LO2 Identify and describe the types of temporary differences that cause deferred tax assets.
- LO3 Describe when and how a valuation allowance is recorded for deferred tax assets.
- LO4 Explain why nontemporary differences have no deferred tax consequences.
- LO5 Explain how a change in tax rates affects the measurement of deferred tax amounts.
- LO6 Determine income tax amounts when multiple temporary differences exist.
- LO7 Describe when and how an operating loss carryforward and an operating loss carryback are recognized in the financial statements.
- LO8 Explain how deferred tax assets and deferred tax liabilities are classified and reported in a classified balance sheet and describe related disclosures.
- LO9 Explain intraperiod tax allocation.

# FINANCIAL REPORTING CASE

## What's the Difference?

The board of directors for Times-Lehrer Industries is meeting for the first time since Laura Lynn was asked to join the board. Laura was the director of the regional office of United Charities. Although she has broad experience with the tax advantages of charitable giving and the vast array of investment vehicles available to donors, her 30 years of experience with not-for-profit organizations has not exposed her to the issues involved with corporate taxation. This gap in her considerable business knowledge causes her to turn to you, Times-Lehrer's CFO and long-time friend, who recommended Laura for appointment to the board.

"I must say," Laura confided, "I've looked long and hard at these statements, and I can't quite grasp why the amount reported for income tax expense is not the same as the amount of income taxes we paid. What's the difference?"

**By the time you finish this chapter, you should be able to respond appropriately to the questions posed in this case. Compare your response to the solution provided at the end of the chapter.**

### QUESTIONS

1. What's the difference? Explain to Laura how differences between financial reporting standards and income tax rules might cause the two tax amounts to differ. (page 774)
2. What is the conceptual advantage of determining income tax expense as we do? (page 774)
3. Are there differences between financial reporting standards and income tax rules that will not contribute to the difference between income tax expense and the amount of income taxes paid? (page 786)

# PART A DEFERRED TAX ASSETS AND DEFERRED TAX LIABILITIES

FINANCIAL REPORTING CASE
Q1, p. 773

A manufacturer of leather accessories in the Midwest is obligated to pay the Internal Revenue Service $24 million in income taxes as determined by its 2006 income tax return. Another $9 million in income taxes also is attributable to 2006 activities. Conveniently, though, tax laws permit the company to defer paying the additional $9 million until subsequent tax years by reporting certain revenues and expenses on the tax return in years other than when reported on the income statement. Does the company have only a current income tax liability of $24 million? Or does it also have a deferred income tax liability for the other $9 million? To phrase the question differently: Should the company report a 2006 income tax expense of the $24 million tax payable for the current year, or $33 million to include the future tax effects of events already recognized? For perspective on this question, we should look closer at the circumstances that might create the situation. Such circumstances are called *temporary differences.*

## Conceptual Underpinning

FINANCIAL REPORTING CASE
Q2, p. 773

**The goals of financial accounting and tax accounting are not the same.**

When a company prepares its tax return for a particular year, the revenues and expenses (and losses) included on the return are, by and large, the same as those reported on the company's income statement for the same year. However, in some instances tax laws and financial accounting standards differ. The reason they differ is that the fundamental objectives of financial reporting and those of taxing authorities are not the same. Financial accounting standards are established to provide useful information to investors and creditors. Congress, through the Internal Revenue Service, on the other hand, is primarily concerned with raising public revenues in a socially acceptable manner and, frequently, with influencing the behavior of taxpayers. In pursuing the latter objective, Congress uses tax laws to encourage activities it deems desirable, such as investment in productive assets, and to discourage activities it deems undesirable, such as violations of law.

**Accounting for income taxes is consistent with the accrual concept of accounting.**

A consequence of differences between GAAP and tax rules is that tax payments frequently occur in years different from when the revenues and expenses that cause the taxes are generated. The financial reporting issue is *when* the tax expense should be recognized. The issue has generated considerable controversy for decades. In 1967 the profession, through *APB 11,* embraced the concept of reporting income tax expense in the same period as events that give rise to the expense, regardless of when the tax actually is paid.[1] You may recognize this approach as being consistent with the accrual concept of accounting. The primary focus of that pronouncement was the matching principle. Income tax expense was calculated on the basis of pretax income reported on the income statement. Differences between the expense and the tax currently paid were reported on the balance sheet not as deferred tax liabilities (or assets) but as nebulous deferred credits (or debits).[2]

***APB 11*** **focused on the income statement and the matching principle.**

*APB 11* was replaced in 1987 by *SFAS 96,* which reiterated the objective of reporting deferred taxes but redirected the focus to an asset-liability approach.[3] This balance sheet focus emphasizes reporting the future tax sacrifice or benefit attributable to temporary differences between the reported amount of an asset or liability in the financial statements and its tax basis.[4] Plagued by implementation complexities, *SFAS 96* was delayed three times and then replaced in 1992 with *SFAS 109* before ever becoming mandatory.[5] The current standard modified some of the more troublesome measurement and recognition requirements but retained the essential flavor of *SFAS 96.* That is, the objective of accounting for income taxes is to recognize a deferred tax liability or deferred tax asset for the tax consequences of amounts that will become taxable or deductible in future years as a result of transactions or

***SFAS 109*** **focuses on the balance sheet and the recognition of liabilities and assets.**

---

[1] "Accounting for Income Taxes," *Accounting Principles Board Opinion No. 11* (New York: AICPA, 1967).

[2] Some critics at the time referred to these amounts as "UGOs: Unidentified Growing Objects."

[3] "Accounting for Income Taxes," *Statement of Financial Accounting Standards No. 96* (Stamford, Conn.: FASB, 1987).

[4] Research supports the notion that deferred tax liabilities are, in fact, viewed by investors as real liabilities.

[5] "Accounting for Income Taxes," *Statement of Financial Accounting Standards No. 109* (Norwalk, Conn.: FASB, 1992).

events that already have occurred. Future taxable amounts and future deductible amounts arise as a result of temporary differences. We discuss those now.

## Temporary Differences

● LO1

The differences in the rules for computing taxable income and those for financial reporting often cause amounts to be included in taxable income in a year later—or earlier—than the year in which they are recognized for financial reporting purposes, or not to be included in taxable income at all. For example, you learned in Chapter 4 that income from selling properties on an installment basis is reported for financial reporting purposes in the year of the sale. But tax laws permit installment income to be reported on the tax return as it actually is received (by the installment method). This means taxable income might be less than accounting income in the year of an installment sale but higher than accounting income in later years when installment income is collected.

The situation just described creates what's referred to as a **temporary difference** between pretax *accounting* income and *taxable* income and, consequently, between the reported amount of an asset or liability in the financial statements and its tax basis. In our example, the asset for which the temporary difference exists is the installment receivable that's recognized for financial reporting purposes, but not for tax purposes.

## Deferred Tax Liabilities

It's important to understand that a temporary difference *originates* in one period and *reverses,* or turns around, in one or more subsequent periods. The temporary difference described above originates in the year the installment sales are made and are reported on the *income statement* and then reverses when the installments are collected and income is reported on the *tax return.* An example is provided in Illustration 16–1.

**ILLUSTRATION 16–1**

Revenue Reported on the Tax Return after the Income Statement

Kent Land Management reported pretax income in 2006, 2007, and 2008 of $100 million, plus additional 2006 income of $40 million from installment sales of property. However, the installment sales income is reported on the tax return when collected, in 2007 ($10 million) and 2008 ($30 million).* The enacted tax rate is 40% each year.†

| ($ in millions) | **Temporary Difference** | | | |
|---|---|---|---|---|
| | **Originates** | **Reverses** | | |
| | **2006** | **2007** | **2008** | **Total** |
| **Accounting income** | $140 | $100 | $100 | $340 |
| Installment sale income on the income statement | (40) | 0 | 0 | (40) |
| Installment sale income on the tax return | 0 | 10 | 30 | 40 |
| **Taxable income** | $100 | $110 | $130 | $340 |

In 2006, taxable income is less than accounting income because income from installment sales is not reported on the tax return until 2007–2008.

*The installment method is not available to accrual method taxpayers. H.R. 1180, sec. 536, 1999.
†The enacted rate refers to the tax rate indicated by currently enacted tax legislation (as distinguished from anticipated legislation). This is discussed later in the chapter.

Notice that accounting income and taxable income total the same amount over the three-year period but are different in each individual year. In 2006, taxable income is $40 million *less* than accounting income because it does not include income from installment sales. The difference is temporary, though. That situation reverses over the next two years. In 2007 and 2008 taxable income is *more* than accounting income because income on the installment sales, reported on the income statement in 2006, becomes taxable during the next two years as installments are collected.

Because tax laws permit the company to delay reporting this income as part of taxable income, the company is able to defer paying the tax on that income. The tax is not avoided, just

**The 2006 tax liability is paid in the next two years.**

deferred. In the meantime, the company has a liability for the income tax deferred. The liability originates in 2006 and is paid over the next two years as follows:

**Deferred Tax Liability**

| ($ in millions) | | | |
|---|---|---|---|
| | | 16 | 2006 ($40 × 40%) |
| 2007 ($10 × 40%) | 4 | | |
| 2008 ($30 × 40%) | 12 | | |
| | | 0 | Balance after 3 years |

At the end of 2006, financial and taxable income for 2007 and 2008 are, of course, not yet known. We assumed knowledge of that information above so we could compare the three-year effect of the temporary difference, but seeing the future is unnecessary to determine amounts needed to record income taxes in 2006. This is demonstrated in Illustration 16–1A.

**ILLUSTRATION 16–1A**
Determining and Recording Income Taxes—2006

| ($ in millions) | Current Year 2006 | Future Taxable Amounts 2007 | Future Taxable Amounts 2008 | Future Taxable Amounts (total) |
|---|---|---|---|---|
| **Accounting income** | $140 | | | |
| Temporary difference: | | | | |
| Installment income | (40) | $10 | $30 | $40 |
| **Taxable income** | $100 | | | |
| Enacted tax rate | 40% | | | 40% |
| Tax payable currently | $ 40 | | | |
| Deferred tax liability | | | | $16 |
| **Deferred Tax Liability** | | | | ↓ |
| Desired ending balance | | | | $16 |
| Less: Beginning balance | | | | 0 |
| Change in balance | | | | $16 |

**Journal Entry at the End of 2006**

| | | |
|---|---|---|
| Income tax expense (to balance) | 56 | |
| Income tax payable (determined above) | | 40 |
| Deferred tax liability (determined above) | | 16 |

With **future taxable amounts** of $40 million, taxable at 40%, a $16 million **deferred tax liability** is indicated. Since no previous balance exists, this amount is added to the liability.

Each year, income tax expense comprises both the current and the deferred tax consequences of events and transactions already recognized. This means we:

1. Calculate the income tax that is payable currently.
2. Separately calculate the change in the deferred tax liability (or asset).
3. Combine the two to get the income tax expense.

Using the 2007 and 2008 income numbers, the journal entries to record income taxes those years would be:

**At the end of 2007, the deferred tax liability should have a balance of $12 million. Because the balance from 2006 is $16 million, we reduce it by $4 million.**

| **2007** | ($ in millions) | |
|---|---|---|
| Income tax expense (to balance) | 40 | |
| Deferred tax liability [($30 million × 40%) − 16 million] | 4 | |
| Income tax payable ($110 million × 40%) | | 44 |

| **2008** | | |
|---|---|---|
| Income tax expense (to balance) . . . . . . . . . . . . . . . . . . . . . . . . . . | 40 | |
| Deferred tax liability ($0 million − 12 million) . . . . . . . . . . . . . . . . . | 12 | |
| Income tax payable ($130 million × 40%) . . . . . . . . . . . . . . . . . . | | 52 |

At the end of 2008, the deferred tax liability should have a balance of zero. So, we eliminate the $12 million balance.

## THE FASB'S BALANCE SHEET APPROACH

Our perspective in this example so far has centered around the income effects of the installment sales and thus on the changes in the deferred tax liability as the temporary difference reverses. Another perspective is to consider the balance sheet effect. From this viewpoint, we regard a deferred tax liability (or asset) to be the tax effect of the temporary difference between the *financial statement carrying amount* of an asset or liability and its *tax basis.* The tax basis of an asset or liability is its original value for tax purposes reduced by any amounts included to date on tax returns. In our example, a temporary book-tax difference exists for a receivable from installment sales that's recognized for financial reporting purposes but not for tax purposes. When a company sells something on an installment basis, it reports a receivable. From a tax perspective, though, there is no receivable because a "taxable sale" doesn't occur until installments are collected. This is shown in Illustration 16–1B.

An installment receivable has no tax basis.

**ILLUSTRATION 16–1B**
Balance Sheet Perspective

**December 31**
($ in millions)

| | **2006** | | **2007** | | **2008** | |
|---|---|---|---|---|---|---|
| Receivable from installment sales: | | | | | | |
| **Accounting basis** | $40 | $40 | $(10) | $30 | $(30) | $0 |
| **Tax basis** | (0) | (0) | (0) | (0) | (0) | (0) |
| Temporary difference | $40 | $40 | $(10) | $30 | $(30) | $0 |
| Tax rate | | × 40% | | × 40% | | × 40% |
| Deferred tax liability | | $16 | | $12 | | $0 |
| | Originating Difference | | Reversing Differences | | | |

The deferred tax liability each year is the tax rate times the temporary difference between the financial statement carrying amount of the receivable and its tax basis.

Of course, the income statement view and the balance sheet view are two different perspectives on the very same event. In this example, we derive the same deferred tax liability whether we view it as a result of a temporary difference (a) between accounting and taxable income or (b) between the financial statement carrying amount of an installment receivable and its tax basis. Conceptually, though, the balance sheet approach strives to establish deferred tax assets and liabilities that meet the definitions of assets and liabilities provided by the FASB's conceptual framework. As specified by *SFAC 6,* assets represent "probable future economic benefits obtained or controlled by a particular entity as a result of past transactions or events," and liabilities are "probable future sacrifices of economic benefits as a result of past transactions or events."[6] In our example, the probable future sacrifices of economic benefits are the payments of $4 million in 2007 and $12 million in 2008. The past transactions or events resulting in the future tax payments are the installment sales in 2006.

*SFAS 109* takes a balance sheet approach to establishing deferred tax assets and liabilities that meet the definitions of assets and liabilities provided by the FASB's conceptual framework.

## TYPES OF TEMPORARY DIFFERENCES

Examples of temporary differences are provided in Graphic 16–1.

[6]"Elements of Financial Statements," *Statement of Financial Accounting Concepts No. 6* (Stamford, Conn.: FASB, 1985), par. 25, 35.

**GRAPHIC 16–1**

Types of Temporary Differences

| | Revenues (or gains) | Expenses (or losses) |
|---|---|---|
| Items reported on the tax return *after* the income statement | • Installment sales of property (installment method for taxes).<br>• Unrealized gain from recording investments at fair value (taxable when asset is sold). | • Estimated expenses and losses (tax deductible when paid).<br>• Unrealized loss from recording investments at fair value or inventory at LCM (tax deductible when asset is sold). |
| Items reported on the tax return *before* the income statement | • Rent collected in advance.<br>• Subscriptions collected in advance.<br>• Other revenue collected in advance. | • Accelerated depreciation on tax return (straight-line depreciation in the income statement).<br>• Prepaid expenses (tax deductible when paid). |

- The temporary differences shown in the diagonal purple areas create *deferred tax liabilities* because they result in *taxable* amounts in some future year(s) when the related assets are recovered or the related liabilities are settled (when the temporary differences reverse).
- The temporary differences in the opposite diagonal (blue) areas create *deferred tax assets* because they result in *deductible* amounts in some future year(s) when the related assets are recovered or the related liabilities are settled (when the temporary differences reverse).

**ADDITIONAL CONSIDERATION**

Temporary differences between the reported amount of an asset or liability in the financial statements and its tax basis are primarily caused by revenues, expenses, gains, and losses being included in taxable income in a year earlier or later than the year in which they are recognized for financial reporting purposes as illustrated in Graphic 16–1. Other events also can cause temporary differences between the reported amount of an asset or liability in the financial statements and its tax basis. Three other such events that are beyond the scope of this textbook are briefly described in "Accounting for Income Taxes," *Statement of Financial Accounting Standards No. 109* (Norwalk, Conn.: FASB, 1992), par. 11 e–h. Our discussions in this chapter focus on temporary differences caused by the timing of revenue and expense recognition, but it's important to realize that the concept of temporary differences embraces all differences that will result in taxable or deductible amounts in future years.

Be sure to notice that deferred tax liabilities can arise from either (a) a revenue being reported on the tax return after the income statement or (b) an expense being reported on the tax return before the income statement. Our previous illustration was of the first type. We look at the second in Illustration 16–2.

Notice, too, that this temporary difference originates during more than a single year before it begins to reverse. This usually is true when depreciation is the cause of the temporary difference. Tax laws typically permit the cost of a depreciable asset to be deducted on the tax return sooner than it is reported as depreciation on the income statement.[7] This means taxable income will be less than accounting income during the years the tax deduction is higher

[7]Presently, the accelerated depreciation method prescribed by the tax code is the modified accelerated cost recovery system (MACRS). The method is described in Chapter 11.

**ILLUSTRATION 16–2**
Expense Reported on the Tax Return before the Income Statement

Woods Temporary Services reported pretax income in 2006, 2007, 2008, and 2009 of $100 million. In 2006, an asset was acquired for $100 million. The asset is depreciated for financial reporting purposes over four years on a straight-line basis (no residual value). For tax purposes the asset's cost is deducted (by MACRS) over 2006–2009 as follows: $33 million, $44 million, $15 million, and $8 million. No other depreciable assets were acquired. The enacted tax rate is 40% each year.

| ($ in millions) | Temporary Difference | | | | |
|---|---|---|---|---|---|
| | Originates | | Reverses | | |
| | 2006 | 2007 | 2008 | 2009 | Total |
| **Accounting income** | $100 | $100 | $100 | $100 | $400 |
| Depreciation on the income statement | 25 | 25 | 25 | 25 | 100 |
| Depreciation on the tax return | (33) | (44) | (15) | (8) | (100) |
| **Taxable income** | $ 92 | $ 81 | $110 | $117 | $400 |

**To determine taxable income, we add back to accounting income the actual depreciation taken in the income statement and then subtract the depreciation deduction allowed on the tax return.**

than income statement depreciation, but higher than accounting income in later years when the situation reverses.

2006 income taxes would be recorded as follows in Illustration 16–2A:

**ILLUSTRATION 16–2A**
Determining and Recording Income Taxes—2006

| ($ in millions) | Current Year 2006 | Future Taxable Amounts 2007 | 2008 | 2009 | Future Taxable Amounts (total) |
|---|---|---|---|---|---|
| **Accounting income** | $ 100 | | | | |
| Temporary difference: | | | | | |
| Depreciation | (8) | $(19) | $10 | $17 | $8 |
| **Taxable income** | $ 92 | | | | |
| Enacted tax rate | 40% | | | | 40% |
| Tax payable currently | $36.8 | | | | |
| Deferred tax liability | | | | | $3.2 |

**Deferred Tax Liability**

| | |
|---|---|
| Ending balance | $3.2 |
| Less: Beginning balance | 0.0 |
| Change in balance | $3.2 |

**Journal Entry at the End of 2006**

| | | |
|---|---|---|
| Income tax expense (to balance) | 40 | |
| Income tax payable (determined above) | | 36.8 |
| Deferred tax liability (determined above) | | 3.2 |

**Taxable income is $8 million less than accounting income because that much more depreciation is deducted on the 2006 tax return ($33 million) than is reported on the income statement ($25 million).**

**Income tax expense is comprised of two components: the amount payable now and the amount deferred until later.**

Let's follow the determination of income taxes for this illustration all the way through the complete reversal of the temporary difference. We assume accounting income is $100 million each year and that the only difference between accounting and taxable income is caused by depreciation. 2007 income taxes would be determined as shown in Illustration 16–2B.

Notice that each year the appropriate balance is determined for the deferred tax liability. That amount is compared with any existing balance to determine whether the account must be either increased or decreased.

Income taxes for 2008 would be recorded as shown in Illustration 16–2C.

**ILLUSTRATION 16–2B**

Determining and Recording Income Taxes—2007

The cumulative temporary difference ($27 million) is both (a) the sum of the amounts originating in 2006 ($8 million) and in 2007 ($19 million) and (b) the sum of the amounts reversing in 2008 ($10 million) and in 2009 ($17 million).

Since a balance of $3.2 million already exists, **$7.6** million must be added.

($ in millions)

| | 2006 | Current Year 2007 | Future Taxable Amounts 2008 | Future Taxable Amounts 2009 | Future Taxable Amounts (total) |
|---|---|---|---|---|---|
| **Accounting income** | | $ 100 | | | |
| Temporary difference: | | | | | |
| Depreciation | $(8) | (19) | $10 | $17 | $27 |
| **Taxable income** | | 81 | | | |
| Enacted tax rate | | 40% | | | 40% |
| Tax payable currently | | $32.4 | | | |
| Deferred tax liability | | | | | $10.8 |

**Deferred Tax Liability**

| | |
|---|---|
| Ending balance | $10.8 |
| Less: Beginning balance | (3.2) |
| Change in balance | $7.6 |

**Journal Entry at the End of 2007**

| | | |
|---|---|---|
| Income tax expense (to balance) | 40 | |
| Income tax payable (determined above) | | 32.4 |
| Deferred tax liability (determined above) | | 7.6 |

**ILLUSTRATION 16–2C**

Determining and Recording Income Taxes—2008

A credit balance of $6.8 million is needed in the deferred tax liability account.

Since a credit balance of $10.8 million already exists, **$4** million must be deducted (debited).

A portion of the tax deferred from 2006 and 2007 is now being paid in 2008.

($ in millions)

| | 2006 | 2007 | Current Year 2008 | Future Taxable Amounts 2009 | Future Taxable Amounts (total) |
|---|---|---|---|---|---|
| **Accounting income** | | | $100 | | |
| Temporary difference: | | | | | |
| Depreciation | $(8) | $(19) | 10 | $17 | $17 |
| **Taxable income** | | | $110 | | |
| Enacted tax rate | | | 40% | | 40% |
| Tax payable currently | | | $ 44 | | |
| Deferred tax liability | | | | | $ 6.8 |

**Deferred Tax Liability**

| | |
|---|---|
| Ending balance | $ 6.8 |
| Less: Beginning balance | (10.8) |
| Change in balance | $ (4.0) |

**Journal Entry at the End of 2008**

| | | |
|---|---|---|
| Income tax expense (to balance) | 40 | |
| Deferred tax liability (determined above) | 4 | |
| Income tax payable (determined above) | | 44 |

Income taxes for 2009 would be recorded as shown in Illustration 16–2D. Notice there that the deferred tax liability is increased in 2006–2007 and decreased in 2008–2009.

**Deferred Tax Liability**

| ($ in millions) | Debit | Credit | |
|---|---|---|---|
| | | 3.2 | 2006 ($ 8 × 40%) |
| 2008 ($10 × 40%) | 4.0 | 7.6 | 2007 ($19 × 40%) |
| 2009 ($17 × 40%) | 6.8 | | |
| | | 0 | Balance after 4 years |

The deferred tax liability increases the first two years and is paid over the next two years.

**ILLUSTRATION 16–2D**
Determining and Recording Income Taxes—2009

| ($ in millions) | 2006 | 2007 | 2008 | Current Year 2009 | Future Taxable Amounts (total) |
|---|---|---|---|---|---|
| **Accounting income** | | | | $100 | |
| Temporary difference: | | | | | |
| Depreciation | $(8) | $(19) | $10 | 17 | $ 0 |
| **Taxable income** | | | | $117 | |
| Enacted tax rate | | | | 40% | 40% |
| Tax payable currently | | | | $ 46.8 | |
| Deferred tax liability | | | | | $ 0.0 |

**Deferred Tax Liability**

| | |
|---|---|
| Ending balance | $ 0.0 |
| Less: Beginning balance | (6.8) |
| Change in balance | $(6.8) |

**Journal Entry at the End of 2009**

| | | |
|---|---|---|
| Income tax expense (to balance) | 40.0 | |
| Deferred tax liability (determined above) | 6.8 | |
| Income tax payable (determined above) | | 46.8 |

Because the entire temporary difference has now reversed, there is a zero cumulative temporary difference, and the balance in the deferred tax liability should be zero.

Since a credit balance of **$6.8** million exists, that amount must be deducted (debited).

The final portion of the tax deferred from 2006 and 2007 is paid in 2009.

We can see this result from the alternate perspective of looking at the temporary book–tax difference that exists for the depreciable asset. Its carrying amount is its cost minus accumulated straight-line depreciation. Its tax basis is cost minus the accumulated cost recovery for tax purposes:

($ in millions) December 31

| | | 2006 | | | 2007 | | 2008 | | 2009 |
|---|---|---|---|---|---|---|---|---|---|
| Depreciable asset: | | | | | | | | | |
| **Accounting basis** | $100 | $(25) | $ 75 | $(25) | $ 50 | $(25) | $ 25 | $(25) | $ 0 |
| **Tax basis** | 100 | (33) | 67 | (44) | 23 | (15) | 8 | (8) | 0 |
| Temporary difference | | $ 8 | $ 8 | $ 19 | $ 27 | $(10) | $ 17 | $(17) | $ 0 |
| Enacted tax rate | | | 40% | | 40% | | 40% | | 40% |
| Deferred tax liability | | | $3.2 | | $10.8 | | $6.8 | | $ 0 |
| | | Originating Differences | | | | Reversing Differences | | | |

A balance sheet perspective focuses on the difference between the carrying amount and the tax basis.

## Deferred Tax Assets

• LO2

The temporary differences illustrated to this point produce future taxable amounts when the temporary differences reverse. Future taxable amounts mean taxable income will be increased relative to accounting income in one or more future years. Sometimes, though, the

**Deferred tax assets are recognized for the future tax benefits of temporary differences that create future deductible amounts.**

future tax consequence of a temporary difference will be to decrease taxable income relative to accounting income. Such situations produce what's referred to as **future deductible amounts.** These have favorable tax consequences that are recognized as **deferred tax assets.**

Two examples indicated in Graphic 16–1 are (1) estimated expenses that are recognized on income statements when incurred but deducted on tax returns in later years when actually paid and (2) revenues that are taxed when collected but recognized on income statements in later years when actually earned. An example of the first type is provided in Illustration 16–3.

**ILLUSTRATION 16–3**

Expense Reported on the Tax Return *after* the Income Statement

**In 2006, taxable income is more than accounting income because the warranty expense is not deducted on the tax return until paid.**

Lane Electronics reported pretax income in 2006, 2007, and 2008 of $70 million, $100 million, and $100 million, respectively. The 2006 income statement includes a $30 million warranty expense that is deducted for tax purposes when paid in 2007 ($15 million) and 2008 ($15 million).* The income tax rate is 40% each year.

| ($ in millions) | Temporary Difference | | | |
|---|---|---|---|---|
| | Originates | Reverses | | |
| | 2006 | 2007 | 2008 | Total |
| **Accounting income** | $ 70 | $100 | $100 | $270 |
| Warranty expense on the income statement | 30 | | | 30 |
| Warranty expense on the tax return | | (15) | (15) | (30) |
| **Taxable income** | $100 | $ 85 | $ 85 | $270 |

*Remember from Chapter 13 that warranty expense is estimated for the period the products are sold even though the actual cost isn't incurred until later periods.

At the end of 2006, the amounts needed to record income tax for 2006 would be determined as shown in Illustration 16–3A.

**ILLUSTRATION 16–3A**

Determining and Recording Income Taxes—2006

**Because the warranty expense was subtracted on the 2006 income statement but isn't deductible on the 2006 tax return, it is added back to accounting income to find taxable income.**

**The amounts deductible in 2007 and 2008 will produce tax benefits that are recognized now as a deferred tax asset.**

| ($ in millions) | Current Year 2006 | Future Deductible Amounts 2007 | Future Deductible Amounts 2008 | Future Deductible Amounts (total) |
|---|---|---|---|---|
| **Accounting income** | $ 70 | | | |
| Temporary difference: | | | | |
| Warranty expense | 30 | $(15) | $(15) | $(30) |
| **Taxable income** | $100 | | | |
| Enacted tax rate | 40% | | | 40% |
| Tax payable currently | $ 40 | | | |
| Deferred tax asset | | | | $(12) |

**Deferred Tax Asset**

| | |
|---|---|
| Ending balance | $ 12 |
| Less: Beginning balance | 0 |
| Change in balance | $ 12 |

**Journal Entry at the End of 2006**

| | | |
|---|---|---|
| Income tax expense (to balance) | 28 | |
| Deferred tax asset (determined above) | 12 | |
| Income tax payable (determined above) | | 40 |

At the end of 2006 and 2007, the company reports a deferred tax asset for future income tax benefits.

**Deferred Tax Asset**

| | | | ($ in millions) |
|---|---|---|---|
| 2006 ($30 × 40%) | 12 | | |
| | | 6 | 2007 ($15 × 40%) |
| | | 6 | 2008 ($15 × 40%) |
| Balance after 3 years | 0 | | |

Income taxes payable in 2007 and 2008 are less than otherwise payable because of the taxes "prepaid" in 2006.

If we continue the assumption of $85 million taxable income in each of 2007 and 2008, income tax those years would be recorded this way:

| | | |
|---|---|---|
| **2007** | | |
| Income tax expense (to balance) | 40 | |
| Deferred tax asset ($15 million × 40%) | | 6 |
| Income tax payable ($85 million × 40%) | | 34 |
| **2008** | | |
| Income tax expense (to balance) | 40 | |
| Deferred tax asset ($15 million × 40%) | | 6 |
| Income tax payable ($85 million × 40%) | | 34 |

The deferred tax asset represents the future tax benefit from the reversal of a temporary difference between the financial statement carrying amount of the warranty liability and its tax basis.

| ($ in millions) | December 31 | | | | | |
|---|---|---|---|---|---|---|
| | 2006 | | 2007 | | 2008 | |
| Warranty liability: | | | | | | |
| **Accounting basis** | $30 | $30 | $(15) | $15 | $(15) | $0 |
| **Tax basis** | (0) | (0) | (0) | (0) | (0) | (0) |
| Temporary difference | $30 | $30 | $(15) | $15 | $(15) | $0 |
| Tax rate | | × 40% | | × 40% | | × 40% |
| Deferred tax asset | ↑ Originating Difference | $12 | ↑ Reversing Differences | $ 6 | ↑ | $0 |

A liability is recognized for financial reporting purposes when the guaranteed product is sold:

| | | |
|---|---|---|
| 2006 Warr. exp | 30 | |
| Liability | | 30 |

and reduced when the expense is paid:

| | | |
|---|---|---|
| 2007 Liability | 15 | |
| Cash | | 15 |
| 2008 Liability | 15 | |
| Cash | | 15 |

From a tax perspective, there is no liability.

The preceding was an illustration of an estimated expense that is reported on the income statement when incurred but deducted on tax returns in later years when actually paid. A second type of temporary difference that gives rise to a deferred tax asset is a *revenue* that is taxed when collected but recognized on income statements in later years when actually earned. Illustration 16–4 demonstrates this second type.

Notice that this temporary difference produces future *deductible* amounts. In 2006, taxable income is $20 million *more* than accounting income because it includes the unearned subscriptions revenue not yet reported on the income statement. However, in 2007 and 2008 taxable income is *less* than accounting income because the subscription revenue is earned and reported on the income statements but not on the tax returns of those two years.

A deferred tax asset is recognized when an existing temporary difference will produce future deductible amounts.

In effect, tax laws require the company to prepay the income tax on this revenue, which is a sacrifice now but will benefit the company later when it avoids paying the taxes when the revenue is earned. In the meantime, the company has an asset representing this future income tax benefit.

At the end of 2006, the amounts needed to record income tax for 2006 would be determined as shown in Illustration 16–4A.

**ILLUSTRATION 16–4**

Revenue Reported on the Tax Return *before* the Income Statement

**In 2006, taxable income is more than accounting income because subscription revenue is not reported on the income statement until 2007–2008.**

Tomorrow Publications reported pretax income in 2006, 2007, and 2008 of $80 million, $115 million, and $105 million, respectively. The 2006 income statement does *not* include $20 million of magazine subscriptions received that year for one- and two-year subscriptions. The subscription revenue is reported for tax purposes in 2006. The revenue will be earned in 2007 ($15 million) and 2008 ($5 million). The income tax rate is 40% each year.

| ($ in millions) | Temporary Difference | | | |
|---|---|---|---|---|
| | Originates | Reverses | | |
| | 2006 | 2007 | 2008 | Total |
| **Accounting income** | $ 80 | $115 | $105 | $300 |
| Subscription revenue on the income statement | | (15) | (5) | (20) |
| Subscription revenue on the tax return | 20 | 0 | 0 | 20 |
| **Taxable income** | $100 | $100 | $100 | $300 |

**ILLUSTRATION 16–4A**

Determining and Recording Income Taxes—2006

| ($ in millions) | 2006 | Future Deductible Amounts 2007 | Future Deductible Amounts 2008 | Future Deductible Amounts (total) |
|---|---|---|---|---|
| **Accounting income** | $ 80 | | | |
| Temporary difference: | | | | |
| Subscription revenue | 20 | $(15) | $(5) | $(20) |
| **Taxable income** | $100 | | | |
| Enacted tax rate | 40% | | | 40% |
| Tax payable currently | $ 40 | | | |
| Deferred tax asset | | | | $(8) |

**Deferred Tax Asset**

| | |
|---|---|
| Ending balance | $ 8 |
| Less: Beginning balance | 0 |
| Change in balance | $ 8 |

**Journal Entry at the End of 2006**

| | | |
|---|---|---|
| Income tax expense (to balance) | 32 | |
| Deferred tax asset (determined above) | 8 | |
| Income tax payable (determined above) | | 40 |

At the end of 2006 and 2007, the company reports a deferred tax asset for future tax benefits.

**Income taxes payable in 2007 and 2008 are less than otherwise payable because of the taxes prepaid in 2006.**

**Deferred Tax Asset**

| | Debit | Credit | ($ in millions) |
|---|---|---|---|
| 2006 ($20 × 40%) | 8 | | |
| | | 6 | 2007 ($15 × 40%) |
| | | 2 | 2008 ($ 5 × 40%) |
| Balance after 3 years | 0 | | |

Again, we could also determine the deferred tax asset as the future tax benefit from the reversal of a temporary difference between the financial statement carrying amount of the subscription liability and its tax basis.[8]

A liability is recognized for financial reporting purposes when the cash is received:

| | | |
|---|---|---|
| 2006 Cash | 20 | |
| Liability | | 20 |

and reduced when the revenue is earned:

| | | |
|---|---|---|
| 2007 Liability | 15 | |
| Revenue | | 15 |
| 2008 Liability | 5 | |
| Revenue | | 5 |

From a tax perspective, there is no liability.

($ in millions)

| | December 31 | | | | | |
|---|---|---|---|---|---|---|
| | 2006 | | 2007 | | 2008 | |
| Liability—subscriptions: | | | | | | |
| **Accounting basis** | $20 | $20 | $(15) | $ 5 | $(5) | $ 0 |
| **Tax basis** | (0) | (0) | (0) | (0) | (0) | (0) |
| Temporary difference | $20 | $20 | $(15) | $ 5 | $(5) | $ 0 |
| Tax rate | | × 40% | | × 40% | | × 40% |
| Deferred tax asset | ↑ | $ 8 | ↑ | $ 2 | ↑ | $ 0 |
| | Originating Difference | | Reversing Differences | | | |

## Valuation Allowance

● LO3

Deferred tax assets are recognized for all deductible temporary differences. However, a deferred tax asset is then reduced by a valuation allowance if it is "more likely than not" that some portion or all of the deferred tax asset will not be realized.[9] Remember, a future deductible amount reduces taxable income and saves taxes only if there is taxable income to be reduced when the future deduction is available. So, a **valuation allowance** is needed if taxable income is anticipated to be insufficient to realize the tax benefit.

A valuation allowance is needed if it is more likely than not that some portion or all of a deferred tax asset will not be realized.

For example, let's say that in the previous illustration management determines that it's more likely than not that $3 million of the deferred tax asset will not ultimately be realized. The deferred tax asset would be reduced by the creation of a valuation allowance as follows:

| | ($ in millions) | |
|---|---|---|
| Income tax expense ..................................... | 3 | |
| Valuation allowance—deferred tax asset .................... | | 3 |

The effect is to increase the income tax expense as a result of reduced expectations of future tax savings. On the 2006 balance sheet, the deferred tax asset would be reported at its estimated net realizable value:

A deferred tax asset is reported at its estimated net realizable value.

| | |
|---|---|
| Deferred tax asset | $8 |
| Less: Valuation allowance—deferred tax asset | (3) |
| | $5 |

**ADDITIONAL CONSIDERATION**

The decision as to whether a valuation allowance is needed should be based on the weight of all available evidence. The real question is whether or not there will be sufficient taxable income in future years for the anticipated tax benefit to be realized. The benefit of future deductible amounts can be realized only if future income is at least equal to the deferred deductions. After all, a deduction reduces taxes only if it reduces taxable income.

[8]It is less intuitive to view an unearned revenue (Illustration 16–4) as producing future deductible amounts when the unearned revenue liability is settled than it is to view the future deductibility of an estimated expense (Illustration 16–3) as a future deductible amount. Nevertheless, the recognition of deferred tax assets for the future tax benefits of unearned revenue liability temporary differences is consistent with the asset/liability approach of *SFAS 109* because these unearned revenue liabilities are reported as if they represent future refundable amounts and therefore future deductible amounts. This point is argued persuasively by Hugo Nurnberg, "Deferred Tax Assets under FASB *Statement No. 96*," *Accounting Horizons*, December 1989.

[9]"More likely than not" means a likelihood of more than 50%, "Accounting for Income Taxes," *Statement of Financial Accounting Standards No. 109* (Norwalk, Conn.: FASB, 1992), par. 17.

All evidence—both positive and negative—should be considered. For instance, operating losses in recent years or anticipated circumstances that would adversely affect future operations would constitute negative evidence. On the other hand, a strong history of profitable operations or sizable, existing contracts would constitute positive evidence of sufficient taxable income to be able to realize the deferred tax asset.

Managerial actions that could be taken to reduce or eliminate a valuation allowance when deferred tax assets are not otherwise expected to be realized must be considered. These tax-planning strategies include any prudent and feasible actions management might take to realize a tax benefit while it is available.

This having been said, it should be clear that the decision as to whether or not a valuation allowance is used, as well as how large the allowance should be, rests squarely on managerial judgment. Because that decision directly impacts the amount of income tax expense and therefore reported income, it has obvious implications for earnings quality assessment from an analyst's perspective.

At the end of each reporting period, the valuation allowance is reevaluated. The appropriate balance is decided on and the balance is adjusted—up or down—to create that balance. For instance, let's say that at the end of the following year, 2007, available evidence indicates that $500,000 of the deferred tax asset at the end of 2007 will not be realized. We would adjust the valuation allowance to reflect the indicated amount:

**Each period, the valuation allowance is adjusted to reflect the appropriate balance at the time.**

| | ($ in millions) | |
|---|---|---|
| Valuation allowance—deferred tax asset ($3 million − 0.5 million). . | 2.5 | |
| Income tax expense . . . . . . . . . . . . . . . . . . . . . . . . . . . . . . . . | | 2.5 |

The disclosure note shown in Graphic 16–2 accompanied the 2004 annual report of **Lucent Technologies** indicating that none of its deferred tax asset was expected to be realized:

**GRAPHIC 16–2**
Valuation Allowance—Lucent Technologies

Forming a conclusion that a valuation allowance is not needed is difficult when there is negative objective evidence such as cumulative losses in recent years. Cumulative losses weigh heavily in the overall assessment. We expect to continue to maintain a full valuation allowance until an appropriate level of profitability is sustained or we are able to develop tax strategies that would enable us to conclude that it is more likely than not that a portion of our deferred tax assets would be realizable.

● LO4

## Nontemporary Differences

**FINANCIAL REPORTING CASE**
Q3, p. 773

So far, we've dealt with temporary differences between the reported amount of an asset or liability in the financial statements and its tax basis. You learned that temporary differences result in future taxable or deductible amounts when the related asset or liability is recovered or settled. However, some differences are caused by transactions and events that under existing tax law will never affect taxable income or taxes payable. Interest received from investments in bonds issued by state and municipal governments, for instance, is exempt from taxation. Interest revenue of this type is, of course, reported as revenue on the recipient's income statement but not on its tax return—not now, not later. Accounting income exceeds taxable income. This situation will not reverse in a later year. Taxable income in a later year will not exceed accounting income because the tax-free income will never be reported on the tax return.

**Permanent differences are disregarded when determining both the tax payable currently and the deferred tax asset or liability.**

These permanent differences are disregarded when determining the tax payable currently, the deferred tax effect, and therefore the income tax expense.[10] This is why we adjust

[10]The term permanent difference was used in *APB 11* to describe differences with no deferred tax consequences. Although the term itself is not used in more recent pronouncements (*SFAS 96* and *SFAS 109*), it still is useful to describe nontemporary differences.

**GLOBAL PERSPECTIVE**

The extent of differences between accounting income and taxable income varies widely from country to country. There also is little uniformity as to how to handle these differences. In some countries, income taxes are not deferred. Instead, tax expense is simply the actual tax paid.

accounting income in the illustrations that follow to eliminate any permanent differences from taxable income. Graphic 16–3 provides examples of differences with no deferred tax consequences.

**GRAPHIC 16–3**
Differences without Deferred Tax Consequences

- Interest received from investments in bonds issued by state and municipal governments (not taxable).
- Investment expenses incurred to obtain tax-exempt income (not tax deductible).
- Life insurance proceeds on the death of an insured executive (not taxable).
- Premiums paid for life insurance policies when the payer is the beneficiary (not tax deductible).
- Compensation expense pertaining to some employee stock option plans (not tax deductible).
- Expenses due to violations of the law (not tax deductible).
- Portion of dividends received from U.S. corporations that is not taxable due to the dividends received deduction.[11]
- Tax deduction for depletion of natural resources (percentage depletion) that permanently exceeds the income statement depletion expense (cost depletion).[12]
- Tax deduction for goodwill amortization over 15 years (goodwill is not amortized for financial reporting purposes).[13]

**Provisions of the tax laws, in some instances, dictate that the amount of a revenue that is taxable or expense that is deductible permanently differs from the amount reported on the income statement.**

To compare temporary and **nontemporary differences**, we can modify Illustration 16–1 to include nontaxable income in Kent Land Management's 2007 pretax accounting income. We do this in Illustration 16–5. Note that the existence of an amount that causes a permanent difference has no effect on income taxes payable, deferred taxes, or income tax expense.

To this point, we've seen that our objective in accounting for income taxes is to recognize the tax consequences of amounts that will become taxable or deductible in future years as a result of transactions or events that already have occurred. To achieve the objective, we record a deferred tax liability or deferred tax asset for future taxable amounts or future deductible amounts that arise as a result of temporary differences. Permanent differences, on the other hand, do not create future taxable amounts and future deductible amounts and therefore have no tax consequences.

**Permanent differences affect a company's effective tax rate.**

You might notice here that because of the permanent difference, Kent's "effective" tax rate is less than its 40% statutory rate. The effective rate is the total tax to be paid (eventually), \$56 million, divided by accounting income, \$145 million, or 38.6%. Without the \$5 million municipal bond interest, the effective rate would have been \$56 million divided by \$140 million, or 40%. Nontaxable revenues and gains, as we have for Kent, cause the effective rate to be *lower* than the statutory rate; whereas, nondeductible expenses and losses would cause the effective rate to be *higher* than the statutory rate. Companies report a comparison of their effective and statutory tax rates in disclosure notes, as in Graphic 16–4's example from **FedEx**'s 2004 financial statements.

**FedEx Corporation**

[11]When a corporation owns shares of another U.S. corporation, a percentage of the dividends from those shares is exempt from taxation due to the dividends received deduction. The percentage is 70% if the investor owns less than 20% of the investee's shares, 80% for 20% to 80% ownership, and 100% for more than 80% ownership.

[12]The cost of natural resources is reported as depletion expense over their extraction period for financial reporting purposes; but tax rules prescribe sometimes different percentages of cost to be deducted for tax purposes. There usually is a difference between the cost depletion and percentage depletion that doesn't eventually reverse.

[13]Recall, though, that goodwill might become "impaired," at which time all or a portion of it will be subtracted from earnings. Because this amount would impact the income statement in a period different from the one in which it is deducted on the tax return, it would represent a temporary difference.

**ILLUSTRATION 16–5**
Temporary and Permanent Differences

Kent Land Management reported pretax income in 2006 of $100 million except for additional income of $40 million from installment sales of property and $5 million interest from investments in municipal bonds in 2006. The installment sales income is reported for tax purposes in 2007 ($10 million) and 2008 ($30 million). The enacted tax rate is 40% each year.

**Because interest on municipal bonds is tax exempt, it is reported only in the income statement. This difference between accounting income and taxable income does not reverse later.**

($ in millions)

| | Current Year 2006 | Future Taxable Amounts 2007 | Future Taxable Amounts 2008 | Future Taxable Amounts (total) |
|---|---|---|---|---|
| **Accounting income** | $145 | | | |
| Permanent difference: | | | | |
| Municipal bond interest | (5) | | | |
| Temporary difference: | | | | |
| Installment income | (40) | $10 | $30 | $40 |
| **Taxable income** | $100 | | | |
| Enacted tax rate | 40% | | | 40% |
| Tax payable currently | $ 40 | | | |
| Deferred tax liability | | | | $16 |

**Deferred Tax Liability**

| | |
|---|---|
| Ending balance | $16 |
| Less: Beginning balance | 0 |
| Change in balance | $16 |

**Journal Entry at the End of 2006**

| | | |
|---|---|---|
| Income tax expense (to balance) | 56 | |
| Income tax payable (determined above) | | 40 |
| Deferred tax liability (determined above) | | 16 |

**GRAPHIC 16–4**
Effective Tax Rate—FedEx Corporation

**Note 9: Income Taxes (in part)**
A reconciliation of the statutory federal income tax rate to FedEx's effective income tax rate for the years ended May 31 is as follows:

| | 2004 | 2003 | 2002 |
|---|---|---|---|
| Statutory U.S. income tax rate | 35.0% | 35.0% | 35.0% |
| Increase resulting from: | | | |
| State income taxes, net of federal benefit | 2.3 | 2.6 | 2.4 |
| Other, net | (0.8) | 0.4 | 0.1 |
| Effective tax rate | 36.5% | 38.0% | 37.5% |

## CONCEPT REVIEW EXERCISE

### TEMPORARY AND PERMANENT DIFFERENCES

Mid-South Cellular Systems began operations in 2006. That year the company reported pretax accounting income of $70 million, which included the following amounts:

1. Compensation expense of $3 million related to employee stock option plans granted to organizers was reported on the 2006 income statement. This expense is not deductible for tax purposes.
2. An asset with a four-year useful life was acquired last year. It is depreciated by the straight-line method on the income statement. MACRS is used on the tax return, causing deductions for depreciation to be more than straight-line depreciation the first two years but less than straight-line depreciation the next two years ($ in millions):

| | Depreciation | | |
|---|---|---|---|
| | **Income Statement** | **Tax Return** | **Difference** |
| 2006 | $150 | $198 | $ (48) |
| 2007 | 150 | 264 | (114) |
| 2008 | 150 | 90 | 60 |
| 2009 | 150 | 48 | 102 |
| | $600 | $600 | $ 0 |

The enacted tax rate is 40%.

**Required:**

Prepare the journal entry to record Mid-South Cellular's income taxes for 2006.

**SOLUTION**

($ in millions)

| | **Current Year 2006** | **Future Taxable Amounts 2007** | **2008** | **2009** | **Future Taxable Amounts (total)** |
|---|---|---|---|---|---|
| **Accounting income** | $70 | | | | |
| Permanent difference: | | | | | |
| Compensation expense | 3 | | | | |
| Temporary difference: | | | | | |
| Depreciation | (48) | $(114) | $60 | $102 | $ 48 |
| **Taxable income** | $25 | | | | |
| Enacted tax rate | 40% | | | | 40% |
| Tax payable | $10 | | | | |
| Deferred tax liability | | | | | $19.2 |

Because the compensation expense is not tax deductible, taxable income does not include that $3 million deduction and is higher by that amount than accounting income.

**Deferred Tax Liability**

| | |
|---|---|
| Ending balance | $19.2 |
| Less: Beginning balance | 0.0 |
| Change in balance | $19.2 |

**Journal Entry at the End of 2006**

| | | |
|---|---|---|
| Income tax expense (to balance) | 29.2 | |
| Income tax payable (determined above) | | 10.0 |
| Deferred tax liability (determined above) | | 19.2 |

Income tax expense is composed of: (1) the tax payable now and (2) the tax deferred until later.

# OTHER TAX ACCOUNTING ISSUES

**PART B**

## Tax Rate Considerations

● LO5

To measure the deferred tax liability or asset, we multiply the temporary difference by the currently *enacted* tax rate that will be effective in the year(s) the temporary difference reverses.[14] We do not base calculations on *anticipated* legislation that would alter the company's tax rate. A conceptual case can be made that expected rate changes should be anticipated when measuring the deferred tax liability or asset. However, this is one of many examples of the frequent trade-off between relevance and reliability. In this case, the FASB chose to favor reliability by waiting until an anticipated change actually is enacted into law before recognizing its tax consequences.

[14]The current U.S. corporate tax rate is 34%, or 35% for corporations with taxable income over $75,000. Most states tax corporate income at rates less than 10%. We use 40% in most of our illustrations to simplify calculations.

## WHEN ENACTED TAX RATES DIFFER

**A deferred tax liability (or asset) is based on enacted tax rates and laws.**

Existing tax laws may call for enacted tax rates to be different in two or more future years in which a temporary difference is expected to reverse. When a phased-in change in rates is scheduled to occur, the specific tax rates of each future year are multiplied by the amounts reversing in each of those years. The total is the deferred tax liability or asset.

To illustrate, let's again modify our Kent Land Management illustration, this time to assume a scheduled change in tax rates. See Illustration 16–6.

**ILLUSTRATION 16–6**
Scheduled Change in Tax Rates

Kent Land Management reported pretax income in 2006 of $100 million except for additional income of $40 million from installment sales of property and $5 million interest from investments in municipal bonds in 2006. The installment sales income is reported for tax purposes in 2007 ($10 million) and 2008 ($30 million). The enacted tax rates are 40% for 2006 and 2007, and 35% for 2008.

($ in millions)

| | Current Year 2006 | Future Taxable Amounts 2007 | Future Taxable Amounts 2008 | (total) |
|---|---|---|---|---|
| **Accounting income** | $145 | | | |
| Permanent difference: | | | | |
| Municipal bond interest | (5) | | | |
| Temporary difference: | | | | |
| Installment income | (40) | $10 | $ 30 | |
| **Taxable income** | $100 | | | |
| Enacted tax rate | 40% | 40% | 35% | |
| Tax payable currently | $ 40 | | | |
| Deferred tax liability | | $ 4 | $10.5 | $14.5 |

**The tax effects of the future taxable amounts depend on the tax rates at which those amounts will be taxed.**

**Deferred Tax Liability**

| | |
|---|---|
| Ending balance | $14.5 |
| Less: Beginning balance | 0.0 |
| Change in balance | $14.5 |

**Journal Entry at the End of 2006**

| | | |
|---|---|---|
| Income tax expense (to balance) | 54.5 | |
| Income tax payable (determined above) | | 40.0 |
| Deferred tax liability (determined above) | | 14.5 |

Be sure to note that the 2007 rate (40%) as well as the 2008 rate (35%) already is enacted into law as of 2006 when the deferred tax liability is established. In the next section we discuss how to handle a change resulting from new legislation.

## CHANGES IN TAX LAWS OR RATES

Tax laws sometimes change. If a change in a tax law or rate occurs, the deferred tax liability or asset must be adjusted. Remember, the deferred tax liability or asset is meant to reflect the amount to be paid or recovered in the future. When legislation changes that amount, the deferred tax liability or asset also should change. The effect is reflected in operating income in the year of the enactment of the change in the tax law or rate.

> As a result of a change [in tax law or rate] deferred tax consequences become larger or smaller.[15]

[15] "Accounting for Income Taxes," *Statement of Financial Accounting Standards No. 109* (Norwalk, Conn.: FASB, 1992), par. 112.

For clarification, reconsider the previous illustration. Without a change in tax rates and assuming that accounting income in 2007 is $100 million (with no additional temporary or permanent differences), the 2007 income tax amounts would be determined as shown in Illustration 16–6A.

**ILLUSTRATION 16–6A**
Reversal of Temporary Difference *without* a Tax Rate Change

**The 40% 2007 rate and the 35% 2008 rate are established by previously enacted legislation.**

| ($ in millions) | 2006 | Current Year 2007 | Future Taxable Amount 2008 | |
|---|---|---|---|---|
| **Accounting income** | | $100 | | |
| Temporary difference: | | | | |
| Installment income | (40) | 10 | $30 | |
| **Taxable income** | | $110 | | |
| Enacted tax rate | | 40% | 35% | |
| Tax payable currently | | $ 44 | | |
| Deferred tax liability | | | $10.5 | $10.5 |

**Deferred Tax Liability**

| | |
|---|---|
| Ending balance | $10.5 |
| Less: Beginning balance | (14.5) |
| Change in balance | $ (4.0) |

**Journal Entry at the End of 2007**

| | | |
|---|---|---|
| Income tax expense (to balance) | 40 | |
| Deferred tax liability (determined above) | 4 | |
| Income tax payable (determined above) | | 44 |

Now assume Congress passed a new tax law in 2007 that will cause the 2008 tax rate to be 30% instead of the previously scheduled 35% rate. Because a deferred tax liability was established in 2006 with the expectation that the 2008 taxable amount would be taxed at 35%, it would now be adjusted to reflect taxation at 30%, instead. This is demonstrated in Illustration 16–6B.

**ILLUSTRATION 16–6B**
Reversal of Temporary Difference *with* a Tax Rate Change

**The deferred tax liability would have been $10.5 million (30 million × 35%) if the tax rate had not changed.**

| ($ in millions) | 2006 | Current Year 2007 | Future Taxable Amount 2008 | |
|---|---|---|---|---|
| **Accounting income** | | $100 | | |
| Temporary difference: | | | | |
| Installment income | (40) | 10 | $30 | |
| **Taxable income** | | $110 | | |
| Enacted tax rate | | 40% | 30%* | |
| Tax payable currently | | $ 44 | | |
| Deferred tax liability | | | $ 9 | $ 9.0 |

*2008 rate enacted into law in 2007.

**Deferred Tax Liability**

| | |
|---|---|
| Ending balance | $ 9.0 |
| Less: Beginning balance | (14.5) |
| Change in balance | $ (5.5) |

**Journal Entry at the End of 2007**

| | | |
|---|---|---|
| Income tax expense (to balance) | 38.5 | |
| Deferred tax liability (determined above) | 5.5 | |
| Income tax payable (determined above) | | 44.0 |

**When a tax rate changes, the deferred tax liability or asset should be adjusted with the effect reflected in operating income in the year of the change.**

Notice that the methods used to determine the deferred tax liability and the change in that balance are the same as without the rate change—the calculation merely uses the new rate (30%) rather than the old rate (35%). So recalculating the desired balance in the deferred tax liability each period and comparing that amount with any previously existing balance automatically takes into account tax rate changes.

Also notice that the income tax expense ($38.5 million) is $1.5 million less than it would have been without the tax rate change ($40 million). The effect of the change is included in income tax expense. In fact, this is highlighted if we separate the previous entry into its component parts: (1) record the income tax expense without the tax rate change and (2) separately record the adjustment of the deferred tax liability for the change:

| **Journal Entries at the End of 2007** | ($ in millions) | |
|---|---|---|
| Income tax expense | 40 | |
| Deferred tax liability | 4 | |
| Income tax payable | | 44 |
| Deferred tax liability [$30 million × (35% − 30%)] | 1.5 | |
| Income tax expense | | 1.5 |

The tax consequence of a change in a tax law or rate is recognized in the period the change is enacted. In this case, the consequence of a lower tax rate is a reduced deferred tax liability, recognized as a reduction in income tax expense in 2007 when the change occurs.

## Multiple Temporary Differences

● LO6

It would be unusual for any but a very small company to have only a single temporary difference in any given year. Having multiple temporary differences, though, doesn't change any of the principles you've learned so far in connection with single differences. All that's necessary is to categorize all temporary differences according to whether they create (a) future taxable amounts or (b) future deductible amounts. The total of the future taxable amounts is multiplied by the future tax rate to determine the appropriate balance for the deferred tax liability, and the total of the future deductible amounts is multiplied by the future tax rate to determine the appropriate balance for the deferred tax asset. This is demonstrated in Illustration 16–7.

Look at Illustration 16–7A on page 794 to see how Eli-Wallace determines the income tax amounts for 2006. Then turn to Illustration 16–7B on page 795 to see how those amounts are determined for 2007.

After the journal entry at the end of 2007, the balances of both the deferred tax asset and the deferred tax liability reflect the desired amounts as follows ($ in millions):

**The deferred tax asset declines and the deferred tax liability increases during 2007.**

| Deferred Tax Asset (Dr.) | Deferred Tax Asset (Cr.) | | Deferred Tax Liability (Dr.) | Deferred Tax Liability (Cr.) |
|---|---|---|---|---|
| 2.8 | | 2006 balance | | 10.0 |
| | 1.2 | Adjustment | | 13.2 |
| 1.6 | | 2007 balance | | 23.2 |

Of course, if a phased-in change in rates is scheduled to occur, it would be necessary to determine the total of the future taxable amounts and the total of the future deductible amounts for each future year as outlined previously. Then the specific tax rates of each future year would be multiplied by the two totals in each of those years. Those annual tax effects would then be summed to get the deferred tax liability and the deferred tax asset.

**ILLUSTRATION 16–7**
Multiple Temporary Differences

**2006**

During 2006, its first year of operations, Eli-Wallace Distributors reported pretax accounting income of $200 million which included the following amounts:

1. Income from installment sales of warehouses in 2006 of $9 million to be reported for tax purposes in 2007 ($5 million) and 2008 ($4 million).
2. Depreciation is reported by the straight-line method on an asset with a four-year useful life. On the tax return, deductions for depreciation will be more than straight-line depreciation the first two years but less than straight-line depreciation the next two years ($ in millions):

| | Income Statement | Tax Return | Difference |
|---|---|---|---|
| 2006 | $ 50 | $ 66 | $(16) |
| 2007 | 50 | 88 | (38) |
| 2008 | 50 | 30 | 20 |
| 2009 | 50 | 16 | 34 |
| | $200 | $200 | $ 0 |

3. Estimated warranty expense that will be deductible on the tax return when actually paid during the next two years. Estimated deductions are as follows ($ in millions):

| | Income Statement | Tax Return | Difference |
|---|---|---|---|
| 2006 | $7 | | $7 |
| 2007 | | $4 | (4) |
| 2008 | — | 3 | (3) |
| | $7 | $7 | $0 |

**2007**

During 2007, pretax accounting income of $200 million included an estimated loss of $1 million from having accrued a loss contingency. The loss is expected to be paid in 2009 at which time it will be tax deductible.

The enacted tax rate is 40% each year.

## Net Operating Losses

LO7

A **net operating loss** is negative taxable income: tax-deductible expenses exceed taxable revenues. Of course, there is no tax payable for the year an operating loss occurs because there's no taxable income. In addition, tax laws permit the operating loss to be used to reduce taxable income in other, profitable years. Offsetting operating profits with operating losses is achieved by either a carryback of the loss to prior years or a carryforward of the loss to later years, or both. In essence, the tax deductible expenses that can't be deducted this year because they exceed taxable revenues can be deducted in other years. Specifically, the operating loss can be carried back 2 years and forward for up to 20 years:

**Carryforward ⟶ Up to 20 Years**

| 2004 | 2005 | LOSS | 2007 | 2008 | 2009 | ⟶ | 2025 | 2026 |
|---|---|---|---|---|---|---|---|---|

**2 years ⟵ Carryback**

Tax laws permit a choice. A company can elect an **operating loss carryback** if taxable income was reported in either of the two previous years. By reducing taxable income of a previous year, the company can receive an immediate refund of taxes paid that year.

If taxable income was not reported in either of the two previous years or higher tax rates are anticipated in the future, a company might elect to forgo the operating loss carryback and carry the loss forward for up to 20 years to offset taxable income of those years. Even if a loss carryback is elected, any loss that remains after the two-year carryback can be carried forward. The carryback election is a choice that must be made in the year of the operating loss and the choice is irrevocable. It usually is advantageous to carry back losses because by

**ILLUSTRATION 16–7A**
Multiple Temporary Differences—2006

Temporary differences are grouped according to whether they create future *taxable* amounts or future *deductible* amounts.

The desired balances in the deferred tax liability and the deferred tax asset are separately determined.

Income tax expense is composed of three components: (1) the tax payable now plus (2) the tax deferred until later, reduced by (3) the deferred tax benefit.

($ in millions)

| | Current Year 2006 | Future Taxable (Deductible) Amounts 2007 | 2008 | 2009 | Future Taxable Amounts (total) | Future Deductible Amounts (total) |
|---|---|---|---|---|---|---|
| **Accounting income** | $ 200 | | | | | |
| Temporary differences: | | | | | | |
| Installment sales | (9) | $ 5 | $ 4 | | $ 9 | |
| Depreciation | (16) | (38) | 20 | $34 | 16 | |
| Warranty expense | 7 | (4) | (3) | | | $(7) |
| **Taxable income** | $ 182 | | | | $25 | (7) |
| Enacted tax rate | 40% | | | | 40% | 40% |
| Tax payable currently | $72.8 | | | | | |
| Deferred tax liability | | | | | $10 ↓ | |
| Deferred tax asset | | | | | | $(2.8) ↓ |
| | | | | | **Deferred Tax Liability** | **Deferred Tax Asset** |
| Ending balances: | | | | | $10 | $2.8 |
| Less: Beginning balances: | | | | | 0 | (0.0) |
| Change in balances | | | | | $10 | $2.8 |

**Journal Entry at the End of 2006**

| | | |
|---|---|---|
| Income tax expense (to balance) | 80.0 | |
| Deferred tax asset (determined above) | 2.8 | |
| Deferred tax liability (determined above) | | 10.0 |
| Income tax payable (determined above) | | 72.8 |

filing an amended tax return to get a refund, a company can realize the benefit much sooner than if the loss is carried forward.

The accounting question is: *When* should the tax benefit created by an operating loss be recognized on the income statement? The answer is: In the year the loss occurs.

## OPERATING LOSS CARRYFORWARD

First consider a loss carryforward. You have learned in this chapter that a deferred tax asset is recognized for the future tax benefit of temporary differences that create future deductible amounts. An operating loss carryforward also creates future deductible amounts. Logically, then, a deferred tax asset is recognized for an operating loss carryforward also. This is demonstrated on the next page in Illustration 16–8.

The income tax benefit of an operating loss carryforward is recognized for accounting purposes in the year the operating loss occurs. The net after-tax operating loss reflects the future tax savings that the operating loss is expected to create:

The income tax benefit of an operating loss carryforward is recognized in the year the operating loss occurs.

**Income Statement (partial)**

| | ($ in millions) |
|---|---|
| Operating loss before income taxes | $125 |
| Less: Income tax benefit—operating loss | (50) |
| Net operating loss | $ 75 |

**Valuation Allowance.** Just as for all deductible temporary differences, deferred tax assets are recognized for any operating loss without regard to the likelihood of having taxable income in future years sufficient to absorb future deductible amounts. However, the deferred tax asset is then reduced by a valuation allowance if it is more likely than not that some

**ILLUSTRATION 16–7B**
Multiple Temporary Differences—2007

($ millions)

| | 2006 | Current Year 2007 | Future Taxable (Deductible) Amounts 2008 | 2009 | Future Taxable Amounts (total)* | Future Deductible Amounts (total)* |
|---|---|---|---|---|---|---|
| **Accounting income** | | $200 | | | | |
| Temporary differences: | | | | | | |
| Installment sales | $ (9) | $ 5 | $ 4 | | $ 4 | |
| Depreciation | (16) | (38) | 20 | $34 | 54 | |
| Warranty expense | 7 | (4) | (3) | | | $(3) |
| Estimated loss | | 1 | | (1) | | (1) |
| **Taxable income** | | $164 | | | $58 | $(4) |
| Enacted tax rate | | 40% | | | 40% | 40% |
| Tax payable currently | | $ 65.6 | | | | |
| Deferred tax liability | | | | | $23.2 | |
| Deferred tax asset | | | | | | $(1.6) |

| | Deferred Tax Liability | Deferred Tax Asset |
|---|---|---|
| Ending balances: | $23.2 | $ 1.6 |
| Less: Beginning balances: | (10.0) | (2.8) |
| Change in balances | $13.2 | $(1.2) |

**Journal Entry at the End of 2007**

| | | |
|---|---|---|
| Income tax expense (to balance) | 80.0 | |
| Deferred tax asset (determined above) | | 1.2 |
| Deferred tax liability (determined above) | | 13.2 |
| Income tax payable (determined above) | | 65.6 |

*Total future taxable and deductible amounts also are equal to the cumulative temporary differences in the related assets and liabilities.

**The future taxable amount of installment sales ($4 million) is equal to the cumulative temporary difference ($9 million − 5 million).**

**Similarly, the total of other future taxable and deductible amounts are equal to the cumulative temporary differences in the related assets and liabilities.**

**Analysis indicates that the deferred tax liability should be increased further and the deferred tax asset should be reduced.**

**ILLUSTRATION 16–8**
Operating Loss Carryforward

During 2006, its first year of operations, American Laminating Corporation reported an operating loss of $125 million for financial reporting and tax purposes. The enacted tax rate is 40%.

($ in millions)

| | Current Year 2006 | Future Deductible Amounts (total) |
|---|---|---|
| **Operating loss** | $(125) | |
| Loss carryforward | 125 | $(125) |
| | $ 0 | |
| Enacted tax rate | 40% | 40% |
| Tax payable | $ 0 | |
| Deferred tax asset | | $ (50) |

| | Deferred Tax Asset |
|---|---|
| Ending balance | $50 |
| Less: Beginning balance | 0 |
| Change in balance | $50 |

**Journal Entry at the End of 2006**

| | | |
|---|---|---|
| Deferred tax asset (determined above) | 50 | |
| Income tax benefit—operating loss (to balance) | | 50 |

**An *operating loss carryforward* can be deducted from taxable income in future years.**

**The tax benefit of being able to deduct amounts in the future represents a deferred tax asset.**

portion or all of the deferred tax asset will not be realized. Remember, a valuation allowance both reduces the net deferred tax asset and increases the income tax expense just as if that portion of the deferred tax asset had not been recognized.

## OPERATING LOSS CARRYBACK

An operating loss must be applied to the earlier year first and then brought forward to the next year.

To compare the treatment of an operating loss carryback, let's modify the illustration to assume that there was taxable income in the two years prior to the operating loss and that American Laminating elected a loss carryback (see Illustration 16–9). Note that the operating loss must be applied to the earlier year first and then brought forward to the next year. If any of the loss remains after reducing taxable income to zero in the two previous years, the remainder is carried forward to future years as an operating loss carryforward.

**ILLUSTRATION 16–9**
Operating Loss Carryback and Carryforward

An *operating loss carryback* can be deducted from taxable income in the two prior years, creating a refund of taxes paid those years.

The portion of an operating loss that remains after a carryback is carried forward.

The income tax benefit of an operating loss carryback, like a carryforward, is recognized in the year the operating loss occurs.

During 2006, American Laminating Corporation reported an operating loss of $125 million for financial reporting and tax purposes. The enacted tax rate is 40% for 2006. Taxable income, tax rates, and income taxes paid in the two previous years were as follows:

| | Taxable Income | Taxable Rates | Income Taxes Paid |
|---|---|---|---|
| 2004 | $20 million | 35% | $ 7 million |
| 2005 | 55 million | 40% | 22 million |

Here's how the income tax benefit of the operating loss carryback and the operating loss carryforward is determined:

($ in millions)

| | Prior Years | | Current Year | Future Deductible Amounts |
|---|---|---|---|---|
| | 2004 | 2005 | 2006 | (total) |
| **Operating loss** | | | $(125) | |
| Loss carryback | $(20) | $(55) | 75 | |
| Loss carryforward | | | 50 | $(50) |
| | | | $ 0 | |
| Enacted tax rate | 35% | 40% | 40% | 40% |
| Tax payable (refundable) | $ (7) | $(22) | $ 0 | |
| Deferred tax asset | | | | $(20) |
| **Deferred Tax Asset** | | | | |
| Ending balance | | | | $ 20 |
| Less: Beginning balance | | | | 0 |
| Change in balance | | | | $ 20 |

**Journal Entry at the End of 2006**

| | | |
|---|---|---|
| Receivable—income tax refund ($7 + 22) | 29 | |
| Deferred tax asset (determined above) | 20 | |
| Income tax benefit—operating loss (to balance) | | 49 |

The income tax benefit of both an operating loss carryback and an operating loss carryforward is recognized for accounting purposes in the year the operating loss occurs. The net after-tax operating loss reflects the reduction of past taxes from the loss carryback and future tax savings that the loss carryforward is expected to create:

| | | ($ in millions) |
|---|---|---|
| Operating loss before income taxes | | $125 |
| Less: Income tax benefit: | | |
| Tax refund from loss carryback | $29 | |
| Future tax savings from loss carryforward | 20 | 49 |
| Net operating loss | | $ 76 |

Notice that the income tax benefit ($49 million) is less than it was when we assumed a carryforward only ($50 million). This is because the tax rate in one of the carryback years (2004) was lower than the carryforward rate (40%).

Let's carry the illustration forward one year (see Illustration 16–9A) and assume a performance turnaround in 2007 resulted in pretax accounting income of $15 million.

**ILLUSTRATION 16–9A**
Determining and Recording Income Taxes—2007

| ($ in millions) | 2006 | Current Year 2007 | Future Deductible Amounts (total) |
|---|---|---|---|
| **Accounting income** | | $15 | |
| Temporary difference: | | | |
| Loss carryforward | $50 | (15) | $ (35) |
| **Taxable income** | | $ 0 | |
| Enacted tax rate | | 40% | 40% |
| Tax payable currently | | $ 0 | |
| Deferred tax asset | | | $ (14) |
| **Deferred Tax Asset** | | | ↓ |
| Ending balance | | | $ 14.0 |
| Less: Beginning balance | | | (20.0) |
| Change in balance | | | $ (6.0) |

**Journal Entry at the End of 2007**

| | | |
|---|---|---|
| Income tax expense (to balance) | 6 | |
| Deferred tax asset (determined above) | | 6 |

$15 million of the carryforward can be used to offset 2007 income. The remaining $35 million is carried forward up to 19 more years.

The $20 million deferred tax asset is reduced to $14 million.

# Financial Statement Presentation

## BALANCE SHEET CLASSIFICATION

● LO8

In a classified balance sheet, deferred tax assets and deferred tax liabilities are classified as either current or noncurrent according to how the related assets or liabilities are classified for financial reporting. For instance, a deferred tax liability arising from different depreciation methods being used for tax and book purposes would be classified as noncurrent because depreciable assets are reported as noncurrent. A deferred tax asset or deferred tax liability is considered to be related to an asset or liability if reduction (including amortization) of that asset or liability will cause the temporary difference to reverse.

Most companies will have several different types of temporary differences that give rise to deferred tax amounts. The several deferred tax assets and liabilities should not be reported individually but combined instead into two summary amounts. Current deferred tax assets and liabilities should be offset (netted together). The resulting *net current* amount is then reported as either a current asset (if deferred tax assets exceed deferred tax liabilities) or current liability (if deferred tax liabilities exceed deferred tax assets). Similarly, a single *net noncurrent* amount should be reported as a net noncurrent asset or a net noncurrent liability. This is demonstrated in Illustration 16–10.

A net current amount and a net noncurrent amount are reported as either an asset or a liability.

**Deferred Tax Amount Not Related to a Specific Asset or Liability.** Sometimes, a deferred tax asset or a deferred tax liability cannot be identified with a specific asset or liability. When that's the case, it should be classified according to when the underlying temporary difference is expected to reverse. For instance, some organization costs are recognized as expenses for financial reporting purposes when incurred, but are deducted for tax purposes in later years. When such expenditures are made, an expense is recorded, but no asset or liability is recognized on the balance sheet. The deferred tax asset recognized for the future deductible amounts is classified as a current asset for the tax effect of the deduction expected next year, and as a noncurrent asset for the tax effect of the deductions expected in later years.

A deferred tax asset or liability that is not related to a specific asset or liability should be classified according to when the underlying temporary difference is expected to reverse.

**ILLUSTRATION 16–10**
Balance Sheet Classification and Presentation

The current or noncurrent classification of deferred tax assets and deferred tax liabilities is the same as that of the related assets or liabilities.

Warren Properties, Inc. had future taxable amounts and future deductible amounts relating to temporary differences between the tax bases of the assets and liabilities indicated below and their financial reporting amounts:

($ in millions)

| Related Balance Sheet Account | Classification Current—C Noncurrent—N | Future Taxable (Deductible) Amounts | Tax Rate | Deferred Tax (Asset) Liability C | N |
|---|---|---|---|---|---|
| Receivable—installment sales of land | C | $ 10 | × 40% | $ 4 | |
| Receivable—installment sales of land | N | 5 | × 40% | | $ 2 |
| Depreciable assets | N | 105 | × 40% | | 42 |
| Allowance—uncollectible accounts | C | (15) | × 40% | (6) | |
| Liability—subscriptions received | C | (20) | × 40% | (8) | |
| Estimated warranty liability | C | (30) | × 40% | (12) | |
| Net current liability (asset) | | | | $(22) | |
| Net noncurrent liability (asset) | | | | | $44 |
| **Balance Sheet Presentation** | | | | | |
| *Current Assets:* | | | | | |
| Deferred tax asset | $22 | | | | |
| *Long-Term Liabilities:* | | | | | |
| Deferred tax liability | $44 | | | | |

Note: Before offsetting assets and liabilities within the current and noncurrent categories, the **total** of deferred tax assets is $26 ($6 + 8 + 12) and the **total** of deferred tax liabilities is $48 ($4 + 2 + 42).

Operating loss carryforwards also are unrelated to a specific asset or liability and so are classified as current or noncurrent according to when future income is expected to be sufficient to realize the benefit of the carryforward.

A valuation allowance is allocated between current and noncurrent on a pro rata basis.

**Valuation Allowance.** Any valuation allowance for deferred tax assets should be allocated between the current and noncurrent amount in proportion to the amounts of deferred tax assets that are classified as current and noncurrent. In our illustration, all three deferred tax assets were classified as current, so any valuation allowance would be reported with the net current deferred tax asset.

## DISCLOSURE NOTES

**Deferred Tax Assets and Deferred Tax Liabilities.** Additional disclosures are required pertaining to amounts reported on the balance sheet. Disclosure notes should reveal the:

- Total of all deferred tax liabilities ($48 million in our Illustration 16–10 Note).
- Total of all deferred tax assets ($26 million in our Illustration 16–10 Note).
- Total valuation allowance recognized for deferred tax assets.
- Net change in the valuation allowance.
- Approximate tax effect of each type of temporary difference (and carryforward).

In its 2004 balance sheet, the **Colgate Palmolive Company** reported net noncurrent deferred tax liabilities of $456 million. The composition of this amount was provided in the disclosure note shown in Graphic 16–5.

**Operating Loss Carryforwards.** In addition, the amounts and expiration dates should be revealed for any operating loss carryforwards. Remember, operating losses can be carried forward for reduction of future taxable income for 20 years. This potential tax benefit can foreshadow desirable cash savings for the company if earnings sufficient to absorb the loss

**GRAPHIC 16–5**
Disclosure of Deferred Taxes—Colgate Palmolive Co.

**Note 11: Income Taxes (in part)**
The components of deferred tax assets (liabilities) are as follows at December 31:

| | 2004 | 2003 |
|---|---|---|
| **Deferred Taxes—Current:** | | |
| Accrued liabilities | $ 71.7 | $ 76.7 |
| Other, net | 49.9 | 59.7 |
| Total deferred taxes, current | 121.6 | 136.4 |
| **Deferred Taxes—Long-Term:** | | |
| Intangible assets | (278.0) | (231.1) |
| Property, plant, and equipment | (288.9) | (280.4) |
| Tax loss and tax credit carryforwards | 178.6 | 166.2 |
| Other, net | (2.5) | .9 |
| Valuation allowance | (118.8) | (111.6) |
| Total deferred taxes, long term | 509.6 | 456.0 |
| Net deferred taxes | $(388.0) | $ 319.6 |

carryforwards are anticipated before their expiration date. The presence of large operating loss carryforwards also can make an unprofitable company an attractive target for acquisition by a company that could use those loss carryforwards to shelter its own earnings from taxes with that loss deduction. If the IRS determines that an acquisition is made solely to obtain the tax benefits of operating loss carryforwards, the deductions will not be allowed. However, motivation is difficult to determine, so it is not uncommon for companies to purchase operating loss carryforwards.

**Income Tax Expense.** Disclosures also are required pertaining to the income tax expense reported on the income statement. Disclosure notes should reveal the:

- Current portion of the tax expense (or tax benefit).
- Deferred portion of the tax expense (or tax benefit), with separate disclosure of amounts attributable to:
  - Portion that does not include the effect of the following separately disclosed amounts.
  - Operating loss carryforwards.
  - Adjustments due to changes in tax laws or rates.
  - Adjustments to the beginning-of-the-year valuation allowance due to revised estimates.
  - Tax credits.

## Intraperiod Tax Allocation

LO9

You should recall that an income statement reports certain items separately from income (or loss) from continuing operations when such items are present. Specifically, (a) discontinued operations and (b) extraordinary items are given a place of their own on the income statement to better allow the user of the statement to isolate irregular components of net income from those that represent ordinary, recurring business operations. Presumably, this permits the user to more accurately project future operations without neglecting events that affect current performance.[16] Following this logic, each component of net income should reflect the income tax effect directly associated with that component.

[16]This was discussed in Chapter 3.

Consequently, the total income tax expense for a reporting period should be allocated among the income statement items that gave rise to it. Each of the following items should be reported net of its respective income tax effects:

- Income (or loss) from continuing operations.
- Discontinued operations.
- Extraordinary items.

The related tax effect can be either a tax expense or a tax benefit. For example, an extraordinary gain adds to a company's tax expense, while an extraordinary loss produces a tax reduction because it reduces taxable income and therefore reduces income taxes. So a company with a tax rate of 40% would report $100 million pretax income that includes a $10 million extraordinary gain this way:

A gain causes an increase in taxes.

| | ($ in millions) |
|---|---|
| Income before tax and extraordinary item ($100 − 10) | $90 |
| Less: Income tax expense ($90 × 40%) | (36) |
| Income before extraordinary item | 54 |
| Extraordinary gain (net of $4 income tax) | 6 |
| Net income | $60 |

If the $100 million pretax income included a $10 million extraordinary loss rather than an extraordinary gain, the loss would be reported net of associated tax savings:

A loss causes a reduction in taxes.

| | ($ in millions) |
|---|---|
| Income before tax and extraordinary item ($100 + 10) | $110 |
| Less: Income tax expense ($110 × 40%) | (44) |
| Income before extraordinary item | 66 |
| Extraordinary loss (net of $4 income tax benefit) | (6) |
| Net income | $ 60 |

**ADDITIONAL CONSIDERATION**

If the extraordinary gain in the earlier example had been of a type taxable at a capital gains tax rate of 30%, it would have been reported net of the specific tax associated with that gain:

Extraordinary gain (net of $3 income tax) $7

Allocating income taxes within a particular reporting period is intraperiod tax allocation.

Allocating income taxes among financial statement components in this way within a particular reporting period is referred to as *intraperiod tax allocation.* You should recognize the contrast with *inter*period tax allocation—terminology sometimes used to describe allocating income taxes between two or more reporting periods by recognizing deferred tax assets and liabilities. While interperiod tax allocation is challenging and controversial, intraperiod tax allocation is relatively straightforward and substantially free from controversy.

## Conceptual Concerns

Some accountants disagree with the FASB's approach to accounting for income taxes. Some of the most persistent objections are outlined below.

**Should Deferred Taxes Not Be Recognized?** Some feel the income tax expense for a reporting period should be the income tax actually payable currently. Reasons often cited include the contentions that the legal liability for taxes is determined only by the tax return and that taxes are based on aggregate taxable income, not individual components of the aggregate amount. The FASB counters that it is not only possible, but desirable, to separate the tax consequences of individual components of income from the financial reporting of those events. If tax laws permit a company to defer paying tax on a particular event, it is only when, not whether, the tax will be paid that is impacted. Recognizing the tax effect when the event occurs, regardless of when the tax will be paid is consistent with accounting on an accrual rather than a cash basis.

**Should Deferred Taxes Be Recognized for Only Some Items?** Critics sometimes argue that the tax liability for certain recurring events will never be paid and therefore do not represent a liability.[17] An example often cited is the temporary difference due to depreciation. Because the temporary difference recurs frequently (as new assets are acquired), new originating differences more than offset reversing differences causing the balance in the deferred tax liability account to continually get larger. The contention is that no future tax payment will be required, so no liability should be recorded. The FASB's counter argument is that, although the aggregate amount of depreciation differences may get larger, the deferred tax liability for a particular depreciable asset usually does require payment. This is analogous to specific accounts payable requiring payment even though the total balance of accounts payable may grow larger year by year.

**Should Deferred Taxes Be Discounted?** Some accountants contend that deferred tax assets and liabilities should reflect the time value of money by determining those amounts on a discounted (present value) basis.[18] For some deferred tax amounts such as operating loss carryforwards that might be realized after perhaps 20 years in some cases, the time value might be significant. Practical considerations weighed heavily in the FASB's decision not to permit discounting. Discounting usually would require detailed scheduling of the reversals of all differences reversing in the future, and the selection of appropriate discount rates would pose practical difficulties.

**Should Classification Be Based on the Timing of Temporary Difference Reversals?** Some feel that deferred tax assets and liabilities should be classified in a balance sheet as current or noncurrent according to the timing of the reversal of the temporary differences that gave rise to them. By this view, those deferred tax assets and liabilities related to temporary differences that will reverse within the coming year should be classified as current, others as noncurrent. Advocates of this view consider it to be consistent with the asset-liability perspective on deferred tax amounts. Again, practical considerations are reflected in the FASB's requirement that a deferred tax asset or deferred tax liability should be classified in a balance sheet as current or noncurrent according to the classification of the asset or liability to which it is related. Classifying a deferred tax liability related to depreciation as noncurrent because the depreciable asset is classified as noncurrent, for example, does not require detailed scheduling of the year-by-year originations and reversals of temporary differences related to depreciation.

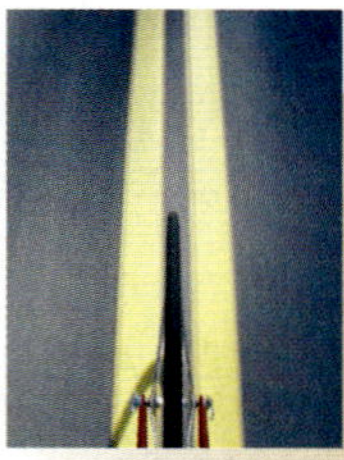

## DECISION MAKERS' PERSPECTIVE

Income taxes represent one of the largest expenditures that many firms incur. When state, local, and foreign taxes are considered along with federal taxes, the total bite can easily consume 40% of income. A key factor, then, in any decision that managers make should be the impact on taxes. Decision makers must constantly be alert to options that minimize or delay taxes. During the course of this chapter, we encountered situations that avoid taxes (for example, interest on municipal bonds) and those that delay taxes (for example, using accelerated depreciation on the tax return). Astute managers make investment decisions that consider the tax effect of available alternatives. Similarly, outside analysts should consider

[17]For example, see Paul Chaney and Debra Jeter, "Accounting for Deferred Taxes: Simplicity? Usefulness?" *Accounting Horizons,* June 1989, pp. 7–8.

[18]For example, see Harry Wolk, Dale Martin, and Virginia Nichols, "*Statement of Financial Standards No. 96*: Some Theoretical Problems," *Accounting Horizons,* June 1989, p. 4.

how effectively management has managed its tax exposure and monitor the current and prospective impact of taxes on their interests in the company.

**Investment patterns and other disclosures can indicate potential tax expenditures.**

Consider an example. Large, capital-intensive companies with significant investments in buildings and equipment often have sizable deferred tax liabilities from temporary differences in depreciation. If new investments cause the level of depreciable assets to at least remain the same over time, the deferred tax liability can be effectively delayed indefinitely. Investors and creditors should be watchful for situations that might cause material paydowns of that deferred tax liability, such as impending plant closings or investment patterns that suggest declining levels of depreciable assets. Unexpected additional tax expenditures can severely diminish an otherwise attractive prospective rate of return.

**Operating loss carryforwards can indicate significant future tax savings.**

You also learned in the chapter that deferred tax assets represent future tax benefits. One such deferred tax asset that often reflects sizable future tax deductions is an operating loss carryforward. When a company has a large operating loss carryforward, a large amount of future income can be earned tax free. This tax shelter can be a huge advantage, not to be overlooked by careful analysts.

**Deferred tax liabilities increase risk as measured by the debt to equity ratio.**

Managers and outsiders are aware that increasing debt increases risk. Deferred tax liabilities increase reported debt. As discussed and demonstrated in the previous chapter, financial risk often is measured by the debt to equity ratio, total liabilities divided by shareholders' equity. Other things being equal, the higher the debt to equity ratio, the higher the risk. Should the deferred tax liability be included in the computation of this ratio? Some analysts will argue that it should be excluded, observing that in many cases the deferred tax liability account remains the same or continually grows larger. Their contention is that no future tax payment will be required. Others, though, contend that is no different from the common situation in which long-term borrowings tend to remain the same or continually grow larger. Research supports the notion that deferred tax liabilities are, in fact, viewed by investors as real liabilities and they appear to discount them according to the timing and likelihood of the liabilities' settlement.[19]

Anytime managerial discretion can materially impact reported earnings, analysts should be wary of the implications for earnings quality assessment. We indicated earlier that the decision as to whether or not a valuation allowance is used, as well as the size of the allowance, is largely discretionary. Alert investors should not overlook the potential for "earnings management" here. In fact, recent empirical evidence indicates that some companies do use the deferred tax asset valuation allowance account to manage earnings upward to meet analyst forecasts.[20]

In short, managers who make decisions based on estimated pretax cash flows and outside investors and creditors who make decisions based on pretax income numbers are perilously ignoring one of the most important aspects of those decisions. Taxes should be a primary consideration in any business decision. ■

## CONCEPT REVIEW EXERCISE

### MULTIPLE DIFFERENCES AND OPERATING LOSS

Mid-South Cellular Systems began operations in 2006. That year the company reported taxable income of $25 million. In 2007, its second year of operations, pretax accounting income was $88 million, which included the following amounts:

1. Insurance expense of $14 million, representing one-third of a $42 million, three-year casualty and liability insurance policy that is deducted for tax purposes entirely in 2007.
2. Insurance expense for a $1 million premium on a life insurance policy for the company president. This is not deductible for tax purposes.

[19]See Dan Givoly and Carla Hayn, "The Valuation of the Deferred Tax Liability: Evidence from the Stock Market," *The Accounting Review,* April 1992, pp. 394–410.

[20]Rego, Sonja O., and Mary Margaret Frank, "Do Managers Use the Valuation Allowance Account to Manage Earnings Around Certain Earnings Targets?" (April 16, 2004). Darden Business School Working Paper No. 03-09.

3. An asset with a four-year useful life was acquired last year. It is depreciated by the straight-line method on the income statement. MACRS is used on the tax return, causing deductions for depreciation to be more than straight-line depreciation the first two years but less than straight-line depreciation the next two years ($ in millions):

| | Income Statement | Tax Return | Difference |
|---|---|---|---|
| 2006 | $150 | $198 | $ (48) |
| 2007 | 150 | 264 | (114) |
| 2008 | 150 | 90 | 60 |
| 2009 | 150 | 48 | 102 |
| | $600 | $600 | 0 |

4. Equipment rental revenue of $80 million, which does not include an additional $20 million of advance payment for 2008 rent. $100 million of rental revenue is reported on the 2007 income tax return.

The enacted tax rate is 40%.

**Required:**

1. Prepare the journal entry to record Mid-South Cellular's income taxes for 2007.
2. What is Mid-South Cellular's 2007 net income?
3. Show how any deferred tax amount(s) should be reported on the 2007 balance sheet. Assume taxable income is expected in 2008 sufficient to absorb any deductible amounts carried forward from 2007.

**SOLUTION**

1. Prepare the journal entry to record Mid-South Cellular's income taxes for 2007.

($ in millions)

| | 2006 | Current Year 2007 | Future Taxable (Deductible) Amounts 2008 | 2009 | Future Taxable Amounts (total) | Future Deductible Amounts (total) |
|---|---|---|---|---|---|---|
| **Accounting income** | | $ 88 | | | | |
| Permanent difference: | | | | | | |
| Life insurance premium | | 1 | | | | |
| Temporary differences: | | | | | | |
| Prepaid insurance | | (28) | $ 14 | $ 14 | $ 28 | |
| Depreciation | $(48) | (114) | 60 | 102 | 162 | |
| Advance rent | | 20 | (20) | | | $(20) |
| **Operating loss** | | $ (33) | | | | |
| Loss carryback | (25) | 25 | | | | |
| Loss carryforward | | 8 | | | | (8) |
| | | $ 0 | | | $190 | $(28) |
| Enacted tax rate | 40% | 40% | | | 40% | 40% |
| Tax payable (refundable) | $(10) | $ 0 | | | | |
| Deferred tax liability | | | | | $76.0 | |
| Deferred tax asset | | | | | | $(11.2) |

| | Deferred Tax Liability | Deferred Tax Asset |
|---|---|---|
| Ending balances: | $76.0 | $11.2 |
| Less: Beginning balance ($48* × 40%) | (19.2) | (0.0) |
| Change in balances | $56.8 | $11.2 |

*2006's only temporary difference.

Differences in tax reporting and financial reporting of both the prepaid insurance and the depreciation create future taxable amounts.

Both the advance rent and the operating loss carryforward create future deductible amounts.

**Income tax expense is composed of three components: (1) the tax deferred until later, reduced by (2) the deferred tax benefit and (3) the refund of 2006 taxes paid.**

**Journal Entry at the End of 2007**

| | | |
|---|---|---|
| Income tax expense (to balance) | 35.6 | |
| Receivable—income tax refund (determined above) | 10.0 | |
| Deferred tax asset (determined above) | 11.2 | |
| Deferred tax liability (determined above) | | 56.8 |

Note: Adjusting accounting income by the nontemporary difference and the three temporary differences creates a negative taxable income, which is a net operating loss.

2. What is Mid-South Cellular's 2007 net income?

| | |
|---|---|
| Pretax accounting income | $88.0 |
| Income tax expense | (35.6) |
| Net income | $52.4 |

3. Show how any deferred tax amount(s) should be reported on the 2007 balance sheet. Assume taxable income is expected in 2008 sufficient to absorb any deductible amounts carried forward from 2007.

($ in millions)

| | Classification Current—C Noncurrent—N | Future Taxable (Deductible) Amounts | Tax Rate | Deferred Tax (Asset) Liability C | N |
|---|---|---|---|---|---|
| **Related balance sheet account** | | | | | |
| Prepaid insurance | C | 28 | × 40% | 11.2 | |
| Depreciable assets | N | 162 | × 40% | | 64.8 |
| Liability—rent received in advance | C | (20) | × 40% | (8.0) | |
| **Unrelated to any balance sheet account** | | | | | |
| Operating loss carryforward | C* | (8) | × 40% | (3.2) | |
| Net current liability (asset) | | | | 0.0 | |
| Net noncurrent liability (asset) | | | | | 64.8 |

*Deferred tax asset classified entirely as current because 2008 income is expected to be sufficient to realize the benefit of the carryforward.

**No net current amount**

***Long-term liabilities:***

Deferred tax liability $64.8

Note: These net amounts ($0.0 + 64.8 = $64.8) sum to the net **total** deferred tax liabilities and deferred tax assets from requirement 1 ($76.0 − 11.2 = $64.8).

## FINANCIAL REPORTING CASE SOLUTION

1. **What's the difference? Explain to Laura how differences between financial reporting standards and income tax rules might cause the two tax amounts to differ.** *(p. 774)* The differences in the rules for computing taxable income and those for financial reporting often cause amounts to be included in taxable income a different year(s) from the year in which they are recognized for financial reporting purposes. Temporary differences result in future taxable or deductible amounts when the temporary differences reverse. As a result, tax payments frequently occur in years different from the years in which the revenues and expenses that cause the taxes are generated.
2. **What is the conceptual advantage of determining income tax expense as we do?** *(p. 774)* Income tax expense is the combination of the current tax effect and the deferred tax consequences of the period's activities. Under the asset-liability approach, the objective

of accounting for income taxes is to recognize a deferred tax liability or deferred tax asset for the tax consequences of amounts that will become taxable or deductible in future years as a result of transactions or events that already have occurred. A result is to recognize both the current and the deferred tax consequences of the operations of a reporting period.

3. **Are there differences between financial reporting standards and income tax rules that will not contribute to the difference between income tax expense and the amount of income taxes paid?** *(p. 786)* Yes. Some differences between accounting income and taxable income are caused by transactions and events that will never affect taxable income or taxes payable. These differences between accounting income and taxable income do not reverse later. These are permanent differences which are disregarded when determining (a) the tax payable currently, (b) the deferred tax effect, and therefore (c) the income tax expense. ■

## THE BOTTOM LINE

1. Temporary differences produce future taxable amounts when the taxable income will be increased relative to accounting income in one or more future years. These produce deferred tax liabilities for the taxes to be paid on the future taxable amounts. Income tax expense for the year includes an amount for which payment (or receipt) is deferred in addition to the amount for which payment is due currently. The deferred amount is the change in the tax liability (or asset).
2. When the future tax consequence of a temporary difference will be to decrease taxable income relative to accounting income, future deductible amounts are created. These have favorable tax consequences that are recognized as deferred tax assets.
3. Deferred tax assets are recognized for all deductible temporary differences. However, a deferred tax asset is then reduced by a valuation allowance if it is more likely than not that some portion or all of the deferred tax asset will not be realized.
4. Nontemporary differences between the reported amount of an asset or liability in the financial statements and its tax basis are those caused by transactions and events that under existing tax law will never affect taxable income or taxes payable. These are disregarded when determining both the tax payable currently and the deferred tax effect.
5. The deferred tax liability (or asset) for which payment (or receipt) is deferred is based on enacted tax rates applied to the taxable or deductible amounts. If a change in a tax law or rate occurs, the deferred tax liability or asset is adjusted to reflect the change in the amount to be paid or recovered. That effect is reflected in operating income in the year of the enactment of the change in the tax law or rate.
6. When multiple temporary differences exist, the total of the future **taxable** amounts is multiplied by the future tax rate to determine the appropriate balance for the deferred tax liability, and the total of the future **deductible** amounts is multiplied by the future tax rate to determine the appropriate balance for the deferred tax asset.
7. Tax laws permit an operating loss to be used to reduce taxable income in other, profitable years by either a carryback of the loss to prior years (2) or a carryforward of the loss to later years (up to 20). The tax benefit of an operating loss carryback or an operating loss carryforward is recognized in the year of the loss.
8. Deferred tax assets and deferred tax liabilities are classified as either current or noncurrent according to how the related assets or liabilities are classified for financial reporting. Disclosure notes should reveal additional relevant information needed for full disclosure pertaining to deferred tax amounts reported on the balance sheet, the components of income tax expense, and available operating loss carryforwards.
9. Through intraperiod tax allocation, the total income tax expense for a reporting period is allocated among the financial statement items that gave rise to it; specifically, income (or loss) from continuing operations, discontinued operations, extraordinary items, and prior period adjustments (to the beginning retained earnings balance). ■

## QUESTIONS FOR REVIEW OF KEY TOPICS

**Q 16–1** A member of the board of directors is concerned that the company's income statement reports income tax expense of $12.3 million, but the income tax obligation to the government for the year is only $7.9 million. How might the corporate controller explain this apparent discrepancy?

**Q 16–2** A deferred tax liability (or asset) is described as the tax effect of the temporary difference between the financial statement carrying amount of an asset or liability and its tax basis. Explain this tax effect of the temporary difference. How might it produce a deferred tax liability? A deferred tax asset?

**Q 16–3** Sometimes a temporary difference will produce future deductible amounts. Explain what is meant by future deductible amounts. Describe two general situations that have this effect. How are such situations recognized in the financial statements?

**Q 16–4** The benefit of future deductible amounts can be achieved only if future income is sufficient to take advantage of the deferred deductions. For that reason, not all deferred tax assets will ultimately be realized. How is this possibility reflected in the way we recognize deferred tax assets?

**Q 16–5** Temporary differences result in future taxable or deductible amounts when the related asset or liability is recovered or settled. Some differences, though, are not temporary. What events create nontemporary or permanent differences? What effect do these have on the determination of income taxes payable? Of deferred income taxes?

**Q 16–6** Identify three examples of differences with no deferred tax consequences.

**Q 16–7** The income tax rate for Hudson Refinery has been 35% for each of its 12 years of operation. Company forecasters expect a much-debated tax reform bill to be passed by Congress early next year. The new tax measure would increase Hudson's tax rate to 42%. When measuring this year's deferred tax liability, which rate should Hudson use?

**Q 16–8** Suppose a tax reform bill is enacted that causes the corporate tax rate to change from 34% to 36%. How would this affect an existing deferred tax liability? How would the change be reflected in income?

**Q 16–9** An operating loss occurs when tax-deductible expenses exceed taxable revenues. Tax laws permit the operating loss to be used to reduce taxable income in other, profitable years by either a carryback of the loss to prior years or a carryforward of the loss to later years. How are loss carrybacks and loss carryforwards recognized for financial reporting purposes?

**Q 16–10** How are deferred tax assets and deferred tax liabilities reported in a classified balance sheet?

**Q 16–11** Additional disclosures are required pertaining to deferred tax amounts reported on the balance sheet. What are the needed disclosures?

**Q 16–12** Additional disclosures are required pertaining to the income tax expense reported on the income statement. What are the needed disclosures?

**Q 16–13** What is intraperiod tax allocation?

**Q 16–14** Some accountants believe that deferred taxes should be recognized only for some temporary differences. What is the conceptual basis for this argument? What is the counter argument that serves as the basis for the FASB's requirement that deferred taxes should be recognized for all temporary differences?

## BRIEF EXERCISES

**BE 16–1**
Temporary difference; deferred tax liability
● LO1

A company reports *pretax accounting income* of $10 million, but because of a single temporary difference, *taxable income* is only $7 million. No temporary differences existed at the beginning of the year, and the tax rate is 40%. Prepare the appropriate journal entry to record income taxes.

**BE 16–2**
Temporary difference; deferred tax asset
● LO2

A company reports *pretax accounting income* of $10 million, but because of a single temporary difference, *taxable income* is $12 million. No temporary differences existed at the beginning of the year, and the tax rate is 40%. Prepare the appropriate journal entry to record income taxes.

**BE 16–3**
Single temporary difference; income tax payable given
● LO2

In 2006, Ryan Management collected rent revenue for 2007 tenant occupancy. For financial reporting, the rent is recognized as income in the period earned, but for income tax reporting it is taxed when collected. The unearned portion of the rent collected in 2006 was $50 million. Taxable income is $180 million. No temporary differences existed at the beginning of the year, and the tax rate is 40%. Prepare the appropriate journal entry to record income taxes.

**BE 16–4**
Single temporary difference; income tax payable given
● LO2

Refer to the situation described in BE 16–3. Suppose the unearned portion of the rent collected was $40 million at the end of 2007. Taxable income is $200 million. Prepare the appropriate journal entry to record income taxes.

**BE 16–5**
Valuation allowance
● LO2 LO3

At the end of the year, the deferred tax asset account had a balance of $12 million attributable to a cumulative temporary difference of $30 million in a liability for estimated expenses. Taxable income is $35 million. No temporary differences existed at the beginning of the year, and the tax rate is 40%. Prepare the journal entry(s) to record income taxes assuming it is more likely than not that one-fourth of the deferred tax asset will not ultimately be realized.

**BE 16–6**
Valuation allowance
● LO2 LO3

Hypercom Corporation is a provider of electronic card payment terminals, peripherals, network products, and software. In its 2003 annual report, it reported current and long-term deferred tax assets totaling $56.6 million. The company also reported valuation allowances totaling $56.6 million. What would motivate Hypercom to have a valuation allowance equal to its deferred tax assets?

**BE 16–7**
Single temporary difference; determine taxable income; determine prior year deferred tax amount
● LO2 LO3

Kara Fashions uses straight-line depreciation for financial statement reporting and MACRS for income tax reporting. Three years after its purchase, one of Kara's buildings has a carrying value of $400,000 and a tax basis of $300,000. There were no other temporary differences and no nontemporary differences. Taxable income was $4 million and Kara's tax rate is 40%. What is deferred tax liability to be reported in the balance sheet? Assuming that balance was $32,000 the previous year, prepare the appropriate journal entry to record income taxes this year.

**BE 16–8**
Temporary and nontemporary differences; determine deferred tax consequences
● LO1 LO4

Differences between financial statement and taxable income were as follows:

| | ($ in millions) |
|---|---|
| Pretax accounting income | $300 |
| Permanent difference | (24) |
| | 276 |
| Temporary difference | (18) |
| Taxable income | $258 |

The cumulative temporary difference to date is $40 million (also the future taxable amount). The enacted tax rate is 40%. What is deferred tax asset or liability to be reported in the balance sheet?

**BE 16–9**
Single temporary difference; nontemporary difference; calculate taxable income
● LO1 LO4

Shannon Polymers uses straight-line depreciation for financial reporting purposes for equipment costing $800,000 and with an expected useful life of four years and no residual value. For tax purposes, the deduction is 40%, 30%, 20%, and 10% in those years. Pretax accounting income the first year the equipment was used was $900,000, which includes interest revenue of $20,000 from municipal bonds. Other than the two described, there are no differences between accounting income and taxable income. The enacted tax rate is 40%. Prepare the journal entry to record income taxes.

**BE 16–10**
Single temporary difference; multiple tax rates
● LO5

J-Matt, Inc. had pretax accounting income of $291,000 and taxable income of $300,000 in 2006. The only difference between accounting and taxable income is estimated product warranty costs for sales this year. Warranty payments are expected to be in equal amounts over the next three years. Recent tax legislation will change the tax rate from the current 40% to 30% in 2008. Determine the amounts necessary to record J-Matt's income taxes for 2006 and prepare the appropriate journal entry.

**BE 16–11**
Change in tax rate; single temporary difference
● LO5

Superior Developers sells lots for residential development. When lots are sold, Superior recognizes income for financial reporting purposes in the year of the sale. For some lots, Superior recognizes income for tax purposes when collected. In the *prior* year, income recognized for financial reporting purposes for lots sold this way was $20 million, which would be collected equally over the next two years. The enacted tax rate was 40%. This year, a new tax law was enacted, revising the tax rate from 40% to 35% beginning next year. Calculate the amount by which Superior should reduce its deferred tax liability this year.

**BE 16–12**
Operating loss carryforward
● LO7

During its first year of operations, Nile.com reported an operating loss of $15 million for financial reporting and tax purposes. The enacted tax rate is 40%. Prepare the journal entry to recognize the income tax benefit of the operating loss.

**BE 16–13**
Operating loss carryback
● LO7

AirParts Corporation reported an operating loss of $25 million for financial reporting and tax purposes. Taxable income last year and the previous year, respectively, was $20 million and $15 million. The enacted tax rate each year is 40%. Prepare the journal entry to recognize the income tax benefit of the operating loss. AirParts elects the carryback option.

**BE 16–14**
Intraperiod tax allocation
● LO9

Southeast Airlines had pretax earnings of $65 million, including an extraordinary gain of $10 million. The company's tax rate is 40%. What is the amount of income tax expense that Southeast should report in its income statement? How should the extraordinary gain be reported?

# EXERCISES

available with McGraw-Hill's Homework Manager www.mhhe.com/spiceland4e

**An alternate exercise and problem set is available on the text website: www.mhhe.com/spiceland4e**

**E 16–1**
Single temporary difference; taxable income given
● LO1

Alvis Corporation reports *pretax accounting income* of $400,000, but due to a single temporary difference, *taxable income* is only $250,000. At the beginning of the year, no temporary differences existed.

**Required:**
Assuming a tax rate of 35%, prepare the appropriate journal entry to record Alvis's income taxes.

**E 16–2**
Single temporary difference; income tax payable given
● LO1 LO2

In 2006, Alworth Corporation collected rent revenue for 2007 tenant occupancy. For income tax reporting, the rent is taxed when collected. For financial statement reporting, the rent is recognized as income in the period earned. The unearned portion of the rent collected in 2006 amounted to $300,000 at December 31, 2006. Alworth had no temporary differences at the beginning of the year.

**Required:**
Assuming an income tax rate of 40% and 2006 income tax payable of $950,000, prepare the journal entry to record income taxes for 2006.

**E 16–3**
Single temporary difference; future deductible amounts; taxable income given
● LO2

Lance Lawn Services reports bad debt expense using the allowance method. For tax purposes, the expense is deducted when accounts prove uncollectible (the direct write-off method). At December 31, 2006, Lance has accounts receivable and an allowance for uncollectible accounts of $20 million and $1 million, respectively, and taxable income of $75 million. At December 31, 2005, Lance reported a deferred tax asset of $435,000 related to this difference in reporting bad debts, its only temporary difference. The enacted tax rate is 40% each year.

**Required:**
Prepare the appropriate journal entry to record Lance's income tax provision for 2006.

**E 16–4**
Deferred tax asset; income tax payable given; valuation allowance
● LO2 LO3

At the end of 2005, Payne Industries had a deferred tax asset account with a balance of $30 million attributable to a temporary book–tax difference of $75 million in a liability for estimated expenses. At the end of 2006, the temporary difference is $70 million. Payne has no other temporary differences and no valuation allowance for the deferred tax asset. Taxable income for 2006 is $180 million and the tax rate is 40%.

**Required:**
1. Prepare the journal entry(s) to record Payne's income taxes for 2006, assuming it is more likely than not that the deferred tax asset will be realized.
2. Prepare the journal entry(s) to record Payne's income taxes for 2006, assuming it is more likely than not that one-half of the deferred tax asset will not ultimately be realized.

**E 16–5**
Deferred tax asset; income tax payable given; previous balance in valuation allowance
● LO2 LO3

(This is a variation of the previous exercise, modified to assume a previous balance in the valuation allowance.)

At the end of 2005, Payne Industries had a deferred tax asset account with a balance of $30 million attributable to a temporary book-tax difference of $75 million in a liability for estimated expenses. At the end of 2006, the temporary difference is $70 million. Payne has no other temporary differences. Taxable income for 2006 is $180 million and the tax rate is 40%.

Payne has a valuation allowance of $10 million for the deferred tax asset at the beginning of 2006.

**Required:**
1. Prepare the journal entry(s) to record Payne's income taxes for 2006, assuming it is more likely than not that the deferred tax asset will be realized.
2. Prepare the journal entry(s) to record Payne's income taxes for 2006, assuming it is more likely than not that one-half of the deferred tax asset will not ultimately be realized.

**E 16–6**
Single temporary difference; determine taxable income; determine prior year deferred tax amount

● LO1 LO2

On January 1, 2003, Ameen Company purchased a building for $36 million. Ameen uses straight-line depreciation for financial statement reporting and MACRS for income tax reporting. At December 31, 2005, the carrying value of the building was $30 million and its tax basis was $20 million. At December 31, 2006, the carrying value of the building was $28 million and its tax basis was $13 million. There were no other temporary differences and no nontemporary differences. Pretax accounting income for 2006 was $20 million.

**Required:**

1. Prepare the appropriate journal entry to record Ameen's 2006 income taxes. Assume an income tax rate of 40%.
2. What is Ameen's 2006 net income?

**E 16–7**
Multiple choice; CPA exam; determining deferred tax amounts

● LO1 LO7 LO8

The following questions dealing with various topics in this chapter are adapted from prior CPA examinations. Determine the response that best completes the statements or questions.

1. Because Jab Co. uses different methods to depreciate equipment for financial statement and income tax purposes, Jab has temporary differences that will reverse during the next year and add to taxable income. Deferred income taxes that are based on these temporary differences should be classified in Jab's balance sheet as a
   a. Contra account to current assets.
   b. Contra account to noncurrent assets.
   c. Current liability.
   d. Noncurrent liability.

*Items 2 and 3 are based on the following:*

Kent, Inc.'s, reconciliation between financial statement and taxable income for 2006 follows:

| | |
|---|---|
| Pretax financial income | $150,000 |
| Permanent difference | (12,000) |
| | 138,000 |
| Temporary difference—depreciation | (9,000) |
| Taxable income | $129,000 |

*Additional information:*

| | At 12/31/05 | At 12/31/06 |
|---|---|---|
| Cumulative temporary differences (future taxable amounts) | $11,000 | $20,000 |

The enacted tax rate was 34% for 2005, and 40% for 2006 and years thereafter.

2. In its December 31, 2006, balance sheet, what amount should Kent report as deferred income tax liability?
   a. $3,600
   b. $6,800
   c. $7,340
   d. $8,000
3. In its 2006 income statement, what amount should Kent report as current portion of income tax expense?
   a. $51,600
   b. $55,200
   c. $55,860
   d. $60,000
4. Mobe Co. reported the following operating income (loss) for its first three years of operations:

| | |
|---|---|
| 2004 | $ 300,000 |
| 2005 | (700,000) |
| 2006 | 1,200,000 |

For each year, there were no deferred income taxes, and Mobe's effective income tax rate was 30%. In its 2005 income tax return, Mobe elected to carry back the maximum amount of loss possible. In its 2006 income statement, what amount should Mobe report as total income tax expense?
   a. $120,000
   b. $150,000
   c. $240,000
   d. $360,000

**E 16–8**
Single temporary difference; taxable income given; calculate deferred tax liability
● LO1

Ayres Services acquired an asset for $80 million in 2006. The asset is depreciated for financial reporting purposes over four years on a straight-line basis (no residual value). For tax purposes the asset's cost is depreciated by MACRS. The enacted tax rate is 40%. Amounts for pretax accounting income, depreciation, and taxable income in 2006, 2007, 2008, and 2009 are as follows:

| | ($ in millions) | | | |
|---|---|---|---|---|
| | **2006** | **2007** | **2008** | **2009** |
| **Accounting income** | $330 | $350 | $365 | $400 |
| Depreciation on the income statement | 20 | 20 | 20 | 20 |
| Depreciation on the tax return | (25) | (33) | (15) | (7) |
| **Taxable income** | $325 | $337 | $370 | $413 |

**Required:**
For December 31 of each year, determine (a) the temporary book–tax difference for the depreciable asset and (b) the balance to be reported in the deferred tax liability account.

**E 16–9**
Identifying future taxable amounts and future deductible amounts
● LO1 LO2

Listed below are 10 causes of temporary differences. For each temporary difference, indicate (by letter) whether it will create future deductible amounts (D) or future taxable amounts (T).

**Temporary Difference**

____ 1. Accrual of loss contingency, tax-deductible when paid.
____ 2. Newspaper subscriptions; taxable when received, recognized for financial reporting when earned.
____ 3. Prepaid rent, tax-deductible when paid.
____ 4. Accrued bond interest expense, tax-deductible when paid.
____ 5. Prepaid insurance, tax-deductible when paid.
____ 6. Unrealized loss from recording investments available for sale at fair market value (tax-deductible when investments are sold).
____ 7. Bad debt expense; allowance method for financial reporting; direct write-off for tax purposes.
____ 8. Advance rent receipts on an operating lease (as the lessor), taxable when received.
____ 9. Straight-line depreciation for financial reporting; accelerated depreciation for tax purposes.
____ 10. Accrued expense for employee postretirement benefits, tax-deductible when subsequent payments are made.

**E 16–10**
Identifying future taxable amounts and future deductible amounts
● LO2

(This is a variation of the previous exercise, modified to focus on the balance sheet accounts related to the deferred tax amounts.)

Listed below are 10 causes of temporary differences. For each temporary difference indicate the balance sheet account for which the situation creates a temporary difference.

**Temporary Difference**

1. Accrual of loss contingency, tax-deductible when paid.
2. Newspaper subscriptions; taxable when received, recognized for financial reporting when earned.
3. Prepaid rent, tax-deductible when paid.
4. Accrued bond interest expense, tax-deductible when paid.
5. Prepaid insurance, tax-deductible when paid.
6. Unrealized loss from recording investments available for sale at fair market (tax-deductible when investments are sold).
7. Bad debt expense; allowance method for financial reporting; direct write-off for tax purposes.
8. Advance rent receipts on an operating lease (as the lessor), taxable when received.
9. Straight-line depreciation for financial reporting; accelerated depreciation for tax purposes.
10. Accrued expense for employee postretirement benefits, tax-deductible when subsequent payments are made.

**E 16–11**
Single temporary difference; nontemporary difference; calculate taxable income
● LO1 LO4

Southern Atlantic Distributors began operations in January 2006 and purchased a delivery truck for $40,000. Southern Atlantic plans to use straight-line depreciation over a four-year expected useful life for financial reporting purposes. For tax purposes, the deduction is 50% of cost in 2006, 30% in 2007, and 20% in 2008. Pretax accounting income for 2006 was $300,000, which includes interest revenue of $40,000 from municipal bonds. The enacted tax rate is 40%.

**Required:**
Assuming no differences between accounting income and taxable income other than those described above:
1. Prepare the journal entry to record income taxes in 2006.
2. What is Southern Atlantic's 2006 net income?

**E16–12**
Single temporary difference; nontemporary difference (goodwill); calculate taxable income
● LO1 LO4

Peridot Developers, Inc. began operations in December 2006. Peridot sells plots of land for industrial development. Peridot recognizes income for financial reporting purposes in the year it sells the plots. For some of the plots sold, Peridot recognizes the income for tax purposes when collected. Income Peridot recognized for financial reporting purposes in 2006 for plots sold this way was $40 million. The company expected to collect this amount over the next two years as follows:

| | |
|---|---|
| 2007 | $24 million |
| 2008 | 16 million |
| | $40 million |

Peridot's pretax *accounting* income for 2006 was $63 million. On its tax return, Peridot is amortizing $45 million of goodwill over the 15-year period permitted by tax laws. Goodwill is not amortizable for financial reporting purposes and thus is not reflected in pretax accounting income. The enacted tax rate is 40 percent.

**Required:**
1. Assuming no differences between accounting income and taxable income other than those described above, prepare the journal entry to record income taxes in 2006.
2. What is Peridot's 2006 net income?

**E 16–13**
Single temporary difference; multiple tax rates
● LO2 LO5

Allmond Corporation, organized on January 3, 2006, had pretax accounting income of $14 million and taxable income of $20 million for the year ended December 31, 2006. The 2006 tax rate is 35%. The only difference between accounting income and taxable income is estimated product warranty costs. Expected payments and scheduled tax rates (based on recent tax legislation) are as follows:

| | | |
|---|---|---|
| 2007 | $2 million | 30% |
| 2008 | 1 million | 30% |
| 2009 | 1 million | 30% |
| 2010 | 2 million | 25% |

**Required:**
1. Determine the amounts necessary to record Allmond's income taxes for 2006 and prepare the appropriate journal entry.
2. What is Allmond's 2006 net income?

**E 16–14**
Change in tax rates; calculate taxable income
● LO1 LO5

Arnold Industries has pretax accounting income of $33 million for the year ended December 31, 2006. The tax rate is 40%. The only difference between accounting income and taxable income relates to an operating lease in which Arnold is the lessee. The inception of the lease was December 28, 2006. An $8 million advance rent payment at the inception of the lease is tax-deductible in 2006 but, for financial reporting purposes, represents prepaid rent expense to be recognized equally over the four-year lease term.

**Required:**
1. Determine the amounts necessary to record Arnold's income taxes for 2006 and prepare the appropriate journal entry.
2. Determine the amounts necessary to record Arnold's income taxes for 2007 and prepare the appropriate journal entry. Pretax accounting income was $50 million for the year ended December 31, 2007.
3. Assume a new tax law is enacted in 2007 that causes the tax rate to change from 40% to 30% beginning in 2008. Determine the amounts necessary to record Arnold's income taxes for 2007 and prepare the appropriate journal entry.
4. Why is Arnold's 2007 income tax expense different when the tax rate change occurs from what it would be without the change?

**E 16–15**
Deferred taxes; change in tax rates
● LO1 LO5

Bronson Industries reported a deferred tax liability of $8 million for the year ended December 31, 2005, related to a temporary difference of $20 million. The tax rate was 40%. The temporary difference is expected to reverse in 2007 at which time the deferred tax liability will become payable. There are no other temporary differences in 2005–2007. Assume a new tax law is enacted in 2006 that causes the tax rate to change from 40% to 30% beginning in 2007. (The rate remains 40% for 2006 taxes.) Taxable income in 2006 is $30 million.

**Required:**
Determine the effect of the change and prepare the appropriate journal entry to record Bronson's income tax expense in 2006. What adjustment, if any, is needed to revise retained earnings as a result of the change?

**E 16–16**
Multiple temporary differences; record income taxes
● LO6

The information that follows pertains to Esther Food Products:
a. At December 31, 2006, temporary differences were associated with the following future taxable (deductible) amounts:

| | |
|---|---|
| Depreciation | $60,000 |
| Prepaid expenses | 17,000 |
| Warranty expenses | (12,000) |

b. No temporary differences existed at the beginning of 2006.
c. Pretax accounting income was $80,000 and taxable income was $15,000 for the year ended December 31, 2006.
d. The tax rate is 40%.

**Required:**
Determine the amounts necessary to record income taxes for 2006 and prepare the appropriate journal entry.

**E 16–17**
Multiple temporary differences; record income taxes
● LO6

The information that follows pertains to Richards Refrigeration, Inc.:
a. At December 31, 2006, temporary differences existed between the financial statement carrying amounts and the tax bases of the following:

| | ($ in millions) | | |
|---|---|---|---|
| | Carrying Amount | Tax Basis | Future Taxable (Deductible) Amount |
| Buildings and equipment (net of accumulated depreciation) | $120 | $90 | $30 |
| Prepaid insurance | 50 | 0 | 50 |
| Liability—loss contingency | 25 | 0 | (25) |

b. No temporary differences existed at the beginning of 2006.
c. Pretax accounting income was $200 million and taxable income was $145 million for the year ended December 31, 2006. The tax rate is 40%.

**Required:**
1. Determine the amounts necessary to record income taxes for 2006 and prepare the appropriate journal entry.
2. What is the 2006 net income?

**E 16–18**
Calculate income tax amounts under various circumstances
● LO1 LO2

Four independent situations are described below. Each involves future deductible amounts and/or future taxable amounts produced by temporary differences:

| | ($ in thousands) Situation | | | |
|---|---|---|---|---|
| | 1 | 2 | 3 | 4 |
| Taxable income | $85 | $215 | $195 | $260 |
| Future deductible amounts | 15 | | 20 | 20 |
| Future taxable amounts | | 15 | 15 | 30 |
| Balance(s) at beginning of the year: | | | | |
| Deferred tax asset | 2 | | 9 | 4 |
| Deferred tax liability | | 2 | 2 | |

The enacted tax rate is 40%.

**Required:**
For each situation, determine the:
a. Income tax payable currently.
b. Deferred tax asset—balance.
c. Deferred tax asset—change (dr) cr.
d. Deferred tax liability—balance.
e. Deferred tax liability—change (dr) cr.
f. Income tax expense.

**E 16–19**
Determine taxable income
● LO1 LO2

Eight independent situations are described below. Each involves future deductible amounts and/or future taxable amounts produced by:

| | ($ in millions) Temporary Differences Reported First on: | | | |
|---|---|---|---|---|
| | The Income Statement | | The Tax Return | |
| | Revenue | Expense | Revenue | Expense |
| 1. | | $20 | | |
| 2. | $20 | | | |
| 3. | | | $20 | |
| 4. | | | | $20 |
| 5. | 15 | 20 | | |
| 6. | | 20 | 15 | |
| 7. | 15 | 20 | | 10 |
| 8. | 15 | 20 | 5 | 10 |

**Required:**

For each situation, determine taxable income assuming pretax accounting income is $100 million.

**E 16–20**
Two temporary differences; nontemporary difference
● LO1 LO2 LO4

For the year ended December 31, 2006, Fidelity Engineering reported pretax accounting income of $977,000. Selected information for 2006 from Fidelity's records follows:

| | |
|---|---|
| Interest income on municipal bonds | $32,000 |
| Depreciation claimed on the 2006 tax return in excess of depreciation on the income statement | 55,000 |
| Carrying amount of depreciable assets in excess of their tax basis at year-end | 85,000 |
| Warranty expense reported on the income statement | 26,000 |
| Actual warranty expenditures in 2006 | 16,000 |

Fidelity's income tax rate is 40%. At January 1, 2006, Fidelity's records indicated balances of zero and $12,000 in its deferred tax asset and deferred tax liability accounts, respectively.

**Required:**

1. Determine the amounts necessary to record income taxes for 2006 and prepare the appropriate journal entry.
2. What is Fidelity's 2006 net income?

**E 16–21**
Operating loss carryforward
● LO7

During 2006, its first year of operations, Baginski Steel Corporation reported an operating loss of $375,000 for financial reporting and tax purposes. The enacted tax rate is 40%.

**Required:**

1. Prepare the journal entry to recognize the income tax benefit of the operating loss. Assume the weight of available evidence suggests future taxable income sufficient to benefit from future deductible amounts from the operating loss carryforward.
2. Show the lower portion of the 2006 income statement that reports the income tax benefit of the operating loss.

**E 16–22**
Operating loss carryback
● LO7

Wynn Sheet Metal reported an operating loss of $100,000 for financial reporting and tax purposes in 2006. The enacted tax rate is 40%. Taxable income, tax rates, and income taxes paid in Wynn's first four years of operation were as follows:

| | Taxable Income | Tax Rates | Income Taxes Paid |
|---|---|---|---|
| 2002 | $60,000 | 30% | $18,000 |
| 2003 | 70,000 | 30 | 21,000 |
| 2004 | 80,000 | 40 | 32,000 |
| 2005 | 60,000 | 45 | 27,000 |

**Required:**

1. Prepare the journal entry to recognize the income tax benefit of the operating loss. Wynn elects the carryback option.
2. Show the lower portion of the 2006 income statement that reports the income tax benefit of the operating loss.

**E 16–23**
Operating loss carryback and carryforward
● LO7

(This exercise is based on the situation described in the previous exercise, modified to include a carryforward in addition to a carryback.)

Wynn Sheet Metal reported an operating loss of $160,000 for financial reporting and tax purposes in 2006. The enacted tax is 40%. Taxable income, tax rates, and income taxes paid in Wynn's first four years of operation were as follows:

| | Taxable Income | Tax Rates | Income Taxes Paid |
|---|---|---|---|
| 2002 | $60,000 | 30% | $18,000 |
| 2003 | 70,000 | 30 | 21,000 |
| 2004 | 80,000 | 40 | 32,000 |
| 2005 | 60,000 | 45 | 27,000 |

**Required:**

1. Prepare the journal entry to recognize the income tax benefit of the operating loss. Wynn elects the carryback option.
2. Show the lower portion of the 2006 income statement that reports the income tax benefit of the operating loss.

**E 16–24**
Balance sheet classification
● LO8

At December 31, 2006, DePaul Corporation had a $16 million balance in its deferred tax asset account and a $68 million balance in its deferred tax liability account. The balances were due to the following cumulative temporary differences:

1. Estimated warranty expense, $15 million: expense recorded in the year of the sale; tax-deductible when paid (one-year warranty).
2. Depreciation expense, $120 million: straight-line on the income statement; MACRS on the tax return.

3. Income from installment sales of properties, $50 million: income recorded in the year of the sale; taxable when received equally over the next five years.
4. Bad debt expense, $25 million: allowance method for accounting; direct write-off for tax purposes.

**Required:**

Show how any deferred tax amounts should be classified and reported on the 2006 balance sheet. The tax rate is 40%.

**E 16–25**
Single temporary difference; nontemporary difference; multiple tax rates; balance sheet classification

● LO1 LO4 LO5 LO8

Case Development began operations in December 2006. When property is sold on an installment basis, Case recognizes installment income for financial reporting purposes in the year of the sale. For tax purposes, installment income is reported by the installment method. 2006 installment income was $600,000 and will be collected over the next three years. Scheduled collections and enacted tax rates for 2007–2009 are as follows:

| | | |
|---|---|---|
| 2007 | $150,000 | 30% |
| 2008 | 250,000 | 40 |
| 2009 | 200,000 | 40 |

Pretax accounting income for 2006 was $810,000, which includes interest revenue of $10,000 from municipal bonds. The enacted tax rate for 2006 is 30%.

**Required:**

1. Assuming no differences between accounting income and taxable income other than those described above, prepare the appropriate journal entry to record Case's 2006 income taxes.
2. What is Case's 2006 net income?
3. How should the deferred tax amount be classified in a classified balance sheet?

**E 16–26**
Two temporary differences; nontemporary difference; multiple tax rates; balance sheet classification

● LO1 LO2 LO4 LO5 LO6 LO8

(This exercise is a variation of the previous exercise, modified to include a second temporary difference.)

Case Development began operations in December 2006. When property is sold on an installment basis, Case recognizes installment income for financial reporting purposes in the year of the sale. For tax purposes, installment income is reported by the installment method. 2006 installment income was $600,000 and will be collected over the next three years. Scheduled collections and enacted tax rates for 2007–2009 are as follows:

| | | |
|---|---|---|
| 2007 | $150,000 | 30% |
| 2008 | 250,000 | 40 |
| 2009 | 200,000 | 40 |

Case also had product warranty costs of $80,000 expensed for financial reporting purposes in 2006. For tax purposes, only the $20,000 of warranty costs actually paid in 2006 was deducted. The remaining $60,000 will be deducted for tax purposes when paid over the next three years as follows:

| | |
|---|---|
| 2007 | $20,000 |
| 2008 | 25,000 |
| 2009 | 15,000 |

Pretax *accounting* income for 2006 was $810,000, which includes interest revenue of $10,000 from municipal bonds. The enacted tax rate for 2006 is 30%.

**Required:**

1. Assuming no differences between accounting income and taxable income other than those described above, prepare the appropriate journal entry to record Case's 2006 income taxes.
2. What is Case's 2006 net income?
3. How should the deferred tax amounts be classified in a classified balance sheet?

**E 16–27**
Identifying income tax deferrals

● LO1 LO2 LO4 LO7

Listed below are ten independent situations. For each situation indicate (by letter) whether it will create a deferred tax asset (A), a deferred tax liability (L), or neither (N).

**Situation**

_____ 1. Advance payments on an operating lease deductible when paid.
_____ 2. Estimated warranty costs, tax deductible when paid.
_____ 3. Rent revenue collected in advance; cash basis for tax purposes.
_____ 4. Interest received from investments in municipal bonds.
_____ 5. Prepaid expenses tax deductible when paid.
_____ 6. Operating loss carryforward.
_____ 7. Operating loss carryback.
_____ 8. Bad debt expense; allowance method for accounting; direct write-off for tax.
_____ 9. Organization costs expensed when incurred, tax deductible over 15 years.
_____ 10. Life insurance proceeds received upon the death of the company president.

**E 16–28**
Concepts; terminology
• LO1 through LO8

Listed below are several terms and phrases associated with accounting for income taxes. Pair each item from List A (by letter) with the item from List B that is most appropriately associated with it.

| List A | List B |
|---|---|
| ____ 1. No tax consequences. | a. Deferred tax liability. |
| ____ 2. Originates, then reverses. | b. Deferred tax asset. |
| ____ 3. Revise deferred tax amounts. | c. 2 years. |
| ____ 4. Operating loss. | d. Current and deferred tax consequence combined. |
| ____ 5. Future tax effect of prepaid expenses tax deductible when paid. | e. Temporary difference. |
| ____ 6. Loss carryback. | f. Specific tax rates times amounts reversing each year. |
| ____ 7. Future tax effect of estimated warranty expense. | g. Nontemporary differences. |
| | h. When enacted tax rate changes. |
| ____ 8. Valuation allowance. | i. Same as related asset or liability. |
| ____ 9. Phased-in change in rates. | j. "More likely than not" test. |
| ____ 10. Balance sheet classifications. | k. Intraperiod tax allocation. |
| ____ 11. Individual tax consequences of financial statement components. | l. Negative taxable income. |
| ____ 12. Income tax expense. | |

**E 16–29**
Intraperiod tax allocation
• LO9

The following income statement does not reflect intraperiod tax allocation.

**Required:**
Recast the income statement to reflect intraperiod tax allocation.

**INCOME STATEMENT**
**For the Fiscal Year Ended March 31, 2006**
($ in millions)

| | |
|---|---|
| Revenues | $830 |
| Cost of goods sold | (350) |
| Gross profit | 480 |
| Operating expenses | (180) |
| Income tax expense | (86) |
| Income before discontinued operations and extraordinary item | 214 |
| Loss from discontinued operations | (10) |
| Extraordinary casualty loss | (75) |
| Net income | $129 |

The company's tax rate is 40%.

**E 16–30**
Multiple choice; CMA exam; deferred taxes
• LO1 LO2 LO5

The following questions dealing with deferred taxes are adapted from questions that previously appeared on Certified Management Accountant (CMA) examinations. The CMA designation sponsored by the Institute of Management Accountants (**www.imanet.org**) provides members with an objective measure of knowledge and competence in the field of management accounting. Determine the response that best completes the statements or questions.

1. Which one of the following temporary differences will result in a deferred tax asset?
   a. Use of the straight-line depreciation method for financial statement purposes and the modified Accelerated Cost Recovery System (MACRS) for income tax purposes.
   b. Installment sale profits accounted for on the accrual basis for financial statement purposes and on a cash basis for income tax purposes.
   c. Advance rental receipts accounted for on the accrual basis for financial statement purposes and on a cash basis for tax purposes.
   d. Investment gains accounted for under the equity method for financial statement purposes and under the cost method for income tax purposes.

Questions 2 and 3 are based on the following information. Bearings Manufacturing Company Inc. purchased a new machine on January 1, 2007 for $100,000. The company uses the straight-line depreciation method with an estimated equipment life of 5 years and a zero salvage value for financial statement purposes, and uses the 3-year Modified Accelerated Cost Recovery System (MACRS) with an estimated equipment life of 3 years for income tax reporting purposes. Bearings is subject to a 35% marginal income tax rate. Assume that the deferred tax liability at the beginning of the year is zero and that Bearings has a positive earnings tax position. The MACRS depreciation rates for 3-year equipment are shown below.

| Year | Rate |
|---|---|
| 1 | 33.33% |
| 2 | 44.45 |
| 3 | 14.81 |
| 4 | 7.41 |

2. What is the deferred tax liability at December 31, 2007 (rounded to the nearest whole dollar)?
   a. $ 7,000
   b. $33,330
   c. $11,666
   d. $ 4,666
3. For Bearings Manufacturing Company Inc., assume that the following new corporate income tax rates will go into effect:

| | |
|---|---|
| 2008–2010 | 40% |
| 2011 | 45% |

   What is the amount of the deferred tax asset/liability at December 31, 2007 (rounded to the nearest whole dollar)?
   a. $0
   b. $9,000
   c. $2,668
   d. $6,332

## PROBLEMS

available with McGraw-Hill's Homework Manager www.mhhe.com/spiceland4e

**An alternate exercise and problem set is available on the text website: www.mhhe.com/spiceland4e**

**P 16–1**
Determine deferred tax assets and liabilities
● LO1 LO2

Corning-Howell reported taxable income in 2006 of $120 million. At December 31, 2006, the reported amount of some assets and liabilities in the financial statements differed from their tax bases as indicated below:

| | Carrying Amount | Tax Basis |
|---|---|---|
| **Assets** | | |
| Current | | |
| Accounts receivable (net of allowance) | $ 10 million | $ 12 million |
| Prepaid insurance | 20 million | 0 |
| Prepaid rent expense (operating lease) | 6 million | 0 |
| Noncurrent | | |
| Buildings and equipment (net) | 360 million | 280 million |
| **Liabilities** | | |
| Current | | |
| Liability—subscriptions received | 14 million | 0 |
| Long-term | | |
| Liability—postretirement benefits | 594 million | 0 |
| **Shareholders' Equity** | | |
| Unrealized gain from recording investments available for sale at fair market value* | 4 million | 0 |

*Taxable when investments are sold.

The total deferred tax asset and deferred tax liability amounts at January 1, 2006, were $250 million and $40 million, respectively. The enacted tax rate is 40% each year.

**Required:**

1. Determine the total deferred tax asset and deferred tax liability amounts at December 31, 2006.
2. Determine the increase (decrease) in the deferred tax asset and deferred tax liability accounts at December 31, 2006.
3. Determine the income tax payable currently for the year ended December 31, 2006.
4. Prepare the journal entry to record income taxes for 2006.
5. Show how the deferred tax amounts should be classified and reported in the 2006 balance sheet.

**P 16–2**
Temporary difference; determine deferred tax amount for three years; balance sheet classification
● LO2 LO8

Times-Roman Publishing Company reports the following amounts in its first three years of operation:

| ($ in 000s) | 2006 | 2007 | 2008 |
|---|---|---|---|
| Pretax accounting income | $250 | $240 | $230 |
| Taxable income | 290 | 220 | 260 |

The difference between pretax accounting income and taxable income is due to subscription revenue for one-year magazine subscriptions being reported for tax purposes in the year received, but reported on the income statement in later years when earned. The income tax rate is 40% each year. Times-Roman anticipates profitable operations in the future.

**Required:**

1. What is the balance sheet account for which a temporary difference is created by this situation?
2. For each year, indicate the cumulative amount of the temporary difference at year-end.
3. Determine the balance in the related deferred tax account at the end of each year. Is it a deferred tax asset or a deferred tax liability?
4. How should the deferred tax amount be classified and reported on the balance sheet?

**P 16–3**
Change in tax rate; single temporary difference

● LO5

Dixon Development began operations in December 2006. When lots for industrial development are sold, Dixon recognizes income for financial reporting purposes in the year of the sale. For some lots, Dixon recognizes income for tax purposes when collected. Income recognized for financial reporting purposes in 2006 for lots sold this way was $12 million, which will be collected over the next three years. Scheduled collections for 2007–2009 are as follows:

| | |
|---|---|
| 2007 | $ 4 million |
| 2008 | 5 million |
| 2009 | 3 million |
| | $12 million |

Pretax accounting income for 2006 was $16 million. The enacted tax rate is 40%.

**Required:**

1. Assuming no differences between accounting income and taxable income other than those described above, prepare the journal entry to record income taxes in 2006.
2. Suppose a new tax law, revising the tax rate from 40% to 35%, beginning in 2008, is enacted in 2007, when pretax accounting income was $15 million. Prepare the appropriate journal entry to record income taxes in 2007.
3. If the new tax rate had not been enacted, what would have been the appropriate balance in the deferred tax liability account at the end of 2007? Why?

**P 16–4**
Change in tax rate; record taxes for four years

● LO5

*eXcel*

Zekany Corporation would have had identical income before taxes on both its income tax returns and income statements for the years 2006 through 2009 except for differences in depreciation on an operational asset. The asset cost $120,000 and is depreciated for income tax purposes in the following amounts:

| | |
|---|---|
| 2006 | $39,600 |
| 2007 | 52,800 |
| 2008 | 18,000 |
| 2009 | 9,600 |

The operational asset has a four-year life and no residual value. The straight-line method is used for financial reporting purposes.

Income amounts before depreciation expense and income taxes for each of the four years were as follows.

| | 2006 | 2007 | 2008 | 2009 |
|---|---|---|---|---|
| Accounting income before taxes and depreciation | $60,000 | $80,000 | $70,000 | $70,000 |

Assume the average and marginal income tax rate for 2006 and 2007 was 30%; however, during 2007 tax legislation was passed to raise the tax rate to 40% beginning in 2008. The 40% rate remained in effect through the years 2008 and 2009. Both the accounting and income tax periods end December 31.

**Required:**

Prepare the journal entries to record income taxes for the years 2006 through 2009.

**P 16–5**
Change in tax rate; permanent and temporary differences; record taxes for four years

● LO1 LO2 LO4 LO5 LO6

*eXcel*

The DeVille Company reported pretax accounting income on its income statement as follows:

| | |
|---|---|
| 2006 | $350,000 |
| 2007 | 270,000 |
| 2008 | 340,000 |
| 2009 | 380,000 |

Included in the income of 2006 was an installment sale of property in the amount of $50,000. However, for tax purposes, DeVille reported the income in the year cash was collected. Cash collected on the installment sale was $20,000 in 2007, $25,000 in 2008, and $5,000 in 2009.

Included in the 2008 income was $15,000 interest from investments in municipal bonds.

The enacted tax rate for 2006 and 2007 was 30%, but during 2007 new tax legislation was passed reducing the tax rate to 25% for the years 2008 and beyond.

**Required:**

Prepare the year-end journal entries to record income taxes for the years 2006–2009.

**P 16–6**
Multiple temporary differences; multiple tax rates; balance sheet classification

● LO5 LO6 LO8

The following information relates to Barry Transport Company:

a. Pretax accounting income was $41 million and taxable income was $8 million for the year ended December 31, 2006.
b. Temporary differences at December 31, 2006, were related to:

| | | Future Taxable (Deductible) Amounts |
|---|---|---|
| Depreciation | 2007 | ($60 million) |
| | 2008 | 50 million |
| | 2009 | 40 million |
| | | $30 million |
| Prepaid insurance, 2007 coverage | | 9 million |
| Loss contingency, to be paid in 2008 | | (6 million) |

c. No temporary differences existed at the beginning of 2006.
d. The tax rate is 40%.

**Required:**

1. Determine the amounts necessary to record income taxes for 2006 and prepare the appropriate journal entry.
2. How should the deferred tax amounts be classified in a classified balance sheet?
3. Assume the enacted federal income tax law specifies that the tax rate will change from 40% to 35% as of 2008. Determine the amounts necessary to record income taxes for 2006 and prepare the appropriate journal entry.

**P 16–7**
Multiple temporary differences; nontemporary difference; calculate taxable income; balance sheet classification

● LO1 LO2 LO4 LO6 LO8

Sherrod, Inc., reported pretax accounting income of $76 million for 2006. The following information relates to differences between pretax accounting income and taxable income:

a. Income from installment sales of properties included in pretax accounting income in 2006 exceeded that reported for tax purposes by $3 million. The installment receivable account at year-end had a balance of $4 million (representing portions of 2005 and 2006 installment sales), expected to be collected equally in 2007 and 2008.
b. Sherrod was assessed a penalty of $2 million by the Environmental Protection Agency for violation of a federal law in 2006. The fine is to be paid in equal amounts in 2006 and 2007.
c. Sherrod rents its operating facilities but owns one asset acquired in 2005 at a cost of $80 million. Depreciation is reported by the straight-line method assuming a four-year useful life. On the tax return, deductions for depreciation will be more than straight-line depreciation the first two years but less than straight-line depreciation the next two years ($ in millions):

| | Income Statement | Tax Return | Difference |
|---|---|---|---|
| 2005 | $20 | $26 | $ (6) |
| 2006 | 20 | 35 | (15) |
| 2007 | 20 | 12 | 8 |
| 2008 | 20 | 7 | 13 |
| | $80 | $80 | $ 0 |

d. Bad debt expense is reported using the allowance method, $3 million in 2006. For tax purposes, the expense is deducted when accounts prove uncollectible (the direct write-off method), $2 million in 2006. At December 31, 2006, the allowance for uncollectible accounts was $2 million (after adjusting entries). The balance was $1 million at the end of 2005.
e. In 2006, Sherrod accrued an expense and related liability for estimated paid future absences of $7 million relating to the company's new paid vacation program. Future compensation will be deductible on the tax return when actually paid during the next two years ($4 million in 2007; $3 million in 2008).
f. During 2005, accounting income included an estimated loss of $2 million from having accrued a loss contingency. The loss is paid in 2006 at which time it is tax deductible.

Balances in the deferred tax asset and deferred tax liability accounts at January 1, 2006, were $1.2 million and $2.8 million, respectively. The enacted tax rate is 40% each year.

**Required:**

1. Determine the amounts necessary to record income taxes for 2006 and prepare the appropriate journal entry.
2. What is the 2006 net income?
3. Show how any deferred tax amounts should be classified and reported on the 2006 balance sheet.

**P 16–8**
Multiple temporary differences; nontemporary difference; taxable income given; two years; balance sheet classification

● LO1 LO2 LO4 LO6 LO8

Arndt, Inc., reported the following for 2005 and 2006 ($ in millions):

| | 2005 | 2006 |
|---|---|---|
| Revenues | $888 | $983 |
| Expenses | 760 | 800 |
| Pretax accounting income (income statement) | $128 | $183 |
| Taxable income (tax return) | $120 | $200 |
| Tax rate: 40% | | |

a. Expenses each year include $30 million from a two-year casualty insurance policy purchased in 2005 for $60 million. The cost is tax-deductible in 2005.
b. Expenses include $2 million insurance premiums each year for life insurance on key executives.
c. Arndt sells one-year subscriptions to a weekly journal. Subscription sales collected and taxable in 2005 and 2006 were $33 million and $35 million, respectively. Subscriptions included in 2005 and 2006 financial reporting revenues were $25 million ($10 million collected in 2004 but not earned until 2005) and $33 million, respectively. Hint: View this as two temporary differences—one reversing in 2005; one originating in 2005.
d. 2005 expenses included a $17 million unrealized loss from reducing investments (classified as trading securities) to fair value. The investments were sold in 2006.
e. During 2004, accounting income included an estimated loss of $5 million from having accrued a loss contingency. The loss was paid in 2005 at which time it is tax deductible.
f. At January 1, 2005, Arndt had a deferred tax asset of $6 million and no deferred tax liability.

**Required:**

1. Which of the five differences described are temporary and which are nontemporary differences? Why?
2. Prepare a schedule that (a) reconciles the difference between pretax accounting income and taxable income and (b) determines the amounts necessary to record income taxes for 2005. Prepare the appropriate journal entry.
3. Show how any 2005 deferred tax amounts should be classified and reported on the 2005 balance sheet.
4. Prepare a schedule that (a) reconciles the difference between pretax accounting income and taxable income and (b) determines the amounts necessary to record income taxes for 2006. Prepare the appropriate journal entry.
5. Explain how any 2006 deferred tax amounts should be classified and reported on the 2006 balance sheet.

**P 16–9**
Single temporary difference originates each year for four years

● LO2

Alsup Consulting sometimes performs services for which it receives payment at the conclusion of the engagement, up to six months after services commence. Alsup recognizes service revenue for financial reporting purposes when the services are performed. For tax purposes, revenue is reported when fees are collected. Service revenue, collections, and pretax accounting income for 2005–2008 are as follows:

| | Service Revenue | Collections | Pretax Accounting Income |
|---|---|---|---|
| 2005 | $650,000 | $620,000 | $186,000 |
| 2006 | 750,000 | 770,000 | 250,000 |
| 2007 | 715,000 | 700,000 | 220,000 |
| 2008 | 700,000 | 720,000 | 200,000 |

There are no differences between accounting income and taxable income other than the temporary difference described above. The enacted tax rate for each year is 40%.

**Required:**

1. Prepare the appropriate journal entry to record Alsup's 2006 income taxes.
2. Prepare the appropriate journal entry to record Alsup's 2007 income taxes.
3. Prepare the appropriate journal entry to record Alsup's 2008 income taxes.

(Hint: You may find it helpful to prepare a schedule that shows the balances in service revenue receivable at December 31, 2005–2008.)

**P 16–10**
Operating loss carryback and carryforward; temporary difference; nontemporary difference

● LO2 LO4 LO7

eXcel

Fores Construction Company reported a pretax operating loss of $135 million for financial reporting purposes in 2006. Contributing to the loss were (a) a penalty of $5 million assessed by the Environmental Protection Agency for violation of a federal law and paid in 2006 and (b) an estimated loss of $10 million from accruing a loss contingency. The loss will be tax deductible when paid in 2007.

The enacted tax rate is 40%. There were no temporary differences at the beginning of the year and none originating in 2006 other than those described above. Taxable income in Fores's two previous years of operation was as follows:

| | |
|---|---|
| 2004 | $75 million |
| 2005 | 30 million |

**Required:**

1. Prepare the journal entry to recognize the income tax benefit of the operating loss in 2006. Fores elects the carryback option.
2. Show the lower portion of the 2006 income statement that reports the income tax benefit of the operating loss.
3. Prepare the journal entry to record income taxes in 2007 assuming pretax accounting income is $60 million. No additional temporary differences originate in 2007.

**P 16–11**
Integrating problem—bonds, leases, taxes

● LO2 LO5

eXcel

The following is the long-term liabilities section of Tempo Co.'s December 31, 2005, balance sheet:

| | | |
|---|---|---|
| **Long-Term Liabilities:** | | |
| Note payable—bank; 15 principal payments of $5,000, plus 10% interest due annually on September 30 | $75,000 | |
| Less current portion | (5,000) | $ 70,000 |
| Capital lease obligation—16 payments of $9,000 due annually on January 1 | $76,600 | |
| Less current portion | (1,340) | 75,260 |
| Deferred income tax liability | | 15,750 |
| Total long-term liabilities | | $161,010 |

a. Tempo's incremental borrowing rate on the date of the lease was 11% and the lessor's implicit rate, which was known by Tempo, was 10%.

b. The only difference between Tempo's taxable income and pretax accounting income is depreciation on a machine acquired on January 1, 2005, for $250,000. The machine's estimated useful life is five years, with no salvage value. Depreciation is computed using the straight-line method for financial reporting purposes and the MACRS method for tax purposes. Depreciation expense for tax and financial reporting purposes for 2006 through 2009 is as follows:

| Year | Tax Depreciation | Financial Depreciation | Tax Depreciation Over (Under) Financial Depreciation |
|---|---|---|---|
| 2006 | $80,000 | $50,000 | $ 30,000 |
| 2007 | 40,000 | 50,000 | (10,000) |
| 2008 | 35,000 | 50,000 | (15,000) |
| 2009 | 30,000 | 50,000 | (20,000) |

The enacted federal income tax rates are 30% for 2005 and 2006, and 35% for 2007 through 2009.

c. Included in Tempo's December 2005 balance sheet was a deferred tax asset of $9,000.

d. For the year ended December 31, 2006, Tempo's income before income taxes was $430,000.

e. On July 1, 2006, Tempo received proceeds of $459,725 from a $500,000 bond issuance. The bonds mature in 30 years and interest of 11% is payable each January 1 and July 1. The bonds were issued at a price to yield the investors 12%. Tempo uses the effective interest method to amortize the bond discount.

**Required:**

1. Prepare a schedule showing Tempo's income before income taxes, current income tax expense, deferred income tax expense, and net income for 2006. Show supporting calculations for current and deferred income tax amounts.
2. Prepare a schedule showing the calculations of Tempo's interest expense for the year ended December 31, 2006.
3. Prepare the long-term liabilities section of Tempo's December 31, 2006, balance sheet. Show supporting calculations.

*(AICPA adapted)*

## BROADEN YOUR PERSPECTIVE

**Apply your critical-thinking ability to the knowledge you've gained. These cases will provide you an opportunity to develop your research, analysis, judgment, and communication skills. You also will work with other students, integrate what you've learned, apply it in real world situations, and consider its global and ethical ramifications. This practice will broaden your knowledge and further develop your decision-making abilities.**

**Analysis Case 16–1**
Basic concepts

● LO1 through LO8

One of the longest debates in accounting history is the issue of deferred taxes. The controversy began in the 1940s and has continued, even after the FASB issued *Statement of Financial Accounting Standards No. 109* in 1992. At issue is the appropriate treatment of tax consequences of economic events that occur in years other than that of the events themselves.

**Required:**

1. Distinguish between temporary differences and permanent differences. Provide an example of each.
2. Distinguish between intraperiod tax allocation and interperiod tax allocation (deferred tax accounting). Provide an example of each.
3. How are deferred tax assets and deferred tax liabilities classified and reported in the financial statements?

**Integrating Case 16–2**
Postretirement benefits

● LO2

*Statement of Financial Accounting Standards No. 106* establishes accounting standards for postretirement benefits other than pensions, most notably postretirement health care benefits. Essentially, the standard requires companies to accrue compensation expense each year employees perform services, for the expected cost of providing future postretirement benefits that can be attributed to that service. Typically, companies do not prefund these costs for two reasons: (a) unlike pension liabilities, no federal law requires companies to fund nonpension postretirement benefits and (b) funding contributions, again unlike for pension liabilities, are not tax deductible. (The costs aren't tax deductible until paid to, or on behalf of, employees.)

**Required:**

1. As a result of being required to record the periodic postretirement expense and related liability, most companies now report lower earnings and higher liabilities. How might many companies also report higher assets as a result of *SFAS 106?*
2. One objection to *SFAS 109,* "Accounting for Income Taxes," as cited in the chapter is the omission of requirements to discount deferred tax amounts to their present values. This objection is inappropriate in the context of deferred tax amounts necessitated by accounting for postretirement benefits. Why?

**Judgment Case 16–3**
Intraperiod tax allocation

● LO9

Russell-James Corporation is a diversified consumer products company. During 2006, Russell-James discontinued its line of cosmetics, which constituted discontinued operations for financial reporting purposes. As vice president of the food products division, you are interested in the effect of the discontinuance on the company's profitability. One item of information you requested was an income statement. The income statement you received was labeled *preliminary* and *unaudited:*

**RUSSELL-JAMES CORPORATION**
**Income Statement**
**For the Year Ended December 31, 2006**
($ in millions, except per share amounts)

| | | |
|---|---|---|
| Revenues | | $300 |
| Cost of goods sold | | 90 |
| Gross profit | | 210 |
| Selling and administrative expenses | | (60) |
| Income from continuing operations before income taxes | | 150 |
| Income taxes | | (22) |
| Income from continuing operations | | 128 |
| Discontinued operations: | | |
| Loss from operations of cosmetics division | $(100) | |
| Gain from disposal of cosmetics division | 15 | (85) |
| Income before extraordinary item | | 43 |
| Extraordinary loss from earthquake | | (10) |
| Net income | | $ 33 |
| **Per Share of Common Stock (100 million shares):** | | |
| Income from continuing operations | | $1.28 |
| Loss from operations of cosmetics division | | (1.00) |
| Gain from disposal of cosmetics division | | .15 |
| Income before extraordinary item | | .43 |
| Extraordinary loss from earthquake | | (.10) |
| Net income | | $ .33 |

You are somewhat surprised at the magnitude of the loss incurred by the cosmetics division prior to its disposal. Another item that draws your attention is the apparently low tax rate indicated by the statement ($22 ÷ 150 = 15%). Upon further investigation you are told the company's tax rate is 40%.

**Required:**

1. Recast the income statement to reflect intraperiod tax allocation.
2. How would you reconcile the income tax expense shown on the statement above with the amount your recast statement reports?

**International Case 16–4**
Accounting for income taxes in other countries

● LO1 LO2 LO8 LO9

The primary objective of the International Accounting Standards Board (IASB) is to narrow worldwide differences in accounting practices and the presentation of financial information. Although the IASB has worked toward uniformity since 1973, harmonization has by no means been achieved. In the area of accounting for income taxes, significant differences exist from country to country that impact reported earnings and financial position.

**Required:**

Choose a country other than the United States and:

1. Locate a recent annual report of a company located in that country.
2. Determine the way that country accounts for income taxes. Include in your analysis:
   a. The extent of variations between accounting income and taxable income.
   b. Whether these differences create deferred taxes.
   c. Whether tax deferral depends on expectations as to when differences are expected to reverse.
3. Prepare a short report highlighting the similarities and differences between the United States and your chosen country in the way income taxes are accounted for.

Note: You can obtain copies of annual reports from the company's website, a friendly stockbroker, Public Register's Annual Report Service at www.PRARS.com or from EDGAR, the Electronic Data Gathering and Retrieval service of the SEC, from EdgarScan at: **edgarscan.pwcglobal.com/**.

**Judgment Case 16–5**
Analyzing the effect of deferred tax liabilities on firm risk; Southwest Airlines

● LO8

The following is a portion of the 2004 balance sheet of **Southwest Airlines**.

| | 2004 | 2003 |
|---|---|---|
| Liabilities and Stockholders' Equity | | |
| Current liabilities | | |
| Accounts payable | $ 420 | $ 405 |
| Accrued liabilities | 1,047 | 650 |
| Air traffic liability | 529 | 462 |
| Current maturities of long-term debt | 146 | 206 |
| Total current liabilities | 2,142 | 1,723 |
| Long-term debt less current maturities | 1,700 | 1,332 |
| Deferred income taxes | 1,610 | 1,420 |
| Deferred gains from sale and leaseback of aircraft | 152 | 168 |
| Other deferred liabilities | 209 | 183 |
| Commitments and contingencies | | |
| Stockholders' equity: | | |
| Common stock, $1 par | 790 | 789 |
| Capital in excess of par | 299 | 258 |
| Retained earnings | 4,089 | 3,883 |
| Accumulated other comprehensive income | 417 | 122 |
| Treasury stock | (71) | — |
| | 5,524 | 5,052 |
| Total stockholders' equity | $11,337 | $9,878 |

Southwest's debt to equity ratio was 1.05, calculated as $5,813 ÷ $5,524. Some analysts argue that long-term deferred tax liabilities should be excluded from liabilities when computing the debt to equity ratio.

**Required:**

1. What is the rationale for the argument that long-term deferred tax liabilities should be excluded from liabilities when computing the debt to equity ratio?
2. What would be the effect on Southwest's debt to equity ratio of excluding deferred tax liabilities from its calculation? What would be the percentage change?
3. What might be the rationale for not excluding long-term deferred tax liabilities from liabilities when computing the debt to equity ratio?

**Integrating Case 16–6**
Income taxes and investment securities

● LO1 LO2 LO8

The **Wrigley Company** is the world's largest manufacturer of chewing gum. The following disclosure note appeared in Wrigley's 2004 annual report.

INVESTMENTS IN DEBT AND EQUITY SECURITIES (IN PART, $ IN 000S)

The Company's investments in marketable equity securities are held for an indefinite period. Application of *Statement of Financial Accounting Standards (SFAS) No. 115,* "Accounting for Certain Investments in Debt and Equity Securities," resulted in unrealized holding gains of $15,351 at December 31, 2004, and $14,555 at December 31, 2003. Unrealized holding gains, net of the related tax effect, of $9,979 and $9,461 at December 31, 2004 and 2003, respectively, are included as components of Accumulated Other Comprehensive Income in stockholders' equity.

**Required:**

1. Explain how investment securities available for sale are accounted for.
2. What would have been Wrigley's journal entry to reflect the 2004 fair value of the investments?

**Communication Case 16–7**
Notes, leases, bonds

● LO1 LO2 LO4 LO6

Chris Green, CPA, is auditing Rayne Co.'s 2006 financial statements. The controller, Ben Dunn, has provided Green with the following information:

a. At December 31, 2005, Rayne had a note payable to Federal Bank with a balance of $90,000. The annual principal payment of $10,000, plus 8% interest on the unpaid balance, was paid when due on March 31, 2006.
b. On January 2, 2006, Rayne leased two automobiles for executive use under a capital lease. Five annual lease payments of $15,000 are due beginning January 3, 2006. Rayne's incremental borrowing rate on the date of the lease was 11% and the lessor's implicit rate, which was known by Rayne, was 10%. The lease was properly recorded at $62,500, before the first payment was made.
c. On July 1, 2006, Rayne received proceeds of $538,000 from a $500,000 bond issuance. The bonds mature in 15 years and interest of 11% is payable semiannually on June 30 and December 31. The bonds were issued at a price to yield investors 10%. Rayne uses the effective interest method to amortize bond premium.
d. For the year ended December 31, 2006, Dunn has prepared a schedule of all differences between financial statement and income tax return income. Dunn believes that as a result of pending legislation, the enacted tax rate at December 31, 2006, will be increased for 2007. Dunn is uncertain which differences to include and which rates to apply in computing deferred taxes under *SFAS 109*. Dunn has requested an overview of *SFAS 109* from Green.

**Required:**

1. Prepare a schedule of interest expense for the year ended December 31, 2006.
2. Prepare a brief memo to Dunn from Green:
   a. Identifying the objectives of accounting for income taxes.
   b. Defining temporary differences.
   c. Explaining how to measure deferred tax assets and liabilities.
   d. Explaining how to measure deferred income tax expense or benefit.

*(AICPA adapted)*

**Integrating Case 16–8**
Accounting changes and error correction; six situations; tax effects considered

● LO1 LO2 LO8

Williams-Santana, Inc., is a manufacturer of high-tech industrial parts that was started in 1994 by two talented engineers with little business training. In 2006, the company was acquired by one of its major customers. As part of an internal audit, the following facts were discovered. The audit occurred during 2006 before any adjusting entries or closing entries were prepared. The income tax rate is 40% for all years.

a. A five-year casualty insurance policy was purchased at the beginning of 2004 for $35,000. The full amount was debited to insurance expense at the time.
b. On December 31, 2005, merchandise inventory was overstated by $25,000 due to a mistake in the physical inventory count using the periodic inventory system.
c. The company changed inventory cost methods to FIFO from LIFO at the end of 2006 for both financial statement and income tax purposes. The change will cause a $960,000 increase in the beginning inventory at January 1, 2005.
d. At the end of 2005, the company failed to accrue $15,500 of sales commissions earned by employees during 2005. The expense was recorded when the commissions were paid in early 2006.
e. At the beginning of 2004, the company purchased a machine at a cost of $720,000. Its useful life was estimated to be 10 years with no salvage value. The machine has been depreciated by the double-declining-balance method. Its carrying amount on December 31, 2005, was $460,800. On January 1, 2006, the company changed to the straight-line method.
f. Additional industrial robots were acquired at the beginning of 2003 and added to the company's assembly process. The $1,000,000 cost of the equipment was inadvertently recorded as repair expense. Robots have 10-year useful lives and no material salvage value. This class of equipment is depreciated by the straight-line method for both financial reporting and income tax reporting.

**Required:**

For each situation:

1. Identify whether it represents an accounting change or an error. If an accounting change, identify the type of change.

2. Prepare any journal entry necessary as a direct result of the change or error correction as well as any adjusting entry for 2006 related to the situation described. Any tax effects should be adjusted for through the deferred tax liability account.
3. Briefly describe any other steps that should be taken to appropriately report the situation.

**Real World Case 16–9**
Disclosure issues; balance sheet classifications

● LO1 LO2 LO8

The income tax disclosure note accompanying the 2004 financial statements of the **Walgreen Company** is reproduced below:

**Income Taxes**

The provision for income taxes consists of the following (in millions):

| | 2004 | 2003 | 2002 |
|---|---|---|---|
| Current provision | | | |
| Federal | $632.5 | $574.0 | $510.2 |
| State | 111.4 | 80.1 | 85.0 |
| | 743.9 | 654.1 | 595.2 |
| Deferred provision | | | |
| Federal | 71.1 | 48.4 | 24.0 |
| State | 1.1 | 10.5 | (1.1) |
| | 72.2 | 58.9 | 22.9 |
| | $816.1 | $713.0 | $618.1 |

The deferred tax assets and liabilities included in the consolidated balance sheets consist of the following (in millions):

| | 2004 | 2003 |
|---|---|---|
| Deferred tax assets | | |
| Employee benefit plans | $212.0 | $181.3 |
| Accrued rent | 52.5 | 56.1 |
| Insurance | 136.0 | 108.0 |
| Inventory | 39.6 | 29.1 |
| Bad debt | 15.4 | 10.2 |
| Other | 29.4 | 34.7 |
| | 484.9 | 419.4 |
| Deferred tax liabilities | | |
| Accelerated depreciation | 621.5 | 486.2 |
| Inventory | 115.1 | 103.0 |
| Other | 18.6 | 28.3 |
| | 755.2 | 617.5 |
| Net deferred tax liabilities | $270.3 | $198.1 |

Income taxes paid were $734.1 million, $625.2 million and $528.0 million during the fiscal years ended August 31, 2004, 2003 and 2002, respectively. The difference between the statutory income tax rate and the effective tax rate is principally due to state income tax provisions.

**Required:**
1. On its 2004 balance sheet, Walgreen reported as a noncurrent liability, "Deferred income taxes" of $327.6 million. Why is this different from the $270.3 million "net deferred tax liability" reported in the disclosure note?
2. Re-create the journal entry that summarizes the entries Walgreen used to record its 2004 income taxes.

**Research Case 16–10**
Researching the way tax deductions are reported on a corporation tax return; retrieving a tax form from the Internet

● LO1 LO2 LO3 LO8

The U.S. Treasury maintains an information site on the Internet. As part of this site the Internal Revenue Service provides tax information and services. Among those services is a server for publications and forms which allows a visitor to download a variety of IRS forms and publications.

**Required:**
1. Access the Treasury site on the Internet. The web address is **www.ustreas.gov**. After exploring the information available there, navigate to the IRS server for forms and publications via the IRS home page.
2. Download the corporation tax return, Form 1120.
3. Note the specific deductions listed that are deductible from total income to arrive at taxable income. Are any deductions listed that might not also be included among expenses on the income statement?
4. One of the deductions indicated is "net operating loss deduction." Under what circumstances might a company report an amount for this item?
5. Based on how taxable income is determined, how might temporary differences be created between taxable income and pretax income on the income statement?

**Analysis Case 16–11**
Reporting deferred taxes

● LO1 LO2 LO3 LO7 LO8

**FedEx Corporation**

Refer to the financial statements and related disclosure notes of **FedEx Corporation** in Appendix B at the end of the book. On FedEx's balance sheet, deferred income taxes are reported as both an asset ($489 million in 2004) and a liability ($1,181 million in 2004).

**Required:**

1. Explain why deferred income taxes can be reported as both an asset and a liability. Why is the deferred tax asset reported as current and the deferred tax liability as long term?
2. Note 11 in the disclosure notes indicates that deferred tax assets are $1,265 million in 2004 and deferred tax liabilities are $1,957 million. How can that be explained in light of the two amounts reported in the balance sheet?
3. Does FedEx feel the need to record a valuation allowance for its deferred tax assets?

**Analysis Case 16–12**
Consult financial statements; analyze tax disclosures; recreate journal entry

● LO1 LO2 LO3 LO7 LO8

**Kroger Co.** is one of the largest retail food companies in the United States as measured by total annual sales. The Kroger Co. operates supermarkets, convenience stores, and manufactures and processes food that its supermarkets sell. Kroger's stores operate under names such as Dillon Food Stores, City Market, Sav-Mor, Kwik Shop, and Mini Mart.

Like most corporations, Kroger has significant deferred tax assets and liabilities resulting from accounting for income taxes in accordance with *SFAS 109.* Using EdgarScan, (**edgarscan. pwcglobal.com/**) check the company's annual report for the year ended February 1, 2005.

**Required:**

1. From the income statement, determine the income tax expense for the year. What is the current portion and the deferred portion of the expense? (See the "Taxes Based on Income" note in the Notes to Consolidated Financial Statements.) Why is the income tax expense from the income statement different from the "provision for income taxes in the disclosure note"?
2. How are the deferred taxes classified on Kroger's balance sheet? (See the "Taxes Based on Income" note in the Notes to Consolidated Financial Statements.) What amounts are reported among current assets or liabilities and among noncurrent assets or liabilities? Why?

## CPA SIMULATION 16–1

**Kerry Oil**
Deferred Taxes

KAPLAN
**CPA Review**

Test your knowledge of the concepts discussed in this chapter, practice critical professional skills necessary for career success, and prepare for the computer-based CPA exam by accessing our CPA simulations at the text website: **www.mhhe.com/spiceland4e**.

The Kerry Oil simulation tests your knowledge of the financial reporting implications of income taxes.

As on the CPA exam itself, you will be asked to use tools including a spreadsheet, a calculator, and professional accounting standards, to conduct research, derive solutions, and communicate conclusions related to these issues in a simulated environment headed by the following interactive tabs:

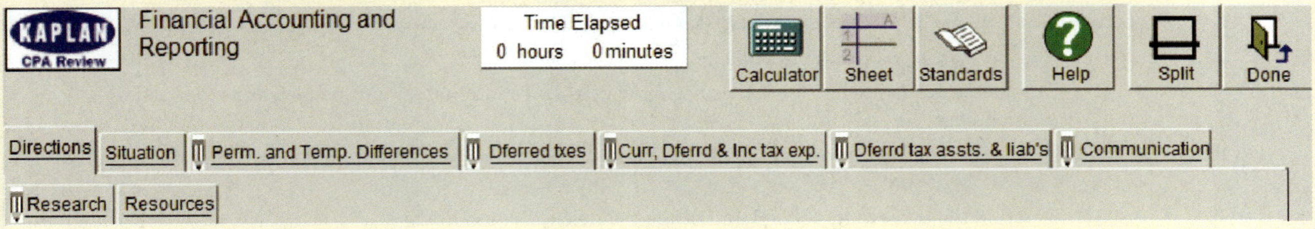


Specific tasks in the simulation include:

- Demonstrating an understanding of temporary and nontemporary differences.
- Analyze transactions for their deferred tax reporting implications.
- Calculating the current and deferred tax components of income tax expense for multiple temporary differences.
- Applying judgment in deciding the deferred tax effects of a variety of transactions.
- Communicating the deferred tax effects of the two deferred tax reporting issues.
- Researching factors that might influence whether a valuation allowance might not be required in spite of evidence to the contrary.

# 17
CHAPTER

# Pensions and Other Postretirement Benefits

## OVERVIEW

Employee compensation comes in many forms. Salaries and wages, of course, provide direct and current payment for services provided. However, it's commonplace for compensation also to include benefits payable after retirement. We discuss pension benefits and other postretirement benefits in this chapter. Accounting for pension benefits recognizes that they represent deferred compensation for current service. Accordingly, the cost of these benefits is recognized on an accrual basis during the years that employees earn the benefits.

### LEARNING OBJECTIVES

**After studying this chapter, you should be able to:**

- LO1 Explain the fundamental differences between a defined contribution pension plan and a defined benefit pension plan.
- LO2 Distinguish among the vested benefit obligation, the accumulated benefit obligation, and the projected benefit obligation.
- LO3 Describe the five events that might change the balance of the PBO.
- LO4 Explain how plan assets accumulate to provide retiree benefits and understand the role of the trustee in administering the fund.
- LO5 Describe the funded status of pension plans and how that amount is reported.
- LO6 Describe how pension expense is a composite of periodic changes that occur in both the pension obligation and the plan assets.
- LO7 Record for pension plans the periodic expense and funding as well as new gains and losses and new prior service cost as they occur.
- LO8 Understand the interrelationships among the elements that constitute a defined benefit pension plan.
- LO9 Describe the nature of postretirement benefit plans other than pensions and identify the similarities and differences in accounting for those plans and pensions.
- LO10 Explain how the obligation for postretirement benefits is measured and how the obligation changes.
- LO11 Determine the components of postretirement benefit expense.

# FINANCIAL REPORTING CASE

## United Dynamics

You read yesterday that many companies in the United States have pension plans that are severely underfunded. This caught your attention in part because you have your office interview tomorrow with United Dynamics. You hadn't really thought that much about the pension plan of your potential future employer, in part because your current employer has a defined contribution 401K plan, for which funding is not a concern. However, United Dynamics is an older firm with a defined benefit plan, for which funding is the employer's responsibility.

To prepare for your interview, you obtained a copy of United Dynamics' financial statements. Unfortunately, the financial statements themselves are of little help. You are unable to find any pension liability on the balance sheet, but the statement does report a relatively small "pension asset." The income statement reports pension expense for each of the years reported. For help, you search the disclosure notes. In part, the pension disclosure note reads as follows:

**Note 7: Pension Plan**

United Dynamics has a defined benefit pension plan covering substantially all of its employees. Plan benefits are based on years of service and the employee's compensation during the last three years of employment. The company's funding policy is consistent with the funding requirements of federal law and regulations. The net periodic pension expense for the company included the following components. The company's pension expense was as follows ($ in millions):

| | 2007 | 2006 | 2005 |
|---|---|---|---|
| Current service costs | $ 43 | $ 47 | $ 42 |
| Interest cost on projected benefit obligation | 178 | 164 | 152 |
| Return on assets | (213) | (194) | (187) |
| Amortization of prior service cost | 43 | 43 | 43 |
| Amortization of net gain | (2) | (1) | – |
| Net pension costs | $ 49 | $ 59 | $ 50 |

The following table describes the change in projected benefit obligation for the plan years ended December 31, 2007, and December 31, 2006 ($ in millions):

| | 2007 | 2006 |
|---|---|---|
| Projected benefit obligation at beginning of year | $2,194 | $2,121 |
| Service cost | 43 | 47 |
| Interest cost | 178 | 164 |
| Actuarial (gain) loss | 319 | (40) |
| Benefits paid | (106) | (98) |
| Projected benefit obligation at end of year | $2,628 | $2,194 |

The weighted-average discount rate and rate of increase in future compensation levels used in determining the actuarial present value of the projected benefit obligations in the above table were 8.1% and 4.3%, respectively,

(continued)

(concluded)

at December 31, 2007, and 7.73% and 4.7%, respectively, at December 31, 2006. The expected long-term rate of return on assets was 9.1% at December 31, 2007 and 2006.

The following table describes the change in the fair value of plan assets for the plan years ended December 31, 2007 and 2006 ($ in millions):

| | 2007 | 2006 |
|---|---|---|
| Fair value of plan assets at beginning of year | $2,340 | $2,133 |
| Actual return on plan assets | 215 | 178 |
| Employer contributions | 358 | 127 |
| Benefits paid | (106) | (98) |
| Fair value of plan assets at end of year | $2,807 | $2,340 |

"Ouch! I can't believe how much of my accounting I forgot," you complain to yourself. "I'd better get out my old intermediate accounting book."

**By the time you finish this chapter, you should be able to respond appropriately to the questions posed in this case. Compare your response to the solution provided at the end of the chapter.**

## QUESTIONS

1. Why is underfunding not a concern in your present employment? (page 831)
2. Were you correct that the pension liability is not reported on the balance sheet? What is the liability? (page 833)
3. What is the amount of the plan assets available to pay benefits? What are the factors that can cause that amount to change? (page 839)
4. What does the "pension asset" represent? Are you interviewing with a company whose pension plan is severely underfunded? (page 841)
5. How is the pension expense influenced by changes in the pension liability and plan assets? (page 842)

# PART A THE NATURE OF PENSION PLANS

Over 60 million American workers are covered by pension plans. The United States' pension funds tripled in size during the previous two decades and now are roughly the size of Japan's gross national product. This powerful investment base now controls about one-fourth of the stock market. At the company level, the enormous size of pension funds is reflected in a periodic pension cost that constitutes one of the largest expenses many companies report. The corporate liability for providing pension benefits, though largely off-balance-sheet, is huge. Obviously, then, the financial reporting responsibility for pensions has important social and economic implications.

Pension plans are designed to provide income to individuals during their retirement years. This is accomplished by setting aside funds during an employee's working years so that at retirement the accumulated funds plus earnings from investing those funds are available to replace wages. Actually, an individual who periodically invests in stocks, bonds, certificates of deposit (CDs), or other investments for the purpose of saving for retirement is establishing a personal pension fund. Often, such individual plans take the form of individual retirement accounts (IRAs) to take advantage of tax breaks offered by that arrangement. In employer plans, some or all of the periodic contributions to the retirement fund often are provided by the employer.

**Pension plans often enhance productivity, reduce turnover, satisfy union demands, and allow employers to compete in the labor market.**

Corporations establish pension plans for a variety of reasons. Sponsorship of pension plans provides employees with a degree of retirement security and fulfills a moral obligation felt by many employers. This security also can induce a degree of job satisfaction and perhaps loyalty that might enhance productivity and reduce turnover. Motivation to sponsor a plan sometimes comes from union demands and often relates to being competitive in the labor market.

## ADDITIONAL CONSIDERATION

When established according to tight guidelines, a pension plan gains important tax advantages. Such arrangements are called *qualified plans* because they qualify for favorable tax treatment. In a qualified plan, the employer is permitted an immediate tax deduction for amounts paid into the pension fund (within specified limits). The employees, on the other hand, are not taxed at the time employer contributions are made—only when retirement benefits are received. Moreover, earnings on the funds set aside by the employer are not taxed while in the pension fund, so the earnings accumulate tax free. If you are familiar with the tax advantages of IRAs, you probably recognize the similarity between those individual plans and corporate pension arrangements.

**Qualified pension plans offer important tax benefits.**

For a pension plan to be qualified for special tax treatment it must meet these general requirements.

1. It must cover at least 70% of employees.
2. It cannot discriminate in favor of highly compensated employees.
3. It must be funded in advance of retirement through contributions to an irrevocable trust fund.
4. Benefits must vest after a specified period of service, commonly five years. (We discuss this in more detail later.)
5. It complies with specific restrictions on the timing and amount of contributions and benefits.

● LO1

Sometimes, employers agree to annually contribute a specific (defined) amount to a pension fund on behalf of employees but make no commitment regarding benefit amounts at retirement. In other arrangements, employers don't specify the amount of annual contributions but promise to provide determinable (defined) amounts at retirement. These two arrangements describe defined contribution pension plans and defined benefit pension plans, respectively:

- **Defined contribution pension plans** promise fixed annual contributions to a pension fund (say, 5% of the employees' pay). Employees choose (from designated options) where funds are invested—usually stocks or fixed-income securities. Retirement pay depends on the size of the fund at retirement.
- **Defined benefit pension plans** promise fixed retirement benefits defined by a designated formula. Typically, the pension formula bases retirement pay on the employees' (a) years of service, (b) annual compensation (often final pay or an average for the last few years), and sometimes (c) age. Employers are responsible for ensuring that sufficient funds are available to provide promised benefits.

Today, more than two-thirds of workers covered by pension plans are covered by defined contribution plans, fewer than one-third by defined benefit plans. This represents a radical shift from previous years when the traditional defined benefit plan was far more common. However, very few new pension plans are of the defined benefit variety. In fact, many companies are terminating long-standing defined benefit plans and substituting defined contribution plans. Why the shift? There are three main reasons:

**Virtually all new pension plans are defined contribution plans.**

1. Government regulations make defined benefit plans cumbersome and costly to administer.
2. Employers are increasingly unwilling to bear the risk of defined benefit plans; with defined contribution plans, the company's obligation ends when contributions are made.
3. There has been a shift among many employers from trying to "buy long-term loyalty" (with defined benefit plans) to trying to attract new talent (with more mobile defined contribution plans).

**GRAPHIC 17–1**
Defined Contribution and Defined Benefit Pension Plans

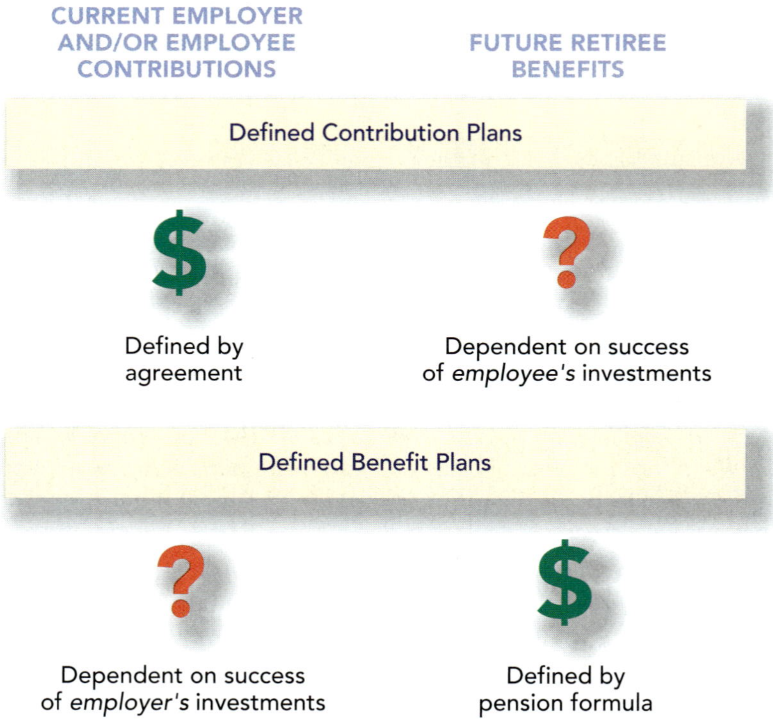


The two categories of pension plans are depicted in Graphic 17–1.

Both types of plans have a common goal: to provide income to employees during their retirement years. Still, the two types of plans differ regarding who bears the risk—the employer or the employees—for whether the retirement objectives are achieved. The two types of plans also have entirely different implications for accounting and financial reporting. Our discussion of defined contribution plans will be brief. Although these are now the most popular type of corporate pension plan, their relative simplicity permits a rather straightforward accounting treatment that requires little explanation. On the other hand, defined benefit plans require considerably more complex accounting treatment and constitute the primary focus of this chapter.

## Defined Contribution Pension Plans

***Defined contribution plans* promise defined periodic contributions to a pension fund, without further commitment regarding benefit amounts at retirement.**

Defined contribution pension plans are becoming increasingly popular vehicles for employers to provide retirement income without the paperwork, cost, and risk generated by the more traditional defined benefit plans. Defined contribution plans promise fixed periodic contributions to a pension fund. Retirement income depends on the size of the fund at retirement. No further commitment is made by the employer regarding benefit amounts at retirement.

These plans have several variations. In money purchase plans, employers contribute a fixed percentage of employees' salaries. Thrift plans, savings plans, and 401(k) plans (named after the Tax Code section that specifies the conditions for the favorable tax treatment of these plans) permit voluntary contributions by employees. These contributions typically are matched to a specified extent by employers. Over 70% of American workers participate in 401(k) plans. More than two trillion dollars are invested in these plans.

When plans link the amount of contributions to company performance, labels include profit-sharing plans, incentive savings plans, 401(k) profit-sharing plans, and similar titles. When employees make contributions to the plan in addition to employer contributions, it's called a *contributory* plan. Sometimes the amount the employer contributes is tied to the amount of the employee contribution.[1] Variations are seemingly endless. An example from a recent annual report of **Cisco Systems** is re-created in Graphic 17–2.

[1]One popular way for employer companies to provide contributions is with shares of its own common stock. If so, the arrangements usually are designed to comply with government requirements to be designated an employee stock ownership plan (ESOP).

**Note 10: Employee Benefit Plans (in part)**
**Employee 401(k) Plans** The Company sponsors the Cisco Systems, Inc. 401(k) Plan to provide retirement benefits for its employees. As allowed under Section 401(k) of the Internal Revenue Code, the Plan provides tax-deferred salary deductions for eligible employees. Employees can contribute from 1% to 25% of their annual compensation to the Plan. Employee contributions are limited to a maximum annual amount as set periodically by the Internal Revenue Service. Through December 31, 2002, the Company matched employee contributions dollar for dollar up to a maximum of $1,500 per person per year. Effective January 1, 2003, the new matching structure is 50% of the first 6% of eligible earnings that are contributed by employees. All matching contributions vest immediately. The Company's matching contributions to the Plan totaled $84 million, $81 million, and $40 million in fiscal 2005, 2004, and 2003, respectively.

**GRAPHIC 17–2**
Defined Contribution Plan—Cisco Systems

Accounting for these plans is quite easy. Each year, the employer simply records pension expense equal to the amount of the annual contribution. Suppose a plan promises an annual contribution equal to 3% of an employee's salary. If an employee's salary is $110,000 in a particular year, the employer would simply recognize compensation expense in the amount of the contribution:

**FINANCIAL REPORTING CASE**
Q1, p. 828

**For defined contribution plans, the employer simply records pension expense equal to the cash contribution.**

| | | |
|---|---|---|
| Pension expense ...................................... | 3,300 | |
| Cash ($110,000 × 3%) ................................ | | 3,300 |

The employee's retirement benefits are totally dependent upon how well investments perform. Who bears the risk (or reward) of that uncertainty? The employee would bear the risk of uncertain investment returns and, potentially, settle for far less at retirement than at first expected.[2] On the other hand, the employer would be free of any further obligation. Because the actual investments are held by an independent investment firm, the employer is free of that recordkeeping responsibility as well.

Risk is reversed in a defined benefit plan. Because specific benefits are promised at retirement, the employer would be responsible for making up the difference when investment performance is less than expected. We look at defined benefit plans next.

## Defined Benefit Pension Plans

When setting aside cash to fund a pension plan, the uncertainty surrounding the rate of return on plan assets is but one of several uncertainties inherent in a defined benefit plan. Employee turnover affects the number of employees who ultimately will become eligible for retirement benefits. The age at which employees will choose to retire as well as life expectancies will impact both the length of the retirement period and the amount of the benefits. Inflation, future compensation levels, and interest rates also have obvious influence on eventual benefits.

***Defined benefit plans* promise fixed retirement benefits defined by a designated formula.**

This is particularly true when pension benefits are defined by a pension formula, as usually is the case. A typical formula might specify that a retiree will receive annual retirement benefits based on the employee's years of service and annual pay at retirement (say, pay level in the final year, highest pay achieved, or average pay in the last two or more years). For example, a pension formula might define annual retirement benefits as:

**Uncertainties complicate determining how much to set aside each year to ensure that sufficient funds are available to provide promised benefits.**

$$1\tfrac{1}{2}\% \times \text{Years of service} \times \text{Final year's salary}$$

By this formula, the annual benefits to an employee who retires after 30 years of service, with a final salary of $100,000, would be:

[2]Of course, this is not entirely unappealing to the employee. Defined contribution plans allow an employee to select investments in line with his or her own risk preferences and often provide greater retirement benefits and flexibility than defined benefit plans.

A pension formula typically defines retirement pay based on the employees' (a) years of service, (b) annual compensation, and sometimes (c) age.

$$1\frac{1}{2}\% \times 30 \text{ years} \times \$100{,}000 = \$45{,}000$$

Typically, a firm will hire an **actuary**, a professional trained in a particular branch of statistics and mathematics, to assess the various uncertainties (employee turnover, salary levels, mortality, etc.) and to estimate the company's obligation to employees in connection with its pension plan. Such estimates are inherently subjective, so regardless of the skill of the actuary, estimates invariably deviate from the actual outcome to one degree or another.[3] For instance, the return on assets can turn out to be more or less than expected. These deviations are referred to as *gains* and *losses* on pension assets. When it's necessary to revise estimates related to the pension obligation because it's determined to be more or less than previously thought, these revisions are referred to as *losses* and *gains,* respectively, on the pension liability. Later, we will discuss the accounting treatment of gains and losses from either source. The point here is that the risk of the pension obligation changing unexpectedly or the pension funds being inadequate to meet the obligation is borne by the employer with a defined benefit pension plan.

Pension gains and losses occur when the *pension obligation* is lower or higher than expected.

Pension gains and losses occur when the *return on plan assets* is higher or lower than expected.

The key elements of a defined benefit pension plan are:

1. The *employer's obligation* to pay retirement benefits in the future.
2. The *plan assets* set aside by the employer from which to pay the retirement benefits in the future.
3. The *periodic expense* of having a pension plan.

As you will learn in this chapter, the first two of these elements are not reported directly in the financial statements. This may seem confusing at first because it is inconsistent with the way you're accustomed to treating assets and liabilities. Even though they are not recorded in the formal accounts, it's critical that you understand the composition of both the pension obligation and the plan assets because (a) they affect amounts that actually are reported on the balance sheet, and (b) their balances are reported in disclosure notes. And, importantly, the pension expense reported on the income statement is a direct composite of periodic changes that occur in both the pension obligation and the plan assets.

Neither the pension obligation nor the plan assets are reported in the balance sheet.

The pension expense is a direct composite of periodic changes that occur in both the pension obligation and the plan assets.

For this reason, we will devote a considerable portion of our early discussion to understanding the composition of the pension obligation and the plan assets before focusing on the derivation of pension expense and required financial statement disclosures. We will begin with a quick overview of how periodic changes that occur in both the pension obligation and the plan assets affect pension expense. Next we will explore how those changes occur, beginning with changes in the pension obligation followed by changes in plan assets. We'll then return to pension expense for a closer look at how those changes influence its calculation. After that, we will bring together the separate but related parts by using a simple spreadsheet to demonstrate how each element of the pension plan articulates with the other elements.

In applying accrual accounting to pensions, this *Statement (87)* retains three fundamental aspects of past pension accounting: *delayed recognition* of certain events, reporting *net cost,* and *offsetting* liabilities and assets. Those three features of practice have shaped financial reporting for many years . . . and they conflict in some respects with accounting principles applied elsewhere.[4]

## Pension Expense—An Overview

The annual pension expense reflects changes in both the pension obligation and the plan assets. Graphic 17–3 provides a brief overview of how these changes are included in pension expense. After the overview, we'll look closer at each of the components.

Next we explore each of these pension expense components in the context of its being a part of either (a) the pension obligation or (b) the plan assets. After you learn how the expense components relate to these elements of the pension plan, we'll return to explore further how they are included in the pension expense.

[3]We discuss changes in more detail in Chapter 20.

[4]"Employers' Accounting for Pensions," *Statement of Financial Accounting Standards No. 87* (Stamford, Conn.: FASB, 1985).

**Graphic 17–3**
Components of Pension Expense

| Components of Pension Expense | |
|---|---|
| + | **Service cost** ascribed to employee service during the period |
| + | **Interest** accrued on the pension liability |
| − | **Return** on the plan assets* |
| | *Amortized portion of:* |
| + | **Prior service cost** attributed to employee service before an amendment to the pension plan |
| + or (−) | **Losses or (gains)** from revisions in the pension liability or from investing plan assets |
| = | **Pension expense** |

*The actual return is adjusted for any difference between actual and expected return, resulting in the *expected* return being reflected in pension expense. This loss or gain from investing plan assets is combined with losses and gains from revisions in the pension liability for deferred inclusion in pension expense. (See the last component of pension expense.)

**Interest and investment return are financing aspects of the pension cost.**

**The recognition of some elements of the pension expense is delayed.**

**Part B**

# THE PENSION OBLIGATION AND PLAN ASSETS

## The Pension Obligation

**Financial Reporting Case**
Q2, p. 828

Now we consider more precisely what is meant by the pension obligation. Unfortunately, there's not just one definition, nor is there uniformity concerning which definition is most appropriate for pension accounting. Actually, three different ways to measure the pension obligation have meaning in pension accounting, as shown in Graphic 17–4.

**Graphic 17–4**
Ways to Measure the Pension Obligation

1. **Accumulated benefit obligation (ABO)** The actuary's estimate of the total retirement benefits (at their discounted present value) earned so far by employees, applying the pension formula using existing compensation levels.
2. **Vested benefit obligation (VBO)** The portion of the accumulated benefit obligation that plan participants are entitled to receive regardless of their continued employment.
3. **Projected benefit obligation (PBO)** The actuary's estimate of the total retirement benefits (at their discounted present value) earned so far by employees, applying the pension formula using estimated future compensation levels. (If the pension formula does not include future compensation levels, the PBO and the ABO are the same.)

Later you will learn that the projected benefit obligation is the basis for some elements of the periodic pension expense. Remember, there is but one obligation; these are three ways to measure it. The relationship among the three is depicted in Graphic 17–5.

Now let's look closer at how the obligation is measured in each of these three ways. Keep in mind, though, that it's not the accountant's responsibility to actually derive the measurement; a professional actuary provides these numbers. However, for the accountant to effectively use the numbers provided, she or he must understand their derivation.

● LO2

### VESTED BENEFIT OBLIGATION

Suppose an employee leaves the company to take another job. Will she still get earned benefits at retirement? The answer depends on whether the benefits are vested under the terms of this particular pension plan. If benefits are fully vested—yes. **Vested benefits** are those that employees have the right to receive even if their employment were to cease today.

Pension plans typically require some minimum period of employment before benefits vest. Before the Employee Retirement Income Security Act (ERISA) was passed in 1974, horror stories relating to lost benefits were commonplace. It was possible, for example, for an employee to be dismissed a week before retirement and be left with no pension benefits. Vesting requirements were tightened drastically to protect employees. These requirements

**GRAPHIC 17–5**

Alternative Measures of the Pension Obligation

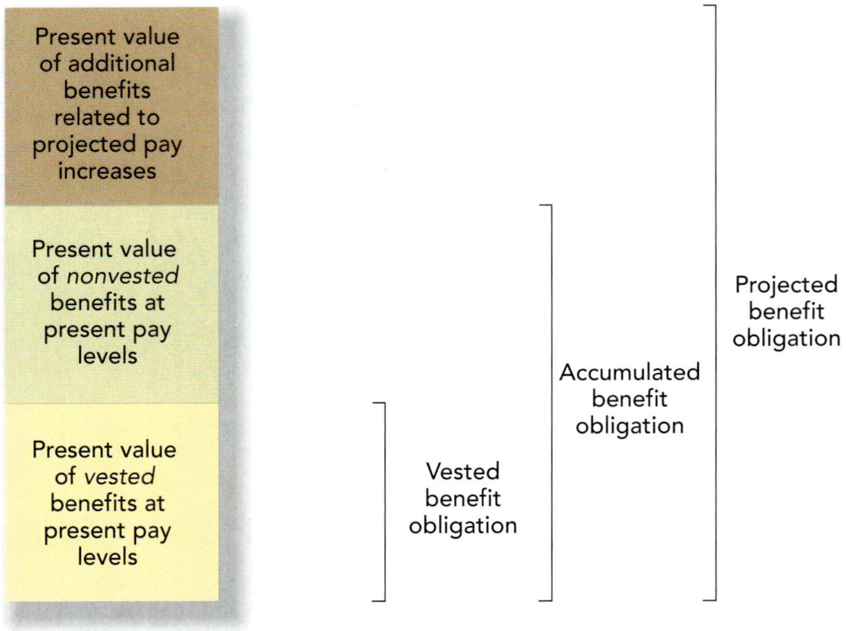


The benefits of most pension plans vest after five years.

have been changed periodically since then. Beginning in 1989, benefits must vest (a) fully within five years or (b) 20% within three years with another 20% vesting each subsequent year until fully vested after seven years. Five-year vesting is most common. ERISA also established the Pension Benefit Guaranty Corporation (PBGC) to impose liens on corporate assets for unfunded pension liabilities in certain instances and to administer terminated pension plans. The PBGC is financed by premiums from employers equal to specified amounts for each covered employee. It makes retirement payments for terminated plans and guarantees basic vested benefits when pension liabilities exceed assets.

## ACCUMULATED BENEFIT OBLIGATION

The *accumulated benefit obligation* ignores possible pay increases in the future.

The **accumulated benefit obligation (ABO)** is an estimate of the discounted present value of the retirement benefits earned so far by employees, applying the plan's pension formula using existing compensation levels. When we look at a detailed calculation of the projected benefit obligation below, keep in mind that simply substituting the employee's existing compensation in the pension formula for her projected salary at retirement would give us the accumulated benefit obligation.

## PROJECTED BENEFIT OBLIGATION

● LO3

As described earlier, when the ABO is estimated, the most recent salary is included in the pension formula to estimate future benefits, even if the pension formula specifies the final year's salary. No attempt is made to forecast what that salary would be the year before retirement. Of course, the most recent salary certainly offers an objective number to measure the obligation, but is it realistic? Since it's unlikely that there will be no salary increases between now and retirement, a more meaningful measurement should include a projection of what the salary might be at retirement.[5] Measured this way, the liability is referred to as the **projected benefit obligation (PBO)**. The PBO measurement may be less reliable than the ABO but is more relevant and representationally faithful.

The *PBO* estimates retirement benefits by applying the pension formula using projected future compensation levels.

To understand the concepts involved, it's helpful to look at a numerical example. We'll simplify the example (Illustration 17–1) by looking at how pension amounts would be determined for a single employee. Keep in mind though, that in actuality, calculations would be made (by the actuary) for the entire employee pool rather than on an individual-by-individual basis.

[5]To project future salaries for a group of employees, actuaries usually assume some percentage rate of increase in compensation levels in upcoming years. Recent estimates of the rate of compensation increase have ranged from 4.5% to 10% with 4.5% being the most commonly reported expectation (AICPA, *Accounting Trends and Techniques,* 2004).

**ILLUSTRATION 17–1**
Projected Benefit Obligation

Jessica Farrow was hired by Global Communications in 1996. The company has a defined benefit pension plan that specifies annual retirement benefits equal to:

1.5% × Service years × Final year's salary

Farrow is expected to retire in 2035 after 40 years service. Her retirement period is expected to be 20 years. At the end of 2005, 10 years after being hired, her salary is $100,000. The interest rate is 6%. The company's actuary projects Farrow's salary to be $400,000 at retirement.*

What is the company's projected benefit obligation with respect to Jessica Farrow?

**Steps to calculate the projected benefit obligation:**

1. Use the pension formula (including a projection of future salary levels) to determine the retirement benefits earned to date.
2. Find the present value of the retirement benefits as of the retirement date.
3. Find the present value of retirement benefits as of the current date.

**3.** Present value ($n$ = 30, $i$ = 6% of retirement benefits at 2005 is $688,195 × .17411 = **$119,822 (PBO)**

**1.** Actuary estimates employee has earned (as of 2005) retirement benefits of 1.5% × 10 years × $400,000 = **$60,000 per year**

1996 — 2005 — 2035 — 2055

10 years | 30 years | 20 years

**Service period** | **Retirement**

**2.** Present value ($n$ = 20, $i$ = 6%) of the retirement annuity at the retirement date is $60,000 × 11.46992 = **$688,195**

**The actuary includes projected salaries in the pension formula. The projected benefit obligation is the present value of those benefits.**

**The lump-sum equivalent at retirement of annuity payments during the retirement period is the present value of those payments.**

*This salary reflects an estimated compound rate of increase of about 5% and should take into account expectations concerning inflation, promotions, productivity gains, and other factors that might influence salary levels.

If the actuary's estimate of the final salary hasn't changed, the PBO a year later at the end of 2006 would be $139,715 as demonstrated in Illustration 17–1A.

**ILLUSTRATION 17–1A**
PBO in 2006

**3.** Present value ($n$ = 29, $i$ = 6% of retirement benefits at 2006 is $757,015 × .18456 = **$139,715 (PBO)**

**1.** Actuary estimates employee has earned (as of 2006) retirement benefits of 1.5% × 11 years × $400,000 = **$66,000 per year**

1996 — 2006 — 2035 — 2055

11 years | 29 years | 20 years

**Service period** | **Retirement**

**2.** Present value ($n$ = 20, $i$ = 6%) of the retirement annuity at the retirement date is $66,000 × 11.46992 = **$757,015**

**In 2006 the pension formula includes one more service year.**

**Also, 2006 is one year closer to the retirement date for the purpose of calculating the present value.**

**Changes in the PBO.** Notice that the PBO increased during 2006 (Illustration 17–1A) from $119,822 to $139,715 for two reasons:

1. One more service year is included in the pension formula calculation (service cost).
2. The employee is one year closer to retirement, causing the present value of benefits to increase due to the time value of future benefits (interest cost).

These represent two of the events that might possibly cause the balance of the PBO to change. Let's elaborate on these and the three other events that might change the balance of the PBO. The five events are (1) service cost, (2) interest cost, (3) prior service cost, (4) gains and losses, and (5) payments to retired employees.

Each year's service adds to the obligation to pay benefits.

**1. Service cost.** As we just witnessed in the illustration, the PBO increases each year by the amount of that year's **service cost.** This represents the increase in the projected benefit obligation attributable to employee service performed during the period. As we explain later, it also is the primary component of the annual pension expense.

Interest accrues on the PBO each year.

**2. Interest cost.** The second reason the PBO increases is called the **interest cost.** Even though the projected benefit obligation is not formally recognized as a liability in the company's balance sheet, it is a liability nevertheless. And, as with other liabilities, interest accrues on its balance as time passes. The amount can be calculated directly as the assumed discount rate multiplied by the projected benefit obligation at the beginning of the year.[6]

### ADDITIONAL CONSIDERATION

We can verify the increase in the PBO as being caused by the service cost and interest cost as follows:

| | | | | | |
|---|---|---|---|---|---|
| PBO at the beginning of 2006 (end of 2005) | | | | | $119,822 |
| **Service cost:** (1.5% × 1 yr. × $400,000) | × | 11.46992 | × | .18456 | 12,701 |
| Annual retirement benefits from 2006 service | | To discount to 2035* | | To discount to 2006† | |
| **Interest cost:** $119,822 × 6% | | | | | 7,189 |
| PBO at the end of 2006 | | | | | $139,712‡ |

*Present value of an ordinary annuity of $1: $n = 20$, $i = 6\%$.

†Present value of $1: $n = 29$, $i = 6\%$.

‡Differs from $139,715 due to rounding.

**3. Prior service cost.** Another reason the PBO might change is when the pension plan itself is *amended* to revise the way benefits are determined. For example, Global Communications in our illustration might choose to revise the pension formula by which benefits are calculated. Let's back up and assume the formula's salary percentage is increased in 2006 from 1.5% to 1.7%:

**1.7%** × Service years × Final year's salary
(revised pension formula)

Obviously, the annual service cost from this date forward will be higher than it would have been without the amendment. This will cause a more rapid future expansion of the PBO. But it also might cause an immediate increase in the PBO as well. Here's why.

When a pension plan is amended, credit often is given for employee service rendered in prior years. The cost of doing so is called *prior service cost.*

Suppose the amendment becomes effective for future years' service only, without consideration of employee service to date. As you might imagine, the morale and dedication of long-time employees of the company could be expected to suffer. So, for economic as well as ethical reasons, most companies choose to make amendments retroactive to prior years. In other words, the more beneficial terms of the revised pension formula are not applied just to future service years, but benefits attributable to all prior service years also are recomputed under the more favorable terms. Obviously, this decision is not without cost to the company. Making the amendment retroactive to prior years adds an extra layer of retirement benefits, increasing the company's benefit obligation. The increase in the PBO attributable to making a plan amendment retroactive is referred to as **prior service cost.**[7] For instance, Graphic 17–6 presents an excerpt from an annual report of **Ecolab, Inc.** describing the increase in its PBO as a result of making an amendment retroactive:

[6]Assumed discount rates should reflect rates used currently in annuity contracts. Discount rates recently reported have ranged from 4.5% to 7%, with 6.5% being the most commonly assumed rate (AICPA, *Accounting Trends and Techniques,* 2004).

[7]Prior service cost also is created if a defined benefit pension plan is initially adopted by a company that previously did not have one, and the plan itself is made retroactive to give credit for prior years' service. Prior service cost is created by plan amendments far more often than by plan adoptions because most companies already have pension plans, and new pension plans in recent years have predominantly been defined contribution plans.

**Note 1: Retirement Plans (in part)**
. . . The Company amended its U.S. pension plan to change the formula for pension benefits and to provide a more rapid vesting schedule. The plan amendments resulted in a $6 million increase in the projected benefits obligation.

**GRAPHIC 17–6**
Prior Service Cost—Ecolab, Inc.

Let's put prior service cost in the context of our illustration.

At the end of 2005, and therefore the beginning of 2006, the PBO is $119,822. If the plan is amended on January 3, 2006, the PBO could be recomputed as:

| | PBO *without* Amendment | | PBO *with* Amendment | |
|---|---|---|---|---|
| 1. | 1.5% × 10 yrs. × $400,000 | = $ 60,000 | 1.7% × 10 yrs. × $400,000 | = $ 68,000 |
| 2. | $60,000 × 11.46992 | = 688,195 | $68,000 × 11.46992 | = 779,955 |
| 3. | $688,195 × .17411 | = 119,822 | $779,955 × .17411 | = 135,798 |

**$15,976**
Prior service cost

Retroactive benefits from an amendment add additional costs, increasing the company's PBO. This increase is the prior service cost.

The $15,976 increase in the PBO attributable to applying the more generous terms of the amendment to prior service years is the prior service cost. And, because we assumed the amendment occurred at the beginning of 2006, both the 2006 service cost and the 2006 interest cost would change as a result of the prior service cost. This is how:

| | |
|---|---|
| PBO at the beginning of 2006 (end of 2005) | $119,822 |
| **Prior service cost** (determined above) | 15,976 |
| PBO including prior service cost at the beginning of 2006 | 135,798 |
| **Service cost:** (1.7% × 1 yr. × $400,000) × 11.46992 × .18456<br>(Annual retirement benefits from 2006 service; To discount to 2035*; To discount to 2006†) | 14,395 |
| **Interest cost:** $135,798‡ × 6% | 8,148 |
| PBO at the end of 2006 | $158,341 |

*Present value of an ordinary annuity of $1: $n = 20$, $i = 6\%$.
†Present value of $1: $n = 29$, $i = 6\%$.
‡Includes the beginning balance plus the prior service cost because the amendment occurred at the beginning of the year.

Prior service cost increased the PBO at the beginning of the year.

## ADDITIONAL CONSIDERATION

We can verify the PBO balance by calculating it directly:

**3.** Present value ($n = 29$, $i = 6\%$) of retirement benefits at 2006 is $857,950 × .18456 = **$158,341* (PBO)**

**1.** Actuary estimates employee has earned (as of 2006) retirement benefits of 1.7% × 11 years × $400,000 = **$74,800 per year**

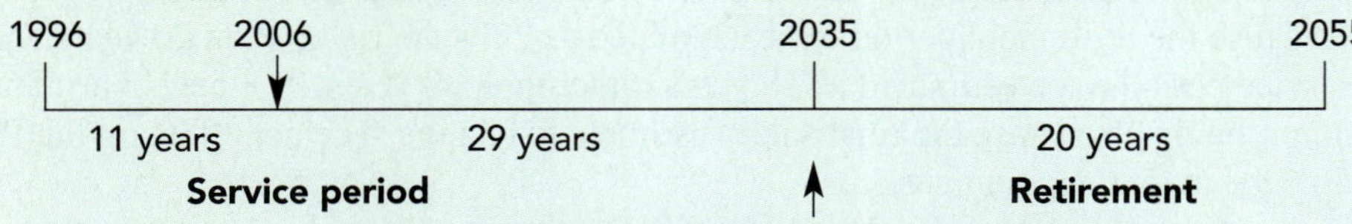


**2.** Present value ($n = 20$, $i = 6\%$) of the retirement annuity at the retirement date is $74,800 × 11.46992 = **$857,950**

*Adjusted by $2 to compensate for the rounding of present value factors.

The pension formula reflects the plan amendment.

The plan amendment would affect not only the year in which it occurs, but also each subsequent year because the revised pension formula determines each year's service cost. Continuing our illustration to 2007 demonstrates this:

During 2007, the PBO increased as a result of service cost and interest cost.

| | | | | |
|---|---|---|---|---|
| PBO at the beginning of 2007 (end of 2006) | | | | $158,341 |
| **Service cost:** (1.7% × 1 yr. × $400,000) | × 11.46992 | × .19563 | | 15,258 |
| Annual retirement benefits from 2007 service | To discount to 2035* | To discount to 2007† | | |
| **Interest cost:** $158,341 × 6% | | | | 9,500 |
| PBO at the end of 2007 | | | | $183,099 |

*Present value of an ordinary annuity of $1: $n = 20$, $i = 6\%$.
†Present value of $1: $n = 28$, $i = 6\%$.

Decreases and increases in estimates of the PBO because of periodic reevaluation of uncertainties are called gains and losses.

**4. Gain or loss on the PBO.** We mentioned earlier that a number of estimates are necessary to derive the PBO. When one or more of these estimates requires revision, the estimate of the PBO also will require revision. The resulting decrease or increase in the PBO is referred to as a *gain* or *loss,* respectively. Let's modify our illustration to imitate the effect of revising one of the several possible estimates involved. Suppose, for instance, that new information at the end of 2007 about inflation and compensation trends suggests that the estimate of Farrow's final salary should be increased by 5% to $420,000. This would affect the estimate of the PBO as follows:

Changing the final salary estimate changes the PBO.

| PBO *without* Revised Estimate | | PBO *with* Revised Estimate | |
|---|---|---|---|
| 1. 1.7% × 12 yrs. × $400,000 | = $ 81,600 | 1.7% × 12 yrs. × **$420,000** | = $ 85,680 |
| 2. $81,600 × 11.46992 | = 935,945 | $85,680 × 11.46992 | = 982,743 |
| 3. $935,945 × .19563 | = 183,099 | $982,743 × .19563 | = 192,254 |

**$9,155**
Loss on PBO

The difference of $9,155 represents a loss on the PBO because the obligation turned out to be higher than previously expected. Now there would be three elements of the increase in the PBO during 2007.[8]

The revised estimate caused the PBO to increase.

| | |
|---|---|
| PBO at the beginning of 2007 | $158,341 |
| **Service cost** (calculated above) | 15,258 |
| **Interest cost** (calculated above) | 9,500 |
| **Loss on PBO** (calculated above) | 9,155 |
| PBO at the end of 2007 | $192,254 |

If a revised estimate causes the PBO to be lower than previously expected, a gain would be indicated. Consider how a few of the other possible estimate changes would affect the PBO:

- A change in life expectancies might cause the retirement period to be estimated as 21 years rather than 20 years. Calculation of the present value of the retirement annuity would use $n = 21$, rather than $n = 20$. The estimate of the PBO would increase.
- The expectation that retirement will occur two years earlier than previously thought would cause the retirement period to be estimated as 22 years rather than 20 years and the service period to be estimated as 28 years rather than 30 years. The new expectation would probably also cause the final salary estimate to change. The net effect on the PBO would depend on the circumstances.
- A change in the assumed discount rate would affect the present value calculations. A lower rate would increase the estimate of the PBO. A higher rate would decrease the estimate of the PBO.

**5. Payment of retirement benefits.** We've seen how the PBO will change due to the accumulation of service cost from year to year, the accrual of interest as time passes, making

[8]The increase in the PBO due to amending the pension formula (prior service cost) occurred in 2006.

plan amendments retroactive to prior years, and periodic adjustments when estimates change. Another change in the PBO occurs when the obligation is reduced as benefits actually are paid to retired employees.

Payment of retirement benefits reduces the PBO.

The payment of such benefits is not applicable in our present illustration because we've limited the situation to calculations concerning an individual employee who is several years from retirement. Remember, though, in reality the actuary would make these calculations for the entire pool of employees covered by the pension plan. But the concepts involved would be the same. Graphic 17–7 summarizes the five ways the PBO can change.

**GRAPHIC 17–7**
Components of Change in the PBO

**The Projected Benefits Obligation Changes as a Result of:**

| Cause | Effect | Frequency |
|---|---|---|
| Service cost | + | Each period |
| Interest cost | + | Each period (except the first period of the plan, when no obligation exists to accrue interest) |
| Prior service cost | + | Only if the plan is amended (or initiated) that period |
| Loss or gain on PBO | + or − | Whenever revisions are made in the pension liability estimate |
| Retiree benefits paid | − | Each period (unless no employees have yet retired under the plan) |

## ILLUSTRATION EXPANDED TO CONSIDER THE ENTIRE EMPLOYEE POOL

For our single employee, the PBO at the end of 2007 is $192,254. Let's say now that Global Communications has 2,000 active employees covered by the pension plan and 100 retired employees receiving retirement benefits. Illustration 17–2 expands the numbers to represent all covered employees.

The PBO is not formally recognized in the balance sheet.

**ILLUSTRATION 17–2**
The PBO Expanded to Include All Employees

The changes in the PBO for Global Communications during 2007 were as follows:

| | ($ in millions)* |
|---|---|
| PBO at the beginning of 2007† (amount assumed) | $400 |
| **Service cost, 2007** (amount assumed) | 41 |
| **Interest cost:** $400 × 6% | 24 |
| **Loss (gain) on PBO** (amount assumed) | 23 |
| **Less: Retiree benefits paid** (amount assumed) | (38) |
| PBO at the end of 2007 | $450 |

*Of course, these expanded amounts are not simply the amounts for Jessica Farrow multiplied by 2,000 employees because her years of service, expected retirement date, and salary are not necessarily representative of other employees. Also, the expanded amounts take into account expected employee turnover and current retirees.
†Includes the prior service cost that increased the PBO when the plan was amended in 2006.

# Pension Plan Assets

● LO4

So far our focus has been on the employer's obligation to provide retirement benefits in the future. We turn our attention now to the resources with which the company will satisfy that obligation—the **pension plan assets.** Like the PBO, the pension plan assets are not formally recognized on the balance sheet but are actively monitored in the employer's informal records. Its balance, too, must be reported in disclosure notes to the financial statements, and as explained below, the return on these assets is included in the calculation of the periodic pension expense.

FINANCIAL REPORTING CASE
Q3, p. 828

We assumed in the previous section that Global Communications' obligation is $450 million for service performed to date. When employees retire, will there be sufficient funds to provide the anticipated benefits? To ensure sufficient funding, Global will contribute cash each year to a pension fund.

A *trustee* manages pension plan assets.

The assets of a pension fund must be held by a **trustee.** A trustee accepts employer contributions, invests the contributions, accumulates the earnings on the investments, and pays benefits from the plan assets to retired employees or their beneficiaries. The trustee can be an individual, a bank, or a trust company. Plan assets are invested in stocks, bonds, and other income-producing assets. The accumulated balance of the annual employer contributions plus the return on the investments (dividends, interest, market price appreciation) must be sufficient to pay benefits as they come due.

When an employer estimates how much it must set aside each year to accumulate sufficient funds to pay retirement benefits as they come due, it's necessary to estimate the return those investments will produce. This is the **expected return on plan assets.** The higher the return, the less the employer must actually contribute. On the other hand, a relatively low return means the difference must be made up by higher contributions. In practice, recent estimates of the rate of return have ranged from 4.5% to 11%, with 8.5% being the most commonly reported expectation.[9] In Illustration 17–3, we shift the focus of our numerical illustration to emphasize Global's pension plan assets.

**ILLUSTRATION 17–3**
How Plan Assets Change

Global Communications funds its defined benefit pension plan by contributing each year the year's service cost plus a portion of the prior service cost. Cash of $48 million was contributed to the pension fund at the end of 2007.

Plan assets at the beginning of 2007 were valued at $300 million. The expected rate of return on the investment of those assets was 9%, but the actual return in 2007 was 10%. Retirement benefits of $38 million were paid at the end of 2007 to retired employees.

What is the value of the company's pension plan assets at the end of 2007?

A trustee accepts employer contributions, invests the contributions, accumulates the earnings on the investments, and pays benefits from the plan assets.

| | ($ in millions) |
|---|---|
| Plan assets at the beginning of 2007 | $300 |
| **Return on plan assets** (10% × $300) | 30 |
| **Cash contributions** | 48 |
| **Less: Retiree benefits paid** | (38) |
| Plan assets at the end of 2007 | $340 |

Recall that Global's PBO at the end of 2007 is $450 million. Because the plan assets are only $340 million, the pension plan is said to be *underfunded.* One reason is that we assumed Global incurred a $60 million prior service cost from amending the pension plan at the beginning of 2006, and that cost is being funded over several years. Another factor is the loss from increasing the PBO due to the estimate revision, since funding has been based on the previous estimate. Later, we'll assume earlier revisions also have increased the PBO. Of course, actual performance of the investments also impacts a plan's funded status.

An *underfunded* pension plan means the PBO exceeds plan assets.

An *overfunded* pension plan means plan assets exceed the PBO.

It is not unusual for pension plans today to be underfunded. Historically the funded status of pension plans has varied considerably. Prior to the Employee Retirement Income Security Act (ERISA) in 1974, many plans were grossly underfunded. The new law established minimum funding standards among other matters designed to protect plan participants. The new standards brought most plans closer to full funding. Then the stock market boom of the 1980s caused the value of plan assets for many pension funds to swell to well over their projected benefit obligations. More than 80% of pension plans were overfunded. As a result, managers explored ways to divert funds to other areas of operations. Today a majority of plans again are underfunded. Many of the underfunded plans are with troubled companies, placing employees at risk. The PBGC guarantees are limited to about $3,400 per month, often less than promised pension benefits.

[9]AICPA, *Accounting Trends and Techniques,* 2004.

### REPORTING THE FUNDED STATUS OF THE PENSION PLAN

● LO5

**FINANCIAL REPORTING CASE**

Q4, p. 828

A company's PBO is not reported among liabilities in the balance sheet. Similarly, the plan assets a company sets aside to pay those benefits are not reported among assets in the balance sheet. However, beginning in 2006 (for most companies), firms must report the net difference between those two amounts, referred to as the "funded status" of the plan.[10] From our previous discussion, we see the funded status for Global to be the following at Dec. 31, 2007, and Dec. 31, 2006:

| ($in millions) | 2007 | 2006 |
|---|---|---|
| Projected benefit obligation (PBO) | $450 | $400 |
| Fair value of plan assets | 340 | 300 |
| Underfunded status | $110 | $100 |

**A company must report in its balance sheet a liability for the underfunded (or asset for the overfunded) status of its postretirement plans.**

Because the plan is underfunded, Global reports a pension liability of $110 million in its 2007 balance sheet and $100 million in 2006. If the plan becomes overfunded in the future, Global will report a pension asset instead.

Now, let's look at all the ways that changes in the pension liability and the pension plan assets affect pension expense.

# DETERMINING PENSION EXPENSE

**PART C**

## The Relationship between Pension Expense and Changes in the PBO and Plan Assets

● LO6

Like wages, salaries, commissions, and other forms of pay, pension expense is part of a company's compensation for employee services each year. Accordingly, the accounting objective is to achieve a matching of the costs of providing this form of compensation with the benefits of the services performed. However, the fact that this form of compensation actually is paid to employees many years after the service is performed means that other elements in addition to the annual service cost will affect the ultimate pension cost. These other elements are related to changes that occur over time in both the pension liability and the pension plan assets. Graphic 17–8 provides a summary of how some of these changes influence pension expense.

**The matching principle and the time period assumption dictate that the costs be allocated to the periods the services are performed.**

We've examined each of the components of pension expense from the viewpoint of its effect on the PBO or on plan assets, using the Global Communications illustration to demonstrate that effect. Now, let's expand the same illustration to see how these changes affect *pension expense.* Illustration 17–4 provides this expanded example.

### COMPONENTS OF PENSION EXPENSE

Illustration 17–4 demonstrates the relationship between some of the changes in the PBO and in plan assets and the components of pension expense: service cost, interest cost, the return on plan assets, prior service cost amortization, and net gain or loss amortization. Let's look at these five components of pension expense one at a time.

**1. Service Cost.** The $41 million service cost represents the increase in the projected benefit obligation attributable to employee service performed during 2007 (benefits earned by employees during the year). Each year this is the first component of the pension expense.

**2. Interest Cost.** The interest cost is calculated as the interest rate (actuary's discount rate) multiplied by the projected benefit obligation at the beginning of the year. In 2007, this is 6% times $400 million, or $24 million.

**Interest cost is the discount rate times the PBO balance at the beginning of the year.**

The PBO is not formally recognized as a liability in the company's balance sheet, but it is a liability nevertheless. The interest expense that accrues on its balance is not separately reported on the income statement but is instead combined with the service cost (and other amounts) as the second component of the annual pension expense.

[10]"Employers' Accounting for Defined Benefit Pension and Other Postretirement Plans—an amendment of FASB Statements No. 87, 88, 106, and 132(R)," *Statement of Financial Accounting Standards No. 158* (Stamford, Conn.: FASB, 2006).

**GRAPHIC 17–8**
Components of the Periodic Pension Expense

**FINANCIAL REPORTING CASE**
Q5, p. 828

The pension expense reported in the income statement is a composite of periodic changes that occur in both the pension obligation and the plan assets.

**Changes in the PBO**

**Service cost**—increase in the employer's obligation attributed to employee service during the current period

**Interest cost**—interest accrued on the obligation during the current period (balance at the beginning of the period multiplied by the interest rate)

**Prior service cost**—increase in the employer's obligation due to giving credit to employees for years of service provided before the pension plan is amended (or initiated)

**Losses or (gains) on the PBO**—increases or (decreases) in the estimate of the PBO from revisions in underlying assumptions

**Less: Payments to retirees**

**Pension Expense**

*Included currently:*
- **Service cost**
- **Interest cost**
- **(Expected return on the plan assets)**

*Delayed recognition:*
Amortized portion of:
- **Prior service cost**
- **Net loss or (gain)**

**Changes in Plan Assets**

**Expected return on the plan assets**—estimated long-term return from changes in the value of plan assets, due to dividends, interest, and market price changes, plus (minus):

**Gains or (losses) on the plan assets**—return on plan assets lower or (higher) than expected

**Cash contributions**—payments into the fund by the employer

**Less: Payments to retirees**

**ILLUSTRATION 17–4**
Pension Expense

These are the changes in the PBO and in the plan assets we previously discussed (Illustration 17–2 and Illustration 17–3).

Reports from the actuary and the trustee of plan assets indicate the following changes during 2007 in the PBO and plan assets of Global Communications.

| ($ in millions) | PBO | | Plan Assets |
|---|---|---|---|
| *Beginning* of 2007 | $400 | *Beginning* of 2007 | $300 |
| Service cost | 41 | Return on plan assets,* | |
| Interest cost, 6% | 24 | 10% (9% expected) | 30 |
| Loss (gain) on PBO | 23 | Cash contributions | 48 |
| Less: Retiree benefits | (38) | Less: Retiree benefits | (38) |
| *End* of 2007 | $450 | *End* of 2007 | $340 |

A *prior service cost* of $60 million was incurred at the beginning of the previous year (2006) due to a plan amendment increasing the PBO. At the beginning of 2007 Global had a *net loss–pensions* of $55 million (previous losses exceeded previous gains). The average remaining service life of employees is estimated at 15 years.

2007 Pension Expense

| **Global's 2007 Pension Expense Is Determined as Follows:** | ($ in millions) |
|---|---|
| Service cost | $41 |
| Interest cost | 24 |
| Expected return on the plan assets ($30 actual, less $3 gain) | (27) |
| Amortization of prior service cost (calculated later) | 4 |
| Amortization of net loss–pensions (calculated later) | 1 |
| **Pension expense** | $43 |

*Expected rates of return anticipate the performance of various investments of plan assets. This is not necessarily the same as the discount rate used by the actuary to estimate the pension obligation. Assumed rates of return recently reported have ranged from 4.5% to 11%, with 8.5% being the most commonly assumed rate (AICPA, *Accounting Trends and Techniques*, 2004).

**3. Return on Plan Assets.** Remember, plan assets comprise funds invested in stocks, bonds, and other securities that presumably will generate dividends, interest, and capital gains. Each year these earnings represent the return on plan assets during that year. When accounting for the return, we need to differentiate between its two modes: the *expected* return and the *actual* return.

The return earned on investment securities increases the plan asset balance.

Actual versus expected return. We've assumed Global's expected rate of return is 9%, so its expected return on plan assets in 2007 was 9% times $300 million, or $27 million. But, as previously indicated, the actual rate of return in 2007 was 10%, producing an actual return on plan assets of 10% times $300 million, or $30 million.

Obviously, investing plan assets in income-producing assets lessens the amounts employers must contribute to the fund. So, the return on plan assets reduces the net cost of having a pension plan. Accordingly, the return on plan assets each year *reduces* the amount recorded as pension expense. Just as the interest expense that accrues on the PBO is included as a component of pension expense rather than being separately reported, the investment revenue on plan assets is not separately reported either. In actuality, both the interest and return-on-assets components of pension expense do not directly represent employee compensation. Instead, they are financial items created only because the pension payment is delayed while the obligation is funded currently.

The interest and return-on-assets components are financial items created only because the compensation is delayed and the obligation is funded currently.

Adjustment for loss or gain. A controversial question is *when* differences between the actual and expected return should be recognized in pension expense. It seems logical that since the net cost of having a pension plan is reduced by the actual return on plan assets, the charge to pension expense should be the actual return on plan assets. However, the FASB concluded that the actual return should first be adjusted by any difference between that return and what the return had been expected to be. So, it's actually the *expected* return that is included in the calculation of pension expense. In our illustration, Global's pension expense is reduced by the expected return of $27 million.

The return on plan assets reduces the net cost of having a pension plan.

The difference between the actual and expected return is considered a loss or gain on plan assets. Although we don't include these losses and gains as part of pension expense when they occur, it's possible they will affect pension expense at a later time. On the next page, we will discuss how that might happen.

Any loss or gain is not included in pension expense right away.

**4. Amortization of Prior Service Cost.** Recall that the $60 million increase in Global's PBO due to recalculating benefits employees earned in prior years as a result of a plan amendment is referred to as the prior service cost. Obviously, prior service cost adds to the cost of having a pension plan. But when should this cost be recognized as pension expense? An argument can be made that the cost should be recognized as expense in the year of the amendment when the cost increases the company's pension obligation. In fact, some members of the FASB have advocated this approach. At present, though, we amortize the cost gradually to pension expense. Here's the rationalization.

Prior service cost is recognized as pension expense over the future service period of the employees whose benefits are recalculated.

Amending a pension plan, and especially choosing to make that amendment retroactive, typically is done with the idea that future operations will benefit from those choices. For that reason, the cost is not recognized as pension expense in the year the plan is amended. Instead, it is recognized as pension expense over the time that the employees who benefited from the retroactive amendment will work for the company in the future. Presumably, this future service period is when the company will receive the benefits of its actions.

In our illustration, the amendment occurred in 2006, increasing the PBO at that time. For the individual employee, Jessica Farrow, the prior service cost was calculated to be $15,976. Our illustration assumes that, for all plan participants, the prior service cost was $60 million at the beginning of 2006. The prior service cost at the beginning of 2007 is $56 million. The following section explains how this amount was computed.

One assumption in our illustration is that the average remaining service life of the active employee group is 15 years. To recognize the $60 million prior service cost in equal annual amounts over this period, the amount amortized as an increase in pension expense each year is $4 million:[11]

[11]An alternative to this straight-line approach, called the *service method,* attempts to allocate the prior service cost to each year in proportion to the fraction of the total remaining service years worked in each of those years. This method is described in the chapter appendix.

By the straight-line method, prior service cost is recognized over the average remaining service life of the active employee group.

| **Amortization of Prior Service Cost:** | ($ in millions) |
|---|---|
| Service cost | $41 |
| Interest cost | 24 |
| Expected return on the plan assets | (27) |
| Amortization of prior service cost | 4 |
| Amortization of net loss–pensions | 1 |
| **Pension expense** | $43 |

Prior service cost is not expensed as it is incurred. Instead, it is reported as a component of *accumulated other comprehensive income* to be amortized over time.

Be sure to note that, even though we're amortizing it, the prior service cost is not an asset, but instead a part of *accumulated other comprehensive income*, a shareholders' equity account. This is a result of the FASB's current disinclination to treat the cost as an expense as it is incurred. The Board, instead, prefers to ascribe it the off-the-income-statement designation as *other comprehensive income* in the same manner as the handful of losses and gains also categorized the same way and not reported among the gains and losses in the traditional income statement. You first learned about comprehensive income in Chapter 4 and again in Chapter 12. We'll revisit it again later in this chapter.

The prior service cost declines by $4 million each year:

| **Prior Service Cost** | ($ in millions) |
|---|---|
| Prior service cost at the beginning of 2007 | $56 |
| Less: 2007 amortization | (4) |
| Prior service cost at the end of 2007 | $52 |

**5. Amortization of a Net Loss or Net Gain.** You learned previously that gains and losses can occur when expectations are revised concerning either the PBO or the return on plan assets. Graphic 17–9 summarizes the possibilities.

**GRAPHIC 17–9**
Gains and Losses

Gains and losses occur when either the PBO or the return on plan assets turns out to be different than expected.

| | Projected Benefit Obligation | Return on Plan Assets |
|---|---|---|
| Higher than expected | Loss | Gain |
| Lower than expected | Gain | Loss |

Like the prior service cost we just discussed, we don't include these gains and losses as part of pension expense in the income statement, but instead report them as *other comprehensive income* in the statement of comprehensive income as they occur. We then report the gains and losses on a cumulative basis as a net loss–pensions or a net gain–pensions, depending on whether we have greater losses or gains over time. We report this amount in the balance sheet as a part of *accumulated other comprehensive income*, a shareholders' equity account.

There is no conceptual justification for not including losses and gains in earnings. After all, these increases and decreases in either the PBO or plan assets immediately impact the net cost of providing a pension plan and, conceptually, should be included in pension expense as they occur.

Nevertheless, The FASB requires that income statement recognition of gains and losses from either source be delayed. Why?—for practical reasons.

## INCOME SMOOTHING

The FASB acknowledged the conceptual shortcoming of delaying the recognition of a gain or a loss while opting for this more politically acceptable approach. Delayed recognition was favored by a dominant segment of corporate America that was concerned with the effect of allowing gains and losses to immediately impact reported earnings. In 2006, the FASB decided to formally reconsider all aspects of accounting for postretirement benefit plans, including this treatment of gains and losses.[14] The project will consider overhauling the entire system for accounting for and reporting on postretirement benefits. This result might include immediately including gains and losses in pension expense, thereby eliminating income smoothing.

The Board believes that it would be conceptually appropriate and preferable to [have] . . . no delay in recognition of gains and losses, or perhaps [to have] . . . gains and losses reported currently in comprehensive income but not in earnings. However, it concluded that those approaches would be too great a change from past practice to be adopted at the present time.[12]

Delayed recognition of gains and losses achieves income smoothing at the expense of conceptual integrity.

The practical justification for delayed recognition is that, over time, gains and losses might cancel one another out. Given this possibility, why create unnecessary fluctuations in reported income by letting temporary gains and losses decrease and increase (respectively) pension expense? Of course, as years pass there may be more gains than losses, or vice versa, preventing their offsetting one another completely. So, if a net gain or a net loss gets "too large," pension expense must be adjusted.

*SFAS 87* defines too large rather arbitrarily as being when a net gain or a net loss at the beginning of a year exceeds an amount equal to 10% of the PBO, or 10% of plan assets, whichever is higher.[15] *SFAS 87* refers to this threshold amount as the "corridor." When the corridor is exceeded, the excess is not charged to pension expense all at once. Instead, as a further concession to income smoothing, only a portion of the excess is included in pension expense. The minimum amount that should be included is the excess divided by the average remaining service period of active employees expected to receive benefits under the plan.[16]

The Board acknowledges that the delayed recognition included in this Statement results in excluding the most current and most relevant information.[13]

A net gain or a net loss affects pension expense only if it exceeds an amount equal to 10% of the PBO, or 10% of plan assets, whichever is higher.

In our illustration, we're assuming a net loss–pensions of $55 million at the beginning of 2007. Also recall that the PBO and plan assets are $400 million and $300 million, respectively, at that time. The amount amortized to 2007 pension expense is $1 million, calculated as follows:

| **Determining Net Loss Amortization—2007** | ($ in millions) |
|---|---|
| Net loss (previous losses exceeded previous gains) | $55 |
| 10% of $400 ($400 is greater than $300): the "corridor" | (40) |
| Excess at the beginning of the year | $15 |
| Average remaining service period | ÷ 15 years |
| Amount amortized to 2007 pension expense | $ 1 |

Because the net loss exceeds an amount equal to the greater of 10% of the PBO or 10% of plan assets, part of the excess is amortized to pension expense.

The pension expense is increased because a net loss is being amortized. If a net *gain* were being amortized, the amount would be *deducted* from pension expense because a gain would indicate that the net cost of providing the pension plan had decreased.

[12]FASB, "Employers' Accounting for Pension and Other Postretirement Benefits," *Preliminary Views,* November 1982, par. 107.

[13]Ibid., par. 88.

[14]"Employers' Accounting for Defined Benefit Pension and Other Postretirement Plans—an amendment of FASB Statements No. 87, 88, 106, and 132(R)," *Statement of Financial Accounting Standards No. 158* (Stamford, Conn.: FASB, 2006), par. B16.

[15]For this purpose the FASB specifies the market-related value of plan assets. This can be either the fair market value or a weighted-average fair market value over a period not to exceed five years. We will uniformly assume fair market value in this chapter.

[16]Companies are permitted to amortize the entire net loss (or gain) rather than just the excess, but few choose that option. (*SFAS 87,* par. 33.)

Amortization of a net gain would decrease pension expense.

Amortization of a net loss increases pension expense.

| **Amortization of the Net Loss–Pensions:** | ($ in millions) |
|---|---|
| Service cost | $41 |
| Interest cost | 24 |
| Expected return on the plan assets | (27) |
| Amortization of prior service cost | 4 |
| Amortization of net loss–pensions | 1 |
| **Pension expense** | $43 |

This amortization reduces the net loss in 2007 by $1 million. Also recall that Global incurred (a) a $23 million loss in 2007 from revising estimates relating to the PBO and (b) a $3 million gain when the 2007 return on plan assets was higher than expected. These three changes affected the net loss–pensions in 2007 as follows:

New losses add to a net loss; new gains reduce a net loss.

| **Net Loss–Pensions** | ($ in millions) |
|---|---|
| Net loss–pensions at the beginning of 2007 | $55 |
| Less: 2007 amortization | (1) |
| Plus: 2007 loss on PBO | 23 |
| Less: 2007 gain on plan assets | (3) |
| Net loss–pensions at the end of 2007 | $74 |

## ADDITIONAL CONSIDERATION

The $74 million balance at the end of 2007 would be the beginning balance in 2008. It would be compared with the 2008 beginning balances in the PBO and plan assets to determine whether amortization would be necessary in 2008. If you were to look back to our analyses of the changes in those two balances, you would see the 2008 beginning balances in the PBO and plan assets to be $450 million and $340 million, respectively. The amount amortized to 2008 pension expense will be $1.93 million, calculated as follows:

| | ($ in millions) |
|---|---|
| Net loss (previous losses exceeded previous gains) | $74 |
| 10% of $450 ($450 is greater than $340) | (45) |
| Excess at the beginning of the year | $29 |
| Average remaining service period | ÷ 15 years* |
| **Amount amortized to 2008 pension expense** | **$1.93** |

*Assumes the average remaining service period of active employees is still 15 years in 2008 due to new employees joining the firm.

## GLOBAL PERSPECTIVE

Most large companies in Japan sponsor pension plans that are funded through financial institutions. Contributions to pension funds are tax deductible. Because the taxes levied by the government are reported as income tax expense on the income statement, most Japanese companies report annual pension expense equal to cash contributions to the pension fund.

In other countries, such as France, Belgium, Finland, India, and New Zealand, pension costs are not covered by accounting standards. In still other countries pension accounting is irrelevant because the occurrence of pension plans is rare (Korea, Argentina, and Brazil, for example).

# REPORTING ISSUES

PART D

## Recording the Pension Expense

• LO7

Recall from Illustration 17–4 that Global's 2007 pension expense is $43 million. Three of the five components of that expense affect the pension liability. Here's why. The expense includes the $41 million service cost and the $24 million interest cost, both of which add to Global's PBO. Since the pension liability is the difference between the PBO and plan assets, when the PBO goes up, so does the pension liability. Similarly, the expense includes a $27 million reduction for the expected return on plan assets. Since the pension liability is the difference between the PBO and plan assets, when the plan assets goes up, the pension liability goes down.[17] These changes are reflected in the following entry:

65 ↑ PBO
27 ↑ Less: plan assets
38 ↑ Pension liability

| To Record Pension Expense | ($ in millions) | |
|---|---|---|
| Pension expense (total) | 43 | |
| Pension liability ($41 + 24 – 27) | | 38 |
| Amortization of prior service cost–OCI* (2007 amortization) | | 4 |
| Amortization of net loss–OCI* (2007 amortization) | | 1 |

*Other comprehensive income (reported in the Statement of Comprehensive Income)

**The pension liability (PBO minus plan assets) is affected only by the three components of pension expense that change either the PBO or plan assets.**

The pension expense also includes the $4 million prior service cost amortization and the $1 million amortization of the net loss–pensions as we calculated earlier. Unlike the other three components, though, these amortization amounts affect neither the PBO nor the plan assets and therefore don't change the pension liability. Of course, amortization reduces the two balances being amortized; the prior service cost decreases by $4 million and the net loss–pensions by $1 million, thus the credits to those accounts.

## Recording the Funding of Plan Assets

When Global adds its annual cash investment to its plan assets, the value of those plan assets increases by $48 million. Since the pension liability is the excess of the PBO over plan assets, that liability is reduced when plan assets increase:

| To Record Funding | ($ in millions) | |
|---|---|---|
| Pension liability | 48 | |
| Cash (contribution to plan assets) | | 48 |

PBO
48 ↑ Less: plan assets
48 ↓ Pension liability

It is not unusual for the cash contribution to differ from that year's pension expense. After all, the determination of the periodic pension expense and the funding of the pension plan are two separate processes. Pension expense is an accounting decision. How much to contribute each year is a financing decision affected by cash flow and tax considerations, as well as minimum funding requirements of ERISA. Subject to these considerations, cash contributions are actuarially determined with the objective of accumulating (along with investment returns) sufficient funds to provide promised retirement benefits.

The pension expense is, of course, reported in the income statement. In addition, the composition of that amount must be reported in disclosure notes. For instance, Northwest Air Lines described the composition of its pension expense in the disclosure note in its 2004 annual report, shown in Graphic 17–10.

## Recording Gains and Losses

As we discussed earlier, gains and losses (either from changing assumptions regarding the PBO or from the return on assets being higher or lower than expected) are deferred and not

[17]The increase in plan assets is the $30 million *actual* return, but the $27 million *expected* return is the reduction in pension expense because the $3 million gain isn't included in expense. We see in the next section that the $3 million gain is reflected in the funded status of the plan (pension liability) and is recorded as other comprehensive income.

**GRAPHIC 17–10**
Disclosure of Pension Expense—Northwest Air Lines

The components of pension expense are itemized in the disclosure note.

**Note 12: Pension and Other Postretirement Health Care Benefits**
The components of net periodic cost of defined benefit plans included the following (in millions):

| | 2004 | 2003 | 2002 |
|---|---|---|---|
| Service cost | $ 239 | $ 248 | $ 218 |
| Interest cost | 534 | 531 | 503 |
| Expected return on plan assets | (503) | (476) | (538) |
| Amortization of prior service cost | 75 | 77 | 80 |
| Recognized net actuarial loss | 99 | 111 | 46 |
| Net periodic benefit cost | $ 444 | $ 491 | $ 309 |

immediately included in pension expense and net income. Instead, we report them as *other comprehensive income* in the statement of comprehensive income. So Global records a *loss–other comprehensive income* for the $23 million loss that occurs in 2007 when it revises its estimate of future salary levels causing its PBO estimate to increase as well as a $3 million *gain–other comprehensive income* that occurred when the $30 million actual return on plan assets exceeded the $27 million expected return. Here's the entry:

Losses and gains (as well as any new prior service cost should it occur) are reported as OCI and cause a change in the pension liability.

23 ↑ PBO
3 ↑ Less: plan assets
20 ↑ Pension liability

| To Record Gains and Losses as Other Comprehensive Income (OCI) | ($ in millions) | |
|---|---|---|
| Loss–OCI (from change in assumption) | 23 | |
| Gain–OCI (from actual return exceeding expected return) | | 3 |
| Pension liability (to balance) | | 20 |

The loss increases the PBO, and the gain increases plan assets. Since the pension liability is the excess of the PBO over the plan assets, when the PBO goes up by $23 million, the pension liability goes up. But when the plan assets go up by $3 million, the pension liability goes down. As a result, the pension liability increases by $20 million.

Remember, gains and losses become part of either a net loss–pensions or a net gain–pensions account (net loss–pensions in Global's case), which is a component of *accumulated other comprehensive income*, a shareholders' equity account.

**ADDITIONAL CONSIDERATION**

Just as we record new losses and gains as they occur, we also will record a change in the prior service cost account for any new prior service cost should it occur. For instance, if Global revised its pension formula again and recalculated its PBO using the more generous formula, causing a $40 million increase in the PBO, the company would record the new prior service cost this way:

| To Record New Prior Service Cost as Other Comprehensive Income (OCI) | ($ in millions) | |
|---|---|---|
| Prior service cost–OCI (increase in PBO due to plan amendment) | 40 | |
| Pension liability | | 40 |

If an amendment *reduces* rather than increases the PBO, the *negative prior service cost* would reduce both the prior service cost and pension liability.

## Comprehensive Income

Comprehensive income, as you may recall from Chapter 4, is a more expansive view of income than traditional net income. In fact, it encompasses all changes in equity other than from transactions with owners.[18] So, in addition to net income, comprehensive income includes up to four other changes in equity. A statement of comprehensive income is demonstrated in Illustration 17–5, highlighting the presentation of the components of other comprehensive income pertaining to Global's pension plan.

**ILLUSTRATION 17–5**
Statement of Comprehensive Income

| | ($ in millions) | |
|---|---|---|
| Net income | | $xxx |
| Other comprehensive income: | | |
| Net unrealized holding gains (losses) on investments | $ x | |
| Loss on pensions—due to revising a PBO estimate* | (23) | |
| Gain on pensions—return on plan assets exceeds expected* | 3 | |
| Amortization of net loss—pensions | 1 | |
| Amortization of prior service cost | 4 | |
| Deferred gains (losses) from derivatives | x | |
| Gains (losses) from foreign currency translation | x | xx |
| Comprehensive income | | $xxx |

*From Illustration 17–4 on p. 842
Note: These amounts are shown without considering taxes. Actually each of the elements of comprehensive income *should be reported net of tax.* For instance, if the tax rate is 40%, the gain would be reported as $13.8 million: $23 million less a $9.2 million tax benefit.

**Gains and losses, as well as any new prior service cost should it arise, are among the other comprehensive income items reported in the period they occur.**

*Other comprehensive income* (OCI) items are reported both (a) as they occur and (b) as an accumulated balance as shown in Illustrations 17–6 and 17–7.[19]

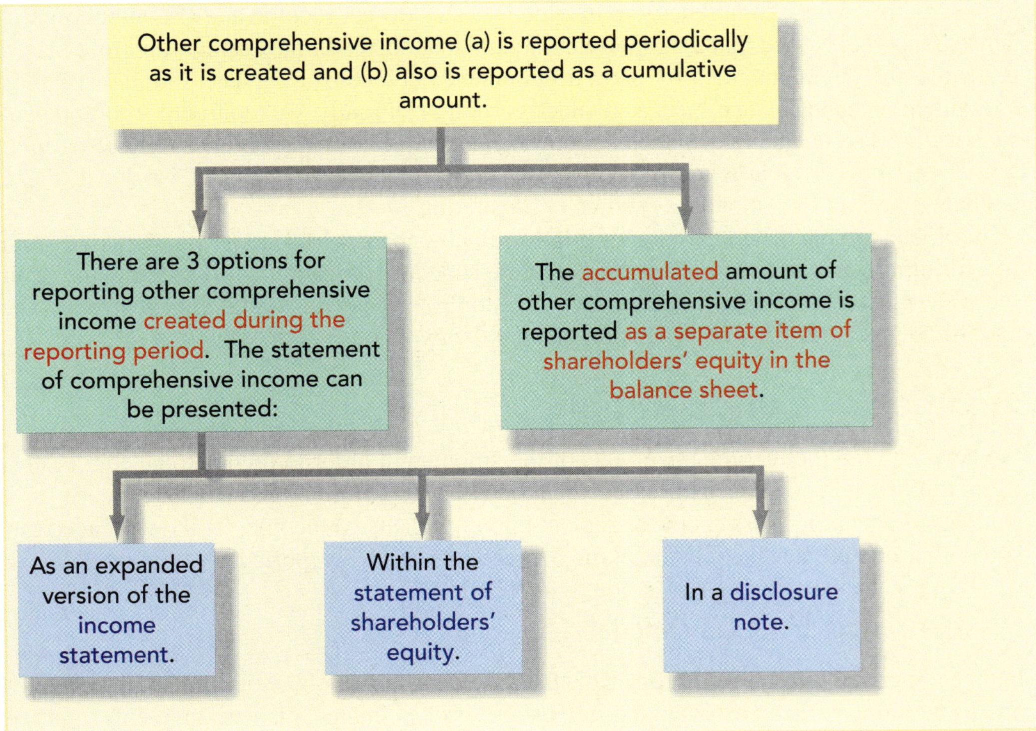


**ILLUSTRATION 17–6**
Reporting Comprehensive Income

In addition to reporting the gains or losses (and other elements of comprehensive income) that occur in the current reporting period, we also report these amounts on a *cumulative* basis

[18]Transactions with owners primarily include dividends and the sale or purchase of shares of the company's stock.
[19]The statement of comprehensive income can be reported either (a) as an extension of the income statement, (b) in a disclosure note, or (c) as part of the statement of shareholders' equity.

**ILLUSTRATION 17–7**
Balance Sheet Presentation of Pension Amounts

If the plan had been overfunded, Global would have reported a pension asset among its assets rather than this pension liability.

The net loss–pensions and prior service cost reduce shareholders' equity.

**Global Communication**
**Balance Sheets**
**For Years Ended December 31**

| | **2007** | **2006** |
|---|---|---|
| **Assets** | | |
| Current assets | $xxx | $xxx |
| Property, plant, and equipment | xxx | xxx |
| **Liabilities** | | |
| Current Liabilities | $xxx | $xxx |
| Pension liability | 110 | 100 |
| Other long-term liabilities | xxx | xxx |
| **Shareholders' Equity** | | |
| Common stock | $xxx | $xxx |
| Retained earnings | xxx | xxx |
| Accumulated other comprehensive income: | | |
| Net unrealized holding gains on investments | xxx | xxx |
| Net loss–pensions* | (74) | (55) |
| Prior service cost* | (52) | (56) |

*These are debit balances and therefore negative components of accumulated other comprehensive income; a net gain–pensions would be a credit balance and a positive component of accumulated other comprehensive income.

Reporting OCI as it occurs and also as an accumulated balance is consistent with the way we report net income and its accumulated counterpart, retained earnings.

in the balance sheet. Comprehensive income includes (a) net income and (b) other comprehensive income. Notice that we report net income that occurs in the current reporting period in the income statement and also report accumulated net income (that hasn't been distributed as dividends) in the balance sheet as retained earnings. Similarly, we report other comprehensive income as it occurs in the current reporting period (see Illustration 17–5) and also report *accumulated other comprehensive income* in the balance sheet. In its 2007 balance sheet, Global will report the amounts as shown in Illustration 17–7.

Look back to the schedule on page 846 to see how the net loss–pensions increased from $55 million to $74 million during 2007 and the schedule on page 844 to see how the prior service cost decreased from $56 million to $52 million. The pension liability represents the underfunded status of Global's pension plan on the two dates.

## Income Tax Considerations

Other comprehensive income items are reported net of tax, in both the (a) statement of comprehensive income and (b) accumulated other comprehensive income.

We have ignored the income tax effects of the amounts in order to focus on the core issues. Note, though, that as gains and losses occur, they are reported net of tax (tax expense for a gain, tax savings for a loss) in the statement of comprehensive income.[20] Likewise, accumulated other comprehensive income in the balance sheet also is reported net of tax.

## Putting the Pieces Together

● LO8

In preceding sections, we've discussed (1) the projected benefit obligation (including changes due to periodic service cost, accrued interest, revised estimates, plan amendments, and the payment of benefits); (2) the plan assets (including changes due to investment returns, employer contributions, and the payment of benefits); (3) prior service cost; (4) gains and losses; (5) the periodic pension expense (comprising components of each of these); and (6) the funded status of the plan. These elements of a pension plan are interrelated. It's helpful to see how each element relates to the others. One way is to bring each part together in a *pension spreadsheet*. We do this for our 2007 Global Communications Illustration in Graphic 17–11.

[20]Similarly, if any new prior service cost should arise due to a plan amendment, it too would be reported net of tax.

**GRAPHIC 17–11**
Pension Spreadsheet

| | Informal Records | | Formal Records | | | | |
|---|---|---|---|---|---|---|---|
| ($ in millions)<br>Note: ( )s indicate credits; debits otherwise | **PBO** | **Plan Assets** | **Prior Service Cost** | **Net Loss–Pensions** | **Pension Expense** | **Cash** | **Prepaid (Liability) / Asset** |
| ***Balance, Jan. 1, 2007*** | (400) | 300 | 56 | 55 | | | (100) |
| Service cost | (41) | | | | 41 | | (41) |
| Interest cost | (24) | | | | 24 | | (24) |
| Expected return on assets | | 27 | | | (27) | | 27 |
| *Adjust for:* Gain on assets | | 3 | | (3) | | | 3 |
| *Amortization of:* | | | | | | | |
| Prior service cost | | | (4) | | 4 | | |
| Net loss | | | | (1) | 1 | | |
| Loss on PBO | (23) | | | 23 | | | (23) |
| Prior service cost | 0 | | 0 | | | | 0 |
| Contributions to fund | | 48 | | | | (48) | 48 |
| Retiree benefits paid | 38 | (38) | | | | | |
| ***Balance, Dec. 31, 2007*** | (450) | 340 | 52 | 74 | 43 | | (110) |

When the PBO exceeds plan assets, we have a pension liability. If plan assets exceed the PBO, we have a pension asset.

Each change in one of the accounts in the formal records (the blue-shaded area) affects exactly two such accounts.

You should spend several minutes studying this spreadsheet, focusing on the relationships among the elements that constitute a postretirement benefit pension plan. Notice that the first numerical column simply repeats the actuary's report of how the PBO changed during the year, as explained previously (Illustration 17–2). Likewise, the second column reproduces the changes in plan assets we discussed earlier (Illustration 17–3). We've also previously noted the changes in the prior service cost (page 844) and the net loss–pensions (page 846) that are duplicated in the third and fourth columns. The fifth column repeats the calculation of the 2007 pension expense we determined earlier (page 842), and the cash contribution to the pension fund is the sole item in the next column.

The last column shows the changes in the funded status of the plan. Be sure to notice that the funded status is the difference between the PBO (column 1) and the plan assets (column 2). That means that each of the changes we see in either of the first two columns also is reflected as a change in the funded status in the last column. For example, we noted earlier that when Global added $48 million to its plan assets, the pension liability decreased since it's the excess of the PBO over plan assets. We see that result in our spreadsheet.

Notice that each change in a formal account (blue-shaded columns) is reflected in exactly two of those columns. Any of the changes that affect the pension liability (or asset) also is reported in one of the first two (pink) columns due to the relationship described in the previous paragraph.

## DECISION MAKERS' PERSPECTIVE

Although financial statement items are casualties of the political compromises of *SFAS 87,* information provided in the disclosure notes fortunately makes up for some of the deficiencies. *SFAS 132* revised the pension disclosure requirements.[21] Foremost among the useful disclosures are changes in the projected benefit obligation, changes in the fair value of plan assets, and a breakdown of the components of the annual pension expense. Other information also is made available to make it possible for interested analysts to reconstruct the financial statements with pension assets and liabilities included. We'll look at specific disclosures after we discuss postretirement benefits other than pensions because the two types of plans are reported together.

[21]"Employers' Disclosures about Pensions and Other Postretirement Benefits," *Statement of Financial Accounting Standards No. 132* (revised 2003), (Stamford, Conn.: FASB, 2003).

Pension amounts reported in the disclosure notes fill a reporting gap left by the minimal disclosures in the primary financial statements.

Investors and creditors must be cautious of the nontraditional treatment of pension information when developing financial ratios as part of an analysis of financial statements. The various elements of pensions that are not reported separately on the balance sheet and income statement (PBO, plan assets, gains and losses) can be included in ratios such as the debt to equity ratio or return on assets, but only by deliberately obtaining those numbers from the disclosure notes and adjusting the computation of the ratios. Similarly, without adjustment, profitability ratios and the times interest earned ratio will be distorted because pension expense includes the financial components of interest and return on assets.

Earnings quality (as defined in Chapter 4 and discussed in other chapters) also can be influenced by amounts reported in pension disclosures. Companies with relatively sizeable unrecognized pension costs (prior service cost, net gain or loss) can be expected to exhibit a relatively high "transitory" earnings component. Recall that transitory earnings are expected to be less predictive of future earnings than the "permanent" earnings component. ■

## Settlement or Curtailment of Pension Plans

Companies sometimes terminate defined benefit plans to reduce costs and lessen risk.

Companies sometimes terminate defined benefit plans to siphon off excess pension fund assets for other purposes.

To cut down on cumbersome paperwork and lessen their exposure to the risk posed by defined benefit plans, many companies are providing defined contribution plans instead. Sometimes the motivation to terminate a plan is to take advantage of the excess funding position of many plans that was created by the stock market boom of the 1980s and 1990s and to divert these assets to another purpose. This trend was given impetus in 1982 when **Tengelmann Group** took over ailing **A&P** and used the acquired company's excess pension plan assets to finance its turnaround. Since then, so-called reversion assets have been used, not only in takeovers, but by existing management as well. **Exxon** (now **ExxonMobil**), for instance, used $1.6 billion from its $5.6 billion pension fund to bolster operations during a period of depressed oil prices in 1986. Asset reversions are not as common now as in the 1980s, largely because of excise taxes on amounts recovered when plans are terminated and other restrictive legislation taken by Congress to limit terminations.

When a plan is terminated, *SFAS 88* requires a gain or loss to be reported at that time.[22] For instance, **Melville Corporation** described the termination of its pension plan in the following disclosure note:

**GRAPHIC 17–12**
Gain on the Termination of a Defined Benefit Plan—Melville Corporation

**Retirement Plans (in part)**
. . . As a result of the termination of the defined benefit plans, and after the settlement of the liability to plan participants through the purchase of nonparticipating annuity contracts or lump-sum rollovers into the new 401(k) Profit Sharing Plan, the Company recorded a nonrecurring gain of approximately $4,000,000 which was the amount of plan assets that reverted to the Company. This was accounted for in accordance with *Statement of Financial Accounting Standards No. 88,* "Employers' Accounting for Settlements and Curtailments of Defined Benefit Pension Plans and for Termination Benefits."

## CONCEPT REVIEW EXERCISE

### PENSION PLANS

Allied Services, Inc. has a noncontributory, defined benefit pension plan. Pension plan assets had a fair market value of $900 million at December 31, 2006.

On January 3, 2007, Allied amended the pension formula to increase benefits for each service year. By making the amendment retroactive to prior years, Allied incurred a prior service cost of $75 million, adding to the previous projected benefit obligation of $875 million. The prior service cost is to be amortized (expensed) over 15 years. The service cost is $31 million for 2007. Both the actuary's discount rate and the expected rate of return on plan assets were 8%. The actual rate of return on plan assets was 10%.

[22]"Employers' Accounting for Settlements and Curtailments of Defined Benefit Pension Plans and for Termination Benefits," *Statement of Financial Accounting Standards No. 88* (Stamford, Conn.: FASB, 1985).

At December 31, 2007, $16 million was contributed to the pension fund and $22 million was paid to retired employees. Also, at that time, the actuary revised a previous assumption, increasing the PBO estimate by $10 million. The net loss at the beginning of the year was $13 million.

**Required:**

Determine each of the following amounts as of December 31, 2007, the fiscal year-end for Allied: (1) projected benefit obligation; (2) plan assets; and (3) pension expense.

**SOLUTION**

| ($ in millions) | Projected Benefit Obligation | Plan Assets | Pension Expense |
|---|---|---|---|
| Balances at Jan. 1 | $ 875 | $900 | $ 0 |
| Prior service cost | 75 | | |
| Service cost | 31 | | 31 |
| Interest cost [($875 + 75)* × 8%] | 76 | | 76 |
| Return on plan assets: | | | |
| Actual ($900 × 10%) | | 90 | |
| Expected ($900 × 8%) | | | (72) |
| Amortization of prior service cost ($75 ÷ 15) | | | 5 |
| Amortization of net loss pensions | | | 0† |
| Loss on PBO | 10 | | |
| Cash contribution | | 16 | |
| Retirement payments | (22) | (22) | |
| Balance at Dec. 31 | $1,045 | $984 | $40 |

Note: The $18 million gain on plan assets ($90 − 72 million) is not recognized yet; it is carried forward to be combined with previous and future gains and losses, which will be recognized only if the net gain or net loss exceeds 10% of the higher of the PBO or plan assets.

*Since the plan was amended at the beginning of the year, the prior service cost increased the PBO at that time.

†Since the net loss ($13) does not exceed 10% of $900 (higher than $875), no amortization is required for 2007.

# POSTRETIREMENT BENEFITS OTHER THAN PENSIONS

**PART E**

As we just discussed, most companies have pension plans that provide for the future payments of retirement benefits to compensate employees for their current services. Many companies also furnish *other postretirement benefits* to their retired employees. These may include medical coverage, dental coverage, life insurance, group legal services, and other benefits. By far the most common is health care benefits. One of every three U.S. workers in medium- and large-size companies participates in health care plans that provide for coverage that continues into retirement. The aggregate impact is considerable; the total obligation for all U.S. corporations is about $500 billion.

Prior to 1993, employers accounted for postretirement benefit costs on a pay-as-you-go basis, meaning the expense each year was simply the amount of insurance premiums or medical claims paid, depending on the way the company provided health care benefits. *SFAS 106* requires a completely different approach. The expected future health care costs for retirees now must be recognized as an expense over the years necessary for employees to become entitled to the benefits.[23] This is the accrual basis that also is the basis for pension accounting.

● LO9

In fact, accounting for postretirement benefits is similar in most respects to accounting for pension benefits. This is because the two forms of benefits are fundamentally similar. Each is a form of deferred compensation earned during the employee's service life and each can be estimated as the present value of the cost of providing the expected future benefits. **General Motors** described its plan as shown in Graphic 17–13.

[23]"Employers' Accounting for Postretirement Benefits Other Than Pensions," *Statement of Financial Accounting Standards No. 106* (Norwalk, Conn.: FASB, 1990). The Standard became effective (with some exceptions) in 1993.

**GRAPHIC 17–13**
Disclosures—General Motors

**Note 5: Other Postretirement Benefits (in part)**
The Corporation and certain of its domestic subsidiaries maintain hourly and salaried benefit plans that provide postretirement medical, dental, vision, and life insurance to retirees and eligible dependents. These benefits are funded as incurred from the general assets of the Corporation. Effective January 1, 1992, the Corporation adopted *SFAS No. 106,* Employers Accounting for Postretirement Benefits Other Than Pensions. This Statement requires that the cost of such benefits be recognized in the financial statements during the period employees provide service to the Corporation.

Despite the similarities, though, there are a few differences in the characteristics of the benefits that necessitate differences in accounting treatment. Because accounting for the two types of retiree benefits is so nearly the same, our discussion in this portion of the chapter will emphasize the differences. This will allow you to use what you learned earlier in the chapter regarding pension accounting as a foundation for learning how to account for other postretirement benefits, supplementing that common base only when necessary. Focusing on the differences also will reinforce your understanding of pension accounting.

## What Is a Postretirement Benefit Plan?

Before addressing the accounting ramifications, let's look at a typical retiree health care plan.[24] First, it's important to distinguish retiree health care benefits from health care benefits provided during an employee's working years. The annual cost of providing *preretirement* benefits is simply part of the annual compensation expense. However, many companies offer coverage that continues into retirement. It is the deferred aspect of these *postretirement* benefits that creates an accounting issue.

**Eligibility usually is based on age and/or years of service.**

Usually a plan promises benefits in exchange for services performed over a designated number of years, or reaching a particular age, or both. For instance, a plan might specify that employees are eligible for postretirement benefits after both working 20 years and reaching age 62 while in service. Eligibility requirements and the nature of benefits usually are specified by a written plan, or sometimes only by company practice.

### POSTRETIREMENT HEALTH BENEFITS AND PENSION BENEFITS COMPARED

Keep in mind that retiree health benefits differ fundamentally from pension benefits in some important respects:

1. The amount of *pension* benefits generally is based on the number of years an employee works for the company so that the longer the employee works, the higher are the benefits. On the other hand, the amount of *postretirement health care* benefits typically is unrelated to service. It's usually an all-or-nothing plan in which a certain level of coverage is promised upon retirement, independent of the length of service beyond that necessary for eligibility.
2. Although coverage might be identical, the cost of providing the coverage might vary significantly from retiree to retiree and from year to year because of differing medical needs.
3. Postretirement health care plans often require the retiree to share in the cost of coverage through monthly contribution payments. For instance, a company might pay 80% of insurance premiums, with the retiree paying 20%. The net cost of providing coverage is reduced by these contributions as well as by any portion of the cost paid by Medicare or other insurance.
4. Coverage often is provided to spouses and eligible dependents.

### DETERMINING THE NET COST OF BENEFITS

To determine the postretirement benefit obligation and the postretirement benefit expense, the company's actuary first must make estimates of what the postretirement benefit costs will

[24]For convenience, our discussion focuses on health care benefits because these are by far the most common type of postretirement benefits other than pensions. But the concepts we discuss apply equally to other forms of postretirement benefits.

| Estimated medical costs in each year of retirement | − | Retiree share of costs | − | Medicare payments | = | Estimated *net* cost of benefits |
|---|---|---|---|---|---|---|

**GRAPHIC 17–14**
Estimating the Net Cost of Benefits

be for current employees. Then, as illustrated in Graphic 17–14 above, contributions to those costs by employees are deducted, as well as Medicare's share of the costs (for retirement years when the retiree will be 65 or older), to determine the estimated net cost of benefits to the employer:

Remember, postretirement health care benefits are anticipated actual costs of providing the promised health care, rather than an amount estimated by a defined benefit formula. This makes these estimates inherently more intricate, particularly because health care costs in general are notoriously difficult to forecast. And, since postretirement health care benefits are partially paid by the retiree and by Medicare, these cost-sharing amounts must be estimated as well.

On the other hand, estimating postretirement benefits costs is similar in many ways to estimating pension costs. Both estimates entail a variety of assumptions to be made by the company's actuary. Many of these assumptions are the same; for instance, both require estimates of:

1. A discount rate.
2. Expected return on plan assets (if the plan is funded).
3. Employee turnover.
4. Expected retirement age.
5. Expected compensation increases (if the plan is pay-related).
6. Expected age of death.
7. Number and ages of beneficiaries and dependents.

**Many of the assumptions needed to estimate postretirement health care benefits are the same as those needed to estimate pension benefits.**

Of course, the relative importance of some estimates is different from that for pension plans. Dependency status, turnover, and retirement age, for example, take on much greater significance. Also, additional assumptions become necessary as a result of differences between pension plans and other postretirement benefit plans. Specifically, it's necessary to estimate:

1. The current cost of providing health care benefits at each age that participants might receive benefits.
2. Demographic characteristics of plan participants that might affect the amount and timing of benefits.
3. Benefit coverage provided by Medicare, other insurance, or other sources that will reduce the net cost of employer-provided benefits.
4. The expected health care cost trend rate.[25]

**Some additional assumptions are needed to estimate postretirement health care benefits besides those needed to estimate pension benefits.**

Taking these assumptions into account, the company's actuary estimates what the net cost of postretirement benefits will be for current employees in each year of their expected retirement. The discounted present value of those costs is the expected postretirement benefit obligation.

**The postretirement benefit obligation is the discounted present value of the benefits during retirement.**

## Postretirement Benefit Obligation

● LO10

There are two related obligation amounts. As indicated in Graphic 17–15, one measures the total obligation and the other refers to a specific portion of the total:

1. **Expected postretirement benefit obligation (EPBO):** The actuary's estimate of the *total* postretirement benefits (at their discounted present value) expected to be received by plan participants.
2. **Accumulated postretirement benefit obligation (APBO):** The portion of the EPBO attributed to employee service to date.

**GRAPHIC 17–15**
Two Views of the Obligation for Postretirement Benefits Other Than Pensions

[25]Health care cost trend rates recently reported have ranged from 5.5% to 14%, with 10% being the most commonly assumed rate. AICPA, *Accounting Trends and Techniques,* 2004.

The accumulated postretirement benefit obligation (APBO) is analogous to the projected benefit obligation (PBO) for pensions. Like the PBO, the APBO is an off-balance-sheet obligation, reported only in the disclosure notes.

## MEASURING THE OBLIGATION

To illustrate, assume the actuary estimates that the net cost of providing health care benefits to Jessica Farrow (our illustration employee from earlier in the chapter) during her retirement years has a present value of $10,842 as of the end of 2005. This is the EPBO. If the benefits (and therefore the costs) relate to an estimated 35 years of service[26] and 10 of those years have been completed, the APBO would be:

$3,098 represents the portion of the EPBO related to the first 10 years of the 35-year service period.

| | | | | |
|---|---|---|---|---|
| $10,842 EPBO | × | 10/35 Fraction attributed to service to date | = | $3,098 APBO |

If the assumed discount rate is 6%, a year later the EPBO will have grown to $11,493 simply because of a year's interest accruing at that rate ($10,842 × 1.06 = $11,493). Notice that there is no increase in the EPBO for service because, unlike the obligation in most pension plans, the total obligation is not increased by an additional year's service.

The APBO, however, is the portion of the EPBO related to service up to a particular date. Consequently, the APBO will have increased both because of interest and because the service fraction will be higher (service cost):

$3,612 represents the portion of the EPBO related to the first 11 years of the 35-year service period.

| | | | | |
|---|---|---|---|---|
| $11,493 EPBO | × | 11/35 Fraction attributed to service to date | = | $3,612 APBO |

The two elements of the increase in 2006 can be separated as follows:

The APBO increases each year due to (a) interest accrued on the APBO and (b) the portion of the EPBO attributed to that year.

| | |
|---|---|
| APBO at the beginning of the year | $3,098 |
| Interest cost: $3,098 × 6% | 186 |
| Service cost: ($11,493 × 1/35) portion of EPBO attributed to the year | 328 |
| APBO at the end of the year | $3,612 |

## ATTRIBUTION

The cost of benefits is attributed to the years during which those benefits are assumed to be earned by employees.

Attribution is the process of assigning the cost of benefits to the years during which those benefits are assumed to be earned by employees. The approach required by *SFAS 106* is to assign an equal fraction of the EPBO to each year of service from the employee's date of hire to the employee's full eligibility date.[27] This is the date the employee has performed all the service necessary to have earned all the retiree benefits estimated to be received by the employee.[28] In our earlier example, we assumed the attribution period was 35 years and accordingly accrued 1/35 of the EPBO each year. The amount accrued each year increases both the APBO and the postretirement benefit expense. In Illustration 17–8 we see how the 35-year attribution (accrual) period was determined.

The attribution period does not include years of service beyond the full eligibility date even if the employee is expected to work after that date.

Some critics of *SFAS 106* feel there is a fundamental inconsistency between the way we measure the benefits and the way we assign the benefits to specific service periods. The benefits (EPBO) are measured with the concession that the employee may work beyond the full eligibility date; however, the attribution period does not include years of service after that date. The counterargument is the fact that at the full eligibility date the employee will have

[26]Assigning the costs to particular service years is referred to as the *attribution* of the costs to the years the benefits are assumed earned. We discuss attribution in the next section.

[27]If the plan specifically grants credit only for service from a date after employee's date of hire, the beginning of the attribution period is considered to be the beginning of that credited service period, rather than the employee's date of hire.

[28]Or any beneficiaries and covered dependents.

**ILLUSTRATION 17–8**
Determining the Attribution Period

Jessica Farrow was hired by Global Communications at age 22 at the beginning of 1996 and is expected to retire at the end of 2035 at age 61. The retirement period is estimated to be 20 years.*

Global's employees are eligible for postretirement health care benefits after both reaching age 56 while in service and having worked 20 years.

Since Farrow becomes fully eligible at age 56 (the end of 2030), retiree benefits are attributed to the 35-year period from her date of hire through that date. Graphically, the situation can be described as follows:

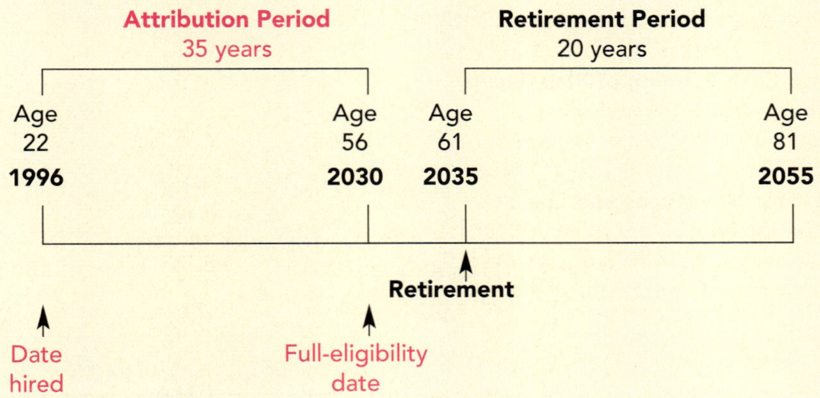


*You probably recognize this as the situation used earlier in the chapter to illustrate pension accounting.

**The attribution period spans each year of service from the employee's date of hire to the employee's full eligibility date.**

earned the right to receive the full benefits expected under the plan and the amount of the benefits will not increase with service beyond that date.[29]

## Accounting for Postretirement Benefit Plans Other Than Pensions

● LO11

**We account for pensions and for other postretirement benefits essentially the same way.**

As we just discussed, it's necessary to attribute a portion of the accumulated postretirement benefit obligation to each year as the service cost for that year as opposed to measuring the actual benefits employees earn during the year as we did for pension plans. That's due to the fundamental nature of these other postretirement plans under which employees are ineligible for benefits until specific eligibility criteria are met, at which time they become 100% eligible. This contrasts with pension plans under which employees earn additional benefits each year until they retire.

**GRAPHIC 17–16**
Measuring Service Cost

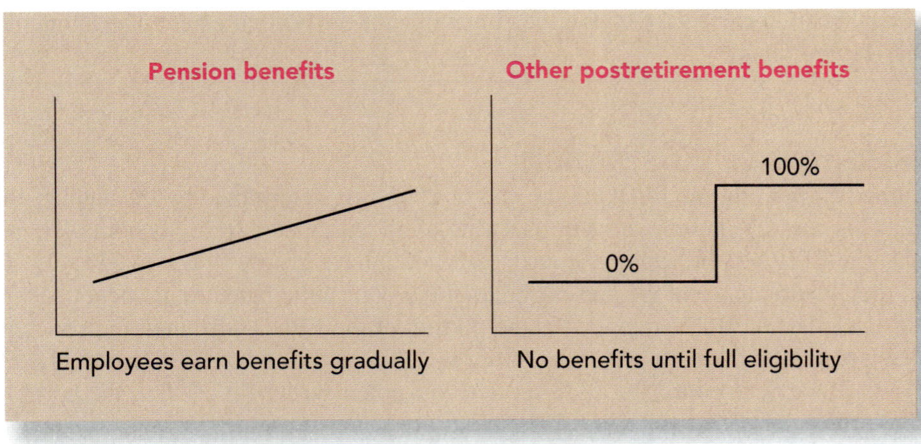


**Measuring the service cost differs, though, due to a fundamental difference in the way employees acquire benefits under the two types of plans.**

The way we measure service cost is the primary difference between accounting for pensions and for other postretirement benefits. Otherwise, though, accounting for the two is virtually

[29] "Employers' Accounting for Postretirement Benefits Other Than Pensions," *Statement of Financial Accounting Standards No. 106* (Norwalk, Conn.: FASB, 1990), par. 219–239.

identical. For example, a company with an underfunded postretirement benefit plan with existing prior service cost and net loss–postretirement benefits would record the following journal entries annually:

| | | |
|---|---|---|
| **To Record Postretirement Benefit Expense** | | |
| Postretirement expense (total) | xx | |
| Postretirement benefit liability (service cost + interest cost – expected return on assets) | | xx |
| Prior service cost[30] (current amortization) | | xx |
| Net loss–postretirement benefits (current amortization) | | xx |
| **To Record Cash Funding of Plan Assets** | | |
| Postretirement benefit liability | xx | |
| Cash (contribution to plan assets) | | xx |
| **To Adjust for New Gains and Losses** | | |
| Loss–OCI (loss on APBO or plan assets) | xx | |
| Gain–OCI (gain on APBO or plan assets) | | xx |
| Postretirement benefit liability (to balance) | | xx |

**We record the annual expense and funding for other postretirement benefit plans the same way we do for pensions.**

**We record losses and gains (as well as any new prior service cost should it occur) as adjustments to other comprehensive income accounts and the postretirement benefit liability.**

**ETHICAL DILEMMA**

Earlier this year, you were elected to the board of directors of Champion International, Inc. Champion has offered its employees postretirement health care benefits for 35 years. The practice of extending health care benefits to retirees began modestly. Most employees retired after age 65, when most benefits were covered by Medicare. Costs also were lower because life expectancies were shorter and medical care was less expensive. Because costs were so low, little attention was paid to accounting for these benefits. The company simply recorded an expense when benefits were provided to retirees. *SFAS 106* changed all that. Now, the obligation for these benefits must be anticipated and reported in the annual report. Worse yet, the magnitude of the obligation has grown enormously, almost unnoticed. Health care costs have soared in recent years. Medical technology and other factors have extended life expectancies. Of course, the value to employees of this benefit has grown parallel to the growth of the burden to the company.

Without being required to anticipate future costs, many within Champion's management were caught by surprise at the enormity of the company's obligation. Equally disconcerting was the fact that such a huge liability now must be exposed to public view. Now you find that several board members are urging the dismantling of the postretirement plan altogether. What do you think?

## A COMPREHENSIVE ILLUSTRATION

We assumed earlier that the EPBO at the end of 2005 was determined by the actuary to be \$10,842. This was the present value on that date of all anticipated future benefits. Then we noted that the EPBO at the end of the next year would have grown by 6% to \$11,493. This amount, too, would represent the present value of the same anticipated future benefits, but as of a year later. The APBO, remember, is the portion of the EPBO attributed to service performed to a particular date. So, we determined the APBO at the end of 2006 to be \$11,493 × $^{11}/_{35}$, or \$3,612. We determined the \$328 service cost noted earlier for 2006 as the portion of the EPBO attributed to that year: \$11,493 × $^{1}/_{35}$.

Now, let's review our previous discussion of how the EPBO, the APBO, and the postretirement benefit expense are determined by calculating those amounts a year later, at the end

[30]The prior service cost for other postretirement benefits is amortized over the average remaining time until "full eligibility" for employees rather than until retirement as is the case for pension plans. This is consistent with recording "regular" service cost over the time to full eligibility.

of 2007. Before doing so, however, we can anticipate (a) the EPBO to be \$11,493 × 1.06, or \$12,182, (b) the APBO to be 12/35 of that amount, or \$4,177, and (c) the 2007 service cost to be 1/35 of that amount, or \$348. In Illustration 17–9 we see if our expectations are borne out by direct calculation.

**ILLUSTRATION 17–9**
Determining the Postretirement Benefit Obligation

Assume the actuary has estimated the net cost of retiree benefits in each year of Jessica Farrow's 20-year expected retirement period to be the amounts shown in the calculation below. She is fully eligible for benefits at the end of 2030 and is expected to retire at the end of 2035.

Calculating the APBO and the postretirement benefit expense at the end of 2007, 12 years after being hired, begins with estimating the EPBO.

Steps to calculate (a) the EPBO, (b) the APBO, and (c) the annual service cost at the end of 2007, 12 years after being hired, are:

(a). 1. Estimate the cost of retiree benefits in each year of the expected retirement period and deduct anticipated Medicare reimbursements and retiree cost-sharing to derive the net cost to the employer in each year of the expected retirement period.
2. Find the present value of each year's net benefit cost as of the *retirement date.*
3. Find the present value of the total net benefit cost as of the *current date*. This is the EPBO.

(b). Multiply the EPBO by the attribution factor, (service to date/total attribution period). This is the APBO. The service cost in any year is simply one year's worth of the EPBO.

(c). Multiply the EPBO by 1/total attribution period.

**The EPBO is the discounted present value of the total benefits expected to be earned.**

**The fraction of the EPBO considered to be earned this year is the service cost.**

**The fraction of the EPBO considered to be earned so far is the APBO.**

The steps are demonstrated in Illustration 17–9A.

**ILLUSTRATION 17–9A**
EPBO, APBO, and Service Cost in 2007

(a.1). Actuary estimates the net cost of benefits paid during retirement years:

(a.2). Present value [$n$ = 1, 2, 3, 4, . . . 19, 20: $i$ = 6%] of the net benefits as of the retirement date:

| Year | Age | Net Benefit | Present Value at 2035 |
|---|---|---|---|
| 2036 | 62 | 5,000 | 4,717 |
| 2037 | 63 | 5,600 | 4,984 |
| 2038 | 64 | 6,300 | 5,290 |
| 2039 | 65 | 3,000 | 2,376 |
| ~ | ~ | ~ | ~ |
| 2054 | 80 | 9,550 | 3,156 |
| 2055 | 81 | 10,300 | 3,212 |
| | | | \$62,269 |

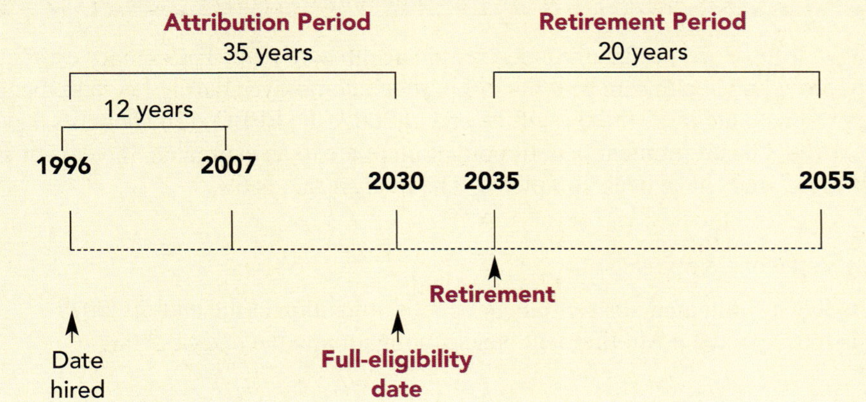


**The actuary estimates the net cost to the employer in each year the retiree is expected to receive benefits.**

**As of the retirement date, the lump-sum equivalent of the expected yearly costs is \$62,269.**

**The EPBO in 2007 is the present value of those benefits.**

**The APBO is the portion of the EPBO attributed to service to date.**

**The service cost is the portion of the EPBO attributed to a particular year's service.**

**ILLUSTRATION 17–9A** concluded

(a.3). Present value ($n = 28$, $i = 6\%$) of postretirement benefits at 2007 is $62,269 × .19563 = $12,182 (EPBO)

(b). $12,182 × $^{12}/_{35}$ = $4,177 (APBO)

(c). $12,182 × $^{1}/_{35}$ = $348 (Service Cost)

## DECISION MAKERS' PERSPECTIVE

Postretirement benefit amounts reported in the disclosure notes fill a reporting gap left by the minimal disclosures in the primary financial statements.

When they analyze financial statements, investors and creditors should be wary of the nonstandard way companies report pension and other postretirement information. Recall that in the balance sheet, firms do not separately report the benefit obligation and the plan assets. Also, companies have considerable latitude in making the several assumptions needed to estimate the components of postretirement benefit plans. Fortunately, information provided in the disclosure notes makes up for some of the deficiency in balance sheet information and makes it possible for interested analysts to modify their analysis. As for pensions, the choices companies make for the discount rate, expected return on plan assets, and the compensation growth rate can greatly impact postretirement benefit expense and earnings quality. The disclosures required are very similar to pension disclosures. In fact, disclosures for the two types of retiree benefits typically are combined.[31] Disclosures include:

- Descriptions of the plans.
- Estimates of the obligations (PBO, ABO, vested benefit obligation, EPBO, and APBO).
- The percentage of total plan assets for each major category of assets (equity securities, debt securities, real estate, other) as well as a description of investment strategies, including any target asset allocations and risk management practices.
- A breakdown of the components of the annual pension and postretirement benefit expenses for the years reported.
- The discount rates, the assumed rate of compensation increases used to measure the PBO, the expected long-term rate of return on plan assets, and the expected rate of increase in future medical and dental benefit costs.
- Estimated benefit payments presented separately for the next five years and in the aggregate for years 6–10.
- Estimate of expected contributions to fund the plan for the next year.
- Disclosures related to the modifications *SFAS 158* introduced, including (a) any changes to the net gain or net loss and prior service cost arising during the period, (b) the accumulated amounts of these components of accumulated other comprehensive income, and (c) the amounts of those balances expected to be amortized in the next year.
- Other information to make it possible for interested analysts to reconstruct the financial statements with plan assets and liabilities included. ■

# CONCEPT REVIEW EXERCISE

### OTHER POSTRETIREMENT BENEFITS

Technology Group, Inc., has an unfunded retiree health care plan. The actuary estimates the net cost of providing health care benefits to a particular employee during his retirement years to have a present value of $24,000 as of the end of 2007 (the EPBO). The benefits and therefore the expected postretirement benefit obligation relate to an estimated 36 years of service and 12 of those years have been completed. The interest rate is 6%.

**Required:**

Pertaining to the one employee only:

1. What is the accumulated postretirement benefit obligation at the end of 2007?
2. What is the expected postretirement benefit obligation at the end of 2008?

---

[31] "Employers' Disclosures about Pensions and Other Postretirement Benefits," *Statement of Financial Accounting Standards No. 132* (Stamford, Conn.: FASB, 1998).

3. What is the service cost to be included in 2008 postretirement benefit expense?
4. What is the interest cost to be included in 2008 postretirement benefit expense?
5. What is the accumulated postretirement benefit obligation at the end of 2008?
6. Show how the APBO changed during 2008 by reconciling the beginning and ending balances.
7. What is the 2008 postretirement benefit expense, assuming no net gains or losses and no prior service cost?

**SOLUTION**

1. What is the accumulated postretirement benefit obligation at the end of 2007?

| | | | | |
|---|---|---|---|---|
| $24,000 | × | 12/36 | = | $8,000 |
| EPBO 2007 | | Fraction earned | | APBO 2007 |

2. What is the expected postretirement benefit obligation at the end of 2008?

| | | | | |
|---|---|---|---|---|
| $24,000 | × | 1.06 | = | $25,440 |
| EPBO 2007 | | To accrue interest | | EPBO 2008 |

3. What is the service cost to be included in 2008 postretirement benefit expense?

| | | | | |
|---|---|---|---|---|
| $25,440 | × | 1/36 | = | $707 |
| EPBO 2008 | | Earned in 2008 | | Service cost |

4. What is the interest cost to be included in 2008 postretirement benefit expense?

$8,000 (beginning APBO) × 6% = $480

5. What is the accumulated postretirement benefit obligation at the end of 2008?

| | | | | |
|---|---|---|---|---|
| $25,440 | × | 13/36 | = | $9,187 |
| EPBO 2008 | | Fraction earned | | APBO 2008 |

6. Show how the APBO changed during 2008 by reconciling the beginning and ending balances.

| | |
|---|---|
| APBO at the beginning of 2008 (from req. 1) | $8,000 |
| Service cost: (from req. 3) | 707 |
| Interest cost: (from req. 4) | 480 |
| APBO at the end of 2008 (from req. 5) | $9,187 |

7. What is the 2008 postretirement benefit expense, assuming no net gains or losses and no prior service cost?

| | |
|---|---|
| Service cost | $ 707 |
| Interest cost | 480 |
| Actual return on the plan assets | (not funded) |
| Adjusted for: gain or loss on the plan assets | (not funded) |
| Amortization of prior service cost | none |
| Amortization of net gain or loss | none |
| **Postretirement benefit expense** | $1,187 |

## GLOBAL PERSPECTIVE

In the United States, postretirement benefits are accrued in a manner similar to pensions. In the United Kingdom, accounting is similar to the United States. In most other countries, little official guidance is offered.

In many countries, postretirement benefits other than pensions are rare. In Japan, for instance, the prevalence of government-sponsored plans has encouraged most Japanese companies not to provide separate benefits.

## FINANCIAL REPORTING CASE SOLUTION

1. **Why is underfunding not a concern in your present employment?** *(p. 831)* In a defined contribution plan, the employer is not obliged to provide benefits beyond the annual contribution to the employees' plan. No liability is created. Unlike retirement benefits paid in a defined benefit plan, the employee's retirement benefits in a defined contribution plan are totally dependent on how well invested assets perform in the marketplace.
2. **Were you correct that the pension liability is not reported on the balance sheet? What is the liability?** *(p. 833)* Yes. The pension liability is measured (in three ways) and tracked informally, but not reported on the balance sheet. It is disclosed, however, in the notes. For United Dynamics, the PBO in 2007 is $2,628 million.
3. **What is the amount of the plan assets available to pay benefits? What are the factors that can cause that amount to change?** *(p. 839)* The plan assets at the end of 2007 total $2,807 million. A trustee accepts employer contributions, invests the contributions, accumulates the earnings on the investments, and pays benefits from the plan assets. So the amount is increased each year by employer cash contributions and (hopefully) a return on assets invested. It is decreased by amounts paid out to retired employees.
4. **What does the "pension asset" represent? Are you interviewing with a company whose pension plan is severely underfunded?** *(p. 841)* The pension asset is not the plan assets available to pay pension benefits. Instead, it's the net difference between those assets and the pension obligation. United Dynamics' plan assets exceed the pension obligation in each year presented.
5. **How is the pension expense influenced by changes in the pension liability and plan assets?** *(p. 842)* The pension expense reported on the income statement is a composite of periodic changes that occur in both the pension obligation and the plan assets. For United Dynamics in 2007, the pension expense included the service cost and interest cost, which are changes in the PBO, and the return on plan assets. It also included an amortized portion of prior service costs (a previous change in the PBO) and of net gains (gains and losses result from changes in both the PBO and plan assets). ■

## THE BOTTOM LINE

1. Pension plans are arrangements designed to provide income to individuals during their retirement years. *Defined contribution* plans promise fixed annual contributions to a pension fund, without further commitment regarding benefit amounts at retirement. *Defined benefit* plans promise fixed retirement benefits defined by a designated formula. The employer sets aside cash each year to provide sufficient funds to pay promised benefits.
2. The *accumulated benefit obligation* is an estimate of the discounted present value of the retirement benefits earned so far by employees, applying the plan's pension formula to *existing* compensation levels. The vested benefit obligation is the portion of the accumulated benefit obligation that plan participants are entitled to receive regardless of their continued employment. The *projected benefit obligation* estimates retirement benefits by applying the pension formula to *projected future* compensation levels.
3. The PBO can change due to the accumulation of *service cost* from year to year, the accrual of *interest* as time passes, making plan amendments retroactive to prior years (prior service cost), and periodic adjustments when estimates change (gains and losses). The obligation is reduced as benefits actually are paid to retired employees.
4. The plan assets consist of the accumulated balance of the annual employer contributions plus the return on the investments less benefits paid to retirees.
5. The difference between an employer's obligation (PBO for pensions, APBO for other postretirement benefit plans) and the resources available to satisfy that obligation (plan assets) is the funded status of the pension plan. The employer must report the "funded status" of the plan in the balance sheet as a pension liability if the obligation exceeds the plan assets or as a pension asset if the plan assets exceed the obligation.
6. The pension expense is a composite of periodic changes in both the pension obligation and the plan assets. Service cost is the increase in the PBO attributable to employee service and

is the primary component of pension expense. The interest and return-on-assets components are financial items created only because the pension payment is delayed and the obligation is funded currently. Prior service cost is recognized over employees' future service period. Also, neither a loss (gain) on the PBO nor a loss (gain) on plan assets is immediately recognized in pension expense; they are recognized on a delayed basis to achieve income smoothing.

7. Recording pension expense causes the pension liability/asset to change by the service cost, the interest cost, and the expected return on plan assets. Any amortization amounts included in the expense will reduce the *accumulated other comprehensive income* balances being amortized, e.g., net loss, prior service cost. Similarly, the pension liability is reduced (or pension asset increased) by the annual cash investment to plan assets. New losses and gains (as well as any new prior service cost should it occur) are recognized as other comprehensive income and change the pension liability.
8. The various elements of a pension plan—projected benefit obligation, plan assets, prior service cost, gains and losses, pension expense, and the funded status of the plan—are interrelated. One way to see how each element relates to the other is to bring each part together in a *pension spreadsheet.*
9. Accounting for postretirement benefits is similar in most respects to accounting for pension benefits. Like pensions, other postretirement benefits are a form of deferred compensation. Unlike pensions, their cost is attributed to the years from the employee's date of hire to the full eligibility date.
10. The expected postretirement benefit obligation (EPBO) is the actuary's estimate of the total postretirement benefits (at their discounted present value) expected to be received by plan participants. The accumulated postretirement benefit obligation (APBO) is the portion of the EPBO attributed to employee service to date.
11. The components of postretirement benefit expense are essentially the same as those for pension expense. ■

APPENDIX 17

# SERVICE METHOD OF ALLOCATING PRIOR SERVICE COST

When amortizing prior service cost, our objective is to match the cost with employee service. The straight-line method described in this chapter allocates an equal amount of the prior service cost to each year of the 15-year average service period of affected employees. But consider this: fewer of the affected employees will be working for the company toward the end of that period than at the beginning. Some probably will retire or quit in each year following the amendment.

An allocation approach that reflects the declining service pattern is called the **service method.** This method allocates the prior service cost to each year in proportion to the fraction of the total remaining service years worked in each of those years. To do this, it's necessary to estimate how many of the 2,000 employees working at the beginning of 2006 when the amendment is made will still be employed in each year after the amendment.

Let's suppose, for example, that the actuary estimates that a declining number of these employees still will be employed in each of the next 28 years as indicated in the abbreviated schedule below. The portion of the prior service cost amortized to pension expense each year is $60 million times a declining fraction. Each year's fraction is that year's service divided by the 28-year total (30,000). This is demonstrated in Graphic 17A–1.

Conceptually, the service method achieves a better matching of the cost and benefits. In fact, this is the FASB's recommended approach. However, *SFAS 87* permits the consistent use of any method that amortizes the prior service cost at least as quickly.[32] The straight-line method meets this condition and is the approach most often used in practice. In our illustration, the cost is completely amortized over 15 years rather than the 28 years required by the

**The service method amortized an equal amount *per employee* each year.**

[32]"Employers' Accounting for Pensions," *Statement of Financial Accounting Standards No. 87* (Stamford, Conn.: FASB, 1985), par. 26.

service method. The 15-year average service life is simply the total estimated service years divided by the total number of employees in the group:

| 30,000 years | ÷ | 2,000 | = | 15 years |
|---|---|---|---|---|
| Total number of service years | | Total number of employees | | Average service years |

**GRAPHIC 17A–1**
Service Method of Amortizing Prior Service Cost

By the service method, prior service cost is recognized each year in proportion to the fraction of the total remaining service years worked that year.

| Year | Number of Employees Still Employed (assumed for the illustration) | Fraction of Total Service Years | | Prior Service Cost ($ in millions) | | Amount Amortized ($ in millions) |
|---|---|---|---|---|---|---|
| 2006 | 2,000 | 2,000/30,000 | × | $60 | = | $ 4.0 |
| 2007 | 2,000 | 2,000/30,000 | × | 60 | = | 4.0 |
| 2008 | 1,850 | 1,850/30,000 | × | 60 | = | 3.7 |
| 2009 | 1,700 | 1,700/30,000 | × | 60 | = | 3.4 |
| 2010 | 1,550 | 1,550/30,000 | × | 60 | = | 3.1 |
| — | — | — | | — | | — |
| 2031 | 400 | 400/30,000 | × | 60 | = | .8 |
| 2032 | 250 | 250/30,000 | × | 60 | = | .5 |
| 2033 | 100 | 100/30,000 | × | 60 | = | .2 |
| Totals | 30,000 Total number of service years | 30,000/30,000 | | | | $60.0 Total amount amortized |

## QUESTIONS FOR REVIEW OF KEY TOPICS

**Q 17–1** What is a pension plan? What motivates a corporation to offer a pension plan for its employees?

**Q 17–2** Qualified pension plans offer important tax benefits. What is the special tax treatment and what qualifies a pension plan for these benefits?

**Q 17–3** Lamont Corporation has a pension plan in which the corporation makes all contributions and employees receive benefits at retirement based on the balance in their accumulated pension fund. What type of pension plan does Lamont have?

**Q 17–4** What is the vested benefit obligation?

**Q 17–5** Differentiate between the accumulated benefit obligation and the projected benefit obligation.

**Q 17–6** Name five events that might change the balance of the PBO.

**Q 17–7** Name three events that might change the balance of the plan assets.

**Q 17–8** What are the components that might be included in the calculation of net pension cost recognized for a period by an employer sponsoring a defined benefit pension plan?

**Q 17–9** Define the service cost component of the periodic pension expense.

**Q 17–10** Define the interest cost component of the periodic pension expense.

**Q 17–11** The return on plan assets is the increase in plan assets (at fair value), adjusted for contributions to the plan and benefits paid during the period. How is the return included in the calculation of the periodic pension expense?

**Q 17–12** Define prior service cost. How is it reported in the financial statements? How is it included in pension expense?

**Q 17–13** How should gains or losses related to pension plan assets be recognized? How does this treatment compare to that for gains or losses related to the pension obligation?

**Q 17–14** Is a company's PBO reported in the balance sheet? Its plan assets? Explain.

**Q 17–15** What two components of pension expense may be negative (i.e., reduce pension expense)?

**Q 17–16** Which are the components of pension expense that involve delayed recognition?

**Q 17–17** Evaluate this statement: The excess of the actual return on plan assets over the expected return decreases the employer's pension cost.

**Q 17–18** When accounting for pension costs, how should the payment into the pension fund be recorded?

**Q 17–19** TFC, Inc. revises its estimate of future salary levels, causing its PBO estimate to increase by $3 million. How is the $3 reflected in TFC's financial statements?

**Q 17–20** A pension plan is underfunded when the employer's obligation (PBO) exceeds the resources available to satisfy that obligation (plan assets) and overfunded when the opposite is the case. How is this funded status reported on the balance sheet if plan assets exceed the PBO? If the PBO exceeds plan assets?

**Q 17–21** What are two ways to measure the obligation for postretirement benefits other than pensions? Define these measurement approaches.

**Q 17–22** How are the costs of providing postretirement benefits other than pensions expensed?

**Q 17–23** The components of postretirement benefit expense are similar to the components of pension expense. In what fundamental way does the service cost component differ between these two expenses?

**Q 17–24** The EPBO for Branch Industries at the end of 2007 was determined by the actuary to be $20,000 as it relates to employee Will Lawson. Lawson was hired at the beginning of 1993. He will be fully eligible to retire with health care benefits in 15 years but is expected to retire in 25 years. What is the APBO as it relates to Will Lawson?

## BRIEF EXERCISES

**BE 17–1**
Changes in the projected benefit obligation
● LO3

The projected benefit obligation was $80 million at the beginning of the year. Service cost for the year was $10 million. At the end of the year, pension benefits paid by the trustee were $6 million and there were no pension-related other comprehensive income accounts requiring amortization. The actuary's discount rate was 5%. What was the amount of the projected benefit obligation at year-end?

**BE 17–2**
Changes in the projected benefit obligation
● LO3

The projected benefit obligation was $80 million at the beginning of the year and $85 million at the end of the year. At the end of the year, pension benefits paid by the trustee were $6 million and there were no pension-related other comprehensive income accounts requiring amortization. The actuary's discount rate was 5%. What was the amount of the service cost for the year?

**BE 17–3**
Changes in the projected benefit obligation
● LO3

The projected benefit obligation was $80 million at the beginning of the year and $85 million at the end of the year. Service cost for the year was $10 million. At the end of the year, there was no prior service cost and a negligible net loss–pensions. The actuary's discount rate was 5%. What was the amount of the retiree benefits paid by the trustee?

**BE 17–4**
Changes in the projected benefit obligation
● LO3

The projected benefit obligation was $80 million at the beginning of the year and $85 million at the end of the year. Service cost for the year was $10 million. At the end of the year, pension benefits paid by the trustee were $6 million. The actuary's discount rate was 5%. At the end of the year, the actuary revised the estimate of the percentage rate of increase in compensation levels in upcoming years. What was the amount of the gain or loss the estimate change caused?

**BE 17–5**
Changes in pension plan assets
● LO4

Pension plan assets were $80 million at the beginning of the year. The return on plan assets was 5%. At the end of the year, retiree benefits paid by the trustee were $6 million and cash invested in the pension fund was $7 million. What was the amount of the pension plan assets at year-end?

**BE 17–6**
Changes in pension plan assets
● LO4

Pension plan assets were $80 million at the beginning of the year and $83 million at the end of the year. The return on plan assets was 5%. At the end of the year, cash invested in the pension fund was $7 million. What was the amount of the retiree benefits paid by the trustee?

**BE 17–7**
Changes in pension plan assets
● LO4

Pension plan assets were $100 million at the beginning of the year and $104 million at the end of the year. At the end of the year, retiree benefits paid by the trustee were $6 million and cash invested in the pension fund was $7 million. What was the percentage rate of return on plan assets?

**BE 17–8**
Pension expense
● LO6

The projected benefit obligation was $80 million at the beginning of the year. Service cost for the year was $10 million. At the end of the year, pension benefits paid by the trustee were $6 million and there were no pension-related other comprehensive income accounts requiring amortization. The actuary's discount rate was 5%. The actual return on plan assets was $5 million although it was expected to be only $4 million. What was the pension expense for the year?

**BE 17–9**
Pension expense; prior service cost
● LO6

The pension plan was amended last year, creating a prior service cost of $20 million. Service cost and interest cost for the year were $10 million and $4 million, respectively. At the end of the year, there was a negligible balance in the net gain–pensions account. The actual return on plan assets was $4 million although it was expected to be $6 million. On average, employees' remaining service life with the company is 10 years. What was the pension expense for the year?

**BE 17–10**
Net gain
● LO6

The projected benefit obligation and plan assets were $80 million and $100 million, respectively, at the beginning of the year. Due primarily to favorable stock market performance in recent years, there also was a net gain of $30 million. On average, employees' remaining service life with the company is 10 years. As a result of the net gain, what was the increase or decrease in pension expense for the year?

**BE 17–11**
Reporting the funded status of pension plans
● LO5

JDS Foods' projected benefit obligation, accumulated benefit obligation, and plan assets were $40 million, $30 million, and $25 million, respectively, at the end of the year. What, if any, pension liability must be reported in the balance sheet? What would JDS report if the plan assets were $45 million instead?

**BE 17–12**
Recording pension expense
● LO7

The Warren Group's pension expense is $67 million. This amount includes a $70 million service cost, a $50 million interest cost, a $55 million reduction for the expected return on plan assets, and a $2 million amortization of a prior service cost. How is the pension liability affected when the pension expense is recorded?

**BE 17–13**
Recording pension expense
● LO7

Andrews Medical reported a net loss–pensions in last year's balance sheet. This year, the company revised its estimate of future salary levels causing its PBO estimate to decline by $4 million. Also, the $8 million actual return on plan assets fell short of the $9 million expected return. How does this gain and loss affect Andrews' income statement, statement of comprehensive income, and balance sheet?

**BE 17–14**
Postretirement benefits; determine the APBO and service cost
● LO9, LO10

Prince Distribution, Inc., has an unfunded postretirement benefit plan. Medical care and life insurance benefits are provided to employees who render 10 years service and attain age 55 while in service. At the end of 2007, Jim Lukawitz is 31. He was hired by Prince at age 25 (6 years ago) and is expected to retire at age 62. The expected postretirement benefit obligation for Lukawitz at the end of 2007 is $50,000 and $54,000 at the end of 2008. Calculate the accumulated postretirement benefit obligation at the end of 2007 and 2008 and the service cost for 2007 and 2008 as pertaining to Lukawitz.

**BE 17–15**
Postretirement benefits; changes in the APBO
● LO11

On January 1, 2007, Medical Transport Company's accumulated postretirement benefit obligation was $25 million. At the end of 2007, retiree benefits paid were $3 million. Service cost for 2007 is $7 million. Assumptions regarding the trend of future health care costs were revised at the end of 2007, causing the actuary to revise downward the estimate of the APBO by $1 million. The actuary's discount rate is 8%. Determine the amount of the accumulated postretirement benefit obligation at December 31, 2007.

## EXERCISES

available with McGraw-Hill's Homework Manager www.mhhe.com/spiceland4e

**An alternate exercise and problem set is available on the text website: www.mhhe.com/spiceland4e**

**E 17–1**
Changes in the PBO
● LO3

Indicate by letter whether each of the events listed below increases **(I)**, decreases **(D)**, or has no effect **(N)** on an employer's projected benefit obligation.

**Events**

____ 1. Interest cost.
____ 2. Amortization of prior service cost.
____ 3. A decrease in the average life expectancy of employees.
____ 4. An increase in the average life expectancy of employees.
____ 5. A plan amendment that increases benefits is made retroactive to prior years.
____ 6. An increase in the actuary's assumed discount rate.
____ 7. Cash contributions to the pension fund by the employer.
____ 8. Benefits are paid to retired employees.
____ 9. Service cost.

____ 10. Return on plan assets during the year are lower than expected.
____ 11. Return on plan assets during the year are higher than expected.

**E 17–2**
Determine the projected benefit obligation
● LO3

On January 1, 2007, Burleson Corporation's projected benefit obligation was $30 million. During 2007 pension benefits paid by the trustee were $4 million. Service cost for 2007 is $12 million. Pension plan assets (at fair value) increased during 2007 by $6 million as expected. At the end of 2007, there was no prior service cost and a negligible balance in net loss–pensions. The actuary's discount rate was 10%.

**Required:**
Determine the amount of the projected benefit obligation at December 31, 2007.

**E 17–3**
Components of pension expense
● LO6

Indicate by letter whether each of the events listed below increases (**I**), decreases (**D**), or has no effect (**N**) on an employer's periodic pension expense in the year the event occurs.

**Events**

____ 1. Interest cost.
____ 2. Amortization of prior service cost.
____ 3. Excess of the expected return on plan assets over the actual return.
____ 4. Expected return on plan assets.
____ 5. A plan amendment that increases benefits is made retroactive to prior years.
____ 6. Actuary's estimate of the PBO is increased.
____ 7. Cash contributions to the pension fund by the employer.
____ 8. Benefits are paid to retired employees.
____ 9. Service cost.
____ 10. Excess of the actual return on plan assets over the expected return.
____ 11. Amortization of net loss–pensions.
____ 12. Amortization of net gain–pensions.

**E 17–4**
Recording pension expense
● LO6 LO7

Harrison Forklift's pension expense includes a service cost of $10 million. Harrison began the year with a pension liability of $28 million (underfunded pension plan).

**Required:**
Prepare the appropriate general journal entries to record Harrison's pension expense in each of the following independent situations regarding the other components of pension expense ($ in millions):

1. Interest cost, $6; expected return on assets, $4; amortization of net loss–pensions, $2.
2. Interest cost, $6; expected return on assets, $4; amortization of net gain–pensions, $2.
3. Interest cost, $6; expected return on assets, $4; amortization of net loss–pensions, $2; amortization of prior service cost, $3 million.

**E 17–5**
Determine pension plan assets
● LO4

The following data relate to Voltaire Company's defined benefit pension plan during 2007:

| | ($ in millions) |
|---|---|
| Plan assets at fair value, January 1 | $600 |
| Expected return on plan assets | 60 |
| Actual return on plan assets | 48 |
| Contributions to the pension fund (end of year) | 100 |
| Amortization of net loss | 10 |
| Pension benefits paid (end of year) | 11 |
| Pension expense | 72 |

**Required:**
Determine the amount of pension plan assets at fair value on December 31, 2007.

**E 17–6**
Changes in the pension obligation; determine service cost
● LO3 LO6

Pension data for Millington Enterprises include the following:

| | ($ in millions) |
|---|---|
| Discount rate, 10% | |
| Projected benefit obligation, January 1, 2007 | $360 |
| Projected benefit obligation, December 31, 2007 | 465 |
| Accumulated benefit obligation, January 1, 2007 | 300 |
| Accumulated benefit obligation, December 31, 2007 | 415 |
| Cash contributions to pension fund, December 31, 2007 | 150 |
| Benefit payments to retirees, December 31, 2007 | 54 |

**Required:**
Assuming no change in actuarial assumptions and estimates, determine the service cost component of pension expense for 2007.

**E 17–7**
Changes in plan assets; determine cash contributions

● LO4

Pension data for Fahy Transportation, Inc. include the following:

| | ($ in millions) |
|---|---|
| Discount rate, 7% | |
| Expected return on plan assets, 10% | |
| Actual return on plan assets, 11% | |
| Projected benefit obligation, January 1, 2007 | $730 |
| Plan assets (fair market value), January 1, 2007 | 700 |
| Plan assets (fair market value), December 31, 2007 | 750 |
| Benefit payments to retirees, December 31, 2007 | 66 |

**Required:**
Assuming cash contributions were made at the end of the year, what was the amount of those contributions for 2007?

**E 17–8**
Components of pension expense

● LO6

Pension data for Sterling Properties include the following:

| | ($ in 000s) |
|---|---|
| Service cost, 2007 | $112 |
| Projected benefit obligation, January 1, 2007 | 850 |
| Plan assets (fair market value), January 1, 2007 | 900 |
| Net prior service cost (2007 amortization, $8) | 80 |
| Net loss–pensions (2007 amortization, $1) | 101 |
| Discount rate, 6% | |
| Expected return on plan assets, 10% | |
| Actual return on plan assets, 11% | |

**Required:**
Determine pension expense for 2007.

**E 17–9**
Determine pension expense

● LO6 LO7

Abbott and Abbott has a noncontributory, defined benefit pension plan. At December 31, 2007, Abbott and Abbott received the following information:

| **Projected Benefit Obligation** | ($ in millions) |
|---|---|
| Balance, January 1 | $120 |
| Service cost | 20 |
| Interest cost | 12 |
| Benefits paid | (9) |
| Balance, December 31 | $143 |
| **Plan Assets** | |
| Balance, January 1 | $80 |
| Actual return on plan assets | 9 |
| Contributions 2007 | 20 |
| Benefits paid | (9) |
| Balance, December 31 | $100 |

The expected long-term rate of return on plan assets was 10%. There was no prior service cost and a negligible net loss–pensions on January 1, 2007.

**Required:**
1. Determine Abbott and Abbott's pension expense for 2007.
2. Prepare the journal entries to record Abbott and Abbott's pension expense and funding for 2007.

**E 17–10**
Components of pension expense; journal entry

● LO6 LO7

Pension data for Barry Financial Services, Inc. include the following:

| | ($ in 000s) |
|---|---|
| Discount rate, 7% | |
| Expected return on plan assets, 10% | |
| Actual return on plan assets, 9% | |
| Service cost, 2007 | $ 310 |
| **January 1, 2007:** | |
| Projected benefit obligation | 2,300 |
| Accumulated benefit obligation | 2,000 |
| Plan assets (fair market value) | 2,400 |
| Prior service cost (2007 amortization, $25) | 325 |
| Net gain–pensions (2007 amortization, $6) | 330 |
| **December 31, 2007:** | |
| Cash contributions to pension fund, December 31, 2007 | 245 |
| Benefit payments to retirees, December 31, 2007 | 270 |

**Required:**

1. Determine pension expense for 2007.
2. Prepare the journal entries to record pension expense and funding for 2007.

**E 17–11**
PBO calculations; ABO calculations; present value concepts

● LO1 LO2 LO3

Clark Industries has a defined benefit pension plan that specifies annual retirement benefits equal to:

$$1.2\% \times \text{Service years} \times \text{Final year's salary}$$

Stanley Mills was hired by Clark at the beginning of 1988. Mills is expected to retire at the end of 2032 after 45 years of service. His retirement is expected to span 15 years. At the end of 2007, 20 years after being hired, his salary is $80,000. The company's actuary projects Mills's salary to be $270,000 at retirement. The actuary's discount rate is 7%.

**Required:**

1. Estimate the amount of Stanley Mills's annual retirement payments for the 15 retirement years earned as of the end of 2007.
2. Suppose Clark's pension plan permits a lump-sum payment at retirement in lieu of annuity payments. Determine the lump-sum equivalent as the present value as of the retirement date of annuity payments during the retirement period.
3. What is the company's projected benefit obligation at the end of 2007 with respect to Stanley Mills?
4. What is the company's accumulated benefit obligation at the end of 2007 with respect to Stanley Mills?
5. If we assume no estimates change in the meantime, what is the company's projected benefit obligation at the end of 2008 with respect to Stanley Mills?
6. What portion of the 2008 increase in the PBO is attributable to 2008 service (the service cost component of pension expense) and to accrued interest (the interest cost component of pension expense)?

**E 17–12**
Determining the amortization of net loss or net gain

● LO6

Hicks Cable Company has a defined benefit pension plan. Three alternative possibilities for pension-related data at January 1, 2007, are shown below:

| | ($ in 000s) | | |
|---|---|---|---|
| | **Case 1** | **Case 2** | **Case 3** |
| Net loss (gain), Jan. 1 | $ 320 | $ (330) | $ 260 |
| 2007 loss (gain) on plan assets | (11) | (8) | 2 |
| 2007 loss (gain) on PBO | (23) | 16 | (265) |
| Accumulated benefit obligation, Jan. 1 | (2,950) | (2,550) | (1,450) |
| Projected benefit obligation, Jan. 1 | (3,310) | (2,670) | (1,700) |
| Fair value of plan assets, Jan. 1 | 2,800 | 2,700 | 1,550 |
| Average remaining service period of active employees (years) | 12 | 15 | 10 |

**Required:**

1. For each independent case, calculate any amortization of the net loss or gain that should be included as a component of pension expense for 2007.
2. For each independent case, determine the net loss or gain as of January 1, 2008.

**E 17–13**
Pension spreadsheet

● LO8

A partially completed pension spreadsheet showing the relationships among the elements that comprise the defined benefit pension plan of Universal Products is given below. The actuary's discount rate is 5%. At the end of 2005, the pension formula was amended, creating a prior service cost of $120,000. The expected rate of return on assets was 8%, and the average remaining service life of the active employee group is 20 years in the current year as well as the previous two years.

**Required:**

Copy the incomplete spreadsheet and fill in the missing amounts.

| ( )s indicate credits; debits otherwise ($ in 000s) | **Informal Records** | | **Formal Records** | | | | |
|---|---|---|---|---|---|---|---|
| | **PBO** | **Plan Assets** | **Prior Service Cost** | **Net Loss–Pensions** | **Pension Expense** | **Cash** | **Prepaid (Liability) / Asset** |
| *Balance, Jan. 1, 2007* | **(800)** | **600** | **114** | **80** | | | **(200)** |
| Service cost | | | | | 84 | | |
| Interest cost, 5% | (40) | | | | | | |
| Expected return on assets | | | | | (48) | | |
| *Adjust for:* | | | | | | | |
| Loss on assets | | | | 6 | | | |
| *Amortization:* | | | | | | | |
| Prior service cost | | | | | | | |
| *Amortization:* | | | | | | | |
| Net loss | | | | | | | |

| | | | | |
|---|---|---|---|---|
| Gain on PBO | | | | 12 |
| Prior service cost | 0 | | | |
| Cash funding | | | (68) | |
| Retiree benefits | | | | |
| *Balance, Dec. 31, 2007* | **(862)** | **108** | | |

**E 17–14**
Effect of pension expense components on balance sheet accounts

● LO7 LO8

Warrick Boards calculated pension expense for its underfunded pension plan as follows:

| | ($ in 000s) |
|---|---|
| Service cost | $224 |
| Interest cost | 150 |
| Expected return on the plan assets ($100 actual, less $10 gain) | (90) |
| Amortization of prior service cost | 8 |
| Amortization of net loss–pensions | 2 |
| Pension expense | $294 |

**Required:**
Which elements of Warrick's balance sheet are affected by the components of pension expense? What are the specific changes in these accounts?

**E 17–15**
Determine and record pension expense, funding, and gains and losses

● LO6 LO7

Actuary and trustee reports indicate the following changes in the PBO and plan assets of Douglas-Roberts Industries during 2007:

| | |
|---|---|
| Prior service cost at Jan. 1, 2007, from plan amendment at the beginning of 2004 (amortization: $4 million per year) | $28 million |
| Net loss–pensions at Jan.1, 2007 (previous losses exceeded previous gains) | $80 million |
| Average remaining service life of the active employee group | 10 years |
| Actuary's discount rate | 7% |

| ($ in millions) PBO | | | Plan Assets |
|---|---|---|---|
| *Beginning* of 2007 | $600 | *Beginning* of 2007 | $400 |
| Service cost | 80 | Return on plan assets, | |
| Interest cost, 7% | 42 | 8% (10% expected) | 32 |
| Loss (gain) on PBO | (14) | Cash contributions | 90 |
| Less: Retiree benefits | (38) | Less: Retiree benefits | (38) |
| *End* of 2007 | $670 | *End* of 2007 | $484 |

**Required:**
1. Determine Douglas-Roberts' pension expense for 2007 and prepare the appropriate journal entries to record the expense as well as the cash contribution to plan assets.
2. Prepare the appropriate journal entry to record any 2007 gains and losses.

**E 17–16**
Concepts; terminology

● LO2 through LO8

Listed below are several terms and phrases associated with pensions. Pair each item from List A (by letter) with the item from List B that is most appropriately associated with it.

| List A | List B |
|---|---|
| ____ 1. Future compensation levels estimated. | a. Actual return exceeds expected |
| ____ 2. All funding provided by the employer. | b. Net gain–pensions |
| ____ 3. Credit to accumulated OCI and debit to pension liability. | c. Vested benefit obligation |
| | d. Projected benefit obligation |
| ____ 4. Retirement benefits specified by formula. | e. Choice between PBO and ABO |
| ____ 5. Trade-off between relevance and reliability. | f. Noncontributory pension plan |
| ____ 6. Cumulative gains in excess of losses. | g. Accumulated benefit obligation |
| ____ 7. Current pay levels implicitly assumed. | h. Plan assets |
| ____ 8. Created by the passage of time. | i. Interest cost |
| ____ 9. Not contingent on future employment. | j. Delayed recognition in earnings |
| ____ 10. Risk borne by employee. | k. Defined contribution plan |
| ____ 11. Increased by employer contributions. | l. Defined benefit plan |
| ____ 12. Caused by plan amendment. | m. Prior service cost |
| ____ 13. Loss on plan assets. | n. Amortize net loss–pensions |
| ____ 14. Excess over 10% of plan assets or PBO. | |

**E 17–17**
Record pension expense, funding, and gains and losses; determine account balances

● LO6 LO7 LO8

Beale Management has a noncontributory, defined benefit pension plan. On December 31, 2007 (the end of Beale's fiscal year), the following pension-related data were available:

| **Projected Benefit Obligation** | ($ in millions) |
|---|---|
| Balance, January 1, 2007 | $480 |
| Service cost | 82 |
| Interest cost, discount rate, 5% | 24 |
| Gain due to changes in actuarial assumptions in 2007 | (10) |
| Pension benefits paid | (40) |
| Balance, December 31, 2007 | $536 |
| **Plan Assets** | |
| Balance, January 1, 2007 | $500 |
| Actual return on plan assets | 40 |
| (Expected return on plan assets, $45) | |
| Cash contributions | 70 |
| Pension benefits paid | (40) |
| Balance, December 31, 2007 | $570 |
| **January 1, 2007, balances:** | |
| Pension asset | $ 20 |
| Prior service cost (amortization $8 per year) | 48 |
| Net gain–pensions (any amortization over 15 years) | 80 |

**Required:**
1. Prepare the 2007 journal entry to record pension expense.
2. Prepare the 2007 journal entry to record the contribution to plan assets.
3. Prepare the journal entry to record any 2007 gains and losses.
4. Determine the balances at December 31, 2007, in the pension asset, the net gain–pensions, and prior service cost and show how the balances changed during 2007. [Hint: You might find T-accounts useful.]

**E 17–18**
Pension spreadsheet

● LO8

Refer to the data provided in E 17–17.

**Required:**
Prepare a pension spreadsheet to show the relationship among the PBO, plan assets, prior service cost, the net gain–pensions, pension expense, and the pension asset.

**E 17–19**
Multiple choice; CPA exam

● LO6

The following questions dealing with pensions are adapted from questions that appeared on previous CPA examinations. Determine the response that best completes the statements or questions.

1. The following information pertains to Lee Corp.'s defined benefit pension plan for 2007:

| | |
|---|---|
| Service cost | $160,000 |
| Actual and expected return on plan assets | 35,000 |
| Unexpected loss on plan assets related to a 2007 disposal of a subsidiary | 40,000 |
| Amortization of prior service cost | 5,000 |
| Annual interest on pension obligation | 50,000 |

   What amount should Lee report as pension expense in its 2007 income statement?
   a. $250,000
   b. $220,000
   c. $210,000
   d. $180,000
2. Interest cost included in the net pension cost recognized by an employer sponsoring a defined benefit pension plan represents the
   a. Amortization of the discount on unrecognized prior service costs.
   b. Increase in the fair value of plan assets due to the passage of time.
   c. Increase in the projected benefit obligation due to the passage of time.
   d. Shortage between the expected and actual returns on plan assets.

**E 17–20**
Classifying accounting changes and errors

● LO8

Indicate with the appropriate letter the nature of each adjustment described below:

**Type of Adjustment**

A. Change in principle
B. Change in estimate
C. Correction of an error
D. Neither an accounting change nor an error

____ 1. Change in actuarial assumptions for a defined benefit pension plan.

____ 2. Determination that the projected benefit obligation under a pension plan exceeded the fair value of plan assets at the end of the previous year by $17,000. The only pension-related amount on the balance sheet was pension a liability of $30,000.

____ 3. Pension plan assets for a defined benefit pension plan achieving a rate of return in excess of the amount anticipated.

____ 4. Instituting a pension plan for the first time and adopting *Statement of Financial Accounting Standards No. 158*, "Employers' Accounting for Defined Benefit Pension and Other Postretirement Plans."

**E 17–21**
Postretirement benefits; determine APBO, EPBO

● LO10

Classified Electronics has an unfunded retiree health care plan. Each of the company's three employees has been with the firm since its inception at the beginning of 2006. As of the end of 2007, the actuary estimates the total net cost of providing health care benefits to employees during their retirement years to have a present value of $72,000. Each of the employees will become fully eligible for benefits after 28 more years of service but aren't expected to retire for 35 more years. The interest rate is 6%.

**Required:**

1. What is the expected postretirement benefit obligation at the end of 2007?
2. What is the accumulated postretirement benefit obligation at the end of 2007?
3. What is the expected postretirement benefit obligation at the end of 2008?
4. What is the accumulated postretirement benefit obligation at the end of 2008?

**E 17–22**
Postretirement benefits; determine APBO, service cost, interest cost; prepare journal entry

● LO10 LO11

The following data are available pertaining to Household Appliance Company's retiree health care plan for 2007:

| | |
|---|---|
| Number of employees covered | 2 |
| Years employed as of January 1, 2007 | 3 [each] |
| Attribution period | 25 years |
| Expected postretirement benefit obligation, Jan. 1 | $50,000 |
| Expected postretirement benefit obligation, Dec. 31 | $53,000 |
| Interest rate | 6% |
| Funding | none |

**Required:**

1. What is the accumulated postretirement benefit obligation at the beginning of 2007?
2. What is interest cost to be included in 2007 postretirement benefit expense?
3. What is service cost to be included in 2007 postretirement benefit expense?
4. Prepare the journal entry to record the postretirement benefit expense for 2007.

**E 17–23**
Postretirement benefits; determine EPBO; attribution period

● LO10 LO11

Lorin Management Services has an unfunded postretirement benefit plan. On December 31, 2007, the following data were available concerning changes in the plan's accumulated postretirement benefit obligation with respect to one of Lorin's employees:

| | |
|---|---|
| APBO at the beginning of 2007 | $16,364 |
| Interest cost: ($16,364 × 10%) | 1,636 |
| Service cost: ($44,000 × 1/22) | 2,000 |
| Portion of EPBO attributed to 2007 | |
| APBO at the end of 2007 | $20,000 |

**Required:**

1. Over how many years is the expected postretirement benefit obligation being expensed (attribution period)?
2. What is the expected postretirement benefit obligation at the *end* of 2007?
3. When was the employee hired by Lorin?
4. What is the expected postretirement benefit obligation at the *beginning* of 2007?

**E 17–24**
Postretirement benefits; components of postretirement benefit expense

● LO11

Data pertaining to the postretirement health care benefit plan of Sterling Properties include the following for 2007:

| | ($ in 000s) |
|---|---|
| Service cost | $124 |
| Accumulated postretirement benefit obligation, January 1 | 700 |
| Plan assets (fair market value), January 1 | 50 |
| Prior service cost | none |
| Net gain–postretirement benefit plan (2007 amortization, $1) | 91 |
| Retiree benefits paid (end of year) | 87 |
| Contribution to health care benefit fund (end of year) | 185 |
| Discount rate, 7% | |
| Return on plan assets (actual and expected), 10% | |

**Required:**

1. Determine the postretirement benefit expense for 2007.
2. Prepare the appropriate journal entries to record the postretirement benefit expense and funding for 2007.

**E 17–25**
Postretirement benefits; amortization of net loss

● LO11

Cahal-Michael Company has a postretirement health care benefit plan. On January 1, 2007, the following plan-related data were available:

| | ($ in 000s) |
|---|---|
| Net loss–postretirement benefit plan | $ 336 |
| Accumulated postretirement benefit obligation | 2,800 |
| Fair value of plan assets | 500 |
| Average remaining service period to retirement | 14 years (same in previous 10 yrs.) |
| Average remaining service period to full eligibility | 12 years (same in previous 10 yrs.) |

The rate of return on plan assets during 2007 was 10%, although it was expected to be 9%. The actuary revised assumptions regarding the APBO at the end of the year, resulting in a $39,000 increase in the estimate of that obligation.

**Required:**

1. Calculate any amortization of the net loss that should be included as a component of postretirement benefit expense for 2007.
2. Assume the postretirement benefit expense for 2007, not including the amortization of the net loss component, is $212,000. What is the expense for the year?
3. Determine the net loss or gain as of December 31, 2007.

**E 17–26**
Postretirement benefits; determine and record expense

● LO11

Gorky-Park Corporation provides postretirement health care benefits to employees who provide at least 12 years of service and reach age 62 while in service. On January 1, 2007, the following plan-related data were available:

| | ($ in millions) |
|---|---|
| Accumulated postretirement benefit obligation | $130 |
| Fair value of plan assets | none |
| Average remaining service period to retirement | 25 years (same in previous 10 yrs.) |
| Average remaining service period to full eligibility | 20 years (same in previous 10 yrs.) |

On January 1, 2007, Gorky-Park amends the plan to provide certain dental benefits in addition to previously provided medical benefits. The actuary determines that the cost of making the amendment retroactive increases the APBO by $20 million. Management chooses to amortize the prior service cost on a straight-line basis. The service cost for 2007 is $34 million. The interest rate is 8%.

**Required:**

1. Calculate the postretirement benefit expense for 2007.
2. Prepare the journal entry to record the expense.

**E 17–27**
Postretirement benefits; negative plan amendment

● LO11

Southeast Technology provides postretirement health care benefits to employees. On January 1, 2007, the following plan-related data were available:

| | ($ in 000s) |
|---|---|
| Prior service cost—originated in 2002 | $ 50 |
| Accumulated postretirement benefit obligation | 530 |
| Fair value of plan assets | none |
| Average remaining service period to retirement | 20 years (same in previous 10 yrs.) |
| Average remaining service period to full eligibility | 15 years (same in previous 10 yrs.) |

On January 1, 2007, Southeast amends the plan in response to spiraling health care costs. The amendment establishes an annual maximum of $3,000 for medical benefits that the plan will provide. The actuary determines that the effect of this amendment is to decrease the APBO by $80,000. Management amortizes prior service cost on a straight-line basis. The interest rate is 8%. The service cost for 2007 is $114,000.

**Required:**

1. Calculate the prior service cost amortization for 2007.
2. Calculate the postretirement benefit expense for 2007.

**E 17–28**
Multiple choice; CPA exam

● LO10

The following question dealing with postretirement benefit plans appeared on a previous CPA examination. Enter the letter corresponding to the response which *best* completes the question.

An employer's obligation for postretirement health benefits that are expected to be provided to or for an employee must be fully accrued by the date the

a. Employee is fully eligible for benefits.
b. Employee retires.

c. Benefits are utilized.
d. Benefits are paid.

**E 17–29**
Multiple choice; CMA exam; pensions
● LO2 LO3 LO6

The following questions dealing with pensions are adapted from questions that previously appeared on Certified Management Accountant (CMA) examinations. The CMA designation sponsored by the Institute of Management Accountants (**www.imanet.org**) provides members with an objective measure of knowledge and competence in the field of management accounting. Determine the response that best completes the statements or questions.

1. According to SFAS 87, *Employer's Accounting for Pension Plans,* the projected benefit obligation (PBO) is best described as the?
   a. Present value of benefits accrued to date based on future salary levels.
   b. Present value of benefits accrued to date based on current salary levels.
   c. Increase in retroactive benefits at the date of the amendment of the plan.
   d. Amount of the adjustment necessary to reflect the difference between actual and estimated actuarial returns.
2. On November 30, the Board of Directors of Baldwin Corporation amended its pension plan giving retroactive benefits to its employees. The information below is provided at November 30.

| | |
|---|---|
| Accumulated benefit obligation (ABO) | $825,000 |
| Projected benefit obligation (PBO) | 900,000 |
| Plan assets (fair value) | 307,500 |
| Market-related asset value | 301,150 |
| Prior service cost | 190,000 |
| Average remaining service life of employees | 10 years |
| Useful life of pension goodwill | 20 years |

   Using the straight-line method of amortization, the amount of prior service cost charged to expense during the year ended November 30 is
   a. $9,500.
   b. $19,000.
   c. $30,250.
   d. $190,000.

**E 17–30**
Prior service cost; service method; straight-line method (Based on Appendix)

Frazier Refrigeration amended its defined benefit pension plan on December 31, 2007, to increase retirement benefits earned with each service year. The consulting actuary estimated the prior service cost incurred by making the amendment retroactive to prior years to be $110,000. Frazier's 100 present employees are expected to retire at the rate of approximately 10 each year at the end of each of the next 10 years.

**Required:**
1. Using the service method, calculate the amount of prior service cost to be amortized to pension expense in each of the next 10 years.
2. Using the straight-line method, calculate the amount of prior service cost to be amortized to pension expense in each of the next 10 years.

## PROBLEMS

available with McGraw-Hill's Homework Manager www.mhhe.com/spiceland4e

**An alternate exercise and problem set is available on the text website: www.mhhe.com/spiceland4e**

**(Note: Problems 1–5 are variations of the same situation, designed to focus on different elements of the pension plan.)**

**P 17–1**
ABO calculations; present value concepts
● LO2 LO3

Sachs Brands' defined benefit pension plan specifies annual retirement benefits equal to: 1.6% × service years × final year's salary, payable at the end of each year. Angela Davenport was hired by Sachs at the beginning of 1993 and is expected to retire at the end of 2027 after 35 years' service. Her retirement is expected to span 18 years. Davenport's salary is $90,000 at the end of 2007 and the company's actuary projects her salary to be $240,000 at retirement. The actuary's discount rate is 7%.

**Required:**
1. Draw a time line that depicts Davenport's expected service period, retirement period, and a 2007 measurement date for the pension obligation.
2. Estimate by the accumulated benefits approach the amount of Davenport's annual retirement payments earned as of the end of 2007.
3. What is the company's accumulated benefit obligation at the end of 2007 with respect to Davenport?

4. If no estimates are changed in the meantime, what will be the accumulated benefit obligation at the end of 2010 (three years later) when Davenport's salary is $100,000?

**P 17–2**
PBO calculations; present value concepts

● LO3

Sachs Brands' defined benefit pension plan specifies annual retirement benefits equal to: 1.6% × service years × final year's salary, payable at the end of each year. Angela Davenport was hired by Sachs at the beginning of 1993 and is expected to retire at the end of 2027 after 35 years' service. Her retirement is expected to span 18 years. Davenport's salary is $90,000 at the end of 2007 and the company's actuary projects her salary to be $240,000 at retirement. The actuary's discount rate is 7%.

**Required:**

1. Draw a time line that depicts Davenport's expected service period, retirement period, and a 2007 measurement date for the pension obligation.
2. Estimate by the projected benefits approach the amount of Davenport's annual retirement payments earned as of the end of 2007.
3. What is the company's projected benefit obligation at the end of 2007 with respect to Davenport?
4. If no estimates are changed in the meantime, what will be the company's projected benefit obligation at the end of 2010 (three years later) with respect to Davenport?

**P 17–3**
Service cost, interest, and PBO calculations; present value concepts

● LO3

Sachs Brands' defined benefit pension plan specifies annual retirement benefits equal to: 1.6% × service years × final year's salary, payable at the end of each year. Angela Davenport was hired by Sachs at the beginning of 1993 and is expected to retire at the end of 2027 after 35 years' service. Her retirement is expected to span 18 years. Davenport's salary is $90,000 at the end of 2007 and the company's actuary projects her salary to be $240,000 at retirement. The actuary's discount rate is 7%.

**Required:**

1. What is the company's projected benefit obligation at the beginning of 2007 (after 14 years' service) with respect to Davenport?
2. Estimate by the projected benefits approach the portion of Davenport's annual retirement payments attributable to 2007 service.
3. What is the company's service cost for 2007 with respect to Davenport?
4. What is the company's interest cost for 2007 with respect to Davenport?
5. Combine your answers to requirements 1, 3, and 4 to determine the company's projected benefit obligation at the end of 2007 (after 15 years' service) with respect to Davenport.

**P 17–4**
Prior service cost; components of pension expense; present value concepts

● LO3 LO6

Sachs Brands' defined benefit pension plan specifies annual retirement benefits equal to: 1.6% × service years × final year's salary, payable at the end of each year. Angela Davenport was hired by Sachs at the beginning of 1993 and is expected to retire at the end of 2027 after 35 years' service. Her retirement is expected to span 18 years. Davenport's salary is $90,000 at the end of 2007 and the company's actuary projects her salary to be $240,000 at retirement. The actuary's discount rate is 7%.

At the beginning of 2008, the pension formula was amended to:

1.75% × Service years × Final year's salary

The amendment was made retroactive to apply the increased benefits to prior service years.

**Required:**

1. What is the company's prior service cost at the beginning of 2008 with respect to Davenport after the amendment described above?
2. Since the amendment occurred at the *beginning* of 2008, amortization of the prior service cost begins in 2008. What is the prior service cost amortization that would be included in pension expense?
3. What is the service cost for 2008 with respect to Davenport?
4. What is the interest cost for 2008 with respect to Davenport?
5. Calculate pension expense for 2008 with respect to Davenport, assuming plan assets attributable to her of $150,000 and a rate of return (actual and expected) of 10%.

**P 17–5**
Gain on PBO; present value concepts

● LO3 LO6

Sachs Brands' defined benefit pension plan specifies annual retirement benefits equal to: 1.6% × service years × final year's salary, payable at the end of each year. Angela Davenport was hired by Sachs at the beginning of 1993 and is expected to retire at the end of 2027 after 35 years' service. Her retirement is expected to span 18 years. Davenport's salary is $90,000 at the end of 2007 and the company's actuary projects her salary to be $240,000 at retirement. The actuary's discount rate is 7%.

At the beginning of 2008, changing economic conditions caused the actuary to reassess the applicable discount rate. It was decided that 8% is the appropriate rate.

**Required:**

Calculate the effect of the change in the assumed discount rate on the PBO at the beginning of 2008 with respect to Davenport.

**P 17–6**
Determine the PBO; plan assets; pension expense; two years

● LO3 LO4 LO6

Stanley-Morgan Industries adopted a defined benefit pension plan on April 12, 2007. The provisions of the plan were not made retroactive to prior years. A local bank, engaged as trustee for the plan assets, expects plan assets to earn a 10% rate of return. A consulting firm, engaged as actuary, recommends 6% as the appropriate discount rate. The service cost is $150,000 for 2007 and $200,000 for 2008. Year-end funding is $160,000 for 2007 and $170,000 for 2008. No assumptions or estimates were revised during 2007.

**Required:**

Calculate each of the following amounts as of both December 31, 2007, and December 31, 2008:

1. Projected benefit obligation
2. Plan assets
3. Pension expense
4. Pensoin asset/liability

**P 17–7**
Determining the amortization of net gain

● LO6

Herring Wholesale Company has a defined benefit pension plan. On January 1, 2007, the following pension-related data were available:

| | ($ in 000s) |
|---|---|
| Net gain–pensions | $ 170 |
| Accumulated benefit obligation | 1,170 |
| Projected benefit obligation | 1,400 |
| Fair value of plan assets | 1,100 |
| Average remaining service period of active employees (expected to remain constant for the next several years) | 15 years |

The rate of return on plan assets during 2007 was 9%, although it was expected to be 10%. The actuary revised assumptions regarding the PBO at the end of the year, resulting in a $23,000 decrease in the estimate of that obligation.

**Required:**

1. Calculate any amortization of the net gain that should be included as a component of net pension expense for 2007.
2. Assume the net pension expense for 2007, not including the amortization of the net gain component, is $325,000. What is pension expense for the year?
3. Determine the net loss or gain as of January 1, 2008.

**P 17–8**
Pension spreadsheet; record pension expense and funding; new gains and losses

● LO7 LO8

A partially completed pension spreadsheet showing the relationships among the elements that constitute Carney, Inc.'s defined benefit pension plan follows. Six years earlier, Carney revised its pension formula and recalculated benefits earned by employees in prior years using the more generous formula. The prior service cost created by the recalculation is being amortized at the rate of $5 million per year. At the end of 2007, the pension formula was amended again, creating an additional prior service cost of $40 million. The expected rate of return on assets and the actuary's discount rate were 10%, and the average remaining service life of the active employee group is 10 years.

| | Informal Records | | Formal Records | | | | |
|---|---|---|---|---|---|---|---|
| ( )s indicate credits: debits otherwise ($ in millions) | PBO | Plan Assets | Prior Service Cost | Net Loss–Pensions | Pension Expense | Cash | Prepaid (Liability) / Asset |
| *Balance, Jan. 1, 2007* | (830) | 680 | 20 | 93 | | | (150) |
| Service cost | ? | | | | 74 | | ? |
| Interest cost | ? | | | | ? | | ? |
| Expected return on asset | | ? | | | ? | | ? |
| *Adjust for:* | | | | | | | |
| Loss on assets | | (7) | | ? | | | ? |
| *Amortization of:* | | | | | | | |
| Prior service cost | | | ? | | ? | | |
| Net loss | | | | ? | ? | | |
| Loss on PBO | ? | | | ? | | | (13) |
| Prior service cost | ? | | ? | | | | ? |
| Cash funding | | ? | | | | ? | 84 |
| Retiree benefits | ? | ? | | | | | |
| *Balance, Dec. 31, 2007* | ? | 775 | ? | ? | ? | | ? |

**Required:**

1. Copy the incomplete spreadsheet and fill in the missing amounts.
2. Prepare the 2007 journal entry to record pension expense.

3. Prepare the 2007 journal entry to record the cash contribution to plan assets.
4. Prepare the journal entry to record any 2007 gains and losses and new prior service cost in 2007.

**P 17–9**
Determine pension expense; PBO; plan assets; pension asset/liability; journal entries

● LO3 through LO8

U.S. Metallurgical, Inc. reported the following balances in its financial statements and disclosure notes at December 31, 2006.

| | |
|---|---|
| Plan assets | $ 400,000 |
| Projected benefit obligation | 320,000 |

U.S.M.'s actuary determined that 2007 service cost is $60,000. Both the expected and actual rate of return on plan assets are 9%. The interest (discount) rate is 5%. U.S.M. contributed $120,000 to the pension fund at the end of 2007, and retirees were paid $44,000 from plan assets.

**Required:**

Determine the following amounts at the end of 2007.

1. Pension expense
2. Projected benefit obligation
3. Plan assets
4. Pension asset/liability
5. Prepare journal entries to record the pension expense and funding of plan assets to verify the change in the pension asset/liability.

**P 17–10**
Determine pension expense; journal entries; two years

● LO3 through LO8

The Kollar Company has a defined benefit pension plan. Pension information concerning the fiscal years 2007 and 2008 are presented below ($ in millions):

**Information Provided by Pension Plan Actuary:**

a. Projected benefit obligation as of December 31, 2006 = $1,800.
b. Prior service cost from plan amendment on January 2, 2007 = $400 (straight-line amortization for 10-year average remaining service period).
c. Service cost for 2007 = $520.
d. Service cost for 2008 = $570.
e. Discount rate used by actuary on projected benefit obligation for 2007 and 2008 = 10%.
f. Payments to retirees in 2007 = $400.
g. Payments to retirees in 2008 = $450.
h. No changes in actuarial assumptions or estimates.

**Information Provided by Pension Fund Trustee:**

a. Plan asset balance at fair value on January 1, 2007 = $1,600.
b. 2007 contributions = $540.
c. 2008 contributions = $590.
d. Expected long-term rate of return on plan assets = 12%.
e. 2007 actual return on plan assets = $180.
f. 2008 actual return on plan assets = $210.
g. Net gain–pensions on January 1, 2007 = $230.
h. Net gains and losses are amortized for 10 years for 2007 and 2008.

**Required:**

1. Calculate pension expense for 2007 and 2008.
2. Prepare the journal entries for 2007 and 2008 to record pension expense.
3. Prepare the journal entries for 2007 and 2008 to record the cash contribution to plan assets.
4. Prepare the journal entries for 2007 and 2008 to record any gains and losses and new prior service cost.

**P 17–11**
Determine the PBO, plan assets, pension expense; prior service cost

● LO3 LO4 LO6

Lewis Industries adopted a defined benefit pension plan on January 1, 2007. By making the provisions of the plan retroactive to prior years, Lewis incurred a prior service cost of $2 million. The prior service cost was funded immediately by a $2 million cash payment to the fund trustee on January 2, 2007. However, the cost is to be amortized (expensed) over 10 years. The service cost—$250,000 for 2007—is fully funded at the end of each year. Both the actuary's discount rate and the expected rate of return on plan assets were 9%. The actual rate of return on plan assets was 11%. At December 31, the trustee paid $16,000 to an employee who retired during 2007.

**Required:**

Determine each of the following amounts as of December 31, 2007, the fiscal year-end for Lewis:

1. Projected benefit obligation
2. Plan assets
3. Pension expense

**P 17–12**
Relationship among pension elements

● LO3 through LO8

The funded status of Hilton Paneling, Inc.'s defined benefit pension plan and the balances in prior service cost and the net gain–pensions, are given below.

| | ($ in 000s) | |
|---|---|---|
| | **2007 Beginning Balances** | **2007 Ending Balances** |
| Projected benefit obligation | $2,300 | $2,501 |
| Plan assets | 2,400 | 2,591 |
| Funded status | 100 | 90 |
| Prior service cost | 325 | 300 |
| Net gain–pensions | 330 | 300 |

Retirees were paid $270,000 and the employer contribution to the pension fund was $245,000 at the end of 2007. The expected rate of return on plan assets was 10%, and the actuary's discount rate is 7%. There were no changes in actuarial estimates and assumptions regarding the PBO.

**Required:**

Determine the following amounts for 2007:

1. Actual return on plan assets
2. Loss or gain on plan assets
3. Service cost
4. Pension expense
5. Average remaining service life of active employees (used to determine amortization of the net gain)

**P 17–13**
Comprehensive—pension elements; spreadsheet

● LO8

The following pension-related data pertain to Metro Recreation's noncontributory, defined benefit pension plan for 2007:

| | ($ in 000s) | |
|---|---|---|
| | **Jan. 1** | **Dec. 31** |
| Projected benefit obligation | $4,100 | $4,380 |
| Accumulated benefit obligation | 3,715 | 3,950 |
| Plan assets (fair value) | 4,530 | 4,975 |
| Interest (discount) rate, 7% | | |
| Expected return on plan assets, 10% | | |
| Prior service cost (from Dec. 31, 2006, amendment) | 840 | |
| Net loss–pensions | 477 | |
| Average remaining service life: 12 years | | |
| Gain due to changes in actuarial assumptions | | 44 |
| Contributions to pension fund (end of year) | | 340 |
| Pension benefits paid (end of year) | | 295 |

**Required:**

Prepare a pension spreadsheet that shows the relationships among the various pension balances, shows the changes in those balances, and computes pension expense for 2007.

**P 17–14**
Comprehensive—reporting a pension plan; pension spreadsheet; determine changes in balances; two years

● LO3 through LO8

Actuary and trustee reports indicate the following changes in the PBO and plan assets of Lakeside Cable during 2007:

| | |
|---|---|
| Prior service cost at Jan. 1, 2007, from plan amendment at the beginning of 2005 (amortization: $4 million per year) | $32 million |
| Net loss–pensions at Jan.1, 2007 (previous losses exceeded previous gains) | $40 million |
| Average remaining service life of the active employee group | 10 years |
| Actuary's discount rate | 8% |

| ($ in millions) | **PBO** | | **Plan Assets** |
|---|---|---|---|
| *Beginning* of 2007 | $300 | *Beginning* of 2007 | $200 |
| Service cost | 48 | Return on plan assets, 7.5% (10% expected) | 15 |
| Interest cost, 8% | 24 | Cash contributions | 45 |
| Loss (gain) on PBO | (2) | Less: Retiree benefits | (20) |
| Less: Retiree benefits | (20) | | |
| *End* of 2007 | $350 | *End* of 2007 | $240 |

**Required:**

1. Determine Lakeside's pension expense for 2007 and prepare the appropriate journal entries to record the expense as well as the cash contribution to plan assets.

2. Determine the new gains and/or losses in 2007 and prepare the appropriate journal entry to record them.
3. Prepare a pension spreadsheet to assist you in determining end of 2007 balances in the PBO, plan assets, prior service cost, the net loss–pensions, and the pension liability.
4. Assume the following actuary and trustee reports indicating changes in the PBO and plan assets of Lakeside Cable during 2008:

| ($ in millions) | PBO | | Plan Assets |
|---|---|---|---|
| *Beginning* of 2008 | $350 | *Beginning* of 2008 | $240 |
| Service cost | 38 | Return on plan assets, | |
| Interest cost at 8% | 28 | 15% (10% expected) | 36 |
| Loss (gain) on PBO | 5 | Cash contributions | 30 |
| Less: Retiree benefits | (16) | Less: Retiree benefits | (16) |
| *End* of 2008 | $405 | *End* of 2008 | $290 |

Determine Lakeside's pension expense for 2008 and prepare the appropriate journal entries to record the expense and the cash funding of plan assets.
5. Determine the new gains and/or losses in 2008 and prepare the appropriate journal entry to record them.
6. Using T-accounts, determine the balances at December 31, 2008, in the pension liability, the net loss–pensions, and prior service cost.
7. Confirm the balances determined in Requirement 6 by preparing a pension spreadsheet.

**P 17–15**
Integrating Problem—Deferred tax effects of pension entries; integrate concepts learned in Chapter 16

● LO7

To focus on the core issues, we ignored the income tax effects of the pension amounts we recorded in the chapter. Reproduced below are the journal entries from the chapter that Global Communications used to record its pension expense and funding in 2007 and the new gain and loss that occurred that year.

| | ($ in millions) | |
|---|---|---|
| **To Record Pension Expense** | | |
| Pension expense (total) | 43 | |
| Pension liability ($41 + 24 – 27) | | 38 |
| Prior service cost (2007 amortization) | | 4 |
| Net loss–pensions (2007 amortization) | | 1 |
| **To Record Funding** | | |
| Pension liability | 48 | |
| Cash (contribution to plan assets) | | 48 |
| **To Record Gains and Losses as Other Comprehensive Income (OCI)** | | |
| Loss–OCI (from change in assumption) | 23 | |
| Gain–OCI (from actual return exceeding expected return) | | 3 |
| Pension liability (to balance) | | 20 |

**Required:**

1. Recast these journal entries to include the income tax effects of the events being recorded. Assume that Global's tax rate is 40%. [Hint: Costs are incurred and recognized for financial reporting purposes now, but the tax impact comes much later—when these amounts are deducted for tax purposes as actual payments for retiree benefits occur in the future. As a result, the tax effects are deferred, creating the need to record deferred tax assets and deferred tax liabilities. So, you may want to refer back to Chapter 16 to refresh your memory on these concepts.]
2. Prepare a statement of comprehensive income for 2007 assuming Global's only other sources of comprehensive income were net income of $300 million and a $20 million net unrealized holding gain on investments in securities available for sale.

**P 17–16**
Postretirement benefits; EPBO calculations; APBO calculations; components of postretirement benefit expense; present value concepts

● LO9 LO10

Century-Fox Corporation's employees are eligible for postretirement health care benefits after both being employed at the end of the year in which age 60 is attained and having worked 20 years. Jason Snyder was hired at the beginning of 1985 by Century-Fox at age 34 (he turned 35 during 1985) and is expected to retire at the end of 2012 (age 62). His retirement is expected to span five years (unrealistically short to simplify calculations). The company's actuary has estimated the net cost of retiree benefits in each retirement year as shown below. The discount rate is 6%. The plan is not prefunded.

| Year | Expected Age | Net Cost |
|---|---|---|
| 2013 | 63 | $4,000 |
| 2014 | 64 | 4,400 |
| 2015 | 65 | 2,300 |
| 2016 | 66 | 2,500 |
| 2017 | 67 | 2,800 |

**Required:**

1. Draw a time line that depicts Snyder's attribution period for retiree benefits and expected retirement period.
2. Calculate the present value of the net benefits as of the expected retirement date.
3. With respect to Snyder, what is the company's expected postretirement benefit obligation at the end of 2007?
4. With respect to Snyder, what is the company's accumulated postretirement benefit obligation at the end of 2007?
5. With respect to Snyder, what is the company's accumulated postretirement benefit obligation at the end of 2008?
6. What is the service cost to be included in 2008 postretirement benefit expense?
7. What is the interest cost to be included in 2008 postretirement benefit expense?
8. Show how the APBO changed during 2008 by reconciling the beginning and ending balances.

**P 17–17**
Postretirement benefits; schedule of postretirement benefit costs

● LO9 through LO11

Stockton Labeling Company has a retiree health care plan. Employees become fully eligible for benefits after working for the company eight years. Stockton hired Misty Newburn on January 1, 2007. As of the end of 2007, the actuary estimates the total net cost of providing health care benefits to Newburn during her retirement years to have a present value of $18,000. The actuary's discount rate is 10%.

**Required:**

Prepare a schedule that shows the EPBO, the APBO, the service cost, the interest cost, and the postretirement benefit expense for each of the years 2007–2014.

**P 17–18**
Postretirement benefits; relationship among elements of postretirement benefit plan

● LO9 through LO11

The information below pertains to the retiree health care plan of Thompson Technologies:

| | ($ in 000s) | |
|---|---|---|
| | **2007 Beginning Balances** | **2007 Ending Balances** |
| Accumulated postretirement benefit obligation | $460 | $485 |
| Plan assets | 0 | 75 |
| Funded status | (460) | (410) |
| Prior service cost | 120 | 110 |
| Net gain–postretirement benefit plan | (50) | (49) |

Thompson began funding the plan in 2007 with a contribution of $127,000 to the benefit fund at the end of the year. Retirees were paid $52,000. The actuary's discount rate is 5%. There were no changes in actuarial estimates and assumptions.

**Required:**

Determine the following amounts for 2007:

1. Service cost.
2. Postretirement benefit expense.
3. Postretirement benefit liability at December 31.

# BROADEN YOUR PERSPECTIVE

**Apply your critical-thinking ability to the knowledge you've gained. These cases will provide you an opportunity to develop your research, analysis, judgment, and communication skills. You also will work with other students, integrate what you've learned, apply it in real world situations, and consider its global and ethical ramifications. This practice will broaden your knowledge and further develop your decision-making abilities.**

**Judgment Case 17–1**
Choose your retirement option

● LO1 LO3 LO4 LO5

"I only get one shot at this?" you wonder aloud. Mrs. Montgomery, human resources manager at Covington State University, has just explained that newly hired assistant professors must choose between two retirement plan options. "Yes, I'm afraid so," she concedes. "But you do have a week to decide."

Mrs. Montgomery's explanation was that your two alternatives are: (1) the state's defined benefit plan and (2) a defined contribution plan under which the university will contribute each year an amount equal to 8% of your salary. The defined benefit plan will provide annual retirement benefits determined by the following formula: 1.5% × years of service × salary at retirement.

"It's a good thing I studied pensions in my accounting program," you tell her. "Now let's see. You say the state is currently assuming our salaries will rise about 3% a year, and the interest rate they use in their calculations is 6%? And, for someone my age, you say they assume I'll retire after 40 years and draw retirement pay for 20 years. I'll do some research and get back to you."

**Required:**

1. You were hired at the beginning of 2007 at a salary of $100,000. If you choose the state's defined benefit plan and projections hold true, what will be your annual retirement pay? What is the present value of your retirement annuity as of the anticipated retirement date (end of 2046)?
2. Suppose instead that you choose the defined contribution plan. Assuming that the rate of increase in salary is the same as the state assumes and that the rate of return on your retirement plan assets will be 6% compounded annually, what will be the future value of your plan assets as of the anticipated retirement date (end of 2046)? What will be your annual retirement pay (assuming continuing investment of remaining assets at 6%)?
3. Based on this numerical comparison, which plan would you choose? What other factors must you also consider in making the choice?

*Hint:* The calculations are greatly simplified using an electronic spreadsheet such as Excel. There are many ways to set up the spreadsheet. One relatively easy way is to set up the first few rows with the formulas as shown below, then use the "fill down" function to fill in the remaining 38 rows, and use the Insert: Name: Define: function to name column A "n". Note that multiplying each contribution by $(1.06)^n$, where $n$ equals the remaining number of years to retirement, calculates the future value of each contribution invested at 6% until retirement.

| | A | B | C | D |
|---|---|---|---|---|
| 1 | Years to | | | Future Value |
| 2 | Retirement | Salary | Contribution | at Retirement |
| 3 | 40 | 100000 | =B3*0.08 | =C3*1.06^n |
| 4 | =A3-1 | =B3*1.03 | =B4*0.08 | =C4*1.06^n |

**Communication Case 17–2**
Pension concepts

● LO2 through LO8

Noel Zoeller is the newly hired assistant controller of Kemp Industries, a regional supplier of hardwood derivative products. The company sponsors a defined benefit pension plan that covers its 420 employees. On reviewing last year's financial statements, Zoeller was concerned about some items reported in the disclosure notes relating to the pension plan. Portions of the relevant note follow:

**Note 8: Pensions**
The company has a defined benefit pension plan covering substantially all of its employees. Pension benefits are based on employee service years and the employee's compensation during the last two years of employment. The company contributes annually the maximum amount permitted by the federal tax code. Plan contributions provide for benefits expected to be earned in the future as well as those earned to date. The following reconciles the plan's funded status and amount recognized in the balance sheet at December 31, 2007 ($ in 000s).

| **Actuarial Present Value Benefit Obligations:** | |
|---|---|
| Accumulated benefit obligation (including vested benefits of $318) | $(1,305) |
| Projected benefit obligation | (1,800) |
| Plan assets at fair value | 1,575 |
| Projected benefit obligation in excess of plan assets | $ (225) |

Kemp's comparative income statements reported net periodic pension expense of $108,000 in 2007 and $86,520 in 2006. Since employment has remained fairly constant in recent years, Zoeller expressed concern over the increase in the pension expense. He expressed his concern to you, a three-year senior accountant at Kemp. "I'm also interested in the differences in these liability measurements," he mentioned.

**Required:**

Write a memo to Zoeller. In the memo:

1. Explain to Zoeller how the composition of the net periodic pension expense can create the situation he sees. Briefly describe the components of pension expense.
2. Briefly explain how pension gains and losses are recognized in earnings.
3. Describe for him the differences and similarities between the accumulated benefit obligation and the projected benefit obligation.

4. Explain how the "Projected benefit obligation in excess of plan assets" is reported in the financial statements.

**Judgment Case 17–3**
Barlow's wife; relationship among pension elements

● LO8

LGD Consulting is a medium-sized provider of environmental engineering services. The corporation sponsors a noncontributory, defined benefit pension plan. Alan Barlow, a new employee and participant in the pension plan, obtained a copy of the 2007 financial statements, partly to obtain additional information about his new employer's obligation under the plan. In part, the pension footnote reads as follows:

**Note 8: Retirement Benefits**
The Company has a defined benefit pension plan covering substantially all of its employees. The benefits are based on years of service and the employee's compensation during the last two years of employment. The company's funding policy is consistent with the funding requirements of federal law and regulations. Generally, pension costs accrued are funded. Plan assets consist primarily of stocks, bonds, commingled trust funds, and cash.

The change in projected benefit obligation for the plan years ended December 31, 2007, and December 31, 2006:

| ($ in 000s) | 2007 | 2006 |
|---|---|---|
| Projected benefit obligation at beginning of year | $3,786 | $3,715 |
| Service cost | 103 | 94 |
| Interest cost | 287 | 284 |
| Actuarial (gain) loss | 302 | (23) |
| Benefits paid | (324) | (284) |
| Projected benefit obligation at end of year | $4,154 | $3,786 |

The weighted average discount rate and rate of increase in future compensation levels used in determining the actuarial present value of the projected benefit obligations in the above table were 7.0% and 4.3%, respectively, at December 31, 2007, and 7.75% and 4.7%, respectively, at December 31, 2006. The expected long-term rate of return on assets was 10.0% at December 31, 2007 and 2006.

The change in the fair value of plan assets for the plan years ended December 31, 2007 and 2006:

| ($ in 000s) | 2007 | 2006 |
|---|---|---|
| Fair value of plan assets at beginning of year | $3,756 | $3,616 |
| Actual return on plan assets | 1,100 | 372 |
| Employer contributions | 27 | 52 |
| Benefits paid | (324) | (284) |
| Fair value of plan assets at end of year | $4,559 | $3,756 |

Included in the Consolidated Balance Sheets are the following components of accumulated other comprehensive income:

| ($ in 000s) | 2007 | 2006 |
|---|---|---|
| Net actuarial gain | $(620) | $(165) |
| Prior service cost | 44 | 46 |

Net periodic defined benefit pension cost for fiscal 2007, 2006, and 2005 included the following components:

| ($ in 000s) | 2007 | 2006 | 2005 |
|---|---|---|---|
| Service cost | $ 103 | $ 94 | $ 112 |
| Interest cost | 287 | 284 | 263 |
| Expected return on plan assets | (342) | (326) | (296) |
| Amortization of prior service cost | 2 | 2 | 1 |
| Recognized net actuarial (gain) loss | (2) | 2 | 4 |
| Net periodic pension cost | $ 48 | $ 56 | $ 84 |

In attempting to reconcile amounts reported in the footnote with amounts reported in the income statement and balance sheet, Barlow became confused. He was able to find the pension expense on the income statement but was unable to make sense of the balance sheet amounts. Expressing his frustration to his wife, Barlow said, "It appears to me that the company has calculated pension expense as if they have the pension liability and pension assets they include in the footnote, but I can't seem to find those amounts in the balance sheet. In fact, there are several amounts here I can't seem to account for. They also say they've made some assumptions about interest rates, pay increases, and profits on invested assets. I wonder what difference it would make if they assumed other numbers,"

Barlow's wife took accounting courses in college and remembers most of what she learned about pension accounting. She attempts to clear up her husband's confusion.

**Required:**

Assume the role of Barlow's wife. Answer the following questions for your husband.

1. Is Barlow's observation correct that the company has calculated pension expense on the basis of amounts not reported in the balance sheet?
2. What amount would the company report as a pension liability on the balance sheet?
3. What amount would the company report as a pension asset on the balance sheet?
4. Which of the other amounts reported in the disclosure note would the company report in the balance sheet?
5. The disclosure note reports a net actuarial gain as well as an actuarial loss. How are these related? What do the amounts mean?
6. Which components of the pension expense represent deferred recognition? Where are these deferred amounts reported prior to amortization?

**Communication Case 17–4**
Barlow's wife; relationship among pension elements

● LO8

The focus of this case is question 1 in the previous case. Your instructor will divide the class into two to six groups, depending on the size of the class. The mission of your group is to assess the correctness of Barlow's observation and to suggest the appropriate treatment of the pension obligation. The suggested treatment need not be that required by GAAP.

**Required:**

1. Each group member should deliberate the situation independently and draft a tentative argument prior to the class session for which the case is assigned.
2. In class, each group will meet for 10 to 15 minutes in different areas of the classroom. During that meeting, group members will take turns sharing their suggestions for the purpose of arriving at a single group treatment.
3. After the allotted time, a spokesperson for each group (selected during the group meetings) will share the group's solution with the class. The goal of the class is to incorporate the views of each group into a consensus approach to the situation.

**International Case 17–5**
Accounting for pensions in other countries

● LO8

Since its inception in 1973, the primary objective of the International Accounting Standards Board (IASB) has been to narrow differences worldwide in accounting practices and the presentation of financial information. While progress has been made, the goal is far from having been met. Significant differences exist from country to country in the area of accounting for pensions. These differences impact on reported earnings and financial position in countries where these benefits are significant.

**Required:**

Choose a country other than the United States and:

1. Locate a recent annual report of a company from that country.
2. Determine the way that country accounts for pensions. Include in your analysis:
   a. Whether and how the cost of providing pension benefits is reported in disclosure notes.
   b. Whether the obligation for the pension benefits is accrued in the balance sheet.
   c. The impact on the income statement, if any.
3. Prepare a short report highlighting the similarities and differences between the United States and your chosen country in the way pension benefits are accounted for.

Note: You can obtain copies of annual reports from the company's website, a friendly stockbroker, or EDGAR, the Electronic Data Gathering, Analysis, and Retrieval service of the SEC, at **www.sec.gov**, or you can use EdgarScan at **edgarscan.pwcglobal.com**.

**Ethics Case 17–6**
401(k) plan contributions

● LO1

You are in your third year as internal auditor with VXI International, manufacturer of parts and supplies for jet aircraft. VXI began a defined contribution pension plan in 2004. The plan is a so-called 401(k) plan (named after the Tax Code section that specifies the conditions for the favorable tax treatment of these plans) that permits voluntary contributions by employees. Employees' contributions are matched with one dollar of employer contribution for every two dollars of employee contribution. Approximately $500,000 of contributions are deducted from employee paychecks each month for investment in one of three employer-sponsored mutual funds.

While performing some preliminary audit tests, you happen to notice that employee contributions to these plans usually do not show up on mutual fund statements for up to two months following the end of pay periods from which the deductions are drawn. On further investigation, you discover that when the plan was first begun, contributions were invested within one week of receipt of the funds. When you question the firm's investment manager about the apparent change in the timing of investments, you are told, "Last year Mr. Maxwell (the CFO) directed me to initially deposit the contributions in the corporate investment account. At the close of each quarter, we add the employer matching contribution and deposit the combined amount in specific employee mutual funds."

**Required:**
1. What is Mr. Maxwell's apparent motivation for the change in the way contributions are handled?
2. Do you perceive an ethical dilemma?

**Research Case 17–7**
Researching pension disclosures; retrieving information from the Internet
● LO1 LO3 LO4

All publicly traded domestic companies use EDGAR, the Electronic Data Gathering, Analysis, and Retrieval system, to make the majority of their filings with the SEC. You can access EDGAR on the Internet at **www.sec.gov**, or you can use EdgarScan at **edgarscan.pwcglobal.com**.

**Required:**
1. Search for a company with which you are familiar and which you believe is likely to have a pension plan. (Older, established firms are good candidates.) Access the company's most recent 10-K filing. Search or scroll to find the financial statements and related notes.
2. From the disclosure notes, determine the type of pension plan(s) the company has.
3. For any defined contribution plans, determine the contributions the company made to the plans on behalf of employees during the most recent three years.
4. For any defined benefit plans, determine the projected benefit obligation for the most recent year. Compare this obligation with the company's total long-term debt. What interest rate was used in estimating the PBO?
5. Repeat steps 2 through 4 for a second firm. Compare and contrast the types of pension plans offered. Are actuarial assumptions the same for defined benefit plans?

**Analysis Case 17–8**
Pension disclosures
**FedEx Corporation**
● LO5

Refer to the financial statements and related disclosure notes of **FedEx Corporation** in Appendix B at the end of the book. FedEx sponsors pension plans covering substantially all employees. The largest plan covers U.S. domestic employees age 21 and over, with at least one year of service, and provides benefits based on average earnings and years of service. The plans are described in Note 12.

**Required:**
1. Are FedEx's pension plans overfunded or underfunded?
2. FedEx reports three actuarial assumptions used in its pension calculations. Did the reported changes in those assumptions from 2003 to 2004 increase or decrease the projected benefit obligation? Why?

**Real World Case 17–9**
Pension amendment
● LO5 LO8

Charles Rubin is a 30-year employee of **General Motors**. Charles was pleased with recent negotiations between his employer and the United Auto Workers. Among other favorable provisions of the new agreement, the pact also includes a 13% increase in pension payments for workers under 62 with 30 years of service who retire during the agreement. Although the elimination of a cap on outside income earned by retirees has been generally viewed as an incentive for older workers to retire, Charles sees promise for his dream of becoming a part-time engineering consultant after retirement. What has caught Charles's attention is the following excerpt from an article in *the financial press:*

> **General Motors Corp.** will record a $170 million charge due to increases in retirement benefits for hourly United Auto Workers employees.
>
> The charge stems from GM's new tentative labor contract with the UAW. According to a filing with the Securities and Exchange Commission, the charge amounts to 22 cents a share and is tied to the earnings of GM's Hughes Electronics unit.
>
> The company warned that its "unfunded pension obligation and pension expense are expected to be unfavorably impacted as a result of the recently completed labor negotiations."

Taking advantage of an employee stock purchase plan, Charles has become an active GM stockholder as well as employee. His stockholder side is moderately concerned by the article's reference to the unfavorable impact of the recently completed labor negotiations.

**Required:**
1. When a company modifies its pension benefits the way General Motors did, what name do we give the added cost? How is it accounted for?
2. What does GM mean when it says its "unfunded pension obligation and pension expense are expected to be unfavorably impacted as a result of the recently completed labor negotiations"?

**Real World Case 17–10**
Effect of pensions on earnings; quest for profits
● LO6

While doing some online research concerning a possible investment in **Qwest Communications International** you spot a February 19, 2004, news release that indicates results less than expectations. Your enthusiasm is dampened more when you access Qwest's 2003 annual report and notice a net loss from continuing operations for the year of $1.3 billion. This prompts you to dig deeper for what might have contributed to the reported numbers. You come across an article that mentions in passing that a representative of Morgan Stanley had indicated that Qwest's pension plan had benefited its reported earnings. Curiosity piqued, you search further.

**Required:**

1. Can the net periodic pension "cost" cause a company's reported earnings to increase?
2. Access EDGAR on the Internet at **www.sec.gov**, or through EdgarScan at **edgarscan.pwcglobal.com**. Find Qwest's 2003 annual report and look at the income statement. What if anything is indicated concerning the effect of pensions on earnings?
3. Look at the disclosure notes. What effect of the pension plan on earnings does the note on employee benefits indicate? What is the major contributor to this effect?
4. Companies must report the actuarial assumptions used to make estimates concerning pension plans. Do any of the changes reported by Qwest impact the effect of the pension plan on reported earnings? Explain.

**Research Case 17–11**
Researching the way employee benefits are tested on the CPA Exam; retrieving information from the Internet

● LO9 LO10 LO11

The board of examiners of the American Institute of Certified Public Accountants (AICPA) is responsible for preparing the CPA examination. The boards of accountancy of all 50 states, the District of Columbia, Guam, Puerto Rico, and the U.S. Virgin Islands use the examination as the primary way to measure the technical competence of CPA candidates. The content for each examination section is specified by the AICPA and described in outline form.

**Required:**

1. Access the AICPA web site on the Internet. The web address is **www.aicpa.org**.
2. Access the CPA exam section within the site. Locate the exam content portion of the section.
3. In which of the four separately graded sections of the exam are postretirement benefits tested?
4. From the AICPA site, access the Board of Accounting for your state. What are the education requirements in your state to sit for the CPA exam?

**Analysis Case 17–12**
Reporting postretirement benefits

**FedEx Corporation**

● LO9 LO10 LO11

Refer to the financial statements and related disclosure notes of **FedEx Corporation** in Appendix B at the end of this text.

**Required:**

1. What types of postretirement benefits other than pensions does FedEx provide its retirees? What are the eligibility requirements?
2. Is the postretirement benefit plan funded? Explain.

## CPA SIMULATION 17–1

**Schachter Company**
Liabilities and Postretirement Benefits

KAPLAN CPA Review

Test your knowledge of the concepts discussed in this chapter, practice critical professional skills necessary for career success, and prepare for the computer-based CPA exam by accessing our CPA simulations at the text website: **www.mhhe.com/spiceland4e**.

The Schachter Company simulation tests your knowledge of contingencies, bonds, leases, deferred income taxes, transferring accounts receivables in a secured borrowing, and postretirement benefits.

As on the CPA exam itself, you will be asked to use tools including a spreadsheet, a calculator, and professional accounting standards to conduct research, derive solutions, and communicate conclusions related to these issues in a simulated environment headed by the following interactive tabs:

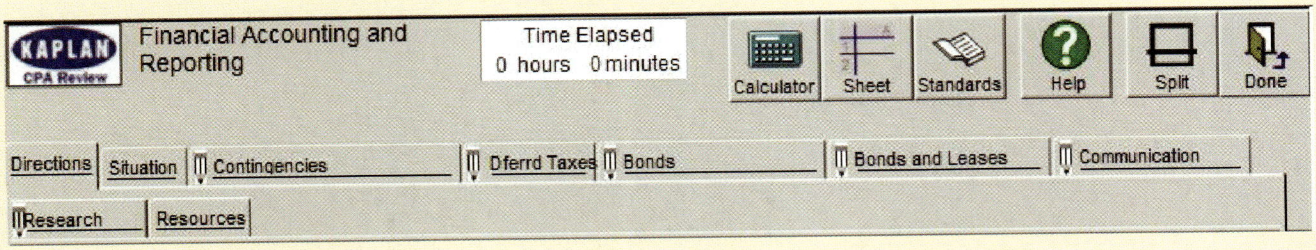


Specific tasks in the simulation include:

- Demonstrating an understanding of financial reporting effects of various contingencies.
- Applying judgment in deciding the deferred tax effects of a variety of transactions.
- Calculating interest and liabilities relating to bonds and leases.
- Communicating the way to calculate financial ratios related to liabilities and what they attempt to measure.
- Researching appropriate accounting for the transfer of accounts receivable to a third party.

**Pages 886–891 have been intentionally omitted.**

**Pages 886–891 have been intentionally omitted.**

**Pages 886–891 have been intentionally omitted.**

**Pages 886–891 have been intentionally omitted.**

**Pages 886–891 have been intentionally omitted.**

**Pages 886–891 have been intentionally omitted.**

18

CHAPTER

# Shareholders' Equity

## OVERVIEW

We turn our attention from liabilities, which represent the creditors' interests in the assets of a corporation, to the shareholders' residual interest in those assets. The discussions distinguish between the two basic sources of shareholders' equity: (1) *invested* capital and (2) *earned* capital. We explore the expansion of corporate capital through the issuance of shares and the contraction caused by the retirement of shares or the purchase of treasury shares. In our discussions of retained earnings, we examine cash dividends, property dividends, stock dividends, and stock splits.

## LEARNING OBJECTIVES

**After studying this chapter, you should be able to:**

- LO1 Describe the components of shareholders' equity and explain how they are reported in a statement of shareholders' equity.
- LO2 Describe comprehensive income and its components.
- LO3 Record the issuance of shares when sold for cash, for noncash consideration, and by share purchase contract.
- LO4 Describe what occurs when shares are retired and how the retirement is recorded.
- LO5 Distinguish between accounting for retired shares and for treasury shares.
- LO6 Describe retained earnings and distinguish it from paid-in capital.
- LO7 Explain the basis of corporate dividends, including the similarities and differences between cash and property dividends.
- LO8 Explain stock dividends and stock splits and how they are accounted for.

# FINANCIAL REPORTING CASE

## Temple-Inland, Inc.

Finally, you have some uninterrupted time to get back on the net. Earlier today you noticed on the Internet that the market price of Temple-Inland's common stock was up almost 10%. You've been eager to look into why but have had one meeting after another all day.

Temple-Inland, based in Austin, Texas, manufactures corrugated packaging and building products and offers financial services. The company employs 19,500 nationwide. You've been a stockholder of Temple-Inland since the beginning of the year when your home improvement contractor bragged to you about the company's products. The dividends of 36 cents a share that you receive quarterly are nice, but that's not why you bought the stock; you were convinced at the time that the stock price was poised to rise rapidly. That hasn't really happened. A few well-placed clicks of the mouse and you come across the following news article:

> AUSTIN, Texas, Feb. 4, 2005 (Business Wire)—At its regularly scheduled meeting, the Board of Directors today declared a regular quarterly dividend of $0.45 per common share, payable March 15, 2005, to shareholders of record March 1, 2005.
>
> This $0.45 per share dividend is a 25% increase over the prior quarterly dividend of $0.36 per share, and is the third consecutive annual dividend increase. Temple-Inland paid a special dividend of $1.00 per share in December 2004.
>
> Temple-Inland, Inc. also announced today that its Board of Directors has authorized the repurchase of up to six million shares of its common stock (12 million shares after considering the stock split discussed below). This represents over 10% of the company's current outstanding shares. The repurchases will be accomplished from time to time through open market or privately negotiated transactions.
>
> In addition to the dividend increase and share repurchase authorization, the Board of Directors approved a two-for-one stock split effected in the form of a stock dividend for shareholders of record on March 1, 2005. For every one share of the Company's common stock held on the record date, the holder will receive one additional share. The additional shares resulting from the split will be distributed on April 1, 2005.

*Source:* "Temple-Inland increases dividend, approves share repurchases and announces stock split," *Business Wire*, February, 4, 2005.

**By the time you finish this chapter, you should be able to respond appropriately to the questions posed in this case. Compare your response to the solution provided at the end of the chapter.**

### QUESTIONS

1. Do you think the stock price increase is related to Temple-Inland's share repurchase plan? (page 909)
2. What are Temple-Inland's choices in accounting for the share repurchases? (page 910)
3. What effect does the quarterly cash dividend of 45 cents a share have on Temple-Inland's assets? Its liabilities? Its shareholders' equity? (page 915)
4. What effect did the stock split have on Temple-Inland's assets? Its liabilities? Its shareholders' equity? (page 918)

# PART A THE NATURE OF SHAREHOLDERS' EQUITY

A corporation raises money to fund its business operations by some mix of debt and equity financing. In earlier chapters, we examined debt financing in the form of notes, bonds, leases, and other liabilities. Amounts representing those liabilities denote *creditors' interest* in the company's assets. Now we focus on various forms of equity financing. Specifically, in this chapter we consider transactions that affect shareholders' equity—those accounts that represent the *ownership interests* of shareholders.

● LO1

In principle, shareholders' equity is a relatively straightforward concept. Shareholders' equity is a residual amount—what's left over after creditor claims have been subtracted from assets (in other words, net assets). You probably recall the residual nature of shareholders' equity from the basic accounting equation:

**Net assets equal shareholders' equity.**

$$\underbrace{\text{Assets} - \text{Liabilities}}_{\text{Net Assets}} = \text{Shareholders' equity}$$

**Shareholders' equity accounts denote the ownership interests of shareholders.**

Ownership interests of shareholders arise primarily from two sources: (1) amounts *invested* by shareholders in the corporation and (2) amounts *earned* by the corporation on behalf of its shareholders. These two sources are reported as (1) paid-in capital and (2) retained earnings.

Despite being a seemingly clear-cut concept, shareholders' equity and its component accounts often are misunderstood and misinterpreted. As we explore the transactions that affect shareholders' equity and its component accounts, try not to allow yourself to be overwhelmed by unfamiliar terminology or to be overly concerned with precise account titles. Terminology pertaining to shareholders' equity accounts is notoriously diverse. To give you one example—retained earnings is reported variously as *retained income* (**Smucker**), *reinvested earnings* (**Verizon**), *earnings reinvested* (**ExxonMobil**), *earnings retained in the business* (**Campbell Soup**), *retained earnings reinvested and employed in the business* (**L.S. Starret Company**), *accumulated* equity (**Federated Department Stores**), and *accumulated earnings* (**Intel**). Every shareholders' equity account has several aliases. Indeed, shareholders' equity itself is often referred to as *stockholders' equity, shareowners' equity, shareholders' investment,* and many other similar titles.

**GAAP permits many choices in accounting for transactions affecting shareholders' equity.**

Complicating matters, transactions that affect shareholders' equity are influenced by corporation laws of individual states in which companies are located. And, as we see later, generally accepted accounting principles provide companies with considerable latitude when choosing accounting methods in this area.

**Legal requirements and disclosure objectives make it preferable to separate a corporation's capital into several separate shareholders' equity accounts.**

Keeping this perspective in mind while you study the chapter should aid you in understanding the essential concepts. At a very basic level, each transaction we examine can be viewed simply as an increase or decrease in shareholders' equity, per se, without regard to specific shareholders' equity accounts. In fact, for a business organized as a single proprietorship, all capital changes are recorded in a single owner's equity account. The same concepts apply to a corporation. But for corporations, additional considerations make it desirable to separate owners' equity into several separate shareholders' equity accounts. These additional considerations—legal requirements and disclosure objectives—are discussed in later sections of this chapter. So, as you study the separate effects of transactions on retained earnings and specific paid-in capital accounts, you may find it helpful to ask yourself frequently "What is the net effect of this transaction on shareholders' equity?" or, equivalently, "By how much are net assets (assets minus liabilities) affected by this transaction?"

## Financial Reporting Overview

Before we examine the events that underlie specific shareholders' equity accounts, let's overview how individual accounts relate to each other. The condensed balance sheet of Exposition Corporation, a hypothetical company, in Graphic 18–1 provides that perspective.

**GRAPHIC 18–1**
Detailed Shareholders' Equity Presentation

**EXPOSITION CORPORATION**
**Balance Sheet**
**December 31, 2006**

($ in millions)

**Assets**
$3,000

**Liabilities**
$1,000

**Shareholders' Equity**

| | | |
|---|---|---|
| **Paid-in capital:** | | |
| Capital stock (par): | | |
| Preferred stock, 10%, $10 par, cumulative, nonparticipating | $100 | |
| Common stock, $1 par | 55 | |
| Common stock dividends distributable | 5 | |
| Additional paid-in capital: | | |
| Paid-in capital—excess of par, preferred | 50 | |
| Paid-in capital—excess of par, common | 300 | |
| Receivable from share purchase contract | (40) | |
| Paid-in capital—reacquired shares | 8 | |
| Paid-in capital—conversion of bonds | 7 | |
| Paid-in capital—stock options | 9 | |
| Paid-in capital—stock award plan | 5 | |
| Paid-in capital—lapse of stock options | 1 | |
| Total paid-in capital | | $ 500 |
| **Retained earnings (Note A)** | | 1,670 |
| **Accumulated other comprehensive income:** | | |
| Net unrealized holding gains (losses) on investments | (85) | |
| Net unrecognized loss on pensions | (75) | |
| Deferred gains (losses) from derivatives* | (4) | |
| Gains (losses) from foreign currency translation** | –0– | (164) |
| **Treasury stock (at cost)** | | (6) |
| Total shareholders' equity | | $2,000 |

**Note A:** Assets represented by $300 million of retained earnings are restricted from distribution as dividends in order to facilitate expansion of manufacturing facilities.

Assets *minus* Liabilities *equals* Shareholders' Equity.

The primary source of paid-in capital is the investment made by shareholders when buying preferred and common stock.

Several other events affect paid-in capital.

Retained earnings represents earned capital.

*When a derivative designated as a cash flow hedge is adjusted to fair value, the gain or loss is deferred as a component of other comprehensive income and included in earnings later, at the same time as earnings are affected by the hedged transaction (described in Appendix A at the end of the book).
**Gains or losses from changes in foreign currency exchange rates. This item is discussed elsewhere in your accounting curriculum. The amount could be an addition to or reduction in shareholders' equity. Also see the Global Perspective on page 894.

Graphic 18–1 depicts a rather comprehensive situation. It's unlikely that any one company would have shareholders' equity from all of these sources at any one time. Remember that, at this point, our objective is only to get a general perspective of the items constituting shareholders' equity. You should, however, note a few aspects of the statement shown in Graphic 18–1. First, the four components of Exposition Corporation's shareholders' equity are paid-in capital, retained earnings, accumulated other comprehensive income, and treasury stock.

## PAID-IN CAPITAL

The two primary components of shareholders' equity are paid-in capital and retained earnings.

**Paid-in capital** consists primarily of amounts invested by shareholders when they purchase shares of stock from the corporation. In addition, amounts sometimes are invested (or disinvested) by others on behalf of the shareholders. For Exposition Corporation, shareholders invested $470 million ($100 + 55 + 5 + 300 + 50 − $40). An additional $30 million

**GLOBAL PERSPECTIVE**

Ours is truly a global economy. Most large U.S. companies are, in fact, multinational companies that may derive only a fraction of their revenues in this country. As a result, many operations are located abroad and foreign operations frequently are denominated in the currency of the foreign country (Japanese yen, Swiss franc, Euro, and so on). When exchange rates change, the dollar equivalent of the foreign currency changes.

Currency rate changes that affect cash flows because they require settlement in a currency other than the entity's functional currency result in foreign currency transaction adjustments. These are reported as gains and losses in the earnings of the period the changes occur. Those that do not require settlement and thus don't affect cash flows are translation adjustments. These are accumulated in a separate component of shareholders' equity: Other comprehensive income.

($8 + 7 + 9 + 5 + 1) of paid-in capital arose from financing activities, bringing the total to $500 million. Later in this chapter, we consider in more detail the events and transactions that affect paid-in capital.

## RETAINED EARNINGS

**Retained earnings** is reported as a single amount, $1,670 million, but a disclosure note provides additional information about a specific restriction on dividends.

● LO2

## ACCUMULATED OTHER COMPREHENSIVE INCOME

Some accounts can be viewed as contra-shareholders' equity accounts.

Also notice that shareholders' equity of Exposition Corporation is adjusted for three events that are not included in net income and so don't affect retained earnings but are part of "other comprehensive income" and therefore are included as separate components of shareholders' equity.[1] **Comprehensive income** provides a more expansive view of the change in shareholders' equity than does traditional net income. It is the total *nonowner* change in equity for a reporting period. In fact, it encompasses all changes in equity other than those from transactions with owners. Transactions between the corporation and its shareholders primarily include dividends and the sale or purchase of shares of the company's stock. Most nonowner changes are reported in the income statement. So, the changes other than those that are part of traditional net income are the ones reported as "other comprehensive income."

Comprehensive income extends our view of income beyond conventional net income to include four types of gains and losses that traditionally haven't been included in income statements:

Comprehensive income includes net income as well as other gains and losses that change shareholders' equity but are not included in traditional net income.

1. Net holding gains (losses) on investments.
2. Net unrecognized loss on pensions.
3. Deferred gains (losses) from derivatives.
4. Gains (losses) from foreign currency translation.

The first of these are the gains and losses on securities "available-for-sale" that occur when the fair values of these investments increase or decrease. As you learned in Chapter 12, these gains and losses aren't included in earnings until they are realized through the sale of the securities but are considered a component of *other comprehensive income* in the meantime. Similarly, as we discussed in Chapter 17, net unrecognized losses on pensions sometimes reduce other comprehensive income but not net income. You have not yet studied the third and fourth potential components of other comprehensive income. As described in Appendix A, "Derivatives" at the back of this textbook, when a derivative designated as a "*cash flow hedge*" is adjusted to fair value, the gain or loss is deferred as a component of other comprehensive income and included in earnings later, at the same time as earnings are affected by the hedged transaction. Gains and losses from changes in foreign currency ex-

[1]Comprehensive income was introduced in Chapter 4 and revisited in Chapter 12.

change rates are discussed elsewhere in your accounting curriculum, but also are included in other comprehensive income but not net income.

Other comprehensive income shares another trait with net income. Just as net income is reported periodically and also on a cumulative basis as part of retained earnings, other comprehensive income, too, is reported periodically as it is created and also as **accumulated other comprehensive income** in the balance sheet along with retained earnings. In other words, we report two attributes of other comprehensive income: (1) components of comprehensive income *created during the reporting period* and (2) the comprehensive income *accumulated* over the current and prior periods.

The first attribute—components of comprehensive income *created during the reporting period*—can be reported either as (a) an additional section of the income statement, (b) part of the statement of shareholders' equity, or (c) a separate statement, usually included in the financial statements in a disclosure note. Regardless of the placement a company chooses, the presentation is similar. It will report net income, other components of comprehensive income, and total comprehensive income, similar to the presentation in Graphic 18–2. Note that each component is reported net of its related income tax expense or income tax benefit.

**GRAPHIC 18–2**
Comprehensive Income

| | | ($ in millions) |
|---|---|---|
| Net income | | $xxx |
| Other comprehensive income: | | |
| Net unrealized holding gains (losses) from investments (net of tax)* | $ x | |
| Gains (losses) from and amendments to postretirement benefit plans (net of tax)† | (x) | |
| Deferred gains (losses) from derivatives (net of tax)‡ | (x) | |
| Gains (losses) from foreign currency translation (net of tax)§ | x | xx |
| Comprehensive income | | $xxx |

*Changes in the market value of securities available-for-sale (described in Chapter 12).
†Gains and losses due to revising assumptions or market returns differing from expectations and prior service cost from amending the plan (described in Chapter 17).
‡When a derivative designated as a cash flow hedge is adjusted to fair value, the gain or loss is deferred as a component of comprehensive income and included in earnings later, at the same time as earnings are affected by the hedged transaction (described in the Derivatives Appendix to the text).
§Gains or losses from changes in foreign currency exchange rates. The amount could be an addition to or reduction in shareholders' equity. (This item is discussed elsewhere in your accounting curriculum.)

**Comprehensive income includes net income as well as other gains and losses that change shareholders' equity but are not included in traditional net income.**

The second measure—the comprehensive income *accumulated* over the current and prior periods—is reported as a separate component of shareholders' equity following retained earnings, similar to the presentation by Exposition Corporation in Graphic 18-1. Note that amounts reported here—accumulated other comprehensive income—represent the *cumulative* sum of the changes in each component created during each reporting period (Graphic 18–2) throughout all prior years.

## TREASURY STOCK

We discuss the final component of shareholders' equity—treasury stock—later in the chapter. It indicates that some of the shares previously sold were bought back by the corporation from shareholders.

You seldom if ever will see this degree of detail reported in the presentation of paid-in capital. Instead, companies keep track of individual additional paid-in capital accounts in company records but ordinarily report these amounts as a single subtotal—additional paid-in capital. Pertinent rights and privileges of various securities outstanding such as dividend and liquidation preferences, call and conversion information, and voting rights are summarized in disclosure notes.[2] The shareholders' equity portion of the balance sheet of **Southwest Airlines,** shown in Graphic 18–3 is a typical presentation format.

**Ordinarily, less detail is reported than is kept in company records.**

[2] "Disclosure of Information about Capital Structure," *Statement of Financial Accounting Standards No. 129* (Norwalk, Conn.: FASB, 1997).

**GRAPHIC 18–3**

Typical Presentation Format—Southwest Airlines

Details of each class of stock are reported on the face of the balance sheet or in disclosure notes.

**SOUTHWEST AIRLINES, INC.**
**Balance Sheet**
**[Shareholders' Equity Section]**
($ in millions)

| | 2004 | 2003 |
|---|---|---|
| **Stockholders' equity:** | | |
| Common stock, $1.00 par value: 2,000,000,000 shares authorized; 790,181,982 and 789,390,678 shares issued in 2004 and 2003, respectively | 790 | 789 |
| Capital in excess of par value | 299 | 258 |
| Retained earnings | 4,089 | 3,883 |
| Accumulated other comprehensive income | 417 | 122 |
| Treasury stock, at cost: 5,199,192 shares in 2004 | (71) | — |
| Total stockholders' equity | 5,524 | 5,052 |

● LO1

*A statement of shareholders' equity* reports the transactions that cause changes in its shareholders' equity account balances.

The balance sheet reports annual balances of shareholders' equity accounts. However, companies also should disclose the sources of the changes in those accounts.[3] This is the purpose of the **statement of shareholders' equity**. To illustrate, Graphic 18–4 on the next page shows how Southwest Airlines reported the changes in its shareholders' equity balances (shown in Graphic 18–3).

The changes that Southwest Airlines's statements of shareholders' equity reveal are net income and two other items of comprehensive income, the purchase of treasury stock and the issuance of common stock.

## The Corporate Organization

A company may be organized in any of three ways: (1) a single proprietorship, (2) a partnership, or (3) a corporation. In your introductory accounting course, you studied each form. In this course we focus exclusively on the corporate form of organization.

Corporations are the dominant form of business organization.

Most well-known companies, such as **Microsoft**, **IBM**, and **General Motors**, are corporations. Also, many smaller companies—even one-owner businesses—are corporations. Although fewer in number than proprietorships and partnerships, in terms of business volume, corporations are the predominant form of business organization.

Accounting for most transactions is the same regardless of the form of business organization.

In most respects, transactions are accounted for in the same way regardless of the form of business organization. Assets and liabilities are unaffected by the way a company is organized. The exception is the method of accounting for capital, the ownership interest in the company. Rather than recording all changes in ownership interests in a single capital account for each owner, as we do for single proprietorships and partnerships, we use the several capital accounts overviewed in the previous section to record those changes for a corporation. Before discussing how we account for specific ownership changes, let's look at the characteristics of a corporation that make this form of organization distinctive and require special accounting treatment.

### LIMITED LIABILITY

A corporation is a separate legal entity—separate and distinct from its owners.

The owners are not personally liable for debts of a corporation. Unlike a proprietorship or a partnership, a corporation is a separate legal entity, responsible for its own debts. Shareholders' liability is limited to the amounts they invest in the company when they purchase shares (unless the shareholder also is an officer of the corporation). The limited liability of shareholders is perhaps the single most important advantage of corporate organization. In other forms of business, creditors may look to the personal assets of owners for satisfaction of business debt.

[3]"Omnibus Opinion," *APB Opinion No. 12* (New York: AICPA, 1967).

**GRAPHIC 18–4** Changes in Stockholders' Equity—Southwest Airlines

**SOUTHWEST AIRLINES**
**Consolidated Statements of Stockholders' Equity**

| (In millions, except per share amounts) | Common Stock | Capital in Excess of Par Value | Retained Earnings | Accumulated Other Comprehensive Income (Loss) | Treasury Stock | Total |
|---|---|---|---|---|---|---|
| **Balance at December 31, 2001** | **$767** | **$ 51** | **$3,228** | **$ (32)** | **$ —** | **$4,014** |
| Issuance of common stock pursuant to employee stock plans | 10 | 47 | — | — | — | 57 |
| Tax benefit of options exercised | — | 38 | — | — | — | 38 |
| Cash dividends, $ .018 per share | — | — | (14) | — | — | (14) |
| *Comprehensive income (loss)* | | | | | | |
| Net income | — | — | 241 | — | — | 241 |
| Unrealized gain on derivative instruments | — | — | — | 88 | — | 88 |
| Other | — | — | — | (2) | — | (2) |
| Total comprehensive income | | | | | | 327 |
| **Balance at December 31, 2002** | **777** | **136** | **3,455** | **54** | **—** | **4,422** |
| Issuance of common stock pursuant to employee stock plans | 12 | 81 | — | — | — | 93 |
| Tax benefit of options exercised | — | 41 | — | — | — | 41 |
| Cash dividends, $ .018 per share | — | — | (14) | — | — | (14 ) |
| *Comprehensive income (loss)* | | | | | | |
| Net income | — | — | 442 | — | — | 442 |
| Unrealized gain on derivative instruments | — | — | — | 66 | — | 66 |
| Other | — | — | — | 2 | — | 2 |
| Total comprehensive income | | | | | | 510 |
| **Balance at December 31, 2003** | **789** | **258** | **3,883** | **122** | **—** | **5,052** |
| Purchase of shares of treasury stock | — | — | — | — | (246) | (246) |
| Issuance of common and treasury stock pursuant to employee stock plans | 1 | 6 | (93) | — | 175 | 89 |
| Tax benefit of options exercised | — | 35 | — | — | — | 35 |
| Cash dividends, $.018 per share | — | — | (14) | — | — | (14) |
| *Comprehensive income (loss)* | | | | | | |
| Net income | — | — | 313 | — | — | 313 |
| Unrealized gain on derivative instruments | — | — | — | 293 | — | 293 |
| Other | — | — | — | 2 | — | 2 |
| Total comprehensive income | | | | | | 608 |
| **Balance at December 31, 2004** | **$790** | **$299** | **$4,089** | **$417** | **$ (71)** | **$5,524** |

## EASE OF RAISING CAPITAL

A corporation is better suited to raising capital than is a proprietorship or a partnership. All companies may raise capital by operating at a profit or by borrowing. However, attracting equity capital is easier for a corporation. Because corporations sell ownership interest in the form of shares of stock, ownership rights are easily transferred. An investor can sell his/her ownership interest at any time and without affecting the corporation or its operations.

**Ownership interest in a corporation is easily transferred.**

From the viewpoint of a potential investor, another favorable aspect of investing in a corporation is the lack of mutual agency. Individual partners in a partnership have the power to bind the business to a contract. Therefore, an investor in a partnership must be careful regarding the character and business savvy of fellow co-owners. On the other hand, shareholders' participation in the affairs of a corporation is limited to voting at shareholders' meetings (unless the shareholder also is a manager). Consequently, a shareholder needn't exercise the same degree of care that partners must in selecting co-owners.

**Shareholders do not have a mutual agency relationship.**

Obviously, then, a corporation offers advantages over the other forms of organization, particularly in its ability to raise investment capital. As you might guess, though, these benefits do not come without a price.

## DISADVANTAGES

Corporations are subject to expensive government regulation.

Paperwork! To protect the rights of those who buy a corporation's stock or who loan money to a corporation, the state in which the company is incorporated and the federal government impose expensive reporting requirements. Primarily the required paperwork is intended to ensure adequate disclosure of information needed by investors and creditors.

Corporations create double taxation.

You read earlier that corporations are separate legal entities. As such, they also are separate taxable entities. Often this causes what is referred to as *double taxation.* Corporations first pay income taxes on their earnings. Then, when those earnings are distributed as cash dividends, shareholders pay personal income taxes on the previously taxed earnings. Proprietorships and partnerships are not taxed at the business level; each owner's share of profits is taxed only as personal income.

## TYPES OF CORPORATIONS

When referring to corporations in this text, we are referring to corporations formed by private individuals for the purpose of generating profits. These corporations raise capital by selling stock. There are, however, other types of corporations.

Not-for-profit corporations may be owned:
1. By the public sector.
2. By a governmental unit.

Some corporations such as churches, hospitals, universities, and charities do not sell stock and are not organized for profit. Also, some not-for-profit corporations are government-owned—the **Federal Deposit Insurance Corporation (FDIC)**, for instance. Accounting for not-for-profit corporations is discussed elsewhere in the accounting curriculum.

Corporations organized for profit may be:
1. Publicly held and traded:
   a. On an exchange.
   b. Over-the-counter.
2. Privately held.

Corporations organized for profit may be publicly held or privately (or closely) held. The stock of publicly held corporations is available for purchase by the general public. You can buy shares of **General Electric**, **Ford Motor Company**, or **ExxonMobil** through a stockbroker. These shares are traded on the New York Stock Exchange. Other publicly held stock, like **Intel** and **Microsoft**, are available through Nasdaq (National Association of Securities Dealers Automated Quotations).

Privately held companies' shares are held by only a few individuals and are not available to the general public.

On the other hand, shares of privately held companies are owned by only a few individuals (perhaps a family) and are not available to the general public. Corporations whose stock is privately held do not need to register those shares with the Securities and Exchange Commission and are spared the voluminous, annual reporting requirements of the SEC. Of course, new sources of equity financing are limited when shares are privately held, as is the market for selling existing shares.

Frequently, companies begin as smaller, privately held corporations. Then as success broadens opportunities for expansion, the corporation goes public. For example, in 2004 **Google** decided to take public the privately held company. The result was the largest technology initial public offering ever.

## HYBRID ORGANIZATIONS

A corporation can elect to comply with a special set of tax rules and be designated an **S corporation**. S corporations have characteristics of both regular corporations and partnerships. Owners have the limited liability protection of a corporation, but income and expenses are passed through to the owners as in a partnership, avoiding double taxation.

Two relatively recent business structures have evolved in response to liability issues and tax treatment—limited liability companies and limited liability partnerships.

A **limited liability company** offers several advantages. Owners are not liable for the debts of the business, except to the extent of their investment. Unlike a limited partnership, all members of a limited liability company can be involved with managing the business without losing liability protection. Like an S corporation, income and expenses are passed through to the owners as in a partnership, avoiding double taxation, but there are no limitations on the number of owners as in an S corporation.

A **limited liability partnership** is similar to a limited liability company, except it doesn't offer all the liability protection available in the limited liability company structure. Partners are liable for their own actions but not entirely liable for the actions of other partners.

## THE MODEL BUSINESS CORPORATION ACT

Corporations are formed in accordance with the corporation laws of individual states. State laws are not uniform, but share many similarities, thanks to the widespread adoption of the

**Model Business Corporation Act.**[4] This act is designed to serve as a guide to states in the development of their corporation statutes. It presently serves as the model for the majority of states.

**The *Model Business Corporation Act* serves as the model for the corporation statutes of most states.**

State laws regarding the nature of shares that can be authorized, the issuance and repurchase of those shares, and conditions for distributions to shareholders obviously influence actions of corporations. Naturally, differences among state laws affect how we account for many of the shareholders' equity transactions discussed in this chapter. For that reason, we will focus on the normal case, as described by the Model Business Corporation Act, and note situations where variations in state law might require different accounting. Your goal is not to learn diverse procedures caused by peculiarities of state laws, but to understand the broad concepts of accounting for shareholders' equity that can be applied to any specific circumstance.

**Variations among state laws influence GAAP pertaining to shareholders' equity transactions.**

The process of incorporating a business is similar in all states. The **articles of incorporation** (sometimes called the *corporate charter*) describe (a) the nature of the firm's business activities, (b) the shares to be issued, and (c) the composition of the initial **board of directors**. The board of directors establishes corporate policies and appoints officers who manage the corporation.

At least some of the shares authorized by the articles of incorporation are sold at the inception of the corporation. Frequently, the initial shareholders include members of the board of directors or officers (who may be one and the same). Ultimately, it is the corporation's shareholders that control the company. Shareholders are the owners of the corporation. By voting their shares, it is they who determine the makeup of the board of directors—who in turn appoint officers, who in turn manage the company.

Shareholders' investment in a corporation ordinarily is referred to as paid-in capital. In the next section, we examine the methods normally used to maintain records of shareholders' investment and to report such paid-in capital in financial statements.

# PAID-IN CAPITAL

**PART B**

## Fundamental Share Rights

In reading the previous paragraphs, you noted that corporations raise equity funds by selling shares of the corporation. Shareholders are the owners of a corporation. If a corporation has only one class of shares, no designation of the shares is necessary, but they typically are labeled *common shares*. Ownership rights held by common shareholders, unless specifically withheld by agreement with the shareholders, are:

a. The right to vote on matters that come before the shareholders, including the election of corporate directors. Each share represents one vote.
b. The right to share in profits when dividends are declared. The percentage of shares owned by a shareholder determines his/her share of dividends distributed.
c. The right to share in the distribution of assets if the company is liquidated. The percentage of shares owned by a shareholder determines his/her share of assets after creditors and preferred shareholders are paid.

Another right sometimes given to common shareholders is the right to maintain one's percentage share of ownership when new shares are issued. This is referred to as a *preemptive right*. Each shareholder is offered the opportunity to buy a percentage of any new shares issued equal to the percentage of shares he/she owns at the time. In most states this right must be specifically granted; in others, it is presumed unless contractually excluded.

This right usually is withheld because of the inconvenience it causes corporations when they issue new shares. The exclusion of the preemptive right ordinarily is inconsequential because few shareholders own enough stock to be concerned about their ownership percentage.

**For reasons of practicality, the preemptive right usually is excluded.**

[4] *Revised Model Business Corporation Act,* the American Bar Association, 1994.

## Distinguishing Classes of Shares

It is not uncommon for a firm to have more than one, and perhaps several, classes of shares, each with different rights and limitations. To attract investors, companies have devised quite a variety of ownership securities.

If more than one class of shares is authorized by the articles of incorporation, the specific rights of each (for instance, the right to vote, residual interest in assets, and dividend rights) must be stated. Also, some designation must be given to distinguish each class.

Some of the distinguishing designations often used are:

1. Class A, class B, and so on (**Tyson Foods**).
2. Preferred stock, common stock, and class B stock (**Hershey Foods**).
3. Common and preferred (**Hewlett Packard**).
4. Capital stock (**Reader's Digest**).
5. Common and serial preferred (**Smucker**).

Terminology varies in the way companies differentiate among share types.

It often is difficult to predict the rights and privileges of shares on the basis of whether they are labeled *common* or *preferred.*

In your introductory study of accounting, you probably became most familiar with the common stock–preferred stock distinction. That terminology has deep roots in tradition. Early English corporate charters provided for shares that were preferred over others as to dividends and liquidation rights. These provisions were reflected in early American corporation laws. But as our economy developed, corporations increasingly felt the need for innovative ways of attracting investment capital. The result has been a gradual development of a wide range of share classifications that cannot easily be identified by these historical designations.

To reflect the flexibility that now exists in the creation of equity shares, the Model Business Corporation Act, and thus many state statutes, no longer mention the words common and preferred. But the influence of tradition lingers. Most corporations still designate shares as common or preferred. For consistency with practice, the illustrations you study in this chapter use those designations. As you consider the examples, keep in mind that the same concepts apply regardless of the language used to distinguish shares.

### TYPICAL RIGHTS OF PREFERRED SHARES

An issue of shares with certain preferences or features that distinguish it from the class of shares customarily called common shares may be assigned any of the several labels mentioned earlier. Very often the distinguishing designation is **preferred shares**. The special rights of preferred shareholders usually include one or both of the following:

a. Preferred shareholders typically have a preference to a specified amount of dividends (stated dollar amount per share or % of par value per share). That is, if the board of directors declares dividends, preferred shareholders will receive the designated dividend before any dividends are paid to common shareholders.
b. Preferred shareholders customarily have a preference (over common shareholders) as to the distribution of assets in the event the corporation is dissolved.

Shares may be:
1. *Convertible* into a specified number of another class of shares.
2. *Redeemable* at the option of:
   a. Shareholders.
   b. The corporation.

Preferred shareholders sometimes have the **right of conversion** which allows them to exchange shares of preferred stock for common stock at a specified conversion ratio. Alternatively, a **redemption privilege** might allow preferred shareholders the option, under specified conditions, to return their shares for a predetermined redemption price. For instance, in 2003, **Xerox Corporation** had outstanding 6.4 million shares of convertible preferred stock. Preferred shareholders have preference over common stockholders in dividends and liquidation rights. Each preferred share is convertible into common shares or an equivalent amount of cash. Similarly, shares may be redeemable at the option of the issuing corporation (sometimes referred to as *callable*).

Preferred shares may be **cumulative** or **noncumulative**. Typically, preferred shares are cumulative, which means that if the specified dividend is not paid in a given year, the unpaid dividends (called *dividends in arrears*) accumulate and must be made up in a later dividend year before any dividends are paid on common shares.

Preferred shares may be **participating** or **nonparticipating**. A participating feature allows preferred shareholders to receive additional dividends beyond the stated amount. If the preferred shares are fully participating, the distribution of dividends to common and preferred shareholders is a pro rata allocation based on the relative par value amounts of common and preferred stock outstanding. Participating preferred stock, previously quite common, is rare today.

**If preferred shares are not cumulative, dividends not declared in any given year need never be paid.**

Remember that the designations of common and preferred imply no necessary rights, privileges, or limitations of the shares so designated. Such relative rights must be specified by the contract with shareholders. A corporation can create classes of preferred shares that are indistinguishable from common shares in voting rights and/or the right to participate in assets (distributed as dividends or distributed upon liquidation). Likewise, it is possible to devise classes of common shares that possess preferential rights, superior to those of preferred shares.

### IS IT EQUITY OR IS IT DEBT

You probably also can imagine an issue of preferred shares that is almost indistinguishable from a bond issue. Let's say, for instance, that preferred shares call for annual cash dividends of 10% of the par value, dividends are cumulative, and the shares must be redeemed for cash in 10 years. Although the declaration of dividends rests in the discretion of the board of directors, the contract with preferred shareholders can be worded in such a way that directors are compelled to declare dividends each year the company is profitable. For a profitable company, it would be difficult to draw the line between this issue of preferred shares and a 10%, 10-year bond issue. Even in a more typical situation, preferred shares are somewhat hybrid securities—a cross between equity and debt.

**The line between debt and equity is hard to draw.**

Sometimes the similarity to debt is even more obvious. Suppose shares are mandatorily redeemable—the company is obligated to buy back the shares at a specified future date. The fact that the company is obligated to pay cash (or other assets) at a fixed or determinable date in the future makes this financial instrument tantamount to debt. A mandatorily redeemable financial instrument must be reported in the balance sheet as a liability, not as shareholders' equity.[5] **Kmart**, for instance, reported its mandatorily redeemable preferred shares as a liability in its 2004 balance sheet.

**Mandatorily redeemable shares are classified as liabilities.**

## The Concept of Par Value

Another prevalent practice (besides labeling shares as common and preferred) that has little significance other than historical is assigning a par value to shares. The concept of par value dates back as far as the concept of owning shares of a business. Par value originally indicated the real value of shares. All shares were issued at that price.

**We have inherited the archaic concept of par value from early corporate law.**

During the late 19th and early 20th centuries, many cases of selling shares for less than par value—known as *watered shares*—received a great deal of attention and were the subject of a number of lawsuits. Investors and creditors contended that they relied on the par value as the permanent investment in the corporation and therefore net assets must always be at least that amount. Not only was par value assumed to be the amount invested by shareholders, but it also was defined by early corporation laws as the amount of net assets not available for distribution to shareholders (as dividends or otherwise).

Many companies began turning to par value shares with very low par values—often pennies—to escape the watered shares liability of issuing shares below an arbitrary par value and to limit the restrictions on distributions. This practice is common today.

**Shares with nominal par value became common to dodge elaborate statutory rules pertaining to par value shares.**

Accountants and attorneys have been aware for decades that laws pertaining to par value and legal capital not only are bewildering but fail in their intent to safeguard creditors from payments to shareholders. Actually, to the extent that creditors are led to believe that they are afforded protection, they are misled. Like the designations of common and preferred shares, the concepts of par value and legal capital have been eliminated entirely from the Model Business Corporation Act.[6]

[5] "Accounting for Certain Financial Instruments with Characteristics of Both Liabilities and Equity," *Statement of Financial Accounting Standards No. 150* (Norwalk, Conn.: FASB, 2003).

[6] *Revised Model Business Corporation Act,* the American Bar Association, 1994, official comment to Section 6.21.

Most shares continue to bear arbitrarily designated par values.

Many states already have adopted these provisions of the Model Act. But most established corporations issued shares prior to changes in the state statutes. Consequently, most companies have par value shares outstanding and continue to issue previously authorized par value shares. The evolution will be gradual to the simpler, more meaningful provisions of the Model Act.

In the meantime, accountants must be familiar with the outdated concepts of par value and legal capital in order to properly record and report transactions related to par value shares. For that reason, most of the discussion in this chapter centers around par value shares. Largely, this means only that proceeds from shareholders' investment is allocated between stated capital and additional paid-in capital. Be aware, though, that in the absence of archaic laws that prompted the creation of par value shares, there is no theoretical reason to do so.

## Accounting for the Issuance of Shares

### SHARES ISSUED FOR CASH

● LO3

When shares are sold for cash, the capital stock account (usually common or preferred) is credited for the amount representing stated capital. When shares have a designated par value, that amount denotes stated capital and is credited to the stock account. Proceeds in excess of this amount are credited to paid-in capital—excess of par.

**ILLUSTRATION 18–1**
Shares Sold for Cash

Dow Industrial sells 100,000 of its common shares, $1 par per share, for $10 per share:

| | ($ in 000s) | |
|---|---|---|
| Cash (100,000 shares at $10 price per share) | 1,000 | |
| Common stock (100,000 shares at $1 par per share) | | 100 |
| Paid-in capital—excess of par (remainder) | | 900 |

The total amount received from the sale of no-par shares is credited to the stock account.

The entire proceeds from the sale of no-par stock are deemed stated capital and recorded in the stock account. If the shares are no-par, the entry is as follows:

| | | |
|---|---|---|
| Cash (100,000 shares at $10 price per share) | 1,000 | |
| Common stock | | 1,000 |

### SHARES ISSUED ON CREDIT

**Preincorporation Subscription Agreements.** In times past, capital to finance new ventures ordinarily was raised by obtaining subscriptions for shares of the impending corporation. These preincorporation subscription agreements typically specified that the subscriber would purchase a certain number of shares if a specified amount of venture capital was obtained.

The classic method of new venture financing by subscription rarely is used today.

A difficult issue was determining what, if any, legal recourse the new company had if a subscriber defaulted. That issue seldom is encountered today. State and federal laws that require elaborate procedures for the registration of new securities make subscription agreements impractical for new ventures. Venture financing by subscription is virtually an activity of the past. Simple contracts to sell shares have replaced preincorporation subscription agreements.

**Share Purchase Contracts and Stock Subscriptions.** After incorporation, a subscription agreement is a contract between the subscriber and the corporation. When shares are sold by **share purchase contract**, shares ordinarily are sold in exchange for a promissory note from the subscriber. In essence, the shares are sold on credit. Recording the sale of shares is modified only by including a receivable for the portion of the selling price not yet received.

For illustration, assume the shares described in Illustration 18–1 are sold by share purchase contract, with 60% of the selling price to be received after six months.

Dow Industrial sells and issues 100,000 of its common shares, $1 par per share. The shares are sold by share purchase contract for $10 per share, with 60% of the selling price to be received after six months: Shares have been issued but are restricted from being resold and from voting privileges until paid in full.

| | ($ in 000s) | |
|---|---|---|
| Cash | 400 | |
| Receivable from share purchase contract | 600 | |
| Common stock | | 100 |
| Paid-in capital—excess of par | | 900 |

**ILLUSTRATION 18–2**
Share Purchase Contracts

A receivable is recorded for the $600,000 not yet received.

Enron now believes that, under generally accepted accounting principles, the note receivable should have been presented as a reduction to shareholders' equity. . . The net effect of this initial accounting entry was to overstate both the note receivable and shareholders' equity. . .[7]

**Reporting the Receivable.** How should the receivable be reported? Your initial response probably is that this account is an *asset,* similar to accounts receivable. Why should the receivable be precluded from being an asset merely because it is exchanged for shares rather than assets?

We can look to an infamous event in accounting history for a persuasive answer. For much of 2000 and the first part of 2001, **Enron Corporation** invested Enron stock in (and committed Enron stock to) "special purpose entities" that were created by Enron. To record these investments and commitments, Enron debited notes receivable and credited shareholders equity as described above. The problem, though, that contributed to Enron's collapse was that it then reported the result as an increase in both assets and shareholders' equity, creating a $1.2 billion asset that didn't really exist. Enron eventually restated its financial statements, referring to its actions as an "accounting error." Rules in place at the time prohibited such accounting. Instead, a receivable from issuing shares is not an asset, but should be reported as a *reduction in paid-in capital.*[8] Dow Industrial's paid-in capital, immediately after the stock subscription described in Illustration 18–2, would be reported by this approach as:

| | ($ in 000s) |
|---|---|
| **Paid-in capital:** | |
| Common stock, 100,000 shares at $1 par | $100 |
| Paid-in capital—excess of par | 900 |
| Less: Receivable from share purchase contract | (600) |
| Total paid-in capital | $400 |

A receivable from issuing stock is a contra equity account until collected.

Reporting the receivable as a contra equity account results in reporting total paid-in capital only to the extent that capital actually has been contributed. This is the prevalent practice.

## SHARES ISSUED FOR NONCASH CONSIDERATION

Occasionally, a company might issue its shares for consideration other than cash. It is not uncommon for a new company, yet to establish a reliable cash flow, to pay for promotional and legal services with shares rather than with cash. Similarly, shares might be given in payment for land, or for equipment, or for some other noncash asset.

Even without a receipt of cash to establish the fair market value of the shares at the time of the exchange, the transaction still should be recorded at fair market value. Best evidence of fair market value might be:

Shares should be issued at fair market value.

- A quoted market price for the shares.
- A selling price established in a recent issue of shares for cash.

[7] Enron's November 2001 8-K filing with the SEC.

[8] This accounting treatment is specified by *EITF Issue 85-1,* "Classifying Notes Received for Capital Stock," and SEC Regulation S-X, Article 5-02.30, *Commons Stocks, and Staff Accounting Bulletin Topic 4-E,* "Receivables from Sale of Stock."

- The amount of cash that would have been paid in a cash purchase of the asset or service.
- An independent appraisal of the value of the asset received.
- Other available evidence.

Whichever evidence of fair market value seems more clearly evident should be used.[9]

Illustration 18–3 demonstrates a situation where the quoted market price is the best evidence of fair value.

**ILLUSTRATION 18–3**

Shares Sold for Noncash Consideration

**The quoted market price for the shares issued might be the best evidence of fair market value.**

DuMont Chemicals issues 1 million of its common shares, $1 par per share, in exchange for a custom-built factory for which no cash price is available. Today's issue of *The Wall Street Journal* lists DuMont's stock at $10 per share:

| | ($ in millions) | |
|---|---|---|
| Property, plant, and equipment (1 million shares at $10 per share) . . . | 10 | |
| Common stock (1 million shares at $1 par per share) . . . . . . . . . . . | | 1 |
| Paid-in capital—excess of par (remainder) . . . . . . . . . . . . . . . . . . | | 9 |

## MORE THAN ONE SECURITY ISSUED FOR A SINGLE PRICE

Although uncommon, a company might sell more than one security—perhaps common shares and preferred shares—for a single price. As you might expect, the cash received usually is the sum of the separate market values of the two securities. Of course, each is then recorded at its market value. However, if only one security's value is known, the second security's market value is inferred from the total selling price as demonstrated in Illustration 18–4.

**ILLUSTRATION 18–4**

More than One Security Sold for a Single Price

**When only one security's value is known ($40 million), the second security's market value ($60 million) is assumed from the total selling price ($100 million).**

AP&P issues 4 million of its common shares, $1 par per share, and 4 million of its preferred shares, $10 par, for $100 million. Today's issue of *The Wall Street Journal* lists AP&P's common at $10 per share. There is no established market for the preferred shares:

| | ($ in millions) | |
|---|---|---|
| Cash . . . . . . . . . . . . . . . . . . . . . . . . . . . . . . . . . . . . . . . . . . . . | 100 | |
| Common stock (4 million shares × $1 par) . . . . . . . . . . . . . . . . . . . | | 4 |
| Paid-in capital—excess of par, common . . . . . . . . . . . . . . . . . . . . | | 36 |
| Preferred stock (4 million shares × $10 par) . . . . . . . . . . . . . . . . . | | 40 |
| Paid-in capital—excess of par, preferred. . . . . . . . . . . . . . . . . . . . | | 20 |

Because the shares sell for a total of $100 million, and the market value of the common shares is known to be $40 million (4 million × $10), the preferred shares are inferred to have a market value of $60 million.

**ADDITIONAL CONSIDERATION**

In the unlikely event that the total selling price is not equal to the sum of the two market prices (when both market values are known), the total selling price is allocated between the two securities, in proportion to their relative market values. You should note that this is the same approach we use (a) when more than one asset is purchased for a single purchase price to allocate the single price to the various assets acquired, (b) when detachable warrants and bonds are issued for a single price, and (c) in any other situation when more than one item is associated with a single purchase price or selling price.

[9] Although stock issuances are not specifically mentioned in *APB Opinion No. 29*, this treatment is consistent with the general rule for accounting for noncash transactions as described in that pronouncement, pars. 18 and 25.

## SHARE ISSUE COSTS

When a company sells shares, it obtains the legal, promotional, and accounting services necessary to effect the sale. The cost of these services reduces the net proceeds from selling the shares. Since paid-in capital—excess of par is credited for the excess of the proceeds over the par value of the shares sold, the effect of share issue costs is to reduce the amount credited to that account. For example, on completing a public offering of 825,000 shares at a price of $17.75 per share, the **Duriron Company, Inc.**, noted in its financial statements: "The proceeds of the offering, after deducting all associated costs, were $13,491,000 or $16.35 per newly issued share." Duriron's entry to record the sale was:

**Share issue costs reduce the net cash proceeds from selling the shares and thus paid-in capital—excess of par.**

| | ($ in millions) | |
|---|---|---|
| Cash (825,000 shares at $16.35 net price per share) . . . . . . . . . . . . . | 13.49 | |
| Common stock (825,000 shares at $1.25 par per share) . . . . . . . . . | | 1.03 |
| Paid-in capital—excess of par (remainder) . . . . . . . . . . . . . . . . . . | | 12.46 |

**The cash proceeds is the net amount received after paying share issue costs.**

You should notice that not separately reporting issue costs differs from how *debt* issue costs are recorded. In Chapter 14 you learned that the costs associated with a debt issue are recorded in a separate debt issue costs account and amortized to expense over the life of the debt.

**Like interest, debt issue costs are an expense of borrowing funds.**

It can be argued that share issue costs and debt issue costs are fundamentally different. That view would argue that a debt issue has a fixed maturity and, like interest expense, debt issue costs are part of the expense of borrowing funds for that period of time (even though it's recorded in a separate expense account—debt issue expense). Selling shares, on the other hand, represents a perpetual equity interest. Dividends paid on that capital investment are not an expense; neither are the costs of obtaining that capital investment (share issue costs).

**Like dividends, share issue costs are not an expense.**

Although expensing debt issue costs presently is required by GAAP, the FASB has suggested in *Concept Statement 6* that those costs should be treated the same way as share issue costs. That is, the recorded amount of the debt would be reduced by the debt issue costs instead of recording the costs separately as an asset. Remember, though, that concept statements do not constitute GAAP, so until a new FASB standard is issued to supersede *APB Opinion 21*, the prescribed practice is to record debt issue costs as assets and expense the asset over the maturity of the debt.

## CONCEPT REVIEW EXERCISE

### EXPANSION OF CORPORATE CAPITAL

**Situation:** The shareholders' equity section of the balance sheet of National Foods, Inc. included the following accounts at December 31, 2004:

| **Shareholders' Equity** | ($ in millions) |
|---|---|
| **Paid-in capital:** | |
| Common stock, 120 million shares at $1 par | $ 120 |
| Paid-in capital—excess of par | 836 |
| **Retained earnings** | 2,449 |
| Total shareholders' equity | $3,405 |

**Required:**

1. During 2005, several transactions affected the stock of National Foods. Prepare the appropriate entries for these events.
   a. On March 11, National Foods sold 10 million of its 9.2% preferred shares, $1 par per share, for $44 per share by share purchase contract. 50% of the selling price was received at the time of sale, a five-year note was received for the remainder. The shares were not issued but held in escrow until the note was paid.
   b. On November 22, 1 million common shares, $1 par per share, were issued in exchange for eight labeling machines. Each machine was built to custom specifications so no cash price was available. National Food's stock was listed at $10 per share.
   c. On November 23, 1 million of the common shares and 1 million preferred shares were sold for $60 million. The preferred shares had not traded since March and their market value was uncertain.

2. Prepare the shareholders' equity section of the comparative balance sheets for National Foods at December 31, 2005 and 2004. Assume that net income for 2005 was $400 million and the only other transaction affecting shareholders' equity was the payment of the 9.2% dividend on the 11 million preferred shares ($1 million).

**SOLUTION**

1. During 2005 several transactions affected the stock of National Foods. Prepare the appropriate entries for these events.
   a. On March 11, National Foods sold 10 million of its preferred shares, $1 par per share, for $44 per share by share purchase contract:

$220 million cash (50% × $440 million) was received at the time of sale. The remaining $220 million was to be received later.

| | ($ in millions) | |
|---|---|---|
| Cash | 220 | |
| Receivable from share purchase contract | 220 | |
| Preferred stock (10 million shares × $1 par per share) | | 10 |
| Paid-in capital—excess of par, preferred | | 430 |

   b. On November 22, 1 million common shares, $1 par per share, were issued in exchange for 8 labeling machines:

The transaction was recorded at the fair market value of the shares exchanged for the machinery.

| | | |
|---|---|---|
| Machinery (fair value of shares) | 10 | |
| Common stock (1 million shares × $1 par per share) | | 1 |
| Paid-in capital—excess of par, common (1 million shares × $9) | | 9 |

   c. On November 23, 1 million of the common shares and 1 million preferred shares were sold for $60 million:

Since the value of only the common stock was known, the preferred stock's market value ($50/share) was inferred from the total selling price.

| | | |
|---|---|---|
| Cash | 60 | |
| Common stock (1 million shares × $1 par per share) | | 1 |
| Paid-in capital—excess of par, common | | 9 |
| Preferred stock (1 million shares × $1 par per share) | | 1 |
| Paid-in capital—excess of par, preferred (to balance) | | 49 |

2. Prepare the shareholders' equity section of the comparative balance sheets for National Foods at December 31, 2005 and 2004.

**NATIONAL FOODS, INC.**
**Balance Sheet**
**[Shareholders' Equity Section]**

| | ($ in millions) | |
|---|---|---|
| | **2005** | **2004** |
| **Shareholders' Equity** | | |
| Preferred stock, 9.2%, $1 par (2005: $10 million + 1 million) | $ 11 | $ — |
| Common stock, $1 par (2005: $120 million + 1 million + 1 million) | 122 | 120 |
| Paid-in capital—excess of par, preferred (2005: $430 million + 49 million) | 479 | — |
| Paid-in capital—excess of par, common (2005: $836 million + 9 million + 9 million) | 854 | 836 |
| Less: Receivable from share purchase contract | (220) | — |
| Retained earnings (2004: $2,449 million + 400 million − 1 million) | 2,848 | 2,449 |
| *Total shareholders' equity* | $4,094 | $3,405 |

Note: This situation is continued in the next Concept Review Exercise on page 913.

## Share Buybacks

● LO4

In the previous section we examined various ways stock might be issued. In this section, we look at situations in which companies reacquire shares previously sold. Most medium- and large-size companies occasionally buy back their own shares. Many have formal share repurchase plans. The motivation often is to support the market price of the shares.

## DECISION MAKERS' PERSPECTIVE

When a company's management feels the market price of its stock is undervalued, it may attempt to support the price by decreasing the supply of stock in the marketplace. A **Johnson & Johnson** announcement that it planned to buy back up to $5 billion of its outstanding shares triggered a buying spree that pushed the stock price up by more than 3 percent.

When announcing plans to repurchase up to $1 billion of its shares, **Compaq** chairman and chief executive officer Michael Capellas explained, "At current price levels, we believe Compaq's stock offers a tremendous investment opportunity for the company."[10] Although clearly a company may attempt to increase net assets by buying its shares at a low price and selling them back later at a higher price, that investment is not viewed as an asset. Similarly, increases and decreases in net assets from that activity are not reported as gains and losses in the company's income statement. Instead, buying and selling its shares are transactions between the corporation and its owners, analogous to retiring shares and then selling previously unissued shares. You should note the contrast between a company's purchasing of its own shares and its purchasing of shares in another corporation as an investment.

**Decreasing the supply of shares in the marketplace supports the price of remaining shares.**

**FINANCIAL REPORTING CASE**

Q1, p. 893

Though not considered an investment, the repurchase of shares often is a judicious use of a company's cash. By increasing per share earnings and supporting share price, shareholders benefit. When **IBM** announced its second $3.5 billion buyback of common stock the same year, **Merrill Lynch & Co.** commented, "I think it's a reasonable use of cash. How many investment opportunities do they have that can return cost of capital? They should be investing up to that point, and beyond that they should return cash to the shareholders."[11]

**Unlike an investment in another firm's shares, the acquisition of a company's own shares does not create an asset.**

To the extent this strategy is effective, a share buyback can be viewed as a way to "distribute" company profits without paying dividends. Capital gains from any stock price increase are taxed at lower capital gains tax rates than ordinary income tax rates on dividends.

Perhaps the primary motivation for most stock repurchases is to offset the increase in shares that routinely are issued to employees under stock award and stock option compensation programs. **Microsoft**'s 2004 financial statements reported its stock buyback program designed to offset the effect of its stock option and stock purchase plans as shown in Graphic 18–5.

**Companies buy back shares to offset the increase in shares issued to employees.**

**Note 11: Stockholders' Equity (in part)**
Our board of directors has approved a program to repurchase shares of our common stock to reduce the dilutive effect of our stock option and stock purchase plans.

**GRAPHIC 18–5**
Disclosure of Share Repurchase Program—Microsoft

Similarly, shares might be reacquired to distribute in a stock dividend, a proposed merger, or as a defense against a hostile takeover.[12]

Whatever the reason shares are repurchased, a company has a choice of how to account for the buyback:

1. The shares can be formally retired.
2. The shares can be called treasury stock.

Unfortunately, the choice is not dictated by the nature of the buyback, but by practical motivations of the company. ■

---

[10] "HP, Compaq Resume Stock Buyback," *CNET News.com,* September 17, 2001.

[11] "IBM Sets Another Big Buyback of Its Shares," *The New York Times,* October 28, 1998.

[12] A corporate takeover occurs when an individual or group of individuals acquires a majority of a company's outstanding common stock from present shareholders. Corporations that are the object of a hostile takeover attempt—a public bid for control of a company's stock against the company's wishes—often take evasive action involving the reacquisition of shares.

**FINANCIAL REPORTING CASE**

Q2, p. 893

## SHARES FORMALLY RETIRED OR VIEWED AS TREASURY STOCK

When a corporation retires its own shares, those shares assume the same status as authorized but unissued shares, just the same as if they never had been issued. We saw earlier in the chapter that when shares are sold, both cash (usually) and shareholders' equity are increased; the company becomes larger. Conversely, when cash is paid to **retire stock**, the effect is to decrease both cash and shareholders' equity; the size of the company literally is reduced.

**Reacquired shares are equivalent to authorized but unissued shares.**

Out of tradition and for practical reasons, companies usually reacquire shares of previously issued stock without formally retiring them.[13] Shares repurchased and not retired are referred to as **treasury stock**. Because reacquired shares are essentially the same as shares that never were issued at all, treasury shares have no voting rights nor do they receive dividends. Like the concepts of par value and legal capital, the concept of treasury shares no longer is recognized in most state statutes.[14] Some companies, in fact, are eliminating treasury shares from their financial statements as corporate statutes are modernized.

## ACCOUNTING FOR RETIRED SHARES

When shares are formally retired, we should reduce precisely the same accounts that previously were increased when the shares were sold, namely, common (or preferred) stock and paid-in capital—excess of par. The first column of Illustration 18–5 demonstrates this. The paid-in capital—excess of par account shows a balance of $900 million while the common

**ILLUSTRATION 18–5**

Comparison of Share Retirement and Treasury Stock Accounting—Share Buybacks

American Semiconductor's balance sheet included the following:

| Shareholders' Equity | ($ in millions) |
|---|---|
| Common stock, 100 million shares at $1 par | $ 100 |
| Paid-in capital—excess of par | 900 |
| Paid-in capital—share repurchase | 2 |
| Retained earnings | 2,000 |

**Formally retiring shares restores the balances in both the Common stock account and Paid-in capital—excess of par to what those balances would have been if the shares never had been issued.**

**When we view a buyback as treasury stock the cost of acquiring the shares is "temporarily" debited to the treasury stock account.**

| Retirement | | | Treasury Stock | | |
|---|---|---|---|---|---|
| Reacquired 1 million of its common shares | | | | | |
| **Case 1: Shares repurchased at $7 per share** | | | | | |
| Common stock ($1 par × 1 million shares) . . . . . | 1 | | Treasury stock (cost). . . . . . | 7 | |
| Paid-in capital—excess of par | | | | | |
| ($9 per shares) . . . . . . . . . . . . . . . . . . . . . . . . | 9 | | | | |
| Paid-in capital—share repurchase | | | | | |
| (difference). . . . . . . . . . . . . . . . . . . . . . . . | | 3 | | | |
| Cash . . . . . . . . . . . . . . . . . . . . . . . . . . . . . | | 7 | Cash . . . . . . . . . . . . . . . . | | 7 |
| **OR** | | | | | |
| **Case 2: Shares repurchased at $13 per share** | | | | | |
| Common stock ($1 par × 1 million shares) . . . . . | 1 | | Treasury stock (cost). . . . . . | 13 | |
| Paid-in capital—excess of par | | | | | |
| ($9 per shares) . . . . . . . . . . . . . . . . . . . . . . . . | 9 | | | | |
| Paid-in capital—share repurchase . . . . . . . . . . . | 2* | | | | |
| Retained earnings (difference) . . . . . . . . . . . . . . | 1 | | | | |
| Cash . . . . . . . . . . . . . . . . . . . . . . . . . . . . . | | 13 | Cash . . . . . . . . . . . . . . . . | | 13 |

*Because there is a $2 million credit balance.

[13]The concept of treasury shares originated long ago when new companies found they could sell shares at an unrealistically low price equal to par value to incorporators, who then donated those shares back to the company. Since these shares already had been issued (though not outstanding), they could be sold at whatever the real market price was without adjusting stated capital.

Because treasury shares are already issued, different rules apply to their purchase and resale than to unissued shares. Companies can:

a. Issue shares without regard to preemptive rights of shareholders.

b. Distribute shares as a dividend to shareholders even without a balance in retained earnings.

[14]*The Revised Model Business Corporation Act* eliminated the concept of treasury shares in 1984 after 1980 revisions had eliminated the concepts of par value and legal capital. Most state laws have since followed suit.

stock account shows a balance of $100 million. Thus the 100 million outstanding shares were originally sold for an average of $9 per share above par, or $10 per share. Consequently, when 1 million shares are retired (regardless of the retirement price), American Semiconductor should reduce its common stock account by $1 per share and its paid-in capital—excess of par by $9 per share. Another way to view the reduction is that because 1% of the shares are retired, both share account balances (common stock and paid-in capital—excess of par) are reduced by 1%.

How we treat the difference between the cash paid to buy the shares and the amount the shares originally sold for (amounts debited to common stock and paid-in capital—excess of par) depends on whether the cash paid is *less* than the original issue price (credit difference) or the cash paid is *more* than the original issue price (debit difference):

1. If a *credit* difference is created (as in Case 1 of Illustration 18–5), we credit paid-in capital—share repurchase.
2. If a *debit* difference is created (as in Case 2 of Illustration 18–5), we debit paid-in capital—share repurchase, but only if that account already has a credit balance. Otherwise, we debit retained earnings. (Reducing the account beyond its previous balance would create a negative balance.)

***Paid-in capital—share repurchase*** **is debited to the extent of its credit balance before debiting retained earnings.**

Why is paid-in capital credited in Case 1 and retained earnings debited in Case 2? The answer lies in the fact that the payments made by a corporation to repurchase its own shares are a distribution of corporate assets to shareholders.

**Payments made by a corporation to retire its own shares are viewed as a distribution of corporate assets to shareholders.**

In Case 1, only $7 million is distributed to shareholders to retire shares that originally provided $10 million of paid-in capital. Thus, some of the original investment ($3 million in this case) remains and is labeled *paid-in capital—share repurchase.*

In Case 2, more cash ($13 million) is distributed to shareholders to retire shares than originally was paid in. The amount paid in comprises the original investment of $10 million for the shares being retired plus $2 million of paid-in capital created by previous repurchase transactions—$12 million total. Thirteen million is returned to shareholders. The additional $1 million paid is viewed as a dividend on the shareholders' investment, and thus a reduction of retained earnings.[15]

## ACCOUNTING FOR TREASURY STOCK

● LO5

We view the purchase of treasury stock as a temporary reduction of shareholders' equity, to be reversed later when the treasury stock is resold. The cost of acquiring the shares is "temporarily" debited to the treasury stock account (second column of Illustration 18–5).

**When a share repurchase is viewed as treasury stock, recording the effects on specific shareholders' equity accounts is delayed until the shares are reissued.**

Recording the effects on specific shareholders' equity accounts is delayed until later when the shares are reissued. In the meantime, the shares assume the fictional status we discussed earlier of being neither unissued nor outstanding. Effectively, we consider the purchase of treasury stock and its subsequent resale to be a "single transaction."

### ADDITIONAL CONSIDERATION

The approach to accounting for treasury stock we discuss in this chapter is referred to as the "cost method." Another permissible approach is the "par value method." It is essentially identical to formally retiring shares, which is why it sometimes is referred to as the *retirement method of accounting for treasury stock.* In fact, if we substitute Treasury stock for Common stock in each of the journal entries we used to account for retirement of shares in Illustrations 18–5 and 18–6, we have the par value method. Because the method has virtually disappeared from practice, we do not discuss it further in this chapter.

**Balance Sheet Effect.** Formally retiring shares restores the balances in both the Common stock account and Paid-in capital—excess of par to what those balances would have

[15]In the next section of this chapter, you will be reminded that dividends reduce retained earnings. (You first learned this in your introductory accounting course.)

been if the shares never had been issued at all. As discussed above, any net increase in assets resulting from the sale and subsequent repurchase is reflected as Paid-in capital—share repurchase. On the other hand, any net decrease in assets resulting from the sale and subsequent repurchase is reflected as a reduction in retained earnings.

In contrast, when a share repurchase is viewed as treasury stock, the cost of the treasury stock is simply reported as a reduction in total shareholders' equity. Reporting under the two approaches is compared in Graphic 18–6 using the situation described above for American Semiconductor after the purchase of treasury stock in Illustration 18–5 (Case 2) on page 910. Notice that either way total shareholders' equity is the same.

**GRAPHIC 18–6**
Reporting Share Buyback in the Balance Sheet

Retirement reduces common stock and associated shareholders' equity accounts.

Treasury stock reduces total shareholders' equity.

| | ($ in millions) | |
|---|---|---|
| | **Shares Retired** | **Treasury Stock** |
| **Shareholders' Equity** | | |
| Paid-in capital: | | |
| Common stock, 100 million shares at $1 par | $ 99 | $ 100 |
| Paid-in capital—excess of par | 891 | 900 |
| Paid-in capital—reacquired shares | | 2 |
| Retained earnings | 1,999 | 2,000 |
| Less: Treasury stock, 1 million shares (at cost) | | (13) |
| Total shareholders' equity | $2,989 | $2,989 |

## RESALE OF SHARES

When shares are retired or the par value method is used, we view any subsequent sale as the sale of new shares.

After shares are formally retired, any subsequent sale of shares is simply the sale of new, unissued shares and is accounted for accordingly. This is demonstrated in the first column of Illustration 18–6.

Allocating the cost of treasury shares occurs when the shares are resold.

The resale of treasury shares is viewed as the consummation of the single transaction begun when the treasury shares were repurchased. The effect of the single transaction of purchasing treasury stock and reselling it for more than cost (Case 2 of Illustration 18–5 and Case A of Illustration 18–6) is to *increase* both cash and shareholders' equity (by $1 million). The effect of the single transaction of purchasing treasury stock and reselling it for less than cost (Case 2 of Illustration 18–5 and Case B of Illustration 18–6) is to *decrease* both cash and shareholders' equity (by $3 million).

**ILLUSTRATION 18–6**
Comparison of Share Retirement and Treasury Stock Accounting—Subsequent Sale of Shares

After formally retiring shares, we record a subsequent sale of shares exactly like any sale of shares.

The resale of treasury shares is viewed as the consummation of the "single transaction" begun when the treasury shares were purchased.

American Semiconductor sold 1 million shares after reacquiring shares at $13 per share (Case 2 in Illustration 18–5).

| **Retirement** | | | **Treasury Stock** | | |
|---|---|---|---|---|---|
| Sold 1 million shares | | | | | |
| **Case A: Shares sold at $14 per share** | | | | | |
| Cash | 14 | | Cash | 14 | |
| Common stock (par) | | 1 | Treasury stock (cost) | | 13 |
| Paid-in capital—excess of par | | 13 | Paid-in capital—share repurchase | | 1 |
| **OR** | | | | | |
| **Case B: Shares sold at $10 per share** | | | | | |
| Cash | 10 | | Cash | 10 | |
| Common stock (par) | | 1 | Retained earnings (to balance) | 1 | |
| Paid-in capital—excess of par | | 9 | Paid-in capital—share repurchase | 2* | |
| | | | Treasury stock (cost) | | 13 |

*Because there is a $2 million credit balance.

Note that retained earnings may be debited in a treasury stock transaction, but not credited. Also notice that transactions involving treasury stock have no impact on the income statement. This follows the reasoning discussed earlier that a corporation's buying and selling of its own shares are transactions between the corporation and its owners and not part of the earnings process.

**ADDITIONAL CONSIDERATION**

**Treasury Shares Acquired at Different Costs**

Notice that the treasury stock account always is credited for the cost of the reissued shares ($13 million in Illustration 18–6). When shares are reissued, if treasury stock on hand has been purchased at different per share prices, the cost of the shares sold must be determined using a cost flow assumption—FIFO, LIFO, or weighted average—similar to determining the cost of goods sold when inventory items are acquired at different unit costs.

Determining the cost of treasury stock sold is similar to determining the cost of goods sold.

## CONCEPT REVIEW EXERCISE

**TREASURY STOCK**

**Situation:** The shareholders' equity section of the balance sheet of National Foods, Inc. included the following accounts at December 31, 2005.

| **Shareholders' Equity** | ($ in millions) |
|---|---|
| **Paid-in capital:** | |
| Preferred stock, 11 million shares at $1 par | $ 11 |
| Common stock, 122 million shares at $1 par | 122 |
| Paid-in capital—excess of par, preferred | 479 |
| Paid-in capital—excess of par, common | 854 |
| Less: Receivable from share purchase contract | (220) |
| **Retained earnings** | 2,848 |
| Total shareholders' equity | $4,094 |

**Required:**

1. National Foods reacquired common shares during 2006 and sold shares in two separate transactions later that year. Prepare the entries for both the purchase and subsequent sale of shares during 2006 assuming that the shares were (a) retired and (b) considered to be treasury stock.
   a. National Foods purchased 6 million shares at $10 per share.
   b. National Foods sold 2 million shares at $12 per share.
   c. National Foods sold 2 million shares at $7 per share.
2. Prepare the shareholders' equity section of National Foods' balance sheet at December 31, 2006, assuming the shares were both (a) retired and (b) viewed as treasury stock. Net income for 2006 was $400 million, and preferred shareholders were paid $1 million cash dividends.

**SOLUTION**

1. National Foods reacquired common shares during 2006 and sold shares in two separate transactions later that year. Prepare the entries for both the purchase and subsequent sale of shares during 2006 assuming that the shares were (a) retired and (b) considered to be treasury stock.
   a. National Foods purchased 6 million shares at $10 per share:

| **Retirement** ($ in millions) | | |
|---|---|---|
| Common stock (6 million shares × $1) . . . | 6 | |
| Paid-in capital—excess of par . . . . . . . . . (6 million shares × $7*) . . . . . . . . . . . . . . | 42 | |
| Retained earnings (to balance) . . . . . . . . . | 12 | |
| Cash . . . . . . . . . . . . . . . . . . . . . . . . . . . | | 60 |

*$854 million ÷ 122 million shares

| **Treasury Stock** ($ in millions) | | |
|---|---|---|
| Treasury stock (6 million shares × $10) . . . . . | 60 | |
| Cash . . . . . . . . . . . . . . . . . . . | | 60 |

b. National Foods sold 2 million shares at $12 per share: ($ in millions)

| | | | | | |
|---|---|---|---|---|---|
| Cash | 24 | | Cash | 24 | |
| Common stock (2 million shares × $1) | | 2 | Treasury stock (2 million shares × $10) | | 20 |
| Paid-in capital—excess of par | | 22 | Paid-in capital—reacquired shares | | 4 |

c. National Foods sold 2 million shares at $7 per share: ($ in millions)

| | | | | | |
|---|---|---|---|---|---|
| Cash | 14 | | Cash | 14 | |
| Common stock (2 million shares × $1 par) | | 2 | Paid-in capital—reacquired shares | 4 | |
| Paid-in capital—excess of par | | 12 | Retained earnings (to balance) | 2 | |
| | | | Treasury stock (2 million shares × $10) | | 20 |

2. Prepare the shareholders' equity section of National Foods' balance sheet at December 31, 2006, assuming the shares were both (a) retired and (b) viewed as treasury stock.

**NATIONAL FOODS, INC.**
**Balance Sheet**
**[Shareholders' Equity Section]**
**At December 31, 2006**

($ in millions)

| | Shares Retired | Treasury Stock |
|---|---|---|
| **Shareholders' Equity** | | |
| Preferred stock, 11 million shares at $1 par | $ 11 | $ 11 |
| Common stock, 122 million shares at $1 par | 120 | 122 |
| Paid-in capital—excess of par, preferred | 479 | 479 |
| Paid-in capital—excess of par, common | 846* | 854 |
| Less: Receivable from share purchase contract | (220) | (220) |
| Retained earnings | 3,235† | 3,245‡ |
| Treasury stock, at cost; 2 million common shares | — | (20) |
| Total shareholders' equity | $4,471 | $4,471 |

*$854 − 42 + 22 + 12
†$2,848 − 12 + 400 − 1
‡$2,848 − 2 + 400 − 1

Note: This situation is continued in the next Concept Review Exercise on page 922.

# PART C RETAINED EARNINGS

## Characteristics of Retained Earnings

In the previous section we examined *invested* capital. Now we consider *earned* capital, that is, retained earnings. In general, retained earnings represents a corporation's accumulated, undistributed net income (or net loss). A more descriptive title used by some companies is reinvested earnings. A credit balance in this account indicates a dollar amount of assets previously earned by the firm but not distributed as dividends to shareholders. We refer to a debit balance in retained earnings as a **deficit**.

● LO6

You saw in the previous section that the buyback of shares (as well as the resale of treasury shares in some cases) can decrease retained earnings. We examine the effect on retained earnings of dividends and stock splits in this section.

# Dividends

● LO7

Shareholders' initial investments in a corporation are represented by amounts reported as paid-in capital. One way a corporation provides a return to its shareholders on their investments is to pay them a **dividend**, typically cash.[16]

Dividends are distributions of assets the company has earned on behalf of its shareholders. If dividends are paid that exceed the amount of assets earned by the company, then management is, in effect, returning to shareholders a portion of their investments, rather than providing them a return on that investment. So most companies view retained earnings as the amount available for dividends.[17]

## LIQUIDATING DIVIDEND

In unusual instances in which a dividend exceeds the balance in retained earnings, the excess is referred to as a **liquidating dividend** because some of the invested capital is being liquidated. This might occur when a corporation is being dissolved and assets (not subject to a superior claim by creditors) are distributed to shareholders. Any portion of a dividend not representing a distribution of earnings should be debited to additional paid-in capital rather than retained earnings.

**Any dividend not representing a distribution of earnings should be debited to paid-in capital.**

## RETAINED EARNINGS RESTRICTIONS

Sometimes the amount available for dividends purposely is reduced by management. A restriction of retained earnings designates a portion of the balance in retained earnings as being *unavailable for dividends.* A company might restrict retained earnings to indicate management's intention to withhold for some specific purpose the assets represented by that portion of the retained earnings balance. For example, management might anticipate the need for a specific amount of assets in upcoming years to repay a maturing debt, to cover a contingent loss, or to finance expansion of the facilities. Be sure to understand that the restriction itself does not set aside cash for the designated event but merely communicates management's intention not to distribute the stated amount as a dividend.

**A restriction of retained earnings communicates management's intention to withhold assets represented by a specified portion of the retained earnings balance.**

A restriction of retained earnings normally is indicated by a disclosure note to the financial statements. Although instances are rare, a formal journal entry may be used to reclassify a portion of retained earnings to an "appropriated" retained earnings account.

**Normally a restriction of retained earnings is indicated by a disclosure note.**

## CASH DIVIDENDS

Microsoft Corp. today announced that its Board of Directors declared a regular quarterly dividend of $0.08 per share. The dividend is payable March 10, 2005, to shareholders of record on Feb. 17, 2005.[18]

FINANCIAL REPORTING CASE

Q3, p. 893

You learned in Chapter 14 that paying interest to creditors is a contractual obligation. No such legal obligation exists for paying dividends to shareholders. A liability is not recorded until a company's board of directors votes to declare a dividend. In practice, though, corporations ordinarily try to maintain a stable dividend pattern over time.

When directors declare a cash dividend, we reduce retained earnings and record a liability. Before the payment actually can be made, a listing must be assembled of shareholders entitled to receive the dividend. A specific date is stated as to when the determination will be made of the recipients of the dividend. This date is called the **date of record**. Registered owners of shares of stock on this date are entitled to receive the dividend—even if they sell those shares prior to the actual cash payment. To be a

**The name of an investor who buys shares on the *ex-dividend date* or later will not appear on the company's list of registered owners until after the *date of record.***

[16]Dividends are not the only return shareholders earn; when market prices of their shares rise, shareholders benefit also. Indeed, many companies have adopted policies of never paying dividends but reinvesting all assets they earn. The motivation is to accommodate more rapid expansion and thus, presumably, increases in the market price of the stock.

[17]Ordinarily, this is not the legal limitation. Most states permit a company to pay dividends so long as, after the dividend, its assets would not be "less than the sum of its total liabilities plus the amount that would be needed, if the corporation were to be dissolved at the time of the distribution, to satisfy the preferential rights upon dissolution of shareholders whose preferential rights are superior to those receiving the distribution." (Revised Model Business Corporation Act, American Bar Association, 1994.) Thus, legally, a corporation can distribute amounts equal to total shareholders' equity less dissolution preferences of senior equity securities (usually preferred stock).

[18]Microsoft press release, December 8, 2004.

registered owner of shares on the date of record, an investor must purchase the shares before the **ex-dividend date**. This date usually is two business days before the date of record. Shares purchased on or after that date are purchased ex dividend—without the right to receive the declared dividend. As a result, the market price of a share typically will decline by the amount of the dividend, other things being equal, on the ex-dividend date. Consider Illustration 18–7.

**ILLUSTRATION 18–7**
Cash Dividends

At the declaration date, retained earnings is reduced and a liability is recorded.

Registered owners of shares on the date of record are entitled to receive the dividend.

On June 1, the board of directors of Craft Industries declares a cash dividend of $2 per share on its 100 million shares, payable to shareholders of record June 15, to be paid July 1:

| | ($ in millions) | |
|---|---|---|
| **June 1—Declaration Date** | | |
| Retained earnings | 200 | |
| Cash dividends payable (100 million shares at $2/share) | | 200 |
| **June 13—Ex-Dividend Date** | | |
| No entry | | |
| **June 15—Date of Record** | | |
| No entry | | |
| **July 1—Payment Date** | | |
| Cash dividends payable | 200 | |
| Cash | | 200 |

A sufficient balance in retained earnings permits a dividend to be declared. Remember, though, that retained earnings is a shareholders' equity account representing a dollar claim on assets in general, but not on any specific asset in particular. Sufficient retained earnings does not ensure sufficient cash to make payment. These are two separate accounts having no necessary connection with one another. When a dividend is "paid from retained earnings," this simply means that sufficient assets previously have been earned to pay the dividend without returning invested assets to shareholders.

### PROPERTY DIVIDENDS

The *fair market value* of the assets to be distributed is the amount recorded for a property dividend.

Because cash is the asset most easily divided and distributed to shareholders, most corporate dividends are cash dividends. In concept, though, any asset can be distributed to shareholders as a dividend. When a noncash asset is distributed, it is referred to as a **property dividend** (often called a *dividend in kind*).

In 2004, **MobilePro Corp.** declared to its shareholders a property dividend in shares of **STI** stock that MobilePro was holding as an investment. Securities held as investments are the assets most often distributed in a property dividend due to the relative ease of dividing these assets among shareholders and determining their fair market values.

A property dividend should be recorded at the fair market value of the assets to be distributed. This may require revaluing the asset to fair market value prior to recording the dividend. If so, a gain or loss is recognized for the difference between book value and fair market value. This is demonstrated in Illustration 18–8 on the next page.

## Stock Dividends and Splits

### STOCK DIVIDENDS

● LO8

A **stock dividend** is the distribution of additional shares of stock to current shareholders of the corporation. Be sure to note the contrast between a stock dividend and either a cash or property dividend. A stock dividend affects neither the assets nor the liabilities of the firm. Also, because each shareholder receives the same percentage increase in shares, shareholders' proportional interest in (percentage ownership of) the firm remains unchanged.

On October 1 the board of directors of Craft Industries declares a property dividend of 2 million shares of Beaman Corporation's preferred stock that Craft had purchased in March as an investment (book value: $9 million). The investment shares have a fair market value of $5 per share, $10 million, and are payable to shareholders of record October 15, to be distributed November 1:

| | ($ in millions) | |
|---|---|---|
| **October 1—Declaration Date** | | |
| Investment in Beaman Corporation preferred stock | 1 | |
| Gain on appreciation of investment ($10 − 9) | | 1 |
| Retained earnings (2 million shares at $5 per share) | 10 | |
| Property dividends payable | | 10 |
| **October 15—Date of Record** | | |
| No entry | | |
| **November 1—Payment Date** | | |
| Property dividends payable | 10 | |
| Investment in Beaman Corporation preferred stock | | 10 |

**ILLUSTRATION 18–8**
Property Dividends

**Before recording the property dividend, the asset first must be written up to fair market value.**

The prescribed accounting treatment of a stock dividend requires that shareholders' equity items be reclassified by reducing one or more shareholders' equity accounts and simultaneously increasing one or more paid-in capital accounts. The amount reclassified depends on the size of the stock dividend. For a small stock dividend, typically less than 25%, the fair market value of the additional shares distributed is transferred from retained earnings to paid-in capital as demonstrated in Illustration 18–9.[19]

Craft declares and distributes a 10% common stock dividend (10 million shares) when the market value of the $1 par common stock is $12 per share.

| | ($ in millions) | |
|---|---|---|
| Retained earnings (10 million shares at $12 per share) | 120 | |
| Common stock (10 million shares at $1 par per share) | | 10 |
| Paid-in capital—excess of par (remainder) | | 110 |

**ILLUSTRATION 18–9**
Stock Dividend

**A small stock dividend requires reclassification to paid-in capital of retained earnings equal to the fair value of the additional shares distributed.**

## ADDITIONAL CONSIDERATION

The entry above is recorded on the declaration date. Since the additional shares are not yet issued, some accountants would prefer to credit "common stock dividends issuable" at this point, instead of common stock. In that case, when the shares are issued, common stock dividends issuable is debited and common stock credited. The choice really is inconsequential; either way the $10 million amount would be reported as part of paid-in capital on a balance sheet prepared between the declaration and distribution of the shares.

**Stock Market Reaction to Stock Distributions.** As a Craft shareholder owning 10 shares at the time of the 10% stock dividend, you would receive an 11th share. Since each is worth $12, would you benefit by $12 when you receive the additional share from Craft? Of course not. If the value of each share were to remain $12 when the 10 million new shares are

[19] The Committee on Accounting Procedure prescribes this accounting treatment in "Restatement and Revision of Accounting Research Bulletins," *Accounting Research Bulletin No. 43* (New York: AICPA, 1961), Chap. 7, sec. B, pars. 10–14. In this pronouncement, a small stock dividend is defined as one 20 to 25% or less. For filings with that agency, the SEC has refined the definition to comprise stock distributions of less than 25%.

distributed, the total market value of the company would grow by $120 million (10 million shares × $12 per share).

The market price per share will decline in proportion to the increase in the number of shares distributed in a stock dividend.

A corporation cannot increase its market value simply by distributing additional stock certificates. Because all shareholders receive the same percentage increase in their respective holdings, you, and all other shareholders, still would own the same percentage of the company as before the distribution. Accordingly, the per share value of your shares should decline from $12 to $10.91 so that your 11 shares would be worth $120—precisely what your 10 shares were worth prior to the stock dividend. Any failure of the stock price to actually adjust in proportion to the additional shares issued probably would be due to information other than the distribution reaching shareholders at the same time.

Early rulemakers felt that per share market prices do not adjust in response to an increase in the number of shares.

Then, what justification is there for recording the additional shares at market value? In 1941 (and reaffirmed in 1953), accounting rulemakers felt that many shareholders are deceived by small stock dividends, believing they benefit by the market value of their additional shares.[20] Furthermore they erroneously felt that these individual beliefs are collectively reflected in the stock market by per share prices that remain unchanged by stock dividends. Consequently, their prescribed accounting treatment is to reduce retained earnings by the same amount as if cash dividends were paid equal to the market value of the shares issued.

This obsolete reasoning is inconsistent with our earlier conclusion that the market price per share will decline in approximate proportion to the increase in the number of shares distributed. Our intuitive conclusion is supported also by formal research.[21]

Capitalizing retained earnings for a stock dividend artificially reclassifies earned capital as invested capital.

Besides being based on fallacious reasoning, accounting for stock dividends by artificially reclassifying "earned" capital as "invested" capital conflicts with the reporting objective of reporting shareholders' equity by source. Despite these limitations, this outdated accounting standard still applies.

Companies sometimes declare a stock dividend in lieu of a real dividend.

**Reasons for Stock Dividends.** Since neither the corporation nor its shareholders apparently benefits from stock dividends, why do companies declare them?[22] Occasionally, a company tries to give shareholders the illusion that they are receiving a real dividend.

Companies sometimes declare a stock dividend so they can capitalize retained earnings.

Another reason is merely to enable the corporation to take advantage of the accepted accounting practice of capitalizing retained earnings. Specifically, a company might wish to lower an existing balance in retained earnings—otherwise available for *cash* dividends—so it can reinvest the earned assets represented by that balance without carrying a large balance in retained earnings.

## STOCK SPLITS

FINANCIAL REPORTING CASE

Q4, p. 893

A frequent reason for issuing a stock dividend is actually to induce the per share market price decline that follows. For instance, after a company declares a 100% stock dividend on 100 million shares of common stock, with a per share market price of $12, it then has 200 million shares, each with an approximate market value of $6. The motivation for reducing the per share market price is to increase the stock's *marketability* by making it attractive to a larger number of potential investors.

### ADDITIONAL CONSIDERATION

No cash dividends are paid on treasury shares. Usually stock dividends aren't paid on treasury shares either. Treasury shares are essentially equivalent to shares that never have been issued. In some circumstances, though, the intended use of the repurchased shares will give reason for the treasury shares to participate in a stock dividend. For instance, if the treasury shares have been specifically designated for issuance to executives in a stock option plan or stock award plan it would be appropriate to adjust the number of shares by the stock distribution.

[20] "Restatement and Revision of Accounting Research Bulletins," *Accounting Research Bulletin No. 43* (New York: AICPA, 1961), chap. 7.

[21] Foster and Vickrey, "The Information Content of Stock Dividend Announcements," *Accounting Review* (April 1978), and Spiceland and Winters, "The Market Reaction to Stock Distributions: The Effect of Market Anticipation and Cash Returns," *Accounting and Business Research* (Summer 1986).

[22] After hitting a high in the 1940s, the number of stock dividends has declined significantly. Currently, about 3% of companies declare stock dividends in any given year.

A stock distribution of 25% or higher, although often called a "large" stock dividend, is more often referred to as a **stock split**.[23] Thus, a 100% stock dividend could be labeled a 2-for-1 stock split. Conceptually, the proper accounting treatment of a stock dividend or a stock split is to make no journal entry, avoiding the reclassification of earned capital as invested capital. This, in fact, is the prescribed accounting treatment for a stock split.

**A large stock dividend is known as a *stock split.***

Following on the heels of an enormous run up in price in shares, Apple Computer announced Friday a two-for-one stock split. Each share held on Feb. 18 gets an additional share. The company plans to start trading on a split-adjusted basis at the end of February. "It potentially makes it more attractive to individual investors," said Steve Lidberg, an analyst at Pacific Crest Securities, who doesn't own shares of Apple. "Outside of that, it doesn't impact at all the way I think of the company."[24]

Since the same common stock account balance (total par) represents twice as many shares, the par value per share should be reduced by one-half. In the previous example, if the par were $1 per share before the stock distribution, then after the 2-for-1 stock split, the par would be $.50 per share.

## STOCK SPLITS EFFECTED IN THE FORM OF STOCK DIVIDENDS (LARGE STOCK DIVIDENDS)

If the per share par value of the shares is not changed, the stock distribution is referred to as a *stock split effected in the form of a stock dividend,* or simply a *stock dividend.* In that case, a journal entry increases the common stock account by the par value of the additional shares. To avoid reducing retained earnings in these instances, most companies reduce (debit) paid-in capital—excess of par to offset the credit to common stock (Illustration 18–10).

Craft declares and distributes a 2-for-1 stock split effected in the form of a 100% stock dividend (100 million shares) when the market value of the $1 par common stock is $12 per share:

| | ($ in millions) | |
|---|---|---|
| Paid-in capital—excess of par . . . . . . . . . . . . . . . . . . . . . . . . . . . . . | 100 | |
| Common stock (100 million shares at $1 par per share) . . . . . . . . . . | | 100 |

**ILLUSTRATION 18–10**
Stock Split Effected in the Form of a Stock Dividend

**If the *per share* par value of the shares is *not* changed, a stock distribution is referred to as a *stock split effected in the form of a stock dividend.***

Notice that this entry does not reclassify earned capital as invested capital. Some companies, though, choose to debit retained earnings instead.[25]

| | ($ in millions) | |
|---|---|---|
| Retained earnings . . . . . . . . . . . . . . . . . . . . . . . . . . . . . . . . . . . . | 100 | |
| Common stock (100 million shares at $1 par per share) . . . . . . . . . | | 100 |

**Some companies capitalize retained earnings when recording a stock split effected in the form of a stock dividend.**

Symantec Corporation described its recent stock split in its disclosure notes as shown in Graphic 18–7.

[23]"Restatement and Revision of Accounting Research Bulletins," *Accounting Research Bulletin No. 43* (New York: AICPA, 1961), Chap. 7, sec. B, par. 11.

[24]"Apple's Share Price Surge Results in Stock Split," *CNN Money*, February 11, 2005.

[25]The 2004 *Accounting Trends & Techniques* reports that 19 of its 600 sample companies reported a stock split. Of those, 7 debited additional paid-in capital, 5 debited retained earnings, and 7 made no entry. Thus all but 7 were handled as stock splits effected in the form of stock dividends.

**GRAPHIC 18–7**
Stock Split Disclosure—Symantec Corporation

**Note 8—Stock Transactions (in part)**
On October 19, 2004, our Board of Directors approved a two-for-one stock split to be effected as a stock dividend. Stockholders of record at the close of business on November 11, 2004 were issued one additional share of common stock for each share owned as of that date.

**ADDITIONAL CONSIDERATION**

A company choosing to capitalize retained earnings when recording a stock split effected in the form of a stock dividend may elect to capitalize an amount other than par value. Accounting guidelines are vague in this regard, stating only that legal amounts are minimum requirements and do not prevent the capitalization of a larger amount per share.

Source: "Restatement and Revision of Accounting Research Bulletins," *Accounting Research Bulletin No. 43* (New York: AICPA, 1961), Chap. 7, sec. B, par. 14.

**Reverse Stock Split.** A **reverse stock split** occurs when a company decreases, rather than increases, its outstanding shares. After a 1-for-4 reverse stock split, for example, 100 million shares, $1 par per share, would become 25 million shares, $4 par per share. No journal entry is necessary. Of course the market price per share theoretically would quadruple, which usually is the motivation for declaring a reverse stock split. Companies that reverse split their shares frequently are struggling companies trying to accomplish with the split what the market has been unwilling to do—increase the stock price.

**Fractional Shares.** Typically, a stock dividend or stock split results in some shareholders being entitled to fractions of whole shares. For example, if a company declares a 25% stock dividend, or equivalently a 5-for-4 stock split, a shareholder owning 10 shares would be entitled to $2\frac{1}{2}$ shares. Another shareholder with 15 shares would be entitled to $3\frac{3}{4}$ shares.

**Cash payments usually are made when shareholders are entitled to fractions of whole shares.**

Cash payments usually are made to shareholders for **fractional shares**. In the situation described above, for instance, if the market price at declaration is $12 per share, the shareholder with 15 shares would receive 3 additional shares and $9 in cash ($\$12 \times \frac{3}{4}$).

## DECISION MAKERS' PERSPECTIVE

**The return on shareholders' equity is a popular measure of profitability.**

Profitability is the key to a company's long-run survival. A summary measure of profitability often used by investors and potential investors, particularly common shareholders, is the return on shareholders' equity. This ratio measures the ability of company management to generate net income from the resources that owners provide. The ratio is computed by dividing net income by average shareholders' equity. A variation of this ratio often is used when a company has both preferred and common stock outstanding. The return to common shareholders' equity is calculated by subtracting dividends to preferred shareholders from the numerator and using average common shareholders' equity as the denominator. The modified ratio focuses on the profits generated on the assets provided by common shareholders.

**Book value measures have limited use in financial analysis.**

Although the ratio is useful when evaluating the effectiveness of management in employing resources provided by owners, analysts must be careful not to view it in isolation or without considering how the ratio is derived. Keep in mind that shareholders' equity is a measure of the book value of equity, equivalent to the book value of net assets. Book value measures quickly become out of line with market values. An asset's book value usually equals its market value on the date it's purchased; the two aren't necessarily the same after that. Equivalently, the market value of a share of stock (or of total shareholders' equity) usually is different from its book value. As a result, to supplement the return on shareholders' equity ratio, analysts often relate earnings to the market value of equity, calculating the earnings-price ratio. This ratio is simply the earnings per share divided by the market price per share.

To better understand the differences between the book value ratio and the market value ratio, let's consider the following condensed information reported by Sharp-Novell Industries for 2006 and 2005:

| ($ in 000s except per share amounts) | 2006 | 2005 |
|---|---|---|
| Sales | $3,500 | $3,100 |
| Net income | 125 | 114 |
| Current assets | $ 750 | $ 720 |
| Property, plant, and equipment (net) | 900 | 850 |
| Total assets | $1,650 | $1,570 |
| Current liabilities | $ 550 | $ 530 |
| Long-term liabilities | 540 | 520 |
| Paid-in capital | 210 | 210 |
| Retained earnings | 350 | 310 |
| Liabilities and shareholders' equity | $1,650 | $1,570 |
| Shares outstanding | 50,000 | 50,000 |
| Stock price (average) | $42.50 | $42.50 |

The 2006 return on shareholders' equity is computed by dividing net income by average shareholders' equity:

$$\$125 \div [(\$560 + 520)/2] = \underline{\underline{23.1\%}}$$

The earnings-price ratio is the earnings per share divided by the market price per share:

$$\text{Earnings per share (2006)} = \$125 \div 50 = \$2.50$$
$$\text{Earnings-price ratio} = \$2.50 \div 42.50 = \underline{\underline{5.9\%}}$$

Obviously, the return on the market value of equity is much lower than on the book value of equity. This points out the importance of looking at more than a single ratio when making decisions. While 23.1% may seem like a desirable return, 5.9% is not nearly so attractive. Companies often emphasize the return on shareholders' equity in their annual reports. Alert investors should not accept this measure of achievement at face value. For some companies this is a meaningful measure of performance; but for others, the market-based ratio means more, particularly for a mature firm whose book value and market value are more divergent.

**Share retirement and treasury stock transactions can affect the return to owners.**

Decisions managers make with regard to shareholders' equity transactions can significantly impact the return to shareholders. For example, when a company buys back shares of its own stock, the return on shareholders' equity goes up. Net income is divided by a smaller amount of shareholders' equity. On the other hand, the share buyback uses assets, reducing the resources available to earn net income in the future. So, managers as well as outside analysts must carefully consider the decision to reacquire shares in light of the current economic environment, the firm's investment opportunities, and cost of capital to decide whether such a transaction is in the long-term best interests of owners.

**Dividend decisions should be evaluated in light of prevailing circumstances.**

The decision to pay dividends requires similar considerations. When earnings are high, are shareholders better off receiving substantial cash dividends or having management reinvest those funds to finance future growth (and future dividends)? The answer, of course, depends on the particular circumstances involved. Dividend decisions should reflect managerial strategy concerning the mix of internal versus external financing, alternative investment opportunities, and industry conditions. High dividends often are found in mature industries and low dividends in growth industries. ■

**ETHICAL DILEMMA**

Interworld Distributors has paid quarterly cash dividends since 1975. The dividends have steadily increased from $.25 per share to the latest dividend declaration of $2.00 per share. The board of directors is eager to continue this trend despite the fact that revenues fell significantly during recent months as a result of worsening economic conditions and increased competition. The company founder and member of the board proposes a solution. He suggests a 5% stock dividend in lieu of a cash dividend to be accompanied by the following press announcement:

"In lieu of our regular $2.00 per share cash dividend, Interworld will distribute a 5% stock dividend on its common shares, currently trading at $40 per share. Changing the form of the dividend will permit the Company to direct available cash resources to the modernization of physical facilities in preparation for competing in the 21st century."

What do you think?

# CONCEPT REVIEW EXERCISE

## CHANGES IN RETAINED EARNINGS

**Situation:** The shareholders' equity section of the balance sheet of National Foods, Inc., included the following accounts at December 31, 2006:

| **Shareholders' Equity** | ($ in millions) |
|---|---|
| **Paid-in capital:** | |
| Preferred stock, 9.09%, 11 million shares at $1 par | $ 11 |
| Common stock, 122 million shares at $1 par | 122 |
| Paid-in capital—excess of par, preferred | 479 |
| Paid-in capital—excess of par, common | 854 |
| Less: Receivable from share purchase contract | (220) |
| **Retained earnings:** | 3,245 |
| Treasury stock, at cost, 2 million common shares | (20) |
| *Total shareholders' equity* | $4,471 |

**Required:**

1. During 2007, several events and transactions affected the retained earnings of National Foods. Prepare the appropriate entries for these events.
   a. On March 1, the board of directors declared a cash dividend of $1 per share on its 120 million outstanding shares (122 million − 2 million treasury shares), payable on April 3 to shareholders of record March 11.
   b. On March 5, the board of directors declared a property dividend of 120 million shares of **Kroger** common stock that National Foods had purchased in February as an investment (book value: $900 million). The investment shares had a fair market value of $8 per share and were distributed March 30 to shareholders of record March 15.
   c. On April 13, a 3-for-2 stock split was declared and distributed. The stock split was effected in the form of a 50% stock dividend. The market value of the $1 par common stock was $20 per share.
   d. On October 13, a 10% common stock dividend was declared and distributed when the market value of the $1 par common stock was $12 per share. Fractional share rights for 1 million equivalent whole shares were paid in cash.
   e. On December 1, the board of directors declared the 9.09% cash dividend on the 11 million preferred shares, payable on December 23 to shareholders of record December 11.
2. Prepare a statement of shareholders' equity for National Foods reporting the changes in shareholders' equity accounts for 2005, 2006, and 2007. Refer to the previous two Concept Reviews in this chapter for the 2005 and 2006 changes. For 2006, assume that shares were reacquired as treasury stock. Also, look back to the statement of shareholders' equity in Graphic 18–4 on page 899 for the format of the statement. Assume that net income for 2007 is $225 million.

1. During 2007, several events and transactions affected the retained earnings of National Foods. Prepare the appropriate entries for these events.

**SOLUTION**

a. Cash dividend of $1 per share on its 120 million *outstanding* common shares (122 million − 2 million treasury shares), payable on April 3 to shareholders of record March 11 (Note: Dividends aren't paid on treasury shares.):

| | ($ in millions) | |
|---|---|---|
| **March 1—Declaration Date** | | |
| Retained earnings | 120 | |
| Cash dividends payable (120 million shares at $1/share) | | 120 |
| **March 11—Date of Record** | | |
| No entry | | |
| **April 3—Payment Date** | | |
| Cash dividends payable | 120 | |
| Cash | | 120 |

The declaration of a dividend reduces retained earnings and creates a liability.

b. Property dividend of 120 million shares of Kroger common stock:

| | ($ in millions) | |
|---|---|---|
| **March 5—Declaration Date** | | |
| Investment in Kroger common stock | 60 | |
| Gain on appreciation of investment ($960 − 900) | | 60 |
| Retained earnings (fair value of asset to be distributed) | 960 | |
| Property dividends payable | | 960 |
| **March 15—Date of Record** | | |
| No entry | | |
| **March 30—Payment Date** | | |
| Property dividends payable | 960 | |
| Investment in Kroger common stock | | 960 |

The investment first must be written up to the $960 million fair market value ($8 × 120 million shares).

The liability is satisfied when the Kroger shares are distributed to shareholders.

c. 3-for-2 stock split effected in the form of a 50% stock dividend:

| | ($ in millions) | |
|---|---|---|
| **April 13** | | |
| Paid-in capital—excess of par* | 60 | |
| Common stock (60 million shares at $1 par per share) | | 60 |

*Alternatively, retained earnings may be debited.

120 million shares times 50% equals 60 million new shares—recorded at par.

d. 10% common stock dividend—fractional share rights for 1 million equivalent whole shares:

| | ($ in millions) | |
|---|---|---|
| **October 13** | | |
| Retained earnings (18 million shares* at $12 per share) | 216 | |
| Common stock (17 million shares at $1 par per share) | | 17 |
| Paid-in capital—excess of par (17 million shares at $11 per share above par) | | 187 |
| Cash (1 million shares at $12 market price per share) | | 12 |

*(120 million + 60 million) × 10% = 18 million shares

The stock dividend occurs after the 3-for-2 stock split; thus 18 million shares are distributed.

The $12 fair market value of the additional shares is capitalized in this small stock dividend.

e. 9.09% cash dividend on the 11 million preferred shares, payable on December 23 to shareholders of record December 11:

| | ($ in millions) | |
|---|---|---|
| **December 1—Declaration Date** | | |
| Retained earnings | 1 | |
| Cash dividends payable ($11 million par × 9.09%) | | 1 |
| **December 11—Date of Record** | | |
| NO ENTRY | | |

Preferred shareholders annually receive the designated percentage (9.09%) of the preferred's par value ($1 million), if dividends are declared.

**December 23—Payment Date**

| | | |
|---|---|---|
| Cash dividends payable . . . . . . . . . . . . . . . . . . . . . . . . . . . . . . . . . . | 1 | |
| Cash . . . . . . . . . . . . . . . . . . . . . . . . . . . . . . . . . . . . . . . . . . . . | | 1 |

2. Prepare a statement of shareholders' equity for National Foods reporting the changes in shareholders' equity accounts for 2005, 2006, and 2007.

**These are the transactions from Concept Review Exercise—Expansion of Corporate Capital.**

**These are the transactions from Concept Review Exercise—Treasury Stock.**

**These are the transactions from Concept Review Exercise—Changes in Retained Earnings.**

**NATIONAL FOODS**
**Statement of Shareholders' Equity**
**For the Years Ended December 31, 2007, 2006, and 2005**

| ($ in millions) | Preferred Stock | Common Stock | Additional Paid-In Capital | Receivable from Share Purchase Contract | Retained Earnings | Treasury Stock (at cost) | Total Share-holder's Equity |
|---|---|---|---|---|---|---|---|
| Balance at January 1, 2005 | | 120 | 836 | | 2,449 | | 3,405 |
| Sale of preferred shares | 10 | | 430 | (220) | | | 220 |
| Issuance of common shares | | 1 | 9 | | | | 10 |
| Issuance of common and preferred shares | 1 | 1 | 58 | | | | 60 |
| Net income | | | | | 400 | | 400 |
| Cash dividends, preferred | | | | | (1) | | (1) |
| Balance at December 31, 2005 | 11 | 122 | 1,333 | (220) | 2,848 | | 4,094 |
| Purchase of treasury shares | | | | | | (60) | (60) |
| Sale of treasury shares | | | 4 | | | 20 | 24 |
| Sale of treasury shares | | | (4) | | (2) | 20 | 14 |
| Net income | | | | | 400 | | 400 |
| Cash dividends, preferred | | | | | (1) | | (1) |
| Balance at December 31, 2006 | 11 | 122 | 1,333 | (220) | 3,245 | (20) | 4,471 |
| Cash dividends, common | | | | | (120) | | (120) |
| Property dividends, common | | | | | (960) | | (960) |
| 3-for-2 split effected in the form of a stock dividend | | 60 | (60) | | | | |
| 10% stock dividend | | 17 | 187 | | (216) | | (12) |
| Preferred dividends | | | | | (1) | | (1) |
| Net income | | | | | 225 | | 225 |
| Balance at December 31, 2007 | 11 | 199 | 1,460 | (220) | 2,173 | (20) | 3,603 |

## FINANCIAL REPORTING CASE SOLUTION

1. **Do you think the stock price increase is related to Temple-Inland's share repurchase plan?** (p. 909) The stock price increase probably is related to Temple-Inland's buyback plan. The marketplace realizes that decreasing the supply of shares supports the price of remaining shares. However, the repurchase of shares is not necessarily the best use of a company's cash. Whether it is in the shareholders' best interests depends on what other opportunities the company has for the cash available.
2. **What are Temple-Inland's choices in accounting for the share repurchases?** (p. 910) When a corporation reacquires its own shares, those shares assume the same status as authorized but unissued shares, just as if they never had been issued. However, for exactly the same transaction, companies can choose between two accounting alternatives: (a) formally retiring them or (b) accounting for the shares repurchased as treasury stock. In actuality, Temple-Inland uses alternative (b).
3. **What effect does the quarterly cash dividend of 45 cents a share have on Temple-Inland's assets? Its liabilities? Its shareholders' equity?** (p. 915) Each quarter, when directors declare a cash dividend, retained earnings are reduced and a liability is recorded. The

liability is paid with cash on the payment date. So, the net effect is a decrease in Temple-Inland 's assets and its shareholders' equity. The effect on liabilities is temporary.

4. **What effect did the stock split have on Temple-Inland 's assets? Its liabilities? Its shareholders' equity?** (p. 918) Conceptually, the proper accounting treatment of a stock split is to make no journal entry. However, since Temple-Inland refers to the stock distribution as a "stock split effected in the form of a stock dividend," a journal entry would increase the common stock account by the par value of the additional shares and would reduce paid-in capital—excess of par. This merely moves an amount from one part of shareholders' equity to another. Regardless of the accounting method, there is no change in Temple-Inland 's assets, liabilities, or total shareholders' equity. ■

## THE BOTTOM LINE

1. Shareholders' equity is the owners' residual interest in a corporation's assets. It arises primarily from (1) amounts invested by shareholders and (2) amounts earned by the corporation on behalf of its shareholders. These are reported as (1) paid-in capital and (2) retained earnings. A statement of shareholders' equity reports the sources of the changes in individual shareholders' equity accounts.
2. Comprehensive income encompasses all changes in equity except those caused by transactions with owners (like dividends and the sale or purchase of shares). It includes traditional net income as well as "other comprehensive income."
3. Shares sold by share purchase contract in essence are sold on credit. Shares sold for consideration other than cash (maybe services or a noncash asset) should be recorded at the fair market value of the shares or the noncash consideration, whichever seems more clearly evident.
4. When a corporation retires previously issued shares, those shares assume the same status as authorized but unissued shares—just the same as if they had never been issued. Payments made to retire shares are viewed as a distribution of corporate assets to shareholders.
5. When reaquired shares are viewed as treasury stock, the cost of acquiring the shares is temporarily debited to the treasury stock account. Recording the effects on specific shareholders' equity accounts is delayed until later when the shares are reissued.
6. Retained earnings represents, in general, a corporation's accumulated, undistributed or reinvested net income (or net loss). Distributions of earned assets are dividends.
7. Most corporate dividends are paid in cash. When a noncash asset is distributed, it is referred to as a property dividend. The fair market value of the assets to be distributed is the amount recorded for a property dividend.
8. A stock dividend is the distribution of additional shares of stock to current shareholders. For a small stock dividend (25% or less), the fair value of the additional shares distributed is transferred from retained earnings to paid-in capital. For a stock distribution of 25% or higher, the par value of the additional shares is reclassified within shareholders' equity if referred to as a stock split effected in the form of a stock dividend, but if referred to merely as a stock split, no journal entry is recorded. ■

## QUASI REORGANIZATIONS

APPENDIX 18

A firm undergoing financial difficulties, but with favorable future prospects, may use a **quasi reorganization** to write down inflated asset values and eliminate an accumulated deficit (debit balance in retained earnings). To effect the reorganization the following procedures are followed:

1. The firm's assets (and perhaps liabilities) are revalued (up or down) to reflect fair market values, with corresponding credits or debits to retained earnings. This process typically increases the deficit.
2. The debit balance in retained earnings (deficit) is eliminated against additional paid-in capital. If additional paid-in capital is not sufficient to absorb the entire deficit, a reduction in capital stock may be necessary (with an appropriate restating of the par amount per share).

3. Retained earnings is dated. That is, disclosure is provided to indicate the date the deficit was eliminated and when the new accumulation of earnings began.

The procedure is demonstrated in Illustration 18A–1. The shareholders approved the quasi reorganization effective January 1, 2006. The plan was to be accomplished by a reduction of inventory by $75 million, a reduction in property, plant, and equipment (net) of $175 million, and appropriate adjustments to shareholders' equity.

**ILLUSTRATION 18A–1**
Quasi Reorganization

The Emerson-Walsch Corporation has incurred operating losses for several years. A newly elected board of directors voted to implement a quasi reorganization, subject to shareholder approval. The balance sheet, on December 31, 2005, immediately prior to the restatement, includes the data shown below.

| | ($ in millions) |
|---|---|
| Cash | $ 75 |
| Receivables | 200 |
| Inventory | 375 |
| Property, plant, and equipment (net) | 400 |
| | $1,050 |
| Liabilities | $ 400 |
| Common stock (800 million shares at $1 par) | 800 |
| Additional paid-in capital | 150 |
| Retained earnings (deficit) | (300) |
| | $1,050 |

When assets are revalued to reflect fair market values, the process often increases the deficit.

The deficit, $550 ($300 + 75 + 175), can be only partially absorbed by the balance of additional paid-in capital.

The remaining deficit, $400 ($300 + 75 + 175 − 150), must be absorbed by reducing the balance in common stock.

| | ($ in millions) | |
|---|---|---|
| **To Revalue Assets:** | | |
| Retained earnings | 75 | |
| Inventory | | 75 |
| Retained earnings | 175 | |
| Property, plant, and equipment | | 175 |
| **To Eliminate a Portion of the Deficit against Available Additional Paid-In Capital:** | | |
| Additional paid-in capital | 150 | |
| Retained earnings | | 150 |
| **To Eliminate the Remainder of the Deficit against Common Stock:** | | |
| Common stock | 400 | |
| Retained earnings | | 400 |

The balance sheet immediately after the restatement would include the following:

Assets and liabilities reflect current values.

Because a reduced balance represents the same 800 million shares, the par amount per share must be reduced.

The deficit is eliminated.

| | ($ in millions) |
|---|---|
| Cash | $ 75 |
| Receivables | 200 |
| Inventory | 300 |
| Property, plant, and equipment (net) | 225 |
| | $800 |
| Liabilities | $400 |
| Common stock (800 million shares at $.50 par) | 400 |
| Additional paid-in capital | 0 |
| Retained earnings (deficit) | 0 |
| | $800 |

**Note A:** Upon the recommendation of the board of directors and approval by shareholders a quasi reorganization was implemented January 1, 2006. The plan was accomplished by a reduction of inventory by $75 million, a reduction in property, plant, and equipment (net) of $175 million, and appropriate adjustments to shareholders' equity. The balance in retained earnings reflects the elimination of a $300 million deficit on that date.

## QUESTIONS FOR REVIEW OF KEY TOPICS

**Q 18–1** Identify and briefly describe the two primary sources of shareholders' equity.

**Q 18–2** The balance sheet reports the balances of shareholders' equity accounts. What additional information is provided by the statement of shareholders' equity?

**Q 18–3** What is comprehensive income? How does comprehensive income differ from net income? Where do companies report it in a balance sheet?

**Q 18–4** Identify the three common forms of business organization and the primary difference between the way they are accounted for.

**Q 18–5** Corporations offer the advantage of limited liability. Explain what is meant by that statement.

**Q 18–6** Distinguish between not-for-profit and for-profit corporations.

**Q 18–7** Distinguish between publicly held and privately (or closely) held corporations.

**Q 18–8** How does the Model Business Corporation Act affect the way corporations operate?

**Q 18–9** The owners of a corporation are its shareholders. If a corporation has only one class of shares, they typically are labeled common shares. Indicate the ownership rights held by common shareholders, unless specifically withheld by agreement.

**Q 18–10** What is meant by a shareholder's preemptive right?

**Q 18–11** Terminology varies in the way companies differentiate among share types. But many corporations designate shares as common or preferred. What are the two special rights usually given to preferred shareholders?

**Q 18–12** Most preferred shares are cumulative. Explain what this means.

**Q 18–13** The par value of shares historically indicated the real value of shares and all shares were issued at that price. The concept has changed with time. Describe the meaning of par value as it has evolved to today.

**Q 18–14** When shares are sold by share purchase contract, shares ordinarily are issued in exchange for a promissory note from the subscriber and a receivable is recorded for the portion of the selling price not yet received. How is this receivable reported in financial statements?

**Q 18–15** At times, companies issue their shares for consideration other than cash. What is the measurement objective in those cases?

**Q 18–16** Companies occasionally sell more than one security for a single price. How is the issue price allocated among the separate securities?

**Q 18–17** The costs of legal, promotional, and accounting services necessary to effect the sale of shares are referred to as share issue costs. How are these costs recorded? Compare this approach to the way debt issue costs are recorded.

**Q 18–18** When a corporation acquires its own shares, those shares assume the same status as authorized but unissued shares, as if they never had been issued. Explain how this is reflected in the accounting records if the shares are formally retired.

**Q 18–19** Discuss the conceptual basis for accounting for a share buyback as treasury stock.

**Q 18–20** The prescribed accounting treatment for stock dividends implicitly assumes that shareholders are fooled by small stock dividends and benefit by the market value of their additional shares. Explain this statement. Is it logical?

**Q 18–21** Brandon Components declares a 2-for-1 stock split. What will be the effects of the split, and how should it be recorded?

**Q 18–22** What is a reverse stock split? What would be the effect of a reverse stock split on one million $1 par shares? On the accounting records?

**Q 18–23** Suppose you own 80 shares of IBM common stock when the company declares a 4% stock dividend. What will you receive as a result?

**Q 18–24** (based on Appendix 18) A quasi reorganization is sometimes employed by a firm undergoing financial difficulties, but with favorable future prospects. What are two objectives of this procedure? Briefly describe the procedural steps.

# BRIEF EXERCISES

**BE 18–1**
Comprehensive income
• LO1

Schaeffer Corporation reports $50 million accumulated other comprehensive income in its balance sheet as a component of shareholders' equity. In a related disclosure note reporting comprehensive income for the year, the company reveals net income of $400 million and other comprehensive income of $15 million. What was the balance in accumulated other comprehensive income in last year's balance sheet?

**BE 18–2**
Stock issued
• LO3

Penne Pharmaceuticals sold 8 million shares of its $1 par common stock to provide funds for research and development. If the issue price is $12 per share, what is the journal entry to record the sale of the shares?

**BE 18–3**
Stock issued
• LO3

Lewelling Company issued 100,000 shares of its $1 par common stock to the Michael Morgan law firm as compensation for 4,000 hours of legal services performed. Morgan's usual rate is $240 per hour. By what amount should Lewelling's paid-in capital—excess of par increase as a result of this transaction?

**BE 18–4**
Retirement of shares
• LO4

Horton Industries' shareholders' equity included 100 million shares of $1 par common stock and a balance in paid-in capital—excess of par of $900 million. Assuming that Horton retires shares it reacquires (restores their status to that of authorized but unissued shares), by what amount will Horton's total paid-in capital decline if it reacquires 2 million shares at $8.50 per share?

**BE 18–5**
Retirement of shares
• LO4

Agee Storage issued 35 million shares of its $1 par common stock at $16 per share several years ago. Last year, for the first time, Agee reacquired 1 million shares at $14 per share. Assuming that Agee retires shares it reacquires (restores their status to that of authorized but unissued shares), by what amount will Agee's total paid-in capital decline if it now reacquires 1 million shares at $19 per share?

**BE 18–6**
Treasury stock
• LO5

The Jennings Group reacquired 2 million of its shares at $70 per share as treasury stock. Last year, for the first time, Jennings sold 1 million treasury shares at $71 per share. By what amount will Jennings' retained earnings decline if it now sells the remaining 1 million treasury shares at $67 per share?

**BE 18–7**
Treasury stock
• LO5

In previous years, Cox Transport reacquired 2 million treasury shares at $20 per share and, later, 1 million treasury shares at $26 per share. By what amount will Cox's paid-in capital—share repurchase increase if it now sells 1 million treasury shares at $29 per share and determines cost as the weighted-average cost of treasury shares?

**BE 18–8**
Treasury stock
• LO5

Refer to the situation described in BE 18–7. By what amount will Cox's paid-in capital—share repurchase increase if it determines the cost of treasury shares by the FIFO method?

**BE 18–9**
Cash dividend
• LO7

Following is a Microsoft press release:

---

In March 2005 Microsoft Corp. today announced that its Board of Directors declared a regular quarterly dividend of $0.08 per share. The dividend is payable March 10, 2005, to shareholders of record on Feb. 17, 2005.

---

Prepare the journal entries Microsoft used to record the declaration and payment of the cash dividend for its 10,862 million shares.

**BE 18–10**
Property dividend
• LO7

LaRoe Moving and Storage, a family-owned corporation, declared a property dividend of 1,000 shares of GE common stock that LaRoe had purchased in February for $37,000 as an investment. GE's shares had a market value of $35 per share on the declaration date. Prepare the journal entries to record the property dividend on the declaration and payment dates.

**BE 18–11**
Stock dividend
• LO8

On June 13, the board of directors of Siewert, Inc. declared a 5% stock dividend on its 60 million, $1 par, common shares, to be distributed on July 1. The market price of Siewert common stock was $25 on June 13. Prepare the journal entry to record the stock dividend.

**BE 18–12**
Stock split
• LO8

Refer to the situation described in BE 18–11, but assume a 2-for-1 stock split instead of the 5% stock dividend. Prepare the journal entry to record the stock split if it is *not* to be effected in the form of a stock dividend. What is the par per share after the split?

**BE 18–13**
Stock split
• LO8

Refer to the situation described in BE 18–11, but assume a 2-for-1 stock split instead of the 5% stock dividend. Prepare the journal entry to record the stock split if it is to be effected in the form of a 100% stock dividend. What is the par per share after the split?

# EXERCISES

available with McGraw-Hill's Homework Manager www.mhhe.com/spiceland4e

**An alternate exercise and problem set is available on the text website: www.mhhe.com/spiceland4e**

**E 18–1**
Comprehensive income
● LO2

The following is an excerpt from a disclosure note from the 2006 annual report of Kaufman Chemicals, Inc:

**COMPREHENSIVE INCOME (LOSS)**
The components of comprehensive income, net of tax, are as follows (in millions):

| Years Ended December 31 | 2006 | 2005 | 2004 |
|---|---|---|---|
| Net income | $856 | $766 | $594 |
| Other comprehensive income: | | | |
| Change in net unrealized gains on available-for-sale investments, net of tax of $22, ($14), and $15 in 2006, 2005, and 2004, respectively | 34 | (21) | 23 |
| Other | (2) | (1) | 1 |
| Total | $888 | $744 | $618 |

Kaufman reports Accumulated other comprehensive income in its balance sheet as a component of shareholders' equity as follows:

| | ($ in millions) | |
|---|---|---|
| | **2006** | **2005** |
| Shareholders' equity: | | |
| Common stock | 355 | 355 |
| Additional paid-in capital | 8,567 | 8,567 |
| Retained earnings | 6,544 | 5,988 |
| Accumulated other comprehensive income | 107 | 75 |
| *Total shareholders' equity* | $15,573 | $14,985 |

**Required:**

1. What is comprehensive income and how does it differ from net income?
2. How is comprehensive income reported in a balance sheet?
3. Why is Kaufman's 2006 balance sheet amount different from the 2006 amount reported in the disclosure note? Explain.
4. From the information provided, determine how Kaufman calculated the $107 million Accumulated other comprehensive income in 2006.

**E 18–2**
Stock issued for cash; Wright Medical Group
● LO3

The following is a news item reported by Reuters:

**WASHINGTON,** Jan 29 (Reuters)—**Wright Medical Group,** a maker of reconstructive implants for knees and hips, on Tuesday filed to sell 3 million shares of common stock.

In a filing with the U.S. Securities and Exchange Commission, it said it plans to use the proceeds from the offering for general corporate purposes, working capital, research and development, and acquisitions.

After the sale there will be about 31.5 million shares outstanding in the Arlington, Tennessee-based company, according to the SEC filing.

Wright shares closed at $17.15 on Nasdaq.

The common stock of Wright Medical Group has a par of $.01 per share.

**Required:**

Prepare the journal entry to record the sale of the shares assuming the price existing when the announcement was made and ignoring share issue costs.

**E 18–3**
Issuance of shares; share purchase contract
● LO3

During the first year of operations, Bekon International, Inc., sold and issued 28 million of its common shares, $1 par per share. During the first year, which ended December 31, 2006, net income was $50 million and no dividends were paid.

**Required:**

1. Prepare the journal entry to record the sale of the shares for cash at a price of $20 per share.
2. Prepare the journal entry to record the sale of the shares if sold by share purchase contract for $20 per share, with 50% of the selling price to be received after 14 months.
3. Show how shareholders' equity would be reported in Bekon's balance sheet at December 31, 2006, assuming the shares were sold by share purchase contract.
4. Prepare the journal entry to record the collection of the receivable from the share purchase contract during the second year of operations.
5. Show how shareholders' equity would be reported in Bekon's balance sheet at December 31, 2007, assuming no additional changes to shareholders' equity other than 2007 net income of $65 million.

**E 18–4**
Issuance of shares; noncash consideration
● LO3

During its first year of operations, Eastern Data Links Corporation entered into the following transactions relating to shareholders' equity. The articles of incorporation authorized the issue of 8 million common shares, $1 par per share, and 1 million preferred shares, $50 par per share.

**Required:**

Prepare the appropriate journal entries to record each transaction.

| | |
|---|---|
| Feb. 12 | Sold 2 million common shares, for $9 per share. |
| 13 | Issued 40,000 common shares to attorneys in exchange for legal services. |
| 13 | Sold 80,000 of its common shares and 4,000 preferred shares for $945,000. |
| Nov. 15 | Issued 380,000 of its common shares in exchange for equipment for which the cash price was known to be $3,688,000. |

**E 18–5**
Redeemable shares
● LO3

Williams Industries has outstanding 30 million common shares, 20 million Class A shares, and 20 million Class B shares. Williams has the right but not the obligation to repurchase the Class A shares if a change in ownership of the voting common shares causes J. P. Williams, founder and CEO, to have less than 50% ownership. Williams has the unconditional obligation to repurchase the Class B shares upon the death of J. P. Williams.

**Required:**

Which, if any, of the shares should be reported in Williams's balance sheet as liabilities? Explain.

**E 18–6**
Share issue costs; issuance
● LO3

ICOT Industries issued 15 million of its $1 par common shares for $424 million on April 11. Legal, promotional, and accounting services necessary to effect the sale cost $2 million.

**Required:**

1. Prepare the journal entry to record the issuance of the shares.
2. Explain how recording the share issue costs differ from the way debt issue costs are recorded (discussed in Chapter 14).

**E 18–7**
Retirement of shares
● LO4

Borner Communications' articles of incorporation authorized the issuance of 130 million common shares. The transactions described below effected changes in Borner's outstanding shares. Prior to the transactions, Borner's shareholders' equity included the following:

| **Shareholders' Equity** | ($ in millions) |
|---|---|
| Common stock, 100 million shares at $1 par, | $100 |
| Paid-in capital—excess of par | 300 |
| Retained earnings | 210 |

**Required:**

Assuming that Borner Communications retires shares it reacquires (restores their status to that of authorized but unissued shares), record the appropriate journal entry for each of the following transactions:

1. On January 7, 2006, Borner reacquired 2 million shares at $5.00 per share.
2. On August 23, 2006, Borner reacquired 4 million shares at $3.50 per share.
3. On July 25, 2007, Borner sold 3 million common shares at $6 per share.

**E 18–8**
Retirement of shares
● LO4

In 2006, Borland Semiconductors entered into the transactions described below. In 2003, Borland had issued 170 million shares of its $1 par common stock at $34 per share.

**Required:**

Assuming that Borland retires shares it reacquires, record the appropriate journal entry for each of the following transactions:

1. On January 2, 2006, Borland reacquired 10 million shares at $32.50 per share.
2. On March 3, 2006, Borland reacquired 10 million shares at $36 per share.
3. On August 13, 2006, Borland sold 1 million shares at $42 per share.
4. On December 15, 2006, Borland sold 2 million shares at $36 per share.

**E 18–9**
Treasury stock

● LO5

In 2006, Western Transport Company entered into the treasury stock transactions described below. In 2004, Western Transport had issued 140 million shares of its $1 par common stock at $17 per share.

**Required:**
Prepare the appropriate journal entry for each of the following transactions:
1. On January 23, 2006, Western Transport reacquired 10 million shares at $20 per share.
2. On September 3, 2006, Western Transport sold 1 million treasury shares at $21 per share.
3. On November 4, 2006, Western Transport sold 1 million treasury shares at $18 per share.

**E 18–10**
Treasury stock; weighted-average and FIFO cost

● LO5

At December 31, 2005, the balance sheet of Meca International included the following shareholders' equity accounts:

| **Shareholders' Equity** | ($ in millions) |
|---|---|
| Common stock, 60 million shares at $1 par | $ 60 |
| Paid-in capital—excess of par | 300 |
| Retained earnings | 410 |

**Required:**
Assuming that Meca International views its share buybacks as treasury stock, record the appropriate journal entry for each of the following transactions:
1. On February 12, 2006, Meca reacquired 1 million common shares at $13 per share.
2. On June 9, 2007, Meca reacquired 2 million common shares at $10 per share.
3. On May 25, 2008, Meca sold 2 million treasury shares at $15 per share—determine cost as the weighted-average cost of treasury shares.
4. For the previous transaction, assume Meca determines the cost of treasury shares by the FIFO method.

**E 18–11**
Reporting shareholders' equity after share repurchase

● LO4 LO5

On two previous occasions, the management of Dennison and Company, Inc. repurchased some of its common shares. Between buyback transactions, the corporation issued common shares under its management incentive plan. Shown below is shareholders' equity following these share transactions, as reported by two different methods of accounting for reacquired shares.

| | ($ in millions) | |
|---|---|---|
| | **Method A** | **Method B** |
| Shareholders' Equity | | |
| Paid-in capital: | | |
| Preferred stock, $10 par | $ 150 | $ 150 |
| Common stock, $1 par | 200 | 197 |
| Additional paid-in capital | 1,204 | 1,201 |
| Retained earnings | 2,994 | 2,979 |
| Less: Treasury stock | (21) | |
| *Total shareholders' equity* | $4,527 | $4,527 |

**Required:**
1. Infer from the presentation which method of accounting for reacquired shares is represented by each of the two columns.
2. Explain why presentation formats are different and why some account balances are different for the two methods.

**E 18–12**
Change from treasury stock to retired stock

● LO4 LO5

In keeping with a modernization of corporate statutes in its home state, UMC Corporation decided in 2006 to discontinue accounting for reacquired shares as treasury stock. Instead, shares repurchased will be viewed as having been retired, reassuming the status of unissued shares. As part of the change, treasury shares held were reclassified as retired stock. At December 31, 2005 UMC's balance sheet reported the following shareholders' equity:

| | ($ in millions) |
|---|---|
| Common stock, $1 par | $200 |
| Paid-in capital—excess of par | 800 |
| Retained earnings | 956 |
| Treasury stock (4 million shares at cost) | (25) |
| Total shareholders' equity | $1,931 |

**Required:**
Identify the type of accounting change this decision represents, and prepare the journal entry to effect the reclassification of treasury shares as retired shares.

**E 18–13**
Multiple choice; CPA exam; paid-in capital

● LO3 LO5

The following questions dealing with paid-in capital are adapted from prior CPA examinations. Determine the response that best completes the statements or questions.

1. East Co. issued 1,000 shares of its $5 par common stock to Howe as compensation for 1,000 hours of legal services performed. Howe usually bills $160 per hour for legal services. On the date of issuance, the stock was trading on a public exchange at $140 per share. By what amount should the additional paid-in capital account increase as a result of this transaction?
   a. $135,000
   b. $140,000
   c. $155,000
   d. $160,000
2. If a corporation sells some of its treasury stock at a price that exceeds its cost, this excess should be
   a. Reported as a gain in the income statement.
   b. Treated as a reduction in the carrying amount.
   c. Credited to additional paid-in capital.
   d. Credited to retained earnings.

**E 18–14**
Transactions affecting retained earnings

● LO6 LO7

Shown below in T-account format are the changes affecting the retained earnings of Brenner-Jude Corporation during 2006. At January 1, 2006, the corporation had outstanding 105 million common shares, $1 par per share.

**Retained Earnings** ($ in millions)

| Debit | | Credit | |
|---|---|---|---|
| | | 90 | Beginning balance |
| Retirement of 5 million common shares for $22 million | 2 | | |
| | | 88 | Net income for the year |
| Declaration and payment of a $.33 per share cash dividend | 33 | | |
| Declaration and distribution of a 4% stock dividend | 20 | | |
| | | 123 | Ending balance |

**Required:**

1. From the information provided by the account changes you should be able to recreate the transactions that affected Brenner-Jude's retained earnings during 2006. Prepare the journal entries that Brenner-Jude must have recorded during the year for these transactions.
2. Prepare a statement of retained earnings for Brenner-Jude for the year ended 2006.

**E 18–15**
Effect of cumulative, nonparticipating preferred stock on dividends—3 years

● LO7

The shareholders' equity of WBL Industries includes the items shown below. The board of directors of WBL declared cash dividends of $8 million, $20 million, and $150 million in its first three years of operation—2006, 2007, and 2008, respectively.

| | ($ in millions) |
|---|---|
| Common stock | $100 |
| Paid-in capital—excess of par, common | 980 |
| Preferred stock, 8% | 200 |
| Paid-in capital—excess of par, preferred | 555 |

**Required:**

Determine the amount of dividends to be paid to preferred and common shareholders in each of the three years, assuming that the preferred stock is cumulative and nonparticipating.

| | Preferred | Common |
|---|---|---|
| 2006 | | |
| 2007 | | |
| 2008 | | |

**E 18–16**
Stock dividend

● LO8

The shareholders' equity of Core Technologies Company on June 30, 2005, included the following:

| | |
|---|---|
| Common stock, $1 par; authorized, 8 million shares; issued and outstanding, 3 million shares | $ 3,000,000 |
| Paid-in capital—excess of par | 12,000,000 |
| Retained earnings | 14,000,000 |

On April 1, 2006, the board of directors of Core Technologies declared a 10% stock dividend on common shares, to be distributed on June 1. The market price of Core Technologies' common stock was $30 on April 1, 2006, and $40 on June 1, 2006.

**Required:**

Prepare the journal entry to record the distribution of the stock dividend on the declaration date.

**E 18–17**
Stock split; Hanmi Financial Corporation
● LO8

**Hanmi Financial Corporation** is the parent company of Hanmi Bank. The company's 2005 stock split was announced in the following Business Wire:

---

LOS ANGELES (BUSINESS WIRE) Jan. 20, 2005—Hanmi Financial Corporation (Nasdaq), announced that the Board of Directors has approved a two-for-one stock split, to be effected in the form of a 100 percent common stock dividend. Hanmi Financial Corporation stockholders of record at the close of business on January 31, 2005 will receive one additional share of common stock for every share of common stock then held. Distribution of additional shares issued as a result of the split is expected to occur on or about February 15, 2005.

---

At the time of the stock split, 24.5 million shares of common stock, $.001 par per share, were outstanding.

**Required:**

1. Prepare the journal entry, if any, that Hanmi recorded at the time of the stock split.
2. What is the probable motivation for declaring the 2-for-1 stock split to be effected by a dividend payable in shares of common stock?
3. If Hanmi's stock price had been $36 at the time of the split, what would be its approximate value after the split (other things equal)?

**E 18–18**
Cash for fractional share rights
● LO8

Douglas McDonald Company's balance sheet included the following shareholders' equity accounts at December 31, 2005:

| | ($ in millions) |
|---|---|
| **Paid-in capital:** | |
| Common stock, 900 million shares at $1 par | $ 900 |
| Paid-in capital—excess of par | 15,800 |
| **Retained earnings** | 14,888 |
| **Total shareholders' equity** | $31,588 |

On March 16, 2006, a 4% common stock dividend was declared and distributed. The market value of the common stock was $21 per share. Fractional share rights represented 2 million equivalent whole shares. Cash was paid in place of the fractional share rights.

**Required:**

1. What is a fractional share right?
2. Prepare the appropriate entries for the declaration and distribution of the stock dividend.

**E 18–19**
Transactions affecting retained earnings
● LO6 through LO8

The balance sheet of Consolidated Paper, Inc. included the following shareholders' equity accounts at December 31, 2005:

| | ($ in millions) |
|---|---|
| **Paid-in capital:** | |
| Preferred stock, 8.8%, 90,000 shares at $1 par | $ 90,000 |
| Common stock, 364,000 shares at $1 par | 364,000 |
| Paid-in capital—excess par, preferred | 1,437,000 |
| Paid-in capital—excess of par, common | 2,574,000 |
| **Retained earnings** | 9,735,000 |
| Treasury stock, at cost; 4,000 common shares | (44,000) |
| **Total shareholders' equity** | $14,156,000 |

During 2006, several events and transactions affected the retained earnings of Consolidated Paper.

**Required:**

1. Prepare the appropriate entries for these events:
   a. On March 3 the board of directors declared a property dividend of 240,000 shares of Leasco International common stock that Consolidated Paper had purchased in January as an investment (book value: $700,000). The investment shares had a fair market value of $3 per share and were distributed March 31 to shareholders of record March 15.
   b. On May 3 a 5-for-4 stock split was declared and distributed. The stock split was effected in the form of a 25% stock dividend. The market value of the $1 par common stock was $11 per share.
   c. On July 5 a 2% common stock dividend was declared and distributed. The market value of the common stock was $11 per share.

d. On December 1 the board of directors declared the 8.8% cash dividend on the 90,000 preferred shares, payable on December 28 to shareholders of record December 20.
e. On December 1 the board of directors declared a cash dividend of $.50 per share on its common shares, payable on December 28 to shareholders of record December 20.

2. Prepare the shareholders' equity section of the balance sheet for Consolidated Paper, Inc. for the year ended at December 31, 2006. Net income for the year was $810,000.

**E 18–20**
Multiple choice; CPA exam; retained earnings

● LO6 LO7

The following questions dealing with retained earnings are adapted from prior CPA examinations. Determine the response that best completes the statements or questions.

1. At December 31, 2005, and December 31, 2006, Apex Co. had 3,000 shares of $100 par, 5% cumulative preferred stock outstanding. No dividends were in arrears as of December 31, 2004. Apex did not declare a dividend during 2005. During 2006 Apex paid a cash dividend of $10,000 on its preferred stock. Apex should report dividends in arrears in its 2006 financial statements as a (an)
   a. Accrued liability of $15,000.
   b. Disclosure of $15,000.
   c. Accrued liability of $20,000.
   d. Disclosure of $20,000.
2. On January 2, 2006, Lake Mining Co.'s board of directors declared a cash dividend of $400,000 to shareholders of record on January 18, 2006, payable on February 10, 2006. The dividend is permissible under law in Lake's state of incorporation. Selected data from Lake's December 31, 2005, balance sheet are as follows:

| | |
|---|---|
| Accumulated depletion | $100,000 |
| Capital stock | 500,000 |
| Additional paid-in capital | 150,000 |
| Retained earnings | 300,000 |

   The $400,000 dividend includes a liquidating dividend of
   a. $0
   b. $100,000
   c. $150,000
   d. $300,000
3. When a company declares a cash dividend, retained earnings is decreased by the amount of the dividend on the date of
   a. Declaration.
   b. Record.
   c. Payment.
   d. Declaration or record, whichever is earlier.

**E 18–21**
Profitability ratio

● LO1

Comparative balance sheets for Softech Canvas Goods for 2006 and 2005 are shown below. Softech pays no dividends, instead reinvesting all earnings for future growth.

**Comparative Balance Sheets**
($ in 000s)

| | December 31 | |
|---|---|---|
| | **2006** | **2005** |
| **Assets:** | | |
| Cash | $ 50 | $ 40 |
| Accounts receivable | 100 | 120 |
| Short-term investments | 50 | 40 |
| Inventory | 200 | 140 |
| Property, plant, and equipment (net) | 600 | 550 |
| | $1,000 | $890 |
| **Liabilities and Shareholders' Equity:** | | |
| Current liabilities | $ 240 | $210 |
| Bonds payable | 160 | 160 |
| Paid-in capital | 400 | 400 |
| Retained earnings | 200 | 120 |
| | $1,000 | $890 |

**Required:**

1. Determine the return on shareholders' equity for 2006.
2. What does the ratio measure?

**E 18–22**
New equity issues; offerings announcements
● LO3

When companies offer new equity security issues, they publicize the offerings in the financial press and on Internet sites. Assume the following were among the equity offerings reported in December 2006:

**NEW SECURITIES ISSUES**

**Equity**

**American Materials Transfer Corporation (AMTC)**—7.5 million common shares, $.001 par, priced at $13.546 each through underwriters led by Second Tennessee Bank N.A. and Morgan, Dunavant & Co., according to a syndicate official.

**Proactive Solutions Inc. (PSI)**—Offering of nine million common shares, $.01 par, was priced at $15.20 a share via lead manager Stanley Brothers, Inc., according to a syndicate official.

**Required:**

Prepare the appropriate journal entries to record the sale of both issues to underwriters. Ignore share issue costs.

**E 18–23**
Stock buyback; ConocoPhillips Corporation; press announcement
● LO4 LO5

The following excerpts are from an article reported in the February 4, 2005, online issue of *Yahoo Finance*.

HOUSTON (BUSINESS WIRE) Feb. 4, 2005—**ConocoPhillips** (NYSE) announced today that it plans to repurchase up to $1 billion of the company's common stock over a period of up to two years. Consistent with previous guidance, the company will use the program as a means of offsetting dilution to existing shareholders from the company's stock-based compensation programs.

The par amount per share for ConocoPhillips common stock is $.01. Paid-in capital—excess of par is $36.12 per share on average. The market price was $95 on February 4, 2005.

**Required:**

1. Suppose ConocoPhillips retires the 10.5 million shares ($1 billion ÷ $95) through repurchase on the open market at $95 per share. Prepare the appropriate journal entry to record the purchase, assuming ConocoPhillips retires the shares it buys back rather than accounting for them as treasury stock.
2. What does the company mean by saying that the buyback will serve "as a means of offsetting dilution to existing shareholders from the company's stock-based compensation programs"?

**E 18–24**
Multiple choice; CMA exam; shareholders' equity
● LO1 LO8

The following questions dealing with shareholders' equity are adapted from questions that previously appeared on Certified Management Accountant (CMA) examinations. The CMA designation sponsored by the Institute of Management Accountants (**www.imanet.org**) provides members with an objective measure of knowledge and competence in the field of management accounting. Determine the response that best completes the statements or questions.

1. The par value of common stock represents
   a. the estimated fair value of the stock when it was issued.
   b. the liability ceiling of a shareholder when a company undergoes bankruptcy proceedings.
   c. the total value of the stock that must be entered in the issuing corporation's records.
   d. the amount that must be recorded on the issuing corporation's record as paid-in capital.
2. The equity section of Smith Corporation's statement of financial position is presented below.

| | |
|---|---|
| Preferred stock, $100 par | $12,000,000 |
| Common stock, $5 par | 10,000,000 |
| Paid-in capital in excess of par | 18,000,000 |
| Retained earnings | 9,000,000 |
| Shareholders' equity | $49,000,000 |

   The common shareholders of Smith Corporation have preemptive rights. If Smith Corporation issues 400,000 additional share of common stock at $6 per share, a current holder of 20,000 shares of Smith Corporation's common stock must be given the option to buy
   a. 1,000 additional shares.
   b. 3,774 additional shares.
   c. 4,000 additional shares.
   d. 3,333 additional shares.
3. A stock dividend
   a. increases the debt to equity ratio of a firm.
   b. decreases future earnings per share.

c. decreases the size of the firm.
d. increases shareholders' wealth.

## PROBLEMS

available with McGraw-Hill's Homework Manager www.mhhe.com/spiceland4e

**An alternate exercise and problem set is available on the text website: www.mhhe.com/spiceland4e**

**P 18–1**
Various stock transactions; correction of journal entries
● LO3

**Part A**

During its first year of operations, the McCollum Corporation entered into the following transactions relating to shareholders' equity. The corporation was authorized to issue 100 million common shares, $1 par per share.

**Required:**

Prepare the appropriate journal entries to record each transaction.

| | |
|---|---|
| Jan. 9 | Issued 40 million common shares for $20 per share. |
| Mar. 11 | Issued 5,000 shares in exchange for custom-made equipment. McCollum's shares have traded recently on the stock exchange at $20 per share. |

**Part B**

A new staff accountant for the McCollum Corporation recorded the following journal entries during the second year of operations. McCollum retires shares that it reacquires (restores their status to that of authorized but unissued shares).

| | | ($ in millions) | |
|---|---|---|---|
| Jan. 12 | Land | 2 | |
| | Paid-in capital—donation of land | | 2 |
| Sept. 1 | Common stock | 2 | |
| | Retained earnings | 48 | |
| | Cash | | 50 |
| Dec. 1 | Cash | 26 | |
| | Common stock | | 1 |
| | Gain on sale of previously issued shares | | 25 |

**Required:**

Prepare the journal entries that should have been recorded for each of the transactions.

**P 18–2**
Share buyback—comparison of retirement and treasury stock treatment
● LO4 LO5

The shareholders' equity section of the balance sheet of TNL Systems, Inc. included the following accounts at December 31, 2005:

| Shareholders' Equity | ($ in millions) |
|---|---|
| Common stock, 240 million shares at $1 par, | $ 240 |
| Paid-in capital—excess of par | 1,680 |
| Paid-in capital—share repurchase | 1 |
| Retained earnings | 1,100 |

**Required:**

1. During 2006, TNL Systems reacquired shares of its common stock and later sold shares in two separate transactions. Prepare the entries for both the purchase and subsequent resale of the shares assuming the shares are (a) retired and (b) viewed as treasury stock.
   a. On February 5, 2006, TNL Systems purchased 6 million shares at $10 per share.
   b. On July 9, 2006, the corporation sold 2 million shares at $12 per share.
   c. On November 14, 2008, the corporation sold 2 million shares at $7 per share.
2. Prepare the shareholders' equity section of TNL Systems' balance sheet at December 31, 2008, comparing the two approaches. Assume all net income earned in 2006–2008 was distributed to shareholders as cash dividends.

**P 18–3**
Reacquired shares—comparison of retired shares and treasury shares
● LO4 LO5
eXcel

National Supply's shareholders' equity included the following accounts at December 31, 2005:

| Shareholders' Equity | ($ in millions) |
|---|---|
| Common stock, 6 million shares at $1 par | $ 6,000,000 |
| Paid-in capital—excess of par | 30,000,000 |
| Retained earnings | 86,500,000 |

**Required:**

1. National Supply reacquired shares of its common stock in two separate transactions and later sold shares. Prepare the entries for each of the transactions under each of two separate assumptions: the shares are (a) retired and (b) accounted for as treasury stock.

| | |
|---|---|
| February 15, 2006 | Reacquired 300,000 shares at $8 per share. |
| February 17, 2007 | Reacquired 300,000 shares at $5.50 per share. |
| November 9, 2008 | Sold 200,000 shares at $7 per share (assume FIFO cost). |

2. Prepare the shareholders' equity section of National Supply's balance sheet at December 31, 2008, assuming the shares are (a) retired and (b) accounted for as treasury stock. Net income was $14 million in 2006, $15 million in 2007, and $16 million in 2008. No dividends were paid during the three-year period.

**P 18–4**
Statement of retained earnings

● LO4 through LO7

Comparative statements of retained earnings for Renn-Dever Corporation were reported in its 2006 annual report as follows.

**RENN-DEVER CORPORATION**
**Statements of Retained Earnings**

| For the Years Ended December 31, | 2006 | 2005 | 2004 |
|---|---|---|---|
| **Balance at beginning of year** | $6,794,292 | $5,464,052 | $5,624,552 |
| Net income (loss) | 3,308,700 | 2,240,900 | (160,500) |
| Deductions: | | | |
| Stock dividend (34,900 shares) | 242,000 | | |
| Common shares retired (110,000 shares) | | 212,660 | |
| Common stock cash dividends | 889,950 | 698,000 | 0 |
| **Balance at end of year** | $8,971,042 | $6,794,292 | $5,464,052 |

At December 31, 2003, common shares consisted of the following:

| | |
|---|---|
| Common stock, 1,855,000 shares at $1 par | $1,855,000 |
| Paid-in capital—excess of par | 7,420,000 |

**Required:**
Infer from the reports the events and transactions that affected Renn-Dever Corporation's retained earnings during 2004, 2005, and 2006. Prepare the journal entries that reflect those events and transactions.

**P 18–5**
Shareholders' equity transactions; statement of shareholders' equity

● LO1 LO6 through LO8

eXcel

Listed below are the transactions that affected the shareholders' equity of Branch-Rickie Corporation during the period 2006–2008. At December 31, 2005, the corporation's accounts included:

| | ($ in 000s) |
|---|---|
| Common stock, 105 million shares at $1 par | $105,000 |
| Paid-in capital—excess of par | 630,000 |
| Retained earnings | 970,000 |

a. November 1, 2006, the board of directors declared a cash dividend of $.80 per share on its common shares, payable to shareholders of record November 15, to be paid December 1.
b. On March 1, 2007, the board of directors declared a property dividend consisting of corporate bonds of Warner Corporation that Branch-Rickie was holding as an investment. The bonds had a fair market value of $1.6 million, but were purchased two years previously for $1.3 million. Because they were intended to be held to maturity, the bonds had not been previously written up. The property dividend was payable to shareholders of record March 13, to be distributed April 5.
c. On July 12, 2007, the corporation declared and distributed a 5% common stock dividend (when the market value of the common stock was $21 per share). Cash was paid for fractional share rights representing 250,000 equivalent whole shares.
d. On November 1, 2007, the board of directors declared a cash dividend of $.80 per share on its common shares, payable to shareholders of record November 15, to be paid December 1.
e. On January 15, 2008, the board of directors declared and distributed a 3-for-2 stock split effected in the form of a 50% stock dividend when the market value of the common stock was $22 per share.
f. On November 1, 2008, the board of directors declared a cash dividend of $.65 per share on its common shares, payable to shareholders of record November 15, to be paid December 1.

**Required:**
1. Prepare the journal entries that Branch-Rickie recorded during the three-year period for these transactions.
2. Prepare comparative statements of shareholders' equity for Branch-Rickie for the three-year period ($ in 000s). Net income was $330 million, $395 million, and $455 million for 2006, 2007, and 2008, respectively.

**P 18–6**
Statement of shareholders' equity

● LO1 LO3 through LO8

Comparative statements of shareholders' equity for Anaconda International Corporation were reported as follows for the fiscal years ending December 31, 2006, 2007, and 2008.

**ANACONDA INTERNATIONAL CORPORATION**
**Statements of Shareholders' Equity**
**For the Years Ended Dec. 31, 2006, 2007, and 2008**
($ in millions)

| | Preferred Stock $10 par | Common Stock $1 par | Additional Paid-In Capital | Receivable from Share Purchase Contract | Retained Earnings | Total Share-holders' Equity |
|---|---|---|---|---|---|---|
| **Balance at January 1, 2006** | | 55 | 495 | | 1,878 | 2,428 |
| Sale of preferred shares | 10 | | 470 | (360) | | 120 |
| Sale of common shares | | 7 | 63 | | | 70 |
| Cash dividend, preferred | | | | | (1) | (1) |
| Cash dividend, common | | | | | (16) | (16) |
| Net income | — | — | — | — | 290 | 290 |
| **Balance at December 31, 2006** | **10** | **62** | **1,028** | **(360)** | **2,151** | **2,891** |
| Received balance from share purchase contract | | | | 360 | | 360 |
| Retirement of shares | | (3) | (27) | | (20) | (50) |
| Cash dividend, preferred | | | | | (1) | (1) |
| Cash dividend, common | | | | | (20) | (20) |
| 3-for-2 split effected in the form of a dividend | 5 | | (5) | | | |
| Net income | — | — | — | — | 380 | 380 |
| **Balance at December 31, 2007** | **15** | **59** | **996** | **0** | **2,490** | **3,560** |
| Common stock dividend | | 6 | 59 | | (65) | |
| Cash dividend, preferred | | | | | (1) | (1) |
| Cash dividend, common | | | | | (22) | (22) |
| Net income | — | — | — | — | 412 | 412 |
| **Balance at December 31, 2008** | **15** | **65** | **1,055** | **0** | **2,814** | **3,949** |

**Required:**
Infer from the statements the events and transactions that affected Anaconda International Corporation's shareholders' equity during 2006, 2007, and 2008. Prepare the journal entries that reflect those events and transactions.

**P 18–7**
Reporting shareholders' equity; comprehensive income; Hewlett-Packard

● LO1 through LO4

**Hewlett-Packard** is a leading provider of computing and imaging solutions and services for business and home. The following is the 2004 Statement of Shareholders' Equity from HP's 2004 annual report. Remember that for comparative purposes, three years are reported in these statements. The 2003 and 2002 portions of the statement are not shown here for brevity of presentation.

**HEWLETT-PACKARD COMPANY AND SUBSIDIARIES**
**Consolidated Statement of Stockholders' Equity (in part)**

| ($ in millions)<br>Shares in 000s | Number of Shares | Par Value | Add'l Paid-in Capital | Retained Earnings | Accum. Other Compr. Income | Total |
|---|---|---|---|---|---|---|
| **Balance October 31, 2003** | **3,042,761** | **30** | **24,587** | **13,332** | **(203)** | **37,746** |
| Net earnings | — | — | — | 3,497 | — | 3,497 |
| Net unrealized loss on available-for-sale securities | — | — | — | — | (20) | (20) |
| Net unrealized loss on cash flow hedges | — | — | — | — | (28) | (28) |
| Minimum pension liability, net of taxes | — | — | — | — | (13) | (13) |
| Cumulative translation adjustment | — | — | — | — | 21 | 21 |
| Comprehensive income | | | | | | 3,457 |
| Assumption of stock options with business acquisitions | | — | 15 | — | — | 15 |
| Issuance of common stock—employee stock plans | 40,467 | — | 592 | — | — | 592 |
| Repurchase of common stock | (172,468) | (1) | (3,100) | (208) | — | (3,309) |
| Tax benefit on employee stock options | — | — | 35 | — | — | 35 |
| Dividends | — | — | — | (972) | — | (972) |
| **Balance October 31, 2004** | **2,910,760** | **29** | **22,129** | **15,649** | **(243)** | **37,564** |

**Required:**

1. What is the purpose of the statement of shareholders' equity?
2. How does HP account for its share buybacks?
3. For its share buybacks in 2004, was the price HP paid for the shares repurchased more or less than the average price at which HP had sold the shares previously? Reconstruct the journal entry HP used to record the buyback.
4. What is comprehensive income? What is other comprehensive income?
5. What caused the change in HP's comprehensive income in 2004? What was the amount of Accumulated other comprehensive income (loss) that HP reported in its 2004 balance sheet?

**P 18–8**
Share issue costs; issuance; dividends; early retirement

● LO3 LO4 LO7

During its first year of operations, Cupola Fan Corporation issued 30,000 of $1 par Class B shares for $385,000 on June 30, 2006. Share issue costs were $1,500. One year from the issue date (July 1, 2007), the corporation retired 10% of the shares for $39,500.

**Required:**

1. Prepare the journal entry to record the issuance of the shares.
2. Prepare the journal entry to record the declaration of a $2 per share dividend on December 1, 2006.
3. Prepare the journal entry to record the payment of the dividend on December 31, 2006.
4. Prepare the journal entry to record the retirement of the shares.

(Note: You may wish to compare your solution to this problem with that of Problem 14–16, which deals with parallel issues of debt issue costs and the retirement of debt.)

**P 18–9**
Effect of preferred stock characteristics on dividends

● LO7

The shareholders' equity of Kramer Industries includes the data shown below. During 2006, cash dividends of $150 million were declared. Dividends were not declared in 2004 or 2005.

| | ($ in millions) |
|---|---|
| Common stock | $200 |
| Paid-in capital—excess of par, common | 800 |
| Preferred stock, 10%, nonparticipating | 100 |
| Paid-in capital—excess of par, preferred | 270 |

**Required:**

Determine the amount of dividends payable to preferred shareholders and to common shareholders under each of the following two assumptions regarding the characteristics of the preferred stock.

**Assumption A**—The preferred stock is noncumulative.
**Assumption B**—The preferred stock is cumulative.

**P 18–10**
Transactions affecting retained earnings

● LO3 through LO8

Indicate by letter whether each of the transactions listed below increases (**I**), decreases (**D**), or has no effect (**N**) on retained earnings. Assume the shareholders' equity of the transacting company includes only common stock, paid-in capital—excess of par, and retained earnings at the time of each transaction.

**Transactions**

Example _N_ 1. Sale of common stock
____ 2. Purchase of treasury stock at a cost *less* than the original issue price
____ 3. Purchase of treasury stock at a cost *greater* than the original issue price
____ 4. Declaration of a property dividend
____ 5. Sale of treasury stock for *more* than cost
____ 6. Sale of treasury stock for *less* than cost
____ 7. Net income for the year
____ 8. Declaration of a cash dividend
____ 9. Payment of a previously declared cash dividend
____ 10. Issuance of convertible bonds for cash
____ 11. Declaration and distribution of a 5% stock dividend
____ 12. Retirement of common stock at a cost *less* than the original issue price
____ 13. Retirement of common stock at a cost *greater* than the original issue price
____ 14. A stock split effected in the form of a stock dividend
____ 15. A stock split in which the par value per share is reduced (not effected in the form of a stock dividend)
____ 16. A net loss for the year

**P 18–11**
Stock dividends received on investments; integrative problem

Ellis Transport Company acquired 1.2 million shares of stock in L&K Corporation at $44 per share. They are classified by Ellis as available for sale. Ellis sold 200,000 shares at $46, received a 10% stock dividend, and then later in the year sold another 100,000 shares at $43.
*Hint:* There is no entry for the stock dividend, but a new investment per share must be calculated for use later when the shares are sold.

• LO8

**Required:**
Prepare journal entries to record these transactions.

**P 18–12**
Various shareholders' equity topics; comprehensive

• LO1 LO3 through LO8

eXcel

**Part A**
In late 2005, the Nicklaus Corporation was formed. The corporate charter authorizes the issuance of 5,000,000 shares of common stock carrying a $1 par value, and 1,000,000 shares of $5 par value, noncumulative, nonparticipating preferred stock. On January 2, 2006, 3,000,000 shares of the common stock are issued in exchange for cash at an average price of $10 per share. Also on January 2, all 1,000,000 shares of preferred stock are issued at $20 per share.

**Required:**
1. Prepare journal entries to record these transactions.
2. Prepare the shareholders' equity section of the Nicklaus balance sheet as of March 31, 2006. (Assume net income for the first quarter 2006 was $1,000,000.)

**Part B**
During 2006, the Nicklaus Corporation participated in three treasury stock transactions:
a. On June 30, 2006, the corporation reacquires 200,000 shares for the treasury at a price of $12 per share.
b. On July 31, 2006, 50,000 treasury shares are reissued at $15 per share.
c. On September 30, 2006, 50,000 treasury shares are reissued at $10 per share.

**Required:**
1. Prepare journal entries to record these transactions.
2. Prepare the Nicklaus Corporation shareholders' equity section as it would appear in a balance sheet prepared at September 30, 2006. (Assume net income for the second and third quarter was $3,000,000.)

**Part C**
On October 1, 2006, Nicklaus Corporation receives permission to replace its $1 par value common stock (5,000,000 shares authorized, 3,000,000 shares issued, and 2,900,000 shares outstanding) with a new common stock issue having a $.50 par value. Since the new par value is one-half the amount of the old, this represents a 2-for-1 stock split. That is, the shareholders will receive two shares of the $.50 par stock in exchange for each share of the $1 par stock they own. The $1 par stock will be collected and destroyed by the issuing corporation.

On November 1, 2006, the Nicklaus Corporation declares a $.05 per share cash dividend on common stock and a $.25 per share cash dividend on preferred stock. Payment is scheduled for December 1, 2006, to shareholders of record on November 15, 2006.

On December 2, 2006, the Nicklaus Corporation declares a 1% stock dividend payable on December 28, 2006, to shareholders of record on December 14. At the date of declaration, the common stock was selling in the open market at $10 per share. The dividend will result in 58,000 (.01 × 5,800,000) additional shares being issued to shareholders.

**Required:**
1. Prepare journal entries to record the declaration and payment of these stock and cash dividends.
2. Prepare the December 31, 2006, shareholders' equity section of the balance sheet for the Nicklaus Corporation. (Assume net income for the fourth quarter was $2,500,000.)
3. Prepare a statement of shareholders' equity for Nicklaus Corporation for 2006.

**P 18–13**
Quasi reorganization (based on Appendix 18)

• LO1

eXcel

A new CEO was hired to revive the floundering Champion Chemical Corporation. The company had endured operating losses for several years, but confidence was emerging that better times were ahead. The board of directors and shareholders approved a quasi reorganization for the corporation. The reorganization included devaluing inventory for obsolescence by $105 million and increasing land by $5 million. Immediately prior to the restatement, at December 31, 2005, Champion Chemical Corporation's balance sheet appeared as follows (in condensed form):

**CHAMPION CHEMICAL CORPORATION**
**Balance Sheet**
**At December 31, 2005**
($ in millions)

| | |
|---|---|
| Cash | $ 20 |
| Receivables | 40 |
| Inventory | 230 |
| Land | 40 |
| Buildings and equipment (net) | 90 |
| | $420 |
| Liabilities | $240 |
| Common stock (320 million shares at $1 par) | 320 |
| Additional paid-in capital | 60 |
| Retained earnings (deficit) | (200) |
| | $420 |

**Required:**

1. Prepare the journal entries appropriate to record the quasi reorganization on January 1, 2006.
2. Prepare a balance sheet as it would appear immediately after the restatement.

# BROADEN YOUR PERSPECTIVE

**Apply your critical-thinking ability to the knowledge you've gained. These cases will provide you an opportunity to develop your research, analysis, judgment, and communication skills. You also will work with other students, integrate what you've learned, apply it in real world situations, and consider its global and ethical ramifications. This practice will broaden your knowledge and further develop your decision-making abilities.**

**Real World Case 18–1**
Initial public offering of common stock; Dolby Laboratories

● LO3

Ray Dolby started **Dolby Laboratories** nearly 40 years ago and since then has been a leader in the entertainment industry and consumer electronics. Closely held since its founding in 1965, Dolby decided to go public in 2005. Here's an AP news report:

---

FEB. 14, 2005
**DOLBY'S IPO EXPECTED TO PLAY SWEET MUSIC**
The initial public offering market is hoping for a big bang this week from Dolby Laboratories Inc. The San Francisco company, whose sound systems and double-D logo are ubiquitous in the movie industry as well as in consumer electronics, plans to sell 27.5 million shares for $13.50 to $15.50 each. Founded by Cambridge-trained scientist Ray Dolby 39 years ago, the company started out manufacturing noise-reduction equipment for the music industry that eliminated the background "hiss" on recordings, and has since expanded to encompass everything from digital audio systems to Dolby Surround sound. The company's IPO, which is lead-managed by underwriters Morgan Stanley and Goldman Sachs Group Inc., is expected to do well not only because of its brand recognition, but also because of its strong financials. *(AP)*

---

**Required:**

1. Assuming the shares are issued at the midpoint of the price range indicated, how much capital did the IPO raise for Dolby Laboratories before any underwriting discount and offering expenses?
2. If the par amount is $.01 per share, what journal entry did Dolby use to record the sale?

**Analysis Case 18–2**
Statement of shareholders' equity

● LO1 LO3 LO6 LO7

The shareholders' equity portion of the balance sheet of Sessel's Department Stores, Inc., a large regional specialty retailer, is as follows:

**SESSEL'S DEPARTMENT STORES, INC.**
**Comparative Balance Sheets**
**Shareholders' Equity Section**

| ($ in 000s, except per share amounts) | Dec. 31, 2006 | Dec. 31, 2005 |
|---|---|---|
| **Shareholders' Equity** | | |
| Preferred stock—$1 par value; 20,000 total shares authorized, | | |
| Series A—600 shares authorized, issued, and outstanding, $50 per share liquidation preference | $ 57,700 | $ — |
| Series B—33 shares authorized, no shares outstanding | | |
| Common stock—$.10 par; 200,000 shares authorized, 19,940 and 18,580 shares issued and outstanding at Dec. 31, 2006, and Dec. 31, 2005, respectively | 1,994 | 1,858 |
| Additional paid-in capital | 227,992 | 201,430 |
| Retained income | 73,666 | 44,798 |
| **Total shareholders' equity** | $361,352 | $248,086 |

Disclosures elsewhere in Sessel's annual report revealed the following changes in shareholders' equity accounts for 2006, 2005, 2004:

**2006:**

1. The only changes in retained earnings during 2006, were preferred dividends on preferred stock of $3,388,000 and net income.
2. The preferred stock is convertible. During the year, 6,592 shares were issued. All shares were converted into 320,000 shares of common stock. No gain or loss was recorded on the conversion.

3. Common shares were issued in a public offering and upon the exercise of stock options. On the statement of shareholders' equity, Sessel's reports these two items on a single line entitled: "Issuance of shares."

**2005:**
1. Net income: $12,126,000.
2. Issuance of common stock: 5,580,000 shares at $112,706,000.

**2004:**
1. Net income: $13,494,000.
2. Issuance of common stock: 120,000 shares at $826,000.

**Required:**
From these disclosures, prepare comparative statements of shareholders' equity for 2006, 2005, and 2004.

**Communication Case 18–3**
Is a receivable for stock issued or to be issued a recognizable asset, or should it be deducted from equity? Group interaction

● LO3

An unsettled question in accounting for stock is: Should a receivable for stock issued or to be issued, such as a note receivable for stock already issued or a stock subscription receivable, be recognized as an asset, or should it be deducted from equity? The prevalent practice is reporting the receivable as a contra equity account. This results in reporting total paid-in capital only to the extent that unrestricted shares are outstanding. However, many accountants believe receivables for stock fit the definition of assets.

Two opposing viewpoints are:

**View 1:** Receivables for stock should be deducted from equity.
**View 2:** Receivables for stock should be reported as assets.

In considering this question, focus on conceptual issues regarding the practicable and theoretically appropriate treatment, unconstrained by GAAP.

**Required:**
1. Which view do you favor? Develop a list of arguments in support of your view prior to the class session for which the case is assigned.
2. In class, your instructor will pair you (and everyone else) with a classmate (who also has independently developed an argument).
   a. You will be given three minutes to argue your view to your partner. Your partner likewise will be given three minutes to argue his or her view to you. During these three-minute presentations, the listening partner is not permitted to speak.
   b. Then after each person has had a turn attempting to convince his or her partner, the two partners will have a three-minute discussion in which they will decide which view is more convincing and arguments will be merged into a single view for each pair.
3. After the allotted time, a spokesperson for each of the two views will be selected by the instructor. Each spokesperson will field arguments from the class in support of that view's position and list the arguments on the board. The class then will discuss the merits of the two lists of arguments and attempt to reach a consensus view, though a consensus is not necessary.

**Research Case 18–4**
Comprehensive income; locate and extract relevant information and authoritative support for a financial reporting issue; integrative; Cisco Systems

● LO2

Titan Networking became a public company through an IPO (initial public offering) two weeks ago. You are looking forward to the challenges of being assistant controller for a publicly owned corporation. One such challenge came in the form of a memo in this morning's in-box. "We need to start reporting comprehensive income in our financials," the message from your boss said. "Do some research on that, will you? That concept didn't exist when I went to school." In response, you sought out the financial statements of **Cisco Systems**, the networking industry leader. The following is an excerpt from a disclosure note from Cisco's 2004 annual report:

**Comprehensive Income (Loss) (in part)**
The components of comprehensive income (loss), net of tax, are as follows (in millions):

| | Years Ended | | |
|---|---|---|---|
| | July 31, 2004 | July 26, 2003 | July 27, 2002 |
| Net income (loss) | $4,401 | $3,578 | $1,893 |
| Other comprehensive income (loss): | | | |
| Change in net unrealized gains and losses on investments net of tax benefit (expense) of $42, $(150), and $9 in fiscal 2004, 2003, and 2002, respectively | (77) | 352 | 224 |
| Other | 19 | 29 | 24 |
| Less: Minority interest | (84) | — | — |
| Total | $4,259 | $3,959 | $2,141 |

**Required:**

1. Use EdgarScan (edgarscan.pwcglobal.com) or Cisco's website to locate the financial statements of Cisco. Search the 2004 annual report for information about how Cisco accounts for comprehensive income. What does Cisco report in its balance sheet regarding comprehensive income?
2. Consult the FASB pronouncements at www.fasb.org/st/ or from some other source. What authoritative literature does Cisco rely on when reporting comprehensive income? When did the requirement become effective?
3. What is comprehensive income? How does it differ from net income? Where is it reported in a balance sheet? Why does Cisco's 2004 balance sheet amount differ from the 2004 amount reported in the disclosure note? Explain.
4. The primary component of Other comprehensive income for Cisco is "Change in net unrealized gains on investments." What does this mean? From the information Cisco's financial statements provide, determine how the company calculated the $212 million accumulated other comprehensive loss in fiscal 2004.
5. What might be possible causes for the "Other" component of Cisco's Other comprehensive income?

**Judgment Case 18–5**
Treasury stock; stock split; cash dividends; Alcoa

● LO5 through LO8

Alcoa is the world's leading producer of primary aluminum, fabricated aluminum, and alumina. The following is a press release from the company:

---

**Alcoa Announces 33% Increase in Base Dividend, 2-for-1 Stock Split**

PITTSBURGH—Alcoa today announced that its Board of Directors approved a base quarterly dividend increase of 33.3%, to 25 cents per common share from 18.75 cents per share. For a full year, base dividends will now total $1.00 compared with 75 cents before the increase.

**2-for-1 Stock Split**

The Board declared a two-for-one split of Alcoa's common stock. The stock split is subject to approval of Alcoa shareholders who must approve an amendment to the company's articles to increase the authorized shares of common stock at Alcoa's annual meeting. Shareholders of record on May 26 will receive an additional common share for each share held, which will be distributed on June 9.

**Commitment to Stock Repurchase Program**

Alcoa restated its commitment to its previously authorized share repurchase program which it announced last year.

---

**Required:**

1. What are the two primary reporting alternatives Alcoa has in accounting for the repurchase of its shares? What would be the effect of the optional courses of action on total shareholders' equity? Explain. What would be the effect of the optional courses of action on how stock would be presented in Alcoa's balance sheet? If the shares are later resold for an amount greater than cost, how should Alcoa account for the sale?
2. What are the two primary courses of action Alcoa has in accounting for the stock split, and how would the choice affect Alcoa's shareholders' equity? Why?
3. How should Alcoa account for the cash dividend, and how would it affect Alcoa's balance sheet? Why?

**Communication Case 18–6**
Issuance of shares; share issue costs; prepare a report

● LO3

You are the newest member of the staff of Brinks & Company, a medium-size investment management firm. You are supervised by Les Kramer, an employee of two years. Les has a reputation as being technically sound but has a noticeable gap in his accounting education. Knowing you are knowledgeable about accounting issues, he requested you provide him with a synopsis of accounting for share issue costs.

"I thought the cost of issuing securities is recorded separately and expensed over time," he stated in a handwritten memo. "But I don't see that for IBR's underwriting expenses. What gives?"

He apparently was referring to a disclosure note on a page of IBR's annual report, photocopied and attached to his memo. To raise funds for expansion, the company sold additional shares of its $.10 par common stock. The following disclosure note appeared in the company's most recent annual report:

---

NOTES TO CONSOLIDATED FINANCIAL STATEMENTS
**Note 10—Stock Transactions (in part)**

In February and March, the Company sold 2,395,000 shares of Common Stock at $22.25 per share in a public offering. Net proceeds to the Company were approximately $50.2 million after the underwriting discount and offering expenses.

---

**Required:**

Write a formal memo to your supervisor. Briefly explain how share issue costs are accounted for and how that accounting differs from that of debt issue costs. To make sure your explanation is understood in context of the footnote, include in your memo the following:

a. At what total amount did the shares sell to the public? How is the difference between this amount and the $50.2 million net proceeds accounted for?
b. The appropriate journal entry to record the sale of the shares.

**Analysis Case 18–7**
Analyzing financial statements; price-earnings ratio; dividend payout ratio

● LO1

IGF Foods Company is a large, primarily domestic, consumer foods company involved in the manufacture, distribution, and sale of a variety of food products. Industry averages are derived from Troy's *The Almanac of Business and Industrial Financial Ratios* and Dun and Bradstreet's *Industry Norms and Key Business Ratios*. Following are the 2006 and 2005 comparative income statements and balance sheets for IGF. The market price of IGF's common stock is $47 during 2006. (The financial data we use are from actual financial statements of a well-known corporation, but the company name used in our illustration is fictitious and the numbers and dates have been modified slightly to disguise the company's identity.)

**IGF FOODS COMPANY**
**Years Ended December 31, 2006 and 2005**

| ($ in millions) | 2006 | 2005 |
|---|---|---|
| **Comparative Income Statements** | | |
| Net sales | $6,440 | $5,800 |
| Cost of goods sold | (3,667) | (3,389) |
| Gross profit | 2,773 | 2,411 |
| Operating expenses | (1,916) | (1,629) |
| Operating income | 857 | 782 |
| Interest expense | (54) | (53) |
| Income from operations before tax | 803 | 729 |
| Income taxes | (316) | (287) |
| Net income | $ 487 | $ 442 |
| Net income per share | $2.69 | $2.44 |
| Average shares outstanding | 181 million | 181 million |
| **Comparative Balance Sheets** | | |
| **Assets** | | |
| Current assets: | | |
| Cash | $ 48 | $ 142 |
| Accounts receivable | 347 | 320 |
| Marketable securities | 358 | — |
| Inventories | 914 | 874 |
| Prepaid expenses | 212 | 154 |
| Total current assets | $1,879 | $1,490 |
| Property, plant, and equipment (net) | 2,592 | 2,291 |
| Intangibles (net) | 800 | 843 |
| Other assets | 74 | 60 |
| *Total assets* | $5,345 | $4,684 |
| **Liabilities and Shareholders' Equity** | | |
| Current liabilities: | | |
| Accounts payable | $ 254 | $ 276 |
| Accrued liabilities | 493 | 496 |
| Notes payable | 518 | 115 |
| Current portion of long-term debt | 208 | 54 |
| Total current liabilities | 1,473 | 941 |
| Long-term debt | 534 | 728 |
| Deferred income taxes | 407 | 344 |
| Total liabilities | 2,414 | 2,013 |
| Shareholders' equity: | | |
| Common stock, $1 par | 180 | 180 |
| Additional paid-in capital | 21 | 63 |
| Retained earnings | 2,730 | 2,428 |
| Total shareholders' equity | 2,931 | 2,671 |
| *Total liabilities and shareholders' equity* | $5,345 | $4,684 |

Profitability is the key to a company's long-run survival. Profitability measures focus on a company's ability to provide an adequate return relative to resources devoted to company operations.

**Required:**

1. Calculate the return on shareholders' equity for IGF. The average return for the stocks listed on the New York Stock Exchange in a comparable period was 18.8%. What information does your calculation provide an investor?
2. Calculate IGF's earnings per share and earnings-price ratio. The average return for the stocks listed on the New York Stock Exchange in a comparable time period was 5.4%. What does your calculation indicate about IGF's earnings?

**International Case 18–8**
Accounting for shareholders' equity in other countries

● LO1

In the United States, shareholders' equity represents a residual amount: assets minus liabilities. It is reported in two primary categories: paid-in (or invested) capital and retained earnings (or earned capital). Worldwide, there is little uniformity in how capital or shareholders' equity is defined or reported on the balance sheet. Significant differences exist from country to country.

**Required:**

1. Choose a country other than the United States and research the way that country accounts for shareholders' equity. Include in your analysis:
   a. How shareholders' equity is defined.
   b. The categories by which it is reported in the financial statements.
   c. What if any requirements exist to separately maintain legal capital.
   d. Restrictions on dividend payments and how dividends are reported.
   e. Whether a statement of shareholders' equity, or equivalent, is reported.
2. Prepare a short report highlighting the similarities and differences between the United States and your chosen country in the way shareholders' equity is accounted for. Optionally, the report might compare (a) the degree of conservatism in the approaches taken by the two countries or (b) whether cultural differences are likely contributors to the differences observed.

**Ethics Case 18–9**
The Swiss label maker; value of shares issued for equipment

● LO3

Bricker Graphics is a privately held company specializing in package labels. Representatives of the firm have just returned from Switzerland, where a Swiss firm is manufacturing a custom-made high speed, color labeling machine. Confidence is high that the new machine will help rescue Bricker from sharply declining profitability. Bricker's chief operating officer, Don Benson, has been under fire for not achieving the company's performance goals of achieving a rate of return on assets of at least 12%.

The afternoon of his return from Switzerland, Benson called Susan Sharp into his office. Susan is Bricker's Controller.

**Benson:** I wish you had been able to go. We have some accounting issues to consider.
**Sharp:** I wish I'd been there, too. I understand the food was marvelous. What are the accounting issues?
**Benson:** They discussed accepting our notes at the going rate for a face amount of $12.5 million. We also discussed financing with stock.
**Sharp:** I thought we agreed, debt is the way to go for us now.
**Benson:** Yes, but I've been thinking. We can issue shares for a total of $10 million. The labeler is custom-made and doesn't have a quoted selling price, but the domestic labelers we considered went for around $10 million. It sure would help our rate of return if we keep the asset base as low as possible.

**Required:**

1. How will Benson's plan affect the return measure? What accounting issue is involved?
2. Is the proposal ethical?
3. Who would be affected if the proposal is implemented?

**Research Case 18–10**
Researching the way shareholders' equity transactions are reported; retrieving financial statements from the Internet

● LO1 LO6

EDGAR, the Electronic Data Gathering, Analysis, and Retrieval system, performs automated collection, validation, indexing, and forwarding of submissions by companies and others who are required by law to file forms with the U.S. Securities and Exchange Commission (SEC). All publicly traded domestic companies use EDGAR to make the majority of their filings. (Filings by foreign companies are not required to be filed on EDGAR, but some of these companies do so voluntarily.) Form 10-K or 10-KSB, which includes the annual report, is required to be filed on EDGAR. The SEC makes this information available on the Internet.

**Required:**

1. Access EDGAR on the Internet at **www.sec.gov**, or through EdgarScan at **edgarscan.pwcglobal.com/**.
2. Search for a public company with which you are familiar. Access its most recent 10-K filing. Search or scroll to find the statement of shareholders' equity and related note(s). If a statement of shareholders' equity is not provided, try another company.
3. Determine from the statement the transactions that occurred during the most recent three years that affected retained earnings.
4. Determine from the statement the transactions that occurred during the most recent three years that affected common stock. Were any of these transactions identified in requirement 3 also?
5. Cross-reference your findings with amounts reported on the balance sheet. How do these two statements articulate with one another?

**Real World Case 18–11**
Reporting preferred shares; AMCON Distributing Co.

● LO1 LO3

**AMCON Distributing Company** is primarily engaged in the wholesale distribution of consumer products in the Great Plains and Rocky Mountain regions. The following disclosure note appeared in the company's 2004 annual report.

---

**4. SHAREHOLDERS' EQUITY**

In June 2004, the Company issued $2.5 million of Series A Convertible Preferred Stock representing 100,000 shares at a purchase price of $25 per share (the "Liquidation Preference"). The Series A Convertible Preferred Stock is convertible at any time by the holders into a number of shares of AMCON common stock equal to the number of Preferred Shares being converted times a fraction equal to $25.00 divided by the conversion price. The conversion price is initially $30.31 per share, but is subject to customary adjustments in the event of stock splits, stock dividends and certain other distributions on the Common Stock. Cumulative dividends on the Series A Convertible Preferred Stock are payable at a rate of 6.785% per annum and are payable in arrears, when, as and if declared by the Board of Directors, on March 31, June 30, September 30 and December 31 of each year. Upon liquidation of the Company, the holders of the Series A Preferred Stock are entitled to receive the Liquidation Preference plus any accrued and unpaid dividends prior to the distribution of any amount to the holders of the Common Stock. The Series A Convertible Preferred Stock is redeemable at the option of the Company beginning June 17, 2006 at a redemption price equal to 112% of the Liquidation Preference. The redemption price decreases 1% annually thereafter until June 16, 2018, after which date it remains the liquidation preference.

---

**Required:**

1. The $25 selling price is the base amount for calculating preferred dividends. What amount of dividends is paid annually to a preferred shareholder owning 100 shares?
2. If dividends are not paid in 2005 and 2006 but are paid in 2007, what amount of dividends will the shareholder receive?
3. If the investor chooses to convert the shares in 2005, how many shares of common stock will the investor receive for his or her 100 shares?
4. If AMCON chooses to redeem the shares in 2006, what amount will the investor be paid for his or her 100 shares?

**Communication Case 18–12**
Should the present two-category distinction between liabilities and equity be retained? group interaction.

● LO1

The current conceptual distinction between liabilities and equity defines liabilities independently of assets and equity, with equity defined as a residual amount. The present proliferation of financial instruments that combine features of both debt and equity and the difficulty of drawing a distinction have led many to conclude that the present two-category distinction between liabilities and equity be eliminated. Two opposing viewpoints are:

**View 1:** The distinction should be maintained.
**View 2:** The distinction should be eliminated and financial instruments should instead be reported in accordance with the priority of their claims to enterprise assets.

One type of security that often is mentioned in the debate is convertible bonds. Although stock in many ways, such a security also obligates the issuer to transfer assets at a specified price and redemption date. Thus it also has features of debt. In considering this question, focus on conceptual issues regarding the practicable and theoretically appropriate treatment, unconstrained by GAAP.

**Required:**

1. Which view do you favor? Develop a list of arguments in support of your view prior to the class session for which the case is assigned.
2. In class, your instructor will pair you (and everyone else) with a classmate (who also has independently developed an argument).
   a. You will be given three minutes to argue your view to your partner. Your partner likewise will be given three minutes to argue his or her view to you. During these three-minute presentations, the listening partner is not permitted to speak.
   b. Then after each person has had a turn attempting to convince his or her partner, the two partners will have a three-minute discussion in which they will decide which view is more convincing and arguments will be merged into a single view for each pair.
3. After the allotted time, a spokesperson for each of the two views will be selected by the instructor. Each spokesperson will field arguments from the class in support of that view's position and list the arguments on the board. The class then will discuss the merits of the two lists of arguments and attempt to reach a consensus view, though a consensus is not necessary.

# CPA SIMULATION 18–1

**Hanson Corporation**
Shareholders' Equity

KAPLAN CPA Review

Test your knowledge of the concepts discussed in this chapter, practice critical professional skills necessary for career success, and prepare for the computer-based CPA exam by accessing our CPA simulations at the text website: **www.mhhe.com/spiceland4e**.

The Hansen Corporation simulation tests your knowledge of a variety of shareholders' equity reporting issues.

As on the CPA exam itself, you will be asked to use tools including a spreadsheet, a calculator, and professional accounting standards, to conduct research, derive solutions, and communicate conclusions related to these issues in a simulated environment headed by the following interactive tabs:

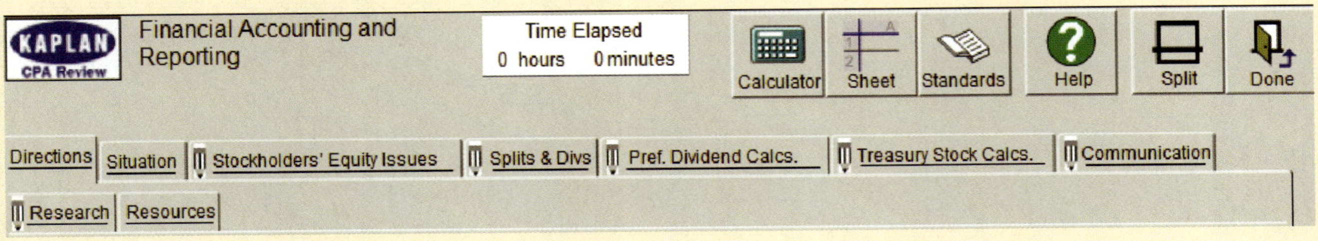


Specific tasks in the simulation include:

- Applying judgment in deciding the financial reporting implications of a variety of shareholders' equity transactions.
- Determining the financial statement effects of stock dividends and stock splits.
- Calculating dividends on preferred stock.
- Demonstrating an understanding of financial reporting effects of treasury stock transactions.
- Communicating the benefits of a stock buyback.
- Researching appropriate accounting for manditorily redeemable preferred stock.

# Additional Financial Reporting Issues

4

SECTION

19

CHAPTER

# Share-Based Compensation and Earnings Per Share

## OVERVIEW

We've discussed a variety of employee compensation plans in prior chapters, including pension and other postretirement benefits in Chapter 17. In this chapter we look at some common forms of compensation in which the amount of the compensation employees receive is tied to the market price of company stock. We will see that these *share-based* compensation plans—stock awards, stock options, and stock appreciation rights—create shareholders' equity, the topic of the previous chapter and also often affect the way we calculate earnings per share, the topic of the second part of the current chapter. Specifically, we view these as *potential common shares* along with convertible securities and calculate earnings per share as if they already had been exercised or converted into additional common shares.

## LEARNING OBJECTIVES

**After studying this chapter, you should be able to:**

- LO1 Explain and implement the accounting for stock award plans.
- LO2 Explain and implement the accounting for stock options.
- LO3 Explain and implement the accounting for stock appreciation rights.
- LO4 Explain and implement the accounting for employee share purchase plans.
- LO5 Distinguish between a simple and a complex capital structure.
- LO6 Describe what is meant by the weighted-average number of common shares.
- LO7 Differentiate the effect on EPS of the sale of new shares, a stock dividend or stock split, and the reacquisition of shares.
- LO8 Describe how preferred dividends affect the calculation of EPS.
- LO9 Describe how options, rights, and warrants are incorporated in the calculation of EPS.
- LO10 Describe how convertible securities are incorporated in the calculation of EPS.
- LO11 Explain the way contingently issuable shares are incorporated in the calculation of EPS.
- LO12 Describe the way EPS information should be reported in an income statement.

# Financial Reporting Case

## Proper Motivation?

The coffee room discussion Thursday morning was particularly lively. Yesterday's press release describing National Electronic Ventures' choice of Sandra Veres as its president and chief operating officer was today's hot topic in all the company's departments. The press release noted that Ms. Veres's compensation package includes elements beyond salary that are intended to not only motivate her to accept the offer, but also to remain with the company and work to increase shareholder value. Excerpts from the release follow:

> National Electronic Ventures, Inc. today announced it had attracted G. Sandra Veres, respected executive from the wireless communications industry to succeed chairman Walter Kovac. Veres will assume the new role as CEO on Jan. 1, 2006. Ms. Veres will receive a compensation package at NEV of more than $1 million in salary, stock options to buy more than 800,000 shares and a grant of restricted stock.

**By the time you finish this chapter, you should be able to respond appropriately to the questions posed in this case. Compare your response to the solution provided at the end of the chapter.**

### QUESTIONS

1. How can a compensation package such as this serve as an incentive to Ms. Veres? (page 952)
2. Ms. Veres received a "grant of restricted stock." How should NEV account for the grant? (page 952)
3. Included were stock options to buy more than 800,000 shares. How will the options affect NEV's compensation expense? (page 954)
4. How will the presence of these and other similar stock options affect NEV's earnings per share? (page 970)

# PART A SHARE-BASED COMPENSATION

Employee compensation plans frequently include share-based awards. These may be outright awards of shares, stock options, or cash payments tied to the market price of shares. Sometimes only key executives participate in a stock benefit plan. Typically, an executive compensation plan is tied to performance in a strategy that uses compensation to motivate its recipients. Some firms pay their directors entirely in shares. Actual compensation depends on the market value of the shares. Obviously, that's quite an incentive to act in the best interests of shareholders.

**FINANCIAL REPORTING CASE**

Q1, p. 951

The accounting objective is to record compensation expense over the periods in which related services are performed.

Although the variations of share-based compensation plans are seemingly endless, each shares common goals. Whether the plan is a stock award plan, a stock option plan, a stock appreciation rights (SARs) plan, or one of the several similar plans, the goals are to provide compensation to designated employees, while sometimes providing those employees with some sort of performance incentive. Likewise, our goals in accounting for each of these plans are the same for each: (1) to determine the fair value of the compensation and (2) to expense that compensation over the periods in which participants perform services. The issue is not trivial. The median total compensation of chief executives of the 188 largest U.S. businesses, including salary, bonuses, present value of stock options, long-term incentive payouts and the value of restricted stock at the time of grant, was $6.4 million in 2003.

## Stock Award Plans

Usually, restricted shares are subject to forfeiture if the employee doesn't remain with the company.

LO1

Executive compensation sometimes includes a grant of shares of stock. Usually, such shares are restricted in such a way as to provide some incentive to the recipient. Typically, restricted stock award plans are tied to continued employment. In a **restricted stock** plan, shares actually are awarded in the name of the employee, although the company might retain physical possession of the shares. The employee has all rights of a shareholder, subject to certain restrictions or forfeiture. Ordinarily, the shares are subject to forfeiture by the employee if employment is terminated within some specified number of years from the date of grant. The employee usually is not free to sell the shares during the restriction period and a statement to that effect often is inscribed on the stock certificates. These restrictions give the employee incentive to remain with the company until rights to the shares vest. Graphic 19–1 describes the restricted award plan for the **Kmart Holding Co**.

**GRAPHIC 19–1**
Restricted Stock Award Plan—Kmart

**Restricted Stock (in part)**
During the 39 weeks ended January 28, 2004, we issued 111,540 shares of restricted stock at market prices ranging from $23.00 to $29.65. . . . The restricted stock generally vests over three years, during which time we will recognize total compensation expense of approximately $3 million.

**FINANCIAL REPORTING CASE**

Q2, p. 951

The compensation associated with a share of restricted stock (or nonvested stock) is the market price at the grant date of an unrestricted share of the same stock. This amount is accrued as compensation expense over the service period for which participants receive the shares, usually from the date of grant to when restrictions are lifted (the vesting date).[1] This is demonstrated in Illustration 19–1.

**ADDITIONAL CONSIDERATION**

An alternative way of accomplishing the same result is to debit deferred compensation for the full value of the restricted shares ($60 million in the illustration) on the date they are granted:

[1]Restricted stock plans usually are designed to comply with Tax Code Section 83 to allow employee compensation to be nontaxable to the employee until the year the shares become substantially vested, which is when the restrictions are lifted. Likewise, the employer gets no tax deduction until the compensation becomes taxable to the employee.

| | | |
|---|---|---|
| Deferred compensation (5 million shares at $12) | 60 | |
| Common stock (5 million shares at $1 par) | | 5 |
| Paid-in capital—excess of par (difference) | | 55 |

If so, deferred compensation is reported as a reduction in shareholders' equity, resulting in a zero net effect on shareholders' equity. Then, deferred compensation is credited when compensation expense is debited over the service period. Just as in Illustration 19–1, the result is an increase in both compensation expense and shareholders' equity each year over the vesting period.

**ILLUSTRATION 19–1**
Restricted Stock Award Plan

Under its restricted stock award plan, Universal Communications grants five million of its $1 par common shares to certain key executives at January 1, 2006. The shares are subject to forfeiture if employment is terminated within four years. Shares have a current market price of $12 per share.

**January 1, 2006**
No entry

Calculate total compensation expense:

| | |
|---|---|
| $12 | Fair value per share |
| × 5 million | Shares awarded |
| = $60 million | Total compensation |

The total compensation is to be allocated to expense over the four-year service (vesting) period: 2006–2009

$60 million ÷ 4 years = $15 million per year

| **December 31, 2006, 2007, 2008, 2009** | ($ in millions) | |
|---|---|---|
| Compensation expense ($60 million ÷ 4 years) | 15 | |
| Paid-in capital—restricted stock | | 15 |
| **December 31, 2009** | | |
| Paid-in capital—restricted stock (5 million shares at $12) | 60 | |
| Common stock (5 million shares at $1 par) | | 5 |
| Paid-in capital—excess of par (difference) | | 55 |

The total compensation is the market value of the shares ($12) times five million shares.

The $60 million is accrued to compensation expense over the four-year service period.

When restrictions are lifted, paid-in capital—restricted stock, is replaced by common stock and paid-in capital—excess of par.

Once the shares vest and the restrictions are lifted, paid-in capital—restricted stock is replaced by common stock and paid-in capital—excess of par.

The amount of the compensation is measured at the date of grant—at the market price on that date. Any market price changes that might occur after that don't affect the total compensation.

If restricted stock is forfeited because, say, the employee leaves the company, related entries previously made would simply be reversed. This would result in a decrease in compensation expense in the year of forfeiture. The total compensation, adjusted for the forfeited amount, is then allocated over the remaining service period.

## Stock Option Plans

More commonly, employees aren't actually awarded shares, but rather are given the option to buy shares in the future. In fact, **stock options** have become an integral part of the total compensation package for key officers of most medium and large companies.[2] As with any compensation plan, the accounting objective is to report compensation expense during the period of service for which the compensation is given.

[2]In a recent survey of 600 corporations, 590 companies disclosed the existence of stock option plans (AICPA, *Accounting Trends and Techniques*, 2004).

## EXPENSE—THE GREAT DEBATE

Stock option plans give employees the option to purchase (a) a specified number of shares of the firm's stock, (b) at a specified price, (c) during a specified period of time. One of the most heated controversies in standard-setting history has been the debate over the amount of compensation to be recognized as expense for stock options. At issue is how the value of stock options is measured, which for most options determines whether any expense at all is recognized.

Historically, options have been measured at their **intrinsic values**—the simple difference between the market price of the shares and the option price at which they can be acquired. For instance, an option that permits an employee to buy $25 stock for $10 has an intrinsic value of $15. However, plans in which the exercise price equals the market value of the underlying stock at the date of grant (which describes most executive stock option plans) have no intrinsic value and therefore result in zero compensation when measured this way, even though the fair value of the options can be quite significant. About half of the chief executives of the largest U.S. companies cashed in stock options in 2000 for a median gain of over $8.7 million. In 2000, **Citigroup**'s chairman Sanford Weill exercised enough stock options to realize a pretax profit of $196 million from selling shares. To many, it seems counterintuitive to not recognize compensation expense for plans that routinely provide executives with a substantial part of their total compensation.

FINANCIAL REPORTING CASE

Q3, p. 951

**Failed Attempt to Require Expensing.** This is where the controversy ensues. In 1993, the FASB issued an Exposure Draft of a new standard that would have required companies to measure options at their *fair values* at the time they are granted and to expense that amount over the appropriate service period. To jump straight to the punch line, the FASB bowed to public pressure and agreed to withdraw the requirement before it became a standard. The FASB consented to encourage, rather than require, that fair value compensation be recognized as expense. Companies were permitted to continue accounting under *APB Opinion 25* (the intrinsic value method referred to in the previous paragraph).[3] Before we discuss the details of accounting for stock options, it's helpful to look back at what led the FASB to first propose fair value accounting and later rescind that proposal.

After lengthy debate, the FASB consented to encourage, rather than require, that the fair value of options be recognized as expense.

As the 1990s began, the public was becoming increasingly aware of the enormity of executive compensation in general and compensation in the form of stock options in particular. The lack of accounting for this compensation was apparent, prompting the SEC to encourage the FASB to move forward on their stock option project. Even Congress got into the fray when, in 1992, a bill was introduced that would require firms to report compensation expense based on the fair value of options. Motivated by this encouragement, the FASB issued its exposure draft in 1993. The real disharmony began then. Opposition to the proposed standard was broad and vehement; and that perhaps is an understatement. Critics based their opposition on one or more of three objections:

1. *Options with no intrinsic value at issue have zero fair value and should not give rise to expense recognition.* The FASB, and even some critics of the proposal, were adamant that options provide valuable compensation at the grant date to recipients.
2. *It is impossible to measure the fair value of the compensation on the grant date.* The FASB argued vigorously that value can be approximated using one of several **option pricing models**. These are statistical models that use computers to incorporate information about a company's stock and the terms of the stock option to estimate the options' fair value. We might say the FASB position is that it's better to be approximately right than precisely wrong.
3. *The proposed standard would have unacceptable economic consequences.* Essentially, this argument asserted that requiring this popular means of compensation to be expensed would cause companies to discontinue the use of options.

There were consistent criticisms of the FASB's requirement to expense option compensation.

The opposition included corporate executives, auditors, members of Congress, and the SEC.[4] Ironically, the very groups that provided the most impetus for the rule change initially—the SEC and Congress—were among the most effective detractors in the end. The

[3]"Accounting for Stock Issued to Employees," *Opinions of the Accounting Principles Board No. 25* (New York: AICPA, 1972).

[4]All of the "Big Six" CPA firms lobbied against the proposal. Senator Lieberman of Connecticut introduced a bill in Congress that if passed would have forbidden the FASB from passing a requirement to expense option compensation.

only group that offered much support at all was the academic community, and that was by-and-large nonvocal support. In reversing its decision, the FASB was not swayed by any of the specific arguments of any opposition group. Dennis Beresford, chair of the FASB at the time, indicated that it was fear of government control of the standard-setting process that prompted the Board to modify its position. The Board remained steadfast that the proposed change was appropriate.

**Voluntary Expensing.** Prior to 2002, only two companies—**Boeing** and **Winn-Dixie**—reported stock option compensation expense at fair value. However, in 2002 public outrage mounted amid high-profile accounting scandals at **Enron**, **WorldCom**, **Tyco**, and others. Some degree of consensus emerged that greed on the part of some corporate executives contributed to the fraudulent and misleading financial reporting at the time. In fact, many in the media were pointing to the proliferation of stock options as a primary form of compensation as a culprit in fueling that greed. An episode of the PBS series *Frontline* argued that not expensing the value of stock options contributed to the collapse of Enron. For these reasons, renewed interest surfaced in requiring stock option compensation to be reported in income statements. At least partly in response to this public sentiment, **Coca-Cola** announced in 2002 that it would begin reporting the fair value of its stock options as an expense. Perhaps seeing the "writing on the wall," other companies soon followed suit. By the end of 2004, nearly 500 firms were voluntarily expensing options.

**FRANK PARTNOY—AUTHOR, INFECTIOUS GREED**
. . . the increase in the use of stock options coincided with a massive increase in accounting fraud by corporate executives, who benefited from short-term increases in their stock prices.[5]

**Nearly 500 U.S. companies voluntarily reported the fair value of stock options as an expense.**

**Current Requirement to Expense.** Emerging from the rekindled debate was an FASB Standard that now requires fair value accounting for employee stock options, eliminating altogether the intrinsic value approach.[6] As you might expect, the proposal did not come without opposition. Many of the same groups that successfully blocked the FASB from enacting a similar requirement in 1995 led the opposition. Not surprisingly, at the forefront of the resistance were the high-tech companies that extensively use stock options as a primary form of compensating employees and thus are most susceptible to a reduction in reported earnings when that compensation is included in income statements. For example, consider **Apple Computer**'s earnings for the 12 months ending March 27, 2004. Reported net income of $179 million would have been only $56 million, or 69% less, if the Standard had been in effect then.[7]

● LO2

**An FASB Standard now requires companies to record the value of options in their income statements.**

**Mandatory expensing of stock options causes lower net income, but the extent of the effect varies from company to company.**

It's important to note that the way we account for stock options has no effect whatsoever on cash flows, only on whether the value of stock options is included among expenses. This is not to say that companies haven't altered their compensation strategies. Already, we have seen a shift in the way some companies compensate their employees. Partly due to the negative connotation that has become associated with executive stock options and partly due to the stock market decline of recent years that caused millions of options to become worthless, we've seen fewer options and more bonuses and restricted stock awards. For its fiscal year ending June 30, 2004, for instance, technology company **JDS Uniphase** awarded stock options to employees worth only 11% of the $1.25 billion value of its 2001 options. Let's examine the way stock options are accounted for now.

**We've witnessed a discernable shift in the way executives are compensated – fewer options, more stock awards and bonuses.**

## RECOGNIZING THE FAIR VALUE OF OPTIONS

Accounting for stock options parallels the accounting for restricted stock we discussed in the first part of this chapter. That is, we measure compensation as the fair value of the stock options at the grant date and then record that amount as compensation expense over the service period for which employees receive the options. Estimating the fair value requires the use of one of several option pricing models. These mathematical models assimilate a variety of

---

[5]Frank Partnoy, *Infectious Greed: How Deceit and Risk Corrupted the Financial Markets* (Henry Holt/Times Books, Spring 2003, p. 159).
[6]"Share-Based Payment," *Statement of Financial Accounting Standards No. 123 (revised 2004)*, (Norwalk, Conn.: FASB 2004).
[7]Alex Salkever, "What Could Crunch Apple Shares," *BusinessWeek*, July 12, 2004, p. 11.

The fair value of a stock option can be determined by employing a recognized option pricing model.

information about a company's stock and the terms of the stock option to estimate the option's fair value. The model should take into account the:

An option pricing model takes into account several variables.

- Exercise price of the option.
- Expected term of the option.
- Current market price of the stock.
- Expected dividends.
- Expected risk-free rate of return during the term of the option.
- Expected volatility of the stock.

The techniques for estimating fair value have been among the most controversial issues in the debate.

The FASB's new Standard modified the way companies actually measure fair value. It calls for using models that permit greater flexibility in modeling the ways employees are expected to exercise options and their expected employment termination patterns after options vest.[8] Option-pricing theory, on which the pricing models are based, is a topic explored in depth in finance courses and is subject to active empirical investigation and development. A simplified discussion is provided in Appendix 19.[9]

An interesting approach to determining fair value was suggested by **Cisco Systems** just prior to the company being required to expense its options for the first time. A major reason why we use option pricing models to *estimate* fair value is that employee stock options are non-transferable; the recipient cannot sell those options. As a result, they are not traded on organized exchanges like shares of stock, so we cannot find an actual market-determined price. Cisco suggests creating a mechanism to establish an actual market-determined fair value and avoid the need to estimate a fair value. Cisco proposes creating a new financial instrument each time it issues options that is designed to mirror the terms of the options and then actually sell that financial instrument to institutional investors. The price the investor is willing to pay in this arms-length transaction would then serve as the per share fair value of the employee options that the financial instrument mimics. At the time of this writing the SEC had not yet approved this approach.

The total compensation as estimated by the options' fair value is reported as compensation expense over the period of service for which the options are given. Recipients normally are not allowed to exercise their options for a specified number of years. This delay provides added incentive to remain with the company. The time between the date options are granted and the first date they can be exercised is the vesting period and usually is considered to be the service period over which the compensation expense is reported. The process is demonstrated in Illustration 19–2.

**ILLUSTRATION 19–2**
Stock Options

At January 1, 2006, Universal Communications grants options that permit key executives to acquire 10 million of the company's $1 par common shares within the next eight years, but not before December 31, 2009 (the vesting date). The exercise price is the market price of the shares on the date of grant, $35 per share. The fair value of the options, estimated by an appropriate option pricing model, is $8 per option.

**January 1, 2006**
No entry

Fair value is estimated at the date of grant.

Calculate total compensation expense:

| | |
|---|---|
| $ 8 | Estimated fair value per option |
| × 10 million | Options granted |
| = $80 million | Total compensation |

The total compensation is to be allocated to expense over the four-year service (vesting) period: 2006–2009

$80 million ÷ 4 years = $20 million per year

The value of the award is expensed over the service period for which the compensation is provided.

| **December 31, 2006, 2007, 2008, 2009** | ($ in millions) | |
|---|---|---|
| Compensation expense ($80 million ÷ 4 years) | 20 | |
| Paid-in capital—stock options | | 20 |

[8]"Share-Based Payment," *Statement of Financial Accounting Standards No.123 (revised 2004)*, (Norwalk, Conn.: FASB 2004), par. A27-A29.
[9]An expanded discussion is provided in *SFAS 123* (revised 2004).

**Estimated Forfeitures.** If previous experience indicates that a material number of the options will be forfeited before they vest (due to employee turnover or violation of other terms of the options), we adjust the fair value estimate on the grant date to reflect that expectation. For instance, if a forfeiture rate of 5% is expected, Universal's estimated total compensation would be 95% of $80 million, or $76 million. In that case, the annual compensation expense in Illustration 19–2 would have been $19 million ($76/4) instead of $20 million. We see the effect of that possibility in Illustration 19–2A.

Option compensation expense is based on the number of options expected to vest.

**ILLUSTRATION 19–2A**
Estimated Forfeitures

| | ($ in millions) | |
|---|---|---|
| **2006** | | |
| Compensation expense ($80 × 95% ÷ 4) | 19 | |
| Paid-in capital—stock options | | 19 |
| **2007** | | |
| Compensation expense ($80 × 95% ÷ 4) | 19 | |
| Paid-in capital—stock options | | 19 |
| **2008** | | |
| Compensation expense [($80 × 90% × 3/4) – ($19 + 19)] | 16 | |
| Paid-in capital—stock options | | 16 |
| **2009** | | |
| Compensation expense [($80 × 90% × 4/4) – ($19 + 19 + 16)] | 18 | |
| Paid-in capital—stock options | | 18 |

The value of the compensation is estimated to be $76 million, or $19 million per year.

The expense each year is the current estimate of total compensation that should have been recorded to date less the amount already recorded.

What if that expectation changes later? Universal should adjust the cumulative amount of compensation expense recorded to date in the year the estimate changes.[10] Suppose, for instance, that during 2008, the third year, Universal revises its estimate of forfeitures from 5% to 10%. The new estimate of total compensation would then be $80 million × 90%, or $72 million. For the first three years, the portion of the total compensation that should have been reported would be $72 million × 3/4, or $54 million, and since $38 million ($19 × 2) of that was recorded in 2006–2007 before the estimate changed, an additional $16 million would now be recorded in 2008. Then if the estimate isn't changed again, the remaining $18 million ($72 – 54) would be recorded in 2009.

When forfeiture estimates change, the cumulative effect on compensation is reflected in current earnings.

**ADDITIONAL CONSIDERATION**

Notice that the $18 million is the amount that would have been reported in each of the four years if Universal had assumed a 10% forfeiture rate from the beginning. Also be aware that this approach is contrary to the usual way companies account for changes in estimates. For instance, assume a company acquires a four-year depreciable asset having an estimated residual value of 5% of cost. The $76 million depreciable cost would be depreciated straight line at $19 million over the four-year useful life. If the estimated residual value changes after two years to 10%, the new estimated depreciable cost of $72 would be reduced by the $38 million depreciation recorded the first two years, and the remaining $34 million would be depreciated equally, $17 million per year, over the remaining two years.

## WHEN OPTIONS ARE EXERCISED

If half the options in Illustration 19–2 (five million shares) are exercised on July 11, 2012, when the market price is $50 per share, the following journal entry is recorded:

[10] "Share-Based Payment," *Statement of Financial Accounting Standards No.123 (revised 2004)*, (Norwalk, Conn.: FASB 2004), par. 43.

Recording the exercise of options is not affected by the market price on the exercise date.

| **July 11, 2012** | ($ in millions) | |
|---|---|---|
| Cash ($35 exercise price × 5 million shares) | 175 | |
| Paid-in capital—stock options (½ account balance) | 40 | |
| Common stock (5 million shares at $1 par per share) | | 5 |
| Paid-in capital—excess of par (to balance) | | 210 |

Notice that the market price at exercise is irrelevant. Changes in the market price of underlying shares do not influence the previously measured fair value of options.

## WHEN UNEXERCISED OPTIONS EXPIRE

If options that have vested expire without being exercised, the following journal entry is made (assuming none of the options in our illustration was exercised):

*Paid-in capital—stock options* becomes *paid-in capital—expiration of stock options*, when options expire without being exercised.

| | ($ in millions) | |
|---|---|---|
| Paid-in capital—stock options (account balance) | 80 | |
| Paid-in capital—expiration of stock options | | 80 |

In effect, we rename the paid-in capital attributable to the stock option plan. Compensation expense for the four years' service, as of the measurement date, is not affected.

### ADDITIONAL CONSIDERATION

**Tax Consequences of Stock-Based Compensation Plans**

In Illustration 19–2 we ignored the tax effect. To illustrate the effect of taxes, let's assume Universal Communications' income tax rate is 40%.

Because an incentive plan provides no tax deduction, it has no deferred tax consequences.

**Case 1.** Recall from our earlier discussion that with an incentive plan, the employer receives no tax deduction at all. If Universal's plan qualifies as an incentive plan, the company will receive no tax deduction upon exercise of the options and thus no tax consequences.

**Case 2.** On the other hand, if we assume the plan does not qualify as an incentive plan, Universal will deduct from taxable income the difference between the exercise price and the market price at the exercise date. Recall from Chapter 16 that this creates a temporary difference between accounting income (for which compensation expense is recorded currently) and taxable income (for which the tax deduction is taken later upon the exercise of the options). We assume the temporary difference is the cumulative amount expensed for the options. The following entries would be recorded on the dates shown:

A deferred tax asset is recognized now for the future tax savings from the tax deduction when the options are exercised.

| **December 31, 2006, 2007, 2008, 2009** | ($ in millions) | |
|---|---|---|
| Compensation expense ($80 million ÷ 4 years) | 20 | |
| Paid-in capital—stock options | | 20 |
| Deferred tax asset (40% × $20 million) | 8 | |
| Income tax expense | | 8 |

The after-tax effect on earnings is thus $12 million each year ($20 − 8).

If all of the options (ten million shares) are exercised in April 2011:

| | | |
|---|---|---|
| Cash ($35 exercise price × 10 million shares) | 350 | |
| Paid-in capital—stock options (account balance) | 80 | |
| Common stock (10 million shares at $1 par per share) | | 10 |
| Paid-in capital—excess of par (to balance) | | 420 |

If the eventual tax savings exceed the deferred tax asset, the difference is recognized as equity.

a. Options exercised when the tax benefit *exceeds* the deferred tax asset:
**If the market price is $50 per share:**

| | | |
|---|---|---|
| Income taxes payable [($50 − 35) × 10 million shares × 40%] | 60 | |
| Deferred tax asset (4 years × $8 million) | | 32 |
| Paid-in capital—tax effect of stock options (remainder)* | | 28 |

b. Options exercised when the tax benefit is *less than* the deferred tax asset:
**If the market price is $40 per share:**

| | | |
|---|---|---|
| Income taxes payable [($40 − 35) × 10 million shares × 40%] . . . . | 20 | |
| Income tax expense or paid-in capital—tax effect of stock options† (remainder) . . . . . . . . . . . . . . . . . . . . . . . . . . . . | 12 | |
| Deferred tax asset (4 years × $8 million) . . . . . . . . . . . . . . . . . . | | 32 |

The tax consequences of all nonqualifying stock options as well as restricted stock plans also are accounted for in the manner demonstrated above.

*This treatment is consistent with a provision of *SFAS 109* (par. 36C) that requires the tax effect of an increase or decrease in equity (paid-in capital—stock options, in this case) be allocated to equity.
†Paid-in capital—tax effect of stock options is debited only if that account has a sufficient credit balance from previous transactions in which the tax benefit exceeded the deferred tax asset.

## PLANS WITH PERFORMANCE OR MARKET CONDITIONS

Stock option (and other share-based) plans often specify a performance condition or a market condition that must be satisfied before employees are allowed the benefits of the award. The objective is to provide employees with additional incentive for managerial achievement. For instance, an option might not be exercisable until a performance target is met. The target could be divisional revenue, earnings per share, sales growth, or rate of return on assets. The possibilities are limitless. On the other hand, the target might be market-related, perhaps a specified stock price or a stock price change exceeding a particular index. The way we account for such plans depends on whether the condition is performance-based or market-based.

**The terms of performance options vary with some measure of performance to tie rewards to productivity.**

**Plans with Performance Conditions.** Whether we recognize compensation expense for performance-based options depends (a) initially on whether it's probable[11] that the performance target will be met and (b) ultimately on whether the performance target actually is met. Accounting is as described earlier for other stock options. Initial estimates of compensation cost as well as subsequent revisions of that estimate take into account the likelihood of both forfeitures and achieving performance targets. For example, in Illustration 19–2, if the options described also had included a condition that the options would become exercisable only if sales increase by 10% after four years, we would estimate the likelihood of that occurring; specifically, is it probable? Let's say we initially estimate that it is probable that sales will increase by 10% after four years. Then, our initial estimate of the total compensation would have been unchanged at:

**If compensation from a stock option depends on meeting a performance target, compensation is recorded only if we feel it's probable the target will be met.**

| $10 million | × | $8 | = | $80 million |
|---|---|---|---|---|
| Options expected to vest | | Fair value | | Estimated total compensation |

Suppose, though, that after two years, we estimate that it is *not* probable that sales will increase by 10% after four years. Then, our new estimate of the total compensation would change to:

| 0 | × | $8 | = | 0 |
|---|---|---|---|---|
| Options expected to vest | | Fair value | | Estimated total compensation |

In that case, we would reverse the $40 million expensed in 2006–2007 because no compensation can be recognized for options that don't vest due to performance targets not being met, and that's our expectation.

**If it later becomes probable that a performance target will *not* be met, we reverse any compensation expense already recorded.**

### ADDITIONAL CONSIDERATION

It's interesting to note that some companies have reacted to the "reversibility" of performance plans by revising their compensation plans to substitute performance-based stock awards or performance-based options for traditional stock options. As discussed

[11] "Probable" means the same as it did in Chapter 13 when we were estimating the likelihood that payment would be made for a loss contingency.

earlier, compensation for traditional employee stock options is measured at the grant date and expensed over the appropriate service period. If the options become worthless because the share price fails to exceed the exercise price, recorded compensation is not adjusted. On the other hand, as we just saw, compensation for a similar performance-based option is recorded, but if the options become worthless because the performance condition isn't met, we would reverse any compensation already recorded.

Of course if all goes well—share prices rise; performance exceeds expectations—compensation is the same under either approach, other things equal. But, if results are disappointing—share prices fall; performance falls short of expectations—compensation expense is higher for traditional options than for performance options. It's the more favorable effect on reported earnings that attracts companies to performance plans.

As an example, First Horizon National Corporation in Memphis began in 2005 to replace employee stock options with "performance share units" with vesting conditional on the company's earnings growth meeting or exceeding that of peer financial institutions, expressly to avoid the more stringent expensing requirements of the former plan.

When we revise our estimate of total compensation because our expectation of probability changes, we record the effect of the change in the current period.

Conversely, assume that our initial expectation is that it is *not* probable that sales will increase by 10% after four years and so we record no annual compensation expense. But then, after two years, we estimate that it *is* probable that sales will increase by 10% after four years. At that point, our revised estimate of the total compensation would change to $80 million, and we would reflect the cumulative effect on compensation in 2008 earnings and record compensation thereafter:

If we had begun with our new estimate of total compensation, $60 million would have been expensed in the first three years.

This leaves $20 million to be expensed the fourth year.

| | | |
|---|---|---|
| **2008** | | |
| Compensation expense [($80 × ¾) − $0] | 60 | |
| Paid-in capital—stock options | | 60 |
| **2009** | | |
| Compensation expense [($80 × 4/4) − $60] | 20 | |
| Paid-in capital—stock options | | 20 |

If the target is based on changes in the market rather than on performance, we record compensation as if there were no target.

**Plans with Market Conditions.** If the award contains a market condition (e.g., a share option with an exercisability requirement based on the stock price reaching a specified level), then no special accounting is required. The fair value estimate of the share option already implicitly reflects market conditions due to the nature of share option pricing models. So, we recognize compensation expense regardless of when, if ever, the market condition is met.

## Stock Appreciation Rights

LO3

**Stock appreciation rights (SARs)** overcome a major disadvantage of stock option plans that require employees to actually buy shares when the options are exercised. Even though the options' exercise price may be significantly lower than the market value of the shares, the employee still must come up with enough cash to take advantage of the bargain. This can be quite a burden if the award is sizable. In a nonqualified stock option plan, income taxes also would have to be paid when the options are exercised.[12]

In an SAR plan, the employer pays compensation equal to the increase in share price from a specified level.

SARs offer a solution. Unlike stock options, these awards enable an employee to benefit by the amount that the market price of the company's stock rises without having to buy shares. Instead, the employee is awarded the share appreciation, which is the amount by which the market price on the exercise date exceeds a prespecified price (usually the market price at the date of grant). For instance, if the share price rises from $35 to $50, the employee receives $15 cash for each SAR held. The share appreciation usually is payable in cash or the recipient has the choice between cash and shares. A plan of this type offered by IBM is described in Graphic 19–2.

[12]The tax treatment of share-based plans is discussed in an earlier section.

**GRAPHIC 19–2**
Stock Appreciation Rights—IBM Corporation

> **Long-Term Performance Plan (in part)**
> SARs offer eligible optionees the alternative of electing not to exercise the related stock option, but to receive payment in cash and/or stock, equivalent to the difference between the option price and the average market price of IBM stock on the date of exercising the right.

## IS IT DEBT OR IS IT EQUITY?

If an employer can elect to settle in shares of stock rather than cash, the award is considered to be equity.

In some plans, the employer chooses whether to issue shares or cash at exercise. In other plans, the choice belongs to the employee.[13] Who has the choice determines the way it's accounted for. More specifically, the accounting treatment depends on whether the award is considered an equity instrument or a liability. If the employer can elect to settle in shares of stock rather than cash, the award is considered to be equity. On the other hand, if the employee will receive cash or can elect to receive cash, the award is considered to be a liability.

If an employee can elect to receive cash, the award is considered to be a liability.

The distinction between share-based awards that are considered equity and those that are considered liabilities is based on the definition of liabilities in *SFAC 6*.[14] That statement classifies an instrument as a liability if it obligates the issuer to transfer its assets to the holder. A stock option is an equity instrument if it requires only the issuance of stock. A cash SAR, on the other hand, requires the transfer of assets, and therefore is a liability. This does not mean that a stock option whose issuer may later choose to settle in cash is not an equity instrument. Instead, cash settlement would be considered equivalent to repurchasing an equity instrument for cash.

## SARS PAYABLE IN SHARES (EQUITY)

The cash settlement of an equity award is considered the repurchase of an equity instrument.

When an SAR is considered to be equity (because the employer can elect to settle in shares of stock rather than cash), we estimate the fair value of the SARs at the grant date and accrue that compensation to expense over the service period. Normally, the fair value of an SAR is the same as the fair value of a stock option with the same terms. The fair value is determined at the grant date and accrued to compensation expense over the service period the same way as for other share-based compensation plans. The total compensation is not revised for subsequent changes in the price of the underlying stock. This is demonstrated in Case 1 of Illustration 19–3 on the next page.

## SARS PAYABLE IN CASH (LIABILITY)

Compensation expense reported to date is the estimated total compensation multiplied by the fraction of the service period that has expired.

When an SAR is considered to be a liability (because the employee can elect to receive cash upon settlement), we estimate the fair value of the SARs and recognize that amount as compensation expense over the requisite service period consistent with the way we account for options and other share-based compensation. However, because these plans are considered to be liabilities, it's necessary to periodically re-estimate the fair value in order to continually adjust the liability (and corresponding compensation) until it is paid. Be sure to note that this is consistent with the way we account for other liabilities. Recall from our discussions in Chapter 16, for instance, that when a tax rate change causes a change in the eventual liability for deferred income taxes, we adjust that liability.

The periodic expense (and adjustment to the liability) is the fraction of the total compensation earned to date by recipients of the SARs (based on the elapsed fraction of the service period) reduced by any amounts expensed in prior periods. For example, if the fair value of SARs at the end of a period is $8, the total compensation would be $80 million if 10 million SARs are expected to vest. Let's say two years of a four-year service period have elapsed, and $21 million was expensed the first year. Then, compensation expense the second year would be $19 million, calculated as (2/4 of $80 million) minus $21. An example spanning several years is provided in Illustration 19–3, case 2.

We make up for incorrect previous estimates by adjusting expense in the period the estimate is revised.

Note that the way we treat changes in compensation estimates entails a catch-up adjustment in the period of change, *inconsistent* with the usual treatment of a change in estimate.

[13]Many such plans are called tandem plans and award an employee both a cash SAR and an SAR that calls for settlement in an equivalent amount of shares. The exercise of one cancels the other.

[14]"Elements of Financial Statements," *Statement of Financial Accounting Concepts No. 6* (Stamford, Conn.: FASB 1985).

**ILLUSTRATION 19–3**
Stock Appreciation Rights
Case 1: Equity
Case 2: Liability

At January 1, 2006, Universal Communications issued SARs that, upon exercise, entitle key executives to receive compensation equal in value to the excess of the market price at exercise over the share price at the date of grant. The SARs vest at the end of 2009 (cannot be exercised until then) and expire at the end of 2013. The fair value of the SARs, estimated by an appropriate option pricing model, is $8 per SAR at January 1, 2006. The fair value re-estimated at December 31, 2006, 2007, 2008, 2009, and 2010, is $8.40, $8, $6, $4.30, and $5, respectively.

**Case 1: SARs considered to be equity because Universal can elect to settle in shares of Universal stock at exercise**

**January 1, 2006**
No entry
*Calculate total compensation expense:*

**Fair value is estimated at the date of grant.**

| | |
|---|---|
| $8 | Estimated fair value per SAR |
| × 10 million | SARs granted |
| = $80 million | Total compensation |

The total compensation is allocated to expense over the four-year service (vesting) period: 2006–2009

**The value of the award is expensed over the service period for which the compensation is provided.**

$80 million ÷ 4 years = $20 million per year

| **December 31, 2006, 2007, 2008, 2009** | ($ in millions) | |
|---|---|---|
| Compensation expense ($80 million ÷ 4 years) | 20 | |
| Paid-in capital—SAR plan | | 20 |

**Case 2: SARs considered to be a liability because employees can elect to receive cash at exercise**

**The value of the compensation is estimated each year at the fair value of the SARs.**

**January 1, 2006**
No entry

**The expense each year is the current estimate of total compensation that should have been recorded to date less the amount already recorded.**

**If the fair value falls below the amount expensed to date, both the liability and expense are reduced.**

| | ($ in millions) | |
|---|---|---|
| **December 31, 2006** | | |
| Compensation expense ($8.40 × 10 million × 1/4) | 21 | |
| Liability—SAR plan | | 21 |
| **December 31, 2007** | | |
| Compensation expense [($8 × 10 million × 2/4) − 21] | 19 | |
| Liability—SAR plan | | 19 |
| **December 31, 2008** | | |
| Compensation expense [($6 × 10 million × 3/4) − 21 − 19] | 5 | |
| Liability—SAR plan | | 5 |
| **December 31, 2009** | | |
| Liability—SAR plan | 2 | |
| Compensation expense [($4.30 × 10 million × 4/4) − 21 − 19 − 5] | | 2 |

Remember that for most changes in estimate, revisions are allocated over remaining periods, rather than all at once in the period of change. The treatment is, however, consistent with the way we treat changes in forfeiture rate estimates as we discussed earlier in the chapter.

The liability continues to be adjusted after the service period if the rights haven't been exercised yet.

**Compensation expense and the liability continue to be adjusted until the SARs expire or are exercised.**

| **December 31, 2010** | ($ in millions) | |
|---|---|---|
| Compensation expense [($5 × 10 million × all) − 21 − 19 − 5 + 2] | 7 | |
| Liability—SAR plan | | 7 |

**Adjustment continues after the service period if the SARs have not yet been exercised.**

It's necessary to continue to adjust both compensation expense and the liability until the SARs ultimately either are exercised or lapse.[15] Assume for example that the SARs are exercised on October 11, 2011, when their fair value is $4.50, and executives choose to receive the market price appreciation in cash:

[15]Except that the cumulative compensation expense cannot be negative; that is, the liability cannot be reduced below zero.

| **October 11, 2011** | ($ in millions) | |
|---|---|---|
| Liability—SAR plan | 5 | |
| Compensation expense [($4.50 × 10 million × all) − 50] | | 5 |
| Liability—SAR plan (balance) | 45 | |
| Cash | | 45 |

Let's look at the changes in the liability—SAR plan account during the 2006–2011 period:

**Liability—SAR Plan**

| | | | |
|---|---|---|---|
| | | ($ in millions) | |
| | | 21 | 2006 |
| | | 19 | 2007 |
| | | 5 | 2008 |
| 2009 | 2 | | |
| | | 7 | 2010 |
| 2011 | 5 | | |
| 2011 | 45 | | |
| | | 0 | Balance after exercise |

The liability is adjusted each period as changes in the fair value estimates cause changes in the liability.

## Employee Share Purchase Plans

Share purchase plans permit employees to buy shares directly from the corporation.

**Employee share purchase plans** often permit all employees to buy shares directly from their company at favorable terms. The primary intent of these plans is to encourage employee ownership of the company's shares. Presumably loyalty is enhanced among employee-shareholders. The employee also benefits because, typically, these plans allow employees to buy shares from their employer without brokerage fees and, perhaps, at a slight discount. Some companies even encourage participation by matching or partially matching employee purchases.

As long as (a) substantially all employees can participate, (b) employees have no longer than one month after the price is fixed to decide whether to participate, and (c) the discount is no greater than 5% (or can be justified as reasonable), accounting is straightforward. Simply record the sale of new shares as employees buy shares.

If these criteria for the plan being noncompensatory are not met, say the discount is 15%, accounting is similar to other share-based plans. The 15% discount to employees, then, is considered to be compensation, and that amount is recorded as expense.[16] Compensation expense replaces the cash debit for any employer-paid portion. Say an employee buys shares (no par) under the plan for $850 rather than the current market price of $1,000. The $150 discount is recorded as compensation expense:

| | | |
|---|---|---|
| Cash (discounted price) | 850 | |
| Compensation expense ($1,000 × 15%) | 150 | |
| Common stock (market value) | | 1,000 |

Analysts should be aware of the possibility of earnings management as a way to increase managers' compensation.

### DECISION MAKERS' PERSPECTIVE

In several previous chapters, we have revisited the concept of "earnings quality" (as first defined in Chapter 4). We also have noted that one rather common practice that negatively influences earnings quality is earnings management, which refers to companies' use of one or more of several techniques designed to artificially increase (or decrease) earnings. A frequent objective of earnings management is to meet analysts' expectations regarding projections of income. The share-based compensation plans we discuss in this chapter suggest another motive managers sometimes have to manipulate income. If a manager's personal

[16] "Share-Based Payment," *Statement of Financial Accounting Standards No.123 (revised 2004)*, (Norwalk, Conn.: FASB 2004), par. 12–13.

compensation includes company stock, stock options, or other compensation based on the value of the firm's stock, it's not hard to imagine an increased desire to ensure that market expectations are met and that reported earnings have a positive effect on stock prices. In fact, as we discussed earlier, that is precisely the reaction these incentive compensation plans are designed to elicit. Investors and creditors, though, should be alert to indications of attempts to artificially manipulate income and realize that the likelihood of earnings management is probably higher for companies with generous share-based compensation plans.

One way managers might manipulate numbers is to low-ball the data that go into the option-pricing models. The models used to estimate fair value are built largely around subjective assumptions. That possibility emphasizes the need for investors to look closely at the assumptions used as reported in the stock option footnote, and particularly at how those assumptions change from year to year. ■

## CONCEPT REVIEW EXERCISE

### SHARE-BASED COMPENSATION PLANS

Listed below are transactions dealing with various stock benefit plans of Fortune-Time Corporation during the period 2006–2008. The market price of the stock is $45 at January 1, 2006.

a. On January 1, 2006, the company issued 10 million common shares to divisional managers under its restricted stock award plan. The shares are subject to forfeiture if employment is terminated within three years.
b. On January 1, 2006, the company granted incentive stock options to its senior management exercisable for 1.5 million common shares. The options must be exercised within five years, but not before January 1, 2008. The exercise price of the stock options is equal to the fair market value of the common stock on the date the options are granted. An option pricing model estimates the fair value of the options to be $4 per option. All recipients are expected to remain employed through the vesting date.
c. On January 1, 2006, the company granted 4 million SARs to its junior managers. The SARs entitle managers to receive their choice of cash or stock equal in value to the excess of the market price at exercise over the share price at the date of grant. The SARs vest at the end of 2007 (cannot be exercised until then) and expire at the end of 2009. The fair value of the SARs is $4 at January 1, 2006. The fair value is $4 and $5 at December 31, 2006 and 2007, respectively.
d. Recorded compensation expense on December 31, 2006.
e. A divisional manager holding 1 million of the restricted shares left the company to become CEO of a competitor on September 15, 2007, before the required service period ended.
f. Recorded compensation expense on December 31, 2007.

**Required:**

Prepare the journal entries that Fortune-Time recorded for each of these transactions. (Ignore any tax effects.)

### SOLUTION

**January 1, 2006**

**Restricted Stock Award Plan**

No entry.

Total compensation is measured as 10 million shares × $45 = $450 million

**Stock Options**

No entry.

Total compensation is measured as 1.5 million shares × $4 = $6 million

**SARs**

No entry.

**December 31, 2006**

| **Restricted Stock** | ($ in millions) | |
|---|---|---|
| Compensation expense ($450 million ÷ 3 years) | 150 | |
| Paid-in capital—restricted stock | | 150 |

| | | |
|---|---|---|
| **Stock Options** | | |
| Compensation expense ($6 million ÷ 2 years) | 3 | |
| Paid-in capital—stock options | | 3 |
| **SARs** | | |
| Compensation expense ($4 × 4 million × 1/2) | 8 | |
| Liability—SAR plan | | 8 |
| **September 15, 2007** | | |
| **Restricted Stock** | | |
| Paid-in capital—restricted stock (10% × $150) | 15 | |
| Compensation expense | | 15 |
| **December 31, 2007** | | |
| **Restricted Stock** | | |
| Compensation expense [($450 − 150 − 15 million) ÷ 2 years] | 142.5 | |
| Paid-in capital—restricted stock | | 142.5 |
| **Stock Options** | | |
| Compensation expense ($6 million ÷ 2 years) | 3 | |
| Paid-in capital—stock options | | 3 |
| **SARs** | | |
| Compensation expense ([$5 × 4 million × 2/2] − 8) | 12 | |
| Liability SAR plan | | 12 |

# EARNINGS PER SHARE

**PART B**

A typical corporate annual report contains four comparative financial statements, an extensive list of disclosure notes and schedules, and several pages of charts, tables, and textual descriptions. Of these myriad facts and figures, the single accounting number that is reported most frequently in the media and receives by far the most attention by investors and creditors is **earnings per share**. The reasons for the considerable attention paid to earnings per share certainly include the desire to find a way to summarize the performance of business enterprises into a single number.

> Information . . . gains greatly in usefulness if it can be compared with similar information about other enterprises and with similar information about the same enterprise for other time periods.[17]

***Earnings per share* is the single accounting number that receives the most media attention.**

Summarizing performance in a way that permits comparisons is difficult because the companies that report the numbers are different from one another. And yet, the desire to condense performance to a single number has created a demand for EPS information. The profession has responded with rules designed to maximize the comparability of EPS numbers by minimizing the inconsistencies in their calculation from one company to the next.[18]

**GLOBAL PERSPECTIVE**

The International Accounting Standards Board (IASB) has as a stated objective to narrow worldwide differences in accounting practices and the presentation of financial information. The IASB has worked toward uniformity since 1973, but harmonization has by no means been achieved. The EPS requirements you see in this chapter are a result of cooperation between the FASB and the IASB to develop common requirements for earnings per share. Significant differences still exist among countries that do not choose to follow the international standards in this area.

[17] "Qualitative Characteristics of Accounting Information," *FASB Statement of Concepts No. 2*, FASB, 1980, par. 111.
[18] "Earnings per Share," *Statement of Financial Accounting Standards No. 128* (Norwalk, Conn.: FASB, 1977).

**Comparability is a qualitative characteristic of relevant accounting information (*Concept Statement 2*).**

Keep in mind as you study the requirements that a primary goal is comparability. As a result, many of the rules devised to achieve consistency are unavoidably arbitrary, meaning that other choices the FASB might have made in many instances would be equally adequate.

## Basic Earnings Per Share

**A firm has a simple capital structure if it has no *potential* common shares.**

LO5

A firm is said to have a **simple capital structure** if it has no outstanding securities that could potentially dilute earnings per share. In this context, to dilute means to *reduce* earnings per share. For instance, if a firm has convertible bonds outstanding and those bonds are converted, the resulting increase in common shares could decrease (or dilute) earnings per share. That is, the new shares represented by the bonds might participate in future earnings. So convertible bonds are referred to as **potential common shares**. Other potential common shares are convertible preferred stock, stock options, and contingently issuable shares. We will see how the potentially dilutive effects of these securities are included in the calculation of EPS later in this chapter. Now, though, our focus is on the calculation of EPS for a simple capital structure—when no potential common shares are present. In these cases, the calculation is referred to as **basic EPS,** and is simply earnings available to common shareholders divided by the weighted-average number of common shares outstanding.

***Basic EPS* reflects no dilution, only shares now outstanding.**

In the most elemental setting, earnings per share (or net loss per share) is merely a firm's net income (or net loss) divided by the number of shares of common stock outstanding throughout the year. The calculation becomes more demanding (a) when the number of shares has changed during the reporting period, (b) when the earnings available to common shareholders are diminished by dividends to preferred shareholders, or (c) when we attempt to take into account the impending effect of potential common shares (which we do in a later section of the chapter). To illustrate the calculation of EPS in each of its dimensions, we will use only one example in this chapter. We'll start with the most basic situation and then add one new element at a time until we have considered all the principal ways the calculation can be affected. In this way you can see the effect of each component of earnings per share, not just in isolation, but in relation to the effects of other components as well. The basic calculation is shown in Illustration 19–4.

**EPS expresses a firm's profitability on a per share basis.**

**ILLUSTRATION 19–4**
Fundamental Calculation

Sovran Financial Corporation reported net income of $154 million in 2006 (tax rate 40%). Its capital structure consisted of:

**Common Stock**

Jan. 1 60 million common shares outstanding

(amounts in millions, except per share amount)

**Basic EPS:**

$$\frac{\underset{\text{Net income}}{\$154}}{\underset{\text{Shares outstanding}}{60}} = \$2.57$$

**In the most elemental setting, earnings per share is simply a company's earnings divided by the number of shares outstanding.**

### ISSUANCE OF NEW SHARES

Because the shares discussed in Illustration 19–4 remained unchanged throughout the year, the denominator of the EPS calculation is simply the number of shares outstanding. But if the number of shares has changed, it's necessary to find the weighted average of the shares outstanding during the period the earnings were generated. For instance, if an additional 12 million shares had been issued on March 1 of the year just ended, we calculate the weighted-average number of shares to be 70 million as demonstrated in Illustration 19–5 on the next page.

LO6

Because the new shares were outstanding only 10 months, or 10/12 of the year, we increase the 60 million shares already outstanding by the additional shares—weighted by the fraction of the year (10/12) they were outstanding. The weighted average is 60 + 12 (10/12) = 60 + 10 = 70 million shares. The reason for time-weighting the shares issued is that the

**ILLUSTRATION 19–5**
Weighted Average

Sovran Financial Corporation reported net income of $154 million for 2006 (tax rate 40%). Its capital structure included:

**Common Stock**

| | |
|---|---|
| Jan. 1 | 60 million common shares outstanding |
| Mar. 1 | 12 million new shares were sold |

(amounts in millions, except per share amount)

**Basic EPS:**

$$\frac{\overset{\text{Net income}}{\$154}}{\underset{\text{Shares at Jan. 1}}{60} + \underset{\text{New Shares}}{12\,(10/12)}} = \frac{\$154}{70} = \$2.20$$

Any new shares issued are time-weighted by the fraction of the period they were outstanding and then added to the number of shares outstanding for the entire period.

resources the stock sale provides the company are available for generating income only after the date the shares are sold. So, weighting is necessary to make the shares in the fraction's denominator consistent with the income in its numerator.

## STOCK DIVIDENDS AND STOCK SPLITS

Recall that a stock dividend or a stock split is a distribution of additional shares to existing shareholders. But there's an important and fundamental difference between the increase in shares caused by a stock dividend and an increase from selling new shares. When new shares are sold, both assets and shareholders' equity are increased by an additional investment in the firm by shareholders. On the other hand, a stock dividend or stock split merely increases the number of shares without affecting the firm's assets. In effect, the same pie is divided into more pieces. The result is a larger number of less valuable shares.[19] This fundamental change in the nature of the shares is reflected in a calculation of EPS by simply increasing the number of shares.

In Illustration 19–6, notice that the additional shares created by the stock dividend are *not* weighted for the time period they were outstanding. Instead, the increase is treated as if it occurred at the beginning of the year.

**ILLUSTRATION 19–6**
Stock Dividends and Stock Splits

Sovran Financial Corporation reported net income of $154 million in 2006 (tax rate 40%). Its capital structure included:

**Common Stock**

| | |
|---|---|
| Jan. 1 | 60 million common shares outstanding |
| Mar. 1 | 12 million new shares were sold |
| June 17 | A 10% stock dividend was distributed |

(amounts in millions, except per share amount)

**Basic EPS:**

$$\frac{\overset{\text{Net income}}{\$154}}{\underset{\text{Shares at Jan. 1}}{60}\,(1.10) + \underset{\text{New Shares}}{12\,(10/12)}\,(1.10)} = \frac{\$154}{77} = \$2.00$$

Stock dividend adjustment

Shares outstanding prior to the stock dividend are retroactively restated to reflect the 10% increase in shares—that is, treated as if the distribution occurred at the beginning of the period.

The number of shares outstanding after a 10% stock dividend is 1.10 times higher than before. This multiple is applied to both the beginning shares and the new shares sold before the stock distribution. If this had been a 25% stock dividend, the multiple would have been 1.25; a 2-for-1 stock split means a multiple of 2; and so on.

[19]For a more complete discussion of why the market price per share declines in proportion to the increase in the number of shares see Chapter 18.

● LO7

Notice that EPS without the 10% stock dividend ($2.20) is 10% more than it is with the stock distribution ($2). This is caused by the increase in the number of shares. But, unlike a sale of new shares, this should not be interpreted as a "dilution" of earnings per share. Shareholders' interests in their company's earnings have not been diluted. Instead, each shareholder's interest is represented by more—though less valuable—shares.

A simplistic but convenient way to view the effect is to think of the predistribution shares as having been "blue." After the stock dividend, the more valuable "blue" shares are gone, replaced by a larger number of, let's say, "green" shares. From now on, we compute the earnings per "green" share, whereas we previously calculated earnings per "blue" share. We restate the number of shares retroactively to reflect the stock dividend, as if the shares always had been "green." After all, our intent is to let the calculation reflect the fundamental change in the nature of the shares.

**ADDITIONAL CONSIDERATION**

When last year's EPS is reported again for comparison purposes in the current year's comparative income statements, it too should reflect the increased shares from the stock dividend. For instance, suppose last year's EPS were $2.09: $115 million net income divided by 55 million weighted-average shares. When reported again for comparison purposes in the 2006 comparative income statements, that figure would be restated to reflect the 10% stock dividend [$115 ÷ (55 × 1.10) = $1.90]:

| Earnings per Share: | 2006 | 2005 |
|---|---|---|
| | $2.00 | $1.90 |

The EPS numbers now are comparable—both reflect the stock dividend. Otherwise we would be comparing earnings per "green" share with earnings per "blue" share; this way both are earnings per "green" share.

## REACQUIRED SHARES

If shares were reacquired during the period (either retired or as treasury stock), the weighted-average number of shares is reduced. The number of reacquired shares is time-weighted for the *fraction of the year they were **not** outstanding,* prior to being *subtracted* from the number of shares outstanding during the period. Let's modify our continuing illustration to assume 8 million shares were reacquired on October 1 as treasury stock (Illustration 19–7).

**ILLUSTRATION 19–7**
Reacquired Shares

The 8 million shares reacquired as treasury stock are weighted by (3/12) to reflect the fact they were not outstanding the last three months of the year.

Sovran Financial Corporation reported net income of $154 million in 2006 (tax rate 40%). Its capital structure included:

**Common Stock**

| | |
|---|---|
| Jan. 1 | 60 million common shares outstanding |
| Mar. 1 | 12 million new shares were sold |
| June 17 | A 10% stock dividend was distributed |
| Oct. 1 | 8 million shares were reacquired as treasury stock |

(amounts in millions, except per share amounts)

**Basic EPS:**

$$\frac{\text{Net income } \$154}{60\,(1.10) + 12\,(10/12)\,(1.10) - 8\,(3/12)} = \frac{\$154}{75} = \$2.05$$

60 = Shares at Jan. 1; 12 (10/12) = New Shares; 8 (3/12) = Treasury shares; (1.10) = Stock dividend adjustment*

*Not necessary for the treasury shares since they were reacquired after the stock dividend and thus already reflect the adjustment (that is, the shares repurchased are 8 million "new green" shares).

Compare the adjustment for treasury shares with the adjustment for new shares sold. Each is time-weighted for the fraction of the year the shares were or were not outstanding. But also notice two differences. The new shares are added, while the reacquired shares are subtracted. The second difference is that the reacquired shares are not multiplied by 1.10 to adjust for the 10% stock dividend. The reason is the shares were repurchased after the June 17 stock dividend; the reacquired shares are 8 million of the new post-distribution shares. (To use our earlier representation, these are 8 million "green" shares.) To generalize, when a stock distribution occurred during the reporting period, any sales or purchases of shares that occurred *before* the distribution are increased by the distribution. But the stock distribution does not increase the number of shares sold or purchased, if any, *after* the distribution.

**The adjustment for reacquired shares is the same as for new shares sold except the shares are deducted rather than added.**

**Any sales or purchases of shares that occurred before, but not after, a stock dividend or split are affected by the distribution.**

## EARNINGS AVAILABLE TO COMMON SHAREHOLDERS

● LO8

The denominator in an EPS calculation is the weighted-average number of common shares outstanding. Logically, the numerator should similarly represent earnings available to common shareholders. This was automatic in our illustrations to this point because the only shares outstanding were common shares. But when a senior class of shareholders (like preferred shareholders) is entitled to a specified allocation of earnings (like preferred dividends), those amounts are subtracted from earnings before calculating earnings per share.[20] This is demonstrated in Illustration 19–8.

**ILLUSTRATION 19–8**
Preferred Dividends

Sovran Financial Corporation reported net income of $154 million in 2006 (tax rate 40%). Its capital structure included:

**Common Stock**

| | |
|---|---|
| January 1 | 60 million common shares outstanding |
| March 1 | 12 million new shares were sold |
| June 17 | A 10% stock dividend was distributed |
| October 1 | 8 million shares were reacquired as treasury stock |

**Preferred Stock, Nonconvertible**

January 1–December 31 5 million 8%, $10 par, shares

(amounts in millions, except per share amount)

**Basic EPS:**

$$\frac{\underset{\text{Net income}}{\$154} \;\; \underset{\text{Preferred dividends}}{-\$4^{*}}}{\underset{\text{Shares at Jan. 1}}{60}\;(1.10) + \underset{\text{New Shares}}{12\,(10/12)}\;(1.10) - \underset{\text{Treasury shares}}{8\,(3/12)}} = \frac{\$150}{75} = \$2.00$$

(1.10) — Stock dividend adjustment

*8% × $10 par × 5 million shares.

**Preferred dividends are subtracted from net income so that "earnings available to common shareholders" is divided by the weighted-average number of common shares.**

Suppose no dividends were declared for the year. Should we adjust for preferred dividends? Yes, if the preferred stock is cumulative—and most preferred stock is. This means that when dividends are not declared, the unpaid dividends accumulate to be paid in a future year when (if) dividends are subsequently declared. Obviously, the presumption is that, although the year's dividend preference isn't distributed this year, it eventually will be paid.

**Preferred dividends reduce earnings available to common shareholders unless the preferred stock is noncumulative and no dividends were declared that year.**

We have encountered no potential common shares to this point in our continuing illustration. As a result, we have what is referred to as a simple capital structure. (Although, at this point, you may question this label.) For a simple capital structure, a single presentation of basic earnings per common share is appropriate. We turn our attention now to situations described as complex capital structures. In these situations, two separate presentations are required: basic EPS and diluted EPS.

[20]You learned in Chapter 18 that when dividends are declared, preferred shareholders have a preference (over common shareholders) to a specified amount.

# Diluted Earnings Per Share

## POTENTIAL COMMON SHARES

Imagine a situation in which convertible bonds are outstanding that will significantly increase the number of common shares if bondholders exercise their options to exchange their bonds for shares of common stock. Should these be ignored when earnings per share is calculated? After all, they haven't been converted as yet, so to assume an increase in shares for a conversion that may never occur might mislead investors and creditors. On the other hand, if conversion is imminent, not taking into account the dilutive effect of the share increase might mislead investors and creditors. The profession's solution to the dilemma is to calculate earnings per share twice.

In a complex capital structure, a second EPS computation takes into account the assumed effect of *potential common shares*, essentially a "worst case scenario."

Securities like these convertible bonds, while not being common stock, may become common stock through their exercise or conversion. Therefore, they may dilute (reduce) earnings per share and are called **potential common shares**. A firm is said to have a **complex capital structure** if potential common shares are outstanding. Besides convertible bonds, other potential common shares are convertible preferred stock, stock options, rights, or warrants, and contingently issuable securities. (We'll discuss each of these shortly.) A firm with a complex capital structure reports two EPS calculations. **Basic EPS** ignores the dilutive effect of such securities, **diluted EPS** incorporates the dilutive effect of all potential common shares.

## OPTIONS, RIGHTS, AND WARRANTS

● LO9

Stock options, stock rights, and stock warrants are similar. Each gives its holders the right to exercise their option to purchase common stock, usually at a specified exercise price. The dilution that would result from their exercise should be reflected in the calculation of diluted EPS, but not basic EPS.

Stock options are assumed to have been exercised when calculating diluted EPS.

To include the dilutive effect of a security means to calculate EPS *as if* the potential increase in shares already has occurred (even though it hasn't yet). So, for a stock option (or right, or warrant), we pretend the option has been exercised. In fact, we assume the options were exercised at the beginning of the reporting period, or when the options were issued if that's later. We then assume the cash proceeds from selling the new shares at the exercise price are used to buy back as many shares as possible at the shares' average market price during the year. This is demonstrated in Illustration 19–9 on the next page.

FINANCIAL REPORTING CASE

Q4, p. 951

When we simulate the exercise of the stock options, we calculate EPS as if 15 million shares were sold at the beginning of the year. This obviously increases the number of shares in the denominator by 15 million shares. But it is insufficient to simply add the additional shares without considering the accompanying consequences. Remember, if this hypothetical scenario had occurred, the company would have had $300 million cash proceeds from the exercise of the options (15 million shares × $20 exercise price per share). What would have been the effect on earnings per share? This depends on what the company would have done with the $300 million cash proceeds. Would the proceeds have been used to buy more equipment? Increase the sales force? Expand facilities? Pay dividends?

Obviously, there are literally hundreds of choices, and it's unlikely that any two firms would spend the $300 million exactly the same way. But remember, our objective is to create some degree of uniformity in the way firms determine earnings per share so the resulting numbers are comparable. So, standard-setters decided on a single assumption for all firms to provide some degree of comparability.

For diluted EPS, we assume the proceeds from exercise of the options were used to reacquire shares as treasury stock at the average market price of the common stock during the reporting period. Consequently, the weighted-average number of shares is increased by the difference between the shares assumed issued and those assumed reacquired—in our illustration: 15 million shares issued minus 12 million shares reacquired ($300 million ÷ $25 per share) equals 3 million net increase in shares.

The way we take into account the dilutive effect of stock options is called the *treasury stock method* because of our assumption that treasury shares are purchased with the cash proceeds of the exercise of the options. Besides providing comparability, this assumption actually is plausible because, if the options were exercised, more shares would be needed to issue

**ILLUSTRATION 19–9**
Stock Options

Sovran Financial Corporation reported net income of $154 million in 2006 (tax rate 40%). Its capital structure included:

**Common Stock**

| | |
|---|---|
| Jan. 1 | 60 million common shares outstanding |
| Mar. 1 | 12 million new shares were sold |
| June 17 | A 10% stock dividend was distributed |
| Oct. 1 | 8 million shares were reacquired as treasury stock |

(The average market price of the common shares during 2006 was $25 per share.)

**Preferred Stock, Nonconvertible**

January 1–December 31 5 million 8%, $10 par, shares

**Executive Stock Options**

Options granted in 2004, exercisable for 15 million common shares* at an exercise price of $20 per share

(amounts in millions, except per share amounts)

**Basic EPS (unchanged)**

$$\frac{\overset{\text{Net income}}{\$154} \quad \overset{\text{Preferred dividends}}{-\$4}}{\underset{\text{Shares at Jan. 1}}{60}\,(1.10) + \underset{\text{New Shares}}{12\,(10/12)}\,(1.10) - \underset{\text{Treasury shares}}{8\,(3/12)}} = \frac{\$150}{75} = \$2$$

(1.10) ... (1.10): Stock dividend adjustment

Stock options give their holders (company executives in this case) the right to purchase common stock at a specified exercise price ($20 in this case).

The stock options do not affect the calculation of basic EPS.

**Diluted EPS**

$$\frac{\overset{\text{Net income}}{\$154} \quad \overset{\text{Preferred dividends}}{-\$4}}{\underset{\text{Shares at Jan. 1}}{60}\,(1.10) + \underset{\text{New Shares}}{12\,(10/12)}\,(1.10) - \underset{\text{Treasury shares}}{8\,(3/12)} + \underset{\text{Exercise of options}}{(15^{*} - 12^{\dagger})}} = \frac{\$150}{78} = \$1.92$$

(1.10) ... (1.10): Stock dividend adjustment

The calculation of diluted EPS assumes that the shares specified by stock options were issued at the exercise price and that the proceeds were used to buy back (as treasury stock) as many of those shares as can be purchased at the average market price during the period.

*Adjusted for the stock dividend. Prior to the stock dividend, the options were exercisable for 13 7/11 million of the "old" shares which became 15 million (13 7/11 × 1.10) of the "new" shares after the stock dividend.

**†Shares Reacquired for Diluted EPS**

| | |
|---|---|
| 15 | million shares |
| × $ 20 | (exercise price) |
| $300 | million |
| ÷ $ 25 | (average market price) |
| 12 | million shares reacquired |

to option-holders. And, as discussed in the previous chapter, many firms routinely buy back shares either to issue to option-holders or, equivalently, to offset the issuance of new shares.

## ADDITIONAL CONSIDERATION

Technically, the number of shares represented by options or warrants should be determined on a quarter by quarter basis. As a result, the net increase in shares is determined for the first quarter for which the market price has been above the exercise price for 11 weeks and for each quarter thereafter (for which the effect is dilutive). Of course, the shares would be appropriately weighted for the time they are assumed outstanding. For example, let's say the $25 average market price in our illustration was the average price for the third and fourth quarters, but the average price for the first two quarters was less than the $20 exercise price. In that case, the share adjustment would have been:

$$+ (15 - 12)\,(2/4)$$

## CONVERTIBLE SECURITIES

● LO10

Sometimes corporations include a conversion feature as part of a bond offering, a note payable, or an issue of preferred stock. Convertible securities can be converted into (exchanged for) shares of stock at the option of the holder of the security. For that reason, convertible securities are potentially dilutive. EPS will be affected if and when such securities are converted and new shares of common stock are issued. In the previous section you learned that the potentially dilutive effect of stock options is reflected in diluted EPS calculations by assuming the options were exercised. Similarly, the potentially dilutive effect of convertible securities is reflected in diluted EPS calculations by assuming they were converted.

**When we assume conversion, the denominator of the EPS fraction is increased by the additional common shares that would have been issued upon conversion.**

By the *if converted method* as it's called, we assume the conversion into common stock occurred at the beginning of the period (or at the time the convertible security is issued, if that's later). We increase the denominator of the EPS fraction by the additional common shares that would have been issued upon conversion. We increase the numerator by the interest (after-tax) on bonds or other debt or preferred dividends that would have been avoided if the convertible securities had not been outstanding due to having been converted.

**Convertible Bonds.** Now, let's return to our continuing illustration and modify it to include the existence of convertible bonds (Illustration 19–10). We increase the denominator by the 12 million shares that would have been issued if the bonds had been converted. However, if that hypothetical conversion had occurred, the bonds would not have been outstanding during the year. What effect would the absence of the bonds have had on income? Obviously, the bond interest expense (10% × $300 million = $30 million) would have been saved, causing income to be higher. But saving the interest paid would also have meant losing a $30 million tax deduction on the income tax return. With a 40% tax rate that would mean paying $12 million more income taxes. So, to reflect in earnings the $18 million after-tax interest that would have been avoided in the event of conversion, we add back the $30 million of interest expense, but deduct 40% × $30 million for the higher tax expense.

**The numerator is increased by the after-tax interest that would have been avoided.**

**ILLUSTRATION 19–10**
Convertible Bonds

Sovran Financial Corporation reported net income of $154 million in 2006 (tax rate 40%). Its capital structure included:

**Common Stock**

| | |
|---|---|
| Jan. 1 | 60 million common shares outstanding |
| Mar. 1 | 12 million new shares were sold |
| June 17 | A 10% stock dividend was distributed |
| Oct. 1 | 8 million shares were reacquired as treasury stock |

(The average market price of the common shares during 2006 was $25 per share.)

**Preferred Stock, Nonconvertible**

January 1–December 31 5 million 8%, $10 par, shares

**Executive Stock Options**

Options granted in 2004, exercisable for 15 million common shares* at an exercise price of $20 per share

**Convertible Bonds**

10%, $300 million face amount issued in 2005, convertible into 12 million common shares)*

(amounts in millions, except per share amounts)

**Basic EPS (unchanged)**

**The convertible bonds do not affect the calculation of basic EPS.**

$$\frac{\overset{\text{Net income}}{\$154} \quad \overset{\text{Preferred dividends}}{-\$4}}{\underset{\text{Shares at Jan. 1}}{60}\ (1.10) + \underset{\text{New Shares}}{12\,(10/12)}\ (1.10) - \underset{\text{Treasury shares}}{8\,(3/12)}} = \frac{\$150}{75} = \$2.00$$

Stock dividend adjustment (applies to both (1.10) factors)

**Diluted EPS**

$$\frac{\underset{\text{Net income}}{\$154} \quad \underset{\text{Preferred dividends}}{-\$4} \quad \underset{\text{After-tax interest savings}}{+\$30 - 40\%\,(30)}}{\underset{\substack{\text{Shares}\\\text{at Jan. 1}}}{60}\,(1.10) + \underset{\substack{\text{New}\\\text{Shares}}}{12}\,(10/12)\,(1.10) - \underset{\substack{\text{Treasury}\\\text{shares}}}{8\,(3/12)} + \underset{\substack{\text{Exercise}\\\text{of options}}}{(15 - 12)} \underset{\substack{\text{Conversion}\\\text{of bonds}}}{+ 12}} = \frac{\$168}{90} = \$1.87$$

(1.10): Stock dividend adjustment

**ILLUSTRATION 19–10**
Concluded

**If the bonds had been converted, 12 million more common shares would have been issued, and net income would have been higher by the interest saved (after tax) from not having the bonds outstanding.**

*Adjusted for the stock dividend. For example, prior to the stock dividend, the bonds were exercisable for $10\frac{10}{11}$ million of the "old" shares which became 12 million ($10\frac{10}{11} \times 1.10$) of the "new" shares after the stock dividend.

## ADDITIONAL CONSIDERATION

The $300 million of convertible bonds in our illustration were issued at face value. Suppose the bonds had been issued for $282 million. In that case, the adjustment to earnings would be modified to include the amortization of the $18 million bond discount. Assuming straight-line amortization and a 10-year maturity, the adjustment to the diluted EPS calculation would have been:

$$\frac{+\,[\$30 + \mathbf{(\$18 \div 10\ years)}] \times (1 - 40\%)^{*}}{+\,12}$$

to reflect the fact that the interest expense would include the $30 million stated interest plus one-tenth of the bond discount.†

*This is an alternative way to represent the after-tax adjustment to interest since subtracting 40% of the interest expense is the same as multiplying interest expense by 60%.
†See Chapter 14 if you need to refresh your memory about bond discount amortization.

Our illustration describes the treatment of convertible bonds. The same treatment pertains to other debt that is convertible into common shares such as convertible notes payable. Remember from our discussion of debt in earlier chapters that all debt is similar whether in the form of bonds, notes, or other configurations.

## ADDITIONAL CONSIDERATION

Notice that we assumed the bonds were converted at the beginning of the reporting period since they were outstanding all year. However, if the convertible bonds had been issued during the reporting period, we would assume their conversion occurred on the date of issue. It would be illogical to assume they were converted before they were issued. If the convertible bonds in our illustration had been sold on September 1, for instance, the adjustment to the EPS calculation would have been:

$$\frac{+\,[\$30 - 40\%\,(\$30)]\,(4/12)}{+\,12\,(4/12)}$$

to reflect the fact that the after-tax interest savings and the net increase in shares would have been effective for only four months of the year.

This is our approach not just for convertible bonds, but for any potential common shares. For example, we assumed the options in our illustration were exercised at the beginning of the reporting period so the net increase in shares was not weighted for a fraction of the year outstanding. If the options had been granted to company executives on April 1 the adjustment to the weighted-average number of shares would have been:

$$+\,(15 - 12)\,(9/12)$$

to reflect the fact that the net increase in shares would have been effective for only nine months of the year.

**We assume convertible securities were converted (or options exercised) at the beginning of the reporting period or at the time the securities are issued, if later.**

**Convertible Preferred Stock.** The potentially dilutive effect of convertible preferred stock is reflected in EPS calculations in much the same way as convertible debt. That is, we calculate EPS as if conversion already had occurred. Specifically, we add shares to the denominator of the EPS fraction and add back to earnings available to common shareholders the preferred dividends that would have been avoided if the preferred stock had been converted. Illustration 19–11 offers an example.

The adjustment for the conversion of the preferred stock should be applied only to diluted EPS computations. However, the existence of another issue of preferred stock also will affect the calculation of basic EPS. The effect on basic EPS is the same as the effect of the first

**ILLUSTRATION 19–11**
Convertible Preferred Stock

Sovran Financial Corporation reported net income of $154 million in 2006 (tax rate 40%). Its capital structure included:

**Common Stock**

| | |
|---|---|
| Jan. 1 | 60 million common shares outstanding |
| Mar. 1 | 12 million new shares were sold |
| June 17 | A 10% stock dividend was distributed |
| Oct. 1 | 8 million shares were reacquired as treasury stock |

(The average market price of the common shares during 2006 was $25 per share.)

**Preferred Stock, Nonconvertible**

January 1–December 31 5 million 8%, $10 par, shares

**Executive Stock Options**

Options granted in 2004, exercisable for 15 million common shares* at an exercise price of $20 per share

**Convertible Bonds**

10%, $300 million face amount issued in 2005, convertible into 12 million common shares*

**Preferred Stock, Convertible**

10 million, 8%, cumulative, $10 par, shares issued in 2002, convertible into 5 million shares*

(amounts in millions, except per share amounts)

**Basic EPS**

$$\frac{\underset{\text{Net income}}{\$154} \; \underset{\text{Preferred dividends}}{-\$4} \; \underset{\text{Preferred dividends}}{-\$8}}{\underset{\text{Shares at Jan. 1}}{60}\,(1.10) + \underset{\text{New Shares}}{12\,(10/12)}\,(1.10) - \underset{\text{Treasury shares}}{8\,(3/12)}} = \frac{\$142}{75} = \$1.89$$

(1.10) = Stock dividend adjustment

Since diluted EPS is calculated *as if* the preferred shares had been converted, there are no dividends. Earnings available to common shareholders is increased by the dividends that otherwise would have been distributed to preferred shareholders.

**Diluted EPS**

$$\frac{\underset{\text{Net income}}{\$154} \; \underset{\text{Preferred dividends}}{-\$4} \; \underset{\text{Preferred dividends}}{-\$8} \; \underset{\text{After-tax interest savings}}{+\$30 - 40\%(\$30)} \; \underset{\text{Preferred dividends}}{+\$8}}{\underset{\text{Shares at Jan. 1}}{60}\,(1.10) + \underset{\text{New Shares}}{12\,(10/12)}(1.10) - \underset{\text{Treasury shares}}{8\,(3/12)} + \underset{\text{Exercise of options}}{(15-12)} + \underset{\text{Conversion of bonds}}{12} + \underset{\text{Conversion of preferred shares}}{5}} = \frac{\$168}{95} = \$1.77$$

(1.10) = Stock dividend adjustment

*Adjusted for the stock dividend. For example, prior to the stock dividend, the preferred shares were convertible into 4 6/11 million of the "old" shares which became 5 million (4 6/11 × 1.10) of the "new" shares after the stock dividend.

(nonconvertible) issue of preferred stock: the numerator is reduced by the preferred dividends in order to derive earnings available to common shareholders.

This second issue of preferred stock would reduce earnings available to common shareholders by $8 million (8% × $100 million par). However, when diluted EPS is calculated, we hypothetically assume the convertible preferred stock was *not* outstanding. Accordingly, no preferred dividends on these shares would have been paid. So we add back the $8 million preferred dividends in much the same way we added back the interest saved when we assumed convertible bonds were converted. An important difference, though, is that, unlike interest expense, dividends have no tax effect. Dividends are not an expense and no income tax deduction is lost when dividends are not paid. Of course, adding back the preferred dividends that otherwise would have been deducted is equivalent to simply not deducting them in the first place.

## Antidilutive Securities

At times, the effect of the conversion or exercise of potential common shares would be to increase, rather than decrease, EPS. These we refer to as **antidilutive securities.** Such securities are ignored when calculating both basic and diluted EPS.

### OPTIONS, WARRANTS, RIGHTS

For illustration, recall the way we treated the stock options in our continuing illustration. In applying the treasury stock method, the number of shares assumed repurchased is fewer than the number of shares assumed sold. This is the case any time the buyback (average market) price is higher than the exercise price. Consequently, there will be a net increase in the number of shares, so earnings per share will decline.

On the other hand, when the exercise price is *higher* than the market price, to assume shares are sold at the exercise price and repurchased at the market price would mean buying back *more* shares than were sold. This would produce a net decrease in the number of shares. EPS would increase, not decrease, if we were to assume the exercise of stock options, stock warrants, or their equivalent. These would have an antidilutive effect and would not be considered exercised. In fact, a rational investor would not exercise options at an exercise price higher than the current market price anyway. Let's look at the example provided by Illustration 19–12 on the next page.

**Antidilutive securities are ignored when calculating both basic and diluted EPS.**

To assume 4 million shares were sold at the $32.50 exercise price and repurchased at the lower market price ($25) would mean reacquiring 5.2 million shares—more shares than were assumed sold. Because the effect would be antidilutive, we would simply ignore the warrants in the calculations.

In our continuing illustration, only the stock warrants were antidilutive. The other potential common shares caused EPS to decline when we considered them exercised or converted. In the case of the executive stock options, it was readily apparent that their effect would be dilutive because the exercise price was less than the market price, indicating that fewer shares could be repurchased (at the average market price) than were assumed issued (at the exercise price). As a result, the denominator increased. When only the denominator of a fraction increases, the fraction itself decreases. On the other hand, in the case of the warrants, it was apparent that their effect would be antidilutive because the exercise price was higher than the market price, which would have decreased the denominator and therefore increased the fraction.

When a company has a net loss, rather than net income, it reports a loss per share. In that situation, stock options that otherwise are dilutive will be antidilutive. Here's why. Suppose we have a loss per share of $2.00 calculated as ($150 million) ÷ 75 million shares = ($2.00). Now suppose stock options are outstanding that, if exercised, will increase the number of shares by 5 million. If that increase is included in the calculation, the loss per share will be $1.88 calculated as ($150 million) ÷ 80 million shares = ($1.88). The *loss* per share *declines.* This represents an *increase* in performance—not a dilution of performance. The options would be considered antidilutive, then, and not included in the calculation of the net loss per share. Any potential common shares not included in dilutive EPS because they are antidilutive should be revealed in the disclosure notes.

**ILLUSTRATION 19–12**
Antidilutive Warrants

Sovran Financial Corporation reported net income of $154 million in 2006 (tax rate 40%). Its capital structure included:

**Common Stock**

| | |
|---|---|
| Jan. 1 | 60 million common shares outstanding |
| Mar. 1 | 12 million new shares were sold |
| June 17 | A 10% stock dividend was distributed |
| Oct. 1 | 8 million shares were reacquired as treasury stock |

(The average market price of the common shares during 2006 was $25 per share.)

**Preferred Stock, Nonconvertible**

January 1–December 31 5 million 8%, $10 par, shares

**Executive Stock Options**

Options granted in 2004, exercisable for 15 million common shares* at an exercise price of $20 per share

**Convertible Bonds**

10%, $300 million face amount issued in 2005, convertible into 12 million common shares*

**Preferred Stock, Convertible**

10 million, 8%, cumulative, $10 par, shares issued in 2002, convertible into 5 million shares*

**Stock warrants**

Warrants granted in 2005, exercisable for 4 million common shares* at an exercise price of $32.50 per share

**Calculations:**

The calculations of both basic and diluted EPS are unaffected by the warrants because the effect of exercising the warrants would be antidilutive.

*Adjusted for the stock dividend. For example, prior to the stock dividend, the bonds were convertible into $10\frac{10}{11}$ million of the "old" shares which became 12 million ($10\frac{10}{11}$ 1.10) of the "new" shares after the stock dividend.

The $32.50 exercise price is higher than the market price, $25, so to assume shares are sold at the exercise price and repurchased at the market price would mean reacquiring more shares than were sold.

## CONVERTIBLE SECURITIES

For convertible securities, though, it's not immediately obvious whether the effect of their conversion would be dilutive or antidilutive because the assumed conversion would affect both the numerator and the denominator of the EPS fraction. We discovered each was dilutive only after including the effect in the calculation and observing the result—a decline in EPS. But there's an easier way.

To determine whether convertible securities are dilutive and should be included in a diluted EPS calculation, we can compare the incremental effect of the conversion (expressed as a fraction) with the EPS fraction before the effect of any convertible security is considered. This, of course is our basic EPS. Recall from Illustration 19–11 that basic EPS is $1.89.

For comparison, we determine the "earnings per incremental share" of the two convertible securities:

The incremental effect (of conversion) of the bonds is the after-tax interest saved divided by the additional common shares from conversion.

**Conversion of Bonds**

$$\frac{\overset{\text{After-tax interest savings}}{+\$30 - 40\%\ (\$30)}}{\underset{\text{Conversion of bonds}}{+12}} = \frac{\$18}{12} = \$1.50$$

The incremental effect (of conversion) of the preferred stock is the dividends that wouldn't be paid divided by the additional common shares from conversion.

**Conversion of Preferred Stock**

$$\frac{\overset{\text{Preferred dividends}}{+\$8}}{\underset{\text{Conversion of preferred shares}}{+5}} = \$1.60$$

## GLOBAL PERSPECTIVE

Earnings per share receives more attention in the United States than in most other countries. In countries that do require EPS disclosures, requirements differ widely. For instance, earnings for the numerator of the EPS calculation are defined in the United States as earnings available for common shareholders, and separate calculations are required for ordinary income and net income when differences exist. In some countries, though, earnings is defined as continuing income from operations only (Norway, for example).

In the United States, basic and diluted EPS are reported. Other countries have similar requirements but define the two calculations differently than the United States (that is, the potential common shares included are different). Japan requires basic and diluted EPS to be reported in disclosure notes. Some countries (Switzerland, for instance) require no EPS disclosure at all, but disclosure may be provided anyway.

If the incremental effect of a security is *higher* than basic EPS, it is antidilutive. That's not the case in our illustration.

## ORDER OF ENTRY FOR MULTIPLE CONVERTIBLE SECURITIES

A convertible security might seem to be dilutive when looked at individually but, in fact, may be antidilutive when included in combination with other convertible securities. This is because the *order of entry* for including their effects in the EPS calculation determines by how much, or even whether, EPS decreases as a result of their assumed conversion. Because our goal is to reveal the maximum potential dilution that might result, theoretically we should calculate diluted EPS using every possible combination of potential common shares to find the combination that yields the lowest EPS. But that's not necessary.

We can use the earnings per incremental share we calculated to determine the sequence of including securities' effects in the calculation. We include the securities in reverse order, beginning with the lowest incremental effect (that is, most dilutive), followed by the next lowest, and so on. This is, in fact, the order in which we included the securities in our continuing illustration.

## ADDITIONAL CONSIDERATION

Actually, the order of inclusion made no difference in our example, but would in many instances. For example, suppose the preferred stock had been convertible into 4.3 million shares, rather than 5 million shares. The incremental effect of its conversion would have been:

**Conversion of Preferred Stock**

$$\frac{\underset{\text{Preferred dividends}}{+\$8}}{\underset{\text{Conversion of preferred shares}}{+4.3}} = \$1.86$$

On the surface, the effect would seem to be dilutive because $1.86 is less than $1.89, basic EPS. In fact, if this were the only convertible security, it would be dilutive. But, after the convertible bonds are assumed converted first, then the assumed conversion of the preferred stock would be *antidilutive:*

**With Conversion of Bonds**

$$\frac{\underset{\text{Net income}}{\$154} \quad \underset{\text{Preferred dividends}}{-\$4} \quad \underset{\text{Preferred dividends}}{-\$8} \quad \underset{\text{After-tax interest savings}}{+\$30 - 40\%(\$30)}}{\underset{\text{Shares at Jan. 1}}{60}\ (1.10) + \underset{\text{New shares}}{12\ (^{10}/_{12})}\ (1.10) - \underset{\text{Treasury shares}}{8\ (^{3}/_{12})} + \underset{\text{Exercise of options}}{(15-12)} + \underset{\text{Conversion of bonds}}{12}} = \frac{\$160}{90} = \$1.777$$

(1.10) factors: Stock dividend adjustment

Because the incremental effect of the convertible bonds ($1.50) is lower than the incremental effect of the convertible preferred stock ($1.86), it is included first.

A convertible security might seem to be dilutive when looked at individually but may be antidilutive when included in combination with other convertible securities.

**With Conversion of Preferred Stock**

$$\frac{\underset{\text{Net income}}{\$154}\ \underset{\text{Preferred dividends}}{-\$4}\ \underset{\text{Preferred dividends}}{-\$8}\ \underset{\text{After-tax interest savings}}{+\$30 - 40\%(\$30)}\ \underset{\text{Preferred dividends}}{+\$8}}{\underset{\text{Shares at Jan. 1}}{60}\ (1.10) + \underset{\text{New Shares}}{12\ (^{10}\!/_{12})}\ (1.10) - \underset{\text{Treasury shares}}{8\ (^{3}\!/_{12})} + \underset{\text{Exercise of options}}{(15-12)} + \underset{\text{Conversion of bonds}}{12} + \underset{\text{Conversion of preferred shares}}{4.3}} = \frac{\$168}{94.3} = \$1.782$$

Stock dividend adjustment (the (1.10) factors)

Although the incremental effect of the convertible preferred stock ($1.86) is lower than basic EPS ($1.89), when included in the calculation after the convertible bonds the effect is antidilutive (EPS increases).

## CONCEPT REVIEW EXERCISE

### BASIC AND DILUTED EPS

At December 31, 2006, the financial statements of Clevenger Casting Corporation included the following:

| | |
|---|---|
| Net income for 2006 | $500 million |
| Common stock, $1 par: | |
| Shares outstanding on January 1 | 150 million shares |
| Shares retired for cash on February 1 | 24 million shares |
| Shares sold for cash on September 1 | 18 million shares |
| 2-for-1 split on July 23 | |
| Preferred stock, 10%, $60 par, cumulative, nonconvertible | $ 70 million |
| Preferred stock, 8%, $50 par, cumulative, convertible into 4 million shares of common stock | $100 million |
| Common stock warrants outstanding for 4 million shares of common stock; the exercise price is $15 | |
| Bonds payable, 12.5%, convertible into 20 million shares of common stock | $200 million |

*Additional data:*
The market price of the common stock averaged $20 during 2006.
The convertible preferred stock and the bonds payable had been issued at par in 2004. The tax rate for the year was 40%.

**Required:**
Compute basic and diluted earnings per share for the year ended December 31, 2006.

### SOLUTION

(amounts in millions, except per share amounts)

**Basic EPS**

$$\frac{\underset{\text{Net income}}{\$500}\ \underset{\text{Preferred dividends}}{-\$7^{a}}\ \underset{\text{Preferred dividends}}{-\$8^{b}}}{\underset{\text{Shares at Jan. 1}}{150}\ (2.00) - \underset{\text{Retired shares}}{24\ (^{11}\!/_{12})}\ (2.00) + \underset{\text{New shares}}{18\ (^{4}\!/_{12})}} = \frac{\$485}{262} = \$1.85$$

Stock split adjustment* (the (2.00) factors)

**Diluted EPS**

$$\frac{\overset{\text{Net income}}{\$500} \;\overset{\text{Preferred dividends}}{-\$7^{a}} \;\overset{\text{Preferred dividends}}{-\$8^{b}} \;\overset{\text{After-tax interest savings}}{+\,25^{d} - 40\%(\$25^{d})}}{\underset{\text{Shares at Jan. 1}}{150}\,(2.00) - \underset{\text{Retired shares}}{24\left(\tfrac{11}{12}\right)}\,(2.00) + \underset{\text{New shares}}{18\left(\tfrac{4}{12}\right)} + \underset{\text{Exercise of warrants}}{(4-3)^{c}} \;\underset{\text{Conversion of bonds}}{+\,20}} = \frac{\$500}{283} = \$1.77$$

(2.00) = Stock split adjustment

[a]10% × $70 million = $7 million
[b]8% × $100 million = $8 million
[c]**Exercise of warrants:**
4 million shares
× $15 (exercise price)
$60 million
÷ $20 (average market price)
3 million shares

[d]12.5% × $200 million = $25 million

**Dilution:**

**Conversion of Bonds**

$$\frac{\overset{\text{After-tax interest savings}}{+\,\$25 - 40\%(\$25)}}{\underset{\text{Conversion of bonds}}{+\,20}} = \$0.75$$

**Conversion of 8% Preferred Stock**

$$\frac{\overset{\text{Preferred dividends}}{+\,\$8}}{\underset{\text{Conversion of preferred shares}}{+\,4}} = \$2.00^{*}$$

*Because the incremental effect of conversion of the preferred stock ($2) is higher than EPS without the conversion of the preferred stock, the conversion would be *antidilutive* and is *not* considered in the calculation of diluted EPS.

# Additional EPS Issues

## CONTINGENTLY ISSUABLE SHARES

● LO11

Sometimes an agreement specifies that additional shares of common stock will be issued, contingent on the occurrence of some future circumstance. For instance, in the disclosure note reproduced in Graphic 19–3, **Hunt Manufacturing Co.** reported contingent shares in connection with its acquisition of **Feeny Manufacturing Company**.

**GRAPHIC 19–3**
Contingently Issuable Shares—Hunt Manufacturing Company

**Note 12: Acquisitions (in part)**
The Company acquired Feeny Manufacturing Company of Muncie, Indiana, for 135,000 shares of restricted common stock with a value of $7.71 per share. Feeny Manufacturing Company is a manufacturer of kitchen storage products. The acquisition was accounted for as a purchase. The purchase agreement calls for the issuance of up to 135,000 additional shares of common stock in the next fiscal year based on the earnings of Feeny Manufacturing Company. . . .

At times, contingent shares are issuable to shareholders of an acquired company, certain key executives, or others in the event a certain level of performance is achieved. Contingent performance may be a desired level of income, a target stock price, or some other measurable activity level.

When calculating EPS, **contingently issuable shares** are considered to be outstanding in the computation of diluted EPS if the target performance level already is being met (assumed to remain at existing levels until the end of the contingency period). For example, if shares will be issued at a future date if a certain level of income is achieved and that level of income

Contingently issuable shares are considered outstanding in the computation of diluted EPS.

or more was already earned this year, those additional shares are simply added to the denominator of the diluted EPS fraction.[21]

For clarification, refer to our continuing illustration and assume 3 million additional shares will become issuable to certain executives in the following year (2007) if net income that year is $150 million or more. Recall that net income in 2006 was $154 million, so the additional shares would be considered outstanding in the computation of diluted EPS by simply adding 3 million additional shares to the denominator of the EPS fraction. Obviously, the 2007 condition ($150 million net income or more) has not been met yet since it's only year 2006. But because that level of income was achieved in 2006, the presumption is it's likely to be earned in 2007 as well.

If a level of income must be attained before the shares will be issued, and income already is that amount or more, the additional shares are simply added to the denominator.

**Assumed Issuance of Contingently Issuable Shares (diluted EPS):**

$$\frac{\text{No adjustment to the numerator}}{\begin{array}{c}+3\\ \text{Additional shares}\end{array}}$$

On the other hand, if the target income next year is $160 million, the contingent shares would simply be ignored in our calculation.

## SUMMARY OF THE EFFECT OF POTENTIAL COMMON SHARES ON EARNINGS PER SHARE

You have seen that under certain circumstances, securities that have the potential of reducing earnings per share by becoming common stock are assumed already to have become common stock for the purpose of calculating EPS. The table in Graphic 19–4 summarizes the circumstances under which the dilutive effect of these securities is reflected in the calculation of basic and diluted EPS.

**GRAPHIC 19–4**

When Potential Common Shares Are Reflected in EPS

| | Is the Dilutive Effect Reflected in the Calculation of EPS?* | |
|---|---|---|
| **Potential Common Shares** | **Basic EPS** | **Diluted EPS** |
| • Stock options (or warrants, rights) | no | yes |
| • Convertible securities (bonds, notes, preferred stock) | no | yes |
| • Contingently issuable shares | no | yes† |

*The effect is not included for any security if its effect is antidilutive.
†Unless shares are contingent upon some level of performance not yet achieved.

Graphic 19–5 summarizes the specific effects on the diluted EPS fraction when the dilutive effect of a potentially dilutive security is reflected in the calculation.

## ACTUAL CONVERSIONS

When calculating EPS in our example, we "pretended" the convertible bonds had been converted at the beginning of the year. What if they actually had been converted, let's say on November 1? Interestingly, diluted EPS would be precisely the same. Here's why:

1. The actual conversion would cause an actual increase in shares of 12 million on November 1. These would be time-weighted so the denominator would increase by 12 ($^2/_{12}$). Also, the numerator would be higher because net income actually would be increased by the after-tax interest saved on the bonds for the last two months, [$30 − 40% ($30)] × ($^2/_{12}$). Be sure to note that this would not be an adjustment in the EPS calculation. Instead, net income would actually have been higher by [$30 − 40% ($30)] × ($^2/_{12}$) = $3. That is, reported net income would have been $157 rather than $154.

[21]The shares should be included in both basic and diluted EPS if all conditions have actually been met so that there is no circumstance under which those shares would not be issued. In essence, these are no longer contingent shares.

**GRAPHIC 19–5**
How Potential Common Shares Are Reflected in a Diluted EPS Calculation

| Potential Common Shares | Modification to the Diluted EPS Fractions: Numerator | Denominator |
|---|---|---|
| • Stock options (or warrants, rights) | None | Add the shares that would be created by their exercise,* reduced by shares repurchased at the average share price. |
| • Convertible bonds (or notes) | Add the interest (after-tax) that would have been avoided if the debt had been converted. | Add shares that would be created by the conversion* of the bonds (or notes). |
| • Convertible preferred stock | Do not deduct the dividends that would have been avoided if the preferred stock had been converted. | Add shares that would have been created by the conversion* of the preferred stock. |
| • Contingently issuable shares: Issuable upon the mere passage of time or Issuable when specified conditions are met, and those conditions are currently being met | None | Add shares that are issuable. |
| • Contingently issuable shares: Issuable when specified conditions are met, and those conditions are **not** currently being met | None | None |

*At the beginning of the year or when potential common shares were issued, whichever is later (time-weight the increase in shares if assumed exercised or converted in midyear).

2. We would assume conversion for the period before November 1 because they were potentially dilutive during that period. The 12 million shares assumed outstanding from January 1 to November 1 would be time-weighted for that 10-month period: 12 ($^{10}/_{12}$). Also, the numerator would be increased by the after-tax interest assumed saved on the bonds for the first 10 months, [\$30 − 40% (\$30)] × ($^{10}/_{12}$).

Notice that the incremental effect on diluted EPS is the same either way:

**Not Actually Converted:** / **Converted on November 1:**

$$\frac{\overset{\text{Assumed after-tax interest savings}}{+\$30 - 40\%(\$30)}}{\underset{\text{Assumed conversion of bonds}}{+12}} = \frac{\overset{\text{Actual after-tax interest savings}}{+[\$30 - 40\%(\$30)] \times (^{2}/_{12})} + \overset{\text{Assumed after-tax interest savings}}{[\$30 - 40\%(\$30)] \times (^{10}/_{12})}}{\underset{\text{Actual conversion of bonds}}{+12(^{2}/_{12})} \quad \underset{\text{Assumed conversion of bonds}}{+12(^{10}/_{12})}}$$

EPS would be precisely the same whether convertible securities were actually converted or not.

Graphic 19–6 shows the disclosure note **Clorox Company** reported after the conversion of convertible notes during the year.

**Note 1: Significant Accounting Policies—Earnings Per Common Share (in part)**
A \$9,000,000 note payable to Henkel Corporation was converted into 1,200,000 shares of common stock on August 1. . . . Earnings per common share and weighted-average shares outstanding reflect this conversion as if it were effective during all periods presented.

**GRAPHIC 19–6**
Conversion of Notes—The Clorox Company

## OPTIONS OUTSTANDING FOR ONLY PART OF THE PERIOD

Options outstanding for only part of the reporting period are included in the denominator on a time-weighted basis. For example, if options were issued on April 1 the denominator would include the appropriate incremental shares × 9/12. Likewise, if options expired on April 1 the weighted-average shares should include the appropriate incremental shares × 3/12.

Similarly, if options were exercised on April 1 the weighted-average shares should include the appropriate incremental shares × 3/12 for the period prior to actual exercise. The weighted-average shares should include the appropriate actual shares issued × 9/12 for the period after the exercise.

## FINANCIAL STATEMENT PRESENTATION OF EARNINGS PER SHARE DATA

● LO12 Recall from Chapter 4 that the income statement sometimes includes items that require separate presentation within the statement as follows:

**Income from Continuing Operations**
Discontinued operations
Extraordinary items
**Net income**

When the income statement includes one or more of the separately reported items, EPS data (both basic and diluted) must also be reported separately for income from continuing operations and net income. Per share amounts for discontinued operations and extraordinary items would be disclosed either on the face of the income statement or in the notes to financial statements. Presentation on the face of the income statement is illustrated by the partial income statements of **Federated Department Stores** from its 2003 annual report and exhibited in Graphic 19–7.

**GRAPHIC 19–7**
EPS Disclosure—Federated Department Stores

**Consolidated Statements of Operations (partial)**

| | 52 Weeks Ended February 2 ($ in millions, except per share data) | | |
|---|---|---|---|
| | **2003** | **2002** | **2001** |
| Income from continuing operations | $638 | $518 | $821 |
| Discontinued operations, net of tax | 180 | (784) | (1,005) |
| Extraordinary item, net of tax | | (10) | |
| Net income (loss) | $818 | ($276) | ($184) |
| **Basic earnings (loss) per share:** | | | |
| Income from continuing operations | $3.23 | $2.65 | $4.01 |
| Discontinued operations | .92 | (4.01) | (4.91) |
| Extraordinary item | | (.05) | |
| Net income (loss) | $4.15 | ($1.41) | ($.90) |
| **Diluted earnings (loss) per share:** | | | |
| Income from continuing operations | $3.21 | $2.59 | $3.97 |
| Discontinued operations | .91 | (3.92) | (4.86) |
| Extraordinary item | | (.05) | |
| Net income (loss) | $4.12 | ($1.38) | ($.89) |

Basic and diluted EPS data should be reported on the face of the income statement for all reporting periods presented in the comparative statements. Businesses without potential common shares present basic EPS only. Disclosure notes should provide additional disclosures including:

1. A reconciliation of the numerator and denominator used in the basic EPS computations to the numerator and the denominator used in the diluted EPS

**GRAPHIC 19–8**
Reconciliation of Basic EPS Computations to Diluted EPS Computations

**Earnings per Share Reconciliation:**

| | Income (Numerator) | Share (Denominator) | Per Share Amount |
|---|---|---|---|
| Net income | $154 | | |
| Preferred dividends | (12) | | |
| **Basic earnings per share** | $142 | 75 | $1.89 |
| | | | |
| Stock options | None | 3* | |
| Convertible debt | 18 | 12 | |
| Convertible preferred stock | 8 | 5 | |
| **Diluted earnings per share** | $168 | 95 | $1.77 |

Note: Stock warrants to purchase an additional 4 million shares at $32.50 per share were outstanding throughout the year but were not included in diluted EPS because the warrants' exercise price is greater than the average market price of the common shares.
*15 million − [(15 million × $20)/$25] = 3 million net additional shares

computations. An example of this is presented in Graphic 19–8 using the situation described in Illustration 19–11.

2. Any adjustments to the numerator for preferred dividends.
3. Any potential common shares that weren't included because they were antidilutive.
4. Any transactions that occurred after the end of the most recent period that would materially affect earnings per share.

**ADDITIONAL CONSIDERATION**

It is possible that potential common shares would have a dilutive effect on one component of net income but an antidilutive effect on another. When the inclusion of the potential common shares has a dilutive effect on "income from continuing operations," the effect should be included in all calculations of diluted EPS. In other words, the same number of potential common shares used in computing the diluted per-share amount for income from continuing operations is used in computing all other diluted per-share amounts, even when amounts are antidilutive to the individual per-share amounts.

Make sure you pay lots of attention to the man behind the curtain. If any earnings figure says pro forma, you should immediately look for a footnote or explanation telling you just what is and is not included in the calculation.[22]

## DECISION MAKERS' PERSPECTIVE

We noted at the beginning of the chapter that investors and creditors pay a great deal of attention to earnings per share information. Because of the importance analysts attach to earnings announcements, companies are particularly eager to meet earnings expectations. As we first noted in Chapter 4, this desire has contributed to a relatively recent trend, especially among technology firms, to report **pro forma** earnings per share. What exactly are pro forma earnings? Unfortunately there is no answer to that question. Essentially, pro forma earnings are actual (GAAP) earnings reduced by any expenses the reporting company feels are unusual and should be excluded. Always, though, the pro forma results of a company look better than the

[22]Bill Mann, "Qualcomm's Globalstar Headache," *MotleyFool.com,* January 25, 2001.

real results. **Broadcom Corporation**, a provider of broadband and network products, reported 2003 pro forma *earnings* of $0.49 per share. However on a GAAP basis, it actually had a *loss* of $3.29 per share. This is not an isolated example.

When companies report pro forma results, they argue they are trying to help investors by giving them numbers that more accurately reflect their normal business activities, because they exclude unusual expenses. Analysts should be skeptical, though. Because of the purely discretionary nature of pro forma reporting and several noted instances of abuse, analysts should, at a minimum, find out precisely what expenses are excluded and what the actual GAAP numbers are.

Another way management might enhance the appearance of EPS numbers is by massaging the denominator of the calculation. Reducing the number of shares increases earnings *per share.* Some companies judiciously use share buyback programs to manipulate the number of shares and therefore EPS. There is nothing inherently wrong with share buybacks and, as we noted in Chapter 18, they can benefit shareholders. The motivation for buybacks, though, can sometimes be detected in the year-to-year pattern. A *Fortune* article asserts that, "One way Big Blue has kept the fabulous EPS growth going has been by buying back shares of its own stock. Since 1995, **IBM** has spent a stunning $34.1 billion to shrink shares outstanding. Indeed, $34.1 billion is more than IBM reported in net income ($31.3 billion) over the same period."[23]

One way analysts use EPS data is in connection with the price-earnings ratio. This ratio is simply the market price per share divided by the earnings per share. It measures the market's perception of the quality of a company's earnings by indicating the price multiple the capital market is willing to pay for the company's earnings. Presumably, this ratio reflects the information provided by all financial information in that the market price reflects analysts' perceptions of the company's growth potential, stability, and relative risk. The price-earnings ratio relates these performance measures with the external judgment of the marketplace concerning the value of the firm.

**The price-earnings ratio measures the quality of a company's earnings.**

The ratio measures the quality of earnings in the sense that it represents the market's expectation of future earnings as indicated by current earnings. Caution is called for in comparing price-earnings ratios. For instance, a ratio might be low, not because earnings expectations are low, but because of abnormally elevated current earnings. On the contrary, the ratio might be high, not because earnings expectations are high, but because the company's current earnings are temporarily depressed. Similarly, an analyst should be alert to differences among accounting methods used to measure earnings from company to company when making comparisons.

Another ratio frequently calculated by shareholders and potential shareholders is the dividend payout ratio. This ratio expresses the percentage of earnings that is distributed to shareholders as dividends. The ratio is calculated by dividing dividends per common share by the earnings per share.

**The dividend payout ratio indicates the percentage of earnings that is distributed to shareholders as dividends.**

This ratio provides an indication of a firm's reinvestment strategy. A low payout ratio suggests that a company is retaining a large portion of earnings for reinvestment for new facilities and other operating needs. Low payouts often are found in growth industries and high payouts in mature industries. Often, though, the ratio is merely a reflection of managerial strategy concerning the mix of internal versus external financing. The ratio also is considered by investors who, for tax or other reasons, prefer current income over market price appreciation, or vice versa. ■

# CONCEPT REVIEW EXERCISE

## ADDITIONAL EPS ISSUES

At December 31, 2006, the financial statements of Bahnson General, Inc., included the following:

| | |
|---|---|
| Net income for 2006 (including a net-of-tax extraordinary loss of $10 million) | $180 million |
| Common stock, $1 par: | |

[23]"Hocus-Pocus: How IBM Grew 27% a Year," *Fortune,* Bethany McLean, June 26, 2000.

Shares outstanding on January 1 44 million

The share price was $25 and $28 at the beginning and end of the year, respectively.

**Additional data:**

- At January 1, 2006, $200 million of 10% convertible notes were outstanding. The notes were converted on April 1 into 16 million shares of common stock.
- An agreement with company executives calls for the issuance of up to 12 million additional shares of common stock in 2007 and 2008 based on the Bahnson's net income in those years. Executives will receive 2 million shares at the end of each of those two years if the company's stock price is at least $26 and another 4 million shares each year if the stock price is at least $29.50.

The tax rate is 40%.

**Required:**

Compute basic and diluted earnings per share for the year ended December 31, 2006.

**SOLUTION**

(amounts in millions, except per share amounts)

**Basic EPS**

$$\frac{\underset{\text{Net income}}{\$180}}{\underset{\text{Shares at Jan. 1}}{44} + \underset{\text{Actual conversion of notes}}{16\,(9/12)}} = \frac{\$180}{56} = \$3.21$$

**Diluted EPS**

$$\frac{\underset{\text{Net income}}{\$180} \quad \overset{\text{Assumed after-tax interest savings}}{+ [\$20 - 40\%(\$20)] \times (3/12)}}{\underset{\text{Shares at Jan. 1}}{44} + \underset{\text{Actual conversion of notes}}{16\,(9/12)} \; \underset{\text{Assumed conversion of notes}}{+ 16\,(3/12)} \; \underset{\text{Contingent shares}}{+ (2 \times 2)}} = \frac{\$183}{64} = \$2.86$$

**Convertible Notes:** Notice that the effect on diluted EPS would be precisely the same whether the convertible notes were actually converted or not.

**Converted on April 1:**

$$\frac{\overset{\text{Net income including actual after-tax interest savings}}{\$180} \quad \overset{\text{Assumed after-tax interest savings}}{+ [\$20 - 40\%(\$20)] \times (3/12)}}{\underset{\text{Shares at Jan. 1}}{44} + \underset{\text{Actual conversion of notes}}{16\,(9/12)} \; \underset{\text{Assumed conversion of notes}}{+ 16\,(3/12)}} = \frac{\$183}{60}$$

**Not Actually Converted:**

$$\frac{\overset{\text{Net income without actual after-tax interest savings}}{\$171^*} \quad \overset{\text{Assumed after-tax interest savings}}{+ [\$20 - 40\%(\$20)]}}{\underset{\text{Shares at Jan. 1}}{44} + \underset{\text{Assumed conversion of notes}}{16}} = \frac{\$183}{60}$$

*$180 – {[$20 – 40% ($20)] × (9/12)} = $171

After-tax interest from Apr. 1 to Dec. 31

**Contingently Issuable Shares:**

Because the conditions are met for issuing 4 million shares (2 million for each of two years), those shares are simply added to the denominator of diluted EPS. The current share price

($28) is projected to remain the same throughout the contingency period, so the other 8 million shares (4 million for each of two years) are excluded.

**Income Statement Presentation:**

To determine the per share amounts for income before extraordinary items, we substitute that amount for net income in the numerator (in this case, that means adding back the $10 million extraordinary loss):

$$\text{Basic: } \frac{\$180 + 10}{56} = \$3.39 \qquad \text{Diluted: } \frac{\$183 + 10}{64} = \$3.02$$

| **Earnings per Share:** | **Basic*** | **Diluted** |
|---|---|---|
| Income before extraordinary items | $3.39 | $3.02 |
| Extraordinary loss | (.18) | (.16) |
| Net income | $3.21 | $2.86 |

*Only diluted EPS is required on the face of the income statement. Basic EPS is reported in the EPS reconciliation shown in the disclosure note (below).

**Disclosure Note:**

***Earnings per Share Reconciliation:***

| | **Income (Numerator)** | **Shares (Denominator)** | **Per Share Amount** |
|---|---|---|---|
| **Basic Earnings per Share** | | | |
| Income before extraordinary items | $190 | 56 | $3.39 |
| Extraordinary loss | (10) | 56 | (.18) |
| Net income | $180 | 56 | $3.21 |
| Convertible debt | 3 | 4 | |
| Contingently issuable shares | — | 4 | |
| **Diluted Earnings per Share** | | | |
| Income before extraordinary items | $193 | 64 | $3.02 |
| Extraordinary loss | (10) | 64 | (.16) |
| Net income | $183 | 64 | $2.86 |

## FINANCIAL REPORTING CASE SOLUTION

1. **How can a compensation package such as this serve as an incentive to Ms. Veres?** *(p. 952)* Stock-based plans like the restricted stock and stock options that Ms. Veres is receiving are designed to motivate recipients. If the shares awarded are restricted so that Ms. Veres is not free to sell the shares during the restriction period, she has an incentive to remain with the company until rights to the shares vest. Likewise, stock options can be made exercisable only after a specified period of employment. An additional incentive of stock-based plans is that the recipient will be motivated to take actions that will maximize the value of the shares.
2. **Ms. Veres received a "grant of restricted stock." How should NEV account for the grant?** *(p. 952)* The compensation associated with restricted stock is the market price of unrestricted shares of the same stock. NEV will accrue this amount as compensation expense over the service period from the date of grant to when restrictions are lifted.
3. **Included were stock options to buy more than 800,000 shares. How will the options affect NEV's compensation expense?** *(p. 954)* Similar to the method used for restricted stock, the value of the options is recorded as compensation over the service period, usually the vesting period.
4. **How will the presence of these and other similar stock options affect NEV's earnings per share?** *(p. 970)* If outstanding stock options were exercised, the resulting increase in shares would reduce or dilute EPS. If we don't take into account the dilutive effect of the share increase, we might mislead investors and creditors. So, in addition to basic EPS, we also calculate diluted EPS to include the dilutive effect of options and other potential common shares.

This means calculating EPS as if the potential increase in shares already has occurred (even though it hasn't yet). ■

## The Bottom Line

1. We measure the fair value of stock issued in a restricted stock award plan and expense it over the service period, usually from the date of grant to the vesting date.
2. Similarly, we estimate the fair value of stock options at the grant date and expense it over the service period, usually from the date of grant to the vesting date. Fair value is estimated at the grant date using an option-pricing model that considers the exercise price and expected term of the option, the current market price of the underlying stock and its expected volatility, expected dividends, and the expected risk-free rate of return.
3. For stock appreciation rights, the award is considered to be equity if the employer can elect to settle in shares of stock rather than cash. If the employee can elect to receive cash, the award is considered to be a liability. In either case, the amount of compensation is the fair value of the SARs (usually the same as a similar stock option). We continually adjust that amount to reflect changes in fair value until the compensation is finally paid unless the award is considered equity in which case, we measure fair value once—at the grant date.
4. Employee share purchase plans allow employees to buy company stock under convenient or favorable terms. Most such plans are considered compensatory and require any discount to be recorded as compensation expense.
5. A company has a simple capital structure if it has no outstanding securities that could potentially dilute earnings per share. For such a firm, EPS is simply earnings available to common shareholders divided by the weighted-average number of common shares outstanding. When potential common shares are outstanding, the company is said to have a complex capital structure. In that case, two EPS calculations are reported. Basic EPS assumes no dilution. Diluted EPS assumes maximum potential dilution.
6. EPS calculations are based on the weighted-average number of shares outstanding during the period. Any new shares issued during the period are time-weighted by the fraction of the period they were outstanding and then added to the number of shares outstanding for the period.
7. For a stock dividend or stock split, shares outstanding prior to the stock distribution are retroactively restated to reflect the increase in shares. When shares are reacquired, as treasury stock or to be retired, they are time-weighted for the fraction of the period they were not outstanding, prior to being subtracted from the number of shares outstanding during the reporting period.
8. The numerator in the EPS calculation should reflect earnings available to common shareholders. So, any dividends on preferred stock outstanding should be subtracted from reported net income. This adjustment is made for cumulative preferred stock whether or not dividends are declared that period.
9. For diluted EPS, it is assumed that stock options, rights, and warrants are exercised at the beginning of the period (or at the time the options are issued, if later) and the cash proceeds received are used to buy back (as treasury stock) as many of those shares as can be acquired at the average market price during the period.
10. To incorporate convertible securities into the calculation of diluted EPS, the conversion is assumed to have occurred at the beginning of the period (or at the time the convertible security is issued, if later). The denominator of the EPS fraction is adjusted for the additional common shares assumed and the numerator is increased by the interest (after-tax) or preferred dividends that would have been avoided in the event of conversion.
11. Contingently issuable shares are considered outstanding in the computation of diluted EPS when they will later be issued upon the mere passage of time or because of conditions that currently are met.
12. EPS data (both basic and diluted) must be reported for (a) income before any separately reported items, (b) the separately reported items (discontinued operations and extraordinary gains and losses), and (c) net income. Disclosures also should include a reconciliation of the numerator and denominator used in the computations. ■

# APPENDIX 19 OPTION-PRICING THEORY

Option values have two essential components: (1) intrinsic value and (2) time value.

## Intrinsic Value

Intrinsic value is the benefit the holder of an option would realize by exercising the option rather than buying the underlying stock directly. An option that permits an employee to buy \$25 stock for \$10 has an intrinsic value of \$15. An option whose exercise price equals or exceeds the market price of the underlying stock has zero intrinsic value.

### TIME VALUE

In addition to their intrinsic value, options also have a time value due to the fact that (a) the holder of an option does not have to pay the exercise price until the option is exercised and (b) the market price of the underlying stock may yet rise and create additional intrinsic value. All options have time value so long as time remains before expiration. The longer the time until expiration, other things being equal, the greater the time value. For instance, the option described above with an intrinsic value of \$15, might have a fair value of, say, \$22 if time still remains until the option expires. The \$7 difference represents the time value of the option. Time value can be subdivided into two components: (1) the effects of time value of money and (2) volatility value.

### TIME VALUE OF MONEY

An option's value is enhanced by the delay in paying cash for the shares.

The time value of money component arises because the holder of an option does not have to pay the exercise price until the option is exercised. Instead, the holder can invest funds elsewhere while waiting to exercise the option. For measurement purposes, the time value of money component is assumed to be the rate of return available on risk-free U.S. Treasury Securities. The higher the time value of money, the higher the value of being able to delay payment of the exercise price.

The time value of money component is the difference between the exercise price and its discounted present value minus the present value of expected dividends.

When the underlying stock pays no dividends, the time value of money component is the difference between the exercise price (a future amount) and its discounted present value. Let's say the exercise price is \$30. If the present value (discounted at the risk-free rate) is \$24, the time value of money component is \$6. On the other hand, if the stock pays a dividend (or is expected to during the life of the option), the time value of money component is lower. The value of being able to delay payment of the exercise price would be partially offset by the cost of forgoing the dividend in the meantime. For instance, if the stock underlying the options just described were expected to pay dividends and the discounted present value of the expected dividends were \$2, the time value of money component in that example would be reduced from \$6 to \$4.

### VOLATILITY VALUE

The volatility value represents the possibility that the option holder might profit from market price appreciation of the underlying stock while being exposed to the loss of only the value of the option, rather than the full market value of the stock. For example, fair value of an option to buy a share at an exercise price of \$30 might be measured as \$7. The potential profit from market price appreciation is conceptually unlimited. And yet, the potential loss from the stock's value failing to appreciate is only \$7.

Volatility enhances the likelihood of stock price appreciation.

A stock's volatility is the amount by which its price has fluctuated previously or is expected to fluctuate in the future. The greater a stock's volatility, the greater the potential profit. It usually is measured as one standard deviation of a statistical distribution. Statistically, if the expected annualized volatility is 25%, the probability is approximately 67% that the stock's year-end price will fall within roughly plus or minus 25% of its beginning-of-year price. Stated differently, the probability is approximately 33% that the year-end stock price will fall outside that range.

Option-pricing models make assumptions about the likelihood of various future stock prices by making assumptions about the statistical distribution of future stock prices that take into account the expected volatility of the stock price. One popular option pricing model, the

Black–Scholes model, for instance, assumes a log-normal distribution. This assumption posits that the stock price is as likely to fall by half as it is to double and that large price movements are less likely than small price movements. The higher a stock's volatility, the higher the probability of large increases or decreases in market price. Because the cost of large decreases is limited to the option's current value, but the profitability from large increases is unlimited, an option on a highly volatile stock has a higher probability of a large profit than does an option on a less volatile stock.

## Summary

In summary, the fair value of an option is (a) its intrinsic value plus (b) its time value of money component plus (c) its volatility component. The variables that affect an option's fair value and the effect of each are indicated in Graphic 19A–1.

| All Other Factors Being Equal, If the: | The Option Value Will Be: |
|---|---|
| Exercise price is higher | Lower |
| Term of the option is longer | Higher |
| Market price of the stock is higher | Higher |
| Dividends are higher | Lower |
| Risk-free rate of return is higher | Higher |
| Volatility of the stock is higher | Higher |

**GRAPHIC 19A–1**
Effect of Variables on an Option's Fair Value

# QUESTIONS FOR REVIEW OF KEY TOPICS

**Q 19–1** What is restricted stock? Describe how compensation expense is determined and recorded for a restricted stock award plan.

**Q 19–2** Stock option plans provide employees the option to purchase: (a) a specified number of shares of the firm's stock, (b) at a specified price, (c) during a specified period of time. One of the most controversial aspects of accounting for stock-based compensation is how the fair value of stock options should be measured. Describe the general approach to measuring fair value.

**Q 19–3** The Tax Code differentiates between qualified option plans, including incentive plans, and nonqualified plans. What are the major differences in tax treatment between incentive plans and nonqualified plans?

**Q 19–4** The fair value of stock options can be considered to comprise two main components. What are they?

**Q 19–5** Stock option (and other share-based) plans often specify a performance condition or a market condition that must be satisfied before employees are allowed the benefits of the award. Describe the general approach we use to account for performance-based options and options with market-related conditions.

**Q 19–6** LTV Corporation grants SARs to key executives. Upon exercise, the SARs entitle executives to receive either cash or stock equal in value to the excess of the market price at exercise over the share price at the date of grant. How should LTV account for the awards?

**Q 19–7** What is a simple capital structure? How is EPS determined for a company with a simple capital structure?

**Q 19–8** When calculating the weighted average number of common shares, how are stock dividends and stock splits treated? Compare this treatment with that of additional shares sold for cash in midyear.

**Q 19–9** Blake Distributors had 100,000 common shares outstanding at the beginning of the year, January 1. On May 13, Blake distributed a 5% stock dividend. On August 1, 1,200 shares were retired. What is the weighted average number of shares for calculating EPS?

**Q 19–10** Why are preferred dividends deducted from net income when calculating EPS? Are there circumstances when this deduction is not made?

**Q 19–11** Distinguish between basic and diluted EPS.

**Q 19–12** The treasury stock method is used to incorporate the dilutive effect of stock options, stock warrants, and similar securities. Describe this method as it applies to diluted EPS.

**Q 19–13** The potentially dilutive effect of convertible securities is reflected in EPS calculations by the if-converted method. Describe this method as it relates to convertible bonds.

**Q 19–14** How is the potentially dilutive effect of convertible preferred stock reflected in EPS calculations by the if-converted method? How is this different from the way convertible bonds are considered?

**Q 19–15** A convertible security may appear to be dilutive when looked at individually but might be antidilutive when included in combination with other convertible securities. How should the order be determined for inclusion of convertible securities in an EPS calculation to avoid including an antidilutive security?

**Q 19–16** Wiseman Electronics has an agreement with certain of its division managers that 50,000 contingently issuable shares will be issued next year in the event operating income exceeds $2.1 million that year. In what way, if any, is the calculation of EPS affected by these contingently issuable shares assuming this year's operating income was $2.2 million? $2.0 million?

**Q 19–17** Diluted EPS would be precisely the same whether convertible securities were actually converted or not. Why?

**Q 19–18** When the income statement includes one or more of the separately reported items, such as discontinued operations or extraordinary items, which amounts require per share presentation?

**Q 19–19** In addition to EPS numbers themselves, what additional disclosures should be provided concerning the EPS information?

## BRIEF EXERCISES

**BE 19–1**
Restricted stock award
● LO1

First Link Services granted 8 million of its $1 par common shares to executives, subject to forfeiture if employment is terminated within three years. The common shares have a market price of $6 per share on the grant date. Ignoring taxes, what is the total compensation cost pertaining to the restricted shares? What is the effect on earnings in the year after the shares are granted to executives?

**BE 19–2**
Stock options
● LO2

Under its executive stock option plan, National Corporation granted options on January 1, 2006, that permit executives to purchase 12 million of the company's $1 par common shares within the next six years, but not before December 31, 2008 (the vesting date). The exercise price is the market price of the shares on the date of grant, $17 per share. The fair value of the options, estimated by an appropriate option pricing model, is $5 per option. No forfeitures are anticipated. Ignoring taxes, what is the total compensation cost pertaining to the stock options? What is the effect on earnings in the year after the options are granted to executives?

**BE 19–3**
Stock options; forfeiture
● LO2

Refer to the situation described in BE 19–2. Suppose that unexpected turnover during 2007 caused the forfeiture of 5% of the stock options. Ignoring taxes, what is the effect on earnings in 2007? In 2008?

**BE 19–4**
Stock options; exercise
● LO2

Refer to the situation described in BE 19–2. Suppose that the options are exercised on April 3, 2009, when the market price is $19 per share. Ignoring taxes, what journal entry will National record?

**BE 19–5**
Stock options; expiration
● LO2

Refer to the situation described in BE 19–2. Suppose that the options expire without being exercised. Ignoring taxes, what journal entry will National record?

**BE 19–6**
Performance-based options
● LO2

On October 1, 2006, Farmer Fabrication issued stock options for 100,000 shares to a division manager. The options have an estimated fair value of $6 each. To provide additional incentive for managerial achievement, the options are not exercisable unless divisional revenue increases by 5% in three years. Farmer initially estimates that it is probable the goal will be achieved. How much compensation will be recorded in each of the next three years?

**BE 19–7**
Performance-based options
● LO2

Refer to the situation described in BE 19–6. Suppose that after one year, Farmer estimates that it is *not* probable that divisional revenue will increase by 5% in three years. What action will be taken to account for the options in 2007?

**BE 19–8**
Performance-based options
● LO2

Refer to the situation described in BE 19–6. Suppose that Farmer initially estimates that it is *not* probable the goal will be achieved, but then after one year, Farmer estimates that it *is* probable that divisional revenue will increase by 5% by the end of 2008. What action will be taken to account for the options in 2007 and thereafter?

**BE 19–9**
Options with market-based conditions
● LO2

On October 1, 2006, Farmer Fabrication issued stock options for 100,000 shares to a division manager. The options have an estimated fair value of $6 each. To provide additional incentive for managerial achievement, the options are not exercisable unless Farmer Fabrication's stock price increases by 5% in three years. Farmer initially estimates that it is not probable the goal will be achieved. How much compensation will be recorded in each of the next three years?

**BE 19–10**
EPS; shares issued, shares retired
● LO6 LO7

McDonnell-Myer Corporation reported net income of $741 million. The company had 544 million common shares outstanding at January 1 and sold 36 million shares on Feb. 28. As part of an annual share repurchase plan, 6 million shares were retired on April 30 for $47 per share. Calculate McDonnell-Myer's earnings per share for the year.

**BE 19–11**
EPS; nonconvertible preferred shares
● LO8

At December 31, 2005 and 2006, Funk & Noble Corporation had outstanding 820 million shares of common stock and 2 million shares of 8%, $100 par value cumulative preferred stock. No dividends were declared on either the preferred or common stock in 2005 or 2006. Net income for 2006 was $426 million. The income tax rate is 40%. Calculate earnings per share for the year ended December 31, 2006.

**BE 19–12**
EPS; stock options
● LO9

Stock options exercisable at $50 per share to obtain 24,000 shares of common stock were outstanding during a period when the average market price of the common stock was $60 and the ending market price was $55. By how many shares will the assumed exercise of these options increase the weighted-average number of shares outstanding when calculating diluted earnings per share?

**BE 19–13**
EPS; convertible preferred shares
● LO10

Ahnberg Corporation had 800,000 shares of common stock issued and outstanding at January 1. No common shares were issued during the year, but on January 1 Ahnberg issued 100,000 shares of convertible preferred stock. The preferred shares are convertible into 200,000 shares of common stock. During the year Ahnberg paid $60,000 cash dividends on the preferred stock. Net income was $1,500,000. What were Ahnberg's basic and diluted earnings per share for the year?

# EXERCISES

available with McGraw-Hill's Homework Manager www.mhhe.com/spiceland4e

**An alternate exercise and problem set is available on the text website: www.mhhe.com/spiceland4e**

**E 19–1**
Restricted stock award plan
● LO1

Allied Paper Products, Inc. offers a restricted stock award plan to its vice presidents. On January 1, 2006, the company granted 16 million of its $1 par common shares, subject to forfeiture if employment is terminated within two years. The common shares have a market price of $5 per share on the grant date.

**Required:**

1. Determine the total compensation cost pertaining to the restricted shares.
2. Prepare the appropriate journal entries related to the restricted stock through December 31, 2007.

**E 19–2**
Restricted stock award plan
● LO1

On January 1, 2006, VKI Corporation awarded 12 million of its $1 par common shares to key personnel, subject to forfeiture if employment is terminated within three years. On the grant date, the shares have a market price of $2.50 per share.

**Required:**

1. Determine the total compensation cost pertaining to the restricted shares.
2. Prepare the appropriate journal entry to record the award of restricted shares on January 1, 2006.
3. Prepare the appropriate journal entry to record compensation expense on December 31, 2006.
4. Prepare the appropriate journal entry to record compensation expense on December 31, 2007.
5. Prepare the appropriate journal entry to record compensation expense on December 31, 2008.
6. Prepare the appropriate journal entry to record the lifting of restrictions on the shares at December 31, 2008.

**E 19–3**
Restricted stock award plan; forfeitures anticipated
● LO1

Magnetic-Optical Corporation offers a variety of share-based compensation plans to employees. Under its restricted stock award plan, the company on January 1, 2006, granted 4 million of its $1 par common shares to various division managers. The shares are subject to forfeiture if employment is terminated within three years. The common shares have a market price of $22.50 per share on the grant date.

**Required:**

1. Determine the total compensation cost pertaining to the restricted shares.
2. Prepare the appropriate journal entry to record the award of restricted shares on January 1, 2006.
3. Prepare the appropriate journal entry to record compensation expense on December 31, 2006.
4. Suppose Magnetic-Optical expected a 10% forfeiture rate on the restricted shares prior to vesting. Determine the total compensation cost, assuming the company chooses to follow the elective fair value approach for fixed compensation plans and chooses to anticipate forfeitures at the grant date.

**E 19–4**
Stock options

● LO2

American Optical Corporation provides a variety of share-based compensation plans to its employees. Under its executive stock option plan, the company granted options on January 1, 2006, that permit executives to acquire 4 million of the company's $1 par common shares within the next five years, but not before December 31, 2007 (the vesting date). The exercise price is the market price of the shares on the date of grant, $14 per share. The fair value of the 4 million options, estimated by an appropriate option pricing model, is $3 per option. No forfeitures are anticipated. Ignore taxes.

**Required:**

1. Determine the total compensation cost pertaining to the options.
2. Prepare the appropriate journal entry to record the award of options on January 1, 2006.
3. Prepare the appropriate journal entry to record compensation expense on December 31, 2006.
4. Prepare the appropriate journal entry to record compensation expense on December 31, 2007.

**E 19–5**
Stock options; forfeiture of options

● LO2

On January 1, 2006, Adams-Meneke Corporation granted 25 million incentive stock options to division managers, each permitting holders to purchase one share of the company's $1 par common shares within the next six years, but not before December 31, 2008 (the vesting date). The exercise price is the market price of the shares on the date of grant, currently $10 per share. The fair value of the options, estimated by an appropriate option pricing model, is $3 per option.

**Required:**

1. Determine the total compensation cost pertaining to the options on January 1, 2006.
2. Prepare the appropriate journal entry to record compensation expense on December 31, 2006.
3. Unexpected turnover during 2007 caused the forfeiture of 6% of the stock options. Determine the adjusted compensation cost, and prepare the appropriate journal entry(s) on December 31, 2007 and 2008.

**E 19–6**
Stock options exercise; forfeitures

● LO2

Walters Audio Visual, Inc. offers an incentive stock option plan to its regional managers. On January 1, 2006, options were granted for 40 million $1 par common shares. The exercise price is the market price on the grant date—$8 per share. Options cannot be exercised prior to January 1, 2008, and expire December 31, 2012. The fair value of the 40 million options, estimated by an appropriate option pricing model, is $1 per option.

**Required:**

1. Determine the total compensation cost pertaining to the incentive stock option plan.
2. Prepare the appropriate journal entry to record compensation expense on December 31, 2006.
3. Prepare the appropriate journal entry to record compensation expense on December 31, 2007.
4. Prepare the appropriate journal entry to record the exercise of 75% of the options on March 12, 2008, when the market price is $9 per share.
5. Prepare the appropriate journal entry on December 31, 2012, when the remaining options that have vested expire without being exercised.

**E 19–7**
Stock options

● LO2

SSG Cycles manufactures and distributes motorcycle parts and supplies. Employees are offered a variety of share-based compensation plans. Under its nonqualified stock option plan, SSG granted options to key officers on January 1, 2006. The options permit holders to acquire 12 million of the company's $1 par common shares for $11 within the next six years, but not before January 1, 2009 (the vesting date). The market price of the shares on the date of grant is $13 per share. The fair value of the 12 million options, estimated by an appropriate option pricing model, is $3 per option.

**Required:**

1. Determine the total compensation cost pertaining to the incentive stock option plan.
2. Prepare the appropriate journal entries to record compensation expense on December 31, 2006, 2007, and 2008.
3. Record the exercise of the options if all of the options are exercised on May 11, 2010, when the market price is $14 per share.

**E 19–8**
Stock appreciation rights; settlement in shares

● LO3

As part of its stock-based compensation package, International Electronics granted 24 million stock appreciation rights (SARs) to top officers on January 1, 2006. At exercise, holders of the SARs are entitled to receive stock equal in value to the excess of the market price at exercise over the share price at the date of grant. The SARs cannot be exercised until the end of 2009 (vesting date) and expire at the end of 2011. The $1 par common shares have a market price of $46 per share on the grant date. The fair value of the SARs, estimated by an appropriate option pricing model, is $3 per SAR at January 1, 2006. The fair value re-estimated at December 31, 2006, 2007, 2008, 2009, and 2010, is $4, $3, $4, $2.50, and $3, respectively. All recipients are expected to remain employed through the vesting date.

**Required:**

1. Prepare the appropriate journal entry to record the award of SARs on January 1, 2006.
2. Prepare the appropriate journal entries pertaining to the SARs on December 31, 2006–December 31, 2009.
3. The SARs remain unexercised on December 31, 2010. Prepare the appropriate journal entry on that date.

4. The SARs are exercised on June 6, 2011, when the share price is $50. Prepare the appropriate journal entry(s) on that date.

**E 19–9**
Stock appreciation rights; cash settlement
● LO3

(Note: This is a variation of the previous exercise, modified to allow settlement in cash.) As part of its stock-based compensation package, International Electronics granted 24 million stock appreciation rights (SARs) to top officers on January 1, 2006. At exercise, holders of the SARs are entitled to receive cash or stock equal in value to the excess of the market price at exercise over the share price at the date of grant. The SARs cannot be exercised until the end of 2009 (vesting date) and expire at the end of 2011. The $1 par common shares have a market price of $46 per share on the grant date. The fair value of the SARs, estimated by an appropriate option pricing model, is $3 per SAR at January 1, 2006. The fair value re-estimated at December 31, 2006, 2007, 2008, 2009, and 2010, is $4, $3, $4, $2.50, and $3, respectively. All recipients are expected to remain employed through the vesting date.

**Required:**

1. Prepare the appropriate journal entry to record the award of SARs on January 1, 2006.
2. Prepare the appropriate journal entries pertaining to the SARs on December 31, 2006–December 31, 2009.
3. The SARs remain unexercised on December 31, 2010. Prepare the appropriate journal entry on that date.
4. The SARs are exercised on June 6, 2011, when the share price is $50, and executives choose to receive the market price appreciation in cash. Prepare the appropriate journal entry(s) on that date.

**E 19–10**
Employee share purchase plan
● LO4

In order to encourage employee ownership of the company's $1 par common shares, Washington Distribution permits any of its employees to buy shares directly from the company through payroll deduction. There are no brokerage fees and shares can be purchased at a 15% discount. During March, employees purchased 50,000 shares at a time when the market price of the shares on the New York Stock Exchange was $12 per share.

**Required:**

Prepare the appropriate journal entry to record the March purchases of shares under the employee share purchase plan.

**E 19–11**
EPS; shares issued; stock dividend
● LO6 LO7

For the year ended December 31, 2006, Norstar Industries reported net income of $655,000. At January 1, 2006, the company had 900,000 common shares outstanding. The following changes in the number of shares occurred during 2006:

| | |
|---|---|
| Apr. 30 | Sold 60,000 shares in a public offering. |
| May 24 | Declared and distributed a 5% stock dividend. |
| June 1 | Issued 72,000 shares as part of the consideration for the purchase of assets from a subsidiary. |

**Required:**

Compute Norstar's earnings per share for the year ended December 31, 2006.

**E 19–12**
EPS; stock dividend; nonconvertible preferred stock
● LO6 LO7 LO8

Hardaway Fixtures' balance sheet at December 31, 2005, included the following:

| | |
|---|---|
| *Shares issued and outstanding:* | |
| Common stock, $1 par | $800,000 |
| Nonconvertible preferred stock, $50 par | 20,000 |

On July 21, 2006, Hardaway issued a 25% stock dividend on its common stock. On December 12 it paid $50,000 cash dividends on the preferred stock. Net income for the year ended December 31, 2006, was $2,000,000.

**Required:**

Compute Hardaway's earnings per share for the year ended December 31, 2006.

**E 19–13**
EPS; net loss; nonconvertible preferred stock; shares sold
● LO8

At December 31, 2005, Albrecht Corporation had outstanding 373,000 shares of common stock and 8,000 shares of 9.5%, $100 par value cumulative, nonconvertible preferred stock. On May 31, 2006, Albrecht sold for cash 12,000 shares of its common stock. No cash dividends were declared for 2006. For the year ended December 31, 2006, Albrecht reported a net loss of $114,000.

**Required:**

Calculate Albrecht's net loss per share for the year ended December 31, 2006.

**E 19–14**
EPS; treasury stock; new shares; stock dividends; two years
● LO6 LO7

The Alford Group had 202,000 shares of common stock outstanding at January 1, 2006. The following activities affected common shares during the year. There are no potential common shares outstanding.

| **2006** | |
|---|---|
| Feb. 28 | Purchased 6,000 shares of treasury stock. |
| Oct. 31 | Sold the treasury shares purchased on February 28. |
| Nov. 30 | Issued 24,000 new shares. |
| Dec. 31 | Net income for 2006 is $400,000. |

**2007**

| | |
|---|---|
| Jan. 15 | Declared and issued a 2-for-1 stock split. |
| Dec. 31 | Net income for 2007 is $400,000. |

**Required:**

1. Determine the 2006 EPS.
2. Determine the 2007 EPS.
3. At what amount will the 2006 EPS be presented in the 2007 comparative financial statements?

**E 19–15**
EPS; stock dividend; nonconvertible preferred stock; treasury shares; shares sold

● LO7 LO8

On December 31, 2005, Berclair, Inc. had 200 million shares of common stock and 3 million shares of 9%, $100 par value cumulative preferred stock issued and outstanding. On March 1, 2006, Berclair purchased 24 million shares of its common stock as treasury stock. Berclair issued a 5% common stock dividend on July 1, 2006. Four million treasury shares were sold on October 1. Net income for the year ended December 31, 2006, was $150 million.

**Required:**

Compute Berclair's earnings per share for the year ended December 31, 2006.

**E 19–16**
EPS; stock dividend; nonconvertible preferred stock; treasury shares; shares sold; stock options

● LO7 LO8 LO9

(Note: This is a variation of the previous exercise, modified to include stock options.) On December 31, 2005, Berclair, Inc. had 200 million shares of common stock and 3 million shares of 9%, $100 par value cumulative preferred stock issued and outstanding. Berclair issued a 5% common stock dividend on July 1, 2006. On March 1, 2006, Berclair purchased 24 million shares of its common stock as treasury stock. Four million treasury shares were sold on October 1. Net income for the year ended December 31, 2006, was $150 million.

Also outstanding at December 31, 2006, were stock options granted to key executives on September 13, 2005. The options are exercisable for 30 million common shares at an exercise price of $56 per share. During 2006, the market price of the common shares averaged $70 per share, peaking at $80 on December 31.

**Required:**

Compute Berclair's basic and diluted earnings per share for the year ended December 31, 2006.

**E 19–17**
EPS; stock dividend; nonconvertible preferred stock; treasury shares; shares sold; stock options exercised

● LO7 through LO9

(Note: This is a variation of the previous exercise, modified to include the exercise of stock options.) On December 31, 2005, Berclair, Inc. had 200 million shares of common stock and 3 million shares of 9%, $100 par value cumulative preferred stock issued and outstanding. Berclair issued a 5% common stock dividend on July 1, 2006. On March 1, 2006, Berclair purchased 24 million shares of its common stock as treasury stock. Four million treasury shares were sold on October 1. Net income for the year ended December 31, 2006, was $150 million.

Also outstanding at December 31 were stock options granted to key executives on September 13, 2005. The options are exercisable for 30 million common shares at an exercise price of $56 per share. During 2006, the market price of the common shares averaged $70 per share, peaking at $80 on December 31.

The options were exercised on September 1, 2006.

**Required:**

Compute Berclair's basic and diluted earnings per share for the year ended December 31, 2006.

**E 19–18**
EPS; stock dividend; nonconvertible preferred stock; treasury shares; shares sold; stock options; convertible bonds

● LO7 through LO10

(Note: This is a variation of the previous exercise, modified to include convertible bonds).
On December 31, 2005, Berclair, Inc. had 200 million shares of common stock and 3 million shares of 9%, $100 par value cumulative preferred stock issued and outstanding. Berclair issued a 5% common stock dividend on July 1, 2006. On March 1, 2006, Berclair purchased 24 million shares of its common stock as treasury stock. Four million treasury shares were sold on October 1. Net income for the year ended December 31, 2006, was $150 million. The income tax rate is 40%.

Also outstanding at December 31 were stock options granted to key executives on September 13, 2005. The options are exercisable for 30 million common shares at an exercise price of $56 per share. During 2006, the market price of the common shares averaged $70 per share, peaking at $80 on December 31.

$62.5 million of 8% bonds, convertible into 6 million common shares, were issued at face value in 2002.

**Required:**

Compute Berclair's basic and diluted earnings per share for the year ended December 31, 2006.

**E 19–19**
EPS; convertible preferred stock; convertible bonds

● LO8 LO10

Information from the financial statements of the Ames Fabricators, Inc., included the following:

| | December 31 | |
|---|---|---|
| | **2006** | **2005** |
| Common shares | 100,000 | 100,000 |
| Convertible preferred shares (convertible into 32,000 shares of common) | 12,000 | 12,000 |
| 10% convertible bonds (convertible into 30,000 shares of common) | $1,000,000 | $1,000,000 |

Ames's net income for the year ended December 31, 2006, is $500,000. The income tax rate is 40%. Ames paid dividends of $5 per share on its preferred stock during 2006.

**Required:**

Compute basic and diluted earnings per share for the year ended December 31, 2006.

**E 19–20**
EPS; shares issued; stock options

● LO7 through LO10

Stanley Department Stores reported net income of $720,000 for the year ended December 31, 2006.

Additional Information:

| | |
|---|---|
| Common shares outstanding at Jan. 1, 2006 | 80,000 |
| Stock warrants outstanding throughout 2006 | 24,000 |

(Each warrant is exercisable for one common share at an exercise price of $37.50)
During the year, the market price of Stanley's common stock averaged $45, ending 2006 at $50 per share.
On Aug. 30 Stanley sold 15,000 common shares.
Stanley's only debt consisted of $50,000 of 10% short term bank notes.
The company's income tax rate is 40%.

**Required:**

Compute Stanley's basic and diluted earnings per share for the year ended December 31, 2006.

**E 19–21**
EPS; contingently issuable shares

● LO11

During its first year of operations, McCollum Tool Works entered into the following transactions relating to shareholders' equity. The corporation was authorized to issue 100 million common shares, $1 par per share.

| | |
|---|---|
| Jan. 2 | Issued 35 million common shares for cash. |
| 3 | Entered an agreement with the company president to issue up to 2 million additional shares of common stock in 2007 based on the earnings of McCollum in 2007. If net income exceeds $140 million, the president will receive 1 million shares; 2 million shares if net income exceeds $150 million. |
| Mar. 31 | Issued 4 million shares in exchange for plant facilities. |

Net income for 2006 was $148 million.

**Required:**

Compute basic and diluted earnings per share for the year ended December 31, 2006.

**E 19–22**
EPS; new shares; contingent agreements

● LO11

Anderson Steel Company began 2006 with 600,000 shares of common stock outstanding. On March 31, 2006, 100,000 new shares were sold at a price of $45 per share. The market price has risen steadily since that time to a high of $50 per share at December 31. No other changes in shares occurred during 2006, and no securities are outstanding that can become common stock. However, there are two agreements with officers of the company for future issuance of common stock. Both agreements relate to compensation arrangements reached in 2005. The first agreement grants to the company president a right to 10,000 shares of stock each year the closing market price is at least $48. The agreement begins in 2007 and expires in 2010. The second agreement grants to the controller a right to 15,000 shares of stock if she is still with the firm at the end of 2014. Net income for 2006 was $2,000,000.

**Required:**

Compute Anderson Steel Company's basic and diluted EPS for the year ended December 31, 2006.

**E 19–23**
EPS; concepts; terminology

● LO6 through LO12

Listed below are several terms and phrases associated with earnings per share. Pair each item from List A (by letter) with the item from List B that is most appropriately associated with it.

| List A | List B |
|---|---|
| ____ 1. Subtract preferred dividends. | a. Options exercised. |
| ____ 2. Time-weighted by 5/12. | b. Simple capital structure. |
| ____ 3. Time-weighted shares assumed issued plus time-weighted actual shares. | c. Basic EPS. |
| | d. Convertible preferred stock. |
| ____ 4. Midyear event treated as if it occurred at the beginning of the reporting period. | e. Earnings available to common shareholders. |
| | f. Antidilutive. |
| ____ 5. Preferred dividends do not reduce earnings. | g. Increased marketability. |
| ____ 6. Single EPS presentation. | h. Extraordinary items. |
| ____ 7. Stock split. | i. Stock dividend. |
| ____ 8. Potentially dilutive security. | j. Add after-tax interest to numerator. |
| ____ 9. Exercise price exceeds market price. | k. Diluted EPS. |
| ____ 10. No dilution assumed. | l. Noncumulative, undeclared preferred dividends. |
| ____ 11. Convertible bonds. | m. Common shares retired at the beginning of August. |
| ____ 12. Contingently issuable shares. | |
| ____ 13. Maximum potential dilution. | n. Include in diluted EPS when conditions for issuance are met. |
| ____ 14. Per share amounts for net income and for income from continuing operations. | |

**E 19–24**
Multiple choice; CMA exam; share-based compensation

● LO2

The following questions dealing with share-based compensation are adapted from questions that previously appeared on Certified Management Accountant (CMA) examinations. The CMA designation sponsored by the Institute of Management Accountants (**www.imanet.org**) provides members with an objective measure of knowledge and competence in the field of management accounting. Determine the response that best completes the statements or questions.

1. Noncompensatory stock option plans have all of the following characteristics except
   a. participation by substantially all full-time employees who meet limited employment qualifications.
   b. equal offers of stock to all eligible employees.
   c. a limited amount of time permitted to exercise the option.
   d. a provision related to the achievement of certain performance criteria.
2. A stock option plan may or may not be intended to compensate employees for their work. The compensation expense for compensatory stock option plans should be recognized in the periods the
   a. employees become eligible to exercise the options.
   b. employees perform services.
   c. stock is issued.
   d. options are granted.

## PROBLEMS

available with McGraw-Hill's Homework Manager www.mhhe.com/spiceland4e

**An alternate exercise and problem set is available on the text website: www.mhhe.com/spiceland4e**

**P 19–1**
Stock options; forfeiture; exercise

● LO2

On October 15, 2005, the board of directors of Ensor Materials Corporation approved a stock option plan for key executives. On January 1, 2006, 20 million stock options were granted, exercisable for 20 million shares of Ensor's $1 par common stock. The options are exercisable between January 1, 2009, and December 31, 2011, at 80% of the quoted market price on January 1, 2006, which was $15. The fair value of the 20 million options, estimated by an appropriate option pricing model, is $6 per option.

Two million options were forfeited when an executive resigned in 2007. All other options were exercised on July 12, 2010, when the stock's price jumped unexpectedly to $19 per share.

**Required:**

1. When is Ensor's stock option measurement date?
2. Determine the compensation expense for the stock option plan in 2006. (Ignore taxes.)
3. What is the effect of forfeiture of the stock options on Ensor's financial statements for 2007 and 2008?
4. Is this effect consistent with the general approach for accounting for changes in estimates? Explain.
5. How should Ensor account for the exercise of the options in 2010?

**P 19–2**
Stock option plan; deferred tax effect recognized

● LO2

eXcel

Walters Audio Visual, Inc. offers a stock option plan to its regional managers. On January 1, 2006, options were granted for 40 million $1 par common shares. The exercise price is the market price on the grant date, $8 per share. Options cannot be exercised prior to January 1, 2008, and expire December 31, 2012. The fair value of the options, estimated by an appropriate option pricing model, is $2 per option. Because the plan does not qualify as an incentive plan, Walters will receive a tax deduction upon exercise of the options equal to the excess of the market price at exercise over the exercise price. The income tax rate is 40%.

**Required:**

1. Determine the total compensation cost pertaining to the stock option plan.
2. Prepare the appropriate journal entries to record compensation expense and its tax effect on December 31, 2006.
3. Prepare the appropriate journal entries to record compensation expense and its tax effect on December 31, 2007.
4. Record the exercise of the options and their tax effect if *all* of the options are exercised on March 20, 2011, when the market price is $12 per share.
5. Assume the option plan qualifies as an incentive plan. Prepare the appropriate journal entries to record compensation expense and its tax effect on December 31, 2006.
6. Assuming the option plan qualifies as an incentive plan, record the exercise of the options and their tax effect if *all* of the options are exercised on March 20, 2011, when the market price is $11 per share.

**P 19–3**
Stock option plan; deferred tax effect of a nonqualifying plan

● LO2

JBL Aircraft manufactures and distributes aircraft parts and supplies. Employees are offered a variety of share-based compensation plans. Under its nonqualified stock option plan, JBL granted options to key officers on January 1, 2006. The options permit holders to acquire six million of the company's $1 par common shares for $22 within the next six years, but not before January 1, 2009 (the vesting date). The market price of the shares on the date of grant is $26 per share. The fair value of the 6 million options, estimated by an appropriate option pricing model, is $6 per option. Because the plan does not qualify as an incentive plan,

JBL will receive a tax deduction upon exercise of the options equal to the excess of the market price at exercise over the exercise price. The tax rate is 40%.

**Required:**

1. Determine the total compensation cost pertaining to the incentive stock option plan.
2. Prepare the appropriate journal entries to record compensation expense and its tax effect on December 31, 2006, 2007, and 2008.
3. Record the exercise of the options and their tax effect if *all* of the options are exercised on August 21, 2010, when the market price is $27 per share.

**P 19–4**
Performance option plan
● LO2

LCI Cable Company grants 1 million performance stock options to key executives at January 1, 2006. The options entitle executives to receive 1 million of LCI $1 par common shares, subject to the achievement of specific financial goals over the next four years. Attainment of these goals is considered probable initially and throughout the service period. The options have a current fair value of $12 per option.

**Required:**

1. Prepare the appropriate entry when the options are awarded on January 1, 2006.
2. Prepare the appropriate entries on December 31 of each year 2006–2009.
3. Suppose at the beginning of 2008, LCI decided it is not probable that the performance objectives will be met. Prepare the appropriate entries on December 31 of 2008 and 2009.

**P 19–5**
EPS; net loss; stock dividend; nonconvertible preferred stock; treasury shares; shares sold; extraordinary loss
● LO6 through LO8

On December 31, 2005, Ainsworth, Inc. had 600 million shares of common stock outstanding. Twenty million shares of 8%, $100 par value cumulative, nonconvertible preferred stock were sold on January 2, 2006. On April 30, 2006, Ainsworth purchased 30 million shares of its common stock as treasury stock. Twelve million treasury shares were sold on August 31. Ainsworth issued a 5% common stock dividend on June 12, 2006. No cash dividends were declared in 2006. For the year ended December 31, 2006, Ainsworth reported a net loss of $140 million, including an after-tax extraordinary loss of $400 million from a litigation settlement.

**Required:**

1. Determine Ainsworth's net loss per share for the year ended December 31, 2006.
2. Determine the per share amount of income or loss from continuing operations for the year ended December 31, 2006.
3. Prepare an EPS presentation that would be appropriate to appear on Ainsworth's 2006 and 2005 comparative income statements. Assume EPS was reported in 2005 as $.75, based on net income (no extraordinary items) of $450 million and a weighted-average number of common shares of 600 million.

**P 19–6**
EPS from statement of retained earnings
● LO5 through LO7

(Note: Problem 19–6 is based on the same situation described in Problem 18–4 in Chapter 18, modified to focus on EPS rather than recording the events that affected retained earnings.)

Comparative Statements of Retained Earnings for Renn-Dever Corporation were reported as follows for the fiscal years ending December 31, 2004, 2005, and 2006.

**RENN-DEVER CORPORATION**
**Statements of Retained Earnings**

| For the Years Ended December 31 | 2006 | 2005 | 2004 |
|---|---|---|---|
| Balance at beginning of year | $6,794,292 | $5,464,052 | $5,624,552 |
| Net income (loss) | 3,308,700 | 2,240,900 | (160,500) |
| Deductions: | | | |
| Stock dividend (34,900 shares) | 242,000 | | |
| Common shares retired, September 30 (110,000 shares) | | 212,660 | |
| Common stock cash dividends | 889,950 | 698,000 | 0 |
| Balance at end of year | $8,971,042 | $6,794,292 | $5,464,052 |

At December 31, 2003, paid-in capital consisted of the following:

| | |
|---|---|
| Common stock, 1,855,000 shares at $1 par, | $1,855,000 |
| Paid in capital—excess of par | 7,420,000 |

No preferred stock or potential common shares were outstanding during any of the periods shown.

**Required:**

Compute Renn-Dever's earnings per share as it would have appeared in income statements for the years ended December 31, 2004, 2005, and 2006.

**P 19–7**
EPS from statement of shareholders' equity

Comparative Statements of Shareholders' Equity for Locke Intertechnology Corporation were reported as follows for the fiscal years ending December 31, 2004, 2005, and 2006.

● LO5 through LO8

eXcel

**LOCKE INTERTECHNOLOGY CORPORATION**
**Statements of Shareholders' Equity**
**For the Years Ended Dec. 31, 2004, 2005, and 2006**
($ in millions)

| | Preferred Stock, $10 par | Common Stock, $1 par | Additional Paid-In Capital | Retained Earnings | Total Shareholders' Equity |
|---|---|---|---|---|---|
| **Balance at January 1, 2004** | | **55** | **495** | **1,878** | **2,428** |
| Sale of preferred shares | 10 | | 470 | | 480 |
| Sale of common shares, 7/1 | | 9 | 81 | | 90 |
| Cash dividend, preferred | | | | (1) | (1) |
| Cash dividend, common | | | | (16) | (16) |
| Net income | — | — | — | 290 | 290 |
| **Balance at December 31, 2004** | **10** | **64** | **1,046** | **2,151** | **3,271** |
| Retirement of common shares, 4/1 | | (4) | (36) | (20) | (60) |
| Cash dividend, preferred | | | | (1) | (1) |
| Cash dividend, common | | | | (20) | (20) |
| 3-for-2 split effected in the form of a common stock dividend, 8/12 | | 30 | (30) | | |
| Net income | — | — | — | 380 | 380 |
| **Balance at December 31, 2005** | **10** | **90** | **980** | **2,490** | **3,570** |
| 10% common stock dividend, 5/1 | | 9 | 90 | (99) | |
| Sale of common shares, 9/1 | | 3 | 31 | | 34 |
| Cash dividend, preferred | | | | (2) | (2) |
| Cash dividend, common | | | | (22) | (22) |
| Net income | — | — | — | 412 | 412 |
| **Balance at December 31, 2006** | **10** | **102** | **1,101** | **2,779** | **3,992** |

**Required:**

Infer from the statements the events and transactions that affected Locke Intertechnology Corporation's shareholders' equity and compute earnings per share as it would have appeared on the income statements for the years ended December 31, 2004, 2005, and 2006. No potential common shares were outstanding during any of the periods shown.

**P 19–8**
EPS; nonconvertible preferred stock; treasury shares; shares sold; stock dividend

● LO5 through LO8

On December 31, 2005, Dow Steel Corporation had 600,000 shares of common stock and 300,000 shares of 8%, noncumulative, nonconvertible preferred stock issued and outstanding. Dow issued a 4% common stock dividend on May 15 and paid cash dividends of $400,000 and $75,000 to common and preferred shareholders, respectively, on December 15, 2006.

On February 28, 2006, Dow sold 60,000 common shares. In keeping with its long-term share repurchase plan, 2,000 shares were retired on July 1. Dow's net income for the year ended December 31, 2006, was $2,100,000. The income tax rate is 40%.

**Required:**

Compute Dow's earnings per share for the year ended December 31, 2006.

**P 19–9**
EPS; nonconvertible preferred stock; treasury shares; shares sold; stock dividend; options

● LO5 through LO9

eXcel

(Note: This is a variation of the previous problem, modified to include stock options.)

On December 31, 2005, Dow Steel Corporation had 600,000 shares of common stock and 300,000 shares of 8%, noncumulative, nonconvertible preferred stock issued and outstanding. Dow issued a 4% common stock dividend on May 15 and paid cash dividends of $400,000 and $75,000 to common and preferred shareholders, respectively, on December 15, 2006.

On February 28, 2006, Dow sold 60,000 common shares. In keeping with its long-term share repurchase plan, 2,000 shares were retired on July 1. Dow's net income for the year ended December 31, 2006, was $2,100,000. The income tax rate is 40%.

As part of an incentive compensation plan, Dow granted stock options to division managers at December 31 of the current and each of the previous two years. Each option permits its holder to buy one share of common stock at an exercise price equal to market value at the date of grant. Information concerning the number of options granted and common share prices follows:

| Date Granted | Options Granted (adjusted for the stock dividend) | Share Price |
|---|---|---|
| December 31, 2004 | 3,000 | $33 |
| December 31, 2005 | 8,000 | $24 |
| December 31, 2006 | 6,500 | $31 |

The market price of the common stock averaged $32 per share during 2006.

**Required:**

Compute Dow's earnings per share for the year ended December 31, 2006.

**P 19–10**
EPS; nonconvertible preferred stock; treasury shares; shares sold; stock dividend; options; convertible bonds; contingently issuable shares

● LO5 through LO11

(Note: This is a variation of the previous problem, modified to include convertible bonds and contingently issuable shares.)

On December 31, 2005, Dow Steel Corporation had 600,000 shares of common stock and 300,000 shares of 8%, noncumulative, nonconvertible preferred stock issued and outstanding. Dow issued a 4% common stock dividend on May 15 and paid cash dividends of $400,000 and $75,000 to common and preferred shareholders, respectively, on December 15, 2006.

On February 28, 2006, Dow sold 60,000 common shares. Also, as a part of a 2005 agreement for the acquisition of Merrill Cable Company, another 23,000 shares (already adjusted for the stock dividend) are to be issued to former Merrill shareholders on December 31, 2007, if Merrill's 2007 net income is at least $500,000. In 2006, Merrill's net income was $630,000.

In keeping with its long-term share repurchase plan, 2,000 shares were retired on July 1. Dow's net income for the year ended December 31, 2006, was $2,100,000. The income tax rate is 40%.

As part of an incentive compensation plan, Dow granted stock options to division managers at December 31 of the current and each of the previous two years. Each option permits its holder to buy one share of common stock at an exercise price equal to market value at the date of grant. Information concerning the number of options granted and common share prices follows:

| Date Granted | Options Granted | Share Price |
|---|---|---|
| | (adjusted for the stock dividend) | |
| December 31, 2004 | 3,000 | $33 |
| December 31, 2005 | 8,000 | $24 |
| December 31, 2006 | 6,500 | $31 |

The market price of the common stock averaged $32 per share during 2006.

On July 12, 2004, Dow issued $800,000 of convertible 10% debentures at face value. Each $1,000 bond is convertible into 30 common shares (adjusted for the stock dividend).

**Required:**

Compute Dow's basic and diluted earnings per share for the year ended December 31, 2006.

**P 19–11**
EPS; antidilution

● LO5 through LO11

Alciatore Company earned a net income of $150,000 in 2006. The weighted-average number of common shares outstanding for 2006 was 40,000. The average stock price for 2006 was $33. Assume an income tax rate of 40%.

**Required:**

For each of the following independent situations, indicate whether the security is antidilutive for diluted EPS.

1. 10,000 shares of 7.7% of $100 par convertible, cumulative preferred stock. Each share may be converted into two common shares.
2. 8% convertible 10-year, $500,000 of bonds, issued at face value. The bonds are convertible to 5,000 shares of common stock.
3. Stock options exercisable at $30 per share after January 1, 2008.
4. Warrants for 1,000 common shares with an exercise price of $35 per share.
5. A contingent agreement to issue 5,000 shares of stock to the company president if net income is at least $125,000 in 2007.

**P 19–12**
EPS; convertible bonds; treasury shares

● LO5 through LO7 LO10

At December 31, 2006, the financial statements of Hollingsworth Industries included the following:

| | |
|---|---|
| Net income for 2006 | $560 million |
| Bonds payable, 10%, convertible into 36 million shares of common stock | $300 million |
| Common stock: | |
| Shares outstanding on January 1 | 400 million |
| Treasury shares purchased for cash on September 1 | 30 million |

**Additional data:**

The bonds payable were issued at par in 2004. The tax rate for 2006 was 40%.

**Required:**

Compute basic and diluted EPS for the year ended December 31, 2006.

**P 19–13**
EPS; options; convertible preferred; additional shares

On January 1, 2006, Tonge Industries had outstanding 440,000 common shares (par $1) that originally sold for $20 per share, and 4,000 shares of 10% cumulative preferred stock (par $100), convertible into 40,000 common shares.

On October 1, 2006, Tonge sold and issued an additional 16,000 shares of common stock at $33. At December 31, 2006, there were common stock options outstanding, issued in 2005, and exercisable for 20,000

● LO5 through LO10

shares of common stock at an exercise price of $30. The market price of the common stock at year-end was $48. During the year the price of the common shares had averaged $40.

Net income was $650,000. The tax rate for the year was 40%.

**Required:**

Compute basic and diluted EPS for the year ended December 31, 2006.

**P 19–14**
EPS; stock options; nonconvertible preferred; convertible bonds; shares sold

● LO5 through LO10

At January 1, 2006, Canaday Corporation had outstanding the following securities:

600 million common shares
20 million 6% cumulative preferred shares, $50 par
8% convertible bonds, $2,000 million face amount, convertible into 80 million common shares

The following additional information is available:

- On September 1, 2006, Canaday sold 72 million additional shares of common stock.
- Unexercised stock options to purchase 60 million shares of common stock at $12 per share were outstanding at the beginning and end of 2006. The average market price of Canaday's common stock was $18 per share during 2006.
- Canaday's net income for the year ended December 31, 2006, was $1,476 million. The effective income tax rate was 40%.

**Required:**

1. Calculate basic earnings per common share for the year ended December 31, 2006.
2. Calculate the diluted earnings per common share for the year ended December 31, 2006.

# BROADEN YOUR PERSPECTIVE

**Apply your critical-thinking ability to the knowledge you've gained. These cases will provide you an opportunity to develop your research, analysis, judgment, and communication skills. You also will work with other students, integrate what you've learned, apply it in real world situations, and consider its global and ethical ramifications. This practice will broaden your knowledge and further develop your decision-making abilities.**

**Real World Case 19–1**
Restricted stock plan; Dell computer

● LO1

**Dell Computer** is the world's leading computer systems company and a provider of related products and services. Compensation to executives is provided in the form of a variety of incentive compensation plans including restricted stock award grants. The following is an excerpt from a disclosure note from Dell's 2004 annual report:

> **Restricted Stock Grants**—During fiscal years 2004, 2003, and 2002, the Company granted .6 million shares, .3 million shares, and 2.1 million shares, respectively, of restricted stock. For substantially all restricted stock grants, at the date of grant, the recipient has all rights of a stockholder, subject to certain restrictions on transferability and a risk of forfeiture. Restricted shares typically vest over a seven-year period beginning on the date of grant.

**Required:**

1. What is the "incentive" provided by Dell's restricted stock grants?
2. If the fair value of Dell's stock at dates of grant was $28, $25, and $24 per share granted during fiscal years 2004, 2003, and 2002, respectively, what is the compensation expense in 2004 pertaining to the three stock awards? Explain.

**Communication Case 19–2**
Stock options; basic concepts; prepare a memo

● LO2

You are Assistant Controller of Stamos & Company, a medium-size manufacturer of machine parts. On October 22, 2005, the board of directors approved a stock option plan for key executives. On January 1, 2006, a specific number of stock options were granted. The options were exercisable between January 1, 2008, and December 31, 2010, at 100% of the quoted market price at the grant date. The service period is for 2006 through 2008.

Your boss, the controller, is one of the executives to receive options. Neither he nor you have had occasion to deal with the FASB pronouncement on accounting for stock options. He and you are aware of the traditional approach your company used previously but do not know the newer method. Your boss understands how options might benefit him personally but wants to be aware also of how the options will be reported in the financial statements. He has asked you for a one-page synopsis of accounting for stock options under the fair value approach. He instructed you, "I don't care about the effect on taxes or earnings per share—just the basics, please."

**Required:**

Prepare such a report that includes the following:

1. At what point should the compensation cost be measured? How should it be measured?
2. How should compensation expense be measured for the stock option plan in 2006 and later?
3. If options are forfeited because an executive resigns before vesting, what is the effect of that forfeiture of the stock options on the financial statements?
4. If options are forfeited because they are allowed to lapse after vesting, what is the effect of that forfeiture of the stock options on the financial statements?

**Ethics Case 19–3**
Stock options

● LO2

You are in your second year as an auditor with Dantly and Regis, a regional CPA firm. One of the firm's long-time clients is Mayberry-Cleaver Industries, a national company involved in the manufacturing, marketing, and sales of hydraulic devices used in specialized manufacturing applications. Early in this year's audit you discover that Mayberry-Cleaver has changed its method of determining inventory from LIFO to FIFO. Your client's explanation is that FIFO is consistent with the method used by some other companies in the industry. Upon further investigation, you discover an executive stock option plan whose terms call for a significant increase in the shares available to executives if net income this year exceeds $44 million. Some quick calculations convince you that without the change in inventory methods, the target will not be reached; with the change, it will.

**Required:**

Do you perceive an ethical dilemma? What would be the likely impact of following the controller's suggestions? Who would benefit? Who would be injured?

**Real World Case 19–4**
Share-based plans; General Electric Company

● LO1 through LO3

**General Electric Company** offers its employees a variety of share-based compensation plans to employees including stock options, stock appreciation rights (SARs), restricted stock units (RSUs), and performance share units (PSUs). The following is an excerpt from a disclosure note from GE's third-quarter 2004 financial statements:

**Note 12 (in part)**
We first measure the total cost of each grant at the grant date using the Black-Scholes option pricing model. We then recognize each grant's total cost over the period that the options or stock appreciation rights vest. Under this approach, we charged $29 million and $22 million to net earnings in the third quarters of 2004 and 2003, respectively, and $74 million and $66 million in the first nine months of 2004 and 2003, respectively.

**Required:**

1. GE's share-based compensation includes stock options, stock appreciation rights, restricted stock awards, and performance-based awards. What is the general financial reporting objective when recording compensation expense for these forms of compensation?
2. GE reported share-based expense of $29 million in 2004's third quarter. Without referring to specific numbers, describe how this amount reflects the value of stock options in periods prior to the current period.

**Judgment Case 19–5**
Where are the profits?

● LO5 through LO8 LO10

Del Conte Construction Company has experienced generally steady growth since its inception in 1950. Management is proud of its record of having maintained or increased its earnings per share in each year of its existence.

Inflationary pressures in the construction industry have led to disturbing dips in revenues the past two years. Despite concerted cost-cutting efforts, profits have actually declined in each of the two previous years. Net income in 2004, 2005, and 2006 was as follows:

| | |
|---|---|
| 2004 | $145 million |
| 2005 | $134 million |
| 2006 | $ 95 million |

A major shareholder has hired you to provide advice on whether to continue her present investment position or to curtail that position. Of particular concern is the declining profitability, despite the fact that earnings per share has continued a pattern of growth:

| | Basic | Diluted |
|---|---|---|
| 2004 | $2.15 | $1.91 |
| 2005 | $2.44 | $2.12 |
| 2006 | $2.50 | $2.50 |

She specifically asks you to explain this apparent paradox. During the course of your investigation you discover the following events:

- For the decade ending December 31, 2003, Del Conte had 60 million common shares and 20 million shares of 8%, $10 par nonconvertible preferred stock outstanding. Cash dividends have been paid quarterly on both.
- On July 1, 2005, half the preferred shares were retired in the open market. The remaining shares were retired on December 30, 2005.
- $55 million of 8% nonconvertible bonds were issued at the beginning of 2006 and a portion of the proceeds were used to call and retire $50 million of 10% debentures (outstanding since 2001) that were convertible into 9 million common shares.
- In 2004 management announced a share repurchase plan by which up to 24 million common shares would be retired. 12 million shares were retired on March 1 of both 2005 and 2006.
- Del Conte's income tax rate is 40% and has been for the last several years.

**Required:**

Explain the apparent paradox to which your client refers. Include calculations that demonstrate your explanation.

**Communication Case 19–6**
Dilution

- LO10

"I thought I understood earnings per share," lamented Brad Dawson, "but you're telling me we need to pretend our convertible bonds have been converted! Or maybe not?"

Dawson, your boss, is the new manager of the Fabricating division of BVT Corporation. His background is engineering and he has only a basic understanding of earnings per share. Knowing you are an accounting graduate, he asks you to explain the questions he has about the calculation of the company's EPS. His reaction is to your explanation that the company's convertible bonds might be included in this year's calculation.

"Put it in a memo!" he grumbled as he left your office.

**Required:**

Write a memo to Dawson. Explain the effect on earnings per share of each of the following:

1. Convertible securities.
2. Antidilutive securities.

**Real World Case 19–7**
Reporting EPS; discontinued operations; Clorox Company

- LO12

**The Clorox Company** is principally engaged in the production and marketing of nondurable consumer products through grocery stores, mass merchandisers, and other retail outlets. The following is an excerpt from the comparative income statements (beginning with income from continuing operations before extraordinary item) from Clorox's 2004 annual report ($ in millions):

| | Years Ended June 30 | | |
|---|---|---|---|
| | 2004 | 2003 | 2002 |
| Earnings from continuing operations | $546 | $514 | $357 |
| Earnings (losses) from discontinued operations, net of tax benefits of $7, $5 and $28 for the years ended June 30, 2004, 2003 and 2002, respectively | 3 | (21) | (35) |
| Net earnings | $549 | $493 | $322 |

An income statement sometimes includes items that require separate presentation (net of income taxes) within the statement. The two possible "separately reported items" are discontinued operations and extraordinary items.

Clorox reports one of these items. A disclosure note from Clorox's 2004 annual report is shown below:

**21. Earnings per Share**

A reconciliation of the weighted-average number of common shares outstanding (in thousands) used to calculate basic and diluted earnings per common share is as follows for the fiscal years ended June 30:

| | 2004 | 2003 | 2002 |
|---|---|---|---|
| Basic | 211,683 | 218,174 | 231,849 |
| Stock options and other | 2,688 | 2,518 | 2,855 |
| Diluted | 214,371 | 220,692 | 234,704 |

Stock options to purchase 832,815, 1,045,413, and 1,141,797 shares of common stock for the fiscal years ended June 30, 2004, 2003 and 2002, respectively, were not included in the computation of diluted net earnings per common share because . . . the effect would be antidilutive.

**Required:**

1. The disclosure note shows adjustments for "stock options and other." What might constitute the "other"? Explain why and how these adjustments are made to the weighted-average shares outstanding.

2. The disclosure note indicates some of the stock options were not included because they would be antidilutive. What does that mean? Why not include antidilutive securities?
3. Based on the information provided, prepare the presentation of basic and diluted earnings per share for 2004, 2003, and 2002 that Clorox reports in its 2004 annual report.

**Analysis Case 19–8**
Analyzing financial statements; price–earnings ratio; dividend payout ratio

● LO12

IGF Foods Company is a large, primarily domestic, consumer foods company involved in the manufacture, distribution and sale of a variety of food products. Industry averages are derived from Troy's *The Almanac of Business and Industrial Financial Ratios* and Dun and Bradstreet's *Industry Norms and Key Business Ratios*. Following are the 2006 and 2005 comparative income statements and balance sheets for IGF. The market price of IGF's common stock is $47 during 2006. (The financial data we use are from actual financial statements of a well-known corporation, but the company name used in our illustration is fictitious and the numbers and dates have been modified slightly to disguise the company's identity.)

**IGF FOODS COMPANY**
**Years Ended December 31, 2006 and 2005**

| ($ in millions) | 2006 | 2005 |
|---|---|---|
| **Comparative Income Statements** | | |
| Net sales | $6,440 | $5,800 |
| Cost of goods sold | (3,667) | (3,389) |
| Gross profit | 2,773 | 2,411 |
| Operating expenses | (1,916) | (1,629) |
| Operating income | 857 | 782 |
| Interest expense | (54) | (53) |
| Income from operations before tax | 803 | 729 |
| Income taxes | (316) | (287) |
| *Net income* | $ 487 | $ 442 |
| Net income per share | $2.69 | $2.44 |
| Average shares outstanding | 181 million | 181 million |
| **Comparative Balance Sheets** | | |
| **Assets** | | |
| Total current assets | $1,879 | $1,490 |
| Property, plant, and equipment (net) | 2,592 | 2,291 |
| Intangibles (net) | 800 | 843 |
| Other assets | 74 | 60 |
| *Total assets* | $5,345 | $4,684 |
| **Liabilities and Shareholders' Equity** | | |
| Total current liabilities | $1,473 | $ 941 |
| Long term debt | 534 | 728 |
| Deferred income taxes | 407 | 344 |
| Total liabilities | 2,414 | 2,013 |
| Shareholders' equity: | | |
| Common stock | 180 | 180 |
| Additional paid-in capital | 21 | 63 |
| Retained earnings | 2,730 | 2,428 |
| Total shareholders' equity | 2,931 | 2,671 |
| *Total liabilities and shareholders' equity* | $5,345 | $4,684 |

Some ratios express income, dividends, and market prices on a per share basis. As such, these ratios appeal primarily to common shareholders, particularly when weighing investment possibilities. These ratios focus less on the fundamental soundness of a company and more on its investment characteristics.

**Required:**
1. Earnings per share expresses a firm's profitability on a per share basis. Calculate 2006 earnings per share for IGF.
2. Calculate IGF's 2006 price-earnings ratio. The average price-earnings ratio for the stocks listed on the New York Stock Exchange in a comparable time period was 18.5. What does your calculation indicate about IGF's earnings?
3. Calculate IGF's 2006 dividend payout ratio. What information does the calculation provide an investor?

**Ethics Case 19–9**
International Network Solutions

● LO7

International Network Solutions provides products and services related to remote access networking. The company has grown rapidly during its first 10 years of operations. As its segment of the industry has begun to mature, though, the fast growth of previous years has begun to slow. In fact, this year revenues and profits are roughly the same as last year.

One morning, nine weeks before the close of the fiscal year, Rob Mashburn, CFO, and Jessica Lane, controller, were sharing coffee and ideas in Lane's office.

**Lane:** About the Board meeting Thursday. You may be right. This may be the time to suggest a share buyback program.

**Mashburn:** To begin this year, you mean?

**Lane:** Right! I know Barber will be lobbying to use the funds for our European expansion. She's probably right about the best use of our funds, but we can always issue more notes next year. Right now, we need a quick fix for our EPS numbers.

**Mashburn:** Our shareholders are accustomed to increases every year.

**Required:**

1. How will a buyback of shares provide a "quick fix" for EPS?
2. Is the proposal ethical?
3. Who would be affected if the proposal is implemented?

**Real World Case 19–10**
Executive stock options and EPS

● LO9

**Microsoft Corporation** offers compensation to its employees and executives through a variety of compensation plans. One such plan is its stock option plan, which is described in the following disclosure note from its fiscal 2004 annual report:

> **Stock Options (in part)**
> Nonqualified and incentive stock options have been granted to our officers and employees under our employee stock plans. Options granted after 2001 vest over four and one-half years and expire ten years from the date of grant. At June 20, 2004, stock options for 569 million shares were vested.

At June 30, 2004, approximately 949 million outstanding options were exercisable. The financial statements also reported 10,894 million shares of common stock used in calculating diluted earnings per share and the shares used in the basic EPS calculations were 10,803 million.

**Required:**

1. How might the employee stock options described in the disclosure note affect earnings per share?
2. If we assume (a) dilutive potential common shares consist entirely of stock options, and (b) the actual number of common shares and number of options did not change during the year, how could we reconcile the shares used in basic and diluted EPS calculations and the number of options outstanding?

**Research Case 19–11**
Determining and comparing price-earnings ratios; retrieving stock prices and earnings per share numbers from the Internet

● LO12

Many sites on the Internet allow the retrieval of current stock price information. Among those sites are Marketwatch (**cbs.marketwatch.com**) and Quicken (**www.quicken.com**).

**Required:**

1. Access any site on the Internet that permits you to get a current stock quote. Determine the current price of **Microsoft Corporation**'s common stock (MSFT) and that of **Intel Corporation** (INTC).
2. Access EDGAR on the Internet using EdgarScan at: **edgarscan.pwcglobal.com.** Search for Microsoft and access its most recent 10-K filing. Search or scroll to find the income statement and related note(s). Determine the most recent earnings per share. Repeat this step for Intel.
3. Calculate the price-earnings ratio for each company.
4. Compare the PE ratios of Microsoft and Intel. What information might be gleaned from your comparison?

**Analysis Case 19–12**
Kellogg's EPS; PE ratio; dividend payout

● LO12

While eating his **Kellogg**'s Frosted Flakes one October morning, Tony noticed the following article in his local paper:

> **Kellogg Reports Strong Results in 2004**
> BATTLE CREEK, Mich., Jan 31, 2005 /PRNewswire—Kellogg Company (NYSE: K) today reported that its fourth quarter and full-year earnings exceeded its previously increased forecast range. The Company also reaffirmed its earnings forecast range for 2005 of $2.28-2.32 per share.
> Reported net earnings for the full year 2004 were $890.6 million, or a 13% increase from last year's $787.1 million. Earnings were $2.14 per diluted share, an increase of 11% from $1.92 per share in 2003. Reported net earnings in the fourth quarter of 2004 were $186.4 million, or $0.45 per diluted share, compared to $188.0 million, or $0.46 per share in the fourth quarter of 2003. This decline was anticipated and resulted primarily from a higher tax rate.
> PRNewswire

As a shareholder, Tony is well aware that Kellogg pays a regular cash dividend of $.2525 per share quarterly. A quick click on a price quote service indicated that Kellogg's shares closed at $44.66 on December 31. That web page also reported Kellogg's previous year's EPS as $1.45.

**Required:**

1. Using the numbers provided, determine the price/earnings ratio for Kellogg Company for 2004. What information does this ratio impart?
2. What is the dividend payout ratio for Kellogg? What does it indicate?

**Analysis Case 19–13**
EPS concepts

- LO5 through LO9

The shareholders' equity of Proactive Solutions, Inc. included the following at December 31, 2006:

Common stock, $1 par
Paid-in capital—excess of par on common stock
7% cumulative convertible preferred stock, $100 par value
Paid-in capital—excess of par on preferred stock
Retained earnings

**Additional information:**

- Proactive had 7 million shares of preferred stock authorized of which 2 million were outstanding. All 2 million shares outstanding were issued in 2000 for $112 a share. The preferred stock is convertible into common stock on a two-for-one basis until December 31, 2008, after which the preferred stock no longer is convertible. None of the preferred stock has been converted into common stock at December 31, 2006. There were no dividends in arrears.
- Of the 13 million common shares authorized, there were 8 million shares outstanding at January 1, 2006. Proactive also sold 3 million shares at the beginning of September 2006 at a price of $52 a share.
- The company has an employee stock option plan where certain key employees and officers may purchase shares of common stock at the market price at the date of the option grant. All options are exercisable beginning one year after the date of the grant and expire if not exercised within five years of the grant date. On January 1, 2006, options for 2 million shares were outstanding at prices ranging from $45 to $53 a share. Options for 1 million shares were exercised at $49 a share at the end of June 2006. No options expired during 2006. Additional options for 1.5 million shares were granted at $55 a share during the year. The 2.5 million options outstanding at December 31, 2006, were exercisable at $45 to $55 a share.

The only changes in the shareholders' equity for 2006 were those described above, 2006 net income, and cash dividends paid.

**Required:**

Explain how each of the following amounts should be determined when computing earnings per share for presentation in the income statements. For each, be specific as to the treatment of each item.

1. Numerator for basic EPS.
2. Denominator for basic EPS.
3. Numerator for diluted EPS.
4. Denominator for diluted EPS.

**Real World Case 19–14**
Per share data; stock options; antidilutive securities; Sun Microsystems

- LO9

**Sun Microsystems, Inc.,** headquartered in Santa Clara, California, is a prominent provider of products and services for network computing. Sun's 2004 annual report included the following disclosure note:

**Computation of Net Loss per Common Share (in part)**
Basic net loss per common share is computed using the weighted-average number of common shares outstanding during the period. Diluted net loss per common share is computed using the weighted average number of common and dilutive common equivalent shares outstanding during the period. Dilutive common equivalent shares consist primarily of stock options.

The following table sets forth the computation of basic and diluted earnings per share for each of the past three fiscal years (in millions, except per share amounts):

| | Fiscal Years Ended June 30 | | |
|---|---|---|---|
| | 2004 | 2003 | 2002 |
| Net loss | $ (388) | $(3,429) | $ (587) |
| Weighted-average shares outstanding: | | | |
| Basic and diluted | 3,277 | 3,190 | 3,242 |
| Net loss per common share—basic and diluted | $(0.12) | $ (1.07) | $(0.18) |

U.S. GAAP requires all antidilutive securities, including stock options, to be excluded from the diluted earnings per share computation. For fiscal 2004, 2003 and 2002, due to our net loss, all of our outstanding options totaling 603 million, 587 million and 556 million, respectively, were excluded from the diluted loss per share calculation because their inclusion would have been antidilutive. If we had earned a profit during fiscal 2004, 2003 and 2002, we would have added 30 million, 28 million and 97 million equivalent shares to our basic weighted-average shares outstanding to compute the diluted weighted-average shares outstanding.

**Required:**

1. The note indicates that "diluted net loss per common share is computed using the weighted-average number of common and dilutive common equivalent shares outstanding during the period." What are dilutive common equivalent shares?
2. In fiscal 2004, Sun would have added 30 million potential common shares to the "basic weighted-average shares outstanding to compute the diluted weighted-average shares outstanding" for its 603 million stock options. What accounts for the 573 million share difference?
3. Sun does not include potential common shares from employee stock options. Why not? If Sun had included dilutive potential common shares from employee stock options, what would have been the amount of diluted loss per share for fiscal 2004?

**Analysis Case 19–15**
EPS; Sonic Drive-ins

- LO6 through LO9

"I guess I'll win that bet!" you announced to no one in particular.

"What bet?" Meg asked. Meg Forsythe was close enough to overhear you.

"When I bought my **Sonic** stock last year Larry insisted it was a mistake, that they were going downhill. I bet him a Coke he was wrong. This press release says per share earnings are up 24%," you bragged. Meg was looking over your shoulder now at the article you were pointing at:

OKLAHOMA CITY, Jan. 3 /PRNewswire-FirstCall/—Sonic Corp. today announced record results for the first quarter of its 2005 fiscal year, which ended November 30, 2004. Highlights of the company's quarterly report included a 24% increase in diluted net income per share, to $0.26.

Earnings per share for the prior-year period have been adjusted to reflect the company's three-for-two stock split distributed in May 2004.

Continued significant growth in cash flow from operations, is expected to be used to fund capital expenditures and, on an opportunistic basis, reduce outstanding debt, repurchase company stock (the company had $60 million authorized for stock repurchases at the end of the first quarter), or purchase franchise drive-ins.

Excerpt from: "Sonic Reports First Quarter Earnings Up 25%," January 3, 2005.

"Twenty-six cents a share, huh?" Meg asked. "How many shares do you have? When do you get the check?"

**Required:**

1. Meg's questions imply that she thinks you will get cash dividends of 26 cents a share. What does earning per share really tell you?
2. The press release says, "Earnings per share for the prior-year period have been adjusted to reflect the company's three-for-two stock split distributed in May 2004." What does that mean?
3. The press release indicates that Sonic may repurchase up to $60 million of its stock. Would that reduction in shares be taken into account when EPS is calculated? How?
4. You know from statements Sonic mailed you that Sonic grants stock options to company executives. If those options are exercised, you know the resulting increase in shares might reduce earnings per share. Is that possibility taken into account when EPS is calculated? Explain.

# CPA SIMULATION 19–1

**Houston County Energy**

EPS and Share-Based Compensation

CPA Review

Test your knowledge of the concepts discussed in this chapter, practice critical professional skills necessary for career success, and prepare for the computer-based CPA exam by accessing our CPA simulations at the text website: www.mhhe.com/spiceland4e.

The Houston County Energy simulation tests your knowledge of a variety of earnings per share and share-based compensation reporting issues.

As on the CPA exam itself, you will be asked to use tools including a spreadsheet, a calculator, and professional accounting standards, to conduct research, derive solutions, and communicate conclusions related to these issues in a simulated environment headed by the following interactive tabs:

Specific tasks in the simulation include:

- Calculating basic and diluted earnings per share.
- Applying judgment in deciding the financial reporting implications of the issuance, exercise, and expiration of stock rights and the conversion of preferred shares.
- Demonstrating an understanding of appropriate financial statement reporting of earnings per share.
- Analyzing the financial statement effects of treasury stock transactions.
- Communicating the financial reporting implications of stock options.
- Researching the purpose of and procedures for a quasi-reorganization.

# 20 CHAPTER

# Accounting Changes and Error Corrections

## OVERVIEW

Chapter 4 provided an overview of accounting changes and error correction. Later, we discussed changes encountered in connection with specific assets and liabilities as we dealt with those topics in subsequent chapters.

Here we revisit accounting changes and error correction to synthesize the way these are handled in a variety of situations that might be encountered in practice. We see that most changes in accounting principle are reported retrospectively. Changes in estimates are accounted for prospectively. A change in depreciation methods is considered a change in estimate resulting from a change in principle. Both changes in reporting entities and the correction of errors are reported retrospectively.

## LEARNING OBJECTIVES

**After studying this chapter, you should be able to:**

- LO1 Differentiate among the three types of accounting changes and distinguish between the retrospective and prospective approaches to accounting for and reporting accounting changes.
- LO2 Describe how changes in accounting principle typically are reported.
- LO3 Explain how and why some changes in accounting principle are reported prospectively.
- LO4 Explain how and why changes in estimates are reported prospectively.
- LO5 Describe the situations that constitute a change in reporting entity.
- LO6 Understand and apply the four-step process of correcting and reporting errors, regardless of the type of error or the timing of its discovery.

# Financial Reporting Case

## In a Jam

"What the heck!" Martin yelped as he handed you the 2002 annual report of J.M. Smucker he'd received in the mail today. "It looks like Smucker found a bunch of lost jelly. It says here that their inventory was $54 million in 2001. I distinctly remember them reporting that number last year as $52 million because my dad was born in '52, and I did a little wordplay in my mind about him 'taking inventory' of his life when he bought the red Mustang." He had circled the number in the comparative balance sheets. "When I bought Smucker shares last year, I promised myself I would monitor things pretty closely, but it's not as easy as I thought it would be."

As an accounting graduate, you can understand Martin's confusion. Flipping to the footnote on accounting changes, you proceed to clear things up for him.

**By the time you finish this chapter, you should be able to respond appropriately to the questions posed in this case. Compare your response to the solution provided at the end of the chapter.**

### QUESTIONS

1. How can an accounting change cause a company to increase a previously reported inventory amount? (page 1013)
2. Are all accounting changes reported this way? (page 1019)

You learned early in your study of accounting that two of the qualitative characteristics of accounting information that contribute to its relevance and reliability are *consistency* and *comparability.* Though we strive to achieve and maintain these financial reporting attributes, we cannot ignore the forces of change. Ours is a dynamic business environment. The economy is increasingly a global one. Technological advances constantly transform both day-to-day operations and the flow of information about those operations. The accounting profession's response to the fluid environment often means issuing new standards that require companies to change accounting methods. Often, developments within an industry or the economy will prompt a company to voluntarily switch methods of accounting or to revise estimates or expectations. In short, change is inevitable. The question then becomes a matter of how best to address change when reporting financial information from year to year.

In the first part of this chapter, we differentiate among the various types of accounting changes that businesses face, with a focus on the most meaningful and least disruptive ways to report those changes. Then, in the second part of the chapter, we direct our attention to a closely related circumstance—the correction of errors.

# PART A ACCOUNTING CHANGES

Accounting changes fall into one of three categories listed in Graphic 20–1.[1]

**GRAPHIC 20–1**
Types of Accounting Changes

| Type of Change | Description | Examples |
|---|---|---|
| Change in accounting principle | Change from one generally accepted accounting principle to another. | • Adopt a new FASB standard.<br>• Change methods of inventory costing.<br>• Change from cost method to equity method, or vice versa.<br>• Change from completed contract to percentage-of-completion, or vice versa. |
| Change in accounting estimate | Revision of an estimate because of new information or new experience. | • Change depreciation methods.<br>• Change estimate of useful life of depreciable asset.<br>• Change estimate of residual value of depreciable asset.<br>• Change estimate of bad debt percentage.<br>• Change estimate of periods benefited by intangible assets.<br>• Change actuarial estimates pertaining to a pension plan. |
| Change in reporting entity | Change from reporting as one type of entity to another type of entity. | • Consolidate a subsidiary not previously included in consolidated financial statements.<br>• Report consolidated financial statements in place of individual statements. |

A change in depreciation methods is a change in estimate that is achieved by a change in accounting principle.

The correction of an error is another adjustment sometimes made to financial statements that is not actually an accounting change but is accounted for similarly. Errors occur when transactions are either recorded incorrectly or not recorded at all as shown in Graphic 20–2.

[1]"Accounting Changes," *Accounting Principles Board Opinion No. 20* (New York: AICPA, 1971).

| Type of Change | Description | Examples |
|---|---|---|
| Error correction | Correction of an error caused by a transaction being recorded incorrectly or not at all. | • Mathematical mistakes.<br>• Inaccurate physical count of inventory.<br>• Change from the cash basis of accounting to the accrual basis.<br>• Failure to record an adjusting entry.<br>• Recording an asset as an expense, or vice versa.<br>• Fraud or gross negligence. |

**GRAPHIC 20–2**
Correction of Errors

Two approaches to reporting accounting changes and error corrections are used, depending on the situation.

LO1

1. Using the **retrospective approach,** financial statements issued in previous years are revised to reflect the impact of the change whenever those statements are presented again for comparative purposes. An advantage of this approach is that it achieves comparability among financial statements. All financial statements presented are prepared on the same basis. However, some argue that public confidence in the integrity of financial data suffers when numbers previously reported as correct are later superseded. On the other hand, proponents argue the opposite—that it's impossible to maintain public confidence unless the financial statements are comparable.

   For each year in the comparative statements reported, the balance of each account affected is revised. In other words, those statements are made to appear as if the newly adopted accounting method had been applied all along or that the error had never occurred. Then, a journal entry is created to adjust all account balances affected to what those amounts would have been. In addition, if retained earnings is one of the accounts whose balance requires adjustment, that adjustment is made to the beginning balance of retained earnings for the earliest period reported in the comparative statements of shareholders' equity.
2. The **prospective approach** requires neither a modification of prior years' financial statements nor a journal entry to adjust account balances. Instead, the change is simply implemented now, and its effects are reflected in the financial statements of the current and future years only.

The *retrospective approach* offers consistency and comparability.

The effects of a change are reflected in the financial statements of only the current and future years under the *prospective approach.*

Now, let's look at each type of accounting change, one at a time, focusing on the selective application of these approaches.

## Change in Accounting Principle

LO2

Accounting is not an exact science. Professional judgment is required to apply a set of principles, concepts, and objectives to specific sets of circumstances. This means choices must be made. In your study of accounting to date, you've encountered many areas where choices are necessary. For example, management must choose whether to use accelerated or straight-line depreciation. Is FIFO, LIFO, or average cost most appropriate to measure inventories? Would the completed contract or percentage-of-completion method best reflect the performance of our construction operations? Should we adopt a new FASB standard early or wait until it's mandatory? These are but a few of the accounting choices management makes.

You also probably recall that consistency and comparability are two fundamental qualitative characteristics of accounting information. To achieve these attributes of information, accounting choices, once made, should be consistently followed from year to year. This doesn't mean, though, that methods can never be changed. Changing circumstances might make a new method more appropriate. A change in economic conditions, for instance, might prompt a company to change accounting methods. The most extensive voluntary accounting change ever—a switch by hundreds of companies from FIFO to LIFO in the mid-1970s, for example—was a result of heightened inflation. Changes within a specific industry, too, can lead a

Although consistency and comparability are desirable, changing to a new method sometimes is appropriate.

company to switch methods, often to adapt to new technology or to be consistent with others in the industry. And, of course, a change might be mandated. This happens when the FASB issues a new accounting standard. In 1993, all firms were required to switch from accounting for income taxes according to *APB 11*[2] to the method prescribed by *SFAS 109*. For these reasons, it's not uncommon for a company to switch from one accounting method to another. This is called a **change in accounting principle.**

## DECISION MAKERS' PERSPECTIVE—Motivation for Accounting Choices

It would be nice to think that all accounting choices are made by management in the best interest of fair and consistent financial reporting. Unfortunately, other motives influence the choices among accounting methods and whether to change methods. It has been suggested that the effect of choices on management compensation, on existing debt agreements, and on union negotiations each can affect management's selection of accounting methods.[3] For instance, research has suggested that managers of companies with bonus plans are more likely to choose accounting methods that maximize their bonuses (often those that increase net income).[4] Other research has indicated that the existence and nature of debt agreements and other aspects of a firm's capital structure can influence accounting choices.[5] Whether a company is forbidden from paying dividends if retained earnings fall below a certain level, for example, can affect the choice of accounting methods.

A financial analyst must be aware that different accounting methods used by different firms and by the same firm in different years complicate comparisons. Financial ratios, for example, will differ when different accounting methods are used, even when there are no differences in attributes being compared.

Investors and creditors also should be alert to instances in which companies change accounting methods. They must consider not only the effect on comparability but also possible hidden motivations for making the changes. Are managers trying to compensate for a downturn in actual performance with a switch to methods that artificially inflate reported earnings? Is the firm in danger of violating debt covenants or other contractual agreements regarding financial position? Are executive compensation plans tied to reported performance measures? Fortunately, the nature and effect of changes are reported in the financial statements. Although a justification for a change is provided by management, analysts should be wary of accepting the reported justification at face value without considering a possible hidden agenda.

Choices are not always those that tend to increase income. As you learned in Chapter 8, many companies use the LIFO inventory method because it reduces income and therefore reduces the amount of income taxes that must be paid currently. Also, some very large and visible companies might be reluctant to report high income that might render them vulnerable to union demands, government regulations, or higher taxes.[6]

Another reason managers sometimes choose accounting methods that don't necessarily increase earnings was mentioned earlier. Most managers tend to prefer to report earnings that follow a regular, smooth trend from year to year. The desire to "smooth" earnings means that any attempt to manipulate earnings by choosing accounting methods is not always in the direction of higher income. Instead, the choice might be to avoid irregular earnings, particularly those with wide variations from year to year, a pattern that might be interpreted by analysts as denoting a risky situation.

---

[2] *SFAS 96* for those companies that voluntarily adopted that interim standard.

[3] R. L. Watts and J. L. Zimmerman, "Towards a Positive Theory of the Determination of Accounting Standards," *The Accounting Review,* January 1978, and "Positive Accounting Theory: A Ten Year Perspective," *The Accounting Review,* January 1990.

[4] For example, see P. M. Healy, "The Effect of Bonus Schemes on Accounting Decisions," *Journal of Accounting and Economics,* April 1985, and D. Dhaliwal, G. Salamon, and E. Smith, "The Effect of Owner versus Management Control on the Choice of Accounting Methods," *Journal of Accounting and Economics,* July 1992.

[5] R. M. Bowen, E. W. Noreen, and J. M. Lacy, "Determinants of the Corporate Decision to Capitalize Interest," *Journal of Accounting and Economics,* August 1981.

[6] This political cost motive is suggested by R. L. Watts and J. L. Zimmerman, "Positive Accounting Theory: A Ten Year Perspective," *The Accounting Review,* January 1990, and M. Zmijewski and R. Hagerman, "An Income Strategy Approach to the Positive Theory of Accounting Standard Setting/Choice," *Journal of Accounting and Economics,* August 1981.

Obviously, any time managers make accounting choices for any of the reasons discussed here, when the motivation is an objective other than to provide useful information, earnings quality suffers. As mentioned frequently throughout this text, earnings quality refers to the ability of reported earnings (income) to predict a company's future earnings.

Let's turn our attention now to situations involving changes in methods and how we account for those changes. ■

## THE RETROSPECTIVE APPROACH: MOST CHANGES IN ACCOUNTING PRINCIPLE

● LO2

We report most voluntary changes in accounting principles retrospectively.[7] This means reporting all previous period's financial statements as if the new method had been used in all prior periods. An example is provided in Illustration 20–1.

**ILLUSTRATION 20–1**
Change in Accounting Principle

Air Parts Corporation used the LIFO inventory costing method. At the beginning of 2006, Air Parts decided to change to the FIFO method. Income components for 2006 and prior years were as follows ($ in millions):

| | 2006 | 2005 | 2004 | Previous Years |
|---|---|---|---|---|
| Cost of goods sold (LIFO) | $430 | $420 | $405 | $2,000 |
| Cost of goods sold (FIFO) | 370 | 365 | 360 | 1,700 |
| Difference | $ 60 | $ 55 | $ 45 | $ 300 |
| Revenues | $950 | $900 | $875 | $4,500 |
| Operating expenses | 230 | 210 | 205 | 1,000 |

Air Parts has paid dividends of $40 million each year beginning in 1999. Its income tax rate is 40%. Retained earnings on January 1, 2004, was $700 million; inventory was $500 million.

LIFO usually produces higher cost of goods sold than does FIFO because more recently purchased goods (usually higher priced) are assumed sold first.

**FINANCIAL REPORTING CASE**

Q1, p. 1009

**1. Revise Comparative Financial Statements.** For each year reported in the comparative statements, Air Parts makes those statements appear as if the newly adopted accounting method (FIFO) had been applied all along. As you learned in Chapter 1, consistency is one of the important qualitative characteristics of accounting information. When accounting changes occur, the usefulness of the comparative financial statements is enhanced with retrospective application of those changes.

Income statements.

| ($ in millions) | 2006 | 2005 | 2004 |
|---|---|---|---|
| Revenues | $950 | $900 | $875 |
| Cost of goods sold (FIFO) | (370) | (365) | (360) |
| Operating expenses | (230) | (210) | (205) |
| Income before tax | $350 | $325 | $310 |
| Income tax expense (40%) | (140) | (130) | (124) |
| Net income | $210 | $195 | $186 |

The company recasts the comparative statements to appear as if the accounting method adopted in 2006 (FIFO) had been used in 2005 and 2004 as well.

Earnings per share each year, of course, also will be based on the revised net income numbers.

[7] "Accounting Changes and Error Corrections—A Replacement of APB Opinion No. 20 and FASB Statement No. 3," *Statement of Financial Accounting Standards No. 154*, (Norwalk, Conn.: FASB, 2005).

## Balance Sheets.

FIFO usually produces *lower* cost of goods sold and thus *higher* inventory than does LIFO.

*Inventory.* In its comparative balance sheets, Air Parts will report 2006 inventory by its newly adopted method, FIFO, and also will revise the amounts it reported last year for its 2005 and 2004 inventory. Each year, inventory will be higher than it would have been by LIFO. Here's why:

Since the cost of goods *available for sale* each period is the sum of the cost of goods *sold* and the cost of goods *unsold* (inventory), a difference in cost of goods sold resulting from having used LIFO rather than FIFO means there also is an opposite difference in inventory. Because cost of goods sold by the FIFO method is *less* than by LIFO, inventory by FIFO is *greater* than by LIFO. The amounts of the differences and also the cumulative differences over the years are calculated in Illustration 20–1A.

**ILLUSTRATION 20–1A**

Effects of Switch to FIFO

By FIFO, cost of goods sold is lower.

The cumulative income effect increases each year by the annual after-tax difference in COGS.

Inventory, pretax income, income taxes, net income, and retained earnings all are higher.

| | Years Ending Dec. 31: | | | |
|---|---|---|---|---|
| **($ in millions)** | **2006** | **2005** | **2004** | **Previous Years** |
| Cost of goods sold (LIFO) | $430 | $420 | $405 | $2,000 |
| Cost of goods sold (FIFO) | 370 | 365 | 360 | 1,700 |
| Differences | $ 60 | $ 55 | $ 45 | $ 300 |
| *Cumulative differences:* | | | | |
| Cost of goods sold | $460 | $400 | $345 | $ 300 |
| Income taxes (40%) | 184 | 160 | 138 | 120 |
| Net income and retained earnings | $276 | $240 | $207 | $ 180 |

Comparative balance sheets, then, will report 2004 inventory $345 million higher than it was reported in last year's statements. Likewise, 2005 inventory will be increased by $400 million. Inventory for 2006, being reported for the first time, is $460 million higher than it would have been if the switch from LIFO had not occurred.

When costs are rising, FIFO produces *lower* cost of goods sold than does LIFO and thus *higher* net income and retained earnings.

Retained earnings is revised each year to reflect FIFO.

*Retained earnings.* Similarly, Air Parts will report retained earnings by FIFO each year as well. Retained earnings is different because the two inventory methods affect income differently. Because cost of goods sold by FIFO is *less* than by LIFO, income and therefore retained earnings by FIFO are *greater* than by LIFO.

Comparative balance sheets, then, will report retained earnings for 2006, 2005, and 2004 at amounts $276, $240, and $207 million higher than would have been reported if the switch from LIFO had not occurred. These are the cumulative net income differences shown in Illustration 20–1A.

## Statements of shareholders' equity.

Because it's the earliest year reported, 2004's beginning retained earnings is increased by the **$180** million cumulative income effect of the difference in inventory methods that occurred before 2004.

Recall that a statement of shareholders' equity reports changes that occur in each shareholders' equity account starting with the beginning balances in the earliest year reported. So, if retained earnings is one of the accounts whose balance requires adjustment due to a change in accounting principle (and it usually is), we must adjust the beginning balance of retained earnings for the earliest period reported in the comparative statements of shareholders' equity. The amount of the revision is the cumulative effect of the change on years prior to that date. Air Parts will revise its 2004 beginning retained earnings since that's the earliest year in its comparative statements. That balance had been reported in prior statements as $700 million. If FIFO had been used for inventory rather than LIFO, that amount would have been higher by **$180** million as calculated in Illustration 20–1B. The disclosure note pertaining to the inventory change should point out the amount of the adjustment. The January 1, 2004, retained earnings balance reported in the comparative statements of shareholders' equity below has been adjusted from $700 million to **$880** million.

| ($ in millions) | Common Stock | Additional Paid-In Capital | Retained Earnings | Total Shareholders' Equity |
|---|---|---|---|---|
| Jan. 1, 2004 | | | $ 880 | |
| Net income (revised to FIFO) | | | 186 | |
| Dividends | | | (40) | |
| Dec. 31, 2004 | | | $1,026 | |
| Net income (revised to FIFO) | | | 195 | |
| Dividends | | | (40) | |
| Dec. 31, 2005 | | | $1,181 | |
| Net income (using FIFO) | | | 210 | |
| Dividends | | | (40) | |
| Dec. 31, 2006 | | | $1,351 | |

**ILLUSTRATION 20–1B**
Comparative Statements of Shareholders' Equity

A footnote should indicate that the beginning retained earnings balance has been increased by $180 million from $700 million to $880 million.

**2. Adjust Accounts for the Change.** Besides reporting revised amounts in the comparative financial statements, Air Parts must also adjust the book balances of affected accounts. It does so by creating a journal entry to change those balances from their current amounts (from using LIFO) to what those balances would have been using the newly adopted method (FIFO). As discussed in the previous section, differences in cost of goods sold and income are reflected in retained earnings, as are the income tax effects of changes in income. So, the journal entry updates inventory, retained earnings, and the income tax liability for revisions resulting from differences in the LIFO and FIFO methods prior to the switch, pre-2006. Repeating a portion of the calculation we made in Illustration 20–1A, we determine the difference in cost of goods sold and therefore in inventory.

($ in millions)

| | 2005 | 2004 | Cumulative Difference pre-2004 | Cumulative Difference pre-2006 |
|---|---|---|---|---|
| Cost of goods sold (LIFO) . . . . . . . | $420 | $405 | $1,000 | |
| Cost of goods sold (FIFO) . . . . . . . | 365 | 360 | 700 | |
| Difference . . . . . . . . . . . . . . . . . . | $ 55 | $ 45 | $ 300 | $400 |

Cost of goods sold would have been $400 million *less* if FIFO rather than LIFO had been used in years before the change.

The $400 million cumulative difference in cost of goods sold also is the difference between the balance in inventory and what that balance would have been if the FIFO method, rather than LIFO, had been used before 2006. Inventory must be increased by that amount. Retained earnings must be increased also, but by only 60% of that amount because income taxes would have been higher by 40% of the change in pretax income.

**Journal entry to record the change in principle.**

| | | |
|---|---|---|
| **January 1, 2006** | | |
| Inventory (additional inventory if FIFO had been used) . . . . . . . . . | 400 | |
| Retained earnings (additional net income if FIFO had been used) . . . . . . . . . . . . . . . . . . . . . . . . . . . . . . | | 240 |
| Deferred tax liability ($400 × 40%) . . . . . . . . . . . . . . . . . . . . . | | 160 |

Inventory would have been $400 million more and cumulative prior earnings $240 more if FIFO rather than LIFO had been used.

Notice that the income tax effect is reflected in the deferred income tax liability. The reason is that an accounting method used for tax purposes cannot be changed retrospectively for prior years. The Internal Revenue Code requires that taxes saved previously ($160 million in this case) from having used another inventory method must now be repaid (over no longer than six years). Recall from Chapter 16 that in the meantime, there is a temporary difference, reflected in the deferred tax liability.

**ADDITIONAL CONSIDERATION**

What if the tax law did not require a recapture of the tax difference? There still would be a credit to the deferred tax liability. That's because retrospectively increasing accounting income, but not taxable income, creates a temporary difference between the two that will reverse over time as the unsold inventory becomes cost of goods sold. When that happens, taxable income will become higher than accounting income—a future taxable amount, creating a deferred tax liability.

If we were switching *from* FIFO to, say, the average method, we would record a deferred tax asset instead. For financial reporting purposes, but not for tax, we would be retrospectively *decreasing* accounting income, but not taxable income. This creates a temporary difference between the two that will reverse over time as the unsold inventory becomes cost of goods sold. When that happens, taxable income will be less than accounting income. When taxable income will be less than accounting income as a temporary difference reverses, we have a "future deductible amount" and record a deferred tax asset.

Footnote disclosure explains why the change was needed as well as its effects on items not reported on the face of the primary statements.

**3. Disclosure Notes.** To achieve consistency and comparability, accounting choices once made should be consistently followed from year to year. Any change, then, requires that the new method be justified as clearly more appropriate. In the first set of financial statements after the change, a disclosure note is needed to provide that justification. The note also should point out that comparative information has been revised, or that retrospective revision has not been made because it is impracticable, and report any per share amounts affected for the current period and all prior periods presented. Disclosure of a recent change by **Milacron, Inc.** in its 2006 annual report provides us the example shown in Graphic 20–3.

**GRAPHIC 20–3**

Disclosure of a change in inventory method—Milacron, Inc.

**Change in Method of Accounting**

In the fourth quarter of 2004, Milacron changed its valuation method for certain inventories in its North American machinery technologies segment. Those operations previously using the "last in, first out" (LIFO) method were changed to the "first in, first out" (FIFO) method, retroactive to the beginning of the year. The FIFO method is considered preferable because it results in a balance sheet presentation more reflective of current costs and, as a result of the change, all Milacron operations now use FIFO. This change in method of accounting had no impact on 2004 earnings, but prior periods have been restated for consistency.

## THE PROSPECTIVE APPROACH

Although we usually report voluntary changes in accounting principles retrospectively, it's not always practicable or appropriate to do so.

● LO3

Sometimes a lack of information makes it impracticable to report a change retrospectively so the new method is simply applied prospectively.

**The Prospective Approach: When Retrospective Application Is Impracticable.** For some changes in principle, insufficient information is available for retrospective application to be practicable. Revising balances in prior years means knowing what those balances should be. But suppose we're switching from the FIFO method of inventory costing to the LIFO method. Recall from your study of inventory costing methods that LIFO inventory consists of "layers" added in prior years at costs existing in those years. If another method has been used, though, the company likely hasn't kept track of those costs. So, accounting records of prior years usually are inadequate to report the change retrospectively. In that case, a company changing to LIFO usually reports the change prospectively, and the beginning inventory in the year the LIFO method is adopted becomes the base year inventory for all future LIFO calculations. Footnote disclosure should indicate reasons why retrospective application was impracticable.

When the **Books A Million, Inc.** adopted the LIFO cost flow assumption for valuing its inventories, the change was reported in its 2004 annual report as shown in Graphic 20–4.

**Inventories (in part)**
Effective February 2, 2003, the Company changed from the first-in, first-out (FIFO) method of accounting for inventories to the last-in, first-out (LIFO) method. Management believes this change was preferable in that it achieves a more appropriate matching of revenues and expenses. The impact of this accounting change was to increase "Costs of Products Sold" in the consolidated statements of operations by $0.7 million for the fiscal year ended January 31, 2004. This resulted in an after-tax decrease to fiscal 2004 net income of $0.4 million or a decrease in net income per diluted share of $0.02. The cumulative effect of a change in accounting principle from the FIFO method to LIFO method is not determinable. Accordingly, such change has been accounted for prospectively.

**GRAPHIC 20–4**
Disclosure of a Change to LIFO— Books A Million, Inc.

**When it is impracticable to determine some period-specific effects.** A company may have some, but not all, the information it needs to account for a change retrospectively. For instance, let's say a company changes to the LIFO inventory method effective as of the beginning of 2006. It has information that would allow it to revise all assets and liabilities on the basis of the newly adopted method for 2005 in its comparative statements, but not for 2004. In that case, the company should report 2005 statement amounts (revised) and 2006 statement amounts (reported for the first time) based on LIFO, but not revise 2004 numbers. Then, account balances should be retrospectively adjusted at the beginning of 2005 since that's the earliest date it's practicable to do so.

*If it's impracticable to adjust each year reported, the change is applied retrospectively as of the earliest year practicable.*

**When it is impracticable to determine the cumulative effect of prior years.** Another possibility is that the company doesn't have the information necessary to retrospectively adjust retained earnings, but does have information that would allow it to revise all assets and liabilities for one or more specific years. Let's say the records of inventory purchases and sales are not available for some previous years, which would have allowed it to determine the cumulative effect of applying this change to LIFO retrospectively. However, it does have all of the information necessary to apply the LIFO method on a prospective basis beginning in, say, 2004. In that case, the company should report numbers for years beginning in 2004 as if it had carried forward the 2003 ending balance in inventory (measured on the previous inventory costing basis) and then had begun applying LIFO as of January 1, 2004. Of course there would be no adjustment to retained earnings for the cumulative income effect of not using LIFO prior to that.

*If full retrospective application isn't possible, the new method is applied prospectively beginning in the earliest year practicable.*

**The Prospective Approach: When Mandated by Authoritative Pronouncements.** Another exception to retrospective application of voluntary changes in accounting principle is when an FASB Statement or another authoritative pronouncement requires prospective application for specific changes in accounting methods. For instance, for a change from the equity method to another method of accounting for long-term investments, *APB Opinion 18* requires the prospective application of the new method.[8] Recall from Chapter 12 that when an investor's level of influence changes, it may be necessary to change from the equity method to another method. This could happen, for instance, if a sale of shares causes the investor's ownership interest to fall from, say, 25% to 15%, resulting in the equity method no longer being appropriate. When this situation happens, no adjustment is made to the remaining carrying amount of the investment. Instead, the equity method is simply discontinued and the new method applied from then on. The balance in the investment account when the equity method is discontinued would serve as the new "cost" basis for writing the investment up or down to fair value on the next set of financial statements.

*If an authoritative pronouncement specifically requires prospective accounting, that requirement is followed.*

[8]"Reporting Accounting Changes in Interim Financial Statements," *Accounting Principles Board Opinion No. 18* (New York: AICPA, 1971).

**GLOBAL PERSPECTIVE**

A joint goal of the FASB and the International Accounting Standards Board is to increase convergence of U.S. and international financial reporting standards. Requiring retrospective application of changes in accounting principle is an example of adapting U.S. GAAP to achieve uniformity in this area. Prior to 2004, the practice in the U.S. was to present prior financial statements as previously reported and to report the cumulative effect of a change in accounting principle as a line item in the income statement of the change year.

We account for a change in depreciation method as a change in accounting estimate.

**The Prospective Approach: Changing Depreciation, Amortization, and Depletion Methods.** A change in depreciation methods is considered to be a change in accounting estimate that is achieved by a change in accounting principle. As a result, we account for such a change prospectively—precisely the way we account for changes in estimates. We discuss that approach in the next section.

## Change in Accounting Estimate

● LO4

You've encountered many instances during your study of accounting in which it's necessary to make estimates of uncertain future events. Depreciation, for example, entails estimates not only of the useful lives of depreciable assets, but their anticipated residual values as well. Anticipating uncollectible accounts receivable, predicting warranty expenses, amortizing intangible assets, and making actuarial assumptions for pension benefits are but a few of the accounting tasks that require estimates.

Revisions are viewed as a natural consequence of making estimates.

Accordingly, estimates are an inherent aspect of accounting. Unfortunately, though, estimates routinely turn out to be wrong. No matter how carefully known facts are considered and forecasts are prepared, new information and experience frequently force the revision of estimates. Of course, if the original estimate was based on erroneous information or calculations or was not made in good faith, the revision of that estimate constitutes the correction of an error.

A change in estimate is reflected in the financial statements of the current period and future periods.

**Changes in accounting estimates** are accounted for prospectively. When a company revises a previous estimate, prior financial statements are *not* revised. Instead, the company merely incorporates the new estimate in any related accounting determinations from then on. So, it usually will affect some aspects of both the balance sheet and the income statement in the current period and future periods. A disclosure note should describe the effect of a change in estimate on income before extraordinary items, net income, and related per share amounts for the current period.

When **Owens-Corning Fiberglass** revised estimates of the useful lives of some of its depreciable assets, the change was disclosed in its annual report as shown in Graphic 20–5.

**GRAPHIC 20–5**
Change in Estimate—Owens-Corning Fiberglass Corporation

**Note 6: Depreciation of Plant and Equipment (in part)**
. . . the Company completed a review of its fixed asset lives. The Company determined that as a result of actions taken to increase its preventative maintenance and programs initiated with its equipment suppliers to increase the quality of their products, actual lives for certain asset categories were generally longer than the useful lives for depreciation purposes. Therefore, the Company extended the estimated useful lives of certain categories of plant and equipment, effective . . . The effect of this change in estimate reduced depreciation expense for the year ended . . . , by $14 million and increased income before cumulative effect of accounting change by $8 million ($.19 per share).

An example of another change in estimate is provided in Illustration 20–2.

**ILLUSTRATION 20–2**
Change in Accounting Estimate

Universal Semiconductors estimates bad debt expense as 2% of credit sales. After a review during 2006, Universal determined that 3% of credit sales is a more realistic estimate of its collection experience. Credit sales in 2006 are $300 million. The effective income tax rate is 40%.

Neither bad debt expense nor the allowance for uncollectible accounts reported in prior years is restated. No account balances are adjusted. The cumulative effect of the estimate change is not reported in current income. Rather, in 2006 and later years, the adjusting entry to record bad debt expense simply will reflect the new percentage. In 2006, the entry would be:

| | ($ in millions) | |
|---|---|---|
| Bad debt expense (3% × $300 million) . . . . . . . . . . . . . . . . . . . . . . . | 9 | |
| Allowance for uncollectible accounts . . . . . . . . . . . . . . . . . . . . . . | | 9 |

The after-tax effect of the change in estimate is $1.8 million [$300 million × (3% − 2%) = $3 million, less 40% of $3 million]. Assuming 100 million outstanding shares of common stock, the effect is described in a disclosure note to the financial statements as follows:

**Note A: Accounts Receivable**
In 2006, the company revised the percentage used to estimate bad debts. The change provides a better indication of collection experience. The effect of the change was to decrease 2006 net income by $1.8 million, or $.018 per share.

## CHANGING DEPRECIATION, AMORTIZATION, AND DEPLETION METHODS

**FINANCIAL REPORTING CASE**

Q2, p. 1009

When a company acquires an asset that will provide benefits for several years, it allocates the cost of the asset over the asset's useful life. If the asset is a building, equipment, or other tangible operational asset, the allocation process is called *depreciation.* It's referred to as *amortization* if an intangible asset or *depletion* if a natural resource. In each case, estimates are essential to the allocation process. How long will benefits accrue? What will be the value of the asset when its use is discontinued? Will the benefits be realized evenly over the asset's life or will they be higher in some years than in others?

An exception to retrospective application of a change in accounting principle is a change in the method of depreciation (or amortization or depletion).

The choice of depreciation method and application reflects these estimates. Likewise, when a company changes the way it depreciates an asset in midstream, the change would be made to reflect a change in (a) estimated future benefits from the asset, (b) the pattern of receiving those benefits, or (c) the company's knowledge about those benefits. For instance, suppose Universal Semiconductors originally chose an accelerated depreciation method because it expected greater benefits in the earlier years of an asset's life. Then, two years later, when it became apparent that remaining benefits would be realized approximately evenly over the remaining useful life, Universal Semiconductor switched to straight-line depreciation. Even though the company is changing its depreciation method, it is doing so to reflect changes in its estimates of future benefits. As a result, we report a change in depreciation method as a change in estimate, rather than as a change in accounting principle.

Companies report a change in depreciation prospectively.

For this reason, a company reports a change in depreciation method (say to straight line) prospectively; previous financial statements are not revised. Instead, the company simply employs the straight-line method from then on. The undepreciated cost remaining at the time of the change would be depreciated straight-line over the remaining useful life. Illustration 20–3 on the next page provides an example.

A company must justify any change in principle as preferable to the previous method.

Is a change in depreciation method a change in accounting principle, or is it a change in estimate? As we've seen, it's both. Even though it's considered to reflect a change in estimate and is accounted for as such, a change to a new depreciation method requires the company to justify the new method as being preferable to the previous method, just as for any

**ILLUSTRATION 20–3**
Change in depreciation methods

Universal Semiconductors switched from the SYD depreciation method to straight-line depreciation in 2006. The change affects its precision equipment purchased at the beginning of 2004 at a cost of $63 million. The machinery has an expected useful life of five years and an estimated residual value of $3 million.

The depreciation prior to the change is as follows ($ in millions):

| **Sum-of-the-Years'-Digits Depreciation:** | |
|---|---|
| 2004 depreciation | $20 ($60 × 5/15) |
| 2005 depreciation | 16 ($60 × 4/15) |
| Accumulated depreciation | $36 |

A change in depreciation method is considered a change in accounting estimate resulting from a change in accounting principle. So, Universal Semiconductors reports the change prospectively; previous financial statements are not revised. Instead, the company simply employs the straight-line method from 2006 on. The undepreciated cost remaining at the time of the change is depreciated straight-line over the remaining useful life.

The $24 million depreciable cost not yet depreciated is spread over the asset's remaining three years.

| **Calculation of Straight-Line Depreciation:** | ($ in millions) |
|---|---|
| Asset's cost | $63 |
| Accumulated depreciation to date (calculated above) | (36) |
| Undepreciated cost, Jan. 1, 2006 | $27 |
| Estimated residual value | (3) |
| To be depreciated over remaining 3 years | $24 |
| | 3 years |
| Annual straight-line depreciation 2006–2008 | $ 8 |

| **Adjusting entry (2006, 2007, and 2008 depreciation):** | ($ in millions) | |
|---|---|---|
| Depreciation expense (calculated above) | 8 | |
| Accumulated depreciation | | 8 |

other change in principle. A disclosure note should justify that the change is preferable and describe the effect of a change on any financial statement line items and per share amounts affected for all periods reported.

In practice, the situation arises infrequently. Most companies changing depreciation methods do not apply the change to existing assets, but instead to assets placed in service after that date. In those cases, of course, the new method is simply applied prospectively (see Graphic 20–6).

**GRAPHIC 20–6**
Change in depreciation method for newly acquired assets—Rohm and Haas Company

**Note 12: Land, Buildings, and Equipment, Net (in part)**
. . . the company changed its method of depreciation for newly acquired buildings and equipment to the straight-line method. The change had no cumulative effect on prior years' earnings but did increase [current year] net earnings by $9 million, or $.14 per share . . .

When it's not possible to distinguish between a change in principle and a change in estimate, the change should be treated as a change in estimate.

Sometimes, it's not easy to distinguish between a change in principle and a change in estimate. For example, if a company begins to capitalize rather than expense the cost of tools because their benefits beyond one year become apparent, the change could be construed as either a change in principle or a change in the estimated life of the asset. When the distinction is not possible, the change should be treated as a change in estimate. This treatment also is appropriate when both a change in principle and a change in estimate occur simultaneously.

## Change in Reporting Entity

● LO5

A reporting entity can be a single company, or it can be a group of companies that reports a single set of financial statements. For example, the consolidated financial statements of

**Philip Morris Cos., Inc.** report the financial position and results of operations not only for the parent tobacco company but also for its subsidiaries which include **Kraft Foods** and **Miller Brewing Company**. Sometimes, changes occur that cause the financial statements to be those of a different reporting entity. The issuance of *SFAS 94,* "Consolidation of All Majority-Owned Subsidiaries," resulted in hundreds of reporting entities being altered to include previously unconsolidated finance subsidiaries. For instance, **General Motors**' consolidated financial statements now include its finance subsidiary, **GMAC**, as part of the reporting entity. A **change in reporting entity** occurs as a result of (1) presenting consolidated financial statements in place of statements of individual companies or (2) changing specific companies that constitute the group for which consolidated or combined statements are prepared.[9]

**The issuance of *SFAS 94* resulted in many companies consolidating previously unconsolidated subsidiaries.**

A change in reporting entity is reported by recasting all previous periods' financial statements as if the new reporting entity existed in those periods.[10] In the first set of financial statements after the change, a disclosure note should describe the nature of the change and the reason it occurred. Also, the effect of the change on net income, income before extraordinary items, and related per share amounts should be indicated for all periods presented. These disclosures aren't necessary in subsequent financial statements. **Hewlett-Packard Company** changed the composition of its reporting entity in response to *SFAS 94* and described it this way:

**A change in reporting entity requires that financial statements of prior periods be retrospectively revised to report the financial information for the new reporting entity in all periods.**

**Note 12: Accounting and Reporting Changes (in part)**
The Company implemented *Statement of Financial Accounting Standards No. 94 (SFAS 94),* "Consolidation of All Majority-Owned Subsidiaries," in fiscal 1989. With the adoption of *SFAS 94,* the company consolidated the accounts of Hewlett-Packard Finance Company (HPFC), a wholly-owned subsidiary previously accounted for under the equity method, with those of the company. The change resulted in an increase in consolidated assets and liabilities but did not have a material effect on the company's financial position. Since HPFC was previously accounted for under the equity method, the change did not affect net earnings. Prior years' consolidated financial information has been restated to reflect this change for comparative purposes.

**GRAPHIC 20–7**
Change in Reporting Entity—Hewlett-Packard Company

## Error Correction

The correction of an error is not actually an accounting change but is accounted for similarly. In fact, it's accounted for retrospectively like a change in reporting entity and like most changes in accounting principle.

More specifically, previous years' financial statements that were incorrect as a result of the error are retrospectively restated to reflect the correction. And, of course, any account balances that are incorrect as a result of the error are corrected by a journal entry. If retained earnings is one of the incorrect accounts, the correction is reported as a prior period adjustment to the beginning balance in a statement of shareholders' equity (or statement of retained earnings if that's presented instead).[11] And, as for accounting changes, a disclosure note is needed to describe the nature of the error and the impact of its correction on operations. We discuss the correction of errors in more detail in Part B of this chapter. But first, let's compare the two approaches for reporting accounting changes and error corrections (Graphic 20–8).

**Previous years' financial statements are retrospectively restated to reflect the correction of an error.**

---

[9] "Consolidation of All Majority-Owned Subsidiaries," *Statement of Financial Accounting Standards No. 94* (Stamford, Conn.: FASB, 1987).

[10] Any prior periods' statements are recast when those statements are presented again for comparative purposes.

[11] "Prior Period Adjustments," *Statement of Financial Accounting Standards No. 16* (Stamford, CT: FASB, 1977).

**GRAPHIC 20–8**

Approaches to Reporting Accounting Changes and Error Corrections

| Previous Years | Current Year | Later Years |
|---|---|---|

← Retrospective

(most changes in accounting principle)

(change in reporting entity)

(corrections of errors)

Prospective →

(changes in estimate including changes in depreciation)

(changes in accounting principle when retrospective application is impractical)

(changes in accounting principle when prospective application is mandated)

A comparison of accounting treatments is provided by Graphic 20–9.

**GRAPHIC 20–9** Accounting Changes and Errors: A Summary

| | Change in Accounting Principle | | Change in Estimate (including depreciation changes) | Change in Reporting Entity | Error |
|---|---|---|---|---|---|
| | Most Changes* | Exceptions† | | | |
| Method of accounting | Retrospective | Prospective | Prospective | Retrospective | Retrospective |
| • Revise prior years' statements? | Yes | No | No | Yes | Yes |
| • Cumulative effect on prior years' income reported: | As adjustment to retained earnings of earliest year reported.‡ | Not reported. | Not reported. | Not reported. | As adjustment to retained earnings of earliest year reported.‡ |
| • Journal entry | To adjust affected balances to new method. | None, but subsequent accounting is affected by the change. | None, but subsequent accounting is affected by the new estimate. | Involves consolidated financial statements discussed in other courses. | To correct any balances that are incorrect as a result of the error. |
| • Disclosure note? | Yes | Yes | Yes | Yes | Yes |

*Changes in depreciation, amortization, and depletion methods are considered changes in estimates.
†When retrospective application is impracticable such as most changes to LIFO and certain mandated changes.
‡On the statement of shareholders' equity or statement of retained earnings.

# CONCEPT REVIEW EXERCISE

## ACCOUNTING CHANGES

Modern Business Machines recently conducted an extensive review of its accounting and reporting policies. The following accounting changes are an outgrowth of that review:

1. MBM has a patent on a copier design. The patent has been amortized on a straight-line basis since it was acquired at a cost of $400,000 in 2003. During 2006, it was decided that the benefits from the patent would be experienced over a total of 13 years rather than the 20-year legal life now being used to amortize its cost.
2. At the beginning of 2006, MBM changed its method of valuing inventory from the FIFO cost method to the average cost method. At December 31, 2005 and 2004, MBM's inventories were $560 and $540 million, respectively, on a FIFO cost basis but would have totaled $500 and $490 million, respectively, if determined on an average cost basis. MBM's income tax rate is 40%.

**Required:**

Prepare all journal entries needed in 2006 related to each change. Also, briefly describe any other measures MBM would take in connection with reporting the changes.

**SOLUTION**

1. Change in estimate

| | ($ in 000s) | |
|---|---|---|
| Patent amortization expense (determined below) | 34 | |
| Patent | | 34 |

**Calculation of Annual Amortization after the Estimate Change**

| | | |
|---|---|---|
| | $400,000 | Cost |
| $20,000 | | Old annual amortization ($400,000 ÷ 20 years) |
| × 3 years | (60,000) | Amortization to date (2003, 2004, 2005) |
| | 340,000 | Unamortized cost |
| | ÷ 10 | Estimated remaining life (13 years − 3 years) |
| | $ 34,000 | New annual amortization |

A disclosure note should describe the effect of a change in estimate on income before extraordinary items, net income, and related per-share amounts for the current period.

2. Change in principle

MBM creates a journal entry to bring up to date all account balances affected.

| | ($ in millions) | |
|---|---|---|
| Retained earnings (The difference in net income before 2005) | 36 | |
| Deferred tax asset ($60 million × 40%) | 24 | |
| Inventory ($560 million − $500 million) | | 60 |

For financial reporting purposes, but not for tax, MBM is retrospectively *decreasing* accounting income, but not taxable income. This creates a temporary difference between the two that will reverse over time as the unsold inventory becomes cost of goods sold. When that happens, taxable income will be less than accounting income. When taxable income will be less than accounting income as a temporary difference reverses, we have a "future deductible amount" and record a deferred tax asset.

**Prior years' financial statements are revised to reflect the use of the new accounting method.**

Also, MBM will revise all previous period's financial statements (in this case 2005) as if the new method (average cost) were used in those periods. In other words, for each year in the comparative statements reported, the balance of each account affected will be revised to appear as if the average method had been applied all along.

**Since it's the earliest year reported, 2005's beginning retained earnings is adjusted for the portion of the cumulative income effect of the change attributable to prior years.**

Since retained earnings is one of the accounts whose balance requires adjustment (and it usually is), MBM makes an adjustment to the beginning balance of retained earnings for the earliest period (2005) reported in the comparative statements of shareholders' equity. Also, in the first set of financial statements after the change, a *disclosure note* describes the nature of the change, justifies management's decision to make the change, and indicates its effect on each item affected in the financial statements.

## CORRECTION OF ACCOUNTING ERRORS

**PART B**

● LO6

Nobody's perfect. People make mistakes, even accountants. When errors are discovered, they should be corrected.[12] Graphic 20–10 describes the steps to be taken to correct an error, if the effect of the error is material.[13]

[12]Interestingly, it appears that not all accounting errors are unintentional. Research has shown that firms with errors that overstate income are more likely "to have diffuse ownership, lower growth in earnings and fewer income-increasing GAAP alternatives available, and are less likely to have audit committees," suggesting that "overstatement errors are the result of managers responding to economic incentives." M. L. DeFond and J. Jiambaolvo, "Incidence and Circumstances of Accounting Errors," *The Accounting Review,* July, 1991.

[13]In practice, the vast majority of errors are not material with respect to their effect on the financial statements and are, therefore, simply corrected in the year discovered (step 1 only).

**GRAPHIC 20–10**

Steps to Correct an Error

The retrospective approach is used for the correction of errors.

The correction of an error is treated as a prior period adjustment.

1. A journal entry is made to correct any account balances that are incorrect as a result of the error.
2. Previous years' financial statements that were incorrect as a result of the error are retrospectively restated to reflect the correction (for all years reported for comparative purposes).
3. If retained earnings is one of the accounts incorrect as a result of the error, the correction is reported as a prior period adjustment to the beginning balance in a statement of shareholders' equity (or statement of retained earnings if that's presented instead).
4. A disclosure note should describe the nature of the error and the impact of its correction on net income.

## Prior Period Adjustments

Before we see these steps applied to the **correction of an error**, one of the steps requires elaboration. As discussed in Chapter 4, the correction of errors is the more common of only two situations that are considered to be prior period adjustments.[14] A **prior period adjustment** refers to an addition to or reduction in the beginning retained earnings balance in a statement of shareholders' equity (or statement of retained earnings if that's presented instead).

In an earlier chapter we saw that a statement of shareholders' equity is the most commonly used way to report the events that cause components of shareholders' equity to change during a particular reporting period. Some companies, though, choose to report the changes that occur in the balance of retained earnings separately in a statement of retained earnings. When it's discovered that the ending balance of retained earnings in the period prior to the discovery of an error was incorrect as a result of that error, the balance must be corrected when it appears as the beginning balance the following year. However, simply reporting a corrected amount might cause misunderstanding for someone familiar with the previously reported amount. Explicitly reporting a prior period adjustment on the statement itself avoids this confusion. Assume, for example, the following comparative statements of retained earnings:

A statement of retained earnings reports the events that cause changes in retained earnings.

**STATEMENTS OF RETAINED EARNINGS**
**For the Years Ended December 31, 2005 and 2004**

| | 2005 | 2004 |
|---|---|---|
| **Balance at beginning of year** | $600,000 | $450,000 |
| Net income | 400,000 | 350,000 |
| Less: Dividends | (200,000) | (200,000) |
| **Balance at end of year** | $800,000 | $600,000 |

Now suppose that in 2006 it's discovered that an error in 2004 caused that year's net income to be overstated by $20,000 (it should have been $330,000). This means retained earnings both years were overstated. Comparative statements the following year, when the error is discovered, would include a prior period adjustment as shown below:

The incorrect balance as previously reported is corrected by the prior period adjustment.

**STATEMENTS OF RETAINED EARNINGS**
**For the Years Ended December 31, 2006 and 2005**

| | 2006 | 2005 |
|---|---|---|
| **Balance at beginning of year** | $ 780,000 | $600,000 |
| Prior period adjustment | | (20,000) |
| Corrected balance | | $580,000 |
| Net Income | 500,000 | 400,000 |
| Less: Dividends | (200,000) | (200,000) |
| **Balance at end of year** | $1,080,000 | $780,000 |

[14]The other is an adjustment that results from the realization of income tax benefits of preacquisition operating loss carryforwards of purchased subsidiaries. See "Prior Period Adjustments," *Statement of Financial Accounting Standards No. 16* (Stamford, Conn.: FASB, 1977). This situation arises in connection with consolidation which is covered in many advanced accounting courses.

At least two years' (as in our example) and often three years' statements are reported in comparative financial statements. The prior period adjustment is applied to beginning retained earnings for the year following the error, or for the earliest year being reported in the comparative financial statements when the error occurs prior to the earliest year presented.[15]

## Error Correction Illustrated

Now, let's discuss these procedures to correct errors in the context of a variety of the most common types of errors. Since there are literally thousands of possibilities, it's not practical to describe every error in every stage of its discovery. However, by applying the process to the situations described below, you should become sufficiently comfortable with the *process* that you could apply it to whatever situation you might encounter.

As you study these examples, be sure to notice that it's significantly more complicated to deal with an error if (a) it affected net income in the reporting period in which it occurred and (b) it is not discovered until a later period.

**You shouldn't try to memorize how specific errors are corrected; you should learn the *process* needed to analyze whatever errors you might encounter.**

### ERROR DISCOVERED IN THE SAME REPORTING PERIOD THAT IT OCCURRED

If an accounting error is made and discovered in the same accounting period, the original erroneous entry should simply be reversed and the appropriate entry recorded. The possibilities are limitless. Let's look at the one in Illustration 20–4.

G. H. Little, Inc. paid $3 million for replacement computers and recorded the expenditure as maintenance expense. The error was discovered a week later.

| | ($ in millions) | |
|---|---|---|
| **To Reverse Erroneous Entry** | | |
| Cash | 3 | |
| Maintenance expense | | 3 |
| **To Record Correct Entry** | | |
| Equipment | 3 | |
| Cash | | 3 |

**ILLUSTRATION 20–4**
Error Discovered in the Same Reporting Period That It Occurred

Note: These entries can, of course, be combined.

### ERROR AFFECTING PREVIOUS FINANCIAL STATEMENTS, BUT NOT NET INCOME

If an error did *not* affect net income in the year it occurred, it's relatively easy to correct. Examples are incorrectly recording salaries payable as accounts payable, recording a loss as an expense, or classifying a cash flow as an investing activity rather than a financing activity on the statement of cash flows. A 2005 restatement by **Kirklands, Inc.** reproduced in Graphic 20–11 provides an example. Illustration 20–5 provides another.

**Note 2 Restatement of Financial Statements (in part)**
On December 8, 2004, we determined that our accounting for tenant allowances received from landlords in connection with store construction did not comply with FASB Technical Bulletin No. 88-1, Issues Relating to Accounting for Leases (FTB 88-1). . . . Accordingly, we have restated our balance sheet as of January 31, 2004 and the statement of cash flows for the 39-week period ended November 1, 2003. Additionally, this adjustment results in an increase to depreciation and amortization expense and a corresponding decrease to cost of sales as the liability is amortized over the lease term. This change does not have any impact on net income, net sales or shareholders equity.

**GRAPHIC 20–11**
Error Correction; Kirkland's, Inc.

[15]The retained earnings balances in years after the first year also are adjusted to what those balances would be if the error had not occurred, but a company may choose not to explicitly report those adjustments as separate line items.

**ILLUSTRATION 20–5**
Error Affecting Previous Financial Statements, but Not Net Income

MDS Transportation incorrectly recorded a $2 million note receivable as accounts receivable. The error was discovered a year later.

**Step 1**

| To Correct Incorrect Accounts | ($ in millions) | |
|---|---|---|
| Note receivable | 2 | |
| Accounts receivable | | 2 |

**Step 2** When reported for comparative purposes in the current year's annual report, last year's balance sheet would be restated to report the note as it should have been reported last year.

**Step 3** Since last year's net income was not affected by the error, the balance in retained earnings was not incorrect. So no prior period adjustment to that account is necessary.

**Step 4** A disclosure note would describe the nature of the error, but there would be no impact on net income, income before extraordinary items, and earnings per share to report.

## ERROR AFFECTING A PRIOR YEAR'S NET INCOME

Most errors affect net income in some way. When they do, they affect the balance sheet as well. Both statements must be retrospectively restated; the statement of cash flows sometimes is affected, too. As with any error, all incorrect account balances must be corrected. Because these errors affect income, one of the balances that will require correcting is retained earnings. Complicating matters, income taxes often are affected by income errors. In those cases, amended tax returns are prepared either to pay additional taxes or to claim a tax refund for taxes overpaid.

In Illustration 20–6 (except as indicated), we ignore the tax effects of the errors and their correction to allow us to focus on the errors themselves rather than their tax aspects.

**ILLUSTRATION 20–6**
Error Affecting Net Income: Recording an Asset as an Expense

**Sometimes, the analysis is easier if you re-create the entries actually recorded incorrectly and those that would have been recorded if the error hadn't occurred and then compare them.**

In 2006, internal auditors discovered that Seidman Distribution, Inc. had debited an expense account for the $7 million cost of sorting equipment purchased at the beginning of 2004. The equipment's useful life was expected to be five years with no residual value. Straight-line depreciation is used by Seidman.

**Analysis:**

($ in millions)

| | Correct (Should have been recorded) | | | Incorrect (As recorded) | | |
|---|---|---|---|---|---|---|
| 2004 | Equipment | 7.0 | | Expense | 7.0 | |
| | Cash | | 7.0 | Cash | | 7.0 |
| 2004 | Expense | 1.4 | | Depreciation entry omitted | | |
| | Accum. deprec. | | 1.4 | | | |
| 2005 | Expense | 1.4 | | Depreciation entry omitted | | |
| | Accum. deprec. | | 1.4 | | | |

During the two-year period, depreciation expense was understated by $2.8 million, but other expenses were overstated by $7 million, so net income during the period was understated by $4.2 million. This means retained earnings is currently understated by that amount.

Accumulated depreciation is understated by $2.8 million.

**Step 1**

| To Correct Incorrect Accounts | ($ in millions) | |
|---|---|---|
| Equipment | 7.0 | |
| Accumulated depreciation | | 2.8 |
| Retained earnings | | 4.2 |

**Step 2 Restate previous years' financial statements**

The 2004 and 2005 financial statements that were incorrect as a result of the error are retrospectively restated to report the equipment acquired and to reflect the correct amount of depreciation expense and accumulated depreciation, assuming both statements are reported again for comparative purposes in the 2006 annual report.

**Step 3 Prior period adjustment**

Because retained earnings is one of the accounts that is incorrect as a result of the error, a correction to that account of $4.2 million is reported as a prior period adjustment to the 2006 beginning retained earnings balance in Seidman's comparative statements of shareholders' equity. A correction would be made also to the 2005 beginning retained earnings balance. That prior period adjustment, though, would be for the pre-2005 difference: $7 million − 1.4

million = $5.6 million. If 2004 statements also are included in the comparative report, no adjustment would be necessary for that period because the error didn't occur until after the beginning of 2004.

Also, a disclosure note accompanying Seidman's 2006 financial statements should describe the nature of the error and the impact of its correction on each year's net income (understated by $5.6 million in 2004 and overstated by $1.4 million in 2005), income before extraordinary items (same as net income), and earnings per share.

**ILLUSTRATION 20–6**
concluded

**Step 4**
**Disclosure note**

The effect of most errors is different, depending on ***when*** the error is discovered. For example, if the error in Illustration 20–6 is not discovered until 2007, rather than 2006, accumulated depreciation would be understated by another $1.4 million, or a total of $4.2 million. If not discovered until 2010 or after, no correcting entry at all would be needed. By then, the sum of the omitted depreciation amounts ($1.4 million × 5 years) would equal the expense incorrectly recorded in 2004 ($7 million), so the retained earnings balance would be the same as if the error never had occurred. Also, the asset would have been disposed of—if the useful life estimate was correct—so neither the equipment nor accumulated depreciation would need to be recorded. Of course, any statements of prior years that were affected and are reported again in comparative statements still would be restated, and a footnote would describe the error.

Most errors, in fact, eventually self-correct. An example of an uncommon instance in which an error never self-corrects would be an expense account debited for the cost of land. Because land doesn't depreciate, the error would continue until the land is sold.

Some errors correct themselves the following year. For instance, if a company's ending inventory is incorrectly counted or otherwise misstated, the income statement would be in error for the year of the error and the following year, but the balance sheet would be incorrect only for the year the error occurs. After that, all account balances will be correct. This is demonstrated in Illustration 20–7 on the next page.

**Even errors that eventually correct themselves cause financial statements to be misstated in the meantime.**

## ADDITIONAL CONSIDERATION

We ignored the tax impact of the error and its correction in Illustration 20–6. To consider taxes, we need to know whether depreciation was also omitted from the tax return and the depreciation methods used for tax reporting. Let's say that depreciation was omitted from the tax return also, and that straight-line depreciation is used by Seidman for both tax and financial reporting. The tax rate is 40%.

Total operating expenses (nontax) still would have been overstated by $4.2 million over the two-year period. But that would have caused taxable income to be understated and the tax liability and income tax expense to be understated by 40% of $4.2 million, or $1.68 million. So net income and retained earnings would have been understated by only $2.52 million:

| | |
|---|---|
| Operating expenses *overstated* | $4.20 million |
| Income tax expense *understated* | (1.68) million |
| Net income (and retained earnings) *understated* | $2.52 million |

| **To Correct Incorrect Accounts:** | ($ in millions) | |
|---|---|---|
| Equipment | 7.00 | |
| Accumulated depreciation | | 2.80 |
| Income tax payable (40% × $4.2 million) | | 1.68 |
| Retained earnings | | 2.52 |

If depreciation had been omitted from the income statement but not from the tax return, or if accelerated depreciation was used for tax reporting but straight-line depreciation for financial reporting, the credit to income tax payable in the correcting entry would be replaced by a credit to deferred tax liability.

**ILLUSTRATION 20–7**

Error Affecting Net Income: Inventory Misstated

In early 2006, Overseas Wholesale Supply discovered that $1 million of inventory had been inadvertently excluded from its 2004 ending inventory count.

**Analysis:**

U = Understated O = Overstated

| 2004 | | 2005 | |
|---|---|---|---|
| Beginning inventory | | → Beginning inventory | U |
| Plus: Net purchases | | Plus: Net purchases | |
| Less: Ending inventory | U → | Less: Ending inventory | |
| Cost of goods sold | O | Cost of goods sold | U |
| Revenues | | Revenues | |
| Less: Cost of goods sold | O | Less: Cost of goods sold | U |
| Less: Other expenses | | Less: Other expenses | |
| Net income | U | Net income | O |
| ↓ | | ↓ | |
| Retained earnings | U | Retained earnings | *corrected* |

**When analyzing inventory errors or other errors that affect cost of goods sold, you may find it helpful to visualize the determination of cost of goods sold, net income, and retained earnings.**

**Step 1**

**If Error Is Discovered in 2005 (before closing):**

| | ($ in millions) | |
|---|---|---|
| Inventory | 1 | |
| Retained earnings | | 1 |

**If Error Discovered in 2006 or Later:**

No correcting entry needed

**Step 2**

If the error is discovered in 2005, the 2004 financial statements that were incorrect as a result of the error are retrospectively restated to reflect the correct inventory amounts, cost of goods sold, and retained earnings when those statements are reported again for comparative purposes in the 2005 annual report. If the error is discovered in 2006, the 2005 financial statements also are retrospectively restated to reflect the correct inventory amounts and cost of goods sold (retained earnings would not require adjustment), even though no correcting entry would be needed at that point.

**Step 3**

Because retained earnings is one of the accounts incorrect if the error is discovered in 2005, the correction to that account is reported as a prior period adjustment to the 2005 beginning retained earnings balance in Overseas' statement of shareholders' equity. Of course, no prior period adjustment is needed if the error isn't discovered until 2006 or later.

**Step 4**

Also, a disclosure note in Overseas' annual report should describe the nature of the error and the impact of its correction on each year's net income (understated by $1 million in 2004, overstated by $1 million in 2005), income before extraordinary items (same as net income), and earnings per share.

Other error corrections that benefit from a similar analysis are the overstatement of ending inventory, the overstatement or understatement of beginning inventory, and errors in recording merchandise purchases (or returns).

An error also would occur if a revenue or an expense is recorded in the wrong accounting period. Illustration 20–8 on the next page offers an example.

**ETHICAL DILEMMA**

As a second-year accountant for McCormack Chemical Company, you were excited to be named assistant manager of the Agricultural Chemicals Division. After two weeks in your new position, you were supervising the year-end inventory count when the senior manager mentioned that two carloads of herbicides were omitted from the count and should be added. Upon checking, you confirm your understanding that the inventory in question had been deemed to be unsaleable. "Yes," your manager agreed, "but we'll write that off next year when our bottom line won't be so critical to the continued existence of the Agricultural Chemicals Division. Jobs and families depend on our division showing well this year."

**ILLUSTRATION 20–8**
Error Affecting Net Income: Failure to Record Sales Revenue

In 2006, General Paper Company discovered that $3,000 of merchandise (credit) sales the last week of 2005 were not recorded until the first week of 2006. The merchandise sold was appropriately excluded from 2005 ending inventory.

**Analysis:**

**($ in 000s)**

| | **Correct** (Should have been recorded) | | | **Incorrect** (As recorded) | | |
|---|---|---|---|---|---|---|
| 2005 | Accounts receivable . . . . . . | 3 | | No entry | | |
| | Sales revenue . . . . . . . . . | | 3 | | | |
| 2006 | No entry . . . . . . . . . . . . . . . | | | Accounts receivable . . . . . . . . . | 3 | |
| | | | | Sales revenue . . . . . . . . . . . . | | 3 |

2005 sales revenue was incorrectly recorded in 2006, so 2005 net income was understated. Retained earnings is currently understated in 2006. 2006 sales revenue is overstated.

Step 1

| **To Correct Incorrect Accounts** | ($ in 000s) | |
|---|---|---|
| Sales revenue . . . . . . . . . . . . . . . . . . . . . . . . . . . . . . . . . . . . . . | 3 | |
| Retained earnings. . . . . . . . . . . . . . . . . . . . . . . . . . . . . . . . . . . . | | 3 |

**Note:** If the sales revenue had not been recorded at all, the correcting entry would include a debit to accounts receivable rather than sales revenue.

Step 2

The 2005 financial statements that were incorrect as a result of the error are retroactively restated to reflect the correct amount of sales revenue and accounts receivable when those statements are reported again for comparative purposes in the 2006 annual report.

Step 3

Because retained earnings is one of the accounts incorrect as a result of the error, the correction to that account is reported as a prior period adjustment to the 2005 beginning retained earnings balance in General Paper's comparative statements of shareholders' equity.

Step 4

Also, a disclosure note in General Paper's 2006 annual report should describe the nature of the error and the impact of its correction on each year's net income ($3,000 in 2005), income before extraordinary items ($3,000 in 2005), and earnings per share.

Graphic 20–12 illustrates how **Benihana, Inc.** corrected its financial statements for having incorrectly expensed leasehold improvements and assets on leased properties in past years. Benihana was one of hundreds of firms making similar correction in 2005 following a Securities and Exchange Commission letter on February 7, 2005, urging companies to follow long-standing accounting standards in this area. As the note indicates, Benihana's previous

**GRAPHIC 20–12**
Error Correction; Benihana, Inc.

**2. Restatement of Previously Issued Financial Statements (in part)**
Following a February 2005 review . . . we have restated our consolidated financial statements for the fiscal years through 2004 and for the third quarter of fiscal 2004 included herein. Previously, when accounting for leases with renewal options, we recorded rent expense on a straight-line basis over the initial noncancelable lease term, with the term commencing when actual rent payments began. We depreciate our buildings, leasehold improvements and other long-lived assets on those properties over a period that includes both the initial noncancelable lease term and all option periods provided for in the lease (or the useful life of the assets if shorter). We previously believed that these long-standing accounting treatments were appropriate under generally accepted accounting principles. We now have restated our financial statements to recognize rent expense on a straight-line basis over the expected lease term, including cancelable option periods where failure to exercise such options would result in an economic penalty and including the period that commences when the underlying property is made available to us for construction.

The cumulative effect of the Restatement through fiscal 2004 is an increase in deferred rent liability of $3.6 million and a decrease in deferred income tax liability of $1.4 million. As a result, retained earnings at the end of fiscal 2004 decreased by $2.2 million. Rent expense for fiscal year ended 2004 and for the three and ten periods ended January 4, 2004 increased by $0.4 million, and $0.1 million and $0.3, respectively. The Restatement decreased reported diluted net earnings per share $0.01 and $0.03 for the three and ten periods ended January 4, 2004, respectively.

earnings had been overstated by $2.2 million as a result of the error and the balance in retained earnings was accordingly decreased in the correcting journal entry. At about the same time, **McDonald's Corp.** recorded a similar charge of $139 million.

As mentioned at the outset, we've made no attempt to demonstrate the correction process for every kind of error in every stage of its discovery. However, after seeing the process applied to the few situations described, you should feel comfortable that the process is the same regardless of the specific situation you might encounter.

## Concept Review Exercise

### Correction of Errors

In 2006, the following errors were discovered by the internal auditors of Development Technologies, Inc.

1. 2005 accrued wages of $2 million were not recognized until they were paid in 2006.
2. A $3 million purchase of merchandise in 2006 was recorded in 2005 instead. The physical inventory count at the end of 2005 was correct.

**Required:**

Prepare the journal entries needed in 2006 to correct each error. Also, briefly describe any other measures Development Technologies would take in connection with correcting the errors. (Ignore income taxes.)

### Solution

**Step 1:**

1. To reduce 2006 wages expense and reduce retained earnings to what it would have been if the expense had reduced net income in 2005.

| | ($ in millions) | |
|---|---|---|
| Retained earnings | 2 | |
| Wages expense | | 2 |

2. To include the $3 million in 2006 purchases and increase retained earnings to what it would have been if 2005 cost of goods sold had not included the $3 million purchases.

**Analysis**

U = Understated O = Overstated

| 2005 | | 2006 | |
|---|---|---|---|
| Beginning inventory | | Beginning inventory | |
| Purchases | O | Purchases | U |
| Less: Ending inventory | | | |
| Cost of goods sold | O | | |
| Revenues | | | |
| Less: Cost of goods sold | O | | |
| Less: Other expenses | | | |
| Net income | U | | |
| ↓ | | | |
| Retained earnings | U | | |

| | ($ in millions) | |
|---|---|---|
| Purchases | 3 | |
| Retained earnings | | 3 |

**Step 2:**

The 2005 financial statements that were incorrect as a result of the errors would be *retrospectively restated* to reflect the correct wages expense, cost of goods sold (income tax expense if taxes are considered), net income, and retained earnings when those statements are reported again for comparative purposes in the 2006 annual report.

**Step 3:**
Because retained earnings is one of the accounts that is incorrect, the correction to that account is reported as a *"prior period adjustment"* to the 2006 beginning retained earnings balance in the comparative Statements of Shareholders' Equity.

**Step 4:**
Also, a *disclosure note* should describe the nature of the error and the impact of its correction on each year's net income, income before extraordinary items, and earnings per share.

## FINANCIAL REPORTING CASE SOLUTION

1. **How can an accounting change cause a company to increase a previously reported inventory amount?** (page 1013) Smucker didn't find any lost jelly. The company increased the 2004 inventory number by $2 million to reflect its change from LIFO to FIFO in 2005. If it had not revised the number, the 2004 inventory would be based on LIFO and the 2005 inventory on FIFO. Analysts would be comparing apples and oranges (or apple jelly and orange jelly). Retrospective application of an accounting change provides better comparability in accounting information.
2. **Are all accounting changes reported this way?** (page 1019) Not all accounting changes are reported retrospectively. Besides most changes in accounting principle, changes in reporting entity and the correction of errors are reported that way, but some changes are reported prospectively instead. Changes in depreciation method, changes in accounting estimate, and some changes for which retrospective application is either impracticable or prohibited are reported prospectively in current and future periods only. ■

## THE BOTTOM LINE

1. Accounting changes are categorized as:
   a. Changes in *principle,*
   b. Changes in *estimates*, or
   c. Changes in *reporting entity.*
   Accounting changes can be accounted for retrospectively (prior years revised) or prospectively (only current and future years affected).
2. Most voluntary changes in accounting principles are reported retrospectively. This means revising all previous periods' financial statements to appear as if the newly adopted accounting method had been applied all along. A journal entry is created to adjust all account balances affected as of the date of the change. In the first set of financial statements after the change, a disclosure note describes the change and justifies the new method as preferable. It also describes the effects of the change on all items affected, including the fact that the retained earnings balance was revised in the statement of shareholders' equity.
3. Some changes are reported prospectively. These include (a) changes in the method of depreciation, amortization, or depletion, (b) some changes in principle for which retrospective application is impracticable, and (c) a few changes for which an authoritative pronouncement requires prospective application.
4. Changes in estimates are accounted for prospectively. When a company revises a previous estimate, prior financial statements are not revised. Instead, the company merely incorporates the new estimate in any related accounting determinations from then on.
5. A change in reporting entity requires that financial statements of prior periods be retrospectively revised to report the financial information for the new reporting entity in all periods.
6. When errors are discovered, they should be corrected and accounted for retrospectively. Previous years' financial statements that were incorrect as a result of an error are retrospectively restated, and any account balances that are incorrect are corrected by a journal entry. If retained earnings is one of the incorrect accounts, the correction is reported

as a prior period adjustment to the beginning balance in a statement of shareholders' equity. And, a disclosure note should describe the nature of the error and the impact of its correction on operations. ■

## QUESTIONS FOR REVIEW OF KEY TOPICS

**Q 20–1** For accounting purposes, we classify accounting changes into three categories. What are they? Provide a short description of each.

**Q 20–2** There are two basic accounting approaches to reporting accounting changes. What are they?

**Q 20–3** We report most changes in accounting principle retrospectively. Describe this general way of recording and reporting changes in accounting principle.

**Q 20–4** Lynch Corporation changes from the sum-of-the-years'-digits method of depreciation for existing assets to the straight-line method. How should the change be reported?

**Q 20–5** Sugarbaker Designs, Inc. changed from the FIFO inventory costing method to the average cost method during 2006. Which items from the 2005 financial statements should be restated on the basis of the average cost method when reported in the 2006 comparative financial statements?

**Q 20–6** Most accounting principles are recorded and reported retrospectively. In a few situations, though, the changes should be reported prospectively. When is prospective application appropriate?

**Q 20–7** Southeast Steel, Inc. changed from the FIFO inventory costing method to the LIFO method during 2005. How would this change likely be reported in the 2006 comparative financial statements?

**Q 20–8** Direct Assurance Company revised the estimates of the useful life of a trademark it had acquired three years earlier. How should Direct account for the change?

**Q 20–9** It's not easy sometimes to distinguish between a change in principle and a change in estimate. In these cases, how should the change be accounted for?

**Q 20–10** For financial reporting, a reporting entity can be a single company, or it can be a group of companies that reports a single set of financial statements. When changes occur that cause the financial statements to be those of a different reporting entity, we account for the situation as a change in reporting entity. What are the situations deemed to constitute a change in reporting entity?

**Q 20–11** The issuance of *SFAS 94,* "Consolidation of All Majority-Owned Subsidiaries," required Ford Motors to include a previously unconsolidated finance subsidiary as part of the reporting entity. How did Ford report the change?

**Q 20–12** Describe the process of correcting an error when it's discovered in a subsequent reporting period.

**Q 20–13** If merchandise inventory is understated at the end of 2005, and the error is not discovered, how will net income be affected in 2006?

**Q 20–14** If it is discovered that an extraordinary repair in the previous year was incorrectly debited to repair expense, how will retained earnings be reported in the current year's statement of shareholders' equity?

**Q 20–15** What action is required when it is discovered that a five-year insurance premium payment of $50,000 two years ago was debited to insurance expense? (Ignore taxes.)

**Q 20–16** Suppose the error described in the previous question is not discovered until six years later. What action will the discovery of this error require?

## BRIEF EXERCISES

**BE 20–1**
Change in inventory methods
● LO2

In 2006, the Carney Company changed its method of valuing inventory from the FIFO method to the average cost method. At December 31, 2005, Carney's inventories were $32 million (FIFO). Carney's records indicated that the inventories would have totaled $23.8 million at December 31, 2005, if determined on an average cost basis. Ignoring income taxes, what journal entry will Carney use to record the adjustment? Briefly describe other steps Carney should take to report the change.

**BE 20–2**
Change in inventory methods
● LO2

In 2006, DeWash Industries changed its method of valuing inventory from the average cost method to the FIFO method. At December 31, 2005, DeWash's inventories were $47.6 million (average cost). DeWash's records indicated that the inventories would have totaled $64 million at December 31, 2005, if determined on a FIFO basis. Ignoring income taxes, what journal entry will DeWash use to record the adjustment?

**BE 20–3**
Change in inventory methods
● LO3

In 2006, Dorsey Markets changed its method of valuing inventory from the FIFO method to the LIFO method. At December 31, 2005, Dorsey's inventories were $96 million (FIFO). Dorsey's records were insufficient to determine what inventories would have totaled if determined on a LIFO cost basis. Briefly describe the steps Dorsey should take to report the change.

**BE 20–4**
Change in depreciation methods
● LO3

Irwin, Inc. constructed a machine at a total cost of $35 million. Construction was completed at the end of 2002 and the machine was placed in service at the beginning of 2003. The machine was being depreciated over a 10-year life using the sum-of-the-years'-digits method. The residual value is expected to be $2 million. At the beginning of 2006, Irwin decided to change to the straight-line method. Ignoring income taxes, what journal entry(s) should Irwin record relating to the machine for 2006?

**BE 20–5**
Change in depreciation methods
● LO3

Refer to the situation described in BE 20–4. Suppose Irwin has been using the straight-line method and switches to the sum-of-the-years'-digits method. Ignoring income taxes, what journal entry(s) should Irwin record relating to the machine for 2006?

**BE 20–6**
Change in estimate; useful life of patent
● LO4

Van Frank Telecommunications has a patent on a cellular transmission process. The company has amortized the patent on a straight-line basis since 2002, when it was acquired at a cost of $18 million at the beginning of that year. Due to rapid technological advances in the industry, management decided that the patent would benefit the company over a total of six years rather than the nine-year life being used to amortize its cost. The decision was made at the end of 2006 (before adjusting and closing entries). What is the appropriate adjusting entry for patent amortization in 2006 to reflect the revised estimate?

**BE 20–7**
Error correction
● LO6

When DeSoto Water Works purchased a machine at the end of 2005 at a cost of $65,000, the company debited Buildings and credited Cash $65,000. The error was discovered in 2006. What journal entry will DeSoto use to correct the error? What other step(s) would be taken in connection with the error?

**BE 20–8**
Error correction
● LO6

In 2006, internal auditors discovered that PKE Displays, Inc. had debited an expense account for the $350,000 cost of a machine purchased on January 1, 2003. The machine's useful life was expected to be five years with no residual value. Straight-line depreciation is used by PKE. Ignoring income taxes, what journal entry will PKE use to correct the error?

**BE 20–9**
Error correction
● LO6

Refer to the situation described in BE 20–8. Assume the error was discovered in 2008 after the 2007 financial statements are issued. Ignoring income taxes, what journal entry will PKE use to correct the error?

**BE 20–10**
Error correction
● LO6

In 2006, the internal auditors of Development Technologies, Inc. discovered that (a) 2005 accrued wages of $2 million were not recognized until they were paid in 2006 and (b) a $3 million purchase of merchandise in 2006 was recorded in 2005 instead. The physical inventory count at the end of 2005 was correct. Ignoring income taxes, what journal entries are needed in 2006 to correct each error? Also, briefly describe any other measures Development Technologies would take in connection with correcting the errors.

## EXERCISES

available with McGraw-Hill's Homework Manager www.mhhe.com/spiceland4e

**An alternate exercise and problem set is available on the text website: www.mhhe.com/spiceland4e**

**E 20–1**
Change in principle; change in inventory methods
● LO2

During 2004 (its first year of operations) and 2005, Batali Foods used the FIFO inventory costing method for both financial reporting and tax purposes. At the beginning of 2006, Batali decided to change to the average method for both financial reporting and tax purposes.

Income components before income tax for 2006, 2005, and 2004 were as follows ($ in millions):

| | 2006 | 2005 | 2004 |
|---|---|---|---|
| Revenues | $420 | $390 | $380 |
| Cost of goods sold (FIFO) | (46) | (40) | (38) |
| Cost of goods sold (average) | (62) | (56) | (52) |
| Operating expenses | (254) | (250) | (242) |

Dividends of $20 million were paid each year. Batali's fiscal year ends December 31.

**Required:**

1. Prepare the journal entry at the beginning of 2006 to record the change in principle. (Ignore income taxes.)
2. Prepare the 2006–2005 comparative income statements.

3. Determine the balance in retained earnings at January 1, 2005, as Batali reported previously using the FIFO method.
4. Determine the adjustment to the January 1, 2005, balance in retained earnings that Batali would include in the 2006–2005 comparative statements of retained earnings or retained earnings column of the statements of shareholders' equity to revise it to the amount it would have been if Batali had used the average method.

**E 20–2**
Change in principle; change in inventory methods

● LO2

Aquatic Equipment Corporation decided to switch from the LIFO method of costing inventories to the FIFO method at the beginning of 2006. The inventory as reported at the end of 2005 using LIFO would have been $60,000 higher using FIFO. Retained earnings had been reported at the end of 2005 as $780,000 (reflecting the LIFO method). The tax rate is 40%.

**Required:**
1. Calculate the balance in retained earnings at the time of the change (beginning of 2006) as it would have been reported if FIFO had been used in prior years.
2. Prepare the journal entry at the beginning of 2006 to record the change in principle.

**E 20–3**
Change in principle; change to the percentage-of completion method

● LO2

The Long Island Construction Company has used the completed contract method of accounting for construction contracts. At the beginning of 2006, the company decides to change to the percentage-of-completion method for financial reporting purposes, but will continue to use the completed contract method for tax reporting. The following table presents information concerning the change. The income tax rate for all years is 40%.

| | Income before Income Tax | | |
|---|---|---|---|
| | Percentage of Completion Method | Completed Contract Method | Difference |
| Before 2005 | $15 million | $8 million | $7 million |
| 2005 | 8 million | 5 million | 3 million |
| 2006 | 10 million | 9 million | 1 million |

**Required:**
1. Prepare the journal entry to record the change in principle. (All tax effects should be reflected in the deferred tax liability account.)
2. Determine the net income to be reported in the 2006–2005 comparative income statements.
3. Which other 2005 amounts would be reported differently in the 2006–2005 comparative income statements and 2006–2005 comparative balance sheets than they were reported the previous year?
4. How would the change be reflected in the 2006–2005 comparative statements of shareholders' equity? Cash dividends were $1 million each year.

**E 20–4**
Classifying accounting changes

● LO1 through LO5

Indicate with the appropriate letter the nature of each situation described below:

**Type of Change**

| | |
|---|---|
| PR | Change in principle reported retrospectively |
| PP | Change in principle reported prospectively |
| E | Change in estimate |
| EP | Change in estimate resulting from a change in principle |
| R | Change in reporting entity |
| N | Not an accounting change |

_____ 1. Change from declining balance depreciation to straight-line.
_____ 2. Change in the estimated useful life of office equipment.
_____ 3. Technological advance that renders worthless a patent with an unamortized cost of $45,000.
_____ 4. Change from determining lower of cost or market for the inventories by the individual item approach to the aggregate approach.
_____ 5. Change from LIFO inventory costing to the weighted-average inventory costing.
_____ 6. Settling a lawsuit for less than the amount accrued previously as a loss contingency.
_____ 7. Including in the consolidated financial statements a subsidiary acquired several years earlier that was appropriately not included in previous years.
_____ 8. Change by a retail store from reporting bad debt expense on a pay-as-you-go basis to the allowance method.
_____ 9. A shift of certain manufacturing overhead costs to inventory that previously were expensed as incurred to more accurately measure cost of goods sold. (Either method is generally acceptable.)
_____ 10. Pension plan assets for a defined benefit pension plan achieving a rate of return in excess of the amount anticipated.

**E 20–5**
Change from the treasury stock method to retired stock

● LO2

In keeping with a modernization of corporate statutes in its home state, UMC Corporation decided in 2006 to discontinue accounting for reacquired shares as treasury stock. Instead, shares repurchased will be viewed as having been retired, reassuming the status of unissued shares. As part of the change, treasury shares held were reclassified as retired stock. At December 31, 2005, UMC's balance sheet reported the following shareholders' equity:

| | ($ in millions) |
|---|---|
| Common stock, $1 par | $ 200 |
| Paid-in capital—excess of par | 800 |
| Retained earnings | 956 |
| Treasury stock (4 million shares at cost) | (25) |
| Total shareholders' equity | $1,931 |

**Required:**
Identify the type of accounting change this decision represents and prepare the journal entry to effect the reclassification of treasury shares as retired shares.

**E 20–6**
Change in principle; change to the equity method

● LO2

The Trump Companies, Inc. has ownership interests in several public companies. At the beginning of 2006, the company's ownership interest in the common stock of Milken Properties increased to the point that it became appropriate to begin using the equity method of accounting for the investment. The balance in the investment account was $31 million at the time of the change. Accountants working with company records determined that the balance would have been $48 million if the account had been adjusted to reflect the equity method.

**Required:**
1. Prepare the journal entry to record the change in principle. (Ignore income taxes.)
2. Briefly describe other steps Trump should take to report the change.
3. Suppose Trump is changing *from* the equity method rather than *to* the equity method. How would your answers to requirements 1 and 2 differ?

**E 20–7**
Change in inventory methods; incomplete information

● LO3

Moulton Foods has always used the FIFO inventory costing method for both financial reporting and tax purposes. At the beginning of 2006, Moulton decided to change to the LIFO method. Net income in 2006 was $80 million. If the company had used LIFO in 2005, its cost of goods sold would have been higher by $6 million that year. Moulton's records of inventory purchases and sales are not available for 2004 and several previous years. Last year, Moulton reported the following net income amounts in its comparative income statements:

| ($ in millions) | 2005 | 2004 | 2003 |
|---|---|---|---|
| Net income | $84 | $82 | $80 |

**Required:**
1. Prepare the journal entry at the beginning of 2006 to record the change in principle. (Ignore income taxes.)
2. Briefly describe other steps Moulton will take to report the change.
3. What amounts will Moulton report for net income in its 2006–2004 comparative income statements?

**E 20–8**
Change in inventory methods; incomplete information

● LO3

Wolfgang Kitchens has always used the FIFO inventory costing method for both financial reporting and tax purposes. At the beginning of 2006, Wolfgang decided to change to the LIFO method. Net income in 2006 was $90 million. If the company had used LIFO in 2005, its cost of goods sold would have been higher by $7 million that year. Company accountants are able to determine that the cumulative net income for all years prior to 2005 would have been lower by $23 million if LIFO had been used all along, but have insufficient information to determine specific effects of using LIFO in 2004. Last year, Wolfgang reported the following net income amounts in its comparative income statements:

| ($ in millions) | 2005 | 2004 | 2003 |
|---|---|---|---|
| Net income | $94 | $92 | $90 |

**Required:**
1. Prepare the journal entry at the beginning of 2006 to record the change in principle. (Ignore income taxes.)
2. Briefly describe other steps Wolfgang will take to report the change.
3. What amounts will Wolfgang report for net income in its 2006–2004 comparative income statements?

**E 20–9**
Change in depreciation methods

● LO3

For financial reporting, Clinton Poultry Farms has used the declining-balance method of depreciation for conveyor equipment acquired at the beginning of 2003 for $2,560,000. Its useful life was estimated to be six years with a $160,000 residual value. At the beginning of 2006, Clinton decides to change to the straight-line method. The effect of this change on depreciation for each year is as follows ($ in 000s):

| Year | Straight–Line | Declining Balance | Difference |
|---|---|---|---|
| 2003 | $ 400 | $ 640 | $240 |
| 2004 | 400 | 550 | 150 |
| 2005 | 400 | 460 | 60 |
| | $1,200 | $1,650 | $450 |

**Required:**

1. Briefly describe the way Clinton should report this accounting change in the 2005–2006 comparative financial statements.
2. Prepare any 2006 journal entry related to the change.

**E 20–10**
Change in depreciation methods
● LO3

The Canliss Milling Company purchased machinery on January 2, 2004, for $800,000. A five-year life was estimated and no residual value was anticipated. Canliss decided to use the straight-line depreciation method and recorded $160,000 in depreciation in 2004 and 2005. Early in 2006, the company changed its depreciation method to the sum-of-the-years'-digits (SYD) method.

**Required:**

1. Briefly describe the way Canliss should report this accounting change in the 2005–2006 comparative financial statements.
2. Prepare any 2006 journal entry related to the change.

**E 20–11**
Multiple choice; CPA exam; accounting changes
● LO1 through LO3

The following questions dealing with accounting changes are adapted from questions that appeared on previous CPA examinations. Determine the response that best completes the statements or questions.

1. When a company changes from the straight-line method of depreciation for previously recorded assets to the double-declining balance method, which of the following should be reported?

| | Prospectively in Current and Future Statements | Retrospective Application |
|---|---|---|
| a. | No | No |
| b. | No | Yes |
| c. | Yes | Yes |
| d. | Yes | No |

2. A company has included in its consolidated financial statements this year a subsidiary acquired several years ago that was appropriately excluded from consolidation last year. This results in:
   a. An accounting change that should be reported prospectively.
   b. An accounting change that should be reported by revising the financial statements of all prior periods presented.
   c. A correction of an error.
   d. Neither an accounting change nor a correction of an error.

**E 20–12**
Book royalties
● LO4

Dreighton Engineering Group receives royalties on a technical manual written by two of its engineers and sold to William B. Irving Publishing, Inc. Royalties are 10% of net sales, receivable on October 1 for sales in January through June and on April 1 for sales in July through December of the prior year. Sales of the manual began in July 2005, and Dreighton accrued royalty revenue of $31,000 at December 31, 2005, as follows:

| | | |
|---|---|---|
| Receivable—royalty revenue | 31,000 | |
| Royalty revenue | | 31,000 |

Dreighton received royalties of $36,000 on April 1, 2006, and $40,000 on October 1, 2006. Irving indicated to Dreighton on December 31 that book sales subject to royalties for the second half of 2006 are expected to be $500,000.

**Required:**

1. Prepare any journal entries Dreighton should record during 2006 related to the royalty revenue.
2. What adjustments, if any, should be made to retained earnings or to the 2005 financial statements? Explain.

**E 20–13**
Loss contingency
● LO4

The Commonwealth of Virginia filed suit in October 2004, against Northern Timber Corporation seeking civil penalties and injunctive relief for violations of environmental laws regulating forest conservation. When the financial statements were issued in 2005, Northern had not reached a settlement with state authorities, but legal counsel advised Northern Timber that it was probable the ultimate settlement would be $1,000,000 in penalties. The following entry was recorded:

| | | |
|---|---|---|
| Loss—litigation | 1,000,000 | |
| Liability—litigation | | 1,000,000 |

Late in 2006, a settlement was reached with state authorities to pay a total of $600,000 to cover the cost of violations.

**Required:**

1. Prepare any journal entries related to the change.
2. Briefly describe other steps Northern should take to report the change.

**E 20–14**
Warranty expense

● LO4

Woodmier Lawn Products introduced a new line of commercial sprinklers in 2005 that carry a one-year warranty against manufacturer's defects. Because this was the first product for which the company offered a warranty, trade publications were consulted to determine the experience of others in the industry. Based on that experience, warranty costs were expected to approximate 2% of sales. Sales of the sprinklers in 2005 were $2,500,000. Accordingly, the following entries relating to the contingency for warranty costs were recorded during the first year of selling the product:

| | | |
|---|---|---|
| **Accrued liability and expense** | | |
| Warranty expense (2% × $2,500,000) | 50,000 | |
| Estimated warranty liability | | 50,000 |
| **Actual expenditures (summary entry)** | | |
| Estimated warranty liability | 23,000 | |
| Cash, wages payable, parts and supplies, etc. | | 23,000 |

In late 2006, the company's claims experience was evaluated and it was determined that claims were far more than expected—3% of sales rather than 2%.

**Required:**

1. Assuming sales of the sprinklers in 2006 were $3,600,000 and warranty expenditures in 2006 totaled $88,000, prepare any journal entries related to the warranty.
2. Assuming sales of the sprinklers were discontinued after 2005, prepare any journal entry(s) in 2006 related to the warranty.

**E 20–15**
Deferred taxes; change in tax rates

● LO4

Bronson Industries reported a deferred tax liability of $8 million for the year ended December 31, 2005, related to a temporary difference of $20 million. The tax rate was 40%. The temporary difference is expected to reverse in 2007 at which time the deferred tax liability will become payable. There are no other temporary differences in 2005–2007. Assume a new tax law is enacted in 2006 that causes the tax rate to change from 40% to 30% beginning in 2007. (The rate remains 40% for 2006 taxes.) Taxable income in 2006 is $30 million.

**Required:**

Determine the effect of the change and prepare the appropriate journal entry to record Bronson's income tax expense in 2006. What adjustment, if any, is needed to revise retained earnings as a result of the change?

**E 20–16**
Accounting change

● LO4

The Peridot Company purchased machinery on January 2, 2004, for $800,000. A five-year life was estimated and no residual value was anticipated. Peridot decided to use the straight-line depreciation method and recorded $160,000 in depreciation in 2004 and 2005. Early in 2006, the company revised the total estimated life of the machinery to eight years.

**Required:**

1. What type of change is this?
2. Briefly describe the accounting treatment for this change.
3. Determine depreciation for 2006.

**E 20–17**
Change in estimate; useful life and residual value of equipment

● LO4

Wardell Company purchased a mini computer on January 1, 2004, at a cost of $40,000. The computer has been depreciated using the straight-line method over an estimated five-year useful life with an estimated residual value of $4,000. On January 1, 2006, the estimate of useful life was changed to a total of 10 years, and the estimate of residual value was changed to $900.

**Required:**

1. Prepare the appropriate adjusting entry for depreciation in 2006 to reflect the revised estimate.
2. Repeat requirement 1 assuming that the company uses the sum-of-the-years'-digits method instead of the straight-line method.

**E 20–18**
Error correction; inventory error

● LO6

During 2006, WMC Corporation discovered that its ending inventories reported on its financial statements were misstated by the following amounts:

| | | |
|---|---|---|
| 2004 | understated by | $120,000 |
| 2005 | overstated by | 150,000 |

WMC uses the periodic inventory system and the FIFO cost method.

**Required:**

1. Determine the effect of these errors on retained earnings at January 1, 2006, before any adjustments. Explain your answer. (Ignore income taxes.)
2. Prepare a journal entry to correct the error.
3. What other step(s) would be taken in connection with the error?

**E 20–19**
Error corrections; investment
● LO6

On December 12, 2006, an investment costing $80,000 was sold for $100,000. The total of the sale proceeds was credited to the investment account.

**Required:**

1. Prepare the journal entry to correct the error assuming it is discovered before the books are adjusted or closed in 2006. (Ignore income taxes.)
2. Prepare the journal entry to correct the error assuming it is not discovered until early 2007. (Ignore income taxes.)

**E 20–20**
Error in amortization schedule
● LO6

Wilkins Food Products, Inc. acquired a packaging machine from Lawrence Specialists Corporation. Lawrence completed construction of the machine on January 1, 2004. In payment for the machine Wilkins issued a three-year installment note to be paid in three equal payments at the end of each year. The payments include interest at the rate of 10%.

Lawrence made a conceptual error in preparing the amortization schedule which Wilkens failed to discover until 2006. The error had caused Wilkens to understate interest expense by $45,000 in 2004 and $40,000 in 2005.

**Required:**

1. Determine which accounts are incorrect as a result of these errors at January 1, 2006, before any adjustments. Explain your answer. (Ignore income taxes.)
2. Prepare a journal entry to correct the error.
3. What other step(s) would be taken in connection with the error?

**E 20–21**
Multiple choice; CPA exam; errors
● LO6

The following questions dealing with errors are adapted from questions that appeared on previous CPA examinations. Determine the response that best completes the statements or questions.

1. During 2006, Paul Company discovered that the ending inventories reported on its financial statements were incorrect by the following amounts:

| | | |
|---|---|---|
| 2004 | $60,000 | understated |
| 2005 | 75,000 | overstated |

   Paul uses the periodic inventory system to ascertain year-end quantities that are converted to dollar amounts using the FIFO cost method. Prior to any adjustments for these errors and ignoring income taxes, Paul's retained earnings at January 1, 2006, would be
   a. Correct.
   b. $15,000 overstated.
   c. $75,000 overstated.
   d. $135,000 overstated.

2. Terry, Inc. is a calendar-year corporation whose financial statements for 2004 and 2005 included errors as follows:

| Year | Ending Inventory | Depreciation Expense |
|---|---|---|
| 2004 | $15,000 overstated | $12,500 overstated |
| 2005 | 5,000 understated | 4,000 understated |

   Assume that purchases were recorded correctly and that no correcting entries were made at December 31, 2004 or at December 31, 2005. Ignoring income taxes, by how much should Terry's retained earnings be retrospectively adjusted at January 1, 2006?
   a. $13,500 increase.
   b. $3,500 decrease.
   c. $1,500 decrease.
   d. $1,000 decrease.

3. After the issuance of its 2005 financial statements Terry, Inc. discovered a computational error of $150,000 in the calculation of its December 31, 2005, inventory. The error resulted in a $150,000 overstatement in the cost of goods sold for the year ended December 31, 2005. In October 2006, Terry paid $500,000 in settlement of litigation instituted against it during 2005. Ignore income taxes. In the 2006 financial statements the December 31, 2005, retained earnings balance, as previously reported, should be adjusted by a
   a. $150,000 credit.
   b. $350,000 debit.
   c. $500,000 debit.
   d. $650,000 credit.

**E 20–22**
Error correction; accrued interest on bonds
● LO6

At the end of 2005, Majors Furniture Company failed to accrue $61,000 of interest expense that accrued during the last five months of 2005 on bonds payable. The bonds mature in 2019. The discount on the bonds is amortized by the straight-line method. The following entry was recorded on February 1, 2006, when the semiannual interest was paid:

| | | |
|---|---|---|
| Interest expense | 73,200 | |
| Discount on bonds payable | | 1,200 |
| Cash | | 72,000 |

**Required:**

Prepare any journal entry necessary to correct the error as well as any adjusting entry for 2006 related to the situation described. (Ignore income taxes.)

**E 20–23**
Error correction; three errors
● LO6

Below are three independent and unrelated errors.

a. On December 31, 2005, Wolfe-Bache Corporation failed to accrue office supplies expense of $1,800. In January 2006, when it received the bill from its supplier, Wolfe-Bache made the following entry:

| | | |
|---|---|---|
| Office supplies expense | 1,800 | |
| Cash | | 1,800 |

b. On the last day of 2005, Midwest Importers received a $90,000 prepayment from a tenant for 2006 rent of a building. Midwest recorded the receipt as rent revenue.

c. At the end of 2005, Dinkins-Lowery Corporation failed to accrue interest of $8,000 on a note receivable. At the beginning of 2006, when the company received the cash, it was recorded as interest revenue.

**Required:**

For each error:

1. What would be the effect of each error on the income statement and the balance sheet in the 2005 financial statements?
2. Prepare any journal entries each company should record in 2006 to correct the errors.

**E 20–24**
Inventory errors
● LO6

For each of the following inventory errors occurring in 2006, determine the effect of the error on 2006's cost of goods sold, net income, and retained earnings. Assume that the error is not discovered until 2007 and that a periodic inventory system is used. Ignore income taxes.

U = Understated O = Overstated NE = No effect

| | Cost of Goods Sold | Net Income | Retained Earnings |
|---|---|---|---|
| (Example) 1. Overstatement of ending inventory | U | O | O |
| 2. Overstatement of purchases | | | |
| 3. Understatement of beginning inventory | | | |
| 4. Freight in charges are understated | | | |
| 5. Understatement of ending inventory | | | |
| 6. Understatement of purchases | | | |
| 7. Overstatement of beginning inventory | | | |
| 8. Understatement of purchases + understatement of ending inventory by the same amount | | | |

**E 20–25**
Classifying accounting changes and errors
● LO1 through LO6

Indicate with the appropriate letter the nature of each adjustment described below:

**Type of Adjustment**

A. Change in principle (reported retrospectively)
B. Change in principle (exception reported prospectively)
C. Change in estimate
D. Change in estimate resulting from a change in principle
E. Change in reporting entity
F. Correction of an error

____ 1. Change from expensing extraordinary repairs to capitalizing the expenditures.
____ 2. Change in the residual value of machinery.
____ 3. Change from FIFO inventory costing to LIFO inventory costing.
____ 4. Change in the percentage used to determine bad debts.
____ 5. Change from LIFO inventory costing to FIFO inventory costing.
____ 6. Change from reporting an investment by the equity method due to a reduction in the percentage of shares owned.
____ 7. Change in the composition of a group of firms reporting on a consolidated basis.
____ 8. Change from sum-of-the-years'-digits depreciation to straight-line.
____ 9. Change from the percentage-of-completion method by a company in the long-term construction industry.
____ 10. Change in actuarial assumptions for a defined benefit pension plan.

**E 20–26**
Multiple choice; CMA exam; accounting changes and errors

● LO4 LO6

The following questions dealing with accounting changes and errors are adapted from questions that previously appeared on Certified Management Accountant (CMA) examinations. The CMA designation sponsored by the Institute of Management Accountants (www.imanet.com) provides members with an objective measure of knowledge and competence in the field of management accounting. Determine the response that best completes the statements or questions.

1. In a review of the May 31, 2007 financial statements during the normal year-end closing process, it was discovered that the interest income accrual on Simpson Company's notes receivable was omitted. The amounts omitted were calculated as follows:

| | |
|---|---|
| May 31, 2006 | $ 91,800 |
| May 31, 2007 | 100,200 |

The May 31, 2007 entry to correct for these errors, ignoring the effect of income taxes, includes a
   a. credit to retained earnings for $91,800.
   b. credit to interest revenue for $91,800.
   c. debit to interest revenue for $100,200.
   d. credit to interest receivable for $100,200.
2. A change in the liability for warranty costs requires
   a. presenting prior-period financial statements as previously reported.
   b. presenting the effect of pro forma data on income and earnings per share for all prior periods presented.
   c. reporting an adjustment to the beginning retained earnings balance in the statement of retained earnings.
   d. reporting current and future financial statements on the new basis.
3. An example of an item that should be reported as a prior-period adjustment in a company's annual financial statements is
   a. a settlement resulting from litigation.
   b. an adjustment of income taxes.
   c. a correction of an error that occurred in a prior period.
   d. an adjustment of utility revenue because of rate revisions ordered by a regulatory commission.

## PROBLEMS

available with McGraw-Hill's Homework Manager www.mhhe.com/spiceland4e

**An alternate exercise and problem set is available on the text website: www.mhhe.com/spiceland4e**

**P 20–1**
Change in inventory costing methods; comparative income statements

● LO2

eXcel

The Cecil-Booker Vending Company changed its method of valuing inventory from the average cost method to the FIFO cost method at the beginning of 2006. At December 31, 2005, inventories were $120,000 (average cost basis) and were $124,000 a year earlier. Cecil-Booker's accountants determined that the inventories would have totaled $155,000 at December 31, 2005, and $160,000 at December 31, 2004, if determined on a FIFO basis. A tax rate of 40% is in effect for all years.

One hundred thousand common shares were outstanding each year. Pretax income from continuing operations was $400,000 in 2005 and $525,000 in 2006. There were no extraordinary items either year.

**Required:**
1. Prepare the journal entry to record the change in principle. (All tax effects should be reflected in the deferred tax liability account.)
2. Prepare the 2006–2005 comparative income statements beginning with income from continuing operations. Include per share amounts.

**P 20–2**
Change in principle; change in method of accounting for long-term construction

● LO2

The Pyramid Construction Company has used the completed-contract method of accounting for construction contracts during its first two years of operation, 2004 and 2005. At the beginning of 2006, Pyramid decides to change to the percentage-of-completion method for both tax and financial reporting purposes. The following table presents information concerning the change for 2004–2006. The income tax rate for all years is 40%.

| | Income before Income Tax | | | | |
|---|---|---|---|---|---|
| | Percentage of Completion Method | Completed Contract Method | Difference | Income Tax Effect | Difference after Tax |
| 2004 | $ 90,000 | $60,000 | $30,000 | $12,000 | $18,000 |
| 2005 | 45,000 | 36,000 | 9,000 | 3,600 | 5,400 |
| Total | $135,000 | $96,000 | $39,000 | $15,600 | $23,400 |
| 2006 | $ 51,000 | $46,000 | $ 5,000 | $ 2,000 | $ 3,000 |

Pyramid issued 50,000 $1 par, common shares for $230,000 when the business began, and there have been no changes in paid-in capital since then. Dividends were not paid the first year, but $10,000 cash dividends were paid in both 2005 and 2006.

**Required:**

1. Prepare the journal entry to record the change in principle. (All tax effects should be reflected in the deferred tax liability account.)
2. Prepare the 2006–2005 comparative income statements beginning with income before income taxes.
3. Prepare the 2006–2005 comparative statements of shareholders' equity. (Hint: The 2004 statements reported retained earnings of $36,000. This is $60,000 − [$60,000 × 40%]).

**P 20–3**
Change in inventory costing methods; comparative income statements

● LO2 LO3

eXcel

Shown below are net income amounts as they would be determined by Weihrich Steel Company by each of three different inventory costing methods ($ in 000s).

| | FIFO | Average Cost | LIFO |
|---|---|---|---|
| Pre-2005 | $2,800 | $2,540 | $2,280 |
| 2005 | 750 | 600 | 540 |
| | $3,550 | $3,140 | $2,820 |

**Required:**

1. Assume that Weihrich used FIFO before 2006, and then in 2006 decided to switch to average cost. Prepare the journal entry to record the change in principle and briefly describe any other steps Weihrich should take to appropriately report the situation. (Ignore income tax effects.)
2. Assume that Weihrich used FIFO before 2006, and then in 2006 decided to switch to LIFO cost. Weihrich's records of inventory purchases and sales are not available for several previous years. Therefore, it is unable to determine the pre-2005 cumulative effect of applying this change to LIFO retrospectively. However, Weihrich does have the information needed to apply LIFO on a prospective basis beginning in 2005. Prepare the journal entry to record the change in principle and briefly describe any other steps Weihrich should take to appropriately report the situation. (Ignore income tax effects.)
3. Assume that Weihrich used FIFO before 2006, and then in 2006 decided to switch to LIFO. Prepare the journal entry to record the change in principle and briefly describe any other steps Weihrich should take to appropriately report the situation. (Ignore income tax effects.)

**P 20–4**
Change in inventory methods

● LO2

The Rockwell Corporation uses a periodic inventory system and has used the FIFO cost method since inception of the company in 1971. In 2006, the company decided to switch to the average cost method. Data for 2006 are as follows:

| | | |
|---|---|---|
| Beginning inventory, FIFO (5,000 units @ $30.00) | | $150,000 |
| Purchases: | | |
| 5,000 units @ $36.00 | $180,000 | |
| 5,000 units @ $40.00 | 200,000 | 380,000 |
| Cost of goods available for sale | | $530,000 |
| Sales for 2006 (8,000 units @ $70.00) | | $560,000 |

**Additional information:**

1. The company's effective income tax rate is 40% for all years.
2. If the company had used the average cost method prior to 2006, ending inventory for 2005 would have been $130,000.
3. 7,000 units remained in inventory at the end of 2006.

**Required:**

1. Prepare the journal entry at the beginning of 2006 to record the change in principle.
2. In the 2006–2004 comparative financial statements, what will be the amounts of cost of goods sold and inventory reported for 2006?

**P 20–5**
Change in inventory methods

● LO2

Fantasy Fashions has used the LIFO method of costing inventories, but at the beginning of 2006 decided to change to the FIFO method. The inventory as reported at the end of 2005 using LIFO would have been $20 million higher using FIFO.

Retained earnings had been reported at the end of 2004 and 2005 as $240 million and $260 million, respectively (reflecting the LIFO method). Those amounts reflecting the FIFO method would have been $250 million and $272 million, respectively. 2005 net income had been reported at the end of 2005 as $28 million (LIFO method) but would have been $30 million using FIFO. After changing to FIFO, 2006 net income was $36 million. Dividends of $8 million were paid each year. The tax rate is 40%.

**Required:**

1. Prepare the journal entry at the beginning of 2006 to record the change in principle.

2. In the 2006–2005 comparative income statements, what will be the amounts of net income reported for 2005 and 2006?
3. Prepare the 2006–2005 retained earnings column of the comparative statements of shareholders' equity.

**P 20–6**
Change in principle; change in depreciation methods

● LO3

During 2004 and 2005, Faulkner Manufacturing used the sum-of-the-years'-digits (SYD) method of depreciation for its operational assets, for both financial reporting and tax purposes. At the beginning of 2006, Faulkner decided to change to the straight-line method for both financial reporting and tax purposes. A tax rate of 40% is in effect for all years.

For an asset that cost $21,000 with an estimated residual value of $1,000 and an estimated useful life of 10 years, the effect of this change on net income the first year is as follows:

| Year | Straight Line | SYD | Difference |
|---|---|---|---|
| 2004 | $2,000 | $3,200 | $1,200 |
| 2005 | 2,000 | 2,800 | 800 |
| | $4,000 | $6,000 | $2,000 |

**Required:**

1. Describe the way Faulkner should account for the change described. Include in your answer any journal entry Faulkner will record in 2006 related to the change and any required footnote disclosures.
2. Suppose instead that Faulkner had previously used straight-line depreciation and changed to sum-of-the-years'-digits in 2006. Describe the way Faulkner should account for the change. Include in your answer any journal entry Faulkner will record in 2006 related to the change and any required footnote disclosures.

**P 20–7**
Depletion; change in estimate

● LO4

eXcel

In 2006, the Marion Company purchased land containing a mineral mine for $1,600,000. Additional costs of $600,000 were incurred to develop the mine. Geologists estimated that 400,000 tons of ore would be extracted. After the ore is removed, the land will have a resale value of $100,000.

To aid in the extraction, Marion built various structures and small storage buildings on the site at a cost of $150,000. These structures have a useful life of 10 years. The structures cannot be moved after the ore has been removed and will be left at the site. In addition, new equipment costing $80,000 was purchased and installed at the site. Marion does not plan to move the equipment to another site, but estimates that it can be sold at auction for $4,000 after the mining project is completed.

In 2006, 50,000 tons of ore were extracted and sold. In 2007, the estimate of total tons of ore in the mine was revised from 400,000 to 487,500. During 2007, 80,000 tons were extracted.

**Required:**

1. Compute depletion and depreciation of the mine and the mining facilities and equipment for 2006 and 2007. Marion uses the units-of-production method to determine depreciation on mining facilities and equipment.
2. Compute the book value of the mineral mine, structures, and equipment as of December 31, 2007.

**P 20–8**
Accounting changes; six situations

● LO1 LO3 LO4

Described below are six independent and unrelated situations involving accounting changes. Each change occurs during 2006 before any adjusting entries or closing entries were prepared. Assume the tax rate for each company is 40% in all years. Any tax effects should be adjusted through the deferred tax liability account.

a. Fleming Home Products introduced a new line of commercial awnings in 2005 that carry a one-year warranty against manufacturer's defects. Based on industry experience, warranty costs were expected to approximate 3% of sales. Sales of the awnings in 2005 were $3,500,000. Accordingly, warranty expense and a warranty liability of $105,000 were recorded in 2005. In late 2006, the company's claims experience was evaluated and it was determined that claims were far fewer than expected: 2% of sales rather than 3%. Sales of the awnings in 2006 were $4,000,000 and warranty expenditures in 2006 totaled $91,000.
b. On December 30, 2002, Rival Industries acquired its office building at a cost of $1,000,000. It has been depreciated on a straight-line basis assuming a useful life of 40 years and no salvage value. However, plans were finalized in 2006 to relocate the company headquarters at the end of 2010. The vacated office building will have a salvage value at that time of $700,000.
c. Hobbs-Barto Merchandising, Inc. changed inventory cost methods to LIFO from FIFO at the end of 2006 for both financial statement and income tax purposes. Under FIFO, the inventory at January 1, 2007, is $690,000.
d. At the beginning of 2003, the Hoffman Group purchased office equipment at a cost of $330,000. Its useful life was estimated to be 10 years with no salvage value. The equipment has been depreciated by the sum-of-the-years'-digits method. On January 1, 2006, the company changed to the straight-line method.
e. In November 2004, the State of Minnesota filed suit against Huggins Manufacturing Company, seeking penalties for violations of clean air laws. When the financial statements were issued in 2005, Huggins

had not reached a settlement with state authorities, but legal counsel advised Huggins that it was probable the company would have to pay $200,000 in penalties. Accordingly, the following entry was recorded:

| | | |
|---|---|---|
| Loss—litigation | 200,000 | |
| Liability—litigation | | 200,000 |

Late in 2006, a settlement was reached with state authorities to pay a total of $350,000 in penalties.

f. At the beginning of 2006, Jantzen Specialties, which uses the sum-of-the-years'-digits method changed to the straight-line method for newly acquired buildings and equipment. The change increased current year net earnings by $445,000.

**Required:**

For each situation:

1. Identify the type of change.
2. Prepare any journal entry necessary as a direct result of the change as well as any adjusting entry for 2006 related to the situation described.
3. Briefly describe any other steps that should be taken to appropriately report the situation.

**P 20–9**
Accounting changes; identify type and reporting approach
● LO1 through LO4

At the beginning of 2006, Wagner Implements undertook a variety of changes in accounting methods, corrected several errors, and instituted new accounting policies.

**Required:**

On a sheet of paper numbered from 1 to 10, indicate for each item below the type of change and the reporting approach Wagner would use.

| Type of Change (choose one) | Reporting Approach (choose one) |
|---|---|
| P. Change in accounting principle | R. Retrospective approach |
| E. Change in accounting estimate | P. Prospective approach |
| EP. Change in estimate resulting from a change in principle | |
| X. Correction of an error | |
| N. Neither an accounting change nor an accounting error. | |

**Change:**

1. By acquiring additional stock, Wagner increased its investment in Wise, Inc. from a 12% interest to 25% and changed its method of accounting for the investment from an available-for-sale investment to the equity method.
2. Wagner instituted a postretirement benefit plan for its employees in 2006 and adopted *SFAS No. 106*, "Accounting for Postretirement Benefit Plans Other than Pensions." Wagner had not previously had such a plan.
3. Wagner changed its method of depreciating computer equipment from the SYD method to the straight-line method.
4. Wagner determined that a liability insurance premium it both paid and expensed in 2005 covered the 2005–2007 period.
5. Wagner custom-manufactures farming equipment on a contract basis. Wagner switched its accounting for these long-term contracts from the completed-contract method to the percentage-of-completion method.
6. Due to an unexpected relocation, Wagner determined that its office building previously to be depreciated over 45 years should be depreciated over 18 years.
7. Wagner offers a three-year warranty on the farming equipment it sells. Manufacturing efficiencies caused Wagner to reduce its expectation of warranty costs from 2% of sales to 1% of sales.
8. Wagner changed from LIFO to FIFO to account for its materials and work in process inventories.
9. Wagner changed from FIFO to average cost to account for its equipment inventory.
10. Wagner sells extended service contracts on some of its equipment sold. Wagner performs services related to these contracts over several years, so in 2006 Wagner changed from recognizing revenue from these service contracts on a cash basis to the accrual basis.

**P 20–10**
Inventory errors
● LO6

You have been hired as the new controller for the Ralston Company. Shortly after joining the company in 2006, you discover the following errors related to the 2004 and 2005 financial statements:

a. Inventory at 12/31/04 was understated by $6,000.
b. Inventory at 12/31/05 was overstated by $9,000.
c. On 12/31/05, inventory was purchased for $3,000. The company did not record the purchase until the inventory was paid for early in 2006. At that time, the purchase was recorded by debit to purchases and a credit to cash.

The company uses a periodic inventory system.

**Required:**

1. Assuming that the errors were discovered after the 2005 financial statements were issued, analyze the effect of the errors on 2005 and 2004 cost of goods sold, net income, and retained earnings. (Ignore income taxes.)
2. Prepare a journal entry to correct the errors.
3. What other step(s) would be taken in connection with the error?

**P 20–11**
Error correction; change in depreciation method
● LO6

The Collins Corporation purchased office equipment at the beginning of 2004 and capitalized a cost of $2,000,000. This cost included the following expenditures:

| | |
|---|---|
| Purchase price | $1,850,000 |
| Freight charges | 30,000 |
| Installation charges | 20,000 |
| Annual maintenance charge | 100,000 |
| Total | $2,000,000 |

The company estimated an eight-year useful life for the equipment. No residual value is anticipated. The double-declining-balance method was used to determine depreciation expense for 2004 and 2005.

In 2006, after the 2005 financial statements were issued, the company decided to switch to the straight-line depreciation method for this equipment. At that time, the company's controller discovered that the original cost of the equipment incorrectly included one year of annual maintenance charges for the equipment.

**Required:**

1. Ignoring income taxes, prepare the appropriate correcting entry for the equipment capitalization error discovered in 2006.
2. Ignoring income taxes, prepare any 2006 journal entry(s) related to the change in depreciation methods.

**P 20–12**
Accounting changes and error correction; eight situations; tax effects ignored
● LO1 through LO4

Williams-Santana, Inc. is a manufacturer of high-tech industrial parts that was started in 1994 by two talented engineers with little business training. In 2006, the company was acquired by one of its major customers. As part of an internal audit, the following facts were discovered. The audit occurred during 2006 before any adjusting entries or closing entries were prepared.

a. A five-year casualty insurance policy was purchased at the beginning of 2004 for $35,000. The full amount was debited to insurance expense at the time.
b. Effective January 1, 2006, the company changed the salvage value used in calculating depreciation for its office building. The building cost $600,000 on December 29, 1995, and has been depreciated on a straight-line basis assuming a useful life of 40 years and a salvage value of $100,000. Declining real estate values in the area indicate that the salvage value will be no more than $25,000.
c. On December 31, 2005, merchandise inventory was overstated by $25,000 due to a mistake in the physical inventory count using the periodic inventory system.
d. The company changed inventory cost methods to FIFO from LIFO at the end of 2006 for both financial statement and income tax purposes. The change will cause a $960,000 increase in the beginning inventory at January 1, 2007.
e. At the end of 2005, the company failed to accrue $15,500 of sales commissions earned by employees during 2005. The expense was recorded when the commissions were paid in early 2006.
f. At the beginning of 2004, the company purchased a machine at a cost of $720,000. Its useful life was estimated to be 10 years with no salvage value. The machine has been depreciated by the double-declining balance method. Its carrying amount on December 31, 2005, was $460,800. On January 1, 2006, the company changed to the straight-line method.
g. Bad debt expense is determined each year as 1% of credit sales. Actual collection experience of recent years indicates that 0.75% is a better indication of uncollectible accounts. Management effects the change in 2006. Credit sales for 2006 are $4,000,000; in 2005 they were $3,700,000.
h. Additional industrial robots were acquired at the beginning of 2003 and added to the company's assembly process. The $1,000,000 cost of the equipment was inadvertently recorded as repair expense. Robots have 10-year useful lives and no material salvage value. This class of equipment is depreciated by the straight-line method.

**Required:**

For each situation:

1. Identify whether it represents an accounting change or an error. If an accounting change, identify the type of change.
2. Prepare any journal entry necessary as a direct result of the change or error correction as well as any adjusting entry for 2006 related to the situation described. (Ignore tax effects.)
3. Briefly describe any other steps that should be taken to appropriately report the situation.

**P 20–13**
Accounting changes and error correction; eight situations; tax effects considered

● LO1 through LO4 LO6

(Note: This problem is a variation of the previous problem, modified to consider income tax effects.) Williams-Santana, Inc. is a manufacturer of high-tech industrial parts that was started in 1994 by two talented engineers with little business training. In 2006, the company was acquired by one of its major customers. As part of an internal audit, the following facts were discovered. The audit occurred during 2006 before any adjusting entries or closing entries were prepared. The income tax rate is 40% for all years.

a. A five-year casualty insurance policy was purchased at the beginning of 2004 for $35,000. The full amount was debited to insurance expense at the time.
b. Effective January 1, 2006, the company changed the salvage values used in calculating depreciation for its office building. The building cost $600,000 on December 29, 1995, and has been depreciated on a straight-line basis assuming a useful life of 40 years and a salvage value of $100,000. Declining real estate values in the area indicate that the salvage value will be no more than $25,000.
c. On December 31, 2005, merchandise inventory was overstated by $25,000 due to a mistake in the physical inventory count using the periodic inventory system.
d. The company changed inventory cost methods to FIFO from LIFO at the end of 2006 for both financial statement and income tax purposes. The change will cause a $960,000 increase in the beginning inventory at January 1, 2007.
e. At the end of 2005, the company failed to accrue $15,500 of sales commissions earned by employees during 2005. The expense was recorded when the commissions were paid in early 2006.
f. At the beginning of 2004, the company purchased a machine at a cost of $720,000. Its useful life was estimated to be ten years with no salvage value. The machine has been depreciated by the double-declining balance method. Its carrying amount on December 31, 2005, was $460,800. On January 1, 2006, the company changed to the straight-line method.
g. Bad debt expense is determined each year as 1% of credit sales. Actual collection experience of recent years indicates that 0.75% is a better indication of uncollectible accounts. Management effects the change in 2006. Credit sales for 2006 are $4,000,000; in 2005 they were $3,700,000.
h. Additional industrial robots were acquired at the beginning of 2003 and added to the company's assembly process. The $1,000,000 cost of the equipment was inadvertently recorded as repair expense. Robots have 10-year useful lives and no material salvage value. This class of equipment is depreciated by the straight-line method.

**Required:**
For each situation:
1. Identify whether it represents an accounting change or an error. If an accounting change, identify the type of change.
2. Prepare any journal entry necessary as a direct result of the change or error correction as well as any adjusting entry for 2006 related to the situation described. Any tax effects should be adjusted for through the deferred tax liability account.
3. Briefly describe any other steps that should be taken to appropriately report the situation.

**P 20–14**
Errors; change in estimate; change in principle; restatement of previous financial statements

● LO1 LO3 LO4 LO6

eXcel

Whaley Distributors is a wholesale distributor of electronic components. Financial statements for the year ended December 31, 2005, reported the following amounts and subtotals ($ in millions):

| | Assets | Liabilities | Shareholders' Equity | Net Income | Expenses |
|---|---|---|---|---|---|
| 2004 | $740 | $330 | $410 | $210 | $150 |
| 2005 | 820 | 400 | 420 | 230 | 175 |

In 2006 the following situations occurred or came to light:

a. Internal auditors discovered that ending inventories reported on the financial statements the two previous years were misstated due to faulty internal controls. The errors were in the following amounts:

| | |
|---|---|
| 2004 inventory | Overstated by $12 million |
| 2005 inventory | Understated by $10 million |

b. A liability was accrued in 2004 for a probable payment of $7 million in connection with a lawsuit ultimately settled in December 2006 for $4 million.
c. A patent costing $18 million at the beginning of 2004, expected to benefit operations for a total of six years, has not been amortized since acquired.
d. Whaley's conveyer equipment has been depreciated by the sum-of-the-years'-digits (SYD) basis since constructed at the beginning of 2004 at a cost of $30 million. It has an expected useful life of five years and no expected residual value. At the beginning of 2006, Whaley decided to switch to straight-line depreciation.

**Required:**
For each situation:

1. Prepare any journal entry necessary as a direct result of the change or error correction as well as any adjusting entry for 2006 related to the situation described. (Ignore tax effects.)
2. Determine the amounts to be reported for each of the five items shown above from the 2004 and 2005 financial statements when those amounts are reported again in the 2004–2006 comparative financial statements.

**P 20–15**
Correction of errors; six errors
● LO6

Conrad Wholesale Supply underwent a restructuring in 2006. The company conducted a thorough internal audit, during which the following facts were discovered. The audit occurred during 2006 before any adjusting entries or closing entries are prepared.

a. Additional computers were acquired at the beginning of 2004 and added to the company's office network. The $45,000 cost of the computers was inadvertently recorded as maintenance expense. Computers have five-year useful lives and no material salvage value. This class of equipment is depreciated by the straight-line method.
b. Two weeks prior to the audit, the company paid $17,000 for assembly tools and recorded the expenditure as office supplies. The error was discovered a week later.
c. On December 31, 2005, merchandise inventory was understated by $78,000 due to a mistake in the physical inventory count. The company uses the periodic inventory system.
d. Two years earlier, the company recorded a 4% stock dividend (2,000 common shares, $1 par) as follows:

| | | |
|---|---|---|
| Retained earnings | 2,000 | |
| Common stock | | 2,000 |

The shares had a market price at the time of $12 per share.
e. At the end of 2005, the company failed to accrue $104,000 of interest expense that accrued during the last four months of 2005 on bonds payable. The bonds which were issued at face value mature in 2010. The following entry was recorded on March 1, 2006, when the semiannual interest was paid:

| | | |
|---|---|---|
| Interest expense | 156,000 | |
| Cash | | 156,000 |

f. A three-year liability insurance policy was purchased at the beginning of 2005 for $72,000. The full premium was debited to insurance expense at the time.

**Required:**
For each error, prepare any journal entry necessary to correct the error as well as any year-end adjusting entry for 2006 related to the situation described. (Ignore income taxes.)

## BROADEN YOUR PERSPECTIVE

**Apply your critical-thinking ability to the knowledge you've gained. These cases will provide you an opportunity to develop your research, analysis, judgment, and communication skills. You also will work with other students, integrate what you've learned, apply it in real world situations, and consider its global and ethical ramifications. This practice will broaden your knowledge and further develop your decision-making abilities.**

**Judgment Case 20–1**
Accounting changes; independent situations
● LO1 through LO5

Sometimes a business entity will change its method of accounting for certain items. The change may be classified as a change in accounting principle, a change in accounting estimate, or a change in reporting entity.

Listed below are three independent, unrelated sets of facts relating to accounting changes.

**Situation I:** A company determined that the depreciable lives of its fixed assets are presently too long to fairly match the cost of the fixed assets with the revenue produced. The company decided at the beginning of the current year to reduce the depreciable lives of all of its existing fixed assets by five years.

**Situation II:** On December 31, 2005, Gary Company owned 51% of Allen Company, at which time Gary reported its investment on a nonconsolidated basis due to political uncertainties in the country in which Allen was located. On January 2, 2006, the management of Gary Company was satisfied that the political uncertainties were resolved and the assets of the company were in no danger of nationalization. Accordingly, Gary will prepare consolidated financial statements for Gary and Allen for the year ended December 31, 2006.

**Situation III:** A company decides in January 2006 to adopt the straight-line method of depreciation for plant equipment. The straight-line method will be used for new acquisitions as well as for previously acquired plant equipment for which depreciation had been provided on an accelerated basis.

**Required:**
For each of the situations described above, provide the information indicated below. Complete your discussion of each situation before going on to the next situation.

1. Type of accounting change.
2. Manner of reporting the change under current generally accepted accounting principles including a discussion, where applicable, of how amounts are computed.
3. Effect of the change on the balance sheet and income statement.
4. Footnote disclosures that would be necessary.

**Analysis Case 20–2**
Various changes

● LO1 through LO5

DRS Corporation changed the way it depreciates its computers from the sum-of-the-year's-digits method to the straight-line method beginning January 1, 2006, DRS also changed its estimated residual value used in computing depreciation for its office building. At the end of 2006, DRS changed the specific subsidiaries constituting the group of companies for which its consolidated financial statements are prepared.

**Required:**

1. For each accounting change DRS undertook, indicate the type of change and how DRS should report the change. Be specific.
2. Why should companies disclose changes in accounting principles?

**Analysis Case 20–3**
Various changes

● LO1 through LO4

Ray Solutions decided to make the following changes in its accounting policies on January 1, 2006:

a. Changed from the cash to the accrual basis of accounting for recognizing revenue on its service contracts.
b. Adopted straight-line depreciation for all future equipment purchases, but continued to use accelerated depreciation for all equipment acquired before 2006.
c. Changed from the LIFO inventory method to the FIFO inventory method.

**Required:**
For each accounting change Ray undertook, indicate the type of change and how Ray should report the change. Be specific.

**Integrating Case 20–4**
Change to dollar-value LIFO

● LO3

Webster Products, Inc. adopted the dollar-value LIFO method of determining inventory costs for financial and income tax reporting on January 1, 2006. Webster continues to use the FIFO method for internal decision-making purposes. Webster's FIFO inventories at December 31, 2006, 2007, and 2008, were $300,000, $412,500, and $585,000, respectively. Internally generated cost indexes are used to convert FIFO inventory amounts to dollar-value LIFO amounts. Webster estimated these indexes as follows:

| | |
|---|---|
| 2006 | 1.00 |
| 2007 | 1.25 |
| 2008 | 1.50 |

**Required:**

1. Determine Webster's dollar-value LIFO inventory at December 31, 2007 and 2008.
2. Describe how the change should have been reported in Webster's 2006 financial statements.

**Communication Case 20–5**
Change in loss contingency; write a memo

● LO4

Late in 2006, you and two other officers of Curbo Fabrications Corporation just returned from a meeting with officials of The City of Jackson. The meeting was unexpectedly favorable even though it culminated in a settlement with city authorities that your company pay a total of $475,000 to cover the cost of violations of city construction codes. Jackson had filed suit in November 2004 against Curbo Fabrications Corporation, seeking civil penalties and injunctive relief for violations of city construction codes regulating earthquake damage standards. Alleged violations involved several construction projects completed during the previous three years. When the financial statements were issued in 2005, Curbo had not reached a settlement with state authorities, but legal counsel had advised the company that it was probable the ultimate settlement would be $750,000 in penalties. The following entry had been recorded:

| | | |
|---|---|---|
| Loss—litigation . . . . . . . . . . . . . . . . . . . . . . . . . . . . . . . . . . . . . . . . . . . . . . . | 750,000 | |
| Liability—litigation . . . . . . . . . . . . . . . . . . . . . . . . . . . . . . . . . . . . . . . . . . . . | | 750,000 |

The final settlement, therefore, was a pleasant surprise. While returning from the meeting, conversation turned to reporting the settlement in the 2006 financial statements. You drew the short straw and were selected to write a memo to Janet Zeno, the financial vice president, advising the proper course of action.

**Required:**
Write the memo. Include descriptions of any journal entries related to the change in amounts. Briefly describe other steps Curbo should take to report the settlement.

**Analysis Case 20–6**
Two wrongs make a right?

● LO4

Early one Wednesday afternoon, Ken and Larry studied in the dormitory room they shared at Fogelman College. Ken, an accounting major, was advising Larry, a management major, regarding a project for Larry's Business Policy class. One aspect of the project involved analyzing the 2005 annual report of Craft Paper Company. Though not central to his business policy case, a footnote had caught Larry's attention.

**Depreciation and Cost of Timber Harvested (in part)**
($ in millions)

| | 2005 | 2004 | 2003 |
|---|---|---|---|
| Depreciation of buildings, machinery and equipment | $260.9 | $329.8 | $322.5 |
| Cost of timber harvested and amortization of logging roads | 4.9 | 4.9 | 4.9 |
| | $265.8 | $334.7 | $327.4 |

Beginning in 2005, the Company revised the estimated average useful lives used to compute depreciation for most of its pulp and paper mill equipment from 16 years to 20 years and for most of its finishing and converting equipment from 12 years to 15 years. These revisions were made to more properly reflect the true economic lives of the assets and to better align the Company's depreciable lives with the predominant practice in the industry. The change had the effect of increasing net income by approximately $55 million.

"If I understand this right, Ken, the company is not going back and recalculating a lower depreciation for earlier years. Instead they seem to be leaving depreciation overstated in earlier years and making up for that by understating it in current and future years," Larry mused. "Is that the way it is in accounting? Two wrongs make a right?"

**Required:**
What are the two wrongs to which Larry refers? Is he right?

**Ethics Case 20–7**
Softening the blow

● LO1 LO2 LO3

Late one Thursday afternoon, Joy Martin, a veteran audit manager with a regional CPA firm, was reviewing documents for a long-time client of the firm, AMT Transport. The year-end audit was scheduled to begin Monday.

For three months, the economy had been in a down cycle and the transportation industry was particularly hard hit. As a result, Joy expected AMT's financial results would not be pleasant news to shareholders. However, what Joy saw in the preliminary statements made her sigh aloud. Results were much worse than she feared.

"Larry (the company president) already is in the doghouse with shareholders," Joy thought to herself. "When they see these numbers, they'll hang him out to dry."

"I wonder if he's considered some strategic accounting changes," she thought, after reflecting on the situation. "The bad news could be softened quite a bit by changing inventory methods from LIFO to FIFO or reconsidering some of the estimates used in other areas."

**Required:**
1. How would the actions contemplated contribute toward "softening" the bad news?
2. Do you perceive an ethical dilemma? What would be the likely impact of following up on Joy's thoughts? Who would benefit? Who would be injured?

**Research Case 20–8**
Researching the way changes in postretirement benefit estimates are reported; retrieving disclosures from the Internet

● LO4

It's financial statements preparation time at Center Industries where you have been assistant controller for two months. Ben Huddler, the controller, seems to be pleasant but unpredictable. Today, although your schedule is filled with meetings with internal and outside auditors and two members of the board of directors, Ben made a request. "As you know, we're decreasing the rate at which we assume health care costs will rise when measuring our postretirement benefit obligation. I'd like to know how others have reported similar changes. Can you find me an example?" he asked. "I'd bet you could get one off the Internet you're always using." As a matter of fact, you often use EDGAR, the Electronic Data Gathering, Analysis, and Retrieval system (www.sec.gov) to access financial statements filed with the U.S. Securities and Exchange Commission (SEC).

**Required:**
1. Access EDGAR on the Internet. You might want to use one of the EDGAR retrieval sites listed at the course website. Access a recent 10-K filing of a firm you think might have a postretirement health care plan. You may need to look up several companies before you find what you're looking for. Older, established companies are most likely to have such benefit plans.
   (Note: You may be able to focus your search by searching with key words and phrases in one of the several "search engines" available on the Internet.)
2. Copy the portion of the disclosures that reports the effect of a change in health care cost trends.
3. What information is provided about the effect of the change on the company's estimated benefit obligation?

**Analysis Case 20–9**
Change in inventory methods; concepts

Generally accepted accounting principles should be applied consistently from period to period. However, changes within a company, as well as changes in the external economic environment, may force a company

● LO2 LO3

to change an accounting method. The specific reporting requirements when a company changes from one generally accepted inventory method to another depend on the methods involved.

**Required:**

Explain the accounting treatment for a change in inventory method (a) not involving LIFO, (b) from the LIFO method, and (c) to the LIFO method. Explain the logic underlying those treatments. Also, describe how disclosure requirements are designed to address the departure from consistency and comparability of changes in accounting principle.

**Real World Case 20–10**
Change in inventory method

● LO2

On March 3, 2004, **Casey's General Stores, Inc.** made the following announcement:

---

***Casey's General Stores, Inc.***

Ankeny, Iowa, March 3, 2004—Casey's General Stores, Inc. (Nasdaq symbol CASY) today reported earnings for the third quarter ended January 31, 2004, and for the fiscal year to date.

In the third quarter of fiscal 2004, the Company changed to FIFO from LIFO for valuing gasoline inventory. The historical financials presented were adjusted in accordance with GAAP to reflect FIFO valuation, and prior-year third quarter earnings per share were adjusted to $0.16 from $0.14.

---

**Required:**

1. Why does GAAP require Casey's General Stores to retrospectively adjust prior years' financial statements for this type of accounting change?
2. Assuming that the quantity of inventory remained stable during the first nine months of 2003, did the cost of Casey's General Stores' inventory move up or down during that year?

**Communication Case 20–11**
Change in inventory method; disclosure note

● LO2

Mayfair Department Stores, Inc., operates over 30 retail stores in the Pacific Northwest. Prior to 2006, the company used the FIFO method to value its inventory. In 2006, Mayfair decided to switch to the dollar-value LIFO retail inventory method. One of your responsibilities as assistant controller is to prepare the disclosure note describing the change in method that will be included in the company's 2006 financial statements. Kenneth Meier, the controller, provided the following information:

- Internally developed retail price indexes are used to adjust for the effects of changing prices.
- If the change had not been made, cost of goods sold for the year would have been $22 million lower. The company's income tax rate is 40% and there were 100 million shares of common stock outstanding during 2006.
- The cumulative effect of the change on prior years' income is not determinable.
- The reasons for the change were (a) to provide a more consistent matching of merchandise costs with sales revenue, and (b) the new method provides a more comparable basis of accounting with competitors that also use the LIFO method.

**Required:**

1. Prepare for Kenneth Meier the disclosure note that will be included in the 2006 financial statements.
2. Explain why the "cumulative effect of the change on prior years' income is not determinable."

**Judgment Case 20–12**
Inventory errors

● LO6

Some inventory errors are said to be "self-correcting" in that the error has the opposite financial statement effect in the period following the error, thereby "correcting" the original account balance errors.

**Required:**

Despite this self-correcting feature, discuss why these errors should not be ignored and describe the steps required to account for the error correction.

**Ethics Case 20–13**
Overstatement of ending inventory

● LO6

Danville Bottlers is a wholesale beverage company. Danville uses the FIFO inventory method to determine the cost of its ending inventory. Ending inventory quantities are determined by a physical count. For the fiscal year-end June 30, 2006, ending inventory was originally determined to be $3,265,000. However, on July 17, 2006, John Howard, the company's controller, discovered an error in the ending inventory count. He determined that the correct ending inventory amount should be $2,600,000.

Danville is a privately owned corporation with significant financing provided by a local bank. The bank requires annual audited financial statements as a condition of the loan. By July 17, the auditors had completed their review of the financial statements which are scheduled to be issued on July 25. They did not discover the inventory error.

John's first reaction was to communicate his finding to the auditors and to revise the financial statements before they are issued. However, he knows that his and his fellow workers' profit-sharing plans are based on annual pretax earnings and that if he revises the statements, everyone's profit sharing bonus will be significantly reduced.

**Required:**

1. Why will bonuses be negatively affected? What is the effect on pretax earnings?
2. If the error is not corrected in the current year and is discovered by the auditors during the following year's audit, how will it be reported in the company's financial statements?
3. Discuss the ethical dilemma Howard faces.

# 21 CHAPTER

# The Statement of Cash Flows Revisited

## OVERVIEW

The objective of financial reporting is to provide investors and creditors with useful information, primarily in the form of financial statements. The balance sheet and the income statement—the focus of your study in earlier chapters—do not provide all the information needed by these decision makers. Here you will learn how the statement of cash flows fills the information gap left by the other financial statements.

The statement lists all cash inflows and cash outflows, and classifies them as cash flows from (a) operating, (b) investing, or (c) financing activities. Investing and financing activities that do not directly affect cash also are reported.

## LEARNING OBJECTIVES

**After studying this chapter, you should be able to:**

- LO1 Explain the usefulness of the statement of cash flows.
- LO2 Define cash equivalents.
- LO3 Determine cash flows from operating activities by the direct method.
- LO4 Determine cash flows from operating activities by the indirect method.
- LO5 Identify transactions that are classified as investing activities.
- LO6 Identify transactions that are classified as financing activities.
- LO7 Identify transactions that represent noncash investing and financing activities.
- LO8 Prepare a statement of cash flows with the aid of a spreadsheet or T-accounts.

# FINANCIAL REPORTING CASE

## Where's the Cash?

"What do you mean you can't afford a wage increase?" union negotiator Vince Barr insisted. "We've all seen your income statement. You had record earnings this year."

This is the first day of negotiations with the company's union representatives. As company controller, you know it's going to be up to you to explain the company's position on the financial aspects of the negotiations. In fact, you've known for some time that a critical point of contention would be the moderate increase in this year's profits after three years of level or slightly declining earnings. Not helping the situation is that the company has always used accelerated depreciation on its equipment which it began replacing this year at considerably higher prices than it cost several years back.

**By the time you finish this chapter, you should be able to respond appropriately to the questions posed in this case. Compare your response to the solution provided at the end of the chapter.**

### QUESTIONS

1. What are the cash flow aspects of the situation that Mr. Barr may be overlooking in making his case for a wage increase? How can a company's operations generate a healthy profit and yet produce meager or even negative cash flows? (page 1057)
2. What information can a statement of cash flows provide about a company's investing activities that can be useful in decisions such as this? (page 1059)
3. What information can a statement of cash flows provide about a company's financing activities that can be useful in decisions such as this? (page 1060)

# PART A THE CONTENT AND VALUE OF THE STATEMENT OF CASH FLOWS

### DECISION MAKERS' PERSPECTIVE—Usefulness of Cash Flow Information

● LO1

Investors and creditors require cash flows from the corporation.

A fund manager of a major insurance company, considering investing $8,000,000 in the common stock of **The Coca-Cola Company**, asks herself: "What are the prospects of future dividends and market-price appreciation? Will we get a return commensurate with the cost and risk of our investment?" A bank officer, examining an application for a business loan, asks himself: "If I approve this loan, what is the likelihood of the borrower making interest payments on time and repaying the loan when due?" Investors and creditors continually face these and similar decisions that require projections of the relative ability of a business to generate future cash flows and of the risk associated with those forecasts.

To make these projections, decision makers rely heavily on the information reported in periodic financial statements. In the final analysis, cash flows into and out of a business enterprise are the most fundamental events on which investors and creditors base their decisions. Naturally, these decisions focus on the prospects of the decision makers receiving cash returns from their dealings with the firm. However, it is the ability of the firm to generate cash flows to itself that ultimately determines the potential for cash flows from the firm to investors and creditors.

Cash flows to investors and creditors depend on the corporation generating cash flows to itself.

The financial statements that have been the focus of your study in earlier chapters—the income statement and the balance sheet—offer information helpful in forecasting future cash-generating ability. Some important questions, however, are not easily answered from the information these statements provide. For example, meaningful projections of a company's future profitability and risk depend on answers to such questions as:

- In what types of activities is the company investing?
- Are these activities being financed with debt? with equity? by cash generated from operations?
- Are facilities being acquired to accommodate future expansion?
- How does the amount of cash generated from operations compare with net income over time?
- Why isn't the increase in retained earnings reflected as an increase in dividends?
- What happens to the cash received from the sale of assets?
- By what means is debt being retired?

Many decisions benefit from information about the company's underlying cash flow process.

The information needed to answer these and similar questions is found in the continuous series of cash flows that the income statement and the balance sheet describe only indirectly. This underlying cash flow process is considered next. ■

## Cash Inflows and Outflows

Cash continually flows into and out of an active business. Businesses disburse cash to acquire operational assets to maintain or expand productive capacity. When no longer needed, these assets may be sold for cash. Cash is paid to produce or purchase inventory for resale, as well as to pay for the expenses of selling these goods. The ultimate outcome of these selling activities is an inflow of cash. Cash might be invested in securities of other firms. These investments provide cash inflows during the investment period in the form of dividends or interest and at the end of the investment period when the securities are sold. To raise cash to finance their operations, firms sell stock and/or acquire debt. Cash payments are made as dividends to shareholders and interest to creditors. When debt is repaid or stock repurchased, cash flows out of the firm. To help you visualize the continual process of cash receipts and cash payments, that process is diagrammed in Graphic 21–1. The diagram also previews the way we will later classify the cash flows on a statement of cash flows.

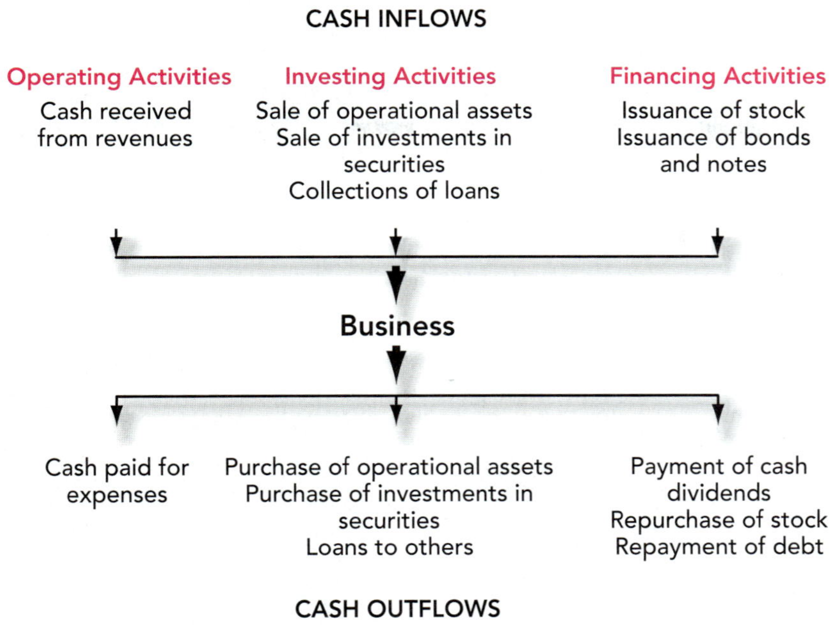


**GRAPHIC 21–1**
Cash Inflows and Cash Outflows

Embodied in this assortment of cash flows is a wealth of information that investors and creditors require to make educated decisions. Much of the value of the underlying information provided by the cash flows is lost when reported only indirectly by the balance sheet and the income statement. Each cash flow eventually impacts decision makers by affecting the balances of various accounts on the balance sheet. Also, many of the cash flows—those related to income-producing activities—are represented on the income statement. However, they are not necessarily reported in the period the cash flows occur because the income statement measures activities on an accrual basis. The statement of cash flows fills the information gap by reporting the cash flows directly.

## Role of the Statement of Cash Flows

● LO2

A statement of cash flows is shown in Graphic 21–2. The statement lists all cash inflows and cash outflows during the reporting period. To enhance the informational value of the presentation, the cash flows are classified according to the nature of the activities that bring about the cash flows. The three primary categories of cash flows are (1) cash flows from operating activities, (2) cash flows from investing activities, and (3) cash flows from financing activities. Classifying each cash flow by source (operating, investing, or financing activities) is more informative than simply listing the various cash flows. Notice, too, that the noncash investing and financing activities—investing and financing activities that do not directly increase or decrease cash—also are reported. *FASB Statement 95,* requiring the statement of cash flows, was issued in direct response to *FASB Concept Statement 1,* which states that the primary objective of financial reporting is to "provide information to help investors and creditors, and others assess the amounts, timing, and uncertainty of prospective net cash inflows to the related enterprise."[1]

**The statement of cash flows provides information about cash flows that is lost when reported only indirectly by the balance sheet and the income statement.**

Many companies have experienced bankruptcy because they were unable to generate sufficient cash to satisfy their obligations. Doubtless, many investors in the stock of these firms would have been spared substantial losses if the financial statements had been designed to foresee the cash flow problems the companies were experiencing. A prominent illustration is the demise of **W. T. Grant** during the 1970s. Grant, a general retailer in the days before malls, was a blue chip stock of its time. Grant's statement of changes in financial position (the predecessor of the statement of cash flows) reported working capital from operations of

[1] "Objectives of Financial Reporting by Business Enterprises," *FASB Statement of Financial Accounting Concepts* No. 1, par 37.

**GRAPHIC 21–2**
Statement of Cash Flows

**UNITED BRANDS CORPORATION**
**Statement of Cash Flows**
**For Year Ended December 31, 2006**
($ in millions)

| | | |
|---|---|---|
| **Cash Flows from Operating Activities** | | |
| Cash inflows: | | |
| From customers | $98 | |
| From investment revenue | 3 | |
| Cash outflows: | | |
| To suppliers of goods | (50) | |
| To employees | (11) | |
| For interest | (3) | |
| For insurance | (4) | |
| For income taxes | (11) | |
| *Net cash flows from operating activities* | | $22 |
| **Cash Flows from Investing Activities** | | |
| Purchase of land | (30) | |
| Purchase of short-term investment | (12) | |
| Sale of land | 18 | |
| Sale of equipment | 5 | |
| *Net cash flows from investing activities* | | (19) |
| **Cash Flows from Financing Activities** | | |
| Sale of common shares | 26 | |
| Retirement of bonds payable | (15) | |
| Payment of cash dividends | (5) | |
| *Net cash flows from financing activities* | | 6 |
| *Net increase in cash* | | 9 |
| Cash balance, January 1 | | 20 |
| Cash balance, December 31 | | $29 |

**Note X:**
**Noncash Investing and Financing Activities**

| | |
|---|---|
| Acquired $20 million of equipment by issuing a 12%, 5-year note. | $20 |

**Reconciliation of Net Income to Cash Flows from Operating Activities:**

| | |
|---|---|
| Net income | $12 |
| *Adjustments for noncash effects:* | |
| Gain on sale of land | (8) |
| Depreciation expense | 3 |
| Loss on sale of equipment | 2 |
| *Changes in operating assets and liabilities:* | |
| Increase in accounts receivable | (2) |
| Decrease in inventory | 4 |
| Increase in accounts payable | 6 |
| Increase in salaries payable | 2 |
| Discount on bonds payable | 2 |
| Decrease in prepaid insurance | 3 |
| Decrease in income tax payable | (2) |
| *Net cash flows from operating activities* | $22 |

$46 million in 1972. Yet, if presented, a statement of cash flows would have reported cash flows from operating activities of negative $10 million. In fact, the unreported cash flow deficiency grew to $114 million in 1973, while working capital from operations was reported as having increased by $1 million. That year, without the benefit of cash flow information, investors were buying Grant's stock at prices that represented up to 20 times its earnings.[2]

More recently, even with cash flow information available, cash flow problems can go unnoticed. An example is the rapid growth and subsequent bankruptcy of the **Wicks 'N' Sticks** franchise. The company's drive for rapid growth led to a dependence on the sale of new franchises in order to generate cash flow instead of doing so in a more healthy way through its operations. As we see shortly, a statement of cash flows can indicate not just the amount of cash flows, but also whether those cash flows are coming from operations or from outside sources. Wicks 'N' Sticks was able to emerge from bankruptcy through restructuring and a new perspective on cash flow management.

The statement of cash flows for United Brands Corporation (UBC), shown in Graphic 21–2, is intended at this point in the discussion to illustrate the basic structure and composition of the statement. Later we will see how the statement of cash flows for UBC is prepared from the information typically available for this purpose. We will refer to UBC's statement of cash flows frequently throughout the chapter as the discussion becomes more specific regarding the criteria for classifying cash flows in the three primary categories and as we identify the specific cash flows to be reported on the statement. We will examine the content of the statement in more detail following a look at how this relatively recent financial statement has evolved to its present form over the course of the last several decades.

## Evolution of the Statement of Cash Flows

LO3

In light of the obvious value of cash flow information, it's interesting to note that the statement of cash flows has been a required financial statement only since 1988. The relatively recent requirement completes a full-cycle movement of accounting thought back to cash flow reporting, which, in different form, was common practice several decades ago.

**Early efforts to instill the standard of accrual accounting intentionally suppressed the widespread practice of cash flow reporting.**

During the early part of this century and continuing into the mid-1930s, the preparation of financial statements on a cash basis was a widely used means of financial reporting, particularly by small and medium-sized companies. It is important to realize, however, that the cash flow reporting requirements of today are quite different from the cash flow reporting practiced during that earlier era, when emphasis was placed on cash-based income determination. The accounting profession was fully aware that accrual accounting (recognizing revenues when earned, expenses when incurred) provides a far better measure of a company's profitability. However, without official standards to ensure the general use of accrual accounting, cash-based reporting flourished. Motivated by the desire to instill the standard of accrual accounting, a concerted effort was exerted to suppress cash-based methods.

As cash-flow reporting abated, the need for some type of funds-flow reporting became apparent and a funds statement began to appear in the annual reports of many companies. Because the statement was not required and there was no officially prescribed format, the definition and presentation of funds varied widely among firms that issued the statement. The mounting bias against cash-based reporting certainly influenced many firms to choose alternate definitions of funds.

**Early official recommendations confessed a noncash bias.**

Prompted by increasing concerns over the lack of uniformity in the reporting of funds flow, the AICPA sponsored a 1961 research study by Perry Mason (the accountant, not the lawyer) entitled "Cash Flow Analysis and the Funds Statement." The study recommended that a funds statement be required.[3] Two years later, *APB Opinion 3* officially recommended, but did not require, a "Statement of Source and Application of Funds."[4] The noncash bias was evident in this opinion. It cautioned against the use of terms such as cash flow and cash earnings and defined funds generally as working capital (current assets minus current liabilities).

**The statement of changes in financial position was the predecessor to the statement of cash flows.**

The first official requirement that a funds statement be included as an integral part of a complete set of financial statements was issued in 1971. *APB Opinion 19* required a statement of changes in financial position that reported funds flows classified as either sources (increases) or applications (decreases) of funds, as well as any significant nonfund investing

[2]Cheryl A. Zega, "The New Statement of Cash Flows," *Management Accounting*, September 1988.
[3]Perry Mason, "Cash Flow Analysis and the Funds Statement," *Accounting Research Study No. 2*, 1961.
[4]"The Statement of Source and Application of Funds," *Opinions of the Accounting Principles Board No. 3*, 1963, par. 8.

and financing activities. Funds could be defined as either cash or working capital.[5] Although defining funds as cash was permitted, a working capital definition predominated practice until the early 1980s. This preference was influenced by the historical bias, described earlier, against cash flow reporting.

Financial Executives International recommended that its members report on a cash basis after being persuaded by many accounting professors and practitioners that a cash-based definition of funds is more meaningful than a working capital definition.[6] This recommendation provided the impetus for a dramatic increase in the number of firms choosing to define funds as cash in their statements of changes in financial position.[7]

The increasingly widespread acceptance of cash-flow reporting, coupled with a recommendation in 1984 of *FASB Concept Statement 5* that a full set of financial statements show cash flows during the period, virtually assured the eventual requirement of a statement of cash flows.[8] In November 1987 the FASB prescribed *SFAS 95* (to supersede *APB Opinion 19*), described in this chapter.

## CASH AND CASH EQUIVALENTS

● LO4

Skilled cash managers will invest temporarily idle cash in short-term investments to earn interest on those funds, rather than maintain an unnecessarily large balance in a checking account. The FASB views short-term, highly liquid investments that can be readily converted to cash, with little risk of loss, as **cash equivalents.** Amounts held as investments of this type are essentially equivalent to cash because they are quickly available for use as cash. Therefore, on the statement of cash flows there is no differentiation between amounts held as cash (e.g., currency and checking accounts) and amounts held in cash equivalent investments. So, when we refer in this chapter to cash, we are referring to the total of cash and cash equivalents.

**There is no differentiation between amounts held as cash and amounts held in cash equivalent investments.**

Examples of cash equivalents are money market funds, Treasury bills, and commercial paper. To be classified as cash equivalents, these investments must have a maturity date not longer than three months from the date of purchase. Flexibility is permitted in designating cash equivalents. Each company must establish a policy regarding which short-term, highly liquid investments it classifies as cash equivalents. The policy should be consistent with the company's customary motivation for acquiring various investments and should be disclosed in the notes to the statement.[9] A recent annual report of **ExxonMobil Corporation** provides this description of its cash equivalents (Graphic 21–3):

**Each firm's policy regarding which short-term, highly liquid investments it classifies as cash equivalents should be disclosed in the notes to the financial statements.**

**GRAPHIC 21–3**

Disclosure of Cash Equivalents—ExxonMobil Corporation

**Note 4: Cash Flow Information (in part)**

The consolidated statement of cash flows provides information about changes in cash and cash equivalents. Highly liquid investments with maturities of three months or less when acquired are classified as cash equivalents.

Transactions that involve merely transfers from cash to cash equivalents (such as the purchase of a three-month Treasury bill), or from cash equivalents to cash (such as the sale of a Treasury bill), should not be reported on the statement of cash flows. The total of cash and cash equivalents is not altered by such transactions.[10] The cash balance reported on the balance sheet also represents the total of cash and cash equivalents, which allows us to compare the change in that balance with the net increase or decrease in the cash flows reported on the statement of cash flows.

[5]"Reporting Changes in Financial Position," *Opinions of the Accounting Principles Board No. 19,* 1971.

[6]See, for example, Lloyd C. Heath, "Let's Scrap the Funds Statement," *The Journal of Accountancy,* October 1978, and Edward Swanson and Richard Vandermeersch, "Statement of Financing and Investing Activities," *The CPA Journal,* November 1981.

[7]Allen H. Seed, III, *The Funds Statement—Structure and Use,* Financial Executives Research Foundation, 1984.

[8]"Recognition and Measurement in Financial Statements of Business Enterprises," *FASB Statement of Financial Accounting Concepts No. 5,* par. 13.

[9]A change in that policy is treated as a change in accounting principle.

[10]An exception is the sale of a cash equivalent at a gain or loss. This exception is described in more detail later in the chapter.

## PRIMARY ELEMENTS OF THE STATEMENT OF CASH FLOWS

This section describes the three primary activity classifications: (1) operating activities, (2) investing activities, and (3) financing activities; and two other requirements of the statement of cash flows: (4) the reconciliation of the net increase or decrease in cash with the change in the balance of the cash account and (5) noncash investing and financing activities.

FINANCIAL REPORTING CASE

Q1, p. 1051

**Cash Flows from Operating Activities.** The income statement reports the success of a business in generating a profit from its operations. Net income (or loss) is the result of netting together the revenues earned during the reporting period, regardless of when cash is received, and the expenses incurred in generating those revenues, regardless of when cash is paid. This is the accrual concept of accounting that has been emphasized throughout your study of accounting. Information about net income and its components, measured by the accrual concept, generally provides a better indication of current operating performance than does information about current cash receipts and payments.[11] Nevertheless, as indicated earlier, the cash effects of earning activities also provide useful information that is not directly accessible from the income statement. The first cash flow classification in the statement of cash flows reports that information.

**Cash flows from operating activities** are both inflows and outflows of cash that result from activities reported on the income statement. In other words, this classification of cash flows includes the elements of net income, but reported on a cash basis. The components of this section of the statement of cash flows, and their relationship with the elements of the income statement, are illustrated in Graphic 21–4.

**The cash effects of the elements of net income are reported as cash flows from operating activities.**

**GRAPHIC 21–4**
Relationship between the Income Statement and Cash Flows from Operating Activities (Direct Method)

| **Income Statement** | **Cash Flows from Operating Activities** |
|---|---|
| Revenues: | Cash inflows: |
| Sales and service revenue | Cash received from customers |
| Investment revenue | Cash revenue received (e.g., dividends, interest) |
| Noncash revenues and gains (e.g., gain on sale of assets) | (Not reported) |
| Less: Expenses: | Less: Cash outflows: |
| Cost of goods sold | Cash paid to suppliers of inventory |
| Salaries expense | Cash paid to employees |
| Noncash expenses and losses (e.g., depreciation, amortization, bad debts, loss on sale of assets) | (Not reported) |
| Interest expense | Cash paid to creditors |
| Other operating expenses | Cash paid to insurance companies and others |
| Income tax expense | Cash paid to the government |
| *Net income* | *Net cash flows from operating activities* |

To see the concept applied, let's look again at the cash flows from operating activities reported by United Brands Corporation. That section of the statement of cash flows is extracted from Graphic 21–2 and reproduced in Graphic 21–5.

Cash inflows from operating activities exceeded cash outflows for expenses by $22 million. We'll see later (in Illustration 21–1) that UBC's net income from the same operating activities was only $12 million. Why did operating activities produce net cash inflows greater than net income? The reason will become apparent when we determine, in a later section, the specific amounts of these cash flows.

You also should be aware that the generalization stated earlier that cash flows from operating activities include the elements of net income reported on a cash basis is not strictly true for all elements of the income statement. Notice in Graphic 21–5 that no cash effects are

[11] *FASB Statement of Financial Accounting Concepts No. 1*, par. 44.

**GRAPHIC 21–5**

Cash Flows from Operating Activities

**Cash flows from operating activities are the elements of net income, but reported on a cash basis.**

| | | |
|---|---|---|
| **Cash Flows from Operating Activities:** | | |
| Cash inflows: | | |
| From customers | $98 | |
| From investment revenue | 3 | |
| Cash outflows: | | |
| To suppliers of goods | (50) | |
| To employees | (11) | |
| For interest | (3) | |
| For insurance | (4) | |
| For income taxes | (11) | |
| *Net cash flows from operating activities* | | $22 |

reported for depreciation and amortization of operational assets, nor for gains and losses from the sale of those assets. Cash outflows occur when operational assets are acquired, and cash inflows occur when the assets are sold. However, as described later, the acquisition and subsequent resale of operational assets are classified as investing activities, rather than as operating activities.

Quite the opposite, the purchase and the sale of inventory are considered operating activities. The cash effects of these transactions—namely, (1) cash payments to suppliers and (2) cash receipts from customers—are included in the determination of cash flows from operating activities. Why are inventories and operational assets treated differently when classifying their cash effects if both are acquired for the purpose of producing revenues? The essential difference is that inventory typically is purchased for the purpose of being sold as part of the firm's current operations, while an operational asset is purchased as an investment to benefit the business over a relatively long period of time.

**Direct Method or Indirect Method of Reporting Cash Flows from Operating Activities.** The presentation by UBC of cash flows from operating activities illustrated in Graphic 21–2 and reproduced in Graphic 21–5 above is referred to as the **direct method**. The method is named for the fact that the cash effect of each operating activity (i.e., income statement item) is reported *directly* on the statement of cash flows. For instance, UBC reports "cash received from customers" as the cash effect of sales activities, "cash paid to suppliers" as the cash effect of cost of goods sold, and so on. Then, UBC simply omits from the presentation any income statement items that do not affect cash at all, such as depreciation expense.

Another way UBC might have reported cash flows from operating activities is by the **indirect method**. By this approach, the net cash increase or decrease from operating activities ($22 million in our example) would be derived *indirectly* by starting with reported net income and working backwards to convert that amount to a cash basis. As we see later in the chapter, UBC's net income is $12 million. Using the indirect method, UBC would replace the previous presentation of net cash flows from operating activities with the one shown in Graphic 21–6.

Be sure to note that the indirect method generates the same $22 million net cash flows from operating activities as did the direct method. Rather than directly reporting only the components of the income statement that *do* represent increases or decreases in cash, by the indirect method we begin with net income—which includes both cash and noncash components—and back out all amounts that *don't* reflect increases or decreases in cash. Later in the chapter, we explore the specific adjustments made to net income to achieve this result. At this point it is sufficient to realize that two alternative methods are permitted for reporting net cash flows from operating activities. Either way, we convert accrual-based income to cash flows produced by those same operating activities.

Notice also that the indirect method presentation is identical to what UBC reported earlier as the "Reconciliation of Net Income to Cash Flows from Operating Activities" in Note X of Graphic 21–2. Whether cash flows from operating activities are reported by the direct method or by the indirect method, the financial statements must reconcile the difference between net income and cash flows from operating activities. When a company uses the *direct*

**GRAPHIC 21–6**
Indirect Method

| | | |
|---|---|---|
| **Cash Flows from Operating Activities:** | | |
| Net income | $12 | |
| *Adjustments for noncash effects:* | | |
| Gain on sale of land | (8) | |
| Depreciation expense | 3 | |
| Loss on sale of equipment | 2 | |
| *Changes in operating assets and liabilities:* | | |
| Increase in accounts receivable | (2) | |
| Decrease in inventory | 4 | |
| Increase in accounts payable | 6 | |
| Increase in salaries payable | 2 | |
| Discount on bonds payable | 2 | |
| Decrease in prepaid insurance | 3 | |
| Decrease in income tax payable | (2) | |
| *Net cash flows from operating activities* | | $22 |

**By the indirect method, UBC derives the net cash increase or decrease from operating activities *indirectly*, by starting with reported net income and working backwards to convert that amount to a cash basis.**

*method*, the company presents the reconciliation in a separate schedule as UBC did. That presentation is precisely the same as the presentation of net cash flows from operating activities by the indirect method. On the other hand, a company choosing to use the indirect method is not required to provide a separate reconciliation schedule because the "cash flows from operating activities" section of the statement of cash flows serves that purpose.[12]

It's important to understand, too, that regardless of which method a company chooses to report *operating* activities, that choice has no effect on the way it identifies and reports cash flows from *investing* and *financing* activities. We turn our attention now to those two sections of the statement of cash flows. Later in Part C, we'll return for a more thorough discussion of the alternative methods of reporting the operating activities section.

**FINANCIAL REPORTING CASE**

Q2, p. 1051

● LO5

**Cash Flows from Investing Activities.** Companies periodically invest cash to replace or expand productive facilities such as property, plant, and equipment. Investments might also be made in other assets, such as securities of other firms, with the expectation of a return on those investments. Information concerning these investing activities can provide valuable insight to decision makers regarding the nature and magnitude of operational assets being acquired for future use, as well as provide clues concerning the company's ambitions for the future.

**Cash outflows and cash inflows due to the acquisition and disposition of assets (other than inventory and assets classified as cash equivalents) are reported as cash flows from investing activities.**

**Cash flows from investing activities** are both outflows and inflows of cash caused by the acquisition and disposition of assets. Included in this classification are cash payments to acquire (1) property, plant, and equipment and other productive assets (except inventories), (2) investments in securities (except cash equivalents and trading securities[13]), and (3) nontrade receivables.[14] When these assets later are liquidated, any cash receipts from their disposition also are classified as investing activities. For instance, cash received from the sale of the assets or from the collection of a note receivable (principal amount only) represents cash inflows from investing activities. Be sure to realize that, unlike the label might imply, any investment revenue like interest, dividends, or other cash return from these investments is not an investing activity. The reason, remember, is that investment revenue is an income statement item and therefore is an operating activity.

For illustration, notice the cash flows reported as investing activities by UBC. That section of the statement of cash flows is extracted from Graphic 21–2 and reproduced in Graphic 21–7.

---

[12]According to the *AICPA, Accounting Trends and Techniques*, 2004, a recent survey of 600 companies showed that 593 companies chose to use the indirect method, only 7 the direct method.

[13]Inflows and outflows of cash from buying and selling trading securities typically are considered operating activities because financial institutions that routinely transact in trading securities consider them an appropriate part of their normal operations.

[14]A nontrade receivable differs from a trade receivable in that it is not one associated with the company's normal trade; that is, it's not received from a customer. A trade receivable, or accounts receivable, is an *operating asset*. A nontrade receivable, on the other hand, might be a loan to an affiliate company or to an officer of the firm. To understand how the creation of a nontrade receivable is an *investing* activity, you might view such a loan as an investment in the receivable.

**GRAPHIC 21–7**

Cash Flows from Investing Activities

**Cash flows from investing activities include investments in assets and their subsequent sale.**

| **Cash Flows from Investing Activities:** | | |
|---|---|---|
| Purchase of land | (30) | |
| Purchase of short-term investment | (12) | |
| Sale of land | 18 | |
| Sale of equipment | 5 | |
| *Net cash flows from investing activities* | | (19) |

UBC reports as investing activities the cash paid to purchase both land and a short-term investment. The other two investing activities reported are cash receipts for the sale of assets—equipment and land—that were acquired in earlier years. The specific transactions creating these cash flows are described in a later section of this chapter.

The purchase and sale of inventories are not considered investing activities. Inventories are purchased for the purpose of being sold as part of the firm's primary operations, so their purchase and sale are classified as operating activities.

Also, the purchase and sale of assets classified as cash equivalents are not reported as investing activities. In fact, these activities usually are not reported on the statement of cash flows. For example, when temporarily idle cash is invested in a money market fund considered to be a cash equivalent, the total of cash and cash equivalents does not change. Likewise, when the cash is later withdrawn from the money market fund, the total remains unchanged. The exception is when cash equivalents are sold at a gain or a loss. In that case, the total of cash and cash equivalents actually increases or decreases in the process of transferring from one cash equivalent account to another cash equivalent account. As a result, the change in cash would be reported as a cash flow from operating activities. This is illustrated later in the chapter.

**FINANCIAL REPORTING CASE**

Q3, p. 1051

● LO6

**Cash inflows and cash outflows due to the external financing of a business are reported as cash flows from financing activities.**

**Cash Flows from Financing Activities.** Not only is it important for investors and creditors to be informed about how a company is investing its funds, but also how its investing activities are being financed. Hopefully, the primary operations of the firm provide a source of internal financing. Information revealed in the cash flows from operating activities section of the statement of cash flows lets statement users know the extent of available internal financing. However, a major portion of financing for many companies is provided by external sources, specifically by shareholders and creditors.

**Cash flows from financing activities** are both inflows and outflows of cash resulting from the external financing of a business. We include in this classification cash inflows from (a) the sale of common and preferred stock and (b) the issuance of bonds and other debt securities. Subsequent transactions related to these financing transactions, such as a buyback of stock (to retire the stock or as treasury stock), the repayment of debt, and the payment of cash dividends to shareholders, also are classified as financing activities.

For illustration, refer to Graphic 21–8 excerpted from Graphic 21–2.

**GRAPHIC 21–8**

Cash Flows from Financing Activities

**Cash flows from financing activities include the sale or repurchase of shares, the issuance or repayment of debt securities, and the payment of cash dividends.**

| **Cash Flows from Financing Activities** | | |
|---|---|---|
| Sale of common shares | 26 | |
| Retirement of bonds payable | (15) | |
| Payment of cash dividends | (5) | |
| *Net cash flows from financing activities* | | 6 |

The cash received from the sale of common stock is reported as a financing activity. Since the sale of common stock is a financing activity, providing a cash return (dividend) to common shareholders also is a financing activity. Similarly, when the bonds being retired were sold in a prior year, that cash inflow was reported as a financing activity. In the current year, when the bonds are retired, the resulting cash outflow is likewise classified as a financing activity.

At first glance, it may appear inconsistent to classify the payment of cash dividends to shareholders as a financing activity when, as stated earlier, paying interest to creditors is classified as an operating activity. But remember, cash flows from operating activities should reflect the cash effects of items that enter into the determination of net income. Interest expense is a determinant of net income. A dividend, on the other hand, is a distribution of net income and not an expense.[15]

**Interest, unlike dividends, is a determinant of net income and therefore an operating activity.**

**Reconciliation with Change in Cash Balance.** One of the first items you may have noticed about UBC's statement of cash flows is that there is a net change in cash of $9 million. Is this a significant item of information provided by the statement? The primary objective of the statement of cash flows is not to tell us that cash increased by $9 million. We can readily see the increase or decrease in cash by comparing the beginning and ending balances in the cash account in comparative balance sheets. Instead, the purpose of the statement of cash flows is to explain *why* cash increased by $9 million.

To reinforce the fact that the net amount of cash inflows and outflows explains the change in the cash balance, the statement of cash flows includes a reconciliation of the net increase (or decrease) in cash with the company's beginning and ending cash balances. Notice, for instance, that on UBC's statement of cash flows, the reconciliation appears as:

| | |
|---|---|
| **Net Increase in Cash** | **$ 9** |
| Cash balance, January 1 | 20 |
| Cash balance, December 31 | $29 |

**The net amount of cash inflows and outflows reconciles the change in the company's beginning and ending cash balances.**

**Noncash Investing and Financing Activities.** Suppose UBC were to borrow $20 million cash from a bank, issuing a long-term note payable for that amount. This transaction would be reported on a statement of cash flows as a financing activity. Now suppose UBC used that $20 million cash to purchase new equipment. This second transaction would be reported as an investing activity.

● LO7

Instead of two separate transactions, as indicated by Graphic 21–2, UBC acquired $20 million of new equipment by issuing a $20 million long-term note payable in a single transaction. Undertaking a significant investing activity and a significant financing activity as two parts of a single transaction does not diminish the value of reporting these activities. For that reason, transactions that do not increase or decrease cash, but which result in significant investing and financing activities, must be reported in related disclosures.

These **noncash investing and financing activities**, such as UBC's acquiring equipment (an investing activity) by issuing a long-term note payable (a financing activity), are reported in a separate disclosure schedule or note. UBC reported this transaction in the following manner:

**Noncash Investing and Financing Activities:**
Acquired $20 million of equipment by issuing a 12%, 5-year note.

**Noncash investing and financing activities are reported also.**

It's convenient to report noncash investing and financing activities on the same page as the statement of cash flows as did UBC only if there are few such transactions. Otherwise, precisely the same information would be reported in disclosure notes to the financial statements.[16]

Examples of noncash transactions that would be reported in this manner are:

1. Acquiring an asset by incurring a debt payable to the seller.
2. Acquiring an asset by entering into a capital lease.
3. Converting debt into common stock or other equity securities.
4. Exchanging noncash assets or liabilities for other noncash assets or liabilities.

Noncash transactions that do not affect a company's assets or liabilities, such as the distribution of stock dividends, are not considered investing or financing activities and are not

[15]Not all accountants are satisfied with the FASB's distinctions among operating, investing, and financing activities. See for example, Hugo Nurnberg, "Inconsistencies and Ambiguities in Cash Flow Statements under *FASB Statement No. 95*," *Accounting Horizons*, June 1993.

[16]"Statement of Cash Flows," *Statement of Financial Accounting Standards No. 95* (Stamford, Conn.: FASB, 1987), par. 74.

reported. Recall from Chapter 18 that stock dividends merely increase the number of shares of stock owned by existing shareholders. From an accounting standpoint, the stock dividend causes a dollar amount to be transferred from one part of shareholders' equity (retained earnings) to another part of shareholders' equity (paid-in capital). Neither assets nor liabilities are affected; therefore, no investing or financing activity has occurred.

**ADDITIONAL CONSIDERATION**

A transaction involving an investing and financing activity may be part cash and part noncash. For example, a company might pay cash for a part of the purchase price of new equipment and issue a long-term note for the remaining amount. In our previous illustration, UBC issued a note payable for the $20 million cost of the equipment it acquired. Suppose the equipment were purchased in the following manner:

| | | |
|---|---|---|
| Equipment | 20 | |
| Cash | | 6 |
| Note payable | | 14 |

In that case, $6 million would be reported under the caption "Cash flows from investing activities," and the noncash portion of the transaction—issuing a $14 million note payable for $14 million of equipment—would be reported as a "noncash investing and financing activity." UBC's statement of cash flows, if modified by the assumption of a part cash/part noncash transaction, would report these two elements of the transaction as follows:

| | | |
|---|---|---|
| **Cash Flows from Investing Activities:** | | |
| Purchase of land | $(30) | |
| Purchase of short-term investments | (12) | |
| Sale of land | 18 | |
| Sale of equipment | 5 | |
| Purchase of equipment | (6) | |
| *Net cash flows from investing activities* | | (25) |
| **Noncash Investing and Financing Activities:** | | |

Acquired $20 million of equipment by paying cash and issuing a 12%, 5-year note as follows:

| | |
|---|---|
| Cost of equipment | $20 million |
| Cash paid | 6 million |
| Note issued | $14 million |

## Preparation of the Statement of Cash Flows

LO8 The objective in preparing the statement of cash flows is to identify all transactions and events that represent operating, investing, or financing activities and to list and classify those activities in proper statement format. A difficulty in preparing a statement of cash flows is that typical accounting systems are not designed to produce the specific information we need for the statement. At the end of a reporting cycle, balances exist in accounts reported on the income statement (sales revenue, cost of goods sold, etc.) and the balance sheet (accounts receivable, common stock, etc.). However, the ledger contains no balances for cash paid to acquire equipment, or cash received from sale of land, or any other cash flow needed for the statement. As a result, it's necessary to find a way of using information that is available to reconstruct the various cash flows that occurred during the reporting period. Typically, the information available to assist the statement preparer includes an income statement for the year and balance sheets for both the current and preceding years (comparative statements). The accounting records also can provide additional information about transactions that caused changes in account balances during the year.

The typical year-end data is provided for UBC in Illustration 21–1. We have referred frequently to the statement of cash flows of UBC to illustrate the nature of the activities the statement reports. Now we will see how that statement is developed from the data provided in that illustration.

In situations involving relatively few transactions, it is possible to prepare the statement of cash flows by merely inspecting the available data and logically determining the reportable activities. Few real-life situations are sufficiently simple to be solved this way. Usually, it is more practical to use some systematic method of analyzing the available data to ensure that all operating, investing, and financing activities are detected. A common approach is to use either a manual or electronic spreadsheet to organize and analyze the information used to prepare the statement.[17]

**Reconstructing the events and transactions that occurred during the period helps identify the operating, investing, and financing activities to be reported.**

Whether the statement of cash flows is prepared by an unaided inspection and analysis or with the aid of a systematic technique such as spreadsheet analysis, the analytical process is the same. To identify the activities to be reported on the statement, we use available data to reconstruct the events and transactions that involved operating, investing, and financing activities during the year. It is helpful to reproduce the journal entries that were recorded at the time of the transaction. Examining reconstructed journal entries makes it easier to visualize whether a reportable activity is involved and how that activity is to be classified.

**ILLUSTRATION 21–1**

Comparative Balance Sheets and Income Statement

**UNITED BRANDS CORPORATION**
**Comparative Balance Sheets**
**December 31, 2006 and 2005**
($ in millions)

| | | |
|---|---|---|
| **Assets** | **2006** | **2005** |
| Cash | $ 29 | $ 20 |
| Accounts receivable | 32 | 30 |
| Short-term investments | 12 | 0 |
| Inventory | 46 | 50 |
| Prepaid insurance | 3 | 6 |
| Land | 80 | 60 |
| Buildings and equipment | 81 | 75 |
| Less: Accumulated depreciation | (16) | (20) |
| | $267 | $221 |
| **Liabilities** | | |
| Accounts payable | $ 26 | $ 20 |
| Salaries payable | 3 | 1 |
| Income tax payable | 6 | 8 |
| Notes payable | 20 | 0 |
| Bonds payable | 35 | 50 |
| Less: Discount on bonds | (1) | (3) |
| **Shareholders' Equity** | | |
| Common stock | 130 | 100 |
| Paid-in capital—excess of par | 29 | 20 |
| Retained earnings | 19 | 25 |
| | $267 | $221 |

[17]The T-account method is a second systematic approach to the preparation of the statement of cash flows. This method is identical in concept and similar in application to the spreadsheet method. The T-account method is used to prepare the statement of cash flows for UBC in Appendix 21B.

**ILLUSTRATION 21–1**
Concluded

**UNITED BRANDS CORPORATION**
**Income Statement**
**For the Year Ended December 31, 2006**
($ in millions)

| | | |
|---|---|---|
| **Revenues** | | |
| Sales revenue | $100 | |
| Investment revenue | 3 | |
| Gain on sale of land | 8 | $111 |
| **Expenses** | | |
| Cost of goods sold | 60 | |
| Salaries expense | 13 | |
| Depreciation expense | 3 | |
| Bond interest expense | 5 | |
| Insurance expense | 7 | |
| Loss on sale of equipment | 2 | |
| Income tax expense | 9 | 99 |
| **Net income** | | $ 12 |

**Additional Information from the Accounting Records**

a. A portion of company land, purchased in a previous year for $10 million, was sold for $18 million.
b. Equipment that originally cost $14 million, and which was one-half depreciated, was sold for $5 million cash.
c. The common shares of Mazuma Corporation were purchased for $12 million as a short-term investment.
d. Property was purchased for $30 million cash for use as a parking lot.
e. On December 30, 2006, new equipment was acquired by issuing a 12%, five-year, $20 million note payable to the seller.
f. On January 1, 2006, $15 million of bonds were retired at maturity.
g. The increase in the common stock account is attributable to the issuance of a 10% stock dividend (1 million shares) and the subsequent sale of 2 million shares of common stock. The market price of the $10 par value common stock was $13 per share on the dates of both transactions.
h. Cash dividends of $5 million were paid to shareholders.

Next, in Part B, we see how a spreadsheet simplifies the process of preparing a statement of cash flows. Even if you choose not to use a spreadsheet, the summary entries described can be used to help you find the cash inflows and outflows you need to prepare a statement of cash flows. For this demonstration, we assume the direct method is used to determine and report cash flows from operating activities. Appreciation of the direct method provides the backdrop for a thorough understanding of the indirect method that we explore in Part C.

# PART B PREPARING AN SCF: THE DIRECT METHOD OF REPORTING CASH FLOWS FROM OPERATING ACTIVITIES

## Using a Spreadsheet

There can be no cash inflow or cash outflow without a corresponding change in a noncash account.

An important advantage gained by using a spreadsheet is that it ensures that no reportable activities are inadvertently overlooked. Spreadsheet analysis relies on the fact that, in order for cash to increase or decrease, there must be a corresponding change in a noncash account. Therefore, if we can identify the events and transactions that caused the change in each noncash account during the year, we will have identified all the operating, investing, and financing activities that are to be included in the statement of cash flows.

The beginning and ending balances of each account are entered on the spreadsheet. Then, as journal entries are reconstructed in our analysis of the data, those entries are recorded on the spreadsheet so that the debits and credits of the spreadsheet entries explain the changes in the account balances. Only after spreadsheet entries have explained the changes in all account balances, can we feel confident that all operating, investing, and financing activities have been identified. The spreadsheet is designed in such a way that, as we record spreadsheet entries that explain account balance changes, we are simultaneously identifying and classifying the activities to be reported on the statement of cash flows.

**Recording spreadsheet entries that explain account balance changes simultaneously identifies and classifies the activities to be reported on the statement of cash flows.**

We begin by transferring the comparative balance sheets and income statement to a blank spreadsheet. For illustration, refer to the 2006 and 2005 balances in the completed spreadsheet for UBC, shown in Illustration 21–1A on the next two pages. Notice that the amounts for elements of the income statement are ending balances resulting from accumulations during the year. Beginning balances in each of these accounts are always zero.

Following the balance sheets and income statement, we allocate space on the spreadsheet for the statement of cash flows. Although at this point we have not yet identified the specific cash flow activities shown in the completed spreadsheet, we can include headings for the major categories of activities: cash flows from operating activities, cash flows from investing activities, and cash flows from financing activities. Leaving several lines between headings allows adequate space to include the specific cash flows identified in subsequent analysis.

The spreadsheet entries shown in the two changes columns, which separate the beginning and ending balances, explain the increase or decrease in each account balance. You will see in the next section how these entries were reconstructed. Although spreadsheet entries are in the form of debits and credits like journal entries, they are entered on the spreadsheet only. They are not recorded in the formal accounting records. In effect, these entries duplicate, frequently in summary form, the actual journal entries used to record the transactions as they occurred during the year.

**Spreadsheet entries duplicate the actual journal entries used to record the transactions as they occurred during the year.**

To reconstruct the journal entries, we analyze each account, one at a time, deciding at each step what transaction or event caused the change in that account. Often, the reason for the change in an account balance is readily apparent from viewing the change in conjunction with that of a related account elsewhere in the financial statements. Sometimes it is necessary to consult the accounting records for additional information to help explain the transaction that resulted in the change.

You may find it helpful to diagram in T-account format the relationship between accounts to better visualize certain changes, particularly in your initial study of the chapter. The analysis that follows is occasionally supplemented with such diagrams to emphasize *why,* rather than merely *how,* specific cash flow amounts emerge from the analysis.

Although there is no mandatory order in which to analyze the accounts, it is convenient to begin with the income statement accounts, followed by the balance sheet accounts. We analyze the accounts of UBC in that order below. Although our analysis of each account culminates in a spreadsheet entry, keep in mind that the analysis described also is appropriate to identify reportable activities when a spreadsheet is not used.[18]

## INCOME STATEMENT ACCOUNTS

As described in an earlier section, cash flows from operating activities are inflows and outflows of cash that result from activities reported on the income statement. Thus, to identify those cash inflows and outflows, we begin by analyzing the components of the income statement. It is important to keep in mind that the amounts reported in the income statement usually do not represent the cash effects of the items reported. For example, UBC reports sales revenue of $100 million. This does not mean, however, that it collected $100 million cash from customers during the year. In fact, by referring to the beginning and ending balances in accounts receivable, we see that cash received from customers could not have been $100 million. Since accounts receivable increased during the year, some of the sales revenue earned must not yet have been collected. This is explained further in the next section.

**Amounts reported in the income statement usually are not the same as the cash effects of the items reported.**

[18]The spreadsheet entries also are used to record the same transactions when the T-account method is used. We refer again to these entries when that method is described in Appendix 21B.

**ILLUSTRATION 21–1A**
Spreadsheet

**UNITED BRANDS CORPORATION**
**Spreadsheet for the Statement of Cash Flows**

| | Dec. 31 2005 | Changes: Debits | | Changes: Credits | | Dec. 31 2006 |
|---|---|---|---|---|---|---|
| **Balance Sheet** | | | | | | |
| **Assets:** | | | | | | |
| Cash | 20 | (19) | 9 | | | 29 |
| Accounts receivable | 30 | (1) | 2 | | | 32 |
| Short-term investments | 0 | (12) | 12 | | | 12 |
| Inventory | 50 | | | (4) | 4 | 46 |
| Prepaid insurance | 6 | | | (8) | 3 | 3 |
| Land | 60 | (13) | 30 | (3) | 10 | 80 |
| Buildings and equipment | 75 | (14) | 20X | (9) | 14 | 81 |
| Less: Accumulated depreciation | (20) | (9) | 7 | (6) | 3 | (16) |
| | 221 | | | | | 267 |
| **Liabilities:** | | | | | | |
| Accounts payable | 20 | | | (4) | 6 | 26 |
| Salaries payable | 1 | | | (5) | 2 | 3 |
| Income tax payable | 8 | (10) | 2 | | | 6 |
| Notes payable | 0 | | | (14) | 20X | 20 |
| Bonds payable | 50 | (15) | 15 | | | 35 |
| Less: Discount on bonds | (3) | | | (7) | 2 | (1) |
| **Shareholders' Equity:** | | | | | | |
| Common stock | 100 | | | (16) | 10 | |
| | | | | (17) | 20 | 130 |
| Paid-in capital—excess of par | 20 | | | (16) | 3 | |
| | | | | (17) | 6 | 29 |
| Retained earnings | 25 | (16) | 13 | | | |
| | | (18) | 5 | (11) | 12 | 19 |
| | 221 | | | | | 267 |
| **Income Statement** | | | | | | |
| **Revenues:** | | | | | | |
| Sales revenue | | | | (1) | 100 | 100 |
| Investment revenue | | | | (2) | 3 | 3 |
| Gain on sale of land | | | | (3) | 8 | 8 |
| **Expenses:** | | | | | | |
| Cost of goods sold | | (4) | 60 | | | (60) |
| Salaries expense | | (5) | 13 | | | (13) |
| Depreciation expense | | (6) | 3 | | | (3) |
| Bond interest expense | | (7) | 5 | | | (5) |
| Insurance expense | | (8) | 7 | | | (7) |
| Loss on sale of equipment | | (9) | 2 | | | (2) |
| Income tax expense | | (10) | 9 | | | (9) |
| **Net income** | | (11) | **12** | | | **12** |
| **Statement of Cash Flows** | | | | | | |
| **Operating Activities:** | | | | | | |
| Cash inflows: | | | | | | |
| From customers | | (1) | 98 | | | |
| From investment revenue | | (2) | 3 | | | |
| Cash outflows: | | | | | | |
| To suppliers of goods | | | | (4) | 50 | |
| To employees | | | | (5) | 11 | |
| To bondholders | | | | (7) | 3 | |
| For insurance expense | | | | (8) | 4 | |
| For income taxes | | | | (10) | 11 | |
| *Net cash flows* | | | | | | 22 |

**ILLUSTRATION 21–1A**
Concluded

| | Dec. 31 2005 | Changes Debits | | Changes Credits | | Dec. 31 2006 |
|---|---|---|---|---|---|---|
| **Investing Activities:** | | | | | | |
| Sale of land | | (3) | 18 | | | |
| Sale of equipment | | (9) | 5 | | | |
| Purchase of S-T investment | | | | (12) | 12 | |
| Purchase of land | | | | (13) | 30 | |
| *Net cash flows* | | | | | | (19) |
| **Financing Activities:** | | | | | | |
| Retirement of bonds payable | | | | (15) | 15 | |
| Sale of common shares | | (17) | 26 | | | |
| Payment of cash dividends | | | | (18) | 5 | |
| *Net cash flows* | | | | | | 6 |
| *Net increase in cash* | | | | (19) | 9 | 9 |
| Totals | | | 376 | | 376 | |

X—As explained later, the X's serve as a reminder to report this noncash transaction.

The cash effects of other income statement elements can be similarly discerned by referring to changes in the balances of the balance sheet accounts that are directly related to those elements. So, to identify cash flows from operating activities we examine, one at a time, the elements of the income statement in conjunction with any balance sheet accounts affected by each element.

**1. Sales Revenue.** Accounts receivable is the balance sheet account that is affected by sales revenue. Specifically, accounts receivable is increased by credit sales and is decreased as cash is received from customers. We can compare sales and the change in accounts receivable during the year to determine the amount of cash received from customers. This relationship can be viewed in T-account format as follows:

**Accounts Receivable**

| | | | |
|---|---|---|---|
| Beginning balance | 30 | | |
| Credit sales | 100 | ? | Cash received |
| *(increases A/R)* | | | *(decreases A/R)* |
| Ending balance | 32 | | |

We see from this analysis that cash received from customers must have been $98 million. Note that even if some of the year's sales were cash sales, say $40 million cash sales and $60 million credit sales, the result is the same:

**Accounts Receivable**

| | | | |
|---|---|---|---|
| Beginning balance | 30 | | |
| Credit sales | 60 | 58 → | |
| Ending balance | 32 | | |

| | |
|---|---|
| Cash sales | $40 |
| Received on account | 58 |
| Cash received | $98 |

Thus, cash flows from operating activities should include cash received from customers of $98 million. The net effect of sales revenue activity during the year can be summarized in the following entry.

**Relating sales and the change in accounts receivable during the period helps determine the amount of cash received from customers.**

| | ($ in millions) | |
|---|---|---|
| **Entry (1)** Cash (received from customers) | 98 | |
| Accounts receivable (given) | 2 | |
| Sales revenue ($100 – 0) | | 100 |

The entry above appears as entry (1) in the completed spreadsheet for UBC, shown in Illustration 21–1A. The entry explains the changes in two account balances—accounts receivable and sales revenue. Since the entry affects cash, it also identifies a cash flow to be reported on the statement of cash flows. The $98 million debit to cash is therefore entered in the statement of cash flows section of the spreadsheet under the heading of cash flows from operating activities.

## ADDITIONAL CONSIDERATION

The preceding discussion describes the most common situation—companies earn revenue by selling goods and services, increase accounts receivable, and then collect the cash and decrease accounts receivable later. Some companies, though, often collect the cash in advance of earning it, record unearned revenue, and then later record revenue and decrease unearned revenue. In those cases, we need to analyze any changes in the unearned revenue account for differences between revenue reported and cash collected. For instance, if UBC also had a $1 million increase in unearned revenue, the summary entry would be modified as follows:

| | ($ in millions) | |
|---|---|---|
| **Entry (1)** Cash (received from customers) | 99 | |
| Accounts receivable (given) | 2 | |
| Unearned revenue (given) | | 1 |
| Sales revenue ($100 − 0) | | 100 |

Notice that we enter the cash portion of entry (1) as one of several cash flows on the statement of cash flows rather than as a debit to the cash account. Only after all cash inflows and outflows have been identified will the net change in cash be entered as a debit to the cash account. In fact, the entry to reconcile the $9 million increase in the cash account and the $9 million net increase in cash on the statement of cash flows will serve as a final check of the accuracy of our spreadsheet analysis.

## ADDITIONAL CONSIDERATION

Notice that bad debt expense does not appear on the income statement and allowance for uncollectible accounts does not appear on the balance sheet. We have assumed that bad debts are immaterial for UBC. When this is not the case, it's necessary to consider the write-off of bad debts as we determine cash received from customers. Here's why.

When using the allowance method to account for bad debts, a company estimates the dollar amount of customer accounts that will ultimately prove uncollectible and records both bad debt expense and allowance for uncollectible accounts for that estimate.

| | | |
|---|---|---|
| Bad debt expense | xxx | |
| Allowance for uncollectible accounts | | xxx |

Then, when accounts actually prove uncollectible, accounts receivable and the allowance are reduced.

| | | |
|---|---|---|
| Allowance for uncollectible accounts | xxx | |
| Accounts receivable | | xxx |

In our illustration, we concluded that UBC received $2 million less cash ($98 million) than sales for the year ($100 million) because accounts receivable increased by that amount. However, if a portion of the change in accounts receivable had been due to write-offs of bad debts, that conclusion would be incorrect. Let's say, for instance, that UBC had bad debt expense of $2 million and its allowance for uncollectible accounts had increased by $1 million. Because the allowance for uncollectible accounts would be credited by $2 million in the adjusting entry for bad debts expense, necessarily there also would have been a $1 million debit to the account in order for there to have been a net increase (credit) in its balance of only $1 million. That debit would occur due to write-offs of bad debts totaling $1 million.

| | ($ in millions) | |
|---|---|---|
| Allowance for uncollectible accounts . . . . . . . . . . . . . . . . . . . . . | 1 | |
| Accounts receivable. . . . . . . . . . . . . . . . . . . . . . . . . . . . . . . . | | 1 |

This would indicate that a portion ($1 million credit) of the total change in accounts receivable ($2 million debit) would have been due to write-offs of bad debts, and the remaining change ($3 million debit) would have been due to cash collections being less than sales revenue. Cash received from customers would have been only $97 million in that case. We can view this in the framework of our T-account analysis as follows:

**Accounts Receivable**

| | | | |
|---|---|---|---|
| Beginning balance | 30 | | |
| Credit Sales | 100 | 97 | Cash received |
| | | 1 | Bad Debt write-offs |
| Ending balance | 32 | | |

The effect of write-offs of bad debts can be explicitly considered by combining all the accounts related to sales and collection activities into a single summary spreadsheet entry:

| | ($ in millions) | |
|---|---|---|
| **Entry (1)** Cash (received from customers) . . . . . . . . . . . . . . . . . . . . | 97 | |
| Accounts receivable ($32 − 30) . . . . . . . . . . . . . . . . . . . . | 2 | |
| Bad debt expense (from income statement) . . . . . . . . . . | 2 | |
| Allowance for uncollectible accounts ($3 − 2) . . . . . . | | 1 |
| Sales revenue ($100 − 0). . . . . . . . . . . . . . . . . . . . . . | | 100 |

This single entry summarizes all transactions related to sales, bad debts expense, write-offs of accounts receivable, and cash collections from sales.

The remaining spreadsheet entries are described in subsections 2 through 19. When including the entries on the spreadsheet, it is helpful to number the entries sequentially to provide a means of retracing the steps taken in the analysis if the need arises. You also may find it helpful to put a check mark (✔) to the right of the ending balance when the change in that balance has been explained. Then, once you have check marks next to every noncash account, you will know you are finished.

**2. Investment Revenue.** The income statement reports investment revenue of $3 million. Before concluding that this amount was received in cash, we first refer to the balance sheets to see whether a change in an account there indicates otherwise. A change in either of two balance sheet accounts, (a) investment revenue receivable or (b) long-term investments, might indicate that cash received from investment revenue differs from the amount reported on the income statement.

Changes in related accounts might indicate that investment revenue reported on the income statement is a different amount from cash received from the investment.

a. If we observe either an increase or a decrease in an *investment revenue receivable* account (e.g., interest receivable, dividends receivable), we would conclude that the amount of cash received during the year was less than (if an increase) or more than (if a decrease) the amount of revenue reported. The analysis would be identical to that of sales revenue and accounts receivable.

b. Also, an unexplained increase in a *long-term investment* account might indicate that a portion of investment revenue has not yet been received in cash. Recall from Chapter 12 that when using the equity method to account for investments in the stock of another corporation, investment revenue is recognized as the investor's percentage share of the investee's income, whether or not the revenue is received currently as cash dividends. For example, assume the investor owns 25% of the common stock of a corporation that reports net income of $12 million and pays dividends of $4 million. This situation would have produced a $2 million increase in long-term investments, which can be demonstrated by reconstructing the journal entries for the recognition of investment and the receipt of cash dividends:

| | ($ in millions) | |
|---|---|---|
| Long-term investments | 3 | |
| Investment revenue ($12 × 25%) | | 3 |
| Cash ($4 × 25%) | 1 | |
| Long-term investments | | 1 |

A combined entry would produce the same results:

| | | |
|---|---|---|
| Long-term investments | 2 | |
| Cash ($4 × 25%) | 1 | |
| Investment revenue ($12 × 25%) | | 3 |

The $2 million net increase in long-term investments would represent the investment revenue not received in cash. This would also explain why there is a $3 million increase (credit) in investment revenue. If these events had occurred, we would prepare a spreadsheet entry identical to the combined entry above. The spreadsheet entry would (a) explain the $2 million increase in long-term investments, (b) explain the $3 million increase in investment revenue, and (c) identify a $1 million cash inflow from operating activities.

However, because neither an investment revenue receivable account nor a long-term investment account appears on the comparative balance sheets, we can conclude that $3 million of investment revenue was collected in cash. Entry (2) on the spreadsheet is:

Because no other transactions are apparent that would have caused a change in investment revenue, we can conclude that $3 million of investment revenue was collected in cash.

| | ($ in millions) | |
|---|---|---|
| **Entry (2)** Cash (received from investment revenue) | 3 | |
| Investment revenue ($3 − 0) | | 3 |

**3. Gain on Sale of Land.** The third item reported on the income statement is an $8 million gain on the sale of land. Recall that our objective in analyzing each element of the statement is to determine the cash effect of that element. To do so, we need additional information about the transaction that caused this gain. The accounting records—item (a) in Illustration 21–1—indicate that land that originally cost $10 million was sold for $18 million. The entry recorded in the journal when the land was sold also serves as our spreadsheet entry:

A gain (or loss) is simply the difference between cash received in the sale of an asset and the book value of the asset—not a cash flow.

| | ($ in millions) | |
|---|---|---|
| **Entry (3)** Cash (received from sale of land) | 18 | |
| Land (given) | | 10 |
| Gain on sale of land ($8 − 0) | | 8 |

The cash effect of this transaction is a cash increase of $18 million. We therefore include the debit as a cash inflow in the statement of cash flows section of the spreadsheet. However, unlike the cash effect of the previous two spreadsheet entries, it is not reported as an operating activity. The sale of land is an *investing* activity, so this cash inflow is listed under that heading of the spreadsheet. The entry also accounts for the $8 million gain on sale of land. The $10 million credit to land does not, by itself, explain the $20 million increase in that account. As we will later discover, another transaction also affected the land account.

It is important to understand that the gain is simply the difference between cash received in the sale of land (reported as an investing activity) and the book value of the land. To report the $8 million gain as a cash flow from operating activities, in addition to reporting $18 million as a cash flow from investing activities, would be to report the $8 million twice.

**4. Cost of Goods Sold.** During the year UBC sold goods that had cost $60 million. This does not necessarily indicate that $60 million cash was paid to suppliers of those goods. To determine the amount of cash paid to suppliers, we look to the two current accounts affected by merchandise purchases—inventory and accounts payable. The analysis can be viewed as a two-step process.

First, we compare cost of goods sold with the change in inventory to determine the cost of goods *purchased* (not necessarily cash paid) during the year. To facilitate our analysis, we can examine the relationship in T-account format:

**Inventory**

| | | | |
|---|---|---|---|
| Beginning balance | 50 | | |
| Cost of goods **purchased** *(increases inventory)* | ? | 60 | Cost of goods **sold** *(decreases inventory)* |
| Ending balance | 46 | | |

From this analysis, we see that $56 million of goods were *purchased* during the year. It is not necessarily true, though, that $56 million cash was paid to suppliers of these goods. By looking in accounts payable, we can determine the cash paid to suppliers:

**Determining the amount of cash paid to suppliers means looking at not only the cost of goods sold, but also the changes in both inventory and accounts payable.**

**Accounts Payable**

| | | | |
|---|---|---|---|
| | | 20 | Beginning balance |
| Cash paid to suppliers *(decreases A/P)* | ? | 56 | Cost of goods *purchased* *(increases A/P)* |
| | | 26 | Ending Balance |

We now see that cash paid to suppliers was $50 million. The spreadsheet entry that summarizes merchandise acquisitions is:

| | ($ in millions) | |
|---|---|---|
| **Entry (4)** Cost of goods sold ($60 – 0) . . . . . . . . . . . . . . . . . . . . . . | 60 | |
| Inventory ($46 – 50) . . . . . . . . . . . . . . . . . . . . . . . . . . . | | 4 |
| Accounts payable ($26 – 20) . . . . . . . . . . . . . . . . . . . . | | 6 |
| Cash (paid to suppliers of goods). . . . . . . . . . . . . . . . . . | | 50 |

**Although $60 million of goods were sold during the year, only $50 million cash was paid to suppliers of these goods.**

**5. Salaries Expense.** The balance sheet account affected by salaries expense is salaries payable. By analyzing salaries expense in relation to the change in salaries payable, we can determine the amount of cash paid to employees:

**Salaries Payable**

| | | | |
|---|---|---|---|
| | | 1 | Beginning balance |
| Cash paid to employees *(decreases salaries payable)* | ? | 13 | Salaries expense *(increases salaries payable)* |
| | | 3 | Ending Balance |

This analysis indicates that only $11 million cash was paid to employees; the remaining $2 million of salaries expense is reflected as an increase in salaries payable.

Viewing the relationship in journal entry format provides the same conclusion and also gives us the entry in our spreadsheet analysis:

| | ($ in millions) | |
|---|---|---|
| **Entry (5)** Salaries expense ($13 – 0) . . . . . . . . . . . . . . . . . . . . . . . | 13 | |
| Salaries payable ($3 – 1). . . . . . . . . . . . . . . . . . . . . . . . | | 2 |
| Cash (paid to employees). . . . . . . . . . . . . . . . . . . . . . . . | | 11 |

**Although salaries expense was $13 million, only $11 million cash was paid to employees.**

**6. Depreciation Expense.** The income statement reports depreciation expense of $3 million. The entry used to record depreciation, which also serves as our spreadsheet entry, is:

**Depreciation expense does not require a current cash expenditure.**

| | ($ in millions) | |
|---|---|---|
| **Entry (6)** Depreciation expense ($3 – 0) . . . . . . . . . . . . . . . . . . . . | 3 | |
| Accumulated depreciation . . . . . . . . . . . . . . . . . . . . . | | 3 |

Depreciation is a noncash expense. It is merely an allocation in the current period of a prior cash expenditure (for the depreciable asset). Therefore, unlike the other entries to this point, the depreciation entry has no effect on the statement of cash flows. However, it does explain the change in the depreciation expense account and a portion of the change in accumulated depreciation.

**7. Interest Expense.** Recall from Chapter 14 that bond interest expense differs from the amount of cash paid to bondholders when bonds are issued at either a premium or a discount. The difference between the two amounts is the reduction of the premium or discount. By referring to the balance sheet, we see that UBC's bonds were issued at a discount. Since we know that bond interest expense is $5 million and that $2 million of the discount was reduced in 2006, we can determine that $3 million cash was paid to bondholders by recreating the entry that summarizes the recording of bond interest expense.

**Bond interest expense is not the same as the amount of cash paid to bondholders when bonds are issued at either a premium or a discount.**

| | ($ in millions) | |
|---|---|---|
| **Entry (7)** Bond interest expense ($5 – 0) . . . . . . . . . . . . . . . . . . . . | 5 | |
| Discount on bonds payable ($1 – 3). . . . . . . . . . . . . . . | | 2 |
| Cash (paid to bondholders) . . . . . . . . . . . . . . . . . . . . . . | | 3 |

Recording this entry on the spreadsheet explains the change in both the bond interest expense and discount on bonds payable accounts. It also provides us with another cash outflow from operating activities. Of course, if a premium were being reduced, rather than a discount, the cash outflow would be *greater* than the expense.

## ADDITIONAL CONSIDERATION

If the balance sheet had revealed an increase or decrease in an accrued bond interest payable account, the entry calculating cash paid to bondholders would require modification. For example, if UBC had a bond interest payable account, and that account had increased (a credit) by $1 million, the entry would have been:

| | ($ in millions) | |
|---|---|---|
| **Entry (7)** Bond interest expense . . . . . . . . . . . . . . . . . . . . . . . . | 5 | |
| (revised) Discount on bonds payable . . . . . . . . . . . . . . . . . . . | | 2 |
| Bond interest payable . . . . . . . . . . . . . . . . . . . . . . . | | 1 |
| Cash (paid to bondholders) . . . . . . . . . . . . . . . . . . . . | | 2 |

If the amount owed to bondholders increased by $1 million, they obviously were paid $1 million less cash than if there had been no change in the amount owed them. Similarly, if bond interest payable decreased by $1 million, the opposite would be true; that is, cash paid to them would have been $1 million more.

**8. Insurance Expense.** A decrease of $3 million in the prepaid insurance account indicates that cash paid for insurance coverage was $3 million less than the $7 million insurance expense for the year. Viewing prepaid insurance in T-account format clarifies this point.

**Prepaid Insurance**

| | | | |
|---|---|---|---|
| Beginning balance | 6 | | |
| Cash paid for insurance *(increases prepaid insurance)* | ? | 7 | Insurance expense *(decreases prepaid insurance)* |
| Ending balance | 3 | | |

From this analysis, we can conclude that $4 million was paid for insurance. We reach the same conclusion by preparing the following spreadsheet entry:

| | ($ in millions) | |
|---|---|---|
| **Entry (8)** Insurance expense ($7 – 0) | 7 | |
| Prepaid insurance ($3 – 6) | | 3 |
| Cash (paid for insurance) | | 4 |

Since $3 million of prepaid insurance was allocated to insurance expense, only $4 million of the expense was paid in cash during the period.

The entry accounts for the change in both the insurance expense and prepaid insurance accounts and also identifies a cash outflow from operating activities.

**9. Loss on Sale of Equipment.** A $2 million loss on the sale of equipment is the next item reported on the income statement. To determine the cash effect of the sale of equipment, we need additional information about the transaction. The information we need is provided in item (b) of Illustration 21–1. Re-creating the journal entry for the transaction described gives us the following entry:

| | ($ in millions) | |
|---|---|---|
| **Entry (9)** Cash (from the sale of equipment) | 5 | |
| Loss on sale of equipment ($2 – 0) | 2 | |
| Accumulated depreciation ($14 × 50%) | 7 | |
| Buildings and equipment (given) | | 14 |

Recreating the journal entry for the sale of equipment reveals a $5 million cash inflow from investing activities.

The $5 million cash inflow is entered in the statement of cash flows section of the spreadsheet as an investing activity. The $2 million debit to the loss on sale of equipment explains the change in that account balance. Referring to the spreadsheet, we see that a portion of the change in accumulated depreciation was accounted for in entry (6). The debit to accumulated depreciation in the entry above completes the explanation for the change in that account. However, the credit to buildings and equipment only partially justifies the change in that account. We must assume that the analysis of a subsequent transaction will account for the unexplained portion of the change.

Recognize too that the loss, like the gain in entry (3), has no cash effect in the current period. Therefore, it is not reported on the statement of cash flows.

**10. Income Tax Expense.** The final expense reported on the income statement is income tax expense. Since income taxes payable is the balance sheet account affected by this expense, we look to the change in that account to help determine the cash paid for income taxes. A T-account analysis can be used to find the cash effect as follows:

**Income Tax Payable**

| | | | |
|---|---|---|---|
| | | 8 | Beginning balance |
| Cash paid for income tax *(decreases the liability)* | **?** | 9 | Income tax expense |
| | | 6 | Ending Balance |

This analysis reveals that $11 million cash was paid for income taxes, $2 million more than the year's expense. The overpayment explains why the liability for income taxes decreased by $2 million.

The same conclusion can be reached from the following spreadsheet entry, which represents the net effect of income taxes on UBC's accounts.

| | ($ in millions) | |
|---|---|---|
| **Entry (10)** Income tax expense ($9 – 0) | 9 | |
| Income tax payable ($6 – 8) | 2 | |
| Cash (paid for income taxes) | | 11 |

## ADDITIONAL CONSIDERATION

Entry (10) would require modification in either of the two independent situations described below.

1. Note that UBC does not have a deferred income tax account. Recall from Chapter 16 that temporary differences between taxable income and pretax accounting income give rise to deferred taxes. If temporary differences had been present, which would be evidenced by a change in a deferred income taxes account, the calculation of cash paid for income taxes would require modification. Assume, for example, that a deferred income tax liability account had experienced a credit change of $1 million for the year. In that case, the previous spreadsheet entry would be revised as follows:

| | | ($ in millions) | |
|---|---|---|---|
| **Entry (10)** | Income tax expense | 9 | |
| (revised) | Income tax payable | 2 | |
| | Deferred income tax liability | | 1 |
| | Cash (paid for income taxes) | | 10 |

   As the revised entry indicates, only $10 million cash would have been paid in this situation, rather than $11 million. The $1 million difference represents the portion of the income tax expense whose payment is deferred to a later year.

2. The spreadsheet entry also would be affected if the income statement includes either an extraordinary gain or an extraordinary loss. Recall from Chapter 3 and Chapter 16 that the income tax effect of an extraordinary item is not reflected in income tax expense, but instead is separately reported as a reduction in the extraordinary item. For example, if UBC's loss on the sale of equipment had been due to an extraordinary event, the tax savings from that loss would be reported as a reduction in the extraordinary loss rather than as a reduction in income tax expense. (Since the loss reduces taxable income by $2 million, assuming a marginal tax rate of 50%, taxes would be reduced by $1 million.) The lower portion of the income statement would have appeared as shown below, in comparison with the presentation in Illustration 21–1:

| **Ordinary Loss** (from Illustration 21–1) | | **Extraordinary Loss** | | |
|---|---|---|---|---|
| | | Income tax expense | | (10) |
| | | **Income before extraordinary items** | | $13 |
| Loss on sale of equipment | (2) | E.O. loss—sale of equipment | $2 | |
| Income tax expense | (9) | Less: Tax savings | (1) | (1) |
| **Net income** | $12 | Net income | | $12 |

Without the tax savings produced by the loss, income tax expense would have been $10 million, rather than $9 million. But the tax savings still reduces the amount of cash paid for income taxes, even though it is reported separately from the income tax expense. Therefore, whether the loss is extraordinary or not, the amount of cash paid for income taxes is the same. If the loss is extraordinary, entry (10) would be modified as follows:

| | | ($ in millions) | |
|---|---|---|---|
| **Entry (10)** | Income tax expense (on ordinary income) | 10 | |
| (revised) | Income tax payable | 2 | |
| | Income tax expense (savings from extraordinary loss) | | 1 |
| | Cash (paid for income taxes) | | 11 |

Entry (9) would be unaffected. Whether or not the loss is extraordinary, it is not reported on the statement of cash flows, and the cash inflow from the sale is reported as an investing activity.

**11. Net Income.** The balance in the retained earnings account at the end of the year includes an increase due to net income. If we are to account for all changes in each of the accounts, we must include the following spreadsheet entry, which represents the closing of net income to retained earnings.

| | | ($ in millions) | |
|---|---|---|---|
| **Entry (11)** | Net income . . . . . . . . . . . . . . . . . . . . . . . . . . . . . . . . . . | 12 | |
| | Retained earnings . . . . . . . . . . . . . . . . . . . . . . . . . . . . | | 12 |

**This entry partially explains the change in the retained earnings account.**

This entry does not affect amounts reported on the statement of cash flows. We include the entry in the spreadsheet analysis only to help explain account balance changes.

## BALANCE SHEET ACCOUNTS

To identify all the operating, investing, and financing activities when using a spreadsheet, we must account for the changes in each account on both the income statement and the balance sheet. Thus far, we have explained the change in each income statement account. Since the transactions that gave rise to some of those changes involved balance sheet accounts as well, some changes in balance sheet accounts have already been explained. We now reconstruct the transactions that caused changes in the remaining balances.

With the exception of the cash account, the accounts are analyzed in the order of their presentation in the balance sheet. As noted earlier, we save the entry that reconciles the change in the cash account with the net change in cash from the statement of cash flows as a final check on the accuracy of the spreadsheet.

**12. Short-Term Investments.** Since the change in accounts receivable was explained previously [in entry (1)], we proceed to the next asset on the balance sheet. The balance in short-term investments increased from zero to $12 million. In the absence of evidence to the contrary, we could assume that the increase is due to the purchase of short-term investments during the year. This assumption is confirmed by item (c) of Illustration 21–1.

The entry to record the investment and our spreadsheet entry is:

| | | ($ in millions) | |
|---|---|---|---|
| **Entry (12)** | Short-term investment ($12 – 0) . . . . . . . . . . . . . . . . . . | 12 | |
| | Cash (purchase of short-term investment). . . . . . . . . . . | | 12 |

**The $12 million increase in the short-term investments account is due to the purchase of short-term investments during the year.**

The $12 million cash outflow is entered in the statement of cash flows section of the spreadsheet as an investing activity.

### ADDITIONAL CONSIDERATION

Recall that some highly liquid, short-term investments such as money market funds, Treasury bills, or commercial paper might be classified as cash equivalents. If the short-term investment above were classified as a cash equivalent, its purchase would have no effect on the total of cash and cash equivalents. In other words, since cash would include this investment, its purchase would constitute both a debit and a credit to cash. We would neither prepare a spreadsheet entry nor report the transaction on the statement of cash flows.

Likewise, a sale of a cash equivalent would not affect the total of cash and cash equivalents and would not be reported.

An exception would be if the cash equivalent investment were sold for either more or less than its acquisition cost. For example, assume a Treasury bill classified as a cash equivalent were sold for $1 million more than its $2 million cost. The sale would constitute both a $3 million increase and a $2 million decrease in cash. We see the effect more clearly if we reconstruct the transaction in journal entry format:

| | ($ in millions) | |
|---|---|---|
| Cash | 3 | |
| Gain on sale of cash equivalent | | 1 |
| Cash (cash equivalent investment) | | 2 |

The spreadsheet entry to reflect the net increase in cash would be:

| | | |
|---|---|---|
| **Entry (X)** Cash (from sale of cash equivalents) | 1 | |
| Gain on sale of cash equivalent | | 1 |

The $1 million net increase in cash and cash equivalents would be reported as a cash inflow from *operating* activities.

**13. Land.** The changes in the balances of both inventory and prepaid insurance were accounted for in previous spreadsheet entries: (4) and (8). Land is the next account whose change has yet to be fully explained. We discovered in a previous transaction that a sale of land caused a $10 million reduction in the account. Yet, the account shows a net *increase* of $20 million. It would be logical to assume that the unexplained increase of $30 million was due to a purchase of land. The transaction described in item (d) of Illustration 21–1 supports that assumption and is portrayed in the following spreadsheet entry:

A $30 million purchase of land accounts for the portion of the $20 million increase in the account that was not previously explained by the sale of land.

| | ($ in millions) | |
|---|---|---|
| **Entry (13)** Land (given) | 30 | |
| Cash (purchase of land) | | 30 |

The $30 million payment is reported as a cash outflow from investing activities.

**14. Buildings and Equipment.** When examining a previous transaction [entry (9)], we determined that the buildings and equipment account was reduced by $14 million from the sale of used equipment. And yet the account shows a net *increase* of $6 million for the year. The accounting records [item (e) of Illustration 21–1] reveal the remaining unexplained cause of the net increase. New equipment costing $20 million was purchased by issuing a $20 million note payable. Recall from the discussion in a previous section of this chapter that, although this is a noncash transaction, it represents both a significant investing activity (investing in new equipment) and a significant financing activity (financing the acquisition with long-term debt).

The journal entry used to record the transaction when the equipment was acquired also serves as our spreadsheet entry:

Investing in new equipment is a significant investing activity and financing the acquisition with long-term debt is a significant financing activity.

| | ($ in millions) | |
|---|---|---|
| **Entry (14)** Buildings and equipment (given) | 20 | |
| Note payable (given) | | 20 |

Remember that the statement of cash flows section of the spreadsheet will serve as the basis for our preparation of the formal statement. But the noncash entry above will not affect the cash flows section of the spreadsheet. Because we want to report this noncash investing and financing activity when we prepare the statement of cash flows, it is helpful to "mark" the spreadsheet entry as a reminder not to overlook this transaction when the statement is prepared. Crosses (*X*) serve this purpose on the spreadsheet in Illustration 21–1A.

## ADDITIONAL CONSIDERATION

### Payments on Debt

When a debt, such as the note payable above, is paid, the payment is reported on a statement of cash flows as a financing activity. However, any interest paid on the debt is reported as a cash outflow from operating activities. The reason is that interest expense is a component of net income, and the cash effects of income statement elements are reported as cash flows from operating activities. If the note is an installment note, each installment payment includes both an amount that represents interest and an amount that represents a reduction of principal. In a statement of cash flows, then, the interest portion is reported as a cash outflow from operating activities and the principal portion as a cash outflow from financing activities.

**Leases**

As we discussed in Chapter 15, lease arrangements vary greatly, in both their purpose and the ways we account for them. Consistent with those differences, we also report leases differently in a statement of cash flows depending on their type. Lease payments for **operating leases,** for instance, represent rent—expense to the lessee, revenue for the lessor. These amounts are included in net income, so both the lessee and lessor report cash payments for operating leases in a statement of cash flows as cash flows from operating activities. **Capital leases,** on the other hand, are agreements that we identify as being formulated outwardly as leases, but which are in reality installment purchases, so we account for them as such. Each rental payment (except the first if paid at inception) includes both an amount that represents interest and an amount that represents a reduction of principal. In a statement of cash flows, then, the lessee reports the interest portion as a cash outflow from operating activities and the principal portion as a cash outflow from financing activities. On the other side of the transaction, the lessor in a **direct financing lease** reports the interest portion as a cash inflow from operating activities and the principal portion as a cash inflow from investing activities. Both the lessee and lessor report the lease at its inception as a noncash investing/financing activity. Remember, though, that a **sales-type lease** differs from a direct financing lease for the lessor in that we assume the lessor is actually selling its product. Consistent with reporting sales of products under installment sales agreements rather than lease agreements, the lessor reports cash receipts from a sales-type lease as cash inflows from operating activities.

**15. Bonds Payable.** The balance in the bonds payable account decreased during the year by $15 million. Illustration 21–1, item (f), reveals the cause. Cash was paid to retire $15 million face value of bonds. The spreadsheet entry that duplicates the journal entry that was recorded when the bonds were retired is:

| | | ($ in millions) | |
|---|---|---|---|
| **Entry (15)** | Bonds payable ($35 − 50) | 15 | |
| | Cash (retirement of bonds payable) | | 15 |

The cash outflow is reported as a financing activity.

**ADDITIONAL CONSIDERATION**

The description of the transaction stipulated that $15 million of bonds were retired at their maturity on the first day of the year. Thus, any discount or premium on the bonds would have been completely amortized before the start of the year. If bonds are retired prior to their scheduled maturity, any unamortized discount or premium would be removed from the accounts at that time. For instance, assume that the bonds above were callable at $16 million and that $1 million of unamortized discount remained when they were retired by a call at that price. The spreadsheet entry would be revised as follows:

| | | ($ in millions) | |
|---|---|---|---|
| **Entry (15)** | Bonds payable | 15 | |
| (revised) | Loss on early extinguishment of bonds | 2 | |
| | Discount on bonds payable | | 1 |
| | Cash (retirement of bonds payable) | | 16 |

The loss, of course, would not be reported on the statement of cash flows. The amortization of the discount, however, would affect a previous spreadsheet entry. In entry (7) we concluded that the decrease in discount on bonds payable was due to the amortization of $2 million of the discount when recording bond interest expense. However, if the early retirement assumed above had occurred, that transaction would have accounted for $1 million of the $2 million decrease in the discount. Entry (7) would be modified as follows:

| | | ($ in millions) | |
|---|---|---|---|
| **Entry (7)** | Bond interest expense | 5 | |
| (revised) | Discount on bonds payable | | 1 |
| | Cash (paid to bondholders) | | 4 |

**16–17. Common Stock.** The comparative balance sheets indicate that the common stock account balance increased by $30 million. We look to the accounting records—Illustration 21–1, item (g)—for an explanation. Two transactions, a stock dividend and a sale of new shares of common stock, combined to cause the increase. To create the spreadsheet entries for our analysis, we replicate the journal entries for the two transactions as described below.

Remember from Chapter 18 that to record a small stock dividend, we capitalize retained earnings for the market value of the shares distributed—in this case, 1 million shares times $13 per share, or $13 million. The entry is:

Although this transaction does not identify a cash flow, nor does it represent an investing or financing activity, we include the spreadsheet entry to help explain changes in the three account balances affected.

| | ($ in millions) | |
|---|---|---|
| **Entry (16)** Retained earnings (1 million shares × $13) | 13 | |
| Common stock (1 million shares × $10 par) | | 10 |
| Paid-in capital—excess of par (difference) | | 3 |

Also recall from the discussion of noncash investing and financing activities earlier in the chapter, that stock dividends do not represent a significant investing or financing activity. Therefore, this transaction is not reported on the statement of cash flows. We include the entry in our spreadsheet analysis only to help explain changes in the account balances affected.

The sale of 2 million shares of common stock at $13 per share is represented by the following spreadsheet entry:

The sale of common shares explains the remaining increase in the common stock account and the remaining increase in paid-in capital—excess of par.

| | ($ in millions) | |
|---|---|---|
| **Entry (17)** Cash (from sale of common stock) | 26 | |
| Common stock ([$130 − 100] − 10) | | 20 |
| Paid-in capital—excess of par ([$29 − 20] − 3) | | 6 |

The cash inflow is reported on the statement of cash flows as a financing activity.

**ADDITIONAL CONSIDERATION**

If cash is paid to retire outstanding shares of stock or to purchase those shares as treasury stock, the cash outflow would be reported on a statement of cash flows as a financing activity.

Together, the two entries above account for both the $30 million increase in the common stock account and the $9 million increase in paid-in capital—excess of par.

**18. Retained Earnings.** The stock dividend in entry (16) above includes a $13 million reduction of retained earnings. Previously, we saw in entry (11) that net income increased retained earnings by $12 million. The net reduction of $1 million accounted for by these two entries leaves $5 million of the $6 million net decrease in the account unexplained.

**Retained Earnings**

| | | | |
|---|---|---|---|
| | | 25 | Beginning balance |
| (16) Stock dividend | 13 | 12 | Net income (11) |
| (18) ? | ? | | |
| | | 19 | Ending balance |

Without additional information about the $5 million decrease in retained earnings, we might assume it was due to a $5 million cash dividend. This assumption is unnecessary, though, because the cash dividend is described in Illustration 21–1, item (h).

**Retained Earnings**

| | | | |
|---|---|---|---|
| | | 25 | Beginning balance |
| (16) Stock dividend | 13 | 12 | Net income (11) |
| (18) Cash dividend | 5 | | |
| | | 19 | Ending balance |

The spreadsheet entry is:

| | ($ in millions) | |
|---|---|---|
| **Entry (18)** Retained earnings. . . . . . . . . . . . . . . . . . . . . . . . . . . . . . | 5 | |
| Cash (payment of cash dividends). . . . . . . . . . . . . . . . . | | 5 |

The cash dividend accounts for the previously unexplained change in retained earnings.

**19. Completing the Spreadsheet.** In preparing the spreadsheet to this point, we have analyzed each noncash account on both the income statement and the balance sheet. Our purpose was to identify the transactions that, during the year, had affected each account. By recreating each transaction in the form of a spreadsheet entry—in effect, duplicating the journal entry that had been used to record the transaction—we were able to explain the change in the balance of each account. That is, the debits and credits in the changes columns of the spreadsheet account for the increase or decrease in each noncash account. When a transaction being entered on the spreadsheet included an operating, investing, or financing activity, we entered that portion of the entry under the corresponding heading of the statement of cash flows section of the spreadsheet. Since, as noted earlier, there can be no operating, investing, or financing activity without a corresponding change in one or more of the noncash accounts, we should feel confident at this point that we have identified all of the activities that should be reported on the statement of cash flows.

To check the accuracy of the analysis, we compare the change in the balance of the cash account with the net change in cash flows produced by the activities listed in the statement of cash flows section of the spreadsheet. The net increase or decrease in cash flows from each of the statement of cash flows categories is extended to the extreme right column of the spreadsheet. By reference to Illustration 21–1A, we see that net cash flows from operating, investing, and financing activities are: $22 million; ($19 million); and $6 million, respectively. Together these activities provide a net increase in cash of $9 million. This amount corresponds to the increase in the balance of the cash account from $20 million to $29 million. To complete the spreadsheet, we include the final spreadsheet entry:

The cash flows section of the spreadsheet provides the information to be reported in the statement of cash flows.

| | ($ in millions) | |
|---|---|---|
| **Entry (19)** Cash . . . . . . . . . . . . . . . . . . . . . . . . . . . . . . . . . . . . . . . . | 9 | |
| Net increase in cash<br>(from statement of cash flows activities). . . . . . . . . . | | 9 |

As a final check of accuracy, we can confirm that the total of the debits is equal to the total of the credits in the changes columns of the spreadsheet.[19]

[19]The mechanical and computational aspects of the spreadsheet analysis are simplified greatly when performed on an electronic spreadsheet such as Microsoft Excel.

The spreadsheet is now complete. The statement of cash flows can now be prepared directly from the spreadsheet simply by presenting the items included in the statement of cash flows section of the spreadsheet in the appropriate format of the statement.

The statements of cash flows from an annual report of **Storage Technology Corporation** are shown in Graphic 21–9. Notice that the reconciliation schedule was reported by Storage Technology on the statement of cash flows itself shown below. Many companies report the schedule separately in the disclosure notes.

**GRAPHIC 21–9** Statement of Cash Flows—Storage Technology Corporation

**STORAGE TECHNOLOGY CORPORATION**
**Consolidated Statements of Cash Flows**

| $ in thousands | 2004 | 2003 | 2002 |
|---|---|---|---|
| **Operating Activities** | | | |
| Cash received from customers | $2,270,300 | $2,258,219 | $2,003,517 |
| Cash paid to suppliers and employees | (1,874,807) | (1,889,154) | (1,636,056) |
| Interest received | 15,231 | 9,912 | 9,956 |
| Interest paid | (1,032) | (1,285) | (1,698) |
| Income taxes paid | (25,177) | (13,115) | (15,430) |
| *Net cash provided by operating activities* | 384,515 | 364,577 | 360,289 |
| **Investing Activities** | | | |
| Purchases of investments | (337,283) | (1,102,244) | (761,305) |
| Proceeds from sale of investments | 339,968 | 957,973 | 584,159 |
| Purchase of property, plant, and equipment | (55,010) | (43,555) | (88,459) |
| Proceeds from sale of P, P & E | 1,661 | 3,752 | 1,274 |
| Other assets | (32,385) | 4,244 | (12,650) |
| *Net cash used in investing activities* | (83,049) | (179,830) | (276,981) |
| **Financing Activities** | | | |
| Repurchases of common stock | (195,353) | — | — |
| Proceeds from employee stock plans | 72,092 | 58,721 | 23,979 |
| Proceeds from other debt | 1,258 | 1,325 | 1,625 |
| Repayments of other debt | (2,194) | (2,372) | (2,577) |
| Repayments of credit | — | — | (73,401) |
| *Net cash provided by (used in) financing activities* | (124,197) | 57,674 | (50,374) |
| Effect of exchange rate changes on cash | (51,213) | 6,484 | (7,702) |
| Increase in cash and cash equivalents | 126,056 | 248,905 | 25,232 |
| Cash and cash equivalents, beg. of year | 727,354 | 478,449 | 453,217 |
| Cash and cash equivalents, end of year | $ 853,410 | $ 727,354 | $ 478,449 |

**Reconciliation of Net Income to Net Cash Provided by Operating Activities**

| | 2004 | 2003 | 2002 |
|---|---|---|---|
| Net income | $ 191,023 | $ 148,912 | $ 110,031 |
| Depreciation and amortization expense | 78,485 | 87,890 | 90,533 |
| Inventory writedowns | 19,716 | 24,064 | 32,571 |
| Translation loss | 53,175 | 21,053 | 8,990 |
| Other noncash adjustments to income | 27,344 | (22,470) | 17,694 |
| *(Increase) decrease in assets:* | | | |
| Accounts receivable | 46,300 | 75,659 | (36,098) |
| Inventories | (16,460) | 959 | 21,403 |
| Other current assets | 945 | 2,297 | (3,550) |
| Spare parts | (22,117) | (16,344) | (22,998) |
| Deferred income tax assets | 15,603 | (13,715) | 4,622 |
| *Increase (decrease) in liabilities:* | | | |
| Accounts payable | (14,650) | (7,191) | 67,337 |
| Accrued liabilities | 19,469 | 17,111 | 39,865 |
| Other current liabilities | (4,850) | 5,020 | 16,869 |
| Income taxes payable | (9,468) | 41,332 | 13,020 |
| Net cash provided by operating activities | $ 384,515 | $ 364,577 | $ 360,289 |

## ETHICAL DILEMMA

"We must get it," Courtney Lowell, president of Industrial Fasteners, roared. "Without it we're in big trouble." The "it" Mr. Lowell referred to is the renewal of a $14 million loan with Community First Bank. The big trouble he fears is the lack of funds necessary to repay the existing debt and few, if any, prospects for raising the funds elsewhere.

Mr. Lowell had just hung up the phone after a conversation with a bank vice-president in which it was made clear that this year's statement of cash flows must look better than last year's. Mr. Lowell knows that improvements are not on course to happen. In fact, cash flow projections were dismal.

Later that day, Tim Cratchet, assistant controller, was summoned to Mr. Lowell's office. "Cratchet," Lowell barked, "I've looked at our accounts receivable. I think we can generate quite a bit of cash by selling or factoring most of those receivables. I know it will cost us more than if we collect them ourselves, but it sure will make our cash flow picture look better."

Is there an ethical question facing Cratchet?

## GLOBAL PERSPECTIVE

A statement of cash flows (or funds flow statement some places) is optional in many countries. However, in some countries many multinational companies voluntarily provide a statement of cash flows either as a primary statement or in disclosure notes. In some countries, such as the United Kingdom, it's required only for firms listed on a stock exchange.

# CONCEPT REVIEW EXERCISE

**COMPREHENSIVE REVIEW**

The comparative balance sheets for 2006 and 2005 and the income statement for 2006 are given below for Beneficial Drill Company. Additional information from Beneficial Drill's accounting records is provided also.

**Required:**

Prepare the statement of cash flows of Beneficial Drill Company for the year ended December 31, 2006. Present cash flows from operating activities by the direct method and use a spreadsheet to assist in your analysis.

**BENEFICIAL DRILL COMPANY**
**Comparative Balance Sheets**
**December 31, 2006 and 2005**
($ in millions)

| **Assets** | **2006** | **2005** |
|---|---|---|
| Cash | $ 20 | $ 40 |
| Accounts receivable | 99 | 100 |
| Less: Allowance for uncollectible accounts | (5) | (4) |
| Investment revenue receivable | 3 | 2 |
| Inventory | 115 | 110 |
| Prepaid insurance | 2 | 3 |
| Long-term investments | 77 | 60 |
| Land | 110 | 80 |
| Buildings and equipment | 220 | 240 |
| Less: Accumulated depreciation | (35) | (60) |
| Patent | 15 | 16 |
| | $621 | $587 |

| | | |
|---|---|---|
| **Liabilities** | | |
| Accounts payable | $ 23 | $ 30 |
| Salaries payable | 2 | 5 |
| Bond interest payable | 4 | 2 |
| Income tax payable | 6 | 7 |
| Deferred income tax liability | 5 | 4 |
| Notes payable | 15 | 0 |
| Bonds payable | 150 | 130 |
| Less: Discount on bonds | (9) | (10) |
| **Shareholders' Equity** | | |
| Common stock | 210 | 200 |
| Paid-in capital—excess of par | 44 | 40 |
| Retained earnings | 178 | 179 |
| Less: Treasury stock (at cost) | (7) | 0 |
| | $621 | $587 |

**BENEFICIAL DRILL COMPANY**
**Income Statement**
**For Year Ended December 31, 2006**
**($ in millions)**

| | | | |
|---|---|---|---|
| **Revenues** | | | |
| Sales revenue | | $200 | |
| Investment revenue | | 6 | |
| Investment revenue—sale of treasury bills | | 1 | $207 |
| **Expenses** | | | |
| Cost of goods sold | | 110 | |
| Salaries expense | | 30 | |
| Depreciation expense | | 5 | |
| Patent amortization expense | | 1 | |
| Bad debts expense | | 4 | |
| Insurance expense | | 3 | |
| Bond interest expense | | 14 | |
| Extraordinary loss on destruction of equipment | $ 10 | | |
| Less: Tax savings | (5) | 5 | |
| Income tax expense | | 12 | (184) |
| **Net income** | | | $ 23 |

*Additional information from the accounting records:*

a. During 2006, $3 million of customer accounts were written off as uncollectible.
b. Investment revenue includes Beneficial Drill Company's $3 million share of the net income of Hammer Company, an equity method investee.
c. Treasury bills were sold during 2006 at a gain of $1 million. Beneficial Drill Company classifies its investments in Treasury bills as cash equivalents.
d. A machine that originally cost $60 million and was one-half depreciated, was rendered unusable by a freak bolt of lightning. Most major components of the machine were unharmed and were sold for $20 million.
e. Temporary differences between pretax accounting income and taxable income caused the deferred income tax liability to increase by $1 million.
f. The common stock of Wrench Corporation was purchased for $14 million as a long-term investment.
g. Land costing $30 million was acquired by paying $15 million cash and issuing a 13%, seven-year, $15 million note payable to the seller.
h. New equipment was purchased for $40 million cash.
i. $20 million of bonds were sold at face value.
j. On January 19, Drill issued a 5% stock dividend (1 million shares). The market price of the $10 par value common stock was $14 per share at that time.

k. Cash dividends of $10 million were paid to shareholders.
l. In November, 500,000 common shares were repurchased as treasury stock at a cost of $7 million. Drill uses the cost method to account for treasury stock.

## SOLUTION

**BENEFICIAL DRILL COMPANY**
**Spreadsheet for the Statement of Cash Flows**

| | Dec. 31 2005 | Changes: Debits | | Changes: Credits | | Dec. 31 2006 |
|---|---|---|---|---|---|---|
| **Balance Sheet** | | | | | | |
| **Assets** | | | | | | |
| Cash | 40 | | | (20) | 20 | 20 |
| Accounts receivable | 100 | | | (1) | 1 | 99 |
| Less: Allowance for uncollectible accounts | (4) | | | (1) | 1 | (5) |
| Investment revenue receivable | 2 | (2) | 1 | | | 3 |
| Inventory | 110 | (4) | 5 | | | 115 |
| Prepaid insurance | 3 | | | (8) | 1 | 2 |
| Long-term investments | 60 | (2) | 3 | | | |
| | | (13) | 14 | | | 77 |
| Land | 80 | (14) | 30X | | | 110 |
| Buildings and equipment | 240 | (15) | 40 | (10) | 60 | 220 |
| Less: Accumulated depreciation | (60) | (10) | 30 | (6) | 5 | (35) |
| Patent | 16 | | | (7) | 1 | 15 |
| | 587 | | | | | 621 |
| **Liabilities** | | | | | | |
| Accounts payable | 30 | (4) | 7 | | | 23 |
| Salaries payable | 5 | (5) | 3 | | | 2 |
| Bond interest payable | 2 | | | (9) | 2 | 4 |
| Income tax payable | 7 | (11) | 1 | | | 6 |
| Deferred income tax liability | 4 | | | (11) | 1 | 5 |
| Notes payable | 0 | | | (14) | 15X | 15 |
| Bonds payable | 130 | | | (16) | 20 | 150 |
| Less: Discount on bonds | (10) | | | (9) | 1 | (9) |
| **Shareholders' Equity** | | | | | | |
| Common stock | 200 | | | (17) | 10 | 210 |
| Paid-in capital—excess of par | 40 | | | (17) | 4 | 44 |
| Retained earnings | 179 | (17) | 14 | | | |
| | | (18) | 10 | (12) | 23 | 178 |
| Less: Treasury stock | 0 | (19) | 7 | | | (7) |
| | 587 | | | | | 621 |
| **Income Statement** | | | | | | |
| **Revenues:** | | | | | | |
| Sales revenue | | | | (1) | 200 | 200 |
| Investment revenue | | | | (2) | 6 | 6 |
| Investment revenue—sale of Treasury bills | | | | (3) | 1 | 1 |
| **Expenses:** | | | | | | |
| Cost of goods sold | | (4) | 110 | | | (110) |
| Salaries expense | | (5) | 30 | | | (30) |
| Depreciation expense | | (6) | 5 | | | (5) |
| Patent amortization expense | | (7) | 1 | | | (1) |
| Bad debts expense | | (1) | 4 | | | (4) |
| Insurance expense | | (8) | 3 | | | (3) |
| Bond interest expense | | (9) | 14 | | | (14) |
| Extraordinary loss | | (10) | 10 | | | (10) |
| Less: Tax savings | | | | (11) | 5 | 5 |
| Income tax expense | | (11) | 12 | | | (12) |
| Net income | | (12) | 23 | | | 23 |

| | Dec. 31 2005 | Changes: Debits | | Changes: Credits | | Dec. 31 2006 |
|---|---|---|---|---|---|---|
| **Statement of Cash Flows** | | | | | | |
| **Operating Activities:** | | | | | | |
| Cash inflows: | | | | | | |
| From customers | | (1) | 198 | | | |
| From investment revenue | | (2) | 2 | | | |
| From sale of Treasury bills | | (3) | 1 | | | |
| Cash outflows: | | | | | | |
| To suppliers of goods | | | | (4) | 122 | |
| To employees | | | | (5) | 33 | |
| For insurance expense | | | | (8) | 2 | |
| For bond interest expense | | | | (9) | 11 | |
| For income taxes | | | | (11) | 7 | |
| *Net cash flows* | | | | | | 26 |
| **Investing Activities:** | | | | | | |
| Sale of equipment | | (10) | 20 | | | |
| Purchase of LT investments | | | | (13) | 14 | |
| Purchase of land | | | | (14) | 15 | |
| Purchase of equipment | | | | (15) | 40 | |
| *Net cash flows* | | | | | | (49) |
| **Financing Activities:** | | | | | | |
| Sale of bonds payable | | (16) | 20 | | | |
| Payment of cash dividends | | | | (18) | 10 | |
| Purchase of treasury stock | | | | (19) | 7 | |
| *Net cash flows* | | | | | | 3 |
| Net decrease in cash | | (20) | 20 | | | (20) |
| Totals | | | 638 | | 638 | |

**BENEFICIAL DRILL COMPANY**
**Statement of Cash Flows**
**For Year Ended December 31, 2006**
($ in millions)

| | | |
|---|---|---|
| **Cash Flows from Operating Activities** | | |
| Cash inflows: | | |
| From customers | $198 | |
| From investment revenue | 2 | |
| From sale of Treasury bills | 1 | |
| Cash outflows: | | |
| To suppliers of goods | (122) | |
| To employees | (33) | |
| For insurance expense | (2) | |
| For bond interest expense | (11) | |
| For income taxes | (7) | |
| *Net cash flows from operating activities* | | $26 |
| **Cash Flows from Investing Activities** | | |
| Sale of equipment | $20 | |
| Purchase of long-term investments | (14) | |
| Purchase of land | (15) | |
| Purchase of equipment | (40) | |
| *Net cash flows from investing activities* | | (49) |

| | | |
|---|---|---|
| **Cash Flows from Financing Activities** | | |
| Sale of bonds payable | $20 | |
| Payment of cash dividends | (10) | |
| Purchase of treasury stock | (7) | |
| *Net cash flows from financing activities* | | 3 |
| *Net decrease in cash* | | ($20) |
| Cash balance, January 1 | | 40 |
| Cash balance, December 31 | | $ 20 |

**Noncash Investing and Financing Activities**

Acquired $30 million of land by paying cash and issuing a 13%, 7-year note as follows:

| | |
|---|---|
| Cost of land | $30 |
| Cash paid | 15 |
| Note issued | $15 |

# PREPARING AN SCF: THE INDIRECT METHOD OF REPORTING CASH FLOWS FROM OPERATING ACTIVITIES

PART C

## Getting There through the Back Door

The presentation of cash flows from operating activities illustrated in Part B is referred to as the *direct method*. By this method, the cash effect of each operating activity (i.e., income statement item) is reported directly on the statement of cash flows. For instance, cash received from customers is reported as the cash effect of sales activities, and cash paid to suppliers is reported as the cash effect of cost of goods sold. Income statement items that have *no* cash effect, such as depreciation expense, bad debt expense, gains, and losses, are simply not reported.

As pointed out previously, a permissible alternative is the *indirect method*, by which the net cash increase or decrease from operating activities is derived indirectly by starting with reported net income and working backwards to convert that amount to a cash basis. The derivation by the indirect method of net cash flows from operating activities for UBC is shown in Illustration 21–1B. For the adjustment amounts, you may wish to refer back to UBC's balance sheets and income statement presented in Illustration 21–1.

**Cash Flows from Operating Activities—Indirect Method**
***and***
**Reconciliation of Net Income to**
**Net Cash Flows from Operating Activities**

| | |
|---|---|
| **Net Income** | $12 |
| Adjustments for noncash effects: | |
| Increase in accounts receivable | (2) |
| Gain on sale of land | (8) |
| Decrease in inventory | 4 |
| Increase in accounts payable | 6 |
| Increase in salaries payable | 2 |
| Depreciation expense | 3 |
| Discount on bonds payable | 2 |
| Decrease in prepaid insurance | 3 |
| Loss on sale of equipment | 2 |
| Decrease in income tax payable | (2) |
| *Net cash flows from operating activities* | $22 |

**ILLUSTRATION 21–1B**
Indirect Method

**The indirect method derives the net cash increase or decrease from operating activities indirectly, by starting with reported net income and "working backwards" to convert that amount to a cash basis.**

Notice that the indirect method yields the same $22 million net cash flows from operating activities as does the direct method. This is understandable when you consider that the indirect method simply reverses the differences between the accrual-based income statement and cash flows from operating activities. We accomplish this as described in the next two sections.

## Components of Net Income that Do Not Increase or Decrease Cash

Amounts that were subtracted in determining net income but did not reduce cash are *added back* to net income to reverse the effect of their having been subtracted. For example, depreciation expense and the loss on sale of equipment are added back to net income. Other things being equal, this restores net income to what it would have been had depreciation and the loss not been subtracted at all.

Similarly, amounts that were added in determining net income but did not increase cash are subtracted from net income to reverse the effect of their having been added. For example, UBC's gain on sale of land is deducted from net income. Here's why. UBC sold for $18 million land that originally cost $10 million. Recording the sale produced a gain of $8 million, which UBC appropriately included in its income statement. But did this gain increase UBC's cash? No. Certainly selling the land increased cash—by $18 million. We therefore include the $18 million as a cash inflow in the statement of cash flows. However, the sale of land is an investing activity. The gain itself, though, is simply the difference between cash received in the sale of land (reported as an investing activity) and the original cost of the land. If UBC also reported the $8 million gain as a cash flow from operating activities, in addition to reporting $18 million as a cash flow from investing activities, UBC would report the $8 million twice. So, because UBC added the gain in determining its net income but the gain had no effect on cash, the gain must now be subtracted from net income to reverse the effect of its having been added.

## Components of Net Income that Do Increase or Decrease Cash

For components of net income that increase or decrease cash, but by an amount different from that reported on the income statement, net income is adjusted for changes in the balances of related balance sheet accounts to *convert the effects of those items to a cash basis.* For example, sales of $100 million are included on the income statement as a component of net income, and yet, since accounts receivable increased by $2 million, only $98 million cash was collected from customers during the reporting period. Sales are converted to a cash basis by subtracting the $2 million increase in accounts receivable. Here's another example:

The income statement reports salaries expense as $13 million. Just because employees earned $13 million during the reporting period, though, doesn't necessarily mean UBC paid those employees $13 million in cash during the same period. In fact, we see in the comparative balance sheets that salaries payable increased from $1 million to $3 million; UBC owes its employees $2 million more than before the year started. The company must not have paid the entire $13 million expense. By analyzing salaries expense in relation to the change in salaries payable, we can determine the amount of cash paid to employees:

**Salaries Payable**

| | | | |
|---|---|---|---|
| | | 1 | Beginning balance |
| Cash paid to employees<br>*(decreases salaries payable)* | ? | 13 | Salaries expense<br>*(increases salaries payable)* |
| | | 3 | Ending balance |

This inspection indicates that UBC paid only $11 million cash to its employees; the remaining $2 million of salaries expense is reflected as an increase in salaries payable. From a cash perspective, then, by subtracting $13 million for salaries in the income statement, UBC has subtracted $2 million more than the reduction in cash. Adding back the $2 million leaves UBC in the same position as if it had deducted only the $11 million cash paid to employees.

Following a similar analysis of the cash effects of the remaining components of net income, those items are likewise converted to a cash basis by adjusting net income for increases and decreases in related accounts.

For components of net income that increase or decrease cash by an amount exactly the same as that reported on the income statement, no adjustment of net income is required. For example, investment revenue of $3 million is included in UBC's $12 million net income amount. Because $3 million also is the amount of cash received from that activity, this element of net income already represents its cash effect and needs no adjustment.[20]

## Comparison with the Direct Method

The indirect method is compared with the direct method in Graphic 21–10, using the data of UBC. To better illustrate the relationship between the two methods, the adjustments to net income using the indirect method are presented parallel to the related cash inflows and cash outflows of the direct method. The income statement is included in the graphic to demonstrate that the indirect method also serves to reconcile differences between the elements of that statement and the cash flows reported by the direct method.

**GRAPHIC 21–10** Comparison of the Indirect Method and the Direct Method of Determining Cash Flows from Operating Activities

| | | Cash Flows from Operating Activities | | | |
|---|---|---|---|---|---|
| **Income Statement** | | **Indirect Method** | | **Direct Method** | |
| | | Net income | $12 | | |
| | | **Adjustments:** | | | |
| Sales | $100 | Increase in accounts receivable | (2) | Cash received from customers | $98 |
| Investment revenue | 3 | (No adjustment—no investment revenue receivable or long-term investments) | | Cash received from investments | 3 |
| Gain on sale of land | 8 | Gain on sale of land | (8) | (Not reported—no cash effect) | |
| Cost of goods sold | (60) | Decrease in inventory | 4 | | |
| | | Increase in accounts payable | 6 | Cash paid to suppliers | (50) |
| Salaries expense | (13) | Increase in salaries payable | 2 | Cash paid to employees | (11) |
| Depreciation expense | (3) | Depreciation expense | 3 | (Not reported—no cash effect) | |
| Interest expense | (5) | Decrease in bond discount | 2 | Cash paid for interest | (3) |
| Insurance expense | (7) | Decrease in prepaid insurance | 3 | Cash paid for insurance | (4) |
| Loss on sale of equipment | (2) | Loss on sale of equipment | 2 | (Not reported—no cash effect) | |
| Income tax expense | (9) | Decrease in income tax payable | (2) | Cash paid for income taxes | (11) |
| Net Income | $12 | **Net cash flows from operating activities** | **$22** | **Net cash flows from operating activities** | **$22** |

As a practical consideration, you might notice that the adjustments to net income using the indirect method follow a convenient pattern. *Increases* in related assets are deducted from net income (i.e., the increase in accounts receivable) when converting to cash from operating activities. Conversely, *decreases* in assets are added (inventory and prepaid insurance in this case). Changes in related liabilities are handled in just the opposite way. Increases in related liabilities are *added* to net income (i.e., the increases in accounts payable and salaries payable) while decreases in liabilities are subtracted (i.e., decrease in income tax payable).[21]

[20]We determined in Part B (subsection 2) that there is no evidence that cash received from investments differs from investment revenue.

[21]The adjustment for the decrease in bond discount is logically consistent with this pattern as well. Bond discount is a contra liability. It's logical, then, that an adjustment for a decrease in this account be added—the opposite of the way a decrease in a liability is treated.

Of course, these are adjustments to net income that effectively convert components of income from reported accrual amounts to a cash basis. The other adjustments to net income (gain, depreciation, loss) as pointed out earlier are to get rid of the three income statement components that have no effect at all on cash. This pattern is summarized in Graphic 21–11.

**GRAPHIC 21–11**

Adjustments to Convert Net Income to a Cash Basis—Indirect Method

| Type of Adjustment | To Adjust for Noncash Effect |
|---|---|
| Income statement components that have *no effect* at all on cash but are *additions* to income | Deduct from net income |
| Income statement components that have *no effect* at all on cash but are *deductions* from income | Add to net income |
| *Increases in assets* related to an income statement component | Deduct from net income |
| *Decreases in assets* related to an income statement component | Add to net income |
| *Increases in liabilities* related to an income statement component | Add to net income |
| *Decreases in liabilities* related to an income statement component | Deduct from net income |

Although either the direct method or the indirect method is permitted, the FASB strongly encourages companies to report cash flows from operating activities by the direct method. The obvious appeal of this approach is that it reports specific operating cash receipts and operating cash payments, which is consistent with the primary objective of the statement of cash flows. Investors and creditors gain additional insight into the specific sources of cash receipts and payments from operating activities revealed by this reporting method. Also, statement users can more readily interpret and understand the information presented because the direct method avoids the confusion caused by reporting noncash items and other reconciling adjustments under the caption *cash flows from operating activities*. Nonetheless, the vast majority of companies choose to use the indirect method. Reasons for this choice range from longstanding tradition to the desire to withhold as much information as possible from competitors.[22]

## Reconciliation of Net Income to Cash Flows from Operating Activities

As we discussed earlier, whether cash flows from operating activities are reported by the direct method or by the indirect method, the financial statements must report a reconciliation of net income to net cash flows from operating activities. When the direct method is used, the reconciliation is presented in a separate schedule and is identical to the presentation of net cash flows from operating activities by the indirect method. In other words, Illustration 21–1B also serves as the reconciliation schedule to accompany a statement of cash flows using the direct method. Obviously, a separate reconciliation schedule is not required when using the indirect method because the cash flows from operating activities section of the statement of cash flows *is* a reconciliation of net income to net cash flows from operating activities.[23]

Remember that the direct and indirect methods are alternative approaches to deriving net cash flows from *operating* activities only. The choice of which method is used for that

[22]Strong arguments are made for the FASB requiring the direct method by Paul R. Bahnson, Paul B. W. Miller, and Bruce P. Budge in "Nonarticulation in Cash Flow Statements and Implications for Education, Research and Practice," *Accounting Horizons*, December 1996, and by G. V. Krishnan and J. A. Largay III in "The Predictive Ability of Direct Method Cash Flow Information," *Journal of Business Finance & Accounting*, January 2000.

[23]It is permissible to present the reconciliation in a separate schedule and to report the net cash flows from operating activities as a single line item on the statement of cash flows.

purpose does not affect the way cash flows from *investing* and *financing* activities are identified and reported.

The statements of cash flows from the annual report of **Hewlett-Packard Company**, which uses the indirect method, are shown in Graphic 21–12.

**GRAPHIC 21–12** Statement of Cash Flows—Indirect Method; Hewlett-Packard

**HEWLETT PACKARD**
**Consolidated Statements of Cash Flows**

| | For the Fiscal Years Ended October 31 | | |
|---|---|---|---|
| $ in millions | 2004 | 2003 | 2002 |
| **Cash Flows from Operating Activities:** | | | |
| Net earnings (loss) | $ 3,497 | $ 2,539 | $ (903) |
| *Adjustments to reconcile net earnings (loss) to net cash provided by operating activities:* | | | |
| Depreciation and amortization | 2,395 | 2,527 | 2,119 |
| Provision for doubtful accounts | 98 | 102 | 299 |
| Provision for inventory | 367 | 391 | 280 |
| Restructuring charges | 114 | 800 | 1,780 |
| Acquisition-related charges | 91 | 281 | 1,494 |
| Deferred taxes on earnings | 26 | (279) | (351) |
| Other, net | 89 | 141 | 234 |
| Changes in assets and liabilities: | | | |
| Accounts and financing receivables | (696) | 88 | 899 |
| Inventory | (1,341) | (638) | 844 |
| Accounts payable | 3 | 2,257 | 395 |
| Taxes on earnings | (32) | 53 | (357) |
| Restructuring | (601) | (1,240) | (790) |
| Other assets and liabilities | 1,078 | (965) | (499) |
| Net cash provided by operating activities | 5,088 | 6,057 | 5,444 |
| **Cash Flows from Investing Activities:** | | | |
| Investment in property, plant, and equipment | (2,126) | (1,995) | (1,710) |
| Proceeds from sale of property, plant, and equipment | 447 | 353 | 362 |
| Purchases of investments | (715) | (596) | (351) |
| Maturities and sales of investments | 1,064 | 875 | 381 |
| Business acquisitions, net of acquisition costs | (1,124) | (149) | 3,557 |
| Dissolution of an equity investee | — | — | 879 |
| Net cash (used in) provided by investing activities | (2,454) | (1,512) | 3,118 |
| **Cash Flows from Financing Activities:** | | | |
| Repayment of commercial paper and notes payable, net | (172) | (223) | (2,402) |
| Issuance of debt | 9 | 749 | 2,529 |
| Payment of long-term debt | (285) | (829) | (472) |
| Repurchase of zero-coupon convertible notes | — | — | (127) |
| Issuance of common stock under employee stock plans | 570 | 482 | 377 |
| Repurchase of common stock | (3,309) | (751) | (671) |
| Dividends | (972) | (977) | (801) |
| Net cash used in financing activities | (4,159) | (1,549) | (1,567) |
| (Decrease) increase in cash and cash equivalents | (1,525) | 2,996 | 6,995 |
| Cash and cash equivalents at beginning of period | 14,188 | 11,192 | 4,197 |
| Cash and cash equivalents at end of period | $12,663 | $14,188 | $11,192 |

**Note 4: Supplemental Cash Flow Information**

| | 2004 | 2003 | 2002 |
|---|---|---|---|
| Cash paid for income taxes, net | $ 609 | $ 464 | $ 139 |
| Cash paid for interest | 305 | 394 | 206 |
| *Noncash investing and financing activities:* | | | |
| Net issuances of restricted stock and other stock benefits | $ 68 | $ 3 | $ 11 |
| Issuance of stock and options in business acquisitions | 15 | — | 24,717 |

For most companies, expenditures for interest and for taxes are significant. Cash payments for interest and for taxes usually are specifically indicated when the direct method is employed as is the case for **Storage Technology Corporation** reported earlier in Graphic 21–9. When the indirect method is used, those amounts aren't readily apparent and should be *separately reported* either on the face of the statement or in an accompanying disclosure note as Hewlett-Packard does.

We use a spreadsheet to help prepare a statement of cash flows by the indirect method in Appendix 21A.

## DECISION MAKERS' PERSPECTIVE—Cash Flow Ratios

We have emphasized the analysis of financial statements from a decision maker's perspective throughout this text. Often that analysis included the development and comparison of financial ratios. Ratios based on income statement and balance sheet amounts enjoy a long tradition of acceptance from which several standard ratios, including those described in earlier chapters, have evolved. To gain another viewpoint, some analysts supplement their investigation with cash flow ratios. Some cash flow ratios are derived by simply substituting cash flow from operations (CFFO) from the statement of cash flows in place of net income in many ratios, not to replace those ratios but to complement them. For example, the times interest earned ratio can be modified to reflect the number of times the cash outflow for interest is provided by cash inflow from operations and any of the profitability ratios can be modified to determine the cash generated from assets, shareholders' equity, sales, etc. Graphic 21–13 summarizes the calculation and usefulness of several representative cash flow ratios.

**GRAPHIC 21–13**
Cash Flow Ratios

| | Calculation | Measures |
|---|---|---|
| **Performance Ratios** | | |
| Cash flow to sales | CFFO ÷ Net sales | Cash generated by each sales dollar |
| Cash return on assets | CFFO ÷ Average total assets | Cash generated from all resources |
| Cash return on shareholders' equity | CFFO ÷ Average shareholders' equity | Cash generated from owner-provided resources |
| Cash to income | CFFO ÷ Income from continuing operations | Cash-generating ability of continuing operations |
| Cash flow per share | (CFFO − preferred dividends) ÷ Weighted-average shares | Operating cash flow on a per share basis |
| **Sufficiency Ratios** | | |
| Debt coverage | Total liabilities ÷ CFFO | Financial risk and financial leverage |
| Interest coverage | (CFFO + interest + taxes) ÷ Interest | Ability to satisfy fixed obligations |
| Reinvestment | CFFO ÷ Cash outflow for noncurrent assets | Ability to acquire assets with operating cash flows |
| Debt payment | CFFO ÷ Cash outflow for LT debt repayment | Ability to pay debts with operating cash flows |
| Dividend payment | CFFO ÷ Cash outflow for dividends | Ability to pay dividends with operating cash flows |
| Investing and financing activity | CFFO ÷ Cash outflows for investing and financing activities | Ability to acquire assets, pay debts, and make distributions to owners |

Cash flow ratios have received limited acceptance to date due, in large part, to the long tradition of accrual-based ratios coupled with the relatively brief time that all companies have published statements of cash flows. A lack of consensus on cash flow ratios by which to make comparisons also has slowed their acceptance. Nevertheless, cash flow ratios offer insight in the evaluation of a company's profitability and financial strength.[24] ■

## FINANCIAL REPORTING CASE SOLUTION

1. **What are the cash flow aspects of the situation that Mr. Barr may be overlooking in making his case for a wage increase? How can a company's operations generate a healthy profit and yet produce meager or even negative cash flows?** *(p. 1057)* Positive net income does not necessarily indicate a healthy cash position. A statement of cash flows provides information about cash flows not seen when looking only at the balance sheet and the income statement. Although cash flows from operating activities result from the same activities that are reported on the income statement, the income statement reports the activities on an accrual basis. That is, revenues reported are those earned during the reporting period, regardless of when cash is received, and the expenses incurred in generating those revenues, regardless of when cash is paid. Thus, the very same operations can generate a healthy profit and yet produce meager or even negative cash flows.
2. **What information can a statement of cash flows provide about a company's investing activities that can be useful in decisions such as this?** *(p. 1059)* Cash flows from investing activities result from the acquisition and disposition of assets. Information about investing activities is useful to decision makers regarding the nature and magnitude of productive assets being acquired for future use. In the union negotiations, for instance, Mr. Barr may not be aware of the substantial investments underway to replace and update equipment and the cash requirements of those investments. Relatedly, the relatively low depreciation charges accelerated depreciation provides in the later years of assets' lives may cause profits to seem artificially high given the necessity to replace those assets at higher prices.
3. **What information can a statement of cash flows provide about a company's financing activities that can be useful in decisions such as this?** *(p. 1060)* Information about financing activities provides insights into sources of a company's external financing. Recent debt issues, for instance, might indicate a need for higher cash flows to maintain higher interest charges. Similarly, recent external financing activity may suggest that a company might be near its practical limits from external sources and, therefore, may need a greater reliance on internal financing through operations. ■

## THE BOTTOM LINE

1. Decision makers focus on the prospects of receiving a cash return from their dealings with a firm. But it is the ability of the firm to generate cash flows to itself that ultimately determines the potential for cash flows to investors and creditors. The statement of cash flows fills an information gap left by the balance sheet and the income statement by presenting information about cash flows that the other statements either do not provide or provide only indirectly. The stipulation that companies present the statement of cash flows is a relatively recent requirement. *SFAS 95* completed a full-cycle movement of accounting thought back to cash flow reporting, which, in different form, was common practice several decades ago.
2. Cash includes cash equivalents. These are short-term, highly liquid investments that can readily be converted to cash with little risk of loss.

[24]Proposals for informative sets of cash flow ratios are offered by Charles Carslaw and John Mills, "Developing Ratios for Effective Cash Flow Analysis," *Journal of Accountancy,* November 1991; Don Giacomino and David Mielke, "Cash Flows: Another Approach to Ratio Analysis," *Journal of Accountancy,* March 1993; and John Mills and Jeanne Yamamura, "The Power of Cash Flows Ratios," *Journal of Accountancy,* October 1998.

3. Cash flows from operating activities are both inflows and outflows of cash that result from activities reported on the income statement.
4. Unlike the direct method, which directly lists cash inflows and outflows, the indirect method derives cash flows indirectly, by starting with reported net income and working backwards to convert that amount to a cash basis.
5. Cash flows from investing activities are related to the acquisition and disposition of assets, other than inventory and assets classified as cash equivalents.
6. Cash flows from financing activities result from the external financing of a business.
7. Noncash investing and financing activities, such as acquiring equipment (an investing activity) by issuing a long-term note payable (a financing activity), are reported in a related disclosure schedule or note.
8. A spreadsheet provides a systematic method of preparing a statement of cash flows by analyzing available data to insure that all operating, investing, and financing activities are detected. Recording spreadsheet entries that explain account balance changes simultaneously identifies and classifies the activities to be reported on the statement of cash flows. ■

## APPENDIX 21A SPREADSHEET FOR THE INDIRECT METHOD

A spreadsheet is equally useful in preparing a statement of cash flows whether we use the direct or the indirect method of determining cash flows from operating activities. The format of the spreadsheet differs only with respect to operating activities. The analysis of transactions for the purpose of identifying cash flows to be reported is the same. To illustrate, Illustration 21A–1 on the next page provides a spreadsheet analysis of the data for UBC.

Two differences should be noted between the spreadsheet in Illustration 21A–1 and the spreadsheet we used earlier for the direct method. First, in the statement of cash flows section of the spreadsheet, under the heading of "cash flows from operating activities," specific cash inflows and cash outflows are replaced by net income and the required adjustments for noncash effects. Second, we do not include an income statement section. This section is unnecessary because, using the indirect method, we are not interested in identifying specific operating activities that cause increases and decreases in cash. Instead, we need from the income statement only the amount of net income, which is converted to a cash basis by adjusting for any noncash amounts included in net income. The spreadsheet entries in journal entry form for the indirect method are illustrated in Illustration 21A–2 on page 1094.

Remember that there is no mandatory order in which the account changes must be analyzed. However, since we determine net cash flows from operating activities by working backwards from net income when using the indirect method, it is convenient to start with the spreadsheet entry that represents the credit to retained earnings due to net income. This entry corresponds to spreadsheet entry (11) using the direct method. By entering the debit portion of the entry as the first item under the cash flows from operating activities (CFOA), we establish net income as the initial amount of cash flows from operating activities, which is then adjusted to a cash basis by subsequent entries. Entries (2)–(4) duplicate the transactions that involve noncash components of net income. Changes in current assets and current liabilities that represent differences between revenues and expenses and the cash effects of those revenues and expenses are accounted for by entries (5)–(11). Spreadsheet entries (12)–(19) explain the changes in the balance sheet not already accounted for by previous entries, and are identical to entries (12)–(19) recorded using the direct method.

**ILLUSTRATION 21A–1**
Indirect Method

**UNITED BRANDS CORPORATION**
**Spreadsheet for the Statement of Cash Flows**

| | Dec. 31 2005 | Changes: Debits | | Changes: Credits | | Dec. 31 2006 |
|---|---|---|---|---|---|---|
| **Balance Sheet** | | | | | | |
| **Assets** | | | | | | |
| Cash | 20 | (19) | 9 | | | 29 |
| Accounts receivable | 30 | (5) | 2 | | | 32 |
| Short-term investments | 0 | (12) | 12 | | | 12 |
| Inventory | 50 | | | (6) | 4 | 46 |
| Prepaid insurance | 6 | | | (8) | 3 | 3 |
| Land | 60 | (13) | 30 | (2) | 10 | 80 |
| Buildings and equipment | 75 | (14) | 20X | (3) | 14 | 81 |
| Less: Accumulated depreciation | (20) | (3) | 7 | (4) | 3 | (16) |
| | 221 | | | | | 267 |
| **Liabilities** | | | | | | |
| Accounts payable | 20 | | | (7) | 6 | 26 |
| Salaries payable | 1 | | | (9) | 2 | 3 |
| Income tax payable | 8 | (11) | 2 | | | 6 |
| Notes payable | 0 | | | (14) | 20X | 20 |
| Bonds payable | 50 | (15) | 15 | | | 35 |
| Less: Discount on bonds | (3) | | | (10) | 2 | (1) |
| **Shareholders' Equity** | | | | | | |
| Common stock | 100 | | | (16) | 10 | |
| | | | | (17) | 20 | 130 |
| Paid-in capital—excess of par | 20 | | | (16) | 3 | |
| | | | | (17) | 6 | 29 |
| Retained earnings | 25 | (16) | 13 | | | |
| | | (18) | 5 | (1) | 12 | 19 |
| | 221 | | | | | 267 |
| **Statement of Cash Flows** | | | | | | |
| **Operating activities:** | | | | | | |
| Net income | | (1) | 12 | | | |
| *Adjustments for noncash effects:* | | | | | | |
| Gain on sale of land | | | | (2) | 8 | |
| Depreciation expense | | (4) | 3 | | | |
| Loss on sale of equipment | | (3) | 2 | | | |
| Increase in accounts receivable | | | | (5) | 2 | |
| Decrease in inventory | | (6) | 4 | | | |
| Decrease in prepaid insurance | | (8) | 3 | | | |
| Increase in accounts payable | | (7) | 6 | | | |
| Increase in salaries payable | | (9) | 2 | | | |
| Decrease in income tax payable | | | | (11) | 2 | |
| Amortization of discount | | (10) | 2 | | | |
| *Net cash flows* | | | | | | 22 |
| **Investing activities:** | | | | | | |
| Purchase of land | | | | (13) | 30 | |
| Purchase of S-T investment | | | | (12) | 12 | |
| Sale of land | | (2) | 18 | | | |
| Sale of equipment | | (3) | 5 | | | |
| *Net cash flows* | | | | | | (19) |
| **Financing activities:** | | | | | | |
| Sale of common shares | | (17) | 26 | | | |
| Retirement of bonds payable | | | | (15) | 15 | |
| Payment of cash dividends | | | | (18) | 5 | |
| *Net cash flows* | | | | | | 6 |
| *Net increase in cash* | | | | (19) | 9 | 9 |
| Totals | | | 198 | | 198 | |

**ILLUSTRATION 21A–2**

Spreadsheet Entries for the Indirect Method

| Entry | Account | Debit | Credit |
|---|---|---|---|
| **Entry (1)** | Net income—CFOA | 12 | |
| | Retained earnings | | 12 |
| | *Establishes net income as the initial amount of cash flows from operating activities, to be adjusted to a cash basis by subsequent entries.* | | |
| **Entry (2)** | Cash (received from sale of land) | 18 | |
| | Land | | 10 |
| | Gain on sale of land—CFOA | | 8 |
| | *Deducts the noncash gain added in determining net income, explains a portion of the change in land, and identifies a cash inflow from investing activities.* | | |
| **Entry (3)** | Cash (received from sale of equipment) | 5 | |
| | Loss on sale of equipment—CFOA | 2 | |
| | Accumulated depreciation | 7 | |
| | Buildings and equipment | | 14 |
| | *Adds back the noncash loss subtracted in determining net income, explains portions of the changes in accumulated depreciation and buildings and equipment, and identifies a cash inflow from investing activities.* | | |
| **Entry (4)** | Depreciation expense—CFOA | 3 | |
| | Accumulated depreciation | | 3 |
| | *Adds back the noncash expense subtracted in determining net income.* | | |
| **Entry (5)** | Accounts receivable | 2 | |
| | Increase in accounts receivable—CFOA | | 2 |
| | *Reduces net income to reflect $98 million cash received from customers rather than $100 million sales.* | | |
| **Entry (6)** | Decrease in inventory—CFOA | 4 | |
| | Inventory | | 4 |
| | *Increases net income to reflect a deduction of $56 million cost of goods purchased rather than $60 million cost of goods sold.* | | |
| **Entry (7)** | Increase in accounts payable—CFOA | 6 | |
| | Accounts payable | | 6 |
| | *Increases net income to reflect a deduction of $50 million cash paid to suppliers rather than $56 million cost of goods purchased.* | | |
| **Entry (8)** | Decrease in prepaid insurance—CFOA | 3 | |
| | Prepaid insurance | | 3 |
| | *Increases net income to reflect a deduction of $10 million cash paid for insurance rather than $13 million insurance expense.* | | |
| **Entry (9)** | Increase in salaries payable—CFOA | 2 | |
| | Salaries payable | | 2 |
| | *Increases net income to reflect a deduction of $11 million cash paid to employees rather than $13 million salaries expense.* | | |
| **Entry (10)** | Amortization of discount on bonds—CFOA | 2 | |
| | Discount on bonds | | 2 |
| | *Increases net income to reflect a deduction of $3 million cash paid for bond interest rather than $5 million bond interest expense.* | | |
| **Entry (11)** | Income taxes payable | 2 | |
| | Decrease in income taxes payable—CFOA | | 2 |
| | *Reduces net income to reflect a deduction of $11 million cash paid for income taxes rather than $9 million income tax expense.* | | |
| **Entry (12)** | Short-term investment | 12 | |
| | Cash (purchase of short-term investment) | | 12 |
| | *Explains the increase in the short-term investment account and identifies a cash outflow from investing activities.* | | |
| **Entry (13)** | Land | 30 | |
| | Cash (purchase of land) | | 30 |
| | *Explains a portion of the change in the land account and identifies a cash outflow from investing activities.* | | |

**ILLUSTRATION 21A–2**
Concluded

| | | |
|---|---|---|
| **Entry (14)** Buildings and equipment | 20 | |
| Note payable | | 20 |
| *Partially explains the changes in the buildings and equipment and notes payable accounts and identifies a noncash investing and financing activity.* | | |
| **Entry (15)** Bonds payable | 15 | |
| Cash (retirement of bonds payable) | | 15 |
| *Explains the decrease in the bonds payable account and identifies a cash outflow from financing activities.* | | |
| **Entry (16)** Retained earnings | 13 | |
| Common stock | | 10 |
| Paid-in capital—excess of par | | 3 |
| *Partially explains the changes in the retained earnings, common stock, and paid-in capital—excess of par accounts.* | | |
| **Entry (17)** Cash (from sale of common stock) | 26 | |
| Common stock | | 20 |
| Paid-in capital—excess of par | | 6 |
| *Partially explains the changes in the common stock and paid-in capital—excess of par accounts and identifies a cash inflow from financing activities.* | | |
| **Entry (18)** Retained earnings | 5 | |
| Cash (payment of cash dividends) | | 5 |
| *Partially explains the change in the retained earnings account and identifies a cash outflow from financing activities.* | | |
| **Entry (19)** Cash | 9 | |
| Net increase in cash (from statement of cash flows activities) | | 9 |
| *Reconciles the net increase in cash from operating, investing, and financing activities to the increase in the cash balance.* | | |

The statement of cash flows presenting net cash flows from operating activities by the indirect method is illustrated in Illustration 21A–3.

**ILLUSTRATION 21A–3**
Statement of Cash Flows—Indirect Method

**All parts of the statement of cash flows except operating activities are precisely the same as in the direct method.**

**UNITED BRANDS CORPORATION**
**Statement of Cash Flows**
**For Year Ended December 31, 2006**
($ in millions)

| | | |
|---|---|---|
| **Cash Flows from Operating Activities** | | |
| Net income | $12 | |
| Adjustments for noncash effects: | | |
| Gain on sale of land | (8) | |
| Depreciation expense | 3 | |
| Loss on sale of equipment | 2 | |
| Increase in accounts receivable | (2) | |
| Decrease in inventory | 4 | |
| Decrease in prepaid insurance | 3 | |
| Increase in accounts payable | 6 | |
| Increase in salaries payable | 2 | |
| Decrease in income tax payable | (2) | |
| Amortization of discount on bonds | 2 | |
| *Net cash flows from operating activities* | | $22 |
| **Cash Flows from Investing Activities** | | |
| Purchase of land | (30) | |
| Purchase of short-term investment | (12) | |
| Sale of land | 18 | |
| Sale of equipment | 5 | |
| *Net cash from investing activities* | | (19) |

**ILLUSTRATION 21A–3**
Concluded

| | | |
|---|---|---|
| **Cash Flows from Financing Activities** | | |
| Sale of common shares | 26 | |
| Retirement of bonds payable | (15) | |
| Payment of cash dividends | (5) | |
| *Net cash flows from financing activities* | | 6 |
| *Net increase in cash* | | 9 |
| Cash balance, January 1 | | 20 |
| Cash balance, December 31 | | $29 |
| **Noncash Investing and Financing Activities** | | |
| Acquired $20 million of equipment by issuing a 12%, 5-year note | | $20 |

## APPENDIX 21B THE T-ACCOUNT METHOD OF PREPARING THE STATEMENT OF CASH FLOWS

**The T-account method serves the same purpose as a spreadsheet in assisting in the preparation of a statement of cash flows.**

This chapter demonstrates the use of a spreadsheet to prepare the statement of cash flows. A second systematic approach to the preparation of the statement is referred to as the T-account method. The two methods are identical in concept. Both approaches reconstruct the transactions that caused changes in each account balance during the year, simultaneously identifying the operating, investing, and financing activities to be reported on the statement of cash flows. The form of the two methods differs only by whether the entries for those transactions are recorded on a spreadsheet or in T-accounts. In both cases, entries are recorded until the net change in each account balance has been explained.

Some accountants feel that the T-account method is less time-consuming than preparing a spreadsheet but accomplishes precisely the same goal. Since both methods are simply analytical techniques to assist in statement preparation, the choice is a matter of personal preference. The following five steps outline the T-account method:

1. Draw T-accounts for each income statement and balance sheet account.
2. The T-account for cash should be drawn considerably larger than other T-accounts because more space is required to accommodate the numerous debits and credits to cash. Also, the cash T-account will serve the same purpose as the statement of cash flows section of the spreadsheet in that the formal statement of cash flows is developed from the cash flows reported there. Therefore, it is convenient to partition the cash T-account with headings for "Operating Activities," "Investing Activities," and "Financing Activities" before entries are recorded.
3. Enter each account's net change on the appropriate side (debit or credit) of the uppermost portion of each T-account. These changes will serve as individual check figures for determining whether the increase or decrease in each account balance has been explained. These first three steps establish the basic work form for the T-account method.
4. Reconstruct the transactions that caused changes in each account balance during the year and record the entries for those transactions directly in the T-accounts. Again using UBC as an example, the entries we record in the T-accounts are exactly the same as the spreadsheet entries we created in the chapter when using the spreadsheet method. The analysis we used in creating those spreadsheet entries is equally applicable to the T-account method. For that reason, that analysis is not repeated here. The complete T-account work form for UBC is presented below. Account balance changes are provided by Illustration 21–1.

## BALANCE SHEET ACCOUNTS

### Cash (statement of cash flows)

| | | Debit | Credit | | |
|---|---|---|---|---|---|
| | | 9 | | | |
| **Operating Activities:** | | | | | |
| From customers | (1) | 98 | 50 | (4) | To suppliers of goods |
| From investment revenue | (2) | 3 | 11 | (5) | To employees |
| | | | 3 | (7) | For interest |
| | | | 4 | (8) | For insurance |
| | | | 11 | (10) | For income taxes |
| **Investing Activities:** | | | | | |
| Sale of land | (3) | 18 | 12 | (12) | Purchase of short-term investment |
| Sale of equipment | (9) | 5 | 30 | (13) | Purchase of land |
| **Financing Activities:** | | | | | |
| Sale of common stock | (17) | 26 | 15 | (15) | Retirement of bonds payable |
| | | | 5 | (18) | Payment of cash dividends |

**Accounts Receivable**

| | | | |
|---|---|---|---|
| | 2 | | |
| (1) | 2 | | |

**Short-Term Investments**

| | | | |
|---|---|---|---|
| | 12 | | |
| (12) | 12 | | |

**Inventory**

| | | | |
|---|---|---|---|
| | | 4 | |
| | | 4 | (4) |

**Prepaid Insurance**

| | | | |
|---|---|---|---|
| | | 3 | |
| | | 3 | (8) |

**Land**

| | | | |
|---|---|---|---|
| | 20 | | |
| (13) | 30 | 10 | (3) |

**Buildings and Equipment**

| | | | |
|---|---|---|---|
| | 6 | | |
| X(14) | 20 | 14 | (9) |

**Accumulated Depreciation**

| | | | |
|---|---|---|---|
| | 4 | | |
| (9) | 7 | 3 | (6) |

**Accounts Payable**

| | | | |
|---|---|---|---|
| | | 6 | |
| | | 6 | (4) |

**Salaries Payable**

| | | | |
|---|---|---|---|
| | | 2 | |
| | | 2 | (5) |

**Income Tax Payable**

| | | | |
|---|---|---|---|
| | 2 | | |
| (10) | 2 | | |

**Notes Payable**

| | | | |
|---|---|---|---|
| | | 20 | |
| | | 20 | (14)X |

**Bonds Payable**

| | | | |
|---|---|---|---|
| | 15 | | |
| (15) | 15 | | |

**Discount on Bonds**

| | | | |
|---|---|---|---|
| | | 2 | |
| | | 2 | (7) |

**Common Stock**

| | | | |
|---|---|---|---|
| | | 30 | |
| | | 10 | (16) |
| | | 20 | (17) |

**Paid-in Capital—excess of par**

| | | | |
|---|---|---|---|
| | | 9 | |
| | | 3 | (16) |
| | | 6 | (17) |

**Retained Earnings**

| | | | |
|---|---|---|---|
| | 6 | | |
| (16) | 13 | | |
| (18) | 5 | 12 | (11) |

X Noncash Investing and Financing Activity

**INCOME STATEMENT ACCOUNTS**

**Sales Revenue**

| | | | |
|---|---|---|---|
| | | 100 | |
| | | 100 | (1) |

**Investment Revenue**

| | | | |
|---|---|---|---|
| | | 3 | |
| | | 3 | (2) |

**Gain on Sale of Land**

| | | | |
|---|---|---|---|
| | | 8 | |
| | | 8 | (3) |

**Cost of Goods Sold**

| | | |
|---|---|---|
| | 60 | |
| (4) | 60 | |

**Salaries Expense**

| | | |
|---|---|---|
| | 13 | |
| (5) | 13 | |

**Depreciation Expense**

| | | |
|---|---|---|
| | 3 | |
| (6) | 3 | |

**Interest Expense**

| | | |
|---|---|---|
| | 5 | |
| (7) | 5 | |

**Insurance Expense**

| | | |
|---|---|---|
| | 7 | |
| (8) | 7 | |

**Loss on Sale of Equipment**

| | | |
|---|---|---|
| | 2 | |
| (9) | 2 | |

**Income Tax Expense**

| | | |
|---|---|---|
| | 9 | |
| (10) | 9 | |

**Net Income (Income Summary)**

| | | |
|---|---|---|
| | 12 | |
| (11) | 12 | |

5. After all account balances have been explained by T-account entries, prepare the statement of cash flows from the cash T-account, being careful also to report noncash investing and financing activities. The statement of cash flows for UBC appears in Graphic 21–2 on page 1052.

## QUESTIONS FOR REVIEW OF KEY TOPICS

**Q 21–1** Effects of all cash flows affect the balances of various accounts reported on the balance sheet. Also, the activities that cause some of these cash flows are reported on the income statement. What, then, is the need for an additional financial statement that reports cash flows?

**Q 21–2** The statement of cash flows has been a required financial statement only since 1988. Is cash flow reporting a totally new concept? Explain.

**Q 21–3** Is an investment in Treasury bills always classified as a cash equivalent? Explain.

**Q 21–4** Transactions that involve merely purchases or sales of cash equivalents generally are not reported on a statement of cash flows. Describe an exception to this generalization. What is the essential characteristic of the transaction that qualifies as an exception?

**Q 21–5** What are the differences between cash flows from operating activities and the elements of an income statement?

**Q 21–6** Do cash flows from operating activities report all the elements of the income statement on a cash basis? Explain.

**Q 21–7** Investing activities include the acquisition and disposition of assets. Provide four specific examples. Identify two exceptions.

**Q 21–8** The sale of stock and the sale of bonds are reported as financing activities. Are payments of dividends to shareholders and payments of interest to bondholders also reported as financing activities? Explain.

**Q 21–9** Does the statement of cash flows report only transactions that cause an increase or a decrease in cash? Explain.

**Q 21–10** How would the acquisition of a building be reported on a statement of cash flows if purchased by issuing a mortgage note payable in addition to a significant cash down payment?

**Q 21–11** Perhaps the most noteworthy item reported on an income statement is net income—the amount by which revenues exceed expenses. The most noteworthy item reported on a statement of cash flows is *not* the amount of net cash flows. Explain.

**Q 21–12** What is the purpose of the "changes" columns of a spreadsheet to prepare a statement of cash flows?

**Q 21–13** Given sales revenue of $200,000, how can it be determined whether or not $200,000 cash was received from customers?

**Q 21–14** When an asset is sold at a gain, why is the gain not reported as a cash inflow from operating activities?

**Q 21–15** Are ordinary losses and extraordinary losses treated alike in preparing a statement of cash flows? Explain.

**Q 21–16** When determining the amount of cash paid for income taxes, what would be indicated by an increase in the deferred income tax liability account?

**Q 21–17** When using the indirect method of determining net cash flows from operating activities, how is bad debt expense reported? Why? What other expenses are reported in a like manner?

**Q 21–18** When using the indirect method of determining net cash flows from operating activities, how are revenues and expenses reported on the statement of cash flows if their cash effects are identical to the amounts reported on the income statement?

**Q 21–19** Why does the FASB recommend the direct method over the indirect method?

**Q 21–20** Compare the manner in which investing activities are reported on a statement of cash flows prepared by the direct method and by the indirect method.

## BRIEF EXERCISES

**BE 21–1**
Determine cash received from customers
● LO3

Horton Housewares' accounts receivable decreased during the year by $5 million. What is the amount of cash Horton received from customers during the reporting period if its sales were $33 million? Prepare a summary entry that represents the net effect of the selling and collection activities during the reporting period.

**BE 21–2**
Determine cash received from customers
● LO3

April Wood Products' accounts receivable increased during the year by $4 million. Its bad debt expense was $2 million, and its allowance for uncollectible accounts increased by $1 million. What is the amount of cash April Wood Products received from customers during the reporting period if its sales were $44 million? Prepare a summary entry that represents the net effect of the selling and collection activities during the reporting period.

**BE 21–3**
Determine cash paid to suppliers
● LO3

LaRoe Lawns' inventory increased during the year by $6 million. Its accounts payable increased by $5 million during the same period. What is the amount of cash LaRoe paid to suppliers of merchandise during the reporting period if its cost of goods sold was $25 million? Prepare a summary entry that represents the net effect of merchandise purchases during the reporting period.

**BE 21–4**
Determine cash paid to employees
● LO3

Sherriane Baby Products' salaries expense was $17 million. What is the amount of cash Sherriane paid to employees during the reporting period if its salaries payable increased by $3 million? Prepare a summary entry that represents the net effect of salaries expense incurred and paid during the reporting period.

**BE 21–5**
Bond interest and discount
● LO3 LO6

Agee Technology, Inc. issued 9% bonds, dated January 1, with a face amount of $400 million on July 1, 2006, at a price of $380 million. For bonds of similar risk and maturity, the market yield is 10%. Interest is paid semiannually on June 30 and December 31. Prepare the journal entry to record interest at December 31. What would be the amount(s) related to the bonds that Agee would report in its statement of cash flows for the year ended December 31, 2006, if it uses the direct method?

**BE 21–6**
Bond interest and discount
● LO4 LO6

Refer to the situation described in BE 21–5. What would be the amount(s) related to the bonds that Agee would report in its statement of cash flows for the year ended December 31, 2006, if it uses the indirect method?

**BE 21–7**
Installment note
● LO3 LO6

On January 1, 2006, the Merit Group issued to its bank a $41 million, five-year installment note to be paid in five equal payments at the end of each year. Installment payments of $10 million annually include interest at the rate of 7%. What would be the amount(s) related to the note that Merit would report in its statement of cash flows for the year ended December 31, 2006?

**BE 21–8**
Sale of land
● LO3 LO4 LO5

On July 15, 2006, M.W. Morgan Distribution sold land for $35 million that it had purchased in 2001 for $22 million. What would be the amount(s) related to the sale that Morgan would report in its statement of cash flows for the year ended December 31, 2006, using the direct method? The indirect method?

**BE 21–9**
Investing activities
● LO5

Carter Containers sold marketable securities, land, and common stock for $30 million, $15 million, and $40 million, respectively. Carter also purchased treasury stock, equipment, and a patent for $21 million, $25 million, and $12 million, respectively. What amount should Carter report as net cash from investing activities?

**BE 21–10**
Financing activities
● LO6

Refer to the situation described in BE 21–9. What amount should Carter report as net cash from financing activities?

**BE 21–11**
Indirect method
● LO4

Sheen Awnings reported net income of $90 million. Included in that number were depreciation expense of $3 million and a loss on the sale of equipment of $2 million. Records reveal increases in accounts receivable, accounts payable, and inventory of $1 million, $4 million, and $3 million, respectively. What were Sheen's cash flows from operating activities?

**BE 21–12**
Indirect method
● LO4

Sunset Acres reported net income of $60 million. Included in that number were trademark amortization expense of $2 million and a gain on the sale of land of $1 million. Records reveal decreases in accounts receivable, accounts payable, and inventory of $2 million, $5 million, and $4 million, respectively. What were Sunset's cash flows from operating activities?

# EXERCISES

available with McGraw-Hill's Homework Manager www.mhhe.com/spiceland4e

**An alternate exercise and problem set is available on the text website: www.mhhe.com/spiceland4e**

**E 21–1**
Classification of cash flows
● LO3 through LO6

Listed below are several transactions that typically produce either an increase or a decrease in cash. Indicate by letter whether the cash effect of each transaction is reported on a statement of cash flows as an operating (**O**), investing (**I**), or financing (**F**) activity.

**Transactions**

F 1. Sale of common stock
____ 2. Sale of land
____ 3. Purchase of treasury stock
____ 4. Merchandise sales
____ 5. Issuance of a long-term note payable
____ 6. Purchase of merchandise
____ 7. Repayment of note payable
____ 8. Employee salaries
____ 9. Sale of equipment at a gain
____ 10. Issuance of bonds
____ 11. Acquisition of bonds of another corporation
____ 12. Payment of semiannual interest on bonds payable
____ 13. Payment of a cash dividend
____ 14. Purchase of a building
____ 15. Collection of nontrade note receivable (principal amount)
____ 16. Loan to another firm
____ 17. Retirement of common stock
____ 18. Income taxes
____ 19. Issuance of a short-term note payable
____ 20. Sale of a copyright

**E 21–2**
Determine cash paid to suppliers of merchandise
● LO3

Shown below in T-account format are the beginning and ending balances ($ in millions) of both inventory and accounts payable.

**Inventory**

| | | | |
|---|---|---|---|
| Beginning balance | 90 | | |
| Ending balance | 93 | | |

**Accounts Payable**

| | | | |
|---|---|---|---|
| | | 14 | Beginning balance |
| | | 16 | Ending balance |

**Required:**

1. Use a T-account analysis to determine the amount of cash paid to suppliers of merchandise during the reporting period if cost of goods sold was $300 million.
2. Prepare a summary entry that represents the net effect of merchandise purchases during the reporting period.

**E 21–3**
Determine cash received from customers
● LO3

Determine the amount of cash received from customers for each of the six independent situations below. All dollars are in millions.

| Situation | Sales Revenue | Accounts Receivable Increase (Decrease) | Bad Debt Expense | Allowance for Uncollectible Accounts Increase (Decrease) | Cash Received from Customers |
|---|---|---|---|---|---|
| 1 | 100 | -0- | -0- | -0- | ? |
| 2 | 100 | 5 | -0- | -0- | ? |
| 3 | 100 | (5) | -0- | -0- | ? |
| 4 | 100 | 5 | 2 | 2 | ? |
| 5 | 100 | (5) | 2 | 1 | ? |
| 6 | 100 | 5 | 2 | (1) | ? |

**E 21–4**
Summary entries for cash received from customers
● LO3

For each of the four independent situations below, prepare journal entries that summarize the selling and collection activities for the reporting period in order to determine the amount of cash received from customers and to explain the change in each account shown. All dollars are in millions.

| Situation | Sales Revenue | Accounts Receivable Increase (Decrease) | Bad Debt Expense | Allowance for Uncollectible Accounts Increase (Decrease) | Cash Received from Customers |
|---|---|---|---|---|---|
| 1 | 200 | -0- | -0- | -0- | ? |
| 2 | 200 | 10 | -0- | -0- | ? |
| 3 | 200 | 10 | 4 | 4 | ? |
| 4 | 200 | 10 | 4 | (2) | ? |

**E 21–5**
Determine cash paid to suppliers of merchandise
● LO3

Determine the amount of cash paid to suppliers of merchandise for each of the nine independent situations below. All dollars are in millions.

| Situation | Cost of Goods Sold | Inventory Increase (Decrease) | Accounts Payable Increase (Decrease) | Cash Paid to Suppliers |
|---|---|---|---|---|
| 1 | 100 | 0 | 0 | ? |
| 2 | 100 | 3 | 0 | ? |
| 3 | 100 | (3) | 0 | ? |
| 4 | 100 | 0 | 7 | ? |
| 5 | 100 | 0 | (7) | ? |
| 6 | 100 | 3 | 7 | ? |
| 7 | 100 | 3 | (7) | ? |
| 8 | 100 | (3) | (7) | ? |
| 9 | 100 | (3) | 7 | ? |

**E 21–6**
Summary entries for cash paid to suppliers of merchandise
● LO3

For each of the five independent situations below, prepare a journal entry that summarizes the purchases, sales, and payments related to inventories in order to determine the amount of cash paid to suppliers and explain the change in each account shown. All dollars are in millions.

| Situation | Cost of Goods Sold | Inventory Increase (Decrease) | Accounts Payable Increase (Decrease) | Cash Paid to Suppliers |
|---|---|---|---|---|
| 1 | 200 | 0 | 0 | ? |
| 2 | 200 | 6 | 0 | ? |
| 3 | 200 | 0 | 14 | ? |
| 4 | 200 | 6 | 14 | ? |
| 5 | 200 | (6) | (14) | ? |

**E 21–7**
Determine cash paid for bond interest
● LO3

Determine the amount of cash paid to bondholders for bond interest for each of the six independent situations below. All dollars are in millions.

| Situation | Bond Interest Expense | Bond Interest Payable Increase (Decrease) | Unamortized Discount Increase (Decrease) | Cash Paid for Interest |
|---|---|---|---|---|
| 1 | 10 | 0 | 0 | ? |
| 2 | 10 | 2 | 0 | ? |
| 3 | 10 | (2) | 0 | ? |
| 4 | 10 | 0 | (3) | ? |
| 5 | 10 | 2 | (3) | ? |
| 6 | 10 | (2) | (3) | ? |

**E 21–8**
Determine cash paid for bond interest
● LO3

For each of the four independent situations below, prepare a single journal entry that summarizes the recording and payment of interest in order to determine the amount of cash paid for bond interest and explain the change (if any) in each of the accounts shown. All dollars are in millions.

| Situation | Bond Interest Expense | Bond Interest Payable Increase (Decrease) | Unamortized Discount Increase (Decrease) | Cash Paid for Interest |
|---|---|---|---|---|
| 1 | 20 | 0 | 0 | ? |
| 2 | 20 | 4 | 0 | ? |
| 3 | 20 | 0 | (6) | ? |
| 4 | 20 | (4) | (6) | ? |

**E 21–9**
Determine cash paid for income taxes
● LO3

Determine the amount of cash paid for income taxes in each of the nine independent situations below. All dollars are in millions.

| Situation | Income Tax Expense | Income Tax Payable Increase (Decrease) | Deferred Tax Liability Increase (Decrease) | Cash Paid for Taxes |
|---|---|---|---|---|
| 1 | 10 | 0 | 0 | ? |
| 2 | 10 | 3 | 0 | ? |
| 3 | 10 | (3) | 0 | ? |
| 4 | 10 | 0 | 2 | ? |
| 5 | 10 | 0 | (2) | ? |
| 6 | 10 | 3 | 2 | ? |
| 7 | 10 | 3 | (2) | ? |
| 8 | 10 | (3) | (2) | ? |
| 9 | 10 | (3) | 2 | ? |

**E 21–10**
Summary entries for cash paid for income taxes
● LO3

For each of the five independent situations below, prepare a single journal entry that summarizes the recording and payment of income taxes in order to determine the amount of cash paid for income taxes and explain the change (if any) in each of the accounts shown. All dollars are in millions.

| Situation | Income Tax Expense | Income Tax Payable Increase (Decrease) | Deferred Tax Liability Increase (Decrease) | Cash Paid for Taxes |
|---|---|---|---|---|
| 1 | 10 | 0 | 0 | ? |
| 2 | 10 | 3 | 0 | ? |
| 3 | 10 | 0 | (2) | ? |
| 4 | 10 | 3 | 2 | ? |
| 5 | 10 | (3) | (2) | ? |

**E 21–11**
Bonds; statement of cash flow effects
● LO3

Most Solutions, Inc. issued 10% bonds, dated January 1, with a face amount of $640 million on January 1, 2006. The bonds mature in 2016 (10 years). For bonds of similar risk and maturity the market yield is 12%. Interest is paid semiannually on June 30 and December 31. Most recorded the sale as follows:

**January 1, 2006**

| | | |
|---|---|---|
| Cash (price) | 566,589,440 | |
| Discount on bonds (difference) | 73,410,560 | |
| Bonds payable (face amount) | | 640,000,000 |

**Required:**

What would be the amount(s) related to the bonds that Most would report in its statement of cash flows for the year ended December 31, 2006?

**E 21–12**
Installment note; statement of cash flow effects
● LO3 LO6

National Food Services, Inc. borrowed $4 million from its local bank on January 1, 2006, and issued a 4-year installment note to be paid in four equal payments at the end of each year. The payments include interest at the rate of 10%. Installment payments are $1,261,881 annually.

**Required:**

What would be the amount(s) related to the note that National would report in its statement of cash flows for the year ended December 31, 2006?

**E 21–13**
Identifying cash flows from investing activities and financing activities
● LO5 LO6

In preparation for developing its statement of cash flows for the year ended December 31, 2006, RapidPac, Inc. collected the following information:

| | ($ in millions) |
|---|---|
| Fair value of shares issued in a stock dividend | $ 65 |
| Payment for the early extinguishment of long-term bonds (carrying amount: $97 million) | 102 |
| Proceeds from the sale of treasury stock (cost: $17 million) | 22 |
| Gain on sale of land | 4 |
| Proceeds from sale of land | 12 |
| Purchase of Microsoft common stock | 160 |
| Declaration of cash dividends | 44 |
| Distribution of cash dividends declared in 2005 | 40 |

**Required:**

1. In RapidPac's statement of cash flows, what were net cash inflows (or outflows) from investing activities for 2006?
2. In RapidPac's statement of cash flows, what were net cash inflows (or outflows) from financing activities for 2006?

**E 21–14**
Identifying cash flows from investing activities and financing activities

● LO5 LO6

In preparation for developing its statement of cash flows for the year ended December 31, 2006, Millennium Solutions, Inc. collected the following information ($ in millions):

| | |
|---|---|
| Payment for the early extinguishments of long-term notes (book value: $50 million) | $ 54 |
| Sale of common shares | 176 |
| Retirement of common shares | 122 |
| Loss on sale of equipment | 2 |
| Proceeds from sale of equipment | 8 |
| Issuance of short-term note payable for cash | 10 |
| Acquisition of building for cash | 7 |
| Purchase of marketable securities (not a cash equivalent) | 5 |
| Purchase of marketable securities (considered a cash equivalent) | 1 |
| Cash payment for 3-year insurance policy | 3 |
| Collection of note receivable with interest (principal amount, $11) | 13 |
| Declaration of cash dividends | 33 |
| Distribution of cash dividends declared in 2005 | 30 |

**Required:**

1. In Millennium's statement of cash flows, what were net cash inflows (or outflows) from investing activities for 2006?
2. In Millennium's statement of cash flows, what were net cash inflows (or outflows) from financing activities for 2006?

**E 21–15**
Capital lease; lessee; statement of cash flows effects

● LO3 LO5 LO6

Wilson Foods Corporation leased a commercial food processor on September 30, 2006. The five-year lease agreement calls for Wilson to make quarterly lease payments of $195,774, payable each September 30, December 31, March 31, June 30, with the first payment at September 30, 2006. Wilson's incremental borrowing rate is 12%. Wilson records depreciation on a straight-line basis at the end of each fiscal year. Wilson recorded the lease as follows:

| **September 30, 2006** | | |
|---|---|---|
| Leased equipment (calculated below) | 3,000,000 | |
| Lease payable (calculated below) | | 3,000,000 |
| Lease payable | 195,774 | |
| Cash (rental payment) | | 195,774 |

**Calculation of the present value of lease payments**

$195,774 × 15.32380* = $3,000,000 (rounded)

*Present value of an annuity due of $1: n = 20, i = 3%

**Required:**

What would be the pretax amounts related to the lease that Wilson would report in its statement of cash flows for the year ended December 31, 2006?

**E 21–16**
Equity method investment; statement of cash flow effects

● LO3 LO5

On January 1, 2006, Beilich Enterprises bought 20% of the outstanding common stock of Wolfe Construction Company for $600 million cash. Wolfe's net income for the year ended December 31, 2006, was $300 million. During 2006, Wolfe declared and paid cash dividends of $60 million. Beilich recorded the investment as follows:

| | ($ in millions) | |
|---|---|---|
| **Purchase** | | |
| Investment in Wolfe Construction shares | 600 | |
| Cash | | 600 |
| **Net income** | | |
| Investment in Wolfe Construction shares (20% × $300 million) | 60 | |
| Investment revenue | | 60 |
| **Dividends** | | |
| Cash (20% × $60 million) | 12 | |
| Investment in Wolfe Construction shares | | 12 |

**Required:**

What would be the pretax amounts related to the investment that Beilich would report in its statement of cash flows for the year ended December 31, 2006?

**E 21–17**
Indirect method; reconciliation of net income to net cash flows from operating activities

● LO4

The accounting records of EZ Company provided the data below. Prepare a reconciliation of net income to net cash flows from operating activities.

| | |
|---|---|
| Net income | $50,000 |
| Depreciation expense | 7,000 |
| Increase in inventory | 1,500 |
| Decrease in salaries payable | 800 |
| Decrease in accounts receivable | 2,000 |
| Amortization of patent | 500 |
| Amortization of premium on bonds | 1,000 |
| Increase in accounts payable | 4,000 |
| Cash dividends | 12,000 |

**E 21–18**
Spreadsheet entries from statement of retained earnings

● LO3 through LO8

The statement of retained earnings of Gary Larson Publishers is presented below.

**GARY LARSON PUBLISHERS**
**Statement of Retained Earnings**
**For the Year Ended December 31, 2006**
($ in millions)

| | | |
|---|---|---|
| **Retained earnings, January 1** | | $200 |
| Add: | Net income | 75 |
| Deduct: | Cash dividend | (25) |
| | Stock dividend (1 million shares of $1 par common stock) | (16) |
| | Property dividend (Garfield Company preferred stock held as a short-term investment) | (12) |
| | Sale of treasury stock (cost $53 million) | (10) |
| **Retained earnings, December 31** | | $212 |

Required:
For the transactions that affected Larson's retained earnings, reconstruct the journal entries for the transactions that affected retained earnings and that can be used to determine cash flows to be reported in a statement of cash flows. Also indicate any investing and financing activities you identify from this analysis that should be reported on the statement of cash flows.

**E 21–19**
Relationship between the income statement and cash flows from operating activities (direct method and indirect method)

● LO3 LO4

The following schedule relates the income statement with cash flows from operating activities, derived by both the direct and indirect methods, in the format illustrated by Graphic 21–10 in the chapter. The amounts for income statement elements are missing.

**Cash Flows from Operating Activities**

| Income Statement | | Indirect Method | | Direct Method | |
|---|---|---|---|---|---|
| | | Net income | $? | | |
| | | Adjustments: | | | |
| Sales | $? | Decrease in accounts receivable | 12 | Cash received from customers | $612 |
| Cost of goods sold | ? | Increase in inventory | (24) | | |
| | | Decrease in accounts payable | (36) | Cash paid to suppliers | (420) |
| Salaries expense | ? | Increase in salaries payable | 12 | Cash paid to employees | (66) |
| Depreciation expense | ? | Depreciation expense | 18 | (Not reported—no cash effect) | |
| Insurance expense | ? | Decrease in prepaid insurance | 18 | Cash paid for insurance | (24) |
| Loss on sale of land | ? | Loss on sale of land | 12 | (Not reported—no cash effect) | |
| Income tax expense | ? | Increase in income tax payable | 12 | Cash paid for income taxes | (42) |
| **Net income** | **$?** | **Net cash flows from operating activities** | $60 | **Net cash flows from operating activities** | $ 60 |

Required:
Deduce the missing amounts and prepare the income statement.

**E 21–20**
Reconciliation of net cash flows from operating activities to net income

● LO3 LO4

The income statement and the cash flows from the operating activities section of the statement of cash flows are provided below for Syntric Company. The merchandise inventory account balance neither increased nor decreased during the reporting period. Syntric had no liability for either insurance, deferred income taxes, or interest at any time during the period.

**SYNTRIC COMPANY**
**Income Statement**
**For the Year Ended December 31, 2006**
($ in 000s)

| | | |
|---|---|---|
| Sales | | $312 |
| Cost of goods sold | | (188) |
| Gross margin | | 124 |
| Salaries expense | $41 | |
| Insurance expense | 22 | |
| Depreciation expense | 11 | |
| Depletion expense | 5 | |
| Bond interest expense | 10 | (89) |
| Gains and losses: | | |
| Gain on sale of equipment | | 25 |
| Loss on sale of land | | (8) |
| Income before tax | | 52 |
| Income tax expense | | (26) |
| **Net income** | | $ 26 |
| **Cash Flows from Operating Activities:** | | |
| Cash received from customers | | $258 |
| Cash paid to suppliers | | (175) |
| Cash paid to employees | | (37) |
| Cash paid for interest | | (9) |
| Cash paid for insurance | | (16) |
| Cash paid for income taxes | | (14) |
| **Net cash flows from operating activities** | | $ 7 |

**Required:**
Prepare a schedule to reconcile net income to net cash flows from operating activities.

**E 21–21**
Cash flows from operating activities (direct method) derived from an income statement and cash flows from operating activities (indirect method)

● LO3 LO4

The income statement and a schedule reconciling cash flows from operating activities to net income are provided below ($ in 000s) for Peach Computers.

**PEACH COMPUTERS**
**Income Statement**
**For the Year Ended December 31, 2006**

| | | |
|---|---|---|
| Sales | | $305 |
| Cost of goods sold | | (185) |
| Gross margin | | 120 |
| Salaries expense | $41 | |
| Insurance expense | 19 | |
| Depreciation expense | 11 | |
| Loss on sale of land | 5 | 76 |
| Income before tax | | 44 |
| Income tax expense | | (22) |
| **Net income** | | $ 22 |

**Reconciliation of Net Income**
**To Net Cash Flows from Operating Activities**

| | |
|---|---|
| Net income | $22 |
| **Adjustments for Noncash Effects** | |
| Depreciation expense | 11 |
| Loss on sale of land | 5 |
| Decrease in accounts receivable | 6 |
| Increase in inventory | (13) |
| Decrease in accounts payable | (8) |
| Increase in salaries payable | 5 |
| Decrease in prepaid insurance | 9 |
| Increase in income tax payable | 20 |
| **Net cash flows from operating activities** | $57 |

**Required:**
1. Calculate each of the following amounts for Peach Computers:
   a. Cash received from customers during the reporting period.
   b. Cash paid to suppliers of goods during the reporting period.
   c. Cash paid to employees during the reporting period.
   d. Cash paid for insurance during the reporting period.
   e. Cash paid for income taxes during the reporting period.
2. Prepare the cash flows from operating activities section of the statement of cash flows (direct method).

**E 21–22**
Indirect method; reconciliation of net income to net cash flows from operating activities

● LO4

The accounting records of Baddour Company provided the data below. Prepare a reconciliation of net income to net cash flows from operating activities.

| | |
|---|---|
| Net loss | $5,000 |
| Depreciation expense | 6,000 |
| Increase in salaries payable | 500 |
| Decrease in accounts receivable | 2,000 |
| Increase in inventory | 2,300 |
| Amortization of patent | 300 |
| Reduction in discount on bonds | 200 |

**E 21–23**
Cash flows from operating activities (direct method)—includes loss on sale of cash equivalents and extraordinary loss

● LO3

Portions of the financial statements for Myriad Products are provided below.

**MYRIAD PRODUCTS COMPANY**
**Income Statement**
**For the Year Ended December 31, 2006**
($ in millions)

| | | |
|---|---|---|
| Sales | | $660 |
| Cost of goods sold | | (250) |
| Gross margin | | 410 |
| Salaries expense | $110 | |
| Depreciation expense | 90 | |
| Patent amortization expense | 5 | |
| Interest expense | 20 | |
| Loss on sale of cash equivalents | 3 | (228) |
| Income before taxes and extraordinary loss | | 182 |
| Income tax expense | | (91) |
| Income before extraordinary loss | | 91 |
| Extraordinary loss (earthquake) | 10 | |
| Less: Tax savings | (5) | (5) |
| Net Income | | $ 86 |

**MYRIAD PRODUCTS COMPANY**
**Selected Accounts from Comparative Balance Sheets**
**December 31, 2006 and 2005**
($ in millions)

| | Year | | |
|---|---|---|---|
| | **2006** | **2005** | **Change** |
| Cash | $102 | $100 | $ 2 |
| Accounts receivable | 220 | 232 | (12) |
| Inventory | 440 | 450 | (10) |
| Accounts payable | 140 | 134 | 6 |
| Salaries payable | 80 | 86 | (6) |
| Interest payable | 25 | 20 | 5 |
| Income taxes payable | 15 | 10 | 5 |

**Required:**
Prepare the cash flows from operating activities section of the statement of cash flows for Myriad Products Company using the *direct method.*

**E 21–24**
Cash flows from operating activities (indirect method) includes loss on sale of cash equivalents and extraordinary loss

● LO4

Refer to the data provided in the previous exercise for Myriad Products Company.

**Required:**
Prepare the cash flows from operating activities section of the statement of cash flows for Myriad Products Company using the *indirect method.*

**E 21–25**
Cash flows from operating activities (direct method)—includes loss on sale of cash equivalents and extraordinary gain

● LO3

Portions of the financial statements for Clear Transmissions Company are provided below.

**CLEAR TRANSMISSIONS COMPANY**
**Income Statement**
**For the Year Ended December 31, 2006** ($ in 000s)

| | | |
|---|---|---|
| Sales | | $1,320 |
| Cost of goods sold | | (500) |
| Gross margin | | 820 |
| Salaries expense | $220 | |
| Depreciation expense | 180 | |
| Patent amortization expense | 10 | |
| Interest expense | 40 | |
| Loss on sale of cash equivalents | 6 | (456) |
| Income before taxes and extraordinary gain | | 364 |

| | | |
|---|---|---|
| Income tax expense | | (182) |
| Income before extraordinary gain | | 182 |
| Extraordinary gain (sale of subsidiary) | 20 | |
| Less: Tax on gain | (10) | 10 |
| Net Income | | $ 192 |

**CLEAR TRANSMISSIONS COMPANY**
**Selected Accounts from Comparative Balance Sheets**
**December 31, 2006 and 2005** ($ in 000s)

| | Year | | |
|---|---|---|---|
| | **2006** | **2005** | **Change** |
| Cash | $102 | $100 | $ 2 |
| Accounts receivable | 220 | 232 | (12) |
| Inventory | 440 | 450 | (10) |
| Accounts payable | 140 | 134 | 6 |
| Salaries payable | 80 | 86 | (6) |
| Interest payable | 25 | 20 | 5 |
| Income taxes payable | 15 | 10 | 5 |

**Required:**
Prepare the cash flows from operating activities section of the statement of cash flows for Clear Transmissions Company using the *direct method.*

**E 21–26**
Cash flows from operating activities (indirect method)—includes loss on sale of cash equivalents and extraordinary gain

● LO4

Refer to the data provided in the previous exercise for Clear Transmissions Company.

**Required:**
Prepare the cash flows from operating activities section of the statement of cash flows for Clear Transmissions Company using the *indirect method.*

**E 21–27**
Statement of cash flows; direct method

● LO3 LO5 LO6 LO8

Comparative balance sheets for 2006 and 2005, a statement of income for 2006, and additional information from the accounting records of Red, Inc. are provided below.

**RED, INC.**
**Comparative Balance Sheets**
**December 31, 2006 and 2005** ($ in millions)

| | **2006** | **2005** |
|---|---|---|
| **Assets** | | |
| Cash | $ 24 | $110 |
| Accounts receivable | 178 | 132 |
| Prepaid insurance | 7 | 3 |
| Inventory | 285 | 175 |
| Buildings and equipment | 400 | 350 |
| Less: Accumulated depreciation | (119) | (240) |
| | $775 | $530 |
| **Liabilities** | | |
| Accounts payable | $87 | $100 |
| Accrued expenses payable | 6 | 11 |
| Notes payable | 50 | 0 |
| Bonds payable | 160 | 0 |
| **Shareholders' Equity** | | |
| Common stock | 400 | 400 |
| Retained earnings | 72 | 19 |
| | $775 | $530 |

**RED, INC.**
**Statement of Income**
**For Year Ended December 31, 2006** ($ in millions)

| | | |
|---|---|---|
| **Revenues** | | |
| Sales revenue | | $2,000 |
| **Expenses** | | |
| Cost of goods sold | $1,400 | |
| Depreciation expense | 50 | |
| Operating expenses | 447 | 1,897 |
| **Net income** | | $ 103 |

*Additional information from the accounting records:*

a. During 2006, $230 million of equipment was purchased to replace $180 million of equipment (95% depreciated) sold at book value.

b. In order to maintain the usual policy of paying cash dividends of $50 million, it was necessary for Red to borrow $50 million from its bank.

**Required:**

Prepare the statement of cash flows of Red, Inc. for the year ended December 31, 2006. Present cash flows from operating activities by the direct method. (You may omit the schedule to reconcile net income with cash flows from operating activities.)

**E 21–28**
Pension plan funding

● LO3

Mayer Corporation has a defined benefit pension plan. Mayer's policy is to fund the plan annually, cash payments being made at the end of each year. Data relating to the pension plan for 2006 are as follows:

| | December 31 ($ in millions) | |
|---|---|---|
| | **2006** | **2005** |
| Prepaid (accrued) pension cost | $ 5 | $ (1) |
| **Net Pension Expense for 2006:** | | |
| Service cost | $112 | |
| Interest cost (6% × $850) | 51 | |
| Actual return on the plan assets (11% × $900 = $99) | | |
| Adjusted for: $9 gain on the plan assets* | (90) | |
| Amortization of prior service cost | 8 | |
| Amortization of net loss | 1 | |
| | $ 82 | |

*(11% × $900) − (10% × $900)

**Required:**

Re-create the journal entry used to record Mayer's 2006 pension expense in order to determine the cash paid to the pension trustee as reported on the statement of cash flows.

**E 21–29**
Multiple choice; CPA exam

● LO1 LO3 LO6

The following questions dealing with cash flows are adapted from questions that appeared on past CPA examinations. Determine the response that best completes the statements or questions.

1. The primary purpose of a statement of cash flows is to provide relevant information about
   a. Difference between net income and associated cash receipts and disbursements.
   b. An enterprise's ability to generate future positive net cash flows.
   c. The cash receipts and cash disbursements of an enterprise during a period.
   d. An enterprise's ability to meet cash operating needs.

Items 2 and 3 are based on the following:

In preparing its cash flow statement for the year ended December 31, 2006, Reve Co. collected the following data:

| | |
|---|---|
| Gain on sale of equipment | $ (6,000) |
| Proceeds from sale of equipment | 10,000 |
| Purchase of A.S., Inc. bonds (par value $200,000) | (180,000) |
| Amortization of bond discount | 2,000 |
| Dividends declared | (45,000) |
| Dividends paid | (38,000) |
| Proceeds from sales of treasury stock (carrying amount $65,000) | 75,000 |

In its December 31, 2006, statement of cash flows,

2. What amount should Reve report as net cash used in investing activities?
   a. $170,000
   b. $176,000

c. $188,000
d. $194,000

3. What amount should Reve report as net cash provided by financing activities?
   a. $20,000
   b. $27,000
   c. $30,000
   d. $37,000

**E 21–30**
Statement of cash flows; indirect method
● LO4 LO5 LO6 LO8

Refer to the data provided in Exercise 21–27 for Red, Inc.

**Required:**
Prepare the statement of cash flows for Red, Inc. using the indirect method to report operating activities.

**E 21–31**
Multiple choice; CMA exam; cash flows
● LO3 through LO6

The following questions dealing with the statement of cash flows are adapted from questions that previously appeared on Certified Management Accountant (CMA) examinations. The CMA designation sponsored by the Institute of Management Accountants (www.imanet.org) provides members with an objective measure of knowledge and competence in the field of management accounting. Determine the response that best completes the statements or questions.

1. When preparing the statement of cash flows, companies are required to report separately as operating cash flows all of the following except
   a. interest received on investments in bonds.
   b. interest paid on the company's bonds.
   c. cash collected from customers.
   d. cash dividends paid on the company's stock.
2. The following information was taken from the accounting records of Oak Corporation for the year ended December 31:

| | |
|---|---|
| Proceeds from issuance of preferred stock | $4,000,000 |
| Dividends paid on preferred stock | 400,000 |
| Bonds payable converted to common stock | 2,000,000 |
| Payment for purchase of machinery | 500,000 |
| Proceeds from sale of plant building | 1,200,000 |
| 2% stock dividend on common stock | 300,000 |
| Gain on sale of plant building | 200,000 |

   The net cash flows from investing and financing activities that should be presented on Oak's statement of cash flows for the year ended December 31 are, respectively
   a. $700,000 and $3,600,000.
   b. $700,000 and $3,900,000.
   c. $900,000 and $3,900,000.
   d. $900,000 and $3,600,000.
3. The net income for Cypress Inc. was $3,000,000 for the year ended December 31. Additional information is as follows:

| | |
|---|---|
| Depreciation on fixed assets | $1,500,000 |
| Gain from cash sale of land | 200,000 |
| Increase in accounts payable | 300,000 |
| Dividends paid on preferred stock | 400,000 |

   The net cash provided by operating activities in the statement of cash flows for the year ended December 31 should be
   a. $4,200,000.
   b. $4,500,000.
   c. $4,600,000.
   d. $4,800,000.

**E 21–32**
Statement of cash flows; T-account method (based on Appendix 21B)
● LO8

Refer to the data provided in Exercise 21–27 for Red, Inc.

**Required:**
Prepare the statement of cash flows (direct method) for Red, Inc. Use the T-account method to assist in your analysis.

# PROBLEMS

available with McGraw-Hill's Homework Manager www.mhhe.com/spiceland4e

**An alternate exercise and problem set is available on the text website: www.mhhe.com/spiceland4e**

**P 21–1**
Classification of cash flows from investing and financing activities

● LO2 LO5 through LO7

Listed below are transactions that might be reported as investing and/or financing activities on a statement of cash flows. Possible reporting classifications of those transactions are provided also.

**Required:**

Indicate the reporting classification of each transaction by entering the appropriate classification code.

| | **Classifications** |
|---|---|
| +I | Investing activity (cash inflow) |
| −I | Investing activity (cash outflow) |
| +F | Financing activity (cash inflow) |
| −F | Financing activity (cash outflow) |
| N | Noncash investing and financing activity |
| X | Not reported as an investing and/or a financing activity |

**Transactions**

Example +I 1. Sale of land.
____ 2. Issuance of common stock for cash.
____ 3. Purchase of treasury stock.
____ 4. Conversion of bonds payable to common stock.
____ 5. Lease of equipment by capital lease.
____ 6. Sale of patent.
____ 7. Acquisition of building for cash.
____ 8. Issuance of common stock for land.
____ 9. Collection of note receivable (principal amount).
____ 10. Issuance of bonds.
____ 11. Issuance of stock dividend.
____ 12. Payment of property dividend.
____ 13. Payment of cash dividends.
____ 14. Issuance of short-term note payable for cash.
____ 15. Issuance of long-term note payable for cash.
____ 16. Purchase of marketable securities (not cash equivalent).
____ 17. Payment of note payable.
____ 18. Cash payment for 5-year insurance policy.
____ 19. Sale of equipment.
____ 20. Issuance of note payable for equipment.
____ 21. Acquisition of common stock of another corporation.
____ 22. Repayment of long-term debt by issuing common stock.
____ 23. Appropriation of retained earnings for plant expansion.
____ 24. Payment of semiannual interest on bonds payable.
____ 25. Retirement of preferred stock.
____ 26. Loan to another firm.
____ 27. Sale of inventory to customers.
____ 28. Purchase of marketable securities (cash equivalents).

**P 21–2**
Statement of cash flows; direct method

● LO3 LO8

eXcel

The comparative balance sheets for 2006 and 2005 and the statement of income for 2006 are given below for Wright Company. Additional information from Wright's accounting records is provided also.

**WRIGHT COMPANY**
**Comparative Balance Sheets**
**December 31, 2006 and 2005**
($ in 000s)

| | **2006** | **2005** |
|---|---|---|
| **Assets** | | |
| Cash | $ 42 | $ 30 |
| Accounts receivable | 73 | 75 |
| Short-term investment | 40 | 15 |
| Inventory | 75 | 70 |
| Land | 50 | 60 |
| Buildings and equipment | 550 | 400 |
| Less: Accumulated depreciation | (115) | (75) |
| | $715 | $575 |

| | | |
|---|---|---|
| **Liabilities** | | |
| Accounts payable | $ 28 | $ 35 |
| Salaries payable | 2 | 5 |
| Interest payable | 5 | 3 |
| Income tax payable | 9 | 12 |
| Notes payable | 0 | 30 |
| Bonds payable | 160 | 100 |
| **Shareholders' Equity** | | |
| Common stock | 250 | 200 |
| Paid-in capital—excess of par | 126 | 100 |
| Retained earnings | 135 | 90 |
| | $715 | $575 |

**WRIGHT COMPANY**
**Income Statement**
**For Year Ended December 31, 2006**
($ in 000s)

| | | |
|---|---|---|
| **Revenues** | | |
| Sales revenue | | $380 |
| **Expenses** | | |
| Cost of goods sold | $130 | |
| Salaries expense | 45 | |
| Depreciation expense | 40 | |
| Interest expense | 12 | |
| Loss on sale of land | 3 | |
| Income tax expense | 70 | 300 |
| **Net income** | | $ 80 |

*Additional information from the accounting records:*

a. Land that originally cost $10,000 was sold for $7,000.
b. The common stock of Microsoft Corporation was purchased for $25,000 as a short-term investment not classified as a cash equivalent.
c. New equipment was purchased for $150,000 cash.
d. A $30,000 note was paid at maturity on January 1.
e. On January 1, 2006, $60,000 of bonds were sold at face value.
f. Common stock ($50,000 par) was sold for $76,000.
g. Net income was $80,000 and cash dividends of $35,000 were paid to shareholders.

**Required:**

Prepare the statement of cash flows of Wright Company for the year ended December 31, 2006. Present cash flows from operating activities by the direct method. (You may omit the schedule to reconcile net income with cash flows from operating activities.)

**P 21–3**
Statement of cash flows; direct method
● LO3 LO8

The comparative balance sheets for 2006 and 2005 and the statement of income for 2006 are given below for National Intercable Company. Additional information from NIC's accounting records is provided also.

**NATIONAL INTERCABLE COMPANY**
**Comparative Balance Sheets**
**December 31, 2006 and 2005**
($ in millions)

| | 2006 | 2005 |
|---|---|---|
| **Assets** | | |
| Cash | $ 72 | $ 55 |
| Accounts receivable | 181 | 170 |
| Less: Allowance for uncollectible accounts | (8) | (6) |
| Prepaid insurance | 7 | 12 |
| Inventory | 170 | 165 |
| Long-term investment | 66 | 90 |
| Land | 150 | 150 |
| Buildings and equipment | 290 | 270 |
| Less: Accumulated depreciation | (85) | (75) |
| Trademark | 24 | 25 |
| | $867 | $856 |

| | | |
|---|---|---|
| **Liabilities** | | |
| Accounts payable | $ 30 | $ 45 |
| Salaries payable | 3 | 8 |
| Deferred income tax liability | 18 | 15 |
| Lease liability | 80 | 0 |
| Bonds payable | 145 | 275 |
| Less: Discount on bonds | (22) | (25) |
| **Shareholders' Equity** | | |
| Common stock | 310 | 290 |
| Paid-in capital—excess of par | 95 | 85 |
| Preferred stock | 50 | 0 |
| Retained earnings | 158 | 163 |
| | $867 | $856 |

**NATIONAL INTERCABLE COMPANY**
**Income Statement**
**For Year Ended December 31, 2006**
($ in millions)

| | | |
|---|---|---|
| **Revenues** | | |
| Sales revenue | $320 | |
| Investment revenue | 15 | |
| Gain on sale of investments | 5 | $340 |
| **Expenses** | | |
| Cost of goods sold | 125 | |
| Salaries expense | 55 | |
| Depreciation expense | 25 | |
| Trademark amortization expense | 1 | |
| Bad debt expense | 7 | |
| Insurance expense | 13 | |
| Bond interest expense | 30 | (256) |
| Income before tax and extraordinary items | | 84 |
| Income tax expense | | (38) |
| Income before extraordinary items | | 46 |
| Extraordinary loss (tornado) | 42 | |
| Less: Tax savings | (21) | (21) |
| **Net income** | | $ 25 |

*Additional information from the accounting records:*

a. During 2006, $5 million of customer accounts were written off as uncollectible.
b. Investment revenue includes National Intercable Company's $6 million share of the net income of Central Fiber Optics Corporation, an equity method investee.
c. A long-term investment in bonds, originally purchased for $30 million, was sold for $35 million.
d. Pretax accounting income exceeded taxable income causing the deferred income tax liability to increase by $3 million.
e. A building that originally cost $60 million, and which was one-fourth depreciated, was destroyed by a tornado. Some undamaged parts were sold for $3 million.
f. A building was acquired by a seven-year capital lease; present value of lease payments, $80 million.
g. $130 million of bonds were retired at maturity.
h. $20 million par value of common stock was sold for $30 million, and $50 million of preferred stock was sold at par.
i. Shareholders were paid cash dividends of $30 million.

**Required:**

1. Prepare a spreadsheet for preparation of the statement of cash flows (direct method) of National Intercable Company for the year ended December 31, 2006.
2. Prepare the statement of cash flows. (A reconciliation schedule is not required.)

**P 21–4**
Statement of cash flows; direct method
● LO3 LO8
excel

The comparative balance sheets for 2006 and 2005 and the statement of income for 2006 are given below for Dux Company. Additional information from Dux's accounting records is provided also.

**DUX COMPANY**
**Comparative Balance Sheets**
**December 31, 2006 and 2005**
($ in 000s)

| | 2006 | 2005 |
|---|---|---|
| **Assets** | | |
| Cash | $ 33 | $ 20 |
| Accounts receivable | 48 | 50 |
| Less: Allowance for uncollectible accounts | (4) | (3) |
| Dividends receivable | 3 | 2 |
| Inventory | 55 | 50 |
| Long-term investment | 15 | 10 |
| Land | 70 | 40 |
| Buildings and equipment | 225 | 250 |
| Less: Accumulated depreciation | (25) | (50) |
| | $420 | $369 |
| **Liabilities** | | |
| Accounts payable | $ 13 | $ 20 |
| Salaries payable | 2 | 5 |
| Interest payable | 4 | 2 |
| Income tax payable | 7 | 8 |
| Notes payable | 30 | 0 |
| Bonds payable | 95 | 70 |
| Less: Discount on bonds | (2) | (3) |
| **Shareholders' Equity** | | |
| Common stock | 210 | 200 |
| Paid-in capital—excess of par | 24 | 20 |
| Retained earnings | 45 | 47 |
| Less: Treasury stock (at cost) | (8) | 0 |
| | $420 | $369 |

**DUX COMPANY**
**Income Statement**
**For the Year Ended December 31, 2006**
($ in 000s)

| | | |
|---|---|---|
| **Revenues** | | |
| Sales revenue | $200 | |
| Dividend revenue | 3 | $203 |
| **Expenses** | | |
| Cost of goods sold | 120 | |
| Salaries expense | 25 | |
| Depreciation expense | 5 | |
| Bad debt expense | 1 | |
| Interest expense | 8 | |
| Loss on sale of building | 3 | |
| Income tax expense | 16 | 178 |
| **Net income** | | $ 25 |

*Additional information from the accounting records:*

a. A building that originally cost $40,000, and which was three-fourths depreciated, was sold for $7,000.
b. The common stock of Byrd Corporation was purchased for $5,000 as a long-term investment.
c. Property was acquired by issuing a 13%, seven-year, $30,000 note payable to the seller.
d. New equipment was purchased for $15,000 cash.
e. On January 1, 2006, $25,000 of bonds were sold at face value.
f. On January 19, Dux issued a 5% stock dividend (1,000 shares). The market price of the $10 par value common stock was $14 per share at that time.
g. Cash dividends of $13,000 were paid to shareholders.
h. On November 12, 500 shares of common stock were repurchased as treasury stock at a cost of $8,000. Dux uses the cost method to account for treasury stock.

**Required:**

Prepare the statement of cash flows of Dux Company for the year ended December 31, 2006. Present cash flows from operating activities by the direct method. (You may omit the schedule to reconcile net income with cash flows from operating activities.)

**P 21–5**
Statement of cash flows; direct method

● LO3 LO8

eXcel

Comparative balance sheets for 2006 and 2005 and a statement of income for 2006 are given below for Metagrobolize Industries. Additional information from the accounting records of Metagrobolize also is provided.

**METAGROBOLIZE INDUSTRIES**
**Comparative Balance Sheets**
**December 31, 2006 and 2005**
($ in 000s)

| | 2006 | 2005 |
|---|---|---|
| **Assets** | | |
| Cash | $ 600 | $ 375 |
| Accounts receivable | 600 | 450 |
| Inventory | 900 | 525 |
| Land | 675 | 600 |
| Building | 900 | 900 |
| Less: Accumulated depreciation | (300) | (270) |
| Equipment | 2,850 | 2,250 |
| Less: Accumulated depreciation | (525) | (480) |
| Patent | 1,200 | 1,500 |
| | $6,900 | $5,850 |
| **Liabilities** | | |
| Accounts payable | $ 750 | $ 450 |
| Accrued expenses payable | 300 | 225 |
| Lease liability—land | 150 | 0 |
| **Shareholders' Equity** | | |
| Common stock | 3,150 | 3,000 |
| Paid-in capital—excess of par | 750 | 675 |
| Retained earnings | 1,800 | 1,500 |
| | $6,900 | $5,850 |

**METAGROBOLIZE INDUSTRIES**
**Income Statement**
**For the Year Ended December 31, 2006**
($ in 000s)

| | | |
|---|---|---|
| **Revenues** | | |
| Sales revenue | $2,645 | |
| Gain on sale of land | 90 | $2,735 |
| **Expenses** | | |
| Cost of goods sold | $ 600 | |
| Depreciation expense—building | 30 | |
| Depreciation expense—equipment | 315 | |
| Loss on sale of equipment | 15 | |
| Amortization of patent | 300 | |
| Operating expenses | 500 | 1,760 |
| **Net income** | | $ 975 |

*Additional information from the accounting records:*

a. During 2006, equipment with a cost of $300,000 (90% depreciated) was sold.
b. The statement of retained earnings reveals reductions of $225,000 and $450,000 for stock dividends and cash dividends, respectively.

**Required:**

Prepare the statement of cash flows of Metagrobolize for the year ended December 31, 2006. Present cash flows from operating activities by the direct method. (You may omit the schedule to reconcile net income with cash flows from operating activities.)

**P 21–6**
Cash flows from operating activities (direct method) derived from an income statement and cash flows from operating activities (indirect method)

● LO3 LO4

The income statement and a schedule reconciling cash flows from operating activities to net income are provided below ($ in millions) for Mike Roe Computers.

**MIKE ROE COMPUTERS**
**Income Statement**
**For the Year Ended December 31, 2006**

| | | |
|---|---|---|
| Sales | | $150 |
| Cost of goods sold | | (90) |
| Gross margin | | 60 |
| Salaries expense | $20 | |
| Insurance expense | 10 | |
| Depreciation expense | 5 | |
| Bad debt expense | 2 | |
| Interest expense | 6 | (43) |
| Gains and losses: | | |
| Gain on sale of equipment | | 12 |
| Loss on sale of land | | (3) |
| Income before tax | | 26 |
| Income tax expense | | (13) |
| **Net income** | | $ 13 |

**Reconciliation of Net Income**
**to Net Cash Flows**
**from Operating Activities**

| | |
|---|---|
| **Net income** | $13 |
| *Adjustments for noncash effects:* | |
| Decrease in accounts receivable | 3 |
| Gain on sale of equipment | (12) |
| Increase in inventory | (6) |
| Increase in accounts payable | 9 |
| Increase in salaries payable | 3 |
| Depreciation expense | 5 |
| Increase in allowance for uncoll. | 2 |
| Decrease in bond discount | 3 |
| Decrease in prepaid insurance | 2 |
| Loss on sale of land | 3 |
| Increase in income tax payable | 6 |
| **Net cash flows from operating activities** | $31 |

**Required:**

1. Calculate each of the following amounts for Mike Roe Computers:
   a. Cash received from customers during the reporting period.
   b. Cash paid to suppliers of goods during the reporting period.
   c. Cash paid to employees during the reporting period.
   d. Cash paid for interest during the reporting period.
   e. Cash paid for insurance during the reporting period.
   f. Cash paid for income taxes during the reporting period.
2. Prepare the cash flows from operating activities section of the statement of cash flows (direct method).

**P 21–7**
Cash flows from operating activities (direct method) derived from an income statement and cash flows from operating activities (indirect method)

● LO3 LO4

The income statement and a schedule reconciling cash flows from operating activities to net income are provided below for Macrosoft Corporation.

**MACROSOFT CORPORATION**
**Income Statement**
**For the Year Ended December 31, 2006**
($ in millions)

| | | |
|---|---|---|
| Sales | | $310 |
| Cost of goods sold | | (120) |
| Gross margin | | $190 |
| Salaries expense | $40 | |
| Insurance expense | 20 | |
| Depreciation expense | 10 | |
| Patent amortization expense | 4 | |
| Interest expense | 12 | (86) |
| Loss on sale of land | | (6) |
| Gain on sale of cash equivalents | | 2 |
| Income before taxes and extraordinary gain | | 100 |
| Income tax expense | | (50) |
| Income before extraordinary gain | | 50 |
| Extraordinary gain (sale of subsidiary) | 24 | |
| Less: Tax on gain | (12) | 12 |
| **Net income** | | $ 62 |

**Reconciliation of Net Income**
**to Net Cash Flows**
**from Operating Activities**

| | |
|---|---|
| **Net income** | $62 |
| Adjustments for noncash effects: | |
| Depreciation expense | 10 |
| Patent amortization expense | 4 |
| Loss on sale of land | 6 |
| Extraordinary gain (sale of subsidiary) | (24) |
| Decrease in accounts receivable | 6 |
| Increase in inventory | (12) |
| Increase in accounts payable | 18 |
| Decrease in bond discount | 1 |
| Increase in salaries payable | 6 |
| Decrease in prepaid insurance | 4 |
| Increase in income tax payable | 10 |
| **Net cash flows from operating activities** | $91 |

**Required:**

Prepare the cash flows from operating activities section of the statement of cash flows (direct method).

**P 21–8**
Cash flows from operating activities (direct method and indirect method)—deferred income tax liability and amortization of bond discount

● LO3 LO4

Portions of the financial statements for Parnell Company are provided below.

**PARNELL COMPANY**
**Income Statement**
**For the Year Ended December 31, 2006**
($ in 000s)

| | | |
|---|---|---|
| Sales | | $800 |
| Cost of goods sold | | (300) |
| Gross margin | | 500 |
| Salaries expense | $120 | |
| Insurance expense | 40 | |
| Depreciation expense | 123 | |
| Interest expense | 50 | (333) |
| Gains and losses: | | |
| Gain on sale of buildings | | 11 |
| Loss on sale of machinery | | (12) |
| Income before tax | | 166 |
| Income tax expense | | (78) |
| **Net income** | | $ 88 |

**PARNELL COMPANY**
**Selected Accounts from Comparative Balance Sheets**
**December 31, 2006 and 2005**
($ in 000s)

| | Year | | |
|---|---|---|---|
| | **2006** | **2005** | **Change** |
| Cash | $134 | $100 | $ 34 |
| Accounts receivable | 324 | 216 | 108 |
| Inventory | 321 | 425 | (104) |
| Prepaid insurance | 66 | 88 | (22) |
| Accounts payable | 210 | 117 | 93 |
| Salaries payable | 102 | 93 | 9 |
| Deferred income tax liability | 60 | 52 | 8 |
| Bond discount | 190 | 200 | (10) |

**Required:**

1. Prepare the cash flows from operating activities section of the statement of cash flows for Parnell Company using the direct method.
2. Prepare the cash flows from operating activities section of the statement of cash flows for Parnell Company using the indirect method.

**P 21–9**
Cash flows from operating activities (direct method and indirect method)—gain on sale of cash equivalents and extraordinary loss

● LO3 LO4

Portions of the financial statements for Hawkeye Company are provided below.

**HAWKEYE COMPANY**
**Income Statement**
**For the Year Ended December 31, 2006**

| | | |
|---|---|---|
| Sales | | $900 |
| Cost of goods sold | | (350) |
| Gross margin | | 550 |
| Salaries expense | $220 | |
| Depreciation expense | 190 | |
| Bad debt expense | 12 | |
| Interest expense | 40 | |
| Gain on sale of cash equivalents | (4) | (458) |
| Income before taxes and extraordinary loss | | 92 |
| Income tax expense | | (46) |
| Income before extraordinary loss | | 46 |
| Extraordinary loss (flood damage) | 12 | |
| Less: Tax savings | (6) | (6) |
| Net Income | | $ 40 |

**HAWKEYE COMPANY**
**Selected Accounts from Comparative Balance Sheets**
**December 31, 2006 and 2005**

| | Year 2006 | Year 2005 | Change |
|---|---|---|---|
| Cash | $212 | $200 | $12 |
| Accounts receivable | 418 | 432 | (14) |
| Allowance for uncollectibles | 23 | 11 | 12 |
| Inventory | 860 | 850 | 10 |
| Accounts payable | 210 | 234 | (24) |
| Salaries payable | 180 | 188 | (8) |
| Interest payable | 55 | 50 | 5 |
| Income taxes payable | 90 | 104 | (14) |

**Required:**

1. Prepare the cash flows from operating activities section of the statement of cash flows for Hawkeye Company using the direct method.
2. Prepare the cash flows from operating activities section of the statement of cash flows for Hawkeye Company using the indirect method.

**P 21–10**
Relationship between the income statement and cash flows from operating activities (direct method and indirect method)

● LO3 LO4

The following schedule relates the income statement with cash flows from operating activities, derived by both the direct and indirect methods, in the format illustrated by Graphic 21–10 in the chapter. Some elements necessary to complete the schedule are missing.

**Cash Flows from Operating Activities**

| Income Statement | | Indirect Method | | Direct Method | |
|---|---|---|---|---|---|
| | | **Net income** | $ ? | | |
| | | Adjustments: | | | |
| Sales | $300 | Decrease in accounts receivable | 6 | Cash received from customers | $ ? |
| Gain on sale of equipment | 24 | Gain on sale of equipment | (24) | (Not reported—no cash effect) | |
| | | Increase in inventory | (12) | | |
| Cost of goods sold | (?) | Increase in accounts payable | 18 | Cash paid to suppliers | (174) |
| Salaries expense | (39) | ? in salaries payable | 6 | Cash paid to employees | (33) |
| Depreciation expense | (9) | Depreciation expense | 9 | Cash paid for depreciation | ? |
| Bad debt expense | (3) | Bad debt expense | 3 | (Not reported—no cash effect) | |
| Interest expense | (?) | Decrease in bond discount | 3 | Cash paid for interest | (9) |
| Insurance expense | (21) | Decrease in prepaid insurance | 9 | Cash paid for insurance | (?) |
| Loss on sale of land | (6) | Loss on sale of land | 6 | (Not reported—no cash effect) | |
| Income tax expense | (27) | Increase in income tax payable | ? | Cash paid for income taxes | (21) |
| **Net Income** | $ ? | **Net cash flows from operating activities** | $57 | **Net cash flows from operating activities** | $57 |

**Required:**

Complete the schedule by determining each of the following missing elements:

1. Cash received from customers
2. Cost of goods sold
3. ? in salaries payable (Increase? or decrease?)
4. Cash paid for depreciation
5. Interest expense
6. Cash paid for insurance
7. Increase in income tax payable
8. Net income

**P 21–11**
Prepare a statement of cash flows; direct method

● LO3 LO8

The comparative balance sheets for 2006 and 2005 and the income statement for 2006 are given below for Arduous Company. Additional information from Arduous's accounting records is provided also.

**ARDUOUS COMPANY**
**Comparative Balance Sheets**
**December 31, 2006 and 2005**
($ in millions)

| | 2006 | 2005 |
|---|---|---|
| **Assets** | | |
| Cash | $ 116 | $ 81 |
| Accounts receivable | 200 | 202 |
| Less: Allowance for uncollectible accounts | (10) | (8) |
| Investment revenue receivable | 6 | 4 |
| Inventory | 205 | 200 |
| Prepaid insurance | 4 | 8 |
| Long-term investment | 156 | 125 |
| Land | 196 | 150 |
| Buildings and equipment | 412 | 400 |
| Less: Accumulated depreciation | (97) | (120) |
| Patent | 30 | 32 |
| | $1,218 | $1,074 |
| **Liabilities** | | |
| Accounts payable | $ 50 | $ 65 |
| Salaries payable | 6 | 11 |
| Bond interest payable | 8 | 4 |
| Income tax payable | 12 | 14 |
| Deferred income tax liability | 11 | 8 |
| Notes payable | 23 | 0 |
| Lease liability | 82 | 0 |
| Bonds payable | 215 | 275 |
| Less: Discount on bonds | (22) | (25) |
| **Shareholders' Equity** | | |
| Common stock | 430 | 410 |
| Paid-in capital—excess of par | 95 | 85 |
| Preferred stock | 75 | 0 |
| Retained earnings | 242 | 227 |
| Less: Treasury stock (at cost) | (9) | 0 |
| | $1,218 | $1,074 |

**ARDUOUS COMPANY**
**Income Statement**
**For Year Ended December 31, 2006**
($ in millions)

| | | | |
|---|---|---|---|
| **Revenues** | | | |
| Sales revenue | | $410 | |
| Investment revenue | | 11 | |
| Gain on sale of treasury bills | | 2 | $423 |
| **Expenses** | | | |
| Cost of goods sold | | 180 | |
| Salaries expense | | 65 | |
| Depreciation expense | | 12 | |
| Patent amortization expense | | 2 | |
| Bad debt expense | | 8 | |
| Insurance expense | | 7 | |
| Bond interest expense | | 28 | |
| Extraordinary loss (flood) | $18 | | |
| Less: Tax savings | (9) | 9 | |
| Income tax expense | | 45 | 356 |
| **Net income** | | | $ 67 |

*Additional information from the accounting records:*

a. During 2006, $6 million of customer accounts were written off as uncollectible.

b. Investment revenue includes Arduous Company's $6 million share of the net income of Demur Company, an equity method investee.

c. Treasury bills were sold during 2006 at a gain of $2 million. Arduous Company classifies its investments in Treasury bills as cash equivalents.

d. A machine originally costing $70 million that was one-half depreciated was rendered unusable by a rare flood. Most major components of the machine were unharmed and were sold for $17 million.
e. Temporary differences between pretax accounting income and taxable income caused the deferred income tax liability to increase by $3 million.
f. The preferred stock of Tory Corporation was purchased for $25 million as a long-term investment.
g. Land costing $46 million was acquired by issuing $23 million cash and a 15%, four-year, $23 million note payable to the seller.
h. A building was acquired by a 15-year capital lease; present value of lease payments, $82 million.
i. $60 million of bonds were retired at maturity.
j. In February, Arduous issued a 4% stock dividend (4 million shares). The market price of the $5 par value common stock was $7.50 per share at that time.
k. In April, 1 million shares of common stock were repurchased as treasury stock at a cost of $9 million. Arduous uses the cost method to account for treasury stock.

**Required:**

Prepare the statement of cash flows of Arduous Company for the year ended December 31, 2006. Present cash flows from operating activities by the direct method. (A reconciliation schedule is not required.)

**P 21–12**
Transactions affecting retained earnings

● LO5 LO6 LO8

Shown below in T-account format are the changes affecting the retained earnings of Brenner-Jude Corporation during 2006. At January 1, 2006, the corporation had outstanding 105 million common shares, $1 par per share.

**Retained Earnings** ($ in millions)

| | | | |
|---|---|---|---|
| | | 90 | Beginning balance |
| Retirement of 5 million common shares for $22 million | 2 | | |
| | | 88 | Net income for the year |
| Declaration and payment of a $.33 per share cash dividend | 33 | | |
| Declaration and distribution of a 4% stock dividend | 20 | | |
| | | 123 | Ending balance |

**Required:**

1. From the information provided by the account changes you should be able to re-create the transactions that affected Brenner-Jude's retained earnings during 2006. Reconstruct the journal entries which can be used as spreadsheet entries in the preparation of a statement of cash flows. Also indicate any investing and financing activities you identify from this analysis that should be reported on the statement of cash flows.
2. Prepare a statement of retained earnings for Brenner-Jude for the year ended 2006. (You may wish to compare your solution to this problem with the parallel situation described in Exercise 18–14.)

**P 21–13**
Various cash flows

● LO3 through LO8

Following are selected balance sheet accounts of Del Conte Corp. at December 31, 2006 and 2005, and the increases or decreases in each account from 2005 to 2006. Also presented is selected income statement information for the year ended December 31, 2006, and additional information.

| Selected Balance Sheet Accounts | 2006 | 2005 | Increase (Decrease) |
|---|---|---|---|
| **Assets** | | | |
| Accounts receivable | $ 34,000 | $ 24,000 | $10,000 |
| Property, plant, and equipment | 277,000 | 247,000 | 30,000 |
| Accumulated depreciation | (178,000) | (167,000) | (11,000) |
| **Liabilities and Stockholders' Equity** | | | |
| Bonds payable | 49,000 | 46,000 | 3,000 |
| Dividends payable | 8,000 | 5,000 | 3,000 |
| Common stock, $1 par | 22,000 | 19,000 | 3,000 |
| Additional paid-in capital | 9,000 | 3,000 | 6,000 |
| Retained earnings | 104,000 | 91,000 | 13,000 |
| **Selected Income Statement Information for the Year Ended December 31, 2006** | | | |
| Sales revenue | $155,000 | | |
| Depreciation | 33,000 | | |
| Gain on sale of equipment | 13,000 | | |
| Net income | 28,000 | | |

**Additional information:**

a. Accounts receivable relate to sales of merchandise.
b. During 2006, equipment costing $40,000 was sold for cash.
c. During 2006, $20,000 of bonds payable were issued in exchange for property, plant, and equipment. There was no amortization of bond discount or premium.

**Required:**

Items 1 through 5 represent activities that will be reported in Del Conte's statement of cash flows for the year ended December 31, 2006. The following two responses are required for each item:

- Determine the amount that should be reported in Del Conte's 2006 statement of cash flows.
- Using the list below, determine the category in which the amount should be reported in the statement of cash flows.
  O. Operating activity
  I. Investing activity
  F. Financing activity

| | Amount | Category |
|---|---|---|
| 1. Cash collections from customers (direct method). | ____ | ____ |
| 2. Payments for purchase of property, plant, and equipment. | ____ | ____ |
| 3. Proceeds from sale of equipment. | ____ | ____ |
| 4. Cash dividends paid. | ____ | ____ |
| 5. Redemption of bonds payable. | ____ | ____ |

*(AICPA adapted)*

**P 21–14**
Statement of cash flows; indirect method; limited information

● LO4 LO8

The comparative balance sheets for 2006 and 2005 are given below for Surmise Company. Net income for 2006 was $50 million.

**SURMISE COMPANY**
**Comparative Balance Sheets**
**December 31, 2006 and 2005**
($ in millions)

| | 2006 | 2005 |
|---|---|---|
| **Assets** | | |
| Cash | $ 45 | $ 40 |
| Accounts receivable | 92 | 96 |
| Less: Allowance for uncollectible accounts | (12) | (4) |
| Prepaid expenses | 8 | 5 |
| Inventory | 145 | 130 |
| Long-term investment | 80 | 40 |
| Land | 100 | 100 |
| Buildings and equipment | 411 | 300 |
| Less: Accumulated depreciation | (142) | (120) |
| Patent | 16 | 17 |
| | $743 | $604 |
| **Liabilities** | | |
| Accounts payable | $ 17 | $ 32 |
| Accrued liabilities | (2) | 10 |
| Notes payable | 35 | 0 |
| Lease liability | 111 | 0 |
| Bonds payable | 65 | 125 |
| **Shareholders' Equity** | | |
| Common stock | 60 | 50 |
| Paid-in capital—excess of par | 245 | 205 |
| Retained earnings | 212 | 182 |
| | $743 | $604 |

**Required:**

Prepare the statement of cash flows of Surmise Company for the year ended December 31, 2006. Use the indirect method to present cash flows from operating activities because you do not have sufficient information to use the direct method. You will need to make reasonable assumptions concerning the reasons for changes in some account balances. A spreadsheet or T-account analysis will be helpful.

**P 21–15**
Statement of cash flows; indirect method
● LO4 LO8

Refer to the data provided in the Problem 21–4 for Dux Company.

**Required:**
Prepare the statement of cash flows for Dux Company using the *indirect method.*

**P 21–16**
Statement of cash flows; indirect method
● LO4 LO8

Refer to the data provided in the Problem 21–5 for Metagrobolize Industries.

**Required:**
Prepare the statement of cash flows for Metagrobolize Industries using the *indirect method.*

**P 21–17**
Statement of cash flows; indirect method
● LO4 LO8
eXcel

Refer to the data provided in the Problem 21–11 for Arduous Company.

**Required:**
Prepare the statement of cash flows for Arduous Company using the *indirect method.*

(Note: The following problems use the technique learned in Appendix 21B.)

**P 21–18**
Statement of cash flows; T-account method
● LO3 LO8

Refer to the data provided in the Problem 21–4 for Dux Company.

**Required:**
Prepare the statement of cash flows for Dux Company. Use the T-account method to assist in your analysis.

**P 21–19**
Statement of cash flows; T-account method
● LO3 LO8

Refer to the data provided in the Problem 21–5 for Metagrobolize Industries.

**Required:**
Prepare the statement of cash flows for Metagrobolize Industries. Use the T-account method to assist in your analysis.

**P 21–20**
Statement of cash flows; T-account method
● LO3 LO8

Refer to the data provided in the Problem 21–11 for Arduous Company.

**Required:**
Prepare the statement of cash flows for Arduous Company. Use the T-account method to assist in your analysis.

## BROADEN YOUR PERSPECTIVE

**Apply your critical-thinking ability to the knowledge you've gained. These cases will provide you an opportunity to develop your research, analysis, judgment, and communication skills. You also will work with other students, integrate what you've learned, apply it in real world situations, and consider its global and ethical ramifications. This practice will broaden your knowledge and further develop your decision-making abilities.**

**Communication Case 21–1**
Distinguish income and cash flows
● LO1 LO3 LO4

"Why can't we pay our shareholders a dividend?" shouted your new boss. "This income statement you prepared for me says we earned $5 million in our first half-year!"

You were hired last month as the chief accountant for Enigma Corporation which was organized on July 1 of the year just ended. You recently prepared the financial statements below:

**ENIGMA CORPORATION**
**Income Statement**
**For the Six Months Ended December 31, 2006**
($ in millions)

| | |
|---|---|
| Sales revenue | $75 |
| Cost of goods sold | (30) |
| Depreciation expense | (5) |
| Remaining expenses | (35) |
| Net income | $ 5 |

**ENIGMA CORPORATION**
**Balance Sheet**
**December 31, 2006** ($ in millions)

| | |
|---|---|
| Cash | $ 1 |
| Accounts receivable (net) | 20 |
| Merchandise inventory | 15 |
| Machinery (net) | 44 |
| Total | $80 |
| Accounts payable | $ 2 |
| Accrued expenses payable | 7 |
| Notes payable | 36 |
| Common stock | 30 |
| Retained earnings | 5 |
| Total | $80 |

You have just explained to your boss, Robert James, that although net income was $5 million, operating activities produced a net decrease in cash. Unable to understand your verbal explanation, he has asked you to prepare a written report.

**Required:**

Prepare a report explaining the apparent discrepancy between Enigma's profitability and its cash flows. To increase the chances of your boss's understanding the situation, include in your report a determination of net cash flows from operating activities by both the direct and indirect methods. Your report should also include a narrative explanation of how it is possible for operating activities to simultaneously produce a positive net income and negative net cash flows.

**Judgment Case 21–2**
Distinguish income and cash flows

● LO3 LO8

You are a loan officer for First Benevolent Bank. You have an uneasy feeling as you examine a loan application from Daring Corporation. The application included the following financial statements.

**DARING CORPORATION**
**Income Statement**
**For the Year Ended December 31, 2006**

| | |
|---|---|
| Sales revenue | $100,000 |
| Cost of goods sold | (50,000) |
| Depreciation expense | (5,000) |
| Remaining expenses | (25,000) |
| Net income | $ 20,000 |

**DARING CORPORATION**
**Balance Sheet**
**December 31, 2006**

| | |
|---|---|
| Cash | $ 5,000 |
| Accounts receivable | 25,000 |
| Inventory | 20,000 |
| Operational assets | 55,000 |
| Accumulated depreciation | (5,000) |
| Total | $100,000 |
| Accounts payable | $ 10,000 |
| Interest payable | 5,000 |
| Note payable | 45,000 |
| Common stock | 20,000 |
| Retained earnings | 20,000 |
| Total | $100,000 |

It is not Daring's profitability that worries you. The income statement submitted with the application shows net income of $20,000 in Daring's first year of operations. By referring to the balance sheet, you see that this net income represents a 20% rate of return on assets of $100,000. Your concern stems from the recollection that the note payable reported on Daring's balance sheet is a two-year loan you approved earlier in the year.

You also recall another promising new company that, just last year, defaulted on another of your bank's loans when it failed due to its inability to generate sufficient cash flows to meet its obligations. Before requesting additional information from Daring, you decide to test your memory of the intermediate accounting class you took in night school by attempting to prepare a statement of cash flows from the information available in the loan application.

**Required:**

Prepare a statement of cash flows using the direct method. Are your concerns justified?

**Integrating Case 21–3**
Lease transaction; lessee and lessor; financial statement effects

● LO3 LO5 LO6

Advanced Equipment leased a protein analyzer to Richards Chemical, Inc. on September 30, 2006. Advanced purchased the machine from Makers, Inc. at a cost of $6 million. The five-year lease agreement calls for Richards to make quarterly lease payments of $391,548, payable each September 30, December 31, March 31, June 30, with the first payment at September 30, 2006. Advanced's implicit interest rate is 12%.

**Required:**

1. What pretax amounts related to the lease would *Richards* report in its statement of cash flows for the year ended December 31, 2006?
2. What pretax amounts related to the lease would *Advanced* report in its statement of cash flows for the year ended December 31, 2006?
3. Assume Makers manufactured the machine at a cost of $5 million and that Richards leased the machine directly from Makers. What pretax amounts related to the lease would *Makers* report in its statement of cash flows for the year ended December 31, 2006?

**Research Case 21–4**
Locate and extract relevant information for a financial reporting issue; integrative; Microsoft Corporation

● LO4

A meeting of your accounting department is scheduled for early tomorrow morning. One topic of discussion is certain to be the appropriate adjustments to net income in your company's statement of cash flows using the indirect method of reporting operating activities. Hallway discussions have suggested some degree of uncertainty, particularly regarding unearned revenues, which are substantial for the company. Because your firm went public only seven months ago, this reporting issue is a new one for you and most other members of the department. In preparation for the meeting, you sought out the financial statements of **Microsoft Corporation**, knowing that it too had substantial unearned revenues. The operating activities section of the comparative statements of cash flows for Microsoft is presented below.

**Cash Flows Statements** (in millions)

| Year Ended June 30 | 2002 | 2003 | 2004 |
|---|---|---|---|
| **Operations** | | | |
| Net income | $ 5,355 | $ 7,531 | $ 8,168 |
| Depreciation, amortization, and other noncash items | 938 | 1,393 | 1,186 |
| Stock-based compensation | 3,784 | 3,749 | 5,734 |
| Net recognized (gains)/losses on investments | 2,424 | 380 | (1,296) |
| Stock option income tax benefits | 1,596 | 1,365 | 1,100 |
| Deferred income taxes | (1,580) | (894) | (1,479) |
| Unearned revenue | 11,152 | 12,519 | 11,777 |
| Recognition of unearned revenue | (8,929) | (11,292) | (12,527) |
| Accounts receivable | (1,623) | 187 | (687) |
| Other current assets | (264) | 412 | 478 |
| Other long-term assets | (9) | (28) | 34 |
| Other current liabilities | 1,449 | 35 | 2,063 |
| Other long-term liabilities | 216 | 440 | 75 |
| Net cash from operations | 14,509 | 15,797 | 14,626 |

**Required:**

1. Use EdgarScan (**edgarscan.pwcglobal.com/**) or another method to locate the financial statements of Microsoft Corporation. Search the disclosure notes for information about how Microsoft accounts for its unearned revenues. What percentage of Microsoft's sales of Windows XP Professional does the company record as unearned revenue initially?
2. Why does the statement of cash flows include "unearned revenue" as an addition to net income in the operations section? Why is "recognition of unearned revenue" included as a deduction from net income? Why do you think Microsoft reported these two items separately rather than just adjusting net income for the change in the unearned revenue account balance?
3. Why is stock-based compensation added to net income?

**Analysis Case 21–5**
Smudged ink; find missing amounts

● LO3 LO4

"Be careful with that coffee!" Your roommate is staring in disbelief at the papers in front of her. "This was my contribution to our team project," she moaned. "When you spilled your coffee, it splashed on this page. Now I can't recognize some of these numbers, and Craig has my source documents."

Knowing how important this afternoon's presentation is to your roommate, you're eager to see what can be done. "Let me see that," you offer. "I think we can figure this out." The statement of cash flows and income statement are intact. The reconciliation schedule and the comparative balance sheets are coffee casualties.

**DISTINCTIVE INDUSTRIES**
**Statement of Cash Flows**
**For the Year Ended December 31, 2006**
($ in millions)

| | | |
|---|---|---|
| **Cash Flows from Operating Activities:** | | |
| Collections from customers | $213 | |
| Payment to suppliers | (90) | |
| Payment of general & administrative expenses | (54) | |
| Payment of income taxes | (27) | |
| Net cash flows from operating activities | | $42 |
| **Cash Flows from Investing Activities:** | | |
| Sale of equipment | | 120 |
| **Cash Flows from Financing Activities:** | | |
| Issuance of common stock | 30 | |
| Payment of dividends | (9) | |
| Net cash flows from financing activities | | 21 |
| *Net increase in cash* | | $183 |
| **Reconciliation of net income to cash flows from operating activities:** | | |
| Net income | $ 84 | |
| *Adjustments for noncash items:* | | |
| Depreciation expense | ☐ | |
| ☐ | ☐ | |
| ☐ | ☐ | |
| ☐ | ☐ | |
| ☐ | ☐ | |
| ☐ | ☐ | |
| Net cash flows from operating activities | | ☐ |

**DISTINCTIVE INDUSTRIES**
**Income Statement**
**For the Year Ended December 31, 2006**

| | | |
|---|---|---|
| Sales revenue | | $240 |
| Cost of goods sold | | 96 |
| Gross profit | | 144 |
| Operating expenses: | | |
| General and administrative | $54 | |
| Depreciation | 30 | |
| Tota operating expenses | | 84 |
| Operating income | | 60 |
| Other income: | | |
| Gain on sale of equipment | | 45 |
| Income before income taxes | | 105 |
| Income tax expense | | 21 |
| Net income | | $ 84 |

**DISTINCTIVE INDUSTRIES**
**Comparative Balance Sheets**
**At December 31**

| | 2006 | 2005 |
|---|---|---|
| **Assets:** | | |
| Cash | $360 | ☐ |
| Accounts receivable (net) | ☐ | 252 |
| Inventory | 180 | ☐ |
| Property, plant, & equipment | 450 | 600 |
| Less: Accumulated depreciation | (120) | ☐ |
| Total assets | ☐ | ☐ |
| **Liabilities and shareholders' equity:** | | |
| Accounts payable | $120 | $ 90 |
| General and administrative expenses payable | 27 | 27 |
| Income taxes payable | 66 | ☐ |
| Common stock | 720 | 690 |
| Retained earnings | ☐ | 141 |
| Total liabilities and shareholders' equity | ☐ | ☐ |

**Required:**

1. Determine the missing amounts.
2. Reconstruct the reconciliation of net income to cash flows from operating activities (operating cash flows using the indirect method).

**Real World Case 21–6**
Analyze cash flow activities; Cingular Wireless

● LO1 through LO8

**Cingular Wireless** is the largest wireless company in the United States, with more than 50 million subscribers who use the nation's largest digital voice and data network.

| ($ in millions) | 2002 | 2003 | 2004 |
|---|---|---|---|
| **Operating Activities** | | | |
| Net income | $1,173 | $ 977 | $ 201 |
| Adjustments to reconcile net income to net cash provided by operating activities: | | | |
| Depreciation and amortization | 1,849 | 2,089 | 3,077 |
| Provision for doubtful accounts | 404 | 259 | 423 |
| Asset impairments | 151 | — | 4 |
| Minority interest in earnings of consolidated entities | 123 | 101 | 86 |
| Equity in net loss of affiliates | 274 | 333 | 415 |
| Cumulative effect of accounting change, net of tax | 32 | — | — |
| Amortization of debt discount (premium), net | 1 | 1 | (43) |
| Deferred income taxes | (3) | (1) | (74) |
| *Changes in operating assets and liabilities* | | | |
| Accounts receivable | (280) | (331) | (336) |
| Inventories | 63 | (147) | (189) |
| Other current assets | (42) | (83) | (18) |
| Accounts payable and other current liabilities | (411) | 278 | (512) |
| Pensions and post-employment benefits | 91 | 55 | 88 |
| Other, net | 167 | 155 | 198 |
| *Net cash provided by operating activities* | 3,592 | 3,686 | 3,320 |
| **Investing Activities** | | | |
| Construction and capital expenditures | (3,085) | (2,734) | (3,449) |
| Investments in and advances to equity affiliates, net | (450) | (616) | (422) |
| Dispositions of assets | 6 | 7 | 188 |
| Acquisition of AT&T Wireless, net of cash received | — | — | (35,543) |
| Acquisitions of other businesses and licenses, net | (6) | (25) | (1,632) |
| Contractor engineering deposit | (50) | — | — |
| Purchases of held-to-maturity investments | — | — | (219) |
| *Net cash used in investing activities* | (3,585) | (3,368) | (41,077) |
| **Financing Activities** | | | |
| Net borrowings under revolving credit agreement | — | — | 1,667 |
| Net repayment of commercial paper | (27) | — | — |
| Net repayment of long-term debt | (59) | (64) | (530) |
| Repayment of long-term debt due to members | — | — | (50) |
| Net distributions to minority interests | (79) | (33) | (141) |
| Contributions from members | 499 | 10 | 36,024 |
| *Net cash provided by (used in) financing activities* | 334 | (87) | 36,970 |
| Net increase (decrease) in cash and cash equivalents | 341 | 231 | (787) |
| Cash and cash equivalents at beginning of period | 567 | 908 | 1,139 |
| Cash and cash equivalents at end of period | $ 908 | $1,139 | $ 352 |

**Required:**

1. In the three years reported, what were Cingular's primary investing activities? How were these activities financed? Be specific.
2. During the most recent fiscal year, Cingular purchased certificates of deposit. How were these purchases reported in the statement of cash flows? (Note: This is not an investing activity.)
3. How are issuances of debt securities and issuances of equity securities classified in a statement of cash flows?
4. How are payments to investors in debt securities (interest) and payments to investors in equity securities (dividends) classified in a statement of cash flows? Is this a conceptual inconsistency? Explain.
5. Cingular's statement of cash flows reports expenditures for acquisition of businesses. It also reports the issuance of debt securities. Suppose the businesses had been acquired, not with cash, but by exchange for debt securities. Would such a transaction be reported? Explain.

**Ethics Case 21–7**
Where's the cash?

● LO1 LO3

After graduating near the top of his class, Ben Naegle was hired by the local office of a Big 4 CPA firm in his hometown. Two years later, impressed with his technical skills and experience, Park Electronics, a large regional consumer electronics chain, hired Ben as assistant controller. This was last week. Now Ben's initial excitement has turned to distress.

The cause of Ben's distress is the set of financial statements he's stared at for the last four hours. For some time prior to his recruitment, he had been aware of the long trend of moderate profitability of his new employer. The reports on his desk confirm the slight, but steady, improvements in net income in recent years. The trend he was just now becoming aware of, though, was the decline in cash flows from operations.

Ben had sketched out the following comparison ($ in millions):

| | 2006 | 2005 | 2004 | 2003 |
|---|---|---|---|---|
| Income from operations | $140.0 | $132.0 | $127.5 | $127.0 |
| Net income | 38.5 | 35.0 | 34.5 | 29.5 |
| Cash flow from operations | 1.6 | 17.0 | 12.0 | 15.5 |

Profits? Yes. Increasing profits? Yes. The cause of his distress? The ominous trend in cash flow which is consistently lower than net income.

Upon closer review, Ben noticed three events in the last two years that, unfortunately, seemed related:

a. Park's credit policy had been loosened; credit terms were relaxed and payment periods were lengthened.
b. Accounts receivable balances had increased dramatically.
c. Several of the company's compensation arrangements, including that of the controller and the company president, were based on reported net income.

**Required:**

1. What is so ominous about the combination of events Ben sees?
2. What course of action, if any, should Ben take?

**Real World Case 21–8**
Cash flow despite losses; Northwest Airlines

● LO3 LO4

"I've been reading that the airline industry is having money problems—big losses and budget cuts," said Bee Del Conte as you walked with her to the library. "How is it, then, that I hear on the radio this morning that **Northwest Airlines** had $270 million cash flow from its operations last year?" Curious, the two of you stop by a computer terminal on the way to the reference section and do a quick search. A few clicks later you're looking at the operating activities section of Northwest's 2004 cash flow statement:

| | Year Ended December 31 | | |
|---|---|---|---|
| ($ in millions) | 2004 | 2003 | 2002 |
| Cash Flows from Operating Activities | | | |
| Net income (loss) | $(862) | $248 | $(798) |
| Adjustments to reconcile net income (loss) to net cash provided by operating activities: | | | |
| Depreciation and amortization | 731 | 586 | 903 |
| Income tax expense (benefit) | 1 | (30) | (422) |
| Net receipts (payments) of income taxes | (3) | 215 | 122 |
| Pension and other postretirement benefit contributions less than expense | 190 | 90 | 139 |
| Net loss (earnings) of affiliates | (8) | (18) | (37) |
| Net loss (gain) on disposition of property, equipment, and other | (95) | (708) | 41 |
| Other, net | 77 | 20 | 83 |
| *Changes in certain assets and liabilities:* | | | |
| Decrease (increase) in accounts receivable | 46 | (20) | (38) |
| Decrease (increase) in flight equipment spare parts | 7 | 31 | (14) |
| Decrease (increase) in supplies, prepaid expenses and other | (60) | 25 | (68) |
| Increase (decrease) in air traffic liability | 191 | 50 | (54) |
| Increase (decrease) in accounts payable | 27 | (103) | (17) |
| Increase (decrease) in other liabilities | 19 | (1) | (164) |
| Increase (decrease) in accrued liabilities | 10 | (10) | 40 |
| *Net cash provided by (used in) operating activities* | 271 | 375 | (284) |

**Required:**

1. Without regard to Northwest specifically, explain to Bee the difference between net income or net loss and cash flows from operating activities.
2. What is the major contributor to Northwest having positive cash flows from operating activities despite a net loss in 2004?
3. Why did Northwest subtract $95 million in the determination of cash flows from operating activities for the gain on disposition of assets?

**Research Case 21–9**
Researching the way cash flows are reported; retrieving information from the Internet

- LO3 through LO8

EDGAR, the Electronic Data Gathering, Analysis, and Retrieval system, performs automated collection, validation, indexing, acceptance, and forwarding of submissions by companies and others who are required by law to file forms with the U.S. Securities and Exchange Commission (SEC). All publicly traded domestic companies use EDGAR to make the majority of their filings. (Filings by foreign companies are not required to be filed on EDGAR, but some of these companies do so voluntarily.) Form 10-K, which includes the annual report, is required to be filed on EDGAR. The SEC makes this information available on the Internet.

**Required:**

1. Access EDGAR on the Internet. The web address is **www.sec.gov** or use **edgarscan.pwcglobal.com**.
2. Search for a public company with which you are familiar. Access its most recent 10-K filing. Search or scroll to find the statement of cash flows and related note(s).
3. Is the direct or indirect method used to report operating activities? What is the largest adjustment to net income in reconciling net income and cash flows from operations in the most recent year?
4. What are the cash payments for interest and for taxes?
5. What has been the most significant investing activity for the company in the most recent three years?
6. What has been the most significant financing activity for the company in the most recent three years?
7. Repeat requirements 2–6 for another company.

**Analysis Case 21–10**
Information from cash flow activities

- LO3 through LO8

**FedEx Corporation**

Refer to the financial statements and related disclosure notes of **FedEx Corporation** in Appendix B at the end of the book. Notice that financing activities created a sizable net reduction in cash in each of the three years reported. Investing activities have required large and increasing amounts of cash over the same period.

**Required:**

1. From the information provided on the statement of cash flows, explain what allows FedEx Corporation to expand its business as evidenced by the investing activities, while at the same time not raising (in fact, decreasing) cash through financing activities for two of the three years shown.
2. Describe the six activities listed under financing activities for the 2004 fiscal year. [*Hint:* FedEx's Statement of Changes in Common Stockholders' Investment (statement of shareholders' equity) will help you determine the nature of the stock activity.] What is the most notable financing activity reported?
3. What are the cash payments FedEx made for interest and for income taxes in two of the three years reported? (*Hint:* See the disclosure notes.)

# CPA SIMULATION 21–1

**Ark Company**
Statement of Cash Flows

KAPLAN
CPA Review

Test your knowledge of the concepts discussed in this chapter, practice critical professional skills necessary for career success, and prepare for the computer-based CPA exam by accessing our CPA simulations at the text website: **www.mhhe.com/spiceland4e**.

The Ark Company simulation tests your knowledge of a variety of statement of cash flows reporting issues.

As on the CPA exam itself, you will be asked to use tools including a spreadsheet, a calculator, and professional accounting standards, to conduct research, derive solutions, and communicate conclusions related to these issues in a simulated environment headed by the following interactive tabs:

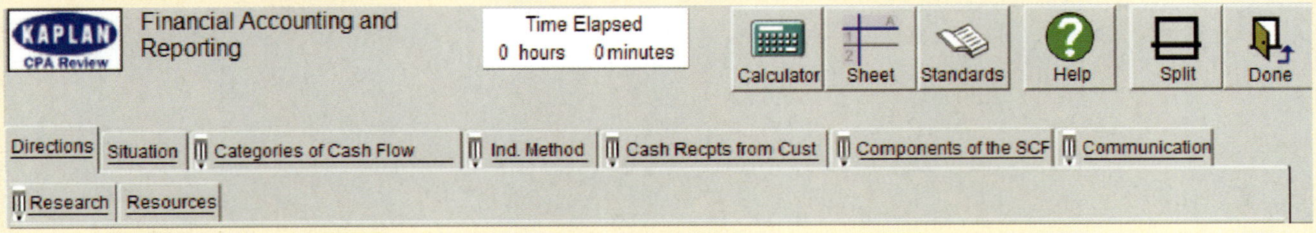


Specific tasks in the simulation include:

- Analyzing accrual transactions to determine their related cash flows.
- Applying judgment in deciding the appropriate financial statement classification of various cash flows.
- Calculating cash flows from operations.
- Determining cash flows from a trial balance.
- Communicating the definition and role of cash equivalents.
- Researching the disclosure requirements for the direct and indirect method of reporting operating activities.

# APPENDIX A Derivatives

In today's global economy and evolving financial markets, businesses are increasingly exposed to a variety of risks, which, unmanaged, can have major impacts on earnings or even threaten a company's very existence. Risk management, then, has become critical. Derivative financial instruments have become the key tools of risk management.[1]

**Derivatives** are financial instruments that "derive" their values or contractually required cash flows from some other security or index. For instance, a contract allowing a company to buy a particular asset (say steel, gold, or flour) at a designated future date, at a predetermined price is a financial instrument that derives its value from expected and actual changes in the price of the underlying asset. Financial futures, forward contracts, options, and interest rate swaps are the most frequently used derivatives. Derivatives are valued as tools to manage or hedge companies' increasing exposures to risk, including interest rate risk, price risk, and foreign exchange risk. The variety, complexity, and magnitude of derivatives have grown rapidly in recent years. Tens of trillions of dollars in derivative contracts are used every year. Accounting standard-setters have scrambled to keep pace.

*Derivatives* are financial instruments that "derive" their values from some other security or *index.*

A persistent stream of headline stories has alerted us to multimillion-dollar losses by **Dell Computer**, **Procter & Gamble**, **Gibson Greetings**, and **Orange County** (California), to name a few. Focusing on these headlines, it would be tempting to conclude that derivatives are risky business indeed. Certainly they can be quite risky, if misused, but the fact is, these financial instruments exist to lessen, not increase, risk. Properly used, they serve as a form of "insurance" against risk. In fact, if a company is exposed to a substantial risk and does not hedge that risk, it is taking a gamble. On the other hand, if a derivative is used improperly, it can be a huge gamble itself.

Derivatives serve as a form of "insurance" against risk.

## Derivatives Used to Hedge Risk

**Hedging** means taking an action that is expected to produce exposure to a particular type of risk that is precisely the *opposite* of an actual risk to which the company already is exposed. For instance, the volatility of interest rates creates exposure to interest-rate risk for companies that issue debt—which, of course, includes most companies. So, a company that frequently arranges short-term loans from its bank under a floating (variable) interest rate agreement is exposed to the risk that interest rates might increase and adversely affect borrowing costs. Similarly, a company that regularly reissues commercial paper as it matures faces the possibility that new rates will be higher and cut into forecasted income. When borrowings are large, the potential cost can be substantial. So, the firm might choose to hedge its position by entering into a transaction that would produce a *gain* of roughly the same amount as the potential loss if interest rates do, in fact, increase.

*Hedging* means taking a risk position that is opposite to an actual position that is exposed to risk.

Hedging is used to deal with three areas of risk exposure: fair value risk, cash flow risk, and foreign currency risk. Let's look at some of the more common derivatives.

### FINANCIAL FUTURES

A futures contract is an agreement between a seller and a buyer that requires the seller to deliver a particular commodity (say corn, gold, or pork bellies) at a designated future date, at a *predetermined* price. These contracts are actively traded on regulated futures exchanges. When the "commodity" is a *financial instrument,* such as a Treasury bond, Treasury bill, commercial paper, or a certificate of deposit, the agreement is referred to as a *financial futures contract*.[2]

A *futures contract* allows a firm to sell (or buy) a financial instrument at a designated future date, at today's price.

[1]Almost all financial institutions and over half of all nonfinancial companies use derivatives.

[2]Note that a financial futures contract meets the definition of a financial instrument because it entails the exchange of financial instruments (cash for Treasury bonds, for instance). But, a futures contract for the sale or purchase of a nonfinancial commodity like corn or gold does not meet the definition because one of the items to be exchanged is not a financial instrument.

To appreciate the way these hedges work, you need to remember that when interest rates rise, the market price of interest-bearing securities goes down. For instance, if you have an investment in a 10% bond and market interest rates go up to, say, 12%, your 10% bond is less valuable relative to other bonds paying the higher rate. Conversely, when interest rates decline, the market price of interest-bearing securities goes up. This risk that the investment's value might change is referred to as *fair value risk*. The company that issued the securities is faced with fair value risk also. If interest rates decline, the fair value of that company's debt would rise, a risk the borrower may want to hedge against. Later in this section, we'll look at an illustration of how the borrower would account for and report such a hedge.

**The seller in a financial futures contract realizes a gain (loss) when interest rates rise (decline).**

Now let's look at the effect on a contract to sell or buy securities (or any asset for that matter) at preset prices. One who is contracted to *sell* securities at a *preset* price after their market price has fallen, benefits from the rise in interest rates. Consequently, the value of the *contract* that gives one the right to sell securities at a preset price goes up as the market price declines. The seller in a futures contract derives a gain (loss) when interest rates rise (decline).[3] Conversely, the one obligated to *buy* securities at a preset price experiences a loss. This risk of having to pay more cash or receive less cash is referred to as *cash flow risk*.

Another example of cash flow risk would be borrowing money by issuing a variable (floating) rate note. If market interest rates rise, the borrower would have to pay more interest. Similarly, the lender (investor) in the variable (floating) rate note transaction would face cash flow risk that interest rates would decline, resulting in lower cash interest receipts.

Let's look closer at how a futures contract can mitigate cash flow risk. Consider a company in April that will replace its $10 million of 8.5% bank notes when they mature in June. The company is exposed to the risk that interest rates in June will have risen, increasing borrowing costs. To counteract that possibility, the firm might enter a contract in April to deliver (sell) bonds in June at their *current* price. Since there are no corporate bond futures contracts, the company buys Treasury bond futures, which will accomplish essentially the same purpose. In essence, the firm agrees to sell Treasury bonds in June at a price established now (April). Let's say it's April 6 and the price of Treasury bond futures on the International Monetary Market of the Chicago Mercantile Exchange is quoted as 95.24.[4] Since the trading unit of Treasury bond futures is a 15-year, $100,000, 8% Treasury bond, the company might sell 105 Treasury bond futures to hedge the June issuance of debt. This would effectively provide a hedge of 105 × $100,000 × 95.24% = $10,000,200.[5]

Here's what happens then. If interest rates rise, borrowing costs will go up for our example company because it will have to sell debt securities at a higher interest cost (or lower price). But that loss will be offset (approximately) by the gain produced by being in the opposite position on Treasury bond futures. Take note, though, this works both ways. If interest rates go down causing debt security prices to rise, the potential benefit of being able to issue debt at that lower interest rate (higher price) will be offset by a loss on the futures position.

A very important point about futures contracts is that the seller does not need to have actual possession of the commodity (the Treasury bonds, in this case), nor is the purchaser of the contract required to take possession of the commodity. In fact, virtually all financial futures contracts are "netted out" before the actual transaction is to take place. This is simply a matter of reversing the original position. A seller closes out his transaction with a purchase. Likewise, a purchaser would close out her transaction with a sale. After all, the objective is not to actually buy or sell Treasury bonds (or whatever the commodity might be), but to incur the financial impact of movements in interest rates as reflected in changes in Treasury bond prices. Specifically, it will buy at the lower price (to reverse the original seller position) at the same time it's selling its new bond issue at that same lower price. The financial futures market is an "artificial" exchange in that its reason for existing is to provide a mechanism to transfer risk from those exposed to it to those willing to accept the risk, not to actually buy and sell the underlying financial instruments.

---

[3]The seller of a futures contract is obligated to sell the bonds at a future date. The buyer of a futures contract is obligated to buy the bonds at a future date. The company in our example, then, is the seller of the futures contract.

[4]Price quotes are expressed as a percentage of par.

[5]This is a simplification of the more sophisticated way financial managers determine the optimal number of futures.

If the impending debt issue being hedged is a short-term issue, the company may attain a more effective hedge by selling Treasury *bill* futures since Treasury bills are 90-day securities, or maybe certificate of deposit (CD) futures that also are traded in futures markets. The object is to get the closest association between the financial effects of interest rate movements on the actual transaction and the effects on the financial instrument used as a hedge.

**The effectiveness of a hedge is influenced by the closeness of the match between the item being hedged and the financial instrument chosen as a hedge.**

## FINANCIAL FORWARD CONTRACTS

A **forward contract** is similar to a futures contract but differs in three ways:

1. A forward contract calls for delivery on a specific date, whereas a futures contract permits the seller to decide later which specific day within the specified month will be the delivery date (if it gets as far as actual delivery before it is closed out).
2. Unlike a futures contract, a forward contract usually is not traded on a market exchange.
3. Unlike a futures contract, a forward contract does not call for a daily cash settlement for price changes in the underlying contract. Gains and losses on forward contracts are paid only when they are closed out.

## OPTIONS

**Options** frequently are purchased to hedge exposure to the effects of changing interest rates. Options serve the same purpose as futures in that respect but are fundamentally different. An option on a financial instrument—say a Treasury bill—gives its holder the right either to buy or to sell the Treasury bill at a specified price and within a given time period. Importantly, though, the option holder has no obligation to exercise the option. On the other hand, the holder of a futures contract must buy or sell within a specified period unless the contract is closed out before delivery comes due.

## FOREIGN CURRENCY FUTURES

Foreign loans frequently are denominated in the currency of the lender (Japanese yen, Swiss franc, Euro, and so on). When loans must be repaid in foreign currencies, a new element of risk is introduced. This is because if exchange rates change, the dollar equivalent of the foreign currency that must be repaid differs from the dollar equivalent of the foreign currency borrowed.

To hedge against "foreign exchange risk" exposure, some firms buy or sell **foreign currency futures** contracts. These are similar to financial futures except specific foreign currencies are specified in the futures contracts rather than specific debt instruments. They work the same way to protect against foreign exchange risk as financial futures protect against fair value or cash flow risk.

**Foreign exchange risk often is hedged in the same manner as interest rate risk.**

## INTEREST RATE SWAPS

Over 70% of derivatives are **interest rate swaps.** These contracts exchange fixed interest payments for floating rate payments, or vice versa, without exchanging the underlying principal amounts. For example, suppose you owe $100,000 on a 10% fixed rate home loan. You envy your neighbor who also is paying 10% on her $100,000 mortgage, but hers is a floating rate loan, so if market rates fall, so will her loan rate. To the contrary, she is envious of your fixed rate, fearful that rates will rise, increasing her payments. A solution would be for the two of you to effectively swap interest payments using an interest rate swap agreement. The way a swap works, you both would continue to actually make your own interest payments, but would exchange the net cash difference between payments at specified intervals. So, in this case, if market rates (and thus floating payments) increase, you would pay your neighbor; if rates fall, she pays you. The net effect is to exchange the consequences of rate changes. In other words, you have effectively converted your fixed-rate debt to floating-rate debt; your neighbor has done the opposite.

**_Interest rate swaps_ exchange fixed interest payments for floating rate payments, or vice versa, without exchanging the underlying notional amounts.**

Of course, this technique is not dependent on happening into such a fortuitous pairing of two borrowers with opposite philosophies on interest rate risk. Instead, banks or other intermediaries offer, for a fee, one-sided swap agreements to companies desiring to be either fixed-rate payers or variable-rate payers. Intermediaries usually strive to maintain a balanced portfolio of matched, offsetting swap agreements.

Theoretically, the two parties to such a transaction exchange principal amounts, say the \$100,000 amount above, in addition to the interest on those amounts. It makes no practical sense, though, for the companies to send each other \$100,000. So, instead, the principal amount is not actually exchanged, but serves merely as the computational base for interest calculations and is called the *notional amount*. Similarly, the fixed-rate payer doesn't usually send the entire fixed interest amount (say 10% × \$100,000 = \$10,000) and receive the entire variable interest amount (say 9% × \$100,000 = \$9,000). Generally, only the net amount (\$1,000 in this case) is exchanged. This is illustrated in Graphic A–1.

**GRAPHIC A–1**
Interest Rate Swap

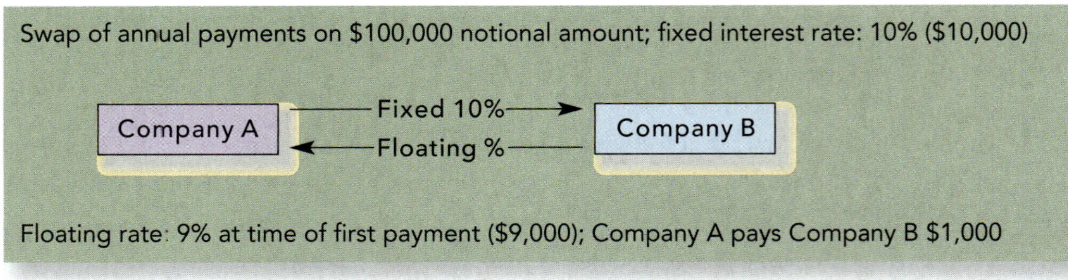


From an accounting standpoint, the central issue is not the operational differences among various hedge instruments, but their similarities in functioning as hedges against risk.

## Accounting for Derivatives

A key to accounting for derivatives is knowing the purpose for which a company holds them and whether the company is effective in serving that purpose. Derivatives, for instance, may be held for risk management (hedging activities). The desired effect, and often the real effect, is a reduction in risk. On the other hand, derivatives sometimes are held for speculative position taking, hoping for large profits. The effect of this activity usually is to increase risk. Perhaps more important, derivatives acquired as hedges and intended to reduce risk may, in fact, unintentionally increase risk instead.

**Derivatives not serving as hedges are extremely speculative due to the high leverage inherent in such investments.**

It's important to understand that, serving as investments rather than as hedges, derivatives are extremely speculative. This is due to the high leverage inherent in derivatives. Here's why. The investment outlay usually is negligible, but, the potential gain or loss on the investment usually is quite high. A small change in interest rates or another underlying event can trigger a large change in the fair value of the derivative. Because the initial investment was minimal, the change in value relative to the investment itself represents a huge percentage gain or loss. Accounting for derivatives is designed to treat differently (a) derivatives designated as hedges and those not designated as hedges as well as (b) the effective portion and the ineffective portion of gains and losses from intended hedges.

**All derivatives are reported on the balance sheet at fair value.**

The basic approach to accounting for derivatives is fairly straightforward, although implementation can be quite cumbersome. All derivatives, no exceptions, are carried on the balance sheet as either assets or liabilities at fair (or market) value.[6] The reasoning is that (a) derivatives create either rights or obligations that meet the definition of assets or liabilities, and (b) fair value is the most meaningful measurement.

Accounting for the gain or loss on a derivative depends on how it is used. Specifically, if the derivative is not designated as a hedging instrument, or doesn't qualify as one, any gain or loss from fair value changes is recognized immediately in earnings. On the other hand, if a derivative is used to hedge against exposure to risk, any gain or loss from fair value changes is either (a) recognized immediately in earnings along with an offsetting loss or gain on the item being hedged or (b) deferred in comprehensive income until it can be recognized in earnings at the same time as earnings are affected by a hedged transaction. Which way

[6]"Accounting for Derivative Instruments and Hedging Activities," *Statement of Financial Accounting Standards No. 133* (Norwalk, Conn.: FASB, 1998).

depends on whether the derivative is designated as a (a) fair value hedge, (b) cash flow hedge, or (c) foreign currency hedge. Let's look now at each of the three hedge designations.

## FAIR VALUE HEDGES

A company can be adversely affected when a change in either prices or interest rates causes a change in the fair value of one of its assets, its liabilities, or a commitment to buy or sell assets or liabilities. If a derivative is used to hedge against the exposure to changes in the fair value of an asset or liability or a firm commitment, it can be designated as a **fair value hedge.** In that case, when the derivative is adjusted to reflect changes in fair value, the other side of the entry recognizes a gain or loss to be included *currently* in earnings. At the same time, though, the loss or gain from changes in the fair value (due to the risk being hedged)[7] of the item being hedged also is included currently in earnings. This means that, to the extent the hedge is effective in serving its purpose, the gain or loss on the derivative will be offset by the loss or gain on the item being hedged. In fact, this is precisely the concept behind the procedure.

**A gain or loss from a *fair value hedge* is recognized immediately in earnings along with the loss or gain from the item being hedged.**

The reasoning is that as interest rates or other underlying events change, a hedge instrument will produce a gain approximately equal to a loss on the item being hedged (or vice versa). These income effects are interrelated and offsetting, so it would be improper to report the income effects in different periods. More critically, the intent and effect of having the hedge instrument is to *lessen* risk. And yet, recognizing gains in one period and counterbalancing losses in another period would tend to cause fluctuations in income that convey an *increase* in risk. However, to the extent that a hedge is ineffective and produces gains or losses different from the losses or gains being hedged, the ineffective portion is recognized in earnings immediately.

**The income effects of the hedge instrument and the income effects of the item being hedged should affect earnings at the same time.**

Some of the more common fair value hedges use:

- An interest rate swap to synthetically convert fixed-rate debt (for which interest rate changes could change the fair value of the debt) into floating-rate debt.
- A futures contract to hedge changes in the fair value (due to price changes) of aluminum, sugar, or some other type of inventory.
- A futures contract to hedge the fair value (due to price changes) of a firm commitment to sell natural gas or some other asset.

## ILLUSTRATION

Because interest rate swaps comprise over 70% of derivatives in use, we will use swaps to illustrate accounting for derivatives. Let's look at the example in Illustration A–1 on the next page.

When the floating rate declined from 10% to 9%, the fair values of both the derivative (swap) and the note increased. This created an offsetting gain on the derivative and holding loss on the note. Both are recognized in earnings at the same time (at June 30, 2006).

| | | |
|---|---|---|
| **January 1, 2006** | | |
| Cash | 1,000,000 | |
| Notes payable | | 1,000,000 |
| *To record the issuance of the note.* | | |
| **June 30, 2006** | | |
| Interest expense (10% × ½ × $1 million) | 50,000 | |
| Cash | | 50,000 |
| *To record interest.* | | |
| Cash ($50,000 − [9% × ½ × $1 million]) | 5,000 | |
| Interest expense | | 5,000 |
| *To record the net cash settlement.* | | |

**The interest rate swap is designated as a fair value hedge on this note at issuance.**

**The swap settlement is the difference between the fixed interest (5%) and variable interest (4.5%).**

[7]The fair value of a hedged item might also change for reasons other than from effects of the risk being hedged. For instance, the hedged risk may be that a change in interest rates will cause the fair value of a bond to change. The bond price might also change, though, if the market perceives that the bond's default risk has changed.

**ILLUSTRATION A–1**
Interest Rate Swap

Wintel Semiconductors issued $1 million of 18-month, 10% bank notes on January 1, 2006. Wintel is exposed to the risk that general interest rates will decline, causing the fair value of its debt to rise. (If the fair value of Wintel's debt increases, its effective borrowing cost is higher relative to the market.) To hedge against this fair value risk, the firm entered into an 18-month interest rate swap agreement on January 1 and designated the swap as a hedge against changes in the fair value of the note. The swap calls for the company to *receive payment* based on a 10% fixed interest rate on a notional amount of $1 million and to *make payment* based on a floating interest rate tied to changes in general rates.[8] As the Illustration will show, this effectively converts Wintel's fixed-rate debt to floating-rate debt. Cash settlement of the net interest amount is made semiannually at June 30 and December 31 of each year with the net interest being the difference between the $50,000 fixed interest [$1 million × (10% × ½)] and the floating interest rate times $1 million at those dates.

Floating (market) settlement rates were 9% at June 30, 2006, 8% at December 31, 2006, and 9% at June 30, 2007. Net interest receipts can be calculated as shown below. Fair values of both the derivative and the note resulting from those market rate changes are assumed to be quotes obtained from securities dealers.

| | 1/1/06 | 6/30/06 | 12/31/06 | 6/30/07 |
|---|---|---|---|---|
| Fixed rate | 10% | 10% | 10% | 10% |
| Floating rate | 10% | 9% | 8% | 9% |
| Fixed payments ($1 million × [10% × ½]) | | $ 50,000 | $ 50,000 | $ 50,000 |
| Floating payments ($1 million × ½ floating rate) | | 45,000 | 40,000 | 45,000 |
| Net interest receipts | | $ 5,000 | $ 10,000 | $ 5,000 |
| Fair value of interest rate swap | 0 | $ 9,363 | $ 9,615 | 0 |
| Fair value of note payable | $1,000,000 | $1,009,363 | $1,009,615 | $1,000,000 |

The fair value of derivatives is recognized in the balance sheet.

The hedged liability (or asset) is adjusted to fair value as well.

| | | |
|---|---|---|
| Interest rate swap[9] ($9,363 − 0) | 9,363 | |
| Holding gain—interest rate swap | | 9,363 |
| *To record change in fair value of the derivative.* | | |
| Holding loss—hedged note | 9,363 | |
| Note payable ($1,009,363 − 1,000,000) | | 9,363 |
| *To record change in fair value of the note due to interest rate changes.* | | |

The net interest settlement on June 30, 2006, is $5,000 because the fixed rate is 5% (half of the 10% annual rate) and the floating rate is 4.5% (half of the 9% annual rate).

As with any debt, interest expense is the effective rate times the outstanding balance.

The settlement is the difference between the fixed interest (5%) and variable interest (4%).

The derivative is increased by the change in fair value.

The note is increased by the change in fair value.

| **December 31, 2006** | | |
|---|---|---|
| Interest expense | 50,000 | |
| Cash (10% × ½ × $1,000,000) | | 50,000 |
| *To record interest.* | | |
| Cash ($50,000 − [8% × ½ × $1 million]) | 10,000 | |
| Interest expense | | 10,000 |
| *To record the net cash settlement.* | | |
| Interest rate swap ($9,615 − 9,363) | 252 | |
| Holding gain—interest rate swap | | 252 |
| *To record the change in fair value of the derivative.* | | |
| Holding loss—hedged note | 252 | |
| Note payable ($1,009,615 − 1,009,363) | | 252 |
| *To record the change in fair value of the note due to interest rate changes.* | | |

[8]A common measure for benchmarking variable interest rates is LIBOR, the London Interbank Offered Rate, a base rate at which large international banks lend funds to each other.

[9]This would be a liability rather than an investment (asset) if the fair value had declined.

The fair value of the swap increased by $252 (from $9,363 to $9,615). Similarly, we adjust the note's carrying value by the amount necessary to increase it to fair value. This produces a holding loss on the note that exactly offsets the gain on the swap. This result is the hedging effect that motivated Wintel to enter the fair value hedging arrangement in the first place.

At June 30, 2007, Wintel repeats the process of adjusting to fair value both the derivative investment and the note being hedged.

| **June 30, 2007** | | |
|---|---|---|
| Interest expense | 50,000 | |
| Cash (10% × ½ × $1,000,000) | | 50,000 |
| *To record interest.* | | |
| Cash [$50,000 − (9% × ½ × $1 million)] | 5,000 | |
| Interest expense | | 5,000 |
| *To record the net cash settlement.* | | |
| Holding loss—interest rate swap | 9,615 | |
| Interest rate swap ($0 − 9,615) | | 9,615 |
| *To record the change in fair value of the derivative.* | | |
| Note payable ($1,000,000 − 1,009,615) | 9,615 | |
| Holding gain—hedged note | | 9,615 |
| *To record the change in fair value of the note due to interest rate changes.* | | |
| Note payable | 1,000,000 | |
| Cash | | 1,000,000 |
| *To repay the loan.* | | |

**The net interest received is the difference between the fixed interest (5%) and floating interest (4.5%).**

**The swap's fair value now is zero.**

The net interest received is the difference between the fixed rate (5%) and floating rate (4.5%) times $1 million. The fair value of the swap decreased by $9,615 (from $9,615 to zero).[10] That decline represents a holding *loss* that we recognize in earnings. Similarly, we record an offsetting holding *gain* on the note for the change in its fair value.

Now let's see how the carrying values changed for the swap account and the note:

| | Swap (Dr.) | Swap (Cr.) | Note (Dr.) | Note (Cr.) |
|---|---|---|---|---|
| *Jan. 1, 2006* | | | | 1,000,000 |
| *June 30, 2006* | 9,363 | | | 9,363 |
| *Dec. 31, 2006* | 252 | | | 252 |
| *June 30, 2007* | | 9,615 | 9,615<br>1,000,000 | |
| | 0 | | | 0 |

The income statement is affected as follows:

| | **Income Statement + (−)** | |
|---|---|---|
| *June 30, 2006* | (50,000) | Interest expense—fixed payment |
| | 5,000 | Interest expense—net cash settlement |
| | 9,363 | Holding gain—interest rate swap |
| | (9,363) | Holding loss—hedged note |
| | (45,000) | Net effect—same as floating interest payment |
| *Dec. 31, 2006* | (50,000) | Interest expense—fixed payment |
| | 10,000 | Interest expense—net cash settlement |
| | 252 | Holding gain—interest rate swap |
| | (252) | Holding loss—hedged note |
| | (40,000) | Net effect—same as floating interest payment |
| *June 30, 2007* | (50,000) | Interest expense—fixed payment |
| | 5,000 | Interest expense—net cash settlement |
| | 9,615 | Holding gain—interest rate swap |
| | (9,615) | Holding loss—hedged note |
| | (45,000) | Net effect—same as floating interest payment |

[10] Because there are no future cash receipts from the swap arrangement at this point, the fair value of the swap is zero.

As this demonstrates, the swap effectively converts fixed-interest debt to floating-interest debt.

**ADDITIONAL CONSIDERATION**

**Fair Value of the Swap**

The fair value of a derivative typically is based on a quote obtained from a derivatives dealer. That fair value will approximate the present value of the expected net interest settlement receipts for the remaining term of the swap. In fact, we can actually calculate the fair value of the swap that we accepted as given in our illustration.

Since the June 30, 2006, floating rate of 9% caused the cash settlement on that date to be $5,000, it's reasonable to look at 9% as the best estimate of future floating rates and therefore assume the remaining two cash settlements also will be $5,000 each. We can then calculate at June 30, 2006, the present value of those expected net interest settlement receipts for the remaining term of the swap:

| | | |
|---|---|---|
| Fixed interest | 10% × ½ × $1 million. . . . . . . . . . | $50,000 |
| Expected floating interest | 9% × ½ × $1 million . . . . . . . . . . | 45,000 |
| Expected cash receipts for both Dec. 31, 2006 and June 30, 2007 | | $ 5,000 |
| | | × 1.87267* |
| Present value. . . . . . . . . . . . . . . . . . . . . . . . . . . . . . . . . . . . . . . . . . . | | $ 9,363 |

*Present value of an ordinary annuity of $1: n = 2, i = 4.5% (½ of 9%)

**Fair Value of the Notes**

The fair value of the note payable will be the present value of principal and remaining interest payments discounted at the *market rate*. The market rate will vary with the designated floating rate but might differ due to changes in default (credit) risk and the term structure of interest rates. Assuming it's 9% at June 30, 2006, we can calculate the fair value (present value) of the notes:

| | | |
|---|---|---|
| Interest | $50,000* × 1.87267† = | $ 93,633 |
| Principal | $1,000,000 × .91573‡ = | 915,730 |
| | | $1,009,363 |

*½ of 10% × $1,000,000
†Present value of an ordinary annuity of $1: n = 2, i = 4.5%
‡Present value of $1: n = 2, i = 4.5%

Note: Often the cash settlement rate is "reset" as of each cash settlement date (thus the floating rate actually used at the *end* of each period to determine the payment is the floating market rate as of the *beginning* of the same period). In our illustration, for instance, there would have been no cash settlement at June 30, 2006, since we would use the beginning floating rate of 10% to determine payment. Similarly, we would have used the 9% floating rate at June 30, 2006, to determine the cash settlement six months later at December 31. In effect, each cash settlement would be delayed six months. Had this arrangement been in effect in the current illustration, there would have been one fewer cash settlement payments (two rather than three), but would not have affected the fair value calculations above because, either way, our expectation would be cash receipts of $5,000 for both Dec. 31, 2006, and June 30, 2007.

## CASH FLOW HEDGES

The risk in some transactions or events is the risk of a change in cash flows, rather than a change in fair values. We noted earlier, for instance, that *fixed-rate* debt subjects a company to the risk that interest rate changes could change the fair value of the debt. On the other hand, if the obligation is *floating-rate* debt, the fair value of the debt will not change when interest rates do, but cash flows will. If a derivative is used to hedge against the exposure to changes in cash inflows or cash outflows of an asset or liability or a forecasted transaction (like a future purchase or sale), it can be designated as a **cash flow hedge.** In that case, when the derivative is adjusted to reflect changes in fair value, the other side of the entry is a gain or loss to be deferred as a **component of Other comprehensive income** and included in earnings later, at the same time as earnings are affected by the hedged transaction. Once again, the effect is matching the earnings effect of the derivative with the earnings effect of the item being hedged, precisely the concept behind hedge accounting.

**A gain or loss from a *cash flow hedge* is deferred as Other comprehensive income until it can be recognized in earnings along with the earnings effect of the item being hedged.**

To understand the deferral of the gain or loss, we need to revisit the concept of comprehensive income. Comprehensive income, as you may recall from Chapters 4, 12, 17, and 18 is a more expansive view of the change in shareholders' equity than traditional net income. In fact, it encompasses all changes in equity other than from transactions with owners.[11] So, in addition to net income itself, comprehensive income includes up to four other changes in equity that don't (yet) belong in net income, namely, net holding gains (losses) on investments (Chapter 12), gain (losses) from and amendments to postretirement benefit plans (Chapter 17), gains (losses) from foreign currency translation, and deferred gains (losses) from derivatives designated as cash flow hedges.[12]

Some of the more commonly used cash flow hedges are:

- An interest rate swap to synthetically convert floating rate debt (for which interest rate changes could change the cash interest payments) into fixed rate debt.
- A futures contract to hedge a forecasted sale (for which price changes could change the cash receipts) of natural gas, crude oil, or some other asset.

## FOREIGN CURRENCY HEDGES

Today's economy is increasingly a global one. The majority of large "U.S." companies are, in truth, multinational companies that may receive only a fraction of their revenues from U.S. operations. Many operations of those companies are located abroad. Foreign operations often are denominated in the currency of the foreign country (the Euro, Japanese yen, Russian rubles, and so on). Even companies without foreign operations sometimes hold investments, issue debt, or conduct other transactions denominated in foreign currencies. As exchange rates change, the dollar equivalent of the foreign currency changes. The possibility of currency rate changes exposes these companies to the risk that some transactions require settlement in a currency other than the entities' functional currency or that foreign operations will require translation adjustments to reported amounts.

**The possibility that foreign currency exchange rates might change exposes many companies to foreign currency risk.**

A **foreign currency hedge** can be a hedge of foreign currency exposure of:

- A firm commitment—treated as a fair value hedge.
- An available-for-sale security—treated as a fair value hedge.
- A forecasted transaction—treated as a cash flow hedge.
- A company's net investment in a foreign operation—the gain or loss is reported in *other comprehensive income* as part of unrealized gains and losses from foreign currency translation.[13]

## HEDGE EFFECTIVENESS

When a company elects to apply hedge accounting, it must establish at the inception of the hedge the method it will use to assess the effectiveness of the hedging derivative as well as the measurement approach it will use to determine the ineffective portion of the hedge.[14] The key criterion for qualifying as a hedge is that the hedging relationship must be highly effective in achieving offsetting changes in fair values or cash flows based on the hedging company's specified risk management objective and strategy.

**To qualify as a hedge, the hedging relationship must be highly effective in achieving offsetting changes in fair values or cash flows.**

An assessment of this effectiveness must be made at least every three months and whenever financial statements are issued. There are no precise guidelines for assessing effectiveness, but it generally means a high correlation between changes in the fair value or cash flows of the derivative and of the item being hedged, not necessarily a specific reduction in risk. Hedge accounting must be terminated for hedging relationships that no longer are highly effective.

## HEDGE INEFFECTIVENESS

In Illustration A–1, the loss on the hedged note exactly offset the gain on the swap. This is because the swap in this instance was highly effective in hedging the risk due to interest rate changes. However, the loss and gain would not have exactly offset each other if the hedging

[11]Transactions with owners primarily include dividends and the sale or purchase of shares of the company's stock.

[12]"Reporting Comprehensive Income," *Statement of Financial Accounting Standards No. 130* (Norwalk, Conn.: FASB, 1997).

[13]This is the same treatment previously prescribed for these translation adjustments by *Statement of Financial Accounting Standards No. 52.*

[14]Remember, if a derivative is not designated as a hedge, any gains or losses from changes in its fair value are recognized immediately in earnings.

arrangement had been ineffective. For instance, suppose the swap's term had been different from that of the note (say a three-year swap term compared with the 18-month term of the note) or if the notional amount of the swap differed from that of the note (say $500,000 rather than $1 million). In that case, changes in the fair value of the swap and changes in the fair value of the note would not be the same. The result would be a greater (or lesser) amount recognized in earnings for the swap than for the note. Because there would not be an exact offset, earnings would be affected, an effect resulting from hedge ineffectiveness. That is a desired effect of hedge accounting; to the extent that a hedge is effective, the earnings effect of a derivative cancels out the earnings effect of the item being hedged. However, even if a hedge is highly effective, all ineffectiveness is recognized currently in earnings.

**Imperfect hedges result in part of the derivative gain or loss being included in current earnings.**

### FAIR VALUE CHANGES UNRELATED TO THE RISK BEING HEDGED

In Illustration A–1, the fair value of the hedged note and the fair value of the swap changed by the same amounts each year because we assumed the fair values changed only due to interest rate changes. It's also possible, though, that the note's fair value would change by an amount different from that of the swap for reasons unrelated to interest rates. Remember from our earlier discussion that the market's perception of a company's creditworthiness, and thus its ability to pay interest and principal when due, also can affect the value of debt, whether interest rates change or not. In hedge accounting, we ignore those changes. We recognize only the fair value changes in the hedged item that we can attribute to the risk being hedged (interest rate risk in this case). For example, if a changing perception of default risk had caused the note's fair value to increase by an additional, say $5,000, our journal entries in Illustration A–1 would have been unaffected. Notice, then, that although we always mark a *derivative* to fair value, the reported amount of the *item being hedged* may not be its fair value. We mark a hedged item to fair value only to the extent that its fair value changed due to the risk being hedged.

**Fair value changes unrelated to the risk being hedged are ignored.**

## Disclosure of Derivatives and Risk

To be adequately informed about the adequacy of a company's risk management, investors and creditors need information about strategies for holding derivatives and specific hedging activities. Toward that end, extensive disclosure requirements provide information that includes:

- Objectives and strategies for holding and issuing derivatives.
- A description of the items for which risks are being hedged.
- For forecasted transactions: a description, time before the transaction is expected to occur, the gains and losses accumulated in other comprehensive income, and the events that will trigger their recognition in earnings.
- Beginning balance of, changes in, and ending balance of the derivative component of other comprehensive income.
- The net amount of gain or loss reported in earnings (representing aggregate hedge ineffectiveness).
- Qualitative and quantitative information about failed hedges: canceled commitments or previously hedged forecasted transactions no longer expected to occur.

The intent is to provide information about the company's success in reducing risks and consequently about risks not managed successfully. Remember, too, that when derivatives are employed ineffectively, risks can escalate. Ample disclosures about derivatives are essential to maintain awareness of potential opportunities and problems with risk management.

Even for some traditional liabilities, the amounts reported on the face of the financial statements provide inadequate disclosure about the degree to which a company is exposed to risk of loss. To provide adequate disclosure about a company's exposure to risk, additional information must be provided about (a) concentrations of credit risk and (b) the fair value of all financial instruments.[15]

[15]"Disclosures About Fair Values of Financial Instruments," *Statement of Financial Accounting Standards No. 107* (Norwalk, Conn.: FASB, 1991) as amended by *Statement of Financial Accounting Standards No. 133,* "Accounting for Derivative Instruments and Hedging Activities" (Norwalk, Conn.: FASB, 1998).

## Extended Method for Interest Rate Swap Accounting

A short-cut method for accounting for an interest rate swap is permitted by *SFAS 133* when a hedge meets certain criteria. In general, the criteria are designed to see if the hedge supports the assumption of "no ineffectiveness." Illustration A–1 of a fair value hedge met those criteria, in particular, (a) the swap's notional amount matches the note's principal amount, (b) the swap's expiration date matches the note's maturity date, (c) the fair value of the swap is zero at inception, and (d) the floating payment is at the market rate.[16] Because Wintel can conclude that the swap will be highly effective in offsetting changes in the fair value of the debt, it can use the changes in the fair value of the swap to measure the offsetting changes in the fair value of the debt. That's the essence of the short-cut method used in Illustration A–1. The extended method required when the criteria are *not* met for the short-cut method is described in this section (Illustration A–2). It produces the same effect on earnings and in the balance sheet as does the procedure shown in Illustration A–1.

**ILLUSTRATION A–2**
Interest Rate Swap—Extended Method

Wintel Semiconductors issued $1 million of 18-month, 10% bank notes on January 1, 2006. Wintel is exposed to the risk that general interest rates will decline, causing the fair value of its debt to rise. (If the fair value of Wintel's debt increases, its effective borrowing cost is higher relative to the market.) To hedge against this fair value risk, the firm entered into an 18-month interest rate swap agreement on January 1 and designated the swap as a hedge against changes in the fair value of the note. The swap calls for the company to *receive payment* based on a 10% fixed interest rate on a notional amount of $1 million and to *make payment* based on a floating interest rate tied to changes in general rates. Cash settlement of the net interest amount is made semiannually at June 30 and December 31 of each year with the net interest being the difference between the $50,000 fixed interest [$1 million × (10% × ½)] and the floating interest rate times $1 million at those dates.

Floating (market) settlement rates were 9% at June 30, 2006, 8% at December 31, 2006, and 8% at June 30, 2007. Net interest receipts can be calculated as shown below. Fair values of both the derivative and the note resulting from those market rate changes are assumed to be quotes obtained from securities dealers.

| | 1/1/06 | 6/30/06 | 12/31/06 | 6/30/07 |
|---|---|---|---|---|
| Fixed rate | 10% | 10% | 10% | 10% |
| Floating rate | 10% | 9% | 8% | 9% |
| Fixed payments [$1 million × (10% × ½)] | | $ 50,000 | $ 50,000 | $ 50,000 |
| Floating payments ($1 million × ½ floating rate) | | 45,000 | 40,000 | 45,000 |
| Net interest receipts | | $ 5,000 | $ 10,000 | $ 5,000 |
| Fair value of interest rate swap | 0 | $ 9,363 | $ 9,615 | 0 |
| Fair value of note payable | $1,000,000 | $1,009,363 | $1,009,615 | $1,000,000 |

When the floating rate declined in Illustration A–2 from 10% to 9%, the fair values of both the derivative (swap) and the note increased. This created an offsetting gain on the derivative and holding loss on the note. Both are recognized in earnings the same period (June 30, 2006).

**January 1, 2006**

| | | |
|---|---|---|
| Cash ........................................ | 1,000,000 | |
| Notes payable ........................................ | | 1,000,000 |
| *To record the issuance of the note.* | | |

**The interest rate swap is designated as a fair value hedge on this note at issuance.**

[16]There is no precise minimum interval, though it generally is three to six months or less. Other criteria are specified by *SFAS 133* (para. 68) in addition to the key conditions listed here.

**The swap settlement is the difference between the fixed interest (5%) and variable interest (4.5%).**

**The fair value of derivatives is recognized in the balance sheet.**

**The hedged liability (or asset) is adjusted to fair value as well.**

| **June 30, 2006** | | |
|---|---|---|
| Interest expense (10% × ½ × $1 million) | 50,000 | |
| Cash | | 50,000 |
| *To record interest.* | | |
| Cash ($50,000 − [9% × ½ × $1 million]) | 5,000 | |
| Interest rate swap ($9,363 − 0) | 9,363 | |
| Interest revenue (10% × ½ × $0) | | 0 |
| Holding gain—interest rate swap (to balance) | | 14,363 |
| *To record the net cash settlement, accrued interest on the swap, and change in the fair value of the derivative.* | | |
| Holding loss—hedged note | 9,363 | |
| Notes payable ($1,009,363 − 1,000,000) | | 9,363 |
| *To record change in fair value of the note due to interest rate changes.* | | |

The net interest settlement on June 30, 2006, is $5,000 because the fixed rate is 5% (half of the 10% annual rate) and the floating rate is 4.5% (half of the 9% annual rate). A holding gain ($14,363) is produced by holding the derivative security during a time when an interest rate decline caused an increase in the value of that asset. A portion ($5,000) of the gain was received in cash and another portion ($9,363) is reflected as an increase in the value of the asset.

We also have holding loss of the same amount. This is because we also held a liability during the same time period, and the interest rate change caused its fair value to increase as well.

**As with any debt, interest expense is the effective rate times the outstanding balance.**

**The cash settlement is the difference between the fixed interest (5%) and variable interest (4%).**

**Interest ($421) accrues on the asset.**

**The note is increased by the change in fair value.**

| **December 31, 2006** | | |
|---|---|---|
| Interest expense (9% × ½ × $1,009,363) | 45,421 | |
| Notes payable (difference)* | 4,579 | |
| Cash (10% × ½ × $1,000,000) | | 50,000 |
| *To record interest.* | | |
| Cash [$50,000 − (8% × ½ × $1 million)] | 10,000 | |
| Interest rate swap ($9,615 − 9,363) | 252 | |
| Interest revenue (9% × ½ × $9,363) | | 421 |
| Holding gain—interest rate swap (to balance) | | 9,831 |
| *To record the net cash settlement, accrued interest on the swap, and change in the fair value of the derivative.* | | |
| Holding loss—hedged note | 4,831 | |
| Notes payable ($1,009,615 − 1,009,363 + 4,579) | | 4,831 |
| *To record the change in fair value of the note due to interest rate changes.* | | |

*We could use a premium on the note to adjust its carrying amount.

We determine interest on the note the same way we do for any liability, as you learned earlier—at the effective rate (9% × ½) times the outstanding balance ($1,009,363). This results in reducing the note's carrying amount for the cash interest paid in excess of the interest expense.

The fair value of the swap increased due to the interest rate decline by $252 (from $9,363 to $9,615). The holding gain we recognize in earnings consists of that increase (a) plus the $10,000 cash settlement also created by the interest rate decline and (b) minus the $421 increase that results not from the interest rate decline, but from interest accruing on the asset.[17] Similarly, we adjust the note's carrying value by the amount necessary to increase it to fair value, allowing for the $4,579 reduction in the note in the earlier entry to record interest.

At June 30, 2007, Wintel repeats the process of adjusting to fair value both the derivative investment and the note being hedged.

[17]The investment in the interest rate swap represents the present value of expected future net interest receipts. As with other such assets, interest accrues at the effective rate times the outstanding balance. You also can think of the accrued interest mathematically as the increase in present value of the future cash flows as we get one period nearer to the dates when the cash will be received.

| | | |
|---|---|---|
| **June 30, 2007** | | |
| Interest expense (8% × ½ × $1,009,615) | 40,385 | |
| Notes payable (difference) | 9,615 | |
| Cash (10% × ½ × $1,000,000) | | 50,000 |
| *To record interest.* | | |
| Cash [$50,000 − (9% × ½ × $1 million)] | 5,000 | |
| Holding loss—interest rate swap (to balance) | 5,000 | |
| Interest rate swap ($0 − $9,615) | | 9,615 |
| Interest revenue (8% × ½ × $9,615) | | 385 |
| *To record the net cash settlement, accrued interest on the swap, and change in the fair value of the derivative.* | | |
| Notes payable ($1,000,000 − 1,009,615 + 9,615) | 0 | |
| Holding gain—hedged note | | 0 |
| *To record the change in fair value of the note due to interest rate changes.* | | |
| Note payable | 1,000,000 | |
| Cash | | 1,000,000 |
| *To repay the loan* | | |

**Interest expense is the effective rate times the outstanding balance.**

**The net interest received is the difference between the fixed interest (5%) and floating interest (4.5%).**

**The swap's fair value now is zero.**

The net interest received is the difference between the fixed rate (5%) and floating rate (4.5%) times $1 million. The fair value of the swap decreased by $9,615 (from $9,615 to zero).[18] The holding loss we recognize in earnings consists of that decline (a) minus the $5,000 portion of the decline resulting from it being realized in cash settlement and (b) plus the $385 increase that results not from the interest rate change, but from interest accruing on the asset.

Now let's see how the carrying values changed for the swap account and the note:

| | Swap (debit) | Swap (credit) | Note (debit) | Note (credit) |
|---|---|---|---|---|
| *Jan. 1, 2006* | | | | 1,000,000 |
| *June 30, 2006* | 9,363 | | | 9,363 |
| *Dec. 31, 2006* | 252 | | 4,579 | 4,831 |
| *June 30, 2007* | | 9,615 | 9,615<br>1,000,000 | |
| | 0 | | | 0 |

The income statement is affected as follows:

| | Income Statement + (−) | |
|---|---|---|
| *June 30, 2006* | (50,000) | Interest expense |
| | 0 | Interest revenue (no time has passed) |
| | 14,363 | Holding gain interest rate swap |
| | (9,363) | Holding loss—hedged note |
| | (45,000) | Net effect—same as floating interest payment |
| *Dec. 31, 2006* | (45,421) | Interest expense |
| | 421 | Interest revenue |
| | 9,831 | Holding gain—interest rate swap |
| | (4,831) | Holding loss—hedged note |
| | (40,000) | Net effect—same as floating interest payment |
| *June 30, 2007* | (40,385) | Interest expense |
| | 385 | Interest revenue |
| | (5,000) | Holding loss—interest rate swap |
| | 0 | Holding gain—hedged note |
| | (45,000) | Net effect—same as floating interest payment |

As this demonstrates, the swap effectively converts Wintel's fixed-interest debt to floating-interest debt.

[18]Because there are no future cash receipts or payments from the swap arrangement at this point, the fair value of the swap is zero.

## The Bottom Line

1. All derivatives are reported in the balance sheet at fair value.
2. *Hedging* means taking a risk position that is opposite to an actual position that is exposed to risk. For a derivative used to hedge against exposure to risk, treatment of any gain or loss from fair value changes depends on whether the derivative is designated as (a) a fair value hedge or (b) a cash flow hedge.
3. We recognize a gain or loss from a *fair value hedge* immediately in earnings along with the loss or gain from the item being hedged. This is so the income effects of the hedge instrument and the income effects of the item being hedged will affect earnings at the same time.
4. We defer a gain or loss from a *cash flow hedge* as part of Other comprehensive income until it can be recognized in earnings along with the earnings effect of the item being hedged.
5. Imperfect hedges result in part of the derivative gain or loss being included in current earnings. We ignore market value changes unrelated to the risk being hedged.
6. Extensive disclosure requirements about derivatives are designed to provide investors and creditors information about the adequacy of a company's risk management and the company's success in reducing risks, including risks not managed successfully. ■

## QUESTIONS FOR REVIEW OF KEY TOPICS

**Q A–1** Some financial instruments are called derivatives. Why?

**Q A–2** Should gains and losses on a fair value hedge be recorded as they occur, or should they be recorded to coincide with losses and gains on the item being hedged?

**Q A–3** Hines Moving Company held a fixed-rate debt of $2 million. The company wanted to hedge its fair value exposure with an interest rate swap. However, the only notional available at the time on the type of swap it desired was $2.5 million. What will be the effect of any gain or loss on the $500,000 notional difference?

**Q A–4** What is a futures contract?

**Q A–5** What is the effect on interest of an interest rate swap?

**Q A–6** How are derivatives reported on the balance sheet? Why?

**Q A–7** When is a gain or a loss from a cash flow hedge reported in earnings?

## EXERCISES

available with McGraw-Hill's Homework Manager www.mhhe.com/spiceland4e

**E A–1**
Derivatives—hedge classification

Indicate (by abbreviation) the type of hedge each activity described below would represent.

**Hedge Type**

FV Fair value hedge
CF Cash flow hedge
FC Foreign currency hedge
N Would not qualify as a hedge

**Activity**

____ 1. An options contract to hedge possible future price changes of inventory.
____ 2. A futures contract to hedge exposure to interest rate changes prior to replacing bank notes when they mature.
____ 3. An interest rate swap to synthetically convert floating rate debt into fixed rate debt.
____ 4. An interest rate swap to synthetically convert fixed rate debt into floating rate debt.
____ 5. A futures contract to hedge possible future price changes of timber covered by a firm commitment to sell.
____ 6. A futures contract to hedge possible future price changes of a forecasted sale of tin.
____ 7. ExxonMobil's net investment in a Kuwait oil field.
____ 8. An interest rate swap to synthetically convert floating rate interest on a stock investment into fixed rate interest.

____ 9. An interest rate swap to synthetically convert fixed rate interest on a held-to-maturity debt investment into floating rate interest.

____ 10. An interest rate swap to synthetically convert floating rate interest on a held-to-maturity debt investment into fixed rate interest.

____ 11. An interest rate swap to synthetically convert fixed rate interest on a stock investment into floating rate interest.

**E A–2**
Derivatives; interest rate swap; fixed rate debt

On January 1, 2006, LLB Industries borrowed $200,000 from Trust Bank by issuing a two-year, 10% note, with interest payable quarterly. LLB entered into a two-year interest rate swap agreement on January 1, 2006, and designated the swap as a fair value hedge. Its intent was to hedge the risk that general interest rates will decline, causing the fair value of its debt to increase. The agreement called for the company to receive payment based on a 10% fixed interest rate on a notional amount of $200,000 and to pay interest based on a floating interest rate. The contract called for cash settlement of the net interest amount quarterly.

Floating (LIBOR) settlement rates were 10% at January 1, 8% at March 31, and 6% June 30, 2006. The fair values of the swap are quotes obtained from a derivatives dealer. Those quotes and the fair values of the note are as indicated below.

| | January 1 | March 31 | June 30 |
|---|---|---|---|
| Fair value of interest rate swap | 0 | $ 6,472 | $ 11,394 |
| Fair value of note payable | $200,000 | $206,472 | $211,394 |

**Required:**

1. Calculate the net cash settlement at March 31 and June 30, 2006.
2. Prepare the journal entries through June 30, 2006, to record the issuance of the note, interest, and necessary adjustments for changes in fair value.

**E A–3**
Derivatives; interest rate swap; fixed rate investment

(This is a variation of Exercise A–2, modified to consider an investment in debt securities.)

On January 1, 2006, S&S Corporation invested in LLB Industries' negotiable two-year, 10% notes, with interest receivable quarterly. The company classified the investment as available-for-sale. S&S entered into a two-year interest rate swap agreement on January 1, 2006, and designated the swap as a fair value hedge. Its intent was to hedge the risk that general interest rates will decline, causing the fair value of its investment to increase. The agreement called for the company to make payment based on a 10% fixed interest rate on a notional amount of $200,000 and to receive interest based on a floating interest rate. The contract called for cash settlement of the net interest amount quarterly.

Floating (LIBOR) settlement rates were 10% at January 1, 8% at March 31, and 6% June 30, 2006. The fair values of the swap are quotes obtained from a derivatives dealer. Those quotes and the fair values of the investment in notes are as follows:

| | January 1 | March 31 | June 30 |
|---|---|---|---|
| Fair value of interest rate swap | 0 | $ 6,472 | $ 11,394 |
| Fair value of the investment in notes | $200,000 | $206,472 | $211,394 |

**Required:**

1. Calculate the net cash settlement at March 31 and June 30, 2006
2. Prepare the journal entries through June 30, 2006, to record the investment in notes, interest, and necessary adjustments for changes in fair value.

**E A–4**
Derivatives; interest rate swap; fixed rate debt; fair value change unrelated to hedged risk

(This is a variation of Exercise A–2, modified to consider fair value change unrelated to hedged risk.)

LLB Industries borrowed $200,000 from Trust Bank by issuing a two-year, 10% note, with interest payable quarterly. LLB entered into a two-year interest rate swap agreement on January 1, 2006 and designated the swap as a fair value hedge. Its intent was to hedge the risk that general interest rates will decline, causing the fair value of its debt to increase. The agreement called for the company to receive payment based on a 10% fixed interest rate on a notional amount of $200,000 and to pay interest based on a floating interest rate.

Floating (LIBOR) settlement rates were 10% at January 1, 8% at March 31, and 6% at June 30, 2006. The fair values of the swap are quotes obtained from a derivatives dealer. Those quotes and the fair values of the note are as indicated below. The additional rise in the fair value of the note (higher than that of the swap) on June 30 was due to investors' perceptions that the creditworthiness of LLB was improving.

| | January 1 | March 31 | June 30 |
|---|---|---|---|
| Fair value of interest rate swap | 0 | $ 6,472 | $ 11,394 |
| Fair value of note payable | $200,000 | $206,472 | $220,000 |

**Required:**

1. Calculate the net cash settlement at June 30, 2006
2. Prepare the journal entries on June 30, 2006, to record the interest and necessary adjustments for changes in fair value.

**E A–5**
Derivatives; interest rate swap; fixed rate debt; extended method

This is a variation of Exercise A–2, modified to consider the extended method.

On January 1, 2006, LLB Industries borrowed $200,000 from Trust Bank by issuing a two-year, 10% note, with interest payable quarterly. LLB entered into a two-year interest rate swap agreement on January 1, 2006, and designated the swap as a fair value hedge. Its intent was to hedge the risk that general interest rates will decline, causing the fair value of its debt to increase. The agreement called for the company to receive payment based on a 10% fixed interest rate on a notional amount of $200,000 and to pay interest based on a floating interest rate. The contract called for cash settlement of the net interest amount quarterly.

Floating (LIBOR) settlement rates were 10% at January 1, 8% at March 31, and 6% at June 30, 2006. The fair values of the swap are quotes obtained from a derivatives dealer. Those quotes and the fair values of the note are as follows:

| | January 1 | March 31 | June 30 |
|---|---|---|---|
| Fair value of interest rate swap | 0 | $ 6,472 | $ 11,394 |
| Fair value of note payable | $200,000 | $206,472 | $211,394 |

**Required:**

Prepare the journal entries through June 30, 2006, to record the issuance of the note, interest, and necessary adjustments for changes in fair value. Use the extended method demonstrated in Illustration A–2.

**E A–6**
Derivatives; interest rate swap; fixed-rate debt; fair value change unrelated to hedged risk; extended method

(Note: This is a variation of Exercise A–5, modified to consider fair value change unrelated to hedged risk.)

On January 1, 2006, LLB Industries borrowed $200,000 from trust Bank by issuing a two-year, 10% note, with interest payable quarterly. LLB entered into a two-year interest rate swap agreement on January 1, 2006, and designated the swap as a fair value hedge. Its intent was to hedge the risk that general interest rates will decline, causing the fair value of its debt to increase. The agreement called for the company to receive payment based on a 10% fixed interest rate on a notional amount of $200,000 and to pay interest based on a floating interest rate. The contract called for cash settlement of the net interest amount quarterly.

Floating (LIBOR) settlement rates were 10% at January 1, 8% at March 31, and 6% June 30, 2006. The fair values of the swap are quotes obtained from a derivatives dealer. Those quotes and the fair values of the note are as indicated below. The additional rise in the fair value of the note (higher than that of the swap) on June 30 was due to investors' perceptions that the creditworthiness of LLB was improving.

| | January 1 | March 31 | June 30 |
|---|---|---|---|
| Fair value of interest rate swap | 0 | $ 6,472 | $ 11,394 |
| Fair value of note payable | $200,000 | 206,472 | 220,000 |

**Required:**

1. Calculate the net cash settlement at June 30, 2006.
2. Prepare the journal entries on June 30, 2006, to record the interest and necessary adjustments for changes in fair value. Use the extended method demonstrated in Illustration A–2.

## PROBLEMS

available with McGraw-Hill's Homework Manager www.mhhe.com/spiceland4e

**P A–1**
Derivatives—interest rate swap

On January 1, 2006, Labtech Circuits borrowed $100,000 from First Bank by issuing a three-year, 8% note, payable on December 31, 2008. Labtech wanted to hedge the risk that general interest rates will decline, causing the fair value of its debt to increase. Therefore, Labtech entered into a three-year interest rate swap agreement on January 1, 2006, and designated the swap as a fair value hedge. The agreement called for the company to receive payment based on an 8% fixed interest rate on a notional amount of $100,000 and to pay interest based on a floating interest rate tied to LIBOR. The contract called for cash settlement of the net interest amount on December 31 of each year.

Floating (LIBOR) settlement rates were 8% at inception and 9%, 7%, and 7% at the end of 2006, 2007, and 2008, respectively. The fair values of the swap are quotes obtained from a derivatives dealer. These quotes and the fair values of the note are as follows:

| | January 1 | December 31 | | |
|---|---|---|---|---|
| | 2006 | 2006 | 2007 | 2008 |
| Fair value of interest rate swap | 0 | $ (1,783) | $ 935 | 0 |
| Fair value of note payable | $100,000 | $98,217 | $100,935 | $100,000 |

**Required:**

1. Calculate the net cash settlement at the end of 2006, 2007, and 2008.
2. Prepare the journal entries during 2006 to record the issuance of the note, interest, and necessary adjustments for changes in fair value.
3. Prepare the journal entries during 2007 to record interest, net cash interest settlement for the interest rate swap, and necessary adjustments for changes in fair value.

4. Prepare the journal entries during 2008 to record interest, net cash interest settlement for the interest rate swap, necessary adjustments for changes in fair value, and repayment of the debt.
5. Calculate the carrying values of both the swap account and the note in each of the three years.
6. Calculate the net effect on earnings of the hedging arrangement in each of the three years. (Ignore income taxes.)
7. Suppose the fair value of the note at December 31, 2006, had been $97,000 rather than $98,217 with the additional decline in fair value due to investors' perceptions that the creditworthiness of Labtech was worsening. How would that affect your entries to record changes in the fair values?

**P A–2**
Derivatives; interest rate swap; comprehensive

CMOS Chips is hedging a 20-year, $10 million, 7% bond payable with a 20-year interest rate swap and has designated the swap as a fair value hedge. The agreement called for CMOS to receive payment based on a 7% fixed interest rate on a notional amount of $10 million and to pay interest based on a floating interest rate tied to LIBOR. The contract calls for cash settlement of the net interest amount on December 31 of each year.

At December 31, 2006, the fair value of the derivative and of the hedged bonds has increased by $100,000 because interest rates declined during the reporting period.

**Required:**
1. Does CMOS have an unrealized gain or loss on the derivative for the period? On the bonds? Will earnings increase or decrease due to the hedging arrangement? Why?
2. Suppose interest rates increased, rather than decreased, causing the fair value of both the derivative and of the hedged bonds to decrease by $100,000. Would CMOS have an unrealized gain or loss on the derivative for the period? On the bonds? Would earnings increase or decrease due to the hedging arrangement? Why?
3. Suppose the fair value of the bonds at December 31, 2006, had increased by $110,000 rather than $100,000, with the additional increase in fair value due to investors' perceptions that the creditworthiness of CMOS was improving. Would CMOS have an unrealized gain or loss on the derivative for the period? On the bonds? Would earnings increase or decrease due to the hedging arrangement? Why?
4. Suppose the notional amount of the swap had been $12 million, rather than the $10 million principal amount of the bonds. As a result, at December 31, 2006, the swap's fair value had increased by $120,000 rather than $100,000. Would CMOS have an unrealized gain or loss on the derivative for the period? On the bonds? Would earnings increase or decrease due to the hedging arrangement? Why?
5. Suppose BIOS Corporation is an investor having purchased all $10 million of the bonds issued by CMOS as described in the original situation above. BIOS is hedging its investment, classified as available-for-sale, with a 20-year interest rate swap and has designated the swap as a fair value hedge. The agreement called for BIOS to make *payment* based on a 7% fixed interest rate on a notional amount of $10 million and to *receive* interest based on a floating interest rate tied to LIBOR. Would BIOS have an unrealized gain or loss on the derivative for the period due to interest rates having declined? On the bonds? Would earnings increase or decrease due to the hedging arrangement? Why?

**P A–3**
Derivatives; interest rate swap; fixed rate debt; extended method

(Note: This is a variation of Problem A–1, modified to consider the extended method demonstrated in Illustration A–2.)

On January 1, 2006, Labtech Circuits borrowed $100,000 from First Bank by issuing a three-year, 8% note, payable on December 31, 2008. Labtech wanted to hedge the risk that general interest rates will decline, causing the fair value of its debt to increase. Therefore, Labtech entered into a three-year interest rate swap agreement on January 1, 2006, and designated the swap as a fair value hedge. The agreement called for the company to receive payment based on an 8% fixed interest rate on a notional amount of $100,000 and to pay interest based on a floating interest rate tied to LIBOR. The contract called for cash settlement of the net interest amount on December 31 of each year.

Floating (LIBOR) settlement rates were 8% at inception and 9%, 7%, and 7% at the end of 2006, 2007, and 2008, respectively. The fair values of the swap are quotes obtained from a derivatives dealer. Those quotes and the fair values of the note are as follows:

| | January 1 | December 31 | | |
|---|---|---|---|---|
| | **2006** | **2006** | **2007** | **2008** |
| Fair value of interest rate swap | 0 | $ (1,783) | $ 935 | 0 |
| Fair value of note payable | $100,000 | 98,217 | 100,935 | $100,000 |

**Required:**
Use the extended method demonstrated in Illustration A–2.
1. Calculate the net cash settlement at the end of 2006, 2007, and 2008.
2. Prepare the journal entries during 2006 to record the issuance of the note, interest, and necessary adjustments for changes in fair value.

3. Prepare the journal entries during 2007 to record interest, net cash interest settlement for the interest rate swap, and necessary adjustments for changes in fair value.
4. Prepare the journal entries during 2008 to record interest, net cash interest settlement for the interest rate swap, necessary adjustments for changes in fair value, and repayment of the debt.
5. Calculate the carrying values of both the swap account and the note in each of the three years.
6. Calculate the net effect on earnings of the hedging arrangement in each of the three years. (Ignore income taxes.)
7. Suppose the fair value of the note at December 31, 2006, had been $97,000 rather than $98,217 with the additional decline in fair value due to investors' perceptions that the creditworthiness of Labtech was worsening. How would that affect your entries to record changes in the fair values?

# BROADEN YOUR PERSPECTIVE

**Apply your critical-thinking ability to the knowledge you've gained. These cases will provide you an opportunity to develop your research, analysis, judgment, and communication skills. You also will work with other students, integrate what you've learned, apply it in real world situations, and consider its global and ethical ramifications. This practice will broaden your knowledge and further develop your decision-making abilities.**

**Real World Case A–1**
Derivative losses; recognition in earnings

The following is an excerpt from a disclosure note of **Johnson & Johnson**:

---

**15. Financial Instruments (in part)**

As of January 2, 2005, the balance of deferred net losses on derivatives included in accumulated other comprehensive income was $150 million after-tax. The Company expects that substantially all of this amount will be reclassified into earnings over the next 12 months as a result of transactions that are expected to occur over that period.

---

**Required:**

1. Johnson & Johnson indicates that it expects that substantially all of the balance of deferred net losses on derivatives will be reclassified into earnings over the next 12 months as a result of transactions that are expected to occur over that period. What is meant by "reclassified into earnings"?
2. What type(s) of hedging transaction might be accounted for in this way?

**Communication Case A–2**
Derivatives; hedge accounting

A conceptual question in accounting for derivatives is: Should gains and losses on a hedge instrument be recorded as they occur, or should they be recorded to coincide (match) with income effects of the item being hedged?

ABI Wholesalers plans to issue long-term notes in May that will replace its $20 million of 9.5% bonds when they mature in July. ABI is exposed to the risk that interest rates in July will have risen, increasing borrowing costs (reducing the selling price of its notes). To hedge that possibility, ABI entered a (Treasury bond) futures contract in May to deliver (sell) bonds in July at their *current* price.

As a result, if interest rates rise, borrowing costs will go up for ABI because it will sell notes at a higher interest cost (or lower price). But that loss will be offset (approximately) by the gain produced by being in the opposite position on Treasury bond futures.

Two opposing viewpoints are:

**View 1:** Gains and losses on instruments designed to hedge anticipated transactions should be recorded as they occur.

**View 2:** Gains and losses on instruments designed to hedge anticipated transactions should be recorded to coincide (match) with income effects of the item being hedged.

In considering this question, focus on conceptual issues regarding the practicable and theoretically appropriate treatment, unconstrained by GAAP. Your instructor will divide the class into two to six groups depending on the size of the class. The mission of your group is to reach consensus on the appropriate accounting for the gains and losses on instruments designed to hedge anticipated transactions.

**Required:**

1. Each group member should deliberate the situation independently and draft a tentative argument prior to the class session for which the case is assigned.

2. In class, each group will meet for 10 to 15 minutes in different areas of the classroom. During that meeting, group members will take turns sharing their suggestions for the purpose of arriving at a single group treatment.
3. After the allotted time, a spokesperson for each group (selected during the group meetings) will share the group's solution with the class. The goal of the class is to incorporate the views of each group into a consensus approach to the situation.

**Real World Case A–3**
Researching the way interest rate futures prices are quoted on the Chicago Mercantile Exchange; retrieving information from the Internet

The **Chicago Mercantile Exchange**, or Merc, at 30 S. Wacker Drive in Chicago, is the world's largest financial exchange, an international marketplace enabling institutions and businesses to trade futures and options contracts including currencies, interest rates, stock indices, and agricultural commodities.

**Required:**

1. Access the Merc on the Internet. The web address is **www.cme.com**.
2. Access the daily settlement prices within the site. Scroll to find the 13-week Treasury bill futures.
3. What are the settlement prices for September and December futures contracts?
4. In terms of dollars, how can we interpret the settlement price?

**Research Case A–4**
Issue related to the derivatives standard; research an article

In an effort to keep up with the rapidly changing global financial markets, the FASB issued a standard—*SFAS 133*—on accounting for derivative financial instruments. A *Journal of Accountancy* article that discusses this standard is "The Decision on Derivatives," by Arlette C. Wilson, Gary Waters and Barry J. Bryan, November 1998.

**Required:**

On the Internet, go to the AICPA site at **www.aicpa.org** and find the article mentioned.

1. What are the primary problems or issues the FASB is attempting to address with the new standard?
2. In considering the issues, the FASB made four fundamental decisions that became the cornerstones of the proposed statement. What are those fundamental decisions? Which do you think is most critical to fair financial reporting?

**Trueblood Case A–5**
Derivatives; definition; embedded derivatives

The following Trueblood case is recommended for use with this appendix. The case provides an excellent opportunity for class discussion, group projects, and writing assignments. The case, along with Professor's Discussion Material, can be obtained from the Deloitte Foundation at its website: **www.deloitte.com/us/truebloodcases**.

**Case 03-8: *Abbey Technologies, Inc.***

This case provides students the opportunity to discuss whether or not a particular issue of redeemable preferred stock can be considered to be a derivative or whether one or more of its features can be considered to be an "embedded" derivative.

APPENDIX B

# FedEx Financial Statements

FEDEX CORPORATION

## CONSOLIDATED STATEMENTS OF INCOME

| (In millions, except per share amounts) | Years ended May 31, 2004 | 2003 | 2002 |
|---|---|---|---|
| **REVENUES** | **$24,710** | $22,487 | $20,607 |
| **Operating Expenses:** | | | |
| Salaries and employee benefits | **10,728** | 9,778 | 9,099 |
| Purchased transportation | **2,407** | 2,155 | 1,825 |
| Rentals and landing fees | **1,918** | 1,803 | 1,780 |
| Depreciation and amortization | **1,375** | 1,351 | 1,364 |
| Fuel | **1,481** | 1,349 | 1,100 |
| Maintenance and repairs | **1,523** | 1,398 | 1,240 |
| Business realignment costs | **435** | – | – |
| Airline stabilization compensation | **–** | – | (119) |
| Other | **3,403** | 3,182 | 2,997 |
| | **23,270** | 21,016 | 19,286 |
| **OPERATING INCOME** | **1,440** | 1,471 | 1,321 |
| **Other Income (Expense):** | | | |
| Interest expense | **(136)** | (124) | (144) |
| Interest income | **20** | 6 | 5 |
| Other, net | **(5)** | (15) | (22) |
| | **(121)** | (133) | (161) |
| **Income Before Income Taxes** | **1,319** | 1,338 | 1,160 |
| **Provision for Income Taxes** | **481** | 508 | 435 |
| **Income Before Cumulative Effect of Change in Accounting Principle** | **838** | 830 | 725 |
| **Cumulative Effect of Change in Accounting for Goodwill, Net of Tax Benefit of $10** | **–** | – | (15) |
| **NET INCOME** | **$ 838** | $ 830 | $ 710 |
| **BASIC EARNINGS PER COMMON SHARE:** | | | |
| Income before cumulative effect of change in accounting principle | **$ 2.80** | $ 2.79 | $ 2.43 |
| Cumulative effect of change in accounting for goodwill | **–** | – | (0.05) |
| **Basic Earnings Per Common Share** | **$ 2.80** | $ 2.79 | $ 2.38 |
| **DILUTED EARNINGS PER COMMON SHARE:** | | | |
| Income before cumulative effect of change in accounting principle | **$ 2.76** | $ 2.74 | $ 2.39 |
| Cumulative effect of change in accounting for goodwill | **–** | – | (0.05) |
| **Diluted Earnings Per Common Share** | **$ 2.76** | $ 2.74 | $ 2.34 |

The accompanying notes are an integral part of these consolidated financial statements.

FEDEX CORPORATION

## CONSOLIDATED BALANCE SHEETS

| (In millions, except share data) | May 31, 2004 | May 31, 2003 |
|---|---|---|
| **ASSETS** | | |
| **Current Assets** | | |
| Cash and cash equivalents | **$ 1,046** | $ 538 |
| Receivables, less allowances of $151 and $149 | **3,027** | 2,627 |
| Spare parts, supplies and fuel, less allowances of $124 and $101 | **249** | 228 |
| Deferred income taxes | **489** | 416 |
| Prepaid expenses and other | **159** | 132 |
| Total current assets | **4,970** | 3,941 |
| **Property and Equipment, at Cost** | | |
| Aircraft and related equipment | **7,001** | 6,624 |
| Package handling and ground support equipment and vehicles | **5,296** | 5,013 |
| Computer and electronic equipment | **3,537** | 3,180 |
| Other | **4,477** | 4,200 |
| | **20,311** | 19,017 |
| Less accumulated depreciation and amortization | **11,274** | 10,317 |
| Net property and equipment | **9,037** | 8,700 |
| **Other Long-Term Assets** | | |
| Goodwill | **2,802** | 1,063 |
| Prepaid pension cost | **1,127** | 1,269 |
| Intangible and other assets | **1,198** | 412 |
| Total other long-term assets | **5,127** | 2,744 |
| | **$19,134** | $15,385 |
| **LIABILITIES AND STOCKHOLDERS' INVESTMENT** | | |
| **Current Liabilities** | | |
| Current portion of long-term debt | **$ 750** | $ 308 |
| Accrued salaries and employee benefits | **1,062** | 724 |
| Accounts payable | **1,615** | 1,168 |
| Accrued expenses | **1,305** | 1,135 |
| Total current liabilities | **4,732** | 3,335 |
| **Long-Term Debt, Less Current Portion** | **2,837** | 1,709 |
| **Other Long-Term Liabilities** | | |
| Deferred income taxes | **1,181** | 882 |
| Pension, postretirement healthcare and other benefit obligations | **768** | 657 |
| Self-insurance accruals | **591** | 536 |
| Deferred lease obligations | **503** | 466 |
| Deferred gains, principally related to aircraft transactions | **426** | 455 |
| Other liabilities | **60** | 57 |
| Total other long-term liabilities | **3,529** | 3,053 |
| **Commitments and Contingencies** | | |
| **Common Stockholders' Investment** | | |
| Common stock, $0.10 par value; 800 million shares authorized; 300 million shares issued for 2004 and 299 million shares issued for 2003 | **30** | 30 |
| Additional paid-in capital | **1,079** | 1,088 |
| Retained earnings | **7,001** | 6,250 |
| Accumulated other comprehensive loss | **(46)** | (30) |
| | **8,064** | 7,338 |
| Less deferred compensation and treasury stock, at cost | **28** | 50 |
| Total common stockholders' investment | **8,036** | 7,288 |
| | **$19,134** | $15,385 |

The accompanying notes are an integral part of these consolidated financial statements.

FEDEX CORPORATION

## CONSOLIDATED STATEMENTS OF CASH FLOWS

| (In millions) | Years ended May 31, 2004 | 2003 | 2002 |
|---|---|---|---|
| **OPERATING ACTIVITIES** | | | |
| Net income | **$ 838** | $ 830 | $ 710 |
| Adjustments to reconcile net income to cash provided by operating activities: | | | |
| Depreciation and amortization | **1,375** | 1,351 | 1,364 |
| Provision for uncollectible accounts | **106** | 105 | 110 |
| Deferred income taxes and other noncash items | **(8)** | 329 | 84 |
| Cumulative effect of change in accounting principle | **–** | – | 15 |
| Tax benefit on the exercise of stock options | **43** | 20 | 18 |
| Changes in operating assets and liabilities, net of the effects of businesses acquired: | | | |
| Receivables | **(307)** | (197) | (88) |
| Other current assets | **10** | 39 | 63 |
| Pension assets and liabilities, net | **155** | (854) | (13) |
| Accounts payable and other operating liabilities | **841** | 252 | (37) |
| Other, net | **(33)** | (4) | 2 |
| Cash provided by operating activities | **3,020** | 1,871 | 2,228 |
| **INVESTING ACTIVITIES** | | | |
| Business acquisitions, net of cash acquired | **(2,410)** | – | (35) |
| Capital expenditures | **(1,271)** | (1,511) | (1,615) |
| Proceeds from asset dispositions | **18** | 22 | 27 |
| Other, net | **1** | (1) | 11 |
| Cash used in investing activities | **(3,662)** | (1,490) | (1,612) |
| **FINANCING ACTIVITIES** | | | |
| Principal payments on debt | **(319)** | (10) | (320) |
| Proceeds from debt issuances | **1,599** | – | – |
| Proceeds from stock issuances | **115** | 81 | 88 |
| Dividends paid | **(66)** | (60) | – |
| Purchase of treasury stock | **(179)** | (186) | (177) |
| Other, net | **–** | 1 | 3 |
| Cash provided by (used in) financing activities | **1,150** | (174) | (406) |
| **CASH AND CASH EQUIVALENTS** | | | |
| Net increase in cash and cash equivalents | **508** | 207 | 210 |
| Cash and cash equivalents at beginning of period | **538** | 331 | 121 |
| Cash and cash equivalents at end of period | **$ 1,046** | $ 538 | $ 331 |

The accompanying notes are an integral part of these consolidated financial statements.

FEDEX CORPORATION

## CONSOLIDATED STATEMENTS OF CHANGES IN STOCKHOLDERS' INVESTMENT AND COMPREHENSIVE INCOME

| (In millions, except share data) | Common Stock | Additional Paid-in Capital | Retained Earnings | Accumulated Other Comprehensive Loss | Treasury Stock | Deferred Compensation | Total |
|---|---|---|---|---|---|---|---|
| **BALANCE AT MAY 31, 2001** | $30 | $1,120 | $4,880 | $(56) | $ (53) | $(21) | $5,900 |
| Net income | – | – | 710 | – | – | – | 710 |
| Foreign currency translation adjustment, net of deferred taxes of $1 | – | – | – | 6 | – | – | 6 |
| Minimum pension liability adjustment, net of deferred tax benefit of $2 | – | – | – | (3) | – | – | (3) |
| Reclassification of deferred jet fuel hedging charges, net of deferred tax benefit of $6 | – | – | – | (9) | – | – | (9) |
| Adjustment for jet fuel hedging charges recognized in expense during period, net of deferred taxes of $6 | – | – | – | 9 | – | – | 9 |
| **Total comprehensive income** | | | | | | | **713** |
| Purchase of treasury stock | – | – | – | – | (177) | – | (177) |
| Cash dividends declared ($0.05 per share) | – | – | (15) | – | – | – | (15) |
| Employee incentive plans and other (4,224,444 shares issued) | – | 24 | (110) | – | 210 | (12) | 112 |
| Amortization of deferred compensation | – | – | – | – | – | 12 | 12 |
| **BALANCE AT MAY 31, 2002** | 30 | 1,144 | 5,465 | (53) | (20) | (21) | 6,545 |
| Net income | – | – | 830 | – | – | – | 830 |
| Foreign currency translation adjustment, net of deferred taxes of $10 | – | – | – | 37 | – | – | 37 |
| Minimum pension liability adjustment, net of deferred tax benefit of $7 | – | – | – | (14) | – | – | (14) |
| **Total comprehensive income** | | | | | | | **853** |
| Purchase of treasury stock | – | – | – | – | (186) | – | (186) |
| Cash dividends declared ($0.15 per share) | – | – | (45) | – | – | – | (45) |
| Employee incentive plans and other (3,268,180 shares issued) | – | (56) | – | – | 181 | (16) | 109 |
| Amortization of deferred compensation | – | – | – | – | – | 12 | 12 |
| **BALANCE AT MAY 31, 2003** | 30 | 1,088 | 6,250 | (30) | (25) | (25) | 7,288 |
| Net income | – | – | 838 | – | – | – | 838 |
| Minimum pension liability adjustment, net of deferred tax benefit of $12 | – | – | – | (16) | – | – | (16) |
| **Total comprehensive income** | | | | | | | **822** |
| Purchase of treasury stock | – | – | – | – | (179) | – | (179) |
| Cash dividends declared ($0.29 per share) | – | – | (87) | – | – | – | (87) |
| Employee incentive plans and other (4,013,182 shares issued) | – | (9) | – | – | 204 | (18) | 177 |
| Amortization of deferred compensation | – | – | – | – | – | 15 | 15 |
| **BALANCE AT MAY 31, 2004** | **$30** | **$1,079** | **$7,001** | **$(46)** | **$ –** | **$(28)** | **$8,036** |

The accompanying notes are an integral part of these consolidated financial statements.

## NOTE 1: DESCRIPTION OF BUSINESS AND SUMMARY OF SIGNIFICANT ACCOUNTING POLICIES

### DESCRIPTION OF BUSINESS

FedEx Corporation ("FedEx") provides a broad portfolio of transportation, e-commerce and business services with companies that operate independently and compete collectively under the respected FedEx brand. Our operations are primarily represented by Federal Express Corporation ("FedEx Express"), the world's largest express transportation company; FedEx Ground Package System, Inc. ("FedEx Ground"), North America's second largest provider of small-package ground delivery service; FedEx Freight Corporation ("FedEx Freight"), a leading U.S. provider of regional less-than-truckload ("LTL") freight services; and FedEx Kinko's Office and Print Services, Inc. ("FedEx Kinko's"), a leading provider of document solutions and business services. These businesses form the core of our reportable segments. Other business units in the FedEx portfolio are FedEx Trade Networks, Inc. ("FedEx Trade Networks"), a global trade services company; FedEx Supply Chain Services, Inc. ("FedEx Supply Chain Services"), a contract logistics provider; FedEx Custom Critical, Inc. ("FedEx Custom Critical"), a critical-shipment carrier; Caribbean Transportation Services, Inc. ("Caribbean Transportation Services"), a provider of airfreight forwarding services, and FedEx Corporate Services, Inc. ("FedEx Services"), a provider of customer-facing sales, marketing and information technology functions, primarily for FedEx Express and FedEx Ground.

The FedEx Kinko's segment was formed in the fourth quarter of 2004 as a result of our acquisition of FedEx Kinko's (formerly known as Kinko's, Inc.). As discussed in Note 2, we acquired FedEx Kinko's on February 12, 2004, and its results of operations have been included in our financial results from the date of acquisition.

### FISCAL YEARS

Except as otherwise specified, references to years indicate our fiscal year ended May 31, 2004 or ended May 31 of the year referenced.

### PRINCIPLES OF CONSOLIDATION

The consolidated financial statements include the accounts of FedEx and its subsidiaries, substantially all of which are wholly owned. All significant intercompany accounts and transactions have been eliminated.

### CREDIT RISK

We routinely grant credit to many of our customers for transportation and business services without collateral. The risk of credit loss in our trade receivables is substantially mitigated by our credit evaluation process, short collection terms and sales to a large number of customers, as well as the low revenue per transaction for most of our services. Allowances for potential credit losses are determined based on historical experience, current evaluation of the composition of accounts receivable and expected credit trends. Historically, credit losses have been within management's expectations.

### REVENUE RECOGNITION

Revenue is recognized upon delivery of shipments or the completion of the service for our office and print services, logistics and trade services businesses. For shipments in transit, revenue is recorded based on the percentage of service completed at the balance sheet date. Estimates for future billing adjustments to revenue and accounts receivable are recognized at the time of shipment for certain discounts, money-back service guarantees and billing corrections. Delivery costs are accrued as incurred.

Our contract logistics and global trade services businesses engage in certain transactions wherein they act as agents. Revenue from these transactions is recorded on a net basis.

### ADVERTISING

Advertising costs are expensed as incurred and are classified in other operating expenses. Advertising expenses were $284 million, $249 million and $226 million in 2004, 2003 and 2002, respectively.

### CASH EQUIVALENTS

Cash equivalents in excess of current operating requirements are invested in short-term, interest-bearing instruments with maturities of three months or less at the date of purchase and are stated at cost, which approximates market value.

### SPARE PARTS, SUPPLIES AND FUEL

Spare parts are stated principally at weighted-average cost. Supplies and fuel are stated principally at standard cost, which approximates actual cost on a first-in, first-out basis. Allowances for obsolescence are provided, over the estimated useful life of the related aircraft and engines, for spare parts expected to be on hand at the date the aircraft are retired from service, and for spare parts currently identified as excess or obsolete. These allowances are based on management estimates, which are subject to change.

### PROPERTY AND EQUIPMENT

Expenditures for major additions, improvements, flight equipment modifications and certain equipment overhaul costs are capitalized when such costs are determined to extend the useful life of the asset. Maintenance and repairs are charged to expense as incurred, except for certain aircraft-related costs on one of our aircraft fleet types, which are capitalized and amortized over their estimated service lives. We capitalize certain direct internal and external costs associated with the development of internal use software. The cost and accumulated depreciation of property and equipment disposed of are removed from the related accounts, and any gain or loss is reflected in the results of operations. Gains and losses on sales of property used in operations are classified with depreciation and amortization.

For financial reporting purposes, depreciation and amortization of property and equipment is provided on a straight-line basis over the asset's service life or related lease term as follows:

| | Range |
|---|---|
| Wide-body aircraft and related equipment | 15 to 25 years |
| Narrow-body and feeder aircraft and related equipment | 5 to 15 years |
| Package handling and ground support equipment and vehicles | 3 to 30 years |
| Computer and electronic equipment | 3 to 10 years |
| Other | 2 to 40 years |

Substantially all property and equipment have no material residual values. The majority of aircraft costs are depreciated on a straight-line basis over 15 to 18 years, while vehicles are depreciated on a straight-line basis over five to ten years. We periodically evaluate the estimated service lives and residual values used to depreciate our aircraft and other equipment. This evaluation may result in changes in the estimated lives and residual values. The changes did not materially affect depreciation expense in any period presented. Depreciation expense, excluding gains and losses on sales of property and equipment used in operations, was $1.361 billion, $1.334 billion and $1.331 billion in 2004, 2003 and 2002, respectively. Depreciation and amortization expense includes amortization of assets under capital lease.

For income tax purposes, depreciation is generally computed using accelerated methods.

### CAPITALIZED INTEREST

Interest on funds used to finance the acquisition and modification of aircraft, construction of certain facilities and development of certain software up to the date the asset is ready for its intended use is capitalized and included in the cost of the asset. Capitalized interest was $11 million in 2004, $16 million in 2003 and $27 million in 2002.

### IMPAIRMENT OF LONG-LIVED ASSETS

Long-lived assets are reviewed for impairment when circumstances indicate the carrying value of an asset may not be recoverable. For assets that are to be held and used, an impairment is recognized when the estimated undiscounted cash flows associated with the asset or group of assets is less than their carrying value. If impairment exists, an adjustment is made to write the asset down to its fair value, and a loss is recorded as the difference between the carrying value and fair value. Fair values are determined based on quoted market values, discounted cash flows or internal and external appraisals, as applicable. Assets to be disposed of are carried at the lower of carrying value or estimated net realizable value.

### PENSION AND POSTRETIREMENT HEALTHCARE PLANS

These defined benefit plans are measured as of the last day of our fiscal third quarter of each year using actuarial techniques that reflect estimates for mortality, turnover and expected retirement. In addition, management makes assumptions concerning future salary increases, future expected long-term returns on plan assets and future increases in healthcare costs. Discount rates are established as of the measurement date using theoretical bond models that select high-grade corporate bonds with maturities or coupons that correlate to the expected payouts of the applicable liabilities. Assets for funded plans are presented at fair value at the measurement date in the accompanying footnotes. A calculated-value method is employed for purposes of determining the expected return on the plan asset component of net periodic pension cost for our qualified U.S. pension plans. Generally, we do not fund defined benefit plans when such funding provides no current tax deduction.

### GOODWILL

Goodwill is recognized for the excess of the purchase price over the fair value of tangible and identifiable intangible net assets of businesses acquired. Goodwill is reviewed at least annually for impairment. Unless circumstances otherwise dictate, we perform our annual impairment testing in the fourth quarter.

### INTANGIBLE ASSETS

Amortizable intangible assets include customer relationships, contract based, technology based and other. Amortizable intangible assets are amortized over periods ranging from 2 to 15 years, either on a straight-line basis or an accelerated basis using the pattern in which the economic benefits are consumed. Non-amortizing intangible assets include the Kinko's trade name. Non-amortizing intangibles are reviewed at least annually for impairment. Unless circumstances otherwise dictate, we perform our annual impairment testing in the fourth quarter.

### INCOME TAXES

Deferred income taxes are provided for the tax effect of temporary differences between the tax basis of assets and liabilities and their reported amounts in the financial statements. The liability method is used to account for income taxes, which requires deferred taxes to be recorded at the statutory rate to be in effect when the taxes are paid.

We have not recognized deferred taxes for U.S. federal income taxes on foreign subsidiaries' earnings that are deemed to be permanently reinvested and any related taxes associated with such earnings are not material. Pretax earnings of foreign operations for 2004 and 2003 were approximately $430 million and $140 million, respectively, which represent only a portion of total results associated with international shipments.

### SELF-INSURANCE ACCRUALS

We are primarily self-insured for workers' compensation claims, vehicle accidents and general liabilities, benefits paid under employee healthcare programs and long-term disability. Accruals are primarily based on the actuarially estimated, undiscounted cost of claims, which includes incurred-but-not-reported claims. Current workers' compensation claims, vehicle and general liability, employee healthcare claims and long-term disability are included in accrued expenses.

**DEFERRED LEASE OBLIGATIONS**

While certain aircraft, facility and retail location leases contain fluctuating or escalating payments, the related rent expense is recorded on a straight-line basis over the lease term. The deferred lease obligation is the net cumulative excess of rent expense over rent payments.

**DEFERRED GAINS**

Gains on the sale and leaseback of aircraft and other property and equipment are deferred and amortized ratably over the life of the lease as a reduction of rent expense. Substantially all of these deferred gains were related to aircraft transactions.

**EMPLOYEES UNDER COLLECTIVE BARGAINING ARRANGEMENTS**

The pilots of FedEx Express, which represent a small number of FedEx Express total employees, are employed under a collective bargaining agreement. Negotiations with the pilots' union began in March 2004, as the current agreement became amendable on May 31, 2004. We will continue to operate under our current agreement while we negotiate with our pilots.

**STOCK COMPENSATION**

We apply Accounting Principles Board Opinion No. ("APB") 25, "Accounting for Stock Issued to Employees," and its related interpretations to measure compensation expense for stock-based compensation plans. We are required to disclose the pro forma effect of accounting for stock options using a valuation method under Statement of Financial Accounting Standards No. ("SFAS") 123, "Accounting for Stock-Based Compensation," for all options granted in 1996 and thereafter. We have currently not elected to adopt this accounting method because it requires the use of subjective valuation models, which we believe are not representative of the real value of the options to either FedEx or our employees. If compensation cost for stock-based compensation plans had been determined under SFAS 123, pro forma net income, stock option compensation expense, and basic and diluted earnings per common share, assuming all options granted in 1996 and thereafter were valued at fair value using the Black-Scholes method, would have been as follows (in millions, except per share amounts):

| | Years ended May 31, | | |
|---|---|---|---|
| | **2004** | 2003 | 2002 |
| Net income, as reported | **$ 838** | $ 830 | $ 710 |
| Add: Stock compensation included in reported net income, net of tax | **10** | – | – |
| Deduct: Total stock-based employee compensation expense determined under fair value based method for all awards, net of tax benefit | **37** | 34 | 37 |
| Pro forma net income | **$ 811** | $ 796 | $ 673 |
| Earnings per common share: | | | |
| Basic – as reported | **$2.80** | $2.79 | $2.38 |
| Basic – pro forma | **$2.71** | $2.67 | $2.26 |
| Diluted – as reported | **$2.76** | $2.74 | $2.34 |
| Diluted – pro forma | **$2.68** | $2.63 | $2.22 |

See Note 9 for a discussion of the assumptions underlying the pro forma calculations above.

**FOREIGN CURRENCY TRANSLATION**

Translation gains and losses of foreign operations that use local currencies as the functional currency are accumulated and reported, net of applicable deferred income taxes, as a component of accumulated other comprehensive loss within common stockholders' investment. Transaction gains and losses that arise from exchange rate fluctuations on transactions denominated in a currency other than the local currency are included in results of operations. Cumulative net foreign currency translation losses in accumulated other comprehensive loss were $13 million, $13 million and $50 million at May 31, 2004, 2003 and 2002, respectively.

**RECLASSIFICATIONS**

Certain reclassifications have been made to prior year financial statements to conform to the current year presentation.

**USE OF ESTIMATES**

The preparation of our consolidated financial statements requires the use of estimates and assumptions that affect the reported amounts of assets and liabilities, the reported amounts of revenues and expenses and the disclosure of contingent liabilities. Management makes its best estimate of the ultimate outcome for these items based on historical trends and other information available when the financial statements are prepared. Changes in estimates are recognized in accordance with the accounting rules for the estimate, which is typically in the period when new information becomes available to management. Areas where the nature of the estimate makes it reasonably possible that actual results could materially differ from amounts estimated include: self-insurance accruals; employee retirement plan obligations; income tax liabilities; accounts receivable allowances; obsolescence of spare parts; airline stabilization compensation; contingent liabilities; and impairment assessments on long-lived assets (including goodwill and indefinite lived intangible assets).

**NOTE 2: BUSINESS COMBINATIONS**

On February 12, 2004, we acquired FedEx Kinko's for approximately $2.4 billion in cash. We also assumed $39 million of capital lease obligations. FedEx Kinko's is a leading provider of document solutions and business services. Its network of worldwide locations offers access to color printing, finishing and presentation services, Internet access, videoconferencing, outsourcing, managed services, Web-based printing and document management solutions.

The allocation of the purchase price to the fair value of the assets acquired, liabilities assumed and goodwill, as well as the assignment of goodwill to our reportable segments, was based primarily on internal estimates of cash flows and independent appraisals. We used an independent appraisal firm to determine the fair value of certain assets and liabilities, primarily property and equipment and acquired intangible assets, including: the value of the Kinko's trade name, customer-related intangibles, technology assets and contract-based intangibles. While the purchase price allocation is substantially complete and we do not expect any material adjustments, we may make adjustments to the purchase price allocation if new data becomes available.

A significant amount of the purchase price was recorded as goodwill, as the acquisition expands our portfolio of business services, while providing a substantially enhanced capability to provide package-shipping services to small- and medium-sized business customers through FedEx Kinko's array of retail store locations. Because this was an acquisition of stock, goodwill is not deductible for tax purposes. Approximately $200 million of the $1.7 billion goodwill balance will be attributed to the FedEx Express segment ($130 million) and the FedEx Ground segment ($70 million) based on the expected increase in each segment's incremental fair value as a result of the acquisition.

Our balance sheet reflects the following allocation of the total purchase price of $2.4 billion (in millions):

| | |
|---|---|
| Current assets, primarily accounts receivable and inventory | $ 236 |
| Property and equipment | 328 |
| Goodwill | 1,739 |
| Indefinite lived intangible asset (trade name) | 567 |
| Amortizable intangible assets | 82 |
| Other long-term assets | 52 |
| Total assets acquired | 3,004 |
| Current liabilities | (282) |
| Deferred income taxes | (266) |
| Long-term capital lease obligations and other long-term liabilities | (36) |
| Total liabilities assumed | (584) |
| Total purchase price | $2,420 |

*Indefinite lived intangible asset.* This intangible asset represents the estimated fair value allocated to the Kinko's trade name. This intangible asset will not be amortized because it has an indefinite remaining useful life based on the length of time that the Kinko's name had been in use, the Kinko's brand awareness and market position and the plans for continued use of the Kinko's brand.

*Amortizable intangible assets.* These intangible assets represent the value associated with business expected to be generated from existing customer relationships and contracts as of the acquisition date. The value of these assets was primarily determined by measuring the present value of the projected future earnings attributable to these assets. Substantially all of these assets are being amortized on an accelerated basis over a weighted-average estimated useful life of approximately seven years. While the useful life of these customer-relationship assets is not limited by contract or any other economic, regulatory or other known factors, the useful life of seven years was determined at the acquisition date based on management's expectations of customer attrition patterns.

The following unaudited pro forma consolidated financial information presents the combined results of operations of FedEx and FedEx Kinko's as if the acquisition had occurred at the beginning of 2003. The unaudited pro forma results have been prepared for comparative purposes only. Adjustments were made to the combined results of operations, primarily related to higher depreciation and amortization expense resulting from higher property and equipment values and acquired intangible assets and additional interest expense resulting from acquisition debt. The accounting literature establishes firm guidelines around how this pro forma information is presented, which precludes the assumption of business synergies. Therefore, this unaudited pro forma information is not intended to represent, nor do we believe it is indicative of the consolidated results of operations of FedEx that would have been reported had the acquisition been completed as of the beginning of 2003. Furthermore, this pro forma information is not representative of the future consolidated results of operations of FedEx.

Pro forma unaudited results were as follows (in millions, except per share data):

| | Years ended May 31, | |
|---|---|---|
| | **2004**[1] | 2003 |
| Revenues | **$26,056** | $24,427 |
| Net income | **836** | 841 |
| Basic earnings per common share | **2.80** | 2.82 |
| Diluted earnings per common share | **2.75** | 2.78 |

*(1) Includes $27 million, net of tax, of nonrecurring expenses at FedEx Kinko's, primarily in anticipation of the acquisition. Also, includes $270 million, net of tax, of business realignment costs and a $37 million, net of tax, nonrecurring tax benefit at FedEx.*

We paid a portion of the purchase price from available cash balances. To finance the remainder of the purchase price, we entered into a six-month credit facility for $2 billion. During February 2004, we issued commercial paper backed by unused commitments under this facility. In March 2004, we issued $1.6 billion of senior unsecured notes in three maturity tranches: one, three and five years at $600 million, $500 million and $500 million, respectively. Net proceeds from the borrowings were used to repay the commercial paper backed by the six-month credit facility. We canceled the six-month credit facility in March 2004. See Note 6 for further discussion.

On March 1, 2002, a subsidiary of FedEx Trade Networks acquired for cash certain assets of Fritz Companies, Inc. that provide essential customs clearance services exclusively for FedEx Express in three U.S. locations, at a cost of $36.5 million. The excess cost over the estimated fair value of the net assets acquired (approximately $35 million) was recorded as goodwill, which was entirely attributed to the FedEx Express segment. Goodwill for tax purposes associated with this transaction will be deductible over 15 years. Pro forma results including this acquisition would not differ materially from reported results.

These acquisitions were accounted for under the purchase method of accounting. The operating results of the acquired businesses are included in our consolidated results of operations from the date of acquisition.

### NOTE 3: GOODWILL AND INTANGIBLES

Effective June 1, 2001, we adopted SFAS 142, "Goodwill and Other Intangible Assets," which establishes new accounting and reporting requirements for goodwill and other intangible assets. Under SFAS 142, material amounts of recorded goodwill attributable to each of our reporting units were tested for impairment by comparing the fair value of each reporting unit with its carrying value (including attributable goodwill). Fair value was determined using a discounted cash flow methodology. Based on our initial impairment tests when the statement was adopted, we recognized an adjustment of $25 million ($15 million or $0.05 per share, net of tax) in 2002 to reduce the carrying value of certain goodwill. Under SFAS 142, the impairment adjustment recognized at adoption of the new rules was reflected as a cumulative effect of accounting change in our 2002 consolidated statement of income.

The carrying amount of goodwill attributable to each reportable operating segment and changes therein follows (in millions):

| | May 31, 2003 | Goodwill Acquired During the Year | **May 31, 2004** |
|---|---|---|---|
| FedEx Express segment | $ 397 | $ 130[1] | **$ 527** |
| FedEx Ground segment | – | 70[1] | **70** |
| FedEx Freight segment | 666 | – | **666** |
| FedEx Kinko's segment | – | 1,539 | **1,539** |
| | $1,063 | $1,739 | **$2,802** |

*(1) These amounts represent goodwill from the FedEx Kinko's acquisition that is attributable to the FedEx Express and FedEx Ground segments.*

The components of our intangible assets were as follows (in millions):

| | **May 31, 2004** | | May 31, 2003 | |
|---|---|---|---|---|
| | Gross Carrying Amount | Accumulated Amortization | Gross Carrying Amount | Accumulated Amortization |
| **Amortizable intangible assets** | | | | |
| Customer relationships | **$ 72** | **$ (3)** | $ – | $ – |
| Contract related | **79** | **(43)** | 73 | (37) |
| Technology related and other | **45** | **(17)** | 40 | (12) |
| Total | **$196** | **$(63)** | $113 | $(49) |
| **Non-amortizing intangible asset** | | | | |
| Trade name | **$567** | **$ –** | $ – | $ – |

Amortization expense for intangible assets was $14 million in 2004, $13 million in 2003 and $14 million in 2002. Estimated amortization expense for the next five years is as follows (in millions):

| | |
|---|---|
| 2005 | $24 |
| 2006 | 23 |
| 2007 | 21 |
| 2008 | 20 |
| 2009 | 17 |

### NOTE 4: BUSINESS REALIGNMENT COSTS

During 2004, voluntary early retirement incentives with enhanced pension and postretirement healthcare benefits were offered to certain groups of employees at FedEx Express who were age 50 or older. Voluntary cash severance incentives were also offered to eligible employees at FedEx Express. These programs, which commenced August 1, 2003 and expired during the second quarter, were limited to eligible U.S. salaried staff employees and managers. Approximately 3,600 employees accepted offers under these voluntary programs, which considerably exceeded our expectations. Costs were also incurred in 2004 for the elimination of certain management positions at FedEx Express and other business units based on the staff reductions from the voluntary programs and other cost reduction initiatives.

Costs for the benefits provided under the voluntary programs were recognized in the period that eligible employees accepted the offer. Other costs associated with business realignment activities were recognized in the period incurred. The savings from these initiatives will be reflected primarily in lower salaries and benefits costs.

The components of our business realignment costs and changes in the related accruals were as follows for the year ended May 31, 2004 (in millions):

| | Voluntary Retirement | Voluntary Severance | Other[1] | Total |
|---|---|---|---|---|
| Beginning accrual balances | $ – | $ – | $ – | $ – |
| Charged to expense | 202 | 158 | 75 | 435 |
| Cash paid | (8) | (152) | (31) | (191) |
| Amounts charged to other assets/liabilities | (194) | – | (22) | (216) |
| Ending accrual balances | $ – | $ 6 | $ 22 | $ 28 |

*(1) Other includes costs for management severance agreements, which are payable over future periods, including compensation related to the modification of previously granted stock options and incremental pension and healthcare benefits. Other also includes professional fees directly associated with the business realignment initiatives and relocation costs.*

Amounts charged to other assets/liabilities relate primarily to incremental pension and healthcare benefits.

FEDEX CORPORATION

## NOTE 5: SELECTED CURRENT LIABILITIES

The components of selected current liability captions were as follows (in millions):

| | May 31, 2004 | 2003 |
|---|---|---|
| **Accrued Salaries and Employee Benefits** | | |
| Salaries | **$ 163** | $ 119 |
| Employee benefits | **496** | 227 |
| Compensated absences | **403** | 378 |
| | **$1,062** | $ 724 |
| **Accrued Expenses** | | |
| Self-insurance accruals | **$ 442** | $ 401 |
| Taxes other than income taxes | **291** | 279 |
| Other | **572** | 455 |
| | **$1,305** | $1,135 |

## NOTE 6: LONG-TERM DEBT AND OTHER FINANCING ARRANGEMENTS

The components of our long-term debt were as follows (in millions):

| | May 31, 2004 | 2003 |
|---|---|---|
| Unsecured debt | **$2,855** | $1,529 |
| Capital lease obligations | **534** | 422 |
| Other debt, interest rates of 2.35% to 9.98% due through 2017 | **198** | 66 |
| | **3,587** | 2,017 |
| Less current portion | **750** | 308 |
| | **$2,837** | $1,709 |

At May 31, 2004, we had two revolving bank credit facilities totaling $1 billion. One revolver provides for $750 million through September 28, 2006. The second is a 364-day facility providing for $250 million through September 24, 2004. Interest rates on borrowings under the agreements are generally determined by maturities selected and prevailing market conditions. Borrowings under the credit agreements will bear interest, at our option, at a rate per annum equal to either (a) the London Interbank Offered Rate ("LIBOR") plus a credit spread, or (b) the higher of the Federal Funds Effective Rate, as defined, plus 1/2 of 1%, or the bank's Prime Rate. The revolving credit agreements contain certain covenants and restrictions, none of which are expected to significantly affect our operations or ability to pay dividends.

From time to time, we finance certain operating and investing activities, including acquisitions, through the issuance of commercial paper. Our commercial paper program is backed by unused commitments under our revolving credit agreements and reduces the amounts available under the agreements. As of May 31, 2004 and 2003, no commercial paper borrowings were outstanding and the entire $1 billion under the revolving credit agreements was available.

The components of unsecured debt (net of discounts) were as follows (in millions):

| | May 31, 2004 | 2003 |
|---|---|---|
| Senior unsecured debt | | |
| Interest rate of three-month LIBOR (1.11% at May 31, 2004) plus 0.28%, due in 2005 | **$ 600** | $ – |
| Interest rate of 7.80%, due in 2007 | **200** | 200 |
| Interest rate of 2.65%, due in 2007 | **500** | – |
| Interest rate of 3.50%, due in 2009 | **499** | – |
| Interest rates of 6.63% to 7.25%, due through 2011 | **499** | 747 |
| Interest rate of 9.65%, due in 2013 | **299** | 299 |
| Interest rate of 7.60%, due in 2098 | **239** | 239 |
| Medium term notes, interest rates of 8.00% to 10.57%, due through 2007 | **19** | 44 |
| | **$2,855** | $1,529 |

To finance our acquisition of FedEx Kinko's, we entered into a six-month credit facility for $2 billion. During February 2004, we issued commercial paper backed by unused commitments under this facility. In March 2004, we issued $1.6 billion of senior unsecured notes in three maturity tranches: one, three and five years, at $600 million, $500 million and $500 million, respectively. Net proceeds from these borrowings were used to repay the commercial paper backed by the six-month credit facility. We canceled the six-month credit facility in March 2004.

In conjunction with the acquisition of FedEx Freight East in February 2001, debt of $240 million was assumed, a portion of which was refinanced subsequent to the acquisition. On April 5, 2002, we prepaid the remaining $101 million. Under the debt agreements, we incurred a prepayment penalty of $13 million, which was included in other nonoperating expense in 2002.

Capital lease obligations include certain special facility revenue bonds that have been issued by municipalities primarily to finance the acquisition and construction of various airport facilities and equipment. These bonds require interest payments at least annually with principal payments due at the end of the related lease agreements. In addition, during 2004, FedEx Express amended two leases for MD11 aircraft and during 2003, FedEx Express amended four leases for MD11 aircraft, which commit FedEx Express to firm purchase obligations for two of these aircraft during both 2005 and 2006. These amended leases were accounted for as capital leases from the date of amendment.

Other long-term debt includes $133 million related to two leased MD11 aircraft that are consolidated under the provisions of Financial Accounting Standards Board Interpretation No. ("FIN") 46, "Consolidation of Variable Interest Entities, an Interpretation of ARB No. 51." The debt requires interest at LIBOR plus a margin and is due in installments through March 30, 2007. See Note 16 for further discussion.

We incur other commercial commitments in the normal course of business to support our operations. Letters of credit at May 31, 2004 were $498 million. The amount unused under our letter of credit facility totaled $114 million at May 31, 2004. This facility expires in May of 2006. These instruments are generally required under certain U.S. self-insurance programs and are used in the normal course of international operations. The underlying liabilities insured by these instruments are reflected in the balance sheet, where applicable. Therefore, no additional liability is reflected for the letters of credit.

Scheduled annual principal maturities of debt, exclusive of capital leases, for the five years subsequent to May 31, 2004, are as follows (in millions):

| | |
|---|---|
| 2005 | $613 |
| 2006 | 265 |
| 2007 | 844 |
| 2008 | – |
| 2009 | 499 |

Long-term debt, exclusive of capital leases, had carrying values of $3.0 billion and $1.6 billion at May 31, 2004 and 2003, respectively, compared with estimated fair values of approximately $3.2 billion and $1.9 billion at those respective dates. The estimated fair values were determined based on quoted market prices or on the current rates offered for debt with similar terms and maturities.

We have a $1.0 billion shelf registration statement with the SEC to provide flexibility and efficiency when obtaining financing. Under this shelf registration statement we may issue, in one or more offerings, either unsecured debt securities, common stock or a combination of such instruments. The entire $1 billion is available for future financings.

## NOTE 7: LEASE COMMITMENTS

We utilize certain aircraft, land, facilities, retail locations and equipment under capital and operating leases that expire at various dates through 2039. In addition, supplemental aircraft are leased under agreements that generally provide for cancelation upon 30 days' notice.

The components of property and equipment recorded under capital leases were as follows (in millions):

| | May 31, 2004 | May 31, 2003 |
|---|---|---|
| Aircraft | **$344** | $221 |
| Package handling and ground support equipment and vehicles | **207** | 207 |
| Other, principally facilities | **230** | 137 |
| | **781** | 565 |
| Less accumulated amortization | **390** | 268 |
| | **$391** | $297 |

Rent expense under operating leases was as follows (in millions):

| | For years ended May 31, 2004 | 2003 | 2002 |
|---|---|---|---|
| Minimum rentals | **$1,560** | $1,522 | $1,453 |
| Contingent rentals | **143** | 107 | 132 |
| | **$1,703** | $1,629 | $1,585 |

Contingent rentals are based on equipment usage.

A summary of future minimum lease payments under capital leases and noncancelable operating leases (principally aircraft, retail locations and facilities) with an initial or remaining term in excess of one year at May 31, 2004 is as follows (in millions):

| | Capital Leases | Operating Leases |
|---|---|---|
| 2005 | $160 | $ 1,707 |
| 2006 | 122 | 1,555 |
| 2007 | 22 | 1,436 |
| 2008 | 99 | 1,329 |
| 2009 | 11 | 1,169 |
| Thereafter | 225 | 7,820 |
| | 639 | $15,016 |
| Less amount representing interest | 105 | |
| Present value of net minimum lease payments | $534 | |

FedEx Express makes payments under certain leveraged operating leases that are sufficient to pay principal and interest on certain pass-through certificates. The pass-through certificates are not direct obligations of, or guaranteed by, FedEx or FedEx Express.

## NOTE 8: PREFERRED STOCK

Our Certificate of Incorporation authorizes the Board of Directors, at its discretion, to issue up to 4,000,000 shares of series preferred stock. The stock is issuable in series, which may vary as to certain rights and preferences, and has no par value. As of May 31, 2004, none of these shares had been issued.

## NOTE 9: COMMON STOCKHOLDERS' INVESTMENT

### TREASURY SHARES

The following table summarizes information about treasury share repurchases for the years ended May 31:

| | 2004 Shares | 2004 Average Price Per Share | 2003 Shares | 2003 Average Price Per Share | 2002 Shares | 2002 Average Price Per Share |
|---|---|---|---|---|---|---|
| Repurchased | **2,625,000** | **$68.14** | 3,275,000 | $56.66 | 3,350,000 | $52.70 |

These repurchases were done under share repurchase programs aggregating 15 million shares. A total of 5.75 million shares remain under existing share repurchase authorizations. At May 31, 2004 and 2003, respectively, 4,760 and 406,304 shares remained outstanding in treasury.

## STOCK COMPENSATION PLANS

### Fixed Stock Option Plans

Under the provisions of our stock incentive plans, key employees and non-employee directors may be granted options to purchase shares of common stock at a price not less than its fair market value at the date of grant. Options granted have a maximum term of 10 years. Vesting requirements are determined at the discretion of the Compensation Committee of our Board of Directors. Option-vesting periods range from one to four years with more than 80% of stock option grants vesting ratably over four years. At May 31, 2004, there were 4,140,440 shares available for future grants under these plans.

The weighted-average fair value of these grants, calculated using the Black-Scholes valuation method under the assumptions indicated below, was $18.02, $17.12 and $12.39 per option in 2004, 2003 and 2002, respectively.

We are required to disclose the pro forma effect of accounting for stock options using such a valuation method for all options granted in 1996 and thereafter (see Note 1). We use the Black-Scholes option-pricing model to calculate the fair value of options for our pro forma disclosures. The key assumptions for this valuation method include the expected life of the option, stock price volatility, risk-free interest rate, dividend yield, forfeiture rate and exercise price. Many of these assumptions are judgmental and highly sensitive in the determination of pro forma compensation expense. Following is a table of the key weighted-average assumptions used in the option valuation calculations for the options granted in the years ended May 31, 2004, 2003 and 2002, and a discussion of our methodology for developing each of the assumptions used in the valuation model:

| | May 31, | | |
|---|---|---|---|
| | **2004** | 2003 | 2002 |
| Expected lives | **4 years** | 4 years | 4 years |
| Expected volatility | **32%** | 35% | 30% |
| Risk-free interest rate | **2.118%** | 4.017% | 4.777% |
| Dividend yield | **0.3102%** | 0.3785% | 0% |

*Expected Lives.* This is the period of time over which the options granted are expected to remain outstanding. Generally, options granted have a maximum term of 10 years. We examine actual stock option exercises to determine the expected life of the options. An increase in the expected term will increase compensation expense.

*Expected Volatility.* Actual changes in the market value of our stock are used to calculate the volatility assumption. We calculate daily market value changes from the date of grant over a past period equal to the expected life of the options to determine volatility. An increase in the expected volatility will increase compensation expense.

*Risk-Free Interest Rate.* This is the U.S. Treasury Strip rate posted at the date of grant having a term equal to the expected life of the option. An increase in the risk-free interest rate will increase compensation expense.

*Dividend Yield.* This is the annual rate of dividends per share over the exercise price of the option. In July 2002, we paid the first dividend in the history of the company. Therefore, the fair value of options prior to 2003 is not affected by the dividend yield. An increase in the dividend yield will decrease compensation expense.

*Forfeiture Rate.* This is the estimated percentage of options granted that are expected to be forfeited or canceled before becoming fully vested. This percentage is derived from historical experience. An increase in the forfeiture rate will decrease compensation expense. Our forfeiture rate is approximately 8%.

The following table summarizes information about our fixed stock option plans for the years ended May 31:

| | 2004 | | 2003 | | 2002 | |
|---|---|---|---|---|---|---|
| | Shares | Weighted-Average Exercise Price | Shares | Weighted-Average Exercise Price | Shares | Weighted-Average Exercise Price |
| Outstanding at beginning of year | **17,315,116** | **$38.88** | 17,306,014 | $34.32 | 17,498,558 | $30.24 |
| Granted | **3,937,628** | **64.96** | 3,261,800 | 53.22 | 4,023,098 | 40.66 |
| Exercised | **(3,724,605)** | **31.05** | (2,951,154) | 27.73 | (3,875,767) | 22.34 |
| Forfeited | **(178,832)** | **46.71** | (301,544) | 40.47 | (339,875) | 35.06 |
| Outstanding at end of year | **17,349,307** | **46.39** | 17,315,116 | 38.88 | 17,306,014 | 34.32 |
| Exercisable at end of year | **8,747,523** | **38.28** | 8,829,515 | 33.58 | 8,050,362 | 29.98 |

The following table summarizes information about fixed stock options outstanding at May 31, 2004:

| | Options Outstanding | | | Options Exercisable | |
|---|---|---|---|---|---|
| Range of Exercise Price | Number Outstanding | Weighted-Average Remaining Contractual Life | Weighted-Average Exercise Price | Number Exercisable | Weighted-Average Exercise Price |
| $14.59 – $21.89 | 970,670 | 1.9 years | $19.15 | 970,670 | $19.15 |
| 21.97 – 32.95 | 2,500,525 | 3.7 years | 29.71 | 2,437,553 | 29.86 |
| 33.02 – 49.52 | 5,635,270 | 6.6 years | 39.58 | 3,248,939 | 39.49 |
| 49.71 – 73.67 | 8,242,842 | 8.0 years | 59.31 | 2,090,361 | 55.09 |
| 14.59 – 73.67 | 17,349,307 | 6.6 years | 46.39 | 8,747,523 | 38.28 |

Total equity compensation shares outstanding or available for grant represented approximately 7.1% and 7.3% of total outstanding common and equity compensation shares and equity compensation shares available for grant at May 31, 2004 and May 31, 2003, respectively.

**Stock Options Expensed**

Under our business realignment programs discussed in Note 4, we recognized approximately $16 million of expense ($10 million, net of tax) during 2004 related to the modification of previously granted stock options. We calculated this expense using the Black-Scholes method.

**Restricted Stock Plans**

Under the terms of our restricted stock plans, shares of common stock are awarded to key employees. All restrictions on the shares expire ratably over a four-year period. Shares are valued at the market price at the date of award. Compensation related to these plans is recorded as a reduction of common stockholders' investment and is amortized to expense as restrictions on such shares expire.

The following table summarizes information about restricted stock awards for the years ended May 31:

| | 2004 | | 2003 | | 2002 | |
|---|---|---|---|---|---|---|
| | Shares | Weighted-Average Fair Value | Shares | Weighted-Average Fair Value | Shares | Weighted-Average Fair Value |
| Awarded | **282,423** | **$67.11** | 343,500 | $47.56 | 329,500 | $43.01 |
| Forfeited | **10,000** | **43.41** | 17,438 | 48.01 | 12,000 | 49.79 |

At May 31, 2004, there were 747,553 shares available for future awards under these plans. Annual compensation cost for the restricted stock plans was approximately $14 million for 2004, and $12 million for 2003 and 2002.

FEDEX CORPORATION

## NOTE 10: COMPUTATION OF EARNINGS PER SHARE

The calculation of basic earnings per common share and diluted earnings per common share for the years ended May 31 was as follows (in millions, except per share amounts):

| | 2004 | 2003 | 2002 |
|---|---|---|---|
| Net income applicable to common stockholders | **$ 838** | $ 830 | $ 710 |
| Weighted-average shares of common stock outstanding | **299** | 298 | 298 |
| Common equivalent shares: | | | |
| Assumed exercise of outstanding dilutive options | **19** | 15 | 16 |
| Less shares repurchased from proceeds of assumed exercise of options | **(14)** | (10) | (11) |
| Weighted-average common and common equivalent shares outstanding | **304** | 303 | 303 |
| Basic earnings per common share | **$2.80** | $2.79 | $2.38 |
| Diluted earnings per common share | **$2.76** | $2.74 | $2.34 |

## NOTE 11: INCOME TAXES

The components of the provision for income taxes for the years ended May 31 were as follows (in millions):

| | 2004 | 2003 | 2002 |
|---|---|---|---|
| Current provision | | | |
| Domestic: | | | |
| Federal | **$371** | $112 | $255 |
| State and local | **54** | 28 | 39 |
| Foreign | **85** | 39 | 41 |
| | **510** | 179 | 335 |
| Deferred (benefit) provision | | | |
| Domestic: | | | |
| Federal | **(22)** | 304 | 99 |
| State and local | **(7)** | 25 | 3 |
| Foreign | **–** | – | (2) |
| | **(29)** | 329 | 100 |
| | **$481** | $508 | $435 |

A reconciliation of the statutory federal income tax rate to the effective income tax rate for the years ended May 31 was as follows:

| | 2004 | 2003 | 2002 |
|---|---|---|---|
| Statutory U.S. income tax rate | **35.0%** | 35.0% | 35.0% |
| Increase resulting from: | | | |
| State and local income taxes, net of federal benefit | **2.3** | 2.6 | 2.4 |
| Other, net | **(0.8)** | 0.4 | 0.1 |
| Effective tax rate | **36.5%** | 38.0% | 37.5% |

The lower effective tax rate in 2004 was primarily attributable to the favorable decision in our U.S. tax case described below, stronger than anticipated international results and the results of tax audits during 2004. Our stronger than anticipated international results, along with other factors, increased our ability to credit income taxes paid to foreign governments on foreign income against U.S. income taxes paid on the same income, thereby mitigating our exposure to double taxation. The 38.0% effective tax rate in 2003 was higher than the 2002 rate primarily due to lower state taxes in 2002.

The significant components of deferred tax assets and liabilities as of May 31 were as follows (in millions):

| | 2004 | | 2003 | |
|---|---|---|---|---|
| | Deferred Tax Assets | Deferred Tax Liabilities | Deferred Tax Assets | Deferred Tax Liabilities |
| Property, equipment, leases and intangibles | **$ 310** | **$1,372** | $ 303 | $ 946 |
| Employee benefits | **386** | **406** | 270 | 407 |
| Self-insurance accruals | **297** | **–** | 259 | – |
| Other | **277** | **179** | 261 | 207 |
| Net operating loss/credit carryforwards | **32** | **–** | 15 | – |
| Valuation allowance | **(37)** | **–** | (14) | – |
| | **$1,265** | **$1,957** | $1,094 | $1,560 |

In 2004, the net deferred tax liability of $692 million is classified in the balance sheet as a current deferred tax asset of $489 million and a noncurrent deferred tax liability of $1.181 billion. In 2003, the net deferred tax liability of $466 million is classified in the balance sheet as a current deferred tax asset of $416 million and a noncurrent deferred tax liability of $882 million.

The valuation allowance primarily represents amounts reserved for operating loss and tax credit carryforwards, which expire over varying periods starting in 2005. As a result of this and other factors, we believe that a substantial portion of these deferred tax assets may not be realized. The net increase in the valuation allowance of $23 million was principally due to net operating loss/credit carryforwards obtained upon the acquisition of FedEx Kinko's during the third quarter of 2004 that are not expected to be realized.

In August 2003, we received a favorable ruling from the U.S. District Court in Memphis over the tax treatment of jet engine maintenance costs. The Court held that these costs were ordinary and necessary business expenses and properly deductible by us. In connection with an Internal Revenue Service ("IRS") audit for the tax years 1993 and 1994, the IRS had proposed adjustments characterizing routine jet engine maintenance costs as capital expenditures that must be recovered over seven years, rather than as expenses that are deducted immediately, as has been our practice. After settlement discussions failed to resolve this matter, in 2001 we paid $70 million in tax and interest and filed suit in Federal District Court for a complete refund of the amounts paid plus interest. Although the IRS has continued to assert its position in audits for the years 1995 through 2000 with respect to maintenance costs for jet engines and rotable aircraft parts, we believe this ruling should also apply to future tax years.

As a result of this ruling, we recognized a one-time benefit in 2004 of $26 million, net of tax, primarily related to the reduction of accruals related to this matter and the recognition of interest earned on the amount we paid in 2001. These adjustments affected both net interest expense ($30 million pretax) and income tax expense ($7 million). Future periods are not expected to be materially affected by the resolution of this matter. On November 19, 2003, the IRS appealed this ruling to the Sixth Circuit Court of Appeals. All briefs have been filed in the case. We believe the District Court's ruling will be upheld on appeal.

## NOTE 12: EMPLOYEE BENEFIT PLANS

### Pension Plans

We sponsor defined benefit pension plans covering a majority of our employees. The largest plan covers certain U.S. employees age 21 and over, with at least one year of service. Eligible employees as of May 31, 2003 were given the opportunity to make a one-time election to accrue future pension benefits under either a new cash balance formula which we call the Portable Pension Account or a traditional pension benefit formula. Benefits provided under the traditional formula are based on average earnings and years of service. Under the Portable Pension Account, the retirement benefit is expressed as a dollar amount in a notional account that grows with annual credits based on pay, age, and years of credited service, and interest on the notional account balance. In either case, employees retained all benefits previously accrued under the traditional pension benefit formula and continue to receive the benefit of future salary increases on benefits accrued as of May 31, 2003. Eligible employees hired after May 31, 2003 receive benefits exclusively under the Portable Pension Account.

Plan funding is actuarially determined and is subject to certain tax law limitations. International defined benefit pension plans provide benefits primarily based on final earnings and years of service and are funded in accordance with local laws and income tax regulations. Substantially all plan assets are actively managed. The weighted-average asset allocation for our primary pension plan at February 29, 2004 was as follows:

| | Actual | Target |
|---|---|---|
| Domestic equities | 54% | 53% |
| International equities | 19 | 17 |
| Private equities | 3 | 5 |
| Long duration fixed income securities | 16 | 15 |
| Other fixed income securities | 8 | 10 |
| | 100% | 100% |

The investment strategy for pension plan assets is to utilize a diversified mix of global public and private equity portfolios, together with public and private fixed income portfolios, to earn a long-term investment return that meets our pension plan obligations. Active management strategies are utilized within the plan in an effort to realize investment returns in excess of market indices.

Our pension cost is materially affected by the discount rate used to measure pension obligations, the level of plan assets available to fund those obligations at the measurement date and the expected long-term rate of return on plan assets. Due to a lower discount rate, a lower expected long-term rate of return and a reduction in the value of plan assets as a result of investment losses at the measurement date for 2004 pension expense (February 28, 2003), our total net pension cost for 2004 increased by approximately $115 million.

An increase in pension cost of approximately $30 million is expected for 2005 based primarily on a continuing decline in the discount rate (to 6.78%). Management reviews the assumptions used to measure pension costs (including the discount rate and the expected long-term rate of return on pension assets) on an annual basis. Economic and market conditions at the measurement date impact these assumptions from year to year and it is reasonably possible that material changes in pension cost may continue to be experienced in the future.

Establishing the expected future rate of investment return on our pension assets is a judgmental matter. Management considers the following factors in determining this assumption:

- the duration of our pension plan liabilities, which drives the investment strategy we can employ with our pension plan assets.
- the types of investment classes in which we invest our pension plan assets and the expected compound return we can reasonably expect those investment classes to earn over the next 10- to 15-year time period (or such other time period that may be appropriate).
- the investment returns we can reasonably expect our active investment management program to achieve in excess of the returns we could expect if investments were made strictly in indexed funds.

We review the expected long-term rate of return on an annual basis and revise it as appropriate. Also, we periodically commission detailed asset/liability studies performed by third-party professional investment advisors and actuaries. These studies project our estimated future pension payments and evaluate the efficiency of the allocation of our pension plan assets into various investment categories. These studies also generate probability-adjusted expected future returns on those assets. The study performed for 2003 supported the reasonableness of our 10.10% return assumption used for 2003 based on our liability duration and market conditions at the time we set this assumption (in 2002). We performed a more recent asset/liability study for 2004, which supported a long-term return on assets of 9.10%. The results of this study were reaffirmed for 2005 by our third-party professional investment advisors and actuaries.

FEDEX CORPORATION

**Postretirement Healthcare Plans**

Certain of our subsidiaries offer medical, dental and vision coverage to eligible U.S. retirees and their eligible dependents. U.S. employees covered by the principal plan become eligible for these benefits at age 55 and older, if they have permanent, continuous service of at least 10 years after attainment of age 45 if hired prior to January 1, 1988, or at least 20 years after attainment of age 35 if hired on or after January 1, 1988.

The following table provides a reconciliation of the changes in the pension and postretirement healthcare plans' benefit obligations and fair value of assets over the two-year period ended May 31, 2004 and a statement of the funded status as of May 31, 2004 and 2003 (in millions):

| | Pension Plans | | Postretirement Healthcare Plans | |
|---|---|---|---|---|
| | **2004** | 2003 | **2004** | 2003 |
| **Changes in Projected Benefit Obligation ("PBO")** | | | | |
| Projected benefit obligation at the beginning of year | **$ 7,117** | $ 6,227 | **$ 382** | $ 329 |
| Service cost | **376** | 374 | **35** | 27 |
| Interest cost | **490** | 438 | **25** | 25 |
| Actuarial loss | **661** | 164 | **36** | 23 |
| Benefits paid | **(136)** | (103) | **(23)** | (21) |
| Special termination benefits(1) | **158** | – | **38** | – |
| Amendments, benefit enhancements and other | **17** | 17 | **3** | (1) |
| Projected benefit obligation at the end of year | **$ 8,683** | $ 7,117 | **$ 496** | $ 382 |
| **Accumulated Benefit Obligation ("ABO")** | **$ 7,427** | $ 6,009 | | |
| **Change in Plan Assets** | | | | |
| Fair value of plan assets at beginning of year | **$ 5,825** | $ 5,510 | **$ –** | $ – |
| Actual return (loss) on plan assets | **1,751** | (663) | **–** | – |
| Company contributions | **335** | 1,072 | **16** | 18 |
| Benefits paid | **(136)** | (103) | **(23)** | (21) |
| Other | **8** | 9 | **7** | 3 |
| Fair value of plan assets at end of year | **$ 7,783** | $ 5,825 | **$ –** | $ – |
| **Funded Status of the Plans** | **$ (900)** | $ (1,292) | **$ (496)** | $ (382) |
| Unrecognized actuarial loss (gain) | **1,694** | 2,247 | **(1)** | (38) |
| Unamortized prior service cost (benefit) | **118** | 123 | **1** | (1) |
| Unrecognized transition amount | **(5)** | (7) | **–** | – |
| Prepaid (accrued) benefit cost | **$ 907** | $ 1,071 | **$ (496)** | $ (421) |
| **Amount Recognized in the Balance Sheet at May 31:** | | | | |
| Prepaid benefit cost | **$ 1,127** | $ 1,269 | **$ –** | $ – |
| Accrued benefit liability | **(220)** | (198) | **(496)** | (421) |
| Minimum pension liability | **(67)** | (42) | **–** | – |
| Accumulated other comprehensive income(2) | **54** | 26 | **–** | – |
| Intangible asset | **13** | 16 | **–** | – |
| Prepaid (accrued) benefit cost | **$ 907** | $ 1,071 | **$ (496)** | $ (421) |

*(1) The special termination benefits reflected in the table above related primarily to early retirement incentives offered to certain groups of our employees at FedEx Express during 2004 (see Note 4 for more information).*

*(2) The minimum pension liability component of Accumulated Other Comprehensive Income is shown in the Statement of Changes in Stockholders' Investment and Comprehensive Income, net of deferred taxes.*

NOTES TO CONSOLIDATED FINANCIAL STATEMENTS

Our pension plans included the following components at May 31, 2004 and 2003 (in millions):

| | U.S. Plans | | | | | | | |
|---|---|---|---|---|---|---|---|---|
| | Qualified | | Nonqualified | | International Plans | | Total | |
| | **2004** | 2003 | **2004** | 2003 | **2004** | 2003 | **2004** | 2003 |
| ABO | **$7,069** | $ 5,725 | **$ 166** | $ 130 | **$ 192** | $ 154 | **$7,427** | $ 6,009 |
| PBO | **$8,274** | $ 6,793 | **$ 179** | $ 144 | **$ 230** | $ 180 | **$8,683** | $ 7,117 |
| Fair Value of Plan Assets | **7,678** | 5,747 | **–** | – | **105** | 78 | **7,783** | 5,825 |
| Funded Status | **$ (596)** | $ (1,046) | **$ (179)** | $ (144) | **$ (125)** | $ (102) | **$ (900)** | $ (1,292) |
| Unrecognized actuarial loss | **1,621** | 2,208 | **32** | 5 | **41** | 34 | **1,694** | 2,247 |
| Unamortized prior service cost | **95** | 105 | **20** | 18 | **3** | – | **118** | 123 |
| Unrecognized transition amount | **(7)** | (8) | **–** | – | **2** | 1 | **(5)** | (7) |
| Prepaid (accrued) benefit cost | **$1,113** | $ 1,259 | **$ (127)** | $ (121) | **$ (79)** | $ (67) | **$ 907** | $ 1,071 |

The projected benefit obligation ("PBO") is the actuarial present value of benefits attributable to employee service rendered to date, including the effects of estimated future pay increases. The accumulated benefit obligation ("ABO") also reflects the actuarial present value of benefits attributable to employee service rendered to date, but does not include the effects of estimated future pay increases. Therefore, the ABO as compared to plan assets is an indication of the assets currently available to fund vested and nonvested benefits accrued through May 31.

The measure of whether a pension plan is underfunded for financial accounting purposes is based on a comparison of the ABO to the fair value of plan assets and amounts accrued for such benefits in the balance sheet. In order to eliminate the need to recognize an additional minimum pension liability (generally required when the ABO exceeds the fair value of plan assets at the measurement date), we made $1.1 billion of tax-deductible contributions to our qualified U.S. pension plans in 2003. In 2004, we made $320 million in tax-deductible contributions. No contributions for 2004 or 2003 were legally required and none are expected to be required in 2005. Based on the substantial improvement in the funded status of our qualified plans, we do not currently expect to contribute any funds to our qualified defined benefit plans in 2005.

We have certain nonqualified defined benefit pension plans that are not funded because such funding would be deemed current compensation to plan participants. Primarily related to those plans and certain international plans, we have ABOs aggregating approximately $356 million at May 31, 2004 and $284 million at May 31, 2003, with assets of $105 million at May 31, 2004 and $78 million at May 31, 2003. Plans with this funded status resulted in the recognition of a minimum pension liability in our balance sheets. This minimum liability was $67 million at May 31, 2004 and $42 million at May 31, 2003.

FEDEX CORPORATION

Net periodic benefit cost for the three years ended May 31 was as follows (in millions):

| | Pension Plans | | | Postretirement Healthcare Plans | | |
|---|---|---|---|---|---|---|
| | 2004 | 2003 | 2002 | 2004 | 2003 | 2002 |
| Service cost | **$ 376** | $ 374 | $ 348 | **$ 35** | $ 27 | $ 27 |
| Interest cost | **490** | 438 | 409 | **25** | 25 | 25 |
| Expected return on plan assets | **(597)** | (594) | (621) | **–** | – | – |
| Net amortization and deferral | **74** | 10 | 13 | **–** | (2) | (2) |
| | **$ 343** | $ 228 | $ 149 | **$ 60** | $ 50 | $ 50 |

Weighted-average actuarial assumptions for our primary U.S. plans, which comprise substantially all of our projected benefit obligations, were as follows:

| | Pension Plans | | | Postretirement Healthcare Plans | | |
|---|---|---|---|---|---|---|
| | 2004 | 2003 | 2002 | 2004 | 2003 | 2002 |
| Discount rate | **6.78%** | 6.99% | 7.11% | **6.57%** | 6.75% | 7.30% |
| Rate of increase in future compensation levels | **3.15** | 3.15 | 3.25 | **–** | – | – |
| Expected long-term rate of return on assets | **9.10*** | 10.10 | 10.90 | **–** | – | – |

**For 2005, the expected long-term rate of return on plan assets will continue to be 9.10%.*

The expected long-term rate of return assumptions for each asset class are selected based on historical relationships between the assets classes and the economic and capital market environments, updated for current conditions.

Benefit payments, which reflect expected future service, as appropriate, are expected to be paid as follows for the years ending May 31 (in millions):

| | Pension Benefits |
|---|---|
| 2005 | $ 216 |
| 2006 | 219 |
| 2007 | 257 |
| 2008 | 283 |
| 2009 | 319 |
| 2010-2014 | 2,389 |

These estimates are based on assumptions about future events. Actual benefit payments may vary significantly from these estimates.

Future medical benefit costs are estimated to increase at an annual rate of 14% during 2005, decreasing to an annual growth rate of 5% in 2019 and thereafter. Future dental benefit costs are estimated to increase at an annual rate of 7% during 2005, decreasing to an annual growth rate of 5% in 2013 and thereafter. Our postretirement healthcare cost is capped at 150% of the 1993 employer cost and, therefore, is not subject to medical and dental trends after the capped cost is attained. Therefore, a 1% change in these annual trend rates would not have a significant impact on the accumulated postretirement benefit obligation at May 31, 2004, or 2004 benefit expense.

**Defined Contribution Plans**

Profit sharing and other defined contribution plans are in place covering a majority of U.S. employees. Profit sharing plans provide for discretionary employer contributions, which are determined annually by our Board of Directors. Other plans provide matching funds based on employee contributions to 401(k) plans. Expense under these plans was $89 million in 2004, $82 million in 2003 and $75 million in 2002.

## NOTE 13: BUSINESS SEGMENT INFORMATION

Our operations for the periods presented are primarily represented by FedEx Express, FedEx Ground, FedEx Freight and FedEx Kinko's. These businesses form the core of our reportable segments. Other business units in the FedEx portfolio are FedEx Trade Networks, FedEx Supply Chain Services, FedEx Custom Critical and Caribbean Transportation Services. Management evaluates segment financial performance based on operating income.

In 2004, we changed the reporting and responsibility relationships of our smaller business units so that they now report directly to a core segment. Prior year amounts have been reclassified to conform to the new segment presentation. As a result, our reportable segments included the following businesses for the periods presented:

| | |
|---|---|
| **FedEx Express Segment** | FedEx Express<br>FedEx Trade Networks |
| **FedEx Ground Segment** | FedEx Ground<br>FedEx Supply Chain Services |
| **FedEx Freight Segment** | FedEx Freight<br>FedEx Custom Critical<br>Caribbean Transportation Services |
| **FedEx Kinko's Segment** | FedEx Kinko's |

NOTES TO CONSOLIDATED FINANCIAL STATEMENTS

The following table provides a reconciliation of reportable segment revenues, depreciation and amortization, operating income (loss) and segment assets to consolidated financial statement totals for the years ended or as of May 31 (in millions):

| | FedEx Express Segment | FedEx Ground Segment | FedEx Freight Segment | FedEx Kinko's Segment[1] | Other and Eliminations[2] | Consolidated Total |
|---|---|---|---|---|---|---|
| Revenues | | | | | | |
| **2004** | **$17,497** | **$3,910** | **$2,689** | **$ 521** | **$ 93** | **$24,710** |
| 2003 | 16,467 | 3,581 | 2,443 | – | (4) | 22,487 |
| 2002 | 15,438 | 2,918 | 2,253 | – | (2) | 20,607 |
| Depreciation and amortization | | | | | | |
| **2004** | **$ 810** | **$ 154** | **$ 92** | **$ 33** | **$ 286** | **$ 1,375** |
| 2003 | 818 | 155 | 88 | – | 290 | 1,351 |
| 2002 | 819 | 136 | 91 | – | 318 | 1,364 |
| Operating income (loss)[3] | | | | | | |
| **2004** | **$ 629** | **$ 522** | **$ 244** | **$ 39** | **$ 6** | **$ 1,440** |
| 2003 | 783 | 494 | 193 | – | 1 | 1,471 |
| 2002 | 801 | 337 | 185 | – | (2) | 1,321 |
| Segment assets[4] | | | | | | |
| **2004** | **$12,443** | **$2,248** | **$1,924** | **$2,903** | **$(384)** | **$19,134** |
| 2003 | 11,188 | 1,846 | 1,825 | – | 526 | 15,385 |
| 2002 | 10,151 | 1,480 | 1,786 | – | 395 | 13,812 |

*(1) Includes the operations of FedEx Kinko's from the formation of the FedEx Kinko's segment on March 1, 2004.*
*(2) Includes the results of operations of FedEx Kinko's from February 12, 2004 (date of acquisition) through February 29, 2004 (approximately $100 million of revenue and $6 million of operating income).*
*(3) Includes business realignment costs of $428 million in the FedEx Express segment, $1 million in the FedEx Ground segment and $6 million in Other and Eliminations.*
*(4) Segment assets include intercompany receivables.*

The following table provides a reconciliation of reportable segment capital expenditures to consolidated totals for the years ended May 31 (in millions):

| | FedEx Express Segment | FedEx Ground Segment | FedEx Freight Segment | FedEx Kinko's Segment | Other | Consolidated Total |
|---|---|---|---|---|---|---|
| **2004** | **$ 592** | **$314** | **$130** | **$36** | **$199** | **$1,271** |
| 2003 | 917 | 252 | 139 | – | 203 | 1,511 |
| 2002 | 1,069 | 214 | 86 | – | 246 | 1,615 |

FEDEX CORPORATION

The following table presents revenue by service type and geographic information for the years ended or as of May 31 (in millions):

**Revenue by Service Type**

| | 2004 | 2003 | 2002 |
|---|---|---|---|
| FedEx Express segment: | | | |
| Package: | | | |
| U.S. overnight box | **$ 5,558** | $ 5,432 | $ 5,338 |
| U.S. overnight envelope | **1,700** | 1,715 | 1,755 |
| U.S. deferred | **2,592** | 2,510 | 2,383 |
| Total domestic package revenue | **9,850** | 9,657 | 9,476 |
| International priority | **5,131** | 4,367 | 3,834 |
| Total package revenue | **14,981** | 14,024 | 13,310 |
| Freight: | | | |
| U.S. | **1,609** | 1,564 | 1,273 |
| International | **393** | 400 | 384 |
| Total freight revenue | **2,002** | 1,964 | 1,657 |
| Other | **514** | 479 | 471 |
| Total FedEx Express segment | **17,497** | 16,467 | 15,438 |
| FedEx Ground segment | **3,910** | 3,581 | 2,918 |
| FedEx Freight segment | **2,689** | 2,443 | 2,253 |
| FedEx Kinko's segment(1) | **521** | – | – |
| Other and Eliminations(2) | **93** | (4) | (2) |
| | **$24,710** | $22,487 | $20,607 |

**Geographical Information(3)**

| | 2004 | 2003 | 2002 |
|---|---|---|---|
| Revenues: | | | |
| U.S. | **$18,643** | $17,277 | $15,968 |
| International | **6,067** | 5,210 | 4,639 |
| | **$24,710** | $22,487 | $20,607 |
| Noncurrent assets: | | | |
| U.S. | **$12,644** | $ 9,908 | $ 8,627 |
| International | **1,520** | 1,536 | 1,520 |
| | **$14,164** | $11,444 | $10,147 |

*(1) Includes the operations of FedEx Kinko's from the formation of the FedEx Kinko's segment on March 1, 2004.*

*(2) Includes the results of operations of FedEx Kinko's from February 12, 2004 (date of acquisition) through February 29, 2004 (approximately $100 million of revenue).*

*(3) International revenue includes shipments that either originate in or are destined to locations outside the United States. Noncurrent assets include property and equipment, goodwill and other long-term assets. Flight equipment is allocated between geographic areas based on usage.*

## NOTE 14: SUPPLEMENTAL CASH FLOW INFORMATION

Cash paid for interest expense and income taxes for the years ended May 31 was as follows (in millions):

| | 2004 | 2003 | 2002 |
|---|---|---|---|
| Interest (net of capitalized interest) | **$151** | $125 | $146 |
| Income taxes | **364** | 53 | 312 |

FedEx Express amended two leases in 2004 and four leases in 2003 for MD11 aircraft, which required FedEx Express to record $110 million in 2004 and $221 million in 2003, in both fixed assets and long-term liabilities.

FedEx Express consolidated an entity that owns two MD11 aircraft under the provisions of FIN 46. The consolidation of this entity on September 1, 2003 resulted in an increase in our fixed assets and long-term liabilities of approximately $140 million. See Note 16.

## NOTE 15: GUARANTEES AND INDEMNIFICATIONS

We adopted FIN 45, "Guarantor's Accounting and Disclosure Requirements for Guarantees, Including Indirect Guarantees of Indebtedness of Others," during 2003, which required the prospective recognition and measurement of certain guarantees and indemnifications. Accordingly, any contractual guarantees or indemnifications we have issued or modified subsequent to December 31, 2002 are subject to evaluation. If required, a liability for the fair value of the obligation undertaken will be recognized.

Substantially all of our guarantees and indemnifications were entered into prior to December 31, 2002 and have not been modified since then. Therefore, no amounts have been recognized in our financial statements for the underlying fair value of these obligations. With the exception of residual value guarantees in certain operating leases, a maximum obligation is generally not specified in our guarantees and indemnifications. As a result, the overall maximum potential amount of the obligation under such guarantees and indemnifications cannot be reasonably estimated. Historically, we have not been required to make significant payments under our guarantee or indemnification obligations.

**Operating Leases**

We have guarantees under certain operating leases, amounting to $43 million as of May 31, 2004, for the residual values of vehicles and facilities at the end of the respective operating lease periods. Under these leases, if the fair market value of the leased asset at the end of the lease term is less than an agreed-upon value as set forth in the related operating lease agreement, we will be responsible to the lessor for the amount of such deficiency. Based upon our expectation that none of these leased assets will have a residual value at the end of the lease term that is materially less than the value specified in the related operating lease agreement, we do not believe it is probable that we will be required to fund any amounts under the terms of these guarantee arrangements. Accordingly, no accruals have been recognized for these guarantees.

Certain of our operating leases contain other indemnification obligations to the lessor, which are considered ordinary and customary (e.g., use and environmental indemnifications). The terms of these obligations range in duration and often are not limited. Such indemnification obligations continue until and, in many cases, after expiration of the respective lease.

**Other Contracts**

In conjunction with certain transactions, primarily sales or purchases of operating assets or services in the ordinary course of business, we sometimes provide routine indemnifications (e.g., environmental, tax and software infringement), the terms of which range in duration and often are not limited.

**Intra-company Guarantees**

FedEx's publicly held debt (approximately $2.3 billion) is guaranteed by our subsidiaries. The guarantees are full and unconditional, joint and several and any subsidiaries that are not guarantors are minor as defined by Securities and Exchange Commission regulations. FedEx, as the parent company issuer of this debt, has no independent assets or operations. There are no significant restrictions on our ability or the ability of any guarantor to obtain funds from its subsidiaries by such means as a dividend or loan.

Special facility revenue bonds have been issued by certain municipalities primarily to finance the acquisition and construction of various airport facilities and equipment. In certain cases, the bond proceeds were loaned to FedEx Express and are included in long-term debt and, in other cases, the facilities were leased to us and are accounted for as either capital leases or operating leases. Approximately $800 million in principal of these bonds (with total future principal and interest payments of approximately $1.5 billion as of May 31, 2004) is unconditionally guaranteed by FedEx Express. Of the $800 million bond principal, $45 million was in long-term debt and $204 million was in capital lease obligations at May 31, 2004 and the remainder was in operating leases.

## NOTE 16: VARIABLE INTEREST ENTITIES

FedEx Express entered into a lease in July 2001 for two MD11 aircraft. These assets are held by a separate entity, which was established and is owned by independent third parties who provide financing through debt and equity participation. The original cost of the assets under the lease was approximately $150 million.

This lease contains residual value guarantees that obligate FedEx Express, not the third-party owners, to absorb the majority of the losses, if any, of the entity. The lease also provides FedEx Express with the right to receive any residual returns of the entity if they occur. At May 31, 2004, the residual value guarantee associated with this lease, which represents the maximum exposure to loss, was $89 million. FIN 46 required us to consolidate the separate entity that owns the two MD11 aircraft. Since the entity was created before February 1, 2003, we measured the assets and liabilities at their carrying amounts (the amounts at which they would have been recorded in the consolidated financial statements if FIN 46 had been effective at the inception of the lease). As a result of this consolidation, the accompanying May 31, 2004 balance sheet includes an additional $126 million of fixed assets and $133 million of long-term liabilities.

## NOTE 17: COMMITMENTS

Annual purchase commitments under various contracts as of May 31, 2004 were as follows (in millions):

| | Aircraft | Aircraft-Related[1] | Other[2] | Total |
|---|---|---|---|---|
| 2005 | $ 22 | $170 | $409 | $ 601 |
| 2006 | – | 136 | 119 | 255 |
| 2007 | 111 | 97 | 44 | 252 |
| 2008 | 131 | 67 | 14 | 212 |
| 2009 | 567 | 63 | 13 | 643 |
| Thereafter | 1,141 | 119 | 179 | 1,439 |

*(1) Primarily aircraft modifications.*
*(2) Primarily vehicles, facilities, computers, printing and other equipment and advertising and promotions contracts.*

The amounts reflected in the table above for purchase commitments represent noncancelable agreements to purchase goods or services. Such contracts include those for certain purchases of aircraft, aircraft modifications, vehicles, facilities, computers, printing and other equipment and advertising and promotions contracts. Open purchase orders that are cancelable are not considered unconditional purchase obligations for financial reporting purposes.

FedEx Express is committed to purchase two A310s, seven ATRs and ten Airbus A380s (a new high-capacity, long-range aircraft). The A310s and ATRs are expected to be delivered in 2005. FedEx Express expects to take delivery of three of the ten A380 aircraft in each of 2009, 2010 and 2011 and the remaining one in 2012. Deposits and progress payments of $25 million have been made toward these purchases and other planned aircraft-related transactions. In addition, we have committed to modify our DC10 aircraft for passenger-to-freighter and two-man cockpit configurations. Payments related to these activities are included in the table above. Aircraft and aircraft-related contracts are subject to price escalations.

## NOTE 18: LEGAL PROCEEDINGS

Operations in 2002 were significantly affected by the terrorist attacks on September 11, 2001. During 2002, we recognized a total of $119 million of compensation under the Air Transportation Safety and System Stabilization Act (the "Act"), of which $101 million had been received as of May 31, 2004. The amounts recognized were for our estimate of losses we incurred as a result of the mandatory grounding of our aircraft and for incremental losses incurred through December 31, 2001. All amounts recognized were reflected as reduction of operating expense under the caption "Airline stabilization compensation."

In the fourth quarter of 2003, the Department of Transportation ("DOT") asserted that we were overpaid by $31.6 million and has demanded repayment. We have filed requests for administrative and judicial review. We received an opinion from the District of Columbia U.S. Court of Appeals stating that most of the determinations that we requested were not yet ripe for decision and the Court will not rule prior to final determination by the DOT and exhaustion of administrative remedies.

Pursuant to the Federal Aviation Administration reauthorization enacted during the third quarter of 2004, the General Accounting Office submitted a report to Congress on June 4, 2004, on the criteria and procedures used by the Secretary of Transportation under the Act. Issuance of the report frees the DOT to make a final determination on our claim and also reinforces the Congressional directive to the DOT to refer any remaining disputed claims to an administrative law judge upon an affected claimant's request.

We agreed to mediation with the DOT, but it did not result in a resolution of the dispute. We will continue to pursue our claim for compensation under the Act.

We believe that we have complied with all aspects of the Act, that it is probable we will ultimately collect the remaining $18 million receivable and that we will not be required to pay any portion of the DOT's $31.6 million demand. We cannot be assured of the ultimate outcome; however, it is reasonably possible that a material reduction to the $119 million of compensation we have previously recognized under the Act could occur. Based on the DOT's assertion, the range for potential loss on this matter is zero to $49.6 million.

We are a defendant in a number of lawsuits filed in California state courts containing various class-action allegations under California's wage and hour laws. The plaintiffs in these lawsuits generally are hourly employees of FedEx operating companies who allege, among other things, that they were forced to work "off the clock" and were not provided work breaks. The plaintiffs generally seek unspecified monetary damages, injunctive relief, or both. To date, only one of these cases has been certified as a class action. We believe that the claims in these cases are without merit. We have denied any liability with respect to these claims and intend to vigorously defend ourselves in these cases. In the opinion of management, the aggregate liability, if any, with respect to these claims will not materially adversely affect our financial position, results of operations or cash flows.

Also, see Note 11 for discussion of other legal proceedings. FedEx and its subsidiaries are subject to other legal proceedings that arise in the ordinary course of their business. In the opinion of management, the aggregate liability, if any, with respect to these other actions will not materially adversely affect our financial position, results of operations or cash flows.

## NOTE 19: RELATED PARTY TRANSACTIONS

In November 1999, FedEx entered into a multi-year naming rights agreement with the National Football League Washington Redskins professional football team. Under this agreement, FedEx has certain marketing rights, including the right to name the Redskins' stadium "FedExField." In August 2003, Frederick W. Smith, Chairman, President and Chief Executive Officer of FedEx, personally acquired an approximate 10% ownership interest in the Washington Redskins and joined its board of directors.

Mr. Smith's son-in-law is a 50% owner of a company that provides insurance brokerage and consulting services in connection with certain insurance and legal services plan benefits offered by FedEx to certain of its employees. Mr. Smith's son-in-law's company is paid commissions and fees directly by the benefit providers and not FedEx. During fiscal 2004, such commissions and fees totaled approximately $497,000.

A member of our Board of Directors, J.R. Hyde, III, and his wife together own approximately 13% of HOOPS, L.P. ("HOOPS"), the owner of the NBA Memphis Grizzlies professional basketball team. Mr. Hyde, through one of his companies, also is the general partner of the minority limited partner of HOOPS. During 2002, FedEx entered into a multi-year, $90 million naming rights agreement with HOOPS that will be amortized to expense over the life of the agreement. Under this agreement, FedEx has certain marketing rights, including the right to name the new arena where the Grizzlies will play. Pursuant to a separate agreement with HOOPS, the City of Memphis and Shelby County, FedEx has agreed to pay $2.5 million a year for the balance of the 25-year term of the agreement if HOOPS terminates its lease for the new arena after 17 years. FedEx also purchased $2 million of municipal bonds issued by the Memphis and Shelby County Sports Authority, the proceeds of which are to be used to finance a portion of the construction costs of the new arena.

On March 26, 2004, FedEx purchased an aggregate of 94 acres of real estate in Olive Branch, Mississippi, for $4.7 million. FedEx proposes to construct a FedEx Ground hub on this site, which is just south of Memphis. The 94-acre site is divided into three parcels, two of which were owned by entities in which Mr. Hyde has a 50% ownership interest. These two parcels total approximately 3.4 acres. An independent appraisal of the property determined its fair market value to be not less than the negotiated purchase price.

## NOTE 20: SUMMARY OF QUARTERLY OPERATING RESULTS (UNAUDITED)

| (In millions, except per share amounts) | First Quarter | Second Quarter | Third Quarter | Fourth Quarter |
|---|---|---|---|---|
| **2004** [1] | | | | |
| Revenues | **$5,687** | **$5,920** | **$6,062** | **$7,041** |
| Operating income | **200** [2] | **183** [4] | **372** | **685** |
| Net income | **128** [2][3] | **91** [4] | **207** | **412** [5] |
| Basic earnings per common share [6] | **0.43** [2][3] | **0.31** [4] | **0.69** | **1.38** [5] |
| Diluted earnings per common share | **0.42** [2][3] | **0.30** [4] | **0.68** | **1.36** [5] |
| 2003 | | | | |
| Revenues | $5,445 | $5,667 | $5,545 | $5,830 |
| Operating income | 283 | 427 | 269 | 492 |
| Net income | 158 | 245 | 147 | 280 |
| Basic earnings per common share [6] | 0.53 | 0.82 | 0.49 | 0.94 |
| Diluted earnings per common share | 0.52 | 0.81 | 0.49 | 0.92 |

*(1) Includes FedEx Kinko's from February 12, 2004 (date of acquisition). See Note 2.*
*(2) Includes $132 million ($82 million, net of tax, $0.28 per share, or $0.27 per diluted share) of business realignment costs described in Note 4.*
*(3) Includes $26 million, net of tax ($0.09 per share or $0.08 per diluted share) related to a favorable ruling on an IRS case described in Note 11.*
*(4) Includes $283 million ($175 million, net of tax, $0.59 per share, or $0.57 per diluted share) of business realignment costs described in Note 4.*
*(5) Includes a $12 million ($0.04 per share and per diluted share) nonrecurring benefit related to the reduction of our effective tax rate. See Note 11.*
*(6) The sum of the quarterly earnings per share may not equal annual amounts due to differences in the weighted-average number of shares outstanding during the respective periods.*

## REPORT OF INDEPENDENT REGISTERED PUBLIC ACCOUNTING FIRM

The Board of Directors and Stockholders
FedEx Corporation

We have audited the accompanying consolidated balance sheets of FedEx Corporation as of May 31, 2004 and 2003, and the related consolidated statements of income, changes in stockholders' investment and comprehensive income, and cash flows for each of the three years in the period ended May 31, 2004. These financial statements are the responsibility of the Company's management. Our responsibility is to express an opinion on these financial statements based on our audits.

We conducted our audits in accordance with the standards of the Public Company Accounting Oversight Board (United States). Those standards require that we plan and perform the audit to obtain reasonable assurance about whether the financial statements are free of material misstatement. An audit includes examining, on a test basis, evidence supporting the amounts and disclosures in the financial statements. An audit also includes assessing the accounting principles used and significant estimates made by management, as well as evaluating the overall financial statement presentation. We believe that our audits provide a reasonable basis for our opinion.

In our opinion, the financial statements referred to above present fairly, in all material respects, the consolidated financial position of FedEx Corporation at May 31, 2004 and 2003, and the consolidated results of its operations and its cash flows for each of the three years in the period ended May 31, 2004, in conformity with U.S. generally accepted accounting principles.

As discussed in Note 3 to the consolidated financial statements, the Company adopted Statement of Financial Accounting Standards No. 142, Goodwill and Other Intangible Assets, in 2002.

Ernst & Young LLP

Memphis, Tennessee
June 22, 2004

# Glossary

**Accounting equation** the process used to capture the effect of economic events; Assets = Liabilities + Owner's Equity.

**Accounting Principles Board (APB)** the second private sector body delegated the task of setting accounting standards.

**Accounts** storage areas to keep track of the increases and decreases in financial position elements.

**Accounts payable** obligations to suppliers of merchandise or of services purchased on open account.

**Accounts receivable** receivables resulting from the sale of goods or services on account.

**Accounts receivable aging schedule** applying different percentages to accounts receivable balances depending on the length of time outstanding.

**Accrual accounting** measurement of the entity's accomplishments and resource sacrifices during the period, regardless of when cash is received or paid.

**Accruals** when the cash flow comes after either expense or revenue recognition.

**Accrued interest** interest that has accrued since the last interest date.

**Accrued liabilities** expenses already incurred but not yet paid (accrued expenses).

**Accrued receivables** the recognition of revenue earned before cash is received.

**Accumulated benefit obligation (ABO)** the discounted present value of estimated retirement benefits earned so far by employees, applying the plan's pension formula using existing compensation levels.

**Accumulated other comprehensive income** amount of other comprehensive income (non-owner changes in equity other than net income) accumulated over the current and prior periods.

**Accumulated postretirement benefit obligation (APBO)** portion of the EPBO attributed to employee service up to a particular date.

**Acid-test ratio** current assets, excluding inventories and prepaid items, divided by current liabilities.

**Acquisition costs** the amounts paid to acquire the rights to explore for undiscovered natural resources or to extract proven natural resources.

**Activity-based method** allocation of an asset's cost base using a measure of the asset's input or output.

**Actuary** a professional trained in a particular branch of statistics and mathematics to assess the various uncertainties and to estimate the company's obligation to employees in connection with its pension plan.

**Additions** the adding of a new major component to an existing asset.

**Adjusted trial balance** trial balance after adjusting entries have been recorded.

**Adjusting entries** internal transactions recorded at the end of any period when financial statements are prepared.

**Allocation base** the value of the usefulness that is expected to be consumed.

**Allocation method** the pattern in which the usefulness is expected to be consumed.

**Allowance method** recording bad debt expense and reducing accounts receivable indirectly by crediting a contra account (allowance for uncollectible accounts) to accounts receivable for an estimate of the amount that eventually will prove uncollectible.

**American Institute of Accountants (AIA)/American Institute of Certified Public Accountants (AICPA)** national organization of professional public accountants.

**Amortization** cost allocation for intangibles.

**Amortization schedule** schedule that reflects the changes in the debt over its term to maturity.

**Annuity** cash flows received or paid in the same amount each period.

**Annuity due** cash flows occurring at the beginning of each period.

**Antidilutive securities** the effect of the conversion or exercise of potential common shares would be to increase rather than decrease, EPS.

**Articles of incorporation** statement of the nature of the firm's business activities, the shares to be issued, and the composition of the initial board of directors.

**Asset retirement obligations (AROs)** obligations associated with the disposition of an operational asset.

**Assets** probable future economic benefits obtained or controlled by a particular entity as a result of past transactions or events.

**Asset turnover ratio** measure of a company's efficiency in using assets to generate revenue.

**Assigning** using receivables as collateral for loans; nonpayment of a debt will require the proceeds from collecting the assigned receivables to go directly toward repayment of the debt.

**Attribution** process of assigning the cost of benefits to the years during which those benefits are assumed to be earned by employees.

**Auditors** independent intermediaries who help ensure that management has appropriately applied GAAP in preparing the company's financial statements.

**Auditor's report** report issued by CPAs who audit the financial statements that informs users of the audit findings.

**Average collection period** indication of the average age of accounts receivable.

**Average cost method** assumes cost of goods sold and ending inventory consist of a mixture of all the goods available for sale.

**Average days in inventory** indicates the average number of days it normally takes to sell inventory.

**Bad debt expense** an operating expense incurred to boost sales; inherent cost of granting credit.

**Balance sheet** a position statement that presents an organized list of assets, liabilities, and equity at a particular point in time.

**Balance sheet approach** determination of bad debt expense by estimating the net realizable value of accounts receivable to be reported in the balance sheet.

**Bank reconciliation** comparison of the bank balance with the balance in the company's own records.

**Bargain purchase option (BPO)** provision in the lease contract that gives the lessee the option of purchasing the leased property at a bargain price.

**Bargain renewal option** gives the lessee the option to renew the lease at a bargain rate.

**Basic EPS** computed by dividing income available to common stockholders (net income less any preferred stock dividends) by the weighted-average number of common shares outstanding for the period.

**Billings of construction contract** contra account to the asset construction in progress; subtracted from construction in progress to determine balance sheet presentation.

**Board of directors** establishes corporate policies and appoints officers who manage the corporation.

**Bond indenture** document that describes specific promises made to bondholders.

**Bonds** A form of debt consisting of separable units (bonds) that obligates the issuing corporation to repay a stated amount at a specified maturity date and to pay interest to bondholders between the issue date and maturity.

**Book value** assets minus liabilities as shown in the balance sheet.

**Callable** allows the issuing company to buy back, or call, outstanding bonds from the bondholders before their scheduled maturity date.

**Capital budgeting** The process of evaluating the purchase of operational assets.

**Capital leases** installment purchases/sales that are formulated outwardly as leases.

**Capital markets** mechanisms that foster the allocation of resources efficiently.

**Cash** currency and coins, balances in checking accounts, and items acceptable for deposit in these accounts, such as checks and money orders received from customers.

**Cash basis accounting/net operating cash flow** difference between cash receipts and cash disbursements during a reporting period from transactions related to providing goods and services to customers.

**Cash disbursements journal** record of cash disbursements.

**Cash discounts** sales discounts; represent reductions not in the selling price of a good or service but in the amount to be paid by a credit customer if paid within a specific period of time.

**Cash equivalents** certain negotiable items such as commercial paper, money market funds, and U.S. Treasury bills that are highly liquid investments quickly convertible to cash.

**Cash equivalents** short-term, highly liquid investments that can be readily converted to cash with little risk of loss.

**Cash flow hedge** a derivative used to hedge against the exposure to changes in cash inflows or cash outflows of an asset or liability or a forecasted transaction ( like a future purchase or sale.

**Cash flows from financing activities** both inflows and outflows of cash resulting from the external financing of a business.

**Cash flows from investing activities** both outflows and inflows of cash caused by the acquisition and disposition of assets.

**Cash flows from operating activities** both inflows and outflows of cash that result from activities reported on the income statement.

**Cash receipts journal** record of cash receipts.

**Certified Public Accountants (CPAs)** licensed individuals who can represent that the financial statements have been audited in accordance with generally accepted auditing standards.

**Change in accounting estimate** a change in an estimate when new information comes to light.

**Change in accounting principle** switch by a company from one accounting method to another.

**Change in reporting entity** presentation of consolidated financial statements in place of statements of individual companies, or a change in the specific companies that constitute the group for which consolidated or combined statements are prepared.

**Closing process** the temporary accounts are reduced to zero balances, and these temporary account balances are closed (transferred) to retained earnings to reflect the changes that have occurred in that account during the period.

**Commercial paper** unsecured notes sold in minimum denominations of $25,000 with maturities ranging from 30 to 270 days.

**Committee on Accounting Procedure (CAP)** the first private sector body that was delegated the task of setting accounting standards.

**Comparability** the ability to help users see similarities and differences among events and conditions.

**Comparative financial statements** corresponding financial statements from the previous years accompanying the issued financial statements.

**Compensating balance** a specified balance (usually some percentage of the committee amount) a borrower of a loan is asked to maintain in a low-interest or noninterest-bearing account at the bank.

**Completed contract method** recognition of revenue for a long-term contract when the project is complete.

**Complex capital structure** potential common shares are outstanding.

**Composite depreciation method** physically dissimilar assets are aggregated to gain the convenience of group depreciation.

**Compound interest** interest computed not only on the initial investment but also on the accumulated interest in previous periods.

**Comprehensive income** traditional net income plus other nonowner changes in equity.

**Conceptual framework** deals with theoretical and conceptual issues and provides an underlying structure for current and future accounting and reporting standards.

**Conservatism** practice followed in an attempt to ensure that uncertainties and risks inherent in business situations are adequately considered.

**Consignment** the consignor physically transfers the goods to the other company (the consignee), but the consignor retains legal title.

**Consistency** permits valid comparisons between different periods.

**Consolidated financial statements** combination of the separate financial statements of the parent and subsidiary each period into a single aggregate set of financial statements as if there were only one company.

**Construction in progress** asset account equivalent to the asset work-in-progress inventory in a manufacturing company.

**Contingently issuable shares** additional shares of common stock to be issued, contingent on the occurrence of some future circumstance.

**Conventional retail method** applying the retail inventory method in such a way that LCM is approximated.

**Convertible bonds** bonds for which bondholders have the option to convert the bonds into shares of stock.

**Copyright** exclusive right of protection given to a creator of a published work, such as a song, painting, photograph, or book.

**Corporation** the dominant form of business organization that acquires capital from investors in exchange for ownership interest and from creditors by borrowing.

**Correction of an error** an adjustment a company makes due to an error made.

**Cost effectiveness** the perceived benefit of increased decision usefulness exceeds the anticipated cost of providing that information.

**Cost of goods sold** cost of the inventory sold during the period.

**Cost recovery method** deferral of all gross profit recognition until the cost of the item sold has been recovered.

**Cost-to-retail percentage** ratio found by dividing goods available for sale at cost by goods available for sale at retail.

**Coupons bonds** name of the owner was not registered; the holder actually clipped an attached coupon and redeemed it in accordance with instructions on the indenture.

**Credits** represent the right side of the account.

**Cumulative** if the specified dividend is not paid in a given year, the unpaid dividends accumulate and must be made up in a later dividend year before any dividends are paid on common shares.

**Current assets** includes assets that are cash, will be converted into cash, or will be used up within one year or the operating cycle, whichever is longer.

**Current liabilities** expected to require current assets and usually are payable within one year.

**Current maturities of long-term debt** the current installment due on long-term debt, reported as a current liability.

**Current ratio** current assets divided by current liabilities.

**Date of record** specific date stated as to when the determination will be made of the recipient of the dividend.

**Debenture bond** secured only by the "full faith and credit" of the issuing corporation.

**Debits** represent the left side of the account.

**Debt issue cost** with either publicly or privately sold debt, the issuing company will incur costs in connection with issuing bonds or notes, such as legal and accounting fees and printing costs, in addition to registration and underwriting fees.

**Debt to equity ratio** compares resources provided by creditors with resources provided by owners.

**Decision usefulness** the quality of being useful to decision making.

**Default risk** a company's ability to pay its obligations when they come due.

**Deferred annuity** the first cash flow occurs more than the one period after the date the agreement begins.

**Deferred tax asset** taxes to be saved in the future when future deductible amounts reduce taxable income (when the temporary differences reverse).

**Deferred tax liability** taxes to be paid in the future when future taxable amounts become taxable (when the temporary differences reverse).

**Deficit** debit balance in retained earnings.

**Defined benefit pension plans** fixed retirement benefits defined by a designated formula, based on employees' years of service and annual compensation.

**Defined contribution pension plans** fixed annual contributions to a pension fund; employees choose where funds are invested—usually stocks or fixed-income securities.

**Depletion** allocation of the cost of natural resources.

**Depreciation** cost allocation for plant and equipment.

**Derivatives** financial instruments usually created to hedge against risks created by other financial instruments or by transactions that have yet to occur but are anticipated and that "derive" their values or contractually required cash flows from some other security or index.

**Detachable stock purchase warrants** the investor has the option to purchase a stated number of shares of common stock at a specified option price, within a given period of time.

**Development costs** for natural resources, costs incurred after the resource has been discovered but before production begins.

**Diluted EPS** incorporates the dilutive effect of all potential common shares.

**Direct financing lease** lease in which the lessor finances the asset for the lessee and earns interest revenue over the lease term.

**Direct method** the cash effect of each operating activity (i.e., income statement item) is reported directly on the statement of cash flows.

**Direct write-off method** an allowance for uncollectible accounts is not used; instead bad debts that do arise are written off as bad debt expense.

**Disclosure notes** additional insights about company operations, accounting principles, contractual agreements, and pending litigation.

**Discontinued operations** The discontinuance of a component of an entity whose operations and cash flows can be clearly distinguished from the rest of the entity.

**Discount** Arises when bonds are sold for less than face amount.

**Discounting** the transfer of a note receivable to a financial institution.

**Distributions to owners** decreases in equity resulting from transfers to owners.

**Dividend** distribution to shareholders of a portion of assets earned.

**Dollar-value LIFO (DVL)** Inventory is viewed as a quantity of value instead of a physical quantity of goods. Instead of layers of units from different purchases, the DVL inventory pool is viewed as comprising layers of dollar value from different years.

**Dollar-value LIFO retail method** LIFO retail method combined with dollar-value LIFO.

**Double-declining-balance (DDB) method** 200% of the straight-line rate is multiplied by book value.

**Double-entry system** dual effect that each transaction has on the accounting equation when recorded.

**Early extinguishment of debt** debt is retired prior to its scheduled maturity date.

**Earnings per share (EPS)** the amount of income earned by a company expressed on a per share basis.

**Earnings quality** refers to the ability of reported earnings (income) to predict a company's future earnings.

**Economic events** any event that directly affects the financial position of the company.

**Effective interest method** recording interest each period as the effective rate of interest multiplied by the outstanding balance of the debt.

**Effective rate** the actual rate at which money grows per year.

**Emerging Issues Task Force (EITF)** responsible for providing more timely responses to emerging financial reporting issues.

**Employee share purchase plans** permit all employees to buy shares directly from their company, often at favorable terms.

**Equity method** used when an investor can't control, but can significantly influence, the investee.

**Equity/net assets** called shareholders' equity or stockholders' equity for a corporation; the residual interest in the assets of an entity that remains after deducting liabilities.

**Estimates** prediction of future events.

**Ethics** a code or moral system that provides criteria for evaluating right and wrong.

**Ex-dividend date** date usually two business days before the date of the record and is the first day the stock trades without the right to receive the declared dividend.

**Executory costs** maintenance, insurance, taxes, and any other costs usually associated with ownership.

**Expected cash flow approach** adjusts the cash flows, not the discount rate, for the uncertainty or risk of those cash flows.

**Expected economic life** useful life of an asset.

**Expected postretirement benefit obligation (EPBO)** discounted present value of the total net cost to the employer of postretirement benefits.

**Expected return on plan assets** estimated long-term return on invested assets.

**Expenses** outflows or other using up of assets or incurrences of liabilities during a period from delivering or producing good, rendering services, or other activities that constitute the entity's ongoing major, or central, operations.

**Exploration costs** for natural resources, expenditures such as drilling a well, or excavating a mine, or any other costs of searching for natural resources.

**External events** exchange between the company and a separate economic entity.

**Extraordinary items** material events and transactions that are both unusual in nature and infrequent in occurrence.

**F.O.B. (free on board) shipping point** legal title to the goods changes hands at the point of shipment when the seller delivers the goods to the common carrier, and the purchaser is responsible for shipping costs and transit insurance.

**F.O.B. destination** the seller is responsible for shipping and the legal title does not pass until the goods arrive at their destination.

**Factor** financial institution that buys receivables for cash, handles the billing and collection of the receivables, and charges a fee for this service.

**Fair value hedge** a derivative is used to hedge against the exposure to changes in the fair value of an asset or liability or a firm commitment.

**Financial accounting** provides relevant financial information to various external users.

**Financial Accounting Foundation (FAF)** responsible for selecting the members of the FASB and its Advisory Council, ensuring adequate funding of FASB activities, and exercising general oversight of the FASB's activities.

**Financial Accounting Standards Board (FASB)** the current private sector body that has been delegated the task of setting accounting standards.

**Financial activities** cash inflows and outflows from transactions with creditors and owners.

**Financial instrument** cash; evidence of an ownership interest in an entity; a contract that imposes on one entity an obligation to deliver cash or another financial instrument, and conveys to the second entity a right to receive cash or another financial instrument; and a contract that imposes on one entity an obligation to exchange financial instruments on potentially unfavorable terms and conveys to a second entity a right to exchange other financial instruments on potentially favorable terms.

**Financial leverage** by earning a return on borrowed funds that exceeds the cost of borrowing the funds, a company can provide its shareholders with a total return higher than it could achieve by employing equity funds alone.

**Financial reporting** process of providing financial statement information to external users.

**Financial statements** primary means of communicating financial information to external parties.

**Finished goods** costs that have accumulated in work in process are transferred to finished goods once the manufacturing process is completed.

**Fiscal year** the annual time period used to report to external users.

**Fixed-asset turnover ratio** used to measure how effectively managers used PP&E;

$$\text{Fixed-asset turnover ratio} = \frac{\text{Net sales}}{\text{Average fixed assets}}$$

**Foreign currency futures contract** agreement that requires the seller to deliver a specific foreign currency at a designated future date at a specific price.

**Foreign currency hedge** if a derivative is used to hedge the risk that some transactions require settlement in a currency other than the entities' functional currency or that foreign operations will require translation adjustments to reported amounts.

**Forward contract** calls for delivery on a specific date; is not traded on a market exchange; does not call for a daily cash settlement for price changes in the underlying contract.

**Fractional shares** a stock dividend or stock split results in some shareholders being entitled to fractions of whole shares.

**Franchise** contractual arrangement under which the franchisor grants the franchisee the exclusive right to use the franchisor's trademark or tradename within a geographical area, usually for specified period of time.

**Franchisee** individual or corporation given the right to sell the franchisor's products and use its name for a specified period of time.

**Franchisor** grants to the franchisee the right to sell the franchisor's products and use its name for a specific period of time.

**Freight-in** transportation-in; in a periodic system, freight costs generally are added to this temporary account, which is added to purchases in determining net purchases.

**Full-cost method** allows costs incurred in searching for oil and gas within a large geographical area to be capitalized as assets and expensed in the future as oil and gas from the successful wells are removed from that area.

**Full-disclosure principle** the financial reports should include any information that could affect the decisions made by external users.

**Funded status** difference between the employer's obligation (PBO) and the resources available to satisfy that obligation (plan assets).

**Future deductible amounts** the future tax consequence of a temporary difference will be to decrease taxable income relative to accounting income.

**Futures contract** agreement that requires the seller to deliver a particular commodity at a designated future date at a specified price.

**Future taxable amounts** the future tax consequence of temporary difference will be to increase taxable income relative to accounting income.

**Future value** amount of money that a dollar will grow to at some point in the future.

**Gain or loss on the PBO** the decrease or increase in the PBO when one or more estimates used in determining the PBO require revision.

**Gains** increases in equity from peripheral, or incidental, transactions of an entity.

**General journal** used to record any type of transaction.

**General ledger** collection of accounts.

**Generally Accepted Accounting Principles (GAAP)** set of both broad and specific guidelines that companies should follow when measuring and reporting the information in their financial statements and related notes.

**Going concern assumption** in the absence of information to the contrary, it is anticipated that a business entity will continue to operate indefinitely.

**Goodwill** unique intangible asset in that its cost can't be directly associated with any specifically identifiable right and it is not separable from the company itself.

**Government Accounting Standards Board (GASB)** responsible for developing accounting standards for governmental units such as states and cities.

**Gross investment in the lease** total of periodic rental payments and residual value.

**Gross method** For the buyer, views a discount not taken as part of the cost of inventory. For the seller, views a discount not taken by the customer as part of sales of revenue.

**Gross profit method (gross margin method)** estimates cost of goods sold which is then subtracted from cost of goods available for sale to estimate ending inventory.

**Gross profit/ratio** highlights the important relationship between net sales revenue and cost of goods sold.

$$\text{Gross profit ratio} = \frac{\text{Gross profit}}{\text{Net sales}}$$

**Group depreciation method** collection of assets defined as depreciable assets that share similar service lives and other attributes.

**Half-year convention** record one-half of a full year's depreciation in the year of acquisition and another half year in the year of disposal.

**Hedging** taking an action that is expected to produce exposure to a particular type of risk that is precisely the opposite of an actual risk to which the company already is exposed.

**Historical costs** original transaction value.

**Horizontal analysis** comparison by expressing each item as a percentage of that same item in the financial statements of another year (base amount) in order to more easily see year-to-year changes.

**Illegal acts** violations of the law, such as bribes, kickbacks, and illegal contributions to political candidates.

**Impairment of value** operational assets should be written down if there has been a significant impairment (fair value less than book value) of value.

**Implicit rate of interest** rate implicit in the agreement.

**Improvements** replacement of a major component of an operational asset.

**Income from continuing operations** revenues, expenses (including income taxes), gain, and losses, excluding those related to discontinued operations and extraordinary items.

**Income statement** statement of operations or statement of earnings is used to summarize the profit-generating activities that occurred during a particular reporting period.

**Income statement approach** estimating bad debt expense as a percentage of each period's net credit sales; usually determined by reviewing the company's recent history of the relationship between credit sales and actual bad debts.

**Income summary** account that is a bookkeeping convenience used in the closing process that provides a check that all temporary accounts have been properly closed.

**Income tax expense** provision for income taxes; reported as a separate expense in corporate income statements.

**Indirect method** the net cash increase or decrease from operating activities is derived indirectly by starting with reported net income and working backwards to convert that amount to a cash basis.

**Initial direct costs** costs incurred by the lessor that are associated directly with originating a lease and are essential to acquire the lease.

**In-process research and development** the amount of the purchase price in a business acquisition that is allocated to projects that have not yet reached technological feasibility.

**Installment notes** Notes payable for which equal installment payments include both an amount that represents interest and an amount that represents a reduction of the outstanding balance so that at maturity the note is completely paid.

**Installment sales method** recognizes revenue and costs only when cash payments are received.

**Institute of Internal Auditors** national organization of accountants providing internal auditing services for their own organizations.

**Institute of Management Accountants (IMA)** primary national organization of accountants working in industry and government.

**Intangible assets** operational assets that lack physical substance; examples include patents, copyrights, franchises, and goodwill.

**Interest** "rent" paid for the use of money for some period of time.

**Interest cost** interest accrued on the projected benefit obligation calculated as the discount rate multiplied by the projected benefit obligation at the beginning of the year.

**Interest rate swap** agreement to exchange fixed interest payments for floating rate payments, or vice versa, without exchanging the underlying principal amounts.

**Internal control** a company's plan to encourage adherence to company policies and procedures, promote operational efficiency, minimize errors and theft, and enhance the reliability and accuracy of accounting data.

**Internal events** events that directly affect the financial position of the company but don't involve an exchange transaction with another entity.

**International Accounting Standards Board (IASB)** objectives are to develop a single set of high-quality, understandable global accounting standards, to promote the use of those standards, and to bring about the convergence of national accounting standards and International Accounting Standards.

**International Accounting Standards Committee (IASC)** umbrella organization formed to develop global accounting standards.

**International Financial Reporting Standards** voluntary IASB standards.

**Intraperiod tax allocation** associates (allocates) income tax expense (or income tax benefit if there is a loss) with each major component of income that causes it.

**Intrinsic value** the difference between the market price of the shares and the option price at which they can be acquired.

**Inventories** goods awaiting sale (finished goods), goods in the course of production (work in process), and goods to be consumed directly or indirectly in production (raw materials).

**Inventory** goods acquired, manufactured, or in the process of being manufactured for sale.

**Inventory turnover ratio** measures a company's efficiency in managing its investment in inventory.

**Investing activities** involve the acquisition and sale of long-term assets used in the business and non-operating investment assets.

**Investments by owners** increases in equity resulting from transfers of resources (usually cash) to a company in exchange for ownership interest.

**Irregularities** intentional distortions of financial statements.

**Journal** a chronological record of all economic events affecting financial position.

**Journal entry** captures the effect of a transaction on financial position in debit/credit form.

**Just-in-time (JIT) system** a system used by a manufacturer to coordinate production with suppliers so that raw materials or components arrive just as they are needed in the production process.

**Land improvements** the cost of parking lots, driveways, and private roads and the costs of fences and lawn and garden sprinkler systems.

**Last-in, first-out (LIFO) method** assumes units sold are the most recent units purchased.

**Leasehold improvements** account title when a lessee makes improvements to leased property that reverts back to the lessor at the end of the lease.

**Lessee** user of a leased asset.

**Lessor** owner of a leased asset.

**Leveraged lease** a third-party, long-term creditor provides nonrecourse financing for a lease agreement between a lessor and a lessee.

**Liabilities** probable future sacrifices of economic benefits arising from present obligations of a particular entity to transfer assets or provide services to other entities in the future as a result of past transactions or events.

**LIFO conformity rule** if a company uses LIFO to measure taxable income, the company also must use LIFO for external financial reporting.

**LIFO inventory pools** simplifies recordkeeping and reduces the risk of LIFO liquidation by grouping inventory units into pools based on physical similarities of the individual units.

**LIFO liquidation** the decline in inventory quantity during the period.

**Limited liability company** owners are not liable for the debts of the business, except to the extent of their investment; all members can be involved with managing the business without losing liability protection; no limitations on the number of owners.

**Limited liability partnership** similar to a limited liability company, except it doesn't offer all the liability protection available in the limited liability company structure.

**Line of credit** allows a company to borrow cash without having to follow formal loan procedures and paperwork.

**Liquidating dividend** when a dividend exceeds the balance in retained earnings.

**Liquidity** period of time before an asset is converted to cash or until a liability is paid.

**Long-term solvency** the riskiness of a company with regard to the amount of liabilities in its capital structure.

**Loss contingency** existing, uncertain situation involving potential loss depending on whether some future event occurs.

**Losses** decreases in equity arising from peripheral, or incidental, transactions of the entity.

**Lower-of -cost-or-market (LCM)** recognizes losses in the period that the value of inventory declines below its cost.

**Management discussion and analysis (MDA)** provides a biased but informed perspective of a company's operations, liquidity, and capital resources.

**Managerial accounting** deals with the concepts and methods used to provide information to an organization's internal users (i.e., its managers).

**Matching principle** expenses are recognized in the same period as the related revenues.

**Materiality** if a more costly way of providing information is not expected to have a material effect on decisions made by those using the information, the less costly method may be acceptable.

**Measurement** process of associating numerical amounts to the elements.

**Minimum lease payments** payments the lessee is required to make in connection with the lease.

**Minimum pension liability** an employer must report a pension liability at least equal to the amount by which its ABO exceeds its plan assets.

**Model Business Corporation Act** designed to serve as a guide to states in the development of their corporation statutes.

**Modified accelerated cost recovery system (MACRS)** The federal income tax code allows taxpayers to compute depreciation for their tax returns using this method.

**Monetary assets** money and claims to receive money, the amount of which is fixed or determinable.

**Monetary liabilities** obligations to pay amounts of cash, the amount of which is fixed or determinable.

**Mortgage bond** backed by a lien on specified real estate owned by the issuer.

**Multiple-step** income statement format that includes a number of intermediate subtotals before arriving at income from continuing operations.

**Natural resources** oil and gas deposits, timber tracts, and mineral deposits.

**Net income/net loss** **revenue + gains – (expenses and losses for a period)** income statement bottom line.

**Net markdown** net effect of the change in selling price (increase, decrease, increase).

**Net markup** net effect of the change in selling price (increase, increase, decrease).

**Net method** For the buyer, considers the cost of inventory to include the net, after-discount amount, and any discounts not taken are reported as interest expense. For the seller, considers sales revenue to be the net amount, after discount, and any discounts not taken by the customer as interest revenue.

**Net operating loss** negative taxable income because tax-deductible expenses exceed taxable revenues.

**Net realizable less a normal profit margin (NRV – NP)** lower limit of market.

**Net realizable value (NRV)** upper limit of market.

**Neutrality** neutral with respect to parties potentially affected.

**Noncash investing and financing activities** transactions that do not increase or decrease cash but that result in significant investing and financing activities.

**Noninterest-bearing note** notes that bear interest, but the interest is deducted (or discounted) from the face amount to determine the cash proceeds made available to the borrower at the outset.

**Nonoperating income** includes gains and losses and revenues and expenses related to peripheral or incidental activities of the company.

**Nontemporary difference** difference between pretax accounting income and taxable income and, consequently, between the reported amount of an asset or liability in the financial statements and its tax basis that will not "reverse" resulting from transactions and events that under existing tax law will never affect taxable income or taxes payable.

**Note payable** A promissory note (essentially an IOU) that obligates the issuing corporation to repay a stated amount at or by a specified maturity date and to pay interest to the lender between the issue date and maturity.

**Notes receivable** receivables supported by a formal agreement or note that specifies payment terms.

**Objectives-oriented/principles-based accounting standards** approach to standard setting stresses professional judgment, as opposed to following a list of rules.

**Operating activities** inflows and outflows of cash related to transactions entering into the determination of net income.

**Operating cycle** period of time necessary to convert cash to raw materials, raw materials to finished product, the finished product to receivables, and then finally receivables back to cash.

**Operating income** includes revenues and expenses directly related to the principal revenue-generating activities of the company.

**Operating leases** fundamental rights and responsibilities of ownership are retained by the lessor and that the lessee merely is using the asset temporarily.

**Operating loss carryback** reduction of prior (up to two) years' taxable income by a current net operating loss.

**Operating loss forward** reduction of future (up to 20) years' taxable income by a current net operating loss.

**Operating segment** a component of an enterprise that engages in business activities from which it may earn revenues and incur expenses (including revenues and expenses relating to transactions with other companies of the same enterprise); whose operating results are regularly reviewed by the enterprise's chief operating decision maker to make decisions about resources to be allocated to the segment and assess its performance; for which discrete financial information is available.

**Operational assets** property, plant, and equipment, along with intangible assets.

**Operational risk** how adept a company is at withstanding various events and circumstances that might impair its ability to earn profits.

**Option** gives the holder the right either to buy or sell a financial instrument at a specified price.

**Option pricing models** statistical models that incorporate information about a company's stock and the terms of the stock option to estimate the option's fair value.

**Ordinary annuity** cash flows occur at the end of each period.

**Other comprehensive income** certain gains and losses that are excluded from the calculation of net income, but included in the calculation of comprehensive income.

**Paid-in capital** invested capital consisting primarily of amounts invested by shareholders when they purchase shares of stock from the corporation.

**Parenthetical comments/modifying comments** supplemental information disclosed on the face of financial statements.

**Participating** preferred shareholders are allowed to receive additional dividends beyond the stated amount.

**Patent** exclusive right to manufacture a product or to use a process.

**Pension plan assets** employer contributions and accumulated earnings on the investment of those contributions to be used to pay retirement benefits to retired employees.

**Percentage-of-completion method** allocation of a share of a project's revenues and expenses to each reporting period during the contract period.

**Periodic inventory system** the merchandise inventory account balance is not adjusted as purchases and sales are made but only periodically at the end of a reporting period when a physical count of the period's ending inventory is made and costs are assigned to the quantities determined.

**Periodicity assumption** allows the life of a company to be divided into artificial time periods to provide timely information.

**Permanent accounts** represent assets, liabilities, and shareholders' equity at a point in time.

**Perpetual inventory system** account inventory is continually adjusted for each change in inventory, whether it's caused by a purchase, a sale, or a return of merchandise by the company to its supplier.

**Pledging** trade receivables in general rather than specific receivables are pledged as collateral; the responsibility for collection of the receivables remains solely with the company.

**Point-of-sale** the goods or services sold to the buyer are delivered (the title is transferred).

**Post-closing trial balance** verifies that the closing entries were prepared and posted correctly and that the accounts are now ready for next year's transactions.

**Posting** transferring debits and credits recorded in individual journal entries to the specific accounts affected.

**Postretirement benefits** all types of retiree benefits; may include medical coverage, dental coverage, life insurance, group legal services, and other benefits.

**Potential common shares** Securities that, while not being common stock may become common stock through their exercise, conversion, or issuance and therefore dilute (reduce) earnings per share.

**Predictive value/feedback value** confirmation of investor expectations about future cash-generating ability.

**Preferred stock** typically has a preference (a) to specified amount of dividends (stated dollar amount per share or percentage of par value per share) and (b) to distribution of assets in the event the corporation is dissolved.

**Premium** arises when bonds are sold for more than face amount.

**Prepaid expense** represents an asset recorded when an expense is paid in advance, creating benefits beyond the current period.

**Prepayments/deferrals** the cash flow precedes either expense or revenue recognition.

**Present value** today's equivalent to a particular amount in the future.

**Prior period adjustment** addition to or reduction in the beginning retained earnings balance in a statement of shareholders' equity due to a correction of an error.

**Prior service cost** the cost of credit given for an amendment to a pension plan to employee service rendered in prior years.

**Product costs** costs associated with products and expensed as cost of goods sold only when the related products are sold.

**Profit margin on sales** net income divided by net sales; measures the amount of net income achieved per sales dollar.

**Pro forma earnings** actual (GAAP) earnings reduced by any expenses the reporting company feels are unusual and should be excluded.

**Projected benefit obligation (PBO)** the discounted present value of estimated retirement benefits earned so far by employees, applying the plan's pension formula using projected future compensation levels.

**Property dividend** when a noncash asset is distributed.

**Property, plant, and equipment** land, buildings, equipment, machinery, autos, and trucks.

**Prospective approach** the accounting change is implemented in the present, and its effects are reflected in the financial statements of the current and future years only.

**Proxy statement** contains disclosures on compensation to directors and executives; sent to all shareholders each year.

**Purchase commitments** contracts that obligate a company to purchase a specified amount of merchandise or raw materials at specified prices on or before specified dates.

**Purchase discounts** reductions in the amount to be paid if remittance is made within a designated period of time.

**Purchase return** a reduction in both inventory and accounts payable (if the account has not yet been paid) at the time of the return.

**Purchases journal** records the purchase of merchandise on account.

**Quasi reorganization** a firm undergoing financial difficulties, but with favorable future prospects, may use a quasi reorganization to write down inflated asset values and eliminate an accumulated deficit.

**Rate of return on stock investment**

$$\frac{\text{Dividends} + \text{Share price appreciation}}{\text{Initial investment}}$$

**Ratio analysis** comparison of accounting numbers to evaluate the performance and risk of a firm.

**Raw materials** cost of components purchased from other manufacturers that will become part of the finished product.

**Real estate lease** involves land—exclusively or in part.

**Realization principle** requires that the earnings process is judged to be complete or virtually complete, and there is reasonable certainty as to the collectibility of the asset to be received (usually cash) before revenue can be recognized.

**Rearrangements** expenditures made to restructure an asset without addition, replacement, or improvement.

**Receivables** a company's claims to the future collection of cash, other assets, or services.

**Receivables turnover ratio** indicates how quickly a company is able to collect its accounts receivable.

**Recognition** process of admitting information into the basic financial statements.

**Redemption privilege** might allow preferred shareholders the option, under specified conditions, to return their shares for a predetermined redemption price.

**Related-party transactions** transactions with owners, management, families of owners or management, affiliated companies, and other parties that can significantly influence or be influenced by the company.

**Relevance** one of the primary decision-specific qualities that make accounting information useful; made up of predictive value and/or feedback value, and timeliness.

**Reliability** the extent to which information is verifiable, representationally faithful, and neutral.

**Rent abatement** lease agreements may call for uneven rent payments during the term of the lease, e.g., when the initial payment (or maybe several payments) is waived.

**Replacement cost (RC)** the cost to replace the item by purchase or manufacture.

**Replacement depreciation method** depreciation is recorded when assets are replaced.

**Representational faithfulness** agreement between a measure or description and the phenomenon it purports to represent.

**Residual value** or salvage value, the amount the company expects to receive for the asset at the end of its service life less any anticipated disposal costs.

**Restoration costs** costs to restore land or other property to its original condition after extraction of the natural resource ends.

**Restricted stock** shares subject to forfeiture by the employee if employment is terminated within some specified number of years from the date of grant.

**Retail inventory method** relies on the relationship between cost and selling price to estimate ending inventory and cost of goods sold; provides a more accurate estimate than the gross profit method.

**Retained earnings** amounts earned by the corporation on behalf of its shareholders and not (yet) distributed to them as dividends.

**Retired stock** shares repurchased and not designated as treasury stock.

**Retirement depreciation method** Records depreciation when assets are disposed of and measures depreciation as the difference between the proceeds received and cost.

**Retrospective approach** financial statements issued in previous years are revised to reflect the impact of an accounting change whenever those statements are presented again for comparative purpose.

**Return on assets (ROA)** indicates a company's overall profitability.

**Return on shareholders' equity** measures the return to suppliers of equity capital.

**Revenues** inflows or other enhancements of assets or settlements of liabilities from delivering or producing goods, rendering services, or other activities that constitute the entity's ongoing major, or central, operations.

**Reverse stock split** when a company decreases, rather than increases, its outstanding shares.

**Reversing entries** optional entries that remove the effects of some of the adjusting entries made at the end of the previous reporting period for the sole purpose of simplifying journal entries made during the new period.

**Right of conversion** shareholders' right to exchange shares of preferred stock for common stock at specified conversion ratio.

**Right of return** customers' right to return merchandise to retailers if they are not satisfied.

**Rules-based accounting standards** a list of rules for choosing the appropriate accounting treatment for a transaction.

**S corporation** characteristics of both regular corporations and partnerships.

***SAB No. 101*** *Staff Accounting Bulletin 101* summarizes the SEC's views on revenue recognition.

**Sale-leaseback transaction** the owner of an asset sells it and immediately leases it back from the new owner.

**Sales journal** records credit sales.

**Sales return** the return of merchandise for a refund or for credit to be applied to other purchases.

**Sales-type lease** in addition to interest revenue earned over the lease term, the lessor receives a manufacturer's or dealer's profit on the sale of the asset.

**Sarbanes-Oxley Act** law provides for the regulation of the key players in the financial reporting process.

**Secondary market transactions** provide for the transfer of stocks and bonds among individuals and institutions.

**Securities and Exchange Commission (SEC)** responsible for setting accounting and reporting standards for companies whose securities are publicly traded.

**Securities available-for-sale** equity or debt securities the investor acquires, not for an active trading account or to be held to maturity.

**Securities to be held-to-maturity** debt securities for which the investor has the "positive intent and ability" to hold the securities to maturity.

**Securitization** the company creates a special purpose entity (SPE), usually a trust or a subsidiary; the SPE buys a pool of trade receivables, credit card receivables, or loans from the company and then sells related securities.

**Serial bonds** more structured (and less popular) way to retire bonds on a piecemeal basis.

**Service cost** increase in the projected benefit obligation attributable to employee service performed during the period.

**Service life (useful life)** the estimated use that the company expects to receive from the asset.

**Service method** allocation approach that reflects the declining service pattern of the prior service cost.

**Share purchase contract** shares ordinarily are sold in exchange for a promissory note from the subscriber—in essence, shares are sold on credit.

**Short-term investments** investments not classified as cash equivalents that will be liquidated in the coming year or operating cycle, whichever is longer.

**Significant influence** effective control is absent but the investor is able to exercise significant influence over the operating and financial policies of the investee (usually between 20% and 50% of the investee's voting shares are held).

**Simple capital structure** a firm that has no potential common shares (outstanding securities that could potentially dilute earnings per share).

**Simple interest** computed by multiplying an initial investment times both the applicable interest rate and the period of time for which the money is used.

**Single-step** income statement format that groups all revenues and gains together and all expenses and losses together.

**Sinking fund debentures** bonds that must be redeemed on a prespecified year-by-year basis; administered by a trustee who repurchases bonds in the open market.

**Source documents** relay essential information about each transaction to the accountant, e.g., sales invoices, bills from suppliers, cash register tapes.

**Special journal** record of a repetitive type of transaction, e.g., a sales journal.

**Specific identification method** each unit sold during the period or each unit on hand at the end of the period to be matched with its actual cost.

**Specific interest method** for interest capitalization, rates from specific construction loans to the extent of specific borrowings are used before using the average rate of other debt.

**Start-up costs** whenever a company introduces a new product or service, or commences business in a new territory or with a new customer, it incurs one-time costs that are expensed in the period incurred.

**Statement of cash flows** change statement summarizing the transactions that caused cash to change during the period.

**Statement of shareholders' equity** statement disclosing the source of changes in the shareholders' equity accounts.

**Stock appreciation rights (SARs)** awards that enable an employee to benefit by the amount that the market price of the company's stock rises above a specified amount without having to buy shares.

**Stock dividend** distribution of additional shares of stock to current shareholders of the corporation.

**Stock options** employees aren't actually awarded shares, but rather are given the option to buy shares at a specified exercise price within some specified number of years from the date of grant.

**Stock split** stock distribution of 25% or higher, sometimes call a *large* stock dividend.

**Straight line** an equal amount of depreciable base is allocated to each year of the asset's service life.

**Straight-line method** recording interest each period at the same dollar amount.

**Subordinated debenture** the holder is not entitled to receive any liquidation payments until the claims of other specified debt issues are satisfied.

**Subsequent event** a significant development that takes place after the company's fiscal year-end but before the financial statements are issued.

**Subsidiary ledger** record of a group of subsidiary accounts associated with a particular general ledger control account.

**Successful efforts method** requires that exploration costs that are known not to have resulted in the discovery of oil or gas be included as expense in the period the expenditures are made.

**Sum-of-the-years'-digits (SYD) method** systematic acceleration of depreciation by multiplying the depreciable base by a fraction that declines each year.

**Supplemental financial statements** reports containing more detailed information than is shown in the primary financial statements.

**T-account** account with space at the top for the account title and two sides for recording increases and decreases.

**Taxable income** comprises revenues, expenses, gains, and losses as measured according to the regulations of the appropriate taxing authority.

**Technological feasibility** established when the enterprise has completed all planning, designing, coding, and testing activities that are necessary to establish that the product can be produced to meet its design specifications including functions, features, and technical performance requirements.

**Temporary accounts** represent changes in the retained earnings component of shareholders' equity for a corporation caused by revenue, expense, gain, and loss transactions.

**Temporary difference** difference between pretax accounting income and taxable income and, consequently, between the reported amount of an asset or liability in the financial statements and its tax basis which will "reverse" in later years.

**Time-based methods** allocates the cost base according to the passage of time.

**Timeliness** information that is available to users early enough to allow its use in the decision process.

**Times interest earned ratio** a way to gauge the ability of a company to satisfy its fixed debt obligations by comparing interest charges with the income available to pay those charges.

**Time value of money** money can be invested today to earn interest and grow to a larger dollar amount in the future.

**Trade discounts** percentage reduction from the list price.

**Trademark (tradename)** exclusive right to display a word, a slogan, a symbol, or an emblem that distinctively identifies a company, a product, or a service.

**Trade notes payable** formally recognized by a written promissory note.

**Trading securities** equity or debt securities the investor (usually a financial institution) acquires principally for the purpose of selling in the near term.

**Transaction analysis** process of reviewing the source documents to determine the dual effect on the accounting equation and the specific elements involved.

**Transaction obligation** the unfunded accumulated postretirement benefit obligation existing when *SFAS 106* was adopted.

**Transactions** economic events.

**Treasury stock** shares repurchased and not retired.

**Troubled debt restructuring** the original terms of a debt agreement are changed as a result of financial difficulties experienced by the debtor (borrower).

**Trustee** person who accepts employer contributions, invests the contributions, accumulates the earnings on the investments, and pays benefits from the plan assets to retired employees or their beneficiaries.

**Unadjusted trial balance** a list of the general ledger accounts and their balances at a particular date.

**Understandability** users must understand the information within the context of the decision being made.

**Unearned revenues** cash received from a customer in one period for goods or services that are to be provided in a future period.

**Units-of-production method** computes a depreciation rate per measure of activity and then multiplies this rate by actual activity to determine periodic depreciation.

**Unqualified opinion** auditors are satisfied that the financial statements present fairly the company's financial position, results of operations, and cash flows and are in conformity with generally accepted accounting principles.

**Valuation allowance** indirect reduction (contra account) in a deferred tax asset when it is more likely than not that some portion or all of the deferred tax asset will not be realized.

**Verifiability** implies a consensus among different measurers.

**Vertical analysis** expression of each item in the financial statements as a percentage of an appropriate corresponding total, or base amount, but within the same year.

**Vested benefits** benefits that employees have the right to receive even if their employment were to cease today.

**Weighted-average interest method** for interest capitalization, weighted-average rate on all interest-bearing debt, including all construction loans, is used.

**Without recourse** the buyer assumes the risk of uncollectibility.

**With recourse** the seller retains the risk of uncollectibility.

**Working capital** differences between current assets and current liabilities.

**Work-in-process inventory** products that are not yet complete.

**Worksheet** used to organize the accounting information needed to prepare adjusting and closing entries and the financial statements.

# Photo Credits

| | |
|---|---|
| page 3 | ©Chuck Savage/CORBIS |
| page 47 | ©Jon Riley/Stone/Getty Images |
| page 101 | ©Colin Young-Wolff/PhotoEdit, Inc. |
| page 153 | ©Stockbyte/Getty Images |
| page 211 | ©Ken Reid/Photographer's Choice/Getty Images |
| page 267 | ©Michael Newman/PhotoEdit, Inc. |
| page 305 | ©Jim Arbogast/Getty Images |
| page 353 | ©Russell Gordon/Aurora Photos |
| page 401 | ©Joel Gordon |
| page 451 | ©Steve Vidler/eStock Photo |
| page 503 | ©Patrick Olear/Photo Edit, Inc. |
| page 557 | ©Justin Sullivan/Getty Images |
| page 611 | ©LWA-Stephen Welstead/CORBIS |
| page 661 | ©Stone/Getty Images |
| page 711 | ©Masterfile |
| page 773 | ©Photodisc Blue/Getty Images |
| page 827 | ©Jennifer Burrell/Masterfile |
| page 893 | ©Photodisc Collection/Getty Images |
| page 951 | ©Rob Lewine/CORBIS |
| page 1009 | ©Michael Newman/PhotoEdit, Inc. |
| page 1051 | ©Bassignac Gilles/GAMMA |

# Subject Index

Note: Page numbers followed by *n* indicate material in footnotes.

## E

## G



## H

## M

## N



## O

## S

## T

# Acounting Standards Index

Note: Page numbers followed by *n* indicate material in footnotes.

## T

# Present and Future Value Tables

This table shows the future value of $1 at various interest rates ($i$) and time periods ($n$). It is used to calculate the future value of any single amount.

**TABLE 1** Future Value of $1
$FV = \$1 (1 + i)^n$

| n/i | 1.0% | 1.5% | 2.0% | 2.5% | 3.0% | 3.5% | 4.0% | 4.5% | 5.0% | 5.5% | 6.0% | 7.0% | 8.0% | 9.0% | 10.0% | 11.0% | 12.0% | 20.0% |
|---|---|---|---|---|---|---|---|---|---|---|---|---|---|---|---|---|---|---|
| 1 | 1.01000 | 1.01500 | 1.02000 | 1.02500 | 1.03000 | 1.03500 | 1.04000 | 1.04500 | 1.05000 | 1.05500 | 1.06000 | 1.07000 | 1.08000 | 1.09000 | 1.10000 | 1.11000 | 1.12000 | 1.20000 |
| 2 | 1.02010 | 1.03022 | 1.04040 | 1.05063 | 1.06090 | 1.07123 | 1.08160 | 1.09203 | 1.10250 | 1.11303 | 1.12360 | 1.14490 | 1.16640 | 1.18810 | 1.21000 | 1.23210 | 1.25440 | 1.44000 |
| 3 | 1.03030 | 1.04568 | 1.06121 | 1.07689 | 1.09273 | 1.10872 | 1.12486 | 1.14117 | 1.15763 | 1.17424 | 1.19102 | 1.22504 | 1.25971 | 1.29503 | 1.33100 | 1.36763 | 1.40493 | 1.72800 |
| 4 | 1.04060 | 1.06136 | 1.08243 | 1.10381 | 1.12551 | 1.14752 | 1.16986 | 1.19252 | 1.21551 | 1.23882 | 1.26248 | 1.31080 | 1.36049 | 1.41158 | 1.46410 | 1.51807 | 1.57352 | 2.07360 |
| 5 | 1.05101 | 1.07728 | 1.10408 | 1.13141 | 1.15927 | 1.18769 | 1.21665 | 1.24618 | 1.27628 | 1.30696 | 1.33823 | 1.40255 | 1.46933 | 1.53862 | 1.61051 | 1.68506 | 1.76234 | 2.48832 |
| 6 | 1.06152 | 1.09344 | 1.12616 | 1.15969 | 1.19405 | 1.22926 | 1.26532 | 1.30226 | 1.34010 | 1.37884 | 1.41852 | 1.50073 | 1.58687 | 1.67710 | 1.77156 | 1.87041 | 1.97382 | 2.98598 |
| 7 | 1.07214 | 1.10984 | 1.14869 | 1.18869 | 1.22987 | 1.27228 | 1.31593 | 1.36086 | 1.40710 | 1.45468 | 1.50363 | 1.60578 | 1.71382 | 1.82804 | 1.94872 | 2.07616 | 2.21068 | 3.58318 |
| 8 | 1.08286 | 1.12649 | 1.17166 | 1.21840 | 1.26677 | 1.31681 | 1.36857 | 1.42210 | 1.47746 | 1.53469 | 1.59385 | 1.71819 | 1.85093 | 1.99256 | 2.14359 | 2.30454 | 2.47596 | 4.29982 |
| 9 | 1.09369 | 1.14339 | 1.19509 | 1.24886 | 1.30477 | 1.36290 | 1.42331 | 1.48610 | 1.55133 | 1.61909 | 1.68948 | 1.83846 | 1.99900 | 2.17189 | 2.35795 | 2.55804 | 2.77308 | 5.15978 |
| 10 | 1.10462 | 1.16054 | 1.21899 | 1.28008 | 1.34392 | 1.41060 | 1.48024 | 1.55297 | 1.62889 | 1.70814 | 1.79085 | 1.96715 | 2.15892 | 2.36736 | 2.59374 | 2.83942 | 3.10585 | 6.19174 |
| 11 | 1.11567 | 1.17795 | 1.24337 | 1.31209 | 1.38423 | 1.45997 | 1.53945 | 1.62285 | 1.71034 | 1.80209 | 1.89830 | 2.10485 | 2.33164 | 2.58043 | 2.85312 | 3.15176 | 3.47855 | 7.43008 |
| 12 | 1.12683 | 1.19562 | 1.26824 | 1.34489 | 1.42576 | 1.51107 | 1.60103 | 1.69588 | 1.79586 | 1.90121 | 2.01220 | 2.25219 | 2.51817 | 2.81266 | 3.13843 | 3.49845 | 3.89598 | 8.91610 |
| 13 | 1.13809 | 1.21355 | 1.29361 | 1.37851 | 1.46853 | 1.56396 | 1.66507 | 1.77220 | 1.88565 | 2.00577 | 2.13293 | 2.40985 | 2.71962 | 3.06580 | 3.45227 | 3.88328 | 4.36349 | 10.69932 |
| 14 | 1.14947 | 1.23176 | 1.31948 | 1.41297 | 1.51259 | 1.61869 | 1.73168 | 1.85194 | 1.97993 | 2.11609 | 2.26090 | 2.57853 | 2.93719 | 3.34173 | 3.79750 | 4.31044 | 4.88711 | 12.83918 |
| 15 | 1.16097 | 1.25023 | 1.34587 | 1.44830 | 1.55797 | 1.67535 | 1.80094 | 1.93528 | 2.07893 | 2.23248 | 2.39656 | 2.75903 | 3.17217 | 3.64248 | 4.17725 | 4.78459 | 5.47357 | 15.40702 |
| 16 | 1.17258 | 1.26899 | 1.37279 | 1.48451 | 1.60471 | 1.73399 | 1.87298 | 2.02237 | 2.18287 | 2.35526 | 2.54035 | 2.95216 | 3.42594 | 3.97031 | 4.59497 | 5.31089 | 6.13039 | 18.48843 |
| 17 | 1.18430 | 1.28802 | 1.40024 | 1.52162 | 1.65285 | 1.79468 | 1.94790 | 2.11338 | 2.29202 | 2.48480 | 2.69277 | 3.15882 | 3.70002 | 4.32763 | 5.05447 | 5.89509 | 6.86604 | 22.18611 |
| 18 | 1.19615 | 1.30734 | 1.42825 | 1.55966 | 1.70243 | 1.85749 | 2.02582 | 2.20848 | 2.40662 | 2.62147 | 2.85434 | 3.37993 | 3.99602 | 4.71712 | 5.55992 | 6.54355 | 7.68997 | 26.62333 |
| 19 | 1.20811 | 1.32695 | 1.45681 | 1.59865 | 1.75351 | 1.92250 | 2.10685 | 2.30786 | 2.52695 | 2.76565 | 3.02560 | 3.61653 | 4.31570 | 5.14166 | 6.11591 | 7.26334 | 8.61276 | 31.94800 |
| 20 | 1.22019 | 1.34686 | 1.48595 | 1.63862 | 1.80611 | 1.98979 | 2.19112 | 2.41171 | 2.65330 | 2.91776 | 3.20714 | 3.86968 | 4.66096 | 5.60441 | 6.72750 | 8.06231 | 9.64629 | 38.33760 |
| 21 | 1.23239 | 1.36706 | 1.51567 | 1.67958 | 1.86029 | 2.05943 | 2.27877 | 2.52024 | 2.78596 | 3.07823 | 3.39956 | 4.14056 | 5.03383 | 6.10881 | 7.40025 | 8.94917 | 10.80385 | 46.00512 |
| 25 | 1.28243 | 1.45095 | 1.64061 | 1.85394 | 2.09378 | 2.36324 | 2.66584 | 3.00543 | 3.38635 | 3.81339 | 4.29187 | 5.42743 | 6.84848 | 8.62308 | 10.83471 | 13.58546 | 17.00006 | 95.39622 |
| 30 | 1.34785 | 1.56308 | 1.81136 | 2.09757 | 2.42726 | 2.80679 | 3.24340 | 3.74532 | 4.32194 | 4.98395 | 5.74349 | 7.61226 | 10.06266 | 13.26768 | 17.44940 | 22.89230 | 29.95992 | 237.37631 |
| 40 | 1.48886 | 1.81402 | 2.20804 | 2.68506 | 3.26204 | 3.95926 | 4.80102 | 5.81636 | 7.03999 | 8.51331 | 10.28572 | 14.97446 | 21.72452 | 31.40942 | 45.25926 | 65.00087 | 93.05097 | 1469.77160 |

This table shows the present value of $1 at various interest rates ($i$) and time periods ($n$). It is used to calculate the present value of any single amount.

**TABLE 2** Present Value of $1

$$PV = \frac{\$1}{(1 + i)^n}$$

| n/i | 1.0% | 1.5% | 2.0% | 2.5% | 3.0% | 3.5% | 4.0% | 4.5% | 5.0% | 5.5% | 6.0% | 7.0% | 8.0% | 9.0% | 10.0% | 11.0% | 12.0% | 20.0% |
|---|---|---|---|---|---|---|---|---|---|---|---|---|---|---|---|---|---|---|
| 1 | 0.99010 | 0.98522 | 0.98039 | 0.97561 | 0.97087 | 0.96618 | 0.96154 | 0.95694 | 0.95238 | 0.94787 | 0.94340 | 0.93458 | 0.92593 | 0.91743 | 0.90909 | 0.90090 | 0.89286 | 0.83333 |
| 2 | 0.98030 | 0.97066 | 0.96117 | 0.95181 | 0.94260 | 0.93351 | 0.92456 | 0.91573 | 0.90703 | 0.89845 | 0.89000 | 0.87344 | 0.85734 | 0.84168 | 0.82645 | 0.81162 | 0.79719 | 0.69444 |
| 3 | 0.97059 | 0.95632 | 0.94232 | 0.92860 | 0.91514 | 0.90194 | 0.88900 | 0.87630 | 0.86384 | 0.85161 | 0.83962 | 0.81630 | 0.79383 | 0.77218 | 0.75131 | 0.73119 | 0.71178 | 0.57870 |
| 4 | 0.96098 | 0.94218 | 0.92385 | 0.90595 | 0.88849 | 0.87144 | 0.85480 | 0.83856 | 0.82270 | 0.80722 | 0.79209 | 0.76290 | 0.73503 | 0.70843 | 0.68301 | 0.65873 | 0.63552 | 0.48225 |
| 5 | 0.95147 | 0.92826 | 0.90573 | 0.88385 | 0.86261 | 0.84197 | 0.82193 | 0.80245 | 0.78353 | 0.76513 | 0.74726 | 0.71299 | 0.68058 | 0.64993 | 0.62092 | 0.59345 | 0.56743 | 0.40188 |
| 6 | 0.94205 | 0.91454 | 0.88797 | 0.86230 | 0.83748 | 0.81350 | 0.79031 | 0.76790 | 0.74622 | 0.72525 | 0.70496 | 0.66634 | 0.63017 | 0.59627 | 0.56447 | 0.53464 | 0.50663 | 0.33490 |
| 7 | 0.93272 | 0.90103 | 0.87056 | 0.84127 | 0.81309 | 0.78599 | 0.75992 | 0.73483 | 0.71068 | 0.68744 | 0.66506 | 0.62275 | 0.58349 | 0.54703 | 0.51316 | 0.48166 | 0.45235 | 0.27908 |
| 8 | 0.92348 | 0.88771 | 0.85349 | 0.82075 | 0.78941 | 0.75941 | 0.73069 | 0.70319 | 0.67684 | 0.65160 | 0.62741 | 0.58201 | 0.54027 | 0.50187 | 0.46651 | 0.43393 | 0.40388 | 0.23257 |
| 9 | 0.91434 | 0.87459 | 0.83676 | 0.80073 | 0.76642 | 0.73373 | 0.70259 | 0.67290 | 0.64461 | 0.61763 | 0.59190 | 0.54393 | 0.50025 | 0.46043 | 0.42410 | 0.39092 | 0.36061 | 0.19381 |
| 10 | 0.90529 | 0.86167 | 0.82035 | 0.78120 | 0.74409 | 0.70892 | 0.67556 | 0.64393 | 0.61391 | 0.58543 | 0.55839 | 0.50835 | 0.46319 | 0.42241 | 0.38554 | 0.35218 | 0.32197 | 0.16151 |
| 11 | 0.89632 | 0.84893 | 0.80426 | 0.76214 | 0.72242 | 0.68495 | 0.64958 | 0.61620 | 0.58468 | 0.55491 | 0.52679 | 0.47509 | 0.42888 | 0.38753 | 0.35049 | 0.31728 | 0.28748 | 0.13459 |
| 12 | 0.88745 | 0.83639 | 0.78849 | 0.74356 | 0.70138 | 0.66178 | 0.62460 | 0.58966 | 0.55684 | 0.52598 | 0.49697 | 0.44401 | 0.39711 | 0.35553 | 0.31863 | 0.28584 | 0.25668 | 0.11216 |
| 13 | 0.87866 | 0.82403 | 0.77303 | 0.72542 | 0.68095 | 0.63940 | 0.60057 | 0.56427 | 0.53032 | 0.49856 | 0.46884 | 0.41496 | 0.36770 | 0.32618 | 0.28966 | 0.25751 | 0.22917 | 0.09346 |
| 14 | 0.86996 | 0.81185 | 0.75788 | 0.70773 | 0.66112 | 0.61778 | 0.57748 | 0.53997 | 0.50507 | 0.47257 | 0.44230 | 0.38782 | 0.34046 | 0.29925 | 0.26333 | 0.23199 | 0.20462 | 0.07789 |
| 15 | 0.86135 | 0.79985 | 0.74301 | 0.69047 | 0.64186 | 0.59689 | 0.55526 | 0.51672 | 0.48102 | 0.44793 | 0.41727 | 0.36245 | 0.31524 | 0.27454 | 0.23939 | 0.20900 | 0.18270 | 0.06491 |
| 16 | 0.85282 | 0.78803 | 0.72845 | 0.67362 | 0.62317 | 0.57671 | 0.53391 | 0.49447 | 0.45811 | 0.42458 | 0.39365 | 0.33873 | 0.29189 | 0.25187 | 0.21763 | 0.18829 | 0.16312 | 0.05409 |
| 17 | 0.84438 | 0.77639 | 0.71416 | 0.65720 | 0.60502 | 0.55720 | 0.51337 | 0.47318 | 0.43630 | 0.40245 | 0.37136 | 0.31657 | 0.27027 | 0.23107 | 0.19784 | 0.16963 | 0.14564 | 0.04507 |
| 18 | 0.83602 | 0.76491 | 0.70016 | 0.64117 | 0.58739 | 0.53836 | 0.49363 | 0.45280 | 0.41552 | 0.38147 | 0.35034 | 0.29586 | 0.25025 | 0.21199 | 0.17986 | 0.15282 | 0.13004 | 0.03756 |
| 19 | 0.82774 | 0.75361 | 0.68643 | 0.62553 | 0.57029 | 0.52016 | 0.47464 | 0.43330 | 0.39573 | 0.36158 | 0.33051 | 0.27651 | 0.23171 | 0.19449 | 0.16351 | 0.13768 | 0.11611 | 0.03130 |
| 20 | 0.81954 | 0.74247 | 0.67297 | 0.61027 | 0.55368 | 0.50257 | 0.45639 | 0.41464 | 0.37689 | 0.34273 | 0.31180 | 0.25842 | 0.21455 | 0.17843 | 0.14864 | 0.12403 | 0.10367 | 0.02608 |
| 21 | 0.81143 | 0.73150 | 0.65978 | 0.59539 | 0.53755 | 0.48557 | 0.43883 | 0.39679 | 0.35894 | 0.32486 | 0.29416 | 0.24151 | 0.19866 | 0.16370 | 0.13513 | 0.11174 | 0.09256 | 0.02174 |
| 24 | 0.78757 | 0.69954 | 0.62172 | 0.55288 | 0.49193 | 0.43796 | 0.39012 | 0.34770 | 0.31007 | 0.27666 | 0.24698 | 0.19715 | 0.15770 | 0.12640 | 0.10153 | 0.08170 | 0.06588 | 0.01258 |
| 25 | 0.77977 | 0.68921 | 0.60953 | 0.53939 | 0.47761 | 0.42315 | 0.37512 | 0.33273 | 0.29530 | 0.26223 | 0.23300 | 0.18425 | 0.14602 | 0.11597 | 0.09230 | 0.07361 | 0.05882 | 0.01048 |
| 28 | 0.75684 | 0.65910 | 0.57437 | 0.50088 | 0.43708 | 0.38165 | 0.33348 | 0.29157 | 0.25509 | 0.22332 | 0.19563 | 0.15040 | 0.11591 | 0.08955 | 0.06934 | 0.05382 | 0.04187 | 0.00607 |
| 29 | 0.74934 | 0.64936 | 0.56311 | 0.48866 | 0.42435 | 0.36875 | 0.32065 | 0.27902 | 0.24295 | 0.21168 | 0.18456 | 0.14056 | 0.10733 | 0.08215 | 0.06304 | 0.04849 | 0.03738 | 0.00506 |
| 30 | 0.74192 | 0.63976 | 0.55207 | 0.47674 | 0.41199 | 0.35628 | 0.30832 | 0.26700 | 0.23138 | 0.20064 | 0.17411 | 0.13137 | 0.09938 | 0.07537 | 0.05731 | 0.04368 | 0.03338 | 0.00421 |
| 31 | 0.73458 | 0.63031 | 0.54125 | 0.46511 | 0.39999 | 0.34423 | 0.29646 | 0.25550 | 0.22036 | 0.19018 | 0.16425 | 0.12277 | 0.09202 | 0.06915 | 0.05210 | 0.03935 | 0.02980 | 0.00351 |
| 40 | 0.67165 | 0.55126 | 0.45289 | 0.37243 | 0.30656 | 0.25257 | 0.20829 | 0.17193 | 0.14205 | 0.11746 | 0.09722 | 0.06678 | 0.04603 | 0.03184 | 0.02209 | 0.01538 | 0.01075 | 0.00068 |

This table shows the future value of an ordinary annuity of $1 at various interest rates ($i$) and time periods ($n$). It is used to calculate the future value of any series of equal payments made at the *end* of each compounding period.

**TABLE 3** Future Value of an Ordinary Annuity of $1

$$FVA = \frac{(1 + i)^n - 1}{i}$$

| n/i | 1.0% | 1.5% | 2.0% | 2.5% | 3.0% | 3.5% | 4.0% | 4.5% | 5.0% | 5.5% | 6.0% | 7.0% | 8.0% | 9.0% | 10.0% | 11.0% | 12.0% | 20.0% |
|---|---|---|---|---|---|---|---|---|---|---|---|---|---|---|---|---|---|---|
| 1 | 1.0000 | 1.0000 | 1.0000 | 1.0000 | 1.0000 | 1.0000 | 1.0000 | 1.0000 | 1.0000 | 1.0000 | 1.0000 | 1.0000 | 1.0000 | 1.0000 | 1.0000 | 1.0000 | 1.0000 | 1.0000 |
| 2 | 2.0100 | 2.0150 | 2.0200 | 2.0250 | 2.0300 | 2.0350 | 2.0400 | 2.0450 | 2.0500 | 2.0550 | 2.0600 | 2.0700 | 2.0800 | 2.0900 | 2.1000 | 2.1100 | 2.1200 | 2.2000 |
| 3 | 3.0301 | 3.0452 | 3.0604 | 3.0756 | 3.0909 | 3.1062 | 3.1216 | 3.1370 | 3.1525 | 3.1680 | 3.1836 | 3.2149 | 3.2464 | 3.2781 | 3.3100 | 3.3421 | 3.3744 | 3.6400 |
| 4 | 4.0604 | 4.0909 | 4.1216 | 4.1525 | 4.1836 | 4.2149 | 4.2465 | 4.2782 | 4.3101 | 4.3423 | 4.3746 | 4.4399 | 4.5061 | 4.5731 | 4.6410 | 4.7097 | 4.7793 | 5.3680 |
| 5 | 5.1010 | 5.1523 | 5.2040 | 5.2563 | 5.3091 | 5.3625 | 5.4163 | 5.4707 | 5.5256 | 5.5811 | 5.6371 | 5.7507 | 5.8666 | 5.9847 | 6.1051 | 6.2278 | 6.3528 | 7.4416 |
| 6 | 6.1520 | 6.2296 | 6.3081 | 6.3877 | 6.4684 | 6.5502 | 6.6330 | 6.7169 | 6.8019 | 6.8881 | 6.9753 | 7.1533 | 7.3359 | 7.5233 | 7.7156 | 7.9129 | 8.1152 | 9.9299 |
| 7 | 7.2135 | 7.3230 | 7.4343 | 7.5474 | 7.6625 | 7.7794 | 7.8983 | 8.0192 | 8.1420 | 8.2669 | 8.3938 | 8.6540 | 8.9228 | 9.2004 | 9.4872 | 9.7833 | 10.0890 | 12.9159 |
| 8 | 8.2857 | 8.4328 | 8.5830 | 8.7361 | 8.8923 | 9.0517 | 9.2142 | 9.3800 | 9.5491 | 9.7216 | 9.8975 | 10.2598 | 10.6366 | 11.0285 | 11.4359 | 11.8594 | 12.2997 | 16.4991 |
| 9 | 9.3685 | 9.5593 | 9.7546 | 9.9545 | 10.1591 | 10.3685 | 10.5828 | 10.8021 | 11.0266 | 11.2563 | 11.4913 | 11.9780 | 12.4876 | 13.0210 | 13.5795 | 14.1640 | 14.7757 | 20.7989 |
| 10 | 10.4622 | 10.7027 | 10.9497 | 11.2034 | 11.4639 | 11.7314 | 12.0061 | 12.2882 | 12.5779 | 12.8754 | 13.1808 | 13.8164 | 14.4866 | 15.1929 | 15.9374 | 16.7220 | 17.5487 | 25.9587 |
| 11 | 11.5668 | 11.8633 | 12.1687 | 12.4835 | 12.8078 | 13.1420 | 13.4864 | 13.8412 | 14.2068 | 14.5835 | 14.9716 | 15.7836 | 16.6455 | 17.5603 | 18.5312 | 19.5614 | 20.6546 | 32.1504 |
| 12 | 12.6825 | 13.0412 | 13.4121 | 13.7956 | 14.1920 | 14.6020 | 15.0258 | 15.4640 | 15.9171 | 16.3856 | 16.8699 | 17.8885 | 18.9771 | 20.1407 | 21.3843 | 22.7132 | 24.1331 | 39.5805 |
| 13 | 13.8093 | 14.2368 | 14.6803 | 15.1404 | 15.6178 | 16.1130 | 16.6268 | 17.1599 | 17.7130 | 18.2868 | 18.8821 | 20.1406 | 21.4953 | 22.9534 | 24.5227 | 26.2116 | 28.0291 | 48.4966 |
| 14 | 14.9474 | 15.4504 | 15.9739 | 16.5190 | 17.0863 | 17.6770 | 18.2919 | 18.9321 | 19.5986 | 20.2926 | 21.0151 | 22.5505 | 24.2149 | 26.0192 | 27.9750 | 30.0949 | 32.3926 | 59.1959 |
| 15 | 16.0969 | 16.6821 | 17.2934 | 17.9319 | 18.5989 | 19.2957 | 20.0236 | 20.7841 | 21.5786 | 22.4087 | 23.2760 | 25.1290 | 27.1521 | 29.3609 | 31.7725 | 34.4054 | 37.2797 | 72.0351 |
| 16 | 17.2579 | 17.9324 | 18.6393 | 19.3802 | 20.1569 | 20.9710 | 21.8245 | 22.7193 | 23.6575 | 24.6411 | 25.6725 | 27.8881 | 30.3243 | 33.0034 | 35.9497 | 39.1899 | 42.7533 | 87.4421 |
| 17 | 18.4304 | 19.2014 | 20.0121 | 20.8647 | 21.7616 | 22.7050 | 23.6975 | 24.7417 | 25.8404 | 26.9964 | 28.2129 | 30.8402 | 33.7502 | 36.9737 | 40.5447 | 44.5008 | 48.8837 | 105.9306 |
| 18 | 19.6147 | 20.4894 | 21.4123 | 22.3863 | 23.4144 | 24.4997 | 25.6454 | 26.8551 | 28.1324 | 29.4812 | 30.9057 | 33.9990 | 37.4502 | 41.3013 | 45.5992 | 50.3959 | 55.7497 | 128.1167 |
| 19 | 20.8109 | 21.7967 | 22.8406 | 23.9460 | 25.1169 | 26.3572 | 27.6712 | 29.0636 | 30.5390 | 32.1027 | 33.7600 | 37.3790 | 41.4463 | 46.0185 | 51.1591 | 56.9395 | 63.4397 | 154.7400 |
| 20 | 22.0190 | 23.1237 | 24.2974 | 25.5447 | 26.8704 | 28.2797 | 29.7781 | 31.3714 | 33.0660 | 34.8683 | 36.7856 | 40.9955 | 45.7620 | 51.1601 | 57.2750 | 64.2028 | 72.0524 | 186.6880 |
| 21 | 23.2392 | 24.4705 | 25.7833 | 27.1833 | 28.6765 | 30.2695 | 31.9692 | 33.7831 | 35.7193 | 37.7861 | 39.9927 | 44.8652 | 50.4229 | 56.7645 | 64.0025 | 72.2651 | 81.6987 | 225.0256 |
| 30 | 34.7849 | 37.5387 | 40.5681 | 43.9027 | 47.5754 | 51.6227 | 56.0849 | 61.0071 | 66.4388 | 72.4355 | 79.0582 | 94.4608 | 113.2832 | 136.3075 | 164.4940 | 199.0209 | 241.3327 | 1181.8816 |
| 40 | 48.8864 | 54.2679 | 60.4020 | 67.4026 | 75.4013 | 84.5503 | 95.0255 | 107.0303 | 120.7998 | 136.6056 | 154.7620 | 199.6351 | 259.0565 | 337.8824 | 442.5926 | 581.8261 | 767.0914 | 7343.8578 |

This table shows the present value of an ordinary annuity of $1 at various interest rates ($i$) and time periods ($n$). It is used to calculate the present value of any series of equal payments made at the *end* of each compounding period.

**TABLE 4** Present Value of an Ordinary Annuity of $1

$$PVA = \frac{1 - \frac{1}{(1+i)^n}}{i}$$

| n/i | 1.0% | 1.5% | 2.0% | 2.5% | 3.0% | 3.5% | 4.0% | 4.5% | 5.0% | 5.5% | 6.0% | 7.0% | 8.0% | 9.0% | 10.0% | 11.0% | 12.0% | 20.0% |
|---|---|---|---|---|---|---|---|---|---|---|---|---|---|---|---|---|---|---|
| 1 | 0.99010 | 0.98522 | 0.98039 | 0.97561 | 0.97087 | 0.96618 | 0.96154 | 0.95694 | 0.95238 | 0.94787 | 0.94340 | 0.93458 | 0.92593 | 0.91743 | 0.90909 | 0.90090 | 0.89286 | 0.83333 |
| 2 | 1.97040 | 1.95588 | 1.94156 | 1.92742 | 1.91347 | 1.89969 | 1.88609 | 1.87267 | 1.85941 | 1.84632 | 1.83339 | 1.80802 | 1.78326 | 1.75911 | 1.73554 | 1.71252 | 1.69005 | 1.52778 |
| 3 | 2.94099 | 2.91220 | 2.88388 | 2.85602 | 2.82861 | 2.80164 | 2.77509 | 2.74896 | 2.72325 | 2.69793 | 2.67301 | 2.62432 | 2.57710 | 2.53129 | 2.48685 | 2.44371 | 2.40183 | 2.10648 |
| 4 | 3.90197 | 3.85438 | 3.80773 | 3.76197 | 3.71710 | 3.67308 | 3.62990 | 3.58753 | 3.54595 | 3.50515 | 3.46511 | 3.38721 | 3.31213 | 3.23972 | 3.16987 | 3.10245 | 3.03735 | 2.58873 |
| 5 | 4.85343 | 4.78264 | 4.71346 | 4.64583 | 4.57971 | 4.51505 | 4.45182 | 4.38998 | 4.32948 | 4.27028 | 4.21236 | 4.10020 | 3.99271 | 3.88965 | 3.79079 | 3.69590 | 3.60478 | 2.99061 |
| 6 | 5.79548 | 5.69719 | 5.60143 | 5.50813 | 5.41719 | 5.32855 | 5.24214 | 5.15787 | 5.07569 | 4.99553 | 4.91732 | 4.76654 | 4.62288 | 4.48592 | 4.35526 | 4.23054 | 4.11141 | 3.32551 |
| 7 | 6.72819 | 6.59821 | 6.47199 | 6.34939 | 6.23028 | 6.11454 | 6.00205 | 5.89270 | 5.78637 | 5.68297 | 5.58238 | 5.38929 | 5.20637 | 5.03295 | 4.86842 | 4.71220 | 4.56376 | 3.60459 |
| 8 | 7.65168 | 7.48593 | 7.32548 | 7.17014 | 7.01969 | 6.87396 | 6.73274 | 6.59589 | 6.46321 | 6.33457 | 6.20979 | 5.97130 | 5.74664 | 5.53482 | 5.33493 | 5.14612 | 4.96764 | 3.83716 |
| 9 | 8.56602 | 8.36052 | 8.16224 | 7.97087 | 7.78611 | 7.60769 | 7.43533 | 7.26879 | 7.10782 | 6.95220 | 6.80169 | 6.51523 | 6.24689 | 5.99525 | 5.75902 | 5.53705 | 5.32825 | 4.03097 |
| 10 | 9.47130 | 9.22218 | 8.98259 | 8.75206 | 8.53020 | 8.31661 | 8.11090 | 7.91272 | 7.72173 | 7.53763 | 7.36009 | 7.02358 | 6.71008 | 6.41766 | 6.14457 | 5.88923 | 5.65022 | 4.19247 |
| 11 | 10.36763 | 10.07112 | 9.78685 | 9.51421 | 9.25262 | 9.00155 | 8.76048 | 8.52892 | 8.30641 | 8.09254 | 7.88687 | 7.49867 | 7.13896 | 6.80519 | 6.49506 | 6.20652 | 5.93770 | 4.32706 |
| 12 | 11.25508 | 10.90751 | 10.57534 | 10.25776 | 9.95400 | 9.66333 | 9.38507 | 9.11858 | 8.86325 | 8.61852 | 8.38384 | 7.94269 | 7.53608 | 7.16073 | 6.81369 | 6.49236 | 6.19437 | 4.43922 |
| 13 | 12.13374 | 11.73153 | 11.34837 | 10.98319 | 10.63496 | 10.30274 | 9.98565 | 9.68285 | 9.39357 | 9.11708 | 8.85268 | 8.35765 | 7.90378 | 7.48690 | 7.10336 | 6.74987 | 6.42355 | 4.53268 |
| 14 | 13.00370 | 12.54338 | 12.10625 | 11.69091 | 11.29607 | 10.92052 | 10.56312 | 10.22283 | 9.89864 | 9.58965 | 9.29498 | 8.74547 | 8.24424 | 7.78615 | 7.36669 | 6.98187 | 6.62817 | 4.61057 |
| 15 | 13.86505 | 13.34323 | 12.84926 | 12.38138 | 11.93794 | 11.51741 | 11.11839 | 10.73955 | 10.37966 | 10.03758 | 9.71225 | 9.10791 | 8.55948 | 8.06069 | 7.60608 | 7.19087 | 6.81086 | 4.67547 |
| 16 | 14.71787 | 14.13126 | 13.57771 | 13.05500 | 12.56110 | 12.09412 | 11.65230 | 11.23402 | 10.83777 | 10.46216 | 10.10590 | 9.44665 | 8.85137 | 8.31256 | 7.82371 | 7.37916 | 6.97399 | 4.72956 |
| 17 | 15.56225 | 14.90765 | 14.29187 | 13.71220 | 13.16612 | 12.65132 | 12.16567 | 11.70719 | 11.27407 | 10.86461 | 10.47726 | 9.76322 | 9.12164 | 8.54363 | 8.02155 | 7.54879 | 7.11963 | 4.77463 |
| 18 | 16.39827 | 15.67256 | 14.99203 | 14.35336 | 13.75351 | 13.18968 | 12.65930 | 12.15999 | 11.68959 | 11.24607 | 10.82760 | 10.05909 | 9.37189 | 8.75563 | 8.20141 | 7.70162 | 7.24967 | 4.81219 |
| 19 | 17.22601 | 16.42617 | 15.67846 | 14.97889 | 14.32380 | 13.70984 | 13.13394 | 12.59329 | 12.08532 | 11.60765 | 11.15812 | 10.33560 | 9.60360 | 8.95011 | 8.36492 | 7.83929 | 7.36578 | 4.84350 |
| 20 | 18.04555 | 17.16864 | 16.35143 | 15.58916 | 14.87747 | 14.21240 | 13.59033 | 13.00794 | 12.46221 | 11.95038 | 11.46992 | 10.59401 | 9.81815 | 9.12855 | 8.51356 | 7.96333 | 7.46944 | 4.86958 |
| 21 | 18.85698 | 17.90014 | 17.01121 | 16.18455 | 15.41502 | 14.69797 | 14.02916 | 13.40472 | 12.82115 | 12.27524 | 11.76408 | 10.83553 | 10.01680 | 9.29224 | 8.64869 | 8.07507 | 7.56200 | 4.89132 |
| 25 | 22.02316 | 20.71961 | 19.52346 | 18.42438 | 17.41315 | 16.48151 | 15.62208 | 14.82821 | 14.09394 | 13.41393 | 12.78336 | 11.65358 | 10.67478 | 9.82258 | 9.07704 | 8.42174 | 7.84314 | 4.94759 |
| 30 | 25.80771 | 24.01584 | 22.39646 | 20.93029 | 19.60044 | 18.39205 | 17.29203 | 16.28889 | 15.37245 | 14.53375 | 13.76483 | 12.40904 | 11.25778 | 10.27365 | 9.42691 | 8.69379 | 8.05518 | 4.97894 |
| 40 | 32.83469 | 29.91585 | 27.35548 | 25.10278 | 23.11477 | 21.35507 | 19.79277 | 18.40158 | 17.15909 | 16.04612 | 15.04630 | 13.33171 | 11.92461 | 10.75736 | 9.77905 | 8.95105 | 8.24378 | 4.99660 |

This table shows the future value of an annuity due of $1 at various interest rates ($i$) and time periods ($n$). It is used to calculate the future value of any series of equal payments made at the *beginning* of each compounding period.

**TABLE 5** Future Value of an Annuity Due of $1

$$FVAD = \left[\frac{(1+i)^n - 1}{i}\right] \times (1+i)$$

| n/i | 1.0% | 1.5% | 2.0% | 2.5% | 3.0% | 3.5% | 4.0% | 4.5% | 5.0% | 5.5% | 6.0% | 7.0% | 8.0% | 9.0% | 10.0% | 11.0% | 12.0% | 20.0% |
|---|---|---|---|---|---|---|---|---|---|---|---|---|---|---|---|---|---|---|
| 1 | 1.0100 | 1.0150 | 1.0200 | 1.0250 | 1.0300 | 1.0350 | 1.0400 | 1.0450 | 1.0500 | 1.0550 | 1.0600 | 1.0700 | 1.0800 | 1.0900 | 1.1000 | 1.1100 | 1.1200 | 1.2000 |
| 2 | 2.0301 | 2.0452 | 2.0604 | 2.0756 | 2.0909 | 2.1062 | 2.1216 | 2.1370 | 2.1525 | 2.1680 | 2.1836 | 2.2149 | 2.2464 | 2.2781 | 2.3100 | 2.3421 | 2.3744 | 2.6400 |
| 3 | 3.0604 | 3.0909 | 3.1216 | 3.1525 | 3.1836 | 3.2149 | 3.2465 | 3.2782 | 3.3101 | 3.3423 | 3.3746 | 3.4399 | 3.5061 | 3.5731 | 3.6410 | 3.7097 | 3.7793 | 4.3680 |
| 4 | 4.1010 | 4.1523 | 4.2040 | 4.2563 | 4.3091 | 4.3625 | 4.4163 | 4.4707 | 4.5256 | 4.5811 | 4.6371 | 4.7507 | 4.8666 | 4.9847 | 5.1051 | 5.2278 | 5.3528 | 6.4416 |
| 5 | 5.1520 | 5.2296 | 5.3081 | 5.3877 | 5.4684 | 5.5502 | 5.6330 | 5.7169 | 5.8019 | 5.8881 | 5.9753 | 6.1533 | 6.3359 | 6.5233 | 6.7156 | 6.9129 | 7.1152 | 8.9299 |
| 6 | 6.2135 | 6.3230 | 6.4343 | 6.5474 | 6.6625 | 6.7794 | 6.8983 | 7.0192 | 7.1420 | 7.2669 | 7.3938 | 7.6540 | 7.9228 | 8.2004 | 8.4872 | 8.7833 | 9.0890 | 11.9159 |
| 7 | 7.2857 | 7.4328 | 7.5830 | 7.7361 | 7.8923 | 8.0517 | 8.2142 | 8.3800 | 8.5491 | 8.7216 | 8.8975 | 9.2598 | 9.6366 | 10.0285 | 10.4359 | 10.8594 | 11.2997 | 15.4991 |
| 8 | 8.3685 | 8.5593 | 8.7546 | 8.9545 | 9.1591 | 9.3685 | 9.5828 | 9.8021 | 10.0266 | 10.2563 | 10.4913 | 10.9780 | 11.4876 | 12.0210 | 12.5795 | 13.1640 | 13.7757 | 19.7989 |
| 9 | 9.4622 | 9.7027 | 9.9497 | 10.2034 | 10.4639 | 10.7314 | 11.0061 | 11.2882 | 11.5779 | 11.8754 | 12.1808 | 12.8164 | 13.4866 | 14.1929 | 14.9374 | 15.7220 | 16.5487 | 24.9587 |
| 10 | 10.5668 | 10.8633 | 11.1687 | 11.4835 | 11.8078 | 12.1420 | 12.4864 | 12.8412 | 13.2068 | 13.5835 | 13.9716 | 14.7836 | 15.6455 | 16.5603 | 17.5312 | 18.5614 | 19.6546 | 31.1504 |
| 11 | 11.6825 | 12.0412 | 12.4121 | 12.7956 | 13.1920 | 13.6020 | 14.0258 | 14.4640 | 14.9171 | 15.3856 | 15.8699 | 16.8885 | 17.9771 | 19.1407 | 20.3843 | 21.7132 | 23.1331 | 38.5805 |
| 12 | 12.8093 | 13.2368 | 13.6803 | 14.1404 | 14.6178 | 15.1130 | 15.6268 | 16.1599 | 16.7130 | 17.2868 | 17.8821 | 19.1406 | 20.4953 | 21.9534 | 23.5227 | 25.2116 | 27.0291 | 47.4966 |
| 13 | 13.9474 | 14.4504 | 14.9739 | 15.5190 | 16.0863 | 16.6770 | 17.2919 | 17.9321 | 18.5986 | 19.2926 | 20.0151 | 21.5505 | 23.2149 | 25.0192 | 26.9750 | 29.0949 | 31.3926 | 58.1959 |
| 14 | 15.0969 | 15.6821 | 16.2934 | 16.9319 | 17.5989 | 18.2957 | 19.0236 | 19.7841 | 20.5786 | 21.4087 | 22.2760 | 24.1290 | 26.1521 | 28.3609 | 30.7725 | 33.4054 | 36.2797 | 71.0351 |
| 15 | 16.2579 | 16.9324 | 17.6393 | 18.3802 | 19.1569 | 19.9710 | 20.8245 | 21.7193 | 22.6575 | 23.6411 | 24.6725 | 26.8881 | 29.3243 | 32.0034 | 34.9497 | 38.1899 | 41.7533 | 86.4421 |
| 16 | 17.4304 | 18.2014 | 19.0121 | 19.8647 | 20.7616 | 21.7050 | 22.6975 | 23.7417 | 24.8404 | 25.9964 | 27.2129 | 29.8402 | 32.7502 | 35.9737 | 39.5447 | 43.5008 | 47.8837 | 104.9306 |
| 17 | 18.6147 | 19.4894 | 20.4123 | 21.3863 | 22.4144 | 23.4997 | 24.6454 | 25.8551 | 27.1324 | 28.4812 | 29.9057 | 32.9990 | 36.4502 | 40.3013 | 44.5992 | 49.3959 | 54.7497 | 127.1167 |
| 18 | 19.8109 | 20.7967 | 21.8406 | 22.9460 | 24.1169 | 25.3572 | 26.6712 | 28.0636 | 29.5390 | 31.1027 | 32.7600 | 36.3790 | 40.4463 | 45.0185 | 50.1591 | 55.9395 | 62.4397 | 153.7400 |
| 19 | 21.0190 | 22.1237 | 23.2974 | 24.5447 | 25.8704 | 27.2797 | 28.7781 | 30.3714 | 32.0660 | 33.8683 | 35.7856 | 39.9955 | 44.7620 | 50.1601 | 56.2750 | 63.2028 | 71.0524 | 185.6880 |
| 20 | 22.2392 | 23.4705 | 24.7833 | 26.1833 | 27.6765 | 29.2695 | 30.9692 | 32.7831 | 34.7193 | 36.7861 | 38.9927 | 43.8652 | 49.4229 | 55.7645 | 63.0025 | 71.2651 | 80.6987 | 224.0256 |
| 21 | 23.4716 | 24.8376 | 26.2990 | 27.8629 | 29.5368 | 31.3289 | 33.2480 | 35.3034 | 37.5052 | 39.8643 | 42.3923 | 48.0057 | 54.4568 | 61.8733 | 70.4027 | 80.2143 | 91.5026 | 270.0307 |
| 25 | 28.5256 | 30.5140 | 32.6709 | 35.0117 | 37.5530 | 40.3131 | 43.3117 | 46.5706 | 50.1135 | 53.9660 | 58.1564 | 67.6765 | 78.9544 | 92.3240 | 108.1818 | 126.9988 | 149.3339 | 566.3773 |
| 30 | 35.1327 | 38.1018 | 41.3794 | 45.0003 | 49.0027 | 53.4295 | 58.3283 | 63.7524 | 69.7608 | 76.4194 | 83.8017 | 101.0730 | 122.3459 | 148.5752 | 180.9434 | 220.9132 | 270.2926 | 1418.2579 |
| 40 | 49.3752 | 55.0819 | 61.6100 | 69.0876 | 77.6633 | 87.5095 | 98.8265 | 111.8467 | 126.8398 | 144.1189 | 164.0477 | 213.6096 | 279.7810 | 368.2919 | 486.8518 | 645.8269 | 859.1424 | 8812.6294 |

This table shows the present value of an annuity due of $1 at various interest rates ($i$) and time periods ($n$). It is used to calculate the present value of any series of equal payments made at the *beginning* of each compounding period.

**TABLE 6** Present Value of an Annuity Due of $1

$$PVAD = \left[\frac{1 - \frac{1}{(1+i)^n}}{i}\right] \times (1 + i)$$

| n/i | 1.0% | 1.5% | 2.0% | 2.5% | 3.0% | 3.5% | 4.0% | 4.5% | 5.0% | 5.5% | 6.0% | 7.0% | 8.0% | 9.0% | 10.0% | 11.0% | 12.0% | 20.0% |
|---|---|---|---|---|---|---|---|---|---|---|---|---|---|---|---|---|---|---|
| 1 | 1.00000 | 1.00000 | 1.00000 | 1.00000 | 1.00000 | 1.00000 | 1.00000 | 1.00000 | 1.00000 | 1.00000 | 1.00000 | 1.00000 | 1.00000 | 1.00000 | 1.00000 | 1.00000 | 1.00000 | 1.00000 |
| 2 | 1.99010 | 1.98522 | 1.98039 | 1.97561 | 1.97087 | 1.96618 | 1.86154 | 1.95694 | 1.95238 | 1.94787 | 1.94340 | 1.93458 | 1.92593 | 1.91743 | 1.90909 | 1.90090 | 1.89286 | 1.83333 |
| 3 | 2.97040 | 2.95588 | 2.94156 | 2.92742 | 2.91347 | 2.89969 | 2.88609 | 2.87267 | 2.85941 | 2.84632 | 2.83339 | 2.80802 | 2.78326 | 2.75911 | 2.73554 | 2.71252 | 2.69005 | 2.52778 |
| 4 | 3.94099 | 3.91220 | 3.88388 | 3.85602 | 3.82861 | 3.80164 | 3.77509 | 3.74896 | 3.72325 | 3.69793 | 3.67301 | 3.62432 | 3.57710 | 3.53129 | 3.48685 | 3.44371 | 3.40183 | 3.10648 |
| 5 | 4.90197 | 4.85438 | 4.80773 | 4.76197 | 4.71710 | 4.67308 | 4.62990 | 4.58753 | 4.54595 | 4.50515 | 4.46511 | 4.38721 | 4.31213 | 4.23972 | 4.16987 | 4.10245 | 4.03735 | 3.58873 |
| 6 | 5.85343 | 5.78264 | 5.71346 | 5.64583 | 5.57971 | 5.51505 | 5.45182 | 5.38998 | 5.32948 | 5.27028 | 5.21236 | 5.10020 | 4.99271 | 4.88965 | 4.79079 | 4.69590 | 4.60478 | 3.99061 |
| 7 | 6.79548 | 6.69719 | 6.60143 | 6.50813 | 6.41719 | 6.32855 | 6.24214 | 6.15787 | 6.07569 | 5.99553 | 5.91732 | 5.76654 | 5.62288 | 5.48592 | 5.35526 | 5.23054 | 5.11141 | 4.32551 |
| 8 | 7.72819 | 7.59821 | 7.47199 | 7.34939 | 7.23028 | 7.11454 | 7.00205 | 6.89270 | 6.78637 | 6.68297 | 6.58238 | 6.38929 | 6.20637 | 6.03295 | 5.86842 | 5.71220 | 5.56376 | 4.60459 |
| 9 | 8.65168 | 8.48593 | 8.32548 | 8.17014 | 8.01969 | 7.87396 | 7.73274 | 7.59589 | 7.46321 | 7.33457 | 7.20979 | 6.97130 | 6.74664 | 6.53482 | 6.33493 | 6.14612 | 5.96764 | 4.83716 |
| 10 | 9.56602 | 9.36052 | 9.16224 | 8.97087 | 8.78611 | 8.60769 | 8.43533 | 8.26879 | 8.10782 | 7.95220 | 7.80169 | 7.51523 | 7.24689 | 6.99525 | 6.75902 | 6.53705 | 6.32825 | 5.03097 |
| 11 | 10.47130 | 10.22218 | 9.98259 | 9.75206 | 9.53020 | 9.31661 | 9.11090 | 8.91272 | 8.72173 | 8.53763 | 8.36009 | 8.02358 | 7.71008 | 7.41766 | 7.14457 | 6.88923 | 6.65022 | 5.19247 |
| 12 | 11.36763 | 11.07112 | 10.78685 | 10.51421 | 10.25262 | 10.00155 | 9.76048 | 9.52892 | 9.30641 | 9.09254 | 8.88687 | 8.49867 | 8.13896 | 7.80519 | 7.49506 | 7.20652 | 6.93770 | 5.32706 |
| 13 | 12.25508 | 11.90751 | 11.57534 | 11.25776 | 10.95400 | 10.66333 | 10.38507 | 10.11858 | 9.86325 | 9.61852 | 9.38384 | 8.94269 | 8.53608 | 8.16073 | 7.81369 | 7.49236 | 7.19437 | 5.43922 |
| 14 | 13.13374 | 12.73153 | 12.34837 | 11.98318 | 11.63496 | 11.30274 | 10.98565 | 10.68285 | 10.39357 | 10.11708 | 9.85268 | 9.35765 | 8.90378 | 8.48690 | 8.10336 | 7.74987 | 7.42355 | 5.53268 |
| 15 | 14.00370 | 13.54338 | 13.10625 | 12.69091 | 12.29607 | 11.92052 | 11.56312 | 11.22283 | 10.89864 | 10.58965 | 10.29498 | 9.74547 | 9.24424 | 8.78615 | 8.36669 | 7.98187 | 7.62817 | 5.61057 |
| 16 | 14.86505 | 14.34323 | 13.84926 | 13.38138 | 12.93794 | 12.51741 | 12.11839 | 11.73955 | 11.37966 | 11.03758 | 10.71225 | 10.10791 | 9.55948 | 9.06069 | 8.60608 | 8.19087 | 7.81086 | 5.67547 |
| 17 | 15.71787 | 15.13126 | 14.57771 | 14.05500 | 13.56110 | 13.09412 | 12.65230 | 12.23402 | 11.83777 | 11.46216 | 11.10590 | 10.44665 | 9.85137 | 9.31256 | 8.82371 | 8.37916 | 7.97399 | 5.72956 |
| 18 | 16.56225 | 15.90765 | 15.29187 | 14.71220 | 14.16612 | 13.65132 | 13.16567 | 12.70719 | 12.27407 | 11.86461 | 11.47726 | 10.76322 | 10.12164 | 9.54363 | 9.02155 | 8.54879 | 8.11963 | 5.77463 |
| 19 | 17.39827 | 16.67256 | 15.99203 | 15.35336 | 14.75351 | 14.18968 | 13.65930 | 13.15999 | 12.68959 | 12.24607 | 11.82760 | 11.05909 | 10.37189 | 9.75563 | 9.20141 | 8.70162 | 8.24967 | 5.81219 |
| 20 | 18.22601 | 17.42617 | 16.67846 | 15.97889 | 15.32380 | 14.70984 | 14.13394 | 13.59329 | 13.08532 | 12.60765 | 12.15812 | 11.33560 | 10.60360 | 9.95011 | 9.36492 | 8.83929 | 8.36578 | 5.84350 |
| 21 | 19.04555 | 18.16864 | 17.35143 | 16.58916 | 15.87747 | 15.21240 | 14.59033 | 14.00794 | 13.46221 | 12.95038 | 12.46992 | 11.59401 | 10.81815 | 10.12855 | 9.51356 | 8.96333 | 8.46944 | 5.86958 |
| 25 | 22.24339 | 21.03041 | 19.91393 | 18.88499 | 17.93554 | 17.05837 | 16.24696 | 15.49548 | 14.79864 | 14.15170 | 13.55036 | 12.46933 | 11.52876 | 10.70661 | 9.98474 | 9.34814 | 8.78432 | 5.93710 |
| 30 | 26.06579 | 24.37608 | 22.84438 | 21.45355 | 20.18845 | 19.03577 | 17.98371 | 17.02189 | 16.14107 | 15.33310 | 14.59072 | 13.27767 | 12.15841 | 11.19828 | 10.36961 | 9.65011 | 9.02181 | 5.97472 |
| 40 | 33.16303 | 30.36458 | 27.90259 | 25.73034 | 23.80822 | 22.10250 | 20.58448 | 19.22966 | 18.01704 | 16.92866 | 15.94907 | 14.26493 | 12.87858 | 11.72552 | 10.75696 | 9.93567 | 9.23303 | 5.99592 |